LARSON SERIES

DUBREUIL'S FLORIDA WORKERS' COMPENSATION HANDBOOK

2007 Edition

JOHN J. DUBREUIL, C.P.C.U.

LexisNexis®

QUESTIONS ABOUT THIS PUBLICATION?

For questions about the **Editorial Content** appearing in these volumes or reprint permission, please call:

Robin Kobayashi, J.D. at .... 1-800-424-0651 (ext. 3352)
Email: .... pi.editor@lexisnexis.com
Serena Wellen, J.D. at .... 1-800-424-0651 (ext. 3261)
Email: .... pi.editor@lexisnexis.com

For assistance with replacement pages, shipments, billing or other customer service matters, please call:

Customer Services Department at .... (800)833-9844
Outside the United States and Canada, please call .... (518)487-3000
Fax Number .... (518)487-3584
Customer Service Website .... http://www.lexisnexis.com/custserv/

For information on other Matthew Bender publications, please call

Your account manager or .... (800)223-1940
Outside the United States and Canada, please call .... (518)487-3000

ISBN: 1–4224–1848–0
ISSN: 1932-1120

Editorial Offices
744 Broad Street, Newark, NJ 07102 (973) 820-2000
201 Mission St., San Francisco, CA 94105-1831 (415) 908-3200
www.lexisnexis.com

MATTHEW BENDER

(Pub. 1130)

Statement on Fair Use

LexisNexis Matthew Bender recognizes the balance that must be achieved between the operation of the fair use doctrine, whose basis is to avoid the rigid application of the copyright statute, and the protection of the creative rights and economic interests of authors, publishers and other copyright holders.

We are also aware of the countervailing forces that exist between the ever greater technological advances for making both print and electronic copies and the reduction in the value of copyrighted works that must result from a consistent and pervasive reliance on these new copying technologies. It is LexisNexis Matthew Bender's position that if the "progress of science and useful arts" is promoted by granting copyright protection to authors, such progress may well be impeded if copyright protection is diminished in the name of fair use. (See *Nimmer on Copyright § 13.05[E][1].*) This holds true whether the parameters of the fair use doctrine are considered in either the print or electronic environment as it is the integrity of the copyright that is at issue, not the media under which the protected work may become available. Therefore, the fair use guidelines we propose apply equally to our print and electronic information, and apply, within §§ 107 and 108 of the Copyright Act, regardless of the professional status of the user.

Our draft guidelines would allow for the copying of limited materials, which would include synopses and tables of contents, primary source and government materials that may have a minimal amount of editorial enhancements, individual forms to aid in the drafting of applications and pleadings, and miscellaneous pages from any of our newsletters, treatises and practice guides. This copying would be permitted provided it is performed for internal use and solely for the purpose of facilitating individual research or for creating documents produced in the course of the user's professional practice and the original from which the copy is made has been purchased or licensed as part of the user's existing in-house collection.

LexisNexis Matthew Bender fully supports educational awareness programs designed to increase the public's recognition of its fair use rights. We also support the operation of collective licensing organizations with regard to our print and electronic information.

No copyright is claimed in the text of statutes, regulation, and excerpts from court opinions quoted within this work.

TABLE OF AMENDMENTS

[The Florida Statutes are updated through Ch. 2007-86 of the 2007 Regular Session. Any further legislative changes in the 2007 Regular Session, as well as revisions by the Division of Statutory Revisions will be covered in an upcoming supplement. At press time, S 992 had not been sent to the Governor yet.]

Florida Statutes

Section	Effect	Status	Bill No.
440.0102	Amended	To enrollment May 4, 2007	S 992

Florida Administrative Code

Section	Effect	Effective Date
59A-30.002	Amended	October 11, 2006
59A-30.003	Amended	October 11, 2005
59A-30.004	Amended	October 11, 2005
59A-30.005	Amended	October 11, 2005
59A-30.006	Amended	October 11, 2006
59A-30.007	Amended	October 11, 2006
59A-30.008	Amended	October 11, 2006
59A-30.009	Repealed	October 11, 2006
59A-30.010	Amended	October 11, 2006
59A-31.002	Repealed	November 28, 2006
59A-31.003	New	November 28, 2006
59A-31.004	New	November 28, 2006
59A-31.005	New	November 28, 2006
59A-31.006	New	November 28, 2006
59A-31.007	New	November 28, 2006
59A-31.008	New	November 28, 2006
59A-31.009	New	November 28, 2006
59A-31.010	New	November 28, 2006
59A-31.011	New	November 28, 2006
59A-31.012	New	November 28, 2006
59A-31.013	New	November 28, 2006
59A-31.014	New	November 28, 2006
59A-31.015	New	November 28, 2006
60Q-6.101	Amended	November 1, 2006
60Q-6.102	Amended	November 1, 2006
60Q-6.103	Amended	November 1, 2006
60Q-6.104	Amended	November 1, 2006

60Q-6.105	Amended	November 1, 2006
60Q-6.106	Amended	November 1, 2006
60Q-6.107	Amended	November 1, 2006
60Q-6.108	Amended	November 1, 2006
60Q-6.110	Amended	November 1, 2006
60Q-6.111	Amended	November 1, 2006
60Q-6.113	Amended	November 1, 2006
60Q-6.114	Amended	November 1, 2006
60Q-6.115	Amended	November 1, 2006
60Q-6.116	Amended	November 1, 2006
60Q-6.117	Amended	November 1, 2006
60Q-6.118	Amended	November 1, 2006
60Q-6.119	Amended	November 1, 2006
60Q-6.120	Amended	November 1, 2006
60Q-6.121	Amended	November 1, 2006
60Q-6.122	Amended	November 1, 2006
60Q-6.123	Amended	November 1, 2006
60Q-6.124	Amended	November 1, 2006
60Q-6.125	Amended	November 1, 2006
60Q-6.127	New	November 1, 2006
60Q-6.128	New	November 1, 2006
69L-5.102	Amended	October 29. 2006
69L-6.009	Amended	February 19, 2007
69L-6.012	Amended	October 30, 2006
69L-6.021	Amended	February 8, 2007
69L-6.025	Amended	February 6, 2007
69L-6.028	Amended	August 31, 2006
69L-6.031	New	October 29, 2006
69L-7.602	Amended	March 8, 2007
69L-7.603	Repealed	December 4, 2005

Rules of Appellate Procedure

Rule	Effect	Effective Date
9.150	New	November 9, 2006

Table of Contents

A DETAILED SYNOPSIS FOR EACH CHAPTER APPEARS AT THE BEGINNING OF THE CHAPTER

Table of Contents

Table of Contents

FOREWORD

This, the 2007 edition of *Dubreuil's Florida Workers' Compensation Handbook*, marks the fourth anniversary of the massive 2003 reforms of Florida's workers' compensation law. Reportedly, the legislature's goal in enacting these reforms was to reduce the cost of workers' compensation insurance for Florida's employers. That goal has been met and has even exceeded expectations. This is also reflected in the legislature's lack of interest in further amendments during the legislative sessions from 2004 through 2007.

On October 31, 2006, the Florida Department of Insurance announced it had approved an amended rate filing submitted by the National Council on Compensation Insurance (NCCI) leading to a *decrease* in workers' compensation insurance rates by a statewide average of minus 15.7 percent effective January 1, 2007.

The Department announced that the overall rate decrease of 15.7 percent would produce a savings of over $400 million for Florida employers. This is the fourth consecutive drop in rates since the 2003 reforms. Without even considering the 2007 rate reduction, current rates are nearly 30 percent lower than 2003 rates.

Summaries of the 2003 amendments, as well as legislative amendments back to 1978, are contained in Chapter 1 of the *Handbook* and are discussed in detail throughout the text, including appellate court decisions interpreting the statutes.

As the Florida Division of Workers' Compensation noted in its 2006 annual report, it is not yet possible to determine with statistical accuracy the specific claims-related amendments that led to the dramatic drop in insurance rates. However, there are some issues that can be anecdotally associated with contributing to the decrease.

It appears that the incidence and extent of litigation has been substantially reduced, probably because of the statutory provision limiting claimant's attorney's fees to the schedule contained in § 440.34, Fla. Stat. That requirement has been challenged in several cases on its constitutional validity; however, the appellate court has consistently upheld the law as written, and so far the Florida Supreme Court has declined further review.

Fraudulent activities appear to have been reduced. § 440.09(4), Fla. Stat. requires the termination of benefits if the evidence shows that the claimant knowingly and intentionally violated the provisions of § 440.105, Fla. Stat.

Effective October 1, 2003, the legislature amended the statute to provide that the termination of benefits applies not only to violations of § 440.105, Fla. Stat., but also to any criminal act committed for the purpose of securing workers' compensation benefits. Now a plea of guilty or *nolo contendere* in criminal matters constitutes evidence of intent. Further, the statute provides that this provision applies to all accident dates. The statute also requires a judge of compensation claims, administrative law judge, or court to take judicial notice of a finding of insurance fraud by a court of competent jurisdiction and to then terminate or otherwise disallow benefits.

In addition, the appellate court has issued decisions that further support a fraud defense. For example, the court held that if the employer/carrier alleges that the claimant violated the provisions of § 440.09, Fla. Stat. and § 440.105, Fla. Stat., it can establish this by a bare preponderance of the evidence that the claimant knowingly or intentionally made any false, incomplete, or misleading statements in an attempt to obtain workers' compensation benefits [*see* Village of North Palm Beach v. McKale, 911 So. 2d 1282 (Fla. 1st DCA, 2005)].

NOTE: The "weight of the evidence" is equivalent to "preponderance of the evidence." It means simply that proof on one side of a cause outweighs the proof on the other side [*see* In re Estate of Brackett, 109 So. 2d 375 (Fla. 2d DCA 1959)].

Litigation has also apparently been reduced by increased specificity requirements in petitions for benefits. For example the 2003 statute requires that a petition must include a listing of the exact statutory classification and time period of benefits requested. Further, a claim for medical benefits must include a statement explaining why the benefit is requested and why the current treatment is not sufficient. Lastly, a claim for alternate medical care must include the name of the physician recommending such treatment and must include a copy of the report making the recommendation [§ 440.02(40), Fla. Stat.].

There are, of course, many other changes to the law that when examined together would have the effect of reducing entitlement to certain benefits and even then reducing the amount of benefits when entitlement has been shown.

Notwithstanding many court decisions interpreting the myriad changes to Ch. 440, Fla. Stat., many of the amendments have yet to undergo judicial review. This *Handbook* is designed to assist workers' compensation professionals in deciding how the law applies to a specific claim.

Comments and suggestions from readers are always welcome.

John J. Dubreuil, CPCU, AIC, ARM

E-mail: Resolution440@aol.com

July 2007

ABOUT THE AUTHOR

John J. Dubreuil has devoted more than thirty-five years to the insurance industry specializing in claims. The past twenty years have been devoted almost exclusively to Florida workers' compensation. He began his career as a field investigator and adjuster and has since held senior management positions with third party administrators, managing general agencies and commercial insurance carriers. In addition, he serves as a consultant and as an expert witness in workers' compensation related litigation.

Mr. Dubreuil is a graduate of Eckerd College in St. Petersburg, Florida, where he earned a B.A. degree in business management. In addition he earned the professional designation of Chartered Property Casualty Underwriter (CPCU) from the American Institute for Property and Liability Underwriters Inc. He also earned the professional designations of Associate in Risk Management (ARM) and Associate in Claims (AIC) from the Insurance Institute of America. He is Board Certified in workers' compensation claims, and in 1994 the Workers' Compensation Claims Professionals Association named him Florida's Claims Professional of the Year.

Mr. Dubreuil is licensed by the State of Florida as an all lines insurance adjuster and general lines insurance agent, and previously as a surplus lines insurance agent. He is a member and past chairman of the Administrative Advisory Committee to the Division of Workers' Compensation. Mr. Dubreuil is a former member of the Florida Statewide Judicial Nominating Commission for judges of compensation claims, and has been certified as a mediator by the Florida Supreme Court.

PUBLISHER'S EDITORIAL STAFF

SERENA WELLEN, J.D.
Director, Practice Area Content

ROBIN E. KOBAYASHI, J.D.
Legal Editor, Practice Area Content

DAVID BENNETT
Primary Sources Editor

KARIN NEWTON
Index Manager

JEAN BERTELSEN
Index Editor

MOHAMMED N. ALI
Senior Publishing Operations Analyst

DEDICATION

This, the 2007 Edition of *Dubrueil's Florida Workers' Compensation Handbook* is dedicated to Sandi, my wife and best friend.

REFERENCE DIRECTORY

FOR ASSISTANCE ON HOW TO READ AND USE THIS HANDBOOK:

Contact Robin Kobayashi, J.D., Practice Area Editor at Matthew Bender, 800-424-0651, ext. 3352, robin.e.kobayashi@lexisnexis.com with questions about:

- Location of analysis of specific workers' compensation topics
- Location of statutes and regulations covered in this edition
- Coverage of recent workers' comp legislation
- Case summaries
- Tables and charts
- Index entries
- Permission to reprint parts of this edition

FOR FURTHER ASSISTANCE REGARDING INTERPRETATION OF THE LAW AND WORKERS' COMP PROCEDURE, CONTACT:

Helpdesk Numbers of Florida Division of Workers' Compensation:

- Bureau of Compliance (Fraud Referral Hotline)
  1-800-742-2214
- Unemployment Compensation (Fraud Hotline)
  1-800-342-9909
- Bureau of Compliance
  850-413-1609
- Employee Assistance Office (Hotline)
  1-800-342-1741
- Office of Data Quality and Collection
  850-413-1607
- Customer Service Center
  850-413-1601
- Bureau of Monitoring & Audit
  850-413-1608
- Vocational Rehabilitation
  850-245-3399
- Reemployment Services
  850-245-3470
- Medical Services
  850-413-1613
- Department of Insurance Bureau of Workers' Compensation Fraud
  850-413-3116

OTHER RESOURCES:

Matthew Bender Publications, CD-ROM Products, and World Wide Web access. To order publications and CD-ROM products, call toll-free ordering at 800-223-1940:

- *Larson's Workers' Compensation Law* (12–volume treatise)
- *Larson's Workers' Compensation, Desk Edition* (3-volume treatise)
- *Occupational Injuries and Illnesses* (3-volume treatise)
- *Social Security Practice Guide* (5-volume treatise)

Websites on the Internet:

- LexisNexis: http://www.lexis.com
- Florida Division of Workers' Compensation: http://www.fldfs.com/WC/
- Florida Division of Administrative Hearings, Office of the Judges of Compensation Claims: http://www.jcc.state.fl.us/jcc/
- Florida Agency for Health Care Administration: http://www.fdhc.state.fl.us
- Florida Office of Insurance Regulation: http://www.floir.com
- Florida Department of Education: http://www.fldoe.org
- National Council on Compensation Insurance (NCCI): http://www.ncci.com
- USDOL, Occupational Safety and Health Administration (OSHA): http://www.osha.gov
- Florida Administrative Weekly: http://faw.dos.state.fl.us
- Florida Legislature On-Line Sunshine: http://www.leg.state.fl.us/
- Florida Workers' Compensation Institute: http://www.fwciweb.org
- Workers' Compensation Claims Professionals Association http://www.wccp.org
- National Organization of Social Security Claimants' Representatives: http://www.nosscr.org
- CDC, National Center for Health Statistics (NCHS): http://www.cdc.gov/nchs
- U.S. Census Bureau: http://www.census.gov

PART I

GUIDE TO WORKERS' COMPENSATION CLAIMS

Guide to Claims

CHAPTER 1

EVOLUTION OF WORKERS' COMPENSATION LAW

SYNOPSIS

§ 1.01 Origins of Workers' Compensation

[1] The Rule

Workers' compensation is a system designed to compensate workers injured on the job without regard to fault. Participation by most employers is required by law and most workers are eligible for benefits. Benefits are limited to those described in the law and essentially provide partial wage replacement and all medically necessary treatment.

[2] Self-Executing System

Books like this usually begin with an obligatory "history of" chapter, and this one will be no exception. Gaining an understanding of the evolution, the intent, the spirit, and the self-executing nature of workers' compensation is an essential first step in handling workers' compensation claims effectively in Florida. Self-executing means that employers and insurance carriers pay benefits without having injured workers resort to legal or administrative proceedings. Put another way the law expects claims adjusters and employers to know what to do and then to do it timely. This chapter is more than a brief history lesson. It also serves as a quick reference to the effective dates of the dozens of legislative amendments enacted over the years.

[3] In the Beginning

At the beginning of the 20th century, Americans witnessed an explosion of industrial growth. Unfortunately, productivity was a far greater concern than was workers' safety. This was true despite many workers suffering industrial injuries. An injured worker's only legal remedy was to show entitlement to damages under tort law. In other words, injured workers had to prove their employers were guilty of having committed a tort. A tort is a civil wrong in violation of a legal duty. A tort has three fundamental elements. First, the defendant (the employer) must owe a legal duty to the plaintiff (the employee). Second, the evidence must show that the defendant violated that duty. Third, the evidence must show that the defendant's conduct caused the plaintiff's injury.

To receive compensation under a tort system, employees had to prove their injuries resulted from their employer's negligence. Employers, however, had the benefit of common-law defenses. Common law is a system of jurisprudence that originated in England and was later applied to the United States. Common law is based on judicial precedent (case law) rather than statutory laws, which are legislative enactments. These defenses included the plaintiff's (employee's) contributory negligence and assumption of risk. Studies done at the time revealed that factors other than employer negligence caused 80 percent of all workplace injuries. As a result, employers rarely compensated their injured workers.

During this period a new idea gained growing support; since industry caused these injuries, industry should pay for them as part of its cost of doing business. In exchange for guaranteeing benefits, the law would grant immunity to employers. The first workers' compensation law in the United States became effective in 1910. Now all states, and the District of Columbia, have workers' compensation laws.

For a detailed discussion of the origins of workers' compensation, see LARSON'S WORKERS' COMPENSATION, DESK EDITION, ch. 2, §§ 2.07, 2.08 (Matthew Bender). For detailed discussion of the common-law background of workers' compensation, see LARSON'S WORKERS' COMPENSATION, DESK EDITION, ch. 2, *Development of Workers' Compensation* (Matthew Bender).

[4] No-Fault System

The means of achieving this goal was workers' compensation, the first true "no-fault" law. Workers' compensation's purpose is to pay workers for their work-related injuries, and upon the worker's death from those injuries, to prevent dependents from becoming public burdens. Instead of placing the burden of providing compensation directly on the workers, the legal system, or the public, the burden is placed on employers. Theoretically, employers pass these costs on to the consumers of their goods and services. Because the law requires this, some people see workers' compensation, incorrectly, as government-provided. This view is wrong because employers bear the system's entire cost and provide all of the benefits. The state simply explains the rules under which employers and employees must deal with each other.

Under this system, fault and negligence are not at issue. Employers must provide benefits for work related injuries without regard to fault. In exchange for providing guaranteed benefits, the law grants employers immunity from lawsuits brought by their employees. In other words, Florida's Workers' Compensation Act mandates and enforces a contractual relationship between employers and employees under which employers provide no-fault compensation for work-related injuries. In exchange for guaranteed benefits, employees surrender their right to bring common law and statutory lawsuits against their employers for such injuries.

For further discussion, see LARSON'S WORKERS' COMPENSATION, DESK EDITION, ch. 1, § 1.03 (Matthew Bender).

[5] System's Purpose and Problems

Some people insist the system's designers devised it as a remedy for social problems. Other people believe the designers simply sought to relieve business of costly, time-consuming, and disruptive lawsuits brought by employees. Many people will argue that both goals failed. Benefits are inadequate, they complain, and the system itself creates social problems. Litigation has become far too frequent as workers try to prove eligibility, entitlement, and injury causation. Litigation is far too common to be sure, but can often be traced to misunderstanding among the parties or to misapplication of the law. Without question, Florida's law is complicated and too often misunderstood and misapplied by insurance adjusters, lawyers, and the courts. For most injured workers, however, the system does work as intended.

For further discussion of the underlying social philosophy of workers' compensation, see LARSON'S WORKERS' COMPENSATION, DESK EDITION, ch. 1, §§ 1.03[2], 1.04 (Matthew Bender).

§ 1.02 Elements of Workers' Compensation Laws

[1] Carriers Pay Benefits Despite Fault

Workers' compensation is the first, true no-fault law. Employers, or their insurance carriers, must provide benefits despite who is at fault, if the facts meet two basic requirements. First, the injury must arise out of the worker's employment. Second, the injury must occur in the course of the worker's employment. (The law's drafters, however, did not foresee that these simple requirements would require a text the size of this one to explain them.)

Disputes over *who* is at fault have, ironically, been replaced with disputes over *what* is at fault. Because legislators and courts have constantly expanded or reduced compensability, today's system is laden with litigation over causation. Examples include toxic exposure claims, cumulative trauma claims, and mental injury claims.

For further discussion, see LARSON'S WORKERS' COMPENSATION, DESK EDITION, ch. 1, § 1.01 (Matthew Bender).

[2] Benefits Are Limited to Measurable Economic Loss

Economic loss includes such benefits as partial wage replacement and medical costs. Workers' compensation differs dramatically from other areas of civil liability, where plaintiffs can seek compensation for damaged personal property, or for pain and suffering. Workers' compensation law does not allow recovery for these damages. Workers can recover two-thirds of their gross wages subject to a statutory maximum and virtually unlimited medical care. While measurable, these items are often left to the courts to calculate. Hundreds of court opinions have tried to explain what may be included in calculating wages and what medical care is necessary and related to a compensable injury.

For further discussion of economic loss, see LARSON'S WORKERS' COMPENSATION, DESK EDITION, ch. 1, § 1.03[4] (Matthew Bender).

[3] Carriers Pay Benefits as Loss Is Incurred

Remember, in workers' compensation deciding fault is not necessary. Therefore, carriers pay expenses such as medical costs, partial wage replacement, and other benefits as the injured worker incurs the loss. In civil liability, the past, present, and future liabilities are often assessed and paid only after a trial. Trial generally takes place months or years after the accident. Meanwhile, the injured person faces escalating unpaid medical bills often coupled with declining or a complete loss of earnings. Even if the parties agree on fault, they usually do not settle the case until the injured person has recovered and all damages are known. In workers' compensation, the carrier pays medical bills directly to the health care providers and pays wage benefits to the injured worker every two weeks.

[4] Special Courts Adjudicate Disputes

Administrative law judges resolve disputes in workers' compensation cases rather than county or circuit court judges. In Florida, these are the judges of compensation claims, or simply JCC. Over the years, the judges have operated under different titles, such as deputy commissioner and judge of industrial claims. The First District Court of Appeal in Tallahassee reviews all appeals from the orders of the judges of compensation claims. From there, a highly limited and discretionary jurisdiction lies with the Florida Supreme Court.

§ 1.03 Genesis: 1935

The Florida Legislature enacted the state's first "Workman's" Compensation Act in 1935. That original version, some say, was in large part copied from the Georgia and New York laws and was a voluntary system. Thus, employers could choose to participate or not. Hardly a year passed since then without legislative change. Substantial change, however, began in 1978.

> *Even when laws have been written down,*
> *they ought not always to remain unaltered.*
> Aristotle, c. 322 B.C.

§ 1.04 The 1978 Amendments

In 1978, the legislature enacted several major revisions to the Workers' Compensation Act. One most important change made participation compulsory for most employers, but specifically excluded certain types of employment. The (then) Bureau of Workman's Compensation had jurisdiction over claims administration. Critics accused the Bureau of loosely administering the system. This may have been because the Bureau had little power.

Injured workers received permanent partial and disability benefits based on a schedule. Schedules, however, did not consider economic loss. Carriers paid these benefits based on a rating provided by a physician who used permanent impairment percentage schedules. The law required carriers to pay these benefits even if the injured worker returned to work. Carriers calculated permanent total disability and other indemnity benefits based on loss of wage-earning capacity. This method was very subjective and often resulted in controversy.

§ 1.05 The 1979 Amendments

In 1979, the legislature enacted sweeping changes. First, the legislature replaced the Bureau of Workman's Compensation with the Division of Workers' Compensation. This was the same agency, only now much bigger and with extensive regulatory powers. In spite of this, its detractors claimed the system was still too loosely administered. Many people believed this was a key to the commonly perceived shortcomings of the 1979 law. The Workers' Compensation Act also granted the new Division authority to issue advisory opinions on benefit entitlement disputes. The new law authorized the Division to conduct medical peer and utilization reviews and to supervise carrier practices.

The now defunct Industrial Relations Commission (IRC) was the first step in the appellate process. The legislature abolished this step effective October 1, 1979. Instead, the 1979 Workers' Compensation Act required the First District Court of Appeal to hear all appellate review of the trial judges' orders.

The Workers' Compensation Act retained the original idea of disability as it applied to temporary and permanent total disability benefits. The law required carriers to calculate benefits for temporary and permanent partial disability under a new and controversial wage loss method.

Initially, injured workers received wage loss benefits on a retrospective monthly basis. Effective October 1, 1989, wage loss benefits became weekly rather than monthly. Beginning January 1, 1994, wage loss—renamed "supplemental benefits"—became monthly again. Besides wage loss benefits, a permanently impaired worker also might be eligible for impairment benefits. This was a special, one time payment for blindness, amputation, or facial scarring.

§ 1.06 The 1980 Amendments

Major legislative rewrites, such as the 1979 reforms, are usually followed the next year with so-called glitch bills. These bills are intended to clean up the inevitable drafting errors that occur with major rewriting. Often, however, these cleanup bills passed with meaty amendments as well. The following amendments were effective July 1, 1980:

- Created apportionment for permanent impairment benefits.
- Ended wage loss benefits at age 65 when the employee becomes eligible for social security benefits.
- Made temporary partial benefits weekly rather than monthly.
- Based claimants' attorney's fees only on the benefits the attorney obtained.

§ 1.07 The 1986 Amendments

By 1986, observers believed the 1979 changes would not be the system's salvation after all. Thus, several years of legislative tinkering with the Workers' Compensation Act began. The most important changes, listed below, were effective July 1, 1986.

- Defined and granted limited immunity to construction design professionals.
- Required a three-member panel to review the medical fee schedule annually. The three-member panel consists of the insurance commissioner and two other members appointed by the governor and confirmed by the senate [*see* § 440.13(12)(a), Fla. Stat.]. Limited non-scheduled hospital charges to 80 percent of a hospital's usual charge. (In 1992, the Division created a controversial hospital reimbursement fee schedule that covered 300 service modalities).
- Provided that commissions or other irregular earnings must be allocated over 12 months when calculating wage loss benefits.
- Added training and education as an additional benefit to the surviving spouse in death cases.

- Increased to 30 days the maximum time by which a carrier must file a first report of injury with the Division.

- Provided for an offset of compensation benefits when the injured worker settled a third-party claim before accepting or claiming workers' compensation benefits [*see* ch. 19, § 19.02[3]].

§ 1.08 The 1987 Amendments

Effective July 1, 1987, the legislature made several significant changes.

- Amended the definition of "wage" to include the value of: uniforms, life, health, accident, and disability insurance, vested pension plans, and anything else considered taxable income under the Internal Revenue Service Code.

- Defined the value of fringe benefits as the actual cost to the employer.

- Provided that injured workers are not personally liable for paying medical bills.

- Increased the time limit for filing a claim against the Special Disability Trust Fund from sixty days to two years.

- Provided a fine of $100 if a carrier deauthorized a health care provider without approval from the employer or a judge of compensation claims. (This section was repealed in 1990.)

§ 1.09 The 1988 Amendments

The legislature enacted several changes during 1988 in both regular and special sessions. The regular session amendments were effective July 1, 1988:

- Authorized physicians to charge injured workers for record copies.

- Added parking, meals, and legal insurance as includable fringe benefits for average weekly wage calculation.

- Defined "minor" as a person under age 22.

- Increased the maximum catastrophic temporary total disability (TTD) benefit from $400 to $700.

- Required wage loss claim forms to contain a provision for reporting job search efforts.

- Required injured workers to sign requests for wage loss, and that such requests contain a fraud statement.

The legislature made additional changes during the subsequent, special legislative session. These became effective October 1, 1988:

- Extended employer immunity for sole proprietors, partners, corporate officers, directors, supervisors, or any other person who acted in a managerial or policy-making capacity.

- Limited fees for attendant care by family members, if not employed, to the federal minimum wage, or to the family member's former wage, or to the cost of the service in the community, whichever was least. The new section also defined the term "family member" [*see* ch. 18, § 18.06[1]].

§ 1.10 The 1989 Amendments

Despite the previous remedial legislative changes, the system's cost continued to rise, increasing premium rates. (In 1988, the Insurance Commissioner approved a 28 percent rate increase.) Of the 29 changes to the 1989 Workers' Compensation Act, the most significant were these:

- Renamed deputy commissioners to judges of compensation claims.
- Allowed the release of AIDS and HIV test information by order of a judge of compensation claims. The requesting party must prove a compelling need for the test results that they cannot satisfy by other means [*see* § 381.004(3)(f)(10), Fla. Stat.].
- Required workers' compensation coverage for construction companies with one or more employees.
- Provided immunity from lawsuits for employers who use the services of a help supply company (employee leasing firm).
- Limited paid attendant care by family members to 12 hours per day.
- Changed wage loss to a weekly, rather than a monthly, benefit. Also provided a procedure to reduce wage loss benefits if the carrier can prove the existence of actual job openings.
- Gave authority to the Division of Workers' Compensation to mediate claim disputes between the carrier and injured workers.
- Repealed bad faith as a basis for awarding injured workers' attorney's fees and replaced it with the 21-day rule.
- Transferred the duty to provide rehabilitation services, from the carrier to the Division of Workers' Compensation.
- Required claim adjusters to complete continuing education to maintain their licenses.
- Required the creation of a permanent Workers' Compensation Oversight Board with members appointed by the governor.

§ 1.11 The 1990 Amendments

[1] Key Changes in Law

Despite the extensive 1989 changes, costs continued to increase. The insurance commissioner approved another large, double digit, rate increase effective January 1,

Guide to Claims

1990. In response, the legislature made dozens of changes to the law:

- Created the Bureau of Workers' Compensation Fraud within the Division of Insurance Fraud, Department of Insurance.
- Recreated the Industrial Relations Commission.
- Removed the exemption option from the Workers' Compensation Act for corporate officers in the construction industry. This also applied to partners and sole proprietors in the construction industry.
- Redefined "wage" as only actual wages, tips, and the cost of housing and health insurance.
- Created a conclusive presumption that blood alcohol of .05 percent or more, or a positive confirmation of controlled drugs, caused the accident if the employer had in place a drug-free work place program as defined by statute and rule. (The court later held this provision unconstitutional.)
- Created special rules regarding compensable accidents.
- Increased the waiting period for compensation for the first 7 days of disability from 14 to 21 days.
- Created the "Super Doc" panel of Division-appointed physicians to resolve medical disputes. Lawyers coined the term "Super Doc" because the law requires courts to give superior weight to testimony by these physicians.
- Provided that supplemental permanent total disability (PTD) benefits stop at age 62.
- Changed wage loss benefit calculation from 85/95 to 80/80 [*see* ch. 14, § 14.06[3]].
- Reduced wage loss maximum eligibility from 525 weeks to 364 weeks.
- Ended wage loss eligibility if the employee, on three or more occasions: (1) resigned employment; (2) refused appropriate employment; or (3) was fired for misconduct.
- Increased the specificity requirements for claims for benefits. (Now called a petition for benefits.)
- Permitted washout settlements of both indemnity and medical benefits if the impairment rating is five percent or less.
- Prohibited injured workers' attorneys from escrowing compensation benefits until the attorney obtains benefits.
- Provided for fines against carriers of $50 for each late payment of compensation.
- Required a premium rate rollback of 25 percent.
- Made filing a fraudulent application for workers' compensation insurance, to avoid or reduce the premiums, a third-degree felony.

Guide to Claims

- Authorized carriers to assess a penalty of $500 against employers who failed to provide records necessary to complete a payroll audit.
- Authorized carriers to assess a 12-percent penalty against an employer who intentionally understated payroll.
- Required employers to indemnify a carrier for all benefits paid if the employer did not list the injured worker on the last quarterly earnings report.
- Authorized carriers to assess a penalty, equal to three times premiums, if the employer failed to provide access to payroll records.

[2] 1990 Law Held Constitutional

The Florida Supreme Court initially declared that the 1990 amendments to the Workers' Compensation Act were unconstitutional because the legislation violated the single subject rule (it addressed both workers' compensation and international trade) [Martinez v. Scanlan, 582 So. 2d 1167, 1174 (Fla. 1991)].

Meanwhile, the legislature met in a special session. It corrected the constitutional problem by separating the law into two distinct bills and reenacted both laws. The legislature expressly provided that the reenactment applied retroactively to the original effective date of July 1, 1990. The *Scanlan* Court agreed, holding that the legislature's reenactment corrected the constitutional problem.

[3] Second Constitutional Challenge Fails

Santos Garcia suffered an injury at work on July 5, 1990. He argued that the carrier should have calculated his wage loss benefits under the old formula of 1989 because the 1990 law was invalid on the date of its passage. The Florida Supreme Court disagreed. The Court held that the legislature's action, and the Court's own opinion in *Scanlan,* [*see* [2], *above*] made the 1991 re-enactment retroactive, constitutional, and effective on the date of Garcia's accident [Garcia v. Carmar Structural, Inc., 629 So. 2d 117, 119 (Fla. 1993)].

> *Constitutions are intended to preserve practical and substantial rights, not to maintain theories.*
> Oliver Wendel Holmes
> Davis v. Mills (1904)

§ 1.12 The 1991 Amendments

In January 1991, the legislature convened a special session and repealed some 1990 changes while altering others. (In addition, the legislature reenacted the 1990 law to overcome constitutional problems as discussed in § 1.11[2]–[3], *above.*) These changes, effective January 25, 1991, included the following:

- Allowed up to three officers of corporations, actively engaged in the construction industry, the option to exempt themselves from the Workers' Compensation Act.

- Allowed sole proprietors, and up to three partners in partnerships actively engaged in the construction industry, the option to exempt themselves from the Workers' Compensation Act.
- Provided that exempt officers, partners, and sole proprietors may not recover benefits.
- Required notification to general contractors if subcontractors become uninsured.
- Repealed the 1990 legislation creating the Industrial Relations Commission. (It never started.)
- Repealed the 1990 legislation creating a permanent Workers' Compensation Oversight Board.

When the regular 1991 session began, the legislature apparently had seen enough of workers' compensation and made no further changes to Chapter 440 of the Florida Statutes.

§ 1.13 The 1992 Amendments

Workers' compensation historians recorded 1992 as a very significant year. For the first year in memory, the legislature made no changes to the Workers' Compensation Act. This lack of change was not due to any lack of trying. Indeed, the Florida House of Representatives passed a massive bill titled "1992 Workers' Compensation Reform Act." It failed to go further because it garnered no interest in the Florida Senate. Perhaps this was because the 1992 legislature had no desire to deal with so complex and controversial a subject in a reapportionment election year.

§ 1.14 The 1993 Amendments

The 1993 legislation is as massive as the 1979 legislation that created the failed, wage loss system. [For background information on this legislation, *see* FLORIDA WORKERS' COMPENSATION HANDBOOK, 1998 Ed. (Matthew Bender).] The 1993 bill effectively repealed wage loss as the means to compensate permanently impaired workers. The list of amendments alone was fourteen pages long! Following are major provisions of the new law, effective January 1, 1994:

- Allowed managed care arrangements.
- Authorized a premium discount of up to 10 percent to employers who participated in a managed care arrangement.
- Defined emergency medical care consistent with the general health care statute [*see* § 395.002, Fla. Stat.].
- Required the Division to certify health care providers before they may treat workers' compensation patients. To qualify, providers must prove they completed training courses covering workers' compensation subjects.

- Allowed the use of HMO's and PPO's as health care delivery systems.
- Limited medical fees and reimbursement increases to growth in the Consumer Price Index.
- Required establishing practice parameters for medical services in workers' compensation.
- Limited health care provider deposition fees to $200 per hour.
- With exceptions, limited chiropractic care to eighteen visits or eight weeks from initial treatment, whichever came first.
- Authorized a two-year pilot program to study twenty-four hour coverage as an alternative to standard workers' compensation.
- Provided that injured workers must pay a $10 per visit co-payment after reaching maximum medical improvement.
- Provided that only persons with a catastrophic injury are eligible for permanent total disability benefits. Catastrophic injury meant only the following:
    - Severe paralysis from a spinal cord injury
    - Amputation and loss of use of an extremity
    - Brain or head injury accompanied with severe motor, cerebral, or neurological disturbances
    - Substantial second- or third-degree burns
    - Blindness
    - Any other injury, severe enough to qualify for Federal disability income benefits
- Limited temporary disability benefits (temporary total and temporary partial combined) to 104 weeks.
- Made impairment benefits payable for all permanent impairment ratings. Eligible injured workers received three weeks' benefits for each percentage point of impairment. The compensation rate was 50 percent of the average weekly, temporary total, disability benefit.
- Repealed existing wage loss provisions. Only injured workers with an impairment rating equal to 20 percent or more could receive wage loss benefits, now called supplemental benefits.
- Authorized carriers to require annual vocational assessments even after permanent total status began.
- Provided that employers with 50 or more employees were subject to a fine of up to $2,000 per violation if they fail to offer re-employment to injured workers.
- Reduced the guideline formula for calculating injured workers' attorney fees

from 25%/20%/15% to 20%/15%/10%.

- Limited injured workers' attorney's fees to 10 percent of indemnity benefits for the first 10 years and 5 percent of indemnity benefits after 10 years.
- Created an Employee Assistance and Ombudsman Office (EAO) as a required first step before an injured worker could file a petition for benefits.
- Required mandatory mediation before a judge of compensation claims could hold a hearing.
- Required the judge to hold and conclude a final hearing within 45 days after a pretrial hearing.
- Created a small claims dispute resolution process for claims involving less than $5,000.
- Created a code of conduct for judges of compensation claims.
- Repealed the Assigned Risk Plan and created a self-funded Joint Underwriting Association (JUA).
- Transferred regulation of self-insurance funds from the Division of Workers' Compensation to the Department of Insurance.
- Created a Guaranty Association to protect against the insolvency of a group self-insurance fund.
- Created a small business workers' compensation insurance purchasing alliance.
- Permitted the Department of Insurance to contract with the state attorney to prosecute fraud.
- Increased penalties for currently illegal activities.
- Increased the fine for employer safety violations to $5,000 per incident.
- Recreated the Workers' Compensation Oversight Board.
- Defined independent contractor.

§ 1.15 The 1994 Amendments

The 1994 legislature made no changes to Chapter 440 of the Florida Statutes in the regular session, at least not directly. It did, however, increase the amount allowed for reimbursement for medical travel expenses when injured workers travel by private car. Mileage reimbursement to workers' compensation claimants would now be the same as the state pays to its employees for official travel. The rate increased to $0.25 per mile on October 1, 1994, and then to $0.29 per mile on July 1, 1995 [*see* § 112.061(7)(d), Fla. Stat.; Division Bulletin #163 (9/1/94); *see also* ch. 16, § 16.03[4][a][i]].

§ 1.16 The 1995 Amendments

Although the 1995 legislature had little interest in workers' compensation, some changes passed anyway. In particular, the legislature:

- Created § 112.181, Fla. Stat. to create a presumption of work causation if public safety workers contract hepatitis, meningococcal meningitis, or tuberculosis. Public safety workers include fire fighters, paramedics, emergency medical technicians, law enforcement officers, and correctional officers.
- Amended § 440.49, Fla. Stat. to freeze the Special Disability Trust Fund assessment until June 30, 1996.
- Amended § 626.989, Fla. Stat. to grant immunity to insurers sharing information relating to fraudulent insurance acts.
- Created § 626.9891, Fla. Stat. to require insurers to set up anti-fraud units within their organizations and to file anti-fraud plans.
- Added § 817.234(1)(a)(3), Fla. Stat. to make the act of presenting false, misleading, or incomplete information supporting an insurance application a third-degree felony. Effective March 1, 1996, all insurers must add an anti-fraud statement to coverage application forms [*see* § 817.234(1)(b), Fla. Stat.].
- Added § 817.234(10), Fla. Stat. to change the definition of insurer to mean an insurer, self-insurer, self-insurance fund, or other similar entity.

§ 1.17 The 1996 Amendments

The 1996 legislature did little more than to reenact the Special Disability Trust Fund. Although this single action created no change, it was still important because the statute creating the Trust Fund was scheduled to expire. This legislation extended the Trust Fund's existence for another four years and maintained the assessment rate at 4.5 percent for one year. Amendments to Chapter 440 of the Florida Statutes, or to other sections that affect workers' compensation, are listed below. Unless otherwise noted these changes became effective on October 1, 1996.

- Designated the Agency for Health Care Administration, rather than the Division of Workers' Compensation as the agency authorized to develop rules activating the drug-free workplace program [*see* § 440.102, Fla. Stat.].
- Allowed using hair samples for drug testing under § 112.0455, Fla. Stat., the Drug-Free Workplace Act.
- Amended § 442.012, Fla. Stat. to require employers, with 20 or more employees, to create a workplace safety committee. Before, this section applied to employers with only 10 or more employees (5/30/96).

§ 1.18 The 1997 Amendments

The 1997 legislature had no interest in changing Chapter 440 of the Florida Statutes, with one significant exception. The legislature closed the Special Disability Trust Fund (SDTF) to new claims occurring on or after January 1, 1998 [*see* Ch. 20]. Key changes to the SDTF section of the Act are as follows:

- Carriers have until July 1, 1998, to submit proof of claim on cases on file as of June 30, 1997. If not, the carrier's claim is barred forever.
- Carriers that are not prepared to submit proof of claim may withdraw the notice and refile if the limitation period has not expired.
- Carriers must pay a $250 notification fee on claims filed or refiled after July 1, 1997. This fee does not apply if the carrier submits proof of claim with the notice.
- Carriers must pay a $500 fee on each proof of claim.
- The Fund will not provide reimbursement of accidents occurring on or after January 1, 1998.

Other, related amendments are as follows:

- Amended § 625.091, Fla. Stat. to restrict the manner in which carriers may take accounting credit for anticipated SDTF recoveries on their financial statements.
- Amended § 624.4621, Fla. Stat. to require that self insurance funds maintain positive surplus. The amendment contains other provisions dealing with insolvencies.
- Created §§ 631.901–631.998, Fla. Stat., the Florida Workers' Compensation Insurance Guaranty Association Act. This merges the Self Insurance Guaranty Fund with the Insurance Guaranty Fund to create a new, single entity.

§ 1.19 The 1998 Amendments

Despite suggestions that the 1998 legislature had no interest in workers' compensation legislation, 247 bills relating to workers' compensation were filed in the House and Senate. Of 130 bills filed in the house and of 117 bills filed in the Senate, only eight passed. These eight bills, however, provide significant changes largely aimed at combating fraud. These amendments, which include the following, became effective on the date indicated:

- Amends § 440.09(7)(b), Fla. Stat. by revising the standard for rebutting the presumption of intoxication and causation in cases where the employer has adopted a formal drug-free workplace program. The presumption may be rebutted only by evidence that there is no reasonable hypothesis that the intoxication or drug influence contributed to the injury. This amendment, by legislative decree, is effective July 1, 1998, and applies to any cause of action or petition for benefits filed on or after that date.
- Amends and/or adds §§ 440.05(7), 440.15(3)(a)6., (3)(b)9., (4)(b), (10)(b), 440.16(10), 440.191(1), (2)(d), 440.20(15)(a), (17), 440.40, 440.42(2), and 440.49(2)(d), (7)(g), (8), Fla. Stat. by granting the Division additional rule-making authority. This amendment became effective upon becoming law.
- Amends § 440.05(10)(b), Fla. Stat. by providing that the Division has first priority in taking any available social security offset on accidents occurring before July 1, 1984.

- Amends § 440.16(1)(a), Fla. Stat. by requiring carriers to pay funeral bills within 14 days after receipt.
- Amends § 440.02(8), Fla. Stat. by defining a "corporate officer" only as one who fills an office provided for in the corporate charter or articles of incorporation as filed with the Department of State. This provision is effective January 1, 1999.
- Amends § 440.02(20), Fla. Stat. by defining a "partner" as one who shares proportionally in the firm's profits and losses, and who participates fully in the management of the firm and who is personally liable for its debts. This has the effect of limiting the number of partners eligible to voluntarily exempt themselves from the Workers' Compensation Act. This provision is effective January 1, 1999.
- Amends § 440.02(24), Fla. Stat. by defining a "sole proprietor" as one who owns a business and all of its assets, and who is solely liable for all of its debts. This provision is effective January 1, 1999.
- Amends § 440.05(3)–(8), Fla. Stat. by requiring additional documentation to accompany a certificate of exemption filed with the division. The amendment gives the division authority to revoke an exemption upon determining that the person does not meet the requirements, and requires the division to notify the carrier of the revocation. Certificates of exemption for persons in the construction industry are valid for two years and expire unless renewed by the person filing the original certificates. This provision is effective January 1, 1999.
- Amends § 440.09, Fla. Stat. by ending entitlement to benefits if a judge of compensation claims determines that the employee willfully committed any of the acts described in § 440.105, Fla. Stat. This provision is effective January 1, 1999.
- Amends § 440.10(1)(g)2., Fla. Stat. by providing that independent contractors are not eligible for benefits if they provide the general contractor with an affidavit certifying that they meet the requirements of an independent contractor in § 440.02(14)(d), Fla. Stat., and if they provide a certification they are not employees under § 440.02(14)(c), Fla. Stat. This provision is effective January 1, 1999.
- Amends § 440.103, Fla. Stat. by requiring contractors to present a certificate of coverage or a valid certificate of exemption each time they apply for a building permit. This provision is effective January 1, 1999.
- Amends § 440.104(1), (3), Fla. Stat. by granting a contractor a cause of action against the winning bidder of a contract if the winning bidder knew or should have known that he or she violated certain provisions of the Workers' Compensation Act, specifically §§ 440.10, 440.105, and 440.38, Fla. Stat. The prevailing party is entitled to liquidated damages equal to 30 percent of the injured party's bid on the contract or $15,000, whichever is greater. This provision is effective January 1, 1999.

Guide to Claims

- Amends § 440.105(4), Fla. Stat. by providing that submitting a false certificate of exemption constitutes insurance fraud. The amendment also ties the degree of the criminal offense to the amount of premiums or benefits involved as follows [*see* § 440.105(4)(f), Fla. Stat.]: Less than $20,000 equals a third degree felony; $20,000 to less than $100,000 equals a second degree felony; $100,000 or more equals a first degree felony. This provision is effective January 1, 1999.

- Amends § 440.107, Fla. Stat. by granting the Division of Workers' Compensation broad powers to enforce compliance with workers' compensation coverage requirements. These powers include issuing subpoenas to compel witness attendance and for the production of business records [*see* § 440.107(3), (4), Fla. Stat.]. This provision is effective January 1, 1999.

- Amends § 440.42(2), Fla. Stat. by allowing workers' compensation policies to contain a provision requiring the insured employer to release certain employment and wage information maintained by the state except to the extent prohibited by federal law. Such information must be kept confidential and used only to verify compliance with the terms of the policy. The practical effect is to allow the state to release information previously prohibited. This provision is effective January 1, 1999.

- Amends § 440.45, Fla. Stat. by limiting the Chief Judge of Workers' Compensation Claims to a term of four years. The Chief Judge must meet the same qualifications as a judge of compensation claims and is subject to review by the Judicial Nominating Commission. The amendment eliminates the requirement that a lawyer be a member of the Florida Bar for five years before being eligible for nomination. This provision is effective January 1, 1999.

- Amends § 440.49(13), Fla. Stat. by creating a special three-member commission to study and determine the feasibility of privatizing the Special Disability Trust Fund. The amendment also authorizes the commission to contract with an administrator to review, allow, deny, compromise, controvert, and litigate claims of the Special Disability Trust Fund. The commission is further authorized to contract with a second entity to administer the claims payment function. This provision is effective October 1, 1998.

- Amends § 440.185(10), Fla. Stat. by exempting first reports of injury from the public records law, i.e., § 119.07(1), Fla. Stat. Thus, members of the public may no longer obtain copies of accident reports from the division. This provision was effective upon becoming law and, unless renewed, stands repealed on October 2, 2003.

§ 1.20 The 1999 Amendments

Despite predictions that Florida's new, Republican-controlled legislature would revamp the system, no noteworthy bills filed survived the 1999 Legislature. Considering that premium rates remained flat, this outcome was not surprising.

§ 1.21 The 2000 Amendments

Although the National Council on Compensation Insurance (NCCI) requested a modest rate increase of 6.5 percent, the Insurance Commissioner approved an increase of only 2.5 percent. This helps explain the Legislature's inability, once again, to enact any changes to Chapter 440 affecting the benefit structure or claims procedures. Legislation that did pass affects only state agencies and carrier, administrative assessments. The amendments are as follows:

- Amends § 19(f), Article III of the State Constitution by recreating the Special Disability Trust Fund. This merely allows the Fund to continue operations until all of its obligations have been satisfied.
- Amends § 19(f), Article III of the State Constitution by recreating the Workers' Compensation Administrative Trust Fund without modification. Current uses and sources of the Trust Fund continue as before.
- Amends § 19(f), Article III of the State Constitution by recreating the Self-Insurance Assessment Trust Fund. Current uses and sources of the Trust Fund continue as before.
- Amends §§ 440.49, 440.51 Fla. Stat., by changing the definition of "net premiums written" for assessment purposes to include ceded reinsurance premiums and full premiums on deductible policies. The amendment prohibits the Division from collecting underpayments from carriers who excluded ceded reinsurance prior to January 1, 2000. The assessment period is changed to a notification date of July 1, to be affective January 1, thus allowing the assessments to be included in the annual rate filing. Lastly, the amendment requires reporting full policy premiums on deductible policies for assessment purposes beginning January 1, 2001.
- Amends §§ 624.460, 624.468, Fla. Stat., by creating a Task Force on Workers' Compensation Administration. Its purpose is to examine the way the workers' compensation system is funded and organized, and to make recommendations to the Governor and to the legislature.
- Amends § 440.38, Fla. Stat., by giving the Division authority to set the financial requirements for qualification as a self-insurer.

By failing to recreate the Division of Safety, this Division will be eliminated effective July 1, 2000, the date the original enabling legislation expires.

§ 1.22 The 2001 Amendments

The 2001 legislature considered adopting several changes that were considered by most observers to be highly controversial such as reducing claimant's attorney fees, changing the requirements for an award of PTD benefits, and eliminating state paid mediators. Whether the amendments that did pass are controversial, depends on individual perception. Unless indicated otherwise, the following amendments are effective October 1, 2001.

- Amends § 61.14(8), Fla. Stat., to provide that a JCC must consider whether a proposed settlement serves the interests of both the injured worker and the worker's family. This includes considering whether the settlement provides for "appropriate recovery of any child-support arrearage."

- Amends § 61.30(2)(a)(5), Fla. Stat., to include workers' compensation settlements as income for child support purposes.
- Amends § 440.02(4), Fla. Stat., by changing the definition of casual employment to mean work anticipated to be completed in 10 days or less when the total labor cost is less than $500.
- Amends § 440.02(14)(d), Fla. Stat., to provide that individuals serving as officials for entities sponsoring amateur sporting events are deemed to be independent contractors. This includes entities sponsoring an interscholastic sports event as well as any public or private nonprofit organization sponsoring an amateur sports event.
- Amends § 440.02(16)(c), Fla. Stat., to provide that the term "employment" does not include state or county inmates with stated exceptions.
- Amends § 440.12(1), Fla. Stat., by providing that, if authorized by the employee, compensation payments may be made by direct deposit.
- Amends § 440.13(2)(f), Fla. Stat., by providing that an injured worker is entitled to one change of physician during the course of treatment for any one accident. Upon written request from the employee, the carrier must provide a list of at least three physicians from which the employee may choose.
- Amends § 440.13(3)(a), Fla. Stat., by repealing the requirement that physicians complete a five-hour course as a prerequisite to obtaining certification from the Division.
- Amends § 440.13(4), Fla. Stat., by requiring that carriers file medical reports and bill with the Division of Workers' Compensation only when requested to do so by the Division.
- Amends § 440.13(4)(c), Fla. Stat., by adding that medical records must be provided upon request by the attorney for the claimant or the attorney for the employer/carrier or by an authorized, qualified rehabilitation provider.
- Amends § 440.134(2)(b), Fla.. Stat., by making the provision of medical care through a managed care arrangement voluntary.
- Amends § 440.14(5)(a), Fla. Stat., by providing that it is the employee's responsibility to provide the carrier with information concerning loss of earning from concurrent employment.
- Amends § 440.14(5)(b), Fla. Stat., by providing that the employee is not entitled to interest, penalties, or attorney's fees for the period in which the employee failed to provide the carrier with information concerning concurrent earnings. Carriers are not subject to penalties by the Division for the incorrect calculation of AWW for the period in which the employee failed to provide the carrier with information concerning concurrent earnings.

- Amends § 440.192(1), Fla. Stat., by repealing the requirement that petitions be filed with Division. Instead, petitions are to be filed by certified mail, or electronically if approved by the Chief Judge, directly with the Office of the Judges of Compensation Claims. Copies must also be served upon the employer, the carrier, and the Division by certified mail or electronically.

- Amends § 440.192(2), Fla. Stat., by requiring the Office of the Judges of Compensation Claims to review each petition upon receipt to ensure compliance with statutory specificity requirements. Upon motion from a party, or upon his or her own motion, the judge must dismiss the entire petition or *any portion* of the petition that fails to meet the specificity requirements. The amendments also add additional specificity requirements of the date or dates of the accident, the specific classifications of compensation not paid timely, and specific travel costs. Petitions for travel costs must include a copy of the request for mileage filed with the carrier and the date the request was filed.

- Amends § 440.192(5), Fla. Stat., by providing that a claimant has 20 days after the date of an order dismissing a portion of a petition to file an amended petition as has been the case when the entire petition was dismissed.

- Amends § 440.192(8), Fla. Stat., by requiring carriers to respond to a petition by either providing the benefits claimed or by filing a response to the petition with the JCC.

- Amends § 440.20(1)(a), Fla. Stat., by providing that a carrier's obligation to pay compensation is satisfied if it makes payment by direct deposit, electronic transfer, or other means directly to the employee's bank. Compensation is considered paid by these means on the date that the funds become available for withdrawal.

- Amends § 440.20(4), Fla. Stat., by providing that the phrase "the initial provision of compensation or benefits" that triggers the commencement of the 120-day rule means "the first installment of compensation or benefits to be paid by the carrier under subsection (2) or pursuant to a petition for benefits."

- Amends § 440.20(11)(a), Fla. Stat., by providing that settlements under this subsection apply to cases in which the carrier has issued a Notice of Denial within 120 days after the employer receives notice of the injury.

- Amends § 440.20(11), Fla. Stat., by adding subsection (c) which provides that settlement of future benefits does not require the approval of the JCC if the claimant is represented by an attorney. JCC approval is still necessary only with regard to fees to be paid to the claimant's attorney by the claimant.

- Amends § 440.20(11), Fla. Stat., by adding subsection (d) providing that the JCC must consider whether all benefits, including settlements, provide for appropriate recovery of any child support arrearage.

- Amends § 440.22, Fla. Stat., to provide the exemption of workers' compensation benefits from the claims of creditors does not apply claims based on an award of child support or alimony.

- Amends § 440.25(1), Fla. Stat., to provide that the claimant and the claims adjuster may appear at a court ordered mediation conference by telephone or other electronic means if the parties and the mediator agree.

- Amends § 440.25(4)(b), Fla. Stat., to provide that if the JCC has already granted a continuance, the JCC may not approve an additional continuance unless the claimant consents in writing.

- Amends § 440.25(4)(d), Fla. Stat., to provide that the JCC must issue a final order within 30 days after the final hearing or closure of the hearing record. The judge may enter an abbreviated final order in cases in which compensability is not disputed. Either party may request findings of fact and conclusions of law.

- Amends § 440.25(5)(b), Fla. Stat., to require the Office of the Judges of Compensation Claims to adopt rules regarding appellate procedure under this section. It also repeals the requirement that a copy of the verified petition be filed with the Division and the Office of the General Counsel, and repeals the JCC's statutory authority to enter an order requiring the petitioner to reimburse the Division for costs incurred when an insolvency petition is denied.

- Amends § 440.271, Fla. Stat., to require the First District Court of Appeal to create a specialized division to hear all appeals of the orders of the judges of compensation claims.

- Amends § 440.34(3)(b), Fla. Stat., to provide that the E/C must pay the claimant's attorney a fee if the attorney successfully prosecutes a claim after the filing of a Response to Petition with the Office of the Judges of Compensation Claims.

- Amends § 440.38(1)(b), Fla. Stat., by authorizing the Division to require a "qualifying security deposit" as a prerequisite to obtaining authorization to self insure. It also repeals the specific requirement that the self insured employer must provide either an indemnity bond or securities only.

- Amends § 440.44(5), Fla. Stat., to provide that the Office of the Judges of Compensation Claims must maintain the 17 district offices, 31 judges of compensation claims, and 31 mediators as they exist on June 30, 2001.

- Amends § 440.442, Fla. Stat., by repealing the statutory code of judicial conduct and instead providing that the judges should be guided by the code of judicial conduct as adopted by the Florida Supreme Court.

- Amends § 440.45, Fla. Stat., by transferring the Office of Judges of Compensation claims to the Department of Management Services. The position of Chief Judge is changed to Deputy Chief Judge and reports to the Director of the Division of Administrative Hearings.

- Amends § 440.45(2)(c), Fla. Stat., to provide that the nominating commission should determine if a judge's performance was satisfactory by determining the extent to which the judge met the requirements of Chapter 440.

- Amends § 440.45(2)(d), Fla. Stat., by adding this new subsection (d), to grant the Governor the authority to appoint any attorney with at least five years experience as a judge of compensation claims *pro hac vice.* An attorney so appointed may not serve for more than 120 successive days.

- Amends § 440.45(2), Fla. Stat., by creating subsection (e) which gives the Director of Administrative Hearings the authority to initiate, receive, and investigate complaints against any judge of compensation claims alleging violations of the code of judicial conduct. The Director may dismiss the complaint or recommend to the Governor that the judge be removed from office or disciplined.

- Amends § 440.45, Fla. Stat., by repealing subsection (3) which eliminates the docketing judge process.

- Amends § 440.45(4), Fla. Stat., by renumbering it as subsection (3) and repealing the chief judge's discretion to require mediation and to designate qualified persons to act as mediators.

- Amends § 440.593, Fla. Stat., to authorize the Division to require carriers to submit data electronically either directly or through a third-party vendor. It also authorizes the Division to require that carriers and vendors be certified to submit data electronically and to revoke the certification for noncompliance with performance standards and to assess a civil penalty of up to $500 for each violation.

- Amends § 440.092, Fla. Stat., to provide that police officers are presumed to be within the course and scope of employment while traveling to or from work in an official law enforcement vehicle. An exception arises if the officer was engaged in a distinct, personal deviation not allowed by the employer's policy or a collective bargaining agreement. This amendment became effective on June 6, 2001, the date the Governor signed it into law.

§ 1.23 The 2002 Amendments

Late in the session, the legislature enacted substantial amendments to the workers' compensation law. In a separate, 151-page bill, the legislature eliminated the Department of Labor and Employment Security and transferred its responsibilities to other agencies. The Division of Workers' Compensation was transferred to the Department of Insurance, but not intact. All of the Division's responsibilities concerning health care and medical services were transferred to the Agency for Health Care Administration. The Division's responsibilities concerning vocational rehabilitation were transferred to the Department of Education. The Division's Bureau of Self-Insurance was transferred separately to the Department of Insurance.

The following amendments are effective July 1, 2002:

- Amends § 440.091, Fla. Stat. to provide that a law enforcement officer "is

Guide to Claims

considered" to be in the course of employment if injured while engaged in law enforcement even while off duty.

- Adds § 440.091(2), Fla. Stat. to provide that firefighters are considered to be in the course of employment if injured while engaged in firefighting or in protecting life and property even if off duty or outside the employer's jurisdiction.
- Adds § 440.091(3), Fla. Stat. to provide that emergency medical technicians or paramedics are considered to be in the course of employment if injured while providing life support services in an emergency situation even if the injury occurs outside the employer's jurisdiction or area of responsibility.
- Amends § 112.18, Fla. Stat. to include correctional officers (with firefighters and law enforcement officers) under the presumption that tuberculosis, heart disease or hypertension are accidental injuries suffered within the course and scope of employment.
- Amends § 440.02(14)(b)2, Fla. Stat. to provide that exempt officer status in the construction industry does not apply with respect to any commercial project estimated to be valued at $250,000 or more.
- Amends § 440.02(14)(c), Fla. Stat. by adding subparagraph 2, which provides that exemption certificates filed by sole proprietors and partners in the construction industry do not apply with respect to work performed at a commercial building project valued at $250,000 or more.
- Amends § 440.02(14)(d)1.i, Fla. Stat. to provide that no person may be in an independent contractor status while engaged in a commercial construction project valued at $250,000 or more. All persons on such projects are either an employer or an employee who may not be exempt from the coverage requirements of the Act.
- Amends § 440.02, Fla. Stat. by creating subsection (40), which provides a definition of the term "Commercial Building."
- Amends § 440.02, Fla. Stat. by creating subsection (41), which provides a definition of the term "Residential Building."
- Amends § 440.05, Fla. Stat. by creating subsection (10), which requires that sole proprietors, partners or corporate officers engaged in the construction industry must maintain specified records if they elect to be exempt from the Workers' Compensation Act, and that the employer must maintain written statements of exempted persons acknowledging their exempt status.
- Amends § 440.05, Fla. Stat. by creating subsection (11), which requires exempt sole proprietors and partners in the construction industry to maintain federal income tax records for the previous three years.
- Amends § 440.05, Fla. Stat. by creating subsection (13), which requires corporate officers claiming exemption to be listed as an officer in the corporate records maintained by the Secretary of State. If not so listed, the officer must

provide a notarized statement from the corporate president of chief operating officer attesting to the individual's status as a corporate officer.

- Amends § 440.107(5), Fla. Stat. by requiring the Division to issue a stop work order within 72 hours after determining that an employer has illegally failed to secure the payment of compensation.
- Amends § 440.107(7), Fla. Stat. by requiring the Division to assess a penalty against an illegally uninsured employer in an amount no less than the amount the employer would have paid for coverage. The maximum penalty is an amount equal to twice the amount the employer would have paid for coverage up to $1,000.
- Amends § 440.13(12), Fla. Stat. by requiring the three-member panel to take testimony and collect data concerning the adequacy of the medical fee schedule and to submit recommendations to the Florida Senate and the House of Representatives every two years.
- Amends § 440.13(14), Fla. Stat. by providing that fee schedule limitations on fees for medical care do not apply to fees for independent medical examinations.
- Amends § 440.134(2)(a), Fla. Stat. to provide that if an employer or carrier elects to provide medical care outside of a managed care arrangement, the managed care provisions do not apply to any claims regardless of the accident date.
- Amends § 440.191, Fla. Stat. by repealing the requirement that a claimant file a Request for Assistance before filling a Petition for Benefits.
- Amends § 440.25(1), Fla. Stat. to provide that the judge of compensation claims must issue an order within 40 days after the filing of a Petition for Benefits directing the parties to attend a mediation conference unless the parties notify the judge that a mediation conference has been held. A mediation conference must be held within 90 days after the filing of a Petition for Benefits. The judge may grant a continuance on motion by a party.
- Amends § 440.25(3)(a)1, Fla. Stat. to provide that the Division of Administrative Hearings will appoint a state mediator if the parties do not conduct a private mediation.
- Amends § 440.25(3)(a)2, Fla. Stat. to provide that beginning with mediations occurring on or after January 1, 2003, the parties must conduct a private mediation, at the carrier's expense, if a state mediator is not available within the 90-day period. The private mediator selected must be certified as a mediator by the Florida Supreme Court. If the parties cannot agree on a private mediator, the judge of compensation claims will appoint one.
- Amends § 440.25(3)(c), Fla. Stat. to provide that the parties must complete the pretrial stipulations before the conclusion of the mediation conference. This applies only if the disputed issues, other than attorney's fees, have not been settled. It also allows the judge of compensation claims to impose sanctions for

non-compliance.

- Amends § 440.25(4)(a), Fla. Stat. to provide that the judge of compensation claims must order a pretrial hearing to occur within 14 days after the mandatory mediation if the parties cannot agree on the issues in dispute at the mediation conference, and that the judge of compensation claims must allow at least 60 days to conduct discovery when setting the final hearing date.
- Amends § 440.25(4)(b), (d), Fla. Stat. to provide that the final hearing must be held within 90 days after the mediation conference and within 210 days after receipt of the Petition for Benefits. It provides that a request for an additional continuance from a claimant's attorney may not be granted without the claimant's written consent. It also requires that a continuance be granted only because of circumstances beyond the control of the parties.
- Amends § 440.25(4)(d), Fla. Stat. to provide that entitlement to a benefit is waived if it was ripe, due and owing at the time of the final hearing, but was not raised.
- Amends § 440.25(4)(h), Fla. Stat. to provide that disputes regarding average weekly wage under § 440.14, Fla. Stat. are to be resolved without oral hearing. The judge may, for good cause, order a hearing.
- Amends § 440.25(4)(i), Fla. Stat. to provide that a claim in a petition for medical benefits only valued at $5,000 or less, or a claim for mileage reimbursement for medical transportation, must be resolved in an expedited hearing. This requirement may be waived only if there is compelling evidence to the contrary.
- Amends § 440.25(4)(j), Fla. Stat. to provide that the judge may dismiss a petition for lack of prosecution without prejudice on the judge's own motion, or on a party's motion.
- Amends § 440.25(4), Fla. Stat. by adding subsection (k), which provides that a judge of compensation claims may not award interest on unpaid medical bills. The new subsection also provides that claimant's attorney's fees do not attach until 30 days after the carrier, or employer if self-insured, receives the Petition for Benefits.
- Amends § 440.381(2), Fla. Stat. to provide that an application for workers' compensation coverage must contain a sworn statement by the agent attesting that the agent explained to the employer the classification codes used to calculate premium.
- Amends § 440.381(3), Fla. Stat. to provide that the employer and auditor must print and sign their names on a premium audit document and attach proof of identification.
- Amends § 440.40, Fla. Stat. to require every employer to post a notice advising that the state will pay cash rewards of up to $25,000 for information leading to a conviction for insurance fraud, including premium fraud or employers who illegally fail to obtain coverage. It provides immunity for persons reporting

violations to the Department of Insurance.

- Amends § 440.13(1)(e), Fla. Stat. by defining a "certified health care provider" as one certified by the Agency for Health Care Administration.
- Amends § 440.13(3)(a), Fla. Stat. by transferring the responsibility to certify health care providers from the Division of Workers' Compensation to the Agency for Health Care Administration.
- Amends § 440.13(7), Fla. Stat. by transferring the responsibility for resolving medical reimbursement disputes from the Division of Workers' Compensation to the Agency for Health Care Administration.
- Amends § 440.13(9), Fla. Stat. by transferring responsibility for certifying Expert Medical Advisors from the Division of Workers' Compensation to the Agency for Health Care Administration.
- Amends § 440.13(11), Fla. Stat. by transferring responsibility for ensuring that carriers pay medical bills correctly and timely from the Division of Workers' Compensation to the Agency for Health Care Administration.
- Amends § 440.15(3)(b)4, Fla. Stat. by repealing the requirement that carriers annually determine if a worker's impairment resulted in an extended period of disability.
- Amends § 440.491, Fla. Stat. by transferring responsibility for the vocational rehabilitation of injured workers from the Division of Workers' Compensation to the Department of Education.
- Amends § 440.525, Fla. Stat. by repealing the requirement that carrier audits must take place at least every three years.
- Created a new act [*see* 2002 Fla. Sess. Law Ch. 2002-194] that affects workers' compensation in the following ways:
  - Transfers the Division of Workers' Compensation from the Department of Labor and Employment Security to the Department of Insurance.
  - Transfers oversight of medical services in workers' compensation provider relations, dispute and complaint resolution, program evaluation, data management and review of medical bill payments from the Division of Workers' Compensation to the Agency for Health Care Administration.
  - Transfers responsibility for rehabilitation and re-employment of injured workers from the Division of Workers' Compensation to the Department of Education.

NOTE: This Act effectively eliminates the Department of Labor and Employment Security.

The following amendment takes effect on October 1, 2002:

- Amends § 440.51, Fla. Stat. by transferring the Bureau of Self Insurance from the Division of Workers' Compensation to the Department of Insurance.

§ 1.24 The 2003 Amendments

The Legislature concluded a special session by approving extensive reforms to the workers' compensation law in a 202-page bill. The amendments are effective on various dates. Some amendments are effective upon becoming law, some are effective on October 1, 2003, and others are effective on January 1, 2004. The following amendments are effective on the dates indicated.

The following amendments are effective upon becoming law on July 15, 2003:
Definitions:

- Amends § 440.02(1), Fla. Stat. by altering the definition of "accident" as follows:
    - Repeals the provision (in this subsection) that a mental or nervous injury due to stress, fright, or excitement only is not an "accident." [This prohibition, however, is reenacted in § 440.093, Fla. Stat., as indicated below].
    - Compensability of the aggravation or acceleration of a preexisting condition is subject to the provisions of § 440.15(5), Fla. Stat., which has been substantially amended.
    - An injury caused by exposure to a toxic substance, including fungus or mold, is not an injury by accident unless there is clear and convincing evidence of exposure to a specific substance at levels that can cause the injury.
- Amends § 440.02(15)(b)2, Fla. Stat. by repealing the provision directing that corporate officer exemptions do not apply to commercial construction projects valued at $250,000 or more.
- Amends § 440.02(15)(c)2, Fla. Stat. by repealing the provision directing that sole proprietor and partner exemptions do not apply to commercial construction projects valued at $250,000 or more.
- Amends § 440.02(15)(d)1.i, Fla. Stat. by repealing the provision directing that independent contractor status does not apply to commercial construction projects valued at $250,000 or more.
- Repeals § 440.02(38), Fla. Stat., defining "catastrophic injury."
- Amends § 440.02(40), Fla. Stat. by providing that the term "statement," for the purposes of § 440.105, Fla. Stat. and § 440.106, Fla. Stat., must include the exact fraud language in § 440.105(7), Fla. Stat.
- Amends § 440.02(41), Fla. Stat. by altering the specificity requirements for a Petition for Benefits as follows:
    - A petition must include a listing of the exact statutory classification and

time period of benefits requested.

- A claim for medical benefits must include a statement explaining why the benefit is requested and why the current treatment is not sufficient.

- A claim for alternate medical care must include the name of the physician recommending such treatment and must include a copy of the report making the recommendation.

The following amendments are effective October 1, 2003:

Medical Evidence and Major Contributing Cause:

- Amends § 440.09(1), Fla. Stat. by providing as follows:

  - The relationship of medical conditions and disability to occupational causation must be established based on objective, relevant medical findings.

  - "Major Contributing Cause" means the cause that is more than 50 percent responsible for the injury.

  - "Major Contributing Cause" must be demonstrated by medical evidence only.

  - Pain or other subjective complaints alone, in the absence of objective relevant findings, are not compensable.

Fraud:

- Amends § 440.105(3)(b), Fla. Stat. by making it unlawful for any employer to knowingly employ any person who has used false, fraudulent statements of identity.

- Amends § 440.09(4)(a), Fla. Stat. by providing that pleas of guilty or nolo contendere constitute an admission of intentional violation of § 440.105, Fla. Stat. or any criminal act for purposes of securing workers' compensation benefits.

- Amends § 440.09(4)(b), Fla. Stat. by requiring the judge of compensation claims to take judicial notice of a finding of insurance fraud by a court and to terminate benefits.

- Amends § 440.09(4)(c), Fla. Stat. by authorizing the judge of compensation claims to order a carrier to pay benefits into the court registry or an escrow account during the pendency of an appeal from an order terminating benefits due to a finding of insurance fraud.

- Amends § 440.105(4)(b), Fla. Stat. by adding subsection 8, which provides that violating a stop-work order constitutes insurance fraud.

- Amends § 440.105(4)(b), Fla. Stat. by adding subsection 9, which provides that providing false or misleading evidence of a person's identity to obtain workers' compensation benefits constitutes insurance fraud.

- Amends § 440.105(7), Fla. Stat. by requiring that any person seeking benefits must personally sign a document attesting to understanding the required "fraud statement." If the person refuses to sign, all benefits must be suspended until the signature is obtained.

Intoxication:

- Amends § 440.09(7)(e), Fla. Stat. by providing that overcoming a presumption of intoxication also requires the injured worker to prove the actual amount of the drug as measured on the initial and confirming test and provide additional evidence of the absence of drug influence other than the worker's denial of being under the influence.

Psychiatric Injury:

- Amends § 440.093(1), Fla. Stat. by providing that mental or nervous injuries unaccompanied by physical injuries requiring treatment are not compensable.
- Amends § 440.093(2), Fla. Stat. by providing as follows:
  - A mental injury is not compensable absent medical evidence from a licensed psychiatrist meeting criteria in the most recent edition of the diagnostic and statistical manual of mental disorders published by the American Psychiatric Association.
  - A mental injury is not compensable unless the physical injury is and remains the major contributing cause of the mental injury, and the physical injury must be at least 50 percent responsible for the mental injury.
  - No compensation is payable for a mental injury arising out of depression from being out of work or losing employment opportunities; or from a preexisting mental condition; or from an emotional condition due to unsubstantiated, subjective complaints of pain.
- Amends § 440.093(3), Fla. Stat. by providing that compensation for a mental injury is not payable for more than six months after maximum medical improvement for the physical injury.

Employers, Premiums, and Coverage:

- Amends § 440.10(1)(g), Fla. Stat. by providing that any employer engaged in work in this state must obtain a Florida endorsement or purchase a Florida workers' compensation policy. Failure to do so constitutes a second-degree felony.
- Amends § 440.1025, Fla. Stat. by making private employers eligible for premium discounts for establishing workplace safety programs.
- Amends § 440.107(2), Fla. Stat. by providing that an employer who understates or conceals payroll to avoid proper premium classification is considered to have failed to secure the payment of compensation and is subject to the same sanctions as an employer who illegally failed to obtain coverage. Such a finding does not alter the employer's duty to provide benefits or alter statutory immunity.

Immunity:

- Amends § 440.11(1)(b), Fla. Stat. to provide that to overcome employer immunity, the employee has the burden to prove his injuries were caused by the employer's intentional tort and not by accident. To do so, the employee must show the following:
  - That the employer deliberately intended to injure the employee; or
  - The employer knew the injury was virtually certain to occur based on the employer's knowledge that similar injuries had occurred in the past or that the employer had received explicit warnings identifying a known danger; and
  - The employee was not aware of the danger because it was not apparent; and
  - The employer deliberately concealed or misrepresented the danger.
- Amends § 440.11(3), Fla. Stat. as follows:
  - Extends immunity from claims by an employer's employees, or the employees of its subcontractor, to a workers' compensation carrier, servicing agent, or safety consultant arising out of the provision of safety consulting services.
  - A "safety consultant" may include an owner or the owner's related, affiliated, or subsidiary companies or their employees.

Experimental Medical Services:

- Amends § 440.13(1)(m), Fla. Stat. by repealing the provision that experimental or investigative medical services are compensable if approved by AHCA.

Overutilization:

- Amends § 440.13(1)(k), Fla. Stat. to provide that medical services in excess of established practice parameters constitutes overutilization.

Chiropractic Care:

- Amends § 440.13(2)(a), Fla. Stat. by increasing the number of chiropractic visits allowed from 18 to 24.

Attendant Care:

- Amends § 440.13(2)(b), Fla. Stat. regarding entitlement to attendant care and fees to family members, as follows:
  - The carrier is not responsible for providing attendant care until it receives a prescription for such care from the physician.
  - Prohibits prescribing attendant care retroactively.
  - If an employed family member provides care during non-working hours, the per-hour rate in the federal minimum wage.

Guide to Claims

- If the family member is not employed, the per-hour rate is the federal minimum wage.
- If the employed family member remains employed while providing attendant care, the per-hour rate is equal to the per-hour value of the family member's employment, not to exceed the hourly rate for such care in the community.

Unauthorized Treatment:

- Amends § 440.13(2)(c), Fla. Stat. to provide that an employee may seek unauthorized care at the carrier's expense if the carrier fails to provide care within a reasonable time after the care is requested. The amendment provides that this applies only to initial treatment.

Changing Physicians:

- Amends § 440.13(2)(f), Fla. Stat. by altering the right to one-time change of physician as follows:
  - The carrier must authorize a change of physician within five days after receiving the request.
  - If the carrier fails to respond within five days, the employee may select the physician, who is then deemed authorized.
  - Once an alternative physician is authorized, the original physician is deauthorized upon written notice from the carrier.
  - If the carrier fails to timely comply with a request for a change of physician, the carrier is subject to penalties as provided in § 440.525, Fla. Stat..

Copy Charges for Medical Records:

- Amends § 440.13(4)(b), Fla. Stat. by providing that medical providers may not charge more than $0.50 per page for producing copies of medical records.

Confidentiality of Medical Records:

- Amends § 440.13(4)(c), Fla. Stat. by providing as follows:
  - An employee claiming a work-related injury waives any physician-patient privilege for conditions relevant to the claimed injury.
  - A medical release from the employee is not required. Physicians must provide records upon request.
  - If the physician is outside the state, and not subject to Florida law, the employee must provide a written medical information release.

Independent Medical Examinations:

- Amends § 440.13(5)(a), Fla. Stat. by altering the independent medical examination requirements as follows:

Guide to Claims

- An independent medical examiner may not be a physician providing treatment, unless the parties agree.
- The employee and the carrier are entitled tc only one independent medical examination for any one accident and not one for each specialty.
- The party requesting and selecting the independent medical examination is responsible for all associated costs.
- The party requesting the independent medical examination must notify all other parties at least 15 days before the examination. Failure to do so renders the examiner's opinions inadmissible.
- The independent medical examiner may not provide follow-up treatment, even if such treatment is held compensable.
- If the employee prevails in a medical dispute, or if benefits are paid or treatment is provided based on the independent medical examination, the carrier must pay for the examination.

- Amends § 440.134(6)(c)9, Fla. Stat. by providing for independent medical examination as follows:
  - A managed care plan must allow the employee to obtain one independent medical examination as provided in § 440.13(5), Fla. Stat.
  - If the physician selected is one in the carrier's managed care arrangement, the carrier is responsible for payment.
  - Such an independent medical examination, requested by the claimant and paid by the carrier, constitutes the claimant's one-time examination.
- Amends § 440.13(5)(b), Fla. Stat. by providing that each party is bound by the opinions of his or her selected independent medical examiner.
- Amends § 440.13(5)(b)4, Fla. Stat. by repealing the provision authorizing the judge of compensation claims to designate an Expert Medical Advisor as an independent medical examiner.
- Amends § 440.13(5)(c), Fla. Stat. by providing that the carrier is not responsible for scheduling an independent medical examination other than its own.
- Amends § 440.13(5)(g), Fla. Stat. by creating the concept of a "consensus independent medical examination." Such an independent medical examination operates as follows:
  - The parties, if they agree, may refer the employee to a mutually acceptable physician specializing in the medical condition at issue.
  - The finding and conclusions of the examiner are binding on the parties and constitute a resolution of the medical dispute.
  - Agreeing to a "consensus independent medical examination" does not alter

the parties' rights to their own, one per accident, independent medical examination.

Expert Medical Advisor:

- Amends § 440.13(9)(f), Fla. Stat. by allocating responsibility for payment of the EMA fee as follows:
  - The party requesting an EMA evaluation is responsible for paying the fee.
  - If the employee requests the EMA evaluation, and prevails based on the report, the carrier is responsible for the fee.
  - If the judge of compensation claims orders the EMA evaluation on his or her own motion, the carrier is responsible for the fee.

Medical Bills:

- Amends § 440.13(11)(b), Fla. Stat. by increasing from 90 to 95 percent the percentage of medical bills that must be paid on time to avoid penalties.

Medical Services:

- Amends § 440.13(12)(a), Fla. Stat. by providing that an outpatient may not remain in observation status for more than 23 hours.

Medical Fees:

- Amends § 440.13(12)(b), Fla. Stat. by increasing maximum medical service fees for selected physicians by decreasing fees payable to hospitals, as follows:
  - Services by hospitals for outpatient physical, occupational, and speech therapy are limited to the amount allowed to non-hospital providers.
  - Services by hospitals for outpatient, non-emergency radiological and laboratory services are limited to the amount allowed to non-hospital providers.
  - Services by hospitals for outpatient, scheduled surgeries are reduced from 75 percent to 60 percent.
  - Maximum fees by M.D.'s and D.O.'s are increased to 110 percent of the amount allowed by Medicare or the Florida fee schedule, whichever is greater.
  - Maximum fees for surgical procedures are increased to 140 percent of the amount allowed by Medicare or the Florida fee schedule, whichever is greater
- Amends § 440.13(12)(c), Fla. Stat. by reducing the amount payable for prescription medication to the wholesale price plus $4.18 for the dispensing fee.
- Amends § 440.13(14)(b), Fla. Stat. by providing that carriers may enter a contract with a health care provider allowing fees in excess of the fee schedule in exchange for enhanced services to injured workers.

Practice Parameters:

- Amends § 440.13(15), Fla. Stat. by repealing existing provisions regarding medical practice parameters and adopting the practice parameters and protocols adopted by the U.S. Agency for Healthcare Research and Quality in effect on January 1, 2003.

Standards of Care:

- Amends § 440.13, Fla. Stat. by adding subsection (16), adopting required standards of medical care, as follows:
  - Abnormal anatomical findings, in the absence of objective relevant medical findings, are not an indicator of injury and cannot be the basis for treatment or physical restrictions.
  - All treatment plans must be based on the premise that return to work is the goal. Work restrictions must be reevaluated at each visit.
  - The treatment plan must be reevaluated every 30 days.
  - Treatment plans may not be based on nondescript diagnostic labels.
- Amends § 440.13, Fla. Stat. by adding subsection (17), providing that health care providers who fail to comply with standard of care requirements are subject to penalties as provided in § 440.525, Fla. Stat.

Managed Care:

- Amends § 440.134(1)(d), Fla. Stat. by defining a "grievance" as a written complaint, other than a Petition for Benefits, filed by an injured worker.
- Amends § 440.134(1)(i), Fla. Stat. by adding chiropractors and podiatrists to the list of physicians qualified to serve as a medical care coordinator.
- Amends § 440.134(6)(c)9, Fla. Stat. by providing that a managed care plan must allow the employee to obtain an independent medical examination as provided in § 440.13(5), Fla. Stat. If the physician selected is one in the carrier's managed care arrangement, the carrier is responsible for payment. Such an independent medical examination, requested by the claimant and paid by the carrier, constitutes the claimant's one-time examination.
- Amends § 440.134(10)(c), Fla. Stat. by limiting a claimant's right to a change of physician to one per accident and in accordance with § 440.13(2)(f), Fla. Stat.
- Amends § 440.134(10), Fla. Stat. by adding subsection (e), requiring that a managed care plan provide for multiple medical care coordinators to supervise care by other physicians in the same license category.
- Amends § 440.134(17), Fla. Stat. by providing that medical care obtained outside the managed care arrangement is not compensable, regardless of the purpose of the treatment. This includes evaluations, diagnostic studies to determine causation, disability, impairments, and the date of maximum medical improvement.

Average Weekly Wage:

- Amends § 440.14(1), Fla. Stat. by providing that average weekly wage is determined based on the accident date.
- Amends § 440.14(1)(a), Fla. Stat. by providing that "13 weeks" means calendar weeks, and that the phrase "substantially the whole of 13 weeks" means 75 percent of the total customary hours of employment.

Permanent Total Disability:

- Amends § 440.15(1), Fla. Stat. by substantially altering the requirements for an award of permanent total disability benefits as follows:
  - An award of permanent total disability is prohibited if the employee is physically capable of engaging in at least sedentary employment.
  - An employee is *presumed* to be permanently and totally disabled if the employee suffered one of the following injuries:
    - Paralysis of an arm, a leg, or the trunk
    - amputation or the effective loss of use of an arm, hand, foot, or leg.
    - Severe brain or closed-head injury, as defined.
    - 2nd or 3rd degree burns of 25 percent or more of the total body surface
    - 3rd degree burns of five percent or more of the face and hands
    - Total or industrial blindness.
  - A carrier may overcome the presumption of permanent total disability with evidence that the employee is able to engage in at least sedentary employment within a 50-mile radius of the employee's residence.
  - In all other cases, permanent total disability may be awarded if the employee is not able to engage in at least sedentary employment within a 50-mile radius of the employee's residence.
  - Permanent total disability benefits end at age 75.
  - The age 75 limitation does not apply if the employee is not eligible for Social Security benefits because the employee's injuries prevented working sufficient quarters to become eligible.
  - If the employee is age 70 or older when the accident occurred, permanent total disability benefits are payable for no more than five years.
- Amends § 440.15(1)(e)1, Fla. Stat. by providing that a carrier may conduct vocational evaluations, even after permanent total disability is established, performed by a rehabilitation provider of the carrier's choice.
- Amends § 440.15(1)(e)3, Fla. Stat. by repealing the requirement that the carrier obtain an order from a judge of compensation claims before withholding

permanent total disability benefits due to the employee's failure to appear for vocational testing.

- Amends § 440.15(1)(f)1, Fla. Stat. by providing that permanent total disability supplemental benefits are not payable after the employee reaches age 62, regardless of whether the employee is eligible for Social Security benefits. This limitation does not apply if the employee is not eligible for Social Security benefits because the employee's injuries prevented working sufficient quarters to become eligible.

Catastrophic Temporary Total Disability Benefits:

- Amends § 440.15(2)(b), Fla. Stat. by providing that an employee is not eligible for catastrophic Temporary Total Disability benefits if the employee is eligible for permanent total disability benefits.

Impairment Income Benefits:

- Amends § 440.15(3), Fla. Stat. by substantially altering eligibility and benefit amounts as follows:
    - Impairment benefits are paid bi-weekly rather than weekly.
    - Increases the benefit amount from 50 percent to 75 percent of the Temporary Total Disability benefit amount
    - Benefits are reduced by 50 percent for each week in which the employee earned wages equal to or in excess of the pre-injury average weekly wage.
    - Impairment benefits are payable only for physical impairments.
    - Impairment benefits for psychiatric impairment are limited to one percent.
    - Entitlement to impairment benefits begins the day after maximum medical improvement, or the expiration of temporary benefits, whichever occurs first.
    - The duration of eligibility increases as the impairment rating increases from a low of two weeks for each percentage point from 1 to 10 percent, to a high of six weeks for impairments of 21 percent or higher.

Supplemental Income (Wage Loss) Benefits:

- Repealed § 440.15(3)(b), Fla. Stat., thus eliminating supplemental income benefits.

Temporary Partial Disability:

- Amends § 440.15(4), Fla. Stat. by altering entitlement, as follows:
    - Benefits are not payable if the employee has achieved overall maximum medical improvement.
    - Benefits are payable only if compensable medical conditions created work restrictions.

- Within five days after the carrier learns of a restricted work release, the carrier must send a letter to the employee, explaining rights and responsibilities.
- If the employee returns to work earning less than 80 percent of the pre-injury wage, the first installment of Temporary Partial Disability benefits is due seven days after the end of the first work week. Subsequent payments are due no later than seven days after the end of each bi-weekly workweek.
- If the employee is not able to work within restrictions, payments are due no later than the last day of each biweekly period.
- If the employee fails to notify the carrier within five days after returning to work, Temporary Partial Disability benefits must be suspended until proper notification is provided.
- No Temporary Partial Disability benefits are payable if the employee's employment is terminated for misconduct.

Aggravation of Preexisting Conditions:

- Amends § 440.15(5), Fla. Stat. by altering compensability of aggravation of preexisting conditions, as follows:
  - Only disability or need for medical treatment associated with the compensable injury is compensable.
  - The degree of disability, or medical treatment required, for preexisting conditions are to be excluded from the impairment rating.
  - The exclusion applies if the prior condition was disabling on the accident date or at the time of the impairment rating.
  - The exclusion applies without considering whether the prior condition would have been disabling without the compensable accident.
  - Impairment ratings must apportion out the preexisting condition.
  - Medical benefits are to be paid apportioning out the percentage attributable to the preexisting condition.

Employee Refuses Employment:

- Amends § 440.15(6), Fla. Stat. to provide that weeks during which benefits were not payable because the employee refused suitable employment are to be counted as part of the maximum number of weeks the employee may receive temporary benefits.

Employee Leaves Employment:

- Amends § 440.15(7), Fla. Stat. to provide that if the judge of compensation claims determines that an employee, receiving Temporary Partial Disability benefits, left his or her employment without just cause, benefits are payable for those weeks based on deemed earnings.

Occupational Disease:

- Amends § 440.151(1)(a), Fla. Stat. by altering compensability of an occupational disease, as follows:
  - The nature of the employment must have been the major contributing cause of the occupational disease.
  - Compensability requires clear and convincing evidence of exposure to a specific, harmful substance shown to be present in the workplace.
- Amends § 440.151(2), Fla. Stat. by defining "occupational disease" as a disease for which there are epidemiological studies showing that exposure to the specific substance, at the levels of actual exposure, can cause the precise disease suffered.

Death Benefits:

- Amends § 440.16(1)(a), Fla. Stat. by increasing funeral benefits from $5,000 to $7,500.
- Amends § 440.16(1)(b), Fla. Stat. by increasing death benefits from $100,000 to $150,000.

Notice of Injury:

- Amends § 440.185(9), Fla. Stat. by increasing the maximum penalty assessed against the employer for late reporting of an accident from $500 to $1,000 for each failure. If the employer failed to timely report more than 10 percent of its industrial accidents during a calendar year, the maximum penalty increases to $2,000 per late report.
- Amends § 440.185(12), Fla. Stat. by requiring the employer, upon receiving an accident report, to provide the employee with a written notice concerning the availability of services from the Employee Assistance Office.

Benefit Disputes:

- Amends § 440.192(1), Fla. Stat. by requiring that a Petition for Benefits may be filed only for benefits that are ripe, due, and owing and that meets the specificity requirements of § 440.02, Fla. Stat.
- Amends § 440.192(2)(i), Fla. Stat. by requiring that a Petition for Benefits seeking an award of medical benefits must have attached a copy of the physician's request, authorization, or recommendation for the treatment sought.
- Amends § 440.192(1), Fla. Stat. by adding subsection (9), providing that a judge of compensation claims may consider only those claims that were ripe, due, and owing when the petition was filed and that have undergone mediation.

Alternate Dispute Resolution; Arbitration:

- Adds § 440.1926, Fla. Stat., allowing the parties to obtain the judge of compensation claims' approval to resolve their dispute via binding arbitration in

Guide to Claims

lieu of any other remedy. The Florida Arbitration Code, Chapter 682, governs arbitration under this provision.

Time for Payment of Compensation:

- Amends § 440.20(2)(a), Fla. Stat. to provide that the first payment for Temporary Total Disability or death is due within 14 calendar days after the employer receives notification of the injury. This applies only when disability is immediate and continuous for eight or more days. If the first seven days of disability are not consecutive, payment is due with six days after the eighth day of disability.

- Amends § 440.20(2)(b), Fla. Stat. to provide that bills for medical, dental, pharmacy, or hospital services must be paid, disallowed, or denied within 45 days after receipt.

- Amends § 440.20(6)(a), Fla. Stat. to provide that the carrier must add a punitive penalty of 20% to any installment of compensation not paid within seven days after it becomes due. Repeals the minimum penalty of $5.00.

- Amends § 440.20(6)(b), Fla. Stat. to provide that all medical bills for services performed on or after January 1, 2002, must be paid or denied within 45 days after receipt. Carriers who fall below the timely performance standard will be assessed penalties as follows:

  - $25.00 for each bill falling between 90 percent and 95 percent timely.

  - $50.00 for each bill falling below a 90 percent timely performance standard.

- Amends § 440.20(8)(b), Fla. Stat. to require a 95 percent timely performance standard for payment of compensation. Carriers who fall below the timely performance standard will be assessed penalties as follows:

  - $50.00 for each late installment of compensation falling between 90 percent and 95 percent timely

  - $100.00 for each late installment falling below 90 percent timely.

- Amends § 440.20(11)(d)1, Fla. Stat. to provide that employers and carriers have no duty to investigate or collect information regarding child support arrearages with regard to lump-sum settlements.

- Amends § 440.20(11)(d), Fla. Stat. by creating subsection 3, providing that the clerk of the court may not assess fees for services of child support documentation regarding lump-sum settlements.

Mediations and Hearings:

- Amends § 440.25(1), Fla. Stat., regarding mediation, as follows:

  - Requires the judge of compensation claims to notify the parties within 40 days after a Petition for Benefits is filed that a mediation conference has been scheduled, unless the parties have notified the judge that a private mediation has been scheduled.

- Increases the deadline for a mediation conference, public or private, from 90 to 130 days after a Petition for Benefits is filed.
- Requires the judge to consolidate multiple pending petitions, including petitions filed after the mediation is scheduled, into one mediation conference.

- Amends § 440.25(2), Fla. Stat. by repealing the requirement that the parties submit any applicable motions to the judge no later than three days before the mediation.
- Amends § 440.25(3), Fla. Stat. by repealing the requirement that the parties complete the pretrial stipulation at the conclusion of the mediation.
- Amends § 440.25(4)(a), Fla. Stat. to provide that if the parties cannot agree to written submission of pretrial stipulations, the judge must conduct a live pretrial hearing, giving the parties at least 14 days' notice of the hearing date.
- Amends § 440.25(4)(d), Fla. Stat. by providing that the final hearing need not be held within 210 days after the petition is filed, if the claimant waives this requirement for good cause.
- Amends § 440.25(4)(h), Fla. Stat. by providing that mediation is not required when a petition is for benefits valued at $5,000 or less, unless requested by a party.

Attorney Fees:

- Amends § 440.34, Fla. Stat. by altering entitlement and the amount of claimant attorney fees as follows:
    - Fees may be awarded based on only benefits secured "on behalf of" a claimant.
    - A judge of compensation claims may not approve any agreement, stipulation, or order for fees in excess of the statutory fee schedule of 20/15/10/5.
    - A judge of compensation claims is not required to approve any retainer agreement between a claimant and his or her attorney.
    - A retainer agreement as to fees and costs may not be for compensation in excess of the amounts allowed in § 440.34, Fla. Stat.
    - An attorney is not entitled to a fee for an issue that was ripe, due, and owing, but was not addressed during the pendency of other issues for the same injury.
    - The term "benefits secured" does not include benefits the carrier offered to provide, including fees, on issues pending before a judge of compensation claims, if the offer was made in writing 30 days before trial. Benefits secured are deemed to be only benefits above the carrier's settlement offer.
    - The prevailing party in a proceeding before a judge of compensation

claims is entitled to recover the costs of such proceedings, not including attorney fees, from the non-prevailing party.

- If the judge of compensation claims determines that the statutory fee schedule will not fairly compensate the attorney for a disputed medical-only claim, the judge may award an alternate fee not to exceed $1,500, based on an hourly rate of $150.00. Such an award is limited to once per accident.

Security for Compensation:

- Amends § 440.38, Fla. Stat. to provide that an employer doing business in Florida, but who has a policy of insurance issued outside the state, must obtain a Florida endorsement to ensure coverage for Florida employees.

Applications for Coverage:

- Amends § 440.381(2), Fla. Stat. by providing that submitting misleading, false, or fraudulent information in an application for workers' compensation coverage constitutes a second-degree felony.

Cancellation of Coverage:

- Amends § 440.42(3), Fla. Stat. by providing that cancellation of a policy for non-payment requires at least 10 days' notice.

Training and Education:

- Amends § 440.491(6)(a), Fla. Stat. by providing that approved training and education for an injured worker includes training at a community college or a vocational-technical school. The phrase "appropriate training and education" includes securing a GED.
- Amends § 440.491(6)(b), Fla. Stat. by providing as follows:
    - Injured workers earning at least 80 percent of the *compensation rate* are not eligible for training and education.
    - Education Temporary Total Disability benefits are *not* in addition to the maximum entitlement of 104 weeks. The carrier, however, may voluntarily pay additional Temporary Total Disability benefits above the maximum.
    - An employee who refuses recommended vocational training forfeits any additional training and education benefits and any additional payment for lost wages.

Examination of Carriers and Claim-Handling Entities:

- Amends § 440.525, Fla. Stat., as follows.
    - Authorizes the department to audit or investigate any carrier, third-party administrator, servicing agent, or other claim-handling entity to ensure compliance with Chapter 440.
    - Such examinations may occur as often as is warranted.

- If the examination is based on the belief that the entity committed a material violation, the audit may cover a period of up to five years prior to the last review.
- Grants the department the power to secure records and documents by subpoena.
- The department may impose penalties, as follows:
  - $2,500 for each pattern or practice of non-willful violation, not to exceed $10,000.
  - Up to $20,000 for each willful violation, up to a maximum of $100,000 for all violations.
  - Prohibits recoupment of penalties in the rate base.

Criminal Punishment:

- Amends § 921.022, Fla. Stat., the Criminal Punishment Code, by adding the following offenses as felonious criminal acts:
  - The following violations constitute a third degree felony:
    - Receiving an attorney fee or consideration without approval by a judge of compensation claims.
    - Making a false report of workers' compensation fraud or retaliation for making such a report.
  - The following violations constitute a second-degree felony.
    - Failing to obtain workers' compensation coverage.
    - Unlawful solicitation for the purpose of making a workers' compensation claim.
    - Submitting false information to avoid or reduce workers' compensation premiums.

Public Records:

- Amends § 443.1715, Fla. Stat. to authorize the division to provide carriers or their representatives with records of a claimant's wages reported to the division by any employer for the quarter that includes the accident date. Releasing such records requires consent by the claimant or by any employer who paid wages subsequent to the accident date.

Insurer Anti-Fraud:

- Amends § 626.9891, Fla. Stat. by requiring carriers to file annual reports with the department regarding implementing and maintaining an anti-fraud unit or plan.

The following amendments are effective January 1, 2004:

Definitions; Employer:

- Amends § 440.02(8), Fla. Stat. by providing that "construction" does not include homeowners' acts of construction on their own premises if the owner does not intend to sell, resell, or lease the premises within one year after construction begins.
- Amends § 440.02(16)(a), Fla. Stat. by providing that the term "employer" includes employment agencies and employee leasing companies.
- Amends § 440.02(16)(b), Fla. Stat. by providing that a homeowner is not the employer of persons hired to carry out construction work on the homeowner's premises if the property is not intended for immediate lease, sale, or resale.

Definitions; Employee:

- Amends § 440.02(15)(a), Fla. Stat. by defining "employee" as any person who receives remuneration from an employer for performing any work or service.
- Amends § 440.02(15)(b)2, Fla. Stat. by limiting to three the number of corporate officers of a corporation or group of affiliated corporations in the construction industry who may elect to be exempt. Provides that such an officer must be a shareholder owning at least 10 percent of the corporation and must be listed as an officer with the Division of Corporations.
- Amends § 440.02(15)(c)1, Fla. Stat. by providing that sole proprietors and partners, not engaged in the construction industry, are not employees but may elect to be included.
- Amends § 440.02(15)(c)1, Fla. Stat. by repealing the provision providing that sole proprietors and partners who are in the construction industry are employees and may not elect to be exempt.
- Amends § 440.02(15)(c), Fla. Stat. by adding subsection 2, providing as follows:
    - The term "employee" includes an independent contractor working in the construction industry.
    - The term "employee" includes a sole proprietor or partner working in the construction industry.
    - The term "employee" includes all persons being paid by a construction contractor as a subcontractor, unless the subcontractor has a valid exemption or has purchased its own workers' compensation coverage.
- Amends § 440.02(15)(d)1, Fla. Stat. by providing as follows:
    - The status of independent contractor applies only to persons not engaged in the construction industry.
    - Independent contractor status applies only if the contractor meets at least four of the six listed criteria defining an independent contractor.
- Amends § 440.02(15)(d)1, Fla. Stat. by adding subsection (b), providing that a

contractor who does not meet at least four of the criteria defining an independent contractor may still be presumed to be an independent contractor by meeting any one of seven listed conditions.

- Amends § 440.02(15)(d)1, Fla. Stat. by adding subsection (c), providing that a person claiming independent contractor status has the burden of proving such status.
- Amends § 440.02(15)(d)7, Fla. Stat. by providing that a validly exempt corporate officer is not an employee under any circumstances, until the exempt officer files a notice of revocation of the election to be exempt and the notice is effective under the provisions of § 440.05, Fla. Stat.
- Amends § 440.02(15)(d), Fla. Stat. by adding subsection 12, providing that a person working under a Medicaid program served by Adult Day Training Services for training purposes and earning less than the federal minimum wage is not an employee for workers' compensation purposes.

Exemptions From Coverage:

- Amends § 440.05(3), Fla. Stat. by requiring that a corporate officer must include a copy of the stock certificate showing the officer has at least a 10 percent owner interest in the corporation when applying for exemption.
- Amends § 440.05, Fla. Stat. by adding subsection (12), providing that exemptions apply only to the business or trade listed on the exemption notice.
- Amends § 440.05(3), Fla. Stat. by adding subsection (13), providing that the department can revoke an exemption if it determines that the officer no longer meets the requirements for exemption.
- Amends § 440.05(3), Fla. Stat. by adding subsection (14), providing that exempt officers may not collect workers' compensation benefits and that the exempt officer's wages may not be included when carriers calculate premium.
- Amends § 440.05(3), Fla. Stat. by adding subsection (15), providing that a corporate officer is not eligible for exemption if he or she is "affiliated" with a person who is delinquent in paying a stop-work order or penalty assessment. Provides a definition of the term "affiliated person."

Subcontractors:

- Amends § 440.10(1)(c), Fla. Stat., by providing that a contractor must require subcontractors to provide evidence of workers' compensation insurance.
- Amends § 440.10(1)(e), Fla. Stat., by providing as follows:
  - A subcontractor is not liable for providing benefits to the employees of the contractor or other subcontractors.
  - A subcontractor is immune under § 440.11, Fla. Stat., from suits brought by the employees of the contractor or other subcontractors if the contractor or the subcontractor secured workers' compensation coverage for the

subcontractor's employees.

- Immunity does not apply if the subcontractor's own gross negligence caused the injury.

§ 1.25 The 2004 Amendments

Although several proposals for additional, substantial changes to Chapter 440 were put forth, the Legislature had little interest in workers' compensation, apparently preferring to allow time for the massive 2003 amendments to take hold. Still, a few changes were enacted as follows:

- The Legislature approved SB 1534, which appears to be a true "glitch" bill that merely corrects statutory references and typographical errors.
- The Legislature also approved SB 1536, which repeals § 440.185(11), Fla. Stat. protecting a report of injury from disclosure if the report revealed the identity of an ill or injured employee. The original provision was scheduled to sunset (stand repealed) on October 1, 2003, unless reenacted. Under this bill, the Legislature formally repealed the provision.

§ 1.26 The 2005 Amendments

Apparently satisfied with the 2003 amendments, the Legislature made only minor technical changes to Chapter 440 during the 2005 legislative session. Effective on July 1, 2005, the Legislature amended § 440.491(6)(a), Fla. Stat.. The previous version of this statute had provided that approved training and education for an injured worker included training at a community college or a "vocational-technical school." The amendment changes "vocational-technical school" to "career center."

Additionally, the legislature amended the definition of "employee" as it relates to truck owner-operator's [*see* ch.3, § 3.05[6]].

§ 1.27 The 2006 Amendments

The 2006 Legislature did not enact any significant legislation affecting workers' compensation claims. Some minor changes to Chapter 440 include:

- Senate Bill S394, effective upon becoming law, removed the sunset provision contained in § 440.02(13), Fla. Stat. that would have repealed this subsection effective on July 1, 2006.
- Senate Bill S388, effective July 5, 2006, amends § 440.13(1)(g), Fla. Stat. to include in the definition of "Health Care Facility," hospitals licensed under Chapter 429, as well as under Chapter 400, Florida Statutes.
- House Bill H561, effective July 1, 2006, amends § 440.105, Fla. Stat. by repealing subparagraph (2)(a)4. This subsection provided that violating a stop work order constitutes a 1st degree misdemeanor. This bill also amends § 440.105(4)(a)3, Fla. Stat. Previously, this subsection provided that the failure

to secure payment of compensation constituted a crime. The amendment changes this to the failure to secure workers' compensation insurance coverage.

§ 1.28 The 2007 Amendments

The legislature made no significant changes to Chapter 440 Florida Statutes affecting claims, but did add other statutes affecting workers' compensation as follows:

- Adds § 627.442, Fla. Stat. to provide that a person who requires a workers' compensation policy under a construction contract may not reject a policy offered by a self-insurance fund merely because the fund is not rated by a nationally recognized insurance rating service. This statute, if it becomes law, is effective July 1, 2007.
- Adds § 112.1815, Fla. Stat. to change certain burden of proof requirements and to extend additional coverage for firefighters, paramedics, emergency medical technicians, and law enforcement officers (all referred to as first responders). This legislation is effective upon becoming law. The Governor signed this legislation on June 8, 2007. The pertinent provisions are as follows:
    - Provides that the new section applies to both paid and volunteer first responders.
    - Creates a presumption that any adverse result or complication caused by a smallpox vaccination administered to a first responder is a compensable accident.
    - Provides that a first responder can demonstrate a compensable mental or nervous injury by clear and convincing evidence.
    - Creates an exception to the requirement that a compensable mental injury must be accompanied by a compensable physical injury. A first responder, who suffers a mental injury arising out of the employment, but no physical injury, is entitled to medical benefits only.
    - Provides that Indemnity benefits for a mental injury are payable only if the first responder suffers a physical injury.
    - Provides that temporary disability benefits for a first responder are not subject to the limitations under § 440.093, Fla. Stat. or to the 1% limitation on permanent psychiatric impairment benefits.
    - Provides that for first responders, exposure to a specific harmful substance can be shown by a preponderance of the evidence, a reduced evidentiary standard.
    - Changes the definition of occupational disease for first responders by deleting language contained in § 440.151, Fla. Stat., which states that an occupational disease means only a disease for which there are epidemiological studies showing that exposure to the specific substance involved, at the levels to which the employee was exposed, may cause the precise

Guide to Claims

disease sustained by the employee.

- Provides that Permanent Total Disability supplemental benefits do not end at age 62 for first responders if their public employer does not participate in the social security program.

NOTE: At press time for the 2007 Edition of this handbook, the Governor had not signed or vetoed SB 1748 (workers' compensation insurance). Be sure to check the status of the bill before citing to this legislation. A good source is the Florida Legislature website at http://www.leg.state.fl.us/Welcome/index.cfm.

The Rules of Procedure for Workers' Compensation Adjudication [*see* Fla. Admin. Code R. Ch. 60Q] was amended, effective 11/1/2006 [*see* Part VI]. Some notable changes include:

- **Exempt Information on Pleadings.** Fla. Admin. Code R. 60Q-1.103(2) was amended to provide that exempt information on pleadings must be appended in a separate document, conspicuously marked "Exempt information," only to the extent it is necessary to the judge's determination of disputed matters or required by statute.

- **Commencement of Claim.** Fla. Admin. Code R. 60Q-1.105(1) was amended to provide that *an employee or claimant* seeking an award of benefits commences a new case by filing a petition for benefits, when there is no existing case pertaining to the same employee and date of accident.

- **Discovery; Surveillance.** Fla. Admin. Code R. 60Q-6.114(4) was amended to delete the provision that evidence in the nature of surveillance is subject to discovery when it will be used at the final hearing. New subsection (4) now refers to responses and objections to discovery that must be made in accordance with the Florida Rules of Civil Procedure.

- **Mediation; Consolidation of Claims.** Fla. Admin. Code R. 60Q-6.110(1) was amended to provide that all petitions and claims pending at the time a mediation conference is held *are deemed consolidated* and will be mediated at that conference.

- **Mediation; Filing of Report, Stipulations, Settlement Agreement.** Fla. Admin. Code R. 60Q-6.110(7) was amended to provide that, following the conclusion of the mediation conference, the mediator must prepare a report stating which issues or claims in dispute are resolved and which remain unresolved, and whether the parties completed a pretrial stipulation, and identifying by filing date each petition mediated. The claimant must file the report and the mediation settlement agreement, if any, together with any pretrial stipulation executed by the parties, with the judge within five days of the mediation conference.

- **Mediation; Request of Party to Appear by Telephone.** Fla. Admin. Code R. 60Q-6.111(1)(c) was amended to provide that the mediator has the discretion to allow any party to appear at the mediation conference by telephone upon the party's written request furnished to the mediator and the opposing party or, if represented, the party's attorney of record, no fewer than five days prior to the mediation conference.

- **Motion Practice; Request for Order or Other Relief.** Fla. Admin. Code R. 60Q-6.115(1), which provides that all motions must be in writing unless made on the record during a hearing and must fully state the relief requested and the grounds relied upon, now also provides that (1) any request for an order or for other relief must be by motion and must have a title describing the relief requested, and (2) the judge may treat a non-standard request for relief from an unrepresented party as a motion.

- **Motion Practice; Filing of Motion.** Fla. Admin Code R. 60Q-1.115(2) was amended to provide that *except for motions to dismiss for lack of prosecution,* prior to filing any motion, the movant must personally confer with the opposing party or parties or, if represented, their attorneys of record, to attempt to amicably resolve the subject matter of the motion.

- **Motion Practice; Unopposed Motion.** Fla. Admin. Code R. 60Q-1.115(3) was substantially revised to provide that a motion that is unopposed must state why an order is necessary to execute the parties' agreement and, unless filed electronically, must be accompanied by a proposed order that has a title describing the action being taken. The motion and proposed order must specify the relief being requested or ordered in reasonable detail and not merely by reference to any other document.

- **Emergency Conferences.** New subsection (2) was added to Fla. Admin. Code R. 60Q-6.117, which provides that, after reviewing the merits of the request, the judge may summarily enter an order denying the request for an emergency conference or, after proper notice, conduct an evidentiary hearing to consider the request.

- **Expedited Hearings.** New subsection (3) in Fla. Admin. Code R. 60Q-6.118 provides that no mediation conference and pretrial hearing will be held, unless requested in writing by a party within 10 days of service of the notice of expedited hearing.

- **Abbreviated Final Orders.** Fla. Admin. Code R. 60Q-6.119 now provides that any party may request that an abbreviated final order be vacated and that a final compensation order containing separate findings of fact and conclusions of law be entered. The request must be made by motion and must be filed within 10 days of the date of the abbreviated final order sought to be vacated.

- **Summary Final Order; Filing of Motion.** Fla. Admin. Code R. 60Q-6.120(2) has been amended to provide that no motion for summary final order may be filed less than *45 days* prior to a scheduled final hearing.

- **Summary Final Order; Filing of Response.** New subsection (3) was added to Fla. Admin. Code R. 60Q-6.120, which provides that the opposing party must file a response to motion for summary final order together with supporting depositions, affidavits, and/or other documents within 30 days of service of the motion for summary final order. The judge must grant an extension for good cause shown.

- **Evidence.** New subsection (2) was added to Fla. Admin. Code R. 60Q-60Q-6.121, which provides that an objection to the admissibility of evidence not ruled on by the judge is deemed adverse to the party making the objection.

- **Motions for Re-hearing.** Fla. Admin. Code R. 60Q-6.122 was amended by deleting the provision allowing for a motion for re-hearing to call attention to typographical or technical errors, and by adding new subsections (4) and (5), which provide that abbreviated final orders are not subject to a motion for re-hearing and that .a judge, on the judge's own initiative or on the motion of any party, may vacate or amend an order not yet final to correct clerical or technical errors, or when due consideration of a motion for re-hearing cannot be made before the order becomes final, respectively.

- **Settlements Under 440.20(11), Fla. Stat.** Fla. Admin. Code R. 60Q-6.123(1)(a) was amended to include additional documentation regarding child support arrearage and any prior attorney's fee lien that must accompany a joint petition.

- **Attorney's Fees and Costs; Response to Motion.** Fla. Admin. Code R. 60Q-6.124(3)(b) was amended to provide that within *30 days* after the motion for attorney's fees and costs is served, the opposing party or parties must file a response to the motion, which includes a detailed recitation of all matters that are disputed in the form outlined in subsection (3)(a) of this rule.

- **Attorney's Fees and Costs; Report to OJCC.** New subsection (4) was added to Fla. Admin. Code R. 60Q-6.124, which provides that no later than October 1 of each year, all self-insurers, third-party administrators, and carriers must report by electronic transmission to the OJCC the amount of all attorney's fees paid to their defense attorneys in connection with workers' compensation claims during the prior July 1 through June 30 fiscal year.

- **Sanctions.** New subsection (1) was added to Fla. Admin. Code R. 60Q-6.125, which provides that generally. failure to comply with the Rules of Procedure for Workers' Compensation Adjudication or any order of the judge may subject a party or attorney to one or more of the following sanctions: striking of claims, petitions, defenses, or pleadings; imposition of costs or attorney's fees; or such other sanctions as the judge may deem appropriate.

- **Appellate Filing Fee and Costs.** New Fla. Admin. Code R. 60Q-6.127 provides that the procedure for relief from payment of the appellate filing fee and from the costs of the preparation of the record on appeal for the review of any order of a judge on the ground of indigency must be in accordance with Fla. R. App. P. 9.180.

§ 1.29 Substantive vs. Procedural Amendments

[1] Understanding the Difference

Sometimes a statutory change affects all existing claims. Other times a change affects only those injuries occurring after its effective date. Which is which, and the difference in treatment, depends on whether the change is substantive or procedural. The First District Court of Appeal explained the difference between substantive and procedural amendments as follows [*see* Paulk v. School Bd. of Palm Beach County, 615 So. 2d 260, 261 (Fla. 1st DCA 1993)]:

> It has long been established that the parties' substantive rights under the Workers' Compensation Law are fixed at the time of the claimant's accident and injury. . . . However, it is also well established that procedural or remedial enactments may apply without regard to the date of accident and injury, as the parties generally do not have a vested entitlement with regard to such matters. . . . As an analysis of the various decisions in this area would suggest, it is sometimes difficult to clearly demarcate the distinction between a substantive right and a procedural or remedial enactment.

The approved rule is that courts will presume the legislature intended a statute to be prospective and not retrospective when a retrospective effect would work injustice and disturb rights acquired under the former law [*see* Robinson v. Johnson, 110 So. 2d 68, 70 (Fla. 1st DCA 1959)].

> *No one can be sure how courts will interpret any new law or amendment.*
> Susan C. Ross, American lawyer
> The Rights of Women, 1973

[2] Substantive Law

A substantive statutory amendment changes entitlement to, or the amount of, benefits. These laws fix duties and establish rights and responsibilities among and for persons. Courts cannot apply substantive changes retroactively. Strictly defined, substantive law is [*see Barron's Law Dictionary,* Third Edition]:

> That part of law that creates, defines, and regulates rights and duties of parties, as opposed to "adjective, procedural, or remedial law," which prescribes methods of enforcing the rights or obtaining redress for their invasion. The basic law of rights and duties (contract law, criminal law, tort law, law of wills, etc.) as opposed to procedural (law of pleading, law of jurisdiction, etc.).

If an amendment changes the benefit amount an injured worker can receive, or changes an injured worker's entitlement to services, then the amendment is substantive and cannot be applied retroactively. Similarly, if an amendment substantially changes the carrier's liability from what it was when the injury occurred, the law cannot be applied retroactively [Southern Bakeries v. Cooper, 659 So. 2d 339, 341 (Fla. 1st DCA 1995)].

[3] Procedural Law

Procedural laws affect only how employers and carriers provide benefits, or the way they calculate the amount of a benefit. Procedural laws merely define how people may exercise their rights and responsibilities, and how they may enforce them in a court. A procedural change applies to all claims, whatever the date of the accident. Strictly defined, procedural law is [*see Barron's Law Dictionary,* Third Edition]:

> That which prescribes methods of enforcing rights or obtaining redress for their invasion, machinery for carrying on procedural aspects of civil or criminal action, e.g., rules of civil, criminal, and appellate procedure as adopted by the Federal and most state courts.

Deciding whether a statutory change is substantive or procedural can be difficult and sometimes even the best lawyers and judges cannot agree. Usually, when the law does not diminish an injured worker's right to a service, a limitation on the amount paid for the service will not alter a substantive right. Thus, for example, a limitation on the medical fees charged can apply to services performed after the effective date of a statutory limitation [*see* Mr. C's TV Rental v. Murray, 559 So. 2d 452, 453 (Fla. 1st DCA 1990); Williams v. Amax Chemical Corp., 543 So. 2d 277, 279 (Fla. 1st DCA 1989)].

> *Let all laws be clear, uniform, and precise; to interpret laws is almost always to corrupt them.*
> Voltaire, 1764

§ 1.30 Statutory Construction

[1] Statutes Are Construed Liberally

Many appellate decisions have held that the legislature intended the courts to interpret the law liberally in favor of injured workers. Some legislators, however, believed such liberal construction had gone too far. Some legal scholars believed that the most important change for 1990 would be not what the legislature put into the Act, but what it took out. Before the change, the law granted an injured worker significant legal presumptions:

1. That the claim comes within the provisions of this chapter.
2. That sufficient notice of such claim has been given.
3. That the injury was not occasioned by the willful intention of the injured employee to injure or kill himself/herself or another [*see* former § 440.26, Fla. Stat.].

During the 1990 session the legislature repealed that section and created § 440.015, Fla. Stat. This new section required that the facts in workers' compensation cases were not "to be given broad liberal construction." The legislature intended to create a level playing field on which judges could resolve disputes on their merits with neither side having an advantage.

[2] Attempt to Require Conservative Construction Fails

A judge of compensation claims held that § 440.015, Fla. Stat. abolished liberal construction favoring injured workers. One judge also held that the amendment required injured workers to show a prima facie case. The worker must base such a case, said the judge, on a preponderance of competent, substantial evidence to show a causal relationship between an injury and the employment. Disagreeing, the First District Court of Appeal reversed, holding that the amendments did nothing to alter the prevailing law on burden of proof. The state of the law had been (and continues to be) that an injured worker needs only to prove or show a state of facts from which it may be reasonably inferred that the worker suffered an injury during the course and scope of employment [*see* Johnson v. Koffee Kettle Restaurant, 125 So. 2d 297, 299 (Fla. 1960)]. Thus, injured workers need only allege a reasonable set of facts to explain the cause of the injury. Disproving the allegations then becomes the carrier's burden. The court said [*see* Schafrath v. Marco Bay Resort, Ltd., 608 So. 2d 97, 103–104 (Fla. 1st DCA 1992)]:

> In the final analysis, this section [§ 440.015, Fla. Stat.] accomplishes nothing more than a statutory recognition of long-standing legal principles enunciated by Florida courts in workers' compensation cases. This section is obviously directed to precluding a judge of compensation claims from giving a 'benefit of the doubt' to either the claimant or the employer when drawing inferences from predicate facts, a practice heretofore condemned by this court.

Neither the deletion of § 440.26, Fla. Stat., nor the addition of § 440.015, Fla. Stat., said the court, had any affect on the operative burden of proof in workers' compensation cases. Apparently this was not the result that the legislature expected. Effective January 1, 1994, the legislature amended § 440.015, Fla. Stat. again. Now the section provides that the *laws* concerning workers' compensation are to be construed according to the basic principles of statutory construction, and not liberally in favor of either the employee or the employer.

The principles of statutory construction require that courts decide statutory meaning by drawing conclusions about subjects that lie beyond the direct expression of the text from elements known from and given in the text. Courts must look to extraneous connected circumstances, laws, writings, or legislative history bearing on the same or connected matters by seeking and applying the probable aim and purpose of the statute. This provision is clearly the legislative reaction to a long history of perceived judicial legislation. To help guide the courts, the legislature added several statements of its legislative intent throughout Chapter 440 of the Florida Statutes. For example, § 440.015, Fla. Stat. now contains this statement from the legislature:

> It is the intent of the legislature to ensure the prompt delivery of benefits to the injured worker. Therefore, an efficient and self-executing system must be created which is not an economic or administrative burden. The Division of Workers' Compensation shall administer the Workers' Compensation Law in a manner which facilitates the self-execution of the system and the process of ensuring a prompt and cost-effective delivery of payments.

The terms "litigation" and "self-executing" are, of course, mutually exclusive. Perhaps the courts will keep this in mind as they review and figure out the meaning of the Florida Workers' Compensation Act.

[3] Doctrine of Last Antecedent

A basic rule of statutory interpretation is that courts should construe statutes to give meaning to all of the provisions. Put another way, courts should not interpret a statute in such a way as to render it meaningless [*see* Unruh v. State, 669 So. 2d 242, 245 (Fla. 1996)].

Another basic rule, adopted by Florida courts, is the doctrine of last antecedent. This doctrine holds that qualifying words or phrases within a statute are to be applied to the words or phrases immediately preceding them. That is to say, qualifiers should not be applied to words or phrases in other more remote parts of the statute [*see* Southeastern Staffing Servs. v. Florida Dep't of Ins., 728 So. 2d 248, 250 n.7 (Fla. 1st DCA 1998)].

For example, § 440.15(3)(a)3, Fla. Stat. deals with the subject of impairment income benefits. That section provides that the benefits payable are "not to exceed the maximum weekly benefit under s.440.12." Under the doctrine of last antecedent, that phrase must be construed to refer only to impairment income benefits [*see* City of St. Petersburg v. Nasworthy, 751 So. 2d 772, 774–775 (Fla. 1st DCA 2000); *see* Ch 15, § 15.03[6], for a discussion of the practical application of this decision].

The best laws should be constructed as to leave as little as possible to the decision of the judge.
Aristotle c. 322 B.C.

CHAPTER 2

REPORTING: EMPLOYEE, EMPLOYER, AND CARRIER

Guide to Claims

SYNOPSIS

Guide to Claims

§ 2.01 Introduction to Reporting Requirements

This chapter explains administrative reporting requirements for injured workers, employers, and insurance carriers. It includes the method and the time deadlines for employees to report injuries to their employers. Also included are the legal requirements for employers to report employees' injuries to their insurance carriers. Lastly, the chapter explains carriers' duty to report injuries and claim details to the Division of Workers' Compensation. The various requirements are contained in the Workers' Compensation Act and as refined in the Florida Administrative Code.

§ 2.02 Employee Reporting

[1] In General

Employees must report injuries to their employers within 30 days. The Workers' Compensation Act extends this 30-day period to 90 days in occupational disease cases [*see* ch. 8, § 8.01[7]].

Previously, the Act required that "within 30 days after the date of an injury, the employee shall give notice of such injury to the employer." Effective January 1, 1994, the legislature amended this section to read as follows [§ 440.185(1), Fla. Stat. (1994)]:

> An employee who suffers an injury arising out of and in the course of employment shall advise his or her employer of the injury within 30 days after the date of or initial manifestation of the injury. Failure to so advise the employer shall bar a petition under this chapter. . . .

[2] Effect of Failing to Report

If no statutory exceptions to the reporting requirement apply, an employee's failure to report the accident and injury within 30 days will automatically bar a claim. For accidents occurring before January 1, 1994, the key to a defense based on late reporting is proof of prejudice to the employer. Even if the employer can prove it had no knowledge, the defense will fail if the late report did not prejudice the employer. This requirement is often a difficult burden for the employer and carrier to overcome. Apparently, the legislature believed this burden to be an unnecessary one. The legislature repealed the prejudice requirement effective with accidents occurring on or after January 1, 1994.

An injured worker's failure to follow the reporting requirement often lacked any effective punitive result, the reason being that the judges of compensation claims had unlimited authority to forgive any failure to report. The legislature repealed the original statutory authority. Effective January 1, 1994, only the following four statutory exceptions to the reporting requirement exist [§ 440.185(1), Fla. Stat. (1994)]:

1. The employer had actual knowledge of the injury.
2. The employee could not have known the injury was work related without a medical opinion.
3. The employer did not put its employees on notice of the statutory requirements.
4. The judge of compensation claims finds exceptional circumstances outside numbered items one and two, above, that justify such failure.

NOTE: ch. 9, § 9.01, contains a detailed review of the requirements for defending claims using a failure to report argument.

§ 2.03 Employer Reporting

[1] The Rule

For reporting purposes, the administrative rules divide injury severity into four classes: first aid; medical only; lost time; and death. The reporting requirements depend on the severity of the injury.

[2] First Report of Injury or Illness: DFS-F2-DWC-1

Employers must be certain to give a copy of the First Report of Injury or Illness (DFS-F2-DWC-1) to the injured employee for each class of injury described in [3]–[5] and [7], *below* [*see* Fla. Admin. Code R. 69L-24.0231(1)(a) (11/28/2001)].

If the employer reports the accident to the carrier by telephone, the carrier must complete the form and send a copy to the employer and the injured worker within three business days. However, if the claims-handling entity is electronically sending the first report of injury information required in Rule 69L-3.0045, F.A.C., Form IA-1 may be sent to the employee and employer [Fla. Admin. Code R. 69L-3.0045(1) (12/5/96, 01/10/2005)].

SPECIAL ALERT: Previously, the Act provided that all information contained in the first report of injury was confidential and was exempt from the public records law, i.e., § 119.07(1), Fla. Stat. [§ 440.185(11), Fla. Stat. (1998)]. The Act provided that disclosing personal information about an employee was an invasion of that person's privacy. The initial effect was, apparently, to prevent lawyers from using these records for soliciting clients and to prevent employers from using an applicant's accident history as a basis for hiring. However, this provision was repealed on October 1, 2003.

[3] First Aid Cases

First aid cases involve injuries that are treated on the job without paid medical treatment and that do not disable the injured employee for more than one shift [Fla. Admin. Code R. 69L-3.002(13) (1/10/2005)]. Employers need not report first aid cases to their carriers but must record and maintain the following information [Fla. Admin. Code R. 69L-3.004(1)(a) (1/10/2005)]:

1. The employee's name.
2. The employee's Social Security number or other identifying number pursuant to Fla. Admin. Code R. 69L-3.003(3)(b).
3. Date and time of the accident or injury.
4. Occupation of the employee.
5. Who the injury was reported to and when.
6. Description of the accident or illness, including the cause of injury.
7. The injury or illness that occurred and the affected body part.
8. Location address of the injury if different from the employer's address.

[4] Medical Only Cases

Employers must report medical only cases to their carriers within seven days after knowledge of the injury. Medical only cases involve injuries that do require paid medical treatment, but do not cause the employee to lose more than seven days of work [Fla. Admin. Code R. 69L-3.002(20) (1/10/2005)]. Employers must report medical only injuries to their carriers on the First Report of Injury form (DFS-F2-DWC-1), as adopted in Fla. Admin. Code R. 69L-3.025, or report the information regarding the injury or illness by other means, as provided by the claims-handling entity. Employers must report to their carriers within seven days after they know about the injury [Fla. Admin. Code R. 69L-3.004(1)(b), (2)(a) (1/10/2005)]. Failure to file the First Report of Injury with the carrier within the seven-day time limit will subject the employer to a fine of up to $500, assessed by the Division. The amount of the fine depends on the degree of lateness. The minimum fine is $100 for up to a seven-day delay in reporting. If the filing is more than 28 days late, the maximum $500 fine applies [*see* Fla. Admin. Code R. 69L-24.0231(1)(a), (b) (7/21/2004)].

[5] Lost Time Cases

Lost time cases involve injuries that cause the employee to lose more than seven days from work. Lost time cases include any injury entitling the injured employee to indemnity benefits, whether the carrier pays compensation or the employer continues salary instead of compensation. These cases also include disabling injuries to covered volunteer workers, although such workers are ineligible for indemnity benefits because they have no earnings [Fla. Admin. Code R. 69L-3.002(19) (1/10/2005)].

Employers must report lost time cases to their carriers within seven days after knowledge of the injury, using the First Report of Injury form (DFS-F2-DWC-1) and providing a copy to the injured worker. If the employer reports an accident to the claims-handling entity by other means, the claims-handling entity must provide the employee and the employer a completed Form DFS-F2-DWC-1, within three business days after the claims-handling entity's notification of the injury or illness. Form IA-1 (the wage statement) may be sent to the employee and the employer, if the claims-handling entity is electronically sending the first report of injury information required in Fla. Admin. Code R. 69L-3.0045 to the Division [Fla. Admin. Code R. 69L-3.004(1)(b), (2)(a) (1/10/2005); Fla. Admin. Code R. 69L-3.0045(1)(b) (12/5/96, 01/10/2005)].

[6] Wage Statement: DFS-F2-DWC-1a

Besides the First Report of Injury (DWC-1), employers also must file the 13-week wage statement, form DFS-F2-DWC-1a, within 14 days after knowledge of the accident or injury involving lost time as defined in [5], *above*, or when a medical only case becomes lost time. Upon receipt, the carrier must compare the First report of Injury (DWC-1) with the Wage Statement DWC-1a to confirm that the employee name, Social Security number or other identifying information, and the date of injury on the two forms are consistent [Fla. Admin. Code R. 69L-3.0046 (1/10/2005)].

Whenever possible, however, employers should submit the wage statement with the First Report of Injury. Delays in submitting wage information often cause carriers to calculate benefits incorrectly. This not only deprives the injured worker of benefits, but may subject the carrier to assessments of interest, penalties, and attorney's fees. Not sending the DWC-1a to the carrier on time subjects the employer to an additional fine [Fla. Admin. Code R. 69L-24.0231(1)(b) (6/4/97)].

[7] Death Cases

When an injury results in death, the employer must, before filing the First Report of Injury (DFS-F2-DWC-1), notify the Division of Workers' Compensation by telephone or other means within 24 hours after the employer has knowledge of the death. The mailing address for reporting of death cases is: Department of Financial Services, Division of Workers' Compensation, Occupational Safety and Health Unit, 200 East Gaines Street, Tallahassee, Florida 32399-4222. The telephone number for reporting death cases is (800) 219-8953, (850) 413-1611, or by facsimile at (850) 922-0024. In addition, the employer must report the accident to its carrier within seven days after knowledge of the accident [Fla. Admin. Code R. 69L-3.004(2)(d) (1/10/2005)].

§ 2.04 Employer Failure to Report

[1] Causes of Failure to Report

Occasionally, employers do not report injuries to their insurance carriers because the injured worker was not able or available to sign the First Report of Injury (DWC-1). The employee's signature is preferred, but not at the cost of a late report. Employers should send the form to their carriers without the signature and simply write "not available" in the employee signature box [*see* Fla. Admin. Code R. 69L-3.004(2)(a)(1) (1/10/2005)].

[2] Effect of Failure to Report

An employer may create problems for itself and its carrier by refusing to file the First Report of Injury (DWC-1), believing the injury is not work-related. This is an extremely unfortunate error. The workers' compensation law is so complex that most employers are ill equipped to decide compensability. The courts are likely to consider a refusal to accept an employee's accident report, whatever the reason, as equivalent to denying the claim. This may lead to assessment of interest, penalties, and attorney's fees, besides subjecting the employer to fines for late reporting. As the name implies, the First Report of Injury (DWC-1) is required to be filed immediately, even when an employee alleges a farfetched story about a job-related injury or illness—not just when the employer believes the employee was injured.

[3] Penalty for Late Reporting

If an employer fails or refuses to report an accident, the employer is subject to an administrative fine of up to $1,000 for each such failure. If during one calendar year the employer fails to timely submit more than 10 percent of its notices of injury, the fine increases to $2,000 for each such failure. Thus, if an employer reported 10 accidents, and two of them were late, 20 percent would have been reported late, subjecting the employer to the maximum fine [§ 440.185(9) Fla. Stat. (10/1/2003)].

§ 2.05 Coercing Employees

[1] Coercion Defined

Coercion as used here means threatening or firing an employee in retaliation for filing a workers' compensation claim. The legislature intended to prevent such action when it added a new section to the Workers' Compensation Act. This section is brief and provides as follows [§ 440.205, Fla. Stat. (1979)]:

> No employer shall discharge, threaten to discharge, intimidate, or coerce any employee by reason of such employee's valid claim for compensation or attempt to claim compensation under the Workers' Compensation Law.

Note that the section refers to a "valid" claim. The court has held that the word "valid" means meritorious and not frivolous, and that the word does not mean compensable. The effect is that this section applies even if the judge of compensation claims determines that the underlying claim for workers' compensation benefits is not compensable [*see* Smalbein v. Volusia County Sch. Bd., 801 So. 2d 169, 170 (Fla. 5th DCA 2001)].

For further discussion of retaliatory discharge, see LARSON'S WORKERS' COMPENSATION, DESK EDITION, Ch. 104, § 104.07 (Matthew Bender).

Guide to Claims

[2] Coercion Is Criminal Offense and Intentional Tort

Violating § 440.205, Fla. Stat. exposes employers to civil actions as well as to criminal penalties. As of January 1, 1994, violation of § 440.205, Fla. Stat. is a second degree misdemeanor that also creates a cause of action for retaliatory discharge [§ 440.105(2), Fla. Stat. (1/1/94)]. What is worse, the Florida Supreme Court held that this violation is also an *intentional* tort. The extent of possible damage awards is still uncertain and potentially unlimited. A wrongfully fired employee can sue for not only special damages, such as future lost wages, but general damages for emotional distress as well [*see* Scott v. Otis Elevator Co., 572 So. 2d 902, 903 (Fla. 1990)].

Are such awards covered under the Employer's Liability section of the workers' compensation policy? Probably not, since most insurance contracts contain exclusions for intentional acts [*see* ch. 3, § 3.01[2][b][iv]]. Carriers base these exclusions on the logical theory that intentional acts are not accidents.

[3] Employees' Remedies Limited

Florida does not recognize a common-law tort for retaliatory discharge. Instead, the legislature created § 440.205, Fla. Stat. to allow a statutory cause of action for wrongful discharge. Courts must narrowly construe a statute in derogation of the common law. Plaintiffs, therefore, cannot use this section as authority to sue co-employees in their individual capacities. This is because the statute refers to *employers* only [*see* Superior Brands, Inc. v. Rogers, 646 So. 2d 257, 258 (Fla. 1st DCA 1994)].

A question arises as to whether plaintiffs cannot use this section in cases beyond retaliatory discharge. We know, for example, that this section does not allow civil actions to resolve disputes over failing to offer a job or in refusing to accept a job. In other words, workers cannot use this section as a platform to launch allegations of intimidation or coercion [*see* De Oca v. Orkin Exterminating Co., 692 So. 2d 257, 260 (Fla. 3d DCA 1997), *rev. den.,* 699 So. 2d 1374 (Fla. 1997)].

While the statute clearly creates a cause of action for retaliatory discharge, it has not been clear whether the statute creates a cause of action for retaliatory intimidation or coercion where the plaintiff has not been discharged. In a case of first impression, the Fifth District Court of Appeal held that such a cause of action does exist. In a lengthy dissenting opinion, Judge Cobb noted that this decision will allow a companion civil action in Circuit Court alleging intimidation or coercion in every case in which there is a dispute involving rehiring under § 440.15(6), Fla. Stat. [*see* Chase v. Walgreen Co., 750 So. 2d 93, 98–99, 101 (Fla. 5th DCA 1999)].

> **NOTE:** Effective October 1, 2003, the Legislature repealed the "obligation to rehire" provision of § 440.15(6), Fla. Stat.

[4] Evidence and Burden of Proof

Plaintiffs are not required to produce evidence demonstrating the employer's motivation or timing of the decision to fire them relative to the filing of a workers' compensation claim. Courts should allow the case to go before a jury if plaintiffs present evidence showing that their employer and supervisors knew they were applying for workers' compensation benefits when they fired plaintiffs. This is, of course, only an inference of wrongdoing, but an inference is enough to allow a jury to decide the issue. This is true even if such evidence is minimal and largely circumstantial. Additionally, courts should allow testimony by other former employees who claim to have been fired for bogus reasons after they applied for workers' compensation benefits [*see* Silvers v. Timothy J. O'Donnell Corp., 751 So. 2d 747, 748 (Fla. 5th DCA 2000)].

A motion for summary judgment should not be granted unless the pleadings, depositions, answers to interrogatories, and admissions on file, together with affidavits, if any, show that there is no genuine issue of material fact and that the moving party is entitled to a judgment as a matter of law. Further, an appellate court should indulge all *proper inferences* in favor of the party against whom summary judgment is sought [*see* Hodges v. Citrus World, Inc., 850 So. 2d 648, 649–650 (Fla. 2d DCA 2003)].

§ 2.06 Carrier Reporting to the Division

[1] Administrative Procedure

Previously, Division rules required carriers to file only the original of any document. The 2005 Rules allow reproductions that are complete and legible. However, when forms are reproduced, they must be reproduced in their entirety, including instructions [*see* Fla. Admin. Code R. 69L-3.003(1) (1/10/2005)]. In addition, the rules allow carriers to file computer-generated versions of any form if they are substantially the same as the original. However, if the Division finds that a computer-generated form is not the same as the promulgated form, the Division will return the form and the claims-handling entity must make the correction, include a revised "Sent to Division Date," and resubmit a corrected form to the Division. The document will be considered completed and in compliance with this section when the corrected document is resent to the Division and is accepted [*see* Fla. Admin. Code R. 69L-3.003(5) (1/10/2005)].

SPECIAL NOTE: Any insurer or claims-handling entity failing to timely send documents promulgated under this chapter is subject to administrative fines assessed by the Division [Fla. Admin. Code R. 69L-3.003(6) (1/10/2005)].

Carriers must file all forms as described in §§ 2.07 and 2.08. Carriers must ensure that they legibly date-stamp every form upon receipt. All forms must contain the employee's name and social security number and the accident date. Additionally, the carrier section must be complete and must bear the Division-assigned carrier or service company code-number where required.

What happens if the injured worker is an alien and does not have a social security number? In such a case, use the number on the Arrival and Departure Card (Form I-94), or the number on the Alien Registration Card (Form I-151). If the carrier cannot discover the numbers, it must send a written request to the Division's Information Management

Guide to Claims

Unit. The unit will then assign a temporary internal file number until the required identity numbers become available.

What should the carrier do if it finds out the original filing contained an incorrect claimant name, social security number, or other key element? Simply report the correct information by filing form DWC-4, Notice of Action/Change. File this form within 14 days after discovering the error. Be sure to use the old, incorrect information at the top of the form, using only the correct information below. The Division needs the old information as a cross-reference for the new information.

The Division will return any form that is illegible or incomplete. Carriers must return the corrected form or respond to any request for information within 14 days. Note that the document will not be considered completed and in compliance with this section until the corrected document is resent to the Division and is accepted [Fla. Admin. Code R. 69L-3.003(1), (2), (5) (11/8/94)].

> **SPECIAL ALERT:** The terms "file" and "filed" mean the date a party received a document, not the document's mailing date. If the Division returns a document for proper completion, it is not filed until the Division receives the corrected version. Submitting poorly completed forms will likely result in late filing, subjecting the carrier to fines [Fla. Admin. Code R. 69L-3.003(11) (1/10/2005); *see* [2], *below*].

[2] Fines for Late Filing

Rule Chapter 69L of the Florida Administrative Code decrees special fines for late filing of both the First Report of Injury (DWC-1) and the Wage Statement (DWC-1a). These fines apply to each incident of late filing by either the employer or the carrier. The fines for late filing of the DWC-1, for example, range from a minimum of $100 to a maximum of $500, depending on the degree of lateness [*see* Fla. Admin. Code R. 69L-24.0231(1)(a) (1/8/2004)].

For all other forms, the rules do not assign specific fines. Instead the Division assesses fines based on the total filing timeliness. Carriers must file all other forms on time at least 90 percent of the time. If not, the minimum fine is $250. The amount increases depending on how far below 90 percent a carrier's filings fall. If a carrier's timely filing falls below 50 percent, the fine soars to $2,500. If, on a follow-up audit, the carrier is still not in compliance, the minimum fine doubles to $500 and the maximum rises to $2,750 [Fla. Admin. Code R. 69L-24.0231(1)(c), (2) (1/10/2005)].

§ 2.07 Carrier Reporting—First Report of Injury

[1] Medical Only Cases

Carriers need not file medical only accident reports unless the Division asks for them in writing. If the Division requests a report, the carrier must send it within 14 days after it receives the request. The notation "MO Filed Pursuant to Division Request" must be provided in the "Remarks" field of the form [Fla. Admin. Code R. 69L-3.0045(2)(h) (1/10/2005)].

[2] Lost Time and Death Cases

A statutory amendment enacted in 1994 requires that carriers file the DWC-1, Notice of Injury, with the Division "within fourteen days after the *employer's* receipt of the form reporting the injury" [§ 440.185(2), Fla. Stat. (1/1/94)]. This implies that the 14-day filing deadline begins on the day the employee reports an injury to the employer. The Division's rules, however, require carriers to file the DWC-1 form within 14 days after the *carrier's* receipt from the employer, or after receipt of a petition for benefits from the employee.

The rules allow telephone reporting by the employer to the carrier. If the employer notifies the carrier of the injury by telephone or electronic data interchange, the carrier must produce and mail to the employee and the employer a paper copy of Form DFS-F2-DWC-1, within three business days of the carrier's knowledge of the injury [Fla. Admin. Code R. 69L-3.0045(1)(b) (1/10/2005)].

[3] Medical Becomes Lost Time

If a medical only case later involves more than seven days of disability for work, the carrier must file the First Report of Injury form (DWC-1). The same is true if the injured worker files a formal petition for benefits despite no disability for work. In either case, the carrier must file the First Report of Injury form with the Division within 14 days after the *employer* learns about the event. The carrier must be certain that all required sections are complete [Fla. Admin. Code R. 69L-3.045(2)(c) (1/10/2005)].

[4] Denied Claims

If the carrier denies a claim, or entitlement to any benefit, or rescinds a previous denial, it must send the DWC-1 form (Notice of Denial) to the Division within 14 days after the carrier decides to deny or rescind the denial of benefits. The notice must show the benefits sought or previously provided, and the reason for the denial [*see* Fla. Admin. Code R. 69L-3.012 (1/10/2005)].

> **NOTE:** If a doctor or other health care provider had been authorized, a copy of the denial should go there, too, so that the provider is put on notice that the carrier, from that point on, will not pay for any subsequent services.

[5] Electronic Filing

When the First Report of Injury is filed electronically, different rules regarding timeliness apply.

1. If disability is immediate and continuous for eight or more calendar days after the injury, the first report is timely filed if the Division receives it on or before the 21st day after the carrier's knowledge of the injury and is assigned an acknowledgment code of Transaction Accepted (TA).

2. If the first seven days of disability are nonconsecutive or delayed, the electronic filing of the first report is timely if the Division receives it on or before the 13th

day after the carrier's knowledge of the eighth day of disability and is assigned a TA [*see* Fla. Admin. Code R. 69L-24.0231(1)(a) (1/08/2004)].

§ 2.08 Carrier Reporting: Other Documents

[1] Controverted Claims: DWC-12

[a] Initial Denial

Carriers must report a controverted (denied) case, including controverted medical only cases, to the Division. Carriers must file both forms—the DWC-1 form (with Box 1 marked) and the DWC-12, Notice of Denial—within 14 days after receiving the first report of injury or a petition for benefits [Fla. Admin. Code R. 69L-3.012 (1/10/2005)].

When responding to a petition for benefits, list on the DWC-12 only those benefits being denied. If benefits claimed are not in dispute and the carrier has or will pay them, explain this in a separate letter to the party filing the petition.

Remember, carriers must pay or deny claimed benefits within 14 days after receiving a valid petition for benefits. The carrier must send a copy of the Notice of Denial to the employer and the injured worker.

[b] Denial After Benefits Begin

If the carrier originally accepted the claim as compensable and filed the DWC-1 form, but denies compensability later, it should now file only the Notice of Denial (DWC-12). The carrier must do so within 14 days after the date it issues the denial [Fla. Admin. Code R. 69L-3.012 (1/10/2005)].

[c] Denial Rescinded

If after filing a denial (DWC-12) the carrier decides to pay benefits voluntarily, or a judge of compensation claims orders the carrier to pay, the carrier must report this to the Division. Within 14 days after beginning payments, the carrier must do the following [Fla. Admin. Code R. 69L-3.012 (1/10/2005)]:

1. Send a copy of the original DWC-12 to the Division with the "date denial rescinded" section completed.
2. Send form DWC-4, Notice of Action/Change to the Division. The DWC-4 must show the effective date disability began and the injured worker's average weekly wage. Report the average weekly wage in the "previous average weekly wage" section. Report the injured worker's compensation rate in the "previous comp. rate" section on the form.

[d] Denying Wage Loss Benefits

Injured workers request pre-1993 wage loss benefits by sending form DWC-3, Request for Wage Loss/Temporary Partial Benefits, to the carrier. If the calculation shows benefits payable, but the carrier disputes entitlement, it must do the following [Fla. Admin. Code R. 69L-3.012 (1/10/2005)]:

1. Send both the DWC-3 and the DWC-12 to the Division.
2. Attach any documents relating to the injured worker's job search.
3. Send copies of the DWC-3 and DWC-12 to the injured worker.

[e] Denying Supplemental Income Benefits

To claim supplemental income benefits, injured workers must send form DWC-40 to the carrier. This is the Statement of Quarterly Earnings for Supplemental Income Benefits. If the calculation shows benefits payable, but the carrier disputes entitlement, it must send both the DWC-40 and the DWC-12 to the Division with a copy to the injured worker [Fla. Admin. Code R. 69L-3.012 (1/10/2005)].

[2] Medical Bills: DWC-9, DWC-11, and DWC-90

Carriers must date-stamp all medical bills upon receipt and pay or deny them within 45 days [*see* Fla. Admin. Code. R. 69L-7.602(5)]. Effective March 16, 2005, all required medical reports must be electronically filed with the Division by all insurers. The rules are complex and should be consulted [*see* Fla. Admin. Code. R. 69L-7.602(6)].

[3] Pharmacy and Medical Supply Bills: DWC-10

Pharmacy and medical supply providers must bill for their services on form DWC-10. As with all medical bills, carriers must date-stamp the bills upon receipt and pay or deny them within 45 days [*see* Fla. Admin. Code. R. 69L-7.602(5)]. Effective March 16, 2005, all required medical reports must be electronically filed with the Division by all insurers. The rules are complex and should be consulted [*see* Fla. Admin. Code. R. 69L-7.602(6)].

[4] Miscellaneous Medical Bills

This class of bills includes all other providers, such as home health agencies and nursing homes. As with all medical bills, carriers must date-stamp the bills upon receipt and pay or deny them within 45 days [*see* Fla. Admin. Code. R. 69L-7.602(5)]. Effective March 16, 2005, all required medical reports must be electronically filed with the Division by all insurers. The rules are complex and should be consulted [*see* Fla. Admin. Code. R. 69L-7.602(6)].

[5] Funeral Bills

Previously, the Administrative Rules required that carriers pay or deny funeral bills within 14 days after receipt. In addition, the former Rules required that carriers report the payment to the Division on form DWC-13, Claim Cost Report. However, the Rule was repealed, effective 01/10/2005 [*see former* Fla. Admin. Code R. 69L-3.0085 (11/8/94)].

[6] Rehabilitation Bills: DWC-21

Carriers must pay or deny rehabilitation bills within 45 days after receipt and report the payment to the Division on form DWC-21, the Rehabilitation Services Reporting form [Fla. Admin. Code R. 6A-22.010(9)(b) (7/1/96)]. Carriers must send this form to the

Division within 30 days after payment [Fla. Admin. Code R. 6A-22.010(9)(d) (6/26/01)].

[7] Annual Case Status Review: DWC-22

If the injured worker receives impairment income benefits or supplemental income benefits, the carrier must determine "at least annually whether any extended unemployment or underemployment is a direct result of the employee's impairment" [§ 440.15(3)(b)(4), Fla. Stat. (1994)].

If an injured worker, who is receiving permanent total disability benefits, elects to begin a trial work period, the carrier must report this to the Division on form DWC-22. The report is due within 15 days after the carrier approves the trial work period. Within 10 business days after filing the report with the Division, the carrier must mail a copy of the report to the injured worker and the employer [Fla. Admin. Code R. 38F-55.004 (6/26/01)].

[8] Carrier Referral for Division Services: DWC-23

The Act allows and encourages carriers to provide reemployment services voluntarily to injured workers [§ 440.491, Fla. Stat. (1994)]. If the carrier discontinues voluntary services, it must make referrals to the Division for reemployment services on a Request for Screening form DWC-23.

A carrier may make a referral of an injured employee at anytime to the Division to be considered for the Division-provided reemployment services program. Such referrals must also be on form DWC-23. Note that the Division will not consider the form to be complete until it is signed by the injured employee [Fla. Admin. Code R. 6A-22.005 (6/26/2001)].

[9] Notice of Action/Change: DWC-4

Administrative rules require carriers to use specific codes when reporting disability types, reasons for suspending benefits, and adjustments in benefits [Fla. Admin. Code R. 69L-3.0091 (1/10/2005)]. The codes are extensive, so consult the rules before completing the DWC-4 form. Essentially, the DWC-4, must be completed and filed whenever a change in benefits occurs.

SPECIAL NOTE: The Rules require that the carrier send a copy of each DWC-4 form filed to the employer and to the employee/claimant.

[10] Petition for Benefits

The original Claim for Benefits, form DWC-16, and the Application for Hearing, form DWC-17, became obsolete effective January 1, 1994. While the Division has not officially adopted replacement forms, the Office of the Judges of Compensation Claims (OJCC) adopted a format and required its use, effective January 2, 2002. The Petition for Benefits is presently discussed in the Division of Administrative Hearing (DOAH) rules [*see* Fla. Admin. Code R. 60Q-6.101 et seq.]. A copy of the form may be downloaded from the

OJCC website at: http://www.jcc.state.fl.us/jcc/.

[11] Quarterly Payment Report: DWC-50

The 1990 Workers' Compensation Act requires the Division to assess a $50 penalty against carriers for each late payment of compensation. This penalty is in addition to any other penalties or interest [§ 440.20(9)(c), Fla. Stat. (7/1/90)].

The legislature repealed the $50 per late payment requirement, effective January 1, 1994 (this section is now found at § 440.20(8)(c), Fla. Stat. (1/1/94)). The Division will now assess a fine only if the carrier falls below a 90 percent timely payment level. If the carrier makes timely payments at least 90 percent of the time, no penalty is due. If, however, timely payments fall below 90 percent generally, the carrier must pay a penalty of $50 for each late payment. Penalties are due, however, only for those *unjustified* late payments that fall below the 90-percent level.

The maximum total fine for a single quarter is one percent of the carrier's prior year administrative assessment [Fla. Admin. Code R. 69L-24.0231(3) (1/10/2005)]. The Division repealed the Quarterly Payment Report form (DWC-50) and stopped requiring it beginning in the second quarter of 1997. Instead, the Division will discover late payments during audits.

[12] Aggregate Defense Attorney Fee Report: DWC-51

Previously, carriers were required to file an annual report on defense attorney's fees paid during the prior year. This report (DWC-51) was required to be filed with the Division by March 31, each year [Fla. Admin. Code R. 69L-3.0214 (11/25/96)]. The Division repealed this rule, effective January 10, 2005. Because of legislation passed in the 2001 legislative session, the responsibility for collecting and reporting data about attorney's fees was transferred to the Division of Administrative Hearings (DOAH). Therefore, carriers are no longer required to file form DWC-51 with the Division of Workers Compensation [*see* Division of Workers Compensation Bulletin No. 230].

[13] Claim Cost Report: DWC-13

[a] Background

Division rules require that the Claim Cost Report (DWC-13) be filed with the Division of Workers' Compensation for the following cases [Fla. Admin. Code R. 69L-3.016 (1/10/2005)]:

(a) Lost time cases, which include lost time cases in which no indemnity benefits have been paid for compensable volunteers and compensable death cases with no dependents.

(b) Lost time cases in which the employee has received full salary in lieu of compensation for eight or more days of disability.

(c) Cases in which the only indemnity benefits paid were for impairment income benefits, a lump sum settlement, or a final settlement.

Guide to Claims

(d) Denied cases in which indemnity benefits were paid.

[b] Initial Report

Carriers must send the Claim Cost Report to the Division within six months after the accident's date if they pay indemnity benefits. (If the case involves lost time longer than six months after the accident, carriers must file within 30 days after the anniversary date.) Carriers should show that this is the initial report [Fla. Admin. Code R. 69L-3.016 (1/10/2005)].

If the case is closed within six months of the date of accident, the carrier must submit Form DWC-13 and indicate the type of report as "Initial Report Summarizing First Six Months" and "Final Report—Case Closed—No Activity in Past Year or Case Settled."

[c] Annual Report

Follow-up reports are due within 30 days after the accident's anniversary date. Carriers should continue filing the Claim Cost Report every 12 months until they close the case. Carriers should show that this is an annual report [Fla. Admin. Code R. 69L-3.016 (1/10/2005)].

[d] Final Report

When the carrier closes the case, it must file form DWC-13 showing this is a final report. If, after this, the carrier makes additional payments, it must refile, showing this is a "final report-case closed."

Whatever the status of the report, carriers must include the following information [Fla. Admin. Code R. 69L-3.016 (1/10/2005)]:

1. The type of report.
2. The average weekly wage and compensation rate used.
3. The "salary end date" if the employer paid salary instead of compensation. This is the date the employer stopped paying the salary. If the employer continues to pay, the carrier must note that "salary continues in lieu of compensation."
4. The weeks and days paid. This does not apply to pre-1994 impairment benefits or wage loss.
5. The total amount paid including amounts previously reported.
6. Any recoveries the carrier received. This does not include recovery of overpayments.
7. The total paid for lump sum settlement of indemnity and medical benefits. The carrier must report medical only settlements separately.

[14] Request for Wage Loss Benefits: DWC-3 (Accident Dates Through December 31, 1993)

Within five days after its knowledge of the date of maximum medical improvement, the carrier must inform the injured worker about possible entitlement to wage loss benefits. In addition, the carrier must give the worker at least four copies of form DWC-3, Request for Wage Loss Benefits.

When the carrier receives a completed DWC-3, the form must be date-stamped and the request paid or denied within 14 days. If the carrier pays the benefits requested, it must send a copy to the employer and the injured worker with replacement forms. The Rules no longer require carriers to send a copy to the Division [*see* Fla. Admin. Code R. 69L-3.016 (1/10/2005)].

If the carrier denies the request for wage loss benefits, it must report this action on the DWC-3 and distribute copies as above. The carrier must also complete and file form DWC-12, Notice of Denial [Fla. Admin. Code R. 69L-3.016 (1/10/2005)].

[15] Employee Earnings Report

[a] Accident Dates January 1, 1994, to September 30, 2003

Injured workers receiving temporary partial disability benefits must, upon request from the carrier, report any earnings. Earnings include wages, unemployment compensation, and social security benefits. Carriers should request a report by sending form DWC-19, Employee Earnings Report, to the worker. Carriers may not require injured workers to complete the form more than once per month. The injured worker must return the completed form to the carrier within 21 days after receiving it. If not, the carrier can suspend benefits until it receives the form [*see* Fla. Admin. Code R. 69L-3.0191 (1/10/2005); *see also* ch. 14, § 14.01[5][b]].

[b] Accident Dates On or After October 1, 2003

The administrative rules require the carrier to mail an informational letter to the employee and the employer within five business days after the carrier's knowledge of the employee's release to restricted work. This letter must explain the employee's eligibility for temporary partial disability benefits and the obligation to report earnings. These earnings would include the receipt of any of the following: salary, wages, unemployment compensation benefits, or Social Security benefits. The rule describes the required format [*see* Fla. Admin. Code R. 69L-3.01915 (1/10/2005)].

[16] Statement of Quarterly Earnings: DWC-40

Injured workers otherwise eligible for supplemental income benefits must send a report of any earnings and job search activity to the carrier. This information must be included on form DWC-40. Within seven days after paying benefits, the carrier must send the completed DWC-40 to the Division, the worker, and the employer. Simultaneously, the carrier must give the worker at least two blank DWC-40 forms. If the carrier denies benefits, it must attach form DWC 12, Notice of Denial [Fla. Admin. Code R. 69L-3.0193 (1/10/2005)].

[17] Monthly Risk Class/SIC Code Report: DWC-48

Previously, Fla. Admin. Code R. 69L-3.0212 required that, when the carrier did not report the Risk Class Code and the Standard Industrial Code (SIC) on the DWC-1 or the DWC-4, it had to do so on the DWC-48. However, that requirement was repealed, effective January 10, 2005.

[18] Claims Administration Change Report: DWC-49

When a new carrier or service company takes over many claims previously handled by another, the new organization must report this to the Division via the DWC-49 form. If the new carrier or service agent takes over only a single case, notice of change can be submitted on DWC-4, Notice of Action/Change. The report must include a list of all claims affected by the change in administration. The new organization must file this report within 30 days after taking over the claim files [Fla. Admin. Code R. 69L-3.0213 (1/10/2005)].

[19] Social Security Benefits Information: DWC-14

When injured workers collect social security disability benefits, workers' compensation carriers may be entitled to take an offset. Carriers can obtain social security disability benefits information by asking the injured worker to complete and return form DWC-14. Upon receipt of the signed form, the carrier may send it to the Social Security Administration. If this information results in a change in the injured worker's compensation rate, the carrier must send a copy of the DWC-14 to the Division. In addition, the carrier must send a completed form DWC-4 [Fla. Admin. Code R. 69L-3.021 (1/10/2005)].

For more information on social security disability law, see SOCIAL SECURITY PRACTICE GUIDE (Matthew Bender).

[20] Unemployment Compensation Information: DWC-30

When injured workers collect unemployment compensation benefits, they cannot collect any form of total disability workers' compensation benefit. This includes, of course, temporary total and permanent total disability [§ 440.15(10)(a), Fla. Stat.]. If the injured worker is collecting temporary partial disability, the carrier can take an offset equal to the unemployment compensation received. Unemployment benefits are primary, and temporary partial benefits are supplemental only. The sum of the two benefits may not exceed the amount of temporary partial benefits that otherwise would have been payable [§ 440.15(10)(b), Fla. Stat.].

Since the Act does not address any other class of benefit, carriers will likely be prohibited from taking any offset against impairment benefits or supplemental income benefits for accidents after January 1, 1994.

Carriers can obtain unemployment information by having the injured worker complete a release, Form DWC-30, "Authorization and Request for Unemployment Compensation Information" [Fla. Admin. Code R. 69L-3.025 (1/10/2005)]. Once complete, the release is valid for 12 months. Upon the carrier's request, the injured worker must renew the release. If the worker does not respond within 21 days, the carrier can suspend benefits. If the carrier suspends benefits or takes an offset, it must send the DWC-30 to the Division with form DWC-4 [Fla. Admin. Code R. 69L-3.021 (1/10/2005)].

[21] Reporting MMI and Permanent Impairment: DWC-9A

Physicians must use form DWC-9A (6/5/96), Maximum Medical Improvement/Permanent Impairment Determination Certification, to report to the carrier that an injured worker has reached maximum medical improvement or has been awarded a permanent impairment rating. In turn, the carrier must report these medical findings to the Division on form DWC-4, Notice of Action/Change. In addition, the carrier must give a copy to the employer and the injured employee [Fla. Admin. Code R. 69L-7.603 (1/10/2005)].

§ 2.09 Brochures and Electronic Reporting

[1] Informational Brochure for Injured Workers

Originally, the Act required the Division to give workers an informational brochure explaining their rights and benefits. Beginning January 1, 1994, the Act shifted this burden to carriers [§ 440.185(4), Fla. Stat. (1994)]. Carriers must send the brochure to each injured worker within three days after receiving the First Report of Injury (DWC-1). This rule applies to both lost time and medical only cases. With prior approval, the Division will allow carriers to produce an abbreviated version for medical only cases. If carriers choose this option, and a medical only case becomes a lost time case, the carrier must send the original full version of the brochure to the injured worker.

The English version of the brochure is titled "Important Workers' Compensation Information for Florida's Workers" and is designated as form DFS-F2-DWC-60. The Spanish language version is designated as form DFS-F2-DWC-61 [*see* Fla. Admin. Code R. 69L-3.0035 (1/10/2005)].

[2] Informational Brochure for Employers

Each year, carriers must mail a Division-approved informational brochure to their insured employers. The brochure's purpose is to explain the law, benefits, and criminal penalties as they apply to employers [§ 440.185(4), Fla. Stat. (1994)].

The English version of the brochure is titled "Important Workers' Compensation Information for Florida Employers" and is designated as form DFS-F2-DWC-65. The Spanish language version is designated as form DFS-F2-DWC-66 [*see* Fla. Admin. Code R. 69L-3.0036 (1/10/2005)].

[3] Electronic Reporting

The Division has experimented for many years with electronic filing as an alternative to paper forms and reports. The Act not only authorizes electronic filing, but authorizes the Division to require it [§ 440.593, Fla. Stat. (1/1/94)]. At press time, the Division was in the process of developing administrative rules to implement this provision.

Effective October 1, 2001, the Act was amended to authorize the Division to require carriers to submit data electronically either directly or through a third-party vendor. The amendment also authorizes the Division to require that carriers and vendors be certified to submit data electronically and to revoke the certification for noncompliance with performance standards and to assess a civil penalty of up to $500 for each violation [§ 440.593, Fla. Stat. (10/1/2001)].

Administrative rules effective January 10, 2005, allow carriers, as an alternative to paper filing, to file forms DWC-1 and DWC-13 using Electronic Data Interchange (EDI) [*see* Fla. Admin. Code. R. 69L-3.0033 (1/10/2005)].

Pursuant to the Workers' Compensation Medical Billing, Filing, and Reporting Rule, 69L-7.602, Florida Administrative Code, effective July 4, 2004, all required medical bills must be filed with the division via the new electronic data interchange (EDI) submission method (per new flat file layout, revision B) beginning March 16, 2005.

CHAPTER 3

CONFIRMING COVERAGE: UNDER THE POLICY AND UNDER THE LAW

Guide to Claims

SYNOPSIS

Guide to Claims

§ 3.01 Coverage Under the Policy

[1] General Coverage Issues

The first action required in handling any new claim is deciding if coverage exists. Many people often misuse and misunderstand the term "coverage," especially in workers' compensation cases. Here, we must decide two separate coverage issues: (1) whether the insurance policy applies to the loss; and (2) whether coverage exists under the law.

Coverage under the policy relates to an insurance company's contractual duty to assume its insured employer's legal duty to provide the benefits required by law. Therefore, the first step in handling a claim is deciding if the insurer has a valid insurance contract with the employer for the accident date.

Most insurers today use the standard workers' compensation policy form developed by the National Council on Compensation Insurance (NCCI). However, Florida's self-insurance funds typically issue membership agreements, rather than traditional insurance policies.

Workers' compensation policies generally contain two types of coverage under the headings Part One and Part Two. Coverage Part One provides statutory workers' compensation coverage [*see* [2][a], *below*]. Coverage Part Two provides employer's liability coverage [*see* [2][b], *below*]. Note: Originally the insurance industry called these parts "Coverage Part A" and "Coverage Part B."

For general discussion of policy coverage, see LARSON'S WORKERS' COMPENSATION, DESK EDITION, Ch. 151 (Matthew Bender).

[2] The Workers' Compensation Policy

[a] Coverage Part One: Workers' Compensation

Standard policies contain the following significant sections:

A. Declarations

B. Policy provisions

 1. General Section

  a. Workers' compensation insurance

  b. Employers' liability insurance

  c. Other states insurance

  d. Employer duties if injury occurs

  e. Premium

  f. Conditions

Besides these standard sections, the policy may contain a wide array of endorsements that change basic coverage. The declarations page, or information page, is not standard, but is a most important part of the policy for confirming coverage. It lists the insured employer's name, the business address, locations covered, and the states in which the employer conducts its operations. This page also contains the coverage dates, and lists any endorsements such as an increase in coverage limits for employers' liability (coverage Part Two). Finally, the declarations page lists any subsidiaries insured. Always investigate to be sure the injured worker is the employee of the firm listed on the accident report. Sometimes an employer will suddenly "transfer" a worker from an uninsured subsidiary to an insured one.

The workers' compensation part of the policy promises to pay, on behalf of the insured employer, all compensation and other benefits required under the law. In practice the policy adopts the law as the basic insuring agreement. The policy promises to pay all the benefits that the law requires. In addition, the policy provides coverage for the defense costs in litigated claims. It also grants the carrier the exclusive right to negotiate settlements. Lastly, the policy covers any defense costs the employer incurs at the carrier's request.

[b] Coverage Part Two: Employer's Liability

[i] What Is Employer's Liability Coverage

Employers' liability coverage protects employers from other liability resulting from a workplace injury. This is liability exposure not covered under the Workers' Compensation Act or under a general liability policy. Basic workers' compensation coverage applies to only those injuries that arise out of the employment for which statutory remedies exist. Its crafters designed employers' liability coverage to fill any gaps that may exist in the insurance protection between workers' compensation and general liability policies. At first glance this coverage appears unnecessary because, first, the law provides that workers' compensation is an employee's exclusive remedy and, second, Florida law grants employers almost complete immunity from lawsuits brought by employees. Nevertheless, good reasons for this coverage exist [*see* ch. 19, § 19.04[1]].

One reason for employers' liability coverage is that some states do not make workers' compensation insurance compulsory, thus destroying the exclusive remedy doctrine. A second reason for this coverage is that some states allow an injured worker's spouse or dependents to file lawsuits as derivative actions to the primary workers' compensation claim. For example, an injured man's wife may sue for the loss of his services. A third reason is that employers may be sued in a so-called third-party-over action. The injured worker may sue some third party, such as a machine's manufacturer for example, who in turn sues the employer for indemnification [*see* ch. 19, § 19.07]. The most important reason, however, is that general liability policies exclude coverage for such lawsuits because they arise from a workplace injury. Employers' liability coverage is, therefore, the only protection an employer has in such cases.

The basic employer's liability coverage limit for these claims is $100,000. Many insurers, however, offer higher limits in exchange for increased premiums. This is another good reason for claims adjusters to check coverage as the first step in handling any claim.

[ii] Exclusive Remedy

[A] Required Conditions

Florida employees cannot sue their employers in tort for a workplace injury if three conditions exist.

1. The first protective condition is that the employer must have provided workers' compensation insurance coverage by buying a policy or qualifying as a self-insurer.
2. The second protective condition is that the employee must have suffered an injury covered under the workers' compensation law.
3. The third protective condition is that the employer's actions, or inactions, did not amount to an intent to injure the worker or were not substantially certain to cause injury.

For example, Tyrone Townsend was injured on the job when a wooden railing gave way. He filed a workers' compensation claim and while represented by counsel formally settled his claim and executed a general release. He then sued the employer in the circuit court. The court dismissed the suit via summary judgment. On appeal, the Second DCA affirmed and held that the suit against the employer for injuries was barred by the doctrine of election of remedies. The court also held, however, that the employee's suit against the employer for spoliation of evidence was not barred by the election of remedies doctrine [*see* Townsend v. Conshor, Inc., 832 So. 2d 166, 167–168 (Fla. 2d DCA 2002), *rev. denied,* 2002 Fla. App. LEXIS 20272 (Fla. 2d DCA Dec. 19, 2002)].

[B] The No Coverage Exception

If a nonexempt employer fails to obtain workers' compensation coverage, the law gives the injured employee two choices. First, the employee can claim compensation benefits from the uninsured employer under the workers' compensation statutes, Ch. 440, Fla. Stat. Second, the employee can instead choose to sue the employer for damages in a civil action. The employee must choose one remedy, however, and cannot pursue both [Pearson v. Harris, 449 So. 2d 339, 342–343 (Fla. 1st DCA 1984); Chorak v. Naughton, 409 So. 2d 35, 38 (Fla. 2d DCA 1981); Hume v. Thomason, 440 So. 2d 441, 442 (Fla. 1st DCA 1983); McKee v. Greene, 360 So. 2d 158 (Fla. 3d DCA 1978); Matthews v. G.S.P. Corp., 354 So. 2d 1243, 1244 (Fla. 1st DCA 1978)].

[C] The Non-Work Injury Exception

The exclusive remedy and election of remedy doctrines do not apply if the injury occurs outside the worker's employment. A worker who passively accepts benefits is not making an election of remedy. Therefore, voluntary payments by the employer will not bar a lawsuit against it if the injured worker has not filed a Petition for Benefits under the workers' compensation system [Velez v. Oxford Development Co., 457 So. 2d 1388, 1390–1391 (Fla. 3d DCA 1984); *see* [iii], *below*].

Conversely, denying benefits may allow the employee to maintain an action in tort. This is based on the theory that if the employer and carrier deny that an injury occurred at work, immunity and exclusive remedy cannot apply. For example, Audrey Byerley clocked out at the end of the work day. She tripped and fell while walking to her car. The carrier denied her claim on the basis that she was not in the course and scope of her employment at the time. Based on this denial, Byerley filed a tort action. The employer defended on the grounds that it was immune under the provisions of § 440.11(1), Fla. Stat. (1995). The Fifth District Court of Appeal disagreed. The court, apparently, interpreted the statute's meaning to be that the failure to "secure the payment of compensation" is the same as denying entitlement to benefits. The court held that an employee who has been denied compensation for an injury may either file a petition for workers' compensation benefits or sue the employer for damages. Because the carrier denied that a work-related injury had occurred, the employee was entitled to rely on that assertion. Thus, the act of denying compensation created an estoppel precluding the employer and carrier from raising the immunity defense.

In a footnote, the court noted that the statute prohibits employers from asserting the common-law defenses of negligence of a fellow employee, assumption of risk, and comparative negligence [*see* Byerley v. Citrus Pub., Inc. 725 So. 2d 1230, 1232, n.1 (Fla. 5th DCA 1999)].

[D] The Sexual Harassment Exception

Cases involving sexual harassment at work can create a situation allowing the injured worker to both collect workers' compensation benefits and to sue the employer. For example, Carol Moniz was injured in an attack by her supervisor in which she claimed he bit her and bruised her neck. In addition, she claimed he had persistently harassed her over time with unwanted touching, sexually suggestive comments, and threats of firing her if she did not "do the right thing." Moniz brought a workers' compensation claim for physical injuries suffered in the biting incident and, while that claim was pending, sued her employer and her supervisor for sexual harassment and retaliation.

The court, in ruling for Moniz, held that these occurrences constituted separate events: (1) the biting incident entitling her to economic damages under workers' compensation, and (2) the pattern of harassment entitling her to intangible injuries to her personal rights compensable by tort. Thus, the court held that Moniz could maintain these separate actions, and that claiming workers' compensation benefits did not constitute an election of remedies. If injuries from sexual harassment are separable, as here from injuries inflicted by assault, no election of remedy is necessary because each affords distinct rights [*see* Moniz v. Reitano Enterprises, Inc. 709 So. 2d 150, 153 (Fla. 4th DCA 1998)].

[E] The OSHA Violation Exception

The Workers' Compensation Law itself contains an exception to immunity when the employer has violated a law for which the maximum penalty exceeds 60 days imprisonment [*see* § 775.082, Fla. Stat.]. The question becomes whether this exception applies to violations of the federal law, such as the Occupational Safety and Health Act (OSHA). The answer is that it does. The court has held that a safety regulation violation (whether contained in state or federal law), which is so serious as to subject the violator to imprisonment for more than 60 days, also deprives the employer of workers' compensation immunity [*see* Gerth v. Wilson, 774 So. 2d 5, 7 (Fla. 2d DCA 2000), *rev. denied,* 789 So. 2d 352 (Fla. 2001)].

[iii] Passively Accepting Benefits Is Not an Election

Without an election of benefits, nothing will prevent an employee from later claiming that the injury did not occur on the job. To show remedy election, the employee must actively and consciously prosecute a workers' compensation claim. If so, that employee cannot later sue the employer and claim the injury arose out of the employment [Greene v. Maharajah of India, Inc., 485 So. 2d 1329, 1331–1332 (Fla. 1st DCA 1986)].

Filling out, signing, and submitting wage loss request forms *is not* active prosecution of a workers' compensation claim. As active as this may seem, it is still passive acceptance of benefits. Only literal and formal prosecution counts. Prosecution means the employee must file a formal claim or Petition for Benefits. Otherwise, accepting benefits is passive and the employee can at any time reject these benefits and sue the employer, claiming the injury was not work-related [Holder v. Waldrop, 654 So. 2d 1059, 1061 (Fla. 1st DCA 1995)].

If the injured worker prosecutes a claim and accepts compensation, the law will not allow the worker to deny employee status. For example, the carrier denied Randall Michael's claim, arguing that Michael was an independent contractor and not entitled to benefits. The judge of compensation claims agreed with the carrier and denied benefits. Michael appealed. Before the case reached the court of appeals, however, Michael and the carrier agreed to a lump-sum settlement, which the judge of compensation claims approved. Despite having accepted a workers' compensation settlement, Michael then sued his employer in tort.

The trial court granted the employer's motion for summary judgment and dismissal. The Fourth District Court of Appeal agreed and affirmed the order. Since Michael actively pursued and then accepted workers' compensation benefits, he elected his remedy. Having done so, it became irrelevant whether he was actually an employee [Michael v. Centex-Rooney Const. Co., 645 So. 2d 133, 135–136 (Fla. 4th DCA 1994)].

[iv] Immunity for Intentional Tort

Does employer immunity apply even if the employee's injury results from the employer's intentional tort? The answer is no [Eller v. Shova, 630 So. 2d 537, 539 (Fla. 1993)]. Originally, the courts concluded the statutory immunity was absolute and included intentional actions. For example, in 1985 the Fourth District Court of Appeal held that even an intentional tort does not disturb the statute's exclusive remedy provision. The Court of Appeal, however, certified the question of immunity for intentional torts to the Florida Supreme Court in two cases. In both cases the Supreme Court did not address the question, finding the employers' acts were not intentional torts and thus rendering the certified question moot. For further discussion, see [v], *below*.

[v] What Is an Intentional Tort

[A] Intent Defined

For an employer's actions to amount to an intentional tort, the employer must either exhibit a deliberate intent to injure or engage in conduct that is substantially certain to result in injury or death [*see* Fisher v. Shenandoah Gen. Const. Co., 498 So. 2d 882,

Guide to Claims

884–888 (Fla. 1986); *see also* Lawton v. Alpine Engineered Products, Inc., 498 So. 2d 879, 881–882 (Fla. 1986)].

Note carefully, that *Fisher* and *Lawton* created two alternative bases for an employee to prove an intentional tort. Those alternatives are as follows:

1. That the employer exhibited a deliberate intent to injure, *or*
2. That the employer engaged in conduct which was substantially certain to result in injury or death.

The first alternative is virtually impossible to prove. The second standard is considerably more nebulous and is discussed at length in [B], *below.*

In 1990, the First District Court of Appeal held that the Workers' Compensation Act preserves immunity even against actions based on strict liability. In 1993, the Florida Supreme Court finally answered the certified question. The immunity provision does not apply if the employer has engaged in any intentional act designed or *substantially certain*to result in an employee's injury or death [Eller v. Shova, 630 So. 2d 537, 539 (Fla. 1993)].

Since this opinion, many plaintiffs have seized on the phrase "substantially certain" to support lawsuits against employers. They have been encouraged by cases such as *Connelly v. Arrow Air, Inc.,* 568 So. 2d. 448 (Fla. 3d DCA 1990). Here, the court held that several of the employer's acts constituted substantial certainty of injury or death. These included routinely overloading a passenger aircraft, and withholding information from the employee-pilot about dangerous mechanical problems. (In this case, the airplane crashed.)

Relying on *Connelly,* Pio Timones sued his employer, Excel Industries of Florida. Timones was injured when his chair fell backward, causing him to accidentally place his hand into a buffing machine. The machine's safety switch was out of reach, so he could not turn it off. Timones alleged that Excel required him to use an unsafe machine. This failure, Timones argued, occurred despite the fact that safety advisors had informed Excel about a safety problem with the equipment. As proof, Timones claimed that these machines had caused injury to 48 other employees. Excel defended based on § 440.11, Fla. Stat. immunity. The trial court granted Excel's motion for summary judgment and dismissed the case. On appeal the First District Court of Appeal agreed with the trial court. To state a cause of action for an intentional tort sufficient to avoid § 440.11, Fla. Stat. immunity, the employee must allege ultimate facts showing the employer either exhibited a deliberate intent to injure or that it engaged in conduct substantially certain to result in injury or death. A strong probability, however, is not enough. The law requires virtual certainty, and requiring employees to operate unsafe machinery is not sufficient [Timones v. Excel Industries of Florida, 631 So. 2d 331, 332–333 (Fla. 1st DCA 1994)].

SPECIAL NOTE: The Florida Supreme Court has disapproved of the subjective measurement standard used in *Timones* and has, instead, adopted a "reasonable person" standard, discussed in [B], *below.*

[B] Objective vs. Subjective Standard

As noted in [A], *above,* a plaintiff who cannot show that the employer intended to injure him or her might still prevail if he or she can show that the employer engaged in conduct that was substantially certain to result in injury or death. The question becomes what standard should be used to measure and decide "substantial certainty." Should the standard be objective or subjective?

A subjective standard, and the standard adopted by the courts to this point, requires proof that the employer actually knew or intended the consequences of its conduct. That, of course, is essentially the same as proving that the employer actually intended to cause injury and therefore does not create any real alternative. The Florida Supreme Court now holds that courts must use an objective standard.

An objective standard requires only an analysis of the circumstances to determine whether a reasonable person would understand that the employer's conduct was substantially certain to result in injury or death to the employee. Put another way, this test requires showing that the employer *should have known* that its conduct would cause injury. Therefore, the employer's actual intent is not controlling in deciding whether immunity applies. That is to say, where a reasonable person would believe that a particular result was substantially certain to follow, he or she will be held in the eyes of the law as though he or she intended it.

The Court noted that workers' compensation responds only to workplace accidents that are unexpected or unusual. If a workplace circumstance is substantially certain to produce injury or death, it cannot be said that the result is unexpected or unusual and thus such an event should not be covered under workers' compensation immunity. Showing its distaste for the lower courts' inclination to dismiss such cases, the Court opined that the legislature did not intend workers' compensation immunity to be used to create a shield for employers to block intentional tort suits at the summary judgment phase. All of this can be summed up as follows:

1. Immunity does not apply if the employer actually intended to injure the employee.
2. Immunity does not apply if the employer engaged in conduct substantially certain to result in injury to the employee.
3. An objective standard should be used to decide whether the employer engaged in conduct which was substantially certain to result in injury.
4. If objective evidence shows that injury was substantially certain to occur, intent is imputed to the employer and immunity does not apply [*see* Turner v. PCR, Inc., 754 So. 2d 683, 686–691 (Fla. 2000)].

[C] Burden of Proof

In an apparent effort to overrule the Supreme Court's *Turner v. PCR* decision, the Legislature enacted a burden of proof standard that the employee must meet to establish that an employer's actions or inactions constitute an intentional tort. In *Turner*, the Supreme Court held that if objective evidence shows that injury was *substantially* certain to occur, intent is imputed to the employer, and immunity does not apply [*see* Turner v. PCR, Inc., 754 So. 2d 683, 686–691 (Fla. 2000)]. The Act now provides that *virtual*

Guide to Claims

certainty is required and that the employee has the burden of proof.

The Act provides that to establish that the employer committed an intentional tort resulting in the employee's injuries, the employee must prove the following by clear and convincing evidence:

1. That the employer deliberately intended to injure the employee; or
2. That the employer knew that its conduct was *virtually* certain to result in injury. The employer's knowledge of such virtual certainty must be established by showing the following:
    a. That similar accidents occurred in the past; or
    b. That the employer had received explicit warnings specifically identifying a known danger; and
    c. That the employee was not aware of the risk because the danger was not apparent; and
    d. That the employer deliberately concealed or misrepresented the danger so as to prevent the employee from exercising informed judgment about whether to perform the work.

This will be an extremely difficult burden to overcome. Essentially, the employee must prove that the employer intended to cause the injuries either by direct action or by inaction. Absent pure intent, the employee may overcome immunity only by showing that the employer knew that an injury was virtually certain to occur because of hidden risks, but the employer deliberately concealed or lied about the danger. This is a substantive amendment that applies only to accidents occurring on or after the amendment's effective date of October 1, 2003 [*see* § 440.11(1)(b), Fla. Stat. (10/1/2003); Bombay Co. v. Bakerman, 891 So. 2d 555 (Fla. 3d DCA 2004), *rehg denied*, 2005 Fla. App. LEXIS 2645 (Fla. 3d DCA Feb. 2, 2005)].

[vi] Case History

Following are examples of employees' lawsuits against their employers that failed for lack of evidence of an intentional tort.

SPECIAL NOTE: Some or all of these cases may no longer be good law in light of the Florida Supreme Court's decision in *Turner,* and the burden of proof standard the Legislature enacted in § 440.11(1)(b), Fla. Stat., effective October 1, 2003. Because the amendment apparently overrules *Turner*, it is probably a substantive amendment. For injuries occurring through September 30, 2003, consider whether a jury would conclude that the employer should have known there was substantial certainty that the injury would occur [*see* [v][B], *above*]. For injuries occurring on or after October 1, 2003, consider whether the employee can meet the statutory burden of proof standard, thus establishing that the employer actually knew there was virtual certainty that the injury would occur [*see* [v][C], *above*].

Case 1. Substantial Certainty. An enraged customer went on a shooting rampage and killed or wounded several employees. The estates of two of the deceased employees sued the employer, GMAC, claiming it was grossly negligent in failing to provide proper security for its employees. The trial court denied summary judgment. The District Court of Appeal reversed and remanded, holding GMAC was immune due to lack of substantial certainty under § 440.11, Fla. Stat. [*see* GMAC v. David, 632 So. 2d 123 (Fla. 1st DCA 1994), *rev. dismissed,* 639 So. 2d 976 (Fla. 1994)].

Case 2. Failure to Comply With OSHA Regulations. Dennis Alderman fell from a poorly constructed scaffold. He broke his neck in the fall and was rendered paraplegic. Although the employer built the scaffold, Alderman sued the general contractor. He claimed that the general contractor failed in its duty to ensure that his employer complied with OSHA regulations. He argued that this failure amounted to an intentional tort. The Third District Court of Appeal disagreed and ordered the lawsuit dismissed [*see* Pinnacle Const., Inc., v. Alderman, 639 So. 2d 1061, 1062–1063 (Fla. 3d DCA 1994)].

Case 3. Intentionally Mispresenting Dangerous Conditions. Betty Keffer worked as a detailer, cleaning fire trucks for a company called Emergency One. Evidence showed Keffer had to use a metal-banded detail brush, with flammable lacquer thinner, to clean places on the trucks where her hand would not fit. One such place was the battery compartment that held live 24-volt batteries bearing decals with the warnings, "explosive" and "no smoking." Nearby were drums of lacquer thinner marked "flammable." Besides all these hazards, the live-charged batteries emitted flammable hydrogen gas. Instances existed where electrical arcs had extended from electrical sources to the metal-banded brushes, and Emergency One knew about this. Despite her request for safer plastic brushes, Keffer's supervisor refused to buy them because of the additional expense. Later, Keffer was seriously injured while detailing a battery case. The metal band on her paint brush caused an electrical arc that ignited the lacquer thinner, severely burning Keffer. The court chose to continue the strict interpretation of the workers' compensation immunity provision despite noting earlier, similar cases that held employers liable. In those cases, however, strong evidence showed that the employer tried to deceive or cover up the danger involved. This prevented the employees from learning about the dangers involved and thereby deciding what they should do. In Keffer's case, evidence showed that she worked in a dangerous environment. No competent evidence, however, supported the argument that Emergency One intentionally misrepresented the dangers involved. Another allegation was that Emergency One withheld safety precautions, but the court found no evidence of a concerted intentional effort to do so. Thus, the court reversed the circuit court's refusal to enter summary judgment in Emergency One's favor and remanded the case for further proceedings [*see* Emergency One, Inc. v. Keffer, 652 So. 2d 1233, 1235 (Fla. 1st DCA 1995)].

Case 4. Negligent and Cavalier Attitude About Worker Safety. Blanca Rubio's job required her to work using a meat tenderizing machine. The machine was designed to be bolted down, but the employer left it free-standing on a table top. Someone had removed the machine's hopper cover with the manufacturer's safety warnings. Even worse, the machine had been repaired in a way that bypassed the emergency cut off switch. Compounding all this, Rubio had never been trained on this machine. Predictably, Rubio caught her hand in the tenderizing blades while she was placing meat into the machine, resulting in serious injury. The Court of Appeal held that although the employer had a negligent and cavalier attitude about its employees' safety, this alone is not an intentional tort. The court went further, holding that there was not even sufficient evidence to meet the gross negligence standard such that Rubio could support a cause of action against corporate officers and managers. The Court of Appeal reversed the Circuit Court's refusal to enter summary judgment and ordered it to enter judgment for the employer [*see* Kline v. Rubio, 652 So. 2d 964, 965–966 (Fla. 3d DCA 1995)].

Case 5. Knowledge and Appreciation of Risk. Kenann & Sons Demolition company secured a contract to demolish bleachers at a school in Broward County. Vittorio Forgiarini offered to do the job for free, expecting to profit by reselling the scrap steel. During the demolition operation a crane-truck struck Michael DiPaolo, one of Forgiarini's employees. DiPaolo sued Kenann & Sons and its owners, alleging both intentional tort and gross negligence. The acts alleged included hiring an unskilled, unprofessional, and unlicenced scrap dealer to perform the demolition work. This, DiPaolo claimed, resulted in recklessly performed work, without regard for the workers' safety. The Court of Appeal disagreed. Mere knowledge and appreciation of risk is not intent. If the risk is appreciable, negligence may exist; if the risk is great, the conduct may be reckless or wanton, but it is not an intentional wrong [*see* Kenann & Sons Demolition, Inc. v. DiPaolo, 653 So. 2d 1130, 1131–1132 (Fla. 4th DCA 1995)].

Case 6. Knowingly Subjecting Workers to Dangerous Conditions. Marcel Subileau fell to his death from an elevated construction site. His widow sued his employer, Southern Forming, claiming an intentional tort. Southern Forming admitted that the Occupational Safety and Health Administration had issued several citations for failing to provide guardrails and other safety devices. The company also admitted it knew about injuries suffered by other employees when they fell from elevated work-sites. Although Southern Forming knowingly subjected its employees to dangerous working conditions, the court held this knowledge did not amount to substantial certainty. After all, said the court, the dangers or hazards were obvious and the employees knew about them. The court affirmed the lower court's summary judgment in Southern Forming's favor [*see* Subileau v. Southern Forming, Inc., 664 So. 2d 11, 12 (Fla. 3d DCA 1995)].

Case 7. Removing Safety Devices. Leon Snyder was injured when his riding lawn mower flipped over and ejected him. A few days before, Snyder's supervisor had removed a malfunctioning safety switch. The safety switch was designed to kill the engine when the rider dismounted. When Snyder sued his employer, the trial court refused to grant the employer's motion for summary judgment under § 440.11, Fla. Stat. immunity. On appeal, the Fifth Court of Appeal reversed, holding that removing the safety switch did not amount to an intentional tort [*see* Mekamy Oaks, Inc. v. Snyder, 659 So. 2d 1290, 1291 (Fla. 5th DCA 1995)].

Case 8. Removing Safety Devices and OSHA Violations. John Shafer was working in a trench, 10 to 15 feet deep, when dirt from the side caved in on him. Shafer sued his employer, pointing to several OSHA violations as evidence of the employer's intentional tort. Violations included failing to have a trench shield in place, failing to slope the trench properly, failing to provide an emergency evacuation ladder in the trench, and failing to train the supervisor properly in safety procedures. Based on this, the trial court refused to grant the employer's motion for summary judgment. The Fifth District Court of Appeal reversed, noting the Supreme Court's holding that violating OSHA guidelines is not an intentional tort [*see* J. B. Coxwell Contracting, Inc. v. Shafer, 663 So. 2d 659, 660 (Fla. 5th DCA 1995), *rev. denied,* 673 So. 2d 30 (Fla. 1996) (citing Fisher v. Shenandoah Gen. Const. Co., 498 So. 2d 882, 883 (Fla. 1986))]. The court held that even if the employer did remove safety devices and violate OSHA regulations to speed up completion of the project, none of this amounts to an intentional tort [*see* J. B. Coxwell Contracting, Inc. v. Shafer, 663 So. 2d 659 (Fla. 5th DCA 1995), *rev. denied.* 673 So. 2d 30 (Fla. 1996)].

Case 9. Maintaining Dangerous Instrumentalities. Arthur Clements worked as a maintenance man for the St. Augustine Alligator Farm. He was cleaning drains with a pool skimmer in the pool area of a four-foot high enclosure that housed Cuban crocodiles. His employer had borrowed the animals from the New York Zoological Society. A seven-foot crocodile jumped and seized Clements' left arm in its jaws. The resulting, massive injuries necessitated amputation of his arm. Clements sued the Society as the owner of the crocodile, arguing that it should be held strictly liable for failing to warn of the unusually dangerous and aggressive characteristics of Cuban crocodiles and in failing to provide workers with appropriate safety measures. The Society argued that it was entitled to the same immunity as Clements' employer. The trial court agreed with the Society and granted the Society's motion for summary judgment on the basis of immunity under § 440.11, Fla. Stat., and the 5th DCA affirmed. The court held that the owner of a dangerous instrumentality enjoys the same immunity from a tort action as the employer to whom it is leased, and who controls it. The court explained that the crocodile became a "working tool" of the Alligator Farm when the Society transferred possession to the farm [*see* Clements v. Wildlife Conservation Soc'y, 750 So. 2d 715, 716–717 (Fla. 5th DCA 2000)].

Case 10. Failure to Remove Violent Employee. Stacy Holderbaum was murdered by an employee that she had fired earlier in the day. Upon his dismissal, the employee had publically threatened her life. Coworkers knew that the employee kept a pistol at the workplace. Despite this knowledge, the company's management did not take the employee's threats seriously and took no action. The court held that such inaction may constitute gross negligence or even culpable negligence, but falls short of the intentional tort necessary to overcome the employer's statutory immunity [*see* Holderbaum v. ITCO Holding Co., 753 So. 2d 699, 700 (Fla. 3d DCA 2000)].

[vii] Review of Non-Final Orders Rejecting Immunity

[A] Motions to Dismiss and Summary Judgment

The cases in [vi], *above,* were holdings based on appeals from lower court orders denying summary judgment based on statutory immunity. New rules of procedure and the Florida Supreme Court hold that such orders are now non-final and therefore non-appealable. An exception arises only if the order asserts that the employer is not entitled to immunity as a matter of law [*see* Hastings v. Demming, 694 So. 2d 718 (Fla. 1997)].

The rule provides that "[r]eview of non-final orders of lower tribunals is limited to those that . . . determine . . . that, as a matter of law, a party is not entitled to workers' compensation immunity . . ." [Fla. R. App. P. 9.130(a)(3)(c)(vi)].

In a subsequent case, the First District Court of Appeal held that the Supreme Court's holding in *Hastings* also applies to motions to dismiss. Therefore, orders denying motions to dismiss and motions for summary judgment are non-final orders that cannot be appealed unless the exception applies. As Judge Wolf noted in a concurring opinion, the exception will rarely arise [Martin Electronics Inc., v. Glombowski, 705 So. 2d 26, 31 (Fla. 1st DCA 1997)]:

> As a practical matter, orders denying motions to dismiss or motions for summary judgements will often be drafted by a plaintiff's attorney or by a trial judge who may be gun-shy of an appeal. We can expect that such orders will simply deny the motion without explanation or be drafted to be ambiguous. Thus, many parties entitled to immunity may be forced to go to trial.

If an injured worker can make a case based on an intentional tort, there will likely be no coverage under Part Two, Employer's Liability, of the standard workers' compensation policy. This is because either the policy specifically excludes intentional torts or the employer's actions will not meet the basic requirement of *accidental* injury. Review the particular policy carefully.

[B] Procedure for Review of Summary Judgment

When a party moves for summary judgment, the opposing party must come forward with counter-evidence sufficient to reveal a genuine issue of material fact. For example, the employee claimed that the general contractor, Konover, committed an intentional tort during the construction process by instructing an electrical subcontractor to remove the safety and protective breakers from an electrical outlet station. He then alleged that he was injured when he received a severe electrical shock while attempting to plug an extension cord into that outlet station.

Konover subsequently filed a motion for summary judgment, claiming workers' compensation immunity. In support of that motion, it filed the sworn affidavit of its supervisor for the construction site, who stated that he did not instruct anyone to remove or cause to be removed the safety and protective breakers from the relevant outlet station. The supervisor also explained that he did not know of any individual affiliated with Konover who gave said instruction or removed the breakers. The employee, however, did not file any counter-evidence in response to the supervisor's affidavit.

The court held that this affidavit was sufficient to shift the burden to the employee to come forward with any counter-evidence to show a genuine issue of material fact. Because he failed to meet that burden, the court affirmed summary judgment [*see* Glasspoole v. Konover Constr. Corps., 787 So. 2d 937, 938 (Fla. 1st DCA 2001)].

[viii] Adjuster Action Required

Claims adjusters should treat a summons and complaint as an extremely important document. Immediately assign a defense attorney to respond to the lawsuit properly. Leaving an employer defenseless in such cases can be very dangerous. If the employer does not hire its own attorney, the result may be a default judgment. A default judgment means the court will award damages to the plaintiff without the defendants being heard in their own defense. This is intended as punishment for the defendants' failure to appear at the trial. If a court later decides the carrier did have coverage, the carrier will be liable for the entire judgment. What happens if the court decides the carrier acted in bad faith in refusing to defend? The carrier may be liable for damages in amounts that are more than its policy limits. The law will not allow a carrier to leave its policyholder defenseless and subject to unlimited damages, and then limit its own liability via the policy's coverage limits.

Occasionally, a question will arise about whether coverage applies. If so, the best course may be to defend the suit under a reservation of rights letter or a non-waiver agreement. These agreements provide that the carrier does not, by accepting the defense of the case, waive any of its rights to later deny coverage [*see* ch. 24, § 24.04[1][a]].

In addition, the workers' compensation carrier should inform the employer to place its general liability carrier on notice of the suit immediately. If the workers' compensation carrier chooses to defend the case under Coverage Part Two, it should inform the liability carrier about this decision. Also, the notice should ask the liability carrier to take over defending the claim. This will prevent the liability carrier from later claiming prejudice by lack of notice.

[ix] Coverage Under Employer's Liability

The discussion above begs the question of whether a carrier must defend and indemnify its insured employer in a tort suit brought by an injured worker under the substantial certainty exception to workers' compensation immunity. The Florida Supreme Court has held that coverage might apply, depending on the specific policy language.

As discussed above, in *Turner v. PCR, Inc.* [754 So. 2d 683 (Fla. 2000)], the Florida Supreme Court reaffirmed the existence of an intentional-tort exception to the otherwise exclusive nature of the statutory remedy provided by the workers' compensation law. Under the intentional-tort exception, an injured employee may avoid the exclusive-remedy provision of the workers' compensation law and sue his or her employer in tort if the workplace injury was caused by an intentional tort committed against the employee by the employer. The Supreme Court held in *Turner* that an injured employee could satisfy the intentional-tort exception either by demonstrating that his employer actually intended to injure him or by demonstrating that his employer engaged in conduct that was objectively substantially certain to result in injury.

NOTE: The latter method of satisfying the intentional-tort exception has now been modified by the Legislature [*see* [v][C], *above*]. In 2003, the Legislature codified the intentional-tort exception and, in doing so, modified the standard announced in *Turner*. Under the current version of § 440.11, Fla. Stat., an injured employee may satisfy the intentional tort-exception, and thereby avoid the exclusive-remedy provision of § 440.11(1), Fla. Stat., only by proving by clear and convincing evidence that the employer "deliberately intended to injure.him" or that the employer:

> . . . engaged in conduct that the employer knew, based on prior similar accidents or on explicit warnings specifically identifying a known danger, was virtually certain to result in injury or death to the employee, and the employee was not aware of the risk because the danger was not apparent and the employer deliberately concealed or misrepresented the danger so as to prevent the employee from exercising informed

judgment about whether to perform the work [§ 440.11(1)(b)(2), Fla. Stat. (2003)].

In *Travelers Indemnity Co. v. PCR, Inc.* [889 So. 2d 779 (Fla. 2004)], the Florida Supreme Court answered two questions of Florida law certified by the United States Court of Appeals for the Eleventh Circuit. The questions were whether an employer's liability insurance policy that provides coverage for liability arising from work-related accidental injuries, but excludes from coverage liability arising from injuries intentionally caused by the employer, provides coverage for a tort claim brought under the objectively-substantially-certain prong of the workers' compensation law's intentional-tort exception. The Court answered this question in the affirmative. Furthermore, the Court held that such insurance coverage does not offend, and is not prohibited by, public policy. The certified questions were as follows:

1. Does Florida insurance law require a reading of specific intent into an insurance clause excepting from liability coverage "bodily injury intentionally caused or aggravated" by the insured?
2. Is the employer entitled to liability coverage based on the language of this policy agreement, read in the light of Florida's law of interpreting insurance policies?

The Supreme Court answered the two certified questions in the affirmative and held that Part Two of the Workers Compensation and Employers Liability Policy issued to PCR by Travelers, which covered claims for "bodily injury by accident" and excluded from coverage claims of "bodily injury intentionally caused . . . by [PCR]," extended coverage to a claim brought against PCR under the objectively-substantially-certain standard articulated in *Turner*. A claim brought under *Turner's* standard does not on its own or as a matter of law fall outside the scope of this particular employer's liability insurance policy. However, the court noted that whether a claim brought under the newly enacted virtual-certainty standard would fall outside such a policy is a different question, which the Court declined to answer here.

The Court also held that public policy does not prohibit an employer from insuring against the risk of liability arising under *Turner's* objectively-substantially-certain standard. In a footnote, the Court observed that insurers remain free to craft policies explicitly limiting the scope of a "by accident" coverage clause or broadening the scope of an "intentional injury" exclusionary clause. The Court's task here was simply to interpret the scope of those particular clauses in a policy that left the operative terms undefined [*see* Travelers Indemnity Co. v. PCR, Inc., 889 So. 2d 779 (Fla. 2004)].

§ 3.02 Coverage Under the Law

[1] In General

Having first decided that coverage under the policy exists, the next step is deciding if coverage under the workers' compensation law exists. In other words, is the injured worker a covered employee of the insured employer?

For general discussion of employment status, see LARSON'S WORKERS' COMPENSATION, DESK EDITION, Ch. 60 (Matthew Bender).

[2] Employers Defined

The law defines "employers" as [§ 440.02(14), Fla. Stat. (1994)]:

1. The state and all public and quasi-public corporations;
2. Every person carrying on any employment; and
3. The legal representative of a deceased person or the receiver or trustees of any person.

The term "person" includes both individuals and entities such as corporations [§ 1.01(3), Fla. Stat. (1996); § 440.02(20), Fla. Stat. (1994)]. This definition is important because §§ 440.105 and 440.106, Fla. Stat., contain lists of prohibited activities. Imposing penalties for violations against corporations is often difficult. This is especially true when the penalty involves jail time or the corporation is out of business. To give these penalty provisions more meaningful effect, the legislature amended the definition of "employer" to include corporate officers and others. The law now provides as follows [§ 440.02(14), Fla. Stat. (1994)]:

> If the employer is a corporation, parties in actual control of the corporation, including, but not limited to, the president, officers who exercise broad corporate powers, directors, and all shareholders who directly or indirectly own a controlling interest in the corporation, are considered the employer for the purposes of § 440.105, Fla. Stat., and § 440.106, Fla. Stat.

This amendment means that the state can now impose penalties directly against the individuals in control of the offending corporation.

[3] Employee Defined

The original statutory definition of the term "employee" was as follows [§ 440.02(13)(a), Fla. Stat. (1994)]:

> "Employee" means any person engaged in any employment under any appointment or contract of hire or apprenticeship, express or implied, oral or written, whether lawfully or unlawfully employed and includes, but is not limited to, aliens and minors.

Effective July 15, 2003, the Legislature changed the definition, now found at § 440.02(15)(a), Fla. Stat., as follows:

> "Employee" means any person *who receives remuneration from an employer for the performance of any work or service while* engaged in any employment under any appointment or contract *for* hire or apprenticeship, express or implied, oral or written, whether lawfully or unlawfully employed and includes, but is not limited to, aliens and minors. [*Emphases added*]

This amendment apparently excludes people who perform a service without pay or remuneration. That is essentially the definition of a volunteer However, § 440.02(15)(d)6, Fla. Stat. already specifically excludes volunteers from the definition of "employee." Therefore, the practical effect of this change is not clear.

For accidents occurring on or after January 1, 1994, the law considers an independent contractor who is not employed in the construction industry to be an employee if the person meets the statutory tests described in § 3.05[3], *below*, and in § 440.02(15)(c), Fla. Stat. (7/15/2003)].

§ 3.03 Corporate Officers

[1] General Rule on Employee Status

Officers of corporations are employees and come under the provisions of the Workers' Compensation Act. Some corporate officers may voluntarily remove themselves from coverage. Exceptions to this rule may apply depending on the date of the accident [§ 440.02(13)(b), Fla. Stat. (1994)].

Beginning January 1, 1999, the definition of "corporate officer" changes significantly. After that date, a "corporate officer" is a person who fills an office provided for in the corporate charter or in the articles of incorporation as filed with the Department of State as provided in Chapter 607, Florida Statutes [*see* § 440.02(8), Fla. Stat. (1998)]. This is an obvious attempt to limit the number of officers eligible to exempt themselves from coverage. The amendment may have a far different effect, however, because Chapter 607 does not even mention the term "corporate charter," and the articles of incorporation do not usually contain a list of officer positions.

[2] Exceptions to Rule; Electing Exemption From Coverage

[a] Before July 1, 1990

All officers of any corporation may elect exemption and not come under the Workers' Compensation Act by filing a Notice of Exemption with the Division of Workers' Compensation [§ 440.05, Fla. Stat. (1994)].

[b] July 1, 1990, to January 25, 1991

Officers of corporations in the construction industry may not choose to exempt themselves. Officers in other industries may still choose to exempt themselves without restriction [§ 440.02(13), Fla. Stat. (1994)].

[c] On or After January 25, 1991

Up to three officers of corporations in the construction industry may elect exemption from the Workers' Compensation Act. Officers in other industries may still choose to exempt themselves without restriction [§§ 440.02(13), 440.05, Fla. Stat. (1994)].

[d] On or After July 1, 2002

The "three-officer" limit continues to apply for officers of corporations in the construction industry. The exemption, however, does not apply with respect to any commercial building project valued at $250,000 or greater [*see* 440.02(15)(b)2, Fla. Stat.].

[e] On or After January 1, 2004

The construction industry's three-officer limit for exemption from the Act now applies to a group of affiliated corporations even if only one is in the construction industry. Thus, although a group of affiliated corporations might have dozens of officers, only three may elect to be exempt. The term "affiliated" means one or more corporations or entities, any one of which is engaged in the construction industry, under the same or substantially the same control of a group of business entities that are connected or associated so that one entity controls or has the power to control each of the other business entities. The term "affiliated" also includes the officers, directors, executives, agents, employees, and shareholders active in management. Ownership, or controlling interest, of one entity by another entity is prima facie evidence of "affiliation." Additionally, pooling equipment or income among entities is prima facie evidence of "affiliation."

Corporate officers in the construction industry are not eligible for exemption from the Act unless they are shareholders owning at least 10 percent of the corporation's stock and are listed as corporate officers with the Division of Corporations [*see* § 440.02(15)(b), Fla. Stat. (1/1/2004)].

[3] Abuse of Election for Exemption From Coverage

An employer's payroll is the basis for computing the workers' compensation premium. Exempting highly-paid officers from coverage can result in large premium savings to the employer. Instead of workers' compensation benefits, employers give such officers health and disability insurance. Some employers even continue salary if the exempt officer suffers a disabling injury at work. Abuse of the exemption privilege, however, came to the legislature's attention. Reports of employers "promoting" almost every employee to vice president status and then exempting them out of the system were frequent. The judges of compensation claims often see this as a ruse to avoid the premium at the employee's expense. A judge will likely decide that an injured worker was promoted to officer status only to avoid the premium if the worker had nothing to do with the management of the corporation. If so, the judge is likely to declare the Notice of Exemption invalid and award benefits.

[4] Revoking the Exemption

Whatever the time periods listed in [2][a]–[c], *above,* exempt officers may revoke the exemption by filing a Revocation of Exemption certificate with the Division. By revoking the exemption, the officer then elects to be covered by workers' compensation.

Prior to January 1, 1999, exemption and revocation certificates were not effective until 30 days after mailing to the Division of Workers' Compensation. An exception arose if an injury occurred within the first 30 days after the effective date of the policy. In such a case, the Notice of Exemption was effective the day after mailing [§ 440.05(4), Fla. Stat. (1994); *see also* Speciality Employee Leasing v. Davis, 737 So. 2d 1170, 1773–1174 (Fla. 1st DCA 1999)].

After January 1, 1999, certificates are effective when issued by the division, or 30 days after the division receives an application for an exemption, whichever occurs first [*see* § 440.05(5), Fla. Stat. (1998)].

[5] Immunity of Exempt Officers

All employees, including officers, are immune from suits by co-workers, with two exceptions. The immunity does not apply if the co-employee committed an act amounting to gross negligence or was guilty of an unprovoked physical assault. In 1991, exempt officers were held to have no immunity from lawsuits brought by employees and co-workers [*see* Dobbins v. Weber, 585 So. 2d 1143, 1145 (Fla. 4th DCA 1991)].

Fortunately for exempt corporate officers, the Florida Supreme Court overruled and reversed *Dobbins*. The Supreme Court found the Court of Appeal had correctly interpreted the Workers' Compensation Act, literally speaking, but added: "If the Court applied a literal interpretation of the statutory definition of 'employee' to [§ 440.11, Fla. Stat.], the result would lead to an unreasonable or ridiculous conclusion." Writing for the majority, Justice Harding pointed out that the Court of Appeal's decision would result in unlimited exposure for injured employees' tort liability claims. The Supreme Court held that the Court of Appeal erred in its finding that exemption from coverage removed the immunities granted by § 440.11, Fla. Stat. Thus, under this decision, corporate officers continue to enjoy the same statutory immunity as before [*see* Weber v. Dobbins, 616 So. 2d 956, 959 (Fla. 1993)].

[6] Officers in Construction Industry

[a] Three-Officer Limit for Election of Exemption

Effective July 1, 1990, the legislature ended the exemption for corporate officers in the construction industry as defined by § 440.02(7), Fla. Stat. [*see* [b], *below*]. This amendment does not affect other industries, but it voided all construction industry certificates of exemption on its effective date. Employers challenged this new provision as violating the Equal Protection Clause, claiming it improperly singled out the construction industry. The court held the statute did not violate equal protection and is constitutional [*see* B & B Steel Erectors v. Burnsed, 591 So. 2d 644, 647 (Fla. 1st DCA 1991)].

The legislature amended this section again, effective January 25, 1991. Now, the Act allows up to three officers of corporations engaged in the construction industry to exempt themselves from coverage. Officers in the construction industry who want to exempt themselves must file form DWC-250, Notice of Election to be Exempt, with the Division. An exempt officer can revoke the election by filing LES form DWC-250-R, Revocation of Election to Be Exempt [§ 440.05(3), Fla. Stat. (1994); § 440.02(13)(b)2., Fla. Stat. (1994); Fla. Admin. Code R. 69L-6.012(1), (5) (10/30/2006)]. Certificates issued before January 1, 1994, were effective for two years unless revoked sooner. The legislature repealed this automatic expiration provision effective January 1, 1994. Therefore, all certificates of election with an effective date on or after January 1, 1994, continue in effect until revoked. Beginning in 1999, such certificates will again expire every two years. Any person who received a non-expiring certificate of exemption up to December 31, 1998, must reapply no later than the last day in his or her birth month following December 1, 1998 [*see* § 440.05(6), Fla. Stat. (1998)]. Although the statute does not specifically say so, presumably the original certificate will expire on that date.

Remember, that the three-officer limit applies only to the construction industry. With the exception of limiting the exemption privilege to officers listed in the corporate charter or articles of incorporation, no other limits exist in other industries as to the number of officers that can choose exemption.

The exemption does not apply to an otherwise exempt officer if the corporation was engaged in a commercial building project estimated to be valued at $250,000 or more. The statute provides as follows [§ 440.02(14)(b)2, Fla. Stat. (7/1/2002)]:

> However, any exemption obtained by a corporate officer of a corporation actively engaged in the construction industry is not applicable with respect to any commercial building project estimated to be valued at $250,000 or greater.

This is an unfortunately vague and poorly drafted provision. One interpretation is that all exemptions are suspended while the corporation is involved in a large commercial project, regardless of where the officer was injured. Note, however, the phrase "with respect to any commercial building project." A narrower, but more logical interpretation is that the exemption does not apply to officers injured while working on the large commercial project. There is nothing in the statute to suggest that the accident must occur on the project site itself. It appears that the exemption will not apply even if the officer was merely doing something incidental to the project when the accident occurred.

Conversely, it appears that the exemption *does* apply if the officer was injured while working on a smaller project or on a non-commercial, residential project. If this is the approach the courts adopt, then construction industry officers will move in and out of a covered employee status depending on the nature of the project where the accident occurred and what the officer was doing at the time.

SPECIAL NOTE: The phrase "commercial building" means any building or structure intended for commercial or industrial use. It also includes buildings intended for use as a multifamily dwelling of four or more dwelling units. Additionally, it includes any accessory use structures constructed in conjunction with the principle structures. The term does not include the conversion of a residential building to a commercial building. A residential building is defined as one with four or fewer dwelling units [*see* § 440.02(40), (41), Fla. Stat. (7/1/2002)].

An exempt officer is not an employee for workers' compensation purposes. If a corporate officer of a corporation engaged in the construction industry is injured, it will be necessary to determine the following to decide if the officer is an employee eligible for benefits:

1. Determine if the officer filed a valid Certificate of Exemption.
2. Determine if the exempt officer was engaged in some activity that was related to a commercial building project when the accident occurred.
3. Determine if the estimated value of the project was $250,000 or more.

If the answers to items two and three are "yes," then the exemption does not apply, and the officer is eligible for benefits.

SPECIAL ALERT: The legislature repealed the $250,000 limitation with respect to commercial projects, effective July 15, 2003. Therefore, for accidents occurring on or after this date, an officer remains exempt, regardless of the size or value of the construction project.

[b] Construction Industry Defined

The statutory definition of "construction industry" is as follows [§ 440.02(7), Fla. Stat. (1994)]:

> For-profit activities involving the carrying out of any building, clearing, filling, excavation, or substantial improvement in the size or use of any structure or the appearance of any land. When appropriate to the context, "construction" refers to the act of construction or the result of construction. However, "construction" shall not mean a landowner's act of construction or the result of a construction upon his or her own premises, provided such premises are not intended to be sold or resold.

This definition is obviously poorly drafted and vague. For example, what does "substantial improvement" mean? Another problem is this hypothetical situation. Assume that an insured employer believes it does not fit the definition of construction industry. Five legitimate officers exempt themselves, and one of them is injured. The injured officer claims the employer is in the construction industry and a judge of compensation claims agrees. Now what? Since the Workers' Compensation Act permits only three officers to exempt themselves, are all five certificates void? Is the injured officer entitled to benefits? Does the employer now owe additional premiums?

Effective January 1, 2004, the Legislature amended the statutory definition of "construction industry," now found at § 440.02(8), Fla. Stat., as follows:

> "Construction industry" means for-profit activities involving any building, clearing, filling, excavation, or substantial improvement in the size or use of any structure or the appearance of any land. However, "construction" does not mean a homeowner's act of construction or the result of a construction upon his or her own premises, provided such premises are not intended to be sold, resold, *or leased by the owner within one year after the commencement of construction. The division may, by rule, establish standard industrial classification codes and definitions thereof, which meet the criteria of the term "construction industry" as set forth in this section.* [*Emphasis added*]

To further clarify which businesses qualify as members of the construction industry for workers' compensation purposes, the Division has adopted the classification codes and descriptions that are specified in the Florida Contracting Classification Premium Adjustment Program, and published in the Florida exception pages of the NCCI Basic Manual. The administrative rule lists the classifications and descriptions adopted by the Rule. The definitions that correspond to the classification codes identify the workplace operations that satisfy the criteria of the term "construction industry." These definitions can be obtained by writing to the Division of Workers' Compensation, Bureau of Compliance,

200 East Gaines Street, Tallahassee, Florida 32399–4228 [*see* Fla. Admin. Code R. 69L-0621 (2/08/2007)].

[7] Exemption and Revocation Certificates

In any case involving a corporate officer, check the officer's status in the carrier's underwriting files. More important, however, are the Division records. A Certificate of Exemption is not valid unless filed with the Division of Workers' Compensation. Do not assume that because a copy of the certificate is in the carrier's underwriting file, the certificate is also on file with the Division. Inspect the file and be certain! Remember, construction industry certificates with an effective date before January 1, 1994, are valid for only two years. Check the effective date in the certificate's upper right corner. Other industries did not have an automatic expiration. However, with legislation effective January 1, 1999, even these are valid for only two years. Any certificate with an effective date on or after January 1, 1994, will continue in effect until the last day of the officer's birth month following December 1, 1998 [*see* § 440.05(6), Fla. Stat. (1998)].

Section 440.05(3), Fla. Stat., provides in part that "The notice of election to be exempt from the provisions of this chapter must be notarized and under oath." The court has held that an oath may be undertaken by any unequivocal act in the presence of an officer authorized to administer oaths (such as a notary public) by which the declarant knowingly attests the truth of a statement and assumes the obligation of an oath. Section 1.01(5), Fla. Stat. (2001), provides that "the word 'oath' includes affirmations." Therefore, a person's signed notice of election to be exempt, containing a statement in which he affirms that the information contained on the form is true, is sufficient to meet the "oath" requirement. By signing the Notice before a notary public, a person binds himself or herself to the promise to secure workers' compensation benefits for himself or herself [*see* Battle v. Gentry, 898 So. 2d 263 (Fla. 1st DCA 2005)].

To revoke exemption, the officer must file a Revocation of Election certificate with the Division.

Note that the Act, § 440.02(14)(c), Fla. Stat. (1997), provides that a contractor may require a subcontractor to provide evidence of insurance *or* a copy of his or her certificate of election to be exempt. If the subcontractor does either, he will be in compliance even if the subcontractor has exempt employees. If the subcontractor provides proof of insurance, nothing in the Act requires the subcontractor to also disclose his exemption. On the other hand, there is nothing in the Act that precludes a contractor from requiring both. This is important because without this information, the contractor may not be aware of the existence of one or more exempt individuals. Remember that an exempt person is not subject to the law or entitled to benefits. Therefore, no immunity extends to the contractor if the exempt subcontractor is injured [*see* Contractor's Mgmt Services v. Dixon, 734 So. 2d 435 (Fla. 4th DCA 1999)].

Any organization engaged in the construction industry with exempt sole proprietors, partners or corporate officers must obtain and maintain written acknowledgments from each exempt person acknowledging their exemption status. The law directs the Division of Workers' Compensation to promulgate rules specifying these and other records that must be maintained [*see* § 440.05(10), Fla Stat. (7/1/2002)].

Sole proprietors or partners engaged in the construction industry and claiming an exemption must maintain a copy of their federal income tax records for the previous three years. These records must be produced upon request from the Division together with a notarized statement attesting that the records are true and accurate. The Act requires the Division to issue a stop work order if the sole proprietor or partner fails or refuses to produce these records within three business days after the Division makes the request [*see* § 440.05(11), Fla. Stat. (7/1/2002)].

To qualify for an exemption, officers of corporations engaged in the construction industry must be listed as an officer in the corporate records maintained by the Division of Corporations. If they are not listed, the request for exemption must be accompanied by a notarized affidavit attesting that the person is a bona fide officer of the corporation. The statement must be signed by the corporate president or by the chief operating officer. The Act requires the Division of Workers' Compensation to issue a stop work order if these affidavits are not produced within three business days following the request [*see* § 440.05(13), Fla. Stat. (7/1/2002)].

[8] Exemption's Effect on Required Coverage

The exemption privilege is most important for small employers. Employers in the construction industry with only one employee must have coverage. Employers in all other industries must have workers' compensation coverage only if they have four or more employees [§ 440.02(15)(b)2, Fla. Stat. (1994); *see* ch. 24, § 24.01].

This brings us to the question of who is an employee. An exempted officer is not an employee for workers' compensation coverage purposes. The law does not count an exempted officer when deciding if an employer has the necessary number of employees to invoke the mandatory coverage provisions of the law [*see* Vanvoorst v. Ruble Trucking Co., 456 So. 2d 1289 (Fla. 1st DCA 1984)].

§ 3.04 Sole Proprietors and Partners

[1] General Rule

The law specifically excludes sole proprietors and partners *not in the construction industry* from the definition of "employee." As such, they are not subject to the law nor entitled to benefits. These individuals can, however, voluntarily choose to come under the Workers' Compensation Act. To do so, the sole proprietor or partner must file a Notice of Election of Coverage, LES form BCM-251 with the Division. To withdraw from coverage, the individual must file a Revocation of Election of Coverage, LES form 251-R with the Division [*see* Fla. Admin. Code R. 69L-6.009 (2/19/2007)]. These individuals can, however, voluntarily choose to come under the Workers' Compensation Act. Sole proprietors and partners in the construction industry are specifically included in the definition of employee. Up to three partners in such firms may elect exemption [§ 440.05, Fla. Stat. (1994)].

For workers' compensation purposes, a "partner" means a co-owner of a business who shares proportionally in the firm's profits and losses, and who participates fully in managing the partnership [*see* § 440.02(20), Fla. Stat. (1998)]. A "sole proprietor" means a person who owns all the assets of the business and is solely liable for its debts [*see* § 440.02(24), Fla. Stat. (1998)].

[2] Exceptions to Rule

[a] Before July 1, 1990

Before July 1, 1990, the law specifically excluded sole proprietors and partners from the definition of an employee, except when they worked in the construction industry. Sole proprietors and partners not in the construction industry could choose to come under the Workers' Compensation Act, however, by filing form BCM-205, Notice of Election of Coverage, with the Division. Like corporate officers, partners and sole proprietors could change their decisions and file form BCM-216, Withdrawal of Election of Coverage with the Division [*see* former § 440.02(13)(c), Fla. Stat.].

[b] July 1, 1990, to January 25, 1991

Effective July 1, 1990, the legislature amended the Act to provide in part that, "partners or sole proprietors actively engaged in the construction industry are considered employees in all instances whether or not the right of election is exercised." The law specifically included partners and sole proprietors in the construction industry with no right of exemption. Partners and sole proprietors in other industries could still choose to exempt themselves without restriction [*see* former § 440.02(13)(c), Fla. Stat.].

[c] After January 25, 1991

The legislature amended the Act again, effective January 25, 1991, to read as follows [§ 440.02(13)(c), Fla. Stat.]:

> Partners or sole proprietors actively engaged in the construction industry are considered employees unless they elect to be excluded from the definition of employee by filing written notice of the election with the division. . . . However, no more than three partners . . . may elect to be excluded.

The law now allows sole proprietors, but not more than three partners of partnerships, in the construction industry to exempt themselves by filing a Notice of Election to be Exempt, form BCM-204. Partners and sole proprietors in other industries can still choose exemption without restriction.

Note carefully that if a sole proprietor does not elect to be exempt, he or she is an employee for workers' compensation purposes. An exempt status means that the person has a valid certificate of exemption [*see* [3], *below*]. If the sole proprietor is working as a subcontractor without a valid exemption certificate in place, the general contractor becomes that individual's statutory employer and is responsible for providing workers' compensation coverage [*see* § 3.06, *below*; *see also* Smith v. Larry Rice Construction, 730 So. 2d 336, 339–340 (Fla. 1st DCA 1999)].

[d] On or After July 1, 2002

Exemption certificates do not apply, however, if the exempt sole proprietor or partner was engaged in work performed at a commercial building project with an estimated value of $250,000 or more [*see* § 3.02[6][a], *below,* for further discussion and for a definition of the term "commercial building"]. Presumably, this suspension of the exemption applies only if the sole proprietor or partner was injured while working on the commercial building project. It is also reasonable to assume that this provision will apply if the employee was doing something incidental and associated with the commercial project, such as traveling to obtain supplies or attending a meeting concerning the project. The statute, however, states that the exemption does not apply with respect to work "performed *at* such a commercial building project" (emphasis added). The court may interpret this to mean that the accident must occur on the physical construction job site [*see* § 440.02(14)(c)2, Fla. Stat. (7/1/2002)].

[e] On or After January 1, 2004

Partners and sole proprietors, who are *not* in the construction industry are not employees and therefore not subject to, or entitled to, benefits under the law. Such individuals may, however, elect to be included in the definition of "employee" by filing a notice of election.

Sole proprietors and partners who *are* in the construction industry are deemed to be employees. However, the Legislature repealed the provision allowing these individuals to exempt themselves. The law is now as it was in 1990 [*see* § 440.15(c), Fla. Stat. (1/1/2004)].

[3] Exemption and Revocation Certificates

As with corporate officers, exemption and revocation certificates are not effective until 30 days after mailing to the Division. An exception arises if the exempted person suffers an injury within the first 30 days after the policy's effective date. In such a case, the notice of exemption is effective the day after mailing [§ 440.05(4), Fla. Stat. (1994)].

The application for exemption must include a copy of the stock certificate, showing that the applicant officer owns at least 10 percent of the corporation's stock [§ 440.05(3), Fla. Stat. (1/1/2004)].

A certificate of exemption applies only to the corporate officer named on the certificate and then only within the scope of the business or trade listed on the exemption certificate. The department must revoke an exemption upon learning that the individual no longer meets the requirements for exemption.

A corporate officer is not eligible for exemption if he or she is affiliated with a person who has violated a stop-work order or penalty assessment order. The term "affiliated person" includes any or all of the following people who are delinquent in paying a stop-work order or a penalty assessment [§ 440.05(15), Fla. Stat. (1/1/2004)]:

- The officer's spouse;
- Any person who holds at least 10 percent of the corporation's voting stock;
- Any person directly or indirectly controlled by the officer;
- Any person who directly or indirectly acquires substantially all of the officer's

assets;

- Any of the officer's directors, trustees, officers, partners, or joint venturers; and
- Any person who has an officer, director, trustee, officer, partner, or joint venturer in common with the officer.

§ 3.05 Workers Who Are Not Employees

[1] Casual Labor

[a] Accident Dates Before October 1, 2001

Casual laborers are not employees, and the law does not entitle them to compensation benefits. The statutory definition of casual labor is [§ 440.02(5), Fla. Stat. (1994)]: "Work . . . (which is) . . . to be completed in not exceeding 10 working days without regard to the total number of persons employed, and when the total labor cost of such work is less than $100." A person injured while engaged in casual labor is not eligible for benefits if the work is not performed in the course of the trade, business, profession, or occupation of the employer [§ 440.02(15)(d)5, Fla. Stat. (1994)].

The vague language in the statute provides a four-part test.

Test 1. The work the employee was performing must be work *contemplated* to be finished in no more than 10 days. This may seem clear, but it is not. Using the term "contemplated" suggests the legislature intended to allow some flexibility. If the evidence shows that the employer expected completion in 10 days or less, the exclusion should apply even if the work took longer. Obviously, the farther from the 10th day an accident occurs, the less likely the evidence will support such a conclusion.

Test 2. The total labor cost cannot exceed $100, despite the number of workers involved. Whatever the time contemplated for finishing the work, if the labor costs exceed or are expected to exceed $100, the exclusion cannot apply.

Test 3. The work must be casual. The statute is no help because it defines "casual" only as to time and cost. Dictionary definitions of the term "casual" suggests an event occurring by chance. Common usage dictates that we define the term as work that is irregular, unpredictable, sporadic, and brief.

Test 4. Despite the time, the cost, and the number of workers engaged, the exclusion does not apply if the work was in the course of the employer's trade, business, profession, or occupation. In a New Mexico case, the injured worker was a truck driver who made deliveries only. When he arrived with a delivery for Ford, no one was available to unload the truck, so Ford paid the driver $20 to do it. The court held the injured worker was an employee because the work was for Ford's business [*see* Barger v. Ford Sales Company, Inc., 89 N.M. 25, 546 P.2d 873, 874–875 (1976)]. Under almost identical facts, a Tennessee court arrived at the same conclusion [*see* Butler v. Johnson, 221 Tenn. 366, 426 S.W.2d 515, 518–519 (1968)].

The various state courts disagree, however, when the work involves maintenance, repair, painting, cleaning, and the like. These courts believe such work is expected,

Guide to Claims

routine, and an inherent part of the employer's business activity. If they are correct, imagining what kind of work is casual is difficult.

Regardless of whether an employment situation meets the definition of casual labor, most such situations will likely fail to meet the $100 compensation test. For example, Carl and Ardis Summers owned unimproved property in Volusia County. The couple listed the property for sale and then hired Charles Blanton and another man to clear part of it. Blanton suffered a severe head injury when a tree branch struck him. The Summers argued that they were not responsible for workers' compensation benefits because Blanton was a casual worker. The court found that Blanton's work was to be completed in less than 10 days and that the work was not in the Summers' trade, business, profession, or occupation. Blanton's wages, however, exceeded the $100 limit and, thus, he could not be considered a casual employee. Although the court did not mention it, presumably Blanton did not meet the tests for exemption as an independent contractor [*see* [3], *below*]. Because the work involved land clearing, it constituted construction, thus making the Summers liable for providing workers' compensation coverage and benefits. The court noted that the $100 limit was enacted decades ago, when $100 was a substantial sum. Time and inflation, however, have rendered that amount incongruous. Looked at another way, the court opined that a single worker paid at today's average weekly wage cannot qualify as casual employment if the job lasts as long as nine hours. The court urged the legislature to address this anachronism [*see* Summers v. Blanton, 712 So. 2d 411, 412 (Fla. 1st DCA 1998), *rev. dismissed,* 719 So. 2d 288 (Fla. 1998)].

[b] Accident Dates On or After October 1, 2001

Effective October 1, 2001, the legislature changed the definition of casual as follows [§ 440.02(4), Fla. Stat. (10/1/2001)]:

> "Casual" as used in this section refers only to employments for work that is anticipated to be completed in 10 working days or less, without regard to the number of persons employed, and at a total labor cost of less than $500.

Since this amendment affects the basic entitlement to benefits, it is most likely a substantive amendment that applies only to accidents occurring on or after 10/1/2001.

The still-vague language in the amended statute continues to provide a four–part test:

Test 1. The work the employee was performing must be work *anticipated* to be finished in no more than 10 days. Replacing the term "contemplated" with the term "anticipated" is no help because the two terms are synonyms. If the evidence shows that the employer expected completion in 10 days or less, the exclusion should apply even if the work took longer. Obviously, the farther from the 10th day an accident occurs, the less likely the evidence will support such a conclusion.

Test 2. The total labor cost cannot exceed $500, despite the number of workers involved. Whatever the time contemplated for finishing the work, if the labor costs exceed $500, the exclusion cannot apply.

Test 3. The work must be casual. The amended statute is still no help because it continues to define the term "casual" only as to time and cost without describing the work itself. Dictionary definitions of the term "casual" suggests an event occurring by chance.

Common usage continues to dictate that we define the term as work that is irregular, unpredictable, sporadic, and brief.

Test 4. Despite the time, the cost, and the number of workers engaged, the exclusion does not apply if the work was in the course of the employer's trade, business, profession, or occupation.

For general discussion of casual employment, see LARSON'S WORKERS' COMPENSATION, DESK EDITION, Ch. 73 (Matthew Bender).

[2] Volunteers

[a] Defined

Volunteers are people who serve without payment. An exception arises if substantial evidence shows that both the employee and the employer intended valuable consideration. Without such evidence, the statute presumes that the worker is a volunteer. Volunteers include people who work in private nonprofit agencies and receive no compensation other than expenses [§ 440.02(13)(d)6, Fla. Stat. (1994)].

For general discussion of volunteer workers, see LARSON'S WORKERS' COMPENSATION, DESK EDITION, Ch. 65, § 65.01 (Matthew Bender).

[b] Governmental Volunteers

Volunteers are not employees and are not entitled to compensation. Exceptions to this rule are volunteer workers for the state, county, municipality, or other governmental entity [*see* § 440.02(16)(b)1, Fla. Stat. (1991)]. A "governmental entity" or "agency" includes private or quasi-public corporations exercising a governmental function. It is broadly defined as a state agency, however styled, that independently exercises any type of state or local government function [*see* § 11.45(c), (h), Fla. Stat.]. Thus, people who do volunteer work for a governmental or quasi-governmental entity are considered to be employees. Note, however, that the term "other government entity" is not defined in the statute. A quasi-public corporation may qualify as an "other governmental entity." A quasi-public corporation is a private corporation that has accepted a franchise or contract from the state involving performing public duties. A quasi-public corporation must be privately owned. It must enjoy privileges not bestowed upon the general public because of the benefits such a corporation confers to the public. Lastly, a quasi-public corporation must provide a service necessary to the public's general welfare [*see* 18 Am. Jur. 2d, Corporations § 31 (1985)].

Not all quasi-public corporations, however, qualify as an "other governmental entity." To decide, look to whether the contracting party provides material or services to or for the public body, or in place of services provided by the public body. For workers' compensation purposes, a quasi-public corporation qualifies as an "other governmental entity" if it is under contract to a public body and preforms services that are traditionally performed by government.

It has been argued that a judge of compensation claims does not have the authority to disregard the legal existence of a corporation or to pierce its corporate veil. Thus, under this argument, the judge of compensation claims does not have the authority to decide if a private corporation is acting as a government entity. That is an interesting argument, but it has no merit. Making a determination of a corporation's status under § 440.02(14), Fla. Stat. does not require the judge of compensation claims to pierce the corporate veil or to disregard the corporate form.

The court has held that by using the broad term "other governmental entity," the legislature intended to extend workers' compensation coverage to volunteers of quasi-public corporations that, under contract with a public body, perform services traditionally performed by government [*see* McClung-Gagne v. Harbour City Volunteer 721 So. 2d 799, 803 (Fla. 1st DCA 1998)].

[c] Good Samaritans

Excluded volunteers do not include workers who "volunteer" to help some third party in distress while working on the job for their normal employer. In such situations, the worker continues in the course of employment with the employer and the law entitles the worker to benefits [*see* ch. 7, § 7.11].

[3] Independent Contractors

[a] General Rule

Independent contractors, except those in the construction industry, are not employees. Thus, an independent contractor not in the construction industry is not eligible for benefits from the hiring entity. Real estate agents, entertainers, truck owner-operators, horse exercise riders, and drivers for hire are independent contractors by statute.

The Legislature enacted major changes to the definition of an independent contractor, effective on January 1, 1994, and again, 10 years later, on January 1, 2004. These are substantive amendments that apply only to accidents occurring on or after the effective date.

> **SPECIAL ALERT:** An employer who classifies a person as an independent contractor who does not meet the criteria specified in § 440.02, Fla. Stat. is subject to large punitive penalties assessed by the Division of Workers' Compensation. The fine is $2,500 for the first two misclassified workers. The penalty increases to $5,000 for each misclassified worker above three [*see* Fla. Admin Code R. 4L-6.018 (3/26/03); *see also* [c], *below*, for discussion of the criteria].

For general discussion of contractors, see LARSON'S WORKERS' COMPENSATION, DESK EDITION, Chs. 61, 62, 63 (Matthew Bender).

[b] Definition Before January 1, 1994

An independent contractor means a person whose conduct is not subject to the employer's control and direction [*see* former § 440.02(13)(d)1, Fla. Stat.].

[c] Definition On or After January 1, 1994

The law now provides that independent contractors are employees unless they meet *all* of the following conditions [§ 440.02(13)(d)1, Fla. Stat. (1994)]:

1. Maintains a separate business with its own work facility, truck, equipment, materials, or similar accommodation;

2. Holds or has applied for a federal employer identification number, unless the independent contractor is a sole proprietor who is not required to obtain a federal employer identification number under state or federal requirements;

3. Does, or agrees to do, specific services or work for specific amounts of money and controls the means of doing the services or work;

4. Incurs the principal expenses related to the service or work that it does or agrees to do;

5. Is responsible for the satisfactory completion of work or services that it does or agrees to do and is or could be held liable for a failure to complete the work or services;

6. Receives compensation for work or services done for a commission or on a per-job or competitive-bid basis and not on any other basis;

7. May realize a profit or suffer a loss concerning doing the work or services;

8. Has continuing or recurring business liabilities or obligation; and

9. The success or failure of the independent contractor's business depends on the relationship of business receipts to expenditures.

These requirements strictly limit independent contractor status to those people operating legitimate independent businesses. Remember that a contractor must meet every one of these conditions for the law to consider the contractor independent. If not, the law deems the contractor an employee of the hiring entity and eligible for benefits.

In the past, many contractors presented certificates of exemption to their general contractors and also certified that they were independent contractors as described above. Unfortunately for many general contractors and their insurance carriers, these assertions often proved to be false, making the general contractor liable for workers' injuries. However, beginning January 1, 1999, such assertions, apparently even if they are false, will preclude benefits.

Under this provision, independent contractors are deemed not to be employees if they present a general contractor with both an affidavit certifying that they meet the independent contractor requirements listed above, and a certificate of exemption [*see* § 440.10(1)(g), Fla. Stat. (1998)].

[d] Exceptions

The tests listed in [c], *above,* do not apply to newspaper delivery persons or to specifically listed industry classifications. Courts must decide independent contractor status of the excepted classifications using common-law principles as discussed below. Specifically, the Act states that we must decide if people in the excepted classes are employees by applying common-law principles, considering the individual's business activity [*see* § 440.02(13)(d)1., Fla. Stat. (1994)].

The excepted classifications are as follows:

1. Newspaper delivery persons. (Note: The Florida Supreme Court has ruled on how to decide newspaper delivery status. *See* [h], *below*.)
2. Certain Agricultural services:
   Class 0711–Soil Preparation services
   Class 0721–Crop planting, cultivating and protecting
   Class 0722–Crop Harvesting, primarily by machine
   Class 0751–Livestock services except veterinary
   Class 0761–Farm labor contractors and crew leaders
   Class 0762–Farm machinery services
   Class 0781–Landscape counseling and planning
   Class 0782–Lawn and garden services
   Class 0783–Ornamental tree and shrub services
3. Certain forestry services:
   Class 0811–Timber tracks
   Class 0831–Forest services and gathering of forest products
   Class 0851–Forestry services
4. Certain lumber and wood products services:
   Class 2411–Logging
   Class 2421–Sawmills and planting mills, general
   Class 2435–Hardwood veneer and plywood
   Class 2436–Softwood veneer and plywood
   Class 2448–Wood pallets and skids
   Class 2449–Wood containers, not otherwise classified

NOTE: Effective January 1, 2004, the Legislature repealed the exceptions for the specific industrial classifications listed above. Therefore, the determination of independent contractor status on or after 1/1/2004 is based on the statutory requirements only, and, therefore, common-law principles no longer apply.

[e] Common-Law Tests

For accidents occurring before January 1, 1994, the common-law tests apply in all cases. For accidents occurring between January 1, 1994, and December 31, 2003, with respect to the exceptions listed in [f], *above*, we must use the common-law tests to decide whether a person is an employee or an independent contractor. A very important factor is how much control the employer exercises over the work's details. The following is a generally accepted list of common-law tests:

1. The extent of control the employer exercises over work's details.
2. Whether the person employed is in a distinct occupation or business.
3. The kind of occupation.

4. The skill required.
5. Who supplies the tools.
6. Where the work is done.
7. The length of time the person is engaged.
8. The payment method (by the piece or by the hour).
9. Whether the work is the employer's regular business.
10. Whether the parties intended to create a master-servant relationship.
11. Whether the employer's workers' compensation policy covers the worker by paying premium calculated on the employer's payroll.

Examples of how the courts have applied these tests follows in [f], *below*.

For general discussion of contractors, see LARSON'S WORKERS' COMPENSATION, DESK EDITION, Chs. 61, 62, 63 (Matthew Bender).

[f] Case History of Common-Law Tests

Case 1. The employer, a company that sold garage doors, hired Bethel to install garage doors. The court held that Bethel was an independent contractor and not an employee because of the following [*see* Eighty Four Lumber v. Bethel, 544 So. 2d 1094, 1096 (Fla. 1st DCA 1989)]:

1. He provided his own tools.
2. The employer did not supervise or instruct him on installing doors.
3. The employer did not withhold taxes from Bethel's pay.

Case 2. Charles Saunders was the sole proprietor of Saunders Electric. Boyd-Scarp Enterprises, a general contractor, hired Saunders to rewire a burned-out house. Saunders suffered severe injuries when he fell through the house's attic floor. The court held that Saunders was an independent contractor and ineligible for benefits because of the following [*see* Boyd-Scarp Enterprises, Inc. v. Saunders, 453 So. 2d 161, 164 (Fla. 1st DCA 1984)]:

1. No one with Boyd-Scarp Enterprises actively supervised Saunders.
2. Saunders was a master electrician engaged in a special vocation distinctly different from Boyd-Scarp's.
3. Saunders provided his own materials, tools, and helpers.
4. Saunders was responsible only for the result of his work.

Case 3. Another important test in these cases has been whether the employer has the right to fire the worker without liability for breach of contract. For example, Cueto hired Brewer to paint a multistory building, which Cueto intended to use as a rooming house. Brewer claimed he was a day laborer and, thus, an employee entitled to benefits.

Guide to Claims

No contract existed between them, and Cueto supplied the materials and tools. Cueto paid Brewer at the end of each day. Finally, and what is most important, Cueto had the right to fire Brewer without liability. That is, Brewer could not come back and enforce any contractual right to complete the job. He was, therefore, an employee and not an independent contractor [*see* Brewer v. Cueto, 379 So. 2d 1322, 1323 (Fla. 1st DCA 1980)].

[g] Definition On or After January 1, 2004

[i] Independent Contractors in the Construction Industry

Independent contractors in the construction industry are considered to be the employees of the hiring entity and are eligible for benefits [*see* § 440.02(15)(c), Fla. Stat. (1/1/2004)].

[ii] Independent Contractors Not in the Construction Industry

Independent contractors who are not in the construction industry are not employees of the hiring entity and are not eligible for benefits. To qualify as an independent contractor, the individual must meet *at least four* of the following six criteria [§ 440.02(15)(d), Fla. Stat. (1/1/2004)]:

1. Maintains a separate business with its own work facility, truck, equipment, materials, or similar accommodation;
2. Holds or has applied for a federal employer identification number, unless the independent contractor is a sole proprietor who is not required to obtain a federal employer identification number under state or federal requirements;
3. Receives compensation for services rendered or work performed, and such compensation is paid to a business rather than to an individual;
4. Holds one or more bank accounts in the name of the business entity for purposes of paying business expenses or other expenses related to services rendered or work performed for compensation;
5. Performs work, or is able to perform work, for any entity in addition to or besides the employer at his or her own election without the necessity of completing an employment application or process; or
6. Receives compensation for work or services rendered on a competitive-bid basis or completion of a task or set of tasks as defined by a contractual agreement, unless the contractual agreement expressly states that an employment relationship exists.

A person who cannot meet *at least four* of the above criteria may still be presumed to be an independent contractor, and thus not an employee, based on the nature and circumstances of the situation. In making the analysis, the fact-finder is required to consider whether the person meets *any* of the following conditions:

1. Performs or agrees to perform specific services or work for specific amounts of money and controls the means of doing the services or work;
2. Incurs the principal expenses related to the service or work that he or she

performs or agrees to perform;

3. Is responsible for the satisfactory completion of work or services that he or she performs or agrees to perform;

4. Receives compensation for work or services performed for a commission, or on a per-job or competitive-bid basis and not on any other basis;

5. May realize a profit or suffer a loss in connection with performing work or services;

6. Has continuing or recurring business liabilities or obligations;

7. The success or failure of the independent contractor's business depends on the relationship of business receipts to expenditures.

The exceptions for the specific industrial classifications listed in [d], *above*, no longer apply. Therefore, the determination of independent contractor status is based on the statutory requirements only, and, therefore, common-law principles no longer apply.

The statute now provides that an individual claiming independent contractor status has the burden of proof [§ 440.15(d), Fla. Stat. (1/1/2004)].

[h] Legislative History

An employer may claim—and even believe—that the injured worker is an independent contractor and that the carrier should deny benefits. Frequently, however, the courts conclude that the employer disguised the worker as an independent contractor to avoid paying the proper premium. (It is this practice that likely led to the statutory definition of an independent contractor presently in the law.)

Be especially wary of independent contractor agreements signed by someone poorly equipped to decide the agreement's validity. These documents may look official, but the courts brush them aside with little hesitation. This is even more likely today given the strict statutory definition. The original Governor's Workers' Compensation Oversight Board reported that this type of system abuse was especially prevalent in the construction industry.

The legislature agreed and, temporarily, amended the Workers' Compensation Act effective July 1, 1990. The amendment provided that there is no such status as an independent contractor *engaged in the construction industry* [*see* § 440.02(13)(d)1., Fla. Stat. (7/1/90)].

This change, however, lasted only a brief time. In a special session in January 1991, the legislature repealed the italicized phrase. Effective January 25, 1991, therefore, the Workers' Compensation Act reverted to its original language.

The legislature, apparently, does not intend to cause contractors undue hardship by requiring them to investigate the status of every contractor hired. The law conclusively presumes the contractor to be independent if [§ 440.10(1)(g), Fla. Stat.]:

1. The contractor certifies, by written affidavit that he meets all the requirements of § 440.02(13)(d), Fla. Stat.; and

Guide to Claims

2. Produces a valid certificate of insurance coverage or exemption.

The difficulty, of course, is to be certain that any certificates produced are, in fact, valid. A contractor or adjuster can confirm this by checking with the Division of Workers' Compensation.

[i] Newspaper Delivery Persons

In 1956, the Florida Supreme Court held that "newspaper boys" worked in a distinct occupation and were independent contractors [*see* Miami Herald Publishing Company v. Kendall, 88 So. 2d 276, 279–280 (Fla. 1956)].

Over the years some courts concluded that *Kendall* created a conclusive presumption that newspaper carriers were independent contractors and not entitled to benefits. In 1995, however, the Supreme Court held that its decision in *Kendall* does not create a conclusive presumption. We must decide independent contractor status under common-law principles, considering the individual's business activity. That, of course, is exactly what the 1994 statute provides. Look first at the agreement between the newspaper and the carrier, and then honor that agreement. Without an agreement, and no way to figure out what the parties intended, courts must do an analysis under the Restatement of the Law of Agency [*see* Keith v. News & Sun Sentinel Co., 667 So. 2d 167, 170–174 (Fla. 1995)].

Remember, however, that even if a newspaper carrier is an independent contractor, coverage may exist if the carrier was actually a subcontractor [*see* § 3.06].

For general discussion of newspaper delivery persons, see LARSON'S WORKERS' COMPENSATION, DESK EDITION, Chs. 61, 62 (Matthew Bender).

[j] Penalty for Misclassifying Employees

The legislature received many reports that some employers deliberately misclassified employees as independent contractors to avoid paying the workers' compensation insurance premium. Employers who misclassify employees after January 1, 1994, are subject to a fine of up to $5,000 for each misclassification [§ 440.10(2)(f), Fla. Stat. (1/1/94)].

The Division's rules provide that for *each* employee classified as an independent contractor, who does not meet the criteria for an independent contractor as specified in § 440.02, Fla. Stat., the employer will be assessed a penalty. The penalty amounts are $2,500 per misclassified employee for the first two, and $5,000 each after the first two. Thus, if there are three misclassified employees, the penalty is $10,000. The Division will investigate cases in which the employer, in any way, maintains that a worker is an independent contractor or if the employer holds out the worker as an independent contractor for federal tax purposes [*see* Fla. Admin. Code. R. 69L-6.018 (1/10/2005)].

[4] Real Estate Salespersons

The term "employee" does *not* include "a real estate salesperson or agent, if that person agrees, in writing, to perform for remuneration solely by way of commission" [§ 440.02(13)(d)2, Fla. Stat. (1994)].

For general discussion of real estate salespersons, see LARSON'S WORKERS' COMPENSATION,

Desk Edition, Chs. 61, 62 (Matthew Bender).

[5] Entertainers

The term "employee" does *not* include "Bands, orchestras, and musical and theatrical performers, including disk jockeys, performing in licensed premises as defined in chapter 562, if a written contract evidencing an independent contractor relationship is entered into before the commencement of such entertainment" [§ 440.02(13)(d)3, Fla. Stat. (1994)].

[6] Truck Owner-Operators

The term "employee" does *not* include [§ 440.02(15)(d)4, Fla. Stat. (1994)]:

> An owner-operator of a motor vehicle who transports property under a written contract with a motor carrier which evidences a relationship by which the owner-operator assumes the responsibility of an employer for the performance of the contract, if the owner-operator is required to furnish the necessary motor vehicle equipment and all costs incidental to the performance of the contract, including, but not limited to, fuel, taxes, licenses, repairs, and hired help; and the owner-operator is paid a commission for his transportation service and is not paid by the hour or on some other time-measured basis.

This section was amended, effective July 1, 2005, and now reads as follows [§ 440.02(15)(d)4, Fla. Stat. (2005)]:

> An owner-operator of a motor vehicle who transports property under a written contract with a motor carrier which evidences a relationship by which the owner-operator assumes the responsibility of an employer for the performance of the contract, if the owner-operator is required to furnish motor vehicle equipment as identified in the written contract and the principal costs incidental to the performance of the contract, including, but not limited to, fuel and repairs, provided a motor carrier's advance of costs to the owner-operator when a written contract evidences the owner-operator's obligation to reimburse such advance shall be treated as the owner-operator furnishing such costs and the owner-operator is not paid by the hour or on some other time-measured basis.

Under the 2005 amendment, an owner-operator is excluded from the definition of employee and, thus, excluded from receiving workers' compensation benefits, if the owner-operator transports property under a written contract with the motor carrier that contains all of the following provisions:

1. The owner-operator assumes responsibility of the employer for performance of a contract.
2. The owner-operator is required to furnish the motor vehicle equipment, and the equipment to be furnished is described in the contract.
3. The owner-operator is responsible for the principal costs, including fuel and repairs.
4. The owner-operator is required to reimburse an advance of operating costs by the

Guide to Claims

motor carrier, and the advance is treated as the owner-operator furnishing such costs.

5. The owner-operator is paid on some basis other than hourly or another time-measured basis.

For general discussion of truck owner-operators, see LARSON'S WORKERS' COMPENSATION, DESK EDITION, Chs. 60, 61, 62 (Matthew Bender).

[7] Horse Exercise Riders

The term "employee" does not include "an exercise rider who does not work for a single horse farm or breeder, and who is compensated for riding on a case-by-case basis, provided a written contract is entered into prior to the commencement of such activity which evidences that an employee/employer relationship does not exist." This is a substantive amendment and applies only to accidents occurring on or after January 1, 1994 [§ 440.02(13)(d)9, Fla. Stat. (1994)].

[8] Drivers for Hire

The term "employee" does not include "[a] taxicab, limousine, or other passenger vehicle-for-hire driver who operates said vehicle pursuant to a written agreement with a company which provides any dispatch, marketing, insurance, communications, or other services under which the driver and any fees or charges paid by the driver to the company for such services are not conditioned upon, or expressed as a proportion of, fare revenues." This is a substantive amendment and applies only to accidents occurring on or after January 1, 1994 [§ 440.02(13)(d)10, Fla. Stat. (1994)].

[9] Amateur Sports Officials

Individuals serving as officials for entities sponsoring amateur sporting events are deemed to be independent contractors, and are thus ineligible for benefits from the hiring entity. This includes entities sponsoring an interscholastic sports event as well as any public or private nonprofit organization sponsoring an amateur sports event. The term "sports official" means a person who is a neutral participant in a sports event such as umpires, referees, judges, linespersons, scorekeepers, or timekeepers.

Note, however, that this exclusion does not apply to individuals employed by a district school board who serve as officials *during normal working hours* as part of their job duties. If the injured official is also a school board employee, an investigation will be necessary to determine if officiating at the event where the injury occurred is part of the employee's job duties. If so, it will also be necessary to determine whether the injury occurred during normal working hours. The phrase "normal working hours" should be applied to the individual. Therefore, it will be necessary to determine what was normal for the injured worker. A key test will likely be whether the employee received pay while officiating at the event.

Because independent contractors are not employees, and are not eligible for benefits, this provision is apparently substantive and likely applies only to accidents occurring on or after 10/1/2001 [*see* § 440.02(14)(d), Fla. Stat. (10/1/2001)].

[10] Medicaid-Enrolled Clients

The term "employee" does not included people who are Medicaid-enrolled under Chapter 393, Florida Statutes. If the person is excluded from the definition of "employment" under § 443.036(21)(d)5, Fla. Stat., that person is not an employee for workers' compensation purposes. Generally, this includes people working in a sheltered workshop setting, licensed by the United States Department of Labor, providing rehabilitation employment for people with an impaired physical or mental capacity.

Facilities serving such disabled individuals are considered agents of the Agency for Health Care Administration, as it relates to providing Adult Day Training Services under Medicaid. Such facilities are not employers or third parties for purposes of limiting or denying Medicaid benefits [§ 440.02(16)(a) & (c), Fla. Stat. (1/1/2004)].

§ 3.06 Subcontractors

[1] General Rule

Subcontractors are, by statute, considered the employees of the general contractor who is, therefore, responsible for providing workers' compensation benefits. This law does not apply, however, if the subcontractor provides its own coverage or is exempt. If the law requires the subcontractor to have coverage, but it does not, the general contractor is liable for benefits. In such a case, the general contractor, or its insurance company, has the right to sue the subcontractor. Recovery includes both benefits paid or payable.

Figuring out when an independent contractor is functioning as a subcontractor is essential. The Workers' Compensation Act provides that the law considers the employees of subcontractors the employees of the general contractor for workers' compensation purposes [§ 440.01(1), Fla. Stat.].

In this sense, the general contractor is the "statutory employer." Once any employer is in a statutory employer status it is responsible for providing workers' compensation benefits to its subcontractors. Simultaneously, such an employer enjoys immunity from liability.

For general discussion of subcontractors, see Larson's Workers' Compensation, Desk Edition, Ch. 61 (Matthew Bender).

[2] Applying Statutory Employer Status

Do not make the mistake of assuming the statutory employer provision applies only in construction industries. The provision applies to other industries as well. Any employer becomes a general contractor and, thus, a statutory employer, when it subcontracts any part of its own contractual obligation. What does subcontracting or subletting mean? The Florida Supreme Court gave the following definition [*see* Jones v. Florida Power Corp., 72 So. 2d 285, 289 (Fla. 1954)]:

To 'sublet' means to 'underlet,' *Webster's New International Dictionary*; in the context in which it is here used, the effect of subletting is to pass on to another an obligation under a contract for which the person so 'subletting' is primarily obligated.

Obviously, then, subletting part of one's contractual duty creates a statutory employer situation. Subletting, however, can also extend even to delegating one's rights under the terms of a contract. For example, a resin manufacturer, the Hercules Corporation, entered into a contract with the St. Joseph Land and Development Company (St. Joe) whereby Hercules agreed to purchase pine tree stumps from St. Joe. Under the terms of the contract, Hercules was to remove the stumps and then pay St. Joe an agreed amount for each ton of stumps it removed. Hercules then hired the B.G. Swilley Trucking Company (Swilley) to do the actual removal and to deliver the stumps to the Hercules plant. During the work, Johnny Pullman, a Swilley employee was seriously injured, but Swilley had no workers' compensation coverage. Pullman, therefore, filed a claim against Hercules claiming he was their statutory employee. The judge of compensation claims denied the claim, holding that the statutory employer provision did not apply because Hercules had not subcontracted any duty it owed to St. Joe. The contract was merely an agreement to purchase and remove tree stumps, but Hercules apparently had no obligation to actually do so. The First District Court of Appeal reversed, holding that the only requirement is a showing of "mutuality of obligation," the essential element of any valid contract. St. Joe was obligated to allow Hercules to remove tree stumps, and Hercules was obligated to pay for the stumps. As Judge Benton pointed out in his dissenting opinion, the majority choose to interpret the contract as *requiring* Hercules to harvest and purchase all the tree stumps it wanted. Therefore, the Swilley Company was performing a job or service arising from the contract between Hercules and St. Joe, making Swilley a Hercules subcontractor and the Statutory employer of Swilley's employees [*see* Pullman v. Hercules Inc., 711 So. 2d 72, 74–76, 77 (Fla. 1st DCA 1998)].

Note that statutory employer status flows from the act of subletting part of a contract. If there is no subletting, there is no statutory employer status. Absent such status, the employer is not liable for providing workers' compensation benefits to the employees of other contractors, and, likewise, there is no immunity from suits brought by those employees.

The court has held that the owner/developer of a real estate project is not a general contractor for workers' compensation purposes and, therefore, is not immune from suits brought by workers injured while working on the construction project. Here, Ryland Homes was the owner/developer as well as the general contractor of Bayshore Townhomes, a 10-building, 68-unit town home complex. Ryland entered into a contract with Sunfish Framing and Construction, Inc. (Sunfish), to do framing work on the project. Under this contract, Sunfish was required to maintain workers' compensation coverage for its employees. Sunfish subcontracted a portion of its work to Carlos Maldonado, who in turn contracted with Diego Gallego, to complete the application of the plywood sheathing on the roof. Gallego hired Luis Cuero to assist him. Cuero suffered personal injuries and resulting quadriplegia when he fell from the roof of one of the buildings. Neither Gallego nor Maldonado had any type of workers' compensation insurance, and Sunfish had insurance for listed (leased) employees only, which did not include Cuero. The claimant then filed suit against Ryland, Sunfish, Carlos Maldonado, and Diego Gallego.

Ryland submitted a notice of accident to its workers' compensation carrier, which accepted the accident as compensable and began making workers' compensation payments to Cuero. Cuero filed a second-amended complaint. Ryland and Sunfish both answered, raising as an affirmative defense their immunity from tort liability under § 440.11, Fla. Stat.. Cuero maintained that he was not a statutory employee of the defendants, that the defendants had failed to secure or provide workers' compensation benefits, and that the defendants were estopped or had waived the assertion of the defense.

The 2d DCA found that Ryland was constructing the town homes as a commercial business venture for itself and not as a result of individual contractual obligations to third parties. The decision to construct a building was not dependent upon sales agreements having been executed for the individual units. Furthermore, the court found that if the sales agreement for an individual unit failed for some reason, such as denial of the buyer's mortgage application, the unit would still be constructed for speculative sale. More important, prior to closing, Ryland retained full ownership of, and assumed all risk of loss or damage to the property.

The court noted that these facts make clear that Ryland's primary obligation to construct the town homes in the Bayshore Town home project did not derive from the sales agreements ultimately executed with individual prospective purchasers. Ryland undertook to develop its own property, acting as its own general contractor. It entered into subcontracts to build all of the buildings and units, whether presold or not. It did not enter into subcontracts on a unit-by-unit basis for the purpose of passing on a construction obligation with a potential purchaser for a particular unit. Thus, the only privity of contract or obligation of Sunfish to perform work on the Bayshore Town homes project was with Ryland, the owner of the project. Furthermore, the sales agreements upon which Ryland relied were not construction contracts nor did they give rise to the contractor relationship required by § 440.10(1)(b), Fla. Stat.. The court held that to construe them as such would result in the illogical and untenable conclusion that Ryland was the statutory employer of persons working on units for which a sales agreement had been executed but was not the statutory employer of persons working on the remaining units. Under this view, Ryland's status as a contractor and statutory employer would have to be examined on a unit-by-unit basis, and Ryland's status would be subject to change during the course of construction on an individual unit from day to day or hour to hour as agreements were executed or defaulted.

The court, therefore, held that an owner/developer acting as its own general contractor is not a "contractor" for workers' compensation purposes. Therefore the owner/developer is not a statutory employer required to provide workers' compensation coverage. The definition of a "contractor" under § 440.10(1)(b), Fla. Stat., by clear implication, requires that there be a contractual obligation on the part of the contractor, a portion of which he sublets to another. To "sublet" means to "underlet" in the context in which it is used in § 440.10(1)(b), Fla. Stat.. The effect of subletting is to pass on to another an obligation under a contract for which the person so "subletting" is primarily obligated. If the developer owns the buildings under construction, there is no contract to sublet. The court held that one does not become a contractor under § 440.10, Fla. Stat. merely by entering into a contract with a subcontractor.

It is the obligation to secure workers' compensation that gives the employer immunity from suit as a third-party tortfeasor. This immunity from suit is commensurate with the duty to secure compensation. Since an owner/developer, even when acting as its own general contractor, has no duty to provide workers' compensation coverage for the employees of its contractors, immunity does not apply [*see* Cuero v. Ryland Group, 849 So. 2d 326, 328 (Fla. 2d DCA 2003)].

[3] Case Examples: Non-Construction General Contractors

Case 1. The Miami Herald entered an Independent Dealer Agreement with a newspaper distributor in Broward County. The distributor, in turn, hired several street hawkers to sell newspapers on street corners. A car struck one of these street hawkers while he was selling newspapers. At the time of the accident, the distributor's workers' compensation coverage had expired and the distributor was uninsured. The question became whether the Miami Herald was the injured worker's statutory employer and responsible for benefits. The First District Court of Appeal held that it was. How can this be? What contract had the Herald sublet?

The Herald had a contract with its advertisers, not only to publish their advertisements, but to deliver the advertisements to the recipients as well. It was the delivery portion of its contract the court found the Herald had sublet. Thus, the Herald became the statutory employer of the distributor and its street hawkers. Since the distributor was illegally uninsured, the court held the Miami Herald liable for benefits [*see* Miami Herald Pub. Co. v. Hatch, 617 So. 2d 380, 382–385 (Fla. 1st DCA 1993)].

Case 2. Ocean Suite Hotel leased space on its premises to Juniper's Restaurant. One of Juniper's cooks hurt herself when she slipped and fell in the restaurant's cooler. Unfortunately for the cook, the restaurant's operator was illegally uninsured. Faced with no source of benefits from her direct employer, she then claimed that she was the hotel's statutory employee. The judge of compensation claims denied her claim. The judge held she was neither the hotel's direct nor statutory employee. Also, the restaurant's only relationship to the hotel was as a tenant under a lease agreement. On appeal, the First District Court of Appeal disagreed and reversed, holding that the hotel was the injured worker's statutory employer. What contract had the hotel sublet? As stated by the court, the hotel sublet its contract with its guests. In its marketing, the hotel had offered its guests a package rate that included a free breakfast. In doing so, the hotel had sublet its obligation to provide the breakfast to Juniper's Restaurant. Thus, the court held that the hotel became the statutory employer of Juniper's employees [*see* Antinarelli v. Ocean Suite Hotel, 642 So. 2d 661, 662–664 (Fla. 1st DCA 1994)].

Case 3. The key to statutory employer status is the existence of a contract of which all or part has been subcontracted to another. In this case, the employer was the owner of a shopping center. The property owner, James Batmasian, hired a roofing company to make repairs. When Paul Ballachino was injured, he discovered that his actual employer, All Roofing Metal Systems, did not have workers' compensation coverage. He then sued Batmasian arguing that he should be held liable as the statutory employer because he had a contract with his tenants requiring him to maintain the common roof areas. Ballachino asserted that Batmasian had subcontracted this obligation to All Roofing, thus creating a subcontract and statutory employer status. The lower court agreed, but the 4th DCA disagreed and reversed. The court held that Batmasian would qualify as a statutory employer only if he had agreed by contract to repair the roof himself and then, in turn, subcontracted that repair contract to another [*see* Batmasian v. Ballachino, 755 So. 2d 157, 158 (Fla. 4th DCA 2000)].

[4] Common Carriers and Public Utilities

The law does not exempt corporations that have public responsibilities as common carriers or as public utilities from the Act's statutory employer provisions. The purpose of § 440.10, Fla. Stat. is to insure that a particular industry is financially responsible for injuries to those employees working in it, although the prime contractor employs an independent contractor to do all or part of its contractual undertaking [Gator Freightways, Inc. v. Roberts, 550 So. 2d 1117, 1119 (Fla. 1989)].

If a subcontractor subject to the Workers' Compensation Act does not provide workers' compensation coverage of its own, then the general contractor, as statutory employer, must do so. The *Miami Herald* and *Ocean Suites Hotel* cases now bring virtually every employer into potential general contractor status [*see* [3], *above*]. Employers must be certain to assure that any contractors employed have all required insurance coverage.

While the law may expose all employers to hidden liability for workers' compensation while they are in a general contractor status, they also enjoy immunity from negligence suits. The law in Florida is well settled that employers who provide workers' compensation coverage are immune from suits brought by employees for workplace injuries [*see* § 440.11, Fla. Stat. (1970)]. The immunity applies to general contractors, so they are immune from lawsuits brought by employees of a subcontractor [Motchkavitz v. L.C. Boggs Industries, Inc. 407 So. 2d 910, 912–913 (Fla. 1981); Marco Polo Hotel v. Popielarczyk, 622 So. 2d 104 (Fla. 3d DCA 1993); *see* ch. 19, § 19.04[2][a]].

[5] Independent Contractor or Subcontractor

Confusion often arises when people try to understand the difference between an independent contractor and a subcontractor. As a practical matter, no real difference exists. The distinction is only important when deciding who is responsible or eligible for workers' compensation. An independent contractor becomes a subcontractor when it does all or part of the contractual obligation of another [*see* [2], *above*].

All employers with four or more employees (one or more in the construction industry) must provide workers' compensation coverage [§ 440.02(15)(b)2, Fla. Stat. (1994)]. When an independent contractor is in subcontractor status and does not provide coverage for its employees as required by law, the general contractor becomes liable [§ 440.10(1)(b), Fla. Stat. (1994)]. Even evidence that the subcontractor lied to the general contractor or gave fraudulent certificates of workers' compensation coverage provides no defense. If the subcontractor is subject to the Workers' Compensation Act and is illegally uninsured, the general contractor must provide benefits.

[6] Exempt Officers, Partners, and Sole Proprietors

What happens if a sole proprietor, partner, or corporate officer elects exemption from the Workers' Compensation Act? The general contractor is not responsible for providing workers compensation for these individuals. This is because the law no longer considers them employees under the Workers' Compensation Act. As such, they are not subject to the law or entitled to its benefits [*see* §§ 3.03, 3.04].

[7] Uninsured Subcontractors

[a] Carrier's Recourse

Carriers forced to pay claims for uninsured subcontractors can sue the subcontractor to recover benefits paid. Effective July 1, 1990, the legislature added a statutory recovery right that includes interest. The section provides in part that [§ 440.10(1)(d)1., Fla. Stat.]:

> If a contractor becomes liable for the payment of compensation to the employees of a subcontractor who has failed to secure such payment in violation of [§ 440.38, Fla. Stat.], the contractor or other third-party payor shall be entitled to recover from the subcontractor all benefits paid or payable plus interest unless the contractor and subcontractor have agreed in writing that the contractor will provide coverage.

In addition, it is a third-degree felony for a subcontractor knowingly to mislead anyone concerning workers' compensation coverage [§ 440.105(4), Fla. Stat.]. If an adjuster's investigation reveals evidence of fraud, the adjuster should report the facts to the Division of Insurance Fraud, Bureau of Workers' Compensation Fraud.

[b] Making Certain Subcontractor Is Uninsured

Carriers and self-insured employers should be certain the subcontractor is not insured before accepting responsibility for benefits. Early reports may suggest that the subcontractor is uninsured, but investigate to be certain. Check with the Division's Compliance Unit. This unit maintains records on employer coverage. The law requires every insurance carrier to report new policies and cancellations to the Division. Even if the records show the subcontractor's insurer canceled coverage, further investigation may be warranted. If a carrier should issue a binder or policy by mistake, the carrier may deny coverage but is likely to owe coverage anyway. This will occur under the doctrine of equitable estoppel.

For example, the carrier canceled Atlantic Masonry's coverage for nonpayment of premiums. The carrier then, by mistake, sent out a renewal policy and declarations. Atlantic presented the declarations to Miller as proof of coverage. When an Atlantic employee was injured, Atlantic's insurance carrier denied coverage. The law then required the general contractor, Miller, to provide coverage for its apparently uninsured subcontractor. The court held the carrier's act of issuing the renewal policy estopped it from now denying its promise to provide workers' compensation coverage [*see* Masonry v. Miller Const., 558 So. 2d 433, 434 (Fla. 1st DCA 1990)].

[8] When State Laws Conflict

Recall that statutory employer status confers immunity from negligence suits brought by the subcontractor's employees. Many contractors conduct business in several states and sometimes these state laws are in conflict with Florida's laws. When this happens, Florida law will usually control because Florida will have the greatest interest in the outcome of the case. Florida uses the "significant relationship test," which provides that the state law with the most significant relationship to the occurrence and to the parties will control [Restatement (Second) of Conflict of Laws § 145(1) (1971); *see* Bishop v. Florida Specialty Paint Co., 389 So. 2d 999, 1001 (Fla. 1980) (adopting Restatement)].

For example, Marion Power, a Delaware corporation, agreed to repair drag line equipment in Dade County, Florida. Marion Power then subcontracted part of the work to Industrial Contracting and Erecting, Inc., an Indiana corporation. Industrial hired Michael Hargis, an Illinois resident, to work on the Florida project. After suffering an injury on the job, Hargis began collecting Illinois workers' compensation benefits and also sued Marion Power. Hargis argued that Florida's immunity laws did not apply because Illinois law does not allow such immunity. The trial court agreed and allowed the suit, but was reversed on appeal. Florida law must apply, said the court, because Florida had the most significant contacts with the issue. The injury happened in Florida as did Marion Power's alleged negligence acts. Further, Hargis could have received Florida workers' compensation benefits. The only connection to Illinois was that it was Hargis' home state and the place where he was hired. Because Illinois had only a minor connection to the litigation, Florida law must apply and, under that law, Marion Power was immune [*see* Marion Power Shovel Co. v. Hargis, 698 So. 2d 1246, 1247–1248 (Fla. 3d DCA 1997)].

For general discussion of conflict of laws, see LARSON'S WORKERS' COMPENSATION, DESK EDITION, Ch. 142 (Matthew Bender).

§ 3.07 Borrowed Servants (Loaned Employees)

[1] General Rule

When a general employer lends an employee to a special employer, the special employer must provide workers' compensation if (1) the employee has made a contract of hire, either express or implied, with the special employer; (2) the work being done is essentially that of the special employer; and (3) the special employer has the right to control the details of the work [Interstate Indus. Park v. Afterdeck Restaurant, 478 So. 2d 852, 854 (Fla. 1st DCA 1985) (dicta)].

Note that leased employees are borrowed employees by statutory definition. When an employer leases its workers from an employee leasing company, the act provides that these leased workers "shall be considered a borrowed employee of the employer." The employer is also responsible for providing workers' compensation coverage if the leasing company does not. [*see* § 440.11(2), Fla. Stat.].

For general discussion of borrowed servants, see LARSON'S WORKERS' COMPENSATION, DESK EDITION, Ch. 67 (Matthew Bender).

[2] Application of Rule

The most important question in loaned employee cases is this: Did the employee make a contract of hire with the special employer? If the answer to this question is yes, the investigation is closed and tests of relative control and the like are unnecessary [Interstate Indus. Park v. Afterdeck Restaurant, 478 So. 2d 852, 854 (Fla. 1st DCA 1985)]. The 5th DCA agrees that the most important factor in deciding whether an employee is a borrowed

Guide to Claims

servant is whether a contract of hire, expressed or implied, exists between the employee and the alleged special employer. Indeed, the court noted that the other factors, such as whether the work performed was the work of the alleged special employer and whether the special employer exercised control over the employee, are essentially indicia of the existence of a contract of hire [*see* Sherrill v. Corbett Cranes Servs., 656 So. 2d 181, 185 (Fla. 5th DCA 1995)].

The Florida Supreme Court's decision in one case is particularly instructive on the contract of hire issue. In *Shelby,* the employee originally worked for T&R farms, but the employer transferred him to T&R Packing, a separate corporation. On a day off from work, the employee went to the farm to find a wrench he had left there while working for the packing company. While he was on the premises, an individual who was a principal in both companies asked the employee to perform some work on machinery owned by the farm. While doing so, the employee was killed in an explosion. He had, on occasion, performed small jobs on the farm while working for the packing company, but only received his regular salary. The court held that no express or implied contract existed to substitute the farm for the packing company as the employer at the time of the injury. Therefore, the packing company's insurer was responsible for the entire amount of the death benefits awarded. Here, the Florida Supreme Court declared a presumption in favor of the continuance of the general employment. The presumption can be overcome only by a clear demonstration that a new, temporary employer has been substituted for the old. This demonstration should include proof that the work being done was, essentially, that of the special employer, and proof that the special employer assumed the right to control the details of the work [*see* Shelby Mutual Insurance Co. v. Aetna Insurance Co., 246 So. 2d 98, 101–102 (Fla. 1971)].

In a more recent case, Modern Drywall put its employee on Hoar Construction Company's payroll. This was done under the terms of an agreement among Modern Drywall, Hoar Construction, and Lee County. The purpose of transferring the employee was to avoid a licensure problem. The judge of compensation claims held the injured worker was either Hoar Construction's actual employee, or at least its "special" employee. In disagreeing, the court of appeal held that paying wages is the *least* important factor. The court found that Modern Drywall retained, and continued to exercise, its right to control and direct the employee's work and, thus, he remained an employee of Modern Drywall for all purposes except the administrative task of issuing paychecks. This particular task was clearly administrative only, because Hoar Construction deducted wages paid from Modern Drywall's payment draw. The court held that the injured worker was clearly not the actual employee of Hoar Construction. Also, the injured worker was not a special employee for several reasons. First, Hoar Construction did not assume control over the employee. Second, the employee did not consent to Hoar Construction's control. Third, the work done was Modern Drywall's. These are the elements the law requires for a special employment relationship to exist [*see* Hoar Const. v. Varney, 586 So. 2d 463, 464 (Fla. 1st DCA 1991)].

§ 3.08 Dual Employment

[1] General Rule

Dual employment occurs when a single employee is under a contract of hire with two different employers. The employee must be under the separate control of each employer, and the employee must do largely unrelated services for each employer separately. In dual employment, the two employers may be liable for workers' compensation separately or jointly. Which one applies depends on the severability of the employee's activities at the time of the injury [*see* Julian Consolidated, Inc. v. Conrad, 553 So. 2d 784 (Fla. 1st DCA 1989)].

For general discussion of borrowed servants, see Larson's Workers' Compensation, Desk Edition, Ch. 67 (Matthew Bender).

[2] Application of Rule

When deciding which of two employers is responsible for providing benefits, ask the following questions: Were the employee's activities separable between the employers? Was there a clear distinction between the activity with one employer and the other? If so, the employer whose work the employee was performing at the time of the injury is exclusively liable.

A joint venture can be a good example of dual employment. Assume that an investor and a builder form a joint venture to build a house on speculation. The investor provides the funds and the builder provides the skill and knowledge, and neither party has exclusive control. The investor and the builder agree to share profits and losses. Here, the courts would assess the cost of a worker's injury equally against both the investor and the builder [*see* Julian Consolidated, Inc. v. Conrad, 553 So. 2d 784 (Fla. 1st DCA 1989)].

§ 3.09 Excluded Employments

[1] General Rule

The law excludes certain classes of employments from coverage under the Workers' Compensation Act. These include convicts, certain juveniles, domestic servants in private homes, agricultural labor, and professional athletes [§ 440.02(15)(c), Fla. Stat. (1994)].

[2] Convicts

Jail and prison inmates are not state or local government employees. Since they are not employees, they are not eligible for workers' compensation benefits. This rule does not apply to private employers when they employ prisoners through a work-release program [§ 946.002, Fla. Stat. (1996)].

Prison inmates cannot collect benefits from governmental entities. This is because true employment does not exist. The legal status of a prisoner is that of an individual in a rehabilitative training program. This exclusion also applies to workers performing labor under a sentence of a court. An example is a convicted drunk driver performing a community service. This is punishment as provided by § 316.193, Fla. Stat., and such individuals are not employees.

A prisoner on a work-release program working for a government agency is not an employee of the agency. The law specifically provides that such workers are not employees. Thus, the law does not entitle them to workers' compensation benefits [§ 946.002, Fla. Stat. (1996); *see* State, Dept. of Health, etc. v. O'Neal, 400 So. 2d 28, 29–30 (Fla. 1st DCA 1981)].

Remember that this applies only to government agencies and not to private employers. Prisoners working in a work-release program for a private employer are considered employees of the private employer and are eligible for benefits [§ 946.002, Fla. Stat. (1996)].

This exclusion from coverage also does not include inmates who are injured while working for employers or those described in § 948.03(8)(a), Fla. Stat. That section provides that an offender is considered to be a state employee and eligible for workers' compensation benefits under the following circumstances:

1. When the offender is required by the court to participate in any work program under the provisions of Chapter 948; or
2. When the offender enters into the pretrial intervention program under § 948.08, Fla. Stat.; or
3. When the offender volunteers to work in a supervised work program conducted by a specified state, county, municipal, or community service organization; or
4. When the offender volunteers to work for the victim, either as an alternative to monetary restitution or as a part of the rehabilitative or community control program [*see* § 440.02(16)(c), Fla. Stat. (10/1/2001)].

For general discussion of borrowed servants, see Larson's Workers' Compensation, Desk Edition, Ch. 64, § 64.03 (Matthew Bender).

[3] Juveniles Under Sentence of a Court

The 1977 legislature created a special, partly covered, class of employee. These are juveniles who "volunteer" or are required to work for a governmental authority or a community service organization. The law entitles these individuals to medical benefits, but not disability benefits [§ 39.11(7), Fla. Stat. (1987); § 440.02(15)(c)4, Fla. Stat. (1994)].

Chapter 39, Florida Statutes, deals with juvenile delinquents, and the courts assign the work described here as punishment. § 39.11(7), Fla. Stat. provides that the child, working under the order of the court, is an employee of the state. Any wages received, however, are a gratuity. Thus, the statute provides that the child "shall not be entitled to any benefits otherwise payable under § 440.15, Fla. Stat." § 440.15, Fla. Stat. is the indemnity benefits section of the Workers' Compensation Act.

[4] Domestic Servants

[a] In General

Whether the law requires an employer to purchase workers' compensation coverage for a domestic servant depends on the employee's actual status. We can separate employment status into three categories: First, those domestic servants employed in private homes [*see* [b], *below*]; second, those employed in a corporate setting [*see* [c], *below*]; and third, those employed by a business to provide domestic services for a corporate officer [*see* [d], *below*].

[b] Domestic Servants in Private Homes

The law does not require employers to provide workers' compensation coverage for domestic servants in private homes [§ 440.02(15)(c), Fla Stat. (1994)]. In 1985, the First District Court of Appeal explained it this way [Smith v. Ford, 472 So. 2d 1223, 1227–1228 (Fla. 1st DCA 1985) (citing *Gunter v. Mersereau,* 491 P.2d 1205 (Or. App. 1971))]:

> The motivating philosophy behind worker's compensation acts is that the loss arising from accidents in industry should be distributed between the employer and consumer as a cost of production. The domestic servant exception recognizes that the home owner, who receives no pecuniary profit from maintaining his home, should not be made to bear what would amount to the total burden of compensation protection. The exclusion of domestic servants is in accord with the intent of the Workers' Compensation Law and is to be fairly applied with that intent and purpose in mind. Private homes having domestics who perform a combination of household duties and personal care services for infants, disabled, or elderly persons are not within the intent of the act or required under its terms to be covered by workers' compensation insurance.

[c] Domestic Servants in Corporate Setting

The phrase "in private homes" is important because the law entitles domestic servants to benefits if they work in a corporate setting. The most frequently encountered example is a person hired to provide housekeeping services in a hotel. No cases deal specifically with this, but the conclusion is obvious: a business is not a private home. The distinction, as the court explained in *Smith v. Ford,* 472 So. 2d 1223, 1227 (Fla. 1st DCA 1985), is whether the servant is employed in a for-profit enterprise.

[d] Personal Services for Corporate Officer

A corporation may hire a person to provide housekeeping services for a corporate officer. If the corporation treats the housekeeper as an employee in most respects, it is highly unlikely that the courts will allow the corporation to deny employee status for workers' compensation purposes. What is more common is for the owner of a small business to use its payroll system to simplify compliance with tax withholding laws.

For example, Dr. Mary Schooley hired Mercedes Vargas as a housekeeper and babysitter. At first Dr. Schooley paid Vargas in cash until she learned that federal law required her to withhold taxes. She decided the simplest way to handle this was to use her animal hospital's payroll account. After Vargas hurt herself while working in Dr. Schooley's home, Vargas claimed benefits under the animal hospital's insurance policy. The judge of compensation claims agreed and awarded benefits. The judge viewed Vargas' status as one hired by a corporation to provide domestic services for a corporate officer. On appeal the carrier argued that the corporation carried the injured worker on the payroll merely for convenience. Any nexus between the corporation and the injured worker was illusory. The First District Court of Appeal agreed with the carrier and reversed. The court's decision turned on its finding that there was no evidence that the corporation deducted Vargas' wages as a business expense on its tax return [*see* Community Animal Hosp., Inc. v. Vargas, 642 So. 2d 812, 814 (Fla. 1st DCA 1994)].

[5] Agricultural Labor

An employer is not responsible for workers' compensation benefits under the following conditions:

1. The employer is a bona fide farmer or association of farmers;
2. The employer employs five or fewer regular employees; and
3. The employer employs less than 12 seasonal workers at any one time for work to be completed in less than 30 days and not more than 45 days during the same calendar year.

Agricultural labor cases require a complete investigation into the employment's nature and the injured worker's duties. Remember, a farmer can voluntarily purchase insurance coverage and bring the employees under the Workers' Compensation Act [§ 440.02(15)(c)2, Fla. Stat.].

For the law to exclude them, farm employees must be engaged in literal agricultural work. An employee hired by a farm to repair buildings, for example, is not an agricultural worker, and the Workers' Compensation Act covers someone working in this capacity [Thomas Smith Farms, Inc. v. Alday, 182 So. 2d 405, 411 (Fla. 1966)].

For general discussion of borrowed servants, see LARSON'S WORKERS' COMPENSATION, DESK EDITION, Ch. 75 (Matthew Bender).

[6] Professional Athletes

The law excludes professional athletes from coverage under the Workers' Compensation Act. The employer may, of course, voluntarily provide coverage. The statute lists certain professional athletes, such as boxers, wrestlers, baseball and football players, and motor sports teams [§ 440.02(15)(c)3, Fla. Stat. (1994)]. Motor sports teams include not only drivers, but pit crews as well [§ 549.08, Fla. Stat. (1989)].

All claims involving professional athletes require an investigation to learn what the athlete was doing at the time of the injury. This is because the exclusion applies only while the athlete is engaged in the sport itself. A baseball player injured while attending a press conference is entitled to benefits [Miles v. Montreal Baseball Club, 379 So. 2d 1325, 1326 (Fla. 1st DCA 1980)]. The exclusion applies during tryouts, practice, and actual games [Rudolph v. Miami Dolphins, Ltd., 447 So. 2d 284, 288 (Fla. 1st DCA 1983)].

§ 3.10 Leased Employees

[1] Introduction

With the growing popularity of leasing employees, the practitioner will likely encounter a growing number of claims involving these often complex, dual-employer situations. The employee leasing company and the actual employer are considered co-employers with mutual obligations. More precisely, the leasing company is deemed to be the employer, and the employee is deemed to be the borrowed servant of the client company. The discussion that follows is designed to assist in understanding how these organizations function, how they are regulated, and how such arrangements are treated under the workers' compensation law.

Guide to Claims

[2] Employee Leasing and Regulation

[a] Regulation

Employee leasing companies are regulated by the Board of Employee Leasing Companies, Department of Business and Professional Regulation, created under part XI of chapter 468, Florida Statutes [*see* § 468.521, Fla. Stat. et seq.].

[b] Definition of Employee Leasing Company

The statutory definition of an employee leasing company is as follows:

> The term "employee leasing company" means an employing unit which maintains a valid and active license under chapter 468 and which maintains the records required by § 443.171(7) and, in addition, maintains a listing of the clients of the employee leasing company and of the employees, including their social security numbers, who have been assigned to work at each client company job site. Further, each client company job site must be identified by industry, products or services, and address. The client list shall be provided to the division by June 30 and by December 31 of each year. For purposes of this subsection, "client" means a party who has contracted with an employee leasing company to provide a worker, or workers, to perform services for the client. Leased employees shall include employees subsequently placed on the payroll of the employee leasing company on behalf of the client. The employee leasing company shall notify the division within 30 days of the initiation or termination of the company's relationship with any client company pursuant to chapter 468 [§ 443.036(18), Fla. Stat. (2001)].

The phrase "Employee Leasing Company" does not include [§ 468.520(4), Fla. Stat.]:

1. A temporary help arrangement, whereby an organization hires its own employees and assigns them to a client to support or supplement the client's workforce in special work situations such as employee absences, temporary skill shortages, seasonal workloads, and special assignments and projects.

2. An arrangement in which an organization employs only one category of employees and assigns them to a client to perform a function inherent to that category and which function is separate and divisible from the primary business of the client.

3. A facilities staffing arrangement, whereby an organization assigns its employees to staff a specific client function or functions, on an ongoing, indefinite basis.

4. An arrangement in which an organization assigns its employees only to a

commonly controlled company or group of companies and in which the organization does not hold itself out to the public as an employee leasing company.

5. A home health agency unless otherwise engaged in business as an employee leasing company.

6. A health care services pool unless otherwise engaged in business as an employee leasing company.

[c] Licensing

To operate an employee leasing company in Florida, both the leasing company and the controlling person must be licensed [§ 468.526, Fla. Stat. (2001)]. The controlling person is defined as any natural person who possesses, directly or indirectly, the power to direct or cause the direction of the management or policies of any employee leasing company, including, but not limited to [§ 468.520(7), Fla. Stat. (2001)]:

1. Direct or indirect control of 50 percent or more of the voting securities of the employee leasing company;

2. The general power to endorse any negotiable instrument payable to or on behalf of the employee leasing company or to cause the direction of the management or policies of any employee leasing company; or

3. Any natural person employed, appointed, or authorized by an employee leasing company to enter into a contractual relationship with a client company on behalf of the employee leasing company.

To qualify for a license, the controlling person must meet all of the requirements of § 468.525, Fla. Stat., which includes having a "good moral character" and documentation showing that the applicant has the education or experience necessary to successfully operate a leasing company [*see* § 468.525(1), Fla. Stat.]. Note that conviction of a crime does not automatically bar an applicant from obtaining a license or continuing as a licensee [*see* § 468.525(2)(b), Fla. Stat.].

[d] Change of Ownership

A person or entity seeking to purchase or acquire ownership of an existing leasing company must first obtain approval from the Board and meet all of the requirements of § 468.525, Fla. Stat. [§ 468.5245, Fla. Stat.].

[e] Responsibilities

Under the provisions of § 468.525, Fla. Stat., the leasing agreement must reflect that the leasing company is responsible for:

1. Maintaining accounting and employment records relating to all employee leasing activities for a minimum of 3 calendar years.

2. Reserving a right of direction and control over leased employees assigned to the client's location. However, a client may retain such sufficient direction and

control over the leased employees as is necessary to conduct the client's business and without which the client would be unable to conduct its business, discharge any fiduciary responsibility that it may have, or comply with any applicable licensure, regulatory, or statutory requirement of the client.

3. Assuming responsibility for the payment of wages to the leased employees without regard to payments by the client to the leasing company.
4. Assuming full responsibility for the payment of payroll taxes and collection of taxes from payroll on leased employees.
5. Retaining authority to hire, terminate, discipline, and reassign the leased employees. However, the client company may have the right to accept or cancel the assignment of any leased employee.
6. Retaining a right of direction and control over management of safety, risk, and hazard control at the work site or sites affecting its leased employees.
7. Performing safety inspections of client equipment and premises.
8. Promulgating and administering employment and safety policies.
9. Managing workers' compensation claims, claims filings, and related procedures.
10. Giving written notice of the relationship between the employee leasing company and the client company to each leased employee it assigns to perform services at the client's work site.

NOTE: Because § 468.532, Fla. Stat. authorizes the Board of Employee Leasing Companies to discipline licensees only, unlike most other professional disciplinary statutes, it does not provide the board with jurisdiction to discipline an entity whose license has expired prior to the filing of the administrative complaint [Haggerty v. Department of Bus. & Prof'l Regulation, 716 So. 2d 873, 874 (Fla. 1st DCA 1998)].

[f] Who Is the Employer

The law provides that leased workers are the employees of the leasing company. § 443.036(21)(a)1b, Fla. Stat. provides as follows:

> Any individual who, under the usual common-law rules applicable in determining the employer-employee relationship, has the status of an employee. However, whenever a company, hereafter referred to as "client," which would otherwise be designated as an employing unit has contracted with an employee leasing company to supply it with workers, those workers shall, after December 31, 1986, be considered employees of the employee leasing company. The employee leasing company shall be permitted to lease corporate officers of the client to the client and such other workers where not prohibited by Internal Revenue Service regulations. Employees of the employee leasing company shall be reported under the employee leasing company's tax identification number and tax rate for work performed for the employee leasing company.

Guide to Claims

> **NOTE:** For workers' compensation purposes, leased workers are borrowed servants and the client company is a special employer. *See* [3], *below.*

[g] Unemployment Compensation

When leased workers leave the employment, they owe a duty to both employers for unemployment compensation purposes. Regardless of the reason leased employees terminate employment, they are deemed to have resigned voluntarily and are not entitled to unemployment compensation unless they contact the employee leasing company. The statute provides as follows [§ 443.101(10)(b), Fla. Stat. (2001)]:

> A temporary or leased employee will be deemed to have voluntarily quit employment and will be disqualified for benefits under subparagraph (1)(a)1. if, upon conclusion of his or her latest assignment, the temporary or leased employee, without good cause, failed to contact the temporary help or employee-leasing firm for reassignment, provided that the employer advised the temporary or leased employee at the time of hire and that the leased employee is notified also at the time of separation that he or she must report for reassignment upon conclusion of each assignment, regardless of the duration of the assignment, and that unemployment benefits may be denied for failure to do so.

If the leasing contract has terminated, or if the leasing company failed to submit reports or pay contributions, the actual employer becomes the new employer for unemployment compensation purposes. The statute provides as follows [§ 443.131(3)(g)4, Fla. Stat. (2001)]:

> This paragraph shall not apply to the employee leasing company and client contractual agreement as defined in § 443.036. The client shall, in the event of termination of the contractual agreement or failure by the employee leasing company to submit reports or pay contributions as required by the division, be treated as a new employer without previous employment record unless otherwise eligible for a rate computation.

[3] Employee Leasing Companies and Workers' Compensation

[a] Workers' Status Is Borrowed Employee

When a general employer lends an employee to a special employer, the special employer must provide workers' compensation if (1) the employee has made a contract of hire, either express or implied, with the special employer; (2) the work being done is essentially that of the special employer; and (3) the special employer has the right to control the details of the work [Interstate Indus. Park v. Afterdeck Restaurant, 478 So. 2d 852, 854 (Fla. 1st DCA 1985) (dicta)].

For workers' compensation purposes, the leasing company is the actual employer, but the client company (the "real" employer) takes on the persona of a special employer. Leased employees are borrowed employees by statutory definition. When an employer leases its workers from an employee leasing company, the workers' compensation act provides that these leased workers "shall be considered a borrowed employee of the employer." The actual employer is also responsible for providing workers' compensation coverage if the leasing company does not do so [*see* § 440.11(2), Fla. Stat. (2001)].

[b] Immunity

Workers' compensation is the injured employee's exclusive remedy. When employers properly secure workers' compensation coverage for their employees, the law grants them (almost) total immunity from suits brought by their employees. Effective January 1, 1994, the legislature amended the Act to include county governments specifically under the immunity umbrella. Immunity does not apply, however, if the employer has engaged in any intentional act that causes harm. Such acts are those designed or substantially certain to result in injury or death to the employee [§ 440.11(1), Fla. Stat. (1/1/94)].

Guide to Claims

Statutory immunity extends to employers who lease their workers from employee leasing companies. Leased employees are statutorily considered to be borrowed servants, but for purposes of immunity are treated as any other employee of the employer. Indeed, such employers are required by the same statutory section to provide workers' compensation coverage if the leasing company does not do so [*see* § 440.11(2), Fla. Stat. (2001)].

The fact that the employee leasing company provides the coverage does not alter the actual employer's immunity status. This is true even if the employee signs an affidavit declaring that he or she is an employee of the employee leasing company. This is because the employer in such cases will have paid a fee to the employee leasing company to provide, among other things, such coverage. If the employee is injured and receives benefits from the insurer for the employee leasing company, the worker cannot take a second bite at the apple by suing the employer in tort. Also, note that the Act, § 440.11(2), Fla. Stat., specifically includes the "help supply services" industry under Standard Industry Code Number 7363, which includes employee leasing services, temporary help services, and labor pools [*see* Maxson Const. Co., Inc. v. Welch, 720 So. 2d 588, 590 (Fla. 2d DCA 1998); *see also* Caramico v. Artcraft Industries, Inc., 727 So. 2d 348, 349 (Fla. 5th DCA 1999) (approving *Maxson*)].

For example, Nurse Finders, a temporary employment agency, placed Watson with Job Corp. to work as a nurse. Watson was later injured while on the job at Job Corp. and sued Job Corp. for negligence. The trial court granted summary judgment in Job Corp.'s favor, finding that Job Corp. was entitled to workers' compensation immunity.

On appeal, the 3d DCA agreed and affirmed. The court held that § 440.11(2), Fla. Stat. (2002), extends an employer's immunity from tort liability to work-related injuries of employees obtained through a help supply services company and also applies to companies that hire workers through temporary employment agencies [*see* B.E.T. Plant Servs. v. Dyer, 678 So. 2d 841, 842 (Fla. 3d DCA 1996); Caramico v. Artcraft Indus., Inc., 727 So. 2d 348, 349 (Fla. 5th DCA 1999)]. The court found that it was undisputed that Nurse Finders supplied Job Corp. with temporary help and that Watson was an employee under Job Corp.'s direction and control at the time he was injured. Watson was thus a borrowed servant of Job Corp. Therefore, the court held that Job Corp. was entitled to the statutory employer immunity [Watson v. Job Corp., 840 So. 2d 367 (Fla. 2d DCA 2003)].

[4] Case Law Review

[a] Responsibility for Benefits

If there is no employer/employee relationship between the injured worker and the leasing company, the actual employer becomes liable for benefits. Here, the leasing company challenged a decision of the judge of compensation claims that directed the leasing company to provide any benefits to which the claimant may have been entitled. The leasing company argued that there was no competent, substantial evidence to support the finding that the leasing company was the claimant's employer at the time of the accident.

The claimant was working for a construction subcontractor, who had an employee leasing agreement with Speciality Leasing company. The leasing company agreed to lease employees to the construction company and to provide employee-related services, including paying workers' compensation premiums. The claimant was injured in a work-related accident while working for the construction subcontractor. The claimant filed two petitions seeking a determination of compensability of his claim. The first was filed against the general contractor and its carrier, and the second was filed against the leasing company. The judge of compensation claims found that the claimant was an employee of the leasing company, through its agreement with the subcontractor, and therefore was required to pay benefits. The First District Court of Appeal reversed this decision, holding that the claimant was not an employee of the leasing company. The court found that the leasing company's relationship with the claimant had been terminated several weeks before the accident. Since the actual employer, the subcontractor, did not have coverage of its own, the court held the general contractor liable as the statutory employer of an uninsured subcontractor [Speciality Employee Leasing v. Davis, 737 So. 2d 1170, 1171 (Fla. 1st DCA 1999)].

[b] Immunity

Case 1. The claimant was a leased employee. After his injury at work, the claimant received workers' compensation benefits from the leasing company. The claimant then filed suit against the client company, his actual employer. The court granted summary judgment for the employer, holding that it was immune under § 440.11, Fla. Stat. because of its use of the services of a help supply services company and the provision of workers' compensation benefits by that company [Caramico v. Artcraft Indus., Inc., 727 So. 2d 348, 349 (Fla. 5th DCA 1999)].

Case 2. The claimant was an employee hired by the contractor but also employed by an employee leasing company that provided benefits, including workers' compensation coverage. The claimant was injured and recovered benefits from the leasing company's workers' compensation coverage pursuant to a stipulation that listed the leasing company as the employer. The claimant then filed an action against the contractor, claiming that the contractor was liable because it was the claimant's employer and it had not provided workers' compensation coverage. The trial court denied the contractor's motion for summary judgment and submitted the issue to the jury, which found that the claimant was not an employee of the leasing company. The contractor appealed and the court reversed, stating that the contractor's motion for summary judgment should have been granted.

Employers that use employee leasing companies are immune from suit pursuant to § 440.11(2), Fla. Stat. The employer's potential liability to employees "borrowed" from an employee leasing company was discharged by the provision of workers' compensation benefits by the leasing company. The claimant was not entitled to bring suit against one employer after receiving benefits from another [Maxson Constr. Co. v. Welch, 720 So. 2d 588, 590 (Fla. 2d DCA 1998)].

[c] Terminating Employee/Employer Relationship

Even employment contracts that are terminable at will, and of no specific duration, require some reasonable notice for termination. In one case, the claimant was employed by the employee leasing company and assigned to work for a transport company. The employee was injured while on this assignment. He filed a workers' compensation claim against the transport company. The transport company filed its own claim for benefits, joining appellants, the leasing company and its insurer, as parties to the action. The leasing company argued that, prior to the employee's accident, it had terminated his employment pursuant to a letter to the transport company, with a copy to the insurer. It never notified the employee. The judge of compensation claims ordered the leasing company's insurer to pay workers' compensation benefits to the employee on the ground that the leasing company's notices were ineffective to terminate the employee's employment with the leasing company. The court affirmed. As an employee at will, the employee could be terminated at any time without prior notice. However, some notice to the employee was required. Because the leasing company failed to prove that it had effectively fired the employee prior to his accident, its insurer was responsible to provide workers' compensation benefits to the employee [Payroll, Inc. v. Elicker, 668 So. 2d 1035, 1038 (Fla. 1st DCA 1996)].

[5] Extending Coverage to Employees of Uninsured Subcontractors

[a] Issues

Because employee leasing companies require individual contracts with each leased employee, a question arises as to whether workers' compensation coverage extends to the employees of the client firm's uninsured subcontractors. The same question also applies to coverage under the Employer's Liability coverage regarding suits brought by the employees of the client firm's subcontractors. It could be argued that coverage does not apply because there is no employer/employee relationship and because the leasing company is not a party to the subcontract. This argument, however, is not likely to withstand judicial scrutiny. If it was held to be true, then there would be no way for contractors who lease employees to comply with their statutory duty to secure the payment of compensation for the employees of subcontractors short of purchasing a second policy.

Additionally, the leasing company and its insurer are aware of the statutory employer concept and its application to workers' compensation. The argument that a subcontractor's workers are not listed and, therefore, not paid for, should be of little import considering that insurance carriers of general contractors receive no premium for subcontractors, but are still responsible for providing benefits.

[b] Applying the Law

The law can be summarized as follows:

1. A subcontractors' employees are employees of the contractor as a matter of law and are therefore protected by the workers' compensation law [§ 440.10(1)(b), Fla. Stat.].

2. The effect of § 440.10, Fla. Stat. is that when a subcontractor, performing part of the work of a contractor, fails to secure payment of compensation, the contractor is liable for same. If both the subcontractor and the contractor fail to secure coverage, then the contractor has an employer's liability to the subcontractor's injured employee for purposes of an action for statutory benefits or damages at law or in admiralty.

3. Statutory employees have been treated identically to actual employees in relation to standard employee exclusion clauses in liability policies. The logic in the exclusion from coverage of both types of employees is simple and compelling: the only coverage intended, and for which the premium has been paid, is the liability of the insured to the public, as distinguished from liability to the insured's employees whether or not they are protected by the workers' compensation law. (Thus, if they are excluded from the liability policy by their status as statutory employees, they must be included under the definition of employee for Coverage B, Employer's liability.)

4. Under the provisions of § 440.11(1), Fla. Stat. (1989), a general contractor's liability remains under the workers' compensation law, notwithstanding his or her failure to secure payment of compensation. This is shown by the statute's elimination of a general contractor's ability to plead negligence by another employee, of his or her ability to plead that the claimant assumed the risk of the employment, and of his or her ability to plead that the injury was due to the claimant's comparative negligence. The failure to secure compensation does not extinguish this employer-employee relationship.

Virtually all general liability policies contain the following exclusion:

This insurance does not apply to:

d. Any obligation of the insured under a worker's compensation . . . law.

e. 'Bodily injury' to:

(1) An employee of the insured arising out of and in the course of employment by the insured. . . .

In one case, the General Liability carrier defended on the basis that the deceased employee was a statutory employee and, therefore, the exclusion applied. The court held that statutory employees have been treated identically to actual employees in relation to standard employee exclusion clauses [Dodge v. Fidelity & Cas. Co. of N.Y., 424 So. 2d 39, 40 (Fla. 5th DCA 1982), *rev. denied,* 431 So. 2d 988 (Fla. 1983) (citing Ward v. Curry, 341 S.W.2d 830 (Mo. 1960)); *see also* Michaels v. United States Fidelity & Guar. Co., 129 So. 2d 427, 429–430 (Fla. 2d DCA 1961)].

The logic in the exclusion from coverage of both types of employees is simple and compelling: the only coverage intended, and for which the premium has been paid, is the liability of the insured to the public, as distinguished from liability to the insured's employees whether or not they are protected by the workers' compensation law.

In *Florida Insurance Guaranty Association v. Revoredo* [Florida Insurance Guaranty Association v. Revoredo, 698 So. 2d 890 (Fla. 3d DCA 1997)], Revoredo's estate contended, nonetheless, that neither exclusion applied since (1) Revoredo was not a statutory employee of the employer because the employer did not secure payment of workers' compensation and, thus, (2) the employers liability for wrongful death is an obligation under common law, not under workers' compensation law. The estate was held wrong on both counts. First, § 440.10(1), Fla. Stat. does not make the statutory employer-employee relationship contingent on the securing of workers' compensation for the employee. Rather, it is the creation of the statutory employer-employee relationship that establishes the employer's duty to secure compensation [Florida Insurance Guaranty Association v. Revoredo, 698 So. 2d 890, 892 (Fla. 3d DCA 1997)]. Second, the Fifth District Court of Appeal, in *Lingold v. Transamerica Ins. Co.* [Lingold v. Transamerica Ins. Co., 416 So. 2d 1271, 1272–1273 (Fla. 5th DCA 1982)], noted that it is the act of subletting (subcontracting) that renders the contractor an employer of the subcontractor's employees:

> None of our statutes declare, and none of our courts has decided, that a failure to secure payment of compensation disestablishes the statutory employer-employee relationship. We specifically hold that there is no such disestablishment.

Even more compelling is the Supreme Court's holding [*see* Motchkavitz v. L.C. Boggs Industries, 407 So. 2d 910, 912 (Fla. 1981)]:

> § 440.10 establishes the concept of "statutory employer" for contractors who sublet part of their work to others. Section 440.11 provides that the liability established in § 440.10 is "exclusive." The effect of § 440.10 is that where a subcontractor performing part of the work of a contractor fails to secure payment of compensation, the contractor is liable for same. If both subcontractor and contractor fail to secure coverage, then the contractor has an employer's liability to the subcontractor's injured employee for purposes of an action for statutory benefits or damages at law or in admiralty. Thus, even when a subcontractor agrees to secure coverage for its employees, a prudent contractor will prepare for or insure against its contingent liability as "statutory employer" in case the subcontractor fails to do so.

§ 3.11 Illegal Aliens

The law clearly provides that all employees, including aliens, are eligible for workers' compensation benefits. The court has held that under the statutory definition of "employee," a claimant who is an alien *illegally* in the country is not precluded from benefits for work-related injury [*see* Cenvill Development Corp. v. Candelo, 478 So. 2d 1168, 1170 (Fla. 1st DCA 1985)].

§ 440.02(15)(a), Fla. Stat. (10/1/2003) defines an employee as follows:

> "Employee" means any person who receives remuneration from an employer for the

> performance of any work or service while engaged in any employment under any appointment or contract *for* hire or apprenticeship, express or implied, oral or written, whether lawfully or unlawfully employed and includes, but is not limited to, *aliens* and minors. [*Emphasis added*]

The court held that an exception applies in cases when the claimant's eligibility depends on searching for and finding employment, but he or she is unemployable because of his or her illegal status. Even in such a case, the employer/carrier is estopped from asserting illegal alien status if the employer knew or should have known of the true status of the employee. This holding prevents unauthorized aliens from suffering at the hands of an employer who would knowingly hire the alien and then conveniently use the unauthorized alien status to avoid paying wage loss benefits. It also protects an employer who, through no fault of his own, would end up paying continued wage loss benefits to an employee who cannot legally be employed. The law of Florida does not impose upon an employer the burden of verifying forged or borrowed green cards [*see* Cenvill Development Corp. v. Candelo, 478 So. 2d 1168, 1170 (Fla. 1st DCA 1985)].

§ 440.16(7), Fla. Stat. limits death benefits to dependents who are not residents (or about to become non-residents) of the United States or Canada. As the Supreme Court did with an earlier version of this statute, the 1st DCA declared the monetary limitation of the 1987 version to be unconstitutional [*see* De Ayala v. Florida Farm Bureau Casualty Insurance Co., 543 So. 2d 204, 207–208 (Fla. 1989); Lopez v. Ideal Roofing Systems, 821 So. 2d 453, 454 (Fla. 1st DCA 2002)].

Effective October 1, 2003, the Legislature amended the Act to provide that providing false information about a person's identity to obtain employment constitutes a third-degree felony [*see* § 440.105(2), Fla. Stat.]. The Act continues to provide that aliens are eligible for benefits, but now arguably refers to legal aliens only. It is probably that a person, illegally in the country, will present false documentation about his or her identity to obtain employment. Doing so is now a felony. If a person commits a felony to induce an employer to enter an employment contract, how may it be said that a legal employer/employee relationship ever existed? Additionally, it might be argued that it is against public policy to permit someone to benefit from his crime, specifically to allow a person to collect workers' compensation benefits based on employment feloniously obtained.

The *Cenvill* case was heard in 1985. Perhaps the courts will revisit this issue and reach a different conclusion. Note, however, that the courts are unlikely to change the view that the employer will be estopped from raising such a defense if it knew the worker presented a false identity.

CHAPTER 4

JURISDICTION: ACCIDENTS OUTSIDE THE STATE AND COVERAGE FOR NONRESIDENTS

Guide to Claims

SYNOPSIS

§ 4.01 Accidents Outside the State

[1] The Rule

A worker injured outside the state is eligible for Florida workers' compensation benefits in two situations. The first situation arises if the parties entered the contract of employment in Florida. The second situation arises if the principal location of the employment is in Florida. *Note that the law requires only one of the two situations to exist.*

> **SPECIAL ALERT:** An injured worker may collect compensation from both Florida and another state. The injured worker may not, however, collect under Florida workers' compensation in combination with the other state to a greater extent than the Florida Workers' Compensation Act provides [*see* § 4.03].

[2] General Requirements

Once questions about coverage under the policy and the law have been answered, the next coverage question might concern jurisdiction. When the accident occurs outside the state of Florida, certain entitlement questions arise. Some states keep the decision simple by requiring that the accident occur within the state. Florida is not one of these states.

In 1974, the Legislature amended the controlling section in the statute. This amendment repealed such requirements as residency and place of hire. (This text will not discuss the law before 1974 since claims enduring from those years probably have had jurisdictional questions resolved.) The present statutory language reads as follows [§ 440.09(1)(d), Fla. Stat. (1994)]:

> If an accident happens while the employee is employed elsewhere than in this state, which would entitle the employee or his or her dependents to compensation if it had happened in this state, the employee or his or her dependents are entitled to compensation if the contract of employment was made in this state, or the employment was principally localized in this state. . . .

The section provides further that if the employee does collect compensation from another state, that employee may still be eligible for Florida benefits. The employee may not, however, collect under Florida Workers' Compensation, in combination with the other state, to an extent greater than the limits of the Florida Act. This is, in essence, an offset for the other state's indemnity benefits.

Note carefully that the Workers' Compensation Act does not require the employer's place of business to be in the state of Florida. In addition, the law does not require that the employee live in Florida. The law requires only one of the two alternative conditions. Injured workers are eligible for Florida workers' compensation benefits if either of the following are true:

1. The employment contract was made in Florida and contemplated the performance of services for the employer both in Florida and elsewhere [*see* Johnson v. Florida Senior Residence, 642 So. 2d 104, 106 (Fla. 1st DCA 1994)]; or

2. The employment was principally localized in Florida.

For a general discussion of coverage of accidents occurring outside the state, see LARSON'S WORKERS' COMPENSATION, DESK EDITION, Chs. 140, 141, 142, 143 (Matthew Bender).

[3] The Contract Within the State Requirement

[a] Case History

The first alternative requirement [*see* [2], *above*] is that the parties execute the hiring contract within the state of Florida. Following are case examples.

Case 1. The employee suffered an injury during the course of his employment, but the employer denied the employee's claim. The employer argued that the parties executed the employment contract in the state of New York for work the employee would do in Saudi Arabia. The employer said that although they made the initial hiring agreement in Florida, they had completed the true "final" employment agreement in New York state.

In rejecting this argument, the court held that the parties executed the actual employment contract in Florida. The parties created the second contract in New York only to correct a mistake contained in the first contract. Obviously, identifying the jurisdiction where the parties completed the actual employment contract is crucial [*see* George A. Fuller Co. v. Chastain, 388 So. 2d 284, 285–286 (Fla. 1st DCA 1980)].

Case 2. A Florida corporation telegraphed an Alabama resident requesting him to travel to Jacksonville for a conference about a job. He did so, and the employer hired him during the Jacksonville conference to work primarily in Georgia. He then moved his home to Georgia. Later, the employee died in an auto accident while driving to Jacksonville for a meeting. The Supreme Court awarded benefits to his dependents because the employee and employer made the employment contract in Florida. In addition, the contract was not for service exclusively outside the state. Although the employee was to work principally in Georgia, "his activities were not, in contemplation of the contract, to be confined there" [*see* Lovejoy Co. v. Ackis, 153 Fla. 876, 16 So. 2d 297, 299 (Fla. 1944)].

Case 3. Mr. Ramos initially worked for his employer in Florida, but moved to Utah to supervise a construction project. While on the job in Utah, he suffered an injury. The court held that the parties made the employment contract in Florida. This, said the court, was sufficient to entitle Ramos to benefits under the Florida Workers' Compensation Act [*see* J.L. Manta, Inc. v. Ramos, 526 So. 2d 919, 921 (Fla. 1st DCA 1988)].

Case 4. The employee was hired by the employer to recruit Missouri residents to attend a college in Florida. The employee answered a newspaper ad in Missouri, was interviewed in Missouri, and never came to Florida. The employee was shot and killed in Missouri while attempting to make one of his first calls. The appellate court held that based on the plain language of § 440.091(1)(d), Fla. Stat. (1999), if a contract was formed in Florida, the accident is compensable under Florida's workers' compensation law. The appellate court held the employment contract between the employer and the employee was executed in Florida. It was undisputed that the employee signed the agreement, then sent it to the employer in Florida, where it was signed and executed by the employer's president. The appellate court held that a contract was created where the last act necessary to make a binding agreement took place. Because the last act necessary to complete the agreement—the employer's president's signature—was performed in Florida, the contract was made in Florida [*see* D.L. Peoples Group v. Hawley, 804 So. 2d 561, 563–564 (Fla. 1st DCA 2002)].

Guide to Claims

[b] Union Hall Hiring

A detailed investigation is necessary when employers hire workers through a union hiring hall. Review carefully all the details of the agreement between the union and the employer. When the employer agrees to accept all employees referred by a union, the union may become the employer's hiring agent. For example, the injured worker was a lifelong Florida resident who obtained a job in Alabama through his union office in Florida. He was later injured in an accident on the job in Alabama. The question became whether the employer and the employee executed the employment agreement in Florida or Alabama.

The employee argued that the Florida union office acted as the employer's hiring agent and that they made the employment contract in Florida. A careful examination of the Articles of Agreement between the employer and the union revealed that this was not correct. The agreement said that if the union were unable to fill a requested position within 48 hours, the employer was free to fill the position from other sources. The agreement also said the employer could reject any applicant referred by the union.

Besides these express provisions, a union official testified that actual hiring takes place at the job site. This was sufficient evidence that the employer had not delegated hiring authority to the union. Accordingly, the court held that Florida had no jurisdiction over this claim. Thus, the law did not entitle the injured worker to Florida workers' compensation benefits [*see* Nelson v. McAbee Const., Inc., 591 So. 2d 1015, 1017–1018 (Fla. 1st DCA 1992)].

[4] Employment Principally Localized in Florida

This simple phrase, "principally localized in Florida" [*see* [2], *above*], is not simple to apply. It does not mean that the employer's place of business must physically be in Florida. Nor does it mean that the employee must be a Florida resident. What, then, does the term "principally localized" mean?

An employee cannot meet the "principally localized" employment requirement merely by evidence that the out-of-state employer may have some presence in Florida. Further, an employee cannot satisfy the requirement by showing that the employer does some business in Florida or that it maintains an office in Florida. The test refers to the state in which the employees will principally do their employment duties when done in more than one state. For example, in one case the employer hired the injured worker in Virginia and the employer's principal place of business was outside Florida. The injured worker, however, lived in Jacksonville where he did two-thirds of his work. The court held this was enough to meet the "principally localized" requirement [*see* General Elec. v. DeCubas, 504 So. 2d 1276, 1277 (Fla. 1st DCA 1986)].

Is it logical, then, that employees will meet the test if they do 50 percent or more of their work in Florida? Unfortunately, the court prevented any chance of the question being answered that easily. For example, the injured worker was a flight attendant who spent most of her time out of state. This was not important because "it is the principal location of the claimant's employment and the principal location of the employer's business which is relevant." Here, the injured worker's base of operation was Miami. It logically followed, said the court, that her employment was therefore principally localized in Florida. Under this holding, the "most of the work to be done in Florida" theory is destroyed. An injured worker will meet the principally localized test if Florida is merely the employment's focal point [*see* Johnson v. United Airlines, 550 So. 2d 134, 135 (Fla. 1st DCA 1989)].

Remember that if the contract of employment was made in Florida by a Florida corporation and contemplated the performance of services both in Florida and out of state, it is not necessary to consider whether the dominate purpose of the trip to another state was principally localized in that state [*see* Johnson v. Florida Senior Residence, 642 So. 2d 104, 106 (Fla. 1st DCA 1994)].

§ 4.02 Coverage for Nonresidents

[1] The Rule

The occurrence of an injury in Florida is sufficient for coverage to exist under the Florida Workers' Compensation Act.

[2] Essential Factors

The question here is whether the Florida Act covers an injured worker if the accident's location is the worker's only connection to Florida. Consider this case: Rufus Philyaw lived in Virginia. A Virginia company hired him as a truck driver and he then moved to Georgia. They made the contract of employment in Georgia. The contract called for Philyaw to work principally in Virginia and Georgia. The employer had no locations in Florida. Philyaw was injured in a motor vehicle accident while driving the employer's truck in Florida. He applied for and received Georgia workers' compensation benefits.

Later, Philyaw filed a claim for Florida benefits. The Florida judge of compensation claims denied the claim for two reasons. First, the judge held Philyaw was not qualified for Florida benefits. Second, the judge held he did not have jurisdiction. The First District Court of Appeal reversed on both counts.

Nothing in Florida's law limits a person's rights if injured in Florida during the course of employment. It does not matter that the employee does not live or work in Florida. Nor does it matter that the employer has no business location in Florida. All that matters is that the employee was within the state and was in the course of employment when the accident occurred. In other words, said the court, the injury occurring in Florida is a sufficient state interest for coverage to exist under the Florida Act [*see* Philyaw v. Arthur H. Fulton, Inc., 569 So. 2d 787, 791–792 (Fla. 1st DCA 1990)].

For a general discussion of nonresident coverage, see LARSON'S WORKERS' COMPENSATION, DESK EDITION, Chs. 140, 141, 142, 143 (Matthew Bender).

§ 4.03 Benefits From More Than One State

[1] The Rule

An injured worker can collect benefits from both Florida and another state, but not to an extent greater than allowed by Florida law.

[2] How the Law Applies

What happens if an injured worker is eligible for benefits in more than one state? For example, an injured worker may be eligible for Georgia benefits because the injury occurred there. The worker also may be eligible for Florida benefits because Florida is where the parties made the employment contract. Can the injured worker collect benefits from both states? Yes. Florida's law provides that "[i]f an employee receives compensation or damages under the laws of any other state, the total compensation for the injury may not be greater than is provided in this chapter" [§ 440.09(1)(d), Fla. Stat. (1994)].

This section means that injured workers can initially collect benefits from another state, and then transfer the claim to Florida. If they do so, however, they cannot collect benefits from both states in a greater amount than allowed by Florida Law.

[3] The Supreme Court's Interpretation

The legislature first adopted § 440.09(1)(d), Fla. Stat. in 1937, but it has undergone very little judicial review. The most recent review occurred in 1970, where the Florida Supreme Court had this to say [deCancino v. Eastern Air Lines, 239 So. 2d 15, 17 (Fla. 1970); *see* [4], *below*]:

> A clear interpretation of this statute reveals that it is intended to secure compensation for persons hired or residing in Florida, and that *they shall be entitled to recover total compensation in all forums up to the maximum amount which might be obtained by proceeding in Florida alone.* The implication of the language is clear that an employee is permitted to seek recovery in more than one state, *but may not recover additional benefits in Florida if benefits already received equal what could have been recovered in Florida.* Equally obvious is the legislative intent that persons in whom Florida has an interest should be compensated in the amount deemed desirable in this State, regardless of the fact that another state also may have an interest in the outcome of their case. (Emphasis added)

[4] Applying the Supreme Court's Holding

Linda Brooks, a flight attendant for Eastern Airlines, was injured in a compensable accident while the aircraft was in Florida. Because she was stationed and lived in Virginia, she elected to file her claim there. Brooks received temporary total disability benefits under Virginia law until the carrier paid the maximum amount. She then transferred her case to Florida where she filed a claim for permanent total disability benefits. The carrier, the same one that had paid Virginia benefits, accepted her claim administratively and began paying permanent total disability benefits under Florida law, but claimed entitlement to a credit for overpayment. The carrier paid Brooks a total of $91,043 under Virginia law. Had the carrier initially paid her under Florida law, she would have received only $80,928. The carrier claimed that the law entitled it to an offset for the $10,115 difference, under § 440.09(1), Fla. Stat.

Brooks argued that the offset applied only if the carrier paid benefits simultaneously under the laws of both states. The law does not operate, she claimed, to force a claimant to reimburse benefits received under the law of another state for a completely different class of disability. Both the judge of compensation claims and the First District Court of Appeal disagreed with her.

The key is whether a given state's statute has unmistakable language that forbids supplemental relief under the law of another state. If not, the law allows a successive award in another state for the same injury if the carrier gets credit for any duplication of benefits in the successive award. Our law entitles the injured worker to only the amount available had she filed her entire claim in Florida in the first place.

Brooks also argued that the court should consider the overpayment a gratuity. The court found no merit in this argument. Carriers can recover an overpayment if a reasonable basis for the overpayment exists. Paying benefits as required by Virginia law is such a reasonable basis [Brooks v. Eastern Air Lines, Inc., 634 So. 2d 809, 812–813 (Fla. 1st DCA 1994)].

For a general discussion of successive awards in different states, see LARSON'S WORKERS' COMPENSATION, DESK EDITION, Ch. 141 (Matthew Bender).

Guide to Claims

CHAPTER 5

INVALID CONTRACT OF EMPLOYMENT; THE *MARTIN v. CARPENTER* DEFENSE

Guide to Claims

SYNOPSIS

§ 5.01 Overview

[1] The Rule

If job applicants lie about their physical condition when applying for a job, they are not eligible for workers' compensation benefits for an otherwise compensable injury if the following statements are true [*see* Martin Company v. Carpenter, 132 So. 2d 400, 406 (Fla. 1961)]:

1. Evidence shows a causal relationship between the injury and the false representation;
2. The employee knew the representation was false;
3. The employer relied on the false representation; and
4. Such reliance resulted in consequent damage to the employer.

For a general discussion of false statements made in employment applications, see LARSON'S WORKERS' COMPENSATION, DESK EDITION, Ch. 47, § 47.53 (Matthew Bender).

Applying this defense has changed for those employers subject to the Americans with Disabilities Act (ADA). The ADA, however, does not prevent using this defense. The ADA requires only that employers make information requests about health or workers' compensation and accident history as part of a post-job offer, medical examination, or inquiry [*see* ch. 25, § 25.06[1]].

[2] Coverage Requires a Valid Employment Contract

Entitlement to workers' compensation benefits begins with an employment relationship. This relationship must arise out of a valid employment contract, either express or implied. Logic suggests that if a worker used fraud to obtain a contract of employment, a valid contract never existed. Under such circumstances, no employer/employee relationship exists. This defense takes its name from the landmark Florida Supreme Court decision in *Martin Company v. Carpenter,* 132 So. 2d 400 (Fla. 1961) [*see* [3], *below*]. This case and others have not, however, established a broad general rule. Apply the doctrine carefully.

For a general discussion of the contract requirement, see LARSON'S WORKERS' COMPENSATION, DESK EDITION, Ch. 64, § 64.01 (Matthew Bender).

[3] The *Martin v. Carpenter* Case

Here, Carpenter had completed a pre-employment questionnaire. In it, she denied she had ever been subject to back injury or backache. This was a lie because she had been suffering for several years from a back condition. In fact, her doctors had advised her to wear a back-brace. Further, doctors told her to leave bench work because of her condition. They also told her to take a job that was easier on her back.

Carpenter ignored all this advice and took a job with the Martin Company doing bench work. During her first six months on the job, her back condition gradually but steadily deteriorated. The employer eventually fired her because of her increasingly poor performance. She then filed a claim for workers' compensation benefits. The trial judge denied her claim, holding no employer/employee relationship existed because she falsified her preemployment application.

The Florida Supreme Court eventually affirmed this finding, stating in pertinent part [*see* Martin Company v. Carpenter, 132 So. 2d 400, 406 (Fla. 1961)]:

> [T]his Court, and others, have in construing the Act determined that there is a presumption that the "employer takes the employee as he finds him" . . . [T]his presumption makes the employer responsible for compensation benefits to an employee who at the time of employment suffered a disease or bodily infirmity which is accelerated or aggravated by a compensable injury. In other words the presumption places on the employer the risks attendant upon hiring an infirm employee.
>
> This presumption makes it wise that an employer determine before employment what state of health an employee enjoys in order to avoid the risks which are resultant from hiring an infirm employee. We do not think the misrepresentations of an employee should be allowed to defeat the efforts of the employer to protect himself from this presumption and the assumed risks.
>
> Second, . . . our legislature, in an effort to encourage the employment of those afflicted or disabled in some way, has created a special disability, or second injury, fund which allows an employer to be reimbursed for compensation paid an employee for disability due to a pre-existing condition. To have resort to this fund, however, the employer probably must either have had knowledge of the pre-existing condition when he hired the employee, or have continued the employment after obtaining knowledge thereof. . . .
>
> We therefore adopt the rule that a false representation as to physical condition of health made by an employee in procuring employment will preclude the benefits of the Workers' Compensation Act for an otherwise compensable injury if there is shown to be a causal relationship between the injury and the false representation and if it is also shown that
>
> (1) the employee knew the representation to be false;
>
> (2) the employer relied on the false representation; and
>
> (3) such reliance resulted in consequent injury to the employer.

Misrepresentation can be a strong defense. The carrier, however, must produce a significant degree of evidence. This evidence must show the causal relationship between the employee's misrepresentation and the injury itself.

§ 5.02 False Representation Requirement

[1] Misrepresentation Defined

A misrepresentation and a misstatement are different. A misrepresentation, on the one hand, is an outright lie; specifically, the job applicant knows that responses to questions on an employment application or health questionnaire are not true. The applicant's intent is to deceive the prospective employer. A misstatement, on the other hand, means the applicant simply misunderstands the questions. As used here, a misrepresentation means obtaining employment by false pretense.

For a general discussion of false statements made in an employment application, see LARSON'S WORKERS' COMPENSATION, DESK EDITION, Ch. 66, § 66.03 (Matthew Bender).

[2] Case History

Case 1. When Winfred MacDonald applied for a job with U.S. Home, he completed an application form that asked:

Question 1. "Have you ever received compensation for injuries?"

Question 2. "Do you have any physical handicaps which would prevent you from performing specific kinds of work?"

Although not everyone would agree, the court considered both questions clear and unambiguous. MacDonald answered "no" to both of them. The facts were, however, that MacDonald was still receiving benefits for a 30-percent disability from the United States Navy. In addition, he had suffered a back injury while working as a police officer. Based on these false statements, the carrier denied the claim. At the time of the hearing MacDonald was also receiving disability retirement benefits from the police department. These misrepresentations were sufficient to deny the claim based on the *Martin v. Carpenter* defense. Note, however, that the defense succeeded because the carrier showed a causal connection between the injured worker's preexisting disability and the new injury. Though the carrier won here, a new court could easily hold that the second question calls for an opinion by the employee [*see* U.S. Home Corp. v. MacDonald, 445 So. 2d 636, 637 (Fla. 1st DCA 1984)].

Case 2. On his job application, Robert Smith was asked to "list any physical defects." Smith answered "none," although he knew he had had an abnormal back x-ray several years earlier. The court held this question was ambiguous. Smith could interpret it to refer to defects existing and symptomatic at the time of the application, of which there were none according to him. Despite Smith's knowledge of his prior abnormal x-rays, his negative answer was not a false application that would defeat a claim [*see* Public Gas Company v. Smith, 386 So. 2d 258 (Fla. 1st DCA 1980)].

Case 3. Bruce Collier had a congenitally weak lower back, but answered "no" to the following question on his job application: "Have you ever had problems with . . . back injury?" Evidence showed, however, that a causal connection existed between Collier's congenital condition and his job-related injury. Based on this evidence the judge of compensation claims denied Collier's claim. The First District Court of Appeal reversed the ruling. First, the court held that the question was ambiguous and indefinite. The question asked about back injuries, but not about congenital defects. Second, and perhaps more important, no evidence existed that Collier knew about the defect when he completed the health questionnaire. Thus, the court concluded Collier did not make an intentional misrepresentation, and the *Martin v. Carpenter* defense could not apply [*see* Collier v. Donzi Marine, 596 So. 2d 1175, 1177 (Fla. 1st DCA 1992)].

NOTE: Employers subject to the Americans with Disabilities Act (ADA) have a narrow period of time to ask general questions about an employee's health. Employers may ask these questions only between the time they make a job offer and the work begins [*see* ch. 25, § 25.05[4][c]].

[3] No Duty to Volunteer Information

Every job applicant has a duty to answer honestly all direct, legally-posed questions. However, applicants have *no* duty to make full disclosure of all their medical shortcomings, when such disclosure is not specifically requested. This is especially true when medical experts declare the preexisting problems to be minor and the employee has a release for return to full-duty work with no restrictions [*see* Simmons v. Trinity Industries, 528 So. 2d 1337, 1339–1340 (Fla. 1st DCA 1988)].

[4] No Need to Prove Employer Would Not Hire

Successfully asserting the *Martin v. Carpenter* defense does not require proof that employees would not have been hired but for their misrepresentations. Employers subject to the Americans with Disabilities Act (ADA) cannot obtain this information legally before making a job offer. Nevertheless, the law does require evidence that the employer relied on legally obtained, false statements to its detriment [*see* Doric Food Co. v. Allen, 383 So. 2d 316, 318 (Fla. 1st DCA 1980); Kalbes v. Armour Indus. Sec. & Claims Ctr., 483 So. 2d 124, 126–127 (Fla. 1st DCA 1986)].

Rosemary Norton represented on her employment application that she had never been in the hospital except for childbirth. The facts were, however, that she had undergone several surgeries, including hernia repair. While working for Colonial Care Nursing Home, she suffered another hernia in precisely the same area as the first. The court reversed an award of benefits because Norton's misrepresentation deprived the employer of the opportunity to decide whether it would assume the risk of hiring her. Further, Norton's misrepresentations may have disqualified the employer from Special Disability Trust Fund reimbursement [*see* Colonial Care Nursing Home v. Norton, 566 So. 2d 44, 45–46 (Fla. 1st DCA 1990)].

What must the carrier show to prove detrimental reliance? Carriers will meet the reliance element with evidence supporting an *inference* that the employer would not have hired the employee had it known the truth. Such inference is sufficient even when the employer's witness does not expressly state the employer would not have hired the employee had it known about the prior condition [*see* Florida Min. & Materials v. Perkins, 612 So. 2d 667, 668–669 (Fla. 1st DCA 1993)].

[5] Blank Spaces on Questionnaire Are No Defense

What happens if the applicant simply leaves blank, health-related questions on an application? Blank spaces are not misrepresentations. The employer has an obligation to obtain the answers to the questions.

When faced with unanswered questions, the employer cannot turn a blind eye to these omissions and then claim reliance on the few questions the applicant did answer negatively. This is especially true when one or more answers admit to some past injury or sickness. When an employer contends it relied on a misrepresentation to its detriment in deciding to hire, the employer must show that it exercised some diligence in investigating the misrepresentation or omission. Further, the employer must show that the employee had exclusive or superior knowledge, or prevented further investigation. Without such evidence, a *Martin v. Carpenter* defense will fail. The due diligence standard is expressed in the following statement [*see* Adams v. Prestressed Systems Industries, 625 So. 2d 895, 897 (Fla. 1st DCA 1993)]:

> The right to rely on a representation is closely related to the duty of the representee to use some measure of precaution to safeguard his own interest. In cases of this kind, assuming that the parties are not dealing in some fiduciary or confidential relation, the principle that the representee must exercise reasonable effort or diligence for his own protection will usually be applied, both in law and in equity.

As a matter of law, leaving blank the answer to a particular question is neither a representation nor a misrepresentation. Remember that the basis for a *Martin v. Carpenter* defense is reliance. Without representation there can be no reliance [*see* Landers v. Medical Personnel Pool, 647 So. 2d 173, 174–175 (Fla. 1st DCA 1994)].

§ 5.03 The Causal Connection Requirement

[1] The Rule

The defense can prove medical causal connection only by presenting expert medical testimony.

[2] Medical Relationship Required

Proving that the injured worker lied about a medical condition is not enough to support a *Martin v. Carpenter* defense. The carrier also must prove a medical causal relationship between the present (new) injury and the misrepresented physical condition resulting from an undisclosed prior injury [*see* Cycenas v. Sarasota Coca Cola Bottling Co., 440 So. 2d 39, 40 (Fla. 1st DCA 1983); Dunnell v. Robbins Warehouse, 465 So. 2d 648, 649 (Fla. 1st DCA 1985)].

[3] Expert Medical Testimony Required

Only expert medical testimony can prove a medical causal relationship. Consider Benny Johnson's case. On his job application, Johnson said he had never suffered a back injury. He also said he never had an operation and never had a disability. These statements were not true. In fact, he had undergone several operations because of a work-related injury. He had been off work for two years and had received a workers' compensation settlement. While working for Bender, he suffered another back injury.

The prior undisclosed condition and the new injury both involved Johnson's back. That alone, however, does not of itself show a medical relationship. None of Johnson's physicians testified that a causal relationship existed between his present condition and a prior injury. Without medical testimony to establish a relationship between the injured worker's present injury and the alleged misrepresented physical condition, it is error to deny a worker's claim based on *Martin v. Carpenter* [*see* Johnson v. Bender Const. Co., 538 So. 2d 1305, 1306 (Fla. 1st DCA 1989)].

The relationship must be sufficient to show a medical merger. To show a merger there must be medical evidence of one or both of the following. First, the evidence must show that the second injury would not have occurred but for the existence of the preexisting impairment. Second, the evidence must show that the impairment from the second accident is materially and substantially increased because of the preexisting impairment [§ 440.49(2)(c), Fla. Stat. (1994)].

§ 5.04 Accidents After July 1, 1990

[1] Legislative Changes

Statutory language effective July 1, 1990, and January 1, 1994, may have changed the basic requirements of a *Martin v. Carpenter* defense. The Legislature amended the law in 1990 by, in essence, incorporating the *Martin v. Carpenter* case into the Workers' Compensation Act. The legislature amended this section again in 1994. The 1994 Act provides that aggravation or acceleration of a preexisting condition is compensable ". . . except that no benefits shall be payable if the employee, at the time of entering into the employment of the employer by whom the benefits would otherwise be payable, falsely represents herself or himself in writing as not having previously been disabled or compensated because of such disability, impairment, anomaly or disease . . . *and the employer detrimentally relies on the misrepresentation*" (the italicized phrase is the 1994 language) [§ 440.15(5)(a), Fla. Stat. (1/1/94)].

[2] Applying the Changes in *Martin v. Carpenter* Cases

This section applies only to accidents occurring on or after the effective date of the amendment. Does it change case law? It seems so.

First, nothing in the 1990 language requires the employer's detrimental reliance. Effective January 1, 1994, however, the legislature added detrimental reliance as a requirement [*see* § 440.15(5), Fla. Stat. (1/1/94); [1], *above*].

Second, the misrepresentation requirement ought to be less difficult to overcome if an employee lies about having been disabled or compensated for a previous disability. The provision, though, is ambiguous. Does this mean that only lies about having been disabled or compensated count? Possibly, so employers must carefully construct employment questionnaires.

Another question is whether this legislative change amends or even overrules *Martin.* Recall the statutes refer to lies regarding preexisting conditions for which the claimant had been compensated or disabled. If the employee failed to disclose a preexisting condition which had not been disabling or for which he or she had not been compensated, does the *Martin* defense apply? The answer, in a word, is yes. The court reviewed this language and noted that the *Martin* decision was based, not on this section, but on § 440.151(b), Fla. Stat., which is essentially the same today as it was in 1961 when the *Martin* decision was published. The court found nothing in the preamble to the chapter law or in the final staff analysis to suggest that § 440.15(5)(a), Fla. Stat., was enacted with any intent to affect the holding in *Martin.* Therefore, whether an employee's preexisting condition caused any disability or whether the employee received any compensation for it, is not relevant in deciding whether a *Martin* defense applies [*see* Irving v. Ametek, Inc., 756 So. 2d 1045 (Fla. 1st DCA 2000)].

The courts will still apply the medical connection requirement since this new language is in the "subsequent injury" section of the Workers' Compensation Act. Statutory changes preclude benefits due to misrepresentation only concerning the aggravation or acceleration of a preexisting condition. Thus, if the new injury did not aggravate an undisclosed preexisting condition, the new statutory defense does not apply [*see* Moore v. Williams Co., 622 So. 2d 120, 121 (Fla. 1st DCA 1993)].

[3] Beware Violating the ADA

Information obtained in violation of the Americans with Disabilities Act (ADA) may not be admissible in evidence. Further, raising the defense based on such illegally obtained information may subject the employer to a lawsuit for damages. ADA compliance should be an essential part of any investigation of a possible *Martin v. Carpenter* defense. For further discussion of the ADA and workers' compensation, see ch. 25, § 25.06.

CHAPTER 6

CONFIRMING COMPENSABILITY: ACCIDENT AND INJURY

Guide to Claims

SYNOPSIS

Guide to Claims

§§ 6.09–6.99 Reserved

§ 6.01 Requirements for Compensability

[1] The Rule

The carrier must provide benefits to a worker who has sustained (1) an injury, (2) by accident, (3) that arose out of, (4) and occurred in the course of employment [§ 440.02(17), Fla. Stat.].

[2] Statutory Burden of Proof

The first step in handling any claim is deciding coverage. This includes deciding if coverage exists under both the policy and under the law. It also includes deciding questions about jurisdiction [*see* ch. 3, §§ 3.01, 3.02; ch. 4]. Once done, the second step is to decide if the injured worker has sustained a compensable accident and injury. Compensability requires showing that the employee suffered an accidental injury that arose out of and occurred during the course of employment.

In addition to the above listed requirements, the injured worker must show that "the injury, its occupational cause, and any resulting manifestations or disability shall be established to a reasonable degree of medical *certainty* and by *objective* medical finding" [§ 440.09(1), Fla. Stat. (1/1/94)].

Requiring certainty and objectivity preclude s mere speculation and subjective medical opinions in proving work connection. Indeed, there can be no certainty without objective evidence. To be objective, the evidence must be open and observable to the examiner. The legislature, by its use of the phrase, "shall be established," has given a clear signal that the statute devolves upon workers' compensation claimants a new standard of proof, rather than providing employers with an affirmative defense [*see* Pyram v. Marriott International, 687 So. 2d 351 (Fla. 1st DCA 1997)].

For example, the judge of compensation claims awarded medical and indemnity benefits to Aida Henderson. This was based on her chiropractor's statement in his medical report that "it appeared" that her cervical and lumbar injuries were secondary to her work-related injury. There was no other evidence to support the judge's finding of causation. Apparently because the doctor's statement was so equivocal, the court held that such a statement does not support an award of benefits under the new standard [*see* Family Dollar Stores v. Henderson, 718 So. 2d 931, 932 (Fla. 1st DCA 1998)].

Note, however, that despite statutory language suggesting otherwise, the method of proving causation has not changed. The Act [*see* § 440.09(1), Fla. Stat.] requires that "[t]he injury, its occupational cause, and any resulting manifestations or disability shall be established to a reasonable degree of medical certainty and by objective medical findings."

Note that the statute requires medical *certainty.* Before this language entered the law in 1994, the statute required a finding based on medical *probability.* Although most language students would agree that there is a huge difference between the terms "probability" and "certainty," the court has concluded that these terms are not different, that they mean the same thing, and that they can be used interchangeably. The court adopted the interpretation in *Black's Law Dictionary* 1273 (7th ed. 1998), which indicates that the phrases "reasonable medical probability" and "reasonable medical certainty" are merely different ways of expressing the same concept. Therefore, the court concluded that the legislature's use of the phrase "reasonable medical certainty" does not reflect any change from the established standard of proof [*see* Closet Maid v. Sykes, 763 So. 2d 377 (Fla. 1st DCA 2000)].

In this chapter, we will examine the elements of an *injury* [*see* § 6.02], sustained by *accident* [*see* § 6.05].

Guide to Claims

§ 6.02 Injury—The First Element

[1] The Rule

Injury includes physical injury and psychiatric disorders that result from the physical injury. Injury also includes diseases and virtually any medical problem resulting from a compensable accident [§ 440.02(17), Fla. Stat.].

[2] Injury Defined

To receive compensation a worker must have sustained an injury as defined by the Workers' Compensation Act. Injury means "personal injury or death . . . and such diseases or infection as naturally or unavoidably result from such injury. . ." [§ 440.02(17), Fla. Stat.].

The last part is easy enough to understand. If a cut finger results in infection which culminates in amputation, the law covers all results.

§ 6.03 Psychiatric Injury

[1] The Rule

Psychiatric injury alone, without physical injury, is not compensable. Psychiatric injury, even with physical injury, is not compensable unless the physical injury is a causative factor. The required physical injury need not be serious or even disabling [§ 440.093(1), Fla. Stat. (7/1/90)].

SPECIAL ALERT: Several exceptions apply to first responders, defined as law enforcement officers, firefighters, emergency medical technicians, or paramedics, who claim a psychiatric injury. For example, a physical injury is not required for a first responder to be eligible for medical benefits [*see* § 112.1815(2)(a)3, Fla. Stat.]. Other exceptions are noted throughout this subsection.

[2] Qualified Psychiatric Injury

A mental or nervous injury due to stress, fright, or excitement only, does not qualify as accidental injury. If, however, a physical accident and injury occurs, and then some traumatic neurosis increases or prolongs the injured worker's disability, the full disability including the results of the mental injury is compensable [§ 440.02(1), Fla. Stat. (7/1/90)].

A mental injury that causes fear or dislike of other people, even if caused by physical injury, is not compensable. "[A] disease that manifests itself in the fear of or dislike for an individual because of the individual's race, color, religion, sex, national origin, age, or handicap is not an injury by accident arising out of the employment" [§ 440.02(1), Fla. Stat. (1/1/94)]. Note, however, that while fear of certain people is not compensable, it may be a covered mental disability under the Americans with Disabilities Act (ADA) [*see* ch. 25, § 25.04].

For a general discussion of the compensability of psychiatric injuries, see LARSON'S WORKERS' COMPENSATION, DESK EDITION, Ch. 56 (Matthew Bender).

[3] Tests for Compensability

[a] Direct and Immediate Result

To be compensable, a mental injury must be the direct and immediate result of an industrial injury. Do not, however, take this literally. "Direct" means the mental injury is predicated on an actual physical injury. The term "immediate" simply means that the mental injury is not remote or only incidentally related to the industrial accident.

For example, Dolores Ackley hurt her back at work in 1988. In 1992, tests showed that she suffered from depression that began about two years after the accident. This, however, was not her only problem. She had a long history of being physically and mentally abused, first by her alcoholic father and then by her alcoholic husband. Ackley's doctor admitted that tremendous overlap was present between her pre-injury mental state and the accident-related depression. However, the doctor added that the accident at work was "like the straw that broke the camel's back." The judge of compensation claims denied the claim, holding that this did not meet the "direct and immediate" cause test. On appeal, the court reversed. First, the term "immediate" has nothing to do with a specific period for an injury to manifest itself. On the contrary, the law does not require any particular period. Second, the law does not require that the work injury be the sole cause of the mental injury. Third, aggravation of a preexisting mental condition is compensable if it results from the industrial accident [*see* Ackley v. General Parcel Service, 642 So. 2d 242, 245 (Fla. 1st DCA 1994)].

The court applied these same tests to Charles Hayden's case. Hayden suffered a knee injury that left him with an eight-percent whole body disability. In addition, he suffered from long standing preexisting mental illness. Hayden suffered from personality and character disorders besides alcohol and substance abuse. He had difficulties with the law, and had been involuntarily admitted for mental treatment. Hayden suffered from depression and, following the breakup of his relationship with his lady friend, he attempted suicide. Although most of these problems predated, or were unrelated to Hayden's compensable injury, doctors agreed that the compensable injury was at least a factor in his psychiatric condition. Based on the *Ackley* tests, the court awarded not only psychiatric treatment, but permanent total disability mostly resulting from the mental illness [*see* Pruett-Sharpe Const. v. Hayden, 654 So. 2d 241, 244 (Fla. 1st DCA 1995)].

A compensable mental injury must meet two tests: first, the mental injury must result from some physical trauma; and second, the mental injury must not be remote from the accident. Thus, the mental injury must directly result from the physical injury. Just because the physical injury is not disabling, however, does not alter the compensability of the mental injury.

A long delay in the mental injury's appearance is not necessarily evidence of remoteness and a lack of connection. On the contrary, no specific time applies. Both a nine-month and a one-year delay in the manifestation of a mental condition were held not enough to disprove direct causation [*see*Greater Miami Academy v. Blum, 466 So. 2d 1262, 1264 (Fla. 1st DCA 1985); Wal-Mart Stores v. Tomlinson, 588 So. 2d 276, 277–278 (Fla. 1st DCA 1991)].

Guide to Claims

[b] Standard of Proof: Major Contributing Cause

When an initial industrial injury results in a mental injury, the claimant must demonstrate causation by clear and convincing evidence. This is evidence of a quality and character designed to produce in the judge of compensation claims' mind a firm belief or conviction, without hesitation, as to the truth of the allegations.

The court held that the "major contributing cause" standard applies only to the original physical injury and not to a resulting mental injury. An injured worker need prove only that the work was the major contributing cause of the initial physical injury. The court held it is not necessary to show that the mental injury also arises out of the work. It is enough for compensability to show that the mental injury is directly and proximately linked to the initial injury [*see* Claims Management, Inc. v. Drewno, 727 So. 2d 395, 397–399 (Fla. 1st DCA 1999)]. For a complete discussion of the major contributing cause requirement, *see* ch. 7, § 7.01.

In March 2003 the court repeated this holding, noting that pursuant to § 440.09(1), Fla. Stat. (1997) there is no requirement that an industrial accident constitute the major contributing cause of any alleged psychiatric injuries. It is sufficient if resulting manifestations, diseases, and conditions are shown to be directly and proximately linked to the initial injury. The test for proximate medical causation requires a claimant to demonstrate his or her resultant mental conditions within a reasonable degree of medical certainty and by objective medical findings, with the proof being established by clear and convincing evidence. This test is one of proximate medical causation, not major contributing cause, as mental conditions are manifestations of the original physical injury [*see* Cromartie v. City of St. Petersburg, 840 So. 2d 372, 374–375 (Fla. 1st DCA 2003)].

The holdings in *Claims Management, Inc. v. Drewno* and *Cromartie v. City of St. Petersburg* were apparently not the result the legislature intended. As noted, the courts held in those cases that the major contributing cause standard does not apply to mental injuries. Effective October 1, 2003, the Act provides that the compensable physical injury must be, and continue to remain, the major contributing cause of the mental injury. This causal relationship must be established as a reasonable medical certainty. Additionally, the statute provides that to meet the major-contributing-cause standard, the compensable injury must be at least 50 percent responsible for the mental condition. Because this amendment changes the requirements for compensability of a mental injury described by the courts, it is probably a substantive amendment that applies only to accidents occurring on or after the effective date, October 1, 2003 [*see* § 440.093(2), Fla. Stat. (10/1/2003)].

Note that the psychiatric injury must result from the physical injury and not from stress, fright, or excitement alone. For example, Eddie Goodman was involved in a horrific automobile accident in which another person was killed. Goodman suffered only a minor shoulder injury, but also suffered from post-traumatic stress disorder. The judge of compensation claims denied Goodman's claim for the psychiatric injury. On appeal, the court remanded the case to the judge to determine if Goodman's mental problems arose from stress, fright, or excitement alone, or whether it was increased or prolonged in any manner as a result of his shoulder injury. The court held that to establish the latter, Goodman must show by clear and convincing evidence that the mental injury was a manifestation of the shoulder injury [*see* Goodman v. BFI of Florida Inc., 755 So. 2d 191, 192 (Fla. 1st DCA 2000); *see also* § 440.093(1), Fla. Stat. (10/1/2003)].

SPECIAL ALERT: The major contributing cause standard for compensability apparently does not apply to first responders, defined as law enforcement officers, firefighters, emergency medical technicians, or paramedics. Instead, first responders must demonstrate manifestation of a compensable psychiatric injury only by clear and convincing evidence [*see* § 112.1815(2)(a)3, Fla. Stat.]. "Clear and Convincing" evidence is evidence of a quality and character designed to produce in the judge of compensation claims' mind a firm belief or conviction, without hesitation, as to the truth of the allegations [*Black's Law Dictionary,* 6th Edition].

[4] Physical Injury Requirement

Over the years the courts concluded that the Workers' Compensation Act does not require an actual physical injury. These opinions held that even a mere "touching" is sufficient trauma. This issue eventually came before the Florida Supreme Court. In dicta, the Supreme Court suggested that such decisions "were obviously grounded upon a desire to avoid what was perceived as the harsh results of the statute" [*see* City of Holmes Beach v. Grace, 598 So. 2d 71, 74 (Fla. 1992); [6][a], *below*].

For a general discussion of the nexus between psychiatric and physical injuries, see Larson's Workers' Compensation, Desk Edition, Ch. 56, §§ 56.02, 56.03 (Matthew Bender).

To understand this issue of a mere touching coupled with psychological trauma, a review of the cases is in order [*see* [5], *below*].

[5] History: Case Examples

Case 1. A robber grabbed a necklace from the employee's neck. Although this did not result in any actual physical injury, the mere "touching" was enough trauma to make her resultant mental problems compensable [*see* Popiel v. Broward County School Bd., 432 So. 2d 1374, 1375–1376 (Fla. 1st DCA 1983)].

Case 2. During a robbery, the mugger placed a handgun at the employee's head, pulled the employee's ring from her finger, and forced her to lie on the floor. In spite of the absence of even a bruise or other physical injury, the court approved an award for psychiatric injury [*see* Prahl Bros. Inc. v. Phillips, 429 So. 2d 386, 387 (Fla. 1st DCA 1983)]. (Note: this case was subsequently disapproved by City of Holmes Beach v. Grace, 598 So. 2d 71, 74 (Fla. 1992); *see* [6][a], *below.*)

Case 3. The employee was a police officer. A combative accident victim grabbed him, causing a bruise to his arm and aggravation of a preexisting psychiatric condition. At trial, the judge denied the claim, holding that the disability resulted from fright or excitement alone. The court of appeal disagreed and reversed. The court acknowledged that the Workers' Compensation Act requires underlying physical injury or trauma for neurosis to be compensable. The court held, however, that the trauma itself need not be disabling for the resulting mental or nervous injury to be compensable [*see* Sheppard v. City of Gainesville Police Dept., 490 So. 2d 972, 974 (Fla. 1st DCA 1986)]. (Note: this case was subsequently disapproved by City of Holmes Beach v. Grace, 598 So. 2d 71, 74 (Fla. 1992); *see* [6][a], *below.*)

Case 4. Contrast Case 3, above, with this one. The injured worker was a school teacher who suffered mental problems because of her students. In denying the claim, the court held that a neurosis or mental problem must have physical trauma associated with it to be compensable. No such evidence was presented here [*see* Williams v. Hillsborough County School Board, 389 So. 2d 1218, 1219 (Fla. 1st DCA 1980)].

Case 5. Here, the injured worker suffered mental problems. These were brought on by personal problems, job stress, and the routine consumption of alcohol while at work in the employer's liquor warehouse. Evidence suggested that the employer approved of drinking in the warehouse, in certain situations, as an inducement to the workers. Not even the injured worker, however, contended that drinking on the job is physical impact or trauma. Since no physical trauma occurred, the court denied the claim [Lafave v. Bay Consol. Distributors, 546 So. 2d 78, 80 (Fla. 1st DCA 1989)].

Case 6. In 1985, a Holmes Beach police officer stopped a man who was attempting to steal a car. During the arrest procedure, the officer had the suspect face down on the ground, trying to handcuff him. The suspect resisted and, during the struggle, he struck the officer several times. In response, the officer drew his weapon and during continued attempts to subdue the suspect, shot the suspect twice in the back, "accidentally." The suspect died. Two years later in 1987, the same officer was involved in an altercation with a motorist. At this point, "[i]t became clear to him and others that he had to leave the police force for emotional . . . reasons." He then filed a workers' compensation claim for psychiatric injury. The trial judge awarded benefits and the First District Court of Appeal agreed. The court based the award on a physician's testimony that the officer suffered from post-traumatic stress disorder. The physician related this condition to the shooting incident two years earlier. The court's opinion did not mention any physical injury the injured worker may have suffered. We can infer that no physical injury occurred because of what the court did next.

Apparently, even the First District Court of Appeal began to question the soundness of its own decisions in cases involving little or no physical injury. The court recognized that its decision here conflicted with a Supreme Court decision. Although the court stuck by its decision to award benefits, it certified the following question to the Florida Supreme Court [City of Holmes Beach v. Grace, 570 So. 2d 1011, 1012 (Fla. 1st DCA 1990), *reversed,* 598 So. 2d 71, 74 (Fla. 1992)]:

> Whether section 440.02(1), Florida Statutes (1985), defining "accident," excludes a mental or nervous injury where the injury suffered by the claimant results in only minor physical consequences?

The Supreme Court's response is discussed in [6][a], *below.*

[6] Present State of the Law

[a] *City of Holmes Beach v. Grace*

The Supreme Court in *City of Holmes Beach v. Grace,* 598 So. 2d 71, 73–74 (Fla. 1992), disagreed with the path that the First District Court of Appeal had taken [*see* [5], *above*].

> . . .The district courts of appeal have attempted to circumvent the statutory exclusion by approving compensation awards for mental or nervous injuries caused by accidents in which the claimant suffered some physical touching, but almost no physical trauma. . . . For a mental or nervous injury to be compensable in Florida, there must have been a physical injury. Otherwise, the disability would have been caused only by a mental stimulus, and must be denied coverage under the statutory exclusion. A mere touching cannot suffice as a physical injury.

The Court cautioned, however, that its decision does not create a requirement that the injury be serious or disabling. Even a minor injury may suffice. On the other hand, the Court held the physical injury must cause the mental injury.

The first application of the Supreme Court's holding in *Grace* occurred in 1992. Here, a co-worker pushed or shoved the injured worker onto a chair. The worker suffered a mental injury as a result, but admitted that he did not suffer any physical injury or require medical care because of the co-worker's actions. The First District Court of Appeal, citing *Grace,* reversed the award of benefits and dismissed the claim. "Because there was no physical injury, claimant's mental impairment, even if related to the pushing incident at work, is not compensable" [*see* Harris Corporation v. Forlenza, 605 So. 2d 1310, 1311 (Fla. 1st DCA 1992)].

SPECIAL ALERT: The physical injury requirement does not apply to first responders in regard to medical benefits. First responders are defined as law enforcement officers, firefighters, emergency medical technicians, or paramedics. First responders are entitled to medical benefits (but not to indemnity benefits) for a mental or nervous injury arising out of the employment even when the condition is not accompanied by a physical injury [*see* § 112.1815(2)(a)3, Fla. Stat.].

[b] Physical Injury Must Cause the Mental Injury

For a mental injury to be compensable, the evidence must show that the physical injury caused the mental injury and that the mental injury was not the result of fright or excitement alone.

> **NOTE:** As noted in the Special Alert in [a], *above*, the physical injury requirement does not apply to first responders with regard to medical benefits. First responders are entitled to medical benefits for a mental injury arising out of the employment even if there is no physical injury. However, first responders are not entitled to indemnity benefits for a mental injury unless a physical injury arising out of the employment accompanies the mental injury [*see* § 112.1815(2)(a)3. Fla. Stat.].

An example of the requirement that a physical injury must cause the mental injury appears in the case of *Thames v. Santa Rosa County Jail* [639 So. 2d 95 (Fla. 1st DCA 1994)]. In *Thames*, the employee was doing his regular duties as a prison guard. He unexpectedly collided with a mailbox, injuring his back. Immediately, he thought an inmate was attacking him from behind, but then realized what had happened. Despite this realization, he began having psychiatric problems after this incident. The carrier denied his claim for psychiatric care, as did the judge of compensation claims. The judge based his decision on medical testimony that the injured worker's anxiety and fear were associated with his misapprehension of the incident. A psychiatrist testified that the injured worker's situation would be unchanged even if the employee had sustained no physical injury. The First District Court of Appeal held that based on this evidence, the JCC was correct. Because the mental injury was due to fright or excitement only, the judge properly denied the claim [*see* Thames v. Santa Rosa County Jail, 639 So. 2d 95, 96 (Fla. 1st DCA 1994)].

Often, physicians are unable to state with certainty whether, within a reasonable degree of medical probability, a mental injury is the direct and immediate result of the compensable industrial injury. In such a case, the usual approach is to attempt linking the mental problems with the compensable physical injury. Such attempts often result in testimony that the compensable injury is linked, connected, or related to the mental injury in some fashion. Mere linkage with the accident, however, is not sufficient. The injured worker must prove that the compensable physical injury is a direct cause of the mental injury [*see* Leon County School Board v. Green, 711 So. 2d 86, 88 (Fla. 1st DCA 1998)]. Note: For accidents occurring on or after October 1, 2003, the compensable accident and physical injury must be, and remain, the major contributing cause of the mental or nervous injury, injury rather than merely a direct cause [*see* § 440.093(2), Fla. Stat. (10/1/2003); ch. 7, § 7.01[4]].

The legislature subsequently amended the Act by essentially codifying the Supreme Court's holding in *City of Holmes Beach v. Grace*. The Act now provides that a mental or nervous injury, without an accompanying physical injury requiring medical treatment, is not compensable. Besides meeting the major contributing cause standard, compensability requires showing that the mental injury is a manifestation of the initial physical injury [*see* § 440.093(1) & (2), Fla. Stat. (10/1/2003)].

[c] Physical Injury Need Not Be Concurrent With the Mental Injury

Most readers of *Grace* [*see* [a], *above*] concluded that the Supreme Court intended that the physical injury and the mental injury must have resulted from the same incident. Further they concluded that the mental injury must flow directly from the physical injury. The First District Court of Appeal, however, does not see it quite that way. Even a preexisting injury will apparently suffice if the mental injury results from the physical injury. Further, it is apparently not necessary that the same event cause both the physical injury and the mental injury.

For example, Thomas Karl was a firefighter and paramedic. He sustained minor bites and scratches while helping a combative auto accident victim. Although the scratches bled, Karl did not need medical treatment. The next day he was called to the scene of a shooting. While attending to the shooting victim, he got some blood on his bare hands. Later, Karl learned that the shooting victim had AIDS. Concerned that he might get the disease, Karl developed psychological problems.

Although the two incidents were not directly related, the court concluded that Karl's mental problems "resulted from the combined effect of the two incidents." The court held that the preexisting scratch wounds satisfied the physical injury requirement. Thus, said the court, the "mental or nervous injury was not due to fright or excitement only" [*see* City of Hollywood v. Karl, 643 So. 2d 34, 35 (Fla. 1st DCA 1994)].

This case raises some interesting questions. Is it necessary that the underlying physical injury be work related, or will any injury do? For example, what if Karl's dog had bitten and scratched him at home? This case also suggests that it is not necessary that the physical injury directly cause the mental injury. It appears enough that some link exists between the two.

[d] Compensability and Evidence Requirements; Excluded Conditions

No compensation is payable for a mental or nervous injury unless the evidence shows that the claimant suffered a compensable physical injury requiring treatment. Additionally, the evidence must show that the physical injury is, and remains, at least 50 percent responsible for the manifestation of a mental injury. (The major-contributing-cause standard).

These compensability elements must be shown by clear and convincing evidence by a licensed psychiatrist. Additionally, the physician's opinions must be based on the criteria established in the most recent edition of the Diagnostic and Statistical Manual of Mental Disorders published by the American Psychiatric Association.

Regardless of whether the compensability requirements have been met, the following conditions are not compensable [*see* § 440.093, Fla. Stat. (10/1/2003)]:

1. Depression from being out of work
2. Depression from losing employment opportunities.
3. Preexisting mental conditions
4. Emotional conditions due to pain or other subjective complaints that cannot be

substantiated by objective, relevant medical findings.

> **SPECIAL ALERT:** The major contributing cause standard for compensability apparently does not apply to first responders, defined as law enforcement officers, firefighters, emergency medical technicians, or paramedics. Instead, first responders must demonstrate manifestation of a compensable psychiatric injury only by clear and convincing evidence [*see* § 112.1815(2)(a)3, Fla. Stat.]. "Clear and Convincing" evidence is evidence of a quality and character designed to produce in the judge of compensation claims' mind a firm belief or conviction, without hesitation, as to the truth of the allegations [*Black's Law Dictionary*, 6th Edition].

[e] Benefit Limitations

For accidents occurring on or after October 1, 2003, temporary disability benefits are not payable for disability caused by a compensable mental injury for more than six months after the claimant reaches maximum medical improvement for the physical injury. Such payments are included in the 104-week maximum entitlement to temporary disability described in § 440.15(2) & (4), Fla. Stat. [*see* § 440.093(3), Fla. Stat. (10/1/2003)]. For a discussion of the 104-week limitation, see ch. 14, § 14.01[3][b].

> **SPECIAL ALERT:** The six-month limit on temporary disability benefits after maximum medical improvement does not apply to first responders. First responders are defined as law enforcement officers, firefighters, emergency medical technicians, or paramedics [*see* § 112.1815(2)(a)3, Fla. Stat.].

§ 6.04 Prosthetic Devices

[1] The Rule

The law allows coverage for prosthetic devices such as artificial limbs, eyeglasses, and dentures. The injured worker must show, however, that the damage to the prosthetic device is part of, or in conjunction with, an accident [§ 440.02(19), Fla. Stat.].

[2] Coverage for Prosthetic Devices

The law specifically allows coverage for repair or replacement of a prosthetic device. To be precise, the Act allows coverage for damage to dentures, eyeglasses, prosthetic devices, and artificial limbs. The damage is covered, however, only if it results from a compensable accident in the normal course of employment [§ 440.02(19), Fla. Stat.]. That leads to the question, what is an accident? An accident is simply an unexpected or unusual event or result that happens suddenly during the course and scope of the job [§ 440.02(1), Fla. Stat.]. As we will see in § 6.05, meeting the definition of "accident" is not difficult.

If a worker is struck in the face and this results in broken eyeglasses, most insurance carriers would have no reservation about paying for replacement eyeglasses. What if the

Guide to Claims

employee is doing normal work and snesezes, causing his eyeglasses to fall off and break? Is that a sudden, unexpected event?

No court decisions exist on this issue. Remember, however, that the Workers' Compensation Act does not require a literal physical injury as a prerequisite. It requires only that an event occur as part of or with an accident. Damage to these devices is included in the statutory definition of injury.

Therefore, if a prosthetic device is damaged in an event that meets the criteria of an otherwise compensable accident, the damage should be covered. Due to the lack of appellate review, people disagree on whether sneezing one's glasses off and breaking them is a compensable event. In deciding, carriers should consider that defense attorney's fees alone may be several times the cost of a pair of eyeglasses. If the carrier litigates the issue and loses, it will owe the injured worker's attorney's fee as well. In one case, the injured worker prevailed in a claim for eyeglasses. A witness testified that a reasonable fee would be about $2,500. The judge awarded only $500, but the court of appeal reversed with a remand to decide a proper fee [*see* Bacon v. Broward Employment & Training Admin., 501 So. 2d 724, 726 (Fla. 1st DCA 1987)].

For a general treatment of injury to prosthetic devices, see Larson's Workers' Compensation, Desk Edition, Ch. 55 (Matthew Bender).

§ 6.05 By Accident—The Second Element

[1] The Rule

The term "accident" means only an unexpected *or* unusual event *or* result that happens suddenly. The legislature's use of the word "or" means that the law requires only one or the other. The event need not be unexpected if the result is unexpected or unusual [§ 440.02(1), Fla. Stat.].

[2] Sudden Happening

Although the statutory definition calls for a sudden happening, do not take the term "sudden" too literally. In the so-called exposure cases [*see* § 6.07], the law does not require that the ill effect of an exposure must occur suddenly and be immediately related to an identifiable accident.

[3] Accidental

The definition does not require a physical accident, such as a slip and fall. Because of the liberal interpretations of the definition of injury and accident, defending cases on these two points is difficult. One exception is what some call non-accidents. These non-accidents include the troublesome areas of heart attack cases, exposure and repetitive trauma cases, and negligent or self-inflicted injury. These situations are often the subject of litigation and we will discuss them in §§ 6.06–6.08.

For a general discussion of the accident requirement, see Larson's Workers' Compensation, Desk Edition, Ch. 42 (Matthew Bender).

§ 6.06 Heart Attack Cases

[1] The Rule

If *evidence exists* of a preexisting condition, heart attacks and internal cardiovascular failures are compensable only if the employee was, at the time, subject to unusual physical strain not routine to the type of work the employee was accustomed to performing.

If *no evidence* exists proving a preexisting condition, heart attacks and internal cardiovascular failures are compensable if caused by *any* amount of actual exertion, even if the exertion was minor and routine and even if associated with some degree of stress [*see* Zundell v. Dade County School Bd., 636 So. 2d 8, 11 (Fla. 1994)].

Injuries that occur purely because of a simple disease of life or non work-related emotional strain alone are not compensable. Only those brought on by the employment are compensable [*see* [9], *below,* for fire fighter's exception to this rule].

All cases involving cardiovascular system injury merit particular attention and extensive investigation. Recall the definition of injury includes diseases that are the natural result of a compensable injury. Thus, if a worker suffered a blow to the chest that resulted in a heart attack, the heart attack is compensable. Medical evidence must show, of course, that a causal relationship between the two events exists. The evidence needed to prove compensability in cases where the injured worker suffers from preexisting conditions can be separated into two parts: first, the evidence must show that the worker was subjected to unusual physical exertion [*see* [2], *below*]; and second, the evidence must also show that the exertion was the major contributing cause of the new injury [*see* [5], *below*]. For a complete discussion of the major contributing cause requirement, *see* Part 6, § 7.01.

For a general discussion of heart attack cases, see Larson's Workers' Compensation, Desk Edition, Ch. 43, § 43.03[1] (Matthew Bender).

[2] The Unusual Physical Exertion Requirement

[a] Overview

The problem cases are those without a physical accident. These are often cases where the employee suffers a heart attack during the routine course of work. Heart attacks and other internal failures caused by mental or emotional stress alone are not compensable. Heart attacks and internal failures are compensable only if caused by some physical exertion. The degree or level of exertion required for compensability depends on whether the evidence shows that the employee suffered from a preexisting disease. Without such evidence, a new cardiovascular injury is not compensable unless the employee was at the time subject to unusual physical strain. Physical strain is not unusual if it is routine to the type of work the employee was accustomed to performing [*see* Victor Wine & Liquor, Inc. v. Beasley, 141 So. 2d 581, 588–589 (Fla. 1962)].

[b] Requirement Applies to Entire Cardiovascular System

In 1978, the Florida Supreme Court extended this rule to apply to all general cardiovascular system failures. The Court held [Richard E. Mosca & Co., Inc. v. Mosca, 362 So. 2d 1340, 1342 (Fla. 1978)]:

Guide to Claims

1. Heart attacks and internal failures of the cardiovascular system are to be treated in the same manner for the purposes of establishing the causation element in compensation cases; and

2. Emotional strain alone is too elusive a factor, independent of any physical activity, in determining a causal connection between a heart attack and other failures of the cardiovascular system, and the injured worker's employment.

A large portion of the work force has preexisting heart defects that would result in heart attacks in any event. This fact has led some legal scholars to believe that *Victor Wine* has limited application [*see* [a], *above*]. They believe it stands for the proposition that the requirement of unusual strain applies only when the injured worker has preexisting, non-disabling, heart disease. Proponents base this theory on statements made by the Supreme Court in *Victor Wine* [Victor Wine & Liquor, Inc. v. Beasley, 141 So. 2d 581, 588–589 (Fla. 1962)]:

> [W]e adopt the following rule for heart cases: When disabling heart attacks are involved and where such heart conditions are precipitated by work-connected exertion *affecting a pre-existing non-disabling heart disease,* said injuries are compensable only if the employee was at the time subject to unusual strain or over-exertion not routine to the type of work he was accustomed to performing. (Emphasis added.)

The First District Court of Appeal decided, however, that no Florida precedent suggests that courts should apply *Victor Wine* only where the employer has shown a preexisting condition. In 1993 the District Court of Appeal, sitting *en banc,* expanded the application of the *Victor Wine* tests. The full court held that the tests of unusual physical exertion apply, not only to heart attacks, but to all other internal failures of the cardiovascular system [*see* Zundell v. Dade County School Bd., 609 So. 2d 1367, 1369–1370 (Fla. 1st DCA 1992), *reversed,* 636 So. 2d 8 (Fla. 1994); *see* [d], *below*].

[c] Exception to the Physical Requirement

Arleen McGuire reported to her job as a part time cashier as usual. Earlier, she had sent a letter to the company president complaining about pay raises that other employees received. (She did not get a pay raise.) On this day, the general manager asked McGuire to attend a meeting with the store manager. McGuire feared the manager would fire her for complaining directly to the president. Upset and nervous, McGuire remained standing during the meeting and began experiencing chest pain diagnosed as coronary artery spasms. McGuire had a history of high blood pressure, but never experienced heart problems or chest pain before. The judge of compensation claims awarded benefits based on *Citrus Cent., Inc. v. Gardner,* 466 So. 2d 369, 370 (Fla. 1st DCA 1985).

In *Gardner,* the court held that a coronary artery spasm was not a heart attack so the *Victor Wine* tests did not apply [*see* [a], *above*]. No evidence was presented to show that McGuire suffered from plaque or arterial blockage. From this, the judge concluded that McGuire met the burden of proving the lack of any relevant preexisting condition. On appeal, however, after reviewing medical testimony and case law, the First District Court of Appeal disagreed. Here, the court held that a coronary artery spasm is an internal failure of the cardiovascular system. Because the judge found no evidence of unusual physical exertion, the court reversed the award of benefits. Thus, the court receded from its decision in *Gardner* to the extent that *Gardner* excluded coronary artery spasm. The *Zundell* court [*see* [b], *above*] also held the law does not require evidence that an injured worker suffered from an existing cardiovascular problem to apply the *Victor Wine* test. This is true, said the court, though the Supreme Court did contemplate such a requirement [*see* Publix Super Markets, Inc. v. McGuire, 629 So. 2d 862, 865–866 (Fla. 1st DCA 1993), *reversed and remanded,* 640 So. 2d 1079 (Fla. 1994), *vacated,* 650 So. 2d 151, 154 (Fla. 1st DCA 1995)].

[d] Supreme Court Settles the Question

Recognizing its decision in *McGuire* [*see* [c], *above*] has "potentially broad ramifications" (not to mention conflict with the Supreme Court), the District Court of Appeal certified the following question to the Florida Supreme Court [Publix Super Markets, Inc. v. McGuire, 629 So. 2d 862, 865–866 (Fla. 1st DCA 1993), *reversed and remanded,* 640 So. 2d 1079 (Fla. 1994), *vacated,* 650 So. 2d 151, 154 (Fla. 1st DCA 1995)]:

> Are the *Victor Wine* and *Mosca* tests requiring unusual physical exertion "Applicable to cases in which there is no evidence that the claimant suffered from a 'pre-existing non-disabling' cardiovascular defect, failure, or disease, thereby requiring proof that, at the time of the injury, a claimant was 'subject to unusual strain or over-exertion not routine to the type of work' a claimant was accustomed to performing?

The Supreme Court rephrased the question [Zundell v. Dade County School Bd., 636 So. 2d 8, 9 (Fla. 1994)]:

> Whether the rule announced in *Victor Wine & Liquor, Inc. v. Beasley* . . . ever can apply to cardiovascular injuries occurring on the job when competent substantial medical evidence shows no evidence of a preexisting condition relevant to the injury?

The Supreme Court answered no, and reversed! Warren Zundell was a school teacher who suffered a hemorrhage of the brain following a series of problems with an unruly student. Twice that day, Zundell had to escort the student to the school office for discipline. After the second trip, Zundell began feeling ill. He was taken to the hospital by ambulance where doctors diagnosed the hemorrhage. No medical evidence was presented suggesting Zundell had any preexisting condition that would explain the injury. An expert testified that the hemorrhage was most likely caused by an elevation in blood pressure caused by the incidents with the student. The Court held that it has never extended the *Victor Wine* test to include cases without evidence of a preexisting condition [*see* Zundell v. Dade County School Bd., 636 So. 2d 8, 10 (Fla. 1994)].

The First District Court of Appeal, on remand from the Florida Supreme Court, applied this holding to *McGuire.* This case, then, stands for the proposition that stress induced cardiovascular injury—even without physical exertion—is compensable absent evidence of relevant preexisting disease [*see* Publix Super Markets, Inc. v. McGuire, 650 So. 2d 151, 154 (Fla. 1st DCA 1995)].

[3] When Does Unusual Physical Exertion Requirement Apply

When no evidence of a preexisting condition exists, analyze cases involving workplace cardiovascular injuries like any other workplace injury. Thus, absent evidence of a preexisting condition, cardiovascular injuries are compensable if any exertion caused the injury. The exertion need not be unusual or even at a high level. Any exertion—no matter how slight—will suffice if the medical evidence shows the exertion brought on the injury. Apparently, the only physical exertion Zundell engaged in was to walk, twice, to the school office. McGuire engaged in even less physical exertion. Job-related stress appears to have exclusively caused her injury. Therefore, the fact that a high level of stress accompanies the minor exertion is not important. Note, however, that simply doing normal work combined with a general, non specific, job-related stress may be enough for compensability. In both *Zundell* [*see* [b], *above*] and *McGuire* [*see* [c], *above*], the evidence showed specific, high stress events.

[4] Who Has Burden of Proof

The injured worker has the initial burden to prove a lack of a preexisting condition. The worker must show that no relevant preexisting condition existed, or at least that none can be medically detected if the injury is a type that a preexisting condition can exacerbate. Generally, presenting a physician's statement that no preexisting condition is medically detectable will be sufficient. If the injured worker can produce such evidence, the burden shifts to the carrier to prove that a preexisting condition does exist [*see* Zundell v. Dade County School Bd., 636 So. 2d 8, 12 (Fla. 1994)].

[5] The Major Contributing Cause Requirement

Recall that compensability requires evidence that the employment subjected the worker to unusual physical exertion. In addition, compensability requires evidence that the exertion—the compensable accident—was the major contributing cause, and not just a contributing factor. For example, William Mangold was doing his work when a go-cart struck him and pinned his right leg. Later, he suffered a heart attack brought on, he claimed, by the stress of the accident. This stress may have been a factor, but many other possible causes existed. Mangold was morbidly obese, had a long history of heart disease, and suffered from hypertension. No medical expert could testify that within a reasonable degree of medical certainty the go-cart incident was the major contributing cause of Mangold's heart attack. Based on this, the judge of compensation claims denied the claim and the First District Court of Appeal affirmed [*see* Mangold v. Rainforest Golf Sports Center, 675 So. 2d 639, 642 (Fla. 1st DCA 1996)]. For a complete discussion of the major contributing cause requirement, *see* ch. 7, § 7.01[4].

As noted, under the 2003 amendment to § 440.09(1), Fla. Stat., the major contributing cause standard requires claimants to prove the industrial accident caused more than 50% of the injury and the resulting need for treatment.

The court has not yet addressed whether the amendment supersedes *Victor Wine* for dates of accident occurring after October 1, 2003. However, in dicta, the court said that since all claimants have always been required to meet the applicable industrial causation standard, which post-2003 is the 50% plus major contributing cause standard, placing the additional burden of complying with the court-created *Victor Wine* test seems unduly burdensome and inappropriate. The court noted that the test was originally established to show at least some industrial causation when claimants experience a heart attack while performing their work duties when they suffered from pre-existing heart disease. When *Victor Wine* was decided, there was no statutory test like the major contributing cause standard as a threshold for establishing industrial causation. Now, a claimant must show the major contributing cause of an injury is industrial, and make this showing by medical evidence. In the case of pre-existing heart disease, the claimant would also have to establish an unusual strain or over-exertion. The court indicated that unless otherwise specified by the Legislature, all compensable injuries should be required to meet the same standard of proof [*see generally* Zundell v. Dade County Sch. Bd., 636 So. 2d 8 (Fla. 1994)]. A claimant who establishes his or her work was the major contributing cause of a myocardial infarction should be able to recover, even if on the day of the myocardial infarction, his or her duties were less than normal, or comparable to an "average" day [*see* Coca-Cola Bottling Co. v. Perdue, 2007 Fla. App. LEXIS 5187 (Fla. 1st DCA 2007)].

[6] Establishing Unusual Exertion

[a] The Rule

If the evidence shows that the injured worker suffered from a relevant, preexisting condition, cardiovascular injury is not compensable absent sufficient evidence that the injured worker was involved in non-routine and unusual physical exertion that caused the heart attack [*see* Zundell v. Dade County School Bd., 636 So. 2d 8, 11 (Fla. 1994)].

[b] What Makes the Exertion Unusual

Though an employee is not personally accustomed to doing the work, if the activities were routine to the work and to the job, a resulting heart attack is not compensable. The type of work that the injured worker had been accustomed to doing in previous jobs, whether for the current employer or for another, is not relevant [*see* Wiggs Const. v. Knowles, 497 So. 2d 942, 944 (Fla. 1st DCA 1986)].

This is true even if the injured worker had been unemployed and sedentary for months before beginning a new job. Starting a new job after a period of unemployment creates a different situation. In such cases, the relevant inquiry regarding a heart attack is whether the precipitating work activity was a strain or over exertion that would not be routine *to the new job* [*see* Skinner v. First Florida Bldg. Corp., 490 So. 2d 1367, 1368–1369 (Fla. 1st DCA 1986); Daniels v. Office Mart Holding Corp., 548 So. 2d 828, 829 (Fla. 1st DCA 1989); Batson Cook Co., v. Thomas, 635 So. 2d 991, 993 (Fla. 1st DCA 1994)].

Look at the injured worker's duties rather than those of fellow workers. Examine carefully all of the employee's work, rather than some isolated segment of the work activities. In all the compensable heart cases requiring evidence of unusual exertion, the injured worker produced sufficient evidence of an unusual physical exertion that caused the heart attack. Now, more then ever, all cardiovascular disease cases require a detailed investigation. Before we can find out if a person's activity was unusual, we must first learn what activity was usual.

The activity in question must be specifically identifiable and non-routine. Often, no difficulty arises in determining whether an activity was routine or not for an individual injured worker. The close cases, however, will cause problems. Unfortunately, court decisions have not provided any clear guideline [*see* [c], *below*].

[c] Case History

Case 1. The injured worker went to work alone to cut some sample patterns. He lifted a heavy bolt of material and felt chest pains. He normally delegated such heavy work to others. The court found sufficient evidence of unaccustomed strain and connection of the strain to the heart attack to award benefits [*see* Jamar Sportswear, Inc. v. Miller, 413 So. 2d 811, 812–813 (Fla. 1st DCA 1982)].

Case 2. The employer sent the 74-year-old employee to Guatemala to audit the return of unsold magazines. The employee was supervising the counting, and moved some stacks of magazines himself. He had a heart attack and died. The trial judge held the worker's job was sedentary and moving stacks of magazines was unusual strain. The First District Court of Appeal disagreed and reversed because the employee had done similar tasks on a prior recent trip to Guatemala. In addition, and perhaps more important, the medical opinion linking the employee's work and the heart attack was based on unsupported assumptions [*see* Editorial America S.A. v. Kent, 421 So. 2d 612, 614 (Fla. 1st DCA 1982)].

Case 3. The employer hired the claimant to work in a new store as a floor sales clerk, a job that had little physical requirements. Before the opening, the employer requested the claimant to come in and help with the pre-opening setup, a process that required strenuous work. The court held that the claimant's resultant heart attack was not compensable. The heavy work before the opening would last only a few days before the claimant assumed his sales work. This did not make the activities any less routine [*see* Daniels v. Office Mart Holding Corp., 548 So. 2d 828, 829 (Fla. 1st DCA 1989)].

[d] The Routine Work Standard

Deciding what is routine and what is unusual can be difficult, especially when the courts issue conflicting opinions. For example, the courts held in several cases that routine work applies to the job, not to the employee. This is the majority view. Therefore, a worker's first day on any job is not automatically non-routine. Though an employee is not personally accustomed to doing the work, if the activity was routine to the work and to the job, a resulting heart attack would not be compensable. Therefore, if the job requires occasional heavy work, it is routine. This is true even if the worker rarely, if ever, did such work before [*see* Skinner v. First Florida Bldg. Corp., 490 So. 2d 1367, 1368–1369 (Fla. 1st DCA 1986)].

Look at the injured worker's duties, rather than those of fellow workers. Also examine the injured worker's duties in their entirety, rather than some isolated segment of work activities. Sometimes, employees' job descriptions require that they must eventually do some heavy work. If the facts show that such work is unusual for them, a resultant heart attack may be compensable [*see* Walker v. Friendly Village of Brevard, 559 So. 2d 258, 261–262 (Fla. 1st DCA 1990)].

For example, Mr. Walker worked as a maintenance man. The evidence revealed that Walker was to do 99 percent of his work inside air-conditioned buildings, with the understanding that he would occasionally have to work outdoors. Part of his duties included care of the grounds. Walker was laying sod when he suffered a heart attack. The court concluded that since Walker was to do 99 percent of his work indoors, laying sod was different and therefore non-routine.

This is a new and ambiguous standard set by the court. What happens if only 80 percent of the employee's work was to be done indoors? Would that make a difference? We do not know. This new standard suggests that the activity, even if part of the employee's duties, will be unusual if the employee does not do it very often.

Remember that the unusual exertion requirement does not apply without evidence of a relevant preexisting condition. Usually, however, such evidence can be found. Heart attacks do not often occur without some preexisting disease. The point is to be certain to obtain full medical records before deciding compensability. In many cases this information will not be available soon enough to meet the new, accelerated, time requirements. If so, carriers may be wise to begin benefits under the 120-day rule and continue the investigation [*see* ch. 10, § 10.02[3]].

Guide to Claims

[7] Heart Attacks Caused by Emotional Stress

[a] The Rule

A heart attack caused by work-related emotional stress alone is compensable if no evidence exists that the employee suffered from relevant preexisting cardiovascular disease [*see* Zundell v. Dade County School Bd., 636 So. 2d 8, 11 (Fla. 1994)].

[b] Case History

Decisions by the Florida Supreme Court in *Zundell* and the First District Court of Appeal in *McGuire* appear to have overruled a long line of cases. These cases held that stress alone is not enough for compensability [*see* [2]–[5], *above*].

Case 1. Harassment on the job designed to coerce the employee to resign does not amount to an accident [*see* City of Miami v. Rosenberg, 396 So. 2d 163, 164–165 (Fla. 1st DCA 1981)].

Case 2. A heart attack following a series of stressful meetings, with no physical strain, is not compensable [*see* Verables v. City of Surfside, IRC 2–3674 (Fla. IRC 1979)].

Case 3. A heart attack suffered one week after someone shot at the employee is not compensable [*see* Russell v. State Department of Corrections, 464 So. 2d 1202, 1203 (Fla. 1st DCA 1984)].

Case 4. Stress from undergoing a polygraph test does not create a compensable event [*see* Hammersmith, Inc. v. Zanfardino, 425 So. 2d 80, 81 (Fla. 1st DCA 1982)].

Case 5. Working unusually long hours, even if accompanied by extraordinary stress, is not enough for compensability. Absent actual physical strain or exertion alone, or physical strain with emotional strain, a heart attack is not compensable. For example, Chester Cole was employed by the Department of Business Regulation for many years, working a standard eight-hour day. Cole suffered from long-standing chronic ischemic heart disease.

On the day of his heart attack, he had to attend a stressful administrative hearing that began about 11:00 a.m. The hearing was still underway at 8:00 p.m., when Cole began to feel ill. The judge of compensation claims held that this non-routine workday was sufficient to make the claim compensable. The First District Court of Appeal disagreed and reversed. Staying at work for a few hours beyond normal quitting time is not enough. The test, said the court, is non-routine physical effort [*see* State, Div. Of Hotels/Restaurants v. Cole, 664 So. 2d 291, 293–294 (Fla. 1st DCA 1995)].

> **REMEMBER:** Under the rule announced in *Zundell,* [*see* [2][b], *above*] each of the cases above may be compensable if the evidence showed that the injured worker did not suffer from a relevant, preexisting condition.

[8] The Medical Connection Requirement

[a] The Rule

Medical evidence must show a causal connection between the unusual strain and the heart attack. Medical causal relationship between the strain or over-exertion and the heart attack must be within a reasonable medical probability. However, this reasonable medical probability may be shown by either medical or lay testimony. Although lay testimony cannot be used to establish causal relationship within reasonable medical probability as to conditions and symptoms that are not readily observable, it is of probative value in establishing the sequence of events, actual inability to work, pain, and similar factors within the knowledge and sensory experience of the worker [*see* McCall v. Dick Burns, Inc., 408 So. 2d 787, 791–792 (Fla. 1st DCA 1982)].

For a general discussion of the medical causation requirement, see LARSON'S WORKERS' COMPENSATION, DESK EDITION, Ch. 46, § 46.03[8] (Matthew Bender).

[b] Making the Connection

Although the physical exertion requirement is important, equally important is the requirement that the physical exertion actually caused the heart attack. Also, even if the employee's heart was on its last tick when the physical exertion occurred, the existence of preexisting heart disease alone is not a defense. On the contrary, the Workers' Compensation Act requires carriers to pay benefits to workers suffering aggravation or acceleration of preexisting disease. A good defense is that the worker's job activities were merely coincidental with or unrelated to the heart attack. This defense requires an in-depth investigation into the employee's medical history, combined with expert medical testimony.

The period between the accident and the attack is always important. The longer the period between the alleged precipitating event and the onset of symptoms, the less likelihood a connection exists.

[9] The Firefighters, Police and Correctional Officer's Presumption

[a] The Rule

The statutes create a presumption that heart disease, tuberculosis and hypertension suffered by firefighters, law enforcement officers, correctional officers and probation officers are related to their employment. The burden of proof to the contrary rests with the employer and carrier. The presumption does not apply unless the employee has successfully passed a physical examination upon entering service as a firefighter or state law enforcement officer, and the examination failed to reveal any evidence of any such condition [§ 112.18(1), Fla. Stat.].

As noted, the presumption does not apply unless the employee successfully completed a pre-employment physical examination showing no evidence of heart disease, tuberculosis, and hypertension. However, the court found that the plain language of the statute does *not* require a *correctional officer* to satisfy this condition precedent. The 2002 amendment provided in relevant part:

> (1) Any condition or impairment of health of any Florida state, municipal, county, port authority, special tax district, or fire control district firefighter or any state law enforcement officer or correctional officer as defined in § 943.10(1), (2), or (3) caused by tuberculosis, heart disease, or hypertension resulting in total or partial disability or death shall be presumed to have been accidental and to have been suffered in the line of duty unless the contrary be shown by competent evidence. However, any such *firefighter* or *state law enforcement officer* shall have successfully passed a physical examination upon entering into any such service as a firefighter or state law enforcement officer, which examination failed to reveal any evidence of any such condition.

Because the amended statute does not include corrections officers among those who must first pass a physical examination upon beginning employment, the requirement does not apply to them [*see* State v. Reese, 911 So. 2d 1291 (Fla. 1st DCA 2005)].

Nevertheless, a corrections officer is still entitled to a presumption of compensability even if the officer did not successfully pass a pre-employment physical examination [Gray v. Dep't of Corrections, 918 So. 2d 322 (Fla. 1st DCA 2005)].

SPECIAL ALERT: The 2002 amendment to § 112.18(1), Fla. Stat. is a procedural enactment and applies retroactively without regard to the date of accident and injury. The amendment changes only the *procedure* for establishing entitlement to workers' compensation benefits [*see* Seminole County Sheriff's Office v. Johnson, 901 So. 2d 342 (Fla. 1st DCA 2005)].

[b] The Presumption

A major exception to the general rules applies in heart attack and cardiovascular cases involving firefighters, law enforcement officers, correctional officers and probation officers. As noted on [a], *above,* the legislature created a statutory presumption that heart

Guide to Claims

disease, tuberculosis and hypertension suffered by employees in these occupations are related to their employment. The burden of proof to the contrary rests with the employer and carrier.

Florida Statutes provide that a heart attack, tuberculosis, and hypertension suffered by a firefighter is presumed to have been accidental and to have been suffered in the line of duty unless competent evidence to the contrary exists [*see* Caldwell v. Division of Retirement, etc., 372 So. 2d 438, 441 (Fla. 1979)]:

> The statutory presumption is the expression of a strong public policy that does not vanish when the opposing party submits evidence. Where the evidence is conflicting, the quantum of proof is balanced and the presumption should prevail. This does not foreclose the employer from overcoming the presumption. However, if there is evidence supporting the presumption, *the employer can overcome the presumption only by clear and convincing evidence.* In the absence of cogent proof to the contrary the public policy in favor of job relatedness must be given effect. (Emphasis added)

Note that hypertensive conditions include only arterial or cardiovascular hypertension, as stated by the First District Court of Appeal [*see* City of Miami v. Thomas, 657 So. 2d 927, 928 (Fla. 1st DCA 1995)].

[c] Exceptions to the Presumption

The presumption does not apply unless the qualified firefighter or officer successfully passed a preemployment physical examination [§ 112.18(1), Fla. Stat. (2001)]. Although the Americans with Disabilities Act (ADA) restricts preemployment medical examinations, an employer may offer employment contingent on the results of the examination. According to the Equal Employment Opportunity Commission, Congress did not intend the ADA to override existing state or local laws. These include laws that set standards for doing specific jobs if the state laws are consistent with federal law. Employers may not, however, use the results of a medical examination to discriminate against an otherwise qualified applicant. For further discussion on the ADA and workers' compensation, see ch. 25, § 25.06.

[d] Overcoming the Presumption

The firefighter's presumption merely switches the burden of proof from the claimant to employer/carrier, and may be overcome by, as the statute plainly states, "competent evidence," and the judge of compensation claims may not apply a higher standard or greater burden of proof, so as to require the employer/carrier to establish that some other specific hazard or non-occupational hazard was the cause of claimant's disease. All that the statute requires to overcome the presumption is competent substantial evidence that convinces a JCC that the disease was caused by some non-work-related factor, not that it was caused by any sort of specific hazard or non-occupational hazard [City of Tarpon Springs v. Vaporis, 2007 Fla. App. LEXIS 3630, 2-3 (Fla. 1st DCA 2007)].

§ 6.07 Exposure and Repetitive Trivial Trauma

[1] The Rule

Exposure and repetitive trivial trauma are compensable events if the injured worker can show all of the following: (1) prolonged exposure; (2) the cumulative effect of which is injury or aggravation of a preexisting condition; and (3) the job subjected the injured worker to a hazard greater than that to which the public is exposed [*see* Festa v. Teleflex, Inc., 382 So. 2d 122, 124 (Fla. 1st DCA 1980)].

[2] Intent Defined

Is exposure or exertion over time an accident? Yes. As a well-known defense attorney once put it, these may be long and boring accidents, but they are accidents nonetheless. Florida's Workers' Compensation Act specifically provides for benefits for injuries sustained by accident or by occupational disease. The Act itself does not provide benefits for simple continuous exertion or exposure.

The courts, however, created the so-called exposure doctrine. This includes repetitive trauma events, any of which in themselves is not significant enough to produce a discernible or visible result until the passage of time results in cumulative injury. The result is that the suddenness requirement no longer applies. The law requires only unexpectedness of result. Probably the best way to approach these cases is to apply a "but for" rule. That is, but for the employment the result would not have occurred.

For a general discussion of injury from usual exertion or exposure, see LARSON'S WORKERS' COMPENSATION, DESK EDITION, Ch. 43 (Matthew Bender).

[3] Current State of the Law

[a] *Festa v. Teleflex*

In *Festa v. Teleflex, Inc.* [382 So. 2d 122, 124 (Fla. 1st DCA 1980)], the court announced a three-pronged test required to show compensability for repetitive trauma and exposure injuries [*see* [b], *below*].

[b] Applying the *Festa* Tests

To receive compensation, a claimant must show the following:

Prong 1. Prolonged exposure. How long is "prolonged?" Almost any period will suffice. A lengthy duration will not affect an otherwise qualifying claim, and a short duration sounds more like a conventional sudden accident case. Indeed, this prong of the *Festa* tests does not impose a minimum temporal threshold, and even a period of exposure as short as two weeks may be sufficient [*see* J & J Enterprises v. Oweis, 733 So. 2d 1149, 1150 (Fla. 1st DCA 1999)].

The "prolonged exposure" factor for purposes of worker's compensation benefits based on toxic exposure may be satisfied by either a single-dose exposure or a repeated exposure. Case law does not impose a minimum temporal threshold for determining a "prolonged exposure." The factor of "prolonged exposure" may be satisfied in any given case by a showing of any exposure, either a single dose exposure or a repeated exposure [*see* Moore v. Pasco County Bd. of Comm'rs, 854 So. 2d 256, 257 (Fla. 1st DCA 2003)].

Prong 2. The cumulative effect of which is injury or aggravation of a preexisting condition. This causal relationship requirement is similar to the "arising out of" language in the Workers' Compensation Act that we must always establish.

Prong 3. The employee has been subjected to a hazard greater than that to which the public is exposed. This language sounds like the occupational disease language of § 440.151(2), Fla. Stat., but it is different. Here, it is the hazard exposure, rather than disease, that must be beyond that to which the public is exposed. This is an alternate theory for compensability. Injured workers need to show only a series of occurrences, the cumulative effect of which is injury. The law does not require injured workers to show, additionally, that the job subjected them to a hazard greater than that to which the public is exposed [*see* Rodriquez v. Frito-Lay Inc., 600 So. 2d 1167, 1172 (Fla. 1st DCA 1992)].

In 1992, the Florida Supreme Court added a fourth prong to the test:

Prong 4. For a preexisting condition to be compensable, it must be exacerbated by some non-routine, job related physical exertion, or by some form of repeated physical trauma. This prong is an original *Victor Wine* test [*see* § 6.06[2][a]] announced years ago for heart attack cases. The Court added this to the *Festa* test to preclude compensability for injuries caused by, or aggravated by stress [*see* University of Florida v. Massie, 602 So. 2d 516, 524 (Fla. 1992)].

[c] Demonstrating Increased Hazard

Deciding what constitutes an increased hazard can be tricky. Making the distinction is best done with examples. The first example involves an employee who injured his back from lifting heavy material over a long period. He could not recall a specific incident, but his doctors said that heavy lifting over time was compatible with the claimed back injury. The Supreme Court held that the injury was an accident and awarded benefits [*see* Houle v. Asphalt Sealing & Stripping Co., Inc., 397 So. 2d 669, 670 (Fla. 1981)].

Most people have no difficulty in accepting the theory that the public is not exposed to continuous heavy lifting and that such activity constitutes an increased hazard. Often, however, whether an event or series of events amount to an increased hazard can be a difficult call. The hazard prong of the *Festa* test does not require an injured worker to prove a work condition unique to the employment [*see* [b], *above*]. Instead, the worker must show that the exposure is materially more than the public undergoes. For example, an employee suffered from neck and back pain. This resulted from working directly under an air-conditioning vent while standing on a hardwood floor with her arms raised above shoulder level. The Supreme Court held these activities constituted an increased hazard [*see* Sewell v. J.C. Penney, 569 So. 2d 1335, 1336 (Fla. 1st DCA 1990)].

Regular exposure to common, but excessive downtown noise and air pollution, for example, does not qualify as an occupational disease, but does constitute an increased hazard under the *Festa* test [*see* City of Miami v. Tomberlin, 492 So. 2d 433, 435 (Fla. 1st DCA 1986)].

The law does not always require expert testimony to prove the hazard prong of the *Festa* test [*see* [b], *above*]. For example, June Knight was a truck driver who had undergone a diskectomy seven years before this accident. (A diskectomy is the surgical removal of a herniated intervertebral disk.) Classically, the evidence showed that her job required working long hours riding in a bouncing, vibrating truck. Also, the job required her to move heavy objects in the truck. Knight's chiropractor testified that her present back problems were related to the repetitive "micro-trauma" sustained as a truck driver. The physician also testified that truck drivers have a higher frequency of low back pain than any other profession. While the court did not consider this expert testimony, it did conclude such testimony was "noteworthy." The court considered the chiropractor's testimony to be sufficient evidence to meet the increased hazard prong of the test [*see* Johnson v. Knight, 594 So. 2d 836, 837–838 (Fla. 1st DCA 1992)].

[d] Constant Trauma Not Required

Neither *Festa* [*see* [b], *above*] nor other cases require constant, excessive, and daily minor trauma. Frequency of exposure to minor trauma is not the controlling consideration. It is merely one factor to consider with all the evidence as a whole [*see* Alvarez v. City of Tampa, 647 So. 2d 301, 303 (Fla. 1st DCA 1994)].

[4] Defending Repeated Trauma Cases

No exotic defenses exist here. Conduct an in-depth investigation aimed at disproving one of the four prongs of the *Festa* tests [*see* [b], *above*]. For example, is it medically probable the employee's activities caused the injury, or is the injury the result of some personal problem? Did the truck really buck and shimmy at low speeds or is this a convenient contrivance? Did the job require the employee to punch holes constantly or to do another repetitive motion, or did the job really entail only one or two efforts a day? Often, a successful defense requires explaining facts to the treating doctor, or to the judge of compensation claims, which results in a combined medical and legal opinion of no causation. Investigate the possibility that the doctor based the original medical opinion about the job causing the injury upon incomplete or inaccurate facts.

Following is an example of the *Festa* test at work. Before beginning work, Donald Stuck suffered a series of back injuries that eventually required doctors to perform a lumbar laminectomy. (A laminectomy is the excision of a vertebral posterior arch.) During his employment, Stuck was continuously under medical care for the back problem. He filed what amounted to a repetitive trauma claim. He claimed his injury occurred on the job, but was unable to specify any particular event or series of events. The trial judge found that Stuck's injury occurred as the result of repetitive trauma caused by lifting and moving items at work. The court of appeal reversed the award, citing the *Festa* test, and held [*see* Lowe's of Bradenton v. Stuck, 561 So. 2d 322, 323–324 (Fla. 1st DCA 1990)]:

> Claimant's treating physician acknowledged that "everything" is a contributing factor to the claimant's condition. Contrary to the JCC's finding, neither the claimant nor his supervisor at Lowe's testified that the claimant's sales position entailed prolonged or repetitive lifting and moving of items. Absent evidence of a causal relationship between the claimant's employment and his disability, any award of benefits is unsupportable.

[5] Contribution Between Carriers in Repetitive Trauma Cases

Like occupational disease cases, repetitive trauma may take place over an extended time before symptoms or disabilities appear. This becomes a coverage problem if the employer has changed insurance carriers during this period. In an occupational disease case, the carrier on the risk when the employee was last injuriously exposed is exclusively liable. This is not true in repetitive trauma cases. In one case, the injured worker suffered from carpal tunnel syndrome. (Carpal tunnel syndrome is pain or numbness affecting some part of the median nerve of the hand.) The worker's symptoms and pain first appeared in 1988. By 1990, her condition became progressively worse as she continued to work. Meanwhile, her employer changed insurance carriers. Believing that the last exposure rule applied, the trial judge held that the last carrier was exclusively liable. The First District Court of Appeal reversed the benefit award. Occupational disease and repetitive trauma are separate and distinct. Apportioning disability benefits is proper in repetitive trauma cases when different insurance carriers are involved [*see* Aetna Life & Cas. Co. v. Schmitt, 597 So. 2d 938, 939–940 (Fla. 1st DCA 1992); Tokyo House, Inc. v. Hsin Chu, 597 So. 2d 348, 351–352 (Fla. 1st DCA 1992)].

For a general discussion of apportionment between insurers, see LARSON'S WORKERS' COMPENSATION, DESK EDITION, Ch. 153, § 153.03 (Matthew Bender).

[6] Exposure to Toxic Substances

Effective July 15, 2003, the Legislature amended § 440.02(1), Fla. Stat. to provide that an injury caused by exposure to toxic substances at work is *not* compensable unless a claimant can satisfy an elevated burden of proof. The law provides that an injury or disease caused by exposure to a toxic substance, including but not limited to, fungus and mold, is not an injury by accident arising out of the employment unless the claimant can produce clear and convincing evidence of the following:

1. First, the claimant must show that he or she was in fact exposed to the specific substance.
2. Second, the claimant must demonstrate the level of exposure.
3. Third, the claimant must show that the level of exposure to the specific substance can cause the injury or disease sustained.

This may prove to be a difficult burden to overcome. Note that the amendment creates a presumption, albeit rebuttable, that an injury caused by exposure to any toxic substance is not compensable. Rebuttal will probably require expert testimony from a person qualified to detect and identify the presence of a toxic substance and to measure the levels present. Next, the claimant will be required to present expert medical testimony that exposure to the measured levels of a specific substance can cause the claimant's injury or disease.

This amendment appears to have overruled the holding in *Wiley v. Southeast Erectors, Inc.* [573 So. 2d 946, 948 (Fla. 1st DCA 1991)]. In *Wiley*, the court held that "evidence of causation must be shown by something more than that it is merely logical that the injury arose out of the claimant's employment. . . . [C]ausal relationship must be shown by clear evidence rather than speculation or conjecture. . . . This is not to say that causal relationship requires absolute proof, to the exclusion of reasonable inferences."

The *Wiley* court held that a reasonable inference might be enough for compensability.

The Act now, however, appears to require absolute proof. Because the amendment alters rights and responsibilities, it is probably a substantive amendment that will apply to accidents occurring only on or after the amendment's effective date. The court has held that if an amendment substantially changes the carrier's liability from what it was when the injury occurred, the law cannot be applied retroactively [Southern Bakeries v. Cooper, 659 So. 2d 339, 341 (Fla. 1st DCA 1995)].

PRACTICE POINT: By declaring that an injury caused by exposure to a toxic substance is presumptively not an accidental injury arising out of the employment, the Legislature may have destroyed an employer's immunity against toxic tort suits.

SPECIAL ALERT: Note that the proof required to overcome the non-compensable presumption in § 440.02(1), Fla. Stat. is based on "clear and convincing evidence." In 2007, the Legislature adopted a reduced standard of proof for first responders, defined as firefighters, law enforcement officers, paramedics, or emergency medical technicians. First responders can overcome the presumption based only on a "preponderance of the evidence" [*see* § 112.1815(2)(a), Fla. Stat.].

"Clear and convincing" evidence is evidence of a quality and character designed to produce in the judge of compensation claims' mind a firm belief or conviction, without hesitation, as to the truth of the allegations. "Preponderance of the evidence" means evidence, which is of greater weight, or more convincing than the evidence, which is offered in opposition to it. It is that degree of proof that is more probable than not [*Black's Law Dictionary*, 6th Edition].

§ 6.08 Self-Inflicted Injury

[1] The Rule

No compensation is payable if workers' injuries result from a willful intention to injure themselves or another [§ 440.09(3), Fla. Stat.].

[2] Willful Intent to Injure Oneself

The statute prohibits compensating injuries resulting from a willful intention to injure oneself or another [§ 440.09(3), Fla. Stat.]. The legislature would have simplified things if it had stopped there. However, it also added § 440.26(3), Fla. Stat. This section created a legal presumption that an employee's injury did *not* occur during a willful attempt to injure himself or another. Thus, the burden of proving intent shifted to the carrier. This section meant the law did not require the employee to prove lack of intent. The law presumed lack of intent. The carrier had the burden to overcome this presumption with competent evidence. Effective July 1, 1990, the legislature repealed § 440.26(3), Fla. Stat. Therefore, for accidents occurring on or after that date, no presumptions exist either way.

For a general discussion on intentional self-injury, see LARSON'S WORKERS' COMPENSA-

TION, DESK EDITION, § 38.06 (Matthew Bender).

[3] Willful Intent Defined

[a] The Rule

An injury is intentionally and willfully sustained if the employee's actions are done with premeditation and deliberation, and the employee reasonably understood that the act would cause injury to himself or another [*see* 391st Bomb Group v. Robbins, 654 So. 2d 1200, 1202 (Fla. 1st DCA 1995)].

[b] History

The 1990 Act, by omission, raises an additional obstacle to successfully asserting this defense. The Act does not define "willful intention," but the common maxim is that people must intend the natural results of their actions. Finding no Florida precedent defining willful intention to injure, the First District Court of Appeal in *391st Bomb Group* [*see* [a], *above*] adopted the following holding from the Louisiana Court of Appeal [*see* Relish v. Hobbs, 188 So. 2d 479, 482 (La. Ct. App. 1966) (quoting *Velotta v. Liberty Mutual,* 241 La. 814, 132 So. 2d 51, 54 (1961))]:

> The test [of willful intent to injure] should involve an inquiry into (1) the existence of some premeditation and malice . . . coupled with (2) a reasonable expectation of bringing about a real injury to himself or another. This clearly means that willfulness, as distinguished from impulsiveness, is not the sole test. Every impulsive act is not condoned by the statute. Some acts, even though impulsive, are so serious and so likely to result in real injury, that they must be construed to show a willful intent to injure.

[c] Present State of the Law

Following are the facts as presented to the Florida Court of Appeal. Steven Robbins' supervisor called him into the office and fired him because of unsatisfactory work. Robbins "yelled some profanities, ripped open the office door, punched a wall, and headed for the rear exit door." As he exited, Robbins pushed hard with an open hand on the door's security window. The window was 18 inches square and constructed of wire mesh, encased by layers of glass, thus "pushing hard" is likely an understatement. By whatever description, Robbins pushed hard enough to shatter the glass, seriously injuring himself in the process. The judge of compensation claims held the claim compensable, ruling that Robbins had no willful intention to injure himself. In other words, the judge held that Robbins did not willfully intend the result of his dangerous and deliberate act. Based on the Louisiana court's holding in *Velotta* [*see* [b], *above*], the First District Court of Appeal disagreed and reversed.

An employee's deliberate acts of aggression are tantamount to a willful intent to injure apart from instinct or impulse. The term "willful intention," said the court, is an act that is premeditated and deliberate. Little difference exists between the aggressor injured in a fight case, and an employee injured by willfully striking an inanimate object in anger, especially an object that obviously presents a danger of injury. Even if an employee's acts are impulsive, benefits are not allowed under § 440.09, Fla. Stat. [*see* 391st Bomb Group

v. Robbins, 654 So. 2d 1200, 1202 (Fla. 1st DCA 1995)].

[4] Fight Cases—The Aggressor Doctrine

[a] The Rule

Injuries resulting from fights at work may be compensable if sufficient connection to the employment exists. Despite work connection, the law does not allow the aggressor in the fight to receive benefits. This is based on the statutory prohibition against compensating someone injured while trying to injure another [§ 440.09(3), Fla. Stat.].

[b] Work Connection

[i] In General

The more elements connecting the fight to the job, the less likely a viable defense can be supported. The aggressor in a fight is the one who first made an assault upon the other with the intention to injure or kill the other. Direct an investigation into fight cases at two issues: what started the fight [*see* [ii], *below*], and who started the fight [*see* [iii], *below*].

[ii] What Started the Fight

When employees begin fighting with each other, and the fight has nothing to do with the job, none of the combatants are entitled to compensation. Just because the fight occurs on the employer's premises during working hours does not automatically mean it arose out of the employment. Investigate the on-duty and off-duty relationship of the combatants carefully. Be careful! The courts have greatly expanded the definition of work connection. Following are examples:

Case 1. Lovers triangle. Two female workers were both involved romantically with a male co-worker. Neither woman, however, was aware of the other's involvement. When they discovered that they were both dating the same man, their outrage climaxed in a brawl. Obviously, this is not work-related, right? Wrong. The fight was work-related because:

1. The two women had no personal relationship outside their work together.
2. All three had initially met through their employment.

The court held: "By facilitating an assault which would not otherwise have been made, the employment became a contributing factor" [*see* Tampa Maid Seafood Products v. Porter, 415 So. 2d 883, 884–885 (Fla. 1st DCA 1982)].

Case 2. Lovers quarrel. Andrew Carnegie and a female co-worker had been dating, but broke off the relationship. About a month after the breakup, Andrew confronted his former sweetheart. Their discussion turned to argument, which erupted into a physical fight. Andrew's lady friend grabbed a knife off a workbench and went after Andrew. The lady friend's sister also worked there, and she joined the melee. Soon a supervisor became involved trying to stop the fight. Somewhere in this brawl, someone stabbed the lady friend. The judge of compensation claims refused to award benefits. He held the fight was purely personal and did not arise out of the employment. Good decision, right? Wrong. The appellate court found that:

Guide to Claims

1. The employment placed the workers in close proximity.
2. The personal relationship began at work.
3. The knife used was an "implement of the employment."

Because the work environment directly influenced the fight, the employment was a factor that facilitated the assault [*see* Carnegie v. Pan American Linen, 476 So. 2d 311, 312 (Fla. 1st DCA 1985)].

Imagining anything more personal than a lover's quarrel is difficult, so is everything work related? Following are two cases involving fights over money.

Case 3. Personal debt. Mr. Langford and a co-worker had an ongoing argument about a debt that Langford owed to the other. The next day the co-worker came to the job site and shot Langford. The First District Court of Appeal held that the claim was not compensable because the assault was purely private and personal. Thus, the employment contributed nothing to the episode [*see* San Marco Company, Inc. v. Langford, 391 So. 2d 326, 327 (Fla. 1st DCA 1980), *app. dismissed,* 399 So. 2d 1143 (Fla. 1981)].

Case 4. Car-pool expenses. Their jobs required the injured employee and his co-worker to work out of town, but the employer did not pay the travel expenses. The two workers agreed to form a car-pool to cut costs. Later, while driving home on a Friday, they got into an argument about who owed what. On the following Monday, the co-worker came to the job site and assaulted the claimant. This sounds like a debt that at least had its origins in the employment. The court, however, found an insufficient relationship to the employment and denied the claim [*see* Ivey H. Smith Co. v. Wingo, 404 So. 2d 1118, 1119 (Fla. 1st DCA 1981)].

Obviously, these cases do not provide clear guidance. The best advice is this: The more elements there are to connect the fight to the job, the more likely the case is compensable.

[iii] Who Started the Fight: The Aggressor

Work related or not, the law does not allow the aggressor in the fight to collect compensation. The problem lies in deciding who was the aggressor. Unfortunately, the Act does not define the term "aggressor"; however, the Florida Supreme Court has done so. The aggressor is the one who first made an assault upon the other with the intention to injure or kill the other. Although this decision is decades old, it still holds today [*see* Florida Forest and Park Service v. Strickland, 154 Fla. 472, 18 So. 2d 251, 254 (1944)].

Consider this case: The employee's supervisor was sitting in a pickup truck and the employee was standing outside the truck when they began to argue. The employee grabbed the supervisor's arm, who then got out of the truck and punched the employee. Who was the aggressor? We could consider the employee's action to be an initial act of aggression, but the law does not base aggressor status on a technical battery, such as merely holding the arm of another person through the window of a truck. Thus, the aggressor is not the person who starts the argument, but is the one who first acts with the intent to injure the other [*see* American International Land Corp. v. May, I.R.C. Order 2-3404].

An exception may arise when the employee is intoxicated. For example, the employee became intoxicated at the company Christmas party. A co-worker suggested he was too drunk to drive and offered to take him home. The employee became angry and repeatedly shoved the co-worker. This provoked the co-worker, who punched the employee in the face with a closed fist. Although the employee probably did not intend to cause injury, and the co-worker was probably the legal aggressor, the injury was not compensable because the employee's intoxication was the primary cause of his injury. Absent evidence that something caused the fight other than the injured worker's intoxication, or that a completely sober person would have suffered the same injury, the injury is not compensable. This is true even if the injured worker is not the aggressor. These cases require a thorough investigation with particular emphasis placed on eyewitnesses [*see* Sterling v. Mike Brown, Inc., 580 So. 2d 832, 835–836 (Fla. 1st DCA 1991)].

Guide to Claims

[5] Suicide Cases

[a] The Rule

No compensation is payable if an employee willfully commits suicide. The defense must show, however, that the employee was capable of forming a willful intention to take his or her own life. An intention is not willful if the compensable injury caused a mental disturbance that leads to suicide [§ 440.09(3), Fla. Stat.].

For a general discussion of employee suicide, see LARSON'S WORKERS' COMPENSATION, DESK EDITION, Ch. 38 (Matthew Bender).

[b] Overview of Suicide Cases

The difficulty in a suicide case is in deciding if the act of suicide was willful. For a suicidal act to be willful, the evidence must show that the employee could form a willful intention. If the actual or attempted act of suicide resulted from an uncontrolled impulse, or was done in a delirium of frenzy, we cannot clearly say that the employee could form the required willful intent.

In one case, constant excruciating pain tormented the injured worker. He eventually developed paralysis of the arm. The combination of the injuries and the pain began to weigh heavily upon him emotionally. Three months later, he killed himself by swallowing a mixture of potash and lye. After several reversals through the judicial system, the Florida Supreme Court held the case compensable. The Court held the employee did not willfully kill himself because he was not able to know what he was doing [*see* Whitehead v. Keene Roofing Co., 43 So. 2d 464, 465–466 (Fla. 1949)].

In Whitehead's case, the compensable injury appears to have been the direct cause of his suicide. That, however, is not a requirement. If the injury is merely the triggering event, that is enough. For example, Kimbell Scott suffered a minor back strain at work. A few days later, he was involuntarily admitted to a psychiatric facility under the Baker Act because of his violent behavior at home. Two months later he killed himself. All doctors agreed that the back injury was not the direct cause of his suicide, but two of them agreed it was the triggering event. Other doctors testified the injury and suicide were unrelated. The hearing judge believed the first doctors and awarded death benefits. The First District Court of Appeal agreed and affirmed the order [*see* City of Tampa v. Scott, 397 So. 2d 1220, 1221–1222 (Fla. 1st DCA 1981)].

The standard does not require evidence that the employee be completely without normal judgement such that he or she does not understand the fatal nature of self-inflicted acts. It is enough for compensability if a physical injury leads to depression, for example, and the depression leads to suicide [*see* Estate of Jenkins v. Recchi America, 658 So. 2d 157, 162 (Fla. 1st DCA 1995), *review denied,* 663 So. 2d 628 (Fla. 1995)].

[c] Suicide—Compensability Guidelines

Guidelines for recovery when an employee commits suicide as a direct result of an injury sustained in the employment are as follows:

1. Suicide is compensable if the injury suffered by the deceased results in the inability to use normal judgment, and is dominated by a mental disturbance directly caused by the injury and its results. Under these facts, suicide cannot be considered willful within the meaning and intent of the Workers' Compensation Act [*see* Whitehead v. Keene Roofing Co., 43 So. 2d 464, 465–466 (Fla. 1949)].

2. Suicide is compensable if it was merely an act intervening between the injury and death. Thus, the suicide must be part of an unbroken chain of events from the injury to the death. It cannot be an independent cause, intervening between the injury and death. Furthermore, it is not necessary that the compensable injury be the direct cause. If the injury was merely the triggering event, that is enough [*see* City of Tampa v. Scott, 397 So. 2d 1220, 1221–1222 (Fla. 1st DCA 1981)].

3. Suicide is compensable even if the deceased could willfully decide to commit suicide. The compensability standard is only that a physical injury causes a mental disturbance and the mental disturbance leads to suicide [*see* Estate of Jenkins v. Recchi America, 658 So. 2d 157, 162 (Fla. 1st DCA 1995), *rev. denied,* 663 So. 2d 628 (Fla. 1995)].

Defending a suicide claim is difficult if it follows a compensable injury and any medical evidence exists linking the two. Note, however, that absent a precipitating compensable injury, suicide is not compensable.

SPECIAL ALERT: An allegation that the employee's injury is self-inflicted is an affirmative defense. As such, it is forever waived if not presented with clarity in the Notice of Denial or during the proceedings with the judge of compensation claims [*see* Bay Automotive v. Allaire, 593 So. 2d 589, 591 (Fla. 1st DCA 1992)].

[6] Intentional Exposure to Risk

[a] The Rule

No compensation is due if employees voluntarily expose themselves to a risk that is certain to result in injury [§ 440.09(3), Fla. Stat.; *see* Earnest Waters Const. Co. v. Mills, 51 So. 2d 180, 181–182 (Fla. 1951)].

For a general discussion of employee misconduct, see Larson's Workers' Compensation, Desk Edition, Chs. 32, 33, 34 (Matthew Bender).

[b] Intent Defined

This category is similar to, but different, from self-inflicted injury. Obviously, intentionally exposing oneself to risk may be negligent or even stupid, but negligence and stupidity do not prevent compensability in Florida. This category deals with risks the employee understands to be so dangerous that they are virtually certain to result in injury.

For example, the injured worker filed a claim for compensation due to a dermatitis induced by exposure to damp weeds and stagnant water. He had two prior attacks of dermatitis with two different employers. Each time, physicians told him not to subject himself to such exposure. In spite of these admonitions the employee continued working in the damp environment. The Supreme Court held benefits were not due, pointing out primarily that the attacks [*see* Earnest Waters Const. Co. v. Mills, 51 So. 2d 180, 181–182 (Fla. 1951)]:

> . . . could have been avoided if he had followed doctors advice . . . He was bound to know the probable effect of his disobedience. Subsequent infections were such voluntary acts as to break the line of causation between his original and his subsequent attacks. Workers' Compensation is not contemplated for injuries voluntarily inflicted.

All the cases to date—and there are very few—revolve around the employee's failure to follow a physician's instructions. No cases denying compensation for failure to follow safety instructions from the employer exist. In keeping with the Supreme Court's decision, however, the following rule may apply: if the injured worker understood that failure to follow safety rules would result in injury, the carrier could deny compensation on the theory that the employee sustained a voluntary injury. Showing the certainty of the employee's knowledge, however, may be difficult.

[7] Violation of Safety Rules

[a] The Rule

Carriers may reduce compensation benefits by 25 percent if the employee refused to use a safety appliance or follow a safety rule. Specific application of this provision depends on the date of the accident [§ 440.09(5), Fla. Stat.].

For a general discussion of employee violation of safety rules, see LARSON'S WORKERS' COMPENSATION, DESK EDITION, Ch. 35 (Matthew Bender).

[b] The Statute's History

Since it was first enacted in 1935, the Florida Workers' Compensation Act has contained penalties when employees suffer injuries as the result of failing to follow safety rules. Although the legislature has amended the original version several times, the section has undergone very little judicial review in its entire history. We will begin with a review of the statutory amendments. We will then review the holdings of the appellate courts and the Florida Supreme Court. In its original 1935 form, the safety violation section provided a complete defense and barred all compensation [§ 440.09(4), Fla. Stat.]:

> No compensation shall be payable if the injury was occasioned primarily by the

> refusal of the employee to use a safety appliance or perform a duty required by statute and/or by any rule or regulation of the employer approved by the Industrial Commission and brought prior to the accident to the knowledge of the employee.

In 1937, the legislature enacted an amendment that seemed minor, but it greatly affected the statute's application. The legislature now required that the refusal be willful. It also repealed the "perform a duty required by statute" language and replaced it with the words "observe a safety rule required by statute."

In 1953, the legislature amended the section again to reduce the penalty from a loss of all compensation to a 25-percent reduction in compensation benefits. This version of § 440.09(4), Fla. Stat. provided as follows:

> Where injury is caused by the willful refusal of the employee to use a safety appliance or observe a safety rule required by statute or lawfully promulgated by the division, and brought prior to the accident to his or her knowledge, the compensation as provided in this chapter shall be reduced 25 percent.

[c] The 1989 Amendment

The 1989 legislature amended the section yet again [§ 440.09(4), Fla. Stat.]:

> Where injury is caused by the willful refusal of the employee to use a safety appliance or observe a safety rule required by statute or lawfully promulgated by the division, and brought prior to the accident to his or her knowledge, *or where injury is caused by the willful refusal of the employee to use a safety appliance provided by the employer,* the compensation as provided in this chapter shall be reduced 25 percent. (Emphasis added)

The italicized sentence is the new language. Apparently, the legislature was concerned that the courts would construe the phrase "required by statute or lawfully promulgated by the division" to exclude safety appliances not required by law. This amendment makes it clear that the provision applies to equipment provided by the employer whether or not required by statute and rule.

[d] The 1990 Amendment

In the discussion that follows, the term "willful" was the undoing of the apparent legislative intent. The 1990 legislature amended the section again by substituting the term "willful" with the term "knowing." The present section now reads as follows [§ 440.09(5), Fla. Stat.]:

> If injury is caused by the *knowing* refusal of the employee to use a safety appliance or observe a safety rule required by statute or lawfully adopted by the division, and brought prior to the accident to the employee's knowledge, or if injury is caused by the *knowing* refusal of the employee to use a safety appliance provided by the employer, the compensation as provided in this chapter shall be reduced 25 percent. (Emphasis added)

[e] Invoking the Statute

[i] Willful Refusal

The term "willful," as construed by the courts, made applying this section extremely difficult. The Florida Supreme Court has held that the mere violation of a statute, ordinance, or regulation is not willful misconduct as a matter of law. Mere negligence and even gross negligence, said the Court, fall short of willful misconduct. The Court defined the term as follows: "Willful misconduct involves conduct of a quasi criminal nature, the intentional doing of something either with the knowledge that it is likely to result in serious injury, or with a wanton and reckless disregard of its probable consequences" [*see* Gregory v. McKesson & Robbins, Inc., 54 So. 2d 682, 686 (Fla. 1951)].

Although this holding is now decades old, the courts still observe it today. It is not enough, therefore, that the employee knew about requirements to observe a safety rule and decided not to obey. The carrier must show that the employee also knew refusal would likely lead to injury.

[ii] Safety Rules and Statutes

[A] Employers Safety Rules

Violation of employer-imposed safety rules does not invoke the penalty provision. To apply, a safety rule must be one required by statute or administrative rule. The safety rules referred to in the statute include only those rules adopted by the Division of Workers' Compensation. (Since this decision, all safety rules are now the responsibility of the Division of Safety.) Rules adopted by other government agencies such as the Florida Department of Transportation, may not be used to invoke this provision [*see* Department of Transportation v. Charles, 481 So. 2d 69 (Fla. 1st DCA 1985)].

[B] OSHA Safety Rules

Would violation of an OSHA rule be enough to authorize a reduction? The answer is yes. In 1982, the First District Court of Appeal held that the term "statute" refers both to state and federal statutes. The court said: "[W]e see no reason why the legislature should not have intended for the word 'statute' in section 440.09(4) to include the OSHA provisions of 29 U.S.C. s. 651 et seq., which are the paramount worker safety statutes geared toward the elimination of significant harm to the worker" [*see* McKenzie Tank Lines, Inc. v. McCauley, 418 So. 2d 1177, 1180 (Fla. 1st DCA 1982)].

[C] Automobile Traffic Laws as Safety Rules

The next question is, do state traffic laws amount to safety rules? When such statutes are intended to protect the public from harm, they become a safety rule required by statute. The Supreme Court held that general statutes governing excessive speed and reckless driving on public highways are safety rules within contemplation of the provisions of § 440.09(5), Fla. Stat. [*see* Gregory v. McKesson & Robbins, Inc., 54 So. 2d 682, 685 (Fla. 1951)]. The Court reaffirmed this holding in *White v. C.H. Lyne Foundry & Machine Co.* [74 So. 2d 538, 540 (Fla. 1954)].

Remember, however, that the mere violation of such laws does not automatically amount to willful misconduct. How many of us drive over the posted speed limit, "with the knowledge that it is likely to result in serious injury?" In *Gregory,* the Court affirmed the reduction in benefits where the employee was driving 80 miles per hour because he was in a hurry to get home. But the Court reached a different conclusion in *White*. Yes, the employee was speeding and driving carelessly. That alone, said the Court, would not imply a willful purpose to injure himself or others. The Court reversed an order reducing benefits.

In another case, the Industrial Relations Commission ordered a reduction in benefits based on evidence of reckless driving. The employee was driving between 60 and 70 miles per hour in a 45-mile per hour zone when he crossed the center line and struck an oncoming vehicle head-on. The Florida Supreme Court reversed. The Court repeated its earlier holdings that simply violating a statute or rule is not enough. There must be evidence of "an intentional commission of an act violative of a statute with knowledge that such act is likely to result in serious injury, or the illegal act must be done with a wanton disregard of probable consequences" [*see* Smith v. Geyer Detective Agency, Inc., 130 So. 2d 882, 884 (Fla. 1961)].

This is an extremely difficult burden to overcome. In *Smit,* the Court reversed because no evidence showed that the employee wilfully drove on the wrong side of the road. He may have swerved, said the Court, to avoid a collision with the vehicle ahead. It seems that only the most outrageous acts committed on the highway will provide sufficient willfulness to invoke the provisions of § 440.09(5), Fla. Stat.

[D] Seat Belt Law as a Safety Rule

Florida law requires drivers and front seat passengers of autos and light trucks to wear seat belts. After the legislature enacted the seat belt law, there have been many court decisions allowing the reduction of awards in liability cases. The courts allowed these reductions merely because of the plaintiff's failure to use a seat belt. The workers' compensation appellate courts have yet to address failure to use seat belts as a basis to reduce compensation benefits.

Under the Supreme Court decision discussed above, benefit reduction would not apply unless the carrier can show the employee refused to wear the seat belt with the knowledge such failure would likely result in serious injury. The civil courts, however, have not viewed the issue so narrowly.

The seat belt law, unlike the traffic laws, is a personal safety rule. It is a statute requiring drivers to use safety equipment designed to prevent or reduce injury in a collision. As with all safety equipment, the reduction will not apply if the seat belt was not functional. The question is, who has the burden of proving function?

In an automobile liability case, the court held that to raise a seatbelt defense, it is not enough to prove that seatbelts were available. In addition, the defense must prove that the seat belts were fully operational, but not in use [*see* Smith v. Holy Temple Church of God in Christ, Inc., 566 So. 2d 864, 865 (Fla. 1st DCA 1990), *disapproved by* Bulldog Leasing Co., Inc. v. Curtis, 630 So. 2d 1060, 1065 (Fla. 1994)].

The *Smith* court took note of several recent cases. These cases placed significance upon evidence that the seat belt snapped closed or "clicked" because that evidence is at least some evidence of operability. Other cases have dwelled on evidence that the belts were properly anchored to the vehicle.

The Florida Supreme Court, however, has held that the appellate courts have too narrowly construed its earlier decisions. To raise the seat belt defense, the defendants need only show that the vehicle "contained seat belts that could have been used." Such evidence is a prima facie showing that the seat belts were operational. It then falls to the plaintiff to show that the seat belts were, in fact, not functional [*see* Bulldog Leasing Co., Inc. v. Curtis, 630 So. 2d 1060, 1064–1065 (Fla. 1994), *cert. denied,* 513 U.S. 847, 115 S. Ct. 141, 130 L. Ed. 2d 82 (1994)].

It is not necessary that employers specifically require their employees to use seatbelts. This is because the law requires such use. In *Gregory,* the Supreme Court held that the phrase "and brought prior to the accident to the knowledge of the employee" is of no significance when the statute is not only a general law, but penal in character. Everyone, said the Court, is presumed to know the law [Gregory v. McKesson & Robbins, Inc., 54 So. 2d 682, 684 (Fla. 1951)].

[E] Failure to Use Safety Equipment

Failure to use required safety equipment is a basis for a reduction in benefits if the evidence shows a causal relationship between the failure to use the device and the resulting injury. Such failure, at least before July 1, 1990, must have been willful. This requires showing that the employee refused to use the device or follow the rule knowing such failure was likely to result in injury.

The defense must also show that the device was in proper working order and readily available to the employee. The judge of compensation claims, however, can forgive the failure if the employee has some plausible excuse to explain violating the rule. Even if the employer orders an employee to use a safety device, the reduction will not apply if the employer does not enforce the order or rule, thereby allowing workers to disregard proper safety procedures.

"In addition to mere knowledge, the concept of wilfulness connotes also that the employee understands the rule and realizes that the device involved is in fact a safety device to guard against a danger which has been explained in advance" [*see* LARSON'S WORKERS' COMPENSATION, DESK EDITION, Ch. 33, § 33.20 (Matthew Bender)]. Furthermore, any direction to observe a safety rule must clearly be an order and not merely a cautionary instruction or advice.

It is important that the employer has a record of enforcing its safety rules. The judges of compensation claims will not support a safety rule violation reduction in the light of evidence that the employer ignored its own rules.

[F] Accidents Occurring On or After July 1, 1990

A large part of the problem in safety rule violation cases has been the use of the term "willful" and its ultra conservative judicial definition. The legislature recognized this and effective July 1, 1990, changed the term "willful" to "knowing." The courts have not yet dealt with this new word, but will they construe the term "knowing" to have substantially different meaning than the term "willful"? Not likely. Knowing means to have knowledge or information. The law is well settled that the reduction does not apply unless the employee willfully violated the rule, knowing such violation would likely result in injury. More likely, all that the legislature has done is to codify case law. If the legislature intends for the reduction to apply by the mere violation of a statute, ordinance, or regulation, it should amend this section again and plainly say so.

SPECIAL ALERT: To justify withholding 25 percent of an employee's benefits, carriers must be prepared to prove that there is a causal relationship between failing to use the safety device and the injuries sustained [*see* Escambia Bd. of County Com'rs v. Reeder, 648 So. 2d 222, 225–226 (Fla. 1st DCA 1994)].

CHAPTER 7

CONFIRMING COMPENSABILITY: THE ARISING OUT OF AND IN THE COURSE OF EMPLOYMENT REQUIREMENTS

Guide to Claims

SYNOPSIS

Guide to Claims

Guide to Claims

§ 7.01 Course and Scope of Employment

[1] The Rule

For an injury to arise out of and to occur in the course of one's employment the following elements must be shown:

1. Some causal connection between the injury and the employment must exist;
2. The injury must have its origin in some risk incidental to or connected with the employment;
3. The injury must flow from the employment as a natural result;
4. The injury must occur within the period of employment and occur while employees are where they are supposed to be; and
5. For accidents occurring on or after January 1, 1994, the work done must be the major contributing cause of the injury.

Thus, the injury must occur while employees are doing their jobs, or at least doing something incidental to their jobs [*see* Hill v. Gregg, Gibson & Gregg, Inc., 260 So. 2d 193, 195 (Fla. 1972)].

[2] Course of Employment

The term "in the course of" refers to the time, place, and circumstances under which a work-related accident occurred. Usually, employees can collect benefits if they suffer injuries while doing what they are supposed to be doing, and at the time and place they are supposed to be doing it.

For a detailed discussion on the meaning of the time and place of "course of employment," see LARSON'S WORKERS' COMPENSATION, DESK EDITION, Ch. 12 (Matthew Bender).

For a thorough discussion of the types of activity falling under "course of employment," see LARSON'S WORKERS' COMPENSATION, DESK EDITION, Part 4, *Course of Employment: Activity* (Matthew Bender).

[3] Arising Out of Employment

The term "arising out of" refers to the source of the cause of the accidental injury. Before January 1, 1994, "arising out of" meant only that the employment must, in some way, contribute an increased risk of injury peculiar to that employment. Then, the law required only a mere causal connection between the workplace accident and the subsequent injury. In other words the injured worker had to prove that the employment was only *a* cause rather than *the* cause of the injury. For accidents occurring on or after January 1, 1994, this is no longer true. After that date, the "major contributing cause" requirement applies [*see* [4], *below*].

For a detailed discussion of "arising out of employment," see LARSON'S WORKERS'

COMPENSATION, DESK EDITION, Part 2, *Arising Out of the Employment* (Matthew Bender).

SPECIAL ALERT: Any adverse result or complication caused by a smallpox vaccination suffered by a first responder is deemed to be an injury arising out of and in the course of employment. First responders include firefighters, law enforcement officers, paramedics, and emergency medical technicians [*see* § 112.1815(2)(a)2, Fla. Stat.]. Although the statute is silent on the subject, presumably the administration of a smallpox vaccination must have been required by or provided by the employer as a required incident of the employment. Also, presumably this presumption of compensability is rebuttable.

Guide to Claims

[4] The Major Contributing Cause Requirement

[a] Overview of Statute

The Workers' Compensation Act, effective January 1, 1994, defines the phrase "arising out of" to mean occupational causation. This is nothing new and is a codification of case law. What is new is that the law now provides that an accidental injury or death arises out of the employment only if the work done in the course and scope of employment is *the major contributing cause* of the injury or death. The statute now provides as follows [§ 440.02(32), Fla. Stat. (1/1/94)]:

> "Arising out of" pertains to occupational causation. An accidental injury or death arises out of employment if work performed in the course and scope of employment is *the major contributing cause* of the injury or death (Emphasis added)

Therefore, a worker injured on or after January 1, 1994, must prove that the work was the major contributing cause of the injury and the need for treatment. In deciding the merits of a claim, the judge of compensation claims must apply this standard and make a specific finding about the major contributing cause of the injury [*see* Clay County School Board v. Robison, 725 So. 2d 425, 426–427 (Fla. 1st DCA 1999)].

[b] The Statute's Effect

[i] General Application

Before this amendment, courts have held injuries compensable even if the employee was not doing assigned tasks when the accident occurred. This is still true because the amendment does not change the definition of the phrase "in the course of employment." Some people have argued that the amendment requires that employees must be literally doing assigned work to be in the course of their employment. Although the statute does include the "major contributing cause" language, it specifies that "work performed in the course and scope of employment" must be the major contributing cause of the accident or injury. Thus, under the statutory definition, an accident or injury arises out of an injured worker's employment if two elements exist:

Element 1. The injured worker was doing work in the course and scope of employment;

Element 2. The work done in the course and scope of employment was *the* major contributing cause of the worker's accident and injury.

Note the significance of the legislature's use of the definite article "the" and not "a" before the term "major contributing cause" [*see* § 440.09(1)(b), Fla. Stat. and § 440.02(35), Fla. Stat.]. This shows that the legislature recognizes that there may be many contributing causes leading to an injury or disability, but that the injured worker must show that the employment occurrence is the preponderant cause of the injury [*see* Orange County MIS Department v. Hak, 710 So. 2d 998, 999 (Fla. 1st DCA 1998)].

[ii] Court's Definition of "Major Contributing Cause"

Unfortunately, the Legislature failed to provide a definition, leaving it to the court to do so. In February 2000, the entire 1st DCA, sitting en banc, drafted a definition of the phrase "major contributing cause." The court concluded that the major-contributing-cause standard has been satisfied, and coverage applies, if the workplace accident contributes more to the disability, or to the need for treatment, than any other single cause. This does not mean, however, that the workplace accident must be a greater cause than all other causes combined. It means that the workplace accident must be greater in significance than any other single cause.

Under the court's definition, if there are two causes, the workplace accident and a single, non-industrial condition, the injury is compensable if the workplace accident contributed at least 51 percent to the disability or to the need for treatment. Assume, however, that there are many causes, as noted by Judge Benton in his dissenting opinion. If, as in his example, there are eight non-industrial causes each contributing eleven percent and the workplace accident contributes twelve percent, the injury is compensable because the work place accident will be the greater in significance than any other single cause [*see* Closet Maid v. Sykes, 763 So. 2d 377 (Fla. 1st DCA 2000)].

For accidents occurring between January 1, 1994, and September 30, 2003, the concept of "major contributing cause," as defined by the court, is therefore the standard to be used in deciding compensability. The court has rejected other concepts, such as "necessary condition." Under this theory, an injury is compensable if the initial incident at work was a necessary condition for subsequent manifestations to occur. For example, Alvenia Scott bumped and bruised her leg at work. She did not suffer any adverse effects until several weeks later when she began to experience a series of medical complications at the site of the bruise. These complications were caused by several preexisting conditions, including a prior dog bite with resulting scar tissue at the site of the bruise, diabetes, and a history of smoking. The judge of compensation claims awarded benefits based on a physician's testimony that the bruising incident was a "necessary condition" for the problems to develop. Put another way, Scott's health problems would not have developed but for the incident at work. The court reversed, holding that the concept of "necessary condition" is not the equivalent of "major contributing cause" and remanded the case for reconsideration using the court's construction of the statute as explained in *Closet Maid* [*see* City of Tallahassee v. Scott, 751 So. 2d 1287, 1288 (Fla. 1st DCA 2000)].

[iii] Statutory Definition of "Major Contributing Cause"

Effective October 1, 2003, the Legislature adopted a definition of "Major Contributing Cause" that is apparently intended to overrule the court's decision in *Closet Maid.* The

Legislature did not alter the "arising out of" language of § 440.02(32), Fla. Stat., which was the basis for the *Closet Maid* decision. Instead, the Legislature amended § 440.09, Fla. Stat.

The revision provides that an employer *must* pay compensation for an accidental *compensable* injury. (The italicized words are new language). The revision goes on to provide that the accidental compensable injury must be the major contributing cause of "any resulting injuries." The phrase "major contributing cause" now means the cause that is more than 50 percent responsible for the injury as compared *to all other causes combined.* The statute provides that major contributing cause may be established by only medical evidence.

Additionally, in cases involving occupational disease or repetitive exposure, the claimant must prove both causation and sufficient exposure to support causation by clear and convincing evidence. (Note: Clear and convincing evidence is evidence of a quality and character designed to produce in the judge's mind a firm belief or conviction, without hesitation, as to the truth of the allegations.)

[c] Applying the Statute

If both elements described in [b], *above,* are present, then the accident or injury arose out of the injured worker's employment. By including the phrase "in the course and scope of employment" within the definition of "arising out of" the legislature did not intend to change case law. Instead, the legislature has simply combined the two phrases, one as part of the definition of the other. With the enactment of this definition, however, an injured worker must now show that the employment was the major contributing cause of the accident and injury.

The amendment changes only the term "arising out of." Thus, doctrines and rules such as the personal comfort doctrine and the bunkhouse rule are unaffected. These doctrines hold that injuries can be compensable though not suffered during literal work. The amendment's effect is that even if the accident occurred during the course of employment, the resulting injury may not be compensable because the accident, though suffered in the course and scope of employment, was not the major contributing cause of the injury. The new requirement is that the accident is *the* major contributing cause of the injury [*see* Vigliotti v. K-Mart Corp., 680 So. 2d 466, 468 (Fla. 1st DCA 1996)].

The statutory phrase "arising out of" requires two proof elements: (1) The claimant must have been performing work in the course and scope of employment at the time of the accident or injury; and (2) There must be proof that the employment constituted more than a contributing, competent, precipitating, or accelerating cause of the accident or injury [*see* Claims Mgmt. Inc. v. Drewno, 727 So. 2d 395, 398 (Fla. 1st DCA 1999)].

Note, however, that this legal standard can be established without pronouncement of the magic words, provided that the totality of the evidence demonstrates a causal relationship between the claimant's injury and employment with the appropriate quantum of proof. Thus, expert medical testimony that an injured worker's employment is more likely than not the cause of the injury is the equivalent of the phrase "major contributing cause" [*see* Hunt v. Exxon Co. USA, 747 So. 2d 966, 973 (Fla. 1st DCA 1999), *reh'g denied,* January 5, 2000].

Guide to Claims

This means that not all injuries occurring on the employer's premises are compensable. On the contrary, the Florida Supreme Court expressly rejected any argument that all injuries to employees that occur on an employer's premises are compensable. The evidence must show that the injury resulted from an effort, exertion, risk, or strain beyond that which employees normally encounter in their non-employment life. An injury does not arise out of the employment unless the employment created an increased hazard of the injury [*see* Leon County School Bd. v. Grimes, 548 So. 2d 205, 207–208 (Fla. 1989)].

[d] Evidence and Basis for Judgment

[i] Evidence Based on Reasonable Medical Certainty

The method of proving causation has not changed. The Act [*see* § 440.09(1), Fla. Stat.] requires that "[t]he injury, its occupational cause, and any resulting manifestations or disability shall be established to a reasonable degree of medical certainty and by objective medical findings."

Note that the statute requires medical *certainty.* Before this language entered the law in 1994, the statute required a finding based on medical *probability.* Although most English language students would agree that there is a huge difference between the terms "probability" and "certainty," the court has concluded that these terms are not different, that they mean the same thing, and that they can be used interchangeably. The court adopted the interpretation in *Black's Law Dictionary* 1273 (7th ed. 1998), which indicates that the phrases "reasonable medical probability" and "reasonable medical certainty" are merely different ways of expressing the same concept. Therefore, the court concluded that the legislature's use of the phrase "reasonable medical certainty" does not reflect any change from the established standard of proof [*see* Closet Maid v. Sykes, 763 So. 2d. 377 (Fla. 1st DCA 2000)].

[ii] Expert and Lay Testimony

The law does not always require medical evidence to show that a workplace accident is the major contributing cause of a disability or of the need for treatment. Sometimes, the connection between an accident at work and an injury is so clear that no medical proof is required and lay testimony will suffice. For example, there is no need to present medical evidence of causation if an employee's arm is severed by a machine at work or if an employee's organic brain damage was caused by being struck in the head by a falling timber. Medical evidence is essential, however, when causation cannot be observed by a lay witness. For example, medical evidence will be required to show that a psychiatric condition or hypertension was caused by a workplace accident.

Whether medical evidence is required, as opposed to lay testimony, depends on the particular circumstances of each case, Thus, a judge's decision can be supported by both medical and lay testimony [*see* Closet Maid v. Sykes, 763 So. 2d. 377 (Fla. 1st DCA 2000)].

[iii] Basis for Judgment

As noted, compensability often depends on a determination that the workplace accident was the major contributing cause of the disability or the need for treatment within a reasonable degree of medical probability or certainty. A judge's determination, however, must be based on the totality and substance of the evidence rather than on the use of the "reasonable medical certainty" phrase or other so-called "magic words" by a medical witness. To do otherwise is to turn the resolution of factual issues into a game of semantics. As Judge Benton noted in his dissenting opinion, however, this holding allows the judge of compensation claims to reject uncontroverted medical testimony that the workplace accident was *not* the major contributing cause of the workplace accident based on lay testimony that the employee had not experienced medical symptoms before the accident and that he had an exemplary work history.

Because the resolution of major contributing cause is a fact-based issue, it is subject to review by the appellate court. Note, however, that a finding of major contributing cause will usually be affirmed on appeal if the record contains sufficient, competent substantial evidence that the workplace accident contributed more to the claimant's disability or need for treatment than any other single cause [*see* Closet Maid v. Sykes, 763 So. 2d. 377 (Fla. 1st DCA 2000)].

[5] The Major Contributing Cause Requirement: Idiopathic Accident Cases

The major contributing cause standard is a critical one in aggravation cases where the injured worker's preexisting defects are the major cause of injury rather than the aggravating, work-related accident. Since falls are a common occurrence, it is important to examine the major contributing cause standard and how it applies in such accidents. If an employee falls and is injured, the event is compensable only if *either* of following two conditions exists:

1. An increased hazard caused the employee to fall, or
2. The increased hazard caused the injury.

For example, the employee is merely walking across a carpeted floor, and because of preexisting arthritis, falls to the floor and suffers a broken arm. This injury is not compensable because the arthritis is the major contributing cause of the fall, not the employment. Furthermore, a carpeted floor is not an increased hazard; thus, the employment did not cause the resulting injury either. Just being in the course of employment when the fall happens is not enough [*see* Hernando County School Bd. v. Dokoupil, 667 So. 2d 275, 276–277 (Fla. 1st DCA 1995)]. Where this new language changes the law, it will affect only injuries suffered on or after January 1, 1994.

For a general discussion of the increased risk doctrine, see LARSON'S WORKERS' COMPENSATION, DESK EDITION, Ch. 3, § 3.03 (Matthew Bender).

[6] The Major Contributing Cause Requirement: Aggravation Cases

Before the 1994 statutory amendments, employers were liable for the combined effects of a new injury aggravating an old one. This is no longer true. The 1994 statute now provides [§ 440.09(1)(b), Fla. Stat. (Supp. 1994)]:

> If an injury arising out of and in the course of employment combines with a preexisting disease or condition to cause or prolong disability or need for treatment,

the employer must pay compensation or benefits required by this chapter only to the extent that the injury arising out of and in the course of employment *is and remains the major contributing cause* of the disability or need for treatment. (Emphasis added)

This amendment creates a more stringent evidentiary standard for accidents occurring after January 1, 1994. Now, the injured worker must first prove the following two elements:

1. That the initial work-related accident is compensable.

2. In cases involving aggravation of preexisting conditions, that the accident is the major contributing cause of the injury or aggravation.

For example, William Mangold was doing his work when a go-cart struck him and pinned his right leg. Later, he suffered a heart attack brought on, he claimed, by the stress of the accident. This stress may have been a factor causing his heart attack, but many other possible causes were equally likely. Mangold was morbidly obese, had a long history of heart disease, and suffered from hypertension. No medical expert could testify that, within a reasonable degree of medical certainty, the go-cart incident was the major contributing cause of Mangold's heart attack. Based on this, the judge of compensation claims denied the claim and the First District Court of Appeal affirmed the judge's decision [*see* Mangold v. Rainforest Golf Sports Center, 675 So. 2d 639, 642 (Fla. 1st DCA 1996)].

For a general discussion of subsequent aggravation of an original injury, see LARSON'S WORKERS' COMPENSATION, DESK EDITION, Ch. 10 (Matthew Bender).

§ 7.02 Logical Cause Doctrine

[1] The Rule

Under the logical cause doctrine, the carrier will owe compensation benefits when:

1. The injured worker conclusively shows that a work-related accident has occurred;

2. The injured worker can show an accidental injury; and

3. The evidence presents a sufficiently logical explanation of a causal relationship between the accident and the injury.

The carrier, if seeking to defeat recovery, has the burden of overcoming the established proof. The carrier must do so by showing that another cause for the injury is more logical and consistent with reason. Note, however, that the carrier's burden is greater than merely to suggest another possible explanation for the injury's cause. To defeat the claim, the carrier must show a *more* logical cause for the injury.

For a general discussion of the interpretation of "arising," see LARSON'S WORKERS' COMPENSATION, DESK EDITION, Ch. 3 (Matthew Bender).

[2] Does Doctrine Still Apply

Is the logical cause doctrine still applicable? It very likely is, despite statutory amendments. First, § 440.015, Fla. Stat. provides that courts cannot liberally construe the law for either party. Second, § 440.09(1), Fla. Stat. provides in pertinent part:

> The injury, its occupational cause, and any resulting manifestations or disability shall be established to a reasonable degree of medical *certainty* and by *objective* medical findings. (Emphasis added)

This language requires that the injury, its work relationship, and any resulting disability must be established to a reasonable degree of medical certainty and by *objective* medical findings. The effect of this statutory requirement is to create a new standard of proof for the injured worker rather than an affirmative defense for the carrier. Carriers need not raise the issue of lack of objective medical findings as a defense. Instead, the injured worker must produce such evidence to establish entitlement to benefits [*see* Pyram v. Marriott Intern., 687 So. 2d 351 (Fla. 1st DCA 1997)].

[3] Objective v. Subjective Findings

[a] Definitions

As noted in § 7.01[4][d], *above,* the phrases "medical *certainty*" and "medical *probability*" mean the same thing and can be used interchangeably. Certain cause and logical cause are obviously worlds apart. Still, are subjective findings really no longer acceptable? An objective finding is one that the diagnostician can see, hear, smell, taste, stimulate (or fail to stimulate), measure, or feel. Objective symptoms are apparent to physical diagnosis means. Subjective symptoms, on the other hand, are those that are evident only to the patient and that an observer cannot perceive. Faced with having to finally define these terms, the court turned to dictionaries for help and adopted the following definitions of the terms "complaint" and "subjective" [*see* Gates Energy Products v. Wheeler, 637 So. 2d 1000, 1005 (Fla. 1st DCA 1994)]:

1. *Complaint* means a symptom, disease, or disorder. It is an expression of pain, dissatisfaction, or resentment. Complaint also means a cause of physical pain; a malady.
2. *Subjective* pertains to or is perceived only by the affected individual: not perceptible to the senses of another person. It means proceeding from or taking place within an individual's mind such as to be unaffected by the external world. A subjective complaint is one perceived only by the patient and not by the examiner. It is a complaint that exists only in the patient's mind.

[b] Standard Definitions Held Too Restrictive

Broadly defined, the subjective complaint standard means that conditions which physicians cannot perceive with their own senses, or with diagnostic tests, are not compensable. The problem with such a definition is that real medical conditions like headache, general pain, or vision loss would no longer be compensable because physicians must often rely only on the patient's subjective reports for a diagnosis. So far, no way exists to test heat, cold, touch, pain, pressure, or any other form of sensation objectively, except to ask patients what they feel.

The *Wheeler* court concluded that the legislature did not intend language requiring objective test results to eliminate previously compensable conditions [*see* Gates Energy Products v. Wheeler, 637 So. 2d 1000, 1005–1007 (Fla. 1st DCA 1994)]. On the contrary, language that did so would likely render the law unconstitutional. Therefore, the objectivity standard applies to only those conditions that *can* be confirmed by a physician's observation or diagnostic testing. The standard does not apply to conditions that must rely on the patient's subjective reports.

Although *Wheeler* predates the 1994 amendment, § 440.09(1), Fla. Stat., it clearly applies here. *Wheeler* dealt with a 1990 amendment that specified an injured worker's permanent impairment could not be decided "based solely on subjective complaints" [§ 440.15(3)(a)3, Fla. Stat. (1990)]. The 1994 amendment requires that physicians base their conclusions only on objective medical findings. This, of course, is essentially the same statement rephrased. Viewed in *Wheeler's* light, § 440.09(1), Fla. Stat. appears to have changed nothing.

[c] Effect on Mental Injuries

With its 1994 amendment, the legislature also tried to restrict compensability for mental injuries. For injuries occurring on or after January 1, 1994, mental injuries are compensable only if proved by the apparently higher standard of "clear and convincing" evidence. Although this standard appears momentous, it is unlikely to have a significant impact. Clear and convincing evidence is that quantum of evidence beyond a mere preponderance, but is less than that of "beyond a reasonable doubt." It is evidence that produces in the judge's mind a firm belief or conviction, without hesitancy, about the facts a party seeks to prove. This is a stricter standard than the normally used standard of competent substantial evidence. It is the judge of compensation claims who will decide if clear and convincing evidence exists.

This greater standard, however does not apply to the appellate court. On appeal, the court will determine whether the record contains competent substantial evidence to meet the clear and convincing standard. The court will not conduct a de novo proceeding [*see* McKesson Drug Co. v. Williams, 706 So. 2d 352, 353–354 (Fla. 1st DCA 1998) (rehearing denied March 12, 1998)]. Because the logical cause doctrine may still be with us, a review is in order [*see* [4], *below*].

[4] The Doctrine's History

[a] Invoking the Doctrine

Logical cause is a judicially created doctrine. It holds that an injured worker needs to offer proof of only (1) an accidental injury that, (2) arose out of and in the course of the employment. If the injured worker does so, the employer and carrier have the burden to produce proof that another cause of the injury was more logical. The carrier must show convincingly that the injury did, or at least more probably, occur outside the employment. The carrier may also defeat the claim by showing the injury is a condition personal to the employee. Carriers can do this either through the testimony of lay witnesses or by medical or other evidence. Such evidence will show that the injury could not, or most likely did not, occur as the employee alleges. Simply put, the carrier must show a *more* logical cause. In the end, the result will depend on who the judge believes.

[b] Case History

Often, the causation issue turns on the medical testimony. Until 1993, the cases held that if physicians testified that an injury occurred as the injured worker described it, the judge of compensation claims must accept such evidence. The judge could not disregard such evidence in favor of contradictory lay testimony. Following are case examples.

Case 1. George Bray fell at work and struck his back. He was bleeding, so his supervisor administered first-aid, but did not file an accident report. Bray continued to work. Over the next five or six weeks, he began to develop pain in his legs. He experienced other problems, including difficulty walking. Initially, Bray did not tell his doctor about the accident at work. When asked why, he claimed the doctor did not ask. During his second office visit, Bray did tell the doctor about the accident. Eventually, diagnostic tests revealed a herniated disc.

The judge of compensation claims denied the claim because of inconsistent testimony. The inconsistencies were that Bray initially sought payment from the group health insurer. Furthermore, Bray initially did not give a history of a work-related accidental injury to the doctor. The First District Court of Appeal reversed and awarded benefits, holding that the employee had established a logical cause for his injury. The carrier, on the other hand, did not meet its burden by showing a more logical cause by competent substantial evidence [*see* Bray v. Electronic Door-Lift, Inc., 558 So. 2d 43, 46–47 (Fla. 1st DCA 1989)].

Case 2. Salvatore Fusco was doing his regular job of leveling concrete when he suddenly felt pain in his back. He had suffered back injuries before in 1985 and in 1986. The judge of compensation claims held that Fusco did not suffer an accident during the course and scope of his employment. Further, the judge held that Fusco's injuries did not result from the alleged accident. The judge also ruled that the logical cause doctrine did not apply because Fusco had not shown that his injury occurred when he claimed. Lastly, the judge concluded that even if the logical cause doctrine did apply the carrier had met its burden of showing a more logical explanation (the prior injuries) for Fusco's injuries and physical complaints.

The First District Court of Appeal reversed the judge's order. The court held that Fusco had conclusively proved an injury because his doctor said he had a herniated disc. That took care of the first requirement of proving an injury. In addition, Fusco established a logical cause for his injury. How? He simply claimed that he hurt himself at work and because he had told others about this at the time. That took care of the second, proof requirement. The court found only one reason in the record for the judge's finding. The doctor had nothing in his records of a history of traumatic injury on the date in question. The court held that relying on this was arbitrary and unreasonable. Lastly, the court held that the carrier did not present any evidence in three important areas. First, no evidence existed showing that Fusco had missed work before the accident. Second, no evidence existed showing that the accident scene was not as Fusco described it. Third, no evidence existed showing that the injury was inconsistent with Fusco's story [*see* Fusco v. P & S Const. Co., 564 So. 2d 526, 529–530 (Fla. 1st DCA 1990)].

In the cases above, no one disputed that the employee had suffered an accident. The only dispute was whether the accident caused the injury. The appellate courts reversed the judgments denying benefits because the uncontradicted medical evidence was that the accident did cause the injury. That is not true, however, in the case discussed next.

Case 3. Claude Faucher claimed he injured his back while lifting a bucket filled with heavy steel rollers. The only evidence that such an event occurred was physicians testifying that the story was logical. The carrier believed it had a better explanation and contested the claim. The carrier proved that Faucher had a long history of at least two prior back injuries similar to the injury of which he now complained. The judge of compensation claims made several findings. First, Faucher reported an incorrect medical history to his doctor. Second, Faucher knowingly misled both the treating doctor and the independent medical examiner. Third, Faucher did not initially relate his back problems to the alleged new accident. Based on this evidence, the judge held that Faucher had not suffered an accident on the date claimed. The judge made this finding despite both physicians involved having related the employee's injury to the alleged lifting incident. In a 2-to-1 decision, the First District Court of Appeal reversed, holding [*see* Faucher v. R.C.F. Developers, 569 So. 2d 794, 801–803 (Fla. 1st DCA 1990)]:

> It is now well settled that a doctor's medical opinion cannot be disregarded by the judge of compensation claims because the judge finds that the history given such doctor by the claimant was either false or incomplete, unless appropriate questions are put to the doctor specifically inquiring about the effect of the false or omitted information on the doctor's previously expressed opinion.

NOTE: The court later receded from the *Faucher* line of cases. *See* [5][a], *below.*

[5] Present State of the Law

[a] Court Recedes From *Faucher*

In 1993, the same fact pattern as *Faucher* was again before the court [*see* [4][b], *above*]. From June 6 until about June 15, 1990, James Ullman had been engaged in heavy work, scraping floors and digging up or moving meter boxes. Four or five days later, the employer served Ullman with notice that he was to be the subject of a disciplinary hearing set for June 21, 1990. On the day of the disciplinary hearing, Ullman reported that he had suffered a back injury earlier in the month. The carrier denied the claim, as did the judge of compensation claims. In a deposition, the lawyer asked Ullman's doctor if the employee's back injury was related to the alleged accident. She replied,"I think it's pretty clear cut that he got an injury at work and subsequently suffered some consequence thereof." No other expert contradicted this testimony. Under the rule established in *Faucher,* it seemed the judge of compensation claims had no choice but to find the claim compensable. The judge denied the claim anyway because he found the employee's testimony was inconsistent, self-serving, and lacked credibility. The judge took special note that Ullman did not report any accident until the employer served him with a notice of disciplinary action that resulted in his dismissal. Considering the holding in *Faucher,* the employee understandably appealed.

On appeal the court found itself questioning whether the *Faucher* line of cases, discussed in [4][b], *above,* had established a rule that remained valid and workable in such cases. The court chose to consider the case en banc to involve the entire court. Its mission was to more clearly define the role of the judge of compensation claims as the arbiter of disputed facts in workers' compensation cases. The issue before the court was whether to continue the rule that a judge of compensation claims cannot reject unrefuted medical testimony as to causation as announced in *Faucher* and its progeny. In a unanimous opinion, the court chose to recede from the *Faucher* line of cases [*see* Ullman v. City of Tampa Parks Dept., 625 So. 2d 868, 872 (Fla. 1st DCA 1993)].

The court now reaffirms adherence to the traditional rule defining the role of the fact-finder in workers' compensation cases, noting the Florida Supreme Court's unanimous opinion in *Easkold v. Rhodes,* 614 So. 2d 495, 498 (Fla. 1993). In *Easkold,* a civil case, the Florida Supreme Court held that a jury has the authority to reject even uncontradicted medical testimony that is "flawed by reason of the materially untruthful history given by the claimant." Simply put, the judge can ignore doctors' testimony if the judge believes the employee is lying. The First District Court of Appeal saw no reason not to apply *Easkold* to contested workers' compensation cases. Questions of the occurrence of an accident and medical causation are often intertwined. Cases will arise in which even the question of causation is not a subject for determination solely by reference to medical testimony. In *Easkold* the Supreme Court stated that although the facts testified to by the medical expert were not within the ordinary experience of the members of the jury, the jury was still free to decide their credibility. The jury was also free to decide the weight to be assigned to them in the face of conflicting lay testimony. *Easkold,* and the following cases in [b], *below,* are now controlling [Ullman v. City of Tampa Parks Dept., 625 So. 2d 868, 872–873 (Fla. 1st DCA 1993)].

[b] Controlling Cases

Case 1. The appellate court must sustain the judge's findings if allowed by any view of the evidence and its permissible inferences [*see* Orange City Water Co. v. Barkley, 432 So. 2d 698 (Fla. 1st DCA 1983)].

Case 2. The law does not require the judge of compensation claims as finder of fact to accept an opinion that the facts of record do not support [*see* Mallon v. Florida Rock Industries, Inc., 568 So. 2d 503, 504 (Fla. 1st DCA 1990)].

Case 3. The judges of compensation claims may reject, in whole or in part, uncontroverted testimony that they do not believe [*see* Storage Technology Corp. v. Philbrook, 448 So. 2d 42, 44 (Fla. 1st DCA 1984)].

Case 4. The law does not require fact finders to accept testimony that they do not believe [*see* John Caves Land Development Co. v. Suggs, 352 So. 2d 44, 45 (Fla. 1977)].

Case 5. The law allows the judge of compensation claims to consider and evaluate all evidence. This includes both lay and professional testimony. The judge may give greater weight to physical evidence and lay testimony than to scientific opinions of experts [*see* Jeffers v. Pan American Envelope Company, 172 So. 2d 577, 578 (Fla. 1965)].

[c] Court's New Instructions to JCCs

The cases described in [b], *above,* properly define the role of the judges of

Guide to Claims

compensation claims as finders of fact. The court adopted the standard jury instruction in civil cases and held it now applies to the judge of compensation claims in workers' compensation cases. Therefore, the court's instruction to the judges of compensation claims is this [*see* Ullman v. City of Tampa Parks Dept., 625 So. 2d 868, 873–874 (Fla. 1st DCA 1993)]:

> You may accept such opinion testimony, *reject it,* or give it the weight you think it deserves, considering the knowledge, skill, experience, training, or education of the witness, *the reasons given by the witness for the opinion expressed, and all the other evidence in the case.*

[d] Doctrine Clarified

The *Ullman* court [*see* [c], *above*] also clarified the meaning of the logical cause doctrine. Originally, the cases suggested that the doctrine applied when an employee showed proof of an injury and had any reasonable story (a logical cause) about how it occurred. The burden then shifted to the carrier to show a more logical cause. For example, assume Joe is an employee who tells the doctor he injured his back lifting something at work. The doctor has no reason not to believe Joe, and if asked, will relate the injury to the alleged lifting incident. Under the original logical cause doctrine, the burden will shift to the carrier to prove otherwise. This, of course, was an almost impossible burden because of the line of cases that held the trial judge could not ignore such testimony if it was not contradicted by another physician.

The court now holds this to be an incorrect application of the law. A doctor's assumption about the occurrence of an accident does not replace the employee's burden of proving that an accident occurred. Citing two Florida Supreme Court decisions, the District Court of Appeal held that the logical cause doctrine applies only when the fact that an accident occurred *has already been established.* Thus, the logical cause doctrine applies to only pure medical issues, and not to causation. To do otherwise, said the court, would be illogical and "would betray [the doctrine's] very name" if courts applied the doctrine to facts that do not prove a work-related accident. If a given case presents an issue about whether an accident occurred, the logical cause doctrine does not apply such that medical testimony alone can establish the occurrence of an accident [Ullman v. City of Tampa Parks Dept., 625 So. 2d 868, 874 (Fla. 1st DCA 1993) (citing *Wilhelm v. Westminster Presbyterian Church,* 235 So. 2d 726, 728 (Fla. 1970), and *Johnson v. Koffee Kettle Restaurant,* 125 So. 2d 297, 299 (Fla. 1960)].

When does the logical cause doctrine apply? It applies only to such questions as whether a *proven* work-related accident caused a particular condition.

[6] Showing Prima Facie Case Is Not Enough

Simply establishing a prima facie case is not enough to invoke the logical cause doctrine. A prima facie case is a case sufficient on its face, being supported by at least the requisite minimum of evidence, and is free from palpable defects. A prima facie case is one in which the evidence is sufficient to support, but not to compel, a certain conclusion and does no more than furnish evidence to be considered and weighed, but not necessarily to be accepted, by the judge. Sufficient proof, acceptable to the judge, must be shown because the doctrine does not relieve the employee of the initial burden of being credible.

The doctrine does not apply when the judge rejects the employee's testimony as so lacking in credibility to conclude that even if the cause described is logical, the injured worker telling the tale is unbelievable. Even when the employee presents a prima facie case, the law allows the judge to rely on contrary evidence. If such contrary evidence exits, the law does not require the judge to apply the logical cause doctrine [*see* Alston v. Etcetera Janitorial Services, 634 So. 2d 1133, 1134 (Fla. 1st DCA 1994)].

Guide to Claims

§ 7.03 Going To and Returning From Work

[1] Going and Coming Rule

Workers traveling to or from work are not in the course and scope of employment unless they are on duty, on a special call, or are in transportation provided by the employer. Going and coming begins and ends when the employee enters or leaves the employer's premises. Employees need not be "on the clock" if they were furthering their employers' interests at the time. The 1990 law change partly eliminated the "employer provided transportation" exception [*see* § 7.04[6]].

For a detailed discussion of the going and coming rule, see Larson's Workers' Compensation, Desk Edition, Ch. 13 (Matthew Bender).

[2] The Theory

The theory behind the going and coming rule is simple. Those people with regular work hours share the risk of traveling to and from work with the public. The trip is not, therefore, a hazard of the job. Something must link traveling to or from work to the job. The link must be something other than the trip itself. Absent such a link, an accident suffered during travel to and from work does not arise out of and in the course of employment [§ 440.092(2), Fla. Stat.; *see* George v. Woodville Lumber Co., 382 So. 2d 802, 803 (Fla. 1st DCA 1980)].

§ 7.04 Exceptions to Going and Coming Rule

[1] Employers' Premises—Shopping Malls/Parking Lots

[a] The Rule

Generally, going and coming begin and end when the employee enters or leaves the employer's premises. Therefore, an important first step is to identify what constitutes an employer's premises.

For a detailed discussion of the premises rule, see Larson's Workers' Compensation, Desk Edition, Ch. 13, § 13.04 (Matthew Bender).

[b] Shopping Malls/Public Buildings

Many businesses are found in shopping malls. In such cases, the entire mall, including the parking lot, is the employer's premises for workers' compensation purposes. The decisive factor in these cases is whether the special hazard doctrine, discussed in [7] *below,* applies. Just because the accident occurred on a site leased by the employer and shared by other tenants does not, by itself, prevent compensability [*see* Petroske v. Worth Ave. Burger Place, 416 So. 2d 856, 857 (Fla. 1st DCA 1982)].

[c] Parking Lots

Accidents that occur on a parking lot owned and controlled by the employer meet the premises test. Remember that accidents occurring on the employer's premises might be compensable, although actual work has not begun. Questions arise, however, when accidents occur on parking lots not owned by the employer. Even non-owned lots may be the employer's premises for workers' compensation purposes, but under very limited circumstances. To constitute employers' premises, non-owned parking lots must be under some control or subject to special use by the employer. In other words, the employer's use of the property must be for purposes other than those shared by the public.

For example, Martha Alvarez crushed her finger in her car door after parking her car to go in to work. Although she parked in a public lot, the judge of compensation claims held the injury compensable. The employer did not allow employees to park in its small lot, because these few spaces were reserved for customers. Instead, the employer directed Alvarez and other employees to park in the public lot. In awarding benefits, the trial judge held that the parking lot was "a part of the zone and environment" of Alvarez' employment. The First District Court of Appeal reversed, holding the judge was wrong as a matter of law. The question, said the court, was not whether Alvarez was directed to park in the public lot, but whether the employer was in control of the lot. Here, the employer had no such control [*see* Security Bureau, Inc. v. Alvarez, 654 So. 2d 1024, 1025–1026 (Fla. 1st DCA 1995)].

In another case, the employee was injured in a parking lot across the street from the employer's premises. The employer did not own the lot. The employee's injury was not compensable because he had not yet entered the employer's premises [*see* Sirocco Motor Inn, Inc. v. Prekop, 207 So. 2d 434, 435 (Fla. 1968)].

If, however, the employee must cross a damaged sidewalk or a construction area, the special hazard exception may invoke compensability [*see* Doctor's Business Service, Inc. v. Clark, 498 So. 2d 659, 662–665 (Fla. 1st DCA 1986); Maas Bros. v. Peo, 498 So. 2d 657, 658–659 (Fla. 1st DCA 1986)].

For a detailed discussion of parking lots owned or maintained by the employer, see LARSON'S WORKERS' COMPENSATION, DESK EDITION, Ch. 10 (Matthew Bender).

[2] Employers' Premises—Police Officers

[a] The Rule

A police officer is in the course of employment if the officer is actually engaged in police work. It does not matter if the officer was not officially on-duty [*see* [5], *below*; *see* Hanstein v. City of Ft. Lauderdale, 569 So. 2d 493, 494 (Fla 1st DCA 1990)].

[b] Applying the Rule

For police officers, the law considers the entire city, county, or even all of Florida as the employer's "premises." Premises, however, is not usually the issue in police officer cases. The issue is usually whether or not the officer is on duty The rule today is that a police officer actually engaged in police work is in the course of employment. It does not matter whether or not the officer is officially on duty.

In 1982, the legislature added § 440.091, Fla. Stat. to the Workers' Compensation Act. This section provides that the law deems a police officer to be acting in the course of employment if the officer:

(a) Is employed full-time by a municipality or other governmental unit;

(b) Has the authority to bear arms and make arrests;

(c) Was engaged in discharging those responsibilities; and

(d) Was not being paid by a private employer for those services at the time.

The question of on duty or not most often arises in going and coming cases. This issue is discussed in [5], *below.*

[3] Travel Between Employer Locations

[a] The Rule

Generally, business travel between an employer's locations is in the course of employment and the going and coming rule does not apply.

For a detailed discussion of travel between two parts of the employer's premises, see LARSON'S WORKERS' COMPENSATION, DESK EDITION, Ch. 10 (Matthew Bender).

[b] Business Purpose and Employer Premises

In many occupations, the employer requires the employee to report to the employer's main office first, and then travel to another of the employer's locations, or to a job site. Without question, such travel between the employer's locations is in the course of employment. The going and coming rule does not apply to accidents occurring when the employee is en route between work premises. This assumes, of course, that such travel is for a work purpose and is not purely personal [*see* Dade County School Bd. v. Polite, 495 So. 2d 795, 797 (Fla. 1st DCA 1986)].

This rule also applies to travel between one portion of the employer's premises, such as an employer provided parking lot, to another portion of the premises, such as the employer's office. For example, the employer rented a parking lot for its employees' use. The lot is across a public street from the employer's office. Once employees enter the parking lot, they have entered the employer's premises. In cases like this, the parking lot extends the employer's premises to include the direct route to and from the office, including any public street that may be between them. In such a case, the law deems an injury suffered while on the public street to have occurred on the employer's premises [*see* Ryan v. Boehm, Brown, Rigdon, Seacrest & Fischer, 673 So. 2d 494, 496 (Fla. 1st DCA 1996)].

[4] Arriving Early—Not on the Clock

[a] The Rule

Whether an employee is working for pay at the time of the accident is not relevant. An injury is deemed to have occurred in the course of employment if the employee was on the employer's premises while preparing to begin a day's work [*see* Doctor's Business Service, Inc. v. Clark, 498 So. 2d 659, 662–663 (Fla. 1st DCA 1986)].

[b] On Duty Status Not Required

The cases have established a general rule that employees need not be officially on duty or receiving pay at the time an injury occurs. All the law requires is that the employee was doing some service for the employer. Naturally, compensability hinges on whether the employer directed the activity and had some degree of control over the employee. Therefore, work connection alone is not enough for compensability [*see* [c], *below,* for case history].

[c] Case History

Case 1. Return to former employer to receive final pay. Kyra Phillips quit her job, then returned two weeks later to pick up her final paycheck. (This was the first available date she could pick up her check.) After obtaining her check, she injured herself when she fell down the stairs. The court held this to be in the course of her employment though she was no longer technically employed. The theory is the employment is not fully ended until the employer pays the employee [*see* Phillips v. Unicare Amelia Island, Inc., 458 So. 2d 50, 52 (Fla. 1st DCA 1984)].

Case 2. Undergoing required physical examination or treatment. Leroy Turner's employer required him to undergo a physical examination. He did so on his own time and at his own expense. Turner suffered a back injury while doing pushups during the examination. The court held the claim compensable because the employer required the examination as a condition of employment [*see* Turner v. Rinker Material Corp., 554 So. 2d 647, 649 (Fla. 1st DCA 1989)].

Remember that the only requirement generally is that the employee is doing something incidental to the employment at the time of the accident. Compensability in this case turned on the fact that this examination was required by the employer. In all such cases, the investigation should focus on compulsion and employer control.

Case 3. Undergoing required physical examination or treatment. Ricardo Dickson worked as a police officer for the City of Kissimmee. Because he was overweight, Dickson was unable to satisfy the department's physical fitness requirements. To lose weight, he decided to undergo a stomach stapling surgery. Sadly, Dickson died as a result of complications from the surgery. While this case appears similar to *Turner,* it is different. Although Dickson was required to maintain a prescribed level of fitness, his decision to undergo surgery was his alone. On the contrary, the department did not even order Dickson to lose weight. He had complete autonomy over how to improve his fitness level within a three-year grace period. Because Dickson's choices, including the surgery, were done on his own time and at his own expense, his death was not compensable [*see* City of Kissimmee v. Dickson, 694 So. 2d 143, 144–145 (Fla. 1st DCA 1997)].

Case 4. Attending training courses. Judith Jordan was a school teacher at Palm Harbor Middle School. She suffered an injury while attending a training course at Tarpon High School to get credits that the law required to maintain her teaching certificate. This looks like a perfect scenario for compensability, but it is not automatically so. It is true that the school board required teachers to maintain a teaching certificate. It is also true that the law required teachers to earn continuing education credits to keep their certificates. The school board, however, did not direct how or where the teachers should get their credits. When Jordan suffered her injury she was on her own time, chose this training course herself, and did not receive pay while attending. Because of these facts and because the employer had no control over Jordan while she attended the seminar, her injury was not compensable [*see* Jordan v. Pinellas County School Bd., 680 So. 2d 448, 450 (Fla. 1st DCA 1996)].

Remember that the keys to compensability are employer control and involvement. Ask the following questions. If the answers are yes, the case for compensability gets stronger.

1. Did the employer order the employee to attend?
2. Did the employer provide the training?
3. Did the employee receive pay to attend?
4. Did the training occur during regular working hours?
5. Did the employer dictate the time, place, or manner in which employees must get their training?
6. Did the employer have control over the employee while attending the training session?

[5] On Duty or Dual Purpose

[a] The Rule

Generally, if the employee is on duty during travel time, or is doing a service for the employer, the employee is in the course of employment [*see* Schoenfelder v. Winn & Jorgensen, P.A., 704 So. 2d 136, 137 (Fla. 1st DCA 1997)].

[b] On Duty

[i] Making the Distinction

Most employees have fixed hours of employment at a permanent location. The going and coming rule prevents compensability for injuries sustained during travel to and from such places of employment. If, however, an employee is on duty and engaged in doing a service for the employer, an injury suffered during such travel is compensable. Many employees work outside and do not always report directly to the employer's premises before beginning the work day.

Examples of on-duty travel include insurance adjusters, rehabilitation specialists, or attorneys who start for their first appointment of the workday from home. The law considers such employees on-duty and the going and coming rule does not apply. Although this premise should be obvious, many people have difficulty seeing the difference.

Usually, employers do not pay employees for the time spent getting to work or going home at the end of the work day. Getting to work or going home is a personal trip, and the employee is doing no service for the employer. A different situation arises, however, when the journey itself is part of the service done for the employer. Even an ordinary going and coming trip comes within the course of the employment if the employee is also doing some service for the employer. Obviously then, a trip that is all business is within the course and scope of employment. Professor Larson agrees and says, "[T]raveling employees are generally within the course of employment from the time they leave home on a business trip until they return, for the self-evident reason that the traveling itself is a large part of the job" LARSON'S WORKERS' COMPENSATION, DESK EDITION, Ch. 12 (Matthew Bender)].

[ii] Travel Must Be Necessarily Incident to Employment

Effective January 1, 1994, the Florida legislature amended the traveling employee section of the law. The amendment provides: "This subsection applies to travel *necessarily incident to performance of the employee's job responsibility* but does not include travel to and from work as provided in subsection (2)" [§ 440.092(4), Fla. Stat. (1/1/94) (emphasis added)]. The amendment attempts to assure that the section does not apply to routine travel to and from work. It also specifically includes travel if it is part of the job duties. Note the italicized phrase. For example, assume the employee goes directly from home to a client's place of business to service the client's machines. How can anyone say the travel is not "necessarily incident to performance of the employee's job responsibilities?" Following are case examples applying this statutory provision:

Case 1. Attorney Robert Schoenfelder took a client's case file home to prepare for a deposition the next morning. At about 7:00 a.m., he began his preparation, and while walking to his car to drive to the deposition site, he was struck by a vehicle. His injuries were held compensable because he began his work at home, and was still so engaged when he was hurt. Most important to this analysis, he was not on his way to his regular place of employment. This type of trip was a regular part of his employment, and cannot be equated with an employee's routine travel to the office to begin a workday [*see* Schoenfelder v. Winn & Jorgensen, P.A., 704 So. 2d 136, 137 (Fla. 1st DCA 1997)].

Case 2. Handi-Man Temporary Services furnished temporary labor to other businesses. The company did not require its workers to pick up their pay checks each day, but they could if they chose to do so. Although nothing prevented them from waiting until the end of the work week for their paychecks, about half the employees collected their checks at the end of each day that they worked. To do so, however, the employees had to turn in their time cards and pick up their checks at an alternate site. Danny Evans chose to do just that, but was injured in a car accident while traveling to the other site.

The judge of compensation claims denied the claim, ruling that this trip was not required and that Evans simply chose to do so for his own convenience. As such, the judge held this was not travel necessarily incident to Evans' job responsibilities. The First

Guide to Claims

District Court of Appeal disagreed and reversed. The court held that an employee traveling from a job site to collect a pay check at an employer-designated pickup point is in the course and scope of employment. That the employee has other means of getting a pay check is immaterial so long as the employee is acting in a method and manner that the employer authorized [*see* Evans v. Handi-Man & Riscorp Temporary Services, 710 So. 2d 132, 134–135 (Fla. 1st DCA 1998)].

[c] Police Officers

[i] On Duty Defined

Police officers are on duty anytime they are enforcing the law. More precisely, § 440.091, Fla. Stat. provides that a police officer is acting in the course of employment if the officer:

1. Is employed full-time by a municipality or other governmental unit;
2. Has the authority to bear arms and make arrests;
3. Was engaged in discharging those responsibilities; and
4. Was not being paid by a private employer for those services at the time.

Previously, the Act provided that the officer "shall be deemed" to have been acting withing the course of employment while enforcing the law. Effective July 1, 2002, § 440.091(1), Fla. Stat. provides that the officer "is considered" to have been acting within the course of employment. The significance of that change is not clear. Still, there is a clear legislative intent to create a presumption of coverage under the law if an officer is injured while enforcing the law, whether or not the officer is officially on duty.

The question of on duty or not most often arises in going and coming cases [*see* [ii], *below*].

[ii] Case History

Case 1. Officer Abrams was a forensic detective. Her injury occurred in an auto collision while driving to work in her personal car. Her injury was not compensable because she was not engaged in police work at the time. That is, Abrams was neither investigating a crime nor enforcing the law. Thus, she was not discharging her primary responsibility as a police officer [*see* City of Fort Lauderdale v. Abrams, 561 So. 2d 1294, 1295 (Fla. 1st DCA 1990)].

Case 2. Officer Hanstein was driving to work in his personal car, but was fully uniformed. He saw a tractor-trailer rig making an improper turn and decided to issue a citation for this violation. Before he could do that, however, the tractor-trailer struck his car. The trial judge denied the claim for two reasons. First, Hanstein had not yet tried to stop the driver of the tractor-trailer. Second, Hanstein had not physically begun to issue a citation. The First District Court of Appeal disagreed and reversed. The court noted that the law requires only that an officer be within the state and discharging a primary responsibility. This, said the court, includes enforcing traffic or highway laws. Because Hanstein was a patrol officer, unlike Abrams, he was "discharging this primary responsibility while traveling to the police station, and it was not necessary to actually issue a citation or take any affirmative action in this regard for the officer to be within the course of his employment. . . ." Here, the court held that off-duty officers are on duty the second they think about enforcing the law [*see* Hanstein v. City of Ft. Lauderdale, 569 So. 2d 493, 494 (Fla. 1st DCA 1990)].

Case 3. Officer Levine, like Hanstein, was driving to work in his personal car and was also in uniform. While stopped at an intersection, two other cars collided and one struck Levine's car. He reported the accident via his portable police radio. He then began working the accident scene in the usual manner until the Highway Patrol arrived and took over the investigation. Then, Levine realized he was injured and drove himself to the hospital. Levine's supervisor testified that Levine was just like any employee driving to work and "there was no requirement of law enforcement function until the accident had actually occurred." The judge of compensation claims denied the claim, holding Levine was not discharging his responsibility as a deputy sheriff when the accident happened. The Court of Appeal disagreed and reversed. Just before the collision, Levine saw one of the other cars make an illegal left turn. The moment he saw this crime occur, said the court, he was immediately thrust into an on-duty status [*see* Levine v. Brevard Cty. Sheriff's Dept., 658 So. 2d 1044, 1045–1047 (Fla. 1st DCA 1995)].

Case 4. Officer Ginn's injury also occurred in an auto accident. At the time, Ginn was off-duty and on a personal errand. He was, however, driving a sheriff's office vehicle that the department allowed him to use on personal business. The judge of compensation claims awarded benefits because Ginn "was in a police car and monitoring the radio and a beeper" before the accident. The First District Court of Appeal reversed and held that merely being ready to respond if called is different from carrying out his primary responsibility. This includes the prevention or detection of crime, elements that the officer must show for the injury to be compensable [*see* Palm Beach Cty. Sheriff's Office v. Ginn, 570 So. 2d 1059, 1060–1061 (Fla. 1st DCA 1990)].

[iii] Present State of the Law for Police Officers

The present state of the law, then, is this. If a police officer is not on duty, the officer must be discharging official duties at the time an accident occurs for an injury to be compensable. The officer need not be officially on duty. The officer need not be engaged in police work. It is apparently enough if the officer is merely thinking about it [*see* Hanstein v. City of Ft. Lauderdale, 569 So. 2d 493, 494 (Fla. 1st DCA 1990)].

[iv] Police Officer Exception to the Going and Coming Rule

For accidents occurring on or after June 6, 2001 of the Act, § 440.092, Fla. Stat., provides a presumption that police officers are within the course and scope of employment while traveling to or from work in an official law enforcement vehicle. This exception to the going and coming rule does not apply if the officer was engaged in a "distinct deviation" for a non-essential personal errand. Even a deviation will not preclude compensability if such deviations are allowed by the employer's policy, or in the collective bargaining agreement.

This amendment covers police officers as defined by § 943.10(1), Fla. Stat. That section provides the following definition:

"Law enforcement officer" means any person who is elected, appointed, or employed full time by any municipality or the state or any political subdivision thereof; who is vested with authority to bear arms and make arrests; and whose primary responsibility is the prevention and detection of crime or the enforcement of the penal, criminal, traffic, or highway laws of the state. This definition includes all certified supervisory and command personnel whose duties include, in whole or in part, the supervision, training, guidance, and management responsibilities of full-time law enforcement officers, part-time law enforcement officers, or auxiliary law enforcement officers but does not include support personnel employed by the employing agency.

Because this amendment changes rights and responsibilities, it is most likely a substantive amendment that will apply to accidents occurring on or after the effective date of June 6, 2001.

[d] Firefighters

Firefighters are considered to be within the course and scope of their employment even if they are off-duty or outside the employer's jurisdiction if they were engaged in extinguishing a fire, or protecting life and property due to a fire. This presumption does not apply to injuries suffered outside of Florida or if the firefighter was being paid by another employer or contractor. Therefore, firefighters are entitled to benefits if injured while off-duty or when they are outside the employer's jurisdiction or area of responsibility when the following conditions are met [*see* § 440.091(2), Fla. Stat. (6/1/2002)]:

1. The employee was engaged in extinguishing a fire or in protecting people and property from the hazards of a fire;
2. The accident occurred within the state of Florida; and
3. The injury would otherwise have been compensable if the firefighter had been on duty and within the employer's jurisdiction.

Note that this presumption applies only to those employees who meet the statutory definition of "firefighter" [*see* § 112.191(1)(b), Fla. Stat.]:

The term "firefighter" means any full-time duly employed uniformed firefighter employed by an employer, whose primary duty is the prevention and extinguishing of fires, the protection of life and property therefrom, the enforcement of municipal, county, and state fire prevention codes, as well as the enforcement of any law pertaining to the prevention and control of fires, who is certified pursuant to § 633.35, and who is a member of a duly constituted fire department of such employer or who is a volunteer firefighter.

[e] Paramedics and Emergency Medical Technicians

Paramedics and EMT's are considered to be within the course and scope of their employment, even if they are outside the employer's jurisdiction, if they were engaged in providing basic or advanced life support services. This presumption does not apply to injuries suffered outside of Florida or if the paramedic or EMT was being paid by another employer or contractor.

SPECIAL NOTE: Unlike law enforcement officers and firefighters, this presumption does not include injuries suffered while off-duty.

Therefore, Paramedics and EMT's are entitled to benefits if injured while they are outside the employer's jurisdiction or area of responsibility when the following conditions are met [*see* § 440.091(3), Fla. Stat. (7/1/2002)]:

1. The employee was on-duty;
2. The accident occurred within the state of Florida;
3. The employee was engaged in providing basic or advanced life support services in an emergency situation; and
4. The injury would otherwise have been compensable if it had occurred within the employer's jurisdiction or area of responsibility.

[f] Dual Purpose: Special Errand Exception

[i] The Rule

From the cases that have been heard by the courts we can develop a general rule. If the employee is going to or from work, but is also doing some service or special errand for the employer, the going and coming rule does not apply. In such cases, the law considers the employee to be in the course of employment.

Deciding the relative importance of the personal part of the trip compared with the business part is not necessary. If the business part was at least a concurrent cause of the trip, the carrier may be liable for any injuries that occur. To decide if an employee's trip had a dual purpose, get the answer to this question: Would the employee have made the trip without a personal motive? If the answer is yes, the trip is likely within the course of the employment [*see* El Viejo Arco Iris, Inc. v. Luaces, 395 So. 2d 225, 226 (Fla. 1st DCA 1981); *see also* [ii], *below*, for case history].

When an employee is on a special errand or mission for the employer, the employee remains within the course and scope of employment during the entire round-trip back to the point of origin *see* Canfield v. Weaver, 768 So. 2d 1205,1206 (Fla. 1st DCA 2000).

The "going and coming" rule governing compensability of workers' compensation claims is codified in § 440.092(2), Fla. Stat. (1995), which provides:

> An injury suffered while going to or coming from work is not an injury arising out of and in the course of employment whether or not the employer provided transportation if such means of transportation was available for the exclusive personal use by the employee, unless the employee was engaged in a special errand or mission for the employer.

Note that one of the exceptions to the rule is that the employee was engaged in a special errand or mission. It has been argued that the statute's reference to "special errand or mission" does not incorporate the dual purpose doctrine. It has also been argued that the maxim *expressio unius est exclusio alterius*—express mention of one thing is the exclusion of another—demonstrates that since the dual purpose doctrine does not appear within one of the exceptions specified in the statute, the court cannot infer that the Legislature intended that exception to remain operative [*see* Swartz v. McDonalds Corp., 788 So. 2d 937, 943 (Fla. 2001)].

The Florida Supreme Court, however, disagreed and held that the special errand or mission language contained in the statute encompasses both the special errand and the dual purpose exceptions to the going and coming rule. The special errand exception and dual purpose doctrine can operate either in tandem or independently [*see* Swartz v. McDonalds Corp., 788 So. 2d 937, 943 (Fla. 2001)].

Although the special errand exception and the dual purpose doctrine can be applied independent of each other, they have also become interconnected in case law. In determining whether to apply the special errand exception, courts consider various factors, including the relative burden of the journey on the employee in light of his or her employment duties, the irregularity of the timing and nature of the journey, the suddenness of the employer's request, the time and length of the journey, and any other special circumstances [*see* Swartz v. McDonalds Corp., 788 So. 2d 937, 945 (Fla. 2001)].

Because compensability depends on the circumstances, there is no firm rule and the determination as to whether one of the exceptions applies must be made on a case-by-case basis. The Court, however, has provided some guidance. It is not necessary to determine the relative importance of a concurrent business and personal motive for the trip. So long as the business purpose is at least a concurrent cause of the trip, the employer may be held liable for workers' compensation. Liability can be established on the inference that the trip would have been made though the private errand had been canceled. It is not necessary that the business purpose be the dominate purpose. It is enough if the business motive is merely a concurrent cause of the trip [*see* Swartz v. McDonalds Corp., 788 So. 2d 937, 950 (Fla. 2001)].

Compensability decisions merely recognize a sufficient business purpose, which must be analyzed on a case-by-case basis. If no such purpose is found, the law continues to preclude recovery for employees who were merely carrying tools of employment when injured and, therefore, not performing a legitimate business purpose [*see* Swartz v. McDonalds Corp., 788 So. 2d 937 (Fla. 2001)].

For a general discussion of dual-purpose trips, see LARSON'S WORKERS' COMPENSATION, DESK EDITION, Ch. 16 (Matthew Bender).

[ii] Case History

Case 1. The employer operated his electrical service business from his home. He discovered that a local ordinance prohibited parking commercial vehicles in this residential area. The vans had to be parked somewhere else at night. Thus, the employee began driving one of the vans home. While driving home, the employee was injured in a vehicle accident. Because the employee was driving the van home, at least partly for the employer's convenience, this was a sufficient business purpose to make this a dual purpose trip and, therefore, compensable [*see* Hages v. Hughes Electrical Service, Inc., 654 So. 2d 1280, 1281 (Fla. 1st DCA 1995)].

Case 2. Karl Gulliford's injury occurred while traveling to work, carrying part of the

Guide to Claims

company's cash receipts with him. This act created an exception to the going and coming rule. Gulliford had taken the cash with him for several years and the parties agreed this task was essential to the business. The business could not open until he arrived each day with the cash. Even on his days off, he would still have to make the trip to deliver the cash. Deciding whether business or personal motives are the dominant purpose of the trip is not necessary. No "nice inquiry" will be made to learn the relative importance of a concurrent business and personal motive. If the business purpose is at least a concurrent cause of the trip, the employer will be liable for workers' compensation [*see* Nikko Gold Coast Cruises v. Gulliford, 448 So. 2d 1002, 1004–1005 (Fla. 1984)].

[iii] Special Errand: Case History

A special errand is a notion similar to a dual purpose. Following are case examples.

Case 1. In a classic example of a special errand, the employer requested the employee to stop on his way home to pick up plumbing supplies. The plumbing store was directly on his way home, and the accident occurred after the employee picked up the supplies and had resumed his trip home. The act of picking up supplies was merely incidental to the trip home. Thus, it did not amount to a dual purpose and such a case is not compensable. Had the accident occurred before picking up the supplies, however, the employee would then have been in the course of his employment and his injury would have been compensable. The point is that the employee had completed the special errand and was back on his regular route home [*see* El Viejo Arco Iris, Inc. v. Luaces, 395 So. 2d 225, 226 (Fla. 1st DCA 1981)].

This case seems to suggest that once the errand is complete and the employee is again en route home, the work relationship ends. This is not necessarily so. If the errand is coupled with the burden of a lengthy round-trip, especially during normally non-working hours, the errand cannot be considered complete until the trip ends. Case 2, below, is a good example.

Case 2. The employer required the employee to attend a special meeting during her normal off-duty hours. While driving home after the meeting she suffered an injury in an automobile accident. The case was compensable because the entire trip was a special errand. The key is whether the travel itself is part of the errand. Thus, in *El Viejo, above,* the employee's errand was complete when he made the purchase because nothing remained other than to continue his trip home [*see* Tampa Airport Hilton Hotel v. Hawkins, 557 So. 2d 953, 954–955 (Fla. 1st DCA 1990)].

Case 3. The employee worked unusually long hours because of a backup of service calls. He usually worked no later then 5:30 p.m. On the day of the accident, however, he did not finish his last service call until 10:30 p.m. Though his last call was only 20 minutes from his home, he had to drive back to the shop to drop off a coworker. During the drive from the shop to his home, he was injured in an automobile accident. The claim was compensable because of the length and burdensome nature of the trip. The question in this and other cases is whether the travel itself is an integral part of the special service provided by the employee [*see* Electronic Service Clinic v. Barnard, 634 So. 2d 707, 709–710 (Fla. 1st DCA 1994)].

[6] Employer Provided Transportation

[a] The Rule

When employers pay for or provide transportation, all travel to and from work is in the course and scope of employment. This does not apply after July 1, 1990, if the employer furnished transportation for the employee's exclusive personal use [§ 440.092(2), Fla. Stat.].

For a general discussion of employer's conveyances, see LARSON'S WORKERS' COMPENSATION, DESK EDITION, Ch. 15 (Matthew Bender).

[b] Accident Dates Through June 30, 1990

The theory behind this rule is based on the employer assuming the obligation to furnish transportation. In such cases, the hazards of the highway are inherent in the contract of employment [*see* Swartzer v. Food Fair Stores, Inc., 175 So. 2d 36, 38 (Fla. 1965)].

The courts favor compensability in these cases. The decisions hold that an employer would not agree to provide or pay for transportation to and from work unless it was for the employer's benefit and convenience. This includes cases where the employer provides a cash allowance for transportation or transports workers in company vehicles. This also includes cases where the employer simply allows the employee to use company owned vehicles.

[c] Accident Dates On or After July 1, 1990

[i] Going and Coming Rule Codified

Effective July 1, 1990, the legislature codified the going and coming rule when it added a new section to the Act. That section provides as follows [§ 440.092(2), Fla. Stat.]:

> An injury suffered while going to or coming from work is not an injury arising out of and in the course of employment *whether or not the employer provided transportation if such means of transportation was available for the exclusive personal use by the employee,* unless the employee was engaged in a special errand or mission for the employer. (Emphasis added)

Deciding that accidents are compensable when they occur in the company bus makes sense. Compensability based on an employer's providing a free company car is another matter. Employers often provide company cars for personal use as a "perk." Employers—and the IRS—consider this part of the employee's compensation. Apparently, the legislature did not believe such generosity should result in increased liability to the employer.

[ii] Exclusive Personal Use

[A] Definition is Illusive

The legislature's use of the phrase, "exclusive personal use," may be important. For example, what is the effect if the employer allows the employee to use a company car for travel to and from work, but restricts all other use to company business? Would this be exclusive personal use?

What is the effect if the employer allows the employee to take a company owned pickup truck home occasionally, with no restrictions on its use? Does exclusive personal use have to be permanent or is it decided day by day? The courts have yet to answer these questions. The legislative intent, however, is clear. Just because the employee is traveling in a company vehicle, available for personal use, does not make an otherwise personal trip a business one. The legislature used the term "personal use" in a clear attempt not to exclude travel in company vehicles done at the employer's direction. If an employer arranges to pick up workers from some central point and transport them to the office, construction site, or farm, for example, the going and coming rule does not apply. Such workers are in the course of their employment.

[B] Judicial Interpretation

The employer sent a car and driver to transport the employee to and from work. Usually the employee paid the employer a nominal fee for this. The court reviewed the 1990 amendment and concluded that this was not transportation provided for the employee's exclusive personal use. The court did not define what "exclusive" means, but only that it is more than the degree of possession or control found here. The employer pointed out that it did not allow other employees to be passengers simultaneously with the injured worker. Thus, the employer argued that the transportation was for the employee's exclusive use. The court found no merit in that argument. From the opinion's tone, however, it appears the court will strictly construe the term "exclusive." Thus, an employee's occasional use of a company vehicle will not likely abrogate the employer provided transportation exception to the going and coming rule [*see* Securex, Inc. v. Couto, 627 So. 2d 595, 596–597 (Fla. 1st DCA 1993)].

Remember, the type of transportation, or who provides it, is not an issue if the employee is on-duty. It is also not an issue if the employee is doing a service for the employer at the time of the accident.

[7] Special Hazard Exception

[a] The Rule

Over the years, the courts have developed a general rule that a special hazard on a normal route used by an employee to enter and exit from the place of work can, under certain circumstances, become a hazard of employment. In such a case the going and coming rule does not apply [*see* Toyota of Pensacola v. Maines, 558 So. 2d 1072, 1075–1076 (Fla. 1st DCA 1990); *see also* [c], *below,* for case history].

For a discussion of special hazards on an employee's normal route, see LARSON'S WORKERS' COMPENSATION, DESK EDITION, Ch. 12 (Matthew Bender).

[b] Applying the Doctrine

Defeating the going and coming rule requires a relationship between the special hazard and the employment. First, the employee must show a special hazard at a particular off-premises location. Second, the special hazard must be one the employee is subjected to abnormally and peculiarly. Note, however, that the special hazard exception may not apply if the employee can choose a safer route. Finally, the special hazard must be on the employee's usual or expected route, or on the means of entry to the workplace [*see* Kash-N-Karry v. Johnson, 617 So. 2d 791, 793–794 (Fla. 1st DCA 1993), *rev. denied,* 629 So. 2d 133 (Fla. 1993)].

In *Kash-N-Karry,* the employee argued that in repealing § 440.26, Fla. Stat. (1989), and in creating § 440.015, Fla. Stat. and § 440.092(2), Fla. Stat., the legislature abolished the special hazard doctrine. That argument requires some explanation. First, § 440.26, Fla. Stat. created a presumption that a claim fell within the provisions of Chapter 440 when an injury indisputably occurred on the job and there was no evidence of causation. The legislature repealed this section effective July 1, 1990. Second, § 440.015, Fla. Stat. (1990) is the so called "level playing field" provision because it instructs courts to not construe the law liberally in either party's favor. The courts have held this provision is nothing more than a codification of long standing legal principles. In other words, § 440.015, Fla. Stat. changed nothing. Finally, § 440.092(2), Fla. Stat. (1990) is the codification of the going and coming rule that eliminated employer-provided transportation as an automatic extension of course and scope of employment [*see generally* ch. 1, § 1.20[1]–[2]].

Whether a special hazard existed is a question we must decide case by case [*see, e.g.,* [c], *below*].

[c] Case History

Case 1. While driving at night during a violent rainstorm, the employee crashed into a tree. He was traveling on a dead-end dirt road that ran beside the employer's property. The Court held that the tree was a special hazard of the employee's job [*see* Naranja Rock Co. v. Dawal Farms, 74 So. 2d 282, 286 (Fla. 1954)].

Case 2. As she usually did to go to work, Colleen Petroske was crossing the driveway that abutted her employer's property. This time she stepped in a pothole and fell. The court held that the pothole was a special hazard of her employment and, thus, the going and coming rule did not apply [*see* Petroske v. Worth Ave. Burger Place, 416 So. 2d 856, 857–858 (Fla. 1st DCA 1982)].

Case 3. Buck Maines worked at a car dealership on a crowded highway. When he began to leave the car lot in his car, he tried to turn left onto the highway. He got no farther than the median when he collided with another car. An expert testified that the area was particularly hazardous. The chance of a motorist becoming involved in an accident there, said the expert, was greater than at most comparable areas on other Florida highways. The judge of compensation claims concluded that because this was the employee's only southbound route, it was uniquely hazardous. The judge found the collision occurred on the employer's literal threshold. This, said the judge, is a special hazard and held the accident compensable. The First District Court of Appeal agreed and added it did not matter that the public is also exposed to the hazard [*see* Toyota of Pensacola v. Maines, 558 So. 2d 1072, 1075–1076 (Fla. 1st DCA 1990)].

Case 4. Victor Betancourt enjoyed bicycling to his job at the Ocean Pavilion Hotel. While peddling on a service road beside the hotel's entrance, a truck came from behind and smashed into him. An expert said the road and the entrance were designed poorly. The judge of compensation claims held that the service road was not only a special hazard, it was also "quasi-company property." The appellate court reversed the decision completely. No evidence existed showing that the accident happened because of alleged special hazards at the hotel's entrance, or that the hotel's staff so habitually used the service road that it became quasi-company property [*see* Ocean Pavilion v. Betancourt, 578 So. 2d 467, 468–469 (Fla. 1st DCA 1991).].

[8] Special Errand Exception

[a] The Rule

If an employee receives a sudden call or is doing a special errand for the employer, the going and coming rule does not apply. Applying this exception depends on the irregularity or suddenness of the request [*see* Spartan Food Systems & Subsid. v. Hopkins, 525 So. 2d 987, 988–989 (Fla. 1st DCA 1988); *see also* [b], *below,* for case history].

For a specific discussion of the special errand rule, see LARSON'S WORKERS' COMPENSATION, DESK EDITION, Ch. 12 (Matthew Bender).

[b] Case History

[i] Compensable Cases

Case 1. A nurse was on her way home when she responded to a call from her employer. The call was for a special job that required her to return to a client's home. During the trip back to the client's home, she was injured in an auto accident. Held: Compensable [*see* Eady v. Medical Personnel Pool, 377 So. 2d 693, 696–697 (Fla. 1979)].

Case 2. A fast-food employee received a sudden call from her employer. The employer asked her to pick up coffee cups from another branch on her way to work. This required a 20-mile detour from her normal route. During the trip she suffered an injury in an auto accident. Although she had made such a trip once before, this did not negate the suddenness and irregularity of the trip. The court held the claim compensable though she had returned to her regular route to work when the accident occurred [*see* Spartan Food Systems & Subsid. v. Hopkins, 525 So. 2d 987, 988–989 (Fla. 1st DCA 1988)].

Case 3. The employee had taken cash receipts home with him for years. On the day of his accident, he was en route to work but was also transporting cash for use by ticket sellers. The business could not open until he arrived with the cash. The Court held such a dual purpose trip compensable [*see* Nikko Gold Coast Cruises v. Gulliford, 448 So. 2d 1002, 1004–1005 (Fla. 1984)].

Case 4. When two other employees failed to appear for work, the employer called the employee at home on her regular day off. She agreed to work and the employer told her she needed to arrive as soon as possible. She took about 45 minutes to get ready and left without breakfast. While driving along her regular route, she stopped at a convenience store to purchase breakfast. She intended to eat while driving, to hasten her arrival. As she exited the store's parking lot, she collided with another car. At trial, the judge of compensation claims found that the employee had no advance notice regarding her need to go to work, thus making the employer's phone call both irregular and sudden. The judge also held that stopping at the store was not a substantial deviation and held the employee's injuries were compensable because she was on a special errand for the employer. The First District Court of Appeal agreed and affirmed. Driving along her normal route to do her regular job are irrelevant facts and do not alter the special errand character of the assignment. Short notice alone is now enough to invoke the special errand exception. That the employee was not responding to an emergency or that she was free to refuse to report for work does not matter. Nor does it matter that she was on her normal route, at her normal time, traveling to do her normal job, and that she encountered no unusual hazards. What does matter is that she received an unexpected call to work on her day off [*see* Publix Supermarkets v. Finocchi, 650 So. 2d 1122, 1123–1124 (Fla. 1st DCA 1995)].

[ii] Non-Compensable Cases

Case 1. The employee was a teacher who had been working at a school football game taking tickets and counting money. On his way home from the stadium, he was injured in an auto accident. The claim was not compensable because working at the game was not an irregular activity, nor was it the result of a sudden call [*see* Gray v. Dade County School Bd., 433 So. 2d 1009, 1011 (Fla. 1st DCA 1983)].

Case 2. A bicycle shop employee was working at a different branch on what was normally a day off. He was injured while riding his bicycle home. According to the employment agreement the employee's hours and work location were to be flexible. The claim was not compensable because the trip home was not an integral part of the employment service [*see* Radomski v. Great Bicycle Shop, Inc., 464 So. 2d 1346, 1348–1349 (Fla. 1st DCA 1985)].

> **NOTE:** The distinction, if any, between the compensable and non-compensable cases is muddy.

§ 7.05 Traveling Employee Doctrine

[1] The Rule

Subject to the 1990 [*see* [4], *below*] and the 1994 [*see* [5], *below*] amendments to the Workers' Compensation Act, the law generally covers employees during travel for their employers. An exception arises if the injury results from or during a distinct departure on a nonessential personal mission [§ 440.092(4), Fla. Stat.].

For general discussions of the traveling employee, see LARSON'S WORKERS' COMPENSATION, DESK EDITION, Chs. 14, 25 (Matthew Bender).

> **SPECIAL ALERT:** The cases have generally held that when the job requires an employee to travel on an overnight mission, the hotel becomes the place of employment. If the employee uses the hotel normally, injuries sustained there are compensable. This is, in essence, an extension of the "bunkhouse" rule discussed in § 7.06.

[2] The Test: Essential Activities

The law considers a traveling employee in the continuous conduct of business. This is true even while not literally working, but also while engaged in such normal and necessary activities as eating and sleeping [*see* Leonard v. Dennis, 465 So. 2d 538, 540 (Fla. 2d DCA 1985)]. Eating and sleeping are obvious examples of essential activities, but the definition of the term "essential" is illusive as the following cases show [*see* [3], *below*].

[3] Case History: Essential Activities

Case 1. Charles Gray, a flight attendant for Eastern Airlines, was in New York on a layover between flights. Gray decided to go to a YMCA near his hotel where he joined a game of pick-up basketball. During the game he broke his nose. The court held the injury compensable because Gray was participating in the game for his personal health and recreation [*see* Gray v. Eastern Airlines, Inc., 475 So. 2d 1288, 1289–1290 (Fla. 1st DCA 1985)].

Case 2. James Leonard was on a field trip inspecting construction sites. One evening, he left his hotel and was driving to a restaurant about four miles away. During the trip Leonard was injured in a smash-up. The carrier defended, claiming this trip was a substantial deviation because Leonard's hotel had its own restaurant and several other restaurants were closer to the hotel. The court, however, held this trip was not a substantial deviation and awarded benefits. No doubt a distance that will be deemed too far exists, but four miles is apparently not enough to show substantial deviation. What distance is too far must be decided case-by-case [*see* Leonard v. Dennis, 465 So. 2d 538, 541 (Fla. 2d DCA 1985)].

Case 3. Bonita Wilmot finished her dinner during an extended layover from her job as a flight attendant for Pan American World Airways. When she tried to light an after-dinner cigarette, the entire match book burst into flame burning her hand. The court held her injury compensable under the personal comfort doctrine [*see* Pan American World Airways v. Wilmot, 492 So. 2d 1373, 1374 (Fla. 1st DCA 1986)].

Case 4. Chandler Rigdon, an Eastern Airlines flight attendant, was on a layover in Portland, Oregon. To attend to his personal health and recreation, Rigdon went snow skiing at a lodge 58 miles from his hotel. Rigdon fell while skiing, suffering a serious leg fracture. Relying on *Gray* and other cases, the judge of compensation claims awarded benefits. The First District Court of Appeal disagreed and reversed the order. The court considered Rigdon's 58-mile skiing adventure too dangerous, too far, and too substantial a deviation to fall within the personal comfort doctrine [*see* Eastern Airlines v. Rigdon, 543 So. 2d 822, 823–824 (Fla. 1st DCA 1989)].

Case 5. The claimant was employed as a limo driver. He was assigned to pick up a passenger at the airport at 10:00 p.m. He dropped off a fare at about 8:00 p.m. and notified his dispatcher that he planned to get dinner before picking up the new fare. At about 8:30 p.m., he was involved in an auto accident. The JCC concluded that because the claimant was on an unpaid dinner break at the time of the accident, he was not performing a business purpose on behalf of the employer. Thus, his injuries did not arise out of the employment, and for that reason the employment could not be considered the major contributing cause of the injuries.

The court reversed, holding that employment status fell squarely within the traveling-employee rule because the claimant's work as a limousine driver consisted exclusively of traveling. In that capacity, he was deemed as a matter of law to be in the service of his employer during his dinner break. Moreover, the court considered it entirely reasonable for him to take meal breaks at restaurants during the time he was on duty. Compensability of his injuries logically followed from the above decisional law. As a result, the court held his injuries arose out of and in the course of employment. Therefore, his employment was the major contributing cause of his injuries [*see* Longo v. Associated Limo, 871 So. 2d 943, 944–945 (Fla. 1st DCA 2004)].

[4] 1990 Amendment

The key in these cases is figuring out which activities are designed to attend to normal creature comforts and necessities. A number of cases have held that sleeping, eating, smoking, drinking, swimming, and now playing sports such as basketball, fall within this category. However, more dangerous sports like snow skiing and scuba diving are personal nonbusiness activities that do not fall within the doctrine [*see* Eastern Airlines v. Rigdon, 543 So. 2d 822, 824 (Fla. 1st DCA 1989)]. The courts have not, unfortunately, provided clear guidance. Instead, the cases hold that compensability hinges on the reasonableness of the activity. Obviously, reasonableness depends on the unique facts of an individual case. In an apparent effort to help, the legislature added the following new section to the Workers' Compensation Act effective July 1, 1990 [§ 440.092(4), Fla. Stat.]:

> TRAVELING EMPLOYEES.—An employee who is required to travel in connection with his employment who suffers an injury while in travel status shall be eligible for benefits under this chapter only if the injury arises out of and in the course of his employment while he is *actively engaged in the duties of his employment,* which shall include travel necessary to and from the place where such duties are to be performed and other activities reasonably required by the travel status. (Emphasis added)

The legislature's apparent intent for the italicized phrase was to limit compensable personal comfort activities to the employment duties only. Employees who are exploring the town, or are out on a date, will do so at their own risk. Under the 1990 amendment, an employee who leaves the hotel that has a restaurant to go out to dinner ought to be considered engaged in a nonessential personal mission. Whether employees were actively engaged in their employment duties, however, is a question of fact for the judge of compensation claims to answer. Nothing in this statutory language appears to overrule the decision in *Leonard v. Dennis,* 465 So. 2d 538 (Fla. 2d DCA 1985). If the legislature intended more than merely codifying case law, such as eliminating the personal comfort doctrine, it appears to have failed. For example, consider the following case decided under the 1990 amendment.

Flight attendant Sheree LeFevers was staying in a hotel, which her employer paid for, while she was on a layover. She was severely injured when she dove into the hotel's swimming pool and struck her head on the bottom of the pool. Relying on the 1990 language of § 440.092(4), Fla. Stat., the carrier denied her claim because she was not literally, actively engaged in doing her duties as the statute seemed to require. The judge of compensation claims, however, concluded the injury was compensable under either the personal comfort doctrine or the bunkhouse rule. On appeal, the First District Court of Appeal agreed with the judge. Because the new statute did not specifically reject the personal comfort doctrine, the court believed it still applies [*see* American Airlines v. LeFevers, 674 So. 2d 940, 942 (Fla. 1st DCA 1996)]. (The personal comfort doctrine is discussed in § 7.09.)

Note that in all but one of the cases discussed here and in [3], *above,* the injured workers were flight attendants on layovers. They had no employment duties other than to relax and refresh themselves before their next flights. From the tone of the opinions we can conclude that in such cases, relaxation and recreation *are* the workers' employment duties. We know from the *LeFevers* decision that there is nothing in the 1990 or the 1994 amendments that change the personal comfort doctrine [*see* § 7.09] or the bunkhouse rule [*see* § 7.06]. Therefore, we can conclude that the law still considers employees actively engaged in doing their duties while attending to their personal comfort or while living in employer-provided premises.

Clearly, the amendments have not changed the law for accidents occurring on the premises. It is not clear if off-premises activities, such as going out to dinner, will still be deemed covered, despite the amendment; however, continued compensability seems likely. The legislature appears to have changed nothing with either the 1990 or the 1994 amendment discussed in [5], *below.* From the statute and the cases a reasonable summation of the law is that traveling employees are covered:

1. While traveling to and from their destination.
2. While actively engaged in the mission their employers sent them to do.
3. While using hotel facilities for eating, sleeping, bathing, swimming, or exercising, etc.
4. While entertaining clients or otherwise doing their jobs.

[5] 1994 Amendment

The key words for compensability in the 1990 amendment are, "and other activities reasonably required by the travel status." That, of course, is what the courts have been saying for years. The legislature, apparently, wanted to be sure that the traveling employee provision does not apply to routine travel to and from work, so it amended the section again effective January 1, 1994. The amended section now provides as follows [§ 440.092(4), Fla. Stat.]:

> TRAVELING EMPLOYEES.—An employee who is required to travel in connection with his or her employment who suffers an injury while in travel status shall be eligible for benefits under this chapter only if the injury arises out of and in the course of employment while he or she is actively engaged in the duties of employment. *This subsection applies to travel necessarily incident to performance of the employee's job responsibility but does not include travel to and from work as provided in subsection (2).* (Emphasis added)

The italicized sentence is the 1994 language. The amendment deleted the reference to travel, "to and from the place where such duties are to be performed." Because this provision alters basic entitlement to benefits, it is likely a substantive amendment that applies only to accidents occurring on or after January 1, 1994.

Workers qualify as a traveling employee if they are required to travel in connection with their employment [*see* Florida Hosp. v. Garabedian, 765 So. 2d 987, 989–990 (Fla. 1st DCA 2000)]. When workers are in travel status, the going and coming rule does not apply [*see* Dunnam v. Olsten Quality Care, 667 So. 2d 948, 950 (Fla. 1st DCA 1996)]. The worker remains in travel status even during the trip home at the end of the work day. The court has stated that "We decline to construe the traveling employee statute to allow a going-and-coming exception that would abrogate workers' compensation coverage in every case once the employee begins travel home, no matter how long or hazardous the route, and no matter whether the employee has been compensated for the travel." The facts that the claimant was reimbursed for her travel expenses and that she drove a hazardous route were persuasive to the court. Although not clearly stated, the court implies that the trip home is compensable even if these facts do not apply [*see* McCormick v. Auditor Gen./Div. of Risk Mgmt., 772 So. 2d 612, 614 (Fla. 1st DCA 2000)].

SPECIAL NOTE: The court has held that its case law applying the traveling-employee rule has *not* been superseded by later statutory amendments [*see* Longo v. Associated Limo, 871 So. 2d 943, 944 (Fla. 1st DCA 2004)].

§ 7.06 Live-in Employees—The Bunkhouse Rule

[1] The Rule

Generally, injuries to employees required to live on the employer's premises are compensable. An essential requirement is that the source of the injury was a risk distinctly associated with conditions under which the employee lived. A second requirement is that the employer required that the employee remain on the premises [*see* Carr v. United States Sugar Corporation, 136 So. 2d 638, 640 (Fla. 1962)].

For a general discussion of resident employees, see Larson's Workers' Compensation, Desk Edition, Ch. 24 (Matthew Bender).

[2] Overview: *Carr v. U.S. Sugar*

All the cases have held that while the live-in employee is using the employer's premises, injuries caused or aggravated by the living conditions are compensable. Following is the lead case on this subject, decided by the Florida Supreme Court.

The employee's job required him to live in a barracks that the employer furnished. The employee was going to see a fellow worker, who lived in another barracks, when he fell down his own barracks stairs. The Court held as follows [Carr v. United States Sugar Corporation, 136 So. 2d 638, 639–640 (Fla. 1962)]:

> The law is well settled . . . that when the contract of employment contemplates that

> the employee shall sleep on the employer's premises, as an incident to the employment, and is injured while not engaged on a purely personal mission, the injury is compensable . . .

If visiting a friend is not a purely personal mission, what is? Defending a claim by a live-in employee on a deviation defense is extremely difficult.

[3] Risk Associated With Employment

This theory, however, does not operate to include every injury that may occur, and specifically not idiopathic injury. For example, Richard Grenon worked as a fire fighter for the City of Palm Harbor. On the day he hurt his back, Grenon was working a 24-hour shift and the fire department required him to live at the firehouse while on-call. He had just finished showering and strained his back while putting on his underwear. About four years before, Grenon had suffered a minor back injury that required only a few visits to the doctor and resulted in two weeks off work. In addition, Grenon suffered from some congenital abnormalities and dysfunctional joints in the L4-5 area. Grenon testified that he did not put on his underwear any differently at the firehouse than he would at home. The judge of compensation claims denied the claim, holding that Grenon's injury was an idiopathic condition unrelated to his employment.

On appeal Grenon argued that the *Carr* case [*see* [2], *above*] stands for the proposition that virtually any injury, including idiopathic injury, is compensable under the bunkhouse rule. The First District Court of Appeal disagreed and affirmed the judge's order. An idiopathic condition is not compensable unless the employment in some way contributes an increased risk of injury peculiar to that employment. To apply the bunkhouse rule as Grenon suggests would give the on-call employee greater coverage than a similar employee injured during the course of employment, but whose employment did not cause the injury. The bunkhouse rule merely brings an on-call period within the course of employment. It does not operate, however, to bring everything within the "arising out of" requirement. Thus, even when the bunkhouse rule applies, the law will not allow recovery if the employee's injury is caused by some internal failure unrelated and unconnected to the employment [*see* Grenon v. City of Palm Harbor Fire Dist., 634 So. 2d 697, 699–700 (Fla. 1st DCA 1994)]. (See also the discussion on idiopathic injury in § 7.14.)

SPECIAL ALERT: If the preexisting condition is from a prior compensable injury, a question of apportionment may arise. In such a case the judge of compensation claims must decide whether the new injury represents an aggravation of the prior compensable injury [*see* ch. 8, § 8.03, on apportionment].

§ 7.07 Deviations—In General

[1] The Rule

If an employee suffers an injury while engaged in a deviation from the job duties, the employee is not eligible for compensation benefits [§ 440.092(3), Fla. Stat.].

For a general discussion of deviations, see LARSON'S WORKERS' COMPENSATION, DESK EDITION, Ch. 17 (Matthew Bender).

[2] Investigation Points

If an employee suffers an injury while doing something outside the job duties, the employee has deviated from the job. During such a deviation the employee is no longer in the course and scope of employment. Recognizing that employees do not always give full attention to duties, the courts make a distinction between small and large deviations. An investigation should focus on answers to the following questions:

1. Why did the employee deviate?
2. What was the time extent of the deviation?
3. What was the physical extent of the deviation?
4. For whom, if anyone, did the employee deviate? (A friend, a stranger, a supervisor?)
5. What, if anything, did the employee accomplish by deviating?
6. Whom did the employee benefit by deviating?
7. Has the employer ever condoned such deviations before?

[3] 1990 Amendment

Effective July 1, 1990, the legislature added the following section to the Workers' Compensation Act [§ 440.092(3), Fla. Stat. (7/1/90)]:

> DEVIATION FROM EMPLOYMENT.—An employee who is injured while deviating from the course of his employment, including leaving the employer's premises, is not eligible for benefits unless the deviation is *expressly* approved by the employer, or unless such deviation or act is in response to an emergency and designed to save life or property. (Emphasis added)

In the past, if the employer approved deviations, the employee continued to be in the course of employment. This was true even if the employer only passively condoned the activity. For example, the employer may be aware of the activity but does not object. The courts consider not objecting, the same as approving. The legislature obviously intended to overrule that theory when it added the requirement that the employer must "expressly" approve the deviation. Merely failing to object or prohibit the activity should no longer be enough. The court, however, does not see it that way, at least when personal comfort is involved. Without even commenting on legislative intent, the court held that employees do not need express approval to attend to their personal needs, even if the need is to leave the premises to purchase cigarettes [*see* § 7.09, for discussion on personal comfort doctrine]. Thus, § 440.092(3), Fla. Stat. applies only while the employee is off premises on a temporary personal mission (other than for personal comfort), and there is no showing of any element of benefit to the employer. The addition of this section does not change existing case law on attending to personal comfort, whether on or off premises. Thus, the court does not view attending to personal comfort, on or off the premises, as a deviation in the first place [Bayfront Medical Center v. Harding, 653 So. 2d 1140, 1141–1142 (Fla. 1st DCA 1995)].

Deviation cases will usually fall into one of the several categories, discussed in §§ 7.08–7.12.

§ 7.08 Deviations: Horseplay

[1] The Rule

When horseplay occurs during a lull in the work, the cases have held that the law does not consider the deviation to involve abandonment of any work duties. This may even be an expected result of such a waiting period. To render an injury not compensable, a deviation must amount to a wholesale abandonment of the employee's work [*see* Boyd v. Florida Mattress Factory, Inc., 128 So. 2d 881, 882–883 (Fla. 1961); *see* [3], *below,* for case history].

For a discussion of horseplay, see LARSON'S WORKERS' COMPENSATION, DESK EDITION, Ch. 23 (Matthew Bender).

[2] Test to Decide Deviation

The test in deviation cases is the distinction between a small and a large deviation. A momentary deviation is not enough. To preclude compensability, deviations must be so significant that they amount to a complete abandonment of the employee's job duties [*see* Boyd v. Florida Mattress Factory, Inc., 128 So. 2d 881, 882–883 (Fla. 1961)]. Despite the new language in the Workers' Compensation Act, the courts will likely continue this view.

[3] Case History

Case 1. Larry Boyd worked as a corporate officer for the Florida Mattress Factory, but also skippered a pleasure boat the company owned and used to entertain customers and suppliers. Boyd had just returned to the dock after a fishing trip to entertain a supplier. As a lark, Boyd lit a cherry bomb firecracker and threw it under the dock. The explosion cost Boyd the sight in his left eye. This happened in 1959 and the judge instinctively ruled against Boyd. On appeal, the Industrial Relations Commission understandably agreed. By 1961, however, the case was before the Florida Supreme Court as one of first impression. It was here that the Court created the distinction between substantial and insubstantial deviations, and defined a substantial deviation as one involving a complete abandonment of job duties. Seeing Boyd's act as merely a whimsical way of doing his job, the Supreme Court reversed and awarded benefits. Doing one's job in a whimsical, negligent, thoughtless, inept, or foolish way does not create a defense based on job duty abandonment. In a lone, but poignant dissent, Justice Thornal expressed amazement at the majority's view that throwing a cherry bomb at a supplier somehow advances the employer's business [*see* Boyd v. Florida Mattress Factory, Inc., 128 So. 2d 881, 882–884 (Fla. 1961)].

Case 2. Eugene Walters, a 14-year-old newspaper carrier, arrived at his work station one afternoon to pick up newspapers for delivery. The 9-year-old paper carrier on duty told Walters the papers were not ready. Walters and another boy, to pass the time, got into a foot race where Walters injured himself. Because the deviation happened during a lull in Walter's work and did not involve an abandonment of his work duties, the court awarded benefits [*see* Times Pub. Co. v. Walters, 382 So. 2d 720, 721–722 (Fla. 1st DCA 1980)].

Case 3. John Wortman worked with a grounds maintenance crew. Wortman, and the rest of the crew, traveled from site to site to clean and mow the employer's and customers' grounds. This was hot and dirty work, but there were no facilities for washing off at the work sites. Wortman and the others, with their foreman's knowledge, often cooled off by going swimming at both public and private swimming pools. On a blistering June day, Wortman and two co-workers stopped at one co-worker's parents' home to cool off in the Alafia River. The home was about two miles from the direct route between job sites. Tragically, when Wortman dove into the river, he struck his head on a rock, broke his neck, and became quadriplegic.

Conceding that cooling off on a hot day may fall under the personal comfort doctrine, the carrier still argued that diving head first into the river was so foolish it amounted to a complete abandonment of job duties. The First District Court of Appeal disagreed and awarded benefits. Because the employer at least impliedly tolerated the men's swimming between jobs, it became reasonably foreseeable. As such, going swimming was an insubstantial deviation [*see* B & B Cash Grocery Stores v. Wortman, 431 So. 2d 171, 173–174 (Fla. 1st DCA 1983)].

Case 4. Donald Harrison, in an effort "to get everyone going," tossed a nail playfully at his supervisor which bounced off him harmlessly. The supervisor picked up the nail and threw it back at Harrison. The nail struck Harrison in an eye, causing serious injury. In ruling the claim compensable, the judge noted that this was horseplay, but involved only a momentary deviation and not a wholesale abandonment of job duties. The First District Court of Appeal agreed and affirmed the order [*see* Jean Fluet, Inc. v. Harrison, 652 So. 2d 1209, 1212 (Fla. 1st DCA 1995)].

Case 5. The claimant, a firefighter, was injured during a playful wrestling match with a co-worker. The testimony was that the claimant and the co-worker were simply "wrestling around" and doing what "guys do at the station." The court noted earlier cases holding that the evidence must show a wholesale abandonment of work duties to bar a claim and that a momentary deviation does not rise to that level. Although the claimant's conduct was contrary to department policy, the court concluded that this activity was momentary and insignificant and did not amount to the abandonment of job duties. Therefore, the court reversed the judge of compensation claims's denial of the claim [*see* Dunlevy v. Seminole County Dep't of Public Safety, 792 So. 2d 592, 594 (Fla. 1st DCA 2001)].

As the cases above reveal, the courts usually find a case compensable if it involves only a momentary deviation without obvious danger. This is especially true if the activity occurs during a lull in work with no abandonment of employment duties. Put another way, a case involving "fooling around" is not going to be the basis of a winning defense unless the conduct is almost outrageous. Remember, however, that conduct may appear outrageous to one person, but not to another. Outrageous conduct can be defined as grossly offensive or heinous. Such conduct precludes compensability. On the other hand, merely

Guide to Claims

stupid conduct will not likely disturb an otherwise compensable event. Conduct is stupid if it shows a lack of good sense or intelligence. Injuries resulting from one's own stupidity are compensable.

§ 7.09 Personal Comfort Doctrine

[1] The Rule

Although not specifically addressed in the statute, the cases have consistently held that workers are within the course and scope of employment while reasonably attending to their personal comfort. Lunchtime accidents on the employer's premises, for example, are compensable. However, when employees with fixed time and place of work leave the premises for lunch, they are outside the course of their employment. Accidents occurring while employees are on a rest break or attending to their personal comfort are also compensable. An exception arises only if some substantial deviation during such breaks occurred [*see generally* Citrus Memorial Hospital v. Cabrera, 388 So. 2d 345, 346 (Fla. 1st DCA 1980); City of Miami v. Dwight, 637 So. 2d 981, 983–984 (Fla. 1st DCA 1994); Bayfront Medical Center v. Harding, 653 So. 2d 1140, 1141 (Fla. 1st DCA 1995)].

For a general discussion of the personal comfort doctrine, see LARSON'S WORKERS' COMPENSATION, DESK EDITION, Ch. 21 (Matthew Bender).

[2] Lunch Time Accidents

[a] Lunch Periods on Employer's Premises

Employees who take their lunch periods on the employer's premises are still in the course of employment, and any injury suffered during this time is compensable [*see* Doctor's Business Service, Inc. v. Clark, 498 So. 2d 659, 662 (Fla. 1st DCA 1986)]. An exception arises if the employee was engaged in a substantial deviation when the lunch time injury occurred. We can decide whether the activities are a substantial deviation only on a case-by-case basis.

[b] Lunch Periods Away From Employer's Premises

Florida courts have adopted Professor Larson's theory on the compensability of off-premises accidents, especially when they occur during the trip to and from lunch. Larson's rule is as follows [*see* LARSON'S WORKERS' COMPENSATION, DESK EDITION, Ch. 13, § 13.05 (Matthew Bender)]:

> When the employee has a definite place and time of work, and the time of work does not include the lunch hour, the trip away from and back to the premises for the purpose of getting lunch is indistinguishable in principle from the trip at the beginning and end of the work day, and should be governed by the same rules and exceptions. . . . The same exceptions apply here as in other going and coming cases.

Questions arise when two or more co-workers take their lunch periods together and the almost inevitable job discussion occurs. Does such work-related discussion bring the lunch within the employment? As a rule, job discussions during an otherwise social event do not change the social character of the trip. If job or business discussions occur coincidentally with an otherwise social lunch gathering, an insufficient business purpose exists to make injuries compensable that are suffered during this time. Courts recognize that job discussions are almost inevitable when co-workers gather socially. Simply having work related topics arise during off premises lunch time conversation does not automatically transform an otherwise social event into a "working lunch." Conversely, when the purpose of the trip is business and lunch is coincidental, employees continue to be in the course of employment [*see* City of Miami v. Dwight, 637 So. 2d 981, 982–983 (Fla. 1st DCA 1994)].

[3] Personal Comfort and Rest Breaks

Florida courts have approved Professor Larson's theory of distinguishing between "lunch periods" and "breaks" [*see* [1], [2][b], *above*]. The going and coming rule has so far been treated as substantially identical whether the trip involves the lunch period, or the beginning and end of the work day. This can be justified. Normally the duration of the lunch period, when lunch is taken off the premises, is substantial. The employees' freedom of movement is so complete that the obligations and controls of employment can justifiably be said to be in suspension during this time.

Florida courts have been consistent in awarding benefits for injuries suffered during rest breaks while on the premises. Short duration rest breaks off the premises are also, generally, in the course of employment. Coffee breaks and rest breaks have become common. Therefore, questions will arise about the compensability of injuries occurring off the premises during such breaks. Also, because the circumstances vary so much, the *Dwight* court held that: "It is clear that one cannot announce an all-purpose 'coffee break rule', since there are too many variables that could affect the result." The court did, however, announce the following operative principle we can use to draw the line [*see* City of Miami v. Dwight, 637 So. 2d 981, 983 (Fla. 1st DCA 1994)]:

> If the employer, in all the circumstances, including duration, shortness of the off-premises distance, and limitations on off-premises activity during the interval can be deemed to have retained authority over the employee, the off-premises injury may be found to be within the course of employment.

[4] Case History

Injuries suffered while an employee is attending to personal comfort, especially on the premises, are not deviations and are usually compensable. An employer derives a benefit when employees improve morale by attending to their health and personal comfort. Activities that benefit the employer "arise out of" the employment. Following are case examples of such activities held compensable:

Case 1. The employee became ill following administration of free flu shots the employer provided [*see* Monette v. Manatee Memorial Hosp., 579 So. 2d 195, 196–197 (Fla. 1st DCA 1991)].

Case 2. The employee became ill from drinking a contaminated soft drink purchased on the employer's premises [*see* Louis v. Louis's Amoco, 534 So. 2d 417, 418 (Fla. 1st DCA 1988)].

Case 3. The employee was injured while using a rest room at work [*see* Citrus Memorial Hospital v. Cabrera, 388 So. 2d 345, 346 (Fla. 1st DCA 1980)].

Case 4. The employee was injured by defective electric socks worn to stay warm at work [*see* Baker v. Orange County Bd. of Cty. Com'rs, 399 So. 2d 400, 401 (Fla. 1st DCA 1981)].

[5] 1990 Amendment

In 1990, the legislature created § 440.092(3), Fla. Stat. to require express employer approval for employee deviations, especially off premises [*see* § 7.07]. With this amendment, the legislature tried but failed to abolish coverage during off-premises breaks unless the employer expressly approved of the deviation. The First District Court of Appeal held that § 440.092(3), Fla. Stat. has no such effect when personal comfort is involved. Following are the facts of the case.

Peter Harding left work, apparently to go to a convenience store to buy cigarettes. While crossing the street, a car struck him. Harding's bosses did not expressly approve this trip, but they did not forbid it either. Such travel during breaks was common among other employees. Despite the language in § 440.092(3), Fla. Stat., the court held this was clearly a personal comfort break and the section did not preclude compensability. The section applies only if the injury happens off the employer's premises on a temporary personal mission without a showing of any benefit to the employer. That, of course, has long been the law. Thus, the amendment changes nothing [*see* Bayfront Medical Center v. Harding, 653 So. 2d 1140, 1141–1142 (Fla. 1st DCA 1995)].

Following are two examples of deviations that the court held compensable. These are the kind of deviations that the 1990 amendment tried, but failed to eliminate from compensability. The effort failed because the courts do not consider attending to personal comfort a deviation from work.

In the first case, the employee suffered a serious injury when he went on a swimming excursion between work functions on a hot day. This was, apparently, a common practice. The Court held that the employer's knowledge of this practice was implied consent, making the injury compensable [*see* B&B Cash Grocery Stores v. Wortman, 431 So. 2d 171, 173 (Fla. 1st DCA 1983)].

In the second case, a car struck the employee while he was crossing the street during working hours to buy a package of cigarettes at a convenience store. The court awarded compensation because employees routinely frequented the store and because the employer failed to enforce a policy discouraging such trips [*see* Holly Hill Fruit Products, Inc. v. Krider, 473 So. 2d 829, 830–831 (Fla. 1st DCA 1985)].

In these cases, the employer's consent was implied because the employer did not expressly forbid the deviation. For accidents occurring on or after July 1, 1990, such cases will require express approval by the employer in order to be compensable, unless the trip is to attend to personal comfort.

Note the special treatment given in the Act for responding to an emergency. For example, if during the course of employment, an employee happens upon the scene of an auto accident and is injured while giving aid, the law entitles the employee to compensation [*see* § 7.11, the Positional Risk Doctrine].

§ 7.10 Personal Errands

[1] The Rule

Employees who are engaged on a purely personal errand are not in the course of their employment [*see* Drinnenberg v. State Dept. of Transportation, 481 So. 2d 51, 52 (Fla. 2d DCA 1985)].

[2] Overview

A personal errand must be a substantial deviation to take employees out of the scope of their employment. For example, an employee was working overtime at his employer's request. A co-worker told him that a police officer was ticketing his car. He left his job to make his way to his car when a passing vehicle struck him. The Court awarded compensation because it found the deviation was insubstantial. Further, the Court held that the employee's departure was for the benefit of his employer. How did the employer benefit? In part, said the Court, because the employee would complete additional work as a result of his willingness to work overtime. The real key to these cases is whether the employer benefits in any manner [*see* Pixley v. Packer Pontiac Company, 131 So. 2d 721, 722–723 (Fla. 1961)].

§ 7.11 Positional Risk Doctrine

[1] The Rule

Injuries are compensable if the employment places employees in a position that requires them, by ordinary standards of humanity, to respond to an emergency [§ 440.092(3), Fla. Stat.].

For general discussions of the positional risk doctrine, see LARSON'S WORKERS' COMPENSATION, DESK EDITION, Ch. 3, § 3.05, Ch. 8, § 8.04 (Matthew Bender).

[2] The Doctrine

Discussing the Positional Risk Doctrine is done best with an example. Strangers asked the employee to help push a disabled vehicle from the highway. The employee did so, but was injured in the process. The Florida Supreme Court held as follows [D.L. Cullifer and Son, Inc. v. Martinez, 572 So. 2d 1360, 1363 (Fla. 1990)]:

> When an employee, during the course of his employment, perceives an imminent danger to the public, such as an obstruction in the roadway, an endeavor to alleviate the danger should be considered incidental to his employment.

The Court took note of the 1990 amendment to the Workers' Compensation Act that created § 440.092(3), Fla. Stat. This section codified a public policy of encouraging employees to undertake humanitarian acts designed to prevent harm to the public. The

Guide to Claims

relevant part says that deviations from the employment preclude compensation "unless such deviation is in response to an emergency and designed to save life or property."

Note, however, that the doctrine does not require an act as dramatic as attempting to save lives following a motor vehicle accident. For example, while working as a used car salesman, claimant saw a vehicle pull in front of the dealership where he was working and watched as a female exited the vehicle, walked onto his employer's premises, and took "some property." Claimant testified that he initially was unsure what she had taken, but he instinctively pursued her on foot as she jumped back in the vehicle. In his pursuit of the perpetrator, claimant left the employer's property, crossed the sidewalk, and caught up to the vehicle. Once there, he noticed that the item stolen from the lot was actually a $15 "bubble machine" that claimant had purchased in an attempt to attract customers to the business. Claimant proceeded to lunge inside the passenger window of the vehicle in an attempt to grab the bubble machine. At that moment, the driver sped away, dragging claimant down the street. Claimant was eventually thrown underneath the vehicle and run over. Due to the accident, claimant sustained multiple injuries.

The court noted that if the emergency deviation is designed to save life or property, the injury must be considered one that arises out of and in the course and scope of employment and should be compensable. However, the court held that there is nothing in case law or in the language of § 440.092(3), Fla. Stat. to suggest that the employer must have an interest in the life or property being saved in order for the injury to be compensable. Under a plain reading of the statute, all that is required in order for a deviation to be compensable is: (1) the deviation is an emergency; and (2) the emergency is designed to save life or property. Because both of these prongs were met here, the court reversed the judge of compensation claims' order denying the claim and held that the accident was compensable. Claimant was responding to an emergency, and his response was designed to save property. The court held that nothing in § 440.092(3), Fla. Stat. (2003) precludes a claimant from receiving benefits simply because the property he or she was saving turned out to be his or her own [*see* Deutsch v. Heritage Auto. Enterprises, 939 So. 2d 259 (Fla. 1st DCA 2006)].

§ 7.12 Recreational and Social Activities

[1] The Rule

Injuries suffered during recreational and social activities may be compensable depending on the accident's date and the degree of employer involvement [*see* [2], [3], *below*].

For a general discussion of recreational and social activities, see Larson's Workers' Compensation, Desk Edition, Ch. 22 (Matthew Bender).

[2] Accidents Before July 1, 1990

[a] Recreational Activities and *Brockman* Test

In 1983, the court announced a three-pronged test, commonly called the *Brockman* test. This test decided the circumstances under which recreational or social activities came within the course of one's employment. Injuries suffered before July 1, 1990, during such activities were compensable if [*see* Brockman v. City of Dania, 428 So. 2d 745 (Fla. 1st DCA 1983)]:

1. They happened on the employer's premises during a lunch or recreation period as a regular incident of the employment;
2. The employer, by expressly or impliedly requiring participation, or by making the activity part of the services of an employee, brought the activity within the orbit of the employment; or
3. The employer derived substantial direct benefit from the activity beyond the intangible value of improvement in employee health and morale that is common to all kinds of recreation and social life.

[b] Athletic Events

[i] Factors for Compensability

Generally, if the factors listed below are present, they suggest that an injury suffered during an athletic event is compensable. The more factors present in a particular case, the more likely the accident is compensable.

1. The employee was pressured into participating, especially if the pressure is from management.
2. The team members included employees only.
3. The employee received pay while playing.
4. The employee received time off to play.
5. The employer provided transportation to and from the game.
6. The employer gained benefit from sponsorship via advertising or employee participation. (Are the games attended by potential customers of the employer?)
7. The injury occurred during a lunch or recreation period, on the premises, as a regular incident of the employment.

Case examples follow in [ii], *below*.

[ii] Case History

[A] Non-Compensable Injuries

Case 1. Ray Hutchinson, a school teacher, suffered an injury while participating in a school Wellness Committee softball game. The school designed the program to benefit the employees, and participation was entirely voluntary. The team members included only school faculty, so students were not present. The faculty played games on school grounds on Sundays. The injured employee admitted his job security would not have been affected if he did not participate. Because participation was entirely voluntary, the case did not meet the requirements of the *Brockman* test and was not compensable [*see* Hutchinson v. Dade County School Bd., 561 So. 2d 1291, 1292–1293 (Fla. 1st DCA 1990)].

Case 2. Gilbert Lemon was hurt while playing softball on a team his employer sponsored periodically. Team members included employees, their spouses, and others. Players did not hold any of the games or practice sessions on company time or property. Lemon admitted that his employer did not require him to play, nor did it encourage his participation. He did claim, however, that the employer "benefitted" in several ways. Employees, he claimed, would often discuss business at restaurants and bars after the games, and once he received a sales lead as a result of such discussions. A former employee testified that "thousands" of sales leads were obtained at the games and that the players talked and thought about work.

Holding that the first two prongs of the *Brockman* test did not apply, the court then concentrated on the third prong: substantial direct benefit to the employer. The court then held that none of the alleged benefits to the employer were substantial enough. "A substantial direct benefit to the employer contemplates more than the intangible, undefined benefits referred to here. . . . Advertising, publicity, and financial benefits are examples of those types of benefits that can be shown and found to be sufficient." The court of appeal reversed the order awarding benefits [*see* Copytronics v. Lemon, 588 So. 2d 23, 24 (Fla. 1st DCA 1991)].

[B] Compensable Injuries

Bari Italian Food sponsored a team of its employees in the city softball league by providing the entry fee and team uniforms that bore its name. Participation was voluntary for everyone. No games or practices took place on company property. The company did not schedule the games. Employees held games and practices on their own time, but they did post notices of the games on the company premises. The judge of compensation claims held that the claim was compensable and the First District Court of Appeal agreed. The employer, said the court, received advertising and publicity benefits from the team's efforts. In addition, team members and other employees patronized company clients after the games [*see* Bari Italian Food v. Rittger, 527 So. 2d 255, 256–257 (Fla. 1st DCA 1988)].

[c] Social Events

[i] Overview: *Sterling v. Mike Brown, Inc.*

This section examines social events such as company picnics and company Christmas parties. The same tests as in [a]–[b], *above,* apply here. Look for compulsion to attend. Does the employer benefit? Oddly enough there were no Florida cases dealing with company Christmas parties until the court's ruling in *Sterling v. Mike Brown, Inc.,* 580 So. 2d 832 (Fla. 1st DCA 1991).

In *Sterling,* the employer closed the business for the afternoon to hold a Christmas party for employees and other guests on its premises. By mid-afternoon the boss decided that Walter Sterling was too drunk to drive the company truck home, and took the truck keys from him. By seven o'clock that evening, most of the guests were leaving. A co-worker offered to drive Sterling home and then back to work the next day. Sterling became angry and shoved the co-worker several times. This provoked the co-worker who smashed Sterling in the face with a closed fist. Sterling fell backwards and struck his head on a concrete floor resulting in severe injuries.

[ii] Applying *Brockman* Tests to *Sterling*

Prong 1. The accident must occur on the premises during a lunch or recreation period as a regular incident of the employment. Although the party took place on company property, the employer had closed the business for the day. Further, the employees did not regard a company Christmas party as a fringe benefit to which they were entitled. Although such parties occurred the previous few years, it had not become "a regular incident of the employment" within the meaning of Prong 1 of the test [*Sterling v. Mike Brown, Inc.*, 580 So. 2d 832, 834 (Fla. 1st DCA 1991)].

Prong 2. The employer, by expressly or impliedly requiring participation, or by making the activity part of the services of an employee, brings the activity within the orbit of the employment. The court found no attendance requirement and employees who testified said they felt no compulsion to attend. Not all employees were present. The employees did not receive pay while attending and the employer did not require them to work if they did not attend. No attendance records were kept. The employee had failed Prong 2 of the *Brockman* test (*see* [2][a], *above*) [Sterling v. Mike Brown, Inc., 580 So. 2d 832, 834–835 (Fla. 1st DCA 1991)].

Prong 3. The employer must derive substantial direct benefit from the activity beyond the intangible value of improvement in employee health and morale that is common to all kinds of recreation and social life. No evidence about the employer's motivation for holding the party was presented. Absent such evidence, the court held it could then be implied that the sole purpose was to improve employee morale. The employer had not invited any customers. The employer did not attempt to deduct the cost of the party as a business expense. Finally, the employer did not use the gathering as an opportunity to make speeches, present awards, or conduct other business. Based on these facts, the court held the employee did not meet Prong 3 of the test and held the case not compensable [Sterling v. Mike Brown, Inc., 580 So. 2d 832, 835 (Fla. 1st DCA 1991)].

> **NOTE:** The *Sterling* court also held that even if the injury had arisen out of and in the course of employment, it still would not be compensable because of the employee's intoxication [Sterling v. Mike Brown, Inc., 580 So. 2d 832, 835–836 (Fla. 1st DCA 1991); *see* ch. 9, § 9.02, on the Intoxication Defense, and ch. 6, § 6.08[4], on the Aggressor Doctrine].

[3] Accidents After July 1, 1990

[a] 1990 Amendment

Effective July 1, 1990, the legislature added a new section to the Workers' Compensation Act, apparently intended to overrule *Brockman*. This amendment makes compensability in recreational and social activity cases more restrictive, but somewhat easier to decide. The new section provides as follows [§ 440.092(1), Fla. Stat. (7/1/90)]:

> RECREATIONAL AND SOCIAL ACTIVITIES.—Recreational or social activities are not compensable unless such recreational or social activities are an expressly required incident of employment AND produce a substantial direct benefit to the

employer beyond improvement in employee health and morale that is common to all kinds of recreation and social life. (Emphasis added)

[b] Effect on *Brockman* Test

With this new language the *Brockman* test [*see* [2][a], *above*] no longer applies, at least not in its present form. The *Brockman* test requires that an employee meet only one of the three prongs. The new section requires both an express requirement to participate and that the employer also realizes a "substantial direct benefit" from the employee's involvement. This is not an "either/or" situation. Both an express requirement to participate and substantial benefit to the employer must be shown. This section will not, however, affect the first prong of the test holding that an injury is compensable if it occurs on the premises during a lunch or recreation period as a regular incident of the employment. If a case meets those conditions, the claim will be compensable unless other defenses apply.

In 1992, that Court noted, "It appears that the statutory change was enacted to avoid compensability in situations where the activity in question was neither part of the job duties of an individual or expressly required by the employer." The Court noted that there was nothing in the statute that would indicate a desire to preclude compensation when a person was injured in conducting actual job duties. If the JCC finds that the facts of a case are controlled by § 440.092(1), Fla. Stat., compensability may be found if there is record support for finding of both "an expressly required incident of employment" and "a substantial direct benefit to the employer beyond improvement in employee health and morale" as required by the statute [Highlands County School Bd. v. Savage, 609 So. 2d 133, 135 (Fla. 1st DCA 1992)].

In 2005, the court repeated its holding in *Savage*. The court noted that § 440.092(1), Fla. Stat. (2003), provides that "recreational or social activities are not compensable unless such activities are:

(1) An expressly required incident of employment; and

(2) Produce a substantial direct benefit to the employer beyond improvement in employee health and morale that is common to all kinds of recreation and social life.

The court held that, unless *both* of these statutory criteria are present, regardless of any other circumstance, an injury sustained during recreational or social activities is not compensable [*see* Whitehead v. Orange County Sheriff's Dep't, 909 So. 2d 344 (Fla. 1st DCA 2005)].

§ 7.13 Subsequent Intervening Accidents

[1] The Rule

[a] Before July 1, 1990

Injury is compensable if the accident was the direct and natural result of the original injury [*see* Central Concrete Co., Inc. v. Harris, 475 So. 2d 1300, 1301–1302 (Fla. 1st DCA 1985)].

[b] Between July 1, 1990, and December 31, 1993

Injury is compensable if the accident was the direct and natural result of the original injury or, if caused by an outside agency, was suffered only while traveling to or from a health care provider to get remedial treatment for the original compensable injury [§ 440.092(5), Fla. Stat. (7/1/90)].

[c] On or After January 1, 1994

Besides the provisions of § 440.092(5), Fla. Stat. described in [b], *above,* the Act now provides that even if the subsequent injury is the result of the original compensable injury, the subsequent injury is not compensable unless the original injury is the "major contributing cause" of the subsequent injury [§ 440.09(1)(a), Fla. Stat. (1/1/94)].

[2] Major Contributing Cause Requirement

Occasionally, an injured worker suffers another injury while recovering from the first injury. To be compensable, such intervening accidents before July 1, 1990, must have been only a natural result of the original industrial accident and injury. Effective with accidents occurring on or after January 1, 1994, the original injury also must be the "major contributing cause" of the new injury [§ 440.092(5), Fla. Stat.]. For a complete discussion of the major contributing cause requirement, *see* § 7.01[4]. How these various amendments apply is discussed in [3]–[5], *below.* Each amendment appears to be substantive and should apply to only those accidents occurring on or after the effective date. Subsequent accident cases generally fall into three basic categories [*see* [3][a]–[c], *below*].

[3] Categories of Intervening Accidents

[a] Category 1. Subsequent Accident Occurs While Traveling To or From a Health Care Provider

The law considers injured workers to be in the course and scope of their employment while they are traveling to or from health care providers' offices. This applies, however, only if the trip's purpose is to obtain medical care for work-related injuries.

For example, the employee suffered a second injury in an auto accident while riding as a passenger in a rehabilitation nurse's car. The nurse was transporting him to a store to buy work shoes. Since this trip had nothing to do with medical treatment, the court held the injury not compensable [*see* Central Concrete Co., Inc. v. Harris, 475 So. 2d 1300, 1301–1302 (Fla. 1st DCA, 1985)].

[b] Category 2. The First Injury Causes the Second Accident

[i] Natural Result Test

When a primary injury is shown to have arisen out of and in the course of the employee's employment, every natural result of that injury will also be held to have arisen out of the employment, unless it is the result of an independent, intervening cause [*see* Central Concrete Co., Inc. v. Harris, 475 So. 2d 1300, 1301–1302 (Fla. 1st DCA 1985)].

As an example, assume the employee suffered a compensable knee injury at work.

Later, the injured knee gave way, causing the employee to fall down stairs at home. Under these facts, the subsequent injury resulting from the fall also would be compensable.

[ii] Direct Causation Required

The original injury must be the direct cause and not merely a factor. For example, Rowena Christilles suffered a knee injury at work aggravated by advanced degenerative arthritis. After considerable time, she recovered enough to go back to work, but she still suffered from the effects of the arthritis. While at home, she fell down the stairs resulting in another injury. Christilles claimed that her injured knee gave way, causing her to fall, but the evidence did not support this. The trial judge found that the fall down the stairs was not compensable because the natural progression of Christilles' preexisting (and unrelated) arthritic condition caused her knee to collapse. Thus, the second accident was not the natural result of the first injury. The First District Court of Appeal agreed and affirmed the denial [*see* Christilles v. H.J. Wilson Co., Inc., 513 So. 2d 208, 209 (Fla. 1st DCA 1987)].

[iii] Liability of Replacement Carrier

What happens if the employer changes insurance carriers between the first and second accidents? The courts will allocate responsibility between the carriers based upon the extent to which each accident contributed to the employee's need for medical care and disability benefits [*see* Sauer Indus. Contracting Inc. v. Ditch, 547 So. 2d 276, 277 (Fla. 1st DCA 1989)].

For example, Kemper Insurance Company was the carrier when Dee Gaskill injured his knee and back in 1987. Gaskill returned to work, but had continuing medical problems. In 1989, he was simply walking across the floor when his injured knee gave way, causing him to fall. This happened several times before, always without warning. This time, however, he fractured his wrist and injured his neck and back when he fell. A dispute arose because, at the time of the second accident in 1989, the employer had changed carriers and was now insured by CNA Insurance Company. The judge of compensation claims found that the second injury was the direct and natural result of the 1987 accident. The First District Court of Appeal agreed and held that Kemper, the carrier at the time of the first accident, was exclusively liable [*see* CNA Ins. Co. v. Kemper Ins. Co., 596 So. 2d 81, 83 (Fla. 1st DCA 1992)].

[c] Category 3. Medical Treatment Causes Additional Injury

Occasionally, the nature of the medical care given the employee results in further injury. In such a case, the courts have held that the additional injury is the natural result of the original injury and is compensable [*see* Telcon, Inc. v. Williams, 500 So. 2d 266, 267–270 (Fla. 1st DCA 1986)].

The court carried this third category to extremes in a case where the physician instructed the employee to take walks as part of her therapy. During one of these walks a car struck her. The court held this to be compensable [*see* D.O.T., State of Florida v. King, 554 So. 2d 1192, 1193 (Fla. 1st DCA 1989), *rev. denied,* 563 So. 2d 631 (Fla. 1990)].

[4] 1990 Amendment

In reaction to decisions such as *King* in [3][c], *above,* the legislature added the following section to the Workers' Compensation Act effective for accidents occurring on or after July 1, 1990 [§ 440.092(5), Fla. Stat.]:

> SUBSEQUENT INTERVENING ACCIDENTS.—Injuries caused by a subsequent intervening accident *arising from an outside agency which* are the direct and natural consequence of the original injury are not compensable unless suffered while traveling to or from a health care provider for the purpose of receiving remedial treatment for the compensable injury. (Emphasis added)

This amendment should not affect Category 1 type cases since the section specifically includes travel to and from a health care provider's office [*see* [3][a], *above*]. The amendment also should not affect Category 2 type cases [*see* [3][b], *above*]. The section prevents compensation only for subsequent accidents caused by an outside agency and not by the employee's own internal bodily failures. The new section should, however, eliminate Category 3 cases from compensability [*see* [3][c], *above*].

The legislature enacted this amendment, apparently, to eliminate the "walking therapy" situations as occurred in *King.* One must wonder if it also eliminates further injury caused by the treatment itself such as in a case of medical malpractice. A health care provider is clearly an "outside agency" and the "subsequent accident" could occur in the provider's office and not while traveling to or from the place of treatment. It is unlikely, however, that the legislature intended to remove such subsequent injury from compensability.

In one case, the carrier attempted an imaginative defense of a subsequent injury based on this section. Chris March injured his right foot in a compensable accident. Four months later, with his leg in a cast and while using crutches, his left foot went out from under him and he fell down a flight of stairs. The carrier argued that March's left foot was an outside agency and, as such, the court should deny the claim. The court disagreed and held that the employee himself cannot be considered "an outside agency" [*see* U-Haul of South Florida v. March, 645 So. 2d 581 (Fla. 1st DCA 1994)].

[5] Major Contributing Cause Requirement

Although the legislature did not amend § 440.092(5), Fla. Stat., it did add the following provision effective with accidents occurring on or after January 1, 1994 [§ 440.09(1)(a), Fla. Stat. (1/1/94)]:

> This chapter does not require any compensation or benefits for any subsequent injury the employee suffers as a result of an original injury arising out of and in the course of employment *unless the original injury is the major contributing cause of the subsequent injury.* (Emphasis added)

The effect of this provision on Category 1 cases is unclear. The Act specifically includes travel to and from health care providers in § 440.092(5), Fla. Stat., as discussed in [3][a], *above.* Will the courts hold the travel itself to be the major contributing cause or will they base this determination on the facts of the accident? For example, assume the employee is driving to the doctor and a muscle spasm causes loss of control and the car crashes.

Here, the original injury is clearly the "major contributing cause" of the accident.

Suppose, however, the same employee collides with a drunk driver who ran a red light. Is the travel the major contributing cause or is it the negligence of the other driver? A best bet interpretation is the courts will hold the travel itself is the major contributing cause. If so, the amendment will not affect medical travel cases.

The amendment also will not affect Category 2 cases since the appellate decisions already require direct causation [*see* [3][b], *above*]. This amendment appears to have merely codified case law for this category.

The amendment also does not appear to affect Category 3 cases. The courts have held that further injury caused by medical treatment is a natural consequence of the original injury and is compensable [*see* [3][c], *above*]. Arguing that something which is a natural consequence is not also a major contributing cause will be a difficult argument to support. For a complete discussion of the major contributing cause requirement, *see* § 7.01[4].

[6] Subsequent Injury: On or After October 1, 2003

Effective October 1, 2003, the law requires that, to be compensable, a subsequent injury must meet the same requirements as for the aggravation of a preexisting condition in § 440.15(5)(b), Fla. Stat. (10/1/2003) [*see* § 440.15(5)(a), Fla. Stat. (10/1/2003); ch. 8, § 8.02].

§ 7.14 Idiopathic Falls and Injury

[1] The Rule

When a worker suffers from an idiopathic, or preexisting, condition which results in injury, the injury is compensable only if it arose out of the employment. The employee must show that the employment in some way contributed to the risk or aggravated the injury [*see* Southern Bell Tel. & Tel. Co. v. McCook, 355 So. 2d 1166, 1168 (Fla. 1977)]. The employment circumstances must have presented a risk different from those necessarily encountered in non-employment life to create a causal connection between the new injury and the preexisting condition [*see* Market Food Distrib., Inc. v. Levenson, 383 So. 2d 726, 727 (Fla. 1st DCA 1980)].

In 2004, the court revisited the basis for compensability de novo and now holds that under the 1994 amendments the existence of an increased hazard must be determined case-by-case [*see* Duval County Sch. Bd. v. Golly, 867 So. 2d 491, 494 (Fla. 1st DCA 2004); *see also* [14], *below*].

For a general discussion of an original compensable injury causing subsequent injury, see LARSON'S WORKERS' COMPENSATION, DESK EDITION, Ch. 10, § 10.01 (Matthew Bender).

[2] Idiopathic Defined

The issue here concerns injuries that happen at work, but result from a condition personal to the employee, and not by any condition of the workplace. We refer to these personal conditions as idiopathic. *Webster's Ninth New Collegiate Dictionary* defines "idiopathic" as a condition "arising spontaneously or from an obscure or unknown cause, peculiar to the individual." The *PDR Medical Dictionary*, First Edition, defines idiopathic as "a disease of unknown cause."

Distinguishing between injury suffered solely because of an idiopathic condition and injury suffered because of a combination of the condition and an increased hazard in the workplace is very important. In the first situation, idiopathic condition alone, the injury develops because of routine activity unrelated to the employment in any meaningful way. These cases are not compensable [*see* Southern Bell Tel. & Tel. Co. v. McCook, 355 So. 2d 1166, 1168–1169 (Fla. 1977)].

The second situation involves some unrelated (to the employment) defect in the individual, such as fainting or epileptic seizure. The defect causes the individual to fall or otherwise suffer an accident. This often results in additional injury, but the injury must result from an increased workplace hazard unique to the employment [*see* Market Food Distrib., Inc. v. Levenson, 383 So. 2d 726, 727 (Fla. 1st DCA 1980)]. An example might be an employee who faints from an idiopathic condition and falls onto a piece of machinery. In cases such as this, the unrelated problem is never compensable, but the new injury may be. The debate will revolve around whether a hazard, unique to the employment, caused the new injury.

When carriers intend to defend a claim under this section, they must be prepared to first prove that an idiopathic, or preexisting, condition exists. If the injured worker has no prior weakness or disease, any exertion connected with the employment and causally connected with the injury as a medical fact satisfies the legal test of causation. Absent evidence of a causal relationship with an idiopathic condition, an unexpected injury occurring during the ordinary performance of the worker's duties in the usual manner is a compensable accident. It is not necessary that the injured worker show that there was a slip, fall, or other mishap. Thus, the definition of "accident" includes an internal failure such as a ruptured disc or a snapped knee cap.

For example, Andrea Bryant worked as a housekeeper at David Lawrence Mental Health Center. In the course of her normal duties, she squatted to lift a bag of laundry from the floor. Before she actually lifted the bag, Bryant felt immediate pain from what turned out to be a torn medial meniscus in her right knee. (The meniscus is crescent shaped cartilage. The medial meniscus is in the middle of the knee.) The judge of compensation claims denied her claim on the theory that the injury was idiopathic. Since Bryant did not suffer a literal accident, such as a slip or fall, the judge held that Bryant's employment did not create an increased hazard. No evidence existed, however, that Bryant had any preexisting defect or injury to her knee, so the appeals court reversed the judge's order [*see* Bryant v. David Lawrence Mental Hlth. Ctr., 672 So. 2d 629, 631–632 (Fla. 1st DCA 1996)].

[3] Fall From an Unknown Cause

Sometimes deciding whether an idiopathic fall caused the injury can be difficult. In one case the employee fell to the floor at work. No one knew why he fell. He could have slipped or he could have fallen for strictly idiopathic reasons. The rule of law in these cases is this: when an injury occurs at work, a presumption exists that it is a compensable accident. The burden then shifts to the carrier to show that the injury was not work related.

If, however, there is conflicting evidence about the cause of the injury, then the employee must show a causal connection between the employment and the injury. Here, no evidence showed how the accident occurred, but only that it did occur. Accordingly, under the presumptions as then provided by statute, the Supreme Court held the claim compensable [*see* Hacker v. St. Petersburg Kennel Club, 396 So. 2d 161, 162–163 (Fla. 1981)].

[4] Increased Hazard of Employment

The first problem will be to decide whether workplace conditions present an increased hazard unique to the employment. Often, the existence of an increased hazard is easy to decide. For example, over the years the courts have agreed that falling from high places is an increased hazard, as is falling onto dangerous objects. The courts have held the following to be dangerous objects: a sawhorse, an iron motor box, a hot stove, a spot welding machine, a sharp corner of a wooden table, and a fire built by a co-worker. Falls onto level floors or onto soft objects are not so clear cut. (These situations are discussed in [6]–[12], *below.*)

The second problem is to find out whether an idiopathic condition caused the accident as opposed to one that occurs more conventionally. Generally, an increased hazard is a greater hazard than that found in the employee's personal, off-duty life. This topic has been controversial and the subject of debate for decades. It has been an issue frequently addressed by the Florida Supreme Court.

For a brief discussion of the increased-risk doctrine, see LARSON'S WORKERS' COMPENSATION, DESK EDITION, Ch. 3, § 3.03 (Matthew Bender).

[5] Routine Movements

In the landmark case of *Southern Bell Tel. & Tel. Co. v. McCook* [355 So. 2d 1166, 1169 (Fla. 1977)], McCook experienced a sharp pain in her back when she reached over to pick up tissue paper from the floor. Doctors discovered that McCook had a congenital defect in her lower back. Everyone agreed that the same injury could have happened any time or place she might have made a similar movement. The Florida Supreme Court held such an injury does not arise out of the employment, is peculiar to the worker, and is not compensable.

In another example, Richard Grenon worked as a fire fighter for the City of Palm Harbor. On the day of his injury, Grenon was working a 24-hour shift. He had just finished showering and strained his back while putting on his underwear. About four years before, Grenon suffered a minor back injury that required only a few visits to the doctor and resulted in two weeks off work. In addition, Grenon suffered from some congenital abnormalities and dysfunctional joints in his back. Grenon testified that he did not put on his underwear any differently at the firehouse than he would have at home. The judge of compensation claims denied the claim. The judge held that Grenon's injury was an idiopathic condition unrelated to his employment. On appeal the First District Court of Appeal agreed with the judge. The court held that Grenon's idiopathic condition was not compensable because his job did not contribute an increased risk of injury peculiar to that employment. The court also held that the bunkhouse rule applied, but did not eliminate the requirement that the cause of the injury should be distinctly associated with the conditions with which the employee lived [*see* Grenon v. City of Palm Harbor Fire Dist., 634 So. 2d 697, 699–700 (Fla. 1st DCA 1994)].

[6] Fall Onto a Bare Concrete Floor

At age 67, Walter Cline suffered from heart disease, which caused fainting spells. One day he fainted, fell onto a concrete floor, and struck his head. He died of the resulting skull fracture. This case is one of first impression. It was here that the Florida Supreme Court first announced the following precept: "Our act affords no relief for disease or physical ailment not produced by industry."

The Court held that Cline did not die of his preexisting heart disease. He died of the trauma of the skull fracture and, thus, the injury was compensable. No one raised the idea of an increased hazard and the Court did not mention whether it considered a concrete floor to be an increased hazard. (In 1955, the Court revisited its holding in *Protectu Awning* and now opined that the hardness of a bare concrete floor was an increased hazard attributable to the employment; see the discussion on *Foxworth v. Florida I.R.C.* in [7], *below*.) We must remember though, that this case happened in the middle of World War II and the Court's sympathy for a frail, but dedicated, defense worker was obvious [*see* Protectu Awning Shutter Co. v. Cline, 154 Fla. 30, 16 So. 2d 342, 343 (1944)].

In the same year (i.e., 1944) in another case, the Supreme Court expanded on the idea that industry ought to be responsible for only those injuries it causes. The Court explained that the Workers' Compensation Act was not designed to replace general health and accident insurance [*see* General Properties Co. v. Greening, 154 Fla. 814, 18 So. 2d 908, 911 (1944)].

[7] Fall Onto an Upholstered Chair

Employee Foxworth suffered a stroke, passed out, and fell onto an upholstered chair. Foxworth suffered a fractured hip as a result. The Florida Supreme Court held that an upholstered chair is not a dangerous object and denied the claim [*see* Foxworth v. Florida Industrial Commission, 86 So. 2d 147, 151–152 (Fla. 1955)].

[8] Fall Onto Linoleum-Covered Concrete Floor

The employee fainted because of an idiopathic condition (i.e., scoliosis, which is a lateral curvature of the spine), and fell onto a linoleum-covered concrete floor. The Florida Supreme Court held the injury was compensable for two reasons. First, the employer had required the employee to work overtime and this contributed to the fainting. Second, the hardness of the tiled concrete floor was a special hazard of the employment. The test is whether the injury was as likely to have occurred in the employee's home [*see* Lovett v. Gore Newspapers Co., 419 So. 2d 306, 308 (Fla. 1982)].

[9] Fall Onto a Tile-Covered Wood Floor

The employee suffered an epileptic seizure that caused him to fall to a tile-covered,

Guide to Claims

wood floor. (Epilepsy is a brain disorder characterized by sudden, brief attacks of altered consciousness, motor activities, or sensory phenomena. Convulsive seizures are the most common form of attacks.) The Florida Supreme Court agreed with the trial judge that the employee's neck and back sprains were not compensable. The Court did not address the issue of whether a tile-covered wood floor was an increased hazard, because doctors testified that the employee would have suffered the same injuries even if he had fallen onto something softer. Thus, the employee's accident and injury were personal and unrelated to his employment [*see* Southern Convalescent Home v. Wilson, 285 So. 2d 404, 408 (Fla. 1973)].

[10] Fall Onto a Desk

The employee suffered a seizure and fell, striking his head on an office desk. The Florida Supreme Court denied the claim. No evidence was presented to show that the desk was more a hazard of employment than any ordinary piece of furniture would be [*see* Federal Electric Corporation v. Best, 274 So. 2d 886, 889 (Fla. 1973)].

[11] Fall Onto Carpeted Floor

Thelma Grimes was afflicted with polio and had to wear a full-length leg brace. ("Polio" is an abbreviation for poliomyelitis. Polio is an acute viral disease causing inflammation of the grey matter of the spinal cord. It often results in atrophy of groups of muscles ending in permanent deformity.) One day the brace's locking device failed. This caused her to fall and fracture her ankle. The judge of compensation claims denied the claim, holding the employment did not contribute to the injury in any way other than that she was at work when the injury occurred. On appeal, the First District Court of Appeal reversed the judge, but was itself reversed by the Florida Supreme Court. The Supreme Court refused to adopt the court of appeal's theory that the "actual-risk doctrine" should apply. (The actual-risk doctrine holds that almost any injury suffered at work is compensable.) Under this doctrine it does not matter whether the risk is also common to the public. Ample evidence supported the judge's finding that Grimes' employment in no way contributed to her injury. The Florida Legislature, said the Court, never intended workers' compensation coverage to be so broad [*see* Leon County School Bd. v. Grimes, 548 So. 2d 205, 207–208 (Fla. 1989)].

[12] Fall Onto a Paved Parking Lot

Randy Dokoupil was a substitute school teacher who suffered from anorexia, liver disease, and osteoporosis. (Anorexia is an eating disorder resulting in loss of appetite and often associated with depression. Osteoporosis is a general term used to describe any disease process that results in reduction in the mass of bone.) One morning Dokoupil realized he had forgotten important materials in his car and went out to the parking lot to get them. While walking back toward the building, loose papers from his attendance book fell out. While bending over to pick them up, he lost his balance and fell. Someone helped him up, but when he had walked another 40 feet he slid to the ground unable to walk any further. As a result he suffered a broken hip. The judge of compensation claims awarded benefits because the injury happened in the course of employment, but the First District Court of Appeal reversed. Dokoupil suffered a "trivial" fall and no evidence showed that the employment created an increased hazard of such a fall or of the injuries that resulted [*see* Hernando County School Bd. v. Dokoupil, 667 So. 2d 275, 276–277 (Fla. 1st DCA 1995)].

[13] Automobile Accidents

Scott Deturk was in the usual course of his job, driving to the bank to make a night deposit for his employer. He passed out from an idiopathic condition and crashed into the back of another car. The trial judge denied the claim. He based his decision on evidence that Deturk spent more than half of his driving time for personal reasons rather than work-related reasons. Thus, the judge held that driving a car did not pose an increased hazard.

On appeal, the First District Court of Appeal found itself with the difficult task of reconciling this case with all the previous idiopathic accident cases. The task was difficult because all of the previous cases dealt with falls, and this one, for the first time, dealt with an automobile collision. The court solved its dilemma by holding that driving a car on public highways is an increased hazard of employment and reversed the lower court's denial of the claim. Driving a car must be an increased hazard, the court reasoned, because Florida has long held that an automobile is a dangerous instrumentality. Requiring an employee to operate a dangerous instrumentality automatically subjects the employee to an increased hazard [*see* Deturk v. Charlotte County Bd. of County Com'rs, 642 So. 2d 779, 782 (Fla. 1st DCA 1994), *rev. dismissed,* 651 So. 2d 1192 (Fla. 1995)].

[14] Increased Hazard Determined Case-By-Case

Most of the cases discussed above applied to the Workers' Compensation Act as it existed before the 1994 amendments creating the major-contributing-cause standard. In visiting this issue de novo in 2004, the court now holds that compensability in idiopathic fall and increased-hazard cases must be determined based on the specific facts of each case and that increased hazard cannot be decided as a matter of law.

In *Duval County Sch. Bd. v. Golly* [867 So. 2d 491 (Fla. 1st DCA 2004)], the claimant, Mr. Golly, was employed as a teacher at Terry Parker High School. While standing on a level concrete walkway during a planning period, Mr. Golly fell to the ground and sustained a severe closed head injury and broken left thigh. The medical testimony in the case concluded that Mr. Golly's fall was due to a seizure and syncopal episode. The JCC found, and competent substantial evidence supported the finding, that the seizure and syncopal episode resulted from alcohol withdrawal syndrome unrelated to Mr. Golly's employment as a high school teacher. Mr. Golly's serious injuries did not result simply because he lost consciousness. Instead, these injuries resulted from his impact with the concrete walkway. The question in this case was, thus, whether a workplace impact with a level concrete surface, following a fall precipitated by an idiopathic or pre-existing condition, is compensable as a matter of law. This question has to do with what has been called the increased or special hazard doctrine in Florida law. Because the JCC concluded, as a matter of law, that the concrete floor should be considered a special hazard of employment, the court reviewed this matter de novo.

The JCC relied on *Protectu Awning Shutter Co. v. Cline* [154 Fla. 30, 16 So. 2d 342

(1944)]. In *Cline*, the 67-year-old claimant suffered a fainting spell, apparently related to a heart problem, and fell, striking his head against a concrete floor, causing a skull fracture and death. The Florida Supreme Court characterized the issue as whether "the injury arises out of and in the course of the employment" [Protectu Awning Shutter Co. v. Cline, 154 Fla. 30, 16 So. 2d 342, 343 (1944)]. The Court then described the public policy behind the Workers' Compensation Act in 1944:

> The purpose of the act is to shoulder on industry the expense incident to the hazards of industry; to lift from the public the burden to support those incapacitated by industry and to ultimately pass on to the consumers of the products of industry such expenses.

The Supreme Court built on this pronouncement by observing, "In this critical war period, industry requires the services of the aged and infirm. The Compensation Law is based primarily on social responsibility of one to another." The court sustained recovery. Importantly, the court characterized the appeal as "a border line case" [Protectu Awning Shutter Co. v. Cline, 154 Fla. 30, 16 So. 2d 342, 343 (1944)].

The DCA in *Golly* noted that underlying the ruling is the Court's conclusion, apparently arrived at based on its own knowledge rather than on evidence in the case, that although Mr. Cline might have fallen and sustained a fatal injury in his own house, that would be less likely had he remained "in the quiet of his own home, for without the physical exertion encountered in his work by a man of his age and physical condition, the chances of his falling were less likely" [Protectu Awning Shutter Co. v. Cline, 154 Fla. 30, 16 So. 2d 342, 343 (1944)].

In *Foxworth v. Florida Industrial Commission*, the claimant, an employee of the Industrial Commission, blacked out, fell, and struck a hotel lobby floor. The Florida Supreme Court examined the doctrine of increased hazard as applied to an idiopathic fall onto a level floor and noted that the area was "highly controversial." The *Foxworth* court noted that, following *Cline*, Florida has "favored the more liberal view allowing recovery." Nevertheless, the court characterized the *Cline* facts as "the outer limits of the doctrine." "To extend the rule further would be to eradicate completely the statutory requirement that the injury must be one arising out of the employment. The employment in some manner must contribute an increased hazard peculiar to the employment" [Foxworth v. Florida Industrial Commission, 86 So. 2d 147, 151 (Fla. 1955)]. The Court upheld the denial of benefits [Foxworth v. Florida Industrial Commission, 86 So. 2d 147, 152 (Fla. 1955)].

In *Lovett v. Gore Newspapers*, the Supreme Court upheld recovery for a worker who, while working an overtime shift, felt ill and then fell to a "tiled concrete floor, aggravating a pre-existing back condition. The Supreme Court allowed a recovery, applying the special hazard doctrine. The Court also noted, in a comment (that the *Golly* court did not find extraneous), "petitioner was required to work two hours beyond her normal eight-hour shift despite her protestations that she was not feeling well." This factor, combined with the fall to a concrete floor, led the Court to conclude, "It cannot fairly be said that petitioner would just as likely have sustained an injury such as the one that occurred if she had been in her own home" [Lovett v. Gore Newspapers Co., 419 So. 2d 306, 308 (Fla. 1982)].

In addition to relying on the foregoing Supreme Court cases, the appellee in *Golly* also relied on the DCA's decision in *Haynes v. World Color Press* [794 So. 2d 674 (Fla. 1st DCA 2001)]. Claimant Haynes had a syncopal episode resulting in a fall, apparently, to a concrete floor, resulting also in the entanglement of her leg in a machine. On appeal, Haynes argued that the JCC's finding that the syncopal episode, rather than a slip on water, caused the fall was not supported by competent substantial evidence. The 1st DCA rejected that contention. Haynes also argued that even if she had a syncopal episode, the JCC should have allowed compensation based on the special hazard doctrine of *Cline* and *Foxworth*. The 1st DCA found the second issue to be unpreserved and therefore did not reach it. Here, the court stated that appellee Golly grasped onto the language used by the *Haynes* Court to characterize the unpreserved argument. The court described the unpreserved allegation as an "increased hazard" posed by "the concrete floor upon which she fell, or the machine in which her leg was entangled."

The 1st DCA in *Golly* noted that it continues to recognize the special or increased-hazard doctrine. Discussing *Foxworth*, the 1st DCA has noted, "When the fall is onto a level surface, compensability is justified when the surface itself is an unusual hazard, such as a hard concrete floor" [Hernando County Sch. Bd. v. Dokoupil, 667 So. 2d 275, 276 (Fla. 1st DCA 1995)]. Although the court observed in *Dokoupil* that a concrete floor had been previously held an unusual hazard, the court directed that the JCC must now apply the major-contributing-cause test required by § 440.02(32), Fla. Stat. [Hernando County Sch. Bd. v. Dokoupil, 667 So. 2d 275, 277 (Fla. 1st DCA 1995)]. That statute provides:

> "Arising out of" pertains to occupational causation. An accidental injury or death arises out of employment if work performed in the course and scope of employment is the major contributing cause of the injury or death.

The court stated that "Our cases confirm that the present test is different from that used before the major statutory revision several years ago. 'As this court has recognized, the 1994 amendments to the workers' compensation law changed the prior case law definition of 'arising out of' as used in chapter 440' " [Orange County MIS Dep't v. Hak, 710 So. 2d 998, 999 (Fla. 1st DCA 1998)].

The court has characterized the pre-1994 law as follows:

In the absence of an idiopathic or preexisting condition, a claimant's employment had to constitute only a contributing, competent, precipitating, or accelerating cause of the accident or injury. If the claimant had an idiopathic or preexisting condition, then for the injury to be compensable, the employment had to expose the claimant "to conditions that would substantially contribute to the risk of injury and to which the claimant would not normally be exposed during his non-employment life" [Vigliotti v. K-Mart Corp., 680 So. 2d 466, 468 (Fla. 1st DCA 1996)].

Now, under the terms of § 440.02(32), Fla. Stat., "the claimant must establish that the employment occurrence is the most preponderant cause of the injury" [Orange County MIS Dep't v. Hak, 710 So. 2d 998, 999 (Fla. 1st DCA 1998)]. The court observed that the statutory changes, as the court has construed them, very strongly suggest that a claimant must now make a specialized, fact-based showing in order to succeed under the increased-hazard doctrine.

Applying the major-contributing-cause statute in *Golly*, the court could not say that a fall to a level concrete floor is automatically compensable, irrespective of the cause of the fall. The court held that the statute now directs the JCC to make a determination of whether work performed in the course and scope of employment is the major contributing cause of the injury. The Supreme Court in 1944 had no major-contributing-cause statute with which to contend. The DCA observed that, the Supreme Court, in an admittedly "border line case," applied a paternalistic public policy that is no longer justified under the Florida Workers' Compensation Act [Protectu Awning Shutter Co. v. Cline, 154 Fla. 30, 16 So. 2d 342, 343 (1944)]. The court pointed out that the Legislature, upon amending the Workers' Compensation Act in 1993, set out a legislative intent that differed from that which had prevailed earlier.

Among other things, the Legislature stated:

> It is the specific intent of the Legislature that workers' compensation cases shall be decided on their merits . . . . In addition, it is the intent of the Legislature that the facts in a workers' compensation case are not to be interpreted liberally in favor of either the rights of the injured worker or the rights of the employer . . . . [T]he laws pertaining to workers' compensation are to be construed in accordance with the basic principles of statutory construction and not liberally in favor of either employee or employer [§ 440.015, Fla. Stat.].

The JCC in the *Golly* case did not make a particularized finding of special or increased hazard. Instead, the JCC felt constrained by *Cline* to find that the concrete surface was, as a matter of law, an increased hazard. The major-contributing-cause statute, as applied by the 1st DCA in *Dokoupil*, requires a particularized finding of "whether the claimant's conditions of employment created an increased risk of the injuries he sustained" [Hernando County Sch. Bd. v. Dokoupil, 667 So. 2d 275, 277 (Fla. 1st DCA 1995)].

Accordingly, the court reversed the order on appeal and remanded for further proceedings consistent with its opinion [*see* Duval County Sch. Bd. v. Golly, 867 So. 2d 491, 494 (Fla. 1st DCA 2004)].

NOTE: In a dissenting opinion, Judge Ervin said: "It is unclear from the majority's opinion whether it has concluded that the legislatures [*sic*] enactment of the major-contributing-cause (MCC) statutes has repealed the increased-hazard doctrine, recognized in this jurisdiction for 60 years. If the doctrine remains viable, I see no reason to remand for the judge of compensation claims (JCC) to determine whether the conditions of employment (here, a concrete walkway) created an increased risk to claimant."

There appears to be nothing contained in the opinion (contrary to Judge Ervin's observations) that eliminates the increased-hazard doctrine. Indeed, the majority specifically states that the court continues to recognize the special or increased-hazard doctrine. Instead, the majority opinion appears to stand for the proposition that no particular condition may be automatically deemed an increased hazard, as a matter of law. Instead, the issue must be decided case-by-case. Although Judge Ervin appears to believe that the increased-hazard nature of a concrete walkway is self-evident, the majority view appears to be to the contrary. It appears that deciding compensability in these idiopathic fall cases requires application of the court's *Vigliotti* standard:

> If the claimant had an idiopathic or preexisting condition, then for the injury to be compensable, the employment had to expose the claimant "to conditions that would substantially contribute to the risk of injury *and* to which the claimant would not normally be exposed during his non-employment life" [Vigliotti v. K-Mart Corp., 680 So. 2d 466, 468 (Fla. 1st DCA 1996)].

May it be fairly said that people are not generally exposed to bare concrete walkways in their non-employment lives?

CHAPTER 8

OCCUPATIONAL DISEASE, ACCELERATION OR AGGRAVATION OF DISEASE, AND APPORTIONMENT

Guide to Claims

SYNOPSIS

§ 8.01 Occupational Disease

[1] The Rule

Occupational disease is compensable if [§ 440.151(2), Fla. Stat.]:

1. A condition peculiar to the occupation causes the disease [*see* [8][a], *below*].
2. The employee contracts the disease during employment in the occupation [*see* [8][b], *below*].
3. The occupation presents a particular hazard of the disease [*see* [8][c], *below*].
4. The incidence of ordinary diseases of life is substantially higher in the

occupation than in the public [*see* [8][d], *below*].

5. The nature of the employment was the major contributing cause of the disease [*see* [8][e], *below*].

6. There are epidemiological studies showing that exposure to the specific substance involved, at the levels to which the employee was exposed, may cause the precise disease sustained by the employee [*see* [8][f], *below*].

For a general discussion of occupational disease, see LARSON'S WORKERS' COMPENSATION, DESK EDITION, Ch. 52 (Matthew Bender).

Guide to Claims

[2] Overview

Occupational disease is a separate and distinct idea in workers' compensation law. Do not confuse it with an accident causing a disease or accidental acceleration or aggravation of a preexisting disease. To be compensable, the law requires that the disease result from the nature of the employee's occupation, rather than the specific job. Further, the law requires that the employee contracted the disease while engaged in the particular occupation [§ 440.151, Fla. Stat.].

The occupation, however, must have attached to it a particular hazard of the disease. The hazard must be such that we can distinguish it from the universe of occupations. In the alternative, the occurrence of the disease must be substantially higher in the particular occupation than in other occupations [*see* Broward Indus. Plating, Inc. v. Weiby, 394 So. 2d 1117, 1119 (Fla. 1st DCA 1981)].

[3] Last Employer Liable for Occupational Disease

Many occupational diseases take years to reveal themselves. During this time the employee may have had many jobs with different employers in the same occupation. We need not decide with which employer the employee originally contracted the disease. The employer whose job last injuriously exposed the employee will be liable. The insurance carrier on the risk at the time the employee was last injuriously exposed also will be liable. The intent here is to end debate over who must pay the claim [*see* Wood v. Harry Harmon Insulation, 511 So. 2d 690, 692–693 (Fla. 1st DCA 1987)].

[4] Occupational Disease Defined

Distinguishing between an occupational disease and an ordinary accident is critical. The Workers' Compensation Act gives significantly different treatment to occupational disease cases. For accidents occurring through September 30, 2003, the Act defines occupational disease as follows [§ 440.151(2), Fla. Stat.]:

> [A] disease which is due to causes and conditions which are characteristic of and peculiar to a particular trade, occupation, process, or employment, and to exclude all ordinary diseases of life to which the general public is exposed, unless the incidence of the disease is substantially higher in the particular trade, occupation, process, or employment than for the general public.

Effective October 1, 2003, the Legislature amended the statutory definition of occupational disease as follows [§ 440.151(2), Fla. Stat. (10/1/2003)]:

> [A] disease which is due to causes and conditions which are characteristic of and peculiar to a particular trade, occupation, process, or employment, and to exclude all ordinary diseases of life to which the general public is exposed, unless the incidence of the disease is substantially higher in the particular trade, occupation, process, or employment than for the general public. *"Occupational disease" means only a disease for which there are epidemiological studies showing that exposure to the specific substance involved, at the levels to which the employee was exposed, may cause the precise disease sustained by the employee.* [*Emphasis added*]

Because the amendment creates a new burden of proof for the employee, this is probably a substantive amendment that applies only to accidents occurring on or after October 1, 2003. Indeed, § 440.151(4), Fla. Stat. provides that: "This section shall not apply to cases of occupational disease in which the last injurious exposure to the hazards of such disease occurred before this section shall have taken effect."

We do not look beyond § 440.151, Fla. Stat. to define its relevant terms. The occupational disease provision language of section 440.151, is "plain," and "so long as an occupational disease fits within the criteria enumerated therein, such disease constitutes a compensable injury" (emphasis added) [*see* Watkins Eng'rs & Constructors v. Wise, 698 So. 2d 294, 295 (Fla. 1st DCA 1997)]. A claimant either meets the requirements for coverage under § 440.151, Fla. Stat., or he or she does not.

The court has previously refused to incorporate other subsections of the Act to add to or supplement the clearly delineated requirements set forth in § 440.151, Fla. Stat.. Not every disease or adverse medical condition in which employment is a contributing cause, or even the major contributing cause, qualifies as an occupational disease. Even when a condition of employment causes a permanent disease, failure to meet the statutory requirements of § 440.151, Fla. Stat. means the claimant would not be entitled to compensation or benefits under the Act [*see* Broward Indus. Plating v. Weiby, 394 So. 2d 1117 (Fla. 1st DCA 1981)].

Because the statute requires disablement or death, neither compensation nor benefits are available until the employee suffers disablement or death [*see* Fla. Power Corp. v. Brown, 863 So. 2d 364, 365 (Fla. 1st DCA 2003) (noting that, even though employee was diagnosed with asbestosis, a permanent disease caused by his employment, since he had not suffered "disablement," his disease was not an occupational disease under the Act)].

Based on the statutory definition, a disease must result in disability or death to qualify as an occupational disease. Effective October 1, 2003, the Legislature amended the statute to define "disablement" to mean "disability" as set forth in § 440.02(13), Fla. Stat. [*see* § 440.151(3), Fla. Stat. (2003)]. The statute, § 440.02(13), Fla. Stat., defines disability as follows:

> (13) "Disability" means incapacity because of the injury to earn in the same or any other employment the wages, which the employee was receiving at the time of the injury.

Thus, the statute requires a claimant actually be incapable of performing his work. Until incapacitated, at least partially, no coverage for a disease or medical condition is available under the Act, because a claimant's disease or medical condition has not resulted in disablement as the statute defines that term [*see* City of Mary Esther v. McArtor, 902 So. 2d 942, 944 (Fla. 1st DCA 2005) ("Determining whether a person is disabled for purposes of workers' compensation turns on the person's capacity to earn income . . .")].

Therefore, a claimant's disease, such as hypertension, must have caused him to miss work. If the claimant did not miss work, he cannot demonstrate an incapacity resulting in actual wage loss. Without incapacity resulting in actual wage loss, a claimant cannot show disablement. Without disablement, the claimant's disease does not meet the statutory definition of an occupational disease. Without an occupational disease, the claimant's disease (such as hypertension) cannot be treated as the happening of an injury by accident. Without an injury by accident, a necessary prerequisite to the applicability of Chapter 440, a claimant's disease is not covered under the Act. Without coverage under the Act, a claimant is not eligible for benefits under § 440.15(3), Fla. Stat. [*see* City of Port Orange v. Sedacca, 2007 Fla. App. LEXIS 5196 (Fla. 1st DCA 2007)].

Note: As Judge Benton noted in his concurring opinion, the *City of Port Orange* case may have limited practical significance. This case arose because the statutory public safety workers' presumption [*see* [12], *below*] combined with a routine physical examination to produce a permanent impairment" in an employee who had not experienced symptoms. (The employee, a firefighter, was diagnosed with hypertension).

Judge Benton said, "When employees have been symptomatic and ill enough with occupational diseases to have to miss work, they have thereby suffered 'disablement,' defined by statute as 'an employee's becoming actually incapacitated, partially or totally, because of an occupational disease, from performing her or his work . . . ,' § 440.151(3), Fla. Stat. (2002); or, since October 1, 2003, a 'disability,' statutorily defined as 'incapacity because of the injury to earn in the same or any other employment the wages which the employee was receiving at the time of the injury.' § 440.02(13), Fla. Stat. (2003); see also § 440.151(1)(a), Fla. Stat. (2003) (requiring that 'the disablement or death of an employee resulting from an occupational disease . . . be treated as the happening of an injury by accident[.]')" [*see* City of Port Orange v. Sedacca, 2007 Fla. App. LEXIS 5196 (Fla. 1st DCA 2007)].

SPECIAL ALERT: The current statutory definition of occupational disease does not apply to first responders defined as law enforcement officers, firefighters, emergency medical technicians, or paramedics. In 2007 the legislature deleted the 2003 language requiring epidemiological studies. Therefore, for first responders, the definition of occupation disease is as it was prior to October 1, 2003 [*see* § 112.1815(4), Fla. Stat.].

For a discussion of the definition of occupational disease, see LARSON'S WORKERS' COMPENSATION, DESK EDITION, Ch. 52, § 52.03 (Matthew Bender).

[5] Case History

Case 1: Carpal Tunnel Syndrome. The carpal tunnel is the canal in the wrist through which the median nerve passes. Carpal Tunnel Syndrome is pain or numbness affecting some part of the median nerve distribution of the hands. Often, there is a history of cumulative trauma to the wrist, especially with carpenters, rowers, or those who regularly use vibrating tools or machinery. Here, the court held that carpal tunnel syndrome is not an occupational disease. It is, however, compensable under a repeated trauma theory [*see* Simon Sez, Inc. v. Ferrer, 567 So. 2d 51, 52 (Fla. 1st DCA 1990)]. Carpal tunnel syndrome is not an occupational disease, but is instead a repetitive trauma or exposure and, therefore, apportionment may apply [*see* Associated Indus. Ins. v. Federal Ins., 707 So. 2d 880, 882–883 (Fla. 1st DCA 1998)].

Case 2: Hearing Loss. Hearing loss from excessive noise levels and air pollution in a downtown area does not qualify as an occupational disease. Hearing loss may be compensable, however, under an exposure theory [*see* City of Miami v. Tomberlin, 492 So. 2d 433, 435 (Fla. 1st DCA 1986)].

Case 3: Dermatitis. Dermatitis is an inflamation of the skin evidenced by itching, redness, and various skin lesions. Although not a specific issue in the case, the court described the employee's dermatitis, caused by allergic reaction to wet cement, as an occupational disease [*see* OBS Co., Inc. v. Freeney, 475 So. 2d 947, 949, 951 (Fla. 1st DCA 1985)].

Case 4: Hepatitis. Hepatitis is an inflamation of the liver caused by a variety of agents, including viral infection, bacterial invasion, and physical or chemical agents. Recall that ordinary diseases of life are not usually compensable. An exception arises if the incidence of the disease is higher in the injured worker's occupation. These cases require significant investigation. In one case, the trial judge found sufficient evidence to show that the incidence of hepatitis B is substantially higher in health care workers than in other occupations. The Appellate Court affirmed and held that an injured worker need not prove a specific incident of exposure. The worker needs to show only the elements of the occupational disease test [*see* Wuesthoff Memorial Hosp. v. Hurlbert, 548 So. 2d 771, 775 (Fla. 1st DCA 1989)].

Case 5: Repetitive trauma. The law considers disability resulting from repetitive trauma an occupational disease, at least for purposes of the statute of limitations [*see* ch. 6, § 6.07, for a complete discussion of repetitive trauma]. This is a logical conclusion because disability from a series of trivial traumas, like an actual disease, often develops over a long period of time [*see* Kulick v. Entertainment Publications, Inc., 667 So. 2d 303, 304–305 (Fla. 1st DCA 1995)].

[6] Special Defense in Occupational Disease Cases

Because the employer with whom the employee is last injuriously exposed is liable for compensation, the legislature added an additional defense. The law does not entitle employees to any benefits if they lie about their medical history at the time of entering the employment [§ 440.15(5)(a), Fla. Stat.; *see* ch. 25, § 25.06[1]]. Such statements must be in writing and must be about never having been disabled, laid off, or compensated for the disease in question [*see* § 8.02].

Another distinctive defense in occupational disease cases is that the statute of limitations does not begin to run until the first day of disability [*see* ch. 9, § 9.03[5]].

[7] Special Reporting Requirement

Generally, an employee must report an injury to the employer within 30 days after the accident. In occupational disease cases, however, the law extends the period for reporting to 90 days. The 90-day period does not begin until the employee first becomes incapacitated [§ 440.151(3), (6), Fla. Stat.].

[8] Elements of Compensability

[a] Employment Conditions That Are Characteristic of and Peculiar to a Particular Occupation Must Cause the Disease

This element requires medical evidence. Allergic reaction to wet cement meets the test, whereas general noise in the city does not. Clear evidence of causal connection between the employment and the disease must be shown. Speculation or guessing is not enough [*see* Harris v. Josephs of Greater Miami, Inc., 122 So. 2d 561, 562 (Fla. 1960)].

[b] Employee Must Contract Disease During Employment in the Particular Occupation

The law does not require proof of a specific exposure if the employee meets the basic tests for compensability of an occupational disease as set forth in *Broward Industrial Plating* (*see* § 8.01[2]) [Wuesthoff Memorial Hosp. v. Hurlbert, 548 So. 2d 771, 775 (Fla. 1st DCA 1989)].

[c] Occupation Must Present a Particular Hazard of the Disease

The hazard must occur frequently enough to distinguish the injured worker's occupation from usual occupations; the incidence of the disease must be substantially higher in the injured worker's occupation; or, the incidence of the disease must be substantially higher in the injured worker's occupation than in usual occupations. Good sources of this information might be OSHA, the Florida Division of Safety, or The National Centers for Disease Control [*see* Wuesthoff Memorial Hosp. v. Hurlbert, 548 So. 2d 771, 772, 773–774 (Fla. 1st DCA 1989)].

[d] If Disease Is an Ordinary Disease of Life, Incidence of Disease Must Be Substantially Higher in the Occupation Than in the Public

Be careful not to confuse a particular job or employment with an occupation. For example, coal mining is an occupation; the Ajax Coal Company is a place of employment.

[e] Nature of Employment Is Major Contributing Cause of the Disease

Effective October 1, 2003, the Act provides that occupational disease is not compensable unless the nature of the employment where the disease was contracted was the major contributing cause of the disease. Major contributing cause must be demonstrated by medical evidence based on physical examination findings and diagnostic testing [§ 440.151(1)(c), Fla. Stat. (10/1/2003)]. The phrase "major contributing cause" now means the cause that is more than 50 percent responsible for the injury as compared *to all other causes combined* [*see* ch. 7, § 7.01[4][b][iii]].

Presumably, the Legislature intended that the phrase "the nature of the employment" to mean the same as the generic term "occupation," so that the term does not refer to the specific job where the employee became sick or disabled. Read that way, the employee must show, for example, that the nature of paint manufacturing generally is the major contributing cause of the disease. Otherwise, the employee would be required to show that the nature of the employer's specific employment is the major contributing cause. Such a reading would be illogical, however, because it would render the "last employer liable" doctrine meaningless.

In cases involving occupational disease or repetitive exposure, the claimant must prove both causation and sufficient exposure to support causation by clear and convincing evidence. [Note: Clear and convincing evidence is evidence of a quality and character designed to produce in the judge's mind a firm belief or conviction, without hesitation, as to the truth of the allegations.]

[f] Epidemiological Studies, Exposure to Specific Substance, Causation of Employee's Precise Disease

To establish compensability, the employee must first identify the specific substance causing the disease. Then the claimant must produce evidence of the levels of the substance to which he or she was exposed. Finally, the employee must show that there are epidemiological studies showing that exposure to the specific substance involved, at the levels to which the employee was exposed, may cause the precise disease sustained [§ 440.151(1)(a), Fla. Stat. (10/1/2003)].

SPECIAL ALERT: The degree of evidence required to show compensability for a first responder is different than for all other occupations. First responders are defined as law enforcement officers, firefighters, emergency medical technicians, or paramedics. For first responders, both causation and sufficient exposure to a specific harmful substance shown to be present in the workplace to support causation can be proven by the lower standard of a preponderance of the evidence [*see* § 112.1815(2)(b), Fla. Stat.].

[9] Average Weekly Wage in Occupational Disease Cases

Calculate an injured worker's average weekly wage and compensation rate in occupational disease cases in the same fashion as other cases with one important exception. Make the calculation using wages earned as of the date disability began, rather than as of the date of last injurious exposure (the accident date) [*see* Cote v. Combustion Engineering, Inc. 502 So. 2d 500, 501 (Fla. 1st DCA 1987)].

[10] Permanent Impairment Not Required for Wage Loss

In occupational disease cases, it is not always necessary that the employee have a permanent impairment under the AMA, Minnesota, or Florida guidelines (or apparently any other guidelines), to be eligible for pre 1994 wage loss benefits. For example, the employee suffered from contact dermatitis resulting from contact with cement. His treatment resulted in a complete cure; however, new exposure to cement caused the condition to reappear. Thus, he was all right if he did not go back to his job. The court held the law still entitled him to wage loss benefits even though he did not have a permanent impairment or any limitations with respect to daily living activities. The basis for the award was that the employee's allergy to cement caused an economic loss [*see* OBS Co., Inc. v. Freeney, 475 So. 2d 947, 950–951 (Fla. 1st DCA 1985)].

The Florida Supreme Court has approved this line of thinking and stated that an employee who suffers a permanent disability from an occupational disease is entitled to compensation though he is not affected if he does not return to work under the conditions that caused his disability, provided there is economic loss [*see* Dayron Corp. v. Morehead, 509 So. 2d 930, 932 (Fla. 1987)].

Will this concept still apply for claims occurring after the 1990 and 1994 changes? Both the 1990 and 1994 Workers' Compensation Act amendments added several new requirements for wage loss eligibility. It is conceivable that if the *Dayron Corp.* court could dispense with the basic requirement of permanent impairment so easily, doing so with the new requirements is not likely to be a problem for a new court. The courts will have some difficulty, however, in applying this theory to claims occurring on or after January 1, 1994. For these cases, an injured worker's entitlement to wage loss benefits does not begin until after the carrier has paid impairment benefits. We cannot decide impairment benefits, of course, without a specific impairment rating. The First District Court of Appeal has certified this question to the Florida Supreme Court. The Supreme Court, however, has yet to take up the question.

[11] Burden of Proof

Who has the burden of proof in occupational disease cases? The burden is the employee's. Following is the rule of law [*see* Wiley v. Southeast Erectors, Inc., 573 So. 2d 946, 948 (Fla. 1st DCA 1991)]:

> [I]t is fundamental that a workers' compensation claimant must establish that the injury for which recovery is sought is related to the employment, and when the injury at issue involves disease or physical effect, evidence of causation must be shown by something more than that it is merely logical that the injury arose out of the claimant's employment. . . . [C]ausal relationship must be shown by clear evidence rather than speculation or conjecture. . . . This is not to say that causal relationship requires absolute proof, to the exclusion of reasonable inferences.

An employee can prove causation by showing medical opinion based on evidence of exposure. This includes medical history, medical tests, or studies showing that exposure to the substances at issue can cause the employee's medical problems. From the discussion thus far, we can conclude that the employee must show the following three facts:

1. That the workplace contains a toxic substance;
2. That the work exposed the employee to the substance; and
3. The medical evidence shows that the substance, at the level of actual exposure, can cause whatever is wrong with the employee.
4. That the employment is the major contributing cause the employee's disease.

[12] Exception For Public Safety Workers

[a] In General

Public safety workers include firefighters, paramedics, emergency medical technicians, law enforcement officers, and correctional officers who work for the state or a political subdivision. In the legislature's view, these workers are uniquely exposed to certain infectious diseases because they frequently contact infected body fluids or airborne organisms. The specific diseases are hepatitis A and B, meningococcal meningitis, and tuberculous. Meningitis is an inflamation of the membranes of the spinal cord or brain. Tuberculosis is an infectious disease caused by the tubercle bacillus. It most commonly affects the respiratory system, but other body parts such as the bones, joints, and nervous system may become infected.

If a public safety worker contracts one of these diseases, the statutes create a rebuttable presumption that the infection occurred in the line of duty [§ 112.181(2), Fla. Stat.].

[b] Requirements to Invoke the Presumption

To invoke the presumption, the worker must meet the following tests [§ 112.181, Fla. Stat.]:

1. If the employer requires it, workers must have undergone a preemployment physical examination designed to detect the presence of any infection. Because of its long incubation period, the worker must bank serum for future testing of hepatitis. This testing does not apply to meningococcal meningitis. The law allows employers to require testing existing employees beginning January 1, 1996.
2. If a vaccine exists, employers can require workers to be immunized. An exception arises if a physician declares that immunization would pose a significant risk to the workers' health.
3. In cases of meningococcal meningitis and tuberculous, infected workers must submit written affidavits asserting they were not exposed to persons with the disease during the 10 days before their diagnosis.
4. The compensability presumption does not arise unless the disease creates the need for medical treatment. The statutory language is vague, but also suggests that if the disease is not at least partially disabling, the presumption does not arise. The section provides that disease "that requires medical treatment, and that results in total or partial disability or death shall be presumed to be a disability suffered in the line of duty." This suggests the presumption does not apply to the need for medical care alone.
5. Employees must show on-the-job exposure to potentially infected persons or body fluids. Such exposure need not be direct. The fact that the employees work in a high risk environment is sufficient. For example, if employees can show they handle body fluids or are exposed to body fluids, the Act does not require showing a specific point of infection.

Additionally, to qualify for the statutory presumption, a claimant must, "by written affidavit," verify that, to the best of his or her knowledge and belief, he or she has not [*see* § 112.181(2)(a)1-4, Fla. Stat. (2002)]:

(1) Been exposed, through transfer of bodily fluids, to any person known to have sickness or medical conditions derived from hepatitis, outside the scope of his or her employment.

(2) Had a blood transfusion or blood components, other than a transfusion arising out of an accident or injury happening in connection with his or her present employment, or received any blood products for the treatment of a coagulation disorder since last undergoing medical tests for hepatitis, which tests failed to indicate the presence of hepatitis.

(3) Engaged in unsafe sexual practices or other high-risk behavior, as identified by the Centers for Disease Control and Prevention, or the Surgeon General of the United States, or had sexual relations with a person known to him or her to have engaged in such unsafe sexual practices or other high-risk behavior.

(4) Used intravenous drugs not prescribed by a physician.

The court has held that submitting the affidavit is mandatory and that depositions cannot take the place of the written affidavit required by statute. Not only must a claimant submit the affidavit, he or she must be able to make the assertions required by the affidavit [*see* Seminole County Gov't v. Bartlett, 2006 Fla. App. LEXIS 1026 (Fla. 1st DCA 2006)].

If the claimant is not entitled to the presumption, he or she might still be entitled to benefits if the tests for compensable occupational disease can be met.

[c] Evidence and Record of Exposure

Employers must keep records of suspected exposure to certain infectious diseases and immediately inform workers who may have been so exposed. Similarly, workers must report to the employer if they suspect they have been exposed to certain infectious diseases [§ 112.181(5), Fla. Stat.].

§ 8.02 Acceleration or Aggravation of Preexisting Conditions or Disease

[1] The Rule

Subject to the limitations described in § 440.15(5), Fla. Stat., acceleration or aggravation of a disease is generally compensable; however, aggravation of venereal disease or habitual use of alcohol or narcotics is not compensable [§ 440.02(1), Fla. Stat.].

Effective October 1, 2003, the law provides that only the disabilities and medical treatment associated with the compensable injury are payable. The Act now provides that compensable disability and medical care exclude the degree of disability or medical conditions that existed when the accident occurred.

Additionally, permanent impairment ratings must be made excluding the degree of any preexisting impairment. This applies without considering whether the preexisting condition was disabling when the accident occurred or even whether the prior condition would

Guide to Claims

not have been disabling if the compensable accident had not occurred. Any impairment or disability for the compensable injury must be determined and compensated by first apportioning out the degree of impairment or disability attributable to the preexisting condition. Therefore, based on this language, no compensation or medical care attributable to preexisting conditions is compensable or payable.

Frequently, it is not possible to treat the new injury without simultaneously treating the preexisting condition. The law now requires, however, that medical benefits be paid by apportioning out the percentage of the treatment attributable to the preexisting condition [§ 440.15(5)(b), Fla. Stat. (10/1/2003)].

Previously, the law provided that aggravations of preexisting conditions were generally compensable without considering which part was old and which part was new. Therefore, this amendment appears to be substantive and cannot be applied to accidents occurring before October 1, 2003.

Additionally, the courts have consistently held that treating an unrelated condition is compensable if such treatment is necessary to treat the compensable injury. In 1966, the Florida Supreme Court held that treatment for a condition that existed before an industrial accident is compensable if it will aid the injured worker's recovery. The basis for awarding this care was that it met the medical necessity test [*see* Jordan v. Florida Industrial Commission, 183 So. 2d 529, 530 (Fla. 1966)].

In *Brown v. Steego Auto Parts* [585 So. 2d 401, 402–403 (Fla. 1st DCA 1991)], the court held that the carrier must pay for a weight loss program because the claimant's obesity prevented effective treatment of the compensable injury.

It appears that this amendment is an attempt to overrule this line of cases. Until we have the benefit of judicial review, the black letter law should be applied.

For a brief discussion of subsequent aggravation of original injuries, see LARSON'S WORKERS' COMPENSATION, DESK EDITION, Ch. 10, §§ 10.09–10.12 (Matthew Bender).

[2] Aggravation of Preexisting Disease

It is, of course, possible for an accident to cause a disease. For example, a worker suffers a back injury followed by surgery. The surgery results in an infection or perhaps the worker contracts pneumonia because of the weakened condition. These results would be compensable. This section, however, deals with the situation where the employee has a preexisting disease, symptomatic or not, aggravated or accelerated by an accident. The most common example is a new back injury that aggravates preexisting arthritis. Arthritis is an inflamation of a joint usually accompanied by pain and swelling, and often by changes in structure. Do not confuse this with occupational disease. In the situation here, the accident made an existing disease worse. This situation is compensable under the provisions of § 440.02(1), Fla. Stat.

When a compensable injury aggravates a preexisting condition, the exacerbation of the preexisting condition is, itself, compensable [*see* Castro v. Florida Juice Division, 400 So. 2d 1280, 1282 (Fla. 1st DCA 1981)].

Note, however, that amendments to the Act effective October 1, 2003, appear to have overruled case law and now provide that no compensation or medical care attributable to preexisting conditions is compensable or payable [*see* [1], *above*].

[3] 1994 Amendment: Major Contributing Cause

The legislature may have modified *Castro* [*see* [2], *above*] or even overruled it. Effective January 1, 1994, the legislature added a new section that provides [§ 440.09(1)(b), Fla. Stat. (1/1/94)]:

> If an injury arising out of and in the course of employment combines with a preexisting disease or condition to cause or prolong disability or need for treatment, the employer must pay compensation or benefits required by this chapter only to the extent that the injury arising out of and in the course of employment is and remains the major contributing cause of the disability or need for treatment.

Previously the Act did not define the phrase "major contributing cause," so the court has done so. The court held that "major contributing cause" refers to a cause that contributes more to the claimant's disability or need for medical treatment than any other single cause. This determination could be made based on either expert or lay testimony, depending on the factual circumstances of the case. For a complete discussion of the major contributing cause requirement, see ch. 7, § 7.01[4]. Assume, for example, that a worker suffered an injury that aggravated a preexisting back and neck condition. If the evidence showed that the new injury was the major contributing cause of the need to treat the back and neck condition, such treatment was compensable [*see* Mellon Sec. & Sound v. Custer, 687 So. 2d 1372, 1373 (Fla. 1st DCA 1997)].

[4] 2003 Amendment: Major Contributing Cause

Effective October 1, 2003, the Legislature adopted a definition of "Major Contributing Cause" that is apparently intended to overrule the court's decision in *Closet Maid* and its progeny. The phrase "major contributing cause" now means the cause that is more than 50 percent responsible for the injury as compared *to all other causes combined.* The statute provides that major contributing cause may be established by medical evidence only [*see* § 440.09, Fla. Stat. (1/10/2003); ch. 7, § 7.01[4]].

Such evidence will show that the preexisting condition did not require treatment before the new industrial accident. This is, in a way, a "but for" rule. That is to say, but for the injury at work, the treatment would not have been necessary. Viewed in reverse, this rule will preclude compensation for preexisting conditions if those conditions required treatment before the industrial accident. In this case, the evidence will show that the new injury was not the major contributing cause of the need for treatment.

Regardless of such testimony, the major contributing cause limitation does not apply in occupational disease cases. This is because the Act allows apportionment between such causes with compensation reduced by the percentage of disability attributed to the preexisting or unrelated condition. This apportionment provision does not require that the occupational disease be the major contributing cause [*see* Watkins Engineers & Constructors v. Wise, 698 So. 2d 294, 295–296 (Fla. 1st DCA 1997)].

[5] Treatment for Preexisting Conditions

Subject to judicial interpretation of the 1994 amendment discussed in [3], *above,* and the 2003 amendment discussed in [1], *above*, an employer and carrier may be liable for treatment for a preexisting medical condition that is not directly related to the compensable injury. This liability arises if the preexisting condition interferes with or retards recovery from the compensable injury [*see* Primous v. Flagler Systems, Inc., 477 So. 2d 1057, 1059 (Fla. 1st DCA 1985)].

Consider the example of a employee who suffers a back injury that aggravates preexisting diabetes. Besides the aggravation, the diabetes hinders effective treatment of the back injury. In such a case the judge of compensation claims must make specific findings about whether the diabetes treatment was a necessary adjunct to treating the compensable back injury. If so, the carrier must provide the employee with compensation for the diabetes treatment. Such compensation is due for the limited period in which the accident made the employee's diabetic condition worse. In addition, the carrier also must provide compensation for the period in which stabilizing the diabetes is necessary to aid the employee in attaining maximum recovery from the compensable injury [*see* Urban v. Morris Drywall Spray, 595 So. 2d 60, 61–62 (Fla. 1st DCA 1991)].

The law now requires, however, that medical benefits be paid by apportioning out the percentage of the treatment attributable to the preexisting condition [*see* § 440.15(5)(b), Fla. Stat. (10/1/2003); [1], *above*].

[6] Psychiatric Care for Preexisting Psychosis

As with all other ailments, preexisting psychiatric conditions are compensable only if the evidence shows that the accident aggravated the condition. For example, the employee suffered from preexisting psychiatric problems. These problems were related to the basic biochemistry of her brain, and to physical, mental, and sexual abuse as a child. She originally worked as an emergency medical technician (EMT) aboard an ambulance. Following maximum medical improvement from a compensable accident, she could no longer physically do such work. The employer then gave her a light duty job as a 911 operator. Two physicians testified that the accident itself, and the employee's new job, aggravated her preexisting mental condition. The new job, they said, was inappropriate because of the high level of stress.

Based on such evidence, the court affirmed the hearing judge's award of psychiatric care. Even where the employee has suffered a history of psychiatric problems, an aggravation of the condition may be compensable if it is the direct and proximate result of a compensable accident [*see* Younkman v. Waste Collection Services, 576 So. 2d 801, 803 (Fla. 1st DCA 1991)].

Effective July 1, 1990, no benefits are due for aggravation of a preexisting condition if the employee lies, in writing, as not having been disabled or compensated for such a preexisting condition [§ 440.15(5), Fla. Stat.]. The key words here are "disabled" and "compensated." The question is what does this mean? Assume, for example, an employee lied on the employment application about having never had arthritis. The arthritis, however, had never been disabling and the applicant had never received compensation for it. Will the lie impact entitlement to benefits under this section? If not, is there a *Martin v. Carpenter* defense [*see* ch. 5]? Remember, the Workers' Compensation Act requires only one of the two elements—not having been disabled or not having been compensated—be established to preclude benefits. This new language may be a significant defense if employers use properly worded job applications.

The law now requires, however, that medical benefits be paid by apportioning out the percentage of the treatment attributable to the preexisting condition [*see* § 440.15(5)(b), Fla. Stat. (10/1/2003); [1], *above*].

CAUTION: An employer may ask medical questions only after it has offered employment, but before actual work starts. This restriction applies only if the employer is subject to the provisions of the Americans with Disabilities Act [*see* ch. 25, §§ 25.03[1], 25.05[4][c]].

§ 8.03 Apportionment

[1] The Rule: Accident Dates Up to September 30, 2003

Apportionment is proper only when and to the extent that the preexisting disease was either [*see* Evans v. Florida Industrial Commission, 196 So. 2d 748, 752–753 (Fla. 1967)]:

1. Disabling at the time of the second accident and continues to be so at the time the award is made; or
2. Producing no disability at the time of the second accident, but through its normal progress is doing so at the time permanent disability is determined, and an award is made.

Note: For accident dates up to September 30, 2003, apportionment does not apply to temporary total disability, medical benefits, or wage loss benefits [*see* § 440.15(5)(a), Fla. Stat.].

For a general discussion of apportionment, see ch. 24, § 24.06[3]; *see also* Larson's Workers' Compensation, Desk Edition, Ch. 90, §§ 90.02–90.04 (Matthew Bender).

[a] Apportionment Between the Carrier and Employee

Do not confuse apportionment as discussed here with apportionment, or contribution, between carriers where multiple exposures produce multiple periods of disability. For example, the employee was a flight attendant who developed a bronchial condition caused by exposure to cigarette smoke. She had successive periods of disabilities during which her condition would improve, only to worsen when she returned to work. During this period the employer had changed insurance carriers. The court held benefits should be apportioned between the carriers with each being responsible for benefits accrued during their period of coverage [*see* Eastern Airlines, Inc. v. Crittenden, 596 So. 2d 112, 113 (Fla. 1st DCA 1992)].

NOTE: At this point we must wonder whether § 440.09(1), Fla. Stat. now precludes apportionment in this situation since establishing that more then one employment is the "major contributing cause" of the injury would be difficult. For a complete discussion of the major contributing cause requirement, *see* ch. 7, § 7.01[4].

The discussion here deals with apportionment between the carrier and the employee. Apportionment between carriers for successive accidents is discussed in ch. 24, § 24.06[3]. People frequently misunderstand and misapply apportionment in this context. Here, apportionment deals with separating benefits when a compensable industrial accident aggravates a preexisting disease. When a compensable accident, occurring before October 1, 2003aggravates or accelerates a preexisting disease, only the aggravation is compensable and not the underlying disease [§ 440.02(1), Fla. Stat.].

[b] Apportionment in Disability Cases

Many people become confused when discussing apportionment in workers' compensation cases. Florida has long subscribed to the universally accepted maxim that an employer takes its employees as it finds them. That is to say, an employer is liable for the total result of a compensable accident even if part of the result preexisted the accident. Confusion arises because the maxim of taking employees as the employer finds them conflicts with the idea of apportionment. In 1967, the Florida Supreme Court revisited the issue, having become convinced that the statute and its application required reexamination. The Court held that the Workers' Compensation Act required the judges of compensation claims to apportion out of an award that portion of the disability that resulted from the normal progress of the preexisting disease at the time the judge makes the award. The Court cautioned, however, that not all preexisting disease conditions require apportionment. Disability in aggravation cases should be considered as falling into one of the following three categories [*see* Evans v. Florida Industrial Commission, 196 So. 2d 748, 752 (Fla. 1967)]:

Category 1. Disability that resulted directly and solely from the accident and would have occurred even if no preexisting disease existed.

Category 2. Disability that resulted from the aggravation or acceleration of the preexisting disease by the accident.

Category 3. Disability that resulted from the normal progress of the disease and would have existed even if the accident had never occurred

Only the third category is subject to apportionment for which the employer is not liable. Apportionment is proper only when, and to the extent that the preexisting disease:

1. Was disabling at the time of the accident and continues to be so at the time the award is made; or
2. Was producing no disability at the time of the accident but through its normal progress is doing so at the time the judge decides permanent disability and makes an award.

The judge of compensation claims must decide the degree or extent of disability falling within the three categories listed above. The judge must then apportion out of an award only that portion of the disability attributable to the normal progress of the preexisting disease; that is, the portion that would have occurred even if the accident had never happened [*see* Evans v. Florida Industrial Commission, 196 So. 2d 748, 752–753 (Fla. 1967)].

[c] Evidence Must Support the Apportionment

When judges make an apportionment, the record must support the percentages used. For example, Delbert Cummins suffered physical injuries but also suffered from preexisting mental problems. One doctor said that 60 percent of the mental problems were related to the workplace accident and 40 percent were unrelated. Another doctor said that all of Cummins' mental problems were unrelated. The judge felt that neither opinion was entirely correct and ordered the carrier to pay only 25 percent of the permanent total disability benefits. The court commended the judge for his attempt at apportionment, but remanded the case because the record did not support the percentages the judge used [*see* Cummins v. Walt Disney World Company, 693 So. 2d 129 (Fla. 1st DCA 1997)].

Unless evidence exists as to the percentage of disability caused by the natural progression of a preexisting condition, apportionment is not allowed [*see* Cover v. TG&Y Store 1331, 405 So. 2d 985, 986 (Fla. 1st DCA 1981); *see also* Watkins Engineers & Constructors v. Wise, 698 So. 2d 294, 295 (Fla 1st DCA 1997)].

[2] Accident Dates On or After October 1, 2003

Effective October 1, 2003, the law provides that only the disabilities and medical treatment associated with the compensable injury are payable. The Act now provides that compensable disability and medical care exclude the degree of disability or medical conditions that existed when the accident occurred. Additionally, permanent impairment ratings must be made excluding the degree of any preexisting impairment. This applies without considering whether the preexisting condition was disabling when the accident occurred or even whether the prior condition would not have been disabling if the compensable accident had not occurred. Any impairment or disability for the compensable injury must be determined and compensated by first apportioning out the degree of impairment or disability attributable to the preexisting condition. Therefore, based on this language, no compensation or medical care attributable to preexisting conditions is compensable or payable. The revised statute provides as follows [§ 440.15(5)(b), Fla. Stat.]:

> If a compensable injury, disability, or need for medical care, or any portion thereof, is a result of aggravation or acceleration of a preexisting condition, or is the result of merger with a preexisting condition, only the disabilities and medical treatment associated with such compensable injury shall be payable under this chapter, excluding the degree of disability or medical conditions existing at the time of the impairment rating or at the time of the accident, regardless of whether the preexisting condition was disabling at the time of the accident or at the time of the impairment rating and without considering whether the preexisting condition would be disabling

Guide to Claims

> without the compensable accident. The degree of permanent impairment or disability attributable to the accident or injury shall be compensated in accordance with this section, apportioning out the preexisting condition based on the anatomical impairment rating attributable to the preexisting condition. Medical benefits shall be paid apportioning out the percentage of the need for such care attributable to the preexisting condition. As used in this paragraph, "merger" means the combining of a preexisting permanent impairment or disability with a subsequent compensable permanent impairment or disability which, when the effects of both are considered together, result in a permanent impairment or disability rating which is greater than the sum of the two permanent impairment or disability ratings when each impairment or disability is considered individually.

If the expert medical opinions are that (for example) 30% of the disability and need for medical treatment are caused by the aggravation or acceleration of preexisting injury, it appears the carrier can deduct 30% from medical bills, disability benefits, and any Impairment Income Benefits. The statute is somewhat vague, but appears to include temporary disability benefits in this apportionment. In the first sentence the statute excludes "the degree of disability . . . existing at the time of the accident." But goes on to state that the deduction or apportionment applies "regardless of whether the preexisting condition was disabling at the time of the accident." There is nothing in the statute to indicate that approval by a judge of compensation claims is required and it appears the carrier can take the deduction administratively. Until the courts provide guidance, each carrier is on its own in interpreting and applying this statute. The key will be to obtain firm and consistent percentages with regard to separating the old and new injuries. If a claimant with a preexisting condition was fully employed on the accident date it might be difficult to obtain a convincing medical opinion that any part of the current disability is caused by the preexisting condition. Whether and how to apply this statute should be based and decided case by case.

[3] Apportionment in Occupational Disease Cases

[a] The Rule

Apportionment between the employee and the carrier is permitted in occupational disease cases. Apportionment, or contribution, between employers or between carriers, however, is *never* appropriate in occupational disease cases.

[b] Apportionment Between Employee and Carrier

When the combination of an occupational disease and a non-compensable condition results in disability, compensation must be apportioned between such causes. Benefits should, therefore, be reduced by the percentage amount attributable to the non-compensable condition [*see* § 440.151(1)(c), Fla. Stat.].

Remember, however, that apportionment requires competent, substantial evidence regarding the percentage attributable to the unrelated condition. For example, Charles Wise worked with toxic chemicals for 22 years. During that time, and for years before, he was also a heavy smoker. This combination resulted in Wise contracting chronic obstructive pulmonary disease. Although expert testimony established that the disease resulted from both a work-related and a non work-related exposure, the doctor could not determine the percentage attributable to smoking. Without such evidence, apportionment between the employer and the employee is not proper and the carrier is responsible for the entire amount of compensation due [*see* Watkins Engineers & Constructors v. Wise, 698 So. 2d 694, 294, 295 (Fla. 1st DCA 1997); *see also* § 8.01, *above,* for a full discussion of occupational disease].

[c] Apportionment or Contribution Between Carriers

[i] Distinction Between Repetitive Trauma and Occupational Disease

Note the importance of distinguishing between repetitive trauma/exposure cases and occupational disease cases. In appropriate cases involving different employers or different carriers, the judge of compensation claims has the authority to apportion liability for benefits between them. In occupational disease cases, however, benefits are never apportionable between carriers. This is because the last injurious exposure rule places the liability on the carrier at risk when the worker was last injuriously exposed to the hazards of the disease.

[ii] Burden of Proof

Whichever carrier defends against a claim for contribution or apportionment on the basis that the injury is an occupational disease and, thus, not apportionable, has the burden of proof. Here, the worker suffered carpal tunnel syndrome first while the employer was insured with AIIC. Sometime later, she filed another claim for carpal tunnel syndrome while the employer was insured with Chubb. AIIC (Associated Industries) argued that the claimant suffered from an occupational disease and that Chubb should be exclusively liable. The court held that carpal tunnel is not an occupational disease, but is instead a repetitive trauma or exposure and apportionment may apply [*see* Associated Indus. Ins. v. Federal Ins., 707 So. 2d 880, 882–884 (Fla. 1st DCA 1998)].

[iii] Major Contributing Cause

Under the provisions of § 440.42(3), Fla. Stat., the judge of compensation claims may apportion liability for successive accidents between carriers. A causal connection must exist between a claimant's employment and a second industrial injury in order to justify apportionment of liability among carriers. In deciding whether and to what extent benefits should be apportioned, the judge may consider only the extent to which each accident contributed to the disability and the need for medical care. The concept of major contributing cause is not part of the determination.

SPECIAL ALERT: Major contributing cause does not apply to apportionment between carriers for subsequent accidents. In *B&L Services, Inc. v. Coach USA* [791 So. 2d 1138, 1143 (Fla. 1st DCA 2001)], the court explained: "As we conclude that the legislature did not intend to apply the major contributing cause standard to section 440.42(3), the JCC must evaluate any reimbursement or contribution claim under the preexisting standard. The determinative factor in placing liability under Section

440.42(3) is whether the second compensable accident causes injury which is independent from or an exacerbation of the first compensable accident. Section 440.42(3) thereafter allows the deputy to divide liability according to each carrier's responsibility" [*see* U.S. Elec. Co. v. Sisk Elec. Service, Inc., 417 So. 2d 738, 739 (Fla. 1st DCA 1982)]. A causal connection must exist between the claimant's employment and second industrial injury in order to justify apportionment of liability among carriers [*see* Custom Architectural Metals v. Bradshaw, 623 So. 2d 804, 806 (Fla. 1st DCA 1993)]. § 440.42(4), Fla. Stat. provides: "When there is any controversy as to which of two or more carriers is liable for the discharge of the obligations and duties of one or more employers with respect to a claim for compensation, remedial treatment, or other benefits under this chapter, the judge of compensation claims shall have jurisdiction to adjudicate such controversy; and if one of the carriers voluntarily or in compliance with a compensation order makes payments in discharge of such liability and it is finally determined that another carrier is liable for all any part of such obligations and duties with respect to such claim, the carrier which has made payments either voluntarily or in compliance with a compensation order shall be entitled to reimbursement from the carrier finally determined liable, and the judge of compensation claims shall have jurisdiction to order such reimbursement; . . . " [*see* Pearson v. Paradise Ford, 23 Fla. L. Weekly D373 (Fla. 1st DCA 2007)].

Prior to 1994, the First District Court of Appeal held that the judge of compensation claims must consider the actual extent to which each accident has contributed to a compensable disability in determining contribution between multiple carriers under § 440.42, Fla. Stat. In 1994, the Florida Legislature substantially amended the workers' compensation laws. One of these amendments included "major contributing cause" as a new burden of proof standard for a claimant to prove compensability [§ 440.09, Fla. Stat. (1995)]. However, the Legislature did not include § 440.42, Fla. Stat. in its amendments. When the Legislature fails to make substantive changes to the pertinent statutory language, it is assumed that the Legislature accepted the prior judicial construction of the statute. Therefore, "major contributing cause" is not a factor in apportioning responsibility between employers and carriers.

The determinative factor in placing liability under § 440.42(3), Fla. Stat. is whether the second compensable accident causes injury which is independent from or an exacerbation of the first compensable accident. § 440.42(3), Fla. Stat. thereafter allows the judge of compensation claims to divide liability according to each carrier's responsibility, and the "major contributing cause" doctrine is not a factor in the determination.

The judge of compensation claims must first determine if the claimant's first and second accidents are compensable, based in part on the "major contributing cause" doctrine. If so, the judge must then make a finding as to what extent the two employers or carriers are each liable for the disability and need for treatment, and apportion benefits based on those findings [*see* Handy-Man/Knep, Inc. v. Weinstein, 802 So. 2d 1186, 1188 (Fla. 1st DCA 2002)].

[4] Apportionment in Death Cases

Although the law clearly provides for apportionment in both death and permanent disability cases, the Florida Supreme Court has not directly addressed how apportionment applies in death cases. This issue was not before the Court in *Evans,* but in dicta the Court warned that such a difference exists between death and disability that a different construction may be appropriate. While it can be said that a preexisting disease would have produced part of the employee's disability despite the accident, it of course cannot be said that it would have produced part of the employee's death. Even after all these years this issue remains uncertain [*see* Evans v. Florida Industrial Commission, 196 So. 2d 748, 753 (Fla. 1967)].

[5] Benefits Subject to Apportionment

For accident dates prior to October 1, 2003, the Act specifically prohibits apportioning temporary disability benefits, medical benefits, and wage loss benefits [*see* § 440.15(5)(a), Fla. Stat.]. Obviously, "temporary benefits" includes both temporary total and temporary partial benefits. The term "wage loss benefits," however, is clear only for accidents occurring before January 1, 1994. This is because the legislature repealed wage loss benefits effective on that date and replaced it with impairment income benefits and supplemental income benefits. The question becomes whether these new benefits are subject to apportionment. In 1985, the court was faced with a similar question, and turned to the statute for the answer. Then, as it does today, the statutory definition of the term "accident" included the following [*see* § 440.02(1), Fla. Stat. (emphasis added)]:

> If a preexisting disease or anomaly is accelerated or aggravated by an accident arising out of and in the course of employment, only acceleration of death or acceleration or aggravation of the preexisting condition reasonably attributable to the accident is compensable, *with respect to death or permanent impairment.*

The court concluded that the emphasized phrase above made the section inapplicable to temporary disability and medical benefits [*see* McGarity v. Merit Elec. Co., Inc., 478 So. 2d 1074, 1075–1076 (Fla. 1st DCA 1985)]. We can conclude, therefore, that absent the specific inclusion of a permanent disability benefit, such as wage loss, the Act allows apportionment for all permanent disability and death benefits. Death is certainly clear enough, but what does the phrase "permanent impairment" mean? Permanent impairment means "any anatomic or functional abnormality or loss determined as a percentage of the body as a whole, existing after the date of maximum medical improvement, which results from the injury" [*see* § 440.02(21), Fla. Stat.]. Both impairment income benefits and supplemental income benefits are based on anatomic or functional abnormality or loss determined as a percentage of the body as a whole. Based on this analysis, we can reasonably conclude that apportionment applies to impairment income benefits, supplemental income benefits, permanent total disability benefits, and death benefits. For accidents occurring before January 1, 1994, apportionment applies to permanent total and death benefits only.

For accident dates on or after October 1, 2003, all disability and medical benefits are subject to apportionment.

[6] Present State of the Law

The present state of the law remains unchanged. In 1992, 25 years after the *Evans* decision [*see* [5], *above*], apportionment was again before the court. Here, the employee had preexisting, non-disabling, and asymptomatic arteriosclerosis at the time he suffered a compensable heart attack. The trial judge apportioned 50 percent of awarded benefits based on the preexisting condition. The First District Court of Appeal reversed the order and strictly applied the *Evans* criteria. The court found no evidence that at the time of the final hearing, the normal progress of the preexisting disease would have created any disability, independent of the effects of the compensable heart attack [*see* Tejada v. Collection Chevrolet, Inc., 594 So. 2d 340, 341 (Fla. 1st DCA 1992)].

Often, a preexisting disease will have significant impact on disability, but will not be subject to apportionment. In such cases, however, the law may entitle the carrier to partial reimbursement from the Special Disability Trust Fund. Note that the Special Disability Trust Fund does not apply to accidents occurring on or after January 1, 1998. For a full discussion of the Special Disability Trust Fund, see Ch. 20.

When deciding apportionment, consider the extent to which each condition contributed to the employee's disability. A judge of compensation cannot simply use equal division to decide apportionment of benefits [*see* Sauer Indus. Contracting Inc. v. Ditch, 547 So. 2d 276, 277–278 (Fla. 1st DCA 1989)].

Additionally, the court has held that the major contributing cause standard does not apply in contribution cases. The major contributing cause language of § 440.09(1), Fla. Stat. applies only in determining whether an injury is covered under workers' compensation. Once the injury is determined to be covered, the judge must then decide if the second accident caused an injury independent from the first injury, or if it caused an aggravation of the first injury. If so, the judge must apportion liability according to each carrier's responsibility. If the claimant is entitled to an award of attorney's fees, such an award must be apportioned between the employers and carriers as well [*see* B&L Services Inc. v. Coach USA, 791 So. 2d 1138, 1143 (Fla. 1st DCA 2001)].

Finally, the judge cannot make an apportionment without medical evidence of the disability percentage relating to the preexisting condition [*see* Russell House Movers, Inc., v. Nolin, 210 So. 2d 859, 862 (Fla. 1968)].

CHAPTER 9

ADDITIONAL DEFENSES

Guide to Claims

SYNOPSIS

Guide to Claims

§ 9.01 Failure to Give Notice of Injury

> *There is nothing more horrible than the murder of a beautiful theory by a brutal gang of facts.*
> La Rochefoucauld 1747–1827

Guide to Claims

[1] The Rule

The Act requires an employee to report an accident to the employer. The employee must make this report "within 30 days after the date of injury" (Ninety days after disability begins in occupational disease cases [*see* ch. 8, § 8.01[7]].) If employees do not report an injury at work within these time limitations, they may lose their entitlement to benefits [§ 440.185(1), Fla. Stat.].

[2] Exceptions to the Rule

A defense based on "failure to report" can be difficult to establish given the exceptions listed in the Act. The legislature changed these exceptions effective January 1, 1994. The most significant amendment is that failure to report timely will bar the employee from filing a petition for benefits. Although the statute begins ominously, it provides several exceptions, or escape clauses [§ 440.185(1)(a)–(d), Fla. Stat.]. A detailed discussion of the timely reporting exceptions follows in [3]–[6], *below.*

[3] Exception: Employer Knowledge by Any Means

[a] Formal Report Not Required

The Workers' Compensation Act does not require employees to make an official or formal report. If the employer learns about an accident, by any means, this is sufficient. Effective January 1, 1994, employees need merely "advise" the employer of the injury. The employee's burden to report and the statutory requirements are satisfied whenever the employer has actual knowledge of the accident [§ 440.185(1)(a), Fla. Stat.].

This statutory amendment is not really new law; it merely codifies case law. Following is an example. Judith Alfonso fell inside a walk-in freezer. Although he could not see her, her supervisor heard her exclaim from the freezer. He asked Alfonso if she was all right, and she replied that she thought so. As it turned out she was not all right. These facts showed that the employer was amply supplied with knowledge of Alfonso's accident to comply with the notice provision of § 440.185(1), Fla. Stat. [*see* Alfonso v. Mac Dinton's Restaurant, 515 So. 2d 243, 245 (Fla. 1st DCA 1987)].

Effective January 1, 1994, the law does not require a report from the employee if "the employer or the employer's agent had actual knowledge of the injury."

[b] When Employer Is Also Employee

Occasionally, the injured worker is also the employer. For example, the employee may also be the owner and president of the company. As such, the employee is also the employer. Does a situation like this create instant notice to the employer and thus to the carrier? It does not. There is not necessarily any notice to the carrier when the employee and the employer are the same person [*see* Vicki's Styling, Inc. v. Moberg, 489 So. 2d 194, 195 (Fla. 1st DCA 1986); Leonard Elec. Co. v. Erskine, 634 So. 2d 289, 290–291 (Fla. 1st DCA 1994)].

[4] Exception: Failure to Report Excused

[a] Accident Dates Through December 31, 1993

Judges of compensation claims have the authority to excuse the employee's failure to report. The law requires only that the judge find some satisfactory reason the employee could not give notice [§ 440.185(1)(b), Fla. Stat.].

The number of satisfactory reasons is seemingly endless. For example, Thomas Slater experienced back pain following an unusually hard day's work. He went to an osteopath who said he suffered from stiff muscles due to overwork. Four months later, tests revealed a herniated disc. It was only then that Slater reported the injury to his employer. Because the employee was unaware of the severity of his injury, he acted reasonably under the circumstances, and as a result offered a satisfactory reason for not notifying the employer of the injury within the statutory time [*see* Slater v. United Parcel Service, 507 So. 2d 1146, 1148 (Fla. 1st DCA 1987)].

The court, as it often does, quoted LARSON'S WORKERS' COMPENSATION LAW. "The time period for notice . . . does not begin to run until the claimant, as a reasonable person, should recognize the nature, seriousness, and probable compensation character of his injury or disease" [LARSON'S WORKERS' COMPENSATION LAW, Ch. 126, § 126.05 (Matthew Bender)].

Florida courts subscribe to Larson's theory and apply it regularly. Note the last part of the quotation. Not understanding possible eligibility for benefits is an acceptable excuse for failure to report. The employer, of course, has the right to receive timely notice. The employer needs such notice to conduct a prompt investigation to protect itself against a speculative claim. Remember, for accidents occurring *before 1994,* raising this defense successfully requires evidence showing that the late notice harmed the carrier or the employer.

[b] Accident Dates On or After January 1, 1994

Effective January 1, 1994, the legislature repealed that portion of § 440.185(1), Fla. Stat. which granted the judges of compensation claims authority to excuse failure to report simply upon finding "some satisfactory reason" for such failure. The only exceptions to the reporting requirement for accidents occurring on or after January 1, 1994, are as follows:

1. The employer had actual knowledge that the employee suffered a work-related injury.
2. The employee could not have known the injury was work related without a medical opinion.

3. There is a finding of "exceptional circumstances" outside the scope of the first two exceptions.

The term "exceptional circumstances" is a higher standard than "some satisfactory reason." The latter phrase means a reason acceptable to the judge. The new phrase, "exceptional circumstances," means by common definition, an uncommon or extraordinary event. Also, the legislature has, whether intentionally or not, adopted the holdings of several cases. Effective January 1, 1994, the time to report does not begin to run if the injured worker could not learn the cause of the injury without a medical opinion. In such cases, the Act gives injured workers 30 days to report after getting a medical opinion that the injury is work related [§ 440.185(1)(b), Fla. Stat.].

This new statutory standard requires that the judge of compensation claims must make a specific finding and describe the exceptional circumstances justifying excusing timely notice of injury. Failure to do so constitutes reversible error [*see* Clay County School Board v. Robison, 725 So. 2d 425, 426–427 (Fla. 1st DCA 1999)].

[c] Death Cases

A peculiar exception to the notice requirement arises in death cases. Notice from the employee's agent or estate satisfies the reporting requirement. Documents filed by lawyers, however, do not satisfy the requirement. These documents include notices of appearance, petitions, motions, or complaints [§ 440.185(1), Fla. Stat.].

> **SPECIAL ALERT:** Effective with accidents occurring on or after January 1, 1994, the legislature repealed the requirement in § 440.185(1), Fla. Stat. that the employer show prejudice or harm as the result of a late report. In this context, prejudice means that the employer or carrier has been placed at a disadvantage in asserting and establishing a defense or has suffered other damage caused by the late report.

[5] Exception: Injury Worse For Lack of Treatment

[a] Accident Dates Through December 31, 1993

If the judge excuses the worker's delay in reporting there is still one additional, though limited, defense. Carriers are not responsible for any aggravation of the injury because of the worker's failure to get first aid or proper medical treatment during the delay. Employers must provide medical care, but clearly cannot do so if they have no notice of the accident. If the lack of treatment aggravates the injury, no compensation is due during the disability period caused by the aggravation [§ 440.185(1)(b), Fla. Stat.].

[b] Accident Dates On or After January 1, 1994

The legislature repealed the "aggravation of injury" clause in § 440.185(1)(b), Fla. Stat. Therefore, this provision does not apply to accidents occurring on or after January 1, 1994.

Guide to Claims

[6] Exception: Knowledge Imputed to Carrier

Remember that in most circumstances the law will impute carrier knowledge to the employer and vice versa. Therefore, if the carrier learns about the accident via a telephone call from the injured worker, or even by receiving a medical report, the carrier is on notice. The law will impute such knowledge to the employer [§ 440.41, Fla. Stat.; *see* Auto-Owners Ins. Co. v. American States Ins., 402 So. 2d 560, 561 (Fla. 1st DCA 1981)].

Failure to timely report can be a bar to compensation and is a viable defense, but proving it can be tricky. Based on the statutes and the cases, we can conclude that successfully defending a claim based on late reporting requires the defense to show the following:

1. No one with the employer, in a real or apparent supervisory capacity, had any knowledge that the employee had suffered an injury. If the employer did know of some injury, it had no knowledge that the accident was work related.
2. The employee knew or should have known that he or she suffered an injury in a work-related accident. The employee understood both the severity of the injury and his or her possible entitlement to workers' compensation benefits.
3. Because of the employee's delay in reporting the accident, the employer's or the carrier's rights have been prejudiced. (This requirement applies only to accidents occurring before January 1, 1994.)

[7] Knowledge Imputed to Statutory Employer

As discussed in ch. 3, § 3.06[1], a general contractor is the statutory employer of its subcontractors. If an employee of an illegally uninsured subcontractor suffers an injury on the job, the general contractor is responsible for providing benefits. The question is this; does the injured worker have a duty to report the accident directly to the general contractor? The answer is no.

For example, Lyle Hartly suffered an injury while working. He promptly reported the accident to his direct employer, the subcontractor. The subcontractor, however, did not have the required workers' compensation coverage. The general contractor did not receive direct notice of the injury and defended the claim, arguing a conspiracy existed to deprive it of actual notice. The court found no evidence to prove this. Hartly satisfied his duty to report when he reported the accident to his direct employer. Further, this legal notice can be imputed to the general contractor in its capacity as the statutory employer [*see* T.E. James Construction Co. v. Hartley, 616 So. 2d 548, 549 (Fla. 1st DCA 1993)].

[8] Raising Defense of Late Notice

For accidents occurring before January 1, 1994, carriers must raise the defense of late notice at the *first* hearing. § 440.185(1), Fla. Stat. provided in part:

> . . . [F]ailure to give such notice . . . (the accident report) . . . shall not be a bar to any claim under this chapter unless objection to such failure is raised before the judge of compensation claims *at the first hearing* of a claim for compensation in respect to

such injury or death. . . . (Emphasis added.)

Though defense attorneys must follow this procedural requirement, claim adjusters need to be aware of it, too. Defense attorneys must raise a defense based on lack of timely notice at the first hearing. This includes motion hearings. If the defense is not raised timely, the law forever bars the carrier's right to raise the defense. Obviously defense attorneys cannot raise the defense if the carrier does not ensure that the attorney is aware of it.

SPECIAL ALERT: The legislature repealed the requirement to raise the defense of a late report at the first hearing effective January 1, 1994. Still, the judge of compensation claims will likely require that the carrier raise the defense at the first pretrial hearing.

§ 9.02 Intoxication Defense

[1] The Rule

No compensation is payable if intoxication caused the accident [§ 440.09(3), Fla. Stat.]. Although the statute refers to "compensation" only, the term includes medical and all other benefits [*see* Gustafson's Dairy/Profes. v. Phillips, 656 So. 2d 1386, 1387 (Fla. 1st DCA 1995)].

Evidence proving intoxication creates a legal presumption that the intoxication caused the injury. This presumption, however, is rebuttable. A rebuttable presumption means the injured worker can present evidence to counteract or disprove the presumption. An effective rebuttal will show that, although intoxicated, the worker's state of intoxication did not cause the accident.

SPECIAL ALERT: The 1994 amendments to the Act provide that if an employer sets up a formal, drug-free workplace program, the presumption is conclusive and irrefutable. A conclusive presumption means the employee automatically loses all rights to benefits despite the facts of the case. Because an irrefutable presumption, here at least, deprives injured workers of their rights to due process, the court held that the irrefutable presumption provision is unconstitutional. This holding has no effect, however, on the other provisions of the drug-free workplace statute [*see* Recchi America Inc. v. Hall, 692 So. 2d 153, 154–155 (Fla. 1997); *see* [10][a], *below*].

In reaction to the court's holding in *Hall,* the legislature created a new and difficult standard that workers must meet to rebut the presumption when the employer has a proper, drug-free workplace program in place. To rebut the presumption, the injured worker must show that "there is no reasonable hypothesis that the intoxication or drug influence contributed to the injury." By statutory decree, this applies to all accident dates if the petition for benefits is filed on or after July 1, 1998 [*see*

§ 440.09(7)(b), Fla. Stat. (1998); *see also* [6][f], *below*].

Over the years the legislature enacted several changes to the intoxication defense section of the statutes. Therefore, how the defense applies depends on the accident's date.

For a general discussion of intoxication as a specific statutory defense, see LARSON'S WORKERS' COMPENSATION, DESK EDITION, Ch. 36, § 36.03 (Matthew Bender).

[2] Presumption of Intoxication

The Act creates a rebuttable presumption that intoxication caused the accident if competent evidence shows the employee's blood alcohol level exceeds the statutory limit [*see* [3]–[5], *below*]. In addition, the intoxication presumption arises if the employee has a positive confirmation of a drug as defined in the Act. This, however, is a rebuttable presumption. That is, the employee can overcome the presumption by presenting evidence that the state of intoxication did not cause the injury. Note that the presumption does not apply if the employer "approves" of the presence of an intoxicated employee on the premises [§ 440.09(7)(b), Fla. Stat.]:

> If, before the accident, the employer had actual knowledge of and expressly acquiesced in the employee's presence at the workplace while under the influence of such alcohol or drug, the presumptions specified in this subsection do not apply.

Drugs and intoxicants include any narcotic drug the employee used that was not prescribed by a physician. While the law provided the precise blood alcohol level for intoxication by alcohol, it did not so neatly measure intoxication by drugs. The legislature has corrected that omission. Effective July 1, 1990, any positive confirmation of a drug, as defined in the Act, raises the presumption that the worker was intoxicated and that the intoxication caused the injury [§ 440.09(3), Fla. Stat. (7/1/90)].

NOTE: With the 1994 amendments, § 440.09(3), Fla. Stat. is unchanged, but is now found at § 440.09(7)(b), Fla. Stat.

[3] Presumption: Accidents Before July 1, 1990

Positive confirmation of 0.10 percent blood alcohol creates a presumption of intoxication. The injured worker may present evidence to rebut the presumption. No presumption exists for intoxication by narcotic drug [§ 440.09(3), Fla. Stat. (Supp. 1989)].

[4] Presumption: Accidents Between July 1, 1990, and December 31, 1993

Intoxication by alcohol remains the same. Positive confirmation of any controlled substance, not prescribed by a physician, creates a presumption of intoxication. Injured workers can present evidence to rebut the presumption [§ 440.09(3), Fla. Stat. (7/1/90)].

Remember that the court declared that the conclusive presumption provision is unconstitutional. Therefore, the presumption is rebuttable whether or not the employer has a formal drug-free workplace program [*see* Recchi America Inc. v. Hall, 692 So. 2d 153, 154–155 (Fla. 1997); [1], *above,* for Special Alert; [10][a], *below*].

Carriers do not owe compensation if the employee's intoxication was the primary cause of the injury. Before January 1, 1994, the Act provided that no compensation is due if [§ 440.09(3), Fla. Stat.]:

> [T]he injury was occasioned primarily by the intoxication of the employee; by the influence of any drugs, barbiturates, or other stimulants not prescribed by a physician, *which affected the employee to such an extent that the employee's normal faculties were impaired.* (Emphasis added)

> **SPECIAL ALERT:** For accidents occurring on or after January 1, 1994, the legislature repealed the italicized phrase [*see* [5], *below*].

[5] Presumption: Accident On or After January 1, 1994

The legislature adopted the intoxication level for blood alcohol as provided by § 316.193, Fla. Stat. The present level in that statute is 0.08 percent. In addition, the legislature repealed the statutory requirement that the intoxication impair the employee's normal faculties. Meeting the statutory definition of intoxication is enough to create a presumption of intoxication. The statute also provides that blood serum can be used for testing. This provision appears to overrule the court's holding in *Florida Tile Industries v. Dozier,* discussed in [6], *below*.

Note carefully that the presumption of intoxication does not apply if the employer expressly consented to the employee's presence at work while intoxicated. Thus, if the employer knows an employee is intoxicated and still allows the employee to continue working, the employer cannot raise the intoxication defense.

The Act describes an irrebuttable presumption of intoxication and causation that arises if the employer has a Drug-Free Workplace Program in place [§ 440.09(7), Fla. Stat. (1/1/94)]. In March 1996, the First District Court of Appeal declared this provision unconstitutional [*see* Hall v. Recchi America Inc., 671 So. 2d 197, 200–201 (Fla. 1st DCA 1996), *aff'd,* 692 So. 2d 153, 154–155 (Fla. 1997); [1], *above,* for Special Alert; [10][a], *below*]. On March 13, 1997, the Florida Supreme Court affirmed this decision, stating the irrebuttable presumption language in the statute is unconstitutional and completely invalid. The Court cured the constitutional problem by excising the irrebuttable presumption and judicially removed the words "[i]n the absence of a drug-free workplace program." Without that clause, the law allows an injured worker to rebut the presumption by presenting clear and convincing evidence that the intoxication or influence of drugs did not contribute to the injury [*see* Recchi America Inc. v. Hall, 692 So. 2d 153, 155 (Fla. 1997)].

The rebuttable presumption, then, remains as before.

Guide to Claims

[6] Rebutting Presumption

[a] Employee's Burden of Proof

§ 440.09(7)(b), Fla. Stat. creates a presumption of intoxication if the employee has a positive confirmation of a drug or an alcohol level specified in § 316.193, Fla. Stat.

Effective October 1, 2003, the legislature added a new subsection creating an additional burden for the employee to overcome the presumption. The statute provides that as part of rebutting the presumption, the employee must show the following:

1. The actual quantitative amounts of the drug or its metabolites as measured on the initial and confirmation drug test of the urine sample.
2. Additional evidence regarding the absence of a drug influence other than the workers' denial of being under the influence of a drug.

Additionally, the section provides that a drug test conducted on a urine sample cannot be rejected, or the presumptions overcome, on the basis of the urine being bodily fluid tested [*see* § 440.09(7)(e), Fla. Stat. (1/1/2003)].

[b] Medical Purpose Drug Tests

If the employer does not have a statutorily proper, drug-free workplace program in place, rebutting the presumption of intoxication and causation is often not as difficult as it may appear. The first attack would be against the validity of the test itself. Hospitals usually conduct routine testing as part of the initial admission work up. Injured workers may try to prevent admissibility of this evidence by showing that the testing facility did not properly conduct the test. They also may try to show that the testing facilities did not properly maintain the chain of evidence. Finally, the worker may try to show that the results are inconclusive.

SPECIAL ALERT: While a drug test performed for medical purposes may be admissible to support an intoxication defense, the statutory presumption of intoxication does not arise as a result of a positive confirmation drug test using a medically-drawn sample unless the drug testing rules in Fla. Admin. Code R. 59A-24 are followed. If the testing procedures set out in the rules are not followed, there is no presumption and the carrier must prove by the greater weight of the evidence that the accident was occasioned primarily by the claimant's intoxication or the influence of a drug or alcohol on the claimant [*see* Temporary Labor Source v. E.H., 765 So. 2d 757, 759 (Fla. 1st DCA 2000), *rev. denied,* 2001 Fla. LEXIS 181 (Fla. Jan. 18, 2001)].

The drug testing rules also apply to testing for alcohol. When testing for either drugs or alcohol is not done in accordance with the drug testing rules in 59A-24 Fla. Administrative Code, no presumption exists, and the employer/carrier must prove intoxication by the greater weight of the evidence [*see* European Marble Co. v. Robinson, 885 So. 2d 502 (Fla. 1st DCA 2004)].

[c] Testing Blood Serum Versus Whole Blood

Controversy over testing blood serum instead of whole blood has been resolved by both the legislature and the Florida Supreme Court. The controversy began in a case in which co-workers found the injured worker unconscious. At the hospital, blood tests confirmed a serum alcohol level of 0.16 percent. Blood serum is the liquid portion of the blood that remains after the red blood cells are removed. The District Court of Appeal held the test was improper and could not be used, stating in part [Florida Tile Industries v. Dozier, 561 So. 2d 654, 655 (Fla. 1st DCA 1990)]:

> The statute plainly requires a showing that there was '0.10 percent or more by weight of alcohol in the employee's *blood,*' not in the employee's *blood serum.* The statute further states that [the test] shall be based upon grams of alcohol per 100 milliliters of *blood;* it does not make any provision for a determination based upon blood serum.

In a subsequent case the First District Court of Appeal faced the same issue, but questioned its earlier decision in *Florida Tile.* Unwilling to overrule itself, the District Court of Appeal certified the question to the Florida Supreme Court, which asked whether anything in the statutes precludes using blood serum for alcohol testing. The Supreme Court answered no and disagreed with *Florida Tile's* narrow construction. Nothing in the statute imposes any limitation on the method for proving blood alcohol content. Furthermore, nothing in the statute excludes blood serum test results. Serum blood alcohol tests meet the standard of general scientific acceptance and have been accepted by other courts to establish blood alcohol levels [*see* Domino's Pizza v. Gibson, 668 So. 2d 593, 595–596 (Fla. 1996)].

Meanwhile, the legislature had already reacted to the *Florida Tile* case by amending the statute. Effective with accidents occurring on or after January 1, 1994, the statute specifically approves of the blood serum testing method. This approval, however, is conditional. The defense must show that this method "is proved to be medically and scientifically equivalent to or greater than the comparable blood alcohol level that would have been obtained if the test was based on percent by weight of alcohol in the blood" [§ 440.09(7)(b), Fla. Stat. (1/1/94)]. Defense lawyers can easily show this with the Supreme Court's *Domino's Pizza* decision.

Note that serum test results are from 8 percent to 17 percent higher than whole blood test results. The accepted reduction factor is 15 percent. Thus, a serum test result of .201 translates to a whole blood result of .17 percent. Recall that the minimum whole blood result needed to raise the intoxication presumption is .08 percent. Therefore, using the reduction factor, the minimum blood serum result needed to raise the intoxication presumption is .092 percent [*see* J & J Baker Enterprises v. Gaylord, 676 So. 2d 67 (Fla. 1st DCA 1996)].

[d] Test Results Are Not Privileged

Billy McFalls' estate tried to exclude from evidence a blood alcohol test conducted by a police officer. The estate argued that the test results were privileged information under § 316.066, Fla. Stat., and were not admissible. The court held the results are not privileged and can be used in evidence [*see* C.A. Meyer Pav. & Const. v. McFalls, 453 So. 2d 912, 913 (Fla. 1st DCA 1984)].

Guide to Claims

[e] Showing Inevitability

An injured worker's fall back position would be to show by clear and convincing evidence that a completely sober person would have suffered the same accident. For example, the employee, a painter, was intoxicated. He fell against a defective guard rail of a scaffold on which he was working. The guard rail snapped and he fell to his death. The Florida Supreme Court awarded compensation. The guard rail, said the Court, was defective. It would have snapped, apparently, had anyone fallen against it, drunk or sober [*see* Zee v. Gary, 137 Fla. 741, 189 So. 34, 37–38 (1939)]. (The Court apparently overlooked the likelihood the employee's intoxication caused him to fall against the rail in the first place.)

The carrier can usually overcome this rebuttal with evidence showing that the injured worker placed himself in a position of peril, contrary to company policy, training standards, and common sense. In another case, Bobby Meadows' blood alcohol level was 0.149 percent when the forklift he was driving went off the edge of a loading dock. Meadows' dependents tried to rebut the presumption by showing that he was not really drunk. They did so by presenting witnesses who testified that Meadows could "hold his liquor." The court held this was not enough to overcome the presumption [Orlando Waste Paper Co. v. Meadows, 460 So. 2d 434, 435 (Fla. 1st DCA 1984)].

[f] Business Records Exception to Hearsay Rule

In an automobile accident case, Luz Maria Garcia was struck by a car when she tried to cross an intersection. The car driver tried to get Garcia's blood alcohol tests into evidence, but Garcia succeeded in convincing the trial court to grant her motion to exclude the hospital's laboratory test results. Garcia argued that:

1. There were no witnesses who could provide independent testimony explaining how the tests were done;
2. There was no information detailing what kinds of tests were done;
3. There was no information about who drew the samples; and
4. There was no evidence that the samples tested were hers.

In short, Garcia argued that the hospital records amounted to hearsay and should not be admitted. The trial court agreed and refused to admit the test results. On appeal, the Fourth District Court of Appeal, sitting en banc, agreed with the trial court. The Florida Supreme Court, however, disagreed and reversed, stating such hospital records are admissible under the business records exception to the hearsay rule. Under this statutory exception, the law presumes the trustworthiness of medical records [§ 90.803(6)(a), Fla. Stat. (1991)]. If the facility made the test and records during the ordinary course of business activity as shown by the testimony of the record's custodian, such records and test results are admissible. The burden then shifts to the opposing party to prove that the records are not trustworthy [*see* Love v. Garcia, 634 So. 2d 158, 159–160 (Fla. 1994)].

[g] When Employer Has Drug-Free Workplace Program

If the employer has implemented a statutorily proper, drug-free workplace program as described in [10], *below,* the injured worker faces a daunting standard to overcome the presumption of intoxication and causation. Rebutting the presumption requires that the worker show that "there is no reasonable hypothesis that the intoxication or drug influence contributed to the injury." The legislature declared that this is a procedural amendment applying to all accident dates if the petition for benefits is filed on or after July 1, 1998 [*see* § 440.09(7)(b), Fla. Stat. (1998)].

Recall that the Act originally provided for an irrebuttable presumption, but that the Supreme Court declared that provision unconstitutional in *Recchi America Inc. v. Hall* [692 So. 2d 153 (Fla. 1997)]. In an obvious reaction to that decision, the legislature created a "reasonable hypothesis" standard that may be extremely difficult to overcome. Note that a hypothesis is nothing more than a theory—a basis for argument or reasoning. Under this standard, overcoming the presumption requires showing that the defense has failed to produce a reasonable theory or argument about how the worker's intoxication contributed to the accident and injury. Note that the defense theory need not reasonably argue that the intoxication *caused* the accident, but only that the intoxication was merely a *contributing* factor. By definition, a reasonable theory will be one that is logical, within the bounds of common sense, and is not extreme. Whether no "reasonable hypothesis" exists, of course, will be a question for the judge of compensation claims to decide.

[7] Intoxication in Fight Cases: Case History

The best way to review intoxication in fight cases is to review the key appellate decisions:

Case 1. A co-worker injured Jaime Avalos in a fight. The judge of compensation claims described the event as a "drunken brawl." The judge concluded that, but for Avalos' intoxicated confrontation with the co-worker, the assault would not have occurred. The judge denied the claim. The First District Court of Appeal agreed and affirmed [*see* Avalos v. Williford Farms, Inc., 561 So. 2d 1344, 1346 (Fla. 1st DCA 1990)].

Case 2. Walter Sterling became intoxicated at the company Christmas party. A co-worker pointed out that Sterling was in no condition to drive and offered him a ride home. Sterling became angry and began shoving the co-worker. A fight followed. No evidence was presented of any hard feelings between the two men that might have caused the fight. Further, the court found no evidence that a completely sober man would have suffered the same accident. The fact that Sterling was not the technical aggressor did not sway the court. Focusing on Sterling's intoxicated condition, the court held this caused him to pick a fight in the first place [*see* Sterling v. Mike Brown, Inc., 580 So. 2d 832, 836 (Fla. 1st DCA 1991); *see also* ch. 6, § 6.08[4], the Aggressor Doctrine].

[8] Employer Knowledge and Estoppel

If the employer knows about and "expressly acquiesced" in allowing intoxicated employees to remain at work, the law will preclude the carrier from asserting the intoxication defense [§ 440.09(7)(b), Fla. Stat. (1/1/94)]. The term "expressly acquiesced" is contradictory. "Express" means clear and unmistakable while "acquiescence" means passive acceptance or approval inferred from silence. The court has resolved the problem by holding that the term requires active acceptance. To have expressly acquiesced, the employer must have made some overt expression, either by words or conduct, showing it allowed the employee to remain at work despite knowing the employee was under the influence of intoxicants. Therefore, a supervisor smelling alcohol on an employee's breath and doing nothing is not express acquiescence [*see* Stepanek v. Rinker Materials Corp., 697 So. 2d 200, 202 (Fla. 1st DCA 1997)].

For example, the injured worker was a liquor sales agent who died in an automobile accident. His blood alcohol level at the time of the crash was.22 percent. The court found the employer had encouraged its sales staff to drink with customers. Further, the employer had at least implied that it would not deprive the employee of compensation if he should become intoxicated. The employer was therefore estopped from raising the intoxication defense. The court cautioned, however, that this case was unique and no one should construe it to provide an estoppel in significantly different circumstances [*see* West Florida Distributors v. Laramie, 438 So. 2d 133, 135–136 (Fla. 1st DCA 1983)].

In *Sterling,* cited in [7], *above,* the court noted that the employees often drank a few beers after work. The employer occasionally joined them and took his turn purchasing the beer. The court held that an estoppel did not apply. The evidence did not suggest such specific employer involvement in the drinking practices of the employees as condoning their regular practice of becoming inebriated [Sterling v. Mike Brown, Inc., 580 So. 2d 832, 836 (Fla. 1st DCA 1991)].

[9] Drug And Alcohol Testing

Effective October 1, 1989, employers have the right to require an employee to submit to drug and alcohol testing if the employer believes the employee's intoxication caused the accident. Refusing to submit to testing raises a presumption of intoxication. The Act provides as follows [§ 440.09(7)(b), Fla. Stat. (10/1/89)]:

> If the injured worker refuses to submit to a drug test, it shall be presumed in the absence of clear and convincing evidence to the contrary that the injury was occasioned primarily by the influence of drugs.

NOTE: With the 1994 amendments, § 440.09(7)(b), Fla. Stat. is unchanged, but is now found under § 440.09(7)(c), Fla. Stat.

This statutory provision means that refusal to submit for drug testing is the same as a positive test result. Employers must conduct such testing according to the drug testing rules issued by the Division of Workers' Compensation [*see* Fla. Admin. Code R. 59A-24].

[10] Drug-Free Workplace Program

[a] Presumption of Intoxication

In 1990, the legislature established the Drug-Free Workplace Program. The statutes provide that if an employer implements a Drug-Free Workplace Program, any positive test in the amount prescribed by rule of drugs or alcohol, raises a conclusive presumption that the use of such drugs or alcohol caused the injury. The statute provides as follows [§ 440.101(2), Fla. Stat. (1/1/94)]:

> If an employer implements a drug-free workplace program in accordance with [§ 440.102, Fla. Stat.] which includes notice, education, and procedural requirements for testing for drugs and alcohol pursuant to law or to rules developed by the Agency for Health Care Administration, the employer may require the employee to submit to a test for the presence of drugs or alcohol and, if a drug or alcohol is found to be present in the employee's system at a level prescribed by rule adopted pursuant to this act, *the employee may be terminated and forfeits his or her eligibility for medical and indemnity benefits*. . . (Emphasis added)

In 1997, however, the Florida Supreme Court held that the conclusive presumption provision is unconstitutional and cannot apply. Therefore, the presumption is rebuttable even if the employer has a drug-free workplace program [*see* Recchi America Inc. v. Hall, 692 So. 2d 153, 154–155 (Fla. 1997)]. When the employer has a drug-free workplace program, however, rebutting the presumption requires showing that no reasonable theory can support the notion that the intoxication contributed to the injury [*see* [6][f], *above*].

Although the irrebuttable presumption provision was held unconstitutional, the Supreme Court's holding does not affect the other drug-free workplace provisions. The section goes on to provide that employers must inform all employees that it is a required condition of employment that employees do not report for work or do their work while using drugs or alcohol. This means, of course, that the employer will fire any employee found using drugs or alcohol on the job.

The law gives the employer the right to conduct reasonable suspicion drug testing. The employer can require testing based on only the belief that an employee is using or has used drugs, violating the employer's policy [§ 440.102(1)(n), Fla. Stat.]. This section lists facts and inferences on which an employer may base such belief. These include the following:

1. Observable phenomena while at work, such as direct observation of drug use, physical symptoms, or manifestations of being under the influence of a drug.

2. Abnormal conduct or erratic behavior while at work or a significant deterioration in work performance.

3. A report of drug use, provided by a reliable and credible source.

4. Evidence that an individual has tampered with a drug test during his employment with the current employer.

5. Information that an employee has caused, or contributed to, or been involved in, an accident while at work.

6. Evidence that an employee has used, possessed, sold, solicited, or transferred drugs while working, while on the employer's premises, or while operating the employer's vehicle, machinery, or equipment.

The Drug-Free Workplace statute is complicated. This section alone is more than 10 pages long. The drug-testing rule is more than 30 pages long. Employers intending to carry out this program will be wise to obtain their carriers' or lawyers' help. Before carriers try to defend under this provision, they and their defense attorneys should review the employer's program. Even substantial compliance is not enough. The employer's program

Guide to Claims

must comply fully with all the requirements of §§ 440.101 and 440.102, Fla. Stat. and the Division's rules [*see* Gustafson's Dairy/Profes. v. Phillips, 656 So. 2d 1386, 1387–1388 (Fla. 1st DCA 1995)].

[b] Drug Testing Procedure

[i] Education

Before any drug testing can begin, the employer must give all employees and job applicants a written policy statement. This policy must include a general statement of the employer's drug-use policy. It also must include the steps the employer will take to insure confidentiality. The policy statement must describe what happens if employees refuse to submit to testing. Finally, it must include a statement of the employee's rights and duties under the program.

The employer must give notice to all employees that it intends to carry out a drug testing program. The employer must give this notice at least 60 days before any testing may begin [§ 440.102(3)(b), Fla. Stat.].

[ii] Substances Subject to Testing

The rules in effect on December 31, 1993, set forth the substances for which the employer can test. Interestingly, the rules require that an employer test for all of them. The rules also prohibit testing for some substances. The only hallucinogen that the employer can test for is phencyclidine (PCP). The only synthetic narcotics the employer can test for are methadone and proxyphene. The rule specifically prohibits testing for any designer drugs. Effective January 1, 1994, however, the Workers' Compensation Act plainly allows testing for any or all these substances [§ 440.102(1)(c), Fla. Stat. (1/1/94)].

[iii] Drug Testing Laboratory and Procedures

[A] Initial Test

Approved laboratories can use urine, hair, blood, and other appropriate body specimens to test for drugs. The legislature added hair as an appropriate specimen effective October 1, 1996 [§ 112.0455, Fla. Stat. (1996)]. The amendment also created detailed procedures that apply only to hair sample testing. Therefore, to preserve a drug intoxication defense, carriers must ensure that sample collection, chain of custody, and other statutory testing requirements are followed precisely. Because hair sample testing allows significantly increased precision in drug test results, this amendment may prove significant to both injured workers and to carriers.

The employer can test for any or all of the substances listed below, but only for those listed. Any level equal to or exceeding the level shown to be a positive test result [*see* Fla. Admin. Code R. 59A-24.006(4)(e)1].

FIRST TEST

SUBSTANCE	POS. LEVEL
Alcohol	0.05 g/dl%

FIRST TEST

SUBSTANCE	POS. LEVEL
Amphetamines	1,000 NG/ml
Cannabinoids	100 NG/ml
Cocaine	300 NG/ml
Phencyclidine	25 NG/ml
Methaqualone	300 NG/ml
Opiates	300 NG/ml
Barbiturates	300 NG/ml
Benzodiaz-epines	300 NG/ml
Methadone	300 NG/ml
Propoxyphene	300 NG/ml

SPECIAL NOTE: The law provides different cutoff levels for initial drug screening using hair samples [§ 112.0455(13), Fla. Stat. (1996)].

All testing must be done at a drug testing laboratory certified by the United States Department of Health and Human Services. If not, the laboratory must be licensed by the Florida Agency for Health Care administration. Exception: Employers who are subject to U.S. Department of Transportation (DOT) regulations should follow those rules instead [§ 440.102(1)(e), Fla. Stat. (1/1/94)].

[B] Confirmation Test Required

Any positive test must be retested and confirmed. The level required for a positive confirmation on retest, however, is significantly less than for the initial test. Levels equal to or exceeding those below on retests are confirmations of a positive test result [§ 440.102(6), Fla. Stat. (1/1/94); Fla. Admin. Code R. 59A-24.006(4)(f)].

CONFIRMATION TEST

SUBSTANCE	POS. LEVEL
Alcohol	0.05 g/dl%
Amphetamines	500 NG/ml
Cannabinoids	15 NG/ml
Cocaine	150 NG/ml
Phencyclidine	25 NG/ml
Methaqualone	150 NG/ml
Opiates	300 NG/ml
Barbiturates	150 NG/ml
Benzodiaz-epines	150 NG/ml
Methadone	150 NG/ml

CONFIRMATION TEST	
SUBSTANCE	**POS. LEVEL**
Propoxyphene	150 NG/ml

SPECIAL NOTE: The level for alcohol is 0.10 g/dl% for accidents occurring before January 1, 1994. For accidents occurring after that date, the level is 0.08 g/dl%. When the employer carries out a formal drug-free workplace program, however, note that the level drops to 0.05 g/dl% [*see* Fla. Admin. Code R. 59A-24.006(4)(f)].

[iv] Releasing Test Results

A Medical Review Officer (MRO) must review and verify the results of drug tests, either positive or negative, before the MRO releases them. An MRO must be a licensed physician knowledgeable in substance abuse disorders and in pharmacology and toxicology of illicit drugs. The MRO must have the necessary medical training to interpret and check an employee's positive test result in relation to the employee's medical history or any other relevant biomedical information. In addition, the MRO must be knowledgeable in laboratory testing procedures and chain of custody collection procedures [§ 440.102(1)(k), Fla. Stat.].

It is the employer's responsibility to contract with an MRO. The MRO cannot be the testing laboratory's employee, but licensed laboratories may help employers find a qualified MRO. The MRO need not be employed by or under direct contract with the employer. If the physician contracted with the hospital, which in turn contracted with the employer, that is enough to satisfy the statutory requirement [*see* Stepanek v. Rinker Materials Corp., 697 So. 2d 200, 202 (Fla. 1st DCA 1997)].

The MRO is responsible for verifying the laboratory's results and for checking the chain of custody and specimen collection procedure. Thus, the MRO must be sure that the entire procedure was conducted according to the rules. If the test result is positive, the MRO must inform the individual of this fact within three days after receiving the result. Further, the MRO must explore the possible use of prescription or over-the-counter medications that may have caused the positive test. The MRO must also inform the employer of the test results, whether positive or negative.

SPECIAL ALERT: Effective January 1, 1994, the Act requires that if a test is positive, the testing facility must maintain the specimen for a minimum of 90 days [§ 440.09(7)(b), Fla. Stat.].

[v] Final Caveat

As mentioned several times in this chapter, the First District Court of Appeal held that the irrebuttable presumption provision contained in § 440.09(3), Fla. Stat. is unconstitutional and cannot apply. The court made it clear, however, that all of the other provisions remain intact [*see* Recchi America Inc. v. Hall, 692 So. 2d 153, 154–155 (Fla. 1997)].

SPECIAL ALERT: Effective January 1, 1994, the Workers' Compensation Act requires that carriers pay for all medical care authorized before the date they issue a Notice of Denial. The Act provides as follows [§ 440.102(5)(p), Fla. Stat. (1/1/94)]:

> All authorized remedial treatment, care, and attendance provided by a health care provider to an injured employee before medical and indemnity benefits are denied under this section must be paid for by the carrier or self-insurer. However, the carrier or self-insurer must have given reasonable notice to all affected health care providers that payment for treatment, care, and attendance provided to the employee after a future date certain will be denied. A health care provider, as defined in [§ 440.13(1)(i), Fla. Stat.], that refuses, without good cause, to continue treatment, care, and attendance before the provider receives notice of benefit denial commits a misdemeanor of the second degree . . .

Carriers who intend to deny a claim based on an intoxication defense must send written notice to all health care providers. This notice must announce the future date after which the carrier will no longer pay for medical treatment. The carrier must pay for all charges incurred up to that date. The section does not define the term "reasonable"; however, five days should suffice since that is the time deemed reasonable notice for depositions.

[11] Public Employees in Safety-Sensitive Positions

Effective January 1, 1994, the legislature added new sections to the Workers' Compensation Act dealing with public employees in safety-sensitive positions [§ 440.102(11), Fla. Stat. (1/1/94)]. A safety-sensitive position with a public employer is one in which a drug impairment is an immediate and direct threat to public health or safety. Examples are positions that require the employee to carry firearms, do life-threatening procedures, work with confidential records and information, work with criminal investigations, or work with controlled substances. It includes any position in which a momentary lapse in attention could result in injury or death to another. In addition, a safety-sensitive position includes those described in § 110.1127, Fla. Stat. These are positions of special trust or responsibility. They include all positions with the Division of Treasury and the Department of Insurance. They also include those positions within the Department of Health and Rehabilitative Services which provide care to children [§ 440.102(1)(o), Fla. Stat. (1/1/94)].

If such employees enroll in a drug rehabilitation program, the employer must reassign them to a non-sensitive position. If no such job exists, the employer must place the employee on leave [§ 440.102(11)(b), Fla. Stat. (1/1/94)].

[12] Public Employees in Special Risk Positions

Effective January 1, 1994, the legislature added new sections to the Workers' Compensation Act dealing with public employees in special risk positions [§ 440.102(11), Fla. Stat. (1/1/94)]. For a public employer, a special-risk position is one that requires the State Fire Marshal or the Department of Law Enforcement to certify the employee. As with safety-sensitive positions, employees under this class must be reassigned or placed on leave if they are enrolled in a drug rehabilitation program. In addition, if a drug test confirms the employee is using illicit drugs, even on the first test, the employer may take disciplinary action including dismissal [§ 440.102(1)(p), Fla. Stat. (1/1/94); *see also* Ch. 633, Ch. 943, Fla. Stat.].

§ 9.03 Statute of Limitations Defense

[1] The Rule

For accident dates through December 31, 1993, a claim or petition for benefits is forever barred unless it is filed within two years of (1) the date of injury, or (2) the last payment of compensation or provision of remedial treatment or rehabilitative care.

For accident dates after January 1, 1994, a claim or petition for benefits is forever barred unless it is filed within (1) two years of the date of injury, or (2) after the initial two years, within one year of the last payment of compensation or provision of remedial treatment, care or attendance [§ 440.19(1)(a), (b), (c), Fla. Stat.].

For a general discussion of notice and claim periods, see Larson's Workers' Compensation, Desk Edition, Ch. 126 (Matthew Bender).

SPECIAL ALERT: For claims up to December 31, 1993, no statute of limitations exists for medical care or indemnity benefits relating to prosthetic devices [§ 440.19(1)(b), Fla. Stat.]. Effective January 1, 1994, the legislature repealed that provision. Therefore, for accidents occurring on or after that date, the one-year limitation period applies to prosthetic devices in the same fashion as other medical benefits. See [7], *below,* for further discussion.

[2] What Is a Statute of Limitations

A statute of limitations is a provision that ends a person's right to claim benefits or sue for compensation and damages unless the person meets certain conditions [§ 440.19(1), Fla. Stat.]. Thus, in workers' compensation, injured workers must file a Petition for Benefits before the time expires or their claims are forever barred. Over the years, the legislature has tinkered with this provision, and has alternately increased and decreased the time.

[3] To Which Claims Do Changes in the Time Apply

A question arises about whether a change to the limitations period is a procedural or substantive amendment. That is to say, do changes apply to existing claims or only to those occurring after the effective date of the change? At first, such amendments appear to alter the substantive rights of the parties since they may increase or decrease the time limit within which an injured worker must file a Petition for Benefits. This, however, is a false appearance. Limitations laws simply prescribe the time within which particular rights may be enforced and relate to remedies only. The law is well settled that the legislature has the authority to change the limitations period. Whether they increase or decrease the time, the legislative changes may apply to any existing cause of action. Different rules of construction apply, however, to statutes extending the limitation period from those reducing the period.

If the amendment increases the time, it applies to any pending case unless the original limitations period has already expired. If the amendment reduces the time, it applies to all pending cases only if there is clear legislative intent that it so apply, and even then only if injured workers have a reasonable time to file a petition after enactment of the change [*see* Corbett v. General Engineering & Machinery, Co., 160 Fla. 879, 37 So. 2d 161, 162 (1948)].

The next question is what is a reasonable time? In 1978, the Florida Supreme Court held that a one-year savings period is a reasonable time [*see* Bauld v. J. A. Jones Const. Co., 357 So. 2d 401, 403 (Fla. 1978); *see also* Rabon v. Hardaway Const., 651 So. 2d 179, 180 (Fla. 1st DCA 1995)].

Note, however, for a decrease in the time to apply retroactively, the legislature must clearly say so. Without a clear statement of legislative intent, the presumption is against any intent by the legislature to make a limitations reduction retroactive [*see* Robinson v. Johnson, 110 So. 2d 68, 70 (Fla. 1st DCA 1959)].

Additionally, if a cause of action has not become time barred on the effective date of a statutory amendment extending the statute of limitations, then a party may take advantage of other provisions that may exist in the statutory amendment providing additional time. For example, the Florida legislature amended § 440.19(1), Fla. Stat., which included a provision allowing a claimant to contend that the carrier is estopped from asserting a limitations defense by failing to tell the claimant about his or her rights, benefits, and obligations. A worker whose injury occurred before this amendment can still take advantage of it if the claim is not time barred by the original statute [*see* Gaines v. Orange County Public Utilities, 710 So. 2d 139, 140 (Fla. 1st DCA 1998)].

[4] How the Limitation Applies

[a] Accident Dates Through December 31, 1993

The law forever bars injured workers' rights to compensation benefits unless they timely file a proper Petition for Benefits. The Petition for Benefits must meet the requirements of the Act and the injured worker must file it with the Division of Workers' Compensation within two years after the following three events [§ 440.19, Fla. Stat.]:

1. Within two years after the injury itself;
2. Within two years after the last payment of compensation; or
3. Within two years after the date the carrier last provided remedial medical treatment or rehabilitative services.

Do not confuse a Petition for Benefits with a notice of injury. A Petition for Benefits is the workers' compensation equivalent of a lawsuit (i.e., a complaint). The same limitations apply to health care providers for claims for reimbursement. For accidents occurring before 1994, no limitation period exists for medical care or indemnity benefits relating to a prosthetic device [§ 440.19(1)(b), Fla. Stat.].

In death cases, dependents or other claimants such as health care providers, must file a petition for benefits within two years of the death or within two years after the carrier paid the last death benefit [§ 440.19(1)(d), Fla. Stat.].

[b] Accident Dates On or After January 1, 1994

The 1994 amendments to § 440.19, Fla. Stat. provide a two-tier limitations period. The two-year time limitation, beginning with the accident date, continues as before. If the employee, or the employee's estate in death cases, fails to report the accident in the time frames discussed in § 9.01, the law bars the claim.

To be timely, a petition must be filed within two years of the date of the accident, or even thereafter, if filed within one year after the last date the claimant received medical treatment or indemnity benefits. § 440.19(2), Fla. Stat. states that, "Payment of any indemnity benefit or the furnishing of remedial treatment. . . . shall toll the limitations period set forth above for 1 year from the date of such payment." Because the term "toll" means only to suspend or to stop temporarily, the section has no practical effect until after the initial two-year period expires. Providing medical treatment or indemnity benfits can extend the limitations period, but cannot shorten it [*see* Orange County School Board v. Best, 728 So. 2d 1186, 1188 (Fla. 1st DCA 1999)]. Two exceptions apply to this. The first exception occurs if a legally uninsured employer posted notice of lack of coverage as required by § 440.055, Fla. Stat. [§ 440.19(4), Fla. Stat. (1/1/94)].

The second exception occurs if the carrier can show it sent the injured worker an informational brochure as required by § 440.185, Fla. Stat. If either exception applies, the burden of proof shifts to the injured worker. If the exceptions apply, and injured workers hope to argue successfully that the carrier or employer is estopped from raising the defense, they can do so only by producing clear and convincing evidence [§ 440.19(4), Fla. Stat. (1/1/94)].

In all cases, a claimant will have a minimum of two years from the date of injury within which to file a petition for benefits. In other instances, the period of time will be longer. A petition is time-barred unless it is filed during the *longer* of the following two periods of time:

(1) Within two years from the date of injury; or

(2) Within one year from the payment of indemnity benefits or the furnishing of remedial treatment, care or attendance pursuant to either a notice of injury or a petition for benefits [*see* Claims Mgmt. v. Philip, 746 So. 2d 1180, 1182 (Fla. 1st DCA 1999), *reh'g denied,* January 12, 2000].

> **NOTE:** Because the Act contains no clear statement of legislative intent about how the limitation period applies, the law presumes this partial reduction in the limitations period applies only prospectively. That is, it applies only to accidents on or after January 1, 1994 [*see* Corbett v. General Engineering & Machinery Co., 160 Fla. 879,

37 So. 2d 161, 162 (1948)].

SPECIAL ALERT: The Act provides that the one-year limitation period does not apply to the issues of compensability, the date of maximum medical improvement, and permanent impairment. For these issues, the two-year limitations period applies [§ 440.19(2), Fla. Stat.]. The Act also provides that the carrier may not raise the statute of limitations defense unless it does so in "its initial response to the petition for benefits." This means the carrier must raise the limitations defense in the Notice of Denial. If not, the law prohibits the carrier from raising the defense [§ 440.19(4), Fla. Stat.].

Several events may start or stop the limitations period [*see* [5], [6], *below*].

[5] What Starts the Clock Running

[a] Identifiable Accident

A work-related accident starts the limitation period running. If the case involves an identifiable accident, the statute of limitations begins to run from the date of the accident, not from the date the injury manifested itself [*see* State Dept. of Agriculture v. Hinote, 442 So. 2d 297, 299 (Fla. 1st DCA 1983)].

[b] Reasonable Person Standard

The clock does not begin to run until the injured worker, as a reasonable person, should recognize the "nature, seriousness, and probable compensable character of his injury or disease" [*see* Herb's Exxon v. Whatmough, 487 So. 2d 1169, 1172 (Fla. 1st DCA 1986); *see also* § 9.01, for discussion on the failure to report defense].

Often, a worker suffers from a condition of unknown cause. The statute of limitations does not begin to run until the injured worker receives actual notice that the injury or disease is compensable within a reasonable degree of medical probability. Opposite this is the worker who suffers an apparently minor injury, but does not know the extent of his injury for weeks or months. Before January 1, 1994, the statutes allowed no specific exceptions for these situations. Thinking such a situation is unacceptable, the *Watmough* court created the "reasonable man" exception. Although the exception was created to form the basis for excusing a worker's failure to report an injury within 30 days, the courts have applied it to the statute of limitations as well. The "reasonable man" exception, however, does not apply to long term complications of a known serious injury or compensable procedure after the statute of limitations has expired. For example, if an injured worker develops complications from compensable surgery only after the statute of limitations has expired, the claim is barred. This is true despite the worker's lack of knowledge. Although the worker in such a case may not have foreseen the exact complication that developed, the worker would have been aware of having suffered the injury leading to the compensable surgery. Such knowledge is enough to start the clock [*see* Florida Hosp. v. Williams, 689 So. 2d 1255, 1257 (Fla. 1st DCA 1997), *rev. denied,* 698 So. 2d 840 (Fla. 1997)].

NOTE: Effective January 1, 1994, the legislature codified the "reasonable man" exception for timely reporting within § 440.19(1), Fla. Stat. by adding that the two-year statute does not begin to run until the employee knew or should have known the injury was work related.

On the other hand, if the employer receives information that the injured worker's condition may be work-related, the employer must inform the worker of such information. If not, the law will not allow the employer to raise a limitations defense. Even if the likelihood of work connection is remote, the employer has a duty to inform the injured worker about possible entitlement to benefits. In such cases the employer should send a Notice of Injury to its carrier. Effective October 1, 1989, § 440.19, Fla. Stat. was amended to provide that failure to file a notice of injury with the Division does not toll the running of the statute of limitations. This provision was repealed effective January 1, 1994.

For example, an employee became ill from the effects of aplastic anemia, an extremely rare disease. In 1987, a physician reported the disease could have been caused from chemical exposure at work or from a non work-related viral infection. At the time, scientific knowledge about the disease was very limited. The doctor provided an opinion to both the employee and to the employer. Everyone, apparently, assumed a non work-related viral infection caused the employee's illness. It was not until 1990 that the employee consulted an expert who concluded that chemical exposure at work caused the disease. Upon learning this, the employee filed a Petition for Benefits. The court rejected the employer's limitations defense because in 1987 the employer knew about the possibility that the disease was work related.

When the employer has knowledge of only a *possibility* of compensability, it has a duty to inform the injured employee about such knowledge. If not told, and this lack of knowledge prejudices the employee, the employer cannot raise a limitation defense. The only exception is if the employer can show the employee had actual notice that the condition was compensable within a reasonable degree of medical *probability* [*see* Timmeny v. Tropical Botanicals Corp., 615 So. 2d 811, 814–817 (Fla. 1st DCA 1993)].

[c] Exceptions to the Rule

To some degree the legislature may have adopted much of this case law. Now, the limitation period begins when the employee knew or should have known that the injury or death arose out of work done in the course and scope of employment [§ 440.19(1), Fla. Stat. (1/1/94)]. Two exceptions to this general rule apply.

The first exception occurs if the injured worker is a minor or is mentally incompetent. If so, the limitations period is tolled until a guardian or representative is appointed. If the injured worker is a minor without a guardian, the limitations period does not begin to run until the minor becomes of age [§ 440.19(5), Fla. Stat. (1/1/94)].

The second exception occurs if the injured worker sues the employer, arguing that no employer/employee relationship existed and therefore the immunity does not apply. Here, the limitations period does not begin to run until the suit is ended with a finding that the injured person was an employee, thus making workers' compensation the exclusive remedy. In such a case, the Act allows the employer a credit of $250 toward its cost of defending the suit. The credit can be taken only by deduction from compensation benefits [§ 440.19(6), Fla. Stat. (1/1/94)].

[d] Occupational Disease and Repetitive Trauma Cases

[i] When the Time Begins

If the case involves an occupational disease the time begins to run from the date of disability. If the case involves repetitive trauma, the time begins to run from the date of disability or the date of last injurious exposure, whichever is later. These dates, of course, may be different from the date the injured worker was first exposed or when he or she detected the disease, or even when symptoms first appeared [*see* American Beryllium Co. v. Stringer, 392 So. 2d 1294, 1296 (Fla. 1980); *see also* Barrett v. Douglas Fertilizer and Chem., 702 So. 2d 609, 610 (Fla. 1st DCA 1997)].

[ii] Repetitive Trauma

The most common form of exposure is repetitive trauma. Here, disability results from months or years of minor, but repetitive trauma. Active symptoms and even knowledge of work connection are not enough to start the clock. Until the worker's condition results in disability, the statute of limitations does not begin [*see* Kulick v. Entertainment Publications, Inc., 667 So. 2d 303, 305 (Fla. 1st DCA 1995)].

Further, in exposure cases it is immaterial whether the employee knew or should have known about possible hazards, or of the possibility of a compensable injury in the future. When the worker was last exposed, or when the worker first detected the disease has nothing to do with starting the limitation period. The period begins only on the first day of disability [*see* Hoppe v. City of Lakeland, 691 So. 2d 585, 587 (Fla. 1st DCA 1997)].

[iii] Importance of Making the Distinction

Note the importance of recognizing the difference between an ordinary case and an occupational disease case. Also note that while occupational disease and repetitive trauma are similar, they are not the same. Confusion arises because the courts have injected occupational disease theory into repeated trauma cases and the doctrines often overlap. More confusing is the fact that some repeated trauma cases may also qualify as occupational disease. The confusion began in 1937 when the Florida Supreme Court held that exposure to heat amounted to an accident [*see* Alexander Orr, Jr., Inc. v. Florida Industrial Com'n, 129 Fla. 369, 176 So. 172, 173 (1937)].

[iv] Exposure Theory

Subsequent cases dealing with repeated trauma eliminated the requirement that an accident happen "suddenly." Meanwhile, in 1945, the legislature created a new section in Ch. 440, Fla. Stat. to provide specifically for occupational disease cases. The main elements that distinguish occupational disease are that the suddenness requirement does not apply, and that the disease must be related to a particular trade or occupation.

Exposure theory continued to evolve and develop separately from occupational disease.

In 1957 the Court decided that an "accidental" injury could result from the cumulative effect of multiple exposures [*see* Czepial v. Krohne Roofing Company, 93 So. 2d 84, 85–86 (Fla. 1957)]. In 1971, the Court explained that all of these little traumas were really just repeated accidents which combine to produce the final, compensable injury [*see* Worden v. Pratt and Whitney Aircraft, 256 So. 2d 209, 210–211 (Fla. 1971)].

[v] Establishing the Accident Date

In all cases the statute of limitations begins to run on the date the accident occurred. However, occupational disease, exposure, and repetitive trauma cases have extended or repetitive accident dates. Therefore, the accident date to use is the date the worker first became disabled or the date the worker suffered the last "little" accident producing the injury [*see* Tokyo House, Inc. v. Hsin Chu, 597 So. 2d 348, 350–351 (Fla. 1st DCA 1992)].

[6] What Stops the Clock Running

[a] Restarting the Clock

Several events may stop or "toll" the running of the statute of limitations. Remember that most of these events do not simply freeze the time in place; they start the two-year period over!

[b] Petition for Benefits

[i] Filing a Petition

Filing a Petition for Benefits stops the limitations period from expiring [*see* ch. 22, § 22.03[2]]. The time does not begin to run again unless one of the following occurs: a judge of compensation claims awards benefits or dismisses the petition, or the injured worker voluntarily withdraws the petition.

For accidents occurring before January 1, 1994, if the injured worker filed a Claim for Benefits, but no Application for Hearing, the case simply remained dormant. Unless the injured worker withdrew the claim or a judge dismissed the claim, the statute of limitations would never expire. The 1994 amendments to the Act should solve this problem because the new Petition for Benefits is both a claim and an application for hearing. Once filed, the resolution process begins.

To stop the limitations period from running, however, the Petition for Benefits must be a statutorily proper one. A Petition for Benefits that does not claim any specific type of benefit is not a claim that tolls the statute of limitation [*see* Jones v. K & L Contractors, 392 So. 2d 375, 376–377 (Fla. 1st DCA 1981); *see also* § 440.19(3), Fla. Stat. (1/1/94)].

A so-called shotgun claim for future medical benefits is not enough to toll the statute of limitations. These are petitions that claim every possible class of benefit simultaneously [*see* Florida Structures, Inc. v. Morton, 443 So. 2d 444, 445–446 (Fla. 1st DCA 1984)].

In 1990, the legislature amended § 440.19, Fla. Stat., which mandates that all Petitions for Benefits meet certain specificity requirements. After July 1, 1990, any petition not meeting the specificity requirements will not toll the statute of limitations. Judges of compensation claims must dismiss any claim not in compliance with the specificity requirements [§ 440.19(3), Fla. Stat.]. Not all judges, however, strictly enforced this provision. The specificity review required of docketing judges beginning in 1994 is intended to help solve this problem. The law also prohibits awarding attorney's fees or penalties if the petition does not meet specificity requirements [§ 440.192(7), Fla. Stat.]. Petitions for Benefits must also strictly meet filing requirements and deadlines.

[ii] Petition Dismissed or Withdrawn

There exists a well-established line of authority in civil cases holding that, when an action is dismissed, the statute of limitations is not tolled during the period when the dismissed action was pending. Rather, the statute will run as if the dismissed action had never been filed. The same is generally true when the state enters a nolle prosequi in a criminal prosecution. This rule also applies in workers' compensation cases.

Florida case law states that the filing of a complaint tolls the statute of limitations in civil actions. However, such cases are merely concerned with whether the date on which a complaint is filed, or the date on which a defendant is served, is the crucial date for determining the timeliness of an action and do not address the tolling effect of an earlier dismissed action on the limitations period applicable to a later action.

The statute, § 440.19(3), Fla. Stat., merely states that a workers' compensation petition must be filed in compliance with the specificity requirements of § 440.192, Fla. Stat., to be timely for purposes of the applicable statute of limitations. It does not purport to address the tolling effect of an earlier-filed (and subsequently-dismissed) petition on the limitations period applicable to a later-filed petition. Instead, it appears intended to eliminate a tolling provision in the pre-1994 statute, which stated that, when a claim was dismissed for lack of specificity, the claimant was allowed 60 days from the date of the order of dismissal in which to file an amended claim, regardless of any other limitation in chapter 440 [*see* § 440.19(1)(e)4, Fla. Stat. (1993)].

In short, there is nothing to suggest that § 440.19(3), Fla. Stat., was intended to alter the well-established rule that the statute of limitations is *not* tolled during the period in which a dismissed action was pending. Rather, courts presume that the legislature was aware of this rule when it enacted subsection (3) [*see* McBride v. Pratt & Whitney & Ace USA, 909 So. 2d 386 (Fla. 1st DCA 2005)].

[c] Claim for Benefits Versus Petition for Benefits

Effective January 1, 1994, the legislature changed the procedure for starting litigation from filing a Claim for Benefits and an Application for Hearing to simply filing a Petition for Benefits [*see* ch. 22, § 22.03[2][a]]. Under the 1994 provision, however, an injured worker cannot file a Petition for Benefits without having first filed a Request for Assistance with the Division of Workers' Compensation [§ 440.191(2), Fla. Stat.]. By allowing concurrent applicability of these two procedures the legislature created an anomaly. If an employee filed a Claim for Benefits after January 1, 1994, for a 1992 accident, does that toll the statute of limitations? Does filing a Request for Assistance toll the statute? The answer to both questions is yes.

Edgar Sanchez was injured on July 17, 1992. He filed an old Claim for Benefits and a Request for Assistance on June 27, 1994. Later, he filed a Petition for Benefits on July 22,

1994, five days after the two-year statute of limitations should have expired. The judge of compensation claims held the statute of limitations did expire because Sanchez filed the Petition for Benefits too late. The First District Court of Appeal disagreed and held filing the Claim for Benefits with the Request for Assistance tolled the statute of limitations. Although filing the Claim for Benefits was incorrect procedure, filing the Request for Assistance would have been sufficient. To hold otherwise would shorten the statute of limitations by 30 days, because injured workers cannot file a Petition for Benefits until 30 days after filing a request for assistance [*see* Sanchez v. Acapulco Plasters & Stucco, 668 So. 2d 298, 300 (Fla. 1st DCA 1996)].

[d] Paying Compensation Benefits

Each payment of compensation starts a new limitation period. If the employer or carrier makes a payment after the limitation period expires, the limitation period is revived and begins again. Paying wages instead of compensation will toll the statute of limitations. This is contingent on evidence that the employer intended the wages to replace compensation or if the employee believed they were so intended [*see* Davis v. Kyle, 529 So. 2d 1240, 1242 (Fla. 1st DCA 1988); *see also* § 440.19(2), Fla. Stat. in which the legislature codified *Davis* and other similar holdings].

Paying interest on late payments is the same as paying compensation for purposes of the statute of limitations [*see* Foster Wheeler Energy Group v. Fairhurst, 405 So. 2d 438, 439 (Fla. 1st DCA 1981)].

[e] Failure to File Notice of Injury With the Division

The First District Court of Appeal once held that the statute of limitations does not begin to run until the carrier files a notice of injury with the Division of Workers' Compensation according to § 440.185, Fla. Stat. Apparently, the court believed that such a filing triggered sending an informational brochure to injured workers without which, said the court, they would not know their rights [*see* McCort v. Southland Corp., 543 So. 2d 232, 233–234 (Fla. 1st DCA 1989)].

The court later withdrew this portion of its opinion; however, the decision still drew the attention of the legislature. Effective October 1, 1989, the legislature added the following to the Act [§ 440.19, Fla. Stat.]:

> This limitations period shall not be tolled or extended by the failure of the employer or carrier to file a notice of injury or any other report or notice required to be filed under this chapter or by the failure of the Division, the employer, or the carrier to furnish the employee or other claimant informational materials required under this chapter, unless such omission by the employer or carrier was intentional and done to deprive the employee of benefits due under this chapter.

In 1993, the court of appeal held this is a substantive provision. It therefore applies only to injuries occurring on or after October 1, 1989 [*see* Timmeny v. Tropical Botanicals Corp., 615 So. 2d 811, 817–818 (Fla. 1st DCA 1993)].

SPECIAL ALERT: The legislature repealed this provision effective January 1, 1994. Repeal does not mean that failing to file a report with the Division will toll the limitations period. It does, however, unlock the door for the courts to revisit the issue. Beginning in 1994, providing an informational brochure to injured workers is the carrier's responsibility [*see* ch. 2, § 2.09[1]].

Guide to Claims

[f] Estoppel

[i] Misleading Injured Workers

The statute of limitations does not run if injured workers do not timely file a petition because the employer or carrier misled or lied to them. For example, in one case the injured worker relied on the carrier's statements that he was not entitled to benefits while he was in jail. The carrier told him to call again upon his release. Although obviously not true, the injured worker did not know that, and so did nothing until his release. By then the two-year period had expired. Because of this, the court refused to allow the statute of limitations defense [*see* Boyd v. Florida Memorial College, 475 So. 2d 990, 992 (Fla. 1st DCA 1985)].

[ii] Failure to Inform Injured Workers About Their Rights

Simply not informing injured workers about their rights also will toll the statute of limitations. In *McCort,* the carrier did not inform the injured worker that she might be entitled to wage loss benefits, or at least did not do so in a timely manner. The court held [*see* McCort v. Southland Corp., 543 So. 2d 232, 234 (Fla. 1st DCA 1989)]:

> [The carrier's] conduct effectively misled claimant into believing no legal action was necessary to protect her legal rights. They never informed claimant of possible benefits pursuant to the Workers' Compensation Act, nor did they notify her that her long-term benefits would [at that time] terminate when she turned 70, until a year after the workers' compensation statute of limitations had expired.

Even an unintentional misrepresentation will toll the statute of limitations. Following is an example. The injured worker's supervisor innocently but incorrectly told him the company had no workers' compensation coverage. By the time he discovered coverage existed, the two-year period had expired. Because the employer misled the injured worker, the carrier was estopped from asserting the limitations defense [*see* Raymond v. Rapid Exp. Parcel Delivery, 548 So. 2d 278, 279 (Fla. 1st DCA 1989)].

The statute of limitations cannot operate to bar a claim for benefits when the employer and carrier fail to explain possible entitlement to those benefits [*see* Stines v. Winter Haven Hospital/Self-Insured, 548 So. 2d 818, 819 (Fla. 1st DCA 1989)]. In other words, the statute of limitations cannot bar a claim until the worker has notice of possible entitlement and the carrier has the burden to provide that information [*see* Timmeney v. Tropical Botanicals Corp., 615 So. 2d 811, 814–817 (Fla. 1st DCA 1993)].

Note, however, that if the employee has been told about the right to benefits, the statute of limitations will expire whether or not the employee knew about the statute. Put another way, failing to tell an injured worker about the details of the statute of limitations does not create an estoppel or stop the limitations period from expiring [*see* Solar Pane Insulating Glass v. Hanssen, 727 So. 2d 961, 963 (Fla. 1st DCA 1998)].This may not apply if the employer and carrier have failed to provide the injured worker with the required brochure describing benefits the worker may be entitled to receive. Failing to provide the brochure tolls the running of the two-year statute of limitations [*see* Southern Bell v. MacDonald, 671 So. 2d 207, 209 (Fla. 1st DCA 1996)].

In 2005, the court clarified its holding in *Hanssen*. The court held that, if the employer/carrier does not inform the claimant about the statute of limitations in the informational brochure (or by other means), the statute is not tolled unless the employer/carrier can prove that the worker had actual knowledge of the pertinent limitation period [*see* Fontanills v. Hillsborough County Sch. Bd., 913 So. 2d 28 (Fla. 1st DCA 2005)].

[g] Estoppel Following Lump-Sum Settlement

Sometimes the parties agree to settle only part of a claim such as indemnity benefits, leaving entitlement to medical benefits open. The rules about instructing injured workers change dramatically after a partial settlement agreement [*see* ch. 21, § 21.04[4]]. Carriers' duty to provide benefits to an injured worker, even one represented by a lawyer, is statutorily different from the duty to tell workers about the statute of limitations. When workers are represented by a lawyer upon signing a settlement agreement, the agreement usually shows that the lawyer explained the agreement and its consequences to the employee. This explanation is usually documented in a stipulation in which the employee acknowledges full understanding. In such cases, arguments that the statute of limitations should not apply because the carrier did not explain it will fail [*see* Gulfstream Press, Inc. v. Acle, 697 So. 2d 213, 216 (Fla. 1st DCA 1997)].

[h] Furnishing Remedial Care and Attention

[i] Remedial Care Defined

Without a statutory definition, the issue of what is remedial care has long been a problem. The legislature temporarily corrected that omission and defined "remedial treatment or attention" as the provision of skilled services provided by a physician or any recognized health care provider as defined in § 440.13, Fla. Stat.

This simple definition suggested that anytime licensed medical providers do anything their licenses permit, such professional service is "remedial treatment" and tolls the statute of limitations. This may include actual treatment, diagnostic tests, simple evaluation, or even giving the injured worker medical advice over the telephone. Before the courts had a chance to review this statutory definition, however, the legislature repealed it effective January 1, 1994.

Again, no statutory definition of remedial treatment exists. Therefore, case law controls and is reviewed in [ii], *below.*

[ii] Furnishing Remedial Care Defined

Understanding when a carrier or employer has, legally speaking, "furnished" remedial medical care is essential because that event starts the statute of limitations running. Unfortunately, no absolute standard exists that we can use to decide this issue. A debate will arise about whether treatment was furnished when the doctor administered the treatment or when the carrier paid the doctor's bill. Either event can be the trigger depending on the circumstances.

When a clearly authorized health care provider administers treatment for an undisputed compensable condition, the treatment is "furnished" when the injured worker receives it. Paying the bill late does not change this fact if the carrier has clearly accepted responsibility. When the carrier has not authorized the treatment, or some question arises about whether the carrier has accepted responsibility, the treatment is not "furnished" until the carrier pays the bill or in another way accepts responsibility [*see* Southern Bell v. MacDonald, 671 So. 2d 207, 209–210 (Fla. 1st DCA 1996)].

[iii] Treatment Date Controls

The treatment date itself, not the date that the physician issues a bill, tolls the statute of limitations. It does not matter if the provider ever sends a bill; the statute is tolled on the date of the treatment [*see* Seamco Laboratories, Inc. v. Pearson, 424 So. 2d 898, 899–900 (Fla. 1st DCA 1982); Whiteman v. United Parcel Service, 438 So. 2d 1042, 1043 (Fla. 1st DCA 1983)].

Before considering a denial under a limitations defense, carriers must be sure to find out from the injured worker, preferably in a signed or recorded statement, the date the worker had their last contact with any health care provider. Adjusters should also contact all authorized physicians and find out when they last treated or had contact with the injured worker.

[iv] Literal Treatment Not Required: Skilled Service Is the Test

"Skilled" service, not literal treatment, is the controlling factor. If the carrier authorizes the doctor for evaluation and treatment, the statute of limitations is tolled though the visit involves only an examination [*see* Barnett v. EMR Telemetry, 396 So. 2d 791, 792 (Fla. 1st DCA 1981)].

There is still ambiguity surrounding this issue. In one case, the injured worker received unauthorized care after an 18-month lapse in treatment. Debate arose about whether this was really treatment because the doctor merely gave the injured worker advice about soaking her injured arm. The carrier knew nothing of this visit and the doctor did not charge for it. Such activity does not amount to furnishing medical treatment that would toll the statute of limitations [*see* Gonzalez v. Allure Shoe Corporation, 160 So. 2d 703, 705 (Fla. 1964)].

[v] Active Treatment Not Required

The law does not limit remedial attention to active medical treatment during a particular two-year period. If the carrier authorizes the doctor to provide follow-up care, visits for continuing supervision, and evaluation for possible changes in treatment, the limitation period is tolled [*see* Tower Chemical Co. v. Hubbard, 527 So. 2d 886, 890 (Fla. 1st DCA 1988)].

Also, the law does not require the employee to obtain renewed authorization to see a physician originally authorized by the carrier. This is true even if the treatment occurs after maximum medical improvement and discharge by the physician. Until the limitations period expires, the employee can obtain treatment without additional authorization [*see* Benson v. Okeechobee Cty. Sheriff's Dept., 632 So. 2d 100, 101 (Fla. 1st DCA 1994)].

[vi] Using a Back Brace May Be Remedial Treatment

Even the continued use of a prescribed back brace is remedial treatment. An important factor is whether the injured worker continues employment and the employer has actual knowledge of the worker's use of the back brace [*see* Fuster v. Eastern Airlines, Inc., 545 So. 2d 268, 273–274 (Fla. 1st DCA 1988)].

The employer, however, is not the carrier's alter ego. If the employer and the employee are the same "person," notice to the employer is not necessarily notice to the carrier. For example, assume that the injured worker also owns the company. The worker/owner continues to use a back brace, unsupervised, for years. The worker/owner's own knowledge of this is not the equivalent of knowledge by the carrier [*see* Solar Pane Insulating Glass v. Hanssen, 727 So. 2d 961, 965–966 (Fla. 1st DCA 1998) (rehearing denied January 16, 1999)].

[vii] Unsupervised Self-Help Is Not Remedial Treatment

[A] Self Help

Self-help, even if suggested by a physician, does not automatically extend the limitations period. For example, Geraldine Devilling's physician released her from active medical care for an ankle injury. Upon release, the doctor advised her to use support hose and prescribed shoe inserts for arch support. The court held that Devilling's occasional, at will use of such modalities does not extend the limitations period. The court said: "Although the doctor indicated that the claimant should use the shoe inserts on a permanent basis, such use does not thereby become treatment furnished by the employer" [*see* Devilling v. Rimes, Inc., 591 So. 2d 304, 305 (Fla. 1st DCA 1991)].

[B] Employer or Carrier Knowledge

The only difference between *Devilling* [*see* [A], *above*] and *Fuster* [*see* [vi], *above*] is employer (or carrier) knowledge. Both *Devilling* and *Fuster* place a burden on the injured worker to prove that the employer or the carrier knew the injured worker was using such devices. This is true even if the worker has had no contact with the employer for years. In 1992, the First District Court of Appeal certified to the Florida Supreme Court the question of the effect continued use of such appliances has on the statute of limitations when the employer had no actual knowledge of use. The facts in the case are in [C], *below*.

[C] *Lee v. City of Jacksonville*

Jay Lee's physician prescribed using a TENS unit for an unspecified period. A TENS unit is a battery-powered machine designed to interfere with pain impulses by applying controlled, low voltage pulses of electricity through electrodes attached to the skin. Lee's physicians did not ask about or supervise his using the unit after prescribing it. In addition, Lee did not tell the physicians he continued to use the device. More than two years later he filed a claim for benefits. Both the trial judge and the First District Court of Appeal held Lee's unsupervised use of the device is not remedial treatment because neither Lee's employer nor his physicians were aware of its use. Thus, the District Court of Appeal certified the question to the Florida Supreme Court [*see* Lee v. City of Jacksonville, 598 So. 2d 296, 297 (Fla. 1st DCA 1992), *aff'd,* 616 So. 2d 37 (Fla. 1993)].

The Supreme Court took up the question and agreed with the District Court of Appeal. For treatment to be "furnished by the employer," the employer or carrier must have actual knowledge that the injured worker is receiving medical treatment. Lee's employer clearly did not have actual knowledge that he was using the TENS unit. Since the employer did not furnish the treatment, the limitations period was not tolled [*see* Lee v. City of Jacksonville, 616 So. 2d 37, 38–39 (Fla. 1993)].

Unfortunately, the conflicting cases fail to establish any fixed rule. Attempting a limitations defense is risky if the injured worker had any professional contact with a medical provider during the past year for accidents occurring after January 1, 1994, or the past two years for accidents occurring before that date.

[viii] Simply Trying to Get an Appointment Is Not Enough

Merely attempting to visit with a physician is not enough to toll the statute of limitations. For example, Vivian Wolf tried to schedule a visit with the authorized doctor during the two months before the expiration of the two-year period since her last treatment. She claimed that she repeatedly tried to get an appointment, but each time was told the doctor was out of town or his calendar was booked. The First District Court of Appeal held that trying to get a doctor appointment was not good enough and that the statute of limitations barred her claim. No express or implied good faith exception to the provisions of the limitations statute exists. Allowing exceptions in cases like this would result in an invitation to fraudulent claims and an evisceration of the statute [*see* Watkins v. Wolf, 626 So. 2d 1080, 1081 (Fla. 1st DCA 1993)].

[i] Orders of Judge of Compensation Claims

If the judge of compensation claims issues an order directing the carrier to supply medical care, the statute of limitations is not tolled, despite whether the order is specific or general [*see* General Electric Co. v. Shepard, 440 So. 2d 462 (Fla. 1st DCA 1983)].

The trial judge here refused to bar the claim although more than two years had elapsed since the employer last supplied compensation or medical care. The judge refused because of an outstanding order from 1979 requiring treatment by a particular physician. The court held: "An order which directs the employer and carrier to supply medical care, be it specific or general and continuing, does not toll the two-year statute."

In addition, the *General Electric* hearing judge found that the limitations defense was not available because the court sent the order to the wrong address and the injured worker did not receive it. The First District Court of Appeal reversed and held: "Nor are the employer and carrier responsible for the failure of claimant's lawyer . . . to communicate with his client. . . ."

What happens if the injured worker files a claim after the two-year period has expired, but it is a claim for medical care given during the two-year period? The injured worker will prevail. For example, Harold Thomas last received medical treatment in September of 1984. He received the bills in June 1985 and filed a claim for benefits in October 1986.

The court held [*see* Roy T. Brinson Lathing and Drywall v. Thomas, 530 So. 2d 379, 380 (Fla. 1st DCA 1988)]:

> Merely because the E/C (employer/carrier) chose not to pay for this treatment at the time does not mean the deputy could not later find the E/C's decision to be incorrect and order payment for this care. Having found the medical treatment to be payable as of a date certain (and within two years of the last payment for such care), the claim for subsequent and continuing treatment filed within two years of that date would be timely.

[j] Reviving an Expired Claim

An injured worker cannot revive an expired claim, but the employer or carrier can, whether on purpose or not! Though the statute of limitations has expired, nothing prevents the carrier from voluntarily paying benefits if it chooses to do so.

If the employer/carrier voluntarily pays compensation or furnishes medical treatment after the statute of limitations has expired, the limitations period is thereby revived, and a new limitations period begins [*see* Daniel v. Holmes Lumber Co., 490 So. 2d 1252, 1256 (Fla. 1986)].

However, to raise an estoppel argument successfully, the claimant must show that the provision or payment of benefits was intentional (not mistaken) and that he or she relied on such activity to his or her detriment.

In *Cole v. Fairfield Cmtys.* [908 So. 2d 1105, (Fla. 1st DCA 2005)], the court found that the employer/carrier did not waive its right to deny compensability pursuant to § 440.20(4), Fla. Stat., even though the employer/carrier had mistakenly tendered a payment to the medical provider.

In *Adamides v. City of Miami* [885 So. 2d 955, 957 (Fla. 1st DCA 2004)] and *Mandarin Paint & Flooring, Inc. v. Potura Coatings of Jacksonville, Inc.* [744 So. 2d 482, 485 (Fla. 1st DCA 1999)], the court held that detrimental reliance is necessary for estoppel.

More recently, the court held that, although the employer/carrier made certain medical and indemnity payments after the expiration of the statute, the evidence was controverted that these payments were made mistakenly. The court held that, although the claimant was blameless in his employer's mistaken payments, he was nevertheless not entitled to invoke the doctrine of estoppel in order to avoid the statute of limitations because he could not show that he had detrimentally changed his position as a result of the employer/carrier's mistake [*see* Williams v. Dep't of Corr., 911 So. 2d 890 (Fla. 1st DCA 2005)].

In another case, the doctor's office called the adjuster on a long-closed case, and requested permission to treat the injured worker. The adjuster saw no problem in authorizing treatment; however, the adjuster could not directly answer the doctor's request because the injured worker's file was in storage. When the adjuster finally recovered the file, he realized the statute of limitations had expired and refused to authorize the doctor to provide care. The court held that this activity did not have the effect of authorizing medical care or reviving the statute of limitations period [*see* Eagle Point Mobile Home Estates v. Smith, 475 So. 2d 992, 994 (Fla. 1st DCA 1985)].

Claims adjusters should always verify the limitations date before authorizing treatment or paying benefits on old claims. Limitations defenses are difficult and tricky and require considerable investigation to be certain no activity has occurred to revive the limitations period.

[k] Providing Palliative Care

Palliative medical care is treatment that may alleviate or ease symptoms, but does not improve or cure the condition. The statutory definition is "noncurative medical services that mitigate the conditions, effects, or pain of an injury" [§ 440.13(1)(o), Fla. Stat. (1/1/94)]. However, "remedial,"as used in § 440.19, Fla. Stat., has been defined to include "palliative" care. Accordingly, the limitations period is revived when the employer/carrier provides the claimant with "palliative" treatment [*see* Borneisen v. Home Depot, 917 So. 2d 361 (Fla. 1st DCA 2005)].

[7] Limitations on Prosthetic Devices

[a] The Rule

[i] Accident Dates Through December 31, 1993

For accident dates through December 31, 1993, the Workers' Compensation Act provided that "no statute of limitations shall apply to the right for remedial attention relating to the insertion or attachment of a prosthetic device to any part of the body" [§ 440.19(1)(b), Fla. Stat.]. This statutory language leads us to two questions. Does it apply to both medical and indemnity benefits? Exactly what is a "prosthetic device?" For further information, see [c], *below*.

[ii] Accident Dates On or After January 1, 1994

Effective January 1, 1994, the legislature repealed § 440.19(1)(b), Fla. Stat. Therefore, the Two-year, one-year limitations period applies to prosthetic devices [*see* [b], *below*]. If the carrier does not provide remedial medical treatment for one year following the initial two years after the date of the accident, the limitations period expires. Thus the carrier is not responsible for the insertion, removal, or maintenance of prosthetic devices or for any treatment causally related to such a device. Remember, this is clearly a substantive amendment that applies only to accidents occurring on or after January 1, 1994.

[b] Prosthetic Device Defined

[i] Background

The Workers' Compensation Act does not define "prosthetic devices." *Webster's Ninth New Collegiate Dictionary* defines a prosthesis as "an artificial device to replace a missing part of the body." This includes such items as artificial arms and legs, but what about surgical devices such as Steffee plates? Surgeons use this device as an internal fixation plate that supplements rather than replaces a body part. *Taber's Cyclopedic Medical Dictionary* (1985) agrees with *Webster,* but expands the definition to include "a device to augment performance of a natural function such as a hearing aid."

The Florida Supreme Court, reluctantly, agreed with the lower court's acceptance of the argument that a Steffee plate is a prosthesis for the purposes of the Workers' Compensation

Act. Why reluctantly? Justice McDonald, in a concurring opinion, explained: "I am not confident that a Steffee plate conforms to the definition of a prosthesis. . . I am doubtful that the legislature intended the exemption to encompass items such as the Steffee Plate." Why then did the Court approve the award of benefits? Because, said Justice McDonald, "[The] respondents [the defense] failed to put forth any evidence on this issue." The Court did not, however, say anything to suggest that we must now consider all such devices as a prosthesis. On the contrary, the Court did not deal with the issue of defining a prosthesis since this was never an issue [*see* Roe v. City Investing/General Dev., 587 So. 2d 1323, 1325 (Fla. 1991)].

[ii] Definition

The First District Court of Appeal provided a preliminary definition, later refined by the Florida Supreme Court. A prosthetic device means: "An artificial substitute or replacement, whether external or implanted, for a missing or defective part of the body."

The judge of compensation claims ruled that a surgical staple is a prosthetic device, and as such, the limitations period did not apply. The First District Court of Appeal reversed, finding that the staple is an internal fixation device and not a replacement part. The court found that such a device has the limited function of holding something in place while something is healing. After that, it is superfluous. As such, the staple is not a prosthetic device and the limitations period does apply [*see* Universal Rivet, Inc. v. Cash, 598 So. 2d 154, 157–158 (Fla. 1st DCA 1992), *aff'd,* 616 So. 2d 446 (Fla. 1993)].

The District Court of Appeal, however, certified the question of definition to the Florida Supreme Court. The high court not only agreed with the District Court of Appeal's view but further narrowed the definition of a prosthetic device. Following is the final, judicially approved, definition of a prosthetic device [*see* Cash v. Universal Rivet, Inc., 616 So. 2d 446, 448 (Fla. 1993)]:

> An artificial substitute or replacement, whether external or implanted, for a missing or defective natural part of the body [which serves] a relatively permanent functional or cosmetic purpose.

[iii] Transplanted Living Tissue Is Not a Prosthesis

Key to the definition of a prosthetic device is the word "artificial." Human organs or other living tissue transplants are not artificial replacements for a body part. Therefore, such transplanted tissue does not qualify as a prosthesis [*see* Colonial Oaks Apartment v. Hood, 680 So. 2d 446, 448 (Fla. 1st DCA 1996)].

[iv] Entitlement to Medical and Indemnity Benefits

The real issue in *Roe* [*see* [i], *above*] was not the definition of a prosthesis. The issue was whether the law entitles an injured worker to both medical and indemnity benefits if doctors insert or attach the device *after* the original limitations period has expired. The First District Court of Appeal has been certain that the law entitles injured workers to medical benefits because that is what the Workers' Compensation Act clearly provides. The question is, however, does this apply to indemnity benefits? The First District Court of Appeal certified the question to the Florida Supreme Court.

The Supreme Court answered yes, holding that a new two-year period is created for both medical and indemnity benefits. The Court reasoned that the Workers' Compensation Act allows a claim for disability benefits if the injured worker files it within two years after the date of last remedial treatment. The Court noted the Act does not have a limitations period for medical care for the insertion of a prosthetic device. When such care is rendered, said the Court, compensable remedial treatment has occurred and a new limitations period is created for indemnity benefits. The Court said: "We therefore hold that a claim for disability is not time-barred, despite a two-year gap between the injury and the claim, so long as the claim is filed within two years after the last remedial treatment" [*see* Roe v. City Investing/General Dev., 587 So. 2d 1323, 1325 (Fla. 1991)]. Note, however, that the statute of limitations does apply to prosthetic devices for accidents occurring on or after January 1, 1994.

[c] Extent of Medical Coverage

Many people believed that the limitations exception applied only to the literal insertion and subsequent maintenance of a prosthetic device. That belief is not correct and virtually any treatment related to a prosthesis is included. For example, Winifred Peo underwent a total hip replacement as the result of a compensable hip fracture suffered in 1985. In 1988 she developed bursitis in the same area. She received no further treatment until 1992 for renewed complaints of bursitis. The carrier denied her claim for further medical care, claiming the statute of limitations had expired. The judge of compensation claims agreed and denied the claim. The First District Court of Appeal, however, disagreed and reversed.

Peo's doctor testified that the treatment had nothing to do with the repair, maintenance, or replacement of the device, but did say that the device caused the bursitis. The carrier argued that the statutory exception to the statute of limitations does not apply to all treatment just because it is in some way related to the device. The court disagreed and held that no limitations period applies to any treatment that has a logical or causal relationship to a prosthetic device [*see* Peo v. Maas Bros., 634 So. 2d 1130, 1132–1133 (Fla. 1st DCA 1994)].

§ 9.04 Intervening Cause Defense

[1] Breaking the Chain of Causation

The intervening cause doctrine, frequently misapplied in workers' compensation, is seldom a complete defense. On the contrary, it is more similar to apportionment. The doctrine has its origins in tort law and holds that if an intervening negligent act breaks the chain of causation, the original tortfeasor will be absolved from liability. For example, assume an automobile driver is operating the car at an excessive speed. A passenger suddenly grabs the steering wheel causing the car to go out of control and crash. Here, there would be no evidence to show that the accident would have occurred from the excessive speed alone. The evidence would show that the intervening negligent act (grabbing the steering wheel) is the proximate cause. The law would absolve the driver from liability for the original negligent act.

For a general discussion of the range of compensable consequences, see LARSON'S WORKERS' COMPENSATION, DESK EDITION, Ch. 10 (Matthew Bender).

[2] Application in Workers' Compensation

Many people have incorrectly believed that the doctrine operates in workers' compensation in the same fashion and with the same finality. For example, a worker suffers a minor back injury at work and then is involved in an unrelated auto accident. This results in significant new back injury. A strict application of the doctrine would consider the auto accident an intervening cause that has broken the chain of causation, absolving the employer from further liability for workers' compensation benefits. Such an application, however, would be incorrect.

The courts have repeatedly held that an intervening subsequent accident may not be so strictly applied. For example, the court has held: "It is well settled . . . (that) . . . the occurrence of the second accident does not break the causal chain for all claims, but only those which would not have resulted if the later, non-compensable, accident had not occurred" [*see* Parrish v. Baptist Hosp., 512 So. 2d 1031, 1032 (Fla. 1st DCA 1987)]. This is especially true when there is evidence that on the date of the non-compensable accident the injured worker was still suffering from the effects of the first, compensable accident.

The court's interpretation is logical and fair, although separating the two injuries may be extremely difficult. In such cases, absent the agreement of the parties, it is the job of the judge of compensation claims to separate the two injuries. The judge must decide what medical expenses relate to which injury. It is the second accident alone for which the workers' compensation carrier is not liable [*see* State, Dept. of Public Health v. Wilcox, 483 So. 2d 21, 22 (Fla. 1st DCA 1985)].

Remember that the judges can only decide from the evidence placed before them. Simply arguing that the subsequent injury was massive compared with the original compensable injury is not enough. If any evidence shows that the worker continues to suffer the effects of the original compensable injury, the intervening cause doctrine cannot operate as a complete bar to recovery. This means that the judge must decide what benefits might yet be due based on the original compensable injury. It is, of course, the carrier's duty to investigate and decide before engaging in litigation.

§ 9.05 Doctrine of Res Judicata

[1] The Rule

Once a court decides a matter, the doctrine of res judicata holds that the court's final judgment is conclusive upon the parties. As such, the issue cannot be brought before the court in any subsequent litigation involving the same cause of action. The doctrine of res judicata also prohibits litigating stale claims. The judge must decide claims for compensation benefits at the benefits hearing if the claims are mature. This is because the law does not allow piecemeal litigation of claims after maturity [*see* Hunt v. Intern. Minerals and Chemical Corp., 410 So. 2d 640, 641 (Fla. 1st DCA 1982)].

For a general discussion of the doctrine of res judicata, see LARSON'S WORKERS' COMPENSATION, DESK EDITION, Ch. 127, § 127.07 (Matthew Bender).

[2] Application

By applying the doctrine of res judicata, the judge can waive compensation claims that are not litigated timely. The policy underlying the doctrine is one of repose. That is, it is the same policy reflected in the statute of limitations that outlaws stale claims. Except under limited circumstances, compensation orders are governed by the same principles of res judicata as applied in other courts. The doctrine of res judicata is not a jurisdictional determination, but a defense that must be asserted by a party to the litigation [*see* PLM Florida Hotels, Inc. v. DeMarseul, 611 So. 2d 1360, 1362 (Fla. 1st DCA 1993); Gladstone v. Kling, 182 So. 2d 471, 474–475 (Fla. 1st DCA 1966)].

Properly applying the doctrine may involve factual determinations, including whether applying the doctrine would result in an injustice. For example, the judge of compensation claims denied payment of certain medical bills because they had not been timely filed or timely litigated. The judge concluded that the bills were for services rendered before the date of the last final hearing, and under the doctrine of res judicata, must be denied. On appeal the court reversed the order. First, a question arose about the injured worker's competency. Second, the record was unclear whether this played a role in the worker's failure to litigate the medical claims timely. (The worker represented himself.) The court held that before applying the doctrine of res judicata, the judge must make certain factual determinations. These include when the medical bills were submitted for payment, who paid portions of these bills, when a guardian was appointed, and whether the guardian should have been aware of the bills and submitted them before the first hearing [*see* Artigas v. Winn Dixie Stores, Inc., 578 So. 2d 356, 358–359 (Fla. 1st DCA 1991)].

Injustice can, of course, affect both sides. For example, the carrier began taking a social security offset of $65.86 per week beginning in 1986. In 1997, the claimant filed a petition asserting that the offset should have been $60.81. The judge of compensation claims agreed and ordered the carrier to recalculate the offset and to repay the entire offset taken from 1986 through all of 1997. The 1st DCA reversed, holding that the claim for recalculation and refund was barred by the doctrine of res judicata. The court noted that there had been three prior merits hearings in 1987, 1989, and 1994. Under the doctrine of res judicata, this claim is barred because the issue was ripe and should have been litigated at the earlier hearings. The court opined that to rule otherwise would cause an injustice for the employer and carrier. Note, however, that an exception to this defense will arise if the issue, such as entitlement to wage loss benefits, is a recurring one [*see* Boynton Landscape v. Dickinson, 752 So. 2d 1236, 1237–1238 (Fla. 1st DCA 2000)].

In another case, Leroy Turner filed a claim for temporary partial disability and wage loss benefits for a period before the date of an earlier hearing. The judge of compensation claims denied the claim under the doctrine of res judicata. The judge held that these claims had been ripe at the time of the first hearing and could have and should have been decided at that hearing. The First District Court of Appeal affirmed the judge's order on this particular issue [*see* Turner v. Rinker Material Corp., 622 So. 2d 80, 83 (Fla. 1st DCA 1993)].

The voluntary dismissal of a claim may invoke the principles of res judicata. The rules of procedure indicate that a claim or petition may be voluntarily dismissed without prejudice. The rule allows only one such dismissal of a claim [*see* Fla. Admin. Code R. 60Q-6.116(2)] and defines "claim" as "each assertion of a legal right or benefit under Chapter 440, Florida Statutes" [Fla. Admin. Code R. 60Q-6.102(1)].

The voluntary dismissal of one of several claims under the Rules of Procedure will not, itself, provide the basis for asserting res judicata as to that claim. The rule, however, does not alter the principles of res judicata. If a claimant voluntarily dismisses a claim that is ripe for hearing at the time of the dismissal, the claimant then waives that claim [*see* McLymont v. A Temporary Solution, 738 So. 2d 447, 448–449 (Fla. 1st DCA 1999)].

[3] Exception to Rule

An exception to the rule may arise if a change of condition or a mistake in the judge's determination of the facts occurs. In such a situation a judge of compensation claims can amend the original order. This exception, however, does not allow a judge to retry the case. For discussion of modification of orders, see ch. 22, § 22.10.

For example, subsequent to two earlier merits hearings, the claimant filed a claim seeking an alternate temporomandibular joint (TMJ) specialist. The judge of compensation claims dismissed the claim on res judicata grounds. As a general rule, piecemeal litigation of mature claims is no more permissible in workers' compensation cases than in civil litigation. If a merits hearing occurs and mature claims are not litigated, the claims are considered waived, and later litigation is precluded by application of the doctrine of res judicata. However, when a claim is based on newly discovered evidence, it cannot be barred for failure to raise it at an earlier proceeding, because it was not mature at the earlier proceeding. Here, the claimant obtained an MRI and discovered she had a TMJ injury *after* the two merits hearings. Prior to obtaining the MRI, she had been expressly advised that she had no TMJ problem. Thus, in reliance on this advice, she had no reason to litigate the issue, and did not do so. Because her claim for an alternate TMJ specialist was based on the newly discovered evidence that she had a TMJ injury, as revealed by the positive MRI, the claimant's claim was not mature at the earlier merits hearings and was not barred by res judicata. Therefore, the court reversed and remanded for further proceedings [Correa v. Miami Airport Hilton, 813 So. 2d 1070, 1071 (Fla. 1st DCA 2002)].

SPECIAL NOTE: Effective July 1, 2002, the legislature amended § 440.25(4)(d), Fla. Stat. to provide that entitlement to a benefit is waived if it was ripe, due, and owing at the time of the final hearing, but was not raised. It appears that the amendment merely codifies case law.

[4] Ripe, Due and Owing

As noted above, a benefit is waived if it was ripe, due, and owing at the time of the final hearing, but was not raised. Whether a particular issue was ripe and mature on a particular date is, itself, a question for the judge of compensation claims to decide.

For example, the claimant, Elizabeth Olmo, appealed the denial of her petition for permanent total workers' compensation disability benefits. The order under review addressed the interplay between two important principles.

The first principle, designed to discourage "piecemeal litigation," has been stated this way: "A workers' compensation claimant is barred by the doctrine of res judicata from raising a claim that he was entitled to a benefit, where he could have but failed to litigate the issue of his right to that benefit in prior proceedings."

The second principle, designed to avoid decisions about a claimant's "permanent" status before the picture is clear, was recently stated this way: A claim for impairment or permanent disability benefits made before a claimant has reached MMI or received 98 weeks of temporary benefits is premature.

Here, the claimant sought authorization for back surgery by filing a petition after her entitlement to temporary disability benefits had expired. Because she did not simultaneously request and litigate entitlement to permanent total disability benefits, the judge of compensation claims later ruled she could not raise the claim separately, explaining that "a claim for [permanent total disability benefits] might have been found to have been premature at the previous hearing; however, there was no impediment to bringing it then."

Once a workers' compensation claim has been litigated and decided, the determination stands, absent a change in condition or a mistake in a determination of fact. Even a claim the parties have never litigated and the judge of compensation claims has never considered can be foreclosed. For instance, if a merits hearing occurs and mature claims are not litigated, the claims are considered waived, and later litigation is precluded by application of the doctrine of res judicata.

On the other hand, the court noted that a claim for permanent total disability benefits cannot succeed if the claim is not yet ripe for consideration. Before January 1, 1994, no claim for permanent total disability benefits was ripe for adjudication until the claimant reached maximum medical improvement, the date after which further recovery from, or lasting improvement to, an injury or disease can no longer reasonably be anticipated, based upon reasonable medical probability.

Amendments to the Workers' Compensation Act effective January 1, 1994, limit temporary benefits to 104 weeks, but provide that a permanently injured claimant can begin receiving permanent impairment benefits upon the expiration of 104 weeks, even if maximum medical improvement has not been attained. Unless the date of maximum medical improvement has already been reached, the injured employee's condition is to be evaluated six weeks before temporary benefits expire, so that an impairment rating can be assigned. The statute provides that once the employee reaches the maximum number of weeks allowed, or the employee reaches the date of maximum medical improvement, whichever occurs earlier, temporary disability benefits shall cease and the injured worker's permanent impairment shall be determined [§ 440.15(2)(a), Fla. Stat. (2001)].

The court held the amended statute contemplates an award of permanent impairment benefits once temporary disability benefits cease, even if maximum medical improvement has not been attained by then, but the amendments do not specify when a claim for permanent total disability benefits ripens.

In the present case, the judge of compensation claims found that Ms. Olmo "might" have been able to claim permanent total disability benefits at or prior to the hearing on December 7, 2004, even though she did not, in fact, do so. No claim for permanent total disability benefits was actually litigated in December of 2004, and no reason was shown why Ms. Olmo was under any obligation to litigate a claim for permanent total disability benefits at that time. The parties stipulated that she had not yet reached maximum medical improvement in December of 2004 (or even by the time of the second hearing in August of 2005). The reason she sought the authorization for surgery at issue at the December 2004 hearing was to avoid or alleviate any permanent disability.

The court held it was, therefore, error for the judge of compensation claims to bar the claim for permanent total disability benefits Ms. Olmo stated in her second petition. A claimant who has yet to attain maximum medical improvement is not required to file a claim for permanent total disability benefits before she is in a position to show not only total disability upon the cessation of temporary benefits but also that total disability would be existing after the date of maximum medical improvement. The court noted that the claimant and her physicians are in the best position to know whether circumstances permit a prospective determination as to when she will be at maximum medical improvement and whether any then-existing impairment will be permanent and total.

In short, although she might have elected to do so, if she had been persuaded she could prove she was fated to be permanently totally disabled at maximum medical improvement, Ms. Olmo was not required to claim permanent total disability benefits at or before the hearing held in December of 2004. The judge of compensation claims erred in ruling that the claim for permanent total disability benefits later alleged in her second petition was res judicata. Therefore, the court held her claim for permanent total disability benefits should be decided on the merits [*see* Olmo v. Rehabcare Starmed/SRS, 930 So. 2d 789 (Fla. 1st DCA 2006)].

§ 9.06 Coverage Under Federal Laws

[1] Eligibility for Federal Benefits Precludes Florida Benefits

Florida statutes preclude payment of benefits under the Florida Workers' Compensation Act if the injured worker is an employee covered by any of three federal laws: (1) Federal Employer's Liability Act; (2) Longshore and Harbor Workers' Compensation Act; or (3) The Jones Act [§ 440.09(2), Fla. Stat.].

What happens if a carrier denies a claim because the injured worker is covered by one of these three laws, but files a Petition for Benefits under the Florida Workers' Compensation Act? It will be up to the judge of compensation claims to decide if the carrier is correct. The inherent danger in this is that some judges have no training or experience in applying these federal laws. Worse yet, the attorneys for the parties may be equally inexperienced.

In 1981, the First District Court of Appeal recognized that Florida's workers' compensation judges are not the "ideal tribunal competent to decide all state and federal questions at a single stroke." The court opined that because of this, the judges are not obliged to weigh the evidence as liberally as a federal judge or jury may weigh the evidence. The court then noted the District Court of Appeal itself is not that perfectly sighted and multi-jurisdictional a tribunal. Thus, the court will be inclined to affirm any order by the judges of compensation claims if they provide any plausible basis for a decision. The court said: "It is enough for affirmance that substantial competent evidence supports the deputy's view of things, whether the factual issue is Jones Act coverage or maximum medical improvement." (Note: At the time this case was heard, the judges were known as deputy commissioners) [*see* Florida Farm Bureau Ins. Co. v. Barrett, 399 So. 2d 993, 995 (Fla. 1st DCA 1981)].

Sometimes, application of the federal laws can be perplexing. Following is a discussion of the basic requirements for coverage under the three laws. This review is limited, but it should give the reader sufficient information to suspect at least that federal coverage may apply and, based on this suspicion, start an investigation. The final decision, however, should not be made without the advice of a lawyer who is an expert in the particular federal law involved.

[2] Federal Employers' Liability Act

If injured workers are entitled to coverage under the Federal Employers' Liability Act, they are not eligible for Florida workers' compensation benefits. The Federal Employers' Liability Act (FELA) applies only to employees of interstate rail carriers and is not a workers' compensation law at all. FELA is an employers' liability law that makes it easier for the employees of railroads to sue their employers for damages. Under FELA, railway employers may not raise the defenses of negligence of a fellow employee or assumption of risk. In addition, FELA replaces common-law contributory negligence with comparative negligence.

Under FELA, a railway employer engaged in interstate commerce is liable in damages for injuries suffered by employees if the injuries were caused, even in part, by the negligence of the employer's officers, agents, or employees. FELA became federal law in 1908. Because the original law was unclear on exactly who it covered, litigation continued unabated for many years. In 1939, Congress tried to clarify the issue when it added the following sentence to the statute [*see* 45 U.S.C.S. § 51].

> Any employee of a (railway) carrier, any part of whose duties as such employee shall be the furtherance of interstate or foreign commerce; or shall, in any way directly or closely and substantially, affect such commerce as above set forth shall . . . be considered as entitled to the benefits of this chapter.

Unfortunately, the amendment is also unclear and litigation over its interpretation continued. It was not until 1956 that the United States Supreme Court ended the controversy in two decisions. In these cases, the Supreme Court held both a clerical worker and a construction worker were covered by FELA. These cases made clear that any railway employee is covered if, at any time, the employee did any duty that could be said to affect interstate commerce. That the employee was not so engaged at the time of the accident and injury is not relevant [*see* Reed v. Pennsylvania Railroad Company, 351 U.S. 502, 100 L. Ed. 1366, 1373–1375, 76 S. Ct. 958 (1956); Southern Pacific Company v. Gileo, 351 U.S. 493, 100 L. Ed. 1357, 1365–1366, 76 S. Ct. 952 (1956)].

In spite of these cases, however, deciding coverage may still not be easy. We can decide whether an employee's duties even partially furthered interstate commerce only on a case by case basis.

For further discussion of FELA, see Larson's Workers' Compensation, Desk Edition, Ch. 147 (Matthew Bender).

[3] Jones Act

If injured workers are entitled to coverage under the Jones Act, they are not eligible for Florida workers' compensation benefits [*see* 46 App. U.S.C.S. § 688]. The Jones Act, or more properly the Merchant Seaman Protection and Relief Act, is a quasi workers' compensation and employers' liability law, designed to cover a vessel's crew members. Like the Federal Employers' Liability Act [*see* [2], *above*], the Jones Act eases a seaman's ability to sue the employer for damages. The law does this by removing the employer's common-law defenses of assumption of risk and negligence of a fellow employee. If the employee cannot prove negligence against the employer, the Act still provides small benefits known as maintenance and cure.

Amazingly, the Jones Act does not define the term "seaman." We can, however, get a definition from the Longshore Act because it excludes coverage to a seaman defined as "a master or member of a crew of any vessel." Originally, the term "seaman" was reserved for those actually involved in a vessel's navigation. Today, however, it applies to any member of the crew from the captain to the social activities director. Despite the work done, to be covered the seaman must be permanently assigned to the vessel. The term "vessel" includes not only boats and ships, but any special purpose floating structure such as a drilling barge. For coverage to apply, the seaman must have done a substantial part of his or her work on the vessel. In addition, these duties must have contributed to the vessel's function or welfare [*see* Offshore Company v. Robison, 266 F.2d 769, 779–781 (5th Cir. 1959)].

Originally, the Jones Act covered seamen only while afloat on navigable water. In 1943, however, the United States Supreme Court greatly extended coverage when the Court held coverage applies on land as well. The Jones Act covers inland accidents if the seaman was engaged in the course of employment and the onshore activity related to the activity of the assigned vessel [*see* O'Donnell v. Great Lakes Dredge & Dock Co. 318 U.S. 36, 87 L. Ed. 596, 602, 63 S. Ct. 488 (1943)].

Take care, however, because the cases have given very liberal interpretation to activities deemed related to the vessel's activities. For example, the court held the Act covered a seaman on shore leave simply because he was subject to recall. Many cases finding coverage for inland injuries are similar to Florida workers' compensation cases. Perhaps the best advice is to conclude that if Florida courts would hold the circumstances of the accident arose out of and in the course of employment under Florida's workers' compensation law, so would the federal courts in a Jones Act case.

For further discussion of conflicts involving the Jones Act, see LARSON'S WORKERS' COMPENSATION, DESK EDITION, Ch. 146 (Matthew Bender).

[4] Longshore and Harbor Workers' Compensation Act

[a] Coverage Under the Act

If injured workers are entitled to coverage under the Longshore and Harbor Workers' Compensation Act, they are not entitled to Florida workers' compensation benefits. It is the Longshore Act that is of most concern in considering the exclusion of § 440.09(2), Fla. Stat., because of Florida's extensive shoreline and the thousands of workers who may fall within the Longshore Act's provisions. This includes not only true dock workers and stevedores, but technicians, construction workers, painters, general laborers, and many others.

To be covered by the Longshore Act, a worker must meet a three-pronged test that includes situs [*see* [b], *below*], status [*see* [c], *below*], and employment. The test refers to where the accident happened, what the worker was doing at the time, and the maritime nature of the employment. This is, of course, very similar to the Florida requirements of arising out of employment, course of employment, and covered employment and occupation.

For further discussion of the Longshore Act, see LARSON'S WORKERS' COMPENSATION, DESK EDITION, Ch. 145 (Matthew Bender).

[b] Situs

Situs refers to where the injured worker was when the accident occurred. The situs test is satisfied if the accident occurs upon the navigable waters of the United States. This includes any adjoining pier, wharf, dry dock, terminal, building way, marine railway, or other adjoining area customarily used by an employer in loading, unloading, repairing, dismantling, or building a vessel. Congress added the landward areas in 1972.

As important as the term "navigable water" is, the Longshore Act does not define it. In 1871, however, the United States Supreme Court defined the term as follows: "the navigable waters of the United States when they form a continued highway over which commerce is or may be carried on with other states or foreign countries."

This includes offshore areas such as the Atlantic Ocean, the Gulf of Mexico, and the Intra coastal Waterway. When an employee is actually working on the water, there is no need to show that such work has anything to do with commercial navigation or maritime commerce. Even working on a recreational project such as a residential boat dock creates coverage under the federal law. Thus, the important fact is whether the employee was injured while doing his job upon actual navigable waters [*see* FCCI Fund (FEISCO) v. Cayce's Excavation, 726 So. 2d 778, 780–782 (Fla. 1st DCA 1998)].

As tricky as the definition of a navigable waterway is, it is the landward extension that really expands the coverage area. Many cases exist on this issue and this text is not designed to review them properly. In those cases where the courts found situs, it was not necessary that the site be immediately next to navigable water. The real test is the site's relationship to maritime use. In 1978 the court had this to say [Brady-Hamilton Stevedore Co. v. Herron, 568 F.2d 137, 141 (9th Cir. 1978)]:

> [T]he phrase 'adjoining area' should be read to describe a functional relationship that does not in all cases depend upon physical contiguity. Consideration should be given to the following factors, among others, in determining whether or not a site is an 'adjoining area' under § 903(a): The particular suitability of the site for the maritime uses referred to in the statute; whether adjoining properties are devoted primarily to uses in maritime commerce; the proximity of the site to the waterway; and whether the site is as close to the waterway as is feasible given all of the circumstances in the case.

[c] Status

If an injury occurs upon navigable waters, that is enough and the status test does not apply. Workers who are injured landward, besides meeting the situs test [*see* [b], *above*], must meet the status test as well. Thus, for longshore coverage to apply the worker must have been on a land site suitable for and used for maritime purposes. Put another way, the worker must have been engaged in maritime employment. Remember, longshore coverage applies only to those workers who are in some way engaged in, or furthering maritime commerce [*see* Northeast Marine Terminal Co. v. Caputo, 432 U.S. 249, 53 L. Ed. 2d 320, 338–343, 97 S. Ct. 2348 (1977)].

To be a maritime employee, a worker need spend only some time in maritime activity. Being engaged in such work at the time of the injury is not necessary. In 1984, Congress again amended the Longshore Act to exclude certain classes of workers. These are as follows:

1. **Clerical employees**, including office clerical, secretarial, security, and data processing. An exception arises if the clerical worker's duties include trips to shipyards and container yards.
2. **Recreational employees**, such as those employed by social clubs, restaurants, museums, retail stores, and recreational diving and boating concerns.
3. **Marina workers** in the pleasure boating industry. The exclusion does not apply to workers engaged in work on piers, docks, and slips nor to the construction, replacement, or expansion of marina facilities.
4. **Supply, transport and vendor employees** are excluded if they are on a maritime site only temporarily while delivering or selling goods to maritime workers. It is the temporary nature of the visit that controls. Thus, subcontractors doing maritime work are still covered.
5. **Aquiculture workers** are excluded if the work involves farming aquatic plants and animals. This includes processing and canning seafood.
6. **Recreational boat construction and repair** are excluded if the vessel under construction or repair is less than 65 feet in length. Marinas involved in the construction or repair of small commercial vessels are also excluded. A small commercial vessel means one less than 900 light-ship displacement tons, or work boats (tugs, fishing boats, crew boats, etc.) less than 1,600 tons gross. CAUTION: Other exceptions to this exclusion exist and additional research is necessary.

[5] Defense Base Act

Effective with accidents occurring on or after October 1, 2001, injured workers who are covered by the Defense Base Act are not eligible for Florida workers' compensation benefits [*see* § 440.09, Fla. Stat. (10/1/2001)].

The Defense Base Act (42 U.S.C.S. § 1651 et seq.) is a federal workers' compensation law that covers civilian workers hired by American companies to work on federal projects in other countries. The Defense Base Act requires this form of workers compensation coverage for all U.S. citizens and residents, and all employees hired in the U.S. on contracts with performance outside the United States and Canada.

Even a rudimentary discussion of the provisions and application of the Defense Base Act are beyond the scope of this text. Because coverage under the federal law is so broad, it is unlikely that an eligible worker would seek Florida benefits instead. In that unlikely event, an attorney experienced in the application of the federal law should be consulted.

§ 9.07 Fraud Defense

[1] The Rule

Effective January 1, 1994, the legislature amended the Workers' Compensation Act to preclude benefits to those guilty of fraud. The section provides as follows [§ 440.09(4), Fla. Stat. (1/1/94)]:

> An employee shall not be entitled to compensation or benefits under this chapter if any administrative hearing officer, court, or jury convened in this state determines that the employee has knowingly or intentionally engaged in any of the acts described in [§ 440.105, Fla. Stat.] for the purpose of securing workers' compensation benefits.

Fraudulent and prohibited activities are described in § 440.105, Fla. Stat. (1/1/94). The section does not require a civil proceeding, and mandates that a claimant forfeit *all compensation or benefits* once there has been a finding of knowing or intentional fraud. The section does not limit a claimant's forfeiture to those benefits that may have been obtained by virtue of the claimant's unlawful conduct.

For a general discussion of employee misconduct, see LARSON'S WORKERS' COMPENSATION, DESK EDITION, Part 5, *Misconduct of Employee* (Matthew Bender).

[2] Application

This is a substantive amendment and cannot be applied retroactively. That is to say, the section applies to only those accidents occurring on or after January 1, 1994 [*see* Rustic Lodge v. Escobar, 729 So. 2d 1014, 1015 (Fla. 1st DCA 1999)]. The employee need not be convicted of fraud in a criminal proceeding for the defense to apply. Note that the section includes a finding by any administrative hearing officer. The court has held, however, that a judge of compensation claims does not qualify as an administrative hearing officer. Thus, under the original statute, the JCCs cannot make a § 440.105, Fla. Stat. determination [*see* E.H. v. Temporary Labor Source, Inc., 687 So. 2d 884, 885 (Fla. 1st DCA 1997), *rev. denied,* 701 So. 2d 868 (Fla. 1997); *see also* Horizons Painting v. Lessard, 688 So. 2d 941, 942 (Fla. 1st DCA 1997)].

The legislature has corrected this problem. Beginning January 1, 1999, the Act specifically includes an administrative law judge and a judge of compensation claims as persons authorized to make a determination about whether an employee violated any of the provisions contained in § 440.105, Fla. Stat. [*see* § 440.09(4), Fla. Stat. (1998)]. Besides losing all rights to workers' compensation benefits, such workers also face prosecution for insurance fraud, subjecting them to severe penalties as described in ch. 24, § 24.10.

Note that § 440.09(4), Fla. Stat. requires the termination of benefits if the evidence shows that the claimant knowingly and intentionally violated the provisions of § 440.105, Fla. Stat. Effective October 1, 2003, the legislature amended the section to provide that the termination of benefits applies not only to violations of § 440.105, Fla. Stat. but also to any criminal act committed for the purpose of securing workers' compensation benefits. A plea of guilty or nolo contendere in criminal matters constitutes evidence of intent. The statute provides that this provision applies to all accident dates [*see* § 440.09(a), Fla. Stat. (10/1/2003)].

Additionally, the statute requires a judge of compensation claims, administrative law judge, or court to take judicial notice of a finding of insurance fraud by a court of competent jurisdiction and to then terminate or otherwise disallow benefits [*see* § 440.09(b), Fla. Stat. (10/1/2003)].

If the judge denies further benefits under this section, the judge has the authority to order benefits, otherwise payable, to be paid into the court registry or an escrow account until the time for appeal expires. Presumably, the carrier would continue to pay into such accounts during the pendency of a timely appeal [*see* § 440.09(c), Fla. Stat. (10/1/2003)].

SPECIAL ALERT: The Florida Workers' Compensation Act contains no authority for the suspension of benefits based on a payor's unilateral determination that a claimant has violated §§ 440.09(4) and 440.105, Fla. Stat. (2004). § 440.09(4), Fla. Stat. contemplates that, before benefits may be denied pursuant to § 440.09(4), Fla. Stat., there must be a showing and an official determination that the claimant made oral or written statements concerning facts material to his or her claim that he or she knew were false, misleading, or incomplete at the time the statements were made [Pavilion Apts. v. Wetherington, 943 So. 2d 226, 228 (Fla. 1st DCA 2006)].

[3] Constitutionality

Following his conviction on two counts of workers' compensation fraud, the judge of compensation claims determined that Lawrence Wright was barred from seeking any benefits as a result based on the operation of § 440.09(4), Fla. Stat., and the court's decision in *Rustic Lodge v. Escobar* [*see* Rustic Lodge v. Escobar, 729 So. 2d 1014, 1015 (Fla. 1st DCA 1999)]. Wright appealed, arguing that the statute violated the provisions of both the state and federal constitutions which prohibit double jeopardy and excessive fines. The court held that § 440.09(4), Fla. Stat. does not offend either the state of federal constitutions and is, therefore, constitutional [*see* Wright v. Uniforms for Indus., 772 So. 2d 560, 561 (Fla. 1st DCA 2000)].

[4] Jurisdiction

As noted in [2], *above,* the penalty of forfeiture of benefits is a substantive amendment that does not apply before the effective date of the amendment, January 1, 1994. That is not true with regard to the authority and jurisdiction of the judge of compensation claims. In 1998, the legislature amended § 440.09(4), Fla. Stat. to provide that the judges of compensation claims have the authority decide issues of fraud in workers' compensation cases. Here, the judge of compensation claims declined to rule on the issue believing that he did not have jurisdiction. The judge ruled that the statutory amendment was a substantive change, and the petition in the case had been filed before the amendment became effective. The 1st DCA reversed, holding that the amendment is procedural and that the judges of compensation claims have the authority to rule on issues of fraud regardless of the date the petition was filed [*see* Russell Corp. v. Jacobs, 782 So. 2d 404 (Fla. 1st DCA 2001)]. However, the JCC has no jurisdiction to rule on a fraud defense if there is no pending Petition for Benefits [*see* Polston v. Hurricane Island Outward Bound, 2006 Fla. App. LEXIS 1740 (Fla. 1st DCA 2006)].

[5] Required Fraud Statement

An injured employee, or any other party, making a claim for workers' compensation benefits must provide his or her personal signature attesting that he or she has reviewed, understands, and acknowledges the following statement [Fla. Admin. Code R. 69L-3.0047 (1/10/2005); *see* § 440.105(7), Fla. Stat.]:

> Any person who, knowingly and with intent to injure, defraud, or deceive any employer or employee, insurance company, or self-insured program, files a statement of claim containing any false or misleading information commits insurance fraud, punishable as provided in § 817.234, Fla. Stat. [§ 440.105(7), Fla. Stat.].

However, the Administrative Rules provide that a party who makes claims for services provided to the carrier on a recurring basis may make one personally signed attestation to the claims-handling entity, as required by § 440.105(7), Fla. Stat., which will satisfy the requirement for all claims submitted to the carrier for the calendar year in which the attestation is submitted [Fla. Admin. Code R. 69L-3.0047 (1/10/2005)].

[6] Evidentiary Standard

The JCC does not need to determine whether the claimant was employed or received payment for work while receiving benefits. The JCC is required only to determine whether the claimant knowingly or intentionally made *any* false, fraudulent, incomplete, or misleading statement, whether oral or written, for the purpose of obtaining workers' compensation benefits, or in support of the claim for benefits. Significantly, it is not necessary that a false, fraudulent, or misleading statement be material to the claim; it is sufficient that it be made for the purpose of obtaining benefits.

If the employer/carrier alleges that the claimant violated the provisions of " 440.09 and 440.105, Fla. Stat., it can establish this by a bare preponderance of the evidence that the claimant knowingly or intentionally made any false, incomplete, or misleading statements in an attempt to obtain workers' compensation benefits [*see* Village of North Palm Beach v. McKale, 911 So. 2d 1282 (Fla. 1st DCA, 2005)].

Note: The standard of "preponderance of the evidence" means the employer/carrier must satisfy the JCC that 51 percent of the probabilities are in the employer/carrier's favor.

Put another way, the employer/carrier need only show that it is more likely than not that the claimant's false or misleading statements were made for the purpose of securing benefits. The "weight of the evidence" is equivalent to "preponderance of the evidence." It means simply that proof on one side of a cause outweighs the proof on the other side [*see* In re Estate of Brackett, 109 So. 2d 375 (Fla. 2d DCA 1959)].

[7] Restitution

The preamble to § 440.105(4), Fla. Stat., provides that the violation of any of the provisions of this subsection constitutes insurance fraud. § 775.089, Fla. Stat., provides that, in addition to any punishment, the court *shall* order the defendant to make restitution to the victim for damage or loss caused directly or indirectly by the defendant's offense, and damage or loss related to the defendant's criminal episode. Thus, trial courts are *required* to order restitution, absent a finding of clear and compelling reasons not to order it [State v. Shinall, 899 So. 2d 1219 (Fla. 1st DCA 2005)].

> *Fraud and deceit abound in these days more than in former times.*
> Sir Edward Coke - 1602

§ 9.08 Failure to Minimize Damages

[1] Compensation Precluded

Employers have a legal duty to provide medical care for employees who suffer work-related injuries. Simultaneously, injured workers have a duty to reduce the effects of an injury by obtaining prompt medical care. The law does not allow compensation (indemnity benefits) to injured workers who allow an injury to become worse either intentionally or by inaction. For example, Ms. Lobnitz contracted dermatitis at work. After six weeks of treatment the condition cleared up. Meanwhile, she quit her job. A short time later the condition reappeared, but Lobnitz waited six months before going back to the doctor. The trial judge awarded disability benefits for that six-month period. On appeal, the Industrial Relations Commission reversed, and the Florida Supreme Court agreed. Once Lobnitz realized that her condition was getting worse, she had a duty to return to the employer's doctor for treatment. Injured workers cannot go for months without treatment and then expect the employer to pay compensation [*see* Lobnitz v. Orange Memorial Hospital, 126 So. 2d 739, 741 (Fla. 1961)].

If the judge decides to deny temporary total disability benefits based on the injured worker's failure to obtain or cooperate in prescribed medical treatment, awarding temporary partial disability benefits for the same period is illogical. When unexcused failure to keep scheduled appointments, for example, forms the basis for denial of temporary total disability benefits, it also precludes an award of temporary partial benefits [*see* Hunt-Wilde Corp. v. Kitchen, 452 So. 2d 2, 4 (Fla. 1st DCA 1984)].

[2] Exceptions

The law does not insist that injured workers make the correct decision about what kind of care to obtain. For example, if months or even years of treatment turn out to be palliative rather than curative, the injured worker is still entitled to benefits [*see* Corral v. McCrory Corporation, 228 So. 2d 900, 902–903 (Fla. 1969)].

If an injured worker fails or refuses to follow the doctor's instructions, and this failure makes the injury worse, compensation can be denied. This applies, however, only if the evidence shows that the injured worker refused treatment that would have reduced the injury [*see* Wendy's of Brevard v. Stickney, 436 So. 2d 346, 347–348 (Fla. 1st DCA 1983)].

Remember, that failing to obtain or to cooperate in palliative care is no defense. For example, failing to participate in a pain management program is not likely to preclude benefits because such programs are unlikely to cause an improvement in the injured worker's condition. More important, remember that this defense applies to indemnity benefits only. The basis of this defense is the injured worker could work if he or she had sought or fully cooperated in prescribed medical treatment [*see* Davis v. Marion County, 667 So. 2d 297, 298 (Fla. 1st DCA 1995)].

[3] No Effect on Medical Benefits

Remember, the failure to minimize damages is only a partial defense because it applies to indemnity benefits only. Benefit denial depends on evidence that the injured workers' failure to obtain treatment also resulted in extended disability. Allowing denial of disability benefits but not additional care required because of the worker's failure is illogical. The issue here is that injured workers cannot be allowed to negligently increase an employer's liability. If failure to obtain prompt care results in the need for otherwise unnecessary surgery, for example, logic requires that the surgery should be denied. Perhaps the courts will revisit and clarify this issue. Clearly, if an injured worker fails to cooperate in court-ordered treatment, the carrier can and should petition the judge for modification. This is also true in cases where the injured worker does cooperate, but the court-ordered care fails to produce desired results in a reasonable time [*see* Verdi's Italian Restaurant v. Campanella, 423 So. 2d 582, 583 (Fla. 1st DCA 1982)].

CHAPTER 10

TO PAY OR NOT TO PAY AND ADJUSTER ETHICS

Guide to Claims

SYNOPSIS

§ 10.01 Time Constraints and Penalty for Late Payment

Previously, the Act required that carriers mail the first payment of compensation within 14 days after they have knowledge of the disability or within 14 days after receipt of a Petition for Benefits.

Beginning October 1, 2003, the payment deadline changes, depending on the nature of the disability. The first payment is due within 14 calendar days after the employer receives notification of the injury, when disability is immediate and continuous for eight calendar days or more after the injury. If the first seven days after disability are nonconsecutive or delayed, the first installment of compensation is due on the sixth day after the first eight calendar days of disability.

Penalty: Before January 1, 1994

For late payments made before January 1, 1994, if any installment of benefits was more than 14 days late, the carrier must add an additional punitive penalty. The penalty was 10 percent of the payment or $5, whichever was greater [§ 440.20(7), Fla. Stat.].

Penalty: January 1, 1994, Through September 30, 2003

In promulgating its administrative rules, the Division interpreted the statute to provide that the penalty increases and is different for the first payment than for subsequent payments. Under the rule, if the first installment is late, the penalty is an amount equal to 20 percent of the late installment. The penalty for all subsequent late installments is $5. However, the court has held this to be an incorrect interpretation and that the 20-percent penalty applies to *all* late installments [*see* ch. 12, § 12.04[9][b][i][B]].

Penalty: On or after October 1, 2003

For late payments made on or after October 1, 2003, the penalty is an amount equal to 20 percent of each late installment. This applies to the initial installment and all subsequent installments. The minimum penalty of $5 no longer applies [§ 440.20(6)(a), Fla. Stat. (10/1/2003)].

> **NOTE:** The court previously held that amendments made to the penalty provisions are procedural and apply to late payments made after the amendment's effective date [*see* Bell v. University of Florida, 652 So. 2d 460, 461 (Fla. 1st DCA 1995)].

Interest Due

Additionally, regardless of the accident date, if the carrier fails to make any installment of compensation on time, it must add interest equal to 12 percent per year from the date the payment became due. The minimum interest payment is $5 [§ 440.20(8)(a), Fla. Stat. (1/1/94); *see* ch. 12, § 12.05[9], for a discussion of penalties and interest].

§ 10.02 Factors to Consider

[1] Cost of Defense Versus Cost of Claim

First, consider the simple economics involved. Spending several thousand dollars defending a claim that has an exposure of only a few hundred dollars makes little financial sense. The rare exception is the case involving an important matter of ethics or principle. Winning the case on all issues still involves considerable cost. Defense attorneys' fees range upward from $95 per hour plus expenses. A single medical deposition can cost $1,000 or more, including attorneys' fees, witness fees, court reporter fees, and transcription costs.

Adjusters also must weigh carefully the chance of losing. Besides all the costs mentioned, the carrier must, of course, pay all benefits due. In addition, the carrier will owe the injured worker's attorney's fee, costs, and interest on "late" compensation benefits.

Cases where the benefits claimed are equal to, or less than, the costs of defense are often called "nuisance" claims. Some carriers never defend these cases while a few defend them

Guide to Claims

all. The latter believe they must make clear that they will not pay just because a worker files a Petition for Benefits. The middle ground, deciding options case-by-case, is probably best.

[2] Soundness of Case

The defense theory's soundness is critical to how the adjuster should handle the matter. When the basis for defense is solid (witnesses lined up, conflicts in medical evidence resolved, the injured worker caught in a lie), then defending the case makes sense and is the right thing to do.

This situation, however, is rare. Most often, litigation outcomes depend on credibility. That is, who will the judge believe? When uncertainties exist, an amicable compromise settlement is likely to be in everyone's best interest. Remember that both sides share doubt about the outcome.

[3] Begin Benefits—Continue to Investigate

[a] 120-Day Rule

[i] Time to Respond

As noted in § 10.01, *above*, the carrier has 14 days after disability begins to issue the first indemnity payment. Additionally, carriers have 14 days to respond to a Petition for Benefits. Unfortunately, carriers rarely have a full two weeks to conduct a complete investigation because of delayed reporting by employers. Hasty denials, however, too often result in awards of large attorneys' fees and improper delay in providing benefits to injured workers. If the case involves a serious injury and large exposure, the more the case and the injured worker deserve a full and unhurried investigation. In such cases, adjusters will often be wise to begin benefits timely but continue the investigation. This is especially true after January 1, 1994. Now, the parties may settle claims under a controverted basis even if the employer or carrier has provided benefits [§ 440.20(11)(a), Fla. Stat. (1994)].

If the investigation finally shows that benefits are due, the carrier will have saved interest payments and attorney's fees on the "whole value" of the case. Additionally, and what is more important, the injured worker has not had to bear the burden of delayed benefits. If, on the other hand, the completed investigation reveals that the case is not compensable, the law allows the carrier to suspend benefits and issue a Notice of Denial. The notice of denial must be filed with the Division within 14 days after suspending benefits [§ 440.20(2), Fla. Stat. (1/1/94)].

[ii] Pay and Investigate

Effective January 1, 1994, the law requires that carriers decide compensability within 120 days after starting compensation or medical benefits. § 440.20(4), Fla. Stat., provides in part:

> If the carrier is uncertain of its obligation to provide all benefits or compensation, the carrier shall immediately and in good faith commence investigation of the employee's entitlement to benefits under this chapter and shall admit or deny compensability

> within 120 days after the initial compensation or benefits as required under subsection (2) or § 440.192(8). Additionally, the carrier shall initiate payment and continue the provision of all benefits and compensation as if the claim had been accepted as compensable without prejudice and without admitting liability. . . . A carrier that fails to deny compensability within 120 days after the initial provision of benefits or payment of compensation as required under subsection (2) or § 440.192(8) waives the right to deny compensability, unless the carrier can establish material facts relevant to the issue of compensability that it could not have discovered through reasonable investigation within the 120-day period. . . .

A carrier may deny a claim it has begun paying any time during the 120-day period without prejudice. When the carrier is uncertain of the compensability of the case, it must give the injured worker written notice that it has begun payment pending further investigation. If the carrier does not deny compensability within the 120-day period, it waives its right to do so. An exception applies if the carrier can show it could not have discovered material facts about the issue of compensability through a reasonable investigation within the 120 days [§ 440.20(4), Fla. Stat. (1/1/94)].

The purpose of the 120-day limit is to ensure that a carrier complies with the mandate of § 440.20(4), Fla. Stat., to "immediately and in good faith commence investigation of the employee's entitlement to benefits." The legislative goal is speedy resolution of claims and protection of a claimant from prolonged periods of uncertainty regarding the carrier's position on the claim's compensability.

[iii] Application

[A] Applying the Rule to Specific Claims

The court has held that this 120-day rule applies to any claim that may arise in a case, and not just to the initial claim following the injury. Here, Douglas Snyder injured his head, neck and back in a motor vehicle accident. Later he contracted hepatitis C, but his doctor said in a report dated 3/23/98, that he could not determine whether Snyder contracted the disease from tattoos, prior blood contact, prior hepatitis C contact, or lying with open wounds after the accident in mud that might have been infected. The carrier paid some of the bills, but then stopped payment. The carrier did not issue a denial or send a 120-day letter. Snyder filed a petition for benefits on 7/22/98 seeking a determination of compensability for the hepatitis C. The judge of compensation claims held that the claim was automatically compensable because the carrier had failed to deny the claim within 120 days after it first paid for treatment. The 1st DCA agreed.

The court held that § 440.20(4), Fla. Stat. is not limited to just the initial claim, but applies to all claims that may arise following the accident. When the carrier becomes aware that a claimant has medical needs, said the court, it should either pay for them, pay and investigate under § 440.20(4), Fla. Stat., or deny compensability. By not denying compensability within 120 days from its initial provision of benefits, the carrier accepted compensability by operation of law [*see* Bynum Transp., Inc. v. Snyder, 765 So. 2d 752, 753–754 (Fla. 1st DCA 2000)].

[B] Good Faith Investigation Defined

The requirement of an "immediate and good faith" investigation does not mandate that

Guide to Claims

every investigative act that can be taken is, in fact, taken. It is merely a requirement that the employer/carrier be prepared to decide, within 120 days, what position they wish to take on a given claim, and be accountable for that decision. Obviously, the employer/carrier's decision is not without consequences. If a claim is denied that should have been accepted, the employer/carrier is sanctioned with penalties, interest, and attorney's fees. Similarly, a failure to controvert within 120 days waives the right to controvert the claim, even if a valid defense exists, if the facts giving rise to the defense could have been discovered within the 120-day period.

An inquiry into the investigative steps an employer/carrier took is not necessary unless the carrier fails to timely controvert the claim and alleges that the material relevant facts could not have been discovered within the 120 days. Clearly, if a carrier fails to timely controvert the claim, and has not shown that there were material relevant facts that would establish valid defenses that could not have been discovered within 120 days, it has not conducted a good-faith investigation [*see* Wintz v. Goodwill, 898 So. 2d 1089 (Fla. 1st DCA 2005)].

[iv] Compensability and Benefits Distinguished

In *Snyder*, the court held that the 120-day pay and investigate provision applies to issues concerning the compensability of subsequent medical conditions. The rule does not apply, however, to specific benefits. A claim for temporary partial disability, temporary total disability, permanent total disability, or impairment benefits, for example, may well raise questions quite different from the question of compensability of an accident. The court has refused to read "entitlement to benefits" to mean the same as "compensability." § 440.20(1)(a), Fla. Stat., directly recognizes that a carrier may deny "compensability or entitlement to benefits" [*see* North River Ins. Co. v. Wuelling, 683 So. 2d 1090, 1092 (Fla. 1st DCA 1996) (noting that compensability and entitlement to benefits are separate concepts, and that the then last sentence of § 440.20(4), Fla. Stat., refers to "the issue of compensability," indicating a distinction from other concepts); *see also* Bussey v. Wal-Mart Store # 725, 867 So. 2d 542, 545 (Fla. 1st DCA 2004)].

The court has acknowledged that cases such as *Travelers Ins. Co. v. Collins* [825 So. 2d 451 (Fla. 1st DCA 2002)], and *Hutchinson v. Lykes Smithfield Packing* [870 So. 2d 144 (Fla. 1st DCA 2004)], have at times blurred the distinction between compensability and entitlement to benefits. Other cases such as *Bussey v. Wal-Mart Store # 725* [867 So. 2d 542 (Fla. 1st DCA 2004)] may have further clouded the application of § 440.20(4), Fla. Stat., in discussing the effect of an employer/carrier's failure to respond to a petition for benefits. Because of the apparent confusion in this area and the potential conflict in the application of the court's decisions, the court revisited the issue en banc.

As the earlier en banc opinion in *Wuelling* explained, § 440.192(8), Fla. Stat., must be read in conjunction with § 440.20(4), Fla. Stat., with regard to the statutory waiver of the right to deny compensability. *Wuelling* established that the recitation as to such a waiver in § 440.192(8), Fla. Stat., is merely a reiteration of the waiver provision in § 440.20(4), Fla. Stat., and that the failure to file a notice of denial in response to a claim under § 440.192(8), Fla. Stat., does not in itself result in a waiver. Instead, the waiver arises under § 440.20(4), Fla. Stat., when an employer/carrier provides compensation or other benefits and does not deny compensability within 120 days of the initial provision of such compensation or benefits. And while an employer/carrier's failure to respond to a petition for benefits might be treated as an implicit denial of the petition for certain other purposes, an employer/carrier's failure to respond to a § 440.192, Fla. Stat., petition does not interrupt the 120-day period and does not avoid the § 440.20(4), Fla. Stat., waiver provision. Similarly, a § 440.192(8), Fla. Stat., notice of denial, which challenges entitlement to a claimed benefit but does not dispute compensability (the occurrence of an industrial accident resulting in injury), will not avoid the § 440.20(4), Fla. Stat. waiver. As that statute indicates, it is the payment of compensation or provision of benefits that begins the 120-day period within which the employer/carrier may admit or deny compensability. And, although § 440.20(4), Fla. Stat., directs the employer/carrier to provide written notice when it has elected to pay the claim pending further investigation, an employer/carrier's failure to provide such notice does not negate application of the § 440.20(4), Fla. Stat., waiver when the employer/carrier does not deny compensability within 120 days of the initial provision of benefits.

The court held that, to the extent that cases such as *Collins*, *Hutchinson*, and *Bussey* may have reflected an approach inconsistent with the holdings in the present opinion, the court receded from those cases and reaffirmed the ruling in *Wuelling*, as explained here [*see* Checkers Restaurant & Specialty Risk Servs. v. Wiethoff, 2006 Fla. App. LEXIS 1847 (Fla. 1st DCA 2006)].

As discussed above, the courts have held that a distinction exists between the concept of compensability and a worker's entitlement to either compensation or benefits. Thus, the 120-day rule applies only to the issue of whether an injury arose out of and occurred within the course of the claimant's employment. The 120-day rule does not apply to entitlement to specific benefits initially or to the continuation of benefits.

In 2006, the court once again addressed this issue. The court noted that an employer/carrier who pays compensation or intentionally provides benefits, but fails to deny compensability within 120 days waives their right to contest that an injury "arose out of, and occurred within the course and scope of, the claimant's employment." Thus, the court held that an employer/carrier who does not deny compensability has not waived anything beyond the ability to contest that an injury "arose out of, and in the course of employment." For instance, the employer/carrier has not waived the right to contest that the workplace injury is the major contributing cause of the condition for which treatment is sought, that the employer/carrier has a defense to the claim, such as the statute of limitations, or that a claimant made a false, misleading, or incomplete statement, forfeiting any right to compensation under chapter 440 [*see* City of Ocoee v. Trimble, 929 So. 2d 687 (Fla. 1st DCA 2006)].

In *City of Ocoee v. Trimble*, the employer/carrier paid for a cardiac evaluation when the claimant complained of chest pressure and discomfort. After receiving the cardiologist's report, the employer/carrier wrote to the claimant and advised him that "no further medical treatment will be authorized for this date of injury." Over one year later, the claimant filed a Petition for Benefits seeking benefits for hypertension. The judge of compensation claims concluded claimant's hypertension was, by default, compensable, because the employer/carrier failed to deny compensability within 120 days of providing the cardiac treatment. The employer/carrier argued the judge of compensation claims erred in this conclusion. The court agreed and reversed, noting that the judge of compensation claims' conclusion as to the consequences of waiver would have far reaching negative implications. The court offered a couple of illustrative examples.

First, there would be an adverse impact on the legislative intent that the workers' compensation system be efficient and self-executing, and not an economic or administrative burden. Under the judge of compensation claims' logic, an employer/carrier providing treatment to an injured employee for a known and accepted condition would incur the obligation to provide treatment for any other condition the claimant may suffer then or in the future. The obligation is incurred without any consideration of the relationship between the contested condition and the accepted condition, or between the workplace injury and the contested condition. This sanctions an employer/carrier who accepts the responsibility for uncontested medical conditions that result from workplace injuries. Sanctions in this context would provide negative incentives for a self-executing system.

Second, a blurring of the distinction between the concepts of compensability and entitlement to benefits renders other important statutory provisions meaningless. For example, § 440.09(1)(a), Fla. Stat., concerning subsequent injuries or conditions, and § 440.09(1)(b), Fla. Stat., concerning preexisting conditions, both require the workplace injury remain the major contributing cause of the need for treatment before the employer/carrier is obligated to provide the treatment. Under the logic here, an employer/carrier providing treatment for the initial condition would become obligated to provide treatment for either a subsequent injury or preexisting condition without the requisite showing that the workplace injury is the major contributing cause of the need for treatment. A similar situation could result in occupational disease cases without disability, and mental or nervous disorders without physical injury.

To avoid waiver of the right to deny compensability, the employer/carrier is only required to deny the claim within 120 days of "the initial provision of compensation benefits" [§ 440.20(4), Fla. Stat.]. Once the statute is triggered, § 440.20(4), Fla. Stat. requires the employer/carrier to "advise the employee of claim acceptance or denial." In keeping with the self-executing goal of chapter 440, advising the employee of claim acceptance or denial does not require elaborate, formalistic procedures. Obviously, the continued provision of compensation or benefits past the 120-day limit advises the employee of "claim acceptance" and waives the right to later deny compensability.

Similarly, to "advise the employee of claim . . . denial," does not require a formalistic process, nor does the statute require "magic words" to convey the denial. Just as the actions of the employer/carrier can advise of claim acceptance, the actions of the employer/carrier may advise of claim denial. The determination of whether a claim has been denied can never depend on a claimant's ability to understand that the employer/carrier is denying the claim. Substantive rights in the workers' compensation context cannot depend on the claimant's ability to understand or the claimant's intelligence. If this were so, we would not have a uniform workers' compensation system, but a system that varied from claimant to claimant, providing benefits based on what each claimant understood or the intelligence of each claimant [*see* City of Ocoee v. Trimble, 929 So. 2d 687, 689–690 (Fla. 1st DCA 2006)].

[v] Triggering the 120-Day Period

[A] Initial Provision of Benefits

Under § 440.20(4), Fla. Stat., the 120-day period is measured from the "initial provision of benefits or payment of compensation as required under . . . § 440.192(8)." However, the 120-day period becomes relevant only when an carrier has elected to pursue the "pay and investigate" option. § 440.20(4), Fla. Stat., applies to a carrier that is "uncertain of its obligation to provide all benefits or compensation" and gives the carrier an option to pay benefits while reserving the right to later deny compensability after investigation [*see* North River Ins. Co. v. Wuelling, 683 So. 2d 1090, 1092 (Fla. 1st DCA 1996) (finding that "deemed compensable" language in § 440.192(8), Fla. Stat., "refers to and is a reiteration of the waiver provision of 440.20(4) as it relates to the opportunity to pay and investigate")]. When the carrier is not uncertain and needs no investigation, the 120-day period is never triggered [*see* Bussey v. Wal-Mart Store # 725, 867 So. 2d 542, 545 (Fla. 1st DCA 2004)].

Also note that it is the actual provision of benefits that triggers the 120-day period. The benefit that triggers the 120-day period must actually be provided, not merely authorized. The test in determining whether a benefit was provided when a physician was authorized is what the physician did, not what the parties suspected or believed the physician did [*see* Tomaskovich v. Lapointe, 904 So. 2d 538 (Fla. 1st DCA 2005)].

[B] Independent Medical Examination

An independent medical examination is not medical treatment and does not trigger the 120-day period. Florida Statutes and case law interpreting those statutes clearly show that an IME is not treatment. An IME is defined in § 440.13(5)(a), Fla. Stat. That section provides that an IME is used only when there is a dispute, and provides that either the employer/carrier or the claimant may use an IME to assist in the resolution of the dispute. Although an IME may ultimately assist a claimant in securing necessary medical treatment, it is not, in and of itself, a form of medical treatment. Therefore, an IME does not trigger the 120-day pay and investigate provision of § 440.20(4), Fla. Stat. [*see* Tomaskovich v. Lapointe, 904 So. 2d 538 (Fla. 1st DCA 2005)].

[vi] Effect of Doing Nothing

The carrier that neither denies a petition for benefits within 14 days of receipt nor elects to pay and investigate pursuant to § 440.20(4), Fla. Stat., is placed in the "identical position as the E/C that files a notice of denial" [Russell Corp. v. Brooks, 698 So. 2d 1334, 1336 (Fla. 1st DCA 1997) (Ervin, J., concurring)]. Thus, doing nothing in response to a Petition for Benefits is the procedural equivalent of filing a Notice of Denial. The courts have consistently adhered to this interpretation [*see, e.g.,* Mitchell v. Sunshine Cos., 850 So. 2d 632, 633 (Fla. 1st DCA 2003) (noting that failure to timely respond is procedural equivalent of notice of denial); Denestan v. Miami-Dade County, 789 So. 2d 515, 516 (Fla. 1st DCA 2001) (holding that late filing of notice of denial did not bar E/C from asserting statute of limitations defense); McDonald's Restaurant # 7160 v. Montes, 736 So. 2d 768, 769 (Fla. 1st DCA 1999) (noting that "carrier that fails to respond to a claimant's petition for benefits within 14 days is deemed to have denied the claim"); Alachua County Bd. of County Comm'rs v. Starling, 699 So. 2d 310, 311 (Fla. 1st DCA 1997) (holding that

Guide to Claims

failure to respond does not amount to procedural default)]. This is true even if the carrier issues a 120-day letter but does not provide benefits. Despite an employer/carrier's letter referencing the 120-day provision, that provision is never actually triggered if the employer/carrier never pays or provides benefits. As with an employer/carrier that takes no action, the employer/carrier in this situation is placed in the same position as the employer/carrier that files a notice of denial [*see* Begley's Cleaning Serv. v. Costa, 913 So. 2d 1244 (Fla. 1st DCA 2005)].

Note, however, that the court has held that the waiver provision should not be construed to require carriers to automatically disbelieve a claimant's reports of injury without additional information warranting investigation. If there is nothing in the information the carrier receives that raises, or should have raised, any doubts as to the cause of the injury, the 120-rule does not apply [*see* Dunlevy v. Seminole County Dep't of Public Safety, 792 So. 2d 592, 593–594 (Fla. 1st DCA 2001)].

[vii] Conclusion

With the exceptions noted in [b] and [c], *below,* no obstacles or detriments arise in controverting a previously accepted claim. The few weeks of benefits paid are nothing compared with the penalties and ethical concerns inherent in controverting prematurely.

No real disadvantages exist to preclude beginning payments before the investigation is complete. Some legal bars do exist, however, and carriers should guard against them. These bars are discussed in [b] and [c], *below.*

[b] Waiver

A carrier may not raise a defense if, by its specific acts or general conduct, the carrier waives its right to assert the defense. The term "waiver" means an *intentional* relinquishment or abandonment of a known right or privilege, or conduct that warrants an inference of the intentional relinquishment of a known right. The law, however, will not hold the carrier to have waived a right unless the court finds that the carrier was in possession of all the material facts. Thus, the cases hold that if the carrier has evidence that a claim is not compensable, but chooses to begin payments anyway, the court may hold the carrier to have waived its right to assert the defense later [*see* Destin Sav. Bank v. Summerhouse of FWB, 579 So. 2d 232, 235 (Fla. 1st DCA 1991); Fireman's Fund Insurance Company v. Vogel, 195 So. 2d 20, 24 (Fla. 2d DCA 1967)].

The legislature has partially overruled these cases with its amendment to § 440.20, Fla. Stat. The danger of waiver in the first 120 days has been eliminated; however, after that period expires a rebuttable statutory waiver of defenses arises.

[c] Estoppel

[i] Estoppel Defined

Estoppel is a fairness doctrine that prevents a person from denying the truth of a fact that has been settled by the facts themselves, or by judicial findings. An estoppel also will occur, if a person, by writings or representations, admits something is true. The elements necessary to establish an equitable estoppel are as follows [*see* State Dept. of Revenue v. Anderson, 403 So. 2d 397, 400 (Fla. 1981)]:

1. A representation as to a material fact that is contrary to a position asserted later;
2. Reliance on that representation; and
3. A change in position detrimental to the party claiming estoppel, caused by reliance on the representation.

For example, assume the carrier enters a stipulation that an injured worker's average weekly wage is $300 per week. The doctrine of estoppel would prevent the carrier from later denying that this is true. The law allows only one way that a person can be relieved from the binding effect of a stipulation. The person must show that he or she was induced by fraud, overreaching, misrepresentation, or withholding of facts by the other party or some such element as would render the agreement void [*see* Steele v. A.D.H. Building Contractors, Inc. 174 So. 2d 16, 19 (Fla. 1965)].

The amendment to § 440.20, Fla. Stat. appears to have overruled the *Steele* case, at least for the first 120 days. Regardless, in any case in which compensability is questionable, adjusters must proceed carefully before entering into any agreements. If the carrier stipulates to entitlement to any benefit, the law may operate to prevent the carrier from later denying the claim is compensable. This is true though the carrier did not have possession of all the facts. What happens if, after having entered such an agreement, the carrier obtains evidence supporting a defense? The carrier may be estopped from asserting the defense unless the carrier first moves to have the stipulations set aside. Until now, the judge of compensation claims could not do so without evidence of fraud or mistake of a material fact. The latter does not include facts that the carrier did not know at the time.

[ii] *Fawaz v. Florida Polymers*

The carrier knew the injured worker had a preexisting permanent impairment and had lied in her employment application about the condition's existence. The carrier did not, however, have evidence of a causal connection between the preexisting condition and the new injury. Thus, the carrier concluded it did not have all the elements necessary to establish a *Martin v. Carpenter* defense [*see* ch. 5]. The carrier began paying benefits, and over time, entered stipulations such as authorizing care by a particular physician. Later, the carrier obtained evidence of a causal relationship between the new injury and the undisclosed preexisting condition. The carrier then denied the entire claim. The judge of compensation claims agreed with the carrier that it did not owe benefits based on the *Martin v. Carpenter* defense. On appeal, the First District Court of Appeal reversed, holding the law estopped the carrier from raising the defense. The court acknowledged the lack of any evidence showing that the carrier had any firm knowledge of a causal connection between the work-related injury and the injured worker's false representations. Even if the carrier had clearly established all the necessary elements of the defense, which the judge of compensation claims held they did, the carrier had the burden to show that the court should set aside the stipulations it had entered. Since the carrier had not done so, the law estopped the carrier from asserting the defense. Further, the court held that although the evidence "clearly supports the JCC's finding that the injured worker made a false representation on her employment application, no evidence was produced showing that the stipulations themselves were procured by fraud." Thus, it could not be said that the injured worker's fraudulent statements to the employer in obtaining employment in any way induced the carrier into entering into the stipulation.

Nothing in *Fawaz* suggests that an estoppel will arise by the simple act of paying benefits, absent a formal agreement such as a joint stipulation. Still, *Fawaz* is a troubling case. Judge Webster reacted with a lengthy dissenting opinion. Part of his opinion is as follows [*see* Fawaz v. Florida Polymers, 622 So. 2d 492, 495–496, 500 (Fla. 1st DCA 1993)]:

> I see little justice in punishing the employer and servicing agent for promptly paying some benefits even though their obligation was not entirely clear at the time. Moreover, to do so would appear to be contrary to a principal intent behind the Workers' Compensation Law—to ensure prompt, inexpensive and non-adversarial compensation to employees who sustain injuries arising out of and in the course of their employment . . . reversal will reward deceit and result in a manifest injustice.

[iii] Court Recedes From *Fawaz: Eastern Airlines v. Griffin*

The legislature apparently agreed with Judge Webster in *Fawaz* [*see* [ii], *above*] when it adopted 1994 amendments to § 440.20, Fla. Stat. Had the amendment been in effect for *Fawaz,* the carrier should have won because there was no way a reasonable investigation would have revealed the material facts within the 120-day period. Unfortunately, the statute is silent about the effect of any binding stipulations.

In 1995, the court decided to side with Judge Webster and now recedes from its opinion in *Fawaz.* Recall that the *Fawaz* court held that a stipulation could be set aside only if it was "obtained by fraud, misrepresentation, or mistake of fact." The court now holds that the due diligence requirement imposed in *Fawaz* is inconsistent with Fla. R. Work. Comp. P. 4.142 (formerly Fla. R. Work. Comp. P. 4.130) and the law generally applicable to relief from a stipulation as Judge Webster described in his dissent. The court held:

> We, therefore, recede from our decision in *Fawaz* to the extent it limits the discretion of the judge of compensation claims in granting relief from stipulations beyond that contemplated by [former] Rule 4.130 [see now Rule 4.142]. [Note: The original Rules of Procedure are now located in the Division of Administrative Hearings rules. The rule on stipulations is now found at Fla. Admin. Code R. 60Q-6.116(5)].

Although Judge Zehmer and Judge Ervin wrote lengthy dissenting opinions, this decision is likely to stand because it is an en banc proceeding [*see* Eastern Airlines v. Griffin, 654 So. 2d 1194, 1196 (Fla. 1st DCA 1995)].

[4] Controverted Claim Settlement Dilemma

Before 1994, the Workers' Compensation Act prohibited settling an injured worker's rights to future medical benefits with two exceptions. The parties could settle future medical benefits only on controverted claims, and on claims where the impairment rating was five percent or less. The five-percent impairment exception applied only to injuries occurring on or after July 1, 1990. Effective July 1, 1983, the legislature amended the law to allow the full discharge of the employer's liability, including future medical costs, on fully controverted claims. The law prohibited settlement under this provision, however, if the carrier or employer had provided any benefits to the injured worker. Obviously, if the carrier paid benefits until the investigation was complete the law prevented a complete settlement. This led to many premature denials to preserve the right to a complete settlement [§ 440.20(12)(b), Fla. Stat. (7/1/83)].

This is no longer a concern because the law now allows full settlement of all benefits on controverted claims, even if the carrier has paid benefits, if the carrier issued the denial during the 120-day period after the injury. This is a procedural amendment that applies to all accident dates [§ 440.20(11)(c), Fla. Stat. (1/1/94)].

NOTE: See ch. 21, § 21.03, for a complete discussion of the washout settlement provisions.

§ 10.03 Adjuster Ethics

[1] Ethics Defined

Character is much easier kept than recovered.
Thomas Paine
The Crisis, 1776–1783

Webster's *Ninth New Collegiate Dictionary* defines ethics as the discipline of dealing with what is good and bad and with moral duty and obligation. Ethics also deals with professional standards of conduct. The State of Florida requires that adjusters handling workers' compensation claims obtain an adjuster's license. Effective July 1, 1990, the legislature amended the Workers' Compensation Act to require continuing education to renew an adjuster's license. The amendment specifically requires that adjusters take at least two hours of ethics courses every two years [§ 626.869(5), Fla. Stat.].

[2] Ethics in Claim Handling

Ethics is a major consideration in deciding to pay or deny a claim. Is it ethical to deny an obviously compensable claim? Is it ethical to pay benefits clearly not due? Is it ethical to pay or deny based on an incomplete investigation? An adjuster's duty is not to find some way to pay every claim or to deny every claim. The adjuster's duty is to gain a solid understanding of the law and of the facts of the particular case, then to provide benefits when due or to deny them when not due. In other words, adjusters must do the right thing. Each must follow not only his or her own moral standards, but also the Code of Ethics issued by the Florida Department of Insurance [§ 626.878, Fla. Stat.; *see* former Fla. Admin. Code R. 4-36]. The Code of Ethics is reviewed in § 10.04.

§ 10.04 Code of Ethics—Insurance Adjusters

[1] Administrative Rules

The Department of Insurance issued an administrative rule entitled the Code of Ethics for Insurance Adjusters [§ 626.878, Fla. Stat.; *see* former Fla. Admin. Code R. 4-36]. Effective June 2, 1993, the department repealed this rule and replaced it with Fla. Admin. Code R. 69O-220. The new rule is an expanded version of the original. The rule begins with a declaration that the business of insurance is a public trust. Adjusters must do their duties in a way that serves the best interest of the insuring public. The rule provides that adjusters "must put the duty for fair and honest treatment of the claimant above the adjuster's own interests." Florida Statutes provide that willful failure to follow these, or any other department rules, is grounds for suspension or revocation of license [§ 626.611(13), Fla. Stat.].

[2] Negotiating Directly With Injured Worker

The Rule provides that [Fla. Admin. Code R. 69O-220.201(4)(i)]:

> An adjuster shall not negotiate or effect settlement directly or indirectly with any third-party claimant represented by an attorney, if said adjuster has knowledge of such representation, except with the consent of the attorney. For purposes of this subsection, the term "third-party claimant" does not include the insured or the insured's resident relatives.

This rule clearly forbids adjusters from trying to negotiate settlements directly with represented injured workers. It does not, however, forbid all direct contact especially in workers' compensation cases. Clearly, adjusters have not only the right, but the duty to ensure that injured workers understand their rights and responsibilities. Where this right begins and ends is not clearly marked. Getting permission from the injured worker's attorney is the safe course, especially for personal contact. Letters, depending on their content, are safer, but adjusters should send a copy of the letter to the injured worker's attorney.

[3] Interviewing Witnesses

Insurance adjusters may interview any witness without the worker's attorney's consent. Adjusters cannot, however, make any suggestion calculated to induce the witness to suppress or deviate from the truth. If witnesses request a copy of their own signed or recorded statement, the carrier must comply [Fla. Admin. Code R. 69O-220.201(4)(j)]. Treating physicians and other health care providers qualify as witnesses.

Physicians cannot, by statute, release medical records to anyone except the patient, the patient's attorney, or another physician without the patient's written permission [§ 455.241(2), Fla. Stat.].

Chapter 440, Florida Statutes, however, provides that this restriction does not apply in workers' compensation cases. This exception allows releasing records to the workers' compensation carrier [§ 440.13(4)(c), Fla. Stat. (1/1/94)].

Finally, the new rule prohibits adjusters from taking any witness's statement who "is, or may reasonably be expected to be, in shock or serious mental, or emotional distress as a result of physical, mental, or emotional trauma associated with a loss" [Fla. Admin. Code R. 69O-220.201(4)(h)].

[4] Giving Advice About Legal Representation

The rules provide that adjusters shall not "advise a claimant to refrain from seeking legal advice, nor advise against the retention of counsel to protect the claimant's interest" [Fla. Admin. Code R. 69O-220.201(4)(k)]. Adjusters must take care to avoid even the appearance of suggesting to injured workers that they should not hire an attorney.

[5] Releases

Adjusters cannot draft special releases without the insurer's written permission. Without such insurer approval, adjusters may do no more than fill the blanks of forms approved by the insurer they represent [Fla. Admin. Code R. 69O-220.201(4)(n)]. While this rule is primarily directed at liability claim adjusters, it applies to workers' compensation adjusters as well.

[6] Contacting Incapacitated Injured Workers

Adjusters may not contact incapacitated injured workers to conclude a settlement. This rule, however, applies only if the settlement would not be to the injured worker's advantage [*see* Fla. Admin. Code R. 69O-220.201(4)(*l*)]. The obvious intent is to prohibit taking advantage of injured workers concerning settlements This rule in no way prohibits contacting incapacitated injured workers generally, especially to inform them about their rights and obligations under the Workers' Compensation Act. Remember that the Act is intended to be self-executing, which means that carriers are supposed to figure out what benefits are due and then to deliver those benefits to the injured worker [*see* § 440.015, Fla. Stat. (1/1/94)].

[7] Advising Injured Workers of Their Rights

Adjusters must not knowingly fail to advise injured workers about their rights under the law [Fla. Admin. Code R. 69O-220.201(4)(*l*)]. This is important because it is the right thing to do. It is also important because the courts have repeatedly held that failing to inform injured workers about their rights may toll the running of the statute of limitations [*see, e.g.*, McCort v. Southland Corp., 543 So. 2d 232, 234 (Fla. 1st DCA 1989)]. Additionally, failing to inform an injured worker about legal obligations, such as conducting a job search, will relieve the injured worker of those obligations [*see* Nickolls v. University of Florida, 606 So. 2d 410, 413 (Fla. 1st DCA 1992)].

[8] Financial Disclosure Required

Adjusters may not have any undisclosed financial interest in any direct or indirect aspect of an adjusting transaction. Further, adjusters may not receive, directly or indirectly, any compensation for a referral, or for any resulting business [Fla. Admin. Code R. 69O-220.201(4)(a)]. The rule, however, does not say to whom adjusters should make this disclosure. Adjusters should at least make such disclosure to their employer or service client, and probably to the injured worker.

[9] Dealing With the Elderly

The Rule provides that "an adjuster shall exercise extraordinary care when dealing with elderly clients, to assure that they are not disadvantaged in their claims transactions by failing memory or impaired cognitive processes" [Fla. Admin. Code R. 69O-220.201(4)(s)].

[10] General Principles

The old rule ended with a statement of general principles of conduct. For some reason, they are not present in the new rule. Still, adjusters should follow these principles in their day-to-day claim handling. The guiding principles are as follows:

1. Approach investigations, adjustments, and settlements with an unprejudiced and open mind.
2. Make truthful and unbiased reports of facts as they are found after making a complete investigation.
3. Handle every case with honesty and integrity, be fair and impartial, and accept no compensation except that to which you are legally entitled.
4. Always act with dispatch and due diligence to achieve a proper disposition of the claim.

Complete candor and full disclosure are, perhaps, the greatest defenses to ethics complaints. When an adjuster denies a benefit, he or she should fully explain the reason to the injured worker. Will most workers understand when the adjuster denies a claim because of the operation of some section of the Workers' Compensation Act? Adjusters should give the injured worker a chance to object or rebut. This will in turn give the adjuster a chance to correct any mistakes or misunderstandings. If the adjuster makes a full and fair disclosure and the injured worker does not object or rebut, there is likely an estoppel issue raised. If the injured worker has information that would help the carrier, that knowledge should put a duty on the injured worker or the injured worker's attorney to let the carrier know about such information.

> *Conscience and reputation are two things.*
> *Conscience is due to yourself, reputation to your neighbor.*
> St. Augustine, 354–430

§ 10.05 Adjusters' Personal Liability

[1] Overview

Injured workers may allege that the adjuster's handling of a claim was so outrageously poor that they suffered additional personal injury (i.e., mental anguish) or financial loss as a result. This allegation usually results from unjustified controverts, summarily deauthorizing physicians, or repeatedly paying benefits late. Assuming all the allegations are true, the question is whether such poor claim handling exposes the adjuster and the carrier to any personal liability.

[2] History

Historically, adjusters and insurance carriers have enjoyed relative immunity from personal liability for handling claims unless the adjuster's actions amounted to criminal conduct. The basis for this immunity is statutory. This statute provides in part that activities *by any person* designed to receive or deny benefits fraudulently is a third degree felony. § 440.37, Fla. Stat. further provided that "any person damaged as a result of a violation of any provision of this subsection, when there has been a criminal adjudication of guilt, shall have a cause of action to recover compensatory damages, plus all reasonable investigation and litigation expenses, including attorney's fees" [§ 440.37(2)(c), Fla. Stat.]. § 440.37, Fla. Stat., in other words, contained an express right of action.

The law had been well settled that an injured worker had no cause of action against an adjuster for damages unless a criminal court convicted the adjuster of violating § 440.37, Fla. Stat. Such holdings did not mean, however, that adjusters and carriers could mishandle claims with impunity. If bad faith claim handling somehow harmed an injured worker, the additional injury was considered part of the original compensable injury. As such, the carrier is liable for additional benefits. All of this, however, changed dramatically in 1990 [*see* [3], *below*].

[3] *Sibley v. Adjustco, Inc.*

In 1990, the Second District Court of Appeal held that Florida Statutes prohibit an injured worker from bringing an independent action against the carrier though its adjuster committed intentional, fraudulent, and bad faith acts in handling a claim [*see* Sibley v. Adjustco, Inc., 573 So. 2d 353, 354–356 (Fla. 2d DCA 1990), *reversed,* 596 So. 2d 1048 (Fla. 1992); *see also* § 440.37, Fla. Stat.].

Here, the injured worker had suffered a heart attack. The carrier denied the claim, basing its decision, apparently, on the injured worker's recorded statement. The judge of compensation claims held that the statement was not of credible value and "appears to a large degree to have been edited by the interviewer. . . ." The injured worker sued the adjuster alleging that the adjuster edited the statement he had given. Because of this alleged fraudulent act, the carrier wrongfully denied his claim. Consistent with the cases to this point, the Second District Court of Appeal rejected the complaint. The court held that the carrier and adjuster were immune because no adjudication of criminal misconduct occurred as required by statute. On further appeal, the Florida Supreme Court reversed!

The high court held that the language of § 440.37, Fla. Stat. provides only an alternate cause of action, rather than an exclusive cause of action. In any tort action, the plaintiff must show both liability and damages. With a criminal conviction, the liability question is resolved and the plaintiff must only prove damages. Without a criminal conviction, said the Court, the section means only that the plaintiff must show both liability and damages. The Court's conclusion was, "[T]he legislature [§ 440.37, Fla. Stat.] was providing an alternative cause of action and not eliminating a common law right of action for an intentional tort" [*see* Sibley v. Adjustco, Inc., 596 So. 2d 1048, 1050–1051 (Fla. 1992)].

[4] Legislative Action

Effective January 1, 1994, however, the legislature repealed § 440.37, Fla. Stat. and replaced it with the similarly-worded § 440.105, Fla. Stat. In so doing, the Third District Court of Appeal held that the legislature eliminated the express private right of action that had been in the earlier statute. Therefore, injured workers have no right to sue under § 440.105, Fla. Stat. A compensation claimant, said the court, cannot avoid the exclusivity of the Act and transform a delay in payments into an actionable tort cognizable in the circuit court simply by calling that delay outrageous, fraudulent, deceitful, or an intentional infliction of emotional distress [*see* De Oca v. Orkin Exterminating Co., 692 So. 2d 257, 260 (Fla. 3d DCA 1997), *rev. denied,* 699 So. 2d 1374 (Fla. 1997)].

Florida law does not allow attempts by claimants to transmogrify a workers' compensation claim into an intentional tort within the jurisdiction of the circuit court. Put another way, the law does not allow an action for the tort of intentional infliction of emotional distress, better known as the tort of outrage [*see* Sheraton Key Largo v. Roca,710 So. 2d 1016, 1017 (Fla. 3d DCA 1998)].

[5] Adjuster/Carrier Immunity Not Absolute

Consistent with the discussion in [3], above, in 2002 the 3rd DCA held that all acts and conduct by adjusters and insurance carriers, no matter how intentional, egregious, or injurious, that occur during the claim process, are always afforded absolute immunity [*see* Inservices, Inc. v. Aguilera, 837 So. 2d 464 (Fla. 3d DCA 2002)]. On further review, however, the Florida Supreme Court disagreed and reversed.

The Supreme Court continued to recognize previous holdings that the mere delay of payments or simple bad faith in handling workers' compensation claims are not actionable torts, and that employees are not permitted to transform such simple delays into actionable torts cognizable in the circuit court. However, the Court held that adjusters and carriers are *not* immune from tort actions when their conduct goes beyond simple claim delay or a simple termination of benefits. The Court held that there was *no* immunity when the complaint specifically alleged harm caused subsequent to and distinct from the original workplace injury.

The Court held that the statutes do not contemplate, and the Supreme Court has never permitted compensation insurance carriers to cloak themselves with, blanket immunity in circumstances in which the carrier has not merely breached the duty to timely pay benefits or acted negligently, but has actually committed an intentional tort upon an employee. Adjusters/carriers may be held liable for the tort of intentional infliction of emotional distress when the conduct is more than simply bad faith or a breach of contract, i.e., when the defaulting party's intentional conduct is outrageous.

As a practical matter, trial judges are unlikely to dismiss complaints alleging an intentional tort, and such complaints will be allowed to proceed to trial to analyze an employee's allegations and ascertain whether the allegations amount to a mere delay in payments, simple bad faith, or truly rise to the level of a separate and independent intentional tort [*see* Aguilera v. Inservices, Inc., 905 So. 2d 84 (Fla. 2005)].

As Justice Bell noted in a dissenting opinion, however, how does one identify the point at which a claims-handling dispute, clearly resolvable within the Act, gives birth to an independent tort of intentional infliction of emotional distress? The first effort to do so occurred in the case of *Protegrity Servs. v. Vaccaro* [909 So. 2d 445 (Fla. 4th DCA 2005)]. In *Protegrity*, the claimant, Julie Vaccaro, was severely injured and disabled in a **workers' compensation** accident. Following the accident, she received **workers' compensation** benefits, including medical treatment. Vaccaro received treatment from Dr. Craig Lichtblau for many years after the accident. As part of her treatment, the carrier provided Vaccaro with massage therapy, which was prescribed by Dr. Lichtblau. According to the complaint, the therapy cost was beyond Vaccaro's financial means but was medically necessary to reduce the number and intensity of dangerous and potentially life threatening seizures. In August 2002, the employer/carrier conducted a "utilization review" of Vaccaro's care and determined that the doctor's treatment and massage therapy were no longer necessary. The carrier informed the doctor of its intent to disallow further treatment and to seek reimbursement of some of its previous payments. The doctor subsequently advised Vaccaro that he would no longer be able to treat her.

Vaccaro filed a complaint in circuit court on May 20, 2003, under several theories, alleging intentional and wrongful termination of her **workers' compensation** benefits. She claimed the employer/carrier made misrepresentations to the doctor that the "utilization review" was concluded and further threatened to initiate a utilization review with the Department of Labor and Employment Security (DLES) and the Division of Workers' Compensation(DWC), which would impose penalties on him for over-utilization. Vaccaro further alleged that the carrier knew or should have known that these threats were false, since the administrative rules allowing utilization review had been repealed. In sum, the complaint alleged that: (1) the defendants "falsely threatened Dr. Lichtblau" with a utilization review, which would expose him to significant fines and possible decertification; (2) this was done intentionally to interfere with the plaintiff's relationship with her doctor and to deprive her of medical care; (3) she suffered injuries apart from the initial accident, severe emotional disorders and other damages because of the carrier's conduct; and (4) the carrier was substantially certain that its conduct would cause her serious injury. The carrier filed a motion to dismiss the complaint, claiming that the circuit court was without subject matter jurisdiction to hear the claim. The trial court, however, agreed with Vaccaro that this dispute was within the jurisdiction of the circuit court.

On appeal, The DCA held that these allegations went beyond a mere claim delay or a simple dispute involving benefits. As the Supreme Court made clear in *Aguilera*, insurance carriers will not be permitted to cloak themselves with blanket immunity in circumstances in which the carrier has allegedly committed an intentional tort upon an employee. Here, the lower court was required to accept the factual allegations of the complaint as true and in the light most favorable to the plaintiff, even though the evidence may ultimately not substantiate them. Accordingly, the court held that the trial court properly denied the insurance carrier's motion to dismiss [*see* Protegrity Servs. v. Vaccaro, 909 So. 2d 445 (Fla. 4th DCA 2005)].

§ 10.06 Prohibited Activities

[1] Prohibited Carrier Activities

Florida statutes describe several activities that not only put an insurer's license to operate in jeopardy, but also expose the violator to civil suit. These are:

1. Practicing unfair methods of competition, and unfair or deceptive acts [§ 626.9541, Fla. Stat.].
2. Creating favored agents or insurers, or coercion of debtors [§ 626.9551, Fla. Stat.].
3. Unfair dealings in issuing or renewing life or disability insurance policies [§ 626.9705, Fla. Stat.].
4. Discrimination by life insurance carriers on the basis of sickle-cell traits [§ 626.9706, Fla. Stat.; § 626.9707, Fla. Stat.].
5. Failing to promptly return unearned premium [§ 627.7283, Fla. Stat.].

Because items 2 through 5, above, do not relate to workers' compensation, or do not affect claim handling, they are not discussed here. Item 1 and § 626.9541, Fla. Stat., however, describe claim handling activities that are strictly prohibited [*see* [2], *below*].

[2] Prohibited Claim Handling Activities

The following activities are strictly prohibited in claim handling [§ 626.9541, Fla. Stat.]:

1. Not attempting in good faith to settle claims when, under all the circumstances, it could and should have done so, had it acted fairly and honestly toward its insured and with due regard for its interests;
2. Making claim payments to insureds or beneficiaries not accompanied by a statement setting forth the coverage under which payments are being made; or
3. Except as to liability coverages, failing to promptly settle claims, when the obligation to settle a claim has become reasonably clear, under one portion of the insurance policy coverage in order to influence settlements under other portions of the insurance policy coverage.

On first reading, none of this appears to apply to workers' compensation, or does it? The first item could be construed to mean that not accepting compensability in good faith is the same as not "settling" a claim. Does the third item about settling claims apply? We could argue it does not, because the law does not require anyone to complete lump-sum settlements. Carriers can, if they wish, settle just indemnity benefits, or just medical benefits, or both. Still, does a carrier violate this section if it is willing to settle a claim, but refuses to do so if the injured worker is unwilling to settle the medical portion?

Arguments can be made on both sides, so carriers should act with caution.

[3] Unfair Claim Settlement Practices

Besides the items listed in [2], *above,* the statutes list additional activities that are unfair claim settlement practices. Of those listed, the following are likely to apply to workers' compensation claims [§ 626.9541(1)(I), Fla. Stat.]:

1. Failing to adopt and implement standards for the proper investigation of claims.
2. Misrepresenting pertinent facts or insurance policy provisions relating to coverages at issue.
3. Failing to acknowledge and act promptly upon communications with respect to claims.
4. Denying claims without conducting reasonable investigations based upon available information.

[4] Civil Liability

Besides administrative punishments, such as fines and loss of license, carriers who violate this section face civil lawsuits as well [§ 624.155, Fla. Stat.]. Most people believed that this section restricted lawsuits to insureds only. That belief is wrong. The statute provides that "any person may bring a civil action against an insurer when such person is damaged" as the result of the carrier having committed any of the prohibited acts. The words "any person" means exactly that. All persons are allowed to sue [Auto-Owners Ins. Co. v. Conquest, 658 So. 2d 928, 929–930 (Fla. 1995)].

Here, Bonita Conquest was injured when thrown from a horse she was riding. She eventually sued Auto-Owners' insured, claiming that negligent maintenance of the insured's property caused the accident. A jury awarded Conquest $327,000, but then reduced it to $130,800 because of her comparative negligence.

Conquest then sued Auto-Owners, claiming the insurer violated § 624.155, Fla. Stat. because it (1) failed to acknowledge and act promptly on her claim, and (2) denied her claim without first doing a reasonable investigation of available information.

Auto-Owners defended, arguing that Conquest had no legal right to sue. It based this argument on a 1989 decision by the Third District Court of Appeal [*see*Cardenas v. Miami-Dade Yellow Cab Co., 538 So. 2d 491, 494–496 (Fla. 3d DCA 1989)]. The Florida Supreme Court in *Conquest* disagreed, holding such suits by plaintiffs are allowed under § 624.155, Fla. Stat.

This is one of the Supreme Court's most important claims related decisions in years. It suggests that after injured workers receive full compensation for the underlying accident, they can sue the insurance company claiming additional damages. Such a suit would be based on the carrier's failure to answer promptly or respond to letters, or that it failed to investigate the claim properly.

This case adds yet another reason for prompt, diligent, fair, and well-documented claim handling.

For a thorough discussion of workers' compensation insurance, see Larson's Workers' Compensation, Desk Edition, Part 15, *Insurance* (Matthew Bender).

A man wants no protection
when his conduct is strictly right.
Chief Justice William Murry, English jurist
1785

CHAPTER 11

RESERVES

SYNOPSIS

§ 11.01 Reserves Defined

In a perfect world, employers would report an accident immediately to their insurance carriers. The same day, the carrier claims department would decide compensability, and the total extent of compensation and medical benefits due. In such a perfect world the carrier could simply pay the injured worker at once and close the case. At the end of each day the payment would have reduced the carrier's funds, appear on the company's balance sheets, and accurately reflect the claim's effect on the company's financial standing. If such an unrealistic circumstance existed, there would be no need for the accounting function known as setting reserves. Compensation claims, of course, rarely settle on the same day carriers receive them.

The future cost of compensation and medical benefits is rarely immediately measurable. Although carriers would obviously prefer to pay losses in full as they receive them, this is hardly possible. A carrier's assets are, as a practical matter, constructively diminished when it receives notice of any claim. The amount of the diminution is the probable pay out over the life of the claim. Carriers must record the reduction immediately, although payment of the claim may take weeks, months, and often years. So that the company knows its true financial condition, a carrier's financial record must, in some way, recognize that the company has incurred a loss. Thus, the accounting process of setting reserves is necessary.

A reserve is an estimate of the future, total cost of the claim. Since accountants are not involved in the claims adjusting process, the responsibility for setting a reserve on a particular case falls to the claim department and more often than not with the individual claim adjuster. This responsibility is critical and the financial security of the carrier or self-insured employer may depend on the skill with which adjusters set reserves.

For general discussion of compensation insurance, see LARSON'S WORKERS' COMPENSATION, DESK EDITION, Ch. 150, et seq. (Matthew Bender).

§ 11.02 I.B.N.R. Reserve

In any given month, a claims office will receive notice of about one-third to one-half of the losses that have occurred during that month. Most reports will arrive in the month following the accident. Some will not arrive for months or even years. In addition, insurance companies are well aware of the tendency of a claim to "develop" or to increase in cost beyond original estimates as time goes on. This development of claims is especially true in workers' compensation cases. There comes a time when a company will need to close its books on a given accounting period. This is necessary to declare dividends to stockholders, issue refunds or premium credits, and so on. To consider the known, and the unknown, companies create a general reserve. We call this reserve an "incurred but not reported" or I.B.N.R. reserve. Carriers may set this reserve early in a given year by using a figure equal to one or two months of losses. Other carriers use a flat percentage of the premium. As the year matures, however, carriers usually adopt a reserve figure calculated by an actuary who bases the reserve on the company's loss development history during prior years. This is another reason that consistent reserving by the claims department is essential. If the claims department is inconsistent and reserves constantly vary up and down or are too low or too high, an actuary may assume that this is the real loss development pattern. The actuary's proposed I.B.N.R. reserve, therefore, may be too low, which could lead to insolvency. A reserve that is too high may prevent dividends or cause unnecessary concern among stockholders, thus adversely affecting the stock's value.

§ 11.03 Formula Reserves

A formula reserve is a standard fixed reserve used on all claims of a given class, such as medical-only claims. The company's historical average cost for such claims is the basis for the reserve. For example, a company may use a formula reserve of $350 on all medical-only claims.

Many companies use a formula reserve upon creating all new lost time cases to establish consistency. For example, the company's history may show that on average, soft tissue low back injuries cost $10,000. This figure would then become the automatic starting reserve for all such cases, subject to revision as additional facts become known.

§ 11.04 Individual Case Reserves

Reserving is more an art than science. Reserving is the adjuster's prediction of future events. Adjusters must then set a reserve in an amount equal to the total amount that the carrier will pay over the life of the case. Will the injured worker's disability last two weeks or two years? Will the injured worker require surgery? Can the injured worker return to the pre-injury job or will retraining be required? The adjuster must estimate the likelihood of these events and put a price tag on them.

Adjusters rarely know the answers to these questions upon receipt of a first report of injury. The likely outcome of the case may change over time. Physicians may make new diagnoses. New physicians may appear. Attorneys may become involved. For these reasons, it is critical that adjusters consider the validity of established reserves every time they handle a new item claim file.

Inexperienced adjusters too often fall into the inexcusable practice of "stair stepping" reserves. Perhaps because they fear large numbers, these adjusters set reserves sufficiently to cover only a few payments. Thus, the adjusters increase reserves dozens of times, and the reserves may never accurately reflect the ultimate exposure of the claims. This practice of stair stepping reserves may cause the actuarial projections of the company's present and future financial position to be based on inaccurate data. Adjusters must guard against the tendency to over-reserve small claims and under-reserve the large ones. Management may perceive such adjusters as novices, or worse, as incompetent. Management has the right to expect, indeed demand, that the reserves on each adjuster's cases are at least the best estimate of the total future cost of all benefits and expenses.

Adjusters also must monitor events as they take place and calculate their likely impact on the future cost of the claim. Let us assume an adjuster is handling a minor, soft tissue, back injury case. The injured worker is receiving conservative treatment with medication and physical therapy. One day the adjuster receives a request for authorization from a hospital for serious back surgery, such as a laminectomy. Obviously, if approved, the adjuster must increase the medical reserve to cover the hospital's charges. Remember, this surgery will generate other costs, such as the surgeon and additional medical providers. The surgery will also increase the period of temporary total disability. Will this now result in permanent impairment such that the injured worker will be eligible for additional disability benefits? What about permanent total disability? Thus, a single telephone call may prompt the adjuster to conduct a complete reevaluation of the case and adjust reserves accordingly.

Decreasing reserves is just as important if the original estimate of the total future cost is overstated. Excessive reserves will not only adversely impact the insurer's financial position, but will inaccurately reflect the employer's loss experience, resulting in improperly increased premiums.

Many companies dictate that case reserves should reflect the projected settlement value, not the ultimate payout. This practice usually results in adverse loss development because of too optimistic projections.

§ 11.05 Estimating Reserves

Most lost time cases are predictable in their outcome. Catastrophic claims, such as paraplegia, are obvious at the outset. These claims can be fairly and accurately reserved based on lifetime benefits.

It is the apparently minor case that will sneak up on carriers. These are the cases that just will not go away. One danger sign is intermittent periods of disability. Another is an injury that requires continuous treatment, but does not get better. Perhaps the injured worker makes frequent requests for a change of physicians. Injured workers who have reemployment problems because of advanced age, little or no formal education, no transferable job skills, language barrier problems, criminal records, or alcohol or drug problems merit particular attention. The appearance of an attorney, for no apparent reason, is a sure sign that the case is about to go downhill. Keep a watchful eye on back injury, head injury, and occupational disease cases.

Adjusters should always review the list of all benefits the Act provides and decide if the injured worker is likely to become eligible for them. For example, an adjuster may conclude that the injured worker does not have an injury that will result in permanent physical impairment. This injured worker is not eligible to receive impairment income or wage loss benefits. The case, therefore, may not require a reserve increase. On the contrary, a decrease may be in order. On the other hand, the injury may be one likely to result in significant permanent impairment. In such a case, consider adjusting reserves not only for permanent partial, but for permanent total disability as well. Be sure to include reserves for expenses, such as investigators, attorneys, and the like.

CAVEAT: Adjusters will likely be subject to company policy. Some carriers take a pessimistic stance and direct that adjusters reserve all cases for a worst-case result. Other carriers take the opposite approach. Some carriers take the middle ground and still others have no philosophy at all. Adjuster should follow their company's rules. Most insurers will, however, agree with this final thought: NEVER PICK UP A CLAIM FILE WITHOUT GIVING SOME THOUGHT TO THE APPROPRIATENESS OF THE CURRENT RESERVE.

§ 11.06 Estimating Disability Periods

[1] In General

Following is a guide to help in estimating the treatment required and the periods of total and partial disability for the most common types of injuries. Obviously, adjusters must consider any unusual factors that may increase or decrease these estimates.

[2] Knee Injury: No Surgery

Arthroscopic surgery–diagnostic only–no findings.

First week–Non weight bearing, crutches, no work.

Second to third weeks–Light duty, minimum walking, no climbing, no squatting, no lifting, may drive.

Third to Sixth week–Lifting 40 to 50 pounds, some light stair climbing, no ladders, light squatting.

Sixth week–Full duty.

[3] Knee Injury: With Surgery

Arthroscopy–surgical repair.

First to Second week–No work, crutches.

Second to Third week–Very light duty with crutches.

Third to Sixth week–Light duty, no crutches, minimum walking, no climbing, no squatting, no lifting, may drive, some light stair climbing, no ladders.

Fourth to Sixth week–Light squatting, lift 40 to 50 pounds.

Sixth week–Full duty.

[4] Knee Injury: Major Surgery

Full reconstructive knee surgery, arthrotomy.

Six weeks in a full cast or immobilizer, four weeks no work.

Fourth to Sixth week–May work with crutches, cast or immobilizer.

Sixth to 24th week–Light duty, sitting only, minimum standing. Therapy for three to six months.

Twenty-fifth week–Limited climbing, squatting, may return to full duty.

NOTE: If the knee deteriorates further, the injured worker may remain in a brace for up to two years or even for life. There is significant wage loss exposure, and permanent total disability is a possibility.

[5] Back Injury: Strain, Sprain, or Soft Tissue

First week–Bed rest.

Second to third week–Physical therapy, no work.

Third week–Light duty, lifting 25 to 40 pounds, no prolonged sitting, alternate standing with sitting. May start to drive 1/2 hour at a time.

Fourth to sixth week–Full duty.

Note: Expect about two weeks of physical therapy.

[6] Back Injury: Herniated Disc With No Surgery

First week–Bed rest.

Second to Fourth week–Therapy.

Fourth to sixth week–Light duty, standing 15 minutes at a time. No sitting more than 45 minutes at a time, (sitting may be a problem) Driving may be a permanent problem. No bending.

Sixth to eighth week–Light duty work.

NOTE: This injury nearly always results in permanent impairment.

[7] Back Injury: Herniated Disc With Surgery (Discectomy)

Return to work light duty could occur as early as six weeks, but several months are more likely. Permanent impairment is almost certain. The injured worker will have trouble sitting, standing and driving. Depending on the individual, permanent total disability is a distinct possibility.

[8] Shoulder Injury: Rotator Cuff (Tendinitis)

First to third week–No work, therapy required for range of motion.

Third to sixth week–Return to work, continue therapy, no lifting over 20 pounds and no lifting overhead. Limited use of the injured arm.

[9] Shoulder Injury: Rotator Cuff Tear

One month of conservative treatment, desk work only, therapy required.

If surgery is required: Six weeks to three months–No use of arm, continuous therapy, injured worker can do light work with the other arm and hand.

Three months to one year–Limited lifting. Injured arm will not regain full strength for one year. Unrestricted return to work after one year.

[10] Compression Fracture of Vertebrae

Light duty after three months, no lifting over 20 pounds. Light duty restriction for up to one year. Permanent impairment is likely.

[11] Fracture, Lower Extremities

Six to ten weeks in a cast. Return to light duty in two to three weeks for office work only. The injured worker should return to unrestricted, full-duty work in three to four months.

[12] Fracture, Upper Extremities

Light office work any time. Return to unrestricted, full duty in two to three months.

§ 11.07 Reserving Catastrophic Cases

Catastrophic or lifetime disability cases, such as paraplegia, are easily recognized but can be difficult to reserve since most adjusters' experience with them is infrequent. Indemnity reserves are not too difficult to estimate. The first step is to estimate the injured worker's life expectancy. Once determined, simply multiply the compensation rate by the number of weeks of life expectancy. Be sure to use the most current life expectancy tables [*see* Part VIII, Tables, Table 4]. Also be sure these tables consider the differences in life expectancy between males and females and also among races. Also, remember the standard tables are based on the life expectancy of relatively healthy persons of a given age. By definition, the injured worker is not a normal, healthy person. Carefully examine the medical records. Find out if the results of the injury, or unrelated medical or lifestyle problems, will likely produce a reduction in life expectancy. Since the impact of these factors is not always obvious, a medical consultant may be helpful. Do not forget to include an additional amount for the PTD Supplemental Benefit [*see* ch. 13, § 13.50[3]].

Reserving medical benefits for lifetime care can be difficult. In many such cases, a life-care plan prepared by a specialist will be necessary. The statistical guidelines below may help. However, these are only guidelines and must be adjusted to fit an individual case.

Guide to Claims

CATASTROPHIC INJURY AVERAGE MEDICAL COSTS

Paraplegic at thoracic spine level	
1st year	$155,000
2nd year	$ 45,000
Subsequent years:	
T-1 to T-10	$6,500 to $10,500 Yr.
T-11 & below	$3,500 to $ 7,000 Yr.

Quadriplegic at cervical spine level C-5 to C-8	
1st year	$255,000
2nd year	$ 50,500
Subsequent years:	$ 16,500 to $40,000 Yr.

Quadriplegic at cervical spine level C-4 & up	
1st year	$290,000
2nd year	$ 90,000
Subsequent years:	$ 45,000 to $87,000 Yr.

Brain damage Comatose	
1st year	$300,000
Subsequent years:	$ 75,000 to $125,000 Yr.

Brain damage All other	
1st year	$100,000 to $275,000
2nd year	$ 95,000 to $220,000
3rd year	$ 40,000 to $ 95,000
Subsequent years:	
Supervised:	$ 15,000 to $ 70,000 Yr.
Unsupervised:	$ 5,000 to $ 6,500 Yr.

Burns 3rd degree up to 33% of body:	
1st year	$225,000
2nd year	$ 65,000
3rd year	$ 15,000
Subsequent years:	$ 1,500 Yr.

Burns	3rd degree up to 66% of body:
1st year	$355,000
2nd year	$ 65,000
3rd year	$ 25,000
Subsequent years:	$ 1,500 Yr.

Burns	Major electrical
1st year	$300,000
2nd year	$ 60,000
Subsequent years:	$ 16,500 to $25,000 Yr.

CHAPTER 12

CALCULATING INDEMNITY BENEFITS, AVERAGE WEEKLY WAGE, PENALTIES, AND OFFSETS

Guide to Claims

SYNOPSIS

Guide to Claims

§ 12.01 Average Weekly Wage

[1] Wages Defined

An injured worker's average weekly wage is the basis upon which carriers compute all compensation. The Act defines wages, in part, as follows:

> "Wages" means the money rate at which the service rendered is recompensed under the contract of hiring in force at the time of the injury and includes only the wages earned and *reported for federal income tax purposes* on the job where the employee is injured and *any other concurrent employment* where he or she is also *subject to workers' compensation coverage* and benefits, together with the reasonable *value of housing* furnished to the employee by the employer which is the permanent year-round residence of the employee, *and gratuities* to the extent reported to the employer in writing as taxable income received in the course of employment from others than the employer and employer contributions for *health insurance* for the employee or the employee's dependents (Emphasis added) [*see* § 440.02(28) Fla. Stat. 2004].

Summarized, this section defines "wages" as the pay a person receives on the job where the injury occurred, combined with pay earned from concurrent jobs [*see* [2], *below,* for a discussion of concurrent earnings]. "Wages" also includes tips, but only if the employee reported tips received to the employer and to the Internal Revenue Service as taxable income [*see* [5], *below,* for a discussion of tips and gratuities]. Finally, "wages" includes the value of housing and health insurance provided by the employer [*see* [3][c][iv][A], *below*, for a discussion of housing, and [4][a][i], *below*, for a discussion of health insurance].

An average weekly wage calculation is simply a method of establishing the value of an employee's lost ability to earn future wages during the period of disability attributable to a covered industrial accident. The entire objective of wage calculation is to arrive at a fair approximation of a claimant's probable future earning capacity. The worker's disability reaches into the future, not the past; the loss as a result of injury must be thought of in terms of its impact on probable future earnings, perhaps for the rest of the worker's life. Fairness in determining the appropriate compensation rate is the key consideration in an employee's benefits determination. If an injury occurring on a part-time job disabled an employee from working in his or her full-time job, the worker's capacity as a wage earner is impaired beyond the limits of the part-time employment, and compensation should be based on the combined wages. The purpose of the Florida Workers' Compensation Act is to compensate for loss of wage earning capacity due to work-connected injury. It is the capacity of the whole man, not the capacity of the part-time or full-time worker, that is involved [Gilbreth v. Genesis Eldercare, 821 So. 2d 1226, 1229–1230 (Fla. 1st DCA 2002), *rev. den.*, 842 So. 2d 843 (Fla. 2003)].

For a general discussion of the concept of average weekly wage, see LARSON'S WORKERS' COMPENSATION, DESK EDITION, Ch. 93, § 93.01 (Matthew Bender).

[2] Concurrent Earnings

[a] Defined

Before we can begin to calculate an injured worker's *average* weekly wage, we must first define the basic wage itself and its components. An injured worker's wages, for purposes of calculating benefits, include wages earned in other covered employments for all accident dates. Despite statutory language to the contrary, this includes those accidents occurring between July 1, 1990 and December 31, 1993. For accidents occurring between those dates, the statute provides that wages: "Includes only the wages earned on the job where the employee is injured, and does not include wages from outside or concurrent employment" [§ 440.02(24), Fla. Stat. (7/1/90)].

Almost everyone read this to mean that we should not include wages earned from outside or concurrent employment when calculating a worker's average weekly wage. In early 1993, the First District Court of Appeal held this provision constitutional, but did not comment on its application [*see* Ciancio v. North Dunedin Baptist Church, 616 So. 2d 61, 62–63 (Fla. 1st DCA 1993)].

In late 1993, however, the court held that the new definition of wages does not affect calculating an injured worker's average weekly wage. In other words, the amendment is merely a definition of "wage" and as such does not control computing *average weekly wage* under the statute. That statute, § 440.14(1), Fla. Stat., requires that we decide average weekly wages based on whether the injured employee worked full-time or part-time. If the injured employee worked full-time, we must use full-time wages. A worker with two, four-hour per day jobs is a full-time worker. If the legislature truly intends to eliminate concurrent earnings, it must amend all related sections, such as § 440.14(1), Fla. Stat., which it did not do. Therefore, under this 1993 court decision, we must include concurrent earnings as before [*see* Vegas v. Globe Sec., 627 So. 2d 76, 77–81 (Fla. 1st DCA 1993)].

All concurrent earnings from covered employment, whether from a similar or a dissimilar job, should be included in an average weekly wage calculation [*see* Gilbreth v. Genesis Eldercare, 821 So. 2d 1226, 1230 (Fla. 1st DCA 2002), *rev. den.*, 842 So. 2d 843 (Fla. 2003)].

[b] Not All Concurrent Employment Is Included

The Act describes specific excluded employments. These are employments statutorily excluded from coverage. If the injured worker's concurrent job is excluded from coverage, wages earned there are excluded from the worker's average weekly wage [*see* Putnam County School Bd. v. Debose, 667 So. 2d 447, 449–450 (Fla. 1st DCA 1996)].

Excluded employments include the following [§ 440.02(15)(c), Fla. Stat. (1/24/91)]:

1. Domestic servants in private homes.
2. Agricultural labor on a farm with 5 or fewer regular employees and fewer than 12 other employees for seasonal work to be completed in less than 30 days.
3. Professional athletes.
4. Labor done under the sentence of a court.
5. All private, non construction employments with three or fewer employees.

The law also describes specific excluded employees [§ 440.02(13)(d), Fla. Stat. (7/1/97)]:

1. Independent contractors including:
   a. Real estate salespersons.
   b. Musical or theatrical performers including disc jockeys.
2. Casual employment.
3. Volunteers.
4. Exempt officers of corporations.
5. Exempt sole proprietors and partners.
6. Independent horse exercise riders.
7. Certain drivers-for-hire (taxis and limousines).

The court held that the phrase "any service performed" contained in the definition of "employment" in § 440.02(16)(a), Fla. Stat., is extremely broad and is limited only by the list of specifically excluded employments. Therefore, the court concluded that work for the U.S. postal service could fall within the broad definition of employment. Because a postal service job is not specifically excluded, earnings there should be included in the calculation of the claimant's AWW [*see* Reaves v. United Parcel Service, 792 So. 2d 688, 692 (Fla. 1st DCA 2001); *see also* Bath v. She-Conc Inc., 560 So. 2d 1289, 1292 (Fla. 1st DCA 1990) (holding that wages earned from employment in National Guard are includable in calculation of AWW)].

NOTE: Ch. 3 contains a detailed discussion of covered and excluded employment.

SPECIAL ALERT: If the law excludes concurrent wages from the calculation of the injured worker's average weekly wage, they are also excluded from the calculation of post injury earnings. Remember, however, that carriers may use such excluded wages to calculate wage-earning capacity [*see* Parrott v. City of Fort Lauderdale, 190 So. 2d 326, 330–331 (Fla. 1966); Christian v. Carolina Freight Carrier, 571 So. 2d 524, 525–526 (Fla. 1st DCA 1990)].

[c] Speculation and Intent Are Insufficient

Speculation about a future job, or the intent to obtain such a job, are not enough to establish concurrent earnings. For example, Dawn Stuart was injured on her fourth day at work for the Cato Corporation. She claimed that the carrier incorrectly calculated her average weekly wage by excluding her concurrent employment with a florist shop. At the hearing the judge of compensation claims decided that Stuart had intended to work for the florist shop before she was injured and ordered her average weekly wage calculated based on a 56-hour work week. On appeal, however, the court found that Stuart did not work even one day for the florist shop. The shop's owner testified that Stuart was no longer an employee but was merely placed on an on-call list of experienced people he could call when he was extremely busy. The only evidence of concurrent employment was Stuart's own testimony that she intended to work both jobs. Speculation and intention, however, are not enough to support a finding of concurrent employment, and the court reversed the judge's order [*see* Cato Corp. v. Stuart, 711 So. 2d 1375, 1376 (Fla. 1st DCA 1998)].

The critical inquiry for an award of worker's compensation based on dual employment must be whether the claimant, during the 13-week period, holds concurrent employment that is expected to continue in the future. Thus, if the claimant resigned from her second job before the accident, there was no expectation of future continuance, and the wages from the second job were not includaible in the average weekly wage calculation. Note, however, that there is no requirement that the claimant be actually working at the second job when the accident occurs. Such a situation would arise most often when the second job was seasonal and the accident occurred during the off-season. If the claimant can show that she expected to resume work at her second job, then the wages earned from the second job must be included [*see* Gomez v. Murdoch, 520 So. 2d 600 (Fla. 1st DCA 1987)].

[d] Calculating Average Weekly Wage When Concurrent Earnings Apply

If an employee worked a full-time job concurrently with a part-time job during the 13 weeks before the accident, calculating the average weekly wage is a simple matter of dividing the total earnings from both jobs by 13. What happens, however, if the employee did not work a full 13 weeks in the part-time job?

In 1998 the Florida Supreme Court held that we must use the formula described in § 440.14(1)(a), Fla. Stat. That formula, said the Court, requires adding the wages from all employments and dividing the total by 13. This applies whether the "other" employment is concurrent or successive. For example, assume the worker earned $5,200 during the 13 weeks before the injury and also earned $600 from a part-time job during the six weeks before the injury. In total, the worker earned $5,800. This amount, divided by 13, yields an average weekly wage of $446.15, which is the average weekly wage to use. The Court noted the DCA's concern about allowing the JCC latitude in calculating average weekly wage on an individual basis in the interest of fairness and reasonableness. The Court also recognized the benefit of having a fixed method of calculation so that everyone involved could easily make the calculation without having to resort to a JCC for a decision. The legislature, said the Court, provided a fixed method of calculation in these concurrent employment situations, which method provides a fair and reasonable calculation of average weekly wage [*see* Wal-Mart Stores v. Campbell, 714 So. 2d 436,440 (Fla. 1998) (reversing *Wal-Mart Stores v. Campbell,* 694 So. 2d 136 (Fla. 1st DCA 1997)].

[e] Accidents On or After January 1, 1994

For accidents occurring on or after January 1, 1994, the definition of "wages" changed again. Wages now include only wages "reported for a federal income tax purpose on the job where the employee is injured." In addition, the new definition again includes wages earned on "any other concurrent employment where (the injured worker) is also subject to workers' compensation coverage and benefits." Note the last sentence carefully. If the injured worker's other employment is with an exempt employer or is in an exempt occupation, or otherwise not qualified for workers' compensation benefits, wages earned there are not included [§ 440.02(24), Fla. Stat. (7/1/97)].

Also, the statute requires including only those wages reported as taxable income. The *Vegas* decision [*see* [a], *above*], however, creates a question about whether the taxable income provision has any real effect since the legislature did not amend the section on calculating average weekly wage. *Vegas* held that overruling case law requires the legislature to amend all relevant sections. In addition, case law holds that includable income does not need to be taxable income [*see* Dubois Farms, Inc. v. Paul, 566 So. 2d 923, 925 (Fla. 1st DCA 1990)].

[f] Burden of Proof

It is the employee's responsibility to provide the carrier with information concerning loss of earnings from concurrent employment [§ 440.14(5)(a), Fla. Stat. (10/1/2001].

The employee is not entitled to interest, penalties, or attorney's fees for the period in which the employee failed to provide the carrier with information concerning concurrent earnings. Carriers are not subject to penalties by the Division for the incorrect calculation of average weekly wage for the period in which the employee failed to provide the carrier with information concerning concurrent earnings [§ 440.14(5)(b), Fla. Stat. (10/1/2001)].

For a general discussion of the wage basis in concurrent employment, see LARSON'S WORKERS' COMPENSATION, DESK EDITION, Ch. 93, § 93.03 (Matthew Bender).

[3] Fringe Benefits

[a] Inclusion Determined by Date of Accident

Besides actual wages, the values of certain fringe benefits are includable, but only if the employer stops providing the benefit during disability. Including fringe benefits causes the most problems in calculating a correct average weekly wage. What the law includes as fringe benefits changes, depending on the accident's date. Previously, fringe benefits included everything from the obvious, such as employer-provided health insurance, to the not so obvious. The latter category includes such things as uniforms or even the value of bird seed the employer occasionally allowed the employee to take home. The decade of the 1980s saw the list of acceptable fringe benefits grow, year after year. This potentially unlimited list of fringe benefits led to considerable confusion and litigation. By 1990, the need for legislative remedy was clear. Today, the Act restricts the allowable fringe benefit list to only a few items. Because these legislative amendments change the amounts of benefits, they are substantive and therefore apply to only those accidents occurring on or after the amendment's effective date.

Whatever the accident's date, the values of fringe benefits are not included in calculating the average weekly wage if the employer continues to provide the benefit

Guide to Claims

during disability. This is an essential investigation issue. In [c] and [4], *below,* we will review what fringe benefits apply to which claims and which accident dates. First, a discussion of how we value these benefits is in order.

For a discussion on fringe benefits and what is included in wages, see LARSON'S WORKERS' COMPENSATION, DESK EDITION, Ch. 93, § 93.01[2] (Matthew Bender).

[b] Value of Fringe Benefits

Originally, "value" meant only the reasonable value, and "reasonable" meant the cost the employee would pay to purchase the benefit personally. That sounds simple enough, but figuring out an employee's cost was very difficult, if not impossible. For example, how do we calculate what it would cost an employee to purchase a health insurance policy like the one provided by the employer, when the policy was a group policy and not available to individuals?

Again the legislature came to the rescue and defined reasonable value as the actual cost to the employer. This method of valuation applies only to accidents occurring on or after October 1, 1987 [§ 440.02(21), Fla. Stat. (Supp. 1987)].

A review of the fringe benefits to include and to which claims they apply is contained in [c], *below.*

[c] Application of Fringe Benefits

[i] Accident Dates Through September 30, 1987

Fringe benefits include tips, gratuities, and the following: board, rent, housing, lodging, or similar advantage received from the employer. Thus, fringe benefits include almost anything one can imagine, including concurrent wages earned on other covered jobs.

The value of these benefits is the employee's retail cost. The value that carriers must calculate and add to the average weekly wage is the amount the employee would pay to purchase the benefit directly [§ 440.02(21), Fla. Stat. (Supp. 1986)].

[ii] Accident Dates Between October 1, 1987, and September 30, 1988

For these accident dates, fringe benefits include all of items listed in [i], *above,* plus:

1. Employer contributions for uniforms or cleaning allowances;
2. Employer contributions for life, health, accident, or disability insurance for the employee or dependents, excluding social security benefits;
3. Contributions to pension plans to the extent that the employee's rights have vested; and
4. Any other consideration received from the employer considered income under the Internal Revenue Code in effect on January 1, 1987.

For a detailed discussion of includable fringe benefits for this period, see FLORIDA WORKERS' COMPENSATION HANDBOOK, 1998 Ed. (Matthew Bender).

KEY CHANGE: The valuation of any fringe benefit is now based on the cost of the benefit to the employer.

[iii] Accident Dates Between October 1, 1988, and June 30, 1990

In 1988, the legislature added meals, parking, and legal insurance as items specifically included. Everything else remained the same [§ 440.02(21), Fla. Stat. (10/1/88)].

[iv] Accident Dates Between July 1, 1990, and December 31, 1993

[A] "Wage" Defined

In 1990, the legislature enacted a significant amendment, changing the definition of "wage" to include only wages earned on the job where the injured worker's injury occurred. Additionally, the amendment specifically excluded wages earned from other concurrent employment, except volunteer fire fighters [§ 440.02(24), Fla. Stat. (7/1/90)]. In December 1993, the First District Court of Appeal held this statutory amendment does not operate to exclude concurrent earnings from the calculation of average weekly wage [*see* Vegas v. Globe Sec., 627 So. 2d 76, 77–81 (Fla. 1st DCA 1993), *rev. denied,* 637 So. 2d 234 (Fla. 1994)].

Fringe benefits now include only:

1. Housing the employer furnished to the employee that is the employee's permanent year round home.
2. Gratuities to the extent reported to the employer, in writing, as taxable income.
3. Employer contributions for health insurance for the employee or the employee's dependents.
4. Housing furnished to migrant workers.

[B] Housing Exception

The basis of reasonable value continues to be the employer's cost, except the cost of housing. Housing is valued at the actual cost to the employer or, "based upon the Fair Market Rent Survey promulgated pursuant to section 8 of the Housing and Urban Development Act of 1974, *whichever is less*." Nothing, however, requires injured workers to prove the reasonable value of housing under both methods. They need only prove the value under either method. If the carrier believes the other method is the lesser of the two, it has the burden to prove it [*see* Blickle v. Bradwood Collections, 632 So. 2d 170, 171 (Fla. 1st DCA 1994)].

[C] Effect of Providing Fringe Benefits During Disability

Case law, and the 1990 changes to the Workers' Compensation Act, make clear that carriers should not include the value of fringe benefits if the employer continues to provide the benefit during disability. This is an important point. If the employer will not continue to provide the fringe benefits, the carrier must include the value of those benefits in the calculation of the injured worker's average weekly wage. [*see* § 440.02(27), Fla. Stat. (2001)]

If the employer will continue to provide the benefits, the carrier should not include them; however, if the employer should later stop the benefit, the carrier must recalculate the average weekly wage to include the value of such benefits. Many employers continue the benefits but, when they find out that the employee will be off work for a long time, they later fire the employee and cease all fringe benefits. The problem is that the employer will almost never remember to tell the adjuster! It is the adjuster's responsibility to verify the status of fringe benefits before each indemnity payment.

Claims adjusters must, before each payment, be sure that fringe benefits continue. If not, the carrier will be liable for interest on the underpaid portion. This failure to verify is also a frequent basis for awarding fees to the worker's attorney.

[v] Accident Dates On or After January 1, 1994

The 1993 legislature (effective January 1, 1994) again amended the statute. Although includable fringe benefits remain the same, the definition of "wage" changed in two important ways. First, for the carrier to include them, wages must have been reported to the Internal Revenue Service for federal income tax purposes.

Second, concurrent earnings are again specifically includable in the average weekly wage calculation. For example, if the worker is injured while working on a part-time job, the carrier must include wages earned on the full-time job. This does not apply, however, if the injured worker's other jobs are not subject to workers' compensation coverage. An example is a full-time worker who plays in a band at night. If the job meets the criteria described in ch. 3, § 3.05[3], the law considers the injured worker an independent contractor and wages earned from the band are not includable. The 1994 amendment provides that wages include the compensation earned on the job where the employee was injured, and any other concurrent employment, but only if he or she is also subject to workers' compensation coverage and benefits on the other job [§ 440.02(24), Fla. Stat. (1/1/94)].

Subsection [4], *below,* discusses the most common fringe benefits, including to which accident dates they apply, and the valuation method. We will limit the discussion on valuation to the employer's cost. Carriers should have long ago resolved the average weekly wage question on cases from 1987 or earlier.

[4] Types of Fringe Benefits

[a] Group Insurance, Pension, and Profit Sharing

[i] Health Insurance—All Accident Dates

[A] Calculating Value

If the employer provides health insurance to the employee, include the employer's cost when calculating average weekly wage. How does this work? Let us assume that an employer pays $400 per year for the employee's health insurance. We simply add 1/52 of the annual total or $7.69 to the injured worker's weekly wage.

Remember that we do not include this or any other fringe benefit if the employer was not providing it on the date of the accident. This is true even if the employer did provide it during some part of the 13 weeks before the accident. For example, Ramonita Rosado voluntarily canceled her health insurance coverage effective March 31, 1992. Two days later, on April 2, 1992, she was injured in an accident at work. The value of health insurance could no longer be included in Rosado's average weekly wage. Why? Because the health insurance was no longer a tangible benefit on the date of her industrial accident [*see* Rosado v. J.C. Penney, 647 So. 2d 987, 988 (Fla. 1st DCA 1994)].

What happens when there is no clear evidence of the employer's cost for health insurance, such as when the employer is self-insured? One argument may be that when no record evidence exists, this item should not be included in the calculation. This approach is unreasonable, though, especially if a reasonable solution presents itself. One such solution is to use the claimant's initial premium under the Consolidated Omnibus Budget Reconciliation Act (COBRA) in the average weekly wage calculation [*see* Public Law No. 93-406, 100 Stat. 227 (codified as amended in various sections throughout 29 U.S.C.S.)].

This federal law provides that the first 18 months of COBRA coverage cannot lawfully exceed 102 percent of the reasonable cost of providing coverage to "similarly situated beneficiaries for the same period occurring during the preceding determination period." [*See* 29 U.S.C.S. §§ 1162–1164 (Supp. 1998)].

If the amount of the initial COBRA premium is the best evidence available as to the amount of an employer's contribution for health insurance, then that is the amount that the judge of compensation claims should use in the AWW calculation. Although this may not be a completely accurate amount, it is more accurate than simply using zero [*see* Running W. Citrus Ltd. v. Raggs, 716 So. 2d 839, 841 (Fla. 1st DCA 1998)].

NOTE: The employer must make a health insurance premium contribution to include the cost in the average weekly wage. For example, the employer arranged for its employees to participate in a reduced cost, group health insurance plan. Employees, however, paid the entire premium and the employer made no contribution toward the plan's cost. The discounted premium is not a fringe benefit to be valued as part of the wages the employer pays [*see* LeBlanc v. Harmon Contract Glazing, 548 So. 2d 815 (Fla. 1st DCA 1989)].

[B] Health Insurance Defined

The next question is, what does the term "health insurance" include? The term is not defined in Chapter 440 Fla. Stat. Florida statutes define the term "health insurance" as [§ 627.6482(6), Fla. Stat. (1995)]:

> Any hospital and medical expense incurred policy, minimum premium plan, stop-loss coverage, health maintenance organization contract, prepaid health clinic contract, multiple-employer welfare arrangement contract, or fraternal benefit society health benefits contract, whether sold as an individual or group policy or contract. The term does not include any policy covering medical payment coverage or personal injury protection coverage in a motor vehicle policy, coverage issued as a supplement to liability insurance, or workers' compensation.

The Judge of Compensation Claims ruled that the employee's average weekly wage

Guide to Claims

excluded premiums paid by his employer for his dental insurance. The judge ruled that dental insurance is a fringe benefit separate from health insurance because it is sold separately with separate costs, and that dental insurance is more similar to disability insurance that is not included within the AWW computation. The claimant argued that "health insurance" includes the stand-alone dental coverage paid for by his employer.

The First DCA agreed with the claimant and reversed. The court held that because the legislature did not list dental insurance separately from health insurance along with the other types of coverages available, it could not be treated separately. The court remanded to the Judge of Compensation Claims to calculate the claimant's average weekly wage to include the value of employer-provided dental insurance [Whitner v. Blvd. Tire Ctrs., 812 So. 2d 592, 593 (Fla. 1st DCA 2002)].

[ii] Disability, Legal, and Life Insurance—Accident Dates Through June 30, 1990

Other forms of employer-paid insurance, such as disability, life, and legal, are includable only for accidents before July 1, 1990.

[iii] Profit Sharing and Pension Plans—Accident Dates Through June 30, 1990

Included in the calculation for these older cases are employer contributions to profit sharing or pension plans. These contributions are includable, however, only if the employee has a vested interest in the plan. Without vesting, this is not a tangible benefit of real present-day value. Employer contributions are includable in the same percentage as the employee's vested interest.

For a detailed discussion, see FLORIDA WORKERS' COMPENSATION HANDBOOK, 1998 Ed. (Matthew Bender).

[b] Vacation and Sick Leave Benefits

These items apply only to accidents occurring before July 1, 1990. Vacation and sick leave benefits are includable if the employee's rights to these benefits have vested. For a detailed discussion, see FLORIDA WORKERS' COMPENSATION HANDBOOK, 1998 Ed. (Matthew Bender).

For accidents occurring on or after July 1, 1990, vacation and sick leave benefits are not included in the definition of "wage" in § 440.02(24), Fla. Stat. and are, therefore, not includable in the benefit calculation [*see* Orange County School Bd. v. Muscanell, 705 So. 2d 1026, 1027–1028 (Fla. 1st DCA 1998)].

[c] Employer Contribution for Social Security or Medicare

Social security taxes the employer pays for the employee are not includable since they do not represent a real present day value to the employee [*see* Munroe Regional Medical Center v. Ricker, 489 So. 2d 785, 788 (Fla. 1st DCA 1986)]. Likewise, the employer's contributions for a worker's medicare benefits are not includable [*see* Curry Industries v. Maringer, 691 So. 2d 4 (Fla. 1st DCA 1997)].

[d] Meals, Uniforms, and Parking

For accidents occurring before July 1, 1990, if meals, uniforms, and parking have a real present day value to the employee, they are includable at the employer's cost. For a detailed discussion, see FLORIDA WORKERS' COMPENSATION HANDBOOK, 1998 Ed. (Matthew Bender); [*see* Brownell v. Hillsborough County, 617 So. 2d 803, 804–805 (Fla. 1st DCA 1993)].

[e] Transportation Expenses

Transportation expenses are includable only for accidents occurring before July 1, 1990. The value of employer provided transportation is includable if it represents a real present value to the employee. Transportation is not includable, however, if it is merely a "make whole" reimbursement. Obviously if the employer gives the employee a free company car, real present value exists. For a detailed discussion, see FLORIDA WORKERS' COMPENSATION HANDBOOK, 1998 Ed. (Matthew Bender).

[f] Capital Accumulation Plans

Capital accumulation plans cannot be included in the average weekly wage calculation. For example, when the employer contracted with the United States government to provide services for a specified number of employee hours, the United States Department of Labor set a level of benefits that the employer was required to pay each employee working under the contract. Holiday pay, sick leave pay, and unpaid absences were excluded. The employer then provided various fringe benefits such as medical and sick leave. When the costs of those fringe benefits were calculated and totaled, any differential between that amount and the minimum set by the government was paid into the CAP (Capital Accumulation Plan) of each employee, which was a type of employee savings plan. The JCC concluded that the CAP for each employee was deferred wages and, therefore, had to be included in the AWW computation. The employer argued that the CAP contributions were not included within the definition of wages for purposes of computing AWW pursuant to § 440.02(24), Fla. Stat. (1997). The First DCA agreed with the employer and reversed. The court held that the CAP should have been excluded from AWW computation because it was a fringe benefit not included within the definition of wages pursuant to § 440.02(24) [Lockheed Martin v. Grzegorczyk, 813 So. 2d 227, 228 (Fla. 1st DCA 2002)].

[5] Tips and Gratuities

The statutory definition of wages before July 1, 1990 included "gratuities received in the course of employment from other than the employer . . . (but) . . . only when such gratuities are received with the knowledge of the employer." Effective July 1, 1990, the legislature changed this section to "gratuities to the extent reported to the employer in writing as taxable income" [§ 440.02(24), Fla. Stat. (7/1/90)].

We will first examine the original language and then consider the effect of the change. Tips are not included in the employee's average weekly wage if the employer did not know the amount of the tips that the injured worker received. Include tips in the calculation only when the injured worker receives them with the knowledge of the employer's knowledge. The injured worker's vague statements about average tips received is not competent and substantial evidence compared to the precision of the employer's payroll records. Two exceptions to this general rule are as follows:

Guide to Claims

1. When the employer closes its eyes to the obvious.

2. When the employer fails to try to find out the amount of the tips.

If the employer knows employees receive tips, but does nothing to require reporting, the law will not allow the employer and carrier to claim lack of knowledge.

In summary, then, only tips reported to the employer are includable unless the employer fails to set up reporting procedures when it knows the employees receive tips. Remember that the employer's reporting procedure need not be mandatory. Employees must comply with even an optional reporting policy or risk losing their tips in the calculation of average weekly wage [*see* Mehrer v. Creative Hairdressers, Inc., 659 So. 2d 333, 334–335 (Fla. 1st DCA 1995)]. The written report requirement, however, does not relieve the employer of its responsibility to set a reporting procedure and to instruct employees properly [*see* Denny's Restaurant v. Bell, 659 So. 2d 1374, 1375 (Fla. 1st DCA 1995)].

The change for accidents occurring on or after July 1, 1990, requires reporting to the employer in writing, or to the Internal Revenue Service. In *Mehrer,* the injured worker said he did not earn enough to require filing a tax return and, therefore, did not report his tips to the IRS. The court held the statute does not allow an exception for non-filers. In such a situation, the employee must report to the employer, or tips cannot be included in average weekly wage [*see* Mehrer v. Creative Hairdressers, Inc., 659 So. 2d 333, 334–335 (Fla. 1st DCA 1995)].

Even if the worker reports tips to the employer, they are still not includable as wages if the worker failed to report them as taxable income to the Internal Revenue Service. Any tips not reported for federal income tax purposes cannot qualify as wages [*see* Corkery v. Best Wings of Cape Coral, 707 So. 2d 884, 885 (Fla. 1st DCA 1998)].

[6] Awards and Prizes

A lump sum awarded to a working student for her academic excellence is not includable because it was not based on any services rendered to the university. To qualify as wages, benefits must be provided to the injured worker as consideration for services performed for the employer [*see* University of Miami Medical School v. Singleton, 582 So. 2d 1182, 1183 (Fla. 1st DCA 1990); *see also* Bell Brokerage Co. v. Quintero, 556 So. 2d 793, 794 (Fla. 1st DCA 1990)].

§ 12.02 Calculating Average Weekly Wage

[1] Thirteen Week Average Method

[a] Statutory Formula

[i] Accident Dates Through September 30, 2003

The method we must use in calculating the average weekly wage is described in the Act [§ 440.14(1)(a), Fla. Stat. (7/1/97)]:

If the injured employee has worked in the employment in which she or he was working at the time of the injury, whether for the same or another employer, during substantially the whole of 13 weeks immediately preceding the injury, her or his average weekly wage shall be one-thirteenth of the total amount of wages earned in such employment during the 13 weeks.

[ii] Accident Dates On or After October 1, 2003

The Legislature changed the statutory formula effective October 1, 2003, as follows [§ 440.14(1)(a), Fla. Stat. (10/1/2003)]:

> If the injured employee has worked in the employment in which she or he was working *on the date of the accident*, whether for the same or another employer, during substantially the whole of 13 weeks immediately preceding the accident, her or his average weekly wage shall be one-thirteenth of the total amount of wages earned in such employment during the 13 weeks. [*Emphasis added*]

This amendment is apparently intended to ensure that the accident date is controlling, not the date on which the employee first obtained treatment or became disabled.

Under either statute, the formula sounds simple enough. Find out all the wages and other compensation the employee earned during the 13 weeks before the accident. Add them up and divide the total by 13. This is not, however, as clear-cut as it appears [*see* [b]–[e], *below*].

[b] Employment Defined

The first problem is the phrase, "in the employment in which he was working at the time of the injury, whether for the same or another employer." This phrase means that if the employee worked for different employers during the 13 weeks, we must use the wages from all similar jobs to calculate average weekly wage. Do not confuse this with concurrent employment, which is two or more jobs worked simultaneously. If, for example, the injured worker began work with the insured employer the day before the accident, we must find out if the injured worker had other jobs during the previous 13 weeks.

This does not mean just any job. The previous job must have been one in the same kind of employment as the injured worker's present job. In addition, the wages earned in the previous job must bear a reasonable relationship to the anticipated full-time wages from the injured worker's present employment. Even if the previous job was identical to the present job, the injured worker must still have worked at them both for "substantially the whole of thirteen weeks" before the accident. Following is an example:

The employee was injured after only one week on the job. He had previously been employed by DeSear's Central Air for 10 weeks. This was a job almost identical to his present job. The judge of compensation claims combined the wages from both jobs to arrive at the injured worker's average weekly wage. The First District Court of Appeal reversed, holding that this was the correct theory but could not apply here because both employments together did not meet the "substantially the whole of thirteen weeks" test. No evidence was introduced to show that the wages earned on the previous job bore any relationship to the anticipated earnings of the present job. Under these facts the injured worker's average weekly wage must be decided under the contract of hire with the present employer [*see* [4], *below*; *see* Efficient Systems v. Dept. of Labor, 624 So. 2d 343, 345 (Fla. 1st DCA 1993)].

[c] Thirteen Weeks Defined

[i] Accident Dates Through September 30, 2003

Exactly what does "substantially the whole of thirteen weeks" mean? The statutory definition before October 1, 2003, is as follows [§ 440.14(1)(a), Fla. Stat. (7/1/97)]:

> [A] constructive period of 13 weeks as a whole, which shall be defined as a consecutive period of 91 days, and the term "during substantially the whole of 13 weeks" shall be deemed to mean during not less than 90 percent of the total customary full-time hours of employment within such period considered as a whole.

This language means that to use the 13-week method, the injured worker must have been employed for the full 13 weeks. During that time, he or she must have worked at least 90 percent of customary full-time hours. If 40 hours per week are customary, then 90 percent is 36 hours per week.

[ii] Accident Dates On or After October 1, 2003

The Legislature amended the statutory definition of "substantially the whole of 13 weeks," effective October 1, 2003, as follows [§ 440.14(1)(a), Fla. Stat. (7/1/97)]:

> The calendar period of 13 weeks as a whole, which shall be defined as the 13 calendar weeks before the accident, excluding the week during which the accident occurred. The term "during substantially the whole of 13 weeks" shall be deemed to mean during not less than 75 percent of the total customary hours of employment within such period considered as a whole.

This language means that to use the 13-week method, we first ignore the week during which the accident occurred in determining whether the claimant was employed for 13 weeks before the accident.

The definition of 91 consecutive days no longer applies. Instead, determine if the claimant was employed during the 13 weeks before the week during which the accident occurred. The legislature repealed the phrase "full-time." Therefore, the next step is to decide if the claimant worked his or her customary hours, whether full-time or part-time. The phrase "during substantially the whole of 13 weeks" now means 75 percent of customary hours. If 40 hours per week are customary, then 75 percent is 30 hours per week. Remember that we must examine the 13 weeks taken as a whole. Therefore, if the claimant was employed for 13 full calendar weeks before the accident week and worked an average of at least 75 percent of customary hours, the 13-week method should be used.

For example, assume that a claimant customarily worked 40 hours per week. Over 13 weeks that amounts to 520 hours. To use the 13-week method, the claimant must have worked at least 75 percent of customary hours, or 390 hours, during those weeks. Therefore, if the claimant missed two weeks of work, he or she would have worked 440 hours, which is well within the 75 percent criteria, and the 13-week method will still apply.

[d] Customary Full-Time Hours Defined

Unfortunately, the Workers' Compensation Act does not define "full-time hours."

Consider the situation where a construction worker worked less than 13 weeks or less than a usual 40 hours because of bad weather or a slack season. Situations such as these would not serve to alter the average weekly wage. Whether busy or slack, raining or not, the wages earned during that 13 weeks are that particular worker's customary full-time hours. Therefore, the 13-week average would be the correct wage to use [*see* Coles v. Gainesville Bonded Warehouse, 409 So. 2d 1205, 1206 (Fla. 1st DCA 1982)]. Note, however, that this does not apply when a worker's wages are determined under the "seasonal worker" method [*see* Anstead v. Cox Broadcasting, 500 So. 2d 197 (Fla. 1st DCA 1986), discussed in [3], *below*].

When the injured worker is also the employer, proof of wages can present problems. In one case the injured worker was also the owner of the company. The injured worker himself apparently completed the 13-week wage statement, reporting a wage of $275 per week. He testified that he arrived at that figure by looking through his business checkbook and figuring out which checks he took from the company. No official payroll records existed and the injured worker's accountant testified that he reported no salary on his income tax returns. Therefore, the injured worker failed to produce evidence of any average weekly wage or wage loss. Thus, he was not entitled to compensation benefits [*see* General Repair Service, Inc. v. McKenzie, 577 So. 2d 619, 620 (Fla. 1st DCA 1991)].

[e] Reportable Wages

Interestingly, the Division has not developed a rule describing which wages to use in calculating average weekly wage. The nearest thing to a rule we have are the instructions on the back of the wage statement form, DWC-1a (11/94). The form instructs employers not to use wages earned in the week of the injury unless it paid the employee for the entire week. Instead, employers are told to report only the wages earned during the 13 weeks before the injury. That, however, is not the interpretation the court gives the statute. Recall the statute defines 13 weeks as the 91 days immediately preceding the accident [§ 440.14(1)(a), Fla. Stat. (7/1/97)]. Therefore, using only complete weeks is not the proper method. Using only complete weeks means we must often ignore wages earned during the week of the injury, which is an incorrect interpretation of the statute. Start with the wages earned the day before the accident and work back exactly 91 days. Then, simply divide the total by 13 to arrive at the injured worker's average weekly wage [*see* Pruitt v. Lotspeich Co. of Florida, Inc., 655 So. 2d 1305, 1306 (Fla. 1st DCA 1995)].

For a general discussion of what is included in wages, see Larson's Workers' Compensation, Desk Edition, Ch. 93, § 93.01[2] (Matthew Bender).

[2] Similar Employee Method

[a] Application

If the injured worker does not meet the criteria in [1][a]–[3], *above,* the next step is to learn if another, similar employee worked 13 weeks for the employer. If so, use the similar employee's wages in the calculation [§ 440.14(1)(b), Fla. Stat. (10/1/89)]:

> If the injured employee has not worked in such employment during substantially the whole of 13 weeks immediately preceding the injury, the wages of a similar employee in the same employment who has worked substantially the whole of such 13 weeks

shall be used in making the determination. . . .

[b] "Similar Employee" Defined

The term "similar employee" sounds simple, but what does "similar" mean? A similar employee is one who [*see* Coleman v. Burnup & Sims, Inc., 95 So. 2d 895, 897 (Fla. 1957)]:

1. Does the same type of work as the injured worker.
2. Works in the same place and preferably in the same crew as the injured worker.
3. Receives pay at the same rate as the injured worker.
4. Works substantially the same hours as the injured worker and both work regular hours.

Although the judge of compensation claims can usually consider wages the injured worker would have earned, this is not true here. Remember that here we look to the average wages earned by another, similar employee [*see* City of Miami v. Fernandez, 603 So. 2d 1346, 1348–1349 (Fla. 1st DCA 1992)].

[c] Exception to Definition

Even when two employees do the same type of work at the same wage, they still may not be similar. For example, the injured worker and other employees were free to work as many or as few hours as they wished, or none at all. The court held that while paying the same hourly wage is a strong sign that employees are similar, the facts here create an exception to the rule [*see* Expicare Nursing Services v. Eudaley, 596 So. 2d 126, 128–129 (Fla. 1st DCA 1992)].

[3] Seasonal Worker Method

If the injured worker is a seasonal worker who believes using the 13-week method would not be fair, the injured worker has the option of using the wages earned during the preceding calendar year or the preceding 52 weeks [§ 440.14(1)(c), Fla. Stat. (1989)]. The injured worker, however, must prove that this would be more reasonable and fair than the 13-week or similar employee method.

The dictionary's definition of the word "season" does not exclude a year-round employee, subjected to a variable income, from entitlement to her average annual wages under § 440.14(1)(c), Fla. Stat. (1997). Among other things, "season" is defined as a period of time of a slack season in business. The definition states specifically, as applied to industries, the term "seasonal" means affected or caused by seasonal need or availability. The only statutory conditions to the calculation of a claimant's average weekly wage (AWW) under § 440.14(1)(c), Fla. Stat. (1997) are a satisfactory showing that (1) the claimant is a seasonal employee, and (2) the seasonal employment method is more reasonable and fairer than that provided in § 440.14(1)(a), Fla. Stat. or § 440.14(1)(b), Fla. Stat., the 13-week and similar-employee methods, respectively.

The Court construed the term "seasonal" to mean simply "affected by seasonal need or availability." For example, in *Indus. Fiberglass Mfrs. & Employers Cas. Co. v. Davis* [460

So. 2d 998, 999–1000 (Fla. 1st DCA 1984)], the Court observed that the "seasonal worker" methodology appeared potentially appropriate for an over-the-road truck driver who normally experienced a slowdown in employment during the summer months. Similarly, a college instructor would ordinarily expect a slowdown in employment during the summer months, in that colleges then traditionally offer a reduced number of courses.

Nothing in § 440.14(1)(c), Fla. Stat. remotely suggests that a claimant, once he or she has presented sufficient proof of being in fact a seasonal employee, must have worked in any type of employment for substantially the whole of 13 weeks preceding an injury. Indeed, the method provided under § 440.14(1)(c), Fla. Stat. for calculating a seasonal employee's AWW, by using either the calendar year or the 52 weeks preceding the injury, strongly intimates that the 13-week procedure is irrelevant in such determination [*see* Gilbreth v. Genesis Eldercare, 821 So. 2d 1226, 1228–1229 (Fla. 1st DCA 2002), *rev. den.*, 842 So. 2d 843 (Fla. 2003)].

In addition, the injured worker must prove earnings by producing W-2 tax statements, written wage statements, or income tax returns. If the injured worker chooses this method, the carrier has 30 days after receipt of the injured worker's proof to adjust the compensation rate and to make any additional payments due for prior weeks. Of course, the carrier can deny the claim for an increased rate if it can disprove the proof, including showing that the injured worker is not a seasonal worker.

Although this method of calculating average weekly wage has been in law since 1974, neither the legislature nor the courts have provided a clear definition of seasonal work. The cases suggest that work is seasonal if the person works only during a specific season, or is subject to seasonal layoffs such as a worker in the canning industry [*see* Plymouth Citrus Products v. Woodard, 450 So. 2d 317, 318 (Fla. 1st DCA 1984)]. Just because a worker's wages fluctuate with seasons, however, does not necessarily make the person a seasonal worker [*see* Anstead v. Cox Broadcasting, 500 So. 2d 197, 198–199 (Fla. 1st DCA 1986)].

For a general discussion of seasonal employment, see LARSON'S WORKERS' COMPENSATION, DESK EDITION, Ch. 93, § 93.02[3] (Matthew Bender).

[4] Full-Time Weekly Wage Method

When the injured worker did not work 13 weeks before the accident, no similar employee exists, and the injured worker is not a seasonal employee, use the actual rate of pay or the contract of hire. The statute specifically states [*see* § 440.14(1)(d), Fla. Stat. (1989)]:

> If any of the forgoing methods cannot reasonably and fairly be applied, the full-time weekly wages of the injured employee shall be used, except as otherwise provided in paragraph (e) or paragraph (f).

(Note: the two exceptions referred to in paragraphs (e) and (f) are employees under age 22 and part-time employees.)

In cases in which none of the other methods applies, decide the average weekly wage prospectively. Use either the contract of employment or the injured worker's actual earnings. Base the choice on which method is the most fair and reasonable [*see* Efficient

Guide to Claims

Systems v. Dept. of Labor, 624 So. 2d 343, 345 (Fla. 1st DCA 1993)].

Note carefully that all the forgoing methods calculate average weekly wage retrospectively based on the injured worker's actual earnings before the accident. The full-time weekly wage method calculates average weekly wage prospectively based on the wages the injured worker would have earned but for the accident. For example, if the worker received a pay rate increase before the accident such that earnings would have increased in the future, this must be considered when making the average weekly wage calculation [*see* Mauranssi v. Centerline Utilities Contract, 685 So. 2d 66, 69 (Fla. 1st DCA 1996)].

This means that we cannot automatically decide the average weekly wage simply by dividing the total number of weeks worked into the wages paid. Does the evidence show that this would have been the injured worker's pattern in the future? In other words we must, based on the evidence, decide what average wage is the most reasonable and fair one to use [*see* Orange-Co of Florida v. Waldrop, 454 So. 2d 724, 725 (Fla. 1st DCA 1984)].

For example, assume the employee was injured during the first day at work. Further assume the employer hired the injured worker with the understanding that pay would be at the rate of $300 per week for a 40-hour week. Here then, $300 plus the value of includable fringe benefits is the average weekly wage to use. If the injured worker's contract of hire included potential sales commissions, decide based on competent evidence what the expected value of those commissions would have been. Do so by examining the commission earnings of other, similar, employees.

We must also consider and include other wages, such as overtime wages, which the injured workers might have earned if they had continued working. If the terms of the employment agreement contemplated overtime work, we must include this in the calculation based on the most reasonable estimate of the overtime hours the injured worker would have worked [*see* Sheffield v. Brannen's Land Clearing, 666 So. 2d 981, 983 (Fla. 1st DCA 1996)].

A prospective determination of average weekly wage might also encompass a future raise that is retroactively effective at the time of the injury [*see* Greater Florida Outdoor Advertising v. Dichristina, 591 So. 2d 1090, 1091 (Fla. 1st DCA 1992)].

[5] Exceptions to Methods for Calculating Average Weekly Wage

[a] Minors Under Age Twenty-Two

If the injured worker was under age 22 at the time of the injury, and in the normal course of events the weekly wage would likely have increased during the injured worker's period of disability, this "fact may be considered in arriving at her or his average weekly wage" [§ 440.14(1)(e), Fla. Stat. (7/1/97)]. This section does not apply automatically in every case involving a minor. It applies only where the facts show that the minor's wages were less than other workers because of his age. For example, the worker was a minor, but earned the same as other laborers. Nothing suggested that the injured worker earned less than others because of his age, so the court held § 440.14(1)(e), Fla. Stat. does not apply [*see* City of Miami v. Fernandez, 603 So. 2d 1346, 1349 (Fla. 1st DCA 1992)].

Though few cases on this subject exist, the court did decide that any such increase must occur during disability. Here, the injured worker received higher pay with a new employer when he returned to work after maximum medical improvement. The court held such increases must occur during the disability, not after, and refused to apply the increase retroactively [*see* Florida Ins. Guar. Ass'n v. Valez, 514 So. 2d 395, 397 (Fla. 1st DCA 1987)].

For a general discussion of adjusting the earning capacity of young workers, see LARSON'S WORKERS' COMPENSATION, DESK EDITION, Ch. 93, § 93.02[i][c] (Matthew Bender).

[b] Part-Time Employment

[i] Part-Time Defined

The second exception is the part-time worker. Finding out if the injured employee is a part-time worker is essential. If part-time employment exists, use the average of all wages paid over the 13 weeks. Be careful because not having worked full time during the 13 weeks before the accident does not automatically make the employee a part-time worker. The statutory definition of a part-time worker is one who "customarily works less than the full-time hours or full-time work week of a similar employee in the same employment" [§ 440.14(1)(f), Fla. Stat. (7/1/97)].

Decide part-time worker status based upon the following three findings:

1. The claimant was a part-time worker at the time of the accident;
2. The claimant adopted part-time employment as a customary practice; and
3. The claimant would have remained a part-time worker during the period of disability.

Remember that an employee cannot be a part-time worker unless all three criteria are met. The third item is somewhat nebulous, but we need not rely only on the worker's subjective testimony about future intent. Instead, consider the totality of the circumstances, including the worker's intent, prior work history, economic circumstances, and the duration of any disability period [§ 440.14(1)(f), Fla. Stat.; *see* Perry v. Fire Barrier Systems, 704 So. 2d 559, 560 (Fla. 1st DCA 1997)].

For a specific discussion of the wage basis in part-time employment, see LARSON'S WORKERS' COMPENSATION, DESK EDITION, Ch. 93, § 93.02 (Matthew Bender).

[ii] Period to Review

Give particular emphasis to the 13 weeks before the accident. For example, an injured worker, such as a part-time retail clerk during Christmas, may work two or three full-time, 40-hour weeks during a busy season. This is still considered part-time employment if part-time work has been the pattern [*see* Silver Springs, Inc. v. Scardo, 408 So. 2d 844, 845 (Fla. 1st DCA 1982)].

In another case, Loretta Richardson had been a full-time worker. She was undergoing chemotherapy treatment, however, and could work only part-time. An understanding was reached that she would return to full-time status when she finished the treatment program. Since Richardson intended to return to work full-time when she was able, the court held that full-time, not part-time work, was her usual practice. Additionally, because she did not work 90 percent of her usual full-time hours during the 13 weeks preceding her injury, the court held that the full-time, similar employee method, must be used [*see* Richardson v. Morrell's, Inc., 570 So. 2d 1076, 1077–1078 (Fla. 1st DCA 1990)].

In 2001, the court held that although, normally, the calculation should be based on the 13 weeks before the accident, this is not always true, especially when the period of disability begins much later. For example, Sue Christopher was originally injured on July 25, 1988. She continued working, but her condition continued to deteriorate until she became totally disabled on April 20, 1995. The judge of compensation claims awarded PTD benefits based on Christopher's AWW at the time of her accident in 1988 rather than her AWW at the point she became disabled in 1995. The court held that this was error and reversed, noting earlier cases holding that the commencement of disability is the pertinent time for AWW determination [*see* Hillsborough County School Board v. Christopher, 790 So. 2d 1267, 1268 (Fla. 1st DCA 2001)].

In an apparent effort to overrule the court's decision in *Hillsborough County School Board v. Christopher*, the Legislature amended § 440.14(1), Fla. Stat., effective October 1, 2003. Previously, this section provided that an employee's average weekly wage at the *time of the injury* should be taken as the basis on which to compute compensation. The statute now provides that the basis for computing compensation is the average weekly wage on the *date of the accident*.

In December 2003, the court, while not receding from *Christopher*, modified its meaning by suggesting that because *Christopher* relied on cases dealing with repetitive trauma and occupational disease, its holding applied to only those type of cases [*see* James v. Armstrong World Indus., Inc., 864 So. 2d 1132, 1135 (Fla. 1st DCA 2003)].

The employer, Armstrong World Industries, Inc., hired the claimant in 1967, and he worked until April 18, 2000. The claimant suffered a job-related injury on March 9, 1982. The claimant recalled missing work for approximately one month due to the injury, but he did not undergo surgery. He then returned to work in 1982 and continued working for the employer until April 17, 2000. On April 18, 2000, the claimant underwent lower back surgery related to the 1982 job injury. The claimant had not returned to work since the surgery, and the parties agreed the claimant was permanently and totally disabled.

The issue before the JCC was whether the claimant's average weekly wage should be calculated using the 13 weeks prior to the 1982 date of accident (which results in an AWW of $305.24, with a compensation rate of $ 203.49) or the 13 weeks prior to the surgery in 2000 (which results in an AWW of $ 638.73, with a compensation rate of $ 426.03). The JCC concluded the appropriate AWW was based on the 13 weeks prior to the claimant's accident in 1982.

On appeal, the court agreed and affirmed. The court noted that the goal of the calculation of the AWW is to determine a fair and reasonable AWW. However, appellate courts also recognize the benefit of having a fixed method of calculation to apply in recurring situations, so that employers, employees, and insurers may readily make the calculation without having to resort to a decision by a judge of compensation claims.

The court also noted that in cases of occupational disease, as defined in § 440.151, Fla.

Stat., the average weekly wage is properly calculated using the "date of disability" as the "date of accident."

In asserting that his "date of accident" should be April 18, 2000, because this was the date he became "disabled," the claimant relied on *Hillsborough County School Board v. Christopher* [790 So. 2d 1267 (Fla. 1st DCA 2001)]. The relevant portion of the decision in *Christopher* is as follows:

> On cross-appeal, claimant argues that the JCC erred by directing that her PTD benefits be calculated based upon her average weekly wage (AWW) in effect on July 25, 1988, when she suffered her back injury, rather than on April 20, 1995, when she became disabled because her condition had deteriorated to the point that she could no longer work. We agree. See Cote v. Combustion Engineering, Inc., 502 So. 2d 500 (Fla. 1st DCA 1987) (the commencement of disability is the pertinent time for AWW determination); Reynolds v. Neisner Bros., Inc., 436 So. 2d 1070 (Fla. 1st DCA 1983) (JCC erroneously calculated AWW at time of 1977 accident, rather than at time of disability in1981). We therefore reverse and remand for recalculation of claimant's PTD benefits based upon the stipulated 1995 AWW

The court noted that the underlying facts in *Christopher* are not disclosed in the opinion, but that the panel in *Christopher* relied on decisions involving repetitive trauma or occupational disease [*see* James v. Armstrong World Indus., Inc., 864 So. 2d 1132, 1135 (Fla. 1st DCA 2003)].

Thus, *James* and *Christopher* may be read to mean that, except for cases involving repetitive trauma and occupational disease, the average weekly wage must be calculated based on earnings before the accident date regardless of when the claimant's disability begins, even if that disability does not commence until years later.

[iii] On-Call Part-Time Work

Another exception is the "on-call" part-time worker. Benny Waldorf was a part-time substitute school bus driver who worked on an as-needed basis. During the entire year before his accident, Waldorf worked only 66 hours, earning a total of $430.98. All the work had been done during the four weeks preceding the accident. The judge of compensation claims accepted the carrier's argument that using the average of those four weeks would result in a windfall to Waldorf. Instead, the carrier argued, the judge should use the average of the 13 weeks preceding the accident. The judge agreed and, using the 13-week average method, decided that Waldorf's average weekly wage was $31.16. The First District Court of Appeal affirmed the judge's decision. The court found that none of the statutory methods adequately covered Waldorf's employment as a substitute bus driver. In reviewing its earlier decisions, the court noted that the judge of compensation claims' duty is to decide average weekly wage reasonably and fairly. In performing this task, said the court, the JCC is not a cipher or a calculating robot, but a judge of the injured worker's unique employment situation [*see* Waldorf v. Jefferson County School Bd., 622 So. 2d 515, 516–517 (Fla. 1st DCA 1993)].

The court also affirmed the judge's exclusion of wages that Waldorf earned in his full-time job as the operator of a television repair business. Since § 440.02(24), Fla. Stat. excluded concurrent employment at the time of this accident, wages earned on other jobs were irrelevant. This, however, is another example of inconsistent appellate opinions. As discussed above, the court, in *Vegas v. Globe Security,* held that the statutory language that we and the *Waldorf* court believed excluded concurrent earnings did not really do so [*see* § 12.01[2][a], for discussion of concurrent earnings; *see also* Orange-Co of Florida v. Waldrop, 454 So. 2d 724, 725 (Fla. 1st DCA 1984)].

[c] Independent Contractors

Independent contractors are not employees and, therefore, not entitled to benefits unless they provide their own coverage [*see* ch. 3, § 3.05[3]]. Sometimes, however, an employer may voluntarily include these contractors under its own coverage. For example, a trucking company may employ regular drivers and independent owner-operators. Including the owner-operators under its own insurance policy is common for such an employer. In such cases, the employer may deduct an agreed amount from the operator's pay to cover the premium. In one case, the contract with the owner-operator stipulated to an average weekly wage of $240 per week for workers' compensation purposes. This was the amount the average staff driver earned.

The judge of compensation claims relied on the average weekly wage specified in the contract, rather than upon the injured worker's actual earnings. The First District Court of Appeal agreed with the judge. For this rule to apply, however, the contract rate must bear a rational relationship to the injured worker's actual wages. Further, the injured worker must be one who would not be entitled to any benefits but for the contract. Thus, he must truly be an independent contractor [*see* Fleitas v. Today Trucking, Inc., 598 So. 2d 252, 253–254 (Fla. 1st DCA 1992)].

[d] Corporate Profits

Sometimes the injured worker is also the working owner of the corporation. In most such cases, the injured worker/owner draws a salary and shares the corporate profits. The question is, are corporate profits includable as wages? The general principle of law is that "where a claimant . . . is the sole or primary owner of the business from which he seeks compensation benefits, monies received *by virtue of his status as owner* . . . will not be characterized as 'earnings' or 'wages' for purposes of determining his entitlement to benefits" (emphasis added) [*see* MDM Marble Co. v. Jackson, 512 So. 2d 305, 306 (Fla. 1st DCA 1987) (quoting from *H.G. Boddiford Painting Cons., Inc. v. Boddiford,* 426 So. 2d 1243, 1246 (Fla. 1st DCA 1983))].

In other words, the employee/owner's return on investment is not includable. An exception arises, however, when the business profits are almost entirely the direct result of personal management and endeavor. Figuring out which part of the profits results from personal efforts can be difficult. Profit earned as the result of other employees' work or the sale of materials is not includable. If the carrier cannot agree with the injured worker, a judge of compensation claims must decide the correct amount on a case-by-case basis [*see* Pishotta v. Pishotta Tile & Marble, Inc., 613 So. 2d 1373, 1375–1376 (Fla. 1st DCA 1993)].

§ 12.03 Thirteen Week Wage Statement

Without question, carriers have an ethical and a legal duty to calculate the injured worker's average weekly wage correctly. Doing so requires that carriers receive accurate and timely wage information from the employer. Division rules require employers to use the Thirteen Week Wage Statement, form DWC-1a. Employers should send this to the carrier with the DWC-1, the First Report of Injury form. The Division, however, recognized that wage information is not always immediately available. The rule grants the employer 14 days from its knowledge of the accident to file the wage statement [Fla. Admin. Code R. 69L-3.004(2)(b) (1/10/2005)].

Failure to submit the DWC-1a timely subjects the employer to a fine of up to $100. This is in addition to a fine of up to $500 for late filing of the DWC-1 [Fla. Admin. Code R. 69L-24.0231 (1/10/2005)].

Until the carrier receives the wage statement, adjusters have no option but to make an educated guess about the correct average weekly wage. The best procedure is to use the information contained in the First Report of Injury and to discuss the facts with the injured worker. If upon receipt of the wage statement, the adjuster concludes the original wage figure is too low, he or she should immediately correct the rate and pay the injured worker the difference for the prior weeks, including any interest due. If the original figure was too high, reduce the rate of future payments; however, except accidents occurring on or after January 1, 1994, the carrier may have no right to recover the overpayment [*see* § 12.08].

Review the wage statement carefully. Did the employer use payroll records for the 91 days immediately before the accident? If the spaces on the form for reporting fringe benefits are blank, does this mean that the injured worker did not receive such benefits or does it mean that the employer simply did not fill out the form properly? Adjusters should always confirm all facts and assume nothing. Adjusters also must be certain to obtain a wage statement from any other, concurrent, employers.

§ 12.04 Calculating Compensation

[1] The Formula

Having calculated the injured worker's average weekly wage, we must now calculate the weekly benefit, or the compensation rate. For the rest of this discussion, assume the injured worker has an average weekly wage of $450.

For accidents occurring after July 1, 1979, injured workers are entitled to receive as compensation, 66 2/3 percent of their average weekly wage. Simply multiply the average weekly wage by .6667. For example: $450 x .6667 = $300. Our example worker is therefore entitled to receive $300 per week. Before July 1, 1979, the rate was based on 60 percent of average weekly wage [§ 440.15, Fla. Stat.].

[2] Minimum Compensation Rate

§ 440.12(2), Fla. Stat., provides in relevant part that:

> Compensation for disability . . . shall not be less than $20 per week. However, if the employee's wages at the time of injury are less than $20 per week, he or she shall receive his or her full weekly wages.

The minimum weekly compensation rate is $20 per week unless the injured worker's average weekly wage is less than $20. Then, the injured worker's full wage also will be the compensation rate. If the injured worker's wage was $25 per week, two-thirds would be $17. Then, the injured worker would be entitled to the statutory minimum of $20. If the injured worker's wage is $18 per week, the compensation rate also will be $18 since the full wage is less than the minimum [§ 440.12(2), Fla. Stat. (7/1/97)].

Note, however, that the minimum rate applies only if the claimant earned wages. If there are no wages, as in the case of a volunteer, no compensation is due. Compensation is paid for disability, with disability being defined at § 440.02(13), Fla. Stat., as incapacity "to earn in the same or any other employment the wages which the employee was receiving at the time of the injury." If a claimant received no wages in any employment, there is no basis for an award of compensation for disability. Furthermore, if wages were less than $20 per week, under the above-quoted statutory language the claimant is entitled to only his or her full weekly wages. If there are no wages, the claimant cannot qualify for an award of disability compensation [*see* Osceola County Sch. Bd. v. Boos, 912 So. 2d 667 (Fla. 1st DCA 2005)].

For a discussion of minimum limits on weekly benefits, see LARSON'S WORKERS' COMPENSATION, DESK EDITION, Ch. 93, § 93.04 (Matthew Bender).

[3] Maximum Compensation Rate

The maximum weekly compensation is an amount equal to the statewide average weekly wage for the year of the injured worker's injury. The Agency for Workforce Innovation calculates the statewide average weekly wage every year. Injured workers are entitled to receive the calculated compensation rate or the maximum, whichever is less [§ 440.12(2), Fla. Stat. (7/1/97)]. The statewide average weekly wage and, therefore, the maximum compensation rates for the years since 1980 are contained in Part VIII, Tables, Table 1.

For a discussion of maximum limits on weekly benefits, see LARSON'S WORKERS' COMPENSATION, DESK EDITION, Ch. 93, § 93.04 (Matthew Bender).

[4] Waiting Period

[a] Accident Dates Through June 30, 1990

For injuries occurring up to June 30, 1990, an injured worker is not entitled to compensation for the first seven days of disability unless the injury results in disability lasting more than 14 days [§ 440.12(1), Fla. Stat. (1989)].

[b] Accident Dates On or After July 1, 1990

For injuries occurring on or after July 1, 1990, an injured worker cannot collect compensation for the first seven days of disability unless the injury results in disability lasting more than 21 days [§ 440.12(1), Fla. Stat. (7/1/97)].

[c] Application

These delays discussed in [a]–[b], *above,* are waiting periods, or even deductibles. If the injured worker's disability exceeds the waiting period of 14 or 21 days, depending on the date of the injury, the law entitles the injured worker to payment for the first week. For example, on a pre-July 1, 1990 claim, the waiting period is 14 days. Assume the injured worker is disabled for 12 days. Then, the law entitles the injured worker to compensation only for the 8th through 12th day, or a total of 5 days. If the disability period is 15 days, compensation is due for the entire period.

For accidents occurring on or after July 1, 1990, the waiting period increases to 21 days. Refer to the example above. If the injured worker is disabled for 15 days, he or she can collect compensation only for the 8th through 15th day, or a total of 8 days. If the disability continues for 22 days, compensation is due for the entire period.

This applies despite the class of disability. For example, assume the injured worker is temporarily totally disabled for seven days. The physician then releases the injured worker to light duty work under temporary partial disability for the next 30 days. Now, the injured worker has met the waiting period requirement, and can collect compensation for the first seven days [§ 440.12(1), Fla. Stat. (7/1/90)].

[5] Compensation—When Due

[a] Between January 1, 1994, and September 30, 2003

For many years, the Act required that the first compensation payment was due within 14 days after the employer or carrier knew about the disability. Effective January 1, 1994, the statute required that carriers issue the first payment "no later than the 14th day after the employer receives notice of the injury or death" [§ 440.20(2), Fla. Stat. (1/1/94)].

Carriers must issue subsequent payments at 14-day intervals after the first payment. An exception arises with supplemental wage loss benefits paid monthly for accidents occurring on or after January 1, 1994. [Note: Supplemental wage loss benefits do not apply to accidents occurring on or after October 1, 2003.]

[b] On or After October 1, 2003

Beginning October 1, 2003, the payment deadline changes, depending on the nature of the disability. The first payment is due within 14 calendar days after the employer receives notification of the injury, when disability is immediate and continuous for eight calendar days or more after the injury. If the first seven days after disability are nonconsecutive or delayed, the first installment of compensation is due on the sixth day after the first eight calendar days of disability [§ 440.20(6)(a), Fla. Stat. (10/1/2003)].

Although rarely done, the judges of compensation claims have the authority to order alternate payment schedules. The judge may do so if the parties agree, or if the judge decides that such a change is in the best interest of the injured worker.

If authorized by the injured worker, compensation payments may be made by direct deposit, electronic transfer, or other means directly to the employee's bank [*see* § 440.12(1), Fla. Stat. (10/1/2001)]. Compensation is considered paid by these means on the date when the funds become available for withdrawal [*see* § 440.20(1)(a), Fla. Stat. (10/1/2001)].

Guide to Claims

SPECIAL ALERT: Paying any installment of compensation late may subject the carrier to fines. The definition of "late" changes depending upon the date of the accident. Effective January 1, 1994, a payment is late if not paid within seven days after it was due [*see* [9], *below*].

[6] Daily Compensation Rate

Usually, compensation benefits are due for an entire calendar week. Often, however, benefits for the first and final weeks are only for part of the week. In cases of minor injury, the injured worker may be entitled to only two or three days benefits. To calculate the amount due, we must calculate a daily compensation rate. Calculate the daily rate of compensation by dividing the weekly compensation rate by the number of days worked per week. If the injured worker's compensation rate is $200 for a five-day work week, the daily rate is $40. Thus, for pre-July 1, 1990 claims, if disability lasted for nine days, the law entitles the injured worker to two days' benefits, or $80 [§ 440.14(1)(g), Fla. Stat. (1989)].

[7] Weekly Compensation Rate

"Weekly compensation rate" means seven consecutive calendar days, including weekends and holidays or other non-working days. Thus, in the example in [6], *above*, if the eighth and ninth days of disability were Saturday and Sunday, the law still entitles the injured worker to compensation, though he or she does not ordinarily work on weekends [§ 440.02(29), Fla. Stat.].

[8] Compensation Rate—Successive Accidents

When a worker is injured in successive compensable accidents, deciding the proper compensation rate to use can be difficult. For example, Charles Higgins suffered a disabling injury. He eventually returned to work with the employer despite considerable physical restrictions. He then earned less than his preinjury wage, but did not qualify for wage loss benefits because his new wage was at least 85 percent of his former wage. Higgins suffered a second accident that, when combined with the first, made him permanently and totally disabled. The question became which compensation rate to use.

The carrier argued that it should use the wage earned at the time of the second accident. In disagreeing, the judge of compensation claims concluded that "it would be unfair to penalize the claimant, who attempted to return to work at a lower wage and sustained additional injuries, while allowing the E/C to receive a windfall by paying compensation based on the second and lower average weekly wage." The First District Court of Appeal agreed with the judge and affirmed the award. Under these circumstances the carrier should pay permanent total disability benefits based upon the highest average weekly wage the injured worker earned from the employer [*see* Pinellas County School Bd. v. Higgins, 597 So. 2d 355, 356 (Fla. 1st DCA 1992)].

This does not mean that carriers must always pay the higher of the two wages. Higgins earned less at his new job because of his original injury and impairment; thus, his original, higher, weekly wage was the correct one to use. Otherwise, use the wages earned from the new job. For example, Donald Allen went back to work but averaged less earnings than before. No evidence was presented to show that his first injury hampered his ability to do his regular job. In other words no evidence supported the notion that Allen suffered any reduced earning capacity because of the first injury. Therefore, his average weekly wage when the second injury occurred was the correct one to use [*see* State Department of Agriculture v. Allen, 692 So. 2d 230, 231 (Fla. 1st DCA 1997)].

If a worker's injury was the direct and natural result of an earlier accidental injury, the law will allow the injured worker to collect benefits based on the average weekly wage for the first accident [Mount v. Kash N' Karry, 635 So. 2d 995, 996 (Fla. 1st DCA 1994)].

For a specific discussion of the wage basis in concurrent employment, see LARSON'S WORKERS' COMPENSATION, DESK EDITION, Ch. 93, § 93.03 (Matthew Bender).

Guide to Claims

[9] Late Payments—Interest, Penalties, and Fines

[a] Interest

If carriers fail to pay *any* installment of compensation when due, they must add interest to the payment. The Act, § 440.20(6), Fla. Stat.], contains the following provision:

> . . .When any installment of compensation payable without an award has not been paid within 7 days after it became due and the claimant concludes the prosecution of the claim before a judge of compensation claims without having specifically claimed additional compensation in the nature of a penalty under this section, the claimant will be deemed to have acknowledged that, *owing to conditions over which the employer or carrier had no control*, such installment could not be paid within the period prescribed for payment and to have waived the right to claim such penalty. [Emphasis added].

The court interprets this to mean that the statute will forgive penalties and interest only when neither the employer nor carrier could have prevented the late payment. For example, the employer became confused about the identity of its workers' compensation insurer, which apparently resulted in a late report and a late first payment. The court did not question the employer's or carrier's good faith, but noted that it could not be said that the late payment was due to conditions over which they had no control. Thus, the judge of compensation claims cannot forgive the statutory penalty even in a case such as this one [*see* Corkery v. Best Wings of Cape Coral, 707 So. 2d 884, 885 (Fla. 1st DCA 1998)].

Interest accumulates at the rate of 12 percent per year from the date the installment became due until the carrier pays it. The minimum interest payment is $5. For example, the first payment of compensation is due 14 days after the employer receives a report of the accident and injury. If the carrier makes the payment on the 15th day or later, the carrier must add interest [§ 440.20(8), Fla. Stat. (1/1/94)].

The calculation, however, is not a simple matter of adding 12 percent. The interest due is 12 percent per year for each late installment. Therefore, each installment is 14 days later than the next one, so we must calculate each period separately. Additionally, remember that the rate is 12 percent per year, not per day or per payment. We must, therefore, multiply the daily interest rate by the number of days late. The formula to calculate interest for each late installment is:

(number of days late) x (.0003288) x (amount due) = Interest

> **EXAMPLE:** Assume the compensation rate is $300 per week. A single, two-week installment ($600) is 20 days late. The calculation is as follows: 20 x .0003288 x $600 = $3.94. Since the interest here is only $3.94, the carrier owes the minimum interest payment of $5.

> **SPECIAL ALERT:** A judge of compensation claims may not award interest on unpaid medical bills, and the amount of such bills may not be used to calculate the amount of interest awarded [§ 440.25(4)(k), Fla. Stat. (7/1/2002)].

For a general discussion of interest, see LARSON'S WORKERS' COMPENSATION, DESK EDITION, Ch. 134, § 134.04 (Matthew Bender).

[b] Penalties

[i] Late Payment of Benefit Installments

[A] Late Payments Made Before January 1, 1994

A payment is late if the carrier issues the payment more than 14 days after the due date. If late, the carrier must add a penalty equal to 10 percent of the late payment or $5, whichever is greater [§ 440.20(6), Fla. Stat. (1991)].

[B] Late Payments Made Between January 1, 1994, and September 30, 2003

A payment is late if the carrier issues the payment more than seven days after the due date. The amended 1994 Workers' Compensation Act provides that the carrier owes the injured worker a penalty if "any installment of compensation for death or dependency benefits, disability, permanent impairment, or wage loss is not paid within seven days after it becomes due . . . there shall be added to such unpaid installment a punitive penalty of an amount equal to 20 percent of the unpaid installment or $5" [§ 440.20(6), Fla. Stat. (1/1/94)].

Note that the revised 1994 statute omitted the phrase "whichever is greater" and ambiguously provides for "20% or $5.00," with no explanation as to which alternative applies. The Division's rule adopted an interpretation of the penalty calculation to provide that the penalty amount is different for a late *initial* installment than for late *subsequent* installments. Under the rule, the 20-percent penalty applies to only the first installment. Under the rule, the penalty for subsequent late payments is a flat $5, but the statute makes no such distinction [*see* Fla. Admin. Code R. 69L-24.0231 (former Fla. Admin. Code R. 38F-24.0231(4) (1/10/2005)].

The court now holds that the Division's Rule is an incorrect interpretation of the statute. The court held that the Legislature did not inadvertently leave out the phrase "whichever is greater," but instead inadvertently failed to delete the phrase "or $5.00." The court said: "We conclude, as did the JCC below, that the deletion of the words 'the greater of' in section 440.20(6) rendered the provision ambiguous. We find it also unintelligible. By its literal wording, the amended statute now provides for a percentage penalty and an alternative penalty, with no indication as to the conditions under which the alternative shall be applied, the method for determination, or by whom the determination is to be made. This obviously does not further the legislative goal of creating an 'efficient and self-executing system . . . , which is not an economic or administrative burden.' "

The court held: "Accordingly, because we can only conclude that the legislature inadvertently failed to omit the term 'or $ 5' from section 440.20(6), we read the statute as requiring a payment of twenty percent penalty on *all* non-award compensation installments not paid within the seven-day grace period" [Greenberg v. Cardiology Surgical Ass'n & Claims Ctr.—Lakeland, 855 So. 2d 234, 238 (Fla. 1st DCA 2003)].

This decision means that since January 1, 1994, carriers have been liable for payment of a 20-percent penalty for *every* installment of compensation made more than seven days after it was due.

[C] Late Payments Made On or After October 1, 2003

For late payments made on or after October 1, 2003, the penalty is an amount equal to 20 percent of each late installment. This applies to the initial installment and all subsequent installments. The Minimum penalty of $5 no longer applies [§ 440.20(6)(a), Fla. Stat. (10/1/2003)].

SPECIAL ALERT: The Division (incorrectly) declared by rule that the 1994 amendment is substantive, and applies to only those accidents occurring on or after the effective date. The court, however, held this amendment is procedural, and applies to late payments made on or after January 1, 1994, whatever the date of the accident [*see* Fla. Admin. Code R. 69L-24.0231 (1/10/2005); Bell v. University of Florida, 652 So. 2d 460, 461 (Fla. 1st DCA 1995)].

NOTE: The Act provides that the carrier does not owe a penalty if the late payment "results from conditions over which the employer or carrier had no control" [§ 440.20(6), Fla. Stat. (1/1/94)]. A carrier can no longer avoid penalties simply by filing a notice of denial within 14 days of a claim. Rather, the carrier must either pay the benefits within seven days or exercise the 120-day pay-and-investigate option under § 440.20(4), Fla. Stat. Thus, an unsuccessful denial of indemnity benefits will always result in the assessment of a penalty. Here, the carrier argued that it did not know the claimant had undergone surgery and thus non-payment was beyond its control. The court disagreed. Once the carrier was on notice via the claimant's petition for benefits, it had an obligation to pay, or to begin paying, while continuing the investigation. Since it did neither, penalties are due [*see* Beverly v. Publix Supermarkets, 792 So. 2d 595, 596 (Fla. 1st DCA 2001)].

Guide to Claims

For a general discussion of penalties, see LARSON'S WORKERS' COMPENSATION, DESK EDITION, Ch. 135 (Matthew Bender).

[ii] Late Payment of Award

[A] Through December 31, 1993

Before 1994, failing to pay benefits under the terms of an award within 30 days after it became due resulted in the assessment of a penalty. That penalty equaled 20 percent of the benefits awarded [§ 440.20(8), Fla. Stat. (1991)].

The question is, when are benefits due? The Division's position was that benefits are not due until the order becomes final. A judge of compensation claims' order becomes final 30 days after the court mails the order to the parties. Thus, the Division Rule provides that the 20-percent penalty applies if the carrier does not issue payment within 60 days after the court mails the order. As will be seen in [B], *below,* the Division's interpretation was wrong!

[B] On or After January 1, 1994

Effective January 1, 1994, the legislature amended § 440.20(8), Fla. Stat., now found under § 440.20(7), Fla. Stat. The amended section provides that carriers owe the 20-percent penalty if they do not pay the benefits awarded within 7 days after the benefits awarded are due. Again, it was the Division's position that benefits are not due until the order becomes final. An order is final 30 days after the judge mails the order to the parties. Thus, if the Division is correct, the following rule applies: for accidents occurring on or after January 1, 1994, the carrier must pay a 20-percent penalty if it does not issue the payment within 37 days after the judge mails the order to the parties [Fla. Admin. Code R. 69L-24.0231(5) (1/10/2005)]. Is the Division correct? The answer is no.

Several cases have suggested that payment is due when the judge of compensation claims enters (signs) the order. In one case that is exactly how the judge ruled. The First District Court of Appeal affirmed and said: "We agree with the deputy commissioner that the obligation to pay benefits arose on the date copies of the order were mailed to the parties" [*see* Mendez v. Florida Power & Light Co., 436 So. 2d 309, 310 (Fla. 1st DCA 1983)]. Although *Mendez* is an old case, it was not until 1996 that the First District Court of Appeal changed its view.

In 1992, the court held that because the carrier paid benefits more than 30 days after the judge of compensation claims entered the order, the carrier owed the penalty [*see* Sigg v. Sears Roebuck & Co., 594 So. 2d 329, 330 (Fla. 1st DCA 1992)]. In 1995, the court addressed the question again, holding that it is indisputable that compensation becomes due on the day the judge of compensation claims approves (in this case) the settlement. Thus, if the judge signs the order on January 1 and the carrier makes the payment on January 8, the carrier would owe a 20-percent penalty [*see* Bell v. University of Florida, 652 So. 2d 460, 461 (Fla. 1st DCA 1995)].

Until 1996, however, the courts did not consider the effect of Fla. R. Work. Comp. P. 4.030(c) [subsequently changed to Fla. R. P. Work. Comp. Adj. 60Q-6.108(6) (OJCC) (see now Fla. Admin. Code R. 60Q-6.108(6))]. The former Court Rule, and the OJCC Rule, provide that when service is made by mail, five days are added to the time required for a subsequent act (such as issuing payment) to be done. (Note this extra time does not apply to filing deadlines for appellate proceedings or notices of hearing.) This includes, said the court, orders awarding benefits or approving settlements. Therefore, the court held that payment does not "become due" until five days after the judge mails the approved settlement or the benefits award order to the parties. The carrier then has up to seven days to make payment or incur a mandatory penalty [*see* Palm Beach Cty. School Bd. v. Miller-Neal, 674 So. 2d 759, 760 (Fla. 1st DCA 1996), *rev. denied,* 684 So. 2d 1352 (Fla. 1996)].

Guide to Claims

This five-day extension, however, does not apply every time. For example, if the parties explicitly stipulate that payment is due as of the date the judge enters the order, the carrier must pay the benefits awarded within 14 days and the 5-day extension does not apply. The rules allow an additional five days for mailing, but if the order provides otherwise, the terms of the order control [*see* Ocala Geriatric Center v. Davis, 684 So. 2d 228, 229–230 (Fla. 1st DCA 1996)].

In a workers' compensation context, a judge of compensation claims has the authority and jurisdiction to impose sanctions for a late payment of a settlement reached pursuant to § 440.20(11)(c), Fla. Stat. and Fla. R. Work. Comp. P. 4.150. However, sanctions under this rule may be implemented only on a showing of willfulness. The court noted that, "We write only to dispel the misconception that sanctions in such case can be imposed on a non-fault basis under section 440.20(11)(c), and to dispel any doubt pertaining to a JCC's authority or jurisdiction to impose sanctions for late payment of settlements under such section for a willful violation" [Frix v. All State Ins., 854 So. 2d 258, 259 (Fla. 1st DCA 2003)].

SPECIAL ALERT: The due date for benefits awarded by the appellate courts is different. Benefits affirmed on appeal become due on the date the court issues a mandate. Therefore, for accidents occurring on or after January 1, 1994, carriers have only seven days from the date of the mandate to issue payment. If the carrier seeks further review by the Florida Supreme Court, it must first obtain a stay from the appellate court because seeking such discretionary review does not, by itself, alter the finality of the appellate court order [*see* Thibodeau v. Sarasota Memorial Hosp., 449 So. 2d 297, 298 (Fla. 1st DCA 1984)].

If the Division decides that the employer was responsible for any late payment, it will assess the penalty against the employer rather than the carrier. The Act prohibits the carrier from paying this penalty for the employer.

NOTE: Because the 1994 legislative amendments are procedural, the definition of "late" changes depending on the payment date rather than the accident date. The Division incorrectly holds, via its administrative rule, that the amendment is substantive and applies to only those accidents occurring on or after the effective date [Fla. Admin. Code R. 69L-24.0231(5) (1/10/2005)]. Effective July 1, 1980, the legislature changed the definition of "late" from 20 to 30 days. In 1988, the court held this to be a substantive amendment that did not apply retroactively [*see* Thibodeau v. Sarasota Memorial Hosp., 449 So. 2d 297, 298–299 (Fla. 1st DCA 1984)]. So why is this change not also substantive? Apparently, the court sees *extensions* of time differently than *reductions*. In 1995, the court—without even mentioning *Thibodeau*—held the 1994 amendment to be procedural [*see* Bell v. University of Florida, 652 So. 2d 460, 461 (Fla. 1st DCA 1995)].

[c] Fines

[i] In General

The law provides for substantial penalties when employers, carriers, and third-party administrators fail to comply with statutory claim handling requirements and established performance standards. Penalties or fines for such violations are paid to the Workers' Compensation Trust Fund and are in addition to penalties and interest that might be payable to an injured worker.

[ii] Late Payment of Compensation

The Act provides that carriers must make all payments of compensation on time at least 95 percent of the time. If a carrier falls below this performance standard, punitive penalties apply as follows [*see* § 440.20(8)(b), Fla. Stat. (10/1/2003); Fla. Admin. Code R. 69L-24.0231(3) (1/10/2005)]:

- If the carrier falls below a 95% timely payments standard, but meets at least a 90% standard, the penalty is $50.00 for each late installment.
- If the carrier falls below a 90% timely payments standard, the penalty doubles to $100.00 for each late installment.

[iii] Late Payment of Medical Bills

The act requires that medical be paid within 45 days after receipt, unless the charges are disallowed or denied. Carriers must meet a 95 percent timely payment standard. If a carrier falls below this performance standard, punitive penalties apply as follows:

- For medical services provided on or after January 1, 2004, if the carrier falls below a 95% timely payments standard, but meets at least a 90% standard, the penalty is $25 for each medical bill paid late.
- If the carrier falls below a 90% timely payments standard, the penalty doubles to $50 for each medical bill paid late [*see* § 440.20(6)(b), Fla. Stat. (10/1/2003); Fla. Admin. Code R. 69L-24.0231(2) (1/10/2005)].

Additionally, within 30 days after the carrier has paid, adjusted and paid, or denied a medical bill, it must report its action to the division by filing the completed billing form. [NOTE: Effective March 16, 2005, such filing must be by electronic means only.] If a carrier fails to file a bill timely, an additional administrative fine will be assessed for each bill filed late. The amount of the fine depends on the degree of lateness. A bill filed one to 15 calendar days late carries a fine of $10. The fine increases by $10 for each additional

14 days, so the fine for a bill filed 61 to 75 days late carries a fine of $50 per bill. Bills filed 76 to 190 days late carry a fine of $100 per bill. Bills filed more than 91 days late carry a fine of $500 per bill. Furthermore, the rule allows for the assessment of a fine for late electronic reporting. If the carrier fails to file an electronic report on time, the division will assess a fine of $25 per day, to a maximum fine of $1,000. This is in addition to any other administrative penalty [Fla. Admin. Code R. 69L-7.602(7) (7/4/2004)].

[iv] General Violations

The Act authorizes the department to audit carriers, third-party administrators, and servicing agents to determine if they are in violation of the Act. Such violations include, but are not limited to, the following:

- Patterns or practices of unreasonable delay in claims handling;
- Late or inaccurate payments;
- Late or inaccurate reports;
- Patterns or practices of harassment, coercion, or intimidation of claimants.

For each *non-willful* pattern or practice, the department may impose a fine of up to $2,500 per violation, up to a maximum of $10,000 for all violations.

For each *willful* pattern or practice, the department may impose a fine of up to $20,000 for each violation, up to a maximum of $100,000 for all violations [§ 440.525(4), Fla. Stat. (10/1/2003)].

§ 12.05 Social Security Reduction

[1] Social Security Disability Benefit Reduction

[a] Offset Limits

To prevent injured workers from realizing a windfall by receiving both workers' compensation and social security benefits, the law provides for a reduction or offset. The offset applies differently for social security disability then for social security retirement benefits. The combination of social security disability benefits payable to the employee and workers' compensation benefits may not exceed 80 percent of the employee's average weekly wage [§ 440.15(10)(a), Fla. Stat. (7/1/97)].

For a thorough discussion of social security offset, see Larson's Workers' Compensation, Desk Edition, Ch. 157, § 157.03 (Matthew Bender).

> **SPECIAL ALERT:** At age 62, the Social Security Administration converts disability benefits to retirement benefits. No offset provision for retirement benefits exists. Therefore, the disability benefit reduction does not apply to benefits payable for any week after the injured worker reaches age 62.

[b] Offset Includes Dependent Benefits

Except cost of living increases, all social security benefits received by the injured

Guide to Claims

worker and for any dependents are included in the offset calculation. § 440.15(10)(a), Fla. Stat. makes this clear [*see* Dax & Trim Development Co. v. Mullens, 590 So. 2d 539, 541 (Fla. 1st DCA 1991)].

[c] Offset Does Not Include Cost of Living Increases

Carriers cannot take an offset that is greater than that allowed by federal law. In other words the offset the Social Security Administration would take is also the maximum offset the carrier can take. Federal law does not allow including cost of living increases in the offset calculation. Therefore, workers' compensation carriers cannot deduct social security disability (SSD) cost of living increases under state law [*see* Great Atlantic & Pacific Tea Co. v. Wood, 380 So. 2d 558, 559 (Fla. 1st DCA 1980) (1/10/2005)].

As explained in [5], *below,* carriers must calculate the state offset and the federal offset and use the smaller of the two. Carriers cannot alter this "put and take provision" by basing the offset on the injured worker's average weekly wage. Instead they must use the injured worker's average current earnings (ACE) if the combined benefits are greater under the ACE formula [*see* Trilla v. Braman Cadillac, 527 So. 2d 873, 874–875 (Fla. 1st DCA 1988)].

The prohibition against using cost of living increases, however, does not apply to increases made before the employee's work injury. If an injured worker began receiving SSD benefits before suffering a work-related injury, increases received up to the date of the injury are includable in the offset calculation [*see* Hunter v. South Florida Sod, 666 So. 2d 1018, 1019 (Fla. 1st DCA 1996)].

For a general discussion of cost of living adjustments in existing benefits, see LARSON'S WORKERS' COMPENSATION, DESK EDITION, Ch. 93, § 93.06 (Matthew Bender).

For a specific discussion of whether cost of living increases are included in offset, see LARSON'S WORKERS' COMPENSATION, DESK EDITION, Ch. 157, § 157.03[5][f] (Matthew Bender).

[d] Offset Does Not Include Disabled Widow Benefits

The law does not allow workers' compensation carriers to take an offset against death benefits for social security disability benefits received by a deceased employee's disabled widow [*see* Seibels Bruce v. Elkins, 661 So. 2d 404, 405 (Fla. 1st DCA 1995)].

For a general discussion of disabled widow benefits, see SOCIAL SECURITY PRACTICE GUIDE, Ch. 3, *Family Relationships,* § 3.03; Ch. 12, *Disability Evaluation for Disabled Widows, Widowers and Surviving Divorced Spouses,* § 12.08 (Matthew Bender).

[e] Offset Does Not Include Attorney Fees

Often, the injured worker may not be entitled to carrier-paid attorney's fees, but this does not mean the worker is not personally responsible for such fees. Occasionally in such cases the judges will order the carrier to withdraw part of the injured worker's disability benefit to pay the fee. The fee portion of the benefit must be excluded when computing the offset [*see* National Linen Service v. Tolliver, 686 So. 2d 797, 798 (Fla. 1st DCA 1997)].

[2] Social Security Retirement Benefit Reduction

If the law entitles an injured worker to both wage loss and social security retirement benefits, social security is primary and wage loss benefits are supplemental only. The two benefits together cannot exceed the basic wage loss benefit [§ 440.15(10), Fla. Stat. (7/1/97)]. To calculate the offset under this provision, simply subtract any retirement benefits received from the wage loss benefit.

> **SPECIAL ALERT:** This provision applies only to wage loss benefits, and even then carriers cannot take the offset after the injured worker reaches age 70. The legislature added this provision to the Workers' Compensation Act effective October 1, 1989. It applies only to accidents occurring on or after that date. Before October 1, 1989, there was no age limit.

Guide to Claims

For a thorough discussion of social security retirement benefits, see SOCIAL SECURITY PRACTICE GUIDE, Ch. 4, *Entitlement/Retirement Benefits (Old Age),* §§ 4.01–4.11 (Matthew Bender).

[3] When Offset Can Be Taken

[a] Reverse Offset

Federal statutes allow the Social Security Administration to take an offset if the injured worker is also receiving state workers' compensation benefits. Section 224 of the Social Security Act forbids carriers from taking an offset, known as a reverse offset, unless its state workers' compensation law allowed such an offset as of February 18, 1981. Florida is one of these states. Thus, reverse offsets are available to Florida workers' compensation carriers, but only to the extent provided in Florida's law in effect on February 1, 1981.

For a thorough discussion of the offset of workers' compensation benefits, see SOCIAL SECURITY PRACTICE GUIDE, Ch. 8, *Social Security and Medicare Offset of Workers' Compensation Benefits,* § 8.02 (Matthew Bender).

[b] Offset Does Not Apply to Wage Loss Benefits

Originally, carriers paid Florida wage loss benefits monthly. The federal law, however, provides that carriers are entitled to offset only against weekly benefits [§ 440.15(10), Fla. Stat. (7/1/97)]. Since wage loss was a monthly benefit, the offset did not apply. Effective October 1, 1989, the legislature amended the Act to change wage loss to a weekly benefit. With this change, carriers began taking the offset on weekly wage loss benefits.

In a ruling effective August 27, 1993, the Social Security Administration declared this offset on weekly wage loss benefits improper. Since Florida law did not allow an offset for wage loss benefits as of February 18, 1981, the SSA regulations will not allow it now. States cannot, under this ruling, enact legislation to expand reverse offsets after February 18, 1981. Therefore, the offset applies only to those benefits that were weekly benefits in 1981. This includes all classes except wage loss [Social Security Ruling 93-1].

[c] Offset Applies Only Prospectively

Carriers can take the social security offset only prospectively beginning with the carrier's receipt of reliable information from the Social Security Administration itself [*see*

Horton v. Martin Memorial Hosp., 610 So. 2d 1352, 1355–1356 (Fla. 1st DCA 1992), *rev. denied,* 626 So. 2d 207 (Fla. 1993); *see also* Fla. Admin. Code R. 69L-3.0194 (1/10/2005)].

Can the carrier take the offset if a judge of compensation claims orders the carrier to pay benefits retroactively? In just such a case the carrier argued that it should be entitled to the offset retroactively because it had not paid any benefits to offset. Since it had denied benefits, the carrier argued, it had no opportunity to assert the right of offset. The trial judge agreed and allowed the offset on the past due benefits. On appeal the First District Court of Appeal reversed. The court held that allowing the offset would reward the carrier for failing to pay benefits it was legally obligated to pay [*see* South Florida Water Dist. v. Ciacci, 647 So. 2d 203, 205 (Fla. 1st DCA 1994)].

Upon receipt of benefit information from the Social Security Administration, however, the carrier must move swiftly to calculate and take the offset. The court has held that if the claimant complied with a request to execute a Request for Social Security Disability Benefits Information (LES Form DWC-14), and furnished the completed form to the employer or its workers' compensation insurance carrier in timely fashion, the offset may be taken only prospectively from the date of the calculation. Here, the carrier received the information from the Social Security Administration on April 9, 1998, but did not calculate and begin taking the offset until March 15, 1999. The court held that the carrier was not entitled to an offset retroactive to the date of its receipt of the information from the Social Security Administration. Presumably, a retroactive offset is permissible if the carrier can provide reasonable explanation of its delay in exercising its right to the set-off. If not, allowing a retroactive offset, said the court, would work undue hardship on needy claimants. The court declined to address the situation in which the claimant failed to comply with a request to execute a Request for Social Security Disability Benefits Information [*see* Monroe v. Publix #148, 790 So. 2d 1249, 1252–1253 (Fla. 1st DCA 2001)].

[d] When SSA Is Taking Offset

Be certain to find out if the Social Security Administration is taking an offset in its own right. If so, carriers should advise the agency that they now plan to do so. Why? Because federal law requires that the SSA take an offset if the carrier does not take it under a state workers' compensation program [42 U.S.C.S. § 424a (1935)].

For a thorough discussion of the offset of workers' compensation benefits, see Social Security Practice Guide, Ch. 8, *Social Security and Medicare Offset of Workers' Compensation Benefits,* § 8.02 (Matthew Bender).

[e] Modification of Order Not Required

Can the carrier take the offset and reduce benefits if it is paying benefits under the provisions of a judge of compensation claims' order? Put another way, can the carrier take the offset and reduce benefits without first asking the judge to modify the original order? The answer is yes! In one example, the judge of compensation claims awarded permanent total disability benefits and ordered the carrier to pay benefits at the rate of $130 per week. Before the hearing, the carrier had full information concerning the injured worker's receipt of social security benefits, but did not raise the issue at the hearing. Later, the carrier began taking the offset and reduced benefits to $30.77. The judge held that the carrier had no authority to do so without first obtaining a modification order. The First District Court of Appeal disagreed and reversed. The court held: "It is the . . . (carrier's) . . . responsibility to determine the applicability of the reduction. Once determined, the offset may be taken administratively by an employer/carrier, and need not be determined by the judge of compensation claims in a modification proceeding" [*see* Quail Ridge v. Johnson, 584 So. 2d 199, 200 (Fla. 1st DCA 1991)].

[4] Obtaining Social Security Information

The only place to obtain information on benefits being received by the injured worker is from the Social Security Administration itself. The SSA will not, however, release any information without the injured worker's written permission. Therefore, employees must authorize the release of such information upon demand by the Division, employer, or carrier [§ 440.15(10)(c), Fla. Stat. (7/1/97)].

The proper form for such a demand is the DWC-14, Request for Social Security Disability Information. What happens if the injured worker fails or refuses to authorize releasing this information? Injured workers are not entitled to compensation benefits for temporary or permanent total disability while they continue to fail or refuse to authorize release.

> **SPECIAL ALERT:** Authorizations to release social security information are only effective for 12 months. Read the form carefully. The SSA release will show the maximum family benefit the injured worker is entitled to, but not necessarily the amount received [§ 440.15(10)(c), Fla. Stat.].

[5] Calculating Offset

[a] Offset Applies to Disability Benefits Only

First, remember this offset calculation applies only to Social Security disability benefit recipients and not to retirement benefits. (Retirement benefit offset against wage loss is discussed in [2], *above*.) When the injured worker reaches age 62, the Social Security Administration converts disability benefits to retirement benefits [*see* Social Security Practice Guide, Ch. 4, *Entitlement/Retirement Benefits (Old Age)*, § 4.02 (Matthew Bender)]. A person is not eligible for Social Security disability benefits after reaching early retirement age, which the Social Security Act defines as age 62 [*see* 42 U.S.C.S. § 416(1)]. The court has held an insurer cannot take any reduction in compensation benefits after the claimant reaches the age of 62 years [Upson v. Orange County Sch. Bd., 811 So. 2d 733 (Fla. 1st DCA 2002)]. Therefore, the carrier's right to an offset for temporary total or permanent total disability benefits ends when the injured worker reaches age 62. Also, remember that an injured worker's entitlement to permanent total supplemental benefits ends at age 65 if the worker is eligible for Social Security.

[b] Basic Information Required

The basic data needed to calculate the offset are shown in the chart below. We will use some assumed figures and work through the calculation.

1. Average Weekly Wage **(AWW)**	$495.00
2. Compensation rate **(WCR)**	$330.00
3. Permanent total supplemental benefit **(PTS)**	$115.50
4. The maximum compensation rate	$444.00
5. 80% average weekly wage. (AWW x.80)	$396.00
6. The Social Security Primary Insurance Amount **(PIA)**	$856.20
7. The injured worker's maximum family benefit **(MFB)**	$1,284.30
8. 80% of Average Current Earnings **(ACE)**	$1,677.60

(Remember, divide monthly benefits by 4.3 to reduce these to weekly benefits.)

9. Number of auxiliaries (Dependents getting benefits) 2

(Remember, the DWC-14 gives 80% of the average current earnings (ACE)). Do not reduce by 80% again.

If the DWC-14 shows the auxiliaries as zero or none, the primary insurance amount (PIA) is the weekly social security benefit amount. When the form shows an auxiliary (dependent) is getting benefits, use the maximum family benefit (MFB) as the weekly benefit amount. The form asks for only the maximum amount available and not the amount paid. Yes, the form is defective in this regard. When dependent benefits are involved, verify the amount actually paid. Remember that, for some reason, the injured worker may not be receiving the maximum amount available.

SPECIAL ALERTS: 1. Offset for Permanent Total Disability Supplemental Benefits. Be sure to include any permanent total disability supplemental benefit in the compensation rate [Fla. Admin. Code R. 69L-3.0194 (1/10/2005)]. After the first calculation that includes supplemental benefits, however, carriers cannot recalculate based on later increases. Since the Social Security Administration cannot include cost of living increases, neither can workers' compensation insurance carriers [*see* Hunt v. Stratton, 677 So. 2d 64, 65–66 (Fla. 1st DCA 1996)].

2. Offset Limited to Amount of Federal Benefit. When the preliminary offset amount under the formula in *Hunt v. Stratton* exceeds the total amount of the federal social security offset, the final offset is limited to the federal payment and the benefits *may exceed 80 percent of the average weekly wage* [*see* Cruse Const. v. St. Remy, 704 So. 2d 1100, 1101 (Fla. 1st DCA 1997)].

3. Recalculation Prohibited. Once the initial offset is determined, the judges of compensation claims may not order recalculation based on any cost-of-living increases in the injured worker's collateral benefits thereafter. Only one recalculation of the offset is allowed as of the date the worker began receiving disability retirement benefits. The court's decision in *Hunt* prohibits recalculation of an offset based on any cost-of-living increase in a particular benefit. The case does not, however, forbid recalculation of an existing offset if the worker begins to receive another type of benefit. For example, if the offset was initially calculated based on social security

disability benefits, the carrier can recalculate the offset if the worker begins receiving disability retirement benefits from the employer [*see* Alderman v. Florida Plastering, 748 So. 2d 1038, 1039 (Fla. 1st DCA 1998), *approved,* 755 So. 2d 604 (Fla. 2000)]. On January 20, 2000, the Florida Supreme Court affirmed the 1st DCA's decision in *Alderman* [*see* Florida Plastering v. Alderman, 755 So. 2d 604 (Fla. 2000)].

Although the Supreme Court has not decided the point, the First District Court of Appeal has decided that supplemental benefits payable when an injured worker becomes entitled to permanent total disability benefits are compensation benefits payable under § 440.15(9)(a), Fla. Stat. (1991) [see now § 440.15(10)(a), Fla. Stat. (2001)]. While the existing workers' compensation supplemental benefit is considered in the initial calculation of the workers' compensation offset, the law does not contemplate a recalculation of the offset based upon any increases thereafter. In performing the offset calculation, supplemental benefits payable in the year that the claimant became totally and permanently disabled should be used. This is true, even if the carrier first became entitled to take the Social Security disability offset two or more years later [*see* Jackson v. Hochadel Roofing Co., 794 So. 2d 668, 671 (Fla. 1st DCA 2001)].

[c] Calculation

Now, let us calculate the offset using the figures above.

STEP 1. CALCULATE THE STATE LAW OFFSET

Add:	Weekly S.S. benefit:		$298.67	(#5)
	Weekly W.C. benefit	+	$444.00	(#4)
		Total:	$742.67	
Subtract 80% of AWW or 80% of ACE, whichever is greater		-	$396.00	
		=	$346.67	

$346.67 = MAXIMUM OFFSET UNDER STATE LAW

STEP 2. CALCULATE THE FEDERAL OFFSET

Add:	Weekly S.S. benefit:		$298.67	(#5)
	Weekly W.C. benefit	+	$444.00	(#4)
		Total:	$742.67	
Subtract 80% of ACE:		-	$390.14	
		=	$352.53	

USE THE CALCULATED AMOUNT OR THE BENEFIT PAID, WHICH EVER IS LESS.
$298.67 (the total benefit) = MAXIMUM OFFSET UNDER FEDERAL LAW

STEP 3. CHOOSE THE SMALLER OF THE STATE OR FEDERAL RESULT.

In this example, choose the federal offset of $298.67. Subtract that sum from the compensation rate. $444.00 minus $298.67 = $145.33. Here then, the amount of weekly compensation due the injured worker is $145.33.

Note, however, that depending on a given worker's earning history, either the average current earnings or the average weekly wage may be the larger number. Nothing in either the state or federal statute binds the carrier to the offset taken by social security in years before the worker became eligible for permanent total disability benefits [*see* Irwin Yacht & Marine Corp. v. Piernik, 675 So. 2d 975, 976 (Fla. 1st DCA 1996)].

[d] Official Formula

Oddly enough there was nothing in the Workers' Compensation Act or the Division's rules setting forth a specific formula for the offset. In one case, the injured worker argued that the carrier had not correctly calculated the offset. Two Division witnesses testified to one formula while the carrier argued that its formula was correct. The court refused to rule on which formula was correct, but did hold that the carrier's inclusion of dependent benefits was proper. In fact, the court chastised the Division in a footnote to its decision where it stated: "In that the Division has acknowledged that calculation of [social security] offsets is a grey area, it would be wise for the Division to promulgate a rule setting forth the proper method for calculating such offsets" [*see* Dax & Trim Development Co. v. Mullens, 590 So. 2d 539, 542 n.4 (Fla. 1st DCA 1991)].

The Division has finally adopted a rule that is identical to that discussed in [c], *above.* Interestingly, however, the Division's formula addresses only the offset against permanent total disability. The rule should apply to temporary total benefits as well [Fla. Admin. Code R. 69L-3.0194 (1/10/2005)].

In 1996, believing that the Division had not adopted a rule, the court set out its own formula. Although the court's formula is a bit convoluted, it reaches the same result as in the example in [c], *above.* This case, however, set out two new rules that will result in decreased offsets [*see* Hunt v. Stratton, 677 So. 2d 64, 67 (Fla. 1st DCA 1996)]:

1. The maximum offset carriers can take is the amount of the federal benefit. This is true even if it results in the injured worker collecting more than the original average weekly wage.
2. Carriers can include supplemental benefits in the initial calculation. They cannot, however, recalculate the offset based on increases in the supplemental benefit in future years.

SPECIAL ALERT: The Division Rule provides that the Division has first priority in taking any available offset on permanent total disability cases with accident dates before July 1, 1984, because the Division pays supplemental benefits on these cases [Fla. Admin. Code R. 69L-3.0194(5)(c) (1/10/2005)].

§ 12.06 Unemployment Compensation

[1] The Rule

Injured workers are not entitled to any temporary total or permanent total disability benefits for any week they have received unemployment compensation benefits. This provision applies to all accident dates [§ 440.15(10), Fla. Stat. (7/1/97)].

For a discussion about coordinating workers' compensation with unemployment compensation, see LARSON'S WORKERS' COMPENSATION, DESK EDITION, Ch. 157, § 157.02 (Matthew Bender).

[2] Accident Dates Through December 31, 1993

If the injured worker is receiving temporary partial or permanent partial wage loss benefits and unemployment compensation, the two benefits together may not exceed wage loss benefits that would otherwise be payable. Therefore, the reduction is dollar for dollar. If the injured worker receives $70 per week from unemployment compensation, the carrier should subtract $70 from the weekly wage loss benefits.

[3] Accident Dates On or After January 1, 1994

Effective with accidents occurring on or after January 1, 1994, the unemployment compensation offset does not apply to wage loss benefits. The legislature repealed the original language in this section that allowed an offset against wage loss benefits. The offset continues to apply to temporary partial benefits as before; that is, the combination of the two may not exceed the TPD benefits that would otherwise be payable [§ 440.15(10)(b), Fla. Stat. (7/1/97)].

§ 12.07 Pension and Disability Benefits

[1] Retirement Pension Benefits

The law does not allow an offset against workers' compensation benefits even if the injured worker is also receiving retirement pension benefits. An employer may not offset workers' compensation payments against an employee's pension benefits except to the extent that the total of the two exceeds the employee's average weekly wage. § 440.21, Fla. Stat. prohibits an employer from deducting workers' compensation from an employee's pension benefit [*see* Barragan v. City of Miami, 545 So. 2d 252, 254–255 (Fla. 1989)].

Originally, § 440.15(12), Fla. Stat. allowed governmental employers an offset against pension disability benefits. The legislature repealed that section effective January 1, 1994. Further, the law does not allow the employer to take an offset against the proceeds of any insurance policy to which the employee contributed [*see* Jewel Tea Company v. Florida Industrial Commission, 235 So. 2d 289, 291 (Fla. 1969)].

The basis for disallowing an offset against retirement benefits is that such benefits are due regardless of the individual's physical condition. As the court explained in *Dixon* [*see*

[4], *below*], an offset is allowed only against duplicative disability benefits and not to retirement benefits [*see* Orlando Utils. Comm'n, 767 So 2d 1232, 1232 (Fla. 1st DCA 2000), *cause dismissed,* 776 So. 2d 276 (Fla. 2000)].

[2] Other Collateral Sources: *Escambia County Sheriff's Dept. v. Grice*

[a] 100 Percent Cap

While the Act does provide for an offset of social security benefits against workers' compensation benefits, it does not specifically include an offset against state disability retirement pension benefits. Since the Act is silent about state disability retirement benefits, did the legislature intend to allow an offset? In other words, what happens if the combination of workers' compensation, state disability retirement, and social security disability benefits exceeds the worker's average weekly wage? For example, the injured worker's average weekly wage is $550. The combination of workers' compensation, state disability retirement, and social security disability results in weekly payments of $770. Is there an offset of the $220 difference? The answer is yes.

When an injured worker receives the equivalent of full wages from any employer source, this is the limit of entitlement to compensation. Injured workers may not receive benefits from their employers or other collateral sources that, when totaled, exceed 100 percent of their average weekly wage. To the extent total benefits exceed the average weekly wage, the carrier is entitled to an offset. This does not apply, however, if the employee has been given the right to collect excess benefits under the express terms of a contract [*see* Escambia County Sheriff's Dept. v. Grice, 692 So. 2d 896, 898 (Fla. 1997)].

[b] Cap Based on AWW

Another question arises when an injured worker is receiving Social Security Disability benefits. The question is whether the 100% average weekly wage (AWW) cap applies regardless of the amount of the worker's average current earnings (ACE). This becomes an important issue when the worker's average current earnings (ACE) is significantly greater than the average weekly wage (AWW), because the offset may equal the compensation rate or exceed the federal maximum offset. Because the Florida Supreme Court, in *Grice,* did not mention the ACE, the Court concluded that the 100% cap must be based on the AWW regardless of the worker's ACE. The Court, however, certified the question to the Florida Supreme Court [*see* Gab. Bus. Servs. v. Dixon, 739 So. 2d 637, 638 (Fla. 1st DCA 1999), *reh'g granted,* 761 So. 2d 328 (Fla. 2000)].

[c] Retroactive Application

Yet another question is whether a so-called *Grice* offset can be applied retroactively. Because the law [*see* § 440.15(13), Fla. Stat. (Supp. 1994)] requires a claimant to repay any benefit to which he or she is not entitled, the offset applies to benefits paid on or after May 1, 1997, the date the Florida Supreme Court issued the *Grice* decision [*see* HRS Dist. II v. Pickard, 760 So. 2d 946 (Fla. 1st DCA 1999), *quashed and remanded,* 767 So. 2d 443 (Fla. 2000)].

Although May 1, 1997, is the earliest date after which the offset may be applied, the court has held that carriers may take an offset retroactive to that date regardless of when the calculation is made [*see* Orange County Fire Rescue v. Antonelli, 794 So. 2d 758, 761 (Fla. 1st DCA 2001)].

[d] 80 Percent Cap Applies to SSD Benefits

Subsequently, the First District found that the Supreme Court's holding in *Grice* prevented an injured worker from receiving more than 100 percent of his or her AWW [GAB Bus. Servs. Inc. v. Dixon, 739 So. 2d 637, 640–641 (Fla. 1st DCA 1999)]. The First District recognized, however, that *Grice* did not involve the situation in which a claimant's ACE (average current earnings) exceeded his AWW and certified the following question to the Supreme Court:

> Whether the holding in *Escambia County Sheriff's Department v. Grice,* 692 So. 2d 896 (Fla. 1997), capping total benefits received by a worker at 100 percent of his or her average weekly wage, applies when social security disability is one of the benefits received by the worker, and 80 percent of his or her average current earnings, as computed by the social security administration, are greater than his or her average weekly wage.

The Supreme Court answered the certified question in the negative and quashed the decision of the district court. The Court held that when a claimant is receiving SSD benefits in addition to workers' compensation, thus implicating § 440.15(10)(a), Fla. Stat., an employer/carrier may offset workers' compensation benefits, but only to the extent that the claimant's benefits exceed 80 percent of AWW or ACE, whichever is greater [*see* American Bankers Ins. Co. v. Little, 393 So. 2d 1063, 1064 (Fla. 1980)]. The benefits may not be reduced beyond this amount. This is so even though the claimant may be receiving in excess of 100 percent of AWW at the time of the accident [*see* Dixon v. GAB Bus. Servs., Inc., 767 So. 2d 443, 445 (Fla. 2000)].

[3] Permanent Total Disability Supplemental Benefits

Does the 100 percent limit announced in *Grice* include permanent total supplemental benefits? The answer, in a word, is no. In December 1999, the Florida Supreme Court answered the questions certified by the 1st District Court of Appeal essentially as follows:

> Where the employer takes a workers' compensation offset under § 440.20(15), Fla. Stat. (1985) [now found at § 440.20(14), Fla. Stat.] and initially includes supplemental benefits paid under § 440.15(1)(e), Fla. Stat. (1985) [now found at § 440.15(1)(f), Fla. Stat.] the employer is not entitled to recalculate the offset based on the subsequent yearly 5% increase in supplemental benefits.

The Court reasoned that allowing repeated recalculations would defeat the legislature's intent to provide a hedge against inflation. To rule otherwise, said the Court, would be to render the supplemental benefits statute virtually meaningless. The Court made a point of stating that this opinion should not be read to change the Social Security offset provisions contained in § 440.15(10), Fla. Stat. [*see* City of Clearwater v. Acker, 755 So. 2d 597, 599–602 (Fla. 1999)].

The 1st DCA has noted that the only statutory cap on benefits is contained in § 440.15(1)(f)1., Fla. Stat., which caps benefits at the maximum compensation rate in effect at the time payment is made. The court noted that after the 10th annual increase in supplemental benefits, a disabled worker will receive 150 percent of the initial compensation rate, which is an amount equal to 100 percent of the average weekly wage. The court held that the employer is not entitled to cap benefits in a way that would effectively freeze supplemental benefits 10 years after the accident. Freezing benefits in this way would frustrate the purpose of supplemental benefits which is to provide increases to offset the increasing cost of living [*see* Department of Children & Families v. Monroe, 744 So. 2d 1163, 1164 (Fla. 1st DCA 1999)].

Prior decisions held that while the employer is not entitled to recalculate a *Grice* offset each year based on the yearly five-percent increase in supplemental benefits, the employer is entitled to include in the offset calculation the initial amount of supplemental benefits. Although the Supreme Court has agreed that a *Grice* offset may not be recalculated to take into account increases in supplemental benefits, it has declined to address whether the initial amount of supplemental benefits must be included. The First District Court of Appeal (en banc) now concludes that the initial amount of supplemental benefits *should not* be included in the calculation of a *Grice* offset. The court reasoned that supplemental benefits are designed to provide a cost-of-living adjustment to injured workers to protect the value of their benefits from the effects of inflation. Logic dictates that no supplemental benefits should be included in the *Grice* offset calculation. Otherwise, the very purpose of supplemental benefits would be frustrated [*see* Orange County Fire Rescue v. Antonelli, 794 So. 2d 758, 760 (Fla. 1st DCA 2001)].

The court has held that the prohibition against recalculation described in *Acker* applies retroactively. Thus, if such recalculation was done in the past, benefits must be restored and any underpayments repaid to the injured worker, presumably with statutory interest [*see* Department of Labor & Empl. Sec., Workers' Compensation Admin. Trust Fund v. McGrath, 774 So. 2d 791, 792 (Fla. 1st DCA 2000)].

[4] Social Security Retirement Benefits

Social security retirement benefits are not collateral source benefits as contemplated in *Grice* and therefore do not apply to the 100% AWW cap. Social security benefits are based on advanced years. People are entitled to these benefits without regard to whether the person suffered a disabling injury. Neither the statutes nor the Supreme Court's holding in *Grice* provide authority for applying an offset based on social security retirement benefits. The only ceiling on permanent total disability and supplemental benefits is described in § 440.15(1)(e)(1), Fla. Stat., which is the maximum weekly compensation rate in effect at the time of payment [*see* Dixon v. Pasadena Yacht & Country Club, 731 So. 2d 141, 144 (Fla. 1st DCA 1999)].

For a discussion of coordination with federal pensions, see LARSON'S WORKERS' COMPENSATION, DESK EDITION, Ch. 157, § 157.03 (Matthew Bender).

For a discussion of coordination with state pensions, see LARSON'S WORKERS' COMPENSATION, DESK EDITION, Ch. 157, § 157.04 (Matthew Bender).

§ 12.08 Overpayments

[1] Through December 31, 1993

Without a reasonable basis for an overpayment, carriers are not entitled to any credit. Such overpayments are considered a gratuity. The question is, what is a reasonable basis? Credit is permissible when an overpayment results from a clerical error and the carrier has performed with due diligence [*see* Montgomery Ward v. Wade, 545 So. 2d 410, 411 (Fla. 1st DCA 1989)].

In *Wade,* the carrier received an order from the judge of compensation claims awarding compensation benefits; however, the compensation rate in the order was incorrect. The carrier paid benefits at the incorrect rate for several months before it discovered the error. The carrier was not entitled to offset the overpayment because the error was obvious from the face of the order. The employer/carrier, said the court, could have corrected the error if the carrier had acted with "ordinary care and diligence in ascertaining their responsibility."

From this and other cases we can conclude that the state of the law for overpayments made before January 1, 1994, is this: if the correct amount due is a figure "available" to the carrier, clerical mistakes will not meet the due diligence test. Following are other examples:

1. Incorrect calculation of average weekly wage is not a valid excuse. Wage information was available to the employer [*see* Strickland v. Neil's Painting, 545 So. 2d 333, 334 (Fla. 1st DCA 1989)].
2. The carrier continued to include the value of fringe benefits though the employer continued to provide them. Again, no credit, since the carrier could have easily found out whether the employer continued these fringe benefits [*see* Pardo v. Sun Supermarket, 510 So. 2d 1244, 1245–1246 (Fla. 1st DCA 1987)].
3. A computer malfunction was a valid, excusable error because it occurred during a system change. The court affirmed the JCC's order to allow the carrier to recover 15 percent per week from future payments [*see* Marrero v. FPA Corporation, 511 So. 2d 1008 (Fla. 1st DCA 1987)].

Few cases exist on this subject. Expect the courts to refuse to allow a credit if the carrier could have discovered the error.

[2] On or After January 1, 1994

Effective January 1, 1994, carriers can recover all overpayments without regard to why they were made. The law gives the carrier the right to recover overpaid amounts directly from the injured worker, or by deducting them from the injured worker's compensation benefits. This applies only to indemnity benefits and not to medical benefits. Benefit deductions, however, are limited to 20 percent. The section provides [§ 440.15(12), Fla. Stat. (7/1/97)]:

REPAYMENT. If an employee has received a sum as an *indemnity* benefit under any

> classification or category of benefit under this chapter to which she or he is not entitled, the employee is liable to repay that sum to the employer or the carrier or to have that sum deducted from future benefits, regardless of the classification of benefits, payable to the employee under this chapter; however, a partial payment of the total repayment may not exceed 20 percent of the amount of the biweekly payment. (Emphasis added)

This is a procedural amendment that applies to all overpayments made on or after January 1, 1994, without regard to the accident date [*see* Brown v. L.P. Sanitation, 689 So. 2d 332, 333 (Fla. 1st DCA 1997)].

While this section clearly allows the recovery to be deducted from any class or category of future indemnity benefit, the reference to "biweekly" payment may cause problems. For accidents occurring after January 1, 1994, wage loss is a monthly benefit. Although adjusters should apply this as intended, the language leaves the door open for the courts to rule that deductions cannot be made from monthly wage loss benefits.

§ 12.09 Advanced Payments

[1] Advance Payments by Employer

Effective January 1, 1994, the law allows employers and carriers to recover advanced payments the employer made. If the employer has advanced any compensation or medical benefits to the employee, the carrier must reimburse the employer. The carrier then has the right to recover these sums from the injured worker. The carrier can deduct the repayment from future compensation installments or from benefits awarded by a judge of compensation claims. The law is silent about how much may be deducted from a single compensation installment. Since 20 percent is the limit for recovering overpayments, assuming that amount applies here is reasonable [§ 440.20(5), Fla. Stat. (1/1/94)].

[2] Advance Payments by Carrier

A judge of compensation claims has the authority to approve a voluntary advance payment or to order the carrier to advance payments to the claimant. There is nothing in the statute requiring proof that the injured worker will have some type of permanent disability upon achieving maximum medical improvement. The Act allows the judge to order an advance payment simply upon a showing that the injured worker has suffered either a substantial loss of earning capacity or a physical impairment [*see* Workers of Florida v. Williams, 743 So. 2d 609, 610–611 (Fla. 1st DCA 1999)].

It is, of course, possible that the claimant will not be eligible for sufficient benefits in the future to allow the carrier to fully recover the advance. The statutes, however, do not contain any provision for recovering the advance as one of the conditions to be used in deciding to award an advance. The only conditions pertinent to the inquiry of the appropriateness of such advances are those stated in § 440.20(12)(c), Fla. Stat., and they do not mention the potential of employer prejudice [*see* Workers of Florida v. Williams, 743 So. 2d 609, 610 (Fla. 1st DCA 1999), *on motion for rehearing*].

If the amount sought exceeds $2,000, and the carrier opposes the advance, the judge must hold a hearing and, to award the advance, must find as follows:

1. The advance is in the injured worker's best interest;
2. That the advance will not materially prejudice the rights of the employer or the carrier; and
3. That the advance is reasonable under the circumstances.

Note, however, that in no event may the judge order an advance of more than $7,500 or 26 weeks of benefits in any 48-month period, whichever is greater [*see* § 440.20(12)(d), Fla. Stat.]. As noted, the carrier is entitled to reimbursement for the advance out of any unpaid installments of compensation due [*see* § 440.20(13), Fla. Stat.].

It is, of course, possible that in some cases the injured worker will not remain disabled long enough for the carrier to recover its full advance payment. While such a likelihood constitutes prejudice to the carrier it does not preclude an advance of less than $2,000. This is because the statute does not require an inquiry into the potential for prejudice if the amount is $2,000 or less [*see* Workers of Florida v. Williams, 743 So. 2d 609 (Fla. 1st DCA 1999)]. Note, however, that potential prejudice to the employer is a factor that the judge must consider in awarding an advance payment of more than $2,000.

§ 12.10 Claims of Creditors

[1] Statutory Protection

With some exceptions, the law protects an injured worker's benefits from the claims of creditors and from collection of a debt. The statute provides as follows [§ 440.22, Fla. Stat. (10/1/2001)]:

> [C]ompensation and benefits shall be exempt from all claims of creditors, and from levy, execution and attachments or other remedy for recovery or collection of a debt, which exemption may not be waived. *However, the exemption of workers' compensation claims from creditors does not extend to claims based on an award of child support or alimony.* (Emphasis added).

Ordinarily, the courts would deem such a provision to be substantive and therefore could not be applied to accident dates occurring before the amendment's effective date. Note, however, that the court has previously given child support and alimony a special status and held that § 440.22, Fla. Stat., does not apply to claims based on awards of child support or alimony [*see* Bryant v. Bryant, 621 So. 2d 574, 576 (Fla. 2d DCA 1993)]. Therefore, this legislative amendment is merely a codification of case law and should apply procedurally and retroactively.

Effective October 1, 2001, the legislature amended this provision by adding the following:

> However, the exemption of workers' compensation claims from creditors does not extend to claims based on an award of child support or alimony.

Ordinarily, the courts would deem such a provision to be substantive and therefore could not be applied to accident dates occurring before the amendment's effective date. Note, however, that the court has previously given child support and alimony a special status and held that § 440.22, Fla. Stat. does not apply to claims based on awards of child support or alimony [*see* Bryant v. Bryant, 621 So. 2d 574, 576 (Fla. 2d DCA 1993)]. Therefore, this legislative amendment is merely a codification of case law and applies procedurally and retroactively [*see* [3], *below*].

For a general discussion of the nonassignability of benefits, see LARSON'S WORKERS' COMPENSATION, DESK EDITION, Ch. 89, § 89.07 (Matthew Bender).

[2] Statute's Meaning

Except child support and alimony, discussed in [3], *below,* this statutory provision means a court may not order the attachment of an injured worker's benefits to satisfy a legal debt. More precisely, the Act forbids attaching benefits that are "due or payable." This raises the question about whether benefits already paid, such as a lump-sum settlement, are also protected. Such paid benefits are protected, whether paid to the injured worker or to the worker's beneficiary, if the funds can be traced to the workers' compensation benefits [*see* Broward v. Jacksonville Medical Center, 690 So. 2d 589, 590–591 (Fla. 1997)].

Due to ignorance of this provision, however, circuit courts may issue an order instructing the carrier to withhold part of the injured worker's benefits and to send them to the court clerk for distribution. Although the order might violate the statute, adjusters cannot unilaterally refuse to comply. The court may not always be right, but it is always the court with significant power that will punish those in contempt of its orders. Protecting an injured worker's benefits, at the risk of a contempt citation, is carrying goodwill too far.

The best course is to comply with the court's order immediately, and perhaps point out the possible error to the injured worker or the injured worker's attorney.

[3] Child Support and Alimony

Previously, the statutory exemption of workers' compensation awards from claims of creditors did not extend to a claim based on an award of child support or alimony. Although the statute protects a worker's workers' compensation benefits from creditors, Florida courts have given child support and alimony a special status. "The legislature," said the court, "passed the Workers' Compensation Act to relieve an injured employee and his family from the economic stress resulting from a work–related injury." Interest due on the child support award is restitution for a loss and not a penalty and is also recoverable from the injured worker's workers' compensation benefits. Note, however, that a spouse's attorney's fees and costs are not recoverable from the injured worker's benefits [*see* Bryant v. Bryant, 621 So. 2d 574, 576 (Fla. 2d DCA 1993)].

As noted in [1], *above,* the legislature has codified the holding in *Bryant* by amending § 440.22, Fla. Stat. (effective 10/1/2001) to provide that the exemption of workers' compensation claims from creditors does not extend to claims based on an award of child support or alimony.

NOTE: Federal Statutes restricting garnishment limit the garnishment for spouse or child support to 50 percent of the individual's aggregate disposable income [*see* 15 U.S.C.S. § 1673].

SPECIAL ALERT: Carriers do not have the duty or even the right to pay part of an injured worker's benefits to a spouse for alimony or child support without the injured worker's permission or a court order. When a court order exists, remember it also applies to any washout settlement proceeds. Additionally, the Act makes it clear that an employer or carrier has no duty to investigate or collect information regarding child support arrearages. Further, for settlement purposes, the clerk of the circuit court is prohibited from charging fees for providing child support documentation [§ 440.20(11)(d), Fla. Stat. (10/1/2003)].

For a discussion of exceptions to nonassignability of benefits for children, see LARSON'S WORKERS' COMPENSATION, DESK EDITION, Ch. 89, § 89.07 (Matthew Bender).

SPECIAL ALERT: If the carrier is entitled to reduce an injured worker's benefits because of a subrogation lien under § 440.39, Fla. Stat., the carrier must apply the lien reduction before calculating total benefits and applying the 100-percent average weekly wage cap and resulting offset under § 440.20(15), Fla. Stat., and under the holding in *Escambia County Sheriff's Dept. v. Grice*, 692 So. 2d 896 (Fla. 1997) [*see* City of Hollywood v. Lombardi, 738 So. 2d 491, 494–496 (Fla. 1st DCA 1999), *reh'g granted,* 761 So. 2d 327 (Fla. 2000)].

CHAPTER 13

TEMPORARY TOTAL AND PERMANENT TOTAL DISABILITY

SYNOPSIS

PART A. OVERVIEW

PART C. PERMANENT TOTAL DISABILITY (PTD)

Part A Overview

§ 13.01 Disability Benefits

Insurance carriers must pay compensation (indemnity) benefits during an injured worker's disability. Inability to work and earn wages because of an industrial accident creates eligibility for benefits. Look at an injured worker's loss of wage-earning ability, and not at lost wages or physical impairment. Decide entitlement to indemnity benefits by comparing the injured worker's lost wage earning ability after the accident with the wages earned before the accident. Florida law does not compensate an injured worker for the loss of wages themselves or for functional disability.

For a thorough discussion of disability benefits, see LARSON'S WORKERS' COMPENSATION, DESK EDITION, Part 9, *Disability and Personal Injury Benefits* (Matthew Bender).

§ 13.02 Deciding and Defining Disability

While physicians must decide the degree of any permanent impairment, they cannot decide the degree of any disability. A treating physician cannot testify about an injured worker's disability because such testimony is beyond the physician's competency as a medical expert. Permanent physical impairment is a medical issue. This is to be distinguished from a "disability," which is a legal question. "Disability" is defined in the law as the incapacity because of injury to earn wages the employee was receiving at the time of the injury [§ 440.02(9), Fla. Stat. (1988)]. In construing the provisions of a federal workers' compensation statute, the United States Supreme Court defined disability as follows [*see* Metropolitan Stevedore Co. v. Rambo, 521 U.S. 121, 138 L. Ed. 2d 327, 337, 117 S. Ct. 1953 (1997)]:

> Disability is a measure of earning capacity lost as a result of work-related injury. By distinguishing between the diminished capacity and the injury itself, and by defining capacity in relation both to the injured workers' old job and to other employment, the statute makes it clear that disability is the product of [the work-related] injury and opportunities in the job market.

Permanent impairment is related directly to the employee's health and physical condition. Disability is decided considering the personal, social, and occupational demands that an impairment creates and is therefore not a medical decision. Physicians are qualified to testify only about anatomic or functional impairment within their medical expertise. The judge of compensation claims alone must make the determination of disability [*see* Photo Electronics Corp. v. Glick, 398 So. 2d 900, 901 (Fla. 1st DCA 1981)].

For a discussion of the kinds and elements of disability, see LARSON'S WORKERS' COMPENSATION, DESK EDITION, Ch. 80 (Matthew Bender).

§ 13.03 Compensation for Disability

Within statutory limits, we compensate an injured worker for each day of disability. That the injured worker would not have ordinarily worked on a given day does not matter. All that matters is that the injured worker could not work on that day. Consequently, the Workers' Compensation Act allows compensation benefits during weekends, holidays, and other normally non-work days.

Sometimes, an employee with a work-related disability may become totally disabled by an unrelated condition. Such a worker may still be entitled to compensation if the work-related injury alone would have resulted in an inability to work. For example, Ricardo La Torre returned to full duty work despite a 10-percent impairment from a work-related knee injury. Several months later, an unrelated condition (retinitis pigmentosa) caused him to lose his eyesight. Totally blind, he could no longer work. In such a case, the judge of compensation claims must decide if the worker would have been disabled anyway from the compensable injury alone. If so, the JCC must award compensation accordingly. Here, La Torre's knee injury became worse after he left work, and doctors said this worsening alone would have been disabling. Therefore, the District Court of Appeal affirmed an award of disability benefits [*see* Winn Dixie Stores, Inc. v. La Torre, 702 So. 2d 1267, 1269–1271 (Fla. 1st DCA 1997)].

Florida's workers' compensation system does not compensate injured workers for the kinds of damages available under tort law or common law. These unrecoverable damages include compensation for property damage, personal expense, and pain and suffering.

How much and for how long may an injured worker collect indemnity benefits? The amount and time change, depending on the class of disability and the date of the accident. We will begin to answer this question by reviewing the four basic classes of disability, which are:

1. Temporary Total
2. Temporary Partial
3. Permanent Partial
4. Permanent Total

Usually, an injured worker who becomes entitled to all four classes of disability benefits will do so in the order listed, but not necessarily so. Any class may precede or follow another. This chapter examines the two classes of *total* disability [*see* Part B and Part C, *below*]. Ch. 14, *Temporary Partial and Permanent Partial Disability Benefits,* examines the two classes of *partial* disability.

For a discussion of schedule benefits for disability, see LARSON'S WORKERS' COMPENSATION, DESK EDITION, Ch. 86 (Matthew Bender).

§§ 13.04—13.09 [Reserved]

Part B Temporary Total Disability (TTD)

§ 13.10 Temporary Total Disability

[1] The Rule

The law entitles an injured worker to receive temporary total disability benefits if the medical evidence shows the injured worker is unable to do any gainful work.

SPECIAL ALERT: An injured worker may not collect temporary total disability benefits while simultaneously collecting unemployment compensation [§ 440.15(10), Fla. Stat. (7/1/97)]. Additionally, an injured worker may not collect temporary total disability benefits while confined as an inmate of a public institution, such as a jail. An exception arises if the injured worker has dependents. If so, the carrier must pay benefits to the dependents while the injured worker remains an inmate [§ 440.15(9), Fla. Stat. (7/1/97)].

[2] Defined

Temporary total disability is the healing period during which the injured worker is totally disabled and cannot perform any work. When injured workers recover at least the ability to do some form of work, although limited in kind or amount, the law no longer considers them temporarily totally disabled. This is true even if they have not reached maximum medical improvement [*see* § 13.12].

For a brief discussion of the classification of disabilities, see LARSON'S WORKERS' COMPENSATION, DESK EDITION, Ch. 80 (Matthew Bender).

[3] Weekly Benefits

When authorized doctors declare that an injured worker is temporarily but totally disabled, the law entitles the injured worker to weekly compensation benefits. This weekly benefit equals 66 2/3 percent of the employee's average weekly wages, not to exceed the maximum amount or time limits for the year in which the accident occurred [*see* ch. 12, § 12.04].

Although the maximum weekly benefit amount has increased over the years, the legislature has repeatedly reduced the number of weeks of eligibility. Therefore, the maximum weeks of eligibility changes depending upon the date of the accident [*see* [4], *below*].

[4] Maximum Eligibility Periods

The maximum time for which an injured worker may collect benefits changes depending upon the accident's date. The maximum periods are as follows:

Through June 30, 1990:
350 weeks (6.7 years)

Guide to Claims

Between July 1, 1990, and December 31, 1993:
260 weeks (five years)
On or After January 1, 1994:
104 weeks (two years)

[5] Waiting Periods

Waiting periods serve to eliminate or reduce benefits for minor injuries. If the injury is severe enough, the waiting period does not apply. If an injured worker's disability does not exceed the waiting period, no compensation is due. If the disability lasts longer than seven days, but less than the waiting period, the carrier owes compensation from the eighth day only. When disability exceeds the waiting period, the carrier owes compensation from the first day of disability [*see* ch. 12, § 12.04[4]]. The waiting period changes depending on the date of the accident.

Accident dates up to June 30, 1990. For these accident dates an injured worker cannot collect compensation for the first 7 days of disability unless disability lasts more than 14 days.

Accident dates on or after July 1, 1990. For these accident dates an injured worker cannot collect compensation for the first seven days of disability unless disability lasts for more than 21 days [*see* ch. 12, § 12.04[4][b]].

SPECIAL NOTE: The waiting period applies to all classes of disability [*see* ch. 12, § 12.04[4], for a complete discussion].

[6] Entitlement to Benefits

[a] Events Ending Entitlement

An injured worker's entitlement to temporary total disability benefits begins when the worker is medically unable to work in any capacity. This assumes the disability extends beyond the waiting period. An injured worker's entitlement ends when the first of any of the following four events occurs:

1. When the injured worker's doctor says he or she can do some work.
2. When the injured worker returns to work.
3. When the injured worker reaches maximum medical improvement.
4. When the carrier has paid the maximum weeks of benefits.

[b] Medical Evidence Required

If no medical evidence exists that proves total disability, the injured worker cannot show entitlement to benefits merely by personal testimony. Injured workers cannot show entitlement, for example, by simply claiming they tried to return to work, but did not feel able to do so. Without medical evidence of total disability, the law requires the injured worker to try to go back to work [*see* Cardinal Industries, Inc. v. Dawkins, 392 So. 2d 368, 370 (Fla. 1st DCA 1981)].

In case after case, the courts have held that mere complaints of pain alone are not enough to show temporary total disability. The law requires medical evidence to support such claims. If not, carriers may suspend temporary total benefits.

[c] Worker's Self-Diagnosis Is Not Medical Evidence

An injured worker's self-diagnosis cannot create or defeat entitlement to benefits. Suppose an honest injured worker claims inability to work because of an unrelated condition. The carrier cannot stop benefits based only on the injured worker's statement that an unrelated condition is causing the disability. Benefit suspension must be based on medical evidence that the disabling condition is unrelated, or at least there must be no evidence to the contrary. Without this evidence the carrier has no defense. Following is a good example of this situation.

Sandra Marlowe became disabled following exposure to insecticide at work. She recovered sufficiently to return to work, but for another employer. Ten days later she quit her new job to get treatment for an unrelated foot problem She told the carrier that she thought her foot problem was the only cause of her disability; however, no medical evidence supported this self-diagnosis. On the contrary, the evidence on the record supported the presumption that the continuing effects of the compensable injury caused her subsequent disability. Even the injured worker's own testimony is not sufficient justification for the judge of compensation claims to ignore uncontroverted medical evidence [*see* Marlowe v. Dogs Only Grooming, 589 So. 2d 990, 993 n.1 (Fla. 1st DCA 1991)].

[d] Physician Must Inform Employee About Return to Work

Physicians must inform injured workers they can return to work before carriers may stop benefits. Even if the medical evidence clearly shows that the employee can work, the carrier may not stop temporary total disability benefits until the doctor tells the employee to return to work.

For example, the carrier received a report that doctors had released Ollie Mae Charles to return to work. Understandably, the carrier stopped benefits. The judge of compensation claims agreed with the carrier and denied temporary total benefits. On appeal, the First District Court of Appeal disagreed and reversed. The court held that even assuming Charles could have returned to work, the carrier could not deny benefits without evidence that she knew or should have known that the doctor released her to return to work [*see* Charles v. Suwannee Swifty, 622 So. 2d 114, 115 (Fla. 1st DCA 1993)].

In another example, several doctors testified that Brenda Amburgey was able to return to work during the period she claimed entitlement to temporary total disability benefits. No evidence, however, showed that the doctors told Amburgey this or that she should have known that she was released to return to work. The court has held consistently that evidence showing that a claimant can return to work is not enough to deny temporary total disability benefits. Evidence that the injured worker was informed or should have known that he or she was released to work is also required. Further, the judge of compensation claims must specifically state in the order that benefits were denied because the injured worker knew or should have known that he or she could return to work. If not, the court will remand the case to the judge for further findings as it did here [*see* Amburgey v. Palm Beach County School Board, 712 So. 2d 426, 427 (Fla. 1st DCA 1998)].

Carriers may not stop benefits just because no medical evidence of total disability exists. Even if the injured worker shows a belief in ability to work by job searching, the carrier still cannot stop benefits. Carriers may not stop temporary total benefits until the treating physician tells the employee to return to work.

SPECIAL ALERT: If a doctor puts an injured worker on temporary total status, the carrier must pay temporary total benefits. The carrier must continue to pay until the doctor tells the injured employee to return to work or until maximum entitlement ends [*see* Garcia-Vina v. U.S. Holiday Health and Recreation, 634 So. 2d 200, 201 (Fla. 1st DCA 1994)].

[7] Verifying Disability

[a] Confirm Verbal Reports

Sometimes carriers will receive notice of medical ability to return to work by a written report from the physician. Frequently, however, the first notice of release for work comes by telephone. Often, these verbal reports come from the physician's staff by reading (and sometimes misreading) from the records. Carriers should always confirm verbal work releases in writing. This is especially true when notification of work release comes from a person who is quoting the doctor or the doctor's notes. Also, carriers should always confirm that the doctor has instructed the employee on returning to work.

[b] Inform Division Benefits Have Started

If the carrier begins temporary total benefits, it must notify the Division of Workers' Compensation. Carriers may satisfy this requirement by filing the First Report of Injury form, DWC-1. The Division requires this filing within 14 days after the carrier receives the first report of injury. If not, the carrier is subject to a fine of up to $500 for late filing [*see* ch. 2, § 2.07].

[c] Injured Workers Must Report Earnings

Effective January 1, 1994, the law requires injured workers receiving temporary total disability benefits to report any earnings, including social security benefits, to the carrier. The carrier should request this information from the injured worker by completing the Employee Earnings Report (DWC-19). The injured worker must respond within 21 days after receiving the request. If not, the law allows carriers to suspend benefits until the injured worker supplies the requested information [*see* § 440.15[2](d), Fla. Stat. (7/1/97); *see also* Division Bulletin #94 (12/29/93)].

[8] Payment of Benefits

[a] When Benefits Are Due

Carriers must pay temporary total benefits after each 14-day period of total disability for work. At least every 14 days then, the adjuster should confirm continuing medical disability with the doctor. Adjusters should also check with the employee and employer. This is to find out if the injured worker has returned to work in spite of the lack of medical release. This process should begin on the 12th or 13th day of each disability period since payment is due on the 14th day. When the carrier pays late, it must pay interest to the injured worker. In addition, the carrier may be subject to a penalty.

[b] When Interest Is Due

The carrier owes the injured worker interest when an installment is late. An installment is late if the carrier pays it even one day after it is due. If the disability period is from the 1st through the 14th day of a given month, for example, the payment is due on the 14th day. The law considers an installment paid on the date of mailing. If the carrier mails the check on the 15th, the payment is late and the carrier owes the injured worker interest at the rate of 12 percent per year or $5, whichever is greater. Interest begins to accrue from the date the installment is due until the carrier pays it [§ 440.20(8), Fla. Stat.; *see also* ch. 12, § 12.04[9][a]].

[c] When Penalties Are Due

Besides interest, the carrier will owe the injured worker a penalty if the payment is more than seven days late. Using the example in [b], *above,* assume the carrier mails the payment on or after the 22nd. Here, the carrier will owe a penalty and interest [§ 440.20(6), Fla. Stat.; *see also* ch. 12, § 12.04[9][b]].

For a complete discussion of schedule benefits, see Larson's Workers' Compensation, Desk Edition, Ch. 86 (Matthew Bender).

[9] Unemployment Compensation

Injured workers cannot collect temporary total benefits for any week in which they have collected unemployment compensation. Carriers can obtain unemployment compensation information by having the injured worker sign an Authorization Request for Unemployment Compensation Information (DWC-30). Upon receipt of the signed authorization form, the carrier should send it to the Division of Workers' Compensation. The Act requires the Division to find out if the injured worker is receiving unemployment compensation and to notify the carrier [§ 440.15(10), Fla. Stat. (7/1/97)].

Injured workers have 21 days after receiving the DWC-30 form to sign and return it to the carrier. If not, the rules provide that benefits "shall cease until such time as the employee furnishes the signed form" [Fla. Admin. Code R. 69L-3.021 (1/10/2005)].

For a discussion of physical incapacity and unemployment compensation, see Larson's Workers' Compensation, Desk Edition, Ch. 84, § 84.05 (Matthew Bender).

[10] Injured Worker in Jail

What happens if the injured worker is in jail or confined involuntarily in a public institution such as a mental hospital under the Baker Act? With one exception, the law prohibits incarcerated injured workers from receiving temporary total disability or any other indemnity benefits. The one exception is an injured worker with dependents. Decide dependency in such cases in the same fashion as in death cases [*see* ch. 15, § 15.04].

As in death cases, the burden is on the party seeking benefits to prove actual dependency. If the injured worker's spouse was not living with him when the accident occurred, disability benefits are not awardable unless the worker can show that the spouse was living apart for "justifiable cause" as required by § 440.02(25), Fla. Stat. [*see* Power Plant Maintenance v. Mercado, 720 So. 2d 298, 300 (Fla. 1st DCA 1998)].

If dependents qualify, carriers should pay compensation benefits directly to them while the injured worker remains disabled and confined [§ 440.15(9), Fla. Stat. (7/1/97)].

The next question is whether this prohibition applies to prisoners injured while working for a private employer in a work-release program. In a 1983 case, the court did not directly answer the question but came close enough to allow a conclusion that such workers are eligible for indemnity benefits. The court held that, "work-released prisoners engaged to work in private enterprise, for compensation paid them by private businesses that are 'employers' in every practical sense of the word, are not excluded from chapter 440 coverage" [*see* Courtesy Construction v. Derscha, 431 So. 2d 232, 233 (Fla. 1st DCA 1983) (emphasis added)].

The court did not mention the language in § 440.15(9), Fla. Stat. prohibiting compensation when, "an employee becomes an inmate of a public institution." The opinion does tell us that such prisoners are not excluded from coverage. Also, consider the phrase, "becomes an inmate." Work-released prisoners do not "become" inmates. They were already inmates when the employment began. From this we can logically conclude that work-released prisoners in private employment are eligible for indemnity benefits and that § 440.15(9), Fla. Stat. does not apply to them. To conclude otherwise would allow employers to escape their responsibility for providing a safe workplace and for assuming responsibility for their workers' industrial injuries.

[11] Suspending Benefits

Suspending temporary total disability benefits properly requires the carrier to file a Notice of Action/Change (DWC-4), with the Division. Carriers must clearly state the reason for suspending benefits. The most common reasons for suspension are return to work, medical release for work, maximum medical improvement, or payment of the maximum weeks of benefits [*see* ch. 2, § 2.08[9]].

§ 13.11 Catastrophic Temporary Total Disability

[1] The Rule

When employees suffer a work-related catastrophic injury, they are entitled to increased temporary total disability benefits. The basis for entitlement, and the amount of the benefit, change depending upon the accident date [§ 440.15(2)(b), Fla. Stat. (7/1/97); *see* [4][a], [b], *below*].

Legislative amendments effective October 1, 2003, specifically provide that these enhanced benefits are not due or payable if the employee is eligible for, entitled to, or collecting permanent total disability benefits. Because this amendment precludes benefits the court previously held were payable, this is clearly a substantive amendment that will apply only to accidents occurring on or after the effective date, October 1, 2003 [§ 440.15(2)(b), Fla. Stat. (10/1/2003)].

[2] Amount of Benefits

For accidents occurring before October 1, 1988, qualified injured workers are eligible for enhanced benefits of 80 percent of average weekly wage up to $400. For accidents occurring on or after October 1, 1988, qualified injured workers are eligible for enhanced benefits of 80 percent of average weekly wage up to $700 [§ 440.15(2)(b), Fla. Stat.].

[3] Duration of Benefits

For accidents occurring before July 1, 1990, benefits are payable for no longer than six months from the *date of injury.* For accidents occurring on or after July 1, 1990, benefits are payable for no longer than six months from the *date of accident.* The distinction between the accident and the injury date is not clear and has not been reviewed by the courts [§ 440.15(2)(b), Fla. Stat.].

The best way to start a discussion about catastrophic temporary total disability benefits is to refer to the Workers' Compensation Act. Remember, however, that the legislature enacted significant amendments effective July 1, 1990 [*see* [4][b], *below*].

[4] Catastrophic Benefits

[a] Before July 1, 1990

[i] The Statute

For accidents occurring up to June 30, 1990, the Workers' Compensation Act provides as follows [§ 440.15(2)(b), Fla. Stat.]:

> An employee who has sustained the loss of an arm, leg, hand, or foot, or within a reasonable medical certainty the anticipated permanent and total loss of use of such member because of organic damage to the nervous system, or has lost the sight of both eyes shall be paid temporary total disability of 80 percent of his average weekly wage until such employee has completed his training in the use of artificial members or appliances as necessary and completed training or education under a program pursuant to s. 440.49 [the rehabilitation section], if provided.

[ii] Judicial Interpretation

To most practitioners, the statute seemed clear enough. Workers suffering an extremity amputation can collect increased benefits while training to use an artificial limb. If the extremity were not amputated but useless, workers could still collect benefits while in a physical or vocational rehabilitation program. Right? Not so fast. The courts did not read the statute that way.

Guide to Claims

For example, several pieces of falling lumber struck the injured worker. He suffered a severe vertebral compression fracture that compressed a nerve. This resulted in loss of the use of his legs. Eventually, physicians performed surgery to decompress that nerve. The trial judge denied the claim for catastrophic temporary total disability benefits. The judge held the injured worker had not suffered total loss of use necessitating training or education in the use of artificial members or appliances under a rehabilitation program. Good decision? It seems so, considering the plain statutory language, but the First District Court of Appeal did not agree.

The court held the Workers' Compensation Act referred to temporary, not permanent, total disability. Total loss of use in the workers' compensation context suggests only the inability to function in an industrial setting. The court said [*see* Van Eyk v. R.N. Hicks Const. Co., 377 So. 2d 793, 794 (Fla. 1st DCA 1979)]:

> Loss of use, total or partial, of an organ or member, in workmen's compensation cases, is never determined in the abstract, but rather is always considered in light of the use which a claimant must reasonably make of the organ or member in his or her employment. . . . In other words, it is obvious that a claimant was totally disabled from doing construction work. . . . Nor did the doctor's decision that appellant was not a candidate for a physical rehabilitation program bar appellant from collecting enhanced benefits.

Four years later the court held that the law does not require total amputation of an extremity to entitle an injured worker to catastrophic temporary total disability benefits [*see* Santiago v. Orr Industries, Inc., 407 So. 2d 1026, 1028 (Fla. 1st DCA 1982)].

Under these decisions then, the loss of an arm does not mean amputation; instead, it means only loss of use. Permanent loss of use does not mean permanent, but temporary. Total loss of use does not literally mean total. It means loss of use sufficient to keep the injured worker from working.

Therefore, carriers owed catastrophic temporary total disability benefits, for injuries sustained before July 1, 1990, based on loss of use due to organic nerve damage. This nerve damage need only prevent the injured employee from working.

[b] After July 1, 1990

[i] The Statute

The legislature amended the statute effective July 1, 1990. This is appears to be a substantive amendment that applies to only those accidents occurring after the effective date. The section now reads as follows [§ 440.15(2)(b), Fla. Stat. (2001)]:

> . . . [A]n employee who has sustained the loss of an arm, leg, hand, or foot, has been rendered a paraplegic, paraparetic, quadriplegic, or quadriparetic, or has lost the sight of both eyes shall be paid temporary total disability of 80 percent of her or his average weekly wage. The increased temporary total disability compensation provided for in this paragraph must not extend beyond 6 months from the date of the accident.

[ii] Date of Injury Versus Date of Accident

Note the last sentence in the statutory quotation in [I], *above*. Previously the statute provided that benefits were payable for six months "from the date of injury" and now reads "from the date of the accident." In interpreting the original, pre-1990 statute, the court held that the term "date of injury" as used in § 440.15(2)(b), Fla. Stat. (1985) means the date on which organic damage occurs or manifests itself by causing the total loss of use of the affected limb [*see* Bordo Citrus Products v. Tedcer, 518 So. 2d 367, 371 (Fla. 1st DCA 1987)].

Therefore, the phrase "date of injury" refers to the date the qualifying condition first manifested itself, and the phrase "date of accident" refers to the precipitating industrial accident.

[iii] Qualifying Injuries

[A] Introduction

The July 1, 1990 version of § 440.15(2)(b), Fla. Stat. is substantially different from the original version. Although the revised version has been in effect for more than a decade, it has not undergone judicial review. Therefore, we are left to decide for ourselves when an injured worker qualifies for enhanced temporary total disability benefits. The 1990 statute lists several qualifying conditions, each of which is reviewed individually in [B]–[D], *below.*

[B] Loss of Arm, Leg, Hand or Foot

A worker who suffers the loss of an arm, leg, hand or foot is eligible for enhanced benefits. The key phrase is the "loss of" an extremity. Note that the phrase "loss of use" has been omitted. This plain language compels a conclusion that the Legislature intended this to mean the amputation of the entire arm, leg, hand or foot [*see* Showell Farms v. Carter, 633 So. 2d 477, 480 (Fla. 1st DCA 1994) (dicta)]. This conclusion is supported further by the Legislature's inclusion of conditions [*see* [C], *below*] that describe the loss of use of an extremity.

SPECIAL ALERT: An amputee adjudged to be permanently and totally disabled as of the accident date may also be entitled to catastrophic temporary total disability for the first six months. Under § 440.15(1)(b), Fla. Stat., a workers' compensation claimant with a catastrophic injury, in the absence of a substantial earning capacity, is presumed to have a permanent total disability from the date of the accident. The plain language of amended § 440.15(2)(b), Fla. Stat. (1999) compels the conclusion that an amputation of an entire hand or foot will support enhanced temporary total disability (TTD) benefits. § 440.15(2)(b), Fla. Stat. provides that catastrophically injured employees are entitled to six months of TTD benefits at a special maximum compensation rate [Neavins v. City of St. Petersburg, 823 So. 2d 288, 289–290 (Fla. 1st DCA 2002)].

Effective October 1, 2003, the Legislature amended the Act in an apparent effort to overrule the *Neavins* court. The section now specifically provides that these enhanced benefits are not due or payable if the employee is eligible for, entitled to, or collecting permanent total disability benefits. Because this amendment precludes benefits the court previously held were payable, this is clearly a substantive amendment that will apply only to accidents occurring on or after the effective date, October 1, 2003 [§ 440.15(2)(b), Fla. Stat. (10/1/2003)].

[C] Paraplegic, Paraparetic, Quadriplegic or Quadriparetic

A worker who has been rendered paraplegic, paraparetic, quadriplegic or quadriparetic is eligible for enhanced benefits. These terms may be defined as follows [*see PDR Medical Dictionary,* 1st Edition]:

Paraplegic	refers to a person who has suffered *complete* paralysis in both lower extremities.
Paraparetic	refers to a person who has suffered *incomplete* paralysis in both lower extremities.
Quadriplegic	refers to a person who has suffered complete paralysis in all four limbs.
Quadriparetic	refers to a person who has suffered incomplete paralysis in all four limbs.

This plain language, using precise medical terms, compels the conclusion that only complete or partial paralysis of all four limbs or both legs qualifies. Paralysis of only one leg or one side would not qualify because the term for that is hemiplegia. Also note that the statute contains no requirement that the condition be permanent, although that is usually the case.

[D] Loss of Sight in Both Eyes

A person who has "lost the sight of both eyes" is eligible for enhanced benefits. The Florida Impairment Rating Guide considers blindness of 85 percent or more as total blindness. Note, however, that the statute does not refer to total blindness or "legal" blindness, but refers only to the ambiguous phrase "lost of sight." Whether this requires total loss of sight is not clear. The most reasonable interpretation is that the loss of sight on both eyes sufficient to preclude employment will be enough to qualify for enhanced benefits.

§ 13.12 Maximum Medical Improvement (MMI)

[1] MMI Date Marks End of Temporary Benefits

The date an injured worker reaches maximum medical improvement is important in workers' compensation. This date signals the end of eligibility for temporary disability benefits. Note carefully, however, that this is only a general rule. Surgery or other remedial or curative medical procedures performed after maximum medical improvement may involve temporary total disability. An injured worker is eligible for temporary total disability benefits even after maximum medical improvement during a period of hospitalization and recuperation following compensable *curative* procedures. This does not apply if the treatment is palliative. For example, Linda Melman reached maximum medical improvement in 1994. In 1995 her chiropractor advised her to stay home from work. The court held that Melman was not entitled to temporary total disability benefits for this period because the chiropractic treatments were merely palliative in that they held no prospect for lasting improvement [*see* Orange County School Board v. Melman, 721 So. 2d 1183, 1184 (Fla. 1st DCA 1998)]. Maximum medical improvement also marks the beginning of eligibility for permanent disability benefits, if warranted. Unfortunately, many medical professionals misunderstand the legal significance of the term "maximum medical improvement."

For a brief discussion of maximum medical improvement, see LARSON'S WORKERS' COMPENSATION, DESK EDITION, Ch. 80 (Matthew Bender).

Guide to Claims

[2] Definition

Do not confuse the date of maximum medical improvement with the date that an injured worker can try to return to work. The ability to return to work in some capacity and the date of maximum medical improvement are two separate issues. Maximum medical improvement is: "The date after which further recovery from, or lasting improvement to, an injury or disease can no longer reasonably be anticipated, based upon reasonable medical probability" [§ 440.02(10), Fla. Stat. (2002)].

A simpler, judicial definition is that maximum medical improvement marks the point after which doctors cannot reasonably anticipate further recovery or improvement [*see* Delgado v. Omni Hotel, 643 So. 2d 1185, 1186 (Fla. 1st DCA 1994)]. Put another way, a finding of maximum medical improvement (MMI) is precluded when treatment is being provided with a reasonable expectation that it will bring about some degree of recovery, even if treatment ultimately proves ineffective. The question of whether a claimant has reached maximum medical improvement (MMI) is a medical question that should be based on a clear, explicit expression in the medical records or medical opinion testimony. Because the question of whether a claimant has reached MMI is essentially a medical question, it should be answered by medical experts [Lemmer v. Urban Elec., Inc., 947 So. 2d 1196, 1998 (Fla. 1st DCA 2007)].

[3] MMI Date Can Be Illusive

Deciding whether or when an injured worker has reached maximum medical improvement can sometimes be difficult. An injured worker cannot be at maximum medical improvement when treatment is still underway and the doctor reasonably expects the treatment will cause some improvement. This is true even if the treatment proves ineffective. Thus, when the treatment concludes, the doctor cannot now declare that since the treatment was ineffective, the injured worker had reached maximum medical improvement earlier [*see* Rolle v. Picadilly Cafeteria, 573 So. 2d 94, 97 (Fla. 1st DCA 1991)].

A finding of maximum medical improvement is precluded when treatment is being rendered with a reasonable expectation that it will bring about some degree of recovery, even if that treatment ultimately proves ineffective [*see* Pinellas County Schs. v. Angell, 899 So. 2d 356 (Fla. 1st DCA 2005)].

[4] Curative and Palliative Treatment

We cannot decide the nature of treatment (i.e., curative v. palliative) by the ultimate success or failure of the treatment. Any treatment is (for legal purposes) curative if the doctor begins treatment with a reasonable expectation that it will result in lasting improvement. Therefore, temporary disability benefits must continue if doctors expect recovery or lasting improvement [*see* Utley-James, Inc. v. Lady, 448 So. 2d 1191, 1193 (Fla. 1st DCA 1984)].

[5] Setting the Date Requires Medical Evidence

Judges of compensation claims may not guess or estimate when an injured worker reaches maximum medical improvement. They should usually base their conclusion that an injured worker has reached maximum improvement upon medical evidence. This includes a clear, explicit expression of that fact set forth in medical records or medical opinion testimony [*see* Stewart v. Resort Inns of America, 513 So. 2d 1334, 1335–1336 (Fla. 1st DCA 1987); Gillich v. Park Ave. Night Club, 569 So. 2d 930, 932 (Fla. 1st DCA 1990)].

[6] Multiple Physicians

Part of the problem in deciding overall maximum medical improvement can be traced to multiple physician involvement. Physicians, especially when they treat different body parts or practice in different specialities, often disagree on the MMI date or the degree of overall impairment. To help solve this dilemma, Division rules require carriers to choose a single physician to make this decision. The chosen physician must consider the impairment ratings from each physician involved in the employee's care. In addition, this "umpire" physician must decide the date on which the injured employee reached overall MMI and, based on the other physicians' reports, assign an impairment rating to the whole body. Once complete, the assigned physician must report this decision to the carrier on form DWC-9a within 10 days. Whether the courts will approve this procedure remains to be seen [Fla. Admin. Code R. 69L-7.603 (1/10/2005)].

§§ 13.13—13.49 [Reserved]

Part C Permanent Total Disability (PTD)

§ 13.50 Permanent Total Disability

[1] Overview

[a] Accident Dates Through September 30, 2003

For accident occurring through September 30, 2003, whenever the carrier, or a judge of compensation claims, decides an injured worker is permanently and totally disabled, the Workers' Compensation Act entitles the injured worker to collect benefits for life. These benefits equal 66 2/3 percent of the worker's average weekly wage, up to the maximum compensation rate for the year of the worker's injury. These benefits continue for life if the injured worker remains totally disabled [§ 440.15(1), Fla. Stat. (7/1/97)].

[b] Accident Dates On or After October 1, 2003

For accidents occurring on or after October 1, 2003, entitlement to permanent total disability benefits end at age 75. This age limitation does not apply if the injured worker is not eligible for Social Security disability or retirement benefits only because the compensable injury prevented the worker from working sufficient quarters to be eligible for federal benefits. Therefore, benefits will still end at age 75, even if the injured worker is not eligible for federal benefits for any other reason.

If the injured worker was at least 70 years old when the accident occurred, he or she is eligible to receive permanent total disability benefits for no more than five years after permanent total disability benefits begin. This is regardless of the person's eligibility for federal benefits [§ 440.15[1][b], Fla. Stat. (10/1/2003)].

For discussion of the law that applies to accidents occurring through December 31, 1993, see § 13.51. For discussion of the law that applies to accidents between January 1, 1994, and September 30, 2003, see § 13.52. For discussion of the law that applies to accidents on or after October 1, 2003, see § 13.53.

For a general discussion of permanent total disability, see LARSON'S WORKERS' COMPENSATION, DESK EDITION, Part 9, *Disability and Personal Injury Benefits* (Matthew Bender).

[2] Basic Benefit

The law entitles injured workers to benefits if the court judges them to be permanently and totally disabled, or if the carrier voluntarily accepts them as such. The basic benefits remain the same for all accident dates. The basic benefit is an amount equal to 66 2/3 percent of the injured worker's average weekly wage, up to the maximum compensation rate for the year of the accident. This benefit continues for life unless the injured worker reestablishes a wage-earning capacity [§ 440.15(1), Fla. Stat. (7/1/97)].

Testing their ability to return to employment will not prejudice injured workers' rights to reinstatement of permanent total disability benefits if the test fails. When an injured worker announces an intent to try to return to work, the carrier must file form DWC-22,

Reemployment and Annual Case Status Review with the Division within 10 days after approving the trial period [Fla. Admin. Code R. 38F-55.004(1) (7/1/96)]. The Division's rules also provide that the trial work period can last no longer than 90 days. Presumably this means that the 91st day marks the beginning of return to regular work and an end to permanent total disability benefits. If the trial work period fails, the carrier must report reinstatement of permanent total disability benefits to the Division by filing the Notice of Action/Change, form DWC-4 [Fla. Admin. Code R. 38F-55.004(3)(b) (7/1/96)].

[3] Supplemental Benefit

[a] Calculating Benefits

[i] Accident Dates On or Before September 30, 2003

Besides the basic benefit, the law entitles permanently and totally disabled injured workers to receive an additional supplemental amount. This benefit is equal to five percent of the injured worker's weekly compensation in effect on the date of the injury, multiplied by the number of calendar years since the date of the injury [§ 440.15(1)(f), Fla. Stat. (7/1/97)].

0.05 x compensation rate x number of years since injury = supplemental amount.

When the injury, maximum medical improvement, and a state of permanent total disability all occur in the same calendar year, the supplement will equal zero until January 1 of the next year. Why? Because the multiplier "number of years since injury" will be zero. This yields a product of zero. When, however, the injury occurs in a prior calendar year, the formula will create supplemental benefits beginning on the date of MMI/PTD. This can be confusing because the Workers' Compensation Act refers to a calendar year and not to a period of 12 months.

By the 20th year of permanent total disability, the supplemental benefit alone will equal the basic benefit; however, the basic benefit combined with the supplement may not exceed the maximum compensation rate in effect *at the time of payment.*

Note the italicized phrase carefully. If the carrier issues a permanent total disability check with supplemental benefits in 1994, the maximum compensation rate for 1994 controls the amount, not the rate for the year the injury occurred. For injuries occurring before July 1, 1984, the Division of Worker's Compensation pays these supplemental benefits. For injuries occurring on or after that date, the carrier pays the supplemental benefits.

[ii] Accident Dates On or After October 1, 2003

For accidents occurring on or after October 1, 2003, permanent total disability supplemental benefits are calculated in the same fashion as before, with the major exception that these benefits are now equal to three percent of the claimant's average weekly compensation rather than five percent as before [*see* § 440.15(1)(f) Fla. Stat.; Fla. Admin. Code. R. 69L-3.01945].

[b] Entitlement Limitations

[i] Accident Dates Through September 30, 2003

For injuries occurring on or after July 1, 1990, entitlement to supplemental benefits ends at age 62 if the injured worker is eligible for social security disability and retirement benefits. This is true whether or not the employee has applied for such benefits [§ 440.15(1)(e)1, Fla. Stat. (1991)]. Whether entitlement to supplemental benefits ends forever, or only temporarily, depends on the claimant's age upon reaching permanent total disability.

1. *Under age 62 upon reaching PTD.* If the claimant is under age 62 upon reaching permanent total disability, entitlement to supplemental benefits ends forever at age 62.

> **NOTE:** However, in order to stop paying PTD supplemental benefits to a claimant who turns 62, the employer/carrier must first establish that the claimant is eligible for *both* Social Security retirement and Social Security disability benefits. In the event that the claimant is eligible for both and, thus, no longer entitled to PTD supplemental benefits, the supplemental benefits should not be reinstated after age 65 pursuant to *Wilkins*.

> **NOTE:** To prove that a claimant is "eligible" for Social Security disability benefits, the employer/carrier must show that (1) the claimant is insured for disability insurance benefits, (2) is younger than age 65, and (3) has a qualifying disability [*see* Hillsborough County Sch. Bd. v. Ward, 913 So. 2d 39 (Fla. 1st DCA 2005)].

2. *Between ages 62 and 65 upon reaching PTD.* If the claimant is over age 62, but under age 65, upon reaching permanent total disability, supplemental benefits are suspended between ages 62 and 65. Upon reaching age 65, supplemental benefits must be reinstated. Put another way, claimants over age 62 are not eligible for supplemental benefits until they reach age 65.
3. *Over age 65 upon reaching PTD.* If the claimant is over age 65 upon reaching permanent total disability, supplemental benefits are due uninterruptedly.

This rather convoluted rule is the result of two appellate opinions:

1. The *Burger King* Case. Recall that the suspension of benefits applies if the injured worker is eligible for social security disability and retirement benefits. In 1997, the court held that suspension, however, applies only to injured workers between the ages of 62 and 65, because this is the only period during which a person can be eligible for *both* disability and retirement benefits. No one is eligible for retirement benefits before age 62 and for disability benefits after age 65. Because the statute allows suspending supplemental benefits only while a person is eligible for both benefits, the suspension can occur only between the

Guide to Claims

ages of 62 and 65 [*see* Burger King Corp./Cigna Ins. v. Moreno, 689 So. 2d 288, 289 (Fla. 1st DCA 1997)].

2. The *Wilkins* Case. Virtually all *Burger King* readers interpreted the case to mean that suspension can occur only between the ages of 62 and 65. In January 2000, however, the *Wilkins* court suggested that these readers had confused the court's dicta with its holding. The court explained that Moreno, the claimant in *Burger King,* was 69 years old at the time of her accident and never would have been eligible for, or qualified for, social security disability, but would have presumably continued to work well beyond the traditional retirement age. Here, however, Gracette Wilkins was younger than 62 at the time of her accident and PTD designation. Thus, she was eligible for both disability and retirement benefits and would have presumably retired at the traditional age. The legislature, said the court, legitimately assumed that workers under age 62 would not continue to work after a traditional retirement age. The court held that when a claimant is injured and reaches PTD prior to age 62, the claimant is not entitled to PTD supplemental benefits after age 65 [*see* Wilkins v. Broward County School Board, 754 So. 2d 50 (Fla. 1st DCA 2000)].

3. The *Hillsborough County School Board* Case. The court affirmed an order awarding attorney's fees and costs in which the JCC concluded that supplemental benefits were not due and owing. In doing so, the court noted that the claimant was younger than 62 at the time of her accident and PTD designation. In the order on appeal, the JCC accepted the employer/carrier's argument and distinguished *Moreno* "because of the age difference of the parties at the time of the award." The court held that, in cases in which a claimant is injured and reaches PTD prior to 62, the claimant is not entitled to PTD supplemental benefits after age 65. Here, however, the court held that *Wilkins does not* stand for the proposition that PTD supplemental benefits automatically cease when a claimant reaches age 62 if the claimant was PTD before age 62.

   In *Wilkins*, the court held that a claimant who is PTD prior to age 62 is not entitled to have his or her supplemental benefits reinstated after age 65. In situations such as the case here, in order to stop paying PTD supplemental benefits to a claimant who turns 62, it must first be established that the claimant is eligible for both Social Security retirement and Social Security disability benefits. In the event that the claimant is eligible for both and, thus, no longer entitled to PTD supplemental benefits, the supplemental benefits should not be reinstated after age 65 pursuant to *Wilkins*.

   To prove that a claimant is "eligible" for Social Security disability benefits, the employer/carrier must show that (1) the claimant is insured for disability insurance benefits, (2) is younger than age 65, and (3) has a qualifying disability [*see* Hillsborough County Sch. Bd. v. Ward, 913 So. 2d 39 (Fla. 1st DCA 2005)].

In two separate cases, workers' compensation claimants sought review of orders of the Judges of Compensation Claims, which held that because the claimants were injured and reached permanent total disability (PTD) prior to age 62, they were not entitled to supplemental benefits after age 65. These claimants challenged the constitutionality of

§ 440.15(1)(e)1, Fla. Stat. (1991) and § 440.15(1)(f)1, Fla. Stat. (1995).

The claimants both suffered industrial accidents that rendered them permanently and totally disabled before the age of 62. Both collected disability payments, and the insurance carriers terminated the payment of supplemental PTD benefits on the basis of § 440.15(1)(e)1, Fla. Stat. (1991) and § 440.15(1)(f)1, Fla. Stat. (1995).

The claimants sought supplemental benefits for PTD after they reached 65, and the respective judges of compensation claims denied the claims. On appeal, the court affirmed. The court held that the Supremacy Clause did not preclude the termination of the benefits under the statutes because federal law, specifically 42 U.S.C.S. § 424a(d), did not preempt the statutes. The termination of benefits under the Florida statutes was not a reverse offset pursuant to § 440.15(10), Fla. Stat. and, therefore, was not in conflict with 42 U.S.C.S. § 424a, when the effect of both the state and the federal statutes was to avoid duplication of benefits. Nor did the Florida statutes violate the guarantee of equal protection on the basis of age discrimination because the legislature's statutory objective of reducing premium costs satisfied the rational basis test [Harrell v. Fla. Constr. Specialists/AARLA, 834 So. 2d 352, 356–358 (Fla. 1st DCA 2003)].

[ii] Accident Dates On or After October 1, 2003

Apparently, the confusing rule the courts developed concerning the age 62 limitation was not what the Legislature intended when the provision was enacted on July 1, 1990 [*see* [i], *above*]. Effective October 1, 2003, the Legislature amended the provision to provide that supplemental benefits "shall not be paid or payable after the employee attains age 62." This applies regardless of whether the employee has applied for, or is eligible to apply for, Social Security disability or Social Security retirement benefits.

Note, however, that permanent total disability supplemental benefits continue beyond age 62 if the injured worker is not eligible for Social Security disability or retirement benefits only because the compensable injury prevented the worker from working sufficient quarters to be eligible for federal benefits. Therefore, supplemental benefits will still end at age 62, even if the injured worker is not eligible for federal benefits for any other reason.

> **SPECIAL ALERT:** First responders are eligible for PTD supplemental benefits for so long as they are entitled to PTD basic benefits. Therefore, the age 62 limitation does not apply, but only if the employer does not participate in the social security program. First responders are defined as law enforcement officers, firefighters, emergency medical technicians, or paramedics [*see* § 112.1815(3), Fla. Stat.].

[4] Injured Worker Must Report Earnings

Once permanent total disability begins, the Act requires the injured worker to report all earnings to the carrier and the Division upon request. The injured worker must do so on the Employee's Earnings Report, DWC-19. If the carrier suspects the injured worker may be earning income, the claims adjuster should send this form to the injured worker with instructions. If the injured worker fails or refuses to make this report within 21 days after receiving the request, Division rules require that the carrier stop paying permanent total benefits until the injured worker complies [Fla. Admin. Code R. 69L-3.021(2) (1/10/2005)].

Once permanent total disability benefits begin, it is easy for adjusters to become complacent and to simply issue checks automatically for years. Checking on the injured worker's vocational and medical status at least annually is critical. Adjusters must take care they do not join the embarrassed few who have discovered they have been paying benefits to an employed or deceased worker for months or years.

[5] Temporary Benefits Credited Against PTD Benefits

A carrier may withhold permanent total disability benefits while it conducts a reasonable investigation to find out whether the injured worker can be rehabilitated and returned to work. Further, once the carrier accepts the injured worker as permanently and totally disabled, it may credit any payments of temporary benefits against permanent total disability benefits owed from the date of maximum medical improvement [*see* Prestressed Decking Corp. v. Medrano, 556 So. 2d 406, 408 (Fla. 1st DCA 1989); Harper Mechanical Corporation v. Lantrip, 606 So. 2d 1284, 1285 (Fla. 1st DCA 1992)].

[6] Permanent Disability Not Always Required

Under certain circumstances, it is possible for a claimant to be entitled to permanent total disability benefits even though the state of total disability is not permanent. This has become known a temporary permanent total disability.

The claimant injured his right knee while working for the employer in June 1995, and had not worked since that industrial accident. An MRI and arthroscopic surgery revealed a torn medial meniscus, contusion, and post-traumatic chondromalacia to the medial femoral condyle. The claimant's condition did not improve, and another arthroscopy was performed in late 1995. The claimant reached maximum medical improvement on July 11, 1997, with a 14 percent permanent impairment of the whole body. The claimant continued to complain of pain and restricted extension and flexion in the right leg after that date, and an x-ray revealed post-traumatic degenerative arthritis. The condition of the claimant's knee deteriorated to the point that in August 1998 the claimant's physician recommended a total knee replacement to restore flexibility and reduce pain, and the doctor performed this procedure in October 1998. The surgeon opined that after four months of post-operative recovery from the corrective knee surgery the claimant should be able to work with restrictions.

A claim was made for permanent total disability benefits, and in a March 4, 1999, order the trial judge determined that the claimant was no longer totally disabled after his release to work on February 27, 1999. The judge therefore denied the permanent total claim for the period of time subsequent to that date. The judge found that the claimant was totally disabled from July 11, 1997, when the doctor placed the claimant at maximum medical improvement, until February 27, 1999, when the doctor released the claimant to return to work after the knee surgery. But the judge denied the permanent total claim for this period of time, concluding that because the claimant's total disability ended on February 27, 1999, it could not have been permanent.

On appeal, the court reversed. The court held that once a claimant's medical condition has improved as much as is reasonably expected under available and recommended remedial treatments, the claimant may be considered to be at maximum medical improvement and entitled to permanent benefits for continuing disability even though it is anticipated that the claimant will likely become a candidate for additional remedial treatment at some time in the future. This principle, said the court, was recognized in Holder v. Keller Kitchen Cabinets, 610 So. 2d 1264 (Fla 1992), wherein a claimant was found to have reached maximum medical improvement and was awarded permanent disability benefits in connection with a knee injury even though it was anticipated that he would subsequently become a candidate for a total knee replacement.

The court noted that the record in the present case would support a finding that as of July 11, 1997, the recommended remedial treatments had provided as much improvement of the claimant's condition as was then possible, and that the claimant then remained totally disabled. The trial judge could, therefore, have found that the claimant reached maximum medical improvement as of July 11, 1997, and could have awarded permanent total disability benefits from that date, even though the claimant later became a candidate for a total knee replacement, and even if such remedial treatment eventually restored the claimant's ability to work.

Because there was competent substantial evidence to support the finding that the claimant was no longer totally disabled as of February 27, 1999, the court affirmed the denial of permanent total disability benefits after that date. However, because the trial judge incorrectly believed that an earlier permanent total disability award was not permissible, the denial of permanent total disability benefits from July 11, 1997, through February 27, 1999, and the denial of interest, costs, and attorney's fees was reversed and remanded for reconsideration of those claims [*see* Emanuel v. David Piercy Plumbing, 765 So. 2d 761, 762–763 (Fla. 1st DCA 2000)].

§ 13.51 Accident Dates Through December 31, 1993

[1] Presumptive Permanent Total Disability

For accidents occurring up to December 31, 1993, the law presumes permanent total disability if workers suffer the following injuries: (1) loss of both hands, both arms, both feet, both legs, both eyes, or any two of these; (2) paraplegia; or (3) quadriplegia. This presumption is rebuttable, but only with conclusive proof of a substantial earning capacity. Obviously, if in spite of such a serious injury a worker could return to gainful employment, the Workers' Compensation Act precludes entitlement to lifetime benefits.

The presumption means that the law will automatically presume entitlement unless the carrier can produce conclusive proof to the contrary. Usually, this is a significant burden to overcome. Entitlement to permanent total disability benefits begins "the moment the physical impairments described . . . occur, a presumption of permanent total disability is in being" [*see* Stables v. Rivers, 562 So. 2d 784, 785 (Fla. 1st DCA 1990)].

Carriers must begin benefit payments although the injured worker has not yet reached maximum medical improvement. Thus, if an injured worker is paraplegic on the date of the accident, the law requires payment of permanent total disability benefits beginning on that date. This is important because it hastens when carriers must add supplemental benefits, as discussed in § 13.50[3] [*see* Pinellas Ambulance Service, Inc. v. Gettinger, 504 So. 2d 1386, 1388 (Fla. 1st DCA 1987); Jackson v. Princeton Farms Corporation, 140 So. 2d 570, 574–575 (Fla. 1962)].

For a discussion of non-presumptive permanent total disability, see [2], *below*.

[2] Non-Presumptive Permanent Total Disability

[a] The Rule

For accidents occurring up to December 31, 1993, injuries other than those creating a presumption [*see* [1], *above*] may still entitle the injured worker to permanent total disability benefits based on wage earning capacity. No rigid formula or "bright line" test applies for deciding whether an injured worker is permanently and totally disabled as far as wage earning capacity is concerned.

[b] Tests for Permanent Total Disability

[i] The Tests

For accidents occurring up to December 31, 1993, unless an injured worker's injury falls into a presumptive class, decide permanent total disability according to the following tests. Injured workers alleging permanent total disability have the burden of proving their PTD status. They can meet that burden in one of three ways:

1. Through evidence of permanent medical incapacity to perform even light work uninterruptedly; or
2. Through evidence of permanent work-related physical restrictions coupled with an exhaustive but unsuccessful job search; or
3. Through evidence of permanent work-related physical restrictions that, while not alone totally disabling, do preclude performing light work uninterruptedly, when combined with vocational factors [*see* Herrera v. Hojo Inn Maingate, 680 So. 2d 439, 440–441 (Fla. 1st DCA 1996); Wal-Mart Stores, Inc. v. Liggon, 668 So. 2d 259, 264–265 (Fla. 1st DCA 1996)].

Look for evidence of an exhaustive and lengthy, though unsuccessful job search. When this is coupled with a permanent disability that affects the injured worker's ability to earn, courts usually award permanent total disability benefits [*see* Davis v. Bonded Transp., Inc., 573 So. 2d 373, 375 (Fla. 1st DCA 1991)].

For example, Iran Boles was a 35-year-old laborer when he injured his back in 1993. Upon reaching maximum medical improvement he was discharged with a seven-percent permanent impairment rating and restrictions of no heavy lifting, no repetitive bending, and no long periods of sitting. All medical evidence suggested Boles was capable of at least doing light duty work uninterruptedly. Boles tried unsuccessfully to find work in what the judge of compensation claims described as an adequate job search. Nevertheless, the judge denied permanent total disability benefits because he believed that Boles' inability to get a job had nothing to do with his injury. Boles was functionally illiterate, and his physical appearance was marred by the need for dental work. In addition, Boles had felony convictions and a suspended drivers license. Further, he had nominal dexterity in both his right and left hands. In denying permanent total benefits, the judge said that to adjudicate him permanently and totally disabled considering these facts would be a disservice and not in keeping with the Act's intent. On appeal the First District Court of Appeal disagreed. The court held that even when medical evidence does not support a finding of permanent total disability status, the injured worker can still meet the burden of proof through evidence of an exhaustive, but unavailing job search. The court remanded the case to the judge of compensation claims to make specific findings about Boles' job search and presumably if it was adequate, to award permanent total disability benefits on this alone [*see* Boles v. West Orange Paint & Body, 667 So. 2d 951, 954–955 (Fla. 1st DCA 1996)].

> **NOTE:** Permanent total disability awards based on failed job searches do not appear to apply under the 1994 amendments.

[ii] Evidence Required

The existence and degree of permanent impairment must be based upon medically or scientifically demonstrable findings, and not on the injured worker's complaints or the judge's evaluation of those complaints. Further, the judge cannot base an award merely on observing the injured worker [*see* Frank's Fine Meats v. Sherman, 443 So. 2d 1055, 1056 (Fla. 1st DCA 1984)].

Permanent total disability implies that the injury destroyed the employee's earning power. Look for injuries that are totally disabling such that the disability is so severe that the employee cannot provide any valuable service for an employer. Injured workers may still be totally disabled if the services they can do are so limited in quality, dependability, or quantity that a stable market for them does not exist. Remember, permanent total disability does not mean that a worker is absolutely helpless or physically broken and wrecked for all purposes, except merely to live. It is simply an analysis of the injured worker's ability to earn wages.

[iii] Sheltered Employment

Sheltered employment is work unavailable in the open labor market that an employer, responsible for paying compensation benefits, pays an injured worker to perform. The Florida Supreme Court has described sheltered employment "a specially created job, one light of effort and responsibility but laden with rest and comfort (employment plums that do not often dangle from the tree of everyday economics)" [*see* Port Everglades Terminal Co. v. Canty, 120 So. 2d 596, 601 (Fla. 1960); *see also* Southern Bell Telephone & Telegraph Co. v. Bell, 167 So. 2d 844, 846 (Fla. 1964)].

Employment in a regular job, such as a night watchman, may be considered sheltered when the injured worker is allowed to regulate his own hours to accommodate his disability. An argument that the Americans with Disabilities Act (ADA) has eliminated the concept of sheltered employment will not prevail. The ADA does not apply if no accommodation will enable an employee to perform the essential functions of a job. Sheltered employment is neither conclusive proof of a substantial earning capacity nor is it a substitute for paying benefits properly due under the provisions of the Act [*see* Commercial Carrier Corp. v. LaPointe, 723 So. 2d 912, 917-919 (Fla. 1st DCA 1999)].

[c] Job Search Requirement

For accidents occurring through December 31, 1993, injured workers must test their ability to work by doing a sincere, good faith search for work. Two exceptions to this rule apply. First, a judge of compensation claims may waive the job search requirement. The second exception arises when an injured worker is medically or presumptively totally disabled. Remember that the injured workers' duty to conduct a job search does not begin until the carrier or employer advises them of this duty [*see* Lerman v. Broward County Bd. of Com'rs, 555 So. 2d 419, 422–423 (Fla. 1st DCA 1989)]:

> It is well settled that it is the employer/carrier's responsibility to apprise the claimant of his possible entitlement to benefits and his duty to conduct a work search. . . . Therefore, a work search will be excused where:
>
> [1] The employer and carrier fail to inform the claimant of his obligation to perform and to document such search; or
>
> [2] The record demonstrates that claimant neither knew nor should have known that he was medically released to return to work.

The *Lerman* court also held a doctor's communication concerning an injured worker's release to work must be clear and unequivocal. In addition, an injured worker's mental health may serve to excuse the job search requirement.

> **SPECIAL ALERT:** The job search requirement likely does not apply to accidents occurring on or after January 1, 1994, since meeting the definition of catastrophic injury creates eligibility for permanent total disability. It may be necessary, as a practical matter, that injured workers seeking to qualify under the "eligible for social security disability" test conduct a job search as a means to show lack of employability.

[d] 100-Mile Job Search

One significant problem in pre-1994 cases has been in deciding how far from home injured workers must travel in their search for work. The courts have not provided a precise distance, but have been consistent in not requiring injured workers to search outside their home towns. This, of course, resulted in many permanent total disability awards to injured workers living in small isolated towns with few job opportunities. In response to this, the legislature amended the Act. For accidents occurring between July 1, 1990 and December 31, 1993, the Act provides that "the burden shall be upon the employee to establish that he is not able to uninterruptedly to do even light work available within a 100-mile radius of the injured employee's residence" [§ 440.15(1)(b), Fla. Stat. (1991)].

A quick look at a map of Florida will reveal that nearly all of its small towns are within 100 miles of a large metropolitan area. Note there is nothing explicit here to suggest that an injured worker must actually travel up to 100 miles in a search for work. It is unlikely that the legislature intended, or that the courts will hold, that this provision requires travel up to one hundred miles from home to conduct a job search. The intent here is not to create a long-range job search requirement, but rather to change the proof required to show entitlement to permanent total disability benefits. Note that the legal burden of proof is upon the employee.

Do not take the injured worker's "burden of proof" requirement too literally. All an injured worker needs to do to meet this burden is to conduct an appropriate, but unsuccessful job search. The carrier has the burden to show jobs are available that the injured worker could do within 100 miles of home.

Assume a case where an electrician cannot return to that occupation, and cannot be retrained into a field generating preinjury income. These facts do not necessarily mean that the injured worker is permanently and totally disabled. The question is whether the injured worker can do a legitimate, although entry level, job. The injured worker may have gone from a $15 per hour job before the injury to one paying only $6. This will entitle the injured worker to wage loss benefits. Just as surely, however, our former electrician is not permanently and totally disabled.

[e] PTD From Unrelated Condition

To what benefits are injured workers entitled if they become permanently and totally disabled because of an unrelated condition that combines with a compensable impairment? This question is best answered with an example.

George Curtis injured his shoulder at work. He reached maximum medical improvement in July 1985 with a 15-percent impairment rating. Earlier in April of that same year, he suffered the onset of an unrelated heart condition from which he was found permanently and totally disabled. The trial judge denied wage loss benefits to Curtis, finding his heart condition was the true cause of his inability to work. The First District Court of Appeal reversed, stating [*see* Curtis v. Bordo Citrus Products, 566 So. 2d 328, 329–331 (Fla. 1st DCA 1990)]:

> While disability resulting solely from a second, noncompensable cause is not compensable, if on the date of the noncompensable event the claimant is still suffering from the effects of the first, compensable accident, it does not follow that he is entitled to no compensation.

Because Curtis could not do a job search, no means existed to measure his loss of income. But the compensable injury's contribution to Curtis' permanent total disability was measurable. Since Curtis' compensable impairment rating was 15 percent, the court held he should receive 15 percent of permanent total disability benefits. What effect, if any, this case will have on accidents occurring after January 1, 1994, is uncertain.

[f] Job Search Not Required if Medically PTD

The law does not require injured workers to test their employability if medical evidence shows they are permanently and totally disabled. Obviously, with such evidence, the law does not require a job search. Without medical evidence showing inability to work, injured workers must show they engaged in a bona fide but unsuccessful search for work [*see* Romero v. Waterproofing Systems of Miami, 491 So. 2d 600, 603 (Fla. 1st DCA 1986)].

Following is a more recent example. Dorothy Yeager's various doctors testified she had a 35-percent impairment from her shoulder injury. In addition, she had a 20-percent impairment from psychiatric problems, and 60 to 80 percent from an unrelated heart condition. One physician testified that she was unemployable from the heart condition alone. This testimony was sufficient to waive any need to test employability by job searching. In other words, the medical evidence alone supported an award of permanent total disability [*see* Vista Manor Nursing Home v. Yeager, 605 So. 2d 1311, 1313 (Fla. 1st DCA 1992)].

Sometimes, the job search requirement may not apply even when no medical evidence of permanent total disability exists. For example, the *Yeager* court considered the testimony of Yeager and a vocational rehabilitation expert, both of whom stated Yeager could not work. Such testimony is sufficient if taken in context with doctors' testimony on the extent of physical limitations, the seriousness of the injury, the injured worker's age, and lack of transferable skills.

[g] Total MMI Not Always Required

Generally, injured workers must have achieved overall maximum medical improvement before permanent total disability can be awarded. What happens when an injured worker has suffered both a physical and a psychiatric injury? A judge of compensation claims may not award permanent total disability benefits unless the injured worker has reached maximum medical improvement from both conditions.

An exception to this rule occurs, however, when the evidence clearly shows that an injured worker is permanently and totally disabled from the physical injury alone. That such an injured worker has not yet reached psychiatric maximum medical improvement does not preclude an award of permanent total disability benefits [*see* Amfesco Duramil Division v. Guzman, 596 So. 2d 732, 733 (Fla. 1st DCA 1992)].

§ 13.52 Accident Dates Between January 1, 1994 and September 30, 2003

[1] Requirements for Award of PTD Benefits

For accidents occurring on or after January 1, 1994, injured workers seeking permanent total disability benefits must show the following:

1. That maximum medical improvement has been reached;
2. That the injury meets the statutory definition of a catastrophic injury;
3. That the state of total disability is permanent; and
4. That the inability to earn wages is caused by the compensable injury.

Each of these elements is discussed in detail in the subsections below.

[2] Maximum Medical Improvement Requirement

Legislative amendments that took effect on January 1, 1994, Ch. 93-415, at 62, Laws of Florida, have given rise to a narrow but necessary exception to the venerable rule that, when a "claimant is not yet at MMI, . . . the award of any permanent disability benefits . . . [must] be premature" [*see* Anderson & Padgett Sawmill v. Collins, 686 So. 2d 795, 796 (Fla. 1st DCA 1997)]. Ordinarily, injured employees remain ineligible until they attain maximum medical improvement, for an award of permanent total disability benefits under Florida's Workers' Compensation Law (even if entitled on account of an industrial accident to receive social security disability income benefits under Title II or supplemental security income benefits under Title XVI of the federal Social Security Act).

The phrase, "date of maximum medical improvement" means the date after which further recovery from, or lasting improvement to, an injury or disease can no longer reasonably be anticipated, based upon reasonable medical probability [*see* § 13.12, *above*].

Because of amendments effective January 1, 1994, an injured worker is no longer entitled to receive temporary benefits for more than two years [Ch. 93-415, § 20, at 120, 128, Laws of Fla., amending § 440.15(2), (4), Fla. Stat.].

Effective January 1, 1994, § 440.15(3)(a)4., Fla. Stat., not only maintains the requirement (now applicable only when maximum medical improvement occurs more than six weeks before the two-year limit for temporary benefits expires) that any permanent impairment rating be assigned "after the employee has been certified by a doctor as having reached maximum medical improvement," but also requires, in the event maximum medical improvement has not occurred earlier, that any permanent impairment be assigned a rating "6 weeks before the expiration of temporary benefits" [Ch. 93-415, § 20, at 122, Laws of Fla., amending § 440.15(3)(d)4., Fla. Stat.]. The definition of "permanent impairment" in § 440.02(21), Fla. Stat., although amended effective January 1, 1994, still requires a determination of the status quo once maximum medical improvement is reached.

In assigning a permanent impairment rating because temporary benefits must come to an end, a qualified professional has to anticipate the employee's maximum medical improvement and use professional judgment first to decide whether the employee will be permanently impaired once maximum medical improvement has been attained and, if so, then to assign an impairment rating prospectively.

To be eligible for permanent total disability benefits, an employee whose temporary benefits have run out, or are expected to do so imminently, must be able to show not only total disability upon the cessation of temporary benefits but also that total disability will be "existing after the date of maximum medical improvement" [§ 440.02(21), Fla. Stat.].

That the Workers' Compensation Law provides incentives for permanently totally disabled workers to obtain federal disability income benefits does not speak to whether a worker's disability is properly deemed permanent instead of temporary. A permanent impairment must be proven in order to support an award of permanent total disability indemnity benefits in Florida. To establish entitlement to such benefits, the Workers' Compensation Law requires that a claimant prove total disability on account of an impairment "existing after the date of maximum medical improvement" [§ 440.02(21), Fla. Stat.; *see* City of Pensacola Firefighters v. Oswald, 710 So. 2d 95, 100 (Fla. 1st DCA 1998)].

Guide to Claims

[3] The Catastrophic Injury Requirement

[a] The Statutory Requirement

For accidents occurring on or after January 1, 1994, only injured workers with a catastrophic injury as defined by § 440.02(34), Fla. Stat. are eligible for permanent total disability benefits. This is a substantive amendment and applies only to accidents occurring on or after January 1, 1994 [*see* Merritt Manor Nursing Home v. Caldwell, 667 So. 2d 265 (Fla. 1st DCA 1995)].

If a worker's injuries meet this definition, a state of eligibility exists but not necessarily entitlement to benefits. Despite having a defined, catastrophic injury the worker still has the burden to prove entitlement to PTD benefits. A person claiming PTD benefits must prove every element of the claim, including the most basic element of a causal connection between the compensable injury and inability to earn wages. For example, even receiving Social Security Disability benefits does not prove permanent total disability. In such cases, the injured worker must still prove a connection between the award of those federal benefits and the compensable injury [*see* Bob Wilson Dodge v. Mohammed, 692 So. 2d 287, 288 (Fla. 1st DCA 1997); *see* [4], *below*]. The Act provides as follows [§ 440.15(1)(b), Fla. Stat. (7/1/97)]:

> Only a catastrophic injury as defined in [§ 440.02, Fla. Stat.] shall, in the absence of conclusive proof of a substantial earning capacity, constitute permanent total disability. Only [injured workers] with catastrophic injuries are eligible for permanent total benefits. In no other case may permanent total disability be awarded.

In June 2000, however, the court adopted a different interpretation of § 440.15(1)(b), Fla. Stat. Here, the court held that if a claimant has a catastrophic injury as defined by § 440.02(34)(b), Fla. Stat., the claimant is presumed to be permanently and totally disabled from the date of the accident unless the carrier can produce conclusive proof of a substantial earning capacity [*see* Temporary Labor Source v. E.H., 765 So. 2d 757, 760 (Fla. 1st DCA 2000), *rev. denied,* 786 So. 2d 1189 (Fla. 2001)]. This case is in clear conflict with *Bob Wilson Dodge,* discussed above. As noted, that case stands for the proposition that having an injury meeting the statutory definition of a catastrophic injury merely creates eligibility, but not entitlement to permanent total disability. The *Temporary Labor Source* case, on the other hand, holds that a statutory catastrophic injury creates a presumption of PTD status if there is no conclusive evidence showing that the claimant has a substantial earning capacity. It appears that *Temporary Labor Source* is a misinterpretation of § 440.15(1)(b), Fla. Stat. Which of the two views the court ultimately adopts, however, remains to be seen.

Also, note that the opinion refers to § 440.02(34)(b), Fla. Stat. which describes the amputation of an extremity. Whether the court considers all of the other listed conditions to create a presumption of PTD status is not clear.

Thus, if employees' injuries do not meet the statutory definition, they are not, under any circumstances, entitled to permanent total disability benefits. Meeting the definition, however, may not be as difficult as the legislature seems to have intended [*see* [b], *below*].

[b] Catastrophic Injury Defined

Catastrophic injury is a permanent impairment constituted by [§ 440.02(34), Fla. Stat. (7/1/97)]:

(a) Spinal cord injury involving severe paralysis of an arm, a leg or the trunk.

(b) Amputation of an arm, a hand, a foot, or a leg involving the effective loss of use of that appendage.

(c) Severe brain or closed-head injury as evidenced by:

1. Severe sensory or motor disturbance.
2. Severe communication disturbance.
3. Severe complex integrated disturbances of cerebral function.
4. Severe episodic neurological disorders.
5. Other severe brain and closed-head injury conditions at least as severe in nature as provided in subparagraphs one to four.

(d) Second-degree or third-degree burns of 25 percent or more of the total body surface or third-degree burns of 5 percent or more to the face and hands.

(e) Total or industrial blindness.

(f) Any other injury that would otherwise qualify under this chapter of a nature and severity that would qualify an employee to receive disability income benefits under Title II or supplemental security income benefits under Title XVI of the federal Social Security Act *as the Social Security Act existed on July 1, 1992,* without regard to any time limitation provided under that Act. (Emphasis added)

Except category (f), all of the required injuries—although sometimes ambiguous—are at least demonstrable by objective medical findings.

Category (a), spinal cord injury, appears to refer to such injuries as partial or complete paraplegia and quadriplegia because the legislature used the term "spinal cord." Conversely, this language appears to exclude paralysis due to nervous system damage, absent injury to the spinal cord.

Category (b), amputation, seems clear. Using the term "effective loss of use" should include even a partial amputation if it results in the effective loss of use of the extremity for work purposes.

Category (c), head and brain injury, is unfortunately vague. Most of the subcategories deal with thought processes, speech, and behavioral problems. The key word in each is the term "severe;" however, the statute does not define this term. Consistent application would have been helped considerably if the legislature had equated "severe" with an impairment class used by the *Florida Impairment Rating Guide.* For example, the *Guide* ranks loss of thinking ability into five classes. Class three is moderate to severe, class four is moderately severe, and class five is severe. Does only a class five count or is class three enough to show permanent impairment? The *Guide* defines class three, moderately severe, as a deficit rendering the patient incapable of drawing rational conclusions from single statements. That sounds severe, but is it severe enough? One could make an argument that "severe" means only a class five deficit according to the *Guide;* however, class three should be sufficient to show a severe injury.

Category (d), burns, is likely the only unambiguous condition in the list, but it is peculiar. Few would argue that second-degree burns covering 25 percent of a person's body is a severe injury. We must wonder, however, about the wisdom of creating eligibility for permanent total disability where the total injury is only 5 percent of a person's hands. Most medical experts consider burns over less then 15 percent of the entire body as small in terms of severity.

Category (e), industrial blindness, is ambiguous in part. The *Florida Impairment Rating Guide* considers blindness of 85 percent or more as total blindness. Unfortunately, the statute does not define the term "industrial blindness." Although determinations of industrial blindness are subjective, blindness sufficient to preclude work should be enough to qualify as a severe injury.

[c] Award or Denial of SSD Benefits Alone Is Not Enough

The last category, (f), is also an illusive standard. Note that the Act does not require the injured worker to be personally eligible for Social Security Disability benefits. Only the worker's injury must qualify for such benefits. For example, a worker over age 65 is not eligible for Social Security Disability benefits and the administration would deny an application for benefits on this basis alone. If the worker's injury would otherwise qualify for such benefits, however, the worker is eligible for permanent total disability benefits [*see* Harris Corp. v. Gary, 695 So. 2d 800, 801–802 (Fla 1st DCA 1997)].

Receiving Social Security Disability benefits does not prove permanent total disability. In such cases, the injured worker must still prove a connection between the award of those federal benefits and the compensable injury [*see* Bob Wilson Dodge v. Mohammed, 692 So. 2d 287, 288 (Fla. 1st DCA 1997) The Act does not require that an injured worker actually receive social security disability benefits. Instead, it provides only that, in addition to the specifically described injuries and conditions, a catastrophic injury consists of any other injury that would otherwise qualify the employee to receive social security disability benefits. Obtaining or being denied social security disability benefits is not, itself, the basis for an award of permanent total disability benefits. In the end, it is the judge of compensation claims who must evaluate a claimant's condition and award or deny permanent total disability benefits [*see* Alachua County Adult Detention Center v. Alford, 727 So. 2d 388, 391 (Fla. 1st DCA 1999)], To determine if an injured worker is receiving Social Security Disability benefits requires only a confirmation of this fact with the Social Security Administration. Remember that meeting any of the above conditions, including receiving Social Security Disability benefits, is not proof of permanent total disability, although it is a good place to begin. In [3], *below,* we will review the requirements for an award of SSD benefits based on a qualifying injury and disability.

Likewise, having been denied social security disability benefits does not prove that the claimant is *not* permanently and totally disabled. The court found no requirement within Chapter 440 to indicate that a JCC is bound by the denial of a claim for SSD benefits.

Indeed, the court opined that it be unjust to view federal disability determinations as carrying binding precedential authority in a proceeding under Chapter 440 [*see* Florida Distillers v. Rudd, 751 So. 2d 754 (Fla. 1st DCA 2000)].

[4] Social Security Disability Requirement

[a] Sequential Evaluation, In General

Guide to Claims

To qualify for Social Security Disability benefits, claimants must show that they are unable to engage in any substantial gainful activity because of any medically determinable physical or mental impairment. Additionally, such claimants must show that the disability has lasted, or can be expected to last, for not less than 12 months or is expected to result in death [*see* 42 U.S.C.S. §§ 423(d), 1382c(a)(3)].

To decide if a claimant is eligible for benefits, the SSA must follow a five-step sequential evaluation process. The workers' compensation adjuster, attorney, or judge should follow the same evaluation process to decide if the worker has an *injury* that qualifies for SSD benefits.

Step 1. Determine whether the claimant is working and whether such work is considered substantial gainful activity. If the answer is yes, the claimant does not qualify for SSD benefits and is therefore ineligible for PTD benefits. If the answer is no, proceed to Step 2.

Step 2. Determine whether the claimant suffers from a severe impairment. If the answer is no, the claimant does not qualify for SSD benefits and is therefore ineligible for PTD benefits. If the answer is yes, proceed to Step 3.

Step 3. Determine whether any of the claimant's impairments meet or equal an impairment listed in 20 C.F.R. Part 404, Subpart P, Appendix 1. If the answer is no, the claimant does not qualify for SSD benefits and is therefore ineligible for PTD benefits. If the answer is yes, proceed to Step 4.

Step 4. Determine whether the claimant's impairment prevents him or her from performing his or her past relevant work. If the answer is no, the claimant does not qualify for SSD benefits and is therefore ineligible for PTD benefits. If the answer is yes, proceed to Step 5.

Step 5. Determine whether the impairment prevents the claimant from performing any other type of work. If the answer is no, the claimant does not qualify for SSD benefits and is therefore ineligible for PTD benefits. If the answer is yes, the claimant's injury qualifies for SSD benefits and meets the catastrophic injury requirement to qualify for PTD benefits.

The subsections in [b], *below,* examine each of the five steps in detail.

The primary guide for evaluating physical disability is Social Security Practice Guide, published by Matthew Bender & Company, Inc. This guidebook covers the array of social security disability laws, including the statutory definition of disability, which is [*see* Social Security Practice Guide, ch. 9, Definition of Disability, § 9.02[1] (Matthew Bender), citing 42 U.S.C.S. § 423(d)(1)(A) (1976)]:

> . . . [T]he inability to engage in *any* substantial gainful activity by reason of any medically determinable physical or mental impairment which can be expected to result in death or *has lasted or can be expected to last for a continuous period of not less than 12 months.* (Emphasis added)

SPECIAL ALERT: The applicable law is the Social Security Act of *1992*. This is important because future revision of the federal law will not affect workers' compensation unless the Florida Legislature amends § 440.02(34)(f), Fla. Stat.

[b] Five-Step Sequential Evaluation

[i] Step 1: Substantial Gainful Activity

If injured workers can engage in substantial gainful activity, they are not considered disabled. The regulations define substantial gainful activity as any work that involves doing significant and productive physical or mental duties for pay or profit. Work can be "substantial" even if the injured worker does it part-time and even if the injured worker does less, has less responsibility, or gets paid less than before [20 C.F.R. § 404.1572].

Even sheltered employment may be sufficient to show that the claimant has the necessary skills and ability to engage in substantial gainful activity. Likewise, self-employment in a supervisory, managerial, advisory, or other significant personal service may show that the claimant can perform substantial gainful activity [20 C.F.R. § 404.1573].

In determining whether a claimant is engaged in substantial gainful activity the following factors should be considered:

1. The time spent doing the work
2. The quality of the worker's performance
3. Whether the worker is self-employed. Note: Self-employment earnings are not the test. The test is based on the relationship between the claimant's activities and their value to the business in terms of actual income.
4. The need for special conditions or supervision
5. The worker's use of experience, skills, and responsibilities
6. Whether the worker contributes substantially to the business's operation.
7. Whether the claimant reported taxable income. Note: Earnings reported on income tax returns raise a rebuttable presumption that the claimant is gainfully employed.
8. Whether the claimant's earnings exceed the amounts specified in 20 C.F.R. § 404.1574. Average monthly earnings of more than $500 constitute evidence that the claimant has engaged in substantial gainful activity [*see* Johnson v. Sullivan, 929 F.2d 596, 597–598 (11th Cir. 1991)].

Note, however, that engaging in substantial gainful employment bars entitlement to benefits for only the periods of employment. Put another way, a claimant can pass into and out of eligibility by stopping work or beginning work [*see*Powell on behalf of Powell v. Heckler, 773 F.2d 1572, 1576 (11th Cir. 1985)].

Finally, remember that a disabled claimant is entitled to a nine-month trial work period. During this time, the claimant can engage in substantial gainful activity and still receive SSD benefits. If such a claimant is still working at the end of this trial period, benefits cease. If the claimant stops working, benefits will be reinstated without the need to reapply [*see* 20 C.F.R. § 404.1592]. Once the entitlement period expires, the claimant must file a new application to receive benefits [*see* Johnson v. Sullivan, 929 F.2d 596, 597–599 (11th Cir. 1991)].

[ii] Step 2: Severe Impairment

If the claimant is not engaged in substantial gainful employment, the next step is to determine if he or she has a severe impairment. Generally, if the claimant's impairment is listed in 20 C.F.R. Part 404, Subpart P, Appendix 1, or is equivalent to a listed impairment, the claimant will be considered disabled [*see* [iii], *below*]. If so, the next step is to determine the claimant's residual functional capacity and to decide if it permits return to former work or, if not, to any other work available in the national economy. The Code of Federal Regulations (CFR) requires evidence of a severe impairment. A severe impairment is one that significantly limits a person's ability to do basic work activities [20 C.F.R. § 416.920(c)]. Basic work activities include the following [20 C.F.R. § 416.921(b)]:

1. Physical functions such as standing, sitting, lifting, pushing, pulling, reaching, carrying, or handling;
2. Capacities for seeing, hearing, and speaking;
3. Understanding, carrying out and remembering simple instructions;
4. Using judgment;
5. Responding appropriately to supervision, co-workers and usual work situations; and
6. Dealing with changes in a routine work setting.

Though not clear, the existence of any one of these six factors should be sufficient to establish a "severe impairment."

If injured workers cannot perform their pre-injury work, the CFR, like Florida's Workers' Compensation Law, will consider the injured worker's residual functional capacity. It will also consider vocational factors such as age, education, and work experience to decide if the injured worker can perform other work. By "other work" the regulations mean jobs that exist in significant numbers in the national economy.

When examining the severity of a medically proven disability, measure it in terms of its effect on the claimant's ability to work. Using the severity test as a means to deny benefits to persons unable to work is a violation of the Social Security Act [*see* McCruter v. Bowen, 791 F.2d 1544, 1547 (11th Cir. 1988)]. On the other hand, an impairment is not severe if it is only a slight abnormality which does not interfere with the individual's ability to work, irrespective of age, education, or other work experience. Even a major injury may not qualify as a severe impairment if it does not preclude reemployment. For example, a computer operator may have had both legs amputated as the result of an accident, but could still operate the computer. If such a person can still perform his job, he or she cannot be considered as disabled [*see* Brady v. Heckler, 724 F.2d 914, 920 (11th Cir. 1984)].

Conversely, a far less severe injury may still render the victim disabled. If the claimant can establish the inability to perform work activities, he or she has a severe impairment [*see* Flynn v. Heckler, 768 F.2d 1273, 1275 (11th Cir. 1985)].

[iii] Step 3: Listed Impairment

If the claimant is not working and has been found to have a severe impairment, the third step is to determine if the impairment meets or equals a listed impairment [*see* 20 C.F.R. Part 404, Subpart P, Appendix 1]. If so, the claimant is considered to have an impairment severe enough to prevent engaging in gainful activity. Most of the listed impairments are permanent or are expected to result in death. If not, a specific statement of duration is made. For all others, the claimant must produce evidence that the impairment has or will last for a continuous period of at least 12 months. In addition to producing evidence of a listed diagnoses, a claimant must also show that the impairment meets the listed conditions [*see* 20 C.F.R. § 404.1525].

[iv] Step 4: Return to Past Relevant Work

The fourth step is to determine if the claimant can return to past relevant work despite having a severe impairment. This step assumes, of course, that a disability determination cannot be made on the medical evidence alone. Past relevant work refers to jobs held during the 15-year period prior to the disability. Thus, if a claimant can still do the kind of work he or she has done in the past, he or she will not be considered disabled. If the claimant cannot perform his or her past work, the burden shifts to the SSA to prove that other work exists in the national economy which the claimant can do [*see* Francis v. Heckler, 749 F.2d 1562, 1564 (11th Cir. 1985)]. Obviously this determination requires investigation into all of the jobs that the claimant has held during the past 15 years, including the physical requirements of those jobs. The 15-year guide is intended to insure that remote work experience is not, inappropriately, currently applied.

[v] Step 5: Return to Other Work

If the claimant can show the inability to perform past relevant work, the burden shifts to the SSA to prove that the claimant is capable of engaging in other kinds of substantial gainful employment. In a workers' compensation setting, this burden would shift to the employer/carrier. This determination is made by considering the claimant's age, education, and work experience. Additionally, there must be evidence that such jobs exist in significant numbers in the national economy rather than the location of the claimant's residence [*see* Allen v. Bowen, 816 F.2d 600, 602 (11th Cir. 1987)].

If the evidence shows that claimant can perform unlimited types of work, the final step is to apply the Medical Vocational Guidelines, commonly called the "grids" to show that the claimant can perform other work that exists in the national economy. This final step is discussed next in [c], *below*.

[c] Medical-Vocational Guidelines: The Grids

[i] When the Grids Apply

If a claimant's vocational ability cannot be determined based on an evaluation of medical considerations alone, the final step is an analysis based on the Medical-Vocational Guidelines, better know as the Grids. This is, essentially, an analysis based on vocational factors such as the claimant's age, education, and work experience in combination with the claimant's residual functional capacity. The latter is viewed in terms of light, medium, heavy, or very heavy work. Use of the Grids assumes that the claimant has a medically demonstrable impairment, and that the evidence shows the claimant cannot perform relevant past work. When the findings made with regard to the claimant's vocational factors and residual functional capacity coincide with all of the criteria of a particular rule, the rule directs a conclusion as to whether the individual is or is not disabled. Each of the factors necessary to use the Grids properly are discussed in [ii], *below*.

[ii] Using the Grids

[A] Age Factor

The older injured workers are, the more likely the regulations will conclude they are unemployable. The regulations do not, however, consider age a factor if a person is less than 50 years of age.

Individuals between 50 and 54 years are considered as "approaching advanced age." Individuals in this age group who have a severe impairment and limited work experience are considered to have an impairment that seriously affects their ability to adjust to enough jobs in the national economy.

The CFR considers people 55 or older as having reached "advanced age." It is at this point that the regulations consider age a major factor. People in this age group with severe impairments, who cannot do medium work and have no transferable skills are considered disabled. People near retirement age, 60 to 64, are considered disabled based only on the existence of a severe impairment.

People 60 years of age or greater who meet the definition of severe impairment are presumed unable to do even sedentary or light work. The only exception is if the injured worker possess "highly marketable" skills [20 C.F.R. § 416.963].

Claimants can rebut the age findings by producing evidence that their ability to adapt to other work is less than the level established by the Grids for people of the claimant's age [*see* Reeves v. Heckler, 734 F.2d 519, 525–526 (11th Cir. 1984)].

SPECIAL ALERT: The Grids are not appropriate if the claimant cannot perform a full range of work at a given functional level on a sustained basis [*see* Allen v. Sullivan, 880 F.2d 1200, 1202 (11th Cir. 1989)]. Non-exertional impairments which significantly limit basic work activities also render the Grids inapplicable [*see*

Guide to Claims

Swindle v. Sullivan, 914 F.2d 222, 226 (11th Cir. 1990)]. An exertional limitation is an impairment-caused restriction that affects the capability to perform an exertional activity such as sitting, standing, and walking. A non-exertional limitation is an impairment-caused limitation of function that directly affects the ability to perform work activities other than the primary strength activities. Examples of non-exertional impairments include mental impairments, dizziness, weakness, visual impairments, hypertension, obesity, and atherosclerotic heart disease.

[B] Education Factor

The lack of formal schooling does not automatically mean the SSA will consider a person uneducated. A person's work experience and responsibilities will be considered. The reverse is also true. If a person finished formal education many years ago and has not used it in work activities since then, such education may be considered no longer useful or meaningful. An individual's ability to communicate in English is another important factor.

If a person has a 12th grade education, the CFR considers that person to be able to do all required work in semiskilled and skilled jobs. Those who have completed the 7th grade through the 11th grade are considered to have a limited education and to have the skills necessary to do more complex jobs in semiskilled or skilled jobs. Those who did not progress beyond the 6th grade are considered to have only a marginal education and able to do only simple, unskilled jobs. Individuals with no formal schooling who cannot read or write are considered illiterate and able to do only menial, unskilled jobs.

Despite the level of formal education, if a person cannot read or write in English, the CFR considers the person to have a significant educational deficit. Even if the injured worker has little or no formal education, the SSA will consider the educational value of work experience [20 C.F.R. § 416.964].

[C] Job Classification

To decide if jobs exist in the national economy, the regulations classify jobs into five categories [20 C.F.R. § 416.967]:

1. Sedentary Work, involves lifting no more than 10 pounds and occasionally carrying light objects, files, or small tools. Such jobs involve a certain amount of standing and walking.
2. Light Work, involves lifting no more than 20 pounds with frequent lifting or carrying objects up to 10 pounds. To be capable of this kind of work a person must be able to walk or stand for fairly long periods and do functions like pulling and pushing arm or leg controls.
3. Medium Work, involves lifting up to 50 pounds and carrying objects up to 20 pounds.
4. Heavy Work, involves lifting up to 100 pounds with frequent carrying of objects of up to 50 pounds.
5. Very Heavy Work, involves lifting objects weighing more than 100 pounds with

frequent carrying of objects weighing more than 50 pounds.

[D] Substantial Work Activity

The critical factor, after considering those discussed in [A]–[C], *above,* is whether the injured worker can do substantial work activity. The test is whether work exists in the national economy that the injured worker can do. That such work does not exist in the immediate area of the injured worker's home is not relevant. That no job openings exist or that the injured worker would not have been hired if they did exist is also not relevant. The only relevant test is whether such jobs exist in significant numbers in the national economy. The reason an injured worker remains unemployed is not relevant [20 C.F.R. § 416.966].

How does the SSA find out if jobs exist that the injured worker can do? This same rule provides that the SSA take administrative notice of reliable job information available from various government or other publications. These include the *Dictionary of Occupational Titles,* (U.S. Department of Labor); *Selected Characteristics of Occupations* (SCO); *County Business Patterns and Census Reports,* (Bureau of the Census); *Occupational Analysis,* (Social Security Administration); and *Occupational Outlook Handbook,* (Bureau of Labor Statistics)]. The primary reference is the *Dictionary of Occupational Titles,* which classifies jobs by their physical and vocational requirements. The other references help decide whether such jobs exist in significant numbers.

As noted in [3], *above,* injured workers receiving Social Security Disability benefits must still prove a causal connection between the compensable injury and receiving federal disability benefits. As the discussion above shows, receiving SSD benefits might be based on issues completely unrelated to the compensable injury.

Carriers have been granted a statutory tool that will help in deciding if an injured worker is permanently and totally disabled. That tool is the reemployment assessment [*see* [5], *below*].

[5] Reemployment Assessment

[a] Defined

Florida law provides that a judge of compensation claims may not adjudicate a claimant as permanently and totally disabled "until or unless the carrier is given the opportunity to provide a reemployment assessment" [§ 440.491(9), Fla. Stat. (1/1/94)].

A reemployment assessment means as follows [§ 440.491(1)(d), Fla. Stat. (1/1/94)]:

> A written assessment performed by a qualified rehabilitation provider which provides a comprehensive review of the medical diagnosis, treatment, and prognosis; includes conferences with the employer, physician, and claimant; and recommends a cost-effective physical and vocational rehabilitation plan to assist the employee in returning to suitable gainful employment.

A qualified rehabilitation provider must meet the requirements contained in the Department of Education rules [Fla. Admin. Code R. 6A-22.002 (2/2/2005)]. The rules now allow a registered nurse who is also a Certified Case Manager (CCM) to be qualified

Guide to Claims

as a rehabilitation provider [Fla. Admin. Code R. 6A-22.002 (5/5/2004)]. That such an assessment will produce conclusive evidence about employability seems unlikely. It is the judge of compensation claims, however, who will decide what is conclusive evidence.

[a.1] Requirements for Reemployment Assessments

A request for screening by the Department of Education must be made on form DWC-23, and the injured employee *must* sign the form [*see* Fla. Admin. Code. R. 6A-22.005 (5/5/2004)].

When submitting a case to the Department of Education for a reemployment assessment, the carrier must provide the following information [*see* Fla. Admin. Code R. 6A-22.0031 (5/5/2004)]:

From the injured employee:

1. Discussion of the injured employee's understanding of the injury, treatment, and prognosis.
2. Description of the injured employee's job duties, including physical demands.
3. Discussion about accommodations that might allow the injured employee to return to work.
4. The injured employee's work history.
5. Factors that would impede the injured employee's ability to work.
6. Results of any vocational, interest, academic, psychological, or other testing if conducted with the injured employee.

From the employer:

1. Discussion of the injured employee's job at the time of injury, including a job description with the essential functions and physical demands of the job.
2. Discussion about the ability to return the injured employee to work in the same job, modified job, or different job.
3. Discussion of possible accommodations that could allow the injured employee to return to work in the same job, modified job, or different job.

From the health care provider:

1. Discussion of the injured employee's diagnosis and prognosis.
2. Discussion of factors that could enhance or impede the healing process.
3. Anticipated release to return to work date and anticipated physical limitations.
4. Anticipated maximum medical improvement date and anticipated permanent physical limitations.

Note that the Department will not provide any reemployment services, including vocational evaluation, unless the employee provides identity documentation and employment eligibility. This should be done using the Immigration and Naturalization Service's

Employment Eligibility Verification Form, I-9 [*see* Fla. Admin. Code. R. 6A-22.006(5) (5/5/2004)].

Additionally, the Department will not provide any vocational services if any of the following conditions exists [*see* Fla. Admin. Code. R. 6A-22.006(7) (5/5/2004)]:

1. The carrier is contesting a claim for permanent total disability, and a judge of compensation claims has not yet adjudicated the issue.
2. The employee's medical condition is unresolved or unstable.
3. The employee refuses to accept reemployment services.
4. The employee has returned to gainful employment as a result of placement services.
5. The employee has no documented permanent physical restrictions related to the injury.
6. The employee has transferable skills that would allow a return to work.
7. The employer terminated the employment for good cause unrelated to the injury.
8. The employee terminated suitable employment for reasons unrelated to the injury.

[b] Annual Vocational Evaluation and Testing

The Act gives the carrier the right to conduct vocational testing. Carriers may do this testing even after they begin paying permanent total benefits. The carrier must give the injured worker at least 10 days written notice of the date, time, and place of the evaluation. Further, the notice letter must explain to injured workers what procedures they will be going through and how long the procedures will take. If the injured worker is represented, the carrier must give the attorney the same information at least seven days before the appointment date [§ 440.15(1)(e), Fla. Stat. (1/1/94)].

Note, however, that this section gives the carrier the right to conduct vocational evaluation or testing in accordance with § 440.491, Fla. Stat. Therefore, it is § 440.491, Fla. Stat. that controls the manner of conducting reemployment assessments and vocational evaluations. Citing the FLORIDA WORKERS' COMPENSATION HANDBOOK, the court held that under that section only the Division of Workers' Compensation has the authority to schedule a vocational evaluation. Before an employer or carrier can file a motion compel a vocational evaluation, it must establish the following:

1. That the claimant has been referred to the Division for a vocational evaluation;
2. That the Division had recommended a vocational evaluation; and
3. That the claimant failed or refused to appear for the evaluation.

The court concluded that § 440.15(1)(e)1, Fla. Stat. was written only to ensure that vocational evaluations and testing applied to PTD claimants as well as to claimants suffering temporary total disability, temporary partial disability, or wage loss. Therefore, the employer/carrier's right under this section is limited to referring the claimant to the

Division for testing and to filing a motion to compel attendance if the Division recommends an evaluation, but the claimant fails or refuses to appear [*see* Eckert v. Publix Supermarkets, Inc., 783 So. 2d 1187 (Fla. 1st DCA 2001)].

With the apparent intent to overrule case law, the Legislature amended this section effective October 1, 2003, to provide that the carrier has the right to conduct such annual testing by a rehabilitation provider of the carrier's choice. The amendment further provides that the employer/carrier is responsible for the costs of such testing and evaluations. Lastly, the amendment repeals the requirement that vocational testing be done pursuant to § 440.491, Fla. Stat. Since it was the reference to § 440.491, Fla. Stat. that led to the court's decision in *Eckert*, it appears the court's holding has been effectively overruled.

Note that the court has previously held that the original version of § 440.15(1)(e), Fla. Stat. was a procedural amendment that applied to all accident dates. Therefore, this amendment is logically also procedural and applies to all accident dates.

Citing the Florida Workers' Compensation Handbook, 2005 Edition (LexisNexis Matthew Bender), the court concurred with the above and noted that the legislature amended § 440.15(1)(e)1, Fla. Stat., in 2003 to delete the phrase "pursuant to § 440.491," which the court in *Eckert* had specifically relied on in concluding that only the Division had the authority to schedule a vocational evaluation of a particular claimant [*see* ch. 2003-412, § 18, at 3918, Laws of Fla.].

The court found, moreover, that the legislature also specifically amended the statute to now provide the employer/carrier with the "right to conduct vocational evaluations or testing by the employer's or carrier's chosen rehabilitation advisor or provider" [§ 440.15(1)(e)1, Fla. Stat.]. The court held that the 2003 changes, like the changes that enacted the statutory framework at issue in *Eckert*, were procedural, not substantive, changes in the law, making them applicable in cases involving dates of accident before the effective date of the amendments, October 1, 2003 [*see* Douglas v. Fla. Power & Light, Inc., 2006 Fla. App. LEXIS 2207 (Fla. 1st DCA 2006)].

SPECIAL ALERT: The First District Court of Appeal held that the vocational testing provisions of § 440.15(1)(e), Fla. Stat., are a procedural amendment that applies to all accident dates. The court reasoned that the amendment does not create any new benefit or obligation. Instead, the amendment merely provides an investigatory tool for deciding the injured worker's status and in helping the worker to return to full employment. The section does not create any new burden for the employer or carrier because these procedures are solely at the carrier's option. Therefore, § 440.15(1)(e), Fla. Stat. is a procedural change [*see* Barnett Bank of Volusia County v. Pelle, 684 So. 2d 311, 312 (Fla. 1st DCA 1996)].

SPECIAL ALERT: Previously, the statute provided that, if the injured worker fails to appear for testing, the carrier may petition the JCC to authorize suspension of benefits until the injured worker does comply. Carriers may not suspend benefits administratively. To suspend benefits under this provision, carriers must first obtain an order from a JCC.

The amendment to § 440.15(1)(e), Fla. Stat., (10/1/2003) now provides that: "The employer or carrier may withhold payment of benefits for permanent total disability or supplements for any period during which the employee willfully fails or refuses to appear without good cause for the scheduled vocational evaluation or testing."

[6] Social Security Disability Benefits

[a] The Rule

The Act requires that all injured workers receiving permanent total disability benefits must apply for or cooperate with the carrier in applying for, Social Security Disability benefits. The statute provides as follows [§ 440.15(1)(f)(2), Fla. Stat. (1/1/94)]:

> The employer or carrier is not required to make any payment of benefits for permanent total disability for any period during which the employee willfully fails or refuses to report upon request by the employer or carrier in the manner prescribed by such rules or if any employee who is receiving permanent total disability benefits refuses to apply for or cooperate with the employer or carrier in applying for social security benefits.

The Division, however, repealed its administrative rules requiring that carriers send written notice to the injured worker when requesting cooperation with them in applying for social security benefits. With the repeal of these rules, employers and carriers are left to their own devices in construing the meaning of this statute.

An affirmative response means that injured workers must either (1) apply for social security disability benefits directly, or (2) advise the carrier in writing that they will cooperate with the carrier.

The phrase "refuses to apply for or cooperate" means nothing more than the carrier must tell the injured worker about the requirement to apply for Social Security benefits and that failure to do so will result in suspension of PTD benefits [*see* Ace Disposal v. Holley, 668 So. 2d 645, 648 (Fla. 1st DCA 1996)].

For a general discussion of coordinating compensation with social security, see LARSON'S WORKERS' COMPENSATION, DESK EDITION, Ch. 157, § 157.03 (Matthew Bender).

[b] Application Process

The application process means the entire process including appeals. The process means the initial application "including any needed hearings or appeals necessary for an ultimate determination by the Social Security Administration of the injured worker's entitlement to social security benefits." This means that if the SSA rejects the initial application, the injured worker must appeal to the next level or the carrier may suspend benefits. A yet unanswered question is who has to pay for any costs associated with this appeal? The rules do not address the question and the courts have not reviewed it. A good guess is that if the carrier insists on an appeal, the carrier must pay for it.

SPECIAL ALERT: The requirement to apply for federal disability benefits is a *procedural* amendment and applies to all accident dates [*see* Ace Disposal v. Holley,

668 So. 2d 645, 646–647 (Fla. 1st DCA 1996)].

[c] Offset

The original social security offset provision became Florida law in 1973 [§ 440.15(10), Fla. Stat. (1973)]. The Florida Supreme Court held this is a procedural amendment. Thus, carriers could take the social security offset on all cases, whatever the date of the accident. Merely shifting the source of payments from predominately state-generated payments to predominately federally-generated payments is procedural and does not affect any vested right that an injured employee has because of his or her disability [*see* American Bankers Ins. Co. v. Little, 393 So. 2d 1063, 1065 (Fla. 1980)].

Because the requirement to apply for social security disability benefits does not change substantive rights or impose a penalty, it is a procedural amendment that applies to all accident dates. If the SSA denies the injured worker's application, no change in workers' compensation benefits occurs. If the injured worker receives Social Security Disability benefits, an offset against workers' compensation is available, but the practical effect is that the combination of the two benefits will be the same or greater than workers' compensation benefits alone [*see* Ace Disposal v. Holley, 668 So. 2d 645, 646–647 (Fla. 1st DCA 1996)].

Remember that this offset calculation applies only to social security disability benefit recipients and not to retirement benefits. (We discuss retirement benefit offset against wage loss in ch. 12, § 12.05[2].) When the injured worker reaches age 62, the Social Security Administration converts disability benefits to retirement benefits. Therefore, the carrier's right to an offset for permanent total disability benefits ends when the injured worker reaches age 62. Also remember that injured workers' entitlement to permanent total supplemental benefits ends at age 62 if they are eligible for social security [*see* ch. 12, § 12.05[b], for the basic data needed to calculate the offset].

For a complete discussion of social security offset, see Social Security Practice Guide, ch. 8, *Social Security and Medicare Offset of Workers' Compensation Benefits*, § 8.02 (Matthew Bender).

§ 13.53 Accident Dates On or After October 1, 2003

[1] General Rule

Beginning with accidents occurring on or after October1, 2003, all of the previous requirements of meeting the statutory definition of catastrophic injury have been repealed, including the requirement of establishing that an injury qualifies for Social Security disability benefits. Now the law provides that permanent total disability benefits are not payable if the claimant is engaged in, or is able to engage in, at least sedentary work. Thus, evidence that a claimant is not able to engage in at least sedentary work constitutes evidence of a state of permanent total disability.

The workers' compensation statutes do not provide a definition of "sedentary work." However, the Code of Federal Regulation is instructive on this issue. The federal regulations define "sedentary work" as follows [*see* 20 C.F.R. § 416.967]:

> Sedentary Work, involves lifting no more than 10 pounds and occasionally carrying light objects, files, or small tools. Such jobs involve a certain amount of standing and walking.

The burden of proof for establishing whether a claimant is able to engage in sedentary work shifts, depending on whether the presumption applies. If the employee is presumptively permanently and totally disabled, the carrier has the burden to prove that the employee is not eligible because he or she is able to engage in at least sedentary work. In all other cases, the claimant has the burden to prove that he or is not able to engage in even sedentary work to be eligible for permanent total disability benefits [§ 440.15(1), Fla. Stat. (10/1/2003)].

[2] Presumptive Permanent Total Disability

If a claimant has suffered any of the injuries listed below, as the result of a compensable accident, he or she is presumed to be permanently and totally disabled. The presumptive conditions are as follows [§ 440.15(1)(b), Fla. Stat. (10/1/2003)]:

1. Spinal cord injury involving severe paralysis of an arm, a leg, or the trunk;
2. Amputation of an arm, a hand, a foot, or a leg involving the effective loss of use of that appendage;
3. Severe brain or closed-head injury as evidenced by:
   a. Severe sensory or motor disturbances;
   b. Severe communication disturbances;
   c. Severe complex integrated disturbances of cerebral function;
   d. Severe episodic neurological disorders; or
   e. Other severe brain and closed-head injury conditions at least as severe in nature as any condition provided in sub-subparagraphs a–d.;
4. Second-degree or third-degree burns of 25 percent or more of the total body surface or third-degree burns of five percent or more to the face and hands; or
5. Total or industrial blindness.

A carrier may overcome the presumption of permanent total disability only by presenting evidence that the claimant is "physically capable of engaging in at least sedentary employment within a 50-mile radius of the employee's residence."

The first requirement to overcome the presumption is evidence of "physical ability" to engage in sedentary work. Does this mean that a person who is *physically* able to engage in such work, but is intellectually incapable of learning how to do it, is not entitled to permanent total disability benefits? Literally interpreted, that appears to be the case. A counter argument might be that a person's mental deficiencies or learning deficits are part of his physical make up and must be considered in determining his physical ability. Until

Guide to Claims

the courts decide this issue, carriers should proceed cautiously.

The second requirement to overcome the presumption is evidence that the claimant is not able to engage in sedentary work "within a 50-mile radius" of his or her residence. There is no statutory requirement that the carrier produce evidence of the existence of jobs that the claimant is physically able to perform. By adding the "50-mile radius" requirement, however, evidence of the existence of such jobs is implied. If there are no such jobs available, how can one prove that the claimant is able to engage in sedentary work within 50 miles of his home? Until the courts rule on this issue, carriers will be wise to develop such evidence if they intend to try overcoming the presumption

[3] Non-Presumptive Permanent Total Disability

A claimant who has not suffered any of the injuries listed in [2], *above*, might still be entitled to permanent total disability benefits, but the burden of proof is the claimant's. To be entitled to permanent total disability benefits, the claimant must show that he or she is not able, because of his or her physical limitations, to engage in at least sedentary work within a 50-mile radius of his or her residence. Presumably, the same problems carriers will have in overcoming the presumption will apply to a claimant when the presumption does not apply.

CHAPTER 14

TEMPORARY PARTIAL AND PERMANENT PARTIAL DISABILITY BENEFITS

Guide to Claims

SYNOPSIS

Guide to Claims

§ 14.01 Temporary Partial Disability

[1] The Rule

Injured workers may be entitled to temporary partial wage loss benefits if they (1) are not totally disabled, (2) have not reached maximum medical improvement, (3) are medically able to do some work but not the pre-injury job, and (4) are earning less than 80 percent of pre injury wages, or (5) have conducted an unsuccessful job search [§ 440.15(4), Fla. Stat. (7/1/97)].

With amendments effective October 1, 2003, the legislature made it clear that temporary partial disability benefits are payable only if the claimant has not reached overall maximum medical improvement.

Additionally, the law provides that temporary partial disability benefits are not payable unless the medical conditions resulting from the compensable accident created restrictions on the claimant's ability to return to work. Put another way, temporary partial disability benefits are not payable, even if the claimant is earning less than 80% of the pre-injury average weekly wage, unless the evidence shows that the reduction in earnings is caused by work restrictions that were in turn caused by the compensable accident [§ 440.15(4)(a), Fla. Stat. (10/1/2003)].

To be entitled to temporary partial disability benefits, a claimant must show a causal connection between his or her injury and a subsequent wage loss. To determine whether an injury and a subsequent wage loss are causally connected, a Judge of Compensation Claims is to consider the totality of the circumstances. The claimant's burden to show causation may be met by proof that encompasses medical evidence or evidence of a good-faith work search. Even when a disabled employee does lose a job for an extraneous reason, a good faith job search may serve as important proof that the employee is unable thereafter to find suitable employment on account of the disability. Coupled with medical restrictions, a good faith job search is not infrequently more than adequate proof of eligibility for temporary disability benefits. Workers' compensation benefits are not precluded merely because some portion of the wage loss is attributable to a reason unrelated to the injury. Even when a claimant is terminated from his or her employment for insubordination, the claimant may still be entitled to benefits if he or she satisfies the burden of demonstrating that the injury contributed to the wage loss after the termination. But, under § 440.15(4)(e), Fla. Stat., as amended by ch. 412, § 8 Laws of Fla. (2003), if the employee is terminated from post injury employment based on the employee's misconduct, temporary partial disability benefits are not payable as provided for in this section. Since wage loss involves a periodic inquiry, a claimant's failure to make the required showing for one period does not preclude wage loss benefits for subsequent periods. Indemnity benefits are not automatically foreclosed when an injured employee loses a job for reasons unrelated to her injury. But, the claimant has the burden to prove that the compensable injury caused continued unemployment. Although no longer statutorily required as a precondition to receiving temporary indemnity benefits, an unsuccessful job search may help provide such proof. Whatever temporary period of unemployment might be attributable solely to unrelated dislocation would logically end upon proof of a prima facie injury connection by continued wage loss after a good faith job search by one whose employment status capacity to earn wages has been altered by a compensable impairment that affects his or her competitive position in the labor market [Arnold v. Florida's Blood Ctrs., Inc., 949 So. 2d 242 (Fla. 1st DCA 2007)].

[2] Defined

Recall that temporary total disability (TTD) means that the injured worker is physically unable to work in any capacity. Maximum medical improvement (MMI) is that point at which injured workers are as well as they are ever going to be. Rarely is a person totally disabled for any kind of work one day, and fully recovered, or at maximum medical improvement, the next day. In virtually every case, a transition period occurs in which the worker is only temporarily, partially disabled. The injured worker cannot yet return to the original work, but can do some work. At this point, the injured worker is no longer eligible to receive temporary total disability benefits. Instead, the injured worker is eligible for temporary partial disability benefits.

For a brief discussion of the permanent partial disability classification, see LARSON'S WORKERS' COMPENSATION, DESK EDITION, Part 9, *Disability and Personal Injury Benefits,* ch. 80 (Matthew Bender).

For a general discussion of disability and personal injury benefits, see LARSON'S WORKERS' COMPENSATION, DESK EDITION, Part 9, *Disability and Personal Injury Benefits* (Matthew Bender).

[3] Maximum Benefits

[a] Accident Dates Through December 31, 1993

With respect to accident dates through December 31, 1993, benefits are payable until maximum medical improvement or for five years (260 weeks), whichever comes first [§ 440.15(4)(c), Fla. Stat. (1991)].

[b] Accident Dates On or After January 1, 1994

With respect to accident dates on or after January 1, 1994, benefits are payable until maximum medical improvement or for two years (104 weeks), whichever comes first [§ 440.15(4)(b), Fla. Stat. (1/1/94)]. This eligibility period is not, however, in addition to the 104 weeks of eligibility for temporary total disability benefits. The maximum period for both benefits combined is 104 weeks [*see* Okeechobee Health Care v. Collins, 726 So. 2d 775, 776 (Fla. 1st DCA 1998)]. Thus, if an injured worker received temporary total benefits for 60 weeks and is then released for light duty work, the maximum eligibility for temporary partial benefits is 44 weeks. § 440.15(4)(b), Fla. Stat. provides:

> Once [an injured worker] reaches the maximum number of weeks, temporary disability benefits cease and the injured worker's permanent impairment must be determined.

Similar language appears in the temporary total disability section. The statute is unclear about how the time applies. The court has held that the time does not apply as a strict calendar calculation under which the 104 weeks begins on the first day of disability and ends exactly 104 weeks later. Instead, the statute establishes the number of weeks of eligibility for payment. Thus, if the injured worker has intermittent periods of disability, only those weeks of total or partial temporary disability apply toward the maximum [§ 440.15(2)(a), Fla. Stat. (7/1/97)].

The administrative rule makes this clearer by describing this time as the maximum number of weeks for which the injured worker may receive benefits [Fla. Admin Code R. 69L-3.0191 (1/10/2005)].

The Court, however, has finally settled the issue. Following a hearing, the JCC ruled that the 104-week limitation period contained in §§ 440.15(2)(a) and (4)(b), Fla. Stat. (1997) is a calendar period that expires 104 weeks following the claimant's date of accident and the first receipt of temporary disability benefits.

The 1st DCA disagreed and reversed, holding that the 104-week limitation period is calculated *cumulatively*. The 104-week period establishes the maximum number of weekly payments a claimant may *receive* [Wright v. City Of Rockledge, 813 So. 2d 283, 284–285 (Fla. 1st DCA 2002)].

For a general discussion of maximum and minimum limits on weekly benefits, see LARSON'S WORKERS' COMPENSATION, DESK EDITION, Ch. 93, § 93.04 (Matthew Bender).

[4] Entitlement

[a] Accident Dates Through December 31, 1993

As discussed in Ch. 13, *Temporary Total and Permanent Total Disability,* temporary total disability benefits are automatic, and the injured worker need do nothing to trigger payment. To receive temporary partial disability benefits, however, the burden of proof (technically) is on injured workers. They must show that any wage loss claimed results from a change in employment status caused by the compensable injury. In addition, the injured worker must make a specific request for benefits every two weeks by sending to the carrier a Request for Wage Loss/Temporary Disability Benefits, form DWC-3.

Lastly, the injured worker must show that accident-related disability caused the lack of a job or reduced earnings. The lack of a job or reduced earnings cannot be because of economic conditions, the unavailability of employment, or personal misconduct [§ 440.15(4)(b), Fla. Stat. (1990); *see* § 14.08].

[b] Accident Dates From January 1, 1994, Through September 30, 2003

SPECIAL ALERT: Two significant differences exist for 1994 and later accident dates. First, injured workers need do nothing to trigger payment. Once the carrier is aware the doctor released the injured worker in a partial disability status (return to work light duty), the carrier must calculate the benefits due and begin payments. Second, injured workers are under no obligation to conduct a job search or to report job search activity voluntarily undertaken. An injured worker's only obligation is to report any wages earned if requested by the carrier. Carriers should continue to calculate benefits under the 80/80 rule as described in § 14.06[3].

[5] Required Entitlement Letter

[a] Accident Dates Through December 31, 1993

Upon notification that the physician has released the injured worker for light duty work, the carrier should suspend temporary total benefits. Upon suspending benefits, the carrier must send to the Division a Notice of Action/Change, form DWC-4. The carrier should send copies to the injured worker, injured worker's attorney, and employer. Simultaneously, the carrier must inform injured workers about their rights and duties regarding entitlement to temporary partial wage loss. Failing to follow this procedure violates Division rules. In addition, injured workers are under no obligation to conduct a job search until the carrier instructs them to do so. The carrier must send this notice directly to the injured worker within five working days after learning the first date of temporary partial disability [Fla. Admin Code R. 4L-3.019(2) (11/11/96)]. The carrier must also give the injured worker at least four copies of form DWC-3, Request for Wage Loss/Temporary Partial Benefits, with the following statement:

> Your treating physician has reported that you may return to limited duty work with some temporary physical restrictions. Your temporary total disability benefits have

been suspended but you may be entitled to additional benefit payments under the Florida Worker's Compensation Law.

If you lose wages, you must complete and send a REQUEST FOR WAGE LOSS/TEMPORARY PARTIAL BENEFITS form (DWC-3) to us within 14 days after the end of any two week period for which a loss of wages is claimed. If you fail to send the completed form within that 14-day period, you may be ineligible for temporary partial wage loss benefits during that period.

In addition, to be eligible for temporary partial wage loss benefits, you must demonstrate that you have made a valid effort to obtain suitable gainful employment and that your loss of wages is due to your work-related physical restriction and NOT due to economic conditions, the unavailability of jobs, your unemployment due to misconduct or your failure to accept employment within your capabilities.

To show that you have made a genuine effort to obtain employment, list the dates, names, addresses, type of work, person contacted and the telephone number of the places of employment that you have contacted on the reverse side of the REQUEST FOR WAGE LOSS/TEMPORARY PARTIAL BENEFITS form. You should also list the dates you make contact with the Florida Job Service Office and any other public or private employment agency.

Please note that the Florida Workers' Compensation Law allows us to evaluate your efforts to obtain gainful employment beginning with the thirteenth week after you have received the first payment of a temporary partial wage loss benefit. If it can be shown that there are actual job openings within your geographical area and which are within your physical and vocational capabilities, the amount of earnings you could have earned at those jobs can be deducted from your benefit payment.

Enclosed are REQUEST FOR WAGE LOSS/TEMPORARY PARTIAL BENEFITS forms for your use. Keep them with your other valuable documents until you either use them or your entitlement to these benefits expires. We are also reporting your status to the Division of Worker's Compensation in Tallahassee.

If you desire further information regarding Wage Loss benefits, you may call the Employee Assistance and Ombudsman Office (EAO) of the Division of Workers' Compensation at any of their local offices, or at 1-800-342-1741.

[b] Accident Dates On or After January 1, 1994

For accidents occurring after January 1, 1994, an injured worker is eligible for temporary partial disability benefits under the following conditions:

1. The doctor has given the injured worker a medical release to return to work;
2. The injured worker is unable to earn at least 80 percent of his or her pre-injury average weekly wage;
3. The injured worker has not reached maximum medical improvement; and
4. The injured worker has not received payment for 104 weeks of temporary total disability, temporary partial disability or any combination of these benefits.

Remember that the injured worker has no duty to look for work or to report any job search activity. Carriers cannot require injured workers to submit documentation of a work search as a prerequisite for payment [Fla. Admin Code R. 4L-3.0191(2), (3) (11/8/94)].

Within five days after learning that the doctor has released the employee for work, the carrier must send the following notice to the employee:

> Your doctor has said that you are able to return to work, but you have not reached maximum medical improvement from your injury (maximum medical improvement is the date after which a doctor says you will not get any better from your injury). You are eligible for temporary partial disability benefits if you cannot make at least 80% of the wages you were making at the time of your accident after the doctor says you can return to work. These benefits will continue until one of the following happens:
>
> (a) Your doctor says you have reached maximum medical improvement from your injury; or
>
> (b) You have received 104 weeks of either temporary total or temporary partial disability benefits, or both combined; or
>
> (c) You are making 80% or more of the wages you were making at the time of your accident.
>
> If you earn wages after the doctor says you can return to work, you must immediately contact this office and give us the name or your employer and the amount of money you are making. If you stop making at least 80% of the wages you were making at the time of your accident, you should also contact this office immediately. If you receive unemployment compensation benefits or Social Security benefits, you must immediately contact this office and tell us what kind of benefits you are getting and the amount of those benefits. If the form "Employee Earnings Report" (LES Form DWC-19) was sent with this letter, you must fill it out, sign it and return it within 21 days after you received it. You may be asked to fill out one of these forms once a month. If you do not fill out, sign and return the form, your compensation benefits may be stopped until you return the form. If you turn down an offer of a job that you can do, your compensation benefits may be stopped. For more information about temporary partial disability benefits, please call the Employee Assistance and Ombudsman office (EAO) of the Division of Workers' Compensation at any of its local offices listed in your "Employee's Rights" brochure, or at 1-800-342-1741.

[c] Accident Dates On or After October 1, 2003

The criteria for eligibility remain as before. However, the required entitlement letter has changed. Within five business days after the claim-handling entity learns about a restricted work release, it must send an informational letter to the claimant. The required text of this letter is contained in the Administrative Rules, Fla. Admin. Code. R. 69L- 3.01915 (1/10/2005) [*see* Part VI for the full text of the rule and required letter].

> **NOTE:** Effective October 1, 2003, the Legislature amended the Act to require that the carrier send the required entitlement letter to the employer and well as to the employee. The entitlement letter must be sent within five days after the carrier learns

that the claimant has been released to restricted work [§ 440.15[4][b], Fla. Stat. (10/1/2003)].

[6] Time Limit to Submit Requests and Report Earnings

[a] Accident Dates Through December 31, 1993

As the required entitlement letter states [*see* [5][a], *above*], it is the employee's burden to submit a request for temporary partial benefits to the carrier every two weeks. The injured worker must send the forms to the carrier within 14 days after the end of the two-week period claimed. If not, the injured worker may be permanently ineligible for benefits for that period. The rule specifically states [Fla. Admin Code R. 4L-3.019(1) (11/11/96)].

SPECIAL ALERT: Because this language appears only in the permanent partial section and not in the temporary partial section, it does not apply to temporary partial wage loss [*see* Bridges v. Motorola, Inc., 646 So. 2d 790, 791 (Fla. 1st DCA 1994)].

A question arises due to the extremely poor choice of words used in drafting this provision. Specifically, what does "within 14 days after the time benefits are due" mean? The clear legislative intent here, and now the judicial interpretation, is that if injured workers wait 15 days or more after a given two week period of wage loss to mail the request, they are not eligible for benefits for that particular period.

This amendment is procedural and applies to any wage loss period arising after July 1, 1990, whatever the accident's date [*see* Litvin v. St. Lucie Cty. Sheriff's Dept., 599 So. 2d 1353, 1355–1356 (Fla. 1st DCA 1992), *cert. denied,* 508 U.S. 913, 113 S. Ct. 2350, 124 L. Ed. 2d 258 (1993)].

In the past, the courts have held that late filing of wage loss claim forms was not a basis for denial. An exception arose if the carrier could show it was prejudiced by the delay. This statutory amendment, however, eliminates the need to show prejudice. The court said:

> [A]s we construe the new law, section 440.15(3)(b)2 is mandatory, leaving no room for such considerations as whether a party was prejudiced by the untimely filing. In other words, the new law contains a strict requirement—timely report or waive.

The court cautioned, however, that carriers must take great care in two areas. First, carriers must inform injured workers about their duty to conduct a job search. Second, carriers must explain the 14-day mailing requirement carefully. The court said: "Given this drastic consequence of failure to report, the E/C's duty to notify a claimant of his responsibilities under the Act becomes even more critical" [*see* Turner v. Rinker Materials, 622 So. 2d 80, 85 (Fla. 1st DCA 1993)].

Carriers should examine the wage loss instruction letter to ensure it provides clear instructions the injured worker can understand. Although Division Rules dictate the language of the required instruction letter, carriers should consider highlighting the warning provision concerning the 14-day deadline.

Another question is whether the 14-day deadline applies to temporary partial wage loss. The answer is it does not. Because this restrictive language appears only in the wage loss section [*see* § 440.15(3)(b)2, Fla. Stat.], the court concluded it does not apply. If the legislature intended this to apply to both temporary partial and permanent partial wage loss, said the court, it would have added this language to both sections [*see* Bridges v. Motorola, Inc., 646 So. 2d 790, 791 (Fla. 1st DCA 1994)].

[b] Accident Dates On or After January 1, 1994

Although the law does not require injured workers in temporary partial disability status to conduct a job search, it does require that they report any earnings. Injured workers must submit an affidavit to the carrier if they get a job with another employer. The law allows carriers to suspend benefits until the injured worker does so [§ 440.15(8), Fla. Stat. (7/1/97)].

Carriers can require an injured worker to submit the affidavit no more frequently than once per month. The affidavit is the Employee Earnings Report, LES form DWC-19. The injured worker must fill out the form, sign it, and return it to the carrier within 21 days. If not, the carrier can suspend benefits until the injured worker does so. Carriers can use the same form to request information about unemployment compensation or Social Security benefits the injured worker might be receiving. If getting this information late causes an overpayment, the carrier can recover it by taking a credit against subsequent benefits [Fla. Admin. Code R. 69L-3.0191(9) (1/10/2005)].

[7] TPD and Job Search Requirement: Accidents Through December 31, 1993

For accident dates through December 31, 1993 only, failure to do a valid job search is grounds for denying wage loss benefits. Remember that injured workers have no legal duty to look for work if they are unaware the physician has given a work release. Further, injured workers have no duty to job search unless the employer or carrier tells them to do so [*see* City of Miami v. Jacoby, 599 So. 2d 171, 172–173 (Fla. 1st DCA 1992)].

Remember also that the injured worker is still partially disabled and in the healing process. Claim adjusters should not demand an extensive job search from such injured workers. Could a construction worker with a leg in a cast do some light office work? Probably, but if the employer will not provide such a job, should the adjuster insist that the injured worker hobble around town on crutches to look for a few weeks light work? That is the carrier's right, but is it practical? Common sense and the injured worker's physical restrictions should be the guides. Yes, the injured worker has the burden to show that inability to find work is because of the injury. This is not, however, a substantial burden for an injured worker in a temporary partial disability status.

Simple logic suggests that most injured employees will go through the transition period of temporary partial disability. Some will even start there, because the injury is not severe enough to render them totally disabled. Many physicians are not aware of the various classes of disability in compensation cases. Too often they inappropriately send injured workers home until they have reached maximum medical improvement. Claims adjuster's have the duty to request information about a light duty (restricted) or even unrestricted work release before the injured worker reaches maximum medical improvement.

If the carrier pays temporary total benefits until a physician discharges the injured worker at maximum medical improvement, it will have overpaid benefits often. A worker who returns to work at almost any salary will, frequently, reduce the cost of the claim. Return to work also may do much for the injured worker's mental well-being. Even if the weekly benefit remains unchanged, the carrier will still have achieved the primary goal of return to work.

PRACTICE POINT: With respect to pre-1994 accidents, what should the carrier do if the employee fails to submit evidence of a job search or conducts what the adjuster believes to be an unsatisfactory search? Pay the first two weeks anyway, then write to the injured worker and carefully explain what was wrong. Be specific and explain exactly what was wrong with the job search and how to correct the problem. Clearly explain that failure to comply will put benefits at risk. Offer the assistance of job placement specialists. Such direct communication is proper even when an attorney represents the injured worker. The courts have repeatedly held that it is the carrier's responsibility to inform the employee directly about rights and responsibilities under the Act.

The carrier should, of course, provide the injured worker's attorney with a copy of written correspondence. Carriers should restrict direct communication with the injured worker to contact required to follow the self-executing provisions of the Act.

[8] Case Management Procedure for Adjusters

1. Early in the life of the claim, get a commitment from the employer to provide a light duty job at as high a rate of pay as practicable (at least 80 percent of the pre injury wage).
2. Get a work release from the attending physician with specific details concerning physical restrictions. Give the doctor a detailed description of the physical requirements of the job that the employer will offer. Ask for a specific comment on the employee's physical ability to do the proposed job.
3. Upon receipt of a work release in writing, instruct the employer to present the job offer to the employee by certified mail. The letter should specify the date the job begins, its nature, and its rate of pay. It also should reflect that the employee's physician has approved the job as medically appropriate. Such a job offer letter should be friendly and not threatening or written in legalese.
4. If the employee accepts the job, pay benefits according to the formula discussed below. (See § 14.08 about what to do if the injured worker refuses the job offer.)
5. If suitable employment cannot be found (for accident dates through December 31, 1993) and the employee has done a suitable job search, pay benefits accordingly. Remember that although the doctor may have granted a completely unrestricted work release, the carrier will still be liable for temporary partial

benefits. This is true, of course, only if the injured worker has not reached maximum medical improvement [*see* Citrus Central v. Parker, 423 So. 2d 610, 612 (Fla. 1st DCA 1982)].

For a general and thorough discussion of workers' compensation insurance, see LARSON'S WORKERS' COMPENSATION, DESK EDITION, Part 16, *Insurance* (Matthew Bender).

[9] Requirements on TPD Claims After January 1, 1994

[a] Burden On Carrier

Administering the 1994 version of temporary partial disability at first seems greatly simplified. Carriers no longer need to process endless biweekly claim forms or spend time verifying job searches. The lack of the former structured system, however, increases the error potential for carriers. The new version is simpler, but more so for injured workers than for carriers. Carriers must now be proactive and can no longer simply wait for the injured worker to submit something to trigger payment. Following in [b]–[d], *below,* are the requirements described in the Division's rules.

[b] First Payment

Previously, the law required carriers to issue the first installment of temporary partial disability benefits within 14 days after the doctor released the employee for work. With amendments effective on October 1, 2003, the Legislature changed the time to issue the first payment as follows:

If the employee returns to work, earning less than 80 percent of the pre-injury average weekly wage, the first payment is due seven days "after the last date of the employer's first bi-weekly work week." Apparently, this refers to the employer's pay cycle. The Division's administrative rules define "biweekly work week" as two consecutive seven-day periods coinciding with the post-injury employer's work week. The Rule provides that, in calculating temporary partial disability benefits, the first biweekly work week includes the week the employee returned to work [*see* Fla. Admin Code. R. 69L-3.002(2) (1/10/2005)].

If the employee is unable to return to work within restrictions, and therefore has no income, the first payment of benefits is due no later than the last day of the employer's bi-weekly period. This is apparently intended to ensure that disability payments coincide with the employer's pay cycle. These appear to be procedural amendments that will apply to first payments due on or after the effective date, regardless of the accident date [§ 440.15(4)(c), Fla. Stat. (10/1/2003)].

SPECIAL NOTE: The law now requires a claimant to notify the carrier within five days after returning to work. If the claimant fails to notify the carrier that he has returned to work within that time, the carrier must suspend benefits until proper notification is provided. Although not clear, the statute's phrasing indicates that the claimant is not entitled to retroactive payment of the suspended benefits. It is also not clear if the carrier may or should suspend benefits because the claimant failed to report, but the carrier received notice from the employer. Carriers should apply a reasonableness test if this occurs [§ 440.15(4)(d), Fla. Stat. (10/1/2003)].

Carriers must contact the employer to find out if the injured worker has returned or will return to work. If the injured worker has not gone, and will not go, back to work, the carrier must mail the informational letter discussed in [5], *above*. Carriers must also enclose the Employee's Earnings Report, form DWC-19. Because the carrier has little time to wait for the worker to return the DWC-19, the adjuster should call the injured worker to check on work status. If the employee reports no earnings, and the carrier has no contrary information, the carrier should pay based on zero earnings [Fla. Admin Code R. 69L-3.0191 (1/10/2005)].

Guide to Claims

[c] Subsequent Payments

Because the carrier will often get wage information after it has paid benefits, overpayment and underpayment will result. What happens if the carrier cannot confirm reemployment or cannot get wage information? The carrier should base payments on the last wage information submitted and continue to pay benefits. If the injured worker does not return the DWC-19 form, the carrier can suspend benefits [Fla. Admin Code R. 69L-3.01915 (1/10/2005)].

[d] Overpayment

If new wage information reveals that the carrier has overpaid previous weeks, it can recover the excess through a credit against subsequent benefits. If the carrier does suspend benefits, it must file Notice of Action/Change, form DWC-4, with the Division [*see* ch. 2, § 2.08[10]]. Remember that overpayment credits cannot exceed 20 percent of the weekly benefit [*see* § 440.15(13), Fla. Stat. (7/1/97); Fla. Admin. Code R. 69L-3.0191(9) (1/10/2005)].

[e] Dismissal for Misconduct

If the employee is fired for misconduct, the law provides that temporary partial disability benefits are not payable [§ 440.15(4)(e), Fla. Stat. (10/1/2003)]. Before suspending benefits under this provision, carriers should first conduct sufficient investigation to determine if the claimant's conduct, leading to dismissal, meets the statutory definition of misconduct. The statute defines misconduct as follows [§ 440.02(18), Fla. Stat. (7/1/97)]:

> Misconduct includes, but is not limited to, the following, which shall not be construed in pari materia with each other:
>
> [a] Conduct evincing such willful or wanton disregard of an employer's interests as is found in deliberate violation or disregard of standards of behavior which the employer has the right to expect of the employee; or
>
> [b] Carelessness or negligence of such a degree or recurrence as to manifest culpability, wrongful intent, or evil design, or to show an intentional and substantial disregard of an employer's interests or of the employee's duties and obligations to the employer.

NOTE: The provision in § 440.15(4)(e), Fla. Stat., precluding temporary partial disability benefits if the claimant is fired for misconduct is a substantive amendment that cannot be applied to accident dates before October 1, 2003 [*see* Fardella v. Genesis Health, Inc., 917 So. 2d 276 (Fla. 1st DCA 2005)].

[10] Basis for TPD Entitlement and Evidence Required

[a] Award Based on Causal Relationship

Every claimant must show a causal relationship between the loss of wages and the compensable injury. Whether a claimant shows a causal relationship between the injury and a change in employment status is a factual question to be determined by the JCC from competent substantial evidence. The presence or absence of any particular fact, such as a layoff due to economic conditions, should not be legally determinative of the JCC's finding. Rather, the judge must look to the totality of the circumstances to determine whether a claimant has shown a causal relationship between the injury and the wage loss [*see* Carruth v. Allied Products Co., 452 So. 2d 634 (Fla. 1st DCA 1984)].

Therefore, the fact the employer offered and provided employment initially and that the claimant was subsequently laid off are not relevant. A claimant's entitlement to temporary partial disability benefits will be based entirely on showing that his or her current wage loss is caused by the injury.

Workers' compensation benefits are not precluded merely because some portion of the wage loss is attributable to a reason unrelated to the injury, such as **economic** factors, a discharge for good cause, or seasonal layoffs. A claimant may still be entitled to benefits if the compensable injury left the claimant in a condition that precludes employment within his or her abilities at his or her prior wage. Even though a claimant may be terminated from employment for insubordination, the claimant may still be entitled to benefits if he or she satisfies the burden of demonstrating that the injury contributed to the wage loss after the termination. Whether a claimant has demonstrated a causal connection between his or her compensable injury and the wage loss is a question of fact to be determined by the JCC upon a consideration of the totality of the circumstances [*see* Stewart v. CRS Rinker Materials Corp., 855 So. 2d 1173 (Fla. 1st DCA 2003); *see also* Betancourt v. Sears Roebuck & Co., 693 So. 2d 680 (Fla. 1st DCA 1997) holding that benefits are not precluded simply because some part of the wage loss is attributable to a reason unrelated to the injury, such as economic factors, seasonal layoff, or discharge for good cause].

An injured employee may recover temporary partial disability benefits only if a disability caused by a work-related injury results in a reduction in the employee's earning capacity below the level set by statute. § 440.15(4)(a), Fla. Stat., defines the minimum level in case of temporary partial disability as equal to 80 percent of the difference between 80 percent of the employee's average weekly wage and the salary, wages, and other remuneration the employee is able to earn, as compared weekly. However, the weekly benefits may not exceed an amount equal to 66 2/3 percent of the employee's average weekly wage at the time of injury. Under § 440.15, Fla. Stat., temporary partial disability benefits are compensation for disability.

§ 440.02(13), Fla. Stat., defines the term "disability" as the incapacity because of the injury to earn in the same or any other employment the wages that the employee was receiving at the time of the injury. Consequently, an employee must still prove a causal connection between a work-related injury and a resulting wage loss to recover temporary partial disability benefits.

§ 440.15(4), Fla. Stat., provides that temporary partial disability must be computed as a percentage of the difference between the employee's average weekly wage and the salary, wages, and other remuneration the employee is able to earn after the disability. Thus, the current statute continues to employ the concept of earning capacity, not actual earnings, to measure the extent of a partial disability [*see* Vencor Hosp. v. Ahles, 727 So. 2d 968 (Fla. 1st DCA 1998)].

Note, however, that if a claimant was earning a pre-injury wage when he or she was laid off, resigned, or was fired, showing entitlement to benefits will be difficult. Wages actually being earned after injury is a factor entitled to great weight. It logically follows that post-injury earnings equal to pre-injury earnings are the strongest evidence of non-impairment of wage earning capacity [*see* Miami v. Garrido, 402 So. 2d 564 (Fla. 1st DCA 1981)].

[b] Self-Employment—Voluntary Limitation of Income

The courts have not yet reviewed the issue of entitlement to temporary partial disability benefits for claimants who elect to try self-employment subsequent to January 1, 1994. All of the cases deal with pre-1994 accident dates when claimants were required to conduct a job search. Still, these cases are instructive as to whether seeking self-employment constitutes a voluntary limitation of income. However, pursuing self-employment might preclude benefits if it is shown that the claimant refused or gave up suitable employment in order to start his or her own business, thereby netting a lower income than he or she was shown to be *able* to earn in the suitable employment.

Note, however, that whether a claimant's effort to establish his or her **own business** is bona fide and sufficient to substitute for an adequate job search (or accepting an appropriate job offer), is a question that is dependent on the circumstances [City of W. Palm Beach Fire Dep't v. Norman, 711 So. 2d 628 (Fla. 1st DCA 1998)].

Pursuant to § 440.15(4)(b), Fla. Stat., when a claimant voluntarily limits his or her income, temporary partial disability benefits are based on the amount that would have been earned if the employee had not limited his or her income or had accepted appropriate employment [Edwards v. Caulfield, 560 So. 2d 364 (Fla. 1st DCA 1990)].

Note: The *Edwards* court relied on the statutory provisions allowing benefits to be based on deemed earnings. These provisions were repealed, effective January 1, 1994. However, the court has held that the 1994 amendments did not change the basic requirement that disability caused any resulting loss of wages. The 1994 legislative amendments removed the deemed earnings provision, but this change did not alter the fact that temporary partial disability benefits are compensation for disability. Thus, the current statute continues to use the concept of earning capacity, not actual earnings, to measure the extent of a partial disability [*see* Vencor Hospital v. Ahles, 727 So. 2d 968, 969 (Fla. 1st DCA 1998); *see also* Fardella v. Genesis Health, Inc., 917 So. 2d 276 (Fla. 1st DCA 2005)].

In 1989, the court reversed the judge's finding that the claimant did *not* voluntarily limit

Guide to Claims

his income based on his pursuit of self-employment beginning in August 1986. The court found that the record did not contain competent substantial evidence to support a determination, pursuant to § 440.15(3)(b)2, Fla. Stat., that the claimant's wage loss after that date was due significantly to his compensable injury and not to other factors. Instead, the evidence showed that the claimant voluntarily limited his income by giving up suitable employment in order to start his **own business**, thereby netting a lower income than he was shown to be *able* to earn in the suitable employment [T.G. Lee Foods, Inc. v. Farley, 544 So. 2d 265 (Fla. 1st DCA 1989)].

[c] Lack of Transportation

The courts have not yet addressed the question of whether a claimant is justified in refusing suitable employment for lack of transportation. It appears, however, that lack of transportation is not a valid reason for rejecting or leaving employment, and the following is offered in support of such an argument. Readers are cautioned however, that the courts might reach a different conclusion.

There are endless reasons why a claimant may lack transportation. Perhaps he or she does not own a car, or his or her car is mechanically unsound and the claimant maintains that he or she cannot afford repairs. Perhaps there is a family car, but the claimant and his or her spouse have decided that the spouse should have exclusive use to get to the spouse's job. Take care not to over-think this problem and be tricked into debating questions that are not dispositive of the issue.

While the law requires carriers to pay for or provide transportation to medical providers, this rule developed from case law and was based on the theory that carriers are required to provide medical treatment and that a claimant cannot get treatment if he or she cannot get to the doctor.

There is no requirement, however, that carriers provide employment, and, therefore, there is no requirement that they provide transportation to work. So, what happens if the claimant is able to perform the job offered but cannot accept because of a preexisting financial or other personal problems resulting in the lack of reliable transportation? The employee must still prove a causal connection between a compensable *injury* and a resulting loss of wages to recover disability benefits. Partial disability benefits are computed based on the difference between the employee's pre-injury wage and what he is *able* to earn after the disability [*see* § 440.15(4), Fla. Stat. (1994)]. The 1994 legislative amendments removed the deemed earnings provision. This change, however, did not change the fact that temporary partial disability benefits are compensation for *disability*. Thus, the current statute continues to use the concept of *earning capacity*, not actual earnings, to measure the extent of a partial disability [*see* Vencor Hospital v. Ahles, 727 So. 2d 968, 969 (Fla. 1st DCA 1998); *see also* Fardella v. Genesis Health, Inc., 917 So. 2d 276 (Fla. 1st DCA 2005)].

If the claimant has recovered the ability to earn wages, and his lack of earnings is caused by his unrelated decisions regarding the family car or even no car at all, the lack of reliable transportation does not change the fact that the claimant has regained a wage earning capacity. Unless the claimant's injuries preclude travel, his lack of reliable transportation alone should not entitle him to disability benefits.

If a claimant's injuries preclude driving a car, public transportation might be available. The argument that the claimant's altered gait or use of a straight cane precludes using a public bus requires further investigation because most, if not all, public transportation has been modified to accommodate people with disabilities. For example, the Miami-Dade Transit website contains the following notice:

> "All Miami-Dade Transit buses are now wheelchair accessible. Look for the international accessibility symbol on the front and side of the bus. If any barrier prevents your approaching the bus stop in a wheelchair or interferes with boarding, report the problem at 305-654-6586, Monday through Friday, 8:30 a.m. to 4:30 p.m. Senior citizens and people with disabilities in our community regularly use Miami-Dade Transit's Metrorail, Metromover, and Paratransit services.
>
> Buses with wheelchair lifts and low-floor buses, are available on all Metrobus routes, have raised our transit system to a new level of accessibility, providing increased independence for passengers with mobility impairments."

If a claimant is unwilling to take the bus or pay for a cab, since everyone incurs the costs of transportation to get to work, and the evidence shows the job offered is suitable and within the claimant's restrictions, temporary partial disability benefits should be awardable based on what the claimant would have earned if he or she had accepted the job.

[d] Illegal Aliens

Generally, an award of temporary partial disability benefits requires medical evidence of the claimant's inability to work [Philpot v. Miami, 541 So. 2d 680, 682 (Fla. 1st DCA 1989)].

If a claimant is physically able to work, but cannot work legally because of illegal immigration status, benefits are precluded. The employee must prove a causal connection between a compensable injury and a resulting loss of wages to recover disability benefits. Partial disability benefits are computed based on the difference between the employee's pre-injury wage and what he is *able* to earn after the disability [*see* § 440.15(4), Fla. Stat. (1994)].

As noted in [b], above, the 1994 revision to § 440.15(4), Fla. Stat., removed the deemed earnings provision, which had previously enabled the courts to attribute earnings to an employee, terminated for **misconduct**. Although the 1994 legislative amendments removed the deemed earnings provision, this did not change the fact that temporary partial disability benefits are compensation for *disability*. Thus, the current statute continues to use the concept of earning capacity, not actual earnings, to measure the extent of a partial disability. An injured employee may recover temporary partial **disability** benefits only if a **disability** caused by a work-related injury results in a reduction in the employee's earning capacity below the level set by statute.

Under § 440.15, Fla. Stat. (Supp. 1994), temporary partial disability benefits are compensation for **disability**. § 440.02(11), Fla. Stat. (Supp. 1994), defines the term "**disability**" as the incapacity because of injury to earn in the same or any other employment the wages that the employee was receiving at the time of the injury. Consequently, an employee must still prove a causal connection between a work-related

Guide to Claims

injury and a resulting wage loss to recover temporary partial **disability** benefits. § 440.15(4), Fla. Stat. (Supp. 1994), provides that temporary partial **disability** must be computed as a percentage of the difference between the employee's average weekly wage and the salary, wages, and other remuneration the employee is *able* to earn after the **disability**. Thus, the current statute continues to employ the concept of *earning capacity*, not actual earnings, to measure the extent of a partial **disability** [Vencor Hosp. v. Ahles, 727 So. 2d 968 (Fla. 1st DCA 1998)].

The Workers' Compensation Act's definition of "employee," in § 440.12(11)(a), Fla. Stat., includes aliens not legally entitled to be employed. Illegal aliens are entitled under the statute to workers' compensation benefits. However, entitlement to wage loss benefits is based on proof of a connection between the injury and the alleged wage loss. One method of demonstrating that connection is by an adequate good faith work search. Use of that method is unavailing when the claimant may not legally be employed because of his or her illegal alien status. That is not to say that such a claimant is foreclosed from demonstrating entitlement to wage loss through other allowable means, such as when the injuries are severe enough to excuse a work search [Cenvill Dev. Corp. v. Candelo, 478 So. 2d 1168 (Fla. 1st DCA 1985); *review denied*, Candelo v. Cenvill Dev. Corp., 488 So. 2d 67 (Fla. 1986)].

As noted, performing a good faith job search is a method by which a claimant may demonstrate a causal link between his injury and his alleged wage loss. However, where the claimant may not legally be employed, a work search, no matter how exhaustive, will not adequately demonstrate such a causal link, unless, of course, the employer is estopped from raising the issue of the claimant's unauthorized status. [Cenvill Dev. Corp. v. Candelo, 478 So. 2d 1168 (Fla. 1st DCA 1985); *review denied*, Candelo v. Cenvill Dev. Corp., 488 So. 2d 67 (Fla. 1986)].

The employer is estopped from asserting the status of an unauthorized alien with respect to a workers' compensation claim, however, only when he knew or should have known of the true status of the employee. This holding prevents unauthorized aliens from suffering at the hands of an employer who would knowingly hire the illegal alien and then conveniently use the unauthorized alien status to avoid paying wage loss benefits. It also protects an employer who, through no fault of his or her own, would end up paying continued wage loss benefits to an employee who cannot legally be employed. The law of Florida does not impose on an employer the burden of verifying forged or borrowed green cards [§ 448.09, Fla. Stat.]. Neither is there any such federal requirement [*see* Cenvill Dev. Corp. v. Candelo, 478 So. 2d 1168 (Fla. 1st DCA 1985); *review denied*, Candelo v. Cenvill Dev. Corp., 488 So. 2d 67 (Fla. 1986)].

[e] Refusing Suitable Employment

If an injured employee refuses suitable employment, that employee is not entitled to *any* compensation during the continuance of such refusal unless, in the opinion of the JCC, refusal is justified [§ 440.15(7), Fla. Stat.]. The legislature clearly intends to strongly encourage injured workers, who are capable, to return to the workplace. The method of encouragement chosen by the legislature was to deny all compensation when the claimant refuses suitable employment.

The sanction applies only during the continuance of the refusal. When a claimant accepts suitable employment, the compensation the employer's insurer must pay is determined pursuant to the formula set forth in § 440.15(4)(a), Fla. Stat. (2001). The formula sets temporary partial disability compensation as equal to 80 percent of the difference between 80 percent of the employee's average weekly wage and the salary, wages, and other remuneration the employee is able to earn, as compared weekly [*see* A. Duda & Sons, Inc. v. Kelley, 900 So. 2d 664 (Fla. 1st DCA 2005)].

NOTE: Calculating benefits for permanent and temporary partial wage loss on pre-1994 accidents is essentially the same. Also, no difference exists in calculating temporary partial disability benefits after 1994. Therefore, we will discuss these subjects together in §§ 14.03–14.06.

§ 14.02 Permanent Partial Disability

[1] Legislative History

An injured worker's status changes upon reaching maximum medical improvement. Eligibility for temporary disability benefits ends, and eligibility for permanent disability benefits may begin. The nature, amount, duration, and classification of permanent disability benefits changes substantially, depending on the accident date.

For a brief discussion of the permanent partial disability classification, see LARSON'S WORKERS' COMPENSATION, DESK EDITION, Ch. 80 (Matthew Bender).

[2] The 1994 Amendment

Effective January 1, 1994, the legislature completely rewrote the wage loss sections of the Act. Wage loss benefits, now called supplemental income benefits, apply to only those workers with at least a 20-percent permanent impairment. The law entitles those with impairments from 1 to 19 percent to scheduled benefits similar to the 1978 law (before wage loss.) What was old may be new again, but is sufficiently changed so that the old appellate cases may not apply. Those people involved in administering the system must now, more than ever, be especially wary in applying the correct law to a given case [§ 440.15(3), Fla. Stat.].

§ 14.03 Eligibility Requirements

[1] Eligibility Before October 1, 1989

For accidents occurring before October 1, 1989, injured workers are eligible for wage loss benefits if they have suffered a permanent impairment under the *Guides to the Evaluation of Permanent Impairment,* published by the American Medical Association.

A permanent impairment rating, therefore, is the only requirement. Physician imposed physical restrictions are not necessary if a rating is appropriate. This is because a physical limitation is always implied in an impairment rating. Once a physician awards an impairment rating, the injured worker's only burden is to show a causal connection between the "physical limitation" and any lost earnings. They can do so by merely conducting an extensive but unsuccessful job search [*see* Davis v. Broward County Health Dept., 570 So. 2d 371, 374 (Fla. 1st DCA 1990)].

This was not, apparently what the legislature intended, because in response it added additional requirements discussed in [2]–[4], *below*.

[2] Eligibility Between October 1, 1989, and June 30, 1990

For accidents occurring between these dates, an injured worker must not only have a permanent impairment, but in addition must meet the following tests [§ 440.15(3), Fla. Stat.]:

1. The permanent impairment must result in a work related physical restriction; and
2. These physical restrictions must affect employees' ability to do the activities of their usual or other appropriate employment.

[3] Eligibility Between July 1, 1990, and June 20, 1993

Although no court cases affected the 1989 amendments, the legislature changed the eligibility requirements again. Injured workers with accident dates between July 1, 1990 and October 31, 1992, must show the following: [§ 440.15(3), Fla. Stat.]:

1. A permanent impairment according to the *Minnesota Department of Labor Disability Schedules.* If not covered by the Minnesota schedule, the *Guides to the Evaluation of Permanent Impairment,* published by the American Medical Association apply.
2. The impairment rating is not based solely on subjective complaints.
3. The permanent impairment resulted in a work related physical restriction.
4. The physical restrictions affect the ability to do the activities of the usual or other appropriate employment.
5. The physical restrictions are directly attributable to the injury.

[4] Eligibility Between November 1, 1992, and December 31, 1993

The only change for injuries occurring between November 1, 1992 and December 31, 1993, is that impairments are based on the *Florida Impairment Rating Guide.* When the *Guide* was first introduced in 1992, it was surrounded in such controversy that it was immediately subjected to legal challenge. Although the *Guide* has so far emerged unchanged, the debate continues. An employee group challenged the *Guide* as unconstitutional. The administrative hearing officer decided that the rule and *Guide* were valid and the First District Court of Appeal affirmed that decision. This does not mean, however, that the application of a specific provision of the *Guide* in a particular case will automatically survive a constitutional challenge. The decision *does* mean that the rule and the *Guide* are constitutional on their face.

These legal disputes also resulted in confusion regarding the *Guide's* effective date. In Bulletin No. 148, dated May 26, 1993, the Division announced that the *Florida Impairment Rating Guide* is effective "for all dates of injury November 1, 1992 and after." Some people argued this conflicted with the statute. The court dismissed this notion and held the Division's declared effective date valid [*see* Injured Workers Ass'n v. Dept. of Labor, 630 So. 2d 1189, 1191–1192 (Fla. 1st DCA 1994)].

SPECIAL ALERT: If the Florida *Guides* do not address a particular condition, no alternative guide exists. The Florida *Guides* provide, "if a category applicable to the impairing condition cannot be found in this guide, then the category most resembling the impairment or degree of impairment based on analogy should be chosen." [*see* 1996 Florida Uniform Permanent Impairment Rating Schedule 5 The Florida Workers' Compensation Institute, Inc.]

[5] Eligibility Between January 1, 1994, and September 30, 2003: Supplemental Income Benefits

For accidents occurring between January 1, 1994, and September 30, 2003, the legislature enacted significant changes in repealing and rewriting the original wage loss provisions of § 440.15, Fla. Stat. One change was the benefit's name. Wage loss benefits are now called "Supplemental Income Benefits." A more important change dealt with eligibility. Only those persons with injuries resulting in a permanent impairment rating of 20 percent or more qualify for supplemental income benefits. The legislature repealed previous requirements such as a work-related physical restrictions, but this deletion may be insignificant with so high a rating. Two additional requirements exist. Besides having at least a 20-percent impairment rating, injured workers must be earning less than 80 percent of their pre-injury average weekly wages as a direct result on their impairment. Also, eligibility requires a good faith effort to find work commensurate with their ability [§ 440.15(3)(b)1, Fla. Stat. (Supp. 1994)]. Eligibility requires that an injured worker meet all three of these requirements [*see* Patterson v. Union Correctional Inst., 697 So. 2d 993 (Fla. 1st DCA 1997)].

Restricting supplemental income benefits to only those injured workers with an impairment rating of 20 percent or more is not unreasonable or arbitrary and is constitutional [*see* Bradley v. Hurricane Restaurant, 670 So. 2d 162, 165 (Fla. 1st DCA 1996), *rev. denied,* 678 So. 2d 337 (Fla. 1996)].

[6] Eligibility On or After October 1, 2003

Effective October 1, 2003, the Legislature repealed the provisions creating entitlement to Supplemental Income (wage loss) Benefits. Therefore, for accidents occurring on or after the effective date, no one is eligible for these supplemental, wage loss benefits. A permanently, partially impaired injured worker is eligible for only Impairment Income Benefits [*see* ch. 15]. A permanently, totally disabled injured worker is eligible for only permanent total disability benefits [*see* ch. 13].

SPECIAL NOTE: ALL OF THE SECTIONS BELOW APPLY ONLY TO ACCIDENT DATES OCCURRING *BEFORE* OCTOBER 1, 2003.

[7] Burden of Proof

A significant 1990 amendment to the law shifted the burden of proving lost earning capacity between the employee and the carrier depending on the percent of the impairment rating. The burden of proof is the injured worker's for accident dates before 1994 if the permanent impairment is 20 percent or less. Injured workers must prove that their post-injury earning capacity is less than their pre-injury average weekly wage. Additionally, they must show that this loss of earning capacity does not result from economic conditions or from their own misconduct.

If the impairment rating is 21 percent or more, however, the legal burden is on the employer—or more accurately on the carrier—to demonstrate that the employee's post-injury earning capacity is the same or more than the pre-injury wage [§ 440.15(3)(b)4(e), Fla. Stat. (7/1/90)].

SPECIAL ALERT: The legislature repealed this provision effective January 1, 1994. The 1994 amendments clearly shift the burden of proof to the carrier by simply repealing most of the injured worker's proof requirements.

[8] Exceptions to Impairment Requirement

[a] Psychological Restriction Exception

The law does not always require a literal physical restriction, such as limits on lifting or ladder climbing. A psychological restriction alone will suffice. For example, Delier Diaz, a police officer, suffered from "brief reactive psychosis." This is a temporary condition caused by a specific stressful event. Once the event passes, the patient returns to normal. Because of this psychosis, Diaz's doctor told him not to return to police work. The court considered such a condition a permanent impairment entitling Diaz to wage loss benefits [*see* Diaz v. City of Tampa, 589 So. 2d 370, 372 (Fla. 1st DCA 1991)].

How this case will affect accidents under the 1994 amendments is unclear. Under the law affecting this case, any permanent impairment entitled an injured worker to wage loss benefits. For 1994 and later accidents, the Act specifically requires at least a 20-percent impairment rating. Since Diaz had no actual rating, this situation probably will not apply under the 1994 amendments.

SPECIAL ALERT: For accident dates on or after January 1, 1994, compensation is not allowed for a mental impairment caused by depression from being out of work [§ 440.15(3)(a), Fla. Stat. (1/1/94)].

[b] Allergy Exception

A significant exception to the permanent impairment requirement also exists in occupational disease cases. Injured workers suffering a permanent disability from an occupational disease are entitled to compensation even though they are not affected if they do not return to work under the conditions that caused the disability. This is provided, of course, that the worker suffered economic (wage) loss [*see* Dayron Corp. v. Morehead, 509 So. 2d 930, 931–932 (Fla. 1987)].

An example is an injured worker who suffers from contact dermatitis resulting from contact with wet cement. Treatment results in a complete cure; however, re-exposure to cement causes the condition to reappear. Such injured workers are entitled to wage loss benefits though they have no precise impairment. Why? Entitlement exists because the injured worker's allergy to cement caused economic loss [*see* OBS Co., Inc. v. Freeney, 475 So. 2d 947, 950–951 (Fla. 1st DCA 1985)].

As in the *Diaz* case [*see* [a], *above*], a question arises about whether we can apply *Freeney* to accidents after January 1, 1994. Recall that previously the law required only some degree of permanent impairment. The numerical impairment rating did not affect basic eligibility. The 1994 amendments, however, preclude entitlement to supplemental income benefits unless the injured worker has an impairment rating of at least 20 percent. Absent a specific impairment rating the allergy exception cannot apply. This is because deciding eligibility for wage loss benefits without a rating is impossible. For the same reason, calculating impairment income benefits will be impossible, because carriers must pay this benefit before supplemental income benefits begin [*see* § 14.05].

For a discussion of employment conditions acting on allergies, see LARSON'S WORKERS' COMPENSATION, DESK EDITION, Ch. 52, § 52.07[1] (Matthew Bender).

[c] "No Notice to Injured Worker" Exception

Even when a job search is required, injured workers have no duty to look for work until the attending physician releases them, and the employer or carrier has instructed them to conduct a job search. When such a failure to inform occurs, the law relieves an injured worker of establishing any of the entitlement tests. The law entitles the injured worker to benefits even with an unimpaired ability to work if the carrier has failed in its duty to inform the employee about the job search requirement. An award of benefits in such cases is a sanction against the carrier. This is punishment for failing in its duty rather than the result of an injured worker failing to satisfy the burden of proof. When the evidence shows that carriers failed to inform injured workers of their responsibilities, we need not decide if the injured worker's wage loss relates to the compensable injury [*see* City of Miami v. Jacoby, 599 So. 2d 171, 172–173 (Fla. 1st DCA 1992)].

No exceptions to this rule exist. Even if the injured worker announces an intent to retire, the carrier must still inform the injured worker about the job search obligation. An injured worker's decision to retire cannot be considered a voluntary limitation of income if the carrier does not inform the worker about the right to wage loss benefits and the responsibility to conduct a work search [*see* Roll v. Sebastian Inlet, 609 So. 2d 674, 676–677 (Fla. 1st DCA 1992); *see also* Alberta v. American Freight Systems, 565 So. 2d 378, 379–380 (Fla. 1st DCA 1990); Phillips v. Duval County School Board, 577 So. 2d 630, 631–632 (Fla. 1st DCA 1991)].

Guide to Claims

[9] Stacking Impairments

May impairment ratings to separate body parts be added, or stacked, to arrive at a whole body rating? Yes, sometimes. If the impairments involve separate parts of the body with different manifestations of impairment, such as orthopedic and psychiatric, ratings may be combined [*see* Rinker Materials Corp. v. Hill, 469 So. 2d 233, 234 (Fla. 1st DCA 1985)].

If the impairment is from the same area of the body, but rated by two different physicians, from different specialties, the ratings may not be combined [*see* Florida Dept. of Corrections v. Carro, 410 So. 2d 629, 630 (Fla. 1st DCA 1982)].

These old cases will have new significance under the 1990 and 1994 amendments to the Workers' Compensation Act. These amendments limit entitlement to wage loss benefits depending on the impairment rating. Note that doctors must base impairment ratings on one of three guides, depending on the date of the accident.

1. For injuries occurring before October 1, 1989, use the AMA Guides.
2. For injuries occurring between October 1, 1989, and October 31, 1992, use the *Minnesota Department of Labor and Industry Disability Schedule.* If the Minnesota guides do not address an injury, use the AMA Guides.
3. For injuries occurring on or after November 1, 1992, use the *Florida Impairment Rating Guide.*

NOTE: The *Minnesota Disability Schedule* is available from Print Communications Division, 117 University (Ford Building.), St. Paul, MN. The *Florida Impairment Rating Guide* is available from the Florida Workers' Compensation Press, P.O. Drawer 200, Tallahassee, Florida 32302-0200.

§ 14.04 Eligibility for Benefits

Meeting all of the tests discussed in § 14.03 establishes an injured worker's basic eligibility for benefits but not actual *entitlement.* To collect benefits, the injured worker must show that:

If employed:

1. For accident dates before July 1, 1990, earnings are less than 85 percent of the pre-injury average weekly wage.
2. For accidents on or after July 1, 1990, earnings are less than 80 percent of the pre-injury average weekly wage.

If not employed:

1. For accident dates up to July 1, 1990, there must be a logical job search.
2. For accident dates between July 1, 1990, and December 31, 1993, the job search must include a minimum of five job searches per period claimed.

3. For accident dates between January 1, 1994, and September 30, 2003, the injured worker "in good faith sought employment commensurate with the employee's ability to work." (Note: this is the *only* requirement; *see* § 14.08].

§ 14.05 Starting Benefits

[1] Accident Dates Through December 31, 1993

As with temporary partial wage loss, the carrier has five days to send at least four wage loss claim forms (DWC-3) to the injured worker with an entitlement letter. The time begins to run from the carrier's first knowledge that the injured worker has met the basic eligibility requirements. As with temporary partial disability claims, the Division of Workers' Compensation has prescribed the exact wording of the entitlement letter for permanent partial wage loss. The wording is the same as the temporary partial letter [*see* § 14.01[5]] except the first, two sentences that state [Fla. Admin Code R. 4L-3.018(2) (11/11/96)]:

> Your treating physician has reported that you have reached maximum medical improvement and you may return to work but that you have a permanent impairment which has resulted in a work-related physical restriction which may affect your ability to perform the duties of your usual occupation or other appropriate employment. If this physical restriction causes you to lose wages, you may be entitled to additional benefit payments under the Florida Workers' Compensation Law.

The carrier has 14 days to calculate benefits, make any payments due, and give copies of the completed form to the employee, employer, and Division. This time begins upon receipt of the properly completed form DWC-3 from the injured worker. Simultaneously, the carrier should give the injured worker a new set of DWC-3 forms.

If the carrier decides that benefits are not due, it must report its intention to deny the claim on the carrier section of the DWC-3. In addition, the carrier must notify the injured worker and the Division of its denial of the claim by completing and sending a Notice of Denial, form DWC-12, within 14 days. The carrier's filing with the Division must also include any documents relating to the injured worker's job search [Fla. Admin Code R. 4L-3.018(2) (11/11/96)].

> **REMEMBER:** Injured workers are not eligible for wage loss benefits if they fail to mail the request for benefits to the carrier within 14 days after the end of a biweekly period [*see* § 14.01[5][a]].

[2] Accident Dates Between January 1, 1994, and September 30, 2003

[a] The Formula

As with most other classes of benefits, supplemental income benefits are almost automatic. Supplemental income benefits are now determined quarterly and paid monthly. That is to say, the injured worker need do something only four times per year to trigger payment. This is especially true for the initial wage loss period.

Although a doctor has awarded an injured worker an impairment rating of 20 percent or more, the carrier must pay impairment benefits before supplemental income benefits begin. Thus, if the doctor awards an impairment rating of 20 percent, the carrier must first pay 60 weeks of impairment benefits [*see* Ch. 15, *Impairment Benefits and Death Benefits*]. Wage loss benefits do not begin until the carrier pays the full 60 weeks of benefits. The first payment of supplemental income benefits is due within seven days after the carrier pays the final impairment benefit [§ 440.15(3)(b), Fla. Stat. (1/1/94)].

The carrier has the duty to decide, in advance, the amount of any wage loss benefits that may be due for the next three months and begin payments. Within 15 weeks before impairment income benefits end, the carrier must send an informational letter to the injured worker. The carrier must send the letter by certified mail. The mailing must include two copies of the Statement of Quarterly Earnings for Supplemental Benefits, form DWC-40. The carrier must complete the first two lines on one form showing the beginning and ending dates of the initial filing period [Fla. Admin Code R. 4L-3.0193 (11/8/94)].

[b] Filing Period Defined

Recall that supplemental income benefits are determined quarterly. Therefore, a filing period means 13 consecutive weeks. The second filing period can be less than 13 weeks if the carrier prorated the first period.

[c] Required Entitlement Letter

Within 15 weeks before impairment income benefits end, the carrier must send the following notice to the injured worker by certified mail [Fla. Admin Code R. 4L-3.0193(7) (11/8/94)]:

> Because your doctor found that you have a permanent impairment of 20% or more due to your work injury, you may be eligible to receive additional workers' compensation benefits, known as SUPPLEMENTAL INCOME BENEFITS. However, you must also meet the requirements below in order to receive payment for these benefits:
>
> 1. You must be unable to earn at least 80% of what you earned before your injury for at least 90 days in a row, and
>
> 2. You must try in good faith to find a job you are able to do and cooperate with any reemployment help offered by the employer, carrier or the Division of Workers' Compensation.
>
> To get your first check for supplemental income benefits, you need to complete, sign and return the enclosed "Statement of Quarterly Earnings for Supplemental Benefits" form (DWC-40) to this office. We recommend you return the form no later than 7 days after the end of the filing period, shown in section "A" of the enclosed form. This should enable you to keep your payments coming about every 4 to 6 weeks. Report any wages you earn during the last 13 weeks that you are paid impairment income benefits. Do not include the amount paid to you for your impairment income benefits. Follow the filing instructions on the back of the form to make sure there will not be

a break in your payments. Your supplemental income benefits will be calculated by a formula that is based on the wages you report for every filing period on each "Statement of Quarterly Earnings for Supplemental Income Benefits."

If you already know that you will not be eligible for payment of supplemental income benefits when your impairment income benefits end. keep this letter and the other blank form for possible future use, because you may later become eligible for supplemental benefits.

If you do not work during the filing period, it is suggested that you keep records of all the places you look for work, the dates you look, the type of work you are seeking, and the names of the people you contact. If you turn down the offer of a job that you are able to do, your supplemental income benefits will be calculated on the basis of what that job would have paid you, for as long as the job offer remained open to you. Also, if you refuse to accept training or education offered by the employer, this office, or the Division, your supplemental income benefits may be reduced by one-half. If you have any questions, contact your claims representative at this office, at the address and telephone number listed in this letter. You may also call the Division of Workers' Compensation's Employee Assistance and Ombudsman Office (EAO) at any of its branch offices listed in your employee brochure, or at its toll-free telephone number in Tallahassee at 1-800-342-1741.

§ 14.06 Calculating Wage Loss Benefits

[1] Accident Dates Through December 31, 1993

[a] Partial Week

NOTE: Calculating wage loss benefits is the same for both temporary partial and permanent partial disability.

Usually, the first calendar week of entitlement for wage loss benefits will be a partial week since eligibility begins on the date of maximum medical improvement. Division rules require that all other weeks of entitlement be for full calendar weeks. How do we figure out wage loss benefits due for a partial week? It depends on the date of the accident. For injuries occurring before July 1, 1990, the answer is in the Division's rule, which provides [Fla. Admin. Code R. 4L-3.018(3) (11/11/96)]:

> Divide the pre-injury average weekly wage by the number of days [the injured worker was] employed per week, multiply by the number of days from date of maximum medical improvement through the last working day of that calendar week, multiply by 85 percent, . . . insert the resulting figure on the DWC-3 in the box labeled "ADJ. AWW", and complete the calculations shown on that form.

This is confusing language, so let us make some assumptions and work through the calculation. Assume the injured worker had an average weekly wage of $300 and worked a five-day week. The injured worker reached maximum medical improvement on

Wednesday and the last working day is Friday.

THE FORMULA

1. AWW divided by days worked
   $300.00 ÷ 5 = $ 60.00
2. Multiply by days since MMI
   $ 60.00 x 3 = $180.00
3. Multiply by 85%
   $180.00 x 85% = $153.00

For the first week only, use $153 as the injured worker's pre-injury, adjusted weekly wage.

NOTE: For accidents occurring on or after July 1, 1990, use 80% in Step 3 of the calculation instead of 85%.

[b] Full Week

Except for the first week, calculate wage loss on a full calendar week basis:

1. Multiply the average weekly wage by 85% (80% if the injury occurs on or after July 1, 1990)]. The result is the injured worker's adjusted average weekly wage.
2. Subtract from that sum, any earnings the injured worker may have received.
3. Multiply the result by 95% (80% if injury on or after July 1, 1990)].
4. Subtract any offset such as social security or unemployment compensation (*see* ch. 12, §§ 12.05, 12.06).

The result is the injured worker's actual wage loss benefit subject to the maximum compensation rate.

SPECIAL ALERT: If the carrier did not include part of the pre-injury earnings in calculating average weekly wage because they were earned in excluded employment, such earnings cannot be included as post-injury earnings when calculating wage loss benefits [Parrott v. City of Fort Lauderdale, 190 So. 2d 326, 329–330 (Fla. 1966)].

[2] Accident Dates Between January 1, 1994, and September 30, 2003

[a] The Formula

Under the 1994 amendments, supplemental income benefits are calculated in a significantly different way. First, benefits are paid monthly rather than weekly. Second, benefits are determined and calculated *in advance,* quarterly. Third, eligibility for benefits ends forever if the injured worker's earnings continue at 80 percent or more of the pre-injury wage for 12 consecutive months. § 440.15(3)(b)7, Fla. Stat. (7/1/97) provides as follows:

> Supplemental benefits are calculated quarterly and paid monthly. For purposes of calculating supplemental benefits, 80 percent of the employee's average weekly wage and the average wages the employee has earned per week are compared quarterly.

§ 440.15(3)(b)8, Fla. Stat. (7/1/97) provides as follows:

> Supplemental benefits are payable at the rate of 80 percent of the difference between 80 percent of the employee's average weekly wage determined pursuant to § 440.14 and the weekly wages the employee has earned during the reporting period, not to exceed the maximum income benefit under § 440.12.

Guide to Claims

[b] Calculating Benefits: The First Quarter

Calculating benefits for the first quarter is different from subsequent calculation. As an example, assume the carrier will pay the last impairment benefit during the last week of December. If at that point the injured worker is earning at least 80 percent of the former wage, no supplemental income benefits are due. If earnings continue at this level for 12 consecutive months, eligibility ends forever. If, however, earnings fall below 80 percent during the year after the carrier paid the last impairment benefit, the law entitles the injured worker to collect benefits. Certain conditions exist, however, that injured workers must meet.

1. Earnings must have been below 80 percent for at least 90 days.
2. The injured worker can show that any decrease in earnings is a direct result of the impairment from the compensable injury.
3. The injured worker must meet the basic eligibility requirements such as an impairment rating of 20 percent or greater.

Let us assume, however, that the injured worker has no job. The carrier must issue the first payment of supplemental income benefits within seven days after it pays the last impairment benefit installment. The carrier must decide the monthly benefit using the 80/80 formula described below. A difference arises because the carrier must now pay benefits monthly. Instead of using the injured worker's average weekly wage, use the average monthly wage. Calculate this by multiplying the average weekly wage by 4.3. (This is the method used in the past when wage loss was a monthly benefit.) For example, assume the injured worker has an average weekly wage of $300. The formula is as follows:

SUPPLEMENTAL INCOME BENEFIT FORMULA

Step 1.
Average weekly wage x 4.3 = Average monthly wage

Step 2.
Average monthly wage x .80 = Adjusted monthly wage

Step 3.

Subtract any earnings from the adjusted monthly wage

Step 4.
Multiply the result by .80

Using our assumed figures, here is the result:

Step 1.
$300 x 4.3 = $1,290

Step 2.
$1,290 x .80 = $1,032

Step 3.
$1,032 - $0 Earnings = $1,032

Step 4.
$1,032 x .80 = $825

In this example, the injured worker's monthly wage loss benefit is $825 payable each month for January, February, and March. Even if the injured worker begins work during this period, the carrier must pay the full $825 benefit. We calculate benefits in advance quarterly and pay them monthly. We will use any earnings during this period to calculate the benefit for the next quarter.

The first month's payment, whether for a full or partial month, is due by the seventh day after impairment benefits end. Carriers must issue the first payment with or without the completed DWC-40 form. If the injured worker submits the form on time, the carrier must issue payments for the second and third months on the first day of each month. Since the first month is unlikely to begin on the first day of the month, let us examine how to calculate benefits for a partial month.

[c] Calculating Benefits for Partial Month

Both the first and last months of eligibility are likely to be partial months. The key to calculating a partial month is to reduce the monthly benefit to a daily rate. Once determined, simply multiply the daily rate by the number of days of eligibility in the month. Start with the monthly figure from the calculation in the section just above.

PARTIAL MONTH FORMULA

Step 1.
Monthly Benefit divided by 4.3 = Weekly benefit

Step 2.
Weekly benefit divided by 7 = Daily benefit

Step 3.
Daily benefit x No. days benefits due

Using the example above, the injured worker's monthly benefit is $825. Assume the injured worker has 16 days eligibility for the first month. Using the formula, the results are as follows:

Step 1.
$825.00 ÷ 4.3 = $191.86

Step 2.
$191.86 ÷ 7 = $ 27.40

Step 3.
$ 27.40 x 16 = $438.53

The injured worker's first, partial month benefit is $438.53.

[d] Calculating Benefits: Subsequent Quarters

After the initial quarter, the injured worker must submit a statement to the carrier. This statement must say that any lack of earnings is a direct result of the impairment, and must attest to a good faith effort to find work. In addition, the injured worker must report any income earned during the past three months. The means to make this report is the Statement of Quarterly Earnings for Supplemental Income Benefits, form DWC-40.

Except the initial payment, all payments are contingent upon the injured worker submitting the DWC-40 to the carrier. Injured workers must submit the form within 21 days of their receipt of the form.

Carriers must issue the first payment within seven days of receipt of the completed DWC-40. Then, they must issue the second and third payments on the first day of each month. If the injured worker does not return the form, the carrier can suspend benefits. When the injured worker does send the form, the carrier must bring all payments current within seven days after receiving the form. This assumes, of course, that the form contains all the necessary information [Fla. Admin Code R. 4L-3.0193(3) (11/8/94)].

[e] Average Weekly Earnings

Now, let us look at calculating benefits for subsequent quarters. Assume the injured worker obtained a part-time job during the first quarter, but worked sporadically and never earned the same amount in the weeks worked. To figure out benefits for the next quarter, we must find out the injured worker's average weekly earnings. This includes any gratuities reported to the employer as income and the employer's cost for health insurance or housing. It also includes any deemed earnings.

To calculate the injured worker's current average weekly wage, simply add all earnings during the period and divide by the number of weeks in the period. When dealing with a full period, this will be 13 weeks.

Remember that we calculate average monthly earnings by multiplying the average weekly wage by 4.3. Calculate the average earnings by dividing the total earned in the quarter by 13.

Assume the injured worker earned a total of $900 during the first quarter. Using this formula ($900 divided by 13) we arrive at average weekly earnings of $69.23. We must now convert this to average monthly earnings by multiplying the weekly earnings by 4.3; thus, $69.23 x 4.3 = $297.68. Now let us calculate the injured worker's monthly benefit for April, May, and June.

Guide to Claims

CALCULATING SUBSEQUENT QUARTERS

Step 1: Determine the pre-injury average monthly wage (AMW) by multiplying the average weekly wage by 4.3:

$330 x 4.3 = $1,290.00

Step 2: Determine the adjusted monthly wage by multiplying the AMW by 80%.

$1,290 x .80 = $1,032.00

Step 3: Subtract average monthly earnings ($297.68 in our example) from the figure in Step 2.

$1,032 - $297.68 = $734.32

Step 4: Multiply the figure in Step 3 by 80% to arrive at the monthly benefits.

$734.32 x .80 = $587.46

For the second quarter, the monthly benefit is $587.46. Again, any earnings (or lack of them) in the second quarter do not affect benefits. Use earnings in the second quarter to calculate the third quarter benefit. If, during the second quarter, the injured worker earned an average weekly wage equal to 80 percent of the pre-injury wage, the injured worker collects nothing for the third quarter. If during the third quarter the injured worker's earnings averaged less than 80 percent of the pre-injury average weekly wage, benefits are due for the fourth quarter. § 440.15(3)(b)3, Fla. Stat. (1/1/94) provides:

> If an employee earns wages that are at least 80 percent of the employee's average weekly wage for a period of at least 90 days during which the employee is receiving supplemental benefits, the employee ceases to be entitled to supplemental benefits for the filing period. Supplemental benefits that have been terminated shall be reinstated when the employee satisfies the conditions enumerated in subparagraph 2 and files the statement required under subparagraph 5.

For a specific discussion of average weekly wages, see LARSON'S WORKERS' COMPENSATION, DESK EDITION, Ch. 93, § 93.01 (Matthew Bender).

[f] Overpayment

Wage information will often arrive after the carrier has paid benefits. If this results in overpayment, the carrier can recover it from subsequent payments. The maximum recovery, however, cannot exceed 20 percent of the monthly installment [Fla. Admin Code R. 4L-3.0193(3)(d) (11/8/94)].

[g] Limitations on Eligibility

What happens if the injured worker's earnings for the entire year are less than 80 percent of the pre-injury wage? The carrier must find out if this is the direct result of the injured worker's impairment. The Division can require reports from both the injured worker and the carrier. Based on these reports, the Division may order physical examinations, vocational assessments, or other tests to decide if the carrier is doing its duty. These examinations and tests are at the carrier's expense. The law requires these examinations and tests for each year the injured worker continues to receive supplemental income benefits. Carriers have the right to request the Division, once annually, to review the case to determine whether the injured worker's lack of earnings is the direct result of the impairment. Injured workers have the same right. Unfortunately, this provision is ambiguous because it does not say what happens if the Division decides the lack of earnings is due to factors other than the injured worker's impairment [§ 440.15(3)(b)4, Fla. Stat. (1/1/94)].

If the injured worker receives impairment income benefits or supplemental income benefits, the carrier must find out "at least annually whether any extended unemployment or underemployment is a direct result of the employee's impairment" [§ 440.15(3)(b)4, Fla. Stat.]. Previously, the Division required carriers to report their findings via form DWC-22. However, the Division has repealed the rule containing that requirement.

If an injured worker receiving permanent total disability benefits elects to begin a trial work period, the carrier must report this to the Division on form DWC-22. The report is due within 10 days after the carrier approves the trial work period. Within 10 business days after filing with the Division, the carrier must mail a copy of the report to the injured worker and to the employer [Fla. Admin Code R. 38F-55.004 (7/1/96)].

If the carrier questions the injured worker's basic entitlement or the amount of benefits, it can request a mediation conference [§ 440.15(3)(b)6, Fla. Stat. (1/1/94)].

SPECIAL ALERT: Carriers may not offset supplemental income benefits by Social Security or unemployment compensation that the injured worker received [Fla. Admin Code R. 4L-3.0193(6) (11/8/94)].

[3] 80/80 Rule

For injuries occurring before July 1, 1990, think of this calculation as the 85/95 rule. For injuries occurring on or after July 1, 1990, think of this calculation as the 80/80 rule. The legislature hoped that the original 15-percent reduction would encourage employees to return to work.

Apparently the legislature did not believe the 85/95 rule had that effect. Effective July 1, 1990, it repealed the 85/95 rule calculation and replaced it with the 80/80 rule [§ 440.15(3)(b)2, Fla. Stat. (7/1/90)].

Previously, we used 85 percent of the injured worker's average weekly wage and paid 95 percent of the result. For injuries occurring on or after July 1, 1990, we use only 80 percent of the average weekly wage and pay 80 percent of the result.

For example, assume that under the pre July 1, 1990, formula of 85/95 an injured worker has an average weekly wage of $300. Also, assume post injury earnings of $100. This injured worker will receive $147.25 in weekly wage loss benefits. Under the new 80/80 formula the same injured worker will receive only $112.

Another side effect of the 80/80 rule is a reduction in the maximum benefit in cases where the injured worker has no earnings. When wages earned in a two-week period equal zero, the 80/80 formula has a surprising effect. It limits compensation to 64 percent of the injured worker's average weekly wage rather than 66⅔ percent.

In one case, the trial judge refused to apply the 80/80 formula to an unemployed injured worker because of this result. The judge construed the 80/80 provision to apply only in cases where the injured worker has some earnings. The First District Court of Appeal reversed because the statute contains no such qualifying language. The 80/80 rule applies in all cases without regard to whether the injured worker was employed or had any earnings during a claimed period of wage loss [*see* S.E. Environmental Contr. v. Cayasso, 611 So. 2d 7, 8 (Fla. 1st DCA 1992)].

[4] Irregular Earnings and Commissions

[a] Accident Dates Through December 31, 1993

[i] Commissions

For accidents occurring during this period, deduct any wages the injured worker earns from the adjusted average weekly wage. Commissions and other types of irregular earnings can present problems in calculating wage loss.

Before 1986, if our former $300 per week injured worker earned $10,000 in commissions in a two-week period, the law did not allow wage loss for that period. If, however, in the next two-week period there are no earnings, the law entitled the injured worker to full wage loss benefits. This, of course, allowed injured workers to earn far more in commissions in a year than they earned in the past and still collect wage loss. In 1986, the legislature addressed this by adding the following provision to the statute [§ 440.15(3)(b), Fla. Stat. (7/1/86)]:

> In determining the amount the employee is able to earn in any month after injury, commissions and similar irregular payments shall be allocated first to the week in which they are received, in an amount which when added to other earnings for such week does not exceed the employees average weekly wage, and the balance in the same manner to the subsequent weeks until fully allocated, but not to exceed 52 weeks from the week that the commission or similar irregular payment was received.

Thus, in the example above, allocate $300 of the $10,000 earnings to the first week, leaving $9,700. Then, continue allocating $300 per week for the next 33 weeks. The injured worker, therefore, could not collect wage loss benefit for 33 weeks because "earnings" will have been equal to the pre-injury, average weekly wage.

[ii] Other Irregular Earnings

Remember that the statute addresses not only commissions, but other irregular earnings. This includes piece work. For example, Charles Prescott obtained a job as a process server. The employer paid him $6 for every summons served and $5 for every subpoena served. The trial judge refused to apply § 440.15(3)(b), Fla. Stat., theorizing that this would somehow punish the injured worker "for demonstrating perseverance." On appeal, the court disagreed and reversed. This is not a fairness issue, said the court, because application of the section is mandatory, not discretionary. Payment "by the piece" is an irregular payment analogous to a commission. Since it qualifies as a commission, § 440.15(3)(b), Fla. Stat. applies [*see* Stanley Steemer Intern. v. Prescott, 615 So. 2d 211, 212 (Fla. 1st DCA 1993)].

[b] Accident Dates Between January 1, 1994, and September 30, 2003

The legislature repealed the earnings allocation part of § 440.15, Fla. Stat. effective January 1, 1994. Therefore, despite the amount an injured worker earns in a three-month period, these earnings affect only the supplemental income benefits for the next quarter. Remember that we decide benefits due quarterly, in advance. Calculate benefits for each three-month period in isolation, based on the earnings of the previous three months alone.

> **SPECIAL ALERT:** The legislature repealed the prohibition against collecting both unemployment compensation and wage loss benefits effective January 1, 1994. The prohibition against collecting both benefits, therefore, applies only to temporary total, temporary partial, and permanent total disability benefits.

[5] Wage Loss Discount Factor

[a] Accident Dates Through December 31, 1993

For accidents occurring during this period, carriers must increase wage loss benefits beginning with the 25th month after maximum medical improvement. The increase is by a factor of five percent compounded annually and five percent after that. This is in essence an inflation guard or cost of living provision [§ 440.15(3)(b)(8), Fla. Stat.].

Because of the compounding provision this is not a simple matter of increasing the injured worker's benefits by five percent each year. The Division of Workers' Compensation developed tables for this purpose by the last day of February each year [*see* former Fla. Admin Code R. 38F-3.0185 (repealed 12/19/95)].

How does the calculation work? Simply multiply the injured worker's weekly earnings by the discount factor found in the tables that the Division provides. For example, assume the injured worker's 25th month after maximum medical improvement occurs in 1995, and reported earnings are $80 in a given week in 1995. Multiply the $80 by the 1995 discount factor of .9737. The result is: $80 x .9737 = $77.89. This reduces the reported earnings, thus increasing the wage loss benefit. Note that this provision is of no benefit to an injured worker who has no earnings, because such an injured worker will already be at the maximum rate.

The Division's tables can be found in Part VIII, Tables, Table 2.

[b] Accident Dates Between January 1, 1994, and September 30, 2003

The legislature repealed the discount factor provision effective January 1, 1994. Therefore, the discount factor does not apply to accidents occurring after that date.

[6] Subsequent Injury

[a] Accident Dates Through December 31, 1993

[i] Benefits and Offsets

Occasionally an injured worker who is receiving wage loss benefits will suffer another injury on a new job. The law entitles that injured worker to receive, to some extent, the benefit of both wage loss benefits for the original injury, and temporary total disability benefits for the new one. The combination of the two benefits, of course, may not exceed the maximum compensation rate in effect at the time of the new injury. Carriers must first apply any offset to the wage loss benefits payable for the first injury [§ 440.15(5)(c), (d), Fla. Stat. (1990)].

For a general discussion of successive disabilities, see LARSON'S WORKERS' COMPENSATION, DESK EDITION, Ch. 90 (Matthew Bender).

[ii] Calculating Average Weekly Wage

An important question in subsequent injury cases is how to calculate the injured worker's average weekly wage for the second accident. For accidents occurring before July 1, 1990, use the average weekly wage earned at the time of the first accident [Cooper's Inc. v. Taylor, 556 So. 2d 491, 492–493 (Fla. 1st DCA 1990)].

For accidents occurring on or after July 1, 1990, use the wages earned at the time of the second accident. Why? Because effective July 1, 1990, the legislature amended § 440.15(5)(c), (d), Fla. Stat. by inserting the following provision:

> In calculating the amount of any wage loss benefits due, the average weekly wage for the subsequent accident shall be deemed to be the salary, wages, and other remuneration the employee is able to earn.

This amendment is substantive and applies only to accidents occurring on or after the effective date of the amendment, July 1, 1990 [Meek v. Layne-Western Co., 624 So. 2d 345, 347–348 (Fla. 1st DCA 1993)].

[b] Accident Dates Between January 1, 1994, and September 30, 2003

The legislature repealed § 440.15(5)(c), (d), Fla. Stat. effective January 1, 1994. Therefore, for accidents occurring after that date, stacking benefits is not allowed.

For a thorough discussion of the calculation of wage basis, see LARSON'S WORKERS' COMPENSATION, DESK EDITION, Ch. 93 (Matthew Bender).

§ 14.07 Duration of Eligibility

[1] Through June 30, 1980

The law entitles an injured worker to wage loss benefits for no more than 350 weeks (6.7 years) after maximum medical improvement [§ 440.15(3), Fla. Stat.].

[2] Between July 1, 1980, and June 30, 1983

The law entitles an injured worker to wage loss benefits for no more than 525 weeks (10 years) after maximum medical improvement or until age 65, whichever comes first [§ 440.15(3), Fla. Stat.].

[3] Between July 1, 1983, and June 30, 1990

The law still entitles an injured worker to a maximum of 525 weeks; however, the legislature repealed the age 65 limitation effective July 1, 1983 [§ 440.15(3), Fla. Stat.]. The age limitation is a substantive change. This is important because the age limitation still applies to claims that occurred before July 1, 1983 [*see* Ralston Purina Co. v. Byers, 457 So. 2d 1138, 1140 (Fla. 1st DCA 1984)].

[4] Between July 1, 1990, and December 30, 1993

The injured worker's eligibility depends on the numerical impairment rating, assigned by the physicians, from the appropriate impairment rating guide [§ 440.15(3)(b), Fla. Stat.]. Decide eligibility according to the following schedule:

Impairment Rating	Maximum Eligibility
1% to 3%	26 weeks
4% to 6%	52 weeks
7% to 9%	78 weeks
10% to 12%	104 weeks
13%	120 weeks
14%	135 weeks
15%	150 weeks
16%	170 weeks
17%	190 weeks
18%	210 weeks
19%	230 weeks
20%	250 weeks
21%	275 weeks
22%	300 weeks
23%	325 weeks
24%	350 weeks
25% to 100%	364 weeks

Not only is maximum eligibility restricted by the injured worker's impairment rating, but the amendment reduced the maximum from 525 weeks to 364 weeks. Before, the numerical impairment rating held little importance. An injured worker with a 1-percent impairment rating was eligible for up to 525 weeks of wage loss benefits. That same injured worker with an accident date between July 1, 1990, and December 31, 1993, is limited to only 26 weeks.

SPECIAL ALERT: The maximum weeks of eligibility is not a time limit that begins on the day of maximum medical improvement and ends the specified number of

Guide to Claims

weeks later. The limitations apply only as a cumulative limitation on the total number of weeks that the injured worker can *receive* wage loss benefits [*see* Winn Dixie v. Resnikoff, 659 So. 2d 1297, 1298–1299 (Fla. 1st DCA 1995)].

Injured workers enrolled in a vocational rehabilitation training program are entitled to temporary total disability benefits despite having reached maximum medical improvement. During this time they need not use any of their eligibility for wage loss benefits [*see* Roberson v. Winn Dixie Stores, Inc., 669 So. 2d 294, 297 (Fla. 1st DCA 1996)].

[5] Accident Dates Between January 1, 1994, and September 30, 2003

The maximum number of weeks of wage loss eligibility depends on when it begins and how many weeks of benefits in other classes the carrier has paid. The statute provides that the employee's eligibility for temporary benefits, impairment income benefits, and supplemental benefits terminates on the expiration of 401 weeks after the date of injury [§ 440.15(3)(c), Fla. Stat. (1/1/94)].

Thus, except for permanent total disability, eligibility for all indemnity benefits ends 401 weeks (7.7 years) from the date of injury. Therefore, if the injured worker begins receiving supplemental wage loss on the 300th week after the date of injury, the maximum wage loss eligibility is 101 weeks.

For example, assume the injured worker reached maximum medical improvement just as temporary benefit entitlement expired at 104 weeks. The physician awards a 20-percent impairment rating that entitles the injured worker to 60 weeks of impairment benefits. When impairment benefits expire, 164 weeks will have been paid since the date of the injury, leaving the injured worker with a maximum wage loss eligibility of 237 weeks or 4.5 years.

§ 14.08 Defending Wage Loss Claims

[1] Return to Work

[a] Full Employment

The first and best "defense" to any claim for wage loss or supplemental income benefits is to convince the original employer to return the employee to work. The carrier does not owe wage loss benefits if the new job pays at least 85 percent of the pre-injury average weekly wage for accidents before July 1, 1990. If the accident occurred on or after that date, the carrier does not owe wage loss or supplemental income benefits if the injured worker receives at least 80 percent of the pre-injury, average weekly wage.

If the original employer cannot or will not re-employ the injured worker, the task becomes more difficult. Now, if injured workers cannot find a job, the carrier must help and perhaps convince another employer to hire them.

[b] Retraining

The Act entitles a qualified injured worker to vocational rehabilitation for retraining into a new field. Unfortunately, such formal training is often unsuccessful. Carriers should be creative! For example, the carrier should consider offering a prospective employer some inducement in exchange for hiring injured workers and training them in an actual job. Carriers also should consider paying an employment agency's fee, or hiring a job placement service.

Evaluating an injured worker's potential for retraining should begin well before maximum medical improvement. Why? Because temporary total disability benefits are payable during retraining, for up to a maximum of 52 weeks. Delay in conducting the evaluation could result in increased cost. Rehabilitation temporary total disability benefits are also payable during counseling and program development.

[c] Reemployment Services

The Act allows and encourages carriers to provide reemployment services voluntarily to injured workers [§ 440.491, Fla. Stat. (1994)]. If the carrier discontinues voluntary services, it must make referrals to the Division for reemployment services on a Request for Screening form DWC-23.

A carrier may make a referral of an injured employee at anytime to the Division to be considered for the Division-provided reemployment services program. Such referrals must also be on form DWC-23. Note that the Division will not considered the form to be complete until it is signed by the injured employee [Fla. Admin. Code. R. 6A-22.005 (6/26/2001)].

SPECIAL NOTE: Providing and paying for vocational rehabilitation and retraining is the carrier's responsibility for accidents occurring before October 1, 1989. For accidents occurring on or after October 1, 1989, that burden shifted to the Division of Worker's Compensation [*see* ch. 17, § 17.03].

[d] Fines for Failure to Rehire

Effective January 1, 1994, the legislature added a new inducement for large employers to rehire their injured workers by subjecting such employers to a substantial fine if they do not rehire. Large employers must offer reemployment within 100 miles of the injured worker's home. A large employer is one with more than 50 employees. Such job offers, of course, must be appropriate to the injured worker's physical limitations. The employer must make the offer within 30 days after the carrier notifies it of the date of maximum medical improvement and of any physical restrictions.

This new requirement is subject to rules not yet adopted by the Division. Undaunted by the lack of administrative rules, the Division announced to employers, by letter, that it began enforcing this provision effective May 1, 1996. In that letter, the Division announced it would enforce the penalty in any case in which the injured worker reached maximum medical improvement on or after January 1, 1996. The fine is an amount equal to $250 for every $5,000 of premium or payroll. The maximum fine is $2,000 per violation. The Division has informally announced that this provision applies only to accident dates occurring on or after January 1, 1994. One statutory exception to this rehire requirement is that it does not apply if the injured worker is receiving permanent total disability benefits [§ 440.15(6), Fla. Stat. (1/1/94)].

SPECIAL ALERT: Effective October 1, 2003, the Legislature repealed the "obligation to rehire" provision of § 440.15(6), Fla. Stat.

[2] Statute of Limitations Defense

[a] Accident Dates Through December 31, 1993

[i] Application

An injured worker's right to wage loss benefits ends if at least two years have passed since the date the injured worker reached maximum medical improvement. This statutory provision does not apply if during that time, wage loss benefits *were payable* during at least three consecutive months [§ 440.15(3)(b)3a, Fla. Stat. (Emphasis added)].

The term "payable" allows carriers to stop wage loss benefits only if the injured worker has displayed a capacity to earn as much or more than pre-injury earnings. Carriers cannot stop benefits when, due to circumstances beyond the injured workers' control, they are unable to collect benefits. For the statute of limitations defense to apply then, the evidence must show that wage loss benefits were not payable *solely* because of the income received by the worker, and not for another reason [*see* Monroe Furniture Co. v. Bonner, 509 So. 2d 1264, 1267 (Fla. 1st DCA 1987)].

One year later, the court repeated this holding and, in addition, held the statutory section is not a true limitations period. The limitations sanction applies only if the injured worker does not collect wage loss for three consecutive months during a two-year period. This must, however, be because earnings were too high [*see* Wood v. McTyre Trucking Co., Inc., 526 So. 2d 739, 742 (Fla. 1st DCA 1988)].

[ii] Multiple MMI Dates

An injured worker can have more than one date of maximum medical improvement. Still, neither the Act nor case law provides for reactivation of any of the time limitations. This is true even if the injured worker does reach a subsequent point of maximum medical improvement [*see* American Airlines v. Miller, 575 So. 2d 669, 670 (Fla. 1st DCA 1990)].

In *Miller,* the injured worker reached maximum medical improvement in 1980. She continued to work full time until she had additional surgery with a new maximum medical improvement date in 1986. More than two years had elapsed since the original maximum medical improvement date without wage loss benefits having been payable for at least three consecutive months. The court held the limitations period had expired and a new maximum medical improvement date could not revive it [*see* ch. 9, § 9.03, for a complete discussion of the limitations defense].

[iii] Reduced Earnings Alone Does Not Toll Statute

Just because an injured worker's post-injury income is less than the pre-injury income does not necessarily mean the injured worker continues to be eligible for wage loss benefits. Simply not earning as much as before the accident does not toll the statute. Income must be sufficiently below the pre-injury wage for the statutory formula to trigger entitlement to benefits [*see* Winn Dixie v. Robinson, 657 So. 2d 64, 65–66 (Fla. 1st DCA 1995)].

[iv] Worker Must Be Informed

The two-year limitations period will not apply unless the evidence shows that the injured worker knew about the obligation to conduct a job search. The carrier, or the employer, must either inform an injured worker of entitlement to wage loss benefits or send job search information. A work search is not a prerequisite to wage loss benefits if the carrier does not tell the injured worker to look for work. In such a case, the statute of limitations will not begin to run until the carrier or the employer properly instructs the injured worker about work search obligations [*see* Bass v. Sarasota County Com'rs, 596 So. 2d 1229, 1230–1232 (Fla. 1st DCA 1992)].

[b] Accident Dates Between January 1, 1994, and September 30, 2003

For accidents occurring after January 1, 1994, the limitations period is *one* year. If the injured worker earns wages that are at least 80 percent of the pre-injury average weekly wage for 12 consecutive months, entitlement to supplemental income benefits ends forever [§ 440.15(3)(b)3, Fla. Stat. (1/1/94)].

At the time the carrier pays the final impairment income benefit, the injured worker may not qualify for supplemental wage loss because earnings are too high. If so, the law still may entitle the injured worker to supplemental income benefits in the future. This will occur if the injured worker's earnings fall below the 80-percent level for three consecutive months (90 days) during the one-year period after eligibility begins. This assumes, of course, that the injured worker meets basic eligibility requirements, which include an impairment rating of at least 20 percent and a good faith job search. This law may be legislative intent to codify the holding in *Bonner* and other cases discussed in [a], *above.*

A third requirement is that the injured worker's decrease in earnings must directly result from the impairment [§ 440.15(3)(b)2.c., Fla. Stat. (1/1/94)]. Unfortunately, the phrase "directly resulting from the impairment" is ambiguous. For example, if the injured worker becomes unemployed because the employer's business closes, does the sudden loss of earnings result directly from the impairment? No, but the injured worker may not find a new job because of the impairment. The courts are likely to hold, as they have often, that the reason for loss of employment is not important. If the injured worker's impairment is still a factor in the inability to get a job, this will be sufficient to satisfy the statute.

> **SPECIAL ALERT:** If the employer fires the injured worker within one year after the injured worker loses eligibility for supplemental income benefits, the court may reinstate benefits if the employer did so with the intent to avoid paying benefits [§ 440.15(3)(b)3, Fla. Stat. (1/1/94)].

For a general discussion of waiver of limitations, see Larson's Workers' Compensation,

DESK EDITION, Ch. 126, § 126.12 (Matthew Bender).

[3] Deemed Earnings Defense

[a] Accident Dates Through December 31, 1993

Deemed earnings are wages injured workers could have earned if they had accepted a suitable job offer. The law allows carriers to base wage loss on such deemed earnings if any of the following occurs.

1. The injured worker refused appropriate employment;
2. The employer fired the injured worker for misconduct; or
3. The injured worker voluntarily limits income.

Carriers can, therefore, deem earnings during a period of unemployment if any of the events listed above occur. The law allows a carrier to deem such earnings, however, for only the next three biweekly periods (six weeks) for permanent partial wage loss, and two biweekly periods (four weeks) for temporary partial wage loss. Carriers may do this administratively. That is to say, the law does not require a judge's prior approval [§ 440.15(3)(b)2, Fla. Stat.]

For example, assume the employer fires the injured worker for stealing. At the time, the injured worker earned $300 per week. The carrier may deem $300 to be the unemployed injured worker's earnings for the next six weeks when calculating wage loss benefits.

CAUTION: The courts are unlikely to consider any limitation of income to be voluntary when carriers fail to inform injured workers about their duty to conduct a job search.

[b] Accident Dates Between January 1, 1994, and September 30, 2003

Effective January 1, 1994, the legislature repealed all of the deemed earnings provisions and partially replaced them with new provisions. These changes are reviewed in [4]–[14], *below.*

The 1994 amendments, however, did not change the basic requirement that disability caused any resulting loss of wages. Thus, the employee must still prove a causal connection between a compensable injury and a resulting loss of wages to recover disability benefits. Partial disability benefits are computed based on the difference between the employee's pre-injury wage and what he or she is *able* to earn after the disability [*see* § 440.15(4), Fla. Stat. (1994)]. The 1994 legislative amendments removed the deemed earnings provision. This change, however, did not change the fact that temporary partial disability benefits are compensation for *disability*. Thus, the current statute continues to use the concept of earning capacity, not actual earnings, to measure the extent of a partial disability. For example, assume that the injured worker returned to work earning at least 80% of the pre-injury wage, but is subsequently fired for stealing. Such an employee would not be eligible for temporary disability benefits because the disability would have nothing to do with the resulting loss of wages [*see* Vencor Hospital v. Ahles, 727 So. 2d 968, 969 (Fla. 1st DCA 1998)].

A claimant must show a causal connection between his or her injury and a subsequent wage loss before an award of temporary wage loss benefits is appropriate. To determine whether an injury and a subsequent wage loss are causally connected, a judge of compensation claims must consider the totality of the circumstances. An unsuccessful job search may be a factor in considering the totality of the circumstances as to the causal connection between the injury and wage loss. However, the performance of a job search does not itself establish a causal relationship. Generally, to establish such a causal relationship, a claimant may show that his or her capabilities preclude adequate performance of his or her prior job.

For example, an employee was injured at work but continued to work until she relocated her residence to another state. She was unable to find a position and, consequently, filed a petition for benefits, seeking an award of Temporary Partial Disability benefits. The JCC awarded her TPD benefits but denied her request for impairment and supplemental benefits as premature. The employer appealed the award. The appellate court found that the award of benefits was supported by substantial evidence in the record to the effect that the employee had not yet reached her maximum medical improvement. However, the court found that the employee had failed to show a causal connection between the injury and the subsequent wage loss, which was required prior to an award of temporary wage loss benefits. The court noted that the employee showed that she conducted a job search, which was unsuccessful. That was only one factor to be considered, but it did not establish the causal relationship on its own. In reversing the award of Temporary Partial Disability benefits, the court concluded that the claimant failed to show that her physical capabilities precluded adequate job performance. The court noted that she had worked satisfactorily for 13 months following her injury and that she terminated her job for personal reasons [Interim Servs. v. Levy, 843 So. 2d 915 (Fla. 1st DCA 2003)].

[4] Failure to Accept Employment

[a] Accident Dates Through December 31, 1993

[i] Perfecting the Defense

Perfecting a defense based on an injured worker's refusal to accept employment requires evidence of two facts. First, the carrier must show that the injured worker knew about the offer of employment. Second, the carrier must show that the job was suitable to the injured worker. What does suitable mean? The Act defines "suitable gainful employment" as "employment which is reasonably attainable in light of the individual's age, education, personal aptitudes, previous vocational experience, and physical abilities" [§ 440.15(3)(b)3, Fla. Stat.].

[ii] Medical Evidence Required

If an injured worker refuses to accept employment because of physical inability to do the work, medical evidence must support this claim. For example, when doctors said

Catherine Selmer had recovered, the employer offered her a suitable job. Selmer refused the offer, claiming pain and inability to work. The medical evidence, however, was that she could work and do the job offered. The court held that Selmer's bare complaints of pain and inability to work are insufficient to override the medical evidence that she is capable of working. The court remanded the case to the judge of compensation claims to reduce the wage loss award by using deemed earnings [*see* Paradyne Corp. v. Selmer, 527 So. 2d 285, 286 (Fla. 1st DCA 1988)].

[iii] Proof of Suitable Job Offer Required

Carriers must be prepared to prove that the injured worker knew about any job offered. They must also be sure that the job is within the injured worker's physical restrictions.

For example, when doctors released Julian Lopez, the employer offered him a job, but Lopez refused it. The judge awarded wage loss benefits, but with deemed earnings. The First District Court of Appeal reversed because the job offered to Lopez required him to do substantially the same duties as his regular job. These job requirements exceeded the light duty restrictions imposed by the physician. The court held: "Because the record does not show that claimant refused employment commensurate with his abilities or suitable to his capacity . . . [the Workers' Compensation Act . . . does not preclude] him from receiving benefits" [*see* Lopez v. Nabisco Brands, Inc., 516 So. 2d 993, 994–995 (Fla. 1st DCA 1987)].

Until now, the test for whether an injured worker refused appropriate employment has been that the job offered:

1. Is within the injured worker's physical restrictions.
2. Is commensurate with the injured worker's ability.
3. Is brought to the injured worker's attention.

[iv] *Woods*—Present State of the Law?

Is a job not suitable if the injured worker simply does not want it? For example, Minnie Woods worked as a licensed practical nurse at a hospital. She suffered a back injury that required surgery. Her physician awarded a 15-percent impairment rating and imposed a 20-pound lifting restriction. This, of course, meant she could no longer do her pre injury job. Before the accident she worked only two days per week, but each work day was a 12-hour shift for a total of 24 hours per week. The employer offered Woods a job at the hospital as a care unit registrar. This, however, was a five-day, 40 hours per week job, which paid slightly less than her original job. She accepted the job but later quit, claiming she was "going crazy doing insurance all the time and in a close [*sic*] room without window. And the sitting and standing is driving me crazy."

The medical evidence was that Woods could not work as a licensed practical nurse but could do the job offered. At trial, the judge of compensation claims held the job was within her restrictions. The judge found no evidence to support her resignation and subsequent failure to work.

Surprisingly, the appellate court reversed! The court found that nearly all Woods' experience was in nursing and found nothing in the record to suggest that she was "suited" to clerical work. The court noted the difference in hours between her original job and the new one. Although the court agreed that Woods could do the new job physically, it held she was justified in not accepting it! Why? Because, said the court, the new job required her to work an additional 16 hours in a windowless room filling out insurance forms.

The court then revisited and gave new meaning to its earlier decision in *Viking Sprinkler Co. v. Thomas* [413 So. 2d 816, 818–819 (Fla. 1st DCA 1982)]. *Viking Sprinkler* now means that carriers do not have the right to choose an injured worker's post-injury occupation when an industrial accident has impaired the injured worker's own freedom of choice and job performance ability. No simple test exists to decide if a job offered is suitable. Now, many factors must be considered, not the least of which are the employee's aptitude, interest, desire, or motivation to engage in a certain type of work [*see* Woods v. St. Anthony's Hosp., 586 So. 2d 415, 419–420 (Fla. 1st DCA 1991)].

Apparently, *Woods* stands for the proposition that even if a job is within an injured worker's physical and vocational ability, it is still not suitable if the injured worker has no interest, desire, or motivation to do it! This decision made new law. Defending wage loss claims under a "failure to accept employment" theory will be more difficult.

> *I accede to the authority of that case,*
> *although I think it is a very strong decision.*
> *It does not convince me; it overcomes me.*
> Sir Edward Hall Alderson (1845)

[b] Accident Dates Between January 1, 1994, and September 30, 2003

[i] Temporary Partial Disability

The legislature repealed all of the provisions describing deemed earnings for temporary partial disability cases effective January 1, 1994. A provision first enacted in 1977, however, remains. § 440.15(7), Fla. Stat. provides that if an employee refuses suitable employment, the employee may not collect compensation while the refusal continues. (This section was renumbered with the 1994 amendments. It was originally found at § 440.15(6), Fla. Stat.) With the 2003 amendments, it is once again found at subsection (6).

Effective October 1, 2003, the Legislature amended this section to provide that the weeks during which the claimant refuses employment are to be counted as part of the 104 weeks of maximum entitlement for temporary disability benefits.

[ii] Frequency of Job Offer

Before January 1, 1994, the Act allowed carriers to apply deemed earnings for the next three biweekly periods, or a total of six weeks for wage loss. Almost everyone assumed that this meant the law required employers to offer the job every six weeks to continue deeming earnings. No statutory or case law authority supports this theory. The employer need only show the continued availability of the job to trigger its right to apply the deemed earnings defense [*see* Hyatt Regency Westshore v. Robinson, 629 So. 2d 1088, 1089 (Fla. 1st DCA 1994)].

Legally, employers must offer the job only once. Still, repeating the job offer periodically may be important to more convincingly establish evidence of its continued availability. With the repeal of § 440.15(3)(b)2, Fla. Stat., the only statutory authority for deeming earnings is § 440.15(7), Fla. Stat. The *Robinson* court declined to address the applicability of this section because the defense did not timely raise the issue.

[iii] Supplemental Wage Loss

If the injured worker refuses to accept a suitable job, the law deems the wages offered as the injured worker's post-injury average weekly wages for purposes of calculating supplemental income benefits. The statute specifically states [§ 440.15(3)(b)7, Fla. Stat. (7/1/97)]:

> If the employee is offered a bona fide position of employment that the employee is capable of performing, given the physical condition of the employee and the geographic accessibility of the position, the employee's weekly wages are considered equivalent to the weekly wages for the position offered to the employee.

The question, of course, is how long can the carrier deem wages? We calculate supplemental income benefits in advance for a three-month period, so this "deeming" of a wage equal to the wage offered applies for three months. Presumably, in keeping with the decision in *Robinson,* the employer need only establish that the job remains open and available to the injured worker. Again, re-offering the job every three months (although not required), may be a good practice.

[5] Voluntary Limitation of Income Defense

[a] Accepting Employment Below Capacity

Working at less than capacity may be a voluntary limitation of income. For example, Samuel Kirkland took a job working only 25 to 28 hours per week. He did not look for full-time work. The court found that the medical evidence did not justify his working part-time as opposed to full-time. Additionally, the court held the carrier could deem earnings for the 15 to 18 hours the injured worker was short of a full 40-hour week. In such a case, base the deemed earnings on the hourly pay-rate the injured worker earned at the part-time hours [*see* Kirkland v. Harold Pratt Paving, Inc., 518 So. 2d 1320, 1324 (Fla. 1st DCA 1987)].

NOTE: No statutory authority exists to deem earnings for supplemental income benefits under accident dates after January 1, 1994. The law does require, however, that the injured worker conduct a good faith job search. Unfortunately, the statute is silent about what happens if the injured worker does not do a job search or accepts employment below capacity. The law is well settled that it does not follow that an injured worker who does no job search is entitled to nothing. Courts will likely continue to apply deemed earnings to the new supplemental income benefits. Remember, however, that injured workers in a temporary partial disability status have no duty to conduct a job search. Their only duty is to report any earnings. Still, employees must prove a causal connection between a compensable injury and a resulting loss of wages to recover disability benefits. Partial disability benefits are computed based on the difference between the employee's pre-injury wage and what he or she is *able* to earn after the disability [*see* § 440.15(4), Fla. Stat. (1994)]. Thus, the current statute continues to use the concept of earning capacity, not actual earnings, to measure the extent of a partial disability [*see* Vencor Hospital v. Ahles, 727 So. 2d 968, 969 (Fla. 1st DCA 1998)]. For accidents occurring after January 1, 1994, the following in [b] and [c], *below,* should apply to supplemental income benefits, but not to temporary partial benefits.

Guide to Claims

[b] Carrier Has Burden of Proof

In another case, almost identical to *Kirkland* [*see* [a], *above*], the court reached a far different conclusion. Deemed earnings does not apply to an injured worker who worked part-time if the carrier fails to show that other, more lucrative, employment is available. The court said [*see* Myers v. Holiday House, 578 So. 2d 349, 350 (Fla. 1st DCA 1991)].

> While a part-time work effort may sometimes constitute a voluntary limitation of earnings, once the claimant's initial burden is satisfied it becomes incumbent upon the employer/carrier to establish the necessary elements for the application of deemed earnings . . . in connection with a voluntary limitation of income. The employer/carrier's burden in this regard requires affirmative proof as to the specific availability of more lucrative employment commensurate with the claimant's skills and capabilities.

[c] Part-Time Job Problem

What happens when an injured worker, who could work full-time, chooses part-time work instead? A carrier may deem earnings in such cases if it can show the following facts:

1. The injured worker took a part-time job contrary to medical evidence of ability to work full-time.
2. The evidence proves the existence of full-time, more lucrative, jobs that the injured worker has the skill to do.

For example, Nancy Braithwaite decided to work part-time in her husband's business, rather than look for full-time work. The judge denied wage loss benefits, holding this is a voluntary limitation of income. On appeal the First District Court of Appeal reversed. The court held the judge should not have denied all benefits, but should have awarded wage loss based on deemed earnings [*see* Braithwaite v. Department of Transp., 622 So. 2d 109, 111 (Fla. 1st DCA 1993)].

REMEMBER: This does not apply to temporary partial disability for accidents occurring on or after January 1, 1994.

[6] Deemed Earnings Seen as Benefit to Injured Worker

Florida courts see deemed earnings not as a defense for the carrier, but as a benefit to the employee. What happens if the injured worker does a poor job search or no job search at all? The law may still entitle the injured worker to wage loss benefits based on deemed earnings.

The rule of law is as follows: the deemed earnings provision is applicable not only to those months in which a work search is inadequate, but also to those months when no work search has been performed [*see* Baggett v. Mulberry Const. Co., 549 So. 2d 1386, 1389 (Fla. 1st DCA 1989)].

For example, three expert witnesses testified that Michael Jerry could not perform his former job. Jerry, however, admitted that he did no job search at all but still claimed wage loss benefits. The judge of compensation claims denied wage loss benefits because of Jerry's failure to look for work. On appeal, the court reversed and held the judge should have awarded wage loss benefits on a deemed earnings basis. In other words, the judge should have decided what Jerry could have earned had he conducted a job search [*see* Jerry v. Farm Stores, Inc., 576 So. 2d 405, 406 (Fla. 1st DCA 1991)].

The effect is this: the burden is on the carrier to prove what the employee could have earned had a good faith (or any) job search been conducted. Despite these and many other cases, carriers continue litigating this issue and continue to lose. The First District Court of Appeal consistently holds that a lack of a job search does not automatically preclude entitlement to wage loss benefits.

This means that failure to conduct a job search is a complete bar to compensation under only one condition. That condition arises when a job search is the only way to decide if the employee can work and how much the employee can earn. If there is evidence the injured worker can work and evidence about earning ability, the carrier must pay wage loss using deemed earnings. This applies whether the injured worker actually conducts a work search.

> *Fools and stubborn men make wealthy lawyers.*
> Spanish proverb. H.L. Mencken,
> A new Dictionary of Quotations, 1946

[7] Income Limitation Must Be Voluntary

[a] No Job Search Due to Illness

Is an ill injured worker, who does no job search, voluntarily limiting income? "Voluntarily" is the operative word. What happens if the injured worker cannot conduct a job search because a completely unrelated medical condition temporarily causes total disability? Although the exacerbation of an injured worker's preexisting disease may have been independently disabling, this does not necessarily preclude an award of wage loss benefits.

For example, Wayne Zellers did not look for work for two months because of an unrelated, but disabling, medical condition. The court held the law still entitled him to wage loss benefits with deemed earnings. Why? Because he experienced the effects of his compensable injury both before and after the two-month period. The court held that "insofar as claimant is otherwise entitled to wage-loss benefits, such a claim should not have been denied during the brief exacerbation of the preexisting disease" [*see* Commercial Carrier Corp. v. Zellers, 579 So. 2d 157, 159 (Fla. 1st DCA 1991)].

[b] No Job Search by Choice

Wayne Zellers had a good excuse for not conducting a job search [*see* [a], *above*]. What happens, though, if the injured worker has no excuse or, at least, not a good one? Such an injured worker can still collect wage loss benefits with deemed earnings. For example, the judge of compensation claims found that McCarthy had voluntarily limited his income. The evidence proved that plenty of jobs were available within his restrictions that would pay between $5 and $6 an hour. The judge, therefore, imputed or deemed McCarthy's income to be $200 per week. The First District Court of Appeals affirmed the judge's order [*see* McCarthy v. Bay Area Signs, 639 So. 2d 1114, 1116 (Fla. 1st DCA 1994)].

[c] No Job Search to Return to School

Sometimes an injured worker can work, but elects not to conduct a job search to pursue full-time education. Pursuing schooling rather than looking for work may be a voluntary limitation of income that triggers the application of the deemed earnings provision. In such a case, the carrier's burden is to prove that appropriate employment was available. The carrier must also show that the injured worker refused an available job within restrictions during the period in question [*see* Church's Fried Chicken v. Maloney, 599 So. 2d 706, 710 (Fla. 1st DCA 1992)].

[d] Employee Leaves Employment

Previously, the law provided that if an injured worker voluntarily quit a job, the carrier did not owe temporary partial benefits. Effective October 1, 2003, the Legislature amended this section to provide that if the claimant quits without just cause, temporary partial disability benefits are payable based on deemed earnings. Put another way, the claimant is entitled to only the benefits that would have been paid if the claimant had remained at work. Although it is the carrier who must first decide if the claimant's departure was not justified, ultimately, it will be for the judge of compensation claims to decide if the claimant's resignation was justified [§ 440.15(7), Fla. Stat. (10/1/2003)].

CAUTION: The peculiar wording of the amendment might be interpreted to mean that the carrier must first obtain a ruling from the judge of compensation claims before altering benefits. The statute provides if the employee leaves his employment "without just cause *as determined* by the judge of compensation claims," benefits are paid based on deemed earnings. [*Emphasis added*]

The key terms are "voluntarily" and "just cause." If an injured worker leaves employment because of physical limitations from the compensable injury, the resignation cannot be considered an unjustified voluntary limitation of income.

Case 1. The injured worker quit her job because the employer did not give her assistance required by her work restrictions [*see* Dyer v. Lakeland Health Care Center, 582 So. 2d 760, 762 (Fla. 1st DCA 1991)].

Case 2. The injured worker quit her job because of physical difficulties in doing the work due to physical restrictions [*see* Mackin v. Olde World Cheese Shop, 536 So. 2d 301, 302–303 (Fla. 1st DCA 1988)].

Case 3. After returning to work on light duty, the injured worker experienced neck pain after falling a second time. He left the job and never returned. Because the employer did not offer a new, and presumably lighter duty job, his limitation of income was not voluntary [*see* Valdez v. Entenmann's Bakery, 632 So. 2d 253, 254 (Fla. 1st DCA 1994)].

[8] Dismissal for Misconduct

If the employer fires the worker because of misconduct, the carrier may deem earnings. The misconduct in question, however, must meet the statutory definition as follows [§ 440.02(16), Fla. Stat. (7/1/97)]:

> Misconduct includes, but is not limited to, the following, which shall not be construed in pari materia with each other:
>
> [a] Conduct evincing such willful or wanton disregard of an employer's interests as is found in deliberate violation or disregard of standards of behavior which the employer has the right to expect of the employee; or
>
> [b] Carelessness or negligence of such a degree or recurrence as to manifest culpability, wrongful intent, or evil design, or to show an intentional and substantial disregard of an employer's interests or of the employee's duties and obligations to the employer.

These dire definitions are also vague. We must, therefore, decide on a case-by-case basis whether the dismissed injured worker was guilty of misconduct.

Except temporary partial disability, this statute should apply to accidents occurring on or after January 1, 1994, because the Act entitles an injured worker to supplemental income benefits only if the lack of earnings is the direct result of the employee's impairment.

[9] Availability of Jobs

[a] Accident Dates Through December 31, 1993

For the first 12 weeks after maximum medical improvement, the law presumes that an unemployed injured worker's wage-earning capacity is zero. This changes, however, beginning with the 13th week after maximum medical improvement. At this point, the Act allows the carrier to show that the injured worker's wage earning ability is more than zero. How? The carrier can show this by proving the existence of actual job openings [§ 440.15(3)(b)2, Fla. Stat. (1991)].

These jobs must be within a reasonable geographical area. Also, these must be jobs that the injured worker is physically and vocationally able to perform. The judge of compensation claims must decide what the injured worker could earn in such jobs. This is the amount used as deemed earnings. Note there is no requirement that the injured worker knew about these jobs or applied for them.

The type and degree of evidence required to prove the existence of such jobs is uncertain. The obvious legislative intent is to give to the carrier the opportunity to show there are many jobs that injured workers could get if they really wanted to work. An independent vocational placement firm might help.

SPECIAL ALERT: The "actual job openings" defense described in Florida Statutes, § 440.15(3)(b)2, Fla. Stat. (1991) is a procedural amendment because it relates to the method carriers may use to prove voluntary limitation of income. It therefore applies to all wage-loss periods after July 1, 1990, whatever the accident date [*see* McCarthy v. Bay Area Signs, 629 So. 2d 1114, 1116 (Fla. 1st DCA 1994)].

[b] Accident Dates Between January 1, 1994, and September 30, 2003

The legislature repealed all the "actual job opening" language. This defense does not appear available for accidents occurring on or after January 1, 1994—at least not on a statutory basis.

[10] Three Strikes and You're Out!

[a] Accident Dates Through December 31, 1993

A significant problem with the system has been full employment that did not necessarily end entitlement to wage loss benefits. Injured workers have walked off their jobs for reasons unrelated to their injuries. They have refused suitable employment offers. They have even spent time in jail and were still eligible for wage loss benefits!

To put a stop to such abuses, the legislature enacted what some call the "three strikes and you're out" rule. Others prefer to call this the 4/3/2 rule. By whatever name, it works like this. If an injured worker commits one or more of *four* offenses, *three* times over a *two*-year period, that injured worker is out of the wage loss system, forever. The statute provides as follows [§ 440.15(3)(b)(5), Fla. Stat. (7/1/90)]:

> The right to wage loss benefits shall terminate if, within a 2-year period there are three occurrences of any of the following incidents:
>
> a. The employee voluntarily terminates his employment for reasons unrelated to his compensable injury.
>
> b. The employee refuses an offer of suitable or reasonable employment within his restrictions and abilities.
>
> c. The employee is terminated from employment due to his own misconduct as defined in s. 440.02(16).

d. The employee voluntarily limits his income.

Provided these measures govern a given claim, note that each occurrence must take place during a different biweekly period. For each occurrence, the carrier may still deem earnings for the next three biweekly periods (six weeks).

> **SPECIAL ALERT:** The "three strikes" defense is a substantive amendment, so carriers cannot apply it retroactively. It is substantive because it may shorten an injured worker's entitlement to benefits. The defense, therefore, applies to accident dates occurring only between the effective date of the amendment, July 1, 1990, and the date of its repeal, December 31, 1993 [*see* McCarthy v. Bay Area Signs, 639 So. 2d 1114, 1116 (Fla. 1st DCA 1994); Smith v. Crest Products, 643 So. 2d 672, 673 (Fla. 1st DCA 1994). The *Smith* court noted that even when this defense applies, it would preclude only wage loss and not other classes of benefits.

[b] Accident Dates Between January 1, 1994, and September 30, 2003

The legislature repealed the "three strikes" provisions. Therefore, it does not apply to accidents occurring on or after January 1, 1994.

[11] One Strike and You're Out

[a] Accident Dates Through December 31, 1993

Besides the three strikes rule [*see* [10], *above*], the legislature also created what some call the "one strike and you're out" rule. This statutory rule became effective July 1, 1990 [§ 440.15(3)(b)6, Fla. Stat. (1990)]:

> The right to wage loss benefits shall terminate if an employee is convicted of conduct punishable under § 775.082 or § 775.083 or is subjected to imprisonment under Chapter 316 which directly affects the employee's ability to perform the activities of his usual or other appropriate employment.

This statutory rule operates independently of the three strikes rule. It provides that an injured worker's right to wage loss ends forever if either of two events occurs. The first event is that the injured worker is convicted of criminal conduct punishable under § 775.082, Fla. Stat. or § 775.083, Fla. Stat. These are the sections that explain maximum jail time and fines for felonies and misdemeanors. The second event is that the injured worker is subjected to imprisonment under Ch. 316, Fla. Stat., the motor vehicle section of the law. The conviction or imprisonment, however, must directly affect the injured worker's ability to perform the activities of his usual or other appropriate employment in order for the statutory rule to apply.

This is another ambiguous and controversial provision that raises some interesting possibilities. For example, under Ch. 316, Fla. Stat., the first offense of reckless driving carries a punishment of up to 90 days in jail. If convicted and sentenced under this provision, would the injured worker's right to wage loss benefits end? Not necessarily.

For example, Gregory Beach, an assembly line worker, was convicted and jailed for driving while intoxicated. This occurred while Beach was receiving temporary total disability benefits. A few days after his release from jail, Beach reached maximum medical improvement with a permanent impairment. The question became whether Beach could collect wage loss benefits because of the operation of § 440.15, Fla. Stat. In spite of this provision, the judge of compensation claims awarded wage loss benefits. The carrier appealed, arguing that the phrase "shall terminate" is plain and unambiguous on its face. The carrier also argued that the judge of compensation claims had no authority to place a limiting construction on the statute. The First District Court of Appeal agreed with the judge and affirmed.

The court stated that to end an employee's right to wage loss benefits because of confinement for driving under the influence (DUI), the carrier must show evidence that the imprisonment affected the employee's ability to perform the activities of his usual or other appropriate employment. The court found that this particular conviction and imprisonment did not affect the injured worker's ability to do his pre-injury employment as an assembly-line worker. Thus, the carrier has the burden to show affirmatively that the confinement directly affected the employee's job performance after release [*see* Deep South Products v. Beach, 616 So. 2d 156, 158 (Fla. 1st DCA 1993)].

If an injured worker drives for a living and a DUI conviction results in a revocation of license, this clearly affects the injured worker's ability to do the driving job. Remember, however, that this must also affect the injured worker's ability to do "other appropriate employment." This defense will have rare application.

[b] Accident Dates Between January 1, 1994, and September 30, 2003

The legislature repealed the "one strike" provision. Therefore, it does not apply to accidents occurring on or after January 1, 1994.

[12] Insincere, Illogical, or No Job Search

[a] Overview

To be eligible for wage loss benefits for accidents occurring before 1994, an injured worker must conduct a logical and adequate job search. An injured worker, however, has no obligation to do so until instructed by the employer or carrier. Conducting an inadequate, illogical, and insincere job search, if medical evidence of disability exists, does not create an automatic bar to recovery. Even an injured worker who conducts no job search may collect wage loss benefits using deemed earnings. Failure to conduct a good job search is a complete defense and bar to recovery under only one condition, i.e., a job search is the only way to show an inability to earn pre-injury wages.

[b] Adequacy of Job Search: Accident Dates Through December 31, 1993

An injured worker who fails to conduct an adequate job search is, in certain cases, not entitled to wage loss benefits for the period in question. Not conducting a job search bars eligibility for wage loss benefits, but only when a job search is the only way to prove inability to earn pre injury wages. When there is medical evidence of inability to earn wages, the lack of a job search does not preclude all compensation. When the medical evidence shows that an injured worker cannot perform the pre-injury job, and the injured worker does not conduct a good job search, the law still allows wage loss benefits but with deemed earnings.

The courts have declined to define any specific test to decide job search adequacy. Decide each case on its own merits. When carriers and injured workers disagree, the decision is ultimately the responsibility of a judge of compensation claims. The judge must decide whether an injured worker's efforts were reasonable and done in good faith in light of all the existing circumstances.

[c] Five Job Search Minimum

Effective July 1, 1990, the legislature amended the job search section of the Workers' Compensation Act. The law now requires a minimum of five job searches in each biweekly period. An exception arises if a judge decides fewer job searches are justified due to the availability of suitable employment. There are two reasons not to construe this amendment too literally. First, the statutory language gives the judge discretion whether or not to apply the minimum requirement. Second, the courts have consistently held there cannot be any absolute number of minimum or maximum weekly contacts as a threshold requirement for an adequate job search [§ 440.15(3)(b)2, Fla. Stat.].

The judges of compensation claims have great leeway in deciding the adequacy of a job search. For example, James Finke completed five job searches during a two-week period, but all those contacts were during the first week. Finke did nothing during the second. The judge of compensation claims decided that this was not a good faith effort and denied wage loss benefits for the second week. Having completed five job searches does not mean an injured worker is entitled to benefits as a matter of law [*see* Finke v. Pasadena Yacht & Tennis Club, 697 So. 2d 994, 995 (Fla. 1st DCA 1997)].

In *Stoffel Plumbing, Inc. v. Smith* [570 So. 2d 1099, 1100 (Fla. 1st DCA 1990)], the court (temporarily) held the five-job search minimum is a substantive change. Thus, it could not apply the statutory requirement to *Stoffel Plumbing* or other cases that occurred before July 1, 1990. Since the new provision did not apply to *Stoffel Plumbing* the court did not directly address the issue of a minimum number of job searches. The court did, however, suggest in dicta that future courts might not construe the five-job search minimum as creating a numerical threshold requirement.

SPECIAL ALERT: In 1992, the court reconsidered the statute's application and receded from the suggestion in *GCC Beverages v. Simmons,* 571 So. 2d 59 (Fla. 1st DCA 1990), that the amendment is substantive. The court now considers the job search amendments to § 440.15, Fla. Stat. procedural. This means they apply to all periods of wage loss occurring after July 1, 1990, despite when the accident and injury occurred [*see* Litvin v. St. Lucie Cty. Sheriff's Dept., 599 So. 2d 1353, 1355–1356 (Fla. 1st DCA 1992), *cert. denied,* 508 U.S. 913 (1993)].

[d] Accident Dates Between January 1, 1994, and September 30, 2003

The legislature repealed all of the detailed job search requirements effective January 1, 1994. All the Act now requires is that "the employee in good faith attempted to obtain employment commensurate with the employee's ability to work" [§ 440.15(3)(b)1, Fla. Stat.]. This may be a codification of many appellate cases. These cases hold generally that, despite statutory provisions, we must decide what is a good faith job search on a case-by-case basis. Since the legislature repealed all the statutory definitions of a good faith job search, the following discussion in [e], *below,* of judicially created guidelines takes on increased importance.

[e] Factors to Decide Adequate Job Search

[i] Job Search Factors

What are the factors the courts require a judge of compensation claims to consider in deciding the adequacy of a job search? They are the injured worker's:

1. Physical impairment
2. Age
3. Industrial history
4. Training and education
5. Motivation
6. Work experience
7. Due diligence and the like

[ii] Carrier Provided Job Search Assistance

The court has since added the additional factor of the carrier's provision of job search assistance or rehabilitation. For example, Howard Gill did not dispute that during a 10-month period he repeatedly contacted the same four prospective employers. After that, Gill contacted only one new employer every three or four months. Gill testified that his injured foot made driving a vehicle very difficult. Despite this, most of the employers he contacted were courier services. These jobs required driving and handling packages or luggage. This, of course, is the quintessential example of an illogical and insincere job search.

The court, however, saw these facts in a considerably different light. "Gill's contacts with a limited number of employers whose work was clearly beyond his abilities should have put the [employer/carrier] on notice that claimant was in need of some direction in this area."

The carrier, said the court, "bears the responsibility of monitoring a claimant's job search to ensure its effectiveness." This means that, initially at least, evidence of a poor and illogical job search does not create a defense to a claim for wage loss benefits. Instead, it is a sign that the injured worker does not know how to conduct a good job search. In such a case the carrier must provide job search help. The court noted that a carrier's failure to help an injured worker to find work may be regarded as an abdication of its duty. The court further pointed out that an employer can end its liability for wage loss benefits by simply giving the injured worker a job [*see* Gill V. USX Corp., 588 So. 2d 1035, 1038 (Fla. 1st DCA 1991)].

[iii] Illogical Job Search: Case History

Following are other examples of illogical job searches that still resulted in an award of benefits.

Case 1. Alfred Grace limited his job applications to employers whose work was beyond his physical ability. The judge of compensation claims denied wage loss benefits, holding such a job search lacked good faith. In its written opinion, the First District Court of Appeal reminded the judge that the employer did not provide other employment to the injured worker. "An employer," said the court, "who fails in this material obligation risks a judge's consideration of such factor when determining the adequacy of a good faith job search" [*see* Grace v. Collier County School Bd., 552 So. 2d 961, 963–964 (Fla. 1st DCA 1989)].

Case 2. James Roll looked only for work that he was incapable of performing. The judge of compensation claims held that such a job search is impermissibly inadequate and denied wage loss benefits. On appeal, the First District Court of Appeals held this finding is incorrect and is a misstatement of the law. The carrier had a chance to decide whether Roll had applied for positions that were beyond his physical or vocational capacities. Considering the carrier's duty to monitor a job search to ensure its effectiveness, it should have helped the injured worker if it became apparent that he was making unrealistic contacts. If the carrier issued notices of denial based on such unrealistic contacts, denying such knowledge would be difficult for the carrier [*see* Roll v. Sebastian Inlet, 609 So. 2d 674, 676–677 (Fla. 1st DCA 1992)].

Case 3. Juanita Ankeny claimed she applied for many jobs, but most of these prospective employers said they had never heard of her. Whether she applied or not was irrelevant because the jobs she listed were not within her limitations anyway. She even admitted that her job search was inadequate. When the judge of compensation claims denied all wage loss benefits, Ankeny appealed and the First District Court of Appeal reversed the judge's order. Everyone agreed that Ankeny did not conduct an adequate job search. Still, said the court, doing a poor job search does not per se preclude all benefits. Instead, the law entitles the employee to wage loss benefits reduced by deemed earnings. Though stated several times in prior cases, the court's holding bears repeating [*see* Ankeny v. Palm Beach County School Bd., 643 So. 2d 1127, 1128–1129 (Fla. 1st DCA 1994)].

Lack of a good job search is a complete bar to compensation under only one condition, i.e., when there is no un controverted medical evidence that the injured worker's inability to work is related to the compensable injury. With such evidence, lack of a job search simply results in reduced wage loss benefits based on deemed earnings [*see* Ankeny v. Palm Beach County School Bd., 643 So. 2d 1127, 1129 (Fla. 1st DCA 1994)].

Perhaps now, the law is sufficiently settled and well known that carriers will avoid such futile litigation.

> *Lawyers' houses are built on the heads of fools.*
> Proverb. Thomas Fuller, Gnomologia, 1732

[iv] Poor Job Search Is Incomplete Defense

A poor job search itself is not a complete defense. Carriers must prove that they at least offered to provide job search assistance. If accepted, carriers may base a sound defense on evidence that the injured worker's inability to get a job is due to malingering and a deliberate sabotage of the job search effort. If injured workers refuse such help, they are on their own, and the traditional inappropriate job search defense should apply.

The carrier, however, is under no duty to provide vocational rehabilitation or retraining services after October 1, 1989. After that date, this became the Division's responsibility. In one case, the judge of compensation claims awarded temporary partial wage loss benefits solely on the basis that the employer and carrier neither offered nor recommended any type of rehabilitation or retraining to help the injured worker in finding work outside his experience. The First District Court of Appeal reversed. Carriers have no responsibility to provide such services after October 1, 1989. Basing an award of wage loss benefits on a requirement that the carrier offer rehabilitation benefits is impermissible [*see* Hyatt Hotel v. Lalu, 605 So. 2d 965, 966 (Fla. 1st DCA 1992)]. This does not, however, negate the court's opinions in *Gill* [*see* [ii], *above*] and other cases. There, the court held the carrier has the duty to provide job search assistance. This, of course, is different from rehabilitation and retraining.

> **CAVEAT:** A carrier's expert and diligent, but unsuccessful, long term effort to help an injured worker find employment may form evidence that the injured worker is permanently and totally disabled.

[13] No Job Search at All

[a] Notice to Conduct Job Search Is Mandatory

The carrier or the employer must be sure tell the injured worker to conduct a job search; otherwise, an injured worker has no duty to do a job search Effective July 1, 1990, notice from the servicing agent or the injured worker's attorney satisfies this requirement. The legal effect of failing to inform is to relieve the injured worker of the need to conduct a work search. This failure does not, however, conclusively entitle the injured worker to benefits. Sometimes, the judge may decide that the injured worker's injuries do not prevent doing prior job duties. If so, then the fact of an unsuccessful job search, real or presumed, is not relevant [*see* Nickolls v. University of Florida, 606 So. 2d 410, 413 (Fla. 1st DCA 1992)].

Merely sending the injured worker a letter, however, is no guarantee. Carriers must prove that the injured worker received it. For example, Jacoby admitted he received a letter from the carrier informing him that the doctor released him to work. He denied, however, receiving the carrier's letter concerning work search requirements. The judge of compensation claims believed him and waived the job search requirement. The First District Court of Appeal affirmed and held the judge may accept such testimony [*see* Scotty's v. Jacoby, 611 So. 2d 101, 102–103 (Fla. 1st DCA 1992)].

If judges in future cases accept simple denials of receipt, a carrier's only rebuttal will be production of registered or certified mail receipts. For periods after July 1, 1990, the legislature created an additional defense. Evidence that the injured worker's attorney advised the injured worker of work search requirements disproves allegations of lack of knowledge.

Simply conducting a job search is not evidence that injured workers understand their legal burden to do so. In one case, the carrier failed to tell the injured worker properly about the duty to job search. The injured worker conducted a job search anyway. When the judge of compensation claims awarded wage loss benefits for a period during which the injured worker did no job search, the carrier appealed. The carrier argued that by conducting a job search, the injured worker displayed actual knowledge of his responsibility to do so. The court disagreed. Simply conducting a job search is not evidence that injured workers understand such issues as the five-job search minimum, or the duty to timely submit wage loss requests. "It is not sufficient," said the court, "for the employer to come before this court and merely argue that the employee must have known of the statutory requirements because a work search of sorts was conducted" [*see* Mac Papers, Inc. v. Cruz, 658 So. 2d 108, 109–110 (Fla. 1st DCA 1995)].

[b] Notice to Attorney Alone Is Not Enough

Telling the injured worker's attorney about the job search requirement is not enough. The carrier must tell the injured worker directly or the law will operate to waive the job search requirement [*see* Morris v. Metal Industries, 491 So. 2d 312, (Fla. 1st DCA 1986)].

An exception arises if the injured worker's attorney directs that all communications go to the attorney rather than to the injured worker. In such a case, notice to the attorney with job-search forms is enough to inform the injured worker of the obligation to conduct a work search [*see* Saavedra v. Cedars Medical Center, 584 So. 2d 197, 198 (Fla. 1st DCA 1991)].

Effective July 1, 1990, the legislature amended § 440.15(3)(b)2, Fla. Stat. The section now provides that an injured worker's obligation to job search begins with knowledge of the requirement to do so. This applies whether notice comes from the employer, carrier, servicing agent, or the injured worker's attorney.

This section means that if the attorney tells the injured worker about the duty to job search, it does not matter that the carrier did not do so. The court dismissed the notion that this somehow offends the attorney-client privilege or that it violates any constitutional rights. Further, the court held these amendments are evidentiary in nature. They are, therefore, procedural changes that apply to all wage loss periods occurring after the effective date of the amendment, whatever the date of the accident [*see* Litvin v. St. Lucie Cty. Sheriff's Dept., 599 So. 2d 1353, 1355–1356 (Fla. 1st DCA 1992), *cert. denied,* 508 U.S. 913 (1993)].

Carriers must be prepared to produce clear evidence that the attorney properly instructed the injured worker. The judge of compensation claims may not assume the attorney gave proper instruction. The court held the amendment to § 440.15(3)(b)2, Fla. Stat. "is an obvious legislative response to case law of this court. . . . We are of the view, nonetheless, that this amendment does not transform the workers' compensation law into a claimant-attorney monitored system. The Workers' Compensation Act remains a presumptively self-executing, but fundamentally employer/carrier monitored, system" [*see* Turner v. Rinker Materials, 622 So. 2d 80, 84 (Fla. 1st DCA 1993)].

In other words, the amendment does not relieve carriers of their duty in the administration of claims. Adjusters must not depend on the injured worker's attorney to do the adjuster's job.

Guide to Claims

SPECIAL ALERT: The legislature repealed § 440.15(3)(b)2, Fla. Stat. effective January 1, 1994. This section provided that notice from the injured worker's attorney is enough. Again, carriers must insure that they communicate notification of job search requirements directly to the injured worker. As discussed above, an exception still arises if the attorney instructs that all communications go through the attorney. In such a case, notice to the attorney is enough.

[c] Excused Job Search Does Not Create Automatic Entitlement

A judge of compensation claims can excuse an injured worker from the job search requirement, but this does not create automatic entitlement to wage loss benefits. Also, conducting an unsuccessful job search does not itself bring automatic entitlement. All relevant evidence must be considered. Whether the evidence shows that the compensable accident caused the loss of wages depends on all the circumstances. Whether or not an injured worker does a job search, the evidence must show that physical limitations are a factor in the loss of wages. If an injured worker's capabilities allow doing the pre-injury job, the injured worker cannot collect wage loss benefits even if the judge excuses the job search requirement.

For example, David Thompson was a certified public accountant with a master's degree in business administration. He received notice that his services as Public Safety Director for the City of Jacksonville were no longer needed. Twelve days later he hurt his back while moving boxes as he packed his office belongings. Because the carrier failed to tell Thompson about his duty to conduct a job search, the judge of compensation claims excused this requirement. Despite this, the judge denied wage loss benefits because Thompson was physically able to perform his former City Hall job. He did not return only because the job was not available. Thus, the judge concluded that Thompson had failed to prove a causal connection between his injury and his later wage loss. On appeal, the court agreed and affirmed the order [*see* Thompson v. City of Jacksonville, 654 So. 2d 1178, 1180–1181 (Fla. 1st DCA 1995)].

[d] Injured Worker Must Be Capable of Job Search

Carriers must be certain the injured worker is medically able to conduct a job search. One physician may have released the injured worker, but another physician may say the injured worker's mental health is such that total disability continues. Also, carriers should be sure the physician tells the injured worker to go back to work. Injured workers are under no duty to return to work or to look for work until instructed by the doctor [*see* Strauss v. City of Sarasota, 556 So. 2d 417, 418 (Fla. 1st DCA 1989)].

[e] Complaints of Pain Generally No Excuse

Usually, complaints of pain alone will not excuse a work search without medical evidence that the injured worker cannot work. A medical expert's testimony, however, does not always constrain a judge of compensation claims. The judge may, in certain cases, disregard the doctor's testimony in favor of the injured worker's testimony [*see* Square G. Const. Co. v. Grace, 412 So. 2d 397, 399 (Fla. 1st DCA 1982); Crowell v. Messana Contractors, 180 So. 2d 329, 330 (Fla. 1965); Lakeside Health Care v. Fox, 584 So. 2d 627, 629–630 (Fla. 1st DCA 1991)].

In *Fox,* the physician said the injured worker needed back surgery, but the injured worker refused surgery, apparently out of fear. The doctor released her for light duty, with restrictions. About two months later, she got a job but quit after only one week because of pain in her back. She returned to the doctor and requested that he schedule the surgery. The doctor performed the surgery three months later. Fox claimed she looked for work meanwhile, but had no documentation. Although the doctor testified the injured worker could work before surgery, she claimed she could not. The court held that the fact the injured worker underwent major surgery supported her claim that she quit because of pain. The court concluded the trial judge was justified in ignoring the doctor in favor of the injured worker and affirmed an award of wage loss benefits.

Always look at such a case entirely and examine all the facts. This is especially true when the medical evidence is limited. If several physicians dispute the injured worker's testimony, the injured worker will have far less credibility.

[f] Settling Subsequent Injury Changes Burden of Proof for First Injury

It is not unusual for an injured worker to suffer another accident while recovering from the first one. It is also not unusual that different carriers are involved for each accident. If an injured worker's wage loss arises from the combination of both injuries, what happens if the injured worker settles with only one carrier? Here is an example. Manuel Almeida hurt his back at work. Eleven days later, he suffered a second back injury in a new accident. By this time the employer had changed carriers. Later, Almeida reached maximum medical improvement from both injuries with a 15-percent impairment rating. Although the first injury was relatively minor, doctors could not separate the injuries and generally attributed Almeida's impairment to the combination of the two. The second carrier settled Almeida's claim, thereby securing a release from liability for wage loss benefits. Almeida then filed a claim for wage loss benefits against the first carrier. The court held that by accepting the settlement, Almeida placed himself in the position of having to prove that his ongoing wage loss resulted from the first injury alone. Since there was no such evidence, the court held he was not entitled to wage loss benefits from the first carrier [*see* Almeida v. Longleaf Forest Products, 648 So. 2d 1235, 1236–1237 (Fla. 1st DCA 1995)].

For a general discussion of the inability to search for work, see LARSON'S WORKERS'

Compensation, Desk Edition, Ch. 84 (Matthew Bender).

> **NOTE:** Do not confuse the *Almeida* case with apportionment between carriers. Because the parties resolved the second carrier's liability by settlement agreement, this case is simply a contest between the injured worker and the first carrier. For a discussion on apportionment between carriers, see ch. 24, § 24.06[3].

> *Facts do not cease to exist because they are ignored.*
> Aldous Huxley, 1894–1963

Guide to Claims

[14] Incomplete or Untimely Request for Wage Loss

[a] Accident Dates Through December 31, 1993

Originally, late filing or other irregularities in wage loss forms were not necessarily fatal to the claim. Such defects were not a valid defense unless they resulted in prejudice to the carrier. Further, the carrier had to show that lack of a signature or job search evidence was more than a mere technical error [*see* Stahl v. Mike Gordon's Seafood Restaurant, 408 So. 2d 808, 809 (Fla. 1st DCA 1982); Ardmore Farms v. Smith, 423 So. 2d 1039, 1043–1044 (Fla. 1st DCA 1982)].

Since the courts decided these cases, there have been several legislative changes that render them moot. First, the Act now requires that the employee report his efforts, if any, to obtain employment, including contacts with prospective employers. In addition, the same section requires that the employee must sign the form [§ 440.185(10), Fla. Stat.].

Second, the Division's administrative rules require the injured worker to furnish the carrier with a work search report, including the name and address of the person contacted at each business [Fla. Admin Code R. 4L-3.018 (11/11/96)].

Third, the Act requires that wage loss forms and job search reports are to be mailed to the employer, carrier, or servicing agent within 14 days after the time benefits are due. The section further provides that failure to submit wage loss requests timely and properly "shall result in benefits not being payable during the time that the employee fails to timely file his request for wage loss and the job search reports" [§ 440.15(3)(b)(2), Fla. Stat.].

The third requirement is a controversial provision, mainly because it is so poorly drafted, but also because it creates a mini, two-week, statute of limitations. No benefits are payable "during the time that the employee fails to timely file." Obviously, the legislature intended this provision to put a stop to the practice of filing multiple wage loss requests simultaneously. Now, an injured worker must file requests within 14 days after the period claimed. Mailing wage loss requests on the 15th day is too late. When filed too late, the law allows the carrier to deny wage loss benefits for that period. The "fifteen days is too late" theory is a correct interpretation of this amendment. In addition, the statutory amendment no longer requires a showing of prejudice The court said [*see* Turner v.

Rinker Materials, 622 So. 2d 80, 85 (Fla. 1st DCA 1993)]:

> . . . [A]s we construe the new law, section 440.15(3)(b)2 is mandatory, leaving no room for such considerations as whether a party was prejudiced by the untimely filing. In other words, the new law contains a strict requirement—timely report or waive. . . .

Carriers must take great care in not only informing an injured worker of the duty to job search, but must carefully explain the 14-day mailing requirement. The court said that "given this drastic consequence of failure to report, the E/C's duty to notify an injured worker of his responsibilities under the Act becomes even more critical."

In *Litvin,* the court held this provision is a procedural change. As such, it applies to any wage loss period occurring after July 1, 1990, whatever the date of the accident and injury [*see* Litvin v. St. Lucie Cty. Sheriff's Dept., 599 So. 2d 1353, 1355–1356 (Fla. 1st DCA 1992), *cert. denied,* 508 U.S. 913 (1993); *see* § 14.01[2]].

The 14-day filing requirement applies whether or not the law requires the injured worker to conduct a job search. For example, Pedro Raga returned to work, but at a reduced wage. He submitted several wage loss benefit requests well after the 14-day period expired. He claimed the filing deadline did not apply to him because he was employed and thus did not have to do a job search. The court disagreed, stating the statutory language is clear and unambiguous. Nothing in the statute suggests that the 14-day period applies to only those requests accompanied by a job search list. Each wage loss request form is governed by the 14-day mailing requirement [*see* Atlantic Sugar Association v. Raga, 652 So. 2d 508 (Fla. 1st DCA 1995)].

SPECIAL ALERT: The 14-day time limit does not apply to temporary partial wage loss benefits because it appears only in the permanent partial wage loss section. The court held that if the legislature intended this to apply to both classes of benefits, it would have put the restriction in both statutory sections [*see* Bridges v. Motorola, Inc., 646 So. 2d 790, 791 (Fla. 1st DCA 1994)].

[b] Accident Dates Between January 1, 1994, and September 30, 2003

Effective January 1, 1994, the legislature repealed § 440.185(10), Fla. Stat. For accidents occurring after that, the Act simply requires supplemental wage loss claimants to file a quarterly affidavit or statement with the carrier. This affidavit is form DWC-40. Injured workers must return it to the carrier within 21 days of receipt. If not, the carrier can suspend benefits until the injured worker complies. The only statutory requirement is that the injured worker certifies any wages earned and makes a good faith effort to find work. No statutory requirement to produce any job search list exists [§ 440.15(3)(b)5, Fla. Stat.; Fla. Admin Code R. 4L-3.0193 (11/8/94)].

For a general discussion of notice and claim periods, see Larson's Workers' Compensation, Desk Edition, Ch. 126 (Matthew Bender).

CHAPTER 15

IMPAIRMENT BENEFITS AND DEATH BENEFITS

SYNOPSIS

§ 15.01 Impairment Benefits

[1] The Rule

[a] Accidents Through December 31, 1993

The law entitles an injured worker to specifically scheduled, one time, lump-sum impairment benefits for a permanent impairment due to (1) amputation, (2) loss of 80 percent or more of vision of either eye after correction, or (3) serious head or facial disfigurement.

[b] Accidents On or After January 1, 1994

The law entitles an injured worker to scheduled weekly impairment benefits, paid over a scheduled number of weeks, for any injury that results in a permanent impairment rating.

[2] History

Before the legislature created the wage loss benefit system in 1979, a permanently impaired worker received a cash award based on several classes of scheduled and non scheduled permanent injuries. This was an entitlement based only on a permanent impairment rating. Carriers made these payments despite an injured worker's ability to work. The legislature repealed this method of calculating compensation when it enacted the wage loss idea in 1979. For accidents occurring up to December 31, 1993, three types or classes of permanent impairment still entitle an injured worker to a scheduled benefit. This is a special, one-time, lump-sum cash benefit besides all other benefits, except permanent total disability benefits [§ 440.15(3)(a), Fla. Stat.].

§ 15.02 Entitlement

[1] When Due

Beginning October 1, 2003, carriers must pay impairment benefits, for all accident dates, within 14 days after the carrier has knowledge of the impairment rating [§ 440.15(3)(a), Fla. Stat. (10/1/2003)].

Remember that for accidents occurring before 1994, an injured worker who is entitled to permanent total disability benefits cannot collect impairment benefits simultaneously. This provision was challenged as unconstitutional on the basis that it unfairly discriminates. Does it discriminate? Yes, but not unfairly, and that is the key to constitutionality. For example, if a worker loses one leg to amputation, which does not result in a state of permanent total disability, the injured worker can collect impairment benefits. If the same injured worker loses both legs to amputation, a statutory presumption of permanent total disability arises that precludes entitlement to impairment benefits. The court held the statute does not discriminate irrationally against amputees. The statute, said the court, "simply provides differently with respect to the indemnity benefits available, depending upon the extent of the injury and its presumed relation to wage-earning ability" [*see* Brownell v. Hillsborough County, 617 So. 2d 803, 805–806 (Fla. 1st DCA 1993)].

[2] Permanent Total Disability Exclusion: Accidents Before January 1, 1994

[a] The Overpayment Problem

For accident dates before 1994, the carrier does not owe impairment benefits if the injured worker is permanently and totally disabled. Excluding impairment benefits in cases of permanent total disability can be good or bad news for the carrier in a given claim. Waiting for a proper and total finding of maximum medical improvement may delay significantly the time when the carrier will owe these benefits. On the other hand, if the maximum medical improvement date escapes the carrier's notice and it pays late, the carrier may be liable for interest and penalties.

For accident dates before 1994, claims adjusters were advised not to be too hasty in paying impairment benefits before maximum medical improvement (MMI). Adjusters often know what the impairment rating will be before MMI. These benefits, however, are not due until 20 days after knowledge of MMI. If the carrier pays before MMI, and the carrier, or a judge of compensation claims, decide the injured worker was permanently and totally disabled at MMI (and thus ineligible for impairment benefits), the carrier would have paid thousands of dollars to the injured worker for which there was no legal liability. This was a problem because the carrier may not have the right to recover the overpayment.

[b] Recovering Overpayments

Originally, the law presumed that an overpayment of benefits in workers' compensation was a gratuity unless a reasonable basis existed for such overpayment [*see* Strickland v. Neil's Painting, 545 So. 2d 333, 334 (Fla. 1st DCA 1989)].

The courts did not consider ignorance of the law as a reasonable basis for overpayment and have held the carrier's premature payment to be a gift. The legislature overruled this line of cases effective January 1, 1994. The Act now provides that employees must repay any indemnity benefit the law did not entitle them to receive [§ 440.15(13), Fla. Stat.]. This is a procedural change that applies to overpayments made after January 1, 1994 [*see* ch. 12, § 12.08[2]].

[c] Maximum Medical Improvement Required

Ordering permanent benefits without a proper determination of the date of maximum medical improvement is improper. Further, where the injured worker has both orthopedic and psychiatric injuries, courts may not award permanent benefits until the injured worker has reached maximum medical improvement for both disorders [*see* Crown Carpentry,

Inc. v. Guillen, 547 So. 2d 1042 (Fla. 1st DCA 1989)].

[d] Effect of Failure to Explain Benefits

Claims adjusters must inform injured workers about possible entitlement to impairment benefits. This is essential because the statute of limitations does not apply if the carrier does not give the injured worker adequate notice of possible entitlement to benefits.

In one case, the trial judge denied impairment benefits because the statute of limitations had expired before the injured worker filed a claim. The First District Court of Appeal reversed. The court found the carrier sent the injured worker a letter that provided a detailed explanation of his rights to wage loss benefits. The letter, however, provided only a vague reference to other benefits. This failure, said the court, defeats the self-executing nature of the Workers' Compensation Act. Therefore, the court held the limitations statute of the act did not bar the claim [*see* Riggs v. Al Raska Contracting/Mission Nat. Ins. F.I.G.A., 537 So. 2d 155, 156 (Fla. 1st DCA 1991)].

[3] Qualifying Injuries

[a] Accident Dates Through December 31, 1993

[i] Amputation

[A] Defined

Unfortunately the Act does not define the term "amputation." Most people would construe the term to mean cutting off all or part of an extremity. The definition proved more illusive for the courts, however, and caused considerable confusion.

In one case, doctors removed the injured worker's testicle. His urologist awarded a 10-percent impairment rating based on the American Medical Association Guides. The physician admitted, however, that the impairment did not affect the injured worker's personal life or ability to work. In spite of this testimony, the court held that the law still entitled him to permanent impairment benefits and said [*see* Morris v. C.A. Meyer Paving & Const., 516 So. 2d 302, 304 (Fla. 1st DCA 1987)]:

> [W]e construe the term "amputation" as used in Section 440.15(3)(a), in context with the definition of permanent impairment in Section 440.02(16), to mean that special benefits for "permanent impairment due to amputation" shall become payable as a consequence of the *severance of any part of the body or limb* that results in a permanent impairment rating. (Emphasis added)

[B] Internal Organs

Does amputation include removing internal organs? It does not. Surgically removing part of a cervical disc, for example, is not an amputation for the purposes of impairment benefits. In rejecting a claim for impairment benefits for removing a cervical disc, the court admitted that its holding in *Morris* [*see* [A], *above*] was unique. Removing a testicle, said the court, is not as clearly an amputation as is the removal of an arm or leg. "A testicle is part of an external body organ which protrudes from the body as does a limb." This statement suggested that the court viewed only removal of protruding external body parts, resulting in permanent impairment, to be eligible for impairment benefits [*see* Zebley v. Stuart Nissan, 576 So. 2d 851, 852 (Fla. 1st DCA 1991)].

[C] Protruding External Body Part

This issue was again before the court in a third case that finally settled the question. Here, the judge of compensation claims awarded impairment benefits for the amputation of the injured worker's patella. The patella is a bone situated in the front of the knee. The judge believed this qualified as an amputation because the patella is a protruding body part. The First District Court of Appeal reversed and announced a definition of amputation that should end the controversy. The court said [*see* James Lewis Drywall v. Davis, 627 So. 2d 1302, 1303 (Fla. 1st DCA 1993)]:

> Only distal portions of the body can be amputated in the ordinary sense of the term. Thus, to be amputated, a body part must be remote or at an extremity. Entering the body itself, in this case in the middle of the leg, to remove a part of the knee cannot reasonably be deemed an amputation.

[ii] Blindness

The second qualifying condition is loss of 80 percent or more of vision in either eye after correction. There have not been any cases regarding this issue since 1983, and all of them dealt with the constitutionality of the statute. The argument was that the change in the Workers' Compensation Act greatly reduced an injured worker's benefits and that this was somehow unconstitutional. The Florida Supreme Court settled the issue when it held the statute is constitutional [*see* Mahoney v. Sears, Roebuck & Co., 440 So. 2d 1285, 1286 (Fla. 1983)].

The best interpretation of the application of this section is that if the injured worker's vision in either eye is 20 percent or less, after correction, the law entitles the injured worker to impairment benefits.

[iii] Serious Head or Facial Disfigurement

The third and final condition is serious head or facial disfigurement. The clear language suggests that any scarring or disfigurement to the face or head that results in a permanent impairment rating, assigned by a physician, entitles the injured worker to impairment benefits.

[b] Accident Dates On or After January 1, 1994

[i] Major Change

For accidents occurring on or after January 1, 1994, all injuries resulting in a permanent impairment rating qualify for impairment benefits, now renamed "impairment income benefits." For accidents occurring between January 1, 1994, and September 30, 2003, the legislature intended this benefit to replace wage loss partially since only those injured workers with an impairment rating of 20 percent or greater may collect wage loss benefits. (Wage loss benefits are now called "supplemental income benefits.") Effective with accidents occurring on or after October 1, 2003, the Legislature repealed the supplemental income benefits provision. Impairment benefits are not necessarily paid in a lump sum.

Instead, effective October 1, 2003, they are paid periodically as bi-weekly benefits [§ 440.15(3)(c), Fla. Stat. (10/1/2003)].

The law requires that doctors base the impairment ratings on objective medical findings and on the Florida Impairment Rating Guide. Only licensed physicians may decide the degree of permanent impairment. Medical doctors, doctors of osteopathy, chiropractors, podiatrists, optometrists, and dentists are considered "physicians" under this section. No other person may give an opinion about the degree of permanent impairment [§ 440.15(3)(b), Fla. Stat. (10/1/2003)].

[ii] Collecting Both Impairment Income Benefits and PTD Benefits

The legislature repealed the statutory prohibition against collecting both impairment benefits and permanent total disability benefits for accident dates on or after January 1, 1994. The question is, can injured workers collect both permanent total disability benefits and impairment income benefits concurrently? Judges of compensation claims have issued orders both ways. In 1998 the First District Court of Appeal settled the issue, holding that an injured worker cannot collect both permanent impairment benefits and permanent total disability benefits simultaneously. The court reasoned that these are two separate classes of benefits and, therefore, cannot be collected simultaneously. Permanent impairment benefits, said the court, is an alternative to permanent total disability benefits [*see* Brannon v. Tampa Tribune, 711 So. 2d 97, 98-100 (Fla. 1st DCA 1998)].

SPECIAL ALERT: A permanent impairment rating cannot include a mental injury caused by depression from being out of work [§ 440.15(3)(a), Fla. Stat. (1/1/94)].

[iii] When Evaluation Must Occur

The physician must evaluate the injured worker and assign an impairment rating when either of two events occurs. The first is the injured worker has reached maximum medical improvement. The second event occurs six weeks before the injured worker's entitlement to temporary benefits ends. At this point, maximum medical improvement or not, the physician must decide an appropriate impairment rating. What happens if a physician, other than the treating physician, does the rating? The doctor must send the evaluation and rating to the treating physician. The treating physician must then agree or disagree. At this point the certifying doctor must issue a written report to the Division, the employee, and the carrier. The report must certify that the injured worker has reached maximum medical improvement, and report the amount of any permanent impairment rating.

Recall that for post-1994 accidents, the law limits an injured worker to only 104 weeks of temporary benefits. What happens if the treating physician has not announced that the injured worker has reached maximum medical improvement before this period expires? The carrier must notify the physician that the law requires an impairment assessment at 104 weeks, whether or not the physician is ready to do so. In essence, this section requires virtual MMI if actual MMI has not been achieved. The practical problems inherent in a forced, premature assessment are obvious. For example, what rating will a physician assign to a patient that is in a hospital's intensive care unit? Will the physician issue an impairment rating based on the patients present totally disabling condition or simply guess about the patient's future?

[iv] When Entitlement to Impairment Income Benefits Begins

Entitlement to benefits begins the day after maximum medical improvement, or the day after the expiration of 104 weeks of temporary benefits, whichever comes first. The first payment is due within 14 days after the carrier has knowledge of the impairment. Carriers owe these benefits even if the injured worker is employed.

SPECIAL ALERT: If the employee has a preexisting impairment, and the new impairment is the result of an aggravation of an old injury or results from a merger with an old impairment, benefits are payable only for that portion of the total impairment attributable to the compensable injury. This applies only to impairment income benefits and does not affect entitlement to supplemental income benefits [§ 440.15(5)(b), Fla. Stat. (1/1/94)].

For a general discussion of Disability and Personal Injury Benefits, see LARSON'S WORKERS' COMPENSATION, DESK EDITION, Part 9, *Disability and Personal Injury Benefits* (Matthew Bender).

§ 15.03 Calculating Impairment Benefits

[1] Accident Dates Before May 1, 1982

Doctors must base a rating on the *American Medical Association Guides to Permanent Impairment.* The benefits are $50 for each percent of permanent impairment from 1 percent through 50 percent, and $100 for each percentage point more than 50 percent. Assume the injured worker has a 20-percent impairment rating. In this example the total benefit is $50 x 20 = $1,000.

[2] Accident Dates Between May 1, 1982, and June 30, 1990

For this period, doctors still must use the AMA Guides, but the legislature increased the benefits. The new rate is $250 for each percent of impairment through 10 percent and $500 for each percent over 10 percent. Using the same example in [1], *above,* the injured worker would receive $7,500.

$250 x 10	=	$2,500 (The first 10%)
+ $500 x 10	=	$5,000 (The second 10%)
Total	=	$7,500

[3] Accident Dates Between July 1, 1990, and October 31, 1992

Only one difference exists for accidents occurring between July 1, 1990 and October 31, 1992. Doctors must now use the *Minnesota Disability Guides* in deciding the impairment rating, rather than the American Medical Association Guides.

[4] Accident Dates Between November 1, 1992, and January 7, 1997

Only one difference exists for accidents occurring between November 1, 1992, and January 7, 1997. Doctors must now use the 1993 *Florida Impairment Rating Guide* rather than the Minnesota or American Medical Association Guides [*see* Division Bulletin No.166, 10/24/94; ch. 14, § 14.03[4]].

[5] Accident Dates On or After January 8, 1997

For accidents occurring on or after January 8, 1997, the 1996 Florida Impairment Rating Guide must be used [*see* Fla. Admin. Code R. 69L-7.604 (1/10/2005)].

QUICK REFERENCE–Assessing Permanent Impairment

Before 7/1/1990	AMA Guides to Permanent Impairment
7/1/1990 to 10/31/1992	Minnesota Disability Guide
11/1/1992 to 1/7/1997	1993 Florida Impairment Rating Guide
1/8/1997 to Present	1996 Florida Impairment Rating Guide

[6] Accident Dates Between January 1, 1994, and September 30, 2003

For accidents occurring on or after January 1, 1994, the law entitles an injured worker to three weeks of Impairment Income Benefits for each percentage point of impairment. The weekly benefit is an amount equal to 50 percent of the employee's average weekly temporary total disability benefit not to exceed the maximum benefit.

To calculate the injured worker's average weekly temporary total disability benefit, simply divide all the temporary total disability benefits by the number of weeks and days paid. Usually, this simply means one-half of the injured workers' compensation rate. If the injured worker has an average weekly wage of $300, the compensation rate is 66²/₃ of that, or $200. This injured worker's weekly impairment income benefit is therefore $100 [*see* Fla. Admin. Code R. 69L-3.002(1) (1/10/2005)].

The legislature's use of the term "average" temporary total disability benefit is curious. If an injured worker's compensation rate is $200, for example, is the average rate automatically $100? Not necessarily. Suppose an injured worker received catastrophic temporary total disability benefits for several weeks immediately following the accident [*see* ch. 13, § 13.11, for a complete discussion of catastrophic temporary total disability benefits]. In such a case, the average of catastrophic TTD and the regular compensation would be greater than the basic rate. The reverse might also be true. The carrier may have paid less than the compensation rate because of some offset such as a safety rule violation reduction.

What happens if the injured worker started in temporary partial status and never received total disability benefits? In such a case the benefit is simply 50 percent of the injured worker's maximum compensation rate [*see* Fla. Admin. Code R. 69L-3.002(1) (1/10/2005)].

Note, however, that the maximum benefit is the individual claimant's compensation rate as described in § 440.12, Fla. Stat. This can become an issue when, as discussed above, the injured worker received catastrophic temporary total disability benefits. The average of those benefits would exceed the maximum rate. This issue will also arise in cases where the claimant's earnings are so high that the maximum rate is less than the claimant's calculated rate. For example, Carlos Nasworthy had an average weekly wage of $1,249.96, which resulted in a compensation rate of $833.35. The maximum rate for this 1995 accident, however, was $465. When Nasworthy reached maximum medical improvement, the carrier paid impairment income benefits at 50 percent of that, or $232.50.

Nasworthy argued that was incorrect and that he should receive 50 percent of his calculated rate, or 50 percent of $833.35. The judge of compensation claims agreed and ordered an increase. The judge accepted Nasworthy's argument that the statutory phrase "not to exceed the maximum weekly benefits under s. 440.12" referred to impairment income benefits rather than to the employee's average weekly temporary total disability benefit. Under this interpretation, a claimant would receive 50 percent of *his* or *her* compensation rate up to the maximum rate. If so, Nasworthy's weekly impairment income benefits would be $416.68 rather than the $232.50 that the carrier paid. The 1st DCA disagreed and reversed, holding that the carrier's calculation was correct.

The court interpreted the statutory provision using the doctrine of the last antecedent [*see* ch. 1, § 1.26, for a discussion of statutory construction]. The court held that the phrase "not to exceed the maximum weekly benefits under s. 440.12" in § 440.15(3)(a)3, Fla. Stat., is intended to make clear that, for purposes of computing the rate of impairment benefits, the amount of temporary total disability benefits is capped at the maximum compensation rate set by § 440.12(2), Fla. Stat. That amount, of course, is an amount equal to 100 percent of the state wide average weekly wage as determined by the Florida Department of Labor. This maximum rate applies even if the claimant had received catastrophic temporary total disability benefits under § 440.15(2)(b), Fla. Stat., which exceeded the maximum rate described in § 440.12(2), Fla. Stat. Although the court did not mention it, presumably the minimum amount ($20) specified in § 440.12(2), Fla. Stat. also applies [*see* City of St. Petersburg v. Nasworthy, 751 So. 2d 772, 774–775 (Fla. 1st DCA 2000)].

The first payment is due within 14 days after the carrier knows the impairment rating. The first payment must be for all full weeks of entitlement since the date of maximum medical improvement, up to the date the carrier makes the payment.

Carriers can issue Impairment Income Benefits either weekly or biweekly at their option. If they choose biweekly, they must issue payment for both weeks at the end of the first week. To ensure a biweekly schedule, carriers must issue payment for the first and second weeks at the end of the first week, and then the third and fourth weeks at the end of the third week and so on. Thus, injured workers will receive payments one week in advance.

Carriers cannot pay periodic benefits in a lump sum without permission from either the Division or a judge of compensation claims. The Division, however, has not developed a procedure for requesting such approval. Unofficially, the Division has no objection to carriers' paying Impairment Income Benefits in a lump sum, and many carriers do so.

Impairment benefits are payable until the carrier pays the maximum number of weeks or the injured worker dies. Carriers owe benefits even if the injured worker is employed. As stated, the benefit is three weeks compensation for each percentage point of impairment. If the impairment rating, for example, is 10 percent, the carrier owes 30 weeks at a rate equal to one-half the injured worker's average temporary total disability compensation benefit. If the injured worker did not receive temporary total disability benefits, the rate is 50 percent of the worker's maximum compensation rate.

Using the initial example in [1], *above,* assume the injured worker has an average weekly wage of $300, and an average compensation rate of $200. At maximum medical improvement the physician awards a 10-percent permanent impairment rating. The total benefit is 30 weeks of impairment benefits at $100 per week or $3,000. This reduction in permanent impairment benefits is reasonable and therefore constitutional [*see* Bradley v. The Hurricane Restaurant, 670 So. 2d 162, 165 (Fla. 1st DCA 1996), *rev. denied,* 678 So. 2d 237 (Fla. 1996)].

[7] Accident Dates On or After October 1, 2003

Effective with accidents occurring on or after October 1, 2003, the number of weeks payable depends on the impairment rating as follows:

- From 1% to 10%–Two weeks for each percentage point from 1 to 10.
- From 11% to 15%–Three weeks for each percentage point from 11 to 15.
- From 16% to 20%–Four weeks for each percentage point from 16 to 20.
- 21% and higher–Six weeks for each percentage point above 20.

The statute's phrasing indicates that benefits are to be calculated in a stair-step fashion, rather than assigning the highest number of weeks based on the overall rating. The statute's language supports the conclusion that the stair-step method applies. For example, the statute states, "two weeks of benefits are to be paid to the employee for each percentage point of impairment from 1 percent up to and including 10 percent." This phrasing is repeated for each grouping, indicating that the number of weeks allowed applies only to the percentage points in the "from and to" range.

Under the overall rating method of assigning the highest number weeks to the entire rating, a rating of 25 percent would create entitlement to six weeks for each percentage point (6 x 25), or a total of 150 weeks.

Under the stair-step method, the maximum entitlement for a 25 percent rating would be 85 weeks. This calculation works as follows:

For that part of the rating from	1% to 10% (2 x 10)	=	20 weeks
For that part of the rating from	11% to 15% (3 x 5)	=	15 weeks
For that part of the rating from	16% to 20% (4 x 5)	=	20 weeks
For that part of the rating from	21% to 25% (6 x 5)	=	30 weeks

Total = 85 weeks

Which method the courts will adopt remains to be seen [*see* § 440.15(3)(g), Fla, Stat. (10/1/2003)].

In addition to altering the number of weeks of entitlement, the amounts of the weekly benefits payable have been increased. Previously, the weekly benefit payable was 50 percent of the claimant's average weekly temporary total disability benefit. Effective with accidents occurring on or after October 1, 2003, the benefit increases to 75 percent of the claimant's average weekly temporary total disability benefit. [Note: The method for calculating a claimant's "average weekly temporary total disability benefit" is unchanged and is described in [6], *above.*]

Previously, if the claimant returned to work, he or she was still entitled to receive the full impairment income benefit, regardless of the amount of income earned. Effective October 1, 2003, the biweekly rate is 75 percent of the employee's average weekly temporary total disability benefit, provided, however, that the biweekly benefit is reduced by 50 percent for each week in which the claimant's earned income is equal to or greater than the claimant's established average weekly wage [§ 440.15(3)(c), Fla. Stat. (10/1/2003)]. Reducing 75 percent by half results in a benefit equal to 38 percent of the claimant's average weekly disability benefits.

For a general discussion of benefit calculation, see LARSON'S WORKERS' COMPENSATION, DESK EDITION, Ch. 93 (Matthew Bender).

§ 15.04 Death Cases and Dependent's Benefits

[1] The Rule

If a worker dies because of a compensable injury, the worker's dependents are entitled to certain fixed benefits. Basic benefits are compensation up to $100,000, funeral expenses, and educational benefits for the spouse. To be compensable, death must result from the accident within one year. If death occurs after one year, benefits are awarded only if death follows continuous disability and occurs within five years after the accident. In occupational disease cases, death must occur within 350 weeks (6.76 years) after the date of last exposure [§ 440.16(1), Fla. Stat.].

[2] Death Must Follow Continuous Disability

Carriers owe death benefits if death follows a period of continuous disability. The question is, what does "continuous disability" mean? Does it mean continuous disability for work or merely continuous suffering to some degree from the effects of the injury? The courts construe the term to require only continuous suffering. In one case, the physician's report said the injured worker was "never the same since the accident." The Florida Supreme Court held this was sufficient for a finding of continuous disability although the injured worker had returned to work [*see* In re Lupola, 293 So. 2d 354, 357–358 (Fla. 1974)]!

[3] When Death Must Occur

In non-occupational disease cases, death must occur within one year after the accident. In occupational disease cases, the law does not allow benefits if death occurs more than five years after the date of the accident, or more than 350 weeks (6.76 years) after the date of last exposure [§§ 440.151(1)(a), 440.16[1], Fla. Stat.].

What happens if the worker's death is clearly related to the compensable injury, but occurs more than five years after the accident? Despite causal relationship, the death claim is not compensable. For example, Leslie Newton suffered a compensable injury in 1973. In the years that followed he underwent multiple surgeries. After nine years of continuous disability he died as the result of a cerebral hemorrhage. The trial judge awarded benefits, believing the five-year limitation to be unconstitutional. The First District Court of Appeal disagreed and reversed. The provision is constitutional and no benefits were due [*see* Newton v. McCotter Motors, Inc., 475 So. 2d 230, 231 (Fla. 1985), *cert. denied,* 475 U.S. 1021, 106 S. Ct. 1210, 89 L. Ed. 2d 323 (1986)].

§ 15.05 Death Benefits

The amount and nature of death benefits changes, depending on the accident date, as follows [§ 440.16, Fla. Stat.]:

- **Accident dates up to April 30, 1982.**
  Funeral Benefits–$1,000
  Death Benefit–$50,000

- **Accident dates between May 1, 1982, and December 31, 1993.**
  Funeral benefits–$2,500
  Death Benefits–$100,000

- **Accident dates between January 1, 1994, and September 30, 2003.**
  Funeral Benefits–$5,000
  Death Benefits–$100,000
  Plus: A lump sum payment to the spouse upon remarriage equal to 26 weeks of benefits;
  Plus: Retraining/Education benefits to the spouse.

- **Accident dates on or after October 1, 2003.**
  Funeral Benefits–$7,500
  Death Benefits–$150,000
  Plus: A lump sum payment to the spouse upon remarriage equal to 26 weeks of benefits;
  Plus: Retraining/Education benefits to the spouse.

SPECIAL ALERT: § 440.16(7), Fla. Stat. limits death benefits to dependents who are residents (or about to become residents) of other countries, *except Canada*. As the Supreme Court did with an earlier version of this statute, the 1st DCA declared the monetary limitation of the 1987 version to be unconstitutional [*see* De Ayala v. Fla. Farm Bureau Cas. Ins. Co., 543 So. 2d 204, 207–208 (Fla. 1989); Lopez v. Ideal Roofing Sys., 821 So. 2d 453, 454 (Fla. 1st DCA 2002)]. In apparent reaction to the court's holding that § 440.16(7), Fla. Stat. is unconstitutional, the Legislature repealed this section effective July 1, 2004.

SPECIAL NOTE: Carriers are not liable for penalties and interest for late payment of funeral expenses because these expenses are not "compensation." Penalties and interest apply only for late payment of compensation [*see* Whiskey Creek Country Club v. Rizer, 599 So. 2d 734, 735 (Fla. 1st DCA 1992)].

Entitlement and calculation of benefits change depending on the class a beneficiary falls into. A review of each class follows in § 15.06.

For a detailed discussion of death benefits, see LARSON'S WORKERS' COMPENSATION, DESK EDITION, Ch. 98 (Matthew Bender).

§ 15.06 Beneficiaries

[1] The Rule

To qualify for benefits an individual must be both a dependent of the deceased and related as the deceased's spouse, child, parent, brother, sister, or grandchild. To be a dependent, a person must have received substantial and regular support from the deceased, the absence of which would materially alter the person's lifestyle [§ 440.16, Fla. Stat.].

[2] Dependent Defined

[a] Actual Dependence Required

The first requirement a claimant must meet is to show actual dependence on the deceased worker. Nowhere in the Workers' Compensation Act is the term "dependent" defined. Case law, however, provides some guidance. The burden of proving dependency is the claimant's, and this burden requires that claimants meet a three-pronged test [*see* General Elec. v. DeCubas, 504 So. 2d 1276, 1278 (Fla. 1st DCA 1986)]:

1. The claimant was dependent upon the deceased for support;
2. The claimant received substantial support from the deceased; and
3. The deceased provided such support regularly and the claimant reasonably expected that the deceased would have provided it in the future.

[b] Substantial Support

The next question is how much support is "substantial"? The court did not provide any neat mathematical formula such as 50 percent of income. Instead, the court offered the following, subjective and ambiguous, measurement [*see* General Elec. v. DeCubas, 504 So. 2d 1276, 1278 (Fla. 1st DCA 1986)]:

> The test is whether the claimant relies on the contributions to maintain his or her customary standard of living and, whether in the absence of continuance of support,

the lifestyle of the claimant would be materially altered.

This test will often require significant investigation into a claimant's other sources of income and lifestyle. Decide dependency, therefore, case-by-case.

SPECIAL ALERT: Check for receipt of substantial life insurance or other benefits. Even if the claimant can prove dependency at the time of the employee's death, the claimant's receipt of a large sum of life insurance or other monetary benefit may result in the end of dependency [*see* Carroll Steel Erectors v. Alderman, 599 So. 2d 181, 185 (Fla. 1st DCA 1992)].

[c] Qualified Relationships

Even if claimants meet the dependency test, they cannot collect benefits unless they were related to the deceased employee as:

1. Spouse
2. Child
3. Parent
4. Brother, sister, or grandchild

No one else is eligible. The above list is not only a list of eligible beneficiaries, it is also the order of priority. [3]–[6], *below,* will examine the classes in detail, including benefit limits by class, but first we will discuss the critical importance of paying benefits by priority.

Although it is the claimant's burden to prove dependency, it is the carrier's burden to be sure it pays the correct people. If the carrier pays the wrong people, the carrier does so at its peril. This problem usually arises where the deceased had multiple marriages and children. For example, Karen was the deceased employee's first wife and the mother of his two children. Nadine was his second wife and his widow. The judge of compensation claims approved an agreement that the two women would share benefits. Half would go to Karen as mother and guardian of the children, and half to Nadine as widow.

The law in effect at the time dictated that a widow's entitlement ended upon her remarriage, so the carrier routinely checked on Nadine's marital status. These investigations, which included checking marriage records at various courthouses, always showed that she was still single. When asked, she denied having remarried. On March 2, 1984, the carrier received a letter from Nadine reporting that she had remarried in August of 1982! The carrier immediately stopped benefits to Nadine and increased them to Karen. The court held, however, that the carrier had not done enough to find out Nadine's true marital status. (The one courthouse they did not check was the one with the marriage certificate on file.) The court ordered the carrier to pay full benefits to Karen, retroactive to the date of Nadine's remarriage. Further, the court held the law did not entitle the carrier to any credit toward the maximum death benefit. The court ended its opinion with the following caveat [*see* Clay Hyder Trucking Lines, Inc. v. Manis, 471 So. 2d 1329, 1331–1332 (Fla. 1st DCA 1985)]:

> By our holding today, we caution that we are not placing an absolute burden on the employer to investigate and 'monitor the system.' We recognize that there may arise circumstances so obfuscated by fraud or collusion that nothing short of clairvoyance on the employer's part would reveal the truth. However, the evidence herein would show that this is not such a case.

All of this means that if the carrier does not pay benefits to the proper dependent, in the proper order, and in the proper amount, the law requires that the carrier make up underpayment. In such a case, carriers may not take any credit for the incorrect payment unless it can show it was the victim of an undetectable fraud.

[d] Overpayments

This raises a question about whether the 1994 amendment providing for recovery of overpayments will apply here. The answer is probably no. The 1994 Act does provide that carriers may recover benefits paid to which the recipient was not entitled. The statute, however, refers only to cases in which the "employee" was overpaid. Dependents are not employees, and the repayment provision may not apply to them [§ 440.15(13), Fla. Stat.].

[3] Spouse Defined and Benefits

[a] Spouse Defined

To define the term "spouse," begin by examining the statute. It defines "spouse" as someone who is "substantially dependent for financial support upon the decedent and living with the decedent at the time of the decedent's injury and death, or substantially dependent upon the decedent for financial support and living apart at that time for a justifiable cause" [§ 440.02(22), Fla. Stat.].

This definition does not do the job because it fails to define the term "spouse" itself. The court solved the problem by simply turning to Webster's dictionary and concluded the term "spouse" means a man or woman joined in wedlock [*see* Hopkins v. E-Systems, Commercial Div., 423 So. 2d 981, 982 (Fla. 1st DCA 1982)].

Therefore, to be an eligible spouse, the person must have been married to the deceased worker, both at the time of the accident and at the time of death. Further, the person must have been dependent upon the deceased for support, whether they lived together or not. Remember that Florida no longer recognizes common-law marriage. The legislature abolished common-law marriage effective January 1, 1968. In *Hopkins,* the deceased worker divorced his wife before his accident and death. Although divorced, she was still living with him and was dependent upon him. Still, the court held the law did not entitle her to benefits because she was no longer his spouse.

In a reverse situation, the court came to the same conclusion. The worker and his spouse had lived together for more than 16 years but had never married. The worker was injured in October 1986, and the couple were legally married in January 1988. The worker died in November 1989. Although they were married at the time of death, the statute clearly requires the injured worker to have been the decedent's spouse, living with and financially dependent upon him or her. This status must have existed both at the time of the initial work-related accident and at the time of the decedent's death [*see* Crews v. Department of

Transp., 591 So. 2d 291, 293–294 (Fla. 1st DCA 1991)].

[b] Spouse Benefits

[i] Basic Benefits

The law entitles a qualified spouse to receive weekly compensation in an amount equal to 50 percent of the deceased worker's average weekly wage not to exceed the compensation rate. If the deceased's average weekly wage was $300, the normal compensation rate would be $200. The spouse, however, would receive only 50 percent of the average weekly wage or $150. These benefits continue until the carrier has paid the maximum benefit of $100,000, or the spouse dies [§ 440.16(1), Fla. Stat.; *see* [iii], *below* (partial suspension occurs if spouse remarries)].

[ii] Retraining

A dependent spouse is entitled to post-secondary student fees at any area vocational or technical school. Maximum eligibility is 1,800 class room hours or student fees at any community college for up to 80 semester hours. If the deceased was a state employee, the law waives all such fees. This educational or retraining benefit is besides all other benefits.

The right to these educational benefits expires seven years after the employee's death or the carrier pays the full death benefit, whichever occurs first. To qualify for these additional benefits, the dependent spouse must meet admission requirements and enroll. For the benefit to continue, the student spouse must make satisfactory academic progress as defined by the school [§ 440.16(1)(c), Fla. Stat.].

[iii] Remarriage

If the spouse remarries, continuing entitlement to death benefits depends on the date of the accident [§ 440.16(1)(b)2, Fla. Stat.]:

1. For accidents occurring before October 1, 1989, entitlement to compensation ends upon remarriage.

2. For accidents occurring between October 1, 1989, and June 30, 1990, remarriage has no effect and entitlement continues.

3. For accidents occurring on or after July 1, 1990, a spouse is entitled to a lump-sum payment upon remarriage. The benefit is 26 weeks of compensation unless this would exceed the maximum limit. Then, the spouse would receive only the remaining available benefits. Note, however, that accepting a lump-sum payment does not affect paying benefits to other dependents.

[4] Children Defined and Benefits

[a] Child Defined

[i] Basic Definition

The statutory definition of "child" includes a posthumous child, a child legally adopted before the injury, and a stepchild. The definition also includes an acknowledged

Guide to Claims

illegitimate child dependent upon the deceased [§ 440.02(5), Fla. Stat.].

A child's legal dependency ends when he or she attains age 18 unless the child is a student in an accredited educational institution. In such cases, dependency ends at age 22. If a child marries, entitlement ends despite age, unless the child is still wholly dependent. None of these limitations applies if the child is physically or mentally unable to earn a living.

[ii] Presumption of Legitimacy

Most cases involve typical family relationships, but it is the atypical case that can really confuse things. For example, George Theis was divorced at the time of his accident, but a child was born while he was still married to his ex-wife, Marie. Ordinarily, this would not create an entitlement question except that another man fathered the child!

Apparently, Theis knew this, but treated the child as his own by providing support and maintaining a parental relationship. The First District Court of Appeal held that in spite of this, the child did not meet the definition of "child" and was not entitled to benefits. The Florida Supreme Court reversed the District Court of Appeal and held the law did entitle the child to benefits, stating it was not necessary that the child be the deceased's biological child. If an individual claims benefits as a legitimate child, by law then, post injury biological proof of paternity is irrelevant. In other words, if a child is born during a legitimate marriage, it does not matter if the child is not the product of the union. A legal presumption exists that the child is the product of both partners of the marriage. That presumption is not subject to challenge in workers' compensation cases [*see* Theis v. City of Miami, 564 So. 2d 117, 119 (Fla. 1990)].

[iii] Adopted Children

Recall that adopted children qualify for benefits. What about children described under the doctrine of "virtual adoption?" This situation arises, for example, when a person marries another who has children from a previous marriage. The newcomer supports the children and cares for them, and treats them as his own, but never goes through the legal procedure of adoption. In November 1988, the Florida Supreme Court held that [*see* Tarver v. Evergreen Sod Farms, Inc., 533 So. 2d 765, 767 (Fla. 1988)]:

> [T]he doctrine of virtual adoption was not intended to create the legal relationship of parent and child. Its purpose is to avoid unfair results from the application of intestacy statutes. . . . [T]he statute contemplates that there not only be a legal adoption but that it occur prior to the injury of the employee.

[b] Child Benefits

Without a spouse, the law entitles a qualified child to receive a weekly benefit equal to $33\frac{1}{3}$ percent of the deceased's average weekly wage. With a spouse, the benefit to the child is $16\frac{2}{3}$ percent of the average weekly wage. This appears complicated, but really is not. Let us take a typical example of a dependent spouse with two minor children. The deceased's average weekly wage is $300. The most they can receive in total, however, is $66\frac{2}{3}$ of that or $200 or the maximum compensation rate for the year in question. In this example, the spouse receives 50 percent or $150 and the children receive the remaining

16⅔ percent, or $50 [§ 440.16(1)(b)3, Fla. Stat.].

With two children, each would receive $25. When the first child reaches age 18 and is not a student or otherwise disqualified, benefits cease. Simultaneously the carrier must increase benefits to the remaining child to the full 16⅔ percent or $50.

If the average weekly wage was $1,000, the spouse's 50 percent would equal $500; however, the maximum compensation rate is $382. The law entitles the spouse, theoretically, to the entire $382 maximum, leaving nothing for the children or other dependents. The judge of compensation claims, however, may apportion the benefits in any manner the judge decides to be just and proper. This includes paying the entire amount to the child or children. In such cases, carriers should consider having a judge approve the benefit disbursement. If the spouse dies, the carrier must increase the children's benefit to 33⅓ percent each [§ 440.16(1)(b)(2), Fla. Stat.].

Remember, start with the order of priority. When more than one eligible dependent exists within a class, then the class members share and share alike.

[5] Parents Defined and Benefits

[a] Parent Defined

In 1960, the Florida Supreme Court established a six-pronged test that those claiming to be dependent parents must meet. The tests apply to all those claiming dependency, but the case dealt specifically with parents. Although the case is more than three decades old, the courts still observe it today. The Supreme Court held that in order for a parent to be entitled to dependency benefits under the act, the parent must bear the burden of proving, by competent substantial evidence which accords with logic and reason, the following essential elements [*see* MacDon Lumber Co. v. Stevenson, 117 So. 2d 487 (Fla. 1960)]:

1. The claimant is a dependent.
2. The claimant was a dependent at the time of the employee's death.
3. The deceased employee must have made substantial contributions toward the claimant's support. The mere expectation of future contributions is not enough.
4. The deceased must have made these contributions regularly with reasonable expectation that they would continue in the future.
5. When the deceased lived with a parent and received board, lodging, or other accommodations of value, the parent must show that the deceased's contributions exceed, in substantial amount, the reasonable value of accommodations.
6. Whether a contribution is substantial enough to create dependency must be decided by the extent to which the contributions of the deceased employee enabled the dependent to maintain his or her accustomed standard of living.

In 1994 the First District Court of Appeal applied prong five of the test. Here, the deceased employee's mother claimed dependency benefits. Thirty-year-old Steven Reid was shot and killed in a robbery while working at a Seven-Eleven store. As he had for most of his life, Reid was living with his 64-year-old mother when he died. He had

Guide to Claims

consistently paid his mother $35 per week for rent and $18 per month for cable TV. He did odd jobs around the house and occasionally bought food. His mother testified that she relied on these contributions and budgeted them to meet her expenses.

Reid's mother, however, held a part time job and received additional income from alimony payments and interest earnings. Despite this, the judge of compensation claims decided that she was dependent upon Reid and awarded benefits. The First District Court of Appeal disagreed and reversed.

Reid's mother had not met prong five of the *MacDon* tests. No evidence was introduced showing that Reid's contributions exceeded the value of his housing, food, and other accommodations as required. The court, quoting *Macdon,* held that "if the decedent's contribution is offset by the value of the board and room received, he is doing no more than to 'pull his own weight'; he is merely supporting himself, with nothing leftover to represent support of dependents" [*see* Southland Corp. v. Reid, 647 So. 2d 146, 148 (Fla. 1st DCA 1994)].

Parents include stepparents and parents by adoption. The definition also includes parents-in-law. Even those with no legal relationship may qualify. Persons will qualify if they "stood in the place of a parent" before the employee's death. The Workers' Compensation Act includes as parents, "any persons who for more than three years prior to the death of the deceased employee stood in the place of a parent to him and were dependent on the injured employee."

The definition of parent is ambiguous in that it is unclear if the state of dependency must have existed for three years as well. Courts could easily interpret the statute either way. The definition requires functioning both as parents and being dependent. The dependency requirement, however, applies to natural parents and is in the same sentence in the statute. A logical interpretation is that dependency need exist only at the time of the accident [§ 440.02(18), Fla. Stat.].

[b] Parent Benefits

If money remains after paying the spouse and children, the next eligible class of dependent is the deceased's parents. If they qualify as dependents, the law entitles them to 25 percent each [§ 440.16(1)(b)4, Fla. Stat.].

[6] Brothers, Sisters, Grandchildren

[a] Brothers and Sisters Defined

Brothers and sisters include stepbrothers and stepsisters. This also includes half brothers and sisters, and adopted brothers and sisters. Married brothers and sisters do not qualify unless they were wholly dependent upon the deceased employee. Lastly, brothers and sisters do not qualify unless, at the time of the employee's death, they are under age 18, or age 22 if a full-time student [§ 440.02(5), Fla. Stat.].

In one case, the deceased's 31-year-old sister challenged the age restriction in the definition. She argued the provision is unconstitutional. She claimed it denied her access to courts, and that it violated her equal protection and due process rights. The First District

Court of Appeal found no merit in that argument and held the provision constitutional [*see* Rodriguez v. Prestress Decking Corp., 611 So. 2d 59, 60–61 (Fla. 1st DCA 1992)].

[b] Grandchildren Defined

Dependent grandchildren qualify if one of their parents meets the definition of "child." Grandchildren, however, do not qualify unless, at the time of the employee's death, they are under age 18, or age 22 if a full-time student [§ 440.02(5), Fla. Stat.].

[c] Benefits

If brothers sisters, and grandchildren were dependent upon the deceased, they are entitled to 15 percent each [§ 440.16(1)(b)5, Fla. Stat.].

[7] Decedent's Estate

What is the estate entitled to if no dependents exist? The estate, with only one exception, can collect only the funeral allowance. The exception is that the deceased worker's personal representative can claim any benefits that accrued before the worker's death, but that the carrier did not pay [*see* D.C. General Contractors v. Blount, 588 So. 2d 674 (Fla. 1st DCA 1991)].

For a detailed discussion of dependency, see LARSON'S WORKERS' COMPENSATION, DESK EDITION, Ch. 97 (Matthew Bender).

CHAPTER 16

MEDICAL BENEFITS

Guide to Claims

SYNOPSIS

Guide to Claims

Guide to Claims

§ 16.01 Overview

Employers must furnish remedial treatment, care, and attendance to the injured worker. Such services must be under the direction and supervision of a qualified physician or other recognized practitioner, nurse, or hospital. The employer must furnish these services for as long as necessary, even for the injured worker's lifetime [§ 440.13, Fla. Stat. (7/1/97)].

The medical component of workers' compensation claims is so large and important that the discussion on the subject is spread across three chapters. This chapter covers managed care, individual benefits, eligibility requirements, and issues regarding health care providers. Ch. 17, *Rehabilitation Benefits,* continues with a discussion of rehabilitation benefits, followed by a discussion of attendant care benefits in Ch, 18, *Attendant Care.*

§ 16.02 Managed Care

SPECIAL ALERT: Beginning October 1, 2001, providing medical treatment through a managed care arrangement is optional [§ 440.134(2), Fla. Stat.] Therefore, this section applies only if the employer has elected the managed care option.

Because managed care was mandatory for injuries occurring between July 1, 1997, and October 1, 2001, there is a presumption that each employer and carrier had a managed care arrangement in place. Therefore, the employer/carrier has no burden to prove that a managed care arrangement is in place. For accidents occurring during this period, the claimant has the burden to prove otherwise.

Before managed care became mandatory, however, the court held that the carrier must establish that a managed care arrangement was, in fact, in place [*see* Florida Distillers v. Rudd, 751 So. 2d 754, 757 (Fla. 1st DCA 2000)]. Since managed care is again voluntary effective October 1, 2001, *Florida Distillers* has renewed relevance, and carriers will again be required to prove that a managed care arrangement is in place in order for its provisions to apply. From the phrasing in *Jefferson v. Wayne Dalton Corp. Hartford,* it appears that the court considers the managed care statutes to be substantive. If so, they apply based on the date of the accident [*see* Jefferson v. Wayne Dalton Corp./Hartford, 793 So. 2d 1081 (Fla. 1st DCA 2001)].

If an employer or carrier elects to provide medical care outside of a managed care arrangement, the managed care provisions do not apply to any claims regardless of the accident date [*see* § 440.134(2)(a), Fla. Stat. (7/1/2002)].

[1] Beginnings of Managed Care In Florida

For 62 years Florida's employers and insurance carriers furnished medical care to injured workers under a statutory fiat that changed little over that time. During those years, the courts issued approximately 400 decisions interpreting the statutes and explaining how employers and carriers are to deliver medical benefits under the statutory directives. While this huge body of law seems daunting to the new practitioner, it has resulted in consistency and predictability. Beginning in 1997, however, Florida abandoned this system and replaced it with Managed Care.

Managed Care has its origins in the health insurance industry and has shown its potential to reduce health care costs. Encouraged by this, Florida's legislature mandated that all employers must furnish health care to injured workers solely through managed care arrangements beginning January 1, 1997 [*see* [2], *below*]. This first step toward merging group health insurance with workers' compensation has many advocates and detractors. Whether managed care will aid or injure the workers' compensation system remains to be seen.

Besides the myriad questions raised by trying to carry out the administrative side of managed care, two broad legal questions must also be addressed. First, are those portions of the managed care statute that affect medical care delivery and claim handling procedural or substantive? That is to say, do these statutory changes apply to all accident

Guide to Claims

dates or only to those that happen after January 1, 1997? The second question is whether the hundreds of appellate decisions on medical benefits will continue to apply. This section begins with a review of the managed care statute [*see* [2]–[4], *below*], followed by detailed discussion of carriers' and injured workers' rights and responsibilities regarding medical care and treatment [*see* [5], *below*]. Each discussion offers an opinion about the answers to these two broad questions whenever there is a lack of judicial review. The managed care section of the statute, however, is so vague and poorly drafted that deciding whether the old appellate decisions still apply is difficult. Therefore, the text first reviews the case law as it existed before Managed Care, then offers suggestions about whether and how case law applies under Managed Care.

[2] The 1997 and 2001 Law

Beginning January 1, 1997, employers were required to provide all medically necessary treatment solely through managed care arrangements. Beginning on October 1, 2001, providing medical treatment through a managed care arrangement is strictly voluntary [§ 440.134(2)(b), Fla. Stat. (1/1/1994) & (10/1/2001)]. These are arrangements under which health care providers and facilities have entered written agreements, directly or indirectly, with a carrier to provide medical care to workers' compensation patients. Carriers may create their own arrangements, or contract with existing Preferred Provider Organizations (PPO) or Health Maintenance Organizations (HMO). Additionally, carriers may arrange for capitated (fixed fees) contracts rather than the traditional fee–for–service arrangement [§ 440.134, Fla. Stat. (1/1/94)].

[3] Regulatory Agency

The Agency for Health Care Administration (AHCA) must approve, in advance, all managed care arrangements before carriers can use them. The Act contains several pages of requirements that carriers must meet before AHCA will grant approval. The approval process and managed care procedures are further refined by the agency's administrative rules [Fla. Admin. Code R. 59A-23 et seq. (amended 4/30/98)]. With the introduction of managed care, workers' compensation insurers find themselves regulated by three state government agencies: the Department of Insurance, the Division of Workers' Compensation, and the Agency for Health Care Administration.

[4] Purpose and Effect of Managed Care

Managed Care represents a significant departure from the way Florida's employers and carriers delivered and managed workers' compensation health care in the past. The legislature clearly intended to end the decades long, tug-of-war between carriers on one end, claimants' attorneys on the other end, and physicians serving as the prize in the middle. This law intends to remove medical decision making from claims adjusters and put this responsibility in a physician's hands, i.e., the Medical Care Coordinator (MCC) [*see* [5][a], *below*].

[5] Claim Administration in Managed Care Environment

[a] Medical Care Coordinator (MCC)

[i] Role of MCC

The key to managed care is the Medical Care Coordinator (MCC), or as some prefer to call them, the medical gatekeeper. The MCC is a primary care physician within the carrier's provider network and is the individual responsible for managing the injured worker's medical care. The MCC decides what care the worker will receive, who will provide it, and at which facilities [§ 440.134(1)(i), Fla. Stat. (7/1/97)]. Previously, the law provided that only medical doctors (M.D.) and osteopathic doctors (D.O.) could serve as a Medical Care Coordinator. An amendment effective October 1, 2003, adds chiropractors and podiatrists as physicians qualified to serve as the MCC [§ 440.134(1)(i), Fla. Stat. (10/1/2003)].

[ii] Primary Care Provider as MCC

A Primary Care Provider is, unless giving emergency treatment, the initial treating physician and when appropriate, the continuing treating physician. Under these definitions, therefore, is the initial or continuing treating physician is also the Medical Care Coordinator? This is a critical question because under managed care treatment approval is transferred from the carrier to the MCC. For example, the Act requires carriers to review and approve in advance a physician's proposed treatment plan. Note, however, that this requirement does not apply to treatment rendered by a managed care arrangement [§ 440.13(2)(e), Fla. Stat. (1/1/94)].

Unfortunately, the courts have yet to answer the question and convincing arguments can be made supporting both positions. An argument supporting the notion that the Primary Care Provider (PCP) and the Medical Care Coordinator (MCC) are the same person begins with the definitions. The Act defines a PCP as the "initial treating physician and, when appropriate the continuing treating physician . . . ." [*see* § 440.134(1)(k), Fla Stat.]. The Act defines the MCC as "a primary care provider . . . ." [*see* § 440.134(1)(i). Fla. Stat.]. If the PCP is the treating physician, is the PCP also the MCC? Perhaps, but note that the definition refers to the MCC as *a* PCP and not *the* PCP. Clearly, only one physician can be primary. Also note that the Act requires that the carrier's managed care plan assure that "all continuing care services be received from the same primary care provider . . . except when services from another provider are authorized by the medical care coordinator" [*see* § 440.134(10)(b), Fla. Stat.]. This clearly suggests that the legislature intended that the PCP and the MCC are to be different individuals. Otherwise, the effect would be to allow the primary care provider to self-authorize medical services. Such a conclusion would render the very name "managed care" meaningless.

The most logical conclusion is that the MCC and the PCP are *not* the same individual.

[iii] Authority of MCC

The MCCs have the authority to refer patients to other physicians within the network as they deem appropriate. The statute is unclear, but it appears to give the MCC the authority to refer outside the network if the medically necessary care is not available within it. The Act provides that all managed care plans must contain the following [§ 440.134(10)(d), Fla. Stat. (1/1/94)]:

> The process for assuring that all referrals authorized by a medical care coordinator are made to the participating network providers, unless medically necessary treatment, care, and attendance are not available and accessible to the injured worker in the provider network.

[iv] Assignment of MCC

Effective October 1, 2003, the law requires that a managed care plan must contain a provision to assign a medical care coordinator to manage care by physicians with the same or similar license. This applies only if requested by the injured worker. Essentially, this requires multiple MCC's if a claimant is receiving treatment from physicians in multiple specialties and requests multiple medical care coordinators. Therefore, upon the injured worker's request, the carrier must assign an MCC as follows [§ 440.134(10)(e), Fla. Stat. (10/1/2003)]:

- Upon request, a medical doctor must be assigned as the MCC to manage care by other medical doctors or osteopathic physicians.
- Upon request, a chiropractic physician must be assigned as the MCC to supervise care by other chiropractors.
- Upon request, a podiatrist must be assigned as the MCC to manage care by other podiatrists.

[b] Carrier's Role in Case Management

Although the Medical Care Coordinator has the authority to initiate a treatment plan and to make referrals, this does not mean that carriers have no say in managing the injured worker's course of medical treatment. On the contrary, carriers have not only the right, but the duty to monitor the treatment constantly and to conduct peer and utilization review. Carriers must maintain an ongoing quality assurance program to monitor the quality and appropriateness of patient care. Carriers also have the right and the duty to prevent inappropriate or excessive treatment. This includes conducting pre-certification review of all elective admissions, and of non-emergency surgeries. Summed up, this means that the MCC now makes the medical decisions, but under carrier oversight [§ 440.134(6), Fla. Stat. (1/1/94); Fla. Admin. Code R. 59A-23.004 (1/22/2002)].

Carriers must review all bills and other claims, which health care providers submit for payment, to identify overutilization and billing errors. Effective October 1, 2003, carriers must also review such billing to determine if the charges are in compliance with required practice parameters and protocols [*see* § 16.17, *below*]. If the carrier determines that billing errors exist, or that overutilization occurred, or that the provider violated the practice parameters, the carrier must disallow or adjust payment accordingly. Carriers may do so unilaterally and do not require prior approval by a judge of compensation claims or AHCA [*see* § 440.13(6), Fla. Stat. (10/1/2003)].

[c] Who Chooses the MCC

[i] Choosing the MCC

Do injured workers have the right to choose the Medical Care Coordinator? Probably not, however, this question has not yet been the subject of judicial review. The most logical conclusion is that the carrier selects and appoints the MCC in each case. Note, however, that the MCC must meet the criteria to qualify as a primary care provider [*see* [a][ii], *above*].

[ii] Choosing the PCP

Every managed care plan must contain a "provision for the selection of a primary care provider by the employee from among primary care providers in the provider network" [§ 440.134(6)(c)10, Fla. Stat. (1/1/94)]. Also, the Act requires that carriers give the injured worker a list of the names, addresses, and telephone numbers of the medical care providers in its network. This includes primary care physicians, specialty physicians, hospitals, and other providers [§ 440.134(14)(a), Fla. Stat. (1/1/94)].

[d] Complying With Statutory Requirements

Employers and carriers who provide medical care by a managed care arrangement are statutorily deemed to have complied fully with the provisions of § 440.13(2)(a) and (b), Fla. Stat. These are the sections that describe the medical care injured workers can receive and the employer's duty to provide it. Simultaneously, the law deems injured workers treated in the managed care arrangement to have received all the medical benefits they are entitled to under the law [§ 440.134(16), Fla. Stat. (1/1/94)] In other words, when carriers offer their managed care arrangements to injured workers, they have fulfilled their statutory duty. It logically follows that the other sections of § 440.13, Fla. Stat. continue to apply as before, and carriers *are not* deemed in compliance with these sections simply because a managed care arrangement exists. Carriers must give the following information to injured workers [§ 440.134(14), Fla. Stat. (1/1/94)]:

> An insurer must make full and fair disclosure in writing of the provisions, restrictions, and limitations of the workers' compensation managed care arrangement to affected workers, including at least:
>
> (a) A description, including address and phone number, of the providers, including primary care physicians, specialty physicians, hospitals, and other providers.
>
> (b) A description of coverage for emergency and urgently needed care provided within and outside the service area.
>
> (c) A description of limitations on referrals.
>
> (d) A description of the grievance procedure.

While notice of the grievance procedures must be given at the time the managed care system is "implemented" [*see* § 440.134(15)(c), Fla. Stat. (1997)], no time frame for disclosure of the remaining aspects of the managed care arrangement is specifically provided in the statute. The judge of compensation claims, however, has no statutory authority to enforce this provision or to impose sanctions. That authority rests solely with

Guide to Claims

the Agency for Health Care Administration (AHCA) [*see* Farhangi v. Dunkin Donuts, 728 So. 2d 772, 773–774 (Fla. 1st DCA 1999), *reh'g denied,* March 22, 1999]. Unfortunately, the AHCA rules are also silent about when these disclosures should be made.

The obvious intent is that disclosure should occur on at least two occasions. The first occasion is at the time an employer enters a carrier's managed care arrangement. The second occasion is immediately upon the carrier's receipt of the First Notice of Injury.

[e] Staying in Managed Care Network

[i] Treatment Outside the Network

Generally, any medical treatment given outside the carrier's network is not compensable. The law, however, allows injured workers to obtain medical treatment outside the carrier's network if the carrier gives permission. Carriers should give this permission if the network cannot provide required, medically necessary treatment. Injured workers can also receive treatment outside the network if the carrier fails in its duty to inform the worker properly about the managed care requirements. Failing to provide the information described in [d], *above,* will result in freeing the injured worker from remaining in the carrier's network. That is to say, the injured worker can obtain medical care at the carrier's expense outside the network without carrier authorization. The statute, prior to October 1, 2003, provided as follows [§ 440.134(17), Fla. Stat. (1/1/94)]:

> Notwithstanding any other provisions of this chapter, when a carrier provides medical care through a workers' compensation managed care arrangement, pursuant to this section, those workers who are subject to the arrangement must receive medical services for work-related injuries and diseases as prescribed in the contract, provided the employer and carrier have provided notice to the employees of the arrangement in a manner approved by the agency. Treatment received outside the workers' compensation managed care arrangement is not compensable unless authorized by the carrier prior to the treatment date.

Effective October 1, 2003, the legislature amended the section to reiterate and clarify that treatment received outside the workers' compensation managed care arrangement is not compensable, regardless of the purpose of the treatment. This includes, but is not limited to, evaluations, examinations, and diagnostic studies to determine the following:

- Causation between medical findings and a compensable accident;
- The existence or extent of impairments or disabilities, and
- Whether the injured employee has reached maximum medical improvement.

As before, such medical services are compensable if the carrier grants authorization before the treatment date [§ 440.134(17), Fla. Stat. (10/1/2003)].

Note that a judge of compensation claims has no statutory authority to award treatment outside of an authorized managed care arrangement or to "strike" the managed care arrangement because the carrier failed to comply with statutory provisions. This is because the statute clearly places the authorization and supervision of managed care arrangements within the authority of the Agency for Health Care Administration [*see* Farhangi v. Dunkin

Donuts, 728 So. 2d 772, 773–774 (Fla. 1st DCA 1999), *reh'g denied,* March 22, 1999]. Although the *Farhangi* court did not address the issue, presumably the judge of compensation claims would have the authority to award care outside the arrangement if appropriate care is not available within it.

[ii] Unanswered Questions

The Agency for Health Care Administration has not developed rules about how carriers should provide notice. Until it does, however, the statutory notice requirement reviewed in [d], *above,* should be enough to invoke this section.

Another important question is whether, despite the statutory prohibition to the contrary, injured workers can obtain treatment outside Florida and, thus, outside the carrier's network. This issue usually arises in two situations. The first situation is an injured worker seeking care by an out-of-state specialist. In 1986 the First District Court of Appeal decided that this is compensable if the out-of-state specialist is more skilled than any other specialist within Florida [*see* Layne-Western Co. v. Cox, 497 So. 2d 955, 956 (Fla. 1st DCA 1986); *see also* § 16.03]. It appears that the managed care legislation overrules this decision since it prohibits care outside the network without the carrier's permission. Courts will likely create an exception, however, if the evidence shows that the specialist's care is medically necessary and unavailable within the network.

The second situation arises when injured workers decide to move their homes out-of-state. Again, this was permissible before managed care, and carriers were required to pay for care by doctors in the workers' new hometown. The statute clearly states, however, that treatment outside the carrier's network is not compensable, but whether this is an absolute prohibition is a question for the courts to answer. For example, if an injured worker presents medical testimony that moving out-of-state will somehow contribute to the worker's recovery, the court could easily justify approving it. On the other hand, the courts may order that if injured workers must remain in the network, carriers must pay for their transportation. Carriers should consider carefully before denying out-of-state treatment.

[f] Changing Doctors

[i] Controlling Statutes

The extent of an injured workers' right to a change of physician depends on the accident date and on whether managed care applies to the claim. Beginning October 1, 2001, providing medical services under a managed care arrangement is voluntary [*see* § 440.134(2)(b), Fla. Stat. (10/1/2001)]. When managed care applies, the right to medical care is governed by the provisions of § 440.134, Fla. Stat. When managed care does not apply, the provisions of § 440.13, Fla. Stat. are controlling.

[ii] Under Managed Care

[A] Accident Dates Through September 30, 2003

Under managed care, an injured worker is allowed one change to another medical provider within the same specialty and within the network during treatment for the work-related injury [§ 440.134(10)(c), Fla. Stat. (1/1/94)]. The injured worker should make the request for a change to the Medical Care Coordinator (MCC), who will refer the worker to another physician within the network. Remember that the MCC is the physician responsible for managing the worker's medical care, which includes determining other health care providers and facilities to which the worker will be referred for evaluation or treatment. Also remember that the one–time change is not an absolute limit. The legislature recognized that occasions will arise when more than one change of physicians may be appropriate. Carriers must arrange for additional changes as part of their grievance procedures. The employer/carrier has the right to select a treating physician for a claimant. A claimant may choose a substitute physician only if the E/C fails to provide the treatment or care requested within a reasonable time [*see* § 440.13(2)(c), Fla. Stat.; Soriano v. Gold Coast Aerial Lift, 705 So. 2d 636, 638 (Fla. 1st DCA 1998), *reh'g denied,* February 19, 1998].

[B] Accident Dates On or After October 1, 2003

Effective October 1, 2003, the Legislature repealed the provision requiring that a carrier's managed plan must contain a provision that an injured worker is allowed one change to another medical provider within the same specialty and within the network during treatment for the work-related injury. It is not clear whether this is a substantive or a procedural amendment, but it appears to be substantive because it creates a statutory limitation on treatment, at least when managed care applies. Until the courts clarify this issue, it will be prudent to treat this as a substantive amendment that applies only to accidents occurring on or after October 1, 2003.

The amendment now provides that the procedures for allowing a change of physician under managed care are the same as those in § 440.13(2)(f), Fla. Stat. That section provides that an injured worker is entitled to one change of physician during the course of treatment for any one accident. Upon written request from the employee, or presumably the employee's attorney, the carrier must authorize an alternative physician who cannot be professionally affiliated with the previous physician. If the carrier fails to provide an alternative physician within five days after receiving the request, the employee may then make the selection, and the physician becomes authorized as a matter of law. Additionally, the statute provides that the treatment rendered is deemed compensable and medically necessary. Thus, if the carrier fails to provide the alternative physician in a timely fashion, it not only loses the right to select the physician, it loses the right to challenge the medical necessity of such treatment [*see* § 440.13(2)(f), Fla. Stat. (10/1/2003)].

[iii] Outside Managed Care

The legislature enacted a provision providing that an injured worker is entitled to *one* change of physician during the course of treatment *for any one accident.* Upon written request from the employee, or presumably the employee's attorney, the carrier must provide a list of at least three physicians from which the employee may choose one. Note that the physicians listed must be independent of one another and not professionally affiliated [*see* § 440.13(2)(f), Fla. Stat. (10/1/2001)].

Effective October 1, 2003, the Legislature amended the section again. The law now provides that upon granting a change of physician, the original authorized physician is deauthorized upon written notification from the carrier. This deauthorization applies only if the original physician is in the same specialty as the replacement physician. Therefore, if the replacement is in a different specialty, the original physician presumably will remain authorized.

Note that the replacement or alternative physician provided cannot be professionally affiliated with the original physician. The right to a change of physician is virtually automatic. The carrier *must* respond to a written request for a change within five days after receiving the request. If the carrier fails to respond within five days, the employee may choose the physician, and the law deems that physician to be authorized. Thus, during the first five days after receipt of the request for a change, the carrier has the right to choose the physician. If the carrier does not authorize a replacement within five days, the employee has the right of selection.

Also note that, besides losing the right to select the physician, failing to authorize the replacement physician within five days constitutes a violation of Chapter 440, subjecting the carrier to penalties under § 440.525, Fla. Stat. [*see* § 440.13(2)(f), Fla. Stat. (10/1/2003)].

Section 440.13(2)(f), Fla. Stat. allows a claimant to select the replacement physician if the carrier does not respond within five days. This provision has not yet undergone judicial review. An unanswered question is whether the section applies when a managed care arrangement is in place. Apparently, it does to some extent, because § 440.134(10)(c), Fla. Stat. was also amended to provide that the authorization of a change of physician must be done in accordance with the procedures provided in § 440.13(2)(f), Fla. Stat. However, § 440.134(10)(c), Fla. Stat., also provides that the change of physician is limited to those participating in the provider network.

Although the provision clearly states that an injured worker may have only one change per accident, it is conceivable that the court will conclude that the phrase "course of treatment" refers to treatment in each specialty. Obviously, this limitation will not apply in situations in which the initial treating physician has retired, is deceased, or simply refuses to treat the claimant. Consideration should also be given to authorizing more than one change in situations in which the attending physician declares that he or she has nothing further to offer the claimant by way of treatment. Refusing an additional change under these circumstances is essentially the same as denying medical care.

[g] Second Opinions

[i] Accident Dates Through September 30, 2003

Carriers must allow employees to obtain *one* second opinion in the same specialty and within the network [§ 440.134(6)(c)9, Fla. Stat. (1/1/94)]. Again, a request for a second opinion should be made to the carrier's MCC for appropriate referral.

Although the statute clearly requires the carrier to allow the injured worker one second opinion, the carrier's plan could presumably allow more or even allow the employer or carrier to have a second opinion.

For example, in addition to allowing a claimant to obtain a second opinion as required by § 440.134(6)(c)9, Fla. Stat. the Wal-Mart Managed Care Plan allowed a second opinion to be initiated by a case manager, the managed care coordinator, or any authorized treating physician. When the claimant refused to submit to such an examination the employer moved to compel the claimant's attendance. The judge of compensation claims refused, holding that the statute allows only the claimant to obtain a second opinion and not the E/C [Wal-Mart Stores, Inc. v. Capuano, 800 So. 2d 652, 653 (Fla. 1st DCA 2001)].

On review, the court noted that the judge's decision effectively struck part of the E/C's AHCA-approved managed care plan and that such an action was beyond the authority or jurisdiction of the judge of compensation claims [Wal-Mart Stores, Inc. v. Capuano, 800 So. 2d 652, 654 (Fla. 1st DCA 2001); *see* Farangi v. Dunkin Donuts, 728 So. 2d 772, 773 (Fla. 1st DCA 1999]. The court, however, denied certiorari because the dispute involved the validity of and enforcement of a managed care arrangement. The *Farhangi* court had held that § 440.134, Fla. Stat. clearly placed the authorization and supervision of managed care arrangements within the authority of AHCA. Therefore, the matter belonged in another arena, and the First District Court of Appeal declined to accept jurisdiction. The question therefore remains unsettled as to whether can employer or carrier can add requirements to its managed plan that are not specifically allowed or required by statute [*see* Wal-Mart Stores, Inc. v. Capuano, 800 So. 2d 652, 654 (Fla. 1st DCA 2001)].

[ii] Accident Dates On or After October 31, 2003

Effective October 1, 2003, the Legislature repealed the requirement that a managed care plan contain a provision allowing a claimant to have one second opinion in each specialty [§ 440.134(6)(9), Fla. Stat. (10/1/2003)].

Note, however, that this amendment merely deletes second opinions as a requirement. If carriers do not amend their plans, they might still be responsible for providing second opinions in accordance with the plan.

This raises the question of whether a claimant is ever entitled to a second opinion if the employer/carrier does not participate in managed care, or if the managed care plan does not provide for second opinions. The answer is that, despite the lack of any statutory provision for a second opinion, a claimant may be entitled to a second opinion as part of his or her medically necessary care.

Occasions may arise when the "nature of the injury or the process of recovery" renders a second medical opinion medically necessary. The court has refused to read § 440.13, Fla. Stat., as evincing a legislative intent to deny a claimant the opportunity to demonstrate the medical necessity of a second opinion. The court was unable to define in advance the universe of possible situations in which a second opinion would be medically necessary. The court did, however, conclude that the claimant's request for a second opinion presents a question of fact, similar to any other request under § 440.13(2)(a), Fla. Stat.

Thus, the judge of compensation claims must resolve such questions after an evidentiary hearing at which the claimant will bear the burden of demonstrating entitlement [*see* Lombardi v. Southern Wine & Spirits, 890 So. 2d 1128 (Fla. 1st DCA 2004), *rehg. denied*, 2005 Fla. App. LEXIS 1440 (Jan. 14, 2005)].

[h] Dispute Resolution

Another significant statutory requirement is a separate dispute resolution procedure.

The parties must resolve all medical disputes by the grievance procedure set forth in the carrier's approved plan [§ 440.192(3), Fla. Stat. (1/1/94)]. Furthermore, a Petition for Benefits must contain a certificate that all managed care grievance procedures have been exhausted before filing the petition [Fla. R. Work. Comp. P. 4.028(5)(D)]. The statute's plain language requires this procedure for any medical benefit. The general requirements for a proper grievance procedure are contained in the AHCA rules [Fla. Admin. Code R. 59A-23.006 (1/22/2002)]. Each carrier is allowed to design its own grievance procedure within guidelines set by AHCA.

Because each carrier's procedures will differ, explaining these procedures carefully to each injured worker is necessary. AHCA rules allow carriers 60 days to resolve disputes. This time extends to 90 days if the process requires gathering information outside the service area. If the parties elect to arbitrate the dispute, the time extends to 210 days from receipt of the injured worker's written request for arbitration.

Effective October 1, 2003, the Act defines a "grievance" as follows [§ 440.134(1)(d), Fla. Stat. (10/1/2003)]:

> "Grievance" means a written complaint, other than a petition for benefits, filed by the injured worker pursuant to the requirements of the managed care arrangement, expressing dissatisfaction with the insurer's workers' compensation managed care arrangement's refusal to provide medical care or the medical care provided.

This appears to be an effort to end the practice of including a grievance as part of a Petition for Benefits.

For a general discussion of dispute resolution in workers' compensation, see LARSON'S WORKERS' COMPENSATION, DESK EDITION, Part 14, *Adjective Law* (Matthew Bender).

[i] Independent Medical Examinations

Beginning October 1, 2003, every managed care plan must contain a provision for allowing the independent medical examination provided for in § 440.13(5), Fla. Stat. Section 440.13(5) provides that each party is entitled to only one independent medical examination for any one accident and that the requesting party is responsible for payment. However, if the claimant's selection of an independent medical examiner is in the carrier's managed care network, the carrier is responsible for payment.

The fact that the claimant's selection is made through the managed care arrangement, and the fact that the carrier paid for the examination, does not alter the limitation of one independent medical examination per accident. Therefore, if the claimant obtains a carrier-paid independent medical examination under the managed care provisions of § 440.134, Fla. Stat., that will constitute his or her one-per-accident examination under § 440.13(5), Fla. Stat. [*see* § 440.134(9), Fla. Stat. (10/1/2003)].

§ 16.03 Medical Benefits

[1] Medical Necessity

[a] Compensable Treatment

To be compensable, the law requires that the treatment, device, or aid be medically necessary. The basis for awarding a benefit must be the injured worker's medical need. A judge of compensation claims may award only those medical benefits that are a medical necessity. An award of a benefit that would not improve or aid the injured worker's recovery is invalid [*see* Stables v. Rivers, 562 So. 2d 784, 785–786 (Fla. 1st DCA 1990); Diamond R. Fertilizer v. Davis, 567 So. 2d 451, 455 (Fla. 1st DCA 1990); Delong v. 3015 West Corp., 558 So. 2d 108, 109 (Fla. 1st DCA 1990)].

Distinguishing between medically necessary benefits and those that are merely pleasant or convenient is essential. Simple convenience to the injured worker will not suffice to support an award [*see* Aino's Custom Slip Covers v. DeLucia, 533 So. 2d 862, 865 (Fla. 1st DCA 1988)].

[b] Medical Necessity Defined

Effective January 1, 1994, the Act defines the term "medically necessary" as [§ 440.13(1)(m), Fla. Stat.]:

> [A]ny medical service or medical supply which is used to identify or treat an illness or injury, is appropriate to the patient's diagnosis and status of recovery, and is consistent with the location of service, the level of care provided, and applicable practice parameters. The service should be widely accepted among practicing health care providers, based on scientific criteria, and determined to be reasonably safe. The service must not be of an experimental, investigative, or research nature, except in those instances in which prior approval of the Agency for Health Care Administration has been obtained.

Effective October 1, 2003, the Legislature amended this section by repealing the provision that investigative or experimental medical services are compensable if they are approved by the Agency for Health Care Administration. Therefore, treatments that are experimental or investigative are not compensable under any circumstance because they no longer meet the statutory definition of "medically necessary." Presumably, this will apply to such services rendered on or after the amendment's effective date [*see* § 440.13(1), Fla. Stat. (10/1/2003)]. The revised definition is now as follows:

> [A]ny medical service or medical supply which is used to identify or treat an illness or injury, is appropriate to the patient's diagnosis and status of recovery, and is consistent with the location of service, the level of care provided, and applicable practice parameters. The service should be widely accepted among practicing health care providers, based on scientific criteria, and determined to be reasonably safe. The service must not be of an experimental, investigative, or research nature.

Remember that a service or device is not rendered unnecessary just because a physician does not utter the phrase "medically necessary." We must examine all the evidence. Conversely, just because a physician declares a service or device medically necessary does not make it automatically so. A kindly physician, for example, may declare it is medically necessary that an injured worker have a jet airplane, but the medical evidence is unlikely to support that opinion. Because the new statutory definition is so broad, it has not altered or overruled case law on what is medically necessary. A review of specific application of the term follows in [c], *below*.

[c] Applying the Medical Necessity Test

[i] Swimming Pools and Spas

Sometimes a doctor will say that the only effective treatment for an injury is exercise, and that the only effective exercise is swimming. Must the carrier build a pool in the injured worker's back yard? In certain cases, yes! In cases like this, swimming is the "medically necessary" issue. The issue is not "a pool in the injured worker's back yard." The courts consider installing a pool at the injured worker's home to be "highly extraordinary relief" [*see* Haga v. Clay Hyder Trucking Lines, 397 So. 2d 428, 429, 431–432 (Fla. 1st DCA 1981)].

Therefore, if a facility exists nearby, such as a YMCA, the carrier would only be responsible for the dues at the YMCA. This general rule does not apply, however, in three situations. The first situation is the injured worker is unable to travel. The second is the facility is not appropriate or available when needed. The third situation is that no facility is available [*see* Sacred Heart Hosp. v. Grafton, 451 So. 2d 1018, 1020 (Fla. 1st DCA 1984)].

In *Grafton,* the doctor prescribed swimming as part of the injured worker's therapy. The doctor testified this was necessary, not only to treat the injury, but to prevent recurrence. The nearest public pool to the injured worker's home, however, was 56 miles distant, and the doctor testified that long-distance driving would worsen the injured worker's condition. The doctor concluded that a swimming pool at the injured worker's home was medically necessary, and the court ordered the carrier to pay for its construction.

The court was silent on several issues. Must the carrier pay for electricity to run the pump, pay for chemicals or a pool service, repair the pool as it aged, or pay for routine maintenance? Presumably, the court would consider the pool a medical device that the carrier must maintain while it remains medically necessary. Indeed, the decisions have held that after a court decides an item is medically necessary, the court may require the carrier to provide for insurance and maintenance to assure its continued availability. The carrier, however, is not responsible for all expenses of operation, although costs uniquely attributable to the provision of a facility or service which is necessitated by an accident and found to be medically necessary, may be awarded [*see* Firestone Tire & Rubber Co. v. Vaughn, 381 So. 2d 740, 742 (Fla. 1st DCA 1980); Applegate Drywall Company v. Patrick, 559 So. 2d 736, 737 (Fla. 1st DCA 1990)].

[ii] Handicapped Equipped Housing

[A] When House Cannot Be Modified

Clearly, a severely injured worker confined to a wheelchair, for example, has special needs at home such as ramps, wide doorways, and so forth. In such a case, the law requires the carrier to modify the injured worker's home according to medical needs. What happens, however, if the injured worker's home cannot be modified? The carrier must provide modified housing, but only for the difference between the cost of the injured worker's current home and the cost of a home fully equipped [*see* Ramada Inn South Airport v. Lamoureux, 565 So. 2d 376, 377 (Fla. 1st DCA 1990)].

For example, Roy Skinner's injury rendered him quadriplegic. On his own authority, he

Guide to Claims

constructed a new, 2,300 square foot, wheelchair-accessible home at a cost of $310,000. Skinner filed a petition, demanding that the carrier pay this amount. Evidence showed that Skinner's impairment required only an additional 527 square feet of living space to adapt to his impairment. The evidence also showed that the cost of construction was $50 per square foot so the judge awarded Skinner $26,350. In addition, the judge awarded the cost of a wheelchair ramp and additional garage space of 96 square feet at $25 per square foot. The total award was $28,950. The First District Court of Appeal affirmed the award [*see* Skinner v. Florida Power Corp., 580 So. 2d 614, 615–616 (Fla. 1st DCA 1991)].

The award of a new house must be based on competent substantial evidence showing the medical necessity. Without evidence establishing why a new house is medically necessary, there can be no competent, substantial evidence to support the award of a new house. Note that economic considerations cannot be the basis for awarding a new home. While circumstances may exist that would entitle a claimant to an award of a new house, the new house must be medically necessary and awarded only when an existing home cannot be modified [*see* Adams Bldg. Materials, Inc. v. Brooks, 892 So. 2d 527 (Fla. 1st DCA 2004)].

[B] Additional Housing for Family Members

Vincent Kowalski suffered severe brain damage and required constant care provided by his parents. The trial judge awarded housing to include a second bedroom and bathroom to accommodate Kowalski's parents. The judge based the award on the physician's testimony that such accommodation was medically necessary. The physician testified that the parents living with the injured worker would provide a very positive, caring, and supportive relationship. This was care, said the doctor, that an outside care-giver could not provide. On appeal, the court reversed. A judge of compensation claims may not award such additional housing based on testimony that this would be merely beneficial, helpful, or convenient. Just because a physician uses the phrase "medically necessary" does not mean it is necessarily so. Further, the court held that the *preference* of a medical witness does not meet the statutory requirement of medical necessity [*see* Timothy Bowser Const. Co. v. Kowalski, 605 So. 2d 885, 888–889 (Fla. 1st DCA 1992)].

[C] Home Owners Insurance

Home insurance is a normal living expense. An injured worker can collect the cost of insurance only to the extent that the cost exceeds the cost of insuring the injured worker's former home [*see* Southern Industries v. Chumney, 613 So. 2d 74, 77 (Fla. 1st DCA 1993)].

[d] Automobiles, Custom Vans, or Other Transportation

[i] Transportation To and From Medical Providers

In certain cases involving severe permanent disability, the injured worker may need a vehicle for transportation to and from medical treatment. Note, however, that compensable transportation is only for travel to and from health care providers. Clearly, a $30,000 custom van complete with color T.V., C.B. radio, and a wet bar would be more comfortable and convenient. Comfort and convenience, however, are not the basis of the entitlement. All that the law allows is transportation to and from medical providers. If an ordinary vehicle will do, or a medical transport service is available, this is all that the courts may award [*see* Aino's Custom Slipcovers v. DeLucia, 533 So. 2d 862, 865 (Fla. 1st DCA 1988)].

Supportive services such as driving the claimant to the store and to other places, other than transportation necessary for medical treatment under § 440.13, Fla. Stat., constitute quality-of-life activities. The claimant is indemnified under disability compensation benefits for such services rather than attendant care service that is medically necessary [*see* Kraft Dairy Group v. Cohen, 645 So. 2d 1072 (Fla. 1st DCA 1994)].

In *Kowalski,* the trial judge awarded an appropriately equipped vehicle. The award included not only medical transport, but transport for other activities as well. These included visits with friends, and trips to the grocery store, the mall, the beach, relatives' homes, and the movies. The judge of compensation claims based the award on medical testimony that such trips were medically necessary to provide the brain injured worker with socialization and reintegration into the community. The judge believed this met the medical necessity test. The First District Court of Appeal disagreed and reversed the non-medical travel portion. The court held that § 440.13(2)(a) and (5), Fla. Stat. (Supp. 1988) provides for an award of transportation only for authorized medical care. Despite how welcome and beneficial social and recreational activities may be, they are not awardable under the Act [*see* Timothy Bowser Const. Co. v. Kowalski, 605 So. 2d 885, 887–888 (Fla. 1st DCA 1992)].

A claimant's need for a van must be clearly established. The test for whether a van may be awarded as "other apparatus" under § 440.13, Fla. Stat., is whether the award would improve the condition caused by the accident or would aid in the recovery from the accident [*see* Kraft Dairy Group v. Cohen, 645 So. 2d 1072 (Fla. 1st DCA 1994)].

When the employer/carrier offers convenient 24-hour per day transportation as an alternative, the claimant must prove that a van is more appropriate, a difficult burden to overcome [*see* Montgomery Ins. & Adm. Farragut Acad. v. Deyo, 876 So. 2d 697 (Fla. 1st DCA 2004)].

[ii] Vehicles as Medical Apparatus

Cars, vans, and trucks are, in effect, medical apparatus. As with the home, a carrier may modify an injured worker's existing car if such modification will suffice. For example, Donna Cremeens suffered the partial amputation of her hand. As a result she could no longer operate her car because it lacked an automatic transmission and power steering. The carrier first tried to modify the car by installing the required equipment, but the effort failed. It was clear a replacement vehicle was necessary. The judge of compensation claims ordered the carrier to pay the entire purchase price of a replacement car.

On appeal, the court reversed. Ordinarily the award should be the difference between the book value of the prior vehicle and the cost of a similar replacement vehicle equipped with the medically necessary apparatus. This case was unusual, however, because Cremeens traded in her car for the replacement. The court held she was entitled to the difference between the trade-in value and the cost of the replacement. In the court's view, the automatic transmission and the power steering were the medically necessary apparatus, not the car itself. Therefore, the carrier was not responsible for the entire cost of expenses such as insurance, repair, gasoline, license tag, and so forth. Because this was a replacement vehicle, the accident did not create the need for such expense items. Therefore, the carrier was responsible for only those expenses uniquely attributable to providing the medically necessary options (the steering and transmission). The court also held that Cremeens should bear the initial cost of these expenses and the carrier should reimburse her upon receipt of proper documentation [*see* Temps & Co. Services v. Cremeens, 597 So. 2d 394, 396–397 (Fla. 1st DCA 1992)].

[iii] Vehicle Ownership

[A] Carrier Has Option of Holding Title

If the carrier does purchase a vehicle, who holds the title? The statutory requirement to provide medically necessary apparatus is not an unconditional mandate for vesting title in the injured worker's name. Therefore, the judge of compensation claims may not require the carrier to place title in the injured worker's name. On the other hand, vesting of title in the injured worker is not, per se, prohibited. This means that a carrier has the option of holding title or transferring it to the injured worker.

[B] Potential Liability for Carrier

As a practical matter, transferring title to the injured worker is likely in the carrier's best interest because of the dangerous instrumentality doctrine. This doctrine holds the owner of a motor vehicle liable for its negligent operation. The Florida Supreme Court applied the doctrine to motor vehicles when it held [*see* Susco Car Rental System of Florida v. Leonard, 112 So. 2d 832, 836 (Fla. 1959) (citing *Anderson v. Southern Cotton Oil Co.*, 73 Fla. 432, 74 So. 975, 978 (1917))]:

> The principles of the common law do not permit the owner of an instrumentality that is . . . peculiarly dangerous in its operation, to authorize another to use such instrumentality on the public highways without imposing upon such owner liability for negligent use. The liability grows out of the obligation of the owner to have the vehicle . . . properly operated when it is by his authority on the public highway.

In 1990, the Florida Supreme Court added the following [*see* Kraemer v. General Motors Acceptance Corp., 572 So. 2d 1363 (Fla. 1990)]:

> [The dangerous instrumentality doctrine] is premised upon the theory that one who originates the danger by entrusting the automobile to another is in the best position to make certain there will be adequate resources with which to pay the damages caused by its negligent operation.

All of this means that the workers' compensation carrier may be responsible for the safe operation of the vehicle if it elects to retain ownership. The risks seem to outweigh any benefit.

NOTE: If injured workers' injuries require a vehicle as a medically necessary apparatus and they do not own one of their own, the carrier will be responsible for the entire cost. If the car itself is the medically necessary apparatus, the carrier must pay for operating expenses because such costs cannot be apportioned. If a special vehicle cannot be apportioned, the carrier is responsible for total maintenance expenses and the cost of insurance [*see* Southern Industries v. Chumney, 613 So. 2d 74, 76 (Fla. 1st DCA 1993)].

Guide to Claims

[iv] Merely Beneficial Is Not Enough

No matter how beneficial a device may be, beneficence alone may not be enough. For example, the carrier gave James Mapes a Pacesaver scooter that everyone agreed was medically necessary. The carrier also modified Mapes' car by providing a lift for the scooter. The judge of compensation claims, however, ordered the carrier to give the injured worker a mini-van equipped with a lift that would hold the scooter. The judge based the award on the recommendation of Mapes' physician. The First District Court of Appeal reversed. Testimony made it abundantly clear that a mini-van would be beneficial, but no evidence was submitted showing that the van, as opposed to the modified car, was medically necessary [*see* Brigham & Winningham v. Mapes, 610 So. 2d 623 (Fla. 1st DCA 1992)].

[v] Vehicle Modifications to Accommodate Medical Attendant

Occasionally, vehicle modifications may be necessary to help the attendant rather than the injured worker. In *Southern Industries,* the court approved an award of running boards for the injured worker's van. This was medically necessary, although the running boards were installed as a convenience to the injured worker's wife. She provided attendant care services and needed the running boards to care for her husband [*see* Southern Industries v. Chumney, 613 So. 2d 74, 76 (Fla. 1st DCA 1993)].

[vi] Automobile Club Membership

In *Southern Industries* the court approved an award of membership in the American Automobile Association. The court found that the injured worker's disability was such that he could not maintain a proper body temperature. The injured worker, stated the court, would be presented with a health risk if he became stranded on the highway. Thus, membership in the automobile club, here, was medically necessary [*see* Southern Industries v. Chumney, 613 So. 2d 74, 76 (Fla. 1st DCA 1993)].

[e] Palliative Medical Care

Palliative medical care is treatment that may alleviate or ease symptoms, but does not improve or cure the condition. The statutory definition is "noncurative medical services that mitigate the conditions, effects, or pain of an injury" [§ 440.13(1)(o), Fla. Stat. (1/1/94)].

As such, palliative care would not seem to meet the definition of medical necessity in that it does not aid recovery or provide progressive and sustained benefit. In spite of this, the law entitles an injured worker to palliative treatment that mitigates the conditions or effects of an injury. The cases suggest that any care is compensable if it will relieve pain or otherwise make the injured worker feel better. Devices, apparatus, and general services, however, must meet the medical necessity test [*see* Clements v. Morrow's Nut House, 598 So. 2d 279, 280 (Fla. 1st DCA 1992)].

[f] Water, Sewer, and Electrical Charges

These items are not compensable, absent a showing of medical necessity. "Utilities are generally considered basic necessities in every home in our society, and a claimant will have a difficult time demonstrating that necessity for such items is caused by the compensable accident, such that they could be properly awarded as medical benefits" [*see* Polk County Bd. of Com'rs v. Varnado, 576 So. 2d 833, 838 (Fla. 1st DCA 1991)].

In *Southern Industries,* however, the injured worker did show such a need. Medical testimony showed the injured worker required an environment that was controlled as to temperature and humidity. Therefore, maintaining home air conditioning was medically necessary. In addition, the court held the carrier responsible for that portion of the injured worker's electric bill attributable to operating the air conditioning [*see* Southern Industries v. Chumney, 613 So. 2d 74, 77 (Fla. 1st DCA 1993)].

Always, the judge of compensation claims must decide what part of utility expense is uniquely attributable to the compensable injury. It is only this part for which the carrier is responsible [*see* Fredrick Electronics v. Pettijohn, 619 So. 2d 14, 16 (Fla. 1st DCA 1993)].

[g] Telephones

In *Varnado,* the court upheld the award of the base payment of a telephone in the injured worker's home. The evidence showed that the injured worker, who was paralyzed in a compensable accident, needed the telephone to contact his wife to receive necessary attendant care. The court, however, made a point of noting the uniqueness of this case [*see* Polk County Bd. of Com'rs v. Varnado, 576 So. 2d 833, 838–839 (Fla. 1st DCA 1991)]. The court approved a similar award in *Southern Industries* [*see* Southern Industries v. Chumney, 613 So. 2d 74, 77 (Fla. 1st DCA 1993)].

[h] Lawn and Yard Maintenance

Evidence that the worker's injuries make it necessary for someone else to mow the lawn is not enough. Compensability turns, first, on medical evidence that the injured worker did this chore before the accident. Second, the evidence must show that avoiding yard work will, itself, improve the injured worker's condition or aid recovery [*see* Delong v. 3015 West Corp., 558 So. 2d 108, 109 (Fla. 1st DCA 1990)].

Imagining such a case is difficult, yet the court approved an award of lawn maintenance in *Southern Industries.* With little comment, the court approved the award based on, "substantial evidence to show that the environment outside the injured worker's home should be reasonably well cared for" [*see* Southern Industries v. Chumney, 613 So. 2d 74, 77 (Fla. 1st DCA 1993)].

With even less comment, the court approved a similar award in *Frederick Electronics.* Here, as in *Southern Industries* [*see* [f], *above*], the worker's injuries rendered him quadriplegic. His treating physician testified that a clean yard was medically necessary. The judge of compensation claims agreed, as did the First District Court of Appeal [*see* Fredrick Electronics v. Pettijohn, 619 So. 2d 14, 16 (Fla. 1st DCA 1993)].

[i] Child Care

Child care, under special circumstances, may be compensable. As always, the test is medical necessity. For example, Faye Robinson suffered from a back injury. Because of her injury and the nature of her medical treatment (frequent traction), she was unable to care for her four-year-old child. Additionally, doctors diagnosed her as having moderate to severe depressive neurosis. Robinson's psychiatrist testified that her inability to care for her child caused a significant stress in her life that made the condition worse. Further, the doctor testified that if the child could attend nursery school (at the carrier's expense), this would lessen Robinson's frustrations and aid her recovery. Under these facts, the court approved an award of child care. The court pointed out strongly that this was an unusual case and stated: "[W]e caution against anyone's misconstruing this opinion as an acceptance of the medical necessity of child care in cases involving circumstances less extreme than those specifically presented here" [*see* Doctors Hospital of Lake Worth v. Robinson, 411 So. 2d 958, 959 (Fla. 1st DCA 1982)].

[j] Postnatal Child Care

The issue here is whether the carrier is responsible for the postnatal care of a child for pregnancy complications brought on by an industrial accident. For example, Margaret Pringle's child was born prematurely as the result of an accident at work. The infant required extra medical treatment and specialized attendant care. The trial judge awarded benefits on the theory that the fetus was an integral part Pringle's body, and that the industrial accident caused the medical costs.

The First District Court of Appeal reversed and refused to award benefits to the child. The court based this refusal on the theory that the child was not an employee, and only employees can receive benefits [*see* Globe Sec. v. Pringle, 559 So. 2d 720, 722 (Fla. 1st DCA 1990)].

[k] Psychological Treatment for Spouse and Children

Imagining that an injured worker's spouse and children may suffer emotional problems is not difficult. The question, however, is whether the carrier must pay for this treatment. As the court pointed out in *Pringle,* only an employee can receive benefits. An exception will arise, however, if the injured worker can show that treating family members will somehow aid or improve the worker's own condition. In one case, the court found that the evidence supported awarding psychological evaluation and counseling for the injured worker's husband and children. The court based the award on evidence that this would help the injured worker's own psychological treatment [*see* Stables v. Rivers, 562 So. 2d 784, 786 (Fla. 1st DCA 1990)].

[l] Garbage Collection

So far the courts have been unable to imagine a case where it could find garbage collection to be a medically necessary benefit. In *Southern Industries,* the court stated that the cost of garbage collection was an ordinary living expense. No evidence even remotely suggested that the need for garbage collection was uniquely attributable to the employee's injury [*see* Southern Industries v. Chumney, 613 So. 2d 74, 77 (Fla. 1st DCA 1993)].

[m] Cleaning Services and Supplies

Usually, routine home maintenance is not compensable. The law requires evidence of medical necessity. In *Southern Industries,* the injured worker suffered from respiratory problems. This condition required him to live in a dust-free and odor-free environment. Thus, the court held the cost of house cleaning service and cleaning supplies to be a medically necessary benefit [*see* Southern Industries v. Chumney, 613 So. 2d 74, 77 (Fla. 1st DCA 1993)].

[n] Life Care Planning

In *Southern Industries,* the injured worker hired a rehabilitation counselor as an expert witness to support his claims for various services discussed in [c]–[*l*], *above.* The charge for developing the life care plan was $5,647.33. The court refused to award reimbursement, stating that the injured worker's testimony and that of his primary care physician, supported all the benefits awarded. Thus, the expert's testimony was not necessary to the procurement of benefits [*see* Southern Industries v. Chumney, 613 So. 2d 74, 78 (Fla. 1st DCA 1993)].

In *Frederick Electronics,* the court went even further. Here, the court held that all a judge may award is medically necessary remedial care and attendance by a health care provider. The life care planner did not meet the requirements of a health care provider as defined by § 440.13 (2)(a), Fla. Stat. [*see now* § 440.13(1)(i), Fla. Stat. (1/1/94)]. The life care planner was not a licensed physician or under the supervision or direction of one. Therefore, the carrier was not responsible for payment for his services [*see* Fredrick Electronics v. Pettijohn, 619 So. 2d 14, 16 (Fla. 1st DCA 1993)].

[2] Prostheses

The law provides that an injured worker is entitled to "medical supplies, durable medical equipment, orthoses, prostheses, and other medically necessary apparatus" [§ 440.13(2)(a), Fla. Stat. (1/1/94)]. This includes just about anything imaginable. Originally, the law did not cover damage to such devices because the courts concluded they were personal property. Today, the law does cover damage to dentures, eyeglasses, prosthetic devices, and artificial limbs when the damage is part of, or with, an accident.

Take special note that for accident dates through December 31, 1993, no statute of limitations applies to the right for remedial attention relating to the insertion or attachment of a prosthetic device to any part of the body. This section also applies to the maintenance and repair of such devices, including a back brace [§ 440.19(1)(b), Fla. Stat.].

> **SPECIAL ALERT:** Effective January 1, 1994, the legislature repealed § 440.19(1)(b), Fla. Stat. Therefore, for accidents occurring on or after that date, the one-year limitation period applies to prosthetic devices in the same fashion as all other medical care [*see* ch. 9, § 9.03[7][ii]].

[3] Transportation Expenses

[a] Accident Dates Through December 31, 1993

[i] The Rule on Reimbursement

The law provides that as part of medical care, an injured worker is entitled to "reasonable actual cost of transportation to and from the doctor's office, hospital, or other place of treatment by the most economical means of transportation available and suitable in the individual case" [§ 440.13(6), Fla. Stat.].

If the injured worker uses a private automobile for transportation, there is a statutory presumption that the cost is the amount allowed by the state to its employees for official travel. The 1994 legislature increased the reimbursement amount for official travel beginning in October 1994, and again in 1995 [§ 112.061(7)(d), Fla. Stat. (10/1/94)]. Therefore, the reimbursement amount changes depending upon the date of travel. The amounts are as follows:

Up to September 30, 1994	$0.20 per mile
Between October 1, 1994 and June 30, 1995	$0.25 per mile
On or after July 1, 1995	$0.29 per mile

The Division's official position is that these increases are procedural amendments and apply to the date of travel, whatever the date of the accident [Division Bulletin #163 (9/1/94)]. The Division is likely correct because the courts have held that changes in the cost of a service are procedural and apply to the date of service.

Sometimes, the injured worker cannot drive a car, does not own a car, or is medically unable to travel alone. In such a case, the law entitles the injured worker to whatever alternative is the most reasonable and economical. Usually this will be bus or cab fare.

[ii] Lost Wages for Driver

Cheryl Mills claimed reimbursement for $0.20 per mile plus $50 per day, per trip to cover her husband's lost wages. Mills was unable to operate a car because of her wrist injury. Is she entitled to recover? Maybe. Here, the judge of compensation claims denied the claim. On appeal, the court did not make a specific finding. Instead, the court found the judge's order was not sufficiently detailed to figure out why the judge ruled as he did. The court remanded the case to the judge with the following instruction.

> We point out that if the most reasonable way to be transported was to have someone drive her, the amount of the person's lost wages incurred when acting as a driver for the claimant is not necessarily an appropriate measure for transportation costs. . . . If it was not reasonable to be transported in the manner undertaken by claimant, claimant should be awarded as much of her actual costs as would have provided the most economical, suitable transportation available.

The injured worker has the burden to show that the mode of transportation taken was reasonable and economical under the circumstances. The carrier's burden is then to show that a more reasonable and economical transportation method existed. For example, if

Guide to Claims

using a commercial taxi was reasonable, and the round trip fare was $20, then this would be all the carrier would have to pay [*see* Mills v. Walden-Sparkman, Inc., 493 So. 2d 64, 66 (Fla. 1st DCA 1986)].

[iii] Treatment Out-of-State

Sometimes, the law entitles the injured worker to treatment by an out-of-state physician as described in § 16.07. If so, the law also entitles the injured worker to transportation costs using the "reasonable and economical" tests described in [ii], *above*.

[iv] Family Emergency

Consider the following case. While the injured worker was confined to a hospital following a compensable injury, his father died. The worker's physician would not allow him to travel to attend the funeral in anything other than an ambulance.

Is the carrier responsible for this? No! The statute does not require the carrier to pay for travel undertaken for reasons unrelated to the treatment of injuries sustained in a compensable industrial accident [*see* State, Hendry County Correctional Institute, Division of Risk Management v. Hughes, 412 So. 2d 922, 923 (Fla. 1st DCA 1982)].

[v] Supportive Services

Supportive services, such as driving the injured worker to the store and other places (other than for medical treatment), are quality of life activities. As such, they are not compensable as attendant care. Instead, the injured worker is compensated for these costs as part of the disability indemnity benefits, and is not entitled to additional reimbursement [*see* Dade County School Bd. v. Grier, 648 So. 2d 805, 806 (Fla. 1st DCA 1994)].

[b] Accident Dates On or After January 1, 1994

Effective January 1, 1994, the legislature repealed § 440.13(6), Fla. Stat. For accidents occurring on or after that date, the Act no longer specifically entitles an injured worker to reimbursement for medical transportation expenses. Despite this, injured workers are still eligible for reimbursement of medical travel costs.

Many people believed that repealing § 440.13(6), Fla. Stat. meant injured workers were no longer entitled to reimbursement for medical travel expenses. This belief is not correct. Recall that this section entitled an injured worker to:

> Reasonable actual cost of transportation to and from the doctor's office, hospital, or other place of treatment by the most economical means of transportation available and suitable in the individual case.

Most workers' compensation "insiders" have no doubt that the legislature intended to eliminate transportation as a benefit. If this was the legislature's intent, it failed. The reason it failed is that § 440.13(6), Fla. Stat. did not create entitlement to travel expense benefits in the first place. That section merely codified case law; thus, repealing the section did nothing to alter case law.

In 1964, the Florida Supreme Court reviewed the issue of medical transportation for the first time. When this case occurred, § 440.13(6), Fla. Stat. was not part of the law. Then, as it does now, the Act did not specifically require or authorize payment of travel expenses. § 440.13, Fla. Stat., however, did exist.

Then, as it does now, the Act required employers to furnish remedial treatment, care, and attendance. The Florida Supreme Court held that this must be interpreted to include reasonable travel expenses. The Court reasoned that the legislature intended that injured workers obtain medical care paid for by the carrier. This legislative intent, according to the Court, cannot be fully accomplished if workers must pay their own travel expenses. Thus, medical travel expenses are simply part of the medical care and treatment described in the statute. Therefore, the carrier must either furnish transportation or reimburse the injured worker's reasonable actual cost.

Another issue here was what is reasonable cost? Then, the Industrial Relations Commission had rule making authority. The IRC Rules limited reimbursement for travel by private automobile to 7 1/2 cents per mile. The Court, although reluctant to do so, held that the IRC rule was improper, stating the IRC did not have authority to set a limit on travel expenses. The Court was reluctant to make this ruling because setting such a limit served "an excellent purpose by making proof unnecessary." Since the limit could not apply, the actual cost of transportation, absent agreement of the parties, requires proof just as any other factual issue [*see* Mobley v. Jack & Son Plumbing, 170 So. 2d 41, 46–48 (Fla. 1964)].

Nineteen years later, a similar issue was before the First District Court of Appeal. This time, the issue was entitlement to travel costs related to vocational rehabilitation. As with medical travel costs, the law did not expressly require a carrier to pay for an injured worker's travel expenses to a rehabilitation program. The law then provided for a 50-percent reduction in benefits if an injured worker failed to participate in a rehabilitation program. The court concluded that reason and fairness required carriers to pay for travel expenses. Otherwise, an offer of rehabilitation services would often be meaningless [*see* Gulfstar, Inc. v. Shuman, 440 So. 2d 1327, 1328 (Fla. 1st DCA 1983)].

In 1996, the First District Court of Appeal held that when the legislature enacted § 440.13(6), Fla. Stat. in 1977, it merely codified *Mobely.* Therefore, repealing the section did nothing to change the case law that held medical transportation is an implicit part of medical care and attendance. The court concluded that by reenacting the requirement that carriers furnish remedial care and treatment, the 1993 legislature must still approve of the *Mobely* decision, which allows reimbursement of medical transportation costs [*see* Sam's Club v. Bair, 678 So. 2d 902, 903–904 (Fla. 1st DCA 1996)].

Repealing § 440.13(6), Fla. Stat., therefore, simply returns the law where it was in 1964. These old cases hold that when the law requires a carrier to pay for a service, it automatically requires the carrier to pay for any related travel expense. Clearly, if the legislature intends to eliminate travel expenses as a benefit, it must try again and plainly say so.

[4] Prescription Drugs

The Act defines the term "medicine" as [§ 440.13(1)(n), Fla. Stat. (1/1/94)]:

A drug prescribed by an authorized health care provider and includes only generic

> drugs or single-source patented drugs for which there is no generic equivalent, unless the authorized health care provider writes or states that the brand-name drug as defined in § 465.025 is medically necessary, or is a drug appearing on the schedule of drugs created pursuant to § 465.025(6), or is available at a cost lower than its generic equivalent.

A "brand-name" is the registered trademark name given to a drug product by its manufacturer, labeler, or distributor. A generic drug is not equivalent if, when substituted for the brand-name drug, it would pose a threat to the health and safety of patients as determined by the Board of Pharmacy and the Board of Medicine. The addition of this language is an obvious attempt by the legislature to preclude physicians from prescribing more expensive brand-names merely as a personal preference.

For drugs dispensed prior to December 31, 2003, the law limits reimbursement for prescription drugs to "the average wholesale price times 1.2 plus $4.18 for the dispensing fee *except where the carrier has contracted for a lower amount.*" Simply put, the maximum rate is 120% of the wholesale price plus the dispensing fee [§ 440.13(12)(b), Fla. Stat. (1/1/94) (Emphasis added)]. The italicized phrase is the 1994 language.

For drugs dispensed on or after January 1, 2004, the maximum allowance is 100% of the wholesale price plus a dispensing fee of $4.18 [§ 440.13(12)(c), Fla. Stat. (10/1/2003)].

Beginning in 1994, the Act grants injured workers an absolute right to choose a pharmacy for filling prescriptions for medicines. Further, the Act expressly forbids anyone, including the Division, from requiring injured workers to use a particular pharmacy or in any other way interfering with the injured worker's selection [§ 440.13(3)(j), Fla. Stat. (1/1/94)].

What one section gives, however, another may take away. A different section provides that the carrier is not responsible for prescription charges higher than its agreed contract price with another pharmacy. The 1994 provision provides, "where the employer or carrier has contracted for such services and the employee elects to obtain them through a provider not a party to the contract, the carrier shall reimburse at the schedule, negotiated, or contract price, whichever is lower" [§ 440.13(12)(b), Fla. Stat. (1/1/94)]. Beginning on October 1, 2003, however, the law provides that the carrier's contract rate cannot be with a provider that is not reasonably accessible to the employee [§ 440.13(12)(c), Fla. Stat. (10/1/2003)].

Many carriers have contracts for discounts with statewide chains or with drug supply service companies. These new provisions mean that a carrier may not force an injured worker to use its contract vendor. However, if the injured worker elects to use another, the carrier is only responsible for its contracted fees. Carriers will be wise to inform injured workers carefully about these statutory rights and traps.

Despite language in the Fee Schedule Reimbursement manual to the contrary, the court held that vitamins and nutritional supplements are compensable if prescribed by a physician and found to be medically necessary. Here the claimant's physician prescribed various nutritional supplements asserting that they would enhance the claimant's healing and accelerate the effectiveness of prescription medications. Although the judge of compensation claims found the supplements to be medically necessary, she denied the claim because the Fee Schedule provides that reimbursement shall not be made for oral vitamins, nutrient preparations, and other dietary supplements.

The 1st DCA reversed, holding that the Fee Schedule deals with reimbursement and utilization issues only. The Judge still has the authority to resolve disputes regarding the need for medical care in the first place. This case means that over-the-counter vitamins and nutritional supplements are compensable if found to be medically necessary [*see* Tiznado v. Orlando Regional Healthcare Sys., 773 So. 2d 584, 585–586 (Fla. 1st DCA 2000)].

[5] Cosmetic Surgery

Compensable medical care includes care that is primarily cometic in nature. The test is not whether medical treatment will improve an injured worker's employability. The test is simply whether the treatment is medically necessary. Florida courts agree with the Supreme Court of Tennessee, which held that when reconstructive surgery or other treatment will be reasonably effective in improving permanent disfigurement, then such treatment is reasonably required even in the absence of vocational impairment [*see* Wilkes v. Resource Auth. Of Sumner Cty., 932 S.W. 2d 458, 461 (Tenn. 1996)].

Generally, treatment is considered medically necessary and, thus, compensable, if it is appropriate to the patient's diagnoses and status of recovery. The purpose of any surgical procedure is to return the employee, as nearly as possible, to his or her normal condition. This includes surgery designed to make the employee more physically presentable [*see* Perez v. United Parcel Service, 725 So. 2d 423, 424 (Fla. 1st DCA 1999)].

§ 16.04 Treatment Resulting in New Injuries

The law entitles an injured worker to medical benefits for any new injury that results from authorized treatment of the compensable injury. If the carrier authorizes surgery or other treatment, it then becomes responsible for any treatment required because of complications arising from the authorized care. For example, the carrier authorized Reba Spacal to undergo a stomach stapling procedure. Later, Spacal developed serious complications from this surgery. At the hearing, the judge of compensation claims denied her claim for treatment of these complications. The judge found no evidence to show a causal relationship to the original injury. On appeal, the First District Court of Appeal reversed. The court held that a carrier is responsible for any new injury that results from authorized treatment. Note that it is not clear from the court's opinion that even the stomach stapling procedure was related to the compensable injury. Because the carrier authorized the procedure, however, the complicating conditions were also compensable [*see* Spacal (Sutton) v. Marietta, 642 So. 2d 46, 47 (Fla. 1st DCA 1994)].

§ 16.05 Treatment for Unrelated Conditions

The law entitles an injured worker to medical benefits for preexisting conditions if the treatment will aid or improve recovery. This entitlement may apply to conditions existing before the accident, and to conditions that arise after the accident.

Injured workers may suffer from a preexisting condition that prevents effective treatment, or increases their pain. For example, Karlton Brown suffered an injury to his back at work. At the time, he weighed 278 pounds, which complicated his recovery. Brown's doctor opined that a weight loss program would relieve his pain. The court approved the program, although the need for it existed before the accident [*see* Brown v. Steego Auto Parts, 585 So. 2d 401, 402–403 (Fla. 1st DCA 1991)].

As noted, the employer/carrier will be responsible for providing treatment for an unrelated condition, even when there is no evidence of a connection to the compensable accident, if the condition interferes with treating the compensable injury. For example, an employee was injured in an industrial accident. At the conclusion of the physical therapy that the employee was undergoing, the employee reported chest pains. The authorized treating physician, who was supervising the physical therapy, referred the employee to an emergency room for an immediate cardiac evaluation. Testimony that the employee would not have been allowed to continue physical therapy without receiving cardiac clearance was uncontroverted. On appeal, the court found that, while it was true that no evidence was presented that a connection existed between the employee's symptoms and the work injury sustained, the evaluation was in the normal progression of authorized treatment. Therefore, the medical expenses the employee incurred in undergoing diagnostic testing were the responsibility of the employer and its servicing agent [*see* Rolle v. City of Riviera Beach/Gallagher Bassett Serv., 826 So. 2d 1075, 1076 (Fla. 1st DCA 2002)].

This is not a new theory. In 1966, the Florida Supreme Court held that treatment for a condition that existed before an industrial accident is compensable if it will aid the injured worker's recovery. The basis for awarding this care is that it meets the medical necessity test [*see* Jordan v. Florida Industrial Commission, 183 So. 2d 529, 530 (Fla. 1966)].

Carriers are responsible when physicians agree that treatment for preexisting conditions, such as high blood pressure or obesity, is medically necessary to the injured worker's treatment and recovery from compensable injuries.

Effective October 1, 2003, however, the legislature amended the Act to provide that no compensation or medical care attributable to preexisting conditions is compensable or payable. It appears that this amendment is an attempt to overrule the line of cases discussed above. Until we have the benefits of judicial review, the black letter law should be applied [§ 440.15(5)(b), Fla. Stat. (10/1/2003); ch. 8, § 8.02].

SPECIAL NOTE: The 1994 amendments to Chapter 440 do not change the carrier's responsibility in this respect [*see* Mellon Sec. & Sound v. Custer, 687 So. 2d 1372, 1373 (Fla. 1st DCA 1997)].

§ 16.06 Diagnostic Testing

Diagnostic testing is always compensable if the purpose is to find out the cause of the injured worker's symptoms. This is true even if the tests prove the symptoms are unrelated to the compensable injury. Following is the court's holding [*see* Kenneth Perry v. Ridgecrest Intern., 548 So. 2d 826, 827–828 (Fla. 1st DCA 1989); *see also* Superior Concrete Construction v. Olsen, 616 So. 2d 183 (Fla. 1st DCA 1993)]:

> Whenever the purpose of the diagnostic test is to determine the cause of a claimant's symptoms, which symptoms may be related to a compensable accident, the cost of the diagnostic test is compensable, even if it should later be determined that the claimant suffered from both compensable and noncompensable conditions.

Testing is compensable even if the tests are inconclusive, or even if they confirm that symptoms are unrelated to the compensable injury. If doctors order tests because they suspect the condition may be related, this is enough to award compensation. For example, Freddie Martinez suffered a work-related injury to his wrist. Later, he developed pain in his chest and neck. After several doctors failed to diagnose Martinez' problem, one of them referred him to the Mayo Clinic. A clinic doctor suspected Martinez had developed reflex sympathetic dystrophy (RSD) and ordered diagnostic tests. These tests were inconclusive and did not confirm the doctor's theory. On appeal, the court reversed the trial judge's order denying the claim for reimbursement of the cost of the tests. The court held the results of the tests are not relevant. It is the purpose of the tests in the first place that controls compensability [*see* Martinez v. Association of Poinciana, 642 So. 2d 118, 119 (Fla. 1st DCA 1994)].

§ 16.07 Treatment by Out-of-State Physicians

What happens if the injured worker has seen two, three, or more physicians in Florida, but now insists that the carrier authorize an out-of-state physician, especially under Managed Care? Does the answer change if the injured worker wants the transfer simply because the out-of-state physician is regarded as the best in the country? Does the carrier owe this extraordinary cost? Following is the court's holding [*see* Layne-Western Co. v. Cox, 497 So. 2d 955, 956 (Fla. 1st DCA 1986)]:

> [T]he controlling issue to be decided in determining whether out-of-state treatment should be directed at the carrier's expense is not the *availability* of facilities within the state, but whether such facilities as are available "can afford equally beneficial treatment."

Here, a Florida hand surgeon treated Earl Cox. His rheumatologist testified that the hand surgeon was as good as or better than any hand surgeon in Florida. The doctor did not, however, consider the surgeon quite as good as a world-renowned hand surgeon who practiced in another state. The court agreed that ordering the carrier to pay for treatment by the out-of-state hand surgeon was appropriate. In a dissenting opinion, Judge Thompson pointed out that the majority view allows any injured worker whose injury requires specialized treatment, and whose treating physician believed that some out-of-state specialist was the best in the field, to obtain such out-of-state evaluation or treatment at the expense of the employer, despite the availability of expert care within the state [Layne-Western Co. v. Cox, 497 So. 2d 955, 957 (Fla. 1st DCA 1986)].

Given the restrictive language in the Act regarding Managed Care, such extraordinary care should not be allowed unless appropriate care is not available within the carrier's network.

§ 16.08 Emergency Medical Treatment

An injured worker has no duty or obligation to get prior authorization for emergency

Guide to Claims

medical treatment, even under Managed Care. The test will be whether the treatment was a genuine emergency [*see* Teimer v. Pixie Playmates, 532 So. 2d 37, 40 (Fla. 1st DCA 1988)].

Effective January 1, 1994, the Act provides a definition of emergency services and care as follows [§§ 395.002(9), 440.13(1)(g), Fla. Stat. (1/1/94)]:

> Medical screening, examination, and evaluation by a physician, or, to the extent permitted by applicable law, by other appropriate personnel under the supervision of a physician, to determine if an emergency medical condition exists and, if it does, the care, treatment, or surgery by a physician necessary to relieve or eliminate the emergency medical condition, within the service capability of the facility.

Whether the treatment was an emergency is a medical question for the treating physician. Carriers should not be too hasty in controverting unauthorized care until after questioning the physician. It does not matter that the physician, when seeking authorization, failed to mention that proposed treatment is an emergency. Further, the reasonableness of the injured worker's choice for emergency care is also irrelevant. It does not matter whether the injured worker could have obtained the care closer to home or from the authorized physician. In an emergency, injured workers have full authority to obtain medical care wherever they choose, and at the carrier's expense [*see* Sieracki v. Pizza Hut, 599 So. 2d 678, 679 (Fla. 1st DCA 1992)].

If a health care provider does render emergency care, the provider must submit a report to the carrier within three business days. If the emergency is such that the employee is admitted to a hospital, the provider must notify the carrier, by telephone, within 24 hours of the initial treatment. Even emergency care, of course, is not compensable unless the need results from a work-related accident [§ 440.13(3)(b), Fla. Stat. (1/1/94)].

> **SPECIAL ALERT:** The legislature amended the Act to make emergency treatment by physicians mandatory! Refusing to provide emergency care to workers' compensation patients is cause for revocation of the provider's license [§ 440.13(3)(i), Fla. Stat. (1/1/94)].

§ 16.09 Work Hardening and Pain Management

Beginning January 1, 1994, the Act specifically includes limited entitlement to work-hardening programs and pain-management programs, but only on referral from an authorized physician. Under Managed Care, the only physician authorized to do so is the Medical Care Coordinator. In addition, the Commission on Accreditation of Health Organizations must accredit the program. If not, the program must at least be a pain management program associated with a medical school. Further, the law requires each facility to maintain outcome data, including work status at discharge, total program charges, total number of visits, and length of the stay. The Division must collect this information and report the cost effectiveness of such programs to the Florida Senate and the House of Representatives. Presumably, if the results show these programs are not cost effective, the legislature will outlaw them from compensability under workers' compensation [§ 440.13(2)(a), Fla. Stat. (1/1/94)].

§ 16.10 Chiropractic Care

[1] Unique and Specific Medical Specialty

The law does not view orthopedic care as equivalent to chiropractic care. On the contrary, the law considers a request for chiropractic care as a request for a unique and specific medical specialty. Carriers must act promptly on an injured worker's request for any medical care. Offering treatment in another discipline does not discharge the carrier's duty to respond promptly to an injured worker's request for chiropractic care [*see* Jackson v. Publix Supermarkets, Inc., 520 So. 2d 50, 51 (Fla. 1st DCA 1987)].

[2] Responding to Requests for Care

How quickly must carriers respond to such requests? If an injured worker requests, in writing, authorization for any medical treatment, then the carrier must respond within three business days after receiving such request [§ 440.13(3)(d), Fla. Stat. (1/1/94)].

If an injured worker submits a written request for chiropractic care, and the carrier does not respond specifically and timely, the carrier will be responsible for any unauthorized care if the court decides the treatment was reasonable and necessary [*see* Bissen v. Smalley Transportation, 653 So. 2d 494, 495 (Fla. 1st DCA 1995)].

[3] Limits on Chiropractic Care

[a] Accidents Occurring Between January 1, 1994, and September 30, 2003

For accidents occurring between January 1, 1994, and September 30, 2003, the law limits chiropractic care to 18 treatments, or eight weeks from the date of first chiropractic treatment, whichever occurs first.

[b] Accidents Occurring On or After October 1, 2003

For accidents occurring on or after October 1, 2003, the law increases the limit on chiropractic care to 24 treatments, or 12 weeks from the date of first chiropractic treatment, whichever occurs first.

NOTE: The court has held that statutory amendments limiting chiropractic care are substantive amendments and, therefore, apply to only those accidents and injuries occurring on or after the amendment's effective date. No statutory limitation applies to chiropractic treatment for accidents occurring before January 1, 1994 [*see* Russell v. P.I.E. Nationwide, 668 So. 2d 696, 697 (Fla. 1st DCA 1996)].

[c] Constitutionality

The Florida Supreme Court has held that the statutory limitation on chiropractic care does not restrict an injured worker's right to receive appropriate treatment. Instead, it merely diminishes, after a certain point in time, the range of providers who may offer such treatment under the law. Therefore, the Court held that the law limiting chiropractic care is constitutional [*see* Strohm v. Hertz Corp., 685 So. 2d 37, 39 (Fla. 1st DCA 1996), *rev. denied,* 697 So. 2d 512 (Fla. 1997)].

[4] Exceptions to the Limits

[a] Additional Treatment Authorized by Carrier

The treatment limitation [*see* [3], *above*] does not apply if the carrier has authorized additional treatment [§ 440.13(2)(a), Fla. Stat. (1/1/94)].

Some claim adjusters will scoff at the idea of voluntarily authorizing additional chiropractic treatments. Thoughtlessly applied, denial will often be a counterproductive decision. Unless the carrier is prepared to prove the injured worker needs no further medical care, the carrier must authorize alternate treatment by another physician. Typically, this will be an orthopedic physician. Despite specialty, new physicians are unlikely to simply accept the diagnosis of their predecessors. Further, the new doctor will likely conduct a complete initial visit and examination with a fresh set of diagnostic tests. Unless the carrier can show the patient requires no further treatment, chiropractic treatment may be replaced with medication prescriptions and physical therapy. The wise adjuster will discuss these cases with the treating chiropractic physician. The physician's treatment plan may require only a few more treatments before maximum medical improvement and complete discharge. If so, why start the entire process over with a new physician?

Carriers should be sure to respond timely to any request for an extension of the treatment limit. Under the *Bissen* decision [*see* [2], *above*], a new court might hold that lack of an appropriate and timely response is passive acceptance. The *Bissen* court held that although the injured worker began chiropractic care without authorization, the law did not compel him to stop treatment because the carrier failed to respond to his request. The same logic will likely apply to requests for extension to the statutory limit.

[b] Catastrophic Injury

The chiropractic treatment limitation [*see* [3], *above*] does not apply if the employee is catastrophically injured [*see* § 440.13(2)(a), Fla. Stat. (1/1/94)]. Previously, § 440.02(38), Fla. Stat. defined and limited catastrophic injury to spinal cord paralysis, amputation of an extremity, brain damage, severe burns, blindness, and other injuries qualifying for Social Security disability benefits. Effective October 1, 2003, the Legislature repealed § 440.02(38), Fla. Stat. Therefore, there is no longer a statutory definition. Whether a claimant is catastrophically injured, and thus eligible for unlimited chiropractic care, must be decided case by case, presumably based on expert medical testimony.

§ 16.11 Experimental Treatment or Services

[1] The Rule

Compensable medical care does not include services or products that are experimental, investigative, or rendered as part of a research project. An exception arises if the Agency for Health Care Administration gives prior approval. The agency must decide each situation on a case-by-case basis. Before January 1, 1994, this task was the Division's responsibility.

Effective October 1, 2003, the Legislature repealed the AHCA-approved exception. Thereafter, experimental or investigative treatments and services are not compensable.

[2] Experimental Defined

The term "experimental" includes medical services, procedures, drugs, equipment, or supplies. These are considered experimental if their efficacy has not been proven for a particular diagnosis, or if their safety and validity are unclear or unknown. The term "investigative" includes these same services and devices when they are known to be safe, but their efficacy is still under investigation. Before denying a claim for medical treatment on the argument that the treatment is experimental or investigative, the carrier must first refer the request for treatment to the Agency for Health Care Administration [*see* Arizona Chemical Corp. v. Hanlon, 605 So. 2d 938, 940–941 (Fla. 1st DCA 1992)].

§ 16.12 Health Care Providers

[1] Procedure for Determining Health Care Provider

[a] Effect of Managed Care Legislation

The Act provides that "the employer shall furnish to the employee such medically necessary remedial treatment, care, and attendance for such period as the nature of the injury or the process of recovery may require . . ." [§ 440.13(2)(a), Fla. Stat. (1/1/94)]. Beginning January 1, 1997, carriers are deemed to have fully complied with this section by providing medical care through their managed care arrangements [§ 440.134(2)(b), Fla. Stat. (1/1/94)].

Before Managed Care, furnishing medical care meant more then simply agreeing to a particular physician. Before a health care provider could provide medical treatment, the carrier must have told the provider about the authorization. This was true even if the parties agreed that the injured worker would make an appointment to see the doctor. Until the carrier directly authorized the provider, the carrier had not complied with its duty to furnish health care services [*see* Pardo v. Denny's, Inc., 631 So. 2d 388, 389 (Fla. 1st DCA 1994)].

Under Managed Care, injured workers have the right to choose their primary care physicians from a list supplied by the carrier [§ 440.134(6)(c)10, Fla. Stat. (1/1/94)]. Carriers should assume that *Pardo* still applies and be certain to notify doctors of their selection as the primary care provider and, thus, as the Medical Care Coordinator.

[b] Provider Eligibility

[i] Health Care Provider Defined

Although the statute allows care only by physicians, non-physicians can also be authorized if a physician prescribes it. The statute allows care by "health care providers," which includes "a physician or any recognized practitioner who provides skilled services pursuant to a prescription or under the supervision or direction of a physician" [§ 440.13(1)(i), Fla. Stat. (1/1/94)].

Thus, a psychologist, although not a "physician," is a recognized practitioner who provides skilled services. If a physician recommends care by a psychologist, for example, such care could be authorized under that prescription. This applies to other non-physicians, such as acupuncturists [*see* Smith v. General Parcel Service, Inc., 699 So. 2d 741, 743 (Fla. 1st DCA 1997)].

[ii] Certification

Only licensed and AHCA–certified health care providers may treat workers' compensation patients. What is a certified health care provider? This simply means a physician, medical practitioner, or hospital that the Agency has certified, or one who has entered an agreement with a licensed managed care organization. In either case, physicians must document that they have read and are familiar with the portions of the statutes, impairment guides, and rules that govern medical treatment [§§ 440.13(1)(e), 440.13(3)(a), Fla. Stat. (1/1/94)]. Effective October 1, 2001, the legislature repealed the requirement that health care providers must complete a five–hour course [§ 440.13(3)(a), Fla. Stat. (10/1/2001)]. This is important because carriers may not authorize any uncertified health care providers. The Act also requires certification as a precondition to receiving payment for services.

[iii] Decertification

Apparently, the purpose of certification is not so much to ensure medical competence, but to give the Agency the power to decertify physicians who violate utilization and cost containment procedures. The Agency can decertify those health care providers who are guilty of certain violations. Decertification means the provider may no longer treat workers' compensation patients. Following is a summary of the violations that can lead to decertification [§ 440.13(13), Fla. Stat. (1/1/94)]:

1. Professional misconduct or incompetence in providing medical service.
2. Making false statements of qualification to be a certified health care provider or exceeding the limits of professional competence.
3. Failing to submit complete and timely medical reports to the employer or carrier as required.
4. Soliciting workers' compensation patients.
5. Refusal to cooperate with the Division or a state official.
6. Illegal or prohibited self-referral.
7. Engaging in a pattern or practice of over utilization as defined by statute and rule, including failure to adhere to practice parameters and protocols established under Chapter 440, Florida Statutes.

[iv] Sanctions

Besides decertification, the Division can also impose the following sanctions [§ 440.13(8), Fla. Stat. (1/1/94)]:

1. Deauthorization of care under review.
2. Denial of payment for care rendered in the future.
3. A fine of up to $5,000 for instances of over utilization.
4. Referral of the offending provider to the appropriate licensing authority for further sanctions, including loss of license.

[c] Objection to Authorized Physician

[i] Before Managed Care

Before Managed Care, injured workers had the right to object to a provider offered by the carrier. If a reasonable basis for the objection existed, the law required the carrier to offer an alternative. If the carrier did not authorize an alternative, the judge of compensation claims ultimately decided the reasonableness of the injured worker's objection. Nevertheless, merely requesting to receive treatment by a physician of the injured worker's own choosing did not meet the requirement. Following is the court's holding [*see* Marcy v. Charlotte Cty. Sheriff's Office, 599 So. 2d 1319, 1321 (Fla. 1st DCA 1992)]:

> The law is clear that while the claimant has the right to dispute the E/C's [Employer/carrier's] selection for good cause, it is equally clear that where there is no emergency, and where there has been no breach by the E/C of its duty to provide an alternative physician, it is incumbent upon the claimant to formally initiate a claim for a change in physicians and to present the matter to the judge for determination.

[ii] Under Managed Care

Under Managed Care, injured workers are allowed to choose their primary care providers. They are also allowed to make one change to another provider within the same specialty and within the network during treatment for the work-related injury [§ 440.134(10)(c), Fla. Stat. (1/1/94)]. The injured worker must make the request to the Medical Care Coordinator, who has the authority to refer the worker to another physician within the network. This is not, however, an absolute limit. The legislature recognized that occasions will arise when more than one change of a physician may be appropriate. Carriers must arrange for additional changes as part of their grievance procedures.

> **SPECIAL ALERT:** If an authorized health care provider makes a written request for authorization of a referral for medical treatment, the carrier must respond within three business days of receipt of the request. If the carrier does not respond within this time, the law deems consent to the request. Thus, doing nothing is the same as granting authorization for the requested referral. Although the Act requires a response by telephone or in writing, carriers will be wise always to put refusals in writing [§ 440.13(3)(d), Fla. Stat. (1/1/94)].

This requirement conflicts with the Managed Care section of the Act that transfers responsibility for referrals to the MCC. That section, however, does not impose any time limits on the MCC. The best advice here is to conclude that the three-day time limit still applies and that someone, the carrier or the MCC, must respond timely or the request will be deemed approved.

[d] Deauthorizing Authorized Physician

[i] Employee or JCC Approval Needed

In 1983, the legislature enacted a provision that prohibited a carrier from unilaterally deauthorizing a physician whom the employer authorized. The amendment required that the carrier first obtain the employer's agreement or a judge's order. The legislature repealed that provision effective July 1, 1990. Do carriers now have the authority to substitute doctors without court or employer approval? The answer is yes, but with a strong caveat. If the injured worker objects to the deauthorization, the carrier may be forced to defend its action before a judge of compensation claims and risk a reversal of its attempted unilateral deauthorization. In such cases, the best course may be to continue authorization while seeking a ruling from the judge [*see* Furtick v. William Shults Contractor, 664 So. 2d 288, 290 (Fla. 1st DCA 1995) (dicta)].

Note that this does not apply in a situation in which the carrier timely authorizes a change of physician. The law now provides that upon granting a change of physician, the original authorized physician is deauthorized upon written notification by the carrier. This deauthorization applies only if the original physician is in the same specialty as the replacement physician. Therefore, if the replacement is in a different specialty, the original physician presumably will remain authorized, and deauthorization is subject to challenge before a judge of compensation claims [§ 440.13(2)(f), Fla. Stat. (10/1/2003)].

[ii] Physician-Patient Relationship

Once an injured employee establishes a satisfactory physician-patient relationship with an authorized physician, the carrier may not deauthorize that physician. What happens if a carrier does attempt to deauthorize a physician without the injured worker's agreement or a judge's approval? The court will require the carrier to "show good cause" for such action. Focus on why an authorized physician should no longer provide care. The law requires a sound basis for severing an established, physician-patient relationship [*see* Stuckey v. Eagle Pest Control Co., Inc., 531 So. 2d 350, 351 (Fla. 1st DCA 1988)].

Further, the carrier must show that such a change is in the injured worker's best interest. If the judge of compensation claims disagrees with the carrier's position, the judge will require the carrier to pay the bills of the doctor it tried to fire. In addition, the carrier may be liable for attorney's fees [*see* Cal Kovens Const. v. Lott, 473 So. 2d 249, 252–254 (Fla. 1st DCA 1985)].

Once the carrier and the injured worker have agreed on a doctor and they establish a satisfactory (i.e., satisfactory to the injured worker) physician-patient relationship, carriers face considerable risk in unilaterally firing that doctor. If the carrier believes it has a good reason for a change and a change is in the injured worker's best interest, then the carrier should get the judge's approval first. Carriers will have trouble proving that the change is in the injured worker's best interest. Such evidence may include expert testimony that further care by a particular physician is of no benefit to the injured worker, or that it may even be harmful. Absent expert testimony, convincing most judges that severing the relationship is in the injured worker's best interest will be difficult. Remember, the law does not require the judge's approval if the injured worker agrees to a proposed change of physicians.

[iii] Deauthorization Based on Overutilization

A frequent reason for deauthorizing a physician is overutilization. The Agency for Health Care Administration has the authority to investigate health care providers to find out if they are requiring unjustified treatment, hospitalization, or office visits [§ 440.13(4)(c), Fla. Stat. (1/1/94)]. Effective October 1, 2003, "overutilization" includes providing treatment in excess of established practice parameters. These are the practice parameters and protocols adopted by the United States Agency for Healthcare Research and Quality in effect on January 1, 2003 [*see* § 440.13(1)(k), Fla. Stat.; § 440.13(15), Fla. Stat. (10/1/2003)].

The judges of compensation claims do not have the authority to settle disputes over the amount of medical fees. When properly submitted, only the Division may resolve a utilization dispute. The judges, however, still have the authority to rule on the need for the treatment itself. In other words, the judge may decide if an injured worker is entitled to chiropractic care, for example, but cannot decide how much the chiropractor will be paid [*see* Beasley v. M & E Pieco, 678 So. 2d 519, 520 (Fla. 1st DCA 1996)].

Therefore, while utilization review is underway, carriers must continue to provide the prescribed care. Further, carriers cannot unilaterally stop care based on another physician's opinion that overutilization is taking place. Refusing to pay for medication or services ordered by a physician amounts to a defacto deauthorization of the doctor. Carriers may not interfere in this way in an established, patient-physician relationship. Carriers must either take their chances in court or wait for the Division's conclusions [*see* Williams v. Triple J Enterprises, 650 So. 2d 1114, 1117 (Fla. 1st DCA 1995)].

[iv] Deauthorization Based on Inappropriate Progress

Carriers can transfer the injured worker's care from the authorized doctor to another doctor if an independent medical examiner decides that the injured worker is "not making appropriate progress" in recuperation [*see* § 440.13(2)(d), Fla. Stat.]. Although the statute allows carriers to transfer medical care based solely on the opinion of an IME physician, without prior approval from a judge of compensation claims, the judge retains the authority to determine the appropriateness of the transfer after the fact. Claimants who object to such a unilateral transfer may seek a review by a judge of compensation claims to determine whether the deauthorization was, in fact, in the claimant's best interest [*see* Terners of Miami Corp. v. Busot, 764 So. 2d 701, 703–704 (Fla. 1st DCA 2000)].

This procedural amendment applies to all accident dates because it does not adversely affect the parties' substantive rights. This is because the carrier's unilateral deauthorization is subject to later review by the judge as to whether a change in care was in the claimant's best interest [*see* State Atty. v. Johnson, 770 So. 2d 187, 188 (Fla. 1st DCA 2000)].

Remember that an independent medical examiner may not render an opinion outside the area of expertise shown by the physician's license [§ 440.13(5)(a), Fla. Stat. (1/1/94)].

[2] Authorized v. Unauthorized Medical Care

[a] Authorized Medical Care

[i] Approving Treatment Plan

Effective January 1, 1994, after initial examination and diagnosis by the authorized physician, the Act requires the physician to submit a proposed course of treatment to the carrier. The carrier must review the proposal and decide if the treatment is prudent and in accord with any applicable practice parameters [*see* § 16.17]. If the carrier has any objection to the proposed treatment plan, it must notify the physician of this fact within 10 business days or the law deems the plan approved. Note, however, that this requirement does not apply to emergencies or for treatment rendered by a managed care arrangement [§ 440.13(2)(d), Fla. Stat. (1/1/94)]. Under Managed Care, the Medical Care Coordinator has the responsibility for approving treatment plans.

[ii] Approving Consultations and Tests

Claims for certain procedures, consultations, and tests that cost $1,000 or more are not valid unless the carrier grants prior approval. These include surgical operations, physiotherapeutic or occupational therapy procedures, x-ray examinations, or special diagnostic laboratory tests. The Division can expand this list by Rule, but has not done so. The law does not require prior approval in emergencies [§ 440.13(3)(i), Fla. Stat. (1/1/94)].

Requests for any of the listed procedures must be in writing. If the carrier fails to respond within 10 days, the law deems the request approved. Authorization of the treatment plan is not, however, automatic approval of these procedures. Although the Act is not clear about where the approval responsibility rests under Managed Care, it probably remains with the carrier. This may, however, be irrelevant. The right to refuse any of these procedures is limited only to those cases where the provider is not certified or where an Expert Medical Advisor (EMA) has decided the procedure is not medically necessary. Absent these two events, carriers may not refuse approval. These exceptions do not limit the carrier's right and duty to refuse payment due to overutilization or billing errors.

Effective October 1, 2003, the Legislature amended the section to provide that the time limitation to respond to a request for authorization applies only to requests for authorization from an authorized health care provider. Additionally, the section does not apply if the requested treatment is not in accordance with practice parameters and protocols. It also does not apply if the judge of compensation claims determines that the treatment is not medically necessary or is not in accordance with practice parameters and protocols [*see* § 440.13(3)(i), Fla. Stat. (10/1/2003)].

[iii] Approving Referrals

Before July 1, 1990, if injured workers convinced their doctors to refer them to another physician, the carrier became liable for such care. This was true even if done without authorization from the employer or carrier. An exception occurred if the request, by itself, was the only reason for the referral. Referral by an authorized physician in the exercise of his or her own judgment, and not the injured worker's request, places the referral in the normal progression of authorized treatment for which the carrier is responsible [*see* McKinney v. McKinney Farms, 380 So. 2d 469, 470 (Fla. 1st DCA 1980)].

The court modified this rule in a subsequent case, and held that this referral authority extends only to evaluation, not to treatment [*see* Atkins v. Greenhut Const. Co., 447 So. 2d 268, 270–271 (Fla. 1st DCA 1983)].

The legislature responded to these decisions by amending the Act to require physicians to obtain approval first. The legislature added the following language effective July 1, 1990, then changed it again effective January 1, 1994 [§ 440.13(3)(c), Fla. Stat. (1/1/94)]:

> A health care provider may not refer the employee to another health care provider, diagnostic facility, therapy center, or other facility without the prior authorization from the carrier [or the employer if self-insured], except when emergency care is rendered. *Any referral must be to a health care provider that has been certified by the division, unless the referral is for emergency treatment.* (Emphasis added)

The italicized sentence is the 1994 language. So far, the courts have treated the statutory authorization requirement as a strict one. Under Managed Care, responsibility for referral rests with the Medical Care Coordinator acting for the carrier. Even the judges of compensation claims do not have unlimited discretion to excuse authorization. There must be a true emergency or another recognized exception.

[iv] Emergency Treatment

Injured workers do not need authorization from either the carrier or the MCC in emergencies. Deciding whether a true emergency existed, though, is often difficult. For example, Carmella Geurtze was on the operating table about to undergo hand surgery. When doctors injected a local anesthetic, she suffered an immediate myocardial ischemia. The doctor canceled the surgery and called in an osteopath. The next day the osteopath performed a cardiac catheterization and an angioplasty. During this procedure, the surgeon nicked an artery, requiring emergency bypass surgery. The carrier denied payment for all of this treatment, stating such treatment was not an emergency and not authorized by the carrier. On appeal the First District Court of Appeal agreed with the carrier. The issue is whether, even in cases like this, the injured worker must obtain authority first. The answer, said the court, is yes! The treating doctor referred Geurtze to the osteopath without authority. The osteopath performed the surgery, also without authority. Since the authorized treating doctor did not specifically request this treatment, and the carrier did not authorize it, the carrier is not responsible for paying for it. Since the bypass surgery resulted directly from the unauthorized angioplasty, it, too, is not compensable [*see* Ben Franklin Crafts v. Geurtze, 646 So. 2d 773, 744–775 (Fla. 1st DCA 1994)].

Remember, however, that if the evidence shows all this is emergency treatment, it is compensable without carrier authorization. Also remember that this situation is compensable under Managed Care if the referring physician is also the Medical Care Coordinator.

[v] Effect of No Authorization

Surprisingly, the Act provides no penalty if a physician fails to get prior approval when required. The clear intent, however, is that if the authorized physician does not obtain carrier or MCC approval before referral, such referral is unauthorized and at the injured

Guide to Claims

worker's own expense. An exception arises, however, if the carrier and the MCC fail to respond or refuse the request. The rule is that "[i]f the employer . . . (or the carrier/MCC) . . . fails to provide such treatment, care and attendance after request by the injured employee, the employee may do so at the expense of the employer, the reasonableness and necessity to be approved by a judge of compensation claims" [*see* Lowry v. Jim Bassitts Auto, 566 So. 2d 303, 304 (Fla. 1st DCA 1990)].

> **SPECIAL ALERT:** Carriers must adopt procedures for receiving, reviewing, documenting, and responding to requests for authorization by certified health care providers. The Division will likely include compliance with this statute in its carrier audits [§ 440.13(3)(e), Fla. Stat. (1/1/94)].

[b] Unauthorized Medical Care

[i] Emergency Treatment; Failure to Provide Proper Care

A carrier must pay for unauthorized care under two conditions: first, for emergency treatment; and second, when the carrier fails to provide care properly, or to respond to requests for care. In both conditions, the care must be medically necessary and related to the compensable injury. Carriers must pay for unauthorized medical treatment if a judge of compensation claims decides the treatment was medically necessary and related to the compensable injury. Except in an emergency, however, if the carrier or Medical Care Coordinator offers alternate medical care, the injured worker cannot unilaterally obtain treatment from an unauthorized provider. Even if the judge finds that the unauthorized treatment was reasonable and necessary, this does not excuse an injured worker's failure to obtain authorization for treatment [*see* Norrell Temporary Services v. Baxter, 645 So. 2d 1068, 1071–1072 (Fla. 1st DCA 1994)].

[ii] Treatment for Unrelated Conditions

Under certain circumstances a carrier may be liable for unauthorized treatment even if the treatment is unrelated to the compensable injury. In one case, the carrier authorized treatment by a chiropractor. The injured worker filed a petition for benefits seeking treatment by another chiropractor. The court held the petition for benefits was sufficient notice that the injured worker wanted such care. "Once a claimant specifies to an (employer or carrier) that chiropractic treatment is desired, it must be provided or the (employer or carrier) must obtain a ruling that such care was not in the claimant's best interest."

The carrier did not authorize the second chiropractor. On the other hand, the carrier did not specifically tell the injured worker that the chiropractor was not authorized. Although the judge later found that the second chiropractor treatment did not relate to the compensable accident, the District Court of Appeal held the carrier had to pay the bills anyway, stating [*see* Irigoyen v. Aircraft Services, Inc., 544 So. 2d 1054, 1055–1056 (Fla. 1st DCA 1989)]:

> The [carrier's] failure to indicate to claimant . . . that it considered there to be an authorization problem with [the second chiropractor], estopped it to deny payment of

[second chiropractor's] bills . . ., notwithstanding their necessity, reasonableness, or causal relationship to the compensable accident, because its actions . . . amount to tacit authorization of the doctor's treatments.

In other words, if the carrier authorizes treatment, either actively or by inaction, it is liable for payment even if the treatment is unrelated to the compensable injury.

SPECIAL NOTE: A judge of compensation claims may not order a carrier to provide medical management type services by anyone who does not qualify as a health care provider under § 440.13, Fla. Stat. Prohibited awards, for example, include services traditionally provided by private rehabilitation providers [*see* K-9 of Orlando v. Davenport, 605 So. 2d 587 (Fla. 1st DCA 1992)].

§ 16.13 Physicians' Medical Reports and Bills

[1] Reporting Form

All physicians must use *only* form DWC-25, Florida Workers' Compensation Uniform Medical Treatment/Status Reporting Form, to report an injured worker's medical treatment and status. This reporting form, DWC-25, replaces all other reporting forms, and no other forms may be used. Note, however, that form DWC-25 does not replace physician notes, medical records, or division-required medical billing reports [Fla. Admin. Code R. 69L-7.602(4) (7/4/2004)].

The physician's preliminary report is due within three business days after the first treatment. Within 15 days after that, the physician must submit a complete and detailed report [§ 440.13(4)(a), Fla. Stat. (1/1/94)].

[2] Reporting Frequency

At the carrier's request, physicians must submit subsequent reports at least every three weeks. The carrier has the right to require reporting at even more frequent intervals. The physician must also supply medical records upon demand to the employee, employee's attorney, or Division of Workers' Compensation [§ 440.13(4)(a), Fla. Stat. (1/1/94)].

[3] Effect of Failure to Report

If the physician fails to submit these reports, any claim for treatment is not valid or enforceable. Thus, it is error to require the carrier to pay for medical treatment if the physician fails to comply with the reporting requirements of § 440.13(4)(a), Fla. Stat. (1/1/94) [*see* Miami-Dade County v. Mitchell, 754 So. 2d 773, 774 (Fla. 1st DCA 2000), *reh'g granted,* March 30, 2000]. The judge of compensation claims, however, has the authority to forgive these failures if the carrier cannot show it was prejudiced as a result. How can the injured worker satisfy the burden of establishing a good cause excuse for a health care provider's failure to honor reporting requirements? The injured worker can do so with evidence showing that the carrier conducted itself so inconsistently that it waived its right to rely on those requirements as a defense. Such evidence will show the following [*see* Watson v. Freeman Decorating Co., 455 So. 2d 1097, 1100–1101 (Fla. 1st DCA 1984)]:

1. The carrier knew about the injured worker's condition and it provided benefits by a specific health care provider;
2. The carrier's acquiesced in the treatment; and
3. The carrier disavowed its responsibility to furnish medical benefits because of a violation of the reporting provisions.

The carrier then has the burden to show how it was prejudiced by the reporting failure. Note, however, that the three-pronged *Watson* test is not the only method an injured worker can use to show good cause. It is only one of several. The type of evidence necessary to meet the burden may vary in a given case [*see* Simon v. Developmental Preschool, 572 So. 2d 538, 539–540 (Fla. 1st DCA 1990)].

For example, a carrier or employer may unintentionally waive the reporting requirement by its own pattern of conduct. This includes the carrier's failure to do any of the following [*see* Ringling Bros.-Barnum & Bailey Comb. Shows v. Jones, 134 So. 2d 244, 246 (Fla. 1961)]:

1. File certain reports required by law;
2. Provide medical treatment;
3. Pay weekly benefits; and
4. File a notice to controvert.

§ 16.14 Price Controls

[1] Medical/Surgical Fee Schedules

Florida regulates the price of individual services under several medical/surgical fee schedules. No cost or time limits apply to medical care generally. Drugs and medicines are, of course, included, but the Act limits them to generic drugs or single-source patented drugs for which there is no generic equivalent. An exception arises if the physician states that a brand name drug is medically necessary.

The 1994 amendments require the creation of statewide schedules of maximum reimbursement that must be revised each year [§ 440.13(12)(a), Fla. Stat. (1/1/94)].

[2] Limitations on Medical Fees

[a] Strict Enforcement of Fee Schedule Limits

Administrative rules, with fee schedules, regulate most services performed by health care providers and medical facilities. A health care provider may receive the lesser of the usual and customary charge for the service or the maximum reimbursement allowance in the schedule [§§ 440.13(12) and 440.13(14), Fla. Stat. (1/1/94)]. Florida courts have strictly enforced fee schedule limits against health care providers who have sought higher fees for their services [*see* Easter Elevator Company v. Hedman, 290 So. 2d 56, 58 (Fla. 1974)].

Although the Act generally prohibits carriers from paying medical service charges in excess of the amounts allowed in the fee schedule, the Legislature adopted exceptions to this rule, effective October 1, 2003. The Act allows carriers and health care providers to agree in writing to depart from the fee schedule if the provider agrees to follow specific procedures aimed at providing quality medical care. These agreements may include, but are not limited to, the following:

1. To ensure the timely scheduling of appointments;
2. Participating in return-to-work programs with the claimant's employer;
3. Expediting medical reports; and
4. Participating in continuing education, utilization review, quality assurance, pre-certification, and case management systems.

This is apparently intended to ensure authorized physicians will work more closely with carriers in managing an employee's treatment by allowing carriers to compensate them for the additional time spent [§ 440.13(14)(b), Fla. Stat. (10/1/2003)].

[b] Collecting From Injured Worker Prohibited

The law prohibits health care providers from collecting or receiving fees directly from injured employees. The employer and carrier are exclusively liable [§ 440.13(14)(a), Fla. Stat. (1/1/94)]. Any contract between the health care provider and the injured employee requiring that the employee pay the difference between the schedule and the usual fee is void as a matter of law. This even applies to contracts agreeing to pay amounts above the schedules from the proceeds of a third-party action [*see* Sun Bank/South Florida, N.A. v. Baker, 632 So. 2d 669, 673 (Fla. 4th DCA 1994), *app. dismissed,* 639 So. 2d 982 (Fla. 1994)].

For example, Steven Baker was seriously injured when a tire exploded in his face. He received full workers' compensation benefits and also recovered $300,000 from a negligent third party. Dr. Felix Freshwater sued the worker, claiming entitlement to the difference between his regular fee and the fee schedule on the basis that Baker had included the full amount of Dr. Freshwater's fees in his demand, and that Baker's lawyer sent a letter to Dr. Freshwater stating that any obligation to him would be protected. The trial court rejected that argument and granted Baker summary judgment.

Sitting en banc, the Third District Court of Appeal agreed with the trial court and held that a health care provider cannot receive fees in workers' compensation cases in excess of the fee schedule even if the worker recovers an additional amount from a third party for medical expenses [*see* Freshwater v. Baker, 707 So. 2d 937, 939 (Fla. 3d DCA 1998)].

[c] Effect of Non-Compliance With Fee Schedule

[i] Health Care Providers

The Division of Workers' Compensation produces the fee schedules subject to final

Guide to Claims

approval by the Three Member Panel. This panel consists of the Insurance Commissioner and two other members appointed by the Governor. Physicians and other health care providers who routinely over-treat or overcharge are subject to decertification and removal from the list of authorized health care providers.

[ii] Insurance Carriers

For many years, extensive fee schedules have limited medical service charges for physicians, hospitals, and ambulatory surgical centers. These schedules, discussed in [3]–[5], *below,* are detailed and sometimes tricky to apply. Correct application, however, is mandatory. Failure to apply the schedules properly subjects carriers to fines assessed by the Division. Even those adjusters who rely on independent bill processing companies must be familiar with the details of the schedules. The fact that an independent service company misapplied the schedule is unlikely to relieve claim handlers of responsibility. In other words, carriers can delegate the work, but not the responsibility for performing the work correctly.

If the carrier makes an overpayment, the medical provider must refund the overpaid amount within 30 days of notification. If not, the Division may fine the provider up to $500 for each overpayment. Similarly, the carrier must repay any disallowed amount within 30 days after notification from the Division.

Carriers and their adjusters should not assume that this means they may now be more relaxed and less diligent in paying medical bills. Beginning on October 1, 2003, carriers must, at a minimum, pay all medical bills timely and in the correct amount in 95 percent of cases. If not, the offending carrier or self-insured employer is subject to a fine of up to one percent of its prior year's administrative assessment [§ 440.13(11)(b), Fla. Stat. (10/1/2003)].

In addition, carriers who engage in a practice of arbitrarily or unreasonably disallowing or reducing payments are subject to additional sanctions. These sanctions include repaying the underpaid amount, fines of up to $5,000 for each violation, and an award of attorney's fees and costs [Fla. Admin. Code R. 69L-24.0231 (1/10/2005)].

SPECIAL ALERT: By administrative rules adopted on 9/17/98 and 5/9/2005, many of the pages in the Health Care Provider Reimbursement Manual were replaced or changed. All of these replacement pages apply to medical treatment or services provided on or after September 1, 1997, the rules' effective date.

Also note that health care providers must use the coding provided in the CPT-4, CDT-2 or HCPCS. These refer to the following:

1. Physician's Current Procedural Terminology (CPT-4), 2004 Edition;
2. Current Dental Terminology CDT-2, 2nd Edition, 2002; and
3. Health Care Financing Administration's Common Procedural Coding (HCPCS, Level II, 2004, 16th Edition) [*see* Fla. Admin. Code R. 69L-7.020 (5/9/2005)].

[3] Limitations on Hospital Fees

[a] General Requirements

Effective July 4, 2004, the Division issued a revision of its Reimbursement Manual for Hospitals [*see* Fla. Admin. Code. R. 69L-7.501 (7/4/2004)]. In addition to describing limitations on reimbursement, the rules address several other issues as follows:

1. **Authorization**

   Hospitals must obtain carrier approval before providing non-emergency treatment or admitting a patient for treatment of work-related injuries. The hospital's records must show the name and title of the carrier representative granting authorization. At the time of seeking such authorization, the hospital must tell the carrier about any treatment proposed for conditions unrelated to the compensable injury [*see* Fla. Admin. Code. R. 69L-7.501 (1/10/2005)].

SPECIAL NOTE: The rules are silent as to the effect of failing to secure authorization before providing treatment. Presumably such failure will preclude payment as with all unauthorized care.

2. **Precertification**

   Carriers are required to precertify the length of stay in accordance with national standards. The rules do not provide for any penalty for failure to do so. Presumably, such failure will create a presumption that the length of stay was appropriate. If additional days are required, the hospital must obtain carrier approval first [*see* Fla. Admin. Code. R. 69L-7.501 (1/10/2005)].

3. **Releasing Medical Records**

   Upon admission, the hospital must obtain a medical information release form from the patient, or from the patient's guardian or representative. If the patient refuses, the hospital must inform the carrier. This does not necessarily preclude releasing treatment records; however, without a signed release, certain records cannot be disclosed. These include records dealing with mental health, substance abuse and HIV [*see* Fla. Admin. Code. R. 69L-7.501 (1/10/2005)].

4. **Medical Records**

   In addition to the records ordinarily maintained, hospital records must also contain documentation sufficient to substantiate the medical necessity of the treatment rendered and for the length of stay [*see* Fla. Admin. Code. R. 69L-7.501 (1/10/2005)].

5. **Copy Charges**

   Copy charges are limited to $.50 per page for paper copies and to actual cost for other media. The rule provides as follows [*see* § 440.13(4)(b), Fla. Stat. (10/1/2003); Fla. Admin. Code. R. 69L-7.601 (1/10/2005)]:

"Health care providers and health care facilities shall upon demand furnish an injured employee or his attorney a copy of his office chart, records and reports. The health care provider or health care facility furnishing the records may charge the employee for copying the records up to $.50 per page or the actual direct cost to the health care provider or health care facility for x-rays, microfilm, or other non-paper records."

Effective October 1, 2003, the legislature amended § 440.13(4)(b), Fla. Stat. to provide that a health care provider may change no more than the actual direct cost for x-rays, microfilm, or other non-paper records. The charge for paper copies may be no more than $0.50 per copy. The amendment also requires health care providers to furnish records, on demand, by the employer or carrier or their attorney, besides furnishing records to the claimant and claimant's attorney.

Also effective October 1, 2003, the law provides that there must be reasonable access to medical records by all parties. When an employee reports an injury alleged to be work-related, the employee waives any physician-patient privilege with respect to any condition, or complaint, reasonably related to the condition for which the employee seeks compensation. Health care providers must provide the parties and their lawyers with records and reports relevant to the condition for which the claimant seeks compensation. The law provides that these records and reports must be produced upon demand and that a release of information by the claimant is not required. If the physician is outside the state, and not subject to Florida law, the claimant must provide the carrier with authorization to release the records [*see* § 440.13(4)(c), Fla. Stat. (10/1/2003)].

[b] Fee Limitations

The rules provide different procedures and limitations on fees depending on the nature and location of the facility as follows:

1. Out of State Facilities

Except for the limitations on fees, the rules apply in their entirety to hospitals located out of the State of Florida. Fees are limited to the amount negotiated between the carrier and the hospital. If no agreement was reached, the state with the highest fee schedule reimbursement amount controls. Presumably, if the other state has no fee schedule, the Florida schedule controls [*see* Fla. Admin. Code. R. 69L-7.501 (1/10/2005)].

2. Federal Facilities

Except for the limitations on fees, the rules apply in their entirety to federal facilities. Federal facilities may use their own billing form and are not subject to any reimbursement limitations [*see* Fla. Admin. Code. R. 69L-7.501 (1/10/2005)].

3. Acute Care Hospitals and Trauma Centers

Inpatient care is reimbursed on a per diem basis. For hospitals, the rate for surgical stays is $3,213.73. The rate for non-surgical stays is $1,906.89. For trauma centers, the rate for surgical stays is $3,214.66. The rate for non-surgical stays is $1,931.96 [*see* Fla. Admin. Code. R. 69L-7.501 (1/10/2005)].

If the charges exceed $50,000, the per diem rates do not apply. Instead, the facility is paid 75% of usual and customary charges [*see* Fla. Admin. Code. R. 69L-7.501 (1/10/2005)].

4. **Psychiatric Hospitals**

Per diem rates do not apply to psychiatric hospitals. Such facilities are paid 75% of usual and customary charges [*see* Fla. Admin. Code. R. 69L-7.501 (1/10/2005)].

5. **Outpatient Services**

All outpatient services are paid at 75% of usual and customary rate [*see* Fla. Admin. Code. R. 69L-7.501 (1/10/2005)].

SPECIAL ALERT: AHCA's administrative rule, Fla. Admin. Code R. 69L-7.100, provides that an ambulatory surgical center is to be reimbursed 70% of that individual service provider's usual and customary charge. However, the court found that the rule is based on the 1992 version of the statute that provided "when a procedure is performed which is not listed in the manual, . . . carriers must reimburse ambulatory surgical centers 70% of the ambulatory surgical center's usual and customary charge." However, the court found that the statute was amended, effective July 15, 2003, to remove all reference to the charges of any individual service provider [Ch. 2003-412, § 15, at 3905-08, Laws of Fla.]. This amendment reveals the legislative intent to eliminate calculation of a "usual and customary charge" based on the fees of any one provider, in favor of a calculation of such charge based on average fees of all providers in a given geographical area. By so doing, the amendment created a conflict between the statute and the administrative rule. In cases of conflict, a statute takes precedence over an administrative rule [One Beacon Ins. v. Agency for Health Care Admin., 2007 Fla. App. LEXIS 4533, 3-4 (Fla. 1st DCA March 28, 2007)]. NOTE: Presumably this holding will apply to hospitals and other facilities as well. Unfortunately, the court did not define the term "Community" other than to make reference to "a given geographically area." So, it is not clear if "community" means individual counties, regions, or the entire state.

SPECIAL NOTE: The 2003 Legislature amended the Act regarding maximum fee allowances as follows [§ 440.13(12), Fla. Stat. (10/1/2003)]:

For services rendered on or after October 1, 2003:

- A patient may not remain in observation status for more than 23 hours.
- The maximum percentage of increase in individual reimbursement allowances is no longer controlled by the Consumer Price Index.
- Reimbursement is based on the agreed upon contract price or the fee

schedule. The Legislature repealed the phrase "whichever is less." Therefore, it appears the carrier may pay either amount at its option.

For services rendered on or after January 1, 2004:

- Payment allowances to hospitals for outpatient services for physical therapy, occupational therapy, and speech therapy are to be reimbursed in the same amounts as for non-hospital providers.
- Payment allowances to hospitals for scheduled outpatient, non-emergency services for radiological and laboratory services not done in conjunction with a surgical procedure are to be reimbursed in the same amounts as for non-hospital providers.
- Payment allowances to hospitals for scheduled surgeries are reduced from 75 percent of charges to 60 percent of charges.
- Payment allowances to medical doctors and osteopathic doctors for non-surgical treatment, are increased to 110 percent of the Medicare rate or the Florida fee schedule in effect on January 1, 2003, whichever is greater.
- Payment allowances to medical doctors and osteopathic doctors for surgical treatment, are increased to 140 percent of the Medicare rate or the Florida fee schedule in effect on January 1, 2003, whichever is greater.
- Reimbursement allowances for prescription medicines are limited to the wholesale price plus $4.18 for the dispensing fee. [Previously, the allowance was for 120 percent of the wholesale price.]

[c] Disallowing Charges

Carriers may not disallow charges for the length of stay unless the stay exceeded the precertified days or the stay exceeded the median length of stay based on national standards. An exception arises if the patient also received services for treatment of a non-compensable condition. In such a case, the portion of the stay attributable to the non-compensable condition is not reimbursable [*see* Fla. Admin. Code. R. 69L-7.501 (1/10/2005)].

The rules allow carriers to conduct on-site audits to justify the length of the patient's stay and the services delivered. As a precondition, however, the carrier must notify the hospital of its intent to conduct an audit, in writing, within 30 days after receiving billing Form DWC-90. Upon receipt of such notice, the hospital must schedule the audit, without charge or requiring prepayment, within 30 days after receiving the notice of intent. Presumably, no payment is due until after the audit is complete, but the rules are silent about the effect of the audit being completed after the 45-day deadline to pay the bill. Claims for overpayments or underpayments must be made during this time. Otherwise, the affected party waives its right to reimbursement. This may be a difficult provision to enforce since the time frames are so ambiguous. Lastly, a new provision in the rules prohibits delaying payment because the carrier has not received copies of medical records [*see* Fla. Admin. Code. R. 69L-7.501 (1/10/2005)].

[d] Explanation of Bill Review (EOBR)

The rules provide that carriers must provide an EBOR when disallowing any charges. Carriers must use the codes listed in the rule to explain any reductions. Note, however, that the rules allow carriers to create additional codes to help explain the reasons for disallowing charges [*see* Fla. Admin. Code. R. 69L-7.501 (1/10/2005)].

For a streamlined discussion of medical benefits, see LARSON'S WORKERS' COMPENSATION, DESK EDITION, Ch. 94 (Matthew Bender).

[4] Resolving Disputes on Medical Fees

[a] Jurisdiction

A judge of compensation claims has no jurisdiction to resolve disputes about the amount due for individual medical services. The Agency for Health Care Administration *alone* must resolve such disputes. Authority for this exclusive jurisdiction can be found in § 440.13, Fla. Stat., Fla. Admin. Code R. 59A-31.001 and Fla. Admin. Code R. 69L-7.605 (1/10/2005) [*see also* Atlantic Foundation v. Gurlacz, 582 So. 2d 10, 11 (Fla. 1st DCA 1991); Carswell v. Broderick Const., 583 So. 2d 803, 804 (Fla. 1st DCA 1991)].

NOTE: The legislative amendment to § 440.13(2)(i)1, Fla. Stat. (7/1/90) is procedural and applies to all claims whatever the date of the accident [*see* Terners of Miami Corp. v. Freshwater, 599 So. 2d 674, 675 (Fla. 1st DCA 1992)].

The Agency's exclusive jurisdiction applies only to reimbursement issues. All other issues, such as medical necessity, are within the jurisdiction of the judges of compensation claims. Reimbursement issues means issues dealing with the amount of a provider's charges only, and not whether the carrier owes payment overall [*see* Williams v. Triple Enterprises, 650 So. 2d 1114, 1116–1117 (Fla. 1st DCA 1995)].

SPECIAL ALERT: The statutes and rules dealing with utilization review and fee schedule reimbursement disputes also apply to out-of-state providers [*see* Furtick v. William Shults Contractor, 664 So. 2d 288, 290–291 (Fla. 1st DCA 1995)]. Note: On April 9, 1996, the Florida Supreme Court declined to accept jurisdiction [*see* Furtick v. Shults, 673 So. 2d 29 (Fla. 1996)].

[b] Dispute Resolution Procedure

Usually, the provider and the carrier manage to resolve disputes over the correct amount of a medical provider's fee. When they reach an impasse, however, Administrative rules prescribe the dispute resolution procedure. When a dispute arises, the provider may ask the Agency to resolve it. The parties must follow preliminary steps as follows [Fla. Admin. Code R. 69L-7.605 (1/10/2005)]:

1. If a carrier pays less than the amount billed, the carrier must provide the physician or facility with a Written Explanation of Medical Benefits. This is

commonly called an EOMB and explains the basis for the reduction.

2. If the provider does not agree, the provider may petition the Agency to resolve the dispute, but must do so within 30 days of receipt of the EOMB. The petition should include all pertinent documentation, such as invoices, the EOMB, correspondence, and written authorizations.

3. Within 10 days after receiving a copy of the provider's petition, the carrier must file its documentation with the Agency. If the carrier fails to do so, it waives all objections to the petition. Documentation should include the following:

   a. The specific policy from the reimbursement manual on which the carrier relies.

   b. An explanation of the method used to decide the proposed reimbursement amount if the disputed fee is for a "by report" or "Allowance Not Established" procedure.

   c. A copy of the consultant's opinion if the carrier relied on a medical consultant.

   d. A description of any adjustments to the original reimbursement.

   e. Notice that a carrier medical consultant reviewed the charges and the issue referred to the Agency for policy clarification, if applicable.

4. The Agency, assuming the parties have followed all required preliminary steps, must respond within 60 days. Either party may dispute the Agency's position and request further reconsideration through a physician peer review. After peer review, the parties have the right to further appeal the dispute as provided by Ch. 120, Fla. Stats. This Chapter describes rights and procedures for appealing the decisions of governmental agencies to the Division of Administrative Hearings.

For a general discussion of dispute resolution in workers' compensation, see LARSON'S WORKERS' COMPENSATION, DESK EDITION, Part 14, *Adjective Law* (Matthew Bender).

[5] Providers' Rights

Physicians and other health care providers have an independent right of action against the employer and carrier for collecting their fees. In 1983, the legislature added language to the Act that prohibits providers from billing or receiving payment directly by injured workers. The legislature amended this section effective January 1, 1994, but its meaning is unchanged. The section now provides that "the employee is not liable for payment for medical treatment or services provided pursuant to this section except as otherwise provided in this section" [§ 440.13(3)(g), Fla. Stat. (1/1/94)].

The various fee schedules list the maximum amount a provider may receive for a particular service. If the provider's usual charge exceeds the fee schedule amount, the provider may not collect the difference from the employee or anyone else. If carriers or servicing agents do not pay medical bills timely, and in the correct amounts, they are subject to the sanctions discussed in [2][c][ii], *above*.

A detailed review of the various fee schedules is beyond the scope of this book. Adjusters, health care providers, and others should carefully read the schedules' instructions and provisions. The proper titles of the fee schedules are as follows:

Florida Workers' Compensation Health Care Provider Reimbursement Manual.
(Effective June 1, 1991)

Florida Workers' Compensation Health Care Provider Fee for Service Reimbursement Manual.
(Effective September 1, 1997)

Florida Workers' Compensation Reimbursement Manual for Hospitals.
(Effective June 1, 1992)

Florida Workers' Compensation Reimbursement Manual for Ambulatory Surgical Centers.
(Effective August 7, 1991)

Florida Workers' Compensation Reimbursement Manual for Work Hardening Programs and Pain Programs.
(Effective February 18, 1993)

The manuals are available from the Division of Workers' Compensations. To order, write to:

Division of Workers' Compensation
Rehabilitation and Medical Services Unit
2728 Centerview Drive
354 Forrest Building
Tallahassee, Florida 32399-0664

§ 16.15 Ex Parte Communication: Physicians

[1] Historical Background

The issue here is whether the employer or carrier has the right to hold private or "ex parte" conversations with the injured worker's physician. The term "ex parte" means outside the presence of one or more parties. Before January 1, 1994, the Act required that doctors give the medical records of an injured worker to the parties [§ 440.13(2)(f), Fla. Stat.]. This includes the employer, the carrier, the attorney for the employer or carrier, and the rehabilitation provider. The statute also required that the injured worker's medical condition "shall be discussed with such persons." In two key cases, discussed in [2]–[3], *below,* the First District Court of Appeal held that a carrier's right to unrestricted private conferences ended with the filing of a petition for benefits. The court held that after the injured worker files a petition for benefits, the carrier can hold such conferences only after giving the injured worker's attorney an opportunity to be present. However, these cases were essentially overruled by 1994 legislation [*see* [4], *below*].

[2] *Perez v. Eastern Airlines*

Injured worker Perez objected when his employer tried to have a private (ex parte) discussion with his internist. The judge of compensation claims ruled that such ex parte communication was permissible under § 440.13(2)(f), Fla. Stat. The District Court of Appeals, however, disagreed.

In a brief opinion, the court held that the statute does allow an employer or carrier to discuss an injured worker's medical condition. Nevertheless, the court also held there is nothing in the statute that allows or requires that such discussion occur without the injured worker's attorney.

The brevity of the opinion was unfortunate. The court developed this new rule regarding ex parte communication inadequately, which provoked considerable confusion and litigation [*see* Perez v. Eastern Airlines, Inc., 569 So. 2d 1290, 1291 (Fla. 1st DCA 1990)].

This court decision was effectively overruled, though, by 1994 legislation [*see* [4], *below*].

[3] *Adelman Steel v. Winter*

Predictably, interpretations of the *Perez* decision [*see* [2], *above*] ran the gamut from ultra conservative to extremely liberal. In 1992, the court again visited the issue, but this time in a lengthy decision.

In essence, the court held that the prohibition against ex parte communication with an injured worker's physicians applies only when an adversarial relationship exists. Filing a formal petition for benefits creates such a relationship [*see* Adelman Steel Corp. v. Winter, 610 So. 2d 494, 504–505 (Fla. 1st DCA 1992)].

This court decision was effectively overruled, though, by 1994 legislation [*see* [4], *below*].

[4] Statutory Amendment

The legislature enacted amendments to the Act effective July 1, 1997 and October 1, 2001. The 1997 amendment was an obvious and successful effort to overrule the court's holding in *Perez* [*see* [2], *above*] and *Adelman Steel* [*see* [3], *above*]. The 1997 amendment, however, did not include rehabilitation providers as persons authorized to receive medical reports or to discuss the claimant's medical condition with the physician. Presumably, that omission was unintentional because effective 10/1/2001 rehabilitation providers have been added to the list. The legislature amended the Act to provide as follows [§ 440.13(4)(c), Fla. Stat. (10/1/2001)]:

> Notwithstanding the limitations in § 456.057 and subject to the limitations in § 381.004, upon the request of the employer, the carrier, *an authorized qualified rehabilitation provider, or the attorney for the employer or carrier,* the medical records of an injured employee must be furnished to those persons and the medical condition of the injured employee must be discussed with those persons, if the records and the discussions are restricted to conditions relating to the workplace injury. Any such discussions may be held before or after the filing of a claim without the knowledge, consent, or presence of any other party or his or her agent or representative. A health care provider who willfully refuses to provide medical

records or to discuss the medical condition of the injured employee, after a reasonable request is made for such information pursuant to this subsection, shall be subject by the division to one or more of the penalties set forth in paragraph (8)(b). (Emphasis added).

NOTE: The italicized phrase in the first sentence is the language added in the 2001 amendment.

This language not only allows free discussion, but also provides penalties for physicians who refuse to cooperate. Note that § 455.241, Fla. Stat. does not apply in workers' compensation cases. This section prohibits physicians from revealing medical records without the patient's authorization. Also note that the provisions of § 381.004, Fla. Stat. do apply. This section prohibits disclosure of HIV or AIDS test results except by written authorization of the patient or by court order. The section, as amended on July 1, 1990, authorizes a judge of compensation claims to order release of HIV or AIDS information, contingent upon finding a compelling need that cannot be accommodated by other means. Even with the 1994 amendments, this restriction remains the same.

The question becomes whether this new language now gives carriers, employers, and defense attorneys free contact with physicians. The answer to the question is yes. The statutory amendment grants carriers, employers, and attorneys the right to hold ex parte communications with physicians and effectively reverses the holdings in *Perez* and *Adelman Steel* [*see* [2]–[3], *above*]. Further, the amendment is procedural and applies to all accident dates [*see* Vickers v. Unity of Lake Worth, 693 So. 2d 62, 63 (Fla. 1st DCA 1997)].

The court has held that a logical review of the 1994 statutory amendments gives the appearance that the legislature intended that the records and opinions of treating and examining physicians should be freely available to employers and carriers. Claimants no longer have the right to be present during discussions between employers and carriers and those physicians [*see* Pierre v. Handi Van, Inc., 717 So. 2d 1115, 1117 (Fla. 1st DCA 1998)]. Note: Ex parte communication with an expert medical advisor (EMA) is not allowed. *See* § 16.18[8].

Additionally, the court has held that such ex parte communication with physicians does not infringe on the employees' right to privacy under the Florida constitution.This is because the workers' compensation system transposes dispute resolution from the private law of torts to a publicly administered and regulated system. By presenting themselves to physicians, not only for treatment, but for evaluation and assessment of an injury's relationship to work, injured workers consent to the disclosure of medical information relating to the claim. The ex parte discussions allowed by § 440.13(4)(c), Fla. Stat., simply further that disclosure system. Additionally, the court held that the ex parte conference with the physician here was permissible under the holding in *Pierre,* because there had been no EMA appointment at the time. This suggests that ex parte conferences with physicians are not allowed once an EMA appointment has been made [*see* S&A Plumbing v. Kimes, 756 So. 2d 1037 (Fla. 1st DCA 2000), *reh'g denied,* May 3, 2000].

Guide to Claims

§ 16.16 Independent Medical Examination (IME)

[1] Definitions

The Act defines an "Independent Medical Examination" as "an objective evaluation of the injured employee's medical condition, including, but not limited to, impairment or work status, performed by a physician or an expert medical advisor at the request of a party, a judge of compensation claims, or the division to assist in the resolution of a dispute arising under this chapter" [§ 440.13(1)(k), Fla. Stat. (1/1/94)].

The Act also defines the term "Independent Medical Examiner" as "a physician selected by either an employee or a carrier to render one or more independent medical examinations in connection with a dispute arising under this chapter" [§ 440.13(1)(j), Fla. Stat. (1/1/94)].

[2] Purposes of IME

[a] Resolution of Disputes

The Workers' Compensation Act now gives both the carrier and the employee the right to an IME. The purpose of such an examination is to resolve disputes, and the issues to be resolved are not limited by the Act. Either party may have an IME to resolve disputes about overutilization, medical benefits, compensability, or disability.

This raises the question of what constitutes a dispute, thus invoking the right to an independent medical examination. § 440.13(5)(a), Fla. Stat., sets forth the basic criteria for obtaining an IME:

> In any dispute concerning overutilization, medical benefits, compensability, or disability under this chapter, the carrier or the employee may select an independent medical examiner.

Under § 440.13(5)(a), Fla. Stat., the only condition required for a party to request an IME is a dispute. Under relevant case law, there are two ways to create a § 440.13(5)(a), Fla. Stat., dispute. First, when an employer denies a claim for benefits, the employer is clearly disputing the claimant's right to benefits. Because a request for an IME could be treated as a request for benefits, a denial of that request may also create a dispute. Second, when an employer authorizes evaluation and treatment of a claimant, but the claimant, after receiving the diagnosis of the treating physician, disagrees with it, a dispute is created, and the claimant may request an IME.

For example, a dispute arose in a case in accordance with the second method, entitling the claimant to a psychiatric IME pursuant to § 440.13(5)(a), Fla. Stat.. The claimant disagreed not only with the medical care she received by the authorized psychiatrist provided, but with his determination that she had achieved MMI. Because the employer/carrier denied the claim for temporary partial disability benefits in part on the basis that the claimant had achieved overall MMI, the claimant's request to present medical opinion evidence from a psychiatric IME was directly related to demonstrating her entitlement to TPD benefits. The court, therefore, reversed for the denial of a psychiatric independent medical examination [*see* Cortina v. Dep't of HRS, 901 So. 2d 273 (Fla. 1st DCA 2005)].

[b] Limits on Conducting IME

The right to an independent medical examination is discussed in the statute as follows [§ 440.13(5)(a), Fla. Stat.]:

> In any dispute concerning overutilization, medical benefits, compensability, or disability under this chapter, the carrier or the employee may select an independent medical examiner. *The examiner may be a health care provider treating or providing other care to the employee.* An independent medical examiner may not render an opinion outside his or her area of expertise, as demonstrated by licensure and applicable practice parameters. (Emphasis added)

Note that the statute specifically allows a treating physician to serve as an independent medical examiner.

Effective October 1, 2003, the Legislature substantially altered the parties' rights to independent medical examinations as follows [*see* § 440.13(5), Fla. Stat. (10/1/2003)]:

1. The employer/carrier and the claimant are each limited to only one independent medical examination per accident. There is no longer any entitlement to an independent medical examination for each medical specialty.
2. The party requesting the examination and choosing the examiner is responsible for all costs associated with the examination. This includes costs associated with diagnostic testing and the physician's fees. Thus, claimants must pay for their own independent medical examinations.
3. The party selecting the independent medical examiner must notify all other parties of their choice within 15 days *after* the date the examination is to take place. If the notification is not timely, the independent medical examiner's findings cannot be submitted into evidence.
4. The independent medical examiner cannot be a treating physician, unless the parties agree.
5. The independent medical examiner is prohibited from providing follow-up care, even if such care is found to be medically necessary.
6. If the employee prevails in a medical dispute, as determined in an order by a judge of compensation claims, the carrier must pay for the claimant's independent medical examination.
7. If the carrier pays benefits, or provides treatment, based on the examiner's findings, the carrier must pay for the independent medical examination. [Note: The statute's vaguely worded language implies that the carrier must pay for the claimant's IME even if it was no help to the claimant and benefits were awarded or provided based on the carrier's IME.]
8. Each party is bound by the opinions of its independent medical examiner.
9. The provision allowing the judge of compensation claims to designate an Expert Medical Advisor as an independent medical examiner is repealed.

10. The carrier is not responsible for scheduling an independent medical examination, other than its own examination.

An exception to the "claimant pay" provision arises if the claimant's choice of an independent medical examiner is in the carrier's managed care network. It that case, the carrier is obligated to pay for the costs of the examination [*see* § 440.134(6), Fla. Stat. (10/1/2003)].

It is also important to note that this section, § 440.13(5), Fla. Stat., refers only to an independent medical examination to resolve disputes about overutilization, medical benefits, compensability, or disability. It does not apply to disputes concerning the date of maximum medical improvement or the degree of permanent impairment. The right to an independent medical examination to resolve those issues is controlled by § 440.1925, Fla. Stat. Therefore, it appears that a claimant might be entitled to a second, carrier-paid independent medical examination to resolve MMI and impairment disputes.

Because this amendment substantially changes the parties' rights and responsibilities, it is probably a substantive amendment that will apply to accidents occurring only on or after the amendment's effective date, October 1, 2003.

SPECIAL NOTE: The following discussion will probably apply to accidents occurring only before October 1, 2003. After that date, as noted, each party is entitled to an independent medical examination by a physician of their choice and at their own expense.

Although the right to conduct an independent medical examination is not restricted to the four issues in the statute, the right to an IME itself is not without limits, and the statute does impose a "reasonableness" requirement subject to the scrutiny of the judge of compensation claims [*see* Wal-Mart Stores, Inc. v. Liggon, 668 So. 2d 259, 263–264 (Fla. 1st DCA 1996)].

Note that item 2 in the statute allows an IME to decide whether overutilization has occurred. In one case, the judge of compensation claims refused to allow the carrier to conduct an IME to assess alleged overutilization. Besides the provision above, another statutory section addresses this issue and provides as follows [§ 440.13(5)(a), Fla. Stat. (1994)]:

> In any dispute concerning overutilization, medical benefits, compensability, or disability under this chapter, the carrier or the employee may select an independent medical examiner.

Given such plain language, the court reversed and ordered the JCC to allow the carrier to proceed with an independent medical examination [*see* Compcare of Florida, Inc. v. Cason, 693 So. 2d 127, 128 (Fla. 1st DCA 1997)]. This section, however, is a double-edged blade. Note, for example, that either party may "select an independent medical advisor" if there is a dispute about "medical benefits." § 440.13(2), Fla. Stat. allows the injured worker to have an IME to "determine whether treatment is necessary." § 400.13(5), Fla. Stat. allows an IME when disputes about medical benefits arise.

Ironically, the court has held that a carrier's refusal to allow an evaluation under § 440.13(2), Fla. Stat. creates a right to an IME under § 440.13(5), Fla. Stat.

Julio Flores requested an IME with a psychiatrist. The carrier refused, apparently because no physician had suggested that Flores needed such care and, therefore, an IME was unnecessary. The court held that Flores' request was essentially a request for authorization of a psychiatrist to evaluate his symptoms and need for treatment under § 440.13(2), Fla. Stat. The carrier's denial created a dispute over a medical benefit, thus creating a right to an IME under § 440.13(5), Fla. Stat. This case will likely result in a flood of requests for an IME under § 440.13(2), Fla. Stat. If carriers deny that request, the injured worker, or rather his or her lawyer, can obtain it anyway under § 440.13(5), Fla. Stat. [*see* ABC Liquors, Inc. v. Flores, 700 So. 2d 102 (Fla. 1st DCA 1997)].

The court has held that when a managed care plan exists, under § 440.134(16), Fla. Stat. (1997), the JCC "*must deny a claimant's request for an IME*", if the purpose of the IME is to resolve a dispute regarding the provision of medical treatment, care, and attendance. Such disputes, said the court, are to be resolved through a request for change of provider [*see* § 440.134(10)(c), Fla. Stat. (1997)], or a grievance under procedures established pursuant to § 440.134(15), Fla. Stat. When the dispute does not concern the provision of medical treatment, care, and attendance, however, the managed care provisions do not govern the selection and use of medical expert witnesses under § 440.13(5), Fla. Stat. Here, the court allowed the IME because its purpose was to determine the cause of the claimant's condition. Note also, that IMEs by a provider of the claimant's choice are allowed for such issues as a determination of disability status, impairment, and so forth. Obviously, this makes it essential that carriers determine the purpose of an IME before agreeing to provide it. This case also leaves a critical question unanswered. Specifically, does this mean that the E/C is also not entitled to an IME for purposes of resolving a dispute about medical treatment [*see* Claims Mgmt., Inc. v. Grenier, 777 So. 2d 1039, 1040–1041 (Fla. 1st DCA 2000)]?

Until the claimant has exhausted the carrier's managed care procedures, including the grievance procedures, the judge of compensation claims has no authority to order medical benefits, including an IME [*see* Weather Eng'rs v. Presgraves, 774 So. 2d 938, 939 (Fla. 1st DCA 2001)].

[3] Choosing an Independent Medical Examiner

[a] Right of Selection

Before January 1, 1994, the law prohibited the examining physician from providing treatment or subsequent care unless both the carrier and the employee agreed. Effective January 1, 1994, the Legislature amend the Act to provide that the treating physician may serve as an independent medical examiner at a party's option. Effective October 1, 2003, the Legislature again amended the Act by restoring it to its pre-1994 state. Once again, the law provides that the examiner cannot be a treating physician unless the parties agree. When in an independent medical examiner status, however, physicians may not give an opinion outside their area of licensure and expertise [§ 440.13(5)(a), Fla. Stat. (1/1/94) and (10/1/2003)].

Beginning in 1994, both the carrier and the injured worker have the right to an independent medical examination. Carriers and injured workers can invoke their right to an independent medical examination, if done reasonably, and in a reasonable time [*see* Roberts v. Ben Hill Griffin, Inc., 629 So. 2d 236, 238 (Fla. 1st DCA 1993); Farm Stores, Inc. v. Fletcher, 621 So. 2d 706, 708 (Fla. 1st DCA 1993)].

[b] Examiner Is Expert Witness

Because the courts consider an independent medical examiner an expert witness, one party cannot choose the examiner for the other. For example, the carrier wanted Yvonne Reed to submit to an independent medical examination. Reed refused, so the carrier filed a motion to compel. The judge of compensation claims granted the carrier's motion, but ordered the carrier to give Reed a list of physicians from which to choose. This, in effect, gave the injured worker the right to choose the carrier's expert witness, which amounts to an undue limitation of the carrier's right of selection [*see* Reed v. Reed, 643 So. 2d 1180, 1182 (Fla. 1st DCA 1994)].

[c] Choose Appropriate Speciality

Select the examining physician with care, especially one with the appropriate specialty. Over the years, the courts have required that the examiner be in the same specialty as the treating physician. That is to say, only a chiropractor could testify about chiropractic care, an orthopedist about orthopedic care, and so forth. In 1993, however, the First District Court of Appeal reversed this line of thinking. In one case, the court held an orthopedist, who had enough knowledge about chiropractic care, qualified to testify about the effect of manipulation upon the injured worker's spine, and the need for continued chiropractic care. If the selected physician is outside the specialty, it is essential to learn the physician's qualifications to give expert testimony [*see* Alford v. G. Pierce Woods Memorial Hosp., 621 So. 2d 1380, 1382–1383 (Fla. 1st DCA 1993)].

In a later, similar case, the carrier selected an orthopedist to conduct an independent medical examination and to testify about the need for continued chiropractic care. The court repeated its earlier holding in *Alford,* that being an orthopedist does not automatically disqualify a doctor from rendering an opinion on chiropractic care. Apparently the carrier here did not choose its independent medical examiner wisely. The court held the doctor disqualified himself when he testified that he knew little about chiropractic care. The doctor also admitted his inability to give an opinion on the need for chiropractic care [*see* Spears v. Gates Energy Products, 621 So. 2d 1386, 1387 (Fla. 1st DCA 1993)].

[d] Legislative Action and Supreme Court Resolution

At first, the legislature appeared to have overruled the *Alford* decision [*see* [c], *above*]. The Act now prohibits examiners from rendering an opinion outside their area of expertise, as shown by licensure and applicable practice parameters [§ 440.13 (5)(a), Fla. Stat. (1/1/94)].

The Florida Supreme Court, however, has finally settled the issue. Nothing in the law prevents a physician, certified in one field, from testifying about care provided by another physician certified in the same field, but licensed under a different regulatory statute. Medical doctors and osteopathic physicians are qualified and licensed in the broadest manner. Their qualifications and licensure encompass those areas of practice allowed for podiatrists and chiropractors. The statutes do not, then, automatically disqualify medical doctors from giving testimony about the necessity of care provided in a different, but related specialty. They must, of course, have sufficient knowledge about the other specialty to qualify as an expert [*see* Clair v. Glades County Bd. of Com'rs, 649 So. 2d 224, 225–227 (Fla. 1995)].

[e] Alternate Examiner Limited

Careful selection is also critical because once the choice is made, the selecting party—the carrier or the injured worker—is not entitled to an alternate examiner unless one of the following is true:

1. The examiner turns out not to be qualified to render an opinion on the issues in dispute.
2. The examiner is no longer in practice.
3. The examiner is unavailable because he has moved far from the area, is ill, or is deceased.
4. The parties agree to another examiner.

The first exception does not mean that the parties are entitled to multiple IMEs by physicians of different specialties. A second IME is allowed only if some aspect of the employee's illness is outside the initial examiner's field. For example, assume an orthopedic surgeon performed the first IME, and the requesting party now wants a chiropractic IME. This second examination is allowed only if the orthopedic surgeon is not qualified to give an opinion about chiropractic care [*see* Watkins Engineers & Constructors v. Wise, 698 So. 2d 294, 296 (Fla. 1st DCA 1997)].

[4] Scheduling IME

Carriers have the statutory right to contact the injured worker directly to schedule a reasonable time for an independent medical examination, even if a lawyer represents the injured worker. If the carrier gives the injured worker notice of the appointment by telephone, the carrier must confirm the appointment in writing within five days. Carriers must inform the injured worker's lawyer about the appointment at least seven days before the appointment date. The section prohibits an injured worker's lawyer from scheduling the carrier's independent medical examination [§ 440.13(5)(c), Fla. Stat. (1/1/94)].

> **SPECIAL ALERT:** Occasionally, the injured worker may oppose the carrier's independent medical examination and attempt to preclude it by motions for protective order or other legal actions. Even if successful, the injured worker cannot recover attorney's fees from the carrier for such actions [§ 440.13(5)(f), Fla. Stat. (1/1/94)].

[5] Failure to Appear for IME

[a] IME at Carrier's Request

What happens if the injured worker fails to appear for an independent medical examination without good cause? If the injured worker fails to advise both the carrier and the physician at least 24 hours before the appointment, the injured worker cannot collect any compensation while refusing to submit to the examination [§ 440.13(5)(d), Fla. Stat. (1/1/94)].

A 24-hour cancellation alone is not, itself, a good cause failure to appear for the examination. If injured workers cannot show good cause, they must reimburse the carrier 50 percent of the doctor's no-show fee. The carrier may recover the no-show fee by deducting up to 20 percent of the injured worker's biweekly compensation. The only exception is if the carrier fails to give the injured worker timely written notice of the details of the appointment [*see* § 440.13(5)(d), Fla. Stat.; *see also* Fla. Admin. Code R. 69L-24.0241 (1/10/2005)]. The change to § 440.13(5)(d), Fla. Stat. is a substantive amendment to the Act and, therefore, applies to only those accidents occurring on or after January 1, 1994 [*see* Anderson v. City of Leesburg, 695 So. 2d 711 (Fla. 1st DCA 1995)].

[b] IME by Court Order

A judge of compensation claims can compel an injured worker to attend an independent medical examination only if the injured worker has filed a petition for benefits. In other words, the judge of compensation claims has no jurisdiction to order an injured worker to attend an IME. This is true even while a dispute is pending with the Employee Assistance and Ombudsman Office if the injured worker has not filed a petition [*see* Karell v. Miami Airport Hilton/Miami Hilton Corp., 668 So. 2d 227, 228–229 (Fla. 1st DCA 1996), *rev. denied,* 675 So. 2d 928 (Fla. 1996)].

What happens if an injured worker fails to attend an independent medical examination when a judge of compensation claims ordered the examination? Workers' compensation judges have broad, but limited powers to impose sanctions besides those provided by statute.

For example, the judge ordered Larry McConnell to an independent medical examination with a specific clinic. The clinic, however, declined to perform the examination. On its own, the carrier set up another IME with a different physician. McConnell did not attend and the judge of compensation claims imposed the maximum sanction: she dismissed the claim with prejudice! Dismissal of a claim *with prejudice,* operates as a bar to any further action, and is considered an adjudication upon the merits of the claim. On appeal, the court did not consider this a judge-ordered IME because it was not the precise one ordered, so the court reversed the dismissal order. The court held dismissal with prejudice is too harsh a sanction to impose for failure to attend an IME not ordered by the judge of compensation claims. Does this mean that dismissal with prejudice is proper if the judge of compensation claims did order the IME? We do not know because the court did not say. In a concurring opinion, Judge Barfield stated [*see* McConnell v. Florida Furniture Center, 611 So. 2d 65, 66 (Fla. 1st DCA 1992)]:

> Without passing on the issue, I suggest that it is fairly debatable that the only sanction that may be taken with or without an order of the judge of compensation claims is the suspension of proceedings and payment of compensation for any period during which the employee refuses to submit to an examination.

It is difficult to predict what the majority view will be in some future case.

Note, however, that the judge of compensation claims' order must contain a specific finding of the claimant's willful noncompliance with a previous order compelling attendance at an independent medical examination. Failure to include specific, written finding of facts of wilfulness in the order of dismissal constitutes reversible error [*see* Hamilton v. Alumax Extrusions, Inc., 724 So. 2d 195 (Fla. 1st DCA 1999)].

[6] Injured Worker's Lawyer May Attend Carrier's IME

Nothing in the Florida Statutes or in the Florida Rules of Workers' Compensation Procedure deals with whether an injured worker may have a lawyer present during an independent medical examination. The Florida Rules of Civil Procedure, however, do contain a provision for the examination of injured workers in civil cases, but do not address whether a person may have a lawyer present at such examination [Fla. R. Civ. P. 1.360(a)]. The courts, however, settled the question first in civil cases. Absent a showing of a valid reason why a lawyer should not be there, a lawyer may accompany the person being examined. The courts have found no merit in the argument that by making groundless objections, the lawyer may hinder the examination and by doing so deprive the defendant of the benefit of an informed medical opinion [*see* Toucet v. Big Bend Moving & Storage, 581 So. 2d 952, 953–954 (Fla. 1st DCA 1991); Collins By & Through Burton v. Skinner, 576 So. 2d 1377, 1378 (Fla. 2d DCA 1991)].

The court has now settled the question in workers' compensation cases. A lawyer may observe the examination, monitor any discussions between the physician and the injured worker, and advise the injured worker when necessary and proper. The court's rationale is this: when a doctor selected by the carrier conducts a physical examination of the injured worker, a possibility exists that the doctor will ask improper questions. The injured worker, said the court, should not be expected to evaluate the propriety of every question at his peril. The court brushed aside the carrier's concern that such ex parte discussion with its expert witness is improper and is prohibited by the holding in *Adelman Steel Corp. v. Winter* [*see* McClennan v. American Building Maintenance/CNA, 648 So. 2d 1214, 1215 (Fla. 1st DCA 1995); [3], *above*].

Conversely, carriers may not have their attorney present during the claimant's independent medical examination. If an unsupported assertion that the claimant's attorney will be distracting or disruptive during an independent medical examination cannot support the denial of the claimant's request to have his or her counsel present at the examination, then the same unsupported assertion cannot constitute a ground for permitting an employer/carrier's counsel to attend a claimant's medical examination against that claimant's wishes. The policy reasons behind permitting a workers' compensation claimant's attorney to attend an independent medical examination, i.e., assistance and protection, do not support an employer/carrier's counsel's attendance at an IME based upon a mere allegation that his or her presence is necessary to ensure against disruption. A workers' compensation judge of compensation claims may bar a claimant's attorney from attending an independent medical examination if an employer/carrier makes a showing that a claimant's attorney will disrupt the examination [Chavez v. J&L Drywall, 858 So. 2d 1266, 1269 (Fla. 1st DCA 2003)].

Guide to Claims

[7] Admissible Medical Testimony

Only the following people can offer medical opinions in a proceeding before a judge of compensation claims. They are [§ 440.13(5)(e), Fla. Stat. (1/1/94)]:

1. An Expert Medical Advisor (EMA) appointed by either the judge of compensation claims or the Division of Workers' Compensation.

2. An independent medical examiner.

3. An authorized treating provider.

NOTE: The limitation on admissible medical testimony under § 440.13(5), Fla. Stat., is a substantive amendment that cannot be applied to accidents occurring before the effective date, January 1, 1994 [*see* Southern Bakeries v. Cooper, 659 So. 2d 339 (Fla. 1st DCA 1995)].

[8] Establishing MMI Date or Impairment Rating

The most frequent uses of independent medical examinations are to establish the date the injured worker reached maximum medical improvement or the percentage of permanent impairment. Effective January 1, 1994, the Act partially limits this determination of maximum medical improvement and impairment rating by providing that the party (i.e., the injured worker or the employer/carrier) who selects the treating physician is not entitled to an alternate opinion. Since the carrier usually selects the physician, it will not be entitled to an independent medical examination to decide the maximum medical improvement date or the impairment rating. Under Managed Care, the injured worker can select the primary care provider, but from a list provided by the carrier. An important question for the courts to answer is whether the carrier or the employee selected the treating physician.

When the law allows an independent medical examination, take care in selecting the examiner when used to decide the date of maximum medical improvement or the impairment rating. The Act allows only one such examination. The legislature appears to have anticipated attempts at getting around this measure. The Act prohibits obtaining an additional opinion by requesting an alternate treating physician by either the employee or the carrier. The legislature established a dispute resolution procedure when the issue is the maximum medical improvement date or the impairment rating [§ 440.1925, Fla. Stat. (1/1/94)].

The law allows only one of three classes of physicians to decide the date of maximum medical improvement and any impairment rating. These classes are as follows:

1. The treating physician;

2. An independent medical examiner; or

3. A Division Expert Medical Advisor.

If the injured worker and the carrier still do not agree, a judge of compensation claims must resolve the dispute. An exception to this arises if the carrier's managed care arrangement contains a procedure for resolving these issues.

Judges must first decide the date of maximum medical improvement. Then, based on the evidence, select either the highest or the lowest estimate In other words, the judge has very little discretion. This procedure applies in two situations. The first occurs if the carrier has obtained an independent medical examiner's opinion that differs from the treating physician's opinion. The second situation occurs if the carrier denies a claim based on a disputed maximum medical improvement date or impairment rating [§ 440.1925(3), Fla. Stat. (1/1/94)].

[9] Injured Worker's IME

[a] The Rule

Injured workers have the right to select an independent medical examiner under the same restrictions as carriers [§ 440.13(5), Fla. Stat. (1/1/94)]. For accidents occurring before October 1, 2003, questions still arise, such as who pays for the examination, whether a second opinion counts as an IME, and what happens if the carrier denies the worker's request for an IME?

The court has settled issue of whether an independent medical examination and a second opinion are the same thing. The court has held they are not the same and has explained the distinction. The court noted that it has long recognized that an IME is a means of obtaining expert medical testimony. The Court held that, although an IME may ultimately assist a claimant in securing necessary medical treatment, it is not, in and of itself, a form of medical treatment.

On the other hand, the court noted that occasions may arise in which the "nature of the injury or the process of recovery" renders a second medical opinion medically necessary. The court refused to read § 440.13, Fla. Stat., as evincing a legislative intent to deny a claimant the opportunity to demonstrate the medical necessity of a second opinion. The court was unable to define in advance the universe of possible situations in which a second opinion may be medically necessary. The court did, however, conclude that the claimant's request for a second opinion presents a question of fact, similar to any other request under § 440.13(2)(a), Fla. Stat.

Thus, the court held the JCC must resolve such questions after an evidentiary hearing, in which the claimant will bear the burden of demonstrating entitlement [*see* Lombardi v. S. Wine & Spirits, 890 So. 2d 1128 (Fla. 1st DCA 2004), *rehg. denied*, 2005 Fla. App. LEXIS 1440 (Jan. 14, 2005)].

Such issues are essentially moot for accidents on or after October 1, 2003, because each party has the right to only one independent medical examination and the obligation to pay for it.

[b] Responsibility for Payment

For accidents occurring before October 1, 2003, the Act did not directly obligate the carrier to pay for the injured worker's chosen examination. The court held, however, that the Act plainly provides that injured workers are never under any obligation to pay for medical services. Since the independent medical examination section of the Act was silent about who pays—and the Act required carriers to pay for all medical service—this silence meant that an injured worker could obtain an independent examination at the carrier's expense [*see* Southern Bakeries v. Cooper, 659 So. 2d 339, 340–341 (Fla. 1st DCA 1995)].

Effective October 1, 2003, the Legislature amend the Act to plainly provide that each party must pay for its own independent medical examination. The carrier becomes responsible for the costs of the claimant's independent medical examination only if the claimant prevails in a dispute resolved by the order of a judge of compensation claims or if the carrier provides benefits based on the results of the independent medical examination. The carrier must also pay for the examination if the claimant chooses a physician from the carrier's managed care network [*see* § 440.13(5), Fla. Stat. (10/1/2003); *see also* [2][b], *above*].

[c] IME Outside Managed Care Network

The issue here is whether an injured workers' IME physician must be one in the carrier's managed care network. The answer is, essentially, no. If the injured worker wants an IME to resolve a dispute about indemnity benefits, he or she is entitled to choose a physician outside the network. If the issues in dispute are medical, the injured worker must first exhaust the carrier's grievance procedure. This means that the worker can request a change of physician from the MCC. The worker can also obtain a second opinion from within the carrier's network. If, after this, the worker is still not satisfied with the medical treatment, he or she can file a petition for medical benefits. At that point, the worker can seek an IME outside the carrier's network to resolve the dispute [*see* Wiggins v. B&L Services, Inc., 701 So. 2d 570, 572 (Fla. 1st DCA 1997)].

If the issues in dispute are not related to the medical care provided by the carrier's managed care plan, the managed care language of § 440.134, Fla. Stat. does not apply. Therefore, if the claimant seeks an IME to help decide such issues as the date of maximum medical improvement or the degree of any permanent impairment, none of the managed care provisions, such as the grievance procedure, apply. In such a case, the claimant's entitlement to an IME is controlled by § 440.1925, Fla. Stat. [*see* Johnson v. Orange County Corrections, 786 So. 2d 678 (Fla. 1st DCA 2001)].

Regardless of the issue in dispute, a claimant might be better served by selecting an independent medical examiner from the carrier's managed care network. This is because an exception to the "claimant pay" provision arises if the claimant's choice of an independent medical examiner is in the carrier's network. It that case, the carrier is obligated to pay for the costs of the examination. If the claimant's choice of physician is not in the network, the claimant is responsible for the costs [*see* § 440.134(6), Fla. Stat. (10/1/2003)].

> **NOTE:** *Johnson* provides a clear indication that none of the provisions of § 440.134, Fla. Stat. will apply to employers electing to provide medical care outside of managed care.

[d] Denying IME Request

For accidents occurring before October 1, 2003, if the carrier, directly or through inaction, denies an injured worker's request for an IME, the worker cannot simply get the examination and then ask the court to approve the action after the fact. For example, Marsha Murphy requested an independent medical examination with Dr. McClane. The carrier did not respond, so Murphy's lawyer set up the examination unilaterally. The judge of compensation claims ruled that because a dispute existed about Murphy's disability status, she was entitled to the examination. The judge also held that the carrier's inaction amounted to a denial of her request. In ordering the carrier to pay for the examination, the judge ruled that when a carrier denies a request for an IME, the injured worker has the right to proceed with the examination subject to a judge's determining the reasonableness and medical necessity of the examination. This holding, of course, is incorrect.

§ 440.13(5)(c), Fla. Stat. provides that an "attorney representing a claimant is not authorized to schedule independent medical examinations under this subsection." In such a situation the worker must file a Petition for Benefits, if the issue is not resolved. Thus, the appellate court reversed the judge's order awarding payment for the IME. It also reversed the award of other benefits based on Dr. McClane's inadmissible testimony. The testimony was not admissible because the doctor was not authorized by a carrier or a judge of compensation claims [*see* Lakeland Regional Med. Center v. Murphy, 695 So. 2d 895, 897 (Fla. 1st DCA 1997)].

[e] Entitlement to IME on Controverted Claim

For accidents occurring before October 1, 2003, a claimant is entitled to an IME paid by the carrier even if it has denied the entire claim and has not provided any medical or indemnity benefits. This is true only if the purpose is to determine the cause or etiology of the claimant's condition.

The court held that if the carrier controverts the claim in its entirety, disputing the threshold question of causation, and the E/C has not offered any medical care, the employee is entitled to an IME by an examiner of his or her choice. Additionally, there is no requirement that the examiner be one in the carrier's managed care grievance procedures [*see* Kohout v. Benefit Administrators, 781 So. 2d 1164, 1165 (Fla. 1st DCA 2001)].

For accidents occurring on or after October 1, 2003, this issue is essentially moot. This is because claimants must now pay for their own independent medical examinations. Note, however, that if the claimant prevails on the issue of compensability, the carrier must then pay the costs of the examination [*see* § 440.13(5), Fla. Stat. (10/1/03)].

[10] Division's Procedures Do Not Apply to Requests for IME

Usually, injured workers must first seek the Division's help in resolving a dispute by filing a Request for Assistance before they can file a Petition for Benefits. This is not so, however, when the dispute is about the carrier paying for the injured worker's independent medical examination. If other issues are already properly before the judge, such as entitlement to medical care or indemnity benefits, the injured worker need not start the process over by filing another Request for Assistance if the independent medical

Guide to Claims

examination is designed to resolve the dispute. This is because the statute does not require the second filing of a Request for Assistance, and because there is no explicit language contained in the Act requiring the application of the Employee Assistance Office process to the IME statute [*see* Kimmins Corp. v. Collier, 664 So. 2d 299, 300 (Fla. 1st DCA 1995)].

[11] Physician Deposition and Witness Fees

Originally, the law limited physicians' deposition fees to a flat rate of $200 [§ 440.13(2)(*l*), Fla. Stat.]. Effective January 1, 1994, the maximum increased to $200 per hour [§ 440.13(10), Fla. Stat. (1/1/94)]. Before January 1, 1994, the limitation did not apply if the physician testified as an expert witness and had never directly provided professional services to the injured worker. In other words, such independent experts could charge what the market would bear. With the 1994 amendments, however, the reverse is true. Deposition fees for non-treating physicians are limited to $200 per day. This includes the following:

1. An expert witness who has never provided direct professional services, but has merely reviewed medical records and provided an opinion.
2. A physician who has provided direct services, but for a condition unrelated to the workers' compensation case.

The $200 per day limit applies only to cases where the physician merely reviewed medical records or testified about unrelated conditions. If the physician treated the injured worker for the compensable injury, or performed an independent physical examination, the $200 per hour limit applies. The increased limit applies to an independent medical examination because a physical examination is a professional service related to the compensation case [*see* Purcell v. Padgett, 658 So. 2d 1237, 1238 (Fla. 1st DCA 1995)].

The original (1990) provision is a procedural change. The 1994 provision is also procedural and applies to all depositions taken on or after January 1, 1994, whatever the accident's date. The original provision applies to depositions taken between July 1, 1990, and December 31, 1993. Also, the court held the 1990 provision does not impermissibly encroach on the Supreme Court's rule-making authority under Article V of Florida's Constitution [*see* Paulk v. School Bd. of Palm Beach County, 615 So. 2d 260, 261–262 (Fla. 1st DCA 1993)]. This holding should apply to the 1994 amendment as well.

Both the 1990 and 1994 amendments are attempts to stop perceived abuse by physicians who demanded hundreds of dollars in fees to give depositions. In response to the 1990 measures, several evasive ploys emerged. Some physicians began demanding pre-deposition consultation fees of several hundreds of dollars. Others imposed a strict one-hour time limit. Although the Act now prohibits carriers from paying more then the amounts provided, the Act does not explicitly preclude payment for the pre-deposition conferences held in the past. Whether these tactics violate the spirit of the law remains for the courts to decide.

[12] Consensus Independent Medical Examination

If they agree, the parties may resolve a medical dispute via a "consensus independent medical examination" rather than proceeding to a hearing before a judge of compensation claims. The parties may agree to refer the employee to a physician specializing in the diagnosis and treatment of the condition at issue. The physician's opinions will then be binding upon both parties and will constitute a resolution of the dispute [*see* § 440.13(5)(g), Fla. Stat. (10/1/2003)].

This is essentially binding arbitration with the chosen physician serving as an arbitrator. The statute specifically provides that using this provision will have no effect on the parties' right to a one time independent medical examination. The statute is silent as to who must pay for the examination, so this issue must be worked out between the parties. The statue is also silent as to entitlement to an attorney fee if the claimant prevails. Presumably, a fee would be due.

Guide to Claims

[13] IME Physician as Treating Physician

Before January 1, 1994, the law prohibited the examining physician from providing treatment or subsequent care unless both the carrier and the employee agreed. The pre-1994 statute, § 440.13(2)(b), Fla. Stat., provided that: "The health care provider performing the independent medical examination shall *not* be the health care provider to provide the treatment or follow-up care, unless the carrier or self-insurer and the employee so agree or unless an emergency exists." (*Emphasis added*)

Effective January 1, 1994, the Legislature amend the Act to provide that the treating physician may serve as an independent medical examiner at a party's option. The 1994 statute, § 440.13(5)(a), Fla. Stat., provided that: "The examiner may be a health care provider treating or providing other care to the employee."

Effective October 1, 2003, the Legislature again amended the Act to prohibit the independent examiner from providing follow-up care. The statute provides as follows: "The independent medical examiner may *not* provide follow-up care if such recommendation for care is found to be medically necessary" [§ 440.13(5)(a), Fla. Stat. (10/1/2003)]. (*Emphasis added*)

[14] Distinction Between Independent Medical Examination and Second Opinion

The court has settled the issue of whether an independent medical examination and a second opinion are the same thing. The court has held they are not the same and has explained the distinction. The court noted that it has long recognized that an IME is a means of obtaining expert medical testimony. The Court held that, although an IME may ultimately assist a claimant in securing necessary medical treatment, it is not, in and of itself, a form of medical treatment. On the other hand, the court noted that occasions may arise in which the "nature of the injury or the process of recovery" renders a second opinion medically necessary. The court refused to read § 440.13, Fla. State., as evincing a legislative intent to deny a claimant the opportunity to demonstrate the medical necessity of a second opinion. The court was unable to define in advance the universe of possible situations in which a second opinion may be medically necessary. The court did, however, conclude that the claimant's request for a second opinion presents a question of fact, similar to any other request under § 440.13(2)(a), Fla. Stat. Thus, the court held the JCC must resolve such questions after an evidentiary hearing, in which the claimant will bear the burden of demonstrating entitlement [*see* Lombardi v. S. Wine & Spirits, 890 So. 2d 1128 (Fla. 1st DCA 2004), *rehg. denied*, 2005 Fla. App. LEXIS 1440 (Jan. 14, 2005)].

[15] IME Before Petition Filed

Although the 2003 version of the statute underwent significant change, the enabling language of § 440.13(5)(a), Fla. Stat., is the same. Prior to the amendment, the court held the employer/carrier *does* have a right to an IME before a petition is filed. However, without a petition the JCC has no authority to compel attendance. Instead, the employer/carrier must rely on the provisions of § 440.13(5)(d), Fla. Stat., to compel the claimant to attend. An IME may be scheduled in any dispute concerning over-utilization, medical benefits, compensability, or disability. Unlike § 440.30, Fla. Stat., dealing with the taking of depositions, and unlike § 440.33(1), Fla. Stat., providing for the pre-claim production of documents if the claimant is represented by an attorney, § 440.13(5), Fla. Stat., contains no authority for the JCC to issue an order to compel an IME prior to the filing of a petition for benefits. Nevertheless, the employer/carrier is not without remedy. The court noted that it is abundantly clear that § 440.13(5)(d), Fla. Stat., provides remedies for the employee's failure to appear for a properly scheduled and noticed IME by providing, among other things, that if the employee fails to appear "without good cause" and "fails to advise the physician at least 24 hours before the scheduled date for the examination that he cannot appear," the employee is barred from recovering compensation for any period during which he has refused to submit to such examination. The employee's failure to appear may also result in his or her being required to reimburse the carrier for 50 percent of the physician's cancellation fee. As may be seen from the above review, the IME provisions are largely self-executing, the one exception being that the employee is given the right to "appeal" to the JCC in the event the employer/carrier withholds payments in excess of the authority granted by this section [§ 440.13(5)(d), Fla. Stat.; *see* Karell v. Miami Airport Hilton/ Miami Hilton Corp., 668 So. 2d 227, 229 (Fla. 1st DCA 1996)].

§ 16.17 Practice Parameters and Standards of Care

[1] Practice Parameters

Previously, the law required the Agency for Health Care Administration to produce practice parameters for workers' compensation patients. Effective October 1, 2003, the Legislature repealed existing requirements regarding medical practice parameters and adopted the practice parameters and protocols as adopted by the U.S. Agency for Healthcare Research and Quality in effect on January 1, 2003. All medical service must now be delivered in accordance with these guidelines [*see* § 440.13(15), Fla. Stat. (10/1/2003)].

Practice parameters are guidelines used by medical providers to decide the appropriate course and level of treatment for a given injury. The Act contains no statutory definition, but Florida's Health Care Administration Law defines practice parameters as "strategies for patient management that are developed to assist physicians in clinical decision making."

The primary goal of practice parameters is to contain costs by ensuring consistent delivery of treatment and appropriate use of medical services. Absent extenuating circumstances, treatment rendered within the parameters is considered appropriate and is evidence that the treatment provided was correct under the circumstances. Carriers and the regulatory agencies must use the established practice parameters in evaluating treatment for appropriateness and overutilization [§ 440.13(15), Fla. Stat. (1/1/94)].

[2] Standards of Care

In addition to requiring physicians and other healthcare providers to adhere to the practice parameters and protocols developed by the U.S. Department of Health, Agency for Healthcare Research and Quality, providers must comply with the following standards of care [§ 440.13(16), Fla. Stat. (10/1/2003)]:

A physician cannot use abnormal anatomical findings alone, in the absence of objective relevant medical findings, as an indicator of any of the following:

- Injury or illness; or
- As a justification for providing medical care; or
- As the basis for assigning restrictions; or
- As a foundation for limitations.

At all times during evaluation and treatment, the provider must act on the premise that returning to work is an integral part of the treatment plan. The goal of removing all restrictions and limitations as early as appropriate must be part of the treatment plan on a continuous basis.

The physician must review the assignment of restrictions and limitations with each patient exam. Upon receipt of new information, such as progress reports from physical therapists and other providers, the physician must give consideration to upgrading or removing the restrictions and limitations with each patient exam. This consideration must be based upon the presence or absence of objective relevant medical findings.

Reasonable necessary medical care, in all situations, must include the following

- Utilization of a high intensity, short duration treatment approach that focuses on early activation and restoration of function whenever possible.
- Include reassessment of the treatment plans, regimes, therapies, prescriptions, and functional limitations or restrictions prescribed by the provider every 30 days.
- Be focused on treatment of the individual employee's specific clinical dysfunction or status and shall not be based upon nondescript diagnostic labels.

All treatment must be inherently scientifically logical and the evaluation or treatment procedure must match the documented physiologic and clinical problem. Treatment must match the type, intensity, and duration of service required by the problem identified.

If physicians or other health care providers fail to comply with these requirements, the law will consider them to be in violation of Chapter 400 Florida Statutes, subjecting them to the penalties provided for in § 440.525.

§ 16.18 Expert Medical Advisor (EMA)

[1] The Rule

The Act requires the Agency for Health Care Administration to certify selected physicians as Expert Medical Advisors. This requirement is a rewrite of the 1990 "Super Doc" provision, but this time with razor sharp teeth [§ 440.13(9), Fla. Stat. (1/1/94)]. The Agency can employ these advisors directly, or it may certify physicians in private practice. The EMAs are the medical experts who will provide peer review or medical consultation to the Agency and to the judges of compensation claims to resolve disagreement between and among physicians. Note carefully, however, that these physicians are much more than mere advisors. Their purpose is to resolve disagreement on medical issues.

[2] Certification as EMA

Before the Agency will certify a physician as an Expert Medical Advisor, the physician must file a formal application and meet specific requirements. Besides being board certified, or at least board eligible, physicians must show experience in workers' compensation cases. For example, applicants must demonstrate expertise in the assignment of permanent impairment ratings and in performing independent medical examinations [Fla. Admin. Code R. 59A-30.004(3) (10/11/06)].

[3] EMA's Opinion Presumed Correct

One of the teeth in this statute provides a legal presumption that the EMA's opinion is correct. The judges of compensation claims must accept the EMA's opinion, unless a party presents clear and convincing evidence to the contrary. This may not be as difficult as it first appears [*see* [5], *below*].

[4] EMA Resolution Required

With little question, the legislature enacted this provision to reduce litigation. Rather than having medical opinion disputes resolved by a judge, such disagreement is to be resolved by an Expert Medical Advisor. Another tooth in the statute is that the judges have little, if any, discretion in ordering an EMA evaluation. The statute imposes a duty, not only on the parties, but also on the judge of compensation claims to have medical disagreements resolved by an EMA. If a material disagreement arises between health care providers, the judge must, even upon his or her own motion, appoint an EMA to resolve the issue. Even without a request from the parties, the judge must appoint an EMA if the required disagreement in physicians' opinions is apparent only at the time of the pretrial hearing. This is also true even if the disagreement becomes apparent only after the merits hearing has begun. The statutes do not impose any time restrictions on requesting an EMA evaluation; however, such requests must be made reasonably soon after becoming aware of the disagreement. This suggests that the judge can reject a request for an EMA evaluation if not made timely, but the judge's degree of discretion is not clear [*see* Palm

Springs General Hosp. v. Cabrera, 698 So. 2d 1352, 1354 (Fla. 1st DCA 1997); *see also* Claims Management, Inc. v. Lake, 717 So. 2d 140, 141 (Fla. 1st DCA 1998) (overturning award because JCC refused carrier's request for expert medical evaluation)].

The court has held that § 440.13(9)(c), Fla. Stat. (1997) is mandatory and binding on the judge of compensation claims and that the statutory language provides no support for the view that the statute is directory only, or that evaluation by expert medical advisors is to be left to the discretion of the judge of compensation claims. The legislature's intent in enacting § 440.13(9)(c), Fla. Stat., was to create a mechanism by which an independent medical expert would offer assistance to the judge of compensation claims when he or she is faced with conflicting medical evidence from the parties' experts. The court also noted that it is apparent that the legislature intended for the provisions of § 440.13(9)(c), Fla. Stat., to be mandatory.

The court said that there is nothing in the plain language of the statute to suggest that a judge of compensation claims need make only one attempt to appoint an expert medical advisor in order to satisfy its mandate. When the only certified expert medical advisor in an area has declined appointment, that area of expertise is not represented among the available expert medical advisors [*see* Fla. Admin. Code R. 59A-30.006(1)], and pursuant to Fla. Admin. Code R. 59A-30.006, the Florida Agency for Health Care Administration has the authority to select a qualified individual to serve as a temporary expert medical advisor [Fla. Admin. Code R. 59A-30.006(1), (3)]. The court held that the clear intent of § 440.13(9)(c), Fla. Stat., is to require participation of an expert medical advisor in *every case* when a disagreement exists between healthcare providers [Broward Children's Ctr., Inc. v. Hall, 859 So. 2d 623, 628 (Fla. 1st DCA 2003)].

The judges, however, are not required to order an EMA evaluation *sua sponte* in every case. On the contrary, failure to order an EMA evaluation in the absence of a timely request by a party is not a fundamental error. The lawyers for the parties have an obligation to diligently defend their clients. It is an abrogation of that duty to raise this issue for the first time on appeal [*see* Arvida River Hills Club v. Van Slyke, 728 So. 2d 1213, 1214 (Fla. 1st DCA 1999)].

[5] Authority and Jurisdiction

Essentially, under the *Cabrera* decision [*see* [4], *above*], the judges seem to no longer have the authority to resolve disagreement between medical providers. The judge's role is to decide if clear and convincing evidence exists to overcome the presumption that the EMA's opinion is correct, only if, of course, one of the parties is willing to try to overcome this presumption. The degree of evidence necessary to meet the "clear and convincing" standard is not clear. Generally, this standard of evidence is beyond a mere preponderance, but below that of "beyond a reasonable doubt." In other words, this standard is less than that required in criminal cases, but more than that required in civil cases. EMAs are to resolve situations in which [§ 440.13(9)(c), Fla. Stat. (1/1/94)]:

1. Doctors disagree on medical evidence supporting the employee's complaints.
2. Doctors disagree on the need for additional treatment.
3. Doctors disagree that the employee is able to return to work.

Note that this list is not inclusive and there may be other disagreements which call for an EMA.

Recall that the judge of compensation claims has the authority to disregard the opinion of an EMA if there is clear and convincing evidence to the contrary. For example, the judge rejected an EMA's opinion choosing instead to accept the opinions of two treating physicians based in part on their greater expertise and familiarity with the claimant's condition. The judge's decision was affirmed on appeal. The court noted that such determinations will not be disturbed on appeal so long as there is evidence in the record that the judge could reasonably find to be clear and convincing. Unfortunately, the court did not provide any guidance in defining what constitutes clear and convincing evidence. [*see* Jacaranda Manor & Crawford & Co. v. Randolph, 755 So. 2d 781, 782 (Fla. 1st DCA 2000)].

Note, however, that although the court's function is not to conduct a de novo proceeding, the appellate court does have to decide whether there was a reasonable basis for rejecting an EMA's opinion as clearly and convincingly disproven [*see* Walgreen Co. v. Carver, 770 So. 2d 172, 175 (Fla. 1st DCA 2000)].

Apparently, offering any reason for rejecting the EMA's opinion will be sufficient. The court has held that in workers' compensation cases the findings of a Judge of Compensation Claims (JCC) must be sustained if supported by *any view* of the evidence and its permissible inferences. The JCC, as the trier of fact, has the right to determine the credibility of witnesses, including a claimant. It is also within the province of the JCC to determine whether the claimant's medical history is credible or not, and the JCC may give greater weight to lay testimony than to scientific opinions of experts. Here, the EMA opined that the claimant's compensable injury was the major contributing cause of the claimant's mental condition. The judge of compensation claims rejected that opinion because he simply did not believe the claimant, and denied benefits. The appellate court affirmed. In a dissenting opinion, Judge Evrin opined that the court's affirmance of the JCC's rejection effectually eviscerates the EMA process and ignores a body of case law this court has developed in defining the respective roles of EMA's and JCC's in resolving conflicting medical opinions [Prather v. Process Sys., 867 So. 2d 479, 482 (Fla. 1st DCA 2004) (as corrected March 4, 2004)].

Although any reason might suffice for rejecting the EMA's opinion, competent substantial evidence must exist to support the reason given. A JCC's rejection of the opinion of an EMA will not be disturbed on appeal when it is based on competent and substantial evidence, which the JCC could reasonably find clear and convincing. Contradiction between the EMA and one of the disagreeing physicians, however, is not, by itself, a reasonable basis for the JCC to reject the EMA's opinion since, under § 440.13(9), Fla. Stat. (2001), the EMA is appointed with the expectation that the EMA's testimony will contradict the record testimony of one of the health care providers.

[6] Assigning an EMA

If any of the circumstances in set forth in [5], *above,* exist, the Agency may, and the judge of compensation claims shall, order an evaluation by an EMA. Within 15 days after receipt of a written request, the judge must order the evaluation. Once ordered, the Agency will assign an EMA, on a rotating basis. If an EMA with the expertise required is not available, the Agency will select a non certified physician based on the recommendation of a state or national organization. These temporary EMAs serve only on the specific case assigned.

[7] EMA Fees

[a] Fee Limitations and Timely Payment

The rules allow EMA's to charge up to $200 per hour and up to $1,600 per case. In addition, they may charge for any reasonable travel expenses. The party responsible for payment must make payment within 45 days after receipt of the bill [*see* Fla. Admin. Code R. 59A-30.007].

[b] Responsibility for Payment: Accident Dates Through September 30, 2003

For accident dates through September 30, 2003, the carrier is responsible for payment, regardless of who requests the examination. Carriers must pay the bill within 45 days after receipt of the EMA's evaluation [*see* § 440.13(9), Fla. Stat. (1/1/1994); Fla. Admin. Code R. 59A-30.007 (10/11/06)].

[c] Responsibility for Payment: Accident Dates On or After October 1, 2003

For accidents occurring on or after October 1, 2003, responsibility for paying the EMA's fees depends on the circumstances, as follows [§ 440.13(9)(f), Fla. Stat. (10/1/2003)]:

- If the employee requests the examination, he or she is responsible for payment.
- If the carrier requests the examination, the carrier is responsible for payment.
- If the judge of compensation claims orders the examination upon his or her own motion, the carrier is responsible for payment.
- If the employee prevails in a dispute based on the EMA's findings as determined by the judge of compensation claims' order, the carrier is responsible for payment

[d] Penalty for Late Payment of EMA Fee

If the carrier does not pay the bill timely, it is subject to a fine of up to $500 assessed by the Division [§ 440.13(9)(f), Fla. Stat. (1/1/1994)]. The administrative rules provide that the term "timely" means the carrier must pay the EMA's bill within 45 days after receipt. The fine increases, depending on the degree of lateness. For up to five days late, the fine is $200. If the payment is six through ten days late, the fine is $400. For payments more than 10 days late, the maximum fine of $500 applies [*see* Fla. Admin. Code R. 59A-30.007 (10/11/06)].

There is no indication in the statutes or rules that a claimant is subject to fines for late payment. The 2003 version of the statute continues to provide that the $500 penalty applies to carriers only.

[e] Time for Submitting EMA Report

Effective October 1, 2003, the legislature shortened the deadline for submission of the

EMA's report to ACHA or to the judge of compensation claims from 45 days to 15 days.

> **SPECIAL ALERT:** Injured workers who fail to cooperate with the EMA forfeit all rights to compensation until they comply fully [§ 440.13(9)(c), Fla. Stat. (1/1/94)].

[8] Ex Parte Communication With an EMA

The law is now clear that the parties have the right to conduct ex parte conferences with treating and examining physicians [*see* § 16.15]. This does not, however, apply to expert medical advisors. The EMA is, essentially, the state's expert witness appointed to give a definitive opinion about the claimant's injuries in the event of disagreement between health care providers. As such, the EMA must remain completely neutral. Because the EMS's opinion is nearly conclusive, impartiality is essential and the expert chosen must avoid even the appearance of impropriety. Therefore, ex parte discussions with an EMA are not appropriate [*see* Pierre v. Handi Van, Inc., 717 So. 2d 1115, 1117 (Fla 1st DCA 1998)].

[9] Failure to Cooperate With EMA

A claimant who fails to cooperate with the EMA is subject to forfeiture of benefits. For example, the Judge of Compensation Claims ordered the claimant's examination by an expert medical advisor (EMA) due to a conflict in the opinions of the treating physician and the independent medical examiner regarding whether the claimant was permanently impaired. The claimant failed to timely schedule the appointment with the EMA, and when the JCC scheduled it for him, his attorney informed the EMA that the claimant was out of the country and would not likely return for several months. The JCC's term of office was due to terminate prior to the time the claimant would be available for the EMA examination. The judge re-evaluated the evidence and found that there was no conflict in the doctors' opinions. Over the claimant's objection, she decided the case without benefit of the EMA's examination. The court held that this constituted reversible error. The court has held previously that if there is conflict in the expert testimony with regard to the degree of permanent impairment, the JCC *must* order examination by an EMA, even if neither party requests an EMA [*see* Palm Springs Gen. Hosp. v. Cabrera, 698 So. 2d 1352, 1356 (Fla. 1st DCA 1997)]. Here, the court held that § 440.13(9)(c), Fla. Stat. (Supp. 1996) provides that the sanction for a claimant's failure to cooperate with the EMA evaluation order is forfeiture of entitlement to compensation during the period of failure to cooperate, not withdrawal of the EMA order. The JCC's impending unavailability cannot be considered a justification for circumventing the mandatory provisions of this statute. The JCC's finding that there was no conflict in the medical testimony was unsupported by the record, which indicated clear disagreement regarding the fact of permanent impairment [Martinez v. HealthSouth Doctor's Hosp., 817 So. 2d 1080, 1081 (Fla. 1st DCA 2002)].

§ 16.19 Co-Payments

[1] Co-Payment Applies Only After MMI

This co-payment provision does not apply until the injured worker has achieved maximum medical improvement for all conditions. Also, the co-payment never applies to emergency treatment, despite whether the injured worker has reached maximum medical improvement. After the injured worker has reached MMI for all conditions, carriers should first apply all applicable fee schedules and then simply deduct an additional $10 from the payment. Although other sections of the Act prohibit health care providers from billing injured workers for services, this particular statute is an exception. Providers are allowed to collect the deductible from the injured worker [§ 440.13(14)(c), Fla. Stat. (1/1/94)].

[2] Effect of New MMI Date

What happens if the injured worker has a medical relapse followed by a new date of maximum medical improvement? Must the carrier refund co-payments the employee made between the first and subsequent MMI dates? No certainty exists here because the statutes do not provide the answer and this issue has not undergone judicial review. The first step should be to decide if the first declaration of maximum medical improvement was made properly, based on all information available at the time. If physicians declare they made a mistake, then no actual MMI existed. If so, carriers should reimburse the injured worker. If, however, the first MMI declaration was fairly made, reimbursement does not appear appropriate. As stated, no cases on point exist. Some precedent exists, however, on whether a new MMI date has any effect upon the statute of limitations. For example, if the limitations period expires following the date of maximum medical improvement, a new MMI date cannot revive the claim [*see* American Airlines v. Miller, 575 So. 2d 669, 670 (Fla. 1st DCA 1990)].

Neither the Act nor case law provides for reimbursing an employee for co-payment because of a subsequent MMI date. Until we have legislative or judicial guidance, carriers should consider each case based on the individual circumstances. In most cases the sum of the $10 co-payments made will be small.

CHAPTER 17

REHABILITATION BENEFITS

Guide to Claims

SYNOPSIS

§ 17.01 Entitlement to Rehabilitation

When the legislature created the wage loss concept in 1979, it recognized the critical importance of returning an injured worker to full employment. To help ensure that injured workers would return to work, the legislature enacted a provision requiring carriers to provide vocational rehabilitation services. Before January 1, 1994, the law entitled qualified injured workers to training and education. This entitlement applied based on the mere appearance that the injury would prevent the employee from earning pre-injury wages. Note that the law does not require a permanent impairment as a prerequisite for entitlement to rehabilitation benefits [*see* Walker v. New Fern Restorium, 409 So. 2d 1201, 1204–1205 (Fla. 1st DCA 1982)].

Originally, the carrier provided training and education at its own expense. Today, the Department of Education provides and pays for this benefit [§ 440.491, Fla. Stat. (7/1/2002)]. Beginning January 1, 1994, the law entitled a qualified injured worker to retraining only upon reaching maximum medical improvement. Note, however, that the law still does not require permanent impairment. With the 1994 amendments, the Department apparently will not begin the assessment and counseling process until the injured worker reaches maximum medical improvement [§ 440.491(6)(b), Fla. Stat. (7/1/97) (note: the rehabilitation section of the Act is § 440.491, Fla. Stat. (7/1/97))].

Effective October 1, 2003, an injured worker is not entitled to retraining benefits if he or she able to earn at least 80 percent of the compensation rate. Because the statute refers to "*the* compensation rate," it is not clear if it refers to the maximum rate generally or the workers' specific rate. Presumably, the intent is to compare the injured worker's earning ability against his or her compensation rate. Since the department determines who is eligible for retraining, this is an issue that should be addressed by administrative rule.

Additionally, if the department determines that vocational training is appropriate, and the claimant refuses to participate, the claimant forfeits any additional training and education benefits as well as any additional payments for lost wages [§ 440.491(6)(b), Fla. Stat. (10/1/2003)].

For a general discussion of rehabilitation and theory, see Larson's Workers' Compensation, Desk Edition, Ch. 96, § 96.02 (Matthew Bender).

§ 17.02 Disability Benefits During Retraining

[1] Jurisdiction to Award Benefits

Before January 1, 1994, the judges of compensation claims decided entitlement to vocational rehabilitation, usually based on a recommendation from the Division of Workers' Compensation. Since that date, the Division has had exclusive jurisdiction to decide entitlement to vocational benefits. Put another way, the 1994 Act ended the role that judges of compensation claims played in deciding entitlement to training and education. If the carrier disagrees with the Division's decision to award retraining benefits, the carrier cannot raise the issue before a judge of compensation claims. Instead, the carrier must seek a section 120.57 hearing under the Administrative Procedures Act (APA). If the Division approves retraining for an injured worker, the carrier must pay temporary total disability benefits for 26 weeks. Note that paying temporary total disability benefits during this period is mandatory [§ 440.491(6)(b), Fla. Stat. (7/1/97); *see* Ring Power Corp. v. Campbell, 697 So. 2d 203, 204–205 (Fla. 1st DCA 1997); *see also* Workman v. Joe Brown Aluminum, 816 So. 2d 1182, 1184–1185 (Fla. 1st DCA 2002)].

Effective July 1, 2002, responsibility for overseeing training and education was transferred to the Department of Education.

The first 26 weeks are virtually automatic. If the training program will exceed 26 weeks, the Department can order an extension or a second 26-week period. Carriers can protest the additional 26-week award to the judge of compensation claims, but only for the additional compensation. Again, defending the additional 26 weeks of training itself must be done via an administrative hearing under section 120 of the APA. Carriers can voluntarily provide an extension without judicial approval [*see* Ring Power Corp. v. Campbell, 697 So. 2d 203, 205 (Fla. 1st DCA 1997)].

[2] When Benefits Begin

Injured workers enrolled in vocational rehabilitation programs are entitled to receive temporary total disability benefits. This is in spite of having reached maximum medical improvement from a medical standpoint. Further, these workers need not use any of their eligibility for wage loss benefits during the training program [*see* Roberson v. Winn Dixie Stores, Inc., 669 So. 2d 294, 297 (Fla. 1st DCA 1996)].

Eligibility begins during counseling and program development necessary for the rehabilitation process, not when the actual classroom program begins. In other words, temporary disability benefits begin when the injured worker begins his or her efforts to enroll in a training program. This does not mean, however, that the injured worker is eligible for temporary total disability benefits in the entire interim before enrollment [*see* Cenvill Communities, Inc. v. Brown, 409 So. 2d 1147, 1148–1149 (Fla. 1st DCA 1982)].

SPECIAL ALERT: The court has held that the 104-week limit on collecting temporary total disability and temporary partial disability benefits does not apply to rehabilitation temporary total disability benefits. Rehabilitation temporary total disability benefits are in addition to the 104-weeks of disability allowed before maximum medical improvement [*see* Bober v. Bush Air Conditioning, 826 So. 2d 487 (Fla. 1st DCA 2002)].

Effective October 1, 2003, the Legislature appears to have overruled the court by amending the Act to provide that rehabilitation temporary total disability benefits are not in addition to the 104-week limitation on temporary disability benefits specified in § 440.15, Fla. Stat. [§ 440.491(6)(b), Fla. Stat. (10/1/2003)]. Since this amendment changes rights and responsibilities, it is probably a substantive amendment that

Guide to Claims

applies to accident dates occurring only on or after the effective date.

§ 17.03 Training and Education

Beginning October 1, 1989, responsibility for providing training and education transferred from the insurance carriers to the Division of Workers' Compensation. This is a substantive amendment and applies only to accidents occurring on or after October 1, 1989 [*see* Ardmore Farms v. Wallace, 571 So. 2d 47, 48 (Fla. 1st DCA 1990) (citing § 440.49, Fla. Stat.)]. Carriers, therefore, remain liable for vocational rehabilitation for accidents occurring before October 1, 1989. For accidents occurring on or after that date, the Division of Workers' Compensation pays the costs of training and education from its administrative trust fund. Effective July 1, 2002, the legislature transferred this responsibility to the Department of Education. This also includes housing near the school facility, food, and travel expenses. The carrier, however, remains liable for temporary total disability benefits during retraining as discussed in § 17.02[2].

Nothing prevents a carrier from voluntarily providing retraining. On the other hand, the judge of compensation claims may not compel a carrier to do so. A carrier has no responsibility to offer rehabilitation benefits to an injured worker if the accident occurred on or after October 1, 1989. For example, a judge of compensation claims awarded temporary partial wage loss benefits to Eduardo Lalu. The judge did so only because the carrier failed to offer the injured worker any type of rehabilitation or retraining to help him find work [*see* Hyatt Hotel v. Lalu, 605 So. 2d 965, 966 (Fla. 1st DCA 1992)]. This ruling was improper because the carrier had no such responsibility in this case.

§ 17.04 Formal Notification Required

[1] When Required

If an injured employee remains unemployed 180 days after the date of accident and is receiving compensation, the carrier most notify the injured employee in writing within 190 days of the date of accident of the availability of a Department screening. The written notice must contain the following language [Fla. Admin. Code R. 6A-22.004 (3/1/2005)]:

> Your continuing disability indicates you may be unable to perform the duties of the job held at the time of your work-related injury. If this is correct and you are unable to return to work in any capacity with your current employer or find other employment which would allow you to earn your pre-injury wages, you may be eligible for a screening for reemployment services from the State of Florida, Department of Education. Upon receipt of your request, the Department will assess your case to determine what services are necessary to return you to suitable gainful employment. Reemployment services that you may be eligible for include job seeking skills training, counseling, referrals to other agencies, job market information, transferable skills analysis, job development, job placement, job analysis, job modification, vocational testing, vocational evaluation, on-the-job training, or formal training and education. Additionally, if you have reached maximum medical improvement, the carrier shall pay temporary total disability benefits for a period up

to 26 weeks upon beginning a Department approved retraining program or the carrier may elect to pay temporary partial disability/wage loss benefits if you earn wages as the result of on-the-job training or work while enrolled in a program. An additional 26 weeks may be approved if deemed necessary by the judge of compensation claims. To request a screening, contact your local state Workers' Compensation Bureau of Rehabilitation and Medical Services District Office or the Central Office in Tallahassee at 850-488-3431 and ask to speak with a staff person in the Reemployment Services Section of the Bureau of Rehabilitation and Medical Services.

The carrier must send a copy of this notification to the Bureau of Rehabilitation and Reemployment Services, Department of Education, 101A Forrest Building, 2728 Centerview Drive, Tallahassee, Florida 32399-0664, within 10 days of mailing the notification to the injured employee.

[2] Failure to Comply

No specific penalty applies for failure to comply with this requirement other than certification to the Department of Insurance for poor carrier practices. Perhaps this is enough, however, since the Department has the power to revoke the carrier's and the adjuster's licenses.

§ 17.05 Starting Vocational Rehabilitation

[1] Assignment of Evaluator

For an injured worker to obtain retraining, the carrier or the employee must file a request with the Department. Within 10 days after receiving the request, the Department will assign an evaluator. An exception arises if the injured worker and the employer have already agreed on an evaluator. The evaluator's job is to decide if training and education is appropriate. Once assigned, the evaluator has 30 days to submit the results to the Department, employer, and employee [*see* § 440.491(6), Fla. Stat. (7/1/97)].

[2] Reemployment Status Reviews

Carriers who have not voluntarily provided medical care coordination services must report their opinion to the Department on whether the injured worker is likely to return to work. The first report is due when the employee has been unemployed for 60 days. After that, the carrier must report every 90 days while the injured worker is receiving indemnity benefits and remains unemployed [§ 440.491(3)(a), Fla. Stat. (7/1/97)]. Remember that this reporting requirement does not apply if the carrier is voluntarily providing medical care coordination services.

[3] Reemployment Assessments

[a] Generally

Although not required, the Act allows and encourages carriers to obtain a reemployment assessment. Carriers should do so when the injured worker appears unlikely to return to work, is underemployed, or has suffered a catastrophic or serious injury [§ 440.491(4), Fla. Stat. (7/1/97)]. In other words, the statute allows carriers to require an injured worker to undergo a reemployment assessment if it considers one appropriate. A qualified rehabilitation provider must conduct all such assessments. A "qualified" provider is one approved by the Department.

> **SPECIAL ALERT:** This is a procedural amendment and therefore applies to all accident dates [*see* Lockheed Space Operations v. Langworthy, 686 So. 2d 665, 666–667 (Fla. 1st DCA 1996)].

[b] Provider Selection

The carrier can choose the assessment provider if it provided voluntary medical care coordination and reemployment services within 60 days after the accident. The provider, however, must be one the Department has approved. If the carrier has not provided voluntary services, and the assessment takes place more than 60 days after the accident, the assessment provider cannot provide the services recommended [*see* § 440.491(4), Fla. Stat. (7/1/97)].

At its option, the carrier can refer the injured worker to the Department. To do so, the carrier must file a Request for Screening (DWC-23) along with the reemployment assessment and documented work restrictions.

[c] Reemployment Assessment Defined

A reemployment assessment is a comprehensive review of the medical diagnosis, treatment, and prognosis [§ 440.491(a)(d), Fla. Stat.; § 440.491(4), Fla. Stat. (7/1/97)]. It includes conferences with the employer, the physician, and the injured worker. Based on this reemployment assessment, the rehabilitation specialist must make a recommendation on a cost-effective, physical and vocational rehabilitation plan to help the employee return to work. Rehabilitation providers must submit this report to the carrier within 30 days after the assessment is complete. Carriers must inform the injured worker if the report recommends that the worker should receive medical care coordination or reemployment services. The injured worker then has 15 days to accept these services. If the injured worker accepts, the carrier must make the assignment to a rehabilitation provider within 15 days after acceptance. The provider, of course, must be a qualified one, but regardless may not be the provider that recommended the services in the assessment. Assuming the carrier is willing to provide the service, and the injured worker accepts, the rehabilitation provider's first step is to develop a reemployment plan. The provider must submit the plan to both the carrier and the injured worker for approval.

Carriers will find this provision useful in cases involving potential permanent total disability. This is because the judge of compensation claims cannot adjudicate an injured worker as permanently and totally disabled, until or unless the carrier is given the opportunity to provide a reemployment assessment [§ 440.491(9), Fla. Stat. (7/1/97)].

[d] Closing Cases

If the injured worker will not cooperate, or the injured worker's lawyer prohibits the service, the rehabilitation provider should close the case by sending a Reemployment Services Reporting Form (DWC-21) to the carrier [Fla. Admin. Code R. 6A-22.010(6)(c) (6/26/2001)].

§ 17.06 Limits on Rehabilitation Services

[1] Reemployment Services

Reemployment services include vocational counseling, job-seeking skills training, ergonomic job analysis, transferable skills analysis, selective job placement, and labor-market surveys. It also includes arranging training, education, and on-the-job vocational training. What happens if the rehabilitation provider decides that the injured worker requires retraining to return to work? Reemployment services must stop, and the carrier must refer the injured worker to the Department.

If retraining is not recommended, then rehabilitation efforts must stop when the following events occur: (1) the injured worker has not returned to work within 180 days; or (2) the injured worker receives $2,500 worth of reemployment services. At this point the carrier must refer the injured worker to the Department for a vocational evaluation.

Although the Act strongly encourages carriers to provide these services, it also adds discouragement to do so. Specifically, carriers cannot treat the cost of the assessment, or the $2,500 worth of reemployment services, as loss adjustment expenses for rate making purposes [§ 440.491(5)(b), Fla. Stat. (7/1/97)].

[2] Medical Care Coordination

Medical care coordination means coordinating such services as medical, psychiatric, or therapeutic treatment. This also includes health training to the employee and family, and monitoring the employee's recovery. The legislative purpose is to reduce the disability period and to assure that carriers provide timely, logical, and cost-effective medical treatment. The Division can monitor and regulate this voluntary service by requiring periodic reports [§ 440.491(5)(c), Fla. Stat. (7/1/97)].

While carriers may not include payments for reemployment services as expenses for rate making, certain medical coordination services can be included. For rate making purposes, voluntary services for the following injuries are considered medical benefits:

1. Traumatic brain injury
2. Spinal cord injury
3. Amputation
4. Loss of an eye
5. Burns involving five percent or more of the body

[3] Screening Process and Approval Requirements

[a] Screening Process

The screening process consists of the following [Fla. Admin. Code. R. 6A-22.006(2)]:

(a) A review of all available medical and vocational documentation relevant to the compensable injury to determine whether the injured employee is able to perform the duties of the pre-injury occupation; and

(b) A review of the documentation which supports the payment of temporary partial disability and wage loss benefits to determine the injured employee's inability to obtain suitable gainful employment because of his or her injury; and

(c) An interview with the injured employee.

> **NOTE:** The Department will not provide a vocational evaluation or any reemployment services when Form DWC-23 is received by the Department more than one year from the date of last payment of indemnity benefits or the furnishing of remedial treatment, care, or attendance from the employer or carrier [Fla. Admin. Code R. 6A-22.006(5)].

[b] Approval Requirements

The rules provide that the Department will not approve a training program if any of the following is true [Fla. Admin. Code R. 6A-22.006(6), (7)]:

1. The claimant has filed a claim for permanent total disability benefits under § 440.15(1), Fla. Stat., which the carrier has denied, in which case the Department will take no action until such time as the Judge of Compensation Claims adjudicates the injured employee's claim; or
2. The injured employee's medical condition is unresolved or unstable; or
3. The injured employee has reached maximum medical improvement and returned to and maintained suitable gainful employment for at least 90 calendar days; or
4. The injured employee refuses to accept reemployment services from the Department; or
5. The claimant has returned to suitable gainful employment as a result of placement services provided by the Department; or
6. The claimant has no documented permanent physical restrictions related to the injury; or
7. The claimant has transferable skills that would allow return to work in suitable gainful employment; or
8. The claimant was terminated by the employer for good cause unrelated to the injury or any restrictions or limitations resulting therefrom; or
9. The claimant terminated suitable gainful employment for reasons unrelated to the injury.

> **NOTE:** "Good cause" is termination resulting from employee conduct [Fla. Admin. Code R. 6A-22.001(6)]:

(a) Evincing such willful or wanton disregard of an employer's interests as is found in deliberate violation or disregard of standards of behavior which the employer has the right to expect of his or her employee; or

(b) Carelessness or negligence of such a degree or recurrence as to manifest culpability, wrongful intent, or evil design, or to show an intentional and substantial disregard of an employer's interests or of the employee's duties and obligations to his or her employer.

Although the extent of a claimant's formal education, such as having a high school diploma, might be a factor for some training programs, (such as college level courses), it is not a requirement generally. Sometimes, such retraining might be no more formal than placing a claimant in an on-the-job training program.

SPECIAL NOTE: Effective with accidents occurring on or after October 1, 2003, rehabilitation and retraining temporary total disability benefits are included as part of the 104-week maximum entitlement to temporary disability benefits [§ 440.491(6)(b), Fla. Stat. (10/1/03)].

§ 17.07 Tactical Considerations

An employer or carrier can provide the benefits mentioned above at its own expense if it chooses to do so. Often, providing training and education directly will favorably affect the outcome of a case. Also, voluntarily providing medical management, job placement, job search help, and the like will frequently reduce an employer's exposure. What is most important is that such activity will enhance a motivated employee's return-to-work potential. Remember, however, that retraining and medical management services are purely voluntary. In one case, the court reversed the JCC's order requiring the carrier to hire a rehabilitation service, and found that a judge of compensation claims has no authority to order a carrier to pay for the services of a standard rehabilitation provider [*see* K-9 of Orlando v. Davenport, 605 So. 2d 587, 588 (Fla. 1st DCA 1992)].

Whether carriers use the services of staff rehabilitation specialists or outside providers, adjusters should be sure to involve them early in serious injury cases. Rehabilitation and medical management services do not come cheaply. Often, however, adjusters will find that the cost of such services more than offset the savings realized from an early return to work. Remember that the longer a person remains away from work due to a disability, the less likely it is that the person will return to work. In any case likely to involve either total disability lasting eight weeks or more or the likelihood of permanent impairment, adjusters should consider placing the case in the hands of an expert case management specialist.

§ 17.08 The Big Loss

[1] Emotional Effect of Disability

Disability has a significant impact upon a patient's self image, including physical appearance, bodily sensations, and beliefs and emotions about the patient's own body. The case manager's first goal should be to note the factors influencing the injured worker's behavior and to help the injured worker feel worthwhile. A desk-bound claims adjuster can easily overlook the human side of workers' compensation cases. This is probably the greatest single cause of "big cases going bad."

In cases of serious injury, a person may go through several phases. First comes a period of confusion, disorganization, and denial. A seriously injured worker must often cope with an almost immediate state of conflict. The injury forces the person to cope with problems of forced dependence, loss of self-esteem, and feeling of threat to self and family integrity.

[2] Emotional Stages

Typically, a newly disabled worker employs mechanisms of denial by refusing to accept the new physical limitations. Injured workers may have false hopes for a speedy and complete recovery. The person is likely to become self-centered and childlike, and may try to remain normal and non-disabled. Denial is a mechanism used by those who have placed great value on strength and attractive appearance.

Following this, a period of depression and grief often follows. A period of mourning for a lost function or body part is also common. Body image distortions occur and depression often sets in due to sensory deprivation and restricted environmental stimulation. Limited mobility may produce behavioral disruptions.

A final stage may involve a redirection of energies into channels concerning physical functioning. Some injured workers will have a revised body image and may change their former picture of themselves, resulting in a reorientation of values. The injured worker may eventually accept a degree of dependency and begin to create a self-image as a permanently disabled person.

Prompt activity by a case manager will help the injured worker accept limitations imposed by disability. A key to the outcome of the case is to help the injured worker begin to develop realistic goals for the future. Alert case managers will constantly talk with the injured worker concerning return to work. The goal is to prevent premature thoughts of permanent disability and inability to work.

[3] Case Manager's Role

Look for a case manager who is also a registered nurse trained in medical case management. Also be certain the Department has authorized the person to provide these services. Whether we call the service rehabilitation, case management, or medical coordination, the provider must be on the Department's approved list.

Adjusters should seek the specialist's counsel in coordinating the injured worker's course of medical care. Adjusters should look to the specialist for recommendations about an appropriate physician or to arrange examinations. Specialists must have all current medical information, including information about prescription drugs. Often, two or more physicians may prescribe drugs without any knowledge of the other prescribing physicians.

When considering reserves on a case, a constant flow of information from the medical case manager is essential. Adjusters should insist on reports at least every 30 days. The specialist should give the adjuster constantly updated information on the injured worker's medical and return-to-work prognosis.

The adjuster must make it clear to both the specialist and the injured worker that the specialist has no authority to order the commencement or suspension of benefits. This is a claim adjuster's function, and the medical manager must concentrate on appropriate medical care and the return to gainful employment. During a claim, problems may arise about paying benefits. The case manager may be the only person representing the carrier that the injured worker sees. Understandably, the injured worker will often want to discuss these problems with the specialist. Unfortunately, medical issues are often complicated with legal ones. The specialist should do nothing more than make note of any complaints and relay them to the claim adjuster for proper response.

Adjusters should take care to select a qualified person to provide these services and should never relinquish control of the case. Properly managed, a rehabilitation specialist or medical case manager can be of great help to both the carrier and the injured worker.

CHAPTER 18

ATTENDANT CARE

Guide to Claims

SYNOPSIS

§ 18.01 Attendant Care Defined

> **SPECIAL ALERT:** The applicable statute for awarding compensation for attendant care is the statute in effect at the time the compensable care is given [*see* Socolow v. Flanigans Enters., 877 So. 2d 742 (Fla. 1st DCA 2004)].

Nursing services include nursing in a hospital setting, but also include home health care by a private duty nurse. Often a private nurse in the injured worker's home is more effective and less expensive than confinement in a hospital. Home health care may do much for the injured worker's physical and mental well-being. Besides these professional services, an injured worker may require nonprofessional or custodial care, commonly called attendant care. The Act defines attendant care as follows [§ 440.13(1)(b), Fla. Stat. (1994)]:

> [C]are rendered by trained professional attendants which is beyond the scope of household duties. Family members may provide nonprofessional attendant care, but may not be compensated under this chapter for care that falls within the scope of household duties and other services normally and gratuitously provided by family members.

For a general discussion of attendant care, see Larson's Workers' Compensation, Desk Edition, Ch. 94, § 94.03[4] (Matthew Bender).

§ 18.02 Entitlement to Attendant Care

[1] Statutory Requirements

[a] Before 1994

Originally, the Act required that compensable attendant care must meet the following tests [§ 440.13(2)(g), Fla. Stat.]:

1. A physician declared attendant care is necessary because of the accident.

2. The physician has described the nature and extent of the duties to be done.

3. The prescription does not include services that go beyond the scope of household duties ordinarily done gratuitously by a family member.

[b] Between January 1, 1994, and September 30, 2003

Effective January 1, 1994, attendant care is compensable only when done at the direction and control of a physician, and only when medically necessary. The law now requires that the physician supervise the care [§ 440.13(2)(b), Fla. Stat. (1994)].

Regardless of the accident date the prescribing physician need not declare that attendant care is medically necessary such that it would improve the injured worker's condition. The law requires only that the nature of the injury requires attendant care. This includes palliative care that relieves the conditions or the effects of the injury. The court has held that the statute embraces services required by the nature of the injury, as well as those that improve an injured worker's condition [*see* Rodriguez v. Howard Industries, 588 So. 2d 646, 650 (Fla. 1st DCA 1991)].

Despite how reasonable services may be, they are not compensable unless the physician specifically prescribed them. For example, in one case the attendant administered medication, helped the injured worker to the bathroom, prepared lunch, gave the injured worker leg and back massages, and retrieved drinks. These are classic active attendant care services, but here they were not compensable. Why not? Because the physician did not specify that the injured worker needed help for these tasks [*see* Dade County School Bd. v. Grier, 648 So. 2d 805, 806 (Fla. 1st DCA 1994)].

[c] On or After October 1, 2003

In addition to the requirements described above, the law now requires that a physician prescribe attendant care in writing. The prescription must include the time frames for such care and must describe the level of care and the type of assistance required. The law now prohibits prescribing attendant care retroactively [*see* § 440.13(2)(b), Fla. Stat. (10/1/2003)].

[2] Open-Ended Award Not Allowed

No matter who provides the care, a judge may not make an open-ended award. For example, a judge of compensation claims awarded around-the-clock care "until further order of this court." The First District Court of Appeal reversed. Such an order improperly places the judge of compensation claims in the position of supervising the provision of future care. This is improper because it violates the self-executing nature of the Workers' Compensation Act [*see* Ramada Inn South Airport v. Lamoureux, 578 So. 2d 48, 49 (Fla. 1st DCA 1991)].

[3] Proof of Medical Necessity Required Even at Emergency Hearing

To receive attendant care paid by the carrier, the injured worker must offer proof that a physician has prescribed it. This requirement is absolute and a judge of compensation claims cannot waive it, even at an emergency hearing [*see* ch. 22, § 22.04, for a discussion on emergency hearing procedure]. For example, the judge granted Karen Frank's request for an emergency hearing on her petition for an award of attendant care

Guide to Claims

benefits. Apparently, her need for attendant care was so obvious to the judge that he awarded the benefit, despite her physician's testimony that she did not need it. The First District Court of Appeal reversed, holding that the injured worker must always provide the competent substantial evidence of a physician's testimony about the medical necessity for attendant care. Absent this testimony, the judge of compensation claims cannot award the benefit [*see* Winn Dixie Stores, Inc. v. Frank, 665 So. 2d 271, 272 (Fla. 1st DCA 1995)].

[4] Statute Interpretation and Application

In an opinion issued on July 9, 2004, the court held that it was not necessary that a physician issue a prescription for attendant care to be compensable. The court held that it was sufficient that the physician provide the necessary testimony at the hearing [*see* Rockette v. Space Gateway Support, 877 So. 2d 852 (Fla. 1st DCA 2004)].

The court cited *Attitudes & Trends v. Arsuaga* [616 So. 2d 1103, 1103 (Fla. 1st DCA 1993)] as authority for this opinion. However, *Arsuaga* dealt with the attendant care statute as it existed in 1990. At that time, the statutory requirement was simply that a physician declare that attendant care was necessary because of the accident. The *Arsuaga* court rejected the employer/carrier's contention that § 440.13(2)(f), Fla. Stat. (Supp. 1990) precluded an award of attendant care for services rendered *before* a physician prescribed such care or stated that it was medically necessary. The court noted that the claimant presented the required medical testimony at a hearing on the claim and held that the statute did not mandate that the physician state an opinion or provide a prescription *before* the care commenced. Furthermore, the court held the circumstances were sufficient to put the employer/carrier on notice of the need to investigate the claimant's possible entitlement to such benefits. The court noted: "It is well established that the employer/carrier may not avoid payment by hiding behind a 'wall of willful ignorance.'"

The *Rockette* court did not mention the date on which the accident occurred or the statutory revisions enacted effective January 1, 1994. The 1994 revision provided that attendant care was compensable only when done at the direction and control of a physician [*see* § 440.13(2)(b), Fla. Stat.]. The 1994 statute still did not specifically say that attendant care was not compensable before the physician prescribed the care. Still, it seemed unlikely that the physician would have controlled and supervised such care before actually prescribing it.

The legislature again amended the statute, effective October 1, 2003, to require that the physician prescribe the care in writing. Additionally, the new statute provides that the carrier is not responsible for attendant care until it receives the written prescription. Lastly, the statue now precludes prescribing attendant care retroactively.

> **NOTE:** If the carrier becomes aware that the claimant's physician is prescribing or recommending attendant care, but has not done so in writing, an employer/carrier may not avoid payment by willful ignorance. § 440.13(2)(b), Fla. Stat. (2004), by its plain meaning, simply ensures that a doctor will memorialize the medical justification for attendant care; it does not authorize an employer/carrier to willfully ignore an employee's need for treatment by failing to disclose the statutory requirement of the treating physician. The E/C has a burden to properly investigate and inform the

claimant or his or her doctor concerning the assisted care requirements [*see* James W. Windham Builders, Inc. v. Van Overloop, 2007 Fla. App. LEXIS 3270 (Fla. 1st DCA 2007)].

It is not clear if the court's decision in *Rockette* applies to accidents occurring after January 1, 1994, and its application is even more problematic for accidents occurring after October 1, 2003. However, it appears that the 2003 amendment effectively overrules both *Arsuaga* and *Rochette* because the statute now requires a *written* prescription and precludes prescribing attendant care retroactively. Most importantly, the 2003 statute provides that the employer/carrier is not responsible for attendant care before receiving the written prescription.

The *Arsuaga* court held the 1990 amendment was procedural in those circumstances as a burden of proof enactment. This appears to apply to the 1994 amendment because the revision requires the claimant to show that the attendant care was done under the physician's supervision. Thus, this should also be construed as a burden-of-proof enactment.

NOTE: In *Adams Bldg. Materials, Inc. v. Brooks* [892 So. 2d 527 (Fla. 1st DCA 2004)], the court stated in a footnote that the amendment applied to any attendant care performed on or after its effective date of October 1, 2003. Although placing this statement in a footnote may create debate over whether it is the court's holding or merely dicta, it is a clear indication of how the court will rule in the future.

Regardless of how the court will eventually apply these statutory amendments, carriers should remain mindful of the court's warning and avoid an obvious need for attendant care by hiding behind a "wall of willful ignorance."

§ 18.03 Choosing the Attendant

As with physicians, the right to choose an attendant, or nurse, rests with the carrier. The injured worker, however, has the right to reject the carrier's choice and request an alternate authorization. If the carrier refuses, injured workers may seek authorization from the judge of compensation claims for an attendant of their own choice. The judge of compensation claims may not, however, grant blanket authority to injured workers to select future attendants as the need arises. This is because such an award would be premature [*see* Polk County Bd. of Com'rs v. Varnado, 576 So. 2d 833, 841 (Fla. 1st DCA 1991)].

The carrier may choose a professional service to provide attendant care. More often than not, however, the carrier and the injured worker will prefer a family member. A family member is a spouse, father, mother, brother, sister, child, grandchild, father-in-law, mother-in-law, aunt, or uncle. This list is very important. A family member not on the list, such as a cousin, is not subject to the limitations discussed below [§ 440.13(1)(b), Fla. Stat. (1994)]. Note that the law does not require that the family member live in the same household with the injured worker [*see* Lemus v. Ocala Star Banner, 672 So. 2d 76, 77 (Fla. 1st DCA 1996)].

Guide to Claims

§ 18.04 Active and Passive Attendant Care

[1] Active Attendant Care and Household Services

The law limits payment to family members for only those services beyond ordinary household services. In certain cases, however, ordinary household services may be medically necessary. Usually, attendant care is an active service. That is to say, the attendant changes the patient's bandages, administers medications, or provides similar services. Active attendant care is necessary when injured workers cannot care for themselves properly.

Remember that ordinary household work, such as cooking and cleaning, is not compensable unless such work is inseparable from the required care. For example, the carrier accepted Isabel Santana as permanently and totally disabled. Her doctor testified that she could take her own medication, as well as bathe, dress, and feed herself. In spite of this, she hired a housekeeper for five months; after that, her husband did the housework. The judge awarded reimbursement for the housekeeper and $210 per week to Santana's husband as attendant care. The First District Court of Appeal reversed the award [*see* Barkett Computer Service v. Santana, 568 So. 2d 520, 521 (Fla. 1st DCA 1990)]:

> Attendant care benefits for family members who are performing ordinary household chores has only been found to be proper when the extent of the attendant care being furnished by the family members is inseparably intertwined with household duties which they would be performing regardless. In such situations, the family members are usually performing sitter/custodial or on-call, attendant care which requires them to be in constant attendance on the claimant but which does not preclude their contemporaneous performance of usual household duties. However, the general rule remains that ordinary household duties performed by a family member are not the responsibility of the [employer].

The *Santana* court also held the law did not entitle the injured worker to the house cleaning service either. Purely domestic services are not compensable. Just because the injured worker's injury precludes doing housework, the need for such services is not automatically medically necessary. Compensable attendant care, based on medical necessity, includes bathing, dressing, administering medication, and helping with sanitary functions [*see* Sealey Mattress Co. v. Gause, 466 So. 2d 399, 400 (Fla. 1st DCA 1985)].

General supportive services, no matter how beneficial, are not compensable. These include driving the injured worker to the store and other places, other than for medical treatment. These are quality of life services and are not compensable. In one case, the injured worker's doctor testified that without household help for cleaning and shopping, the injured worker risked aggravating her back condition. The judge of compensation claims awarded attendant care for these services and the First District Court of Appeal reversed, holding these to be ordinary household services and, thus, not compensable [*see* Montgomery Ward v. Lovell, 652 So. 2d 509, 511–512 (Fla. 1st DCA 1995)].

In one case, the JCC awarded the claimant two hours of attendant-care services per week. Specifically, the award involved assistance in "carrying groceries and laundry up the three flights of stairs to her apartment." Given the facts stated in the JCC's order, the court reversed and concluded that the definition of "attendant care" in § 440.13(1)(b), Fla. Stat. (2000), construed with § 440.13(2)(a)-(b), Fla. Stat. (2000), does not encompass the types of services for which attendant care was awarded to the claimant. The court refused to construe the statute or the applicable case law as designating a special blanket exception to the ordinary "household duties" rule for claimants who live alone and do not have family members or friends available to provide dependable, convenient assistance with domestic chores when needed. The court noted that such "quality of life activities" and "supportive services" might well be "indemnified under disability compensation benefits rather than attendant care service that is medically necessary," but held that they are *not* covered under the attendant-care provision at issue here. Finally, the court noted that the claimant misplaced her reliance on certain language in *Allied Discount Tires v. Cook*, 587 So. 2d 626 (Fla. 1st DCA 1991) (discussed below), which might support affirmance here if *Cook* had not been decided pursuant to an earlier, different version of § 440.13, Fla. Stat. [*see* Palm Beach County Sch. Bd. v. Zabik, 906 So. 2d 362 (Fla. 1st DCA 2005)].

In *Allied Discount Tires v. Cook*, the claimant, George Cook, was rendered permanently and totally disabled in a compensable accident. There was evidence that Cook, who lived alone, was physically unable to do such routine chores as housekeeping, laundry, and shopping. The court held that in such a case an award of ordinary housekeeping services was proper. As indicated above, however, this case was decided in 1991, under the pre-1994 version of § 440.13, Fla. Stat., and as indicated in the *Zabik* decision, above, is no longer good law.

[2] Passive Attendant Care

Note carefully the distinction between ordinary, active, attendant care and so-called passive or on-call care. Passive attendant care involves situations in which injured workers may be a danger to themselves or to others. For example, Norman Caron's physicians testified that his head injury had hampered his ability to think clearly. Because of this, Caron required 24-hour attendant care. This care was passive supervision since Caron was apparently able to generally care for himself. The trial judge concluded that Caron's parents devoted only about two hours per day to active, exclusive supervision and awarded $100 per week. The First District Court of Appeal reversed and held that "[O]n-call attendant care provided by a family member is not subject to reduction merely because the family member is involved in other household activities while simultaneously monitoring the activities of a claimant" [*see* Caron v. Systematic Air Services, 576 So. 2d 372, 374 (Fla. 1st DCA 1991)].

Not all attendant care services are compensable. As the court explained in *AT&T Wireless Servs. v. Castro* [896 So. 2d 828, 831 (Fla. 1st DCA 2005)]:

> "Generally, attendant care considered medically necessary includes only bathing, dressing, administering medication, and assisting with sanitary functions." . . .On the other hand, "housekeeping, transportation other than to a doctor, and other normal household duties that reflect on quality of life rather than medical necessity are generally considered gratuitous and not compensable." . . .Household services may, in limited circumstances, be compensable if the caretaker (family member or not) substantially departs from his or her daily routine to provide care, or if the claimant

is completely prevented from doing such activities on his or her own.

In *Indus. Blowpipe v. Capps* [2006 Fla. App. LEXIS 4379 (Fla. 1st DCA 2006)], The JCC awarded attendant care benefits after the MMI date, in part because the claimant removed his prosthesis at night and the claimant's spouse was on-call and available at night to evacuate the claimant from their house in the event of an emergency. The court has recognized that, when the claimant is unable to respond to life-threatening situations relating to the injury, the claimant may be entitled to 24-hour attendant care. Here, however, the potential emergency for which the JCC awarded attendant care was not related to the claimant's injuries, but was related to the possible need to evacuate the claimant's home in the event of an emergency such as a fire. Such stand-by care is not compensable. Accordingly, the court reversed that portion of the post-MMI attendant care benefits that related solely to stand-by care at night for the purpose of responding to an emergency requiring the evacuation of the home.

In another case, the judge of compensation claims awarded Karen Kuring 12 hours of on-call attendant care per day, which her husband was to provide. The facts produced little question that Mrs. Kuring required periodic assistance. On the surface this award seemed in order. The appellate court, however, noted that the judge did not explain how Mr. Kuring could provide 12 hours of attendant care while still working at his full-time job! The court reversed, finding error in an award based only on the need for care without regard to the services done. Though the court has approved on-call care in the past, this case went too far. The court held there is no authority permitting payment for time the attendant was employed outside the injured worker's presence [*see* Bojangles v. Kuring, 598 So. 2d 250, 251 (Fla. 1st DCA 1992)].

More recently, the court repeated its holding that a caretaker cannot be compensated for time spent employed outside of the claimant's presence, even if the caretaker is considered "on call" [*see* AT & T Wireless Servs. v. Castro, 896 So. 2d 828 (Fla. 1st DCA 2005)].

§ 18.05 The 12-Hour Limit

[1] Family Members as Attendants

A family member, or a combination of family members, may not be paid for more than 12 hours per day. § 440.13(1)(b), Fla. Stat. (1997) defines "family member" as follows: "Family member" means a spouse, father, mother, brother, sister, child, grandchild, father-in-law, mother-in-law, aunt, or uncle. The court has held that the statute clearly defines family members to include certain enumerated blood relatives and in-laws of a workers' compensation claimant. The court rejected the notion that the term "family member" should include only those members of the claimant's family living in her household, which would have allowed the claimant's non-resident son to be paid more than the federal minimum wage. Thus, family members include those not living with the claimant [*see* Lemus v. Ocala Star Banner, 672 So. 2d 76, 77 (Fla. 1st DCA 1996)].

Because the statute is so specific, the definition of "family member" in § 440.13, Fla. Stat. does not include a nephew for the simple reason that a nephew is not listed. Thus, a nephew would not be subject to the time limitations [*see* King Lumber Co. v. Bloomfield, 560 So. 2d 389, 390–391 (Fla. 1st DCA 1990)].

Additionally, the term "child" does not include a stepdaughter or stepson. This is because the legislature did not include the term "stepchild" within the definition of "family member," and the terms "child" and "stepchild" are legally distinct. Therefore, the 12-hour limitation does not apply to a stepchild [*see* Walt Disney World Co. v. McCrea, 754 So. 2d 196, 198 (Fla. 1st DCA 2000)].

The 12 hours per day limit on family members does not in any way, however, affect an injured worker's basic entitlement to attendant care. Cases will arise where injured workers are so severely injured that they will need care 24 hours per day. The limitation only affects the number of paid hours per day, and then only for family members [§ 440.13(2)(b)2., Fla. Stat. (1994)]. *There is no limit on attendant care done by professional attendants.*

For example, in a 1992 case the judge of compensation claims limited attendant care by the injured worker's wife to 12 hours per day. This was in spite of medical testimony that the injured worker required care 24 hours per day. The court held that the statute does not impose any limit on an injured worker's right to receive 24-hour attendant care. The statute, said the court, "merely limits the number of hours for which the injured worker's wife may be paid" [*see* Collura v. Multi Line Can Co., 598 So. 2d 1072, 1074 (Fla. 1st DCA 1992)].

Also note that a family member may be entitled to compensation during the time spent receiving training to care for the disabled employee [*see* Johnson v. Superior Nat'l Ins., 819 So. 2d 249, 250 (Fla. 1st DCA 2002)].

[2] Professional Attendants

In a reverse situation, the judge awarded 18 hours of attendant care per day. The judge based this on the injured worker's wife providing care at a level greater than that of the average nurse's aide. The judge concluded she was entitled to professional level compensation. The court reversed, holding that the wife was a nonprofessional since she was neither licensed nor trained as an attendant. The curt adopted the definition of "professional" found in Webster's dictionary as one who (1) is engaged in specific activity for their livelihood, (2) possesses great skill or experience in a field or activity, and (3) works with assured competence in their field. This means that if a family member does qualify as a professional, the 12-hour limit will not apply [*see* Standard Blasting & Coating v. Hayman, 597 So. 2d 392, 393–394 (Fla. 1st DCA 1992)].

[3] Family Members as Professional Attendants

If a family member qualifies as a professional, the limits do not apply. For example, Abraham Cohen required attendant care. His wife, who was a Certified Nursing Assistant, agreed to provide the care. The question became whether she should be paid the prevailing rate in the community for a CNA ($10 per hour), or her actual salary as a CNA ($5 per hour). The court agreed with the carrier that even a professional cannot collect professional rates for nonprofessional service. Here, however, the court found Mr. Cohen needed professional level services and affirmed the award of $10 per hour [*see* Kraft Dairy Group v. Cohen, 645 So. 2d 1072, 1074–1075 (Fla. 1st DCA 1994)].

[4] 24-Hour Attendant Care

If the injured worker needs care 24 hours per day, and the spouse (or other family member) wants to provide it and the physician prescribed it, then the law allows 24 hours of care. The law does not allow that family member, however, to be paid for more than 12 hours at the maximum rates [*see* § 18.06]. If the family member is not interested in providing 24 hours of care for only 12-hours' pay, then the carrier must arrange for a professional service. In such a case, the carrier may wish to volunteer full payment if this becomes an attractive option. Professional care may be far more expensive.

[5] No Employer-Employee Relationship Between Medical Attendant and Carrier

Contracting with a family member to provide attendant care services does not create an employer-employee relationship between the attendant and the carrier. For six years, the carrier paid the claimant's wife to provide attendant care for her husband. She then sued the carrier, claiming that she was the carrier's employee and therefore entitled to the federal minimum wage and overtime pay under the Fair Labor and Standards Act (FLSA). The 3d DCA held that a contractual agreement did exist, but that there was no employment relationship between the attendant and the carrier. The court held further that once the terms of the contract have been met, no claim for other non agreed upon benefits could be added [*see* Marin v. Travelers Ins. Co., 771 So. 2d 625, 626–627 (Fla. 3d DCA 2000)].

[6] Burden of Proof and Documentation of Time Spent

The law is clear that the carrier is not responsible to pay for time not actually expended in providing attendant care, regardless of the claimant's need for such services. While the claimant is entitled to reimbursement for the actual performance of attendant care services by family members going beyond those household services that would normally be provided by family members on a gratuitous basis, "[t]he burden is on the claimant to prove by competent, substantial evidence the quantity, quality, and duration of the attendant services claimed" [Walt Disney World Co. v. Harrison, 443 So. 2d 389, 393 (Fla. 1st DCA 1983); *see also* Jones v. McGhee, 502 So. 2d 509 (Fla. 1st DCA 1987)].

A blanket award of attendant care or services without regard to the actual performance of those services is error [*see* Perez v. Pennsuco Cement & Aggregates, 504 So. 2d 1274, 1275–1276 (Fla. 1st DCA 1986)]. In *Perez*, the court found that the record did not contain competent substantial evidence that Perez's wife actually spent eight hours a day performing necessary services for the claimant for the period of time at issue. Therefore, the court reversed the judge's order and remanded for further proceedings so that testimony could be taken on the issue of how much time was actually spent by Perez's wife or any other person performing attendant services.

In *Ramada Inn South Airport v. Lamoureux* [578 So. 2d 48, 49 (Fla. 1st DCA 1991), *rev. den.*, 587 So. 2d 1328 (Fla. 1991)] the claimant sought payment for attendant care services provided by her son following her move to Massachusetts in June 1988. The claimant presented a contract, which she and her son had entered into, in which she agreed to pay him $ 12 per hour for sleeping in her apartment, helping her with hygiene, and running various errands. The claimant testified that her son lived with her, but the only evidence of his assistance was her testimony that he emptied bedpans and helped her change clothes and bedding when she frequently became incontinent. The son did not testify, and the court's review of the voluminous record failed to uncover evidence as to the amount of time the son spent assisting the claimant. Although competent substantial evidence supported the need for 12 hours of attendant care per day during the period in question, the court held that the JCC erred in ordering payment without regard to the services actually performed. The court held that it is improper to order payment for past attendant care based solely on the claimant's need for care and without regard to the services actually performed. Therefore, the court reversed the award of attendant care and remanded for further proceedings so that testimony could be taken on the issue of how much time was actually spent by the son in performance of attendant care services for which reimbursement may be had.

Similarly, the court in *Bojangles v. Kuring* [598 So. 2d 250, 251 (Fla. 1st DCA 1992)] held that it is in error to base an award of compensation to a caregiver solely on the claimant's need for attendant care without regard to the services actually performed by the caregiver. Although the JCC's order cited competent substantial evidence establishing the claimant's *need* for care 12 hours per day, no mention was made of the hours expended by the husband. In fact, the husband's own testimony indicated that only six hours per day were spent caring for his wife and, when ordinary household tasks were excluded, he only spent three hours per day. Therefore, the court reversed and remanded for a determination of the time actually spent in providing care.

The law is now well settled that the carrier is entitled to documentation of the time actually expended before making payment for attendant care services. It is the claimant's burden to prove by competent, substantial evidence the quantity, quality, and duration of attendant services claimed. The judge of compensation claims may not make a blanket award of attendant care or services without regard to the actual performance of those services.

§ 18.06 Limits on Fees for Family Members

[1] Determining Rate of Pay

If the family member is not employed, or if the family member is employed but provides attendant care services during his or her non-working hours, the per-hour rate for attendant care is the federal minimum wage.

If the family member quits a job to provide attendant care, the hourly rate is the same as the family member's per hour value of the former job. This rate may not exceed the hourly rate for such care in the community [§ 440.13(2)(b), Fla. Stat. (1994)]. Once injured workers have met their initial burden of establishing the family member's former wage, it becomes the carrier's burden to produce evidence showing entitlement to a lesser amount.

Effective October 1, 2003, the Act provides that if the family member remains employed while providing attendant care, the per-hour value of that care equals the per-hour value of the attendant's regular job. The per-hour value, or hourly rate, cannot exceed the hourly rate available in the community [*see* § 440.13(2)(b), Fla. Stat. (10/1/2003)].

> **NOTE:** The use of the phrase "per-hour value" suggests that the rate is to be based on the family member's wages and fringe benefits.

Sometimes a family member can continue outside employment and still provide attendant care. If so, the prevailing market rate for the service is the basis for payment and not the attendant's hourly wage or the federal minimum wage [*see* Buena Vida Townhouse Ass'n v. Parciak, 603 So. 2d 26, 27–28 (Fla. 1st DCA 1992); Frederick Electronics v. Pettijohn, 619 So. 2d 14, 17 (Fla. 1st DCA 1993)].

[2] Proof of Wage Raises Presumption

Establishing the family member's former wage raises a rebuttable presumption that the former wage is the correct rate for attendant care. It then becomes the carrier's burden to produce evidence to rebut the presumption. The carrier may use evidence showing that the income from the family member's former employment exceeded the per hour value of attendant care available in the particular community [*see* Hunter v. Hernando County Bd. of Com'rs, 578 So. 2d 798, 800 (Fla. 1st DCA 1991)].

[3] Calculating Family Member's Wage

Calculating the family member's correct total wage is essential. Unfortunately, the Act does not provide a method and there has been little appellate review. The best course is to calculate a family member's wage in the same fashion as the injured worker. Include any fringe benefits the family member received in the former employment [*see* F.W. Woolworth v. Spann, 596 So. 2d 529, 530 (Fla. 1st DCA 1992)].

The courts have not said which fringe benefits to include or how to value them. The safe position will be to calculate the wage under the same criteria as for an injured worker before July 1, 1990. After that date the legislature deleted most fringe benefits from the calculation for injured workers. It is unlikely the courts would so restrict a family member. Since the calculation before the 1990 change was the most liberal, the courts are likely to agree this is a fair way to calculate a family member's wage.

[4] Procedure When There Is No Wage

Where there is no former wage to use as a basis for the rate, the burden to establish the market rate is the injured worker's [*see* Walt Disney World Co. v. Harrison, 443 So. 2d 389, 392–393 (Fla. 1st DCA 1983)]. In 1991, the trial judge awarded $10 per hour based on the injured worker's wife's testimony alone. She testified that registered nurse friends told her $10 was the rate they received for work in doctors' offices and hospitals. The First District Court of Appeal reversed and held that such testimony is hearsay. Work in doctors' offices, said the court, has little to do with the market rate for nonprofessional attendant care. The court rejected the theory that the trial judge could rely on such testimony because the carrier had not produced contrary evidence. Injured workers have the burden to prove by competent substantial evidence the quantity, quality, and duration of claimed attendant care, as well as the market rate for such attendant care [*see* Commercial Carrier Corp. v. Beck, 580 So. 2d 334, 335 (Fla. 1st DCA 1991)].

[5] Requirements to Apply Minimum Wage

A judge of compensation claims may set the per hour value of attendant care at the federal minimum wage level only if one of the following circumstances exists [*see* Hunter v. Hernando County Bd. of Com'rs, 578 So. 2d 798, 801 (Fla. 1st DCA 1991)]:

1. The family member was not employed at the time the care was provided.
2. The family member was employed at the federal minimum wage rate.
3. The per hour value of attendant care available in the community was equal to the federal minimum wage, which was an amount less than that earned by the family member.

If the family member leaves a part-time job to provide attendant care, fees for such services are not limited to the federal minimum wage, though the hours of attendant care exceed the hours worked in the former, part-time job. For example, Philip King's wife quit a 20-hour per week job to provide attendant care to her husband. She was to care for him for 5 hours per day, 7 days per week, or a total of 35 hours per week. The judge awarded attendant care at Mrs. King's hourly rate from her part-time job. The carrier argued she was entitled to her former rate for only the first 20 hours of care, and to the federal minimum wage rate for the balance. The court disagreed, and in affirming the order, held neither the Workers' Compensation Act nor the cases support such a position [*see* Winn Dixie Stores, Inc. v. King, 579 So. 2d 313, 315 (Fla. 1st DCA 1991)].

[6] Increases in Federal Minimum Wage

If the carrier pays a family member based on the federal minimum wage, is the attendant entitled to an increase whenever the minimum increases? The court (almost) answered this question in a 1991 case. Unfortunately, the court declined to answer the question directly because the issue was not raised before the judge of compensation claims. In dicta, however, the court observed that an upward adjustment in the compensation rate for attendant care, due to an increase in the federal minimum wage, can be the subject of new claim upon remand of the case [*see* Artigas v. Winn Dixie Stores, Inc., 578 So. 2d 356, 358 (Fla. 1st DCA 1991)]. This is a solid clue suggesting how the court will rule in the future.

[7] Fee Limitations Before October 1, 1989

The limits on attendant care by family members became effective on October 1, 1989. This is a procedural change and applies to all claims, despite the date of the accident. Take care, however, because the new statute did not revoke prior awards based on stipulations that were valid when made and approved by the judge of compensation claims. Assume, for example, that before the amendment the carrier agreed to pay a spouse 16 hours attendant care per day. Also assume that a judge of compensation claims approved the agreement. If the judge approved or awarded the level of attendant care, the carrier may not unilaterally reduce it. Proper procedure requires filing a motion for modification of the original order; however, not much by way of law exists to convince a judge to modify the original order in such cases.

§ 18.07 When Duty to Provide Begins

[1] The Rule

A carrier must provide attendant care services when it knows, or reasonably should have known, that the injured worker needs such services. Carriers must provide nursing care benefits, if needed, although not requested [*see* Honeycutt v. R.G. Butlers Dairy, 525 So. 2d 984, 986 (Fla. 1st DCA 1988)].

Effective October 1, 2003, the Legislature overruled the court's holding in *Honeycutt* by providing that the employer or carrier is not responsible for providing attendant care until it receives the physician's written prescription. Presumably, the duty to provide such care does not begin if the prescription does not meet the statutory requirements of including a description of the time frames for which attendant care is needed as well as the level of care and the type of assistance required [*see* § 440.13(2)(b), Fla. Stat. (10/1/2003)].

[2] Limits on Retroactive Awards

In one case, the carrier told the injured worker that if he felt he needed attendant care services, all he needed to do was ask and it would be provided. Even this was not sufficient for the carrier to fulfill its duty to provide such services. An offer couched in these terms is "an impermissible attempt by the employer/carrier to avoid its continuing obligation, once it has knowledge of an employee's injury, to place needed benefits in the hands of the injured worker" [Smith v. DRW Realty Services, 569 So. 2d 462, 464 (Fla. 1st DCA 1990)].

The effect of this holding is that a judge of compensation claims may award attendant care or nursing service benefits retroactively to the date of the carrier's knowledge of need. The JCC may not, however, order payment for past attendant care based solely upon the injured worker's need for care, but without regard to the services actually done [*see* Orange County Sheriff's Dept. v. Perez, 541 So. 2d 652, 654 (Fla. 1st DCA 1989)].

Additionally, a judge of compensation claims may not retroactively award attendant care benefits unless evidence exists that the carrier had actual, or at least constructive, knowledge of the need for such care. The judge, however, is under no such restriction unless the carrier raises lack of knowledge as a defense. Additionally, the nature of the injury alone may be enough to impute knowledge of need to the carrier [*see* Wee Wisdom Montessori School v. Vickers, 584 So. 2d 132, 133 (Fla. 1st DCA 1991)].

In a similar case, the court repeated the requirement that the judge of compensation claims decides whether the nature of the injury was sufficient to impute knowledge of the need for attendant care to the carrier. Here, however, the carrier denied all entitlement to attendant care. The judge of compensation claims awarded attendant care retroactively, beginning two years before the injured worker filed the petition for benefits. The judge, however, made no finding of the carrier's knowledge of the injured worker's need for such care. Since the carrier did not raise the issue of pre-claim benefits, the issue was not preserved for appellate review [Merritt Sea Wall v. Revels, 594 So. 2d 855, 856 (Fla. 1st DCA 1992)].

[3] Interest, Penalties, and Attorney's Fees

A judge of compensation claims may not assess interest or penalties on an award of past attendant care. § 440.20, Fla. Stat. limits interest and penalties to awards of compensation only. Attendant care, of course, is not compensation [*see* Williams v. Amax Chemical Corp., 543 So. 2d 277, 279 (Fla. 1st DCA 1989)].

The judge may, however, award attorney's fees based on the present value of all future attendant care on accidents occurring before October 1, 1989. For accidents occurring after October 1, 1989, the law limits the value, for purposes of fee calculation, to five years worth of future benefits [§ 440.34(2), Fla. Stat. (1994); *see* Sir Elec., Inc. v. Borlovan, 582 So. 2d 22, 23 (Fla. 1st DCA 1991)].

Lastly, attorney's fee awards may not include an inflation factor in quantifying future attendant care benefits for the purposes of deciding the amount of fees [*see* A.G. Holly State Hospital and Division of Risk Management v. Kaiser, 577 So. 2d 612, 613 (Fla. 1st DCA 1991)].

CHAPTER 19

SUBROGATION

SYNOPSIS

§ 19.01 Subrogation Defined

[1] The Rule

Subrogation describes an insurance carrier's right to recover from a wrongdoer all sums paid to, or for, its policy holder. The right of subrogation has its basis in common law. A person who negligently causes loss to another is responsible for damages to the person injured. In Florida, an injured employee's exclusive remedy against the employer is the right to collect workers' compensation benefits. In additicn the employee has a statutory right to sue the wrongdoer (other than the employer) for damages [§ 440.39(1), Fla. Stat. (7/1/97)].

For a general discussion of subrogation, see Larson's Workers' Compensation, Desk Edition, Chs. 116–122 (Matthew Bender).

[2] Extent of Lien

Obviously, if workers recover most of their wages and all of their medical expenses from the employer or the insurance carrier, and recover them again from the wrongdoer,

Guide to Claims

a considerable profit will result. Profiting from an insurance claim is against public policy in virtually every jurisdiction.

In addition, most if not all insurance policies contain subrogation clauses. These are provisions that transfer to the insurer the right to recover its payments from the wrongdoer. This includes payments the insurer has paid, or will pay, to the covered worker under the policy. Further, the law preserves this right in Florida workers' compensation cases. It does so by granting carriers a statutory lien against the proceeds of any settlement the employee may receive. This lien includes a right of set-off against future workers' compensation benefits the carrier will pay to the injured employee [§ 440.39, Fla. Stat. (7/1/97)].

SPECIAL NOTE: Most of the cases reviewed in this chapter are from the various Florida appellate courts. If there is no inter-district conflict, district court decisions are binding on all Florida trial courts. If the only appellate decision on point is from a district other than the one in which the trial court is located, the trial court must follow that decision [*see* Special's Trading v. Intern. Consumer, 679 So. 2d 369, 370 (Fla. 4th DCA 1996)]. Until the Florida Supreme Court resolves any conflict between district courts, the result is a confusion of differing applications of the law depending on the jurisdiction.

§ 19.02 Subrogation and Lien Rights

[1] Extent of Lien

Despite language in § 440.39, Fla. Stat. suggesting that carriers may recover 100 percent of their liens, this is rarely the case. A workers' compensation carrier's rights of subrogation and lien against third-party settlement recoveries is *not* total and absolute. The discussion that follows in [2]–[6], *below,* describes the limitations on the carrier's right of subrogation recovery.

[2] Injury Not in Course of Employment

[a] Unrelated Accident Aggravating Compensable Injury

The statutory right of subrogation does not apply when the injured worker recovers for injuries suffered in an accident that occurred outside the course of employment. This is true, even if the off-duty accident aggravated a work-related injury [*see* Nationwide Mut. Ins. Co. v. Jacoby, 505 So. 2d 471, 472 (Fla. 2d DCA 1987)].

[b] Medical Malpractice Aggravating Compensable Injury

Does the carrier have a lien if medical malpractice makes the employee's injuries worse? The answer is yes. The workers' compensation carrier has a valid lien against the employee's settlement proceeds in a medical malpractice case [*see* Liberty Mutual Insurance Co. v. Chambers, 526 So. 2d 66, 67 (Fla. 1988)].

[3] Settlement Before Workers' Compensation Benefits Paid

Occasionally, an injured worker receives a settlement from a third-party tortfeasor before making a claim for, or accepting, workers' compensation benefits. A tort is a private or civil wrong or injury resulting from a breach of a legal duty. The essential elements of a tort are a duty owed, a breach of that duty, and resulting damage to the plaintiff. A tortfeasor is one who commits a tort. If the employee has settled a claim against the responsible tortfeasor, disbursement of the proceeds extinguishes the carrier's lien rights. This situation was common until the legislature enacted a partial repair. The law now entitles the workers' compensation carrier to a set off against any compensation benefits paid or payable. The set off, however, does not apply to medical or rehabilitation benefits. In addition, the set off is reduced further by all of the injured worker's attorney's fees and court costs paid to obtain the settlement [§ 440.39(2), Fla. Stat. (7/1/97)].

[4] Vocational Rehabilitation

A workers' compensation carrier is not entitled to recover any portion of vocational rehabilitation benefits paid. The statutory right to a lien is explicit in granting the right of subrogation only for compensation and medical benefits paid or to be paid. Vocational rehabilitation is neither compensation nor a medical benefit. As such, neither an equitable nor statutory basis exists to justify a recovery to the carrier [*see* § 440.39(3)(a), Fla. Stat. (7/1/97); Associated Home Health Agency, Inc. v. Lore, 484 So. 2d 1389, 1390 (Fla. 4th DCA 1986)].

[5] Adjusting, Investigation, and Other Expenses

The same logic used in disallowing recovery for vocational rehabilitation costs applies to miscellaneous claims expenses, such as the use of investigators or experts. Since these expenses do not qualify as compensation or medical benefits, they are not recoverable [§ 440.39(3)(a), Fla. Stat. (7/1/97)].

[6] Settlement Paid to Children of Deceased Worker

The Florida Supreme Court held that the law did not entitle the carrier to recover any portion of the separate settlement it made with the deceased worker's children. The Court's logic was that the workers' compensation death benefits were awarded in the name of the deceased's wife, and not the children. Thus, the children were not the direct beneficiaries of the compensation payments. The settlement they received from the third party was not, therefore, subject to the carrier's lien [*see* Coon v. Continental Ins. Co., 511 So. 2d 971, 974 (Fla. 1987)]. Such an unfair and harsh result may be avoided if documents and compensation payments are properly directed.

[7] Spoliation of Evidence Settlement

The issue here is whether a workers' compensation carrier is entitled to a portion of a settlement or judgment against the claimant's employer because of the employer's spoliation of evidence. The answer, in a word, is no.

A spoliation claim compensates the plaintiff for the loss of recovery in the underlying

Guide to Claims

case due to the plaintiff's inability to prove the case because of the lost or destroyed evidence and not for the "bodily injury" actually sustained.

For example, the injured employee had sued the manufacturer of a ladder as a third party tortfeasor. The employer, however, destroyed the allegedly defective ladder, and the employee settled with the ladder manufacturer for less than the full measure of his damages caused by the ladder's failure. He then sued his employer for spoliation of evidence, and the jury awarded him damages. The jury's award in the spoliation action simply made up the difference between the full amount of the damages caused by the defective ladder and the settlement received from the manufacturer.

The workers' compensation insurer contended that, pursuant to § 440.39(3)(a), Fla. Stat., it was entitled to recover a pro rata share of the damages awarded by the jury. The insurer argued that it was entitled to such a recovery as subrogee because the employer "essentially stood in the shoes of the third-party ladder manufacturer by being liable for the same tort and the same damages [for which] the ladder manufacturer would have been [liable] in the products liability claim." The appellate court disagreed.

The court noted the workers compensation rule allows an employer's insurer to have a specified share of any recovery in an employee's action against a third party tortfeasor. However, the court concluded that the rule did not apply when an employee recovered damages from the employer itself for destroying evidence essential to prove the injured employee's claim against a third party tortfeasor who manufactured a defective product causing the employee's injuries.

In short, the court held the insurer was not entitled to recover a share of the damages its own insured was forced to pay for the insured's negligent destruction of evidence [*see* Shaw v. Cambridge Integrated Servs. Group, Inc., 888 So. 2d 58 (Fla. 4th DCA 2004)].

> **NOTE:** In Shaw v. Cambridge Integrated Servs. Group, Inc. [2004 Fla. App. LEXIS 19119 (Fla. 4th DCA Dec. 15, 2004)], the court denied rehearing, but certified the following question to the Florida Supreme Court:
>
> May an employer who has been found guilty of destroying evidence critical to its employee's right to recover from a third party tortfeasor, and who has been forced to pay the employee damages for such destruction, be deemed a third party tortfeasor for purposes of a carrier's subrogation rights under § 440.39(3)(a)?

§ 19.03 Right to Sue Tortfeasor

[1] The First Year

During the first year after the injury, the law gives the injured employee the exclusive right to sue the third-party tortfeasor [§ 440.39(4)(a), Fla. Stat. (7/1/97)].

[2] The Second Year

[a] The Carrier's Rights

If the injured employee does not sue the tortfeasor within the first year, the carrier may do so during the second year [§ 440.39(4)(a), Fla. Stat. (7/1/97)]. Carriers must, however, give 30 days notice to the employee, dependents if deceased, or their attorney. During this second year, both the employee and the carrier have the right to sue the tortfeasor directly. The carrier, however, can preempt the employee's right to sue by providing 30 days notice to the employee and then actually filing suit. Once carriers give the required 30 days notice of their intention to sue and then actually file suit, the law bars employees from bringing their own separate suits [*see* Kimbrell v. Paige, 448 So. 2d 1009, 1011–1012 (Fla. 1984)].

The *Kimbrel* court noted that it is clear that the *right* to institute suit is concurrent during the second year after the accrual of the cause of action, but if the carrier does file suit first, the only sensible interpretation of the intent of the statute is that it precludes the employee from also being able to maintain suit at that time.

As noted, the right of action is concurrent during the second year after accrual of the cause of action. To hold otherwise would be to take from the injured employee or his or her dependents that very right of action, the encouragement toward diligent exercise [*see* Zurich Ins. Co. v. Renton, 189 So. 2d 492 (Fla. 2d DCA 1966)].

Both the statute and the court are silent on whether the claimant has the right to file suit during the carrier's 30-day notice period. A reasonable interpretation is that the 30-day notice period is intended to give the claimant a last chance to do so. Otherwise, the carrier could preempt the injured employee's rights even if the carrier did not actually file a suit during the second year. Thus, the notice letter, with no further action, would force the injured worker to wait an entire year until the beginning of the third year before being able to file his or her own suit.

The statute specifies the carrier's right of damage recovery as follows [§ 440.39(4)(a), Fla. Stat. (7/1/97)]:

> [I]n the event suit is so instituted [the employer/carrier] shall be subrogated to and entitled to retain from any judgment recovered against, or settlement made with, such third party, the following: All amounts paid as compensation and medical benefits under the provisions of this law and the present value of all future compensation benefits payable, to be reduced to its present value, and to be retained as a trust fund from which future payments of compensation are to be made, together with all court costs, including attorneys' fees expended in the prosecution of such suit, to be prorated as provided by subsection (3). *The remainder of the moneys derived from such judgment or settlement shall be paid to the employee or his or her dependents, as the case may be.* (Emphasis added)

[b] Refunding the Remainder

Carriers seldom exercise their right to sue. As a result, the law is still unsettled. For example, the law is clear that once a carrier files suit, the injured worker's right to do so is extinguished. A carrier may recover only amounts paid or payable as medical or indemnity benefits. What happens then, to the injured worker's right to claim damages for

Guide to Claims

pain and suffering or loss of consortium. Must the carrier claim these damages for the injured worker as well? The Supreme Court was silent on this issue in its holding in *Kimbrell v. Paige* [*see* [a], *above*].

In a dissenting opinion, however, Justice Ehrlich opined that the carrier does have such a duty. Read the last sentence from the quotation in [a], *above,* again. The section provides that the carrier must pay any remainder from the settlement or judgment to the injured employee or dependents. If the carrier sues only for benefits it has paid, how can there be a remainder? Does this language suggest the carrier must also include a claim for the injured worker's pain and suffering? Justice Ehrlich, at least, believes it does [*see* Kimbrell v. Paige, 448 So. 2d 1009, 1012–1013 (Fla. 1984)]. A counter argument may be that the carrier has the right to sue, not only for benefits paid, but for benefits payable in the future as well. The statute provides that any recovery for future benefits must be "retained as a trust fund." It is possible that a judgment for future benefits may exceed the carrier's payments. If so, this may be the remainder to which the legislature referred.

The advantage to the carrier in bringing its own suit is that the carrier can recover all of the benefits paid, and not just its pro rata share. Another unanswered question, however, is whether the law entitles the injured worker to only a pro rata share of any remainder. In all fairness, the answer should be yes, since recovery would not have occurred if the carrier had not financed the lawsuit.

[3] The Third Year

If, by the end of the second year, the carrier has not brought its own suit, the exclusive right to sue reverts to the employee. The employee's right to sue continues until the applicable statute of limitations expires [§ 440.39(4)(b), Fla. Stat. (7/1/97)].

[4] Duty to Cooperate

Employees, employers, and carriers must cooperate with each other in investigating and prosecuting potential claims against third-party tortfeasors. This cooperation includes producing non-privileged documents and allowing inspection of the premises. Presumably, the employee cannot use evidence obtained from documents and inspections against the employer, because the act also provides that "such documents and the results of such inspections shall not be used or disclosed for any other purpose" [§ 440.39(7), Fla. Stat. (7/1/97)].

In 1990, the First District Court of Appeal held that an injured worker cannot use this provision to go on a fishing expedition to establish employer liability. The court pointed out that it did not consider other important questions. Specifically, does the section allow discovery of documents beyond those specified in the Workers' Compensation Act? Does it allow inspection of the premises? Does the employer's duty to cooperate extend to the injured worker's fellow employees [*see* Suburban Propane v. Estate of Pitcher, 564 So. 2d 1118, 1120–1121 (Fla. 1st DCA 1990)]? Due to this uncertainty, and in spite of apparent safeguards, carriers and employers should consider having an attorney present during such an inspection.

The *Suburban Propane* case, however, does not suspend the duty to cooperate before filing a third-party lawsuit. That no legal action is pending, in either the compensation case or a potential third-party liability case, does not matter. The legislature clearly intended the statute to allow the injured worker an opportunity to gather information necessary to decide if a potential third-party recovery exists. To successfully resist requests or court orders to allow inspection of the employer's records, premises, and equipment, the defense must show that the injured worker's real intent is to prove employer liability [*see* Southeast Recycling Corporation v. McClure, 658 So. 2d 670, 671 (Fla. 1st DCA August 1995)].

Guide to Claims

> **CAUTION:** If the court decides that the employer or carrier did not cooperate, the court can reduce the lien by any amount it deems appropriate.

[5] Duty to Preserve Evidence

[a] Spoliation of Evidence

Although the statute speaks only about producing documents and allowing inspection of the premises, the employer also has a specific duty to preserve evidence. The purpose of § 440.39, Fla. Stat. is to preserve causes of action against third-party tortfeasors and, therefore, impose a duty of cooperation to that end. This includes a duty to preserve evidence, at least when the injured worker has made a timely request to do so. If physical evidence comes into the employer's possession, such as a defective saw, for example, the employer has a statutory duty to preserve it. If not, the employer exposes itself to a lawsuit claiming the damages the injured worker would have recovered if the employer had saved the evidence [*see* General Cinema Beverages v. Mortimer, 689 So. 2d 276, 278–279 (Fla. 3d DCA 1995)].

[b] Requirements to Establish Spoliation Claim

A complaint must contain the "ultimate facts" necessary to support a claim for relief [*see* Fla. R. Civ. P. 1.110(b)(2)]. To plead a cause of action properly for spoliation of evidence, the complainant must plead facts that could establish the essential elements of the claim. The essential elements of spoliation of evidence claim are as follows [*see* Hagopian v. Publix Supermarkets, Inc., 788 So. 2d 1088, 1091 (Fla. 4th DCA 2001), quoting Cont'l Ins. Co. v. Herman, 576 So. 2d 313, 315 (Fla. 3d DCA 1990)]:

1. The existence of a potential civil action.
2. A legal or contractual duty to preserve evidence, which is relevant to the potential civil action.
3. Destruction of that evidence.
4. Significant impairment in the ability to prove the lawsuit.
5. A causal relationship between the evidence destruction and the inability to prove the lawsuit.

6. Damages.

A duty to preserve evidence may arise by contract, by statute, or by a properly served discovery request (after a lawsuit has already been filed) [Silhan v. Allstate Ins. Co., 236 F. Supp. 2d 1303, 1309 (N.D. Fla. 2002), citing Bondu v. Gurvich, 473 So. 2d 1307, 1312 (Fla. 3d DCA 1984); Miller v. Allstate, 573 So. 2d 24, 27 (Fla. 3d DCA 1990)].

As noted in subsection [a], *above,* the duty to preserve evidence in a workers' compensation context is statutory.

[c] No Coverage Under Part 2, Employer's Liability

If the employer is sued for spoliation of evidence, the question is whether coverage applies under Part 2, Employers' Liability, of the workers' compensation policy. The Florida Supreme Court has held the employers' liability part does *not* provide coverage for the tort of spoliation of evidence.

Here, the claimant was an employee of Home Emergency Services (HES) and was injured when he fell from a ladder during the course of his employment. The claimant, Milian, received workers' compensation benefits, which were paid pursuant to Part One of HES's policy. HES then agreed to maintain the ladder in its possession for Milian, who intended to pursue a claim against the ladder's manufacturer and distributor. The ladder was subsequently misplaced or destroyed. When Milian later filed suit against the manufacturer and distributor for product liability, he also sued HES for negligent spoliation of evidence. Milian's complaint contained two counts against HES, one alleging that HES breached a contractual duty to maintain the evidence and a second alleging breach of a statutory duty. The complaint averred that the contractual duty arose from HES's agreement to maintain the ladder, while the statutory duty arose from § 440.39(7), Fla. Stat. (1995), which imposes a duty on an employer to cooperate with an employee in the prosecution of claims and potential claims against third-party tortfeasors [*see* General Cinema Bevs. v. Mortimer, 689 So. 2d 276, 278–279 (Fla. 3d DCA 1995) (holding § 440.39(7), Fla. Stat. imposes duty to preserve evidence)]. The question became whether the employer's liability part (Part 2) of the workers' compensation policy applies to a claim for spoliation of evidence. The trial court granted summary judgment in favor of Humana, concluding that Milian's spoliation claim against HES was not a "bodily injury" claim covered by the policy.

HES appealed to the Third DCA, which reversed and held that the spoliation claim was covered by Part Two of the policy. On further appeal, the Florida Supreme Court reversed the 3d DCA. Negligent spoliation of evidence is a tort claim based on a defendant's breach of a duty to preserve evidence. The damage that flows from such a breach is the resulting inability to prove a cause of action. Milian's spoliation claim sought compensation not for the bodily injury he sustained in falling from the ladder, but for his loss of a probable expectancy of recovery in the underlying suit. The Supreme Court held that Part 2, (Employer's Liability) of the workers' compensation policy applying to "bodily injury by accident" does not provide coverage for claims against an insured for negligent spoliation of evidence. The Court noted that its holding here was consistent with the Fourth District's decision in *Norris v. Colony Ins. Co.* [760 So. 2d 1010, 1011–1012 (Fla. 4th DCA 2000)] as well as decisions of other jurisdictions [*see* Johnson v. Evan Hall Sugar Coop., Inc., La.

App. 2001-2956, 836 So. 2d 484, 488 (2002) (holding spoliation claim was not derived from plaintiff's bodily injuries but rather from "completely separate incident" when evidence was destroyed); Fremont Cas. Ins. Co. v. Ace-Chicago Great Dane Corp., 317 Ill. App. 3d 67, 75–76, 739 N.E.2d 85, 91–92, 250 Ill. Dec. 624 (2000) (holding damage suffered in spoliation claim is inability to prove underlying action, which does not fall within plain and ordinary meaning of term "bodily injury")]. Accordingly, The Supreme Court quashed the DCA's decision and remanded to the district court for proceedings consistent with this decision [Humana Workers' Comp. Servs. v. Home Emergency Servs., 842 So. 2d 778 (Fla. 2003)].

On the other hand, the statute does not impose a duty on an employer or carrier to preserve and produce evidence that was never in its possession. The court refused to expand the employer's and the carrier's duty to obtain, and then to preserve evidence that is not in their custody. This is especially true when nothing prevents injured workers from making their own inspection [§ 440.39(7), Fla. Stat. (7/1/97); *see* Barbosa v. Liberty Mut. Ins. Co., 617 So. 2d 1129, 1130 (Fla. 3d DCA 1993)].

§ 19.04 Immunity and Exclusive Remedy

[1] Injured Worker's Employer

[a] Immune Employers

Workers' compensation is the injured employee's exclusive remedy. When employers properly secure workers' compensation coverage for their employees, the law grants them (almost) total immunity from suits brought by their employees. Effective January 1, 1994, the legislature amended the Act to include county governments specifically under the immunity umbrella. Immunity does not apply, however, if the employer has engaged in any intentional act that causes harm. Such acts are those designed or substantially certain to result in injury or death to the employee [§ 440.11(1), Fla. Stat. (1/1/94)].

Also note that statutory immunity extends to employers who lease their workers from employee leasing companies. Leased employees are statutorily considered to be borrowed servants, but for purposes of immunity are treated as any other employee of the employer. Indeed, such employers are required by the same statutory section to provide workers' compensation coverage if the leasing company does not do so [*see* § 440.11(2), Fla. Stat.].

The fact that the employee leasing company provides the coverage does not alter the employer's immunity status. This is true even if the employee signs an affidavit declaring that he or she is an employee of the employee leasing company. This is because the employer in such cases will have paid a fee to the employee leasing company to provide, among other things, such coverage. If the employee is injured and receives benefits from the insurer for the employee leasing company, the worker cannot take a "second bite at the apple" by suing the employer in tort. Also, note that the Act, § 440.11(2), Fla. Stat., specifically includes the "help supply services" industry under Standard Industry Code Number 7363, which includes employee leasing services, temporary help services, and labor pools [*see* Maxson Const. Co., Inc. v. Welch, 720 So. 2d 588, 590 (Fla. 2nd DCA

1998); *see also* Caramico v. Artcraft Industries, Inc., 727 So. 2d 348, 349 (Fla. 5th DCA 1999) (approving *Maxson*)].

We now turn to those general circumstances where the employer's immunity does not apply, whatever the degree of employer negligence [*see* [b]–[e], *below*].

For a general discussion of the exclusive remedy rule, see LARSON'S WORKERS' COMPENSATION, DESK EDITION, Ch. 100 (Matthew Bender).

[b] No Workers' Compensation Coverage

The basis for granting immunity to employers is their guarantee of benefits via workers' compensation. If the employer fails to provide coverage, either by an insurance policy or qualifying as a self-insurer, the employer's immunity is gone. Even worse, the employer loses the right to raise the common-law defenses of assumption of risk, comparative negligence, and negligence of a fellow employee. The employer's only defense under such circumstances is that it was not negligent in any way [§ 440.11(1), Fla. Stat. (1/1/94)].

[c] Estoppel

[i] Misleading Employee

The law may prevent an employer from raising the immunity defense when it attempts to mislead employees about their rights. In one case, the employer told the injured employee that no workers' compensation benefits were available to him when, in fact, the employer was fully insured. When the employee sued, the employer asked the court to dismiss the action based on workers' compensation immunity. The circuit court refused and held the law estopped the employer from raising the immunity defense because of its actions in misleading the injured worker. The First District Court of Appeal affirmed this decision [*see* Quality Shell Homes & Supply Company v. Roley, 186 So. 2d 837, 840–841 (Fla. 1st DCA 1966)].

In another case, the employer paid medical bills directly and gave the injured worker money for rent and food. The insurance company sent compensation checks, but the employer deposited them into its own business account. Such conduct, calculated to convey a misleading impression, is sufficient to constitute a misrepresentation. The trial court had granted a summary judgment for the employer based on exclusive remedy. The appellate court remanded to decide if the employee was led to believe that no workers' compensation benefits were available. Presumably, if he were misled, then the immunity defense would not be allowed [*see* Francoeur v. Pipers, Inc., 560 So. 2d 244, 245 (Fla. 3d DCA 1990)].

[ii] Denying Benefits

Denying benefits may create an estoppel that opens the door to allowing the employee to maintain an action in tort. For example, Audrey Byerley clocked out at the end of the work day. She tripped and fell while walking to her car. The carrier denied her claim on the basis that she was not in the course and scope of her employment when she was injured. Based on this denial, Byerley filed a tort action. The employer defended on the grounds that it was immune under the provisions of § 440.11(1), Fla. Stat. (1995). The Fifth District Court of Appeal disagreed. The court, apparently, interpreted the statute's meaning to be that the failure "to secure the payment of compensation" is the same as denying entitlement to benefits. The court held that an employee who has been denied compensation for an injury may either file a petition for workers' compensation benefits *or* sue the employer for damages. Because the carrier denied that a work-related injury had occurred, the employee was entitled to rely on that assertion. Thus, the act of denying compensation created an estoppel precluding the employer and carrier from raising the immunity defense.

In a footnote, the court noted that the statute also prohibits employers from asserting the common-law defenses of negligence of a fellow employee, assumption of risk, and comparative negligence [*see* Byerley v. Citrus Publ., Inc., 725 So. 2d 1230, 1232, n.1 (Fla. 5th DCA 1999)].

[d] Employer in Dual Capacity or Dual Persona

[i] Dual Capacity Theory

If a manufacturer's negligently made product injures someone, the individual may sue for damages. What happens, however, if the manufacturer is also the injured person's employer? Is the manufacturer/employer immune? Under the sparsely accepted dual capacity theory, immunity does not apply. Dual capacity theory holds that an employer may have a dual capacity. The first capacity is that of a manufacturer of products for sale to the public. The second capacity is that of an employer. If a product manufactured by the employer injures an employee, the employee may sue the employer. Under this theory, the employee would sue the company in its manufacturer capacity.

The dual capacity theory is based upon the manufacturer assuming a liability toward the employee as it would toward the public. This theory does not hold favor around the country today and even the California courts have rejected it [*see* Shook v. Jacuzzi, 59 Cal. App. 3d 978, 980, 129 Cal. Rptr. 496 (1976)].

[ii] Dual Persona Theory

Florida courts subscribe to Professor Larson's theory on dual persona. This theory holds that an employer may become a third person, vulnerable to a tort suit by an employee if, and only if, it possesses a second persona, so completely independent from and unrelated to its status as employer that the law recognizes the other persona as a separate legal person [*see* Larson's Workers' Compensation, Desk Edition, Ch. 113, § 113.01 (Matthew Bender)].

[iii] Applying Theory in Florida

Florida courts dealt with the dual persona theory for the first time in 1991. Here, the worker was injured by a machine whose manufacturer had merged with the injured worker's employer. The court held the theory of dual persona does create a narrow exception to the exclusive remedy of workers' compensation. Immunity does not preclude a third-party action against the corporate successor of a third-party tortfeasor when the corporate successor happens to be the injured worker's employer. Thus, the injured worker's employer assumed the manufacturer's liability when the two companies merged. The court said: "We . . . hold that an injured employee may sue her employer in tort when that employer is the corporate successor of the manufacturer of the defective product that caused the injury, and the product was manufactured before the corporate merger" [*see* Percy v. Falcon Fabricators, Inc., 584 So. 2d 17, 18 (Fla. 1st DCA 1991)].

[iv] Employer's Liability Coverage

In such cases, employers' liability coverage—coverage part 2 of the workers' compensation policy—should apply unless precluded by the "liability assumed under contract" exclusion [*see* ch. 3, § 3.01]. Often, the owner of a business also owns the building. The owner then leases the building to the owned corporation. Assume that the worker's injury resulted from a negligently maintained building. In such a case, the injured worker may have a right to bring an action against the landlord, even if the landlord is also the injured worker's employer. The employer's liability as a landowner is not eliminated by his status as the owner and manager of the injured worker's employer. Employers' liability coverage would not likely apply here since it is the "landlord" the employee sued and not the employer. Check the declarations page of the policy carefully [*see* Perkins v. Scott, 554 So. 2d 1220, 1221–1222 (Fla. 2d DCA 1990)].

[v] Immunity Does Not Extend to Corporate Parent

The building occupied by the injured worker's employer was owned by its parent corporation. The court held the parent corporation of the injured worker's employer was not statutorily immune. Though the corporate employer had paid workers' compensation benefits, and the same insurance company insured both corporations, immunity did not apply. The logic here is that the parent corporation is not the injured worker's employer and has no immunity. Under the same theory, employers' liability coverage may not apply either [*see* Wilkerson v. Gulfstream Land and Development Corp. 402 So. 2d 550, 551 (Fla. 4th DCA 1981), *aff'd,* 420 So. 2d 587 (Fla. 1982)].

[e] No Immunity for Sexual Harassment

The Act's immunity provisions do not apply to claims based on sexual harassment in the workplace. Obviously, if such actions resulted in physical injury, workers' compensation benefits would apply. Usually, however, any resulting injury is psychological only and such mental injury, absent physical injury, is not compensable. Workplace injuries rob a person of resources while sexual harassment robs the person of dignity and self esteem. From a legal perspective, sexual harassment is a violation of the Civil Rights Act of 1964. To allow immunity would be to nullify federal law and, furthermore, defy the constitution. Since mental injury alone is not compensable, the employer's liability portion of the workers' compensation policy may not cover suits for such injury [*see* Byrd v. Richardson-Greenshields Securities, 552 So. 2d 1099, 1102–1105 (Fla. 1989)].

[f] Migrant Workers

In 1990, the United States Supreme Court held that the exclusive remedy provisions of state workers' compensation laws do not apply if the employer intentionally violated certain provisions of The Migrant and Seasonal Agricultural Worker Protection Act (AWPA) [*see* Adams Fruit Co. v. Barrett, 494 U.S. 638, 108 L. Ed. 2d 585, 595–600, 110 S. Ct. 1384 (1990)].

In response to this decision, the Florida legislature amended the Act to entitle workers' compensation carriers to a 100-percent offset against any recovery an employee may receive under the AWPA. Application of employers' liability coverage here is a close question. Many policies exclude coverage for this exposure [§ 440.39, Fla. Stat. (7/1/90)].

[2] General Contractors, Subcontractors, and Independent Contractors

[a] General Contractors and Subcontractors

Immunity from suit depends on whether the employer fulfilled its duty to secure compensation coverage [*see* Jones v. Florida Power Corp., 72 So. 2d 285, 287–289 (Fla. 1954)]. When a contractor sublets any part of its contract work, the law deems all employees of the subcontractors as the employees of the general contractor. The general contractor is therefore responsible for securing the payment of compensation for all the employees on the job [*see* ch. 3, § 3.06].

Employees of a subcontractor cannot sue the general contractor, because the law considers the general contractor to be the employee's statutory employer. Immunity applies even if the immediate (actual) employer secured compensation for its employees [*see* § 440.10(1), Fla. Stat. (1/1/94); Fred G. Wright, Inc. v. Edwards, 642 So. 2d 808, 809 (Fla. 2d DCA 1994)].

This immunity does not, however, apply between subcontractors because they have no liability to secure compensation for each other. Remember that the employer's immunity arises from its duty to obtain workers' compensation coverage. If the employer does not discharge this duty, it has no immunity.

[b] Independent Contractors

Sometimes, a general contractor may employ a legitimate, independent contractor. Since the general contractor has no duty to provide coverage to an independent contractor, automatic immunity does not apply. Many general contractors, however, provide such coverage voluntarily. They frequently do this by entering an agreement under which the contractor deducts coverage premiums from the independent contractor's fees. The question is, does such voluntarily provided coverage create immunity? In 1992, the Florida Supreme Court held that in such a case, the independent contractor, in effect, elects coverage. This election binds the contractor to the provisions of Ch. 440, Fla. Stat., including the exclusiveness of liability and immunity clauses. Some independent contractors claim they are coerced into such contracts, and the premium paid is improperly deducted from fees due. Requiring an employee to pay any part of the premium is illegal for an employer; however, an independent contractor, by definition, is not an employee. Accordingly, the Supreme Court held [*see* Mandico v. Taos Const., Inc., 605 So. 2d 850, 852–853 (Fla. 1992)]:

> A general contractor who employs an independent contractor insulates itself from civil liability when, in accordance with the parties' contract, it procures a workers' compensation policy for the benefit of the independent contractor by deducting the policy premiums from payments due the independent contractor.

Guide to Claims

[3] Fellow Employees

[a] General Immunity

An injured worker's co-workers have the same statutory immunity as their employer, but with three significant exceptions reviewed in [b], *below.*

[b] Exceptions to Immunity

[i] No Immunity for Gross Negligence

Immunity does not apply to fellow workers if their actions constitute willful and wanton disregard, unprovoked physical aggression, or gross negligence [§ 440.11(1), Fla. Stat. (1/1/94)]. Gross negligence means, "a conscious and voluntary act or omission which is likely to result in injury when in the face of a clear and present danger of which the alleged tortfeasor is aware" [*see* Gerentine v. Coastal Sec. Systems, 529 So. 2d 1191, 1193 (Fla. 5th DCA 1988)].

Another definition of gross negligence is an act or omission that a reasonable, prudent person would know is likely to result in injury to another. Gross negligence is difficult to prove because it is conduct so outrageous it is almost an intentional tort. Proving gross negligence requires evidence that the co-worker engaged in conduct substantially certain to result in injury or death.

[ii] No Immunity if Engaged in Unrelated Works

Immunity does not apply to employees of the same employer even when they are serving the employer's interests if they are assigned *primarily to unrelated works* within private or public employment. For example, no immunity exists between two state employees when one works for the Department of Insurance, and the other works for the Department of Transportation. Although loss of immunity is likely in this example, it is not certain. It is conceivable that the two employees may be involved in related work. Unfortunately, the legislature failed to define the term "unrelated works," and so far the courts have declined to correct this failure. Instead, they regard this as a question of fact to be decided on a case-by-case basis [*see* Lake v. Ramsay, 566 So. 2d 845, 848 (Fla. 4th DCA 1990)].

Section 440.11(1), Fla. Stat., provides as follows:

> The same immunities from liability enjoyed by an employer shall extend as well to each employee of the employer when such employee is acting in furtherance of the employer's business and the injured employee is entitled to receive benefits under this chapter. Such fellow-employee immunities shall not be applicable to an employee who acts, with respect to a fellow employee, with willful and wanton disregard or unprovoked physical aggression or with gross negligence when such acts result in injury or death or such acts proximately cause such injury or death,*nor shall such immunities be applicable to employees of the same employer when each is operating in the furtherance of the employer's business but they are assigned primarily to unrelated works within private or public employment.* (*Emphasis provided*)

Simply having different skills or different jobs does not automatically make work unrelated. Following are examples. Charles Johnson worked as a laborer for the general contractor and claimed that a subcontractor's employee caused his injuries. Johnson argued the subcontractor's employee had no immunity because he worked as a welder for a different employer. In quickly dismissing the argument about different employers, the court held that the subcontractor was the statutory employee of the general contractor. Just because Johnson was a laborer, and the subcontractor was a welder, their work was not unrelated [Johnson v. Comet Steel Erection, Inc., 435 So. 2d 908, 909 (Fla 3d DCA 1983)].

In a similar case, 12 years later, the Second District Court of Appeal reached the same conclusion. Here, Alex Abraham and Adam Dzafic both worked for A&K Service Corporation. They were both traveling between job sites in different vans when Abraham's van collided with Dzafic's van. Because they both worked for the same employer on the same construction site, Abraham was immune from Dzafic's lawsuit despite the fact one was a painter and the other was a lighting technician [*see* Abraham v. Dzafic, 666 So. 2d 232, 233 (Fla. 2d DCA 1995)].

Why the legislature created this exception to immunity is unclear. In a 1996 case, Judge Miner offered this theory of the legislature's intent [*see* Vause v. Bay Medical Center, 687 So. 2d 258, 267 (Fla. 1st DCA 1996)]:

> The purpose for the exception could have been "to remove workers' compensation immunity as a disincentive to employers assigning employees, primarily assigned to full-time duties in a particular area of employment, occasional, non-routine duties because of a legislative assumption that the danger of injury might be increased if workers were expected to perform such tasks on a relatively infrequent basis."

The 3d DCA has held that the "unrelated works" exception to workers' compensation immunity did not apply between a teacher and a custodian. The fact that employees have different duties does not necessarily mean they are involved in "unrelated works" [*see* Dade County Sch. Bd. v. Laing, 731 So. 2d 19, 20 (Fla. 3d DCA 1999)].

For example, Caridad Sanchez, a middle school teacher, sued the Dade County School Board for negligence after she was sexually assaulted and beaten during her lunch period by a trespasser in the teacher's parking lot. The trial court granted summary judgment in favor of the School Board based on its workers' compensation immunity. The 3d DCA agreed that by accepting workers' compensation benefits, Sanchez was precluded from asserting a tort claim against her employer. Because both were engaged in activities primarily related to the provision of education related services, the "unrelated works" exception to the School Board's immunity under § 440.11(1), Fla. Stat. did not apply. The court saw no distinction between the teacher-custodian relationship in *Laing* and the teacher-security personnel relationship in this case [*see* Sanchez v. Dade County Sch. Bd., 784 So. 2d 1172 (Fla. 3d DCA 2001)].

As noted earlier, a recurring problem in these cases is that the legislature failed to define the term "unrelated works." Thus, the courts have addressed the issue based on the facts of the case rather than trying to fashion a broad standard. The court has now concluded that crafting a definition is a task best left to the legislature. As a guideline however, unrelated works may apply if the workers' physical location is separate and the specific

Guide to Claims

purpose of their work is distinct, but with a unity of purpose. Until the legislature amends the statute, we must decide this issue on a case-by-case basis [*see* Lopez v. Vilches, 734 So. 2d 1095, 1096–1097 (Fla. 2d DCA 1999), *rev. denied,* 749 So. 2d 504 (Fla. 1999)].

In *Taylor v. Sch. Bd.* [790 So. 2d 1156 (Fla. 5th DCA 2001)], the employee, Taylor, was injured in the course of his work as a bus attendant, when a wheelchair lift affixed to the bus fell on him. On the day of the accident, the emergency release pin plate on the mechanism was loose because the rivets had worn off. This caused the lift to fall as soon as the doors opened. The lock assembly on the lift had been repaired, four months earlier. A week before the accident, the lift was re-positioned by a school board mechanic. The lift was last inspected and lubricated in the shop two days before the accident. A school board mechanic testified the rivets might have worn out due to stress on the lift.

The trial court granted a summary judgment in favor of school board on the grounds that the alleged negligent workers were assigned to related works. (These workers included school board mechanics and a school bus attendant whose duties included operation of the wheelchair lift.) Because both the former and the latter were employees of the school board involved in the same project, they had in common the provision of transportation services to county school children. Thus, the court held the unrelated works exception to the immunity provision of § 440.11, Fla. Stat. did not apply and affirmed the lower court's ruling.

In 2004 the Florida Supreme Court reviewed the 5th DCA's decision in *Taylor*. The Supreme Court was faced with different outcomes on similar facts in the conflicting district court decisions. On the one hand, in *Taylor*, the school bus attendant and the school bus mechanic were both employed by the school board, and both had jobs that dealt with the bus: the attendant interacted with students who rode the bus, and the mechanic maintained and repaired the bus. The 5th DCA found that the key elements of the two employees' jobs were the facts that they worked "out of the same transportation facility" and that their jobs both involved the wheelchair lift, resulting in their both being involved in the "same project" of providing transportation services to Brevard County school children [*see* Taylor v. Sch. Bd., 790 So. 2d 1156, 1157 (Fla. 5th DCA 2001)]. On the other hand, in *Lopez,* the court determined that the funeral home employee and the mechanic responsible for maintaining the work vehicles had different work locations and that their "specific purposes" were different [*see* Lopez v. Vilches, 734 So. 2d 1095, 1097 (Fla. 2d DCA 1999)].

The resolution of the issue before the Court turned largely on whether the Legislature intended that the unrelated works exception be construed liberally or narrowly. The Court noted its task was not made easier by the Legislature's admonition that the worker's compensation law was not to be construed liberally in favor of the employee or the employer. Rather, the Legislature had cautioned that the system was based on "a mutual renunciation of common-law rights and defenses by employers and employees alike" [*see* § 440.015, Fla. Stat. (1999)]. The Court noted that the Legislature had also mandated that the ordinary rules of statutory construction be invoked.

Hence, the Court noted it was bound to apply these principles in its analysis. The Court initially noted that, in one sense, all employees of the same employer could always be considered engaged in related works since they are all charged to carry out the mission of the employer. At the same time, however, some distinction could always be drawn between the work of most employees so as to make their work unrelated. Because the unrelated works exception set out in § 440.11(1), Fla. Stat., represented an exception to the broad exclusive remedy provisions of Florida's workers' compensation law, The Supreme Court concluded that under the ordinary rules of statutory construction it must interpret it narrowly.

The Court noted that since virtually all workplace injuries are caused by the actions of fellow workers, applying the unrelated works exception liberally would substantially handicap the underlying purpose of the compensation scheme to compensate employees for workplace injuries regardless of fault.

The Court also noted that in the ordinary case, when faced with a situation in which an employee was injured on the job, there existed a natural inference that the injury was covered by the Legislature's workers' compensation scheme. That is the fundamental purpose of the law, to provide benefits for workplace injuries in place of common-law remedies.

Correspondingly, the Court concluded that the exception to this scheme for unrelated works should be applied only when it can clearly be demonstrated that a fellow employee whose actions caused the injury was engaged in works unrelated to the duties of the injured employee. While the Court indicated a preference to be more precise in providing guidance to those initially charged with deciding disputes based on this exception, the Court indicated it was limited by its lack of precise knowledge of the legislative intent behind the exception and the reality that it could not hope to contemplate the myriad factual circumstances that may give rise to the issue.

The Court observed that a contrary holding giving wide breadth to the rare exceptions to workers' compensation immunity would merely erode the purpose and function of the workers'compensation law as established by the Legislature. The Court also agreed with the observations of the 4th DCA in its recent decision in *Fitzgerald v. South Broward Hospital District* [840 So. 2d 460, 463 (Fla. 4th DCA 2003)], that the unrelated works exception should be narrowly construed because "an expansive construction would obliterate the legislative intent that the system operate at 'a reasonable cost' to the employer" and that to decide otherwise would "erode the immunity provided under the worker's compensation law . . . leading to a profusion of suits and a proliferation of costs."

Accordingly, the Supreme Court disapproved the 2d DCA's holding in *Lopez* and approved the 5th DCA's decision in *Taylor* [*see* Taylor v. Sch. Bd., 888 So. 2d 1 (Fla. 2004)].

[iii] No Immunity Beyond Employment

Remember that co-workers' immunity applies only while they are in the course and scope of employment.

[c] Officers, Managers, and Supervisors

[i] General Immunity

In 1988, the legislature created an even higher level of immunity for co-workers who serve as officers, directors, or supervisors. This also includes any other person while acting in a managerial or policymaking capacity, including sole proprietors and partners. The law gives these individuals immunity from liability for workplace injuries only while acting in their capacity as managers or policymakers. An example is an allegation of failing to provide a safe workplace [§ 440.11(1), Fla. Stat.].

[ii] No Immunity for Culpable Negligence

A single exception arises when the actions alleged are a violation of law and constitute a first degree misdemeanor. A first degree misdemeanor occurs when a person, through culpable negligence, inflicts actual personal injury on another [§ 440.11(1), Fla. Stat. (1/1/94)]. Culpable negligence means, "reckless indifference" or "grossly careless disregard" of human life [*see* State v. Greene, 348 So. 2d 3, 4 (Fla. 1977)].

In 1993, the Florida Supreme Court held the provision constitutional. This section is merely a clarification regarding the immunity afforded managerial employees. Excepting unlawful conduct, managerial employees enjoy the same immunity as the employer [*see* Eller v. Shova, 630 So. 2d 537, 542–543 (Fla. 1993)].

> **NOTE:** Whether an employee was acting in a managerial or supervisory capacity is a question of fact for the jury to decide. Thus, courts will not be inclined to grant motions to dismiss based on statutory immunity if any question about the defendant's status arises [*see* Hawkins v. Cordy, 642 So. 2d 1115, 1116–1117 (Fla. 3d DCA 1994)].

[iii] *Weber v. Dobbins*

In 1991, the Fourth District Court of Appeal dropped a bombshell. The court held that exempt corporate officers did not meet the definition of "employee." If they are not employees, the court reasoned, immunity cannot apply. Had this case stood, an employee could have sued an exempt officer based only on simple or ordinary negligence [*see* Dobbins v. Weber, 585 So. 2d 1143, 1144–1145 (Fla. 4th DCA 1991), *reversed,* 616 So. 2d 956 (Fla. 1993)].

Recognizing the significant impact its decision would have, the District Court of Appeal certified the question to the Florida Supreme Court. The Florida Supreme Court reversed, and found the District Court of Appeal correctly applied a literal interpretation of the Workers' Compensation Act, but ignored legislative intent. Exemption from coverage does not remove the immunities granted by § 440.11, Fla. Stat., and the Court quashed the District Court of Appeal's decision [*see* Weber v. Dobbins, 616 So. 2d 956, 958–959 (Fla. 1993)].

[iv] No Immunity When Federal Maritime Law Applies

Unlike Florida's workers' compensation law, federal maritime law does not provide immunity to employers for work-related injuries, thus placing the two laws in conflict. In 1917, the United States Supreme Court resolved this conflict under what is now called the Jensen doctrine. The Court held that state law must yield to federal maritime law if it works material prejudice to the characteristic features of the general maritime law or interferes with the proper harmony and uniformity of that law in its international and interstate regulations [*see* Southern Pacific Co. v. Jensen, 244 U.S. 205, 216, 61 L. Ed. 1086, 1098, 37 S. Ct. 524 (1917)].

Based on *Jensen* and other cases, Florida's Fourth District Court of Appeal rejected the notion that Florida's act is not in conflict with federal maritime law. State law remedies for wrongful death admiralty cases have been allowed only when the state law is more generous than federal law. Noting that Florida's workers' compensation death benefits are not more generous, the court held that federal law must apply, thereby eliminating immunity under the Florida law [*see* Flying Boat, Inc. v. Alberto, 723 So. 2d 866, 869 (Fla. 4th DCA 1998)].

[4] Employer's Lessor

[a] Extension of Immunity

When an employer leases cars, trucks, and other equipment, generally the lessor enjoys the same immunity as the employer. Such items are the equivalent of vehicles owned by the employer. Thus, they are the vehicles or working tools used in carrying out the employer's business [*see* Morales v. Ryder Truck Rental, 559 So. 2d 317, 318 (Fla. 3d DCA, 1990)].

For example, Scott & Jobalia Construction Company borrowed a crane and operator from Halifax Paving Inc. Although Halifax employed the operator, Scott & Jobalia employees directed his activities by using hand signals. During the work a pipe fell from a sling attached to the crane and injured an employee. The injured worker settled his compensation claim against the employer, Scott & Jobalia, and then sued Halifax. The Florida Supreme Court held that workers' compensation was the injured worker's exclusive remedy, and that Halifax enjoyed the same immunity as Scott & Jobalia [*see* Halifax Paving v. Scott & Jobalia Const., 565 So. 2d 1345, 1347–1348 (Fla. 1990)].

[b] No Immunity for Negligent Maintenance

An exception arises, however, when the lessor negligently maintains or repairs leased equipment. The lessor of defective or negligently maintained equipment is not immune when such defects are the proximate cause of the injury [*see* Litton v. Saf-T-Green of Orlando, Inc., 608 So. 2d 908, 910–911 (Fla. 5th DCA 1992)].

[5] Safety Services Providers

The law grants limited immunity to insurance companies, service agents, and safety consultants. This immunity is limited to liability arising out of their efforts to help an employer by furnishing safety inspections, safety consultative services, or any other safety services incidental to workers' compensation. Immunity does not apply if injury is caused by a willful and unprovoked physical aggression, or by the negligent operation of a motor vehicle [§ 440.11(3), Fla. Stat. (1/1/94)].

Effective October 1, 2003, the Legislature amended this section to provide that immunity applies to suits brought by the employer's employees and the employer's subcontractor's employees. Additionally, the section provides that a "safety consultant" may include an owner or an owner's related, affiliated, or subsidiary companies and their employees [*see* § 440.11(3), Fla. Stat. (10/1/2003)].

[6] Immunity Under Florida's Automobile "No Fault" Law

Though outside our topic, remember that Florida owners, operators, and occupants of motor vehicles are immune from lawsuits for bodily injury damages unless the worker's injuries involve one of the following:

1. Significant and permanent loss of an important bodily function.
2. Permanent injury within a reasonable degree of medical probability.
3. Significant and permanent scarring or disfigurement.

The term "motor vehicle" includes private passenger motor vehicles and commercial motor vehicles. The statutory definition requires four or more wheels. Thus, motorcycles and mopeds do not meet the definition. The statute expressly excludes mobile homes, government-owned mass transit, and public school vehicles designed to carry at least five passengers plus the operator [§ 627.732, Fla. Stat. (10/1/97)].

Defined motor vehicles are, therefore, subject to the no-fault statute. If the injured worker has no right to sue as a matter of law, the carrier has no right of subrogation either.

[7] Property Owner

In 1994, the Third DCA held that a property owner who hires a general contractor is a statutory employer and enjoys workers' compensation immunity against a negligence suit. The court also held that a property owner's act of hiring an inspector to observe the work and enforce the construction contract does not alter the owner's immunity [*see* Univision Holdings v. Ramos, 638 So. 2d 130, 131–132 (Fla. 3d DCA 1994), *quashed and remanded,* 655 So. 2d 89 (Fla. 1995)].

The Florida Supreme Court disagreed and reversed. The Court held that only when an owner assumes the role of contractor and employer and, consequently, the duty to provide workers' compensation benefits is the owner entitled to workers' compensation immunity [Ramos v. Univision Holdings, 655 So. 2d 89, 90–91 (Fla. 1995)].

[8] Construction Design Professionals

The law grants immunity to construction design professionals providing professional services on a construction site for injuries to construction workers arising out of the employer's failure to comply with safety standards [§ 440.09(5), Fla. Stat. (1/1/94)]. This immunity, however, does not apply under two circumstances. The first exception arises if the person injured is not entitled to workers' compensation benefits. The second exception applies if the construction design professional assumed responsibility for safety practices in a services contract.

In one case, an injured worker sued the engineering consultant along with several others. The worker argued that the engineering firm, by its conduct, assumed the duty to monitor safety and, therefore, the immunity should not apply. The Fourth District Court of Appeal found no merit in this argument. To impose a common-law theory of assumption of duty, said the court, would be to render the statute meaningless. Here, the firm did not agree to this responsibility in its contract, and the contract specifically forbade the firm from advising or issuing directions about safety precautions [*see* Williams, Hatfield & Stoner v. Malcolm, 687 So. 2d 295, 296 (Fla. 4th DCA 1997)].

In order for a construction design professional to lose its statutory immunity, there must be a provision in the contract by which the construction engineer specifically assumed responsibility for the safety practices of the employer [*see* § 440.09(6), Fla. Stat. (2001)]. The contract must specifically provide that the engineering contractor assumed responsibility for employer safety practices or worker safety. Put another way, the responsibility for worker safety must be undertaken by plain words in the contract. The question whether the engineer undertook responsibility for safety practices specifically in the contract is a question of law for the court [*see* Estate of Reyes v. Parsons Brinckerhoff Constr. Services, 784 So. 2d 514, 516 (Fla. 3d DCA 2001)].

[9] Immunity Between Subcontractors

Effective January 1, 2004, the Legislature amended the Act to grant immunity to employers, in a subcontractor status, from suits brought by the employees of the general contractor, or by the employees of another subcontractor. This immunity applies only if the following requirements are met [*see* § 440.10(1)(e), Fla. Stat. (1/1/2004)]:

1. The general contractor provided worker's compensation insurance on behalf of the subcontractor, or
2. The subcontractor purchased its own workers' compensation insurance, and
3. The injury was not the result of the subcontractor's own gross negligence.

Because this amendment alters a person's right to bring suit against a co-subcontractor, it is probably a substantive amendment that applies to injuries suffered only on or after the amendment's effective date, January 1, 2004.

§ 19.05 Preserving the Subrogation Lien

[1] Requirements

Both the carrier and the employee have duties and obligations regarding the subrogation lien. First, to preserve its lien, the carrier must give written notice of its subrogation rights to the third-party tortfeasors. Second, when injured workers sue, they do so not only for themselves individually, but for the use and benefit of the employer or carrier as well. Third, the law obligates injured workers to notify the carrier that they have filed a lawsuit. Fourth, the carrier has the statutory right to file with the court a notice of payment of compensation and medical benefits. This filing is a lien upon any judgment or settlement. Finally, injured workers cannot settle their third-party claims, either before or after suit, without the agreement of the workers' compensation carrier [§ 440.39, Fla. Stat. (7/1/97)].

Take the first requirement of written notice literally. Carriers must be certain to notify everyone involved, in writing, of the existence of the lien. This includes the tortfeasor, the tortfeasor's insurer, the injured employee, and the employee's attorney. The requirement that the injured worker inform the carrier about filing a suit is also mandatory. For example, the carrier put the injured worker on notice of its lien by letter. The injured worker later sued the third party without notifying the workers' compensation carrier. After he settled the claim, the injured worker tried to avoid the lien. He argued the carrier waived its rights because the carrier failed to file notice of its lien in the suit. This argument failed. The carrier's duty to file notice of its lien in the suit does not apply unless the injured worker first complies with his own duty to notify the carrier that he has filed a suit [*see* C & L Trucking v. Corbitt, 546 So. 2d 1185, 1186 (Fla. 5th DCA 1989)].

Once suit is filed against a tortfeasor, the employer or carrier may file in the suit a "Notice of Payment of Compensation Benefits" to the employee [*see* § 440.39(3)(a), Fla. Stat.]. When a case is settled either before a suit is filed or while a suit is pending, the settlement should not be concluded without the consent of the employer or its workers' compensation carrier. This assumes, of course, that the tortfeasor is on notice of the employer's subrogation claim. If the parties cannot agree on the employer's pro rata share of the settlement, the circuit court will determine the amount to be paid to each in an equitable distribution hearing [*see* Circle K Corp. v. Webster, 747 So. 2d 1010, 1011 (Fla. 5th DCA 1999)].

[2] Notice of Lien and Statute of Limitations

Florida law provides a four-year time limit to sue for bodily injury. This limitation, however, does not apply to filing a notice of lien. The best way to explain this is with a case example. The employee was injured in February 1986, and sued the third-party tortfeasor in December 1989. In June 1990, the workers' compensation carrier filed notice of its lien with the court. The injured worker sought to have the lien dismissed. He argued that the carrier filed its lien more than four years after the injury and that the statute of limitations on personal injury claims had expired. The Fifth District Court of Appeal held that the right to file a notice of lien is not a new cause of action. Filing a lien merely asserts a right in an existing claim. In other words, no time limit applies to filing a notice of lien in the employee's tort action against a third party [*see* Sun Bank v. Jakubowski, 583 So. 2d 782, 783 (Fla. 5th DCA 1991)].

[3] Shake the Trees and See If Any Money Falls Out

Workers' compensation carriers should be certain to conduct a good investigation into every case of possible subrogation. Always look beyond the obvious cases, such as automobile rear-end collisions. Was the machine defective in some manner? Was it poorly designed? Should someone have covered the hole into which the injured worker fell? Did some third party fail to repair the brakes properly? Were the boards sold for use on the scaffold appropriate for such use? Was the power company supposed to turn off the electricity?

The possibilities seem endless. If some physical object is involved, have it inspected by an expert. If the object is defective, the carrier must be certain to preserve it as it was at the time of the accident. Adjusters should consult with an attorney on the proper procedure to maintain the chain of custody of such physical evidence.

Even when the subrogation potential is weak, carriers should put third parties on notice anyway. Sometimes it pays to shake the trees and see if any money falls out.

§ 19.06 Recovery Limits

[1] Lien Reduction Factors

The law entitles workers' compensation carriers to recover 100 percent of paid and future benefits. The same law, however, reduces this recovery by the carrier's proportionate share of the injured worker's attorney's fees and costs, and any reductions in the injured worker's settlement. A court may reduce an injured worker's recovery because of the injured worker's own negligence. Further, reductions may result because the third party had inadequate insurance limits, or no insurance at all. § 440.39(3)(a), Fla. Stat. provides:

> In determining the employer's or carrier's pro rata share of those costs and attorney's fees, the employer or carrier shall have deducted from its recovery a percentage amount equal to the percentage of the judgment or settlement which is for costs and attorneys' fees. Subject to this deduction, the employer or carrier shall recover from the judgment or settlement, after costs and attorney's fees incurred by the employee or dependent in that suit have been deducted, 100 percent of what it has paid and future benefits to be paid, except, if the employee or dependent can demonstrate to the court that he or she did not recover the full value of damages sustained, the employer or carrier shall recover . . . a percentage of what it has paid and future benefits to be paid equal to the percentage that the employee's net recovery is of the full value of the employee's damages. . . .

Note that one of the factors used to reduce the amount of the lien is the employer's pro rata share of the employees' "costs." The question is does "costs" include all costs or only taxable costs incurred on behalf of the employee. The 2d DCA held that only taxable costs apply [*see* ETS of New Orleans Inc. v. Jones, 738 So. 2d 958, 959–960 (Fla. 2d DCA 1999), *reh'g granted,* 761 So. 2d 329 (Fla. 2000)]. However, the Florida Supreme Court disagreed and quashed the 2d DCA's decision in *ETS*. The question before the Supreme Court was whether, under § 440.39(3)(a), Fla. Stat., the term "court costs" meant "taxable costs" or meant "all costs" incurred by the claimant in preparing the claim against the third party, subject to the determination that the costs were reasonable. The Supreme Court concluded the term "all court costs," when viewed within the totality of § 440.39(3)(a), Fla. Stat., is not limited to taxable costs [Jones v. ETS of New Orleans, Inc., 793 So. 2d 912 (Fla. 2001)].

Although the employer is immune, a jury's verdict form must show the employer's percentage of negligence, if any. The Florida Supreme Court held that, "It [is] necessary to consider the percentage of fault of the plaintiff's employer even though the employer was immune from tort liability under workers' compensation laws" [*see* Allied Signal, Inc. v. Fox, 623 So. 2d 1180, 1182 (Fla. 1993)].

If the employer's negligence contributes to the accident, the injured worker's recovery

Guide to Claims

and, thus, the workers' compensation carrier's lien, will be reduced. For example, assume a defective machine caused the worker's injury. The jury then finds as follows. The injured worker is 20 percent at fault, the employer is 20 percent at fault, and the manufacturer of the machine is 60 percent at fault. Before the *Allied Signal* decision, a jury would ignore the immune employer's negligence and assign 80 percent of the blame to the manufacturer. Damages awarded would be reduced by 20 percent. Under *Allied Signal,* the plaintiff's award would be reduced by 40 percent because the employer's portion would not be recoverable [*see also* Fabre v. Marin, 623 So. 2d 1182, 1185–1186 (Fla. 1993)].

[2] The *Manfredo* Formula

The Third District Court of Appeal gave us the proper formula to use in calculating the distribution of settlement proceeds. Following are the facts of the case:

The workers' compensation carrier paid $44,465.05 in benefits. The Court decided the claim against the third party was worth $1,500,000, but the injured worker received only $900,000 because of his own comparative negligence. His attorney's fees and costs were $409,500. Now let us apply the formula:

THE MANFREDO FORMULA

Value of claim	$1,500,000
Actual recovery	$ 900,000
Minus fees and costs	$ 409,500
= Net recovery	$ 490,500
Percent recovered	$490,500/$1,500,000 = 0.327

The injured worker's actual recovery, after deductions for his own comparative negligence and his attorney's fees and costs, amounted to only 32 percent of the value of his claim. The carrier could therefore recover only 32 percent of what it had already paid. In addition, however, the Court held the carrier could reduce future benefits by 32 percent as well [*see* Cas. Ins. Co. v. Manfredo, 542 So. 2d 1365, 1366–1367 (Fla. 3d DCA 1989), *aff'd,* 560 So. 2d 1162 (Fla. 1990)].

In 1999, however, the 1st DCA reached a different conclusion about how the percentage should be applied. If the employee recovers, for example, 25 percent of the full value of his claim, the carrier may recover only 25 percent as well. The question is, 25 percent of what? Until now, there existed a general assumption that *Manfredo* stood for the proposition that the carrier could recover 25% of what it had paid and what it would pay in the future. The court noted that this could result in the carrier recovering the entire amount paid to the injured worker which would include that portion attributable to compensation for pain and suffering. For example, assume that the worker's claim was worth $100,000 and that the recovery amounted to $25,000 or 25 percent. Assume further that the carrier had paid $120,000 in benefits. The lien's value then would be 25 percent of that, or $30,000, an amount greater than the total received by the worker.

The court has held, therefore, that the carrier's lien is limited to a percentage of the amount recovered by the worker rather than of the benefits it paid. In this example, the carrier's lien is worth 25 percent of the $25,000 recovered or a total of $6,250. Put another way, the carrier is entitled to a percentage of the percentage recovered by the worker [*see* City of Hollywood v. Lombardi, 738 So. 2d 491, 495–496 (Fla. 1st DCA 1999) (Benton dissenting), *reh'g granted,* 761 So. 2d 327 (Fla. 2000)].

The Florida Supreme Court, however, disagreed with the "percentage of a percentage" formula and quashed the First District's decision, holding that the legislature did not intend to so drastically limit the lien rights of carriers. Therefore, the maximum amount a carrier can recover, both directly and by offsetting future benefits, is the full amount that the claimant recovered. This is true even if it results in a claimant's net tort recovery being consumed by the repayment of the carrier's lien [*see* City of Hollywood v. Lombardi, 770 So. 2d 1196, 1199–1202 (Fla. 2000)].

Guide to Claims

[3] Recovery and Offset Apply to Both Medical and Indemnity Benefits

In 1990, the trial court held that the carrier's recovery for future benefits applies to indemnity benefits only. The Second District Court of Appeal affirmed the order [*see* Payless Oil Co. v. Reynolds, 565 So. 2d 737, 738 (Fla. 2d DCA 1990)].

In 1992, the issue was again before the appellate court, but this time in the Fifth District Court of Appeal. Relying on *Payless,* the trial judge approved a 34-percent set off. The judge held, however, that the set off applied only against future indemnity benefits and not health care benefits. Instead of a direct set off against both classes of benefits, the judge granted the carrier a credit of 34 percent of medical benefits, but only as a set off against future indemnity benefits. Thus, if indemnity benefits cease, so does the set off. The appellate court disagreed with the lower court and reversed. The appellate court held that the trial court erred in relying on *Payless.* The carrier's pro rata recovery applies equally to both compensation and medical benefits for both past and future payments. The court acknowledged its opinion conflicted with the Second District Court of Appeal in *Payless,* but did not certify the question to the Florida Supreme Court [*see* Tarmac of Fla./Liberty Mut. v. Gwaltney, 604 So. 2d 907, 908 (Fla. 5th DCA 1992)].

Since the *Gwaltney* decision, however, the Second District Court of Appeal revisited the issue. The court noted the Fifth District Court of Appeal's holding and receded from its earlier view in *Payless.* The Second District Court of Appeal, in agreeing with the Fifth District Court of Appeal, said: "We now agree the applicable statute does not allow the trial court the discretion to exclude future medical benefits and limit recovery of the workers' compensation lien to only future indemnity benefits" [*see* City of Lakeland v. Morris, 627 So. 2d 572, 573 (Fla. 2d DCA 1993)].

[4] Full Value Often Difficult to Decide

[a] Jurisdiction

Another problem in these cases is figuring out the full value of the injured worker's damages. When a case goes through a jury trial to conclusion, the jury will award full damages. The jury will then reduce the award by the amount of any comparative negligence. Without a judicial determination of full value, however, the debate begins.

Often, when a case settles before trial, the injured worker's attorney will argue that the injured worker did not receive full value. What happens if the carrier and the injured worker's attorney cannot agree on the amount of full value? The parties must resolve the issue in circuit court rather than by a judge of compensation claims.

The statute makes it clear that a judge of compensation claims has no jurisdiction to resolve a dispute over a third-party tortfeasor's lien. Such jurisdiction rests with the appropriate circuit court [*see* § 440.39(3)(b), Fla. Stat. (7/1/97); University of Cent. Florida v. Gleaves, 586 So. 2d 458, 459 (Fla. 1st DCA 1991)].

If the case goes up to the circuit court, the parties should be prepared with expert testimony about the value of the claim. According to the Fourth DCA, the injured worker's attorney is qualified to testify as to the true value of the injured worker's case [*see* Arone v. Sherwood, 561 So. 2d 1269, 1271 (Fla. 4th DCA 1990)].

[b] Burden of Proof

It is the claimant's burden to prove that he or she did not receive full value for the settlement of his or her claim. § 440.39, Fla. Stat., requires the employee to demonstrate to the court that he or she did not receive the full value of damages sustained because of comparative negligence or because of limits of insurance coverage and collectibility. Note, however, that the claimant's attorney is qualified to testify as to the value of the case, and the attorney's sworn testimony is competent substantial evidence, which the court should consider [*see* American States Ins. Co. v. Rozier, 450 So. 2d 547 (Fla. 4th DCA 1984); *see also* Arone v. Sherwood, 561 So. 2d 1269 (Fla. 4th DCA 1990)].

[5] Recovery of Interest on the Judgment

The law provides that defendants owe interest on a judgment at the rate of 12 percent per year. Interest accrues from the date a court enters an order until the date the defendant pays it. This can be a substantial sum if the judgment is large and a significant time passes from the date of the judgment to the date of payment. The most common cause for a long delay is an appeal. The question becomes whether the law entitles a workers' compensation carrier to a pro rata share of any interest paid. The answer is yes! *Commercial Union Ins. Co. v. Fallen,* 603 So. 2d 610, 613 (Fla. 5th DCA 1992), provides:

> The lien of the employer or its compensation carrier attaches when the amount is liquidated through judgment or settlement. The right to distribution of the proceeds of the judgment or settlement is after the funds are collected and the employees and carrier either agree on the pro rata share due the carrier or a court awards the pro rata share. It is immaterial whether the proceeds from the judgment or settlement include interest since the proceeds represent a fund to be shared by Employees and the carrier.

[6] Recovery From Uninsured Motorist Policy

Automobile uninsured motorist coverage is first-party coverage. That is to say, its purpose is to protect the insured in the event the liable motorist is not insured, or does not carry adequate limits. Subject to policy limits, uninsured or under-insured coverage pays the policy holder those amounts he or she would have recovered had the at-fault driver been properly insured. The first question is, does the workers' compensation carrier have a right of lien against the proceeds of the uninsured motorist policy? The answer is no. § 627.727(1), Fla. Stat. provides:

> Such coverage . . . [uninsured motorist] . . . shall not inure directly or indirectly to the benefit of any workers' compensation or disability benefits carrier or any person or organization qualifying as a self-insurer under any workers' compensation or disability benefits law or similar law.

The second question is, can we include the uninsured motorist recovery as part of the total recovery in calculating the percentage amount of the compensation carrier's lien? Again, the answer is no.

1. The law provides that a workers' compensation carrier may recover only in claims or actions at law against a third-party tortfeasor. The uninsured motorist carrier is not a third party [§ 440.39(3)(a), Fla. Stat. (7/1/97)].
2. The law does not allow uninsured motorist coverage to benefit any workers' compensation carrier. To include the amount recovered under uninsured motorist coverage would clearly benefit the compensation carrier and, therefore, cannot be allowed [§ 627.727(1), Fla. Stat. (7/1/97); *see* Volk v. Gallopo, 585 So. 2d 1163, 1166 (Fla. 4th DCA 1991)].

[7] Settlement for Other Than Cash

Finally, be aware that the parties can settle a lien for other than cash. For example, the carrier may agree to waive all or part of its lien in exchange for a settlement of the injured worker's future compensation benefits.

§ 19.07 Beware of Creating Employer's Liability

[1] Suits for Contribution and Indemnity

Carriers must be careful when pursuing a third-party recovery to avoid exposing the employer and the carrier to an end-run lawsuit. As discussed, employees cannot sue their employers but, by suing a third party, they may end with the same result. For example, the employee may sue the manufacturer of the machine that caused the injury. The manufacturer then sues the employer for indemnity.

The chance of setting events in motion that result in an employer's liability exposure has often made claims departments reluctant to pursue sound subrogation claims.

[2] Contribution v. Indemnity

[a] Contribution

Under the principle of contribution, a court may enter a judgment against a tortfeasor. This principle allows the tortfeasor to recover proportional shares of the judgment from other tortfeasors whose negligence contributed to the injury and who were also liable to the plaintiff. Contribution, then, is the principle of apportioning the burden of loss among two or more joint tortfeasors. This principle, however, has no application to an employer's

Guide to Claims

liability in workers' compensation. Since the employer does not share a common duty or liability to the injured worker with a third-party tortfeasor, contribution does not apply. Contribution assesses relationships such as between the negligent parties and the injured employee. Indemnification, on the other hand, assesses the relationships such as between the third party and the employer.

An employer, however, is subject to strict liability to its workers for workplace injuries despite fault. Because of this, the employer's liability is different from that of a third-party tortfeasor. Assume the employer's negligence was the primary cause of the accident. If the third-party tortfeasor was actively negligent, even to a minor degree, contribution between the parties cannot apply. The third party will bear the entire loss [*see* United Gas Pipeline Company v. Gulf Power Company, 334 So. 2d 310, 313–314 (Fla. 1st DCA 1976)].

[b] Indemnity

The Court defined the term "indemnity" as follows [*see* Houdaille Industries, Inc. v. Edwards, 374 So. 2d 490, 493 (Fla. 1979)]:

> Indemnity is a right which inures to one who discharges the duty owed by him, but which, as between himself and another, should have been discharged by the other and is allowable only where the *whole* fault is in the one against whom indemnity is sought. . . . It shifts the entire loss from one who, although without active negligence or fault, has been obligated to pay, because of some vicarious, constructive, derivative, or technical liability, to another who should bear the costs because it was the latter's wrongdoing for which the former is held liable. . . . Indemnity rests upon the fault of another which has been imputed to or constructively fastened upon the one seeking indemnity, and there can be no indemnity between joint tortfeasors. . . . A weighing of the relative fault of tortfeasors has no place in the concept of indemnity for the one seeking indemnity must be without fault.

[3] The *Houdaille* Test

The Houdaille Court [*see* [2][b], *above*] set forth an implicit two-part test.

1. A party seeking indemnity must be wholly without fault. As a logical corollary, the other party (the employer) must be at fault.

2. Although faultless, the party seeking indemnity has become obligated to pay. This obligation results from some vicarious, constructive, derivative, or technical liability, and it may arise from a special relationship with the blameworthy party.

As this test suggests, indemnity allows such a constructively liable, but faultless, party to shift the whole loss against the actual wrongdoer. As should be clear by now, injured workers can support claims for indemnity only in extraordinary situations.

[4] Active v. Passive Negligence: Applying the Tests

One problem in these cases has been abuses in terminology that led to confusing decisions in the past. The *Houdaille* Court [*see* [2][b], [3], *above*] clarified the issue by saying [Houdaille Industries, Inc. v. Edwards, 374 So. 2d 490, 493 (Fla. 1979)]:

"Regardless of what specific terms are employed—whether the courts say active-passive or primary-secondary—what they are really speaking of is fault or no fault."

Further, the court said: "We will look to the party seeking indemnity to determine whether he is without fault . . . [I]t is immaterial whether the (other party) is also without fault."

It does not matter whether or not the employer is negligent as far as the first part of the test is concerned. The court is initially interested only in whether the party seeking indemnification is wholly without fault. If there is fault, even to some small degree, then indemnification does not apply.

Assume that the first part of the test has been satisfied and that the party seeking indemnity is wholly without fault. This is still not enough. The second part of the test is that the party seeking indemnification, although faultless, is vicariously, constructively, derivatively, or technically liable.

The "vicarious" language encompasses unique circumstances where some special relationship or duty owed by one party to the party seeking indemnity exists. An example may be the common practice of general contractors lending their contractor's license to another. Usually, this occurs because the borrowing general contractor is not authorized to work in the particular county. It may be because, for one reason or another, the borrowing general contractor simply does not have a contractor's license. Assume an employee of the subcontractor is injured on the job where the borrowing general contractor is in charge. The general contractor has a duty to assure the safety of the construction site. A check of the records will make it appear that the loaning contractor is responsible for the job though he has absolutely nothing to do with the project. That contractor may be held liable although clearly without fault regarding the accident.

The loaning contractor is technically liable for the judgment because his name is recorded as the general contractor on the project; however, the negligence was solely that of the person who borrowed the license. Thus, the relationship of the parties makes the named general contractor vicariously or technically liable.

PRACTICE POINT: The mere suggestion of a possible indemnity situation should not give employers or carriers undue concern. Many imaginative attempts may occur to show vicarious liability. The *Houdaille* Court [*see* [2][b], [3], *above*], however, clearly suggested that it will not allow the ruse of vicarious, constructive, or derivative liability to be applied in mundane or otherwise inapplicable situations. In short, carriers and adjusters need not become alarmed about the prospects of indemnity simply because the employer appears to have acted with gross or active negligence. The third party must be wholly (100 percent) blameless. Simultaneously, it must occupy some peculiar posture where the courts will compel it to pay for wrongful actions of the employer in question. Focus an investigation on these points. If present, carriers should consult with an attorney before encouraging or starting litigation.

Regardless of what specific terms are employed—whether the courts say active-passive or primary-secondary—what they are really speaking of is fault or no fault."

Further, the court said: "We will look to the party seeking indemnity to determine whether he is without fault. . . . [I]t is immaterial whether the (other party) is also without fault."

It does not matter whether or not the employer is negligent as far as the first part of the test is concerned. The court is initially interested only in whether the party seeking indemnification is wholly without fault. If there is fault, even to some small degree, then indemnification does not apply.

Assume that the first part of the test has been satisfied and that the party seeking indemnity is wholly without fault. This is still not enough. The second part of the test is that the party seeking indemnification, although faultless, is vicariously, constructively, derivatively, or technically liable.

The "vicarious" language encompasses unique circumstances where some special relationship or duty owed by one party to the party seeking indemnity exists. An example may be the common practice of general contractors lending their contractor's license to another. Usually, this occurs because the borrowing general contractor is not authorized to work in the particular county. It may be because, for one reason or another, the borrowing general contractor simply does not have a contractor's license. Assume an employee of the subcontractor is injured on the job where the borrowing general contractor is in charge. The general contractor has a duty to assure the safety of the construction site. A check of the records will make it appear that the loaning contractor is responsible for the job though he has absolutely nothing to do with the project. That contractor may be held liable although clearly without fault regarding the accident.

The loaning contractor is technically liable for the judgment because his name is recorded as the general contractor on the project; however the negligence was solely that of the person who borrowed the license. Thus, the relationship of the parties makes the named general contractor vicariously or technically liable.

PRACTICE POINT: The mere suggestion of a possible indemnity situation should not give employers or carriers undue concern. Many imaginative attorneys may occur to show vicarious liability. The *Rossmoor* Court [see [2][b], [3], *above*], however, clearly suggested that it will not allow the use of vicarious, constructive, or derivative liability to be applied in mundane or otherwise inapplicable situations. In short, carriers and adjusters need not become alarmed about the prospects of indemnity simply because the employer appears to have acted with gross or active negligence. The third party must be wholly (100 percent) blameless. Simultaneously, it must occupy some peculiar posture where the courts will compel it to pay for wrongful actions of the employer in question. Focus an investigation on these points. If present, carriers should consult with an attorney before encouraging or starting litigation.

CHAPTER 20

THE SPECIAL DISABILITY TRUST FUND

Guide to Claims

SYNOPSIS

§ 20.01 Purpose and Legislative Intent

[1] The Rule

> **SPECIAL ALERT:** The Special Disability Trust Fund does not apply to accidents occurring on or after January 1, 1998 [*see* § 20.04, *below*].

If an impaired worker is injured again, the preexisting condition may result in increased disability. The carrier or self-insured employer remains liable for the cumulative effects, but may, however, be eligible for reimbursement for that portion of benefits paid as the result of the increased injury and disability.

[2] Purpose

The purpose of the Special Disability Trust Fund (SDTF) is to encourage the hiring of disabled workers. It also serves to relieve an employer of excess liability if an impaired worker is injured on the job. For example, an employer may hire an applicant with only one eye. The employer does so with the knowledge that should the employee lose the remaining eye in an industrial accident, the employee will become permanently and totally disabled. As a result, the employer will be liable for workers' compensation benefits for the cumulative effects of the combined injuries. Due to this increased exposure and liability, employers could be reluctant to hire or rehire such an individual. In response to this concern, the legislature created the SDTF in 1955. Its original purpose was to encourage the hiring of "disabled" workers by providing reimbursement for that portion of benefits paid as the result of the increased injury and disability. Financing for the SDTF comes from taxes assessed against insurance companies and self-insured employers.

> **SPECIAL NOTE:** The Special Disability Trust Fund provisions in the Workers' Compensation Act underwent a significant rewrite effective January 1, 1994. This is a substantive amendment that applies only to accidents occurring on or after that date. We will first review the law as it applies to accident dates in and before 1993. We will follow this with a review of the law as it applies to accidents occurring during and after 1994. Accidents occurring on or after January 1, 1998, are not eligible for reimbursement [*see* § 20.04].

For a general survey of second injury funds, see LARSON'S WORKERS' COMPENSATION, DESK EDITION, Ch. 91 (Matthew Bender).

§ 20.02 Application Through December 31, 1993

[1] Legislative Intent

The legislature's intent comes directly from the statute, which provides [§ 440.49(2)(a), Fla. Stat.]:

Guide to Claims

It is the purpose of this subsection to encourage the employment of the physically handicapped by protecting employers from excess liability for compensation and medical expense when an injury to a handicapped worker merges with his preexisting permanent physical impairment to cause a greater disability, permanent impairment, or wage loss than would have resulted from the injury alone.

[2] Reemployment Benefit for Employers

The Special Disability Trust Fund's primary purpose is to encourage the hiring of impaired workers, and to encourage the rehiring of such workers after an injury as well. Effective July 1, 1990, the legislature created a new rehiring program [§ 440.49(2)(k), Fla. Stat. (7/1/90)], the purpose of which is to encourage the hiring of workers who suffered a permanent impairment from a workplace injury. The SDTF promised to pay an employer who hired such a worker, 50 percent of that employee's wages for up to 6 months. As it turns out, the experiment failed miserably. Only a half dozen or fewer employers applied for reimbursement, and the Fund denied all of them. Understandably, the legislature repealed the program effective January 1, 1994.

[3] Criteria for Perfecting a Claim

Carriers must satisfy four fundamental elements before obtaining reimbursement from the Special Disability Trust Fund. Those elements are as follows:

1. The injured worker must have had a preexisting permanent impairment [§ 440.49(4), Fla. Stat. (5/30/97)].

2. The employer must have known of the preexisting permanent impairment before the accident [§ 440.49(6), Fla. Stat. (5/30/97)].

3. The new injury must result in a new disability and the new disability must merge with the preexisting disability. This merger must result in a new disability or wage loss that is greater than that which would have occurred from the new disability alone [§ 440.49(2)(c), (d), Fla. Stat. (5/30/97)].

4. Payment of permanent compensation, such as impairment benefits, wage loss, permanent total disability, or death benefits must be made [*see* former § 440.49(2)(g), Fla. Stat. (1991) (the legislature repealed this requirement effective 1/1/94; *see* § 20.03[5], for discussion of § 440.49(2)(c)3, Fla. Stat. (5/30/97))].

[4] Preexisting Impairment Required

To qualify for reimbursement, carriers must show that the injured worker had a preexisting permanent impairment. This impairment may be due to a previous accident or disease, or even a congenital condition. The impairment must be, or at least is likely to be, a hindrance or obstacle to employment. The impairment or condition, however, cannot be due to the natural aging process.

What does permanent impairment mean? For the purposes of the Special Disability

Trust Fund, permanent impairment means "any permanent condition due to previous accident or disease or any congenital condition which is, or is likely to be, a hindrance or obstacle to employment, but not due to the natural aging process" [*see* former § 440.49(2)(b)1, Fla. Stat. (1991)]. The preexisting condition need not have arisen out of a previous workers' compensation loss. Any preexisting disability will do, unless it is from old age.

The carrier's first step is to prove the preexisting condition exists. This will require that the claims adjuster carefully question the injured worker concerning medical history. If evidence of a preexisting condition exists, the next step is to obtain the medical records. The emphasis should be on the permanent nature of the condition. Often the old records may not be available. This is not necessarily fatal to the carrier's claim. Disabilities should be obvious to the present treating physician. The physician can probably testify that the condition preexisted the present injury and is permanent.

[5] Employer Knowledge Required

[a] Purpose

Remember that the SDTF's purpose is to encourage hiring. If the employer did not know about the preexisting condition, the employer could not have been encouraged to hire the employee in spite of it. Therefore, the law requires that the employer not only knew about the condition, but knew it was permanent and likely to be a hindrance to employment [*see* former § 440.49(2)(f)1, Fla. Stat. (1991)].

[b] When Knowledge Must Exist

The employer's knowledge need only have existed before the accident and injury. The Act provides that the employer must have known about the preexisting condition "prior to the occurrence of the subsequent injury or occupational disease" [§ 440.49(6)(a), Fla. Stat. (5/30/97)]. If the employer hired an individual without knowing about a preexisting impairment, but learned of it before the accident, this is enough to satisfy the knowledge requirement. Remember that employer knowledge does not refer to any particular person. This is especially true with a corporate employer. If a supervisor, manager, or anyone in management with hiring and firing authority knew about the impairment, then the corporate employer will be held to have the requisite knowledge. Thus, do not give up simply because the company's president had no knowledge.

[c] Employer Must Know Condition Is Permanent

The second part of the knowledge requirement is that the employer knew the condition was permanent in character. The Act lists 24 conditions. Employer knowledge of these conditions creates a "conclusive presumption that the employer considered the condition to be both permanent and . . . a hindrance to employment" [*see* former § 440.49(2)(f)1, Fla. Stat. (7/1/90)]. Note, however, that the mere existence of one of these conditions does not create a presumption that the condition is permanent, but only that the employer considered it so. This language does not change the employer's burden to prove that the condition was, in fact, permanent [*see* D.A. Netzel, Inc. v. Trust Fund, 681 So. 2d 874, 875–876 (Fla. 1st DCA 1996)].

For example, although an employer can show that the injured worker was obese, the employer must still show that this worker's obesity amounts to a preexisting permanent impairment. (Note: The 1994 amendments create a presumption of both knowledge and permanence; *see* § 20.03).

The presumptive conditions are as follows:

1. Epilepsy
2. Diabetes
3. Cardiac disease
4. Marie-Strumpell disease
5. Amputation of foot, leg, arm, or hand
6. Total loss of sight of one or both eyes or a partial loss of corrected vision of more than 75 percent bilaterally
7. Residual disability from poliomyelitis
8. Cerebral palsy
9. Multiple sclerosis
10. Parkinson's disease
11. Vascular disorder
12. Psychoneurotic disability following confinement for treatment in a recognized medical or mental institution for more than six months
13. Hemophilia
14. Chronic osteomyelitis
15. Ankylosis of a major weight bearing bone
16. Hyperinsulinism
17. Muscular dystrophy
18. Herniated intervertebral disk
19. Surgical removal of an intervertebral disk
20. Total deafness
21. Mental retardation
22. Any condition resulting in a 20-percent impairment of the body as a whole
23. Thrombophlebitis
24. Obesity in which the employee is 30 percent or more overweight (The legislature added obesity as one of these conditions effective July 1, 1990)

PRACTICE POINT: Establishing the existence of preexisting conditions often requires expert testimony. For his or her testimony to be admissible, a physician must qualify as an expert on the specific topic, such as the cause for the claimant's obesity. Otherwise, such testimony does not constitute competent substantial evidence upon which a judge of compensation claims can base a ruling [*see* Special Disability Trust Fund, Dep't of Labor & Empl. Sec. v. South Florida Board Marriot/Marriot Cas. Claim, 775 So. 2d 423 (Fla. 1st DCA 2001)].

For all other conditions, the carrier also must show that the employer knew the condition was both permanent and likely to be a hindrance to employment. It is therefore critical, and required by rule, to obtain an affidavit or deposition from the employer (i.e., someone with hiring and firing authority). The affidavit must attest to this knowledge and that, moreover, in spite of this knowledge, the employer hired the individual or continued the employment. Affidavits must contain the following statement [Fla. Admin. Code R. 69L-10.011(3), (4) (1/10/2005)]:

> Under penalty of perjury, I declare that I have read the foregoing; that the facts as alleged are true, to the best of my knowledge and belief; and that a representative of the Special Disability Trust Fund is authorized to contact me to confirm the truthfulness of this statement.

[6] The Merger Requirement

[a] Definition of Merger

Once having produced evidence that the employer knew about a preexisting condition [*see* [5], *above*], the carrier must now show that the employee has suffered a new disability. The carrier also must show that the two conditions have merged to create a new, greater, disability. The Act, before 1994, defines a merger as follows [§ 440.49(2)(b)2, Fla. Stat.]:

> a. Had the permanent physical impairment not existed, the subsequent accident or occupational disease would not have occurred;
>
> b. The permanent disability, permanent impairment, or wage loss resulting from the subsequent accident or occupational disease is materially and substantially greater than that which would have resulted had the permanent physical impairment not existed and the employer has been required to pay, and has paid, permanent total disability, permanent impairment, or wage loss benefits for that materially and substantially greater disability; or
>
> c. Death would not have been accelerated had the permanent physical impairment not existed.

[b] Direct Medical Merger Not Required

Direct medical relationship between the two impairments is not necessary to have a merger. The law requires only that the previous disability interact with the effects of a new compensable injury. This interaction must result in an increase in the residual disability beyond the new injury alone [*see* Flowers Baking v. Special Disability Tr., 550 So. 2d 135, 137 (Fla. 1st DCA 1989)].

The Act does not intend the term "merger" to be a merger in a medical sense. Instead, "merger" means, in the more general sense, a combination of all factors that influence the injured worker's employability. These factors include the injured worker's physical disabilities, age, education, job skills, and rehabilitation prospects [*see* Wright v. Gulf and Western Food Products, 401 So. 2d 1316, 1317 (Fla. 1981)].

A physician may not simply add the old and new disability ratings together. Such evidence does not establish a merger. For example, assume the original rating is 2 percent and the new rating (for the new injury alone) is 8 percent. The combined rating is 10 percent. Just because the new combined rating is greater than the new rating alone does not establish a merger. The impairment rating for the second accident alone must be increased because of the effects of the preexisting impairment. "To establish a merger, there must be evidence that the claimant's overall disability rating is greater than the sum of [the] permanent partial disability ratings" [*see* Bd. of Cty. Com'rs v. Spec. Disability Trust, 417 So. 2d 1075 (Fla. 1st DCA 1982); Special Disability Trust v. Florida Power, 593 So. 2d 1178, 1179–1180 (Fla. 1st DCA 1992)].

[7] The Permanent Compensation Requirement

The final requirement to perfect an SDTF claim is paying permanent benefits. These benefits include permanent impairment benefits, wage loss benefits, permanent total disability benefits, or death benefits [§ 440.49(2)(b)3, Fla. Stat. (1990)]. The reasoning is that if injured workers recover to the point that they return to work without wage loss, there cannot be any increased disability as the result of a merger. Thus, no recovery is allowed when the carrier pays only temporary benefits, no matter how high the costs.

[8] Recovery Limits

The maximum recovery limits are as follows:

1. Temporary Total and Medical
   50% of the first $10,000
   100% of benefits paid above $10,000

2. Permanent Impairment
   60% of impairment benefits paid

3. Wage Loss
   60% of wage loss paid in the first five years
   75% of wage loss paid after five years

4. Permanent Total
   100% of permanent total disability benefits paid after the first 175 weeks

5. Death
   75% of all death benefits paid
   75% of all funeral expenses paid

Remember that these percentages of recovery are maximums. The SDTF may say that less than the maximum is due. For example, assume the merger of the two conditions caused increased wage loss. Also assume that this did not contribute in any way to the period of temporary total disability or to the need for medical care. In such a case, the law entitles the carrier to reimbursement only for the increased permanent benefits. There is no entitlement to recover the temporary benefits or the medical expenses.

The law specifically excludes reimbursement for any portion of the carrier's costs, interest, penalties, or attorney's fees [§ 440.49(2)(f)2, Fla. Stat. (1990)]. The law specifically includes reimbursement for rehabilitation benefits. Rehabilitation is remedial attendance for the purposes of SDTF reimbursement. Also, remember that this applies only to education and training, and not to such services as medical management, job placement, and the like. Beginning on July 1, 1990, vocational rehabilitation (training and education) became the Division's responsibility for accidents occurring on or after that date. The law does allow carriers to provide such rehabilitation benefits voluntarily. The SDTF, however, is unlikely to voluntarily reimburse any benefits paid but not required under the Act [§ 440.49(2)(f)4, Fla. Stat. (6/30/83)].

§ 20.03 Accidents Between January 1, 1994, and January 1, 1998

[1] Legislative Intent

The legislature's intent comes directly from the statute [§ 440.49(1), Fla. Stat. (5/30/97)]:

> Whereas it is often difficult for workers with disabilities to achieve employment or to become reemployed following an injury, and it is the desire of the Legislature to facilitate the return of these workers to the workplace, it is the purpose of this section to encourage the employment, reemployment, and accommodation of the physically disabled by reducing an employer's insurance premium for reemploying an injured worker, to decrease litigation between carriers on apportionment issues, and to protect employers from excess liability for compensation and medical expense when an injury to a physically disabled worker merges with, aggravates, or accelerates her or his preexisting permanent physical impairment to cause either a greater disability or permanent impairment, or an increase in expenditures for temporary compensation or medical benefits than would have resulted from the injury alone.

[2] Criteria for Perfecting a Claim

The legislature enacted significant changes to the basic criteria for reimbursement. For all injuries occurring on or after January 1, 1994, the carrier need establish only that: (1) the injured worker suffered from a preexisting permanent impairment; and (2) the employer had knowledge of the preexisting impairment before the occurrence of the new accident [*see* § 440.49(6)(a), Fla. Stat. (5/30/97)]. The requirement that the new injury resulted in an increased impairment no longer exists. Showing the new injury aggravated the preexisting condition is enough.

[3] Preexisting Impairment Required

As before, the injured worker must have had a preexisting permanent impairment listed in the statute. *No other impairments qualify.* The qualifying impairments are as follows [§ 440.49(6)(a), Fla. Stat. (5/30/97)]:

1. Epilepsy
2. Diabetes
3. Cardiac disease
4. Amputation of foot, leg, arm or hand
5. Total loss of sight of one or both eyes or a partial loss of corrected vision of more than 75 percent bilaterally
6. Residual disability from poliomyelitis
7. Cerebral palsy
8. Multiple sclerosis
9. Parkinson's disease
10. Meniscectomy
11. Patellectomy
12. Ruptured cruciate ligament
13. Hemophilia
14. Chronic osteomyelitis
15. Surgical or spontaneous fusion of a major weight-bearing joint
16. Hyperinsulinism
17. Muscular dystrophy
18. Thrombophlebitis
19. Herniated intervertebral disk
20. Surgical removal of an intervertebral disk
21. One or more back injuries or a disease process of the back; this must result in disability over a total of 120 or more days, if proved by a doctor's opinion that there was a preexisting impairment to the injured worker's back
22. Total deafness
23. Mental retardation where the intelligence quotient is within the lowest two percentiles of the general population; it is not necessary that the employer knew the actual I.Q. ranking
24. Any condition resulting in a 20-percent impairment of the body as a whole

25. Obesity in which the employee is 30 percent or more overweight
26. Any permanent impairment that is the result of a prior workplace injury with the same or affiliated employer

SPECIAL ALERT: As noted, only the listed impairments qualify, with one significant exception. If the impairment resulted from a prior compensable injury with the same employer, any impairment will qualify despite whether it is a listed impairment [§ 440.49(6)(a)26, Fla. Stat. (5/30/97)]. This includes the same employer, parent company, subsidiary, sister company, or affiliate located within the State of Florida. Clearly, the legislature created this exception as an added incentive to an employer to rehire its own injured workers.

As before the 1994 amendment, the carrier's first task is to show the existence of the preexisting condition as a fact. This will still require that the adjuster carefully question the injured worker concerning medical history.

[4] Employer Knowledge Required

The employer's knowledge need only have existed before the accident and injury. If the employer hired an individual without knowing about any preexisting impairment, but learned of it before the accident, this is enough to show the requisite knowledge. The law still requires an affidavit attesting to the employer's knowledge [§ 440.49(6), Fla. Stat. (5/30/97)].

Remember, the SDTF's purpose is to encourage hiring or rehiring impaired workers both before and after an industrial accident.

The law presumes knowledge that the condition was permanent and likely to be a hindrance to employment [*see* [3], *above*].

One of the statutory conditions under § 440.49(6)(a)(21), Fla. Stat. entitling the carrier to reimbursement from the SDTF is as follows:

> One or more back injuries or a disease process of the back resulting in disability over a total of 120 or more days, if substantiated by a doctor's opinion that there was a preexisting impairment to the claimant's back.

The court held that the employer must have knowledge, not only of the preexisting back injury, but that it had resulted in disability of at least 120 days. Here, the employer knew only that the claimant had previously incurred back injuries which prevented him from performing certain physically demanding jobs. The employer did not know the extent of the employee's preexisting impairment or the length of any prior disability caused by those back injuries. Thus, the court affirmed the Judge of Compensation Claims' order denying reimbursement [Staff Leasing v. Special Disability Trust Fund, 784 So. 2d 512, 513–514 (Fla. 1st DCA 2001)].

NOTE: The legislature repealed the requirement that the employer show it knew the condition was permanent and likely to be a hindrance to employment. Instead, the

Act defines the listed impairments as permanent ones [*see* [3], *above*]. For example, the 1994 statute [§ 440.49(6)25, Fla. Stat. (5/30/97)] strongly implies that obesity, despite cause, is a permanent physical impairment for reimbursement purposes [*see* D.A. Netzel, Inc. v. Trust Fund, 681 So. 2d 874, 875 (Fla. 1st DCA 1996)].

[5] The Merger Requirement

It is still necessary that a merger exist; however, the legislature changed the definition of the term "merger." Establishing evidence of a preexisting condition and the fact that the employer had knowledge of the condition is enough to show a merger. Showing that the employee has suffered a new, increased, permanent disability is no longer necessary. Evidence that the preexisting condition merged with the new injury is also enough to show a merger. The evidence must show either a greater disability, or simply an increase in payments for temporary compensation (TTD or TPD) or for medical benefits. In other words, if the carrier can show that it has paid more benefits because of the preexisting condition than it would have otherwise, this is enough to show a merger. The Act now defines "merger" as follows [§ 440.49(2)(c), Fla. Stat. (5/30/97)]:

1. If the permanent physical impairment had not existed, the subsequent accident or occupational disease would not have occurred;
2. The permanent disability or permanent impairment resulting from the subsequent accident or occupational disease is materially and substantially greater than that which would have resulted had the permanent physical impairment not existed, and the employer has been required to pay, and has paid, permanent total disability or permanent impairment benefits for that materially and substantially greater disability;
3. The preexisting permanent physical impairment is aggravated or accelerated as a result of the subsequent injury or occupational disease, or the preexisting impairment has contributed, medically and circumstantially, to the need for temporary compensation, medical, or attendant care and the employer has been required to pay, and has paid, temporary compensation, medical, or attendant care benefits for the aggravated preexisting permanent impairment; or
4. Death would not have been accelerated had the permanent physical impairment not existed.

SPECIAL NOTE: Item number three is the new language added to the definition of "merger" effective January 1, 1994. Also, the Act refers to "merger" as defined by § 440.49(1)(*b*)(2), Fla. Stat. Unfortunately that section does not exist. § 440.49(2)(*c*), Fla. Stat. is the section that defines "merger" and that is the section we must use [*see* Sp. Disability Trust Fund v. Fla. Hosp., 692 So. 2d 260, 262 (Fla. 1st DCA 1997)].

As discussed in § 20.02, no requirement exists for direct medical relationship between the two impairments to have a merger. The fact that the previous disability interacted with the effects of a new compensable injury is enough to show a merger. The appellate decisions reviewed above should apply to cases after January 1, 1994.

[6] Paying Permanent Compensation

The legislature repealed the requirement of actual payment of permanent benefits. Carriers need only show that the preexisting condition aggravated or accelerated the new injury [§ 440.49(2)(c), Fla. Stat. (5/30/97)].

[7] Recovery Limits

Maximum recovery limits have changed substantially. A $10,000 deductible applies to most claims. An exception is that the $10,000 deductible does not apply "to claims by employers for reimbursement under subparagraph (b)3." The problem is that subparagraph (b)3 does not exist within § 440.49, Fla. Stat. This is obviously a bill drafting error. We can speculate that the intent was to apply this to subparagraph (c)3. This section describes cases of aggravated, preexisting conditions resulting in increased payments for temporary compensation, medical care, or attendant care. The SDTF's (unofficial) position is that the $10,000 deductible exception refers to subparagraph [b], the Preferred Worker Program. Until the courts rule on this issue, it will remain mere speculation [§ 440.49(3), Fla. Stat. (5/30/97)].

Except the first $10,000, unless the deductible waiver applies, the maximum recovery is as follows [§ 440.49(4), (5), Fla. Stat. (5/30/97)]:

1. Temporary Total, Temporary partial, Medical and attendant care: 50% of all payments.
2. Impairment benefits: 50% of impairment benefits paid.
3. Supplemental Wage Loss: 50% of wage loss benefits paid.
4. Permanent Total: 50% of permanent total disability benefits paid.
5. Death: 50% of all death benefits paid and 50% of all funeral expenses paid.

SPECIAL ALERT: The legislature deleted wage loss benefits from the definition of "excess permanent compensation." The new definition includes only permanent impairment, permanent total disability, or death benefits. It is conceivable that because the legislature now refers to wage loss as "supplemental benefits," it intended to include them with permanent impairment benefits. Unfortunately, the statute does not plainly say so. How the SDTF attorneys and the courts will view this remains to be seen. The early indication is that the SDTF will consider both impairment benefits and supplemental wage loss benefits in the term "permanent impairment" benefit.

Remember that, as before, these percentages of recovery are maximums. The SDTF may still say that less than the maximum is due. Also remember that the Workers'

Compensation Act still specifically excludes reimbursement for any portion of the carrier's costs, interest, penalties, or attorney's fees [§ 440.49(6)(b), Fla. Stat. (5/30/97)].

SPECIAL ALERT: Formerly, the statutes specifically included reimbursement for voluntary vocational rehabilitation expenses and for medical care coordination [§ 440.49(2)(f)4, Fla. Stat. (1983)]. The legislature repealed that section effective January 1, 1994. Therefore, for accidents occurring on or after that date, the law does not allow reimbursement for voluntary rehabilitation expense. Although the statutes provide that voluntary rehabilitation services for some catastrophic injuries are to be considered benefits, this will not apply for SDTF reimbursement [§ 440.491(5)(c), Fla. Stat. (7/1/97)]. Why? Because the section plainly provides that such services are considered benefits for rate-making purposes only.

§ 20.04 Accidents On or After January 1, 1998

Faced with mounting claims that will take decades to pay, the legislature concluded that the SDTF no longer serves a useful purpose. On the contrary, it had become a drain on carriers faced with growing assessments. Therefore, the legislature enacted changes to shut the program down.

The SDTF will not provide reimbursement for any accident occurring on or after January 1, 1998. Also, the Fund will not provide reimbursement in occupational disease cases if the disability or death occurs on or after that date. The Fund will continue to reimburse employers and carriers for accidents occurring between July 1, 1955 and December 31, 1997.

Once payment for claims occurring between these dates has been completed, the SDTF will cease operating and close forever [§ 440.49(11), Fla. Stat. (5/30/97)].

§ 20.05 General Issues: All Accident Dates

[1] Attorney's Fees

Generally, the SDTF is not responsible for reimbursing claimant attorney's fees paid by the carrier. Often, settlement agreements provide that injured workers are responsible for paying their own attorney's fees. Settlement orders usually include an attorney's fee provision. This provision describes the agreement between the injured worker and the attorney about paying the fee from the settlement proceeds. As a convenience to the parties, carriers often agree to issue separate checks for benefits and fees. The Division took the position, however, that the law did not entitle the carrier to reimbursement for the attorney's fee distribution. The Division concluded that since it was not responsible for any attorney's fees, it made no difference whether the injured worker alone is responsible for paying fees. The Division looked solely to the form of the settlement checks. If a portion appeared as a check payable to the injured worker's attorney, the Division argued that the SDTF had no liability to reimburse the carrier.

The First District Court of Appeal strongly disagreed and reversed. The court held a carrier may issue two checks without jeopardizing its statutory rights to reimbursement from the SDTF. This will be true, however, only when the carrier has no responsibility for attorney's fees and no evidence exists of collusion between the carrier and the injured worker [*see* FEISCO v. Special Disability Trust Fund, 615 So. 2d 859, 861 (Fla. 1st DCA 1993)].

[2] Imputing Knowledge

Recall that the law always requires employer knowledge of the preexisting impairment. What happens if the owner sells the businesses? Will the law impute the seller's knowledge to the new owner? The answer is no. In one case the new owner admitted that he had no actual knowledge of the worker's preexisting condition before the injury. The carrier tried to impute knowledge from the former owner to the new owner. The court held that the former owner's knowledge is not sufficient to perfect a claim for reimbursement [*see* Special Disability Trust Fund v. Siesta Lago Mobile Homes, 473 So. 2d 8, 9 (Fla. 1st DCA 1985)].

If, however, an employer relies on an outside agency to do its hiring, the law will impute the agency's knowledge to the employer. For example, the employer delegated hiring to the injured worker's union. The court held that where an employer "relies for hiring upon another, the other is the employer's veritable agent for that purpose, and the other's knowledge should be held to satisfy the employer's need for knowledge in order to claim [Special Disability Trust Fund reimbursement]" [*see* Special Disability Trust Fund v. Wheeler, 440 So. 2d 460, 461 (Fla. 1st DCA 1983)].

[3] Permanent Total Supplemental Benefits

Reimbursement for permanent total disability benefits includes the supplemental benefit. In two cases, combined for the court's review, the SDTF argued that PTD supplemental benefits are separate and distinct benefits and are not recoverable. The court disagreed and held there is a clear and unambiguous legislative intent that "additional" or "supplemental" benefits are compensation for permanent total disability and, as such, are recoverable [*see* Sp. Disability Fund v. Stephens, Lynn et al., 595 So. 2d 206, 209 (Fla. 1st DCA 1992)].

§ 20.06 Time and Procedure for Filing Claims

[1] Time Limitations

[a] Date of Accident

For accidents occurring before July 1, 1987, the Act bars a claim against the SDTF if it is not filed within 60 days after the date of the first payment of permanent benefits.

For accidents occurring on or after July 1, 1987, the Act extends this period. The new deadline is two years after the injured worker first reached maximum medical improvement, or the first payment of permanent benefits, whichever is later [*see* former § 440.49(2)(g), Fla. Stat. (1990)]. The two-year time limit is not retroactive and applies only to accidents occurring on or after July 1, 1987 [*see* Special Disability Tr. v. Southern

Bell, 551 So. 2d 575, 576 (Fla. 1st DCA 1989)].

If the employer/carrier timely places the Fund on notice of claim, there is no deadline or separate limitations period within which a proof of claim (SDF-1) must be filed. The filing of the proof of claim does not institute a separate cause of action. Instead, there is only one cause of action for entitlement to reimbursement from the Special Disability Trust Fund, followed by a second cause of action for the amount of that reimbursement (the "request" for reimbursement) if the Fund approves the initial claim. Proof of claim is nothing more than evidence required or requested in support of the initial claim for reimbursement filed by an employer/carrier. The Florida statute of limitations is met when an action is commenced within the applicable limitations period [*see* Special Disability Trust Fund v. Rescare Home Health, Inc./Liberty Mutual Group, 930 So. 2d 746, 747 (Fla. 1st DCA 2006)].

[b] When Time Begins

The time to file a claim with the SDTF begins to run on either the date the claimant last reached MMI or the date the carrier mails the first check for excess permanent compensation benefits, whichever is later [*see* Special Disab. Trust Fund v. Robbins Mfg. Co., 484 So. 2d 54, 56 (Fla. 1st DCA 1986)]. The term "excess permanent compensation" means permanent impairment, permanent total disability, wage loss benefits, or death benefits [§ 440.49(2)(b)3, Fla. Stat. (1981), § 440.49(2)(d), Fla. Stat. (1994)]. If the carrier misses the deadline, nothing will restart the clock.

As noted above, § 440.49(7)(a), Fla. Stat. provides that employer/carriers may seek reimbursement from the SDTF if they file a written notice of the claim "within 2 years after the date the employee last reached maximum medical improvement, or within 2 years after the date of the first payment of compensation for permanent total disability, wage loss, or death, whichever is later." This time period cannot be waived because, rather than a statute of limitations, this is a non-claim statute.

The phrase "whichever is later" refers to the later of two dates as between the MMI date and the date of the first compensation payment, whether it be for permanent total disability, wage loss, or death.

For example, claimant's workers' compensation claim was affirmed on appeal in 1991, the employer/carrier sent claimant a check in 1992, and claimant reached MMI in 1994. When the employer/carrier filed a notice of reimbursement with the SDTF in 1995, SDTF denied the claim as untimely, characterizing the 1992 check as the first payment of benefits. However, because claimant reached MMI after the 1992 check, employer/carrier had until two years from the date of MMI to seek reimbursement. Thus, the court held the employer/carrier's claim for reimbursement was timely [*see* Lockheed Martin v. Special Disability Trust Fund, 943 So. 2d 811, 812 (Fla. 1st DCA 2006)].

Note, however, that § 440.49(7), Fla. Stat. (Supp. 1994) provides that a claim is time barred unless the carrier submits written notice of claim within two year after the claimant last reached maximum medical improvement or within two years after the carrier issued the first payment for permanent total disability, wage loss, or death, whichever is later. The court has held that because the statute does not mention impairment income benefits, paying that class of benefit does not trigger the running of the limitations period [*see*

Manatee Mem'l Hosp. v. Special Disability Trust Fund, Dep't of Labor & Empl. Sec., 774 So. 2d 876, 878 (Fla. 1st DCA 2000)].

[c] New MMI Date Cannot Restart Clock

Assume the injured worker resumes active medical care after medical release. The doctor then releases the injured worker again with a new date of maximum medical improvement. In such a case, the 60-day or two-year clock does not restart. Similarly, the clock does not restart each time the injured worker makes a wage loss request [*see* Jake's Restaurant v. Special Disability Trust Fund, 596 So. 2d 498 (Fla. 1st DCA 1992)]. In another situation, the carrier and the injured worker entered an agreement to settle the case. In the court approved joint stipulation, they agreed upon an MMI date. More than two years later, the carrier filed its claim for reimbursement. The judge of compensation claims awarded reimbursement because the actual MMI date was later than the stipulated date. The First District Court of Appeal reversed and held that the judge's revised MMI date could not revive the carrier's stale claim [*see* Special Disability Trust Fund v. Collier Enterpr., 676 So. 2d 45, 46 (Fla. 1st DCA 1996)].

Even if an injured worker returns to a temporary total disability status after having reached maximum medical improvement, a new maximum medical improvement date does not restart the clock. This is true despite the language of § 440.49(7), Fla. Stat. That section provides that a claim must be filed "within two years after the date the employee *last* reached maximum medical improvement." Once a carrier accepts the original maximum medical improvement date by beginning the payment of permanent benefits, the two-year clock has started. A new, subsequent maximum medical improvement date, even with an intervening period of temporary total disability, cannot revive an untimely claim. Once the two-year period following the date of maximum medical improvement has expired, a claim for reimbursement cannot be revived by a finding of a new maximum medical improvement date. Once the carrier accepts an assigned date by beginning to pay permanent benefits, it has a responsibility to adhere to that date in filing for reimbursement from the Fund [*see* Special Disability Fund v. Low Cost Transmission, 725 So. 2d 1218, 1220 (Fla. 1st DCA 1999)].

[d] Payment Errors Cannot Restart Clock

Making a mistake is no excuse. For example, the carrier began paying wage loss benefits, but did not request reimbursement until long after the deadline expired. Later, the carrier realized the injured worker had not reached MMI and converted the wage loss payments to temporary partial disability. The court, however, held that this changed nothing. The fact that the carrier paid wage loss benefits by mistake was irrelevant, as was the fact that no evidence existed showing that the injured worker had reached MMI when the carrier began payments. The only relevant fact was that the carrier knew that stopping temporary benefits and beginning permanent disability benefits triggered its duty to request reimbursement or else it would risk losing reimbursement altogether [*see* Sp. Disability Fund v. Westwind Transp., 648 So. 2d 830, 832 (Fla. 1st DCA 1995)].

Remember that either the date of maximum medical improvement or the date of first payment of permanent disability benefits triggers the time to file a claim with the SDTF. Everyone is presumed to know that an injured worker is not entitled to any form of permanent benefits until a state of maximum medical improvement has been reached. Paying permanent total disability benefits, for example, before MMI creates an implied concession of MMI. Thus, if a carrier misses the filing deadline, it cannot salvage its claim by arguing that the injured worker had not reached MMI when payments began. This precept is similar to the doctrine of equitable estoppel [*see* American Exp. v. Special Disability Trust, 694 So. 2d 59, 60 (Fla 1st DCA 1997)].

SPECIAL ALERT: The cases above dealt with accidents occurring before the statute was amended in 1984. § 440.49(7), Fla. Stat. was amended to provide that the two-year statute of limitations began to run on the date of maximum medical improvement or the date the carrier paid compensation for permanent total disability, wage loss, or death, whichever is later. Note that the statute does not include Impairment Income Benefits as one of the payments that will trigger the running of the limitations period. This omission is evidence of a legislative intent to exclude the payment of such benefits from § 440.49(7), Fla. Stat. Therefore, paying Impairment Income Benefits has no effect on the limitations period for filing a claim for reimbursement [*see* Menatee Mem'l Hosp. v. Special Disability Trust Fund, Dep't of Labor & Empl. Sec., 774 So. 2d 876, 878 (Fla. 1st DCA 2000)].

[e] Notice of Receipt of Claim From SDTF

[i] Before January 1, 1994

If the SDTF does not serve notice of its receipt of the carrier's claim within 120 days, the law before January 1, 1994, provides that such failure should be deemed a denial of the claim [§ 440.49(2)(g), Fla. Stat. (1990)]. This is an important provision because the carrier has only 60 days after denial of a claim to file an application for hearing. If not, the law forever bars its claim.

Note, however, that the 60-day period does not begin to run until the carrier pays permanent benefits. Therefore, if the carrier files its claim before having paid permanent benefits and the Fund denies the claim, a subsequent claim is not barred once the carrier pays permanent disability benefits. Obviously, upon denial the carrier must either apply for a hearing or abandon the claim. The carrier could not proceed to a hearing, however, since the claim would not be ripe until it had actually paid permanent disability benefits [*see* Polk County Bd. of County Comm'rs v. Special Disability Trust Fund, 753 So. 2d 769 (Fla. 1st DCA 2000)].

As a practical matter, the SDTF has never enforced this provision because its work backlog prevented it from supplying timely notice. The 120-day period does not begin to run until the SDTF receives a fully completed Notice of Claim for Reimbursement Against the Special Disability Fund, form SDF-1. Further, the Fund must acknowledge that the form is complete and contains the required documents. The Fund must send notice within 14 days of receipt of form SDF-1 [Fla. Admin. Code R. 69L-10.015 (1/10/2005)].

[ii] On or After January 1, 1994

For accident dates on or after January 1, 1994, the 120-day period to serve notice of acceptance of the claim does not begin until the carrier pays more than $10,000 in benefits. In addition, failure to serve notice timely is no longer a deemed denial of the claim. Effective January 1, 1994, such failure simply gives the carrier the right to request a hearing. If the SDTF formally denies the claim, however, the 60-day time limit to file a request for hearing still applies [§ 440.49(7), Fla. Stat. (5/30/97)].

[2] Procedure for Filing Claim

[a] Notice of Claim: SDF-1

The carrier should put SDTF on written notice of the claim when it has confirmed a preexisting permanent impairment. The carrier should do this by filing a Notice of Claim for Reimbursement Against the Special Disability Fund, form SDF-1.

Guide to Claims

SPECIAL ALERT: Carriers must submit a proof of claim on each notice of claim on file as of June 30, 1997, within one year after July 1, 1997. If carriers fail to submit proof of claim by July 1, 1998, the claim will be forever barred. If carriers are not prepared to submit proof of claim, they may withdraw the claim and refile later. This assumes, of course, that the limitation period has not expired. Refiling has no effect on the limitation period applicable to that claim [§ 440.49(7)(c), Fla. Stat. (1997)].

The question here is what constitutes a "proof of claim," since that term is not defined in the statute. The Florida Administrative Code, however, defines a proof of claim as a properly completed LES Form SDF-1 with all required documents to support the claim [*see* Fla. Admin. Code. R. 69L-10.006(4) (1/10/2005)]. Filing a supporting document, such as the employer's affidavit of knowledge, is not enough. Therefore, if a Notice of Claim was filed before July 1, 1997, it must have been withdrawn or an SDF-1 with supporting documents must have been filed by July 1, 1998. If not, the claim for reimbursement is time-barred [*see* Special Disability Trust Fund v. City of Tampa, 783 So. 2d 339, 341 (Fla. 1st DCA 2001)].

Even a simple letter announcing an intent to file a claim may be construed as a Notice of Claim. For example, the employer sent the following letter to the Fund:

> This is to inform you of our intent to file a claim against the Special Disability Trust Fund, in regard to the above captioned case in accordance with 440.49(2). Additional evidence supporting our claim will be forthcoming at the proper time. Thank you for acknowledging our claim.

The court held that the judge of compensation claims properly found that this letter, sent to Fund prior to June 30, 1997, was a notice of claim, and not a letter of intent to file a future notice of claim. The court also held that the statute which shortened the limitation period for filing proof of claim could properly be applied retroactively to an accident that occurred prior to the effective date of the amendment [*see* Polk County BOCC v. Special Disability Trust Fund, 791 So. 2d 581, 582–583 (Fla. 1st DCA 2001)].

In addition, carriers must pay a $250 notification fee on each notice of claim filed or refiled after July 1, 1997. Also, carriers must pay a $500 fee on each proof of claim filed. The notification fee does not apply if carriers submit the proof of claim with the notice of claim [§ 440.49(7)(d), Fla. Stat. (1997)].

Naturally, the SDTF will not consider the claim until the carrier presents evidence of employer knowledge, merger and, when applicable, payment of permanent benefits. The Fund will, however, acknowledge receipt of the Notice of Claim. If the carrier wants acknowledgment of receipt of any other documents, it must provide a self-addressed, stamped envelope with a copy of such documents.

[b] Requesting Reimbursement: SDF-2

[i] General Requirements

Once the carrier pays permanent benefits, it should file a request for reimbursement with the Fund on a Request for Reimbursement, form SDF-2. The carrier must properly document its claim with copies of paid bills, computer printouts, ledger sheets, check copies, and other relevant documents. If the carrier claims reimbursement for pre-1994 wage loss benefits, the carrier must provide either copies of checks or the Request for Wage Loss/Temporary Partial Benefits, form DWC-3. If the carrier paid benefits under a judge's order, it should attach a copy of the order. If the claim involves different rates of compensation, include copies of the First Report of Injury, form DWC-1, or the Notice of Action/Change, form DWC-4 [Fla. Admin. Code R. 69L-10.016 (1/10/2005)].

If the Fund accepts the claim, it will usually notify the carrier of the terms of the acceptance in writing. The Fund will usually serve notice of acceptance of the claim within 180 days after receipt of the proof of claim. Occasionally, the acceptance may be only for partial reimbursement. If the carrier agrees with the offer, it should accept in writing. Such acceptance may mean automatic agreement to all terms specified in the offer without modification. Exercise caution! If the carrier does not agree with the offer, it should avoid counter proposals. Even a partial acceptance may be deemed full acceptance. If the offer is not acceptable, the carrier should file a claim for determination by a judge of compensation claims.

SPECIAL NOTE: A request for reimbursement, SDF-2, is barred if not filed within four years after the Fund accepts a claim and offers some reimbursement. In *Associated Coca Cola v. Special Disability Trust Fund*, the court described the request for reimbursement from the Fund as a two-step process. The first step was described as follows [Associated Coca Cola v. Special Disability Trust Fund, 508 So. 2d 1305 (Fla. 1st DCA 1987)]:

> . . . The notice of claim is the first step in obtaining reimbursement from the Fund. The filing of a notice of claim is intended to result in a determination by the Fund that the e/c are or are not entitled to reimbursement in some amount. . . .

The court determined that § 440.49(2)(g), Fla. Stat. prescribed filing requirements for notice of claims. The court described the second step of the process as follows:

> In contrast, reimbursement requests are filed after the Fund determines the employer/carrier are entitled, generally, to reimbursement. These requests are the

second step in the reimbursement process, and their purpose is to trigger reimbursement for specific amounts of compensation and medical benefits paid the injured employee by the e/c. Section 440.49(2)(g) places no time limitation on the filing of reimbursement requests. . . .

The court determined that the general statute of limitations is applicable to the second step: "[A]n e/c's request for a hearing before a deputy commissioner to contest a denial of reimbursement from the Fund is an action founded on a statutory liability" [Associated Coca Cola v. Special Disability Trust Fund, 508 So. 2d 1305, 1306 (Fla. 1st DCA 1987)]. Thus, the court found that the four-year limitations period contained in § 95.11(3)(f), Fla. Stat. is applicable to the second step of the process.

[ii] Specific Requirements

[A] Payments for Medical Benefits

Payments for medical benefits must be properly documented to ensure reimbursement. This requires submitting copies of medical bills paid showing that required utilization review procedures have been followed and that all applicable fee schedule deductions have been taken. These bills must be submitted with corroborating documentation of the amount paid. This may include computer printouts, ledger sheets, or copies of checks. Note, however, that computer records or ledger sheets are not acceptable unless accompanied by medical bills marked "paid" or by form SDF-6. The Fund may request copies of medical reports to substantiate that the payments were for treatment related to the injury. Therefore, carriers should voluntarily submit such documentation if there is likely to be debate about the relationship of the treatment to the compensable injury [*see* Fla. Admin. Code R. 69L-10.016(1) (1/10/2005)].

[B] Payment for Compensation Payments

Payments for temporary or permenent disability compensation, permanent impairment benefits, or death benefits may be documented by submitting a copy of form DWC-13, Claim Cost Report, or with copies of the checks issued. If the DWC-13's were not completed contemporaneously with the payments, computer printouts or ledger sheets may be used to corroborate payment. Wage loss benefits may be documented only with copies of checks or copies of form DWC-3, Request for Wage Loss/Temporary Partial Benefits. Benefits paid in compliance with the order of a judge of compensation claims may be documented by submitting a copy of the order [*see* Fla. Admin. Code R. 69L-10.016(2), (3) (1/10/2005)].

[C] Miscellaneous

Changes in the rate of compensation paid may be documented by submitting a copy of form DWC-4, Notice of Action/Change or with copies of the checks issued. Likewise, changes in the class of benefits paid should be documented by submitting a copy of form DWC-4 [*see* Fla. Admin. Code R. 69L-10.016(4) (1/10/2005)].

[iii] Subsequent Reimbursement

If all is in order, carriers should file subsequent reimbursement requests every 12 months while the carrier continues to make benefit payments. Note: Annual reimbursement is the frequency specified in the statute effective January 1, 1994 [§ 440.49(7)(f), Fla. Stat. (1/10/2005)].

§ 20.07 The Preferred Worker Program

[1] Purpose

Effective January 1, 1994, the legislature created a new program as an additional incentive to hire "preferred workers" [§ 440.49(8), Fla. Stat. (5/30/97)]. A preferred worker is anyone unable to return to regular employment because of a permanent impairment resulting from a compensable, workplace injury [§ 440.49(2)(b), Fla. Stat. (5/30/97)].

The Act requires the Division, upon the request of such a worker, to issue an identity card that certifies the applicant as a preferred worker [*see* [2], *below*]. If an employer hires a preferred worker, the law may entitle the employer to reimbursement for that part of its workers' compensation premium that relates to the preferred worker [*see* [3], *below*].

[2] Obtaining an Identity Card

To obtain an Identity Card, form PW-1, an injured worker must send a Request for Screening, form DWC-23, to the Division's local office of Rehabilitation and Medical Services. If the Division confirms that the worker suffered a compensable injury resulting in a permanent impairment, it will issue an Identity Card within 60 days [Fla. Admin. Code R. 69L-11.003 (1/10/2005)]. The worker must make this request within two years after a doctor assigns a permanent impairment rating [Fla. Admin. Code R. 69L-11.006 (1/10/2005)].

[3] Claiming Premium Reimbursement

As discussed in § 20.04, the SDTF will not accept any claims for reimbursement that occur on or after January 1, 1998. Although not specifically addressed in the statute or rules, the Division's position is that this cut-off period applies to the Preferred Worker Program as well. That is to say, the disabling accident causing the permanent impairment must have occurred before January 1, 1998. Therefore, the SDTF will not accept any claims for premium reimbursement if the worker's disabling injury occurred on or after January 1, 1998.

To claim reimbursement for the preferred worker's portion of its workers' compensation premium, the employer must send the worker's Identity Card [*see* [2], *above*] to the SDTF within 60 days after hiring the worker. The worker and the employer must sign the card and certify the hire date. In addition, the employer must send a completed Request for Reimbursement of Premium, form PW-2. The completed form must have additional documentation attached. This documentation includes the Payroll and Job Classification, form UCT-6, a copy of the Premium Calculation Sheet, and a copy of the Premium Audit. As noted, a qualified employer is entitled to reimbursement for three years, but the employer must refile form PW-2 annually within six months after the end of the year claimed [Fla. Admin. Code R. 69L-11.005, 69L-11.007, 69L-11.008 (1/10/2005)].

CHAPTER 21

WASHOUT SETTLEMENTS

Guide to Claims

SYNOPSIS

§ 21.01 Introduction

[1] Washout Defined

A "washout" settlement in workers' compensation refers to the lump-sum payment of all future indemnity benefits and, depending on the legal posture of the case and the date of the accident, all or part of liability for future medical benefits.

For general discussion of settlements, see LARSON'S WORKERS' COMPENSATION, DESK EDITION, Ch. 132 (Matthew Bender).

[2] Historical Perspective

For accidents before 1977, the law allowed complete, lump-sum settlements of all benefits. The law also allowed even partial settlement of selected benefits any time following an accident. The only statutory requirement was that a judge of compensation claims must find that the settlement was in the interests of the person entitled to compensation.

In 1977, the legislature added a new provision. This required the judge, before considering full settlement, to decide whether the settlement would aid the injured worker's rehabilitation.

In 1979, the legislature amended the law again. This new provision barred all lump-sum settlements except future compensation. In addition, the legislature made the following expression of its intent [§ 440.20(12)(a), Fla. Stat.]: "It is the stated policy for the administration of the workers' compensation system that it is in the best interests of the injured worker that he receives disability or wage loss payments periodically."

With this amendment, the legislature expressed a clear intent to discourage lump-sum settlements under the then-new wage loss law. The hope was that the wage loss idea would eliminate the need for such settlements. In addition, the legislature believed that allowing sufficient time to pass was important to discern whether the wage loss idea had the desired effect. The legislature, in effect, forced the parties in a workers' compensation case to continue periodic payments. This provision also forced the parties to litigate or pay all questionable cases. The amendment removed the ability to abort litigation by means of settlement, or to reduce the time during which periodic benefits were payable.

Over the years, the legislature frequently amended the Workers' Compensation Act, with each amendment expanding the parties' rights to conclude lump-sum settlements of future benefits. Effective January 1, 1994, the legislature repealed all the previous settlement provisions, returning the system to the unrestricted days before 1977. The 1994 amendments were procedural, for the most part, and applied to all claims whatever the accident date. Because of certain restrictions, and for comparison purposes, reviewing the pre-1994 procedure is important [*see* § 21.02].

§ 21.02 Limitations Through December 31, 1993

[1] Three Categories

Previously, the law allowed lump-sum settlements under three distinct categories. These were found in the Workers' Compensation Act under §§ 440.20(12)(a), 440.20(12)(b), and 440.20(12)(c), Fla. Stat., and became known as "12(a), 12(b), and 12(c) settlements." All settlements both previously and now, regardless of citation, require a judge of compensation claims' approval before they are final.

[2] 12(a) Settlements—The Routine Case Washout

The law allowed settlement under this provision only for indemnity benefits. § 440.20(12)(a), Fla. Stat. prohibited settlement of future medical entitlement. The law did allow this, however, under subsections 12(b) and 12(c) [*see* [3] and [4], *below*].

Settlements under subsection 12(a) required the approval of a judge of compensation claims. To give such approval, the judge must have found that:

1. A lump-sum payment would aid in rehabilitation, or is otherwise clearly in the best interest of the injured worker;
2. A lump-sum payment would avoid undue expense or undue hardship to any party; or
3. The injured worker had or was about to move from the state; and
4. At least three months elapsed since the date of injured worker's maximum medical improvement. (Note: This three-month, post-MMI requirement did not apply to nonresident aliens of the United States or Canada. Originally, 12(a) had a six-month requirement; however, it was reduced to three months in 1987.)

Guide to Claims

[3] 12(b) Settlements—The Controverted Claim Washout

Beginning in 1983, the legislature recognized that disputes often arose on the issue of basic compensability. This section simplified resolution of such cases without litigation by allowing compromise settlements. This section allowed settlement of all benefits (except training and education for accidents on or after July 1, 1990).

Before approving a 12(b) settlement, however, the judge must have found a justiciable controversy. This controversy must have related to legal or medical compensability of the claimed injury or the alleged accident. The reason for this was to prevent carriers from controverting everything to obtain complete settlements. This is still the requirement today.

If the carrier initially accepted a claim as compensable, or if the carrier provided any benefits, the 12(b) provision did not apply. Lastly, subsection 12(b) required that injured workers be responsible for their own attorney's fees under such a settlement. In practice, however, most injured workers' attorneys, then as now, would not agree to any settlement that is insufficient to cover a fee.

[4] 12(c) Settlements—The Minor Claim Washout

[a] The Provision

Effective July 1, 1990 the legislature added a third provision under which carriers could settle all benefits, including training and education. Some called this the "minor claim washout." Settlements under this provision applied only to cases in which the injured worker had a permanent impairment rating up to and including five percent. The law did not allow a complete washout settlement under this provision if the injured worker's impairment rating was greater than five percent.

Besides the correct impairment rating, the judge also must have found that the injured worker had not received any medical treatment for at least three months. Further, the judge could not approve the settlement unless at least three months had elapsed since the injured worker reached maximum medical improvement. Under this section, and for the first time, the legislature dictated the settlement amount.

[b] The Formula

The section provided that a 12(c) settlement should equal: (Compensation Rate) x (3) x (Impairment Rating).

For example, assume a weekly compensation rate of $300 and an impairment rating of five percent. Under the statutory formula, the settlement would be calculated as follows:

$300 x 3 = $900: $900 x 5 = $4,500

Statutorily, the settlement in this example could be no more and no less than $4,500. The section also provided that injured workers were responsible for their own attorney's fees. Because this provision did not incorporate attorney's fees, judges approved settlements where the impairment rating was zero or greater than five percent. This was risky because the courts could overturn such settlements in the future on the basis that they violated the statutory provision. There was mixed opinion on what the consequences of straying from the statutory formula would be. Most likely, as a matter of law, the courts would deem such a settlement to be a 12(a) settlement, leaving future medical open. Concern arose, however, that the courts would consider a set-aside 12(c) settlement to be a gratuity. As such, the injured worker would not be required to repay the money, and the settlement would be void.

[c] Medical Settlement Prohibited

For accidents occurring up to January 1, 1994, the Act allowed the parties to conclude the carrier's obligations via a lump-sum settlement only for indemnity benefits. The statute provided as follows [§ 440.20(12)(a), Fla. Stat.]: "In no case may a lump-sum payment be allowed in exchange for the release of the employer's or carrier's liability for future medical expenses and training and education."

[d] Training Settlement Prohibited

Note that the Act also prohibited lump-sum settlement of the carrier's obligation for training and education. This seemed to have no real effect because, in 1989, the legislature made the Division of Workers' Compensation responsible for providing training and education. Recall, however, that carriers must still pay temporary total disability benefits for up to 52 weeks during the training period. This payment is therefore part of the training and education benefit. In other words, the legislature split the obligation between the carrier and the state. The carrier pays temporary total disability benefits, and the state pays for the training. Since the disability benefits are part of the training and education benefit, the law prohibits lump-sum settlement of the carrier's obligation for temporary total disability benefits during retraining [*see* Hertz Rent-A-Car v. Sosa, 670 So. 2d 73, 76 (Fla. 1st DCA 1996)]. This does not apply to accidents occurring on or after January 1, 1994, because the legislature repealed the prohibiting section.

§ 21.03 Limitations On or After January 1, 1994

[1] Procedural Amendments

Effective January 1, 1994, the legislature repealed all the settlement provisions previously found under § 440.20(12)(a), (b) and (c), Fla. Stat. It initially replaced them with only two provisions, now found under § 440.20(11)(a) and (b), Fla. Stat. Effective October 1, 2001, the legislature added new subsection (11)(c). An 11(a) settlement applies to controverted claims, but only when the claimant is *not* represented by an attorney. An 11(b) settlement applies to compensable claims, but only when the claimant is *not* represented by an attorney. An (11)(c) settlement applies to all claims, controverted or not, and whether or not the claimant has reached maximum medical improvement, but only if the claimant *is* represented by an attorney. Settlements concluded under (11)(a) and (b) where the claimant is not represented by an attorney require the approval of a JCC. Settlements concluded under (11)(c) where the claimant is represented by an attorney do not require JCC approval. All three provisions are procedural amendments. As such, they apply to all claims, whatever the date of the accident.

[2] 11(a) Settlements—The Controverted Claim Washout

If the injured worker is *not* represented by an attorney, carriers and injured workers may settle all benefits on a controverted claim at any time, but on one condition. The carrier must have filed its notice of denial within 120 days after the employer receives notice of the injury. Settlement may take place even before the worker's injury has reached maximum medical improvement. Although this is a procedural provision, the 120-day requirement will likely apply only to accidents occurring on or after January 1, 1994.

All of the original requirements remain the same, such that the judge of compensation claims must find a justiciable controversy, and the settlement must serve the interests of the injured worker. Even if the carrier initially accepts the claim as compensable and pays benefits, this provision applies if the denial meets the 120-day requirement.

[3] 11(b) Settlements—The Routine Case Washout

[a] Significant Changes

If the injured worker is *not* represented by an attorney, the parties may settle all other claims in full, any time after the date of maximum medical improvement. Carriers and injured workers may settle all benefits including medical, indemnity, and rehabilitation. The law no longer requires that the parties wait until three months after the injured worker reaches maximum medical improvement. As before, the Act prohibits carriers from paying an attorney's fee for a washout settlement. This is, of course, meaningless since a represented injured worker will not agree to a settlement that is not large enough to cover fees.

Another important change is that the judge of compensation claims no longer must wait for the Division's file before holding a settlement hearing. This now repealed requirement often did nothing more than needlessly delay most settlements for weeks.

[b] Claims Previously Settled

§ 440.20(11)(a) and (b), Fla. Stat. applies to all accident dates, with one significant exception. The Act provides that settlement under this provision does not apply to "claims that the parties have previously settled." What seemed a clear provision created controversy even before it became law. Recall that most settlements before 1994 were for indemnity benefits only, leaving medical benefits open. Many people believe the intent of this provision is to prohibit the parties from now settling the medical portion. Many others disagree. They maintain that the use of the term "claims" previously settled is the key. The claim we settled before, they say, was a claim for indemnity benefits. Now, we can settle our claim for medical benefits. If they are correct, then what did the legislature intend? Some people believe the intent was to prevent the resurrection of old claims. The Division, however, believes the intent is only to preclude injured workers from attempting to renegotiate settlements for any class of benefits under the new statute. In a declaratory statement issued March 17, 1994, the Division announced that its official position is that § 440.20(11)(c), Fla. Stat. operates only to preclude resettlement of benefits previously settled. It is now the Division's official position that the 1994 amendments allow settlement of all claims, including claims for future medical benefits that the parties have not previously settled. The Division's theory applies whatever the date of the accident, or whether the parties have already settled indemnity benefits.

[c] Partial Settlements

Another early controversy caused conflict and confusion among the judges. Many judges, even before the amendment in § 440.20(11)(a) and (b), Fla. Stat. took effect, maintained that the law now required that settlements must include all benefits and that the law prohibits partial settlements. This is startling when we consider that the Florida Supreme Court resolved this issue in 1963. In 1963, the settlement language of the Act was very similar to the language in 1994. The Supreme Court held that the law allowed an injured worker to waive all rights to future benefits. Therefore, no logical reason suggests that the injured worker could not waive part of those rights [*see* Westinghouse Electric Supply Co. v. Reagan, 159 So. 2d 222, 225 (Fla. 1963)].

Guide to Claims

[4] 11(c) Settlements—Represented Claimants

Effective October 1, 2001, the legislature amended § 440.20, Fla. Stat. by adding subsection (c). This subsection provides that lump-sum settlements of benefits do not require the approval of the judge of compensation claims *if the claimant is represented by an attorney.* The amendment does not impose any other restrictions such as requiring that the injured worker has reached MMI. To settle a claim, the parties simply need to execute a settlement agreement releasing the employer and carrier from further liability in exchange for the agreed upon settlement amount. Judicial approval is still necessary, however, with regard to fees to be paid to the claimant's attorney by the claimant. Under this provision, there is no longer any requirement to submit any documentation to the JCC except for documentation supporting the amount of attorney fees. Payment of the lump-sum settlement is be due within 14 days after the judge mails the order approving the attorney fees. Fees approved in this fashion are not considered an award. Thus, the order approving fees is not subject to modification or review.

> **SPECIAL ALERT:** The statute plainly provides that this is a procedural amendment that applies to all accident dates. Additionally, the court held that the addition of § 440.20(11)(c), Fla. Stat., does not impact the amount of benefits or services that a claimant may receive or change the liability of the employer/carrier. Moreover, the statutory change affects only the means of approval of a settlement agreement. Thus, it is a procedural change that should be applied retroactively. Thus, the JCC no longer has jurisdiction to approve settlements. Additionally, the JCC no longer has jurisdiction to vacate settlements, regardless of the date the settlement agreement was executed and regardless of whether the settlement had been judicially approved under the earlier statue [*see* Flamily v. City of Orlando, 2006 Fla. App. LEXIS 2443 (Fla. 1st DCA 2006)].

The following are important points to remember:

1. If the claimant is not represented by an attorney, settlement may be concluded only under the provisions of § 440.20(11)(a) & (b), Fla. Stat. and JCC approval

is still required as before.

2. Without the benefit of judicial approval, the requirements to set aside such a settlement remain to be developed by the courts. For this reason, and because workers' compensation settlements are often complicated, it will still be wise to have settlement agreements prepared by an attorney with the same specificity and detail as contained in a typical joint petition. Adjusters cannot draft special releases without the insurer's written permission. Without such insurer approval, adjusters may do no more than fill the blanks of forms approved by the insurer they represent [Fla. Admin. Code R. 69O-220.201(4)(g)]. While this rule is primarily directed at liability claim adjusters, it now has relevance to workers' compensation adjusters as well.

3. Be especially careful in drafting settlement agreements when the following circumstances exist:

   a. Under (11)(a) with regard to whether the 120 day rule applies.

   b. When the claimant is a minor.

   c. When the claimant is suffering from any mental impairment or disease. In some cases, it may be wise to secure an affidavit from the claimant's psychiatrist attesting to the claimant's ability to understand the nature, details, and consequences of a washout settlement.

   d. In death cases in which the dependents include minor children or in which the identity of qualified dependents is not clear.

   e. When attempting to settle multiple accident dates.

   f. When attempting to settle issues outside the scope of Chapter 440, such as claims based on violations of the ADA.

The 2001 Act also amends § 440.20(11), Fla. Stat. by adding subsection (d) providing that the judge of compensation claims must consider whether all benefits, including settlements, provide for appropriate recovery of any child support arrearage. The significance of this provision is not clear since settlements no longer require the JCC's approval when the claimant is represented by an attorney. Perhaps this provision is intended to apply to those cases in which the claimant is not represented by an attorney and which still require judicial approval. In any event, the 2003 Act makes it clear that an employer or carrier has no duty to investigate or collect information regarding child support arrearages. Further, for settlement purposes, the clerk of the circuit court is prohibited from charging fees for providing child support documentation [§ 440.20(11)(d), Fla. Stat. (10/1/2003)].

As noted, under the 2000 amendments to § 440.20(11)(c), Fla. Stat., a lump sum settlement agreement requires approval by the JCC *only* as to the attorney's fees paid to the claimant's attorney by the claimant. However, the court held the plain language of § 440.20(11)(c), Fla. Stat., did not extinguish the JCC's previously existing jurisdiction to determine whether a settlement agreement was entered, or to construe or give effect to settlement agreements. Rather, except for the amount of attorney's fees, the statute simply permits parties represented by counsel to enter lump sum settlement agreements without obtaining the JCC's approval of the settlement actually reached [*see* Jacobsen v. Ross Stores, 882 So. 2d 431 (Fla. 1st DCA 2004)].

In *Gerow v. Yesterday's* [881 So. 2d 94 (Fla. 1st DCA 2004)], the court was again asked to determine whether the amendments adopted by the 2000 Florida Legislature to § 440.20(11)(c), Fla. Stat. (2001), eliminated the JCC's jurisdiction to determine whether a settlement agreement was reached or to determine the terms of such an agreement. Based on the reasoning in *Jacobsen v. Ross Stores*, the court concluded they did not. The court held it was within the province of the JCC to determine whether a settlement agreement was reached and, if so, to establish its terms.

In *Borque v. Trugreen, Inc.* [389 F.3d 1354 (11th Cir. 2004)], the U.S. Court of Appeals for the 11th Circuit (citing *Jacobsen*) also recognized the authority of a judge of compensation claims to determine whether a settlement agreement in a workers' compensation case is binding on the parties.

§ 21.04 Amount and Procedure

[1] Washout Settlements

Generally, the value of any claim is an amount equal to or less than the present value of future benefits, and any past due benefits. Precise calculation of the present value of future benefits can be tricky. Figuring out what future benefits will be is even more difficult. Should injured workers and carriers settle at all? Often a washout settlement is the best result for all concerned. If washout settlements could be placed into only three categories, they would be the cases where (1) the decision is purely financial, as in lump-sum settlements of permanent total or death cases [*see* [2][a], *below*]; (2) the carrier has failed in the primary task of returning the injured employee to work [*see* [3], *below*]; and (3) continued defense of a controverted claim is no longer as attractive as it once was [*see* [3], *below*].

[2] The Purely Financial Decision Cases

[a] Which Cases Are Included

This category includes cases where predicting future benefits is reasonably elementary [*see* [1], *above*]. This includes death or permanent total disability cases. In death cases, the adjuster must consider the likelihood the surviving spouse will remarry or die before the carrier has paid the statutory limit of $100,000.

In permanent total disability cases the adjuster must accurately estimate the injured worker's life expectancy. The primary source for this information is life expectancy tables produced by the United States Department of Health and Human Services [*see* Part VIII, Tables, Table 4]. Note that these tables will reflect a significant difference in life expectancy between males and females, and among racial groups. Do not rely strictly on life expectancy tables. Remember that these are only averages. They do not consider life-expectancy-reducing factors, such as the nature of the disabling compensable injury, unrelated chronic illness, or abusive lifestyle habits. For example, does the injured worker have high blood pressure, diabetes, or history of cardiac problems? Is the person a heavy smoker or drinker? Consider all such factors when estimating life expectancy. Usually, carriers will be wise to have the injured worker's medical history reviewed by a medical consultant for an expert opinion.

For simplicity, we will use a death case as an example. First, we will assume there is no reason to believe the spouse will remarry or die before the carrier pays statutory death benefits. Further, we will assume that at the point the carrier is considering a settlement, it has already paid $20,000, leaving a maximum but likely exposure of $80,000. The present value of $80,000 then, is the maximum settlement that should be considered.

[b] Calculating Present Value

Assume the weekly compensation rate is $200. Paying out $80,000 will take 400 weeks, or 7.67 years, at the rate of $400 every two weeks. Present value is the amount we must invest today to earn a specific sum ($80,000), within a specific period (7.67 years). Tables of present value can be helpful in making the calculation.

In our example, the compensation rate is $200 per week projected over the next 400 weeks ($200 x 400 = $80,000). From the table, find the present worth factor. Here, the present worth factor is 301.6541. Now simply multiply the weekly compensation rate ($200) by the present worth factor. The result is $200 x 301.6541 = $60,330. Thus, the $80,000 balance in our example has a present value that rounds off to $60,000.

Note, however, that the tables use an eight-percent discount factor because this is the amount formerly required by statute [*see* former § 440.20(12)(d), Fla. Stat.]. The legislature repealed this requirement effective January 1, 1994; thus, the mandated discount rate no longer exists. Most carriers still use the eight-percent discount factor, probably from force of habit [*see* Part VIII, Tables, Table 5].

If a carrier enjoys a higher rate of return on its investments, a settlement based on an eight-percent discount factor may not be desirable. If a particular carrier prefers to use a discount factor other than eight percent, the tables will be of no use. Personal computer programs such as Lotus 1-2-3, Microsoft Excel, and many hand-held calculators have built in functions to make these calculations. In addition, several firms have developed software designed specifically to calculate present value in workers' compensation cases.

Remember, however, that the calculation becomes much more complex when the projected future payments are not an even and consistent stream of payments. For example, in permanent total disability cases, the benefits change each year with the addition of supplemental benefits. If the carrier's entitlement to a social security offset will end, for example, the calculation must allow for this. Many of the software products take these complexities into account.

[3] The Uncertain Future Cases

This category includes the second and third classes [*see* [1], *above*]. These are the cases that the carrier denied, or cases where the injured worker is on wage loss, but unable to find work. These are the most difficult cases to price for settlement because the future value of benefits is so uncertain.

In such cases, take the time to estimate the cost of future benefits such as wage loss and medical care. A theory developed that wage loss claims should settle for one to three years' worth of wage loss benefits. That is not the way to price these cases, especially under the wage loss maximums and restrictions contained in the 1990 and 1994 amendments to the Act. Unfortunately, no easy mathematical formula exists. Here, accurate reserving may be helpful. As discussed in ch. 11, carriers must base case reserves on all available data. The reserve should always reflect the adjuster's best estimate of the total future benefits the carrier will pay. If the adjuster has properly reserved the case, the settlement value would be no more than the present value of the reserve.

Controverted cases are another matter because, by definition, the claim may or may not be compensable. Obviously, a carrier would not be considering an 11(a) type settlement unless the carrier believed it would lose at trial, or that it can settle the case for an amount equal to or less than future defense costs. At the point of reaching that conclusion, the adjuster must first calculate what will be due for past benefits and then the value of future benefits, if the case is lost on all counts. The latter calculation would be the reserve the adjuster would set, tempered by the relative likelihood of winning or losing. Such cases settle for anywhere from an insignificant amount to the entire present value of the exposure. Assuming the case is not a "total loser," a 50–50 chance of winning or losing is likely. If so, the settlement value should be approximately the present value of 50 percent of the total value of the case. When considering past medical costs, remember to apply the fee schedule first. Adjusters should not simply accept someone's estimate of the amount. Demand copies of the bills claimed.

For accidents occurring before 1998, also consider the impact that recoveries, via subrogation or the Special Disability Trust Fund, may have on the claim [*see* ch. 19; ch. 20, § 20.02]. If the Fund makes a full offer on a pre-1994 permanent total disability case, the carrier's maximum exposure is 175 weeks of indemnity benefits. After that, the Fund will repay the carrier 100 percent. Therefore, the settlement value of the indemnity benefit should generally be no more than the present value of 175 weeks of benefits, less any of the 175 weeks already paid. That is the extent of the carrier's exposure, but the carrier should also keep the Fund's interest in mind. At the point of considering settlement, the carrier may have already paid more than 175 weeks of benefits. Carriers should submit any settlement request to the Fund for consideration and settlement authority.

[4] Procedure

A judge of compensation claims must approve all settlements if the injured worker is not represented by an attorney. Although a partial advance payment of $2,000 or less is not a washout settlement, the judge can informally approve it. The judge can do so by letter; thus, a formal hearing is not necessary [§ 440.20(12)(c), Fla. Stat. (7/1/97)].

When the injured worker is not represented by counsel, the standard procedure to obtain a release of liability for future payments is formal, and the judge will usually hold a hearing. Some judges allow liberalized use of mail-in stipulations with an affidavit. Upon agreeing on a settlement with an unrepresented injured worker, the carrier should send the necessary documents to its attorney with the details of the settlement. The carrier's attorney will then prepare a joint petition and stipulation that sets out the details [*see* Fla.

Guide to Claims

Admin. Code R. 60Q-6.123]. If approved, the judge will then enter a formal order.

The legislature amended § 61.14(8), Fla. Stat., effective October 1, 2001, to provide that a judge of compensation claims must consider whether a proposed settlement serves the interests of both the injured worker and the worker's family. This includes considering whether the settlement provides for "appropriate recovery of any child-support arrearage" [*see* ch. 12, § 12.10[3], for additional discussion]. This is a vaguely worded provision. It is illogical to conclude that this provision requires considering whether the settlement amount is large enough to cover an arrearage. Such a conclusion would require rejecting settlements that are too small to cover the arrearage. Viewed from its flip side, this would sometimes require carriers to pay excess amounts in order to secure a settlement, and that in itself would violate the requirements of § 440.20(11), Fla. Stat. That section requires the JCC to ensure that a settlement is in the interest of all interested parties and that the amount of the settlement is not in excess of the value of benefits the claimant would be entitled to receive under the Act. The intent, therefore, appears to be to require that the settlement agreement contains a provision that part or all of the settlement will be directed to satisfying any child-support arrearage. If so, it appears that the carrier or its attorney must provide documentary evidence to verify if any arrearage exists and if so, the exact amount. How this section is to be applied is even more problematic when considering that the law no longer requires JCC approval of settlements when the claimant is represented by an attorney.

[5] Voidable Settlements

Ensuring that the judge has all information relating to the injured worker's medical and vocational status is essential. If not, the settlement agreement is subject to being set aside. In one case, for example, the judge approved a settlement based on an eight-percent impairment rating resulting from the worker's knee injury. Neither attorney told the judge that the injured worker continued to suffer from mental problems. In fact, the injured worker had attempted suicide just six days before the settlement hearing. These facts went unmentioned because everyone assumed the mental condition was unrelated to the original compensable injury. Later, a different lawyer succeeded not only in having the settlement set aside because of this omission, but also in having the judge declare the mental condition compensable and award permanent total disability benefits. It did not matter that the injured worker's original lawyer knew about the mental problems and failed to inform the judge [*see* Pruett-Sharpe Const. v. Hayden, 654 So. 2d 241, 243 (Fla. 1st DCA 1995)].

[6] Penalty for Late Payment of Settlement Order

[a] Statutory Mandate

Adjusters must be certain to pay, on time, any settlement approved by a judge's order. If not, the carrier will be subject to a penalty equal to 20 percent of the settlement amount. The statute provides as follows [§ 440.20(7), Fla. Stat. (7/1/97) (emphasis added)]:

> If any compensation, payable under the terms of an award, is not paid *within 7 days* after it becomes due, there shall be added to such unpaid compensation an amount equal to 20 percent thereof, which shall be paid at the same time as, but in addition

to, such compensation, unless review [appeal] of the compensation order making such an award is had as provided in § 440.25.

Note the italicized phrase carefully. Previously, carriers had 30 days to pay. The legislature reduced the time to just seven days! Most judges "enter" an order the day they mail it to the parties. If carriers wait until they receive the order in the mail, they will have very little time, if any, to make payment. This is a procedural amendment that applies to all orders entered on or after January 1, 1994 [*see* Bell v. University of Florida, 652 So. 2d 460, 461 (Fla. 1st DCA 1995)].

[b] Knowledge Presumed

In a pre-1994 case, the carrier and the injured worker agreed to settle the claim. The judge approved the settlement and entered an order on April 6. The carrier, however, did not issue the payment until May 17. The judge declined to assess a penalty because he concluded the carrier had not received notice of the order's entry. On appeal, the First District Court of Appeal reversed, holding that the carrier was at least on constructive notice. How? Because first, the carrier knew the joint stipulation had been presented to the judge on April 5. Second, the carrier knew that the Act required the judge to enter an order within seven days, or by April 12. Thus, the court concluded that the carrier was on constructive notice that the judge must have entered the order by the April 12 deadline. This required payment within 30 days after that date. This conclusion, of course, presumes that all judges always issue orders within the statutory time constraints. Remember, when the court heard this case, carriers had 30 days to make payment [*see* Sigg v. Sears, Roebuck & Co., 594 So. 2d 329, 330 (Fla. 1st DCA 1992)].

[c] Penalty Assessment Mandatory

Over the years the cases on the issue of penalties have been in conflict. Many cases have held that a judge of compensation claims has full discretion whether to assess a penalty. Several other cases held that the judges have no judicial discretion and that assessing a penalty is mandatory. The court has resolved the conflict by concluding that a mandatory penalty is the preferred position [*see* Steinbrecher v. Better Const. Co., 587 So. 2d 492, 494 (Fla. 1st DCA 1991); Bell v. University of Florida, 652 So. 2d 460, 461 (Fla. 1st DCA 1995)].

§ 21.05 Medicare and Washout Settlements

EDITOR'S NOTE: The following discussion on medicare was originally printed in NEW YORK WORKERS' COMPENSATION HANDBOOK (LexisNexis). Some minor changes have been made to the text.

In any case in which the claimant is eligible to receive Social Security Disability Insurance (SSDI) benefits at the time of a workers' compensation settlement or might be reasonably expected to become eligible in the future, the settlement agreement must address any Medicare issues in addition to the SSDI benefit allocation problem discussed in ch. 13, § 13.52[4]. Generally speaking, a claimant receiving SSDI will become entitled to Medicare within 24 months of the date Social Security found the claimant to be disabled. With regard to medical benefits causally related to a workers' compensation injury, Medicare is always a "secondary payer," with all causally related medical bills being the primary responsibility of the compensation carrier unless the carrier can justify an objection [*see* Haines & Campbell, *Protecting the Disabled Individual Through the Use of a Medicare Set-Aside Trust*, 33 Clearinghouse Rev. 305 (Sept.–Oct. 1999)].

It is impermissible to attempt to shift the compensation carrier's primary responsibility for causally related medical expenses to Medicare by settlement of the workers' compensation claims. Further, any settlement in which Medicare is an issue must account for any claim Medicare may have for medical bills it has already paid as "conditional payments" in its role of "secondary payer." The relevant statute is 42 U.S.C.S. § 1395y. The regulations governing these provisions may be found at 42 C.F.R. Part 411.1 et seq. The effective date of these regulations is 11/13/89, and they do not apply to settlements prior to that date [*see* Health Ins. Ass'n of Am., Inc. v. Shalala, 23 F.3d 412, 423–424 (D.C. Cir. 1994), *cert. denied sub nom.* Shalala v. Health Ins. Ass'n of Am., Inc., 513 U.S. 1147, 130 L. Ed. 2d 1064, 115 S. Ct. 1095 (1995)].

The applicable regulations are complex. Suffice it to say that at the present time the Department of Health and Human Services, through its Centers for Medicare and Medicaid Services (CMS), is engaged in a major Coordination of Benefits program reaching to all states. The aim of this program is to identify workers' compensation cases in which Medicare benefits have been paid that should have been paid by the workers' compensation carrier. When such cases are identified, CMS generally advises both the injured worker and his or her counsel.

Neither carriers nor claimants nor their representatives should enter into a workers' compensation settlement agreement in which Medicare is potentially an issue without careful review of the applicable regulations and without appropriate acknowledgment in the agreement. Not to account for Medicare's potential interest may be fatal to the finality of the agreement and may expose both parties to significant future financial liability. Anyone contemplating a settlement agreement in which Medicare is potentially involved should begin by reviewing the CMS memorandum to all CMS Regional Administrators dated July 23, 2001, available at www.hcfa.gov/medicare/mspmain.htm [*see also* SOCIAL SECURITY PRACTICE GUIDE, Ch. 8, *Social Security and Medicare Offset of Workers' Compensation Benefits*, App. § 8B[3] (LexisNexis)].

It is beyond the scope of this section to fully address the complexities involved in settling a case in which past or future Medicare benefits are at issue. All practitioners are strongly advised to make themselves aware of the applicable federal regulations and practices in this area. Failure to properly do so under the current law is improper. That being said, the following points are offered as guidance:

1. An injured worker who is *not yet a Medicare beneficiary* need consider Medicare's interests only when the injured worker has a "reasonable expectation" of Medicare enrollment within 24 months of the settlement date and the anticipated total settlement amount for future medical expenses and disability/lost wages over the life or duration of the settlement agreement is expected to be greater than $250,000. The "24-month/$250,000" standard is set

forth only in the CMS memorandum of July 23, 2001, referenced above, and is, therefore, the agency's interpretation of the statute and regulations. Unlike rules and regulations promulgated in the C.F.R., informal agency opinion letters, manuals, and enforcement guidelines lack "force of law" [*see, e.g.,* Spirit Lake Tribe v. North Dakota, 262 F.3d 732, 741–742 (8th Cir. 2001), *cert. denied,* 535 U.S. 988 (2002)]. However, CMS is entitled to considerable deference in the interpretation of the Social Security Act and its own regulations [*see, e.g.,* Visiting Nurse Ass'n v. Bullen, 93 F.3d 997, 1002 (1st Cir. 1996), *cert. denied,* 519 U.S. 1114, 136 L. Ed. 2d 842, 117 S. Ct. 955 (1997)].

2. In any case in which the claimant *is already a Medicare beneficiary*, a settlement must provide for total repayment or compromise of any and all Medicare "conditional payments" related to the compensable injury. Conditional payments may occur in any case in which the workers' compensation carrier did not pay the medical provider "promptly." In many cases the claimant may not even be aware such payments were made, but this information may be obtained from the Centers for Medicare and Medicaid Services (CMS) with a proper release from the claimant.

3. In any case in which the claimant *is already a Medicare beneficiary*, CMS will consider the *entire* amount of the settlement to be *allocated* for the payment of future medical bills unless the settlement provides otherwise.

4. Medicare divides workers' compensation settlements into those that provide for a "commutation" of established lifetime workers' compensation benefits and those that "compromise" controverted benefits. The proper method to allocate a settlement depends entirely on which type of settlement applies to the situation. Unless Medicare approves of the allocation, it considers the entire settlement to be allocated for future medical expenses and will not pay future Medicare benefits until there is proof the settlement has been spent on Medicare-eligible medical expenses. In a worst-case scenario, should Medicare find, on the facts of the particular case, that the settlement agreement was designed to improperly shift liability to Medicare, all future Medicare coverage for that condition may be denied.

5. In commutation cases any allocation of future causally related medical costs must account for the realistic value of causally related medical for the remainder of the claimant's life.

6. In compromise cases any allocation must bear a reasonable relationship to the value of the settlement. That is, if the liability settlement is for 10% of the value of the case, the medical settlement should be 10% of the value of the anticipated future medical.

7. If a compromise settlement includes a disallowance of the workers' compensation case, Medicare will recognize that disallowance only if the evidence indicates there was a real possibility the case would not be established.

There are various methods within the settlement agreement to accommodate Medicare's interests. One successful method is simply to agree that the workers' compensation carrier remains liable for future causally related medical treatment. If, however, the parties intend to settle entitlement to future medical care as part of the agreement, the options range from applying to CMS for pre-settlement approval to crafting a proper allocation of future medical costs such that CMS will approve the allocation when and if it reviews it. Failure to account for Medicare's past or future interest in a settlement may result in unintended financial liabilities for either the claimant or the carrier or both.

§ 21.06 Effect of Settlement on Subsequent Claims by Others

A question arises as to the extent of the protection a carrier receives by virtue of a lump sum settlement, especially as to possible claims for contribution or reimbursement from another employer and carrier when the claimant's medical needs and disability are attributable to more than one accident. Essentially, a settlement agreement between an employer/carrier and the claimant will have no effect on such a potential claim brought by others who are not parties to the settlement agreement.

In *Standard Fire Ins. Co. v. U-Haul Co. of Eastern Florida* [551 So. 2d 580 (Fla. 1st DCA 1989)], the claimant sustained a back injury while working for U-Haul. He received benefits and ultimately reached maximum medical improvement and received a disability rating. He then went to work for Taylor Rental and re-injured his back a few months later. Taylor paid the claimant medical benefits and then reached a settlement agreement with him. Taylor was then ordered to reimburse U-Haul, which had been paying temporary total disability benefits during this period, but Taylor argued that the reimbursement order conflicted with its settlement with the claimant. The court disagreed, holding that the settlement dealt with the liability between Taylor and the claimant, while the reimbursement dealt with the liability between the two employers.

A settlement covers only those claims or rights that are specifically mentioned in the agreement. Thus, claims for a latent injury unknown at the time of settlement, for subsequent injuries, or for prior injuries not covered in the agreement have been held not barred by a settlement agreement. Similarly, a claim for silicosis disability benefits has been held not barred because of a previous settlement that did not mention silicosis or any occupational disease. An agreement that states that it is a settlement of all claims has been held to be broad enough to bar a later claim of bad faith in terminating benefits. Georgia has held that such an agreement will bar a later claim for rehabilitation benefits [*see* Purdy v. American Mut. Liability Ins. Co., 148 Ga. App. 864, 253 S.E.2d 250 (1979)].

However, New Mexico reached the opposite result on the ground that the stipulation on which the agreement was based had not expressly mentioned rehabilitation benefits [*see* Ruiz v. City of Albuquerque, 91 N.M. 526, 577 P.2d 424 (Ct. App. 1978)]. A claim under the Maryland Compensation Act for abusive retaliatory discharge was held not barred by a release, since the claim stemmed not from the claimant's compensable injury, but from the employer's violation of an anti-retaliation statute. Even a very broadly worded settlement agreement will not cover issues that are clearly peripheral to the settlement, such as release of third-party tortfeasors, the employer's derivative liability for a different injury, or the rights of lien claimants [*see* LARSON'S WORKERS' COMPENSATION, DESK EDITION, Ch. 132, § 132.05[1] (Matthew Bender)].

§ 21.07 Enforcing Settlement Agreements

[1] General Rules

Contract law governs settlement agreements [*see* Robbie v. City of Miami, 469 So. 2d 1384, 1385 (Fla. 1985)]. Such agreements "are highly favored and will be enforced whenever possible" [Robbie v. City of Miami, 469 So. 2d 1384, 1385 (Fla. 1985)]. Contracts, including settlement agreements, are to be construed according to the parties' intent, as demonstrated by the words used [*see* Gendzier v. Bielecki, 97 So. 2d 604, 608 (Fla. 1957); Ross v. Savage, 66 Fla. 106, 63 So. 148, 155 (Fla. 1913)]. An objective test is to be used to determine whether the claimant accepted the employer/carrier's offer and whether the settlement is enforceable [*see* Robbie v. City of Miami, 469 So. 2d 1384, 1385 (Fla. 1985); King v. Bray, 867 So. 2d 1224, 1227 (Fla. 5th DCA 2004)].

For a settlement agreement to be valid and enforceable against a claimant, counsel for claimant must have the client's clear and unequivocal authority to settle on his or her behalf [*see* Dixie Operating Co. v. Exxon Co., U.S.A., 493 So. 2d 61, 63–64 (Fla. 1st DCA 1986); Nehleber v. Anzalone, 345 So. 2d 822, 823 (Fla. 4th DCA 1977)].

[2] Intent of the Parties

When two parties enter into a contract, there must be a mutual intent—a meeting of the minds—concerning which there can be a mutual mistake subject to certain legal corrections [*see* Brown v. Brown, 501 So. 2d 24, 27 (Fla 5th DCA 1986)].

It is axiomatic that the clear and unambiguous words of a contract are the best evidence of the intent of the parties. Lack of mutuality of contract is not a defense in the case of an executed contract [*see* Murry v. Zynyx Mktg. Communs., Inc., 774 So. 2d 714 (Fla. 3rd DCA 2000)].

In construing a contract, the legal effect of its provisions should be determined from the words of the entire contract. It is well established that the language in a release is the best evidence of the parties' intent and that when the language is clear and unambiguous, the courts cannot indulge in construction or interpretation of its plain meaning [*see* Vermut v. GMC, 773 So. 2d 126, 128 (Fla. 4th DCA 2000)].

However, it is universally recognized that parole evidence is admissible to alter the terms of a written agreement, when it is shown that by reason of mutual mistake the true intention of the parties is not expressed in the agreement [*see* Abernethy v. National Union Fire Ins. Co., 717 So. 2d 196 (Fla. 5th DCA 1998)].

[3] Mutuality of Obligation

Mutuality of obligation means that both parties are bound or neither is bound. In other words, there must be a valid consideration. Without a valid consideration, a contract cannot be enforced in law or in equity [*see* Hope v. National Airlines, Inc., 99 So. 2d 244, 247 (Fla. 3rd DCA 1957)].

The so-called requirement of mutuality of obligation is now widely discredited. "It is consideration . . . that is necessary, not mutuality of obligation" [Arthur Linton Corbin,

Corbin on Contracts § 6.1, at 197 (Joseph M. Perillo ed., rev. ed. 1995); *see also* Restatement (Second) of Contracts § 79 ("If the requirement of consideration is met, there is no additional requirement of . . . 'mutuality of obligation.' ")].

Even if there had been a lack of mutuality at the inception, an executed contract would nevertheless be enforceable. The court has held that lack of mutuality of contract is not a defense in the case of an executed contract [*see* Wright & Seaton, Inc. v. Prescott, 420 So. 2d 623, 627 (Fla. 4th DCA 1982) (quoting 17 C.J.S. Contracts § 100(3), at 799–800 (1963))].

[4] Enforcement of General Release

Settlement agreements are governed by the same legal principles applied to other contracts. In contract interpretation there is a basic rule, which is that the intention of parties to a contract is ascertained from a consideration of the whole agreement.

The making of a contract depends not on an agreement of two minds in one intention, but on an agreement of two sets of external signs, that is, not on the parties having meant the same thing, but on their having said the same thing. An agreement must be sufficiently specific and mutually agreeable as to every essential element [*see* Grimsley v. Inverrary Resort Hotel, Ltd., 748 So. 2d 299, 301 (Fla. 4th DCA 1999)].

Generally, Florida courts enforce general releases to further the policy of encouraging settlements. Numerous Florida cases have upheld general releases, even when the releasing party is unaware of the defect at the time the agreement was executed. More importantly, other courts recognize this principle even in the face of a fraudulent inducement claim. The execution of all-encompassing general releases prohibits plaintiffs from suing defendants for fraudulent inducement. The court will construe a release for "any and all" causes of action as barring a fraudulent inducement claim [*see* Mazzoni Farms, Inc. v. E. I. DuPont De Nemours & Co., 761 So. 2d 306, 314 (Fla. 2000)].

Under Florida law, a general release will ordinarily be regarded as embracing all claims or demands, which had matured at the time of its execution. Conversely, a general release does not bar a claim, which had not yet accrued when the release was executed. When the language of the release is clear and unambiguous, a court cannot indulge in construction or interpretation of its plain meaning [*see* Hold v. Manzini, 736 So. 2d 138, 141 (Fla. 3rd DCA 1999)].

The court recognizes that it is the duty of the court to give effect to the intention of the parties, even if every contingency may not be specifically covered by an agreement, and that an alleged contract should not be voided due to uncertainty unless there is no alternative [*see* Woodfield Plaza by & Through Straub Capital Corp. v. Stiles Construction Co., 687 So. 2d 856, 857 (Fla. 4th DCA 1997)].

[5] Authority of JCC to Enforce Settlement Agreement

A workers' compensation claimant represented by counsel may enter into a lump sum settlement agreement [§ 440.20(11)(c), Fla. Stat.]. However, pursuant to the year 2000 amendments to § 440.20(11)(c), Fla. Stat. such settlement agreement requires approval by a judge of compensation claims only as to the attorney's fees paid to the claimant's attorney by the claimant. The parties need not submit any information or documentation in support of the settlement, except as needed to justify the amount of the attorney's fees. The plain language of § 440.20(11)(c), Fla. Stat. does not extinguish a judge of compensation claims' previously existing jurisdiction to determine whether a settlement agreement was entered, or to construe, or give effect to settlement agreements. Rather, except for the amount of attorney's fees, it simply permits parties represented by counsel to enter lump sum settlement agreements without obtaining the judge of compensation claim's approval of the settlement actually reached. A judge of compensation claims' jurisdiction relating to settlement agreements is well settled. Construction of a settlement agreement is a matter clearly within the province of the judge of compensation claims. The judge of compensation claims has authority to determine whether a valid, binding settlement agreement was reached, and, if so, to give effect to the settlement agreement [*see* Jacobsen v. Ross Stores, 882 So. 2d 431, 433 (Fla. 1st DCA 2004)].

The *Jacobsen* case has been followed in two subsequent cases. In *Gerow v. Yesterday's* [881 So. 2d 94 (Fla. 1st DCA 2004)], the court was asked to determine whether the amendments adopted by the 2000 Florida Legislature to § 440.20(11)(c), Fla. Stat. (2001) eliminated the judge of compensation claims' jurisdiction to determine whether a settlement agreement was reached, or to determine the terms of such an agreement. Based on the reasoning discussed in *Jacobsen*, the court concluded they do not. The court held it is within the province of the judge of compensation claims to determine whether a settlement agreement was reached, and, if so, to establish its terms.

In *Borque v. Trugreen, Inc.* [389 F.3d 1354, 1357 (11th Cir. 2004)], the Eleventh Circuit, citing *Jacobsen*, recognized the authority of a judge of compensation claims to determine whether a settlement agreement in a workers' compensation case is binding upon the parties.

CHAPTER 22

THE LEGAL ENVIRONMENT AND DISPUTE RESOLUTION

SYNOPSIS

Guide to Claims

§ 22.01 Overview of Dispute Resolution Process

> *We should get away from the idea that a court is the only place in which to settle disputes. People with claims are likely people with pains. They want relief and results and they don't care whether it's in a courtroom with lawyers and judges, or somewhere else.*
> Warren E. Burger
> 1978

Workers' compensation disputes are not resolved at the trial level in the regular courts, but through a somewhat informal, administrative law system. Beginning January 1, 1994, the procedure for dispute resolution changed dramatically. Dispute resolution is now a multi-step process.

Step one begins with the Division of Workers' Compensation and, when a managed care arrangement is in place, with the carrier [*see* § 22.03[1]]. Injured workers, or their lawyers, must first refer disputes involving indemnity benefits to the Division's Office of Employee Assistance [*see* § 22.03[1]]. If the dispute involves medical benefits, injured workers must first refer the dispute to the carrier's managed care grievance procedure. This is a mandatory first step before formal litigation may begin.

If the Division cannot bring the issue in dispute to resolution within 30 days, the injured worker may begin the second step by filing a Petition for Benefits [*see* § 22.03[2]]. Interestingly, carriers have 60 days to resolve a medical benefit dispute before a Petition for Benefits can be filed.

Upon filing a Petition for Benefits, the next step in the process is a mandatory, but non-binding, mediation unless the chief judge waives this requirement [*see* § 22.03[3]].

If mediation fails to resolve the issue, the next step, following a pretrial conference [*see* § 22.03[4]] is a formal hearing before a judge of compensation claims [*see* § 22.03[5]]. (Note: Judges of compensation claims do not have the authority to enforce their own orders. This authority rests with the circuit courts. See ch. 23, § 23.06, on rule nisi proceedings.)

Finally, appeals from the orders of the judges of compensation claims go to the First District Court of Appeal in Tallahassee. Under highly limited circumstances the final stop in the appellate process is the Florida Supreme Court [*see* § 22.11].

For general commentary on informal compensation procedure, see LARSON'S WORKERS' COMPENSATION, DESK EDITION, Ch. 124 (Matthew Bender).

> **SPECIAL ALERT:** Because the 1994 amendments change only the procedure for dispute resolution, they apply to all claims whatever the accident date.

§ 22.02 Judges of Compensation Claims (JCC)

[1] Relationship to Department of Labor and Employment Security

Effective October 1, 2001, the legislature transferred the Office of Judges of Compensation Claims from the Florida Department of Labor and Employment Security, to the Department of Management Services, Division of Administrative Hearings. The position of Chief Judge is changed to Deputy Chief Judge and reports to the Director of the Division of Administrative Hearings [§ 440.45(1), Fla. Stat. (10/1/2001)].

[2] Judicial Qualifications and Appointment

To qualify as a judge of compensation claims, the applicant must have be a member of the Florida Bar, and must be knowledgeable in the practice of workers' compensation law [§ 440.45(2)(a), Fla. Stat.]. The Governor appoints the judges from a list of three nominees submitted by the Statewide Nominating Commission. The term of office is four years. The Statewide Nominating Commission consists of 15 members. The Florida Bar appoints five members, the Governor appoints an additional five members, and these 10 members appoint the remaining five by majority vote. The Workers' Compensation Act now prohibits a lawyer from serving on the commission if the lawyer appears before a judge of compensation claims more then four times per year [§ 440.45(2)(b), Fla. Stat. (11/4/96)].

[3] Appointment and Reappointment Procedure

The Governor can remove a judge from office at any time for cause. At least six months before the expiration of a judge's four-year term, the Nominating Commission must hold a public hearing to review the judge's conduct in office. If the commission finds the judge's performance satisfactory, the commission must then report its findings to the Governor. If, after reviewing the commission's report, the Governor decides not to reappoint the judge, the commission will be informed and it must then send the names of three nominees from which the Governor will select a replacement. If the commission determines that the judge's performance was not satisfactory, it must submit the names of three nominees from which the Governor will select a replacement [§ 440.45(2)(c), Fla. Stat.].

The Act requires the nominating commission to determine if a judge's performance was satisfactory by determining the extent to which the judge met the requirements of Chapter 440. The new language specifically refers to certain statutory provisions as part of this performance review. These are the provisions requiring the JCC to dismiss petitions lacking specificity, to set mediation conferences, pretrials, and trials in a timely manner, as well as to issue final orders within the time frames specified in the Act. It also directs the commission to give particular attention to the judges performance in awarding attorney fees. The obvious intent is to instruct the members of the nominating commission to give greater weight to these specific issues in evaluating a judge's performance [§ 440.45(2)(c), Fla. Stat. (10/1/2001)].

[4] Docketing Judges

Previously, the Act required the chief judge must appoint two or more judges, among all the sitting judges, to serve as docketing judges on a rotating basis. The primary function of the docketing judge is to review Petitions for Benefits and to dismiss those that do not meet the statutory specificity requirements. The legislature amended § 440.45, Fla. Stat., by repealing subsection (3) which eliminates the docketing judge process.

[5] Deputy Chief Judge

[a] Organization and Qualifications

Effective October 1, 2001, the judges of compensation, as part of agency reorganization, were transferred from the Division of Workers' Compensation to the Office of the Judges of Compensation Claims (OJCC) under the direction of the Division of Administrative Hearings (DOAH). The position of Chief Judge was reclassified as Deputy Chief Judge.

Like the judges, the deputy chief judge must be a member of the Florida Bar and knowledgeable in the practice of workers' compensation law. The deputy chief judge also serves a four–year term of office and is selected and appointed by the Governor from a list of three nominees submitted by the nominating commission [*see* § 440.45, Fla. Stat.].

[b] Rules of Procedure

Previously, all the judges and lawyers followed the Workers' Compensation Rules of Procedure (WCRP) as approved by the Florida Supreme Court. The 2002 law transferred rule- making authority to the Division of Administrative Hearings [§ 440.45(5), Fla. Stat. (11/4/2002)].

The Division of Administrative Hearings (DOAH) promulgated and adopted the Rules of Procedure for Workers' Compensation Adjudication. under Rule Chapter 60Q-6, effective February 23, 2003.

Although not everyone agreed, the statutory revisions effectively repealed the original Court-approved rules of procedure and replaced them with the DOAH rules. In 2004, this issue was before the Florida Supreme Court. On December 2, 2004, the Court issued an analysis of its role in promulgating workers' compensation rules of procedure as it has done since 1977. The Court noted that its authority is limited to promulgating rules for courts, but the Office of the Judges of Compensation Claims is a quasi-judicial body and not a court. The JOCC is part of the executive branch rather than the judicial branch. Therefore, the Supreme Court concluded it has *never* had authority to promulgate rules of procedure for workers' compensation and repealed the Florida Rules of Workers' Compensation Procedure, effective December 2, 2004.

To avoid the possibility of confusion or upheaval within the workers' compensation system, the Court declared this repeal is prospective, beginning on December 2, 2004; therefore, this repeal has no effect on any workers' compensation proceedings that are final.

As the Supreme Court noted, in 2001 the Legislature amended § 440.45, Fla. Stat., to provide that: "The workers' compensation rules of procedure approved by the Supreme

Court shall apply *until* rules promulgated by the [OJCC] . . . become effective."

As noted, the agency (DOAH) adopted Rules of Procedure for Workers' Compensation Adjudications, under Rule Chapter 60Q-6, effective February 23, 2003. Since then, lawyers and the judges of compensation claims have been guided by these rules [*see* Amendments to the Fla. Rules of Workers' Comp. Procedure, 891 So. 2d 474 (Fla. 2004)].

[6] Code of Judicial Conduct

Effective January 1, 1994, the legislature enacted a lengthy and detailed Code of Judicial Conduct for the Chief Judge and all the judges of compensation claims. Effective October 1, 2001, the legislature repealed the statutory code of judicial conduct and providing instead that the judges should be guided by the code of judicial conduct as adopted by the Florida Supreme Court [§ 440.442, Fla. Stat. (10/01/2001); *see* Part VII, Code of Judicial Conduct].

In addition, the legislature granted the Director of Administrative Hearings the authority to initiate, receive, and investigate complaints against any judge of compensation claims alleging violations of the code of judicial conduct. The Director may dismiss the complaint or recommend to the Governor that the judge be removed from office or disciplined [§ 440.45(2)(e), Fla. Stat. (10/1/2001)].

> *Four things belong to a judge:*
> *to hear courteously, to answer wisely, to consider soberly,*
> *and to decide impartially.*
> Socrates, 470–399 B.C.

§ 22.03 Dispute Resolution Procedure

[1] Step One: Employee Assistance and Ombudsman Office (EAO)

[a] Purpose

To help resolve disputes without costly and time-consuming litigation, the legislature created the Employee Assistance and Ombudsman Office within the Division of Workers' Compensation. An ombudsman is a government official appointed to receive and investigate complaints and to help to achieve equitable settlements. When employees believe the law entitles them to benefits that the carrier disputes, they may contact the Employee Assistance and Ombudsman Office and request help in resolving the dispute [*see* § 440.191(1)(c), Fla. Stat. (7/1/2002)].

Upon receiving notice of an injury from an employee, the employer or carrier must provide the employee with a written notice of the availability of services from the Employee Assistance and Ombudsman Office. The substance of the notice to the employee must include the following [§ 440.185(12), Fla. Stat. (10/1/2003)]:

(a) A description of the scope of services provided by the office.

(b) A listing of the toll-free telephone number of, the email address, and the postal address of the office.

(c) A statement that the informational brochure will be mailed to the employee within 3 days after the carrier receives notice of the injury.

(d) Any other information regarding access to assistance that the department finds is immediately necessary for an injured employee.

NOTE: The statute provides that the notice is to be in the form and manner determined by the department by rule. Presumably, this requirement will not take effect until the department develops the required rule.

[b] Request for Assistance

The requirement for filing a Request for Assistance was repealed, effective July 1, 2002 [*see* § 440.191, Fla. Stat.].

[c] Powers of EAO

Although using the Division's dispute resolution services is voluntary, once these services are requested, the statutes require the parties to participate in good faith [*see* § 440.191(1)(a), Fla. Stat.]. The rules describe a good faith effort as cooperation with the Division's efforts and include responding to requests for information within five working days [*see* Fla. Admin. Code. R. 69L-26.002(6)(c) (1/10/2005)]. Despite the voluntary nature of this informal process, once it is initiated, the Division has authority to compel the parties to attend conferences in person or by telephone [*see* § 440.191(2)(b), Fla. Stat. (July 1, 2002)].

[d] Failure to Act in Good Faith

Although the Act requires the parties to cooperate with the Division, it contains no penalty for either the employee or E/C for failing to do so [§ 440.191, Fla. Stat. (7/1/97)]. The legislature also failed to grant even the judges of compensation claims authority to impose sanctions for a party's failure to try to resolve a dispute in good faith, or to cooperate with EAO efforts to resolve disagreement between the parties. Neither the Workers' Compensation Rules of Procedure nor Ch. 440, Fla. Stat. contain authority to allow a judge of compensation claims to impose sanctions for failure to cooperate in the informal dispute resolution process. In dicta, the court suggested that this omission renders the EAO process ineffective and meaningless, and urged the legislature to address this issue [*see* Plouffe v. Lake County Sheriff's Office, 653 So. 2d 507, 508–509 (Fla. 1st DCA 1995)].

[e] Assistance With Petition for Benefits

If the injured worker does not have a lawyer, the ombudsman may help in preparing the Petition for Benefits [*see* [a], *above*]. The ombudsman, however, may not represent the injured worker before a judge of compensation claims. Once this phase is complete, the process is on a fast track. Carriers should consider the first contact by an ombudsman as a red flag for the possible need to involve a defense lawyer. This is especially true when the injured worker does not have a lawyer. Once the more formal dispute resolution process begins, the time for discovery and defense development is very short.

[f] Carrier Action Required: The 120-Day Rule

[i] The 120-Day Rule

Often, the carrier may not have sufficient information to decide if the claim is compensable. If so, the carrier may begin benefits without prejudice and without admitting liability. Within 120 days, however, the carrier must issue a notice of denial or waive the right to deny compensability later. An exception will arise if the carrier can show that it could not have discovered evidence supporting a denial through reasonable investigation during the 120–day period. In such cases, the carrier must provide written notice to the employee that it is paying all or part of the claim pending further investigation and that the carrier will advise the injured worker of its final decision within 120 days. § 440.20(4), Fla. Stat. as amended effective October 1, 2001, specifically provides:

> If the carrier is uncertain of its obligation to provide benefits or compensation, it may initiate payment without prejudice and without admitting liability. The carrier shall immediately and in good faith commence investigation of the employee's entitlement to benefits under this chapter and shall admit or deny compensability within 120 days after the initial provision of compensation or benefits as required under subsection (2) or § 440.192(8). Upon commencement of payment as required under subsection (2) or § 440.192(8), the carrier shall provide written notice to the employee that it has elected to pay all or part of the claim pending further investigation, and that it will advise the employee of claim acceptance or denial within 120 days. A carrier that fails to deny compensability within 120 days after the initial provision of benefits or payment of compensation as required under subsection (2) or § 440.192(8) waives the right to deny compensability, unless the carrier can establish material facts relevant to the issue of compensability that it could not have discovered through reasonable investigation within the 120–day period. The initial provision of compensation or benefits, for purposes of this subsection, means the first installment of compensation or benefits to be paid by the carrier under subsection (2) or pursuant to a petition for benefits under § 440.192(8).

[ii] Triggering the 120-Day Period: Indemnity Benefits

The statute provides that the right to deny a claim expires 120 days after "the initial provision of compensation or benefits." The amendment to § 440.20(4), Fla. Stat. effective October 1, 2001, provides that the phrase "the initial provision of compensation or benefits" means "the first installment of compensation or benefits *to be paid* by the carrier under subsection (2) or pursuant to a petition for benefits." § 440.20(2)(a) Fla. Stat., refers to paying or denying indemnity benefits within 14 days after the employer receives a notice of injury or death. § 440.20(2)(b) Fla. Stat., refers to paying medical bills within 45 days after receipt [*see* [iii], *below*]. Note that the statute refers to compensation or benefits "to be paid" rather than actually paid. This suggests strongly that the 120-day period begins with the *obligation* to pay indemnity benefits or to pay medical bills rather than the actual payment. Therefore, with regard to indemnity benefits it is logical to conclude that the 120-day period begins to run 14 days after the employer receives notice of the accident and disability, or after a petition for benefits is filed, whether or not benefits have been paid. If so, the 120-day cut-off for denying a claim will occur 134 days after the employer receives notice of the injury and disability.

This, however, is not certain. The uncertainty is created by § 440.20(11)(a), Fla. Stat., which now precludes a settlement of a controverted case if the Notice of Denial was not issued within 120 days after the employer received notice of the injury [*see* [iv], *below*]. Because of this ambiguity, carriers should ensure that any Notice of Denial be issued within 120 days from the date the employer received the notice of injury. Obviously, determining the date on which the employer received notice will be critical. If the employer maintains that it never received notice, then it appears that filing a petition will trigger the running of the 120-day period. Because of the statute's phrasing, it may also be argued that filing a Petition for Benefits triggers a second 120-day period, even if the initial period has expired.

[iii] Triggering the 120-Day Period: Medical Benefits

The next issue is what triggers the 120-day period with regard to providing medical benefits. The court concluded that the "initial provision of benefits" occurs on the date a claimant visits an authorized physician. Authorization makes a doctor's visit, and payment for that visit, possible, but it does not obligate the employer and carrier to pay for that visit until the visit takes place. Furthermore, such a visit may produce the first available information useful to the employer and carrier to determine whether the injury is compensable, which is one of the reasons for the 120-day period. Therefore, the court held the first authorized doctor's visit by a claimant is the "initial provision of benefits," beginning the 120-day pay-and-investigate period [*see* Osceola County Sch. Bd. v. Arace, 884 So. 2d 1003 (Fla. 1st DCA, 2004)].

[iv] Invoking the 120-Day Period: Written Notice Required

The statute, § 440.20(4), Fla. Stat., requires the carrier to provide a claimant with written notice if it intends to invoke the 120-day pay-and- investigate provision. Note carefully the following sentence from the statute [§ 440.20(4), Fla. Stat. (7/1/97)]:

> Upon commencement of payment, the carrier shall provide written notice to the employee that it has elected to pay all or part of the claim pending further investigation, and that it will advise the employee of claim acceptance or denial within 120 days.

The main section begins with a statement that if the carrier is uncertain about its obligation, it may begin payments without prejudice. The question is whether the written notice is mandatory every time. Apparently, the notice letter is required only in cases where the carrier is not certain about compensability. If the carrier is certain, how does it announce its acceptance of compensability? If the carrier does announce acceptance, but does not send the written notice, will the carrier be estopped from asserting a defense even within the 120-day period? As Judge Kahn noted in *Waffle House,* this is a poorly written statute [*see* [2][e][i][B], *below*]. Carriers should consider sending the notice always.

[2] Step Two: Petition for Benefits

[a] Procedure

The injured worker may file a Petition for Benefits at any time, but only for benefits that are ripe, due, and owing.

Petitions for Benefits are to be filed by certified mail or electronically, if approved by the Chief Judge, directly with the office of the judges of compensation claims. Copies must be served on the employer, the carrier, and the Division of Workers' Compensation, also by certified mail or electronically. The Chief Judge will then refer the petition to the appropriate judge of compensation claims [§ 440.192(1), Fla. Stat. (10/1/2001)]. If the petition lacks the required specificity, the Office of the Judges of Compensation Claims must dismiss the entire petition or only the part lacking specificity [§ 440.192(2), Fla. Stat. (10/1/2003)].

[b] Specificity Requirements

The purpose of the specificity requirements is to ensure that the carrier has the information necessary to figure out exactly what the injured worker believes is due. This is obviously essential to make a timely and informed decision. Effective January 1, 1994, the legislature expanded the requirements and did so again effective October 1, 2001. A judge must dismiss the entire petition or any portion of a petition that does not, on its face, specifically identify or itemize the following [§ 440.192(2), Fla. Stat. (10/1/2001)]:

1. The name, address, telephone number, and social security number of the injured worker.

> **NOTE:** The court has held the requirement that a petition must contain the claimant's Social Security number is a violation of section 7 of the federal Privacy Act of 1974, at 5 U.S.C.S. § 552a. Therefore, including the Social Security number is not required [*see* Cagnoli v. Tandem Staffing & Specialty Risk Servs., 888 So. 2d 79 (Fla. 1st DCA 2004), *rehg denied*, 2004 Fla. App. LEXIS 20840 (Fla. 1st DCA 2004)].

2. The name, address, and telephone number of the employer.
3. A detailed description of the injury and cause of the injury, including the location of the occurrence and the date or dates of the accident.
4. A detailed description of the employee's job, work responsibilities, and the work the employee was doing when the injury occurred.
5. The time for which compensation and the specific classification of compensation were not timely provided.
6. The date of maximum medical improvement, character of disability, and a specific statement of all benefits or compensation that the employee is seeking.
7. All specific travel costs to which the employee believes he or she is entitled, including the dates of travel, purpose of travel, the means of transportation, and

mileage, and including the date the request for mileage was filed with the carrier and a copy of the request filed with the carrier.

8. A specific listing of all medical charges alleged to be unpaid, including the name and address of the medical provider, the amounts due, and the specific dates of treatment.

9. The type or nature of treatment care or attendance sought and the justification for such treatment. If the employee is under the care of a physician, a copy of the physician's request, authorization, or recommendation for treatment, care, or attendance must accompany the petition.

10. A specific explanation of any other disputed issue upon which a judge of compensation claims will be called upon to rule.

While the law is specific about the form and information required in a legally sufficient Petition for Benefits, minor defects are not likely to destroy a petition's validity. Until 1998, the courts had not directly addressed this issue under the 1994 statutory language, as they have done in the earlier versions of the law. While courts expected lawyers to be well versed in preparing formal pleadings, exacting formality had not been the requirement in workers' compensation. In the past, any paper suggesting even the probability that the injured worker has not received compensation when due has been treated as a proper "claim" [*see* A.B. Taff & Sons v. Clark, 110 So. 2d 428, 433 (Fla. 1st DCA 1959)].

Until the 1994 amendment to § 440.19, Fla. Stat. and the simultaneous creation of § 440.192, Fla. Stat., the law on specificity has been liberally applied. Courts accepted petitions (formerly known as Claims for Benefits) as complete if they provided enough information for the employer or carrier to determine the accident referred to in the claim and the benefits sought by the injured worker. If the claim or petition provided enough information for the carrier to make these determinations, the carrier could not support a defense based on the deficient petition itself. This was true even if the petition gave no clue about specific benefits, but the carrier already had the facts. For example, the injured worker or the worker's lawyer might show an incorrect accident date on the petition. This did not disturb the petition's validity if the carrier already knew the correct date, or if the correct date was discernable from the petition or its attachments [*see* Mays v. Packers, 677 So. 2d 992, 994–995 (Fla. 1st DCA 1996)].

Note that when the courts were formulating these rules, the statute was quite different than it is today. The statute before 1994 required specificity of a sort, but also allowed "equivalent information."

Under the 1994 amendments, however, § 440.192(2), Fla. Stat. and § 440.192(4), Fla. Stat. set forth basic information that the petition must identify or contain on its face. Under these statutes, the judge of compensation claims is not obligated to decide if the information is sufficient to place the carrier on notice of the benefits that the injured worker seeks. Instead, the judge's responsibility is to decide only if the petition meets the statutory requirements. If it does not, the law mandates that the judge dismiss the petition without prejudice, allowing the injured worker to file a corrected and proper petition. Carriers are not required to file a motion to dismiss to trigger the judge's review of the petition, but may do so if they wish [*see* § 440.192(5), Fla. Stat.]. Filing a petition properly is important to injured workers and their lawyers seeking carrier-paid attorney's fees, because § 440.192(7), Fla. Stat. prohibits an award of carrier-paid attorney's fees for services rendered before filing a statutorily proper petition. This is true even if the carrier initially denied the claim, but reversed itself within the 14-day period provided by § 440.192(8), Fla. Stat. [*see* Kennedy v. Orlando Shader Realty, 711 So. 2d 156, 157-158 (Fla. 1st DCA 1998)].

PRACTICE POINT: Unless the parties have agreed, expressly or by their conduct, issues not framed by the pleadings cannot be litigated at the merits hearing. § 440.192(2), Fla. Stat. (Supp. 1994), requires specificity in listing the issues that the judge of compensation claims is expected to rule upon. Likewise, § 440.192(8), Fla. Stat. (Supp. 1994), requires carriers to list all benefits requested but not paid and explain its justification for nonpayment in a formal notice of denial. Note that these claim or defense omissions can be cured in a pretrial stipulation or by consent of the parties. The purpose of these provisions is to enforce a fundamental principle of law that the parties receive reasonable notice of the issues to be adjudicated [*see* Lakeside Baptist Church v. Jones, 714 So. 2d 1188, 1189-1190 (Fla. 1st DCA 1998)].

The Act, § 440.02(40), Fla. Stat., defines the term "specificity" as information on the Petition for Benefits sufficient to put the employer or carrier on notice of the exact statutory benefits requested. To meet the specificity requirements, a petition must contain the following:

1. The exact statutory classification of benefit requested
2. The outstanding time period of benefits requested.
3. A detailed explanation of any benefits received that should be increased, decreased, changed, or otherwise modified.
4. Requests for medical benefits must include specific details as to why such benefits are requested.
5. Requests for medical benefits must include specific details as to why such benefits are medically necessary.
6. Requests for medical benefits must include specific details as to why current treatment, if any, is not sufficient.
7. Requests for alternate or other medical care, including psychiatric, must specifically identify the physician recommending such treatment. Additionally, a copy of the physician's report making the recommendation must be attached to the petition.

The statute further provides that the judge of compensation claims may not order treatment not recommended by a physician. Presumably, the judge of compensation claims will dismiss a petition that does not include the required information. If not, carriers should consider having counsel file a Motion to Dismiss rather than try to respond to vague and non-specific requests. Conversely, carriers must proceed cautiously before denying benefit requests meeting these requirements. This is especially true of medical requests that the petition documents as having been recommended by an authorized physician.

NOTE: These requirements are in addition to the specificity requirements described in § 440.192(1), Fla. Stat.

[c] Other Requirements for a Valid Petition

A Petition for Benefits may claim both past and future benefits, but must be limited to only those benefits that are in default and are ripe, due, and owing on the date the petition is filed. This means, for example, that a petition for impairment benefits filed before a determination of maximum medical improvement is premature and invalid [§ 440.192(3), Fla. Stat. (7/1/97)].

[d] Requirements for Dismissal

[i] Specificity and Technical Details

The primary basis for dismissing a Petition for Benefits is that the petition does not meet the specificity requirements of § 440.192(2), Fla. Stat. Additionally, a judge may dismiss a Petition for Benefits that is not ripe, due, and owing at the time the injured worker files it. A judge also may dismiss a petition when it was not served by certified mail, or does not contain the required certification of a good–faith attempt to resolve the issues, or when the judge finds the certification is not supported by the facts. Finally, the judge may dismiss a petition if the injured worker filed it without first having exhausted the informal dispute resolution procedures.

In the past, the judges were required to dismiss the entire petition even if only one portion was technically deficient. That is no longer true. Effective October 1, 2001, the judges have the authority to dismiss not only the entire petition, but any portion that does not meet the requirement. The judge may do so on his or her own motion, or upon the motion of either party [§ 440.192(5), Fla. Stat. (10/1/2001)].

All motions to dismiss must state with particularity the basis for the motion. The judge must enter an order on all such motions without a hearing unless the parties can show good cause for a hearing. If the judge does dismiss the claim under these provisions, the order must allow the injured worker 20 days to file an amended petition. If the injured worker does not have a lawyer, the judge may request the Employee Assistance Office to help the injured worker in preparing a petition that meets all the technical requirements [§ 440.192(5), Fla. Stat. (7/1/97)].

SPECIAL ALERT: A motion for dismissal on the grounds the petition does not meet the statutory specificity requirements must be asserted within 30 days after receipt of the petition. If not, the carrier waives its right to file a dismissal motion [§ 440.192(5), Fla. Stat. (7/1/97)].

[ii] Lack of Prosecution

On the judge's own motion, or on the motion of a party, the judge of compensation claims may dismiss a petition for lack of prosecution. A dismissal for lack of prosecution is without prejudice and does not require a hearing. Dismissal for lack of prosecution is appropriate if a petition, response, motion, order, request for hearing, or notice of deposition has not been filed during the previous 12 months [§ 440.25(4)(j), Fla. Stat. (7/1/2002)].

[e] Carrier Action Required

[i] The 14-Day Rule

[A] General Rule

§ 440.192(8), Fla. Stat. (10/1/2001) specifically provides:

> Within 14 days after receipt of a petition for benefits by certified mail, the carrier must either pay the requested benefits without prejudice to its right to deny within 120 days from receipt of the petition or file a Response to Petition with the Office of the Judges of Compensation Claims. The carrier must list all benefits requested but not paid and explain its justification for nonpayment in the Response to Petition. A carrier that does not deny compensability in accordance with § 440.22(4) is deemed to have accepted the employee's injuries as compensable, unless it can establish material facts relevant to the issue of compensability that could not have been discovered through reasonable investigation within the 120–day period. The carrier shall provide copies of the response to the filing party, employer, and claimant by certified mail.

Note that the statute now requires carriers to respond to a petition by either providing the benefits claimed, or by filing a "Response to Petition with the Office of the Judges of Compensation Claims." Previously, the statute required carriers to respond by either paying or filing a Notice of Denial with the Division. As with a Notice of Denial, the Response to Petition must list the benefits claimed and the justification for non payment. Obviously, this change provides a more suitable vehicle when the response is that the benefit claimed was provided previously or when some response other than outright denial is appropriate. Also, as with the Notice of Denial, the Response to Petition must be served upon the filing party, the employer, and the claimant by certified mail. The amendment does not require any particular format for the response. Still, carriers should considering developing a standardized format to ensure uniformity.

[B] *Waffle House v. Hutchinson*

SPECIAL ALERT: The First District Court of Appeal receded from its decision in *Waffle House v. Hutchinson,* 673 So. 2d 883, 884–885 (Fla. 1st DCA 1996), *rev. denied,* 683 So. 2d 486 (Fla. 1996). This decision held that a carrier's failure to file a Notice of Denial with the Division within 14 days after receipt of a Petition for Benefits created an irrebuttable presumption that the carrier accepted compensability. This failure meant the carrier waived any defenses and may have owed the benefits claimed by operation of law, without any evidence the injured worker was entitled to the benefits.

In *Waffle House,* the carrier initially denied the entire claim. Later, Hutchinson filed a Petition for Benefits. The carrier, believing it had already denied the claim properly, did nothing in response. At the trial, the judge of compensation claims held that the carrier, by its inaction, was deemed to have accepted compensability under the provisions of the statute. Therefore, holding a merits hearing was unnecessary and the judge awarded benefits based on the operation of § 440.192(8), Fla. Stat. alone. On appeal the First District Court of Appeal affirmed the judge's order.

In late 1996, however, the First District Court of Appeal, sitting en banc, receded from its decision in *Waffle House* to the extent that it precluded a carrier from contesting compensability when it failed to file a Notice of Denial within 14 days after receiving a Petition for Benefits. Instead, the court held that the third sentence of § 440.192(8), Fla. Stat. [*see* [A], *above*] merely refers to, and is a repetition of, the 120-day waiver rule described in § 440.20(4), Fla. Stat. [*see* [1][*l*], *above*]. Neither section, said the court, contains anything that imposes a penalty for failure to timely file a Notice of Denial. The court also held that neither section bars a carrier from asserting a defense and defending a Petition for Benefits within the rules of procedure for workers' compensation claims.

The court explained that the phrase "the issue of compensability" in § 440.20(4), Fla. Stat. refers only to determining whether the claimed injury arose out of, and occurred within the course of, the claimant's employment [*see* North River Ins. Co. v. Wuelling, 683 So. 2d 1090, 1092 (Fla. 1st DCA 1996)].

[C] Presumption of Denial of Benefits

In 1997, however, the court modified its decision in *Wuelling* [*see* [B], *above*]. *Wuelling* still stands for the proposition that failing to file a notice of denial on time does not mean that the carrier loses all its defenses. However, it does not mean that doing nothing has no consequence. If a carrier does not pay the benefits claimed within 14 days after receiving a Petition for Benefits, the carrier is deemed to have denied every allegation in the petition. The penalty for being late is, of course, liability for attorney's fees. Carriers may also be subjected to statutory penalties under § 440.20, Fla. Stat. [*see* Russell Corp. v. Brooks, 698 So. 2d 1334, 1335 (Fla. 1st DCA 1997)].

[ii] Applicability of 120-Day Rule

As with the first report of accident, carriers must either pay or deny benefits requested in a Petition for Benefits within 14 days after receipt by certified mail [§ 440.192(8), Fla. Stat. (7/1/97)]. Although § 440.192(8), Fla. Stat. does not specifically require the carrier to send a 120-day letter as set forth in § 440.20(4), Fla. Stat. [*see* [1][*l*], *above*], such a requirement is implied in that the statute references § 440.20(4), Fla. Stat. Carriers should err on the side of caution and send the 120-day letter anyway if they pay all or part of the benefits requested in the petition. The carrier must send a new Response to Petition in response to each new Petition for Benefits if it does not intend to pay [§ 440.192(8), Fla. Stat. (7/1/97)].

[3] Step Three: Mediation

[a] Background and Procedure

After the filing of a Petition for Benefits, a mediation conference is the required third step. The judge of compensation claims must issue an order within 40 days after the filing of a Petition for Benefits, notifying the parties that a mediation conference must be held. The order must specify the date by which the mediation conference must be held. Such an order is not required, however, if the parties notify the judge that a private mediation conference has been scheduled or has already been held.

The mediation conference, whether public or private, must take place within 130 days after the date the injured worker filed the Petition for Benefits. The judge may grant a continuance if the requesting party can demonstrate to the judge that the continuance is required for reasons beyond the requesting party's control. If multiple petitions are pending, or if additional petitions are filed after the mediation is scheduled, the judge must consolidate all of the petitions into one mediation conference. A continuance may be granted upon the agreement of the parties. If there is no agreement, a judge of compensation claims may grant a continuance if the requesting party can demonstrate that the need for a continuance is for reasons beyond the party's control [§ 440.25(1), Fla. Stat. (10/1/2003)].

Effective October 1, 2003, holding a mediation conference prior to a hearing on a petition for benefits valued at $5,000 or less is not required unless requested by one of the parties [§ 440.25(4)(h), Fla. Stat. (10/1/2003)].

If the parties do not conduct a private mediation, the Division of Administrative Hearings will appoint a state mediator [§ 440.25(3)(a)1, Fla. Stat. (7/1/2002)].

Beginning with mediations occurring on or after January 1, 2003, the parties must conduct a private mediation, at the carrier's expense, if a state mediator is not available within the 90-day period. The private mediator selected must be certified as a mediator by the Florida Supreme Court. If the parties cannot agree on a private mediator, one will be appointed by the judge of compensation claims [§ 440.25(3)(a)2, Fla. Stat. (7/1/2002)].

Mediation, for informal dispute resolution, began as a voluntary system. The 1989 legislature amended the Workers' Compensation Act to provide for mediation conferences as an alternate vehicle for dispute resolution to reduce expensive litigation [§ 440.25, Fla. Stat. (7/1/97)]. Mediation, then as now, is an informal but structured dispute resolution conference in which the mediator acts as an impartial and neutral facilitator. Mediation, under this provision, is not binding on the parties unless they agree that it should be. These conferences are informal; however, they are subject to the rules of procedure [*see* Fla. Admin. Code R. 60Q-6.110, Fla. Admin. Code R. 60Q-6.111].

All communications and materials used at the conference are privileged and confidential. Thus, the mediator may not reveal anything without the written consent of all parties to the conference. Any conduct or statements made during a mediation conference, or in negotiations concerning the conference, are not admissible in evidence at subsequent hearings. This does not, however, preclude discovery of information not protected by statute or rule.

If injured workers elect to have a lawyer present at the conference, they may do so; however, the carrier may then have its lawyer present as well. Put another way, if the injured worker does not have a lawyer, the carrier cannot have one either.

Unlike the judges during a trial, the mediators may meet privately with a party during the mediation. The mediators have full authority to allow any party to appear at the conference by telephone upon request by a party or, if represented, the party's attorney of record, no fewer than five days prior to the mediation conference [*see* Fla. Admin. Code R. 60Q-6.111(1)(b), (c)].

Guide to Claims

NOTE: Effective October 1, 2001, the Act specifically provides that the claimant and the claims adjuster may appear at a court ordered mediation conference by telephone or other electronic means if the parties and the mediator agree [§ 440.25(1), Fla. Stat. (10/1/2001)].

SPECIAL ALERT: Attendance at mediation is mandatory when the initial mediation conference has not been waived or when the judge of compensation claims has entered an order referring a case to mediation. The judge can impose sanctions on any party who fails to appear for a mediation conference without good cause [Fla. Admin. Code R. 60Q-6.110(6); *see* Feldman v. Deal's Seafood/CIGNA, 694 So. 2d 870, 871 (Fla. 1st DCA 1997)].

Agree, for the law is costly.
William Camden, 1605

[b] Mediators

State mediators are either full-time employees from the Office of the Judges of Compensation Claims, or lawyers in private practice serving as adjunct mediators. To qualify as a state mediator, an individual must be a lawyer with a minimum of five years as a member of the Florida Bar. In addition the applicant must complete mediation training as the Chief Judge requires. In addition, the adjunct mediator must be independent of all parties involved in the mediation [§ 440.25(3), Fla. Stat. (7/1/97)].

Mediation is now a required prerequisite to a formal hearing by a judge of compensation claims. Still, cases will arise in which the parties wish to mediate voluntarily, such as to ease a settlement. Formerly, the procedure for requesting mediation required sending an Application for Mediation, form DWC-18, to the Office of the Judges of Compensation Claims in Tallahassee. That form, however, is now obsolete. Beginning January 1, 1994, the proper procedure to initiate mediation is to file the Petition for Benefits form. If the carrier requests mediation, it should send a copy to the injured worker and the injured worker's lawyer.

It is both prudent and required by the Rules of Procedure that the persons attending the conference have full authority to settle the issues without further consultation. If the carrier does not appear, or if the representative who does appear has insufficient authority, the carrier is subject to sanctions [Fla. Admin. Code R. 60Q-6.110(6)]. These sanctions may include reprimand, striking of defenses or pleadings, or imposition of costs or attorney's fees. The Rules of Procedure provide that the judge may impose any sanction, but the sanction must be limited to what is sufficient to deter repetition. In other words, the sanction must be reasonable [*see* Fla. Admin. Code R. 60Q-6.125]. The problem is that neither the statute nor the rules define the phrase "sufficient authority." If the injured worker demands a settlement of $1,000,000, must the adjuster appear at the mediation with the authority to approve a monetary settlement at that level? The adjuster must at least appear with the authority to settle the issues or to refuse settlement. Carriers must guard against putting an adjuster or representative in the position of being unable to respond to a proposal.

[c] When to Mediate

Although mediation is a required step in the dispute resolution process, the Chief Judge has the authority to waive the mediation requirement. Some cases will be far too complex to resolve in mediation. Other cases may already be at a complete impasse. Either party may file a motion to waive mediation, but they must do so within three days before the date of the conference. Such motions should not be hastily filed because mediation has a proven record of success. Virtually any issue in dispute lends itself to mediation; however, following is a list of claim types that have been the most responsive to effective mediation:

1. Cases in which the parties seek to negotiate a washout settlement [*see* ch. 21, for further discussion of washout settlements].
2. Cases with a close question of compensability and the parties have completed sufficient investigation or discovery to assess the likelihood of prevailing at trial properly.
3. Cases in which injured workers have unrealistic expectations or when they may fail to follow the recommendations of their lawyers. Mediators have frequently been effective in bringing these people down to earth.
4. Cases involving multiple employers and carriers. Mediation brings the parties together, which helps foster agreement and settlement.
5. Cases with misconceptions, misunderstandings, or lack of communication between the parties. Often, simply scheduling the conference can bring the parties to resolution.

Mediation, of course, will have no value when the parties are unwilling to compromise.

[d] Mediation Confidentiality

Effective July 1, 2004, the Legislature enacted the "Mediation Confidentiality and Privilege Act" within Chapter 44, Florida Statutes. The key provisions are as follows:

The statute applies to any mediation required by statute, court rule, agency rule or order, oral or written case-specific court order, or court administrative order [§ 44.402, Fla. Stat.].

All mediation communications are confidential and may not be disclosed to a person other than a mediation participant or counsel. A breach of the confidentiality requirements creates a cause of action for damages, as discussed below. Additionally, if the mediation is court-ordered, the violator is subject to sanctions by the court, including but not limited to costs, attorney fees, and mediator's fees [§ 44.405(1), Fla. Stat.].

A mediation participant has a privilege to refuse to testify and to prevent others from testifying in a subsequent proceeding regarding mediation communications [§ 44.405(2), Fla. Stat.].

There is no confidentiality or privilege attached to a signed written agreement reached during mediation, unless the parties agree otherwise [§ 44.405(4), Fla. Stat.].

Information that is otherwise admissible or subject to discovery does not become inadmissible or protected from discovery by reason of its disclosure or use in mediation [§ 44.405(5), Fla. Stat.].

A party that discloses or makes a representation about a privileged communication waives the privilege, but only to the extent necessary for the other party to respond to the disclosure or representation [§ 44.405(6), Fla. Stat.].

A breach of the confidentiality requirements creates a cause of action for civil remedy, including:

- Equitable relief.
- Compensatory damages.
- Attorney and mediator fees and costs.

The limitations period for bringing an action under this section is two years after the date when a party had a reasonable opportunity to discover the breach of confidentiality, but no more than four years after the date of the breach [§ 44.406, Fla. Stat.].

[4] Step Four: Pretrial

[a] Notice Requirement

Previously, the Act required that if the issues, except for attorney's fees and costs, had not been settled by the conclusion of the mediation, the parties attorneys had to complete the pretrial stipulations before the mediation conference ended. The judge of compensation claims was authorized to impose sanctions if the parties failed to complete the pretrial stipulations before the mediation's conclusion [§ 440.25(3)(c), Fla. Stat. (7/1/2002)].

With amendments effective October 1, 2003, completing the pretrial stipulation at the conclusion of the mediation conference is no longer required. If issues remain unresolved, and if the parties cannot agree to written submission of a pretrial stipulation, the judge must issue an order setting a live pretrial hearing, giving the parties at least 14 days' notice [§ 440.25(4)(a), Fla. Stat. (10/1/2003)].

[b] Procedure

Usually, only the lawyers for the parties attend the pretrial conference. The purpose of the pretrial conference is to decide several issues, including the details of the dispute and the issues on which the parties agree. The pretrial also includes the listing of witnesses and evidence each side intends to present. Based on all of this, the judge can decide the time needed for the final hearing.

The rules of procedure require the parties at a pretrial conference to do the following [Fla. Admin. Code R. 60Q-6.113(2)]:

1. State and simplify the issues.
2. Stipulate to such facts and documents as will avoid unnecessary proof.
3. Examine and mark for identification, all exhibits. Impeachment and rebuttal exhibits need not be revealed.
4. Furnish the opposing party with the names and addresses of all witnesses. Identify those who will testify by telephone. Impeachment witnesses and rebuttal witnesses need not be revealed.
5. Exchange all available written reports of experts to be offered at trial.
6. Consider and decide other matters that may help in the disposition of the case.

If the deputy chief judge has waived mediation, the parties must file a pretrial stipulation no later than 30 days before the final hearing. Witness lists, exhibit lists, supplements, and amendments served less than 30 days before the final hearing are not admissible unless approved by the judge or stipulated to by the parties [Fla. Admin. Code R. 60Q-6.113(3), (4)].

[c] Pretrial Required

Before July 1, 1990, the Act contained nothing that specifically allowed, much less required, a pretrial hearing. Effective July 1, 1990, the law required that the judge hold a pretrial hearing no sooner than 30 days, and no later than 60 days, after the filing of a request for hearing. Furthermore, the judge was required to give the parties at least 15 days notice of the pretrial hearing, and to set a date for the final hearing far in advance so that the parties had at least 90 days to conduct discovery, unless they agreed to an earlier date [§ 440.25, Fla. Stat.].

Effective January 1, 1994, the legislature dramatically reduced the time frames. The judge must now hold the pretrial within 10 days after mediation begins, and set the trial itself within 30 days after the pretrial. Thus, the time to conduct discovery has been reduced by two-thirds. In addition, the 1994 amendment reduced the minimum trial notice period from 15 to only 7 days [§ 440.25(4)(a), Fla. Stat. (7/1/97)].

Effective July 1, 2002, the legislature changed the time frames again. Now, the pretrial must be held within 14 days after the mediation if issues remain unresolved. The final hearing must be set to occur within 90 days after the mediation, but must allow 60 days for discovery. The minimum notice requirement for the final hearing remains seven days [§ 440.25(4), Fla. Stat. (7/1/2002)].

Law is not justice
and a trial is not a scientific inquiry into truth.
A trial is the resolution of a dispute.
Edison Haines, 1977

[5] Step Five: Trial

[a] Notice

The law requires that "the judge of compensation claims give the interested parties at least 14 days' advance notice of the final hearing, served on the interested parties by mail" [§ 440.25(4)(c), Fla. Stat. (10/1/2003)]. Serving notice to the service agent places the carrier on notice as well. If the carrier or service agent receives notice from another source, such as the employer, this, too, may place the carrier on notice, unless the carrier objects before the final hearing that it did not receive the notice directly from the judge of compensation claims [*see* Guarantee Mutual Life Company v. McCartney, 672 So. 2d 636, 637 (Fla. 1st DCA 1996)].

[b] Trial Date

Beginning July 1, 2002 the law requires the judge of compensation claims to hold the final hearing within 90 after the mediation conference and within 210 days after receipt of the Petition for Benefits. The judge must set a hearing date that allows at least 60 days to conduct discovery. The judge may grant a continuance of the hearing on motion by either party, but only if the need for the delay is due to circumstances beyond the control of the requesting party. An additional continuance requested by the claimant's attorney may be granted only if the claimant consents in writing. The judge must report to the chief judge if the judge grants two or more continuances [§ 440.25(4), Fla. Stat. (7/1/2002)].

Note, however, that the law allows the claimant to waive the statutory timeframes, if he or she can show good cause [§ 440.25(4)(d), Fla. Stat. (10/1/2003)].

SPECIAL ALERT: If a benefit claimed was ripe, due and owing at the time of the final hearing, but was not raised at the hearing, entitlement to that benefit is waived [§ 440.25(4)(d), Fla. Stat. (7/1/2002)].

Generally the judges resolve issues raised in motions, without holding an oral hearing, based on written statements filed by the parties in support and in opposition. The law now requires that the judges resolve disputes concerning the claimant's average weekly wage raised in a petition without an oral hearing. Presumably, if the claimant disputes the average weekly wage used to calculate indemnity benefits, each side will be required to submit memorandums in support and in opposition. The judge will then decide the issue independent of other issues raised in the petition. The judge may, for good cause, order the parties to attend a final hearing on this issue [§ 440.25(4)(h), Fla. Stat. (7/1/2002)].

[c] Effect of Failure to Appear

The carrier cannot raise arguments on appeal that were not raised at the trial. Obviously, if the carrier does not appear at the trial level, it cannot raise any arguments on appeal and, thus, essentially losses its right to appeal [*see* Guarantee Mutual Life Company v. McCartney, 672 So. 2d 636, 637 (Fla. 1st DCA 1996)].

[d] Resolution Deadline

The judge must issue an order resolving the case within 30 days after the hearing, unless the parties agree to allow a delay. If the judge does not timely enter the order, the judge must file a report explaining the delay to the chief judge [§ 440.25(4)(d), Fla. Stat. (7/1/97)]. One reason for trial delays in the past was a statutory requirement that a judge could not hold a hearing without the Division's file, which often took weeks to obtain. The legislature repealed this requirement of the need for the Division's file effective January 1, 1994.

[e] Procedure

In workers' compensation practice, we do not hold actual trials as most people think of them. The procedure is a semiformal hearing. The rules of procedure allow a judge to hold a hearing by telephone conference, but telephone testimony is allowed only if the parties agree and the judge approves [Fla. Admin. Code R. 60Q-6.116(3)]. Judges usually hold hearings in their office conference rooms or in the local courthouse. The hearing is usually in the county where the accident occurred. If the accident occurred out of the state, the hearing must be in the county where the employer's place of business is located. If both parties agree (i.e., a party cannot have venue changed against their will), the judge may transfer the case to another county if it is more convenient.

The hearing procedure is similar to a traditional trial in that each side presents its evidence including the live testimony of witnesses. Whenever possible, adjusters and employers should try to attend such hearings, particularly on their own cases. Some judges appreciate the employer and carrier's active interest. If nothing else, the educational benefit alone is worth the effort.

The judge of compensation claims has no authority to consider claims that were not properly raised in a Petition for Benefits. The law prohibits raising any issue in a Petition for Benefits that was not ripe, due, and owing when the petition was filed. Additionally, the judge of compensation claims cannot consider any issue that has not undergone mediation. The law does allow adjudication of issues that were not ripe at the time of filing, or that have not been mediated, but only with the written agreement of the parties [§ 440.192(9), Fla. Stat. (10/1/2003)].

SPECIAL ALERT: If the JCC has already granted a continuance, the judge may not approve an additional continuance unless the claimant consents in writing. Presumably, this applies even if it is the claimant's attorney who is seeking a continuance since the statute is silent concerning the identity of the requesting party [§ 440.25(4)(b), Fla. Stat. (10/1/2001)].

§ 22.04 Emergency Hearing

[1] Bona Fide Emergency Required

In special cases, a judge of compensation claims may hold an emergency hearing *without written notice* [*see* [4], *below*] if a bona fide emergency exists involving the health, safety, or welfare of an employee. The judge can resolve an emergency hearing by entering an order. This is a procedural amendment and applies to any case pending after January 1, 1994 [§ 440.25(4)(h), Fla. Stat. (7/1/97)].

The Rules of Procedure require that a written request for an emergency conference be filed with the judge and served on all other parties or, if represented, their attorneys of record. The request must set forth in detail the facts giving rise to the request, its legal basis, the factual or medical basis for the claim that there is a bona fide emergency involving the health, safety, or welfare of an employee, and the specific relief sought. Any documents relied upon should be specifically referenced and attached. The judge may then summarily deny the request or, after proper notice, conduct an emergency hearing to consider the request. Under the rule, the judge may not simply grant the request and then conduct an emergency hearing [Fla. Admin. Code R. 60Q-6.117].

[2] Emergency Not Defined

The legislature intended the emergency hearing provision to provide immediate relief in cases where a bona fide emergency exists. The problem, of course, is that it did not precisely define the term "emergency." What is an emergency depends on the perception of individual judges. Because the law allows the judges of compensation claims to resolve issues by entering an appealable order, they must include a finding, based on competent substantial evidence, that an actual emergency exists. More importantly, they must state sufficient facts to support this finding. For example, the judge of compensation claims agreed to an emergency hearing, finding that the carrier jeopardized Billy Rue's health, safety, and welfare. The First District Court of Appeal reversed for two reasons. First, the record contained no evidence about Rue's financial situation. Second, Rue's doctor could not be certain that the requested surgery would help. Judges must reserve emergency hearings for cases of verified urgency. Otherwise, the standard dispute resolution procedures will be subsumed and obliterated [*see* Dayco Products v. Rue, 676 So. 2d 58, 60–61 (Fla. 1st DCA 1996)].

[3] Good Faith Required

Both the carrier and the injured worker should act in good faith and not abuse the appeal process to frustrate compliance with orders entered on genuine emergencies. When judges fail to describe the facts leading to their conclusion that an emergency exists, carriers should first try to correct the problem on a motion for rehearing. Judges, too, have a responsibility to ensure that technical deficiencies do not make the emergency hearing process a pointless exercise [*see* Owens-Illinois v. DeLoach, 686 So. 2d 1387, 1388–1389 (Fla. 1st DCA 1997)].

Guide to Claims

[4] Notice

Although the statute allows the judges to hold emergency hearings without written notice, it does not allow such hearings without any notice. Due process requires notice, but it does not require *written* notice. Because of the statute's nature, however, the law requires only "reasonable" notice. What is reasonable depends on the circumstances. The judges must consider all factors and give notice reasonably calculated to simplify the ability of the opposing party to appear and be heard. To be reasonable, notice must include the nature of the relief the injured worker seeks and information about the witnesses to be called, and the evidence to be presented to prove entitlement to relief. The emergency hearing must be limited to the emergency involved [*see* Town of Jupiter v. Andreff, 656 So. 2d 1374, 1377–1378 (Fla. 1st DCA 1995)].

> **CAUTION:** The appellate court will not disturb the JCC's finding of reasonable notice absent evidence of abuse of discretion.

[5] Emergency Issues Only

If several issues are pending, the judge can address only those issues determined to be an emergency. All others issues and claims are therefore not ripe, and cannot be adjudicated at an emergency hearing [*see* Bradley v. Hurricane Restaurant, 652 So. 2d 443, 444 (Fla. 1st DCA 1995)]. If the judge decides and rules on all emergency issues, the judge's order is a final order. This is significant because a final order is subject to appellate review.

> *Whatever disagreement there may be as to the scope of the phrase "due process of law" there can be no doubt that it embraces the fundamental conception of a fair trial, with opportunity to be heard.*
> Oliver Wendell Holmes (1915)

§ 22.05 Expedited Hearings

A new and mandatory statutory rule of procedure applies to all claims that have a value of less than $5,000 [§ 440.25(4)(h), Fla. Stat. (7/1/97)]. Beginning January 1, 1994, the law requires the judges to speed up the resolution process for claims valued at $5,000 or less. Although the Act says nothing about procedure, the parties must stipulate to the estimated value of the benefits claimed. In cases involving these small claims, the parties must exchange and file with the judge a pretrial outline of all issues, defenses, and witnesses within 15 days of the hearing.

Warning: The minimum notice period for such hearings is 15 days. However, the rules of procedure provide that the parties have at least 30 days to conduct discovery, which must be completed 15 days before the hearing [*see* Fla. Admin. Code R.

60Q-6.118(2)]. Following are the key features:

1. To speed up the small claims adjudication process further, the Act provides that the judge may not hold a pretrial. However, as noted above, the parties must submit a pretrial outline at least 15 days before the final hearing [*see* Fla. Admin. Code R. 60Q-6.118(4)].
2. At the hearing, all argument and presentation of evidence is limited to a maximum of 30 minutes. Indeed, the entire hearing may not exceed 30 minutes. This means, of course, that each side should have no more than 15 minutes to present its case.
3. Neither party is required to have a lawyer. The Act specifically provides that the carrier may be represented by an adjuster or other qualified representative.
4. The employer, the carrier, and any witnesses may appear by telephone. Because the litigants may not be represented by a lawyer, the Act requires the judges to relax the rules on introduction of evidence.
5. Remember, this procedure is mandatory on claims valued at or below $5,000.
6. Claims valued at more than $5,000 may be granted this expedited process if both parties submit a written agreement and application.

Effective July 1, 2002, a claim in a petition for medical benefits only valued at $5,000 or less, or a claim for mileage reimbursement for medical transportation, must be resolved in an expedited hearing. This requirement may be waived only if there is compelling evidence to the contrary [§ 440.25(4)(i), Fla. Stat. (7/1/2002)].

Effective October 1, 2003, holding a mediation conference prior to a hearing on a petition for benefits valued at $5,000 or less is not required unless requested by one of the parties [§ 440.25(4)(h), Fla. Stat. (10/1/2003)].

§ 22.06 Frivolous Claims and Defenses

[1] Penalties and Fines May Be Assessed by JCC

A judge of compensation claims can punish lawyers if they frivolously maintain any claim or defense. In such cases, the judge may assess the cost of the proceedings and an attorney's fee against the offending lawyer *personally,* and not the attorney's client. In addition, the judge must send a copy of the penalty order to the appropriate Florida Bar grievance committee. The Act forbids a lawyer from recovering these penalties from the client. Remember that this law applies to both defense and claimants' lawyers [§ 440.32, Fla. Stat. (1994)]. Thus, insurance adjusters should not be surprised to see defense lawyers refuse to proceed with motions or to attend a hearing that advances indefensible positions. Adjusters must adopt a more conciliatory approach in hearing out defense lawyers' concerns. This will be most necessary in cases where the adjuster or the employer feels strongly about proceeding with the case, but the lawyer urges caution, citing the Act's provisions on penalties and fines for frivolous claims or defenses. With possible fines and even a license to practice law at stake, patience on the adjusters' part will help to avoid potentially serious conflict between defense lawyers and claims adjusters.

[2] Frivolous Defined

A claim or defense is frivolous if it is one clearly lacking in substance, or is insufficient as a matter of law because it presents no debatable question. Following is a formal definition [*Barrons' Law Dictionary,* Third Edition]:

> A claim is frivolous if it clearly appears either that it is insufficient because it is not supported by the facts or that it is one for which the law recognizes no remedy.

Lawyers must sign each pleading and motion, and other papers. The signature is a certificate that the lawyer has read the document and that, to the best of the lawyer's knowledge after reasonable inquiry, it is well grounded in fact, warranted by existing law, and not interposed for any improper purpose. Examples of improper purpose are to harass or to cause unnecessary delays or needless increases in the cost of litigation. If the lawyer fails to sign such documents, the judge must strike the document from evidence, unless the lawyer promptly signs it after notification of the omission. If the judge decides that any document or motion is filed in violation of this provision, the judge may on personal motion or the motion of any party impose sanctions against the lawyer who signed the document or motion. Such sanctions may include an order to pay the other party's reasonable expenses incurred because of the filing, including an attorney's fee [§ 440.32(3), Fla. Stat. (1994)].

§ 22.07 Alternative Dispute Resolution

[1] Collective Bargaining Agreements

Individual employers can bypass litigation and dispute resolution procedures under Ch. 440, Fla. Stat. entirely. They may do so by entering a collective bargaining agreement. The agreement, however, requires approval by both the carrier and the Division of Workers' Compensation. The filing of the agreement with the division must include a list of all registered bargaining representatives and the groups they represent. If approved, the agreement may require an alternate dispute resolution system that is valid and binding upon the carrier, employer, and employee. The agreement may supplement, modify, or completely replace the dispute resolution procedure described in Ch. 440, Fla. Stat. The agreement may include, but is not limited to, conciliation, mediation, and arbitration. If the agreement requires arbitration, it must be binding on the parties [§ 440.211, Fla. Stat. (1/1/94)].

In one case, the employee argued that the JCC should not have dismissed a petition for benefits because a collective bargaining agreement was in place. The employee claimed that federal case law precluded his union and his employer from bargaining away his rights under Florida Statutes, Chapter 440 (1997). The court held that the legislature both established the workers' compensation system and enacted § 440.211, Fla. Stat. expressly approving the development by employers and unions of alternative systems of resolving compensation disputes. The right to utilize Chapter 440 is not an inviolable right. The CBA validly supplants the provisions of Chapter 440 without diminishing an employee's entitlement to benefits [*see* Ariston v. Allied Bldg. Crafts. 825 So. 2d 435, 436–437 (Fla. 1st DCA 2002)].

[2] Exclusive Medical Treatment Source

The collective bargaining agreement also may include a specific list of health care providers. Such list may be the exclusive source of all medical treatment. The agreement may also include a list of independent medical examination physicians as the exclusive source of IMEs. The agreement may describe a binding, light duty, modified job, or return to work program, and required vocational rehabilitation and retraining programs. However, the agreement may not diminish in any way an employee's entitlement to benefits. Any attempt to do so renders the entire agreement void [§ 440.211, Fla. Stat.].

In one case, an employee argued that the failure of his CBA did not provide for independent medical examinations constituted a *per se* diminution of a claimant's entitlement to benefits, which should render the agreement void. The JCC agreed and denied the employer's motion to dismiss. In reversing the order, the court noted that by definition at least some of the procedures in a workers' compensation alternative dispute resolution system must differ from the dispute resolution procedures set out in Florida Statutes, Chapter 440 (1995). Identical procedures do not constitute an alternative. When, as § 440.211, Fla. Stat. contemplates, a collective bargaining agreement establishes an alternative dispute resolution system, new means and methods are brought into existence to deliver the same statutory benefits.

The court noted that although the agreement did not explicitly afford an employee the benefit of an IME, it did provide him with the right to a second opinion, which, while not identical to the procedure afforded by § 440.13(5), Fla. Stat., is somewhat comparable because, if the employee is dissatisfied with the opinion of the physician selected, he or she has the right to seek the opinion of a different physician designated in the list. Although the employee does not have the broader range of care available under § 440.13(5), Fla. Stat., the court considered it important to observe once again that the alternative procedure afforded by a CBA need not be identical to that provided by the remainder of Florida Statutes, Chapter 440 in order to avoid offending the provision in § 440.211(2), Fla. Stat. precluding diminishment of an employee's entitlement to benefits. If, as the claimant argued, the agreement creates procedural requirements for the receipt of benefits that Florida Statutes, Chapter 440 does not impose, the agreement also creates procedural opportunities for the provision of benefits that Florida Statutes, Chapter 440 does not afford. As long as the benefits themselves are undiminished, the requirements of § 440.211, Fla. Stat. (1995) are met. The court agreed that although the CBA made no explicit provision for an independent medical examination, it nonetheless adequately complied with § 440.211(1)(b), Fla. Stat. by providing the claimant with a list of medical providers agreed upon by his employer and his union, and it thereby supplants—without diminishing—the provisions of Florida Statutes, Chapter 440. Therefore, the court reversed the order denying the employer's motion to dismiss [*see* Ulico Cas. Co. v. Fernandez, 825 So. 2d 988, 990–993 (Fla. 1st DCA 2002)].

[3] Agreements Displace Jurisdiction of JCC

The legislature's clear intention was to offer a means to curtail or displace the jurisdiction of the Division and its judges of compensation claims. Collective bargaining agreements do just that when they meet the statutory criteria. The statutory language that prohibits the diminishing of benefits in these agreements does not preclude alternative procedures. By definition, at least some of the procedures in an alternative dispute resolution system must differ from those described in Ch. 440, Fla. Stat. Procedures identical to those in the Act do not constitute an alternative dispute resolution system. The Act contemplates a wide range of possible alternative dispute resolution systems. Such systems can completely replace the statutory system, or defeat only a portion of the statutory provisions that would otherwise apply. In many cases, these alternative dispute resolution systems will remove jurisdiction from the judges of compensation claims to resolve disputes. Allowing private parties to create their own dispute resolution procedures by agreement in no way violates Florida's constitution [*see* Gassner v. Bechtel Const., 702 So. 2d 548, 553–556 (Fla. 1st DCA 1997)].

For example, the JCC dismissed the claimant's petition for benefits on the basis that the judge lacked jurisdiction because a collective bargaining agreement was in place between the claimant's union and the employer. The JCC ruled that this agreement supplanted the provisions of Florida Statutes, Chapter 440, and the 1st DCA agreed and affirmed [*see* Maribona v. S. Pan Servs., 825 So. 2d 434 (Fla. 1st DCA 2002)].

Note, however that a collective bargaining agreement will not be controlling if it goes beyond the dispute resolution procedure or has the effect of diminishing the employee's substantive right to workers' compensation benefits. A collective bargaining agreement is invalid to the extent that it purports to regulate the method of recovering workers' compensation benefits. An example is an agreement requiring that injured workers use all of their personal and sick leave time before collecting workers' compensation benefits [*see* Heric v. City of Ormond Beach, 728 So. 2d 1247, 1249 (Fla. 1st DCA 1999)].

[4] Voluntary Binding Arbitration

If the judge of compensation claims approves, the parties may bypass the litigation process required by the workers' compensation law, Chapter 440 Florida Statutes, and agree to resolve a dispute by binding arbitration.

If the parties agree to arbitration, the provisions of the Florida Arbitration Code, Chapter 682 Florida Statutes, govern the process. For workers' compensation purposes, the term "court" in the Arbitration Code is deemed to mean a judge of compensation claims. An arbitration award is enforceable in the same manner and with the same powers as a final compensation order [§ 440.1926, Fla. Stat. (10/1/2003)].

§ 22.08 Discovery

[1] Depositions

Depositions are nothing more than a series of questions and answers under oath. Depositions of the parties and witnesses may be taken before a Petition for Benefits at the request of any party, or prospective party, or upon the order of a judge of compensation claims [§ 440.30, Fla. Stat. (1991); *see* § 22.03[2], for discussion of Petition for

Benefits]. Taking depositions during the 30-day ombudsman dispute resolution period may be necessary to decide the carrier's responsibility. The judge of compensation claims has the authority, under the rules, to require the taking of a deposition by phone if the judge finds good cause.

SPECIAL NOTE: If a carrier insists on a deposition before the injured worker files a Petition for Benefits, the carrier must pay the injured worker's lawyer a fee for attending the deposition [§ 440.30, Fla. Stat. (1991)]. A Request for Assistance is not a Petition for Benefits. If the injured worker's attorney files a Request for Assistance but does not file a Petition for Benefits, the carrier must pay the attorney's fee for preparing for and attending the deposition [*see* Wright v. Industrial Automotive, 662 So. 2d 1321, 1322 (Fla. 1st DCA 1995)].

The discovery phase of a workers' compensation claim can be very costly. While defense lawyers are expert at what they do, they will look to the carrier for some guidance. Depositions can be very expensive because they include the cost of the lawyer's fee, witness fees, court reporter fees, and transcript fees. A single medical deposition can easily cost $1,000 or more. Full transcripts will add another few hundred dollars to the cost, but are usually unnecessary. Most defense lawyers summarize the results of depositions taken. Adjusters should review these summaries carefully and consider if the original defense position is still sound. As each phase of discovery proceeds, the carrier's defense costs and exposure for interest payments and claimant attorney's fees move inexorably upward. Adjusters who have never attended a deposition should do so. This will not only give adjusters some first hand experience, but will enable them to judge the skills of both lawyers.

SPECIAL ALERT: Recognizing that many adjusters dislike having their depositions taken, some claimants' lawyers will subpoena the adjuster as a harassment tactic to encourage a settlement offer before the deposition. Adjusters should take care not to fall into that trap. If the defense can establish that the adjuster's deposition was set merely to harass the adjuster, the offending lawyer may be subject to sanctions as discussed in § 22.06.

[2] Records and Documents

[a] Carrier's Response to Requests to Produce

Carriers must produce certain records. Some records should (almost) never be produced, and others may have to be produced under certain circumstances. The carrier's defense lawyer is the best authority here on this subject, but we can make some general statements.

Under the category of "always-required" are hospital and medical reports, rehabilitation reports, records about the injured worker's average weekly wage, transcripts of the injured worker's recorded or written statement, and Division claim forms such as the First Report of Injury. Carriers should produce on demand any document that they have filed with the state. If the carrier has any doubt about what the law entitles the claimant's lawyer to discover, it should send all requests to produce documents to a defense lawyer for proper response.

Adjusters must take care to respond promptly to requests to produce. The rules require a response within 30 days, unless a judge of compensation claims has extended the time. If the carrier does not respond timely, the judge not only has the authority to compel the carrier to do so, but may impose sanctions as well.

[b] Privileged Communication

[i] General Rule

Communication deemed privileged is generally not discoverable. Correspondence to and from the carrier's lawyer is privileged and should never be given to the injured worker or to the injured worker's lawyer. Confidential communications between a lawyer and client during a professional relationship cannot be revealed without the client's consent, absent extraordinary circumstances as discussed in [ii]–[iii], *below.* Florida statutes provide that attorney-client communication is confidential if not intended to be disclosed to third parties [§ 90.502(1)(c), Fla. Stat. (1976)]. The privilege to prohibit disclosure, however, belongs to the client and, as such, the client can waive it. If the carrier voluntarily provides copies to third parties, it has likely destroyed the privilege [*see* [ii], *below*].

[ii] Tests for Voluntary Disclosure

Voluntary disclosure is key, so that generally inadvertent disclosure does not destroy the attorney-client privilege. Whether disclosure is voluntary depends, however, on the result of a "relevant circumstances" test. The result of this test determines whether the disclosing party took reasonable precautions to prevent the disclosure. Under this test, the court considers the following factors:

1. The reasonableness of the precautions taken to prevent an inadvertent disclosure in view of the extent of the document production;
2. The number of inadvertent disclosures;
3. The extent of the disclosure;
4. Any delay and measures taken to rectify the disclosures; and
5. Whether the overriding interest of justice could be served by relieving a party of its error.

Essentially, this test measures negligence in attempting to protect the privileged documents. In other words, negligently disclosed documents will not be protected [*see* Abamar Housing v. Lisa Daly Lady Decor, 698 So. 2d 276, 278–279 (Fla. 3d DCA 1997), *rev. denied,* 704 So. 2d 520 (Fla. 1997)].

[iii] Bad Faith Exception

An exception to the attorney-client privilege arises in bad faith proceedings in excess liability cases. The plaintiff in a bad faith action is a third-party beneficiary of the defendant's inusrance policy. As such, the court may compel disclosure of the insurer's entire case file [*see* Boston Old Colony Insurance Company v. Gutierrez, 325 So. 2d 416, 417 (Fla. 3d DCA 1976)].

The First District Court of Appeal, however, rejected this third-party beneficiary theory in workers' compensation bad faith proceedings. This does not mean the courts will never order production. They may do so, but only under compelling circumstances [*see* Brevard Community College v. Barber, 488 So. 2d 93, 97 (Fla. 1st DCA 1986)].

Guide to Claims

[c] Work Product

Work product is work done by or at the direction of a lawyer while representing a client, and is ordinarily not subject to discovery. We can generally define the term "work product" to encompass writings, statements, or testimony that would reflect or invade a lawyer's legal impressions or legal theories as to pending or even anticipated litigation. Documents such as statements of witnesses or other investigation are usually considered work product and are not discoverable unless the injured worker can show compelling necessity. An injured worker can establish compelling necessity by showing that [*see* Agri-Business, Inc. v. Bridges, 397 So. 2d 394, 395 (Fla. 1st DCA 1981)]:

> [The] underlying evidence has been damaged, disassembled, changed, or is inaccessible to the same examination by [the party seeking disclosure]; . . . that the withholding of the information and the documents sought would defeat interest of justice; or . . . that the information is not as readily available to [such party as to the opposing party].

The key factor in deciding whether the privilege applies is in deciding whether the documents requested were prepared "in anticipation of litigation." Meeting this test does not require that such documents be prepared for imminent or ongoing litigation. Even preliminary investigative materials are privileged if compiled in response to some foreseeable event that could be the basis for a claim. Note carefully, though, that the work product privilege attaches only to documents prepared in contemplation of litigation and not for the mere likelihood of litigation. If materials are gathered or prepared in anticipation of litigation, a limited privilege attaches to them. Such materials may qualify as work product despite the fact that no specific litigation is pending at the time the materials are compiled. To determine if the privilege attaches, focus on whether there is some foreseeable event that could be the basis of future litigation which compels the creation of the documents [*see* National Union Fire Ins. v. FCCI, 720 So. 2d 535, 537 (Fla. 2d DCA 1998)].

In its 1947 opinion in *Hickman v. Taylor* [329 U.S. 495, 91 L. Ed. 451, 67 S. Ct. 385 (1947)] the United States Supreme Court originated what has become known as the "attorney work-product privilege." The Court concluded:

> In performing his various duties, . . . it is essential that a lawyer work with a certain degree of privacy, free from unnecessary intrusion by opposing parties and their counsel. Proper preparation of a client's case demands that he assemble information, sift what he considers to be the relevant from the irrelevant facts, prepare his legal theories and plan his strategy without undue and needless interference. That is the

> historical and the necessary way in which lawyers act within the framework of our system of jurisprudence to promote justice and to protect their clients' interests. This work is reflected, of course, in interviews, statements, memoranda, correspondence, briefs, mental impressions, personal beliefs, and countless other tangible and intangible ways—aptly though roughly termed . . . the "work product of the lawyer." Were such materials open to opposing counsel on mere demand, much of what is now put down in writing would remain unwritten. An attorney's thoughts, heretofore inviolate, would not be his own. Inefficiency, unfairness and sharp practices would inevitably develop in the giving of legal advice and in the preparation of cases for trial. The effect on the legal profession would be demoralizing. And the interests of the clients and the cause of justice would be poorly served.

The Florida Supreme Court has provided an in-depth analysis of the work product privilege in *Northup v. Herbert W. Acken, M.D., P.A.* [865 So. 2d 1267 (Fla. 2004)]. The Court noted that the United States Supreme Court (in *Hickman*) has established the privacy of an attorney's professional activities and foreclosed discovery of materials created by an attorney in preparation for litigation, absent adequate reasons to justify production. A primary purpose in the adoption of the Florida Rules of Civil Procedure is to prevent the use of surprise, trickery, bluff, and legal gymnastics. Revelation through discovery procedures of the strengths and weaknesses of each side before trial encourages settlement of cases and avoids costly litigation. Each side may make an intelligent evaluation of the entire case and may better anticipate the ultimate results.

Generally, those documents, pictures, statements, and diagrams, which are to be presented as evidence, are not work products anticipated by the rule for exemption from discovery. Personal views of the attorney as to how and when to present evidence, his or her evaluation of its relative importance, his or her knowledge of which witness will give certain testimony, personal notes and records as to witnesses, jurors, legal citations, proposed arguments, jury instructions, diagrams and charts the attorney may refer to at trial for convenience, but not to be used as evidence, come within the general category of work product.

The scope of the attorney work product privilege protection is specifically bounded and limited to materials that are not intended for use as evidence or as an exhibit at trial. Any work product privilege that existed ceases once the materials or testimony are intended for trial use. More simply, if the materials are only to aid counsel in trying the case, they are work product. But if they will be used as evidence, the materials cease to be work product and become subject to an adversary's discovery. In Florida, when a party reasonably expects or intends to utilize an item before the court at trial, for impeachment or otherwise, the video recording, document, exhibit, or other piece of evidence is fully discoverable and is not privileged work product.

In essence, Florida litigants must make a simple and discrete decision prior to entry of a pretrial case management order by the trial court. An attorney must evaluate whether he or she intends to use evidence in his or her possession for strategy and trial preparation purposes only, which would qualify the selection of the particular items as a protected product of the thought processes and mental impressions of an attorney. On the other hand, if the evidence or material is reasonably expected or intended to be disclosed to the court or jury at trial, it must be identified, disclosed, and copies provided to the adverse party in accordance with the trial court's order and the discovery requests of the opposing party.

All materials reasonably expected or intended to be used at trial, including documents intended solely for witness impeachment, are subject to proper discovery requests and are not protected by the work product privilege. Florida's dedication to the prevention of surprise, trickery, bluff, and legal gymnastics at trial holds no exception for impeachment materials. In Florida, litigants are entitled to evaluate the strength and weaknesses of each side before trial and have the ability to make an intelligent evaluation of the entire case to better anticipate the ultimate results.

An attorney may not be compelled to disclose the mental impressions resulting from his or her investigations, labor, or legal analysis unless the product of such investigation itself is reasonably expected or intended to be presented to the court or before a jury at trial. Only at such time as the attorney should reasonably ascertain in good faith that the material may be used or disclosed at trial is he or she expected to reveal it to the opposing party.

SPECIAL ALERT: With the creation of the Division's Office of Employee Assistance, a question arises about whether the ombudsman may require a carrier to submit privileged or work product documents. The statute provides that "the carrier shall cooperate with the office and shall timely provide the office with any documents or other information that it may require . . ." [§ 440.191(2)(b), Fla. Stat. (7/1/97)]. Whether this provision extends to protected documents and other information is not clear. If a carrier voluntarily provides such documents, will it be held to have waived the privilege? Another question is whether documents supplied to the ombudsman become public records. Adjusters should consult with a lawyer before releasing any communications or documents considered work product to the Division.

[d] Surveillance Evidence

[i] When Subject to Discovery

Fla. Admin. Code R. 60Q-6.114(4) was amended 11/1/2006 to delete the provision that surveillance evidence is subject to discovery only if the carrier will use it at trial.

Prior court decisions have held that surveillance evidence is subject to discovery only if the carrier will use it at trial. The Florida Supreme Court stated that the existence of surveillance movies and photographs is discoverable in every instance. The contents are discoverable if the materials will be used as evidence either substantively or for impeachment. If the movies or photographs will not be used as evidence by the holder, the contents are discoverable only upon a showing of exceptional circumstances. The party seeking discovery must be afforded a reasonable opportunity to observe the movies or photographs before their presentation as evidence. Within the trial court's discretion, the surveilling party has the right to depose the party or witness filmed before being required to produce the contents of the surveillance information for inspection [*see* Dodson v. Persell, 390 So. 2d 704, 707–708 (Fla. 1980); *see also* Williams v. Walt Disney World Co., 583 So. 2d 794, 795 (Fla. 1st DCA 1991)].

[ii] Continuing Effect of Request to Produce

A question has perplexed both sides for some time about whether a request to produce has a continuing effect. In other words, if the carrier has no surveillance at the time the injured worker makes the request to produce, must the carrier reveal surveillance evidence obtained later?

In one case, the injured worker argued that the carrier had a continuing obligation to produce surveillance evidence. The carrier maintained that the law did not require it to list either surveillance witnesses or surveillance films on the pretrial stipulation because the carrier intended to use the witnesses and films solely for impeachment or rebuttal purposes. Further, the carrier argued it had no duty to supplement its response to the request to produce. When the carrier received the injured worker's request to produce, it answered truthfully that it had no such evidence. Later, however, the carrier did obtain surveillance evidence and used it at the trial.

The First District Court of Appeal reluctantly agreed with the carrier. Former Fla. R. Work. Comp. P. 4.090 (repealed May 16, 1996) contained nothing to suggest that either party who has made a truthful and complete response to a request to produce has any legal duty to supplement that response to reflect information found later. Further, no duty exists to correct a response that, because of subsequent developments, is no longer accurate.

The court, however, italicized the term "legal" duty several times in the written opinion, suggesting that the court believes a moral duty exists to supplement or correct a response to a request to produce. As stated by the court: "[w]e do not mean to suggest by this opinion that we approve of tactics such as that employed below, which, as the judge noted, result in trial by ambush."

In dicta, the court advised injured workers' lawyers to serve a request to produce such films shortly before the hearing and to ask the judge to shorten the time for compliance [*see* Ogden Allied Services v. Panesso, 619 So. 2d 1024, 1026–1027 (Fla. 1st DCA 1993)].

[iii] Using Surveillance Evidence to Influence Physicians

[A] Doctor-Patient Relationship

Doctors are trained to believe what their patients tell them. Their mission is not to try to figure out if a patient is lying for reason of secondary gain. Their mission is to try to fix the patient's medical problem. Often, carriers provide injured workers' doctors with surveillance videotape to show that the injured workers may not have been truthful in describing symptoms and physical limitations. Sometimes, after viewing these films, doctors change their minds about the need for further treatment or the degree of impairment. The First District Court of Appeal, however, has condemned this practice of showing surveillance videotape to doctors [*see* [C], *below*].

[B] Confidentiality of Medical Records

Florida law provides for the strict confidentially of a person's medical records [§ 455.667(5), Fla. Stat. (7/1/97)]. Health care providers are prohibited by law from furnishing records or even discussing a patient's case without the patient's permission. This does not apply, however, in workers' compensation practice [§ 440.13(4), Fla. Stat.

(7/1/97)]. Doctors must supply carriers with medical information, and the law requires them to discuss the case upon request. The court has held that in enacting § 440.13(4), Fla. Stat., the legislature intended that the records and opinions of treating and examining physicians and other practitioners be freely available to employer/carriers and that claimants no longer enjoy the right to be present during discussions between employer/carriers and those providers. § 440.13(4)(c), Fla. Stat. furthers the self-executing nature of the compensation system by ensuring that the cmployer/carrier has ready access to medical information involving the claimant [*see* S & A Plumbing v. Kimes, 756 So. 2d 1037, 1041 (Fla. 1st DCA 2000)]. The *Kimes* court held that the workers' compensation system transposed dispute resolution for workplace injuries from the private law of torts to a publicly administered and regulated system. The very foundation of an employee's right to receive benefits under the self-executing system in Florida Statutes, Chapter 440 requires a healthcare provider to assess the injury, establish a causal connection to the workplace accident, and communicate that information to the employer's insurance carrier [*see* § 440.13, Fla. Stat.]. By presenting himself to be examined by a health care provider for not only treatment of an injury, but also for evaluation of the injury and assessment of whether it is attributable to his employment, a claimant consents to the provider's disclosing to the carrier medical information relating to the claim. The discussions authorized by § 440.13(4)(c), Fla. Stat. simply further that disclosure system.[*see* S & A Plumbing v. Kimes, 756 So. 2d 1037, 1042 (Fla. 1st DCA 2000)]. The question is, does this allow the carrier to visit with the doctor to view surveillance videotape?

[C] Showing Surveillance Evidence to Physicians

In one case the carrier showed its surveillance tapes to the doctor. At trial, the judge held that the carrier failed to advise the injured worker's lawyer that it intended to show the videotape to the doctor in order to try to change the doctor's opinion. This, said the judge, violated the rules of discovery. The judge not only refused to allow the videotape into evidence, but refused to allow that part of the doctor's testimony based on it. The First District Court of Appeal affirmed the order.

In dicta, the court added that the workers' compensation exception to the confidentiality requirements does not allow the ex parte showing of surveillance videotapes to the injured worker's physician. The court said: "In our view, the statute obviously contemplates the receipt of medical information *from the physician* or other medical care provider, and it just as obviously does not contemplate an *ex parte* 'mini trial' before the health care provider, or the deliberate undermining of the doctor-patient relationship" [*see* Holiday Inn v. Re, 643 So. 2d 13, 15 (Fla. 1st DCA 1994) (emphasis added)].

This is a surprising statement because it suggests the court views the free flow of information to flow in only one direction, i.e., from the doctor to the carrier. It also suggests that the exception does not allow the carrier to supply the doctor with relevant information.

Previously, the court held that carriers may not hold ex parte meetings with an injured worker's doctor after the beginning of an adversarial relationship without inviting the injured worker's lawyer to attend [*see* Adelman Steel Corp. v. Winter, 610 So. 2d 494, 504–505 (Fla. 1st DCA 1992)]. The court has held that the 1994 legislative amendments have overruled *Adelman* [*see* Vickers v. Unity of Lake Worth, 693 So. 2d 62, 63 (Fla. 1st DCA 1997)]. For discussion on ex parte conferences with injured worker's doctors, see ch. 16, § 16.15. The *Holiday Inn* court decided that filing a Petition for Benefits marked the beginning of an adversarial relationship. In dicta, the court opined that carriers who show surveillance videotape to injured workers' doctors "might also evidence the beginning of an adversarial relationship." This, of course, creates a "catch-22" situation. The carrier may show a videotape to the doctor only if no adversarial relationship exists, but showing a videotape to the doctor creates an adversarial relationship and is therefore prohibited.

[D] Effect of *Holiday Inn v. Re*

In summary, the following is what the *Holiday Inn* case [*see* Holiday Inn v. Re, 643 So. 2d 13 (Fla. 1st DCA 1994); *see* [C], *above*] appears to mean:

1. The ex parte showing of surveillance videotape to the injured worker's doctor is forbidden by *Adelman Steel v. Winter* [*see* [C], *above*].

2. Even if *Adelman* has been overruled by the 1994 legislative amendments, ex parte showing of videotape is still prohibited because it falls outside the workers' compensation exception to the confidentially requirements of former § 455.241(2), Fla. Stat. (*see now* § 455.667(5), Fla. Stat. (7/1/97)) [*see* § 440.13(4)(c), Fla. Stat. (7/1/97)]. That is to say, the exception allows doctors to furnish records and information to the carrier, but does not allow the carrier to give information to the doctor.

3. The discovery rule that carriers need not produce videotape unless it will be used at trial should not be taken literally. If the carrier uses the videotape to influence the outcome of the case, this is the same as using it at trial. Thus, the carrier must produce the tape on demand. If not, the judge may refuse to allow the videotape into evidence and any testimony influenced by it. (Note: this is the only holding in *Holiday Inn.*)

The state of the law is uncertain because the *Holiday Inn* opinion is so equivocal, and because separating the court's holding from its dicta is difficult. Dicta are merely remarks or observations and are not binding on courts in subsequent cases. This makes it tempting to dismiss these dicta as unimportant. Since the same district court of appeal will hear all subsequent cases, however, this is a clear predictor of future holdings. Carriers, apparently, may now use surveillance evidence only at trial and only to rebut medical testimony.

[E] Excluding Evidence Not Produced Timely

Although a judge has broad discretion in determining whether to exclude evidence due to a party's failure to disclose the evidence within the time required by a pretrial order, the exclusion of such evidence is a drastic remedy that should pertain in only the most compelling circumstances and only after the judge has made a case-specific determination as to whether admission of the evidence would result in actual procedural prejudice to the objecting party. Three factors to be considered by the judge in making a determination regarding the exclusion of evidence are as follows: (i) the objecting party's ability to cure the prejudice or, similarly, that party's independent knowledge of the existence of the evidence; (ii) the calling party's possible intentional, or bad faith, noncompliance with the pretrial order; and (iii) the possible disruption of the orderly and efficient trial of the case. A judge should not exclude the evidence if consideration of these and other relevant factors reveals that use of the evidence would not substantially endanger the fairness of the proceeding [*see* Med. Logistics, Inc. v. Marchines, 911 So. 2d 823 (Fla. 1st DCA 2005)].

[3] Admissibility of Medical Reports

Effective January 1, 1994, the judges of compensation claims must receive all medical reports of authorized treating health care providers into evidence. To be admissible, however, these reports must be served on the opposing party at least 30 days before the final hearing. Adjusters must be alert when they receive medical reports from an injured worker's lawyer since the lawyer may intend to submit them into evidence. This provision on medical reports in no way limits the right to further discovery, including depositions [§ 440.29(4), Fla. Stat. (1/1/94)].

[4] Testimony by Unauthorized Physicians

[a] Authorized Medical Witnesses

Effective January 1, 1994, the legislature amended the Act to limit the admission of testimony to only three classes of health care providers [§ 440.13(5)(e), Fla. Stat. (7/1/97) (emphasis added)]:

> No medical opinion other than the opinion of a *medical advisor* appointed by the judge of compensation claims or division, an *independent medical examiner,* or an *authorized treating provider* is admissible in proceedings before the judges of compensation claims.

Excluding possible witnesses affects a party's substantive rights; thus, the above restriction applies only to accidents occurring on or after January 1, 1994, the effective date of the amendment [*see* Merritt Manor Nursing Home v. Caldwell, 667 So. 2d 265 (Fla. 1st DCA 1995)].

As noted, independent medical examiners are qualified to provide trial testimony unless something happens to change their status. For example, the 1997 edition of the Florida Workers' Compensation Health Care Provider Fee for Service Reimbursement Manual provides that the maximum fee to be paid for an IME is $200 per hour, for a maximum of two hours, or a total maximum payment of $400. The carrier, however, agreed to pay $700 for an IME by Dr. Leighton. The claimant objected to the admission of the doctor's testimony and the judge of compensation claims agreed [*see* City of Riviera Beach v. Napier, 791 So. 2d 1160, 1161 (Fla 1st DCA 2001)].

On appeal, the First District Court of Appeal affirmed the judge's order. The court held that Dr. Leighton's action in charging in excess of the allowable amount, and the E/C's action in acquiescing to and paying that charge, took Dr. Leighton out of the statutory category of independent medical examiner. Under the limiting provisions of § 440.13(5)(e), Fla. Stat., only authorized treating physicians, expert medical advisors and independent medical examiners may offer testimony. Since Dr. Leighton did not qualify under any of these categories, the judge of compensation claims properly excluded

Dr. Leighton's testimony as an inadmissible medical opinion [*see* City of Riviera Beach v. Napier, 791 So. 2d 1160, 1161 (Fla 1st DCA 2001)].

SPECIAL ALERT: It appears, however, that the legislature has overruled the court. The Act now provides that the prohibition against paying medical fees in excess of the fee schedule does not apply to independent medical examinations [*see* § 440.13(14)(b), Fla. Stat. (7/1/2002)].

The amendment to § 440.13(14)(b), Fla. Stat., does not apply to IMEs taken before its effective date, July 1, 2002. It does, however, apply to all IMEs taken after that date, including those taken in cases in which the injury occurred before July 1, 2002 [DeCuba v. Indian River Cmty. College, 867 So. 2d 1257, 1258 (Fla. 1st DCA 2004)].

PRACTICE POINT: Absent a proper and timely objection, the judge of compensation claims may allow testimony from physicians other than those in the classes listed above. Failing to object to testimony at or before the deposition precludes objecting for the first time at the hearing. Failure to object timely may create admissibility for otherwise inadmissable testimony. For example, under *Clairson* (below), designating a physician as an independent medical examiner *after* the physician's deposition is not allowed. Note, however, that to be effective under *Clairson,* an objection must be made before the deposition or, at the latest, before the physician gives medical opinion testimony [*see* § 440.13(5)(e), Fla. Stat.] The court has suggested that the objecting party send the following letter before the deposition [*see* Shea v. Durty Two, Inc., 738 So. 2d 510, 511 (Fla. 1st DCA 1999)]:

Dear Counsel:

You have noticed the deposition of Dr. Smith, an unauthorized physician. I do not know whether this deposition is for discovery purposes or for use at trial. Please be advised that because you have not designated Dr. Smith as an IME physician, I object to the admission of his medical opinion testimony at trial pursuant to section 440.13(5)(e), Florida Statutes.

Sincerely,

[Name and Signature of Opposing Counsel]

Note also that the statute restricts only medical *opinion* testimony. Testimony adduced on purely factual matters is admissible even if the witness does not qualify as one of the three listed classes of physicians [*see* Clairson International v. Rose, 718 So. 2d 210, 212–215 (Fla. 1st DCA 1998)]. Regardless of the physician's status, his or her testimony is admissible for the purpose of adducing the physician's factual observations and diagnoses.

For example, the judge of compensation claims awarded chiropractic treatment to Sally Sweikata based on the chiropractor's testimony that Sweikata's back pain was caused by the sequella of her compensable injury. The judge, however, made the award without the benefit of the deposition testimony of an osteopath who, before the accident, had diagnosed Sweikata with congenital scoliosis. Although the doctor was not within one of the defined classes eligible to give opinion testimony, excluding his deposition was error because it dealt only with facts. His deposition consisted of a factual report of the information contained in his office records about her visits to him for back pain. He described her complaints, his diagnoses, and the treatment he gave her, but offered no medical opinion about any of these issues. The court held that such testimony is admissible because it deals with facts and not opinion. Excluding the testimony, however, was not harmless because the existence of a preexisting back condition could affect the compensability of a current back condition. The court reversed the award of benefits and remanded the case [*see* Office Depot, Inc v. Sweikata, 737 So. 2d 1189, 1191 (Fla. 1st DCA 1999)].

Guide to Claims

[b] Expert Medical Advisors

Many physicians may be considered as experts and advisors to the court, but they are not necessarily the "expert medical advisors" referred to in the statute. Note that the qualifying term "expert" is missing from the statutory quotation in [a], *above.* That omission, however, is mere legislative oversight. When taken in context with Ch. 440, Fla. Stat. in its entirety, it clearly refers to "expert" or "division" appointed medical advisors [*see* Washington v. Orange County School Board, 702 So. 2d 1356, 1357 (Fla. 1st DCA 1997); *see also* ch. 16, § 16.18, for a discussion on qualified Expert Medical Advisors (EMAs)].

Note carefully that being an "expert" is not enough to qualify as an expert medical advisor. The designation "expert medical advisor" means a physician who has been certified by the division and who has contracted with the division to provide peer review or medical consultation to the division or to a judge of compensation claims [*see* Fla. Admin. Code R. 59A-30.002(10)]. As noted in Ch. 16, § 16.18, an expert medical advisor may be appointed by either the division or a judge of compensation claims. In either case, however, the selection must be made from those physicians who are certified by the division. Thus, if a judge of compensation claims appoints a physician as an expert medical advisor who is not on the division's approved list, that physician's testimony is not admissible. An exception will arise, of course, if the doctor qualifies as a treating physician or as an IME physician [*see* Johns Eastern Co., Inc. v. Matta, 717 So. 2d 91, 92 (Fla. 1st DCA 1998)].

[c] Authorized Treating Physician Defined

The phrase "authorized treating physician" is not defined in the Act, but the court held it means a physician authorized by the employer or carrier. If the employer or carrier did not authorize a particular physician to provide treatment, the physician is not allowed to testify if the injured worker has the opportunity for a meaningful hearing appropriate to the nature of the case. Thus, an unauthorized chiropractor cannot testify about the necessity for treatment if the injured worker has the opportunity to present other evidence, such as from an authorized physician or an IME physician. This provision is constitutional and does not deny access to courts or to equal protection [*see* Rucker v. City of Ocala, 684 So. 2d 836, 839–842 (Fla. 1st DCA 1996), *rev. dismissed,* 689 So. 2d 1071 (Fla. 1997)].

For example, the carrier denied further benefits to Charles Hurst based upon an independent medical examiner's report finding no injury related to the industrial accident. Without asking for or receiving authorization, Hurst was evaluated by a psychiatrist who diagnosed related depression and anxiety. Also without authorization, Hurst was examined by a neurologist who believed Hurst's medical problems were related to the workplace accident. Relying on the testimony of these unauthorized physicians, the judge of compensation claims awarded benefits. On appeal, the court reversed, holding that the judge made his findings and conclusions based upon inadmissible evidence. Hurst, said the court, was under an affirmative obligation to request an independent medical examination by a physician of his choice if he objected to the carrier's decision to controvert based on its independent examination [*see* Union Camp Corp. v. Hurst, 696 So. 2d 873, 875 (Fla. 1st DCA 1997)].

[d] Exception to Unauthorized Physician Rule

Testimony from unauthorized physicians is allowed if the parties agree. Since an unauthorized physician's testimony will usually favor one party or the other, agreement is unlikely. Inadvertent agreement is more likely. For example, the parties in a case stipulated that "all depositions properly noticed and filed, of witnesses, either expert or non-expert, will be stipulated into evidence." No one argued that the depositions in question had not been properly noticed and filed. Absent unusual circumstances, all stipulations are usually binding. The problem here was that the depositions stipulated into evidence included those of unauthorized physicians. Having so stipulated, however, the testimony became admissible [*see* Citrus World, Inc. v. Mullins, 704 So. 2d 128 (Fla. 1st DCA 1997)].

[5] Testimony of Unqualified Physicians

Clearly, physicians must be qualified to testify about a given subject based on their training and experience. It is the judge of compensation claim's province, as the trier of fact, to decide a witness' credibility, including experts, and to resolve evidentiary conflicts. Although it is the judge of compensation claims who must decide if a physician is qualified, the judge may not disallow testimony on this basis absent an objection from the lawyers for the parties. If neither lawyer objects, the judge of compensation claims should assume that there is no challenge to a physician's qualifications to give opinions on a given issue [*see* Fields v. S.O.S. Drivers, Inc., 736 So. 2d 773, 774 (Fla. 1st DCA 1999)].

[5A] Testimony by Non-Physician Health Care Providers

As previously noted, § 440.13(5)(e), Fla. Stat., limits admissible medical opinion testimony to that of an authorized treating physician, an independent medical examiner, and an expert medical advisor. Although deciding whether a physician qualifies as being in one of these three categories may sometimes be problematic, the statute appears to preclude opinion testimony from non-physician health care providers. The court, however, apparently disagrees with that conclusion.

In *Peckham v. Speegle Constr., Inc.* [896 So. 2d 815 (Fla. 1st DCA 2005)], the judge of compensation claims relied on the testimony of a physician assistant in determining that the claimant was not entitled to Temporary Total Disability benefits. A Physician Assistant (PA) is a non-physician health care provider working under a licensed physician's supervision. Here, the claimant asserted that he was entitled to TTD benefits, beginning on February 23, 2003. The Judge determined that the PA was in the best position to determine the claimant's work status since only he examined and/or interacted with the claimant on that date. With little comment and no explanation, the appellate court approved the Judge's findings, saying only that the order was supported by competent substantial evidence.

Guide to Claims

CAUTION: Because the court did not specifically discuss admissibility of non-physician testimony, relying on *Peckham* as authority for the admission of such evidence is problematic. This is especially true in light of Judge Ervin's lengthy and well-reasoned dissenting opinion that, because the PA was not an authorized treating physician, his medical opinion testimony should not be admissible.

[6] Admissibility of Novel Scientific Evidence

[a] *Frye v. United States*

Many workers' compensation cases turn on the weight of medical evidence. Sometimes, that involves novel scientific evidence, or as some prefer to call it, "junk science." The court has held that the standards of *Frye v. United States* [Frye v. United States, 93 F. 1013 (D.C. Cir. 1923)] apply to the admissibility of novel scientific evidence in workers' compensation cases [United States Sugar Corp. v. Henson, 787 So. 2d 3 (Fla. 1st DCA 2000)].

[b] Novel Scientific Evidence and *Frye* Reliability Standard

The *Frye* test is applied only to novel scientific evidence, which is defined as evidence in the twilight zone of evidence and is somewhere between the experimental and demonstrable stages. Thus, under *Frye,* courts may take judicial notice of a scientific theory, methodology, or technique only after it has emerged from the twilight zone and has taken on uncontroverted validity. Therefore, medical theories are admissible only after they are so firmly established as to have attained the status of scientific law, such as the law of thermodynamics [United States Sugar Corp. v. Henson, 787 So. 2d 3 (Fla. 1st DCA 2000)].

[c] Rationale for *Frye* Standard

The Florida Supreme Court discussed the rationale for using the *Frye* standard in *Stokes v. State* [Stokes v. State, 548 So. 2d 188, 193–194 (Fla. 1989)], as follows:

The underlying theory for this rule [*Frye*] is that a courtroom is not a laboratory, and as such it is not the place to conduct scientific experiments. If the scientific community considers a procedure or process unreliable for its own purposes, then the procedure must be considered less reliable for courtroom use.

NOTE: *Frye* does not apply to "pure opinion testimony" based solely on the expert's personal experience and training [*see* Flanagan v. State, 625 So. 2d 827, 828 (Fla.

1993) ("[P]ure opinion testimony . . . does not have to meet *Frye,* because this type of testimony is based on the expert's personal experience and training"); Florida Power & Light Co. v. Tursi, 729 So. 2d 995, 997 (Fla. 4th DCA 1999) (ophthalmologist's opinion on causation not required to meet *Frye* standard because opinion was not based on novel scientific evidence, but rather expert's experience and training)].

[d] Preserving the Objection

[i] *Frye* Objection Must Be Raised in Pretrial Stipulation

Because a *Frye* objection goes to the heart of the claimant's case and may require the judge of compensation claims to conduct a separate evidentiary hearing, it is an issue that is required to be listed in the pretrial stipulation [United States Sugar Corp. v. Henson, 787 So. 2d 3 (Fla. 1st DCA 2000)].

[ii] *Frye* Objection Must Be Raised at Deposition

It is necessary to make an express *Frye* objection at the depositions. Fla. R. Civ. P. 1.330(d)(3)(A), provides:

> Objections to the competency of a witness or to the competency, relevancy, or materiality of testimony are not waived by failure to make them before or during the taking of the deposition *unless the ground of the objection is one that might have been obviated or removed if presented at that time.* (emphasis added).

Ensure that the parties and the expert witnesses are on notice that a *Frye* test will be sought as to the admissibility of the expert testimony. This is to alert counsel and the witnesses of the need to have available texts, scientific literature, or studies that would support a conclusion that the scientific principles on which their testimony is based is generally accepted in the relevant scientific community.

[e] Burden of Proof

The burden is on the proponent of the evidence to establish by a preponderance of the evidence the general acceptance of the underlying scientific principles and methodology [*see* Murray v. State, 692 So. 2d 157, 161 (Fla. 1997); E.I. du Pont de Nemours & Co. v. Castillo, 748 So. 2d 1108, 1114 (Fla. 3d DCA 2000)].

[f] Four-Step Process for Applying *Frye*

The four steps for applying *Frye* are [United States Sugar Corp. v. Henson, 787 So. 2d 3 (Fla. 1st DCA 2000)]:

1. The trial judge must determine whether such expert testimony will assist the jury (or judge) in understanding the evidence or in determining a fact in issue. . . .

2. The trial judge must decide whether the expert's testimony is based on a scientific principle or discovery that is "sufficiently established to have gained general acceptance in the particular field in which it belongs." [Frye v. United States, 293 F. 1013, 1014 (D.C. Cir. 1923)]

3. The trial judge must determine whether a particular witness is qualified as an expert to present opinion testimony on the subject in issue. . . .

4. The judge may then allow the expert to render an opinion on the subject of his or her expertise, and it is then up to the jury (or judge) to determine the credibility of the expert's opinion, which it may either accept or reject. . . . [Ramirez v. State, 651 So. 2d 1164, 1167 (Fla. 1995)]

[g] Determining General Acceptance

Determining general acceptance requires a court to evaluate both the quality and quantity of the literature and other evidence supporting the principle or technique. It is clear that scientific unanimity is not a precondition to a finding of general acceptance in the scientific community. Instead, general acceptance in the scientific community can be established if use of the technique is supported by a clear majority of the members of that community. Of course, the trial courts, in determining the general acceptance issue, must consider the quality, as well as quantity, of the evidence supporting or opposing a new scientific technique. Mere numerical majority support or opposition by persons minimally qualified to state an authoritative opinion is of little value. Therefore, while a "nose count" is not alone sufficient to establish general acceptance in the scientific community, such acceptance likewise need not be predicated upon a unanimous view [Brim v. State, 695 So. 2d 268, 272 (Fla. 1997)].

The *Frye* standard does not call upon the trial judge to read the scientific literature to understand or access the scientific reliability or validity of a principle or procedure. The trial judge reviews this literature merely to determine whether there is quantitative and qualitative acceptance of the science. The trial judge is determining legal reliability, as a threshold test of legal relevance, by judging—as an objective outsider—the level of acceptance that a principle or procedure has achieved within a scientific community. Thus, although the judge must develop at least a solid, layperson's understanding of the science, he or she is not expected to perform the superhuman task of transforming himself or herself into an expert within the community. The judge is merely to position himself or herself to determine the level of agreement or dissension within it [Brim v. State, 779 So. 2d 427, 434–435 (Fla. 2d DCA 2000)].

[h] Separate Evidentiary Hearing

While a separate evidentiary hearing is the usual practice, *it is not mandatory.* The four-step process for applying *Frye* set forth by the Supreme Court in *Ramirez v. State* [Ramirez v. State, 651 So. 2d 1164, 1167 (Fla. 1995)]. does not mandate a separate evidentiary hearing [United States Sugar Corp v. Henson, 787 So. 2d 3, 21 (Fla. 1st DCA 2001) (on rehearing), *aff.* United States Sugar Corp. v. Henson, 823 So. 2d 104, 106–109 (Fla. 2002)].

[7] Application of the *Frye* Standard to Florida Workers' Compensation

In workers' compensation cases, when determining the admissibility of expert opinion testimony based on new or novel scientific principles or methodology, the Judge of Compensation Claims must determine whether such evidence is sufficiently reliable under the *Frye* admissibility standards.

It is only on proper objection that the novel scientific evidence offered is unreliable that a trial court must make the determination of whether evidence meets the *Frye* standards. Unless the party against whom the evidence is being offered makes this specific objection, the trial court will not have committed error in admitting the evidence.

The *Frye* standard applies only when an expert attempts to render an opinion that is based on new or novel scientific techniques. Thus, the Judge of Compensation Claims must make the threshold determination of whether the scientific principle or methodology underlying the expert's opinion is "new or novel." When a scientific principle has been established and generally accepted in the relevant scientific community, and has also been *Frye*-tested in the legal community, it is no longer new or novel, and there is simply no need to reapply a *Frye* analysis.

If new or novel scientific principles are at issue, the Judge of Compensation Claims should perform a *Frye* analysis following the four-step process set forth in *Ramirez v. State*.

In workers' compensation cases, *Frye* issues should generally be set forth in the pretrial stipulation and raised at the deposition of the expert. This procedural requirement is based on the nature of the trial procedure in a workers' compensation proceeding. Nevertheless, when the expert's medical report did not disclose that the opinion was based on scientific studies, no deposition of the expert was taken, and the final hearing was the first time the claimant knew or reasonably should have known that the expert's opinion testimony would present a *Frye* issue, a *Frye* motion at the hearing was timely [*see* Dirling v. Sarasota County Gov't, 871 So. 2d 303 (Fla. 1st DCA 2004)].

[8] Cross-Examination of Medical Witnesses

To satisfy due process considerations, parties must be given a meaningful opportunity to present evidence and be heard. Indeed, the right to call witnesses is one of the most important due process rights of a party, and accordingly the exclusion of the testimony of expert witnesses must be carefully considered and sparingly done.

One of the purposes of cross-examination of an expert is to suggest the existence of a hypothesis contrary to that adopted by the expert. For that reason, parties are permitted wide latitude in cross-examination. Failure to permit full and fair cross-examination of matters testified to on direct examination is harmful error.

It is true that an injury, its cause, and any manifestations must be established by competent, substantial evidence within a reasonable degree of medical probability or certainty. However, the fact finder, when deciding whether a party has proven its case, makes this determination. There is no statutory requirement that every question asked of an expert on cross-examination be phrased in the rigid terms of "reasonable degree of medical probability or certainty." Such an inflexible requirement would be completely at odds with the practice of permitting wide latitude on cross-examination and testing the conclusions drawn by the experts. The statutory standard for a doctor's expert testimony contained in § 440.09(1), Fla. Stat., may be established without using magic words [*see* AT & T Wireless Servs. v. Castro, 896 So. 2d 828 (Fla. 1st DCA 2005)].

§ 22.09 Judges' Orders

[1] Issuing Orders Timely

[a] Statutory Requirements

Justice and the law require that the judges of compensation claims issue their orders promptly. In the past, waiting a year or more for an order, despite the statutory requirement that the judge enter the order within 30 days, was common. Effective January 1, 1994, this statutory time requirement was cut in half to only 15 days. The judge could take longer to issue an order, but only with the agreement of the parties [§ 440.25(4)(d), Fla. Stat. (7/1/97)]. When judges miss the deadline, they must file a written explanation with the Chief Judge. If the judges did not comply with these time constraints before, why would they bother now? The answer is simple. The Governor now has statutory authority to fire a judge who does not comply with these rules. Judges' orders become final within 30 days after mailing copies of the order to the parties, unless a party files a notice of appeal [§ 440.25(5)(a), Fla. Stat. (7/1/97)].

Effective October 1, 2001, the deadline was increased to the original 30 days.

> **PRACTICE POINT:** The JCC must issue a final order within 30 days after the final hearing or closure of the hearing record. The judge may enter an abbreviated final order in cases in which compensability is not disputed. Either party may request findings of fact and conclusions of law [§ 440.25(4)(d), Fla. Stat. (10/1/2001)].

[b] Effect of Stale Orders

Excessive delay in issuing an order may be the basis for a trial de novo. For example, the judge of compensation claims held a trial in Steven Greenwell's case on March 4, 1995. The outcome of the case turned on Greenwell's credibility. Thirteen months later, on April 13, 1995, the judge issued an order denying the claim. On appeal the court reversed and remanded for a new trial because Greenwell's credibility was critical to the outcome of the case, and there was excessive delay between his live testimony and the entry of the final order [*see* Greenwell v. Bellsouth Telecoms., 732 So. 2d 333 (Fla. 1st DCA 1998); *see also* Harrington v. Vida Appliance Corp., 542 So. 2d 1006, 1007 (Fla. 1st DCA 1988) (order reversed and remanded for de novo hearing when JCC entered order 245 days after hearing and testimony of live witnesses was critical to outcome); Maddox v. Rinaldi's Expressway Lanes, 459 So. 2d 421, 422 (Fla. 1st DCA 1984) (new hearing required "in the interest of justice" when deputy entered order five months after final hearing and nine months after claimant testified and entire case was determined based on claimant's credibility)].

[2] Paying Awarded Benefits Timely

Effective January 1, 1994, carriers must pay any benefits awarded, including washout settlements [*see* ch. 21], within seven days after benefits become due. If not, and the carrier has not filed a notice of appeal within 30 days, the carrier is subject to a penalty equal to 20 percent of the benefits awarded [§ 440.20(7), Fla. Stat. (7/1/97)]. In a serious injury case, such a penalty could be very large. Adjusters should treat all orders of the judges of compensation claims as top priority items [*see* ch. 12, § 12.04[9], for a detailed discussion about how penalties apply].

[3] Disqualifying a JCC

A motion for disqualification of a judge of compensation claims is to be made and determined pursuant to Fla. R. Jud. Admin. 2.160 [Fla. Admin. Code R. 60Q-6.126(1)]. "Any party" can seek disqualification of the judge of compensation claims assigned to the case "on grounds provided by rule, by statute, or by the Code of Judicial Conduct" [*see* Fla. R. Jud. Admin. 2.160(b)]. As to the issue of timeliness, the pertinent rule requires the motion to be made "within a reasonable time not to exceed 10 days after discovery of the facts constituting the grounds for the motion and . . . promptly presented to the court for an immediate ruling" [Fla. R. Jud. Admin. 2.160(e); *see* Amato v. Winn Dixie Stores, 810 So. 2d 979, 981 (Fla. 1st DCA 2002)].

For example, in *Amato v. Winn Dixie Stores,* the judge held a final merits hearing on July 27, 2000. At the hearing's conclusion, the judge of compensation claims granted leave for the employer/carrier to take a post-hearing deposition of their vocational expert. Before all the evidence had been presented (and before the vocational expert had been deposed), the judge of compensation claims reviewed what evidence had been submitted and entered a final order on the merits, denying the claimant's entire claim. Apparently, the judge had forgotten about allowing the additional evidence. When the carrier brought this to his attention, the judge of compensation claims vacated the premature final order. The claimant then filed a motion to disqualify the judge, alleging that she "reasonably believed it would be futile to present evidence to rebut the carrier's vocational expert when the judge of compensation claims denied the entire claim without even considering that evidence in the first place." Likewise, the claimant contended it would be unavailing to respond to the carrier's trial memorandum in light of the judge of compensation claims's already having denied the claim without affording the claimant an opportunity to respond in writing. The judge of compensation claims denied the motion, stating that the premature final order on the merits had been entered based on "the mistaken assumption that all evidence had been presented." The judge of compensation claims concluded that his prior adverse ruling was not an adequate ground for disqualification [Amato v. Winn Dixie Stores, 810 So. 2d 979, 983 (Fla. 1st DCA 2002)].

On appeal, the First District Court of Appeal stated that the court must determine whether the facts alleged (which must be taken as true) would prompt a reasonably prudent person to fear that he or she could not get a fair and impartial trial. It is not a question of how the judge feels; rather, it is a question of what feeling resides in the affiant's mind, and the basis for such feeling. The court concluded that the claimant's motion to disqualify the judge of compensation claims was legally sufficient, in that the facts alleged would place a reasonably prudent person in fear of not receiving a fair and impartial proceeding because the trial judge had prejudged the case before all the evidence was presented. Therefore, the court reversed and remanded with instructions that a different judge of compensation claims be assigned to all further proceedings. The court cautioned its conclusion should not be construed as adopting a *per se* rule mandating disqualification solely upon the allegation that the trial court ruled on a matter without having heard from the other side [Amato v. Winn Dixie Stores, 810 So. 2d 979, 983 (Fla. 1st DCA 2002)].

In a dissenting opinion Judge Padovano noted that when the judge of compensation claims learned of his mistake, he promptly vacated the order and prepared to consider the case again in light of the additional evidence. He opined that a reasonable person would take this to mean that the judge was willing to start over with an open mind. That was not the case here, according to Judge Padovano [*see* Amato v. Winn Dixie Stores, 810 So. 2d 979, 984 (Fla. 1st DCA 2002)]:

> . . . The claimant says that the error in rendering the decision prematurely reveals a potential bias on the part of the judge. It seems more likely to me, however, that this is an argument of convenience that merely capitalizes on the judge's error. What the claimant really wants is a chance to try the case before a judge who might be more receptive to her claim.

§ 22.10 Modification of Orders

[1] When Modification Is Proper

Once a judge of compensation claims enters an order awarding benefits, the carrier cannot stop paying those benefits without a judge's approval. The courts strictly enforce this rule because the judges of compensation claims do not have the authority to enforce their own orders. That authority rests with the circuit court in a rule nisi proceeding [*see* ch. 23, § 23.06]. Before stopping any benefit, carriers must be certain this action will not violate an outstanding order. If so, they should seek a modification of the order.

For example, the carrier administratively accepted the injured worker as permanently and totally disabled. Later, the injured worker filed a petition for permanent total supplemental benefits, and the judge awarded the benefits. Later still, the carrier claimed it caught the employee working and stopped paying PTD benefits. The District Court of Appeal held the carrier had no right to do this. Although the judge of compensation claims had not issued an order awarding PTD benefits, he did award supplemental benefits. The court held that modification is not required where prior orders do not adjudicate the issue on the merits. Here, however, the judge did adjudicate entitlement to PTD supplemental benefits. He could not have done so without an underlying right to PTD benefits. In such a case the carrier can stop benefits only with the approval of a judge in a modification proceeding [*see* Knapp v. Florida Min. and Materials, 662 So. 2d 983, 984–985 (Fla. 1st DCA 1995)].

[2] Basis for Modification

On either the judge's own initiative, or upon application of either party, the judge may materially alter an order's effect. This is true even after the order becomes final. Modification is appropriate when a change of condition occurred or when there is a mistake in the judge's determination of the facts. Judges may not modify an order after the statute of limitations has expired, unless the limitations statute itself has been waived.

The new order may stop, continue, reinstate, increase, or decrease compensation. If the order decreases the compensation rate effective to the date of the accident, the carrier may deduct any overpayment from future payments. The judge will decide the rate and method of the deduction. The statute provides as follows [§ 440.28, Fla. Stat. (1/1/94)]:

> Modification of orders–Upon a judge of compensation claims' own initiative, or upon the application of any party in interest, on the ground of a change in condition or because of a mistake in a determination of fact, the judge of compensation claims may, at any time prior to 2 years after the date of the last payment of compensation pursuant to the compensation order the party seeks to modify, or at any time prior to 2 years after the date copies of an order rejecting a claim are mailed to the parties at the last known address of each, review a compensation case in accordance with the procedure prescribed in respect of claims in § 440.25 and, in accordance with such section, issue a new compensation order which may terminate, continue, reinstate, increase, or decrease such compensation or award compensation.

[3] Time Limitations

In interpreting § 440.28, Fla. Stat. [*see* [2], *above*], the District Court of Appeal held that a petition for modification that seeks specific benefits denied in a prior compensation order must be filed within two years of that order [*see* Ford v. Alexander Cabinet Co., 467 So. 2d 1050, 1052 (Fla. 1st DCA 1985)].

The courts have, however, rejected this theory. Now, petitions filed within two years of the last voluntary compensation payment are timely within the meaning of § 440.28, Fla. Stat. [*see* Santa Rosa County Bd. of Com'rs v. Stephens, 585 So. 2d 1067, 1068 (Fla. 1st DCA 1991)]. Note: Under the 1994 amendments this time is reduced to one year [*see* Daniel v. Holmes Lumber Co., 490 So. 2d 1252, 1256 (Fla. 1986)].

[4] Change of Condition

A long list of decisions from the First District Court of Appeal gave the impression that a change of condition must have been unanticipated at the time of the original hearing to support modification. This seems strange, considering the Florida Supreme Court ruling that: "The so-called change of condition provision is available to bring relief to a claimant whose condition becomes progressively worse *even though not anticipated* by the original diagnosis" [*see* Soloff v. U-Totem, Inc. of Broward, 257 So. 2d 31, 32 (Fla. 1971) (emphasis added) (quoting *Saunder v. Coast Cities Coaches, Inc.*, 156 So. 2d 162, 165 (Fla. 1963))].

The First District Court of Appeal now holds that the rule announced in *Saunder* does not preclude an order of modification where the injured worker's changed condition, though anticipated, was not considered when the judge issued the original order. Even an anticipated substantial change of condition will support a modification order when there is "new and positive evidence that the claimant's condition has changed so that the conditions which were the foundation of the prior order no longer operate" [*see* Starkman v. Bechtel Power Corporation, 588 So. 2d 304, 305 (Fla. 1st DCA 1991)].

[5] Finding of Different Tribunal

To establish entitlement to modification, the carrier has the burden of presenting the judge of compensation claims with new evidence that could not have been discovered during the earlier proceeding. The mere fact that a different tribunal subsequently reached a different conclusion does not constitute such new evidence.

For example, the judge of compensation claims determined that Phillip Alford's injuries qualified for social security disability benefits. Based on this and other factors, the judge awarded permanent total disability benefits. The carrier appealed and the First District Court of Appeal issued a per curiam affirmance. While the appeal was pending, Alford was twice denied social security disability benefits. Based on this, the carrier filed an application for modification, arguing that the judge had made a mistake of fact in deciding that Alford's injuries qualified for social security disability benefits.

The court noted that the carrier made no showing that the Legislature intended to delegate the authority of the judge of compensation claims to the Social Security Administration. Additionally, the court found no provision for obliteration of a permanent total disability award if the claimant does not in the future qualify for social security disability payment [*see* Alachua County Adult Detention Center v. Alford, 727 So. 2d 388, 391 (Fla. 1st DCA 1999)].

§ 22.11 Appeals

[1] Deciding Whether to Appeal

Simply losing an issue before a judge of compensation claims should not be the basis for an appeal. In a typical case each side will put forth evidence supporting its position. The judge must decide which evidence is the most persuasive and rule accordingly. While it is tempting to appeal an adverse ruling on the theory that the judge failed to choose the most persuasive evidence, doing so is to do nothing more than to seek a new trial. An appellate court will not retry a case and substitute its judgment for that of the judge of compensation claims on factual issues supported by competent, substantial evidence. Asking the court to do so amounts to filing a frivolous appeal. The legal standard for appellate review includes such issues as lack of competent substantial evidence to support the judge's order, abuse of discretion, and erroneous application of a rule of law [*see* Swanigan v. Dobbs House, 442 So. 2d 1026, 1027 (Fla. 1st DCA 1983)].

Appeals can be very costly, not to mention the potential for an adverse opinion. If the court rules against the carrier, paying the benefits originally awarded is only the beginning. The carrier will also owe interest on those benefits and an additional claimant's attorney's fee for successful prosecution or defense of the appeal. Even worse, both sides risk a holding by the court that may change the state of the law. Such cases must be chosen carefully. Carriers should be sure the defense lawyer, or at least the lawyer's firm, has a good grasp of appellate work (and not just rely on their "say-so"). Several cases causing system-wide problems because of surprising appellate results may have been attributed to a lackluster appellate presentation from the defense. Even the best firms have cases backfire at times. Carriers, however, should help improve the odds by not placing a poorly chosen case before the court, especially when the situation can become worse when marginal appellate presentation is made.

SPECIAL ALERT: Remember that the time to decide whether to appeal is very short. Although the carrier may file a notice of appeal any time within 30 days of the date the judge enters the order, the carrier has only 7 days to pay the benefits awarded. If the carrier struggles with the decision too long and decides not to appeal, the price of the delay will be a 20-percent penalty.

[2] Notice of Appeal

[a] When Appeal Is Proper

The parties have the right to appeal the final orders of the judge of compensation claims. With narrow exceptions, non-final orders in workers' compensation cases are not immediately appealable. By definition, a workers' compensation order that decides all issues ripe for adjudication is a final order that can be appealed [Emro Marketing v. Schwier, 670 So. 2d 1141, 1142 (Fla. 1st DCA 1996)].

Technical errors in a judge's order that are readily correctable by a motion for rehearing are not a proper subject for appeal. The court explained that, "[I]n workers' compensation appeals,. . .we will not reverse for a readily correctable technical error that the [judge] was not asked to correct within the time available for correction" [*see* Sunland Hospital/State of Fla. v. Garrett, 415 So. 2d 783, 785 (Fla. 1st DCA 1982)].

For example, the judge awarded the claimant 108 weeks of temporary benefits despite the statutory maximum of 104 weeks. On appeal, the court held the issue had not been preserved for appellate review. The question of an excess award was not raised before the judge, nor did the carrier file a motion for rehearing to correct what the court saw as a readily correctable, technical error [*see* Wal-Mart Stores v. Lopez, 742 So. 2d 301, 302 (Fla. 1st DCA 1998).

[b] Time Constraints and Appealable Issues

The First District Court of Appeal in Tallahassee hears all workers' compensation appeals. To preserve the right of appeal, the appellant must file the notice with the court or the judge, "within thirty days of the date copies of the order were mailed to the parties" [Fla. R. App. P. 9.180 (1997)]. This rule gives the district court discretionary jurisdiction to review even a non-final order on the following issues:

1. Jurisdiction
2. Venue
3. Compensability of accidents or occupational disease
4. Insurance coverage

Note carefully that the deadline for filing a notice of appeal with the judge of compensation claims or the First District Court of Appeal is 30 days from the date the judge mails the order to the parties. The term "filed" means *received* by the court, not mailed to the court. In one case, the appellant mailed a notice of appeal to the judge of compensation claims within the 30-day period, but apparently the judge did not receive it. By the time the appellant discovered this problem, the 30-day period had expired. The court held that mailing the notice within the period is not sufficient. The fact and date of mailing is irrelevant. The only date that counts is the date the notice of appeal was filed with the JCC. In dismissing the appeal for lack of timely filing, the court issued the following warning: "We cannot stress strongly enough that counsel must insure the notice of appeal is *filed* in a timely manner. Reliance upon the mail is not well founded" [*see* Coca Cola Foods v. Cordero, 589 So. 2d 961, 962 (Fla. 1st DCA 1991)].

Carriers should be certain the defense lawyer confirms receipt of the notice of appeal by the judge of compensation claims before the 30-day period expires. Hand delivery is the prudent and preferred method of filing.

Also, note that "filed" means received. The absolute deadline is midnight on the 30th day, but someone must be at the judge's office to receive the filing. Therefore, the effective deadline is before the close of business on the 30th day [*see* Metropolitan Dade County v. Vasquez, 659 So. 2d 355, 356 (Fla. 1st DCA 1995)].

PRACTICE POINT: Unlike other classes of cases, a motion for rehearing a workers' compensation case does not toll the time for initiating an appeal [*see* Betancourt v. Sears Roebuck & Co., 693 So. 2d 680, 683 (Fla. 1st DCA 1997)]. The proper exercise of the judge's authority to vacate an order requires that the order be vacated unconditionally and that a new order be entered once proceedings on rehearing are concluded, whereupon the time for instituting an appeal begins anew. Of course, if rehearing is denied, the original order may simply be republished, and in such a case, the time for filing a notice of appeal runs from the date of mailing of the order that republishes the original [*see* Fla. R. App. P. 9.180(b)(2)].

Orders that seem to be intended to resurrect previously entered and conditionally vacated orders without any further action by the JCC cannot be reconciled with the provisions of Fla. R. App. P. 9.180(b)(2) relating to the time limits for commencing an appeal in workers' compensation proceedings [*see* W & W Lumber of Palm Beach, Inc. v. Marrero, 780 So. 2d 291, 292 (Fla. 1st DCA 2001)].

[3] Payment of Benefits While Appeal Pending

The rules provide that benefits awarded by the judge of compensation claims, but challenged on appeal, may be withheld pending the outcome of the appeal [Fla. R. App. P. 9.180 (1997)]. Carriers should be sure, however, that they timely pay any benefits awarded but not certified as part of the appeal.

[4] Filing Fees and Costs

[a] Cost of Transcript

The appellant has 60 days after the filing of a notice of appeal to send a transcript of the record of the hearing to the court and to the parties [Fla. R. App. P. 9.180 (1997)]. Before doing so, however, the judge will notify the appellant of the cost of the transcript, which can run several hundred dollars. If the appellant does not pay for the transcript within the allotted time, the court may dismiss the appeal [Fla. R. App. P. 9.180 (1997)].

[b] Effect of Insolvency

The injured worker (if he or she is the appellant) may be spared costs. The injured worker may file a Verified Petition of Indigency, attesting that he or she is impoverished. These petitions ask the court to waive payment. In the past, courts usually granted these requests based only on the injured worker's "say so." Actually, the court does not waive the cost. The Division pays it from its administrative trust fund. Evidently the Division was picking up the cost on many cases in which the appellant (the injured worker) was not truly insolvent. The law now requires the appellant to file a verified petition to be relieved of costs [§ 440.25(5)(b), Fla. Stat. (7/1/97)]. Petitions must contain a sworn statement that the appellant is insolvent with a complete, detailed, and sworn financial affidavit showing all of the appellant's assets. If the injured worker fails to show all assets and income, including marital assets and income, the judge may deny the petition with prejudice. Dismissal "with prejudice" means the petition may not be refiled.

In addition, the 1994 amendment defines insolvency. To be relieved of the filing costs, appellants must show that they (1) have ceased to pay their debts in the ordinary course of business and cannot pay debts as they become due, or (2) have been adjudicated as insolvent pursuant to the Federal Bankruptcy law [§ 440.02(31)(b), Fla. Stat. (7/1/97)]. This means nothing more than that the person cannot afford to pay both the costs of the record and personal bills. The determination of insolvency must be based on the injured worker's financial condition after including the cost of the record as a liability. Unless the injured worker's financial condition is such that the injured worker can pay this additional liability as well as other expenses as they become due, the statutory definition of "insolvent" is satisfied [*see* Furtick v. Shults, 640 So. 2d 123, 125 (Fla. 1st DCA 1994)].

In *Furtick,* the injured worker's petition showed income of $640 per month and expenses of $620 per month. His assets consisted of $200 in cash and 30-year-old pickup truck. The cost of preparing the trial record was $1,250, but this was money Furtick did not have. Part of the statutory definition requires that to be insolvent the petitioner must have "ceased to pay his debts as they become due." Clearly, Furtick was paying his debts but had nothing left over. The court found that Furtick could not continue to pay his debts if he was forced to pay the cost of the record. "In effect," said the court, "Furtick will be compelled to choose between paying his monthly support expenses or abandoning his appeal." The court would not accept the argument that the legislature intended such a harsh result.

Another issue in *Furtick* was whether the statute has substantive or procedural application. The amendment became effective on January 1, 1994, but the accident occurred in 1985. The court did not decide the question. Since the court found that the injured worker was insolvent, reaching the question of retroactive application was unnecessary.

[c] Insolvency Hearing Required

The judge of compensation claims must hold a hearing on the injured worker's petition of insolvency, giving all interested parties 15 days' notice. If no one objects to the petition, the judge may enter an order without a hearing. If the judge grants the petition, the order will direct the Division to pay the record cost and any filing fees. At its option, the Division may transcribe the record itself or contract with a transcription service.

> **NOTE:** Effective October 1, 2001, the legislature repealed the JCC's statutory authority to enter an order requiring the petitioner to reimburse the Division for costs incurred when an insolvency petition is denied [§ 440.25(5)(b), Fla. Stat. (10/1/2001)].

No matter who pays the bill, the costs can be charged against the carrier if the injured worker prevails. The statute specifically provides that "if the [injured worker] should prevail in any proceedings before a judge . . . or court, there shall be taxed against the employer the reasonable costs of such proceedings . . ." [§ 440.34(3), Fla. Stat. (7/1/97)].

If the Division has paid the costs for the injured worker, the rules of procedure require the carrier to reimburse the Division within 30 days of the mandate issued by the District Court of Appeal or the Supreme Court [Fla. R. App. P. 9.180(g)(3)(J) (1997)]. The carrier will still be liable for these costs, even if the case is settled while the appeal is pending. The parties should include in the settlement agreement a provision for paying the costs of the appeal. If not, the judge of compensation claims has the authority to issue an order compelling the carrier to reimburse the Division for sums it has paid for an indigent injured worker [*see* Dept. of Labor v. Circle T-Bone Ranch, 439 So. 2d 993, 994 (Fla. 1st DCA 1983); Boswell IH Trucks v. Div. of Workers' Comp., 498 So. 2d 1042, 1044 (Fla. 1st DCA 1986)].

[5] Appellate Process

The appellant's lawyer has 30 days after filing the record to prepare and serve a copy of the brief upon the other party and the court. The appellee has 20 days after receipt of the appellant's brief to file a reply brief. Then, the appellant may file an answer brief. Note that the appellee also may file a cross appeal [Fla. R. App. P. 9.180(h) (1997)]. The lawyers may, besides the required briefs, file various motions for consideration by the court. At its discretion, the court may allow the lawyers to appear in person and present oral argument. This is usually limited to 10 or 15 minutes to each side. A panel of three appellate court judges hears workers' compensation cases. The panel members change on a rotating, periodic basis.

Frequently, the court simply affirms the order per curiam, which means the appellate court approves the lower court's ruling, but without a written opinion. In other cases, the appellate court may write an opinion designed to guide and instruct future litigants on the issues. Frequently, if the court reverses all or part of an award, it will send back or remand the case to the judge for further determinations. When the court reverses a judgment, it usually remands the matter for a new trial consistent with the principles announced in its written opinion. For example, if the judge denied a claim, and the court reverses, it will remand the case to the judge to decide the benefits to which the injured worker is entitled, consistent with the court's order.

Upon remand, a workers' compensation case goes back to the same condition as if the judge had not entered the order reviewed. Unless the appellate court expressly restricts the judge on remand, the judge may exercise sound quasi-judicial discretion to allow additional testimony. The judge may reconsider the evidence previously received, giving due consideration to the appellate decision. In other words, the judge may exercise discretion. The judge may confine the inquiry on remand to matters and issues taken up in the first hearing. The judge can, however, choose to allow new evidence about matters occurring subsequently to the first hearing [*see* Dade County School Bd. v. Jackson, 473 So. 2d 1356, 1357 (Fla. 1st DCA 1985); Turner v. Rinker Materials, 622 So. 2d 80, 83 (Fla. 1st DCA 1993)].

Occasionally, the appellate court, upon proper motion of a party, may agree to a rehearing or reconsideration of its original decision. Such a rehearing may be by the same panel or by the entire court. We call the latter a rehearing en banc. The court, however, does not always approve these motions. The court will require the moving litigant to show substantial good cause to obtain a rehearing.

[6] Appealing Non-Final Interlocutory Orders

A judge of compensation claims may issue a non-final or interlocutory order. Such orders decide intermediate issues, but do not dispose of the case. Instead, interlocutory orders direct further legal proceedings. An example is an order finding the injured worker is entitled to reimbursement for attorney's fees, but the order reserves jurisdiction to decide the fee later. Usually, interlocutory orders are not appealable until the entire matter has been disposed of by order or by judgment.

In workers' compensation cases, however, the rules of procedure allow the district court to review non-final orders in specific categories [Fla. R. App. P. 9.180(b) (1997)]. Those categories are:

1. Jurisdiction
2. Venue
3. Compensability
4. Insurance Coverage
5. Discovery issues (but only if it appears the order will cause irreparable harm and there is no adequate legal remedy)

Any non-final order dealing with an issue not on the list—such as reserving jurisdiction on the amount of attorney's fees—is a non-appealable order [*see* Wometco Enterprises v. Cordoves, 650 So. 2d 1117, 1118 (Fla. 1st DCA 1995)]. Put another way, if the JCC expressly reserves jurisdiction on a fully tried issue that is ripe for adjudication, such reservation renders the order non-final and non-appealable. Trying to appeal such an order will result in a dismissal for lack of jurisdiction. Conversely, failing to rule on a ripe, fully tried issue and failing to reserve jurisdiction is the same as a denial for jurisdictional purposes. Failing to rule in such cases is reversible error. Sometimes, judges do not rule on an issue because the injured worker failed to produce evidence supporting the claim. When this happens, the appellate court considers the claim abandoned and the issue waived. Such an order is final and therefore appealable. Any subsequent claim for the same benefits will be barred by the principle of res judicata [*see* Betancourt v. Sears Roebuck & Co., 693 So. 2d 680, 683 (Fla. 1st DCA 1997)].

When judges fail to do their duty by not ruling on ripe, fully tried issues, the proper response is a motion for rehearing rather than appeal [*see* Betancourt v. Sears Roebuck & Co., 693 So. 2d 680, 683 (Fla. 1st DCA 1997)]. Unfortunately, filing such a motion does not toll the 30-day time limit for filing an appeal as it does in other classes of cases.

Appealing a non-final, interlocutory order on the issue of compensability is allowed [*see* Fla. R. App. P. 9.180(b)(1)(C)]:

> Provided that the order expressly finds that an injury occurred within the scope and course of employment and that claimant is entitled to receive causally related benefits in some amount, and provided further that the lower tribunal certifies in the order that determination of the exact nature and amount of benefits due to claimant will require substantial expense and time.

To make a non-final order on compensability alone appealable, the judge of compensation claims must certify that determination of the nature and amount of benefits due to the claimant will require substantial expense and time. In one case, the parties agreed to bifurcate the hearing proceedings and to try only the issue of compensability to save the cost of further litigation on the issue of benefits. The judge ruled in the claimant's favor on the compensability issue and the carrier appealed. The judge noted that the benefits in dispute were substantial, but did not expressly certify that deciding those benefits would require substantial expense and time. On appeal, the court held that the rule (Fla. R. App. P. 9.180(b)(1)(C)) must be strictly construed and that the judge must make a certification as required. Since the judge did not do so in this case, the court dismissed the appeal, holding that the order was not appealable and that the court lacked jurisdiction to review it [*see* Cadco Builders, Inc. v. Roberts, 712 So. 2d 457, 458 (Fla. 1st DCA 1998)].

[7] Appellate Attorney's Fees

When deciding whether to appeal, carriers should take into account their exposure to appellate attorney's fees. § 440.34, Fla. Stat. contains nothing to require a judge of compensation claims to calculate an appellate attorney's fee using the statutory percentage-based formula. Calculating appellate attorney's fees does not lend itself to one inflexible rule and must necessarily be left to the discretion of the JCC.

Thus, the judge can award anything deemed appropriate. In addition, the courts have rejected the notion that evidence of the hourly rate charged by defense lawyers should influence or control the injured worker's attorney's fee. Why? Because defense lawyers always get paid, win or lose. This is not so with lawyers who represent indigent injured workers. If the injured worker's lawyer loses, the carrier will not pay the fee. Absent

Guide to Claims

ongoing compensation payments, the injured worker will not likely pay the fee either. On the other hand, the court has cautioned that employers and carriers should not subsidize claimant lawyers' ("fee-less") losses on unrelated cases. That is to say, the fact that claimants' lawyers lose half their cases does not mean they should be awarded twice as much on the cases they do win.

The court also rejected the notion that the judges of compensation claims should decide the fee based on a lodestar figure multiplied by a contingency risk factor. Injured workers' lawyers often complain that their hourly rate should be high because they handle cases on a contingency basis and receiving a fee is uncertain. The court appears to agree with this theory. Since injured workers lawyers do not get paid every time in each case, they contend their hours are worth more than defense lawyers' hours. However, the law does not require the judge to consider statistics on the injured worker's chances for success on appeal.

Also, remember that carriers owe interest on fees not paid timely. Frequently, a long time passes from the date the appellate court holds the lawyer is entitled to a fee and the date the judge makes the award. In one case, the lawyer argued that interest should begin to run from the date the court holds the lawyer is entitled to a fee. The First District Court of Appeal disagreed and held, as it has several times, that interest on an award of appellate lawyers' fees is payable as of the date the judge decides the fee amount and makes the award [*see* Spaulding v. Albertson's, Inc. 610 So. 2d 721, 724 (Fla. 1st DCA 1992); *see also* ch. 23, § 23.01, for a complete discussion of interest on fees].

[8] JCC's Jurisdiction During Appeal

Judges of compensation claims retain jurisdiction to decide issues that have not been adjudicated and are not the subject of a pending appeal [*see* Fla. R. App. P. 9.180(c)(1) (1997)]. Therefore, if basic compensability of a case is pending appeal, the judge of compensation claims has no jurisdiction to award benefits. For example, the carrier denied Leta Collier's claim in its entirety. Following a hearing, the JCC held that the claim was compensable. The carrier filed an appeal. While the appeal was pending, Collier requested an emergency hearing after which the JCC awarded psychiatric care. The judge, however, had no authority to make this award because the issue of compensability had been adjudicated and was the subject of a pending appeal [*see* CRIMS/PCA Solutions v. Collier, 700 So. 2d 1231, 1232 (Fla. 1st DCA 1997)].

[9] Trial Record Lost—Trial de Novo

What happens if the notes or tapes of the final hearing have been misplaced and constructing a transcript is not possible? In such a case the appellant may prepare a statement of the evidence or proceedings from the best available means including recollection. The appellee may file objections or proposed amendments. Once done and agreed, the stipulated statement is submitted to the judge of compensation claims for approval. If approved, the appeal may go forward [*see* Fla. R. App. P. 9.200(b)(4); *see also* Bay Medical Center v. Haynes, 667 So. 2d 216, 217 (Fla 1st DCA 1995)]. If, however, the parties and the judge of compensation claims certify to the court that they are unable to prepare a transcript, the judge of compensation claims must hold a trial de novo [*see*

Brascom v. General Furniture Leasing, 717 So. 2d 615 (Fla. 1st DCA 1998)].

When recording equipment problems preclude a complete transcript of a final hearing resulting in an inability to develop a statement of the evidence for appeal, the remedy is to vacate the final order and hold a hearing de novo [Orange County Sch. Bd. v. Shoemaker, 782 So. 2d 529 (Fla. 1st DCA 2001)].

CHAPTER 23

LAWYERS AND THEIR FEES

Guide to Claims

SYNOPSIS

Guide to Claims

§ 23.01 Overview of Attorney's Fees

> *The business of the advocate, simply stated,*
> *is to win if possible without violating the law.*
> Marvin Frankel, Judge, U.S. District Court.
> 1975

[1] Who Must Pay Attorney's Fees

Florida's workers' compensation system is self-executing. As such, philosophically speaking, the system requires that injured workers pay their own lawyers. The statute provides that "[an injured worker] shall be responsible for the payment of his own attorney's fees . . ." [§ 440.34(3), Fla. Stat. (7/1/97)]. However, there are exceptions to this "injured worker pay" system, which exceptions are discussed throughout this chapter.

For a general discussion of attorney's fees, see LARSON'S WORKERS' COMPENSATION, DESK EDITION, Ch. 133 (Matthew Bender).

[2] Carrier-Paid Costs

[a] When Injured Worker Prevails

Despite whether the law entitles injured workers to carrier-paid attorney's fees, the carrier must pay the injured worker's costs if the injured worker [§ 440.34(3), Fla. Stat. (7/1/97)]:

> . . . should prevail in any proceedings before a judge of compensation claims, or court, there shall be taxed against the employer [or the carrier] the reasonable costs of such proceedings, not to include the attorney's fees of the [injured worker].

[b] Taxable Costs

Costs include all the legitimate expenses of prosecuting a claim. These include expenses such as court reporters' fees, deposition transcript costs, filing fees, and so forth. Recoverable costs include the fees of expert witnesses, but only if the judge accepts their testimony as admissible evidence. In one case, the judge refused to award expert witness fees to the injured worker. Witnesses included a registered nurse and a rehabilitation specialist. The judge allowed their testimony, but rejected the claim for their fees because he did not rely on their testimony in making his decision. The First District Court of

Appeal disagreed with the judge, stating that when the trial judge receives expert testimony as admissible, and the testimony is used for an issue on which the injured worker prevails, the witnesses' fees should be taxed as costs, despite whether the JCC relies upon the testimony [*see* Raska v. Glasgow Contracting Co., 588 So. 2d 307, 308 (Fla. 1st DCA 1991)].

Under the Statewide Uniform Guidelines for Taxation of Costs in Civil Actions, civil filing fees are not assessable as costs against the non-prevailing party. Under the Guidelines, mailing costs are considered office expenses and are not recoverable as taxable costs to the prevailing party [*see, e.g.*, Seminole County v. Chandrinos, 816 So. 2d 1241, 1246 (Fla. 5th DCA 2002); In re Estate of Williams, 771 So. 2d 7, 8 (Fla. 2d DCA 2000); Dep't of Transp. v. Skidmore, 720 So. 2d 1125, 1130 (Fla. 4th DCA 1998)].

The Guidelines, however, do not apply to workers' compensation. The court found that, although no provision under chapter 440 explicitly approves the taxing as costs of pleadings required to be served by certified mail, § 440.34(3), Fla. Stat., permits a prevailing claimant to tax against the employer "the reasonable costs of such proceedings." The court could not conceive it to be the legislative intent that an injured worker who successfully prosecutes a claim against his or her employer should not be made whole for all costs necessary to maintain the claim. Any conclusion to the contrary would obfuscate the expressed purpose to ensure the prompt delivery of benefits to the injured worker and to create an efficient and self-executing system. It would ignore as well the fundamental purpose of the workers' compensation law, which is that the cost of employment injuries should be placed on the industry served, rather than on society.

The court, therefore, concluded that the legislative refusal to tax certain expenses as costs to successful litigants in the civil arena has no materiality whatsoever to the question of their taxation in workers' compensation proceedings. The court observed that Florida's workers' compensation law has long been imbued with its own unique policy considerations that are entirely unlike those in any other legal setting [*see* Morris v. Dollar Tree Store, 869 So. 2d 704 (Fla. 1st DCA 2004)].

[c] Only Relevant Costs Taxable

To be taxable, costs must be relevant. In workers' compensation law, "relevant" also means "necessary." In a 1993 decision, the court applied the relevancy test. Here, the injured worker hired a rehabilitation counselor as an expert witness to support his claim for various services. The judge of compensation claims accepted this testimony and apparently relied on it because the judge ordered the carrier to pay the expert's bill. On appeal, the First District Court of Appeal reversed. The court held the testimony was unnecessary—and the costs not recoverable—because the judge could have awarded benefits based on the testimony of the injured worker and the physicians alone [*see* Southern Industries v. Chumney, 613 So. 2d 74, 78 (Fla. 1st DCA 1993)].

[d] Medical Expert's Services Must Be Medically Necessary

Despite the relevancy of a cost, judges cannot award the costs of medical experts' services if the services do not qualify as medical benefits. Life care planning costs provide a good example. Life care planning experts are not usually licensed physicians. To qualify as medical service providers, they must work under the direction of a physician. Courts cannot order carriers to pay for services by non-medical providers [*see* Frederick Electronics v. Pettijohn, 619 So. 2d 14, 16 (Fla. 1st DCA 1993)].

[e] Unnecessary Testimony

Under certain circumstances the costs that an expert incurs in preparing testimony may be taxed, even though the testimony proves unnecessary because a party took a voluntary dismissal. If the carrier decides to pay benefits claimed before trial, the JCC can order the carrier to pay the injured worker's costs incurred in preparing for trial. This is, of course, a matter left to the judge of compensation claims to decide [*see* Coastal Petroleum Co. v. Mobil Oil Corp., 583 So. 2d 1022, 1025 (Fla. 1991)].

All costs, however, are not automatically included. For example, Dr. Gary Weiss canceled several patients' appointments in anticipation of testifying at a workers' compensation hearing. The day before the hearing, the carrier agreed to pay the benefits claimed and the petition was voluntarily dismissed and the hearing canceled. Besides his regular fee for having completed an examination of the injured worker, Dr. Weiss sought to recover fees lost because of the canceled appointments. The court agreed he was entitled to his fee for the IME, but rejected the remainder of the doctor's costs. Revenue lost by an expert witness because his testimony proved unnecessary cannot be taxed as costs [*see* Wuesthoff Memorial Hospital v. Tapia, 687 So. 2d 1370, 1371 (Fla. 1st DCA 1997)].

PRACTICE POINT: Once a claimant elects to seek remedies through the Florida Workers' Compensation Insurance Guaranty Association (FWCIGA), he or she is not entitled to recover attorney fees, penalties, or interest from either the employer or from FWCIGA [*see* § 631.929, Fla. Stat. (1997); Shear Homes, Inc. v. Sheppard, 764 So. 2d 705, 707 (Fla. 1st DCA 2000)].

SPECIAL ALERT: Effective with accidents occurring on or after October 1, 2003, the Act provides that whoever prevails in a proceeding before a judge of compensation claims is responsible for paying the prevailing party's costs. Put another way, if the claimant files a Petition for Benefits and loses, he or she must pay the carrier's costs. Note that "costs" do not include attorney fees [§ 440.34(3), Fla. Stat. (10/1/2003)].

[3] Interest on Fees

[a] When Interest Begins to Run

Despite the category under which a judge awards a fee, interest on the amount awarded begins to run from the time the judge enters an order awarding a fee. An attorney's fee award is a "judgment" within the meaning of § 55.03, Fla. Stat. Originally, the workers' compensation act did not specifically provide for interest on attorney's fees. The Florida Supreme Court, however, held that interest awards are proper [*see* Stone v. Jeffres, 208 So.

2d 827, 829 (Fla. 1968)]. The legislature has since corrected that omission, and the statutory rate for workers' compensation purposes is 12 percent per year [§ 440.20(8), Fla. Stat. (7/1/97)].

An award of benefits (including attorney's fees) carries with it an award of interest by operation of law. This means that carriers owe interest on a late payment despite whether the judge's order includes a statement specifically awarding interest [Thompson v. Dept. of Health & Rehab. Serv., 618 So. 2d 333, 335 (Fla. 5th DCA 1993), *rev. denied,* 626 So. 2d 204 (Fla. 1993)].

Guide to Claims

[b] Prejudgment Interest

Sometimes, the judges will enter an order finding that the attorney is entitled to a fee, but reserve jurisdiction to decide the amount later. No legal basis exits to award prejudgment interest for the time between the initial order of entitlement and the order awarding a specific amount. Since the First District Court of Appeal was uncertain whether its decision conflicted with the Supreme Court's decision in *Quality Engineered Inst. v. Higley South,* 670 So. 2d 929, 930–931 (Fla. 1996), it certified the question to the high court [*see* Wells Fargo Armored Services v. Lee, 692 So. 2d 284, 287 (Fla. 1st DCA 1997); *see also* Riviera Beach v. Deliso, 713 So.2d 426, 427–428 (Fla. 1st DCA 1997)]. In *Quality,* the Supreme Court approved an award of prejudgment interest. *Quality* though, was not a workers' compensation case, but a matter pertaining to a fee arising from a contract.

In 1998, the Florida Supreme Court affirmed the District Court of Appeal, and held that an attorney's fee cannot be paid until it is approved as reasonable by a judge of compensation claims or a court. Logically then, there is no entitlement to interest on attorney's fees in a workers' compensation case until a judge of compensation claims has approved the amount of the fee. Therefore, interest cannot begin to accrue until the JCC actually determines the fee amount [*see* Lee v. Wells Fargo Armored Services, 707 So. 2d 700, 702 (Fla. 1998); *see also* Mims v. Lipton Toyota, Inc., 709 So. 2d 106 (Fla. 1998) (Supreme Court reached the same holding)].

In 2001, the 3d DCA reconfirmed that there is no entitlement to prejudgment interest until the amount of the fee has been approved by the judge of compensation claims [*see* Public Health Trust/Jacksonville Mem'l Hosp. v. Spencer, 826 So. 2d 995, 996 (Fla. 3d DCA 2001)].

[c] Interest on Appellate Fees

Usually, carriers do not owe interest on a fee award reversed on appeal with one exception. If a fee award is reversed and then increased on remand, interest continues to accrue. This is especially true if no one argued against entitlement to a fee in the first place. For example, the judge of compensation claims awarded Wille Rolle an attorney's fee of $210,000. On appeal the court reversed and sent the case back to the judge to recalculate the fee. The judge did so, and this time awarded $341,250. The court held that the carrier must pay interest on the original $210,000 award [*see* Metropolitan Dade County v. Rolle, 678 So. 2d 904, 905–906 (Fla. 1st DCA 1996)].

Carriers can protect themselves from this added cost in either of two ways. During the pendency of the appeal the carrier can (1) make an unconditional tender of the full amount due on the judgment, or (2) place the funds in the court's registry [*see* Devolder v. Sandage, 575 So. 2d 312, 314 (Fla. 2d DCA 1991)].

§ 23.02 Fees on Controverted Claims

[1] The Rule

An injured worker is entitled to recover a reasonable attorney's fee from a carrier or employer in a proceeding in which the employer or carrier denies that an accident occurred for which compensation benefits are payable, and the injured worker prevails on the issue of compensability [§ 440.34, Fla. Stat. (7/1/97)].

Except for claims involving medical benefits only [*see* § 23.03[4], *below*], a claimant is not entitled to an attorney's fee award, however, even if the carrier denies the claim so long as the carrier subsequently pays the claim within 14 days after the claimant files a petition for benefits. This is true even if the notice of denial is issued after the claimant files a request for assistance with the division. The request for assistance procedure is part of the informal dispute resolution process. § 440.191(2)(d), Fla. Stat. exempts employers and carriers from liability for attorney's fees for services rendered in connection with the Ombudsman's informal dispute resolution process. Neither the filing of a request for assistance, nor the denial of the request, entitles the judge of compensation claims to award attorney's fees. There must be a successful prosecution of a claim. The judge of compensation claims' jurisdiction in an informal dispute resolution process is limited to proceedings after the filing of a petition for benefits. A petition for benefits, not a request for assistance, invokes the judge's jurisdiction [*see* Fla. P. Workers' Comp. P. 4.020(u), (y)]. If the carrier denies a claim during the RFA process, but pays the benefits within 14 days after the claimant files a petition for benefits, the claim was never controverted [*see* Integrated Health Services v. Hyde, 721 So. 2d 1217, 1218 (Fla. 1st DCA 1998)].

The most basic foundation for an award of attorney fees is that the claimant prevailed on the issue of compensability. Awarding fees is proper, even if the finding of compensability does not result in an award of benefits.

For example, the claimant returned to work for a new employer, where she suffered a second accident in which she reinjured her knee. The carrier denied all further benefits, arguing that the need for medical care and any disability were the result of the new accident alone. The judge of compensation claims disagreed, holding that the original injury was the major contributing cause of the claimant's knee condition. Entitlement to indemnity benefits was not an issue at the final hearing. The only issue was the claimant's entitlement to ongoing physical therapy. Because the claim had been denied, the claimant did not obtain professional medical care and, instead, treated herself with home remedies. By the time of the hearing, the claimant was well, and no longer needed care, so no actual benefits were awarded. Despite the lack of an award of benefits, the judge of compensation claims awarded an attorney's fee, based on the claimant's having prevailed on the issue of basic compensability [Florida Hospital v. Taylor, 784 So. 2d 601, 602 (Fla. 1st DCA 2001)].

On appeal, the court noted that the carrier transformed what would otherwise have been straightforward litigation over the need for medical benefits into a much more expansive proceeding. Before the carrier raised compensability as a threshold issue, the only question before the judge of compensation claims was the medical necessity of the medical benefits sought by the claimant. Contesting compensability significantly increased the complexity of the case. Because the carrier then lost on the issue of compensability, the judge of compensation claims was correct in awarding attorney's fees under § 440.34(3)(c), Fla. Stat. (1997) [*see* Florida Hospital v. Taylor, 784 So. 2d 601, 603–604 (Fla. 1st DCA 2001)].

[2] Partial Denials

If the carrier denies an entire claim on the issue of compensability and does not prevail at a trial, the carrier will owe the injured worker's attorney's fees and costs. This applies beyond cases in which the carrier has denied entitlement to all benefits. It also applies if the carrier denies entitlement to benefits resulting from a second injury, such as a subsequent heart attack. Put another way, the law entitles the injured worker to carrier-paid attorney's fees if the carrier unsuccessfully denies any identifiable specific injury. This is true though the carrier may have accepted compensability of the underlying claim. If the carrier accepts the fact of a compensable injury, but unsuccessfully denies compensability of other injuries due to an alleged lack of causal relationship, the court can award fees [Occidental Chemical Co. v. Neely, 490 So. 2d 59 (Fla. 1st DCA 1985)].

For example, the carrier accepted compensability of Kennedy Walker's initial foot injury. The carrier, however, specifically denied any injury by way of the accident's acceleration of a preexisting spinal cyst that resulted in paraplegia. The court concluded that the carrier "therefore denied that the claimant's subsequent paraplegia was causally related to the accident." In essence, said the court, the carrier denied the occurrence of an injury for which compensation is payable and, thus, the injured worker was entitled to attorney's fees [*see* Publix Supermarkets, Inc. v. Walker, 576 So. 2d 904, 905 (Fla. 1st DCA 1991)].

[3] Incidental Benefits

Carriers do not owe attorney's fees under § 440.34, Fla. Stat., however, when the litigation issue concerns the average weekly wage or another incidental benefit. This assumes, of course, that the carrier does not deny that an injury occurred for which benefits are payable. It also assumes that the carrier did not force the injured worker to prove the injury and entitlement to compensation [*see* Hillsborough County School Bd. v. Hilburn, 472 So. 2d 1309, 1310–1312 (Fla. 1st DCA 1985)].

[4] Paying One of Two Alternative Claims May Preclude Award of Fees

Frequently, an injured worker will file a petition, claiming permanent total disability benefits, or in the alternative, temporary total disability benefits. The Act, § 440.192(8), Fla. Stat. does not require the carrier to file a notice of denial when it pays one of two alternative claims for indemnity benefits made in a single petition. If the carrier agrees, for example, to pay temporary total disability benefits on the basis that the injured worker has not reached maximum medical improvement, it has no obligation to formally deny the request for permanent total disability benefits. If the carrier later timely accepts the worker as permanently and totally disabled, after learning of the date of maximum medical improvement, an award of an attorney's fee would be improper based on the lack of a successful prosecution of the case as required by § 440.34(3)(b), Fla. Stat. (1995) [*see* Volusia County Fire Services v. Eaby, 725 So. 2d 415, 417 (Fla. 1st DCA 1999)].

§ 23.03 Fees on Medical Only Cases

[1] The Rule

The law entitles an injured worker to attorney's fees paid by the carrier if "she or he successfully asserts a claim for medical benefits only, if the [injured worker] has not filed or is not entitled to file at such time a claim for disability, permanent impairment, wage-loss, or death benefits, arising out of the same accident" [§ 440.34(3)(a), Fla. Stat. (7/1/97)].

[2] Terminology Explained

The wording of § 440.34(3)(a), Fla. Stat. is vague. The statute does not apply if injured workers are "entitled" to file a claim for disability benefits "at the time" they file a claim for medical benefits. This raises two questions.

First, what does "at the time" mean? Is it at the time the injured worker files the claim, or is it at the time of the trial? The phrase "at the time" means when the injured worker files the claim. For claims filed up to December 31, 1993, "filed" means filed with the Division. For claims or petitions for benefits filed on or after January 1, 1994, "filed" means filed with the carrier by certified mail. § 440.34(3)(a), Fla. Stat. applies only if the injured worker has not filed, or is not entitled to file, a claim for any disability benefits.

Second, what does the phrase "entitled to file" mean? This means that, at the time the injured worker files the claim with the Division (or the carrier after January 1, 1994), there is no matter in controversy other than medical benefits. § 440.34(3)(a), Fla. Stat. applies even if the carrier is paying indemnity benefits. It also applies if the injured worker files the medical claim after filing and withdrawing a claim for disability benefits.

Therefore, a claim is a "claim for medical benefits only" if, at the time the injured worker files the claim, it is unconnected with and in isolation from other claims [*see* Gunn's Quality Glass & Mirrors v. Strode, 425 So. 2d 73, 75–76 (Fla. 1st DCA 1982)].

[3] Proof of Status Required

To prevail under § 440.34(3)(a), Fla. Stat., injured workers must prove that when they filed a claim for medical benefits, they were not entitled to file a claim, for example, for wage loss benefits. The statute specifically provides that a fee award under this section is proper only when the injured worker has not filed and is not entitled to file a claim for disability, permanent impairment, wage loss, or death benefits. Thus, a fee award under this section is proper only if the evidence shows that the worker was not entitled to file a claim for disability or death benefits arising out of the same accident [*see* City of Lakeland v. Loveland, 647 So. 2d 997, 998 (Fla. 1st DCA 1994)].

[4] When Fees Are Due

As a general rule, carriers will owe a fee if the injured worker prevails on the following issues: (1) when the medical provider that the carrier is offering is a different specialty than the one requested; (2) when the provider is too far away from the injured worker; (3) when offered providers report they have nothing more to offer the injured worker in the way of treatment; (4) when the carrier denies requests for evaluation and treatment, medical devices, such as wheel chairs, attendant care, and so on. If the carrier does not promptly pay or provide medical benefits requested, and a judge later decides that the carrier should have done so, the carrier will owe a fee.

When a specific request for reasonable and necessary medical care is made, the carrier has an obligation to provide the benefits within a reasonable time, whether or not a petition for medical benefits is ever filed. Therefore, authorizing medical benefits within 14 days of the filing of a petition for medical benefits only, does not preclude an award of attorney's fees [*see* Allen v. Tyrone Square 6 AMC Theaters, 731 So. 2d 699, 700–701 (Fla. 1st DCA 1999)].

What is a "reasonable time?" A carrier must respond to a request for authorization, by telephone or in writing, by the close of the third business day after receiving the request [*see* § 440.13(3)(d), Fla. Stat.]. An exception to this rule applies to claims for specialist consultations, surgical operations, physiotherapeutic or occupational therapy procedures, X-ray examinations, or special diagnostic laboratory tests that cost more than $1,000. For these procedures, the carrier has 10 days to respond to a written request [*see* § 440.13(3)(i), Fla. Stat].

Effective October 1, 2003, the Legislature amended the section to provide that the time limitation to respond to a request for authorization applies only to requests for authorization from an authorized health care provider. Additionally, the section does not apply if the requested treatment is not in accordance with practice parameters and protocols. It also does not apply if the judge of compensation claims determines that the treatment is not medically necessary or is not in accordance with required practice parameters and protocols [*see* § 440.13(3)(i), Fla. Stat. (10/1/2003)].

Also note that a claimant may prevail on a medical-benefits petition if he or she succeeds in causing the carrier to retract its *intention* to transfer care, regardless of the timing of the de-authorization. For example, in *Mylock v. Champion Int'l* [906 So. 2d 363 (Fla. 1st DCA 2005)], the employer/carrier forwarded a letter to the claimant's counsel informing him that, pursuant to § 440.13(2)(d), Fla. Stat., it was transferring the claimant's care from his authorized physician, Dr. Mangieri, to that of his "replacement physician," Dr. Spruill, because an independent medical examination disclosed that the claimant was not making appropriate progress under Dr. Mangieri. The letter also scheduled an appointment with Dr. Spruill. The claimant filed a petition for benefits, seeking the continued authorization of Dr. Mangieri. Thereafter, the employer/carrier replied by letter that it did not intend to de-authorize Dr. Mangieri, who remained claimant's physician. Four days thereafter, the carrier filed a formal reply to the petition, again referring to its rights under § 440.13(2)(d), Fla. Stat., to transfer the care of an injured employee to a health-care provider, if the IME confirmed that the employee was not making adequate progress. The next event occurred when a mediation conference was held, and a report thereafter filed, agreeing that all pending issues had been resolved, including Dr. Mangieri's authorization, and a medical bill paid. The court found that any uncertainty as to what the carrier may have intended by its earlier letters to the claimant's attorney was clarified by its actions, continuing through the mediation. Because the claimant prevailed on his medical benefits claim, he was entitled to the payment of a fee at the carrier's expense. Rather than proceeding to an evidentiary hearing, the parties participated in mediation, and the carrier thereafter agreed to accept the claim. While this acceptance avoided the necessity of a merits hearing, the attorney's efforts in obtaining the benefits constituted a successful prosecution of the claim for purposes of an attorney's fee award.

[5] Fees Based on Opposition to Independent Medical Examination

The Act, § 440.13(5)(f), Fla. Stat., provides as follows:

> Attorneys' fees incurred by an injured employee in connection with delay of or opposition to an independent medical examination, including, but not limited to, motions for protective orders, are not recoverable under this chapter.

The court has held that this section precludes an attorney's fee only when the injured employee opposes and delays the carrier's effort to obtain an independent medical examination. Conversely, when the carrier opposes and delays an injured employee's effort to obtain an independent medical examination, and the employee incurs attorney's fees because of the carrier's opposition, the injured employee is entitled to recovery of an attorney's fee. In such a case, the carrier will have forced the claimant to incur attorney's fees in litigation of the independent medical examination issue. Thus, the statutory provision may not be construed to preclude an award of a fee to the claimant's attorney [*see* Richardson v. Showell Farms, 734 So. 2d 590, 593 (Fla. 1st DCA 1999)].

[6] Fees Based on Emergency Hearings

Usually, a judge of compensation claims may not hold a hearing until the conclusion of the informal dispute resolution process and the filing of a proper Petition for Benefits. Emergency hearings are an exception to that rule. For example, the judge of compensation claims awarded medical treatment following an emergency conference although an RFA and PFB had not been filed. The court held that the carrier was responsible for attorney's fees because it refused to authorize the requested care even after the Motion for Emergency Conference was filed [*see* Smurfit-Stone Container Corp v. Taylor, 786 So. 2d 1207, 1208 (Fla. 1st DCA 2001)].

§ 23.04 Fees on Petitions for Modification

Either party may petition for a change in an order of a judge of compensation claims [*see* ch. 22, § 22.10, for a discussion on modification of orders]. The parties must base such a petition on either of two issues: the first is a change in the injured worker's condition; the second is that the judge made a mistake in deciding the facts [§ 440.28, Fla. Stat. (1/1/94); Crews v. Sanderlin and Associates, 290 So. 2d 487, 491 (Fla. 1974)]. Usually, if the injured worker initiates the petition and wins, the carrier will owe a fee. If the carrier initiates the petition and loses, it will owe a fee.

§ 23.05 Fees for Appeals

[1] The Rule

If the injured worker appeals the order of a judge of compensation claims, the court can award a fee in any amount, even if the injured worker loses the appeal. The statute provides that "[i]f any proceedings are had for review of any claim, award, or compensation order before any court, the court may award the injured employee or dependent an attorney's fee to be paid by the employer or carrier, *in its discretion,* which shall be paid as the court may direct" [§ 440.34(5), Fla. Stat. (7/1/97) (emphasis added)].

[2] Application of Rule

This general rule applies to any proceeding for review by the Court of Appeal or by the Supreme Court. Even if the court did not award fees for the initial dispute, it may award fees for the appeal itself. Because the law allows fee awards "in the discretion of the reviewing body," it is not even necessary that the injured worker win. Such a result is rare, but it does happen. In one case, for example, the court said, "While we have seldom have awarded fees when the claimant did not prevail, there is no limitation as such in the statute." Here, the carrier made no objection or challenge to the injured worker's motion for award of attorney's fees. The court concluded that the carrier must approve of such an award or it would have objected if it believed it did not owe a fee [*see* City of Miami v. Burnett, 596 So. 2d 478, 479 (Fla. 1st DCA 1992)].

The court can and will award fees, even when the injured worker loses, in "important" cases and where the court's decision will serve as precedent for resolving pending cases. If the carrier loses at the trial level, at the appellate level, and again before the Florida Supreme Court, the carrier is responsible for all the injured worker's attorney's fees at each level. This, of course, is besides the injured worker's costs and interest on the benefits and fees originally awarded. On top of all this, the carrier will also owe its own attorney's fees and costs. This is a significant factor to weigh in considering an appeal in the first place.

[3] Procedure for Review of Appellate Fee Award

If a party is dissatisfied with the appellate fee award, the correct procedure is to file a Motion for Review [*see* Fla. R. App. P. 9.180(i)(4); Fla. R. App. P. 9.400]. For example, the claimant prevailed at trial and again on appeal. The court granted the claimant's motion for appellate attorney's fees and remanded the case to the judge of compensation claims to determine the amount. The judge awarded a fee of $10,000. The attorney, apparently, was dissatisfied with that and filed another appeal to which the court assigned a new case number. The court held that this was improper procedure under Fla. R. App. P. 9.180(i)(4) and Fla. R. App. P. 9.400. Those rules require that a request for review of an order on appellate attorney's fees be made by Motion for Review. The court declined to treat the claimant's Notice of Appeal as a Motion for Review and dismissed the appeal on the basis that the court lacked jurisdiction [*see* Browning v. New Hope South, 785 So. 2d 732, 733 (Fla. 1st DCA 2001)].

A party seeking attorney's fees in an appellate court must specify the particular contractual, statutory, or other substantive basis for an award of fees on appeal. Although here the court affirmed an award of permanent total benefits in all respects, the court denied the claimant's request for appellate attorney's fees, because the motion for fees was substantively deficient. The motion cited Fla. R. Workers' Comp. P. 4.265, which was deleted in 1997. The motion further cited "chapter 440," without specifying the particular statutory section and subsection forming the basis for an award of fees in this case. Because the motion failed to comply with the requirement to state the particular basis for the requested award, it was denied [*see* Home Depot v. Ferreira, 827 So. 2d 371 (Fla. 1st DCA 2002)].

> *[Appeal:] In law, to put the dice into the box for another throw.*
> *Ambrose Bierce*
> *The Devil's Dictionary, 1906*

§ 23.06 Fees in Rule Nisi Proceedings

[1] The Rule

Carriers must comply with the judge of compensation claims' order within seven days after the order becomes final. If not, the injured worker may petition the circuit court to issue a writ of execution or other process to enforce the judge's order [§ 440.24, Fla. Stat.]. The law entitles injured workers to attorney's fees if they win in a rule nisi proceeding [§ 440.34(3)(d), Fla. Stat. (7/1/97)].

[2] Rule Nisi Defined

Rule nisi is a procedure used by one party (usually the injured worker in workers' compensation cases) to petition the circuit court to order the other party (usually the carrier) to show cause why it has not complied with the order of a judge of compensation claims. What happens if the carrier cannot show cause? The court will enter an order that makes the JCC's order absolute and requires the carrier's compliance. If the carrier still fails to obey, it will face serious punitive action by the court, including a charge of contempt. If the injured worker can show the carrier failed to obey the JCC's order, the carrier must pay the injured worker's attorney's fees for the proceeding. Even worse, the Act requires the Department of Insurance to suspend the carrier's or self-insurer's license until it complies with the court's order. Additionally, the JCC is authorized to strike the carrier's defenses in the underlying action. Injured workers, on the other hand, who do not comply with a court's order, risk having their benefits suspended and claims dismissed [§ 440.24, Fla. Stat. (1991)].

[3] Misunderstanding Is No Excuse

Sometimes the noncompliance of a party may be innocent because the judge's order is vague. However, this is not an acceptable excuse or defense. A perceived lack of clarity in the compensation order is not a proper basis for denial of a rule nisi [*see* Lidholm v. Aetna Life & Cas., 569 So. 2d 905, 906 (Fla. 2d DCA 1990)].

[4] Unilateral Modification of Order Prohibited

Once a judge issues an order, the carrier cannot unilaterally modify the order. If it does, the carrier may find itself defending a rule nisi proceeding. For example, the judge of compensation claims awarded benefits in a controverted case. The judge specifically ordered the carrier to pay temporary total disability benefits until the injured worker reached maximum medical improvement. Sometime later, the carrier unilaterally decided the injured worker had reached maximum medical improvement. Without the judge's approval, the carrier stopped temporary total disability benefits. The injured worker did not agree that he had reached maximum medical improvement and sought a rule nisi proceeding in circuit court. The circuit court held that if a JCC's order is still viable, the carrier may not unilaterally cease compliance, unless the parties agree. On appeal, the First District Court of Appeal agreed with the lower court. The First District Court of Appeal instructed the circuit court to issue the rule nisi and require compliance until the judge of compensation claims modifies or cancels the order [*see* Pierce v. Aetna Ins. Co., 519 So. 2d 754, 755–756 (Fla. 4th DCA 1988)].

An exception to this general rule arises in the case of a set-off for Social Security benefits. The court has held that a carrier is entitled to unilaterally calculate the set-off following the order of a judge of compensation claims [*see* Merritt v. Promo Graphics, Inc., 691 So. 2d 632, 634 (Fla. 5th DCA 1997)]. Similarly, the 1st DCA has held that the section permitting a set-off for unemployment compensation, like the section allowing a set-off for Social Security benefits, is self executing, giving rise to a continuing right and responsibility on the part of carriers to compute the correct set-off at the time a payment of compensation is due [*see* Borden, Inc. v. Butler, 377 So. 2d 795 (Fla. 1st DCA 1979)].

[5] Authority of Circuit Court

The law limits the authority of the circuit court in a rule nisi proceeding to deciding whether the JCC's workers' compensation order is in effect. If the JCC's order is in effect, the court can enforce the order. The circuit court, however, cannot decide the merits of the order itself. Injured workers cannot use a rule nisi proceeding to resolve factual disputes. Besides awarding attorney's fees, the circuit court can award the appropriate value of services or benefits the JCC ordered the carrier to provide [*see* Alvarez v. Kendall Associates, 590 So. 2d 518, 519–520 (Fla. 3d DCA 1991); Benedict v. Executive Risk Consultants, 616 So. 2d 525, 526 (Fla. 4th DCA 1993)].

When considering a request for rule nisi relief, the circuit court is limited to a two-prong inquiry: (1) Whether there is a final order in full force and effect, and (2) whether there has been a default under that order. Importantly, the procedure is not to be used to determine the merits of the underlying compensation order or to resolve factual disputes between the parties [*see* Merritt v. Promo Graphics, Inc., 691 So. 2d 632, 634 (Fla. 5th DCA 1997)].

[6] Recovering Interest on Delayed Benefits

Injured workers can use a rule nisi proceeding to recover interest on the delayed benefits. Any award carries interest by operation of law. This means every award, including attorney's fees, automatically includes interest even though the judge of compensation did not specifically award interest. Indeed, the court implicitly approved the use of a rule nisi proceeding to recover such interest [*see* Mander v. Concreform Company, 212 So. 2d 631 (Fla. 1968); *see also* Thompson v. Dept. of Health & Rehab. Serv., 618 So. 2d 333, 335 (Fla. 5th DCA 1993), *rev. denied,* 626 So. 2d 204 (Fla. 1993)].

§ 23.07 Fees Based on Bad Faith: Up to October 1, 1989

[1] The Rule

For accidents occurring before October 1, 1989, carriers owe attorney's fees if the judge decides that the carrier (or the employer) handled the claim in bad faith. The judge must also find that this caused economic loss to the injured worker [*see* [5], *below*].

The legislature repealed the "bad faith" claim handling basis for awarding attorney's fees effective October 1, 1989. This is a substantive amendment; therefore, the bad faith test still applies to all accidents that occurred before the effective date.

[2] "Bad Faith" Defined

What does "bad faith" mean? The statute defines it as "conduct which amounts to fraud; malice; oppression; or willful, wanton, or reckless disregard of the rights of the injured worker" [*see* former § 440.34(3)(b), Fla. Stat.].

This statutory definition is "very strong stuff." The language describes a carrier that is deliberately trying to harm an injured worker, which is what the legislature exactly intended when it enacted this law. By 1989, however, court decisions interpreted these very plain words to mean the guilty carrier did not pay a benefit that it knew, or should have known, it owed to the injured worker under the law [*see* Hernando County Bd. of County Com'rs v. Gleaton, 449 So. 2d 935, 936 (Fla. 1st DCA 1984)].

Today, bad faith includes almost any delay in providing benefits. Bad faith also includes a carrier's failure to investigate properly an injured worker's entitlement to benefits [*see* T.J. Chastain Farms v. Kusiak, 414 So. 2d 1187, 1188 (Fla. 1st DCA 1982)]. Even late payment of medical bills is bad faith claim handling [*see* Legal Aid Services of Broward County v. Logsdon, 421 So. 2d 1, 2 (Fla. 1st DCA 1982)]. Failure to investigate and pay benefits based on a correct average weekly wage is bad faith [*see* King Motor Co. v. Parisi, 445 So. 2d 1074, 1076 (Fla. 1st DCA 1984)]. Failing to give the injured worker information and wage loss forms is also bad faith claim handling. Employers are guilty of bad faith if they fail to give the carrier accurate wage information. Employer guilt is no defense for the carrier, though, because the law imputes the employer's bad faith to the carrier [*see* Sam Rogers Enterprises v. Williams, 401 So. 2d 1388, 1391 (Fla. 1st DCA 1981)]. Stopping benefits prematurely or incorrectly is bad faith claim handling. When the court awards benefits, the carrier is guilty of bad faith if it could have found out the injured worker's entitlement with a proper investigation [*see* Celtics Mobile Home Mfg. v. Butler, 460 So. 2d 486, 488 (Fla. 1st DCA 1984)].

[3] Defending Against Claims of Bad Faith

The best defense against bad faith attorney's fees is a prompt and complete investigation. Suspending benefits based on sound evidence and a good investigation is not bad faith. For example, the carrier received a report from a physician saying the injured worker reached maximum medical improvement with no permanent impairment. Based on this, the carrier stopped benefits. Although the judge later found the injured worker did have a permanent impairment, the District Court of Appeal held the carrier acted reasonably. A carrier's reliance on the opinion of one doctor over another doctor's contradicting opinion may be reasonable [*see* Orlando Precast Products v. Ciofalo, 537 So. 2d 1043, 1046 (Fla. 1st DCA 1989)].

In another example, the carrier received a letter from the injured worker's physician saying the worker had reached maximum medical improvement two weeks earlier. To that point, all reports suggested the injured worker would have permanent physical restrictions, but that this would disable him from heavy labor only. In his MMI letter, the physician said rehabilitation would be useless because the injured worker was not motivated. For about the next five weeks, the carrier concentrated on determining whether the injured worker could be rehabilitated or if placement in sedentary employment was more appropriate. At the end of this period, the carrier concluded neither was appropriate and began paying permanent total disability benefits. The judge of compensation claims decided the carrier acted appropriately and refused to award bad faith attorney's fees. The First District Court of Appeal agreed that the carrier acted appropriately and affirmed the JCC's order [*see* Smith v. U.S. Sugar Corp., 624 So. 2d 315, 317 (Fla. 1st DCA 1993)].

In *Smith,* however, the carrier conceded bad faith in its failure to pay certain wage loss benefits timely. The court held that just because the carrier does not owe bad faith fees on one set of benefits, does not mean it does not owe them on another set.

[4] Limitations on Bad Faith Fees

Courts must limit such fees to the time the lawyer spent in securing the specific benefit. In *Smith,* the carrier was held to owe Smith's attorney's fees from the date it suspended wage loss benefits until it reinstated them. In some cases, like *Smith,* accurately separating hours spent on specific benefits may be impossible for the judge and, if so, the court may award a fee for the entire period. Additionally, the *Smith* court held the carrier owed a fee on the entire time Smith's lawyer spent in preparing for the bad faith hearing [*see* Smith v. U.S. Sugar Corp., 624 So. 2d 315, 318 (Fla. 1st DCA 1993)].

An injured worker can recover for the lawyer's time spent preparing for, traveling to, and attending a fee hearing if the time is related to proving the substantive issues of bad faith, rather than proving the fee amount [*see* Crittenden Orange Blossom Fruit v. Stone, 514 So. 2d 351, 353 (Fla. 1987)].

[5] Economic Loss

Recall that economic loss is the second element required to support a claim for bad faith attorney's fees [*see* [1], *above*]. This is often easy to prove because denied benefits are usually the issue. Not receiving benefits can obviously cause economic loss. But what about having to pay costs such as attorney's fees? In one case the judge of compensation claims awarded permanent total disability benefits to the injured worker. Five years later, the carrier filed a motion for modification, claiming it had evidence the injured worker was no longer permanently and totally disabled and no longer needed attendant care. The judge denied the motion. The injured worker then filed a claim to recover attorney's fees incurred in defending himself against the carrier's motion. At the attorney's fee hearing, the judge held the carrier acted in bad faith by filing its motion. Further, the judge held this resulted in the injured worker suffering economic loss because he was forced to hire a lawyer and incur litigation costs. The First District Court of Appeal disagreed and reversed. The court did not address the question of any bad faith action on the carrier's part because the injured worker, contrary to the JCC's order, had not suffered any economic loss. The judge of compensation claims, said the court, was wrong as a matter of law on the economic loss issue. The court said: "We have consistently held that litigation costs do not constitute 'economic loss' for purposes of the statute" [*see* Kraft Dairy Group v. Sorge, 634 So. 2d 720, 722 (Fla. 1st DCA 1994); *see also* Swift & Co.; Winter Garden Citrus v. Parrish, 438 So. 2d 472, 473–474 (Fla. 1st DCA 1983)].

Carriers still handling these old cases should ensure their claim files include a solid and well-documented basis for not providing benefits. This is a good policy to follow even on claims where bad faith is not an issue.

§ 23.08 Attorney's Fees and the 21-Day Rule: October 1, 1989, to January 1, 1994

[1] The Rule

Beginning with accidents occurring *on or after October 1, 1989,* the legislature repealed the bad faith basis for deciding an injured worker's entitlement to attorney's fees and replaced it with the so-called 21-day rule. Beginning with accidents occurring on or after January 1, 1994, the legislature repealed the 21-day rule [*see* [3][c], *below*]. Therefore, the 21-day rule applies only to accident dates between October 1, 1989, and December 31, 1993. For accidents occurring between these dates, the law provides that a carrier will owe a fee "in any case in which the employer or carrier fails or refuses to pay a claim filed with the Division that meets the requirements of s. 440.19(1)(d), Fla. Stat., on or before the 21st day after receiving notice of the claim, and the injured person has employed an attorney in the successful prosecution of his claim" [§ 440.34(3)(b), Fla. Stat. (10/1/89)].

[2] Determining Whether Proper Claim Has Been Filed

[a] Claim Defined

For accidents occurring between October 1, 1989, and December 31, 1993, the Workers' Compensation Act requires that carriers pay a claim within 21 days after receipt of such claim. For attorney's fee purposes, a claim is a Claim for Benefits—now called a Petition for Benefits—if it meets all the statutory specificity requirements and the injured worker has properly filed it with the Division of Workers' Compensation [§ 440.19, Fla. Stat.; *see* ch. 22, § 22.03[2]].

A Request for Assistance, however, is not a Petition for Benefits [*see* ch. 22, § 22.03[2]]. On the contrary, it is a procedure designed to avoid the need for lawyers and litigation. When the law mentions the term "claim" (usually concerning triggering entitlement to attorney's fees), it means filing a Petition for Benefits under § 440.192, Fla.

Stat. [*see* Wright v. Industrial Automotive, 662 So. 2d 1321, 1322–1323 (Fla. 1st DCA 1995)].

[b] Benefits Must Be Ripe, Due, and Owing

Further, to be valid, the petition must claim benefits due when the injured worker files the claim. This requirement is an important restraint on "fishing line" claims that are cast into the water and then used to justify entitlement to fees on benefits that "bite" much later. Thus, speculative fishing for future benefits is no longer a valid Petition for Benefits for attorney's fee purposes.

For example, Thomas Linehan filed a petition for permanent total disability benefits beginning September 15, 1993. The carrier denied the claim, asserting that Linehan was not totally disabled. Based on Linehan's job search evidence, the judge of compensation claims awarded benefits, but beginning on the date of the hearing, July 13, 1995. In addition, based on the 21-day rule, the judge also awarded attorney's fees. The First District Court of Appeal reversed the award of attorney's fees. Since the judge found that Linehan was not permanently and totally disabled until July 13, 1995, PTD benefits were not ripe, due, and owing on the day Linehan filed the claim as required by § 440.19(1)(e), Fla. Stat. (1991) [*see* Daytona Beach Geriatric Center v. Linehan, 673 So. 2d 548, 549–550 (Fla. 1st DCA 1996)].

[c] Requirement of Specificity for Claim Filed

Lack of specificity in preparing Petitions for Benefits has been a significant problem for years. The legislature intended the 1990 amendments to the law to cure this problem. For example, the Act now requires that a specific claim for unpaid medical charges must include the name and address of the doctor, amounts due, and specific dates of treatment in dispute.

A Petition for Benefits will meet the statutory requirements if it is specific enough to put the carrier on notice about the exact nature of the claim once the Division has acknowledged it. Beginning January 1, 1994, injured workers can meet the "notice to the carrier" requirement by sending the petition to the carrier by certified mail. Before, the Division decided specificity and carriers simply waited for a copy of the approved petition from the Division. Now, carriers must decide specificity correctly or risk exposure to liability for attorney's fees. Obviously then, we must decide specificity on a case-by-case basis [*see* ch. 22, § 22.03[2], for a discussion on specificity].

[d] Dismissing Non-Specific Claims

The law requires judges of compensation claims to dismiss petitions that do not meet the statutory requirements [§ 440.19, Fla. Stat.]. When carriers receive vague or speculative Petitions for Benefits, they should consider having their attorney file a motion to dismiss the petition. A motion granted by the judge will toll the 21-day period, giving the carrier more time to evaluate its position. The 21-day period, however, will start over if the injured worker files a corrected petition.

[e] When Presumption of Specificity Arises

Carriers should respond to a nonspecific petition with a Motion to Dismiss, because if the carrier simply denies and litigates the petition on its merits, the law will presume the claim was specific enough. Even if the initial claim fails to comply with the statutory specificity requirements, the carrier will owe a fee if it litigates the claim to resolution (i.e., trial or settlement). If the judge grants a motion to dismiss, the injured worker must refile the petition. The injured worker, however, cannot collect an attorney's fee for the time spent defending the motion to dismiss or the time spent refiling the petition to comply with the specificity requirements [*see* Straw v. Steve Moore Chevrolet, 651 So. 2d 708, 713 (Fla. 1st DCA 1995)].

[f] When Carrier Pays Benefits Within 21-Day Period

The courts have consistently held that if the carrier pays benefits claimed within the 21-day period, the carrier does not owe a fee, despite its activities before the injured worker filed the claim. In an "old" 21-day rule case, the Florida Supreme Court held that even if the carrier's refusal to pay benefits forces the employee to file a petition, the carrier may avoid paying attorney's fees by accepting the claim within 21 days [*see* Carillon Hotel v. Rodriguez, 124 So. 2d 3, 8 (Fla. 1960)]. In 1994, the District Court of Appeal held that this also applies to the "new," i.e., 1989, 21-day rule as well. Following is the court's holding [*see* National Distributing Co. v. Campbell, 632 So. 2d 647, 649 (Fla. 1st DCA 1994)]:

> Even though it may be argued that the [carrier] unjustifiably suspended claimant's benefits . . . and forced intervention by claimant's attorney in order to secure these benefits, an attorney's fee is not awardable because the [carrier] paid these benefits within 21 days of claimant's . . . claim.

[3] Starting the 21-Day Period

[a] Requirement of Actual Notice

The 21-day period begins when the carrier receives notice of a claim. In the past, a carrier was deemed to have notice of a claim when it received sufficient information to begin investigating the status of the employee's condition. The courts have receded from this view and now hold that the 21-day rule requires actual notice of the claim to start the clock [*see* Indian River County Sch. Bd. v. Baker, 695 So. 2d 898, 900 (Fla. 1st DCA 1997), *review denied,* 703 So. 2d 475 (Fla. 1997)].

In *Baker,* the judge of compensation claims awarded attorney's fees because the carrier failed to pay the claim within 21 days after receiving notice of the claim. The judge acknowledged that the claim for permanent total disability benefits was premature because Baker had not reached maximum medical improvement. The judge held that the carrier was on notice of a ripened claim when it called Baker's doctor and could have learned that Baker was at MMI, had the carrier asked the right questions. The court disagreed and determined that the operative date was instead the date that the doctor actually informed the carrier that Baker was at MMI [Indian River County Sch. Bd. v. Baker, 695 So. 2d 898, 899 (Fla. 1st DCA 1997), *review denied,* 703 So. 2d 475 (Fla. 1997)].

The 21-day period is the carrier's time to investigate the injured worker's entitlement to benefits. If the carrier does not pay claimed benefits within the 21-day period and a judge of compensation claims decides the carrier owes the claimed benefits, the carrier will owe an attorney's fee.

Under the 1994 amendments, a claimant cannot file a Petition for Benefits until having first exhausted the informal dispute resolution process outlined in § 440.191, Fla. Stat. This requirement is a procedural amendment and therefore applies to injuries occurring before 1994 [*see* FCCI Mut. Ins. Co. v. Schnupp, 697 So 2d 1234, 1238 (Fla. 1st DCA 1997)].

Although a Request for Assistance may contain all the information required to be included in a "claim," an RFA does not constitute a claim for purposes of triggering a claimant's right to attorney's fees under the 21-day rule described in § 440.34(3)(b), Fla. Stat. (Supp. 1990). Thus, apparently, only a Petition for Benefits is sufficient to place the carrier on actual notice of its obligation to make a decision about accepting a claim within 21 days [*see* Vilches v. City of Dunedin, 738 So. 2d 990, 992 (Fla. 1st DCA 1999)].

Guide to Claims

[b] Notice From Any Source

The Act provides that the carrier (or the employer) must pay or deny a claim for benefits, "within twenty-one days of receipt of the *acknowledged claim from the division*" [§ 440.19(1)(e)7, Fla. Stat. (10/1/89) (emphasis added)]. § 440.34, Fla. Stat. is the statute dealing with attorney's fees, with § 440.34(3)(b), Fla. Stat. (10/1/89) containing the 21-day rule. This subsection, however, does not mention the phrase, "*acknowledged claim from the division.*" It merely requires that injured workers file their claims with the division and that carriers owe an attorney's fee if they fail to provide benefits claimed on or before the 21st day after receiving notice of the claim.

Many attorneys, and some judges, have argued that the statute requires only notice by any means or source, including receiving a copy of the petition directly from the attorney or the employer. The court agreed with the "any source" theory, holding that the 21-day period begins the day the carrier receives a claim or petition for benefits from any source. The logic behind this conclusion is that the provisions of § 440.19, Fla. Stat. mean that the 21-day period, beginning with the receipt of an acknowledged claim from the Division, deals with penalties only. § 440.34, Fla. Stat. does not limit the application of the 21-day period to receipt of an acknowledged claim. For purposes of awarding attorney's fees, the 21-day period begins upon the carrier's actual notice of the filed claim [*see* Gunter v. Sauer, Inc., 629 So. 2d 1086, 1087 (Fla. 1st DCA 1994)].

SPECIAL ALERT: The 21-day period does not begin until the injured worker files the petition with the Division. For example, if the injured worker gives the carrier a copy of the petition on June 1 and files it with the Division on June 15, the 21 days do not begin until June 15 [*see* Ralston v. Circle K, 659 So. 2d 1380 (Fla. 1st DCA 1995)].

[c] 21-Day Rule Repealed

Almost as though anticipating the decision in *Gunter v. Sauer, Inc.*, 629 So. 2d 1086 (Fla. 1st DCA 1994) [*see* [b], *above*], the legislature repealed the 21-day rule effective

January 1, 1994. For Petitions for Benefits filed on or after January 1, 1994, the proper procedure is to send the petition to the carrier, the employer, and the Division by certified mail [§ 440.192(1), Fla. Stat. (7/1/97)].

Because the 21-day rule deals with entitlement to a fee paid by the carrier, its repeal is a substantive amendment. A fee statute affects the respective rights and responsibilities of the parties. Therefore, it is substantive, and we cannot retroactively apply substantive amendments to the statute that occur after a worker's injury. Thus, the 21-day rule still applies to accidents occurring between October 1, 1989 and December 31, 1993. This is true even if an injured worker files a Petition for Benefits relating to these dates after January 1, 1994 [*see* Kraft Dairy Group v. Sorge, 634 So. 2d 720, 721 (Fla. 1st DCA 1994)].

A new question arises about whether the time starts only upon receipt of the petition by certified mail. The certified mail requirement appears to be a procedural amendment that applies to all petitions filed on or after January 1, 1994. Remember, however, that the law requires only "actual notice" to trigger the 21-day period. This is consistent with legislative statements characterizing the Workers' Compensation Act as a self-executing system that requires quick and efficient delivery of benefits. It seems, then, that the notice by any means standard will continue to apply.

[4] Stopping the 21-Day Period

[a] Definitive Action Needed

Providing claimed benefits stops the 21-day clock. If the claim is for payment of temporary total disability, for example, mailing the check stops the clock. Requesting a check from the accounting department, or entering a payment request into a computer, does not stop the clock. Good intentions have nothing to do with avoiding attorney's fees.

Claims adjusters and defense attorneys must be careful not to allow communications problems with authorized doctors to occur while the 21-day clock is ticking. Doctors' delays in providing requested information are no excuse. Courts will likely blame the carrier, rather than the injured worker, for such delays.

[b] Effect of "Super Doc" Provision

[i] "Super Doc" Wild Card

The legislature created a wild card when it enacted the so-called "Super Doc" provision. Requesting a "Super Doc" evaluation stops the 21-day clock and does not start it again until the carrier receives the doctor's report [§ 440.13(2)(j)3.c, Fla. Stat. (10/1/89)]. This section required that the Division certify physicians in each medical specialty [§ 440.13(2)(j)3.a, Fla. Stat.]. The Division gathered its list of "Super Docs" by simply including any licensed physician who asked to be included.

[ii] "Super Doc" Repealed

The original "Super Doc" provision became effective on July 1, 1990, and no cases exist on this issue yet. This may be a moot point, however, because the legislature repealed all the "Super Doc" language, along with the 21-day rule, effective January 1, 1994. This section was replaced with a new provision that calls these physicians Expert Medical Advisors (EMAs). Whether this new class of "Super Docs" can be used to toll the 21-day rule is questionable and unresolved. No clear statutory authority exists to support the argument that requesting an EMA evaluation has any effect on entitlement to attorney's fees [*see* ch. 16, § 16.18, for a complete discussion of the EMA provision].

[c] Rescinding a Denial of Benefits

What happens if the carrier denies a claimed benefit on day 10 of the 21-day period, then reverses its position and pays the benefit on day 20? Does the carrier owe an attorney's fee? Maybe, because the pre-1979, 21-day rule cases went both ways. A carrier-paid fee is likely if the injured worker's lawyer takes some steps in reaction to the initial refusal.

[d] Interference by Injured Workers or Their Lawyers

What happens if injured workers or their lawyers do something to impede the carrier's efforts to investigate the claim properly? In such a case, it is unlikely the court will consider the 21 days to have begun to run in the first place. In a 1981 case dealing with the pre-1979, 21-day rule, the carrier wanted to depose the injured worker as part of its investigation. Because the injured worker's lawyer was on an extended vacation, the deposition was delayed far beyond the 21 days. The court held that the lawyer could not raise the original 21-day period as the basis for an attorney's fee because the lawyer prevented the carrier from conducting a proper investigation [*see* Latt Maxcy Corp. v. Mann, 393 So. 2d 1128, 1131–1132 (Fla. 1st DCA 1981)].

§ 23.09 Attorney's Fees and the 14-Day Rule: January 1, 1994, to July 1, 2002

[1] When Carrier Must Pay Attorney's Fee

Beginning with accidents occurring on or after January 1, 1994, the legislature repealed the 21-day rule [*see* § 23.08]. All the other statutory provisions for awarding attorney's fees, such as claims for medical only, modification proceedings, appeals, and rule nisi proceedings remain unchanged. In addition, the Act now provides that carriers must pay the injured worker's attorney's fee if the carrier files a notice of denial with the division and the claimant's attorney prevails on the issue of compensability [*see* § 440.34(3)(b), (c), Fla. Stat. (7/1/97)].

> **SPECIAL ALERT:** Note that the Act does not provide specific authority for awarding an attorney's fee because the carrier missed a time deadline. The court, however, has created a 14-day rule [*see* [2], *below*].

[2] 14-Day Rule

[a] Creation of Rule

Carriers must pay benefits claimed or issue a Response to Petition within 14 days after

Guide to Claims

receiving a Petition for Benefits by certified mail [§ 440.192(8), Fla. Stat. (7/1/97)]. The 14-day period begins to run on the date the carrier receives the petition [*see, e.g.*, Allen v. Tyrone Square 6 AMC Theaters, 731 So. 2d 699 (Fla. Dist. Ct. App. 1999)]. § 440.192(8), Fla. Stat., provides that "Within 14 days after receipt of a petition for benefits by certified mail, the carrier must either pay the requested benefits without prejudice to its right to deny within 120 days from receipt of the petition or file a response to petition with the Office of the Judges of Compensation Claims." What happens if the carrier misses this deadline and pays the benefits on day 15 or even day 30? Has the legislature, intentionally or inadvertently, created a 14-day rule? In a way they have because, when the carrier does nothing in response to a Petition for Benefits either before or after this statutory amendment, the carrier has constructively denied all benefits claimed in the petition. The basis for this rule lies with a 1981 case, which held that an actual denial is not necessarily required to entitle the claimant to an award of attorney's fees [*see* Dolphin Tire Co. v. Ellison, 402 So. 2d 36, 37 (Fla. 1st DCA 1981); *see also* [c], *below*]. Many people, though, argued that *Dolphin Tire* would not apply after 1994 because the legislature enacted law, which states: "A carrier that does not deny compensability in accordance with § 440.20(4) is deemed to have accepted the employee's injuries as compensable" [§ 440.192(8), Fla. Stat. (7/1/97)]. For discussion of § 440.20(4), Fla. Stat., see [b], *below.*

[b] Provisional Acceptance: 120-Day Rule

If the carrier is unsure of its responsibility to provide benefits, it may begin benefits provisionally without admitting liability and while continuing to investigate [§ 440.20(4), Fla. Stat. (7/1/97)]. Within 120 days after beginning benefits, the carrier must admit liability or deny the claim [*see* ch. 22, § 22.03[2], for further discussion of the 120-day rule].

A provisional acceptance requires that the carrier give the injured worker written notice that compensability of the injuries is uncertain, but that the carrier will provide benefits anyway while continuing its investigation. The notice must state that the carrier will inform the injured worker of its final decision within 120 days. If the carrier does not deny the claim within the 120-day period, it waives its right ever to do so, with one exception. The exception arises if the carrier can show that it could not have discovered material facts about compensability through reasonable investigation during the 120-day period [*see* § 440 20(4), Fla. Stat. (7/1/97)].

[c] Effect of Missing 14-Day Deadline

Does simply being late in paying benefits create an automatic entitlement to an attorney's fee as it does under the 21-day rule [*see* § 23.08]? In *Howard*, the judge of compensation claims held that repeal of the 21-day rule was a procedural amendment and that now, a new 14-day rule applied. The First District Court of Appeal disagreed with the judge on both counts. The 1994 statute is not only substantive, but contains no provision for attorney's fees if the carrier fails to pay benefits within 14 days. In dicta the court said: "Section 440.192(8) does not include the additional 'stick' of attorney's fees comparable to those provided by section 440.34(3)(b), Florida Statutes [1989]." This suggested that there may be no punitive consequence if the carrier does nothing in response to a Petition for Benefits [see City of Crestview v. Howard, 657 So. 2d 73, 74–75 (Fla. 1st DCA 1995)].

However, the court now holds that failing to respond to a petition for benefits within 14 days operates as a denial of every allegation in the petition. Therefore, if the carrier neither pays nor files a Response to Petition in a timely manner. the carrier is deemed to have denied compensability of the worker's injuries. Thus, doing nothing is the same as issuing a denial, subjecting the carrier to liability for attorney's fees and even penalties for late payment [*see* Russell Corp. v. Brooks, 698 So. 2d 1334, 1335 (Fla. 1st DCA 1997)].

§ 23.10 Attorney's Fees and The 30-Day Rule

Beginning with accidents occurring on or after July 1, 2002, the carrier, or self-insured employer, must provide the benefits requested within 30 days after receiving the petition. Regardless of the date that benefits were originally requested, attorney's fees do not attach until the expiration of this 30-day period [*see* §§ 440.25(4)(k), 440.34(3)(d), Fla. Stat. (7/1/2002)].

Without commenting on the meaning of the phrase "regardless of the date benefits were originally requested," the court held that the amendment increasing the time to respond to a petition from 14 to 30 days was a substantive amendment that could not be applied retroactively. Therefore, the 30-day attachment period for fees applies only to accidents occurring on or after July 1, 2002 [*see* Stolzer v. Magic Tilt Trailer, Inc., 878 So. 2d 437 (Fla. 1st DCA 2004), *rehg denied*, 2004 Fla. App. LEXIS 12617 (Fla. 1st DCA 2004)].

Therefore, if the carrier provides the benefits requested within 30 days after receiving the petition, no attorney's fees are due. This will make it necessary that carriers carefully record the date on which petitions were received. Claimants' attorneys should consider filing petitions with carriers via certified or registered mail.

If the carrier had previously denied benefits, but provides them within 30 days after receiving a Petition for Benefits, no fee is due. This is true even if it was the carrier's denial that forced the claimant to hire a lawyer and file a petition [*see* Carrillon Hotl v. Rodriquez, 124 So. 2d 3, 7–8 (Fla. 1960); *see also* National Distributing Co. v. Campbell, 632 So. 2d 647, 649 (Fla. 1st DCA 1994)].

If the carrier denies entitlement to benefits claimed in its response to the petition, and the claimant later secures an award of the benefits denied. fees will be due. If the carrier denies benefits, but later rescinds the denial before trial and provides the benefits, fees will be due if the benefits were provided more than 30 days after the carrier received the Petition for Benefits [§ 440.34(3)(d), Fla. Stat. (7/1/2002)].

If the carrier issues a denial in response to a petition, but then provides the benefits claimed within the 30-day period, entitlement to a fee is not clear. A strong argument for entitlement can be made if the attorney took actions in response to the carrier's denial. Conversely, the statute plainly provides that fees do not attach until after the 30-day period has expired [§ 440.34(3)(d), Fla. Stat. (7/1/2002)].

Remember that simply doing nothing in response to a Petition for Benefits has been held to be the same as denying each allegation in the petition. Therefore, doing nothing is the same as issuing a denial [*see* Russell Corp. v. Brooks, 698 So. 2d 1334, 1335 (Fla. 1st DCA 1997)].

§ 23.11 Calculating Fees

[1] General Rule and Procedure

A judge of compensation claims must approve any fee paid to an injured worker's lawyer whether the carrier or the injured worker pays it. Much of the time, carriers will negotiate fees directly. Adjusters should use the same procedure [*see* [2]–[3], *below*] to decide a proper fee that the law requires a judge to use. Any order awarding fees should, of course, include the amount. In addition, the order must include the statutory basis for fee entitlement. Most important, the order must state the type of benefits secured as the result of the attorney's legal service. When carriers are dealing directly with the injured worker's lawyer, they should insist that the lawyer explain these items. Calculate the fee based only on the benefits the lawyer was responsible for securing, not on everything the carrier has paid [§ 440.34(2), Fla. Stat. (7/1/97); *see* [2], *below*].

[2] Benefits Secured

[a] Defined

Benefits secured means benefits obtained by successfully prosecuting a claim. In other words, these are the benefits the injured worker received because of the lawyer's efforts. If the claimant's attorney succeeds in securing a different classification of benefits, but the award does not change the amount of the benefit the claimant is already receiving, no fee is due. For example, assume that the carrier begins paying permanent total disability on September 1. Until then, it had paid temporary total disability benefits without interruption since the day of the accident. The claimant's attorney then succeeds in securing an award for permanent total disability beginning on January 1. In such a case, no fee would be due because the attorney's actions would not have secured any benefit for the claimant that she was not already receiving [*see* Crawford & Co. v. Nash, 754 So. 2d 145, 145–146 (Fla. 1st DCA 2000)].

Benefits, however, include more than measurable monetary compensation. For example, benefits may also include successfully securing medical evaluations [*see* Chery v. Southeast Service Corp., 644 So. 2d 148, 149 (Fla. 1st DCA 1994)]. The first step is to decide if the law entitles the lawyer to a carrier-paid fee based on the criteria described in §§ 23.01–23.09. The second step is to decide the value of the benefits, both past and future, which the lawyer secured for the injured worker. The third step is to reduce the value of benefits secured to present value [*see* [3], *below*]. The fourth and last step is to apply the statutory sliding scale formula [*see* [4], *below*].

[b] Limit on Future Medical Care

The Act prohibits including the value of future medical care beyond five years. The medical limitation provision applies only to claims occurring on or after October 1, 1989 [*see* Sir Elec., Inc. v. Borlovan, 582 So. 2d 22, 23 (Fla. 1st DCA 1991)]. This five-year period begins on the date the petition for benefits is filed, not when the injured worker's lawyer files a claim for attorney's fees [*see* Riviera Beach v. Deliso,713 So. 2d 426, 427–428 (Fla. 1st DCA 1997)].

Judges may not project an inflation factor in quantifying the value of future attendant care benefits to decide attorney's fees. Judges can and should, however, base attorney's fees on the present value of future attendant care [*see* Tri-State Motor Transit Co. v. Judy, 566 So. 2d 537, 540 (Fla. 1st DCA 1990); A.G. Holly State Hospital and Division of Risk Management v. Kaiser, 577 So. 2d 612, 613 (Fla. 1st DCA 1991)]. See [3], *below,* for a discussion of present value.

[3] Present Value

The third step in calculating attorney's fees is to reduce the value of benefits secured to their present value. Before 1994, the Act required using an eight-percent interest or discount factor to calculate the present value of future benefits for washout settlements [*see* ch. 21, for discussion of washout settlements]. That requirement applied only to settlements, however, and not to calculating attorney's fees. The legislature repealed the language in § 440.20(12)(d), Fla. Stat. requiring an eight-percent discount factor for settlements effective January 1, 1994. The law does not require a mandatory rate to use in calculating present value for attorney's fee purposes. Decide the proper rate either by agreement or by evidence and expert testimony on an individual case basis [*see* Rolle v. Metropolitan Dade County, 642 So. 2d 100, 102–103 (Fla. 1st DCA 1994)].

Before *Rolle*, the cases could have been read to require the judge of compensation claims to calculate the present value of future benefits themselves. *Rolle,*however, renders calculation by the judge of compensation claims unnecessary. Calculating the present value of future benefits is strictly a matter of proof to be established by evidence and expert testimony [*see* Sistrunk v. City of Dunedin, 715 So. 2d 375, 376 (Fla. 1st DCA 1998)].

[4] Fee Schedule: Sliding Scale Formula

The fourth and last step in calculating attorney's fees is to apply the statutory sliding scale formula. Note, however, the formula changes depending on the date of the accident.

For accident dates through December 31, 1993, the statutory formula for a typical case is as follows: 25 percent of the first $5,000 of benefits secured; 20 percent of the second $5,000; and 15 percent of the remainder. For accidents occurring on or after October 1, 1989, there is no entitlement to a fee based on the value of medical benefits beyond five years from the date on which the injured worker files the petition.

For accident dates on or after January 1, 1994, the statutory formula for a typical case is as follows: 20 percent of the first $5,000 of benefits secured; 15 percent of the second $5,000; 10 percent of the remaining benefits secured up to 10 years from the date the injured worker filed the petition; and 5 percent of the benefits secured after 10 years. The five-year limitation on medical benefits secured still applies [*see* [2][b], *above*].

[5] Exceptions to Scheduled Fees

[a] Accident Dates Through September 30, 2003

[i] Factors to Consider

The law provides no automatic entitlement or restriction to a scheduled fee as set forth in [4], *above*. Instead, the law allows the judge of compensation claims to increase or decrease the fee after considering the following factors [§ 440.34(1), Fla. Stat. (7/1/97)]:

1. The time and labor required, the novelty and difficulty of the questions involved, and the skill required to do the legal service properly.
2. The likelihood, if apparent to the injured worker, that accepting the particular employment will preclude employment of the lawyer by others or cause antagonisms with other clients. (Note: The legislature repealed this factor effective January 1, 1994.)
3. The customary fee charged in the locality for similar services.
4. The amount of benefits resulting to the injured worker.
5. The time limitation imposed by the injured worker or the circumstances.
6. The nature and length of the professional relationship with the injured worker. (Note: The legislature repealed this provision effective January 1, 1994.)
7. The experience, reputation, and ability of the lawyer.
8. The contingency or certainty of a fee.

[ii] Exceptional Circumstances Required

As stated, the JCC's have authority to depart from the schedule as set forth in [4], *above*. The court has held, however, that "the statutory fee schedule embodies a legislative intent to standardize the method of assessing fees; departures from its percentage formula should be made *only in exceptional circumstances*" [*see* Tri-State Motor Transit Co. v. Judy, 566 So. 2d 537, 539 (Fla. 1st DCA 1990); Marsh v. Benedetto, 566 So. 2d 324, 326 (Fla. 1st DCA 1990) (emphasis added)].

When such an exceptional circumstance arises, the order of a judge of compensation claims must contain an analysis of each factor listed in [a], *above*. This analysis must be sufficient to decide whether, when considered as a whole, the general effect of these factors demonstrably justifies an increase or decrease in the formula fee [*see* Marsh v. Benedetto, 566 So. 2d 324, 325–326 (Fla. 1st DCA 1990); *see also* General Kinetics v. Butts, 586 So. 2d 1331, 1332 (Fla. 1st DCA 1991); Dobbs v. Suncoast Acoustics, 590 So. 2d 7, 8 (Fla. 1st DCA 1991)].

[iii] Increasing the Fee

Whether the circumstances in a particular case are exceptional enough to allow departure from the schedule [*see* [4], *above*] is a question for the JCC to decide. Unfortunately, clear guidelines do not exist. If the carrier mounts an aggressive defense, forcing the worker's lawyer to spend a great deal of time prosecuting the case, the judge may be justified in increasing the fee. Carriers may also be assessed fees for paralegal services, but only for meaningful legal work. The time spent by the paralegal staff on clerical work is not recoverable [Dayco Products v. McLane, 690 So. 2d 654, 656 (Fla. 1st DCA 1997)].

[iv] Decreasing the Fee

Conversely, the judge should reduce the scheduled fee [*see* [4], *above*] if the carrier took steps to shorten the litigation process by making concessions or similar actions. If the judge does not take such actions into consideration, the implication is that each side would aggressively defend or prosecute every issue without regard for the injured worker's needs [*see* Johnson v. Ocala Geriatric Center, 695 So. 2d 802 (Fla. 1st DCA 1997)].

[v] Fees Based on Time Spent

The time an attorney spends on a case is frequently the main issue in dispute. The hourly rate and time spent is only one statutory factor that courts must consider in deciding whether to deviate from the statutory guideline fee [*see* [4], *above*] based on benefits secured [*see* Barco Vending Company v. Villalonga, 608 So. 2d 128, 129 (Fla. 1st DCA 1992); *see also* [f], *below*].

When a fee is awardable based on the time spent, this includes the time expended both before and after a petition is filed. The court considered the provisions of § 440.192(7), Fla. Stat., which states:

> Notwithstanding the provisions of s. 440.34, a judge of compensation claims may not award attorney's fees payable by the carrier for services expended or costs incurred prior to the filing of a petition that does not meet the requirements of this section.

The court found it difficult to conclude that the above language clearly and unambiguously bars compensation for any attorney time expended before a petition is filed, and particularly so in view of the qualification therein specifically linking the preclusion of fees to a petition that fails to satisfy the statute's requirements. The court held that, under the circumstances, the provisions of subsection (7) obviously cannot be considered in isolation from other pertinent statutory specifications, namely, those in § 440.34, Fla. Stat., relating to the factors to be considered in awarding the claimant's attorney fees, and those in § 440.192(2), Fla. Stat., setting out the requisites of a petition for benefits.

Because of subsection (7)'s reference to other statutes, the court deemed it necessary to apply the *in pari materia* canon of statutory construction, which recognizes that statutes will be considered together when two different statutory provisions deal with the same specific subject or with subjects so connected that the meaning of the one informs the other.

The court concluded that subsection (7) is so interconnected with the subsection (2) criteria that the meaning of the former cannot be ascertained without reference to the latter. Section 440.192(2), Fla. Stat., clearly states that a petition is to be dismissed if it fails to comply with its filing requirements. The 1st DCA, moreover, in construing the provisions of the two subsections *in pari materia*, has previously concluded that no attorney fee may be awarded to a claimant's counsel for time expended before the filing of a petition that is later dismissed on the ground that it did not satisfy the subsection (2) requisites [*see* Kennedy v. Orlando Shader Realty, 711 So. 2d 156, 158 (Fla. 1st DCA 1998)].

The court held that the logical inference from *Kennedy* is that services performed before a proper petition is filed may be included in a fee awarded to a prevailing claimant. Therefore, the order denying fees for time spent before the petition was filed was reversed and remanded [*see* Morris v. Dollar Tree Store, 869 So. 2d 704 (Fla. 1st DCA 2004)].

As noted, it is well settled that the employer/carrier is not obligated to pay expert

Guide to Claims

witness fees charged by an attorney testifying as to the reasonableness of a requested attorney's fee in a workers' compensation case. The court saw no reason this rule should not be equally applied to medical expert witnesses.

In any workers' compensation case in which the necessity of medical benefits is contested, expert medical testimony will be required. It would be a simple matter to elicit the expert's opinion as to the value of the medical treatment recommended when the expert is giving his medical opinion as to the necessity of treatment. The court could not conceive of any circumstance in which such testimony could not be elicited at this time, and doing so is consistent with the philosophy of the workers' compensation law to provide an expeditious result at a minimum cost.

The court noted that if, for some reason, those questions cannot be asked in the primary proceeding, the judge of compensation claims can often ascertain the value of medical benefits obtained without a hearing, based upon a medical expert's affidavit. Although it is within the judge of compensation claims' discretion to hold collateral proceedings to determine the amount of attorney's fees, medical expert witness fees incurred during such proceedings are not taxable against the employer/carrier [*see* Tucker v. FedEx, 931 So. 2d 222, 223(Fla. 1st DCA 2006)].

[vi] Fee Must Be Based on Benefits Secured

A judge of compensation claims must base the fee award only on the benefits the lawyer secured [*see* [2][a], *above*]. In other words, the judge must apply the statutory factors to only those benefits the carrier did not pay timely. Even if an injured worker formerly and properly claimed a benefit, the judge may not include these benefits if the carrier paid them voluntarily and timely [*see* Corporate Service, Inc. v. Justus, 648 So. 2d 844 (Fla. 1st DCA 1995)].

[vii] No Fee for Proving Amount of Fees

If the judge decides that the statutory fee schedule [*see* [4], *above*] would result in an inequitable fee, the judge may base the award on the time the lawyer spent in proving entitlement to benefits and entitlement to a fee. The judge may not, however, include the time the lawyer spent in proving the amount of the fee, unless entitlement itself is in dispute [*see* Spiker's All Amer. Custom Acces. v. Spiker, 647 So. 2d 201 (Fla. 1st DCA 1994)]. This is true even if the carrier's resistance forces the lawyer to spend additional time [*see* Hyatt Regency Grand Cypress v. Williams, 639 So. 2d 1119 (Fla. 1st DCA 1994)]. Likewise, none of the lawyer's time spent proving the hours worked in obtaining the benefits is includable in the fee award. Once the judge enters an order awarding benefits and entitlement to a carrier-paid fee, the judge cannot include the time the lawyer spent proving the amount [*see* Crittenden Orange Blossom Fruit v. Stone, 514 So. 2d 351, 353 (Fla. 1987)].

[viii] Fees Based on Complexity of Case

Great skill and years of experience do not, themselves, create an exception and, thus, automatic entitlement to an increase from the scheduled fee amount [*see* [4], *above*]. The exception is a case so complex that it requires an extraordinary level of skill. Another increasing factor is the time limitation imposed by the injured worker, or by the general circumstances. To collect an increased fee based on novelty or complexity, the lawyer must show a need to act quickly due to the injured worker's condition. This includes cases involving brain damage, quadriplegia, suicidal tendency, and so forth. It may also include evidence showing the lawyer was forced to give up weekends and vacations to pursue the claim. Another factor is a case so urgent or complex that the lawyer cannot handle other cases [*see* Regal Wood Products v. Baschansci, 603 So. 2d 551, 553–554 (Fla. 1st DCA 1992)].

Guide to Claims

[ix] Verified Petition—Time Limits for Filing

The judge of compensation claims does not have the authority to impose time limits on the submission of a verified petition for attorney's fees. For example, the claimant filed several petitions for benefits. The parties eventually resolved all of the claims. The parties then advised the judge of compensation claims' office that there was no need for a final hearing, but reserved on the issue of attorney's fees entitlement. The judge of compensation claims served Notices of Administrative Closure of Case, which indicated the case would be administratively closed unless a verified petition for attorney's fees was filed within 45 days. The notices also advised that all pending petitions for benefits would be subject to dismissal without a hearing unless a party filed an objection.

On October 29, 2004, the judge of compensation claims entered an order closing the file. In the order, the judge of compensation claims noted that all of the issues between the parties, other than attorney's fees entitlement, had been resolved. Accordingly, the judge of compensation claims dismissed all of the petitions for benefits pending prior to February 3, 2004.

The claimant's attorney filed his verified petition for attorney's fees on March 2, 2005. The employer/carrier filed a motion to dismiss the verified petition with prejudice. The employer/carrier alleged the petition had to be dismissed because it was not timely filed within the dictates of the October 29, 2004 Order. After a hearing was held on the motion to dismiss, the judge of compensation claims granted the employer/carrier's motion and dismissed the petition with prejudice. The judge of compensation claims reasoned that because the October 29, 2004 Order was not appealed within 30 days, he was without jurisdiction to modify the earlier Order.

The court found that the portion of the October 29, 2004 Order relating to attorney's fees was not final. Further, the court held that the judge of compensation claims did not have authority, pursuant to either statute or rule, to set a time limitation for filing the verified petition for fees. The employer/carrier's argument that the judge of compensation claims had authority to set such a time limitation pursuant to § 440.33(1), Fla. Stat., was not persuasive. Accordingly, the Order was reversed [Villazano v. Horace Bell Honey Co., 928 So. 2d 515 (Fla. 1st DCA 2006)].

[b] Accident Dates On or After October 1, 2003

For accidents occurring on or after October 1, 2003, an attorney is entitled to a fee based only on the statutory fee schedule [*see* [4], *above*], with one exception. The exception arises in a dispute in a medical-only case. A "medical-only" case is defined in § 440.34(3)(a), Fla. Stat. as a petition filed for medical benefits only and, at the time, the claimant is not entitled to file a claim for disability benefits [*see* § 23.03, *above*].

In such a medical-only case the judge may, as an alternative, award fees calculated on time spent if the judge decides that the statutory schedule would not compensate the attorney fairly. The maximum hourly rate for such a fee is $150. Additionally, the total hourly fee awarded cannot exceed $1,500.

The law prohibits a judge of compensation claims from awarding an hourly fee more than once per accident [§ 440.34(7), Fla. Stat. (10/1/2003)]. Note, however, that the hourly fee applies if *the* attorney cannot be otherwise fairly compensated. Since the statute uses the definite article "the" rather "an," it appears that this fee method may apply more than once if the claimant changes lawyers.

The statute is silent concerning the method to be used in calculating the amount of a fee due under the provisions of § 440.30, Fla. Stat. Under that section, a carrier is allowed to depose a represented claimant even if there is no petition for benefits pending. In such a case, however, the statute provides that the carrier must pay the claimant's attorney a fee for attending the deposition. Since there are no benefits secured, the statutory schedule cannot apply. Since, by definition, there is no medical-only claim pending, the restriction on hourly fees cannot apply. Therefore, it appears that, under the provisions of § 440.24(1), Fla. Stat., the attorney is entitled to his or her regular hourly rate for attending the deposition. That section provides that the judge cannot approve a fee outside the statutory limits for issues related to benefits under the Act. Since attending a deposition required by the carrier has nothing to do with benefits, the fee limitations should not apply.

As noted above, for accidents occurring on or after October 1, 2003, a claimant's attorney's fee is generally limited to the sliding scale formula described in § 440.34(1), Fla. Stat.

The court has held that when statutory language is clear and unambiguous, courts will not look beyond the plain language for legislative intent, nor resort to external rules of statutory construction to ascertain intent, because doing so would constitute an abrogation of legislative power. When the legislature makes substantial, material changes to the language of a statute, it is presumed to have intended some specific objective or alteration of law, unless a contrary indication is clear. In 2003, the legislature amended § 440.34(1), Fla. Stat., effecting three material changes. First, the amount of an attorney's fee award is no longer based on *services rendered*, but instead is based on the value of the *benefits secured* on behalf of the claimant. Second, language permitting the JCC to increase or decrease the statutory attorney's fee by considering six enumerated factors if, in the JCC's judgment, the circumstances warrant such action, was deleted. Third, the legislature added language specifically prohibiting a JCC from awarding a fee in excess of the percentage fee, but did not, with the same specificity, prohibit a lower fee. In the amended § 440.34, Fla. Stat., the legislature defined a "reasonable" fee. The statute requires JCC approval of any attorney's fee. A JCC is permitted to approve a fee only if it is "reasonable." All approved fees *must* equal a statutorily enumerated percentage based on the value of the *benefits secured* on behalf of the claimant. Therefore, a JCC may approve a fee as "reasonable" only when it equals a statutorily established percentage of the value of benefits secured on behalf of the claimant. The court found the statutory language to be clear and unambiguous and that the court must presume the legislature intended the amended statute to mean what it clearly says. In workers' compensation cases, a fee award must be based on the value of the benefits actually obtained on behalf of the claimant. The statute expressly prohibits the JCC from awarding an attorney's fee greater than that provided by the statute, except under certain conditions in medical only cases [*see* Wood v. Fla. Rock Indus., 2006 Fla. App. LEXIS 1752 (Fla. 1st DCA 2006)].

[6] Offer to Settle

If the carrier offers to settle issues raised in a petition and that are pending before a judge of compensation claims, the judge cannot award a fee based on the benefits offered. A fee awarded in such a case must be based on only the benefits the attorney secured in excess of the benefits offered. Such an "offer to settle" must meet the following requirements [§ 440.34(2), Fla. Stat. (10/1/2003)]:

- The offer to settle must be in writing.
- The offer to settle must be communicated to the claimant's attorney at least 30 days before the trial date.
- The offer to settle must address each disputed issue separately.
- The offer to settle must specify whether the offer on each issue is severable.
- The offer to settle must state unequivocally whether it includes witness fees and expenses and all other costs associated with the claim.

Note that the offer must have been *communicated* to the claimant's attorney at least 30 days before trial. This clearly indicates that the attorney must have actually received the written offer 30 days before trial. Therefore, carriers should send such offers both by facsimile and by registered mail. Additionally, the precise wording of the offer letter is likely to become the subject of debate based on an argument that the offer letter does not meet the statutory requirements. Therefore, carriers should consider having their attorneys draft and send settlement offers.

> **PRACTICE POINT:** Since the judge must consider the factors discussed in [a]–[h], *above,* carriers should consider them, too. An injured worker's lawyer may argue that the statutory guideline fee [*see* [4], *above*] is just a starting point and that the fee can only go up from there. Do not be misled by such arguments because they are simply not true. In one case, the court affirmed a fee award that was 57 percent *less* than the statutory schedule [*see* Fumigation Dept. v. Pearson, 559 So. 2d 587, 590 (Fla. 1st DCA 1989)].
>
> If the law does not allow the injured worker's lawyer a carrier-paid fee, the lawyer must still obtain the judge's approval for any fee the client will pay. Once approved, the judge will issue an order and send the carrier a copy.

§ 23.12 Defense Lawyers

[1] Strategic Considerations for Carrier and Attorney Relationship

Always remember that defense lawyers get paid, win or lose. Following are some observations on the carrier and attorney relationship, and on legal-fee cost containment. Carriers and individual adjusters must give guidance and direction to the defense lawyer. Otherwise, adjusters are in a poor position to complain about too much or too little work done by the defense lawyer.

Always remember that lawyers must follow ethical and professional standards of conduct. They owe a duty to their client, the Bar, and the public. The lawyers' ethical duty requires that they act aggressively and in their client's best interests. They may not divulge a client confidence. Further, they may not advance a client's cause if this would violate ethical responsibilities in the process. Lawyers may not knowingly allow a client to give false testimony or engage in any activity that even appears illegal.

Carriers can and should criticize their defense lawyers if they have not done essential trial preparation, and when they charge for excessive or unnecessary work. Adjusters are not, however, in a very good position to criticize a lawyer's work if they do not stay involved in the process.

While adjusters should always defer to their lawyer's legal expertise, they must stay actively involved. Adjusters should insist that the defense lawyer telephone, or at least write, shortly after receipt of a new assignment to review and agree on the issues involved. Carriers should agree on the legal basis for a defense and the evidence the lawyer must produce to support that defense. This meeting of the minds should then form the lawyer's guidelines for discovery. Defense lawyers cannot control the number of depositions or motion hearings that the other side may request. Even so, there is nothing wrong with requiring lawyers to prepare a defense budget. They should closely follow this budget, unless the carrier and the lawyer become convinced that the case requires more time and work. Both the carrier and the lawyer should always consider the cost of further defense compared with the benefits in dispute.

Carriers should be wary of law firms that continually transfer files from one lawyer to the next. This is an expensive process since each new lawyer that becomes involved must take time to become familiar with the case.

Usually, carriers should not allow the firm to use a team of lawyers. This may consist of a partner and one or more associates, each of whom handles a different portion of the case. This is an approach that inflates costs.

To avoid defense fees from building excessive accounts receivable for the firm, carriers should consider asking for at least quarterly interim billing. Consider whether charging the same rate as senior lawyers is appropriate for secretaries and paralegal staff.

Adjusters must always carefully read correspondence from the defense lawyer. Constant reminders to the adjuster needlessly increase the bill. Simultaneously, defense lawyers should help by avoiding long-winded reports and specifically highlight important passages. This is especially important when the lawyer needs the adjuster to complete a task.

Adjusters must be sure to tell the defense attorney the whole story. Nothing will get adjusters and their lawyers into more trouble than surprises at trial.

For further discussion on legal cost containment, see [3], *below*.

[2] Defense Fee Approval by JCC Not Required

Based on some peculiar language in the Workers' Compensation Act, it first appeared that defense attorneys must get court approval of their fees just like injured workers' lawyers. The section, in part, provides that, "it shall be unlawful for *any attorney* . . . to receive any fee . . . from a person on account of services rendered for a person in connection with any proceedings arising under this chapter, unless such fee . . . is approved by a judge of compensation claims or by the Chief Judge of Compensation Claims" [§ 440.105(3)(b), Fla. Stat. (7/1/97) (emphasis added)].

The Chief Judge resolved the issue by declaring that this section applies only to claimant's attorney's fees. In Administrative Order I, issued March 16, 1994, the Chief Judge held:

1. That Fla. Stat. Section 440.105(3)(b) requires judicial approval of fees to injured workers' attorneys payable under Fla. Stat. Section 440.34 and does not require judicial approval of any other fees; and
2. That Judges of Compensation Claims are hereby advised that they are not required by Fla. Stat. Section 440.105(3)(b) to approve fees other than those fees payable to injured workers' attorneys under Fla. Stat. Section 440.34.

[3] Legal Cost Containment

[a] In General

Most lawyers and law firms deal competently, honestly, and fairly with their clients. A few, sad to say, seem to have missed more than a few ethics courses along the way. In a large claim department, legal fees can become a significant cost. Containing these costs is an important claims management function. Not all excessive costs are the fault of lawyers. Inattentive claim departments must also shoulder some blame. The following discussion in [b]–[k], *below,* are a few legal cost containment measures that carriers and self-insured employers should consider.

[b] Padding

Padding is simply the practice of charging for more time then the lawyer worked. An example of the thoroughly dishonest version of padding is charging three hours for one hour's work. More subtle is the practice of minimum charges. A particular firm may have a billing practice of always charging a minimum of 15 minutes or more, whatever the time spent. Sound business reasons for this may exist, but business ethics, at least, require that the firm clearly reveal the practice.

[c] Churning

Churning is the practice of increasing charges by performing unnecessary work. This happens because these lawyers either are dishonest or do not know how to proceed, so they subpoena everything and everyone remotely connected to the case. Adjusters must decide which is worse: dishonesty or incompetency.

[d] Case Loads and Geography

Excessive case loads or large geographical territories make lawyers ineffective. Some "red flags" include constantly late or inadequate reporting and inability to easily contact the lawyer. In such a case, consider replacing the lawyer or firm. Simply adding a second firm in the area may be the best option.

[e] Case Managers or Litigators

Too often, lazy or inexperienced adjusters abandon claims to their lawyers. In effect, they ask the lawyer to take over managing the case rather than concentrating on the litigation. This will always result in excessive legal fees, and carriers will have only themselves to blame.

[f] Aggressiveness

Aggressiveness is a desirable quality in a defense lawyer. Defense lawyers are, of course, aware of this, but adjusters should guard against lawyers who simply put on a show. In this context, aggressiveness means making things happen.

[g] Penny-Wise

Adjusters must, of course, control spending defense dollars. In doing so, however, they should take care not to confuse control with handcuffing the lawyer. When adjusters find themselves frequently distrusting the lawyer's judgment, it is time to obtain a new lawyer.

[h] Shape of the File

One of the first cost containment steps is giving the defense attorney a clean, well-documented file. Making the attorney review a messy file is very expensive. First, eliminate all duplicate correspondence. Always include the following:

1. A detailed payment ledger
2. Medical reports (do not include bills, unless important)
3. All DWC forms
4. Rehabilitation reports
5. Surveillance reports
6. Correspondence to and from the injured worker or his or her attorney
7. Correspondence to and from the employer
8. Legible adjusters' notes

Explain in the cover letter what the attorney is supposed to do. An assignment to "handle to conclusion" is far too little and will likely result in excessive legal fees. On the other hand, avoid explaining too much. The attorney does not need a history of the world. Highlight all scheduled legal events such as pretrials and depositions. Explain any limits on authority. Avoid paying lawyers for adjuster work.

Find out how large law firms assign cases and be sure the assigned lawyer has the needed expertise in difficult cases, such as those dealing with occupational disease. On the other hand, do not be afraid of new or young lawyers if senior lawyers are available to consult with them. Also, be aware that individual lawyers may do better with specific judges and claimants' lawyers than other members of the firm.

[i] Reducing Costs in Discovery

In most claims, injured workers' depositions are important. Injured workers are, after all, the focal point of the case and it is important for the defense lawyer to know what the injured worker is all about. All other depositions, however, should be kept to a minimum. Ask what the defense plan is and how the proposed discovery fits into this plan. Doctors' depositions should not be necessary just to obtain general information. In such a case, the lawyer should simply subpoena the medical records if such records are not voluntarily forthcoming.

[j] Trial or Settlement

Adjusters must decide early if the carrier's goal is a complete defense or settlement of the case. Direct all discovery and litigation toward that goal. The defense lawyer should provide a constant evaluation of the progress of the case. Avoid getting a reputation as a "settler" based on fear of trial. This will only invite and encourage increased litigation on less meritorious cases. Look for the "sweet spot," i.e., the prime time to open the case for settlement.

[k] The Partnership Approach

Because of continuing pressure to contain legal costs, a tendency exists for the carrier and attorney relationship to become adversarial. This is counterproductive. Instead, carriers should form a "partnership" with defense lawyers. A good lawyer will listen and help the adjuster, not only in the litigation, but in the cost reduction effort as well. Do not expect to win every case. One defense lawyer suggests that adjusters evaluate lawyers by applying the "seed pack test." Not every seed will sprout, but look for the most blooms per lawyer.

> *The public regards lawyers with great distrust.*
> *They think lawyers are smarter than the average guy*
> *but use their intelligence deviously.*
> *Well, they're wrong; usually, they are not smarter.*
> F. Lee Bailey
> *Los Angeles Times,* January 9, 1972

CHAPTER 24

INSURANCE AND REGULATION IN WORKERS' COMPENSATION

Guide to Claims

SYNOPSIS

Guide to Claims

§ 24.01 Introduction

[1] Insurance Required

[a] Securing Payment of Compensation

Florida's Workers' Compensation Act requires employers to "secure the payment of compensation" in two ways. The first way is buying an insurance policy from an authorized insurance company, either directly or through the Joint Underwriting Association. The second way is qualifying as a self-insurer, either individually or as a member of a self-insurance fund [§ 440.38, Fla. Stat. (7/1/97)].

"Securing the payment of workers' compensation" means obtaining coverage that meets the requirements of the workers' compensation statutes, Ch. 440, Fla. Stat., and the Florida Insurance Code. The law provides, however, that an employer who purchased an insurance policy will still be deemed to have failed to secure payment of workers' compensation, and therefore subject statutory sanctions, if any of the following is true:

1. The employer materially understates or conceals payroll, or
2. The employer materially misrepresents or conceals employee duties so as to avoid proper classification for premium calculations, or

3. The employer materially misrepresents or conceals information pertinent to the computation and application of an experience rating modification factor.

If the department determines that an employer is guilty of any of the listed offenses, a stop-work order may be issued. A stop-work order issued for these reasons, however, will have no effect on an employer's or a carrier's duty to provide benefits or on any of the employer's or carrier's rights and defenses, including exclusive remedy [*see* § 440.107(2), Fla. Stat. (10/1/2003)].

The Legislature has vested the department with broad powers to enforce workers' compensation requirements. These include entering and inspecting any place of business, administering oaths, issuing subpoenas, enforcing stop-work orders, assessing penalties, and pursuing actions to enforce penalty orders, including seeking injunctions [*see* § 440.107(3), Fla. Stat. (10/1/2003)].

If a person refuses to obey a subpoena to appear before the department, or produce requested evidence, or to give testimony about the matter under investigation, a court has jurisdiction to issue an order requiring compliance with the subpoena. Failure to obey such a court order may be punished by the court as contempt, either civilly or criminally. Costs, including reasonable attorney's fees, incurred by the department to obtain an order granting a petition to enforce a subpoena, or a subpoena duces tecum, will be taxed against the subpoenaed party [*see* § 440.107(6), Fla. Stat. (10/1/2003)].

For a general discussion of the requirement of insurance, see LARSON'S WORKERS' COMPENSATION, DESK EDITION, Ch. 150, § 150.01[1] (Matthew Bender).

[b] Carrier Substituted for Employer

Communication failure between carriers and employers frequently results in delayed or miscalculated benefits. Placing blame is a worthless self-defense exercise because the law effectively places the employer and the carrier in each other's shoes. When an employer buys an insurance policy, the law, for purposes of imposing liability for benefits, substitutes the carrier for the employer. The law presumes that each has the knowledge of the other. The courts even refer to the two parties as single entity, i.e., the employer/carrier. The Act provides as follows [§ 440.41, Fla. Stat. (1991)]:

1. Notice to or knowledge of an employer of the occurrence of the injury shall be notice to or knowledge of the carrier.

2. Jurisdiction of the employer by the Judges of Compensation Claims, the Division, or any court under this chapter shall be jurisdiction of the carrier.

3. Any requirement by the Judges of Compensation Claims, the Division, or any court under any compensation order, finding or decision shall be binding upon the carrier in the same manner and to the same extent as upon the employer.

[2] Employers Required to Insure

[a] Non-Construction Employers

All private, non-construction industry employers with four or more employees must

Guide to Claims

have workers' compensation coverage [§ 440.02(15)(b)2, Fla. Stat. (7/1/97)]. A non-construction employer with less than four employees may voluntarily come under the Workers' Compensation Act by buying workers' compensation coverage. These "voluntary" employers enjoy the same immunities as other employers who are subject to the law.

A *legally* uninsured employer must post a clear written notice of this fact to all employees. This notice announces to employees their lack of entitlement to workers' compensation benefits. The original 1990 statute required the employer to file an annual affidavit with the Division, reporting that it had not obtained coverage, but this is no longer required [§ 440.055, Fla. Stat. (1/1/94)].

The court noted that this provision does not apply to private employers who are not in the construction industry and who have fewer than four employees. This is because such businesses are not "employers" for purposes of workers' compensation in the first place. The statute speaks of employers who have the legal right to elect not to be covered by Chapter 440. The Act automatically relieves such employers of any obligation to secure compensation, and no separate election is required [*see* Larry K. Meyer P.A. v. Kimberly, 765 So. 2d 951, 953 (Fla. 1st DCA 2000)].

[b] Construction Industry Employers

Employers in the construction industry must obtain workers' compensation coverage if they have even one employee. Employers may not, however, include exempt officers, partners, and sole proprietors when deciding if it has enough employees to require coverage. An important question is, what kinds of businesses does the construction industry include? Following is the statutory definition of construction [§ 440.02(7), Fla. Stat. (7/1/97)]:

> [F]or-profit activities involving the carrying out of any building, clearing, filling, excavation, or substantial improvement in the size or use of any structure or the appearance of any land. When appropriate to the context, 'construction' refers to the act of construction or the result of construction. However, 'construction' shall not mean a landowner's act of construction or the result of a construction upon his or her own premises, provided such premises are not intended to be sold or resold.

This is vague and ambiguous language. Employers, who doubt their status, should obtain a ruling from the Division before deciding not to buy coverage.

[c] Out-of-State Contractors

The Legislature amended the Act in an apparent attempt to ensure that contractors, both in and out of the state, bidding on a job are on an equal footing, at least with regard to the cost of providing workers' compensation insurance coverage. Effective January 1, 2004, any employer who has employees engaged in work in Florida must either purchase a Florida workers' compensation insurance policy or obtain a Florida endorsement to an out-of-state policy. Both the policy and the endorsement must be based on Florida class codes, rates, rules, and manuals used to determine premium. The policy and the endorsement must be approved under the provisions of Ch. 440, Fla. Stat. and by the Florida Insurance Code.

SPECIAL NOTE: Violation of this requirement constitutes a second-degree felony.

The amendment requires the department to develop rules defining what activities will constitute being "engaged in work" in Florida for both construction and non-construction industries. In developing the administrative rules, the department must use the following standards [*see* § 440.10(1)(g), Fla. Stat. (1/1/2004)]:

1. For employees of non-construction-industry employers who have their headquarters outside Florida and also operate in Florida and who are routinely crossing state lines, but usually return to their homes each night, the employee must be assigned to the headquarters' state. However, construction industry employees performing new construction or alterations in Florida must be assigned to Florida, even if the employees return to their home state each night.

2. The payroll of executive supervisors who may visit a Florida location, but who are not in direct charge of a Florida location, must be assigned to the state in which the headquarters is located.

3. For construction contractors who maintain a permanent staff of employees and superintendents, if any of these employees or superintendents is assigned to a job located in Florida, either for the duration of the job or any portion thereof, their payroll must be assigned to Florida rather than the headquarters' state.

4. Employees who are hired for a specific project in Florida must be assigned to Florida.

[3] Penalty for Failure to Insure

Failure to buy a policy of insurance or to qualify as a self-insurer will result in severe penalties [§ 440.107, Fla. Stat. (7/1/97)]. After 30 days, unpaid fines accrue interest at the rate of one percent per month. In addition, the state obtains a lien against the business. An employer who illegally fails to obtain workers' compensation coverage faces the following penalties [§§ 440.06, 440.105, Fla. Stat. (1997)]:

1. The employer may be found guilty of a second degree misdemeanor, a crime punishable by 60 days in jail, a fine of $500, or both.

2. The Division must issue a stop-work order. An employer who violates a stop-work order is subject to a penalty of $1,000 per day. In addition, an illegally uninsured employer is subject to a penalty of an amount equal to 1.5 times the premium the employer would have paid for the period it was without coverage. The minimum penalty is $1,000 [*see* § 440.107, Fla. Stat. (10/1/2003)].

3. If the employer cannot prove coverage upon written notice from the Division, the Division will impose an additional fine. This fine is equal to twice the premium the employer would have paid had it obtained coverage or $1,000, whichever is greater. The law bases this stiff penalty on the offending employer's payroll for the past three years.

Guide to Claims

4. If the employer is a contractor, the Division will report the violation to the appropriate state licensing board for unspecified disciplinary action.
5. An employer who fails to obtain coverage becomes subject to suits filed by injured workers in circuit court. Worse yet, such an employer not only loses its immunity but loses its common-law defense rights as well. If sued by an employee, an illegally uninsured employer may not raise the following common-law defenses:
   a. That of negligence of a fellow employee.
   b. That the injured employee assumed the risk.
   c. That the worker's own comparative or contributory negligence caused the injury.

An uninsured employer's *only* remaining defense is that it was not negligent.

In addition, the legislature has granted the division broad powers to investigate and to enforce compliance. The division has the authority to enter a business to examine its records, administer oaths, and to issue subpoenas [*see* § 440.107(1)–(4), Fla. Stat. (1998)].

[4] 24-Hour Coverage Alternative

Employers can meet their insurance coverage obligation by buying a 24-hour health and disability policy [§ 440.38(1)(e), Fla. Stat. (7/1/90), amended (1/1/94)]. Employers who purchase such coverage enjoy the same immunity under the law as employers who purchase traditional workers' compensation coverage [§ 440.11, Fla. Stat.]. Such a policy must provide medical and indemnity benefits that are comparable to those required by Chapter 440, Florida Statutes. The employer must pay the entire premium, except any portion relating to dependents. These policies may employ deductibles and coinsurance provisions that require the injured worker to pay part of the health care benefits. If the 24-hour policy covers both work-related and non-work-related injuries, the carrier may base the indemnity benefit on only 60 percent of the injured worker's average weekly wage as opposed to $66^2/_3$ percent under standard coverage. The policy must also provide for life insurance with a death benefit of $100,000.

Initially, the Department of Insurance stated that it would allow only life and health insurers to underwrite such coverage. The 1994 amendments now make it clear that property and casualty insurers may do so as well.

For now, this idea is still in the pilot project stage. At press time the Department of Insurance had not issued any administrative rules. The Department has stated that it will not approve any 24-hour policy filings until the rules are in place. This idea may be the wave of the future, but for now it is merely an interesting, yet unavailable alternative [§ 440.38, Fla. Stat. (1/1/94)].

§ 24.02 Self-Insurance

[1] Self-Insurance Option

Buying an insurance policy from an insurance company is not an employer's only option. The law allows employers to meet the coverage requirement by joining a self-insurance fund or by qualifying as an individual self-insurer. The statutory definition of the term "carrier" includes an insurance company, a self-insurer, and a commercial self-insurance fund [§ 440.02(4), Fla. Stat. (7/1/97)].

For a general discussion of self-insurance, see LARSON'S WORKERS' COMPENSATION, DESK EDITION, Ch. 150, § 150.01[2] (Matthew Bender).

Guide to Claims

[2] Self-Insurance Funds

[a] Private Employers

[i] Creation

Two or more employers can pool their workers' compensation liabilities by forming a group self-insurers fund. An administrator, reporting to a board of trustees, manages the program. Staff employees sometimes carry out all the self-insurance funds' work, but many funds contract with independent service companies. Florida's self-insurance funds look and function like more conventional insurers, but there are significant differences [*see* [iii], *below*].

[ii] Regulation

Before July 1, 1994, two classes of funds operated in Florida: those regulated by the Department of Labor [§ 440.57, Fla. Stat.]; and those funds regulated by the Department of Insurance [§ 624.462, Fla. Stat.]. Funds regulated by the Department of Labor were limited to workers' compensation. Funds regulated by the Department of Insurance, however, could obtain approval to underwrite property and liability coverage besides workers' compensation. Effective July 1, 1994, the legislature transferred regulation of all self-insurance funds to the Department of Insurance under § 624.462, Fla. Stat. The legislature repealed § 440.57, Fla. Stat. on January 1, 1994, and transferred its provisions to § 624.4621, Fla. Stat.

[iii] Operation

Florida's self-insurance funds function as not-for-profit pools. They return premium and investment income dollars, which were not used to pay claims and operating expenses, to their members. The funds usually decide the amount of refunds to individual members based on each member's loss experience and pro rata share contribution of premiums. Generally, the fewer accidents an employer suffers, the greater its share of the refund.

One potential problem with membership in self-insurance funds has been the possibility of an additional assessment of premiums, which can occur if the total premiums collected are insufficient to pay claims. This is especially true for those self-insurance funds with inadequate reinsurance. Beginning January 1, 1994, the legislature created a guaranty association for self-insurance funds. The guaranty association provides protection to injured workers by assuring that it will pay claims if a self-insurance fund becomes insolvent. This, however, does not necessarily protect the employers in the fund. The employers are still subject to a possible assessment [§ 631.901, Fla. Stat. (5/30/97)].

When a self-insurance fund becomes insolvent, the Department of Insurance acts as the

Receiver. In such a case, the department has the right to make assessments against the fund's members under the terms of the indemnity agreement [*see* Southeastern Staffing v. Fl. Dept. of Ins. 728 So. 2d 248, 250 (Fla. 1st DCA 1998) (question certified)].

As commercial insurers became less interested in Florida workers' compensation, the self-insurance funds experienced explosive growth. By 1995, 34 self-insurance funds and assessable mutual companies operated in Florida. The funds, with individual self-insurers, represented approximately 60 percent of the workers' compensation premiums in the state. Beginning in 1994, however, the larger self-insurance funds began converting to standard stock or mutual insurance companies. Several of the funds either ceased operations voluntarily or became insolvent. By 1997, only 10 self-insurance funds remained in Florida, and a few of these were in danger of financial collapse.

[b] Public Employers

Two or more local governmental entities can enter an agreement to pool their resources to provide workers' compensation coverage to employees. To qualify, the total annual premiums must be more than $5 million and excess insurance (reinsurance) must be in place. The governing body, the trustees, must be locally elected officials. Each year, the pool must file an audited financial statement. If the pool meets these basic requirements, it is exempt from the requirement to file reports required of private employer funds [§ 624.4622, Fla. Stat. (1991)].

[3] Individual Self-Insurers

[a] Private Employers

Employers can individually self-insure their duty to "secure the payment of compensation" if they can meet stringent financial requirements. The Division of Workers' Compensation has extensive rules dealing with self-insurers [Fla. Admin. Code R. Ch. 69L-5 (1/10/2005)]. A basic requirement is that an employer must have, and will continue to have, the financial strength to pay claims. The Division may require a self-insurance applicant to post a surety bond. A surety bond is a bond guaranteeing performance of a contract or obligation. The Division also may require the applicant to purchase an excess insurance policy. Further, all self-insurers must join the Florida Self-Insurers Guaranty Association, which is more commonly called the Guaranty Fund. In the event a self-insured employer becomes insolvent, the Guaranty Fund takes over handling and paying the employer's claims. Thus, injured workers are assured they will continue to receive benefits [§ 440.385, Fla. Stat. (1997)].

> **PRACTICE POINT:** Once a claimant elects to seek remedies through the Florida Workers' Compensation Insurance Guaranty Association (FWCIGA), he or she is not entitled to recover attorney fees, penalties, or interest from either the employer or from FWCIGA [*see* § 631.929, Fla. Stat. (1997); Shear Homes, Inc. v. Sheppard, 764 So. 2d 705, 707 (Fla. 1st DCA 2000)].

The law allows self-insurers to employ their own staff adjusters and safety engineers.

Most, however, contract for these services from licensed service companies. To qualify, self-insurance service companies must file an application with the Division and meet all the Division's requirements. In addition, the third-party service company must maintain a claim adjuster within the state while claims remain open [§ 440.38(4)(b), Fla. Stat.; Fla. Admin. Code R. 69L-5.113 (1/10/2005)].

An authorized self-insured employer can cover the employees of another employer under its self-insured plan [§ 440.38(1)(f), Fla. Stat. (7/1/91)]. If a second employer enters such an agreement with an authorized self-insurer, the law deems the second employer to have met its coverage obligations.

[b] Public Utilities

Self-insured public utilities can cover contractors and subcontractors under their self-insurance plans. This applies, however, only when the contractor performs its work on or next to property owned or used by the utility [§ 624.46225, Fla. Stat. (1993); *see* Cartier v. Florida Power & Light Co., 594 So. 2d 755, 756 (Fla. 3d DCA 1991)].

Note, however, that voluntarily providing coverage to contractors, or providing coverage under the terms of a contract, does not result in immunity under § 440.11, Fla. Stat. Put another way, a self-insured public utility that provides coverage to independent contractors under § 440.571, Fla. Stat. has no immunity from suits filed by an employee of the independent or subcontractor. Additionally, the Supreme Court disapproved of the 3d DCA's decision in *Cartier* (above) to the extent that it conflicts with the Court's opinion here [*see* Deen v. Quantum Resources, 750 So. 2d 616, 621–622 (Fla. 1999)].

[4] Servicing Agent—Liability for Benefits for Bankrupt Self-Insured Employer

Third party administrators providing claim-handling services to self-insured employers must proceed carefully to ensure that they do not become liable for providing benefits to injured workers if the self-insured employer becomes bankrupt. For example, A JCC entered a compensation order finding the injured worker had sustained a compensable injury and directed the servicing agent to pay workers' compensation benefits, personally. The servicing agent appealed. The servicing agent argued that the JCC erred in ruling it was a carrier and was responsible for paying benefits. The appellate court found nothing in the order holding that the servicing agent was obligated to pay on the basis it was a carrier. The JCC decided that the servicing agent failed to establish its affirmative defense that it did not have sufficient funds from the employer with which to pay the benefits awarded. The servicing agent had proceeded to a hearing at which it raised various defenses to the merits of the claim, but not the termination of coverage. The parties' stipulations included an admission that workers' compensation coverage was in effect, that temporary benefits had been paid in a certain amount, and that the servicing agent would pay medical bills incurred. After the employer's bankruptcy, the servicing agent did not seek to withdraw as a party to the proceeding. No one appeared on behalf of either the employer or the servicing agent at the final hearing. The JCC found that the servicing agent did not prove its affirmative defense that no coverage existed. The court held that competent, substantial evidence supported the determination and affirmed the order [*see* Crawford & Co.—Orlando v. Connors, 840 So. 2d 1060, 1062–1063 (Fla. 1st DCA 2003), *reh'g den.,* 2003 Fla. App. LEXIS 6038 (Fla. 1st DCA Mar. 20, 2003)].

Guide to Claims

In a dissenting opinion, Judge Wolf noted that the legal effect of the majority's affirmance is to hold servicing agents (third party administrators) jointly and severally liable along with the self-insured employer for payment of compensation benefits. Judge Wolf noted that the majority cited no precedent for this result. In fact, he said, there is no precedent for converting a servicing agent into an insurer. Although entitlement to compensation benefits is based on statute, the majority also cited no section of the statute that supports this result. The only possible justification for this decision, said Judge Wolf, is to find a deep pocket for an employee who cannot collect benefits because his or her self-insured employer has gone bankrupt. Judge Wolf went on to say that "the majority espouses a unique theory of liability. It is based on the servicing agent's failure to prove that it did not have any funds belonging to the bankrupt employer. This conclusion is unsupportable for a number of reasons. The majority wrongly placed the burden of proof on the servicing agent to demonstrate that it was not holding any of the employer's funds. In addition, the remedy of joint and severable liability chosen by the JCC and affirmed by the majority is not tailored to suit the alleged failure of the servicing agent to meet its burden of proof. If liability was imposed at all, such liability should have been limited to the amount of money actually held by the servicing agent. The imposition of joint and several liability upon both the servicing agency and bankrupt employer for all compensation benefits is unsupportable. In fact, as previously noted, such a result is in direct contravention of departmental rules which state that a servicing agency shall not be liable for unpaid claims of a self-insurer" [*see* Crawford & Co.—Orlando v. Connors, 840 So. 2d 1060, 1063–1064 (Fla. 1st DCA 2003), *reh'g den.*, 2003 Fla. App. LEXIS 6038 (Fla. 1st DCA Mar. 20, 2003)].

§ 24.03 Insurance Policies

[1] Employer Insolvent or Bankrupt

If an insured employer becomes insolvent or bankrupt, the insurance carrier is not relieved of its obligation to pay benefits to injured workers. This assumes that the policy remained in force on the date of the accident [§ 440.42(1)(b), Fla. Stat. (1991)].

[2] Cancellation

[a] Notice Requirement

Originally, § 627.4133, Fla. Stat. required that carriers must give 45 days advance notice of cancellation for property and casualty policies. This section expressly provided, however, that it did not apply to workers' compensation. The workers' compensation statute, § 440.42(2), Fla. Stat., requires only 30 days notice. Beginning January 1, 1994, the legislature amended § 627.4133, Fla. Stat. by bringing workers' compensation within its provisions. The legislature did not amend § 440.42, Fla. Stat., which still requires only 30 days notice. This, of course, created immediate controversy because the two statutes now provide for different periods of times. The Department of Labor has stated that § 627.4133, Fla. Stat. overrides § 440.42, Fla. Stat., but many people disagree. Until the courts resolve the issue, carriers will be wise to assume the 45-day period applies. The discussion in [b]–[c], *below,* however, is based on the 30-day rule.

Cancellation notices must be filed with the Division electronically either directly or through a third-party vendor. The cancellation does not take effect until 30 days have elapsed after the electronic filing. The 30-day notice period begins the day *after* the Division receives the electronic notice [*see* Fla. Admin. Code. R. 69L-6.008(1) (3/11/2004)].

For a general discussion of insurance cancellation and notice, see LARSON'S WORKERS' COMPENSATION, DESK EDITION, Ch. 150, § 150.03 (Matthew Bender).

[b] Effect of Improper Cancellation Date

A cancellation notice is meaningless unless the notice states the date of the cancellation. More important, the date must be at least 45 days in the future. When the following cases were heard, the time requirement was 30 days. We can assume, however, that the holdings will apply to the 45-day period. For example, the carrier sent a notice of cancellation that purported to be effective immediately. This, stated the court, did not meet the 30-day notice requirement though the employer received it more than 30 days before the accident. The result was that the policy was still in full force [*see* Young v. Travelers Ins. Co., 496 So. 2d 232, 233 (Fla. 1st DCA 1986)].

The effective date of cancellation stated in the notice must be at least 30 days after the date the carrier sends the notice. If not, the notice is void. As such, coverage is still in full force and will continue until the carrier sends a proper notice [*see* Employers Self Insurers Fund v. Torres, 565 So. 2d 395, 396–397 (Fla. 1st DCA 1990)].

[c] Notice to Division Required

Timely notice to the employer, however, is still not enough. The cancellation is not effective unless the carrier also timely sends a copy to the Division. For example, the carrier did not send the cancellation notice to the Division until the day after the accident. The court held the policy could not be considered canceled since the carrier had not met the statutory requirement [*see* Travelers Ins. Co. v. Nettles, 528 So. 2d 1291, 1292 (Fla. 1st DCA 1988)].

Later, the court held that *Torres* and other cases should not be construed to mean that coverage continues indefinitely just because the carrier files an improper cancellation notice. The policy will expire on its normal expiration date if the carrier does nothing to suggest it has renewed the policy [*see* Curtis-Hale, Inc. v. Geltz, 610 So. 2d 558, 561 (Fla. 1st DCA 1992)].

[3] Dual Coverage

[a] Replacement Policy

If two carriers issue a policy to the same employer for the same period, how does coverage apply? This situation occurs most often near the end of the term of the original policy. With only a few weeks or less before the policy expires, the employer decides to change carriers and buys a new policy. For a time, both policies appear in effect. As a matter of law, however, the policy with the later effective date is the only one in force. By statute, the earlier policy automatically canceled when the second policy became effective [§ 440.42(3), Fla. Stat. (1993)].

[b] Two Policies in Effect

A situation may arise where both policies are in effect. In such a case both carriers are liable. For example, the employer had two policies. One, issued by USF&G, covered the Florida employees. The other, issued by Hanover, covered the employees in the Bahamas. When an employee in the Bahamas injured himself, a dispute arose about which carrier owed benefits. The employer hired the worker in Florida, but he worked both in the Bahamas and in Florida. The Supreme Court held both carriers were liable and ordered them to pay the benefits jointly and equally [*see* Hanover Insurance Co. v. Florida Industrial Com'n, 234 So. 2d 661, 663 (Fla. 1970)].

[c] Wrap-Up Programs

So called "wrap-up" programs are often used on large construction projects. Under these programs a single carrier provides coverage for all the contractors involved. A basic requirement is that the total standard premiums for the project, for all entities, must be $250,000 or more. Usually, the individual contractors already have their own policies, thus creating a situation of dual coverage. Which carrier is liable? The carrier that provides the wrap-up coverage on the project is the one on the risk. This applies despite the effective date of any other policies. State guidelines require the wrap-up carrier to notify the other carriers of the various contractors about the coverage it will provide in order to give the other carriers the opportunity to issue endorsements excluding coverage for the project. The fact that the other carrier issues such an endorsement after an accident has no bearing on the matter. Why? Because the wrap-up carrier knows the other carriers would exclude coverage eventually. Thus, it has no expectation that it will not be required to provide coverage [*see* McRae Fire Protection v. McRae, 493 So. 2d 1105, 1107 (Fla. 1st DCA 1986)].

[4] Deductibles and Coinsurance

Upon receipt of a written request from their insured employers, carriers must offer deductibles and coinsurance in exchange for a premium discount. The deductible amounts are $500, $1,000, $1,500, $2,000, and $2,500 per claim. In addition, carriers must offer a coinsurance provision of 80/20. Under the 80/20 plans the carrier pays 80 percent of the benefits over the deductible up to $21,000. The carrier must first pay the benefits and then seek reimbursement from the employer. Employers who purchase a deductible policy are entitled to discounts ranging from 3.3 percent to 10.3 percent, depending on the size of the deductible selected [§ 440.38(5), Fla. Stat. (7/1/90)].

Interestingly, the legislature changed the statutes, not by amending § 440.38, Fla. Stat., but by amending § 440.20(1)(b), Fla. Stat. Beginning January 1, 1994, all insurers, including self-insurance funds and the Joint Underwriting Association, must offer deductible programs in writing. The amendment clearly provides that carriers cannot reimburse employers for any part of their deductible payments, but employers must still report claims as the statutes and rules require. Also beginning January 1, 1994, carriers may not charge the deductible portion the employer pays to the employer's experience rating [§ 420.20(1)(b), Fla. Stat. (1/1/94)].

[5] Information Release Provision

To help carriers collect the proper premiums due, the Act allows insurers to include a policy provision requiring the employer to release employment and wage information maintained by the state pertaining to unemployment. By accepting such a policy, the employer is deemed to consent to release the information unless such release violates federal law. Because these records are sensitive, the law requires insurers to safeguard them and to maintain confidentiality. Carriers may use this information only to verify compliance with the terms of the policy [*see* § 440.42(2), Fla. Stat. (1998)].

§ 24.04 Coverage Disputes

[1] Requirements for Coverage Defense

[a] Reservation of Rights

The law imposes certain requirements on carriers when coverage disputes occur. Coverage defenses most often arise out of the insured employer's failure to comply with one or more of the conditions contained in the policy, or in making fraudulent applications for coverage. The law describes the steps carriers must take to raise a coverage defense. First, the carrier must give the insured employer written notice of its reservation of rights. The carrier must do so within 30 days after it knew, or should have known, about the possible coverage defense. A reservation of rights letter is notice that the carrier will defend the insured employer, but reserves its right to deny coverage or raise policy defenses later. This is a critical step because it is the best way for an insurer to protect itself against waiver or estoppel [*see* [2], *below*].

Carriers must send the reservation of rights letter to the insured's last known address by registered or certified mail. A lawyer should draft a reservation of rights letter to avoid the possibility that a court may find the letter technically deficient. Next, within 60 days of sending the reservation of rights letter, or of receipt of a summons and complaint (but never longer than 30 days before trial), the insurer must do one of the following:

1. Advise the insured employer in writing of the carrier's refusal to defend.
2. Obtain a signed non-waiver agreement from the insured employer. This is a formal document in which the employer acknowledges that the carrier does not waive any of its rights by investigating or defending a claim.
3. Hire an independent attorney, one agreeable to both sides, to defend the action.

[b] Employer's Options

At this point the insured employer has some choices to make. The employer can agree that coverage does not exist and hire a private lawyer to defend against the claim. If the insured does not agree, the next step is usually filing a motion for declaratory judgment. This is a motion that asks the court to resolve the question of coverage. As a practical matter, requesting declaratory judgment itself is probably wiser for the insurer than risking an award of damages for breach of contract [§ 627.426, Fla. Stat. (1983)].

[c] Requests for Declaratory Judgment

Insurers should weigh carefully the decision to file a declaratory judgment action because they can be very expensive. If the insurer loses, it must pay not only the award under the policy, but the employer's legal fees and costs as well [§ 627.428, Fla. Stat. (1982)]. Worse, the insurer also faces the risk of a bad faith claim if the judgment exceeds the policy limits [*see* ch. 23, § 23.07]. This is a particular concern in employers' liability coverage cases. Beside all this, the insurer will, of course, be responsible for its own attorney's fees and costs.

The courts have so far applied this only to coverage defenses based on a breach of a policy condition or on a material misrepresentation in the insurance application. Misrepresentations are outright lies designed to mislead an insurer into issuing a policy.

Coverage defenses are rare in workers' compensation, but may occur more frequently under coverage part two, employers' liability [*see* ch. 3, § 3.01[2][b]]. Carriers face harsh sanctions for failure to follow this section of the statutes, but compliance is not complicated. Still, claim adjusters should consult with management and defense lawyers before attempting a coverage defense.

[2] Estoppel and Waiver

[a] Definitions

A waiver is the voluntary or intentional relinquishment of a right. Equitable estoppel is the loss of a right that would otherwise be available to an insurer but, under the circumstances, would be inequitable to allow. More precisely, this is a doctrine by which a persons may be precluded by their act or conduct, or silence when it is their duty to speak, from asserting a right that they otherwise would have had [*see Black's Law Dictionary,* Sixth Edition (West 1990)].

Even when a valid coverage defense does apply, a carrier may be estopped from asserting it if the carrier's actions create an inequitable situation. Estoppel is a fairness doctrine that operates to prevent someone from misleading another and then using the misrepresentation as a defense. Estoppel based on the carrier's conduct does not operate to create coverage for risks or losses not covered by the policy's terms. Estoppel also cannot operate to create coverage for losses that the policy specifically excludes [*see* Criterion Leasing v. Gulf Coast Plastering, 582 So. 2d 799, 800 (Fla. 1st DCA 1991)].

[b] Exception to Equitable Estoppel

The Florida Supreme Court, however, approved a narrow exception to the doctrine of equitable estoppel. The Court held that the doctrine of promissory estoppel may be used to create insurance coverage when refusing to do so would sanction fraud or other injustice. The Court held that a party will be estopped from denying liability under the principle of promissory estoppel when the party makes a promise which the promisor should reasonably expect to induce action or forbearance of a definite and substantial character on the part of the promisee and which does induce such action or forbearance, and injustice can be avoided only by enforcement of the promise [*see* Crown Life Ins. Co. v. McBride, 517 So. 2d 660, 662 (Fla. 1987)].

[c] Creating Coverage Via Estoppel

Sole proprietor Michael Newsbaum failed to file a notice of election to be covered by the Workers' Compensation Act. When Newsbaum injured himself, he reported the accident to his insurance agent who correctly told him that he was not covered. In spite of this, Newsbaum filed a claim with the carrier who mistakenly began paying benefits. Two years later the carrier discovered its error, suspended benefits, and raised a coverage defense. Newsbaum argued that the carrier should be estopped from raising the defense based on detrimental reliance. Had the carrier denied coverage immediately, Newsbaum complained, he could have sought medical benefits from the Veterans Administration Hospital and disability benefits from the Social Security Administration.

The First District Court of Appeal disagreed. The court found that the insurance policy clearly did not cover Newsbaum because he failed to file a Notice of Election, although he did pay the premium to cover his employees. The court held that the doctrine of equitable estoppel cannot be used to create coverage under these facts [*see* Tradewinds Construction v. Newsbaum, 606 So. 2d 708, 709 (Fla. 1st DCA 1992)].

[d] Promissory Estoppel

Promissory estoppel requires proof that one party relied to its detriment on an affirmative representation made by another [*see* Crown Life Ins. Co. v. McBride, 517 So. 2d 660, 662 (Fla. 1987)]. It cannot apply in a case where one party made an assumption based on the other party's failure to act. For example, the employer asked the carrier to add Florida to its list of covered states, but the carrier never responded. The employer, apparently, assumed that the carrier had done so. When an injury occurred in Florida, the carrier denied the claim for lack of coverage in Florida. The judge of compensation claims determined that coverage did exist under the doctrine of promissory estoppel. On appeal, the court reversed, finding that the carrier never made any representation to the employer that it would provide coverage for accidents occurring in Florida. The employer simply made an assumption [*see* Travelers Indem. Co. v. Billue, 763 So. 2d 1204 (Fla. 1st DCA 2000), *reh'g denied,* May 22, 2000].

[3] Fraudulent Insurance Application

[a] Requirements to Void the Policy

Misrepresentations, omissions, concealment of facts, and incorrect statements on insurance applications do not void the policy and prevent recovery unless the following is true [§ 627.409(1), Fla. Stat. (1992)]:

1. The misstatements are fraudulent; and
2. They are material either to accepting the risk or to the hazard assumed by the insurer; or
3. The insurer in good faith would not have issued the policy, or at least not at the same price or at the same coverage amount, if the insurer knew the facts.

Even an unintentional misstatement in an insurance application will preclude recovery when the misstatement materially affects the risk or the insurer's willingness to accept that risk on the agreed terms [*see* Guerrero v. John Hancock Mutual Life Insurance Company, 522 So. 2d 1032, 1033 (Fla. 3d DCA 1988)].

For a general discussion of fraudulent insurance application, see LARSON'S WORKERS' COMPENSATION, DESK EDITION, Ch. 150, § 150.02[2] (Matthew Bender).

[b] Misstatements Cannot Void Workers' Compensation Policy

The question is whether fraudulent misstatements in an insurance application have the effect of voiding coverage in workers' compensation. The answer, in a word, is no. First, the courts subscribe to the generally recognized rule of workers' compensation insurance that, "[a]s between the insurer and the employee . . . defenses based upon the misconduct or omissions of the employer are of no relevance. . . . Fraudulent statements by the employer preceding and inducing the issuance of a policy are no defenses against the employee . . ." [*see* LARSON'S WORKERS' COMPENSATION, DESK EDITION, Ch. 150, § 150.02[2] (Matthew Bender)].

The District Court of Appeal agreed with Professor Larson and held that since chapter 440 specifically addresses the carrier's remedies, the legislature did not intend § 627.409[1], Fla. Stat. to apply in workers' compensation [*see* Perkins v. A. Perkins Drywall, 615 So. 2d 187, 191–192 (Fla. 1st DCA 1993)]. This does not mean, however, that Florida employers can mislead carriers with impunity. Recognizing that fraudulent applications cannot void the policy, the legislature provided for severe penalties instead [*see* [c], *below*]. This is the remedy the court mentions in *Perkins.*

[c] Penalty for Fraudulent Application in Workers' Compensation

If misstatements lead to understated premiums, the law imposes a severe penalty on the employer. Beginning January 1, 1994, the penalty is *10 times* the understated amount. The Act provides as follows [§ 440.381(6), Fla. Stat. (7/1/97)]:

> If an employer intentionally understates or conceals payroll or misrepresents or conceals employee duties so as to avoid proper classification for premium calculations, or misrepresents or conceals information pertinent to the computation and application of an experience rating modification factor, the employer, or the employer's agent or attorney, shall pay to the insurance carrier a penalty of 10 times the amount of the difference in premium paid and the amount the employer should have paid and reasonable attorneys' fees. The penalty may be enforced in the circuit courts of this state.

NOTE: Filing an application containing false, misleading, or incomplete information for the purpose of avoiding or reducing premiums is a second-degree felony [§ 440.381(2), Fla. Stat. (10/1/2003)].

[4] Carrier Liability for Acts of Agent

[a] Agents and Brokers: General Rule

When coverage disputes arise, a question frequently asked is whether an insurance carrier is liable for the acts or omissions of an independent insurance agent or broker with regard to creation of coverage under a policy.

Under the general rule, an insurance broker is the agent of the insured in matters connected with the procurement of insurance. An insured is bound by its broker's acts, even though fraudulent, and is charged with such broker's knowledge and cannot challenge the validity of the contract that the broker makes for it. Consequently, a misrepresentation or breach of warranty by such broker is, in law, the act of the insured. According to general principles of both contract and insurance law, in the absence of express provisions to the contrary, the application of one seeking insurance constitutes an offer, and the insurance company creates a legally enforceable contract upon acceptance of the application. Generally, an insurance policy becomes effective when the application is received and accepted by the insurance company [Liberty Mut. Ins. Co. v. Scalise, 627 So. 2d 87 (Fla. 1st DCA 1993)].

Ordinarily, issues of agency are to be resolved by the trier of fact [Underwriters of Lloyd's of London v. CZX Prods., 686 So. 2d 706 (Fla. 2d DCA 1996)].

[b] Broker Defined

An insurance broker is one who acts as middleman between the insured and the insurer, who solicits insurance from the public under no employment from any special company, and who, upon securing an order, places it with a company selected by the insured or, in the absence of such a selection, with a company selected by the broker [Auto-Owners Ins. Co. v. Yates, 368 So. 2d 634 (Fla. 2d DCA 1979)].

[c] Insurance Agent Defined

An insurance agent is one who represents an insurer under an employment by it. Whether a person acts as a broker or as an agent is not determined by what that person is called but is to be determined from what he or she does. The general rule that an insurance broker is the agent of the insured rather than of the insurer is not altered simply because the broker receives compensation out of the premium. The mere fact that the insurance broker receives compensation from the insurer, such as by retention of all or part of the commissions paid from premiums received from the insured, cannot change his or her relation from that of agent for the policyholder to that of an agent for the insurance company [Auto-Owners Ins. Co. v. Yates, 368 So. 2d 634 (Fla. 2d DCA 1979)].

[d] Broker as Statutory Agent

In Florida, an insurance broker may become a statutory agent for the insurer under § 626.342(2), Fla. Stat., if the insurance company furnishes to the broker company materials, such as blank forms, applications, stationery, or other supplies used in soliciting or negotiating insurance contracts, and the insurance company subsequently accepts business from that broker. In this instance, the acts of the broker make the insurance company civilly liable to the insured in the same manner as if the insurer had specifically designated the broker as its agent, unless the insured knew or was put on notice of inquiry regarding limitations that may have been placed on the broker's actual authority. The insured may be put on notice if the application for insurance executed by the insured contains provisions that state the limitations placed on the broker's actual authority [Amstar Ins. Co. v. Cadet, 862.So. 2d 736 (Fla. 5th DCA 2003)].

[e] Requirements for Actual Agency

In Florida, the essential elements necessary to establish an actual agency relationship are (1) acknowledgment by the principal that the agent will act for him or her, (2) acceptance by the agent of the undertaking, and (3) control by the principal over the agent's actions. Generally, a principal may be held vicariously liable for the acts of his or her agent committed within the scope of the agent's real authority [Amstar Ins. Co. v. Cadet, 862 So. 2d 736 (Fla. 5th DCA 2003)].

[f] Requirements for Apparent Agency

In Florida, in order to determine the existence of apparent agency, it must be determined that (1) there was a representation by the principal, (2) the injured party relied on that representation, and (3) the injured party changed position in reliance on the representation and suffered detriment. A principal may be liable for the acts of his or her apparent agent that are committed within the scope of the apparent agency [Amstar Ins. Co. v. Cadet, 862 So. 2d 736 (Fla. 5th DCA 2003)].

§ 24.05 Rate and Premium Calculation

[1] Rating Organizations

The law allows workers' compensation insurers to use the services of rating organizations. Carriers and self-insurance funds may delegate to them the responsibility for filing manuals of classification, rules, and rates. In Florida, the organization used most often is the National Council on Compensation Insurance (NCCI). NCCI's member companies submit claim loss data sorted by payroll classification. The NCCI divides all occupations into payroll classes. NCCI then decides a separate rate for each class and bases this rate principally on loss experience [§ 624.482, Fla. Stat. (1993)].

For a general discussion of rate making, see LARSON'S WORKERS' COMPENSATION, DESK EDITION, Ch. 150, § 150.06 (Matthew Bender).

[2] Premium Calculation

There are more than 500 payroll or occupational classes used. The rate is a unit price that, when multiplied by each $100 of the payroll within the class, results in the calculation of the premium. For example, in 1998 the clerical class has a rate of $0.56 per $100 of the payroll and the rate for roofers is $52.53 per $100 of the payroll. An employer may have more than one payroll class. Certain classes, such as clerical and sales for example, are standard classes that may be applied to all employers. Employers in the construction industry may avail themselves of many classes, given certain restrictions. Note, however, that the goal of classification is the classifying of the employer generally and not classifying each employer activity. Following is the premium calculation formula based on a $50,000 payroll:

PREMIUM CALCULATION FORMULA

[Payroll] / [100] x [rate] = Manual premium

PAYROLL	RATE	MANUAL PREMIUM
CLERICAL	/ 100 x $0.56	$280.00
ROOFER	/ 100 x $52.53	$26,265

We call this manual premium because we base the calculations only on the rates listed in the Manual on Compensation as approved by the State of Florida.

[3] Premium Calculation and the Modification Factor

We base manual premiums on the loss experience of all employers in a given class. The actual premium assigned to an employer considers the employer's individual loss experience as compared with all other employers within that class. We call this procedure experience rating. Each employer is thus assigned a modification factor, commonly called the "mod." The Division of Workers' Compensation calculates the mod for self-insured employers. The National Council on Compensation Insurance calculates the mod for commercially insured employers.

Employers with better than average loss experience receive a credit mod, and those with worse than average experience receive a debit mod. The appropriate agency calculates the mod based on an employer's three-year loss experience, not including the most recently completed year. For example, an employer's mod for 1999 is based on the employer's losses for 1995, 1996, and 1997. An employer who has not been in business long enough or whose premium is too small will be assigned a 1.0 mod. Experience rating has a dramatic effect because the manual premium is multiplied by the mod. The formula is as follows:

MODIFICATION FACTOR CALCULATION

[Manual Premium] x [Mod] = Modified Premium

MANUAL PREMIUM	RATE	MOD FACTOR	MODIFIED PREMIUM	MOD TYPE
$24,265	$41.53	1.00	$24,265	NEUTRAL
$24,265	$41.53	.70	$16,985	CREDIT MOD
$24,265	$41.53	1.50	$36,397	DEBIT MOD

Frequently, the employer's insurance agent initially classifies the payroll, and carriers usually accept this on face value. Most carriers later verify the classifications, with auditors, after the policy's inception.

SPECIAL ALERT: The data used in the modification factor calculation includes reserves. Improperly reserved claims can, therefore, have a significant affect on an employer's premium.

[4] Premium Discounts and Surcharges

[a] Drug-Free Workplace Discount Program

An employer who creates a formal drug-free workplace program as defined by statute and rule and approved by the carrier, may be entitled to a five-percent premium discount. Beginning January 1, 1994, the discount entitlement ceases if the employer fails to maintain the program according to required procedures and standards [§ 440.102(2), Fla. Stat. (7/1/97)].

[b] Managed Care Discount Program

Initially, employers who participated in a carrier's managed care program were eligible for a premium discount of up to 10 percent. To qualify, the managed care plan must have been one approved by the Agency for Health Care Administration. Next, the carrier must have submitted the approved plan to the Department of Insurance for permission to offer a discount. Managed care, as a means to supply required medical treatment to injured workers, was voluntary until January 1, 1997. Then, participation by all carriers became mandatory. Simultaneously, the discount program ended [§ 440.134, Fla. Stat. (1/1/94); § 627.091, Fla. Stat. (1993)].

[c] Safety Program Surcharge

Carriers may voluntarily impose a surcharge of no more than 10 percent on the premium of a policyholder or fund member if that policyholder or fund member has been identified by the department as having been required to implement a safety program but has failed to do so [§ 627.212, Fla. Stat.].

[d] Safety Credit

A private or public employer may be eligible for premium credits for implementing a workplace safety program. At a minimum, the employer's safety program must include a written safety policy and safety rules, and make provision for safety inspections, preventative maintenance, safety training, first-aid, accident investigation, and necessary record keeping [*see* § 440.1025, Fla. Stat.].

[5] Cheating on Payroll

The 1990 Legislature concluded that part of the problem with Florida's workers' compensation system is that carriers do not collect all the premium due. The legislature believed that if they could deal with payroll cheaters and lazy carriers, perhaps the rate adequacy problem would go away. Cheaters and lazy carriers now face fines and criminal charges.

Applications for coverage must now contain the employer's sworn statement attesting to the accuracy of the information submitted. Further, anyone who knowingly submits false or misleading information to a carrier to avoid or improperly reduce premiums is guilty of a third-degree *felony.* This applies to anyone, including insurance agents and consultants [§ 440.381, Fla. Stat. (7/1/90); § 440.105(4), Fla. Stat. (7/1/97)].

[6] Payroll Audits Required

The legislature apparently believed that some carriers did not do a very good job auditing payroll. The law requires carriers to conduct employer audits in the construction classes at least once every year. Carriers must audit employers in all other classes at least every two years. Knowingly accepting incorrect classifications can result in a fine of up to $1,000 [§ 440.381(3), Fla. Stat. (7/1/90); § 440.52(4), Fla. Stat. (1991)].

[7] Hiding Employees

Another way to reduce premiums improperly is to "hide" employees. The law requires all employers to submit a quarterly earnings report to the Department of Unemployment Compensation. Employers must send a copy of that report to their workers' compensation carriers. The law imposes a severe penalty if the employer did not report an injured worker on the last quarterly report and the employer cannot prove it hired the injured worker after filing the report. In such a case, the employer must reimburse the carrier for all benefits paid or payable.

The law requires the Division of Workers' Compensation to notify carriers if this situation occurs. Apparently, the Division does not yet have the means to do this. If the employer fails to reimburse the carrier within 21 days after a demand for payment, the carrier may cancel coverage immediately. Further, the carrier may bring an action against the employer in circuit court. The carrier is entitled to recover its attorney fees "if it recovers any portion of the benefits paid" [§ 440.381(4), (7), Fla. Stat. (7/1/90)].

[8] Employer Penalty for Understating Payroll

[a] Insured Employers

An employer who intentionally understates its payroll or misrepresents its employee's duties to avoid proper classification for premium calculations is subject to a penalty. In such an event, the employer must first pay the correct premium. In addition, the employer must pay an additional 12-percent penalty to the carrier on the underpaid amount [§ 440.381(6), Fla. Stat. (7/1/90)].

Beginning January 1, 1994, the legislature increased this penalty. The penalty for concealing or misrepresenting the payroll is an amount equal to 10 times the difference in the premium paid and the amount the employer should have paid. In addition, the employer must pay the carrier's attorney fees [§ 440.381(6), Fla. Stat. (1/1/94)].

[b] Self-Insured Employers

Self-insured employers, of course, do not pay premiums. However, the premiums the employer would pay, if insured, must be calculated anyway. The state uses this to calculate a self-insurer's tax or assessment that goes to the Division's operating fund, the Special Disability Trust Fund, and the Self-Insurer's Guaranty Fund. The law authorizes the Division to conduct an audit of the employer's payroll records. If the audit reveals a deficiency in the amounts reported to the Division, or in the amounts paid to the Division, the entire cost of the audit is assessed against the employer [Fla. Admin. Code R. 69L-5.116 (1/10/2005)].

[9] Employer Interference With Audit

Many reports reached the legislature stating that some employers try to impede audits by suddenly discovering that necessary records are not available. In response, the legislature amended the law to impose a penalty if an employer fails, upon request of the auditor, to provide access to the documents specified in the Act. If, as a result, the carrier cannot complete the audit, the employer must pay a $500 penalty to the carrier to compensate the carrier for the cost of the audit [§ 440.381(5), Fla. Stat. (7/1/90)].

[10] Employer Failure to Allow Audit

If the employer "fails to provide reasonable access to payroll records for a payroll verification audit," the carrier can assess a severe penalty. In such an event, the employer must pay the carrier a penalty not to exceed three times the most recent estimated annual premium [§ 440.381(8), Fla. Stat. (7/1/90)].

§ 24.06 Disputes Between Carriers

[1] Recovery From Another Carrier

Frequently, two or more carriers will acknowledge that a worker's injuries are compensable, but then engage in debate over which of them owes the benefits. In such a case, no moral, ethical, or even financial basis exists for both carriers to refuse to pay. The Act allows either carrier to furnish benefits and be reimbursed for any sums later found not to be its responsibility [*see* Iowa National Mutual Insurance Co. v. Webb, 174 So. 2d 21, 25 (Fla. 1965)]. Note: If the other carrier can show that it has been prejudiced by lack of knowledge, it will not be liable for benefits paid before it received notice [§ 440.42(3), Fla. Stat. (1991)].

Interestingly, the term "reimbursement" is not defined in the statute. Faced with providing a definition, the court simply adopted the one found in Black's Law Dictionary (5th Edition), which is, "to pay back, to make restoration, to repay that expended; to indemnify, to make whole." This means that the judge of compensation claims can award reimbursement not only for benefits paid, but for prejudgment interest on those payments. Although not specifically mentioned, this should also include attorney's fees and costs [*see* Eastern Airlines v. Planet-Reliance Ins. Co., 695 So. 2d 732, 734 (Fla. 1st DCA 1996)].

[2] New Accident Versus Aggravation

The most common dispute arises over whether an injured worker's present complaints result from a new injury or from aggravating an old injury at a time when the employer was insured with a different carrier. If the judge of compensation claims decides that the injury is clearly one or the other, then obviously only one carrier will be responsible. Pending that determination, however, one carrier should voluntarily provide benefits. If the carrier providing benefits is ultimately held liable, it will have been managing the case since the outset and will have lost nothing. If the court holds the other carrier responsible, the law entitles the first carrier to reimbursement [§ 440.42(3), Fla. Stat. (1991)]. Again no harm is done. If the judge decides that the injured worker's present problems are a combination of both the old injury and a new one, the judge may allocate benefits between the carriers.

When one compensable injury follows another compensable injury, and merger is inapplicable, the courts will apportion the injured worker's compensation between the carriers. Apportionment depends on the extent to which each accident contributed to the injured worker's disability and to the need for medical care. If, in a worst case scenario, the parties cannot find the doctor who will venture an opinion on relative contribution, the carrier for the second accident must pay the entire claim. What happens if the injured worker suffers both a compensable injury and a non-compensable injury? In such a case, the judge must apportion or carve-out the effect of the non-compensable injury and award benefits only for the compensable one [*see* Atkins Const. Co. v. Wilson, 509 So. 2d 1185, 1187–1188 (Fla. 1st DCA 1987); Flagship Nat. Bank of Broward Cty. v. Hinkle, 479 So. 2d 828, 831 (Fla. 1st DCA 1985); Newhouse v. Volusia County School Bd., 474 So. 2d 1222, 1224 (Fla. 1st DCA 1985)].

Guide to Claims

[3] Contribution Between Carriers

[a] Requirements

The judges of compensation claims have authority to decide and apportion liability between carriers and employers for successive accidents. If the judge can identify the effects of successive accidents and injuries as to particular employers or carriers, the judge can apportion the cost of such injuries among them.

If an injured worker suffers a second accident and injury with a new employer, or with the same employer insured with a different carrier, contribution may apply if the first accident was the direct, immediate, and proximate cause of the second accident. This is especially true if the employment, at the time of the second accident, created an increased risk to the injured worker that contributed to causing the accident [§ 440.42(3), Fla. Stat. (1991)].

For a general discussion of contribution between carriers, see Larson's Workers' Compensation, Desk Edition, Ch. 153, § 153.03 (Matthew Bender).

[b] Case Examples

[i] Contribution Based on Medical Evidence

Ernest Tolvanen worked as a mechanic for Eastern Air Lines. He suffered two back injuries at work, 14 months apart. During the period between accidents, Eastern changed insurance carriers. Doctors testified that Tolvanen's herniated disc resulted from the combination of the two accidents. The doctors could not, however, accurately apportion Tolvanen's disability to the individual accidents. The judge, therefore, simply apportioned liability 50/50 between the two carriers. Florida's Supreme Court held this 50/50 apportionment was proper because the medical evidence was conflicting and inconclusive [*see* Tolvanen v. Eastern Air Lines, 287 So. 2d 299, 301 (Fla. 1973)].

The judges of compensation claims must base an allocation between employers and carriers upon the extent to which each accident contributes to any resulting disability or the need for medical care [*see* Sauer Indus. Contracting Inc. v. Ditch, 547 So. 2d 276, 277 (Fla. 1st DCA 1989)].

[ii] Multiple Accidents and Employers

Richard Berry suffered three different disabling accidents with three different employers and carriers. In the third accident, he suffered a fractured wrist that was the least serious of the three injuries. The combination of the three injuries, however, left Berry permanently and totally disabled. The trial judge held that the last employer was solely responsible. The First District Court of Appeal reversed, stating this was impermissible. The court ordered the judge to allocate benefits between the carriers because injured worker's state of permanent total disability resulted from the cumulative effect of all three injuries [*see* Oaks Farm v. Berry, 500 So. 2d 175, 176–177 (Fla. 1st DCA 1986)].

[iii] Apportioning Attorney's Fees in Contribution Cases

If attorney's fees are an issue in such a case, the judge must apportion fees between and among the carriers as well [*see* Champion Intern. v. St. Regis Paper Co., 562 So. 2d 416, 417–418 (Fla. 1st DCA 1990)].

[iv] Old Injury Causing New Accident

Vernon Bradshaw suffered a disabling knee injury. Although left with permanent impairment, he returned to work but later the employer fired him. He obtained a new job with a retail store assembling bicycles. One day he fell off a ladder while balancing a bicycle that he was attempting to hang on a ceiling hook. Bradshaw testified that he fell because his injured knee just "gave way." The judge of compensation claims refused to apportion the injury between the two employers. The judge believed that the first injury directly caused the second one and that the new job did not contribute to it. The First District Court of Appeal disagreed and reversed.

The court held that common sense suggests that the strain of climbing a ladder would increase the strain on Bradshaw's knee. Climbing a ladder under the weight of an assembled bicycle, said the court, dramatically increased the likelihood of a knee failure. The court remanded the case to the JCC to apportion liability between the two employers [*see* Custom Architectural Metals v. Bradshaw, 623 So. 2d 804, 806–807 (Fla. 1st DCA 1993)].

Irwin Dort injured his lower back in 1975. Initially, he missed very little time from work, but his back condition deteriorated over the next several years. By 1980, corrective disc surgery became necessary. After several months recovering, Dort returned to work, but for a different employer where he earned more than he had with the original employer. Over the years he continued to work, but also continued to have problems with his lower back. In 1983, he was involved in an accident injuring his neck, arm, and shoulders. He underwent extensive treatment and was twice hospitalized in 1984. A physician connected the two injuries when he opined that awkward positioning required by the subsequent new shoulder injury had aggravated the old back injury.

The combination of the injuries rendered Dort permanently and totally disabled. The JCC apportioned permanent total disability benefits against both employers: two-thirds against the first employer; and one-third against the second employer. The First District Court of Appeal affirmed the judge's order [*see* Wood & Wood v. Dort, 625 So. 2d 42, 44–45 (Fla. 1st DCA 1993)].

[c] Washout Settlements in Contribution Cases

In *Dort* [*see also* [b], *above*], the second employer settled the case with Dort for $125,000 before the apportionment hearing took place. On appeal, the first employer argued that the second employer's lump-sum settlement barred any recovery of further permanent total disability benefits from them. The court held this was not necessarily so. A settlement agreement is like any other contract. If the terms of the agreement are susceptible to more than one construction, this presents an issue of fact. The settlement agreement with the second employer was unclear about whether or not it extinguished the injured worker's right to recover further benefits from the first employer. Accordingly, the court remanded the case to the JCC to decide the intended effect of the settlement agreement [*see* Wood & Wood v. Dort, 625 So. 2d 42, 45 (Fla. 1st DCA 1993)].

Look at these cases like liability cases involving joint tortfeasors. If claims are pending against multiple carriers and employers, a joint stipulation releasing only one employer or carrier may show lack of intent to settle the injured worker's entire claim. Adjudicating contribution before a washout settlement by one carrier is another indication the carrier did not intend to settle the entire claim against all parties. Carriers must craft washout settlements in contribution cases carefully [*see* ch. 21, for discussion on washout settlements].

[d] Allocating Benefits in Contribution Cases

The cases hold that the judges of compensation claims must precisely allocate benefits even though this task is difficult. A judge may not simply use equal division between two carriers as a fallback position for apportioning benefits. Instead, the judge must consider the extent to which each accident contributed to the injured worker's compensable disability after maximum medical improvement from the last accident [*see* Copeland Steel Erectors v. McCollom, 587 So. 2d 658, 659–660 (Fla. 1st DCA 1991)].

Recall, however, that the Florida Supreme Court has held such equal division may be proper when the evidence is conflicting and inconclusive [*see* Tolvanen v. Eastern Air Lines, 287 So. 2d 299, 301 (Fla. 1973)].

SPECIAL ALERT: In contribution cases, the second employer likely has a viable claim for reimbursement from the Special Disability Trust Fund. Carriers, however, must weigh this against the uncertain savings they may realize in a contribution proceeding. If the judge correctly apportions the cost of the injury between the carriers, the second carrier may be unable to show it has paid excess benefits entitling it to Special Disability Trust Fund reimbursement because of the first impairment.

[e] Contribution in Occupational Disease Cases

As noted in [3][a], *above*, in appropriate cases involving different employers or different carriers, the JCC has the authority to apportion liability for benefits between them. In occupational disease cases, however, benefits are never apportionable because the last injurious exposure rule places the liability on the carrier at risk when the worker was last injuriously exposed to the hazards of the disease.

Whichever carrier defends against a claim for contribution or apportionment on the basis that the injury is an occupational disease and thus not apportionable, has the burden of proof. Here, the worker suffered carpal tunnel syndrome first while the employer was insured with AIIC. Sometime later, she filed another claim for carpal tunnel while the employer was insured with Chubb. AIIC argued that the claimant suffered from an occupational disease and that Chubb should be exclusively liable. The court held that carpal tunnel is not an occupational disease, but is instead a repetitive trauma or exposure and that apportionment may apply [*see* Associated Indus. Ins. v. Federal Ins., 707 So. 2d 880, 882–884 (Fla. 1st DCA 1998); *see also* Ch. 8, for a complete discussion of occupational disease cases].

§ 24.07 Jurisdiction in Carrier/Employer Disputes

Disputes between an employer and its workers' compensation carrier are usually over the contract of insurance. Does jurisdiction lie with the judge of compensation claims or the circuit court? Jurisdiction depends on whether the dispute will affect an injured worker's ability to collect benefits. A judge of compensation claims has full authority to decide all questions about workers' compensation claims [§ 440.25, Fla. Stat. (7/1/97)]. This means that a JCC has authority to resolve contractual disputes involving insurance coverage if the real issue is whether the policy applies to a particular claim. If the dispute does not involve a pending claim, jurisdiction is with the circuit court [*see* Kent Ins. Co. v. Hobbs, 421 So. 2d 658, 659 (Fla. 1st DCA 1982)].

For a general discussion of jurisdictional issues regarding insurance disputes, see LARSON'S WORKERS' COMPENSATION, DESK EDITION, Ch. 150, § 150.04 (Matthew Bender).

§ 24.08 Reinsurance

[1] Defined

An oversimplified definition of reinsurance is insurance for insurance companies. A more formal definition is the practice under which one party, called the reinsurer, in consideration of a premium paid, agrees to indemnify another party, called the reinsured, for part or all of the liability assumed by the latter party under a policy or policies of insurance that it has issued. The reinsured party is often called the Primary Insurer or the Ceding Company.

[2] Purpose

A primary carrier will purchase reinsurance coverage for a variety of reasons, but the most important and common are as follows:

1. Reinsurance coverage is required by law.
2. To increase sales capacity.

3. For protection against catastrophic loss.
4. To stabilize financial results.

Whether a carrier achieves these goals depends on the type of reinsurance program purchased and on the financial strength of the reinsurer. If the reinsurer cannot or will not pay its claims when called upon, the primary carrier will often find itself in serious financial trouble.

[3] Types of Reinsurance

[a] In General

Usually, we can describe reinsurance in two types: "pro rata share" and "excess of loss." Under a pro rata share arrangement the reinsurer agrees to pay the primary insurer for losses above an agreed upon percentage. Excess of loss arrangements come in four types as described in [b]–[e], *below.*

[b] Per Occurrence

This coverage is designed to protect the primary carrier against excess loss arising out of a single event. The primary carrier agrees to retain part of a given loss, typically anywhere from $100,000 to $500,000. The reinsurer agrees to reimburse the primary carrier for losses over this retention up to an agreed limit, for example, $1,000,000. If the loss exceeds this limit, the remainder is the primary carrier's responsibility. For example, assume the primary carrier has a $500,000 retention and a $1,000,000 reinsurance limit. An accident occurs that renders the injured worker quadriplegic, and the total cost is $2,000,000. The primary carrier pays the first $500,000. The reinsurer reimburses the next $1,000,000, but the remaining $500,000 remains with the primary carrier. Consequently, the primary carrier may purchase two or more reinsurance policies. The second policy, for example, may start at $1,000,000, to begin when the first policy is exhausted.

[c] Aggregate

Having protected itself against a catastrophic loss in a single occurrence, a carrier may wish to cap its total losses in a given year by purchasing an aggregate reinsurance policy. Under this arrangement, the reinsurer agrees to reimburse the primary carrier if losses in a given year exceed an agreed dollar amount or an agreed percentage of the carrier's premiums.

[d] Stop Loss

This is another form of aggregate coverage under which the primary carrier receives reimbursement if losses exceed an agreed loss ratio.

[e] Per Risk

Under this arrangement the primary carrier is protected if losses on each insured employer exceed an agreed amount.

[4] Basic Forms of Reinsurance

Reinsurance contracts are usually in one of two basic forms: treaty reinsurance and

Guide to Claims

facultative reinsurance. Under a treaty arrangement, the reinsurer agrees to cover the primary carrier's entire book of business. In other words, the reinsurer is willing to trust the judgment of the primary carrier's underwriters. In a facultative arrangement the companies negotiate the reinsurance coverage on a risk-by-risk basis.

[5] Reinsurance Policy Provisions

[a] Rules of Construction

Unlike the basic workers' compensation policy, reinsurance policies are not standard and may vary widely in the terms of coverage. If an insurance policy contains ambiguous language, the courts will always resolve such doubt in favor of the insured. The law considers insurance contracts between an insurance company and members of the public as "contracts of adhesion." That is, the carrier dictates all the terms and conditions of the contract and the insured has no say in its construction. Because an insurer has such a significant advantage in drawing up the contract, and in its superior knowledge, the courts have long held that doubts about meaning will be resolved in favor of the insured party. This is not so in reinsurance policies, which are negotiated between two insurance companies. The general rules of construction of insurance contracts do not apply between two insurance companies [*see* Great American Ins. Co. v. Fireman's Fund Ins. Co., 481 F.2d 948, 954 (2d Cir. 1973)].

[b] Tips and Traps

The most frequent and serious problem reinsurers have with primary carriers is their failure to report required losses timely. Adjusters should become familiar with the terms and conditions of any reinsurance contracts, in particular the reporting requirements. Typically, these include both numerical and verbal reporting triggers. For example, one large reinsurer requires a report from the primary carrier if its incurred loss (paid plus reserves) on a case is equal to or greater than one-third of the retention. Carriers must report other cases, such as serious head injuries, multiple fractures, and serious burns, whatever the incurred loss amount. Another reinsurer's policy is more vague. It requires a report "when an injury occurs that appears reasonably likely to involve liability on the part of the reinsurer."

Failure to comply with the reporting requirement will likely result in the reinsurer denying the carrier's claim.

[c] Contract of Utmost Good Faith

Reinsurance contracts are usually drawn in clear language and do not contain the confusing legalese found in many primary policies. The parties to reinsurance contracts are theoretically highly sophisticated and possess sufficient expertise so that they do not require verbose contracts.

The reinsurer's knowledge of the facts of a case is limited to reports from the primary carrier. Primary carriers, therefore, have a duty to act with utmost good faith. This duty requires the primary carrier to act with the interests of the reinsurer in mind.

Adjusters should never make any ex-gratia payments without conferring with the reinsurer, including payments for benefits not required under the law and, in particular, washout settlements. Adjusters must always inform the reinsurer immediately about significant case developments. Finally, a word of advice to adjusters: spend every dollar for both expense and benefits as if it were your own. The attitude that "it is the reinsurer's money" can lead to inconsistent claim handling and conflict.

§ 24.09 Workers' Compensation Fraud

[1] Division of Insurance Fraud

Fraud is an unfortunate part of insurance claims and is as old as the industry itself. Florida's first major effort to combat fraudulent claims created the Division of Insurance Fraud in 1976. Over the years the Division's size and its powers have increased significantly. Fraud Division investigators not only have the authority to issue search warrants, but are empowered to make arrests as well.

Insurers, self-insurance funds, insurance agents, medical review committees, and individual professionals licensed by the Department of Professional Regulation must report any suspected fraud to the Division of Insurance Fraud. Any person making such a report is immune from civil liability for libel, slander, or any other relevant tort. Immunity does not apply, of course, if the report is intentionally false. Knowingly filing a false report or retaliating against someone who files a report is a first-degree misdemeanor. This tort immunity extends to ordinary citizens as well. Upon receipt of a report, the Division of Insurance Fraud will decide if further investigation is warranted [§ 440.1051, Fla. Stat.; § 626.989, Fla. Stat. (7/1/97)].

If the Division does begin an investigation, the carrier is unlikely to know the status unless the authorities make an arrest. The Division records are not subject to public inspection or even to subpoena. This is to protect the person under investigation. If the investigation results in an adjudication of guilt, the insurer is entitled to recover compensatory damages, including attorney's fees and costs.

[2] Bureau of Workers' Compensation Fraud

As part of its sweeping reforms, the 1990 Legislature created a special workers' compensation fraud bureau within the Division of Insurance Fraud. This bureau is dedicated to the investigation and prosecution of workers' compensation fraud cases. While fraud by workers is a serious problem, fraud is not unique to them. Temptation can infect anyone involved in the system. When they succumb, they are subject to arrest, fines, and even jail.

Employers may try to show they have workers' compensation coverage using forged or altered certificates of coverage. They may submit deliberately understated payroll records or mis-classify employees to reduce premiums illegally.

Insurance agents violate the law when they issue insurance certificates and then pocket the premiums. Some may help an employer in schemes designed to skirt the law. Even highly compensated professionals, such as doctors and lawyers, are not immune from temptation to defraud. Fraud in all its forms and sources is subject to investigation and

Guide to Claims

criminal arrest by the Bureau of Workers' Compensation Fraud.

[3] Special Investigation Units

All carriers licensed in Florida must create antifraud investigation units if they have at least $10 million in written premiums. The law allows insurers to either employ their own investigators or to contract with an outside firm. Insurers must file a description of their staff units, or a copy of their contract with an outside agency, with the Division of Insurance Fraud. The law does not compel smaller insurers to set up such units, but if they do not, they must file an antifraud plan with the Division [§ 626.9891, Fla. Stat. (7/1/95)].

[4] Penalty for Insurance Fraud

Any person who violates the provision of § 440.105(4), Fla. Stat. is guilty of insurance fraud. Beginning January 1, 1999, the severity of the crime depends on the amount of money involved [*see* § 24.10].

Any person convicted of workers' compensation fraud and, thus, of committing a felony, is subject to fines and imprisonment [§§ 775.082, 775.083, 775.084, Fla. Stat.]. Fraudulent activity, as the statute defines it, is not restricted to workers. Florida statutes provide that fraudulent activity in workers' compensation is a felony [§ 440.105(4)(f), Fla. Stat. (7/1/97)]. Fraudulent activities include making false or misleading statements or representations to obtain or deny benefits or payments.

Physicians who help or even urge a person to commit fraud are themselves guilty of fraud. Besides fines and jail, physicians face professional sanctions, including losing their licenses. The statute defines misleading or deceptive statements to include doctors' reports and bills.

Lawyers who help or urge an injured worker to collect benefits fraudulently are guilty of a third-degree felony. This includes unlawfully soliciting clients in hospitals, courthouses, or other public institutions. Besides possible fines and jail, lawyers face sanctions by the Bar and possible disbarment by the Florida Supreme Court.

The statute grants the damaged party the right to sue the guilty parties for damages and costs. These provisions apply to employers, insurance companies, and claim adjusting companies. It is a criminal act to deceive or cheat any injured worker regarding any claim.

[5] Referral Procedure

The Bureau of Workers' Compensation Fraud suggests the following procedures when adjusters suspect they have received a fraudulent claim:

1. Send a cover letter to the bureau explaining your suspicions.

2. Give the bureau copies of any documents that establish statements made in applications for workers' compensation benefits.

3. Provide copies of documents on which a claim was submitted, with evidence of payments made.

4. Provide copies of any other documents that support the suspicion that fraudulent activity has occurred. Keep all original documents in the claim file.

[6] Fraud Bureau Regions and Offices

The Bureau of Workers' Compensation Fraud operates from regional offices.

NORTH REGION
CAPTAIN BRUCE ASHLEY
850.413.3115

PENSACOLA FIELD OFFICE
850.453.7802
610 Burgess Road
Pensacola, FL 32504
LT. DAVID P. BOYD
Counties: Gulf, Bay, Calhoun, Escambia, Holmes, Jackson, Okaloosa, Santa Rosa, Walton, Washington

PANAMA CITY FIELD OFFICE
850.872.4552
429 S. Tyndall Parkway, Suite. G
Panama City, FL 32404
Vacant

TALLAHASSEE FIELD OFFICE
850.413.3115
200 East Gaines Street
Tallahassee, FL 32399-0324
LT. DAVID P. BOYD
Counties: Franklin, Gadsden, Jefferson, Lafayette, Leon, Liberty, Madison, Taylor, Wakulla

JACKSONVILLE FIELD OFFICE
904.348.2604
1965 Beachway Road, Suite 105
Jacksonville, FL 32207-2340
LT. DONALD F. TAYLOR
Counties: Baker, Bradford, Clay, Columbia, Duval, Hamilton, Nassau, St. Johns, Suwannee, Union

OCALA OFFICE
352.732.1746
11655 NW Gainesville Road
Ocala, FL 34482
INV. II. TONY DEFALCO
Counties: Dixie, Martin, Citrus, Putnam, Flagler, Alachua, Gilchrist, Levy

CENTRAL REGION
CAPTAIN VINCE MAZZARA
813.890.1902

ORLANDO – FIELD OFFICE
407.835.4402
400 West Robinson Street, Suite S-823
Hurston Building, Orlando, FL 3280l
LT. CARLOS FERNANDEZ
Counties: Brevard, Citrus, Lake, Orange, Osceola, Seminole, Sumter, Volusia

HILLSBOROUGH FIELD OFFICE
8l3.890.1902
6800 North Dale Mabry Highway, Suite 232
Tampa, FL 33614
LT. IRA WARDER
Counties: Hardee, Hernando, Hillsborough, Pasco, Polk

PINELLAS FIELD OFFICE
727.563.1142
St. Lucie Building, 9800 4th St., Suite 100
St. Petersburg, FL 33702
LT. VINCE PICCIOLO
Counties: DeSoto, Manatee, Pinellas, Sarasota

SOUTH REGION
CAPTAIN SIMON BLANK
561.242.5442

WEST PALM BEACH FIELD OFFICE
561.242.5442
1655 Palm Beach Lakes Blvd., Suite 721
West Palm Beach, Florida 3340l
LT. RICHARD S. DWYER
LT. VANCE AKINS
Counties: Indian River, Martin, Okeechobee, Palm Beach, St. Lucie

FORT MYERS FIELD OFFICE
239.461.4002
2295 Victoria Avenue, Suite l78
Fort Myers, FL 3390l
LT. VANCE AKINS
Counties: Charlotte, Collier, Glades, Hendry, Highlands, Lee

BROWARD REGION
CAPTAIN BILL SANTNER
954.321.2902

PLANTATION FIELD OFFICE
954.321.2902
499 N.W. 70 Avenue, Suite 309
Plantation, FL 33317
LT. EVELYN VALLES
LT. MARK DEE
LT. KATHY CLARK-SCOTT
Counties: Broward

MIAMI DADE REGION
CAPTAIN STEVEN SMITH
305.536.0302

MIAMI FIELD OFFICE
305.536.0302
401 N. W. 2 Avenue, Suite N-321
Miami, FL 33128
LT. JOHN DYGON
LT. MIKE SHEA
Counties: Dade, Monroe

The Bureau now operates a toll-free fraud hotline from 8:00 a.m. to 5:00 p.m. weekdays. The number is: 1-800-378-0445. The number outside of Florida is: 1-850-413-3261.

§ 24.10 Prohibited Activities

[1] Crimes and Penalties

The Workers' Compensation Act contains many prohibited activities. Previously, these were scattered about within Chapter 440 in no particular order. The legislature has consolidated these various provisions into newly-created sections, § 440.105, Fla. Stat. and § 440.106, Fla. Stat. For offenses committed before January 1, 1999, the various prohibited acts carry penalties ranging from second degree misdemeanors to third degree felonies. For the felony offenses listed in § 440.105(4), Fla. Stat., the severity depends on the amount of premiums or benefits involved. Formerly, the offenses listed in this subsection constituted a third degree felony. Now, as the amount of benefits or premiums involved increases, the severity increases as follows [*see* § 440.105(4)(f), Fla. Stat. (1998)]:

1. If the amount is less than $20,000, the offense constitutes a third degree felony.
2. If the amount is $20,000 or more, but less than $100,000, the offense constitutes a second degree felony.
3. If the amount involved is $100,000 or more, the offense constitutes a first degree felony.

The maximum penalties are as follows [§§ 775.082, 775.083, 775.084, Fla. Stat.]:

Second degree misdemeanors–$500 fine and 60 days in jail

First degree misdemeanors–1,000 fine and one year in jail

Third degree felonies–$5,000 fine and five years in jail

Second degree felonies–$10,000 fine and 15 years in jail

First degree felonies–$10,000 fine and 30 years in jail

The prohibited acts are listed below in order of severity for offenses occurring before January 1, 1999. Remember that severity for offenses after that date depends on the amount of money involved. For the purposes of this section, the term "statement" includes notices, representations, statements, proof of injury, bills for service, diagnosis, prescriptions, hospital and doctor records, x-rays, test results, and any other evidence of loss, injury, or expense. In addition, all claim forms must bear the following statement [§ 440.105(7), Fla. Stat. (7/1/97)]:

> Any person who, knowingly and with intent to injure, defraud, or deceive any employer or employee, insurance company, or self-insured program, files a statement of claim containing any false or misleading information is guilty of a felony of the third degree.

[2] Employers

[a] First-Degree Misdemeanors

Employers who commit the following acts are guilty of first-degree misdemeanors [§ 440.105(2), Fla. Stat. (10/1/2003)]:

1. Coercing or attempting to coerce an employee to obtain a certificate of exemption from coverage as a precondition of employment.

2. Discharging or refusing to hire someone because the person has filed a workers' compensation claim for benefits.

3. Discharging or disciplining an employee for reporting violations of any of the provisions of the Workers' Compensation Act.

4. Violating a stop-work order issued by the Division of Workers' Compensation.

5. Knowingly failing to update an application for coverage within seven days after the reporting date or failing to post notice of coverage as required by § 440.40, Fla. Stat.

6. Knowingly participating in the creation of the employment relationship in which the employee has used any false, fraudulent, or misleading oral or written statement as evidence of identity.

[b] Insurance Fraud and Third-Degree Felonies

An employer who commits any of the following acts is guilty of insurance fraud, a third-degree felony. The severity of punishment increases, depending on the amount of money involved [§ 440.105(4)(a), Fla. Stat. (7/1/97); *see* [1], *above*]:

1. Presenting false or fraudulent or even misleading statements, oral or written, as evidence of compliance with § 440.38, Fla. Stat., which requires employers to obtain workers' compensation coverage.

2. Requiring an employee to pay part of the workers' compensation premium or to contribute to a benefit fund by payroll deduction.

3. Failing to obtain workers' compensation coverage if required by law to do so.

In addition, the Division may refer contractors to the appropriate licensing agency for further disciplinary action [§ 440.106(4), Fla. Stat. (7/1/97)].

[3] Insurance Carriers

The following act is a second-degree misdemeanor [§ 440.105(2)(b), Fla. Stat. (7/1/97)]:

Revoking or canceling a workers' compensation policy because the employer rehired an injured worker or because an employee filed a workers' compensation claim.

Besides other penalties, carriers and self-insurers are subject to revocation of their certificate of authority. Insurance agents face possible revocation or suspension of license [§ 440.106(3), Fla. Stat. (7/1/97)].

[4] Lawyers

The following act is a first-degree misdemeanor. After that date, the severity of punishment increases depending on the amount of money involved [§ 440.105(3)(b), Fla. Stat. (7/1/97); *see* [1], *above*]:

Failing to have a fee approved by a judge of compensation claims.

The following act, if committed before January 1, 1999, is a third degree felony. After that date, the severity increases depending on the amount of money involved [§ 440.105(4)(f), Fla. Stat. (7/1/97)]:

Unlawfully soliciting clients to make workers' compensation claims.

Besides possible criminal prosecution, lawyers face sanctions imposed by bar association grievance committees and possible disbarment by the Florida Supreme Court.

[5] Physicians

The following, if committed prior to January 1, 1999, is a third-degree felony. After that date, the severity of punishment increases depending on the amount of money involved [§ 440.105(4)(c), Fla. Stat. (7/1/97); *see* [1], *above*]:

To help or conspire with any person to violate the provisions of the Workers' Compensation Act.

Besides possible criminal prosecution, physicians face administrative sanctions by the appropriate licensing agency [§ 440.106(2), Fla. Stat. (7/1/97)].

[6] All Persons

Any of the following acts, if committed prior to January 1, 1999, constitutes insurance fraud and, as such, is a third-degree felony. After that date, the severity of punishment increases, depending on the amount of money involved [§ 440.105(4), Fla. Stat. (7/1/97); *see* [1], *above*]:

1. Making, or causing to be made, false or misleading oral or written statements to obtain or deny benefits.

2. Presenting, or causing to be presented, any oral or written statement, knowing it contains false or misleading information material to a claim for the purpose of obtaining or denying benefits.

3. Preparing, or causing to be prepared, any oral or written statement intended to be presented to an employer or insurance carrier in support of a claim, knowing it contains false, incomplete, or misleading information.

4. Helping or even urging a person to engage in prohibited activities.

5. Making false or misleading oral or written statements to obtain workers' compensation coverage or to reduce premiums. This includes knowingly omitting or concealing material information.

6. Knowingly misrepresenting or concealing payroll, classification of workers, or loss history to diminish or avoid premiums.

7. Knowingly presenting, or causing to be presented, false or misleading oral or written statements as evidence of eligibility for a certificate of exemption.

The following were added, effective October 1, 2003 [*see* § 440.105(4)(b), Fla. Stat. (10/1/2003)]:

8. Knowingly violating a stop-work order issued by the department pursuant to § 440.107, Fla. Stat.

9. Knowingly presenting, or causing to be presented, any false, fraudulent, or misleading oral or written statement to any person as evidence of identity for the purpose of obtaining employment or filing or supporting a claim for workers' compensation benefits.

CHAPTER 25

THE AMERICANS WITH DISABILITIES ACT AND ITS EFFECT ON WORKERS' COMPENSATION

SYNOPSIS

§ 25.01 Purpose of Americans With Disabilities Act (ADA)

. . . most people, no doubt, when they espouse human rights, make their own mental reservations about the proper application of the word human.
Suzanne LaFollette, American feminist and writer
"The beginnings of Emancipation," 1926

The Americans with Disabilities Act—or the ADA as most people call it—is the most significant federal anti-discrimination legislation since the Civil Rights Act of 1964 [*see* Americans with Disabilities Act of 1990, Pub. L. No. 101-336, 104 Stat. 327 (1990), codified at 42 U.S.C.S. § 12101 et seq.]. The ADA's broad purpose is to prevent discrimination against disabled persons in hiring and other employment activities [42 U.S.C.S. § 12101(b)]. The law protects not only those people with typical disabilities such as blindness, but also covers less obvious disabilities such as recovering drug abusers, AIDS victims, and people with mental impairments.

Although probably not intended, a possible side effect is some significant change—or at least attempts to change—the administration of Florida's and other states' workers' compensation laws. Some people have even claimed that Florida's workers' compensation law itself violates the ADA [*see* § 25.02].

For detailed coverage of the ADA, see Ogletree, et al., AMERICANS WITH DISABILITIES ACT (Matthew Bender).

§ 25.02 Florida's Workers' Compensation Act Does Not Violate ADA

In 1995, Morton Barry argued that the 1994 Florida Workers' Compensation Act is discriminatory and therefore violates the federal law. Barry claimed that by reducing certain benefits, the new Florida law discriminates against people disabled in work accidents after the law took effect on January 1, 1994. In *Cramer v. State of Florida,* the federal court heard and rejected a similar argument [*see* Cramer v. State of Florida, 885 F. Supp. 1545, 1550–1553 (M.D. Fla. 1995), *aff'd,* 117 F.3d 1258 (11th Cir. 1997)].

A Florida judge of compensation claims rejected Barry's argument, and the First District Court of Appeal agreed and affirmed the lower court's order. Recognizing the significance of the issue, however, the First District Court of Appeal certified the question to the Florida Supreme Court as one of great public importance [*see* Barry v. Burdines and the Travelers, 667 So. 2d 241, 242 (Fla. 1st DCA 1995)].

In 1996 the Florida Supreme Court, agreeing with the First District Court of Appeal, held that Florida's Workers' Compensation Act does not violate the ADA [*see* Barry v. Burdines, 675 So. 2d 587, 589–590 (Fla. 1996), *cert. denied,* 519 U.S. 966, 136 L. Ed. 2d 306, 117 S. Ct. 390 (1996)].

In a Massachusetts case, William McDonald suffered a severe injury in an industrial accident. The insurer, however, denied his workers' compensation claim. Undaunted, McDonald sued the insurer and the state, claiming both violated his rights under the ADA. How? McDonald argued that denying workers' compensation benefits to a disabled person violated the ADA. The state was also guilty, said McDonald, because it failed to force the insurer to pay benefits. The court dismissed the suit, concluding neither allegation had merit, nor was there coverage under the ADA [*see* McDonald v. Com. of Mass., 901 F. Supp. 471, 478–479 (D. Mass. 1995)].

CAVEAT: The following discussion is not a comprehensive treatise on the ADA. Instead, it is a summary designed to help decide the effect the ADA may have on a Florida workers' compensation claim. For an in-depth review of the law, see Olgletree, et al., AMERICANS WITH DISABILITIES ACT (Matthew Bender), *The Americans With Disabilities Act Desk Manual 1992* (Florida Workers' Compensation Institute, Inc.), and *EEOC Technical Assistance Manual* (ADA Technical Assistance Center, Atlanta, Georgia). Be sure to keep up with the EEOC's statements of its interpretations of the ADA statutes. Although the EEOC's statements are not legal precedent, courts give them significant consideration [*see* Little v. F.B.I., 1 F.3d 255, 258 (4th Cir. 1993)].

§ 25.03 Scope and Coverage of ADA

[1] ADA Basics

This chapter's purpose is to discuss possible effects the ADA may have on the Florida Workers' Compensation system. First, however, we must understand the basics of the federal law.

Title I of the ADA contains the employment provisions. It became fully effective on July 26, 1990, and applies to all employers with 15 or more employees. In other words, the law does not apply to employers with 14 or fewer workers [42 U.S.C.S. § 12111(5)(A); 29 C.F.R. § 1630.2(e)(1)]. Thus, the ADA cannot affect the workers' compensation claims of small employers, i.e., those with 14 or fewer workers. The ADA prohibits covered employers from discriminating against a person with a disability who can do the essential job functions with or without reasonable accommodation [42 U.S.C.S. § 12112(b); 29 C.F.R. § 1630.9(a)]. An exception arises if accommodation is unreasonable in that it creates an undue hardship to the employer [42 U.S.C.S. § 12112(b)(5)(A)]. We will define and discuss these terms in §§ 25.04 and 25.05.

[2] Enforcement and Penalties

The Equal Employment Opportunity Commission (EEOC) is the federal agency charged with both the administration and enforcement of the ADA [42 U.S.C.S. § 2000e-6]. All workers can file a complaint against employers suspected of violating their individual rights under the ADA. An employer guilty of violating the ADA faces substantial penalties, including assessments of awards for compensatory and punitive damages. These assessments and awards, however, are limited. The award's size depends on the employer's size. The larger the employer, the larger the penalty. The maximum award against employers with 16 to100 employees is $50,000. For companies with up to 200 workers, the amount doubles to $100,000. Employers with up to 500 workers face awards of up to $200,000. Finally, employers with more than 500 workers are subject to a maximum award of $300,000 [42 U.S.C.S. § 1981a(c)(1)]. In addition, the court may assess litigation costs against the employer, and the aggrieved employee can sue the employer for damages, including reinstatement and back pay [42 U.S.C.S. § 2000e-5(g)]. All other aspects of the Civil Rights Act of 1991 apply, including the right to a jury trial [*see* 42 U.S.C.S. § 1981A(b)(4)(c)(1)]. On top of all this, many employers have no insurance coverage to defend and indemnify them against such lawsuits.

§ 25.04 Disability Defined

[1] Disability Tests

Remember that the ADA does not apply to all workers. It applies only to workers with disabilities. The ADA's definition of "disability" is extremely broad. However, the EEOC's Technical Assistance Manual makes it clear that just because a worker is receiving disability benefits under workers' compensation, Social Security, or other disability laws does not mean the worker automatically meets the ADA's definition of "disabled" [*see* EEOC Technical Assistance Manual at IX-3; *see, e.g.,* Harding v. Winn-Dixie Stores, Inc., 907 F. Supp. 386, 390 (M.D. Fla. 1995) (workers' compensation considers an individual to be disabled based upon incapacity to earn wages commensurate to those received prior to any injury, while same impairment under ADA may or may not substantially limit a major life activity)].

To determine if the ADA considers a person disabled, we must apply a three-pronged test. People are disabled and entitled to the protection of the ADA if they [42 U.S.C.S. § 12102(2)]:

1. Have a physical or mental impairment that substantially limits a major life

activity;

2. Have a record of having an impairment; *or*
3. Are regarded as having an impairment.

[2] Physical or Mental Impairment

[a] Impairment Defined

The Equal Employment Opportunity Commission regulations provide that a physical or mental impairment is any physiological disorder or condition, cosmetic disfigurement, or anatomical loss affecting one or more of the following body systems [29 C.F.R. § 1630.2(h)]:

- Neurological
- Musculoskeletal
- Special sense organs
- Respiratory, including speech organs
- Cardiovascular
- Reproductive
- Digestive
- Genitourinary
- Hemic and lymphatic
- Skin
- Endocrine

Mental or psychological disorders, including mental retardation, organic brain disorders, emotional or mental illness, and learning disabilities may qualify as disabilities under the ADA. However, a person who suffers from general stress, even if work-related, is not disabled under the ADA. If a physician diagnoses the person as suffering from an identifiable stress disorder, however, that person does have an impairment that may be a covered disability [*see* Lucero v. Hart, 915 F.2d 1367, 1371–1372 (9th Cir. 1990)].

[b] EEOC Guidelines

It is not possible to create a comprehensive list of all possible disorders; however, the EEOC has given us guidance in some cases. For example, the EEOC has stated the ADA includes conditions like HIV infection and AIDS. Obviously, covered disorders also include cancer, diabetes, and so forth. The ADA does not cover general physical characteristics such as hair color, height, and weight [29 C.F.R. App. § 1630.2(h)]. An exception arises if these characteristics are outside the "normal" range and some physiological disorder caused them.

The statute does not consider homosexuality and bisexuality as impairments [42

Guide to Claims

U.S.C.S. § 12211(a); 29 C.F.R. § 1630.3(e)]. On the contrary, the statute specifically excludes them, as well as transvestism and kleptomania, for example [42 U.S.C.S. § 12211(b)(1); 29 C.F.R. § 1630.3(d)(1)], and disorders resulting from illegal drug use [42 U.S.C.S. § 12211(b)(3); 29 C.F.R. § 1630.3(d)(3)] from the definition of impairment. Having a prison record or simply being poor does not qualify as an impairment [*see* EEOC Interpretive Guidance of 29 C.F.R. § 1630.2(h)].

[c] Judicial Definitions

Following are examples of medical conditions that the federal courts held are not disabilities under the ADA:

- Pregnancy, absent unusual circumstances, is not a disability [*see* Jessie v. Carter Health Care Center, Inc., 926 F. Supp. 613, 616 (E.D. Ky. 1996)].
- Allergies and asthma may not be disabilities if they can be successfully controlled and if they do not prevent the employee from doing the essential functions of the job [*see* Suttles v. U.S Postal Service, 927 F. Supp. 990, 1003–1005 (S.D. Tex. 1996)].
- Cancer history itself is not a disability if the employer does not regard it as such or if the cancer does not affect the employee's ability to do the job [*see* Ellison v. Software Spectrum, Inc., 85 F.3d 187, 192–193 (5th Cir. 1996)].
- High blood pressure and angina are not themselves disabilities. To qualify, the employee must show that these conditions substantially interfere with major life activities [*see* Aucutt v. Six Flags Over Mid-America, Inc., 85 F.3d 1311, 1318–1319 (8th Cir. 1996)].

[3] Substantial Limitation of a Major Life Activity

Even if a person has an impairment, it does not automatically constitute a disability. To qualify as a disability for purposes of the ADA, the impairment must "substantially limit a major life activity." EEOC regulations define major life activities as the following functions [29 C.F.R. § 1630.2(i)]:

- Caring for oneself
- Doing manual tasks
- Walking
- Seeing
- Hearing
- Speaking
- Breathing
- Learning
- Working

In other words, major life activities are those basic life functions that the average person can do with little difficulty. What, however, does the phrase "substantial limitation" mean? The term "substantial limitation" means the inability to do a major life activity that the average person can do. It also means the person's condition significantly restricts the manner or duration under which he or she can do a major life activity compared with the way the average person can do the same activity [29 C.F.R. § 1630.2(j)(1)]. To decide if a "substantial limitation" exists, compare the individual with a hypothetical average person. It is not necessary that the condition be permanent. The regulations provide a three-pronged test to determine whether a person's impairment substantially limits a major life activity. Under this test, examine the following [29 C.F.R. § 1630.2(j)(2)]:

1. The nature and severity of the impairment;
2. How long the impairment will last; *and*
3. The impairment's permanent or long-term impact

Remember that the condition's name is not important. What is important is the effect the condition has on the individual's life. In a Rehabilitation Act case, the court held that a person with a back injury that lasted for one year was disabled [*see* Perez v. Philadelphia Housing Authority, 677 F. Supp. 357, 360–361 (E.D. Pa. 1987), *aff'd,* 841 F.2d 1120 (3rd Cir. 1988)].

On the other hand, a short-term disability such as a sprained joint or a hernia will likely not qualify under the ADA. A broken leg is probably a short-term disability under the ADA, unless it does not heal correctly and causes a permanent limp. A temporary impairment is not a disability covered under Section 504 of the Rehabilitation Act. For example, the employee was a police officer who suffered a back injury. Although this prevented the officer from performing his full duties temporarily, it was not a disabling condition under the Rehabilitation Act [*see* Paegle v. Department of Interior, 813 F. Supp. 61, 63–65 (D.D.C. 1993)]. Similarly, the ADA does not automatically protect workers just because they are receiving workers' compensation disability benefits. This is true even if the worker has a high impairment rating. The reason for this is simple. The definition of disability under the workers' compensation law is different from the definition under the ADA, because the two laws have a different purpose. State legislatures designed workers' compensation to provide financial assistance, while Congress designed the ADA to protect people from discrimination [42 U.S.C.S. § 12101(b)(1)].

The United States Supreme Court has stated that to be substantially limited in the activity of working, a person must be precluded from more than one type of job, a specialized job, or a particular job of choice. If jobs exist that can use a person's skills, then the person is not precluded from a substantial class of jobs. Likewise, if a host of different jobs are available, a person is not precluded from a broad range of jobs.

Additionally, whether a person has a disability is not the issue. The issue is whether the disability substantially limits a major life activity. If corrective measures, such as eyeglasses or medication, eliminates the individual's limitations, then the person is not disabled for purposes of the ADA. Put another way, a person whose physical or mental impairment is corrected by mitigating measures still has an impairment, but if the impairment is corrected it does not substantially limit a major life activity. Thus, for

Guide to Claims

example, a person whose vision is corrected by eyeglasses, or a diabetic whose condition is controlled with medication, is not disabled for purposes of the ADA. Note, however, that if in spite of such corrective measures a person is still substantially limited in a major life activity, the disability is not relieved and such a person is still protected by the ADA. In essence then, it is not the use or nonuse of a corrective device that forms the basis of the test. The test is based on the limitations that a person with a disability actually faces and not where the disability might, could or would be substantially limiting if corrective measures were not taken [*see* Sutton v. United Airlines, 527 U.S. 471, 144 L. Ed. 2d 450, 119 S. Ct. 2139 (1999); *see also* Albertsons, Inc. v. Kirkinburg (1999) 527 U.S. 555, 144 L. Ed. 2d 518, 119 S. Ct. 2162; Murphy v. UPS (1999) 527 U.S. 516, 144 L. Ed. 2d 484, 119 S. Ct. 2133].

Subsequently, the U.S. Supreme Court held that each claim must be reviewed case-by-case on its own merits. The analysis must focus on individuals' inability, not only to do their jobs, but also whether they are unable to do the variety of tasks central to most people's daily lives. The Court noted that the definition of "disability" is intended to cover individuals with substantially disabling impairments regardless of whether they have any connection to a workplace. Because the manual tasks unique to any particular job are not necessarily important parts of most people's lives, occupation-specific tasks may have only limited relevance to the manual task inquiry. Evidence of a medical impairment is not enough. The impairment must be so substantial that it prevents doing tasks important to daily life such as household chores, walking, seeing, bathing, and brushing one's teeth [*see* Toyota Motor Mfg. v. Williams, 534 U.S. 184, 151 L. Ed. 2d 615, 633, 122 S. Ct. 681, 693 (2002)].

[4] Record of Impairment

Having an existing disability is not necessary to qualify under the ADA. Individuals who have a record of past disability may still qualify under the ADA if they continue to be treated as disabled because of their history of disability [29 C.F.R. App. § 1630.2(k)]. This is true even if they have fully recovered from their past disability. For example, when individuals have recovered from mental illness, but others still treat them as if they were still disabled, they may qualify under the ADA.

It is also possible that a person may never have been disabled, but was misclassified as such [29 C.F.R. § 1630.2(k)]. If so, that person may qualify for protection under the ADA. For example, a person with a prior drug addiction or who has previously suffered from hepatitis may qualify for protection under the ADA.

[5] Being Regarded as Having an Impairment

If an employer merely regards someone as impaired, that person qualifies for protection under the ADA [*see* 29 C.F.R. § 1630.2(*l*)]. Remember that this part of the test examines the employer's perception of the person. Examples include former drug addicts, persons suspected of having AIDS, or even those living with a person infected with HIV.

All of these rules can be vague and confusing. Just remember that the ADA intends to prevent employers from failing to hire an otherwise qualified applicant because of a real or perceived disability that would not prevent the applicant from performing essential job duties, given reasonable accommodation.

§ 25.05 Qualified Individuals

[1] Qualified Person

> *Experience tells us that sometimes, when minorities insist on their rights, they ultimately prevail.*
> Robert George Kekewich
> English Jurist, 1926

The ADA, on the one hand, allows an employer to determine if an applicant is physically or mentally qualified to perform the job. On the other hand, the ADA also ensures that the hiring process does not unfairly discriminate against a person with a disability. A qualified person then is someone with a disability who can do the essential functions of the job either alone or with reasonable accommodation. Such a person must also meet necessary skill, experience, education, or other qualifications [29 C.F.R. § 1630.2(m)]. A person may fall under the definition of being "regarded as having a disability" in two ways:

1. A covered entity mistakenly believes that a person has a physical impairment that substantially limits one or more major life activities; or
2. A covered entity mistakenly believes that an actual, nonlimiting impairment substantially limits one or more major life activities.

To qualify under this provision, it must be shown that a covered entity entertained misperceptions about the individual. The entity must believe either that the person has a substantially limiting impairment that does not actually exist, or one that is not as limiting as believed [*see* Sutton v. United Airlines, 527 U.S. 471, 144 L. Ed. 2d 450, 119 S. Ct. 2139 (1999)].

[2] Essential Job Functions

It is, of course, critical that employers carefully determine the essential functions of any job. The EEOC regulations define essential functions as "the fundamental job duties of the employment position the individual holds or desires." The key word is "essential"; the term does not include marginal functions. Further, employers must apply the job requirements uniformly to all applicants. EEOC regulations list three standards employers and courts can use to determine if a particular function is an essential requirement. These standards are [29 C.F.R. § 1630.2(n)]:

1. The reason the position exists is to do that particular function.
2. There are only a few employees available among whom the employer can distribute the job functions.

Guide to Claims

3. The function is highly specialized so that the incumbent in the position is hired for his or her expertise or ability to do the particular function.

> **SPECIAL ALERT:** Experts suggest strongly that employers prepare written job descriptions. Such job descriptions should focus on the functions of the job and the result the employer intends these functions to accomplish. Properly done, these may form evidence in legal actions concerning what the essential functions of a particular job are. In other words, employers should identify what functions are important in accomplishing the purpose of the job. Employers should prepare job descriptions before they advertise a job or interview applicants. Courts may not allow job descriptions prepared after hiring into evidence. This does not mean that, once written, the employer cannot change the job description. On the contrary, if the functions of the job change, the employer should immediately update the job description.

[3] Reasonable Accommodation v. Undue Hardship

[a] Reasonable Accommodation

Occasionally, individual applicants cannot do the essential functions of the job because of physical or mental disabilities. The ADA will not protect such individuals unless they could do the job with reasonable, employer-provided accommodation. For example, an applicant for a typist position may not qualify because of a hearing impairment that would prevent the applicant from understanding dictation. A reasonable accommodation, however, may be supplying such a person with an amplifier. Other examples of reasonable accommodation include [42 U.S.C.S. § 12111(9)]:

- Making existing facilities accessible and usable by individuals with a disability
- Job restructuring
- Modifying work schedules
- Reassignment to a vacant position
- Getting or modifying equipment
- Adjusting or modifying examinations, training materials, or policies
- Providing qualified readers or interpreters

The United States Supreme Court has held that an accommodation that conflicts with the employer's seniority rules might not be reasonable. An employee injured his back while working as a cargo handler for petitioner US Airways, Inc. He then transferred to a less physically demanding mailroom position. His new position later became open to seniority-based employee bidding under US Airways' seniority system, and employees senior to him planned to bid on the job. US Airways refused his request to accommodate his disability by allowing him to remain in the mailroom, and he lost his job. He then filed suit under the Americans with Disabilities Act of 1990, which prohibits an employer from discriminating against "an individual with a disability" who with "reasonable accommodation" can perform a job's essential functions [42 U.S.C.S. § 12112(a), (b)], unless the employer "can demonstrate that the accommodation would impose an undue hardship on the operation of [its] business" [42 U.S.C.S. § 12112(b)(5)(A)]. Finding that altering a seniority system would result in an "undue hardship" to both US Airways and its non-disabled employees, the District Court granted the company summary judgment. The Ninth Circuit, en banc, reversed, holding that the seniority system was merely a factor in the undue hardship analysis and that a case-by-case, fact intensive analysis is required to determine whether any particular assignment would constitute an undue hardship.

The United States Supreme Court reversed and held that an employer's showing that a requested accommodation conflicts with seniority rules is ordinarily sufficient to show, as a matter of law, that an "accommodation" is not "reasonable." However, the employee remains free to present evidence of special circumstances that makes a seniority rule exception reasonable in the particular case [US Airways, Inc. v. Barnett, 535 U.S. 391, 405–406, 152 L. Ed. 2d 589, 122 S. Ct. 1516 (2002)]. Essentially, the Court has created a rebuttable presumption.

In a dissenting opinion, Justice Scalia said, "the Court's opinion leaves the question whether a seniority system must be disregarded in order to accommodate a disabled employee in a state of uncertainty that can be resolved only by constant litigation." The Court's opinion, he said, " . . . adopts an interpretation of the ADA that incorrectly subjects all employer rules and practices to the requirement of reasonable accommodation" [US Airways, Inc. v. Barnett, 535 U.S. 391, 420, 152 L. Ed. 2d 589, 122 S. Ct. 1516 (2002)].

[b] Undue Hardship

With respect to the reasonable accommodation requirement, the ADA does not define the term "reasonable," leaving us to decide the meaning of this requirement on a case-by-case basis. Employers do not have to provide an accommodation that would create an undue hardship on them [29 C.F.R. § 1630.15(d)]. A significant criterion is the cost involved. What would be unreasonable for a small auto repair shop may be completely reasonable for a large national chain. An accommodation that may greatly affect the morale of co-workers does not amount to undue hardship. The ADA defines undue hardship as an action that is excessively costly, extensive, substantial, or disruptive, or that would fundamentally alter the nature of the operation of the business [42 U.S.C.S. § 12111(10); EEOC Technical Assistance Manual at III-12].

Undue hardship can include indirect or non economic issues, including the effect—other than low morale—an accommodation has on other employees. For example, a qualified person may require that the work area be very warm. Raising the thermostat, however, may make it uncomfortably hot for other employees or customers. This would likely be seen as an unreasonable accommodation. What may be reasonable is giving the employee a space heater or a room that has its own thermostat.

[c] The Health or Safety Defense

An employer can deny employment to individuals who pose a direct threat to the health or safety of themselves or others [42 U.S.C.S. § 12101 et seq.]. The threat, however, must pose a significant risk of substantial harm [42 U.S.C.S. § 12111(3)]. Slightly increased risk is not enough to deny employment. This safety defense does not apply if the employer can remove the risk with reasonable accommodation [29 C.F.R. §§ 1630.2(r), 1630.15(b)(2)].

[4] Preemployment Inquiries

[a] Stages in the Employment Process

The ADA entitles an employer to obtain all necessary information to learn an applicant's qualifications for the job. In addition, the employer may obtain sufficient medical information, not only to decide qualifications, but also to insure the safety and health of both the applicant and co-workers on the job. What the employer may ask, however, depends on the stage of the employment process. For purposes of the ADA this employment process has three stages [*see* EEOC Technical Assiatance Manual, Ch. 5, § 5.5; *see also* 29 C.F.R. § 1630.4]:

Stage one. Before making a conditional job offer.

Stage two. After making a job offer, but before the job begins.

Stage three. After the job begins and the applicant starts work.

[b] Stage One: Pre Offer

At stage one, the employer can ask questions about the applicant's ability to do specific job functions. For example, an employer can explain the physical requirements of a job and then ask applicants if they can satisfy those requirements. In addition, employers can ask applicants to describe or show how they would do these tasks. Employers can also ask about an applicant's non-medical qualifications and skills such as education, work history, and required certifications and licenses.

The employer may not, however, ask about disabilities or about prior workers' compensation accidents and claims. The employer cannot require a medical examination, but can make the job offer conditioned upon a satisfactory, post-offer, medical examination. Employers may need to review and revise their job application forms, especially since the ADA does not allow questions about prior hospitalizations and accidents at the pre-offer stage.

What is a disability-related question? It is a question that is likely to elicit information about a disability. We know an employer cannot directly ask whether an applicant has a particular disability. The prohibition, however, also applies to questions closely related to disability [*see* EEOC Technical Assistance Manual, Chs. 5, 6; *see also* 29 C.F.R. §§ 1630.13, 1630.14].

[c] Stage Two: Post Offer

Once having offered the applicant a job, but before the actual work begins, the employer can require a medical examination or ask health-related questions. This applies, however, only if the employer requires the same of all candidates for the same job class. If, because of such inquiry or examination, the employer withdraws the job offer, the reasons must be job-related. Reasons for refusing to hire must be consistent with the essential functions of the job. None of this applies if the employer can correct the problem by providing reasonable accommodation. Mere speculation that the applicant poses some future risk is not a legal basis for withdrawing the offer [*see* EEOC Technical Assistance Manual, Chs. 5, 6; *see also* 29 C.F.R. § 1630.14(c)].

[d] Stage Three: During Employment

Once actual work begins, the ADA limits the employer's right to conduct examinations and make medical inquires. The ADA allows medical examinations at this stage only if there is evidence of a job performance or safety problem.

Employers must keep all medical information obtained strictly confidential. An employer must keep medical information in separate files apart from the regular personnel file. Supervisors and managers may use this information only to decide necessary work restrictions and accommodations [*see* EEOC Technical Assistance Manual, Ch. 6, § 6.1; *see also* 29 C.F.R. § 1630.14(c)].

Guide to Claims

§ 25.06 Interaction of ADA and Florida Workers' Compensation Law

[1] The *Martin v. Carpenter* Defense

CAUTIONARY NOTE: The Florida legislature codified, but also altered this case law defense as a formal part of the Workers' Compensation Act [*see* ch. 5].

Recall that the *Martin v. Carpenter* case provides a complete defense to a workers' compensation claim if the employee falsified medical and health information upon entering employment [*see* Martin Company v. Carpenter, 132 So. 2d 400, 403–407 (Fla. 1961); *see* ch. 5, § 5.01[3]]. In addition, the legislature codified the case under the 1990 amendments to the Workers' Compensation Act and amended it further effective January 1, 1994. The 1994 amendment provides that no compensation is due under the following circumstances [§ 440.15(5)(a), Fla. Stat. (7/1/97)]:

> [I]f the employee, at the time of entering into the employment of the employer by whom the benefits would otherwise be payable, falsely represents himself in writing as not having previously been disabled or compensated because of such previous disability, impairment, anomaly, or disease *and the employer detrimentally relies on the misrepresentation.* (Emphasis added; the italicized phrase is the 1994 addition)

Some people believe that, under the ADA, the classic *Martin v. Carpenter* defense no longer exists. Others believe it still applies, but is limited in its application. Neither view is correct. First, the ADA does not apply to any employer with fewer then 14 workers. Therefore, there is no change in the law for these small employers.

Second, there is nothing in the ADA to prevent employers and carriers from using this defense. The ADA requires only that employers make informational requests about health or workers' compensation history as part of a stage two, post-offer, medical examination or inquiry. Therefore, all information legally obtained may be used. Is the defense then available only during stage two? Generally speaking, yes, but not necessarily. Every employer under the ADA has the right to make sufficient inquiry to decide if an applicant is physically able to do the job offered. Recall that physicians had warned Carpenter to avoid bench work because of her previous back injuries. Today, the ADA does not allow inquiry about previous back injuries at stage one. The employer may, however, ask if the applicant is physically able to work long hours performing bench work. In Carpenter's case, a "yes" answer at this stage would be a lie that would form the basis for a defense.

Even if the employer asks questions illegally, the *Martin v. Carpenter* defense may still apply. For example, suppose that an employment application violates the ADA by blatantly asking whether the applicant has a history of back injury. This is exactly what happened in Julius Caldwell's case in Georgia. He answered the question, "no," which was a lie because he had suffered a disabling back injury just three months earlier. The Georgia court held that a false representation defense is not inconsistent with the ADA. Caldwell's remedy for the improper application question was the ADA, not the loss of the defense in workers' compensation. The court's dilemma was in deciding the greater wrong. Should it refuse to allow the employer to be rewarded for its use of an improper question, or should it refuse to allow the employee to be improperly rewarded for his lie? The court decided to affirm the order denying benefits [*see* Caldwell v. Aarlin/Holcombe Armature, 267 Ga. 613, 481 S.E.2d 196, 197–199 (1997)]. How Florida courts will answer this question, however, remains to be seen.

[2] The Special Disability Trust Fund

NOTE: The Special Disability Trust Fund does not apply to any accident occurring on or after January 1, 1998 [*see* ch. 20, § 20.04].

Recall that a major requirement for perfecting a claim against the Special Disability Trust Fund is that the employer has knowledge of the existence of the prior impairment. Having such knowledge is necessary only before the accident and injury. The ADA allows employers to make medical inquires and require physical examinations after they make a job offer. It is at stage two that employers should obtain Special Disability Trust Fund questionnaires from the individual.

There was early concern that the confidentiality requirements of the ADA would prevent employers and carriers from submitting required medical information to the Special Disability Trust Fund. The EEOC regulations make it clear that Congress did not intend for the ADA to disrupt the orderly operations of state workers' compensation laws or related insurance principles. In its guidelines the EEOC stated [Guidelines to 20 C.F.R. § 1630.14(b) (1991)]:

> State workers' compensation laws are not preempted by the ADA or this part [29 C.F.R. Part 1630]. These laws require the collection of information from individuals for state administrative purposes that do not conflict with the ADA . . . Consequently, employers or other covered entities may submit information to state workers'

compensation offices or second injury funds in accordance with state workers' compensation laws without violating this part.

> **SPECIAL ALERT:** Employers must obtain this medical information only at stage two in the hiring process. The opportunity to obtain this information at stage three, after employment begins, is very limited. At stage three the ADA does not allow general Special Disability Trust Fund questionnaires and there can be no general inquiries or medical examinations [*see* ch. 20, for a complete discussion of the Special Disability Trust Fund].

For a general discussion of the interaction of second injury funds and the ADA, see LARSON'S WORKERS' COMPENSATION, DESK EDITION, Ch. 91 (Matthew Bender).

[3] Wage Loss and Return to Work Under the ADA

[a] Rehiring

Clearly, rehiring recovered injured workers will always have a positive financial effect on the outcome of a workers' compensation case. The question here, however, is whether the ADA requires employers to rehire. The answer depends on whether the injury has caused the worker to become a "qualified individual with a disability." As discussed in §§ 25.03–25.05, such a person must have an impairment that "substantially limits a major life activity, has a record of having an impairment or is regarded as having such an impairment." Obviously, not everyone injured on the job will meet the ADA definition. Just as obviously, the ADA will not protect a worker left with a permanent impairment that prevents doing any of the essential functions of the original job. Employers can fire injured workers only if they cannot make reasonable accommodation without undue hardship. Remember that it is the employer's burden to prove undue hardship. Remember also that the definition of "reasonable" accommodation is elusive. In individual cases the EEOC will decide the question, frequently followed by a federal judge. Guessing incorrectly can be very expensive. Employers will be wise to seek legal advice before firing an injured worker.

For a general discussion of reemployment and the ADA, see LARSON'S WORKERS' COMPENSATION, DESK EDITION, Ch. 95 (Matthew Bender).

[b] Accommodation

Under the EEOC regulations, accommodation may take the form of a change in job duties. This includes giving the disabled worker a new and perhaps light-duty job or allowing more flexible hours [EEOC Technical Assistance Manual at 111-23]. Accommodation may even require providing mechanical or even human assistance to enable the worker to do the job [29 C.F.R. App. § 1630.2(o)]. The ADA does not require an employer to provide a light-duty job, unless the heavy-duty tasks the worker can no longer perform are only marginal and not essential job functions the employer might assign to other workers. The ADA does not, however, require the employer to create a new job or promote the worker to a new position [*see, e.g.,* Weiler v. Household Fin. Corp. (N.D. Ill. 1995) 11

Guide to Claims

ADD 848 (employer does not have to create new position to accommodate disabled worker); Kuehl v. Wal-Mart Stores (D.C. Colo. 1995) 13 ADD 19, 5 AD Cases (BNA) 91, 94]. As always, ordinary workers' compensation exposure may, under the circumstances, warrant such a dramatic assist to the injured worker.

[c] Failure to Rehire

All employers who fail to rehire disabled workers are potentially liable for full disability benefits under workers' compensation. This is because in some cases, such as those involving wage loss, unemployment caused even in part by disability makes the employee eligible for benefits [*see* ch. 14, § 14.03]. In other cases, inability to find employment may constitute evidence of permanent total disability [*see* ch. 13, § 13.51]. In addition, those employers subject to the ADA face the possibility of becoming the target of a lawsuit, both by the EEOC as an enforcement measure, and by the employee seeking damages for violation of the ADA [*see* 29 C.F.R. §§ 1601.24, 1601.28].

Even if a worker fully recovers from a workplace injury and is ineligible for permanent disability benefits, the ADA may still protect the worker. For example, a worker may suffer a serious injury that causes total disability for one year. Though the worker recovers fully with no permanent impairment, there would still be a record of having had a substantially limiting impairment. Refusing to rehire or promote the worker because of that record, in spite of full recovery, violates the ADA [*see* § 24.04[4]].

What happens if the employee did not suffer a serious, substantially limiting injury but the employer still regarded the worker as having an impairment? Firing the employee because of this perception would violate the ADA [*see* § 24.04[5]].

[d] Mutual Exclusivity

Workers cannot claim complete disability for workers' compensation purposes and then sue the employer under the ADA for failure to provide reasonable accommodation. For example, Daryl Cheatwood testified at his workers' compensation trial that his injury disabled him to the point where he could no longer do the essential functions of his job. Later, he sued his employer for not letting him come back to work in violation of the ADA. The court rejected Cheatwood's argument, finding he was not a qualified person with a disability. Remember, qualified people have a disability, but are still employable at least with reasonable accommodation. The court held that Cheatwood's statements at his workers' compensation trial were binding admissions that he could not do even the essential functions of his former job. Cheatwood did not tell the employer that he could do another job, or that he wanted or needed accommodation. The court held it was therefore reasonable for the employer to conclude that Cheatwood could not do any of its jobs, even with accommodation [*see* Cheatwood v. Roanoke Industries, 891 F. Supp. 1528, 1537–1539 (N.D. Ala. 1995)].

> *If you will think about what you ought to do for other people,*
> *your character will take care of itself.*
> Woodrow Wilson, 1914

PART II

CASE SUMMARIES

Part II of this handbook contains summaries of workers' compensation-related cases decided from approximately April 2006 through April 2007. Practitioners should check for subsequent history and publication status before citing to a case.

Case Summaries

SYNOPSIS

§ 50.23 **Immunity**

§ 50.01 Jurisdiction: In General

Editor's Note: No cases were reported on this topic during the time period covered for the 2007 Edition.

§ 50.02 Jurisdiction: Accidents Outside the State and Coverage for Non-residents

Editor's Note: No cases were reported on this topic during the time period covered for the 2007 Edition.

§ 50.03 Confirming Coverage: Under the Policy and the Law

[1] Election of Remedy

Dispute Over Attendant Care Benefits. The employee suffered a serious burn when an explosion occurred on the employer's premises. From the beginning, the employer provided workers' compensation benefits. The only petition filed by the employee involved a dispute over the amounts that should be paid for attendant care benefits. In preparing the petition, the employee used a pre-printed form containing a stipulation that his injury was compensable. Petitioners, the employee and his wife, filed an action to obtain damages in tort. The employer filed a motion for summary judgment, which was denied by the district court. However, the appellate court reversed, finding that petitioners were precluded from bringing a tort action when they had actively pursued their workers' compensation claim. The first district certified for review by the Florida Supreme Court the question of whether petitioners could pursue a civil action against the employer at the same time they were receiving workers' compensation benefits for the same injury. Reversing, the Florida Supreme Court noted that the only affirmative act by petitioners was the request for a change in attendant care benefits. That act did not constitute an inconsistent election of remedies that precluded petitioners from pursuing a tort action. There had not been a conclusion on the merits in the workers' compensation action. The employer continued to be protected from a double recovery under § 440.39, Fla. Stat.. The Court answered the certified question in the negative, quashed the decision of the intermediate appellate court and remanded the matter with instructions to return the case to the trial court for further proceedings. [Jones v. Martin Elecs., Inc., 932 So. 2d 1100 (Fla. 2006)].

NOTE: It is not clear if the civil action would have been barred if the petitioners had filed a petition for attendant care benefits themselves, rather than on a pre-printed standard form, which the carrier had denied.

Case Summaries

§ 50.04 Invalid Contract of Employment: The *Martin v. Carpenter* Defense

Editor's Note: No cases were reported on this topic during the time period covered for the 2007 Edition.

§ 50.05 Confirming Compensability: Accident and Injury

[1] Causation

Causation—Competent, Substantial Evidence. Claimant suffered two injuries during her employment with the employer, the first occurring on March 1, 2003, and the second occurring on August 13, 2003. Her petition for workers' compensation benefits was based solely on her first injury and listed the date of injury as March 1, 2003. In the petition, claimant alleged injuries to her back, neck, hands, and wrist. The IME concluded that claimant suffered from an underlying degenerative disk disease and that she had herniated a disk on August 13, 2003, after picking up seven or eight 20 pound boxes of tile. The Judge of Compensation Claims awarded claimant treatment for all medically necessary and causally related cervical spinal conditions stemming from the March 1, 2003 injury. Claimant, her employer and its carrier (E/C), sought further review.

The appeals court first held that because the claimant's herniated disk and neck pain were not readily observable injuries, she was required to produce medical evidence as to the cause of those injuries. The JCC found that the independent medical examiner was in the best position to provide an opinion as to the major contributing cause of the claimant's injury, and he opined that her continued work could have made her condition worse. Moreover, he stated that, hypothetically, an injury such as the claimant's could be due to repetitive trauma. But, from how she described her injury, lifting seven or eight boxes of 20-pound tiles and the immediate onset of increasing and significant pain on August 13, 2003, it was likely that was when she actually ruptured her disk. No other medical evidence rebutted this testimony. Hence, because the record did not contain competent, substantial evidence to support the treatment award relative to the claimant's March, 2003 injury, and because the parties did not try by consent the issue of the claimant's August injury, an award for the claimant's cervical condition could not be upheld. The judgment was reversed. [Dollar Gen. Corp. v. MacDonald, 928 So. 2d 464 (Fla. 1st DCA 2006)].

Major Contributing Cause—Apportionment/Contribution Between Carriers. Clamant sustained industrial injuries to his back first in 1999 and then again in 2004, both of which combined to cause his need for compensation benefits. Each of claimant's injuries involved different employers/carriers. Based on the medical evidence, the JCC determined that 80 percent of claimant's condition was related to the first accident and 20 percent was related to the second accident. The JCC further determined that since the second accident was not greater than 50 percent responsible for the worker's condition, that accident was not compensable pursuant to § 440.09(1)(b), Fla. Stat., and that, therefore, the subsequent employer/carrier (E/C) at risk for the second accident was not responsible for any contribution. The JCC further determined that the earlier E/C at risk for the first accident was required to pay the worker 80 percent of the benefits due through the date of an MRI.

On appeal, the court held that § 440.42(4), Fla. Stat., rather than § 440.09(1)(b), Fla. Stat., applied as the issue involved two or more compensable accidents and that he JCC erred in not assessing liability 80 percent to the earlier employer and 20 percent to the subsequent employer in accordance with his findings of responsibility. Because the JCC found that the worker was not aware he was to return to work before the date of the merits hearing, there was no support for the JCC's determination not to award benefits through the date of that hearing. The court affirmed the JCC's allocation of responsibility between the two different E/Cs, but reversed the ruling that the subsequent E/C was absolved of liability for workers' compensation benefits. The court also reversed the JCC's finding that benefits were due for the period ending when the MRI occurred, rather than the date of the merits hearing. [Pearson v. Paradise Ford, 951 So. 2d 12 (Fla. 1st DCA 2007)].

[2] Heart Attack—Cardiovascular Disease

Heart Attack—Firefighters Presumption. Claimant began employment as a firefighter on January 27, 1986. His pre-employment physical was partially completed ten days before he began working, and completed fifteen days after he started work. On February 14, 2005, claimant suffered a heart attack. In awarding workers' compensation benefits, the Judge of Compensation Claims applied the presumption set forth in § 112.18, Fla. Stat. The employer challenged the award based on application of the firefighter's presumption. The appellate court held that the firefighter had successfully passed his physical examination upon starting his employment. In addition, the court held that the firefighter's presumption merely switches the burden of proof from the claimant to the employer/carrier, and may be overcome by, as the statute plainly states, "competent evidence." The JCC may not apply a higher standard or greater burden of proof so as to require the E/C to establish that some other specific hazard or non-occupational hazard was the cause of claimant's disease. All that the statute require to overcome the presumption was competent substantial evidence that convinced the JCC that the disease was caused by some non-work-related factor, not that it was caused by any sort of specific hazard or non-occupational hazard, as the JCC in this case concluded. The JCC's decision was reversed and the matter remanded for the JCC to consider the evidence under the proper burden of proof. [City of Tarpon Springs v. Vaporis, 953 So. 2d 597 (Fla. 1st DCA 2007)].

§ 50.06 Confirming Compensability: The Arising Out of and In the Course of Employment Requirements

[1] Course and Scope of Employment

Self-Inflicted Injury. Claimant sustained injuries following an altercation with a co-worker. The first injury occurred when the co-worker struck claimant with a hammer, causing him to fall and strike his right hand. After the altercation, claimant discussed the incident with a supervisor and was told to leave the job site. Out of anger over being sent away, claimant stuck a table and sustained a separate injury to his finger. Claimant sought workers' compensation for both injuries. The JCC found that both injuries were the result of the altercation and, therefore, were compensable. The employer appealed. The appellate court found that the act of striking the table occurred after a temporal break and a change

Case Summaries

in location, not during the fight. Claimant was responding in an aggressive manner to his supervisor's command and, as the aggressor, would not be entitled to benefits if the act of aggression amounted to a willful intent to injure himself. Thus, even if the JCC were correct in her finding that claimant's injuries were the result of an altercation with a co-worker in which the claimant was not an aggressor, the injury would still remain non-compensable. The court concluded that the act of punching a hard object, even though impulsive, was so serious and so likely to result in real injury that it must be construed to show willful intent. The JCC's order was affirmed as to her finding of compensability with regard to the first injury, but reversed as to the second injury. [Restoration Tech. v. Reyes, 936 So. 2d 1187 (Fla. 1st DCA 2006)].

Deviation From Employment—Emergency. Claimant was injured while attempting to retrieve a $15 bubble machine he had purchased in an effort to attract business to the used car lot where he was working, after the machine was stolen from the lot by a female assailant. In trying to grab the machine, claimant lunged inside the passenger window of the assailant's vehicle. The vehicle sped away, dragging claimant down the street. The Judge of Compensation Claims held that, once claimant had left his employer's property, he was no longer in the course of his employment and, therefore, was not eligible for workers' compensation benefits.

On appeal, the court found that claimant was responding to an emergency, and his response was designed to save property, thereby entitling him to benefits under § 440.092(3), Fla. Stat. According to the appellate court, the plain language of § 440.092(3), Fla. Stat. allows recovery in cases of deviation from employment when 1) the deviation is an emergency; and 2) the emergency is designed to save life or property. Nothing § 440.092(3), Fla. Stat. precludes a claimant from receiving benefits simply because the property he was saving turned out to be his own. The JCC's order was reversed and the matter remanded. [Deutsch v. Heritage Auto. Enterprises, 939 So. 2d 259 (Fla. 1st DCA 2006)].

Going and Coming Rule. Claimant was injured in a car accident when he was driving home from work in a company car on March 2, 2005. After a hearing on his entitled to workers' compensation, the Judge of Compensation Claims denied compensation benefits based on the going and coming rule, § 440.092(2), Fla. Stat. Claimant appealed, contending that (1) the traveling employee exception, § 440.092(4), Fla. Stat. precluded application of the going and coming rule, (2) there was no competent substantial evidence to support the finding that he was operating an employer-provided vehicle available for his exclusive personal use, and (3) there was no substantial evidence to support the JCC's finding that the dual purpose doctrine, an exception to the going and coming rule, did not apply in this case.

The appellate court affirmed the JCC's decision. The court first found that claimant failed to preserve his first argument at the final hearing. In addition, there was substantial competent evidence provided by the employer's president indicating that the company vehicle was provided as part of the claimant's compensation package, supporting the JCC's finding on that issue. The JCC had also determined that there were no practical restrictions on the claimant's use of the vehicle, and the employer made no effort to enforce its personal use policy or to monitor personal use of its vehicles in any meaningful way. Finally, the employer testified that it did not benefit from claimant having the company vehicle at home. Under the circumstances, the court concluded that there was no dual purpose for the claimant's trip home at the time he was injured. [Wilcox v. AG Mart Produce, 942 So. 2d 959 (Fla. 1st DCA 2006)].

§ 50.07 Occupational Disease, Acceleration or Aggravation of Disease, and Apportionment

[1] Occupational Disease

Firefighter—Hepatitis C. Claimant sought workers' compensation benefits stemming from his hepatitis C. The JCC found the hepatitis C compensable. On appeal, the court noted that claimant could establish the compensability of his hepatitis C in one of two ways: (1) he could meet the criteria necessary to qualify for the statutory presumption of compensability pursuant to § 112.181(2), Fla. Stat.; or (2) he could present clear evidence to meet the elements necessary to establish his hepatitis C was an occupational disease pursuant to § 440.151(2), Fla. Stat. The court concluded that the claimant failed to present evidence sufficient to establish compensability on either basis. First, claimant was not entitled to the statutory presumption because he failed to submit the required affidavit and testified that, during the relevant time, he had engaged in unprotected sex with approximately 20 women. In addition, claimant failed to present clear evidence that he more likely than not contracted hepatitis C during his employment as a firefighter, or that the disease was actually caused by employment conditions characteristic of and particular to his employment as a firefighter. Thus, the record lacked competent, substantial evidence to support the JCC's finding that the claimant's hepatitis C was compensable. The JCC's order was reversed. [Seminole County Gov't v. Bartlett, 933 So. 2d 550 (Fla. 1st DCA 2006)].

§ 50.08 Additional Defenses: Late Notice; Intoxication; Statute of Limitations; Intervening Cause; Res judicata; Federal Laws; and Fraud

[1] Late Notice

Knowledge of Industrial Causation. Claimant's employment ended in1994 and, on April 3, 2002, she filed a petition for workers' compensation benefits, claiming hepatitis C. The employer/carrier contended that claimant knew she was infected as early as 1995. Claimant responded that she notified the E/C within 30 days of obtaining a medical opinion connecting her disease to her employment. The JCC found that claimant timely reported her injury, and that the injury was compensable. The E/C appealed. The appellate court held that, since there was no medical causation prior to the date that an expert hepatologist gave claimant a clear and definitive opinion as to the cause and factors of her disease, competent substantial evidence existed in the record to support the judge's factual finding that the employee gave timely notice under § 440.185(1)(b), Fla. Stat. The JCC's order was affirmed. [Polk County Bd. of County Comm'rs v. Ross, 911 So. 2d 854 (Fla. 1st DCA 2005)].

Case Summaries

[2] Statute of Limitations

Taking Prescription Drugs. Claimant received compensation benefits after injuring both knees. In June 2002, a surgeon recommended a knee replacement and prescribed a 30-day course of pain killers. In July 2002, claimant filed a petition for pain management treatment, which he dismissed after receiving authorization. When claimant requested another visit with the surgeon in July 2003, his request was denied as untimely. Claimant saw the surgeon on his own and, within one year of that visit, filed a second petition for benefits. The JCC granted the employer/carrier's motion for summary order, and denied and dismissed applicant's pending claims based on the running of the statute of limitations in § 440.19, Fla. Stat.

On appeal, claimant argued that the JCC erred by basing the date the statute began to run on the date he was prescribed pain medication as remedial treatment for his injury, and instead should have used the date he finished the course of treatment. Based on the particular facts of this case, the court agreed with claimant's contention. There was no dispute that the medication was prescribed for treatment of claimant's injury and that only one 30-day supply was allowed. However, because the claimant dismissed his first petition after receiving authorization for pain management treatment, the first petition did not toll the limitations period. [Ginsberg v. ChemMED Corp., 929 So. 2d 633 (Fla. 1st DCA 2006)].

Petition for Benefits—Dismissal. Claimant was injured in a compensable accident in 1994, and his indemnity benefits ceased in 1999. In 2001 and again in 2002, claimant filed petitions seeking authorization for an orthopedic surgeon to evaluate and treat specified injuries and for reimbursement of certain medical bills. The following year, claimant voluntarily dismissed the petitions and filed a third petition, seeking authorization of a physician for evaluation and treatment. The JCC denied his petition on the ground that it was barred by the statute of limitations set forth in § 440.19, Fla. Stat. Claimant appealed, asserting that the statute was tolled during the period that his two earlier petitions were pending. The appellate court held that absent a clear statement from the legislature to the contrary, the one-year statute of limitations specified in § 440.19(2), Fla. Stat., was not tolled during the period that the earlier-filed petitions were pending before they were voluntarily dismissed. Consequently, the JCC properly dismissed the claimant's petition for additional benefits as untimely. [McBride v. Pratt & Whitney, 909 So. 2d 386 (Fla. 1st DCA 2005)].

Petition for Benefits—Dismissal. Claimant injured his back on the job on both March 18, 2000, and April 3, 2000. On September 4, 2003, which was within one year of the date claimant received authorized medical treatment, claimant filed a petition for benefits for his April 3, 2000 injury. He filed a second petition for benefits dated January 8, 2004, also for the April 3 accident. On March 10, 2004, claimant voluntarily dismissed his first petition, filed September 4, 2003. On March 12, 2004, claimant filed a third petition for benefits for the April 3, 2000 accident. Finally, on April 12, 2004, claimant voluntarily dismissed his second petition, dated January 8, 2004. At all times between September 4, 2003, and the hearing before the JCC, at least one petition was pending regarding the April 3 accident date. Claimant appealed the final compensation order entered by the Judge of compensation Claims dismissing with prejudice his petition for benefits on grounds that the statute of limitations barred his claims for treatment. The appellate court concluded that, as the claimant had at least one petition pending at all times between the filing of the first petition and the hearing on the last petition filed, the claimant's voluntary dismissal of the first petition did not operate to dismiss the entire case regarding the April 3 accident date. The dismissal of the claim for the March 18, 2000 accident was affirmed however. [Rice v. Reedy Creek Improvement Dist., 924 So. 2d 882 (Fla. 1st DCA 2006)].

Failure to Give Notice to Claimant. The claimant sought review of a decision of a Judge of Compensation Claims who determined that claimant's petition for continuing medical benefits was barred by the limitation period in § 440.19(2), Fla. Stat. The statute required claimant to file his petition within one year from the time he had been provided remedial treatment. On appeal, claimant argued that the employer/carrier was estopped from relying on the limitations period because it had failed to provide him with information about the limitations period as required by chs. 440.19(4) and 440.185, Fla. Stat. Claimant also asserted that he otherwise had no knowledge of the limitations period. The appellate court reversed and found that, in rejecting claimant's estoppel argument, the JCC erred in relying on a prior appellate decision that was issued before the enactment of § 440.19(4), Fla. Stat. Under the amended version of the statute, the E/C had the burden of showing that it had given claimant notice of his rights and the procedures for obtaining benefits as provided by § 440.185, Fla. Stat. Claimant's evidence clearly disclosed that he was unaware of the statute of limitations and that the lack of such knowledge was the cause of his failure to seek the requested remedial care within the applicable time required by the statute. Because his evidence was not contradicted by the E/C, the JCC erred in holding the E/C was not estopped from raising the statute of limitations defense. [Fontanills v. Hillsborough County Sch. Bd., 913 So. 2d 28 (Fla. 1st DCA 2005)].

Palliative Care. Claimant appealed the order of the Judge of Compensation Claims, which denied his 2002 claim arising from injuries sustained during industrial accidents in 1991 and 1992. Specifically, the JCC held that the two-year statute of limitations period for filing such a claim had run, and that the continued provision of "palliative" treatment to the claimant by the employer/carrier through 2001, had not revived the limitations period. On appeal, the claimant argued that the JCC erred in denying his claim. The appellate court agreed with the claimant that the JCC erred. The JCC found that the claimant's prescriptions filled as recently as September 12, 2001, and September 18, 2001, were related to claimant's 1991 and 1992 industrial accidents. The JCC also found that these prescriptions constituted "palliative" treatment and were paid for by the employer/carrier on December 19, 2001. The appellate court concluded that the JCC based her ruling upon an erroneous legal distinction between "remedial" and "palliative" treatment. Both "remedial" and "palliative" treatment were capable of reviving the limitations period under § 440.19, Fla. Stat. Thus, the limitations period on claimant's 1991 and 1992 industrial accidents was revived when the employer/carrier provided the claimant with "palliative" treatment in 2001. [Borneisen v. Home Depot, 917 So. 2d 361 (Fla. 1st DCA 2005)].

[3] Fraud

Jurisdiction—No Pending Petition. Claimant filed a petition for benefits, which she voluntarily dismissed. Subsequently, the employer/carrier filed a petition for benefits, requesting that the Judge of Compensation Claims issue a determination pursuant to

§ 440.09(4), Fla. Stat., regarding whether claimant knowingly made false, fraudulent or misleading oral or written statements for the purposes of obtaining workers' compensation benefits in violation of § 440.105(4)(b). Claimant filed a motion to dismiss the E/C's petition, arguing that the JCC had no jurisdiction. The JCC found that claimant had violated § 440.105(4)(b)2, Fla. Stat., and was not entitled to compensation or benefits pursuant to § 440.09(4), Fla. Stat. Claimant appealed. The appellate court found that the JCC lacked jurisdiction to rule on the defense in the absence of a pending petition for benefits filed by the employee. [Polston v. Hurricane Island Outward Bound, 920 So. 2d 766 (Fla. 1st DCA 2006)].

Evidentiary Standard—Preponderance of the Evidence. The employer alleged that claimant violated §§ 440.09(4) and 440.105(4)(b)2., Fla. Stat., by providing false, incomplete or misleading statements regarding his employment status while he was receiving temporary total disability benefits from an industrial injury. In its order, the JCC found that the employer failed to prove by clear and convincing evidence that claimant committed fraud. On appeal, the court found that the employer was only required to prove that claimant committed one of the prohibited acts by a preponderance of the evidence. The JCC did not need to determine whether the employee was employed or received payment for work while he was receiving benefits. Further, the JCC was only required to determine whether the employee knowingly or intentionally made any false, fraudulent, incomplete, or misleading statement, whether oral or written, for the purpose of obtaining workers' compensation benefits, or in support of his claim for benefits. Significantly, it was not necessary that a false, fraudulent, or misleading statement be material to the claim; it only had to be made for the purpose of obtaining benefits. [Vill. of N. Palm Beach v. McKale, 911 So. 2d 1282 (Fla. 1st DCA 2005)].

The Knowing and Intentional Standard. The employer/carrier appealed an order by the the Judge of Compensation Claims that determined claimant suffered an industrial accident that was the major contributing cause of his neck condition and that the need for cervical surgery was compensable. The appellate court upheld the JCC's decision, finding that §§ 440.09(4) and 440.105(4)(b), Fla. Stat., required a showing of "knowing" or "intentional" activity before the "fraud" defense applied to the worker's claim. Because some competent substantial evidence supported the JCC's denial of the "fraud" defense, it would not be disturbed. It did not matter that other persuasive evidence might have supported a contrary ruling. To the extent that some discrepancies appeared between the employee's deposition and live testimony, the JCC correctly deemed them immaterial or inconsequential. Pursuant to § 440.13(9)(c), Fla. Stat., the JCC could exercise his authority in accepting an expert medical advisor's opinions over those of the other physicians. [Pinnacle Benefits, Inc. v. Alby, 913 So. 2d 756 (Fla. 1st DCA 2005)].

Finding of Fraud Precludes All Benefits. After suffering an injury while at work, claimant sought disability benefits and continuing medical care. The JCC found that claimant intended to mislead by testifying at his deposition that his symptoms appeared after the accident, when in fact he had complained of them prior to the accident. However, because the E/C's independent medical examiner (IME) found a causal connection between the injury and the workplace accident, the JCC granted claimant's claim for continuing medical care. The appellate court held that once the JCC found that claimant intended to mislead by making false or misleading statements about his symptoms that were designed to advance his claims, the statements fell within the scope of § 440.105(4)(b)2, Fla. Stat. Consequently, § 440.09(4), Fla. Stat. precluded claimant from receiving workers' compensation benefits regardless of whether the IME later opined that the statements had no effect on his determination of a causal connection. [Citrus Pest Control v. Brown, 913 So. 2d 754 (Fla. 1st DCA 2005)].

False Statements Made in Other Unrelated Claims. Claimant sought workers' compensation benefits for three work-related accidents in three years. The third accident allegedly occurred when the chair claimant was sitting in gave way suddenly, causing the injuries complained of. The employer and the workers' compensation insurance carrier (E/C) had provided benefits for the first two accidents and did not contend that the claimant had committed any of the acts prohibited by § 440.105(4)(b), Fla. Stat.. However, the E/C denied that the third accident actually occurred, and argued that the claimant did not suffer any injury within the course and scope of his employment, pursuant to § 440.09(1), Fla. Stat. After a hearing, the Judge of Compensation Claims dismissed the claimant's application for workers' compensation benefits, finding that the claimant had given false, fraudulent, incomplete, or misleading statements to obtain benefits in an unconnected workers' compensation case. Claimant sought review of the order. The appellate court held that it was error for the JCC to bar the claimant from receiving workers' compensation benefits based on § 440.09(4), Fla. Stat. when the allegedly false statements at issue were not made in the case that was being addressed by the JCC, but were allegedly made in an earlier case. The court reversed the judgment of the JCC and remanded the matter for further findings. [Paulson v. Dixie County Emergency Med. Servs., 936 So. 2d 1109 (Fla. 1st DCA 2006)].

Res Judicata. The employer/carrier challenged an award of benefits made to a workers' compensation claimant by a Judge of Compensation Claims in which the JCC found that the doctrine of res judicata prevented the employer from raising the defense of § 440.09(4), Fla. Stat. With respect to claimant's first claim for benefits, the employer had claimed that claimant failed to disclose to his treating physicians two motor vehicle accidents that might have played a role in his claim. The first claim for benefits was settled. Claimant then brought the present claim for benefits. The reviewing court held that the employer did not simply argue that claimant made misrepresentations prior to the settlement. If that were the sole argument, res judicata would bar the defense. However, the employer argued that claimant, after the settlement and after seeking additional benefits, made subsequent misrepresentations to his treating physicians. As the employer's § 440.09, Fla. Stat., defense was based upon facts that allegedly arose after the settlement and concerned new petitions for benefits, the defense was not barred by the earlier settlement. The court observed that, although the JCC seemed less than impressed with the evidence supporting the employer's fraud defense, the JCC failed to make an alternative finding based upon a lack of evidence. [Nelco Cos. v. Lott, 937 So. 2d 1219 (Fla. 1st DCA 2006)].

Carrier Cannot Unilaterally Suspend Benefits. The employer/carrier made permanent total disability payments and furnished medical benefits to claimant due to compensable accidents. After several years, the E/C put claimant under videotaped surveillance, took his deposition, and unilaterally cut off medical and indemnity benefits, then filed a notice of denial under §§ 440.105 and 440.09(4), Fla. Stat., alleging claimant

Case Summaries

had made false statements to obtain benefits. The JCC ordered the E/C to reinstate benefits, with penalties and interest, and to furnish the prescribed medical benefits sought by claim. The E/C sought review. The appellate court held that appellants failed to meet their burden to prove fraud. The court pointed out that, after seeing the videotapes, claimant's physicians testified that claimant did not misrepresent anything to them, and that he had informed them that he regularly attempted to perform several of the very household activities about which appellants were concerned. The JCC found that claimant's deposition testimony was truthful and consistent with his hearing testimony. Neither the doctors nor the JCC found anything in the videotapes demonstrating that claimant had exaggerated his limitations during his deposition or that he had made any materially false statement about his activities, including the use of a cane his wife had given him. Further, and most important, the court held that the Florida Workers' Compensation Act contains no authority for the suspension of benefits based on a payor's unilateral determination that a claimant has violated §§ 440.09 and 440.105, Fla. Stat. Section 440.09(4), Fla. Stat. contemplates that, before benefits may be denied pursuant to § 440.09(4), Fla. Stat., there must be a showing and an official determination that the claimant made oral or written statements concerning facts material to his claim that he knew were false, misleading or incomplete at the time the statements were made. [Pavilion Apts. v. Wetherington, 943 So. 2d 226 (Fla. 1st DCA 2006)].

§ 50.09 Adjuster Ethics

> **Editor's Note:** No cases were reported on this topic during the time period covered for the 2007 Edition.

§ 50.10 Calculating Benefits, Average Weekly Wage, Penalties, and Offsets

[1] Average Weekly Wage and Compensation Rate

Full Time Weekly Wage Method. The Judge of Compensation Claims adopted as the claimant's average weekly wage (AWW) the determination of the employer/carrier (E/C) that such should be based on a 20-hour work week. However, nothing in the record supported this determination. The parties agreed that claimant had worked 32 hours during his four days of employment and that § 440.14(1)(d), Fla. Stat. (the full-time weekly wage method), governed the calculation of the AWW in this case. On appeal, the court found that the JCC abused her discretion in adopting the E/C's determination of the AWW. When there is no contractual provision governing the number of hours the claimant will work per week, the JCC must calculate the AWW based upon the actual wages earned. Full-time weekly wages, therefore, should have been determined using claimant's actual earnings as set out in the wage statement furnished by the E/C and admitted into evidence without objection. Accordingly, the court reversed and remanded for the JCC to use the claimant's actual wages in determining his AWW. [Taylor v. Labor Finders, 928 So. 2d 435 (Fla. 1st DCA 2006)].

Valuation of Health Insurance. Claimant appealed the Judge of Compensation

Claims' order, which held the Employer/Carrier correctly adjusted claimant's average weekly wage. The E/C adjusted claimant's AWW by valuing the employer-provided group health insurance as of January 29, 1987, the date of the accident, rather than June 29, 2004, the date claimant's position as an employee terminated and provision of health insurance ceased. The court held that it is well established that a claimant's AWW is calculated as of the date of the accident, not the date a claimant's employment terminated as a result of the accident. Because the JCC's ruling was consistent with the requirements of § 440.14(1), Fla. Stat., the order was affirmed. [Rotstein v. Publix Supermarkets, Inc., 933 So. 2d 1256 (Fla. 1st DCA 2006)].

[2] Penalties

Notice of Denial—Time to File. Office Depot, the employer/carrier (E/C), appealed a final workers' compensation order directing it to pay claimant permanent total disability (PTD) benefits, together with supplemental benefits. Claimant, cross-appealed the denial of her claim for penalties, contending the Judge of Compensation Claims erred in finding the E/C timely filed its notice of denial within the statutory period provided in § 440.192(8), Fla. Stat. The court summarily affirmed the award of PTD benefits, concluding that the JCC's findings were based on competent, substantial evidence, and his interpretation of the applicable statutes governing a determination of PTD was correct. As to his denial of the claim for penalties, the court found that the record showed the employer did not file its notice of denial within 14 days after its receipt of the petition for benefits, as required by § 440.192(8), Fla. Stat., and the denial was reversed. [Office Depot v. Ortega, 931 So. 2d 1051 (Fla. 1st DCA 2006)].

§ 50.11 Temporary Total Disability and Permanent Total Disability Benefits

[1] Temporary Total Disability

Claimant Not Informed About Return to Work By Physician. Claimant alleged that she sustained a work-related back injury. She experienced pain in her lower back while rising from a chair at work, and reported the injury to her employer. The record disclosed that, on July 3, 2003, immediately after she had experienced pain in her lower back while rising from a chair in the course of her employment, claimant reported the injury to her employer, and the employer shortly thereafter considered, based on the description claimant provided of the injury, that the injury was caused by claimant's idiopathic, personal condition, and it denied compensability of the claim.

After consulting a physician, claimant asserted that the injury came about when she was required to lift x-ray aprons at work. The JCC found that the injury was compensable, but denied the claimant's request for temporary total disability (TTD) benefits. The E/C appealed the JCC's order, and claimant cross-appealed. The appellate court held that it was error for the JCC to deny claimant TTD benefits for the period when claimant's treating physician advised claimant that she should not work because of the injury. The court further held that, even in the absence of medical evidence that a claimant is temporarily totally disabled or that the claimant searched for but could not find work, TTD benefits should nevertheless be awarded where it is shown that the claimant's physicians never communicated to the claimant that he or she was released to return to work. Indeed, TTD

Case Summaries

benefits may be awarded despite the testimony of a claimant's physician that the claimant was able to perform work with certain restrictions. Once claimant's physicians failed to inform her of her release to return to work, claimant could not be denied TTD benefits, even assuming retrospective testimony that claimant could have worked during this period. Based upon the information given to claimant at the time, claimant could not reasonably have been expected to ignore the directions of her treating physician to remain off work. It was also error for the JCC to deny the medical bills of two treating physicians when the services they provided complied with § 440.13(2)(a), Fla. Stat.. That section provides, in part, that the employer shall furnish to the employee such medically necessary remedial treatment, care, and attendance for such period as the nature of the injury or the process of recovery may require. Additionally, the statute's definition of the term centers on the provision of a medical service or supply, and says nothing about a treating physician's actual knowledge of the cause of a patient's injury. Section 440.13(1)(l), Fla. Stat., provides, in part, that "medically necessary" or "medical necessity" means any medical service or medical supply which is used to identify or treat an illness or injury, is appropriate to the patient's diagnosis and status of recovery, and is consistent with the location of service, the level of care provided, and applicable practice parameters. Indeed, the appellate case law mirrors the above statutory provisions by recognizing that the appropriate test for the authorization of medical benefits is whether the award would improve the condition caused by the accident or would aid in the recovery. [Fla. Hosp. Deland v. Van Wagner-Vick, 940 So. 2d 588 (Fla. 1st DCA 2006)].

[2] Permanent Total Disability

After 104 Weeks, But Before Actual MMI. The employer/carrier appealed an order awarding permanent total disability benefits to claimant. On appeal, the court reversed. The record showed that the claimant had not reached actual maximum medical improvement. Where a claimant has not reached MMI by the expiration of the temporary benefit period and has presented no competent substantial evidence that she will be totally disabled when she does reach MMI, any claim for PTD benefits is premature. In this case, claimant had not provided any competent substantial evidence that she would be totally disabled when she reached MMI. Therefore, the award of PTD benefits constitute error, notwithstanding that claimant was no longer entitled to temporary benefits. [Palm Beach Dermatology v. Mikan, 936 So. 2d 671 (Fla. 1st DCA 2006)].

Supplemental Benefits After Age 62. The district court held that in order to terminate the claimant's supplemental benefits, the E/C had the burden of showing, pursuant to § 440.15(1)(e), Fla. Stat., that claimant would be eligible for both social security retirement benefits and social security disability benefits. Because the E/C failed in this burden, it was ordered to reinstate claimant's supplemental benefits. On appeal, the E/C argued that (1) claimant's entitlement to supplemental benefits automatically ceased when she turned age 62 because she became permanently and totally disabled prior to reaching age 62, and (2) even if claimant's entitlement did not automatically cease at age 62, she was no longer entitled to supplemental benefits because she was eligible for social security disability benefits.

The appeals court held that a claimant is eligible, as that term is used in § 440.15(1)(e)1., Fla. Stat., for social security disability benefits, if he or she is insured for disability insurance benefits, is younger than age 65, and is under a disability. Although the social security law also requires that a claimant apply for disability benefits to be entitled to such benefits, § 440.5(1)(e)1., Fla. Stat., prescribes that a claimant may be eligible for social security benefits whether or not the employee has applied for such benefits. Thus, as the JCC found, the E/C failed to show that the claimant was eligible for social security disability benefits and declined a continuance so that the issue could be addressed in more detail. [Hillsborough County Sch. Bd. v. Ward, 913 So. 2d 39 (Fla. 1st DCA 2005)].

Job Search After Award of Permanent Total Disability. The employee was accepted by the employer and the carrier as permanently and totally disabled. The JCC ordered him to submit to monthly job interviews as part of vocational rehabilitation, but the employee appealed. The employee argued that there was no provision in ch. 440, Fla. Stat. authorizing the JCC to order him to conduct such interviews after he was accepted as permanently and totally disabled. The court agreed. Section 440.15(1)(e), Fla. Stat., explicitly provided that the employer's right to conduct vocational evaluations had to be carried out under § 440.491, Fla. Stat., which allowed reemployment assessments for permanently and totally disabled employees only if the rehabilitation provider recommended such services. After that recommendation and conduct of interviews, § 440.491, Fla. Stat., further stated that the employee could be subjected to no more than annual interviews. Since there was no showing that a reemployment assessment or recommendation was ever made, that statutory law did not allow the JCC to order interviews. The JCC erred as a matter of law. The court reversed the order directing the employee to submit to monthly job interviews. [Delgado v. A. Garcia Harvesting, Inc., 913 So. 2d 78 (Fla. 1st DCA 2005)].

Vocational Evaluation. In July 2004, the employee filed a petition for benefits in which he sought, among other things, permanent and total disability benefits from March 30, 2004 in connection with a work-related accident that occurred in 1972. The parties stipulated that the case not only involved the 1972 accident, but also an accident that occurred in July 2001. The JCC granted respondents' motion to compel the employee to submit to a vocational evaluation by respondents' retained expert. The employee sought certiorari review of the JCC's order. The court found that the Florida Legislature had amended § 440.15(1)(e)1, Fla. Stat. in 2003 to provide that a carrier had the right to conduct testing by a rehabilitation provider of the carrier's choice. The amendment was procedural and applied to all accident dates. Hence, the amendment was applicable to the employee's case, and the court denied review. [Douglas v. Fla. Power & Light, Inc., 921 So. 2d 750 (Fla. 1st DCA 2006)].

§ 50.12 Temporary Partial Disability and Permanent Partial Disability Benefits

[1] Temporary Partial Disability

Deemed Earnings—Fired for Misconduct. Claimant appealed an order from the Judge of Compensation Claims denying certain temporary indemnity benefits. The appeals court affirmed the denial of temporary total or temporary partial disability (TPD) benefits from August 12, 2003 through September 16, 2003, as claimant was at maximum medical improvement (MMI) with no permanent impairment and no work restrictions as of July

Case Summaries

21, 2003. The court also upheld the denial of additional TPD benefits from September 17, 2003 through February 14, 2004, as claimant had the capacity to earn no less than the amount of temporary indemnity benefits paid to her during such time. But, denial of benefits from February 14, 2004 through June 1, 2004 was reversed, as the court found that the JCC erroneously relied on § 440.15(4)(e), Fla. Stat., which did not take effect until October 1, 2003, after the date of claimant's injury. According to the court, the JCC further erred in relying on § 440.15(6), Fla. Stat. Following her termination from employment, claimant no longer continued to refuse work the employer had offered her. Even if claimant had been terminated for misconduct, she might have still been entitled to TPD benefits if she were able to show a causal connection between the compensable injury and the loss of income. [Fardella v. Genesis Health, Inc., 917 So. 2d 276 (Fla. 1st DCA 2005)].

§ 50.13 Impairment Income Benefits and Death Benefits

[1] Impairment Income

Apportionment of Impairment Rating. Claimant/firefighter had a history of ventricular ectopy, which began while she was employed with the city. The city accepted the condition as compensable. An expert medical advisor (EMA) appointed by the Judge of Compensation Claims assigned the firefighter an eight percent impairment rating for the condition, but apportioned half of that rating because some activities, such as lack of sleep, caffeine, smoking, and stress, could have triggered increased arrhythmia. The JCC accepted the EMA's testimony and apportioned the condition to four percent. The appellate court held that this was error because the city had previously accepted the condition as compensable pursuant to §112.18(1), Fla. Stat. The city did not rebut the §112.18(1), Fla. Stat. presumption through the EMA's testimony because it had previously acknowledged the compensable nature of the condition pursuant to the statute. It was unreasonable to apportion a part of the firefighter's impairment rating for the ventricular ectopy as being part non-work-related when the city had previously accepted the entire condition as compensable. The condition was not pre-existing nor caused by an intervening circumstance. [Potter v. City of Ormond Beach, 913 So. 2d 710 (Fla. 1st DCA 2005)].

§ 50.14 Medical Benefits

[1] Independent Medical Examination

New vs. Alternate Examiner. Claimant argued that the JCC departed from the essential requirements of law resulting in a miscarriage of justice by permitting respondents, the employer and the carrier (E/C), to select a physician who practiced outside claimant's county of residence, rather than the same IME physician selected by the E/C who performed the IME on claimant in 2004. The court concluded that a surgery issue was a new dispute entitling the E/C to an IME with the physician of its choice. § 440.13(5)(a), Fla. Stat., does not require a party to repeatedly use the same IME physician for every dispute that arises within the scope of the physician's specialty during the course of a claimant's injury and treatment. Because the claimant made a new request for surgery following her 2004 IME and the E/C disputed whether the need for surgery was related to the industrial injury or a later, non-work-related cause, and there had been no IME addressing what the E/C asserted was a shoulder condition that was attributable to an event post-dating the IME, the E/C was entitled to select a new—not an alternate—IME physician. In addition, there is no statutory limitation regarding the geographical location of the IME. [Miller v. Jupiter Med. Ctr., 928 So. 2d 485 (Fla. 1st DCA. 2006)].

[2] Diagnostic Testing

Competent Substantial Evidence. Claimant sought payments for (1) surgery for treatment of an upper spine injury, (2) a urological consultation, (3) a bone scan, and (4) a discogram. The Judge of Compensation Claims denied claimant's request for payment of these medical benefits. Claimant appealed. The appellate court found that, as to the surgery, the opinions of the worker's treating physician and two independent medical examiners (IME) constituted substantial evidence in support of the JCC's determination that the surgery was unneeded. While the JCC's reason for denying the discogram lacked evidentiary support, the denial was proper. Whether the spine injury was caused by the work-related accident was not at issue. The only other purpose of the discogram was to ascertain if surgery would benefit the worker, but since the worker proceeded with the surgery before the hearing, a post-operative evaluation would have served no purpose. However, the JCC erred in denying the claims for a urological consultation and a bone scan, both of which were recommended by the worker's IME. The record did not support the JCC's finding that the IME's recommendation was the result of a misstatement by the worker as to the time he had experienced the onset of his incontinence. [Roberts v. Spartan Premier Staffing, Inc., 909 So. 2d 529 (Fla. 1st DCA 2005)].

[3] Expert Medical Advisor

Rejection of Expert Medical Advisor's Opinion. Claimant challenged the final order entered against her, arguing that the Judge of Compensation Claims erred in rejecting the opinion of an expert medical advisor (EMA). The appeals court agreed, as contradiction between the EMA and one of the disagreeing physicians was not, by itself, a reasonable basis for the JCC to reject the EMA's opinion since, under § 440.13(9), Fla. Stat., the EMA was appointed with the expectation that its testimony would contradict the record testimony of one of the health care providers. Hence, after a review of the record on appeal, the court found that it did not contain competent and substantial evidence to support a determination by the JCC that clear and convincing evidence existed sufficient to reject the opinion of the EMA. [Manuel v. Amstaff, 915 So. 2d 679 (Fla. 1st DCA 2005)].

Conflicting Medical Opinion. Because it was clear in this workers' compensation case that a conflict existed between the opinion of claimant's treating physician and the opinion of the employer's and servicing agent's independent medical examiner, on the issue of causation, the Judge of Compensation Claims committed reversible error when he denied the employer's and servicing agent's request for appointment of an expert medical advisor. *See, e.g.,* Broward Children's Ctr., Inc. v. Hall, 859 So. 2d 623, 627 (Fla. 1st DCA 2003) ("the clear intent of § 440.13(9)(c), Fla. Stat. is to require participation of an expert medical advisor in every case where a disagreement exists between healthcare providers"). Accordingly, the appellate court reversed the final order awarding benefits and remanded

Case Summaries

with instructions that the JCC appoint an expert medical advisor as requested by the employer and servicing agent. [City of Tampa v. Thompson, 923 So. 2d 558 (Fla. 1st DCA 2006)].

[4] Physician Selection

Managed Care. The court affirmed the dismissal of claimant's petitions for benefits. Because claimant had exhausted the grievance process under her managed care arrangement (MCA), the Judge of Compensation Claims had jurisdiction over claimant's petitions. However, the resolution of the petitions continued to be governed by the MCA. *See* § 440.134(16), Fla. Stat. The court found that the employer/carrier did not deny the treatment requested by claimant. Rather, the E/C had only dictated which provider would provide the treatment. Under the terms of the MCA, the E/C had sole authority to select a specialist and although the E/C could negotiate with the claimant on the matter, it was not required to do so. Therefore, the JCC properly dismissed claimant's petitions because the E/C acted in compliance with the terms of the MCA. [Mack v. Westminster Suncoast Manor, Travelers Ins., 929 So. 2d 610 (Fla. 1st DCA 2006)].

[5] Changing Physicians

One-Time Change. Claimant sought treatment from a specific pain management physician. The E/C had timely authorized treatment with a different pain management physician and scheduled an appointment for claimant, which claimant refused to attend. After a hearing, the Judge of Compensation Claims denied claimant's petition for treatment from a specific pain management physician, finding that the E/C had no duty to authorize the pain management physician requested by the claimant when the claimant had refused to attend the earlier appointment. On appeal, the court found that the JCC's finding that the E/C's authorization was timely was supported by substantial evidence. The JCC was, therefore, not able to award treatment with the specific physician requested by the claimant, pursuant to § 440.13(2)(c), Fla. Stat. Claimant could not request a change of treatment under § 440.13(2)(f), Fla. Stat., because claimant had not yet initiated treatment with the appointed physician. According to the court, claimant may request "one change of physician during the course of treatment for any one accident." [§ 440.13(2)(f), Fla. Stat.]. The legislature's use of the language "change . . . during the course of treatment" indicates a claimant must be currently receiving treatment by a physician before she may request a "change." If a claimant never even attended the initial appointment with the authorized physician, then she cannot "change" that physician because she was never treated by the physician. If never treated, the procedural right to request a one-time "change of physician during the course of treatment" does not attach. Therefore, before requesting another authorized physician, a claimant must at least begin treatment with the physician the claimant seeks to change. [Butler v. Bay Center/ Chubb Ins. Co., 947 So. 2d 570 (Fla. 1st DCA 2006)].

Right to Choose Alternative Physician. A claimant is entitled to see the physician of her choice if the E/C failed to provide another physician within five days of receiving her request for another authorized physician. *See* § 440.13(2)(f), Fla. Stat. However, under the 2005 version of the workers' compensation law, the E/C is no longer statutorily required to provide a claimant with the choice of three physicians. Moreover, the language of the statute plainly indicates a claimant may request a change of treating physician only once, no matter the number and variety of treatments needed by a claimant arising from the original accident. The choice of a claimant's authorized treating physician is not a substantive right, but a procedural one gratuitously granted by the Legislature. Consequently, in requesting a one-time change of physician, a claimant risks receiving another physician with whom she may also be unsatisfied. [Butler v. Bay Center/ Chubb Ins. Co., 947 So. 2d 570 (Fla. 1st DCA 2006)].

Second Change of Physician. The employer/carrier appealed an order by the Judge of Compensation Claims that awarded certain indemnity and medical benefits to the employee, claiming that § 440.13(2)(f), Fla. Stat. denied the employee the right to seek a second change of physician. The JCC found that the change in treatment was brought about by the employee's initially authorized hand specialist, not the employee. The JCC then authorized the employee to change her orthopedic care from one physician to another. The court held that the JCC's findings were supported by competent, substantial evidence. However, the JCC failed to heed the provisions of § 440.13(2)(f), Fla. Stat., which required the employee to first request the E/C's authorization from a list selected by it of no fewer than three physicians. The order was reversed insofar as it authorized the employee to substitute orthopedists, and the matter was remanded for further proceedings; the order was affirmed in all other respects. [Hillsborough County Sch. Bd. v. Suarez, 920 So. 2d 167 (Fla. 1st DCA 2006)].

Medical Authorization Statutes Apply Procedurally. Statutory provisions regarding authorization of physicians, including changing physicians, are procedural enactments. Therefore, the provisions of § 440.13, Fla. Stat. apply without regard to the accident date. [Butler v. Bay Center/ Chubb Ins. Co., 947 So. 2d 570 (Fla. 1st DCA 2006)].

[6] Functional Capacity Evaluation

Order Resulting in Irreparable Harm. Claimant appealed from the order of the Judge of Compensation Claims compelling her to attend a Functional Capacity Evaluation at the facility selected by the employer/carrier. The appellate court held that on certiorari review, the order of the lower tribunal will be quashed only if it departs from the essential requirements of law. Prior to considering whether the order departs from the essential requirements of law, however, the petitioner must establish that the order results in irreparable harm. In this case, the court found that claimant had failed to demonstrate that the functional capacity evaluation would result in irreparable harm. Accordingly, the petition for writ of certiorari was denied. [Vazquez v. Wendy's & Ace-USA, 931 So. 2d 152 (Fla. St DCA 2006)].

[7] Housing

Imposition of Lien. Claimant was injured in a workers' compensation accident and is now a quadriplegic. The employer/carrier accepted claimant's injury as compensable, provided treatment at an in-patient facility, and agreed that it was responsible for modifying claimant's home to meet his medical needs under Fla. Stat. § 440.13(2)(a), Fla. Stat. The E/C sought to impose a lien to prevent unjust enrichment or repetitive expenses from a variety of causes, including, but not limited to, claimant's sale of his home. The

Case Summaries

appellate court held the E/C was not entitled to involuntarily impose a lien because there is no statutory authorization for a lien. Section 440.13(2)(a), Fla. Stat., does not provide for a lien, nor does any other section cited by the E/C. In addition, because the legislature used the term of imposing a lien in other areas of Chapter 440 but not in § 440.13(2)(a), Fla. Stat., the court refused to read this term into § 440.13(2)(a), Fla. Stat. [Sunshine Towing, Inc. v. Fonseca, 933 So. 2d 594 (Fla. 1st DCA 2006)].

[8] Medical Transportation

Travel To and From Pharmacy. Claimant sought to prove that he, or sometimes his wife, drove back and forth to the pharmacy nearest his home to obtain prescriptions authorized by his treating physicians to treat his compensable injuries. The Judge of Compensation Claims ruled that it was not necessary to address the rate of travel reimbursement requested because he ruled that transportation expenses for obtaining pharmaceuticals was not reimbursable as a matter of law. Reversing, the appellate court held that the statutory obligation on the employer/carrier to provide medical care, pursuant to § 440.13(2)(a) Fla. Stat., includes medicine. Construing the language of § 440.13(2)(a), Fla. Stat., the employer/carrier was also obligated to reimburse travel expenses or provide transportation for the expenses incurred. The court found that there was no basis in the statute or the case law for a distinction between transportation expenses incurred to obtain treatment from healthcare professionals and transportation expenses incurred to obtain treatment from the pharmacy. Because the JCC did not address questions surrounding the admissibility of some of claimant's evidence on this issue, or the evidence itself, that matter was remanded for further proceedings. [Remington v. City of Ocala/United Self Insured, 940 So. 2d 1207 (Fla. 1st DCA 2006)].

[9] Medical Reimbursement

Usual and Customary Charges. On August 15, 2003, an Ambulatory Surgery Center (ASC) performed a service and charged appellant $6,025. Appellant paid only $651.51 in reimbursement, calculating the amount by noting that the service was not listed in the Florida Workers' Compensation Reimbursement Manual for Ambulatory Surgical Centers, and then determining the usual and customary charges for that service in the community., ASC requested dispute resolution from the Agency for Health Care Administration (AHCA), which found that appellant should have reimbursed $4,217.50 because the applicable version of the ASCRM required it to reimburse 70% of that service provider's usual and customary charge. The appellate court reversed, noting that Because the ASCRM was not amended between 1992 and 2005, the applicable version in the instant case is the 1992 version. It was adopted by reference in what was numbered, at that time, to Fla. Admin. Code R. 38F-7.100, which provides that "when a procedure is performed which is not listed in the manual, . . . carriers must reimburse ambulatory surgical centers 70% of the ambulatory surgical center's usual and customary charge." The rule was codified in § 440.13(4)(b)5., Fla. Stat. However, the court found that the statute was amended, effective July 15, 2003, to remove all reference to the charges of any individual service provider. [Ch. 2003-412, § 15, at 3905-08, Laws of Fla.]. According to the court, this amendment reveals the legislative intent to eliminate calculation of a "usual and customary charge" based on the fees of any one provider, in favor of a calculation of such charge based on average fees of all providers in a given geographical area. By so doing, the amendment created a conflict between the statute and the administrative rule. In cases of conflict, a statute takes precedence over an administrative rule. [One Beacon Ins. v. Agency for Health Care Admin., 2007 Fla. App. LEXIS 4533, 32 Fla. L. Weekly D 806 (Fla. 1st DCA 2007)].

NOTE: Presumably this holding applies to hospitals and other facilities as well. Unfortunately, the court did not define the term "community" other than to make reference to "a given geographical area." So, it is not clear if the term community means individual counties, regions, or the entire state.

§ 50.15 Rehabilitation Benefits

Editor's Note: No cases were reported on this topic during the time period covered for the 2007 Edition.

§ 50.16 Attendant Care

Guardian's Fees. The employer and carrier appealed a final order directing them to reimburse claimant for the fees and expenses of claimant's court-appointed guardian. Claimant, Linda Lavoy, was totally incapacitated by an injury she sustained on April 28, 1980, in the course of her employment with Florida Cypress Gardens. A guardianship was established for her in a separate proceeding in the circuit court. The appointed guardian, Kathleen Foust, performed a variety of services for claimant in addition to pursuing her claim for workers' compensation benefits, and the circuit court ordered that she be paid $ 8,534.25, from the guardianship estate.

Following the award of fees in the guardianship case, the claimant filed a petition for reimbursement. She argued that the fees and expenses of the guardianship should be assessed against the employer and carrier, because the need for the appointment of a guardian came about solely as a result of the accident. The employer and carrier agreed to pay for the services the guardian rendered in connection with claimant's earlier claim for workers' compensation benefits, but maintained the petition should be denied to the extent that it sought reimbursement for other fees and expenses of the guardianship.

The Judge of Compensation Claims agreed with claimant and, with one minor exception, approved of all the fees and costs relating to all of the guardian's services, including those that were unrelated to the pursuit of workers' compensation benefits. Based on the court's decision in *Sanchez v. Woerner Management, Inc.*, 867 So. 2d 1173 (Fla. 1st DCA 2004), the judge concluded that the employer and carrier had failed to present any evidence that would justify a reduction in the guardian's bill.

The court found that the question in this case was not whether the guardian performed all of the services listed in her bill. There was apparently no dispute about that. Rather, the question was whether some or all of these services qualified for reimbursement in a claim against the employer and carrier. The court held that this is an issue of law.

The court noted that in *Southeastern Concrete Floor v. Charlton*, 584 So. 2d 574, 576

(Fla. 1st DCA 1991), the only case addressing the point, the court held that an employer is obligated to pay for the services of a guardian only to the extent that those services were "incurred in and about the handling of the claimant['s] rights, duties, and responsibilities under Chapter 440." The court opined that it might be more equitable to make an employer pay for all of the expenses of a guardianship necessitated by a workplace injury, but the issue is not directly addressed in the Workers' Compensation Law, and the court felt bound by its own decisions on the subject. The rule in *Charlton* required the court to reverse the order in this case. The court directed that on remand, the employer and carrier should be ordered to reimburse the guardianship estate only for the services the guardian performed in the course of pursuing claimant's claims for workers' compensation benefits. [Florida Cypress Gardens & Specialty Risk Servs. v. Lavoy, 932 So. 2d 542 (Fla. 1st DCA 2006)].

Written Prescription for Attendant Care. Claimant severely injured his ankle in a workplace accident, which required emergency surgery. At the time of claimant's hospital discharge, his treating physician orally prescribed attendant care from claimant's wife. Seven months after the accident, at the claimant's request, the physician wrote a prescription for attendant care, which was intended to be a memorialization of his initial oral prescription at the time of the injury. The E/C denied coverage because § 440.13(2)(b), Fla. Stat., required a written prescription before the attendant care was actually provided. The Judge of Compensation Claims found that the oral prescription was sufficient. The appellate court found that the JCC's interpretation of the statute was in error. However, the E/C did not meet its burden in properly investigating and informing claimant or his doctor concerning the assisted care requirements. Therefore, the JCC properly awarded the benefits to claimant. [James W. Windham Builders, Inc. v. Van Overloop, 951 So. 2d 40 (Fla. 1st DCA 2007)].

§ 50.17 Subrogation

Failure to Assert Notice of Lien. After an injured worker received workers' compensation benefits for a traffic accident, he sued the tortfeasor, which was insured by the liability insurer. Neither party complied with the notice requirements of § 440.39, Fla. Stat. The appellate court found, however, that the record indicated the workers' compensation insurer had actual notice of the third-party suit. The tort action was settled, and then the workers' compensation insurer sued the tortfeasor and the liability insurer, seeking to impose a lien on the settlement proceeds pursuant to § 440.39, Fla. Stat. The appellate court held that the § 440.39(3)(a), Fla. Stat. notice needed to have been filed before any settlement or judgment was recovered. Any other interpretation would have led to the inequitable result where parties could reach a settlement that did not include the amount later sought to be asserted as a lien. The workers' compensation insurer had actual knowledge of the suit against the tortfeasor but failed to assert its right of subrogation in accordance with § 440.39(3)(a), Fla. Stat. Any claims or liens not raised in accordance with the statute were waived. [Summit Claims Mgmt. v. Lawyers Express Trucking, Inc., 913 So. 2d 1182 (Fla. 4th DCA 2005)].

§ 50.18 Special Disability Trust Fund

Limitations Period. The filing of the proof of claim does not institute a separate cause of action. Instead, there is only one cause of action for entitlement to reimbursement from the Special Disability Trust Fund, followed by a second cause of action for the amount of that reimbursement (the "request" for reimbursement) if the Fund approves the initial claim. Proof of claim is nothing more than evidence required or requested in support of the initial claim for reimbursement filed by an employer/carrier. The Florida statute of limitations is met when an action is commenced within the applicable limitations period. [Special Disability Trust Fund v. Rescare Home Health, Inc./Liberty Mutual Group, 930 So. 2d 746 (Fla. 1st DCA 2006)].

Limitations Period—Maximum Medical Improvement. Section 440.49(7)(a), Fla. Stat. provides that employer/carriers may seek reimbursement from the SDTF if they file a written notice of the claim "within 2 years after the date the employee last reached maximum medical improvement, or within 2 years after the date of the first payment of compensation for permanent total disability, wage loss, or death, whichever is later." This time period cannot be waived because, rather than a statute of limitations, this is a non-claim statute.

The phrase "whichever is later" refers to the later of two dates as between the MMI date and the date of the first compensation payment, whether it be for permanent total disability, wage loss, or death.

In the instant case, claimant's workers' compensation claim was affirmed on appeal in 1991, E/C sent claimant a check in 1992, and claimant reached MMI in 1994. When E/C filed a notice of reimbursement with the SDTF in 1995, SDTF denied the claim as untimely, characterizing the 1992 check as the first payment of benefits. However, because claimant reached MMI after the 1992 check, E/C had until two years from the date of MMI to seek reimbursement. Thus, the court held the E/C's claim for reimbursement was timely. [Lockheed Martin v. Special Disability Trust Fund, 943 So. 2d 811 (Fla. 1st DCA 2006)].

§ 50.19 Settlements

Attorney's Authority. The employee's attorney asked the employee what her position was on a settlement purportedly reached at a mediation session held on the previous day. The employee answered, "I don't have any choice." The attorney testified that she understood this to mean that the employee would accept the offer. After negotiating a somewhat larger payment and without consulting the employee, she told appellees' attorney that the matter was settled. The employee refused to sign settlement papers, explaining that her comment to the attorney meant that she had no choice but to turn down the settlement proposal because it would not cover needed medical treatment. The JCC found that the employee accepted the agreement through her attorney, that the parties agreed upon the additional amount, and that a valid settlement contract existed. The court reversed the order. The attorney's testimony that she did not consult the employee showed that she did not have clear and unequivocal authority to accept the settlement agreement. The matter was remanded for a determination of whether equitable relief was required because appellees had relied to their detriment on the attorney's representations. [Fivecoat v. Publix Super Mkts., Inc., 928 So. 2d 402 (Fla. 1st DCA 2006)].

Enforcement of Settlement Agreement—Fulfillment of Contingencies. The deceased claimant's personal representative appealed from an order of the Judge of

Case Summaries

Compensation Claims denying her motion to enforce a proposed settlement agreement. The proposed agreement was based on the terms of a Mediation Settlement Agreement that the parties had reached as to claimant's compensable industrial accident. Because the contingencies to final settlement set forth in the Mediation Settlement Agreement had not occurred, the court agreed with the JCC's ruling that a final and enforceable agreement was never made.

The Mediation Settlement Agreement was expressly not final and was contingent upon both parties' approval of a Medicare set-aside amount for future medical care. It was also expressly contingent upon resolution of any Medicare lien(s) that may be determined to exist. Neither of these contingencies had come to pass at the time that the claimant signed a draft proposed settlement agreement prepared by the carrier's attorney. Nor did the employer/carrier ever execute the proposed agreement. Although the proposed settlement agreement contained a recommended figure for the Medicare set-aside amount, that amount had yet to be approved by the Centers for Medicaid and Medicare Services ("CMMS") at the Department of Health & Human Services. Such approval was required before the employer/carrier could sign off on the amount. Further, the parties agreed that the existence and amount of any Medicare liens had yet to be determined at the time claimant signed the proposed agreement. Claimant died less than a month after signing the draft documents.

The appellate court agreed with the JCC's conclusion that the express contingencies set forth in the Mediation Settlement Agreement were not satisfied at the time claimant signed the proposed agreement or by the time she died. The court rejected claimant's argument that the mere inclusion in the draft agreement of the recommended set-aside amount and discussion of responsibility for any liens therein amounted to resolution of these issues and fulfillment of the contingencies. Competent substantial evidence in the record supported the judge's finding that the parties intended for finality of the settlement agreement to hinge on both approval of the set-aside amount by CMMS and actual resolution of any Medicare liens after the existence and amount thereof had been determined.

The judge in this case found that the parties did not intend that the Mediation Settlement Agreement was to be final and enforceable, and that they instead intended that its finality would depend upon the subsequent provision and execution of additional documents. The court found that this finding was supported by the language of the Mediation Settlement Agreement itself, which expressly stated, "The parties acknowledge that this document does not represent the final agreement & that subsequent documents will be prepared & signed by the parties."

The court held that, based on the record, the JCC correctly ruled that the necessary and express contingencies to finality set forth in the Mediation Settlement Agreement had not yet occurred at the time claimant signed the draft proposed settlement agreement. Therefore, the court affirmed the judgment. [Quinlan v. Ross Stores & Sedgwick Claims Mgmt. Servs., 932 So. 2d 428 (Fla. 1st DCA 2006)].

Enforcement of Settlement Agreement—Conditions. Claimant's widow appealed the order of the Judge of Compensation Claims denying the widow's request to enforce a settlement agreement signed by the decedent and the former employer. The decedent and the employer entered into a settlement of a workers' compensation claim before the decedent's passing. The agreement required the decedent to execute a general release and voluntary resignation and stated that it was effective and binding upon the entry of an order approving a motion for attorney's fees. The decedent failed to execute a general release or sign a voluntary resignation prior to his death. The widow sought and received an order approving her motion for attorney's fees as personal representative of her husband's estate and later executed a general release and voluntary resignation on her husband's behalf. The court found that the employer was obligated to perform under the agreement. The decedent's execution of the general release and voluntary resignation were neither conditions precedent nor conditions subsequent, as the disputed provision did not condition formation of the contract and or performance of the contract on the completion of the conditions. Further, the court held that the contract could be performed by the widow and that the widow had authorization under § 733.612(2), (24), Fla. Stat. to perform contracts and to satisfy and settle claims. [Gunderson v. Sch. Dist, 937 So. 2d 777 (Fla. 1st DCA 2006)].

General Release. While driving a truck for the employer, the employee was struck from behind by a truck driven by another of the employer's drivers. Almost two years later, the employee filed suit in circuit court against the employer and others, alleging that the other driver's negligence had injured him. Shortly thereafter, the parties settled the action and the employee executed a general release. Despite the settlement, the employee filed a petition for workers' compensation benefits. Although the petition for benefits was filed outside the statutory limitations period in § 440.19(1), Fla. Stat., the employer failed to raise the statute of limitations as a defense. The appellate court held that the employee's general release was broad enough to cover his petition for workers' compensation benefits. The parties settled all claims that might have been the subject matter of the complaint, including workers' compensation claims. Therefore, pursuant to 440.20(11)(c), Fla. Stat., the employee was not entitled to workers' compensation benefits in excess of the parties' settlement. [Patco Transp., Inc. v. Estupinan, 917 So. 2d 922 (Fla. 1st DCA 2005)].

Mediation Settlement Agreement. The Judge of Compensation Claims found that the parties intended to settle claimant's claim by the agreement they reached in mediation convened for that purpose. The court stated it was bound by that finding. Since claimant later refused to sign releases even though, represented by counsel, he had agreed in writing to execute "any releases E/C may require," the agreement was voidable at the other parties' election, but not void. Claimant could not escape the binding effect of the settlement agreement by breaching his obligation to execute a release. The employer and carrier were within their rights simply to overlook his breach, and insist on the other benefits of the bargain they struck in the settlement agreement. [Calderon v. J. B. Nurseries, Inc., 933 So. 2d 553 (Fla. 1st DCA 2006)].

Construction and Enforcement of Settlement Agreements. Claimant sought review of an order of the Judge of Compensation Claims denying his "Motion to Enforce Settlement Agreement," which sought construction and enforcement of the parties' washout settlement agreement. The court agreed that the JCC erred in concluding that she was without jurisdiction to construe the agreement. Nonetheless, the court affirmed the denial of the motion because claimant was not entitled to the relief sought.

The intent of the parties governs in contract construction, and that intent is to be

Case Summaries

ascertained from the agreement itself where its terms are clear and unambiguous. The initial determination of whether a contract is ambiguous presents a question of law. Absent any ambiguity, the construction of the contract also presents a question of law.

In this case, the terms of the settlement agreement unequivocally provided that (1) the settlement payment was in full settlement of any and all claims, (2) the employer and carrier would be released from liability for past and future medical benefits upon payment of the settlement amount, and (3) the E/C would not be liable for the payment of any medical bills upon execution of the agreement. Based upon the unambiguous terms of the agreement, the E/C's liability was completely extinguished without any limitation. Therefore, the court held that the claimant was not entitled to payment of the medical bills that were outstanding at the time the agreement was executed. [Cartaya v. Coastline Distrib., 937 So. 2d 700 (Fla. 1st DCA 2006)

§ 50.20 The Legal Environment and Dispute Resolution

[1] The 120-Day Rule

Paying Benefits Triggers the 120-Day Rule. After an employee fell to the ground while trimming a palm tree at work, the Employer/Carrier sent the employee a letter advising that it would pay the claim, but was reserving the right to deny the benefits after further investigation, within 120 days, if the claim or benefit was determined not to be compensable. Despite the letter, the E/C never paid any indemnity or medical benefits. Therefore, the employee filed a petition for benefits. The Judge of Compensation Claims found that the E/C was estopped to deny compensability of the employee's claim. The E/C appealed, claiming that they denied the employee's claim by never providing benefits..The appellate court held that by doing nothing in response to a request for benefits, the E/C effectively denied the claim. Despite the E/C's letter referencing the 120-day provision in § 440.20 (4), Fla. Stat., it was never actually triggered because the E/C never paid anything. Accordingly, the judge of compensation claims erred in finding the E/C estopped to deny compensability of the accident. [Begley's Cleaning Serv. v. Costa, 913 So. 2d 1244 (Fla. 1st DCA 2005)].

Untimely Denial. The employee appealed an order by the Judge of Compensation Claims that denied his claims for compensability of a back condition and for authorization of a neurologist.

After the carrier accepted the compensability of the employee's injury and commenced the payments of benefits, the employee's doctor informed the carrier that the employee's need for medical treatment was caused by preexisting degenerative changes to the employee's personal condition. The appellate court found that the doctor's surgery notes should have reasonably brought to the carrier's attention the fact that the employee's condition preexisted the accident, thereby alerting it to the necessity of beginning an investigation. However, the carrier failed to take any action within 120 days from the notice. The carrier presented no evidence that Dr. Scharf did not provide his office notes to them, that he misled them, or that his notes were lost or misplaced. The only evidence offered by the carrier as an excuse for its failure to deny within the 120-day period was that it only actually became aware as of November 15, 2004, that the industrial accident was not the major contributing cause of the injury. The statute does not, however, provide that the carrier have nothing less than actual notice, but rather that it have sufficient information to enable it to deny compensability within 120 days. Therefore, the carrier's subsequent denial of compensability was a waiver of its right to contest the compensability of the back condition by reason of the expiration of the requisite 120-day period.

The court agreed, however, that the JCC correctly denied the claim seeking authorization of a neurologist. While § 440.20(4), Fla. Stat. does bar the carrier from denying compensability after the expiration of the 120-day pay-and-investigate period, it does not have the effect of precluding the carrier from denying a specific claim for benefits on the ground that the injuries resulting from the compensable accident were not the major contributing cause of the claimant's need for such benefits. [Mims v. Confederated Staffing, 940 So. 2d 518 (Fla. 1st DCA 2006)].

Payments Made Pending Resolution of Compensability. The employer/carrier appealed an order of the Judge of Compensation Claims finding the employee's alleged workplace injuries compensable because the employer and carrier had not denied her claim within the 120-day period prescribed in § 440.20(4), Fla. Stat.

The employer and the carrier argued from the beginning that the injury was not compensable. They responded to the employee's initial claim with the standard letter that normally, pursuant to § 440.20(4), Fla. Stat. would have commenced the running of a 120-day time limit for granting or denying coverage. A failure to grant or deny within that time frame normally precludes an employer or carrier from raising the issue of compensability later on. The court held that the instant case was distinguishable, however, in that all parties understood that compensability was at issue, so that all payments made to the employee were pursuant to a mediated interim settlement pending final resolution of compensability. Under these circumstances, the employer and the carrier had not waived their defenses. [Long John Silver's/Yum! Brands, Inc. v. Holcombe, 924 So. 2d 66 (Fla. 1st DCA 2006)].

120-Day Rule Application Clarified. The Judge of Compensation Claims held that the employer/carrier were estopped from denying claimant's request for additional treatment, including surgery, even though the JCC found that claimant's preexisting condition was the major contributing cause (MCC) of any need for further treatment or surgery. The E/C, claiming error, appealed from the order, while claimant cross-appealed.

The E/C contended that claimant failed to prove that her injury remained the MCC of her need for continued treatment and surgery, and that the JCC erred in authorizing this medical care because, although § 440.20(4), Fla. Stat. barred the E/C from denying compensability after the expiration of the 120-day pay and investigate period, it did not preclude the E/C from challenging claimant's entitlement to benefits. The appeals court agreed. The E/C's failure to respond to the § 440.192, Fla. Stat. petition requesting medical treatment with surgery did not constitute a denial of compensability. But, the E/C's failure to deny compensability warranted application of a § 440.20(4), Fla. Stat. waiver. While the E/C was precluded from contending that there was no industrial accident resulting in injury, it could still contend that the injuries resulting from the industrial accident were not the MCC of claimant's need for further treatment or surgery. The JCC's finding that claimant reached maximum medical improvement with no

Case Summaries

permanent impairment rating, and that her industrial injuries were no longer the MCC of any continuing need for treatment or surgery, was upheld.

The finding that the E/C was precluded from challenging claimant's entitlement to benefits, as well as the JCC's authorization of additional medical care, were reversed, but the court found that claimant's issues on cross-appeal lacked merit. The court also affirmed the denial of other benefits. [Checkers Rest. v. Wiethoff, 925 So. 2d 348 (Fla. 1st DCA 2006)].

120-Day Rule Does Not Apply to Continued Medical Treatment. The Judge of Compensation Claims applied the 120-day pay and investigate provision of § 440.20(4), Fla. Stat., to claimant's entitlement to further benefits under § 440.09(1)(b), Fla. Stat. The court held this was error. Section 440.20(4), Fla. Stat. does not preclude the E/C from challenging claimant's entitlement to benefits, by contending that the injuries resulting from the industrial accident were not the MCC of claimant's need for further treatment or surgery. Indeed, the JCC found that claimant had reached maximum medical improvement with no permanent impairment rating, and that the industrial injuries were no longer the MCC of any continuing need for treatment or surgery. Therefore, claimant was no longer entitled to medical benefits.

Here, the JCC properly found the industrial accident was not the major contributing cause of claimant's need for further treatment. Instead, the facts credited by the JCC showed that such treatment was attributable to a pre-existing condition. Therefore, the order was reversed. [Citrus County Sch. Bd. v. Carlucci, 928 So. 2d 468 (Fla. 1st DCA 2006)].

Waiver of Right to Deny Compensability Does Not Establish Entitlement to Any Benefits Claimant May Seek. The Judge of Compensation Claims concluded that appellee claimant's hypertension was, by default, compensable, as appellants, the employer and its carrier (E/C), failed to deny compensability within 120 days of providing cardiac treatment. The E/C appealed. The E/C argued that the JCC's finding regarding the compensability of claimant's hypertension was erroneous. The appeals court agreed, and reversed the judgment. Since the E/C waived the right to deny compensability, the JCC erroneously concluded that all benefits sought for hypertension had to be provided. Under the JCC's logic, an E/C providing treatment to an injured employee for a known and accepted condition would incur the obligation to provide treatment for any other condition the claimant might suffer then, or in the future. The obligation would then be incurred without any consideration of the relationship between the contested condition and the accepted condition, or between the workplace injury and the contested condition. Such action sanctioned an E/C who accepted the responsibility for uncontested medical conditions that resulted from workplace injuries and provided negative incentives for a self-executing system. Second, a blurring of the distinction between the concepts of compensability and entitlement to benefits rendered other important statutory provisions meaningless. [City of Ocoee v. Trimble, 929 So. 2d 687 (Fla. 1st DCA 2006)].

[2] Petition for Benefits

Social Security Number Not Required. Section 440.192, Fla. Stat., provides that a Petition for Benefits that does not contain the claimant's social security number is invalid.

The first district court of appeal held that this statutory requirement of including a social security number violates section 7 of the federal Privacy Act of 1974, at 5 U.S.C. § 552a and is therefore invalid.

On further review, the Florida Supreme Court agreed and adopted the first district's opinion. The Court found that the exception provided in section 7(a)(2)(B) of the Privacy Act would not apply to § 440.192, Fla. Stat., requiring injured workers to list their social security number, because § 440.192, Fla. Stat., was not enacted until 1980. The Court reviewed other exceptions to the Privacy Act, including those contained in section 42 U.S.C. § 405, and found none to be applicable. [Fla. Div. of Workers' Comp. v. Cagnoli, 914 So. 2d 950, 951 (Fla. 2005)].

NOTE: Presumably, this decision invalidates any other statute or administrative rule enacted after July 1, 1975, requiring a claimant to disclose his or her social security number.

[3] Jurisdiction

Compulsion to Sign Social Security Administration Release Forms. Claimant received permanent and total disability benefits from the Employer/Carrier (E/C) for a work-related injury sustained in 1999. After the Social Security Administration (SSA) denied claimant disability benefits a second time, the E/C sought access to his SSA records pursuant to § 440.15(9)(c), Fla. Stat. Historically, an E/C could access these records by providing SSA with a signed DWC-14 Form referenced in to Fla. Admin. Code R. 69L-3.0194(3)(d)(5); however, the SSA recently began requiring an additional signed consent form which they developed. Claimant signed the DWC-14 Form, but refused to sign the SSA form.

Claimant's refusal to sign the SSA form resulted in the E/C filing a motion to compel. The JCC subsequently granted the motion and ordered claimant to execute the SSA form. Claimant filed a petition for a writ of certiorari to quash a JCC's order of the Judge of Compensation Claims compelling claimant to execute forms authorizing the SSA to release claimant's records to the E/C. Claimant contended that (1) the JCC never had jurisdiction over the dispute because there was no pending petition for benefits, and (2) the JCC could not compel him to sign a form that was not referenced in to Fla. Admin. Code R. 69L-3.0194(d)(5). The court held the claimant erred in both contentions.

As to the first contention, claimant erroneously implied that an E/C has no remedy to enforce any of its substantive rights under ch. 440, Fla. Stat. unless a claimant first files a petition for benefits. An E/C has a statutory right to access a claimant's social security disability benefit records pursuant to § 440.15(9)(c), Fla. Stat. The JCC has jurisdiction, pursuant to § 440.33(1), Fla. Stat., to "do all things conformable to law which may be necessary to enable the [JCC] effectively to discharge the duties of her or his office." Here, the JCC compelling claimant to sign the SSA form was conformable, or based on, § 440.15(9)(c), Fla. Stat. and therefore necessary to discharge the duties of his office.

As to the second contention, the court found that nowhere does § 440.15(9)(c), Fla. Stat., or to Fla. Admin. Code R. 69L-3.0194(d)(5) expressly limit the forms a claimant must sign. Even if, as claimant suggested, the rule implicitly limits his responsibility to execute only the DWC-14 Form, it is axiomatic that an administrative rule cannot

Case Summaries

contravene the provisions of a statute. The court found that here, the statute allowed the E/C access and affirmed the Order. [Canovas v. Sugar Supply, Inc., 921 So. 2d 26 (Fla. 1st DCA 2006)].

[4] Discovery

Psychiatric Medical Records. A claimant's medical records concerning preexisting mental conditions are not discoverable unless the condition has been placed at issue. Although the psychiatric records might contain information that would be relevant for impeachment purposes or in connection with a defense that fatigue and neurological symptoms are the result of some mental or emotional condition unrelated to the injuries of which claimant complains, the § 90.503(4)(c), Fla. Stat. exception applies only when the patient, rather than some party who opposes the patient in litigation, places his mental or emotional condition at issue. Therefore, because the patient in the present litigation, claimant, had not placed his mental or emotional condition at issue, the court held that the § 90.503(4)(c), Fla. Stat. exception to the privilege did not apply. The petition was accordingly granted and the discovery order was quashed. [Bandorf v. Volusia County Dep't of Corr., 939 So. 2d 249 (Fla. 1st DCA 2006)].

[5] Admissible Evidence

Evidence Not Timely Produced. The employer/carrier sought review of a decision of the Judge of Compensation Claims, which denied their fraud defense and awarded workers' compensation benefits to claimant. Pursuant to a pretrial order, the parties were to notice and submit all discovery at least 30 days prior to the date of the final hearing. Twenty-one days prior to the hearing, claimant's counsel received surveillance tapes from counsel for the employer/carrier. Based on his uniform policy that the failure to provide notice of surveillance evidence at least 30 days prior to the final hearing always resulted in a finding of procedural prejudice to the claimant, the JCC refused to allow the employer/carrier to introduce the tapes at the final hearing. The appellate court reversed. Prior case law required a three factor, case-specific analysis of whether evidence that was not timely provided should be excluded. Because the per se rule applied by the JCC was antithetical to that case-specific analysis, the exclusion of the surveillance tapes was an abuse of discretion and could not be sustained. [Med. Logistics, Inc. v. Marchines, 911 So. 2d 823 (Fla. 1st DCA 2005)].

Medical Opinions Based on Otherwise Inadmissible Facts or Data. On appeal from an order of the Judge of Compensation Claims, claimant argued that the JCC's admission of her treating physician's opinion testimony that she had no need for attendant care was an abuse of discretion in that the facts or data that the physician relied on in reaching his opinion were not the facts or data that experts in his field reasonably relied on. Claimant urged that this was so because the JCC had previously excluded the evidence supporting the physician's opinion, namely, a surveillance videotape and a typewritten surveillance report. However, the court noted that the JCC excluded the evidence solely because of discovery violations. Even if the JCC erred in allowing the physician's opinion into evidence, the error was harmless because the physician did not base his opinion solely on the surveillance tape and report. The physician reported that claimant never expressed to him any difficulty in engaging in the activities of daily living. Claimant herself testified that the surveillance tape was an accurate depiction of her activities during the time in question. The JCC did not abuse her discretion in admitting into evidence the physician's opinion testimony pursuant to § 90.704, Fla. Stat. [King v. Auto Supply of Jupiter, Inc., 917 So. 2d 1015 (Fla. 1st DCA 2006)].

Unauthorized Chiropractor. The employee, a bus driver, was injured in a work-related accident. After seeing various physicians, the employee, without seeking authorization for chiropractic care, saw a chiropractor, who released her from work for two weeks. The employer/servicing agent objected to the admissibility of the chiropractor's opinions on the basis that he was not an authorized treating provider. The Judge of Compensation Claims decided that the chiropractor was an authorized provider because the E/SA denied the employee's request for orthopedic care, and awarded temporary disability. The E/SA appealed the order that awarded temporary total disability benefits to the employee. The E/SA claimed that because the order was erroneously based on an unauthorized provider's opinion, no competent, substantial evidence supported the award. The court found that, while the employee might have sought further orthopedic care, she did not seek authorization for chiropractic care. Thus, because the chiropractor was not an authorized treating provider, pursuant to § 440.13(5)(e), Fla. Stat., the JCC erred in relying upon his opinion regarding the employee's work status in support of the award. However, because the JCC properly relied upon the employee's testimony that she was unable to work during the period in question and the fact that she was never advised that she could return to work, there was other substantial evidence to support the award. The order was affirmed. [Seminole County Sch. Bd. v. Tweedie, 922 So. 2d 1011 (Fla. 1st DCA 2006)].

[6] Frivolous Claims

Award of Attorney Fees to Carrier. Claimant sought review of a final order granting fees to the carrier, Travelers Insurance Co., pursuant to § 440.32(2), Fla. Stat. Claimant raised three points: (1) the Judge of Compensation Claims lacked jurisdiction to award fees under this statute because claimant had served a Notice of Voluntary Dismissal as to Travelers; (2) the evidence was not sufficient to support the JCC's award of fees; and (3) the JCC abused his discretion in allowing Travelers' witnesses to testify at the evidentiary hearing on attorney's fees.

The appellate court affirmed the latter two points without further discussion. The court also found no merit to the claimant's first point. According to Florida law, "after a voluntary dismissal by a plaintiff the trial court does have jurisdiction to award attorney's fees where the fees are authorized by statute or a contract between the parties." Moreover, although claimant served a Notice of Voluntary Dismissal as to Travelers, the claim pending before the JCC was never dismissed. Any attempt to dismiss less than the entire action is a nullity, and does not terminate the court's jurisdiction. At all relevant times, the JCC here had jurisdiction over the claim, the claimant, and Travelers. [Murillo v. Tri-State Empl. Servs., 925 So. 2d 376, 377 (Fla. 1st DCA 2006)]

[7] Piecemeal Litigation

Res Judicata—Permanent Total Disability. The worker sought authorization for back surgery. After her surgery had been authorized but before the surgery took place, she filed a second petition for permanent total disability benefits. By that time, she was no longer eligible for any temporary indemnity benefits. When the second petition came on for hearing, the parties stipulated that she had not by then reached maximum medical improvement, but that when she did reach maximum medical improvement, she would have a permanent impairment. The injured worker sought review of the order of the JCC which denied her petition for permanent total workers' compensation disability benefits because she did not simultaneously request and litigate entitlement to those benefits when she sought authorization for back surgery by filing a petition after her entitlement to temporary disability benefits had expired.

The appellate court noted that no claim for permanent total disability benefits was actually litigated when the JCC had earlier required the authorization for back surgery. The court held that no reason was shown why the worker was under any obligation to litigate a claim for permanent total disability benefits at that time. It was, therefore, error for the JCC to bar the claim for permanent total disability benefits the worker stated in her second petition. [Olmo v. Rehabcare Starmed/SRS, 930 So. 2d 789 (Fla. 1st DCA 2006)].

Res Judicata. The issue in this case was whether the portion of the claim for the worker's left shoulder injury was precluded by res judicata. The Judge of Compensation Claims found, in an earlier hearing, that to the extent the worker was alleging benefits based on the left shoulder injury, she failed to prove she was entitled to benefits. The appellate court found that the issue of the worker's left shoulder injury was ripe for adjudication at that first merits hearing. Although the worker dismissed her petition for benefits regarding the left shoulder injury before the first merits hearing, she presented testimony on this issue at the hearing. In the order currently on appeal, the JCC awarded benefits for the same time period, finding the left shoulder condition compensable, and authorized treatment for the worker's left shoulder. Because these claims were ripe at the time of the first final merits hearing, they were barred by res judicata. The fact that the deposition of the doctor relied on by the worker to prove causation with regard to the left shoulder injury was not taken until after the first merits hearing did not preclude application of res judicata. [U. S. Block Windows v. Dixon, 943 So. 2d 852 (Fla. 1st DCA 2006)].

[8] Disqualification of Judge of Compensation Claims

Disparaging Remarks by Judicial Assistant. After a dispute arose over scheduling a hearing on a motion to vacate a merits order in claimant's workers' compensation case, a motion to disqualify was filed which was based primarily upon disparaging remarks allegedly made to claimant's counsel by the judicial assistant (JA) to the Judge of Compensation Claims. The court found that the motion for disqualification was facially insufficient, and therefore properly denied, because movant failed to establish why a reasonable person would attribute any negative bias against counsel to the JCC when the JA made the comments. This was particularly important in the instant case, where the JA's comments were made while counsel was communicating with the JA to schedule a hearing, an administrative responsibility generally delegated to judicial assistants by trial judges. In other words, there was nothing on the face of the motion, when the facts were taken as true as required by Fla. R. Jud. Admin. 2.160(f) and to Fla. Admin. Code R. 60Q-6.126(1), to show that a reasonable person hearing these remarks by the JA would have a sound reason to believe that they reflected the views of anyone other that the JA.

Claimant also argued that the JCC violated the requirement that the facts set forth in the motion to disqualify be taken as true in her remarks at a hearing. The court found this argument to be without merit. The petition for writ of prohibition was denied. [Leone v. F.J.M. Constr., 911 So. 2d 1285 (Fla. 1st DCA 2005)].

§ 50.21 Attorney's Fees

[1] Entitlement to Fees

Benefits Secured. Claimant sought review of an order of the Judge of Compensation Claims, which determined that claimant was not entitled to attorney's fees. The JCC determined that claimant suffered a compensable accident by injury arising out of the scope of her employment with appellee employer/carrier (E/C). Claimant came under the care and treatment of an orthopedic surgeon, who was authorized to treat claimant by the E/C. After a hiatus from treatment, the physician's office incorrectly would not allow claimant to see the doctor when she wanted to resume treatment. Claimant retained legal counsel and filed two petitions for benefits. After the petitions were filed, the E/C advised claimant that she could continue ongoing treatment with the physician. Further, the JCC found that there was never any resistance by the E/C to the continuation of claimant's treatment with the physician. The JCC found that there was no award of new benefits, only a clarification of the benefits authorized to claimant, and that claimant was not entitled to attorney's fees or reimbursable taxable costs under § 440.34(3)(a), Fla. Stat. The court found that the JCC's order was well-reasoned and affirmed the decision. [Tipton v. E-Z Serve Convenience Stores, Inc., 936 So. 2d 48 (Fla. 1st DCA 2006)].

Statutory Fee Schedule. Claimant sought review of an order entered by the Judge of Compensation Claims with respect to an award of an attorney's fee to her in strict accordance with the guideline formula set forth in § 440 34(1), Fla. Stat. Claimant also made a motion for an appellate attorney's fee under § 440.34(5), Fla. Stat. Claimant made constitutional challenges to the formula used in § 440.34(1), Fla. Stat.. However, the court found that similar arguments had been considered and rejected in its recent decisions of *Lundy v. Four Seasons Ocean Grand Palm Beach*, 932 So. 2d 506 (Fla. 1st DCA 2006), and *Campbell v. Aramark*, 933 So. 2d 1255 (Fla.1st DCA 2006). Further, based on the language of § 440.34(5), Fla. Stat., the court held that it was discretionary whether or not to award appellate attorney's fees. Because claimant's appeal was unsuccessful, the court found that she had to meet a heavy burden under *Wick Roofing v. Curtis*, 110 So. 2d 385, 387 (Fla. 1959) to justify a discretionary award of appellate attorney's fees; claimant did not meet this burden. The court formulated the following certified question: do the amended provisions of § 440.34(1), Fla. Stat. clearly and unambiguously establish the percentage fee formula provided therein as the sole standard for determining the reasonableness of an attorney's fee to be awarded to a claimant? [Buitrago v. Landry's, 949 So. 2d 1046 (Fla. 1st DCA 2006)].

Verified Petition for Attorney's Fees—Time to File. Claimant filed several petitions for benefits. The parties eventually resolved all of the claims. The parties then advised the Judge of Compensation Claims' office that there was no need for a final hearing, but reserved on the issue of attorney fee entitlement. The JCC served Notices of Administrative Closure of Case, which indicated the case would be administratively closed unless a verified petition for attorney's fees was filed within 45 days. The notices also advised that all pending petitions for benefits would be subject to dismissal without a hearing unless a party filed an objection.

On October 29, 2004, the JCC entered an order closing the file. In the order, the JCC noted that all of the issues between the parties, other than attorney fee entitlement, had been resolved. Accordingly, the JCC dismissed all of the petitions for benefits pending prior to February 3, 2004.

Claimant's attorney filed his verified petition for attorney fees on March 2, 2005. The employer/carrier filed a motion to dismiss the verified petition with prejudice. The employer/carrier alleged the petition had to be dismissed because it was not timely filed within the dictates of the October 29, 2004, order. After a hearing was held on the motion to dismiss, the JCC granted the employer/carrier's motion and dismissed the petition with prejudice. The JCC reasoned that because the October 29, 2004, order was not appealed within 30 days, he was without jurisdiction to modify the earlier order.

The court found that the portion of the October 29, 2004, order relating to attorney's fees was not final. Further, the court held that the JCC did not have authority, pursuant to either statute or rule, to set a time limitation for filing the verified petition for fees. The employer/carrier's argument that the JCC had authority to set such a time limitation pursuant to § 440.33(1), Fla. Stat. was not persuasive. Accordingly, the order was reversed. [Villazano v. Horace Bell Honey Co., 928 So. 2d 515 (Fla. 1st DCA 2006)]

Verified Petition for Attorney's Fees-Time to File. Claimant sought review of an order of the Judge of Compensation Claims, which dismissed his verified petition for attorney's fees with prejudice, after claimant failed to file the petition within the time frame specified by the JCC. The court reversed noting its recent decision in Villazano v. Horace Bell Honey Co., 928 So. 2d 515 (Fla. 1st DCA 2006). In that case, the court held that: "the JCC did not have authority, pursuant to either statute or rule, to set a time limitation for filing the verified petition for fees." Although the court recognized the JCC was merely attempting to govern his own docket, the court held that the Legislature has not yet given JCCs the authority to do so. Consequently, the order was reversed. [Gillislee v. FPL, 929 So. 2d 716, 717 (Fla. 1st DCA 2006)]

[2] Amount of Fees

Statutory Fee Schedule—Reasonable Fee. The Judge of Compensation Claims awarded claimant an additional $1,148.50 in disputed benefits. As a result, claimant's counsel was awarded $229.70 in attorney's fees, pursuant to § 440.34(1), Fla. Stat. Further, the JCC awarded counsel an additional $100.00 in attorney's fees as a sanction due to the employer/carrier's failure to comply with a motion to compel. Counsel appealed. Counsel challenged the judgment entered concerning the attorney's fees awarded. First, he argued that the JCC erred in interpreting the word "reasonable" in § 440.34(1), Fla. Stat., and that he was entitled to a fee of $ 3,340.00, almost three times greater than the value of the benefits he secured for claimant. Second, he claimed that the $ 100.00 attorney's fee was inadequate. The appeals court disagreed, first holding that neither the parties' stipulations nor Fla. R. Bar 4-1.5(b) trumped the interpretation of § 440.34(1), Fla. Stat. Second, acceptance of counsel's arguments that they did would, rendered the 2003 legislative amendments to § 440.34, Fla. Stat., meaningless. Under that section, the JCC was required to approve any attorney's fee, and could only approve a fee if it was reasonable. A JCC may approve a fee as "reasonable" only when it equals a statutorily established percentage of the value of benefits secured on behalf of the claimant. Counsel's second claim was not addressed. [Wood v. Fla. Rock Indus., 929 So. 2d 542 (Fla. 1st DCA 2006)].

Statutory Fee Schedule—Constitutionality. The employer/carrier agreed that claimant was due past benefits in the amount of $1,700.00 and that claimant's attorney was entitled to a fee in the amount of $1,900.00 for securing these benefits. The Judge of Compensation Claims refused to approve the fee because the schedule fee was only $340.00 and she had no authority to approve a fee in excess of that amount. The JCC entered an Order approving a statutory fee in the amount of $340.00. On appeal, the court agreed with the JCC and affirmed the fee award consistent with its decision in *Wood v. Florida Rock Industries*, 929 So. 2d 542 (Fla. 1st DCA 2006) (where the court held that the statutory fee schedule in § 440.34(1), Fla. Stat., for attorney fees based on benefits secured must be strictly applied and that the JCC may not approve fees in excess of the statutory formula).

In addition, the court addressed constitutional challenges. In summary, the court held that § 440.34(1), Fla. Stat. is constitutional. The court further held that (1) the Legislature did not encroach upon the powers of the judiciary by amending the statute to restrict payment of fees to the statutory schedule; (2) § 440.34(1), Fla. Stat. does not violate the equal protection clause or the due process clause; (3) the statute does not deny a claimant the right to be represented by counsel; (4) § 440.34(1), Fla. Stat. does not impermissibly restrict the right to freely contract; and (5) claimant abandoned the issues of the statute denying access to courts during oral argument. The court noted the statute has not been shown to deny access to courts because it impairs a claimant's ability to retain counsel.

As it did in *Wood*, the court also certified this case to the Florida Supreme Court for further review. [Lundy v. Four Seasons Ocean Grand Palm Beach, 932 So. 2d 506 (Fla. 1st DCA 2006)]

Taxable Costs—Expert Witness Fees. Claimant challenged the Judge of Compensation Claims' order, which denied claimant's request that the employer and carrier (E/C) pay the fees and costs resulting from a medical expert's second deposition. The second deposition was conducted solely for the purpose of determining the value of treatments the physician previously recommended. The value of the recommended treatment was necessary to determine the attorney's fee to which claimant was entitled.

The appellate court held that it is well settled that the E/C is not obligated to pay expert witness fees charged by an attorney testifying as to the reasonableness of a requested attorney's fee in a workers' compensation case. The court saw no reason this rule should not be equally applied to medical expert witnesses.

According to the court, in any workers' compensation case where the necessity of medical benefits is contested, expert medical testimony will be required. It would be a

Case Summaries

simple matter to elicit the expert's opinion as to the value of the medical treatment recommended when the expert is giving his medical opinion as to the necessity of treatment. The court could not conceive of any circumstance in which such testimony could not be elicited at this time, and doing so is consistent with the philosophy of the worker's compensation law to provide an expeditious result at a minimum cost.

The court noted that if, for some reason, those questions cannot be asked in the primary proceeding, the JCC can often ascertain the value of medical benefits obtained without a hearing, based upon a medical expert's affidavit. Although it is within the JCC's discretion to hold collateral proceedings to determine the amount of attorney's fees, medical expert witness fees incurred during such proceedings are not taxable against the E/C. [*See* Tucker v. FedEx, 931 So. 2d 222 (Fla. 1st DCA 2006)].

Appellate Attorney Fees—Unverified Petition for Attorney's Fees. In a previous appeal, the appellate court had affirmed an award of fees to the employee's attorney, reversed a denial of costs and remanded that issue for reconsideration, granted the employee's motion for appellate attorney's fees, and relinquished jurisdiction to the Judge of Compensation Claims to determine the amount of the appellate fee award. At a hearing on the appellate fee issue, the employee objected to appellees' response to the employee's verified petition for fees and costs, claiming that it was unverified, untimely, and did not provide sufficient detail to give notice of the matters in dispute. The JCC refused to accept the unverified response, placed the attorneys under oath, and allowed them to testify and to cross-examine each other. Subsequently, the JCC awarded appellate attorney's fees to the employee pursuant to order of the Florida Judge of Compensation Claims (JCC) that awarded appellate attorney's fees to the employee pursuant to § 440.34(3)(b), Fla. Stat. and Fla. R. App. P. 9.400(b) pursuant to the previous appellate order. The employee's counsel sought review. The appellate court affirmed the resulting award. No cost award was necessary because the parties had agreed on that issue. Appellees' response was timely and the JCC's approach properly cured its unverified status. The response was sufficiently specific to provide notice of the disputed issues. The employee should have, but did not, move for a continuance to avoid any problems of surprise. The JCC's fee award reasonably construed the appellate court order. [Nash v. AMR Corp., 937 So. 2d 1205 (Fla. 1st DCA 2006)].

Stipulations. Claimant was injured and petitioned for benefits for a stomach/colon condition and an orthopedic condition. The Judge of Compensation Claims petition. While claimant's appeal of that denial was pending, she filed additional petitions for benefits related to two falls that occurred because of foot problems. A remand was ordered from claimant's appeal for an independent medical examination (IME) of the stomach/colon condition. The parties resolved those claims in mediation. Thereafter, the parties executed a stipulation providing attorney's fees under the criteria of § 440.34, Fla. Stat. The parties entered another stipulation allowing claimant appellate attorney's fees. However, the JCC denied claimant's petition for fees related to non-appellate time expended securing the IME. Claimant appealed. The court found that the first stipulation on attorney fees plainly precluded any non-appellate attorney's fees. In that stipulation, the claimant clearly relinquished any additional claim for fees based on time that counsel expended prior to the appeal. Since claimant was bound by the plain language of the stipulation, denial of the non-appellate attorney fees was proper. [Klatt v. Wal-Mart Stores, Inc., 913 So. 2d 79 (Fla. 1st DCA 2005)].

§ 50.22 Insurance and Regulation

Coverage Requirement—Construction Industry. On the date of his accident, claimant was working on the roof of a hanger at the Clearwater/St. Petersburg Airport, applying white sealant coating to the roof when he fell and was injured. The Judge of Compensation Claims found that the employer was not engaged in the construction industry and that, since it did not employ four or more employees, it was not required to provide workers' compensation coverage. It was undisputed that the employer employed fewer than four employees. The JCC concluded that the employer made only "minor" repairs to facilities and, so, its activities did not fall within the definition of "construction industry." The appellate court disagreed. The nature of the employer's business was clearly within the type of "building" activities traditionally included in the construction industry. Further, while the work of the employer did not improve the size of the airport hangers which it serviced, its activities did result in substantial improvement in the use of those hangers. The repairs and sealing of the roof permitted the hangers to continue to function as storage facilities that protected aircraft and other equipment. The activities of the employer were analogous to painting, application of vinyl and asphalt, tile installation, and sheet metal work, which were recognized as part of the construction industry. [*See* Ficocelli v. Just Overlay, Inc., 932 So. 2d 1230 (Fla. 1st DCA 2006)].

§ 50.23 Immunity

Temporary Staffing. Defendant company sought review of a non-final order of the Circuit Court for Miami-Dade County (Florida), which granted summary judgment in favor of plaintiff, personal representative of the deceased's estate, finding that the company was not entitled to workers' compensation immunity. The deceased was employed by a temporary staffing agency. At the company's request, the agency sent the deceased to a construction site where the company was a subcontractor. The deceased was instructed and supervised by the company's personnel while on the site, but was paid directly by the staffing agency. The deceased was killed in a work-related incident on the company's job site. The deceased's estate filed a wrongful death action against the company and the primary contractor. The trial court denied the company's motion for summary judgment based on immunity under § 440.11(2), Fla. Stat. and, based on the hold harmless agreement signed by the agency, determined that the estate was entitled to partial summary judgment. The court held that the company was entitled to workers' compensation immunity as a matter of law, pursuant to § 440.11(2), Fla. Stat. The court rejected the contention that the hold harmless agreement executed by the agency waived the company's statutory entitlement to immunity. The hold harmless agreement was executed only by the agency and there was nothing in that agreement that indicated that the company waived its right to statutory immunity. [Am. Eng'g & Dev. Corp. v. Sanchez, 932 So. 2d 1241 (Fla. 3rd DCA 2006)].

Case Summaries

PART III

FLORIDA STATUTES

SYNOPSIS

TITLE XXXI
LABOR
CHAPTER 440
WORKERS' COMPENSATION

Fla. Stats.

TITLE XXXIX
COMMERCIAL RELATIONS

CHAPTER 682
ARBITRATION CODE

Fla. Stats.

FLORIDA STATUTES*

TITLE XXXI LABOR

CHAPTER 440 WORKERS' COMPENSATION

*Editor's Note

The Florida Statutes are updated through Ch. 2007-86 of the 2007 Regular Session. Any further legislative changes in the 2007 Regular Session, as well as the Division of Stautory Revisions will be covered in an upcoming supplement.

§ 440.01. Short Title.

This chapter may be cited as the "Workers' Compensation Law."

History: s. 1, ch. 17481, 1935; CGL 1936 Supp. 5966(1); s. 23, ch. 78-300; ss. 1, 124, ch. 79-40; s. 21, ch. 79-312; s. 43, ch. 89-289; s. 56, ch. 90-201; s. 52, ch. 91-1.

§ 440.015. Legislative Intent.

It is the intent of the Legislature that the Workers' Compensation Law be interpreted so as to assure the quick and efficient delivery of disability and medical benefits to an injured worker and to facilitate the worker's return to gainful reemployment at a reasonable cost to the employer. It is the specific intent of the Legislature that workers' compensation cases shall be decided on their merits. The workers' compensation system in Florida is based on a mutual renunciation of common-law rights and defenses by employers and employees alike. In addition, it is the intent of the Legislature that the facts in a workers' compensation case are not to be interpreted liberally in favor of either the rights of the injured worker or the rights of the employer. Additionally, the Legislature hereby declares that disputes concerning the facts in workers' compensation cases are not to be given a broad liberal construction in favor of the employee on the one hand or of the employer on the other hand, and the laws pertaining to workers' compensation are to be construed in accordance with the basic principles of statutory construction and not liberally in favor of either employee or employer. It is the intent of the Legislature to ensure the prompt delivery of benefits to the injured worker. Therefore, an efficient and self-executing system must be created which is not an economic or administrative burden. The department, agency, the Office of Insurance Regulation, the Department of Education, and the Division of Administrative Hearings shall administer the Workers' Compensation Law in a manner which facilitates the self-execution of the system and the process of ensuring a prompt and cost-effective delivery of payments.

History: s. 8, ch. 90-201; s. 6, ch. 91-1; s. 1, ch. 93-415; s. 10, ch. 2002-194, effective July 1, 2002; s. 466, ch. 2003-261, effective June 26, 2003.

§ 440.02. Definitions.

When used in this chapter, unless the context clearly requires otherwise, the following terms shall have the following meanings:

(1) "Accident" means only an unexpected or unusual event or result that happens suddenly. Disability or death due to the accidental acceleration or aggravation of a venereal disease or of a disease due to the habitual use of alcohol or controlled substances or narcotic drugs, or a disease that manifests itself in the fear of or dislike for an individual because of the individual's race, color, religion, sex, national origin, age, or handicap is not an injury by accident arising out of the employment. Subject to s. 440.15(5), if a preexisting disease or anomaly is accelerated or aggravated by an accident arising out of and in the course of employment, only acceleration of death or acceleration or aggravation of the preexisting condition reasonably attributable to the accident is compensable, with respect to any compensation otherwise payable under this chapter. An injury or disease caused by exposure to a toxic substance, including, but not limited to, fungus or mold, is not an injury by accident arising out of the employment unless there is clear and convincing evidence establishing that exposure to the specific substance involved, at the levels to which the employee was exposed, can cause the injury or disease sustained by the employee.

(2) "Adoption" or "adopted" means legal adoption prior to the time of the injury.

(3) "Agency" means the Agency for Health

Care Administration.

(4) "Carrier" means any person or fund authorized under s. 440.38 to insure under this chapter and includes a self-insurer, and a commercial self-insurance fund authorized under s. 624.462.

(5) "Casual" as used in this section refers only to employments for work that is anticipated to be completed in 10 working days or less, without regard to the number of persons employed, and at a total labor cost of less than $500.

(6) "Child" includes a posthumous child, a child legally adopted prior to the injury of the employee, and a stepchild or acknowledged child born out of wedlock dependent upon the deceased, but does not include married children unless wholly dependent on the employee. "Grandchild" means a child as above defined of a child as above defined. "Brother" and "sister" include stepbrothers and stepsisters, half brothers and half sisters, and brothers and sisters by adoption, but does not include married brothers or married sisters unless wholly dependent on the employee. "Child," "grandchild," "brother," and "sister" include only persons who at the time of the death of the deceased employees are under 18 years of age, or under 22 years of age if a full-time student in an accredited educational institution.

(7) "Compensation" means the money allowance payable to an employee or to his or her dependents as provided for in this chapter.

(8) "Construction industry" means for-profit activities involving any building, clearing, filling, excavation, or substantial improvement in the size or use of any structure or the appearance of any land. However, "construction" does not mean a homeowner's act of construction or the result of a construction upon his or her own premises, provided such premises are not intended to be sold, resold, or leased by the owner within 1 year after the commencement of construction. The division may, by rule, establish standard industrial classification codes and definitions thereof which meet the criteria of the term "construction industry" as set forth in this section.

(9) "Corporate officer" or "officer of a corporation" means any person who fills an office provided for in the corporate charter or articles of incorporation filed with the Division of Corporations of the Department of State or as permitted or required by chapter 607. As to persons engaged in the construction industry, the term "officer of a corporation" includes a member owning at least 10 percent of a limited liability company created and approved under chapter 608.

(10) "Date of maximum medical improvement" means the date after which further recovery from, or lasting improvement to, an injury or disease can no longer reasonably be anticipated, based upon reasonable medical probability.

(11) "Death" as a basis for a right to compensation means only death resulting from an injury.

(12) "Department" means the Department of Financial Services; the term does not include the Financial Services Commission or any office of the commission.

(13) "Disability" means incapacity because of the injury to earn in the same or any other employment the wages which the employee was receiving at the time of the injury.

(14) "Division" means the Division of Workers' Compensation of the Department of Financial Services.

(15)

(a) "Employee" means any person who receives remuneration from an employer for the performance of any work or service while engaged in any employment under any appointment or contract for hire or apprenticeship, express or implied, oral or written, whether lawfully or unlawfully employed, and includes, but is not limited to, aliens and minors.

(b) "Employee" includes any person who is an officer of a corporation and who performs services for remuneration for such corporation within this state, whether or not such services are continuous.

Fla. Stats.

1. Any officer of a corporation may elect to be exempt from this chapter by filing written notice of the election with the department as provided in s. 440.05.

2. As to officers of a corporation who are engaged in the construction industry, no more than three officers of a corporation or of any group of affiliated corporations may elect to be exempt from this chapter by filing written notice of the election with the department as provided in s. 440.05. Officers must be shareholders, each owning at least 10 percent of the stock of such corporation and listed as an officer of such corporation with the Division of Corporations of the Department of State, in order to elect exemptions under this chapter. For purposes of this subparagraph, the term "affiliated" means and includes one or more corporations or entities, any one of which is a corporation engaged in the construction industry, under the same or substantially the same control of a group of business entities which are connected or associated so that one entity controls or has the power to control each of the other business entities. The term "affiliated" includes, but is not limited to, the officers, directors, executives, shareholders active in management, employees, and agents of the affiliated corporation. The ownership by one business entity of a controlling interest in another business entity or a pooling of equipment or income among business entities shall be prima facie evidence that one business is affiliated with the other.

3. An officer of a corporation who elects to be exempt from this chapter by filing a written notice of the election with the department as provided in s. 440.05 is not an employee. Services are presumed to have been rendered to the corporation if the officer is compensated by other than dividends upon shares of stock of the corporation which the officer owns.

(c) "Employee" includes:

1. A sole proprietor or a partner who is not engaged in the construction industry, devotes full time to the proprietorship or partnership, and elects to be included in the definition of employee by filing notice thereof as provided in s. 440.05.

2. All persons who are being paid by a construction contractor as a subcontractor, unless the subcontractor has validly elected an exemption as permitted by this chapter, or has otherwise secured the payment of compensation coverage as a subcontractor, consistent with s. 440.10, for work performed by or as a subcontractor.

3. An independent contractor working or performing services in the construction industry.

4. A sole proprietor who engages in the construction industry and a partner or partnership that is engaged in the construction industry.

(d) [1] "Employee" does not include:

1. An independent contractor who is not engaged in the construction industry.

a. In order to meet the definition of independent contractor, at least four of the following criteria must be met:

(I) The independent contractor maintains a separate business with his or her own work facility, truck, equipment, materials, or similar accommodations;

(II) The independent contractor holds or has applied for a federal employer identification number, unless the independent contractor is a sole proprietor who is not required to obtain a federal employer identification number under state or federal regulations;

(III) The independent contractor receives compensation for services rendered or work performed and such compensation is paid to a business rather than to an individual;

(IV) The independent contractor holds one or more bank accounts in the name of the business entity for purposes of paying business expenses or other expenses related to services rendered or work performed for compensation;

(V) The independent contractor performs work or is able to perform work for any entity in addition to or besides the employer at his or her own election without the necessity of completing an employment application or process; or

(VI) The independent contractor receives

compensation for work or services rendered on a competitive-bid basis or completion of a task or a set of tasks as defined by a contractual agreement, unless such contractual agreement expressly states that an employment relationship exists.

b. If four of the criteria listed in sub-subparagraph a. do not exist, an individual may still be presumed to be an independent contractor and not an employee based on full consideration of the nature of the individual situation with regard to satisfying any of the following conditions:

(I) The independent contractor performs or agrees to perform specific services or work for a specific amount of money and controls the means of performing the services or work.

(II) The independent contractor incurs the principal expenses related to the service or work that he or she performs or agrees to perform.

(III) The independent contractor is responsible for the satisfactory completion of the work or services that he or she performs or agrees to perform.

(IV) The independent contractor receives compensation for work or services performed for a commission or on a per-job basis and not on any other basis.

(V) The independent contractor may realize a profit or suffer a loss in connection with performing work or services.

(VI) The independent contractor has continuing or recurring business liabilities or obligations.

(VII) The success or failure of the independent contractor's business depends on the relationship of business receipts to expenditures.

c. Notwithstanding anything to the contrary in this subparagraph, an individual claiming to be an independent contractor has the burden of proving that he or she is an independent contractor for purposes of this chapter.

2. A real estate licensee, if that person agrees, in writing, to perform for remuneration solely by way of commission.

3. Bands, orchestras, and musical and theatrical performers, including disk jockeys, performing in licensed premises as defined in chapter 562, if a written contract evidencing an independent contractor relationship is entered into before the commencement of such entertainment.

4. An owner-operator of a motor vehicle who transports property under a written contract with a motor carrier which evidences a relationship by which the owner-operator assumes the responsibility of an employer for the performance of the contract, if the owner-operator is required to furnish motor vehicle equipment as identified in the written contract and the principal costs incidental to the performance of the contract, including, but not limited to, fuel and repairs, provided a motor carrier's advance of costs to the owner-operator when a written contract evidences the owner-operator's obligation to reimburse such advance shall be treated as the owner-operator furnishing such cost and the owner-operator is not paid by the hour or on some other time-measured basis.

5. A person whose employment is both casual and not in the course of the trade, business, profession, or occupation of the employer.

6. A volunteer, except a volunteer worker for the state or a county, municipality, or other governmental entity. A person who does not receive monetary remuneration for services is presumed to be a volunteer unless there is substantial evidence that a valuable consideration was intended by both employer and employee. For purposes of this chapter, the term "volunteer" includes, but is not limited to:

a. Persons who serve in private nonprofit agencies and who receive no compensation other than expenses in an amount less than or equivalent to the standard mileage and per diem expenses provided to salaried employees in the same agency or, if such agency does not have salaried employees who receive mileage and per diem, then such volunteers who receive no compensation other than expenses in an amount less than or equivalent to the customary mileage and per diem paid to salaried workers in the community as determined by the department;

Fla. Stats.

and

b. Volunteers participating in federal programs established under Pub. L. No. 93-113.

7. Unless otherwise prohibited by this chapter, any officer of a corporation who elects to be exempt from this chapter. Such officer is not an employee for any reason under this chapter until the notice of revocation of election filed pursuant to s. 440.05 is effective.

8. An officer of a corporation that is engaged in the construction industry who elects to be exempt from the provisions of this chapter, as otherwise permitted by this chapter. Such officer is not an employee for any reason until the notice of revocation of election filed pursuant to s. 440.05 is effective.

9. An exercise rider who does not work for a single horse farm or breeder, and who is compensated for riding on a case-by-case basis, provided a written contract is entered into prior to the commencement of such activity which evidences that an employee/employer relationship does not exist.

10. A taxicab, limousine, or other passenger vehicle-for-hire driver who operates said vehicles pursuant to a written agreement with a company which provides any dispatch, marketing, insurance, communications, or other services under which the driver and any fees or charges paid by the driver to the company for such services are not conditioned upon, or expressed as a proportion of, fare revenues.

11. A person who performs services as a sports official for an entity sponsoring an interscholastic sports event or for a public entity or private, nonprofit organization that sponsors an amateur sports event. For purposes of this subparagraph, such a person is an independent contractor. For purposes of this subparagraph, the term "sports official" means any person who is a neutral participant in a sports event, including, but not limited to, umpires, referees, judges, linespersons, scorekeepers, or timekeepers. This subparagraph does not apply to any person employed by a district school board who serves as a sports official as required by the employing school board or who serves as a sports official as part of his or her responsibilities during normal school hours.

12. Medicaid-enrolled clients under chapter 393 who are excluded from the definition of employment under s. 443.1216(4)(d) and served by Adult Day Training Services under the Home and Community-Based or the Family and Supported Living Medicaid Waiver program in a sheltered workshop setting licensed by the United States Department of Labor for the purpose of training and earning less than the federal hourly minimum wage.

13. Medicaid-enrolled clients under chapter 393 who are excluded from the definition of employment under s. 443.1216(4)(d) and served by Adult Day Training Services under the Family and Supported Living Medicaid Waiver program in a sheltered workshop setting licensed by the United States Department of Labor for the purpose of training and earning less than the federal hourly minimum wage.

(16)

(a) "Employer" means the state and all political subdivisions thereof, all public and quasi-public corporations therein, every person carrying on any employment, and the legal representative of a deceased person or the receiver or trustees of any person. "Employer" also includes employment agencies, employee leasing companies, and similar agents who provide employees to other persons. If the employer is a corporation, parties in actual control of the corporation, including, but not limited to, the president, officers who exercise broad corporate powers, directors, and all shareholders who directly or indirectly own a controlling interest in the corporation, are considered the employer for the purposes of ss. 440.105, 440.106, and 440.107.

(b) A homeowner shall not be considered the employer of persons hired by the homeowner to carry out construction on the homeowner's own premises if those premises are not intended for immediate lease, sale, or resale.

(c) Facilities serving individuals under subparagraph (15)(d)12. shall be considered agents of the Agency for Health Care Administration as it relates to providing Adult Day Training Services under the Home and Community-Based Medicaid Waiver program and not employers or third parties for the purpose of limiting or denying Medicaid benefits.

(17)

(a) "Employment," subject to the other provisions of this chapter, means any service performed by an employee for the person employing him or her.

(b) "Employment" includes:

1. Employment by the state and all political subdivisions thereof and all public and quasi-public corporations therein, including officers elected at the polls.

2. All private employments in which four or more employees are employed by the same employer or, with respect to the construction industry, all private employment in which one or more employees are employed by the same employer.

3. Volunteer firefighters responding to or assisting with fire or medical emergencies whether or not the firefighters are on duty.

(c) "Employment" does not include service performed by or as:

1. Domestic servants in private homes.

2. Agricultural labor performed on a farm in the employ of a bona fide farmer, or association of farmers, that employs 5 or fewer regular employees and that employs fewer than 12 other employees at one time for seasonal agricultural labor that is completed in less than 30 days, provided such seasonal employment does not exceed 45 days in the same calendar year. The term "farm" includes stock, dairy, poultry, fruit, fur-bearing animals, fish, and truck farms, ranches, nurseries, and orchards. The term "agricultural labor" includes field foremen, timekeepers, checkers, and other farm labor supervisory personnel.

3. Professional athletes, such as professional boxers, wrestlers, baseball, football, basketball, hockey, polo, tennis, jai alai, and similar players, and motorsports teams competing in a motor racing event as defined in s. 549.08.

4. Labor under a sentence of a court to perform community services as provided in s. 316.193.

5. State prisoners or county inmates, except those performing services for private employers or those enumerated in s. 948.036(1).

(18) "Misconduct" includes, but is not limited to, the following, which shall not be construed in pari materia with each other:

(a) Conduct evincing such willful or wanton disregard of an employer's interests as is found in deliberate violation or disregard of standards of behavior which the employer has the right to expect of the employee; or

(b) Carelessness or negligence of such a degree or recurrence as to manifest culpability, wrongful intent, or evil design, or to show an intentional and substantial disregard of an employer's interests or of the employee's duties and obligations to the employer.

(19) "Injury" means personal injury or death by accident arising out of and in the course of employment, and such diseases or infection as naturally or unavoidably result from such injury. Damage to dentures, eyeglasses, prosthetic devices, and artificial limbs may be included in this definition only when the damage is shown to be part of, or in conjunction with, an accident. This damage must specifically occur as the result of an accident in the normal course of employment.

(20) "Parent" includes stepparents and parents by adoption, parents-in-law, and any persons who for more than 3 years prior to the death of the deceased employee stood in the place of a parent to him or her and were dependent on the injured employee.

(21) "Partner" means any person who is a member of a partnership that is formed by two or more persons to carry on as coowners of a business with the understanding that there will be a proportional sharing of the profits and losses between them. For the purposes of this chapter, a partner is a person who participates fully in the management of the partnership and

Fla. Stats.

who is personally liable for its debts.

(22) "Permanent impairment" means any anatomic or functional abnormality or loss determined as a percentage of the body as a whole, existing after the date of maximum medical improvement, which results from the injury.

(23) "Person" means individual, partnership, association, or corporation, including any public service corporation.

(24) "Self-insurer" means:

(a) Any employer who has secured payment of compensation pursuant to s. 440.38(1)(b) or (6) as an individual self-insurer;

(b) Any employer who has secured payment of compensation through a group self-insurance fund under s. 624.4621;

(c) Any group self-insurance fund established under s. 624.4621;

(d) A public utility as defined in s. 364.02 or s. 366.02 that has assumed by contract the liabilities of contractors or subcontractors pursuant to s. 624.46225; or

(e) Any local government self-insurance fund established under s. 624.4622.

(25) "Sole proprietor" means a natural person who owns a form of business in which that person owns all the assets of the business and is solely liable for all the debts of the business.

(26) "Spouse" includes only a spouse substantially dependent for financial support upon the decedent and living with the decedent at the time of the decedent's injury and death, or substantially dependent upon the decedent for financial support and living apart at that time for justifiable cause.

(27) "Time of injury" means the time of the occurrence of the accident resulting in the injury.

(28) "Wages" means the money rate at which the service rendered is recompensed under the contract of hiring in force at the time of the injury and includes only the wages earned and reported for federal income tax purposes on the job where the employee is injured and any other concurrent employment where he or she is also subject to workers' compensation coverage and benefits, together with the reasonable value of housing furnished to the employee by the employer which is the permanent year-round residence of the employee, and gratuities to the extent reported to the employer in writing as taxable income received in the course of employment from others than the employer and employer contributions for health insurance for the employee or the employee's dependents. However, housing furnished to migrant workers shall be included in wages unless provided after the time of injury. In employment in which an employee receives consideration for housing, the reasonable value of such housing compensation shall be the actual cost to the employer or based upon the Fair Market Rent Survey promulgated pursuant to s. 8 of the Housing and Urban Development Act of 1974, whichever is less. However, if employer contributions for housing or health insurance are continued after the time of the injury, the contributions are not "wages" for the purpose of calculating an employee's average weekly wage.

(29) "Weekly compensation rate" means and refers to the amount of compensation payable for a period of 7 consecutive calendar days, including any Saturdays, Sundays, holidays, and other nonworking days which fall within such period of 7 consecutive calendar days. When Saturdays, Sundays, holidays, or other nonworking days immediately follow the first 7 calendar days of disability or occur at the end of a period of disability as the last day or days of such period, such nonworking days constitute a part of the period of disability with respect to which compensation is payable.

(30) "Construction design professional" means an architect, professional engineer, landscape architect, or surveyor and mapper, or any corporation, professional or general, that has a certificate to practice in the construction design field from the Department of Business and Professional Regulation.

(31) "Individual self-insurer" means any employer who has secured payment of compensation pursuant to s. 440.38(1)(b) as an individual self-insurer.

(32) "Domestic individual self-insurer" means an individual self-insurer:

(a) Which is a corporation formed under the laws of this state;

(b) Who is an individual who is a resident of this state or whose primary place of business is located in this state; or

(c) Which is a partnership whose principals are residents of this state or whose primary place of business is located in this state.

(33) "Foreign individual self-insurer" means an individual self-insurer:

(a) Which is a corporation formed under the laws of any state, district, territory, or commonwealth of the United States other than this state;

(b) Who is an individual who is not a resident of this state and whose primary place of business is not located in this state; or

(c) Which is a partnership whose principals are not residents of this state and whose primary place of business is not located in this state.

(34) "Insolvent member" means an individual self-insurer which is a member of the Florida Self-Insurers Guaranty Association, Incorporated, or which was a member and has withdrawn pursuant to s. 440.385(1)(b), and which has been found insolvent, as defined in subparagraph (35)(a)1., subparagraph (35)(a)2., or subparagraph (35)(a)3., by a court of competent jurisdiction in this or any other state, or meets the definition of subparagraph (35)(a)4.

(35) "Insolvency" or "insolvent" means:

(a) With respect to an individual self-insurer:

1. That all assets of the individual self-insurer, if made immediately available, would not be sufficient to meet all the individual self-insurer's liabilities;

2. That the individual self-insurer is unable to pay its debts as they become due in the usual course of business;

3. That the individual self-insurer has substantially ceased or suspended the payment of compensation to its employees as required in this chapter; or

4. That the individual self-insurer has sought protection under the United States Bankruptcy Code or has been brought under the jurisdiction of a court of bankruptcy as a debtor pursuant to the United States Bankruptcy Code.

(b) With respect to an employee claiming insolvency pursuant to s. 440.25(5), a person is insolvent who:

1. Has ceased to pay his or her debts in the ordinary course of business and cannot pay his or her debts as they become due; or

2. Has been adjudicated insolvent pursuant to the federal bankruptcy law.

(36) "Arising out of" pertains to occupational causation. An accidental injury or death arises out of employment if work performed in the course and scope of employment is the major contributing cause of the injury or death.

(37) "Soft-tissue injury" means an injury that produces damage to the soft tissues, rather than to the skeletal tissues or soft organs.

(38) "Insurer" means a group self-insurers' fund authorized by s. 624.4621, an individual self-insurer authorized by s. 440.38, a commercial self-insurance fund authorized by s. 624.462, an assessable mutual insurer authorized by s. 628.6011, and an insurer licensed to write workers' compensation and employer's liability insurance in this state. The term "carrier," as used in this chapter, means an insurer as defined in this subsection.

(39) "Statement," for the purposes of ss. 440.105 and 440.106, shall include the exact fraud statement language in s. 440.105(7). This requirement includes, but is not limited to, any notice, representation, statement, proof of injury, bill for services, diagnosis, prescription, hospital or doctor record, X ray, test result, or other evidence of loss, injury, or expense.

(40) "Specificity" means information on the petition for benefits sufficient to put the employer or carrier on notice of the exact statutory classification and outstanding time period of benefits being requested and includes a detailed

Fla. Stats.

explanation of any benefits received that should be increased, decreased, changed, or otherwise modified. If the petition is for medical benefits, the information shall include specific details as to why such benefits are being requested, why such benefits are medically necessary, and why current treatment, if any, is not sufficient. Any petition requesting alternate or other medical care, including, but not limited to, petitions requesting psychiatric or psychological treatment, must specifically identify the physician, as defined in s. 440.13(1), that is recommending such treatment. A copy of a report from such physician making the recommendation for alternate or other medical care shall also be attached to the petition. A judge of compensation claims shall not order such treatment if a physician is not recommending such treatment.

(41) "Office of Insurance Regulation" means the Office of Insurance Regulation of the Financial Services Commission.

History: s. 2, ch. 17481, 1935; s. 1, ch. 17482, 1935; s. 1, ch. 17483, 1935; CGL 1936 Supp. 5966(2); s. 1, ch. 18413, 1937; s. 1, ch. 20672, 1941; s. 1, ch. 28238, 1953; s. 1, ch. 29778, 1955; s. 1, ch. 57-155; s. 1, ch. 57-225; s. 1, ch. 59-100; s. 1, ch. 65-184; s. 1, ch. 67-554; ss. 17, 35, ch. 69-106; s. 1, ch. 71-80; s. 162, ch. 71-377; s. 1, ch. 72-243; s. 1, ch. 73-127; s. 1, ch. 73-283; s. 116, ch. 73-333; s. 1, ch. 74-46; s. 1, ch. 74-124; s. 1, ch. 74-197; s. 1, ch. 75-209; s. 1, ch. 77-174; s. 1, ch. 77-290; ss. 1, 23, ch. 78-300; s. 15, ch. 79-7; ss. 2, 124, ch. 79-40; s. 21, ch. 79-312; s. 1, ch. 80-236; s. 3, ch. 81-119; ss. 1, 20, ch. 83-305; s. 1, ch. 84-267; s. 6, ch. 86-171; s. 1, ch. 87-330; s. 1, ch. 88-203; s. 2, ch. 89-61; ss. 3, 43, ch. 89-289; ss. 9, 56, ch. 90-201; ss. 7, 52, ch. 91-1; s. 1, ch. 91-2; s. 2, ch. 93-415; s. 117, ch. 94-119; s. 59, ch. 94-218; s. 97, ch. 97-103; s. 1, ch. 98-174; s. 89, ch. 2000-153; s. 7, ch. 2001-91, effective Oct. 1, 2001; s. 11, ch. 2002-194, effective July 1, 2002; s. 5, ch. 2002-236, effective July 1, 2002; s. 54, ch. 2003-164, effective July 1, 2003; s. 1, ch. 412, effective July 15, 2003; s. 2, ch. 412, effective Jan. 1, 2004; s. 467, 2003-261, effective June 26, 2003; s. 2, ch. 2003-422, effective January 1, 2004; s. 59, ch. 2004-5, effective June 29, 2004; s. 32, ch. 2004-373, effective July 1, 2004; s.21, ch. 2005-60; s. 12, ch. 2005-71; s. 1, ch. 2005-78, effective July 1, 2005; s. 4, ch. 2006-15, effective July 5, 2006.

[1]**2005 Note:** Section 12, ch. 2005-71, amended paragraph 15(d) "in order to implement Specific Appropriation 614 of the 2005-2006 General Appropriations Act."

2002 Note: Chapter 2002-194 amended and renumbered subsection (14) to subsection (15); Chapter 2002-236 amended the old subsection (14) which is now subsection (15).

§ 440.021. Exemption of Workers' Compensation from Chapter 120.

Workers' compensation adjudications by judges of compensation claims are exempt from chapter 120, and no judge of compensation claims shall be considered an agency or a part thereof. Communications of the result of investigations by the department pursuant to s. 440.185(4) are exempt from chapter 120. In all instances in which the department institutes action to collect a penalty or interest which may be due pursuant to this chapter, the penalty or interest shall be assessed without hearing, and the party against which such penalty or interest is assessed shall be given written notice of such assessment and shall have the right to protest within 20 days of such notice. Upon receipt of a timely notice of protest and after such investigation as may be necessary, the department shall, if it agrees with such protest, notify the protesting party that the assessment has been revoked. If the department does not agree with the protest, it shall refer the matter to the judge of compensation claims for determination pursuant to s. 440.25(2)–(5). Such action of the department is exempt from the provisions of chapter 120.

History: s. 15, ch. 77-290; s. 23, ch. 78-300; ss. 3, 124, ch. 79-40; ss. 6, 21, ch. 79-312; s. 4, ch. 81-119; s. 2, ch. 83-305; s. 43, ch. 89-289; s. 56, ch. 90-201; s. 52, ch. 91-1; s. 2, ch. 91-46; s. 90, ch. 2000-153; s. 12, ch. 2002-194, effective July 1, 2002.

§ 440.03. Application.

Every employer and employee as defined in s. 440.02 shall be bound by the provisions of this chapter.

History: s. 3, ch. 17481, 1935; CGL 1936 Supp. 5966(3); s. 1, ch. 70-148; s. 23, ch. 78-300; s. 124, ch. 79-40; s. 21, ch. 79-312; s. 43, ch. 89-289; s. 56, ch. 90-201; s. 52, ch. 91-1.

§ 440.04. Waiver of Exemption.

(1) Every employer having in her or his employment any employee not included in the

definition "employee" or excluded or exempted from the operation of this chapter may at any time waive such exclusion or exemption and accept the provisions of this chapter by giving notice thereof as provided in s. 440.05, and by so doing be as fully protected and covered by the provisions of this chapter as if such exclusion or exemption had not been contained herein.

(2) When any policy or contract of insurance specifically secures the benefits of this chapter to any person not included in the definition of "employee" or whose services are not included in the definition of "employment" or who is otherwise excluded or exempted from the operation of this chapter, the acceptance of such policy or contract of insurance by the insured and the writing of same by the carrier shall constitute a waiver of such exclusion or exemption and an acceptance of the provisions of this chapter with respect to such person, notwithstanding the provision of s. 440.05 with respect to notice.

(3) A corporate officer who has exempted herself or himself by proper notice from the operation of this chapter may at any time revoke such exemption and thereby accept the provisions of this chapter by giving notice as provided in s. 440.05.

History: s. 4, ch. 17481, 1935; CGL 1936 Supp. 5966(4); s. 2, ch. 18413, 1937; s. 2, ch. 29778, 1955; s. 4, ch. 70-148; s. 2, ch. 74-197; s. 23, ch. 78-300; s. 124, ch. 79-40; s. 21, ch. 79-312; s. 43, ch. 89-289; s. 56, ch. 90-201; s. 52, ch. 91-1; s. 98, ch. 97-103.

§ 440.05. Election of Exemption; Revocation of Election; Notice; Certification.

(1) Each corporate officer who elects not to accept the provisions of this chapter or who, after electing such exemption, revokes that exemption shall mail to the department in Tallahassee notice to such effect in accordance with a form to be prescribed by the department.

(2) Each sole proprietor or partner who elects to be included in the definition of "employee" or who, after such election, revokes that election must mail to the department in Tallahassee notice to such effect, in accordance with a form to be prescribed by the department.

(3) Each officer of a corporation who is engaged in the construction industry and who elects an exemption from this chapter or who, after electing such exemption, revokes that exemption, must mail a written notice to such effect to the department on a form prescribed by the department. The notice of election to be exempt from the provisions of this chapter must be notarized and under oath. The notice of election to be exempt which is submitted to the department by the officer of a corporation who is allowed to claim an exemption as provided by this chapter must list the name, federal tax identification number, social security number, all certified or registered licenses issued pursuant to chapter 439 held by the person seeking the exemption, a copy of relevant documentation as to employment status filed with the Internal Revenue Service as specified by the department, a copy of the relevant occupational license in the primary jurisdiction of the business, and the registration number of the corporation filed with the Division of Corporations of the Department of State along with a copy of the stock certificate evidencing the required ownership under this chapter. The notice of election to be exempt must identify each corporation that employs the person electing the exemption and must list the social security number or federal tax identification number of each such employer and the additional documentation required by this section. In addition, the notice of election to be exempt must provide that the officer electing an exemption is not entitled to benefits under this chapter, must provide that the election does not exceed exemption limits for officers provided in s. 440.02, and must certify that any employees of the corporation whose officer elects an exemption are covered by workers' compensation insurance. Upon receipt of the notice of the election to be exempt, receipt of all application fees, and a determination by the department that the notice meets the requirements of this subsection, the department shall issue a certification of the election to the officer, unless the department determines that the information contained in the notice is invalid. The department shall revoke a certificate of election to be exempt from coverage upon a determination by the

Fla. Stats.

department that the person does not meet the requirements for exemption or that the information contained in the notice of election to be exempt is invalid. The certificate of election must list the name of the corporation listed in the request for exemption. A new certificate of election must be obtained each time the person is employed by a new or different corporation that is not listed on the certificate of election. A copy of the certificate of election must be sent to each workers' compensation carrier identified in the request for exemption. Upon filing a notice of revocation of election, an officer who is a subcontractor or an officer of a corporate subcontractor must notify her or his contractor. Upon revocation of a certificate of election of exemption by the department, the department shall notify the workers' compensation carriers identified in the request for exemption.

(4) The notice of election to be exempt from the provisions of this chapter must contain a notice that clearly states in substance the following: "Any person who, knowingly and with intent to injure, defraud, or deceive the department or any employer or employee, insurance company, or any other person, files a notice of election to be exempt containing any false or misleading information is guilty of a felony of the third degree." Each person filing a notice of election to be exempt shall personally sign the notice and attest that he or she has reviewed, understands, and acknowledges the foregoing notice.

(5) A notice given under subsection (1), subsection (2), or subsection (3) shall become effective when issued by the department or 30 days after an application for an exemption is received by the department, whichever occurs first. However, if an accident or occupational disease occurs less than 30 days after the effective date of the insurance policy under which the payment of compensation is secured or the date the employer qualified as a self-insurer, such notice is effective as of 12:01 a.m. of the day following the date it is mailed to the department in Tallahassee.

(6) A construction industry certificate of election to be exempt which is issued in accordance with this section shall be valid for 2 years after the effective date stated thereon. Both the effective date and the expiration date must be listed on the face of the certificate by the department. The construction industry certificate must expire at midnight, 2 years from its issue date, as noted on the face of the exemption certificate. A construction industry certificate of election to be exempt may be revoked before its expiration by the officer for whom it was issued or by the department for the reasons stated in this section. At least 60 days prior to the expiration date of a construction industry certificate of exemption issued after December 1, 1998, the department shall send notice of the expiration date and an application for renewal to the certificateholder at the address on the certificate.

(7) Any contractor responsible for compensation under s. 440.10 may register in writing with the workers' compensation carrier for any subcontractor and shall thereafter be entitled to receive written notice from the carrier of any cancellation or nonrenewal of the policy.

(8)

(a) The department must assess a fee of $50 with each request for a construction industry certificate of election to be exempt or renewal of election to be exempt under this section.

(b) The funds collected by the department shall be used to administer this section, to audit the businesses that pay the fee for compliance with any requirements of this chapter, and to enforce compliance with the provisions of this chapter.

(9) The department may by rule prescribe forms and procedures for filing an election of exemption, revocation of election to be exempt, and notice of election of coverage for all employers and require specified forms to be submitted by all employers in filing for the election of exemption. The department may by rule prescribe forms and procedures for issuing a certificate of the election of exemption.

(10) Each officer of a corporation who is actively engaged in the construction industry and who elects an exemption from this chapter shall maintain business records as specified by the [2]department by rule, which rules must in-

clude the provision that any corporation with exempt officers engaged in the construction industry must maintain written statements of those exempted persons affirmatively acknowledging each such individual's exempt status.

(11) Any corporate officer permitted by this chapter to claim an exemption must be listed on the records of this state's Secretary of State, Division of Corporations, as a corporate officer. The [2]department shall issue a stop-work order under [1]s. 440.107(7) to any corporation who employs a person who claims to be exempt as a corporate officer but who fails or refuses to produce the documents required under this subsection to the [2]department within 3 business days after the request is made.

(12) Certificates of election to be exempt issued under subsection (3) shall apply only to the corporate officer named on the notice of election to be exempt and apply only within the scope of the business or trade listed on the notice of election to be exempt.

(13) Notices of election to be exempt and certificates of election to be exempt shall be subject to revocation if, at any time after the filing of the notice or the issuance of the certificate, the person named on the notice or certificate no longer meets the requirements of this section for issuance of a certificate. The department shall revoke a certificate at any time for failure of the person named on the certificate to meet the requirements of this section.

(14) An officer of a corporation who elects exemption from this chapter by filing a certificate of election under this section may not recover benefits or compensation under this chapter. For purposes of determining the appropriate premium for workers' compensation coverage, carriers may not consider any officer of a corporation who validly meets the requirements of this section to be an employee.

(15) Any corporate officer who is an affiliated person of a person who is delinquent in paying a stop-work order and penalty assessment order issued pursuant to s. 440.107, or owed pursuant to a court order, is ineligible for an election of exemption. The stop-work order and penalty assessment shall be in effect against any such affiliated person. As used in this subsection, the term "affiliated person" means:

(a) The spouse of such other person;

(b) Any person who directly or indirectly owns or controls, or holds with the power to vote, 10 percent or more of the outstanding voting securities of such other person;

(c) Any person who directly or indirectly owns 10 percent or more of the outstanding voting securities that are directly or indirectly owned, controlled, or held with the power to vote by such other person;

(d) Any person or group of persons who directly or indirectly control, are controlled by, or are under common control with such other person;

(e) Any person who directly or indirectly acquires all or substantially all of the other assets of such other person;

(f) Any officer, director, trustee, partner, owner, manager, joint venturer, or employee of such other person or a person performing duties similar to persons in such positions; or

(g) Any person who has an officer, director, trustee, partner, or joint venturer in common with such person.

History: s. 5, ch. 17481, 1935; CGL 1936 Supp. 5966(5); ss. 17, 35, ch. 69-106; s. 2, ch. 70-148; s. 1, ch. 70-439; s. 3, ch. 74-197; s. 2, ch. 75-209; s. 23, ch. 78-300; s. 124, ch. 79-40; s. 21, ch. 79-312; s. 43, ch. 89-289; s. 56, ch. 90-201; s. 52, ch. 91-1; s. 2, ch. 91-2; s. 3, ch. 93-415; s. 99, ch. 97-103; s. 1, ch. 98-125; s. 2, ch. 98-174; s. 40, ch. 99-240, effective October 1, 1999; s. 13, ch. 2002-194, effective July 1, 2002; s. 6, ch. 2002-236, effective July 1, 2002; s. 3, ch. 412, effective Jan. 1, 2004; s. 468, ch. 2003-261, effective June 26, 2003; s. 74, ch. 2005-2, effective July 5, 2005; s. 52, ch. 2006-1, effective July 5, 2006.

[1]**2005 Note:** — Section 440.107 contains legislative findings; stop-work orders are addressed in s. 440.107(7).

[2]**Note:** —The Division of Workers' Compensation of the Department of Labor and Employment Security was transferred to the Department of Insurance by s. 1, ch. 2002-194. Section 13, ch. 2002-194, replaced existing references to the division in s. 440.05 with references to the Department of Insurance.

Fla. Stats.

1999 Note: Chapter 99-240 repealed subsection (8)(a). The Division of Statutory Revision redesignated subsection (8)(b) to (8)(a) and subsection (8)(c) to (8)(b).

§ 440.055. Notice Requirements.

An employer who employs fewer than four employees, who is permitted by law to elect not to secure payment of compensation under this chapter, and who elects not to do so shall post clear written notice in a conspicuous location at each worksite directed to all employees and other persons performing services at the worksite of their lack of entitlement to benefits under this chapter.

History: s. 10, ch. 90-201; s. 8, ch. 91-1; s. 4, ch. 93-415.

§ 440.06. Failure to Secure Compensation; Effect.

Every employer who fails to secure the payment of compensation, as provided in s. 440.10, by failing to meet the requirements of s. 440.38 may not, in any suit brought against him or her by an employee subject to this chapter to recover damages for injury or death, defend such a suit on the grounds that the injury was caused by the negligence of a fellow servant, that the employee assumed the risk of his or her employment, or that the injury was due to the comparative negligence of the employee.

History: s. 6, ch. 17481, 1935; CGL 1936 Supp. 5966(6); s. 5, ch. 70-148; s. 23, ch. 78-300; ss. 4, 124, ch. 79-40; s. 21, ch. 79-312, s. 43, ch. 89-289; s. 56, ch. 90-201; s. 52, ch. 91-1, s. 100, ch. 97-103; s.4, ch. 412, effective Oct. 1, 2003.

§ 440.075. When Corporate Officer Rejects Chapter; Effect.

Every corporate officer who elects to reject this chapter shall, in any action to recover damages for injury or death brought against the corporate employer, proceed as at common law, and the employer in such suit may avail itself of all defenses that exist at common law.

History: s. 4, ch. 74-197; s. 23, ch. 78-300; s. 124, ch. 79-40; s. 21, ch. 79-312; s. 43, ch. 89-289; s. 56, ch. 90-201; s. 52, ch. 91-1.

§ 440.077. When a Corporate Officer Rejects Chapter, Effect.

An officer of a corporation who is permitted to elect an exemption under this chapter and who elects to be exempt from the provisions of this chapter may not recover benefits under this chapter.

History: s. 3, ch. 91-2; s. 5, ch. 412, effective Jan. 1, 2004.

§ 440.09. Coverage.

(1) The employer must pay compensation or furnish benefits required by this chapter if the employee suffers an accidental compensable injury or death arising out of work performed in the course and the scope of employment. The injury, its occupational cause, and any resulting manifestations or disability must be established to a reasonable degree of medical certainty, based on objective relevant medical findings, and the accidental compensable injury must be the major contributing cause of any resulting injuries. For purposes of this section, "major contributing cause" means the cause which is more than 50 percent responsible for the injury as compared to all other causes combined for which treatment or benefits are sought. In cases involving occupational disease or repetitive exposure, both causation and sufficient exposure to support causation must be proven by clear and convincing evidence. Pain or other subjective complaints alone, in the absence of objective relevant medical findings, are not compensable. For purposes of this section, "objective relevant medical findings" are those objective findings that correlate to the subjective complaints of the injured employee and are confirmed by physical examination findings or diagnostic testing. Establishment of the causal relationship between a compensable accident and injuries for conditions that are not readily observable must be by medical evidence only, as demonstrated by physical examination findings or diagnostic testing. Major contributing cause must be demonstrated by medical evidence only.

(a) This chapter does not require any compensation or benefits for any subsequent injury the employee suffers as a result of an original injury arising out of and in the course of employment unless the original injury is the major contributing cause of the subsequent injury. Major contributing cause must be demonstrated by medical evidence only.

(b) If an injury arising out of and in the course of employment combines with a preexisting disease or condition to cause or prolong disability or need for treatment, the employer must pay compensation or benefits required by this chapter only to the extent that the injury arising out of and in the course of employment is and remains more than 50 percent responsible for the injury as compared to all other causes combined and thereafter remains the major contributing cause of the disability or need for treatment. Major contributing cause must be demonstrated by medical evidence only.

(c) Death resulting from an operation by a surgeon furnished by the employer for the cure of hernia as required in[1] s. 440.15(6) [F.S. 1981] shall for the purpose of this chapter be considered to be a death resulting from the accident causing the hernia.

(d) If an accident happens while the employee is employed elsewhere than in this state, which would entitle the employee or his or her dependents to compensation if it had happened in this state, the employee or his or her dependents are entitled to compensation if the contract of employment was made in this state, or the employment was principally localized in this state. However, if an employee receives compensation or damages under the laws of any other state, the total compensation for the injury may not be greater than is provided in this chapter.

(2) Benefits are not payable in respect of the disability or death of any employee covered by the Federal Employer's Liability Act, the Longshoremen's and Harbor Worker's Compensation Act, the Defense Base Act, or the Jones Act.

(3) Compensation is not payable if the injury was occasioned primarily by the intoxication of the employee; by the influence of any drugs, barbiturates, or other stimulants not prescribed by a physician; or by the willful intention of the employee to injure or kill himself, herself, or another.

(4)

(a) An employee shall not be entitled to compensation or benefits under this chapter if any judge of compensation claims, administrative law judge, court, or jury convened in this state determines that the employee has knowingly or intentionally engaged in any of the acts described in s. 440.105 or any criminal act for the purpose of securing workers' compensation benefits. For purposes of this section, the term "intentional" shall include, but is not limited to, pleas of guilty or nolo contendere in criminal matters. This section shall apply to accidents, regardless of the date of the accident. For injuries occurring prior to January 1, 1994, this section shall pertain to the acts of the employee described in s. 440.105 or criminal activities occurring subsequent to January 1, 1994.

(b) A judge of compensation claims, administrative law judge, or court of this state shall take judicial notice of a finding of insurance fraud by a court of competent jurisdiction and terminate or otherwise disallow benefits.

(c) Upon the denial of benefits in accordance with this section, a judge of compensation claims shall have the jurisdiction to order any benefits payable to the employee to be paid into the court registry or an escrow account during the pendency of an appeal or until such time as the time in which to file an appeal has expired.

(5) If injury is caused by the knowing refusal of the employee to use a safety appliance or observe a safety rule required by statute or lawfully adopted by the department, and brought prior to the accident to the employee's knowledge, or if injury is caused by the knowing refusal of the employee to use a safety appliance provided by the employer, the compensation as provided in this chapter shall be reduced 25 percent.

(6) Except as provided in this chapter, a construction design professional who is retained to perform professional services on a construction project, or an employee of a construction design professional in the performance of professional services on the site of the construction project, is not liable for any injuries resulting

Fla. Stats.

from the employer's failure to comply with safety standards on the construction project for which compensation is recoverable under this chapter, unless responsibility for safety practices is specifically assumed by contracts. The immunity provided by this subsection to a construction design professional does not apply to the negligent preparation of design plans or specifications.

(7)

(a) To ensure that the workplace is a drug-free environment and to deter the use of drugs and alcohol at the workplace, if the employer has reason to suspect that the injury was occasioned primarily by the intoxication of the employee or by the use of any drug, as defined in this chapter, which affected the employee to the extent that the employee's normal faculties were impaired, and the employer has not implemented a drug-free workplace pursuant to ss. 440.101 and 440.102, the employer may require the employee to submit to a test for the presence of any or all drugs or alcohol in his or her system.

(b) If the employee has, at the time of the injury, a blood alcohol level equal to or greater than the level specified in s. 316.193, or if the employee has a positive confirmation of a drug as defined in this act, it is presumed that the injury was occasioned primarily by the intoxication of, or by the influence of the drug upon, the employee. If the employer has implemented a drug-free workplace, this presumption may be rebutted only by evidence that there is no reasonable hypothesis that the intoxication or drug influence contributed to the injury. In the absence of a drug-free workplace program, this presumption may be rebutted by clear and convincing evidence that the intoxication or influence of the drug did not contribute to the injury. Percent by weight of alcohol in the blood must be based upon grams of alcohol per 100 milliliters of blood. If the results are positive, the testing facility must maintain the specimen for a minimum of 90 days. Blood serum may be used for testing purposes under this chapter; however, if this test is used, the presumptions under this section do not arise unless the blood alcohol level is proved to be medically and scientifically equivalent to or greater than the comparable blood alcohol level that would have been obtained if the test were based on percent by weight of alcohol in the blood. However, if, before the accident, the employer had actual knowledge of and expressly acquiesced in the employee's presence at the workplace while under the influence of such alcohol or drug, the presumptions specified in this subsection do not apply.

(c) If the injured worker refuses to submit to a drug test, it shall be presumed in the absence of clear and convincing evidence to the contrary that the injury was occasioned primarily by the influence of drugs.

(d) The agency shall provide by rule for the authorization and regulation of drug-testing policies, procedures, and methods. Testing of injured employees shall not commence until such rules are adopted.

(e) As a part of rebutting any presumptions under paragraph (b), the injured worker must prove the actual quantitative amounts of the drug or its metabolites as measured on the initial and confirmation post-accident drug tests of the injured worker's urine sample and provide additional evidence regarding the absence of drug influence other than the worker's denial of being under the influence of a drug. No drug test conducted on a urine sample shall be rejected as to its results or the presumption imposed under paragraph (b) on the basis of the urine being bodily fluid tested.

(8) If, by operation of s. 440.04, benefits become payable to a professional athlete under this chapter, such benefits shall be reduced or setoff in the total amount of injury benefits or wages payable during the period of disability by the employer under a collective bargaining agreement or contract for hire.

History: s. 9, ch. 17481, 1935; CGL 1936 Supp. 5966(9); s. 3, ch. 18413, 1937; s. 1, ch. 28236, 1953; s. 1, ch. 57-293; s. 2, ch. 73-127; s. 5, ch. 74-197; s. 3, ch. 75-209; s. 2, ch. 77-290; s. 23, ch. 78-300; s. 124, ch. 79-40; s. 21, ch. 79-312; s. 7, ch. 86-171; ss. 4, 5, 6, 43, ch. 89-289; ss. 11, 56, ch. 90-201; ss. 9, 52, ch. 91-1; ss. 5, 55, ch. 93-415; s. 101, ch. 97-103; s. 1, ch. 98-161; s. 3, ch. 98-174; s. 8, ch. 2001-91, effective Oct. 1, 2001; s. 14, ch. 2002-194, effective July 1,

2002; s. 6, ch. 412, effective Oct. 1, 2003; s. 469, 2003-261, effective June 26, 2003.

[1]**Note:** —Repealed by s. 3, ch. 82-237.

§ 440.091. Law Enforcement Officer, Firefighter, Emergency Medical Technician, or Paramedic; When Acting Within the Course of Employment.

(1) If an employee:

(a) Is elected, appointed, or employed full time by a municipality, the state, or any political subdivision and is vested with authority to bear arms and make arrests and the employee's primary responsibility is the prevention or detection of crime or the enforcement of the penal, criminal, traffic, or highway laws of the state;

(b) Was discharging that primary responsibility within the state in a place and under circumstances reasonably consistent with that primary responsibility; and

(c) Was not engaged in services for which he or she was paid by a private employer, and the employee and his or her public employer had no agreement providing for workers' compensation coverage for that private employment;

the employee is considered to have been acting within the course of employment. The term "employee" as used in this subsection includes all certified supervisory and command personnel whose duties include, in whole or in part, responsibilities for the supervision, training, guidance, and management of full-time law enforcement officers, part-time law enforcement officers, or auxiliary law enforcement officers but does not include support personnel employed by the employing agency.

(2) If a firefighter as defined by s. 112.191(1)(b) is engaged in extinguishing a fire, or protecting and saving life or property due to a fire in this state in an emergency, and such activities would be considered to be within the course of his or her employment as a firefighter and covered by the employer's workers' compensation coverage except for the fact that the firefighter was off duty or that the location of the fire was outside the employer's jurisdiction or area of responsibility, such activities are considered to be within the course of employment. This subsection does not apply if the firefighter is performing activities for which he or she is paid by another employer or contractor.

(3) If an emergency medical technician or paramedic is appointed or employed full time by a municipality, the state, or any political subdivision, is certified under chapter 401, is providing basic life support or advanced life support services, as defined in s. 401.23, in an emergency situation in this state, and such activities would be considered to be within the course of his or her employment as an emergency medical technician or paramedic and covered by the employer's workers' compensation coverage except for the fact that the location of the emergency was outside of the employer's jurisdiction or area of responsibility, such activities are considered to be within the course of employment. The provisions of this subsection do not apply if the emergency medical technician or paramedic is performing activities for which he or she is paid by another employer or contractor.

History: s. 1, ch. 82-146; s. 43, ch. 89-289; s. 56, ch. 90-201; s. 52, ch. 91-1; s. 102, ch. 97-103; s. 1, ch. 2002-236, effective July 1, 2002.

§ 440.092. Special Requirements for Compensability; Deviation From Employment; Subsequent Intervening Accidents.

(1) Recreational and Social Activities.—Recreational or social activities are not compensable unless such recreational or social activities are an expressly required incident of employment and produce a substantial direct benefit to the employer beyond improvement in employee health and morale that is common to all kinds of recreation and social life.

(2) Going or Coming.An injury suffered while going to or coming from work is not an injury arising out of and in the course of employment whether or not the employer provided transportation if such means of transportation was available for the exclusive personal use by the employee, unless the employee was engaged in a special errand or mission for the employer. For the purposes of this subsection and not withstanding any other provisions of

Fla. Stats.

law to the contrary, an injury to a law enforcement officer as defined in s. 943.10(1), during the officer's work period or while going to or coming from work in an official law enforcement vehicle, shall be presumed to be an injury arising out of and in the course of employment unless the injury occurred during a distinct deviation for a non-essential personal errand. If, however, the employer's policy or the collective bargaining agreement that applies to the officer permits such deviations for non-essential errands, the injury shall be presumed to arise out of and in the course of employment.

(3) Deviation From Employment.—An employee who is injured while deviating from the course of employment, including leaving the employer's premises, is not eligible for benefits unless such deviation is expressly approved by the employer, or unless such deviation or act is in response to an emergency and designed to save life or property.

(4) Traveling Employees.—An employee who is required to travel in connection with his or her employment who suffers an injury while in travel status shall be eligible for benefits under this chapter only if the injury arises out of and in the course of employment while he or she is actively engaged in the duties of employment. This subsection applies to travel necessarily incident to performance of the employee's job responsibility but does not include travel to and from work as provided in subsection (2).

(5) Subsequent Intervening Accidents.—Injuries caused by a subsequent intervening accident arising from an outside agency which are the direct and natural consequence of the original injury are not compensable unless suffered while traveling to or from a health care provider for the purpose of receiving remedial treatment for the compensable injury.

History: s. 14, ch. 90-201; s. 10, ch. 91-1; s. 6, ch. 93-415; s. 103, ch. 97-103; s. 1, ch. 2001-168, effective June 6, 2001.

§ 440.093. Mental and Nervous Injuries.

(1) A mental or nervous injury due to stress, fright, or excitement only is not an injury by accident arising out of the employment. Nothing in this section shall be construed to allow for the payment of benefits under this chapter for mental or nervous injuries without an accompanying physical injury requiring medical treatment. A physical injury resulting from mental or nervous injuries unaccompanied by physical trauma requiring medical treatment shall not be compensable under this chapter.

(2) Mental or nervous injuries occurring as a manifestation of an injury compensable under this chapter shall be demonstrated by clear and convincing medical evidence by a licensed psychiatrist meeting criteria established in the most recent edition of the diagnostic and statistical manual of mental disorders published by the American Psychiatric Association. The compensable physical injury must be and remain the major contributing cause of the mental or nervous condition and the compensable physical injury as determined by reasonable medical certainty must be at least 50 percent responsible for the mental or nervous condition as compared to all other contributing causes combined. Compensation is not payable for the mental, psychological, or emotional injury arising out of depression from being out of work or losing employment opportunities, resulting from a preexisting mental, psychological, or emotional condition or due to pain or other subjective complaints that cannot be substantiated by objective, relevant medical findings.

(3) Subject to the payment of permanent benefits under s. 440.15, in no event shall temporary benefits for a compensable mental or nervous injury be paid for more than 6 months after the date of maximum medical improvement for the injured employee's physical injury or injuries, which shall be included in the period of 104 weeks as provided in s. 440.15(2) and (4). Mental or nervous injuries are compensable only in accordance with the terms of this section.

History: s. 7, ch. 412, effective Oct. 1, 2003.

§ 440.10. Liability for Compensation.

(1)

(a) Every employer coming within the provisions of this chapter shall be liable for, and shall secure, the payment to his or her employees, or any physician, surgeon, or pharmacist providing services under the provisions of s. 440.13, of the compensation payable under ss. 440.13, 440.15, and 440.16. Any contractor or subcontractor who engages in any public or private construction in the state shall secure and maintain compensation for his or her employees under this chapter as provided in s. 440.38.

(b) In case a contractor sublets any part or parts of his or her contract work to a subcontractor or subcontractors, all of the employees of such contractor and subcontractor or subcontractors engaged on such contract work shall be deemed to be employed in one and the same business or establishment, and the contractor shall be liable for, and shall secure, the payment of compensation to all such employees, except to employees of a subcontractor who has secured such payment.

(c) A contractor shall require a subcontractor to provide evidence of workers' compensation insurance. A subcontractor who is a corporation and has an officer who elects to be exempt as permitted under this chapter shall provide a copy of his or her certificate of exemption to the contractor.

(d)

1. If a contractor becomes liable for the payment of compensation to the employees of a subcontractor who has failed to secure such payment in violation of s. 440.38, the contractor or other third-party payor shall be entitled to recover from the subcontractor all benefits paid or payable plus interest unless the contractor and subcontractor have agreed in writing that the contractor will provide coverage.

2. If a contractor or third-party payor becomes liable for the payment of compensation to the corporate officer of a subcontractor who is engaged in the construction industry and has elected to be exempt from the provisions of this chapter, but whose election is invalid, the contractor or third-party payor may recover from the claimant or corporation all benefits paid or payable plus interest, unless the contractor and the subcontractor have agreed in writing that the contractor will provide coverage.

(e) A subcontractor providing services in conjunction with a contractor on the same project or contract work is not liable for the payment of compensation to the employees of another subcontractor or the contractor on such contract work and is protected by the exclusiveness-of-liability provisions of s. 440.11 from any action at law or in admiralty on account of injury to an employee of another subcontractor, or of the contractor, provided that:

1. The subcontractor has secured workers' compensation insurance for its employees or the contractor has secured such insurance on behalf of the subcontractor and its employees in accordance with paragraph (b); and

2. The subcontractor's own gross negligence was not the major contributing cause of the injury.

(f) If an employer fails to secure compensation as required by this chapter, the department shall assess against the employer a penalty not to exceed $5,000 for each employee of that employer who is classified by the employer as an independent contractor but who is found by the department to not meet the criteria for an independent contractor that are set forth in s. 440.02. The department shall adopt rules to administer the provisions of this paragraph.

(g) Subject to s. 440.38, any employer who has employees engaged in work in this state shall obtain a Florida policy or endorsement for such employees which utilizes Florida class codes, rates, rules, and manuals that are in compliance with and approved under the provisions of this chapter and the Florida Insurance Code. Failure to comply with this paragraph is a felony of the second degree, punishable as provided in s. 775.082, s. 775.083, or s. 775.084. The department shall adopt rules for construction industry and nonconstruction-industry employers with regard to the activities that define what constitutes being "engaged in work" in this state, using the following standards:

1. For employees of nonconstruction-industry employers who have their headquarters outside

Fla. Stats.

of Florida and also operate in Florida and who are routinely crossing state lines, but usually return to their homes each night, the employee shall be assigned to the headquarters' state. However, the construction industry employees performing new construction or alterations in Florida shall be assigned to Florida even if the employees return to their home state each night.

2. The payroll of executive supervisors who may visit a Florida location but who are not in direct charge of a Florida location shall be assigned to the state in which the headquarters is located.

3. For construction contractors who maintain a permanent staff of employees and superintendents, if any of these employees or superintendents are assigned to a job that is located in Florida, either for the duration of the job or any portion thereof, their payroll shall be assigned to Florida rather than the headquarters' state.

4. Employees who are hired for a specific project in Florida shall be assigned to Florida.

(2) Compensation shall be payable irrespective of fault as a cause for the injury, except as provided in s. 440.09(3).

History: s. 10, ch. 17481, 1935; CGL 1936 Supp. 5966(10); s. 4, ch. 18413, 1937; s. 6, ch. 74-197; s. 23, ch. 78-300; ss. 5, 124, ch. 79-40; s. 21, ch. 79-312; s. 2, ch. 80-236; s. 14, ch. 86-171; ss. 7, 43, ch. 89-289; ss. 15, 56, ch. 90-201; ss. 11, 52, ch. 91-1; s. 4, ch. 91-2; s. 7, ch. 93-415; s. 104, ch. 97-103; s. 4, ch. 98-174, effective Jan. 1, 1999; s. 15, ch. 2002-194, effective July 1, 2002; s. 7, ch. 2002-236, effective July 1, 2002; s. 8, ch. 412, effective Jan. 1, 2004; s. 470, 2003-261, effective June 26, 2003.

[1]**Note:** —The Division of Workers' Compensation of the Department of Labor and Employment Security was transferred to the Department of Insurance by s. 1, ch. 2002-194. Section 15, ch. 2002-194, replaced existing references to the division in s. 440.10 with references to the Department of Insurance.

§ 440.101. Legislative Intent; Drug-Free Workplaces.

(1) It is the intent of the Legislature to promote drug-free workplaces in order that employers in the state be afforded the opportunity to maximize their levels of productivity, enhance their competitive positions in the marketplace, and reach their desired levels of success without experiencing the costs, delays, and tragedies associated with work-related accidents resulting from drug abuse by employees. It is further the intent of the Legislature that drug abuse be discouraged and that employees who choose to engage in drug abuse face the risk of unemployment and the forfeiture of workers' compensation benefits.

(2) If an employer implements a drug-free workplace program in accordance with s. 440.102 which includes notice, education, and procedural requirements for testing for drugs and alcohol pursuant to law or to rules developed by the Agency for Health Care Administration, the employer may require the employee to submit to a test for the presence of drugs or alcohol and, if a drug or alcohol is found to be present in the employee's system at a level prescribed by rule adopted pursuant to this act, the employee may be terminated and forfeits his or her eligibility for medical and indemnity benefits. However, a drug-free workplace program must require the employer to notify all employees that it is a condition of employment for an employee to refrain from reporting to work or working with the presence of drugs or alcohol in his or her body and, if an injured employee refuses to submit to a test for drugs or alcohol, the employee forfeits eligibility for medical and indemnity benefits.

History: s. 12, ch. 90-201; s. 12, ch. 91-1; s. 8, ch. 93-415; s. 2, ch. 96-289; s. 1049, ch. 97-103.

§ 440.102. Drug-Free Workplace Program Requirements.

The following provisions apply to a drug-free workplace program implemented pursuant to law or to rules adopted by the Agency for Health Care Administration:

(1) Definitions.—Except where the context otherwise requires, as used in this act:

(a) "Chain of custody" refers to the methodology of tracking specified materials or substances for the purpose of maintaining control and accountability from initial collection to final disposition for all such materials or substances and providing for accountability at each stage in handling, testing, and storing specimens and reporting test results.

(b) "Confirmation test," "confirmed test," or "confirmed drug test" means a second analytical procedure used to identify the presence of a specific drug or metabolite in a specimen, which test must be different in scientific principle from that of the initial test procedure and must be capable of providing requisite specificity, sensitivity, and quantitative accuracy.

(c) "Drug" means alcohol, including a distilled spirit, wine, a malt beverage, or an intoxicating liquor; an amphetamine; a cannabinoid; cocaine; phencyclidine (PCP); a hallucinogen; methaqualone; an opiate; a barbiturate; a benzodiazepine; a synthetic narcotic; a designer drug; or a metabolite of any of the substances listed in this paragraph. An employer may test an individual for any or all of such drugs.

(d) "Drug rehabilitation program" means a service provider, established pursuant to s. 397.311(27), that provides confidential, timely, and expert identification, assessment, and resolution of employee drug abuse.

(e) "Drug test" or "test" means any chemical, biological, or physical instrumental analysis administered, by a laboratory certified by the United States Department of Health and Human Services or licensed by the Agency for Health Care Administration, for the purpose of determining the presence or absence of a drug or its metabolites.

(f) "Employee" means any person who works for salary, wages, or other remuneration for an employer.

(g) "Employee assistance program" means an established program capable of providing expert assessment of employee personal concerns; confidential and timely identification services with regard to employee drug abuse; referrals of employees for appropriate diagnosis, treatment, and assistance; and followup services for employees who participate in the program or require monitoring after returning to work. If, in addition to the above activities, an employee assistance program provides diagnostic and treatment services, these services shall in all cases be provided by service providers pursuant to s. 397.311(27).

(h) "Employer" means a person or entity that employs a person and that is covered by the Workers' Compensation Law.

(i) "Initial drug test" means a sensitive, rapid, and reliable procedure to identify negative and presumptive positive specimens, using an immunoassay procedure or an equivalent, or a more accurate scientifically accepted method approved by the United States Food and Drug Administration or the Agency for Health Care Administration as such more accurate technology becomes available in a cost-effective form.

(j) "Job applicant" means a person who has applied for a position with an employer and has been offered employment conditioned upon successfully passing a drug test, and may have begun work pending the results of the drug test. For a public employer, "job applicant" means only a person who has applied for a special-risk or safety-sensitive position.

(k) "Medical review officer" or "MRO" means a licensed physician, employed with or contracted with an employer, who has knowledge of substance abuse disorders, laboratory testing procedures, and chain of custody collection procedures; who verifies positive, confirmed test results; and who has the necessary medical training to interpret and evaluate an employee's positive test result in relation to the employee's medical history or any other relevant biomedical information.

(*l*) "Prescription or nonprescription medication" means a drug or medication obtained pursuant to a prescription as defined by s. 893.02 or a medication that is authorized pursuant to federal or state law for general distribution and use without a prescription in the treatment of human diseases, ailments, or injuries.

(m) "Public employer" means any agency within state, county, or municipal government that employs individuals for a salary, wages, or other remuneration.

(n) "Reasonable-suspicion drug testing"

Fla. Stats.

means drug testing based on a belief that an employee is using or has used drugs in violation of the employer's policy drawn from specific objective and articulable facts and reasonable inferences drawn from those facts in light of experience. Among other things, such facts and inferences may be based upon:

1. Observable phenomena while at work, such as direct observation of drug use or of the physical symptoms or manifestations of being under the influence of a drug.

2. Abnormal conduct or erratic behavior while at work or a significant deterioration in work performance.

3. A report of drug use, provided by a reliable and credible source.

4. Evidence that an individual has tampered with a drug test during his or her employment with the current employer.

5. Information that an employee has caused, contributed to, or been involved in an accident while at work.

6. Evidence that an employee has used, possessed, sold, solicited, or transferred drugs while working or while on the employer's premises or while operating the employer's vehicle, machinery, or equipment.

(o) "Safety-sensitive position" means, with respect to a public employer, a position in which a drug impairment constitutes an immediate and direct threat to public health or safety, such as a position that requires the employee to carry a firearm, perform life-threatening procedures, work with confidential information or documents pertaining to criminal investigations, or work with controlled substances; a position subject to s. 110.1127; or a position in which a momentary lapse in attention could result in injury or death to another person.

(p) "Special-risk position" means, with respect to a public employer, a position that is required to be filled by a person who is certified under chapter 633 or chapter 943.

(q) "Specimen" means tissue, hair, or a product of the human body capable of revealing the presence of drugs or their metabolites, as approved by the United States Food and Drug Administration or the Agency for Health Care Administration.

(2) Drug Testing.—An employer may test an employee or job applicant for any drug described in paragraph (1)(c). In order to qualify as having established a drug-free workplace program under this section and to qualify for the discounts provided under s. 627.0915 and deny medical and indemnity benefits under this chapter, an employer must implement drug testing that conforms to the standards and procedures established in this section and all applicable rules adopted pursuant to this section as required in subsection (4). However, an employer does not have a legal duty under this section to request an employee or job applicant to undergo drug testing. If an employer fails to maintain a drug-free workplace program in accordance with the standards and procedures established in this section and in applicable rules, the employer is ineligible for discounts under s. 627.0915. All employers qualifying for and receiving discounts provided under s. 627.0915 must be reported annually by the insurer to the department.

(3) Notice to Employees and Job Applicants.—

(a) One time only, prior to testing, an employer shall give all employees and job applicants for employment a written policy statement which contains:

1. A general statement of the employer's policy on employee drug use, which must identify:

a. The types of drug testing an employee or job applicant may be required to submit to, including reasonable-suspicion drug testing or drug testing conducted on any other basis.

b. The actions the employer may take against an employee or job applicant on the basis of a positive confirmed drug test result.

2. A statement advising the employee or job applicant of the existence of this section.

3. A general statement concerning confiden-

tiality.

4. Procedures for employees and job applicants to confidentially report to a medical review officer the use of prescription or nonprescription medications to a medical review officer both before and after being tested.

5. A list of the most common medications, by brand name or common name, as applicable, as well as by chemical name, which may alter or affect a drug test. A list of such medications as developed by the Agency for Health Care Administration shall be available to employers through the department.

6. The consequences of refusing to submit to a drug test.

7. A representative sampling of names, addresses, and telephone numbers of employee assistance programs and local drug rehabilitation programs.

8. A statement that an employee or job applicant who receives a positive confirmed test result may contest or explain the result to the medical review officer within 5 working days after receiving written notification of the test result; that if an employee's or job applicant's explanation or challenge is unsatisfactory to the medical review officer, the medical review officer shall report a positive test result back to the employer; and that a person may contest the drug test result pursuant to law or to rules adopted by the Agency for Health Care Administration.

9. A statement informing the employee or job applicant of his or her responsibility to notify the laboratory of any administrative or civil action brought pursuant to this section.

10. A list of all drugs for which the employer will test, described by brand name or common name, as applicable, as well as by chemical name.

11. A statement regarding any applicable collective bargaining agreement or contract and the right to appeal to the Public Employees Relations Commission or applicable court.

12. A statement notifying employees and job applicants of their right to consult with a medical review officer for technical information regarding prescription or nonprescription medication.

(b) An employer not having a drug-testing program shall ensure that at least 60 days elapse between a general one-time notice to all employees that a drug-testing program is being implemented and the beginning of actual drug testing. An employer having a drug-testing program in place prior to July 1, 1990, is not required to provide a 60-day notice period.

(c) An employer shall include notice of drug testing on vacancy announcements for positions for which drug testing is required. A notice of the employer's drug-testing policy must also be posted in an appropriate and conspicuous location on the employer's premises, and copies of the policy must be made available for inspection by the employees or job applicants of the employer during regular business hours in the employer's personnel office or other suitable locations.

(4) Types of Testing.—

(a) An employer is required to conduct the following types of drug tests:

1. Job applicant drug testing.—An employer must require job applicants to submit to a drug test and may use a refusal to submit to a drug test or a positive confirmed drug test as a basis for refusing to hire a job applicant.

2. Reasonable-suspicion drug testing.—An employer must require an employee to submit to reasonable-suspicion drug testing.

3. Routine fitness-for-duty drug testing.—An employer must require an employee to submit to a drug test if the test is conducted as part of a routinely scheduled employee fitness-for-duty medical examination that is part of the employer's established policy or that is scheduled routinely for all members of an employment classification or group.

4. Followup drug testing.—If the employee in the course of employment enters an employee assistance program for drug-related problems, or a drug rehabilitation program, the employer

Fla. Stats.

must require the employee to submit to a drug test as a followup to such program, unless the employee voluntarily entered the program. In those cases, the employer has the option to not require followup testing. If followup testing is required, it must be conducted at least once a year for a 2-year period after completion of the program. Advance notice of a followup testing date must not be given to the employee to be tested.

(b) This subsection does not preclude a private employer from conducting random testing, or any other lawful testing, of employees for drugs.

(c) Limited testing of applicants, only if it is based on a reasonable classification basis, is permissible in accordance with law or with rules adopted by the Agency for Health Care Administration.

(5) Procedures and Employee Protection.—All specimen collection and testing for drugs under this section shall be performed in accordance with the following procedures:

(a) A sample shall be collected with due regard to the privacy of the individual providing the sample, and in a manner reasonably calculated to prevent substitution or contamination of the sample.

(b) Specimen collection must be documented, and the documentation procedures shall include:

1. Labeling of specimen containers so as to reasonably preclude the likelihood of erroneous identification of test results.

2. A form for the employee or job applicant to provide any information he or she considers relevant to the test, including identification of currently or recently used prescription or nonprescription medication or other relevant medical information. The form must provide notice of the most common medications by brand name or common name, as applicable, as well as by chemical name, which may alter or affect a drug test. The providing of information shall not preclude the administration of the drug test, but shall be taken into account in interpreting any positive confirmed test result.

(c) Specimen collection, storage, and transportation to the testing site shall be performed in a manner that reasonably precludes contamination or adulteration of specimens.

(d) Each initial drug test and confirmation test conducted under this section, not including the taking or collecting of a specimen to be tested, shall be conducted by a licensed or certified laboratory as described in subsection (9).

(e) A specimen for a drug test may be taken or collected by any of the following persons:

1. A physician, a physician assistant, a registered professional nurse, a licensed practical nurse, or a nurse practitioner or a certified paramedic who is present at the scene of an accident for the purpose of rendering emergency medical service or treatment.

2. A qualified person employed by a licensed or certified laboratory as described in subsection (9).

(f) A person who collects or takes a specimen for a drug test shall collect an amount sufficient for two drug tests as determined by the Agency for Health Care Administration.

(g) Every specimen that produces a positive, confirmed test result shall be preserved by the licensed or certified laboratory that conducted the confirmation test for a period of at least 210 days after the result of the test was mailed or otherwise delivered to the medical review officer. However, if an employee or job applicant undertakes an administrative or legal challenge to the test result, the employee or job applicant shall notify the laboratory and the sample shall be retained by the laboratory until the case or administrative appeal is settled. During the 180-day period after written notification of a positive test result, the employee or job applicant who has provided the specimen shall be permitted by the employer to have a portion of the specimen retested, at the employee's or job applicant's expense, at another laboratory, licensed and approved by the Agency for Health Care Administration, chosen by the employee or job applicant. The second laboratory must test at equal or greater sensitivity for the drug in question as the first laboratory. The first laboratory that performed the test for the employer is responsible for the transfer of the portion of the specimen to be retested, and for the integrity of the chain of custody during such transfer.

(h) Within 5 working days after receipt of a positive confirmed test result from the medical review officer, an employer shall inform an employee or job applicant in writing of such positive test result, the consequences of such results, and the options available to the employee or job applicant. The employer shall provide to the employee or job applicant, upon request, a copy of the test results.

(i) Within 5 working days after receiving notice of a positive confirmed test result, an employee or job applicant may submit information to the employer explaining or contesting the test result, and explaining why the result does not constitute a violation of the employer's policy.

(j) The employee's or job applicant's explanation or challenge of the positive test result is unsatisfactory to the employer, a written explanation as to why the employee's or job applicant's explanation is unsatisfactory, along with the report of positive result, shall be provided by the employer to the employee or job applicant; and all such documentation shall be kept confidential by the employer pursuant to subsection (8) and shall be retained by the employer for at least 1 year.

(k) An employer may not discharge, discipline, refuse to hire, discriminate against, or request or require rehabilitation of an employee or job applicant on the sole basis of a positive test result that has not been verified by a confirmation test and by a medical review officer.

(*l*) An employer that performs drug testing or specimen collection shall use chain-of-custody procedures established by the Agency for Health Care Administration to ensure proper recordkeeping, handling, labeling, and identification of all specimens tested.

(m) An employer shall pay the cost of all drug tests, initial and confirmation, which the employer requires of employees. An employee or job applicant shall pay the costs of any additional drug tests not required by the employer.

(n) An employer shall not discharge, discipline, or discriminate against an employee solely upon the employee's voluntarily seeking treatment, while under the employ of the employer, for a drug-related problem if the employee has not previously tested positive for drug use, entered an employee assistance program for drug-related problems, or entered a drug rehabilitation program. Unless otherwise provided by a collective bargaining agreement, an employer may select the employee assistance program or drug rehabilitation program if the employer pays the cost of the employee's participation in the program.

(o) If drug testing is conducted based on reasonable suspicion, the employer shall promptly detail in writing the circumstances which formed the basis of the determination that reasonable suspicion existed to warrant the testing. A copy of this documentation shall be given to the employee upon request and the original documentation shall be kept confidential by the employer pursuant to subsection (8) and shall be retained by the employer for at least 1 year.

(p) All authorized remedial treatment, care, and attendance provided by a health care provider to an injured employee before medical and indemnity benefits are denied under this section must be paid for by the carrier or self-insurer. However, the carrier or self-insurer must have given reasonable notice to all affected health care providers that payment for treatment, care, and attendance provided to the employee after a future date certain will be denied. A health care provider, as defined in s. 440.13(1)(h), that refuses, without good cause, to continue treatment, care, and attendance before the provider receives notice of benefit denial commits a misdemeanor of the second degree, punishable as provided in s. 775.082 or s. 775.083.

(6) Confirmation Testing.—

(a) If an initial drug test is negative, the

Fla. Stats.

employer may in its sole discretion seek a confirmation test.

(b) Only licensed or certified laboratories as described in subsection (9) may conduct confirmation drug tests.

(c) All positive initial tests shall be confirmed using gas chromatography/mass spectrometry (GC/MS) or an equivalent or more accurate scientifically accepted method approved by the Agency for Health Care Administration or the United States Food and Drug Administration as such technology becomes available in a cost-effective form.

(d) If an initial drug test of an employee or job applicant is confirmed as positive, the employer's medical review officer shall provide technical assistance to the employer and to the employee or job applicant for the purpose of interpreting the test result to determine whether the result could have been caused by prescription or nonprescription medication taken by the employee or job applicant.

(7) Employer Protection.—

(a) An employee or job applicant whose drug test result is confirmed as positive in accordance with this section shall not, by virtue of the result alone, be deemed to have a "handicap" or "disability" as defined under federal, state, or local handicap and disability discrimination laws.

(b) An employer who discharges or disciplines an employee or refuses to hire a job applicant in compliance with this section is considered to have discharged, disciplined, or refused to hire for cause.

(c) No physician-patient relationship is created between an employee or job applicant and an employer or any person performing or evaluating a drug test, solely by the establishment, implementation, or administration of a drug-testing program.

(d) Nothing in this section shall be construed to prevent an employer from establishing reasonable work rules related to employee possession, use, sale, or solicitation of drugs, including convictions for drug-related offenses, and taking action based upon a violation of any of those rules.

(e) This section does not operate retroactively, and does not abrogate the right of an employer under state law to conduct drug tests, or implement employee drug-testing programs; however, only those programs that meet the criteria outlined in this section qualify for reduced rates under s. 627.0915.

(f) If an employee or job applicant refuses to submit to a drug test, the employer is not barred from discharging or disciplining the employee or from refusing to hire the job applicant. However, this paragraph does not abrogate the rights and remedies of the employee or job applicant as otherwise provided in this section.

(g) This section does not prohibit an employer from conducting medical screening or other tests required, permitted, or not disallowed by any statute, rule, or regulation for the purpose of monitoring exposure of employees to toxic or other unhealthy substances in the workplace or in the performance of job responsibilities. Such screening or testing is limited to the specific substances expressly identified in the applicable statute, rule, or regulation, unless prior written consent of the employee is obtained for other tests. Such screening or testing need not be in compliance with the rules adopted by the Agency for Health Care Administration under this chapter or under s. 112.0455. A public employer may, through the use of an unbiased selection procedure, conduct random drug tests of employees occupying safety-sensitive or special-risk positions if the testing is performed in accordance with drug-testing rules adopted by the Agency for Health Care Administration and the department. If applicable, random drug testing must be specified in a collective bargaining agreement as negotiated by the appropriate certified bargaining agent before such testing is implemented.

(h) No cause of action shall arise in favor of any person based upon the failure of an employer to establish a program or policy for drug testing.

(8) Confidentiality.—

(a) Except as otherwise provided in this subsection, all information, interviews, reports, statements, memoranda, and drug test results, written or otherwise, received or produced as a result of a drug-testing program are confidential and exempt from the provisions of s. 119.07(1) and s. 24(a), Art. I of the State Constitution, and may not be used or received in evidence, obtained in discovery, or disclosed in any public or private proceedings, except in accordance with this section or in determining compensability under this chapter.

(b) Employers, laboratories, medical review officers, employee assistance programs, drug rehabilitation programs, and their agents may not release any information concerning drug test results obtained pursuant to this section without a written consent form signed voluntarily by the person tested, unless such release is compelled by an administrative law judge, a hearing officer, or a court of competent jurisdiction pursuant to an appeal taken under this section or is deemed appropriate by a professional or occupational licensing board in a related disciplinary proceeding. The consent form must contain, at a minimum:

1. The name of the person who is authorized to obtain the information.

2. The purpose of the disclosure.

3. The precise information to be disclosed.

4. The duration of the consent.

5. The signature of the person authorizing release of the information.

(c) Information on drug test results shall not be used in any criminal proceeding against the employee or job applicant. Information released contrary to this section is inadmissible as evidence in any such criminal proceeding.

(d) This subsection does not prohibit an employer, agent of an employer, or laboratory conducting a drug test from having access to employee drug test information or using such information when consulting with legal counsel in connection with actions brought under or related to this section or when the information is relevant to its defense in a civil or administrative matter.

(9) Drug-Testing Standards for Laboratories.—

(a) A laboratory may analyze initial or confirmation test specimens only if:

1. The laboratory is licensed and approved by the Agency for Health Care Administration using criteria established by the United States Department of Health and Human Services as general guidelines for modeling the state drug testing program pursuant to this section or the laboratory is certified by the United States Department of Health and Human Services.

2. The laboratory has written procedures to ensure the chain of custody.

3. The laboratory follows proper quality control procedures, including, but not limited to:

a. The use of internal quality controls, including the use of samples of known concentrations which are used to check the performance and calibration of testing equipment, and periodic use of blind samples for overall accuracy.

b. An internal review and certification process for drug test results, conducted by a person qualified to perform that function in the testing laboratory.

c. Security measures implemented by the testing laboratory to preclude adulteration of specimens and drug test results.

d. Other necessary and proper actions taken to ensure reliable and accurate drug test results.

(b) A laboratory shall disclose to the medical review officer a written positive confirmed test result report within 7 working days after receipt of the sample. All laboratory reports of a drug test result must, at a minimum, state:

1. The name and address of the laboratory that performed the test and the positive identification of the person tested.

2. Positive results on confirmation tests only, or negative results, as applicable.

3. A list of the drugs for which the drug analyses were conducted.

Fla. Stats.

4. The type of tests conducted for both initial tests and confirmation tests and the minimum cutoff levels of the tests.

5. Any correlation between medication reported by the employee or job applicant pursuant to subparagraph (5)(b)2. and a positive confirmed drug test result.

A report must not disclose the presence or absence of any drug other than a specific drug and its metabolites listed pursuant to this section.

(c) The laboratory shall submit to the Agency for Health Care Administration a monthly report with statistical information regarding the testing of employees and job applicants. The report must include information on the methods of analysis conducted, the drugs tested for, the number of positive and negative results for both initial tests and confirmation tests, and any other information deemed appropriate by the Agency for Health Care Administration. A monthly report must not identify specific employees or job applicants.

(10) Rules.—The Agency for Health Care Administration shall adopt rules pursuant to s. 112.0455 and criteria established by the United States Department of Health and Human Services as general guidelines for modeling the state drug testing program, concerning, but not limited to:

(a) Standards for licensing drug testing laboratories and suspension and revocation of such licenses.

(b) Urine, hair, blood, and other body specimens and minimum specimen amounts that are appropriate for drug testing.

(c) Methods of analysis and procedures to ensure reliable drug testing results, including standards for initial tests and confirmation tests.

(d) Minimum cutoff detection levels for each drug or metabolites of such drug for the purposes of determining a positive test result.

(e) Chain of custody procedures to ensure proper identification, labeling, and handling of specimens tested.

(f) Retention, storage, and transportation procedures to ensure reliable results on confirmation tests and retests.

(11) Public Employees in Safety-Sensitive or Special-Risk Positions.—

(a) If an employee who is employed by a public employer in a safety-sensitive position enters an employee assistance program or drug rehabilitation program, the employer must assign the employee to a position other than a safety-sensitive position or, if such position is not available, place the employee on leave while the employee is participating in the program. However, the employee shall be permitted to use any accumulated annual leave credits before leave may be ordered without pay.

(b) An employee who is employed by a public employer in a special-risk position may be discharged or disciplined by a public employer for the first positive confirmed test result if the drug confirmed is an illicit drug under s. 893.03. A special-risk employee who is participating in an employee assistance program or drug rehabilitation program may not be allowed to continue to work in any special-risk or safety-sensitive position of the public employer, but may be assigned to a position other than a safety-sensitive position or placed on leave while the employee is participating in the program. However, the employee shall be permitted to use any accumulated annual leave credits before leave may be ordered without pay.

(12) Denial of Benefits.—An employer shall deny an employee medical or indemnity benefits under this chapter, pursuant to this section.

(13) Collective Bargaining Rights.—

(a) This section does not eliminate the bargainable rights as provided in the collective bargaining process if applicable.

(b) Drug-free workplace program requirements pursuant to this section shall be a mandatory topic of negotiations with any certified collective bargaining agent for nonfederal public sector employers that operate under a collective bargaining agreement.

(14) Applicability.—A drug testing policy or

procedure adopted by an employer pursuant to this chapter shall be applied equally to all employee classifications where the employee is subject to workers' compensation coverage.

(15) State Construction Contracts.—Each construction contractor regulated under part I of chapter 489, and each electrical contractor and alarm system contractor regulated under part II of chapter 489, who contracts to perform construction work under a state contract for educational facilities governed by chapter 1013, for public property or publicly owned buildings governed by chapter 255, or for state correctional facilities governed by chapter 944 shall implement a drug-free workplace program under this section.

History: s. 13, ch. 90-201; s. 13, ch. 91-1; s. 1, ch. 91-201; s. 4, ch. 91-429; s. 9, ch. 93-415; s. 3, ch. 95-119; s. 3, ch. 96-289; s. 284, ch. 96-406; s. 198, ch. 96-410; s. 1050, ch. 97-103; s. 99, ch. 97-264; s. 3, ch. 99-186; s. 14, ch. 2000-320; s. 1, ch. 2002-14, effective October 1, 2002; s. 5, ch. 2002-78, effective July 1, 2002; s. 16, ch. 2002-194, effective July 1, 2002; s. 8, ch. 2002-196, effective July 1, 2002. s. 51, ch. 2003-1, effective July 1, 2003; s. 60, ch. 2004-5, effective June 29, 2004; s. 7, ch. 2005-55, effective July 1, 2005.

§ 440.1025. Employer Workplace Safety Program in Rate-Setting; Program Requirements; Rulemaking.

(1) For a public or private employer to be eligible for receipt of specific identifiable consideration under s. 627.0915 for a workplace safety program in the setting of rates, the employer must have a workplace safety program. At a minimum, the program must include a written safety policy and safety rules, and make provision for safety inspections, preventative maintenance, safety training, first-aid, accident investigation, and necessary recordkeeping. The department may adopt rules for insurers to utilize in determining employer compliance with the requirements of this section.

(2) The division shall publicize on the Internet, and shall encourage insurers to publicize, the availability of free safety consultation services and safety program resources.

History: s. 9, ch. 2001-91; s. 9, ch. 412, effective Oct. 1, 2003; s. 471, ch. 2003-261, effective June 26, 2003.

§ 440.103. Building Permits; Identification of Minimum Premium Policy.

Every employer shall, as a condition to applying for and receiving a building permit, show proof and certify to the permit issuer that it has secured compensation for its employees under this chapter as provided in ss. 440.10 and 440.38. Such proof of compensation must be evidenced by a certificate of coverage issued by the carrier, a valid exemption certificate approved by the department, or a copy of the employer's authority to self-insure and shall be presented each time the employer applies for a building permit. As provided in s. 627.413(5), each certificate of coverage must show, on its face, whether or not coverage is secured under the minimum premium provisions of rules adopted by rating organizations licensed pursuant to s. 627.221. The words "minimum premium policy" or equivalent language shall be typed, printed, stamped, or legibly handwritten.

History: s. 10. ch. 93-415; s. 5, ch. 98-174, effective Jan. 1, 1999; s. 17, ch. 2002-194, effective July 1, 2002; s. 10, ch. 412, effective Oct. 1, 2003; s. 472, 2003-261, effective June 26, 2003.

§ 440.104. Competitive Bidder; Civil Actions.

(1) Any person engaged in the construction industry, as provided in s. 440.02, who loses a competitive bid for a contract shall have a cause of action for damages against the person awarded the contract for which the bid was made, if the person making the losing bid establishes that the winning bidder knew or should have known that he or she was in violation of s. 440.10, s. 440.105, or s. 440.38 while performing the work under the contract.

(2) To recover in an action brought under this section, a party must establish a violation of s. 440.10, s. 440.105, or s. 440.38 by a preponderance of the evidence.

(3) Upon establishing that the winning bidder knew or should have known of the violation, the person shall recover as liquidated damages 30 percent of the total amount bid on the contract

Fla. Stats.

by the person bringing the action, or $15,000, whichever is greater.

(4) In any action under this section, the prevailing party is entitled to an award of reasonable attorney's fees.

(5) An action under this section must be commenced within 2 years after the performance of activities involving any building, clearing, filling, or execution contract, or the substantial improvement in the size or use of any structure, or the appearance of any land.

(6) A person may not recover any amounts under this section if the defendant in the action establishes by a preponderance of the evidence that the plaintiff:

(a) Was in violation of s. 440.10, s. 440.105, or s. 440.38 at the time of making the bid on the contract; or

(b) Was in violation of s. 440.10, s. 440.105, or s. 440.38 with respect to any contract performed by the plaintiff within 1 year before making the bid on the contract.

(7) (a)Any person who loses a competitive bid may petition the court to join in a suit brought under this section by another person against the winning bidder on the same contract and shall be joined in such suit. If more than one person is joined against the winning bidder and such persons prevail in the suit, the court must enter judgment dividing damages recoverable under this section between the parties equally.

(b) Any person who receives notice of a suit filed under this section and fails, within 20 days after receipt of such notice, to petition the court to join as a party to the suit is barred from bringing a cause of action under this section against the winning bidder on the contract at issue. For purposes of this subsection, publication in accordance with s. 49.10 constitutes sufficient notice.

History: s. 11, ch. 93-415; s. 6, ch. 98-174, effective Jan. 1, 1999; s. 18, ch. 2002-194, effective July 1, 2002.

§ 440.105. Prohibited Activities; Reports; Penalties; Limitations.

(1) (a) Any insurance carrier, any individual self-insured, any commercial or group self-insurance fund, any professional practitioner licensed or regulated by the Department of Health, except as otherwise provided by law, any medical review committee as defined in s. 766.101, any private medical review committee, and any insurer, agent, or other person licensed under the insurance code, or any employee thereof, having knowledge or who believes that a fraudulent act or any other act or practice which, upon conviction, constitutes a felony or misdemeanor under this chapter is being or has been committed shall send to the Division of Insurance Fraud, Bureau of Workers' Compensation Fraud, a report or information pertinent to such knowledge or belief and such additional information relative thereto as the bureau may require. The bureau shall review such information or reports and select such information or reports as, in its judgment, may require further investigation. It shall then cause an independent examination of the facts surrounding such information or report to be made to determine the extent, if any, to which a fraudulent act or any other act or practice which, upon conviction, constitutes a felony or a misdemeanor under this chapter is being committed. The bureau shall report any alleged violations of law which its investigations disclose to the appropriate licensing agency and state attorney or other prosecuting agency having jurisdiction with respect to any such violations of this chapter. If prosecution by the state attorney or other prosecuting agency having jurisdiction with respect to such violation is not begun within 60 days of the bureau's report, the state attorney or other prosecuting agency having jurisdiction with respect to such violation shall inform the bureau of the reasons for the lack of prosecution.

(b) In the absence of fraud or bad faith, a person is not subject to civil liability for libel, slander, or any other relevant tort by virtue of filing reports, without malice, or furnishing other information, without malice, required by this section or required by the bureau, and no civil cause of action of any nature shall arise against such person:

1. For any information relating to suspected fraudulent acts furnished to or received from

law enforcement officials, their agents, or employees;

2. For any information relating to suspected fraudulent acts furnished to or received from other persons subject to the provisions of this chapter; or

3. For any such information relating to suspected fraudulent acts furnished in reports to the bureau, or the National Association of Insurance Commissioners.

(2) Whoever violates any provision of this subsection commits a misdemeanor of the first degree, punishable as provided in s. 775.082 or s. 775.083.

(a) It shall be unlawful for any employer to knowingly:

1. Coerce or attempt to coerce, as a precondition to employment or otherwise, an employee to obtain a certificate of election of exemption pursuant to s. 440.05.

2. Discharge or refuse to hire an employee or job applicant because the employee or applicant has filed a claim for benefits under this chapter.

3. Discharge, discipline, or take any other adverse personnel action against any employee for disclosing information to the department or any law enforcement agency relating to any violation or suspected violation of any of the provisions of this chapter or rules promulgated hereunder.

4. Violate a stop-work order issued by the department pursuant to s. 440.107.

(b) It shall be unlawful for any insurance entity to revoke or cancel a workers' compensation insurance policy or membership because an employer has returned an employee to work or hired an employee who has filed a workers' compensation claim.

(3) Whoever violates any provision of this subsection commits a misdemeanor of the first degree, punishable as provided in s. 775.082 or s. 775.083.

(a) It shall be unlawful for any employer to knowingly fail to update applications for coverage as required by s. 440.381(1) and the[1] department rules within 7 days after the reporting date for any change in the required information, or to post notice of coverage pursuant to s. 440.40.

(b) It shall be unlawful for any employer to knowingly participate in the creation of the employment relationship in which the employee has used any false, fraudulent, or misleading oral or written statement as evidence of identity.

(c) It is unlawful for any attorney or other person, in his or her individual capacity or in his or her capacity as a public or private employee, or for any firm, corporation, partnership, or association to receive any fee or other consideration or any gratuity from a person on account of services rendered for a person in connection with any proceedings arising under this chapter, unless such fee, consideration, or gratuity is approved by a judge of compensation claims or by the Deputy Chief Judge of Compensation Claims.

(4) Whoever violates any provision of this subsection commits insurance fraud, punishable as provided in paragraph (f).

(a) It shall be unlawful for any employer to knowingly:

1. Present or cause to be presented any false, fraudulent, or misleading oral or written statement to any person as evidence of compliance with s. 440.38.

2. Make a deduction from the pay of any employee entitled to the benefits of this chapter for the purpose of requiring the employee to pay any portion of premium paid by the employer to a carrier or to contribute to a benefit fund or department maintained by such employer for the purpose of providing compensation or medical services and supplies as required by this chapter.

3. Fail to secure payment of compensation if required to do so by this chapter.

(b) It shall be unlawful for any person:

1. To knowingly make, or cause to be made, any false, fraudulent, or misleading oral or written statement for the purpose of obtaining or

Fla. Stats.

denying any benefit or payment under this chapter.

2. To present or cause to be presented any written or oral statement as part of, or in support of, a claim for payment or other benefit pursuant to any provision of this chapter, knowing that such statement contains any false, incomplete, or misleading information concerning any fact or thing material to such claim.

3. To prepare or cause to be prepared any written or oral statement that is intended to be presented to any employer, insurance company, or self-insured program in connection with, or in support of, any claim for payment or other benefit pursuant to any provision of this chapter, knowing that such statement contains any false, incomplete, or misleading information concerning any fact or thing material to such claim.

4. To knowingly assist, conspire with, or urge any person to engage in activity prohibited by this section.

5. To knowingly make any false, fraudulent, or misleading oral or written statement, or to knowingly omit or conceal material information, required by s. 440.185 or s. 440.381, for the purpose of obtaining workers' compensation coverage or for the purpose of avoiding, delaying, or diminishing the amount of payment of any workers' compensation premiums.

6. To knowingly misrepresent or conceal payroll, classification of workers, or information regarding an employer's loss history which would be material to the computation and application of an experience rating modification factor for the purpose of avoiding or diminishing the amount of payment of any workers' compensation premiums.

7. To knowingly present or cause to be presented any false, fraudulent, or misleading oral or written statement to any person as evidence of compliance with s. 440.38, as evidence of eligibility for a certificate of exemption under s. 440.05.

8. To knowingly violate a stop-work order issued by the department pursuant to s. 440.107.

9. To knowingly present or cause to be presented any false, fraudulent, or misleading oral or written statement to any person as evidence of identity for the purpose of obtaining employment or filing or supporting a claim for workers' compensation benefits.

(c) It shall be unlawful for any physician licensed under chapter 458, osteopathic physician licensed under chapter 459, chiropractic physician licensed under chapter 460, podiatric physician licensed under chapter 461, optometric physician licensed under chapter 463, or any other practitioner licensed under the laws of this state to knowingly and willfully assist, conspire with, or urge any person to fraudulently violate any of the provisions of this chapter.

(d) It shall be unlawful for any person or governmental entity licensed under chapter 395 to maintain or operate a hospital in such a manner so that such person or governmental entity knowingly and willfully allows the use of the facilities of such hospital by any person, in a scheme or conspiracy to fraudulently violate any of the provisions of this chapter.

(e) It shall be unlawful for any attorney or other person, in his or her individual capacity or in his or her capacity as a public or private employee, or any firm, corporation, partnership, or association, to knowingly assist, conspire with, or urge any person to fraudulently violate any of the provisions of this chapter.

(f) If the monetary value of any violation of this subsection:

1. Is less than $20,000, the offender commits a felony of the third degree, punishable as provided in s. 775.082, s. 775.083, or s. 775.084.

2. Is $20,000 or more, but less than $100,000, the offender commits a felony of the second degree, punishable as provided in s. 775.082, s. 775.083, or s. 775.084.

3. Is $100,000 or more, the offender commits a felony of the first degree, punishable as provided in s. 775.082, s. 775.083, or s. 775.084.

(5) It shall be unlawful for any attorney or other person, in his or her individual capacity or

in his or her capacity as a public or private employee or for any firm, corporation, partnership, or association, to unlawfully solicit any business in and about city or county hospitals, courts, or any public institution or public place; in and about private hospitals or sanitariums; in and about any private institution; or upon private property of any character whatsoever for the purpose of making workers' compensation claims. Whoever violates any provision of this subsection commits a felony of the second degree, punishable as provided in s. 775.082, s. 775.083, or s. 775.085.

(6) This section shall not be construed to preclude the applicability of any other provision of criminal law that applies or may apply to any transaction.

(7) An injured employee or any other party making a claim under this chapter shall provide his or her personal signature attesting that he or she has reviewed, understands, and acknowledges the following statement: "Any person who, knowingly and with intent to injure, defraud, or deceive any employer or employee, insurance company, or self-insured program, files a statement of claim containing any false or misleading information commits insurance fraud, punishable as provided in s. 817.234." If the injured employee or other party refuses to sign the document attesting that he or she has reviewed, understands, and acknowledges the statement, benefits or payments under this chapter shall be suspended until such signature is obtained.

History: s. 12, ch. 93-415; s. 105, ch. 97-103; s. 7, ch. 98-174, effective Jan. 1, 1999; s. 10, ch. 2001-91, effective Oct. 1, 2001; s. 87, ch. 2001-277, effective July 1, 2001; s. 19, ch. 2002-194, effective July 1, 2002; s. 11, ch. 2003-412, effective Oct. 1, 2003; s. 473, ch. 2003-261, effective June 26, 2003.

[1]**2005 Note:** As amended by s. 11, ch. 2003-412. The amendment by s. 473, ch. 2003-261, substituted a reference to the Financial Services Commission instead of referencing the department (defined as the Department of Financial Services in s. 440.02) in place of the former Department of Insurance.

§ 440.1051. Fraud Reports; Civil Immunity; Criminal Penalties.

(1) The Bureau of Workers' Compensation Insurance Fraud of the Division of Insurance Fraud of the department shall establish a toll-free telephone number to receive reports of workers' compensation fraud committed by an employee, employer, insurance provider, physician, attorney, or other person.

(2) Any person who reports workers' compensation fraud to the Division of Insurance Fraud under subsection (1) is immune from civil liability for doing so, and the person or entity alleged to have committed the fraud may not retaliate against him or her for providing such report, unless the person making the report knows it to be false.

(3) A person who calls and, knowingly and falsely, reports workers' compensation fraud or who, in violation of subsection (2) retaliates against a person making such report, commits a felony of the third degree, punishable as provided in s. 775.082, s. 775.083, or s. 775.084.

History: s. 13 ch. 93-415; s. 106, ch. 97-103; s. 12, ch. 412, effective October 1, 2003; s. 474, ch. 2003-261, effective June 26, 2003.

§ 440.106. Civil Remedies; Administrative Penalties.

(1) Whenever any circuit or special grievance committee acting under the jurisdiction of the Supreme Court finds probable cause to believe that an attorney has violated s. 440.105, such committee may forward to the appropriate state attorney a copy of the findings of probable cause and a copy of the report being filed in the matter.

(2) Whenever a physician, osteopathic physician, chiropractic physician, podiatric physician, or other practitioner is determined to have violated s. 440.105, the Board of Medicine as set forth in chapter 458, the Board of Osteopathic Medicine as set forth in chapter 459, the Board of Chiropractic Medicine as set forth in chapter 460, the Board of Podiatric Medicine as set forth in chapter 461, or other appropriate licensing authority, shall hold an administrative hearing to consider the imposition of administrative sanctions as provided by law against said physician, osteopathic physician, chiropractic physician, or other practitioner.

(3) Whenever any group or individual self-insurer, carrier, rating bureau, or agent or other representative of any carrier or rating bureau is determined to have violated s. 440.105, the agency responsible for licensure or certification may revoke or suspend the authority or certification of the group or individual self-insurer, carrier, agent, or broker.

(4) The department or the Office of Insurance Regulation shall report any contractor determined in violation of requirements of this chapter to the appropriate state licensing board for disciplinary action.

(5) The terms "violation" or "violated" shall include having been found guilty of or having pleaded guilty or nolo contendere to a felony or misdemeanor under the law of the United States of America or any state thereof or under the law of any other country without regard to whether a judgment of conviction has been entered by the court having jurisdiction of such cases.

History: s. 14, ch. 93-415; s. 14, ch. 97-98; s. 44, ch. 97-264; ss. 187, 258, ch. 98-166; s. 20, ch. 2002-194, effective July 1, 2002; s. 475, ch. 2003-261, effective June 26, 2003.

§ 440.107. Department Powers to Enforce Employer Compliance With Coverage Requirements.

(1) The Legislature finds that the failure of an employer to comply with the workers' compensation coverage requirements under this chapter poses an immediate danger to public health, safety, and welfare.

(2) For the purposes of this section, "securing the payment of workers' compensation" means obtaining coverage that meets the requirements of this chapter and the Florida Insurance Code. However, if at any time an employer materially understates or conceals payroll, materially misrepresents or conceals employee duties so as to avoid proper classification for premium calculations, or materially misrepresents or conceals information pertinent to the computation and application of an experience rating modification factor, such employer shall be deemed to have failed to secure payment of workers' compensation and shall be subject to the sanctions set forth in this section. A stop-work order issued because an employer is deemed to have failed to secure the payment of workers' compensation required under this chapter because the employer has materially understated or concealed payroll, materially misrepresented or concealed employee duties so as to avoid proper classification for premium calculations, or materially misrepresented or concealed information pertinent to the computation and application of an experience rating modification factor shall have no effect upon an employer's or carrier's duty to provide benefits under this chapter or upon any of the employer's or carrier's rights and defenses under this chapter, including exclusive remedy.

(3) The department shall enforce workers' compensation coverage requirements, including the requirement that the employer secure the payment of workers' compensation, and the requirement that the employer provide the carrier with information to accurately determine payroll and correctly assign classification codes. In addition to any other powers under this chapter, the department shall have the power to:

(a) Conduct investigations for the purpose of ensuring employer compliance.

(b) Enter and inspect any place of business at any reasonable time for the purpose of investigating employer compliance.

(c) Examine and copy business records.

(d) Administer oaths and affirmations.

(e) Certify to official acts.

(f) Issue and serve subpoenas for attendance of witnesses or production of business records, books, papers, correspondence, memoranda, and other records.

(g) Issue stop-work orders, penalty assessment orders, and any other orders necessary for the administration of this section.

(h) Enforce the terms of a stop-work order.

(i) Levy and pursue actions to recover penalties.

(j) Seek injunctions and other appropriate

relief.

(4) The department shall designate representatives who may serve subpoenas and other process of the department issued under this section.

(5) The department shall specify by rule the business records that employers must maintain and produce to comply with this section.

(6) If a person has refused to obey a subpoena to appear before the department or its authorized representative or produce evidence requested by the department or to give testimony about the matter that is under investigation, a court has jurisdiction to issue an order requiring compliance with the subpoena if the court has jurisdiction in the geographical area where the inquiry is being carried on or in the area where the person who has refused the subpoena is found, resides, or transacts business. Failure to obey such a court order may be punished by the court as contempt, either civilly or criminally. Costs, including reasonable attorney's fees, incurred by the department to obtain an order granting, in whole or in part, a petition to enforce a subpoena or a subpoena duces tecum shall be taxed against the subpoenaed party.

(7)

(a) Whenever the department determines that an employer who is required to secure the payment to his or her employees of the compensation provided for by this chapter has failed to secure the payment of workers' compensation required by this chapter or to produce the required business records under subsection (5) within 5 business days after receipt of the written request of the department, such failure shall be deemed an immediate serious danger to public health, safety, or welfare sufficient to justify service by the department of a stop-work order on the employer, requiring the cessation of all business operations. If the department makes such a determination, the department shall issue a stop-work order within 72 hours. The order shall take effect when served upon the employer or, for a particular employer worksite, when served at that worksite. In addition to serving a stop-work order at a particular worksite which shall be effective immediately, the department shall immediately proceed with service upon the employer which shall be effective upon all employer worksites in the state for which the employer is not in compliance. A stop-work order may be served with regard to an employer's worksite by posting a copy of the stop-work order in a conspicuous location at the worksite. The order shall remain in effect until the department issues an order releasing the stop-work order upon a finding that the employer has come into compliance with the coverage requirements of this chapter and has paid any penalty assessed under this section. The department may issue an order of conditional release from a stop-work order to an employer upon finding that the employer has complied with coverage requirements of this chapter and has agreed to remit periodic payments of the penalty pursuant to a payment agreement schedule with the department. If an order of conditional release is issued, failure by the employer to meet any term or condition of such penalty payment agreement shall result in the immediate reinstatement of the stop-work order and the entire unpaid balance of the penalty shall become immediately due. The department may require an employer who is found to have failed to comply with the coverage requirements of s. 440.38 to file with the department, as a condition of release from a stop-work order, periodic reports for a probationary period that shall not exceed 2 years that demonstrate the employer's continued compliance with this chapter. The department shall by rule specify the reports required and the time for filing under this subsection.

(b) Stop-work orders and penalty assessment orders issued under this section against a corporation, partnership, or sole proprietorship shall be in effect against any successor corporation or business entity that has one or more of the same principals or officers as the corporation or partnership against which the stop-work order was issued and are engaged in the same or equivalent trade or activity.

(c) The department shall assess a penalty of $1,000 per day against an employer for each day that the employer conducts business operations that are in violation of a stop-work order.

Fla. Stats.

(d)

1. In addition to any penalty, stop-work order, or injunction, the department shall assess against any employer who has failed to secure the payment of compensation as required by this chapter a penalty equal to 1.5 times the amount the employer would have paid in premium when applying approved manual rates to the employer's payroll during periods for which it failed to secure the payment of workers' compensation required by this chapter within the preceding 3-year period or $1,000, whichever is greater.

2. Any subsequent violation within 5 years after the most recent violation shall, in addition to the penalties set forth in this subsection, be deemed a knowing act within the meaning of s. 440.105.

(e) When an employer fails to provide business records sufficient to enable the department to determine the employer's payroll for the period requested for the calculation of the penalty provided in paragraph (d), for penalty calculation purposes, the imputed weekly payroll for each employee, corporate officer, sole proprietor, or partner shall be the statewide average weekly wage as defined in s. 440.12(2) multiplied by 1.5.

(f) In addition to any other penalties provided for in this chapter, the department may assess against the employer a penalty of $5,000 for each employee of that employer who the employer represents to the department or carrier as an independent contractor but who is determined by the department not to be an independent contractor as defined in s. 440.02.

(8) In addition to the issuance of a stop-work order under subsection (7), the department may file a complaint in the circuit court in and for Leon County to enjoin any employer who has failed to secure the payment of workers' compensation required by this chapter from employing individuals and from conducting business until the employer presents evidence satisfactory to the department of having secured the payment of workers' compensation required by this chapter and pays a civil penalty assessed by the department under this section.

(9) The department shall adopt rules to administer this section.

(10) The department may bring an action in circuit court to recover penalties assessed under this section, including any interest owed to the department pursuant to this section. In any action brought by the department pursuant to this section in which it prevails, the circuit court shall award costs, including the reasonable costs of investigation and a reasonable attorney's fee.

(11) Any judgment obtained by the department and any penalty due pursuant to the service of a stop-work order or otherwise due under this section shall, until collected, constitute a lien upon the entire interest of the employer, legal or equitable, in any property, real or personal, tangible or intangible; however, such lien is subordinate to claims for unpaid wages and any prior recorded liens, and a lien created by this section is not valid against any person who, subsequent to such lien and in good faith and for value, purchases real or personal property from such employer or becomes the mortgagee on real or personal property of such employer, or against a subsequent attaching creditor, unless, with respect to real estate of the employer, a notice of the lien is recorded in the public records of the county where the real estate is located, and with respect to personal property of the employer, the notice is recorded with the Secretary of State.

(12) Any law enforcement agency in the state may, at the request of the department, render any assistance necessary to carry out the provisions of this section, including, but not limited to, preventing any employee or other person from remaining at a place of employment or job site after a stop-work order or injunction has taken effect.

(13) Agency action by the department under this section, if contested, must be contested as provided in chapter 120. All penalties assessed by the department must be paid into the Workers' Compensation Administration Trust Fund.

(14) If the department finds that an employer who is certified or registered under part I or part II of chapter 489 and who is required to secure

the payment of workers' compensation under this chapter to his or her employees has failed to do so, the department shall immediately notify the Department of Business and Professional Regulation.

History: s. 15, ch. 93-415; s. 107, ch. 97-103; s. 8, ch. 98-174; s. 21, ch. 2002-194, effective July 1, 2002; s. 8, ch. 2002-236, effective July 1, 2002; s. 13, ch. 412, effective Oct. 1, 2003; s. 476, ch. 2003-261, effective June 26, 2003; s. 2, ch. 2004-370, effective July 1, 2004; s. 148, SB 2994, effective July 1, 2004.

§ 440.108. Investigatory Records Relating to Workers' Compensation Employer Compliance; Confidentiality.

(1) All investigatory records made or received pursuant to s. 440.107 and any records necessary to complete an investigation held by the department are confidential and exempt from the provisions of s. 119.07(1) and s. 24(a), Art. I of the State Constitution until the investigation is completed or ceases to be active. For purposes of this section, an investigation is considered "active" while such investigation is being conducted by the department with a reasonable, good faith belief that it may lead to the filing of administrative, civil, or criminal proceedings. An investigation does not cease to be active if the agency is proceeding with reasonable dispatch and there is a good faith belief that action may be initiated by the agency or other administrative or law enforcement agency.

(2) After an investigation is completed or ceases to be active, information in records relating to the investigation remains confidential and exempt from the provisions of s. 119.07(1) and s. 24(a), Art. I of the State Constitution if disclosure of that information would:

(a) Jeopardize the integrity of another active investigation;

(b) Reveal a trade secret, as defined in s. 688.002;

(c) Reveal business or personal financial information;

(d) Reveal personal identifying information regarding the identity of a confidential source;

(e) Defame or cause unwarranted damage to the good name or reputation of an individual or jeopardize the safety of an individual; or

(f) Reveal investigative techniques or procedures.

(3) The department may provide information made confidential and exempt by this section to any law enforcement agency or administrative agency for use in the performance of its official duties and responsibilities. The receiving agency must maintain the confidential and exempt status of such information.

History: s. 1, ch. 98-407, effective Jan. 1, 1999; s. 22, ch. 2002-194, effective July 1, 2002; s. 1, ch. 2003-106, effective Oct. 1, 2003.

1998 Note: Section 2, ch. 98-407 states: "The Legislature finds that it is a public necessity that these investigatory and examination records be held confidential and exempt during an investigation in order not to compromise the investigation and disseminate potentially inaccurate information. To the extent this information is made available to the public, those persons being investigated will not have access to such information which would potentially defeat the purpose of the investigation. This would impede the effective and efficient operation of investigatory governmental functions. Additionally, the Legislature finds that it is a public necessity that trade secrets or business or personal financial records remain confidential and exempt after an investigation is completed or ceases to be active because the disclosure of such information would injure the affected party in the marketplace. Further, information that would defame or cause unwarranted damage to the name or reputation of an individual, or jeopardize the safety of an individual, must remain confidential and exempt after an investigation is completed or ceases to be active to protect that individual's name or reputation or personal safety. As well, information that would jeopardize the integrity of another active investigation or that would reveal investigative techniques or procedures must remain confidential and exempt after an investigation is completed or ceases to be active in order to permit the effective and efficient operation of the program."

§ 440.11. Exclusiveness of Liability.

(1) The liability of an employer prescribed in s. 440.10 shall be exclusive and in place of all other liability, including vicarious liability, of such employer to any third-party tortfeasor and to the employee, the legal representative thereof,

Fla. Stats.

husband or wife, parents, dependents, next of kin, and anyone otherwise entitled to recover damages from such employer at law or in admiralty on account of such injury or death, except as follows:

(a) If an employer fails to secure payment of compensation as required by this chapter, an injured employee, or the legal representative thereof in case death results from the injury, may elect to claim compensation under this chapter or to maintain an action at law or in admiralty for damages on account of such injury or death. In such action the defendant may not plead as a defense that the injury was caused by negligence of a fellow employee, that the employee assumed the risk of the employment, or that the injury was due to the comparative negligence of the employee.

(b) When an employer commits an intentional tort that causes the injury or death of the employee. For purposes of this paragraph, an employer's actions shall be deemed to constitute an intentional tort and not an accident only when the employee proves, by clear and convincing evidence, that:

1. The employer deliberately intended to injure the employee; or

2. The employer engaged in conduct that the employer knew, based on prior similar accidents or on explicit warnings specifically identifying a known danger, was virtually certain to result in injury or death to the employee, and the employee was not aware of the risk because the danger was not apparent and the employer deliberately concealed or misrepresented the danger so as to prevent the employee from exercising informed judgment about whether to perform the work.

The same immunities from liability enjoyed by an employer shall extend as well to each employee of the employer when such employee is acting in furtherance of the employer's business and the injured employee is entitled to receive benefits under this chapter. Such fellow-employee immunities shall not be applicable to an employee who acts, with respect to a fellow employee, with willful and wanton disregard or unprovoked physical aggression or with gross negligence when such acts result in injury or death or such acts proximately cause such injury or death, nor shall such immunities be applicable to employees of the same employer when each is operating in the furtherance of the employer's business but they are assigned primarily to unrelated works within private or public employment. The same immunity provisions enjoyed by an employer shall also apply to any sole proprietor, partner, corporate officer or director, supervisor, or other person who in the course and scope of his or her duties acts in a managerial or policymaking capacity and the conduct which caused the alleged injury arose within the course and scope of said managerial or policymaking duties and was not a violation of a law, whether or not a violation was charged, for which the maximum penalty which may be imposed does not exceed 60 days' imprisonment as set forth in s. 775.082. The immunity from liability provided in this subsection extends to county governments with respect to employees of county constitutional officers whose offices are funded by the board of county commissioners.

(2) The immunity from liability described in subsection (1) shall extend to an employer and to each employee of the employer which utilizes the services of the employees of a help supply services company, as set forth in Standard Industry Code Industry Number 7363, when such employees, whether management or staff, are acting in furtherance of the employer's business. An employee so engaged by the employer shall be considered a borrowed employee of the employer, and, for the purposes of this section, shall be treated as any other employee of the employer. The employer shall be liable for and shall secure the payment of compensation to all such borrowed employees as required in s. 440.10, except when such payment has been secured by the help supply services company.

(3) An employer's workers' compensation carrier, service agent, or safety consultant shall not be liable as a third-party tortfeasor to employees of the employer or employees of its subcontractors for assisting the employer and its subcontractors, if any, in carrying out the employer's rights and responsibilities under this

chapter by furnishing any safety inspection, safety consultative service, or other safety service incidental to the workers' compensation or employers' liability coverage or to the workers' compensation or employer's liability servicing contract. Without limitation, a safety consultant may include an owner, as defined in chapter 713, or an owner's related, affiliated, or subsidiary companies and the employees of each. The exclusion from liability under this subsection shall not apply in any case in which injury or death is proximately caused by the willful and unprovoked physical aggression, or by the negligent operation of a motor vehicle, by employees, officers, or directors of the employer's workers' compensation carrier, service agent, or safety consultant.

(4) Notwithstanding the provisions of s. 624.155, the liability of a carrier to an employee or to anyone entitled to bring suit in the name of the employee shall be as provided in this chapter, which shall be exclusive and in place of all other liability.

History: s. 11, ch. 17481, 1935; CGL 1936 Supp. 5966(11); s. 1, ch. 70-25; s. 1, ch. 71-190; s. 4, ch. 75-209; ss. 2, 23, ch. 78-300; ss. 6, 124, ch. 79-40; s. 21, ch. 79-312; s. 3, ch. 83-305; s. 1, ch. 88-284; ss. 8, 43, ch. 89-289; ss. 16, 56, ch. 90-201; ss. 14, 52, ch. 91-1; s. 16, ch. 93-415; s. 108, ch. 97-103; s. 14, ch. 2003-412, effective Oct. 1, 2003.

§ 440.12. Time for Commencement and Limits on Weekly Rate of Compensation.

(1) No compensation shall be allowed for the first 7 days of the disability, except benefits provided for in s. 440.13. However, if the injury results in disability of more than 21 days, compensation shall be allowed from the commencement of the disability. All weekly compensation payments, except for the first payment, shall be paid by check or, if authorized by the employee, deposited directly into the employee's account at a financial institution. As used in this subsection, the term "financial institution" means a financial institution as defined in s. 655.005(1)(h).

(2) Compensation for disability resulting from injuries which occur after December 31, 1974, shall not be less than $20 per week. However, if the employee's wages at the time of injury are less than $20 per week, he or she shall receive his or her full weekly wages. If the employee's wages at the time of the injury exceed $20 per week, compensation shall not exceed an amount per week which is:

(a) Equal to 100 percent of the statewide average weekly wage, determined as hereinafter provided for the year in which the injury occurred; however, the increase to 100 percent from 66⅔ percent of the statewide average weekly wage shall apply only to injuries occurring on or after August 1, 1979; and

(b) Adjusted to the nearest dollar.

For the purpose of this subsection, the "statewide average weekly wage" means the average weekly wage paid by employers subject to the Florida Unemployment Compensation Law as reported to the Agency for Workforce Innovation for the four calendar quarters ending each June 30, which average weekly wage shall be determined by the Agency for Workforce Innovation on or before November 30 of each year and shall be used in determining the maximum weekly compensation rate with respect to injuries occurring in the calendar year immediately following. The statewide average weekly wage determined by the Agency for Workforce Innovation shall be reported annually to the Legislature.

(3) The provisions of this section as amended effective July 1, 1951, shall govern with respect to disability due to injuries suffered prior to July 1, 1959. The provisions of this section as amended effective July 1, 1959, shall govern with respect to disability due to injuries suffered after June 30, 1959, and prior to January 1, 1968. The provisions of this section as amended effective January 1, 1968, shall govern with respect to disability due to injuries suffered after December 31, 1967, and prior to July 1, 1970. The provisions of this section as amended effective July 1, 1970, shall govern with respect to disability due to injuries suffered after June 30, 1970, and prior to July 1, 1972. The provisions of this section as amended effective July 1, 1972, shall govern with respect to disability due to injuries suffered after June 30, 1972, and prior to July 1, 1973. The provisions of this section, as

Fla. Stats.

amended effective July 1, 1973, shall govern with respect to disability due to injuries suffered after June 30, 1973, and prior to January 1, 1975.

History: s. 12, ch. 17481, 1935; CGL 1936 Supp. 5966(12); s. 5, ch. 18413, 1937; s. 1, ch. 21824, 1943; ss. 1, 3, ch. 26876, 1951; s. 1, ch. 59-151; s. 1, ch. 67-239; s. 1, ch. 70-172; s. 1, ch. 72-198; ss. 3, 4, ch. 73-127; s. 7, ch. 74-197; ss. 3, 23, ch. 78-300; ss. 7, 124, ch. 79-40; s. 21, ch. 79-312; s. 3, ch. 80-236; ss. 9, 43, ch. 89-289; ss. 17, 56, ch. 90-201; ss. 15, 52, ch. 91-1; s. 109, ch. 97-103; s. 11, ch. 2001-91, effective Oct. 1, 2001; s. 23, ch. 2002-194, effective July 1, 2002.

§ 440.125. Medical Records and Reports; Identifying Information in Employee Medical Bills; Confidentiality.

Any medical records and medical reports of an injured employee and any information identifying an injured employee in medical bills which are provided to the department, pursuant to s. 440.13, are confidential and exempt from the provisions of s. 119.07(1) and s. 24(a), Art. I of the State Constitution, except as otherwise provided by this chapter. The department may share any such confidential and exempt records, reports, or information received pursuant to s. 440.13 with the Agency for Health Care Administration and the Department of Education in furtherance of their official duties under ss. 440.13 and 440.134. The agency and the department shall maintain the confidential and exempt status of such records, reports, and information received.

History: s. 1, ch. 93-421; s. 285, ch. 96-406; s. 24, ch. 2002-194, effective July 1, 2002.

§ 440.13. Medical Services and Supplies; Penalty for Violations; Limitations.

(1) Definitions.—As used in this section, the term:

(a) "Alternate medical care" means a change in treatment or health care provider.

(b) "Attendant care" means care rendered by trained professional attendants which is beyond the scope of household duties. Family members may provide nonprofessional attendant care, but may not be compensated under this chapter for care that falls within the scope of household duties and other services normally and gratuitously provided by family members. "Family member" means a spouse, father, mother, brother, sister, child, grandchild, father-in-law, mother-in-law, aunt, or uncle.

(c) "Carrier" means, for purposes of this section, insurance carrier, self-insurance fund or individually self-insured employer, or assessable mutual insurer.

(d) "Certified health care provider" means a health care provider who has been certified by the agency or who has entered an agreement with a licensed managed care organization to provide treatment to injured workers under this section. Certification of such health care provider must include documentation that the health care provider has read and is familiar with the portions of the statute, impairment guides, practice parameters, protocols of treatment, and rules which govern the provision of remedial treatment, care, and attendance.

(e) "Compensable" means a determination by a carrier or judge of compensation claims that a condition suffered by an employee results from an injury arising out of and in the course of employment.

(f) "Emergency services and care" means emergency services and care as defined in s. 395.002.

(g) "Health care facility" means any hospital licensed under chapter 395 and any health care institution licensed under chapter 400 or chapter 429.

(h) "Health care provider" means a physician or any recognized practitioner who provides skilled services pursuant to a prescription or under the supervision or direction of a physician and who has been certified by the agency as a health care provider. The term "health care provider" includes a health care facility.

(i) "Independent medical examiner" means a physician selected by either an employee or a carrier to render one or more independent medical examinations in connection with a dispute arising under this chapter.

(j) "Independent medical examination" means an objective evaluation of the injured employee's medical condition, including, but not limited to, impairment or work status, performed by a physician or an expert medical advisor at the request of a party, a judge of compensation claims, or the agency to assist in the resolution of a dispute arising under this chapter.

(k) "Instance of overutilization" means a specific inappropriate service or level of service provided to an injured employee that includes the provision of treatment in excess of established practice parameters and protocols of treatment established in accordance with this chapter.

(*l*) "Medically necessary" or "medical necessity" means any medical service or medical supply which is used to identify or treat an illness or injury, is appropriate to the patient's diagnosis and status of recovery, and is consistent with the location of service, the level of care provided, and applicable practice parameters. The service should be widely accepted among practicing health care providers, based on scientific criteria, and determined to be reasonably safe. The service must not be of an experimental, investigative, or research nature.

(m) "Medicine" means a drug prescribed by an authorized health care provider and includes only generic drugs or single-source patented drugs for which there is no generic equivalent, unless the authorized health care provider writes or states that the brand-name drug as defined in s. 465.025 is medically necessary, or is a drug appearing on the schedule of drugs created pursuant to s. 465.025(6), or is available at a cost lower than its generic equivalent.

(n) "Palliative care" means noncurative medical services that mitigate the conditions, effects, or pain of an injury.

(o) "Pattern or practice of overutilization" means repetition of instances of overutilization within a specific medical case or multiple cases by a single health care provider.

(p) "Peer review" means an evaluation by two or more physicians licensed under the same authority and with the same or similar specialty as the physician under review, of the appropriateness, quality, and cost of health care and health services provided to a patient, based on medically accepted standards.

(q) "Physician" or "doctor" means a physician licensed under chapter 458, an osteopathic physician licensed under chapter 459, a chiropractic physician licensed under chapter 460, a podiatric physician licensed under chapter 461, an optometrist licensed under chapter 463, or a dentist licensed under chapter 466, each of whom must be certified by the agency as a health care provider.

(r) "Reimbursement dispute" means any disagreement between a health care provider or health care facility and carrier concerning payment for medical treatment.

(s) "Utilization control" means a systematic process of implementing measures that assure overall management and cost containment of services delivered, including compliance with practice parameters and protocols of treatment as provided for in this chapter.

(t) "Utilization review" means the evaluation of the appropriateness of both the level and the quality of health care and health services provided to a patient, including, but not limited to, evaluation of the appropriateness of treatment, hospitalization, or office visits based on medically accepted standards. Such evaluation must be accomplished by means of a system that identifies the utilization of medical services based on practice parameters and protocols of treatment as provided for in this chapter.

(2) Medical Treatment; Duty of Employer to Furnish.—

(a) Subject to the limitations specified elsewhere in this chapter, the employer shall furnish to the employee such medically necessary remedial treatment, care, and attendance for such period as the nature of the injury or the process of recovery may require, which is in accordance with established practice parameters and protocols of treatment as provided for in this chapter, including medicines, medical supplies, durable medical equipment, orthoses, prostheses, and

Fla. Stats.

other medically necessary apparatus. Remedial treatment, care, and attendance, including work-hardening programs or pain-management programs accredited by the Commission on Accreditation of Rehabilitation Facilities or Joint Commission on the Accreditation of Health Organizations or pain-management programs affiliated with medical schools, shall be considered as covered treatment only when such care is given based on a referral by a physician as defined in this chapter. Medically necessary treatment, care, and attendance does not include chiropractic services in excess of 24 treatments or rendered 12 weeks beyond the date of the initial chiropractic treatment, whichever comes first, unless the carrier authorizes additional treatment or the employee is catastrophically injured.

(b) The employer shall provide appropriate professional or nonprofessional attendant care performed only at the direction and control of a physician when such care is medically necessary. The physician shall prescribe such care in writing. The employer or carrier shall not be responsible for such care until the prescription for attendant care is received by the employer and carrier, which shall specify the time periods for such care, the level of care required, and the type of assistance required. A prescription for attendant care shall not prescribe such care retroactively. The value of nonprofessional attendant care provided by a family member must be determined as follows:

1. If the family member is not employed or if the family member is employed and is providing attendant care services during hours that he or she is not engaged in employment, the per-hour value equals the federal minimum hourly wage.

2. If the family member is employed and elects to leave that employment to provide attendant or custodial care, the per-hour value of that care equals the per-hour value of the family member's former employment, not to exceed the per-hour value of such care available in the community at large. A family member or a combination of family members providing nonprofessional attendant care under this paragraph may not be compensated for more than a total of 12 hours per day.

3. If the family member remains employed while providing attendant or custodial care, the per-hour value of that care equals the per-hour value of the family member's employment, not to exceed the per-hour value of such care available in the community at large.

(c) If the employer fails to provide initial treatment or care required by this section after request by the injured employee, the employee may obtain such initial treatment at the expense of the employer, if the initial treatment or care is compensable and medically necessary and is in accordance with established practice parameters and protocols of treatment as provided for in this chapter. There must be a specific request for the initial treatment or care, and the employer or carrier must be given a reasonable time period within which to provide the initial treatment or care. However, the employee is not entitled to recover any amount personally expended for the initial treatment or care unless he or she has requested the employer to furnish that initial treatment or service and the employer has failed, refused, or neglected to do so within a reasonable time or unless the nature of the injury requires such initial treatment, nursing, and services and the employer or his or her superintendent or foreman, having knowledge of the injury, has neglected to provide the initial treatment or care.

(d) The carrier has the right to transfer the care of an injured employee from the attending health care provider if an independent medical examination determines that the employee is not making appropriate progress in recuperation.

(e) Except in emergency situations and for treatment rendered by a managed care arrangement, after any initial examination and diagnosis by a physician providing remedial treatment, care, and attendance, and before a proposed course of medical treatment begins, each insurer shall review, in accordance with the requirements of this chapter, the proposed course of treatment, to determine whether such treatment would be recognized as reasonably prudent. The review must be in accordance with all applicable workers' compensation practice parameters and protocols of treatment established in accordance with this chapter. The insurer must accept any such proposed course of treatment unless the insurer notifies the physician of its specific objections to the proposed course of treatment by the close of the tenth business day after notification by the physician, or a supervised designee of the physician, of the proposed course of treatment.

(f) Upon the written request of the employee, the carrier shall give the employee the opportunity for one change of physician during the course of treatment for any one accident. Upon the granting of a change of physician, the originally authorized physician in the same specialty as the changed physician shall become deauthorized upon written notification by the employer or carrier. The carrier shall authorize an alternative physician who shall not be professionally affiliated with the previous physician within 5 days after receipt of the request. If the carrier fails to provide a change of physician as requested by the employee, the employee may select the physician and such physician shall be considered authorized if the treatment being provided is compensable and medically necessary.

Failure of the carrier to timely comply with this subsection shall be a violation of this chapter and the carrier shall be subject to penalties as provided for in s. 440.525.

(3) Provider Eligibility; Authorization.—

(a) As a condition to eligibility for payment under this chapter, a health care provider who renders services must be a certified health care provider and must receive authorization from the carrier before providing treatment. This paragraph does not apply to emergency care. The agency shall adopt rules to implement the certification of health care providers.

(b) A health care provider who renders emergency care must notify the carrier by the close of the third business day after it has rendered such care. If the emergency care results in admission of the employee to a health care facility, the health care provider must notify the carrier by telephone within 24 hours after initial treatment. Emergency care is not compensable under this chapter unless the injury requiring emergency care arose as a result of a work-related accident. Pursuant to chapter 395, all licensed physicians and health care providers in this state shall be required to make their services available for emergency treatment of any employee eligible for workers' compensation benefits. To refuse to make such treatment available is cause for revocation of a license.

(c) A health care provider may not refer the employee to another health care provider, diagnostic facility, therapy center, or other facility without prior authorization from the carrier, except when emergency care is rendered. Any referral must be to a health care provider that has been certified by the agency, unless the referral is for emergency treatment, and the referral must be made in accordance with practice parameters and protocols of treatment as provided for in this chapter.

(d) A carrier must respond, by telephone or in writing, to a request for authorization from an authorized health care provider by the close of the third business day after receipt of the request. A carrier who fails to respond to a written request for authorization for referral for medical treatment by the close of the third business day after receipt of the request consents to the medical necessity for such treatment. All such requests must be made to the carrier. Notice to the carrier does not include notice to the employer.

(e) Carriers shall adopt procedures for receiving, reviewing, documenting, and responding to requests for authorization. Such procedures shall be for a health care provider certified under this section.

(f) By accepting payment under this chapter for treatment rendered to an injured employee, a health care provider consents to the jurisdiction of the agency as set forth in subsection (11) and to the submission of all records and other information concerning such treatment to the agency in connection with a reimbursement dispute, audit, or review as provided by this section. The health care provider must further agree to comply with any decision of the agency rendered under this section.

(g) The employee is not liable for payment

for medical treatment or services provided pursuant to this section except as otherwise provided in this section.

(h) The provisions of s. 456.053 are applicable to referrals among health care providers, as defined in subsection (1), treating injured workers.

(i) Notwithstanding paragraph (d), a claim for specialist consultations, surgical operations, physiotherapeutic or occupational therapy procedures, X-ray examinations, or special diagnostic laboratory tests that cost more than $1,000 and other specialty services that the agency identifies by rule is not valid and reimbursable unless the services have been expressly authorized by the carrier, or unless the carrier has failed to respond within 10 days to a written request for authorization, or unless emergency care is required. The insurer shall authorize such consultation or procedure unless the health care provider or facility is not authorized or certified, unless such treatment is not in accordance with practice parameters and protocols of treatment established in this chapter, or unless a judge of compensation claims has determined that the consultation or procedure is not medically necessary, not in accordance with the practice parameters and protocols of treatment established in this chapter, or otherwise not compensable under this chapter. Authorization of a treatment plan does not constitute express authorization for purposes of this section, except to the extent the carrier provides otherwise in its authorization procedures. This paragraph does not limit the carrier's obligation to identify and disallow overutilization or billing errors.

(j) Notwithstanding anything in this chapter to the contrary, a sick or injured employee shall be entitled, at all times, to free, full, and absolute choice in the selection of the pharmacy or pharmacist dispensing and filling prescriptions for medicines required under this chapter. It is expressly forbidden for the agency, an employer, or a carrier, or any agent or representative of the agency, an employer, or a carrier to select the pharmacy or pharmacist which the sick or injured employee must use; condition coverage or payment on the basis of the pharmacy or pharmacist utilized; or to otherwise interfere in the selection by the sick or injured employee of a pharmacy or pharmacist.

(4) Notice of Treatment to Carrier; Filing With Department.—

(a) Any health care provider providing necessary remedial treatment, care, or attendance to any injured worker shall submit treatment reports to the carrier in a format prescribed by the department. A claim for medical or surgical treatment is not valid or enforceable against such employer or employee, unless, by the close of the third business day following the first treatment, the physician providing the treatment furnishes to the employer or carrier a preliminary notice of the injury and treatment in a format prescribed by the department and, within 15 days thereafter, furnishes to the employer or carrier a complete report, and subsequent thereto furnishes progress reports, if requested by the employer or insurance carrier, at intervals of not less than 3 weeks apart or at less frequent intervals if requested in a format prescribed by the department.

(b) Upon the request of the department, each medical report or bill obtained or received by the employer, the carrier, or the injured employee, or the attorney for the employer, carrier, or injured employee, with respect to the remedial treatment, care, and attendance of the injured employee, including any report of an examination, diagnosis, or disability evaluation, must be produced by the health care provider to the department pursuant to rules adopted by the department. The health care provider shall also furnish to the injured employee or his or her attorney and the employer or carrier or its attorney, on demand, a copy of his or her office chart, records, and reports, and may charge the injured employee no more than 50 cents per page for copying the records and the actual direct cost to the health care provider or health care facility for X rays, microfilm, or other nonpaper records. Each such health care provider shall provide to the department information about the remedial treatment, care, and attendance which the department reasonably requests.

(c) It is the policy for the administration of

the workers' compensation system that there shall be reasonable access to medical information by all parties to facilitate the self-executing features of the law. An employee who reports an injury or illness alleged to be work-related waives any physician-patient privilege with respect to any condition or complaint reasonably related to the condition for which the employee claims compensation. Notwithstanding the limitations in s. 456.057 and subject to the limitations in s. 381.004, upon the request of the employer, the carrier, an authorized qualified rehabilitation provider, or the attorney for the employer or carrier, the medical records, reports, and information of an injured employee relevant to the particular injury or illness for which compensation is sought must be furnished to those persons and the medical condition of the injured employee must be discussed with those persons, if the records and the discussions are restricted to conditions relating to the workplace injury. Release of medical information by the health care provider or other physician does not require the authorization of the injured employee. If medical records, reports, and information of an injured employee are sought from health care providers who are not subject to the jurisdiction of the state, the injured employee shall sign an authorization allowing for the employer or carrier to obtain the medical records, reports, or information. Any such discussions or release of information may be held before or after the filing of a claim or petition for benefits without the knowledge, consent, or presence of any other party or his or her agent or representative. A health care provider who willfully refuses to provide medical records or to discuss the medical condition of the injured employee, after a reasonable request is made for such information pursuant to this subsection, shall be subject by the department to one or more of the penalties set forth in paragraph (8)(b). The department may adopt rules to carry out this subsection.

(5) Independent Medical Examinations.—

(a) In any dispute concerning overutilization, medical benefits, compensability, or disability under this chapter, the carrier or the employee may select an independent medical examiner. If the parties agree, the examiner may be a health care provider treating or providing other care to the employee. An independent medical examiner may not render an opinion outside his or her area of expertise, as demonstrated by licensure and applicable practice parameters. The employer and employee shall be entitled to only one independent medical examination per accident and not one independent medical examination per medical specialty. The party requesting and selecting the independent medical examination shall be responsible for all expenses associated with said examination, including, but not limited to, medically necessary diagnostic testing performed and physician or medical care provider fees for the evaluation. The party selecting the independent medical examination shall identify the choice of the independent medical examiner to all other parties within 15 days after the date the independent medical examination is to take place. Failure to timely provide such notification shall preclude the requesting party from submitting the findings of such independent medical examiner in a proceeding before a judge of compensation claims. The independent medical examiner may not provide followup care if such recommendation for care is found to be medically necessary. If the employee prevails in a medical dispute as determined in an order by a judge of compensation claims or if benefits are paid or treatment provided after the employee has obtained an independent medical examination based upon the examiner's findings, the costs of such examination shall be paid by the employer or carrier.

(b) Each party is bound by his or her selection of an independent medical examiner, including the selection of the independent medical examiner in accordance with s. 440.134 and the opinions of such independent medical examiner. Each party is entitled to an alternate examiner only if:

1. The examiner is not qualified to render an opinion upon an aspect of the employee's illness or injury which is material to the claim or petition for benefits;

2. The examiner ceases to practice in the specialty relevant to the employee's condition;

Fla. Stats.

3. The examiner is unavailable due to injury, death, or relocation outside a reasonably accessible geographic area; or

4. The parties agree to an alternate examiner.

(c) The carrier may, at its election, contact the claimant directly to schedule a reasonable time for an independent medical examination. The carrier must confirm the scheduling agreement in writing with the claimant and the claimant's counsel, if any, at least 7 days before the date upon which the independent medical examination is scheduled to occur. An attorney representing a claimant is not authorized to schedule the self-insured employer's or carrier's independent medical evaluations under this subsection. Neither the self-insured employer nor the carrier shall be responsible for scheduling any independent medical examination other than an employer or carrier independent medical examination.

(d) If the employee fails to appear for the independent medical examination scheduled by the employer or carrier without good cause and fails to advise the physician at least 24 hours before the scheduled date for the examination that he or she cannot appear, the employee is barred from recovering compensation for any period during which he or she has refused to submit to such examination. Further, the employee shall reimburse the employer or carrier 50 percent of the physician's cancellation or no-show fee unless the employer or carrier that schedules the examination fails to timely provide to the employee a written confirmation of the date of the examination pursuant to paragraph (c) which includes an explanation of why he or she failed to appear. The employee may appeal to a judge of compensation claims for reimbursement when the employer or carrier withholds payment in excess of the authority granted by this section.

(e) No medical opinion other than the opinion of a medical advisor appointed by the judge of compensation claims or the department, an independent medical examiner, or an authorized treating provider is admissible in proceedings before the judges of compensation claims.

(f) Attorney's fees incurred by an injured employee in connection with delay of or opposition to an independent medical examination, including, but not limited to, motions for protective orders, are not recoverable under this chapter.

(g) When a medical dispute arises, the parties may mutually agree to refer the employee to a licensed physician specializing in the diagnosis and treatment of the medical condition at issue for an independent medical examination and report. Such medical examination shall be referred to as a "consensus independent medical examination." The findings and conclusions of such mutually agreed upon consensus independent medical examination shall be binding on the parties and shall constitute resolution of the medical dispute addressed in the independent consensus medical examination and in any proceeding. Agreement by the parties to a consensus independent medical examination shall not affect the employer's, carrier's, or employee's entitlement to one independent medical examination per accident as provided for in this subsection.

(6) Utilization Review.—Carriers shall review all bills, invoices, and other claims for payment submitted by health care providers in order to identify overutilization and billing errors, including compliance with practice parameters and protocols of treatment established in accordance with this chapter, and may hire peer review consultants or conduct independent medical evaluations. Such consultants, including peer review organizations, are immune from liability in the execution of their functions under this subsection to the extent provided in s. 766.101. If a carrier finds that overutilization of medical services or a billing error has occurred, or there is a violation of the practice parameters and protocols of treatment established in accordance with this chapter, it must disallow or adjust payment for such services or error without order of a judge of compensation claims or the agency, if the carrier, in making its determination, has complied with this section and rules adopted by the agency.

(7) Utilization and Reimbursement Disputes.—

(a) Any health care provider, carrier, or employer who elects to contest the disallowance or adjustment of payment by a carrier under subsection (6) must, within 30 days after receipt of notice of disallowance or adjustment of payment, petition the agency to resolve the dispute. The petitioner must serve a copy of the petition on the carrier and on all affected parties by certified mail. The petition must be accompanied by all documents and records that support the allegations contained in the petition. Failure of a petitioner to submit such documentation to the agency results in dismissal of the petition.

(b) The carrier must submit to the agency within 10 days after receipt of the petition all documentation substantiating the carrier's disallowance or adjustment. Failure of the carrier to timely submit the requested documentation to the agency within 10 days constitutes a waiver of all objections to the petition.

(c) Within 60 days after receipt of all documentation, the agency must provide to the petitioner, the carrier, and the affected parties a written determination of whether the carrier properly adjusted or disallowed payment. The agency must be guided by standards and policies set forth in this chapter, including all applicable reimbursement schedules, practice parameters, and protocols of treatment, in rendering its determination.

(d) If the agency finds an improper disallowance or improper adjustment of payment by an insurer, the insurer shall reimburse the health care provider, facility, insurer, or employer within 30 days, subject to the penalties provided in this subsection.

(e) The agency shall adopt rules to carry out this subsection. The rules may include provisions for consolidating petitions filed by a petitioner and expanding the timetable for rendering a determination upon a consolidated petition.

(f) Any carrier that engages in a pattern or practice of arbitrarily or unreasonably disallowing or reducing payments to health care providers may be subject to one or more of the following penalties imposed by the agency:

1. Repayment of the appropriate amount to the health care provider.

2. An administrative fine assessed by the agency in an amount not to exceed $5,000 per instance of improperly disallowing or reducing payments.

3. Award of the health care provider's costs, including a reasonable attorney's fee, for prosecuting the petition.

(8) Pattern or Practice of Overutilization.—

(a) Carriers must report to the agency all instances of overutilization including, but not limited to, all instances in which the carrier disallows or adjusts payment or a determination has been made that the provided or recommended treatment is in excess of the practice parameters and protocols of treatment established in this chapter. The agency shall determine whether a pattern or practice of overutilization exists.

(b) If the agency determines that a health care provider has engaged in a pattern or practice of overutilization or a violation of this chapter or rules adopted by the agency, including a pattern or practice of providing treatment in excess of the practice parameters or protocols of treatment, it may impose one or more of the following penalties:

1. An order of the agency barring the provider from payment under this chapter;

2. Deauthorization of care under review;

3. Denial of payment for care rendered in the future;

4. Decertification of a health care provider certified as an expert medical advisor under subsection (9) or of a rehabilitation provider certified under[1] s. 440.49;

5. An administrative fine assessed by the agency in an amount not to exceed $5,000 per instance of overutilization or violation; and

6. Notification of and review by the appropriate licensing authority pursuant to s. 440.106(3).

(9) Expert Medical Advisors.—

Fla. Stats.

(a) The agency shall certify expert medical advisors in each specialty to assist the agency and the judges of compensation claims within the advisor's area of expertise as provided in this section. The agency shall, in a manner prescribed by rule, in certifying, recertifying, or decertifying an expert medical advisor, consider the qualifications, training, impartiality, and commitment of the health care provider to the provision of quality medical care at a reasonable cost. As a prerequisite for certification or recertification, the agency shall require, at a minimum, that an expert medical advisor have specialized workers' compensation training or experience under the workers' compensation system of this state and board certification or board eligibility.

(b) The agency shall contract with one or more entities that employ, contract with, or otherwise secure expert medical advisors to provide peer review or expert medical consultation, opinions, and testimony to the agency or to a judge of compensation claims in connection with resolving disputes relating to reimbursement, differing opinions of health care providers, and health care and physician services rendered under this chapter, including utilization issues. The agency shall by rule establish the qualifications of expert medical advisors, including training and experience in the workers' compensation system in the state and the expert medical advisor's knowledge of and commitment to the standards of care, practice parameters, and protocols established pursuant to this chapter. Expert medical advisors contracting with the agency shall, as a term of such contract, agree to provide consultation or services in accordance with the timetables set forth in this chapter and to abide by rules adopted by the agency, including, but not limited to, rules pertaining to procedures for review of the services rendered by health care providers and preparation of reports and testimony or recommendations for submission to the agency or the judge of compensation claims.

(c) If there is disagreement in the opinions of the health care providers, if two health care providers disagree on medical evidence supporting the employee's complaints or the need for additional medical treatment, or if two health care providers disagree that the employee is able to return to work, the agency may, and the judge of compensation claims shall, upon his or her own motion or within 15 days after receipt of a written request by either the injured employee, the employer, or the carrier, order the injured employee to be evaluated by an expert medical advisor. The opinion of the expert medical advisor is presumed to be correct unless there is clear and convincing evidence to the contrary as determined by the judge of compensation claims. The expert medical advisor appointed to conduct the evaluation shall have free and complete access to the medical records of the employee. An employee who fails to report to and cooperate with such evaluation forfeits entitlement to compensation during the period of failure to report or cooperate.

(d) The expert medical advisor must complete his or her evaluation and issue his or her report to the agency or to the judge of compensation claims within 15 days after receipt of all medical records. The expert medical advisor must furnish a copy of the report to the carrier and to the employee.

(e) An expert medical advisor is not liable under any theory of recovery for evaluations performed under this section without a showing of fraud or malice. The protections of s. 766.101 apply to any officer, employee, or agent of the agency and to any officer, employee, or agent of any entity with which the agency has contracted under this subsection.

(f) If the agency or a judge of compensation claims orders the services of a certified expert medical advisor to resolve a dispute under this section, the party requesting such examination must compensate the advisor for his or her time in accordance with a schedule adopted by the agency. If the employee prevails in a dispute as determined in an order by a judge of compensation claims based upon the expert medical advisor's findings, the employer or carrier shall pay for the costs of such expert medical advisor. If a judge of compensation claims, upon his or her motion, finds that an expert medical advisor is needed to resolve the dispute, the carrier must compensate the advisor for his or her time in accordance with a schedule adopted by the agency. The agency may assess a penalty not to exceed $500 against any carrier that fails to timely compensate an advisor in accordance with this section.

(10) Witness Fees.—Any health care provider who gives a deposition shall be allowed a witness fee. The amount charged by the witness may not exceed $200 per hour. An expert witness who has never provided direct professional services to a party but has merely reviewed medical records and provided an expert opinion or has provided only direct professional services that were unrelated to the workers' compensation case may not be allowed a witness fee in excess of $200 per day.

(11) Audits.—

(a) The Agency for Health Care Administration may investigate health care providers to determine whether providers are complying with this chapter and with rules adopted by the agency, whether the providers are engaging in overutilization, whether providers are engaging in improper billing practices, and whether providers are adhering to practice parameters and protocols established in accordance with this chapter. If the agency finds that a health care provider has improperly billed, overutilized, or failed to comply with agency rules or the requirements of this chapter, including, but not limited to, practice parameters and protocols established in accordance with this chapter, it must notify the provider of its findings and may determine that the health care provider may not receive payment from the carrier or may impose penalties as set forth in subsection (8) or other sections of this chapter. If the health care provider has received payment from a carrier for services that were improperly billed, that constitute overutilization, or that were outside practice parameters or protocols established in accordance with this chapter, it must return those payments to the carrier. The agency may assess a penalty not to exceed $500 for each overpayment that is not refunded within 30 days after notification of overpayment by the agency or carrier.

(b) The department shall monitor carriers as provided in this chapter and the Office of Insurance Regulation shall audit insurers and group self-insurance funds as provided in s. 624.3161, to determine if medical bills are paid in accordance with this section and rules of the department and Financial Services Commission, respectively. Any employer, if self-insured, or carrier found by the[2] department or office of Insurance Regulation not to be within 90 percent compliance as to the payment of medical bills after July 1, 1994, must be assessed a fine not to exceed 1 percent of the prior year's assessment levied against such entity under s. 440.51 for every quarter in which the entity fails to attain 95-percent compliance. The department shall fine or otherwise discipline an employer or carrier, pursuant to this chapter, or rules adopted by the department, and the Office of Insurance Regulation shall fine or otherwise discipline an insurer or group self-insurance fund pursuant to the insurance code or rules adopted by the Financial Services Commission, for each late payment of compensation that is below the minimum 95-percent performance standard. Any carrier that is found to be not in compliance in subsequent consecutive quarters must implement a medical-bill review program approved by the[2] department or office, and an insurer or group self-insurance fund is subject to disciplinary action by the Office of Insurance Regulation.

(c) The agency has exclusive jurisdiction to decide any matters concerning reimbursement, to resolve any overutilization dispute under subsection (7), and to decide any question concerning overutilization under subsection (8), which question or dispute arises after January 1, 1994.

(d) The following agency actions do not constitute agency action subject to review under ss. 120.569 and 120.57 and do not constitute actions subject to s. 120.56: referral by the entity responsible for utilization review; a decision by the agency to refer a matter to a peer review committee; establishment by a health care provider or entity of procedures by which a peer review committee reviews the rendering of health care services; and the review proceedings, report, and recommendation of the peer review committee.

(12) Creation of Three-Member Panel; Guides of Maximum Reimbursement Allowances.—

(a) A three-member panel is created, consisting of the Chief Financial Officer, or the Chief Financial Officer's designee, and two members to be appointed by the Governor, subject to confirmation by the Senate, one member who, on account of present or previous vocation, employment, or affiliation, shall be classified as a representative of employers, the other member who, on account of previous vocation, employment, or affiliation, shall be classified as a representative of employees. The panel shall determine statewide schedules of maximum reimbursement allowances for medically necessary treatment, care, and attendance provided by physicians, hospitals, ambulatory surgical centers, work-hardening programs, pain programs, and durable medical equipment. The maximum reimbursement allowances for inpatient hospital care shall be based on a schedule of per diem rates, to be approved by the three-member panel no later than March 1, 1994, to be used in conjunction with a precertification manual as determined by the department, including maximum hours in which an outpatient may remain in observation status, which shall not exceed 23 hours. All compensable charges for hospital outpatient care shall be reimbursed at 75 percent of usual and customary charges, except as otherwise provided by this subsection. Annually, the three-member panel shall adopt schedules of maximum reimbursement allowances for physicians, hospital inpatient care, hospital outpatient care, ambulatory surgical centers, work-hardening programs, and pain programs. An individual physician, hospital, ambulatory surgical center, pain program, or work-hardening program shall be reimbursed either the agreed-upon contract price or the maximum reimbursement allowance in the appropriate schedule.

(b) It is the intent of the Legislature to increase the schedule of maximum reimbursement allowances for selected physicians effective January 1, 2004, and to pay for the increases through reductions in payments to hospitals. Revisions developed pursuant to this subsection are limited to the following:

1. Payments for outpatient physical, occupational, and speech therapy provided by hospitals shall be reduced to the schedule of maximum reimbursement allowances for these services which applies to nonhospital providers.

2. Payments for scheduled outpatient nonemergency radiological and clinical laboratory services that are not provided in conjunction with a surgical procedure shall be reduced to the schedule of maximum reimbursement allowances for these services which applies to nonhospital providers.

3. Outpatient reimbursement for scheduled surgeries shall be reduced from 75 percent of charges to 60 percent of charges.

4. Maximum reimbursement for a physician licensed under chapter 458 or chapter 459 shall be increased to 110 percent of the reimbursement allowed by Medicare, using appropriate codes and modifiers or the medical reimbursement level adopted by the three-member panel as of January 1, 2003, whichever is greater.

5. Maximum reimbursement for surgical procedures shall be increased to 140 percent of the reimbursement allowed by Medicare or the medical reimbursement level adopted by the three-member panel as of January 1, 2003, whichever is greater.

(c) As to reimbursement for a prescription medication, the reimbursement amount for a prescription shall be the average wholesale price plus $4.18 for the dispensing fee, except where the carrier has contracted for a lower amount. Fees for pharmaceuticals and pharmaceutical services shall be reimbursable at the applicable fee schedule amount. Where the employer or carrier has contracted for such services and the employee elects to obtain them through a provider not a party to the contract, the carrier shall reimburse at the schedule, negotiated, or contract price, whichever is lower. No such contract shall rely on a provider that is not reasonably accessible to the employee.

(d) Reimbursement for all fees and other charges for such treatment, care, and attendance, including treatment, care, and attendance provided by any hospital or other health care provider, ambulatory surgical center, work-hardening program, or pain program, must not exceed the amounts provided by the uniform schedule of maximum reimbursement allowances as determined by the panel or as otherwise provided in this section. This subsection also applies to independent medical examinations performed by health care providers under this chapter. In determining the uniform schedule, the panel shall first approve the data which it finds representative of prevailing charges in the state for similar treatment, care, and attendance of injured persons. Each health care provider, health care facility, ambulatory surgical center, work-hardening program, or pain program receiving workers' compensation payments shall maintain records verifying their usual charges. In establishing the uniform schedule of maximum reimbursement allowances, the panel must consider:

1. The levels of reimbursement for similar treatment, care, and attendance made by other health care programs or third-party providers;

2. The impact upon cost to employers for providing a level of reimbursement for treatment, care, and attendance which will ensure the availability of treatment, care, and attendance required by injured workers;

3. The financial impact of the reimbursement allowances upon health care providers and health care facilities, including trauma centers as defined in s. 395.4001, and its effect upon their ability to make available to injured workers such medically necessary remedial treatment, care, and attendance. The uniform schedule of maximum reimbursement allowances must be reasonable, must promote health care cost containment and efficiency with respect to the workers' compensation health care delivery system, and must be sufficient to ensure availability of such medically necessary remedial treatment, care, and attendance to injured workers; and

4. The most recent average maximum allowable rate of increase for hospitals determined by the Health Care Board under chapter 408.

(e) In addition to establishing the uniform schedule of maximum reimbursement allowances, the panel shall:

1. Take testimony, receive records, and collect data to evaluate the adequacy of the workers' compensation fee schedule, nationally recognized fee schedules and alternative methods of reimbursement to certified health care providers and health care facilities for inpatient and outpatient treatment and care.

2. Survey certified health care providers and health care facilities to determine the availability and accessibility of workers' compensation health care delivery systems for injured workers.

3. Survey carriers to determine the estimated impact on carrier costs and workers' compensation premium rates by implementing changes to the carrier reimbursement schedule or implementing alternative reimbursement methods.

4. Submit recommendations on or before January 1, 2003, and biennially thereafter, to the President of the Senate and the Speaker of the House of Representatives on methods to improve the workers' compensation health care delivery system.

The agency and the department, as requested, shall provide data to the panel, including but not limited to, utilization trends in the workers' compensation health care delivery system. The department shall provide the panel with an annual report regarding the resolution of medical reimbursement disputes and any actions pursuant to s. 440.13(8). The agency shall provide administrative support and service to the panel to the extent requested by the panel.

(13) Removal of Physicians from Lists of Those Authorized to Render Medical Care.—The agency shall remove from the list of physicians or facilities authorized to provide remedial treatment, care, and attendance under this chapter the name of any physician or facility found after reasonable investigation to have:

(a) Engaged in professional or other misconduct or incompetency in connection with medical services rendered under this chapter;

(b) Exceeded the limits of his or her or its professional competence in rendering medical care under this chapter, or to have made mate-

Fla. Stats.

rially false statements regarding his or her or its qualifications in his or her application;

(c) Failed to transmit copies of medical reports to the employer or carrier, or failed to submit full and truthful medical reports of all his or her or its findings to the employer or carrier as required under this chapter;

(d) Solicited, or employed another to solicit for himself or herself or itself or for another, professional treatment, examination, or care of an injured employee in connection with any claim under this chapter;

(e) Refused to appear before, or to answer upon request of, the agency or any duly authorized officer of the state, any legal question, or to produce any relevant book or paper concerning his or her conduct under any authorization granted to him or her under this chapter;

(f) Self-referred in violation of this chapter or other laws of this state; or

(g) Engaged in a pattern of practice of overutilization or a violation of this chapter or rules adopted by the agency, including failure to adhere to practice parameters and protocols established in accordance with this chapter.

(14) Payment of Medical Fees.—

(a) Except for emergency care treatment, fees for medical services are payable only to a health care provider certified and authorized to render remedial treatment, care, or attendance under this chapter. Carriers shall pay, disallow, or deny payment to health care providers in the manner and at times set forth in this chapter. A health care provider may not collect or receive a fee from an injured employee within this state, except as otherwise provided by this chapter. Such providers have recourse against the employer or carrier for payment for services rendered in accordance with this chapter. Payment to health care providers or physicians shall be subject to the medical fee schedule and applicable practice parameters and protocols, regardless of whether the health care provider or claimant is asserting that the payment should be made.

(b) Fees charged for remedial treatment, care, and attendance, except for independent medical examinations and consensus independent medical examinations, may not exceed the applicable fee schedules adopted under this chapter and department rule. Notwithstanding any other provision in this chapter, if a physician or health care provider specifically agrees in writing to follow identified procedures aimed at providing quality medical care to injured workers at reasonable costs, deviations from established fee schedules shall be permitted. Written agreements warranting deviations may include, but are not limited to, the timely scheduling of appointments for injured workers, participating in return-to-work programs with injured workers' employers, expediting the reporting of treatments provided to injured workers, and agreeing to continuing education, utilization review, quality assurance, precertification, and case management systems that are designed to provide needed treatment for injured workers.

(c) Notwithstanding any other provision of this chapter, following overall maximum medical improvement from an injury compensable under this chapter, the employee is obligated to pay a copayment of $10 per visit for medical services. The copayment shall not apply to emergency care provided to the employee.

(15) Practice Parameters.—The practice parameters and protocols mandated under this chapter shall be the practice parameters and protocols adopted by the United States Agency for Healthcare Research and Quality in effect on January 1, 2003.

(16) Standards of Care.—The following standards of care shall be followed in providing medical care under this chapter:

(a) Abnormal anatomical findings alone, in the absence of objective relevant medical findings, shall not be an indicator of injury or illness, a justification for the provision of remedial medical care or the assignment of restrictions, or a foundation for limitations.

(b) At all times during evaluation and treatment, the provider shall act on the premise that returning to work is an integral part of the treatment plan. The goal of removing all restrictions and limitations as early as appropriate shall be part of the treatment plan on a continuous basis. The assignment of restrictions and limitations shall be reviewed with each patient exam and upon receipt of new information, such as progress reports from physical therapists and other providers. Consideration shall be given to upgrading or removing the restrictions and limitations with each patient exam, based upon the presence or absence of objective relevant medical findings.

(c) Reasonable necessary medical care of injured employees shall in all situations:

1. Utilize a high intensity, short duration treatment approach that focuses on early activation and restoration of function whenever possible.

2. Include reassessment of the treatment plans, regimes, therapies, prescriptions, and functional limitations or restrictions prescribed by the provider every 30 days.

3. Be focused on treatment of the individual employee's specific clinical dysfunction or status and shall not be based upon nondescript diagnostic labels.

All treatment shall be inherently scientifically logical and the evaluation or treatment procedure must match the documented physiologic and clinical problem. Treatment shall match the type, intensity, and duration of service required by the problem identified.

(17) Failure to comply with this section shall be considered a violation of this chapter and is subject to penalties as provided for in s. 440.525.

History: s. 13, ch. 17481, 1935; CGL 1936 Supp. 5966(13); s. 6, ch. 18413, 1937; CGL 1940 Supp. 8135(14-a); s. 2, ch. 20672, 1941; s. 2, ch. 21824, 1943; s. 1, ch. 22814, 1945; s. 1, ch. 25244, 1949; s. 1, ch. 28241, 1953; s. 2, ch. 57-225; ss. 1, 2, ch. 63-91; ss. 17, 35, ch. 69-106; s. 363, ch. 71-136; s. 5, ch. 75-209; s. 3, ch. 77-290; ss. 4, 23, ch. 78-300; s. 16, ch. 79-7; ss. 8, 124, ch. 79-40; ss. 7, 21, ch. 79-312; s. 4, ch. 80-236; s. 1, ch. 82-46; s. 1, ch. 83-45; s. 1, ch. 83-303; s. 4, ch. 83-305; s. 1, ch. 86-171; s. 1, ch. 87-111; s. 2, ch. 87-330; s. 2, ch. 88-203; s. 1, ch. 88-372; ss. 10, 43, ch. 89-289; ss. 18, 56, ch. 90-201; ss. 16, 52, ch. 91-1; s. 3, ch. 91-269; s. 101, ch. 92-33; s. 81, ch. 92-289; s. 17, ch. 93-415; s. 199, ch. 96-410; s. 1051, ch. 97-103; s. 45, ch. 97-264; s. 36, ch. 98-89; ss. 33, 188, 259, ch. 98-166; s. 22, ch. 2000-160; s. 9, ch. 2000-189; s. 12, ch. 2001-91, effective Oct. 1, 2001; s. 25, ch. 2002-194, effective July 1, 2002; s. 9, ch. 2002-236, effective July 1, 2002; s. 15, ch. 2003-412, effective Oct. 1, 2003; s. 477, ch. 2003-261, effective June 26, 2003; s. 91, ch. 2006-197, effective July 1, 2006.

[1]**2003 Note:** Section 440.49(1), relating to rehabilitation, was repealed by s. 43, ch. 93-415.

[2]**Note:** —The Division of Workers' Compensation of the Department of Labor and Employment Security was transferred to the Department of Insurance by s. 1, ch. 2002-194, and substitutions of other entities for the division were made for most existing references to the division by that law.

§ 440.132. Investigatory Records Relating to Workers' Compensation Managed Care Arrangements; Confidentiality.

All investigatory records of the Agency for Health Care Administration made or received pursuant to s. 440.134 and any examination records necessary to complete an investigation are confidential and exempt from the provisions of s. 119.07(1) and s. 24(a), Art. I of the State Constitution until the investigation is completed or ceases to be active, except that portions of medical records which specifically identify patients must remain confidential and exempt. An investigation is considered "active" while such investigation is being conducted by the agency with a reasonable, good faith belief that it may lead to the filing of administrative, civil, or criminal proceedings. An investigation does not cease to be active if the agency is proceeding with reasonable dispatch and there is good faith belief that action may be initiated by the agency or other administrative or law enforcement agency.

History: ss. 1, 2, ch. 93-419; s. 286, ch. 96-406; s. 54, ch. 2004-335, effective Oct. 1, 2004.

§ 440.134. Workers' Compensation Managed Care Arrangement.

(1) As used in this section, the term:

(a) "Agency" means the Agency for Health Care Administration.

Fla. Stats.

(b) "Complaint" means any dissatisfaction expressed by an injured worker concerning an insurer's workers' compensation managed care arrangement.

(c) "Emergency care" means medical services as defined in chapter 395.

(d) "Grievance" means a written complaint, other than a petition for benefits, filed by the injured worker pursuant to the requirements of the managed care arrangement, expressing dissatisfaction with the insurer's workers' compensation managed care arrangement's refusal to provide medical care or the medical care provided.

(e) "Insurer" means an insurance carrier, self-insurance fund, assessable mutual insurer, or individually self-insured employer.

(f) "Service area" means the agency-approved geographic area within which an insurer is authorized to offer a workers' compensation managed care arrangement.

(g) "Workers' compensation managed care arrangement" means an arrangement under which a provider of health care, a health care facility, a group of providers of health care, a group of providers of health care and health care facilities, an insurer that has an exclusive provider organization approved under s. 627.6472 or a health maintenance organization licensed under part I of chapter 641 has entered into a written agreement directly or indirectly with an insurer to provide and to manage appropriate remedial treatment, care, and attendance to injured workers in accordance with this chapter.

(h) "Capitated contract" means a contract in which an insurer pays directly or indirectly a fixed amount to a health care provider in exchange for the future rendering of medical services for covered expenses.

(i) "Medical care coordinator" means a primary care provider within a provider network who is responsible for managing the medical care of an injured worker including determining other health care providers and health care facilities to which the injured employee will be referred for evaluation or treatment. A medical care coordinator shall be a physician licensed under chapter 458, an osteopathic physician licensed under chapter 459, a chiropractic physician licensed under chapter 460, or a podiatric physician licensed under chapter 461.

(j) "Provider network" means a comprehensive panel of health care providers and health care facilities who have contracted directly or indirectly with an insurer to provide appropriate remedial treatment, care, and attendance to injured workers in accordance with this chapter.

(k) "Primary care provider" means, except in the case of emergency treatment, the initial treating physician and, when appropriate, continuing treating physician, who may be a family practitioner, general practitioner, or internist physician licensed under chapter 458; a family practitioner, general practitioner, or internist osteopathic physician licensed under chapter 459; a chiropractic physician licensed under chapter 460; a podiatric physician licensed under chapter 461; an optometrist licensed under chapter 463; or a dentist licensed under chapter 466.

(2)

(a) The self-insured employer or carrier may, subject to the terms and limitations specified elsewhere in this section and chapter, furnish to the employee solely through managed care arrangements such medically necessary remedial treatment, care, and attendance for such period as the nature of the injury or the process of recovery requires and which shall be in accordance with practice parameters and protocols established pursuant to this chapter. For any self-insured employer or carrier who elects to deliver the medical benefits required by this chapter through a method other than a workers' compensation managed care arrangement, the discontinuance of the use of the workers' compensation managed care arrangement shall be without regard to the date of the accident, notwithstanding any other provision of law or rule.

(b) The agency shall authorize an insurer to offer or utilize a workers' compensation managed care arrangement after the insurer files a completed application along with the payment of a $1,000 application fee, and upon the agency's being satisfied that the applicant has the ability to provide quality of care consistent with the prevailing professional standards of care and the insurer and its workers' compensation managed care arrangement otherwise meets the requirements of this section. No insurer may offer or utilize a managed care arrangement without such authorization. The authorization, unless sooner suspended or revoked, shall automatically expire 2 years after the date of issuance unless renewed by the insurer. The authorization shall be renewed upon application for renewal and payment of a renewal fee of $1,000, provided that the insurer is in compliance with the requirements of this section and any rules adopted hereunder. An application for renewal of the authorization shall be made 90 days prior to expiration of the authorization, on forms provided by the agency. The renewal application shall not require the resubmission of any documents previously filed with the agency if such documents have remained valid and unchanged since their original filing.

(3) An insurer may not directly or indirectly enter into a capitated contract with any person who is not a health care provider, a health care facility, a health maintenance organization licensed under part I of chapter 641, or a health insurer that has an exclusive provider organization approved under s. 627.6472. A capitated contract must provide that the capitated amount for rendering of covered medical services be paid directly to the person who has contracted with the insurer. Such contracts excluding the capitated amount must be filed with the agency for approval prior to use.

(4) An insurer may not offer or utilize a workers' compensation managed care arrangement in this state until its managed care plan of operation has been approved by the agency and the insurer is authorized by the agency to offer or utilize a workers' compensation managed care arrangement.

(5) An insurer must file a proposed managed care plan of operation with the agency in a format prescribed by the agency. The plan of operation must contain evidence that all covered services are available and accessible, including a demonstration that:

(a) Such services can be provided with reasonable promptness with respect to geographic location, hours of operation, and after-hour care. The hours of operation and availability of after-hour care must reflect usual practice in the local area. Geographic availability must reflect the usual travel times within the community.

(b) Unless the agency determines that insufficient numbers of providers are available, the number of providers in the workers' compensation managed care arrangement service area are sufficient, with respect to current and expected workers to be served by the arrangement, either:

1. By delivery of all required medical services; or

2. Through the ability to make appropriate referrals within the provider network.

(c) There are written agreements with providers describing specific responsibilities.

(d) Emergency care is available 24 hours a day and 7 days a week.

(e) In the case of covered services, there are written agreements with providers prohibiting such providers from billing or otherwise seeking reimbursement from or recourse against any injured worker.

(6) The proposed managed care plan of operation must include:

(a) A statement or map providing a clear description of the service area.

(b) A description of the grievance procedure to be used.

(c) A description of the quality assurance program which assures that the health care services provided to workers shall be rendered under reasonable standards of quality of care consistent with the prevailing standards of medical practice in the medical community. The program shall include, but not be limited to:

1. A written statement of goals and objectives that stresses health and return-to-work outcomes as the principal criteria for the evaluation of the

quality of care rendered to injured workers.

2. A written statement describing how methodology has been incorporated into an ongoing system for monitoring of care that is individual case oriented and, when implemented, can provide interpretation and analysis of patterns of care rendered to individual patients by individual providers.

3. Written procedures for taking appropriate remedial action whenever, as determined under the quality assurance program, inappropriate or substandard services have been provided or services that should have been furnished have not been provided.

4. A written plan, which includes ongoing review, for providing review of physicians and other licensed medical providers.

5. Appropriate financial incentives to reduce service costs and utilization without sacrificing the quality of service.

6. Adequate methods of peer review and utilization review. The utilization review process shall include a health care facility's precertification mechanism, including, but not limited to, all elective admissions and nonemergency surgeries and adherence to practice parameters and protocols established in accordance with this chapter.

7. Provisions for resolution of disputes arising between a health care provider and an insurer regarding reimbursements and utilization review.

8. Availability of a process for aggressive medical care coordination, as well as a program involving cooperative efforts by the workers, the employer, and the workers' compensation managed care arrangement to promote early return to work for injured workers.

9. A written plan allowing for the independent medical examination provided for in s. 440.13(5). Notwithstanding any provision to the contrary, the costs for the independent medical examination shall be paid by the carrier if such examination is performed by a physician in the provider network. Otherwise, such costs shall be paid in accordance with s. 440.13(5). An independent medical examination requested by a claimant and paid for by the carrier shall constitute the claimant's one independent medical examination per accident under s. 440.13(5).

10. A provision for the selection of a primary care provider by the employee from among primary providers in the provider network.

11. The written information proposed to be used by the insurer to comply with subparagraph 8.

(7) Written procedures to provide the insurer with timely medical records and information including, but not limited to, work status, work restrictions, date of maximum medical improvement, permanent impairment ratings, and other information as required, including information demonstrating compliance with the practice parameters and protocols of treatment established pursuant to this chapter.

(8) Evidence that appropriate health care providers and administrative staff of the insurer's workers' compensation managed care arrangement have received training and education on the provisions of this chapter; the administrative rules that govern the provision of remedial treatment, care, and attendance of injured workers; and the practice parameters and protocols of treatment established pursuant to this chapter.

(9) Written procedures and methods to prevent inappropriate or excessive treatment that are in accordance with the practice parameters and protocols of treatment established pursuant to this chapter.

(10) Written procedures and methods for the management of an injured worker's medical care by a medical care coordinator including:

(a) The mechanism for assuring that covered employees receive all initial covered services from a primary care provider participating in the provider network, except for emergency care.

(b) The mechanism for assuring that all continuing covered services be received from the same primary care provider participating in the provider network that provided the initial covered services, except when services from another provider are authorized by the medical care coordinator pursuant to paragraph (d).

(c) The policies and procedures for allowing an employee one change to another provider within the provider network as the authorized treating physician during the course of treatment for a work-related injury, in accordance with the procedures provided in s. 440.13(2)(f).

(d) The process for assuring that all referrals authorized by a medical care coordinator, in accordance with the practice parameters and protocols of treatment established pursuant to this chapter, are made to the participating network providers, unless medically necessary treatment, care, and attendance are not available and accessible to the injured worker in the provider network.

(e) Assignment of a medical care coordinator licensed under chapter 458 or chapter 459 to manage care by physicians licensed under chapter 458 or chapter 459, a medical care coordinator licensed under chapter 460 to manage care by physicians licensed under chapter 460, and a medical care coordinator licensed under chapter 461 to manage care by physicians licensed under chapter 461 upon request by an injured employee for care by a physician licensed under chapter 458, chapter 459, chapter 460, or chapter 461.

(11) A description of the use of workers' compensation practice parameters and protocols of treatment for health care services.

(12) An insurer must file any proposed changes to the plan of operation, except for changes to the list of providers, with the agency prior to implementing the changes. The changes are considered approved by the agency after 45 days unless specifically disapproved.

(13) An updated list of providers must be filed with the agency at least semiannually.

(14) An insurer must make full and fair disclosure in writing of the provisions, restrictions, and limitations of the workers' compensation managed care arrangement to affected workers, including at least:

(a) A description, including address and phone number, of the providers, including primary care physicians, specialty physicians, hospitals, and other providers.

(b) A description of coverage for emergency and urgently needed care provided within and outside the service area.

(c) A description of limitations on referrals.

(d) A description of the grievance procedure.

(15)

(a) A workers' compensation managed care arrangement must have and use procedures for hearing complaints and resolving written grievances from injured workers and health care providers. The procedures must be aimed at mutual agreement for settlement and may include arbitration procedures. Procedures provided herein are in addition to other procedures contained in this chapter.

(b) The grievance procedure must be described in writing and provided to the affected workers and health care providers.

(c) At the time the workers' compensation managed care arrangement is implemented, the insurer must provide detailed information to workers and health care providers describing how a grievance may be registered with the insurer.

(d) Grievances must be considered in a timely manner and must be transmitted to appropriate decisionmakers who have the authority to fully investigate the issue and take corrective action.

(e) If a grievance is found to be valid, corrective action must be taken promptly.

(f) All concerned parties must be notified of the results of a grievance.

(g) The insurer must report annually, no later than March 31, to the agency regarding its grievance procedure activities for the prior calendar year. The report must be in a format prescribed by the agency and must contain the number of grievances filed in the past year and a summary of the subject, nature, and resolution of such grievances.

(16) When a carrier enters into a managed care arrangement pursuant to this section the

Fla. Stats.

employees who are covered by the provisions of such arrangement shall be deemed to have received all the benefits to which they are entitled pursuant to s. 440.13(2)(a) and (b). In addition, the employer shall be deemed to have complied completely with the requirements of such provisions. The provisions governing managed care arrangements shall govern exclusively unless specifically stated otherwise in this section.

(17) Notwithstanding any other provisions of this chapter, when a carrier provides medical care through a workers' compensation managed care arrangement, pursuant to this section, those workers who are subject to the arrangement must receive medical services for work-related injuries and diseases as prescribed in the contract, provided the employer and carrier have provided notice to the employees of the arrangement in a manner approved by the agency and the medical services are in accordance with the practice parameters and protocols established pursuant to this chapter. Treatment received outside the workers' compensation managed care arrangement is not compensable, regardless of the purpose of the treatment, including, but not limited to, evaluations, examinations, or diagnostic studies to determine causation between medical findings and a compensable accident, the existence or extent of impairments or disabilities, and whether the injured employee has reached maximum medical improvement, unless authorized by the carrier prior to the treatment date.

(18) The agency may suspend the authority of an insurer to offer a workers' compensation managed care arrangement or order compliance within 60 days, if it finds that:

(a) The insurer is in substantial violation of its contracts;

(b) The insurer is unable to fulfill its obligations under outstanding contracts entered into with its employers;

(c) The insurer knowingly utilizes a provider who is furnishing or has furnished health care services and who does not have an existing license or other authority to practice or furnish health care services in this state;

(d) The insurer no longer meets the requirements for the authorization as originally issued; or

(e) The insurer has violated any lawful rule or order of the agency or any provision of this section.

(19) Revocation of an insurer's authorization shall be for a period of 2 years. After 2 years, the insurer may apply for a new authorization by compliance with all application requirements applicable to first-time applicants.

(20) Suspension of an insurer's authority to offer a workers' compensation managed care arrangement shall be for such period, not to exceed 1 year, as is fixed by the agency. The agency shall, in its order suspending the authority of an insurer to offer workers' compensation managed care, specify the period during which the suspension is to be in effect and the conditions, if any, that must be met by the insurer prior to reinstatement of its authority. The order of suspension is subject to rescission or modification by further order of the agency prior to the expiration of the suspension period. Reinstatement shall not be made unless requested by the insurer; however, the agency shall not grant reinstatement if it finds that the circumstances for which the suspension occurred still exist or are likely to recur.

(21) Upon expiration of the suspension period, the insurer's authorization shall automatically be reinstated unless the agency finds that the causes of the suspension have not been rectified or that the insurer is otherwise not in compliance with the requirements of this chapter. If not so automatically reinstated, the authorization shall be deemed to have expired as of the end of the suspension period.

(22) If the agency finds that one or more grounds exist for the revocation or suspension of an authorization issued under this section, the agency may, in lieu of such revocation or suspension, impose a fine upon the insurer. With respect to any nonwillful violation, such fine shall not exceed $2,500 per violation. In no event shall such fine exceed an aggregate

amount of $10,000 for all nonwillful violations arising out of the same action. With respect to any knowing and willful violation of a lawful order or rule of the agency or a provision of this section, the agency may impose a fine upon the insurer in an amount not to exceed $20,000 for each such violation. In no event shall such fine exceed an aggregate amount of $100,000 for all knowing and willful violations arising out of the same action.

(23) The agency shall immediately notify the office whenever it issues an administrative complaint or an order or otherwise initiates legal proceedings resulting in, or which may result in, suspension or revocation of an insurer's authorization.

(24) Nothing in[1] this chapter shall be deemed to authorize any entity to transact any insurance business, assume risk, or otherwise engage in any other type of insurance unless it is authorized as an insurer or a health maintenance organization under a certificate of authority issued under the provisions of the Florida Insurance Code.

(25) The agency shall adopt rules that specify:

(a) Procedures for authorization and examination of workers' compensation managed care arrangements by the agency.

(b) Requirements and procedures for authorization of workers' compensation arrangement provider networks and procedures for the agency to grant exceptions from accessibility of services.

(c) Requirements and procedures for case management, utilization management, and peer review.

(d) Requirements and procedures for quality assurance and medical records.

(e) Requirements and procedures for dispute resolution in conformance with this chapter.

(f) Requirements and procedures for employee and provider education.

(g) Requirements and procedures for reporting data regarding grievances, return-to-work outcomes, and provider networks.

History: s. 18, ch. 93-415; s. 46, ch. 97-264; s. 1, ch. 98-127; ss. 189, 260, ch. 98-166; s. 3, ch. 2000-305; s. 13, ch. 2001-91, effective Oct. 1, 2001; s. 26, ch. 2002-194, effective July 1, 2002; s. 10, ch. 2002-236, effective July 1, 2002; s. 16, ch. 412, effective October 1, 2003; s. 478, ch. 2003-261, effective June 26, 2003.

§ 440.14. Determination of Pay.

(1) Except as otherwise provided in this chapter, the average weekly wages of the injured employee on the date of the accident shall be taken as the basis upon which to compute compensation and shall be determined, subject to the limitations of s. 440.12(2), as follows:

(a) If the injured employee has worked in the employment in which she or he was working on the date of the accident, whether for the same or another employer, during substantially the whole of 13 weeks immediately preceding the accident, her or his average weekly wage shall be one-thirteenth of the total amount of wages earned in such employment during the 13 weeks. As used in this paragraph, the term "substantially the whole of 13 weeks" means the calendar period of 13 weeks as a whole, which shall be defined as the 13 calendar weeks before the date of the accident, excluding the week during which the accident occurred. The term "during substantially the whole of 13 weeks" shall be deemed to mean during not less than 75 percent of the total customary hours of employment within such period considered as a whole.

(b) If the injured employee has not worked in such employment during substantially the whole of 13 weeks immediately preceding the accident, the wages of a similar employee in the same employment who has worked substantially the whole of such 13 weeks shall be used in making the determination under the preceding paragraph.

(c) If an employee is a seasonal worker and the foregoing method cannot be fairly applied in determining the average weekly wage, then the employee may use, instead of the 13 weeks immediately preceding the accident, the calendar year or the 52 weeks immediately preceding the accident. The employee will have the burden of proving that this method will be more reasonable and fairer than the method set forth in paragraphs (a) and (b) and, further, must document prior earnings with W-2 forms, written wage statements, or income tax returns. The employer shall have 30 days following the receipt of this written proof to adjust the compensation rate, including the making of any additional payment due for prior weekly payments, based on the lower rate compensation.

(d) If any of the foregoing methods cannot reasonably and fairly be applied, the full-time weekly wages of the injured employee shall be used, except as otherwise provided in paragraph (e) or paragraph (f).

(e) If it is established that the injured employee was under 22 years of age when the accident occurred and that under normal conditions her or his wages should be expected to increase during the period of disability, the fact may be considered in arriving at her or his average weekly wages.

(f) If it is established that the injured employee was a part-time worker on the date of the accident, that she or he had adopted part-time employment as a customary practice, and that under normal working conditions she or he probably would have remained a part-time worker during the period of disability, these factors shall be considered in arriving at her or his average weekly wages. For the purpose of this paragraph, the term "part-time worker" means an individual who customarily works less than the full-time hours or full-time workweek of a similar employee in the same employment.

(g) If compensation is due for a fractional part of the week, the compensation for such fractional part shall be determined by dividing the weekly compensation rate by the number of days employed per week to compute the amount due for each day.

(2) If, during the period of disability, the employer continues to provide consideration, including board, rent, housing, or lodging, the value of such consideration shall be deducted when calculating the average weekly wage of the employee so long as these benefits continue to be provided.

(3) The department shall establish by rule a form which shall contain a simplified checklist of those items which may be included as "wage" for determining the average weekly wage.

(4) Upon termination of the employee or upon termination of the payment of fringe benefits of any employee who is collecting indemnity benefits pursuant to s. 440.15(2) or (3), the employer shall within 7 days of such termination file a corrected 13-week wage statement reflecting the wages paid and the fringe benefits that had been paid to the injured employee, as provided in s. 440.02(28).

(5)

(a) If the lost wages from concurrent employment are used in calculating the average weekly wage, the employee is responsible for providing information concerning the loss of earnings from the concurrent employment.

(b) The employee waives any entitlement to interest, penalties, and attorney's fees during the period in which the employee has not provided information concerning the loss of earnings from concurrent employment. Carriers are not subject to penalties under s. 440.20(8)(b) for unpaid compensation related to concurrent employment during the period in which the employee has not provided information concerning the loss of earnings from concurrent employment.

History: s. 14, ch. 17481, 1935; CGL 1936 Supp. 5966(14); s. 3, ch. 20672, 1941; s. 2, ch. 28241, 1953; s. 1, ch. 63-160; s. 8, ch. 74-197; s. 1, ch. 77-290; s. 23, ch. 78-300; ss. 9, 124, ch. 79-40; s. 21, ch. 79-312; s. 4, ch. 82-237; s. 3, ch. 88-203; ss. 11, 43, ch. 89-289; s. 56, ch. 90-201; s. 52, ch. 91-1; s. 110, ch. 97-103; s. 91, ch. 2000-153; s. 14, ch. 2001-91, effective Oct. 1, 2001; s. 73, ch. 2002-1, effective May 21, 2002; s. 27, ch. 2002-194, effective July 1, 2002; s. 17, ch. 2003-412, effective Oct. 1, 2003; s. 479, ch. 2003-261, effective June 26, 2003; s. 61, ch. 2004-5, effective June 29, 2004.

§ 440.15. Compensation for Disability.

Compensation for disability shall be paid to the employee, subject to the limits provided in s. 440.12(2), as follows:

(1) Permanent Total Disability.—

(a) In case of total disability adjudged to be permanent, 66²/₃ percent of the average weekly wages shall be paid to the employee during the continuance of such total disability. No compensation shall be payable under this section if the employee is engaged in, or is physically capable of engaging in, at least sedentary employment.

(b) In the following cases, an injured employee is presumed to be permanently and totally disabled unless the employer or carrier establishes that the employee is physically capable of engaging in at least sedentary employment within a 50-mile radius of the employee's residence:

1. Spinal cord injury involving severe paralysis of an arm, a leg, or the trunk;

2. Amputation of an arm, a hand, a foot, or a leg involving the effective loss of use of that appendage;

3. Severe brain or closed-head injury as evidenced by:

a. Severe sensory or motor disturbances;

b. Severe communication disturbances;

c. Severe complex integrated disturbances of cerebral function;

d. Severe episodic neurological disorders; or

e. Other severe brain and closed-head injury conditions at least as severe in nature as any condition provided in sub-subparagraphs a.-d.;

4. Second-degree or third-degree burns of 25 percent or more of the total body surface or third-degree burns of 5 percent or more to the face and hands; or

5. Total or industrial blindness.

In all other cases, in order to obtain permanent total disability benefits, the employee must establish that he or she is not able to engage in at least sedentary employment, within a 50-mile radius of the employee's residence, due to his or her physical limitation. Entitlement to such benefits shall cease when the employee reaches age 75, unless the employee is not eligible for social security benefits under 42 U.S.C. s. 402 or s. 423 because the employee's compensable injury has prevented the employee from working sufficient quarters to be eligible for such benefits, notwithstanding any age limits. If the accident occurred on or after the employee reaches age 70, benefits shall be payable during the continuance of permanent total disability, not to exceed 5 years following the determination of permanent total disability. Only claimants with catastrophic injuries or claimants who are incapable of engaging in employment, as described in this paragraph, are eligible for permanent total benefits. In no other case may permanent total disability be awarded.

(c) Total or industrial blindness.

In cases of permanent total disability resulting from injuries that occurred prior to July 1, 1955, such payments shall not be made in excess of 700 weeks.

(d) If an employee who is being paid compensation for permanent total disability becomes rehabilitated to the extent that she or he establishes an earning capacity, the employee shall be paid, instead of the compensation provided in paragraph (a), benefits pursuant to subsection (3). The department shall adopt rules to enable a permanently and totally disabled employee who may have reestablished an earning capacity to undertake a trial period of reemployment without prejudicing her or his return to permanent total status in the case that such employee is unable to sustain an earning capacity.

(e)

1. The employer's or carrier's right to conduct vocational evaluations or testing by the employer's or carrier's chosen rehabilitation advisor or provider continues even after the employee has been accepted or adjudicated as entitled to compensation under this chapter and costs for such evaluations and testing shall be borne by the employer or carrier, respectively. This right includes, but is not limited to, instances in which such evaluations or tests are recommended by a treating physician or independent medical-examination physician, instances warranted by a change in the employee's medical condition, or instances in which the

Fla. Stats.

employee appears to be making appropriate progress in recuperation. This right may not be exercised more than once every calendar year.

2. The carrier must confirm the scheduling of the vocational evaluation or testing in writing, and must notify the employee and the employee's counsel, if any, at least 7 days before the date on which vocational evaluation or testing is scheduled to occur.

3. The employer or carrier may withhold payment of benefits for permanent total disability or supplements for any period during which the employee willfully fails or refuses to appear without good cause for the scheduled vocational evaluation or testing.

(f)

1. If permanent total disability results from injuries that occurred subsequent to June 30, 1955, and for which the liability of the employer for compensation has not been discharged under s. 440.20(11), the injured employee shall receive additional weekly compensation benefits equal to 5 percent of her or his weekly compensation rate, as established pursuant to the law in effect on the date of her or his injury, multiplied by the number of calendar years since the date of injury. The weekly compensation payable and the additional benefits payable under this paragraph, when combined, may not exceed the maximum weekly compensation rate in effect at the time of payment as determined pursuant to s. 440.12(2). These supplemental payments shall not be paid or payable after the employee attains age 62, regardless of whether the employee has applied for or is eligible to apply for social security benefits under 42 U.S.C. s. 402 or s. 423, unless the employee is not eligible for social security benefits under 42 U.S.C. s. 402 or s. 423 because the employee's compensable injury has prevented the employee from working sufficient quarters to be eligible for such benefits. These supplemental benefits shall be paid by the department out of the Workers' Compensation Administration Trust Fund when the injury occurred subsequent to June 30, 1955, and before July 1, 1984. These supplemental benefits shall be paid by the employer when the injury occurred on or after July 1, 1984. Supplemental benefits are not payable for any period prior to October 1, 1974.

2.

a. The department shall provide by rule for the periodic reporting to the department of all earnings of any nature and social security income by the injured employee entitled to or claiming additional compensation under subparagraph 1. Neither the department nor the employer or carrier shall make any payment of those additional benefits provided by subparagraph 1. for any period during which the employee willfully fails or refuses to report upon request by the department in the manner prescribed by such rules.

b. The department shall provide by rule for the periodic reporting to the employer or carrier of all earnings of any nature and social security income by the injured employee entitled to or claiming benefits for permanent total disability. The employer or carrier is not required to make any payment of benefits for permanent total disability for any period during which the employee willfully fails or refuses to report upon request by the employer or carrier in the manner prescribed by such rules or if any employee who is receiving permanent total disability benefits refuses to apply for or cooperate with the employer or carrier in applying for social security benefits.

3. When an injured employee receives a full or partial lump-sum advance of the employee's permanent total disability compensation benefits, the employee's benefits under this paragraph shall be computed on the employee's weekly compensation rate as reduced by the lump-sum advance.

(2) Temporary Total Disability.—

(a) Subject to subsection (7), in case of disability total in character but temporary in quality, $66^2/_3$ percent of the average weekly wages shall be paid to the employee during the continuance thereof, not to exceed 104 weeks except as provided in this subsection, s. 440.12(1), and s. 440.14(3). Once the employee reaches the maximum number of weeks allowed, or the employee reaches the date of maximum medical improvement, whichever occurs earlier, temporary disability benefits shall cease and the injured worker's permanent impairment shall be determined.

(b) Notwithstanding the provisions of paragraph (a), an employee who has sustained the loss of an arm, leg, hand, or foot, has been rendered a paraplegic, paraparetic, quadriplegic, or quadriparetic, or has lost the sight of both eyes shall be paid temporary total disability of 80 percent of her or his average weekly wage. The increased temporary total disability compensation provided for in this paragraph must not extend beyond 6 months from the date of the accident; however, such benefits shall not be due or payable if the employee is eligible for, entitled to, or collecting permanent total disability benefits. The compensation provided by this paragraph is not subject to the limits provided in s. 440.12(2), but instead is subject to a maximum weekly compensation rate of $700. If, at the conclusion of this period of increased temporary total disability compensation, the employee is still temporarily totally disabled, the employee shall continue to receive temporary total disability compensation as set forth in paragraphs (a) and (c). The period of time the employee has received this increased compensation will be counted as part of, and not in addition to, the maximum periods of time for which the employee is entitled to compensation under paragraph (a) but not paragraph (c).

(c) Temporary total disability benefits paid pursuant to this subsection shall include such period as may be reasonably necessary for training in the use of artificial members and appliances, and shall include such period as the employee may be receiving training and education under a program pursuant to s. 440.491.

(d) The department shall, by rule, provide for the periodic reporting to the department, employer, or carrier of all earned income, including income from social security, by the injured employee who is entitled to or claiming benefits for temporary total disability. The employer or carrier is not required to make any payment of benefits for temporary total disability for any period during which the employee willfully fails or refuses to report upon request by the employer or carrier in the manner prescribed by the rules. The rule must require the claimant to personally sign the claim form and attest that she or he has reviewed, understands, and acknowledges the foregoing.

(3) Permanent Impairment Benefits.—

(a) Once the employee has reached the date of maximum medical improvement, impairment benefits are due and payable within 14 days after the carrier has knowledge of the impairment.

(b) The three-member panel, in cooperation with the department, shall establish and use a uniform permanent impairment rating schedule. This schedule must be based on medically or scientifically demonstrable findings as well as the systems and criteria set forth in the American Medical Association's Guides to the Evaluation of Permanent Impairment; the Snellen Charts, published by the[1] American Medical Association Committee for Eye Injuries; and the Minnesota Department of Labor and Industry Disability Schedules. The schedule must be based upon objective findings. The schedule shall be more comprehensive than the AMA Guides to the Evaluation of Permanent Impairment and shall expand the areas already addressed and address additional areas not currently contained in the guides. On August 1, 1979, and pending the adoption, by rule, of a permanent schedule, Guides to the Evaluation of Permanent Impairment, copyright 1977, 1971, 1988, by the American Medical Association, shall be the temporary schedule and shall be used for the purposes hereof. For injuries after July 1, 1990, pending the adoption by rule of a uniform disability rating agency schedule, the Minnesota Department of Labor and Industry Disability Schedule shall be used unless that schedule does not address an injury. In such case, the Guides to the Evaluation of Permanent Impairment by the American Medical Association shall be used. Determination of permanent impairment under this schedule must be made by a physician licensed under chapter 458, a doctor of osteopathic medicine licensed under chapters 458 and 459, a chiropractic physician licensed under chapter 460, a podiatric physician licensed under chapter 461, an optometrist licensed under chapter 463, or a dentist licensed

Fla. Stats.

under chapter 466, as appropriate considering the nature of the injury. No other persons are authorized to render opinions regarding the existence of or the extent of permanent impairment.

(c) All impairment income benefits shall be based on an impairment rating using the impairment schedule referred to in paragraph (b). Impairment income benefits are paid biweekly at the rate of 75 percent of the employee's average weekly temporary total disability benefit not to exceed the maximum weekly benefit under s. 440.12; provided, however, that such benefits shall be reduced by 50 percent for each week in which the employee has earned income equal to or in excess of the employee's average weekly wage. An employee's entitlement to impairment income benefits begins the day after the employee reaches maximum medical improvement or the expiration of temporary benefits, whichever occurs earlier, and continues until the earlier of:

1. The expiration of a period computed at the rate of 3 weeks for each percentage point of impairment; or

2. The death of the employee.

Impairment income benefits as defined by this subsection are payable only for impairment ratings for physical impairments. If objective medical findings can substantiate a permanent psychiatric impairment resulting from the accident, permanent impairment benefits are limited for the permanent psychiatric impairment to 1-percent permanent impairment.

(d) After the employee has been certified by a doctor as having reached maximum medical improvement or 6 weeks before the expiration of temporary benefits, whichever occurs earlier, the certifying doctor shall evaluate the condition of the employee and assign an impairment rating, using the impairment schedule referred to in paragraph (b). If the certification and evaluation are performed by a doctor other than the employee's treating doctor, the certification and evaluation must be submitted to the treating doctor, the employee, and the carrier within 10 days after the evaluation. The treating doctor must indicate to the carrier agreement or disagreement with the other doctor's certification and evaluation.

1. The certifying doctor shall issue a written report to the employee and the carrier certifying that maximum medical improvement has been reached, stating the impairment rating to the body as a whole, and providing any other information required by the department by rule. The carrier shall establish an overall maximum medical improvement date and permanent impairment rating, based upon all such reports.

2. Within 14 days after the carrier's knowledge of each maximum medical improvement date and impairment rating to the body as a whole upon which the carrier is paying benefits, the carrier shall report such maximum medical improvement date and, when determined, the overall maximum medical improvement date and associated impairment rating to the department in a format as set forth in department rule. If the employee has not been certified as having reached maximum medical improvement before the expiration of 98 weeks after the date temporary disability benefits begin to accrue, the carrier shall notify the treating doctor of the requirements of this section.

(e) The carrier shall pay the employee impairment income benefits for a period based on the impairment rating.

(f) The department may by rule specify forms and procedures governing the method of payment of benefits under this section.

(g) Notwithstanding paragraph (c), for accidents occurring on or after October 1, 2003, an employee's entitlement to impairment income benefits begins the day after the employee reaches maximum medical improvement or the expiration of temporary benefits, whichever occurs earlier, and continues for the following periods:

1. Two weeks of benefits are to be paid to the employee for each percentage point of impairment from 1 percent up to and including 10 percent.

2. For each percentage point of impairment from 11 percent up to and including 15 percent,

3 weeks of benefits are to be paid.

3. For each percentage point of impairment from 16 percent up to and including 20 percent, 4 weeks of benefits are to be paid.

4. For each percentage point of impairment from 21 percent and higher, 6 weeks of benefits are to be paid.

(4) Temporary Partial Disability.—

(a) Subject to subsection (7), in case of temporary partial disability, compensation shall be equal to 80 percent of the difference between 80 percent of the employee's average weekly wage and the salary, wages, and other remuneration the employee is able to earn postinjury, as compared weekly; however, weekly temporary partial disability benefits may not exceed an amount equal to $66^2/_3$ percent of the employee's average weekly wage at the time of accident. In order to simplify the comparison of the preinjury average weekly wage with the salary, wages, and other remuneration the employee is able to earn postinjury, the department may by rule provide for payment of the initial installment of temporary partial disability benefits to be paid as a partial week so that payment for remaining weeks of temporary partial disability can coincide as closely as possible with the postinjury employer's work week. The amount determined to be the salary, wages, and other remuneration the employee is able to earn shall in no case be less than the sum actually being earned by the employee, including earnings from sheltered employment. Benefits shall be payable under this subsection only if overall maximum medical improvement has not been reached and the medical conditions resulting from the accident create restrictions on the injured employee's ability to return to work.

(b) Within 5 business days after the carrier's knowledge of the employee's release to restricted work, the carrier shall mail to the employee and employer an informational letter, adopted by department rule, explaining the employee's possible eligibility and responsibilities for temporary partial disability benefits.

(c) When an employee returns to work with the restrictions resulting from the accident and is earning wages less than 80 percent of the preinjury average weekly wage, the first installment of temporary partial disability benefits is due 7 days after the last date of the postinjury employer's first biweekly work week. Thereafter, payment for temporary partial benefits shall be paid biweekly no later than the 7th day following the last day of each biweekly work week.

(d) If the employee is unable to return to work with the restrictions resulting from the accident and is not earning wages, salary, or other remuneration, temporary partial disability benefits shall be paid no later than the last day of each biweekly period. The employee shall notify the carrier within 5 business days after returning to work. Failure to notify the carrier of the establishment of an earning capacity in the required time shall result in a suspension or nonpayment of temporary partial disability benefits until the proper notification is provided.

(e) Such benefits shall be paid during the continuance of such disability, not to exceed a period of 104 weeks, as provided by this subsection and subsection (2). Once the injured employee reaches the maximum number of weeks, temporary disability benefits cease and the injured worker's permanent impairment must be determined. If the employee is terminated from postinjury employment based on the employee's misconduct, temporary partial disability benefits are not payable as provided for in this section. The department shall by rule specify forms and procedures governing the method and time for payment of temporary disability benefits for dates of accidents before January 1, 1994, and for dates of accidents on or after January 1, 1994.

(5) Subsequent Injury.—

(a) The fact that an employee has suffered previous disability, impairment, anomaly, or disease, or received compensation therefor, shall not preclude her or him from benefits, as specified in paragraph (b), for a subsequent aggravation or acceleration of the preexisting condition or preclude benefits for death resulting therefrom, except that no benefits shall be payable if the employee, at the time of entering into the

Fla. Stats.

employment of the employer by whom the benefits would otherwise be payable, falsely represents herself or himself in writing as not having previously been disabled or compensated because of such previous disability, impairment, anomaly, or disease and the employer detrimentally relies on the misrepresentation.

(b) If a compensable injury, disability, or need for medical care, or any portion thereof, is a result of aggravation or acceleration of a preexisting condition, or is the result of merger with a preexisting condition, only the disabilities and medical treatment associated with such compensable injury shall be payable under this chapter, excluding the degree of disability or medical conditions existing at the time of the impairment rating or at the time of the accident, regardless of whether the preexisting condition was disabling at the time of the accident or at the time of the impairment rating and without considering whether the preexisting condition would be disabling without the compensable accident. The degree of permanent impairment or disability attributable to the accident or injury shall be compensated in accordance with this section, apportioning out the preexisting condition based on the anatomical impairment rating attributable to the preexisting condition. Medical benefits shall be paid apportioning out the percentage of the need for such care attributable to the preexisting condition. As used in this paragraph, "merger" means the combining of a preexisting permanent impairment or disability with a subsequent compensable permanent impairment or disability which, when the effects of both are considered together, result in a permanent impairment or disability rating which is greater than the sum of the two permanent impairment or disability ratings when each impairment or disability is considered individually.

(6) Employee Refuses Employment.—If an injured employee refuses employment suitable to the capacity thereof, offered to or procured therefor, such employee shall not be entitled to any compensation at any time during the continuance of such refusal unless at any time in the opinion of the judge of compensation claims such refusal is justifiable. Time periods for the payment of benefits in accordance with this section shall be counted in determining the limitation of benefits as provided for in paragraphs (2)(a), (3)(c), and[2] (4)(b).

(7) Employee Leaves Employment.—If an injured employee, when receiving compensation for temporary partial disability, leaves the employment of the employer by whom she or he was employed at the time of the accident for which such compensation is being paid, the employee shall, upon securing employment elsewhere, give to such former employer an affidavit in writing containing the name of her or his new employer, the place of employment, and the amount of wages being received at such new employment; and, until she or he gives such affidavit, the compensation for temporary partial disability will cease. The employer by whom such employee was employed at the time of the accident for which such compensation is being paid may also at any time demand of such employee an additional affidavit in writing containing the name of her or his employer, the place of her or his employment, and the amount of wages she or he is receiving; and if the employee, upon such demand, fails or refuses to make and furnish such affidavit, her or his right to compensation for temporary partial disability shall cease until such affidavit is made and furnished. If the employee leaves her or his employment while receiving temporary partial benefits without just cause as determined by the judge of compensation claims, temporary partial benefits shall be payable based on the deemed earnings of the employee as if she or he had remained employed.

(8) Employee Becomes Inmate of Institution.—In case an employee becomes an inmate of a public institution, then no compensation shall be payable unless she or he has dependent upon her or him for support a person or persons defined as dependents elsewhere in this chapter, whose dependency shall be determined as if the employee were deceased and to whom compensation would be paid in case of death; and such compensation as is due such employee shall be paid such dependents during the time she or he remains such inmate.

(9) Employee Eligible for Benefits Under This Chapter and Federal Old-Age, Survivors,

and Disability Insurance Act.—

(a) Weekly compensation benefits payable under this chapter for disability resulting from injuries to an employee who becomes eligible for benefits under 42 U.S.C. s. 423 shall be reduced to an amount whereby the sum of such compensation benefits payable under this chapter and such total benefits otherwise payable for such period to the employee and her or his dependents, had such employee not been entitled to benefits under this chapter, under 42 U.S.C. ss. 402 and 423, does not exceed 80 percent of the employee's average weekly wage. However, this provision shall not operate to reduce an injured worker's benefits under this chapter to a greater extent than such benefits would have otherwise been reduced under 42 U.S.C. s. 424(a). This reduction of compensation benefits is not applicable to any compensation benefits payable for any week subsequent to the week in which the injured worker reaches the age of 62 years.

(b) If the provisions of 42 U.S.C. s. 424(a) are amended to provide for a reduction or increase of the percentage of average current earnings that the sum of compensation benefits payable under this chapter and the benefits payable under 42 U.S.C. ss. 402 and 423 can equal, the amount of the reduction of benefits provided in this subsection shall be reduced or increased accordingly. The department may by rule specify forms and procedures governing the method for calculating and administering the offset of benefits payable under this chapter and benefits payable under 42 U.S.C. ss. 402 and 423. The department shall have first priority in taking any available social security offsets on dates of accidents occurring before July 1, 1984.

(c) Disability compensation benefits payable for any week, including those benefits provided by paragraph (1)(f), may not be reduced pursuant to this subsection until the Social Security Administration determines the amount otherwise payable to the employee under 42 U.S.C. ss. 402 and 423 and the employee has begun receiving such social security benefit payments. The employee shall, upon demand by the department, the employer, or the carrier, authorize the Social Security Administration to release disability information relating to her or him and authorize the Agency for Workforce Innovation to release unemployment compensation information relating to her or him, in accordance with rules to be adopted by the department prescribing the procedure and manner for requesting the authorization and for compliance by the employee. The department or the employer or carrier may not make any payment of benefits for total disability or those additional benefits provided by paragraph (1)(f) for any period during which the employee willfully fails or refuses to authorize the release of information in the manner and within the time prescribed by such rules. The authority for release of disability information granted by an employee under this paragraph is effective for a period not to exceed 12 months and such authority may be renewed, as the department prescribes by rule.

(d) If compensation benefits are reduced pursuant to this subsection, the minimum compensation provisions of s. 440.12(2) do not apply.

(10) Employee Eligible for Benefits Under This Chapter Who Has Received or is Entitled to Receive Unemployment Compensation.—

(a) No compensation benefits shall be payable for temporary total disability or permanent total disability under this chapter for any week in which the injured employee has received, or is receiving, unemployment compensation benefits.

(b) If an employee is entitled to temporary partial benefits pursuant to subsection (4) and unemployment compensation benefits, such unemployment compensation benefits shall be primary and the temporary partial benefits shall be supplemental only, the sum of the two benefits not to exceed the amount of temporary partial benefits which would otherwise be payable.

(11) Full-Pay Status for Certain Law Enforcement Officers.—Any law enforcement officer as defined in s. 943.10(1), (2), or (3) who, while acting within the course of employment as provided by s. 440.091, is maliciously or intentionally injured and who thereby sustains a job-connected disability compensable under this chapter shall be carried in full-pay status rather

Fla. Stats.

than being required to use sick, annual, or other leave. Full-pay status shall be granted only after submission to the employing agency's head of a medical report which gives a current diagnosis of the employee's recovery and ability to return to work. In no case shall the employee's salary and workers' compensation benefits exceed the amount of the employee's regular salary requirements.

(12) Repayment.—If an employee has received a sum as an indemnity benefit under any classification or category of benefit under this chapter to which she or he is not entitled, the employee is liable to repay that sum to the employer or the carrier or to have that sum deducted from future benefits, regardless of the classification of benefits, payable to the employee under this chapter; however, a partial payment of the total repayment may not exceed 20 percent of the amount of the biweekly payment.

History: s. 15, ch. 17481, 1935; CGL 1936 Supp. 5966(15); s. 4, ch. 20672, 1941; s. 2, ch. 22814, 1945; s. 1, ch. 23921, 1947; s. 11, ch. 25035, 1949; s. 1, ch. 26877, 1951; s. 10, ch. 26484, 1951; s. 1, ch. 29803, 1955; s. 3, ch. 29778, 1955; s. 1, ch. 59-103; s. 1, ch. 59-102; s. 2, ch. 61-119; s. 1, ch. 61-188; s. 1, ch. 63-235; s. 1, ch. 65-168; ss. 17, 35, ch. 69-106; s. 1, ch. 70-71; s. 1, ch. 70-312; s. 5, ch. 73-127; s. 9, ch. 74-197; s. 6, ch. 75-209; s. 1, ch. 77-174; s. 4, ch. 77-290; ss. 5, 23, ch. 78-300; ss. 10, 124, ch. 79-40; ss. 8, 21, ch. 79-312; s. 5, ch. 80-236; s. 5, ch. 81-119; s. 275, ch. 81-259; ss. 1, 3, ch. 82-237; s. 8, ch. 83-174; s. 5, ch. 83-305; s. 2, ch. 84-267; s. 3, ch. 86-171; s. 3. ch. 87-330; s. 4, ch. 88-203; ss. 12, 43, ch. 89-289; ss. 20, 56, ch. 90-201; ss. 18, 52, ch. 91-1; s. 20, ch. 93-415; s. 73, ch. 96-418; s. 1052, ch. 97-103; s. 47, ch. 97-264; s. 2, ch. 98-125; ss. 190, 261, ch. 98-166; s. 92, ch. 2000-153; s. 65, ch. 2001-62, effective July 3, 2001; s. 28, ch. 2002-194, effective July 1, 2002; s. 52, ch. 2003-1, effective July 1, 2003; s. 11, ch. 2003-36, effective Oct. 1, 2003; s. 18, ch. 2003-412, effective Oct. 1, 2003; s. 62, ch. 2004-5, effective June 29, 2004.

[1]**2003 Note:** The word "the" was inserted by the editors.

[2]**2003 Note:** Paragraph (4)(b) does not reference time periods for payment of benefits. The appropriate reference may be to paragraph (4)(e).

[3]**Note:** —Repealed by s. 20, ch. 93-415.

§ 440.151. Occupational Diseases.

(1)

(a) Where the employer and employee are subject to the provisions of the Workers' Compensation Law, the disablement or death of an employee resulting from an occupational disease as hereinafter defined shall be treated as the happening of an injury by accident, notwithstanding any other provisions of this chapter, and the employee or, in case of death, the employee's dependents shall be entitled to compensation as provided by this chapter, except as hereinafter otherwise provided; and the practice and procedure prescribed by this chapter shall apply to all proceedings under this section, except as hereinafter otherwise provided. Provided, however, that in no case shall an employer be liable for compensation under the provisions of this section unless such disease has resulted from the nature of the employment in which the employee was engaged under such employer, was actually contracted while so engaged, and the nature of the employment was the major contributing cause of the disease. Major contributing cause must be shown by medical evidence only, as demonstrated by physical examination findings and diagnostic testing. "Nature of the employment" means that in the occupation in which the employee was so engaged there is attached a particular hazard of such disease that distinguishes it from the usual run of occupations, or the incidence of such disease is substantially higher in the occupation in which the employee was so engaged than in the usual run of occupations. In claims for death under s. 440.16, death must occur within 350 weeks after last exposure. Both causation and sufficient exposure to a specific harmful substance shown to be present in the workplace to support causation shall be proven by clear and convincing evidence.

(b) No compensation shall be payable for an occupational disease if the employee, at the time of entering into the employment of the employer by whom the compensation would otherwise be payable, falsely represents herself or himself in writing as not having previously been disabled, laid off or compensated in damages or otherwise, because of such disease.

(c) Where an occupational disease is aggravated by any other disease or infirmity, not itself compensable, or where disability or death from any other cause, not itself compensable, is aggravated, prolonged, accelerated or in anywise contributed to by an occupational disease, the compensation shall be payable only if the occupational disease is the major contributing cause of the injury. Any compensation shall be reduced and limited to such proportion only of the compensation that would be payable if the occupational disease were the sole cause of the disability or death as such occupational disease, as a causative factor, bears to all the causes of such disability or death, such reduction in compensation to be effected by reducing the number of weekly or monthly payments or the amounts of such payments, as under the circumstances of the particular case may be for the best interest of the claimant or claimants. Major contributing cause must be demonstrated by medical evidence based on physical examination findings and diagnostic testing.

(d) No compensation for death from an occupational disease shall be payable to any person whose relationship to the deceased, which under the provisions of this Workers' Compensation Law would give right to compensation, arose subsequent to the beginning of the first compensable disability, save only to afterborn children of a marriage existing at the beginning of such disability.

(e) No compensation shall be payable for disability or death resulting from tuberculosis arising out of and in the course of employment by the Department of Health at a state tuberculosis hospital, or aggravated by such employment, when the employee had suffered from said disease at any time prior to the commencement of such employment.

(2) Whenever used in this section the term "occupational disease" shall be construed to mean only a disease which is due to causes and conditions which are characteristic of and peculiar to a particular trade, occupation, process, or employment, and to exclude all ordinary diseases of life to which the general public is exposed, unless the incidence of the disease is substantially higher in the particular trade, occupation, process, or employment than for the general public. "Occupational disease" means only a disease for which there are epidemiological studies showing that exposure to the specific substance involved, at the levels to which the employee was exposed, may cause the precise disease sustained by the employee.

(3) Except as otherwise provided in this section, "disablement" means disability as described in s. 440.02(13).

(4) This section shall not apply to cases of occupational disease in which the last injurious exposure to the hazards of such disease occurred before this section shall have taken effect.

(5) Where compensation is payable for an occupational disease, the employer in whose employment the employee was last injuriously exposed to the hazards of such disease, and the insurance carrier, if any, on the risk when such employee was last so exposed under such employer, shall alone be liable therefor, without right to contribution from any prior employer or insurance carrier; and the notice of injury and claim for compensation, as hereinafter required, shall be given and made to such employer; provided, however, that in case of disability from any dust disease the only employer and insurance carrier liable shall be the last employer in whose employment the employee was last injuriously exposed to the hazards of the disease for a period of at least 60 days.

(6) The time for notice of injury or death provided in s 440.185(1) shall be extended in cases of occupational diseases to a period of 90 days.

History: s. 1, ch. 22852, 1945; s. 1, ch. 23921, 1947; s. 11, ch. 25035, 1949; s. 3, ch. 28241, 1953; s. 1, ch. 65-116; ss. 19, 35, ch. 69-106; ss. 10, 24, ch. 74-197; s. 23, ch. 78-300; ss. 11, 124, ch. 79-40; s. 21, ch. 79-312; s. 43, ch. 89-289; s. 56, ch. 90-201; s. 52, ch. 91-1; s. 111, ch. 97-103; s. 53, ch. 99-5, effective March 25, 1999; s. 210, ch. 99-8, effective March 25, 1999; s. 19, ch. 2003-412, effective Oct. 1, 2003.

1999 Note: Chapter 99-5 repealed subsection (1)(e); Chapter 99-8 amended subsection (1)(f). The Division of Statutory Revision redesignated the amended subsection (1)(f) to (1)(e).

§ 440.16. Compensation for Death.

(1) If death results from the accident within 1 year thereafter or follows continuous disability and results from the accident within 5 years thereafter, the employer shall pay:

(a) Within 14 days after receiving the bill, actual funeral expenses not to exceed $7,500.

(b) Compensation, in addition to the above, in the following percentages of the average weekly wages to the following persons entitled thereto on account of dependency upon the deceased, and in the following order of preference, subject to the limitation provided in subparagraph 2., but such compensation shall be subject to the limits provided in s. 440.12(2), shall not exceed $150,000, and may be less than, but shall not exceed, for all dependents or persons entitled to compensation, 66²/₃ percent of the average wage:

1. To the spouse, if there is no child, 50 percent of the average weekly wage, such compensation to cease upon the spouse's death.

2. To the spouse, if there is a child or children, the compensation payable under subparagraph 1. and, in addition, 16²/₃ percent on account of the child or children. However, when the deceased is survived by a spouse and also a child or children, whether such child or children are the product of the union existing at the time of death or of a former marriage or marriages, the judge of compensation claims may provide for the payment of compensation in such manner as may appear to the judge of compensation claims just and proper and for the best interests of the respective parties and, in so doing, may provide for the entire compensation to be paid exclusively to the child or children; and, in the case of death of such spouse, 33¹/₃ percent for each child. However, upon the surviving spouse's remarriage, the spouse shall be entitled to a lump-sum payment equal to 26 weeks of compensation at the rate of 50 percent of the average weekly wage as provided in s. 440.12(2), unless the $150,000 limit provided in this paragraph is exceeded, in which case the surviving spouse shall receive a lump-sum payment equal to the remaining available benefits in lieu of any further indemnity benefits. In no case shall a surviving spouse's acceptance of a lump-sum payment affect payment of death benefits to other dependents.

3. To the child or children, if there is no spouse, 33¹/₃ percent for each child.

4. To the parents, 25 percent to each, such compensation to be paid during the continuance of dependency.

5. To the brothers, sisters, and grandchildren, 15 percent for each brother, sister, or grandchild.

(c) To the surviving spouse, payment of postsecondary student fees for instruction at any career center established under s. 1001.44 for up to 1,800 classroom hours or payment of student fees at any community college established under part III of chapter 1004 for up to 80 semester hours. The spouse of a deceased state employee shall be entitled to a full waiver of such fees as provided in ss. 1009.22 and 1009.23 in lieu of the payment of such fees. The benefits provided for in this paragraph shall be in addition to other benefits provided for in this section and shall terminate 7 years after the death of the deceased employee, or when the total payment in eligible compensation under paragraph (b) has been received. To qualify for the educational benefit under this paragraph, the spouse shall be required to meet and maintain the regular admission requirements of, and be registered at, such career center or community college, and make satisfactory academic progress as defined by the educational institution in which the student is enrolled.

(2) The dependence of a child, except a child physically or mentally incapacitated from earning a livelihood, shall terminate with the attainment of 18 years of age, with the attainment of 22 years of age if a full-time student in an accredited educational institution, or upon marriage.

(3) Where, because of the limitation in paragraph (1)(b), a person or class of persons cannot receive the percentage of compensation specified as payable to or on account of such person or class, there shall be available to such person or class that proportion of such percentage as, when added to the total percentage payable to all persons having priority of preference, will not

exceed a total of said 66⅔ percent, which proportion shall be paid:

(a) To such person; or

(b) To such class, share and share alike, unless the judge of compensation claims determines otherwise in accordance with the provisions of subsection (4).

(4) If the judge of compensation claims determines that payments in accordance with paragraph (3)(b) would provide no substantial benefit to any person of such class, the judge of compensation claims may provide for the payment of such compensation to the person or persons within such class who the judge of compensation claims considers will be most benefited by such payment.

(5) Upon the cessation of compensation under this section to any person, the compensation of the remaining persons entitled to compensation, for the unexpired part of the period during which their compensation is payable, shall be that which such persons would have received if they had been the only persons entitled to compensation at the time of the decedent's death.

(6) Relationship to the deceased giving right to compensation under the provisions of this section must have existed at the time of the accident, save only in the case of afterborn children of the deceased.

History: s. 16, ch. 17481, 1935; s. 7, ch. 18413, 1937; CGL 1936 Supp. 5966(16); s. 5, ch. 20672, 1941; s. 1, ch. 26966, 1951; ss. 4-6, ch. 28241, 1953; s. 1, ch. 57-143; s. 2, ch. 67-239; ss. 17, 35, ch. 69-106; s. 6, ch. 73-127; s. 11, ch. 74-197; s. 8, ch. 75-209; s. 23, ch. 78-300; ss. 12, 124, ch. 79-40; ss. 9, 21, ch. 79-312; s. 2, ch. 82-237; s. 11, ch. 86-171; s. 4, ch. 87-330; ss. 13, 43, ch. 89-289; ss. 21, 56, ch. 90-201; ss. 19, 52, ch. 91-1; s. 28, ch. 91-46; s. 62, ch. 92-136; s. 21, ch. 93-415; s. 3, ch. 98-125, effective May 22, 1998; s. 1002, ch. 2002-387, effective Jan. 7, 2003; s. 20, ch. 412, effective Oct. 1, 2003; s. 56, ch. 2004-64, effective July 1, 2004; s. 39, ch. 2004-357, effective July 1, 2004.

[1]**Note:** —The term "area technical center" was substituted for the term "area vocational-technical center" by the editors pursuant to the directive of the Legislature in s. 16, ch. 94-232.

§ 440.17. Guardian for Minor or Incompetent.

Prior to the filing of a claim, the department, and after the filing of a claim, a judge of compensation claims, may require the appointment by a court of competent jurisdiction, for any person who is mentally incompetent or a minor, of a guardian or other representative to receive compensation payable to such person under this chapter and to exercise the powers granted to or to perform the duties required of such person under this chapter; however, the judge of compensation claims, in the judge of compensation claims' discretion, may designate in the compensation award a person to whom payment of compensation may be paid for a minor or incompetent, in which event payment to such designated person shall discharge all liability for such compensation.

History: s. 17, ch. 17481, 1935; CGL 1936 Supp. 5966(17); s. 8, ch 18413, 1937; ss. 17, 35, ch. 69-106; s. 9, ch. 75-209; ss. 13, 124, ch. 79-40; s. 21, ch. 79-312; s. 43, ch. 89-289; s. 56, ch. 90-201; s. 52, ch. 91-1; s. 3, ch. 91-46; s. 480, ch. 2003-261, effective June 26, 2003.

§ 440.185. Notice of Injury or Death; Reports; Penalties for Violations.

(1) An employee who suffers an injury arising out of and in the course of employment shall advise his or her employer of the injury within 30 days after the date of or initial manifestation of the injury. Failure to so advise the employer shall bar a petition under this chapter unless:

(a) The employer or the employer's agent had actual knowledge of the injury;

(b) The cause of the injury could not be identified without a medical opinion and the employee advised the employer within 30 days after obtaining a medical opinion indicating that the injury arose out of and in the course of employment;

(c) The employer did not put its employees on notice of the requirements of this section by posting notice pursuant to s. 440.055; or

(d) Exceptional circumstances, outside the scope of paragraph (a) or paragraph (b) justify

Fla. Stats.

such failure. In the event of death arising out of and in the course of employment, the requirements of this subsection shall be satisfied by the employee's agent or estate. Documents prepared by counsel in connection with litigation, including but not limited to notices of appearance, petitions, motions, or complaints, shall not constitute notice for purposes of this section.

(2) Within 7 days after actual knowledge of injury or death, the employer shall report such injury or death to its carrier, in a format prescribed by the department, and shall provide a copy of such report to the employee or the employee's estate. The report of injury shall contain the following information:

(a) The name, address, and business of the employer;

(b) The name, social security number, street, mailing address, telephone number, and occupation of the employee;

(c) The cause and nature of the injury or death;

(d) The year, month, day, and hour when, and the particular locality where, the injury or death occurred; and

(e) Such other information as the department may require. The carrier shall, within 14 days after the employer's receipt of the form reporting the injury, file the information required by this subsection with the department. However, the department may by rule provide for a different reporting system for those types of injuries which it determines should be reported in a different manner and for those cases which involve minor injuries requiring professional medical attention in which the employee does not lose more than 7 days of work as a result of the injury and is able to return to the job immediately after treatment and resume regular work.

(3) In addition to the requirements of subsection (2), the employer shall notify the department within 24 hours by telephone or telegraph of any injury resulting in death. However, this special notice shall not be required when death results subsequent to the submission to the department of a previous report of the injury pursuant to subsection (2).

(4) Within 3 days after the employer or the employee informs the carrier of an injury the carrier shall mail to the injured worker an informational brochure approved by the department which sets forth in clear and understandable language an explanation of the rights, benefits, procedures for obtaining benefits and assistance, criminal penalties, and obligations of injured workers and their employers under the Florida Workers' Compensation Law. Annually, the carrier or its third-party administrator shall mail to the employer an informational brochure approved by the department which sets forth in clear and understandable language an explanation of the rights, benefits, procedures for obtaining benefits and assistance, criminal penalties, and obligations of injured workers and their employers under the Florida Workers' Compensation Law. All such informational brochures shall contain a notice that clearly states in substance the following: "Any person who, knowingly and with intent to injure, defraud, or deceive any employer or employee, insurance company, or self-insured program, files a statement of claim containing any false or misleading information commits a felony of the third degree."

(5) Additional reports with respect to such injury and of the condition of such employee, including copies of medical reports, funeral expenses, and wage statements, shall be filed by the employer or carrier to the department at such times and in such manner as the department may prescribe by rule. In carrying out its responsibilities under this chapter, the department or agency may by rule provide for the obtaining of any medical records relating to medical treatment provided pursuant to this chapter, notwithstanding the provisions of ss. 90.503 and 395.3025(4).

(6) In the absence of a stipulation by the parties, reports provided for in subsection (2), subsection (4), or subsection (5) shall not be evidence of any fact stated in such report in any proceeding relating thereto, except for medical reports which, if otherwise qualified, may be admitted at the discretion of the judge of com-

pensation claims.

(7) Every carrier shall file with the department within 21 days after the issuance of a policy or contract of insurance such policy information as the department requires, including notice of whether the policy is a minimum premium policy. Notice of cancellation or expiration of a policy as set out in s. 440.42(3) shall be mailed to the department in accordance with rules adopted by the department under chapter 120. The department may contract with a private entity for the collection of policy information required to be filed by carriers under this subsection and the receipt of notices of cancellation or expiration of a policy required to be filed by carriers under s. 440.42(3). The submission of policy information or notices of cancellation or expiration to the contracted private entity satisfies the filing requirements of this subsection and s. 440.42(3).

(8) When a claimant, employer, or carrier has the right, or is required, to mail a report or notice with required copies within the times prescribed in subsection (2), subsection (4), or subsection (5), such mailing will be completed and in compliance with this section if it is postmarked and mailed prepaid to the appropriate recipient prior to the expiration of the time periods prescribed in this section.

(9) Any employer or carrier who fails or refuses to timely send any form, report, or notice required by this section shall be subject to an administrative fine by the department not to exceed $1,000 for each such failure or refusal. If, within 1 calendar year, an employer fails to timely submit to the carrier more than 10 percent of its notices of injury or death, the employer shall be subject to an administrative fine by the department not to exceed $2,000 for each such failure or refusal. However, any employer who fails to notify the carrier of the injury on the prescribed form or by letter within the 7 days required in subsection (2) shall be liable for the administrative fine, which shall be paid by the employer and not the carrier. Failure by the employer to meet its obligations under subsection (2) shall not relieve the carrier from liability for the administrative fine if it fails to comply with subsections (4) and (5).

(10) The department may by rule prescribe forms and procedures governing the submission of the change in claims administration report and the risk class code and standard industry code report for all lost time and denied lost-time cases. The department may by rule define terms that are necessary for the effective administration of this section.

(11) Upon receiving notice of an injury from an employee under subsection (1), the employer or carrier shall provide the employee with a written notice, in the form and manner determined by the department by rule, of the availability of services from the Employee Assistance and Ombudsman Office. The substance of the notice to the employee shall include:

(a) A description of the scope of services provided by the office.

(b) A listing of the toll-free telephone number of, the email address, and the postal address of the office.

(c) A statement that the informational brochure referred to in subsection (4) will be mailed to the employee within 3 days after the carrier receives notice of the injury.

(d) Any other information regarding access to assistance that the department finds is immediately necessary for an injured employee.

History: s. 10, ch. 75-209; s. 1, ch. 77-174; ss. 6, 23, ch. 78-300; ss. 14, 124, ch. 79-40; ss. 10, 21, ch. 79-312; s. 6, ch. 80-236; s. 276, ch. 81-259; s. 6, ch. 83-305; s. 8, ch. 86-171; s. 5, ch. 87-330; s. 5, ch. 88-203; ss. 14, 43, ch. 89-289; ss. 22, 56, ch. 90-201; ss. 20, 52, ch. 91-1; s. 29, ch. 91-46; s. 82, ch. 92-289; s. 22, ch. 93-415; s. 112, ch. 97-103; s. 4, ch. 98-125; s. 9, ch. 98-174; s. 3, ch. 98-407; s. 93, ch. 2000-153; s. 15, ch. 2001-91; s. 29, ch. 2002-194, effective July 1, 2002; s. 21, ch 2003-412, effective Oct. 1, 2003; s. 13, ch. 2004-6, effective Oct. 2, 2003; s. 13, ch. 2004-5, effective Oct. 2, 2004.

§ 440.19. Time Bars to Filing Petitions for Benefits.

(1) Except to the extent provided elsewhere in this section, all employee petitions for benefits under this chapter shall be barred unless the employee, or the employee's estate if the employee is deceased, has advised the employer of

Fla. Stats.

the injury or death pursuant to s. 440.185(1) and the petition is filed within 2 years after the date on which the employee knew or should have known that the injury or death arose out of work performed in the course and scope of employment.

(2) Payment of any indemnity benefit or the furnishing of remedial treatment, care, or attendance pursuant to either a notice of injury or a petition for benefits shall toll the limitations period set forth above for 1 year from the date of such payment. This tolling period does not apply to the issues of compensability, date of maximum medical improvement, or permanent impairment.

(3) The filing of a petition for benefits does not toll the limitations period set forth in this section unless the petition meets the specificity requirements set forth in s. 440.192.

(4) Notwithstanding the provisions of this section, the failure to file a petition for benefits within the periods prescribed is not a bar to the employee's claim unless the carrier advances the defense of a statute of limitations in its initial response to the petition for benefits. If a claimant contends that an employer or its carrier is estopped from raising a statute of limitations defense and the carrier demonstrates that it has provided notice to the employee in accordance with s. 440.185 and that the employer has posted notice in accordance with s. 440.055, the employee must demonstrate estoppel by clear and convincing evidence.

(5) If a person who is entitled to compensation under this chapter is mentally incompetent or a minor, the limitations period is tolled while that person has no guardian or other authorized representative, but the period shall begin to run from the date of appointment of such guardian or other representative, or in the case of a minor, if no guardian is appointed before the minor becomes of age, from the date the minor becomes of age.

(6) When recovery is denied to any person in a suit brought at law or in admiralty to recover damages for injury or death on the ground that such person was an employee, that the defendant was an employer within the meaning of this chapter, and that such employer had secured compensation of such employee under this chapter, the limitations period set forth in this section shall begin to run from the date of termination of such suit; however, in such an event, the employer is allowed a credit of his or her actual cost of defending such suit in an amount not to exceed $250, which amount must be deducted from any compensation allowed or awarded to the employee under this chapter.

History: s. 19, ch. 17481, 1935; CGL 1936 Supp. 5966(19); s. 1, ch. 23908, 1947; s. 10, ch. 26484, 1951; s. 4, ch. 29778, 1955; s. 1, ch. 57-192; s. 1, ch. 65-120; s. 2, ch. 67-554; ss. 17, 35, ch. 69-106; s. 23, ch. 78-300; ss. 15, 124, ch. 79-40; ss. 11, 21, ch. 79-312; s. 7, ch. 80-236; s. 7, ch. 83-305; ss. 15, 43, ch. 89-289; ss. 23, 56, ch. 90-201; ss. 21, 52, ch. 91-1; s. 23, ch. 93-415; s. 113, ch. 97-103.

§ 440.191. Employee Assistance and Ombudsman Office.

(1)

(a) In order to effect the self-executing features of the Workers' Compensation Law, this chapter shall be construed to permit injured employees and employers or the employer's carrier to resolve disagreements without undue expense, costly litigation, or delay in the provisions of benefits. It is the duty of all who participate in the workers' compensation system, including, but not limited to, carriers, service providers, health care providers, attorneys, employers, managed care arrangements, and employees, to attempt to resolve disagreements in good faith and to cooperate with the department's efforts to resolve disagreements between the parties. The department may by rule prescribe definitions that are necessary for the effective administration of this section.

(b) An Employee Assistance and Ombudsman Office is created within the department to inform and assist injured workers, employers, carriers, health care providers, and managed care arrangements in fulfilling their responsibilities under this chapter. The department may by rule specify forms and procedures for administering this section.

(c) The Employee Assistance and Ombudsman Office shall be a resource available to all employees who participate in the workers' compensation system and shall take all steps necessary to educate and disseminate information to employees and employers. Upon receiving a notice of injury or death, the Employee Assistance and Ombudsman Office may initiate contact with the injured employee or employee's representative to discuss rights and responsibilities of the employee under this chapter and the services available through the Employee Assistance and Ombudsman Office.

(2)

(a) If at any time the employer or its carrier fails to provide benefits to which the employee believes she or he is entitled, the employee shall contact the office to request assistance in resolving the dispute. The office may review a petition for benefits filed under s. 440.192 and may attempt to facilitate an agreement between the employee and the employer or carrier. The employee, the employer, and the carrier shall cooperate with the office and shall timely provide the office with any documents or other information that it may require in connection with its efforts under this section.

(b) The office may compel parties to attend conferences in person or by telephone in an attempt to resolve disputes quickly and in the most efficient manner possible. Settlement agreements resulting from such conferences must be submitted to the Office of the Judges of Compensation Claims for approval.

(c) The Employee Assistance and Ombudsman Office may assign an ombudsman to assist the employee in resolving the dispute. The ombudsman may, at the employee's request, assist the employee in drafting a petition for benefits and explain the procedures for filing petitions. The Employee Assistance and Ombudsman Office may not represent employees before the judges of compensation claims. An employer or carrier may not pay any attorneys' fees on behalf of the employee for services rendered or costs incurred in connection with this section, unless expressly authorized elsewhere in this chapter.

History: s. 24, ch. 93-415; s. 114, ch. 97-103; s. 5, ch. 98-125; s. 94, ch. 2000-153; s. 30, ch. 2002-194, effective July 1, 2002; s. 11, ch. 2002-236, effective July 1, 2002.

§ 440.192. Procedure for Resolving Benefit Disputes.

(1) Any employee may, for any benefit that is ripe, due, and owing, file by certified mail, or by electronic means approved by the Deputy Chief Judge, with the Office of the Judges of Compensation Claims a petition for benefits which meets the requirements of this section and the definition of specificity in s. 440.02. The department shall inform employees of the location of the Office of the Judges of Compensation Claims for purposes of filing a petition for benefits. The employee shall also serve copies of the petition for benefits by certified mail, or by electronic means approved by the Deputy Chief Judge, upon the employer and the employer's carrier. The Chief Judge shall refer the petitions to the judges of compensation claims.

(2) Upon receipt, the Office of the Judges of Compensation Claims shall review each petition and shall dismiss each petition or any portion of such a petition that does not on its face specifically identify or itemize the following:

(a) Name, address, telephone number, and social security number of the employee.

(b) Name, address, and telephone number of the employer.

(c) A detailed description of the injury and cause of the injury, including the location of the occurrence and the date or dates of the accident.

(d) A detailed description of the employee's job, work responsibilities, and work the employee was performing when the injury occurred.

(e) The time period for which compensation and the specific classification of compensation were not timely provided.

(f) Date of maximum medical improvement, character of disability, and specific statement of all benefits or compensation that the employee is seeking.

(g) All specific travel costs to which the employee believes she or he is entitled, including dates of travel and purpose of travel, means of transportation, and mileage and including the date the request for mileage was filed with the carrier and a copy of the request filed with the carrier.

(h) Specific listing of all medical charges alleged unpaid, including the name and address of the medical provider, the amounts due, and the specific dates of treatment.

(i) The type or nature of treatment care or attendance sought and the justification for such treatment. If the employee is under the care of a physician for an injury identified under paragraph (c), a copy of the physician's request, authorization, or recommendation for treatment, care, or attendance must accompany the petition.

(j) Specific explanation of any other disputed issue that a judge of compensation claims will be called to rule upon. The dismissal of any petition or portion of such a petition under this section is without prejudice and does not require a hearing.

(3) A petition for benefits may contain a claim for past benefits and continuing benefits in any benefit category, but is limited to those in default and ripe, due, and owing on the date the petition is filed. If the employer has elected to satisfy its obligation to provide medical treatment, care, and attendance through a managed care arrangement designated under this chapter, the employee must exhaust all managed care grievance procedures before filing a petition for benefits under this section.

(4) The petition must include a certification by the claimant or, if the claimant is represented by counsel, the claimant's attorney, stating that the claimant, or attorney if the claimant is represented by counsel, has made a good faith effort to resolve the dispute and that the claimant or attorney was unable to resolve the dispute with the carrier.

(5) All motions to dismiss must state with particularity the basis for the motion. The judge of compensation claims shall enter an order upon such motions without hearing, unless good cause for hearing is shown. When any petition or portion of a petition is dismissed for lack of specificity under this subsection, the claimant must be allowed 20 days after the date of the order of dismissal in which to file an amended petition. Any grounds for dismissal for lack of specificity under this section which are not asserted within 30 days after receipt of the petition for benefits are thereby waived.

(6) If the claimant is not represented by counsel, the Office of the Judges of Compensation Claims may request the Employee Assistance and Ombudsman Office to assist the claimant in filing a petition that meets the requirements of this section.

(7) Notwithstanding the provisions of s. 440.34, a judge of compensation claims may not award attorney's fees payable by the carrier for services expended or costs incurred prior to the filing of a petition that does not meet the requirements of this section.

(8) Within 14 days after receipt of a petition for benefits by certified mail, the carrier must either pay the requested benefits without prejudice to its right to deny within 120 days from receipt of the petition or file a response to petition with the Office of the Judges of Compensation Claims. The carrier must list all benefits requested but not paid and explain its justification for nonpayment in the response to petition. A carrier that does not deny compensability in accordance with s. 440.20(4) is deemed to have accepted the employee's injuries as compensable, unless it can establish material facts relevant to the issue of compensability that could not have been discovered through reasonable investigation within the 120-day period. The carrier shall provide copies of the response to the filing party, employer, and claimant by certified mail.

(9) A petition for benefits must contain claims for all benefits that are ripe, due, and owing on the date the petition is filed. Unless stipulated in writing by the parties, only claims which have been properly raised in a petition for benefits and have undergone mediation may be consid-

ered for adjudication by a judge of compensation claims.

History: s. 25, ch. 93-415; s. 115, ch. 97-103; s. 16, ch. 2001-91, effective Oct. 1, 2001; s. 31, ch. 2002-194, effective July 1, 2002; s. 22, ch. 2003-412, effective Oct. 1, 2003.

§ 440.1925. Procedure for Resolving Maximum Medical Improvement or Permanent Impairment Disputes.

History: s. 13, ch. 93-415; s. 106, ch. 97-103; s. 12, ch. 412, effective October 1, 2003; s. 474, ch. 2003-261, effective June 26, 2003; repealed by s. 45, 2003-412, Laws of Florida, effective October 1, 2003.

§ 440.1926. Alternate Dispute Resolution; Claim Arbitration.

Notwithstanding any other provision of this chapter, the employer, carrier, and employee may mutually agree to seek consent from a judge of compensation claims to enter into binding claim arbitration in lieu of any other remedy provided for in this chapter to resolve all issues in dispute regarding an injury. Arbitrations agreed to pursuant to this section shall be governed by chapter 682, the Florida Arbitration Code, except that, notwithstanding any provision in chapter 682, the term "court" shall mean a judge of compensation claims. An arbitration award in accordance with this section shall be enforceable in the same manner and with the same powers as any final compensation order.

History: s. 23, ch. 412, effective Oct. 1, 2003.

§ 440.20. Time for Payment of Compensation and Medical Bills; Penalties for Late Payment.

(1)

(a) Unless it denies compensability or entitlement to benefits, the carrier shall pay compensation directly to the employee as required by ss. 440.14, 440.15, and 440.16, in accordance with the obligations set forth in such sections. If authorized by the employee, the carrier's obligation to pay compensation directly to the employee is satisfied when the carrier directly deposits, by electronic transfer or other means, compensation into the employee's account at a financial institution. As used in this paragraph, the term "financial institution" means a financial institution as defined in s. 655.005(1)(h). Compensation by direct deposit is considered paid on the date the funds become available for withdrawal by the employee.

(b) Notwithstanding any other provision of this chapter, all insurance carriers, group self-insurance funds, assessable mutual insurers, and the Joint Underwriting Association authorized to write workers' compensation insurance in this state shall make available a notice in writing to the employer the fact that a state-authorized deductible plan is available. Under this plan, an employer may pay, for each injury for which an employee files a claim under this chapter as a deductible, up to the first $2,500 of the total amount payable under compensable claims related to such injury. An employer shall not be reimbursed for any amount paid under this paragraph; however, the reporting requirements of the employer, relating to injuries required under any provision under this chapter, are not altered or alleviated. The rate base of any workers' compensation insurance offered pursuant to this chapter shall include the deductible provision authorized by this paragraph. Any amounts paid by an employer pursuant to this paragraph shall not apply in any way to such employer's experience rating for injury.

(2)

(a) The carrier must pay the first installment of compensation for total disability or death benefits or deny compensability no later than the 14th calendar day after the employer receives notification of the injury or death, when disability is immediate and continuous for 8 calendar days or more after the injury. If the first 7 days after disability are nonconsecutive or delayed, the first installment of compensation is due on the 6th day after the first 8 calendar days of disability. The carrier shall thereafter pay compensation in biweekly installments or as otherwise provided in s. 440.15, unless the judge of compensation claims determines or the parties agree that an alternate installment schedule is in the best interests of the employee.

(b) The carrier must pay, disallow, or deny all

Fla. Stats.

medical, dental, pharmacy, and hospital bills submitted to the carrier in accordance with department rule no later than 45 calendar days after the carrier's receipt of the bill.

(3) Upon making initial payment of indemnity benefits, or upon suspension or cessation of payment for any reason, the carrier shall immediately notify the injured employee, the employer, and the department that it has commenced, suspended, or ceased payment of compensation. The department may require such notification to the injured employee, employer, and the department in a format and manner it deems necessary to obtain accurate and timely notification.

(4) If the carrier is uncertain of its obligation to provide all benefits or compensation, the carrier shall immediately and in good faith commence investigation of the employee's entitlement to benefits under this chapter and shall admit or deny compensability within 120 days after the initial provision of compensation or benefits as required under subsection (2) or s. 440.192(8). Additionally, the carrier shall initiate payment and continue the provision of all benefits and compensation as if the claim had been accepted as compensable, without prejudice and without admitting liability. Upon commencement of payment as required under subsection (2) or s. 440.192 (8), the carrier shall provide written notice to the employee that it has elected to pay the claim pending further investigation, and that it will advise the employee of claim acceptance or denial within 120 days. A carrier that fails to deny compensability within 120 days after the initial provision of benefits or payment of compensation as required under subsection (2) or s. 440.192(8) waives the right to deny compensability, unless the carrier can establish material facts relevant to the issue of compensability that it could not have discovered through reasonable investigation within the 120-day period. The initial provision of compensation or benefits, for purposes of this subsection, means the first installment of compensation or benefits to be paid by the carrier under subsection (2) or pursuant to a petition for benefits under s. 440.192(8).

(5) If the employer has advanced compensation payments or benefits to the employee, the carrier shall reimburse the employer for the advanced payments if the employee is entitled to compensation and benefits pursuant to this chapter. The carrier may deduct such reimbursements from the employee's compensation installments or, if applicable, from payments to the employee ordered by a judge of compensation claims.

(6)

(a) If any installment of compensation for death or dependency benefits, or compensation for disability benefits payable without an award is not paid within 7 days after it becomes due, as provided in subsection (2), subsection (3), or subsection (4), there shall be added to such unpaid installment a penalty of an amount equal to 20 percent of the unpaid installment, which shall be paid at the same time as, but in addition to, such installment of compensation. This penalty shall not apply for late payments resulting from conditions over which the employer or carrier had no control. When any installment of compensation payable without an award has not been paid within 7 days after it became due and the claimant concludes the prosecution of the claim before a judge of compensation claims without having specifically claimed additional compensation in the nature of a penalty under this section, the claimant will be deemed to have acknowledged that, owing to conditions over which the employer or carrier had no control, such installment could not be paid within the period prescribed for payment and to have waived the right to claim such penalty. However, during the course of a hearing, the judge of compensation claims shall on her or his own motion raise the question of whether such penalty should be awarded or excused. The department may assess without a hearing the penalty against either the employer or the carrier, depending upon who was at fault in causing the delay. The insurance policy cannot provide that this sum will be paid by the carrier if the department or the judge of compensation claims determines that the penalty should be paid by the employer rather than the carrier. Any additional installment of compensation paid by the carrier pursuant to this section shall be paid directly to the employee by check or, if authorized by the employee, by direct deposit into the employee's account at a financial institution.

(b) For medical services provided on or after January 1, 2004, the department shall require that all medical, hospital, pharmacy, or dental bills properly submitted by the provider, except for bills that are disallowed or denied by the carrier or its authorized vendor in accordance with department rule, are timely paid within 45 calendar days after the carrier's receipt of the bill. The department shall impose penalties for late payments or disallowances or denials of medical, hospital, pharmacy, or dental bills that are below a minimum 95 percent timely performance standard. The carrier shall pay to the Workers' Compensation Administration Trust Fund a penalty of:

1. Twenty-five dollars for each bill below the 95 percent timely performance standard, but meeting a 90 percent timely standard.

2. Fifty dollars for each bill below a 90 percent timely performance standard.

(7) If any compensation, payable under the terms of an award, is not paid within 7 days after it becomes due, there shall be added to such unpaid compensation an amount equal to 20 percent thereof, which shall be paid at the same time as, but in addition to, such compensation, unless review of the compensation order making such award is had as provided in s. 440.25.

(8)

(a) In addition to any other penalties provided by this chapter for late payment, if any installment of compensation is not paid when it becomes due, the employer, carrier, or servicing agent shall pay interest thereon at the rate of 12 percent per year from the date the installment becomes due until it is paid, whether such installment is payable without an order or under the terms of an order. The interest payment shall be the greater of the amount of interest due or $5.

(b) In order to ensure carrier compliance under this chapter, the office shall monitor, audit, and investigate the performance of carriers. The office shall require that all compensation benefits are timely paid in accordance with this section. The office shall impose penalties for late payments of compensation that are below a minimum 95 percent timely payment performance standard. The carrier shall pay to the Workers' Compensation Administration Trust Fund a penalty of:

1. Fifty dollars per number of installments of compensation below the 95 percent timely payment performance standard and equal to or greater than a 90 percent timely payment performance standard.

2. One hundred dollars per number of installments of compensation below a 90 percent timely payment performance standard. This paragraph does not affect the imposition of any penalties or interest due to the claimant. If a carrier contracts with a servicing agent to fulfill its administrative responsibilities under this chapter, the payment practices of the servicing agent are deemed the payment practices of the carrier for the purpose of assessing penalties against the carrier.

(9) The department may upon its own initiative at any time in a case in which payments are being made without an award investigate same and shall, in any case in which the right to compensation is controverted, or in which payments of compensation have been stopped or suspended, upon receipt of notice from any person entitled to compensation or from the employer that the right to compensation is controverted or that payments of compensation have been stopped or suspended, make such investigations, cause such medical examination to be made, or hold such hearings, and take such further action as it considers will properly protect the rights of all parties.

(10) Whenever the department deems it advisable, it may require any employer to make a deposit with the Chief Financial Officer to secure the prompt and convenient payments of such compensation; and payments therefrom upon any awards shall be made upon order of the department or judge of compensation claims.

(11)

Fla. Stats.

(a) When a claimant is not represented by counsel, upon joint petition of all interested parties, a lump-sum payment in exchange for the employer's or carrier's release from liability for future medical expenses, as well as future payments of compensation expenses and any other benefits provided under this chapter, shall be allowed at any time in any case in which the employer or carrier has filed a written notice of denial within 120 days after the employer receives notice of the injury, and the judge of compensation claims at a hearing to consider the settlement proposal finds a justiciable controversy as to legal or medical compensability of the claimed injury or the alleged accident. The employer or carrier may not pay any attorney's fees on behalf of the claimant for any settlement under this section unless expressly authorized elsewhere in this chapter. Upon the joint petition of all interested parties and after giving due consideration to the interests of all interested parties, the judge of compensation claims may enter a compensation order approving and authorizing the discharge of the liability of the employer for compensation and remedial treatment, care, and attendance, as well as rehabilitation expenses, by the payment of a lump sum. Such a compensation order so entered upon joint petition of all interested parties is not subject to modification or review under s. 440.28. If the settlement proposal together with supporting evidence is not approved by the judge of compensation claims, it shall be considered void. Upon approval of a lump-sum settlement under this subsection, the judge of compensation claims shall send a report to the Chief Judge of the amount of the settlement and a statement of the nature of the controversy. The Chief Judge shall keep a record of all such reports filed by each judge of compensation claims and shall submit to the Legislature a summary of all such reports filed under this subsection annually by September 15.

(b) When a claimant is not represented by counsel, upon joint petition of all interested parties, a lump-sum payment in exchange for the employer's or carrier's release from liability for future medical expenses, as well as future payments of compensation and rehabilitation expenses, and any other benefits provided under this chapter, may be allowed at any time in any case after the injured employee has attained maximum medical improvement. An employer or carrier may not pay any attorney's fees on behalf of the claimant for any settlement, unless expressly authorized elsewhere in this chapter. A compensation order so entered upon joint petition of all interested parties shall not be subject to modification or review under s. 440.28. However, a judge of compensation claims is not required to approve any award for lump-sum payment when it is determined by the judge of compensation claims that the payment being made is in excess of the value of benefits the claimant would be entitled to under this chapter. The judge of compensation claims shall make or cause to be made such investigations as she or he considers necessary, in each case in which the parties have stipulated that a proposed final settlement of liability of the employer for compensation shall not be subject to modification or review under s. 440.28, to determine whether such final disposition will definitely aid the rehabilitation of the injured worker or otherwise is clearly for the best interests of the person entitled to compensation and, in her or his discretion, may have an investigation made. The joint petition and the report of any investigation so made will be deemed a part of the proceeding. An employer shall have the right to appear at any hearing pursuant to this subsection which relates to the discharge of such employer's liability and to present testimony at such hearing. The carrier shall provide reasonable notice to the employer of the time and date of any such hearing and inform the employer of her or his rights to appear and testify. The probability of the death of the injured employee or other person entitled to compensation before the expiration of the period during which such person is entitled to compensation shall, in the absence of special circumstances making such course improper, be determined in accordance with the most recent United States Life Tables published by the National Office of Vital Statistics of the United States Department of Health and Human Services. The probability of the happening of any other contingency affecting the amount or duration of the compensation, except the possibility of the remarriage of a surviving spouse, shall be disregarded. As a condition of approving a lump-sum payment to a surviving spouse, the judge of compensation claims, in the judge of compensation claims' discretion, may require security which will ensure that, in the event of the remarriage of such surviving spouse, any unaccrued future payments so paid may be recovered or recouped by the employer or carrier. Such applications shall be considered and determined in accordance with s. 440.25.

(c) Notwithstanding s. 440.21(2), when a claimant is represented by counsel, the claimant may waive all rights to any and all benefits under this chapter by entering into a settlement agreement releasing the employer and the carrier from liability for workers' compensation benefits in exchange for a lump-sum payment to the claimant. The settlement agreement requires approval by the judge of compensation claims only as to the attorney's fees paid to the claimant's attorney by the claimant. The parties need not submit any information or documentation in support of the settlement, except as needed to justify the amount of the attorney's fees. Neither the employer nor the carrier is responsible for any attorney's fees relating to the settlement and release of claims under this section. Payment of the lump-sum settlement amount must be made within 14 days after the date the judge of compensation claims mails the order approving the attorney's fees. Any order entered by a judge of compensation claims approving the attorney's fees as set out in the settlement under this subsection is not considered to be an award and is not subject to modification or review. The judge of compensation claims shall report these settlements to the Deputy Chief Judge in accordance with the requirements set forth in paragraphs (a) and (b). Settlements entered into under this subsection are valid and apply to all dates of accident.

(d)

1. With respect to any lump-sum settlement under this subsection, a judge of compensation claims must consider at the time of the settlement, whether the settlement allocation provides for the appropriate recovery of child support arrearages. An employer or carrier does not have a duty to investigate or collect information regarding child support arrearages.

2. When reviewing any settlement of lump-sum payment pursuant to this subsection, judges of compensation claims shall consider the interests of the worker and the worker's family when approving the settlement, which must consider and provide for appropriate recovery of past due support.

3. With respect to any lump-sum settlement under this subsection, any correspondence to a clerk of the circuit court of this state regarding child support documentation shall be exempt from any fees or costs ordinarily assessed by the clerk's office.

(e) This section applies to all claims that the parties have not previously settled, regardless of the date of accident.

(12)

(a) Liability of an employer for future payments of compensation may not be discharged by advance payment unless prior approval of a judge of compensation claims or the department has been obtained as hereinafter provided. The approval shall not constitute an adjudication of the claimant's percentage of disability.

(b) When the claimant has reached maximum recovery and returned to her or his former or equivalent employment with no substantial reduction in wages, such approval of a reasonable advance payment of a part of the compensation payable to the claimant may be given informally by letter by a judge of compensation claims or by the department.

(c) In the event the claimant has not returned to the same or equivalent employment with no substantial reduction in wages or has suffered a substantial loss of earning capacity or a physical impairment, actual or apparent:

1. An advance payment of compensation not in excess of $2,000 may be approved informally by letter, without hearing, by any judge of compensation claims or the Chief Judge.

2. An advance payment of compensation not in excess of $2,000 may be ordered by any judge of compensation claims after giving the inter-

Fla. Stats.

ested parties an opportunity for a hearing thereon pursuant to not less than 10 days' notice by mail, unless such notice is waived, and after giving due consideration to the interests of the person entitled thereto. When the parties have stipulated to an advance payment of compensation not in excess of $2,000, such advance may be approved by an order of a judge of compensation claims, with or without hearing, or informally by letter by any such judge of compensation claims, or by the department, if such advance is found to be for the best interests of the person entitled thereto.

3. When the parties have stipulated to an advance payment in excess of $2,000, subject to the approval of the department, such payment may be approved by a judge of compensation claims by order if the judge finds that such advance payment is for the best interests of the person entitled thereto and is reasonable under the circumstances of the particular case. The judge of compensation claims shall make or cause to be made such investigations as she or he considers necessary concerning the stipulation and, in her or his discretion, may have an investigation of the matter made. The stipulation and the report of any investigation shall be deemed a part of the record of the proceedings.

(d) When an application for an advance payment in excess of $2,000 is opposed by the employer or carrier, it shall be heard by a judge of compensation claims after giving the interested parties not less than 10 days' notice of such hearing by mail, unless such notice is waived. In her or his discretion, the judge of compensation claims may have an investigation of the matter made, in which event the report and recommendation will be deemed a part of the record of the proceedings. If the judge of compensation claims finds that such advance payment is for the best interests of the person entitled to compensation, will not materially prejudice the rights of the employer and carrier, and is reasonable under the circumstances of the case, she or he may order the same paid. However, in no event may any such advance payment under this paragraph be granted in excess of $7,500 or 26 weeks of benefits in any 48-month period, whichever is greater, from the date of the last advance payment.

(13) If the employer has made advance payments of compensation, she or he shall be entitled to be reimbursed out of any unpaid installment or installments of compensation due.

(14) When an employee is injured and the employer pays the employee's full wages or any part thereof during the period of disability, or pays medical expenses for such employee, and the case is contested by the carrier or the carrier and employer and thereafter the carrier, either voluntarily or pursuant to an award, makes a payment of compensation or medical benefits, the employer shall be entitled to reimbursement to the extent of the compensation paid or awarded, plus medical benefits, if any, out of the first proceeds paid by the carrier in compliance with such voluntary payment or award, provided the employer furnishes satisfactory proof to the judge of compensation claims of such payment of compensation and medical benefits. Any payment by the employer over and above compensation paid or awarded and medical benefits, pursuant to subsection (13), shall be considered a gratuity.

(15)

(a) The office shall examine on an ongoing basis claims files in accordance with s. 624.3161 and may impose fines pursuant to s. 624.310(5) and this chapter in order to identify questionable claims-handling techniques, questionable patterns or practices of claims, or a pattern of repeated unreasonably controverted claims by carriers, as defined in s. 440.02, providing services to employees pursuant to this chapter. If the office finds such questionable techniques, patterns, or repeated unreasonably controverted claims as constitute a general business practice of a carrier, as defined in s. 440.02, the office shall take appropriate action so as to bring such general business practices to a halt pursuant to s. 440.38(3) or may impose penalties pursuant to s. 624.4211. The office may initiate investigations of questionable techniques, patterns, practices, or repeated unreasonably controverted claims. The Financial Services Commission may by rule establish forms and procedures for corrective action plans and for auditing carriers.

(b) As to any examination, investigation, or hearing being conducted under this chapter, the department and office:

1. May administer oaths, examine and cross-examine witnesses, receive oral and documentary evidence; and

2. Shall have the power to subpoena witnesses, compel their attendance and testimony, and require by subpoena the production of books, papers, records, files, correspondence, documents, or other evidence which is relevant to the inquiry.

(c) If any person refuses to comply with any such subpoena or to testify as to any matter concerning which she or he may be lawfully interrogated, the Circuit Court of Leon County or of the county wherein such examination, investigation, or hearing is being conducted, or of the county wherein such person resides, may, on the application of the department or the office, issue an order requiring such person to comply with the subpoena and to testify.

(d) Subpoenas shall be served, and proof of such service made, in the same manner as if issued by a circuit court. Witness fees, costs, and reasonable travel expenses, if claimed, shall be allowed the same as for testimony in a circuit court.

(e) The department shall publish annually a report which indicates the promptness of first payment of compensation records of each carrier or self-insurer so as to focus attention on those carriers or self-insurers with poor payment records for the preceding year. The department and the office shall take appropriate steps so as to cause such poor carrier payment practices to halt pursuant to s. 440.38(3). In addition, the department shall take appropriate action so as to halt such poor payment practices of self-insurers. "Poor payment practice" means a practice of late payment sufficient to constitute a general business practice.

(f) The Financial Services Commission, in consultation with the department, shall adopt rules providing guidelines to carriers, as defined in s. 440.02, self-insurers, and employers to indicate behavior that may be construed as questionable claims-handling techniques, questionable patterns of claims, repeated unreasonably controverted claims, or poor payment practices.

(16) No penalty assessed under this section may be recouped by any carrier or self-insurer in the rate base, the premium, or any rate filing. The office shall enforce this subsection.

(17) The Financial Services Commission may by rule establish audit procedures and set standards for the Automated Carrier Performance System.

History: s. 20, ch. 17481, 1935; CGL 1936 Supp. 5966(20); s. 9, ch. 18413, 1937; s. 6, ch. 20672, 1941; s. 2, ch. 23921, 1947; s. 2, ch. 26877, 1951; s. 5, ch. 29778, 1955; s. 1, ch. 59-422; ss. 1, 2, ch. 65-203; s. 2, ch. 67-554; ss. 17, 35, ch. 69-106; s. 13, ch. 74-197; s. 11, ch. 75-209; s. 1, ch. 77-174; s. 5, ch. 77-290; ss. 7, 23, ch. 78-300; ss. 16, 124, ch. 79-40; ss. 12, 21, ch. 79-312; s. 179 ch. 79-400; s. 8, ch. 80-236; s. 277, ch. 81-259; s. 31, ch. 83-215; s. 8, ch. 83-305; s. 7, ch. 84-267; s. 9, ch. 86-171; s. 6, ch. 87-330; ss. 6, 7, ch. 88-203; ss. 16 43, ch. 89-289; ss. 24, 56, ch. 90-201; ss. 22, 52, ch. 91-1; s. 30, ch. 91-46; s. 26, ch. 93-415; s. 116, ch. 97-103; s. 6, ch. 98-125; s. 17, ch. 2001-91; s. 48, ch. 2001-158; s. 33, ch. 2002-194, effective July 1, 2002; s. 53, ch. 2003-1, effective July 1, 2003; s. 24, ch. 412, effective Oct. 1, 2003; s. 481, ch. 2003-261, effective June 26, 2003.

§ 440.205. Coercion of Employees.

No employer shall discharge, threaten to discharge, intimidate, or coerce any employee by reason of such employee's valid claim for compensation or attempt to claim compensation under the Workers' Compensation Law.

History: s. 17, ch. 79-40; s. 43, ch. 89-289; s. 56, ch. 90-201; s. 52, ch. 91-1.

§ 440.207. Workers' Compensation System Guide.

(1) The department shall educate all persons providing or receiving benefits pursuant to this chapter as to their rights and responsibilities under this chapter.

(2) The department shall publish an understandable guide to the workers' compensation system which shall contain an explanation of benefits provided; services provided by the Em-

Fla. Stats.

ployee Assistance and Ombudsman Office; procedures regarding mediation, the hearing process, and civil and criminal penalties; relevant rules of the department; and such other information as the department believes will inform employees, employers, carriers, and those providing services pursuant to this chapter of their rights and responsibilities under this chapter and the rules of the department. For the purposes of this subsection, a guide is understandable if the text of the guide is written at a level of readability not exceeding the eighth grade level, as determined by a recognized readability test.

(3) The guide must be updated as necessary and must be available at cost.

(4) The guide does not constitute either rules or agency action for purposes of chapter 120.

History: ss. 41, 43, ch. 89-289; s. 56, ch. 90-201; s. 52, ch. 91-1; s. 27, ch. 93-415; s. 34, ch. 2002-194, effective July 1, 2002.

§ 440.21. Invalid Agreements.

(1) Any agreement by an employee to pay any portion of premium paid by her or his employer to a carrier or to contribute to a benefit fund or department maintained by the employer for the purpose of providing compensation or medical services and supplies as required by this chapter is invalid.

(2) An agreement by an employee to waive her or his right to compensation under this chapter is invalid.

History: s. 21, ch. 17481, 1935; CGL 1936 Supp. 5966(21), 8135(10); s. 364, ch. 71-136; s. 118, ch. 71-355; s. 23, ch. 78-300; s. 124, ch. 79-40; s. 21, ch. 79-312; s. 43, ch. 89-289; s. 56, ch. 90-201; s. 52, ch. 91-1; s. 28, ch. 93-415; s. 117, ch. 97-103.

§ 440.211. Authorization of Collective Bargaining Agreement.

(1) Subject to the limitation stated in subsection (2), a provision that is mutually agreed upon in any collective bargaining agreement filed with the department between an individually self-insured employer or other employer upon consent of the employer's carrier and a recognized or certified exclusive bargaining representative establishing any of the following shall be valid and binding:

(a) An alternative dispute resolution system to supplement, modify, or replace the provisions of this chapter which may include, but is not limited to, conciliation, mediation, and arbitration. Arbitration held pursuant to this section shall be binding on the parties.

(b) The use of an agreed-upon list of certified health care providers of medical treatment which may be the exclusive source of all medical treatment under this chapter.

(c) The use of a limited list of physicians to conduct independent medical examinations which the parties may agree shall be the exclusive source of independent medical examiners pursuant to this chapter.

(d) A light-duty, modified-job, or return-to-work program.

(e) A vocational rehabilitation or retraining program.

(2) Nothing in this section shall allow any agreement that diminishes an employee's entitlement to benefits as otherwise set forth in this chapter. Any such agreement in violation of this provision shall be null and void.

History: s. 29, ch. 93-415; s. 35, ch. 2002-194, effective July 1, 2002.

§ 440.22. Assignment and Exemption From Claims of Creditors.

No assignment, release, or commutation of compensation or benefits due or payable under this chapter except as provided by this chapter shall be valid, and such compensation and benefits shall be exempt from all claims of creditors, and from levy, execution and attachments or other remedy for recovery or collection of a debt, which exemption may not be waived. However, the exemption of workers' compensation claims from creditors does not extend to claims based on an award of child support or alimony.

History: s. 22, ch. 17481, 1935; CGL 1936 Supp. 5966(22); s. 23, ch. 78-300; s. 124, ch. 79-40; s. 21, ch. 79-312; s. 43, ch. 89-289; s. 56, ch. 90-201; s. 52, ch. 91-1; s. 18, ch. 2001-91; s. 49, ch. 2001-158.

§ 440.23. Compensation a Lien Against Assets.

Compensation shall have the same preference of lien against the assets of the carrier or employer without limit of an amount as is now or may hereafter be allowed by law to the claimant for unpaid wages or otherwise.

History: s. 23, ch. 17481, 1935; CGL 1936 Supp. 5966(23); s. 23, ch. 78-300; s. 124, ch. 79-40; s. 21, ch. 79-312; s. 43, ch. 89-289; s. 56, ch. 90-201; s. 52, ch. 91-1.

§ 440.24. Enforcement of Compensation Orders; Penalties.

(1) In case of default by the employer or carrier in the payment of compensation due under any compensation order of a judge of compensation claims or other failure by the employer or carrier to comply with such order within 10 days after the order becomes final, any circuit court of this state within the jurisdiction of which the employer or carrier resides or transacts business shall, upon application by the department or any beneficiary under such order, have jurisdiction to issue a rule nisi directing such employer or carrier to show cause why a writ of execution, or such other process as may be necessary to enforce the terms of such order, shall not be issued, and, unless such cause is shown, the court shall have jurisdiction to issue a writ of execution or such other process or final order as may be necessary to enforce the terms of such order of the judge of compensation claims.

(2) In any case where the employer is insured and the carrier fails to comply with any compensation order of a judge of compensation claims or court within 10 days after such order becomes final, the department shall notify the office of such failure and the office shall suspend the license of such carrier to do an insurance business in this state, until such carrier has complied with such order.

(3) In any case where the employer is a self-insurer and fails to comply with any compensation order of a judge of compensation claims or court within 10 days after such order becomes final, the department may suspend or revoke any authorization previously given to the employer to be a self-insurer, and the Florida Self-Insurers Guaranty Association, Incorporated, may call or sue upon the surety bond or exercise its rights under the letter of credit deposited by the self-insurer with the association as a qualifying security deposit as may be necessary to satisfy the order.

(4) In any case wherein the employee fails to comply with any order of a judge of compensation claims within 10 days after such order becomes final, the judge of compensation claims may dismiss the claim or suspend payments due under said claim until the employee complies with such order. The judge of compensation claims may strike the defenses of the employer, if said employer is self-insured, or of the insurance carrier, if said employer is not self-insured, if said employer or carrier fails to comply with any order of a judge of compensation claims within 10 days after such order becomes final.

History: s. 24, ch. 17481, 1935; CGL 1936 Supp. 5966(24); s. 10, ch. 18413, 1937; s. 7, ch. 28241, 1953; s. 2, ch. 67-554; ss. 13, 17, 35, ch. 69-106; s. 120, ch. 71-355; s. 14, ch. 74-197; s. 23, ch. 78-300; ss. 18, 124, ch. 79-40; ss. 13, 21, ch. 79-312; s. 6, ch. 81-119; s. 43, ch. 89-289; s. 56, ch. 90-201; s. 52, ch. 91-1; s. 4, ch. 91-46; s. 36, ch. 2002-194, effective July 1, 2002; s. 1, ch. 2002-262, effective Oct. 1, 2002; s. 482, ch. 2003-261, effective June 26, 2003.

§ 440.25. Procedures for Mediation and Hearings.

(1) Forty days after a petition for benefits is filed under s. 440.192, the judge of compensation claims shall notify the interested parties by order that a mediation conference concerning such petition has been scheduled unless the parties have notified the judge of compensation claims that a private mediation has been held or is scheduled to be held. A mediation, whether private or public, shall be held within 130 days after the filing of the petition. Such order must give the date the mediation conference is to be held. Such order may be served personally upon the interested parties or may be sent to the interested parties by mail. If multiple petitions are pending, or if additional petitions are filed after the scheduling of a mediation, the judge of compensation claims shall consolidate all peti-

tions into one mediation. The claimant or the adjuster of the employer or carrier may, at the mediator's discretion, attend the mediation conference by telephone or, if agreed to by the parties, other electronic means. A continuance may be granted upon the agreement of the parties or if the requesting party demonstrates to the judge of compensation claims that the reason for requesting the continuance arises from circumstances beyond the party's control. Any order granting a continuance must set forth the date of the rescheduled mediation conference. A mediation conference may not be used solely for the purpose of mediating attorney's fees.

(2) Any party who participates in a mediation conference shall not be precluded from requesting a hearing following the mediation conference should both parties not agree to be bound by the results of the mediation conference. A mediation conference is required to be held unless this requirement is waived by the Deputy Chief Judge.

(3) Such mediation conference shall be conducted informally and does not require the use of formal rules of evidence or procedure. Any information from the files, reports, case summaries, mediator's notes, or other communications or materials, oral or written, relating to a mediation conference under this section obtained by any person performing mediation duties is privileged and confidential and may not be disclosed without the written consent of all parties to the conference. Any research or evaluation effort directed at assessing the mediation program activities or performance must protect the confidentiality of such information. Each party to a mediation conference has a privilege during and after the conference to refuse to disclose and to prevent another from disclosing communications made during the conference whether or not the contested issues are successfully resolved. This subsection and paragraphs (4)(a) and (b) shall not be construed to prevent or inhibit the discovery or admissibility of any information that is otherwise subject to discovery or that is admissible under applicable law or rule of procedure, except that any conduct or statements made during a mediation conference or in negotiations concerning the conference are inadmissible in any proceeding under this chapter.

(a) Unless the parties conduct a private mediation under paragraph (b), mediation shall be conducted by a mediator selected by the Director of the Division of Administrative Hearings from among mediators employed on a full-time basis by the Office of the Judges of Compensation Claims. A mediator must be a member of The Florida Bar for at least 5 years and must complete a mediation training program approved by the Deputy Chief Judge. Adjunct mediators may be employed by the Office of the Judges of Compensation Claims on an as-needed basis and shall be selected from a list prepared by the Director of the Division of Administrative Hearings. An adjunct mediator must be independent of all parties participating in the mediation conference. An adjunct mediator must be a member of The Florida Bar for at least 5 years and must complete a mediation training program approved by the Office of the Judges of Compensation Claims. An adjunct mediator shall have access to the office, equipment, and supplies of the judge of compensation claims in each district.

(b) With respect to any private mediation, if the parties agree or if mediators are not available under paragraph (a), pursuant to notice from the judge of compensation claims, to conduct the required mediation within the period specified in this section, the parties shall hold a mediation conference at the carrier's expense within the 130-day period set for mediation. The mediation conference shall be conducted by a mediator certified under s. 44.106. If the parties do not agree upon a mediator within 10 days after the date of the order, the claimant shall notify the judge in writing and the judge shall appoint a mediator under this[1] paragraph within 7 days. In the event both parties agree, the results of the mediation conference shall be binding and neither party shall have a right to appeal the results. In the event either party refuses to agree to the results of the mediation conference, the results of the mediation conference as well as the testimony, witnesses, and evidence presented at the conference shall not be admissible at any subsequent proceeding on the claim. The mediator shall not be called in to testify or give deposition to resolve any claim for any hearing before the judge of compensation claims. The employer may be represented by an attorney at the mediation conference if the employee is also represented by an attorney at the mediation conference.

(4)

(a) If the parties fail to agree to written submission of pretrial stipulations, the judge of compensation claims shall conduct a live pretrial hearing. The judge of compensation claims shall give the interested parties at least 14 days' advance notice of the pretrial hearing by mail.

(b) The final hearing must be held and concluded within 90 days after the mediation conference is held, allowing the parties sufficient time to complete discovery. Except as set forth in this section, continuances may be granted only if the requesting party demonstrates to the judge of compensation claims that the reason for requesting the continuance arises from circumstances beyond the party's control. The written consent of the claimant must be obtained before any request from a claimant's attorney is granted for an additional continuance after the initial continuance has been granted. Any order granting a continuance must set forth the date and time of the rescheduled hearing. A continuance may be granted only if the requesting party demonstrates to the judge of compensation claims that the reason for requesting the continuance arises from circumstances beyond the control of the parties. The judge of compensation claims shall report any grant of two or more continuances to the Deputy Chief Judge.

(c) The judge of compensation claims shall give the interested parties at least 14 days' advance notice of the final hearing, served upon the interested parties by mail.

(d) The final hearing shall be held within 210 days after receipt of the petition for benefits in the county where the injury occurred, if the injury occurred in this state, unless otherwise agreed to between the parties and authorized by the judge of compensation claims in the county where the injury occurred. However, the claimant may waive the timeframes within this section for good cause shown. If the injury occurred outside the state and is one for which compensation is payable under this chapter, then the final hearing may be held in the county of the employer's residence or place of business, or in any other county of the state that will, in the discretion of the Deputy Chief Judge, be the most convenient for a hearing. The final hearing shall be conducted by a judge of compensation claims, who shall, within 30 days after final hearing or closure of the hearing record, unless otherwise agreed by the parties, enter a final order on the merits of the disputed issues. The judge of compensation claims may enter an abbreviated final order in cases in which compensability is not disputed. Either party may request separate findings of fact and conclusions of law. At the final hearing, the claimant and employer may each present evidence with respect to the claims presented by the petition for benefits and may be represented by any attorney authorized in writing for such purpose. When there is a conflict in the medical evidence submitted at the hearing, the provisions of s. 440.13 shall apply. The report or testimony of the expert medical advisor shall be admitted into evidence in a proceeding and all costs incurred in connection with such examination and testimony may be assessed as costs in the proceeding, subject to the provisions of s. 440.13. No judge of compensation claims may make a finding of a degree of permanent impairment that is greater than the greatest permanent impairment rating given the claimant by any examining or treating physician, except upon stipulation of the parties. Any benefit due but not raised at the final hearing which was ripe, due, or owing at the time of the final hearing is waived.

(e) The order making an award or rejecting the claim, referred to in this chapter as a "compensation order," shall set forth the findings of ultimate facts and the mandate; and the order need not include any other reason or justification for such mandate. The compensation order shall be filed in the Office of the Judges of Compensation Claims at Tallahassee. A copy of such compensation order shall be sent by mail to the parties and attorneys of record at the last known address of each, with the date of

Fla. Stats.

mailing noted thereon.

(f) Notwithstanding any other provision of this section, the judge of compensation claims may require the appearance of the parties and counsel before her or him without written notice for an emergency conference where there is a bona fide emergency involving the health, safety, or welfare of an employee. An emergency conference under this section may result in the entry of an order or the rendering of an adjudication by the judge of compensation claims.

(g) To expedite dispute resolution and to enhance the self-executing features of the Workers' Compensation Law, the Deputy Chief Judge shall make provision by rule or order for the resolution of appropriate motions by judges of compensation claims without oral hearing upon submission of brief written statements in support and opposition, and for expedited discovery and docketing. Unless the judge of compensation claims, for good cause, orders a hearing under paragraph (h), each claim in a petition relating to the determination of the average weekly wage under s. 440.14 shall be resolved under this paragraph without oral hearing.

(h) To further expedite dispute resolution and to enhance the self-executing features of the system, those petitions filed in accordance with s. 440.192 that involve a claim for benefits of $5,000 or less shall, in the absence of compelling evidence to the contrary, be presumed to be appropriate for expedited resolution under this paragraph; and any other claim filed in accordance with s. 440.192, upon the written agreement of both parties and application by either party, may similarly be resolved under this paragraph. A claim in a petition[2] of $5,000 or less for medical benefits only or a petition for reimbursement for mileage for medical purposes shall, in the absence of compelling evidence to the contrary, be resolved through the expedited dispute resolution process provided in this paragraph. For purposes of expedited resolution pursuant to this paragraph, the Deputy Chief Judge shall make provision by rule or order for expedited and limited discovery and expedited docketing in such cases. At least 15 days prior to hearing, the parties shall exchange and file with the judge of compensation claims a pretrial outline of all issues, defenses, and witnesses on a form adopted by the Deputy Chief Judge; provided, in no event shall such hearing be held without 15 days' written notice to all parties. No pretrial hearing shall be held and no mediation scheduled unless requested by a party. The judge of compensation claims shall limit all argument and presentation of evidence at the hearing to a maximum of 30 minutes, and such hearings shall not exceed 30 minutes in length. Neither party shall be required to be represented by counsel. The employer or carrier may be represented by an adjuster or other qualified representative. The employer or carrier and any witness may appear at such hearing by telephone. The rules of evidence shall be liberally construed in favor of allowing introduction of evidence.

(i) A judge of compensation claims may, upon the motion of a party or the judge's own motion, dismiss a petition for lack of prosecution if a petition, response, motion, order, request for hearing, or notice of deposition has not been filed during the previous 12 months unless good cause is shown. A dismissal for lack of prosecution is without prejudice and does not require a hearing.

(j) A judge of compensation claims may not award interest on unpaid medical bills and the amount of such bills may not be used to calculate the amount of interest awarded. Regardless of the date benefits were initially requested, attorney's fees do not attach under this subsection until 30 days after the date the carrier or self-insured employer receives the petition.

(5)

(a) Procedures with respect to appeals from orders of judges of compensation claims shall be governed by rules adopted by the Supreme Court. Such an order shall become final 30 days after mailing of copies of such order to the parties, unless appealed pursuant to such rules.

(b) An appellant may be relieved of any necessary filing fee by filing a verified petition of indigency for approval as provided in s. 57.081(1) and may be relieved in whole or in part from the costs for preparation of the record on appeal if, within 15 days after the date notice of the estimated costs for the preparation is served, the appellant files with the judge of compensation claims a copy of the designation of the record on appeal, and a verified petition to be relieved of costs. A verified petition filed prior to the date of service of the notice of the estimated costs shall be deemed not timely filed. The verified petition relating to record costs shall contain a sworn statement that the appellant is insolvent and a complete, detailed, and sworn financial affidavit showing all the appellant's assets, liabilities, and income. Failure to state in the affidavit all assets and income, including marital assets and income, shall be grounds for denying the petition with prejudice. The Office of the Judges of Compensation Claims shall adopt rules as may be required pursuant to this subsection, including forms for use in all petitions brought under this subsection. The appellant's attorney, or the appellant if she or he is not represented by an attorney, shall include as a part of the verified petition relating to record costs an affidavit or affirmation that, in her or his opinion, the notice of appeal was filed in good faith and that there is a probable basis for the District Court of Appeal, First District, to find reversible error, and shall state with particularity the specific legal and factual grounds for the opinion. Failure to so affirm shall be grounds for denying the petition. A copy of the verified petition relating to record costs shall be served upon all interested parties. The judge of compensation claims shall promptly conduct a hearing on the verified petition relating to record costs, giving at least 15 days' notice to the appellant, the department, and all other interested parties, all of whom shall be parties to the proceedings. The judge of compensation claims may enter an order without such hearing if no objection is filed by an interested party within 20 days from the service date of the verified petition relating to record costs. Such proceedings shall be conducted in accordance with the provisions of this section and with the workers' compensation rules of procedure, to the extent applicable. In the event an insolvency petition is granted, the judge of compensation claims shall direct the department to pay record costs and filing fees from the Workers' Compensation Administration Trust Fund pending final disposition of the costs of appeal. The department may transcribe or arrange for the transcription of the record in any proceeding for which it is ordered to pay the cost of the record.

(c) As a condition of filing a notice of appeal to the District Court of Appeal, First District, an employer who has not secured the payment of compensation under this chapter in compliance with s. 440.38 shall file with the notice of appeal a good and sufficient bond, as provided in s. 59.13, conditioned to pay the amount of the demand and any interest and costs payable under the terms of the order if the appeal is dismissed, or if the District Court of Appeal, First District, affirms the award in any amount. Upon the failure of such employer to file such bond with the District Court of Appeal, First District, along with the notice of appeal, the District Court of Appeal, First District, shall dismiss the notice of appeal.

(6) An award of compensation for disability may be made after the death of an injured employee.

(7) Any interested party shall have the right in any case of death to require an autopsy, the cost thereof to be borne by the party requesting it; and the judge of compensation claims shall have authority to order and require an autopsy and may, in her or his discretion, withhold her or his findings and award until an autopsy is held.

History: s. 25, ch. 17481, 1935; CGL 1936 Supp. 5966(25); s. 11, ch. 18413, 1937; s. 7, ch. 20672, 1941; s. 3, ch. 22814, 1945; s. 1, ch. 26967, 1951; s. 8, ch. 28241, 1953; s. 6, ch. 29778, 1955; s. 1, ch. 57-270; s. 2, ch. 59-100; s. 2, ch. 59-142; s. 2, ch. 65-120; s. 1, ch. 65-119; s. 1, ch. 67-374; s. 2, ch. 67-554; ss. 17, 35, ch. 69-106; s. 120, ch. 71-355; s. 1, ch. 74-48; s. 15, ch. 74-197; s. 12, ch. 75-209; ss. 6, 8, ch. 77-290; ss. 8, 23, ch. 78-300; s. 17, ch. 79-7; ss. 19, 124, ch. 79-40; ss. 14, 21, ch. 79-312; s. 180, ch. 79-400; s. 9, ch. 80-236; s. 7, ch. 81-119; s. 9, ch. 83-305; ss. 17, 43, ch. 89-289; ss. 25, 56, ch. 90-201; ss. 23, 52, ch. 91-1; s. 31, ch. 91-46; s. 1, ch. 91-47; s. 30, ch. 93-415; s. 118, ch. 97-103; s. 95, ch. 2000-153; s. 19, ch. 2001-91; s. 37, ch. 2002-194, effective July 1, 2002; s. 12, ch. 2002-236, effective July 1, 2002; s. 25, ch. 2003-261, effective Oct. 1, 2003; s. 17, ch. 2003-412; s. 63, ch. 2004-5, effective June 29, 2004.

[1]**2003 Note:** Subparagraph 2. was redesignated as paragraph (b) by s. 25, ch. 2003-412.

[2]**2003 Note:** The word "of" was substituted for the word "or" by the editors.

§ 440.271. Appeal of Order of Judge of Compensation Claims.

Review of any order of a judge of compensation claims entered pursuant to this chapter shall be by appeal to the District Court of Appeal, First District. Appeals shall be filed in accordance with rules of procedure prescribed by the Supreme Court for review of such orders. The department shall be given notice of any proceedings pertaining to s. 440.25, regarding indigency, or s. 440.49, regarding the Special Disability Trust Fund, and shall have the right to intervene in any proceedings.

History: s. 1, ch. 79-312; s. 10, ch. 80-236; s. 278, ch. 81-259; s. 43, ch. 89-289; ss. 27, 56, ch. 90-201; ss. 25, 52, ch. 91-1; s. 2, ch. 91-47; s. 38, ch. 2002-194, effective July 1, 2002.

§ 440.2715. Access to Courts Through State Video Teleconferencing Network.

The First District Court of Appeal shall use the state video teleconferencing network established by the Department of Management Services to facilitate access to courts for purposes of workers' compensation actions.

History: s. 103, ch. 93-415.

§ 440.28. Modification of Orders.

Upon a judge of compensation claims' own initiative, or upon the application of any party in interest, on the ground of a change in condition or because of a mistake in a determination of fact, the judge of compensation claims may, at any time prior to 2 years after the date of the last payment of compensation pursuant to the compensation order the party seeks to modify, or at any time prior to 2 years after the date copies of an order rejecting a claim are mailed to the parties at the last known address of each, review a compensation case in accordance with the procedure prescribed in respect of claims in s. 440.25 and, in accordance with such section, issue a new compensation order which may terminate, continue, reinstate, increase, or decrease such compensation or award compensation. Such new order shall not affect any compensation previously paid, except that an award increasing the compensation rate may be made effective from the date of the injury, and, if any part of the compensation due or to become due is unpaid, an award decreasing the compensation rate may be made effective from the date of the injury, and any payment made prior thereto in excess of such decreased rate shall be deducted from any unpaid compensation, in such manner and by such method as may be determined by the judge of compensation claims.

History: s. 28, ch. 17481, 1935; CGL 1936 Supp. 5966(28); s. 9, ch. 20672, 1941; s. 10, ch. 28241, 1953; s. 119, ch. 71-355; s. 13, ch. 75-209; s. 23, ch. 78-300; ss. 21, 124, ch. 79-40; s. 21, ch. 79-312; s. 43, ch. 89-289; s. 56, ch. 90-201; s. 52, ch. 91-1; s. 5, ch. 91-46; s. 31, ch. 93-415.

§ 440.29. Procedure Before the Judge of Compensation Claims.

(1) In making an investigation or inquiry or conducting a hearing, the judge of compensation claims shall not be bound by technical or formal rules of procedure, except as provided by this chapter, but may make such investigation or inquiry, or conduct such hearing, in such manner as to best ascertain the rights of the parties. A declaration of a deceased employee concerning the injury in respect of which the investigation or inquiry is being made or the hearing conducted shall be received in evidence and shall, if corroborated by other evidence, be sufficient to establish the injury.

(2) Hearings before the judge of compensation claims shall be open to the public, and the Deputy Chief Judge is authorized to designate the manner in which particular types of hearings are recorded and reported and, when necessary, to contract for the reporting of such hearings. The Deputy Chief Judge shall arrange for the preparation of a record of the hearings and other proceedings before judges of compensation claims, as necessary, and is authorized to allow for the attendance of court reporters at hearings, for preparation of transcripts of testimony, for copies of any instrument, and for other reporting or recording services. The Deputy Chief Judge

may charge the same fees allowed by law or court rule to reporters, persons preparing transcripts, or clerks of courts of this state for like services.

(3) The practice and procedure before the judges of compensation claims shall be governed by rules adopted by the Supreme Court, except to the extent that such rules conflict with the provisions of this chapter.

(4) All medical reports of authorized treating health care providers relating to the claimant and subject accident shall be received into evidence by the judge of compensation claims upon proper motion. However, such records must be served on the opposing party at least 30 days before the final hearing. This section does not limit any right of further discovery, including, but not limited to, depositions.

History: s. 29, ch. 17481, 1935; CGL 1936 Supp. 5966(29); s. 10, ch. 20672, 1941; s. 8, ch. 29778, 1955; ss. 17, 35, ch. 69-106; s. 16, ch. 74-197; s. 14, ch. 75-209; ss. 9, 23, ch. 78-300; ss. 22, 124, ch. 79-40; s. 21, ch. 79-312; s. 11, ch. 80-236; s. 10, ch. 83-305; s. 43, ch. 89-289; s. 56, ch. 90-201; s. 52, ch. 91-1; s. 6, ch. 91-46; s. 32, ch. 93-415; s. 20, ch. 2001-91, effective Oct. 1, 2001.

§ 440.30. Depositions.

Depositions of witnesses or parties, residing within or without the state, may be taken and may be used in connection with proceedings under the Workers' Compensation Law, either upon order of the judge of compensation claims or at the instance of any party or prospective party to such proceedings, and either prior to the institution of a claim, if the claimant is represented by an attorney, or after the filing of the claim in the same manner, for the same purposes, including the purposes of discovery, and subject to the same rules; all as now or hereafter prescribed by law or by rules of court governing the taking and use of such depositions in civil actions at law in the circuit courts of this state. Such depositions may be taken before any notary public, court reporter, or deputy, and the fees of the officer taking the same and the fees of the witnesses attending the same, including expert witness fees as provided by law or court rule, shall be the same as in depositions taken for such circuit courts. Such fees may be taxed as costs and recovered by the claimant, if successful in such workers' compensation proceedings. If no claim has been filed, then the carrier or employer taking the deposition shall pay the claimant's attorney a reasonable attorney's fee for attending said deposition.

History: s. 30, ch. 17481, 1935; CGL 1936 Supp. 5966(30); s. 13, ch. 18413, 1937; s. 1, ch. 28228, 1953; ss. 17, 35 ch. 69-106; s. 17, ch 74-197; s. 15, ch. 75-209; s. 23, ch. 78-300; ss. 23, 124, ch. 79-40; s. 21, ch. 79-312; s. 43, ch. 89-289; s. 56, ch. 90-201; s. 52, ch. 91-1; s. 7, ch. 91-46.

§ 440.31. Witness Fees.

Each witness who appears in obedience to a subpoena shall be entitled to the same fees as witnesses in a civil action in the circuit court; however, any expert witness, as defined in Rule 1.390(a) of the Florida Rules of Civil Procedure, who shall have testified in any proceeding under this chapter shall be allowed a witness fee, including the cost of any exhibits used by such witness, in such reasonable amount as the judge of compensation claims may determine, not in excess of the rate prevailing in the locality for witness fees for such expert witnesses in workers' compensation proceedings, notwithstanding the limitation provided in s. 92.231.

History: s. 31, ch. 17481, 1935; CGL 1936 Supp. 5966(31); s. 9, ch. 29778, 1955; s. 2, ch. 67-554; s. 23, ch. 78-300; ss. 24, 124, ch. 79-40; s. 21, ch. 79-312; s. 43, ch. 89-289; s. 56, ch. 90-201; s. 52, ch. 91-1; s. 8, ch. 91-46.

§ 440.32. Cost in Proceedings Brought Without Reasonable Ground.

(1) If the judge of compensation claims or any court having jurisdiction of proceedings in respect of any claim or compensation order determines that the proceedings in respect of such claim or order have been instituted or continued without reasonable ground, the cost of such proceedings shall be assessed against the party who has so instituted or continued the proceedings.

(2) If the judge of compensation claims or any court having jurisdiction of proceedings in respect to any claims or defense under this

section determines that the proceedings were maintained or continued frivolously, the cost of the proceedings, including reasonable attorney's fees, shall be assessed against the offending attorney. If a penalty is assessed under this subsection, a copy of the order assessing the penalty must be forwarded to the appropriate grievance committee acting under the jurisdiction of the Supreme Court. Penalties, fees, and costs awarded under this provision may not be recouped from the party.

(3) Every pleading, motion, and other paper of a party represented by an attorney shall be signed by at least one attorney of record in the attorney's individual name, whose address shall be stated. The signature of an attorney constitutes a certificate by the signer that the signer has read the pleading, motion, or other paper; that to the best of the signer's knowledge, information, and belief formed after reasonable inquiry it is well grounded in fact and is warranted by existing law or a good faith argument for the extension, modification, or reversal of existing law, and that it is not interposed for any improper purpose, such as to harass or to cause unnecessary delay or needless increase in the cost of litigation. If a pleading, motion, or other paper is not signed, it shall be stricken unless it is signed promptly after the omission is called to the attention of the pleader or movant. If a pleading, motion, or other paper is signed in violation of this section, the judge of compensation claims or any court having jurisdiction of proceedings, upon motion or upon its own initiative, shall impose upon the person who signed it an appropriate sanction, which may include an order to pay to the other party or parties the amount of the reasonable expenses incurred because of the filing of the pleading, motion, or other paper, including a reasonable attorney's fee.

History: s. 32, ch. 17481, 1935; CGL 1936 Supp. 5966(32); s. 1, ch. 63-283; ss. 17, 35, ch. 69-106; s. 16, ch. 75-209; s. 23, ch. 78-300; ss. 25, 124, ch. 79-40; s. 21, ch. 79-312; s. 12, ch. 80-236; s. 43, ch. 89-289; s. 56, ch. 90-201; s. 52, ch. 91-1; s. 9, ch. 91-46; s. 33, ch. 93-415.

§ 440.33. Powers of Judges of Compensation Claims.

(1) The judge of compensation claims may preserve and enforce order during any such proceeding; issue subpoenas for, administer oaths or affirmations to, and compel the attendance and testimony of witnesses, or the production of books, papers, documents, and other evidence, or the taking of depositions before any designated individual competent to administer oaths; examine witnesses; and do all things conformable to law which may be necessary to enable the judge effectively to discharge the duties of her or his office. Whenever a law requires an order of a court of competent jurisdiction for the obtention of medical or hospital records, an order of a judge of compensation claims entered for such purposes shall be deemed to be an order of a court of competent jurisdiction.

(2) If any person in proceedings before the judge of compensation claims disobeys or resists any lawful order or process, or misbehaves during a hearing or so near the place thereof as to obstruct the hearing, or neglects to produce, after having been ordered to do so, any pertinent book, paper, or document, or refuses to appear after having been subpoenaed, or upon appearing refuses to take oath or affirmation as a witness, or after having taken the oath refuses to be examined according to law, the judge of compensation claims shall certify the facts to the court having jurisdiction in the place in which it is sitting, which shall thereupon in a summary manner hear the evidence as to the acts complained of and, if the evidence so warrants, punish such person in the same manner and to the same extent as for a contempt committed before the court, or commit such person upon the same conditions as if the doing of the forbidden act had occurred with reference to the process of or in the presence of the court.

(3) Before adjudicating a claim for permanent total disability benefits, the judge of compensation claims may request an evaluation pursuant to[1] s. 440.491(6) for the purpose of assisting the judge of compensation claims in the determination of whether there is a reasonable probability that, with appropriate training or education, the employee may be rehabilitated to the extent that such employee can achieve suitable gainful

employment and whether it is in the best interest of the employee to undertake such training or education.

History: s. 33, ch. 17481, 1935; CGL 1936 Supp. 5966(33); ss. 17, 35, ch. 69-106; s. 17, ch. 75-209; s. 23, ch. 78-300; ss. 26, 124, ch. 79-40; s. 21, ch. 79-312; s. 13, ch. 80-236; s. 11, ch. 83-305; ss. 18, 43, ch. 89-289; s. 56, ch. 90-201; s. 52, ch. 91-1; s. 10, ch. 91-46; s. 119, ch. 97-103; s. 64, ch. 2004-5, effective June 29, 2004.

[1]**Note:** —Repealed by s. 43, ch. 93-415.

§ 440.34. Attorney's Fees; Costs.

(1) A fee, gratuity, or other consideration may not be paid for a claimant in connection with any proceedings arising under this chapter, unless approved as reasonable by the judge of compensation claims or court having jurisdiction over such proceedings. Any attorney's fee approved by a judge of compensation claims for benefits secured on behalf of a claimant must equal to 20 percent of the first $5,000 of the amount of the benefits secured, 15 percent of the next $5,000 of the amount of the benefits secured, 10 percent of the remaining amount of the benefits secured to be provided during the first 10 years after the date the claim is filed, and 5 percent of the benefits secured after 10 years. The judge of compensation claims shall not approve a compensation order, a joint stipulation for lump-sum settlement, a stipulation or agreement between a claimant and his or her attorney, or any other agreement related to benefits under this chapter that provides for an attorney's fee in excess of the amount permitted by this section. The judge of compensation claims is not required to approve any retainer agreement between the claimant and his or her attorney. The retainer agreement as to fees and costs may not be for compensation in excess of the amount allowed under this section.

(2) In awarding a claimant's attorney's fee, the judge of compensation claims shall consider only those benefits secured by the attorney. An attorney is not entitled to attorney's fees for representation in any issue that was ripe, due, and owing and that reasonably could have been addressed, but was not addressed, during the pendency of other issues for the same injury. The amount, statutory basis, and type of benefits obtained through legal representation shall be listed on all attorney's fees awarded by the judge of compensation claims. For purposes of this section, the term "benefits secured" does not include future medical benefits to be provided on any date more than 5 years after the date the claim is filed. In the event an offer to settle an issue pending before a judge of compensation claims, including attorney's fees as provided for in this section, is communicated in writing to the claimant or the claimant's attorney at least 30 days prior to the trial date on such issue, for purposes of calculating the amount of attorney's fees to be taxed against the employer or carrier, the term "benefits secured" shall be deemed to include only that amount awarded to the claimant above the amount specified in the offer to settle. If multiple issues are pending before the judge of compensation claims, said offer of settlement shall address each issue pending and shall state explicitly whether or not the offer on each issue is severable. The written offer shall also unequivocally state whether or not it includes medical witness fees and expenses and all other costs associated with the claim.

(3) If any party should prevail in any proceedings before a judge of compensation claims or court, there shall be taxed against the nonprevailing party the reasonable costs of such proceedings, not to include attorney's fees. A claimant shall be responsible for the payment of her or his own attorney's fees, except that a claimant shall be entitled to recover a reasonable attorney's fee from a carrier or employer:

(a) Against whom she or he successfully asserts a petition for medical benefits only, if the claimant has not filed or is not entitled to file at such time a claim for disability, permanent impairment, wage-loss, or death benefits, arising out of the same accident;

(b) In any case in which the employer or carrier files a response to petition denying benefits with the Office of the Judges of Compensation Claims and the injured person has employed an attorney in the successful prosecution of the petition;

(c) In a proceeding in which a carrier or

Fla. Stats.

employer denies that an accident occurred for which compensation benefits are payable, and the claimant prevails on the issue of compensability; or

(d) In cases where the claimant successfully prevails in proceedings filed under s. 440.24 or s. 440.28. Regardless of the date benefits were initially requested, attorney's fees shall not attach under this subsection until 30 days after the date the carrier or employer, if self-insured, receives the petition.

(4) In such cases in which the claimant is responsible for the payment of her or his own attorney's fees, such fees are a lien upon compensation payable to the claimant, notwithstanding s. 440.22.

(5) If any proceedings are had for review of any claim, award, or compensation order before any court, the court may award the injured employee or dependent an attorney's fee to be paid by the employer or carrier, in its discretion, which shall be paid as the court may direct.

(6) A judge of compensation claims may not enter an order approving the contents of a retainer agreement that permits the escrowing of any portion of the employee's compensation until benefits have been secured.

(7) If an attorney's fee is owed under paragraph (3)(a), the judge of compensation claims may approve an alternative attorney's fee not to exceed $1,500 only once per accident, based on a maximum hourly rate of $150 per hour, if the judge of compensation claims expressly finds that the attorney's fee amount provided for in subsection (1), based on benefits secured, fails to fairly compensate the attorney for disputed medical-only claims as provided in paragraph (3)(a) and the circumstances of the particular case warrant such action.

History: s. 34, ch. 17481, 1935; CGL 1936 Supp. 5966(34), 8135(11); s. 11, ch. 20672, 1941; ss. 17, 35, ch. 69-106; s. 365, ch. 71-136; s. 119, ch. 71-355; s. 18, ch. 75-209; s. 9, ch. 77-290; ss. 10, 23, ch. 78-300; ss. 27, 124, ch. 79-40; ss. 15, 21, ch. 79-312; s. 14, ch. 80-236; s. 12, ch. 83-305; s. 4, ch. 86-171; ss. 19, 43, ch. 89-289; ss. 29, 56, ch. 90-201; ss. 27, 52, ch. 91-1; s. 32, ch. 91-46; s. 3, ch. 91-47; s. 252, ch. 91-224; s. 34, ch. 93-415; s. 120, ch. 97-103; s. 21, ch. 2001-91, effective Oct. 1, 2001; s. 13, ch. 2002-236, effective July 1, 2002; s. 26, ch. 412, effective Oct. 1, 2003.

§ 440.345. Reporting of Attorney's Fees.

All fees paid to attorneys for services rendered under this chapter shall be reported to the Office of the Judges of Compensation Claims as the Division of Administrative Hearings requires by rule.

History: s. 35, ch. 93-415; s. 22, ch. 2001-91, effective Oct. 1, 2001; s. 39, ch. 2002-194, effective July 1, 2002.

§ 440.35. Record of Injury or Death.

Every employer shall keep a record in respect of any injury to an employee. Such record shall contain such information of disability or death in respect of such injury as the department may by regulation require, and shall be available to inspection by the department or by any state authority at such time and under such conditions as the department may by regulation prescribe.

History: s. 35, ch. 17481, 1935; CGL 1936 Supp. 5966(35); ss. 17, 35, ch. 69-106; s. 23, ch. 78-300; s. 124, ch. 79-40; s. 21, ch. 79-312; s. 43, ch. 89-289; s. 56, ch. 90-201; s. 52, ch. 91-1; s. 40, ch. 2002-194, effective July 1, 2002.

§ 440.38. Security for Compensation; Insurance Carriers and Self-Insurers.

(1) Every employer shall secure the payment of compensation under this chapter:

(a) By insuring and keeping insured the payment of such compensation with any stock company or mutual company or association or exchange, authorized to do business in the state;

(b) By furnishing satisfactory proof to the Florida Self-Insurers Guaranty Association, Incorporated, created in s. 440.385, that it has the financial strength necessary to ensure timely payment of all current and future claims individually and on behalf of its subsidiary and affiliated companies with employees in this state and receiving an authorization from the department to pay such compensation directly. The association shall review the financial strength of applicants for membership, current members, and former members and make recommendations to the department regarding their qualifications to self-insure in accordance with this section and ss. 440.385 and 440.386. The department shall act in accordance with the recommendations unless it finds by clear and convincing evidence that the recommendations are erroneous.

1. As a condition of authorization under paragraph (a), the association may recommend that the department require an employer to deposit with the association a qualifying security deposit. The association shall recommend the type and amount of the qualifying security deposit and shall prescribe conditions for the qualifying security deposit, which shall include authorization for the association to call the qualifying security deposit in the case of default to pay compensation awards and related expenses of the association. As a condition to authorization to self-insure, the employer shall provide proof that the employer has provided for competent personnel with whom to deliver benefits and to provide a safe working environment. The employer shall also provide evidence that it carries reinsurance at levels that will ensure the financial strength and actuarial soundness of such employer in accordance with rules adopted by the department. The department may by rule require that, in the event of an individual self-insurer's insolvency, such qualifying security deposits and reinsurance policies are payable to the association. Any employer securing compensation in accordance with the provisions of this paragraph shall be known as a self-insurer and shall be classed as a carrier of her or his own insurance. The employer shall, if requested, provide the association an actuarial report signed by a member of the American Academy of Actuaries providing an opinion of the appropriate present value of the reserves, using a 4-percent discount rate, for current and future compensation claims. If any member or former member of the association refuses to timely provide such a report, the association may obtain an order from a circuit court requiring the member to produce such a report and ordering any other relief that the court determines is appropriate. The association may recover all reasonable costs and attorney's fees in such proceedings.

2. If the employer fails to maintain the foregoing requirements, the association shall recommend to the department that the department revoke the employer's authority to self-insure, unless the employer provides to the association the certified opinion of an independent actuary who is a member of the American Academy of Actuaries as to the actuarial present value of the employer's determined and estimated future compensation payments based on cash reserves, using a 4-percent discount rate, and a qualifying security deposit equal to 1.5 times the value so certified. The employer shall thereafter annually provide such a certified opinion until such time as the employer meets the requirements of subparagraph 1. The qualifying security deposit shall be adjusted at the time of each such annual report. Upon the failure of the employer to timely provide such opinion or to timely provide a security deposit in an amount equal to 1.5 times the value certified in the latest opinion, the association shall provide that information to the department along with a recommendation, and the department shall then revoke such employer's authorization to self-insure. Failure to comply with this subparagraph constitutes an immediate serious danger to the public health, safety, or welfare sufficient to justify the summary suspension of the employer's authorization to self-insure pursuant to s. 120.68.

3. Upon the suspension or revocation of the employer's authorization to self-insure, the employer shall provide to the association the certified opinion of an independent actuary who is a member of the American Academy of Actuaries of the actuarial present value of the determined and estimated future compensation payments of the employer for claims incurred while the member exercised the privilege of self-insurance, using a discount rate of 4 percent. The employer shall provide such an opinion at 6-month intervals thereafter until such time as the latest opinion shows no remaining value of claims. With each such opinion, the employer shall deposit with the association a qualifying security deposit in an amount equal to the value certified by the actuary. The association has a cause of action against an employer, and against any successor of the employer, who fails to timely provide such opinion or who fails to

Fla. Stats.

timely maintain the required security deposit with the association. The association shall recover a judgment in the amount of the actuarial present value of the determined and estimated future compensation payments of the employer for claims incurred while the employer exercised the privilege of self-insurance, together with attorney's fees. For purposes of this section, the successor of an employer means any person, business entity, or group of persons or business entities, which holds or acquires legal or beneficial title to the majority of the assets or the majority of the shares of the employer.

4. A qualifying security deposit shall consist, at the option of the employer, of:

a. Surety bonds, in a form and containing such terms as prescribed by the association, issued by a corporation surety authorized to transact surety business by the office, and whose policyholders' and financial ratings, as reported in A.M. Best's Insurance Reports, Property-Liability, are not less than "A" and "V", respectively.

b. Irrevocable letters of credit in favor of the association issued by financial institutions located within this state, the deposits of which are insured through the Federal Deposit Insurance Corporation.

5. The qualifying security deposit shall be held by the association exclusively for the benefit of workers' compensation claimants. The security shall not be subject to assignment, execution, attachment, or any legal process whatsoever, except as necessary to guarantee the payment of compensation under this chapter. No surety bond may be terminated, and no letter of credit may be allowed to expire, without 90 days' prior written notice to the association and deposit by the self-insuring employer of some other qualifying security deposit of equal value within 10 business days after such notice. Failure to provide such written notice or failure to timely provide qualifying replacement security after such notice shall constitute grounds for the association to call or sue upon the surety bond or to exercise its rights under a letter of credit. Current self-insured employers must comply with this section on or before December 31, 2001, or upon the maturity of existing security deposits, whichever occurs later. The department may specify by rule the amount of the qualifying security deposit required prior to authorizing an employer to self-insure and the amount of net worth required for an employer to qualify for authorization to self-insure;

(c) By entering into a contract with a public utility under an approved utility-provided self-insurance program as set forth in s. 624.46225 in effect as of July 1, 1983. The[1] department shall adopt rules to implement this paragraph;

(d) By entering into an interlocal agreement with other local governmental entities to create a local government pool pursuant to s. 624.4622; or

(e) By entering into a contract with an individual self-insurer under an approved individual self-insurer-provided self-insurance program as set forth in s. 624.46225. The[2] department may adopt rules to administer this subsection.

(2)

(a) The department shall adopt rules by which businesses may become qualified to provide underwriting claims-adjusting, loss control, and safety engineering services to self-insurers.

(b) The department shall adopt rules requiring self-insurers to file any reports necessary to fulfill the requirements of this chapter. Any self-insurer who fails to file any report as prescribed by the rules adopted by the department shall be subject to a civil penalty.

(3)

(a) The license of any stock company or mutual company or association or exchange authorized to do insurance business in the state shall for good cause, upon recommendation of the[2] division, be suspended or revoked by the department. No suspension or revocation shall affect the liability of any carrier already incurred.

(b) The department shall suspend or revoke any authorization to a self-insurer for failure to comply with this section or for good cause, as defined by rule of the department. No suspension or revocation shall affect the liability of any self-insurer already incurred.

(c) Violation of s. 440.381 by a self-insurance fund shall result in the imposition of a fine not to exceed $1,000 per audit if the self-insurance fund fails to act on said audits by correcting errors in employee classification or accepted applications for coverage where it knew employee classifications were incorrect. Such fines shall be levied by the[1] department and deposited into the Workers' Compensation Administration Trust Fund.

(4)

(a) A carrier of insurance, including the parties to any mutual, reciprocal, or other association, may not write any compensation insurance under this chapter without a certificate of authority from the office. Such certificate of authority shall be given, upon application therefor, to any insurance or mutual or reciprocal insurance association upon the office's being satisfied of the solvency of such corporation or association and its ability to perform all its undertakings. The office may revoke any certificate of authority so issued for violation of any provision of this chapter.

(b) A carrier of insurance, including the parties to any mutual, reciprocal, or other association, may not write any compensation insurance under this chapter unless such carrier has a claims adjuster, either in-house or under contract, situated within this state. Self-insurers whose compensation payments are administered through a third party and carriers of insurance shall maintain a claims adjuster within this state during any period for which there are any open claims against such self-insurer or carrier arising under the compensation insurance written by the self-insurer or carrier. Individual self-insurers whose compensation payments are administered by employees of the self-insurer shall not be required to have their claims adjuster situated within this state. Individual self-insurers shall not be required to have their claims adjusters situated within this state.

(5) All insurance carriers authorized to write workers' compensation insurance in this state shall make available, at the written request of the employer, an insurance policy containing deductibles in the amount of $500, $1,000, $1,500, $2,000, and $2,500 per claim and a coinsurance provision per claim. Any amount of coinsurance shall bind the carrier to pay 80 percent, and the employer to pay 20 percent, of the benefits due to an employee for an injury compensable under this chapter of the amount of benefits above the deductible, up to the limit of $21,000. One hundred percent of the benefits above the amount of any deductible and coinsurance, as the case may be, due to an employee for one injury shall be paid solely by the carrier. Regardless of any coinsurance or deductible amount, the claim shall be paid by the applicable carrier, which shall then be reimbursed by the employer for any coinsurance or deductible amounts paid by the carrier. No insurance carrier shall be required to offer a deductible or coinsurance to any employer if, as a result of a credit investigation, the carrier determines that the employer is not sufficiently financially stable to be responsible for payment of such deductible or[1] coinsurance amounts.

(6) The state and its boards, bureaus, departments, and agencies and all of its political subdivisions which employ labor, and the state universities, shall be deemed self-insurers under the terms of this chapter, unless they elect to procure and maintain insurance to secure the benefits of this chapter to their employees; and they are hereby authorized to pay the premiums for such insurance.

(7) Any employer who meets the requirements of subsection (1) through a policy of insurance issued outside of this state must at all times, with respect to all employees working in this state, maintain the required coverage under a Florida endorsement using Florida rates and rules pursuant to payroll reporting that accurately reflects the work performed in this state by such employees.

History: s. 38, ch. 17481, 1935; CGL 1936 Supp. 5966(37), 7475(7), 8135(13); s. 13, ch. 22637, 1945; ss. 13, 17, 35, ch. 69-106; s. 367, ch. 71-136; s. 11, ch. 78-95; ss. 12, 23, ch. 78-300; ss. 29, 124, ch. 79-40; ss. 16, 21, ch. 79-312; s. 1, ch. 80-324; s. 2, ch. 82-65; s. 2, ch. 83-303; ss. 13, 14, ch. 83-305; s. 3, ch. 84-267; s. 67, ch. 85-81; s. 7, ch. 87-330; s. 43, ch. 89-289; ss.

31, 56, ch. 90-201; ss. 29, 52, ch. 91-1; s. 36, ch. 93-415; s. 121, ch. 97-103; s. 9, ch. 2000-150; s. 96, ch. 2000-153; s. 1, ch. 2000-368; s. 23, ch. 2001-91, effective Oct. 1, 2001; s. 2, ch. 2002-262, effective Oct. 1, 2002; s. 27, ch. 2003-412, effective Oct. 1, 2003; s. 483, ch. 2003-261, effective June 26, 2003; s. 11, ch. 2003-399, effective July 1, 2003, expires July 1, 2004; s. 12, ch. 2003-399, effective July 1, 2004; s. 11, ch. 2004-41, effective July 1, 2004.

[1]**2003 Note:** —The Division of Workers' Compensation of the Department of Labor and Employment Security was transferred to the Department of Insurance by s. 1, ch. 2002-194, and substitutions of other entities for the division were made for most existing references to the division by that law; ch. 2002-262 substituted other entities for many of the references to the division in s. 440.38.

§ 440.381. Application for Coverage; Reporting Payroll; Payroll Audit Procedures; Penalties.

(1) Applications by an employer to a carrier for coverage required by s. 440.38 must be made on a form prescribed by the Financial Services Commission. The Financial Services Commission shall adopt rules for applications for coverage required by s. 440.38. The rules must provide that an application include information on the employer, the type of business, past and prospective payroll, estimated revenue, previous workers' compensation experience, employee classification, employee names, and any other information necessary to enable a carrier to accurately underwrite the applicant. The rules must include a provision that a carrier or self-insurance fund may require that an employer update an application monthly to reflect any change in the required application information.

(2) Submission of an application that contains false, misleading, or incomplete information provided with the purpose of avoiding or reducing the amount of premiums for workers' compensation coverage is a felony of the second degree, punishable as provided in s. 775.082, s. 775.083, or s. 775.084. The application must contain a statement that the filing of an application containing false, misleading, or incomplete information provided with the purpose of avoiding or reducing the amount of premiums for workers' compensation coverage is a felony of the third degree, punishable as provided in s. 775.082, s. 775.083, or s. 775.084. The application must contain a sworn statement by the employer attesting to the accuracy of the information submitted and acknowledging the provisions of former s. 440.37(4). The application must contain a sworn statement by the agent attesting that the agent explained to the employer or officer the classification codes that are used for premium calculations.

(3) The Financial Services Commission, in consultation with the department, shall establish by rule minimum requirements for audits of payroll and classifications in order to ensure that the appropriate premium is charged for workers' compensation coverage. The rules shall ensure that audits performed by both carriers and employers are adequate to provide that all sources of payments to employees, subcontractors, and independent contractors have been reviewed and that the accuracy of classification of employees has been verified. The rules shall provide that employers in all classes other than the construction class be audited not less frequently than biennially and may provide for more frequent audits of employers in specified classifications based on factors such as amount of premium, type of business, loss ratios, or other relevant factors. In no event shall employers in the construction class, generating more than the amount of premium required to be experience rated, be audited less than annually. The annual audits required for construction classes shall consist of physical onsite audits. Payroll verification audit rules must include, but need not be limited to, the use of state and federal reports of employee income, payroll and other accounting records, certificates of insurance maintained by subcontractors, and duties of employees. At the completion of an audit, the employer or officer of the corporation and the auditor must print and sign their names on the audit document and attach proof of identification to the audit document.

(4) Each employer must submit a copy of the quarterly earning report required by chapter 443 at the end of each quarter to the carrier and submit self-audits supported by the quarterly earnings reports required by chapter 443 and the

rules adopted by the Agency for Workforce Innovation or by the state agency providing unemployment tax collection services under contract with the Agency for Workforce Innovation through an interagency agreement pursuant to s. 443.1316. The reports must include a sworn statement by an officer or principal of the employer attesting to the accuracy of the information contained in the report.

(5) Employers shall make available all records necessary for the payroll verification audit and permit the auditor to make a physical inspection of the employer's operation. If the employer fails upon request of the auditor to provide access to the documents specified in this section and the carrier cannot complete the audit as a result, the employer shall pay $500 to the carrier to defray the costs of the audits.

(6)

(a) If an employer understates or conceals payroll, or misrepresents or conceals employee duties so as to avoid proper classification for premium calculations, or misrepresents or conceals information pertinent to the computation and application of an experience rating modification factor, the employer, or the employer's agent or attorney, shall pay to the insurance carrier a penalty of 10 times the amount of the difference in premium paid and the amount the employer should have paid and reasonable attorney's fees. The penalty may be enforced in the circuit courts of this state.

(b) If the department determines that an employer has materially understated or concealed payroll, has materially misrepresented or concealed employee duties so as to avoid proper classification for premium calculations, or has materially misrepresented or concealed information pertinent to the computation and application of an experience rating modification factor, the department shall immediately notify the employer's carrier of such determination. The carrier shall commence a physical onsite audit of the employer within 30 days after receiving notification from the department. If the carrier fails to commence the audit as required by this section, the department shall contract with auditing professionals to conduct the audit at the carrier's expense. A copy of the carrier's audit of the employer shall be provided to the department upon completion. The carrier is not required to conduct the physical onsite audit of the employer as set forth in this paragraph if the carrier gives written notice of cancellation to the employer within 30 days after receiving notification from the department of the material misrepresentation, understatement, or concealment and an audit is conducted in conjunction with the cancellation.

(7) If an employee suffering a compensable injury was not reported as earning wages on the last quarterly earnings report filed with the Agency for Workforce Innovation or the state agency providing unemployment tax collection services under contract with the Agency for Workforce Innovation through an interagency agreement pursuant to s. 443.1316 before the accident, the employer shall indemnify the carrier for all workers' compensation benefits paid to or on behalf of the employee unless the employer establishes that the employee was hired after the filing of the quarterly report, in which case the employer and employee shall attest to the fact that the employee was employed by the employer at the time of the injury. Failure of the employer to indemnify the insurer within 21 days after demand by the insurer is grounds for the insurer to immediately cancel coverage. Any action for indemnification brought by the carrier is cognizable in the circuit court having jurisdiction where the employer or carrier resides or transacts business. The insurer is entitled to a reasonable attorney's fee if it recovers any portion of the benefits paid in the action.

(8) If an employer fails to provide reasonable access to payroll records for a payroll verification audit, the employer shall pay a premium to the carrier or self-insurer not to exceed three times the most recent estimated annual premium.

History: s. 32, ch. 90-201; s. 30, ch. 91-1; s. 37, ch. 93-415; s. 122, ch. 97-103; s. 66, ch. 2001-62, effective July 3, 2001; s. 41, ch. 2002-194, effective July 1, 2002; s. 14, ch. 2002-236, effective July 1, 2002; s. 12, ch. 2003-36, effective Oct. 1, 2003; s. 28, ch. 412, effective Oct. 1, 2003; s. 484, ch. 2003-261, effective June 26, 2003.

Fla. Stats.

§ 440.385. Florida Self-Insurers Guaranty Association, Incorporated.

(1) Creation of Association.—

(a) There is created a nonprofit corporation to be known as the "Florida Self-Insurers Guaranty Association, Incorporated," hereinafter referred to as "the association." Upon incorporation of the association, all individual self-insurers as defined in[1] ss. 440.02(24)(a) and 440.38(1)(b), other than individual self-insurers which are public utilities or governmental entities, shall be members of the association as a condition of their authority to individually self-insure in this state. The association shall perform its functions under a plan of operation as established and approved under subsection (5) and shall exercise its powers and duties through a board of directors as established under subsection (2). The association shall have those powers granted or permitted corporations not for profit, as provided in chapter 617. The activities of the association shall be subject to review by the department. The department shall have oversight responsibility as set forth in this section. The association is specifically authorized to enter into agreements with this state to perform specified services.

(b) A member may voluntarily withdraw from the association when the member voluntarily terminates the self-insurance privilege and pays all assessments due to the date of such termination. However, the withdrawing member shall continue to be bound by the provisions of this section relating to the period of his or her membership and any claims charged pursuant thereto. The withdrawing member who is a member on or after January 1, 1991, shall also be required to provide to the association upon withdrawal, and at 12-month intervals thereafter, satisfactory proof, including, if requested by the association, a report of known and potential claims certified by a member of the American Academy of Actuaries, that it continues to meet the standards of s. 440.38(1)(b)1. in relation to claims incurred while the withdrawing member exercised the privilege of self-insurance. Such reporting shall continue until the withdrawing member demonstrates to the association that there is no remaining value to claims incurred while the withdrawing member was self-insured. If a withdrawing member fails or refuses to timely provide an actuarial report to the association, the association may obtain an order from a circuit court requiring the member to produce such a report and ordering any other relief that the court determines appropriate. The association is entitled to recover all reasonable costs and attorney's fees expended in such proceedings. If during this reporting period the withdrawing member fails to meet the standards of s. 440.38(1)(b)1., the withdrawing member who is a member on or after January 1, 1991, shall thereupon, and at 6-month intervals thereafter, provide to the association the certified opinion of an independent actuary who is a member of the American Academy of Actuaries of the actuarial present value of the determined and estimated future compensation payments of the member for claims incurred while the member was a self-insurer, using a discount rate of 4 percent. With each such opinion, the withdrawing member shall deposit with the association security in an amount equal to the value certified by the actuary and of a type that is acceptable for qualifying security deposits under s. 440.38(1)(b). The withdrawing member shall continue to provide such opinions and to provide such security until such time as the latest opinion shows no remaining value of claims. The association has a cause of action against a withdrawing member, and against any successor of a withdrawing member, who fails to timely provide the required opinion or who fails to maintain the required deposit with the association. The association shall be entitled to recover a judgment in the amount of the actuarial present value of the determined and estimated future compensation payments of the withdrawing member for claims incurred during the time that the withdrawing member exercised the privilege of self-insurance, together with reasonable attorney's fees. The association is also entitled to recover reasonable attorney's fees in any action to compel production of any actuarial report required by this section. For purposes of this section, the successor of a withdrawing member means any person, business entity, or group of persons or business entities, which holds or acquires legal or beneficial title to the majority of the assets or the majority of the shares of the withdrawing member.

(2) Board of Directors.—The board of directors of the association shall consist of nine persons and shall be organized as established in the plan of operation. All board members shall be experienced in self-insurance in this state. Each director shall serve for a 4-year term and may be reappointed. Appointments after January 1, 2002, shall be made by the department upon recommendation of members of the association. Any vacancy on the board shall be filled for the remaining period of the term in the same manner as appointments other than initial appointments are made. Each director shall be reimbursed for expenses incurred in carrying out the duties of the board on behalf of the association.

(3) Powers and Duties.—

(a) Upon creation of the Insolvency Fund pursuant to the provisions of subsection (4), the association is obligated for payment of compensation under this chapter to insolvent members' employees resulting from incidents and injuries existing prior to the member becoming an insolvent member and from incidents and injuries occurring within 30 days after the member has become an insolvent member, provided the incidents giving rise to claims for compensation under this chapter occur during the year in which such insolvent member is a member of the guaranty fund and was assessable pursuant to the plan of operation, and provided the employee makes timely claim for such payments according to procedures set forth by a court of competent jurisdiction over the delinquency or bankruptcy proceedings of the insolvent member. Such obligation includes only that amount due the injured worker or workers of the insolvent member under this chapter. In no event is the association obligated to a claimant in an amount in excess of the obligation of the insolvent member. The association shall be deemed the insolvent employer for purposes of this chapter to the extent of its obligation on the covered claims and, to such extent, shall have all rights, duties, and obligations of the insolvent employer as if the employer had not become insolvent. However, in no event shall the association be liable for any penalties or interest.

(b) The association may:

1. Employ or retain such persons as are necessary to handle claims and perform other duties of the association.

2. Borrow funds necessary to effect the purposes of this section in accord with the plan of operation.

3. Sue or be sued.

4. Negotiate and become a party to such contracts as are necessary to carry out the purposes of this section.

5. Purchase such reinsurance as is determined necessary pursuant to the plan of operation.

6. Review all applicants for membership in the association to determine whether the applicant is qualified for membership under the law. The association shall recommend to the department that the application be accepted or rejected based on the criteria set forth in s. 440.38(1)(b). The department shall approve or disapprove the application as provided in paragraph (6)(a).

7. Collect and review financial information from employers and make recommendations to the department regarding the appropriate security deposit and reinsurance amounts necessary for an employer to demonstrate that it has the financial strength necessary to ensure the timely payment of all current and future claims. The association may audit and examine an employer to verify the financial strength of its current and former members. If the association determines that a current or former self-insured employer does not have the financial strength necessary to ensure the timely payment of all current and estimated future claims, the association may recommend to the department that the department:

a. Revoke the employer's self-insurance privilege.

b. Require the employer to provide a certified opinion of an independent actuary who is a member of the American Academy of Actuaries as to the actuarial present value of the employer's estimated current and future compensation payments, using a 4-percent discount rate.

Fla. Stats.

c. Require an increase in the employer's security deposit in an amount determined by the association to be necessary to ensure payment of compensation claims. The department shall act on such recommendations as provided in paragraph (6)(a). The association has a cause of action against an employer, and against any successor of an employer, who fails to provide an additional security deposit required by the department. The association shall file an action in circuit court to recover a judgment in the amount of the requested additional security deposit together with reasonable attorney's fees. For the purposes of this section, the successor of an employer is any person, business entity, or group of persons or business entities which holds or acquires legal or beneficial title to the majority of the assets or the majority of the shares of the employer.

8. Charge fees to any member of the association to cover the actual costs of examining the financial and safety conditions of that member.

9. Charge an applicant for membership in the association a fee sufficient to cover the actual costs of examining the financial condition of the applicant.

10. Implement any procedures necessary to ensure compliance with regulatory actions taken by the department.

(c)

1. To the extent necessary to secure funds for the payment of covered claims and also to pay the reasonable costs to administer them, the association, subject to approval by the department, shall levy assessments based on the annual written premium each employer would have paid had the employer not been self-insured. Every assessment shall be made as a uniform percentage of the figure applicable to all individual self-insurers, provided that the assessment levied against any self-insurer in any one year shall not exceed 1 percent of the annual written premium during the calendar year preceding the date of the assessment. Assessments shall be remitted to and administered by the board of directors in the manner specified by the approved plan. Each employer so assessed shall have at least 30 days' written notice as to the date the assessment is due and payable. The association shall levy assessments against any newly admitted member of the association so that the basis of contribution of any newly admitted member is the same as previously admitted members, provision for which shall be contained in the plan of operation.

2. If, in any one year, funds available from such assessments, together with funds previously raised, are not sufficient to make all the payments or reimbursements then owing, the funds available shall be prorated, and the unpaid portion shall be paid as soon thereafter as sufficient additional funds become available.

3. Funds may be allocated or paid from the Workers' Compensation Administration Trust Fund to contract with the association to perform services required by law. However, no state funds of any kind shall be allocated or paid to the association or any of its accounts for payment of covered claims or related expenses except those state funds accruing to the association by and through the assignment of rights of an insolvent employer. The department may not levy any assessment on the association.

(4) Insolvency Fund.—Upon the adoption of a plan of operation, there shall be created an Insolvency Fund to be managed by the association.

(a) The Insolvency Fund is created for purposes of meeting the obligations of insolvent members incurred while members of the association and after the exhaustion of any security deposit, as required under this chapter. However, if such security deposit or reinsurance policy is payable to the association, the association shall commence to provide benefits out of the Insolvency Fund and be reimbursed from the security deposit or reinsurance policy. The method of operation of the Insolvency Fund shall be defined in the plan of operation as provided in subsection (5).

(b) The department shall have the authority to audit the financial soundness of the Insolvency Fund annually.

(c) The department may offer certain amendments to the plan of operation to the board of directors of the association for purposes of assuring the ongoing financial soundness of the Insolvency Fund and its ability to meet the obligations of this section.

(5) Plan of Operation.—The association shall operate pursuant to a plan of operation approved by the board of directors. The plan of operation in effect on January 1, 2002, and approved by the[1] Department of Labor and Employment Security shall remain in effect. However, any amendments to the plan shall not become effective until approved by the Department of Financial Services.

(a) The purpose of the plan of operation shall be to provide the association and the board of directors with the authority and responsibility to establish the necessary programs and to take the necessary actions to protect against the insolvency of a member of the association. In addition, the plan shall provide that the members of the association shall be responsible for maintaining an adequate Insolvency Fund to meet the obligations of insolvent members provided for under this act and shall authorize the board of directors to contract and employ those persons with the necessary expertise to carry out this stated purpose. By January 1, 2003, the board of directors shall submit to the department a proposed plan of operation for the administration of the association. The department shall approve the plan by order, consistent with this section. The department shall approve any amendments to the plan, consistent with this section, which are determined appropriate to carry out the duties and responsibilities of the association.

(b) All member employers shall comply with the plan of operation.

(c) The plan of operation shall:

1. Establish the procedures whereby all the powers and duties of the association under subsection (3) will be performed.

2. Establish procedures for handling assets of the association.

3. Establish the amount and method of reimbursing members of the board of directors under subsection (2).

4. Establish procedures by which claims may be filed with the association and establish acceptable forms of proof of covered claims. Notice of claims to the receiver or liquidator of the insolvent employer shall be deemed notice to the association or its agent, and a list of such claims shall be submitted periodically to the association or similar organization in another state by the receiver or liquidator.

5. Establish regular places and times for meetings of the board of directors.

6. Establish procedures for records to be kept of all financial transactions of the association and its agents and the board of directors.

7. Provide that any member employer aggrieved by any final action or decision of the association may appeal to the department within 30 days after the action or decision.

8. Establish the procedures whereby recommendations of candidates for the board of directors shall be submitted to the department.

9. Contain additional provisions necessary or proper for the execution of the powers and duties of the association.

(d) The plan of operation may provide that any or all of the powers and duties of the association, except those specified under subparagraphs (c)1. and 2., be delegated to a corporation, association, or other organization which performs or will perform functions similar to those of this association or its equivalent in two or more states. Such a corporation, association, or organization shall be reimbursed as a servicing facility would be reimbursed and shall be paid for its performance of any other functions of the association. A delegation of powers or duties under this subsection shall take effect only with the approval of both the board of directors and the department and may be made only to a corporation, association, or organization which extends protection which is not substantially less favorable and effective than the protection provided by this section.

(6) Powers and Duties of Department.— The department shall:

Fla. Stats.

(a) Review recommendations of the association concerning whether current or former self-insured employers or members of the association have the financial strength necessary to ensure the timely payment of all current and estimated future claims. If the association determines an employer does not have the financial strength necessary to ensure the timely payment of all current and future claims and recommends action pursuant to paragraph (3)(b), the department shall take such action as necessary to order the employer to comply with the recommendation, unless the department finds by clear and convincing evidence that the recommendation is erroneous.

(b) Contract with the association for services, which may include, but are not limited to:

1. Processing applications for self-insurance.

2. Collecting and reviewing financial statements and loss reserve information from individual self-insurers.

3. Collecting and maintaining files for original security deposit documents and reinsurance policies from individual self-insurers and, if necessary, perfecting security interests in security deposits.

4. Processing compliance documentation for individual self-insurers and providing copies of such documentation to the department.

5. Collecting all data necessary to calculate annual premium for all individual self-insurers, including individual self-insurers that are public utilities or governmental entities, and providing such calculated annual premium to the department for assessment purposes.

6. Inspecting and auditing annually, if necessary, the payroll and other records of each individual self-insurer, including individual self-insurers that are public utilities or governmental entities, in order to determine the wages paid by each individual self-insurer, the premium such individual self-insurer would have to pay if insured, and all payments of compensation made by such individual self-insurer during each prior period with the results of such audit provided to the department. For purposes of this section, the payroll records of each individual self-insurer shall be open to inspection and audit by the association and the department, or their authorized representatives, during regular business hours.

7. Processing applications and making recommendations with respect to the qualification of a business to be approved to provide or continue to provide services to individual self-insurers in the areas of underwriting, claims adjusting, loss control, and safety engineering.

8. Providing legal representation to implement the administration and audit of individual self-insurers and making recommendations regarding prosecution of any administrative or legal proceedings necessitated by the regulation of the individual self-insurers by the department.

(c) Contract with an attorney or attorneys recommended by the association for representation of the department in any administrative or legal proceedings necessitated by the recommended regulation of the individual self-insurers.

(d) Direct the association to require from each individual self-insurer, at such time and in accordance with such regulations as the department prescribes, reports relating to wages paid, the amount of premiums such individual self-insurer would have to pay if insured, and all payments of compensation made by such individual self-insurer during each prior period and to determine the amounts paid by each individual self-insurer and the amounts paid by all individual self-insurers during such period. For purposes of this section, the payroll records of each individual self-insurer shall be open to annual inspection and audit by the association and the department, or their authorized representative, during regular business hours, and if any audit of such records of an individual self-insurer discloses a deficiency in the amount reported to the association or in the amounts paid to the department by an individual self-insurer for its assessment for the Workers' Compensation Administration Trust Fund, the department or the association may assess the cost of such audit against the individual self-insurer.

(e) Require that the association notify the member employers and any other interested parties of the determination of insolvency and of their rights under this section. Such notification shall be by mail at the last known address thereof when available; but, if sufficient information for notification by mail is not available, notice by publication in a newspaper of general circulation shall be sufficient.

(f) Suspend or revoke the authority of any member employer failing to pay an assessment when due or failing to comply with the plan of operation to self-insure in this state. As an alternative, the department may levy a fine on any member employer failing to pay an assessment when due. Such fine shall not exceed 5 percent of the unpaid assessment per month, except that no fine shall be less than $100 per month.

(g) Revoke the designation of any servicing facility if the department finds that claims are being handled unsatisfactorily.

(7) Effect of Paid Claims.—

(a) Any person who recovers from the association under this section shall be deemed to have assigned his or her rights to the association to the extent of such recovery. Every claimant seeking the protection of this section shall cooperate with the association to the same extent as such person would have been required to cooperate with the insolvent member. The association shall have no cause of action against the employee of the insolvent member for any sums the association has paid out, except such causes of action as the insolvent member would have had if such sums had been paid by the insolvent member. In the case of an insolvent member operating on a plan with assessment liability, payments of claims by the association shall not operate to reduce the liability of the insolvent member to the receiver, liquidator, or statutory successor for unpaid assessments.

(b) The receiver, liquidator, or statutory successor of an insolvent member shall be bound by settlements of covered claims by the association or a similar organization in another state. The court having jurisdiction shall grant such claims priority against the assets of the insolvent member equal to that to which the claimant would have been entitled in the absence of this section. The expense of the association or similar organization in handling claims shall be accorded the same priority as the expenses of the liquidator.

(c) The association shall file periodically with the receiver or liquidator of the insolvent member statements of the covered claims paid by the association and estimates of anticipated claims on the association, which shall preserve the rights of the association against the assets of the insolvent member.

(8) Notification of Insolvencies.—To aid in the detection and prevention of employer insolvencies: Upon determination by majority vote that any member employer may be insolvent or in a financial condition hazardous to the employees thereof or to the public, it shall be the duty of the board of directors to notify the department of any information indicating such condition.

(9) Examination of the Association.—The association shall be subject to examination and regulation by the department. No later than March 30 of each year, the board of directors shall submit an audited financial statement for the preceding calendar year in a form approved by the department.

(10) Immunity.—There shall be no liability on the part of, and no cause of action of any nature shall arise against, any member employer, the association or its agents or employees, the board of directors, or the department or its representatives for any action taken by them in the performance of their powers and duties under this section.

(11) Stay of Proceedings; Reopening of Default Judgments.—All proceedings in which an insolvent employer is a party, or is obligated to defend a party, in any court or before any quasi-judicial body or administrative board in this state shall be stayed for up to 6 months, or for such additional period from the date the employer becomes an insolvent member, as is deemed necessary by a court of competent

Fla. Stats.

jurisdiction to permit proper defense by the association of all pending causes of action as to any covered claims arising from a judgment under any decision, verdict, or finding based on the default of the insolvent member. The association, either on its own behalf or on behalf of the insolvent member, may apply to have such judgment, order, decision, verdict, or finding set aside by the same court or administrator that made such judgment, order, decision, verdict, or finding and shall be permitted to defend against such claim on the merits. If requested by the association, the stay of proceedings may be shortened or waived.

(12) Limitation on Certain Actions.—Notwithstanding any other provision of this chapter, a covered claim, as defined herein, with respect to which settlement is not effected and pursuant to which suit is not instituted against the insured of an insolvent member or the association within 1 year after the deadline for filing claims with the receiver of the insolvent member, or any extension of the deadline, shall thenceforth be barred as a claim against the association.

(13) Corporate Income Tax Credit.—Any sums acquired by a member by refund, dividend, or otherwise from the association shall be payable within 30 days of receipt to the Department of Revenue for deposit with the Chief Financial Officer to the credit of the General Revenue Fund. All provisions of chapter 220 relating to penalties and interest on delinquent corporate income tax payments apply to payments due under this subsection.

History: s. 1, ch. 82-65; ss. 1, 3, ch. 82-410; s. 32, ch. 83-215; s. 4, ch. 84-267; s. 8, ch. 87-330; ss. 20, 43, ch. 89-289; ss. 33, 56, ch. 90-201; ss. 31, 52, ch. 91-1; s. 123, ch. 97-103; s. 97, ch. 2000-153; s. 3, ch. 2002-262, effective Oct. 1, 2002; s. 485, ch. 2003-261, effective June 26, 2003.

[1]**2004 Note:** Section 69, ch. 2004-194, repealed s. 20.171, which created the Department of Labor and Employment Security.

§ 440.3851. Public Records and Public Meetings Exemptions.

(1) The following records of the Florida Self-Insurers Guaranty Association, Incorporated, are confidential and exempt from s. 119.07(1) and s. 24(a), Art. I of the State Constitution:

(a) Claims files, until termination of all litigation and settlement of all claims arising out of the same accident.

(b) Medical records that are part of a claims file and other information relating to the medical condition or medical status of a claimant.

(c) Minutes of exempt portions of meetings, as provided in subsection (3), until termination of all litigation and settlement of all claims with regard to that claim.

(2) Records or portions of records made confidential and exempt by this section may be released, upon written request, to another agency in the performance of that agency's official duties and responsibilities. The receiving agency shall maintain the confidential and exempt status of such record or portion of a record.

(3) That portion of a meeting of the association's board of directors or any subcommittee of the association's board at which records made confidential and exempt by this section are discussed is exempt from s. 286.011 and s. 24(b), Art. I of the State Constitution. All exempt portions of meetings shall be recorded and transcribed. The board shall record the times of commencement and termination of the meeting, all discussion and proceedings, the names of all persons present at any time, and the names of all persons speaking. An exempt portion of any meeting may not be off the record. Subject to this section and 46 s. 119.021(2), the court reporter's notes of any exempt portion of a meeting shall be retained by the association for a minimum of 5 years. A copy of the transcript of any exempt portion of a meeting in which claims files are discussed shall become public as to individual claims after settlement of the claim with any confidential and exempt information redacted.

(4) This section is subject to the Open Government Sunset Review Act of 1995 in accordance with s. 119.15 and shall stand repealed on October 2, 2010, unless reviewed and saved from repeal through reenactment by the Legislature.

History: s.1, ch. 2005-198, effective May 5, 2005.

§ 440.386. Individual Self-Insurers' Insolvency; Conservation; Liquidation.

(1) Jurisdiction of Delinquency Proceeding Venue; Change of Appeal.—

(a) The circuit court shall have original jurisdiction in any delinquency proceeding under this section, and any court with jurisdiction is authorized to make all necessary or proper orders to carry out the purposes of this section.

(b) The venue of a delinquency proceeding or summary proceeding against a domestic or foreign individual self-insurer shall be in the Circuit Court of Leon County.

(c) An appeal shall be to the District Court of Appeal, First District, from an order granting or refusing liquidation or conservation and from every order in a delinquency proceeding having the character of a final order as to the particular portion of the proceeding embraced therein.

(2) Commencement of Delinquency Proceeding.—The department or the Florida Self-Insurers Guaranty Association, Incorporated, may commence a delinquency proceeding by application to the court for an order directing the individual self-insurer to show cause why the department or association should not have the relief sought. On the return of such order to show cause, and after a full hearing, the court shall either deny the application or grant the application, together with such other relief as the nature of the case and the interests of the claimants, creditors, stockholders, members, subscribers, or public may require. The department and the association shall give reasonable written notice to each other of all hearings which pertain to an adjudication of insolvency of a member individual self-insurer.

(3) Grounds for Liquidation.—The department or the association may apply to the court for an order appointing a receiver and directing the receiver to liquidate the business of a domestic individual self-insurer if such individual self-insurer is insolvent.

(4) Grounds for Conservation; Foreign Individual Self-Insurers.—

(a) The department or the association may apply to the court for an order appointing a receiver or ancillary receiver, and directing the receiver to conserve the assets within this state, of a foreign individual self-insurer if such individual self-insurer is insolvent.

(b) An order to conserve the assets of an individual self-insurer shall require the receiver forthwith to take possession of the property of the receiver within the state and to conserve it, subject to the further direction of the court.

(5) Procedure in Liquidations of Individual Self-Insurer by Court.—

(a) In proceedings to liquidate the assets and business of an individual self-insurer, the court shall have power:

1. To issue injunctions.

2. To appoint a receiver or receivers pendente lite with such powers and duties as the court, from time to time, may direct.

3. To take such other proceedings as may be requisite to preserve the individual self-insurer assets, wherever situated, and carry on the business of the individual self-insurer until a full hearing can be held.

(b) After a hearing had upon such notice as the court may direct to be given to all parties to the proceedings and to any other parties in interest designated by the court, the court may appoint a liquidating receiver or receivers with authority to collect the assets of the individual self-insurer. Such liquidating receiver or receivers shall have authority, subject to the order of the court, to sell, convey, and dispose of all or any part of the assets of the individual self-insurer, wherever situated, either at public or private sale. The assets of the individual self-insurer or the proceeds resulting from a sale, conveyance, or other disposition thereof shall be applied to the expenses of such liquidation and to the payment of the liabilities and obligations of the individual self-insurer, and any remaining assets or proceeds shall be distributed among its owners or shareholders according to their respective rights and interests. The order appoint-

Fla. Stats.

ing such liquidating receiver or receivers shall state their powers and duties. Such powers and duties may be increased or diminished at any time during the proceedings.

(c) The court shall have power to allow, from time to time, as expenses of the liquidation, compensation to the receiver or receivers and to the receiver's attorneys in the proceeding and to direct the payment thereof out of the assets of the individual self-insurer or the proceeds of any sale or disposition of such assets.

(d) A receiver of an individual self-insurer appointed under the provisions of this section shall have authority to sue and defend in all courts in her or his own name as receiver of such individual self-insurer. The court appointing such receiver shall have exclusive jurisdiction of the individual self-insurer and its property, wherever situated.

(e) The circuit court shall have jurisdiction to appoint an ancillary receiver for the assets and business of such individual self-insurer, to serve ancillary to the receiver for the assets and business of the individual self-insurer acting under orders of a court having jurisdiction to appoint such a receiver for the individual self-insurer, located in any other state, whenever circumstances exist deemed by the court to require the appointment of such ancillary receiver. Such court, whenever circumstances exist deemed by it to require the appointment of a receiver for all the assets in and out of this state, and the business, of a foreign individual self-insurer doing business in this state, in accordance with the ordinary usages of equity, may appoint such a receiver for all its assets in and out of this state, and its business, even though no receiver has been appointed elsewhere. Such receivership shall be converted into an ancillary receivership when deemed appropriate by such circuit court in the light of orders entered by a court of competent jurisdiction in some other state, providing for a receivership of all assets and business of such individual self-insurer.

(6) Qualifications of Receivers.—A receiver shall in all cases be a natural person or a corporation authorized to act as receiver, which corporation may be a domestic corporation or a foreign corporation authorized to transact business in this state, and shall in all cases give such bond as the court may direct, with such sureties as the court may require.

(7) Filing of Claims in Liquidation Proceedings.—In proceedings to liquidate the assets and business of an individual self-insurer, the court may require all creditors of the individual self-insurer to file with the clerk of the court or with the receiver, in such form as the court may prescribe, proofs under oath of their respective claims. If the court requires the filing of claims, it shall fix a date, which shall be not less than 4 months from the date of the offer, as the last day for filing of claims, and shall prescribe the notice of the date so fixed that shall be given to creditors and claimants. Prior to the date so fixed, the court may extend the time for the filing of claims. Creditors and claimants failing to file proofs of claim on or before the date so fixed may be barred, by order of court, from participating in the distribution of the assets of the individual self-insurer. Nothing in this section affects the enforceability of any recorded mortgage or lien or the perfected security interest or rights of a person in possession of real or personal property.

(8) Discontinuance of Delinquency Proceedings.—The liquidation of the assets and business or other delinquency proceedings of an individual self-insurer may be discontinued at any time during the proceedings when it is established that cause for the delinquency proceeding no longer exists. In such event, the court shall dismiss the proceedings and direct the receiver to redeliver to the individual self-insurer all its remaining property and assets.

(9) Voidable Transfers.—

(a) Any transfer of, or lien upon, the property of an individual self-insurer which is made or created within 4 months prior to the granting of an order to show cause under this section with the intent of giving to any creditor a preference or of enabling the creditor to obtain a greater percentage of her or his debt than any other creditor of the same class, and which is accepted by such creditor having reasonable cause to believe that such preference will occur, shall be voidable.

(b) Every director, officer, employee, stockholder, member, subscriber, and any other person acting on behalf of such individual self-insurer who shall be concerned in any such act or deed and every person receiving thereby any property of such individual self-insurer or the benefit thereof shall be personally liable therefor and shall be bound to account to the court.

(c) The receiver in any proceeding under this section may avoid any transfer of or lien upon the property of an individual self-insurer which any creditor, stockholder, or subscriber of such individual self-insurer might have avoided and may recover the property so transferred unless such person was a bona fide holder for value prior to the date of the entering of an order to show cause under this chapter. Such property or its value may be recovered from anyone who has received it except a bona fide holder for value as herein specified.

(10) Transfers Prior to Petition.—

(a) Every transfer made or suffered and every obligation incurred by an individual self-insurer within 1 year prior to the filing of a successful petition in any delinquency proceeding under this section, upon a showing by the receiver that the same was incurred without fair consideration, or with actual intent to hinder, delay, or defraud either then-existing or future creditors, shall be fraudulent and voidable. However, every such transfer or obligation incurred or suffered within 6 months prior to the filing of the above petition shall be presumed void and fraudulent, with the burden of proof upon the obligee or transferee to show otherwise. This paragraph shall not apply to a person who in good faith is a purchaser, lienor, or obligee, for a present fair equivalent value, but any purchaser, lienor, or obligee who in good faith has given a valuable consideration less than fair for such transfer, lien, or obligation may retain the property, lien, or obligation as a security for repayment. The court may, on due notice, order any such transfer or obligation to be preserved for the benefit of the estate, and in that event the receiver shall succeed to and may enforce the rights of the purchaser, lienor, or obligee.

(b) Transfers shall be deemed to have been made or suffered, or obligations incurred, when perfected according to the following criteria:

1. A transfer of property other than real property shall be deemed to be made or suffered when it becomes so far perfected that no subsequent lien obtainable by legal or equitable proceedings on a simple contract could become superior to the rights of the transferee.

2. A transfer of real property shall be deemed to be made or suffered when it becomes so far perfected that no subsequent bona fide purchaser from the individual self-insurer could obtain rights superior to the rights of the transferee.

3. A transfer which creates an equitable lien shall not be deemed to be perfected if there are available means by which a legal lien could be created.

4. Any transfer not perfected prior to the filing of a petition in a delinquency proceeding shall be deemed to be made immediately before the filing of a successful petition.

Subparagraphs 1.-4. apply whether or not there are or were creditors who might have obtained any liens or persons who might have become bona fide purchasers.

(c) The transferor or obligor individual self-insurer shall record and preserve adequate official memoranda by corporate minutes which shall fully reflect all transactions involving transfers as contemplated by this section of real property or securities of any type and, in the case of all other property or assets, any transfer out of the individual self-insurer's ordinary course of business. Any person, firm, or corporation, or any officer, director, or employee thereof, who violates this paragraph commits a misdemeanor of the first degree, punishable as provided in s. 775.082 or by a fine of not more than $5,000. Each instance of such violation shall be considered a separate offense.

(d) The personal liability of the officers or directors of an insolvent individual self-insurer shall be subject to the provisions of chapter 607 and the penalties provided therein.

(e) Every transaction of the individual self-

Fla. Stats.

insurer with a reinsurer or an excess insurer within 1 year prior to the filing of the petition shall be voidable upon a showing that such transaction was made without fair consideration or with intent to hinder, delay, or defraud either then-existing or future creditors notwithstanding the provisions of subsection (1).

(11) Transfers After Petition.—

(a) After the original petition is filed in any delinquency proceeding, a transfer of any of the real property of the individual self-insurer made to a person acting in good faith shall be valid against the receiver if made for a present fair equivalent value, or, if not made for a present fair equivalent value, then to the extent of the present consideration actually paid therefor, for which amount the transferee shall have a lien on the property so transferred. The recording of a copy of the petition for, or order in, any delinquency proceeding with the clerk of the circuit court in the county where any real property in question is located is constructive notice of the commencement of a delinquency proceeding. The exercise by a court of the United States or any state with jurisdiction to authorize or effect a judicial sale of real property of the individual self-insurer within any county in any state shall not be impaired by the pendency of such a proceeding unless the copy is recorded in the county prior to the consummation of the judicial sale.

(b) After the original petition for a delinquency proceeding has been filed and before an order of conservation or liquidation is granted:

1. A transfer of any of the property of the individual self-insurer, other than real property, made to a person acting in good faith shall be valid against the receiver if made for a present fair equivalent value, or, if not made for a present fair equivalent value, then to the extent of the present consideration actually paid therefor, for which amount the transferee shall have a lien on the property so transferred.

2. A person indebted to the individual self-insurer or holding property of the individual self-insurer may, if acting in good faith, pay the indebtedness or deliver the property or any part thereof to the individual self-insurer or upon her or his order, with the same effect as if the petition were not pending.

(c) A person having actual knowledge of the pending delinquency proceeding shall be deemed not to act in good faith.

(d) A person asserting the validity of a transfer under this subsection has the burden of proof. Except as elsewhere provided in this subsection, any transfer by or in behalf of the individual self-insurer after the date of filing of the original petition in any delinquency proceeding requesting the appointment of a receiver by any person other than the receiver is not valid against the receiver.

(e) Nothing in this section shall impair the negotiability of currency or negotiable instruments.

(12) Judgment of Involuntary Dissolution; Entry; Filing.—

(a) In proceedings to liquidate the assets and business of an individual self-insurer which is a corporation, when the costs and expenses of such proceedings and all debts, obligations, and liabilities of the corporation shall have been paid and discharged and all of its remaining property and assets distributed to its shareholders or, in case its property and assets are not sufficient to satisfy and discharge such costs, expenses, debts, and obligations, all the property and assets have been applied so far as they will go to their payment, the court shall enter a judgment dissolving the corporation, whereupon the existence of the corporation shall cease.

(b) In case the court shall enter a judgment dissolving a corporation, it shall be the duty of the clerk of such court to cause a certified copy of the judgment to be filed with the Department of State. No fee shall be charged by the Department of State for the filing thereof.

(13) Guaranty Fund; Orders of Court.—Any delinquency order issued pursuant to this section shall authorize and direct the receiver to coordinate the operation of the receivership with the operation of the Florida Self-Insurers Guaranty Association, Incorporated. Such authorization

shall include, but not be limited to, release of copies of any of the following:

(a) Workers' compensation claims files, records, or documents pertaining to workers' compensation claims on file with the insolvent individual self-insurer.

(b) Workers' compensation claims filed with the receiver.

History: s. 34, ch. 90-201; s. 32, ch. 91-1; s. 124, ch. 97-103; s. 4, ch. 2002-262, effective Oct. 1, 2002; s. 486, ch. 2003-261, effective June 26, 2003.

[1]**Note:** —Redesignated as s. 440.02(24)(a) by s. 11, ch. 2002-194.

[2]**Note:** —The Department of Labor and Employment Security no longer exists; all divisions, responsibilities, and functions were reassigned effective July 1, 2002, by s. 1, ch. 2002-194.

§ 440.39. Compensation for Injuries When Third Persons Are Liable.

(1) If an employee, subject to the provisions of the Workers' Compensation Law, is injured or killed in the course of his or her employment by the negligence or wrongful act of a third-party tortfeasor, such injured employee or, in the case of his or her death, the employee's dependents may accept compensation benefits under the provisions of this law, and at the same time such injured employee or his or her dependents or personal representatives may pursue his or her remedy by action at law or otherwise against such third-party tortfeasor.

(2) If the employee or his or her dependents accept compensation or other benefits under this law or begin proceedings therefor, the employer or, in the event the employer is insured against liability hereunder, the insurer shall be subrogated to the rights of the employee or his or her dependents against such third-party tortfeasor, to the extent of the amount of compensation benefits paid or to be paid as provided by subsection (3). If the injured employee or his or her dependents recovers from a third-party tortfeasor by judgment or settlement, either before or after the filing of suit, before the employee has accepted compensation or other benefits under this chapter or before the employee has filed a written claim for compensation benefits, the amount recovered from the tortfeasor shall be set off against any compensation benefits other than for remedial care, treatment and attendance as well as rehabilitative services payable under this chapter. The amount of such offset shall be reduced by the amount of all court costs expended in the prosecution of the third-party suit or claim, including reasonable attorney fees for the plaintiff's attorney. In no event shall the setoff provided in this section in lieu of payment of compensation benefits diminish the period for filing a claim for benefits as provided in s. 440.19.

(3)

(a) In all claims or actions at law against a third-party tortfeasor, the employee, or his or her dependents or those entitled by law to sue in the event he or she is deceased, shall sue for the employee individually and for the use and benefit of the employer, if a self-insurer, or employer's insurance carrier, in the event compensation benefits are claimed or paid; and such suit may be brought in the name of the employee, or his or her dependents or those entitled by law to sue in the event he or she is deceased, as plaintiff or, at the option of such plaintiff, may be brought in the name of such plaintiff and for the use and benefit of the employer or insurance carrier, as the case may be. Upon suit being filed, the employer or the insurance carrier, as the case may be, may file in the suit a notice of payment of compensation and medical benefits to the employee or his or her dependents, which notice shall constitute a lien upon any judgment or settlement recovered to the extent that the court may determine to be their pro rata share for compensation and medical benefits paid or to be paid under the provisions of this law, less their pro rata share of all court costs expended by the plaintiff in the prosecution of the suit including reasonable attorney's fees for the plaintiff's attorney. In determining the employer's or carrier's pro rata share of those costs and attorney's fees, the employer or carrier shall have deducted from its recovery a percentage amount equal to the percentage of the judgment or settlement which is for costs and attorney's fees. Subject to this deduction, the employer or carrier shall recover from the judgment or settlement, after

Fla. Stats.

costs and attorney's fees incurred by the employee or dependent in that suit have been deducted, 100 percent of what it has paid and future benefits to be paid, except, if the employee or dependent can demonstrate to the court that he or she did not recover the full value of damages sustained, the employer or carrier shall recover from the judgment or settlement, after costs and attorney's fees incurred by the employee or dependent in that suit have been deducted, a percentage of what it has paid and future benefits to be paid equal to the percentage that the employee's net recovery is of the full value of the employee's damages; provided, the failure by the employer or carrier to comply with the duty to cooperate imposed by subsection (7) may be taken into account by the trial court in determining the amount of the employer's or carrier's recovery, and such recovery may be reduced, as the court deems equitable and appropriate under the circumstances, including as a mitigating factor whether a claim or potential claim against a third party is likely to impose liability upon the party whose cooperation is sought, if it finds such a failure has occurred. The burden of proof will be upon the employee. The determination of the amount of the employer's or carrier's recovery shall be made by the judge of the trial court upon application therefor and notice to the adverse party. Notice of suit being filed shall be served upon the employer and compensation carrier and upon all parties to the suit or their attorneys of record by the employee. Notice of payment of compensation benefits shall be served upon the employee and upon all parties to the suit or their attorneys of record by the employer and compensation carrier. However, if a migrant worker prevails under a private cause of action under the Migrant and Seasonal Agricultural Worker Protection Act (AWPA) 96 Stat. 2583, as amended, 29 U.S.C. ss. 1801 et seq. (1962 ed. and Supp. V), any recovery by the migrant worker under this act shall be offset 100 percent against any recovery under AWPA.

(b) If the employer or insurance carrier has given written notice of his or her rights of subrogation to the third-party tortfeasor, and, thereafter, settlement of any such claim or action at law is made, either before or after suit is filed, and the parties fail to agree on the proportion to be paid to each, the circuit court of the county in which the cause of action arose shall determine the amount to be paid to each by such third-party tortfeasor in accordance with the provisions of paragraph (a).

(4)

(a) If the injured employee or his or her dependents, as the case may be, fail to bring suit against such third-party tortfeasor within 1 year after the cause of action thereof has accrued, the employer, if a self-insurer, and if not, the insurance carrier, may, after giving 30 days' notice to the injured employee or his or her dependents and the injured employee's attorney, if represented by counsel, institute suit against such third-party tortfeasor, either in his or her own name or as provided by subsection (3), and, in the event suit is so instituted, shall be subrogated to and entitled to retain from any judgment recovered against, or settlement made with, such third party, the following: All amounts paid as compensation and medical benefits under the provisions of this law and the present value of all future compensation benefits payable, to be reduced to its present value, and to be retained as a trust fund from which future payments of compensation are to be made, together with all court costs, including attorney's fees expended in the prosecution of such suit, to be prorated as provided by subsection (3). The remainder of the moneys derived from such judgment or settlement shall be paid to the employee or his or her dependents, as the case may be.

(b) If the carrier or employer does not bring suit within 2 years following the accrual of the cause of action against a third-party tortfeasor, the right of action shall revert to the employee or, in the case of the employee's death, those entitled by law to sue, and in such event the provisions of subsection (3) shall apply.

(5) In all cases under subsection (4) involving third-party tortfeasors in which compensation benefits under this law are paid or are to be paid, settlement may not be made either before or after suit is instituted except upon agreement of the injured employee or his or her dependents and the employer or his or her insurance carrier,

as the case may be.

(6) Any amounts recovered under this section by the employer or his or her insurance carrier shall be credited against the loss experience of such employer.

(7) The employee, employer, and carrier have a duty to cooperate with each other in investigating and prosecuting claims and potential claims against third-party tortfeasors by producing nonprivileged documents and allowing inspection of premises, but only to the extent necessary for such purpose. Such documents and the results of such inspections are confidential and exempt from the provisions of s. 119.07(1), and shall not be used or disclosed for any other purpose.

History: s. 39, ch. 17481, 1935; CGL 1936 Supp. 5966(38); s. 14, ch. 18413, 1937; s. 1, ch. 23822, 1947; s. 1, ch. 26546, 1951; s. 1, ch. 59-431; s. 6, ch. 70-148; s. 18, ch. 74-197; s. 11, ch. 77-290; s. 23, ch. 78-300; ss. 30, 124, ch. 79-40; s. 21, ch. 79-312; s. 280, ch. 81-259; s. 15, ch. 83-305; s. 9, ch. 84-267; s. 5, ch. 86-171; ss. 21, 43, ch. 89-289; ss. 35, 56, ch. 90-201; ss. 33, 52, ch. 91-1; s. 5, ch. 91-269; s. 287, ch. 96-406; s. 1053, ch. 97-103.

§ 440.40. Compensation Notice.

Every employer who has secured compensation under the provisions of this chapter shall keep posted in a conspicuous place or places in and about her or his place or places of business typewritten or printed notices, in accordance with a form prescribed by the department, the following:

(1) A notice stating that such employer has secured the payment of compensation in accordance with the provisions of this chapter. Such notices shall contain the name and address of the carrier, if any, with whom the employer has secured payment of compensation and the date of the expiration of the policy. The department may by rule prescribe the form of the notices and require carriers to provide the notices to policyholders.

(2) A notice stating: "Anti-Fraud Reward Program.—Rewards of up to $25,000 may be paid to persons providing information to the Department of Financial Services leading to the arrest and conviction of persons committing insurance fraud, including employers who illegally fail to obtain workers' compensation coverage. Persons may report suspected fraud to the department at . . . (Phone No.). . . . A person is not subject to civil liability for furnishing such information, if such person acts without malice, fraud, or bad faith."

History: s. 40, ch. 17481, 1935; CGL 1936 Supp. 5966(39); ss. 17, 35, ch. 69-106; s. 23, ch. 78-300; s. 124, ch. 79-40; s. 21, ch. 79-312; s. 43, ch. 89-289; s. 56, ch. 90-201; s. 52, ch. 91-1; s. 125, ch. 97-103; s. 7, ch. 98-125, effective May 22, 1998; s. 42, ch. 2002-194, effective July 1, 2002; s. 15, ch. 2002-236, effective July 1, 2002; s. 487, ch. 2003-261, effective June 26, 2003.

§ 440.41. Substitution of Carrier for Employer.

In any case where the employer is not a self-insurer, in order that the liability for compensation imposed by this chapter may be most effectively discharged by the employer, and in order that the administration of this chapter in respect of such liability may be facilitated, the department shall by regulation provide for the discharge, by the carrier for such employer, of such obligations and duties of the employer in respect of such liability, imposed by this chapter upon the employer, as it considers proper in order to effectuate the provisions of this chapter. For such purposes:

(1) Notice to or knowledge of an employer of the occurrence of the injury shall be notice to or knowledge of the carrier.

(2) Jurisdiction of the employer by the judges of compensation claims, the department, or any court under this chapter shall be jurisdiction of the carrier.

(3) Any requirement by the judges of compensation claims, the department, or any court under any compensation order, finding, or decision shall be binding upon the carrier in the same manner and to the same extent as upon the employer.

History: s. 41, ch. 17481, 1935; CGL 1936 Supp. 5966(40); ss. 17, 35, ch. 69-106; s. 19, ch. 75-209; s. 23, ch. 78-300; ss. 31, 124, ch. 79-40; s. 21, ch. 79-312; s. 9, ch. 81-119; s. 43, ch. 89-289; s. 56, ch.

Fla. Stats.

90-201; s. 52, ch. 91-1; s. 11, ch. 91-46; s. 43, ch. 2002-194, effective July 1, 2002.

§ 440.42. Insurance Policies; Liability.

(1) Every policy or contract of insurance issued under authority of this chapter shall contain:

(a) A provision to carry out the provisions of s. 440.41; and

(b) A provision that insolvency or bankruptcy of the employer and discharge therein shall not relieve the carrier from payment of compensation for disability or death sustained by an employee during the life of such policy or contract.

(2) A workers' compensation insurance policy may require the employer to release certain employment and wage information maintained by the state pursuant to federal and state unemployment compensation laws except to the extent prohibited or limited under federal law. By entering into a workers' compensation insurance policy with such a provision, the employer consents to the release of the information. The insurance carrier requiring such consent shall safeguard the information and maintain its confidentiality. The carrier shall limit use of the information to verifying compliance with the terms of the workers' compensation insurance policy. The department may charge a fee to cover the cost of disclosing the information.

(3) No contract or policy of insurance issued by a carrier under this chapter shall expire or be canceled until at least 30 days have elapsed after a notice of cancellation has been sent to the department and to the employer in accordance with the provisions of s. 440.185(7). For cancellation due to nonpayment of premium, the insurer shall mail notification to the employer at least 10 days prior to the effective date of the cancellation. However, when duplicate or dual coverage exists by reason of two different carriers having issued policies of insurance to the same employer securing the same liability, it shall be presumed that only that policy with the later effective date shall be in force and that the earlier policy terminated upon the effective date of the latter. In the event that both policies carry the same effective date, one of the policies may be canceled instanter upon filing a notice of cancellation with the department and serving a copy thereof upon the employer in such manner as the department prescribes by rule. The department may by rule prescribe the content of the notice of retroactive cancellation and specify the time, place, and manner in which the notice of cancellation is to be served.

(4) When there is any controversy as to which of two or more carriers is liable for the discharge of the obligations and duties of one or more employers with respect to a claim for compensation, remedial treatment, or other benefits under this chapter, the judge of compensation claims shall have jurisdiction to adjudicate such controversy; and if one of the carriers voluntarily or in compliance with a compensation order makes payments in discharge of such liability and it is finally determined that another carrier is liable for all or any part of such obligations and duties with respect to such claim, the carrier which has made payments either voluntarily or in compliance with a compensation order shall be entitled to reimbursement from the carrier finally determined liable, and the judge of compensation claims shall have jurisdiction to order such reimbursement; however, if the carrier finally determined liable can demonstrate that it has been prejudiced by lack of knowledge or notice of its potential liability, such reimbursement shall be only with respect to payments made after it had knowledge or notice of its potential liability.

History: s. 42, ch. 17481, 1935; CGL 1936 Supp. 5966(41); s. 11, ch. 29778, 1955; s. 3, ch. 57-225; s. 3, ch. 59-100; s. 1, ch. 65-204; ss. 17, 35, ch. 69-106; s. 1, ch. 73-185; s. 20, ch. 75-209; s. 23, ch. 78-300; ss. 32, 124, ch. 79-40; s. 21, ch. 79-312; s. 43, ch. 89-289; s. 56, ch. 90-201; s. 52, ch. 91-1; s. 12, ch. 91-46; s. 8, ch. 98-125; s. 10, ch. 98-174; s. 44, ch. 2002-194, effective July 1, 2002; s. 29, ch. 412, effective Oct. 1, 2003.

§ 440.44. Workers' Compensation; Staff Organization.

(1) Interpretation of Law.—As a guide to the interpretation of this chapter, the Legislature takes due notice of federal social and labor acts and hereby creates an agency to administer such

acts passed for the benefit of employees and employers in Florida industry, and desires to meet the requirements of such federal acts wherever not inconsistent with the Constitution and laws of Florida.

(2) Intent.—It is the intent of the Legislature that the department, the agency, the Department of Education, and the Division of Administrative Hearings assume an active and forceful role in its administration of this act, so as to ensure that the system operates efficiently and with maximum benefit to both employers and employees.

(3) Expenditures.—The department, the agency, the office, the Department of Education, and the director of the Division of Administrative Hearings shall make such expenditures, including expenditures for personal services and rent at the seat of government and elsewhere, for law books; for telephone services and WATS lines; for books of reference, periodicals, equipment, and supplies; and for printing and binding as may be necessary in the administration of this chapter. All expenditures in the administration of this chapter shall be allowed and paid as provided in s. 440.50 upon the presentation of itemized vouchers therefor approved by the department, the agency, the Department of Education, or the director of the Division of Administrative Hearings.

(4) Personnel Administration.—Subject to the other provisions of this chapter, the department, the agency, the office, the Department of Education, and the Division of Administrative Hearings may appoint, and prescribe the duties and powers of, bureau chiefs, attorneys, accountants, medical advisers, technical assistants, inspectors, claims examiners, and such other employees as may be necessary in the performance of their duties under this chapter.

(5) Office.—The department, the agency, the Department of Education, and the Deputy Chief Judge shall maintain and keep open during reasonable business hours an office, which shall be provided in the Capitol or some other suitable building in the City of Tallahassee, for the transaction of business under this chapter, at which office the official records and papers shall be kept. The office shall be furnished and equipped. The department, the agency, any judge of compensation claims, or the Deputy Chief Judge may hold sessions and conduct hearings at any place within the state. The Office of the Judges of Compensation Claims shall maintain the 17 district offices, 31 judges of compensation claims, and 31 mediators as they exist on June 30, 2001.

(6) Seal.—The department and the judges of compensation claims shall have a seal upon which shall be inscribed the words "State of Florida Department of Financial Services—Seal" and "Division of Administrative Hearings—Seal," respectively.

(7) Destruction of Obsolete Records.—The department is expressly authorized to provide by regulation for and to destroy obsolete records of the department. The Division of Administrative Hearings is expressly authorized to provide by regulation for and to destroy obsolete records of the Office of the Judges of Compensation Claims.

(8) Procedure.—In the exercise of their duties and functions requiring administrative hearings, the department and the agency shall proceed in accordance with the Administrative Procedure Act. The authority of the department and the agency to issue orders resulting from administrative hearings as provided for in this chapter shall not infringe upon the jurisdiction of the judges of compensation claims.

History: s. 44, ch. 17481, 1935; CGL 1936 Supp. 5966(42); s. 15, ch. 18413, 1937; s. 1, ch. 20299, 1941; s. 1, ch. 21875, 1943; s. 4, ch. 22814, 1945; s. 1, ch. 23920, 1947; s. 10, ch. 26484, 1951; s. 11, ch. 28241, 1953; s. 24, ch. 57-1; s. 1, ch. 57-785; s. 1, ch. 57-156; s. 1, ch. 63-274; s. 19, ch. 63-400; s. 2, ch. 67-554; ss. 17, 35, ch. 69-106; s. 163, ch. 71-377; ss. 1, 2, ch. 72-143; s. 2, ch. 72-241; s. 1, ch. 73-283; s. 19, ch. 74-197; s. 21, ch. 75-209; s. 3, ch. 75-237; s. 23, ch. 78-300; s. 4, ch. 78-323; s. 18, ch. 79-7; ss. 33, 124, ch. 79-40; ss. 17, 21, ch. 79-312; s. 15, ch. 80-236; ss. 1, 2, 3, ch. 81-76; s. 10, ch. 81-119; ss. 1, 4, ch. 82-46; ss. 22, 42, 43, ch. 89-289; ss. 37, 56, ch. 90-201; ss. 35, 52, ch. 91-1; s. 33, ch. 91-46; s. 24, ch. 2001-91, effective Oct. 1, 2001; s. 45, ch. 2002-194, effective July 1, 2002; s. 488, ch. 2003-261, effective June 26, 2003.

§440.4416. Workers' Compensation Oversight Board.

History: Enacted 1993. Repealed July 1, 2002 ch. 2002-194.

§ 440.442. Code of Judicial Conduct.

The Deputy Chief Judge and judges of compensation claims shall observe and abide by the Code of Judicial Conduct as adopted by the Florida Supreme Court. Any material violation of a provision of the Code of Judicial Conduct shall constitute either malfeasance or misfeasance in office and shall be grounds for suspension and removal of the Deputy Chief Judge or judge of compensation claims by the Governor.

History: ss. 13, 23, ch. 78-300; ss. 34, 124, ch. 79-40; ss. 18, 21, ch. 79-312; s. 16, ch. 80-236; s. 43, ch. 89-289; s. 56, ch. 90-201; s. 52, ch. 91-1; s. 13, ch. 91-46; s. 39, ch. 93-415; s. 127, ch. 97-103; s. 16, ch. 99-7; s. 8, ch. 2000-243; s. 25, ch. 2001-91, effective Oct. 1, 2001.

§ 440.45. Office of the Judges of Compensation Claims.

(1)

(a) There is created the Office of the Judges of Compensation Claims within the Department of Management Services. The Office of the Judges of Compensation Claims shall be headed by the Deputy Chief Judge of Compensation Claims. The Deputy Chief Judge shall report to the director of the Division of Administrative Hearings. The Deputy Chief Judge shall be appointed by the Governor for a term of 4 years from a list of three names submitted by the statewide nominating commission created under subsection (2). The Deputy Chief Judge must demonstrate prior administrative experience and possess the same qualifications for appointment as a judge of compensation claims, and the procedure for reappointment of the Deputy Chief Judge will be the same as for reappointment of a judge of compensation claims. The office shall be a separate budget entity and the director of the Division of Administrative Hearings shall be its agency head for all purposes, including, but not limited to, rulemaking pursuant to subsection (4) and establishing agency policies and procedures. The Department of Management Services shall provide administrative support and service to the office to the extent requested by the director of the Division of Administrative Hearings but shall not direct, supervise, or control the Office of the Judges of Compensation Claims in any manner, including, but not limited to, personnel, purchasing, budgetary matters, or property transactions. The operating budget of the Office of the Judges of Compensation Claims shall be paid out of the Workers' Compensation Administration Trust Fund established in s. 440.50.

(b) Effective October 1, 2001, the position of Deputy Chief Judge of Compensation Claims is created.

(2)

(a) The Governor shall appoint full-time judges of compensation claims to conduct proceedings as required by this chapter or other law. No person may be nominated to serve as a judge of compensation claims unless he or she has been a member of The Florida Bar in good standing for the previous 5 years and is experienced in the practice of law of workers' compensation. No judge of compensation claims shall engage in the private practice of law during a term of office.

(b) Except as provided in paragraph (c), the Governor shall appoint a judge of compensation claims from a list of three persons nominated by a statewide nominating commission. The statewide nominating commission shall be composed of the following:

1. Five members, at least one of whom must be a member of a minority group as defined in s. 288.703(3), one of each who resides in each of the territorial jurisdictions of the district courts of appeal, appointed by the Board of Governors of The Florida Bar from among The Florida Bar members who are engaged in the practice of law. On July 1, 1999, the term of office of each person appointed by the Board of Governors of The Florida Bar to the commission expires. The Board of Governors shall appoint members who reside in the odd-numbered district court of appeal jurisdictions to 4-year terms each, begin-

ning July 1, 1999, and members who reside in the even-numbered district court of appeal jurisdictions to 2-year terms each, beginning July 1, 1999. Thereafter, each member shall be appointed for a 4-year term;

2. Five electors, at least one of whom must be a member of a minority group as defined in s. 288.703(3), one of each who resides in each of the territorial jurisdictions of the district courts of appeal, appointed by the Governor. On July 1, 1999, the term of office of each person appointed by the Governor to the commission expires. The Governor shall appoint members who reside in the odd-numbered district court of appeal jurisdictions to 2-year terms each, beginning July 1, 1999, and members who reside in the even-numbered district court of appeal jurisdictions to 4-year terms each, beginning July 1, 1999. Thereafter, each member shall be appointed for a 4-year term; and

3. Five electors, at least one of whom must be a member of a minority group as defined in s. 288.703(3), one of each who resides in the territorial jurisdictions of the district courts of appeal, selected and appointed by a majority vote of the other 10 members of the commission. On October 1, 1999, the term of office of each person appointed to the commission by its other members expires. A majority of the other members of the commission shall appoint members who reside in the odd-numbered district court of appeal jurisdictions to 2-year terms each, beginning October 1, 1999, and members who reside in the even-numbered district court of appeal jurisdictions to 4-year terms each, beginning October 1, 1999. Thereafter, each member shall be appointed for a 4-year term. A vacancy occurring on the commission shall be filled by the original appointing authority for the unexpired balance of the term. No attorney who appears before any judge of compensation claims more than four times a year is eligible to serve on the statewide nominating commission. The meetings and determinations of the nominating commission as to the judges of compensation claims shall be open to the public.

(c) Each judge of compensation claims shall be appointed for a term of 4 years, but during the term of office may be removed by the Governor for cause. Prior to the expiration of a judge's term of office, the statewide nominating commission shall review the judge's conduct and determine whether the judge's performance is satisfactory. Effective July 1, 2002, in determining whether a judge's performance is satisfactory, the commission shall consider the extent to which the judge has met the requirements of this chapter, including, but not limited to, the requirements of ss. 440.25(1) and (4)(a)-(e), 440.34(2), and 440.442. If the judge's performance is deemed satisfactory, the commission shall report its finding to the Governor no later than 6 months prior to the expiration of the judge's term of office. The Governor shall review the commission's report and may reappoint the judge for an additional 4-year term. If the Governor does not reappoint the judge, the Governor shall inform the commission. The judge shall remain in office until the Governor has appointed a successor judge in accordance with paragraphs (a) and (b). If a vacancy occurs during a judge's unexpired term, the statewide nominating commission does not find the judge's performance is satisfactory, or the Governor does not reappoint the judge, the Governor shall appoint a successor judge for a term of 4 years in accordance with paragraph (b).

(d) The Governor may appoint any attorney who has at least 5 years of experience in the practice of law in this state to serve as a judge of compensation claims pro hac vice in the absence or disqualification of any full-time judge of compensation claims or to serve temporarily as an additional judge of compensation claims in any area of the state in which the Governor determines that a need exists for such an additional judge. However, an attorney who is so appointed by the Governor may not serve for a period of more than 120 successive days.

(e) The director of the Division of Administrative Hearings may receive or initiate complaints, conduct investigations, and dismiss complaints against the Deputy Chief Judge and the judges of compensation claims on the basis of the Code of Judicial Conduct. The director may recommend to the Governor the removal of the Deputy Chief Judge or a judge of compensation claims or recommend the discipline of a

Fla. Stats.

judge whose conduct during his or her term of office warrants such discipline. For purposes of this section, the term "discipline" includes reprimand, fine, and suspension with or without pay. At the conclusion of each investigation, the director shall submit preliminary findings of fact and recommendations to the judge of compensation claims who is the subject of the complaint. The judge of compensation claims has 20 days within which to respond to the preliminary findings. The response and the director's rebuttal to the response must be included in the final report submitted to the Governor.

(3) The Deputy Chief Judge shall establish training and continuing education for new and sitting judges.

(4) The Office of the Judges of Compensation Claims shall adopt rules to effect the purposes of this section. Such rules shall include procedural rules applicable to workers' compensation claim resolution and uniform criteria for measuring the performance of the office, including, but not limited to, the number of cases assigned and disposed, the age of pending and disposed cases, timeliness of decisionmaking, extraordinary fee awards, and other data necessary for the judicial nominating commission to review the performance of judges as required in paragraph (2)(c). The workers' compensation rules of procedure approved by the Supreme Court apply until the rules adopted by the Office of the Judges of Compensation Claims pursuant to this section become effective.

(5) Not later than December 1 of each year, the Office of the Judges of Compensation Claims shall issue a written report to the Governor, the House of Representatives, the Senate, The Florida Bar, and the statewide nominating commission summarizing the amount, cost, and outcome of all litigation resolved in the previous fiscal year; summarizing the disposition of mediation conferences, the number of mediation conferences held, the number of continuances granted for mediations and final hearings, the number and outcome of litigated cases, the amount of attorney's fees paid in each case according to order year and accident year, and the number of final orders not issued within 30 days after the final hearing or closure of the hearing record; and recommending changes or improvements to the dispute resolution elements of the Workers' Compensation Law and regulations. If the Deputy Chief Judge finds that judges generally are unable to meet a particular statutory requirement for reasons beyond their control, the Deputy Chief Judge shall submit such findings and any recommendations to the Legislature.

History: s. 45, ch. 17481, 1935; CGL 1936 Supp. 5966(43); s. 2, ch. 57-245; s. 1, ch. 61-133; s. 1, ch. 63-179; s. 1, ch. 63-275; s. 1, ch. 65-541; s. 1, ch. 67-515; s. 2, ch. 67-554; s. 1, ch. 69-201; ss. 17, 35, ch. 69-106; s. 1, ch. 70-313; s. 1, ch. 71-290; s. 20, ch. 74-197; s. 3, ch. 74-363; s. 22, ch. 75-209; ss. 14, 23, ch. 78-300; ss. 35, 124, ch. 79-40; ss. 19, 21, ch. 79-312; s. 17, ch. 80-236; s. 16, ch. 83-305; s. 8, ch. 84-267; s. 10, ch. 86-171; ss. 23, 43, ch. 89-289; ss. 39, 56, ch. 90-201; ss. 37, 52, ch. 91-1; s. 34, ch. 91-46; s. 40, ch. 93-415; s. 74, ch. 96-418; s. 11, ch. 98-174; s. 26, ch. 2001-91; s. 46, ch. 2002-194, effective July 1, 2002; s. 16, ch. 2002-236, effective July 1, 2002; s. 66, ch. 2004-5, effective June 29, 2004.

§ 440.47. Travel Expenses.

The Deputy Chief Judge, judges of compensation claims, and employees of the department shall be reimbursed for travel expenses as provided in s. 112.061. Such expenses shall be sworn to by the person who incurred the same and shall be allowed and paid as provided in s. 440.50 upon the presentation of vouchers therefor approved by the director of the Division of Administrative Hearings or the department, whichever is applicable.

History: s. 47, ch. 17481, 1935; CGL 1936 Supp. 5966(45); s. 19, ch. 63-400; ss. 17, 35, ch. 69-106; s. 23, ch. 75-209; s. 23, ch. 78-300; ss. 36, 124, ch. 79-40; s. 21, ch. 79-312; s. 18, ch. 80-236; s. 43, ch. 89-289; s. 56, ch. 90-201; s. 52, ch. 91-1; s. 14, ch. 91-46; s. 27, ch. 2001-91, effective Oct. 1, 2001.

§ 440.49. Limitation of Liability for Subsequent Injury Through Special Disability Trust Fund.

(1) Legislative Intent.—Whereas it is often difficult for workers with disabilities to achieve employment or to become reemployed following an injury, and it is the desire of the Legislature to facilitate the return of these workers to

the workplace, it is the purpose of this section to encourage the employment, reemployment, and accommodation of the physically disabled by reducing an employer's insurance premium for reemploying an injured worker, to decrease litigation between carriers on apportionment issues, and to protect employers from excess liability for compensation and medical expense when an injury to a physically disabled worker merges with, aggravates, or accelerates her or his preexisting permanent physical impairment to cause either a greater disability or permanent impairment, or an increase in expenditures for temporary compensation or medical benefits than would have resulted from the injury alone. The department or the administrator shall inform all employers of the existence and function of the fund and shall interpret eligibility requirements liberally. However, this subsection shall not be construed to create or provide any benefits for injured employees or their dependents not otherwise provided by this chapter. The entitlement of an injured employee or her or his dependents to compensation under this chapter shall be determined without regard to this subsection, the provisions of which shall be considered only in determining whether an employer or carrier who has paid compensation under this chapter is entitled to reimbursement from the Special Disability Trust Fund.

(2) Definitions.—As used in this section, the term:

(a) "Permanent physical impairment" means and is limited to the conditions listed in paragraph (6)(a).

(b) "Preferred worker" means a worker who, because of a permanent impairment resulting from a compensable injury or occupational disease, is unable to return to the worker's regular employment.

(c) "Merger" describes or means that:

1. If the permanent physical impairment had not existed, the subsequent accident or occupational disease would not have occurred;

2. The permanent disability or permanent impairment resulting from the subsequent accident or occupational disease is materially and substantially greater than that which would have resulted had the permanent physical impairment not existed, and the employer has been required to pay, and has paid, permanent total disability or permanent impairment benefits for that materially and substantially greater disability;

3. The preexisting permanent physical impairment is aggravated or accelerated as a result of the subsequent injury or occupational disease, or the preexisting impairment has contributed, medically and circumstantially, to the need for temporary compensation, medical, or attendant care and the employer has been required to pay, and has paid, temporary compensation, medical, or attendant care benefits for the aggravated preexisting permanent impairment; or

4. Death would not have been accelerated if the permanent physical impairment had not existed.

(d) "Excess permanent compensation" means that compensation for permanent impairment, or permanent total disability or death benefits, for which the employer or carrier is otherwise entitled to reimbursement from the Special Disability Trust Fund.

(e) "Administrator" means the entity selected by the department to review, allow, deny, compromise, controvert, and litigate claims of the Special Disability Trust Fund. In addition to the definitions contained in this subsection, the department may by rule prescribe definitions that are necessary for the effective administration of this section.

(3) Deductible.—Reimbursement may not be obtained for the first $10,000 of benefits paid which otherwise qualify for reimbursement under this section. This deductible does not apply to claims by employers for reimbursement under[1] subparagraph (b)3.

(4) Permanent Impairment or Permanent Total Disability. Temporary Benefits, Medical Benefits, or Attendant Care after Other Physical Impairment.—

(a) *Permanent impairment.* —If an employee who has a preexisting permanent physical impairment incurs a subsequent permanent impair-

Fla. Stats.

ment from injury or occupational disease arising out of, and in the course of, her or his employment which merges with the preexisting permanent physical impairment to cause a permanent impairment, the employer shall, in the first instance, pay all benefits provided by this chapter; but, subject to the limitations specified in subsection (6), such employer shall be reimbursed from the Special Disability Trust Fund created by subsection (9) for 50 percent of all impairment benefits which the employer has been required to provide pursuant to s. 440.15(3) as a result of the subsequent accident or occupational disease.

(b) *Permanent total disability.* —If an employee who has a preexisting permanent physical impairment incurs a subsequent permanent impairment from injury or occupational disease arising out of, and in the course of, her or his employment which merges with the preexisting permanent physical impairment to cause permanent total disability, the employer shall, in the first instance, pay all benefits provided by this chapter; but, subject to the limitations specified in subsection (6), such employer shall be reimbursed from the Special Disability Trust Fund created by subsection (9) for 50 percent of all compensation for permanent total disability.

(c) *Temporary compensation and medical benefits; aggravation or acceleration of preexisting condition or circumstantial causation.* —If an employee who has a preexisting permanent physical impairment experiences an aggravation or acceleration of the preexisting permanent physical impairment as a result of an injury or occupational disease arising out of and in the course of her or his employment, or suffers an injury as a result of a merger as defined in paragraph (2)(c), the employer shall provide all benefits provided by this chapter, but, subject to the limitations specified in subsection (7), the employer shall be reimbursed by the Special Disability Trust Fund created by subsection (9) for 50 percent of its payments for temporary, medical, and attendant care benefits.

(5) When Death Results.—If death results from the subsequent permanent impairment contemplated in subsection (4) within 1 year after the subsequent injury, or within 5 years after the subsequent injury when disability has been continuous since the subsequent injury, and it is determined that the death resulted from a merger, the employer shall, in the first instance, pay the funeral expenses and the death benefits prescribed by this chapter; but, subject to the limitations specified in subsection (6), she or he shall be reimbursed from the Special Disability Trust Fund created by subsection (9) for the last 50 percent of all compensation allowable and paid for such death and for 50 percent of the amount paid as funeral expenses.

(6) Employer Knowledge, Effect on Reimbursement.—

(a) Reimbursement is not allowed under this section unless it is established that the employer knew of the preexisting permanent physical impairment prior to the occurrence of the subsequent injury or occupational disease, and that the permanent physical impairment is one of the following:

1. Epilepsy.
2. Diabetes.
3. Cardiac disease.
4. Amputation of foot, leg, arm, or hand.
5. Total loss of sight of one or both eyes or a partial loss of corrected vision of more than 75 percent bilaterally.
6. Residual disability from poliomyelitis.
7. Cerebral palsy.
8. Multiple sclerosis.
9. Parkinson's disease.
10. Meniscectomy.
11. Patellectomy.
12. Ruptured cruciate ligament.
13. Hemophilia.
14. Chronic osteomyelitis.
15. Surgical or spontaneous fusion of a major weight-bearing joint.
16. Hyperinsulinism.

17. Muscular dystrophy.

18. Thrombophlebitis.

19. Herniated intervertebral disk.

20. Surgical removal of an intervertebral disk or spinal fusion.

21. One or more back injuries or a disease process of the back resulting in disability over a total of 120 or more days, if substantiated by a doctor's opinion that there was a preexisting impairment to the claimant's back.

22. Total deafness.

23. Mental retardation, provided the employee's intelligence quotient is such that she or he falls within the lowest 2 percentile of the general population. However, it shall not be necessary for the employer to know the employee's actual intelligence quotient or actual relative ranking in relation to the intelligence quotient of the general population.

24. Any permanent physical condition which, prior to the industrial accident or occupational disease, constitutes a 20-percent impairment of a member or of the body as a whole.

25. Obesity, provided the employee is 30 percent or more over the average weight designated for her or his height and age in the Table of Average Weight of Americans by Height and Age prepared by the Society of Actuaries using data from the 1979 Build and Blood Pressure Study.

26. Any permanent physical impairment as defined in s. 440.15(3) which is a result of a prior industrial accident with the same employer or the employer's parent company, subsidiary, sister company, or affiliate located within the geographical boundaries of this state.

(b) The Special Disability Trust Fund is not liable for any costs, interest, penalties, or attorneys' fees.

(c) An employer's or carrier's right to apportionment or deduction pursuant to ss. 440.02(1), 440.15(5)(b), and 440.151(1)(c) does not preclude reimbursement from such fund, except when the merger comes within the definition of paragraph (2)(c) and such apportionment or deduction relieves the employer or carrier from providing the materially and substantially greater permanent disability benefits otherwise contemplated in those paragraphs.

(7) Reimbursement of Employer.—

(a) The right to reimbursement as provided in this section is barred unless written notice of claim of the right to such reimbursement is filed by the employer or carrier entitled to such reimbursement with the department or administrator at Tallahassee within 2 years after the date the employee last reached maximum medical improvement, or within 2 years after the date of the first payment of compensation for permanent total disability, wage loss, or death, whichever is later. The notice of claim must contain such information as the department by rule requires or as established by the administrator; and the employer or carrier claiming reimbursement shall furnish such evidence in support of the claim as the department or administrator reasonably may require.

(b) For notice of claims on the Special Disability Trust Fund filed on or after July 1, 1978, the Special Disability Trust Fund shall, within 120 days after receipt of notice that a carrier has paid, been required to pay, or accepted liability for excess compensation, serve notice of the acceptance of the claim for reimbursement.

(c) A proof of claim must be filed on each notice of claim on file as of June 30, 1997, within 1 year after July 1, 1997, or the right to reimbursement of the claim shall be barred. A notice of claim on file on or before June 30, 1997, may be withdrawn and refiled if, at the time refiled, the notice of claim remains within the limitation period specified in paragraph (a). Such refiling shall not toll, extend, or otherwise alter in any way the limitation period applicable to the withdrawn and subsequently refiled notice of claim. Each proof of claim filed shall be accompanied by a proof-of-claim fee as provided in paragraph (9)(d). The Special Disability Trust Fund shall, within 120 days after receipt of the proof of claim, serve notice of the acceptance of the claim for reimbursement. This paragraph shall apply to all claims notwithstand-

Fla. Stats.

ing the provisions of subsection (12).

(d) Each notice of claim filed or refiled on or after July 1, 1997, must be accompanied by a notification fee as provided in paragraph (9)(d). A proof of claim must be filed within 1 year after the date the notice of claim is filed or refiled, accompanied by a proof-of-claim fee as provided in paragraph (9)(d), or the claim shall be barred. The notification fee shall be waived if both the notice of claim and proof of claim are submitted together as a single filing. The Special Disability Trust Fund shall, within 180 days after receipt of the proof of claim, serve notice of the acceptance of the claim for reimbursement. This paragraph shall apply to all claims notwithstanding the provisions of subsection (12).

(e) For dates of accident on or after January 1, 1994, the Special Disability Trust Fund shall, within 120 days of receipt of notice that a carrier has been required to pay, and has paid over $10,000 in benefits, serve notice of the acceptance of the claim for reimbursement. Failure of the Special Disability Trust Fund to serve notice of acceptance shall give rise to the right to request a hearing on the claim for reimbursement. If the Special Disability Trust Fund through its representative denies or controverts the claim, the right to such reimbursement shall be barred unless an application for a hearing thereon is filed with the department or administrator at Tallahassee within 60 days after notice to the employer or carrier of such denial or controversion. When such application for a hearing is timely filed, the claim shall be heard and determined in accordance with the procedure prescribed in s. 440.25, to the extent that such procedure is applicable, and in accordance with the workers' compensation rules of procedure. In such proceeding on a claim for reimbursement, the Special Disability Trust Fund shall be made the party respondent, and no findings of fact made with respect to the claim of the injured employee or the dependents for compensation, including any finding made or order entered pursuant to s. 440.20(11), shall be res judicata. The Special Disability Trust Fund may not be joined or made a party to any controversy or dispute between an employee and the dependents and the employer or between two or more employers or carriers without the written consent of the fund.

(f) When it has been determined that an employer or carrier is entitled to reimbursement in any amount, the employer or carrier shall be reimbursed annually from the Special Disability Trust Fund for the compensation and medical benefits paid by the employer or carrier for which the employer or carrier is entitled to reimbursement, upon filing request therefor and submitting evidence of such payment in accordance with rules prescribed by the department, which rules may include parameters for annual audits. The Special Disability Trust Fund shall pay the approved reimbursement requests on a first-in, first-out basis reflecting the order in which the reimbursement requests were received.

(g) The department may by rule require specific forms and procedures for the administration and processing of claims made through the Special Disability Trust Fund.

(8) Preferred Worker Program.—The Department of Education or administrator shall issue identity cards to preferred workers upon request by qualified employees and the Department of Financial Services shall reimburse an employer, from the Special Disability Trust Fund, for the cost of workers' compensation premium related to the preferred workers payroll for up to 3 years of continuous employment upon satisfactory evidence of placement and issuance of payroll and classification records and upon the employee's certification of employment. The Department of Financial Services and the Department of Education may by rule prescribe definitions, forms, and procedures for the administration of the preferred worker program. The Department of Education may by rule prescribe the schedule for submission of forms for participation in the program.

(9) Special Disability Trust Fund.—

(a) There is established in the State Treasury a special fund to be known as the "Special Disability Trust Fund," which shall be available only for the purposes stated in this section; and the assets thereof may not at any time be appropriated or diverted to any other use or purpose. The Chief Financial Officer shall be the custodian of such fund, and all moneys and securities in such fund shall be held in trust by such Chief Financial Officer and shall not be the money or property of the state. The Chief Financial Officer is authorized to disburse moneys from such fund only when approved by the department or corporation. The Chief Financial Officer shall deposit any moneys paid into such fund into such depository banks as the department may designate and is authorized to invest any portion of the fund which, in the opinion of the department, is not needed for current requirements, in the same manner and subject to all the provisions of the law with respect to the deposits of state funds by such Chief Financial Officer. All interest earned by such portion of the fund as may be invested by the Chief Financial Officer shall be collected by her or him and placed to the credit of such fund.

(b)

1. The Special Disability Trust Fund shall be maintained by annual assessments upon the insurance companies writing compensation insurance in the state, the commercial self-insurers under ss. 624.462 and 624.4621, the assessable mutuals as defined in s. 628.6011, and the self-insurers under this chapter, which assessments shall become due and be paid quarterly at the same time and in addition to the assessments provided in s. 440.51. The department shall estimate annually in advance the amount necessary for the administration of this subsection and the maintenance of this fund and shall make such assessment in the manner hereinafter provided.

2. The annual assessment shall be calculated to produce during the ensuing fiscal year an amount which, when combined with that part of the balance in the fund on June 30 of the current fiscal year which is in excess of $100,000, is equal to the average of:

a. The sum of disbursements from the fund during the immediate past 3 calendar years, and

b. Two times the disbursements of the most recent calendar year. Such amount shall be prorated among the insurance companies writing compensation insurance in the state and the self-insurers. Provided however, for those carriers that have excluded ceded reinsurance premiums from their assessments on or before January 1, 2000, no assessments on ceded reinsurance premiums shall be paid by those carriers until such time as the former Division of Workers' Compensation of the[2] Department of Labor and Employment Security or the department advises each of those carriers of the impact that the inclusion of ceded reinsurance premiums has on their assessment. The department may not recover any past underpayments of assessments levied against any carrier that on or before January 1, 2000, excluded ceded reinsurance premiums from their assessment prior to the point that the former Division of Workers' Compensation of the Department of Labor and Employment Security or the department advises of the appropriate assessment that should have been paid.

3. The net premiums written by the companies for workers' compensation in this state and the net premium written applicable to the self-insurers in this state are the basis for computing the amount to be assessed as a percentage of net premiums. Such payments shall be made by each carrier and self-insurer to the department for the Special Disability Trust Fund in accordance with such regulations as the department prescribes.

4. The Chief Financial Officer is authorized to receive and credit to such Special Disability Trust Fund any sum or sums that may at any time be contributed to the state by the United States under any Act of Congress, or otherwise, to which the state may be or become entitled by reason of any payments made out of such fund.

(c) Notwithstanding the Special Disability Trust Fund assessment rate calculated pursuant to this section, the rate assessed shall not exceed 4.52 percent.

(d) The Special Disability Trust Fund shall be supplemented by a $250 notification fee on each notice of claim filed or refiled after July 1, 1997, and a $500 fee on each proof of claim filed in

Fla. Stats.

accordance with subsection (7). Revenues from the fee shall be deposited into the Special Disability Trust Fund and are exempt from the deduction required by s. 215.20. The fees provided in this paragraph shall not be imposed upon any insurer which is in receivership with the department.

(e) The department or administrator shall report annually on the status of the Special Disability Trust Fund. The report shall update the estimated undiscounted and discounted fund liability, as determined by an independent actuary, change in the total number of notices of claim on file with the fund in addition to the number of newly filed notices of claim, change in the number of proofs of claim processed by the fund, the fee revenues refunded and revenues applied to pay down the liability of the fund, the average time required to reimburse accepted claims, and the average administrative costs per claim. The department or administrator shall submit its report to the Governor, the President of the Senate, and the Speaker of the House of Representatives by December 1 of each year.

(10) Department Administration of Fund; Claims; Expenses.—The department or administrator shall administer the Special Disability Trust Fund with authority to allow, deny, compromise, controvert, and litigate claims made against it and to designate an attorney to represent it in proceedings involving claims against the fund, including negotiation and consummation of settlements, hearings before judges of compensation claims, and judicial review. The department or administrator or the attorney designated by it shall be given notice of all hearings and proceedings involving the rights or obligations of such fund and shall have authority to make expenditures for such medical examinations, expert witness fees, depositions, transcripts of testimony, and the like as may be necessary to the proper defense of any claim. All expenditures made in connection with conservation of the fund, including the salary of the attorney designated to represent it and necessary travel expenses, shall be allowed and paid from the Special Disability Trust Fund as provided in this section upon the presentation of itemized vouchers therefor approved by the department.

(11) Effective Dates.—This section does not apply to any case in which the accident causing the subsequent injury or death or the disablement or death from a subsequent occupational disease occurred prior to July 1, 1955, or on or after January 1, 1998. In no event shall the Special Disability Trust Fund be liable for, or reimburse employers or carriers for, any case in which the accident causing the subsequent injury or death or the disablement or death from a subsequent occupational disease occurred on or after January 1, 1998. The Special Disability Trust Fund shall continue to reimburse employers or carriers for subsequent injuries occurring prior to January 1, 1998, and the department shall continue to assess for and the department or administrator shall fund reimbursements as provided in subsection (9) for this purpose.

(12) Reimbursement From the Special Disability Trust Fund.—The applicable law for the purposes of determining entitlement to reimbursement from the Special Disability Trust Fund is the law in effect on the date the accident occurred.

History: s. 49, ch. 17481, 1935; CGL 1936 Supp. 5966(47); s. 13, ch. 28241, 1953; s. 12, ch. 29778, 1955; s. 1, ch. 59-101; s. 2, ch. 63-235; s. 19, ch. 63-400; s. 2, ch. 67-554; ss. 17, 35, ch. 69-106; s. 21, ch. 74-197; s. 24, ch. 75-209; ss. 151, 152, ch. 77-104; ss. 15, 23, ch. 78-300; ss. 37, 124, ch. 79-40; s. 21, ch. 79-312; s. 11, ch. 81-119; s. 17, ch. 83-305; s. 10, ch. 85-61; s. 9, ch. 87-330; ss. 24, 43, ch. 89-289; ss. 40, 56, ch. 90-201; ss. 38, 52, ch. 91-1; s. 43, ch. 93-415; s. 4, ch. 95-285; s. 21, ch. 95-327; s. 12, ch. 96-423; s. 1054, ch. 97-103; s. 1, ch. 97-262; s. 9, ch. 98-125; s. 84, ch. 98-199; s. 2, ch. 2000-150; s. 98, ch. 2000-153; s. 30, ch. 2001-89, effective Jan. 1, 2002; s. 141, ch. 2001-266, effective July 1, 2001; s. 47, ch. 2002-194, effective July 1, 2002; s. 30, ch. 2003-412, effective Oct. 1, 2003; s. 489, ch. 2003-261, effective June 26, 2003.

[1]**2003 Note:** Subsection (3) is not divided into subunits.

[2]**2003 Note:** The Department of Labor and Employment Security no longer exists; all divisions, responsibilities, and functions were reassigned effective July 1, 2002, by s. 1, ch. 2002-194.

[3]**Note:** —Transferred to s. 628.905 by s. 3, ch. 87-127. Section 628.905 is concerned with captive

insurers; assessable mutual insurers are covered by part II of ch. 628.

§ 440.491. Reemployment of Injured Workers; Rehabilitation.

(1) Definitions.—As used in this section, the term:

(a) "Carrier" means group self-insurance funds or individual self-insureds authorized under this chapter and commercial funds or insurance entities authorized to write workers' compensation insurance under chapter 624.

(b) "Department" means the Department of Education.

(c) "Medical care coordination" includes, but is not limited to, coordinating physical rehabilitation services such as medical, psychiatric, or therapeutic treatment for the injured employee, providing health training to the employee and family, and monitoring the employee's recovery. The purposes of medical care coordination are to minimize the disability and recovery period without jeopardizing medical stability, to assure that proper medical treatment and other restorative services are timely provided in a logical sequence, and to contain medical costs.

(d) "Qualified rehabilitation provider" means a rehabilitation nurse, rehabilitation counselor, vocational evaluator, rehabilitation facility, or agency approved by the Department of Education as qualified to provide reemployment assessments, medical care coordination, reemployment services, or vocational evaluations under this chapter.

(e) "Reemployment assessment" means a written assessment performed by a qualified rehabilitation provider which provides a comprehensive review of the medical diagnosis, treatment, and prognosis; includes conferences with the employer, physician, and claimant; and recommends a cost-effective physical and vocational rehabilitation plan to assist the employee in returning to suitable gainful employment.

(f) "Reemployment services" means services that include, but are not limited to, vocational counseling, job-seeking skills training, ergonomic job analysis, transferable skills analysis, selective job placement, labor market surveys, and arranging other services such as education or training, vocational and on-the-job, which may be needed by the employee to secure suitable gainful employment.

(g) "Reemployment status review" means a review to determine whether an injured employee is at risk of not returning to work.

(h) "Suitable gainful employment" means employment or self-employment that is reasonably attainable in light of the employee's age, education, work history, transferable skills, previous occupation, and injury, and which offers an opportunity to restore the individual as soon as practicable and as nearly as possible to his or her average weekly earnings at the time of injury.

(i) "Vocational evaluation" means a review of the employee's physical and intellectual capabilities, his or her aptitudes and achievements, and his or her work-related behaviors to identify the most cost-effective means toward the employee's return to suitable gainful employment.

(2) Intent.—It is the intent of this section to implement a systematic review by carriers of the factors that are predictive of longer-term disability and to encourage the provision of medical care coordination and reemployment services that are necessary to assist the employee in returning to work as soon as is medically feasible.

(3) Reemployment Status Reviews and Reports.—

(a) When an employee who has suffered an injury compensable under this chapter is unemployed 60 days after the date of injury and is receiving benefits for temporary total disability, temporary partial disability, or wage loss, and has not yet been provided medical care coordination and reemployment services voluntarily by the carrier, the carrier must determine whether the employee is likely to return to work and must report its determination to the department. The carrier must thereafter determine the reemployment status of the employee at 90-day intervals as long as the employee remains un-

Fla. Stats.

employed, is not receiving medical care coordination or reemployment services, and is receiving the benefits specified in this subsection.

(b) If medical care coordination or reemployment services are voluntarily undertaken within 60 days of the date of injury, such services may continue to be provided as agreed by the employee and the carrier.

(4) Reemployment Assessments.—

(a) The carrier may require the employee to receive a reemployment assessment as it considers appropriate. However, the carrier is encouraged to obtain a reemployment assessment if:

1. The carrier determines that the employee is at risk of remaining unemployed.

2. The case involves catastrophic or serious injury.

(b) The carrier shall authorize only a qualified rehabilitation provider to provide the reemployment assessment. The rehabilitation provider shall conduct its assessment and issue a report to the carrier, the employee, and the department within 30 days after the time such assessment is complete.

(c) If the rehabilitation provider recommends that the employee receive medical care coordination or reemployment services, the carrier shall advise the employee of the recommendation and determine whether the employee wishes to receive such services. The employee shall have 15 days after the date of receipt of the recommendation in which to agree to accept such services. If the employee elects to receive services, the carrier may refer the employee to a rehabilitation provider for such coordination or services within 15 days of receipt of the assessment report or notice of the employee's election, whichever is later.

(5) Medical Care Coordination and Reemployment Services.—

(a) Once the carrier has assigned a case to a qualified rehabilitation provider for medical care coordination or reemployment services, the provider shall develop a reemployment plan and submit the plan to the carrier and the employee for approval.

(b) If the rehabilitation provider concludes that training and education are necessary to return the employee to suitable gainful employment, or if the employee has not returned to suitable gainful employment within 180 days after referral for reemployment services or receives $2,500 in reemployment services, whichever comes first, the carrier must discontinue reemployment services and refer the employee to the department for a vocational evaluation. Notwithstanding any provision of chapter 289 or chapter 627, the cost of a reemployment assessment and the first $2,500 in reemployment services to an injured employee must not be treated as loss adjustment expense for workers' compensation ratemaking purposes.

(c) A carrier may voluntarily provide medical care coordination or reemployment services to the employee at intervals more frequent than those required in this section. For the purpose of monitoring reemployment, the carrier or the rehabilitation provider shall report to the department, in the manner prescribed by the department, the date of reemployment and wages of the employee. The carrier shall report its voluntary service activity to the department as required by rule. Voluntary services offered by the carrier for any of the following injuries must be considered benefits for purposes of ratemaking: traumatic brain injury; spinal cord injury; amputation, including loss of an eye or eyes; burns of 5 percent or greater of the total body surface.

(d) If medical care coordination or reemployment services have not been undertaken as prescribed in paragraph (3)(b), a qualified rehabilitation service provider, facility, or agency that performs a reemployment assessment shall not provide medical care coordination or reemployment services for the employees it assesses.

(6) Training and Education.—

(a) Upon referral of an injured employee by the carrier, or upon the request of an injured employee, the department shall conduct a training and education screening to determine whether it should refer the employee for a vocational evaluation and, if appropriate, approve training and education or other vocational services for the employee. The department may not approve formal training and education programs unless it determines, after consideration of the reemployment assessment, pertinent reemployment status reviews or reports, and such other relevant factors as it prescribes by rule, that the reemployment plan is likely to result in return to suitable gainful employment. The department is authorized to expend moneys from the Workers' Compensation Administration Trust Fund, established by s. 440.50, to secure appropriate training and education at a community college as designated in s. 1000.21(3) or at a career center established under s. 1001.44, or to secure other vocational services when necessary to satisfy the recommendation of a vocational evaluator. As used in this paragraph, "appropriate training and education" includes securing a general education diploma (GED), if necessary. The department shall establish training and education standards pertaining to employee eligibility, course curricula and duration, and associated costs.

(b) When an employee who has attained maximum medical improvement is unable to earn at least 80 percent of the compensation rate and requires training and education to obtain suitable gainful employment, the employer or carrier shall pay the employee additional training and education temporary total compensation benefits while the employee receives such training and education for a period not to exceed 26 weeks, which period may be extended for an additional 26 weeks or less, if such extended period is determined to be necessary and proper by a judge of compensation claims. The benefits provided under this paragraph shall not be in addition to the 104 weeks as specified in s. 440.15(2). However, a carrier or employer is not precluded from voluntarily paying additional temporary total disability compensation beyond that period. If an employee requires temporary residence at or near a facility or an institution providing training and education which is located more than 50 miles away from the employee's customary residence, the reasonable cost of board, lodging, or travel must be borne by the department from the Workers' Compensation Administration Trust Fund established by s. 440.50. An employee who refuses to accept training and education that is recommended by the vocational evaluator and considered necessary by the department will forfeit any additional training and education benefits and any additional payment for lost wages under this chapter. The department shall adopt rules to implement this section, which shall include requirements placed upon the carrier to notify the injured employee of the availability of training and education benefits as specified in this chapter. The department shall also include information regarding the eligibility for training and education benefits in informational materials specified in ss. 440.207 and 440.40.

(7) Provider Qualifications.—

(a) The department shall investigate and maintain a directory of each qualified public and private rehabilitation provider, facility, and agency, and shall establish by rule the minimum qualifications, credentials, and requirements that each rehabilitation service provider, facility, and agency must satisfy to be eligible for listing in the directory. These minimum qualifications and credentials must be based on those generally accepted within the service specialty for which the provider, facility, or agency is approved.

(b) The department shall impose a biennial application fee of $25 for each listing in the directory, and all such fees must be deposited in the Workers' Compensation Administration Trust Fund.

(c) The department shall monitor and evaluate each rehabilitation service provider, facility, and agency qualified under this subsection to ensure its compliance with the minimum qualifications and credentials established by the department. The failure of a qualified rehabilitation service provider, facility, or agency to provide the department with information requested or access necessary for the department to satisfy its responsibilities under this subsection is grounds for disqualifying the provider, facility, or agency from further referrals.

(d) A qualified rehabilitation service provider, facility, or agency may not be authorized by an employer, a carrier, or the department to provide

Fla. Stats.

any services, including expert testimony, under this section in this state unless the provider, facility, or agency is listed or has been approved for listing in the directory. This restriction does not apply to services provided outside this state under this section.

(e) The department, after consultation with representatives of employees, employers, carriers, rehabilitation providers, and qualified training and education providers, shall adopt rules governing professional practices and standards.

(8) Carrier Practices.—The department shall monitor the selection of providers and the provision of services by carriers under this section for consistency with legislative intent set forth in subsection (2).

(9) Permanent Disability.—The judge of compensation claims may not adjudicate an injured employee as permanently and totally disabled until or unless the carrier is given the opportunity to provide a reemployment assessment.

History: s. 44, ch. 93-415; s. 75, ch. 96-418; s. 1055, ch. 97-103; s. 48, ch. 2002-194, effective July 1, 2002; s. 31, ch. 412, effective Oct. 1, 2003; s. 67, ch. 2004-5, effective June 29, 2004; s. 75, ch. 2005-2, effective July 5, 2005.

[1]**2004 Note:** —Section 69, ch. 2004-194, repealed s. 20.171, which created the Department of Labor and Employment Security.

§ 440.50. Workers' Compensation Administration Trust Fund.

(1)

(a) [1] There is established in the State Treasury a special fund to be known as the "Workers' Compensation Administration Trust Fund" for the purpose of providing for the payment of all expenses in respect to the administration of this chapter, including the vocational rehabilitation of injured employees as provided in s. 440.49 and the payments due under s. 440.15(1)(f), the funding of the fixed administrative expenses of the plan, and the funding of the Bureau of Workers' Compensation Fraud within the Department of Financial Services. Such fund shall be administered by the department.

(b) The department is authorized to transfer as a loan an amount not in excess of $250,000 from such special fund to the Special Disability Trust Fund established by s. 440.49(9), which amount shall be repaid to said special fund in annual payments equal to not less than 10 percent of moneys received for such Special Disability Trust Fund.

(2) The Chief Financial Officer is authorized to disburse moneys from such fund only when approved by the department.

(3) The Chief Financial Officer shall deposit any moneys paid into such fund into such depository banks as the department may designate and is authorized to invest any portion of the fund which, in the opinion of the department, is not needed for current requirements, in the same manner and subject to all the provisions of the law with respect to the deposit of state funds by such The Chief Financial Officer. All interest earned by such portion of the fund as may be invested by the The Chief Financial Officer shall be collected by him or her and placed to the credit of such fund.

(4) All civil penalties provided in this chapter, if not voluntarily paid, may be collected by civil suit brought by the department and shall be paid into such fund.

History: s. 50, ch. 17481, 1935; CGL 1936 Supp. 5966(48); s. 13, ch. 29778, 1955; s. 2, ch. 61-119; ss. 17, 35, ch. 69-106; s. 22, ch. 74-197; s. 23, ch. 78-300; ss. 38, 124, ch. 79-40; s. 21, ch. 79-312; s. 11, ch. 85-61; s. 43, ch. 89-289; s. 56, ch. 90-201; s. 52, ch. 91-1; s. 45, ch. 93-415; s. 72, ch. 96-418; s. 1056, ch. 97-103; s. 36, ch. 98-34; s. 6, ch. 2000-150; s. 49, ch. 2002-194, effective July 1, 2002; s. 490, ch. 2003-261, effective June 26, 2003.

[1]**2005 Note:** Section 2, ch. 2005-58, provides that "[i]n addition to the purpose of the Workers' Compensation Administration Trust Fund specified in section 440.50(1)(a), Florida Statutes, moneys in the Workers' Compensation Administration Trust Fund in the Department of Financial Services may also be appropriated to fund the enforcement of farm labor laws by the Department of Business and Professional Regulation."

§ 440.501. Workers' Compensation Administration Trust Fund within the Department of Business and Professional Regulation.

History: s. 1, ch. 2002-399, effective July 1, 2002. Repealed July 1, 2004.

§ 440.51. Expenses of Administration.

(1) The department shall estimate annually in advance the amounts necessary for the administration of this chapter, in the following manner.

(a) The department shall, by July 1 of each year, notify carriers and self-insurers of the assessment rate, which shall be based on the anticipated expenses of the administration of this chapter for the next calendar year. Such assessment rate shall take effect January 1 of the next calendar year and shall be included in workers' compensation rate filings approved by the office which become effective on or after January 1 of the next calendar year. Assessments shall become due and be paid quarterly.

(b) The total expenses of administration shall be prorated among the carriers writing compensation insurance in the state and self-insurers. The net premiums collected by carriers and the amount of premiums calculated by the department for self-insured employers are the basis for computing the amount to be assessed. When reporting deductible policy premium for purposes of computing assessments levied after July 1, 2001, full policy premium value must be reported prior to application of deductible discounts or credits. This amount may be assessed as a specific amount or as a percentage of net premiums payable as the department may direct, provided such amount so assessed shall not exceed 2.75 percent, beginning January 1, 2001, except during the interim period from July 1, 2000, through December 31, 2000, such assessments shall not exceed 4 percent of such net premiums. The carriers may elect to make the payments required under s. 440.15(1)(f) rather than having these payments made by the department. In that event, such payments will be credited to the carriers, and the amount due by the carrier under this section will be reduced accordingly.

(2) The department shall provide by regulation for the collection of the amounts assessed against each carrier. Such amounts shall be paid within 30 days from the date that notice is served upon such carrier. If such amounts are not paid within such period, there may be assessed for each 30 days the amount so assessed remains unpaid, a civil penalty equal to 10 percent of the amount so unpaid, which shall be collected at the same time and a part of the amount assessed. For those carriers who excluded ceded reinsurance premiums from their assessments prior to January 1, 2000, the department shall not recover any past underpayments of assessments related to ceded reinsurance premiums prior to January 1, 2001, against such carriers.

(3) If any carrier fails to pay the amounts assessed against him or her under the provisions of this section within 60 days from the time such notice is served upon him or her, the office, upon being notified by the department, may suspend or revoke the authorization to insure compensation in accordance with the procedure in s. 440.38(3)(a). The department may permit a carrier to remit any underpayment of assessments for assessments levied after January 1, 2001.

(4) All amounts collected under the provisions of this section shall be paid into the fund established in s. 440.50.

(5) Any amount so assessed against and paid by an insurance carrier, self-insurer authorized pursuant to s. 624.4621, or commercial self-insurance fund authorized under ss. 624.460-624.488 shall be allowed as a deduction against the amount of any other tax levied by the state upon the premiums, assessments, or deposits for workers' compensation insurance on contracts or policies of said insurance carrier, self-insurer, or commercial self-insurance fund. Any insurance carrier claiming such a deduction against the amount of any such tax shall not be required to pay any additional retaliatory tax levied pursuant to s. 624.5091 as a result of claiming such deduction. Because deductions under this subsection are available to insurance carriers, s. 624.5091 does not limit such deductions in any manner.

(6) The department may require from each carrier, at such time and in accordance with such

Fla. Stats.

regulations as the department may prescribe, reports in respect to all gross earned premiums and of all payments of compensation made by such carrier during each prior period, and may determine the amounts paid by each carrier and the amounts paid by all carriers during such period.

(7) The department shall keep accumulated cost records of all injuries occurring within the state coming within the purview of this chapter on a policy and calendar-year basis. For the purpose of this chapter, a "calendar year" is defined as the year in which the injury is reported to the department; "policy year" is defined as that calendar year in which the policy becomes effective, and the losses under such policy shall be chargeable against the policy year so defined.

(8) The department shall assign an account number to each employer under this chapter and an account number to each insurance carrier authorized to write workers' compensation insurance in the state; and it shall be the duty of the department under the account number so assigned to keep the cost experience of each carrier and the cost experience of each employer under the account number so assigned by calendar and policy year, as above defined.

(9) In addition to the above, it shall be the duty of the department to keep the accident experience, as classified by the department, by industry as follows:

(a) Cause of the injury;

(b) Nature of the injury; and

(c) Type of disability.

(10) In every case where the duration of disability exceeds 30 days, the carrier shall establish a sufficient reserve to pay all benefits to which the injured employee, or in case of death, his or her dependents, may be entitled to under the law. In establishing the reserve, consideration shall be given to the nature of the injury, the probable period of disability, and the estimated cost of medical benefits.

(11) The department shall furnish to any employer or carrier, upon request, its individual experience.

(12) In addition to any other penalties provided by this law, the failure to submit any report or other information required by this law shall be just cause to suspend the right of a self-insurer to operate as such or shall be just cause for the department to suspend or revoke the license of such carrier.

(13) As used in s. 440.50 and this section, the term:

(a) "Plan" means the workers' compensation joint underwriting plan provided for in s. 627.311(5).

(b) "Fixed administrative expenses" means the expenses of the plan, not to exceed $750,000, which are directly related to the plan's administration but which do not vary in direct relationship to the amount of premium written by the plan and which do not include loss adjustment premiums.

(14) Before July 1 in each year, the plan shall notify the department of the amount of the plan's gross written premiums for the preceding calendar year. Whenever the plan's gross written premiums reported to the department are less than $30 million, the department shall transfer to the plan, subject to appropriation by the Legislature, an amount not to exceed the plan's fixed administrative expenses for the preceding calendar year.

History: s. 51, ch. 17481, 1935; CGL 1936 Supp. 5966(49); s. 17, ch. 18413, 1937; s. 1, ch. 24081, 1947; s. 14, ch. 28241, 1953; ss. 14, 15, ch. 29778, 1955; ss. 13, 17, 35, ch. 69-106; s. 23, ch. 74-197; s. 25, ch. 75-209; s. 23, ch. 78-300; ss. 39, 124, ch. 79-40; s. 21, ch. 79-312; s. 19, ch. 80-236; s. 281, ch. 81-259; s. 16, ch. 88-206; s. 43, ch. 89-289; s. 56, ch. 90-201; s. 52, ch. 91-1; s. 46, ch. 93-415; s. 128, ch. 97-103; ss. 3, 7, ch. 2000-150; s. 99, ch. 2000-153; s. 50, ch. 2002-194, effective July 1, 2002; s. 5, ch. 2002-262, effective Oct. 1, 2002; s. 2, ch. 2003-108, effective Oct. 1, 2003; s. 491, ch. 2003-261, effective June 26, 2003.

§ 440.515. Reports From Self-Insurers; Confidentiality.

The department shall maintain the reports filed in accordance with former s. 440.51(6)(b) as confidential and exempt from the provisions of s. 119.07(1), and such reports shall be released only for bona fide research or educational purposes or after receipt of consent from the employer.

History: s. 5, ch. 84-267; s. 43, ch. 89-289; s. 56, ch. 90-201; s. 52, ch. 91-1; s. 6, ch. 91-269; s. 47, ch. 93-415; s. 288, ch. 96-406; s. 492, 2003-261, effective June 26, 2003; s. 68, ch. 2004-5, effective June 29, 2004.

§ 440.52. Registration of Insurance Carriers; Notice of Cancellation or Expiration of Policy; Suspension or Revocation of Authority.

(1) Each insurance carrier who desires to write such compensation insurance in compliance with this chapter shall be required, before writing such insurance, to register with the department and pay a registration fee of $100. This shall be deposited by the department in the fund created by s. 440.50.

(2) A carrier or self-insurance fund that receives notice pursuant to s. 440.05 shall notify the contractor of the cancellation or expiration of the insurance.

(3) If the department finds, after due notice and a hearing at which the insurance carrier is entitled to be heard in person or by counsel and present evidence, that the insurance carrier has repeatedly failed to comply with its obligations under this chapter, the department may request the office to suspend or revoke the authorization of such insurance carrier to write workers' compensation insurance under this chapter. Such suspension or revocation shall not affect the liability of any such insurance carrier under policies in force prior to the suspension or revocation.

(4) In addition to the penalties prescribed in subsection (3), violation of s. 440.381 by an insurance carrier shall result in the imposition of a fine not to exceed $1,000 per audit, if the insurance carrier fails to act on said audits by correcting errors in employee classification or accepted applications for coverage where it knew employee classifications were incorrect. Such fines shall be levied by the office and deposited into the Insurance Regulatory Trust Fund.

History: s. 52, ch. 17481, 1935; CGL 1936 Supp. 5966(50); ss. 17, 35, ch. 69-106; s. 1, ch. 70-30; s. 1, ch. 70-439; s. 23, ch. 78-300; ss. 40, 124, ch. 79-40; s. 21, ch. 79-312; s. 43, ch. 89-289; ss 41, 56, ch. 90-201; ss. 39, 52, ch. 91-1; s. 5, ch. 91-2; s. 51, ch. 2002-194, effective July 1, 2002; s. 493, ch. 2003-261, effective June 26, 2003.

§ 440.525. Examination and Investigation of Carriers and Claims-Handling Entities.

(1) The department may examine, or investigate any carrier, third-party administrator, servicing agent, or other claims-handling entity as often as is warranted to ensure that it is fulfilling its obligations under this chapter.

(2) An examination may cover any period of the carrier's, third-party administrator's, servicing agent's, or other claims-handling entity's operations since the last previous examination. An investigation based upon a reasonable belief by the department that a material violation of this chapter has occurred may cover any time period, but may not predate the last examination by more than 5 years. The department may by rule establish procedures, standards, and protocols for examinations and investigations. If the department finds any violation of this chapter, it may impose administrative penalties pursuant to this chapter. If the department finds any self-insurer in violation of this chapter, it may take action pursuant s. 440.38(3). Examinations or investigations by the department may address, but are not limited to addressing, patterns or practices of unreasonable delay in claims handling; timeliness and accuracy of payments and reports under ss. 440.13, 440.16, and 440.185; or patterns or practices of harassment, coercion, or intimidation of claimants. The department may also specify by rule the documentation to be maintained for each claim file.

(3) As to any examination or investigation conducted under this chapter, the department shall have the power to conduct onsite inspections of claims records and documentation of a carrier, third-party administrator, servicing agent, or other claims-handling entity, and conduct interviews, both sworn and unsworn, of

Fla. Stats.

claims-handling personnel. Carriers, third-party administrators, servicing agents, and other claims-handling entities shall make all claims records, documentation, communication, and correspondence available to department personnel during regular business hours. If any person fails to comply with a request for production of records or documents or fails to produce an employee for interview, the department may compel production or attendance by subpoena. The results of an examination or investigation shall be provided to the carrier, third-party administrator, servicing agent, or other claims-handling entity in a written report setting forth the basis for any violations that are asserted. Such report is agency action for purposes of chapter 120, and the aggrieved party may request a proceeding under s. 120.57 with regard to the findings and conclusion of the report.

(4) If the department finds that violations of this chapter have occurred, the department may impose an administrative penalty upon the offending entity or entities. For each offending entity, such penalties shall not exceed $2,500 for each pattern or practice constituting nonwillful violation and shall not exceed an aggregate amount of $10,000 for all nonwillful violations arising out of the same action. If the department finds a pattern of practice that constitutes a willful violation, the department may impose an administrative penalty upon each offending entity not to exceed $20,000 for each willful pattern or practice. Such fines shall not exceed $100,000 for all willful violations arising out of the same action. No penalty assessed under this section may be recouped by any carrier in the rate base, the premium, or any rate filing. Any administrative penalty imposed under this section for a nonwillful violation shall not duplicate an administrative penalty imposed under another provision of this chapter or the Insurance Code. The department may adopt rules to implement this section. The department shall adopt penalty guidelines by rule to set penalties under this chapter.

History: s. 51, ch. 93-415; s. 52, ch. 2002-194, effective July 1, 2002; s. 32, SB 50A, effective Oct. 1, 2003; s. 494, ch. 2003-261, effective June 26, 2003.

§ 440.53. Effect of Unconstitutionality.

If any part of this chapter is adjudged unconstitutional by the courts, and such adjudication has the effect of invalidating any payment of compensation under this chapter, the period intervening between the time the injury was sustained and the time of such adjudication shall not be computed as a part of the time prescribed by law for the commencement of any action against the employer in respect of such injury; but the amount of any compensation paid under this chapter on account of such injury shall be deducted from the amount of damages awarded in such action in respect of such injury.

History: s. 53, ch. 17481, 1935; CGL 1936 Supp. 5966(51); s. 23, ch. 78-300; s. 124, ch. 79-40; s. 21, ch. 79-312; s. 43, ch. 89-289; s. 56, ch. 90-201; s. 52, ch. 91-1.

§ 440.54. Violation of Child Labor Law.

If the judge of compensation claims determines that an injured employee at the time of an accident is a minor employed, permitted, or suffered to work in violation of any of the provisions of the child labor laws of Florida, the employer shall, in addition to the normal compensation and death benefits provided by this chapter, pay such additional compensation as the judge of compensation claims may determine according to the circumstances of the case or the seriousness of the violation; however, the total compensation so payable shall not exceed double the amount otherwise payable under this chapter. The employer alone, and not the insurance carrier, shall be liable for the increased compensation or increased death benefits provided for by this section. Any provision in an insurance policy undertaking to protect an employer from such increased liability shall be void.

History: s. 18, ch. 18413, 1937; CGL 1940 Supp. 5966(54); s. 15, ch. 28241, 1953; ss. 17, 35, ch. 69-106; s. 26, ch. 75-209; s. 23, ch. 78-300; ss. 41, 124, ch. 79-40; s. 21, ch. 79-312; s. 43, ch. 89-289; s. 56, ch. 90-201; s. 52, ch. 91-1; s. 15, ch. 91-46.

§ 440.55. Proceedings Against State.

Any person entitled to compensation benefits by reason of the injury or death of an employee of the state, its boards, bureaus, departments, agencies, or subdivisions employing labor, may maintain proceedings and actions at law against the state, its boards, bureaus, departments, agencies, and subdivisions, for such benefit, said proceedings and action at law to be in the same manner as provided herein with respect to other employers.

History: s. 19, ch. 18413, 1937; CGL 1940 Supp. 5966(55); s. 23, ch. 78-300; s. 124, ch. 79-40; s. 21, ch. 79-312; s. 43, ch. 89-289; s. 56, ch. 90-201; s. 52, ch. 91-1.

§ 440.572. Authorization for Individual Self-Insurer to Provide Coverage.

An individual self-insurer having a net worth of not less than $250 million as authorized by s. 440.38(1)(f) may assume by contract the liabilities under this chapter of contractors and subcontractors, or each of them, employed by or on behalf of such individual self-insurer when performing work on or adjacent to property owned or used by the individual self-insurer by the department. The net worth of the individual self-insurer shall include the assets of the self-insurer's parent company and its subsidiaries, sister companies, affiliated companies, and other related entities, located within the geographic boundaries of the state.

History: s. 43, ch. 90-201; s. 41, ch. 91-1; s. 48, ch. 93-415; s. 53, ch. 2002-194, effective July 1, 2002.

§ 440.585. Workers' Compensation Group Self-Insurance Fund Application Disclosure.

Each application for workers' compensation coverage under a group self-insurance fund authorized under this chapter must contain in contrasting color and in not less than 10-point type, the following statement: "This is a fully assessable policy. If the fund is unable to pay its obligations, policyholders must contribute on a pro rata earned premium basis the money necessary to meet any unfilled obligations." If the application is signed by the applicant, it must be conclusively presumed that there was an informed, knowing acceptance of the assessment liability that exists as a result of participation in the fund.

History: s. 4, ch. 92-328.

§ 440.59. Reporting Requirements.

The department shall annually prepare a report of the administration of this chapter for the preceding calendar year, including a detailed statement of the receipts of and expenditures from the fund established in s. 440.50 and a statement of the causes of the accidents leading to the injuries for which the awards were made, together with such recommendations as the department considers advisable. On or before September 15 of each year, the department shall submit a copy of the report to the Governor, the President of the Senate, the Speaker of the House of Representatives, the Democratic and Republican Leaders of the Senate and the House of Representatives, and the chairs of the legislative committees having jurisdiction over workers' compensation.

History: ss. 17, 23, ch. 78-300; s. 20, ch. 79-7; ss. 45, 124, ch. 79-40; s. 21, ch. 79-312; s. 43, ch. 89-289; ss. 45, 56, ch. 90-201; ss. 43, 52, ch. 91-1; s. 49, ch. 93-415; s. 28, ch. 2001-91; s. 54, ch. 2002-194, effective July 1, 2002.

§ 440.591. Administrative Procedure; Rulemaking Authority.

The department, the Financial Services Commission, the agency, and the Department of Education may adopt rules pursuant to ss. 120.536(1) and 120.54 to implement the provisions of this chapter conferring duties upon them.

History: s. 46, ch. 90-201; s. 44, ch. 91-1; s. 115, ch. 98-200; s. 55, ch. 2002-194, effective July 1, 2002; s. 495, ch. 2003-261, effective June 26, 2003; s. 76, ch. 2005-2, effective July 5, 2005.

§ 440.593. Electronic Reporting.

(1) The department may establish an electronic reporting system requiring or authorizing an employer or carrier to submit required forms, reports, or other information electronically rather than by other means. The department may establish different deadlines for submitting forms, reports, or information to the department, or to its authorized agent, via the electronic reporting system than are otherwise required when reporting information by other means.

(2) The department may require any carrier to submit data electronically, either directly or

through a third-party vendor, and may require any carrier or vendor submitting data to the department electronically to be certified by the department. The department may specify performance requirements for any carrier or vendor submitting data electronically.

(3) The department may revoke the certification of any carrier or vendor determined by the department to be in noncompliance with performance standards prescribed by rule for electronic submissions.

(4) The department may assess a civil penalty, not to exceed $500 for each violation, as prescribed by rule.

(5) The department may adopt rules to administer this section.

History: s. 50, ch. 93-415; s. 29, ch. 2001-91, effective Oct. 1, 2001; s. 56, ch. 2002-194, effective July 1, 2002.

§ 440.60. Application of Laws.

(1) Chapter 79-40, Laws of Florida, shall apply to all claims for injury arising out of accidents occurring on or after August 1, 1979.

(2) Sections 6-20, chapter 79-312, Laws of Florida, shall apply to all claims for injury arising out of accidents occurring on or after August 1, 1979.

(3) All acts or proceedings performed by or on behalf of the former[2] Division of Workers' Compensation of the[1] Department of Labor and Employment Security or the employer, or in which the division or the employer was a party under s. 440.15(1) and (3) between October 1, 1974, and July 10, 1987, are ratified and validated in all respects if such acts or proceedings would have been valid if chapter 87-330, Laws of Florida, had been in effect at the time such acts or proceedings were performed.

History: s. 127, ch. 79-40; ss. 23, 25, ch. 79-312; s. 10, ch. 87-330; s. 43, ch. 89-289; s. 56, ch. 90-201; s. 52, ch. 91-1; s. 69, ch. 2004-5, effective June 29, 2004.

[1]**2004 Note:** —Section 69, ch. 2002-194, repealed s. 20.171, which created the Department of Labor and Employment Security.

[2]**Note:** —The Division of Workers' Compensation of the Department of Labor and Employment Security was transferred to the Department of Insurance by s. 1, ch. 2002-194.

TITLE XXXIX COMMERCIAL RELATIONS

CHAPTER 682 ARBITRATION CODE

§ 682.01. Florida Arbitration Code.

Sections 682.01-682.22 may be cited as the "Florida Arbitration Code."

History: s. 22, ch. 57-402; s. 12, ch. 67-254.

2003 Note: Former s. 57.10

§ 682.02. Arbitration Agreements Made Valid, Irrevocable, and Enforceable; Scope.

Two or more parties may agree in writing to submit to arbitration any controversy existing between them at the time of the agreement, or they may include in a written contract a provision for the settlement by arbitration of any controversy thereafter arising between them relating to such contract or the failure or refusal to perform the whole or any part thereof. This section also applies to written interlocal agreements under ss. 163.01and 373.1962 in which two or more parties agree to submit to arbitration any controversy between them concerning water use permit applications and other matters, regardless of whether or not the water management district with jurisdiction over the subject application is a party to the interlocal agreement or a participant in the arbitration. Such agreement or provision shall be valid, enforceable, and irrevocable without regard to the justiciable character of the controversy; provided that this act shall not apply to any such agreement or provision to arbitrate in which it is stipulated that this law shall not apply or to any arbitration or award thereunder.

History: s. 1, ch. 57-402; s. 12, ch. 67-254; s. 3, ch. 98-402.

2003 Note: Former s. 57.11

§ 682.03. Proceedings to Compel and to Stay Arbitration.

(1) A party to an agreement or provision for arbitration subject to this law claiming the neglect or refusal of another party thereto to comply therewith may make application to the court for an order directing the parties to proceed with arbitration in accordance with the terms thereof. If the court is satisfied that no substantial issue exists as to the making of the agreement or provision, it shall grant the application. If the court shall find that a substantial issue is raised as to the making of the agreement or provision, it shall summarily hear and determine the issue and, according to its determination, shall grant or deny the application.

(2) If an issue referable to arbitration under an agreement or provision for arbitration subject to this law becomes involved in an action or proceeding pending in a court having jurisdiction to hear an application under subsection (1), such application shall be made in said court. Otherwise and subject to s. 682.19, such application may be made in any court of competent jurisdiction.

(3) Any action or proceeding involving an issue subject to arbitration under this law shall be stayed if an order for arbitration or an application therefor has been made under this section or, if the issue is severable, the stay may be with respect thereto only. When the application is made in such action or proceeding, the order for arbitration shall include such stay.

(4) On application the court may stay an arbitration proceeding commenced or about to be commenced, if it shall find that no agreement or provision for arbitration subject to this law exists between the party making the application and the party causing the arbitration to be had. The court shall summarily hear and determine the issue of the making of the agreement or provision and, according to its determination, shall grant or deny the application.

(5) An order for arbitration shall not be refused on the ground that the claim in issue lacks merit or bona fides or because any fault or grounds for the claim sought to be arbitrated have not been shown.

History: s. 2, ch. 57-402; s. 12, ch. 67-254.

2003 Note: Former s. 57.12

§ 682.04. Appointment of Arbitrators by Court.

If an agreement or provision for arbitration subject to this law provides a method for the

Fla. Stats.

appointment of arbitrators or an umpire, this method shall be followed. In the absence thereof, or if the agreed method fails or for any reason cannot be followed, or if an arbitrator or umpire who has been appointed fails to act and his or her successor has not been duly appointed, the court, on application of a party to such agreement or provision shall appoint one or more arbitrators or an umpire. An arbitrator or umpire so appointed shall have like powers as if named or provided for in the agreement or provision.

History: s. 3, ch. 57-402; s. 12, ch. 67-254; s. 724, ch. 97-102.

2003 Note: Former s. 57.13

§ 682.05. Majority Action by Arbitrators.

The powers of the arbitrators may be exercised by a majority of their number unless otherwise provided in the agreement or provision for arbitration.

History: s. 4, ch. 57-402; s. 12, ch. 67-254.

2003 Note: Former s. 57.14

§ 682.06. Hearing.

Unless otherwise provided by the agreement or provision for arbitration:

(1)

(a) The arbitrators shall appoint a time and place for the hearing and cause notification to the parties to be served personally or by registered or certified mail not less than 5 days before the hearing. Appearance at the hearing waives a party's right to such notice. The arbitrators may adjourn their hearing from time to time upon their own motion and shall do so upon the request of any party to the arbitration for good cause shown, provided that no adjournment or postponement of their hearing shall extend beyond the date fixed in the agreement or provision for making the award unless the parties consent to a later date. An umpire authorized to hear and decide the cause upon failure of the arbitrators to agree upon an award shall, in the course of his or her jurisdiction, have like powers and be subject to like limitations thereon.

(b) The arbitrators, or umpire in the course of his or her jurisdiction, may hear and decide the controversy upon the evidence produced notwithstanding the failure or refusal of a party duly notified of the time and place of the hearing to appear. The court on application may direct the arbitrators, or the umpire in the course of his or her jurisdiction, to proceed promptly with the hearing and making of the award.

(2) The parties are entitled to be heard, to present evidence material to the controversy and to cross-examine witnesses appearing at the hearing.

(3) The hearing shall be conducted by all of the arbitrators but a majority may determine any question and render a final award. An umpire authorized to hear and decide the cause upon the failure of the arbitrators to agree upon an award shall sit with the arbitrators throughout their hearing but shall not be counted as a part of their quorum or in the making of their award. If, during the course of the hearing, an arbitrator for any reason ceases to act, the remaining arbitrator, arbitrators or umpire appointed to act as neutrals may continue with the hearing and determination of the controversy.

History: s. 5, ch. 57-402; s. 12, ch. 67-254; s. 725, ch. 97-102.

2003 Note: Former s. 57.15

§ 682.07. Representation by Attorney.

A party has the right to be represented by an attorney at any arbitration proceeding or hearing under this law. A waiver thereof prior to the proceeding or hearing is ineffective.

History: s. 6, ch. 57-402; s. 12, ch. 67-254.

2003 Note: Former s. 57.16

§ 682.08. Witnesses, Subpoenas, Depositions.

(1) Arbitrators, or an umpire authorized to hear and decide the cause upon failure of the arbitrators to agree upon an award, in the course of her or his jurisdiction, may issue subpoenas for the attendance of witnesses and for the production of books, records, documents and other evidence, and shall have the power to administer oaths. Subpoenas so issued shall be served, and upon application to the court by a party to the arbitration or the arbitrators, or the

umpire, enforced in the manner provided by law for the service and enforcement of subpoenas in a civil action.

(2) On application of a party to the arbitration and for use as evidence, the arbitrators, or the umpire in the course of her or his jurisdiction, may permit a deposition to be taken, in the manner and upon the terms designated by them or her or him of a witness who cannot be subpoenaed or is unable to attend the hearing.

(3) All provisions of law compelling a person under subpoena to testify are applicable.

(4) Fees for attendance as a witness shall be the same as for a witness in the circuit court.

History: s. 7, ch. 57-402; s. 12, ch. 67-254; s. 726, ch. 97-102.

2003 Note: Former s. 57.17

§ 682.09. Award.

(1) The award shall be in writing and shall be signed by the arbitrators joining in the award or by the umpire in the course of his or her jurisdiction. They or he or she shall deliver a copy to each party to the arbitration either personally or by registered or certified mail, or as provided in the agreement or provision.

(2) An award shall be made within the time fixed therefor by the agreement or provision for arbitration or, if not so fixed, within such time as the court may order on application of a party to the arbitration. The parties may, by written agreement, extend the time either before or after the expiration thereof. Any objection that an award was not made within the time required is waived unless the objecting party notifies the arbitrators or umpire in writing of his or her objection prior to the delivery of the award to him or her.

History: s. 8, ch. 57-402; s. 12, ch. 67-254; s. 727, ch. 97-102.

2003 Note: Former s. 57.18

§ 682.10. Change of Award by Arbitrators or Umpire.

On application of a party to the arbitration, or if an application to the court is pending under s. 682.12, s. 682.13 or s. 682.14, on submission to the arbitrators, or to the umpire in the case of an umpire's award, by the court under such conditions as the court may order, the arbitrators or umpire may modify or correct the award upon the grounds stated in s. 682.14(1)(a) and (c) or for the purpose of clarifying the award. The application shall be made within 20 days after delivery of the award to the applicant. Written notice thereof shall be given forthwith to the other party to the arbitration, stating that he or she must serve his or her objections thereto, if any, within 10 days from the notice. The award so modified or corrected is subject to the provisions of ss. 682.12-682.14.

History: s. 9, ch. 57-402; s. 12, ch. 67-254; s. 728, ch. 97-102.

2003 Note: Former s. 57.19

§ 682.11. Fees and Expenses of Arbitration.

Unless otherwise provided in the agreement or provision for arbitration, the arbitrators' and umpire's expenses and fees, together with other expenses, not including counsel fees, incurred in the conduct of the arbitration, shall be paid as provided in the award.

History: s. 10, ch. 57-402; s. 12, ch. 67-254.

2003 Note: Former s. 57.20

§ 682.12. Confirmation of an Award.

Upon application of a party to the arbitration, the court shall confirm an award, unless within the time limits hereinafter imposed grounds are urged for vacating or modifying or correcting the award, in which case the court shall proceed as provided in ss. 682.13and 682.14.

2003 Note: Former s. 57.21

§ 682.13. Vacating an Award.

(1) Upon application of a party, the court shall vacate an award when:

(a) The award was procured by corruption, fraud or other undue means.

(b) There was evident partiality by an arbitrator appointed as a neutral or corruption in any of the arbitrators or umpire or misconduct prejudicing the rights of any party.

(c) The arbitrators or the umpire in the course

Fla. Stats.

of her or his jurisdiction exceeded their powers.

(d) The arbitrators or the umpire in the course of her or his jurisdiction refused to postpone the hearing upon sufficient cause being shown therefor or refused to hear evidence material to the controversy or otherwise so conducted the hearing, contrary to the provisions of s. 682.06, as to prejudice substantially the rights of a party.

(e) There was no agreement or provision for arbitration subject to this law, unless the matter was determined in proceedings under s. 682.03 and unless the party participated in the arbitration hearing without raising the objection.

But the fact that the relief was such that it could not or would not be granted by a court of law or equity is not ground for vacating or refusing to confirm the award.

(2) An application under this section shall be made within 90 days after delivery of a copy of the award to the applicant, except that, if predicated upon corruption, fraud or other undue means, it shall be made within 90 days after such grounds are known or should have been known.

(3) In vacating the award on grounds other than those stated in paragraph (1)(e), the court may order a rehearing before new arbitrators chosen as provided in the agreement or provision for arbitration or by the court in accordance with s. 682.04, or, if the award is vacated on grounds set forth in paragraphs (1)(c) and (d), the court may order a rehearing before the arbitrators or umpire who made the award or their successors appointed in accordance with s. 682.04. The time within which the agreement or provision for arbitration requires the award to be made is applicable to the rehearing and commences from the date of the order therefor.

(4) If the application to vacate is denied and no motion to modify or correct the award is pending, the court shall confirm the award.

History: s. 12, ch. 57-402; s. 12, ch. 67-254; s. 729, ch. 97-102.

2003 Note: Former s. 57.22

§ 682.14. Modification or Correction of Award.

(1) Upon application made within 90 days after delivery of a copy of the award to the applicant, the court shall modify or correct the award when:

(a) There is an evident miscalculation of figures or an evident mistake in the description of any person, thing or property referred to in the award.

(b) The arbitrators or umpire have awarded upon a matter not submitted to them or him or her and the award may be corrected without affecting the merits of the decision upon the issues submitted.

(c) The award is imperfect as a matter of form, not affecting the merits of the controversy.

(2) If the application is granted, the court shall modify and correct the award so as to effect its intent and shall confirm the award as so modified and corrected. Otherwise, the court shall confirm the award as made.

(3) An application to modify or correct an award may be joined in the alternative with an application to vacate the award.

History: s. 13, ch. 57-402; s. 12, ch. 67-254; s. 730, ch. 97-102.

2003 Note: Former s. 57.23

§ 682.15. Judgment or Decree on Award.

Upon the granting of an order confirming, modifying or correcting an award, judgment or decree shall be entered in conformity therewith and be enforced as any other judgment or decree. Costs of the application and of the proceedings subsequent thereto, and disbursements may be awarded by the court.

History: s. 14, ch. 57-402; s. 12, ch. 67-254.

2003 Note: Former s. 57.24

§ 682.16. Judgment Roll, Docketing.

(1) On entry of judgment or decree, the clerk shall prepare the judgment roll consisting, to the extent filed, of the following:

(a) The agreement or provision for arbitration and each written extension of the time within which to make the award;

(b) The award;

(c) A copy of the order confirming, modifying or correcting the award; and

(d) A copy of the judgment or decree.

(2) The judgment or decree may be docketed as if rendered in a civil action.

History: s. 15, ch. 57-402; s. 12, ch. 67-254.

2003 Note: Former s. 57.25

§ 682.17. Application to Court.

Except as otherwise provided, an application to the court under this law shall be by motion and shall be heard in the manner and upon the notice provided by law or rule of court for the making and hearing of motions. Unless the parties have agreed otherwise, notice of an initial application for an order shall be served in the manner provided by law for the service of a summons in an action.

History: s. 16, ch. 57-402; s. 12, ch. 67-254.

2003 Note: Former s. 57.26

§ 682.18. Court; Definition; Jurisdiction.

(1) The term "court" means any court of competent jurisdiction of this state. The making of an agreement or provision for arbitration subject to this law and providing for arbitration in this state shall, whether made within or outside this state, confer jurisdiction on the court to enforce the agreement or provision under this law, to enter judgment on an award duly rendered in an arbitration thereunder and to vacate, modify or correct an award rendered thereunder for such cause and in the manner provided in this law.

(2) Any judgment entered upon an award by a court of competent jurisdiction of any state, territory, the Commonwealth of Puerto Rico or foreign country shall be enforceable by application as provided in s. 682.17 and regardless of the time when said award may have been made.

History: s. 17, ch. 57-402; s. 12, ch. 67-254.

2003 Note: Former s. 57.27

§ 682.19. Venue.

Any application under this law may be made to the court of the county in which the other party to the agreement or provision for arbitration resides or has a place of business, or, if she or he has no residence or place of business in this state, then to the court of any county. All applications under this law subsequent to an initial application shall be made to the court hearing the initial application unless it shall order otherwise.

History: s. 18, ch. 57-402; s. 12, ch. 67-254; s. 731, ch. 97-102.

2003 Note: Former s. 57.28

§ 682.20. Appeals.

(1) An appeal may be taken from:

(a) An order denying an application to compel arbitration made under s. 682.03.

(b) An order granting an application to stay arbitration made under s. 682.03(2)-(4).

(c) An order confirming or denying confirmation of an award.

(d) An order modifying or correcting an award.

(e) An order vacating an award without directing a rehearing.

(f) A judgment or decree entered pursuant to the provisions of this law.

(2) The appeal shall be taken in the manner and to the same extent as from orders or judgments in a civil action.

History: s. 19, ch. 57-402; s. 12, ch. 67-254.

2003 Note: Former s. 57.29

§ 682.21. Law not Retroactive.

This law applies only to agreements and provisions for arbitration made subsequent to the taking effect of this law.

History: s. 20, ch. 57-402; s. 12, ch. 67-254.

2003 Note: Former s. 57.30

§ 682.22. Severability.

If any provision of this chapter or the application thereof to any person or circumstance is held invalid, that invalidity shall not affect other provisions or applications of this chapter. In any

Fla. Stats.

action or proceeding in any state or territory of the United States, the Commonwealth of Puerto Rico, or any foreign country, this chapter and any agreement or provision to arbitrate made thereunder shall be classified as substantive within the meaning of that term in the conflict of laws; provided, however, that such substantive classification shall never be intended to derogate the public policy of such other jurisdiction.

History: s. 21, ch. 57-402; s. 12, ch. 67-254.

2003 Note: Former s. 57.31

PART IV

FLORIDA RULES OF PROCEDURE FOR WORKERS' COMPENSATION ADJUDICATIONS

Editor's Note: Chapter 60Q-6 Rules of Procedure for Workers' Compensation Adjudications has been moved to Part VI, Selected Provisions of the Florida Administrative Code.

R. WC. Proc.

PART V

FLORIDA RULES OF APPELLATE PROCEDURE

SYNOPSIS

FLORIDA RULES OF APPELLATE PROCEDURE

Rule 9.010. Effective Date and Scope.

These rules, cited as "Florida Rules of Appellate Procedure," and abbreviated "Fla.R.App.P.," shall take effect at 12:01 a.m. on March 1, 1978. They shall govern all proceedings commenced on or after that date in the supreme court, the district courts of appeal, and the circuit courts in the exercise of the jurisdiction described by rule 9.030(c); provided that any appellate proceeding commenced before March 1, 1978, shall continue to its conclusion in the court in which it is then pending in accordance with the Florida Appellate Rules, 1962 Amendment. These rules shall supersede all conflicting statutes and, as provided in Florida Rule of Judicial Administration 2.135, all conflicting rules of procedure.

History: Amended Oct. 22, 1992, effective Jan. 1, 1993 (609 So.2d 516); Nov. 22, 1996, effective Jan. 1, 1997 (685 So.2d 773).

Committee Notes

1977 Amendment. The rules have been re-numbered to conform with the numbering system adopted by the Florida Supreme Court for all of its rules of practice and procedure, and to avoid confusion with the former rules, which have been extensively revised. The abbreviated citation form to be used for these rules appears in this rule and in rule 9.800.

This rule sets an effective date and retains the substance of former rules 1.1, 1.2, and 1.4. A transition provision has been incorporated to make clear that proceedings already in the appellate stage before the effective date will continue to be governed by the former rules until the completion of appellate review in the court in which it is pending on the effective date. If review is sought after March 1, 1978, of an appellate determination made in a proceeding filed in the appellate court before that date, the higher court may allow review to proceed under the former rules if an injustice would result from required adherence to the new rules. Unnecessary language has been deleted and the wording has been simplified. Specific reference has been made to rule 9.030(c) to clarify those aspects of the jurisdiction of the circuit courts governed by these rules.

1992 Amendment. This rule was amended to eliminate the statement that the Florida Rules of Appellate Procedure supersede all conflicting rules. Other sets of Florida rules contain provisions applicable to certain appellate proceedings, and, in certain instances, those rules conflict with the procedures set forth for other appeals under these rules. In the absence of a clear mandate from the supreme court that only the Florida Rules of Appellate Procedure are to address appellate concerns, the committee felt that these rules should not automatically supersede other rules. See, e.g., *In the Interest of E.P. v. Department of Health and Rehabilitative Services,* 544 So.2d 1000 (Fla.1989).

1996 Amendment. Rule of Judicial Administration 2.135 now mandates that the Rules of Appellate Procedure control in all appellate proceedings.

Rule 9.020. Definitions.

The following terms have the meanings shown as used in these rules:

(a) Administrative Action. Administrative action shall include:

(1) final agency action as defined in the Administrative Procedure Act, chapter 120, Florida Statutes;

(2) non-final action by an agency or administrative law judge reviewable under the Administrative Procedure Act;

(3) quasi-judicial decisions by any administrative body, agency, board or commission not subject to the Administrative Procedure Act; and

(4) administrative action for which judicial review is provided by general law.

(b) Clerk. The person or official specifically designated as such for the court or lower tribunal; if no person or official has been specifically so designated, the official or agent who most closely resembles a clerk in the functions performed.

(c) Court. The supreme court; the district courts of appeal; and the circuit courts in the exercise of the jurisdiction described by rule 9.030(c) including the chief justice of the supreme court and the chief judge of a district court of appeal in the exercise of constitutional, administrative, or supervisory powers on behalf of such courts.

(d) Family Law Matter. A matter governed by the Florida Family Law Rules of Procedure.

(e) Lower Tribunal. The court, agency, of-

R. App. Proc.

ficer, board, commission, judge of compensation claims, or body whose order is to be reviewed.

(f) Order. A decision, order, judgment, decree, or rule of a lower tribunal, excluding minutes and minute book entries.

(g) Parties.

(1) Appellant. A party who seeks to invoke the appeal jurisdiction of a court.

(2) Appellee. Every party in the proceeding in the lower tribunal other than an appellant.

(3) Petitioner. A party who seeks an order under rule 9.100 or rule 9.120.

(4) Respondent. Every other party in a proceeding brought by a petitioner.

(h) Rendition (of an Order). An order is rendered when a signed, written order is filed with the clerk of the lower tribunal. However, unless another applicable rule of procedure specifically provides to the contrary, if a final order has been entered and there has been filed in the lower tribunal an authorized and timely motion for new trial, for rehearing, for certification, to alter or amend, for judgment in accordance with prior motion for directed verdict, for arrest of judgment, to challenge the verdict, to correct a sentence or order of probation pursuant to Florida Rule of Criminal Procedure 3.800(b)(1), to withdraw a plea after sentencing pursuant to Florida Rule of Criminal Procedure 3.170(*l*), or to vacate an order based upon the recommendations of a hearing officer in accordance with Florida Family Law Rule of Procedure 12.491, the following exceptions apply:

(1) If such a motion or motions have been filed, the final order shall not be deemed rendered with respect to any claim between the movant and any party against whom relief is sought by the motion or motions until the filing of a signed, written order disposing of all such motions between such parties.

(2) If such a motion or motions have been filed, a signed, written order granting a new trial shall be deemed rendered when filed with the clerk, notwithstanding that other such motions may remain pending at the time.

(3) If such a motion or motions have been filed and a notice of appeal is filed before the filing of a signed, written order disposing of all such motions, all motions filed by the appealing party that are pending at the time shall be deemed abandoned, and the final order shall be deemed rendered by the filing of the notice of appeal as to all claims between parties who then have no such motions pending between them. However, a pending motion to correct a sentence or order of probation or a motion to withdraw the plea after sentencing shall not be affected by the filing of a notice of appeal from a judgment of guilt. In such instance, the notice of appeal shall be treated as prematurely filed and the appeal held in abeyance until the filing of a signed, written order disposing of such motion.

(i) Rendition of an Appellate Order. If any timely and authorized motion under rule 9.330 or 9.331 is filed, the order shall not be deemed rendered as to any party until all of the motions are either abandoned or resolved by the filing of a written order.

History: Amended July 14, 1988, effective Jan. 1, 1989 (529 So.2d 687); Dec. 30, 1988, effective Jan. 1, 1989 (536 So.2d 240); March 23, 1989 (541 So.2d 1142); Oct. 22, 1992, effective Jan. 1, 1993 (609 So.2d 516); June 27, 1996, effective July 1, 1996 (675 So.2d 1374); Sept. 27, 1996, effective Oct. 1, 1996 (681 So.2d 1132); Nov. 22, 1996, effective Jan. 1, 1997 (685 So.2d 773); Nov. 12, 1999, effective Nov. 12, 1999 (24 Fla. L. Weekly S530); opinion corrected Nov. 23, 1999 (24 Fla. L. Weekly S567); opn. on grant of reh'g Jan. 13, 2000 *Amendment to Florida Rules of Criminal Procedure 3.111(e), 3.800 and Florida Rules of Appellate Procedure 9.020(h), 9.140, and 9.600*, No. 95707 (25 Fla. L. Weekly S37a); opinion corrected Jan. 14, 2000; amended Oct. 12, 2000, effective Jan. 1, 2001 (780 So. 2d 834; 2000 Fla. LEXIS 2273; 25 Fla. L. Weekly S 835); Aug. 29, 2002, effective Jan. 1, 2003.

1999 Note: The amendment at 24 Fla. L. Weekly S530 shall also apply to cases pending on appeal.

Committee Notes

1977 Amendment. This rule supersedes former rule 1.3. Throughout these rules the defined terms have been used in their technical sense only, and are not intended to alter substantive law. Instances may arise in which the context of the rule requires a different meaning for a defined term, but these should be rare.

The term "administrative action" is new and has been defined to make clear the application of these rules to judicial review of administrative agency action. This definition was not intended to conflict with the Administrative Procedure Act, chapter 120, Florida Statutes (1975), but was intended to include all administrative agency action as defined in the Administrative Procedure Act. The reference to municipalities is not intended to conflict with article VIII, section 1(a), Florida Constitution, which makes counties the only political subdivisions of the state.

The term "clerk" retains the substance of the term "clerk" defined in the former rules. This term includes the person who in fact maintains records of proceedings in the lower tribunal if no person is specifically and officially given that duty.

The term "court" retains the substance of the term "court" defined in the former rules, but has been modified to recognize the authority delegated to the chief justice of the supreme court and the chief judges of the district courts of appeal. This definition was not intended to broaden the scope of these rules in regard to the administrative responsibilities of the mentioned judicial officers. The term is used in these rules to designate the court to which a proceeding governed by these rules is taken. If supreme court review of a district court of appeal decision is involved, the district court of appeal is the "lower tribunal".

The term "lower tribunal" includes courts and administrative agencies. It replaces the terms "commission," "board," and "lower court" defined in the former rules.

The term "order" has been broadly defined to include all final and interlocutory rulings of a lower tribunal and rules adopted by an administrative agency. Minute book entries are excluded from the definition in recognition of the decision in *Employers' Fire Ins. Co. v. Continental Ins. Co.,* 326 So.2d 177 (Fla.1976). It was intended that this rule encourage the entry of written orders in every case.

The terms "appellant," "appellee," "petitioner," and "respondent" have been defined according to the rule applicable to a particular proceeding and generally not according to the legal nature of the proceeding before the court. The term "appellee" has been defined to include the parties against whom relief is sought and all others necessary to the cause. This rule supersedes all statutes concerning the same subject matter, such as section 924.03, Florida Statutes (1975). It should be noted that if a certiorari proceeding is specifically governed by a rule that only refers to "appellant" and "appellee," a "petitioner" and "respondent" should proceed as if they were "appellant" and "appellee," respectively. For example, certiorari proceedings in the supreme court involving the Public Service Commission and Industrial Relations Commission are specifically governed by rule 9.110 even though that rule only refers to "appellant" and "appellee". The parties in such a certiorari proceeding remain designated as "petitioner" and "respondent," because as a matter of substantive law the party invoking the court's jurisdiction is seeking a writ of certiorari. The same is true of rule 9.200 governing the record in such certiorari proceedings.

The term "rendition" has been simplified and unnecessary language deleted. The filing requirement of the definition was not intended to conflict with the substantive right of review guaranteed by the Administrative Procedure Act, section 120.68(1), Florida Statutes (Supp.1976), but to set a point from which certain procedural times could be measured. Motions that postpone the date of rendition have been narrowly limited to prevent deliberate delaying tactics. To postpone rendition the motion must be timely, authorized, and one of those listed. However, if the lower tribunal is an administrative agency whose rules of practice denominate motions identical to those listed by a different label, the substance of the motion controls and rendition is postponed accordingly.

The definition of "legal holiday" has been eliminated but its substance has been retained in rule 9.420(e).

The term "bond" is defined in rule 9.310(c)(1).

Terms defined in the former rules and not defined here are intended to have their ordinary meanings in accordance with the context of these rules.

1992 Amendment. Subdivision (a) has been amended to reflect properly that deputy commissioners presently are designated as judges of compensation claims.

Subdivision (g) has been rewritten extensively. The first change in this rule was to ensure that an authorized motion for clarification (such as under rule 9.330) was included in those types of motions that delay rendition.

Subdivision (g) also has been revised in several respects to clarify some problems presented by the generality of the prior definition of "rendition." Although rendition is postponed in most types of cases by the filing of timely and authorized post-judgment motions, some rules of procedure explicitly provide to the contrary. The subdivision therefore has been qualified to provide that conflicting rules shall control over the general rule stated in the subdivision. See *In Re Interest of E.P.,* 544 So.2d 1000 (Fla.1989). The subdivision also has been revised to make explicit a qualification of long standing in the decisional law, that rendition of non-final orders cannot be postponed

R. App. Proc.

by motions directed to them. Not all final orders are subject to postponement of rendition, however. Rendition of a final order can be postponed only by an "authorized" motion, and whether any of the listed motions is an "authorized" motion depends on the rules of procedure governing the proceeding in which the final order is entered. See *Francisco v. Victoria Marine Shipping, Inc.*, 486 So.2d 1986 (Fla. 3d DCA 1986), review denied 494 So.2d 1153.

Subdivision (g)(1) has been added to clarify the date of rendition when post-judgment motions have been filed. If there is only 1 plaintiff and 1 defendant in the case, the filing of a post-judgment motion or motions by either party (or both parties) will postpone rendition of the entire final order as to all claims between the parties. If there are multiple parties on either or both sides of the case and less than all parties file post-judgment motions, rendition of the final order will be postponed as to all claims between moving parties and parties moved against, but rendition will not be postponed with respect to claims disposed of in the final order between parties who have no post-judgment motions pending between them with respect to any of those claims. See, e.g., *Phillips v. Ostrer,* 442 So.2d 1084 (Fla. 3d DCA 1983).

Ideally, all post-judgment motions should be disposed of at the same time. See *Winn-Dixie Stores, Inc. v. Robinson,* 472 So.2d 722 (Fla.1985). If that occurs, the final order is deemed rendered as to all claims when the order disposing of the motions is filed with the clerk. If all motions are not disposed of at the same time, the final order is deemed rendered as to all claims between a moving party and a party moved against when the written order disposing of the last remaining motion addressed to those claims is filed with the clerk, notwithstanding that other motions filed by co-parties may remain pending. If such motions remain, the date of rendition with respect to the claims between the parties involved in those motions shall be determined in the same way.

Subdivision (g)(2) has been added to govern the special circumstance that arises when rendition of a final order has been postponed initially by post-judgment motions, and a motion for new trial then is granted. If the new trial has been granted simply as an alternative to a new final order, the appeal will be from the new final order. However, if a new trial alone has been ordered, the appeal will be from the new trial order. See rule 9.110. According to the decisional law, rendition of such an order is not postponed by the pendency of any additional, previously filed post-judgment motions, nor can rendition of such an order be postponed by the filing of any further motion. See *Frazier v. Seaboard System Railroad, Inc.,* 508 So.2d 345 (Fla.1987). To ensure that subdivision (g)(1) is not read as a modification of this special rule, subdivision (g)(2) has been added to make it clear that a separately appealable new trial order is deemed rendered when filed, notwithstanding that other post-judgment motions directed to the initial final order may remain pending at the time.

Subdivision (g)(3) has been added to clarify the confusion generated by a dictum in *Williams v. State,* 324 So.2d 74 (Fla.1975), which appeared contrary to the settled rule that post-judgment motions were considered abandoned by a party who filed a notice of appeal before their disposition. See *In Re: Forfeiture of $104,591 in U.S. Currency,* 578 So.2d 727 (Fla. 3d DCA 1991). The new subdivision confirms that rule, and provides that the final order is rendered as to the appealing party when the notice of appeal is filed. Although the final order is rendered as to the appealing party, it is not rendered as to any other party whose post-judgment motions are pending when the notice of appeal is filed.

1996 Amendment. Subdivision (a) was amended to reflect the current state of the law. When the term "administrative action" is used in the Florida Rules of Appellate Procedure, it encompasses proceedings under the Administrative Procedure Act, quasi-judicial proceedings before local government agencies, boards, and commissions, and administrative action for which judicial review is provided by general law.

Addition of language in subdivision (i) is intended to toll the time for the filing of a notice of appeal until the resolution of a timely filed motion to vacate when an order has been entered based on the recommendation of a hearing officer in a family law matter. Under the prior rules, a motion to vacate was not an authorized motion to toll the time for the filing of an appeal, and too often the motion to vacate could not be heard within 30 days of the rendition of the order. This rule change permits the lower tribunal to complete its review prior to the time an appeal must be filed.

2000 Amendment. The text of subdivision (i) was moved into the main body of subdivision (h) to retain consistency in the definitional portions of the rule.

Court Commentary

1996 Amendment. Subdivision (h) was amended to ensure that a motion to correct sentence or order of probation and a motion to withdraw the plea after sentencing would postpone rendition. Subdivision (h)(3) was amended to explain that such a motion is not waived by an appeal from a judgment of guilt.

Rule 9.030. Jurisdiction of Courts.

(a) Jurisdiction of Supreme Court.

(1) Appeal Jurisdiction.

(A) The supreme court shall review, by appeal

(i) final orders of courts imposing sentences of death; [1]

(ii) decisions of district courts of appeal declaring invalid a state statute or a provision of the state constitution. [2]

(B) If provided by general law, the supreme court shall review

(i) by appeal final orders entered in proceedings for the validation of bonds or certificates of indebtedness; [3]

(ii) action of statewide agencies relating to rates or service of utilities providing electric, gas, or telephone service. [4]

(2) Discretionary Jurisdiction. The discretionary jurisdiction of the supreme court may be sought to review

(A) decisions of district courts of appeal that [5]

(i) expressly declare valid a state statute;

(ii) expressly construe a provision of the state or federal constitution;

(iii) expressly affect a class of constitutional or state officers;

(iv) expressly and directly conflict with a decision of another district court of appeal or of the supreme court on the same question of law;

(v) pass upon a question certified to be of great public importance;

(vi) are certified to be in direct conflict with decisions of other district courts of appeal;

(B) orders and judgments of trial courts certified by the district court of appeal in which the appeal is pending to require immediate resolution by the supreme court, and [6]

(i) to be of great public importance, or

(ii) to have a great effect on the proper administration of justice;

(C) questions of law certified by the Supreme Court of the United States or a United States court of appeals that are determinative of the cause of action and for which there is no controlling precedent of the Supreme Court of Florida. [7]

(3) Original Jurisdiction. The supreme court may issue writs of prohibition to courts and all writs necessary to the complete exercise of its jurisdiction, and may issue writs of mandamus and quo warranto to state officers and state agencies. The supreme court or any justice may issue writs of habeas corpus returnable before the supreme court or any justice, a district court of appeal or any judge thereof, or any circuit judge. [8]

(b) Jurisdiction of District Courts of Appeal.

(1) Appeal Jurisdiction. District courts of appeal shall review, by appeal

(A) final orders of trial courts, [1, 2] not directly reviewable by the supreme court or a circuit court; including county court final orders declaring invalid a state statute or provision of the state constitution;

(B) non-final orders of circuit courts as prescribed by rule 9.130; [9]

(C) administrative action if provided by general law. [2]

(2) Certiorari Jurisdiction. [8] The certiorari jurisdiction of district courts of appeal may be sought to review

(A) non-final orders of lower tribunals other than as prescribed by rule 9.130;

(B) final orders of circuit courts acting in their review capacity.

(3) Original Jurisdiction. [8]District courts of appeal may issue writs of mandamus, prohibition, quo warranto, and common law certiorari, and all writs necessary to the complete exercise of the courts' jurisdiction; or any judge thereof may issue writs of habeas corpus returnable before the court or any judge thereof, or before

any circuit judge within the territorial jurisdiction of the court.

(4) Discretionary Review. [10]District courts of appeal, in their discretion, may review by appeal

(A) final orders of the county court, otherwise appealable to the circuit court under these rules, that the county court has certified to be of great public importance;

(B) non-final orders, otherwise appealable to the circuit court under rule 9.140(c), that the county court has certified to be of great public importance.

(c) Jurisdiction of Circuit Courts.

(1) Appeal Jurisdiction. The circuit courts shall review, by appeal

(A) final orders of lower tribunals as provided by general law; [1, 2]

(B) non-final orders of lower tribunals as provided by general law;

(C) administrative action if provided by general law. [2]

(2) Certiorari Jurisdiction. [8]The certiorari jurisdiction of circuit courts may be sought to review non-final orders of lower tribunals other than as prescribed by rule 9.130.

(3) Original Jurisdiction. [5]Circuit courts may issue writs of mandamus, prohibition, quo warranto, common law certiorari, and habeas corpus, and all writs necessary to the complete exercise of the courts' jurisdiction. **1.** 9.140: Appeal Proceedings in Criminal Cases. **2.** 9.110: Appeal Proceedings: Final Orders. **3.** 9.110(i): Validation of Bonds. **4.** 9.110: Appeal Proceedings: Final Orders; 9.100: Original Proceedings. **5.** 9.120: Discretionary Review of District Court Decisions. **6.** 9.125: Discretionary Review of Trial Court Orders and Judgments Certified by the District Court. **7.** 9.150: Certified Questions from Federal Courts. **8.** 9.100: Original Proceedings. **9.** 9.130: Appeal Proceedings: Non-Final Orders. **10.** 9.160: Discretionary Review of County Court Decisions.

History: Amended March 27, 1980, effective April 1, 1980 (381 So.2d 1370); Nov. 26, 1980, effective Jan. 1, 1981 (391 So.2d 203); Sept. 13, 1984, effective Oct. 1, 1984 (463 So.2d 1114); Feb. 14, 1985, effective March 1, 1985 (463 So.2d 1124); July 14, 1988, effective Jan. 1, 1989 (529 So.2d 687); Dec. 30, 1988, effective Jan. 1, 1989 (536 So.2d 240); Oct. 22, 1992, effective Jan. 1, 1993 (609 So.2d 516); amended Oct. 12, 2000, effective Jan. 1, 2001 (780 So. 2d 834; 2000 Fla. LEXIS 2273; 25 Fla. L. Weekly S 835).

Committee Notes

1977 Amendment. This rule replaces former rules 2.1(a)(5) and 2.2(a)(4). It sets forth the jurisdiction of the supreme court, district courts of appeal, and that portion of the jurisdiction of the circuit courts to which these rules apply. It paraphrases sections 3(b), 4(b), and, in relevant part, 5(b) of article V of the Florida Constitution. The items stating the certiorari jurisdiction of the supreme court and district courts of appeal refer to the constitutional jurisdiction popularly known as the "constitutional certiorari" jurisdiction of the supreme court and "common law certiorari" jurisdiction of the district courts of appeal. This rule is not intended to affect the substantive law governing the jurisdiction of any court and should not be considered as authority for the resolution of disputes concerning any court's jurisdiction. Its purpose is to provide a tool of reference to the practitioner so that ready reference may be made to the specific procedural rule or rules governing a particular proceeding. Footnote references have been made to the rule or rules governing proceedings invoking the listed areas of jurisdiction.

This rule does not set forth the basis for the issuance of advisory opinions by the supreme court to the governor because the power to advise rests with the justices under article IV, section 1(c), Florida Constitution, and not the supreme court as a body. The procedure governing requests from the governor for advice are set forth in rule 9.500.

The advisory committee considered and rejected as unwise a proposal to permit the chief judge of each judicial circuit to modify the applicability of these rules to that particular circuit. These rules may be modified in a particular case, of course, by an agreed joint motion of the parties granted by the court so long as the change does not affect jurisdiction.

1980 Amendment. Subdivision (a) of this rule has been extensively revised to reflect the constitutional modifications in the supreme court's jurisdiction as approved by the electorate on March 11, 1980. See art. V, § 3(b), Fla. Const. (1980). The impetus for these modifications was a burgeoning caseload and the attendant need to make more efficient use of limited appellate resources. Consistent with this purpose, revised subdivision (a) limits the supreme court's appellate, discretionary, and original jurisdiction to cases that substantially affect the law of the state. The district courts of appeal will constitute the courts of last resort for the vast majority of litigants under amended article V.

Subdivision (a)(1)(A)(i) retains the mandatory appellate jurisdiction of the supreme court to review final orders of trial courts imposing death sentences.

Subdivision (a)(1)(A)(ii) has been substantively changed in accordance with amended article V, section 3(b)(1), Florida Constitution (1980), to eliminate the court's mandatory appellate review of final orders of trial courts and decisions of district courts of appeal initially and directly passing on the validity of a state statute or a federal statute or treaty, or construing a provision of the state or federal constitution. Mandatory supreme court review under this subdivision is now limited to district court decisions "declaring invalid" a state statute or a provision of the state constitution. Jurisdiction to review final orders of trial courts in all instances enumerated in former subdivision (a)(1)(A)(ii) now reposes in the appropriate district court of appeal.

Revised subdivision (a)(1)(B) enumerates the 2 classes of cases that the supreme court may review if provided by general law. See art. V, § 3(b)(2), Fla.Const. (1980). Eliminated from the amended article V and rule is the legislative authority, never exercised, to require supreme court review of trial court orders imposing sentences of life imprisonment.

Subdivision (a)(1)(B)(i), pertaining to bond validation proceedings, replaces former subdivision (a)(1)(B)(ii). Its phraseology remains unchanged. Enabling legislation already exists for supreme court review of bond validation proceedings. See § 75.08, Fla.Stat. (1979).

Subdivision (a)(1)(B)(ii) is new. See art. V, § 3(b)(2), Fla.Const. (1980). Under the earlier constitutional scheme, the supreme court was vested with certiorari jurisdictions (which in practice was always exercised) to review orders of "commissions established by general law having statewide jurisdiction," including orders of the Florida Public Service Commission. See art. V, § 3(b)(3), Fla.Const. (1968); § 350.641, Fla.Stat. (1979). This jurisdiction has been abolished. In its stead, amended article V limits the supreme court's review of Public Service Commission orders to those "relating to rates or services of utilities providing electric, gas, or telephone service." Enabling legislation will be required to effectuate this jurisdiction. Review of Public Service Commission orders other than those relating to electric, gas, or utility cases now reposes in the appropriate district court of appeal. See art. V, § 4(b)(2), Fla. Const. (1968); Fla.R.App.P. 9.030(b)(1)(C); and § 120.68(2), Fla. Stat. (1979).

Subdivision (a)(2) has been substantially revised in accordance with amended article V, section 3(b)(3), Florida Constitution (1980), to restrict the scope of review under the supreme court's discretionary jurisdiction. Under the earlier constitution, this jurisdiction was exercised by writ of certiorari. Constitutional certiorari is abolished under amended article V. Reflecting this change, revised subdivision (a)(2) of this rule substitutes the phrase "discretionary jurisdiction" for "certiorari jurisdiction" in the predecessor rule. This discretionary jurisdiction is restricted, moreover, to 6 designated categories of district court decisions, discussed below. Amended article V eliminates the supreme court's discretionary power to review "any interlocutory order passing upon a matter which upon final judgment would be directly appealable to the Supreme Court" as reflected in subdivision (a)(2)(B) of the predecessor rule. It also eliminates the supreme court's certiorari review of "commissions established by general law having statewide jurisdiction" as reflected in subdivision (a)(2)(C) of the predecessor rule.

Subdivision (a)(2)(A) specifies the 6 categories of district court decisions reviewable by the supreme court under its discretionary jurisdiction.

Subdivisions (a)(2)(A)(i) and (a)(2)(A)(ii) are new and pertain to matters formerly reviewable under the court's mandatory appellate jurisdiction. Under former rule 9.030(a)(1)(A)(ii), the supreme court's mandatory appellate jurisdiction could be invoked if a lower tribunal "inherently" declared a statute valid. See *Harrell's Candy Kitchen, Inc. v. Sarasota-Manatee Airport Auth.*, 111 So.2d 439 (Fla.1959). The 1980 amendments to article V and this subdivision require a district court to "expressly declare" a state statute valid before the supreme court's discretionary jurisdiction may be invoked.

Subdivision (a)(2)(A)(iii), pertaining to supreme court review of district court decisions affecting a class of constitutional or state officers, has been renumbered. It tracks the language of the predecessor constitution and rule, with the addition of the restrictive word "expressly" found in amended article V.

Subdivision (a)(2)(A)(iv) represents the most radical change in the supreme court's discretionary jurisdiction. The predecessor article V vested the supreme court with power to review district court decisions "in direct conflict with a decision of any district court of appeal or of the Supreme Court on the same point of law." These cases comprised the overwhelming bulk of the court's caseload and gave rise to an intricate body of case law interpreting the requirements for

R. App. Proc.

discretionary conflict review. With the enunciation of the "record proper rule" in *Foley v. Weaver Drugs, Inc.,* 177 So.2d 221 (Fla.1965), the supreme court extended its discretionary review in instances of discernible conflict to district court decisions affirming without opinion the orders of trial courts. Amended article V abolishes the Foley doctrine by requiring an "express" as well as a "direct" conflict of district court decisions as a prerequisite to supreme court review. The new article also terminates supreme court jurisdiction over purely intradistrict conflicts, the resolution of which is addressed in rule 9.331.

Subdivision (a)(2)(A)(v) substitutes the phrase "great public importance" for "great public interest" in the predecessor constitution and rule. The change was to recognize the fact that some legal issues may have "great public importance," but may not be sufficiently known by the public to have "great public interest."

Subdivision (a)(2)(A)(vi) is new and tracks the language of article V, section 3(b)(4), Florida Constitution (1980).

Subdivisions (a)(2)(B) and (a)(2)(C) are new. See art. V, §§ 3(b)(5), 3(b)(6), Fla.Const. (1980). Certification procedures under these subdivisions are addressed in rule 9.125 and rule 9.150, respectively.

Subdivision (a)(3) is identical to the predecessor article V and rule, except it limits the issuance of writs of prohibition to "courts" rather than "courts and commissions" and limits the issuance of writs of mandamus and quo warranto to "state agencies" rather than "agencies."

1984 Amendment. Subdivision (b)(4) was added to implement legislation authorizing district courts of appeal discretion to review by appeal orders and judgments of county courts certified to be of great public importance.

1992 Amendment. Subdivision (c)(1)(B) was amended to reflect correctly that the appellate jurisdiction of circuit courts extended to all non-final orders of lower tribunals as prescribed by rule 9.130, and not only those defined in subdivision (a)(3) of that rule.

Subdivision (c)(1)(C) was amended to reflect the jurisdiction conferred on circuit courts by article V, section 5, Florida Constitution, which provides that "[t]hey shall have the power of direct review of administrative action prescribed by general law."

2000 Amendment. Subdivision (c)(1)(B) was amended to reflect that the appellate jurisdiction of circuit courts is prescribed by general law and not by rule 9.130, as clarified in *Blore v. Fierro*, 636 So. 2d 1329 (Fla. 1994).

Rule 9.040. General Provisions.

(a) Complete Determination:In all proceedings a court shall have such jurisdiction as may be necessary for a complete determination of the cause.

(b) Forum.

(1) If a proceeding is commenced in an inappropriate court, that court shall transfer the cause to an appropriate court.

(2) After a lower tribunal renders an order transferring venue, the appropriate court to review otherwise reviewable non-final orders is as follows:

(A) After rendition of an order transferring venue, the appropriate court to review the non-final venue order, all other reviewable non-final orders rendered prior to or simultaneously with the venue order, any order staying, vacating, or modifying the transfer of venue order, or an order dismissing a cause for failure to pay venue transfer fees, is the court that would review non-final orders in the cause, had venue not been transferred.

(B) After rendition of an order transferring venue, the appropriate court to review any subsequently rendered reviewable non-final order, except for those orders listed in subdivision (b)(2)(A), is the court which would review the order, if the cause had been filed in the lower tribunal to which venue was transferred.

(C) The clerk of the lower tribunal whose order is being reviewed shall perform the procedures required by these provisions regarding transfer of venue, including accepting and filing a notice of appeal. If necessary to facilitate non-final review, after an order transferring venue has been rendered, the clerk of the lower tribunal shall copy and retain such portions of the record as are necessary for review of the non-final order. If the file of the cause has been transferred to the transferee tribunal before the notice of appeal is filed in the transferring tribunal, the clerk of the transferee tribunal shall copy and transmit to the transferring tribunal such portions of the record as are necessary for review of the non-final order.

(c) Remedy. If a party seeks an improper remedy, the cause shall be treated as if the proper remedy had been sought; provided that it shall not be the responsibility of the court to seek the proper remedy.

(d) Amendment. At any time in the interest of justice, the court may permit any part of the proceeding to be amended so that it may be disposed of on the merits. In the absence of amendment, the court may disregard any procedural error or defect that does not adversely affect the substantial rights of the parties.

(e) Assignments of Error. Assignments of error are neither required nor permitted.

(f) Filing Fees. Filing fees may be paid by check or money order.

(g) Clerks' Duties. On filing of a notice prescribed by these rules, the clerk shall forthwith transmit the fee and a certified copy of the notice, showing the date of filing, to the court. If jurisdiction has been invoked under rule 9.030(a)(2)(A)(v) or (a)(2)(A)(vi), or if a certificate has been issued by a district court under rule 9.030(a)(2)(B), the clerk of the district court of appeal shall transmit copies of the certificate and decision or order and any suggestion, replies, or appendices with the certified copy of the notice. Notices to review final orders of county and circuit courts in civil cases shall be recorded.

(h) Non-Jurisdictional Matters. Failure of a clerk or a party timely to file fees or additional copies of notices or petitions or the conformed copy of the order or orders designated in the notice of appeal shall not be jurisdictional; provided that such failure may be the subject of appropriate sanction.

History: Amended March 27, 1980, effective April 1, 1980 (381 So.2d 1370); Oct. 22, 1992, effective Jan. 1, 1993 (609 So.2d 516); Nov. 22, 1996, effective Jan. 1, 1997 (685 So.2d 773); amended Oct. 12, 2000, effective Jan. 1, 2001 (780 So. 2d 834; 2000 Fla. LEXIS 2273; 25 Fla. L. Weekly S 835); Aug. 29, 2002, effective Jan. 1, 2003.

Committee Notes

1977 Amendment. This rule sets forth several miscellaneous matters of general applicability.

Subdivision (a) is derived from the last sentence of former rule 2.1(a)(5)(a), which concerned direct appeals to the supreme court. This provision is intended to guarantee that once the jurisdiction of any court is properly invoked, the court may determine the entire case to the extent permitted by substantive law. This rule does not extend or limit the constitutional or statutory jurisdiction of any court.

Subdivisions (b) and (c) implement article V, section 2(a), Florida Constitution. Former rule 2.1(a)(5)(d) authorized transfer if an improper forum was chosen, but the former rules did not address the problem of improper remedies being sought. The advisory committee does not consider it to be the responsibility of the court to seek the proper remedy for any party, but a court may not deny relief because a different remedy is proper. Under these provisions a case will not be dismissed automatically because a party seeks an improper remedy or invokes the jurisdiction of the wrong court. The court must instead treat the case as if the proper remedy had been sought and transfer it to the court having jurisdiction. All filings in the case have the same legal effect as though originally filed in the court to which transfer is made. This rule is intended to supersede *Nellen v. State,* 226 So.2d 354 (Fla. 1st DCA 1969), in which a petition for a common law writ of certiorari was dismissed by the district court of appeal because review was properly by appeal to the appropriate circuit court, and *Engel v. City of North Miami,* 115 So.2d 1 (Fla.1959), in which a petition for a writ of certiorari was dismissed because review should have been by appeal. Under this rule, a petition for a writ of certiorari should be treated as a notice of appeal, if timely.

Subdivision (d) is the appellate procedure counterpart of the harmless error statute, section 59.041, Florida Statutes (1975). It incorporates the concept contained in former rule 3.2(c), which provided that deficiencies in the form or substance of a notice of appeal were not grounds for dismissal, absent a clear showing that the adversary had been misled or prejudiced. Amendment should be liberally allowed under this rule, including pleadings in the lower tribunal, if it would not result in irremediable prejudice.

Subdivision (e) is intended to make clear that assignments of error have been abolished by these rules. It is not intended to extend the scope of review to matters other than judicial acts. If less than the entire record as defined in rule 9.200(a)(1) is to be filed, rule 9.200(a)(3) requires service of a statement of the judicial acts for which review is sought. This requirement also applies under rule 9.140(d). As explained in the commentary accompanying those provisions, such a statement does not have the same legal effect as an

R. App. Proc.

assignment of error under the former rules.

Subdivision (f) permits payment of filing fees by check or money order and carries forward the substance of former rule 3.2(a), which allowed payments in cash.

Subdivision (g) is derived from former rules 3.2(a) and 3.2(e). Under these rules, notices and fees are filed in the lower tribunal unless specifically stated otherwise. The clerk must transmit the notice and fees immediately. This requirement replaces the provision of the former rules that the notice be transmitted within 5 days. The advisory committee was of the view that no reason existed for any delays. The term "forthwith" should not be construed to prevent the clerk from delaying transmittal of a notice of criminal appeal for which no fee has been filed for the period of time necessary to obtain an order regarding solvency for appellate purposes and the appointment of the public defender for an insolvent defendant. This provision requires recording of the notice if review of a final trial court order in a civil case is sought. When supreme court jurisdiction is invoked on the basis of the certification of a question of great public interest, the clerk of the district court of appeal is required to transmit a copy of the certificate and the decision to the court along with the notice and fees.

Subdivision (h) is intended to implement the decision in *Williams v. State,* 324 So.2d 74 (Fla.1975), in which it was held that only the timely filing of the notice of appeal is jurisdictional. The proviso permits the court to impose sanctions if there is a failure to timely file fees or copies of the notice or petition.

The advisory committee considered and rejected as too difficult to implement a proposal of the bar committee that the style of a cause should remain the same as in the lower tribunal.

It should be noted that these rules abolish the practice of permitting Florida trial courts to certify questions to an appellate court. The former rules relating to the internal government of the courts and the creation of the advisory committee have been eliminated as irrelevant to appellate procedure. At its conference of June 27, however, the court unanimously voted to establish a committee to, among other things, prepare a set of administrative rules to incorporate matters of internal governance formerly contained in the appellate rules. The advisory committee has recommended that its existence be continued by the supreme court.

1980 Amendment. Subdivision (g) was amended to direct the clerk of the district court to transmit copies of the district court decision, the certificate, the order of the trial court, and the suggestion, replies, and appendices in all cases certified to the supreme court under rule 9.030(a)(2)(B) or otherwise certified under rule 9.030(a)(2)(A)(v) or (a)(2)(A)(vi).

1992 Amendment. Subdivision (h) was amended to provide that the failure to attach conformed copies of the order or orders designated in a notice of appeal as is now required by rules 9.110(d), 9.130(c), and 9.160(c) would not be a jurisdictional defect, but could be the basis of appropriate sanction by the court if the conformed copies were not included with the notice of appeal.

2000 Amendment. In the event non-final or interlocutory review of a reviewable, non-final order is sought, new subdivision 9.040(b)(2) specifies which court should review such order, after rendition of an order transferring venue to another lower tribunal outside the appellate district of the transferor lower tribunal. It is intended to change and clarify the rules announced in *Vasilinda v. Lozano*, 631 So. 2d 1082 (Fla. 1994), and *Cottingham v. State*, 672 So. 2d 28 (Fla. 1996). The subdivision makes the time a venue order is rendered the critical factor in determining which court should review such non-final orders, rather than the time fees are paid, or the time the file is received by the transferee lower tribunal, and it applies equally to civil as well as criminal cases. If review is sought of the order transferring venue, as well as other reviewable non-final orders rendered before the change of venue order is rendered, or ones rendered simultaneously with it, review should be by the court that reviews such orders from the transferring lower tribunal. If review is sought of reviewable, non-final orders rendered after the time the venue order is rendered, review should be by the court that reviews such orders from the transferee lower tribunal. The only exceptions are for review of orders staying or vacating the transfer of venue order, or an order dismissing the cause for failure to pay fees, which should be reviewed by the court that reviews orders from the transferring lower tribunal. This paragraph is not intended to apply to review of reviewable non-final orders, for which non-final or interlocutory review is not timely sought or perfected.

Rule 9.100. Original Proceedings.

(a) Applicability. This rule applies to those proceedings that invoke the jurisdiction of the courts described in rules 9.030(a)(3), (b)(2), (b)(3), (c)(2), and (c)(3) for the issuance of writs of mandamus, prohibition, quo warranto, certiorari, and habeas corpus, and all writs necessary to the complete exercise of the courts' jurisdiction; and for review of non-final administrative action.

(b) Commencement; Parties. The original jurisdiction of the court shall be invoked by filing a petition, accompanied by a filing fee if prescribed by law, with the clerk of the court deemed to have jurisdiction. If the original jurisdiction of the court is invoked to enforce a private right, the proceeding shall not be brought on the relation of the state. If the petition seeks review of an order entered by a lower tribunal, all parties to the proceeding in the lower tribunal who are not named as petitioners shall be named as respondents.

(c) Exceptions; Petitions for Certiorari; Review of Non-Final Agency Action. The following shall be filed within 30 days of rendition of the order to be reviewed:

(1) A petition for certiorari.

(2) A petition to review quasi-judicial action of agencies, boards, and commissions of local government, which action is not directly appealable under any other provision of general law but may be subject to review by certiorari.

(3) A petition to review non-final agency action under the Administrative Procedure Act.

(4) A petition challenging an order of the Department of Corrections entered in prisoner disciplinary proceedings.

Lower court judges shall not be named as respondents to petitions for certiorari; individual members of the agencies, boards, and commissions of local government shall not be named as respondents to petitions for review of final quasi-judicial action; and hearing officers shall not be named as respondents to petitions for review of non-final agency action. A copy of the petition shall be furnished to the person (or chairperson of a collegial administrative agency) issuing the order.

(d) Exception; Orders Excluding Press or Public.

(1) A petition to review an order excluding the press or public from access to any proceeding, any part of a proceeding, or any judicial records, if the proceedings or records are not required by law to be confidential, shall be filed in the court as soon as practicable following rendition of the order to be reviewed, if written, or announcement of the order to be reviewed, if oral. A copy shall be furnished to the person (or chairperson of the collegial administrative agency) issuing the order, and to the parties to the proceeding.

(2) The court shall immediately consider the petition to determine whether a stay of proceedings in the lower tribunal is appropriate, and on its own motion or that of any party, the court may order a stay on such conditions as may be appropriate.

(3) If requested by the petitioner or any party, or on its own motion, the court may allow oral argument.

(e) Exception; Petitions for Writs of Mandamus and Prohibition Directed to a Judge or Lower Tribunal. When a petition for a writ of mandamus or prohibition seeks a writ directed to a judge or lower tribunal, the following procedures apply:

(1) Caption. The name of the judge or lower tribunal shall be omitted from the caption. The caption shall bear the name of the petitioner and other parties to the proceeding in the lower tribunal who are not petitioners shall be named in the caption of respondents.

(2) Parties. The judge or the lower tribunal is a formal party to the petition for mandamus or prohibition and must be named as such in the body of the petition (but not in the caption). The petition must be served on all parties, including any judge or lower tribunal who is a formal party to the petition.

(3) Response. The responsibility to respond to an order to show cause is that of the litigant opposing the relief requested in the petition. Unless otherwise specifically ordered, the judge or lower tribunal has no obligation to file a response. The judge or lower tribunal retains the discretion to file a separate response should the judge or lower tribunal choose to do so. The absence of a separate response by the judge or lower tribunal shall not be deemed to admit the allegations of the petition.

R. App. Proc.

(f) Review Proceedings in Circuit Court.

(1) Applicability. The following additional requirements apply to those proceedings that invoke the jurisdiction of the circuit court described in rules 9.030(c)(2) and (c)(3) to the extent that the petition involves review of judicial or quasi-judicial action.

(2) Caption. The caption shall contain a statement that the petition is filed pursuant to this subdivision.

(3) Duties of the Circuit Court Clerk. When a petition prescribed by this subdivision is filed, the circuit court clerk shall forthwith transmit the petition to the administrative judge of the appellate division, or other appellate judge or judges as prescribed by administrative order, for a determination as to whether an order to show cause should be issued.

(4) Default. The clerk of the circuit court shall not enter a default in a proceeding where a petition has been filed pursuant to this subdivision.

(g) Petition. The caption shall contain the name of the court and the name and designation of all parties on each side. The petition shall not exceed 50 pages in length and shall contain

(1) the basis for invoking the jurisdiction of the court;

(2) the facts on which the petitioner relies;

(3) the nature of the relief sought; and

(4) argument in support of the petition and appropriate citations of authority. If the petition seeks an order directed to a lower tribunal, the petition shall be accompanied by an appendix as prescribed by rule 9.220, and the petition shall contain references to the appropriate pages of the supporting appendix.

(h) Order to Show Cause. If the petition demonstrates a preliminary basis for relief, a departure from the essential requirements of law that will cause material injury for which there is no adequate remedy by appeal, or that review of final administrative action would not provide an adequate remedy, the court may issue an order directing the respondent to show cause, within the time set by the court, why relief should not be granted. In prohibition proceedings such orders shall stay further proceedings in the lower tribunal.

(i) Record. A record shall not be transmitted to the court unless ordered.

(j) Response. Within the time set by the court, the respondent may serve a response, which shall not exceed 50 pages in length and which shall include argument in support of the response, appropriate citations of authority, and references to the appropriate pages of the supporting appendices.

(k) Reply. Within 20 days thereafter or such other time set by the court, the petitioner may serve a reply, which shall not exceed 15 pages in length, and supplemental appendix.

(*l*) General Requirements; Fonts. The lettering in all petitions, responses, and replies filed under this rule shall be black and in distinct type, double-spaced, with margins no less than 1 inch. Lettering in script or type made in imitation of handwriting shall not be permitted. Footnotes and quotations may be single spaced and shall be in the same size type, with the same spacing between characters, as the text. Computer-generated petitions, responses, and replies shall be submitted in either Times New Roman 14-point font or Courier New 12-point font. All computer-generated petitions, responses, and replies shall contain a certificate of compliance signed by counsel, or the party if unrepresented, certifying that the petition, response, or reply complies with the font requirements of this rule. The certificate of compliance shall be contained in the petition, response, or reply immediately following the certificate of service.

History: Amended March 27, 1980, effective April 1, 1980 (381 So.2d 1370); July 3, 1980, effective Jan. 1, 1981 (387 So.2d 920); Nov. 26, 1980, effective Jan. 1, 1981 (391 So.2d 203); July 14, 1988, effective Jan 1, 1989 (529 So.2d 687); Dec. 30, 1988, effective Jan. 1, 1989 (536 So.2d 240); Oct. 22, 1992, effective Jan. 1, 1993 (609 So.2d 516); Nov. 22, 1996, effective Jan. 1, 1997 (685 So.2d 773); Nov. 24, 1999, effective Jan. 1, 2000 (24 Fla. L. Weekly S561); amended Oct. 12, 2000, effective Jan. 1, 2001 (780 So. 2d 834; 2000 Fla. LEXIS 2273; 25 Fla. L. Weekly S 835).

Committee Notes

1977 Amendment. This rule replaces former rule 4.5, except that the procedures applicable to supreme court review of decisions of the district courts of appeal on writs of constitutional certiorari are set forth in rule 9.120; and supreme court direct review of administrative action on writs of certiorari is governed by rule 9.100. This rule governs proceedings invoking the supreme court's jurisdiction to review an interlocutory order passing on a matter where, on final judgment, a direct appeal would lie in the supreme court. The procedures set forth in this rule implement the supreme court's decision in *Burnsed v. Seaboard Coastline R. R.,* 290 So.2d 13 (Fla.1974), that such interlocutory review rests solely within its discretionary certiorari jurisdiction under article V, section 3(b)(3), Florida Constitution, and that its jurisdiction would be exercised only when, on the peculiar circumstances of a particular case, the public interest required it. This rule abolishes the wasteful current practice in such cases of following the procedures governing appeals, with the supreme court treating such appeals as petitions for the writ of certiorari. This rule requires that these cases be prosecuted as petitions for the writ of certiorari.

This rule also provides the procedures necessary to implement the Administrative Procedure Act, section 120.68(1), Florida Statutes (Supp.1976), which provides for judicial review of non-final agency action "if review of the final agency decision would not provide an adequate remedy." It was the opinion of the advisory committee that such a right of review is guaranteed by the statute and is not dependent on a court rule, because article V, section 4(b)(2), Florida Constitution provides for legislative grants of jurisdiction to the district courts to review administrative action without regard to the finality of that action. The advisory committee was also of the view that the right of review guaranteed by the statute is no broader than the generally available common law writ of certiorari, although the statutory remedy would prevent resort to an extraordinary writ.

Subdivisions (b) and (c) set forth the procedure for commencing an extraordinary writ proceeding. The time for filing a petition for common law certiorari is jurisdictional. If common law certiorari is sought to review an order issued by a lower tribunal consisting of more than 1 person, a copy of the petition should be furnished to the chairperson of that tribunal.

Subdivision (d) sets forth the procedure for appellate review of orders excluding the press or public from access to proceedings or records in the lower tribunal. It establishes an entirely new and independent means of review in the district courts, in recognition of the decision in *English v. McCrary,* 348 So.2d 293 (Fla.1977), to the effect that a writ of prohibition is not available as a means to obtain review of such orders. Copies of the notice must be served on all parties to the proceeding in the lower tribunal, as well as the person who, or the chairperson of the agency that, issued the order.

No provision has been made for an automatic stay of proceedings, but the district court is directed to consider the appropriateness of a stay immediately on the notice being filed. Ordinarily an order excluding the press and public will be entered well in advance of the closed proceedings in the lower tribunal, so that there will be no interruption of the proceeding by reason of the appellate review. In the event a challenged order is entered immediately before or during the course of a proceeding and it appears that a disruption of the proceeding will be prejudicial to 1 or more parties, the reviewing court on its own motion or at the request of any party shall determine whether to enter a stay or to allow the lower tribunal to proceed pending review of the challenged order. See *State ex rel. Miami Herald Publishing Co. v. McIntosh,* 340 So.2d 904, 911 (Fla.1977).

This new provision implements the "strict procedural safeguards" requirement laid down by the United States Supreme Court in *National Socialist Party of America v. Village of Skokie,* 432 U.S. 43, 97 S.Ct. 2205, 53 L.Ed.2d 96 (1977). In that case the Court held that state restraints imposed on activities protected by the First Amendment. must be either immediately reviewable or subject to a stay pending review.

Subdivision (g) sets forth the contents of the initial pleading. The party seeking relief must file a petition stating the authority by which the court has jurisdiction of the case, the relevant facts, the relief sought, and argument supported by citations of authority. This rule does not allow the petitioner to file a brief. Any argument or citations of authority that the petitioner desires to present to the court must be contained in the petition. This change in procedure is intended to eliminate the wasteful current practice of filing repetitive petitions and briefs. Under subdivision (i) no record is required to be filed unless the court so orders, but under subdivision (g) the petitioner must file an appendix to the petition containing conformed copies of the order to be reviewed and other relevant material, including portions of the record, if a record exists. The appendix should also contain any documents that support the allegations of fact contained in the petition. A lack of supporting documents may, of course, be considered by the court in exercising its discretion not to issue an order to show cause.

Under subdivisions (h), (j), and (k), if the allegations

R. App. Proc.

of the petition, if true, would constitute grounds for relief, the court may exercise its discretion to issue an order requiring the respondent to show cause why the requested relief should not be granted. A single responsive pleading (without a brief) may then be served, accompanied by a supplemental appendix, within the time period set by the court in its order to show cause. The petitioner is then allowed 20 days to serve a reply and supplemental appendix, unless the court sets another time. It should be noted that the times for response and reply are computed by reference to service rather than filing. This practice is consistent throughout these rules except for initial, jurisdictional filings. The emphasis on service, of course, does not relieve counsel of the responsibility for filing original documents with the court as required by rule 9.420(b); it merely affects the time measurements.

Except as provided automatically under subdivision (h), a stay pending resolution of the original proceeding may be obtained under rule 9.310.

Transmittal of the record under order of the court under subdivision (i) shall be in accordance with the instructions and times set forth in the order.

1980 Amendment. The rule was amended by deleting its reference to former rule 9.030(a)(2)(B) to reflect the 1980 revisions to article V, section 3(b), Florida Constitution that eliminated supreme court review by certiorari of non-final orders that would have been appealable if they had been final orders. The procedures applicable to discretionary supreme court review of district court decisions under rule 9.030(a)(2)(A) are governed by rule 9.120. The procedures applicable to supreme court discretionary review of trial court orders and judgments certified by the district courts under rule 9.030(a)(2)(B) are set forth in rule 9.125.

Subdivision (d) was amended to delete references to the district courts of appeal as the proper court for review of orders excluding the press and public, because the appropriate court could also be a circuit court or the supreme court.

1992 Amendment. Subdivision (b) was amended to add 2 provisions clarifying designation of parties to original proceedings. The first change eliminates the practice of bringing original proceedings on the relation of the state and instead requires that if a private right is being enforced, an action must be brought in the names of the parties. Second, this subdivision now requires that all parties not named as petitioners be included in the style as respondents, consistent with rules 9.020(f)(3) and (f)(4).

Subdivision (c) was amended to eliminate the practice of naming lower court judges, members of administrative bodies, and hearing officers as respondents in petitions for certiorari and for review of non-final agency action. Such individuals still are to be served a copy of the petition, but the amendment is to eliminate any suggestion that they are parties or adverse to the petitioner.

Subdivision (c) also was amended to reflect that review of final administrative action, taken by local government agencies, boards, and commissions acting in a quasi-judicial capacity, is subject to the requirement that the petition for writ of certiorari be filed within 30 days of rendition of the order to be reviewed.

Subdivision (g) was amended to require that the petition, the jurisdictional document, identify all parties on each side to assist the court in identifying any potential conflicts and to identify all parties to the proceeding as required by subdivision (b) of this rule. Additionally, this subdivision was amended to require, consistent with rule 9.210(b)(3), that the petition make references to the appropriate pages of the appendix that is required to accompany the petition.

Subdivision (h) was amended to add the existing requirement in the law that a petition must demonstrate not only that there has been a departure from the essential requirements of law, but also that that departure will cause material injury for which there is no adequate remedy by appeal. This subdivision, without amendment, suggested that it established a standard other than that recognized by Florida decisional law.

Subdivision (j) was amended to require that any response, like the petition, contain references to the appropriate pages of appendices, consistent with subdivision (f) of this rule and rules 9.210(b)(3) and 9.210(c).

1996 Amendment. The reference to "common law" certiorari in subdivision (c)(1) was removed so as to make clear that the 30-day filing limit applies to all petitions for writ of certiorari.

Subdivision (c)(4) is new and pertains to review formerly available under rule 1.630. It provides that a prisoner's petition for extraordinary relief, within the original jurisdiction of the circuit court under rule 9.030(c)(3) must be filed within 30 days after final disposition of the prisoner disciplinary proceedings conducted through the administrative grievance process under chapter 33, Florida Administrative Code. *See Jones v. Florida Department of Corrections,* 615 So. 2d 798 (Fla. 1st DCA 1993).

Subdivision (e) was added, and subsequent subdivisions re-lettered, in order to alter the procedural requirements placed or apparently placed on lower court judges in prohibition and mandamus proceedings. The duty to respond to an Order to Show Cause is expressly placed on the party opposing the relief requested in the petition, and any suggestion of a duty to respond on the part of the lower court judge is removed. The lower court judge retains the option to file a response. In those circumstances in which a response from the lower tribunal is desirable, the court may so order.

Subdivision (f) was added to clarify that in extraordinary proceedings to review lower tribunal action this rule, and not Florida Rule of Civil Procedure 1.630, applies and to specify the duties of the clerk in such proceedings, and to provide a mechanism for alerting the clerk to the necessity of following these procedures. If the proceeding before the circuit court is or may be evidentiary in nature, then the procedures of the Florida Rules of Civil Procedure should be followed.

Court Commentary

2000. As to computer-generated petitions, re &hardhyph; sponses, and replies, strict font requirements were imposed in subdivision (*l*) for at least three reasons:

First and foremost, appellate petitions, responses, and replies are public records that the people have a right to inspect. The clear policy of the Florida Supreme Court is that advances in technology should benefit the people whenever possible by lowering financial and physical barriers to public record inspection. The Court's eventual goal is to make all public records widely and readily available, especially via the Internet. Unlike paper documents, electronic documents on the Internet will not display properly on all computers if they are set in fonts that are unusual. In some instances, such electronic documents may even be unreadable. Thus, the Court adopted the policy that all computer-generated appellate petitions, responses, and replies be filed in one of two fonts either Times New Roman 14-point or Courier New 12-point that are commonplace on computers with Internet connections. This step will help ensure that the right to inspect public records on the Internet will be genuinely available to the largest number of people.

Second, Florida's court system as a whole is working toward the day when electronic filing of all court documents will be an everyday reality. Though the technology involved in electronic filing is changing rapidly, it is clear that the Internet is the single most significant factor influencing the development of this technology. Electronic filing must be compatible with Internet standards as they evolve over time. It is imperative for the legal profession to become accustomed to using electronic document formats that are most consistent with the Internet.

Third, the proliferation of vast new varieties of fonts in recent years poses a real threat that page-limitation rules can be circumvented through computerized typesetting. The only way to prevent this is to establish an enforceable rule on standards for font use. The subject font requirements are most consistent with this purpose and the other two purposes noted above.

Subdivision (*l*) was also amended to require that immediately after the certificate of service in computer-generated petitions, responses, and replies, counsel (or the party if unrepresented) shall sign a certificate of compliance with the font standards set forth in this rule for computer-generated petitions, responses, and replies.

Rule 9.110. Appeal Proceedings to Review Final Orders of Lower Tribunals and Orders Granting New Trial in Jury and Non-Jury Cases.

(a) Applicability. This rule applies to those proceedings that

(1) invoke the appeal jurisdiction of the courts described in rules 9.030(a)(1), (b)(1)(A), and (c)(1)(A);

(2) seek review of orders entered in probate and guardianship matters that finally determine a right or obligation of an interested person as defined in the Florida Probate Code;

(3) seek review of administrative action described in rules 9.030(b)(1)(C) and (c)(1)(C); and

(4) seek review of orders granting a new trial in jury and non-jury civil and criminal cases described in rules 9.130(a)(4) and 9.140(c)(1)(C).

(b) Commencement. Jurisdiction of the court under this rule shall be invoked by filing 2 copies of a notice, accompanied by filing fees prescribed by law, with the clerk of the lower tribunal within 30 days of rendition of the order to be reviewed.

(c) Exception; Administrative Action. In an appeal to review final orders of lower administrative tribunals, the appellant shall file the

R. App. Proc.

original notice with the clerk of the lower administrative tribunal within 30 days of rendition of the order to be reviewed, and file a copy of the notice, accompanied by the filing fees prescribed by law, with the clerk of the court.

(d) Notice of Appeal. The notice of appeal shall be substantially in the form prescribed by rule 9.900(a). The caption shall contain the name of the lower tribunal, the name and designation of at least 1 party on each side, and the case number in the lower tribunal. The notice shall contain the name of the court to which the appeal is taken, the date of rendition, and the nature of the order to be reviewed. Except in criminal cases, a conformed copy of the order or orders designated in the notice of appeal shall be attached to the notice together with any order entered on a timely motion postponing rendition of the order or orders appealed.

(e) Record. Within 50 days of filing the notice, the clerk shall prepare the record prescribed by rule 9.200 and serve copies of the index on all parties. Within 110 days of filing the notice, the clerk shall transmit the record to the court.

(f) Briefs. Appellant's initial brief shall be served within 70 days of filing the notice. Additional briefs shall be served as prescribed by rule 9.210.

(g) Cross-Appeal. An appellee may cross-appeal by serving a notice within 10 days of service of the appellant's notice or within the time prescribed in subdivision (b) of this rule, whichever is later. No filing fee shall be required for a cross-appeal.

(h) Scope of Review. The court may review any ruling or matter occurring before filing of the notice. Multiple final orders may be reviewed by a single notice, if the notice is timely filed as to each such order.

(i) Exception; Bond Validation Proceedings. If the appeal is from an order in a proceeding to validate bonds or certificates of indebtedness, the record shall not be transmitted unless ordered by the supreme court. Appellant's initial brief, accompanied by an appendix as prescribed by rule 9.220, shall be served within 20 days of filing the notice. Additional briefs shall be served as prescribed by rule 9.210.

(j) Exception; Appeal Proceedings From District Courts of Appeal. If the appeal is from an order of a district court of appeal, the clerk shall transmit the record to the court within 60 days of filing the notice. Appellant's initial brief shall be served within 20 days of filing the notice. Additional briefs shall be served as prescribed by rule 9.210.

(k) Review of Partial Final Judgments. Except as otherwise provided herein, partial final judgments are reviewable either on appeal from the partial final judgment or on appeal from the final judgment in the entire case. If a partial final judgment totally disposes of an entire case as to any party, it must be appealed within 30 days of rendition.

(*l*) Premature Appeals. If a notice of appeal is filed before rendition of a final order, the appeal shall be subject to dismissal as premature. However, if a final order is rendered before dismissal of the premature appeal, the premature notice of appeal shall be considered effective to vest jurisdiction in the court to review the final order. Before dismissal, the court in its discretion may permit the lower tribunal to render a final order.

(m) Exception; Insurance Coverage Appeals. Judgments that determine the existence or nonexistence of insurance coverage in cases in which a claim has been made against an insured and coverage thereof is disputed by the insurer may be reviewed either by the method prescribed in this rule or that in rule 9.130.

History: Amended March 27, 1980, effective April 1, 1980 (381 So.2d 1370); Nov. 26, 1980, effective Jan. 1, 1981 (391 So.2d 203); Sept. 13, 1984, effective Jan. 1, 1985 (463 So.2d 1114); amended effective Oct. 17, 1988 (536 So.2d 198); amended Oct. 22, 1992, effective Jan. 1, 1993 (609 So.2d 516); Nov. 22, 1996, effective Jan. 1, 1997 (685 So.2d 773); June 24, 1999, effective July 1, 1999 (24 Fla. L.Weekly S300); amended Oct. 23, 2003, effective Oct. 23, 2003 (28 Fla. L. Weekly S549).

Committee Notes

1977 Amendment. This rule replaces former rules 3.1, 3.5, 4.1, 4.3, 4.4, and 4.7. It applies when (1) a final order has been entered by a court or administrative agency; (2) a motion for a new trial in a jury case is granted; or (3) a motion for rehearing in a non-jury case is granted and the lower tribunal orders new testimony. It should be noted that certain other non-final orders entered after the final order are reviewable under the procedure set forth in rule 9.130. This rule does not apply to review proceedings in such cases.

Except to the extent of conflict with rule 9.140 governing appeals in criminal cases, this rule governs: (1) appeals as of right to the supreme court; (2) certiorari proceedings before the supreme court seeking direct review of administrative action (for example, Industrial Relations Commission and Public Service Commission); (3) appeals as of right to a district court of appeal, including petitions for review of administrative action under the Administrative Procedure Act, section 120.68, Florida Statutes (Supp.1976); (4) appeals as of right to a circuit court, including review of administrative action if provided by law.

This rule is intended to clarify the procedure for review of orders granting a new trial. Rules 9.130(a)(4) and 9.140(c)(1)(C) authorize the appeal of orders granting a motion for new trial. Those rules supersede *Clement v. Aztec Sales, Inc.,* 297 So.2d 1 (Fla.1974), and are consistent with the decision there. Under subdivision (h) of this rule the scope of review of the court is not necessarily limited to the order granting a new trial. The supreme court has held that "appeals taken from new trial orders shall be treated as appeals from final judgments to the extent possible." *Bowen v. Willard,* 340 So.2d 110, 112 (Fla.1976). This rule implements that decision.

Subdivisions (b) and (c) establish the procedure for commencing an appeal proceeding. Within 30 days of the rendition of the final order the appellant must file 2 copies of the notice of appeal, accompanied by the appropriate fees, with the clerk of the lower tribunal; except that if review of administrative action is sought, 1 copy of the notice and the applicable fees must be filed in the court. Failure to file any notice within the 30-day period constitutes an irremediable jurisdictional defect, but the second copy and fees may be filed after the 30-day period, subject to sanctions imposed by the court. See *Williams v. State,* 324 So.2d 74 (Fla.1975); Fla.R.App.P. 9.040(h).

Subdivision (d) sets forth the contents of the notice and eliminates the requirement of the former rule that the notice show the place of recordation of the order to be reviewed. The rule requires substantial compliance with the form approved by the supreme court. The date of rendition of the order for which review is sought must appear on the face of the notice. See the definition of "rendition" in Florida Rule of Appellate Procedure 9.020, and see the judicial construction of "rendition" for an administrative rule in *Florida Admin. Comm'n v. Judges of the District Court,* 351 So.2d 712 (Fla.1977), on review of *Riley-Field Co. v. Askew,* 336 So.2d 383 (Fla. 1st DCA 1976). This requirement is intended to allow the clerk of the court to determine the timeliness of the notice from its face. The advisory committee intended that defects in the notice would not be jurisdictional or grounds for disposition unless the complaining party was substantially prejudiced.

This rule works significant changes in the review of final administrative action. The former rules required that a traditional petition for the writ of certiorari be filed if supreme court review was appropriate, and the practice under the Administrative Procedure Act, section 120.68, Florida Statutes (Supp.1976), has been for the "petition for review" to be substantially similar to a petition for the writ of certiorari. See *Yamaha Int'l Corp. v. Ehrman,* 318 So.2d 196 (Fla. 1st DCA 1975). This rule eliminates the need for true petitions in such cases. Instead, a simple notice is filed, to be followed later by briefs. It is intended that the notice constitute the petition required in section 120.68(2), Florida Statutes (Supp.1976). There is no conflict with the statute because the substance of the review proceeding remains controlled by the statute, and the legislature directed that review be under the procedures set forth in these rules. Because it is a requirement of rendition that an order be written and filed, this rule supersedes *Shevin ex rel. State v. Public Service Comm'n,* 333 So.2d 9 (Fla.1976), and *School Bd. v. Malbon,* 341 So.2d 523 (Fla. 2d DCA 1977), to the extent that those decisions assume that reduction of an order to writing is unnecessary for judicial review.

This rule is not intended to affect the discretionary nature of direct supreme court review of administrative action taken under the certiorari jurisdiction of that court set forth in article V, section 3(b)(3), Florida Constitution. Such proceedings remain in certiorari with the only change being to replace wasteful, repetitive petitions for the writ of certiorari with concise notices followed at a later date by briefs. The parties to such actions should be designated as "petitioner" and "respondent" despite the use of the terms "appellant" and "appellee" in this rule. See commentary, Fla.R.App.P. 9.020.

Subdivisions (e), (f), and (g) set the times for preparation of the record, serving copies of the index on the parties, serving briefs, and serving notices of cross-appeal. Provision for cross-appeal notices has been made to replace the cross-assignments of error eliminated by these rules. In certiorari proceedings governed by this rule the term "cross-appeal" should be read as equivalent to "cross-petition." It should be noted that if time is measured by service, rule 9.420(b) requires filing to be made before service or immediately thereafter.

Subdivision (h) permits a party to file a single notice of appeal if a single proceeding in the lower tribunal, whether criminal or civil, results in more than 1 final judgment and an appeal of more than 1 is sought. This rule is intended to further the policies underlying the decisions of the supreme court in *Scheel v. Advance Marketing Consultants, Inc.,* 277 So.2d 773 (Fla.1973), and *Hollimon v. State,* 232 So.2d 394 (Fla.1970). This rule does not authorize the appeal of multiple final judgments unless otherwise proper as to each. If a prematurely filed notice is held in abeyance in accordance with *Williams v. State,* 324 So.2d 74 (Fla.1975), the date of filing is intended to be the date the notice becomes effective.

Subdivision (i) provides an expedited procedure in appeals as of right to the supreme court in bond validation proceedings. An appendix is mandatory.

Subdivision (j) provides for an expedited procedure in appeals as of right to the supreme court from an order of a district court of appeal.

1980 Amendment. The rule has been amended to incorporate changes in rule 9.030 and to reflect the abolition of supreme court jurisdiction to review, if provided by general law, final orders of trial courts imposing sentences of life imprisonment.

The reference indicated (2) in the second paragraph of this committee note for 1977 amendment should be disregarded. See amended rule 9.030(a)(1)(B)(ii) and accompanying committee note.

1984 Amendment. Subdivision (k) was added to remedy a pitfall in the application of case law under *Mendez v. West Flagler Family Association,* 303 So.2d 1 (Fla.1974). Appeals may now be taken immediately or delayed until the end of the entire case, under the rationale of *Mendez* .

1992 Amendment. Subdivision (d) was amended to require that the appellant, except in criminals cases, attach to its notice of appeal a conformed copy of any orders designated in the notice of appeal, along with any orders on motions that postponed the rendition of orders appealed. This amendment is designed to assist the clerk in determining the nature and type of order being appealed and the timeliness of any such appeal.

Subdivision (m) was added to clarify the effect of a notice of appeal filed by a party before the lower court renders a final appealable order. Under this subdivision, such a notice of appeal is subject to dismissal as premature, but a final order rendered before the dismissal of the appeal will vest the appellate court with jurisdiction to review that final order. It further provides that the appellate court may relinquish jurisdiction or otherwise allow the lower court to render such a final order before dismissal of the appeal. If the only motion that is delaying rendition has been filed by the party filing the notice of appeal, under rule 9.020(g)(3), such motion is deemed abandoned and the final order is deemed rendered by the filing of a notice of appeal.

1996 Amendment. The addition of new subdivision (a)(2) is a restatement of former Florida Rule of Probate Procedure 5.100, and is not intended to change the definition of final order for appellate purposes. It recognizes that in probate and guardianship proceedings it is not unusual to have several final orders entered during the course of the proceeding that address many different issues and involve many different persons. An order of the circuit court that determines a right, an obligation, or the standing of an interested person as defined in the Florida Probate Code may be appealed before the administration of the probate or guardianship is complete and the fiduciary is discharged.

Subdivision (c) was amended to reflect that in appeals of administrative orders, the appellate court filing fees should be filed in the appellate court, not the administrative tribunal.

Subdivision (n) was added by the committee in response to the opinion in *Canal Insurance Co. v. Reed,* 666 So. 2d 888 (Fla. 1996), suggesting that the Appellate Court Rules Committee consider an appropriate method for providing expedited review of these cases to avoid unnecessary delays in the final resolution of the underlying actions. Expedited review in the manner provided in rule 9.130 is available for such judgments in cases where a claim against the insured is pending and early resolution of the coverage issue is in the best interest of the parties. The notice of appeal should identify whether a party is seeking review pursuant to the procedure provided in this rule or in rule 9.130.

Rule 9.120. Discretionary Proceedings to Review Decisions of District Courts of Appeal.

(a) Applicability. This rule applies to those proceedings that invoke the discretionary jurisdiction of the supreme court described in rule 9.030(a)(2)(A).

(b) Commencement. The jurisdiction of the supreme court described in rule 9.030(a)(2)(A) shall be invoked by filing 2 copies of a notice, accompanied by the filing fees prescribed by law, with the clerk of the district court of appeal within 30 days of rendition of the order to be reviewed.

(c) Notice. The notice shall be substantially in the form prescribed by rule 9.900. The caption shall contain the name of the lower tribunal, the name and designation of at least 1 party on each side, and the case number in the lower tribunal.The notice shall contain the date of rendition of the order to be reviewed and the basis for invoking the jurisdiction of the court.

(d) Briefs on Jurisdiction. Petitioner's brief, limited solely to the issue of the supreme court's jurisdiction and accompanied by an appendix containing only a conformed copy of the decision of the district court of appeal, shall be served within 10 days of filing the notice. Respondent's brief on jurisdiction shall be served within 20 days after service of petitioner's brief. Formal requirements for both briefs are specified in rule 9.210. No reply brief shall be permitted. If jurisdiction is invoked under rules 9.030(a)(2)(A)(v) or (a)(2)(A)(vi) (certifications by the district courts to the supreme court), no briefs on jurisdiction shall be filed.

(e) Accepting or Postponing Decision on Jurisdiction; Record. If the supreme court accepts or postpones decision on jurisdiction, the court shall so order and advise the parties and the clerk of the district court of appeal. Within 60 days thereafter or such other time set by the court, the clerk shall transmit the record.

(f) Briefs on Merits. Within 20 days of rendition of the order accepting or postponing decision on jurisdiction, the petitioner shall serve the initial brief on the merits, accompanied by an appendix that must include a conformed copy of the decision of the district court of appeal. Additional briefs shall be served as prescribed by rule 9.210.

History: Amended March 27, 1980, effective April 1, 1980 (381 So.2d 1370); Nov. 26, 1980, effective Jan. 1, 1981 (391 So.2d 203); Oct. 22, 1992, effective Jan. 1, 1993 (609 So.2d 516); amended Oct. 12, 2000, effective Jan. 1, 2001 (780 So. 2d 834; 2000 Fla. LEXIS 2273; 25 Fla. L. Weekly S 835); Aug. 29, 2002, effective Jan. 1, 2003.

Committee Notes

1977 Amendment. This rule replaces former rule 4.5(c) and governs all certiorari proceedings to review final decisions of the district courts. Certiorari proceedings to review interlocutory orders of the district courts if supreme court jurisdiction exists under article V, section 3(b)(3), Florida Constitution are governed by rule 9.100.

Subdivision (b) sets forth the manner in which certiorari proceedings in the supreme court are to be commenced. Petitions for the writ are abolished and replaced by a simple notice to be followed by briefs. Two copies of the notice, which must substantially comply with the form approved by the supreme court, are to be filed with the clerk of the district court within 30 days of rendition along with the requisite fees. Failure to timely file the fees is not jurisdictional.

Subdivision (c) sets forth the contents of the notice. The requirement that the notice state the date of rendition, as defined in rule 9.020, is intended to permit the clerk of the court to determine timeliness from the face of the notice. The statement of the basis for jurisdiction should be a concise reference to whether the order sought to be reviewed (1) conflicts with other Florida appellate decisions; (2) affects a class of constitutional or state officers; or (3) involves a question of great public interest certified by the district court.

Subdivision (d) establishes the time for filing jurisdictional briefs and prescribes their content. If supreme court jurisdiction is based on certification of a question of great public interest, no jurisdictional briefs are permitted. Briefs on the merits in such cases are to be prepared in the same manner as in other cases. Briefs on the merits are to be served within the time provided after the court has ruled that it will accept jurisdiction or has ruled that it will postpone decision on jurisdiction.

The jurisdictional brief should be a short, concise statement of the grounds for invoking jurisdiction and the necessary facts. It is not appropriate to argue the merits of the substantive issues involved in the case or discuss any matters not relevant to the threshold jurisdictional issue. The petitioner may wish to include a very short statement of why the supreme court should exercise its discretion and entertain the case on the merits if it finds it does have certiorari jurisdiction. An appendix must be filed containing a conformed copy of the decision of the district court. If the decision of the district court was without opinion, or otherwise does not set forth the basis of decision with sufficient clarity to enable the supreme court to deter-

R. App. Proc.

mine whether grounds for jurisdiction exist, a conformed copy of the order of the trial court should also be included in the appendix.

Subdivisions (e) and (f) provide that within 60 days of the date of the order accepting jurisdiction, or postponing decision on jurisdiction, the clerk of the district court must transmit the record to the court. The petitioner has 20 days from the date of the order to serve the initial brief on the merits. Other briefs may then be served in accordance with rule 9.210. Briefs that are served must be filed in accordance with rule 9.420.

It should be noted that the automatic stay provided by former rule 4.5(c)(6) has been abolished because it encouraged the filing of frivolous petitions and was regularly abused. A stay pending review may be obtained under rule 9.310. If a stay has been ordered pending appeal to a district court, it remains effective under rule 9.310(e) unless the mandate issues or the district court vacates it. The advisory committee was of the view that the district courts should permit such stays only when essential. Factors to be considered are the likelihood that jurisdiction will be accepted by the supreme court, the likelihood of ultimate success on the merits, the likelihood of harm if no stay is granted, and the remediable quality of any such harm.

1980 Amendment. The rule has been amended to reflect the 1980 revisions to article V, section 3, Florida Constitution creating the additional categories of certifications by the district courts to the supreme court enumerated in rule 9.030(a)(2)(A).

District court decisions that (a) expressly declare valid a state statute, (b) expressly construe a provision of the state or federal constitution, (c) expressly affect a class of constitutional or state officers, (d) expressly and directly conflict with a decision of another district court or the supreme court on the same point of law, (e) pass upon a question certified to be of great public importance, or (f) are certified to be in direct conflict with decisions of other district courts, are reviewed according to the procedures set forth in this rule. No jurisdictional briefs are permitted if jurisdiction is based on certification of a question of great public importance or certification that the decision is in direct conflict with a decision of another district court.

The mandatory appendix must contain a copy of the district court decision sought to be reviewed and should be prepared in accordance with rule 9.220.

Supreme court review of trial court orders and judgments certified by the district court under rule 9.030(a)(2)(B) is governed by the procedures set forth in rule 9.125.

Reply briefs from petitioners are prohibited, and the court will decide whether to accept the case for review solely on the basis of petitioner's initial and respondent's responsive jurisdictional briefs.

1992 Amendment. Subdivision (d) was amended to provide that jurisdictional briefs must conform to the same requirements set forth in rule 9.210.

Rule 9.125. Review of Trial Court Orders and Judgments Certified by the District Courts of Appeal as Requiring Immediate Resolution by the Supreme Court.

(a) Applicability. This rule applies to any order or judgment of a trial court that has been certified by the district court of appeal to require immediate resolution by the supreme court because the issues pending in the district court are of great public importance or have a great effect on the proper administration of justice throughout the state. The district court of appeal may make such certification on its own motion or on suggestion by a party.

(b) Commencement. The jurisdiction of the supreme court is invoked on rendition of the certificate by the district court of appeal.

(c) Suggestion. Any party may file with the district court and serve on the parties a suggestion that the order to be reviewed should be certified by the district court to the supreme court. The suggestion shall be substantially in the form prescribed by this rule and shall be filed within 10 days from the filing of the notice of appeal.

(d) Response. Any party may file a response within 5 days of the service of the suggestion.

(e) Form. The suggestion shall be limited to 5 pages and shall contain all of the following elements:

(1) A statement of why the appeal requires immediate resolution by the supreme court.

(2) A statement of why the appeal

(A) is of great public importance, or

(B) will have a great effect on the proper administration of justice throughout the state.

(3) A certificate signed by the attorney stat-

ing: I express a belief, based on a reasoned and studied professional judgment, that this appeal requires immediate resolution by the supreme court and (a) is of great public importance, or (b) will have a great effect on the administration of justice throughout the state.

/s/ ______________

Attorney for ______________ (name of party)

______________ (address and phone number)

Florida Bar No. ______________

(4) An appendix containing a conformed copy of the order to be reviewed.

(f) Effect of Suggestion. The district court shall not be required to rule on the suggestion and neither the filing of a suggestion nor the rendition by the district court of its certificate shall alter the applicable time limitations or place of filing. If an order is rendered granting or denying certification, no rehearing shall be permitted.

(g) Procedure When Supreme Court Accepts Jurisdiction. The jurisdiction of the supreme court attaches on rendition of the order accepting jurisdiction. If the supreme court accepts jurisdiction, it shall so order and advise the parties, the clerk of the district court, and the clerk of the lower tribunal. The clerk of the district court shall transfer the record in the case to the supreme court within 10 days thereafter. The time limitations of the applicable jurisdictional rule will continue in effect, except that all papers formerly required to be filed in the district court shall be filed in the supreme court.

History: Adopted March 27, 1980, effective April 1, 1980 (381 So.2d 1370). Amended Nov. 26, 1980, effective Jan. 1, 1981 (391 So.2d 203); Oct. 22, 1992, effective Jan. 1, 1993 (609 So.2d 516); amended Oct. 12, 2000, effective Jan. 1, 2001 (780 So. 2d 834; 2000 Fla. LEXIS 2273; 25 Fla. L. Weekly S 835).

Committee Notes

1980 Amendment. This rule is entirely new and governs all discretionary proceedings to review trial court orders or judgments that have been certified by the district court under rule 9.030(a)(2)(B) to require immediate resolution by the supreme court and to be of great public importance or to have a great effect on the proper administration of justice throughout the state. Final and nonfinal orders are covered by this rule. Discretionary review of other district court decisions if supreme court jurisdiction exists under rule 9.030(a)(2)(A) is governed by rule 9.120.

Subdivision (b) makes clear that certification by the district court is self-executing.

Subdivision (c) sets forth the manner in which a party may file a suggestion that the order to be reviewed should be certified by the district court to the supreme court and requires the suggestion be filed within 10 days from the filing of the notice of appeal. It is contemplated that suggestions under this rule will be rare. A suggestion should be filed only if, under the peculiar circumstances of a case, all the elements contained in subdivision (e) of the rule are present.

Subdivision (d) provides that any other party may file a response to a suggestion within 5 days of the service of the suggestion.

Subdivision (e) provides for the form of the suggestion. All suggestions must be substantially in this form. The suggestion is limited to 5 pages and must contain (1) a statement of why the appeal requires immediate resolution by the supreme court, and (2) a statement of why the appeal either is of great public importance or will have a great effect on the proper administration of justice throughout the state. The suggestion must be accompanied by an appendix containing a copy of the order to be reviewed. The suggestion also must include a certificate signed by the attorney in the form appearing in the rule.

To ensure that no proceeding is delayed because of this rule, subdivisions (f) and (g) provide that the filing of a suggestion will not alter the applicable time limitations or the place of filing. The district court shall not be required to rule on a suggestion. The parties should follow the time limitations contained in the rule through which jurisdiction of the district court was invoked. See rules 9.100, 9.110, 9.130, and 9.140.

Rule 9.130. Proceedings to Review Non-Final Orders and Specified Final Orders.

(a) Applicability.

(1) This rule applies to appeals to the district courts of appeal of the non-final orders authorized herein and to appeals to the circuit court of non-final orders when provided by general law. Review of other non-final orders in such courts and non-final administrative action shall be by the method prescribed by rule 9.100.

(2) Appeals of non-final orders in criminal cases shall be as prescribed by rule 9.140.

R. App. Proc.

(3) Appeals to the district courts of appeal of non-final orders are limited to those that

(A) concern venue;

(B) grant, continue, modify, deny, or dissolve injunctions, or refuse to modify or dissolve injunctions;

(C) determine

(i) the jurisdiction of the person;

(ii) the right to immediate possession of property;

(iii) the right to immediate monetary relief or child custody in family law matters;

(iv) the entitlement of a party to arbitration;

(v) that, as a matter of law, a party is not entitled to workers' compensation immunity;

(vi) that a class should be certified; or

(vii) that, as a matter of law, a party is not entitled to absolute or qualified immunity in a civil rights claim arising under federal law;

(viii) that a governmental entity has taken action that has inordinately burdened real property within the meaning of section 70.001(6)(a), Florida Statutes.

(D) grant or deny the appointment of a receiver, and terminate or refuse to terminate a receivership.

(4) Non-final orders entered after final order on motions that suspend rendition are not reviewable; provided that orders granting motions for new trial in jury and non-jury cases are reviewable by the method prescribed in rule 9.110. Other non-final orders entered after final order on authorized motions are reviewable by the method prescribed by this rule.

(5) Orders entered on motions filed under Florida Rule of Civil Procedure 1.540, Small Claims Rule 7.190, Rule of Juvenile Procedure 8.270, and Florida Family Law Rule of Procedure 12.540 are reviewable by the method prescribed by this rule.

(6) Orders that deny motions to certify a class may be reviewed by the method prescribed by this rule.

(b) Commencement. The jurisdiction to seek review of orders described in subdivisions (a)(3)-(a)(6) shall be invoked by filing 2 copies of a notice, accompanied by the filing fees prescribed by law, with the clerk of the lower tribunal within 30 days of rendition of the order to be reviewed.

(c) Notice. The notice, designated as a notice of appeal of non-final order, shall be substantially in the form prescribed by rule 9.900(c). Except in criminal cases, a conformed copy of the order or orders designated in the notice of appeal shall be attached to the notice.

(d) Record. A record shall not be transmitted to the court unless ordered.

(e) Briefs. Appellant's initial brief, accompanied by an appendix as prescribed by rule 9.220, shall be served within 15 days of filing the notice. Additional briefs shall be served as prescribed by rule 9.210.

(f) Stay of Proceedings. In the absence of a stay, during the pendency of a review of a non-final order, the lower tribunal may proceed with all matters, including trial or final hearing; provided that the lower tribunal may not render a final order disposing of the cause pending such review.

(g) Review on Full Appeal. This rule shall not preclude initial review of a non-final order on appeal from the final order in the cause.

(h) Scope of Review. Multiple non-final orders that are listed in rule 9.130(a)(3) may be reviewed by a single notice if the notice is timely filed as to each such order.

History: Amended March 27, 1980, effective April 1, 1980 (381 So.2d 1370); Nov. 26, 1980, effective Jan. 1, 1981 (391 So.2d 203); Sept. 13, 1984, effective Jan. 1, 1985 (463 So.2d 1114); amended effective July 9, 1992 (605 So.2d 850); amended Oct. 22, 1992, effective Jan. 1, 1993 (609 So.2d 516), amended Nov. 22, 1995, effective Jan. 1, 1996 (663 So.2d 1314); Nov. 22, 1996, effective Jan. 1, 1997 (685 So.2d 773); amended Oct. 12, 2000, effective Jan. 1, 2001 (780 So. 2d 834; 2000 Fla. LEXIS 2273; 25 Fla. L. Weekly S 835); amended Feb.3, 2005, effective Feb. 3, 2005 (2005 Fla. LEXIS 154; 30 Fla. L. Weekly S 84).

Committee Notes

1977 Amendment. This rule replaces former rule 4.2 and substantially alters current practice. This rule applies to review of all non-final orders, except those entered in criminal cases, and those specifically governed by rules 9.100 and 9.110.

The advisory committee was aware that the common law writ of certiorari is available at any time and did not intend to abolish that writ. However, because that writ provides a remedy only if the petitioner meets the heavy burden of showing that a clear departure from the essential requirements of law has resulted in otherwise irreparable harm, it is extremely rare that erroneous interlocutory rulings can be corrected by resort to common law certiorari. It is anticipated that because the most urgent interlocutory orders are appealable under this rule, there will be very few cases in which common law certiorari will provide relief. See *Taylor v. Board of Pub. Instruction,* 131 So.2d 504 (Fla. 1st DCA 1961).

Subdivision (a)(3) designates certain instances in which interlocutory appeals may be prosecuted under the procedures set forth in this rule. Under these rules there are no mandatory interlocutory appeals. This rule eliminates interlocutory appeals as a matter of right from all orders "formerly cognizable in equity," and provides for review of certain interlocutory orders based on the necessity or desirability of expeditious review. Allowable interlocutory appeals from orders in actions formerly cognizable as civil actions are specified, and are essentially the same as under former rule 4.2. Item (A) permits review of orders concerning venue. Item (C)(i) has been limited to jurisdiction over the person because the writ of prohibition provides an adequate remedy in cases involving jurisdiction of the subject matter. Because the purpose of these items is to eliminate useless labor, the advisory committee is of the view that stays of proceedings in lower tribunals should be liberally granted if the interlocutory appeal involves venue or jurisdiction over the person. Because this rule only applies to civil cases, item (C)(ii) does not include within its ambit rulings on motions to suppress seized evidence in criminal cases. Item (C)(ii) is intended to apply whether the property involved is real or personal. It applies to such cases as condemnation suits in which a condemnor is permitted to take possession and title to real property in advance of final judgment. See ch. 74, Fla.Stat. (1975). Item (C)(iii) is intended to apply to such matters as temporary child custody or support, alimony, suit money, and attorneys' fees. Item (C)(iv) allows appeals from interlocutory orders that determine liability in favor of a claimant.

Subdivision (a)(4) grants a right of review if the lower tribunal grants a motion for new trial whether in a jury or non-jury case. The procedures set forth in rule 9.110, and not those set forth in this rule, apply in such cases. This rule has been phrased so that the granting of rehearing in a non-jury case under Florida Rule of Civil Procedure 1.530 may not be the subject of an interlocutory appeal unless the trial judge orders the taking of evidence. Other non-final orders that postpone rendition are not reviewable in an independent proceeding. Other non-final orders entered by a lower tribunal after final order are reviewable and are to be governed by this rule. Such orders include, for example, an order granting a motion to vacate default.

Subdivision (a)(5) grants a right of review of orders on motions seeking relief from a previous court order on the grounds of mistake, fraud, satisfaction of judgment, or other grounds listed in Florida Rule of Civil Procedure 1.540.

Subdivision (a)(6) provides that interlocutory review is to be in the court that would have jurisdiction to review the final order in the cause as of the time of the interlocutory appeal.

Subdivisions (b) and (c) state the manner for commencing an interlocutory appeal governed by this rule. Two copies of the notice must be filed with the clerk of the lower tribunal within 30 days of rendition of the order. Under rule 9.040(g) the notice and fee must be transmitted immediately to the court by the clerk of the lower tribunal.

Subdivision (d) provides for transmittal of the record only on order of the court. Transmittal should be in accordance with instructions contained in the order.

Subdivision (e) replaces former rule 4.2(e) and governs the service of briefs on interlocutory appeals. The time to serve the appellant's brief has been reduced to 15 days so as to minimize interruption of lower tribunal proceedings. The brief must be accompanied by an appendix containing a conformed copy of the order to be reviewed and should also contain all relevant portions of the record.

Subdivision (f) makes clear that unless a stay is granted under rule 9.310, the lower tribunal is only divested of jurisdiction to enter a final order disposing of the case. This follows the historical rule that trial courts are divested of jurisdiction only to the extent that their actions are under review by an appellate court. Thus, the lower tribunal has jurisdiction to proceed with matters not before the court. This rule is intended to resolve the confusion spawned by *De la Portilla v. De la Portilla,* 304 So.2d 116 (Fla.1974), and its progeny

Subdivision (g) was embodied in former rule 4.2(a)

R. App. Proc.

and is intended to make clear that the failure to take an interlocutory appeal does not constitute a waiver of any sort on appeal of a final judgment, although an improper ruling might not then constitute prejudicial error warranting reversal.

1992 Amendment. Subdivisions (a)(3)(C)(vii) and (a)(6) were added to permit appeals from non-final orders that either granted or denied a party's request that a class be certified. The committee was of the opinion that orders determining the nature of an action and the extent of the parties before the court were analogous to other orders reviewable under rule 9.130. Therefore, these 2 subdivisions were added to the other limited enumeration of orders appealable by the procedures established in this rule.

Subdivision (a)(3)(D) was added by the committee in response to the decision in *Twin Jay Chambers Partnership v. Suarez,* 556 So.2d 781 (Fla. 2d DCA 1990). It was the opinion of the committee that orders that deny the appointment of receivers or terminate or refuse to terminate receiverships are of the same quality as those that grant the appointment of a receiver. Rather than base the appealability of such orders on subdivision (a)(3)(C)(ii), the committee felt it preferable to specifically identify those orders with respect to a receivership that were non-final orders subject to appeal by this rule.

Subdivision (c) was amended to require the attachment of a conformed copy of the order or orders designated in the notice of appeal consistent with the amendment to rule 9.110(d).

1996 Amendment. The amendment to subdivision (a)(3)(C)(vi) moves the phrase "as a matter of law" from the end of the subdivision to its beginning. This is to resolve the confusion evidenced in *Breakers Palm Beach v. Gloger*, 646 So. 2d 237 (Fla. 4th DCA 1994), *City of Lake Mary v. Franklin*, 668 So. 2d 712 (Fla. 5th DCA 1996), and their progeny by clarifying that this subdivision was not intended to grant a right of nonfinal review if the lower tribunal denies a motion for summary judgment based on the existence of a material fact dispute.

Subdivision (a)(3)(C)(viii) was added in response to the supreme court's request in *Tucker v. Resha*, 648 So. 2d 1187 (Fla. 1994). The court directed the committee to propose a new rule regarding procedures for appeal of orders denying immunity in federal civil rights cases consistent with federal procedure. Compare *Johnson v. Jones*, 115 S. Ct. 2151, 132 L. Ed. 2d 238 (1995), with *Mitchell v. Forsyth*, 472 U.S. 511, 105 S. Ct. 2806, 86 L. Ed. 2d 411 (1985). The Florida Supreme Court held that such orders are "subject to interlocutory review to the extent that the order turns on an issue of law."

2000 Amendment. The title to this rule was amended to reflect that some of the review proceedings specified in this rule may involve review of final orders.

Subdivision (a)(1) was amended to reflect that the appellate jurisdiction of circuit courts is prescribed by general law and not by this rule, as clarified in *Blore v. Fierro*, 636 So. 2d 1329 (Fla. 1994).

Subdivision (a)(3)(c)(iv) allowing review of orders determining "the issue of liability in favor of a party seeking affirmative relief" was deleted so that such orders are not appealable until the conclusion of the case.

Subdivision (a)(7) was deleted because it is superseded by proposed rule 9.040(b)(2), which determines the appropriate court to review non-final orders after a change of venue.

Rule 9.140. Appeal Proceedings in Criminal Cases.

(a) Applicability. Appeal proceedings in criminal cases shall be as in civil cases except as modified by this rule.

(b) Appeals by Defendant.

(1) Appeals Permitted. A defendant may appeal

(A) a final judgment adjudicating guilt;

(B) a final order withholding adjudication after a finding of guilt;

(C) an order granting probation or community control, or both, whether or not guilt has been adjudicated;

(D) orders entered after final judgment or finding of guilt, including orders revoking or modifying probation or community control, or both, or orders denying relief under Florida Rule of Criminal Procedure 3.800(a), 3.850, or 3.853;

(E) an unlawful or illegal sentence;

(F) a sentence, if the appeal is required or permitted by general law; or

(G) as otherwise provided by general law.

(2) Guilty or Nolo Contendere Pleas.

(A) Pleas. A defendant may not appeal from a

guilty or nolo contendere plea except as follows:

(i) Reservation of Right to Appeal. A defendant who pleads guilty or nolo contendere may expressly reserve the right to appeal a prior dispositive order of the lower tribunal, identifying with particularity the point of law being reserved.

(ii) Appeals Otherwise Allowed. A defendant who pleads guilty or nolo contendere may otherwise directly appeal only

a. the lower tribunal's lack of subject matter jurisdiction;

b. a violation of the plea agreement, if preserved by a motion to withdraw plea;

c. an involuntary plea, if preserved by a motion to withdraw plea;

d. a sentencing error, if preserved; or

e. as otherwise provided by law.

(B) Record.

(i) Except for appeals under subdivision (b)(2)(A) of this rule, the record for appeals involving a plea of guilty or nolo contendere shall be limited to:

a. all indictments, informations, affidavits of violation of probation or community control, and other charging documents;

b. the plea and sentencing hearing transcripts;

c. any written plea agreements;

d. any judgments, sentences, scoresheets, motions, and orders to correct or modify sentences, orders imposing, modifying, or revoking probation or community control, orders assessing costs, fees, fines, or restitution against the defendant, and any other documents relating to sentencing;

e. any motion to withdraw plea and order thereon;

f. notice of appeal, statement of judicial acts to be reviewed, directions to the clerk, and designation to the court reporter.

(ii) Upon good cause shown, the court, or the lower tribunal before the record is transmitted, may expand the record.

(3) Commencement. The defendant shall file the notice prescribed by rule 9.110(d) with the clerk of the lower tribunal at any time between rendition of a final judgment and 30 days following rendition of a written order imposing sentence. Copies shall be served on the state attorney and attorney general.

(4) Cross-Appeal. A defendant may cross-appeal by serving a notice within 10 days of service of the state's notice or service of an order on a motion pursuant to Florida Rule of Criminal Procedure 3.800(b)(2). Review of cross-appeals before trial is limited to related issues resolved in the same order being appealed.

(c) Appeals by the State.

(1) Appeals Permitted. The state may appeal an order

(A) dismissing an indictment or information or any count thereof or dismissing an affidavit charging the commission of a criminal offense, the violation of probation, the violation of community control, or the violation of any supervised correctional release;

(B) suppressing before trial confessions, admissions, or evidence obtained by search and seizure;

(C) granting a new trial;

(D) arresting judgment;

(E) granting a motion for judgment of acquittal after a jury verdict;

(F) discharging a defendant under Florida Rule of Criminal Procedure 3.191;

(G) discharging a prisoner on habeas corpus;

(H) finding a defendant incompetent or insane;

(I) granting relief under Florida Rule of Criminal Procedure 3.853;

(J) ruling on a question of law if a convicted defendant appeals the judgment of conviction;

R. App. Proc.

(K) imposing an unlawful or illegal sentence or imposing a sentence outside the range permitted by the sentencing guidelines;

(L) imposing a sentence outside the range recommended by the sentencing guidelines;

(M) denying restitution; or

(N) as otherwise provided by general law for final orders.

(2) Non-Final Orders. The state as provided by general law may appeal to the circuit court non-final orders rendered in the county court.

(3) Commencement. The state shall file the notice prescribed by rule 9.110(d) with the clerk of the lower tribunal within 15 days of rendition of the order to be reviewed; provided that in an appeal by the state under rule 9.140(c)(1)(J), the state's notice of cross-appeal shall be filed within 10 days of service of defendant's notice or service of an order on a motion pursuant to rule 3.800(b)(2). Copies shall be served on the defendant and the attorney of record. An appeal by the state shall stay further proceedings in the lower tribunal only by order of the lower tribunal.

(d) Withdrawal of Defense Counsel after Judgment and Sentence or After Appeal by State.

(1) The attorney of record for a defendant in a criminal proceeding shall not be relieved of any professional duties, or be permitted to withdraw as defense counsel of record, except with approval of the lower tribunal on good cause shown on written motion, until either the time has expired for filing an authorized notice of appeal and no such notice has been filed by the defendant or the state, or after the following have been completed:

(A) a notice of appeal or cross-appeal has been filed on behalf of the defendant or the state;

(B) a statement of judicial acts to be reviewed has been filed if a transcript will require the expenditure of public funds;

(C) the defendant's directions to the clerk have been filed, if necessary;

(D) designations to the court reporter have been filed for transcripts of those portions of the proceedings necessary to support the issues on appeal or, if transcripts will require the expenditure of public funds for the defendant, of those portions of the proceedings necessary to support the statement of judicial acts to be reviewed; and

(E) in publicly funded defense and state appeals, the lower tribunal has appointed the public defender for the local circuit court, who shall initially remain counsel for the appeal until the record is transmitted to the appellate court. In publicly funded state appeals, defense counsel shall additionally file in the appellate court a copy of the order appointing the local public defender. In nonpublicly funded defense and state appeals, retained appellate counsel shall file a notice of appearance in the appellate court, or defense counsel of record shall file a motion to withdraw in the appellate court, with service on the defendant, that states what the defendant's legal representation on appeal, if any, is expected to be. Documents filed in the appellate court shall be served on the attorney general (or state attorney in appeals to the circuit court).

(2) Orders allowing withdrawal of counsel are conditional and counsel shall remain of record for the limited purpose of representing the defendant in the lower tribunal regarding any sentencing error the lower tribunal is authorized to address during the pendency of the direct appeal pursuant to Florida Rule of Criminal Procedure 3.800(b)(2).

(e) Sentencing Errors. A defendant may not raise a sentencing error on appeal unless the alleged error has first been brought to the attention of the lower tribunal:

(1) at the time of sentencing; or

(2) by motion pursuant to Florida Rule of Criminal Procedure 3.800(b).

(f) Record.

(1) Service. The clerk of the lower tribunal shall prepare and serve the record prescribed by rule 9.200 within 50 days of the filing of the notice of appeal.

(2) Transcripts.

(A) If a defendant's designation of a transcript of proceedings requires expenditure of public funds, trial counsel for the defendant (in conjunction with appellate counsel if possible) shall serve, within 10 days of filing the notice, a statement of the judicial acts to be reviewed, and a designation to the court reporter requiring preparation of only so much of the proceedings as fairly supports the issues raised.

(B) Either party may file motions in the lower tribunal to reduce or expand the transcript.

(C) Except as permitted in subdivision (f)(2)(D) of this rule, the parties shall designate the court reporter to file with the clerk of the lower tribunal the original transcripts for the court and sufficient copies for the state and all indigent defendants.

(D) Non-indigent defendants represented by counsel may designate the court reporter to prepare only original transcripts. Counsel adopting this procedure shall, within 5 days of receipt of the original transcripts from the court reporter, file the original transcripts along with securely bound copies for the state and all defendants. Counsel shall serve notice of the use of this procedure on the attorney general (or the state attorney in appeals to circuit court) and the clerk of the lower tribunal. Counsel shall attach a certificate to each copy certifying that it is an accurate and complete copy of the original transcript. When this procedure is used, the clerk of the lower tribunal upon conclusion of the appeal shall retain the original transcript for use as needed by the state in any collateral proceedings and shall not destroy the transcripts without the consent of the Office of the Attorney General.

(E) In state appeals, the state shall designate the court reporter to prepare and file with the clerk of the lower tribunal the original transcripts and sufficient copies for all separately represented defendants. Alternatively, the state may elect to use the procedure specified in subdivision (f)(2)(D) of this rule.

(F) The lower tribunal may by administrative order in publicly-funded cases direct the clerk of the lower tribunal rather than the court reporter to prepare the necessary copies of the original transcripts.

(3) Retention of Documents. Unless otherwise ordered by the court, the clerk of the lower tribunal shall retain all original documents except the original transcripts designated for appeal which shall be included in the record transmitted to the court.

(4) Service of Copies. The clerk of the lower tribunal shall serve copies of the record to the court, attorney general (or state attorney in appeals to circuit court), and all counsel appointed to represent indigent defendants on appeal. The clerk of the lower tribunal shall simultaneously serve copies of the index to all non-indigent defendants and, upon their request, copies of the record or portions thereof at the cost prescribed by law.

(5) Return of Record. Except in death penalty cases, the court shall return the record to the lower tribunal after final disposition of the appeal.

(6) Supplemental Record for Motion to Correct Sentencing Error Pursuant to Florida Rule of Criminal Procedure 3.800(b)(2).

(A) The clerk of circuit court shall automatically supplement the appellate record with any motion pursuant to Florida Rule of Criminal Procedure 3.800(b)(2), any response, any resulting order, and any amended sentence. The clerk shall transmit the supplement to the appellate court within 5 days of the filing of the order ruling on the motion. If an order is not filed within 60 days from the filing of the motion, this time shall run from the expiration of the 60 day period, and the clerk shall supplement the record with the motion and a statement that no order was timely filed.

(B) If any appellate counsel determines that a transcript of a proceeding relating to such a motion is required to review the sentencing issue, appellate counsel shall, within 5 days from the transmittal of the supplement described in subdivision (A), designate those portions of the proceedings not on file deemed necessary for transcription and inclusion in the record. A copy of the designation shall be filed with the appel-

R. App. Proc.

late court. The procedure for this supplementation shall be in accordance with this subdivision, except that counsel is not required to file a revised statement of judicial acts to be reviewed, the court reporter shall deliver the transcript within 15 days, and the clerk shall supplement the record with the transcript within 5 days of its receipt.

(g) Briefs. Initial briefs shall be served within 30 days of service of the record or designation of appointed counsel, whichever is later. Additional briefs shall be served as prescribed by rule 9.210.

(h) Post-Trial Release.

(1) Appeal by Defendant. The lower tribunal may hear a motion for post-trial release pending appeal before or after a notice is filed; provided that the defendant may not be released from custody until the notice is filed.

(2) Appeal by State. An incarcerated defendant charged with a bailable offense shall on motion be released on the defendant's own recognizance pending an appeal by the state, unless the lower tribunal for good cause stated in an order determines otherwise.

(3) Denial of Post-Trial Release. All orders denying post-trial release shall set forth the factual basis on which the decision was made and the reasons therefor.

(4) Review. Review of an order relating to post-trial release shall be by the court on motion.

(i) Scope of Review. The court shall review all rulings and orders appearing in the record necessary to pass upon the grounds of an appeal. In the interest of justice, the court may grant any relief to which any party is entitled.

History: Amended Nov. 1, 1979, effective Jan. 1, 1980 (376 So.2d 844); March 27, 1980, effective April 1, 1980 (381 So.2d 1370); Dec. 15, 1983 (443 So.2d 972); Sept. 13, 1984, effective Jan. 1, 1985 (463 So.2d 1114); June 8, 1987, effective July 1, 1987 (509 So.2d 276); Oct. 22, 1992, effective Jan. 1, 1993 (609 So.2d 516); effective Aug. 29, 1996 (678 So.2d 1285); Nov. 22, 1996, effective Jan. 1, 1997 (685 So.2d 773); Nov. 12, 1999, effective Nov. 12, 1999 (24 Fla. L. Weekly S530); opinion corrected Nov. 23, 1999 (24 Fla. L. Weekly S567); opn. on grant of reh'g Jan. 13, 2000 *Amendment to Florida Rules of Criminal Procedure 3.111(e), 3.800 and Florida Rules of Appellate Procedure 9.020(h), 9.140, and 9.600*, No. 95707 (25 Fla. L. Weekly S37a); opinion corrected Jan. 14, 2000; amended Oct. 12, 2000, effective Jan. 1, 2001 (780 So. 2d 834; 2000 Fla. LEXIS 2273; 25 Fla. L. Weekly S 835); amended Oct. 18, 2001 (2001 Fla. LEXIS 2083; 26 Fla. L. Weekly S 686); Aug. 29, 2002, effective Jan. 1, 2003; October 31, 2002, effective Jan. 1, 2003.

1999 Note: The amendment at 24 Fla. L. Weekly S530 shall also apply to cases pending on appeal.

Committee Notes

1977 Amendment. This rule represents a substantial revision of the procedure in criminal appeals.

Subdivision (a) makes clear the policy of these rules that procedures be standardized to the maximum extent possible. Criminal appeals are to be governed by the same rules as other cases, except for those matters unique to criminal law that are identified and controlled by this rule.

Subdivision (b)(1) lists the only matters that may be appealed by a criminal defendant, and it is intended to supersede all other rules of practice and procedure. This rule has no effect on either the availability of extraordinary writs otherwise within the jurisdiction of the court to grant, or the supreme court's jurisdiction to entertain petitions for the constitutional writ of certiorari to review interlocutory orders. This rule also incorporates the holding in *State v. Ashby,* 245 So.2d 225 (Fla.1971), and is intended to make clear that the reservation of the right to appeal a judgment based on the plea of no contest must be express and must identify the particular point of law being reserved; any issues not expressly reserved are waived. No direct appeal of a judgment based on a guilty plea is allowed. It was not intended that this rule affect the substantive law governing collateral review.

Subdivision (b)(3) replaces former rule 6.2. Specific reference is made to rule 9.110(d) to emphasize that criminal appeals are to be prosecuted in substantially the same manner as other cases. Copies of the notice, however, must be served on both the state attorney and the attorney general. The time for taking an appeal has been made to run from the date judgment is rendered to 30 days after an order imposing sentence is rendered or otherwise reduced to writing. The former rule provided for appeal within 30 days of rendition of judgment or within 30 days of entry of sentence. The advisory committee debated the intent of the literal language of the former rule. Arguably, under the former rule an appeal could not be taken by a defendant during the "gap period" that occurs when sentencing is postponed more than 30 days after entry of judgment. The advisory committee concluded that no purpose was served by such an interpretation because the full case would be reviewable when the "gap" closed. This modification of the former rule promotes the policies underlying *Williams v. State,* 324 So.2d 74 (Fla. 1975), in which it was held that a notice of appeal prematurely filed should not be dismissed, but held in abeyance until it becomes effective. This rule does not specifically address the issue of whether full review is available if resentencing occurs on order of a court in a collateral proceeding. Such cases should be resolved in accordance with the underlying policies of these rules. Compare *Wade v. State,* 222 So.2d 434 (Fla. 2d DCA 1969), with *Neary v. State,* 285 So.2d 47 (Fla. 4th DCA 1973). If a defendant appeals a judgment of conviction of a capital offense before sentencing and sentencing is anticipated, the district court of appeal (as the court then with jurisdiction) should hold the case in abeyance until the sentence has been imposed. If the death penalty is imposed, the district court of appeal should transfer the case to the supreme court for review. See § 921.141(4), Fla.Stat. (1975); Fla.R.App.P. 9.040(b). Subdivision (f) governs the service of briefs. Filing should be made in accordance with rule 9.420.

Subdivision (c)(1) lists the only matters that may be appealed by the state, but it is not intended to affect the jurisdiction of the supreme court to entertain by certiorari interlocutory appeals governed by rule 9.100, or the jurisdiction of circuit courts to entertain interlocutory appeals of pretrial orders from the county courts. See *State v. Smith,* 260 So.2d 489 (Fla.1972). No provision of this rule is intended to conflict with a defendant's constitutional right not to be placed twice in jeopardy, and it should be interpreted accordingly. If there is an appeal under item (A), a motion for a stay of the lower tribunal proceeding should be liberally granted in cases in which there appears to be a substantial possibility that trial of any non-dismissed charges would bar prosecution of the dismissed charges if the dismissal were reversed, such as in cases involving the so-called "single transaction rule." Item (F) refers to the popularly known "speedy trial rule," and items (G), (H), and (I) track the balance of state appellate rights in section 924.07, Florida Statutes (1975).

Subdivision (c)(3) parallels subdivision (b)(3) regarding appeals by defendants except that a maximum of 15 days is allowed for filing the notice. An appeal by the state stays further proceedings in the lower tribunal only if an order has been entered by the trial court. Subdivision (c)(3) governs the service of briefs.

Subdivision (e) applies rule 9.200 to criminal appeals and sets forth the time for preparation and service of the record, and additional matters peculiar to criminal cases. It has been made mandatory that the original record be held by the lower tribunal to avoid loss and destruction of original papers while in transit. To meet the needs of appellate counsel for indigents, provision has been made for automatic transmittal of a copy of the record to the public defender appointed to represent an indigent defendant on appeal, which in any particular case may be the public defender either in the judicial circuit where the trial took place or in the judicial circuit wherein the appellate court is located. See § 27.51(4), Fla.Stat. (1975). Counsel for a non-Indigent defendant may obtain a copy of the record at the cost prescribed by law. At the present time, section 28.24(13), Florida Statutes (1975), as amended by chapter 77-284, § 1, Laws of Florida, prescribes a cost of $1 per page.

To conserve the public treasury, appeals by indigent defendants, and other criminal defendants in cases in which a free transcript is provided, have been specially treated. Only the essential portions of the transcript are to be prepared. The appellant must file a statement of the judicial acts to be reviewed on appeal and the parties are to file and serve designations of the relevant portions of the record. (This procedure emphasizes the obligation of trial counsel to cooperate with appellate counsel, if the two are different, in identifying alleged trial errors.) The statement is necessary to afford the appellee an opportunity to make a reasonable determination of the portions of the record required. The statement should be sufficiently definite to enable the opposing party to make that determination, but greater specificity is unnecessary. The statement of judicial acts contemplated by this rule is not intended to be the equivalent of assignments of error under former rule 3.5. Therefore, an error or inadequacy in the statement should not be relevant to the disposition of any case. In such circumstances, the appropriate procedure would be to supplement the record under rule 9.200(f) to cure any potential or actual prejudice. Either party may move in the lower tribunal to strike unnecessary portions before they are prepared or to expand the transcript. The ruling of the lower tribunal on such motions is reviewable by motion to the court under rule 9.200(f) if a party asserts additional portions are required.

Subdivision (g) replaces former rule 6.15. Subdivision (g)(1) governs if an appeal is taken by a defendant and permits a motion to grant post-trial release pending appeal to be heard although a notice of appeal has not yet been filed. The lower tribunal may then grant the motion effective on the notice being filed. This rule is intended to eliminate practical difficulties that on

R. App. Proc.

occasion have frustrated the cause of justice, as in cases in which a defendant's attorney has not prepared a notice of appeal in advance of judgment. Consideration of such motions shall be in accordance with section 903.132, Florida Statutes (Supp.1976), and Florida Rule of Criminal Procedure 3.691. This rule does not apply if the judgment is based on a guilty plea because no right to appeal such a conviction is recognized by these rules.

Subdivision (g)(2) governs if the state takes an appeal and authorizes release of the defendant without bond, if charged with a bailable offense, unless the lower tribunal for good cause orders otherwise. The "good cause" standard was adopted to ensure that bond be required only in rare circumstances. The advisory committee was of the view that because the state generally will not be able to gain a conviction unless it prevails, the presumed innocent defendant should not be required to undergo incarceration without strong reasons, especially if a pre-trial appeal is involved. "Good cause" therefore includes such factors as the likelihood of success on appeal and the likelihood the defendant will leave the jurisdiction in light of the current status of the charges against the defendant.

Subdivision (g)(3) retains the substance of former rules 6.15(b) and (c). The lower tribunal's order must contain a statement of facts as well as the reasons for the action taken, in accordance with *Younghans v. State,* 90 So.2d 308 (Fla.1956).

Subdivision (g)(4) allows review only by motion so that no order regarding post-trial relief is reviewable unless jurisdiction has been vested in the court by the filing of a notice of appeal. It is intended that the amount of bail be reviewable for excessiveness.

Subdivision (h) interacts with rule 9.110(h) to allow review of multiple judgments and sentences in 1 proceeding.

Subdivision (i) sets forth the procedure to be followed if there is a summary denial without hearing of a motion for post-conviction relief under Florida Rule of Criminal Procedure 3.850. This rule does not limit the right to appeal a denial of such a motion after hearing under rule 9.140(b)(1)(C).

1980 Amendment. Although the substance of this rule has not been changed, the practitioner should note that references in the 1977 committee notes to supreme court jurisdiction to review non-final orders that would have been appealable if they had been final orders are obsolete because jurisdiction to review those orders no longer reposes in the supreme court.

1992 Amendment. Subdivision (b)(5) was amended to provide that, in cases in which public funds would be used to prepare the record on appeal, the attorney of record would not be allowed to withdraw until substitute counsel has been obtained or appointed.

Subdivision (h) was amended to provide a specific procedure to be followed by the courts in considering appeals from summary denial of Florida Rule of Criminal Procedure 3.800(a) motions. Because such motions are in many respects comparable to Florida Rule of Criminal Procedure 3.850 motions, it was decided to use the available format already created by existing subdivision (h) of this rule. Because a Florida Rule of Criminal Procedure 3.800(a) motion does not have the same detailed requirements as does a Florida Rule of Criminal Procedure 3.850 motion, this subdivision also was amended to require the transmittal of any attachments to the motions in the lower court.

1996 Amendment. The 1996 amendments are intended to consolidate and clarify the rules to reflect current law unless otherwise specified.

Rule 9.140(b)(2)(B) was added to accurately reflect the limited right of direct appeal after a plea of guilty or nolo contendere. See *Robinson v. State*, 373 So. 2d 898 (Fla. 1979), and *Counts v. State*, 376 So. 2d 59 (Fla. 2d DCA 1979).

New subdivision (b)(4) reflects *Lopez v. State*, 638 So. 2d 931 (Fla. 1994). A defendant may cross-appeal as provided, but if the defendant chooses not to do so, the defendant retains the right to raise any properly preserved issue on plenary appeal. It is the committee's intention that the 10-day period for filing notice of the cross-appeal should be interpreted in the same manner as in civil cases under rule 9.110(g).

Rule 9.140(b)(6)(E) adopts Florida Rule of Criminal Procedure 3.851(b)(2) and is intended to supersede that rule. See Fla. R. Jud. Admin. 2.135. The rule also makes clear that the time periods in rule 9.140(j) do not apply to death penalty cases.

The revised rules 9.140(e)(2)(D) and 9.140(e)(2)(E) are intended to supersede *Brown v. State*, 639 So. 2d 634 (Fla. 5th DCA 1994), and allow non-Indigent defendants represented by counsel, and the state, to order just the original transcript from the court reporter and to make copies. However, the original and copies for all other parties must then be served on the clerk of the lower tribunal for inclusion in the record. The revised rule 9.140(e)(2)(F) also allows chief judges for each circuit to promulgate an administrative order requiring the lower tribunal clerk's office to make copies of the transcript when the defendant is indigent. In the absence of such an administrative order, the court reporter will furnish an original and copies for all parties in indigent appeals.

Rule 9.140(j)(3) imposes a two-year time limit on proceedings to obtain delayed appellate review based on either the ineffectiveness of counsel on a prior appeal or the failure to timely initiate an appeal by appointed counsel. The former was previously applied for by a petition for writ of habeas corpus in the appellate court and the latter by motion pursuant to Florida Rule of Criminal Procedure 3.850 in the trial court. Because both of these remedies did not require a filing fee, it is contemplated that no fee will be required for the filing of petitions under this rule. Subdivision (j)(3)(B) allows two years "after the conviction becomes final." For purposes of the subdivision a conviction becomes final after issuance of the mandate or other final process of the highest court to which direct review is taken, including review in the Florida Supreme Court and United States Supreme Court. Any collateral review shall not stay the time period under this subdivision. Subdivision (j)(3)(C) under this rule makes clear that defendants who were convicted before the effective date of the rule will not have their rights retroactively extinguished but will be subject to the time limits as calculated from the effective date of the rule unless the time has already commenced to run under rule 3.850.

Rule 9.140(j)(5) was added to provide a uniform procedure for requesting belated appeal and to supersede *State v. District Court of Appeal of Florida, First District*, 569 So. 2d 439 (Fla. 1990). This decision resulted in there being two procedures for requesting belated appeal: Florida Rule of Criminal Procedure 3.850 when the criminal appeal was frustrated by ineffective assistance of trial counsel, *id* .; and habeas corpus for everything else. See *Scalf v. Singletary*, 589 So. 2d 986 (Fla. 2d DCA 1991). Experience showed that filing in the appellate court was more efficient. This rule is intended to reinstate the procedure as it existed prior to *State v. District Court of Appeal, First District* . See *Baggett v. Wainwright*, 229 So. 2d 239 (Fla. 1969); *State v. Meyer*, 430 So. 2d 440 (Fla. 1983).

In the rare case where entitlement to belated appeal depends on a determination of disputed facts, the appellate court may appoint a commissioner to make a report and recommendation.

2000 Amendment. Subdivision (b)(1)(B) was added to reflect the holding of *State v. Schultz*, 720 So. 2d 247 (Fla. 1998). The amendment to renumber subdivision (b)(1)(D), regarding appeals from orders denying relief under Florida Rules of Criminal Procedure 3.800(a) or 3.850, reflects current practice.

The committee added language to subdivision (b)(6)(B) to require court reporters to file transcripts on computer disks in death penalty cases. Death penalty transcripts typically are lengthy, and many persons review and use them over the years. In these cases, filing lengthy transcripts on computer disks makes them easier to use for all parties and increases their longevity.

The committee deleted the last sentence of subdivision (b)(6)(E) because its substance is now included in rule 9.141(a). The committee also amended and transferred subdivisions (i) and (j) to rule 9.141 for the reasons specified in the committee note for that rule.

Court Commentary

1996. Rule 9.140 was substantially rewritten so as to harmonize with the Criminal Appeal Reform Act of 1996 (CS/HB 211). The reference to unlawful sentences in rule 9.140(b)(1)(D) and (c)(1)(J) means those sentences not meeting the definition of illegal under *Davis v. State*, 661 So. 2d 1193 (Fla. 1995), but, nevertheless, subject to correction on direct appeal.

Rule 9.141. Review Proceedings in Collateral or Post-Conviction Criminal Cases.

(a) Death Penalty Cases. This rule does not apply to death penalty cases.

(b) Appeals from Post-Conviction Proceedings Under Florida Rule of Criminal Procedure 3.800(a), 3.850, or 3.853.

(1) Applicability of Civil Appellate Procedures. Appeal proceedings under this subdivision shall be as in civil cases, except as modified by this rule.

(2) Summary Grant or Denial of Motion Without Evidentiary Hearing.

(A) When a motion for post-conviction relief under rule 3.800(a), 3.850, or 3.853 is granted or denied without an evidentiary hearing, the clerk of the lower tribunal shall transmit to the court, as the record, copies of the motion, response, reply, order on the motion, motion for rehearing, response, reply, order on the motion for rehearing, and attachments to any of the foregoing, together with the certified copy of the notice of appeal.

(B) Unless directed otherwise by the court, the clerk of the lower tribunal shall not index or paginate the record or send copies of the index or record to the parties.

R. App. Proc.

(C) No briefs or oral argument shall be required, but any appellant's brief shall be filed within 15 days of the filing of the notice of appeal. The court may request a response from the appellee before ruling.

(D) On appeal from the denial of relief, unless the record shows conclusively that the appellant is entitled to no relief, the order shall be reversed and the cause remanded for an evidentiary hearing or other appropriate relief.

(3) Grant or Denial of Motion after Evidentiary Hearing.

(A) Transcription. In the absence of designations to the court reporter, the notice of appeal filed by an indigent pro se litigant in a rule 3.850 or 3.853 appeal after an evidentiary hearing shall serve as the designation to the court reporter for the transcript of the evidentiary hearing. Within 5 days of receipt of the notice of appeal, the clerk of the lower tribunal shall request the appropriate court reporter to transcribe the evidentiary hearing and shall send the court reporter a copy of the notice, the date of the hearing to be transcribed, the name of the judge, and a copy of this rule.

(B) Record.

(i) When a motion for post-conviction relief under rule 3.850 or 3.853 is granted or denied after an evidentiary hearing, the clerk of the lower tribunal shall index, paginate, and transmit to the court as the record, within 50 days of the filing of the notice of appeal, copies of the notice of appeal, motion, response, reply, order on the motion, motion for rehearing, response, reply, order on the motion for rehearing, and attachments to any of the foregoing, as well as the original transcript of the evidentiary hearing.

(ii) Appellant may direct the clerk to include in the record any other documents that were before the lower tribunal at the hearing. If the clerk is directed to include in the record a previously prepared appellate record involving the appellant, the clerk need not reindex or repaginate it.

(iii) The clerk of the lower tribunal shall serve copies of the record on the attorney general (or state attorney in appeals to the circuit court), all counsel appointed to represent indigent defendants on appeal, and any pro se indigent defendant. The clerk of the lower tribunal shall simultaneously serve copies of the index on all nonindigent defendants and, at their request, copies of the record or portions of it at the cost prescribed by law.

(C) Briefs. Initial briefs shall be served within 30 days of service of the record or its index. Additional briefs shall be served as prescribed by rule 9.210.

(c) Petitions Seeking Belated Appeal or Alleging Ineffective Assistance of Appellate Counsel.

(1) Treatment as Original Proceedings. Review proceedings under this subdivision shall be treated as original proceedings under rule 9.100, except as modified by this rule.

(2) Forum. Petitions seeking belated appeal or alleging ineffective assistance of appellate counsel shall be filed in the appellate court to which the appeal was or should have been taken.

(3) Contents. The petition shall be in the form prescribed by rule 9.100, may include supporting documents, and shall recite in the statement of facts

(A) the date and nature of the lower tribunal's order sought to be reviewed;

(B) the name of the lower tribunal rendering the order;

(C) the nature, disposition, and dates of all previous proceedings in the lower tribunal and, if any, in appellate courts;

(D) if a previous petition was filed, the reason the claim in the present petition was not raised previously;

(E) the nature of the relief sought; and

(F) the specific acts sworn to by the petitioner or petitioner's counsel that constitute the alleged ineffective assistance of counsel or basis for entitlement to belated appeal, including in the case of a petition for belated appeal whether the petitioner requested counsel to proceed with the appeal.

(4) Time Limits.

(A) A petition for belated appeal shall not be filed more than 2 years after the expiration of time for filing the notice of appeal from a final order, unless it alleges under oath with a specific factual basis that the petitioner

(i) was unaware an appeal had not been timely filed or was not advised of the right to an appeal; and

(ii) should not have ascertained such facts by the exercise of reasonable diligence.

(B) A petition alleging ineffective assistance of appellate counsel shall not be filed more than 2 years after the conviction becomes final on direct review unless it alleges under oath with a specific factual basis that the petitioner was affirmatively misled about the results of the appeal by counsel.

(C) Time periods under this subdivision shall not begin to run prior to January 1, 1997.

(5) Procedure.

(A) The petitioner shall serve copies of the petition on the attorney general and state attorney.

(B) The court may by order identify any provision of this rule that the petition fails to satisfy and, pursuant to rule 9.040(d), allow the petitioner a specified time to serve an amended petition.

(C) The court may dismiss a second or successive petition if it does not allege new grounds and the prior determination was on the merits, or if a failure to assert the grounds was an abuse of procedure.

(D) An order granting a petition for belated appeal shall be filed with the lower tribunal and treated as the notice of appeal, if no previous notice has been filed.

History: Adopted Oct. 12, 2000, effective Jan. 1, 2001 (780 So. 2d 834; 2000 Fla. LEXIS 2273; 25 Fla. L. Weekly S 835); amended Oct. 18, 2001 (2001 Fla. LEXIS 2083; 26 Fla. L. Weekly S 686).

Committee Notes

2000 Amendment. Rule 9.141 is a new rule governing review of collateral or post-conviction criminal cases. It covers topics formerly included in rules 9.140(i) and (j). The committee opted to transfer these subjects to a new rule, in part because rule 9.140 was becoming lengthy. In addition, review proceedings for collateral criminal cases are in some respects treated as civil appeals or as extraordinary writs, rather than criminal appeals under rule 9.140.

Subdivision (a) clarifies that this rule does not apply to death penalty cases. The Supreme Court has its own procedures for these cases, and the committee did not attempt to codify them.

Subdivision (b)(2) amends former rule 9.140(i) and addresses review of summary grants or denials of post-conviction motions under Florida Rules of Criminal Procedure 3.800(a) or 3.850. Amended language in subdivision (b)(2)(A) makes minor changes to the contents of the record in such cases. Subdivision (b)(2)(B) addresses a conflict between *Summers v. State*, 570 So. 2d 990 (Fla. 1st DCA 1990), and *Fleming v. State*, 709 So. 2d 135 (Fla. 2d DCA 1998), regarding indexing and pagination of records. The First District requires clerks to index and paginate the records, while the other district courts do not. The committee determined not to require indexing and pagination unless the court directs otherwise, thereby allowing individual courts to require indexing and pagination if they so desire. Subdivision (b)(2)(B) also provides that neither the state nor the defendant should get a copy of the record in these cases, because they should already have all of the relevant documents. Subdivision (b)(2)(D) reflects current case law that the court can reverse not only for an evidentiary hearing but also for other appropriate relief.

Subdivision (b)(3) addresses review of grants or denials of post-conviction motions under rule 3.850 after an evidentiary hearing. Subdivision (b)(3)(A) provides for the preparation of a transcript if an indigent pro se litigant fails to request the court reporter to prepare it. The court cannot effectively carry out its duties without a transcript to review, and an indigent litigant will usually be entitled to preparation of the transcript and a copy of the record at no charge. *See Colonel v. State*, 723 So. 2d 853 (Fla. 3d DCA 1998). The procedures in subdivisions (b)(3)(B) and (C) for preparation of the record and service of briefs are intended to be similar to those provided in rule 9.140 for direct appeals from judgments and sentences.

Subdivision (c) is a slightly reorganized and clarified

R. App. Proc.

version of former rule 9.140(j). No substantive changes are intended.

Rule 9.142. Procedures for Review in Death Penalty Cases.

(a) Procedure in Death Penalty Appeals.

(1) Record. When the notice of appeal is filed in the supreme court, the chief justice will direct the appropriate chief judge of the circuit court to monitor the preparation of the complete record for timely filing in the supreme court.

(2) Briefs; Transcripts. After the record is filed, the clerk will promptly establish a briefing schedule allowing the defendant 60 days from the date the record is filed, the state 45 days from the date the defendant's brief is served, and the defendant 30 days from the date the state's brief is served to serve their respective briefs. On appeals from orders ruling on applications for relief under Florida Rule of Criminal Procedure 3.851 or 3.853, and on resentencing matters, the schedules set forth in rule 9.140(g) will control. In addition to filing paper copies of transcripts, the court reporter shall file with the clerk of the lower tribunal, on clearly labeled computer disks in a format approved by the supreme court, sufficient copies of these transcripts for the clerk of the lower tribunal to include the disks in the record transmitted to the court and to the parties.

(3) Sanctions. If any brief is delinquent, an order to show cause may issue under Florida Rule of Criminal Procedure 3.840, and sanctions may be imposed.

(4) Oral Argument. Oral argument will be scheduled after the filing of the defendant's reply brief.

(5) Petitions for Extraordinary Relief. In death penalty cases, all petitions for extraordinary relief over which the supreme court has original jurisdiction, including petitions for writ of habeas corpus, shall be filed simultaneously with the initial brief in the appeal from the lower tribunal's order on the defendant's application for relief under Florida Rule of Criminal Procedure 3.851.

(6) Scope of Review. In death penalty cases, whether or not insufficiency of the evidence or proportionality is an issue presented for review, the court shall review these issues and, if necessary, remand for the appropriate relief.

(b) Petition Seeking Review of Nonfinal Orders in Death Penalty Postconviction Proceedings.

(1) Applicability. This rule applies to proceedings that invoke the jurisdiction of the supreme court for review of nonfinal orders issued in postconviction proceedings following the imposition of the death penalty.

(2) Treatment as Original Proceedings. Review proceedings under this subdivision shall be treated as original proceedings under rule 9.100 unless modified by this subdivision.

(3) Commencement; Parties.

(A) Jurisdiction of the supreme court shall be invoked by filing a petition with the clerk of the supreme court within 30 days of rendition of the nonfinal order to be reviewed. A copy of the petition shall be served on the opposing party and furnished to the judge who issued the order to be reviewed.

(B) Either party to the death penalty postconviction proceedings may seek review under this rule.

(4) Contents. The petition shall be in the form prescribed by rule 9.100, and shall contain

(A) the basis for invoking the jurisdiction of the court;

(B) the date and nature of the order sought to be reviewed;

(C) the name of the lower tribunal rendering the order;

(D) the name, disposition, and dates of all previous trial, appellate, and postconviction proceedings relating to the conviction and death sentence that are the subject of the proceedings in which the order sought to be reviewed was entered;

(E) the facts on which the petitioner relies, with references to the appropriate pages of the supporting appendix;

(F) argument in support of the petition, including an explanation of why the order departs from the essential requirements of law and how the order may cause material injury for which there is no adequate remedy on appeal, and appropriate citations of authority; and

(G) the nature of the relief sought.

(5) Appendix. The petition shall be accompanied by an appendix, as prescribed by rule 9.220, which shall contain the portions of the record necessary for a determination of the issues presented.

(6) Order to Show Cause. If the petition demonstrates a preliminary basis for relief or a departure from the essential requirements of law that may cause material injury for which there is no adequate remedy by appeal, the court may issue an order directing the respondent to show cause, within the time set by the court, why relief should not be granted.

(7) Response. No response shall be permitted unless ordered by the court.

(8) Reply. Within 20 days after service of the response or such other time set by the court, the petitioner may serve a reply, which shall not exceed 15 pages in length, and supplemental appendix.

(9) Stay.

(A) A stay of proceedings under this rule is not automatic; the party seeking a stay must petition the supreme court for a stay of proceedings.

(B) During the pendency of a review of a nonfinal order, unless a stay is granted by the supreme court, the lower tribunal may proceed with all matters, except that the lower tribunal may not render a final order disposing of the cause pending review of the nonfinal order.

(10) Other Pleadings. The parties shall not file any other pleadings, motions, replies, or miscellaneous papers without leave of court.

(11) Time Limitations. Seeking review under this rule shall not extend the time limitations in rule 3.851 or 3.852.

History: Adopted Oct. 31, 2002, effective Jan. 1, 2003; amended Feb.3, 2005, effective Feb. 3, 2005 (2005 Fla. LEXIS 154; 30 Fla. L. Weekly S 84).

Rule 9.145. Appeal Proceedings in Juvenile Delinquency Cases.

(a) Applicability. Appeal proceedings in juvenile delinquency cases shall be as in rule 9.140 except as modified by this rule.

(b) Appeals by Child. To the extent adversely affected, a child or any parent, legal guardian, or custodian of a child may appeal

(1) an order of adjudication of delinquency or withholding adjudication of delinquency, or any disposition order entered thereon;

(2) orders entered after adjudication or withholding of adjudication of delinquency, including orders revoking or modifying the community control;

(3) an illegal disposition; or

(4) any other final order as provided by law.

(c) Appeals by the State.

(1) Appeals Permitted. The state may appeal an order

(A) dismissing a petition for delinquency or any part of it, if the order is entered before the commencement of an adjudicatory hearing;

(B) suppressing confessions, admissions, or evidence obtained by search and/or seizure before the adjudicatory hearing;

(C) granting a new adjudicatory hearing;

(D) arresting judgment;

(E) discharging a child under Florida Rule of Juvenile Procedure 8.090;

(F) ruling on a question of law if a child appeals an order of disposition;

(G) constituting an illegal disposition;

(H) discharging a child on habeas corpus; or

(I) finding a child incompetent pursuant to the

R. App. Proc.

Florida Rules of Juvenile Procedure.

(2) Non-Final State Appeals. If the state appeals a pre-adjudicatory hearing order of the trial court, the notice of appeal must be filed within 15 days of rendition of the order to be reviewed and before commencement of the adjudicatory hearing.

(A) A child in detention whose case is stayed pending state appeal shall be released from detention pending the appeal if the child is charged with an offense that would be bailable if the child were charged as an adult, unless the lower tribunal for good cause stated in an order determines otherwise. The lower tribunal retains discretion to release from detention any child who is not otherwise entitled to release under the provisions of this rule.

(B) If a child has been found incompetent to proceed, any order staying the proceedings on a state appeal shall have no effect on any order entered for the purpose of treatment.

(d) References to Child. The appeal shall be entitled and docketed with the initials, but not the name, of the child and the court case number. All references to the child in briefs, other papers, and the decision of the court shall be by initials.

(e) Confidentiality. All papers shall remain sealed in the office of the clerk of court when not in use by the court, and shall not be open to inspection except by the parties and their counsel, or as otherwise ordered.

History: Adopted Nov. 22, 1996, effective Jan. 1, 1997 (685 So.2d 773); amended Feb.3, 2005, effective Feb. 3, 2005 (2005 Fla. LEXIS 154; 30 Fla. L. Weekly S 84).

Committee Notes

1996 Adoption. Subdivision (c)(2) is intended to make clear that in non-final state appeals, the notice of appeal must be filed before commencement of the adjudicatory hearing. However, the notice of appeal must still be filed within 15 days of rendition of the order to be reviewed as provided by rule 9.140(c)(3). These two rules together provide that when an adjudicatory hearing occurs within 15 days or less of rendition of an order to be reviewed, the notice of appeal must be filed before commencement of the adjudicatory hearing. This rule is not intended to extend the 15 days allowed for filing the notice of appeal as provided by rule 9.140(c)(3).

Subdivision (d) requires the parties to use initials in all references to the child in all briefs and other papers filed in the court in furtherance of the appeal. It does not require the deletion of the name of the child from pleadings or other papers transmitted to the court from the lower tribunal.

Rule 9.146. Appeal Proceedings in Juvenile Dependency and Termination of Parental Rights Cases and Cases Involving Families and Children in Need of Services.

(a) Applicability. Appeal proceedings in juvenile dependency and termination of parental rights cases and cases involving families and children in need of services shall be as in civil cases except as modified by this rule.

(b) Appeals Permitted. Any child, any parent, guardian ad litem, or legal custodian of any child, any other party to the proceeding affected by an order of the lower tribunal, or the appropriate state agency as provided by law may appeal to the appropriate court within the time and in the manner prescribed by these rules.

(c) Stay of Proceedings.

(1) Application. Except as provided by general law and in subdivision (c)(2) of this rule, a party seeking to stay a final or non-final order pending review shall file a motion in the lower tribunal, which shall have continuing jurisdiction, in its discretion, to grant, modify, or deny such relief, after considering the welfare and best interest of the child.

(2) Termination of Parental Rights. The taking of an appeal shall not operate as a stay in any case unless pursuant to an order of the court, except that a termination of parental rights order with placement of the child with a licensed child-placing agency or the Department of Children and Family Services for subsequent adoption shall be suspended while the appeal is pending, but the child shall continue in custody under the order until the appeal is decided.

(d) Retention of Jurisdiction. Transmittal of the record to the appellate court does not remove the jurisdiction of the lower tribunal to conduct judicial reviews or other proceedings related to the health and welfare of the child pending appeal.

(e) References to Child or Parents. When the parent or child is a party to the appeal, the appeal shall be docketed and any papers filed in the court shall be titled with the initials, but not the name, of the child or parent and the court case number. All references to the child or parent in briefs, other papers, and the decision of the court shall be by initials.

(f) Confidentiality. All papers shall remain sealed in the office of the clerk of the court when not in use by the court, and shall not be open to inspection except by the parties and their counsel, or as otherwise ordered.

(g) Expedited Review. The court shall give priority to appeals under this rule.

History: Adopted Nov. 22, 1996, effective Jan. 1, 1997 (685 So.2d 773); amended Oct. 12, 2000, effective Jan. 1, 2001 (780 So. 2d 834; 2000 Fla. LEXIS 2273; 25 Fla. L. Weekly S 835).

Committee Notes

1996 Adoption. The reference in subdivision (a) to cases involving families and children in need of services encompasses only those cases in which an order has been entered adjudicating a child or family in need of services under chapter 39, Florida Statutes. Subdivision (c) requires the parties to use initials in all references to the child and parents in all briefs and other papers filed in the court in furtherance of the appeal. It does not require the deletion of the names of the child and parents from pleadings and other papers transmitted to the court from the lower tribunal.

Rule 9.150. Discretionary Proceedings to Review Certified Questions From Federal Courts.

(a) Applicability. On either its own motion or that of a party, the Supreme Court of the United States or a United States court of appeals may certify a question of law to the Supreme Court of Florida if the answer is determinative of the cause and there is no controlling precedent of the Supreme Court of Florida.

(b) Certificate. The certificate shall contain the style of the case, a statement of the facts showing the nature of the cause and the circumstances out of which the questions of law arise, and the questions of law to be answered. The certificate shall be prepared as directed by the federal court. It shall be certified to the Supreme Court of Florida by the clerk of the federal court.

(c) Record. The Supreme Court of Florida, in its discretion, may require copies of all or any portion of the record before the federal court to be filed if the record may be necessary to the determination of the cause.

(d) Briefs. The brief of the party designated by the federal court as the moving party shall be served within 20 days of the filing of the certificate. Additional briefs shall be served as prescribed by rule 9.210.

(e) Costs. The costs of these proceedings shall be divided equally between the parties unless otherwise ordered by the court.

History: Adopted March 27, 1980, effective April 1, 1980 (381 So.2d 1370). Amended Oct. 22, 1992, effective Jan. 1, 1993 (609 So.2d 516).

Committee Notes

1977 Amendment. This rule retains the substance of former rule 4.61. Except for simplification of language, the only change from the former rule is that answer and reply briefs are governed by the same time schedule as other cases. It is contemplated that the federal courts will continue the current practice of directing the parties to present a stipulated statement of the facts.

1980 Amendment. This rule is identical to former rule 9.510. It has been renumbered to reflect the addition to the Florida Constitution of article V, section 3(b)(6), which permits discretionary supreme court review of certified questions from the federal courts. Answer briefs and reply briefs will continue to be governed by the same time schedule as in other cases.

Rule 9.160. Discretionary Proceedings to Review Decisions of County Courts.

(a) Applicability. This rule applies to those proceedings that invoke the discretionary jurisdiction of the district courts of appeal to review county court orders described in rule 9.030(b)(4).

(b) Commencement. Any appeal of an order certified by the county court to be of great public importance must be taken to the district court of appeal. Jurisdiction of the district court of appeal under this rule shall be invoked by filing 2 copies of a notice and a copy of the order containing certification, accompanied by the filing fees prescribed by law, with the clerk or the lower tribunal. The time for filing the appeal shall be the same as if the appeal were being taken to the circuit court.

(c) Notice. The notice shall be in substantially the form prescribed by rule 9.900(a) or rule 9.900(c), depending on whether the order sought to be appealed is a final or a non-final order, except that such notice should refer to the fact of certification. Except in criminal cases, a conformed copy of the order or orders designated in the notice of appeal shall be attached to the notice together with any order entered on a timely motion postponing rendition of the order or orders appealed.

(d) Method of Certification. The certification may be made in the order subject to appeal or in any order disposing of a motion that has postponed rendition as defined in rule 9.020(h). The certification shall include (1) findings of fact and conclusions of law and (2) a concise statement of the issue or issues of great public importance.

(e) Discretion.

(1) Any party may suggest that an order be certified to be of great public importance. However, the decision to certify shall be within the absolute discretion of the county court and may be made by the court on its own motion.

(2) The district court of appeal, in its absolute discretion, shall by order accept or reject jurisdiction. Until the entry of such order, temporary jurisdiction shall be in the district court of appeal.

(f) Scope of Review.

(1) If the district court of appeal accepts the appeal, it will decide all issues that would have been subject to appeal if the appeal had been taken to the circuit court.

(2) If the district court declines to accept the appeal, it shall transfer the case together with the filing fee to the circuit court that has appellate jurisdiction.

(g) Record. The record shall be prepared and filed in accord with rule 9.110(e) or 9.140(f), depending on the nature of the appeal.

(h) Briefs. The form of the briefs and the briefing schedule shall be in accord with rules 9.110(f), 9.140, 9.210, and 9.220, depending on the nature of the appeal.

(i) Cross-Appeal. Cross-appeals shall be permitted according to the applicable rules only in those cases in which a cross-appeal would have been authorized if the appeal had been taken to circuit court.

(j) Applicability of Other Rules. All other matters pertaining to the appeal shall be governed by the rules that would be applicable if the appeal had been taken to circuit court.

History: Adopted Sept. 13, 1984, effective Oct. 1, 1984 (463 So.2d 1114). Amended Feb. 14, 1985, effective March 1, 1985 (463 So.2d 1124); Oct. 22, 1992, effective Jan. 1, 1993 (609 So.2d 516); Nov. 22, 1996, effective Jan. 1, 1997 (685 So.2d 773); Jan. 19, 2006, effective Jan. 19, 2006 (2006 Fla. LEXIS 10).

Committee Notes

1984 Amendment. This rule was added to implement the amendments to sections 26.012 and 924.08 and the adoption of section 34.195 by the 1984 Legislature. Section 34.195 authorizes only the certification of final judgments, but section 924.08 authorizes the certification of non-final orders in criminal cases. Therefore, this rule does not provide for appeals from non-final orders in civil cases. Under the rationale of *State v. Smith,* 260 So.2d 489 (Fla.1972), the authority to provide for appeals from non-final orders may rest in the supreme court rather than in the legislature. However, in keeping with the spirit of the legislation, the rule was drafted to permit certification of those non-final orders in criminal cases that would otherwise be appealable to the circuit court.

Sections 26.012 and 924.08 authorize only the certification of orders deemed to be of great public importance. However, section 34.195 refers to the certification of questions in final judgments if the question may have statewide application and is of great public importance or affects the uniform administration of justice. The committee concluded that any order certified to be of great public importance might have statewide application and that any order that would affect the uniform administration of justice would also be of great public importance. Therefore, the additional statutory language was deemed to be surplusage, and the rule refers only to the requirement of certifying the order to be of great public importance.

The district court of appeal may, in its discretion, decline to accept the appeal, in which event it shall be transferred to the appropriate circuit court for disposition in the ordinary manner. Except as stated in the rule, the procedure shall be the same as would be followed if the appeal were being taken to circuit court. The rule does not authorize review of certified orders by common law certiorari.

It is recommended that in those cases involving issues of great public importance, parties should file suggestions for certification before the entry of the order from which the appeal may be taken. However, parties are not precluded from suggesting certification following the entry of the order except that such suggestion, by itself, will not postpone rendition as defined in rule 9.020(h).

1992 Amendment. Subdivision (c) was amended to require that the appellant, except in criminal cases, attach to its notice of appeal a conformed copy of any orders designated in the notice of appeal, along with any orders on motions that postponed the rendition of orders appealed.

Rule 9.165. Repealed.

History: Repealed Feb. 14, 1985, effective March 1, 1985 (463 So.2d 1124).

Rule 9.180. Appeal Proceedings to Review Workers' Compensation Cases.

(a) Applicability. Appellate review of proceedings in workers' compensation cases shall be as in civil cases except as specifically modified in this rule.

(b) Jurisdiction.

(1) Appeal. The First District Court of Appeal (the court) shall review by appeal any final order, as well as any nonfinal order of a lower tribunal that adjudicates

(A) jurisdiction;

(B) venue; or

(C) compensability, provided that the order expressly finds an injury occurred within the scope and course of employment and that claimant is entitled to receive causally related benefits in some amount, and provided further that the lower tribunal certifies in the order that determination of the exact nature and amount of benefits due to claimant will require substantial expense and time.

(2) Waiver of Review: Abbreviated Final Orders. Unless a request for findings of fact and conclusions of law is timely filed, review by appeal of an abbreviated final order shall be deemed waived. The filing of a timely request tolls the time within which an abbreviated final order becomes final or an appeal may be filed.

(3) Commencement. Jurisdiction of the court shall be invoked by filing two copies of a notice of appeal with the lower tribunal, accompanied by the filing fee prescribed by law unless a verified petition for relief from payment of the fee has been filed with the lower tribunal within 30 days of the date the order to be reviewed is mailed by the lower tribunal to the parties, which date shall be the date of rendition.

(4) Notice of Appeal. The notice shall be substantially in the form prescribed by rule 9.900(a), and shall contain a brief summary of the type of benefits affected, including a statement setting forth the time periods involved which shall be substantially in the following form:

I hereby certify that this appeal affects only the following periods and classifications of benefits and medical treatment: 1. Compensation for ________ (TTD, TPD, wage loss, impairment benefits, PTD, funeral benefits, or death benefits) ________ from ________ (date) to ________ (date) 2. Medical benefits. 3. Rehabilitation. 4. Reimbursement from the SDTF for benefits paid from ________ (date) to ________ (date) 5. Contribution for benefits paid from ________ (date) to ________ (date)

(c) Jurisdiction of Lower Tribunal.

(1) Substantive Issues. The lower tribunal retains jurisdiction to decide the issues that have not been adjudicated and are not the subject of pending appellate review.

(2) Settlement. At any time before the record on appeal is filed with the court, the lower

R. App. Proc.

tribunal shall have the authority to approve settlements or correct clerical errors in the order appealed.

(3) Relinquishment of Jurisdiction by Court to Consider Settlement. If, after the record on appeal is filed, settlement is reached, the parties shall file a joint motion stating that a settlement has been reached and requesting relinquishment of jurisdiction to the lower tribunal for any necessary approval of the settlement. The court may relinquish jurisdiction for a specified period for entry of an appropriate order. In the event the Division of Workers' Compensation has advanced the costs of preparing the record on appeal or the filing fee, a copy of the joint motion shall be furnished to the division by the appellant.

(A) Notice. On or before the date specified in the order relinquishing jurisdiction, the parties shall file a joint notice of disposition of the settlement with a conformed copy of any order entered on the settlement.

(B) Costs. Any order approving a settlement shall provide where appropriate for the assessment and recovery of appellate costs, including any costs incurred by the division for insolvent appellants.

(d) Benefits Affected. Benefits specifically referenced in the notice of appeal may be withheld as provided by law pending the outcome of the appeal. Otherwise, benefits awarded shall be paid as required by law.

(1) Abandonment. If the appellant or cross-appellant fails to argue entitlement to benefits set forth in the notice of appeal in the appellant's or cross-appellant's initial brief, the challenge to such benefits shall be deemed abandoned. If there is a dispute as to whether a challenge to certain benefits has been abandoned, the court upon motion shall make that determination.

(2) Payments of Benefits When Challenged Benefits Are Abandoned. When benefits challenged on appeal have been abandoned under subdivision (d)(1) above, benefits no longer affected by the appeal are payable within 30 days of the service of the brief together with interest as required under section 440.20, Florida Statutes, from the date of the order of the lower tribunal making the award.

(3) Payment of Benefits After Appeal. If benefits are ordered paid by the court on completion of the appeal, they shall be paid, together with interest as required under section 440.20, Florida Statutes, within 30 days after the court's mandate. If the order of the court is appealed to the supreme court, benefits determined due by the court may be stayed in accordance with rule 9.310. Benefits ordered paid by the supreme court shall be paid within 30 days of the court's mandate.

(e) Intervention by Division of Workers' Compensation.

(1) District Court. Within 30 days of the date of filing a notice or petition invoking the jurisdiction of the court the Division of Workers' Compensation may intervene by filing a notice of intervention as a party appellant/petitioner or appellee/respondent with the court and take positions on any relevant matters.

(2) Supreme Court. If review of an order of the court is sought in the supreme court, the division may intervene in accordance with these rules. The clerk of the supreme court shall provide a copy of the pertinent papers to the division.

(3) Division Not a Party Until Notice to Intervene Is Filed. Until the notice of intervention is filed, the division shall not be considered a party.

(f) Record Contents: Final Orders.

(1) Transcript, Order, and Other Documents. The record shall contain the claim(s) or petition(s) for benefits, notice(s) of denial, pretrial stipulation, pretrial order, depositions or exhibits admitted into evidence, transcripts of any hearings before the lower tribunal and the order appealed. The parties may designate other items for inclusion in or omission from the record in accordance with rule 9.200.

(2) Proffered Evidence. Evidence proffered but not introduced into evidence at the hearing shall not be considered unless its admissibility is an issue on appeal and the question is properly

designated for inclusion in the record by a party.

(3) Certification and Transmittal. The lower tribunal shall certify and transmit the record to the court as prescribed by these rules.

(4) Stipulated Record. The parties may stipulate to the contents of the record. In such a case the record shall consist of the stipulated statement and the order appealed which the lower tribunal shall certify as the record on appeal.

(5) Costs.

(A) Notice of Estimated Costs. Within 5 days after the contents of the record have been determined under these rules, the lower tribunal shall notify the appellant of the estimated cost of preparing the record. The lower tribunal also shall notify the Division of Workers' Compensation of the estimated record costs if the appellant files a verified petition to be relieved of costs and a sworn financial affidavit in substantially the same form as form 4.9125 of the Rules of Workers' Compensation Procedure.

(B) Deposit of Estimated Costs. Within 15 days after the notice of estimated costs is served, the appellant shall deposit a sum of money equal to the estimated costs with the lower tribunal.

(C) Failure to Deposit Costs. If the appellant fails to deposit the estimated costs within the time prescribed, the lower tribunal shall notify the court, which may dismiss the appeal.

(D) State Agencies: Waiver of Costs. Any self-Insured state agency or branch of state government, including the division and the Special Disability Trust Fund, need not deposit the estimated costs.

(E) Costs. If additional costs are incurred in correcting, amending, or supplementing the record, the lower tribunal shall assess such costs against the appropriate party. If the division is obligated to pay the costs of the appeal due to appellant's indigency, it must be given notice of any proceeding to assess additional costs. Within 15 days after the entry of the order assessing costs, the assessed party must deposit the sums so ordered with the lower tribunal. The lower tribunal shall promptly notify the court if costs are not deposited as required.

(6) Preparation of Record.

(A) Selection of Reporter by Lower Tribunal. The lower tribunal shall supervise the preparation of the record. The lower tribunal or chief judge of compensation claims shall select the reporter or transcriber to prepare the record. The judge who makes the selection shall give the parties notice of the selection.

(B) Objection to Reporter or Transcriber Selected. Any party may object to the reporter or transcriber selected by filing written objections with the judge who made the selection within 15 days after service of notice of the selection. Within 5 days after filing the objection, the judge shall hold a hearing on the issue. In such a case, the time limits mandated by these rules shall be appropriately extended.

(C) Certification of Record by Court Reporter or Transcriber. The reporter or transcriber designated by the lower tribunal or chief judge of compensation claims shall transcribe, certify, and deliver all necessary copies of the record to the lower tribunal as required under these rules. The record shall be delivered in sufficient time for the lower tribunal to review the record and send it to the court. The reporter or transcriber shall promptly notify all parties in writing when the record is delivered to the lower tribunal.

(D) Certification and Transmittal by Lower Tribunal. The lower tribunal shall review the original record, certify that it was prepared in accordance with these rules, and within 60 days of the notice of appeal being filed transmit the record to the court.

(E) Copies. The lower tribunal shall provide a copy of the record to all counsel of record and all unrepresented parties.

(7) Extensions. For good cause, the lower tribunal may extend by no more than 30 days the time for filing the record with the court. Any further extension of time may be granted by the court.

(8) Applicability of Rule 9.200. Rules 9.200(a)(2), (c), and (f) shall apply to preparation of the record in appeals under this rule.

(g) Relief From Filing Fee and Costs: Indi-

R. App. Proc.

gency.

(1) Indigency Defined. Indigency for the purpose of this rule is synonymous with insolvency as defined by section 440.02, Florida Statutes.

(2) Filing Fee.

(A) Authority. An appellant may be relieved of paying filing fees by filing a verified petition or motion of indigency under section 57.081(1), Florida Statutes, with the lower tribunal.

(B) Time. The verified petition or motion of indigency must be filed with the lower tribunal together with the notice of appeal.

(C) Verified Petition: Contents. The verified petition or motion shall contain a statement by the appellant to be relieved of paying filing fees due to indigency and appellant's inability to pay the charges. The petition shall request that the lower tribunal enter an order or certificate of indigency. One of the following shall also be filed in support of the verified petition or motion:

(i) If the appellant is unrepresented by counsel, a financial affidavit; or

(ii) If the appellant is represented by counsel, counsel shall certify that counsel has investigated (a) the appellant's financial condition and finds appellant indigent; and (b) the nature of appellant's position and believes it to be meritorious as a matter of law. Counsel shall also certify that counsel has not been paid or promised payment of a fee or other remuneration for such legal services except for the amount, if any, ultimately approved by the lower tribunal to be paid by the employer/carrier if such entitlement is determined by the court.

(D) Service. Appellant shall serve a copy of the verified petition or motion of indigency, including appellant's financial affidavit or counsel's certificate, whichever is applicable, on all interested parties, and the clerk of the court.

(E) Order or Certificate of Indigency. The lower tribunal shall review the verified petition or motion for indigency and supporting documents without a hearing, and if the lower tribunal finds compliance with section 57.081(1), Florida Statutes, may issue a certificate of indigency or enter an order granting said relief, at which time appellant may proceed without further application to the court and without payment of any filing fees. If the lower tribunal enters an order denying relief, appellant shall deposit the filing fee with the lower tribunal within 15 days from the date of the order unless timely review is sought by motion filed with the court.

(3) Costs of Preparation of Record.

(A) Authority. An appellant may be relieved in whole or in part from the costs of the preparation of the record on appeal by filing with the lower tribunal a verified petition to be relieved of costs and a copy of the designation of the record on appeal. The verified petition to be relieved of costs shall contain a sworn financial affidavit as described in subdivision (D) in a form substantially the same as form 4.9125 of the Rules of Workers' Compensation Procedure.

(B) Time. The verified petition to be relieved of costs must be filed within 15 days after service of the notice of estimated costs. A verified petition filed prior to the date of service of the notice of estimated costs shall be deemed not timely.

(C) Verified Petition: Contents. The verified petition shall contain a request by appellant to be relieved of costs due to insolvency. The petition also shall include a statement by the appellant's attorney or the appellant, if not represented by an attorney, that the appeal was filed in good faith and the court reasonably could find reversible error in the record and shall state with particularity the specific legal and factual grounds for that opinion.

(D) Sworn Financial Affidavit: Contents. With the verified petition to be relieved of costs, the appellant shall file a sworn financial affidavit listing income and assets, including marital income and assets, and expenses and liabilities. The sworn financial affidavit shall be substantially the same as form 4.9125.

(E) Verified Petition and Sworn Financial Affidavit: Service. The appellant shall serve a copy of the verified petition to be relieved of costs, including the sworn financial affidavit, on all interested parties, including the Division of Workers' Compensation, the office of general counsel of the Department Financial Services, and the clerk of the court.

(F) Hearing on Petition to Be Relieved of Costs. After giving 15 days' notice to the Division of Workers' Compensation and all parties, the lower tribunal shall promptly hold a hearing and rule on the merits of the petition to be relieved of costs. However, if no objection to the petition is filed by the Division or a party within 20 days after the petition is served, the lower tribunal may enter an order on the merits of the petition without a hearing.

(G) Extension of Appeal Deadlines: Petition Granted. If the petition to be relieved of the entire cost of the preparation of the record on appeal is granted, the 60-day period allowed under these rules for the preparation of the record shall begin to run from the date of the order granting the petition.

(H) Extension of Appeal Deadlines: Petition Denied. If the petition to be relieved of the cost of the record is denied or only granted in part, the petitioner shall deposit the estimated costs with the lower tribunal within 15 days from the date the order denying the petition is entered. The 60-day period allowed under these rules for the preparation of the record shall begin from the date the estimated cost is deposited with the lower tribunal.

(I) Payment of Cost for Preparation of Record by Administration Trust Fund. If the petition to be relieved of costs is granted, the lower tribunal may order the Workers' Compensation Administration Trust Fund to pay the cost of the preparation of the record on appeal pending the final disposition of the appeal. The lower tribunal shall provide a copy of such order to all interested parties, including the division, general counsel of the Department of Financial Services, and the clerk of the court.

(J) Reimbursement of Administration Trust Fund If Appeal Is Successful. If the Administration Trust Fund has paid the costs of the preparation of the record and the appellant prevails at the conclusion of the appeal, the appellee shall reimburse the fund the costs paid within 30 days of the mandate issued by the court or supreme court under these rules.

(h) Briefs and Motions Directed to Briefs.

(1) Briefs: Final Order Appeals. Within 30 days after the lower tribunal certifies the record to the court, the appellant shall serve the initial brief. Additional briefs shall be served as prescribed by rule 9.210.

(2) Briefs: Non-Final Appeals. Appellant's initial brief, accompanied by an appendix as prescribed by rule 9.220, shall be served within 15 days of filing the notice. Additional briefs shall be served as prescribed by rule 9.210.

(3) Motions to Strike. Motions to strike a brief or portions of a brief will not be entertained by the court. However, a party, in its own brief, may call to the court's attention a breach of these rules. If no further responsive brief is authorized, noncompliance may be brought to the court's attention by filing a suggestion of noncompliance. Statements in briefs not supported by the record shall be disregarded and may constitute cause for imposition of sanctions.

(i) Attorneys' Fees and Appellate Costs.

(1) Costs. Appellate costs shall be taxed as provided by law. Taxable costs shall include those items listed in rule 9.400 and costs for a transcript included in an appendix as part of an appeal of a nonfinal order.

(2) Attorneys' Fees. A motion for attorneys' fees shall be served in accordance with rule 9.400(b).

(3) Entitlement and Amount of Fees and Costs. If the court determines that an appellate fee is due, the lower tribunal shall have jurisdiction to conduct hearings and consider evidence regarding the amount of the attorney fee and costs due at any time after the mandate is issued.

(4) Review. Review shall be in accordance with rule 9.400(c).

R. App. Proc.

History: Adopted Nov. 22, 1996, effective Jan. 1, 1997 (685 So.2d 773); amended Oct. 12, 2000, effective Jan. 1, 2001 (780 So. 2d 834; 2000 Fla. LEXIS 2273; 25 Fla. L. Weekly S 835); Aug. 29, 2002, effective Jan. 1, 2003; amended Feb.3, 2005, effective Feb. 3, 2005 (2005 Fla. LEXIS 154; 30 Fla. L. Weekly S 84).

Committee Notes

1996 Adoption. Rule 9.180 is intended to supersede rules 4.160, 4.161, 4.165, 4.166, 4.170, 4.180, 4.190, 4.220, 4.225, 4.230, 4.240, 4.250, 4.260, 4.265, 4.270, and 4.280 of the Rules of Workers' Compensation Procedure. In consolidating those rules into one rule and incorporating them into the Rules of Appellate Procedure, duplicative rules have been eliminated. The change was not intended to change the general nature of workers' compensation appeals. It is contemplated there still may be multiple "final orders." See 1980 Committee Note, Fla. R. Work. Comp. P. 4.160.

The orders listed in rules 9.180(b)(1)(A), (B), and (C) are the only nonfinal orders appealable before entry of a final order in workers' compensation cases.

Rule 9.180(b)(2) now limits the place for filing the notice of appeal to the lower tribunal that entered the order and not any judge of compensation claims as the former rule provided.

Rule 9.180(f)(6)(E) provides that the lower tribunal shall provide a copy of the record to all counsel of record and all unrepresented parties. It is contemplated that the lower tribunal can accomplish that in whatever manner the lower tribunal deems most convenient for itself, such as, having copies available that counsel or the parties may pick up.

Rule 9.190. Judicial Review of Administrative Action.

(a) Applicability. Judicial review of administrative action shall be governed by the general rules of appellate procedure except as specifically modified herein.

(b) Commencement.

(1) An appeal from final agency action as defined in the Administrative Procedure Act, chapter 120, Florida Statutes, or other administrative action for which judicial review is provided by general law shall be commenced in accordance with rule 9.110(c).

(2) Review of non-final agency action, including non-final action by an administrative law judge, under the Administrative Procedure Act shall be commenced by filing a petition for review in accordance with rules 9.100(b) and (c).

(3) Review of quasi-judicial decisions of any administrative body, agency, board, or commission not subject to the Administrative Procedure Act shall be commenced by filing a petition for certiorari in accordance with rules 9.100(b) and (c), unless judicial review by appeal is provided by general law.

(c) The Record.

(1) Generally. As further described in this rule, the record shall include only materials furnished to and reviewed by the lower tribunal in advance of the administrative action to be reviewed by the court.

(2) Review of Final Action Pursuant to the Administrative Procedure Act.

(A) In an appeal from any proceeding conducted pursuant to section 120.56 (rule challenges) or sections 120.569 (decisions which affect substantial interests) and 120.57(1), Florida Statutes (decisions which affect substantial interests involving disputed material facts), the record shall consist of all notices, pleadings, motions, and intermediate rulings; evidence admitted; those matters officially recognized; proffers of proof and objections and rulings thereon; proposed findings and exceptions; any decision, opinion, order, or report by the presiding officer; all staff memoranda or data submitted to the presiding officer during the hearing or prior to its disposition, after notice of submission to all parties, except communications by advisory staff as permitted under section 120.66(1), Florida Statutes, if such communications are public records; all matters placed on the record after an ex parte communication; and the official transcript.

(B) In an appeal from any proceeding pursuant to sections 120.569 (decisions which affect substantial interests) and 120.57(2), Florida Statutes (decisions which affect substantial interests involving no disputed issue of material fact), the record shall consist of the notice and summary of grounds; evidence received; all written statements submitted; any decisions overruling objections; all matters placed on the record after an ex parte communication; the official transcript; and any decision, opinion, order, or report by the presiding officer.

(C) In an appeal from any proceeding pursuant to section 120.565, Florida Statutes (declaratory statements), the record shall consist of the petition seeking a declaratory statement and any pleadings filed with the agency; all notices relating to the petition published in the Florida Administrative Weekly; the declaratory statement issued by the agency or the agency's denial of the petition; and all matters listed in subdivision (c)(2)(A) or (c)(2)(B) of this rule, whichever is appropriate, if a hearing is held on the declaratory statement petition.

(D) In an appeal from any proceeding pursuant to section 120.574, Florida Statutes (summary proceeding), the record shall consist of all notices, pleadings, motions, and intermediate rulings; evidence received; a statement of matters officially recognized; proffers of proof and objections and rulings thereon; matters placed on the record after an ex parte communication; the written decision of the administrative law judge presiding at the final hearing; and the official transcript of the final hearing.

(E) In an appeal from a rule adoption pursuant to sections 120.54 (rule adoption) and 120.68(9), Florida Statutes, in which the sole issue presented by the petition is the constitutionality of a rule and there are no disputed issues of fact, the record shall consist only of those documents from the rulemaking record compiled by the agency that materially address the constitutional issue. The agency's rulemaking record consists of all notices given for the proposed rule; any statement of estimated regulatory costs for the rule; a written summary of hearings on the proposed rule; the written comments and responses to written comments as required by sections 120.54 (rule adoption) and 120.541, Florida Statutes (statement of estimated regulatory costs); all notices and findings made pursuant to section 120.54(4), Florida Statues (adoption of emergency rules); all materials filed by the agency with the Administrative Procedures Committee pursuant to section 120.54(3), Florida Statutes (rule adoption procedure); all materials filed with the Department of State pursuant to section 120.54(3), Florida Statutes (rule adoption procedure); and all written inquiries from standing committees of the legislature concerning the rule.

(3) Review of Non-Final Action Pursuant to the Administrative Procedure Act. The provisions of rules 9.100 and 9.220 govern the record in proceedings seeking review of non-final administrative action.

(4) Review of Administrative Action Not Subject to the Administrative Procedure Act. In proceedings seeking review of administrative action not governed by the Administrative Procedure Act, the clerk of the lower tribunal shall not be required to prepare a record or record index. The petitioner or appellant shall submit an appendix in accordance with rule 9.220. Supplemental appendices may be submitted by any party. Appendices may not contain any matter not made part of the record in the lower tribunal.

(5) Videotaped Testimony. In any circumstance in which hearing testimony is preserved through the use of videotape rather than through an official transcript, the testimony from the videotape shall be transcribed and the transcript shall be made a part of the record before the record is transmitted to the court.

(6) Modified Record. The contents of the record may be modified as provided in rule 9.200(a)(3).

(d) Attorneys' Fees.

(1) Attorneys' Fees. A motion for attorneys' fees may be served not later than the time for service of the reply brief and shall state the grounds on which the recovery is sought, citing all pertinent statutes.

(2) Disputes As To Amount. If the court decides to award attorney's fees, the court may either remand the matter to the lower tribunal or to the administrative law judge for determination of the amount, or refer the matter to a special magistrate.

R. App. Proc.

(3) Review. Review of orders entered by the lower tribunal or the administrative law judge rendered under this rule shall be by motion filed in the court within 30 days of rendition of the order. Objections to reports of special magistrates shall be filed with this court within 30 days after the special magistrate's report is filed with the court.

(e) Stays Pending Review.

(1) Effect of Initiating Review. The filing of a notice of administrative appeal or a petition seeking review of administrative action shall not operate as a stay, except that such filing shall give rise to an automatic stay as provided in rule 9.310(b)(2) or when timely review is sought of an award by an administrative law judge on a claim for birth-related neurological injuries.

(2) Application for Stay Under the Administrative Procedure Act.

(A) A party seeking to stay administrative action may file a motion either with the lower tribunal or, for good cause shown, with the court in which the notice or petition has been filed. The filing of the motion shall not operate as a stay. The lower tribunal or court may grant a stay upon appropriate terms. Review of orders entered by lower tribunals shall be by the court on motion.

(B) When an agency has ordered emergency suspension, restriction, or limitation of a license under section 120.60(6), Florida Statutes, a licensee may file with the reviewing court a motion for stay on an expedited basis. The court may issue an order to show cause and, after considering the agency's response, if timely filed, grant a stay on appropriate terms.

(C) When an agency has suspended or revoked a license other than on an emergency basis, a licensee may file with the reviewing court a motion for stay on an expedited basis. The agency may file a response within 10 days of the filing of the motion, or within a shorter time period set by the court. Unless the agency files a timely response demonstrating that a stay would constitute a probable danger to health, safety or welfare of the state, the court shall grant a motion and issue a stay.

(D) When an order suspending or revoking a license has been stayed pursuant to subdivision (2)(C), an agency may apply to the court for dissolution or modification of the stay on grounds that subsequently acquired information demonstrates that failure to dissolve or modify the stay would constitute a probable danger to the public health, safety, or welfare of the state.

(3) Application for Stay or Supersedeas of Other Administrative Action. A party seeking to stay administrative action, not governed by the Administrative Procedure Act, shall file a motion in the lower tribunal, which shall have continuing jurisdiction, in its discretion, to grant, modify, or deny such relief. A stay pending review may be conditioned on the posting of a good and sufficient bond, other conditions, or both. Review of orders entered by lower tribunals shall be by the court on motion.

(4) Duration. A stay entered by a lower tribunal or a court shall remain in effect during the pendency of all review proceedings in Florida courts until a mandate issues, unless otherwise modified or vacated.

History: Adopted Sept. 27, 1996, effective Oct. 1, 1996 (681 So.2d 1132); amended Oct. 12, 2000, effective Jan. 1, 2001 (780 So. 2d 834; 2000 Fla. LEXIS 2273; 25 Fla. L. Weekly S 835); Aug. 29, 2002, effective Jan. 1, 2003; amended Feb.3, 2005, effective Feb. 3, 2005 (2005 Fla. LEXIS 154; 30 Fla. L. Weekly S 84).

Committee Notes

1996 Amendment. Appeals which fall within the exception included in subdivision (b)(3) are commenced in accordance with subdivision (b)(1). Therefore, administrative action by appeal in a circuit court, if prescribed by general law, is commenced pursuant to subdivision (b)(1). Unless review of administrative action in circuit court is prescribed by general law to be by appeal, review in circuit court is by petition for an extraordinary writ commenced pursuant to subdivision (b)(3). See *Board of County Commissioners v. Snyder*, 627 So. 2d 469 (Fla. 1993); *Grace v. Town of Palm Beach*, 656 So. 2d 945 (Fla. 4th DCA 1995). Subdivision (b)(3) supersedes all local government charters, ordinances, rules and regulations which purport to provide a method of review in conflict herewith.

Subdivision (c) was adopted to identify more clearly what constitutes the record in appeals from administrative proceedings. Several sections of the Florida Administrative Procedure Act, as revised in 1996, specifically state what shall constitute the record in certain types of proceedings, and this rule incorporates that statutory language. The rule makes clear that the record shall include only materials that were furnished to and reviewed by the lower tribunal in advance of the administrative action to be reviewed. The intent of this statement is to avoid the inclusion of extraneous materials in the record that were never reviewed by the lower tribunal.

Subdivision (c)(2)(A) is based on provisions of section 120.57(1)(f), Florida Statutes. This subdivision of the rule governs the record from proceedings conducted pursuant to section 120.56 and sections 120.569 and 120.57(1), Florida Statutes. This is because section 120.56(1)(e), Florida Statutes, states that hearings under section 120.56, Florida Statutes, shall be conducted in the same manner as provided by sections 120.569 and 120.57, Florida Statutes.

Subdivision (c)(2)(B) lists the provisions of section 120.57(2)(b), Florida Statutes. Subdivision (c)(2)(B)(vii), which refers to "any decision, opinion, order, or report by the presiding officer," was added by the committee to the list of statutory requirements.

Subdivision (c)(2)(C) addresses the record on appeal from declaratory statement requests pursuant to section 120.565, while subdivision (c)(2)(D) lists the provisions of section 120.574(2)(d), Florida Statutes. Subdivision (c)(2)(E) of the rule addresses proceedings governed by sections 120.54 and 120.68(9), Florida Statutes. The definition of the rulemaking record tracks language in section 120.54 (8), Florida Statutes.

Subdivision (c)(3) makes clear that rules 9.100 and 9.220 govern the record in proceedings seeking review of non-final administrative action, while subdivision (c)(4) governs the record in administrative proceedings not subject to the Administrative Procedure Act.

Subdivision (c)(5) states that if videotape is used to preserve hearing testimony, the videotape shall be transcribed before the record is transmitted to the court.

Subdivision (d) was adopted to conform to the 1996 revisions to the Administrative Procedure Act. Recoupment of costs is still governed by rule 9.400.

2000 Amendment. Subdivision (e) was added to address stays pending judicial review of administrative action. Ordinarily, application for a stay must first be made to the lower tribunal, but some agencies have collegial heads who meet only occasionally. If a party can show good cause for applying initially to the court for a stay, it may do so. When an appeal has been taken from a license suspension or revocation under the Administrative Procedure Act, good cause for not applying first to the lower tribunal is presumed.

Subdivision (e)(2)(B) deals with stays of orders which suspend licenses on an emergency basis. Before entering an emergency suspension order, the agency must make a finding that immediate suspension is necessary to protect the public health, safety, or welfare. § 120.60(6), Fla. Stat. (1999). In effect, the agency makes a finding that would be sufficient to defeat issuance of the "stay as a matter of right" contemplated by section 120.68(3), Florida Statutes. The agency's finding is subject to judicial review, however, on application for a stay under subdivision (e)(2)(B).

Absent an emergency suspension order, the court grants a stay as of right in Administrative Procedure Act license suspension and revocation cases unless the licensing agency makes a timely showing that a stay "would constitute a probable danger to the health, safety, or welfare of the state." § 120.68(3), Fla. Stat. (1999). The court can shorten the 10 day period specified in subdivision (e)(2)(c). If the court stays a nonemergency suspension or revocation, the licensing agency can move to modify or dissolve the stay on the basis of material information that comes to light after the stay is issued.

Nothing in subdivision (e) precludes licensing agencies from making suspension or revocation orders effective 30 days after entry, granting stays pending judicial review, or taking other steps to implement section 120.68(3), Florida Statutes.

2004 Amendment. Subdivision (e)(2)(C) was amended to clarify that the ten days (or shorter period set by the court) within which the agency has to respond run from the filing of the motion for the stay. See *Ludwig v. Dept. of Health*, 778. So.2d 531 (Fla. 1 st DCA 2001).

Rule 9.200. The Record.

(a) Contents.

(1) Except as otherwise designated by the parties, the record shall consist of the original documents, exhibits, and transcript(s) of proceedings, if any, filed in the lower tribunal, except summonses, praecipes, subpoenas, returns, notices of hearing or taking deposition, depositions, other discovery, and physical evidence. The record shall also include a progress docket.

R. App. Proc.

(2) In family law cases the record shall include those items designated in subdivision (a)(1) except that the clerk of the lower tribunal shall retain the original orders, reports and recommendations of masters or hearing officers, and judgments within the file of the lower tribunal and shall include copies thereof within the record.

(3) Within 10 days of filing the notice of appeal, an appellant may direct the clerk to include or exclude other documents or exhibits filed in the lower tribunal. The directions shall be substantially in the form prescribed by rule 9.900(f). If the clerk is directed to transmit less than the entire record or a transcript of trial with less than all of the testimony, the appellant shall serve with such direction a statement of the judicial acts to be reviewed. Within 20 days of filing the notice, an appellee may direct the clerk to include additional documents and exhibits.

(4) The parties may prepare a stipulated statement showing how the issues to be presented arose and were decided in the lower tribunal, attaching a copy of the order to be reviewed and as much of the record in the lower tribunal as is necessary to a determination of the issues to be presented. The parties shall advise the clerk of their intention to rely on a stipulated statement in lieu of the record as early in advance of filing as possible. The stipulated statement shall be filed by the parties and transmitted to the court by the clerk of the lower tribunal within the time prescribed for transmittal of the record.

(b) Transcript(s) of Proceedings.

(1) Within 10 days of filing the notice, the appellant shall designate those portions of the proceedings not on file deemed necessary for transcription and inclusion in the record. Within 20 days of filing the notice, an appellee may designate additional portions of the proceedings. Copies of designations shall be served on the court reporter. Costs of the original and all copies of the transcript(s) so designated shall be borne initially by the designating party, subject to appropriate taxation of costs as prescribed by rule 9.400. At the time of the designation, unless other satisfactory arrangements have been made, the designating party must make a deposit of ½ of the estimated transcript costs, and must pay the full balance of the fee on delivery of the completed transcript(s).

(2) Within 30 days of service of a designation, or within the additional time provided for under subdivision (b)(3) of this rule, the court reporter shall transcribe and deliver to the clerk of the lower tribunal the designated proceedings and shall furnish copies as requested in the designation. If a designating party directs the court reporter to furnish the transcript(s) to fewer than all parties, that designating party shall serve a copy of the designated transcript(s) on the parties within 5 days of receipt from the court reporter. The transcript of the trial shall be securely bound in consecutively numbered volumes not to exceed 200 pages each, and each page shall be numbered consecutively. Each volume shall be prefaced by an index containing the names of the witnesses, a list of all exhibits offered and introduced in evidence, and the pages where each may be found.

(3) On service of a designation, the reporter shall acknowledge at the foot of the designation the fact that it has been received and the date on which the reporter expects to have the transcript(s) completed and shall transmit the designation, so endorsed, to the parties and to the clerk of the appellate court within 5 days of service. If the transcript(s) cannot be completed within 30 days of service of the designation, the reporter shall request such additional time as is reasonably necessary and shall state the reasons therefor. If the reporter requests an extension of time, the court shall allow the parties 5 days in which to object or agree. The appellate court shall approve the request or take other appropriate action and shall notify the reporter and the parties of the due date of the transcript(s).

(4) If no report of the proceedings was made, or if the transcript is unavailable, the appellant may prepare a statement of the evidence or proceedings from the best available means, including the appellant's recollection. The statement shall be served on the appellee, who may serve objections or proposed amendments to it within 10 days of service. Thereafter, the statement and any objections or proposed amendments shall be submitted to the lower tribunal

for settlement and approval. As settled and approved, the statement shall be included by the clerk of the lower tribunal in the record.

(c) Cross-Appeals. Within 20 days of filing the notice, a cross-appellant may direct that additional documents, exhibits, or transcript(s) be included in the record. If less than the entire record is designated, the cross-appellant shall serve, with the directions, a statement of the judicial acts to be reviewed. The cross-appellee shall have 10 days after such service to direct further additions. The time for preparation and transmittal of the record shall be extended by 10 days.

(d) Duties of Clerk; Preparation and Transmittal of Record.

(1) The clerk of the lower tribunal shall prepare the record as follows:

(A) The clerk of the lower tribunal shall not be required to verify and shall not charge for the incorporation of any transcript(s) into the record. The transcript of the trial shall be incorporated at the end of the record, and shall not be renumbered by the clerk. The progress docket shall be incorporated into the record immediately after the index.

(B) The remainder of the record, including all supplements and any transcripts other than the transcript of the trial, shall be consecutively numbered. The record shall be securely bound in consecutively numbered volumes not to exceed 200 pages each. The cover sheet of each volume shall contain the name of the lower tribunal and the style and number of the case.

(2) The clerk of the lower tribunal shall prepare a complete index to the record and shall attach a copy of the progress docket to the index.

(3) The clerk of the lower tribunal shall certify and transmit the record to the court as prescribed by these rules; provided that if the parties stipulate or the lower tribunal orders that the original record be retained, the clerk shall prepare and transmit a certified copy.

(e) Duties of Appellant or Petitioner. The burden to ensure that the record is prepared and transmitted in accordance with these rules shall be on the petitioner or appellant. Any party may enforce the provisions of this rule by motion.

(f) Correcting and Supplementing Record.

(1) If there is an error or omission in the record, the parties by stipulation, the lower tribunal before the record is transmitted, or the court may correct the record.

(2) If the court finds the record is incomplete, it shall direct a party to supply the omitted parts of the record. No proceeding shall be determined, because of an incomplete record, until an opportunity to supplement the record has been given.

(g) Return of Record. In civil cases the record shall be returned to the lower tribunal after final disposition by the court.

History: Amended July 3, 1980, effective Jan. 1, 1981 (387 So.2d 920); Nov. 26, 1980, effective Jan. 1, 1981 (391 So.2d 203); June 8, 1987, effective July 1, 1987 (509 So.2d 276); July 14, 1988, effective Jan. 1, 1989 (529 So.2d 687); Dec. 30, 1988, effective Jan. 1, 1989 (536 So.2d 240); Oct. 22, 1992, effective Jan. 1, 1993 (609 So.2d 516); Nov. 22, 1996, effective Jan. 1, 1997 (685 So.2d 773) amended Oct. 12, 2000, effective Jan. 1, 2001 (730 So. 2d 834; 2000 Fla. LEXIS 2273; 25 Fla. L. Weekly S 835).

Committee Notes

1977 Amendment. This rule replaces former rule 3.6 and represents a complete revision of the matters pertaining to the record for an appellate proceeding. References in this rule to "appellant" and "appellee" should be treated as equivalent to "petitioner" and "respondent," respectively. See Commentary, Fla.R.App.P. 9.020. This rule is based in part on Federal Rule of Appellate Procedure 10(b).

Subdivision (a)(1) establishes the content of the record unless an appellant within 10 days of filing the notice directs the clerk to exclude portions of the record or to include additional portions, or the appellee within 20 days of the notice being filed directs inclusion of additional portions. In lieu of a record, the parties may prepare a stipulated statement, attaching a copy of the order that is sought to be reviewed and essential portions of the record. If a stipulated statement is prepared, the parties must advise the clerk not to prepare the record. The stipulated statement is to be filed and transmitted within the time prescribed for transmittal of the record. If less than a full record is to be used, the initiating party must serve a statement of

R. App. Proc.

the judicial acts to be reviewed so that the opposing party may determine whether additional portions of the record are required. Such a statement is not intended to be the equivalent of assignments of error under former rule 3.5. Any inadequacy in the statement may be cured by motion to supplement the record under subdivision (f) of this rule.

Subdivision (a) interacts with subdivision (b) so that as soon as the notice is filed the clerk of the lower tribunal will prepare and transmit the complete record of the case as described by the rule. To include in the record any of the items automatically omitted, a party must designate the items desired. A transcript of the proceedings in the lower tribunal will not be prepared or transmitted unless already filed, or the parties designate the portions of the transcript desired to be transmitted. Subdivision (b)(2) imposes on the reporter an affirmative duty to prepare the transcript of the proceedings as soon as designated. It is intended that to complete the preparation of all official papers to be filed with the court, the appellant need only file the notice, designate omitted portions of the record that are desired, and designate the desired portions of the transcript. It therefore will be unnecessary to file directions with the clerk of the lower tribunal in most cases.

Subdivision (b)(1) replaces former rule 3.6(d)(2), and specifically requires service of the designation on the court reporter. This is intended to avoid delays that sometimes occur when a party files the designation, but fails to notify the court reporter that a transcript is needed. The rule also establishes the responsibility of the designating party to initially bear the cost of the transcript.

Subdivision (b)(2) replaces former ruled 3.6(e). This rule provides for the form of the transcript, and imposes on the reporter the affirmative duty of delivering copies of the transcript to the ordering parties on request. Such a request may be included in the designation. Under subdivision (e), however, the responsibility for ensuring performance remains with the parties. The requirement that pages be consecutively numbered is new and is deemed necessary to assure continuity and ease of reference for the convenience of the court. This requirement applies even if 2 or more parties designate portions of the proceedings for transcription. It is intended that the transcript portions transmitted to the court constitute a single consecutively numbered document in 1 or more volumes not exceeding 200 pages each. If there is more than 1 court reporter, the clerk will renumber the pages of the transcript copies so that they are sequential. The requirement of a complete index at the beginning of each volume is new, and is necessary to standardize the format and to guide those preparing transcripts.

Subdivision (b)(3) provides the procedures to be followed if no transcript is available.

Subdivision (c) provides the procedures to be followed if there is a cross-appeal or cross-petition.

Subdivision (d) sets forth the manner in which the clerk of the lower tribunal is to prepare the record. The original record is to be transmitted unless the parties stipulate or the lower court orders the original be retained, except that under rule 9.140(d) (governing criminal cases), the original is to be retained unless the court orders otherwise.

Subdivision (e) places the burden of enforcement of this rule on the appellant or petitioner, but any party may move for an order requiring adherence to the rule.

Subdivision (f) replaces former rule 3.6(1). The new rule is intended to ensure that appellate proceedings will be decided on their merits and that no showing of good cause, negligence, or accident is required before the lower tribunal or the court orders the completion of the record. This rule is intended to ensure that any portion of the record in the lower tribunal that is material to a decision by the court will be available to the court. It is specifically intended to avoid those situations that have occurred in the past when an order has been affirmed because appellate counsel failed to bring up the portions of the record necessary to determine whether there was an error. See *Pan American Metal Prods. Co. v. Healy,* 138 So.2d 96 (Fla. 3d DCA 1962). The rule is not intended to cure inadequacies in the record that result from the failure of a party to make a proper record during the proceedings in the lower tribunal. The purpose of the rule is to give the parties an opportunity to have the appellate proceedings decided on the record developed in the lower tribunal. This rule does not impose on the lower tribunal or the court a duty to review on their own the adequacy of the preparation of the record. A failure to supplement the record after notice by the court may be held against the party at fault.

Subdivision (g) requires that the record in civil cases be returned to the lower tribunal after final disposition by the court regardless of whether the original record or a copy was used. The court may retain or return the record in criminal cases according to its internal administration policies.

1980 Amendment. Subdivisions (b)(1) and (b)(2) were amended to specify that the party designating portions of the transcript for inclusion in the record on appeal shall pay for the cost of transcription and shall pay for and furnish a copy of the portions designated for all opposing parties. See rule 9.420(b) and 1980 committee note thereto relating to limitations of number of copies.

1987 Amendment. Subdivision (b)(3) above is patterned after Federal Rule of Appellate Procedure 11(b).

1992 Amendment. Subdivisions (b)(2), (d)(1)(A), and (d)(1)(B) were amended to standardize the lower court clerk's procedure with respect to the placement and pagination of the transcript in the record on appeal. This amendment places the duty of paginating the transcript on the court reporter and requires the clerk to include the transcript at the end of the record, without repagination.

1996 Amendment. Subdivision (a)(2) was added because family law cases frequently have continuing activity at the lower tribunal level during the pendency of appellate proceedings and that continued activity may be hampered by the absence of orders being enforced during the pendency of the appeal.

Subdivision (b)(2) was amended to change the wording in the third sentence from "transcript of proceedings" to "transcript of the trial" to be consistent with and to clarify the requirement in subdivision (d)(1)(B) that it is only the transcript of trial that is not to be renumbered by the clerk. Pursuant to subdivision (d)(1)(B), it remains the duty of the clerk to consecutively number transcripts other than the transcript of the trial. Subdivision (b)(2) retains the requirement that the court reporter is to number each page of the transcript of the trial consecutively, but it is the committee's view that if the consecutive pagination requirement is impracticable or becomes a hardship for the court reporting entity, relief may be sought from the court.

Rule 9.210. Briefs.

(a) Generally. In addition to briefs on jurisdiction under rule 9.120(d), the only briefs permitted to be filed by the parties in any one proceeding are the initial brief, the answer brief, a reply brief, and a cross-reply brief. All briefs required by these rules shall be prepared as follows:

(1) Briefs shall be printed, typewritten, or duplicated on opaque, white, unglossed 8½-by-11 inch paper.

(2) The lettering in briefs shall be black and in distinct type, double-spaced, with margins no less than 1 inch. Lettering in script or type made in imitation of handwriting shall not be permitted. Footnotes and quotations may be single spaced and shall be in the same size type, with the same spacing between characters, as the text. Computer-generated briefs shall be submitted in either Times New Roman 14-point font or Courier New 12-point font. All computer-generated briefs shall contain a certificate of compliance signed by counsel, or the party if unrepresented, certifying that the brief complies with the font requirements of this rule. The certificate of compliance shall be contained in the brief immediately following the certificate of service.

(3) Briefs shall be securely bound in book form and fastened along the left side in a manner that will allow them to lie flat when opened or be securely stapled in the upper left corner. Headings and subheadings shall be at least as large as the brief text and may be single spaced.

(4) The cover sheet of each brief shall state the name of the court, the style of the cause, including the case number if assigned, the lower tribunal, the party on whose behalf the brief is filed, the type of brief, and the name and address of the attorney filing the brief.

(5) The initial and answer briefs shall not exceed 50 pages in length. Reply briefs shall not exceed 15 pages in length; provided that if a cross-appeal has been filed, the reply brief shall not exceed 50 pages, not more than 15 of which shall be devoted to argument replying to the answer portion of the appellee/cross-appellant's brief. Cross-reply briefs shall not exceed 15 pages. Briefs on jurisdiction shall not exceed 10 pages. The table of contents and the citation of authorities shall be excluded from the computation. Longer briefs may be permitted by the court.

(b) Contents of Initial Brief. The initial brief shall contain the following, in order:

(1) A table of contents listing the issues presented for review, with references to pages.

(2) A table of citations with cases listed alphabetically, statutes and other authorities, and the pages of the brief on which each citation appears. See rule 9.800 for a uniform citation system.

R. App. Proc.

(3) A statement of the case and of the facts, which shall include the nature of the case, the course of the proceedings, and the disposition in the lower tribunal. References to the appropriate volume and pages of the record or transcript shall be made.

(4) A summary of argument, suitably paragraphed, condensing succinctly, accurately, and clearly the argument actually made in the body of the brief. It should not be a mere repetition of the headings under which the argument is arranged. It should seldom exceed 2 and never 5 pages.

(5) Argument with regard to each issue including the applicable appellate standard of review.

(6) A conclusion, of not more than 1 page, setting forth the precise relief sought.

(c) Contents of Answer Brief. The answer brief shall be prepared in the same manner as the initial brief; provided that the statement of the case and of the facts may be omitted. If a cross-appeal has been filed, the answer brief shall include the issues in the cross-appeal that are presented for review, and argument in support of those issues.

(d) Contents of Reply Brief. The reply brief shall contain argument in response and rebuttal to argument presented in the answer brief.

(e) Contents of Cross-Reply Brief. The cross-reply brief is limited to rebuttal of argument of the cross-appellee.

(f) Times for Service of Briefs. The times for serving jurisdiction and initial briefs are prescribed by rules 9.110, 9.120, 9.130, and 9.140. Unless otherwise required, the answer brief shall be served within 20 days after service of the initial brief; the reply brief, if any, shall be served within 20 days after service of the answer brief; and the cross-reply brief, if any, shall be served within 20 days thereafter.

(g) Filing With Courts. The filing requirements of the courts are as follows:

(1) Circuit Courts. Original and 1 copy.

(2) District Courts of Appeal. Original and 3 copies.

(3) Supreme Court. Original and 7 copies; except that 5 copies only shall accompany the original jurisdictional briefs prescribed in rule 9.120(d).

(h) Citations. Counsel are requested to use the uniform citation system prescribed by rule 9.800.

History: Amended Nov. 26, 1980, effective Jan. 1, 1981 (391 So.2d 203); Sept. 13, 1984, effective Jan. 1, 1985 (463 So.2d 1114); Oct 22, 1992, effective Jan. 1, 1993 (699 So.2d 516); Nov. 22, 1996, effective Jan. 1, 1997 (685 So.2d 773); amended Oct. 12, 2000, effective Jan. 1, 2001 (780 So. 2d 834; 2000 Fla. LEXIS 2273; 25 Fla. L. Weekly S 835).

Committee Notes

1977 Amendment. This rule essentially retains the substance of former rule 3.7. Under subdivision (a) only 4 briefs on the merits are permitted to be filed in any 1 proceeding: an initial brief by the appellant or petitioner, an answer brief by the appellee or respondent, a reply brief by the appellant or petitioner, and a cross-reply brief by the appellee or respondent (if a cross-appeal or petition has been filed). A limit of 50 pages has been placed on the length of the initial and answer briefs, 15 pages for reply and cross-reply briefs (unless a cross-appeal or petition has been filed), and 20 pages for jurisdictional briefs, exclusive of the table of contents and citations of authorities. Although the court may by order permit briefs longer than allowed by this rule, the advisory committee contemplates that extensions in length will not be readily granted by the courts under these rules. General experience has been that even briefs within the limits of the rule are usually excessively long.

Subdivisions (b), (c), (d), and (e) set forth the format for briefs and retain the substance of former rules 3.7(f), (g), and (h). Particular note must be taken of the requirement that the statement of the case and facts include reference to the record. The abolition of assignments of error requires that counsel be vigilant in specifying for the court the errors committed; that greater attention be given the formulation of questions presented; and that counsel comply with subdivision (b)(5) by setting forth the precise relief sought. The table of contents will contain the statement of issues presented. The pages of the brief on which argument on each issue begins must be given. It is optional to have a second, separate listing of the issues. Subdivision (c) affirmatively requires that no statement of the facts of the case be made by an appellee or respondent unless there is disagreement with the initial brief, and then only to the extent of disagreement. It is unacceptable in an answer brief to make a general statement that the facts in the initial brief are accepted, except as rejected in the argument section of the answer brief. Parties are encouraged to place every fact utilized in the argument section of the brief in the statement of facts.

Subdivision (f) sets forth the times for service of briefs after service of the initial brief. Times for service of the initial brief are governed by the relevant rule.

Subdivision (g) (now rule 9.225) authorizes the filing of notices of supplemental authority at any time between the submission of briefs and rendition of a decision. Argument in such a notice is absolutely prohibited.

Subdivision (g) states the number of copies of each brief that must be filed with the clerk of the court involved—1 copy for each judge or justice in addition to the original for the permanent court file. This rule is not intended to limit the power of the court to require additional briefs at any time.

The style and form for the citation of authorities should conform to the uniform citation system adopted by the Supreme Court of Florida, which is reproduced in rule 9.800.

The advisory committee urges counsel to minimize references in their briefs to the parties by such designations as "appellant," "appellee," "petitioner," and "respondent." It promotes clarity to use actual names or descriptive terms such as "the employee," "the taxpayer," "the agency," etc. See Fed.R.App.P. 28(d).

1980 Amendment. Jurisdictional briefs, now limited to 10 pages by subdivision (a), are to be filed only in the 4 situations presented in rules 9.030(a)(2)(A)(i), (ii), (iii), and (iv).

A district court decision without opinion is not reviewable on discretionary conflict jurisdiction. See *Jenkins v. State,* 385 So.2d 1356 (Fla.1980); *Dodi Publishing Co. v. Editorial Am., S.A.,* 385 So.2d 1369 (Fla.1980). The discussion of jurisdictional brief requirements in such cases that is contained in the 1977 revision of the committee notes to rule 9.120 should be disregarded.

1984 Amendment. Subdivision (b)(4) is new; subdivision (b)(5) has been renumbered from former (b)(4); subdivision (b)(6) has been renumbered from former (b)(5). Subdivision (g) has been amended.

The summary of argument required by (b)(4) is designed to assist the court in studying briefs and preparing for argument; the rule is similar to rules of the various United States courts of appeals.

1992 Amendment Subdivision (a)(2) was amended to bring into uniformity the type size and spacing on all briefs filed under these rules. Practice under the previous rule allowed briefs to be filed with footnotes and quotations in different, usually smaller, type sizes and spacing. Use of such smaller type allowed some overly long briefs to circumvent the reasonable length requirements established by subdivision (a)(5) of this rule. The small type size and spacing of briefs allowed under the old rule also resulted in briefs that were difficult to read. The amended rule requires that all textual material wherever found in the brief will be printed in the same size type with the same spacing.

Subdivision (g) (now rule 9.225) was amended to provide that notices of supplemental authority may call the court's attention, not only to decisions, rules, or statutes, but also to other authorities that have been discovered since the last brief was served. The amendment further provides that the notice may identify briefly the points on appeal to which the supplemental authorities are pertinent. This amendment continues to prohibit argument in such notices, but should allow the court and opposing counsel to identify more quickly those issues on appeal to which these notices are relevant.

1996 Amendment Former subdivision (g) concerning notices of supplemental authority was transferred to new rule 9.225.

Court Commentary

1987. The commission expressed the view that the existing page limits for briefs, in cases other than those in the Supreme Court of Florida, are tailored to the "extraordinary" case rather than the "ordinary" case. In accordance with this view, the commission proposed that the page limits of briefs in appellate courts other than the supreme court be reduced. The appellate courts would, however, be given discretion to expand the reduced page limits in the "extraordinary" case.

2000. As to computer-generated briefs, strict font requirements were imposed in subdivision (a)(2) for at least three reasons:

First and foremost, appellate briefs are public records that the people have a right to inspect. The clear policy of the Florida Supreme Court is that advances in technology should benefit the people whenever possible by lowering financial and physical barriers to public record inspection. The Court's eventual goal is to make all public records widely and readily available, especially via the Internet. Unlike paper documents, electronic documents on the Internet will not display properly on all computers if they are set in fonts that are unusual. In some instances, such electronic documents may even be unreadable. Thus, the Court adopted the policy that all computer-generated appellate briefs be filed in one of two fonts—either Times New Roman 14-point or Courier New 12-point—that are commonplace on computers with Internet connections. This step will help ensure that the right to inspect public records on the Internet will be genuinely available to the largest number of people.

Second, Florida's court system as a whole is working toward the day when electronic filing of all court documents will be an everyday reality. Though the technology involved in electronic filing is changing rapidly, it is clear that the Internet is the single most significant factor influencing the development of this technology. Electronic filing must be compatible with Internet standards as they evolve over time. It is imperative for the legal profession to become accustomed to using electronic document formats that are most consistent with the Internet.

Third, the proliferation of vast new varieties of fonts in recent years poses a real threat that page-limitation rules can be circumvented through computerized typesetting. The only way to prevent this is to establish an enforceable rule on standards for font use. The subject font requirements are most consistent with this purpose and the other two purposes noted above.

Subdivision (a)(2) was also amended to require that immediately after the certificate of service in computer-generated briefs, counsel (or the party if unrepresented) shall sign a certificate of compliance with the font standards set forth in this rule for computer-generated briefs.

Rule 9.220. Appendix.

(a) Purpose. The purpose of an appendix is to permit the parties to prepare and transmit copies of those portions of the record deemed necessary to an understanding of the issues presented. It may be served with any petition, brief, motion, response, or reply; but shall be served as otherwise required by these rules. In any proceeding in which an appendix is required if the court finds that the appendix is incomplete, it shall direct a party to supply the omitted parts of the appendix. No proceeding shall be determined until an opportunity to supplement the appendix has been given.

(b) Contents. The appendix shall contain an index and a conformed copy of the opinion or order to be reviewed and may contain any other portions of the record and other authorities. It shall be separately bound or separated from the petition, brief, motion, response, or reply by a divider and appropriate tab. Asterisks should be used to indicate omissions in documents or testimony of witnesses. If the appendix includes documents filed before January 1991 on paper measuring 8½ by 14 inches, the documents should be reduced in copying to 8½ by 11 inches, if practicable. If impracticable, the appendix may measure 8½ by 14 inches, but it should be bound separately from the document that it accompanies.

History: Amended March 27, 1980, effective April 1, 1980 (381 So.2d 1370); Oct. 22, 1992, effective Jan. 1, 1993 (609 So.2d 516); amended Feb.3, 2005, effective Feb. 3, 2005 (2005 Fla. LEXIS 154; 30 Fla. L. Weekly S 84).

Committee Notes

1977 Adoption. This rule is new and has been adopted to encourage the use of an appendix either as a separate document or as a part of another matter. An appendix is optional, except under rules 9.100, 9.110(i), 9.120, and 9.130. If a legal size (8½ by 14 inches) appendix is used, counsel should make it a separate document. The term "conformed copy" is used throughout these rules to mean a true and accurate copy. In an appendix the formal parts of a document may be omitted if not relevant.

1980 Amendment. The rule has been amended to reflect the requirement that an appendix accompany a suggestion filed under rule 9.125.

1992 Amendment. This amendment addresses the transitional problem that arises if legal documents filed before January 1991 must be included in an appendix filed after that date. It encourages the reduction of 8½ by 14 inch papers to 8½ by 11 inches if practicable, and requires such documents to be bound separately if reduction is impracticable.

Rule 9.225. Notice of Supplemental Authority.

Notices of supplemental authority may be filed with the court before a decision has been rendered to call attention to decisions, rules, statutes, or other authorities that are significant to the issues raised and that have been discovered after the last brief served in the cause. The notice may identify briefly the points argued on appeal to which the supplemental authorities are pertinent, but shall not contain argument. Copies of the supplemental authorities shall be attached to the notice.

History: Adopted Nov. 22, 1996, effective Jan. 1, 1997 (685 So.2d 773).

Committee Notes

1996 Adoption. Formerly rule 9.210(g) with the addition of language that requires that supplemental authorities be significant to the issues raised.

Rule 9.300. Motions.

(a) Contents of Motion; Response. Unless otherwise prescribed by these rules, an application for an order or other relief available under these rules shall be made by filing a motion therefor. The motion shall state the grounds on which it is based, the relief sought, argument in support thereof, and appropriate citations of authority. A motion for an extension of time shall, and other motions if appropriate may, contain a certificate that the movant's counsel has consulted opposing counsel and that the movant's counsel is authorized to represent that opposing counsel either has no objection or will promptly file an objection. A motion may be accompanied by an appendix, which may include affidavits and other appropriate supporting documents not contained in the record. A party may serve 1 response to a motion within 10 days of service of the motion. The court may shorten or extend the time for response to a motion.

(b) Effect on Proceedings. Except as prescribed by subdivision (d) of this rule, service of a motion shall toll the time schedule of any proceeding in the court until disposition of the motion. An order granting an extension of time for any act shall automatically extend the time for all other acts that bear a time relation to it. An order granting an extension of time for preparation of the record or the index to the record, or for filing of the transcript of proceedings, shall extend automatically, for a like period, the time for service of appellant's initial brief. A conformed copy of an order extending time shall be transmitted forthwith to the clerk of the lower tribunal until the record has been transmitted to the court.

(c) Emergency Relief; Notice. A party seeking emergency relief shall, if practicable, give reasonable notice to all parties.

(d) Motions Not Tolling Time.

(1) Motions for post-trial release, rule 9.140(g).

(2) Motions for stay pending appeal, rule 9.310.

(3) Motions relating to oral argument, rule 9.320.

(4) Motions relating to joinder and substitution of parties, rule 9.360.

(5) Motions relating to amicus curiae, rule 9.370.

(6) Motions relating to attorneys' fees on appeal, rule 9.400.

(7) Motions relating to service, rule 9.420.

(8) Motions relating to admission or withdrawal of attorneys, rule 9.440.

(9) Motions relating to expediting the appeal.

(10) All motions filed in the supreme court, unless accompanied by a separate request to toll time.

History: Amended July 3, 1980, effective Jan. 1, 1981 (387 So.2d 920); Oct. 22, 1992, effective Jan. 1, 1993 (609 So.2d 516); Nov. 22, 1996, effective Jan. 1, 1997 (685 So.2d 773).

Committee Notes

1977 Amendment. This rule replaces former rule 3.9.

Subdivision (a) is new, except to the extent it replaces former rule 3.9(g), and is intended to outline matters required to be included in motions. These provisions are necessary because it is anticipated that oral argument will only rarely be permitted. Any matters that formerly would have been included in a brief on a motion should be included in the motion. Although affidavits and other documents not appearing in the record may be included in the appendix, it is to be emphasized that such materials are limited to matter germane to the motion, and are not to include matters related to the merits of the case. The advisory committee was of the view that briefs on motions are cumbersome and unnecessary. The advisory committee anticipates that the motion document will become simple and unified, with unnecessary technical language eliminated. Routine motions usually require only limited argument. Provision is made for a re-

R. App. Proc.

sponse by the opposing party. No further responses by either party are permitted, however, without an order of the court entered on the court's own motion or the motion of a party. To ensure cooperation and communication between opposing counsel, and conservation of judicial resources, a party moving for an extension of time is required to certify that opposing counsel has been consulted, and either has no objection or intends to serve an objection promptly. The certificate may also be used for other motions if appropriate. Only the motions listed in subdivision (d) do not toll the time for performance of the next act. Subdivision (d)(10) codifies current practice in the supreme court, where motions do not toll time unless the court approves a specific request, for good cause shown, to toll time for the performance of the next act. Very few motions filed in that court warrant a delay in further procedural steps to be taken in a case.

The advisory committee considered and rejected as unwise a proposal to allow at least 15 days to perform the next act after a motion tolling time was disposed.

Subdivision (b) replaces former rule 3.9(f).

Subdivision (c) is new and has been included at the requests of members of the judiciary. It is intended to require that counsel make a reasonable effort to give actual notice to opposing counsel when emergency relief is sought from a court.

Specific reference to motions to quash or dismiss appeals contained in former rules 3.9(b) and (c) has been eliminated as unnecessary. It is not intended that such motions be abolished. Courts have the inherent power to quash frivolous appeals, and subdivision (a) guarantees to any party the right to file a motion. Although no special time limitations are placed on such motions, delay in presenting any motion may influence the relief granted or sanctions imposed under rule 9.410.

As was the case under former rule 3.8, a motion may be filed in either the lower tribunal or the court, in accordance with rule 9.600.

1980 Amendment. Subdivision (b) was amended to require the clerk of either court to notify the other clerk when an extension of time has been granted, up to the time that the record on appeal has been transmitted to the court, so that the clerk of the lower tribunal will be able to properly compute the time for transmitting the record on appeal, and that both courts may properly compute the time for performing subsequent acts.

1992 Amendment. Subdivision (b) was amended to clarify an uncertainty over time deadlines. The existing rule provided that an extension of time for performing an act automatically extended for a comparable period any other act that had a time relation thereto. The briefing schedule, however, is related by time only to the filing of the notice of appeal. Accordingly, this amendment provides that orders extending the time for preparation of the record, the index to the record, or a transcript, automatically extends for the same period the time for service of the initial brief. Subdivision (b) also was amended to correlate with rule 9.600(a), which provides that only an appellate court may grant an extension of time.

Rule 9.310. Stay Pending Review.

(a) Application. Except as provided by general law and in subdivision (b) of this rule, a party seeking to stay a final or non-final order pending review shall file a motion in the lower tribunal, which shall have continuing jurisdiction, in its discretion, to grant, modify, or deny such relief. A stay pending review may be conditioned on the posting of a good and sufficient bond, other conditions, or both.

(b) Exceptions.

(1) Money Judgments. If the order is a judgment solely for the payment of money, a party may obtain an automatic stay of execution pending review, without the necessity of a motion or order, by posting a good and sufficient bond equal to the principal amount of the judgment plus twice the statutory rate of interest on judgments on the total amount on which the party has an obligation to pay interest. Multiple parties having common liability may file a single bond satisfying the above criteria.

(2) Public Bodies; Public Officers. The timely filing of a notice shall automatically operate as a stay pending review, except in criminal cases, when the state, any public officer in an official capacity, board, commission, or other public body seeks review; provided that an automatic stay shall exist for 48 hours after the filing of the notice of appeal for public records and public meeting cases. Ords and public meeting cases. On motion, the lower tribunal or the court may extend a stay, impose any lawful conditions, or vacate the stay.

(c) Bond.

(1) Defined. A good and sufficient bond is a

bond with a principal and a surety company authorized to do business in the State of Florida, or cash deposited in the circuit court clerk's office. The lower tribunal shall have continuing jurisdiction to determine the actual sufficiency of any such bond.

(2) Conditions. The conditions of a bond shall include a condition to pay or comply with the order in full, including costs; interest; fees, and damages for delay, use, detention, and depreciation of property, if the review is dismissed or order affirmed; and may include such other conditions as may be required by the lower tribunal.

(d) Judgment Against a Surety. A surety on a bond conditioning a stay submits to the jurisdiction of the lower tribunal and the court. The liability of the surety on such bond may be enforced by the lower tribunal or the court, after motion and notice, without the necessity of an independent action.

(e) Duration. A stay entered by a lower tribunal shall remain in effect during the pendency of all review proceedings in Florida courts until a mandate issues, or unless otherwise modified or vacated.

(f) Review. Review of orders entered by lower tribunals under this rule shall be by the court on motion.

History: Amended Sept. 13, 1984, effective Jan. 1, 1985 (463 So.2d 1114); July 14, 1988, effective Jan. 1, 1989 (529 So.2d 687); Dec. 30, 1988, effective Jan. 1, 1989 (536 So.2d 240); amended effective March 23, 1989 (541 So.2d 1142); amended Oct. 22, 1992, effective Jan. 1, 1993 (609 So.2d 516); amended Nov. 22, 1996, effective Jan. 1, 1997 (685 So.2d 773).

Committee Notes

1977 Amendment. This rule replaces former rules 5.1 through 5.12. It implements the Administrative Procedure Act, section 120.68(3), Florida Statutes (Supp.1976).

Subdivision (a) provides for obtaining a stay pending review by filing a motion in the lower tribunal, and clarifies the authority of the lower tribunal to increase or decrease the bond or deal with other conditions of the stay, even though the case is pending before the court. Exceptions are provided in subdivision (b). The rule preserves any statutory right to a stay. The court has plenary power to alter any requirements imposed by the lower tribunal. A party desiring exercise of the court's power may seek review by motion under subdivision (f) of this rule.

Subdivision (b)(1) replaces former rule 5.7. It establishes a fixed formula for determining the amount of the bond if there is a judgment solely for money. This formula shall be automatically accepted by the clerk. If an insurance company is a party to an action with its insured, and the judgment exceeds the insurance company's limits of liability, the rule permits the insurance company to supersede by posting a bond in the amount of its limits of liability, plus 15 percent. For the insured co-defendant to obtain a stay, bond must be posted for the portion of the judgment entered against the insured co-defendant plus 15 percent. The 15 percent figure was chosen as a reasonable estimate of 2 years' interest and costs, it being very likely that the stay would remain in effect for over 1 year.

Subdivision (b)(2) replaces former rule 5.12. It provides for an automatic stay without bond as soon as a notice invoking jurisdiction is filed by the state or any other public body, other than in criminal cases which are covered by rule 9.140(c)(2), but the lower tribunal may vacate the stay or require a bond. This rule supersedes *Lewis v. Career Service Commission,* 332 So.2d 371 (Fla. 1st DCA 1976).

Subdivision (c) retains the substance of former rule 5.6, and states the mandatory conditions of the bond.

Subdivision (d) retains the substance of former rule 5.11, with an additional provision for entry of judgment by the court so that if the lower tribunal is an agency, resort to an independent action is unnecessary.

Subdivision (e) is new and is intended to permit a stay for which a single bond premium has been paid to remain effective during all review proceedings. The stay is vacated by issuance of mandate or an order vacating it. There are no automatic stays of mandate under these rules, except for the state or a public body under subdivision (b)(2) of this rule, or if a stay as of right is guaranteed by statute. See, e.g., § 120.68(3), Fla.Stat. (Supp.1976). This rule interacts with rule 9.340, however, so that a party has 15 days between rendition of the court's decision and issuance of mandate (unless issuance of mandate is expedited) to move for a stay of mandate pending review. If such motion is granted, any stay and bond previously in effect continues except to the extent of any modifications, by operation of this rule. If circumstances arise requiring alteration of the terms of the stay, the party asserting the need for such change should apply by motion for the appropriate order.

Subdivision (f) provides for review of orders regarding stays pending appeal by motion in the court.

Although the normal and preferred procedure is for the parties to seek the stay in the lower court, this rule is not intended to limit the constitutional power of the court to issue stay orders after its jurisdiction has been invoked. It is intended that if review of the decision of a Florida court is sought in the United States Supreme Court, a party may move for a stay of mandate, but subdivision (e) does not apply in such cases.

1984 Amendment. Because of recent increases in the statutory rate of interest on judgments, subdivision (b)(1) was amended to provide that 2 years' interest on the judgment, rather than 15 percent of the judgment, be posted in addition to the principal amount of the judgment. In addition, the subdivision was amended to cure a deficiency in the prior rule revealed by *Proprietors Insurance Co. v. Valsecchi,* 385 So.2d 749 (Fla. 3d DCA 1980). As under the former rule, if a party has an obligation to pay interest only on the judgment, the bond required for that party shall be equal to the principal amount of the judgment plus 2 years' interest on it. In some cases, however, an insurer may be liable under its policy to pay interest on the entire amount of the judgment against its insured, notwithstanding that the judgment against it may be limited to a lesser amount by its policy limits. See *Highway Casualty Co. v. Johnston,* 104 So.2d 734 (Fla.1958). In that situation, the amended rule requires the insurance company to supersede the limited judgment against it by posting a bond in the amount of the judgment plus 2 years' interest on the judgment against its insured, so that the bond will more closely approximate the insurer's actual liability to the plaintiff at the end of the duration of the stay. If such a bond is posted by an insurer, the insured may obtain a stay by posting a bond in the amount of the judgment against it in excess of that superseded by the insurer. The extent of coverage and obligation to pay interest may, in certain cases, require an evidentiary determination by the court.

1992 Amendment. Subdivision (c)(1) was amended to eliminate the ability of a party posting a bond to do so through the use of 2 personal sureties. The committee was of the opinion that a meaningful supersedeas could be obtained only through the use of either a surety company or the posting of cash. The committee also felt, however, that it was appropriate to note that the lower tribunal retained continuing jurisdiction over the actual sufficiency of any such bond.

Rule 9.315. Summary Disposition.

(a) Summary Affirmance. After service of the initial brief in appeals under rule 9.110, 9.130, or 9.140, or after service of the answer brief if a cross-appeal has been filed, the court may summarily affirm the order to be reviewed if the court finds that no preliminary basis for reversal has been demonstrated.

(b) Summary Reversal. After service of the answer brief in appeals under rule 9.110, 9.130, or 9.140, or after service of the reply brief if a cross-appeal has been filed, the court may summarily reverse the order to be reviewed if the court finds that no meritorious basis exists for affirmance and the order otherwise is subject to reversal.

(c) Motions Not Permitted. This rule may be invoked only on the court's own motion. A party may not request summary disposition.

History: Adopted June 8, 1987, effective July 1, 1987 (509 So.2d 276). Amended Oct. 22, 1992, effective Jan. 1, 1993 (609 So.2d 516); Nov. 22, 1996, effective Jan. 1, 1997 (685 So.2d 773).

Court Commentary

1987. This rule contemplates a screening process by the appellate courts. More time will be spent early in the case to save more time later. The rule is fair in that appellant has an opportunity to file a full brief. The thought behind this proposal is to allow expeditious disposition of nonmeritorious appeals or obviously meritorious appeals.

Rule 9.320. Oral Argument.

Oral argument may be permitted in any proceeding. A request for oral argument shall be a separate document served by a party not later than the time the last brief of that party is due. Each side will be allowed 20 minutes for oral argument, except in capital cases in which each side will be allowed 30 minutes. On its own motion or that of a party, the court may require, limit, expand, or dispense with oral argument.

History: Amended Sept. 13, 1984, effective Jan. 1, 1985 (463 So.2d 1114); Oct. 22, 1992, effective Jan. 1, 1993 (609 So.2d 516).

Committee Notes

1977 Amendment. This rule replaces former rule 3.10. As under the former rules, there is no right to oral argument. It is contemplated that oral argument will be granted only if the court believes its consideration of the issues raised will be enhanced. The time ordinarily allowable to each party has been reduced from 30 minutes to 20 minutes to conform with the prevailing practice in the courts. If oral argument is permitted, the order of the court will state the time and place.

Rule 9.330. Rehearing; Clarification; Certification.

(a) Time for Filing; Contents; Response. A motion for rehearing, clarification, or certification may be filed within 15 days of an order or within such other time set by the court. A motion for rehearing shall state with particularity the points of law or fact that, in the opinion of the movant, the court has overlooked or misapprehended in its decision, and shall not present issues not previously raised in the proceeding. A motion for clarification shall state with particularity the points of law or fact in the court's decision that, in the opinion of the movant, are in need of clarification. A response may be served within 10 days of service of the motion. When a decision is entered without opinion, and a party believes that a written opinion would provide a legitimate basis for supreme court review, the motion may include a request that the court issue a written opinion. If such a request is made by an attorney, it shall include the following statement: I express a belief, based upon a reasoned and studied professional judgment, that a written opinion will provide a legitimate basis for supreme court review because (state with specificity the reasons why the supreme court would be likely to grant review if an opinion were written).

/s/ ____________________
Attorney for ____________________
(name of party) ____________________
____
(address and phone number) ____________________
Florida Bar No. ____________________

(b) Limitation. A party shall not file more than 1 motion for rehearing or for clarification of decision and 1 motion for certification with respect to a particular decision.

(c) Exception; Bond Validation Proceedings. A motion for rehearing or for clarification of a decision in proceedings for the validation of bonds or certificates of indebtedness as provided by rule 9.030(a)(1)(B)(ii) may be filed within 10 days of an order or within such other time set by the court. A reply may be served within 5 days of service of the motion. The mandate shall issue forthwith if a timely motion has not been filed. A timely motion shall receive immediate consideration by the court and, if denied, the mandate shall issue forthwith.

(d) Exception; Review of District Court Decisions. No motion for rehearing may be filed in the supreme court addressed to the grant or denial of a request for the court to exercise its discretion to review a decision described in rule 9.120, or addressed to the dismissal of a petition for an extraordinary writ described in rule 9.100(a) when such writ is used to seek review of a district court decision without opinion.

History: Amended July 14, 1988, effective Jan. 1, 1989 (529 So.2d 687); Dec. 30, 1988, effective Jan. 1, 1989 (536 So.2d 240); Oct. 22, 1992, effective Jan. 1, 1993 (609 So.2d 516); amended Oct. 12, 2000, effective Jan. 1, 2001 (780 So. 2d 834; 2000 Fla. LEXIS 2273; 25 Fla. L. Weekly S 835); Aug. 29, 2002, effective Jan. 1, 2003.

Committee Notes

1977 Amendment. This rule replaces former rule 3.14. Rehearing now must be sought by motion, not by petition. The motion must be filed within 15 days of rendition and a response may be served within 10 days of service of the motion. Only 1 motion will be accepted by the clerk. Re-argument of the issues involved in the case is prohibited.

Subdivision (c) provides expedited procedures for issuing a mandate in bond validation cases, in lieu of those prescribed by rule 9.340.

Subdivision (d) makes clear that motions for rehearing or for clarification are not permitted as to any decision of the supreme court granting or denying discretionary review under rule 9.120.

2000 Amendment. The amendment has a dual purpose. By omitting the sentence "The motion shall not re-argue the merits of the court's order," the amendment is intended to clarify the permissible scope of motions for rehearing and clarification. Nevertheless, the essential purpose of a motion for rehearing remains the same. It should be utilized to bring to the attention of the court points of law or fact that it has overlooked or misapprehended in its decision, not to express mere disagreement with its resolution of the issues on appeal. The amendment also codifies the decisional law's prohibition against issues in post-decision motions that have not previously been raised in the proceeding.

R. App. Proc.

2002 Amendment. The addition of the language at the end of subdivision (a) allows a party to request the court to issue a written opinion that would allow review to the supreme court, if the initial decision is issued without opinion. This language is not intended to restrict the ability of parties to seek rehearing or clarification of such decisions on other grounds.

Rule 9.331. Determination of Causes in a District Court of Appeal En Banc.

(a) En Banc Proceedings: Generally. A majority of the judges of a district court of appeal participating may order that a proceeding pending before the court be determined en banc. A district court of appeal en banc shall consist of the judges in regular active service on the court. En banc hearings and rehearings shall not be ordered unless the case is of exceptional importance or unless necessary to maintain uniformity in the court's decisions. The en banc decision shall be by a majority of the active judges actually participating and voting on the case. In the event of a tie vote, the panel decision of the district court shall stand as the decision of the court. If there is no panel decision, a tie vote will affirm the trial court decision.

(b) En Banc Proceedings by Divisions. If a district court of appeal chooses to sit in subject-matter divisions as approved by the Supreme Court, en banc determinations shall be limited to those regular active judges within the division to which the case is assigned, unless the chief judge determines that the case involves matters of general application and that en banc determination should be made by all regular active judges. However, in the absence of such determination by the chief judge, the full court may determine by an affirmative vote of three-fifths of the active judges that the case involves matters that should be heard and decided by the full court, in which event en banc determination on the merits of the case shall be made by an affirmative vote of a majority of the regular active judges participating.

(c) Hearings En Banc. A hearing en banc may be ordered only by a district court of appeal on its own motion. A party may not request an en banc hearing. A motion seeking the hearing shall be stricken.

(d) Rehearings En Banc.

(1) Generally. A rehearing en banc may be ordered by a district court of appeal on its own motion or on motion of a party. Within the time prescribed by rule 9.330, a party may move for an en banc rehearing solely on the grounds that the case is of exceptional importance or that such consideration is necessary to maintain uniformity in the court's decisions. A motion based on any other ground shall be stricken. A response may be served within 10 days of service of the motion. A vote will not be taken on the motion unless requested by a judge on the panel that heard the proceeding, or by any judge in regular active service on the court. Judges who did not sit on the panel are under no obligation to consider the motion unless a vote is requested.

(2) Required Statement for Rehearing En Banc. A rehearing en banc is an extraordinary proceeding. In every case the duty of counsel is discharged without filing a motion for rehearing en banc unless one of the grounds set forth in (1) is clearly met. If filed by an attorney, the motion shall contain either or both of the following statements:

I express a belief, based on a reasoned and studied professional judgment, that the panel decision is of exceptional importance.

Or

I express a belief, based on a reasoned and studied professional judgment, that the panel decision is contrary to the following decision(s) of this court and that a consideration by the full court is necessary to maintain uniformity of decisions in this court: (citing specifically the case or cases).

/s/ ____________________

Attorney for ____________________

(name of party) ____________________

____

(address and phone number) ____________________

Florida Bar No. ____________________

(3) Disposition of Motion for Rehearing En Banc. A motion for rehearing en banc shall be disposed of by order. If rehearing en banc is granted, the court may limit the issues to be reheard, require the filing of additional briefs,

and may require additional argument.

History: Adopted Sept. 20, 1979, effective Jan. 1, 1980 (374 So.2d 992). Amended Dec. 6, 1979, effective Jan. 1, 1980 (377 So.2d 700); June 24, 1982, effective Oct. 1, 1982 (416 So.2d 1127); Sept. 13, 1984, effective Jan. 1, 1985 (463 So.2d 1114); Oct. 22, 1992, effective, Jan. 1, 1993 (609 So.2d 516); effective December 15, 1994 (646 So.2d 730).

Committee Notes

1982 Amendment. This rule is patterned in part after the en banc rule of the United States Court of Appeals for the Fifth and Eleventh Circuits. The rule is an essential part of the philosophy of our present appellate structure because the supreme court no longer has jurisdiction to review intra-district conflict. The new appellate structural scheme requires the district courts of appeal to resolve conflict within their respective districts through the en banc process. By so doing, this should result in a clear statement of the law applicable to that particular district.

Subdivision (a) provides that a majority vote of the active and participating members of the district court is necessary to set a case for hearing en banc or rehearing en banc. The issues on the merits will be decided by a simple majority of the judges actually participating in the en banc process, without regard to recusals or a judge's absence for illness. All judges in regular active service, not excluded for cause, will constitute the en banc panel. Counsel are reminded that en banc proceedings are extraordinary and will be ordered only in the enumerated circumstances. The ground, maintenance of uniformity in the court's decisions, is the equivalent of decisional conflict as developed by supreme court precedent in the exercise of its conflict jurisdiction. The district courts are free, however, to develop their own concept of decisional uniformity. The effect of an en banc tie vote is self-explanatory, but such a vote does suggest that the matter is one that should be certified to the supreme court for resolution.

Subdivision (b) provides that hearings en banc may not be sought by the litigants; such hearings may be ordered only by the district court sua sponte.

Subdivision (c)(1) governs rehearings en banc. A litigant may apply for an en banc rehearing only on the ground that intra-district conflict of decisions exists, and then only in conjunction with a timely filed motion for rehearing under rule 9.330. The en banc rule does not allow for a separate motion for an en banc rehearing nor does it require the district court to enter a separate order on such request. Once a timely motion for rehearing en banc is filed in conjunction with a traditional petition for rehearing, the 3 judges on the initial panel must consider the motion. A vote of the entire court may be initiated by any single judge on the panel. Any other judge on the court may also trigger a vote by the entire court. Nonpanel judges are not required to review petitions for rehearing en banc until a vote is requested by another judge, although all petitions for rehearing en banc should be circulated to nonpanel judges. The court may on its own motion order a rehearing en banc.

Subdivision (c)(2) requires a signed statement of counsel certifying a bona fide belief that an en banc hearing is necessary to ensure decisional harmony within the district.

Subdivision (c)(3) is intended to prevent baseless motions for en banc rehearings from absorbing excessive judicial time and labor. The district courts will not enter orders denying motions for en banc rehearings. If a rehearing en banc is granted, the court may order briefs from the parties and set the case for oral argument.

1992 Amendment. Subdivision (c)(3) was amended to correct a linguistic error found in the original subdivision.

1994 Amendment. The intent of this amendment is to authorize courts sitting in subject-matter divisions to have cases that are assigned to a division decided en banc by that division without participation by the regular active judges assigned to another division. The presumption is that en banc consideration will usually be limited to the division in which the case is pending. However, recognizing that in exceptional instances it may be preferable for the matter under review to be considered by the whole court, the case can be brought before all regular active judges by the chief judge or by an affirmative vote of three-fifths of the regular active judges on the whole court. Once the matter is before the whole court en banc, a vote on the merits will be a majority of the regular active judges as now provided in rule 9.331.

Rule 9.340. Mandate.

(a) Issuance of Mandate. Unless otherwise ordered by the court or provided by these rules, the clerk shall issue such mandate or process as may be directed by the court after expiration of 15 days from the date of an order or decision. A copy thereof, or notice of its issuance, shall be served on all parties.

(b) Extension of Time for Issuance of Mandate. If a timely motion for rehearing, clarification, or certification has been filed, the time for issuance of the mandate or other process shall be extended until 15 days after rendition of the order denying the motion, or, if granted, until 15 days after the cause has been fully determined.

(c) Entry of Money Judgment. If a judgment of reversal is entered that requires the entry of a money judgment on a verdict, the mandate shall be deemed to require such money judgment to be entered as of the date of the verdict.

History: Amended Sept. 13, 1984, effective Jan. 1, 1985 (463 So.2d 1114); July 14, 1988, effective Jan. 1, 1989 (529 So.2d 687); Dec. 30, 1988, effective Jan. 1, 1989 (536 So.2d 240); Oct. 22, 1992, effective Jan. 1, 1993 (609 So.2d 516).

Committee Notes

1977 Amendment. This rule replaces former rule 3.15. The power of the court to expedite as well as delay issuance of the mandate, with or without motion, has been made express. That part of former rule 3.15(a) regarding money judgments has been eliminated as unnecessary. It is not intended to change the substantive law there stated. The 15-day delay in issuance of mandate is necessary to allow a stay to remain in effect for purposes of rule 9.310(e). This automatic delay is inapplicable to bond validation proceedings, which are governed by rule 9.330(c).

1984 Amendment. Subdivision (c) was added. It is a repromulgation of former rule 3.15(a), which was deleted in 1977 as being unnecessary. Experience proved it to be necessary.

Rule 9.350. Dismissal of Causes.

(a) Dismissal of Causes When Settled. When any cause pending in the court is settled before a decision on the merits, the parties shall immediately notify the court by filing a signed stipulation for dismissal.

(b) Voluntary Dismissal. A proceeding of an appellant or petitioner may be dismissed before a decision on the merits by filing a notice of dismissal with the clerk of the court without affecting the proceedings filed by joinder or cross-appeal; provided that dismissal shall not be effective until 10 days after filing the notice of appeal or until 10 days after the time prescribed by rule 9.110(b), whichever is later.

(c) Clerk's Duty. When a proceeding is dismissed under this rule, the clerk of the court shall notify the clerk of the lower tribunal.

History: Amended Sept. 13, 1984, effective Jan. 1, 1985 (463 So.2d 1114); Oct. 22, 1992, effective Jan. 1, 1993 (609 So.2d 516); amended Oct. 12, 2000, effective Jan. 1, 2001 (780 So. 2d 834; 2000 Fla. LEXIS 2273; 25 Fla. L. Weekly S 835).

Committee Notes

1977 Amendment. Subdivision (a) retains the substance of former rule 3.13(a). On the filing of a stipulation of dismissal, the clerk of the court will dismiss the case as to the parties signing the stipulation.

Subdivision (b) is intended to allow an appellant to dismiss the appeal but a timely perfected cross-appeal would continue. A voluntary dismissal would not be effective until after the time for joinder in appeal or cross-appeal. This limitation was created so that an opposing party desiring to have adverse rulings reviewed by a cross-appeal cannot be trapped by a voluntary dismissal by the appellant after the appeal time has run, but before an appellee has filed the notice of joinder or cross-appeal.

Subdivision (c) retains the substance of former rule 3.13(c).

Rule 9.360. Parties.

(a) Joinder. A party to the cause in the lower tribunal who desires to join in a proceeding as a petitioner or appellant shall file a notice to that effect within 10 days of service of the petition or notice or within the time prescribed by rule 9.110(b), whichever is later.

(b) Attorneys, Representatives, and Guardians Ad Litem. Attorneys, representatives, and guardians ad litem in the lower tribunal shall retain their status in the court unless others are duly appointed or substituted.

(c) Substitution of Parties.

(1) If substitution of a party is necessary for any reason, the court may so order on its own motion or that of a party.

(2) Public officers as parties in their official capacities may be described by their official titles rather than by name. Their successors in office shall be automatically substituted as parties.

(3) If a party dies while a proceeding is pending and that party's rights survive, the court may order the substitution of the proper party on

its own motion or that of any interested person.

(4) If a person entitled to file a notice dies before filing and that person's rights survive, the notice may be filed by the personal representative, attorney of record, or, if none, by any interested person. Following filing, the proper party shall be substituted.

History: Amended Oct. 22, 1992, effective Jan. 1, 1993 (609 So.2d 516).

Committee Notes

1977 Amendment. This rule is intended as a simplification of the former rules with no substantial change in practice.

Subdivision (a) is a simplification of the provisions of former rule 3.11(b), with modifications recognizing the elimination of assignments of error.

Subdivision (b) retains the substance of former rule 3.11(d).

Subdivision (c)(1) substantially simplifies the procedure for substituting parties. This change is in keeping with the overall concept of this revision that these rules should identify material events that may or should occur in appellate proceedings and specify in general terms how that event should be brought to the attention of the court and how the parties should proceed. The manner in which these events shall be resolved is left to the courts, the parties, the substantive law, and the circumstances of the particular case.

Subdivision (c)(2) is new and is intended to avoid the necessity of motions for substitution if the person holding a public office is changed during the course of proceedings. It should be noted that the style of the case does not necessarily change.

Subdivision (c)(4) is new, and is intended to simplify the procedure and avoid confusion if a party dies before an appellate proceeding is instituted. Substitutions in such cases are to be made according to subdivision (c)(1).

Rule 9.370. Amicus Curiae.

(a) When Permitted.

(b) Contents and Form. An amicus brief must comply with Rule 9.210(b) but shall omit a statement of the case and facts and may not exceed 20 pages. The cover must identify the party or parties supported. An amicus brief must include a concise statement of the identity of the amicus curiae and its interest in the case.

(a) When Permitted. An amicus curiae may file a brief only by leave of court. A motion for leave to file must state the movant's interest, the particular issue to be addressed, how the movant can assist the court in the disposition of the case, and whether all parties consent to the filing of the brief.

(b) Contents and Form. An amicus brief must comply with Rule 9.210(b) but shall omit a statement of the case and facts and may not exceed 20 pages. The cover must identify the party or parties supported. An amicus brief must include a concise statement of the identity of the amicus curiae and its interest in the case.

(c) Time for Filing. An amicus curiae must serve its brief no later than 5 days after the first brief of the party being supported is served. An amicus curiae that does not support either party must serve its brief no later than 5 days after the initial brief or petition is filed. A court may grant leave for later service, specifying the time within which an opposing party may respond. An amicus curiae may not file a reply brief.

History: Amended Oct. 22, 1992, effective Jan. 1, 1993 (609 So.2d 516); Aug. 29, 2002, effective Jan. 1, 2003; amended Feb.3, 2005, effective Feb. 3, 2005 (2005 Fla. LEXIS 154; 30 Fla. L. Weekly S 84).

Committee Notes

1977 Amendment. This rule replaces former rule 3.7(k) and expands the circumstances in which amicus curiae briefs may be filed to recognize the power of the court to request amicus curiae briefs.

Rule 9.400. Costs and Attorneys' Fees.

(a) Costs. Costs shall be taxed in favor of the prevailing party unless the court orders otherwise. Taxable costs shall include

(1) fees for filing and service of process;

(2) charges for preparation of the record;

(3) bond premiums; and

(4) other costs permitted by law.

Costs shall be taxed by the lower tribunal on motion served within 30 days after issuance of the mandate.

(b) Attorneys' Fees. A motion for attorneys' fees may be served not later than the time for

R. App. Proc.

service of the reply brief and shall state the grounds on which recovery is sought. The assessment of attorneys' fees may be remanded to the lower tribunal. If attorneys' fees are assessed by the court, the lower tribunal may enforce payment.

(c) Review. Review of orders rendered by the lower tribunal under this rule shall be by motion filed in the court within 30 days of rendition.

History: Amended Oct. 22, 1992, effective Jan. 1, 1993 (609 So.2d 516); Nov. 22, 1996, effective Jan. 1, 1997 (685 So.2d 773).

Committee Notes

1977 Amendment. Subdivision (a) replaces former rules 3.16(a) and (b). It specifies allowable cost items according to the current practice. Item (3) is not intended to apply to bail bond premiums. Item (4) is intended to permit future flexibility. This rule provides that the prevailing party must move for costs in the lower tribunal within 30 days after issuance of the mandate.

Subdivision (b) retains the substance of former rule 3.16(e). The motion for attorneys' fees must contain a statement of the legal basis for recovery. The elimination of the reference in the former rule to attorneys' fees "allowable by law" is not intended to give a right to assessment of attorneys' fees unless otherwise permitted by substantive law.

Subdivision (c) replaces former rules 3.16(c) and (d). It changes from 20 days to 30 days the time for filing a motion to review an assessment of costs or attorneys' fees by a lower tribunal acting under order of the court.

Rule 9.410. Sanctions.

After 10 days' notice, on its own motion, the court may impose sanctions for any violation of these rules, or for the filing of any proceeding, motion, brief, or other paper that is frivolous or in bad faith. Such sanctions may include reprimand, contempt, striking of briefs or pleadings, dismissal of proceedings, costs, attorneys' fees, or other sanctions.

History: Amended July 14, 1988, effective Jan. 1, 1989 (529 So.2d 687); Dec. 30, 1988, effective Jan. 1, 1989 (536 So.2d 240); Oct. 22, 1992, effective Jan. 1, 1993 (609 So.2d 516).

Committee Notes

1977 Amendment. This rule replaces former rule 3.17. This rule specifies the penalties or sanctions that generally are imposed, but does not limit the sanctions available to the court. The only change in substance is that this rule provides for 10 days notice to the offending party before imposition of sanctions.

Rule 9.420. Filing; Service of Copies; Computation of Time.

(a) Filing.

(1) Generally. Filing may be accomplished by filing with the clerk; provided that a justice or judge may accept the documents for filing, and shall note the filing date and immediately transmit them to the office of the clerk.

(2) Inmate Filing. A document filed by a pro se inmate confined in an institution is timely filed if the inmate places the document in the hands of an institution official for mailing on or before the last day for filing. Such a document shall be presumed to be timely filed if it contains a certificate of service certifying that the inmate placed the document in the hands of an institution official for mailing on a particular date, and if the document would have been timely filed had it been received and file-stamped by the court on that date.

(b) Service. All original papers shall be filed either before service or immediately thereafter. A copy of all documents filed under these rules shall, before filing or immediately thereafter, be served on each of the parties. The lower tribunal, before the record is transmitted, or the court, on motion, may limit the number of copies to be served.

(c) Method of Service. If service is required or permitted to be made on a party represented by an attorney, service shall be made on the attorney unless service on the party is ordered by the court. Service on the attorney or party shall be made by delivering a copy to the attorney or party or by mailing it to the attorney or party at the last known address or, if no address is known, by leaving it with the clerk of the court. Delivery of a copy within this rule shall mean (A) handing it to the attorney or to the party, or (B) leaving it at the attorney's or party's office with the clerk or other person in charge thereof, or (C) if there is no one in charge, leaving it in a conspicuous place therein, or (D) if the office is closed or the person to be served has no office, leaving it at the attorney's or party's usual place of abode with some person of the attorney's or party's family above 15 years of age and informing such person of the contents. Service by mail shall be complete on mailing.

(d) Proof of Service. A certificate of service that complies in substance with the appropriate form below shall be taken as prima facie proof of service in compliance with these rules. The certificate shall specify the party each attorney represents.

(1) By Attorney:

I certify that a copy hereof has been furnished to ______________ (here insert name or names) by ______________(delivery) (mail) on ______________ (date)______________ Attorney for __________ (name of party) ______________

______________(address and phone number) ______________ Florida Bar Number ______________

(2) By Pro Se Inmate:

I certify that I placed this document in the hands of ______________(here insert name of institution official) __________ for mailing to ______________(here insert name or names) on ______________(date)______________

______________ (name) ______________

______________ (address) ______________

______________ (prison identification number) __________

(3) By Other Pro Se Litigants:

I certify that a copy hereto has been furnished to ______________(here insert name or names) ______________ by ______________(delivery) (mail) on ______________ (date)______________

______________ (name) ______________

______________ (address) ______________

______________ (phone number) ______________

(e) Additional Time After Service by Mail. If a party, court, reporter, or clerk is required or permitted to do an act within some prescribed time after service of a document, and the document is served by mail, 5 days shall be added to the prescribed period.

(f) Computation. In computing any period of time prescribed or allowed by these rules, by order of the court, or by any applicable statute, the day of the act, event, or default from which the designated period of time begins to run shall not be included. The last day of the period so computed shall be included unless it is a Saturday, a Sunday, or a holiday described below, in which event, the period shall run until the end of the next day that is neither a Saturday, Sunday, nor holiday. If the period of time prescribed or allowed is less than 7 days, intermediate Saturdays, Sundays, and holidays shall be excluded in the computation. As used in this rule, holiday means

(1) New Year's Day;

(2) Martin Luther King, Jr.'s Birthday, the third Monday in January;

(3) Washington's Birthday, the third Monday in February;

(4) Good Friday;

(5) Memorial Day, the last Monday in May;

(6) Independence Day;

(7) Labor Day, the first Monday in September;

(8) Columbus Day, the second Monday in October;

(9) Veterans' Day;

(10) General Election Day;

(11) Thanksgiving Day, the fourth Thursday in November;

(12) Christmas Day;

(13) any statewide primary day;

(14) any Monday immediately following a Sunday on which one of the foregoing holidays falls; and

(15) any other day when the clerk's office is closed.

History: Amended July 3, 1980, effective Jan. 1, 1981 (387 So.2d 920); amended effective March 19, 1987 (505 So.2d 1087); amended June 8, 1987, effective July 1, 1987 (509 So.2d 276); Oct. 22, 1992, effective Jan. 1, 1993 (609 So.2d 516); Nov. 22, 1996, effective Jan. 1, 1997 (685 So.2d 773); amended Oct. 12, 2000, effective Jan. 1, 2001 (780 So. 2d 834; 2000 Fla. LEXIS 2273; 25 Fla. L. Weekly S 835); amended Feb.3, 2005, effective Feb. 3, 2005 (2005 Fla. LEXIS 154; 30 Fla. L. Weekly S 84); amended January 19, 2006, effective January 19, 2006 (2006 Fla. LEXIS 10).

Committee Notes

1977 Amendment. Subdivision (a) replaces former rule 3.4(a). The last sentence of former rule 3.4(a) was eliminated as superfluous. The filing of papers with a judge or justice is permitted at the discretion of the judge or justice. The advisory committee recommends that the ability to file with a judge or justice be exercised only if necessary, and that care be taken not to discuss in any manner the merits of the document being filed. See Fla.Code Prof.Resp., DR 7-110(B) (now R. Regulating Fla. Bar 4-3.5(b)); Fla.Code Jud.Conduct, Canon 3(A)(4).

Subdivision (b) replaces and simplifies former rules 3.4(b)(5) and 3.6(i)(3). The substance of the last sentence of former rule 3.4(b)(5) is preserved. It should be noted that except for the notices or petitions that invoke jurisdiction, these rules generally provide for service by a certain time rather than filing. Under this provision filing must be done before service or immediately thereafter. Emphasis has been placed on service so as to eliminate the hardship on parties caused by tardy service under the former rules and to eliminate the burden placed on the courts by motions for extension of time resulting from such tardy service. It is anticipated that tardy filing will occur less frequently under these rules than tardy service under the former rules because the parties are unlikely to act in a manner that would irritate the court. The manner for service and proof thereof is provided in subdivision (c).

Subdivision (d) replaces former rule 3.4(b)(3) and provides that if a party or clerk is required or permitted to do an act within a prescribed time after service, 5 days (instead of 3 days under the former rule) shall be added to the time if service is by mail.

Subdivision (e) replaces former rule 3.18, with no substantial change. "Holiday" is defined to include any day the clerk's office is closed whether or not done by order of the court. The holidays specifically listed have been included, even though many courts do not recognize them as holidays, to not place a burden on practitioners to check whether an individual court plans to observe a particular holiday.

1980 Amendment. Subdivision (b) was amended to provide that either the lower tribunal or the court may limit the number of copies to be served. The rule contemplates that the number of copies may be limited on any showing of good cause, for example, that the number of copies involved is onerous or that the appeal involves questions with which some parties have no interest in the outcome or are so remotely involved as not to justify furnishing a complete record to them at appellant's initial cost. The availability of the original record at the clerk's office of the lower tribunal until due at the appellate court is a factor to be considered.

Court Commentary

2000. Subdivision (a)(2) codifies the Florida Supreme Court's holding in *Thompson v. State*, 761 So. 2d 324 (Fla. 2000).

Rule 9.430. Proceedings by Indigents.

(a) Motion and Affidavit. A party who has the right to seek review by appeal without payment of costs shall, unless the court directs otherwise, file a motion in the lower tribunal, with an affidavit showing the party's inability either to pay fees and costs or to give security therefor. For review by original proceedings under rule 9.100, unless the court directs otherwise, the party shall file a motion and affidavit with the court. If the motion is granted, the party may proceed without further application to the court and without either the prepayment of fees or costs in the lower tribunal or court or the giving of security therefor. Reasons for denying the motion shall be stated in writing. Review of decisions by the lower tribunal shall be by motion filed in the court.

(b) Incarcerated Parties.

(1) Presumptions.

(A) assertions in an affidavit filed by an incarcerated party under this rule are true, and

(B) in cases involving criminal or collateral criminal proceedings, an incarcerated party who has been declared indigent for purposes of proceedings in the lower tribunal remains indigent.

(2) Non-Criminal Proceedings.

Except in cases involving criminal or collateral proceedings, a motion and affidavit under this rule by a person who has been convicted of a crime and is incarcerated for that crime or who is being held in custody pending extradition or sentencing shall contain substantially the same information as required by rule 9.900(i). The determination of whether the case involves an appeal from an original criminal or collateral proceeding depends on the substance of the issues raised and not on the form or title of the petition or complaint. In these non-criminal cases, the court may require the party to make continued partial payments until the full amount is paid.

History: Amended Oct. 22, 1992, effective Jan. 1, 1993 (609 So.2d 516); amended effective April 25, 1996 (21 Fla. L. Weekly 183); amended Nov. 22, 1996, effective Jan. 1, 1997 (685 So.2d 773); amended Feb.3, 2005, effective Feb. 3, 2005 (2005 Fla. LEXIS 154; 30 Fla. L. Weekly S 84).

Committee Notes

1977 Adoption. This rule governs the manner in which an indigent may proceed with an appeal without payment of fees or costs and without bond. Adverse rulings by the lower tribunal must state in writing the reasons for denial. Provision is made for review by motion. Such motion may be made without the filing of fees as long as a notice has been filed, the filing of fees not being jurisdictional. This rule is not intended to expand the rights of indigents to proceed with an appeal without payment of fees or costs. The existence of such rights is a matter governed by substantive law.

Rule 9.440. Attorneys.

(a) Foreign Attorneys. An attorney who is an active member in good standing of the bar of another state may be permitted to appear in a proceeding upon compliance with Florida Rule of Judicial Administration 2.061.

(b) Withdrawal of Attorneys. An attorney shall not be permitted to withdraw unless the withdrawal is approved by the court. The attorney shall file a motion for that purpose stating the reasons for withdrawal and the client's address. A copy of the motion shall be served on the client and adverse parties.

History: Amended Oct. 22, 1992, effective Jan. 1, 1993 (609 So.2d 516); Aug. 29, 2002, effective Jan. 1, 2003.

Committee Notes

1977 Amendment. This rule replaces former rule 2.3 with unnecessary subdivisions deleted. The deletion of former rule 2.3(c) was not intended to authorize the practice of law by research aides or secretaries to any justice or judge or otherwise approve actions inconsistent with the high standards of ethical conduct expected of such persons.

Subdivision (a) permits foreign attorneys to appear on motion filed and granted at any time. See Fla.Bar Integr. Rule By-Laws, art. II, § 2. There is no requirement that the foreign attorney be from a jurisdiction giving a reciprocal right to members of The Florida Bar. This rule leaves disposition of motions to appear to the discretion of the court.

Subdivision (b) is intended to protect the rights of parties and attorneys, and the needs of the judicial system.

This rule does not affect the right of a party to employ additional attorneys who, if members of The Florida Bar, may appear at any time.

2002 Amendment. The amendments to subdivision (a) are intended to make that subdivision consistent with Florida Rule of Judicial Administration 2.061, which was adopted in 2001, and the amendments to subdivision (b) are intended to make that subdivision consistent with Florida Rule of Judicial Administration 2.060(i).

Rule 9.500. Advisory Opinions to Governor.

(a) Filing. A request by the governor for an advisory opinion from the justices of the supreme court on a question affecting gubernatorial powers and duties shall be in writing. The original and 7 copies shall be filed with the clerk of the supreme court.

(b) Procedure. As soon as practicable after the filing of the request, the justices shall determine whether the request is within the purview of article IV, section 1(c), Florida Constitution, and proceed as follows:

(1) If 4 justices concur that the question is not within that purview, the governor shall be advised forthwith in writing and a copy shall be filed in the clerk's office.

(2) If the request is within that purview, the court may permit persons whose substantial

R. App. Proc.

interests may be affected to be heard on the questions presented through briefs, oral argument, or both. If the court determines to receive briefs or hear oral argument, it shall set the time for filing briefs, the date of argument, and the time allotted. The court may appoint amicus curiae and prescribe their duties.

(3) The justices shall file their opinions in the clerk's office. Copies shall be delivered to the governor.

History: Amended Oct. 22, 1992, effective Jan. 1, 1993 (609 So.2d 516).

Committee Notes

1977 Amendment. This rule simplifies former rule 2.1(h) without material change.

Rule 9.510. Advisory Opinions to Attorney General.

(a) Filing. A request by the attorney general for an advisory opinion from the justices of the supreme court concerning the validity of an initiative petition for the amendment of the Florida Constitution shall be in writing. The original and 7 copies shall be filed with the clerk of the supreme court.

(b) Contents of Request. In addition to the language of the proposed amendment, the request referenced in subdivision (a) must contain the following information:

(1) the name and address of the sponsor of the initiative petition;

(2) the name and address of the sponsor's attorney, if the sponsor is represented;

(3) a statement as to whether the sponsor has obtained the requisite number of signatures on the initiative petition to have the proposed amendment put on the ballot;

(4) if the sponsor has not obtained the requisite number of signatures on the initiative petition to have the proposed amendment put on the ballot, the current status of the signature-collection process;

(5) the date of the election during which the sponsor is planning to submit the proposed amendment to the voters;

(6) the last possible date that the ballot for the target election can be printed in order to be ready for the election;

(7) a statement identifying the date by which the Financial Impact Statement will be filed, if the Financial Impact Statement is not filed concurrently with the request; and

(8) the names and complete mailing addresses of all of the parties who are to be served.

(c) Procedure. The justices must initially determine whether the request is within the purview of article V, section 3(b)(10), Florida Constitution, and proceed as follows:

(1) If 4 justices concur that the request is not within that purview, the attorney general will be advised immediately in writing and a copy will be filed in the clerk's office.

(2) If the request is within the purview, the court may permit the attorney general and other interested persons to be heard on the questions presented through briefs, oral argument, or both. If the court decides to receive briefs or hear oral argument, it will establish the time for filing briefs, the date of argument, and the time allotted.

History: Adopted November 9, 2006, effective November 9, 2006 (942 So.2d 406).

Rule 9.520. Deleted.

History: Former Rule 9.520, concerning Judicial Qualifications Commission, deleted Sept. 13, 1984, effective Jan. 1, 1985 (458 So.2d 1110) and relocated to Rule of Judicial Administration 2.140 (463 So.2d 1114).

Rule 9.600. Jurisdiction of Lower Tribunal Pending Review.

(a) Concurrent Jurisdiction. Only the court may grant an extension of time for any act required by these rules. Before the record is transmitted, the lower tribunal shall have concurrent jurisdiction with the court to render orders on any other procedural matter relating to the cause, subject to the control of the court.

(b) Further Proceedings. If the jurisdiction of

the lower tribunal has been divested by an appeal from a final order, the court by order may permit the lower tribunal to proceed with specifically stated matters during the pendency of the appeal.

(c) Family Law Matters. In family law matters:

(1) The lower tribunal shall retain jurisdiction to enter and enforce orders awarding separate maintenance, child support, alimony, attorneys' fees and costs for services rendered in the lower tribunal, temporary attorneys' fees and costs reasonably necessary to prosecute or defend an appeal, or other awards necessary to protect the welfare and rights of any party pending appeal.

(2) The receipt, payment, or transfer of funds or property under an order in a family law matter shall not prejudice the rights of appeal of any party. The lower tribunal shall have the jurisdiction to impose, modify, or dissolve conditions upon the receipt or payment of such awards in order to protect the interests of the parties during the appeal.

(3) Review of orders entered pursuant to this subdivision shall be by motion filed in the court within 30 days of rendition.

(d) Criminal Cases. The lower tribunal shall retain jurisdiction to consider motions pursuant to Florida Rules of Criminal Procedure 3.800(b)(2) and in conjunction with post-trial release pursuant to rule 9.140(g).

History: Amended July 3, 1980, effective Jan. 1, 1981 (387 So.2d 920); June 8, 1987, effective July 1, 1987 (509 So.2d 276); Oct. 22, 1992, effective Jan. 1, 1993 (609 So.2d 516); June 15, 1995 (657 So.2d 897); Nov. 22, 1996, effective Jan. 1, 1997 (685 So.2d 773); Nov. 12, 1999, effective Nov. 12, 1999 (24 Fla. L. Weekly S530); opinion corrected Nov. 23, 1999 (24 Fla. L. Weekly S567); opn. on grant of reh'g Jan. 13, 2000 *Amendment to Florida Rules of Criminal Procedure 3.111(e), 3.800 and Florida Rules of Appellate Procedure 9.020(h), 9.140, and 9.600,* No. 95707 (25 Fla. L. Weekly S37a); opinion corrected Jan. 14, 2000.

1999 Note: The amendment at 24 Fla. L. Weekly S530 shall also apply to cases pending on appeal.

Committee Notes

1977 Amendment. This rule governs the jurisdiction of the lower tribunal during the pendency of review proceedings, except for interlocutory appeals. If an interlocutory appeal is taken, the lower tribunal's jurisdiction is governed by rule 9.130(f).

Subdivision (b) replaces former rule 3.8(a). It allows for continuation of various aspects of the proceeding in the lower tribunal, as may be allowed by the court, without a formal remand of the cause. This rule is intended to prevent unnecessary delays in the resolution of disputes.

Subdivision (c) is derived from former rule 3.8(b). It provides for jurisdiction in the lower tribunal to enter and enforce orders awarding separate maintenance, child support, alimony, temporary suit money, and attorneys' fees. Such orders may be reviewed by motion.

1980 Amendment. Subdivision (a) was amended to clarify the appellate court's paramount control over the lower tribunal in the exercise of its concurrent jurisdiction over procedural matters. This amendment would allow the appellate court to limit the number of extensions of time granted by a lower tribunal, for example.

1994 Amendment. Subdivision (c)(1) was amended to conform to and implement section 61.16(1), Florida Statutes (1994 Supp.), authorizing the lower tribunal to award temporary appellate attorneys' fees, suit money, and costs.

1996 Amendment. New rule 9.600(d) recognizes the jurisdiction of the trial courts, while an appeal is pending, to rule on motions for post-trial release, as authorized by rule 9.140(g), and to decide motions pursuant to Florida Rule of Criminal Procedure 3.800(a), as authorized by case law such as *Barber v. State*, 590 So. 2d 527 (Fla. 2d DCA 1991).

Rule 9.700. Deleted.

History: Deleted Nov. 22, 1996, effective Jan. 1, 1997 (685 So.2d 773).

Rule 9.800. Uniform Citation System.

This rule applies to all legal documents, including court opinions. Except for citations to case reporters, all citation forms should be spelled out in full if used as an integral part of a sentence either in the text or in footnotes. Abbreviated forms as shown in this rule should be used if the citation is intended to stand alone either in the text or in footnotes.

(a) Florida Supreme Court.

R. App. Proc.

(1) 1846-1886: *Livingston v. L'Engle,* 22 Fla. 427 (1886).

(2) 1948-date: *Fenelon v. State,* 594 So.2d 292 (Fla. 1992).

(3) For recent opinions not yet published in the Southern Reporter, cite to Florida Law Weekly: *Traylor v. State,* 17 Fla. L. Weekly S42 (Fla. Jan. 16, 1992). If not therein, cite to the slip opinion: *Medina v. State,* No. SC00-280 (Fla. Mar. 14, 2002).

(b) Florida District Courts of Appeal.

(1) *Sotolongo v. State,* 530 So.2d 514 (Fla. 2d DCA 1988); *Buncayo v. Dribin,* 533 So.2d 935 (Fla. 3d DCA 1988).

(2) For recent opinions not yet published in Southern Reporter, cite to Florida Law Weekly: *Myers v. State,* 16 Fla. L. Weekly D1507 (Fla. 4th DCA June 5, 1991). If not therein, cite to the slip opinion: *Fleming v. State,* No. 1D01-2734 (Fla. 1st DCA Mar. 6, 2002).

(c) Florida Circuit Courts and County Courts.

(1) *Whidden v. Francis,* 27 Fla. Supp. 80 (Fla. 11th Cir. Ct. 1966).

(2) *State v. Alvarez,* 42 Fla. Supp. 83 (Fla. Dade Cty. Ct. 1975).

(3) For opinions not published in Florida Supplement, cite to Florida Law Weekly: *State v. Campeau,* 16 Fla. L. Weekly C65 (Fla. 9th Cir. Ct. Nov. 7, 1990). If not therein, cite to the slip opinion: *State v. Campeau,* No. 90-4363 (Fla. 9th Cir. Ct. Nov. 7, 1990).

(d) Florida Administrative Agencies. (Cite if not in Southern Reporter.)

(1) For decisions of the Public Employees Relations Commission: *Indian River Educ. Ass'n v. School Bd.,* 4 F.P.E.R. ¶ 4262 (1978).

(2) For decisions of the Florida Public Service Commission: *In re Application of Tampa Elec. Co.,* 81 F.P.S.C. 2:120 (1981).

(3) For decisions of all other agencies: *Insurance Co. v. Department of Ins.,* 2 F.A.L.R. 648-A (Fla. Dept. of Insurance 1980).

(e) Florida Constitution. (Year of adoption should be given if necessary to avoid confusion.) Art. V, § 3(b)(3), Fla. Const.

(f) Florida Statutes (Official). § 350.34, Fla. Stat. (1973). § 120.53, Fla. Stat. (Supp. 1974).

(g) Florida Statutes Annotated. (To be used only for court-adopted rules, or references to other nonstatutory materials that do not appear in an official publication.) 32 Fla. Stat. Ann. 116 (Supp. 1975).

(h) Florida Laws. (Cite if not in Fla. Stat. or if desired for clarity or adoption reference.)

(1) After 1956: Ch. 74-177, § 5, at 473, Laws of Fla.

(2) Before 1957: Ch. 22000, Laws of Fla. (1943).

(i) Florida Rules. Fla. R. Civ. P. 1.180. Fla. R. Jud. Admin. 2.035. Fla. R. Crim. P. 3.850. Fla. R. Work. Comp. P. 4.113. Fla. Prob. R. 5.120. Fla. R. Traf. Ct. 6.165. Fla. Sm. Cl. R. 7.070. Fla. R. Juv. P. 8.070. Fla. R. App. P. 9.100. Fla. R. Med. 10.010 Fla. R. Arb. 11.010 Fla. Fam. L. R. P. 12.010 Fla. Admin. Code 62D-2.014. R. Regulating Fla. Bar 4-1.10. Fla. Bar Found. By-Laws, art. 2.19(b). Fla. Bar Found. Charter, art. III §3.4. Fl. Bar Integr. R., art. XI, § 11.09. Fla. Jud. Qual. Comm'n R. 9. Fla. Std. Jury Instr. (Civ.) 6.4(c). Fla. Std. Jury Instr. (Crim.) 2.03. Fla. Std. Jury Instr. (Crim.) Robbery. Fla. Stds. Imposing Law. Sancs. 9.32(a). Fla. Bar Admiss. R. 3-23.1.

(j) Florida Attorney General Opinions. Op. Att'y Gen. Fla. 73-178 (1973).

(k) United States Supreme Court. *Sansone v. United States,* 380 U.S. 343 (1965). Cite to United States Reports, if published therein; otherwise cite to Supreme Court Reporter, Lawyer's Edition, or United States Law Week, in that order of preference. For opinions not published in these reporters, cite to Florida Law Weekly Federal: *California v. Hodari D.,* 13 Fla. L. Weekly Fed. S249 (U.S. Apr. 23, 1991).

(*l*) Federal Courts of Appeals. *Gulf Oil Corp. v. Bivins,* 276 F. 2d 753 (5th Cir. 1960). For opinions not published in the Federal Reporter, cite to Florida Law Weekly Federal: *Cunningham v. Zant,* 13 Fla. L. Weekly Fed. C591 (11th Cir. March 27, 1991).

(m) Federal District Courts. *Pugh v. Rainwater,* 332 F. Supp. 1107 (S.D. Fla. 1971).

For opinions not published in the Federal Supplement, cite to Florida Law Weekly Federal: *Wasko v. Dugger,* 13 Fla. L. Weekly Fed. D183 (S.D. Fla. Apr. 2, 1991).

(n) United States Constitution.

Art. IV, § 2, cl. 2, U.S. Const. Amend. V, U.S. Const.

(o) Other Citations. When referring to specific material within a Florida court's opinion, pinpoint citation to the page of the Southern Reporter where that material occurs is optional, although preferred. All other citations shall be in the form prescribed by the latest edition of The Bluebook: A Uniform System of Citation, The Harvard Law Review Association, Gannett House, Cambridge, MA 02138. Citations not covered in this rule or in The Bluebook shall be in the form prescribed by the Florida Style Manual published by the Florida State University Law Review, Tallahassee, FL 32306.

(p) Case Names. Case names shall be underscored (or italicized) in text and in footnotes.

History: Amended Sept. 13, 1984, effective Jan. 1, 1985 (463 So.2d 1114); Oct. 22, 1992, effective Jan. 1, 1993 (609 So.2d 516); Oct. 12, 1995 (661 So.2d 815); Nov. 22, 1996, effective Jan. 1, 1997 (685 So.2d 773); amended Oct. 12, 2000, effective Jan. 1, 2001 (780 So. 2d 834; 2000 Fla. LEXIS 2273; 25 Fla. L. Weekly S 835); Aug. 29, 2002, effective Jan. 1, 2003.

Committee Notes

1977 Adoption. This rule is new and is included to standardize appellate practice and ease the burdens on the courts. It is the duty of each litigant and counsel to assist the judicial system by use of these standard forms of citation. Use of these citation forms, however, has not been made mandatory.

1992 Amendment. Rule 9.800 was updated to reflect changes in the available reporters. Additionally, the citations to new rules have been added and citations to rules no longer in use have been deleted.

Rule 9.900. Forms.

(a) Notice of Appeal.

Notice of Appeal

IN THE ______________
(NAME OF LOWER TRIBUNAL
WHOSE ORDER IS TO
BE REVIEWED)
Case No. __________

______________,

Defendant/Appellant,

v.

______________,

Plaintiff/Appellee.

NOTICE OF APPEAL

NOTICE IS GIVEN that ______________, Defendant/Appellant, appeals to the ______________ (name of court that has appellate jurisdiction), the order of this court rendered [see rule 9.020(h)] ____________ (date). [Conformed copies of orders designated in the notice of appeal shall be attached in accordance with rules 9.110(d), and 9.160(c).] The nature of the order is a final order ____________ (state nature of the order).

Attorney for ______________________________ (name of party)

____

(address and phone number)

Florida Bar No. ______________________________

(b) Notice of Cross-Appeal.

Notice of Cross-Appeal

IN THE ___________
(NAME OF LOWER TRIBUNAL
WHOSE ORDER IS TO
BE REVIEWED)
Case No. ___________

___________,

Defendant/Appellant,
Cross-Appellee,

v.

___________,

Plaintiff/Appellee.
Cross-Appellant.

NOTICE OF
CROSS APPEAL

NOTICE IS GIVEN that ___________, Plaintiff/Cross-Appellant, appeals to the ___________ (name of court that has appellate jurisdiction), the order of this court rendered [see rule 9.020(h)] ___________ (date). The nature of the order is a final order ___________ (state nature of the order).

Attorney for ___________ (name of party)

____
(address and phone number)

Florida Bar No. ___________

R. App. Proc.

(c) Notice of Appeal of Non-Final Order.

Notice of Appeal of Non-Final Order

IN THE ____________
(NAME OF LOWER TRIBUNAL
WHOSE ORDER IS TO
BE REVIEWED)
Case No. ____________

____________ ,
Defendant/Appellant,

v.

____________ ,
Plaintiff/Appellee.

NOTICE OF APPEAL OF A NON-FINAL ORDER

NOTICE IS GIVEN that ____________ , Defendant/Appellant, appeals to the ____________ (name of court that has appellate jurisdiction), the order of this court rendered [see rule 9.020(h)] ____________ (date). Conformed copies of orders designated in the notice of appeal shall be attached in accordance with rules 9.110(d), 9.130(c), and 9.160(c).] The nature of the order is a non-final order ____________ (state nature of the order).

Attorney for ____ (name of party)

____
(address and phone number)

Florida Bar No. ____

(d) Notice to Invoke Discretionary Jurisdiction of Supreme Court.

Notice to Invoke Discretionary Jurisdiction of Supreme Court

IN THE DISTRICT COURT
OF APPEAL OF FLORIDA,
__________ DISTRICT
Case No. __________

__________,

Defendant/Petitioner,

v.

__________,

Plaintiff/Respondent.

NOTICE TO INVOKE DISCRETIONARY JURISDICTION

NOTICE IS GIVEN that __________, Defendant/Petitioner, invokes the discretionary jurisdiction of the supreme court to review the decision of this court rendered [see rule 9.020(h)] __________ (date). The decision __________ (state why the decision is within the supreme court's jurisdiction). [1]

Attorney for __________ (name of party)

__________ (address and phone number)

Florida Bar No. __________

1. The choices are:

a. expressly declares valid a state statute.

b. expressly construes a provision of the state or federal constitution.

c. expressly affects a class of constitutional or state oficers.

d. expressly and directly conflicts with a decision of another district court of appeal or of the supreme court on the same question of law.

e. passes on a question certified to be of great public importance.

f. is certified to be in direct conflict with decisions of other district courts of appeal.

See rule 9.030(a)(2)(a).

Rule 9.900.

E.g., "Order Denying Plaintiff's Motion for Summary Judgment," "Defendant's Motion to Compel," "Order Denying Defendant's Motion to Dismiss," "Final Judgment for Plaintiff," etc.

(e) Notice of Administrative Appeal.

Notice of Administrative Appeal

IN THE ____________
(NAME OF AGENCY, OFFICER,
BOARD, COMMISSION, OR
BODY WHOSE ORDER
IS TO BE REVIEWED)
Case No. ____________

____________,
Defendant*/Appellant,

v.

____________,
Plaintiff*/Appellee.

NOTICE OF ADMINISTRATIVE APPEAL

NOTICE IS GIVEN that ____________, Appellant, appeals to the ____________ (name of court that has appellate jurisdiction), ____________ the order of this ____________ (name of agency, officer, board, commission, or body whose order is to be reviewed) rendered [see rule 9.020(h)] ____________ (date). [Conformed copies of orders designated in the notice of appeal shall be attached in accordance with rules 9.110(d) and 9.130(c).] The nature of the order is ____________ (state nature of the order).

Attorney for ________________________________ (name of party)

____

(address and phone number)

Florida Bar No. ________________________________

*or other appropriate designation.

(f) Directions to Clerk.

Directions to Clerk

IN THE ____________
(NAME OF LOWER TRIBUNAL
WHOSE ORDER IS TO
BE REVIEWED)
Case No. ____________

____________ ,

Plaintiff/Appellant,

v. DIRECTIONS TO CLERK

____________ ,

Defendant/Appellee.

Plaintiff/Appellant, ____________ , directs the clerk to ____________ (include/exclude) the following items ____________ (in/from) the original record described in rule 9.200(a)(1):

ITEM DATE FILED

1.

[List of Desired Items]

2.

Note: This form is necessary only if a party does not wish to rely on the record that will be automatically prepared by the clerk under rule 9.200(a)(1).

R. App. Proc.

(g) Designation to Reporter.

Designation to Reporter

IN THE ____________
(NAME OF LOWER TRIBUNAL
WHOSE ORDER IS TO
BE REVIEWED)
Case No. ____________

____________ ,

Plaintiff/Appellant,

v.

____________ ,

Defendant/Appellee.

DESIGNATION TO REPORTER AND REPORTER'S ACKNOWLEDGMENT

I.

DESIGNATION

Plaintiff/Appellant, ____________ , files this Designation to Reporter and directs ____________ (name of court reporter) to transcribe an original and ______ copies of the following portions of the trial proceedings to be used in this appeal:

1. The entire trial proceedings recorded by the reporter on ____________ (date), before the Honorable ____________ (judge), except ____________ .

2. [Indicate all other portions of reported proceedings.]

3. The court reporter is directed to file the original with the clerk of the lower tribunal and to serve one copy on each of the following:

1.

2.

3.

I, counsel for Appellant, certify that satisfactory financial arrangements have been made with the court reporter for preparation of the transcript.

Attorney for ____ (name of party)

____

(address and phone number)

Florida Bar No. ____

II.

REPORTER'S ACKNOWLEDGMENT

1. The foregoing designation was served on ____________ (date), and received on ____________ (date).

2. Satisfactory arrangements have ( ) have not ( ) been made for payment of the transcript cost. These financial arrangements were completed on ____________ (date).

3. Number of trial or hearing days _______ .

4. Estimated number of transcript pages _______ .

5a. The transcript will be available within 30 days of service of the foregoing designation and will be filed on or before ____________ (date).

OR

5b. For the following reason(s) the court reporter requests an extension of time of days for preparation of the transcript that will be filed on or before ____________ (date).

6. Completion and filing of this acknowledgment by the court reporter constitutes submission to the jurisdiction of the court for all purposes in connection with these appellate proceedings.

7. The undersigned court reporter certifies that the foregoing is true and correct and that a copy has been furnished by mail ( ) hand delivery ( ) on ____________ (date), to each of the parties or their counsel.

____

Court Reporter

____

(address)

Note: The foregoing court reporter's acknowledgment to be placed "at the foot of" or attached to a copy of the designation, shall be properly completed, signed by the court reporter, and filed with the clerk of the appellate court within 5 days of service of the designation on the court reporter. A copy shall be served on all parties or their counsel, who shall have 5 days to object to any requested extension of time. See Fla.R.App.P. 9.200(b)(1), (2), & (3).

(h) Civil Supersedeas Bond.

Civil Supersedeas Bond

____
(Title of Court)
Case No. ______________

______________ ,

Plaintiff,

v. CIVIL SUPERSEDEAS BOND

______________ ,

Defendant.

We, ______________ as Principal, and ______________ as Surety, are held and firmly bound unto ______________ in the principal sum of $ ______________ , for the payment of which we bind ourselves, our heirs, personal representatives, successors, and assigns, jointly and severally.

The condition of this obligation is: the above-named Principal has entered an appeal to the ______________ (court) to review the ______________ (judgment or order) entered in the above case on ______________ (date), and filed in the records of said court in book ______________ at page ________ .

NOW THEREFORE, if the Principal shall satisfy any money judgment contained in the judgment in full, including, if allowed by law, costs, interest, and attorneys' fees, and damages for delay in the event said appeal is dismissed or said judgment is affirmed, then this obligation shall be null and void; otherwise to remain in full force and effect.

Signed on ______________ (date), at ______________ (place).

/s/ ____

Principal

Signed on ______________ (date), at ______________ (place).

/s/ ______________
Surety

(i) Prisoner's Motion and Affidavit to Proceed Without Prepayment of Court Costs and Fees.

Prisoner's Motion and Affidavit to Proceed Without Prepayment of Court Costs and Fees

IN THE (name of court)

Case No. ________

________________________________,

Appellant(s)/Plaintiff(s)/Petitioner(s),

v.

________________________________,

Appellee(s)/Defendant(s)/Respondent(s).

PRISONER'S MOTION AND AFFIDAVIT TO PROCEED WITHOUT PREPAYMENT OF COURT COSTS AND FEES

I, ____________ , am a plaintiff/petitioner/appellant in the above-styled action. I have been convicted of a crime and am currently incarcerated for that crime, or I am being held in custody pending extradition or sentencing. Pursuant to § 57.085, Fla. Stat., I hereby apply for leave to proceed in this action without prepayment of court costs and fees.

I acknowledge that the custodian or the custodian's designee for my inmate trust account may withdraw funds from my account and transmit these funds to the clerk of the court, as directed by order of the court. These funds will be applied to any court costs or fees that the court requires me to pay in connection with this case. This acknowledgment applies to any institution in which I am or will be confined.

I am unable to pay court costs and fees. Under penalty of perjury, I swear or affirm that all statements in this affidavit are true and complete.

1. State your inmate number and the place and address of the institution where you are in prison or in custody.

____

2. Are you presently employed? Yes ( ) No ( )

a. If yes, state your occupation, the amount of your monthly salary or wages, and your employer's address.

b. If no, state the time period of your last employment, your occupation, and the amount of monthly salary or wages received.

3. Have you received within the past twelve months any money from any of the following sources?

a. Business, profession, or self-employment? Yes ( ) No ( )

b. Rent, payments, interest, or dividends? Yes ( ) No ( )

c. Pensions, annuities, or life insurance? Yes ( ) No ( )

R. App. Proc.

d. Gifts or inheritances? Yes ( ) No ( )

e. Any other source? Yes ( ) No ( )

If you answered yes to any of the above, describe each source and state amount received from each. ______________ .

4. Do you own any cash, or do you have money in a checking, savings, or money market account? (Include funds in prison account.) Yes ( ) No ( )

If yes, state the amount of cash owned and the current balance(s) in each checking, savings, or money market account.

____ .

5. Do you own any real estate, stocks, bonds, notes, automobiles, or other tangible or intangible thing of value worth more than $100? Yes ( ) No ( )

If yes, describe each item of property and state its approximate value.

____ .

6. List the persons who are dependent upon you for support, state their ages and their relationship to you, and indicate how much you contribute toward their support.

7. State the nature and amount of any significant monthly expenses that you must pay, such as mortgage payments or rent.

____ .

8. List all of your significant debts, including the name of each person or entity to whom you owe the debt, the total amount owed, and monthly payment, if any.

____ .

9. During the past three years, have you been permitted two or more times to proceed without prepayment of court costs or fees in Florida or federal courts or adjudicatory forums, or to intervene in actions in these courts or adjudicatory forums without prepayment of court costs or fees, pursuant to sections 57.081 or 57.085, Florida Statutes, or 28 U.S.C. § 1915?

Yes ( ) No ( )

If yes, list below all suits, actions, claims, proceedings, or appeals that you have brought or intervened in during the past five years in any court or adjudicatory forum.

Name of Court	Case Number	Nature of the Action
Disposition		

If necessary, attach additional pages that reflect the required information.

____

Signature of Appellant/Plaintiff/

Petitioner

State of Florida

County of ____________

Sworn to and subscribed before me on ________ (date) ________ by ______________________________ (name)

____

Notary Public — State of Florida
(Print, Type, or Stamp Commissioned Name Of Notary Public)

Personally known ____________ OR Produced Identification ____________

Type of Identification Produced ____________

FINANCIAL CERTIFICATE

(To be completed by authorized official of institution where prisoner is confined)

The prisoner must attach computer printout(s) reflecting all transactions in the prisoner's inmate trust account(s) for the preceding six months or for the period of incarceration, whichever is shorter. The prisoner has the responsibility to obtain the required printout(s) from each institution where the prisoner was or is confined and to provide the printout(s) to the official completing this certificate.

1. Name of prisoner ____________

2. Current available account balance ____________

3. Average highest available ____________ monthly balance for the preceding six months or for the period of incarceration, whichever is shorter.

4. Average available monthly ____________ deposits for preceding six months or for the period of incarceration, whichever is shorter.

If printout(s) or the above calculations do not represent the preceding six month period in its entirety, the official completing this certificate should explain here:

I hereby certify that, as of this date, the above information for the inmate trust account of the prisoner named above is correct.

Date: ____________ ____________

Authorized official of institution

ORDER REQUIRING FURTHER INFORMATION FOR DETERMINATION OF PRISONER'S INDIGENCY

Based on a claim of indigency, Petitioner (Plaintiff) seeks a waiver of the filing fee in this matter of $ ____________ . Petitioner (Plaintiff) appears to be incarcerated for conviction of a crime or pending extradition or sentencing. The documents filed by Petitioner (Plaintiff) are insufficient to determine whether the Petitioner (Plaintiff) is

R. App. Proc.

indigent under Section 57.085, Florida Statutes. Petitioner (Plaintiff) must either pay the filing fee stated above or file the following items (as marked) with this tribunal within 45 days of the date of this order:

_______ 1. Affidavit of indigency containing Petitioner's (Plaintiff's) identity and the financial information required by Section 57.085(2), Florida Statutes.

_______ 2. Statement in the affidavit regarding whether the Petitioner (Plaintiff) has been determined to be indigent under Sections 57.081 or 57.085, Florida Statutes, or 28 U.S.C. § 1915 two or more times during the past three years and, if yes, a listing of all suits, actions, claims, proceedings, or appeals brought by the prisoner or intervened in by the prisoner in any court or adjudicatory forum during the past five years.

_______ 3. Statement in the affidavit that "I am unable to pay court costs and fees. Under penalty of perjury, I swear or affirm that all statements in this affidavit are true and complete."

_______ 4. Acknowledgment that funds will be withdrawn from the Petitioner's (Plaintiff's) inmate trust account.

_______ 5. A copy of the Petitioner's (Plaintiff's) inmate trust account records for the past 6 months or the length of the Petitioner's (Plaintiff's) incarceration, whichever period is shorter. If Petitioner (Plaintiff) has not had an inmate trust account during this time period, the Petitioner (Plaintiff) must submit signed documentation from prison or jail officials for each institution confirming that the Petitioner(Plaintiff) did not have a trust account.

_______ 6. A financial certificate, signed by an authorized official of the Petitioner's (Plaintiff's) place of confinement, reflecting the current available account balance of the Petitioner's (Plaintiff's) inmate trust account and the average highest available monthly balance and average available monthly deposits in the trust account for the past 6 months or the length of the Petitioner's (Plaintiff's) incarceration, whichever period is shorter.

Completion of the enclosed or attached form will satisfy all of these requirements. Failure either to pay the filing fee in full or to comply with this order within 45 days from the date of this order may result in dismissal of this case. If the Petitioner (Plaintiff) has filed or intervened in more than one action, separate documents must be supplied for each action and the case number must appear on each submission.

ORDER ON PRISONER'S INDIGENCY

Based on a claim of indigency, Petitioner (Plaintiff) seeks waiver of prepayment of court costs and fees, pursuant to Section 57.085, Florida Statutes. Having reviewed the documents filed by Petitioner (Plaintiff), this tribunal finds that Petitioner (Plaintiff) is a prisoner as defined by Section 57.085(1), Florida Statutes, and orders as follows:

I. DETERMINATION OF INDIGENCY (check one)

_______ A. NOT INDIGENT. The Petitioner (Plaintiff) is found not indigent because _______________. The filing fee of $ _______________ must be paid in full or this case will be dismissed. (skip Section II) *(Note that Fla. R. App. P. 9.430 requires a statement of reasons for denying a request for indigency status.)*

_______ B. FULL WAIVER. Petitioner (Plaintiff) is indigent and unable to prepay court costs and fees. Petitioner (Plaintiff) is obligated to pay court costs and fees as specified in Section II below.

_______ C. PARTIAL WAIVER. Petitioner (Plaintiff) is indigent but able to prepay part of the court costs and fees. Petitioner (Plaintiff) shall make, prior to any further proceedings, an initial partial payment of the greater of either (1) 80% of the current available balance of the Petitioner's (Plaintiff's) inmate trust account or (2) the greater of 20% of the average highest available monthly balance or the average available monthly deposits of the Petitioner's (Plaintiff's) inmate trust account for the preceding 6 months or the period of incarceration, whichever period is shorter. This tribunal determines this amount to be $ _____________ . Payment must be made within 45 days of the date of this order, or this case may be dismissed. Petitioner (Plaintiff) shall make monthly payments of the remaining court costs and fees as specified in Section II below.

II. PAYMENT OF COURT COSTS AND FILING FEES

The initial filing fee in this case is $ _______ . The Department of Corrections or the local detention facility shall place a lien on the inmate's trust account for the full amount owed, withdraw money maintained in the trust account, and transmit the money to the clerk of the court until the Petitioner's (Plaintiff's) court costs and fees are paid in full. When the balance in the inmate's account is less than $10, the Department of Corrections or local detention facility shall accumulate the funds and not transmit them to the clerk until the balance exceeds $10. Any dismissal of this case, transfer of the Petitioner (Plaintiff) to a different detention facility, or release of the Petitioner (Plaintiff) from custody shall not extinguish the lien or the Petitioner's (Plaintiff's) responsibility to pay the full amount owed.

History: Amended Nov. 26, 1980, effective Jan. 1, 1981 (391 So.2d 203); Sept. 13, 1984, effective Jan. 1, 1985 (463 So.2d 1114); June 8, 1987, effective July 1, 1987 (509 So.2d 276); July 14, 1988, effective Jan. 1, 1989 (529 So.2d 687); Dec. 30, 1988, effective Jan. 1, 1989 (536 So.2d 240); Oct. 22, 1992, effective Jan. 1, 1993 (609 So.2d 516); Nov. 22, 1996, effective Jan. 1, 1997 (685 So.2d 773); amended Oct. 12, 2000, effective Jan. 1, 2001 (780 So. 2d 834; 2000 Fla. LEXIS 2273; 25 Fla. L. Weekly S 835); amended Feb.3, 2005, effective Feb. 3, 2005 (2005 Fla. LEXIS 154; 30 Fla. L. Weekly S 84).

Committee Notes

1980 Amendment. Forms 9.900(a) and (b) under the 1977 rules are modified, and additional forms are provided.

1992 Amendment. Forms 9.900(a), (c), and (e) were revised to remind the practitioner that conformed copies of the order or orders designated in the notice of appeal should be attached to the notice of appeal as provided in rules 9.110(d), 9.130(c), and 9.160(c).

PART VI

SELECTED PROVISIONS OF THE FLORIDA ADMINISTRATIVE CODE

SYNOPSIS

Drug-Free Workplace Standards

59A-24.003. **Definitions.**

59A-24.004. **Drugs to be Tested/Body Specimens.**

59A-24.005. **Collection Site and Specimen Collection Procedures.**

59A-24.006. **Drug Testing Laboratories.**

59A-24.008. **Review of Test Results.**

CHAPTER 59A-29
Health Care Provider Certification

59A-29.001. **Definitions.**

59A-29.002. **Requirements for Certification.**

59A-29.003. **Certification Time Frames.**

59A-29.004. **Occasional Health Care Providers.**

59A-29.005. **Decertification of a Health Care Provider.**

59A-29.006. **Decertification Process.**

59A-29.007. **Recertification Process.**

59A-29.008. **Determining Certification Status.**

59A-29.009. **Carrier Responsibilities.**

59A-29.010. **Health Care Provider Responsibilities.**

59A-29.011. **Workers' Compensation Certification Training Courses.**

CHAPTER 59A-30
Expert Medical Advisors

59A-30.002. **Definitions.**

59A-30.003. **Qualifications for Expert Medical Advisor Certification.**

59A-30.004. **Application for Expert Medical Advisor Certification.**

59A-30.005. **Selection of Expert Medical Advisors.**

59A-30.006. **Temporary Expert Medical Advisors.**

59A-30.007. **Expert Medical Advisor Responsibilities.**

59A-30.008. **Billing and Reimbursement for Expert Medical Advisor Services.**

59A-30.010. **Expert Medical Advisor Decertification.**

CHAPTER 59A-31
Disputed Reimbursement

59A-31.003 **Petition Form.**

59A-31.004 **Carrier Response Form.**

59A-31.005 **Petition Requirements.**

59A-31.006 **Consolidation of Petitions.**

59A-31.007 **Service of Petition on Carrier and Affected Parties.**

59A-31.008 **Computation of Time.**

59A-31.009 **Carrier Response Requirements.**

59A-31.010 **Effect of Non-Response by Carrier.**

59A-31.011 **Complete Record.**

59A-31.012 **Joint Stipulation of the Parties.**

59A-31.013 **Petition Withdrawal.**

59A-31.014 **Overutilization Issues Raised in Reimbursement Dispute Resolution.**

59A-31.015 **Managed Care Arrangements.**

59B
COST MANAGEMENT AND CONTROL

CHAPTER 59B-6

TITLE 69
FINANCIAL SERVICES

CHAPTER 69L-3
Workers' Compensation Claims

Workers' Compensation Medical Reimbursement and Utilization Review

69L-7.020. Florida Workers' Compensation Health Care Provider Reimbursement Manual.

69L-7.100. Florida Workers' Compensation Reimbursement Manual for Ambulatory Surgical Centers (ASCs).

69L-7.501. Florida Workers' Compensation Reimbursement Manual for Hospitals.

69L-7.601. Copying Charges for Medical Records.

69L-7.602. Florida Workers' Compensation Medical Services Billing, Filing and Reporting Rule.

69L–7.604. Permanent Impairment.

CHAPTER 69L-9
Drug Testing Rule.

69L-9.015. Drug Testing Criteria.

CHAPTER 69L-10
Claim for Reimbursement Against the Special Disability Trust Fund

69L-10.006. Definitions.

69L-10.0065. Filing; Facsimile Transmissions.

69L-10.007. Notice of Claim.

69L-10.009. Claimant's Representatives.

69L-10.011. Informed Conclusion of Pre-Existing Conditions for Proof of Claim.

69L-10.012. Review of Proof of Claim.

69L-10.013. Acknowledgements by SDTF.

69L-10.014. Procedure for Accepting an Offer of Reimbursement.

69L-10.015. Deemed Denial—120 Day Time Period.

69L-10.016. Documenting Expenditures for Purposes of Obtaining Reimbursement.

69L-10.0165. On-site Audit Criteria.

69L-10.017. Reimbursement to Subsequent Employer.

69L-10.018. Attorneys' Fees, Costs, Penalties and Interest.

69L-10.019. Forms.

CHAPTER 69L-11
Preferred Worker Program

69L-11.002. Definitions.

69L-11.003 Procedure for Obtaining Identity Card.

69L-11.004. Time and Procedure for Notifying Injured Employees.

69L-11.005. Documentation of Placement of a Preferred Worker.

69L-11.006. Time for Filing Application for Identity Card.

69L-11.007. Documentation for Reimbursement of Premium.

69L-11.008. Time for Requesting Reimbursement.

69L-11.009. Procedure When Eligibility for a Card Is Denied.

69L-11.010. Procedure When Request for Reimbursement of Premium is Denied.

69L-11.011. Forms.

CHAPTER 69L-24
Insurers Standards and Practices

69L-24.021. Minimum Performance Standards.

FLORIDA ADMINISTRATIVE CODE

TITLE 6 DEPARTMENT OF EDUCATION

6A-22.001. Definitions.

(1) "Cooperative working agreement" means a written contractual agreement between the Department and a qualified rehabilitation provider or a public or private agency to provide comprehensive reemployment services such as on-the-job training development, job placement and follow up.

(2) "Customary residence" is the injured employee's place of permanent residence.

(3) "Customary vicinity" is the distance traveled by the injured employee from his customary residence to his place of employment at the time of injury.

(4) "Education program" means a formal course of study or a certificate program in a training and education facility, agency or institution operating under Chapters 1004, Parts II, III, and IV, 1005 F.S., or a career and technical education program defined in Section 1003.01(4)(c), F.S., which states: "At the post secondary education level, courses of study that provide vocational competencies needed for entry into specific occupations or for advancement within an occupation." Outside of the State of Florida, an education program shall be approved as governed by comparable statutes of that state.

(5) "Ergonomic job analysis" is the objective study of the relationship among job demands, environmental conditions and human functional characteristics.

(6) "Good cause" is termination resulting from employee conduct:

(a) Evincing such willful or wanton disregard of an employer's interests as is found in deliberate violation or disregard of standards of behavior which the employer has the right to expect of his employee; or

(b) Carelessness or negligence of such a degree or recurrence as to manifest culpability, wrongful intent, or evil design, or to show an intentional and substantial disregard of an employer's interests or of the employee's duties and obligations to his employer.

(7) "Individualized written rehabilitation program" (IWRP) is an individualized written rehabilitation program as defined in the Rehabilitation Act of 1973, 29 U.S.C. §§ 701, et seq.

(8) "Labor market" means an area not to exceed a 50 mile radius of the injured employee's customary vicinity.

(9) "On-the-job training (OJT) contractor" is a qualified rehabilitation provider or employee of a public or private agency which has entered into a cooperative working agreement with the Department for the provision of on-the-job development and follow-up services.

(10) "On-the-job training (OJT) contract" is a contract between an employer, injured employee and the Department in which an employer agrees to hire an injured employee subject to the same working conditions and benefits as all other similarly situated employees. Pursuant to the contract, the employer shall provide training and adequate supervision to enable the injured employee to achieve predetermined competencies to ensure a return to suitable gainful employment with the contract employer at the end of the contract period.

(11) "Rehabilitation Company" means a business entity such as a corporation or partnership, or sole proprietorship which employs or contracts to provide services pursuant to Section 440.491, F.S. All services provided by a carrier or a rehabilitation company under Section 440.491, F.S., shall be provided only by an individual who is a qualified rehabilitation provider or a facility that is a qualified rehabilitation provider. Neither the employment status of the person providing the services, nor the main method of communication in providing the services negates the statutory requirement that a person requiring such services must be a qualified rehabilitation provider.

(12) "Rehabilitation Facility" means an institution or agency accredited by the Commission on Accreditation of Rehabilitation Facilities (CARF) for a specific vocational rehabilitation program.

(13) "Test-site" is a Department approved location that may be inspected by the Department, to be used by a qualified rehabilitation provider for vocational evaluation and assessment services.

(14) "Vocational evaluator" is a qualified individual employed by the Department or who holds the designation of a certified vocational evaluator and is approved by the Department to perform vocational evaluations.

(15) "Vocational specialist" means an individual who possesses:

(a) A master's degree in vocational rehabilitation (counseling, evaluation, adjustment); or

(b) Is certified by the Commission on Rehabilitation Counselor Certification, or by the Commission on Certification of Work Adjustment and Vocational Evaluation Specialists; and

(c) Is employed by a CARF-accredited facility.

Specific Authority 440.491(5), (6), (7), Fla. Stat.
Law Implemented 440.491 Fla. Stat.

History: New 7-1-96, Amended 2-9-2000, 6-26-2001, Formerly 38F-55.001, Amended 5-5-04.

6A-22.002. Rehabilitation Provider Qualifications.

(1) The Department shall approve qualified rehabilitation providers who submit proof of meeting the following requirements:

(a) Rehabilitation nurse:

1. A current Florida license as a registered professional nurse, and

2. A current C.R.R.N. certificate as a Certified Rehabilitation Registered Nurse from the Association of Rehabilitation Nurses, or

3. A current C.O.H.N. certificate as a Certified Occupational Health Nurse from the American Board for Occupational Health Nurses, or

4. A current C.R.C. certificate as a Certified Rehabilitation Counselor from the Commission on Rehabilitation Counselor Certification, or

5. A current C.D.M.S. certificate as a Certified Disability Management Specialist from the Certification of Disability Management Specialists Commission, or

6. A current C.C.M. certificate as a Certified Case Manager from the Commission for Case Management Certification.

(b) Rehabilitation counselor:

1. A current C.R.C. certificate as a Certified Rehabilitation Counselor from the Commission on Rehabilitation Counselor Certification, or

2. A current C.D.M.S. certificate as a Certified Disability Management Specialist from the Certification of Disability Management Specialists Commission.

(c) Vocational evaluator: A current C.V.E. certificate as a Certified Vocational Evaluator from the Commission on Certification of Work Adjustment and Vocational Evaluation Specialists.

(d) Facilities, other than hospitals:

1. Current accreditation by CARF in a specific vocational rehabilitation program in which the facility will provide services, and

2. Designation on the application of the qualified rehabilitation counselor or vocational specialist who will be a member of the core team to provide services to injured employees.

(e) Companies:

1. Employ only qualified rehabilitation providers for the purpose of providing all services under Section 440.491, F.S., and are,

2. Incorporated under Chapters 607 and 617, F.S., or are a partnership under Chapter 620, F.S.

3. Submit a non-refundable twenty-five (25) dollar biennial renewal fee, and a signed, typed and completed qualified rehabilitation provider application on form DWC-96, which is incorporated by reference and made a part of this rule to become effective April 2004, for each business address providing any services under Section 440.491, F.S.

(2) Applicants applying for renewal shall submit a non-refundable twenty-five (25) dollar

biennial renewal fee, and a signed, typed and completed qualified rehabilitation provider application on form DWC-96 and a copy of current certification and applicable licensure.

(a) Attendance at a qualified rehabilitation provider workshop conducted by the Department within the prior two (2) years is required before the initial application and also before each renewal.

(b) An applicant for initial listing in the directory or an applicant whose qualified rehabilitation provider number has expired shall not provide services to injured employees until notification of an assigned provider number or renewal is received from the Department.

(3) Each applicant shall submit a signed, typed and completed form DWC-96, proof of attendance at a Department sponsored or approved qualified rehabilitation provider workshop, and a non-refundable check or money order in the amount of twenty-five (25) dollar payable to Workers' Compensation Administrative Trust Fund to the Department of Education, Bureau of Rehabilitation and Reemployment Services, Provider Relations Section, 2728 Centerview Drive, 101A Forrest Building, Tallahassee, Florida 32399-0400. Illegible or unsigned applications and applications submitted without the application fee shall be returned. Facilities and companies must attach to this application a listing of all individuals listed in the directory as qualified rehabilitation providers who provide services under Section 440.491, F.S., for the facility or company.

(4) Department approval of a qualified rehabilitation provider, facility or company shall be revoked for a period of six (6) months for one or more of the following:

(a) Revocation of credentials or certification by the applicable certification or credentialing board.

(b) Misrepresentation of credentials or certification.

(c) Allowing a non-qualified rehabilitation provider to report and bill for services using an individual's, company's and/or facility's qualified rehabilitation provider number.

(5) Employees of the Department are exempt from the requirements of subsections 6A-22.002(2) and (3), F.A.C.

Specific Authority 440.491(7) Fla. Stat.

Law Implemented 440.491(7) Fla. Stat.

History: New 7-1-96, Amended 6-26-2001, Formerly 38F-55.002, Amended 5-5-04, 2-22-05.

6A-22.003 Reemployment Status Review.

(1) The carrier shall conduct a reemployment status review by completing a reemployment status review form on the DWC-22, which is incorporated by reference in Rule 6A-22.011, Florida Administrative Code.

(2) The carrier shall complete form DWC-22 within 15 days of the reporting requirement deadlines set forth in Section 440.491(3)(a), Florida Statutes, and

(a) Shall retain a copy in the carrier's file, and

(b) Shall submit form DWC-22 to the Department within 15 business days of completion.

Specific Authority 440.491(3), (5), (6), (8) Fla. Stat.

Law Implemented 440.491 Fla. Stat.

History: New 7-1-96, Amended 6-26-2001, Formerly 38F-55.005.

6A-22.0031. Reemployment assessments.

Reemployment assessments shall include documentation of the following:

(1) From the injured employee:

(a) Discussion of the injured employee's understanding of their injury, treatment and prognosis,

(b) Description of the injured employee's job duties, including physical demands,

(c) Discussion about accommodations that might allow the injured employee to return to work,

(d) The injured employee's work history,

(e) Factors that would impede the injured employee's ability to return to work, and

(f) Results of any vocational, interest, academic, psychological, or other testing if conducted with the injured employee.

(2) From the employer:

(a) Discussion of the injured employee's job of injury, including a job description with the essential functions and physical demands of the job,

(b) Discussion about the ability to return the injured employee to work in either the same job, modified job or different job, and

(c) Discussion of possible accomodations that could allow the injured employee to work in either the same job, modified job or different job.

3 From the Health Care Provider(s):

(a) Discussion of the injured employee's diagnosis and prognosis,

(b) Discussion of factors that could enhance or impede the healing process,

(c) Anticipated release to return-to-work date and anticipated physical limitations, and

(d) Anticipated Maximum Medical Improvement date and anticipated permanent physical limitations.

Specific Authority 440.491(7)(e) Fla. Stat.

Law Implemented 440.491 Fla. Stat.

History: New 5-5-04.

6A-22.004. Notice Requirements.

(1) If an injured employee remains unemployed 180 days after the date of accident and is receiving compensation, the carrier shall notify the injured employee in writing within 190 days of the date of accident of the availability of a Department screening.

(2) A carrier shall use the following written notice: "Your continuing disability indicates you may be unable to perform the duties of the job held at the time of your work-related injury. If this is correct and you are unable to return to work in any capacity with your current employer or find other employment which would allow you to earn your pre-injury wages, you may be eligible for a screening for reemployment services from the State of Florida, Department of Education. Upon receipt of your request, the Department will assess your case to determine what services are necessary to return you to suitable gainful employment. Reemployment services that you may be eligible for include job seeking skills training, counseling, referrals to other agencies, job market information, transferable skills analysis, job development, job placement, job analysis, job modification, vocational testing, vocational evaluation, on-the-job training, or formal training and education. Additionally, if you have reached maximum medical improvement, and subject to the overall limitation of one hundred four (104) weeks of temporary total disability benefits payable in a workers' compensation case with a date of accident which falls on or after October 1, 2003, the carrier shall pay temporary total disability benefits for a period up to 26 weeks upon beginning a Department approved retraining program or the carrier may elect to pay temporary partial disability/wage loss benefits if you earn wages as the result of on-the-job training or work while enrolled in a program. An additional 26 weeks may be approved if deemed necessary by the Judge of Compensation Claims. To request a screening, contact your local state Division of Vocational Rehabilitation District Office or the Central Office in Tallahassee at (850) 245-3470 and ask to speak with a staff person in the Reemployment Services Section of the Bureau of Rehabilitation and Reemployment Services." The carrier shall send a copy of this notification to the Bureau of Rehabilitation and Reemployment Services, Department of Education, 101A Forrest Building, 2728 Centerview Drive, Tallahassee, Florida 32399-0400 within ten days of mailing the notification to the injured employee.

Specific Authority 440.491(5), (6), (8) Fla. Stat.

Law Implemented 440.491 Fla. Stat.

History: New 7-1-96, Amended 6-26-2001, Formerly 38F-55.006, Amended 3-1-05.

6A-22.005. Carrier Referrals for Services.

(1) A carrier may make a referral of an injured employee at anytime to the Department to be considered for the Department provided

reemployment services program. The carrier shall make referrals to the Department for reemployment services on a request for screening form DWC-23, which is incorporated by reference in Rule 6A-22.011, Florida Administrative Code.

(2) Upon discontinuation of carrier sponsored services pursuant to Section 440.491(5), Florida Statutes, the carrier shall make referrals to the Department for reemployment services on a request for screening form DWC-23, which is incorporated by reference in Rule 6A-22.011, Florida Administrative Code.

(3) A Form DWC-23 submitted by the carrier to the Department shall not be considered complete until signed by the injured employee.

Specific Authority 440.491(5), (6), (8) Fla. Stat.

Law Implemented 440.491 Fla. Stat.

History: New 7-1-96, Amended 6-26-2001, Formerly 38F-55.008.

6A-22.006 Screening Process.

(1) A request for screening is made using a form DWC-23. Before the Department will consider a request complete and initiate a screening, the injured employee must sign the form DWC-23.

(2) The screening process shall consist of:

(a) A review of all available medical and vocational documentation relevant to the compensable injury to determine whether the injured employee is able to perform the duties of the pre-injury occupation; and

(b) A review of the documentation which supports the payment of temporary partial disability and wage loss benefits to determine the injured employee's inability to obtain suitable gainful employment because of his injury; and

(c) An interview with the injured employee.

(3) The carrier shall provide, within 10 business days of receipt of a request from the Department, any medical, vocational, and other requested documents or reports related to the injured employee's workers' compensation case.

(4) The Department may request the information directly from the authorized treating physician(s), or qualified rehabilitation provider(s), or obtain the services of an expert medical adviser to identify the injured employee's ability to return to work, permanent impairment rating, and permanent work restrictions.

(5) The Department shall not provide any reemployment services, including a vocational evaluation unless the injured employee provides documentation to establish identity and employment eligibility. Such documentation shall be consistent with the acceptable documents for verifying identity and employment eligibility as required by the U.S. Department of Justice, Immigration and Naturalization Service's Employment Eligibility Verification Form I-9 (Rev. 11-21-91).

(6) The Department shall not provide a vocational evaluation or any reemployment services when form DWC-23, which is signed by the injured employee, is received by the Department more than one (1) year from the date of last payment of indemnity benefits or the furnishing of remedial treatment, care or attendance from the employer or carrier.

(7) Following a Department screening the Department shall not provide any additional reemployment services

(a) If the injured employee has filed a claim for permanent total disability benefits under Section 440.15(1), Florida Statutes, which the carrier has denied, wherein either the injured employee's medical condition or vocational capabilities are in dispute, until such time as an Office of the Judge of Compensation Claims adjudicates the injured employee's claim; or

(b) If the injured employee's medical condition is unresolved or unstable, until such time as the medical condition becomes stable; or

(c) If the injured employee has reached maximum medical improvement and returned to and maintained suitable gainful employment for at least 90 calendar days; or

(d) If the injured employee refuses to accept reemployment services from the Division.

(8) The Department shall not refer the injured

employee for a vocational evaluation if the injured employee:

(a) Has returned to suitable gainful employment as a result of placement services provided by the Division; or

(b) Has no documented permanent physical restrictions related to the injury; or

(c) Has transferable skills which would allow return to work in suitable gainful employment; or

(d) Was terminated by the employer for good cause unrelated to the injury or any restrictions or limitations resulting therefrom; or

(e) Terminated suitable gainful employment for reasons unrelated to the injury.

Specific Authority 440.491(5) Fla. Stat.

Law Implemented 440.491 Fla. Stat.

History: New 7-1-96, Amended 6-26-2001, Formerly 38F-55.009, Amended 5-5-04.

6A-22.007. Vocational Evaluations.

(1) The provision of Department sponsored vocational evaluations shall be limited to one per injured employee, per date of accident. Vocational evaluations shall be adapted to the specific needs of an injured employee to insure validity.

(2) The Department shall accept a vocational evaluation only if the vocational evaluation meets the requirements of and contains the information identified in paragraph 6A-22.010(2)(e), Florida Administrative Code.

Specific Authority 440.491(5), (6) Fla. Stat.

Law Implemented 440.491 Fla. Stat.

History: New 7-1-96, Formerly 38F-55.010.

6A-22.008. Reemployment Services and Programs.

(1) The Department shall approve sponsorship of reemployment services provided through an on-the-job training program, vocational assessment, job placement or a training and education program when recommended and approved as part of a Department reemployment plan.

(2) The Department will approve and sponsor retraining services if:

(a) The vocational evaluation is completed by a Department approved vocational evaluator, and

(b) The vocational evaluation contains the information identified in paragraph 6A-22.010(2)(e). F.A.C.; and

(c) The vocational evaluation demonstrates that the injured employee:

1. Has no transferable skills which would allow for return to suitable gainful employment with the same employer, same job; same employer, different or modified job; new employer, same job; new employer, modified or different job; or

2. Requires additional Department sponsored reemployment services to enable the injured employee to return to suitable gainful employment.

(3) The Department shall sponsor retraining programs which exceed 52 weeks only when there is no program shorter than 52 weeks which would enable the injured employee to return to suitable gainful employment, the injured employee provides a plan for living expenses during the period in excess of 52 weeks, and one of the following conditions apply:

(a) The injured employee has no formal marketable vocational training and education; or

(b) The injured employee has documented physical restrictions as a result of the injury.

(4) If the Department determines a training program is necessary to return an injured employee to suitable gainful employment, the Department shall have the exclusive right to determine the educational programs and facilities at which to sponsor the injured employee.

(a) For all dates of accidents, training programs which only accept students from an applicant pool after the students complete a prerequisite curriculum may be approved only if the injured employee presents evidence of acceptance into such program.

(b) For dates of accident October 1, 1989 through and including September 30, 2003, training at private education facilities shall not be approved unless such recommended training is not offered at a public educational facility or provides an overall cost/time savings to the Workers' Compensation System, which can be justified.

1. Baccalaureate or Graduate level studies may be approved only if the program capitalizes on prior education and/or aptitudes, and

2. The program under consideration firmly establishes marketability toward suitable gainful employment for that injured employee, and

3. The injured employee presents evidence of acceptance into a degree program prior to the Department's Disposition letter of approval, and

4. The program does not exceed the level of a Master's degree.

(c) For dates of accident on or after October 1, 2003, only programs which are consistent with the requirements found in Section 440.491(6)(a), Florida Statutes, shall be approved.

(5) The Department shall not transfer its sponsorship of reemployment services outside the range of the labor market survey unless a labor market survey for the new area supports the specific recommendation of the vocational evaluation.

(6) The Department shall not sponsor reemployment services if the vocational evaluation does not recommend reemployment services.

Specific Authority 440.491(5), (6) Fla. Stat.

Law Implemented 440.491 Fla. Stat.

History: New 7-1-96, Amended 2-9-2000, 6-26-2001, Formerly 38F-55.011, Amended 3-1-05.

6A-22.009. Employee Responsibilities.

(1) Upon approval of Department sponsored reemployment services, the injured employee and Department staff shall sign and date a Department and student agreement for sponsorship of training and education form DWC-24, which is incorporated by reference in Rule 6A-22.011, F.A.C.

(2) An employee who refuses retraining and education after the recommendation of a vocational evaluator and approval by the Department, will forfeit his or her entitlement to further training and education benefits, as well as additional payment for lost wages under Chapter 440, Florida Statutes. The following shall not be deemed a refusal of training and education:

(a) Failure to participate in a recommended retraining program due to medical instability;

(b) Failure to participate in a recommended retraining program due to an adverse change in the employee's medical status;

(c) Failure to participate in a recommended retraining program due to the school's failure to offer the approved program; and

(d) Failure to participate in a recommended retraining program due to a family medical emergency.

Specific Authority 440.491(5), (6) Fla. Stat.

Law Implemented 440.491 Fla. Stat.

History: New 7-1-96, Amended 6-26-2001, Formerly 38F-55.012, Amended 3-1-05.

6A-22.010. Reporting Services and Costs: Qualified Rehabilitation Provider and Employer or Carrier Responsibilities.

(1) A qualified rehabilitation provider providing employer or carrier sponsored reemployment services shall:

(a) Submit a properly completed individualized written rehabilitation program within 30 days of referral which specifies the recommended services and associated costs necessary to return the injured employee to suitable gainful employment, using terminology consistent with Department service code descriptions to the employer or carrier for approval when recommending:

1. Reemployment services as a result of a reemployment assessment, or

2. Three or more counseling sessions, or

3. A vocational evaluation, or

4. A work evaluation, or

5. Training and education, including on-the-job training, or

6. Placement services, or

7. Changes to the initial individualized written rehabilitation program.

(b) Maintain a copy of the properly completed individualized written rehabilitation program in the injured employee's file.

(2) A certified vocational evaluator providing Department sponsored vocational evaluations shall:

(a) Ensure any test site used for Department sponsored vocational evaluations meets the definition of "test site" set forth in subsection 6A-55.001(13), Florida Administrative Code; and

(b) Be responsible for the administration, scoring and interpretation of all testing instruments and work samples used as part of the vocational evaluation process; and

(c) Remove or cure conditions that invalidate test results; and

(d) Provide adaptive evaluation tools or techniques to accommodate any physical or functional disability or language barrier; and

(e) Submit to the Department, within 30 calendar days of Department approval of services, a written report which shall:

1. Include an interpretation of testing instruments and work samples used, specifying the form and level of tests, percentile scores, norm groups, grade levels, standard scores and stanine scores as applicable to the test instrument; and

2. Identify the injured employee's physical and intellectual capabilities, aptitudes, achievements, work related behaviors, and interests. The interests of the injured employee alone cannot be the only basis for the vocational evaluator's recommendation; and

3. Identify residual or transferable skills; and

4. Identify the most appropriate vocational objectives; and

5. Identify which reemployment service(s) are necessary for the injured employee to return to suitable gainful employment; and

6. Discuss how the provision of the recommended service(s) will facilitate reemployment; and

7. When a retraining program is recommended, include the rationale for the recommended program, the entrance, enrollment and exit requirements of the program, the anticipated program costs and the proximity of the program to the injured employee's customary residence; and

8. Include an individualized labor market survey which supports the injured employee's ability to compete for employment in the identified vocational goal(s) and shall include information documenting:

a. The potential wage earning capacity,

b. The physical demands of the identified vocational goal as identified by potential employers,

c. The minimum educational requirements and work experience required by potential employers, and

d. Each potential employer's job openings for the six months prior to the survey and projected openings for the upcoming six months.

(f) Submit to the Department, within 10 days of submission of the written report, the original receipt statement signed by the injured employee and the vocational evaluator.

(3) Any qualified rehabilitation provider providing any employer or carrier or Department sponsored reemployment services, reemployment assessments or medical care coordination shall submit with each DWC-21, which is incorporated by reference into this rule, a written report which reports services provided and expected outcomes, covering the following points:

(a) Summary by date of contacts with the injured employee and other pertinent parties; and

(b) Problems or issues adversely affecting the reemployment process and the corrective actions taken in that process; and

(c) Continuing feasibility of the reemployment plan; and

(d) Vocational activities planned for the subsequent month; and

(e) Justification for change or modification of current plan.

(4) Upon request a qualified rehabilitation provider providing a Department sponsored reemployment service, including a vocational evaluation, shall make available to the Department information and documentation to certify that the authorized service that was rendered is complete pursuant to Rule 6A-22.010, Florida Administrative Code, if such information or documentation is identified by the Department.

(5) Failure of a qualified rehabilitation provider providing Department sponsored reemployment services to submit the written report and additional information and documentation as required by this rule shall result in the:

(a) Reassignment of the case,

(b) Termination of the contract,

(c) Forfeiture of any monies owing at the time of termination of contract.

(6) A qualified rehabilitation provider providing either employer or carrier or Division sponsored reemployment services, reemployment assessments, medical care coordination and vocational evaluations, shall:

(a) Report on form DWC-21 only those services provided by or through the authorized qualified rehabilitation provider. Services not rendered by or through the qualified rehabilitation provider may not be billed or reimbursed.

(b) Submit a properly completed form DWC-21 listing the specific service(s) provided, utilizing only valid service codes and descriptors for those direct services rendered to the injured employee. Direct services are those services provided or required by an individualized written rehabilitation program. Other services are to be billed in the manner agreed upon by the employer or carrier and the qualified rehabilitation provider.

1. The initial form DWC-21 shall be submitted to the Department within 30 days of the contract approval date for Department sponsored services or to the employer or carrier within 30 days of the date of the referral for employer or carrier sponsored services.

2. An interim DWC-21 shall be submitted at 30-day intervals thereafter during which the authorized services are provided. The DWC-21 should not be filed if services are not provided within any 30-day period.

3. A final DWC-21 shall be submitted within 30 days of the date of the last service provided or according to the terms of a contract with the Department for vocational evaluation services.

(c) Close a file and submit a final DWC-21 when attorney involvement interferes with the provision of direct services.

(7) Any qualified rehabilitation provider or employee of the Department or other public or private agencies administering, scoring and interpreting testing instruments shall have the training and education required by the publisher of the testing instrument.

(8) Testing instruments, including work samples, used in vocational evaluations, reemployment assessments or other reemployment service activities may be administered and scored under the supervision of a qualified rehabilitation provider. Testing instruments shall be interpreted by the qualified rehabilitation provider with whom the contact for services is authorized.

(9) The employer or carrier shall:

(a) Ensure that the information required in this rule is provided on the form DWC-21 prior to payment and filing with the Department, and

(b) Approve or deny the provision of services recommended as part of an individualized written rehabilitation program within 15 calendar days of receipt of the same; and pay or deny form DWC-21 bills within 45 calendar days after receipt of a bill for services provided to an injured employee, and

(c) Complete items 20, 21 and 23 on every form DWC-21 filed with the Department. In item 20 it is necessary to legibly enter the date the form DWC-21 was received. In item 21 it is necessary to legibly enter the date the form DWC-21 was reimbursed. In item 23 it is necessary to enter the amount reimbursed only if it is different from the amount billed by the qualified rehabilitation provider or facility, and

(d) File form DWC-21 with the Department of Education at its office in Tallahassee, Florida within 30 days after the full or partial payment of form DWC-21 (A DWC-21 filed with the Department shall have a date stamp in the upper right hand corner indicating the date the DWC-21 is sent to the Department), and

(e) Be responsible for the legibility, accuracy and completeness of the social security number, date of accident, the employer or carrier's and servicing company/TPA's Department of Insurance, Division of Workers' Compensation's assigned four digit carrier code number and Federal Employer Identification Number (FEIN), and those areas that the employer or carrier completes on form DWC-21.

(10) If an employer or carrier is submitting to the Department and retaining DWC-21s on electronic media, that employer or carrier need not retain paper copies of those forms, but may treat the electronic media as the original documentation.

(11) A form DWC-21 filed with the Department which is not completed according to these rules will be returned by the Department to the employer or carrier. Upon receipt of the returned form, the employer or carrier shall properly complete and refile the form with the Department within 15 days.

(12) Form DWC-21 is incorporated by reference in Rule 6A-22.011, F.A.C.

Specific Authority 440.491(5), (6), (7) Fla. Stat.

Law Implemented 440.491 Fla. Stat.

History: New 7-1-96, Amended 6-26-2001, Formerly 38F-55.013, Amended 5-5-04.

6A-22.011. List of Forms.

(1) Forms DWC-21, DWC-22, DWC-23, DWC-24 and DWC-96 and accompanying instructions are incorporated by reference as part of this rule to become effective April, 2004. Each form shall be typed or legibly completed in order for the form to be considered properly filed or submitted with the Department.

(a) Department reemployment services billing form shall be submitted to the Department on form DWC-21.

(b) Reemployment status review form shall be submitted to the Department on Form DWC-22.

(c) Request for screening form shall be submitted to the Department on form DWC-23.

(d) Department and student agreement for sponsorship of training and education form shall be completed on form DWC-24.

(e) Qualified rehabilitation provider application shall be submitted to the Division on form DWC-96.

(2) A copy of the forms and accompanying instructions incorporated by subsection 6A-22.011(1) may be obtained from the Department of Education, Bureau of Rehabilitation and Reemployment Services, 2728 Centerview Drive, Suite 101, Forrest Building, Tallahassee, Florida 32399-0400. Copies are also available on the Deparment's web page on the Internet at http://www.firn.edu/doe/rules/rules.htm.

Specific Authority 440.491(5), (6), (7) Fla. Stat.

Law Implemented 440.491 Fla. Stat.

History: New 7-1-96, Amended 6-26-2001, Formerly 38F-55.014, Amended 5-5-04.

6A-22.012. Expenditures from the Workers' Compensation Administrative Trust Fund.

(1) Upon receipt of the completed evaluation report, the Department shall authorize reimbursement for the evaluation from the Workers' Compensation Administration Trust Fund at a maximum rate of $ 55.00 per hour, not to exceed $ 1,100.00 per evaluation.

(2) The Department shall expend funds from the Workers' Compensation Administration Trust Fund only:

(a) for vocational evaluations and retraining for dates of accident on or after October 1, 1989 through December 31, 1993, and

(b) for reemployment services authorized by the Department pursuant to rule chapter 38F-55, Florida Administrative Code, for dates of accident on or after January 1, 1994.

(3) The maximum cost the Department shall expend for an approved retraining plan shall not exceed 85% of the injured employee's pre-injury average weekly wages as calculated on an annual basis, which amount shall include:

(a) Pre-approved costs for fees, tuition, books and special supplies required by the program curriculum, and

(b) Pre-approved costs for board, lodging, and travel at the rate currently allowed for state employees when an approved program requires temporary relocation for participation, or

(c) Pre-approved mileage reimbursement at the rate currently allowed for state employees for mileage to the training facility in excess of 50 miles, one-way, using the most direct route from the injured employee's customary residence. Mileage expense will not be reimbursed or paid by the Department when the training facility is less than 50 miles from the injured employee's customary residence at the time of approval for training.

(4) The Department shall pay from the Workers' Compensation Administration Trust Fund the direct costs to employers for on-the-job training according to the reimbursement schedule negotiated in the on-the-job training contract.

(5) The Department shall not reimburse or pay for any reemployment services independently initiated or obtained by the injured employee without prior written approval from the Division of the proposed reemployment plan recommending such reemployment services, including any expenses associated with retraining or education.

(6) The Department shall reimburse travel associated with the provision of reemployment services at a rate not to exceed one-half (1/2) the professional rate at which the services were contracted.

(7) The Department shall have exclusive jurisdiction over any dispute involving a claim made against it or the Workers' Compensation Administration Trust Fund for reemployment services, vocational evaluations, training and education, and rehabilitation.

(8) The Office of the Judge of Compensation Claims shall have jurisdiction over claims relating to additional temporary total disability compensation provided in Section 440.491(6)(b), Florida Statutes (Supp. 1994).

Specific Authority 440.491(5), (6), (7), (8) Fla. Stat.

Law Implemented 440.491 Fla. Stat.

History: New 7-1-96, Amended 12-2-98, 6-26-2001, Formerly 38F-55.015.

TITLE 38 DEPARTMENT OF LABOR AND EMPLOYMENT SECURITY

38F DIVISION OF WORKERS' COMPENSATION

CHAPTER 38F-55 Reemployment Services

38F-55.004. Trial Period of Reemployment.

(1) The trial period of reemployment shall:

(a) Automatically commence on the date of hire, and

(b) Be within the physical capabilities of the injured employee, and

(c) Not be a result of coercion or intimidation, and

(d) Automatically terminate:

1. When the injured employee is unable to perform the duties as a result of the permanently disabling condition, or

2. One year from the date of hire if the injured employee is able to work 50 percent (50%) of his normal pre-injury working hours with an earning capacity of at least 80% of his previous wage.

(2) Following termination of the trial period

of reemployment the carrier shall file a notice of action/change form DWC-4 with the Division to report whether the return to work was successful. Form DWC-4 is incorporated by reference in Rule 38F-3.025, F.A.C.

Specific Authority 440.15(1), (3), 440.491(5), (6), (8) Fla. Stat.

Law Implemented 440.15, 440.491 Fla. Stat.

History: New 7-1-96, Amended 6-26-2001.

TITLE 59 AGENCY FOR HEALTH CARE ADMINISTRATION

59A HEALTH FACILITY AND AGENCY CERTIFICATION

CHAPTER 59A-23 Workers' Compensation Managed Care Arrangements

59A-23.001. Scope.

The following rules developed by the Agency for Health Care Administration govern the authorization of workers' compensation managed care arrangements pursuant to the Authority set forth in Chapter 440, Florida Statutes (F.S.).

Specific Authority 440.134(2)(a) Fla. Stat.

Law Implemented 440.134 Fla. Stat.

History: New 9-12-94.

59A-23.002. Definitions.

(1) Agency means the Agency for Health Care Administration.

(2) Case files means a system for managing medical information and return to work information regarding the injured employee, whether in electronic or paper format.

(3) Complaint means any dissatisfaction expressed by an injured worker as defined in Section 440.134(1)(b), F.S. An initial request for services, such as a request for medical services, second opinions, or a change in providers, is not considered a complaint.

(4) "Delegated entity" means a unit or single organization authorized by written agreement to act on behalf of the insurer to provide managed care services.

(5) Credentialing means the process for validating and evaluating the qualifications of a licensed health care provider to participate in a workers compensation managed care arrangement provider network.

(6) Division means the Division of Workers Compensation of the Florida Department of Labor and Employment Security.

(7) External case management means face-to-face medical care coordination performed by a qualified rehabilitation provider pursuant to Section 440.491, F.S.

(8) Grievance means a written expression of dissatisfaction with medical care by an injured worker as defined in Section 440.134(1)(d), F.S. Initial written requests for medical services, second opinions, or changes in providers are not grievances.

(9) Insurer means an entity which contracts to provide workers compensation insurance coverage as defined under Section 440.134(1)(e), F.S.

(10) Internal case management means a process for telephonically coordinating, facilitating, and monitoring all aspects of the medical care coordination of the injured employee in consultation with the treating physician and the medical care coordinator.

(11) Medical care coordination means active case management and coordination of the health care services for an injured employee involving a medical care coordinator to ensure the delivery of necessary services in a manner which will return the individual to work as soon as feasible.

(12) Peer review means the evaluation of the treatment plan or clinical performance of providers by one or more licensed professionals with the same authority or similar specialty when potential quality of care issues have been identified through case management or quality assurance processes.

(13) Quality assurance means a formal set of activities, which review and safeguard the quality of medical services provided to the injured employee. Quality assurance includes assessment and implementation of corrective actions to address any deficiencies identified in the quality of care and services provided to the

injured employee.

(14) Second medical opinion means a consultation by a health care provider authorized by the medical care coordinator that requires at a minimum a history, an examination, and a straightforward medical decision to confirm or offer alternatives.

(15) Service area means a geographic area consisting of a county or group of counties, which shall not be subdivided for purposes of authorizing a workers compensation managed care arrangement.

(16) Utilization management means the examination and evaluation of health care services to determine the appropriate use of the resources and components available within the workers compensation managed care arrangement including, retrospective, concurrent, and prospective care reviews.

(17) Urgent means that in the judgment of the primary care physician or medical care coordinator, the injured employee's clinical condition requires a response within 72 hours, and the clinical condition is at significant risk of deterioration if a response is not made within that timeframe.

(18) Written agreement means an express, legally executed, written contract between two or more parties which specifies the following: the parties to the contract; the effective date of the contract; duties of the respective parties; reporting and or oversight of the responsibilities to be performed; performance standards; termination and expiration terms of the contract.

(19) Workers compensation managed care arrangement means those arrangements as defined under Section 440.134(1)(g), F.S.

Specific Authority 440.134 Fla. Stat.

Law Implemented 440.134 (1)(g), (5)(a), (6)(b), (c)4., 6. — 9., (9), (10), (14)(b), (d), (16), (17), (25)(b), (c), (d), (g) Fla. Stat.

History: New 9-12-94, Amended 10-8-2001, 1-22-2002.

59A-23.003. Authorization Procedures.

(1) General Provisions.All insurers offering a managed care arrangement for the provision of health services for the treatment of persons filing workers compensation claims shall obtain an authorization from the agency in accordance with the following procedures:

(a) Applications for an initial authorization, amendment of the authorized plan of operation, or renewal shall be submitted with the following:

1. A completed copy of AHCA Form 3160-0004, November 2000, incorporated by reference herein;

2. Required attachments as specified in AHCA Form 3160-0004, November 2000; and

3. Written agreements linking the entities within the managed care arrangement and specifying the duties of each entity.Application forms are available from and shall be submitted to the Agency for Health Care Administration, Division of Managed Care and Health Quality, Bureau of Managed Health Care, 2727 Mahan Drive, Mail Stop 45, Tallahassee, Florida 32308.

(b) An initial application for authorization shall be submitted to the agency at least 90 days prior to the intended date of implementation of services. An amendment application shall be submitted to the agency 60 days prior to the effective date of the proposed change in the plan of operation. Upon receipt of the application the agency shall review the content to determine compliance with the requirements of paragraphs 440.134(5) through (15), F.S.

(c) The agency shall notify applicants for initial or renewal authorization in writing via certified mail of any deficiencies in the application within 30 days of the receipt of the application. The applicant shall provide information necessary to complete the application within 30 days of receipt of the written notice. Failure to timely submit the necessary information shall result in denial of the application unless the applicant needs an extension of time due to circumstances beyond its control and requests the extension within 30 days of its receipt of the written notice of deficiencies. No extensions shall exceed 90 days or the expiration date of the workers compensation managed care arrangement.

(d) The agency shall provide notice to the applicant of its right to administrative review under Sections 120.569 and 120.57, F.S., with its written notice of intent to deny an application.

(e) Applications to amend an approved plan of operation by replacing the delegated managed care organization or provider network shall address the continuity of care and coordination of medical services for injured employees during the transition. The applicant shall submit information that identifies the activities to be conducted, persons involved, and dates for completion of the following tasks:

1. The identification and authorization of out of network services for injured employees whose current primary treating physician is not in the new provider network and who prefer to continue with their current provider;

2. The transfer of injured employees current medical care management information to the newly contracted entity; and

3. The notification of employers and employees of the requirements of the new network arrangements and the contact persons via the educational materials required under Section 440.134(14)(a) through (d), F.S.

(f) Examination. The agency shall conduct an on-site survey of the managed care arrangement, within the first year of operation and no less than every two years thereafter, to determine compliance with the requirements of Section 440.134, F.S. The agency shall verify through subsequent survey that any deficiency identified during a previous survey is corrected. The agency may verify the correction without on-site resurvey if written documentation has been received from the insurer or delegated entity and is accepted by the agency. The agency shall also investigate on-site any alleged pattern of non-compliance with the requirements of Section 440.134, F.S.

(2) Fees.All initial and renewal applications for authorization of a workers compensation managed care arrangement shall be accompanied by a fee of $ 1,000 made payable to the agency. Applications to amend an existing authorized workers compensation managed care arrangement do not require submission of a fee.

(3) Authorization for a workers compensation managed care arrangement shall not be sold, assigned, or otherwise transferred either voluntarily or involuntarily and is valid only for the legal entity to which it was originally issued.

(4) Validity.Each authorization shall be valid for a period of two years only for:

(a) The entity to which it is issued as specified on the authorization letter; and

(b) The service area approved by the agency.

(5) Service Areas.Each application shall indicate the geographic service area or areas in which the insurer or delegated entity will provide managed care services. The insurer shall offer a managed care arrangement only to those employers whose place of business or business operations are located in a service area approved by the agency to provide services under a workers compensation managed care arrangement. A service area shall be approved if there is a sufficient number and type of providers adequate to meet the needs of the geographic area in addition to other requirements specified under Rules 59A-23.003,.004,.005, and.006.

(6) Travel Times.Each application shall provide information which indicates the ability of the insurer or delegated entity to provide geographic access to health services for injured employees. Average travel time for injured employees from the employee's usual employment site to the nearest primary care delivery site and to the nearest general acute care hospital in the provider network shall be no longer than 30 minutes under normal circumstances. Average travel time from the employee's usual employment site to the nearest provider of specialty physician services, ancillary services, specialty inpatient hospital services and all other health services shall be no longer than 60 minutes under normal circumstances.

(7) Provider Network.

(a) Medical services shall be available for injured employees in the geographic area in which they are employed through directly or indirectly contracted network(s) of health care providers. The hours of operation and availability of after-hour care must reflect usual practices in the community and the insurer must demonstrate that:

1. All medically necessary services are available and accessible;

2. Medically necessary referrals are provided within the network or, if unavailable, outside the network;

3. There are written agreements describing specific delegated duties for provision of medical services. Delegation of the provision of medical services by the insurer must be specifically described in the written agreement linking the insurer with the delegated entity;

4. Written agreements for arrangements in which the insurer is indirectly linked with a provider network shall contain language requiring the insurer's approval in advance of a change in the provider network; and

5. There are written agreements with providers prohibiting such providers from billing or otherwise seeking reimbursement from or recourse against any injured employee except as specified under Section 440.13, F.S.

(b) The insurer or delegated entity, shall establish and implement a policy and procedure regarding access to services which reflects usual and customary practices in the community and addresses access times for emergency, initial, and continuing care including referrals to specialty services.

(c) The agency shall examine provider networks at least annually. The insurer or delegated entity, shall file with the agency an updated list of providers by county, by specialty, semiannually. The list shall be submitted within six months of the initial network approval date and every six months thereafter in a format approved or prescribed by the agency.

(d) The insurer or delegated entity shall develop and implement a policy and procedure for credentialing and recredentialing network providers as needed, but at a minimum every two years. The credentialing criteria shall be specified in the policy and shall include the core credentialing data specified under paragraph 455.557(2)(d), F.S., and verification of education of providers as required by Section 440.134(8), F.S.

(e) The recredentialing process shall monitor and incorporate quality assurance findings and information on individual providers including sanctions, complaints and grievances, medical record audits, provider profiling, and employee satisfaction.

(f) If the insurer delegates all or part of the credentialing process to other organizations, the insurer shall specify the activities of the delegated entity and the oversight and reporting requirements in the written agreement. The insurer shall perform oversight of the delegated credentialing activities annually.

(g) The insurer or delegated entity shall designate one or more physicians as a medical care coordinator to manage medical care for injured workers. A medical care coordinator shall be assigned for each injured employee. The medical care coordinator shall be licensed under Chapter 458 or 459, F.S., and be board certified by the American Board of Medical Specialties, or the American Osteopathic Association, or have two years experience as a participating provider in a workers compensation managed care arrangement network. The medical care coordinator shall have experience or training in workers compensation and be responsible for the following:

1. Management of the medical treatment plan;

2. Participation in the quality improvement process and evaluation of outcomes of care;

3. Review of grievances; and

4. Authorization of referrals to specialty providers for second opinions, evaluation of treatment, including changes to another specialty provider pursuant to paragraph 440.134(10)(c), F.S.

(h) Nothing in this rule prohibits the use by a medical or osteopathic physician of advanced registered nurse practitioners licensed under Section 464.012, F.S., or physician's assistants licensed under Chapter 458 or 459, F.S., in accordance with and within the scope of their professional licenses in Florida Statute. An injured employee shall be evaluated or treated by the physician supervising the advanced registered nurse practitioner or physician assistant if specifically requested by the injured employee.

(i) The insurer or delegated entity, may direct injured employees to a single primary care provider or a selected group of primary care providers within the provider network for assessment and initial treatment. However, the employee shall have the right to select a primary care provider and thereafter, to request one change of primary care provider and of each authorized treating specialty provider during the course of treatment for each injury. The injured employee shall select a primary care provider from a current list of all primary care providers in the approved service area within 30 minutes average travel time of the employee's employment site.

(j) Initial and network change applications shall contain information on the numbers, types, and locations of health care providers which are included in the managed care network. The types of providers to be included shall comply with those listed on AHCA Form 3160-0005, November 2000, WCMCA Service Area Network Checklist, incorporated herein by reference. This form is available from the agency by contacting the Agency for Health Care Administration, Division of Managed Care and Health Quality, Bureau of Managed Health Care, 2727 Mahan Drive, Mail Stop 45, Tallahassee, Florida 32308.

(8) Delegation.The insurer shall conduct oversight of the delegated functions of the workers compensation managed care arrangement. The insurer is responsible for the performance of all functions associated with the delivery of medical services to injured employees under Section 440.134(1)(g), F.S., regardless of whether the function has been delegated, by written agreement, to other entities. The insurer shall specify, in the written agreement, the oversight and reporting requirements for monitoring the performance of delegated functions. Reports of subcontractors shall be evaluated no less than quarterly, and the findings incorporated into the insurer's quality assurance program.

Specific Authority 440.134(25) Fla. Stat.

Law Implemented 120.57, 440.134(1)(g), (2)(a), (3), (4), (5), (6), (10), (12), (13), (14) Fla. Stat.

History: New 9-12-94, Amended 4-30-98, 5-8-2001.

59A-23.004. Quality Assurance.

(1) Each insurer or delegated entity shall have an ongoing quality assurance program designed to objectively and systematically monitor and evaluate the quality of patient care, based upon the prevailing standards of medical practice in the community.

(2) The scope of the quality assurance program shall include the following:

(a) Peer review;

(b) Satisfaction survey;

(c) Utilization management;

(d) Case management;

(e) Complaints and grievances;

(f) Credentialing and recredentialing;

(g) Medical records;

(h) Return to work;

(i) Cost analysis;

(j) Data collection;

(k) Outcome studies;

(*l*) Education; and

(m) Provider dispute resolution.

(3) The quality assurance plan shall be in writing, updated annually, and shall describe the program's objectives, organization and problem-solving activities for improvement of medical services. The plan shall specify:

(a) Those specific activities under subsection (1) that will be conducted;

(b) The timeframes and the responsible individual for each quality assurance activity; and

(c) The follow-up activities including written procedures for taking remedial action.

(4) The insurer or delegated entity shall have a quality assurance committee that meets quarterly to review the progress of quality assurance activities, completion of the written work plan, findings, and to develop recommendations for corrective action and follow-up. The committee shall keep minutes of meetings to document the committee's activities. Activities of the committee shall include:

(a) Identification of data to be collected;

(b) Evaluation of data collected;

(c) Recommendation of improvements utilizing data collected;

(d) Communication of the committee's findings to accountable authorities for implementation of improvements; and

(e) Evaluation and documentation of the results of the implementation of improvements.

(5) The insurer or delegated entity shall perform a quality assurance review of the processes and outcomes of care, at least annually, using current state and nationally recognized practice guidelines.

(6) All findings, conclusions, recommendations, actions taken and results of actions taken shall be documented, shared with contracted entities and reported through organizational channels that have been established within the workers compensation managed care arrangement.

(7) The insurer or delegated entity shall provide, as part of the quality assurance program, an ongoing peer review process which:

(a) Resolves issues regarding provision of medical services; and

(b) Evaluates clinical performance at least annually. The evaluation process shall include: medical record audits of a representative sample of providers to evaluate medical necessity; provision of medical service(s) appropriate to the diagnosis; use of current state and nationally accepted practice parameters; timeliness and access to treatment; and the development and use of a plan of care. The insurer or delegated entity shall have a written methodology for determining the size and scope of the medical record audits that shall reflect the volume and complexity of services provided by the provider network.

(8) Utilization Management.The insurer or delegated entity shall have written policies and procedures for approving or denying requests for care in accordance with the agency's practice parameters and with nationally recognized standards based on medical necessity. The program shall evaluate quality of care and services, and provide review prospectively, concurrently, and retrospectively including pre-certification mechanisms for elective admissions and non-emergency surgeries.

(a) The utilization management program shall ensure that:

1. All elective admissions and non-emergency services must be precertified;

2. Utilization management policies and procedures are clearly defined in writing and any advisory responsibilities are assigned to individuals with training and education in a health care field sufficient to evaluate the consistency of the proposed treatment with the relevant standards;

3. The utilization management program uses nationally recognized written criteria based on clinical evidence to determine medical necessity. Treating providers shall have access to the criteria used for determining medical necessity upon request;

4. The medical care coordinator is involved in the decision process and consultation regarding decisions with the treating physician. Any decision to deny a request for treatment shall be made by a licensed medical or osteopathic physician. A physician not involved in the initial decision shall review any denial based on medical necessity;

5. Decisions are made in a timely manner to accommodate the clinical urgency of the situation. There are policies and procedures and a

process for making timely decisions including those involving urgent care;

6. The utilization management program documents and communicates the reasons for each denial of requested medical services to treating providers and the injured employees;

7. The information obtained through the quality assurance program is considered in evaluating the timeliness and necessity of medical services;

8. There is a procedure for handling requests for experimental procedures;

9. There is a procedure for resolution of provider disputes regarding reimbursement and utilization review;

10. There is a procedure for ensuring that referrals are made to network providers who are available and accessible within the service area. The insurer or delegated entity shall monitor the utilization of network and out-of-network services to improve network access; and

11. There is a procedure for authorization of out-of-network services.

(b) Utilization management is responsible for:

1. Selection and application of nationally recognized review criteria and protocols;

2. Recommendation of general utilization management program policies;

3. Overall program monitoring; and

4. Review of all appeals of denials of requests for treatment or referrals.

(9) Case Management.The insurer or delegated entity shall develop and implement policies and procedures for aggressive medical care coordination, which may be provided via internal and external case management services in association with utilization management activities. The insurer or delegated entity shall specify the types and severity of injuries which require internal and external case management.

(a) Internal case management activities shall include:

1. Coordinating, facilitating, and monitoring all aspects of the ongoing medical care of the injured employee;

2. Communicating utilization management decisions to the medical care coordinator and treating providers;

3. Assisting the injured employee in resolving complaints and obtaining medically necessary services;

4. Educating injured employees regarding their rights, responsibilities, and limitations of the workers compensation managed care arrangement;

5. Coordinating, facilitating, and monitoring the injured employee's return to work status including communicating to the claims representative the services required pursuant to Section 440.491, F.S.; and

6. Communicating the injured employee's status to the employer and to the injured employee.

(b) Internal case management activities shall be performed in consultation with the treating physician and the medical care coordinator.

(c) Internal case management services shall be provided by individuals with the experience and training required to perform their assigned responsibilities.

(d) External case management shall be provided for catastrophic injuries as defined under Section 440.02(37), F.S., and for such other injuries as determined by the insurer or delegated entity. External case management services shall be performed by certified rehabilitation providers approved pursuant to Section 440.491, F.S.

(e) The insurer or delegated entity shall develop and implement procedures for communication of information regarding medical services and return to work between internal and external case management, the medical care coordinator, claims administration, the employer, and injured employee.

Specific Authority 440.134(25) Fla. Stat.

Law Implemented 440.134(6)(c)1. — 8., 11., (7),

(9), (10)(d), (11), (14)(a), (d), (15) Fla. Stat.

History: New 9-12-94, Amended 10-8-2001, 1-22-2002.

59A-23.005. Medical Records and Case Files.

(1) The insurer or delegated entity shall implement a system for managing electronic and paper medical information necessary to promote the prompt delivery of medical services in order to return the injured employee to work as soon as medically feasible.

(2) Provider Medical Records.The insurer or delegated entity shall maintain or assure that its providers maintain a medical records system, which is consistent with professional standards, pursuant to Section 456.057, F.S. The insurer or delegated entity shall develop and implement policies and procedures that:

(a) Permit prompt retrieval of legible and timely information, which is accurately documented and readily available if requested by a health care practitioner with written authorization and consent from the patient when required by statute;

(b) Protect the confidentiality and security of paper and electronic patient records including:

1. Transfer, storage, and faxing of records; and

2. Handling of records containing information on HIV, substance abuse, and mental health, in accordance with statutory requirements;

(c) Provide for the training and education of administrative staff and providers on medical record documentation, policies and procedures, storage and confidentiality of patient records;

(d) Document in the medical record a summary related to work injury or illness, of significant procedures, past and current diagnoses or problems and allergies and adverse reactions to current medications;

(e) Identify the patient as follows:

1. Name;

2. Social Security, alien identification number, or other identification number;

3. Date of Birth; Employer; home and work telephone numbers;

4. Sex; and

5. Date of work injury or illness.

(f) Indicate in the medical record for each visit the following information:

1. Date;

2. Chief complaint, unresolved problems or complaints from prior interventions and purpose of visit;

3. Objective findings of practitioner;

4. Diagnosis or medical impression;

5. Studies ordered, for example: lab, x-ray, EKG, and referral reports;

6. Therapies administered and prescribed;

7. Name and profession of practitioner rendering services, for example: M.D., D.O., D.C., D.P.M., R.N., O.D., etc., including signature or initials of practitioner;

8. Disposition, recommendations, instructions, and education to the patient. Evidence of whether there was follow-up and the specific time of return is noted in weeks, months or as needed;

9. Outcome of services;

10. Work status, release for return to work, work restrictions; and

11. Evidence of coordination of care and any injured employee non-compliance with treatment.

(g) Require the insurer or delegated entity to request written consent of patients for release of medical records that are subject to the limitations in Sections 381.004 and 456.057, F.S., and for obtaining and sharing all documents and medical records from providers necessary to carry out the provisions of Section 440.134, F.S.; and

(h) Address transfer and retrieval of records, and provision of copies when requested by the patient, designated representative, or the Agency pursuant to Section 440.13(4)(c), F.S. The insurer or delegated entity shall communicate its policy to providers via provider educational materials.

(3) Case Files.The insurer or delegated entity shall maintain electronic or paper medical information necessary to ensure the efficient functioning of the care coordination process. The insurer or delegated entity shall develop and implement a policy and procedure that protects the confidentiality and security of case file information including the transfer and storage of paper and electronic information, and the handling of information on HIV, substance abuse, and mental health. Case files shall contain necessary information for the coordination of quality patient care between providers, insurers, employees, and employers including:

(a) The information from the notice of injury required by Section 440.13(4)(a), F.S.;

(b) The current primary care physician, primary care physician changes and the designated medical care coordinator;

(c) The treating physician's plan of care;

(d) Medical reports and information necessary to support the coordination of medical care;

(e) The injured employee's work status, work restrictions, date of maximum medical improvement, and permanent impairment ratings; and

(f) Efforts toward rehabilitation and reemployment of the injured employee.

(4) Audits of provider records.The insurer or delegated entity shall implement an ongoing process for conducting medical record audits to determine compliance with the medical record standards specified under paragraphs (2)(d), (e), and (f). The insurer or delegated entity shall have a written methodology for determining the size and scope of the medical record audits that shall reflect the volume and complexity of services provided by the provider network. The insurer or delegated entity shall develop and implement an annual work plan for the medical record audits. The results of the audits shall be reported quarterly to the quality assurance committee and shall include the following:

(a) Number of physicians reviewed by county and by specialty;

(b) Areas where specific improvements in record keeping are indicated;

(c) Results from implementing improvements recommended in prior audits;

(d) Recommendations for education and feedback to providers; and

(e) Extent to which the physician's treatment plan was implemented.

Specific Authority 440.134(25) Fla. Stat.

Law Implemented 440.134(5)(c), (6)(c)1. — 4., 8., (7), (8) Fla. Stat.

History: New 9-12-94, Amended 10-8-2001, 1-22-2002.

59A-23.006. Grievance Procedures.

(1) Each insurer or delegated entity shall develop and implement a grievance procedure to resolve complaints and written grievances by employees and providers.

(2) A detailed description of the employee complaint and grievance procedure shall be provided by the insurer or delegated entity to employees pursuant to Rule 59A-23.009, F.A.C. A detailed description of the employee complaint and written grievance procedures shall be included in educational materials provided to injured employees. A detailed description of the provider complaint and grievance procedure shall be included in educational materials given to providers.

(3) A copy of the grievance procedure and forms for filing a written grievance shall be made available to providers, employees, or their designated representative within seven calendar days of receipt of a request. Copies of the form required for filing a grievance shall also be available at the same location as the compensation notice required under Rule 38F-6.007, F.A.C. The insurer or delegated entity shall not charge the employer, employee, or provider for administering the grievance process.

(4) The grievance procedure shall include the following:

(a) Requests for services.The insurer or delegated entity shall implement a procedure to address initial requests for services. Initial requests for services, such as a request for medical services, second opinions, or a change in providers, are not considered a complaint or grievance. The insurer or delegated entity shall evaluate requests for medical services within seven calendar days of receipt and shall notify the injured employee of the decision to grant the request, to deny it, or to request additional information. When the insurer or delegated entity denies a request it shall notify the injured employee in writing of the denial and the right to file a grievance. The insurer or delegated entity shall provide the employee with a copy of AHCA Form No. 3160-0019 (November 2000) which is incorporated by reference. If the insurer or delegated entity fails to respond within seven calendar days of receipt of the request, the injured employee may make a complaint or file a written grievance;

(b) Complaint Procedure.The insurer or delegated entity shall implement a procedure to address complaints about medical issues and employees rights under Section 440.134, F.S., in a timely manner in order to expedite the resolution of issues of providers and injured employees.

1. The insurer or delegated entity shall investigate and resolve a complaint within ten calendar days of receipt unless the parties and the insurer or delegated entity mutually agree to an extension. The ten days shall commence upon receipt of a personal or telephone contact by the insurer or delegated entity from the injured employee, provider, designated representative, the Agency, or the Division.

2. If a complaint is denied, or remains unresolved after ten days of receipt, the insurer or delegated entity shall notify the affected parties in writing of the right to file a written grievance. If the insurer or delegated entity denies a complaint, it shall notify the injured employee of the reason for the denial. The written notification shall include the name, title, address, and telephone number of the grievance coordinator. In addition, the insurer or delegated entity shall advise the injured employee of the right to contact the Division's Employee Assistance Office for additional information on rights and responsibilities and the dispute resolution process under Chapter 440, F.S., and related administrative rules; and

(c) Written Grievance.The procedure for written grievances shall commence upon receipt of a signed grievance form AHCA Form No. 3160-0019 (November 2000) by the insurer or delegated entity, from the injured employee, provider, or their designated representative. A written grievance may be submitted or withdrawn at any time. The injured employee or provider is not required to make a complaint prior to filing a written grievance. The procedure shall include notice to the employer when a grievance has been filed. The insurer or delegated entity shall notify the injured employee and employer in writing of the resolution of the written grievance, and the reasons therefor within seven days of the final determination.

1. The insurer or delegated entity shall implement an expedited procedure for urgent grievances to render a determination and notify the injured employee within three calendar days of receipt. If the insurer or delegated entity has initiated an expedited grievance procedure, the injured employee shall be considered to have exhausted all managed care grievance procedures after three days from receipt.

2. Upon receipt of a written grievance, the grievance coordinator shall gather and review medical and related information pertaining to the issues being grieved. The grievance coordinator shall consult with appropriate parties and shall render a determination on the grievance within 14 calendar days of receipt. If the determination is not in favor of the aggrieved party the grievance coordinator shall notify the aggrieved party that the grievance is being forwarded to the grievance committee for further consideration unless withdrawn in writing by the employee or provider.

3. The grievance committee shall consist of not less than three individuals, of whom at least one must be a physician other than the injured employee's treating physician, who is licensed under Chapter 458 or 459, F.S., and has profes-

sional expertise relevant to the issue. The committee shall review information pertaining to the issues being grieved and render a determination within 30 calendar days of receipt of the grievance by the committee unless the grieving party and the committee mutually agree to an extension that is documented in writing. If the grievance involves the collection of additional information from outside the service area, the insurer or delegated entity will have 14 additional calendar days to render a determination. The insurer or delegated entity shall notify the employee in writing within seven days of receipt of the grievance by the committee if additional information is required to complete the review of the grievance.

4. The insurer or delegated entity may allow but may not require arbitration as part of the grievance process. A grievance which is arbitrated pursuant to Chapter 682, F.S., is permitted an additional time limitation not to exceed 210 calendar days from the date the insurer or delegated entity receives a written request for arbitration from the injured employee. Arbitration provisions in a workers compensation managed care arrangement shall not preclude the employee from filing a request for assistance with the Division of Workers Compensation relating to non-medical issues.

5. An injured employee or provider grievance shall be submitted on AHCA Form No. 3160-0019 (November 2000). The insurer or delegated entity shall provide assistance to an injured employee unable to complete the grievance form and to those persons who have improperly filed a grievance.

6. The claimant or provider shall be considered to have exhausted all managed care grievance procedures if a determination on a grievance has not been rendered within the required timeframe specified in this section or other timeframe, as mutually agreed to in writing by the grieving party and the insurer or delegated entity.

7. Upon completion of the grievance procedure, the insurer or delegated entity shall provide written notice to the employee of the right to file a petition for benefits with the Division pursuant to Section 440.192, F.S.

(5) The insurer or delegated entity shall designate at least one grievance coordinator who is responsible for the implementation of the grievance procedure. The insurer or delegated entity shall ensure that the grievance coordinator's role in the grievance procedure is identified in the grievance coordinator's job description.

(6) The insurer or delegated entity shall provide specified phone numbers in the provider and employee educational materials for the employee or provider to contact the grievance coordinator. Each phone number shall be toll free within the injured employee's or provider's geographic service area and shall provide access without undue delays. There must be an adequate number of phone lines to handle incoming complaint calls.

(7) The insurer or delegated entity shall provide a current mailing address in employee and provider educational materials that indicate where to file a grievance.

(8) Physician involvement in reviewing medically related grievances. This involvement shall not be limited to the injured employee's primary care physician, but shall include at least one other physician.

(9) A meeting between the insurer or delegated entity and the injured employee or provider during the written grievance process if requested by the injured employee or provider. The insurer or delegated entity shall offer to meet with the injured employee or provider at a location within the service area convenient to the injured employee or provider.

(10) A record of each written grievance. The insurer or delegated entity will maintain a record of each written grievance to include the following:

(a) A description of the grievance, the injured employee's or provider's name and address, the names and addresses of any treating workers compensation providers relevant to the grievance, and the managed care arrangement name and address;

(b) A complete description of the findings,

including supportive documentation, conclusions and final disposition of the grievance; and

(c) A statement as to the current status of the grievance.

(11) The insurer or delegated entity shall maintain a list of all grievance files that contains the identity of the injured employee, the individual filing the grievance, the date filed, the nature of the grievance, the resolution, and the resolution date.

(12) The insurer or delegated entity shall be responsible for regular and systematic review and analysis of all written grievances for the purpose of identifying trends or patterns, and, upon emergence of any pattern, shall develop and implement recommendations for corrective action.

(13) An annual report of all grievances filed by employees and providers shall be submitted to the Agency pursuant to paragraph 440.134(15)(g), F.S. The report shall list the number, nature, and resolution of all written employee and provider grievances. This report shall be submitted no later than March 31 for grievances filed during the previous calendar year in a format prescribed by the Agency on AHCA Form No. 3160-0012 (July 1997). This form is hereby incorporated by reference and is available by contacting AHCA, 2727 Mahan Drive, Tallahassee, Florida 32308, Bureau of Managed Health Care, Workers' Compensation Managed Care Unit. It is also available at www.fdhc.state.fl.us/ManagedHealthCare/WCMC.

Specific Authority 440.134(25) Fla. Stat.

Law Implemented 440.134(1)(b), (d), (5)(c), (e), (6)(b), (c), (7), (8), (10)(c), (14)(d), (15) Fla. Stat.

History: New 9-12-94, Amended 10-8-2001, 1-22-2002.

59A-23.007. Examination by the Agency for Health Care Administration.

The agency shall conduct surveys within the first year of operation and no less than every two years thereafter, and shall conduct examinations, and investigate complaints regarding the quality of health care services being provided by workers' compensation managed care arrangements to ensure the health, safety and welfare of employees and to carry out the provisions of s. 440.134, F.S.

Specific Authority 440.134(2)(a) Fla. Stat.

Law Implemented 440.134(2)(a) Fla. Stat.

History: New 9-12-94.

59A-23.009. Education Procedures.

(1) Employee Education.

(a) The insurer or delegated entity in conjunction with the employer, shall develop and implement procedures for the education of employees about the managed care process and requirements. The education procedures shall include:

1. Orientation of all existing and new employees to the requirements and limitations of the workers compensation managed care arrangement. The employer shall display a telephone number for obtaining information about the workers compensation managed care arrangement in a prominent location in the workplace;

2. Provision of detailed employee education materials about the requirements and limitations of the workers compensation managed care arrangement to the injured employees; and

3. Ongoing education of employees about changes in the workers compensation managed care arrangement.

(b) The insurer or delegated entity shall provide, either directly or indirectly, employee educational materials written in language common to the workforce in the geographic service area. Whether or not the employer has provided educational materials previously, the educational material shall be provided to an injured employee within three calendar days of the date that the notice of injury is filed by the insurance carrier or the employer. The content of the employee educational material shall include:

1. The rights and responsibilities of the injured employee;

2. A description of the process for accessing medical care including the use of network providers, the primary care provider, medical care

coordinator, case management, and the procedure to request a referral to a specialist;

3. The possible effect to the injured employee's health and benefits for failure to use network providers or obtaining authorization for specialty care;

4. A description of the process for changing primary care and other specialty providers once within the same specialty as the authorized treating physician during the course of treatment for a work-related injury;

5. A description of the procedure for obtaining a second opinion;

6. A description of the complaint and grievance process including the procedure to file a complaint or grievance, timeframes for completion of a complaint or grievance, and the availability of a grievance form;

7. The toll free telephone number of the grievance coordinator; and

8. The telephone number of the Division of Workers Compensation, Employee Assistance Office toll free hotline.

(c) The insurer or delegated entity shall ensure that all injured employees are provided a current list of network providers within the service area in which the individual is employed. The insurer or delegated entity shall provide a copy of the list to the employee or designated representative within five calendar days of receipt of a request.

(2) Provider Education.The insurer or delegated entity shall ensure that the health care providers within the provider network have received training and education on the provisions of Chapter 440, F.S., and related administrative rules. This shall be accomplished by a provider education program or verification that providers have previously received certification from the Division pursuant to Section 440.13, F.S.

(a) The provider education program shall address the following:

1. The mission and goals of workers compensation managed care;

2. Roles, rights, and responsibilities;

3. Provider network procedures;

4. Case management procedures;

5. Practice guidelines;

6. Utilization management procedures;

7. Peer review procedures;

8. Dispute resolution and grievance procedures;

9. Communication procedures between managed care components;

10. Medical records and case file procedures;

11. Workers compensation managed care statutes and regulations relating to remedial treatment; and

12. The health care provider's role in successful return to work.

(b) The insurer or delegated entity shall identify those ancillary providers who require training on the provisions of workers compensation medical services and shall provide and document the staff training and education program.

(c) The insurer or delegated entity shall provide such ongoing provider education at least annually to keep providers informed of changes in the processes of the workers compensation managed care arrangement and to correct problems and implement recommendations of the quality assurance program. The insurer or delegated entity shall document the provision of training.

(3) Administrative Staff Education.The insurer or delegated entity shall develop and implement a policy and procedure, and implement a process, to identify and train those administrative staff who require training on the provisions of Chapter 440, F.S., and related administrative rules. Administrative staff shall include case managers, the grievance coordinator, and claims representatives. The insurer or delegated entity shall document the staff training and education program. The program content shall address the following:

(a) The mission and goals of workers compensation managed care;

(b) Roles, rights, and responsibilities;

(c) Provider network procedures;

(d) Case management procedures;

(e) Practice guidelines;

(f) Utilization management procedures;

(g) Peer review procedures;

(h) Dispute resolution and grievance procedures;

(i) Communication procedures between managed care components; and

(j) Medical records and case files procedures.

Specific Authority 440.134(25) Fla. Stat.

Law Implemented 440.134(1)(b), (d), (g), (i), (j), (k), (3), (5)(a), (c), (e), (6)(b), (c)2., 3., 4., 6.-10., (7), (8), (10)(a)-(d), (11), (12), (14)(a)-(d), (15)(a)-(f), (17) Fla. Stat.

History: New 10-8-2001.

CHAPTER 59A-24 Drug-Free Workplace Standards

59A-24.001. Title.

Specific Authority 112.0455(13)(a) Fla. Stat.

Law Implemented 112.0455 Fla. Stat.

History: New 3-15-90, Repromulgated 6-28-91, Formerly 10E-18.001, Repealed 5-1-96.

59A-24.002. Scope of the Rules.

Specific Authority 112.0455(13)(a) Fla. Stat.

Law Implemented 112.0455 Fla. Stat.

History: New 3-15-90, Amended 6-28-91, Formerly 10E-18.002, Amended 5-1-96, Repealed 12-4-96.

59A-24.003. Definitions.

In addition to the definitions set forth in section 112.0455 (5), F.S., as used in this rule chapter the following terms shall mean:

(1) "Agency" means the Agency for Health Care Administration.

(2) "Aliquot" means a portion of a specimen used for testing.

(3) "Approved Proficiency Testing Provider" means a private non-profit proficiency testing organization that meets the following requirements:

(a) Supplies a shipment of no less than 10 drug of abuse proficiency testing samples for screening and confirmation testing at least 3 times per year. Samples shall consist of a combination of negative specimens and a selection of positive specimens containing the drugs or metabolites of the substances listed in section 112.0455 (5)(a), F.S.

(b) Evaluates proficiency testing sample results using statistical methods based on results obtained from participant peer group comparisons.

(c) Provides no communication with the participant laboratory regarding the drug content of the samples prior to the issuance of the proficiency testing report.

(d) Provides explanatory information to assist the participant laboratory in the interpretation of the proficiency testing results.

(4) "Collection Site" means a place owned, operated, or contracted by a laboratory licensed under this rule chapter, or a site prepared by a collector authorized under section 112.0455, F.S., and Chapter 59A-24, F.A.C., where individuals present themselves for the purpose of providing a specimen or specimens to be analyzed for the presence of drugs.

(5) "Collection Site Person" or "Collector" means a person who instructs and assists donors at a collection site and who collects or receives and makes an initial observation of the specimen provided by those donors. The laboratory is responsible to ensure that the collector(s) is trained to carry out his or her responsibilities under this rule chapter.

(6) "Donor" means a job applicant or employee who present themselves to a collection site for the purpose of submitting to a drug test.

(7) "Federal Workplace Drug Testing Programs" means the Department of Health and

Human Services Mandatory Guidelines for Federal Workplace Drug Testing Programs as contained in Volume 59, Number 110, of the Federal Register published June 9, 1994, and the criteria found in the National Laboratory Certification Program Guidance Document for Laboratories and Inspectors as published by the Substance Abuse and Mental Health Services Administration Center for Substance Abuse Prevention, August 29, 1994, each incorporated by reference herein.

(8) "Forensic Toxicology Laboratory" or "Laboratory" means a place where examinations are performed on specimens taken from the human body to provide information regarding the presence or absence of drugs or their metabolites for the purpose of promoting a drug free workplace under the provisions of section 112.0455, F.S.

(9) "Medical Review Officer" or "MRO" means a licensed physician qualified under section 59A-24.008 (1)(a)–(e), F.A.C., who evaluates a donor's test result, together with his or her medical history or any other biomedical information, and makes the final determination of the donor's test results.

(10) "Prescription or Nonprescription Medication" means a drug or medication obtained pursuant to a prescription as defined by s. 893.02 (17), F.S., or a medication that is authorized pursuant to federal or state law for general distribution and use without a prescription in the treatment of human diseases, ailments, or injuries.

(11) "Reason to Believe" means a belief by the collection site person that a particular individual intends to alter or has altered or substituted a specimen. Reason to believe includes, for example:

(a) A urine specimen temperature falling outside the specified range of 90–100 degrees fahrenheit.

(b) Unusual urine color or signs of contaminants in the urine.

(c) A finding of contaminants on the individual.

(d) Unusual behavior or appearance by the individual.

(12) "Peer reviewed literature" includes literature approved for publication.

(13) "Run" or "batch" means an interval in which tests are performed within which the accuracy and precision of a testing system is expected to be stable. This interval shall not exceed 24 hours; nor shall it exceed the stability limits indicated by the instrument manufacturer.

(14) "Split sample" means a specimen that is divided into two separate containers, for the purpose of using one container for immediate testing and the other being tested at the donor's request if the first sample tested results in a confirmed positive test.

Specific Authority 112.0455(13)(a) Fla. Stat.
Law Implemented 112.0455 Fla. Stat.

History: New 3-15-90, Amended 6-28-91, Formerly 10E-18.003, Amended 5-1-96, 3-11-98.

59A-24.004. Drugs to be Tested/Body Specimens.

(1) Notwithstanding the definition of drug in section 112.0455 (5)(a), F.S., the only hallucinogen to be tested for is phencyclidine (PCP), the only synthetic narcotics to be tested for are methadone and propoxyphene, and there will be no designer drugs tested for until standard testing procedures are developed for such drugs.

(2) Body Specimens.

(a) Urine.Urine will be used for the initial test for all drugs except alcohol and for the confirmation for all drugs except alcohol.

(b) Blood.Blood will be used as the initial and confirmation specimen for alcohol.

Specific Authority 112.0455(13)(a) Fla. Stat.
Law Implemented 112.0455 Fla. Stat.

History: New 3-15-90, Amended 6-28-91, Formerly 10E-18.004, Amended 5-1-96.

59A-24.005. Collection Site and Specimen Collection Procedures.

(1) Designation of Collection Sites.For urine and blood specimen collection, each laboratory,

that has a contract or agreement for testing services with an employer, shall provide collection sites under contract and training for collectors, or shall provide a trained collector to collect specimens for the employer at any time designated by the employer in his contract or agreement with the laboratory. The collector shall be responsible to the laboratory for implementing collection procedures and chain of custody procedures as designated in Chapter 59A-24, F.A.C. The laboratory shall provide to the collection site, or collector, specimen collection kits which, as applicable, shall contain chain of custody forms, as incorporated in section 59A-24.005 (2), F.A.C., mailing boxes or containers, specimen identification labels, laboratory address labels, urine specimen bottles, external temperature strips, tamper-proof plastic sealable bags and forensic tamper-proof tape to seal the specimen container(s). Kits for alcohol testing must have a 7ml blood vial that contains an anticoagulant and a preservative of sodium fluoride. Employers who do not use hair testing for their drug-free workplace program shall not be required to maintain collection facilities and personnel as described in section 112.0455 (13)(b)3.a., F.S. Employers that choose to use hair as a specimen for testing shall meet the requirements found in section 112.0455 (13)(b)3.a., F.S.

(2) Chain of Custody Form and Procedures.Chain of custody refers to the methodology of documenting the tracking of specified materials or substances for the purpose of maintaining control and accountability from initial collection to final disposition of all such materials or substances and providing for accountability at each stage in handling, testing, storing and reporting of the test results. The agency chain of custody forms, AHCA Form 3170-5006 July 95; Drug Testing Chain of Custody for urine and AHCA Form 3170-5008, Sept. 97; Drug Testing Chain of Custody —Hair, incorporated by reference herein, shall be utilized for this purpose. These forms will be available from each laboratory licensed under these rules. Each laboratory shall be responsible for obtaining these forms from a vendor of their choosing. The agency shall provide one camera-ready copy of this form to each laboratory upon request.

(a) A chain of custody form shall be completed for each donor tested.

(b) Each laboratory licensed under these rules shall provide legally defensible chain-of-custody forms to be used for each donor. Laboratories licensed prior to the effective date of these rules are permitted to use Drug Testing Chain of Custody, HRS Form 1806, Revised 5/91 (currently AHCA Form 3170-5006 Nov. 94), which is incorporated by reference herein, until 12 months after this rule chapter is effective. Laboratories licensed after the effective date of these rules shall use Drug Testing Chain of Custody form AHCA Form 3170-5006 July 95, for urine and AHCA Form 3170-5008 Sept. 97 for hair.

(c) All chain of custody forms shall provide a unique identifier which shall not be used to identify any other Florida Drug Free Workplace specimen. The employer is permitted to assign an employee identification number for use with each donor tested.

(d) The design of the chain of custody forms shall meet the following requirements:

1. Prominently indicate the name and address of the laboratory performing the drug test(s).

2. A section to be completed by the collector or employer respresentative that solicits the following information:

a. Employer name and address;

b. Medical review officer name and address;

c. Employee identification number;

d. Reason for the test(s); and

e. Test(s) to be performed.

3. A section which indicates the temperature of urine specimens taken within 4 minutes of collection. This shall not be required for chain-of-custody forms for hair specimens.

4. A section to be completed by the collector that indicates the following:

a. The collection facility name, address and telephone number;

b. A designation that a split sample was or

was not collected;

c. A remarks section;

d. A statement for the collector to sign incorporating the following language: I certify that the specimen identified on this form is the specimen presented to me or collected by me from the donor providing certification on Copy 4 of this form, that it bears the same identification number as set forth above, and that it has been collected, labeled and sealed in accordance with the Florida Drug-Free Workplace as found in section 112.0455, Florida Statutes, and Chapter 59A-24, Florida Administrative Code; and

e. A place for the collector to print his name, a place for the collector's signature and the date and time.

5. A section to be initiated by the collector and completed as necessary thereafter that documents the transfer of the specimen for the purpose of maintaining control and accountability for the specimen. At a minimum, this section shall indicate:

a. Date of transfer;

b. Signature and name of the person releasing the specimen;

c. Signature and name of the person receiving the specimen; and

d. Purpose of the transfer.

6. A section to be completed by the laboratory which indicates the following:

a. An indication as to whether the specimen was received with intact specimen seals;

b. The test results;

c. Contains the following statement for the certifying scientist to sign: I certify that the specimen identified by the laboratory accession number on this form is the same specimen that bears the specimen identification number set forth above, that the specimen has been examined upon receipt, handled and analyzed in accordance with the Florida Drug-Free Workplace Program requirements as found in section 112.0455, Florida Statutes, and Chapter 59A-24, Florida Administrative Code, and that the results set forth are for that specimen; and

d. A place for the certifying scientist to print his name, the signature of the certifying scientist and the date.

7. A section to be completed by the Medical Review Officer including the following:

a. The statement: I have reviewed the laboratory test(s) for the specimen identified by this form in accordance with the Florida Drug-Free Workplace Program as found in section 112.0455, Florida Statutes, and Chapter 59A-24, Florida Administrative Code;

b. A space for determination of test results as one of the following:

I. Negative;

II. Positive;

III. Test not performed; and

IV. Test canceled.

c. A place for remarks;

d. The signature of the Medical Review Officer; and

e. The name of the Medical Review Officer and the date.

8. The chain of custody form shall be comprised of the following copies for distribution:

a. Original laboratory copy (Copy 1) which shall be routed to the laboratory with the specimen; the labcratory will retain upon the completion of testing.

b. Second Original Laboratory copy (Copy 2) which shall be routed to the laboratory with the specimen; as a means of reporting the test result, the laboratory will forward the copy to the Medical Review Officer.

c. Split specimen copy (Copy 3) which must accompany the split portion to the laboratory. Split sample testing is optional.

d. Medical Review Officer copy (Copy 4) which shall be routed directly to the MRO by the collection site personnel; this form copy is not to be sent to the laboratory.

e. Donor copy (Copy 5) which shall be given to the donor by the collector. Do not send to the laboratory.

f. Collector copy (Copy 6) which shall be retained by the collector. Do not send to the laboratory.

g. Employer copy (Copy 7) which shall be forwarded to the employer.

(e) AHCA Form 3170-5006 July 95 and AHCA Form 3170-5008 Sept. 97 are permitted to be modified to indicate specialized specimen identification numbering systems, laboratory identification information and logos, and specimen labels provided that:

1. The content of each section of the form is not altered.

2. The instructions are not altered.

3. The sequence, number and color of the copies are not altered.

4. The drugs listed in the reverse of Copy 5 are not altered.

(f) The form shall contain no information which can be traceable to the donor except the unique identifier, the employee identification number, if used, and the laboratory's specimen identification number.

(g) The form shall also contain the following list of over-the-counter and prescription drugs which could alter or affect a test result. Due to the large number of obscure brand names and constant marketing of new products, this list, as follows, is not intended to be all-inclusive.

Alcohol	All liquid medications containing ethyl alcohol (ethanol). Please read the label for alcohol content. As an example, Vick's Nyquil is 25% (50 proof) ethyl alcohol, Comtrex is 20% (40 proof), Contact Severe Cold Formula Night Strength is 25% (50 proof) and Listerine is 26.9% (54 proof).
Amphetamines	Obetrol, Biphetamine, Desoxyn, Dexedrine, Didrex, Ionamine, Fastin.
Cannabinoids	Marinol (Dronabinol, THC).
Cocaine	Cocaine HCl topical solution (Roxanne).
Phencyclidine	Not legal by prescription.
Methaqualone	Not legal by prescription.
Opiates	Paregoric, Parepectolin, Donnagel PG, Morphine, Tylenol with Codeine, Empirin with Codeine, APAP with Codeine, Aspirin with Codeine, Robitussin AC, Guiatuss AC, Novahistine DH, Novahistine Expectorant, Dilaudid (Hydromorphone), M-S Contin and Roxanol (morphine sulfate), Percodan, Vicodin, Tussi-organidin, etc.
Barbiturates	Phenobarbital, Tuinal, Amytal, Nembutal, Seconal, Lotusate, Fiorinal, Fioricet, Esgic, Butisol, Mebaral, Butabarbital, Butalbital, Phrenilin, Triad, etc.
Benzodiazepines	Ativan, Azene, Clonopin, Dalmane, Diazepam, Librium, Xanax, Serax, Tranxene, Valium, Verstran, Halcion, Paxipam, Restoril, Centrax.
Methadone	Dolophine, Metadose.
Propoxyphene	Darvocet, Darvon N, Dolene, etc.

(h) Handling and transportation of a specimen from one authorized individual or place to another shall always be accomplished through the chain of custody form and procedures. The chain of custody form shall be used for maintaining control and accountability of each specimen from the point of collection to final disposition of the specimen at the laboratory. The purpose of the transfer of possession, the name and signature of the person releasing and receiving the specimen, and the date shall be documented on the form each time a specimen is handled or transferred and every individual in the chain shall be identified. Since the specimen and the chain of custody form are sealed in tamper-proof sealable plastic bags that would indicate any tampering during transit to the laboratory, and since couriers, express carriers and postal service personnel do not have access to the chain of custody forms, there is no requirement that such personnel document chain of custody for the shipping container during transit. Nor is there a requirement that there be a chain of custody entry when a specimen which is sealed in such a shipping container is placed in or taken out of secure storage at the collection site prior to pickup by such personnel. A test shall not be canceled because couriers, express carriers, postal service personnel or other persons involved solely with the transportation of a specimen to a laboratory have not documented their participation in the chain of custody or because the chain of custody does not contain entries related to placing the specimen in or removing it from secure temporary storage at the collection site.

(i) Once the specimen has arrived at the laboratory, an internal chain of custody form shall be used by the laboratory until the laboratory has finalized the test results.

(j) Every effort shall be made to minimize the number of persons handling the specimens.

(3) Security Procedures and Specimen Collection.Collection site security and specimen collection security are the responsibility of the collector through contract with the licensed laboratory. Security procedures shall provide for the designated collection site to be secure including the providing of privacy for the donor and the integrity of the specimen.

(a) Access to Authorized Personnel Only. No unauthorized personnel shall be permitted in any part of the designated collection site when specimens are collected or stored.

(b) Privacy. Procedures for collecting urine specimens shall allow individual privacy unless there is reason to believe that a particular individual intends to alter or has altered or substituted the specimen to be provided.

(c) Integrity and Identity of Specimen. The collection site person shall take precautions to ensure that a specimen not be adulterated or diluted during the collection procedure and that information on the collection bottle and on the chain of custody form can identify the individual from whom the specimen was collected. The following minimum precautions shall be taken to ensure that unadulterated specimens are obtained and correctly identified.

1. To prevent specimen contamination at the collection site:

a. For urine specimens, toilet bluing agents shall be placed in toilet tanks so the reservoir of water in the toilet bowl always remains blue. There shall be no other source of water in the enclosure or partitioned area where urination occurs. All other sources of water shall be controlled by the collector.

2. When a donor arrives at the collection site, the collection site person shall request the donor to present a photo identification. If the donor does not have the proper photo identification, the collection site person shall contact the employer who can positively identify the donor. If the donor's identity cannot be established, the collection site person shall not proceed with the collection. The collection site person shall document the reason for not collecting the specimen and provide the donor with a copy of this documentation.

3. Before collecting a specimen, the collection site person shall check to see that the donor has a chain of custody form or has a letter from the employer authorizing the drug test. If a letter is used, the letter shall contain the following information:

a. The name of the individual to be tested;

b. The name of the employer and the employer's address, phone number, and fax number;

c. The name, address and phone number of the laboratory with which the employer has contracted or established an agreement for testing services;

d. The name, address, phone number, and secured fax number of the employer's Medical Review Officer;

e. The reason for the test (i.e., either job applicant, reasonable suspicion, routine fitness, or follow-up to treatment);

f. The drugs for which the laboratory will test; and

g. The signature of the employer's representative authorizing the testing.

4. If a collection time is assigned by the employer or collection site, and the donor fails to arrive at the collection site at the assigned time, the collection site person shall notify the employer of the missed appointment.

5. The collection site person shall ask the individual to remove any unnecessary outer garments, such as a coat or jacket, and to empty all clothing pockets. The collection site person shall ensure that all personal belongings, such as a purse or briefcase, remain with the outer garments. The individual may retain his or her wallet, provided that the collection site person shall check it for possible contaminants.

6. The individual shall be instructed to wash and dry his or her hands prior to urination. After washing hands, the individual shall remain in the presence of the collection site person and shall not have access to any water fountain, faucet, soap dispenser, cleaning agent or any other materials which could be used to adulterate the specimen.

7. The individual may provide his or her urine specimen in a stall or otherwise partitioned enclosure that allows for individual privacy. The collection site person shall remain in the restroom or area, but outside the stall or partitioned enclosure.

8. Upon receiving the specimen from the individual, the collection site person shall determine that:

a. Urine specimens contain at least 30 milliliters (mL) of urine. The approximate volume of the specimen shall be documented by the collector at the time of collection. If there is less than 30 mL of urine in the container, another urine specimen shall be collected in a separate container. Collected specimens which contain less than 30 mL of urine shall not be submitted to the laboratory for testing. Such specimens shall be discarded in the presence of the donor and such procedure shall be annotated by the collector on the chain of custody form. The collector is permitted to give the donor water to drink for the purpose of providing another urine specimen not to exceed an 8 ounce glass of water every 30 minutes for up to 2 hours. If the donor still fails to provide 30 mL of urine, the collection site person shall reschedule another collection within 24 hours and notify the employer as soon as possible of such rescheduling.

b. Blood alcohol specimens shall be collected using aseptic venipuncture technique. The venipuncture site for blood alcohol shall be cleansed with a non-alcoholic antiseptic substance prior to collection. Blood specimens shall contain 7 mL of blood which shall be collected in one tube containing an anticoagulant and a preservative of sodium fluoride. Immediately after collection, the collection site person shall rock the tube gently to mix the anticoagulant and preservative substance with the blood.

c. A quantity of hair shall be collected as described in section 112.0455 (13)(b)3.f.(IV), F.S.

9. After a urine specimen has been provided and submitted to the collection site person, the individual shall be allowed to wash his or her hands.

10. No longer than 4 minutes following collection, the collection site person shall measure and record the temperature of the urine specimen, as indicated, on the chain of custody form. The temperature measuring device must be placed on the outside of the container to prevent contamination. If the temperature measurement exceeds 4 minutes, the specimen shall be ren-

dered invalid and shall be rejected. A second specimen shall be collected and a new chain of custody form generated.

11. If the temperature of a urine specimen is outside the range of 90 —100 degrees fahrenheit, there is reason to believe that the donor may have altered or substituted the specimen and another urine specimen shall be collected under direct observation by an observer of the same gender as the donor, as specified in section 59A-24.005 (3)(c)13. The reason for the observed collection and the identity of the direct observer shall be documented on the chain of custody form.

12. Immediately after a urine specimen is collected, the collection site person shall also inspect the specimen to determine its color and look for any signs of contaminants. Any unusual findings shall be noted on the chain of custody form.

13. Whenever a collection site person has reason to believe that a particular individual may alter or has altered or substituted a urine specimen, a higher level supervisor at the collection site or at the laboratory shall review the decision and concur in advance with the collection of a second specimen under the direct observation of an observer of the same gender as the donor. Once approved by a higher level supervisor, the collector shall require the individual to provide another specimen under direct observation. If the same gendered observer is not the collector, the observer shall be identified on the chain of custody form. The observer, if different from the collector, shall not handle the specimen and the specimen shall be handed to the collector by the donor in the observer's presence. The observer shall keep the specimen in sight at all times prior to it being sealed. A new chain of custody form shall be executed to accompany any specimen collected under direct observation. Information regarding a specimen collected under direct observation shall be included on both the new chain of custody form and on the original form in the remarks section. In addition, the new chain of custody specimen identification number shall be annotated on the original form. Both specimens shall be sent to the laboratory to be analyzed.

14. The individual being tested, the collection site person, and the observer if used for direct observation, shall keep the specimen in view at all times prior to its being sealed and labeled.

15. The collection site person shall place securely on the bottle an identification label containing the donor's specimen number, which matches the specimen number on the chain of custody form, and the date.

16. The employee (donor) and the collector shall initial the identification label on the specimen bottle for the purpose of certifying that it is the specimen collected from the donor.

17. The collector shall enter on the chain of custody form all required information.

18. The individual shall be asked to sign a statement on the chain of custody form certifying that the specimen identified as having been collected from him or her is in fact that specimen he or she provided. It shall be noted and signed on the chain of custody form by the collection site person, with a witness' signature, if the individual refuses to sign this statement.

19. The collection station is permitted to store unrefrigerated urine specimens up to 72 hours after collection, provided they are sealed for shipment as described in section 59A-24.005 (3)(c)21., F.A.C., and kept in locked, secure temporary storage. Hair specimens shall be stored at all times in unrefrigerated locked, secured storage.

20. While any part of the above chain of custody procedures is being performed, it is essential that the specimen and the chain of custody form be under the control of the collection site person. If the collection site person leaves his or her work station momentarily, the specimen and the chain of custody form shall be taken with him or her or shall be secured in a locked room, drawer, file cabinet, etc. After the collection site person returns to the work station, the chain of custody process will continue. If the collection site person is leaving for an extended period of time, the specimen shall be packaged for shipment before he or she leaves the site.

21. The collection site person shall arrange to

send the collected specimens by express shipment, courier, or U.S. Mail to the drug testing laboratory which is designated by the employer. The specimens shall be placed in containers designed to minimize the possibility of damage during shipment. Prior to shipping or storage, the collection site person shall ensure that:

a. The specimen container is sealed with forensic tamper-proof tape;

b. The forensic tamper-proof tape contains the initials of the donor, the date the specimen was sealed in the specimen container; and

c. The completed chain of custody form and specimen container is enclosed and sealed in a tamper-proof sealable plastic bag before packaging for shipment to the drug testing laboratory.

22. This rule chapter does not prohibit the use of split samples provided that such samples are collected in accordance with the provisions of the Mandatory Guidelines for Federal Workplace Drug Testing Programs as defined in section 59A-24.003 (7), F.A.C.

Specific Authority 112.0455(13)(a) Fla. Stat.

Law Implemented 112.0455 Fla. Stat.

History: New 3-15-90, Amended 6-28-91, Formerly 10E-18.005, Amended 5-1-96, 3-11-98, 3-29-00.

59A-24.006. Drug Testing Laboratories.

Laboratories shall be licensed by the agency in accordance with this rule chapter in order to collect or analyze specimens for an employer's drug testing program and shall also comply with the provisions of Chapter 483, Part I, F.S.

(1) Laboratory Personnel.

(a) Qualifications of Director.The laboratory shall have a qualified director to assume professional, technical, educational, and administrative responsibilities for the laboratory's drug testing. The director shall meet one of the following requirements:

1. Is duly licensed as a physician in the state in which he or she practices medicine; and is licensed under Chapter 458 or 459, F.S., if the laboratory is located in the State of Florida; and has had at least four years of experience in forensic analytical toxicology; or

2. Holds a doctoral degree from an accredited institution with Chemistry, Toxicology or Pharmacology as a major subject of study; and has had at least four years of experience in forensic analytical toxicology; and shall be licensed as a director under Chapter 483, Part IV, F.S., in the specialty of clinical chemistry, if the laboratory is located in the State of Florida.

(b) Responsibilities of Director.The director shall be responsible for the following:

1. The director shall be engaged in and responsible for the day-to-day management of the drug testing laboratory.

2. The director shall be engaged in and responsible for ensuring that there are sufficient personnel with adequate training and experience to supervise and conduct the work of the drug testing laboratory. He or she shall assure the continued competency of laboratory personnel by documenting their inservice training, reviewing their work performance, and verifying their skills.

3. The director shall ensure that the laboratory has a procedure manual which is complete, up-to-date, available to the personnel performing tests. All such procedures must, at a minimum, meet the requirements stipulated in this rule chapter. The director shall ensure that the procedures are followed by personnel performing tests. The procedure manual shall be reviewed, signed, and dated by this director whenever procedures are first placed into use, or changed, or when a new director assumes responsibility of the drug testing laboratory. Copies of all procedures and the dates that they are in effect shall be maintained as required in section 59A-7.029 (3)(e), F.A.C.

4. The director shall be responsible for maintaining a quality assurance program to assure the proper performance and reporting of all test results; for maintaining acceptable analytical performance for all controls and standards; for maintaining quality control testing; and for assuring and documenting the validity, reliability, accuracy, precision, and performance characteristics of each test and test system.

5. The director shall be responsible for taking all remedial actions necessary to maintain satisfactory operation and performance of the laboratory. The director shall ensure that sample results are not reported until all corrective actions have been taken and that he or she can assure that the tests results provided are accurate and reliable.

(c) Certifying Scientists.The laboratory shall have a qualified individual who serves as certifying scientist. This individual reviews all pertinent data and quality control results in order to attest to the validity of the laboratory's test reports. A laboratory may designate more than one person to perform this function.

1. The certifying scientist(s) shall have a minimum of 2 years experience in forensic analytical toxicology and be qualified as a director or licensed as a supervisor under the provisions of Chapter 483, Part IV, F.S., in the specialty of clinical chemistry if the laboratory is located in the State of Florida.

2. The laboratory director is permitted to designate technical personnel to certify results that are negative on the initial screening test. These individuals shall be technologists licensed in the specialty of clinical chemistry in accordance with the provisions of Chapter 483, Part IV, F.S., if the laboratory is located in the State of Florida.

(d) Laboratory Operation and Supervision.

1. The laboratory's drug testing facility shall have an individual(s) responsible for day-to-day operation of the laboratory and the supervision of the technical analysts. This individual(s) shall be licensed as a laboratory supervisor in the specialty of clinical chemistry or qualified as a director in accordance with Chapter 483, Part IV, F.S., in the specialty of clinical chemistry if the laboratory is located in the State of Florida; and

2. Have a minimum of 2 years experience in forensic analytical toxicology.

(e) Technical and Non-Technical Personnel.

1. Technical personnel shall have the training and skills to conduct forensic toxicology testing and shall be licensed in accordance with Chapter 483, Part IV, F.S., if the laboratory is located in the State of Florida. Documentation of such training and skills shall be maintained by the laboratory and available upon request by the agency.

2. Non-technical personnel, including all persons collecting specimens under these rules shall have the necessary training and skills for the tasks assigned but shall not perform drug testing.

(f) Collection Site Person or Persons Collecting Specimens.A specimen for a drug test shall be taken or collected by:

1. A physician, a physician's assistant, a registered professional nurse, a licensed practical nurse, a nurse practitioner, or a certified paramedic who is present at the scene of an accident for the purpose of rendering emergency medical service or treatment.

2. A qualified person employed by a licensed laboratory who has the necessary training and skills for the assigned tasks.

(2) Training.The laboratory's drug testing program shall make available continuing education programs to meet the needs of laboratory personnel.

(3) Files.Laboratory personnel files shall include: resume of training and experience; certification or license, if any; references; job descriptions; records of performance evaluations and advancement; incident reports; and results of tests which establish employee competency for the position he or she holds, such as a test for color blindness, if appropriate.

(4) Specimen Security and Analysis Procedures.

(a) Specimen Security and Internal Chain of Custody.

1. Drug testing laboratories shall be secure at all times. They shall have in place sufficient security measures to control access to the premises and to ensure that no unauthorized personnel handle specimens or gain access to the laboratory processes or to areas where records

or specimens are stored. Access to these secured areas shall be limited to specifically authorized individuals whose authorization is documented. For the purposes of section 59A-24.006 (4)(a)1., F.A.C., authorized individuals means those persons designated by the laboratory to have access to the drug testing laboratory. All authorized visitors, including maintenance and service personnel, shall be escorted by laboratory personnel at all times. Documentation of individuals accessing these areas, dates, time of entry and egress, and purpose of entry must be maintained for no less than 2 years.

2. Laboratories shall use internal chain of custody procedures to maintain control and accountability of specimens from receipt through completion of testing, reporting of results, during storage, and continuing until final disposition of specimens. The date and purpose shall be documented on the internal chain of custody form each time a specimen is handled or transferred, and every individual in the chain shall be identified. Accordingly, authorized personnel shall be responsible for each specimen or aliquot in their possession and shall sign and complete internal chain of custody forms for those specimens or aliquots as they are received. Aliquots and internal chain of custody forms shall be used by laboratory personnel for conducting both initial and confirmation tests.

(b) Receiving Specimens.When a shipment of specimens is received, laboratory personnel shall inspect each package for evidence of possible damage or tampering and compare information listed on specimen containers within each package to the information on the accompanying chain of custody forms. The laboratory shall establish written standards for the rejection or acceptance of specimens. In addition, any evidence of tampering, mismatched or omitted specimen identification numbers, spillage, damage or other discrepancies in the information on specimen containers and the chain of custody form shall render a specimen invalid and shall be rejected by the laboratory for testing. The laboratory shall immediately report any rejection to the employer and shall note such rejection on the chain of custody form.

(c) Short-Term Refrigerated Storage.Urine or blood specimens that do not receive an initial test within 72 hours of arrival at the laboratory shall be placed in locked, secure refrigerated units. Temperatures of these units shall not exceed 6 degrees Celsius. Emergency power equipment shall be available and used in case of power failure.

(d) Specimen Testing Requirements.A laboratory must be capable of testing for all drugs listed in section 112.0455 (5)(a), F.S., and be capable of conducting testing to ensure that a specimen has not been diluted or adulterated. The laboratory shall test and report drug test results no more than 3 working days after the receipt of the specimen in the laboratory.

(e) Initial Test.The initial screen for all drugs shall be an immunoassay except that the initial test for alcohol shall be an enzyme oxidation methodology.

1. Levels on initially screened urine specimens which are equal to or exceed the following shall be considered to be presumptively positive and submitted for confirmation testing:

Amphetamines	1,000 ng/mL
Cannabinoids (11-nor-Δ^9 - tetrahydrocannabinol-9-carboxylic acid)	50 ng/mL
Cocaine (benzoylecgonine)	300 ng/mL
Phencyclidine	25 ng/mL
Methaqualone	300 ng/mL
Opiates	2,000 ng/mL
Barbiturates	300 ng/mL
Benzodiazepines	300 ng/mL
Methadone	300 ng/mL
Propoxyphene	300 ng/mL

The only specimen for alcohol testing shall be blood and the intially screened specimen shall be considered presumptively positive and submitted for confirmation testing if the level is equal to or exceeds 0.04 g/dL.

2. Levels which exceed the following for hair specimens shall be considered presumptively positive on initial screening and submitted for confirmation testing:

Marijuana	10 pg/10 mg of hair
Cocaine	5 ng/10 mg of hair
Opiate/synthetic narcotics and metabolites	5 ng/10 mg of hair
Phencyclidine	3 ng/10 mg of hair
Amphetamines	5 ng/10 mg of hair

3. Laboratories are permitted to use multiple screening tests for the same drug or drug class to eliminate any possible presumptive positives due to structural analogs, provided that such tests meet the requirements of this rule chapter.

(f) Confirmation Test.All specimens identified as presumptively positive on the initial test shall be confirmed using mass spectrometry/mass spectrometry (MS/MS) or gas chromatography/mass spectrometry (GC/MS), except that alcohol will be confirmed using gas chromatography. All confirmations shall be done by quantitative analysis.

1. Levels on confirmation testing for urine specimens which are equal to or exceed the following shall be reported as positive:

Amphetamines (amphetamine, methamphetamine)	500 ng/mL
Cannabinoids (11-nor-Δ^9 -tetrahydrocannabinol-9-carboxylic acid)	15 ng/mL
Cocaine (benzoylecgonine)	150 ng/mL
Phencyclidine	25 ng/mL
Methaqualone	150 ng/mL
Opiates	
Codeine	2000 ng/mL
Morphine	2000 ng/mL
6-Acetylmorphine	10 ng/mL
Barbiturates	150 ng/mL
Benzodiazepines	150 ng/mL
Methadone	150 ng/mL
Propoxyphene	150 ng/mL

A laboratory shall not report a specimen positive for methamphetamine only. The specimen must contain amphetamine at a concentration equal to or greater than 200 ng/mL, by the confirmation test. If this criterion is not met, the specimen shall be reported as negative for methamphetamine. Tests for 6-Acetylmorphine when the morphine concentration exceeds 2000 ng/mL. The alcohol level on confirmation testing for blood which is equal to or exceeds 0.04 g/dL shall be reported as positive.

2. Levels for hair specimens on confirmation testing which are equal to or exceed the following shall be reported as positive:

Marijuana Metabolites	1 pg/10 mg of hair
Cocaine	5 ng/10 mg of hair
Opiate/synthetic narcotics and metabolites	5 ng/10 mg of hair
Phencyclidine	3 ng/10 mg of hair
Amphetamines	5 ng/10 mg of hair

(g) Reporting Results.

1. The laboratory shall report all test results to the MRO indicated on the chain of custody form. Before any test result is reported by the laboratory, the results of initial tests, confirmation tests, and quality control data of such tests shall be reviewed by the certifying scientist and the test certified as an accurate report. The report, at a minimum, shall identify the drugs or metabolites tested for, the results of the drug test either positive or negative, the specimen number assigned on the chain of custody form, the name and address of the laboratory performing the testing, and the drug testing laboratory's specimen accession number.

2. The following criteria shall be used when reporting drug testing results.

a. Specimens that test negative as specified in section 59A-24.006 (4)(e)1. and 2., F.A.C., on the initial test shall be reported as negative. If an employer wishes to retest a negative specimen under the provisions of section 112.0455 (9)(a), F.S., such testing is authorized to be conducted only once and must be requested no more than 7 working days from the time the original negative test result was reported to the employer by the MRO. Hair specimens may be re-collected only once to perform repeat confirmation testing under the provisions of section 112.0455 (9)(a), F.S.

b. Specimens that test positive as specified in section 59A-24.006 (4)(e)1., F.A.C., on initial immunoassay tests, but test negative as specified in section 59A-24.006 (4)(f), F.A.C., on confirmation shall be reported as negative.

c. The laboratory is permitted to report drug test results for specimens that do not meet the adulteration/dilution criteria of the laboratory. Reports on specimens that do not meet the laboratory's adulteration/dilution requirements shall not indicate the actual results of the adulteration/dilution tests, but the report shall indicate the adulteration/dilution test results in non-quantitative terms.

d. The laboratory report shall indicate solely that the test(s) resulted in a positive drug test result or resulted in a negative drug test result.

3. The MRO may request from the laboratory, and the laboratory shall provide, detailed quantification of initial and confirmation test results.

4. The laboratory may transmit results to the MRO by various electronic means (for example, teleprinter, facsimile, or computer) in a manner designed to ensure confidentiality of the information. The laboratory and MRO must ensure the security of the data transmission and restrict access to any data transmission, storage, and retrieval system to only those individuals authorized under these rules to obtain such information.

5. The laboratory shall send the MRO a copy of the original chain of custody form (copy 2) signed by the certifying scientist responsible for attesting to the validity of the test report.

6. The laboratory shall make available copies of all analytical results of donor testing upon request by the MRO or the agency.

7. Unless otherwise specified in this rule chapter, all records pertaining to a given specimen shall be retained by the drug testing laboratory for a minimum of 2 years.

(h) Storage of Specimens.Drug testing laboratories shall retain and place all confirmed positive urine specimens in locked, secured long-term frozen storage (-15 degrees Celsius or less) and confirmed positive blood specimens in locked, secured long-term refrigerated storage (2—8 degrees Celsius) for a minimum of 210 days. Within this 210 day period an employer, employee, job applicant, or MRO is permitted to request in writing that the laboratory retain the specimen for an additional period of time. If no such request is received, the laboratory is permitted to discard the specimen after 210 days of storage. When notified in writing, the laboratory shall be required to maintain any specimens under legal challenge until such challenge is resolved. To maintain applicable storage temperatures for stored specimens, emergency power equipment shall be available and used in the case of power failure. After the required retention time has passed, laboratories are permitted to either discard the specimens or pool all or part of these specimens for use in the laboratory's internal quality control program.

1. When an employee or job applicant undertakes an administrative or legal challenge to the test result, it shall be the employee's or job applicant's responsibility to notify the employer and laboratory in writing of such challenge and such notice shall include reference to the chain of custody specimen identification number. After such notification, the sample shall be retained by the laboratory until the case or administrative appeal is settled.

2. During a 180 day period after written notification of a positive test result, the employee or job applicant who has provided the specimen shall be permitted by the employer to have a portion of the specimen retested, at the employee or job applicant's expense. The laboratory which performed the original test for the employer shall be responsible for transferring a portion of the specimen to be retested at a second laboratory licensed under these rules, selected by the employee or job applicant, and shall be responsible for the integrity of the specimen and for the chain of custody during such transfer.

3. Urine specimens that test negative shall be stored in locked, secured refrigerated (2 —8 degrees Celsius) or frozen storage (-15 degrees Celsius or less). Blood specimens that test negative shall be stored in locked, secured, refrigerated storage (2 —8 degrees Celsius). These specimens shall be retained for no less than 7 working days after the test result has been reported to the employer by the MRO. After the

required retention time has passed, laboratories are permitted to either discard the specimens or pool all or part of these specimens for use in the laboratory's internal quality control program.

4. The laboratory is permitted to discard or pool specimens that test negative immediately after the negative test result is transmitted to the MRO, provided that the laboratory has written authorization from the employer that specimens which test negative are not to be retained for retesting under section 112.0455 (9)(a), F.S.

5. Under no circumstances shall a laboratory be required to retain a specimen, which has been reported as negative, for a period longer than 14 working days after receipt of that specimen in the laboratory unless a confirmation test has been requested by the employer under the provisions of section 112.0455 (9)(a), F.S.

(i) Retesting Specimens.As some analytes deteriorate or are lost during freezing, refrigeration, or storage, quantification for a retest is not subject to a specific cutoff requirement but must provide data sufficient to detect the presence of the drug or metabolite.

(5) Subcontracting.Drug testing laboratories shall not subcontract, except for collection sites, and shall perform all analysis with their own personnel and equipment. The laboratory must be capable of performing testing for the classes of drugs defined in section 112.0455 (5)(a), F.S., using the specimens indicated in section 112.0455 (5)(k), F.S., and initial and confirmation methods specified in section 59A-24.006 (4)(e) and (f), F.A.C.

(6) Contracted Collection Sites.Collection sites or collectors shall contract with laboratories licensed under this rule chapter to collect specimens for analysis. Such contracts shall be in writing and include the utilization of all the necessary facilities, personnel, materials, equipment, or other supplies, as needed, to collect specimens as required in section 59A-24.005, F.A.C. For the purposes of section 112.0455 (8)(e), F.S., persons collecting specimens under contract with a forensic drug testing laboratory shall be deemed to be employees of the licensed laboratory. In addition, the collectors shall be trained by, and shall be accountable to, the licensed laboratory. However, after an accident, if an employee is taken to a facility for medical treatment and the facility does not have a contract with the laboratory, an individual authorized in section 59A-24.006 (1)(f), F.A.C., is permitted to collect a specimen provided that this collector utilize, and complete to the fullest extent possible, a chain of custody form. In addition, the collector shall follow the collection procedures found in section 59A-24.005, F.A.C., to the fullest extent possible and shall maintain full control of the specimen until the specimen is sealed and packaged for shipment to the employer's selected laboratory.

(7) Inspections.The agency or the representatives of the Federal Department of Health and Human Services Federal Workplace Drug Testing Program shall conduct announced or unannounced inspections of the laboratory at any reasonable time for the purpose of determining compliance with this rule chapter. The right of entry and inspection shall also be extended to any collection sites under contract with the laboratory. Inspections shall document the overall quality of the laboratory setting for the purpose of licensure to conduct drug free workplace testing. Inspection reports shall also contain any requirements of the laboratory to correct deficiencies noted during the inspections.

(a) Prior to laboratory licensure and at least twice a year after licensure, an on-site inspection of the laboratory shall be conducted.

(b) In order to be considered for licensure renewal, laboratories certified by the federal Department of Health and Human Services Federal Workplace Drug Testing Programs shall submit one inspection report of the federal Department of Health and Human Services Federal Workplace Drug Testing Programs in lieu of one of the two required bi-annual inspections. This provision does not apply to laboratories applying for initial licensure. In addition, such laboratories certified by the federal Department of Health and Human Services Federal Workplace Drug Testing Programs shall:

1. Maintain a policy to conduct the testing of all specimens authorized under section

112.0455, F.S., in the same manner as required for those drugs included under the Mandatory Guidelines for Federal Workplace Drug Testing Programs. This policy must be in writing and contained in the laboratory's policy and procedure manual.

2. Submit to the agency all reports of such inspections, post inspection activities and reports including any corrective action taken by the laboratory within 45 days of the receipt of the initial evaluation report in the laboratory.

3. Request in writing that the inspection report be accepted in lieu of an on-site inspection by the agency.

(8) Documentation.Laboratories shall maintain and make available for at least 2 years all documentation of the testing process. Except that the laboratory shall be required to maintain documents and records for any specimen(s) under legal challenge until such challenge is resolved. The required documentation shall include:

(a) Personnel files on all individuals authorized to have access to specimens;

(b) Chain of custody documents;

(c) Quality assurance records;

(d) Quality control records;

(e) Procedure manuals;

(f) All test data, calibration curves and any calculations used in determining test results;

(g) Donor test reports;

(h) Proficiency testing records;

(i) Computer generated data used for testing and reporting specimen results.

(9) Additional Requirements for Laboratory Licensure.

(a) Procedure Manual.Each laboratory shall have a procedure manual which meets the applicable requirements of section 59A-7.029 (3)(b), (d), and (e), F.A.C.

(b) Standards and Controls.Laboratory standards shall be prepared with pure drug standards which are properly labeled as to content and concentration. The standards shall be labeled with dates indicating when received, when prepared or opened, when placed in service, and the expiration date.

(c) Instruments and Equipment.

1. Volumetric pipettes and measuring devices shall be certified for accuracy or be checked by gravimetric, colorimetric, or other verification procedures on a quarterly basis. Automatic pipettes and dilutors shall be checked for accuracy and reproducibility before being placed in service and checked quarterly thereafter.

2. There shall be written procedures for instrument setup and normal operation, a schedule for checking critical operating characteristics for all instruments, tolerance limits for acceptable function checks and instructions for major trouble shooting, repair, and maintenance in accordance with manufacturer's specifications. Manufacturer's specifications for, and records of preventive and regular maintenance shall be maintained for as long as the instrument is in use and for at least 2 years after the instrument is discontinued from use and shall be available upon request by the agency.

(d) Remedial Actions.There shall be written procedures for the actions to be taken when test systems are not operating correctly or errors are detected. There shall be documentation that these procedures are followed and that all necessary corrective actions are taken. There shall also be in place systems to verify all stages of testing and reporting and documentation that these procedures are followed.

(e) Personnel Available to Testify at Proceedings.A laboratory director shall assure that technical personnel, including the director, be available to testify in an administrative or disciplinary proceeding regarding any employee or a job applicant when that proceeding is based on a test result which was analyzed and reported by the laboratory.

(10) Quality Assurance and Quality Control.Quality assurance and quality control for hair analyses shall be conducted in accordance with section 112.0455 (13)(b)4., F.S.

(a) General.Drug testing laboratories shall have a quality assurance program which encompasses all aspects of the testing process including but not limited to specimen acquisition, chain of custody, security and reporting of results, initial and confirmation testing and validation of analytical procedures. Quality assurance procedures shall be designed, implemented, and reviewed to monitor the conduct of each step of the process of testing for drugs.

(b) Laboratory Quality Control Requirements for Initial and Confirmation Tests.At a minimum, each analytical run of specimens for an initial or confirmation test shall include the following quality control samples:

1. Negative specimens certified to contain no drug;

2. Urine specimens fortified with known standards; and

3. Positive controls with the drug or metabolite at or near the threshold (cutoff).

4. At least 1 percent of each initial screening run, with a minimum of one sample per run, shall consist of a blind sample(s) of known concentration. Such samples shall appear as ordinary test specimens to the laboratory analysts.

(11) Proficiency Testing.Proficiency testing is a part of the initial evaluation of a laboratory seeking licensure and is required as a continuing assessment of laboratory performance necessary to maintain continued licensure.

(a) General Considerations.

1. The laboratory must successfully participate in proficiency testing surveys, as described in section 59A-24.006 (11), F.A.C.

2. Proficiency testing specimens are permitted to consist of negative specimens as specified in section 59A-24.006 (4)(e)1., F.A.C., and positive specimens, as specified in section 59A-24.006 (4)(f), F.A.C.

3. Proficiency testing specimens are permitted to contain interfering substances.

4. Proficiency testing specimens are permitted to be identified for screening or confirmation testing only.

5. All procedures associated with the laboratory's handling and testing of any proficiency testing specimens shall be carried out in the same manner as the laboratory tests donor samples.

6. The laboratory shall report results of proficiency testing samples using the same criteria applied to routine drug testing specimens.

7. Failure to submit the results of each proficiency testing survey within the time frames indicated in section 59A-24.006 (11)(c)1.c., F.A.C., and section 59A-24.006 (11)(c)3.h., F.A.C., is considered unsuccessful participation and will result in a failing score for that proficiency testing survey and administrative action up to and including revocation of licensure, as provided in section 59A-24.006 (12), F.A.C.

8. Failure to participate in any proficiency testing survey is considered unsuccessful participation and will result in a failing score for that proficiency testing survey and administrative action up to and including revocation of licensure as provided in section 59A-24.006 (12), F.A.C.

9. The laboratory shall be permitted to request that the agency supply additional proficiency testing samples to be tested to document whether the source of unsuccessful proficiency testing performance has been corrected. The agency shall permit no more than two such additional shipments of proficiency testing samples. The laboratory will be required to pay the cost of such samples.

10. In addition to the proficiency testing requirements, any licensed laboratory shall be subject to blind performance testing by the agency. Blind performance testing means proficiency test samples which are shipped to a laboratory in a manner such that the samples appear to be actual drug testing samples.

(b) Initial Licensure.Laboratories applying for initial licensure shall be required to successfully complete three proficiency testing surveys supplied by the agency before the laboratory is eligible to be considered for licensure.

1. Two of these proficiency testing surveys shall be completed prior to the initial inspection of the laboratory.

2. The third proficiency testing survey shall be provided so that it arrives prior to the initial inspection. These samples will be analyzed in conjunction with the on-site inspection as directed by the agency.

3. Evaluation of initial proficiency testing surveys shall be in accordance with the requirements set forth in section 59A-24.006 (11)(c)3., F.A.C.

4. Any initial applicant whose proficiency testing evaluation does not meet the requirements of section 59A-24.006 (11)(c)3., F.A.C., on any of the three initial proficiency testing surveys shall automatically be disqualified for licensure. To be considered for future licensure, the laboratory must reapply for licensure and must submit the required licensure fee as a new applicant.

(c) Continued Licensure.In order to remain licensed, the laboratory shall participate in four proficiency testing surveys per year. The laboratory must participate in 3 non-agency proficiency testing surveys supplied by an approved proficiency testing organization as defined in section 59A-24.003 (3), F.A.C., and 1 annual proficiency testing survey supplied by the agency as described below. Failure to meet the applicable grading criteria found in section 59A-24.006 (11)(c)3., F.A.C., shall be considered unsuccessful proficiency testing participation. The agency shall revoke or suspend the laboratory's license or take no further action, taking into consideration the potential for such errors to affect the reporting of reliable drug test results.

1. Non-Agency Supplied Proficiency Testing.

a. Three of the four required proficiency testing surveys shall be obtained at the laboratory's expense from an approved proficiency testing provider, as defined in section 59A-24.003 (3), F.A.C.

b. Proficiency testing results from the approved non-agency providers shall be graded using the grading criteria required in section 59A-24.006 (11)(c)3., F.A.C.

c. The laboratory shall submit the reports of non-agency supplied proficiency testing results and any corrective action taken with regards to unsuccessful results within 14 working days of their receipt in the laboratory.

2. Agency Supplied Proficiency Testing.The remaining proficiency testing survey shall be supplied by the agency and shall be shipped to the laboratory at any time during the licensure year.

3. In order to obtain initial licensure or to remain licensed, the laboratory must meet the following criteria for successful participation on any proficiency testing shipment:

a. Report no false positive drug identifications.

b. Correctly screen 90 percent of the samples in each proficiency testing survey.

c. Achieve a combined score of 90 percent for screening and confirmation testing.

d. Correctly confirm 90 percent of the drug challenges for proficiency samples that screen as positive.

e. For all proficiency samples screened as positive, quantitate 80 percent of all drug challenges at ± 20 percent of the group mean.

f. Detect and quantitate 50 percent of the total drug challenges for any individual drug or drug classes.

g. Submit the results of agency supplied proficiency testing surveys no more than 10 working days from receipt of the samples by the laboratory.

h. Submit any remedial action taken in regard to proficiency testing errors found in agency supplied proficiency testing samples within five days of such notification by the agency.

4. Consequences of Unsuccessful Proficiency Testing Performance.

a. Failure to achieve successful proficiency

testing performance as described in section 59A-24.006 (11), F.A.C., shall result in administrative action up to and including revocation of licensure as provided in section 59A-24.006 (12), F.A.C.

b. In the event that a laboratory's license is suspended due to unsatisfactory proficiency testing performance, re-instatement of licensure shall not be considered until the laboratory can demonstrate:

i. Satisfactory performance on no more than 2 agency supplied proficiency surveys;

ii. That the source of unsuccessful proficiency testing performance has been corrected; and

iii. That payment for any additional proficiency testing samples supplied by the agency has been received.

(12) Administrative Enforcement and Hearings.

(a) The agency shall enforce the provisions of section 112.0455, F.S., and Chapter 59A-24, F.A.C., by administering remedies for statutory and rule violations as provided in section 112.0455 (14), F.S.

(b) Whenever the agency has reason to believe that immediate action is necessary in order to protect the interests of an employer, employee, or job applicant, the agency shall immediately suspend or revoke a laboratory's license to conduct drug testing.

(c) Grounds for Disciplinary Action.The following actions shall result in the agency taking administrative action:

1. Failure to accurately analyze and report donor drug tests;

2. Unsuccessful participation in proficiency testing surveys;

3. A violation of a licensure standard;

4. Participation in a pretrial intervention or other first-offender agreement respecting a charge of, the entering of a plea of nolo contendere or guilty to a charge of, a finding of guilt regardless of adjudication of, or a conviction or any criminal offense under federal law or the law of any state relating to the operation of any laboratory;

5. Making a fraudulent statement on an application for a forensic toxicology license or any other document required by the agency;

6. Permitting unauthorized persons to perform technical procedures or issue reports;

7. Demonstrating incompetence or making consistent errors in the performance and reporting of drug free workplace testing or proficiency testing samples;

8. Performing a test and rendering a report thereon to a person not authorized by law to receive such services;

9. Knowingly having professional connection with or knowingly lending the use of the name of the licensed forensic toxicology laboratory or the license of the director to an unlicensed forensic toxicology laboratory;

10. Violating or aiding and abetting in the violation of any provision of this part or the rules promulgated hereunder;

11. Failing to file any report required by the provisions of this part or the rules promulgated hereunder;

12. Reporting a drug test result when no such test was performed;

13. Knowingly advertising false services or credentials;

14. Failure to correct deficiencies within the time required by the agency;

15. Failing to maintain a secured area for toxicology tests; or

16. Any other cause which affects the ability of the laboratory to ensure the full reliability and accuracy of drug tests and the accurate reporting of results.

17. Failure to submit statistical reports as required in section 59A-24.009 (3), F.A.C.

(d) Hearings.All administrative hearings shall be in accordance with Chapter 120, F.S., and applicable rules and regulations. Those proceedings brought in the circuit courts of Florida to enjoin or restrain the unlawful operation of a forensic laboratory without a valid license under section 112.0455, F.S., shall be governed by section 112.0455, F.S., and the Florida Rules of Civil Procedure.

(13) Re-instatement of Licensure.Upon the submission of evidence to the agency that the laboratory is in compliance with this rule chapter and section 112.0455, F.S., and any other conditions imposed as part of a suspension, the agency shall reinstate the laboratory's license. A laboratory having its license revoked shall be required to reapply for licensure in accordance with the provisions for initial applicants and pay the applicable licensure fee.

(14) Licensure Fee.

(a) Laboratories seeking licensure must complete licensure application form, AHCA Form 3170-5001 July 95, which is hereby incorporated by reference. This form is available from the agency.

1. Initial and annual licensure renewal fees shall be $8,000 and shall be made payable to the agency.

2. For late filing of an application for renewal, the provisions of section 112.0455 (17), F.S., shall apply.

(b) Refunds are authorized pursuant to provisions of section 215.26, F.S., and shall be approved only in the following instances:

1. an overpayment of a fee;

2. a payment where no fee is due; and

3. any payment made into the State Treasury in error.

(c) Applications for refunds shall be filed with the Comptroller within 3 years from the date of the payment into the State Treasury, or else such right shall be barred. Refund claims shall not otherwise be barred under the laws of this state.

(15) Statistical Information Reporting.

(a) The laboratory shall submit statistical information on drug testing to the agency. No statistical information reported to the agency shall reveal the names of the persons tested, nor shall it reveal the employer's identity. This data shall contain the following information on specimens received for all drug testing conducted under section 112.0455, F.S.:

1. The total number of specimens received for testing.

2. The total number of specimens that tested positive on the initial screening.

3. The total number of specimens that were confirmed and reported as positive for each drug class tested.

4. The total number of samples that were received but not tested.

(b) Statistical summaries shall be submitted to the agency on a monthly basis no later than 14 working days after the end of a reporting month. Reporting is required even if no Florida Drug Free Workplace testing has been done for that reporting month.

(c) Failure of a laboratory to submit the statistical reports as authorized in section 112.0455 (12)(c), F.S., shall result in administrative action pursuant to section 59A-24.006 (12)(a), F.A.C.

Specific Authority 112.0455(12)(c), (13)(a) Fla. Stat.

Law Implemented 112.0455 Fla. Stat.

History: New 3-15-90, Amended 6-28-91, Formerly 10E-18.006, Amended 5-1-96, 12-5-96, 3-11-98, 3-29-00.

59A-24.007. Confidentiality.

Specific Authority 112.0455(11)(a) Fla. Stat.

Law Implemented 112.0455 Fla. Stat.

History: New 3-15-90, Repromulgated 6-28-91, Formerly 10E-18.007, Repealed 5-1-96.

59A-24.008. Review of Test Results.

Prior to the transmission of test results to the employer, both positive and negative test results shall be reviewed and verified by a medical review officer (MRO) qualified under subsection 59A-24.008 (1), F.A.C. The MRO is permitted to use a language interpreter to assist in communicating the results of drug tests with employees and job applicants. Such language interpreters are subject to the confidentiality provisions of Section 112.0455 (11), F.S. After the results have been reviewed and verified by the MRO, the test result is reported to the employer.

(1) Qualifications of Medical Review Officers.

(a) Persons serving as medical review officers shall be medical or osteopathic physicians duly licensed in the state in which he or she practices medicine.

(b) The MRO shall have knowledge of substance abuse disorders, laboratory testing procedures, chain of custody procedures, collection procedures, and have the appropriate medical training to interpret and evaluate an individual's drug test result together with the individual's medical history or any other biomedical information.

(c) Beginning January 1, 1998, medical review officers shall be certified as medical review officers by the American Association of Medical Review Officers, American Society of Addiction Medicine or the American College of Occupational and Environmental Medicine.

(d) The MRO shall be employed by or contracted by the employer and shall not be employed or contracted by a drug testing laboratory performing drug free workplace testing under section 112.0455, F.S. The drug testing laboratory is permitted to assist the employer in locating qualified medical review officers.

(e) An employer shall not serve as the MRO for his or her own employees and job applicants.

(2) Responsibilities of Medical Review Officer.The MRO shall evaluate the drug test result(s), which is reported out by the laboratory, to verify by checking the chain of custody form that the specimen was collected, transported, and analyzed under proper procedures, as specified in these rules, and to determine if any alternative medical explanations caused a positive test result. This determination could include conducting a medical interview with the individual, review of the individual's medical history, or the review of any other relevant biomedical factors. The MRO shall review all medical records made available by the tested individual. The MRO shall not consider the results of samples that are not obtained or processed in accordance with these rules.

(a) Negative Results.To verify that a negative test result was properly analyzed and handled according to these rules, the MRO shall:

1. Receive and review the test result(s) from the laboratory;

2. Verify the laboratory report by checking the chain of custody form for required signatures, procedures, and information.

3. Ensure that the donors specimen identification number on copy 2 of the laboratory test report and on copy 4 of the chain of custody form which was sent to the MRO by the collection site accurately identifies the donor with the negative test result; and

4. Notify the employer in writing of the negative test result no more than 7 working days after the specimen was received by the laboratory, and appropriately file copy 2 and 4 of the chain of custody form under confidential procedures for a period of 2 years.

5. Within 24 hours of notification of the employer of a negative test result, notify the testing laboratory that the negative test result has been submitted to the employer.

(b) Positive Results.To verify that a positive test result was properly analyzed and handled according to these rules, the MRO shall:

1. Receive and review the test result(s) from the laboratory;

2. Verify the laboratory report by checking the chain of custody form for required signatures, procedures, and information.

3. Ensure that the donor's specimen identification number on copy 2 of the laboratory test report and on copy 4 of the chain of custody form which was sent to the MRO by the collection site accurately identifies the donor

with the positive test result;

4. Notify the employee or job applicant of a confirmed positive test result, within 3 days of receipt of the test result from the laboratory, and inquire as to whether prescriptive or over-the-counter medications could have caused the positive test result;

5. Within 5 days of notification to the donor of the positive test result, provide an opportunity for employee or job applicant to discuss the positive test result and to submit documentation of any prescriptions relevant to the positive test result;

6. Review any medical records provided by the employee or job applicant, or authorized by the employee or job applicant and released by the individual's physician, to determine if the positive test result was caused by a legally prescribed medication. If the donor does not have prescribed medication, the MRO shall inquire about over-the-counter medications which could have caused the positive test result. The donor shall be responsible for providing all necessary documentation, (i.e., a doctor's report, signed prescription, etc.) within the 5 day period after notification of the positive test result;

7. Notify the employer in writing of the verified test result, either negative, positive, or unsatisfactory, no more than 7 working days after the specimen was received by the laboratory, and appropriately file the chain of custody form under confidential procedures for 2 years;

8. If the MRO determines that there is a legitimate medical explanation for the positive test result, based on the medical judgment of the MRO and accepted standards of practice, the MRO shall report a negative test result to the employer.

9. Process any employee or job applicant requests for a retest of the original specimen, within 180 days of notice of the positive test result, at another licensed laboratory selected by the employee or job applicant. The donor requesting the additional test shall be required to pay for the costs of the retest, including handling and shipping expenses. The MRO shall contact the original testing laboratory to initiate the retest.

10. The MRO shall not declare a confirmed positive as verified, until the MRO receives copy 2 of the chain of custody form from the drug testing laboratory and copy 4 from the collection site.

(3) Chain of Custody Procedures.A strict chain of custody procedure, initiated at the time of specimen collection, is mandatory for the validation of any test result. The MRO shall be responsible, before reporting either positive or negative test result(s) to the employer, to review all signatures, procedures, and information as required on the chain of custody form to determine that the specimen was under authorized control both before and during laboratory analysis. If proper chain of custody procedures have not been followed, the MRO shall declare the test result as unsatisfactory, due to an unacceptable chain of custody procedure.

(4) Verification for Opiates.Before a positive test for opiates is verified, the MRO shall determine that there is clinical evidence in addition to the urine test, of illegal use of any opium, opiate, or opium derivative (e.g., morphine/codeine). This requirement does not apply if the GC/MS confirmation test for opiates confirms the presence of 6-monoacetylmorphine.

(5) Reanalysis Authorized.Should any question arise as to the accuracy or validity of a test result which has been collected and analyzed in accordance with these rules, the MRO may order a reanalysis of the original sample at any licensed laboratory licensed under these rules.

(6) Scientifically Unsatisfactory Results.The MRO, based on a review of the chain of custody form, quality control data, multiple samples and other pertinent results, is permitted to determine that the result is scientifically unsatisfactory for further action and may request the donor to provide another sample or request a reanalysis of the original sample before making such decision. The MRO is permitted to request that the reanalysis be performed by the same laboratory or, that an aliquot of the original specimen be sent to another licensed laboratory. The

laboratory shall assist in this review process as requested by the MRO and shall make available appropriate personnel to provide consultation as required by the MRO. The MRO shall report all findings based on the unsatisfactory specimen, as required by this rule chapter, but shall not include any personal identifying information in such reports.

(7) Contacting Donors Who Test Positive.

(a) If the MRO is unable to contact a donor who tested positive within 3 working days of receipt of the test results from the laboratory, the MRO shall contact the employer and request that the employer direct the donor to contact the MRO as soon as possible. If the MRO has not been contacted by the donor within 2 working days from the request to the employer, the MRO shall verify the report as positive.

(b) As a safeguard to employees and job applicants, once a MRO verifies a positive test result, the MRO may change the verification of the result if the donor presents information to the MRO which documents that a serious illness, injury, or other circumstance unavoidably prevented the employee from contacting the MRO within the specified time frame and if the donor presents information concerning a legitimate explanation for the positive test result.

(c) If the donor declines to talk with the MRO regarding a positive test result, the MRO shall validate the result as positive and annotate such decline in the remarks section.

(8) Identification of Donor.Prior to providing an employee or job applicant with the opportunity to discuss a test result, the MRO shall confirm the identity of the employee or job applicant. At a minimum, to confirm the identity of the donor, the MRO shall ask the donor to respond with the following information:

(a) If the request is in person, the MRO shall request a picture identification.

(b) If the request is over the telephone, the MRO shall request:

1. An employee identification number or social security number;

2. Date of birth;

3. Employer's name; and

4. Work telephone number.

(9) Information for Donor.Once the donor's identification has been established, and before any additional information is solicited from the donor, the MRO shall:

(a) Inform the donor that the MRO is an agent of the employer whose responsibility is to make a determination on test results and report them to the employer;

(b) Inform the donor that medical information revealed during the MRO's inquiry will be kept confidential; unless the donor is in a safety sensitive or special risk position and the MRO believes that such information is relevant to the safety of the donor or to other employees. Any additional release of information shall be solely pursuant to a written consent form signed voluntarily by the donor, except where such release is compelled by a hearing officer or a court of competent jurisdiction pursuant to an appeal, or where deemed appropriate by a professional or occupational licensing board in a related disciplinary proceeding.

(c) Outline the rights and procedures for a retest of the original specimen by the donor.

(d) If the donor voluntarily admits to the use of the drug in question without a proper prescription, the MRO shall advise the donor that a verified positive test report will be sent to the employer.

(10) Verification Signature.After the MRO reviews the chain of custody forms from the laboratory and the collection site (copy 2 from the laboratory and copy 4 from the collection site) and, in the case of a positive test result, has contacted the donor who tested positive, the MRO shall:

(a) On copy 2 of the chain of custody form, mark the appropriate box if the verified result is positive or negative and if positive, write in for which drug(s). If the test was not performed or the test was canceled, mark the appropriate box. The reason for the cancellation or non-performance of the test shall be explained in the remarks section.

(b) On copy 2 of the chain of custody form, sign and date the verification of the final test result.

(c) Prepare and sign a verification letter to the employer revealing the final verified test result. Copies of the laboratory report form or chain of custody are not suitable for this purpose.

Specific Authority 112.0455(13)(a) Fla. Stat.

Law Implemented 112.0455 Fla. Stat.

History: New 6-28-91, Formerly 10E-18.008, Amended 5-1-96, 3-11-98, 2-3-05.

59A-24.009. Statistical Information Reporting.

Specific Authority 112.0455(12)(c) Fla. Stat.

Law Implemented 112.0455 Fla. Stat.

History: New 6-28-91, Formerly 10E-18.009, Amended 5-1-96, Repealed 12-4-96.

CHAPTER 59A-29 Health Care Provider Certification

59A-29.001. Definitions.

(1) "Application" means form DWC-97 required by this rule chapter to be submitted by health care providers to the Division. The DWC-97 application form is incorporated into this rule chapter by reference in rule 38F-53.002 (1), F.A.C.

(2) "Certification training course" is a training and education course approved by the Division to satisfy the minimum five hour course required by section 440.13 (3)(a), Florida Statutes.

(3) "Certified health care provider" is defined in section 440.13 (1)(e), Florida Statutes.

(4) "Certify" is the process through which the Division grants or denies certification status to a health care provider.

(5) "Decertification" means Division revocation of certification.

(6) "Division" is defined in s. 440.02 (12), Florida Statutes.

(7) "Emergency services and care" is defined in section 440.13 (1)(g), Florida Statutes.

(8) "Health care facility" is defined in section 440.13 (1)(h), Florida Statutes.

(9) "Health care provider" is defined in section 440.13 (1)(i), Florida Statutes.

(10) "Non-physician health care provider" means a health care provider licensed pursuant to the Florida Statutes, who is not a physician as defined in section 440.13 (1)(r), Florida Statutes, and who bills for services rendered on form DWC-9 pursuant to rule 38F-7.602, F.A.C.

(11) "Occasional provider" means a health care provider who treats 12 or fewer injured employees in one calendar year.

(12) "Physician" is defined in section 440.13 (1)(r), Florida Statutes.

(13) "Suspension" means Division action to bar for a specified period of time a health care provider's eligibility to receive reimbursement for services rendered under chapter 440, Florida Statutes.

Specific Authority 440.13(3)(a), 440.591 Fla. Stat.

Law Implemented 440.13(3), 440.13(13) Fla. Stat.

History: New 3-14-95, Formerly 38F-53.001.

59A-29.002. Requirements for Certification.

(1) The Division shall certify health care providers who meet the following requirements:

(a) The health care provider holds a valid license issued by the Florida Agency for Health Care Administration or the Department of Business and Professional Regulation, or a Florida medical school teaching certificate pursuant to sections 458.3145, 459.0077, 463.0057 or 466.002, Florida Statutes, or a temporary certificate in an area of critical need pursuant to section 458.315, Florida Statutes.

(b) The health care provider has submitted a signed, typed, and completed application form DWC-97 to the Division of Workers' Compensation, Bureau of Rehabilitation and Medical Services, Provider Relations Section, 2728 Centerview Drive, 100 Forrest Building, Tallahassee, Florida 32399-0664. Illegible or unsigned applications shall be returned. The DWC-97 application form is incorporated by reference into rule chapter 38F-53, F.A.C. The version of the form required to be submitted to the Division shall bear the date October 15, 1994. A copy of the application form DWC-97 may be obtained from the Division.

(c) Physicians shall enroll in and complete a minimum 5 hour Division approved training course, pursuant to 440.13 (3)(a), Florida Statutes. The Division shall not credit a physician for completion of any training course to meet the requirements of section 440.13 (3)(a), Florida Statutes, prior to the date the Division approves the training course for credit.

(2) The Division shall not certify a health care provider when:

(a) The Agency for Health Care Administration has entered an adverse final order imposing an administrative penalty, which revokes or suspends the health care provider's license, or places the health care provider on probation, or the health care provider agrees to such an administrative penalty, within twelve months preceding the date of filing of the application form DWC-97; or

(b) The Division has entered an adverse final order imposing an administrative penalty or fine against the health care provider within twelve months preceding the date of filing of the application form DWC-97; or

(c) The health care provider has been suspended three times pursuant to rule 38F-53.006 (5), F.A.C.

(3) The following are not required to be certified in order to provide services pursuant to section 440.13, Florida Statutes:

(a) Health care providers rendering emergency services and care.

(b) Pharmacists licensed under chapter 465, Florida Statutes.

(c) Medical suppliers who bill on the DWC-10.

(d) Health care providers of medical services rendered outside the State of Florida.

(e) Federal health care providers.

(f) Health care facilities, except that physicians and non-physician health care providers employed as health care providers must be certified under this rule as a condition to eligibility for payment under chapter 440, Florida Statutes.

Specific Authority 440.13(3)(a), 440.591 Fla. Stat.
Law Implemented 440.13(3), 440.13(13) Fla. Stat.
History: New 3-14-95, Formerly 38F-53.002.

59A-29.003. Certification Time Frames.

The Division shall certify health care providers within the following time frames:

(1) Upon the effective date of this rule, the Division shall accept applications for certification from physicians. Within 90 days of receipt of an application for certification, the Division shall return to the physician a notice of approval or denial of certification, or shall request additional required information not previously submitted, and shall state the reasons for denial of certification. The Division shall maintain the original application form DWC-97 in its files. Physicians, as a condition to eligibility for payment under chapter 440, Florida Statutes, shall be certified within 12 months of the effective date of this rule.

(2) Beginning 12 months following the effective date of this rule, the Division shall accept applications for certification from non-physician health care providers. Within 90 days of receipt of an application for certification, the Division shall return to the non-physician health care provider a notice of approval or denial of certification, and shall request additional required information not previously submitted, or shall state the reasons for denial of certification. The Division shall maintain the original application form DWC-97 in its files. Non-physician health care providers, as a condition to eligibility for payment under chapter 440, Florida Statutes, shall be certified within 24 months of the effective date of this rule.

Specific Authority 440.13(3)(a), 440.591 Fla. Stat.

Law Implemented 440.13(3), 440.13(13) Fla. Stat.

History: New 3-14-95, Formerly 38F-53.003.

59A-29.004. Occasional Health Care Providers.

(1) An occasional health care provider shall meet the following requirements in order to provide services under section 440.13, Florida Statutes:

(a) Treat twelve or fewer injured employees annually in the calendar year before and after the date that the health care provider submits application form DWC-97 to the Division.

(b) Meet the requirements of rule 38F-53.002 (1)(a) and (b), F.A.C. Occasional health care providers are not required to meet the requirements of rule 38F-53.002 (1)(c), F.A.C., but are encourage by the Division to do so. Anesthesiologists, radiologists, and pathologists licensed under chapter 458, or chapter 459, Florida Statutes, and who do not and will not submit preliminary notices of injury or treatment plans to a carrier under section 440.13 (4)(a), Florida Statutes, are not required to meet the requirements of rule 38F-53.002 (1)(c), F.A.C., but are encouraged by the Division to do so.

(c) Not be ineligible for certification pursuant to rule 38F-53.002 (2), F.A.C.

(d) Not be decertified pursuant to Rule 38F-53.006 (5), F.A.C.

(2) Occasional health care providers shall comply with all provisions of chapter 440, Florida Statutes, and all administrative rules adopted by the Division.

Specific Authority 440.13(3)(a), 440.591 Fla. Stat.

Law Implemented 440.13(3), 440.13(13) Fla. Stat.

History: New 3-14-95, Formerly 38F-53.004.

59A-29.005. Decertification of a Health Care Provider.

(1) Pursuant to section 440.13 (13), Florida Statutes, the Division shall suspend and remove health care providers from its database of certified health care providers, upon the following:

(a) When the Division enters an adverse final order against the health care provider imposing an administrative fine or penalty upon the health care provider for violations of chapter 440, Florida Statutes, or the administrative rules adopted by the Division; or

(b) When the Agency for Health Care Administration has entered an adverse final order imposing an administrative penalty, which revokes or suspends the health care provider's license, or places the health care provider on probation, or the health care provider agrees to such an administrative penalty.

(2) When a health care provider is suspended or decertified, the health care provider shall notify each carrier from whom he/she has received authorization to treat an injured employee. The carrier shall transfer the care of the injured employee to another certified health care provider.

Specific Authority 440.13(3)(a), 440.591 Fla. Stat.

Law Implemented 440.13(3), 440.13(13) Fla. Stat.

History: New 3-14-95, Formerly 38F-53.005.

59A-29.006. Decertification Process.

(1) The Division shall review a health care provider's certification to determine whether suspension or decertification is required when requested to do so in writing.

(2) All requests to the Division to review a health care provider's certification shall be submitted in writing to the Division. Documentation necessary to substantiate the perceived need for Division review shall accompany the request. Anonymous requests shall not be reviewed. Reports and documentation, except for violations addressed by section 440.13 (8), Florida Statutes, shall be sent to the following address: Division of Workers' Compensation, Bureau of Rehabilitation and Medical Services, Provider Relations Section, 2728 Centerview Drive, 100 Forrest Building, Tallahassee, Florida 32399-0664.

(3) When, upon review of all submitted documentation, the Division finds that a health care provider has engaged in or committed any of the actions set out in rule 38F-53.005 (1), F.A.C., the Division shall suspend certification of that

health care provider for a length of time to be determined as follows:

(a) When suspension of certification is based upon rule 38F-53.005 (1)(a), F.A.C., the duration of suspension shall be:

1. 12 months for one of the violations established in section 440.13 (13)(a) through (f);

2. 24 months for multiple violations of section 440.13 (a) through (f);

(b) When suspension of certification is based upon rule 38F-53.005 (1)(b), F.A.C., the duration of suspension shall be equal to and run concurrently with the duration of revocation, suspension, or probation imposed by the Agency for Health Care Administration, or agreed to by the health care provider.

(4) When a health care provider is suspended a second time, the Division shall revoke certification for a period of time, twice as long in duration as the first period of suspension.

(5) When a health care provider is suspended a third time, the heatlh care provider shall be decertified and shall not be eligible to become recertified.

(6) Suspension and decertification of health care providers for violations of sections 440.13 (8) and 440.13 (13)(g), Florida Statutes, shall be for the duration of time set forth in administrative rules adopted by the Division pursuant to sections 440.13 (8) and 440.13 (13)(g).

Specific Authority 440.13(3)(a), 440.591 Fla. Stat.

Law Implemented 440.13(3), 440.13(8), 440.13(13) Fla. Stat.

History: New 3-14-95, Formerly 38F-53.006.

59A-29.007. Recertification Process.

(1) When the Division suspends a health care provider, the health care provider may apply for recertification upon completion of the following:

(a) Completion of the period of suspension; and

(b) Submission of a current application to the Division; and

(c) Completion of a repeat certification training course.

(2) When a health care provider's license has been revoked, suspended, or the health care provider has been placed on probation, by the Agency for Health Care Administration, proof of reinstatement shall be submitted with the health care provider's request for recertification.

Specific Authority 440.13(3)(a), 440.591 Fla. Stat.

Law Implemented 440.13(3), 440.13(13) Fla. Stat.

History: New 3-14-95, Formerly 38F-53.007.

59A-29.008. Determining Certification Status.

(1) When a carrier or an agent of the carrier requests the certification status of a health care provider, the health care provider shall provide proof of current certification before being authorized to render care. A copy of the notice of approval of certification issued by the Division to the health care provider may be used as proof of current certification.

(2) The Division shall maintain on a quarterly basis a list of health care providers suspended or decertified and the duration of suspension.

(3) The Division shall respond to written requests for certification status within sixty days of receipt of the request. The request shall provide the full name, license number, and mailing address of each health care provider for whom certification status is being requested. No request for certification status shall be answered over the telephone or accepted by facsimile transmission.

Specific Authority 440.13(3)(a), 440.591 Fla. Stat.

Law Implemented 440.13(3), 440.13(13) Fla. Stat.

History: New 3-14-95, Formerly 38F-53.008.

59A-29.009. Carrier Responsibilities.

(1) Beginning 12 months following the effective date of this rule, a carrier shall authorize only certified health care providers to provide services to injured employees.

(2) A carrier shall transfer the care of an injured employee from the care of a suspended or decertified health care provider to the care of

a certified health care provider.

Specific Authority 440.13(3)(a), 440.591 Fla. Stat.

Law Implemented 440.13(3), 440.13(13) Fla. Stat.

History: New 3-14-95, Formerly 38F-53.009.

59A-29.010. Health Care Provider Responsibilities.

Health care providers shall notify the Division in writing of any change in the status of that health care provider's license, or mailing address within 10 days of such change. Such changes shall be sent to: Division of Workers' Compensation, Bureau of Rehabilitation and Medical Services, Providers Relations Section, 2728 Centerview Drive, 100 Forrest Building, Tallahassee, Florida 32399-0664.

Specific Authority 440.13(3)(a), 440.591 Fla. Stat.

Law Implemented 440.13(3), 440.13(13) Fla. Stat.

History: New 3-14-95, Formerly 38F-53.010.

59A-29.011. Workers' Compensation Certification Training Courses.

(1) All certification training courses offered to health care providers to meet the requirements of section 440.13 (3)(a), Florida Statutes, shall be submitted for, and receive, Division approval prior to the presentation of the course.

(2) To receive Division approval, a training course must be a minimum of five (5) hours and must address the following:

(a) Cost containment; and

(b) Ergonomics; and

(c) Practice parameters governing the physician's field of practice; and

(d) Utilization control; and

(e) Return to work.

(3) The Division's certification training course outline contains those components required to be included in each certification training course.

(4) Within 120 days of receipt of a training course proposal the Division shall notify the vendor in writing that the course is approved, specify the additional requirements needed for course approval, or deny approval. No training proposals submitted to the Division for approval shall be returned.

(5) A certification training course approved by the Division shall maintain its course approval status for three (3) years unless the approval is revoked. When a vendor intends to offer the course after the expiration date, the course must be resubmitted.

(6) Section 440.13, Florida Statutes, as well as any revisions or amendments to section 440.13, and Division adopted administrative rules shall be included in all certification courses. Notification of course adjustments shall be made through a Division bulletin.

(7) In order for a certification training course to be approved, the following shall be submitted to the Division as part of the proposed training course:

(a) Name and credentials of instructor(s) or author(s) and copy of license, if applicable, and documentation substantiating the qualifications of the instructor(s). Credentials of at least one substitute instructor(s) per area of instruction must also be included. Instructors must have:

1. Professional license in a health care or related field and 10 years experience in the area in which licensed to practice; or 5 years experience in workers' compensation or safety; or 3 years experience in the specific area of cost containment, ergonomics, practice parameters, or utilization control; or

2. Professional license in a health care or related field and be a current employee of the Agency for Health Care Administration, the Division of Safety, or the Division of Workers' Compensation.

(b) Syllabus and outline of course content including time frames for each component and schedules for any breaks or meals included in the presentation. If audio-visual materials are to be utilized, a qualified and approved instructor must be present, during the audio-visual presentation, to answer questions on the subject matter presented.

(c) Copy of course completion certificate

which shall include name of vendor, instructor(s), date and location of course.

(d) Copies of all texts, brochures, audio-visuals and all other course materials and hand-outs that will be utilized during the course presentation.

(e) The certification training course outline developed by the Division and the Certification Taskforce is hereby incorporated into this rule chapter by reference and shall be distributed to the participants of certification training courses approved by the Division. A copy of the certification training course outline is available from the Division of Workers' Compensation, Bureau of Rehabilitation and Medical Services, Provider Relations Section, 2728 Centerview Drive, Suite 100, Forrest Building, Tallahassee, Florida 32399-0664. The version of certification training course outline required by this rule to be distributed shall bear the date October 15, 1994.

(8) No later than one (1) month prior to offering an approved course, a vendor shall notify the Division in writing of the date(s) and location(s) (city, name of facility) of each course offering. Point of contact and telephone number shall be included. Printed information to be used for promotional or publicity purposes is sufficient to meet the requirements of this paragraph, provided all required information is set forth.

(9) The vendor or certification training course instructor shall send to the Division within ten (10) business days following course completion a roster of attenders including the name, license number, address, telephone number and specialty of each participant. Each participant must sign his/her name next to their typed or computer printed name. The roster must identify the vendor, as well as the date, time, place of the course, and name(s) of instructor(s).

(10) The Division shall monitor and audit approved courses on dates that such courses are presented in order to ensure the quality and content of such courses.

(11) For the purposes of meeting the requirements of section 440.13 (3)(a), Florida Statutes, health care providers shall not receive credit for attending a course prior to the date that the Division approves such course.

(12) The Division shall revoke its approval of a certification training course for any one of the following grounds:

(a) Substitution of course instructor(s) without prior Division approval.

(b) Elimination of course components which were approved by the Division as part of the training course.

(c) Falsification of any course completion record or other document related to the course.

(d) Failure to send a completed roster to the Division as required by paragraph (9) of this rule.

(13) A certification training course that has had its approval revoked shall not be reconsidered for Division approval for a period of no less than six (6) months from the date of notification of revocation. After the six (6) month waiting period, the course may be resubmitted following the requirements set forth in this rule. Proof of corrected deficiencies shall be submitted.

(14) The Division shall not reapprove a course if Division revocation is based upon a violation of paragraph (12)(c) of this rule.

Specific Authority 440.13(3)(a), 440.591 Fla. Stat.
Law Implemented 440.13(3), 440.13(13) Fla. Stat.

History: New 3-14-95, Formerly 38F-53.011.

CHAPTER 59A-30 Expert Medical Advisors

59A-30.002 Definitions.

For purposes of this rule the following definitions apply:

(1) "Board certification" or "board certified" means the physician has been awarded board certification or diplomate status by the American Board of Medical Specialties, American Board of Internal Medicine, American Board of Physician Specialties, American Osteopathic Association, American Board of General Dentistry, American Board of Podiatric Orthopedics and Primary Podiatric Medicine, American Board of Podiatric Surgery, American Chiropractic Rehabilitation Board, American Chiropractic Neurol-

ogy Board, American Board of Chiropractic Internists, American Chiropractic Board of Nutrition, American Chiropractic Board of Occupational Health, American Board of Chiropractic Orthopedists, American Board of Chiropractic Radiology, or American Chiropractic Board of Sports Physicians.

(2) "Board eligible" or "board eligibility" means the physician has been recognized by the applicable national-specialty board as eligible to take the board certification examination.

Specific Authority 440.13(9), 440.591 Fla. Stat.
Law Implemented 440.13(9) Fla. Stat.

History: New 1-23-95, Formerly 38F-54.002, Amended 10-11-06.

59A-30.003 Qualifications for Expert Medical Advisor Certification.

To be certified as an Expert Medical Advisor, a physician shall meet the following qualifications:

(1) Must have been certified as a health care provider by the Agency pursuant to Chapter 59A-29, F.A.C., for a period of not less than twelve months prior to the date of the Expert Medical Advisor application; and

(2) Must hold valid licensure, issued by the Florida Department of Health, with "clear and active" status; and

(3) Must hold specialty-board certification or specialty-board eligibility applicable to the specialty for which the applicant seeks certification. If the applicable national-specialty board does not recognize "board eligible" or "board eligibility" status, the applicant must hold board certification for the specialty; and

(4) Must demonstrate experience in the assignment of permanent impairment ratings greater than zero (0%) to Florida's injured employees, pursuant to Rule 69L-7.604, F.A.C., within the two-year period immediately preceding the date of application; and

(5) Must demonstrate experience in performing independent medical examinations pursuant to Sections 440.13(2) or 440.13(5), Florida Statutes, within the two-year period immediately preceding the date of application; and

(6) Must have completed twenty hours of continuing medical education, specifically related to the practitioner's field of specialty, within the two-year period immediately preceding the date of application. Completion of courses required for licensure by the Florida Department of Health addressing Domestic Violence, HIV-AIDS and Prevention of Medical Errors will not be applied to the medical continuing education requirements for Expert Medical Advisor certification; and

(7) Must possess knowledge of the Florida Statutes related to workers' compensation, specifically Sections 440.02, 440.09, 440.093, 440.102, 440.105, 440.13, 440.134, 440.15(3), 440.15(5), 440.151, 440.20 and 440.491; and possess knowledge of the Florida Administrative Code Rules 69L-7.602 and 69L-7.020 related to workers' compensation.

Specific Authority 440.13(9), 440.591 Fla. Stat.
Law Implemented 440.13(9) Fla. Stat.

History: New 1-23-95, Amended 6-8-95, Formerly 38F-54.003, Amended 10-11-06.

59A-30.004 Application for Expert Medical Advisor Certification.

(1) A physician shall apply for Expert Medical Advisor certification by submitting a signed, legible and accurately completed Expert Medical Advisor Certification Application, AHCA Form 3160-0021, to the following address: AHCA Workers' Compensation Medical Services Unit; c/o Department of Financial Services, Division of Workers' Compensation; 200 E. Gaines Street; Tallahassee, FL 32399-4232. The Expert Medical Advisor Certification Application, AHCA Form 3160-0021, revised May 2006, is incorporated by reference into Chapter 59A-30, F.A.C., and may be obtained from the AHCA Workers' Compensation Medical Services Unit; c/o Department of Financial Services, Division of Workers' Compensation's website: www.fldfs.com/wc/ forms.html#7.

(2) As part of the Expert Medical Advisor certification application, the physician shall agree to provide consultation or services in accordance with the timetables set forth in

Chapter 440, F.S., and abide by rules adopted by the Agency, including, but not limited to, rules pertaining to procedures for review of the services rendered by health care providers and preparation of reports and testimony or recommendations for submission to the Agency or judge of compensation claims.

(3) The application shall be accompanied by the following documentation to establish that the qualifications for Expert Medical Advisor certification set forth in Rule 59A-30.003, F.A.C., have been met:

(a) To document specialty-board certification or specialty-board eligibility, the applicant must submit a copy of a current certificate of national specialty-board certification or written proof of specialty-board eligibility and documentation that indicates any expiration date for specialty-board certification or specialty-board eligibility applicable to the specialty for which the applicant seeks certification.

(b) To demonstrate experience in the assignment of permanent impairment ratings to Florida's injured employees, pursuant to Rule 69L-7.604, F.A.C., the applicant must submit five completed DFS-F5-DWC-25 forms (with all patient identification redacted) indicating assignment of the date of maximum medical improvement and calculation of the permanent impairment rating greater than zero (0%) for injured employee evaluations completed within the two-year period immediately preceding the date of application; and

(c) To demonstrate experience in performing independent medical examinations pursuant to Section 440.13(2) or 440.13(5), F.S., the applicant must submit copies of five independent medical examination reports (with all patient identification redacted) written for workers' compensation injured employees within the two-year period immediately preceding the date of application; and

(d) To demonstrate completion of twenty hours of continuing medical education, specifically related to the practitioner's field of specialty, the applicant must submit copies of certificates of completion for twenty hours of continuing medical education, related to the specialty field of practice, completed within the two-year period immediately preceding the date of application. Certificates for courses required for licensure by the Florida Department of Health addressing Domestic Violence, HIV-AIDS and Prevention of Medical Errors will not be applied to the medical education requirements for Expert Medical Advisor certification; and

(4) To demonstrate knowledge of Florida Workers' Compensation, the physician must attest to knowledge of the Florida Statutes related to workers' compensation, specifically Sections 440.02, 440.09, 440.093, 440.102, 440.105, 440.13, 440.134, 440.15(3), 440.15(5), 440.151, 440.20 and 440.491, F.S.; and knowledge of the Florida Administrative Code Rules 69L-7.602 and 69L-7.020. If an Expert Medical Advisor applicant is not otherwise familiar with the statutes and rules identified above, he/she may attest to familiarity with those rules and statutes upon completion of the Workers' Compensation Health Care Provider Educational Tutorial available on the Department of Financial Services, Division of Workers' Compensation's website: www.fldfs.com/wc.

(5) The Agency will review the Expert Medical Advisor certification application, pursuant to the requirements of Section 120.60, Florida Statutes, and notify the applicant of any deficiencies in the application submitted. If the Agency does not receive, within 30-calendar days of the applicant's receipt of notice of deficiencies, information curing all deficiencies identified by the Agency, the Expert Medical Advisor Certification Application will be denied.

(6) Throughout the certification period, the Expert Medical Advisor shall notify the Agency:

(a) If specialty-board certification has expired.

(b) If Florida Department of Health license status is changed from "clear and active".

(c) Of any change in address or contact information.

(7) Expert Medical Advisor certification shall be for a period of two years. If at any time during the certification period, the physician no longer meets all qualifications for Expert Medical Advisor certification, the Expert Medical Advisor certification shall be revoked.

Specific Authority 440.13(9), 440.591 Fla. Stat.

Law Implemented 440.13(9) Fla. Stat.

History: New 1-23-95, Formerly 38F-54.004, Amended 10-11-06.

59A-30.005 Selection of Expert Medical Advisors.

(1) All individuals contracted to provide services through certification as an Expert Medical Advisor will be placed on an Agency list of certified Expert Medical Advisors eligible for selection as an Expert Medical Advisor by the Agency or a judge of compensation claims.

(2) When Expert Medical Advisor services are needed by the Agency, the Agency shall:

(a) Select an Expert Medical Advisor from the Agency's list of certified Expert Medical Advisors; and

(b) Make the necessary arrangements for the Expert Medical Advisor to provide the Expert Medical Advisor services.

(3) When Expert Medical Advisor services are needed in a proceeding before a judge of compensation claims, the judge of compensation claims shall:

(a) Select an Expert Medical Advisor from the Agency's list of certified Expert Medical Advisors; and

(b) Make the necessary arrangements for the Expert Medical Advisor to provide the Expert Medical Advisor services.

(4) Upon receiving notice of selection by the Agency or judge of compensation claims as an Expert Medical Advisor the physician shall disclose any conflict of interest related to the case for which the physician was selected and shall decline selection as an Expert Medical Advisor.

(5) A physician who has been decertified pursuant to Chapter 59A-29, F.A.C., and/or has ever been decertified pursuant to Rule 59A-30.010, F.A.C., shall not be certified as an Expert Medical Advisor.

Specific Authority 440.13(9), 440.591 Fla. Stat.

Law Implemented 440.13(9) Fla. Stat.

History: New 1-23-95, Formerly 38F-54.005, Amended 10-11-06.

59A-30.006 Temporary Expert Medical Advisors.

(1) When a judge of compensation claims needs Expert Medical Advisor services and there is no Expert Medical Advisor on the Agency's list of certified Expert Medical Advisors who meets the needs of the judge of compensation claims and is available to provide the Expert Medical Advisor services needed, the judge of compensation claims may propose a specific physician for temporary Expert Medical Advisor certification by the Agency.

(2) The Agency will certify the specific physician proposed by the judge of compensation claims as a temporary Expert Medical Advisor if one of the following is met:

(a) All parties in a proceeding before the judge of compensation claims stipulate to the qualifications of the medical-specialty-board certified physician to provide Expert Medical Advisor services in the judge of compensation claims proceeding; or

(b) The physician has a valid and active license to practice medicine, has medical specialty-board certification and the judge of compensation claims has established that the physician has training or experience applicable to the specific medical issue before the judge of compensation claims.

(3) Certification as a temporary Expert Medical Advisor shall be limited to the specific case for which the judge of compensation claims proposed the physician for temporary Expert Medical Advisor certification.

(4) A physician who has been decertified pursuant to Chapter 59A-29, F.A.C., and/or has ever been decertified pursuant to Rule 59A-30.010, F.A.C., shall not be certified as a tem-

porary Expert Medical Advisor.

(5) Upon receiving notice of selection by the judge of compensation claims as a temporary Expert Medical Advisor, the physician shall disclose any conflict of interest related to the case for which the physician was selected and shall decline selection as a temporary Expert Medical Advisor.

Specific Authority 440.13(9), 440.591 Fla. Stat.

Law Implemented 440.13(9) Fla. Stat.

History: New 1-23-95, Formerly 38F-54.006, Amended 10-11-06.

59A-30.007 Expert Medical Advisor Responsibilities.

(1) A physician shall disclose any conflict of interest upon receiving notice of selection as an Expert Medical Advisor and shall not accept selection if a conflict of interest exists. For the purposes of this rule, "conflict of interest" means that any of the following matters may exist, potentially influencing the Expert Medical Advisor's opinions and decisions while fulfilling responsibilities to evaluate the medical care provided the injured employee by the examining physician:

(a) Private, business, financial or ownership interests involving potential gain or benefit based on the outcome of the case; or

(b) Prior knowledge of the injured employee.

(2) When the judge of compensation claims selects an Expert Medical Advisor, the Expert Medical Advisor shall complete and submit a written report to the judge of compensation claims within 15-calendar days following receipt of all medical records and examination of the injured employee. The medical records, which may be submitted to an Expert Medical Advisor shall be within the discretion of the judge of compensation claims.

(3) When the Agency selects an Expert Medical Advisor, the Expert Medical Advisor shall complete and submit a written report to the Agency within 15-calendar days following receipt of all medical records.

(4) The Expert Medical Advisor shall furnish a copy of the written report to the insurer and to the injured employee pursuant to Section 440.13(9)(d), F.S.

Specific Authority 440.13(9), 440.591 Fla. Stat.

Law Implemented 440.13(9) Fla. Stat.

History: New 1-23-95, Formerly 38F-54.007, Amended 10-11-06.

59A-30.008 Billing and Reimbursement for Expert Medical Advisor Services.

(1) Within 30-calendar days following completion of the written report, the physician must submit billing for Expert Medical Advisor services on the Agency approved or judge of compensation claims approved invoice, as applicable, documenting total number of hours and total dollar charges.

(2) In a judge of compensation claims proceeding, if additional diagnostic testing is required for the Expert Medical Advisor to render a medical opinion, charges for diagnostic testing shall:

(a) Require prior authorization from the judge of compensation claims; and

(b) Be billed in accordance with Rule 69L-7.602, F.A.C.; and

(c) Be reimbursed in accordance with the appropriate Florida Workers' Compensation reimbursement manual in effect on the date services were completed.

(3) Within 45-calendar days from receipt of both the Expert Medical Advisor's copy of the written report and invoice, reimbursement shall be rendered to the Expert Medical Advisor pursuant to Section 440.13(9)(f), F.S.

(4) Hourly reimbursement for Expert Medical Advisor services shall include reimbursement for all services rendered except specialty-diagnostic testing.

(5) Reimbursement for Expert Medical Advisor services, pursuant to an Expert Medical Advisor Contract, shall be as follows:

(a) For an Expert Medical Advisor selected by the Agency pursuant to subsection 59A-30.005(2), F.A.C., reimbursement shall not exceed $200.00 per hour for no more than 8 hours per case, not including reasonable expenses associated with travel, when applicable, which will be reimbursed in accordance with Section 112.081, F.S.

(b) For an Expert Medical Advisor selected by a Judge of Compensation Claims pursuant to subsection 59A-30.005(3), F.A.C., reimbursement shall not exceed $300.00 per hour, nor more than 8 hours per case, not including reasonable expenses associated with travel, when applicable, which will be reimbursed in accordance with Section 112.081, F.S.

Specific Authority 440.13(9), 440.591 Fla. Stat.
Law Implemented 440.13(9) Fla. Stat.
History: New 1-23-95, Formerly 38F-54.008, Amended 10-11-06.

59A-30.009 Recertification of Expert Medical Advisors

Specific Authority 440.13(9), 440.591 FS.
Law Implemented 440.13(9) FS.
History: New 1-23-95, Formerly 38F-54.009, Repealed 10-11-06.

59A-30.010 Expert Medical Advisor Decertification.

(1) An Expert Medical Advisor shall be decertified for any one of the following:

(a) The physician is removed from the Agency's list of physicians authorized to provide services to workers' compensation injured employees.

(b) The physician fails to report a conflict of interest and decline selection in a case assignment as required in Rule 59A-30.004, F.A.C.

(2) If an Expert Medical Advisor is decertified by the Agency, the physician shall not be eligible for certification as an Expert Medical Advisor in the future.

Specific Authority 440.13(9), 440.591 Fla. Stat.
Law Implemented 440.13(9) Fla. Stat.
History: New 1-23-95, Formerly 38F-54.010, Amended 10-11-06.

CHAPTER 59A-31 Disputed Reimbursement

59A-31.001. Disputed Reimbursement Avoidance.

Specific Authority 440.13(2)(i)1., 440.591 Fla. Stat.
Law Implemented 440.13(2)(a), (i) Fla. Stat.
History: New 5-15-91, Formerly 38F-7.517, Formerly 4L-7.517, Repealed 3-8-06.

59A-31.002 Disputed Reimbursement Resolution.

Specific Authority 440.13(7), 440.591 FS.
Law Implemented 440.13(7) FS.
History: New 5-15-91, Amended 12-28-97, Formerly 38F-7.518, 38F-7.605, 4L-7.605, 4-2-06, Repealed 11-28-06.

59A-31.003 Petition Form.

(1) The Petition for Resolution of Reimbursement Dispute Form (AHCA Form 3160-0023, effective September 8, 2006) is hereby incorporated by reference. This form may be obtained on the Internet at http://www.fldfs.com/wc/forms.html or by contacting the Agency at (850)413-1613.

(2) A petition to contest carrier disallowance or adjustment of payment pursuant to Section 440.13(7)(a), F.S., must be on the Petition for Resolution of Reimbursement Dispute Form. Any submission seeking to contest the disallowance or adjustment of payment by a carrier pursuant to Section 440.13(7)(a), F.S., must include a completed Petition for Resolution of Reimbursement Dispute Form.

Specific Authority 440.13(7)(e) FS.
Law Implemented 440.13(7)(a) FS
History: New 11-28-06.

59A-31.004 Carrier Response Form.

(1) The Carrier Response to Petition for Resolution of Reimbursement Dispute Form (AHCA Form 3160-0024, effective September 8, 2006) is hereby incorporated by reference. This form may be obtained on the Internet at http://www.fldfs.com/wc/forms.html or by contacting the Agency at (850)413-1613.

(2) The Carrier Response to Petition for Resolution of Reimbursement Dispute Form

shall be considered a required element of the requested documentation to the Agency under Section 440.13(7)(b), F.S. The Carrier Response to Petition for Resolution of Reimbursement Dispute Form shall be the only form accepted by the Agency upon which a carrier may submit to the Agency its response to a Petition for Resolution of Reimbursement Dispute. Any submission by a carrier pursuant to Section 440.13(7)(b), F.S., that does not include a completed Carrier Response to Petition for Resolution of Reimbursement Dispute Form shall result in a notice of deficiency by the Agency. A carrier shall have ten (10) calendar days from receipt of the notice of deficiency to cure the deficiency identified in the Agency's notice of deficiency. Failure to timely cure the deficiency shall constitute failure to submit requested documentation to the Agency.

Specific Authority 440.13(7)(e) Fla Stat.

Law Implemented 440.13(7)(b) Fla Stat.

History: New 11-28-06.

59A-31.005 Petition Requirements.

(1) All documents and records that support the allegations contained in the petition must accompany the petition. A petition that is accompanied by all items specified below will not be dismissed for failure to submit supporting documents and records:

(a) A copy of each Explanation of Bill Review received from the carrier providing notice of disallowance or adjustment of payment in this dispute.

(b) A copy of the medical bill or medical bills or request for reimbursement for which payment was disallowed or adjusted by the carrier on the contested Explanation of Bill Review(s).

(c) One copy set of all medical documentation and records submitted to the carrier in support of the medical bill(s) or request(s) for reimbursement which are the subject of this dispute.

(d) If the answer to question 5 on the Petition for Resolution of Reimbursement Dispute Form is yes, a copy of all applicable provision(s) of the reimbursement contract.

(e) Provider's documentation of authorization by carrier for non-emergency treatment for the date(s) of service covered by the petition.

(f) Documentation of health care provider notification to the carrier, pursuant to Section 440.13(3)(b), F.S., for emergency treatment for the date(s) of service included in the petition.

(2) If the petitioner does not submit a completed Petition for Resolution of Reimbursement Dispute Form, accompanied by all of the items specified in subsection 59A-31.005(1), F.A.C., the petitioner will be notified by the Agency of the deficiency in submission. The petitioner shall have ten (10) calendar days from receipt of the notice of deficiency to cure the deficiency by providing to the Agency the items specified in the Agency's notice along with proof of proper service of the curative documentation upon the carrier. If the Agency does not receive the curative documentation and proof of service of the curative documentation upon the carrier within ten (10) days after petitioner's receipt of the notice of deficiency, the petition will be dismissed with prejudice.

(3) Documents and records accompanying the petition must be submitted in hard copy.

Specific Authority 440.13(7)(e), 440.591 FS.

Law Implemented 440.13(7) FS.

History: New 11-28-06.

59A-31.006 Consolidation of Petitions.

(1) If multiple petitions addressing the same substantive issue(s) have been filed by petitioner contesting disallowance or adjustment of payment by the same carrier, the Agency may, in its discretion, consolidate the petitions into a single determination.

(2) If the Agency consolidates multiple petitions into a single determination, the timetable for rendering a determination upon a consolidated petition shall be expanded to 120 days after Agency receipt of all documentation.

Specific Authority 440.13(7)(e), 440.591 FS.

Law Implemented 440.13(7)(e) FS

History: New 11-28-06.

59A-31.007 Service of Petition on Carrier and Affected Parties.

(1) The petitioner shall effectuate service upon the carrier and on all affected parties by serving a copy of the petition and all documents and records in support of the petition, by United States Postal Service (USPS) certified mail on the entity identified on the Explanation of Bill Review as the entity the carrier designates to receive service on behalf of the carrier and all affected parties. If the Explanation of Bill Review does not specifically identify the name and mailing address of the entity the carrier designates to receive service on behalf of the carrier and all affected parties, as required by paragraph 69L-7.602(5)(q), F.A.C., the petitioner may effectuate service of the petition upon the carrier and all affected parties by serving a copy of the petition and copies of all documents and records in support of the petition by United States Postal Service (USPS) certified mail upon the entity who issued the Explanation of Bill Review at the address from which the Explanation of Bill Review was issued.

(2) A Petition for Resolution of Reimbursement Dispute must be served upon the carrier and all affected parties by United States Postal Service (USPS) certified mail. Service upon the carrier shall include one copy set of all documents and records submitted to the Agency in support of the petition.

(3) Service by certified mail means service by United States Postal Service (USPS) certified mail. Service by United States Postal Service (USPS) delivery other than certified mail or service by common carrier does not constitute service by certified mail, as required by statute, even if carrier delivery and receipt of the petition are confirmed.

(4) If a carrier has not been properly served in accordance with this subsection, the petitioner will be notified by the Agency of the deficiency in service. The petitioner shall have ten (10) calendar days from receipt of the notice of deficiency in service to provide the Agency with proof the deficiency in service identified in the notice of deficiency has been cured by proper service. If the Agency does not receive proof of proper service within ten (10) days after petitioner's receipt of the notice of deficiency, the petition will be dismissed with prejudice. For purposes of this rule, "proof of proper service" means that a copy of the petition and one copy set of all documents and records in support of the petition have been sent by United States Postal Service (USPS) certified mail to the proper entity at the proper address as set forth in this rule, and a certified mail receipt number is provided to the Agency to confirm mailing.

Specific Authority 440.13(7)(e), 440.591 FS.

Law Implemented 440.13(7)(a) FS.

History: New 11-28-06.

59A-31.008 Computation of Time.

(1) Pursuant to paragraph 69L-7.602(5)(q), F.A.C., notice of disallowance or adjustment of payment, which begins the thirty (30) day time period in Section 440.13(7), F.S., shall only be through receipt of an Explanation of Bill Review issued by or on behalf of a carrier. Therefore, the thirty (30) day time period within which a petition must be served upon the Agency begins upon receipt of the Explanation of Bill Review by the health care provider or by an entity designated by the provider to receive such notice on behalf of the health care provider. The health care provider shall document receipt of the Explanation of Bill Review using a date stamp, which clearly reflects date of receipt, or by using a verifiable login process. Documentation of receipt through a date stamp or verifiable login process shall accompany the petition. A date stamped Explanation of Bill Review will be accepted as proof of date of receipt by date stamp. A copy of the applicable portion of the login roster showing the date of login of the Explanation of Bill Review will be accepted as proof of receipt through a verifiable login process. If receipt cannot be established through a date stamp or verifiable login process, the health care provider may provide with the petition a copy of the envelope in which the Explanation of Bill Review was sent which clearly and legibly shows the postmark date, in which case receipt will be deemed to be five (5) calendar days from the postmark date on the envelope in

which the Explanation of Bill Review was sent. If the health care provider does not establish the date of its receipt of the Explanation of Bill Review by any of the methods set forth in this subsection through documentation accompanying the Petition, the health care provider receipt of the Explanation of Bill Review will be deemed to be five (5) calendar days from the issue date on the Explanation of Bill Review. An affidavit attesting to date of receipt will not be accepted as proof of date of receipt.

(2) Petitioning the Agency shall be effectuated upon service of the petition upon the Agency. The timeliness of a Petition for Resolution of Reimbursement Dispute shall be calculated based upon service of the petition upon the Agency. Service upon the Agency shall be by United States Postal Service (USPS) mail, by common carrier, or by hand delivery. If service is by United States Postal Service (USPS) mail, the date of service shall be the postmark date. If service is by common carrier, the date of service shall be the common carrier pick-up date. If service is by hand delivery, the date of service is the date the petition is hand delivered to: Receptionist, Hartman Building, 2012 Capital Circle Southeast, Tallahassee, Florida. Service by hand delivery is available Monday through Friday between 8:00 a.m. and 5:00 p.m., Eastern Time, excluding state holidays.

(3) Carrier date of receipt of the petition by certified mail will be established by reference to the United States Postal Service (USPS) certified mail receipt date. Timely submission by the carrier of the Carrier Response to Petition for Resolution of Reimbursement Dispute Form and accompanying documentation to the Agency shall be determined based upon the date of service of the Carrier Response to Petition for Resolution of Reimbursement Dispute Form and accompanying documentation to the Agency. If service is by United States Postal Service (USPS) mail, the date of service shall be the postmark date. If service is by common carrier, the date of service shall be the common carrier pick-up date. If service is by hand delivery, the date of service is the date the petition is hand delivered to: Receptionist, Hartman Building, 2012 Capital Circle Southeast, Tallahassee, Florida. Service by hand delivery is available Monday through Friday between 8:00 a.m. and 5:00 p.m., Eastern Time, excluding state holidays.

(4) Neither the request for, nor the conducting of, an on-site audit, nor the referral of the health care provider for peer review consultation, nor independent medical examination shall toll the time period for petitioning the Agency for the resolution of a reimbursement dispute as set forth in Section 440.13(7)(a), F.S., or the time period for the carrier to submit requested documentation under Section 440.13(7)(b), F.S.

Specific Authority 440.13(7)(e), 440.591 FS.

Law Implemented 440.13(7)(a), (b) FS.

History: New 11-28-06.

59A-31.009 Carrier Response Requirements.

(1) The Carrier Response to Petition for Resolution of Reimbursement Dispute Form, accompanied by all requested information, must be served upon the Agency within ten (10) days after receipt of a copy of the petition by United States Postal Service (USPS) certified mail. However, where the Carrier has received curative documentation from the Petitioner pursuant to subsection 59A-31.005(2), F.A.C., the Carrier Response to Petition for Resolution of Reimbursement Dispute Form, accompanied by all requested information, must be served upon the Agency within ten (10) calendar days after receipt, by the carrier of the curative documentation from the Petitioner. The carrier's response to the petition must include a completed Carrier Response to Petition for Resolution of Reimbursement Dispute Form (AHCA Form 3160-0024, effective September 8, 2006). Failure of the carrier to meet these requirements constitutes waiver of all objections to the petition.

(2) The carrier shall provide to the petitioner, using a delivery method which provides confirmation of date of delivery, at the petitioner's mailing address on the Petition for Resolution of Reimbursement Dispute Form, a copy of the Carrier Response to Petition for Resolution of Reimbursement Dispute Form, and one copy set of all accompanying information served upon the Agency in response to the petition.

(3) Documents and records accompanying the carrier's Response to Petition for Resolution of Reimbursement Dispute Form must be in hard copy.

Specific Authority 440.13(7)(e), 440.591 FS.
Law Implemented 440.13(7)(b) FS.
History: New 11-28-06.

59A-31.010 Effect of Non-Response by Carrier.

Failure of the carrier to timely submit a Carrier Response to Petition for Resolution of Reimbursement Dispute Form (AHCA Form 3160-0024, effective September 8, 2006) and accompanying documentation substantiating its disallowance or adjustment of payment constitutes a waiver of all objections to the petition. Waiver of all objections to the petition shall result in the Agency determination and final order being based solely upon the allegations and supporting documentation submitted by the petitioner.

Specific Authority 440.13(7), 440.591 FS.
Law Implemented 440.13(7)(b) FS.
History: New 11-28-06.

59A-31.011 Complete Record.

The evidentiary record upon which the Agency's determination will be made shall be the Petition for Resolution of Reimbursement Dispute Form and all supporting documents and records accompanying the petition and the Carrier's Response to Petition for Resolution of Reimbursement Dispute Form and all accompanying documents. However, if the petitioner and carrier enter into a joint stipulation of the parties pursuant to Rule 59A-31.012, F.A.C., the evidentiary record upon which the Agency's determination will be made shall also include all additional supporting documentation submitted to the Agency by the parties within the 10 calendar day period provided for in Rule 59A-31.012, F.A.C.

Specific Authority 440.13(7)(e), 440.591 FS.
Law Implemented 440.13(7)(c) FS.
History: New 11-28-06.

59A-31.012 Joint Stipulation of the Parties.

Within fourteen (14) calendar days subsequent to service upon the Agency of the carrier response, the petitioner and carrier may serve upon the Agency a joint stipulation of the parties, mutually stipulating in writing that the reimbursement dispute be held in abeyance for a specified time period, not to exceed sixty (60) calendar days, for the parties to seek a resolution of the reimbursement dispute without the need for a determination by the Agency. Service of a joint stipulation of the parties upon the Agency shall be by one of the methods by which a petition is served upon the Agency in subsection 59A-31.008(2), F.A.C. At the conclusion of the specified time period in such joint stipulation, or upon earlier notice in writing served upon the Agency and the other party(ies) to the joint stipulation by any party to such joint stipulation that the negotiations to resolve the reimbursement dispute are at an impasse, the Agency will proceed to make a determination on the reimbursement dispute. At the time the abeyance of the dispute is concluded, the Agency will allow the parties to such joint stipulation ten (10) calendar days to serve any additional supporting documentation a party wishes to be considered in making a determination on the dispute. If a reimbursement dispute is held in abeyance pursuant to a joint stipulation of the parties, the 60-day time period for the Agency to issue a determination shall commence when the 10-day period for serving additional documentation ends.

Specific Authority 440.13(7)(e), 440.591 FS.
Law Implemented 440.13(7) FS.
History: New 11-28-06.

59A-31.013 Petition Withdrawal.

(1) Prior to the issuance of a determination, the petitioner may voluntarily withdraw its Petition for Resolution of Reimbursement Dispute.

(2) The withdrawal of a petition shall be in writing and must clearly indicate:

(a) The name of the health care provider or facility requesting withdrawal;

(b) The name of the carrier against whom the petition has been initiated;

(c) The date(s) of service covered by the

petition; and

(d) The identity of the injured employee to whom medical services were delivered.

(3) The result of receipt by the Agency of a request for withdrawal of a petition shall be dismissal of the determination case by the Agency.

Specific Authority 440.13(7)(e), 440.591 FS.

Law Implemented 440.13(7)(a), (c) FS.

History: New 11-28-06.

59A-31.014 Overutilization Issues Raised in Reimbursement Dispute Resolution.

If the carrier, in its Carrier Response to Petition for Resolution of Reimbursement Dispute, asserts and submits documentation substantiating that a basis for disallowing petitioner's claim for payment is overutilization and the Agency, in its discretion, determines that the reimbursement dispute cannot be resolved without addressing the issue, the Agency will issue a determination pursuant to Section 440.13(7), F.S., that the reimbursement dispute cannot be resolved under Section 440.13(7), F.S., and is being converted to a proceeding under Sections 440.13(8) and 440.13(11), F.S.; or both.

Specific Authority 440.13(7)(e), 440.591 FS.

Law Implemented 440.13(7)(b), 440.13(7)(c) FS.

History: New 11-28-06.

59A-31.015 Managed Care Arrangements.

A health care provider may not elect to contest under Section 440.13(7), F.S., disallowance or adjustment of payment by a carrier for services rendered pursuant to a managed care arrangement.

Specific Authority 440.13(7)(e), 440.134(25)(e), 440.591 FS.

Law Implemented 440.13(7) FS.

History: New 11-28-06.

59B COST MANAGEMENT AND CONTROL

CHAPTER 59B-6 Reports Required of Hospitals and Other Facilities

59B-6.008. Health Care Entities Required to Report and Pay Assessment.

Any health care entity included in Section 395.7015, F.S., shall report actual financial and statistical data to the agency in compliance with this Chapter and shall pay an annual assessment as described in Rule 59B-6.022. A health care entity subject to the requirements of Section 395.7015, F.S., shall provide the agency written notification which includes name and address of the entity and fiscal year.

Specific Authority 395.7015(5), 408.15(8), 408 Fla. Stat.

Law Implemented 395.7015 Fla. Stat.

History: New 5-7-92, Formerly 10N-6.008, Amended 2-10-93.

59B-6.009. Definitions.

As used in this Chapter, unless the context requires otherwise:

(1) "Agency" means the Agency for Health Care Administration (AHCA).

(2) "Freestanding" means the health care entity bills and receives revenue which is not directly subject to the hospital PMATF (Public Medical Assistance Trust Fund) assessment described in Section 395.7015, F.S. "Freestanding" means that the health care entity is not a department or other subdivision of a hospital.

(3) "Gross revenue" means the sum of daily service charges, ambulatory service charges, ancillary service charges, and other operating revenue. This amount includes all revenue to the health care entity, excluding documented physician professional fees, revenues received for testing or analysis of samples received from outside the state or from product sales outside the sales, and revenue unrelated to the operation of the health care entity as provided in Rules 59B-6.012 and 59B-6.013.

(4) "Deductions from revenue" means reductions from gross revenue resulting from inability to collect payment of charges. Such reductions include bad debts; contractual adjustments; uncompensated care; administrative, courtesy, and policy discounts and adjustments; and other such revenue deductions and includes the offset of restricted donations and grants for indigent

care.

(5) "Net operating revenue" means gross revenue less deductions from revenue. For health care entities using a cash basis of accounting, net operating revenue means the amount of gross revenue collected.

(6) "Gross patient revenue" means all billed charges including both billed technical and professional or physician fees for patient services.

(7) "Other operating revenue" means all billed charges for health care entity services other than direct patient services.

(8) "Generally accepted auditing standards" means the ten generally accepted auditing standards adopted by the American Institute of Certified Public Accountants, together with interpretations, in the Statements on Auditing Standards as published by the American Institute of Certified Public Accountants in effect as of August 20, 1984 and may be amended by Rule 61H1-20.008, Department of Business and Professional Regulation, Board of Accountancy.

(9) "Generally accepted accounting principles" means accounting principles or standards generally accepted in the United States, including but not limited to, Accounting Principles Board Opinions Numbers 1 to 31 as published by the American Institute of Certified Public Accountants and Statements of Financial Accounting Standards and interpretations as published by the Financial Accounting Standards Board in effect as of August 20, 1984 and as may be amended by Rule 61H1-20.007, Department of Business and Professional Regulation, Board of Accountancy.

(10) "Financial statements" means a presentation of financial data, including accompanying notes, derived from accounting records and intended to communicate a health care entity's economic resources or obligations at a point in time, or changes for a period of time, in accordance with generally accepted accounting principles.

(11) "Change in health care entity ownership" means that a majority of the ownership or the controlling interest of the health care entity is transferred or assigned. A change in ownership includes, but is not limited to, the acquisition of the health care entity by any person by any means; the leasing of the health care entity when the lessee agrees to undertake or provide services at the health care entity to the extent that legal liability for operation of the health care entity rests with the lessee; conversion of the health care entity's type or kind of business organization; the sale, acquisition, assignment or other voluntary or involuntary transfer of a majority of the ownership or the controlling interest of the health care entity; merger of the health care entity into a new corporation; and consolidation of the health care entity with one or more corporations resulting in the creating of a new corporation.

(12) "Physician" means a health professional licensed by the Board of Medicine under Sections 458.311, 458.313, or 458.317, F.S., or by an osteopathic physician licensed by the Board of Osteopathic Medical Examiners under Sections 459.006, 459.007, or 459.0075, F.S.

(13) "Owners" means principal owners of record or known beneficial owners regardless of what percent of voting interest is owned.

(14) "Contractual adjustments" means the differences between the amount, based on the facility's full established rates, of contractual patients' charges for services covered by the contract, and the amount received and due from third party agencies such as Medicare and Medicaid including adjustments made at year end.

(15) "Bad debts" means the difference between billed charges and the amount received or an estimate of the credit losses in accounts receivable using an internally documented methodology.

(16) "Uncompensated care" means the difference between the amount billed to patients for which no payment or less than full payment is expected because of inability to pay and known at the time the services are rendered, and the amount received.

(17) "Administrative adjustments" means the amount of write-offs in which the cost of billings exceeds the amount of the account balance.

(18) "Courtesy adjustments" means to report reductions which occur on a nonroutine and infrequent basis to promote customer satisfaction.

(19) "Policy Discounts" means discounts for staff and their families, physicians and their families or other individuals as a matter of documented policy.

(20) "Restricted donations and grants for indigent care" means voluntary and governmental agency grants or subsidies for the care of nonspecified medically indigent patients.

(21) "Physician professional fee" means the billed charges for professional services provided to or on behalf of patients by physicians.

(22) "Unrelated revenue" means income that is received from environmental air testing, veterinary services, clinical laboratory services performed by another health care entity or hospital subject to s. 395.7015 or s. 395.701, or other income that is unrelated to the operation of an ambulatory surgery center, clinical laboratory, radiation therapy center or diagnostic imaging center.

Specific Authority 395.7015(5), 408.15(8), 408 Fla. Stat.

Law Implemented 395.7015 Fla. Stat.

History: New 5-7-92, Formerly 10N-6.009, Amended 2-10-93.

59B-6.010. Adoption and Establishment of AHCA AMBFAC Report Forms.

The agency adopts and establishes AHCA Ambulatory Health Facility Report Forms AMBFAC01 and AMBFAC02 incorporated by reference herein.

Specific Authority 395.7015(5), 408.15(8), 408 Fla. Stat.

Law Implemented 395.7015 Fla. Stat.

History: New 5-7-92, Formerly 10N-6.010, Amended 2-10-93, 12-11-95.

59B-6.011. Manner for Submitting Reports.

(1) Beginning January 1, 1993, each health care entity shall submit to the agency not more than 120 days subsequent to the end of its fiscal year, its AHCA AMBFAC01 and AMBFAC02 reports for the fiscal year then ended.

(2) Each health care entity is to provide documentation of amounts reported in its AMBFAC report from audited financial statements federal income tax returns, physician orders, patient bills, or records of actual receipts upon audit as provided in Rule 59B-6.020.

(3) Audited financial statements shall be prepared in accordance with generally accepted accounting principles, and shall be examined by an independent, Florida licensed, certified public accountant, in accordance with generally accepted auditing standards, with an auditor's opinion issued.

(4) In the event a health care entity's audited financial statements or federal income tax returns are examined by an agency of federal, state or local government and that examination requires adjustments, in accordance with generally accepted auditing standards, to audited financial statements or federal income tax returns, and adjustments to previously reported AMBFAC reports then the health care entity will report the adjustments to the Agency within 30 days of acceptance of the adjustments by health care entity management.

(5) Where more than one health care entity is operated by the reporting organization, the information required by this section shall be reported for each health care entity separately.

(6) Health care entities shall submit one duplicate copy of all reports required in this section.

(7) Health care entities shall submit AMBFAC reports for a consecutive period of 12 months EXCEPT as described in Rules 59B-6.014 and 59B-6.015.

Specific Authority 395.7015(5), 408.15(8), 408 Fla. Stat.

Law Implemented 395.7015 Fla. Stat.

History: New 5-7-92, Formerly 10N-6.011, Amended 2-10-93, 12-11-95.

59B-6.012. Physician Professional Fees.

(1) Physician professional fees are included in the amount of gross revenue to be assessed

under the provisions of this Chapter unless the amount of physician fees is documented, reconciled to the entity's federal income tax return, audited financial statements, patient bills, physician orders, or records of receipts, and the entity can provide billing documentation if audited by the agency.

(2) Documentation requires that ambulatory surgery centers obtain a separate provider identification number for physician fees.

Specific Authority 395.7015(5), 408.15(8), 408 Fla. Stat.

Law Implemented 395.7015 Fla. Stat.

History: New 5-7-92, Formerly 10N-6.012, Amended 2-10-93.

59B-6.013. Unrelated Revenue.

Revenue unrelated to the operation of the health care entity is included in the amount of gross revenue to be assessed under the provisions of this Chapter unless the amount of unrelated revenue is documented, reconciled to the entity's federal income tax return, audited financial statements, physician orders, patient bills, or records of receipts, and the entity can provide billing documentation if audited by the agency.

Specific Authority 395.7015(5), 408.15(8), 408 Fla. Stat.

Law Implemented 395.7015 Fla. Stat.

History: New 5-7-92, Formerly 10N-6.013, Amended 2-10-93.

59B-6.014. Change of Fiscal Year.

(1) Beginning with fiscal year ending 1993 reports, when a health care entity changes the date of the end of its fiscal year, the health care entity shall file its AMBFAC report for the period then ended, within 120 days of such change.

(2) A health care entity changing its fiscal year shall submit written notification to the Agency within 30 days of the health care entity's change of fiscal year. The notification shall include name of health care entity, AHCA identification number of entity, previous year end, new year end and reason for change.

Specific Authority 395.7015(5), 408.15(8), 408 Fla. Stat.

Law Implemented 395.7015 Fla. Stat.

History: New 5-7-92, Formerly 10N-6.014, Amended 2-10-93.

59B-6.015. Change of Ownership or New Health Care Entity.

(1) When the application for a license required by Sections 395.003 or 483.091, F.S., is filed for a new health care entity or due to a change in ownership of an existing health care facility, the proposed new owner is to advise the Agency in writing of the filing of that application.

(2) A new health care entity shall submit written notification to the Agency within 30 days of the health care entity's first date of operations. The owner shall submit written notification which includes identification of owner, name and address of new entity, first date of operations and fiscal year.

(3) Beginning with fiscal year ending 1993 reports, when a health care entity changes ownership, the health care entity shall file its AHCA AMBFAC report for the period then ended of the last date of ownership, within 120 days of such change. If a new owner provides the Agency with a written statement that such period of prior ownership will be included in the AMBFAC reports to be filed by the new owner within 120 days of the facilities fiscal year end and that the new owner agrees to be responsible for all Agency-related obligations for the entire fiscal year, the Agency may waive the separate reporting requirement of this section.

(4) A health care entity changing its ownership shall submit written notification of such change to the Agency within 30 days of the health care entity's change of ownership. The new owner shall submit written notification which includes name of acquired entity, AHCA identification number of entity, identification of the new owner, date of ownership change, and status of health care entity's license if licensure is required by statute.

(5) Until a health care entity changes owner-

ship as specified in Rule 59B-6.009 (11), it is the responsibility of the then-current owner to comply with this Chapter and Section 395.7015, F.S., and it is the responsibility of the then-current owner to prepare and submit timely reports as required by the Agency.

Specific Authority 395.7015(5), 408.15(8), 408 Fla. Stat.

Law Implemented 395.7015 Fla. Stat.

History: New 5-7-92, Formerly 10N-6.015, Amended 2-10-93.

59B-6.016. Change of Health Care Entity Address.

A health care entity changing its address shall submit written notification of such change to the Agency within 30 days of the health care entity's change of address. The health care entity shall submit written notification which includes the AHCA identification number of the health care entity, name of health care entity, old street address and new street address.

Specific Authority 395.7015(5), 408.15(8), 408 Fla. Stat.

Law Implemented 395.7015 Fla. Stat.

History: New 5-7-92, Formerly 10N-6.016, Amended 2-10-93.

59B-6.017. Extensions.

(1) The Agency shall grant any written request for an extension of the due date for submission to the Agency of the AMBFAC report, provided the written request for an extension is received by the Agency by the due date of the report.

(2) An extension shall be granted for the period requested not to exceed 90 days from the due date described in Rule 59B-6.011.

(3) Extensions shall not be granted for submitting corrections as described in Rule 59B-6.019.

(4) Extension of the due date for assessment payment shall not be granted.

Specific Authority 395.7015(5), 408.15(8), 408 Fla. Stat.

Law Implemented 395.7015 Fla. Stat.

History: New 5-7-92, Formerly 10N-6.017, Amended 2-10-93.

59B-6.018. Information Letters.

(1) The Director of the agency is also authorized to make uniform applicable interpretations or clarifications with respect to instructions contained in the AHCA AMBFAC Report Forms adopted under Rule 59B-6.010. The Director of the Agency is also authorized to make other minor organizational modifications when those corrections and modifications appear to be necessary to facilitate fair, accurate, and efficient reporting of health care entity financial information or other data to the Agency.

(2) Any interpretations, corrections, or modifications shall be in writing and distributed as an attachment to a consecutively numbered information letter. The letter shall describe in detail the changes made by the attached material and shall identify, by number, the AHCA AMBFAC Report Form changed. Each health care entity shall be sent a copy of any information letters together with all attachments.

Specific Authority 395.7015(5), 408.15(8), 408 Fla. Stat.

Law Implemented 395.7015 Fla. Stat.

History: New 5-7-92, Formerly 10N-6.018, Amended 2-10-93.

59B-6.019. Notice of Reporting Deficiencies and Response.

(1) Within 90 days after receipt of any report, the staff shall determine and notify the health care entity whether it is complete and conforms to the applicable statutory, rule, and AHCA AMBFAC Report Forms; and whether the data contained in the reports is verifiable.

(2) Written notification shall be provided by certified mail to a health care entity in the event the staff determines a report is incomplete; fails to conform to applicable statutory, rule, or AHCA AMBFAC Report Forms. The notice shall clearly indicate the deficiencies found, the corrections or modifications that must be made to make it complete or conforming, as well as the time by which a corrected or modified report and certification must be received in the Agen-

cy's office.

(3) A health care entity shall have no fewer than 10 working days following receipt of notice, to return to the Agency's office the requested corrected or modified report.

(4) A health care entity not notified as provided in Rules 59B-6.019 (1) and 59B-6.019 (2), above shall be deemed to have submitted a report that is complete, conforming and verifiable.

(5) If the corrected or modified report is not returned to the Agency within the specified time period, the entire report shall be deemed delinquent from the original due date.

Specific Authority 395.7015(5), 408.15(8), 408 Fla. Stat.

Law Implemented 395.7015 Fla. Stat.

History: New 5-7-92, Formerly 10N-6.019, Amended 2-10-93.

59B-6.020. Audits of Health Care Entities.

(1) The Agency may inspect and audit health care entity books and records, and records of individual or corporate ownership, including books and records of related organizations with which a health care entity had transactions, for compliance with Section 395.7015, F.S., and this Chapter.

(2) Upon presentation of a written request for inspection to a health care entity owner or its staff, the health care entity shall make available to the Agency or Agency staff for inspection, copying and review all books and records documenting compliance or failure to comply with Section 395.7015, F.S., and this Chapter.

Specific Authority 395.7015(5), 408.15(8), 408, 408.08(1) Fla. Stat.

Law Implemented 395.7015 Fla. Stat.

History: New 5-7-92, Formerly 10N-6.020, Amended 2-10-93.

59B-6.021. Certification of PMATF Assessment.

(1) Beginning July 1, 1993 and beginning with 1993 fiscal year end reports, within 6 months after the end of each entity's fiscal year, the agency shall certify the amount of the assessment to each entity.

(2) In the event the health care entity changes fiscal year, the assessment shall be on the actual experience of the entity for the most recent AHCA AMBFAC report received, provided that report contains, at a minimum, 6 months actual data.

(3) In the event an extension is issued as described in Rule 59B-6.017 or the report is incomplete, nonconforming or delinquent as described in Rule 59B-6.019, the Agency shall certify the amount of the assessment to each entity within 10 working days of a determination that the report is complete and conforming.

Specific Authority 395.7015(5), 408.15(8), 408 Fla. Stat.

Law Implemented 395.7015 Fla. Stat.

History: New 5-7-92, Formerly 10N-6.021, Amended 2-10-93.

59B-6.022. Calculation and Payment of Assessment.

(1) Beginning July 1, 1993, the assessment shall be payable to and collected by the Agency in equal quarterly amounts, on or before the first day of each calendar quarter, beginning with the first full calendar quarter.

(2) The current owner of the health care entity is liable for payment of any past due assessments.

(3) In the event an extension is issued as described in Rule 59B-6.017 or the report is incomplete, nonconforming or delinquent as described in Rule 59B-6.019, the assessment shall be based on previous year's annual assessment until the most recent amount of assessment is certified. In the event an extension is issued as described in Rule 59B-6.017, the assessment due April 30, 1992 shall be based on an estimated amount. The Agency will issue an adjustment to the assessment amounts for any difference.

(4) In the event an AHCA audit determines that the net operating revenue previously reported is incorrect or an audit performed by another governmental agency as described in Rule 59B-6.011 (5) results in an adjustment of

net operating revenue, the Agency will issue an adjustment to the assessment amount due from the health care entity for any difference between the amount of the assessment originally payable and the corrected amount.

(5) All moneys collected pursuant to this Chapter shall be deposited into the Public Medical Assistance Trust Fund.

Specific Authority 395.7015(5), 408.15(8), 408 Fla. Stat.

Law Implemented 395.7015 Fla. Stat.

History: New 5-7-92, Formerly 10N-6.022, Amended 2-10-93, 12-11-95.

59B-6.023. Penalties for Reporting Deficiencies.

(1) For purposes of the rule, a report or other information is "incomplete" when it does not contain all data required by the Agency or when it contains inaccurate data and the report is not corrected by the health care entity and timely filed following an Agency correction notice as provided in Rule 59B-6.019. A report or other information is "false" if done or made with the actual knowledge of the preparer or an administrator that it contains information or data which is not true or accurate.

(2) When a health care entity refuses to file, fails to timely file, or files false or incomplete reports or other information required to be filed under the provisions of Sections 395.1015 and 408, F.S., other Florida Law, or a rule adopted thereunder, administrative proceedings to impose fines consistent with this rule shall be commenced. When true and complete information is timely filed in response to an Agency correction notice, no administrative action shall be commenced for reporting deficiencies.

(3) Reports are deemed delinquent on the first working day following the due date.

(4) Delinquent report notices will be sent via certified mail to the attention of "chief executive officer". The notice will indicate that the reporting deficiency will be turned over to agency legal counsel if not received within twenty-one (21) days from the date certified notice is signed for by the facility.

(5) The penalty period will begin on the first working day following the due date in subsection (4) above for purposes of penalty assessments.

(6) Any health care entity which is delinquent for a reporting deficiency other than submission of a false report shall be subject to a fine not to exceed $50.00 per day of violation for the first violation under 59B-6.023, $100.00 per day of violation for the second violation under 59B-6.023, and $500.00 per day of violation for the third or subsequent violations under 59B-6.023 to be fixed, imposed, and collected by the Agency. The maximum fine imposed shall not exceed 300% of the respective annual assessment if the amount of the assessment is reported by the entity under the requirements of this Chapter. Any health care entity which files a false report with the agency or provides false information to the agency under the provisions of s. 395.7015, F.S., and Chapter 408, F.S., shall be subject to a fine of $1,000.00 per day to be fixed, imposed and collected by the agency.

Specific Authority 395.7015(5), 408.15(8), 408 Fla. Stat.

Law Implemented 395.7015, 408.08 Fla. Stat.

History: New 5-7-92, Formerly 10N-6.023, Amended 2-10-93, 12-11-95.

59B-6.024. Penalties for Assessment Payment Deficiencies.

(1) Assessments are deemed delinquent on the first working day following the due date.

(2) Payment deficiency notices will be sent via certified mail to the attention of "chief executive officer." The notice will indicate that the assessment payment deficiency will be turned over to agency legal counsel if not received within twenty-one (21) days from the date the certified notice is signed for by the facility.

(3) The penalty period will begin on the first working day following the due date in subsection (1) above, for purposes of penalty assessments.

(4) Any health care entity which is delinquent for payment of an assessment shall be subject to

a fine not to exceed $100.00 per day of violation for the first violation under 59B-6.024, $500.00 per day of violation for the second violation under 59B-6.024, and $1,000.00 per day of violation for the third or subsequent violations under 59B-6.024 to be fixed, imposed, and collected by the agency. The maximum fine imposed shall not exceed 500% of the respective annual assessment if the amount of the assessment is reported by the entity under the requirements of this Chapter.

Specific Authority 395.7015(5), 408.15(8), 408 Fla. Stat.

Law Implemented 395.7015(5), 408.08 Fla. Stat.

History: New 5-7-92, Formerly 10N-6.024, Amended 2-10-93, 12-11-95.

CHAPTER 59B-9 Ambulatory Patient Data

59B-9.010. Purpose of Ambulatory Patient Data Reporting.

The reporting of ambulatory patient data will provide a statewide integrated database that includes ambulatory surgery and hospital emergency department services for the assessment of variations in utilization, disease surveillance, access to care and cost trends. The amendments appearing herein are effective with the reporting period starting January 1, 2005.

Specific Authority 408.15(8) Fla. Stat.

Law Implemented 408.061, 408.062, 408.063 Fla. Stat.

History: New 9-6-93, Formerly 59B-7.010, Amended 6-29-95, 12-28-98, 2-25-2002, 4-18-04.

59B-9.011. Submission of Ambulatory Patient Data.

(1) The following entities shall submit ambulatory patient data and reports to the Agency for Health Care Administration (AHCA or agency):

(a) All licensed short-term acute care hospitals;

(b) All licensed ambulatory surgical centers as defined in s. 395.002(3), F.S.;

(c) All lithotripsy centers defined in s. 408.07, F.S.;

(d) All cardiac catheterization laboratories defined in s. 408.07, F.S.

(2) For purposes of Rules 59B-9.010 through 59B-9.023, Florida Administrative Code (F.A.C.), "ambulatory centers" refers to the ambulatory patient data reporting facilities and providers in (1) above.

(3) Each facility in (1)(a) above shall submit a separate report for each location per Rule 59A-3.203, F.A.C. Each facility in (1)(b) above shall submit a separate report for each location per Rule 59A-5.003, F.A.C. Each facility or provider in (1)(c) or (1)(d) above shall submit a separate report for each separate location.

(4) All ambulatory centers performing the services set forth in Rules 59B-9.011 through 59B-9.023, F.A.C., shall submit ambulatory patient data as set forth in Rules 59B-9.018 and 59B-9.019, F.A.C., unless the reporting entity meets the criteria listed in Rules 59B-9.011(6), F.A.C., below.

(5) Any ambulatory center which has a total of 200 or more patient visits per Rule 59B-9.014, F.A.C., for the reporting period is required to report data as set forth in Rules 59B-9.018 and 59B-9.019, F.A.C.

(6) Ambulatory Centers with fewer than 200 patient visits in a quarter, must have the entity's Chief Executive Officer certify to the Agency in writing, that the ambulatory center has fewer than 200 patient visits per Rule 59B-9.014, F.A.C., for the reporting period, and the certification is to be received at the Agency office in Tallahassee on or prior to the deadline for submission of the report. This is not a one time letter, but must be submitted for each quarter where there were fewer than 200 visits.

(7) If requested by Agency staff, all ambulatory centers shall provide access to or at the option of Agency staff, information from the medical records underlying and documenting the ambulatory patient data submitted, as well as other patient related documentation deemed necessary by the Agency to conduct complete ambulatory patient data audits subject to the limitations as set forth in s. 408.061(1)(d), F.S.

Specific Authority 408.15(8) Fla. Stat.

Law Implemented 408.061, 408.062, 408.063, 408.07, 408.08 Fla. Stat.

History: New 9-6-93, Formerly 59B-7.011, Amended 6-29-95, 12-28-98, 7-11-2001, 2-25-2002.

59B-9.012. Exemptions.

Specific Authority 408.15(8) Fla. Stat.

Law Implemented 408.006(5), 408.061 Fla. Stat.

History: New 9-6-93, Formerly 59B-7.012, Repealed 6-29-95.

59B-9.013. Definitions.

(1) "CPT" means Current Procedural Terminology and refers to a coding system established by the American Medical Association to describe physician services which is published annually in Physicians' Current Procedural Terminology manual which is incorporated by reference.

(2) "HCPCS" means Health Care Financing Administration Common Procedure Coding System which is published annually by the United States Department of Health and Human Services and is required by the Federal Government for Medicare reporting purposes.

(3) "Charity" means medical care provided by a health care entity to a person who has insufficient resources or assets to pay for needed medical care without utilizing his resources which are required to meet his basic need for shelter, food, or clothing. No patient shall be considered charity care whose family income, as applicable for the twelve (12) months preceding the determination, exceeds 150 percent of the federal poverty guidelines, unless the amount of health care charges due from the patient exceeds 25 percent of annual family income.

(4) "Inpatient" means a patient who has an admission order given by a licensed physician or other individual who has been granted admitting privileges by the hospital. Observation patients are excluded unless they are admitted.

(5) "Visit" means a face to face encounter between a health care provider and a patient who is not formally admitted as an inpatient in an acute care hospital setting at the time of the encounter or who is not admitted to the same facility's acute care hospital setting immediately following the encounter as described in subsection 59B-9.015(3), F.A.C. Visits which require the patient to appear in an ambulatory setting prior to the actual procedure (even if this occurs one or more days before the procedure) shall be counted as one visit.

(6) Each "Ambulatory Center" is required to report ambulatory patient data. For the purposes of this rule, ambulatory center includes free-standing ambulatory surgery centers, short-term acute care hospitals, lithotripsy centers, and cardiac catheterization laboratories.

(7) "Attending Physician" means a licensed medical doctor, osteopathic physician, dentist, podiatrist, chiropractor, or advanced registered nurse practitioner who has primary responsibility for the patient's medical care and treatment during the visit or who certifies as to the medical necessity of the services rendered. The attending physician may be the operating or performing physician. The attending physician may be an emergency room physician or other specialist.

(8) "Operating or Performing Physician" means a licensed medical doctor, osteopathic physician, dentist, podiatrist, chiropractor, or advanced registered nurse practitioner who has primary responsibility for the surgery or procedure performed. The operating or performing physician may be the attending physician.

(9) "Other Physician" means a licensed medical doctor, osteopathic physician, dentist, podiatrist, chiropractor, or advanced registered nurse practitioner who rendered care to the patient other than the attending physician or the operating or performing physician.

(10) "Short-Term Acute Care Hospitals" means a hospital as defined in Section 395.002(12), F.S.

Specific Authority 408.15(8) Fla. Stat.

Law Implemented 395.002, 408.061, 408.062, 408.063 Fla. Stat.

History: New 9-6-93, Formerly 59B-7.013, Amended 6-29-95, 12-28-98, 7-11-2001, 2-25-2002, 4-18-04.

59B-9.014. Schedule for Submission of Am-

bulatory Patient Data and Extensions.

(1) Ambulatory centers shall report ambulatory patient data, as described in subsection 59B-9.015(2) and Rule 59B-9.018, F.A.C., according to the following schedule:

(a) Each report covering patient visits ending between January 1 and March 31, inclusive of each year, shall be submitted no later than June 10 of the calendar year during which the visit occurred.

(b) Each report covering patient visits ending between April 1 and June 30, inclusive of each year, shall be submitted no later than September 10 of the calendar year during which the visit occurred.

(c) Each report covering patient visits ending between July 1 and September 30, inclusive of each year, shall be submitted no later than December 10 of the calendar year during which the visit occurred.

(d) Each report covering patient visits ending between October 1 and December 31, inclusive of each year, shall be submitted no later than March 10 of the calendar year following the year in which the visit occurred.

(2) Extensions to the due dates in subsection 59B-9.014(1), F.A.C., above shall be granted by Agency staff for thirty (30) days in response to a written request if received prior to the due date, and provided that the delay is due to unforeseen and unforeseeable factors beyond the control of the reporting entity. These factors must be specified in the letter requesting the extension together with documentation of efforts undertaken to meet the filing requirements. For re-submissions, a fourteen (14) calendar day extension will be granted if requested in writing prior to the due date as specified in the letter accompanying the resubmitted request.

Specific Authority 408.15(8) Fla. Stat.

Law Implemented 408.006(5), 408.061 Fla. Stat.

History: New 9-6-93, Formerly 59B-7.014, Amended 6-29-95, 4-18-04.

59B-9.015. Reporting Instructions

(1) Ambulatory centers shall submit ambulatory patient data according to Rule 59B-9.018, F.A.C.

(2) Ambulatory centers shall report data for:

(a) All non-emergency visits in which surgery services were performed and the services provided correspond to a Current Procedural Terminology (CPT) code 10000 through 69999 or 93500 through 93599. Codes must be valid in the current or the immediately preceding year's code book to be accepted.

(b) All emergency department visits in which emergency department registration occurs and the patient is not admitted for inpatient care at the reporting entity. Include all visits for which a billing record is created.

(3) Ambulatory centers shall exclude records of any patient visit in which the outpatient and inpatient billing record is combined because the patient was admitted to inpatient care within a facility at the same location per Rule 59A-3.203, F.A.C. Report one record for each visit, except pre-operation visits may be combined with the record of the associated ambulatory surgery visit. See subsection 59B-9.013(5), F.A.C.

(4) For each patient visit, ambulatory centers shall report all services provided using procedural codes specified in subsection 59B-9.018(2), F.A.C.

(5) Ambulatory centers shall submit ambulatory patient data reports to the agency using one of the following methods described in paragraph (a) or in (b) below except that for patient visits ending on or after January 1, 2006, the methods described in paragraph (b) must not be used unless an exception is requested by the ambulatory center due to extraordinary or hardship circumstances and use of method (b) is approved by the agency. Use of method (a) must be approved by the agency for any patient visits ending prior to January 1, 2006.

(a) Internet Transmission. The Internet address established for receipt of ambulatory patient data is www.fdhc.state.fl.us. Reports sent to the Internet address shall be electronically transmitted with the ambulatory data in a text (XML) file using the Ambulatory Patient Data XML

Schema available at www.fdhc.state.fl.us. The Ambulatory Patient Data XML Schema is incorporated by reference. The data in the text file shall contain the data elements, codes, and standards required in Rule 59B-9.018, F.A.C.

(b) CD-ROM or diskettes shall be sent to the agency's mailing address: Agency for Health Care Administration, 2727 Mahan Drive, Tallahassee, Florida 32308. Attention: State Center for Health Statistics. Electronic media specifications are:

1. MS-DOS formatted.

2. Text File (XML) using the Ambulatory Patient Data XML Schema available at www.fdhc.state.fl.us.

3. Type: 3.5" diskette, 1.4MB, hd; or CD-ROM.

4. FILENAME: (e.g., AS10QYY.XML) The 5th position shall contain the quarter (1-4) and the 6th and 7th position shall contain the year. XML indicates an XML text file.

5. Only one (1) file per diskette set or CD-ROM is allowable. Data requiring more than one diskette shall have the same internal file name. Data requiring more than one (1) diskette shall be externally labeled 1 of x, 2 of x, etc. (x = total number of diskettes).

(6) Ambulatory centers submitting diskettes shall affix the following external identification, or for CD-ROM, use a standard CD-ROM external label with the following information:

(a) Ambulatory center name;

(b) AHCA ambulatory center identification number in the AHCA format;

(c) Reporting period;

(d) Number of records excluding the header record and the trailer record;

(e) Diskette or CD-ROM Filename as in subsection 59B-9.015(5), F.A.C., above; and

(f) The description: "AMBULATORY PATIENT DATA".

Specific Authority 408.15(8) Fla. Stat.

Law Implemented 408.061, 408.062, 408.063 Fla. Stat.

History: New 9-5-93, Formerly 59B-7.015, Amended 6-29-95, 12-28-98, 1-4-2000, 7-11-2001, 2-25-2002, 4-18-04.

59B-9.016. Notice of Reporting Deficiencies and Response.

(1) Within sixty (60) days after the due date or date of receipt, whichever is later of ambulatory patient data, agency staff shall determine and notify the ambulatory center whether the report is complete and conforms to the applicable rule instructions and data standards per Rules 59B-9.018–.020, F.A.C.

(2) Written notification shall be provided by certified mail, electronic mail, or FAX to an ambulatory center in the event the staff determines the data is incomplete or nonconforming. The notice shall clearly indicate the deficiencies found, and the time by which a corrected or modified report must be received in the agency's office.

(3) An ambulatory center shall have fourteen (14) calendar days following receipt of notice to return to the agency's office the requested corrected data or completed certification pages.

Specific Authority 408.15(8) Fla. Stat.

Law Implemented 408.006(5), 408.061 Fla. Stat.

History: New 9-6-93, Formerly 59B-7.016, Amended 6-29-95, 7-11-2001.

59B-9.017. Certification and Audit Procedures.

(1) All ambulatory centers submitting data in compliance with Rules 59B-9.010 through 59B-9.022, F.A.C., shall certify that the data submitted for each reporting period is accurate. These certification pages are sent by the agency to the reporting entity with summary reports generated by the agency using submitted data. The certification shall be submitted to the agency's office at the address in (3) below using the Certification of Ambulatory Patient Data Form described in (3) below or the Certification of Ambulatory Patient Data Form shall be submitted by electronic mail to SCHSdata@fdhc.state.fl.us using an agency authorized electronic signature.

(2) The Chief Executive Officer and Chief Financial Officer shall state in writing that a complete review was accomplished to assure the accuracy of the data and that to the best of their knowledge and belief, the data submitted are accurate and complete.

(3) Form APD1 is titled "Certification of Ambulatory Patient Data", and may be obtained by writing to The Agency for Health Care Administration, Ambulatory Patient Data Section, 2727 Mahan Drive, Fort Knox Building #3, Tallahassee, Florida 32308-5403. The effective date of the form is July 1, 1995. Form APD1 is incorporated by reference.

(4) The agency shall to the extent practical, apply the same audit standards and use the same audit procedures for all ambulatory centers or audit a random sample of ambulatory centers. The agency will notify each ambulatory center of any possible errors discovered by audit and request that the ambulatory center either correct the data or verify that the data is complete and correct. The notice shall indicate that the ambulatory center must return corrected data if there are errors and certify the data within ninety (90) days of receipt of the notice, or the ambulatory center Chief Executive Officer must verify by signature that the previously submitted and certified data is complete and correct within ninety (90) days of receipt of the notice. The notice shall clearly indicate that the ambulatory center may be subject to penalties pursuant to Rule 59B-9.022, F.A.C.

Specific Authority 408.15(8) Fla. Stat.

Law Implemented 408.061, 408.08(1), (5), 408.15(11) Fla. Stat.

History: New 9-6-93, Formerly 59B-7.017, Amended 6-29-95, 7-11-2001.

59B-9.018. Ambulatory Patient Data Format — Data Elements, Codes and Standards.

(1) Header Record:The first record in the data file shall be a header record, containing the information described below. If diskettes are submitted, the header record must be placed as the first record on the first diskette of the data set.

(a) Transaction Code — Enter Q for a calendar quarter report or S for a report period other than a calendar quarter where the special report is requested or authorized by the agency to receive data corrections.

(b) Report Year — Enter the year of the data in the format YYYY.

(c) Report Quarter — Enter the quarter of the data, 1, 2, 3 or 4, where 1 corresponds to the first quarter of the calendar year, 2 corresponds to the second quarter of the calendar year, 3 corresponds to the third quarter of the calendar year, and 4 corresponds to the fourth quarter of the calendar year.

(d) Data Type — Enter AS10 for Ambulatory Data.

(e) Submission Type — Enter I, R, or C where I indicates an initial submission of data or resubmission of previously rejected data, R indicates a replacement submission of previously processed and accepted ambulatory patient data, and C indicates an individual record correction or set of individual record corrections where submission of a correction or corrections is requested or authorized by the agency.

(f) Processing Date — Enter the date that the data file was created in the format YYYY-MM-DD where MM represents numbered months of the year from 1 to 12, DD represents numbered days of the month from 1 to 31, and YYYY represents the year in four digits.

(g) AHCA Ambulatory Center Number — Enter the identification number of the ambulatory center as assigned by AHCA for reporting purposes. A valid identification number must contain at least eight digits and no more than 10 digits.

(h) Organization Name — Enter the name of the ambulatory center that performed the ambulatory services represented by the data, and which is responsible for reporting the data. All questions regarding data accuracy and integrity will be referred to thisentity. Up to a forty character field.

(i) Contact Person Name — Enter the name of the contact person at the ambulatory center. Submit name in the Last, First format. Up to a twenty-five character field.

(j) Contact Person Telephone Number — The area code, business telephone number, and if applicable, extension for the contact person. Enter the contact person telephone number in the format (AAA)XXX-XXXX-EEEEE where AAA is the area code, and EEEEE is the extension. Blank fill if no extension.

(k) Contact Person E-Mail Address — The e-mail address of the contact person.

(l) Contact Person Address — Enter the mailing address of the contact person. Up to a forty character field.

(m) Mailing Address City — Enter the city of the address of the contact person. Up to a twenty-five character field.

(n) Mailing Address State — Enter the state of the address of the contact person using the U.S. Postal Service state abbreviation in the format XX. Use the abbreviation FL for Florida.

(o) Mailing Address Zip Code — Enter the zip code of the address of the contact person in the format XXXXX-XXXX. Blank fill if no extension.

(2) Individual Data Records:All data elements and data element codes listed below shall be reported consistent with the records of the reporting entity. Data elements and codes are listed with a description of the data to be reported and data standards.

(a) AHCA Ambulatory Center Number — An identification number assigned by AHCA for reporting purposes. The number must match the ambulatory center number recorded on the CD-ROM or diskette external label and header record. A valid identification number must contain at least eight digits and no more than 10 digits. A required entry.

(b) Record Identification Number — An alpha-numeric code containing standard letters or numbers assigned by the facility as a unique identifier for each record submitted in the reporting period to facilitate storage and retrieval of individual case records. Up to seventeen characters. A required entity. Duplicate record identification numbers are not permitted.

(c) Patient Social Security Number — The social security number (SSN) of the patient. A nine digit field to facilitate retrieval of individual case records, to be used to track multiple patient visits, and for medical research. Reporting 000000000 is acceptable for newborns and infants up to 2 years of age who do not have a SSN. For patients not from the United States, use 555555555 if a SSN is not assigned. For those patients where efforts to obtain the SSN have been unsuccessful or where one is unavailable, and the patient is 2 years of age or older and not known to be from a country other than the United States, use 777777777. A required entry.

(d) Patient Race or Ethnicity — Self-designated by the patient or patient's parent or guardian except code 8 indicating no response may be reported where efforts to obtain the information have been unsuccessful. A required entry. Must be a one digit code as follows:

1. 1 — American Indian or Alaska Native.

2. 2 — Asian or Pacific Islander.

3. 3 — Black or African American.

4. 4 — White.

5. 5 — White Hispanic.

6. 6 — Black Hispanic.

7. 7 — Other. Use if the patient's self-designated race or ethnicity is not described by the above categories.

8. 8 — No response. Use if the patient refuses or fails to disclose.

(e) Patient Birth Date — The date of birth of the patient. A ten character field in the format YYYY-MM-DD where MM represents the numbered months of the year from 1 to 12, DD represents numbered days of the month from 1 to 31, and YYYY represents the year in four digits. Use 9999-99-99 where type of service is "2" and efforts to obtain the patient's birth date have been unsuccessful. Age greater than 120 years is not permitted unless verified by the reporting entity. A birth date after the patient visit ending date is not permitted. A required entry.

(f) Patient Sex — The gender of the patient. A required entry. Must be a one digit code as follows:

1. 1 — Male.

2. 2 — Female.

3. 3 — Unknown shall be reported where efforts to obtain the information have been unsuccessful or where the patient's sex cannot be determined due to a medical condition.

(g) Patient Zip Code — The five digit United States Postal Service ZIP Code of the patient's permanent residence. Use 00009 for foreign residences. Use 00007 for homeless patients. Use 00000 where efforts to obtain the information have been unsuccessful. A required entry.

(h) Type of Service Code — A code designating the type of service, either ambulatory surgery or emergency department visit. A required entry. Must be a one digit code as follows:

1. 1 — Ambulatory surgery, as described in paragraph 59B-9.015(2)(a), F.A.C.

2. 2 — Emergency department visit, as described in paragraph 59B-9.015(2)(b), F.A.C.

(i) Principal Payer Code — Describes the primary source of expected reimbursement for services rendered. A required entry. Must be a one character field using upper case as follows:

1. A — Medicare.

2. B — Medicare HMO.

3. C — Medicaid.

4. D — Medicaid HMO.

5. E — Commercial Insurance.

6. F — Commercial HMO.

7. G — Commercial PPO.

8. H — Workers' Compensation.

9. I — CHAMPUS.

10. J — VA.

11. K — Other State/Local Government.

12. L — Self Pay. No third party coverage.

13. M — Other.

14. N — Charity.

15. O — KidCare. Includes Healthy Kids, MediKids and Children's Medical Services.

16. P — Unknown. Unknown shall be reported if principal payer information is not available and type of service is "2" and patient status is "07".

(j) Principal Diagnosis Code — The code representing the diagnosis chiefly responsible for the services performed during the visit. Must contain a valid ICD-9-CM or ICD-10-CM diagnosis code if type of service is "1" indicating ambulatory surgery. Must contain a valid ICD-9-CM or ICD-10-CM diagnosis code if type of service is "2" indicating an emergency department visit unless patient status is "07" indicating that the patient left against medical advice or discontinued care. A blank field is permitted if type of service is "2" and patient status is "07" consistent with the records of the reporting entity. If not space filled, must contain a valid ICD-9-CM diagnosis code or valid ICD-10-CM diagnosis code for the reporting period. Inconsistency between the principal diagnosis code and patient sex must be verified by the reporting entity. Inconsistency between the principal diagnosis code and patient age must be verified by the reporting entity. A diagnosis code cannot be used more than once as a principal or other diagnosis for each visit reported. The code must be entered with a decimal point that is included in the valid code and without use of a zero or zeros that are not included in the valid code.

(k) Other Diagnosis Code (1), Other Diagnosis (2), Other Diagnosis (3), Other Diagnosis (4), Other Diagnosis (5), Other Diagnosis (6), Other Diagnosis (7), Other Diagnosis (8), Other Diagnosis (9) — A code representing a diagnosis related to the services provided during the visit. If no principal diagnosis code is reported, another diagnosis code must not be reported. No more than nine other diagnosis codes may be reported. Less than nine entries or no entry is permitted consistent with the records of the reporting entity. If not space filled, must contain a valid ICD-9-CM code or valid ICD-10-CM code for the reporting period. Inconsistency between the diagnosis code and patient sex must be verified by the reporting entity. Inconsistency between the diagnosis code and patient age must be verified by the reporting entity. A diagnosis code cannot be used more than once as a principal or other diagnosis for each visit reported. The code must be entered with use of a decimal point that is included in the valid code and without use of a zero or zeros that are not included in the valid code.

(l) Principal CPT or HCPCS Procedure Code — A code representative of the services provided or procedures performed. Must contain a valid CPT code between 10000 and 69999, inclusive, or between 93500 and 93599, inclusive if type of service is "1" indicating ambulatory surgery. Must contain a valid HCPCS or CPT evaluation and management code if type of service is "2" indicating an emergency department visit and patient status is not "07." Must contain a valid HCPCS or CPT evaluation and management code, or a blank field, consistent with the records of the reporting entity, if type of service is "2" indicating an emergency department visit and patient status is "07" indicating that the patient left against medical advice or discontinued care. If not space filled, must contain a valid CPT or HCPCS procedure code. Inconsistency between the principal procedure code and patient sex must be verified by the reporting entity. Inconsistency between the principal procedure code and patient age must be verified by the reporting entity. The code must be five digits and valid for the reporting period.

(m) Other CPT or HCPCS Procedure Code (1), Other CPT or HCPCS Procedure Code (2), Other CPT or HCPCS Procedure Code (3), Other CPT or HCPCS Procedure Code (4), Other CPT or HCPCS Procedure Code (5), Other CPT or HCPCS Procedure Code (6), Other CPT or HCPCS Procedure Code (7), Other CPT or HCPCS Procedure Code (8), Other CPT or HCPCS Procedure Code (9) — A code representing a procedure or service provided during the visit. If no principal CPT or HCPCS procedure is reported, another CPT or HCPCS procedure code must not be reported. No more than nine other CPT or HCPCS procedure codes may be reported. Less than nine entries or no entry is permitted consistent with the records of the reporting entity. If not space filled, must be a valid CPT or HCPCS code. Inconsistency between the procedure code and patient sex must be verified by the reporting entity. Inconsistency between the procedure code and patient age must be verified by the reporting entity. The code must be five digits and valid for the reporting period.

(n) Attending Physician Identification Number — The Florida license number of the attending physician as defined in subsection 59B-9.013(7), F.A.C. Report the medical doctor, osteopathic physician, dentist, podiatrist, chiropractor or advanced registered nurse practitioner who had primary responsibility for the patient's care during the visit. An alpha-numeric field of up to eleven characters. For military physicians not licensed in Florida, use US. Use NA if the patient was not treated by a medical doctor, osteopathic physician, dentist, podiatrist, chiropractor, or advanced registered nurse practitioner. A required entry.

(o) Operating or Performing Physician Identification Number — The Florida license number of the operating or performing physician as defined in subsection 59B-9.013(8), F.A.C. Report the medical doctor, osteopathic physician, dentist, podiatrist, chiropractor, or advanced registered nurse practitioner who had primary responsibility for the surgery or procedure performed. The operating or performing physician may be the person reported in paragraph (n) above. An alpha-numeric field of up to eleven characters. For military physicians not licensed in Florida, use US. A blank or no entry is permitted consistent with the records of the reporting entity.

(p) Other Physician Identification Number — The Florida license number of another physician as defined in subsection 59B-9.013(9), F.A.C. Report a medical doctor, osteopathic physician, dentist, podiatrist, chiropractor, or advanced registered nurse practitioner who rendered care to the patient other than the person reported in paragraph (n) or (o) above. An alpha-numeric field of up to eleven characters. For military physicians not licensed in Florida, use US. A blank or no entry is permitted consistent with the records of the reporting entity.

(q) Pharmacy Charges — Charges for medication, reported in dollars numerically without dollar signs or commas, excluding cents. Report 0 (zero) if there are no pharmacy charges. Negative amounts are not permitted unless verified separately by the reporting entity. A required entry.

(r) Medical and Surgical Supply Charges — Charges for supply items required for patient care, reported in dollars numerically without dollar signs or commas, excluding cents. Report 0 (zero) if there are no medical and surgical supply charges. Negative amounts are not permitted unless verified separately by the reporting entity. A required entry.

(s) Laboratory Charges — Charges for the performance of diagnostic and routine clinical laboratory tests, reported in dollars numerically without dollar signs or commas, excluding cents. Report 0 (zero) if there are no laboratory charges. Negative amounts are not permitted unless verified separately by the reporting entity. A required entry.

(t) Radiology and Other Imaging Charges — Charges for the performance of diagnostic and therapeutic radiology services including computed tomography, mammography, magnetic resonance imaging, nuclear medicine, and chemotherapy administration of radioactive substances, reported in dollars numerically without dollar signs or commas, excluding cents. Report 0 (zero) if there are no radiology or computed tomography charges. Negative amounts are not permitted unless verified separately by the reporting entity. A required entry.

(u) Cardiology Charges — Facility charges for cardiac procedures rendered such as heart catheterization, reported in dollars numerically without dollar signs or commas, excluding cents. Report 0 (zero) if there are no cardiology charges. Negative amounts are not permitted unless verified separately by the reporting entity. A required entry.

(v) Operating Room Charges — Charges for the use of the operating room, reported in dollars numerically without dollar signs or commas, excluding cents. Report 0 (zero) if there are no operating room charges. Negative amounts are not permitted unlessverified separately by the reporting entity. A required entry.

(w) Anesthesia Charges — Charges for anesthesia services by the facility, reported in dollars numerically without dollar signs or commas, excluding cents. Report 0 (zero) if there are no anesthesia charges. Negative amounts are not permitted unless verified separately by the reporting entity. A required entry.

(x) Recovery Room Charges — Charges for the use of the recovery room, reported in dollars numerically without dollar signs or commas, excluding cents. Report 0 (zero) if there are no recovery room charges. Negative amounts are not permitted unless verified separately by the reporting entity. A required entry.

(y) Emergency Room Charges — Charges for medical examinations and emergency treatment, reported in dollars numerically without dollar signs or commas, excluding cents. Report 0 (zero) if there are no emergency room charges. Negative amounts are not permitted unless verified separately by the reporting entity. A required entry.

(z) Treatment or Observation Room Charges — Charges for use of a treatment room or for the room charge associated with observation services, reported in dollars numerically without dollar signs or commas, excluding cents. Report 0 (zero) if there are no treatment or observation room charges. Negative amounts are not permitted unless verified separately by the reporting entity. A required entry.

(aa) Other Charges — Other facility charges not included in paragraphs (q) to (z) above, reported in dollars numerically without dollar signs or commas, excluding cents. Report 0 (zero) if there are no other charges. Negative amounts are not permitted unless verified separately by the reporting entity. A required entry.

(bb) Total Gross Charges — The total of undiscounted charges for services rendered by the reporting entity, reported in dollars numerically without dollar signs or commas, excluding cents. Include charges for services rendered by the ambulatory center excluding professional fees. Zero (0) or negative amounts are not permitted unless verified separately by the reporting entity. Amounts exceeding 50000 must be verified separately by the reporting entity if type of service is "1" indicating ambulatory surgery. Amounts exceeding 100000 must be verified separately by the reporting entity if type of service is "2" indicating an emergency department visit. The sum of pharmacy charges, medical and surgical supply charges, laboratory charges, radiology and other imaging charges, cardiology charges, operating room charges, anesthesia charges, recovery room charges, emergency room charges, treatment or observation room charges, and other charges must equal total charges, plus or minus 10. A required entry.

(cc) Patient Visit Beginning Date — The date at the beginning of the patient's visit for ambulatory surgery or the date at the time of registration in the emergency department. A ten character field in the format YYYY-MM-DD where MM represents the numbered months of the year from 1 to 12, DD represents numbered days of the month from 1 to 31, and YYYY represents the year in four digits. Patient visit beginning date must equal or precede the patient visit ending date. A required entry.

(dd) Patient Visit Ending Date — The date at the end of the patient's visit. A ten character field in the format YYYY-MM-DD where MM represents the numbered months of the year from 1 to 12, DD represents numbered days of the month from 1 to 31, and YYYY represents the year in four digits. Patient visit ending date must equal or follow the patient visit beginning date. Patient visit ending date must occur within the calendar quarter recorded on the CD-ROM or diskette external label and header record. A visit exceeding 2 days as determined by the patient visit beginning date and patient visit ending date must be verified by the reporting entity. A blank field is not permitted unless type of service is "2" indicating an emergency department visit and patient status is "07" indicating the patient left against medical advice or discontinued care.

(ee) Hour of Arrival — The hour on a 24-hour clock during which the patient's visit for ambulatory surgery began or during which registration in the emergency department occurred. A required entry. Use 99 where efforts to obtain the information have been unsuccessful. Must be two digits as follows:

1. 00— 12:00 midnight to 12:59

2. 01 — 01:00 to 01:59

3. 02 — 02:00 to 02:59

4. 03 — 03:00 to 03:59

5. 04 — 04:00 to 04:59

6. 05 — 05:00 to 05:59

7. 06 — 06:00 to 06:59

8. 07 — 07:00 to 07:59

9. 08 — 08:00 to 08:59

10. 09 — 09:00 to 09:59

11. 10 — 10:00 to 10:59

12. 11 — 11:00 to 11:59

13. 12 — 12:00 noon to 12:59

14. 13 — 01:00 to 01:59

15. 14 — 02:00 to 02:59

16. 15 — 03:00 to 03:59

17. 16 — 04:00 to 04:59

18. 17 — 05:00 to 05:59

19. 18 — 06:00 to 06:59

20. 19 — 07:00 to 07:59

21. 20 — 08:00 to 08:59

22. 21 — 09:00 to 09:59

23. 22 — 10:00 to 10:59

24. 23 — 11:00 to 11:59

25. 99 — Unknown.

(ff) Patient's Reason for Visit ICD-CM Code

(Admitting Diagnosis) — The code representing the patient's chief complaint or stated reason for seeking care. Must contain a valid ICD-9-CM code or valid ICD-10-CM code for the reporting period if type of service is "2" indicating an emergency department visit unless the patient fails to disclose or the information is unavailable. A blank field is permitted if the patient fails to disclose or efforts to obtain the information have been unsuccessful consistent with the records of the reporting entity. If not space filled, must contain a valid ICD-9-CM or ICD-10-CM diagnosis code. The code must be entered with use of a decimal point that is included in the valid code and without use of a zero or zeros that are not included in the valid code. Space fill if type of service is "07" indicating ambulatory surgery.

(gg) Principal ICD-CM Procedure Code — The code representing the procedure or service most related to the principal diagnosis. A blank field is permitted if type of service is "1" indicating ambulatory surgery. A blank or no entry is permitted consistent with the records of the reporting entity if type of service is "2" indicating an emergency department visit. If not space filled, must contain a valid ICD-9-CM or ICD-10-CM procedure code for the reporting period. Inconsistency between the principal procedure code and patient sex must be verified by the reporting entity. Inconsistency between the principal procedure code and patient age must be verified by the reporting entity. The code must be entered with use of a decimal point that is included in the valid code and without use of a zero or zeros that are not included in the valid code.

(hh) Other ICD-CM Procedure Code (1), Other ICD-CM Procedure Code (2), Other ICD-CM Procedure Code (3), Other ICD-CM Procedure Code (4) — A code representing a procedure or service provided during the visit. If no principal ICD-CM procedure is reported, another ICD-CM procedure code must not be reported. No more than four other ICD-CM procedure codes may be reported. A blank or no entry is permitted if type of service is "1." Less than four or no entry is permitted if type of service is "2" consistent with the records of the reporting entity. If not space filled, must be a valid ICD-9-CM or ICD-10-CM procedure code for the reporting period. Inconsistency between the procedure code and patient sex must be verified by the reporting entity. Inconsistency between the procedure code and patient age must be verified by the reporting entity. The code must be entered with use of a decimal point that is included in the valid code and without use of a zero or zeros that are not included in the valid code.

(ii) External Cause of Injury Code (1), External Cause of Injury Code (2), and External Cause of Injury Code (3) — A code representing circumstances or conditions as the cause of the injury, poisoning, or other adverse effects recorded as a diagnosis. No more than three external cause of injury codes may be reported. Less than three or no entry is permitted consistent with the records of the reporting entity. If not space filled, must be a valid ICD-9-CM or ICD-10-CM cause of injury code for the reporting period. An external cause of injury code cannot be used more than once for each visit reported. The code must be entered with use of a decimal point that is included in the valid code and without use of a zero or zeros that are not included in the valid code.

(jj) Patient Status — Patient disposition at end of visit. A required entry. Must be a two digit code as follows:

1. 01 — Discharged to home or self care (with or without planned outpatient medical care).

2. 02 — Transferred to a short-term general hospital.

3. 03 — Transferred to a skilled nursing facility.

4. 04 — Transferred to an intermediate care facility.

5. 05 — Transferred to another type of institution (psychiatric, cancer or children's hospital or distinct part unit).

6. 06 — Discharged to home under care of home health care organization.

7. 07 — Left against medical advice or discontinued care.

8. 08 — Discharged to home under care of home IV provider.

9. 20 — Expired.

10. 50 — Discharged to hospice — home.

11. 51 — Transferred to hospice — medical facility.

12. 62 — Transferred to an inpatient rehabilitation facility including distinct part units of a hospital.

(3) Trailer Record: The last record in the data file shall be a trailer record and must accompany each data set. If diskettes are submitted, the trailer record must be placed as the last record on the last diskette of the data set. One data element, number of records, must be entered in the trailer record. Report the total number of patient data records contained in the file, excluding header and trailer records. The number entered must equal the number of records processed.

Specific Authority 408.15(8) Fla. Stat.

Law Implemented 408.061, 408.062, 408.063 Fla. Stat.

History: New 9-6-93, Formerly 59B-7.018, Amended 6-29-95, 12-28-98, 7-11-2001, 2-25-2002, 4-18-04.

59B-9.019. Ambulatory Patient Data Format — Record Layout.

Specific Authority 408.15(8) Fla. Stat.

Law Implemented 408.061, 408.062, 408.063 Fla. Stat.

History: New 9-6-93, Formerly 59B-7.019, Amended 6-29-95, 12-28-98, 7-11-2001, 2-25-2002, Repealed 4-18-04.

59B-9.020. Data Standards.

Specific Authority 408.15(8) Fla. Stat.

Law Implemented 408.061, 408.062, 408.063 Fla. Stat.

History: New 9-6-93, Formerly 59B-7.020, Amended 6-29-95, 12-28-98, 7-11-2001, 2-25-2002, Repealed 4-14-04.

59B-9.021. Manual Submission of Data.

Specific Authority 408.15(8) Fla. Stat.

Law Implemented 408.061 Fla. Stat.

History: New 9-6-93, Formerly 59B-7.021, Amended 6-29-95, 1-4-2000, Repealed 7-11-2001.

59B-9.022. Penalties for Ambulatory Patient Data Reporting Deficiencies.

(1) For purposes of this rule, a report or other information is "incomplete" when it does not contain all data required by the agency or when it contains inaccurate data and the report is not corrected by the ambulatory center and certified timely pursuant to Rule 59B-9.017, F.A.C. A report or other information is "false" if done or made with the knowledge of the preparer or an administrator that it contains information or data which is not true or accurate.

(2) An ambulatory center which refuses to file, fails to timely file, or files false or incomplete reports or other information required to be filed under the provisions of s. 408.08, F.S., other Florida Law, or a rule adopted thereunder, shall be subject to administrative fines pursuant to s. 408.08 (14), F.S.

(3) Reports are deemed delinquent on the first working day following the due date.

(4) Delinquent report notices will be sent via certified mail to the attention of "chief executive officer."

(5) The penalty period will begin on the first working day following the due date for purposes of penalty assessments.

(6) Any ambulatory center which is delinquent for a reporting deficiency other than submission of a false report shall be subject to a fine of $100 per day of violation for the first violation, $350 per day of violation for the second violation, and $1000 per day of violation for the third or subsequent violations to be fixed, imposed, and collected by the agency. Any ambulatory center which files a false report with the agency or provides false information to the agency shall be subject to a fine of $1000 per

day to be fixed, imposed and collected by the agency.

Specific Authority 408.15(8) Fla. Stat.

Law Implemented 408.006(5), 408.061, 408.08(14) Fla. Stat.

History: New 9-6-93, Formerly 59B-7.022, Amended 6-29-95.

59B-9.023. Ambulatory Patient Data Release.

(1) Agency records, public records under Chapter 119, F.S., (Florida's Public Records Law), are available for public inspection during normal business hours. Copies of such records may be obtained upon request and upon payment of the cost of copying. ($0.15 per one-sided page or $0.20 per two-sided page.)

(2) Patient-specific records collected by the Agency pursuant to Rules 59B-9.010 through 59B-9.022, F.A.C., are exempt from disclosure pursuant to s. 408.061 (8), F.S., and shall not be released unless modified to protect patient confidentiality as described in paragraph (2)(a) below and released in the manner described in paragraphs (2)(c) and (2)(d).

(a) The patient-specific record shall be modified to protect patient confidentiality as follows:

1. Record ID Number Delete or Substitute Sequential Number

2. Patient Social Delete or Substitute a Record Linkage Number Security Number

3. Patient Birth Date Substitute Age

4. Patient Zip Code If less than 500 population for zip code per U.S. census, report a code representing a combination set of zip codes; if out of state, report state, U.S. territory or out of country code.

5. Patient Visit Substitute Month Indicator (01 12)

(b) A record linkage number shall be assigned which does not identify an individual patient and cannot reasonably be used to identify individual patients through use of data available through the Agency.

(c) The modified data records described in paragraph (2)(a) shall be released as a set of all records occurring in one calendar quarterly period based on date of visit.

(3) Aggregate reports derived from patient-specific records collected pursuant to Rules 59B-9.010 through 59B-9.022, F.A.C., are public records and shall be released as described in subsections (1) and (4) of this rule, provided the aggregate reports do not include record ID number, patient birth date, patient visit date, patient social security number, or patient zip code or provided the aggregate reports contain the combination of five or more records for any data disclosed.

(4) Requests shall be submitted by users sufficiently in advance to permit the staff to respond without disruption of its duties as provided in s. 119.07 (1)(b), F.S.

Specific Authority 408.15(8) Fla. Stat.

Law Implemented 119.07, 120.53(2)(a), 408.061 Fla. Stat.

History: New 9-6-93, Formerly 59B-7.023, Amended 6-29-95.

CHAPTER 59B-11 Exceptions to 440.13(1)(m), Florida Statutes, Coverage of Experimental and Investigative Procedures and Treatments Under Research

59B-11.001. Purpose.

Specific Authority 440.13(1)(m) Fla. Stat.

Law Implemented 440.13(1)(m), 440.13(2) Fla. Stat.

History: New 3-4-96, Repealed 4-18-04.

59B-11.002. Definitions.

Specific Authority 440.13(1)(m) Fla. Stat.

Law Implemented 440.13(1)(m) Fla. Stat.

History: New 3-4-96, Repealed 4-18-04.

59B-11.003. Request for Agency Review.

Specific Authority 440.13(1)(m) Fla. Stat.

Law Implemented 440.13(1)(m) Fla. Stat.

History: New 3-4-96, Repealed 4-18-04.

59B-11.004. Agency Review.

Specific Authority 440.13(1)(m) Fla. Stat.

Law Implemented 440.13(1)(m) Fla. Stat.

History: New 3-4-96, Repealed 4-18-04.

59B-11.005. Agency Determination.

Specific Authority 440.015, 440.13(1)(m) Fla. Stat.

Law Implemented 120.57, 440.13(1)(m) Fla. Stat.

History: New 3-4-96, Repealed 4-18-04.

59B-11.006. Reimbursement Disputes.

Specific Authority 440.13(1)(m) Fla. Stat.

Law Implemented 440.13(1)(m), 440.13(7) Fla. Stat.

History: New 3-4-96, Repealed 4-18-04.

TITLE 60 DEPARTMENT OF MANAGEMENT SERVICES

CHAPTER 60-Q Rules of Procedure for Workers' Compensation Adjudications

60Q-6.101. Scope.

These rules of procedure apply in all workers' compensation proceedings before the judges of compensation claims.

Specific Authority 440.45(1)(a), (4) Fla. Stat.

Law Implemented 440.45(1)(a), (4) Fla. Stat.

History: New 2-23-03, Amended 11-1-06.

60Q-6.102 Definitions.

(1) "Claim" means each assertion of a legal right or benefit under Chapter 440, Florida Statutes.

(2) "Claimant" means the person asserting a claim.

(3) "Division" means the Division of Workers' Compensation, Department of Financial Services.

(4) "Office of the Judges of Compensation Claims" (OJCC) is the office within the Department of Management Services, Division of Administrative Hearings, where the deputy chief judge and judges of compensation claims preside.

(5) "Electronic transmission" means transmitted through a link on the OJCC website identified for that purpose.

(6) "Filed" means received by the clerk of the Office of the Judges of Compensation Claims in Tallahassee or by the judge as provided in subsection 60Q-6.108(1), F.A.C.

(7) "Judge" means a judge of compensation claims appointed pursuant to Chapter 440, Florida Statutes.

(8) "Parties" may include the petitioner, claimant, employer, carrier, servicing agent, health care provider, and division.

(9) "Petition for benefits" means a pleading invoking the jurisdiction of the OJCC and subject to the requirements of Sections 440.192(1) through (4), Florida Statutes.

(10) "Pleading" means a petition for benefits or an amended petition, a motion, a response to a petition or a motion, a voluntary dismissal, a voluntary agreement to provide benefits, a stipulation changing the issues pending in a case, or a notice.

Specific Authority 440.45(1)(a), (4) Fla. Stat.

Law Implemented 440.192(1), 440.45 (1)(a), (4) Fla. Stat.

History: New 2-23-03, Amended 11-1-06.

60Q-6.103 Pleadings and Proposed Orders.

(1) Pleadings. All documents filed with the OJCC or with the judge shall:

(a) Be typewritten or printed on 8 1/2″ by 11″ unfolded white paper, unless filed by electronic transmission;

(b) Be unstapled;

(c) Contain the signature, or the electronic equivalent of the signature if filed electronically, of the party in interest or, if represented, the party's attorney of record;

(d) Contain the style of the proceeding; the case number, if any; the date of accident; the name of the party on whose behalf the document is filed; the subject matter of the document; and the name, mailing address, and telephone number of the party or, if represented, the party's attorney of record (including the attorney's Florida Bar number) filing the document; and

(e) Contain a certificate of service representing that copies have been served on all parties or, if represented, their attorneys of record.

(2) Exempt information. Except for the employee's social security number or equivalent on petitions for benefits and responses thereto, no pleading shall contain information exempt from public records disclosure. Exempt information shall be supplied in connection with a pleading only to the extent it is necessary to the judge's determination of disputed matters or required by Florida Statutes and shall be appended to a pleading in a separate document conspicuously marked "Exempt Information".

(3) All pleadings filed in paper form shall contain in the bottom 1 1/2 inches of each page only the following: "OJCC Case #" followed by the case number and "page #" followed by the page number.

(4) Proposed Orders. Except as provided in subsection 60Q-6.115(3), F.A.C., proposed orders shall not be submitted unless requested by the judge, and shall be accompanied by preaddressed, postage-paid envelopes. They shall be clearly identified as proposed orders and shall be sent to all other parties or, if represented, their attorneys of record prior to being submitted to the judge. Proposed orders shall be a separate document and not be included as a part of the motion.

Specific Authority 440.45(1)(a), (4) Fla. Stat.

Law Implemented 440.192(1), 440.45(1)(a), (4) Fla. Stat.

History: New 2-23-03, Amended 11-1-06.

60Q-6.104 Representation and Appearance of Counsel.

(1) Appearance of Counsel. An attorney who files a petition or claim on behalf of a party has entered an appearance and shall be deemed the party's attorney of record. All other attorneys appearing for a party in an existing case shall file promptly with the judge a notice of appearance and serve copies on all other parties or, if represented, their attorneys of record. The notice of appearance shall include the style of the proceeding; the case number; the name of the party on whose behalf the attorney is appearing; and the name, mailing address, telephone number, and Florida Bar number of the attorney.

(2) Substitution or Withdrawal of Counsel. During the pendency of any issues before the judge, an attorney of record remains the attorney of record until:

(a) A stipulation for substitution has been filed with the judge and served on all other parties or, if represented, their attorneys of record; or

(b) A motion to substitute or to withdraw, which reflects that it has been served on the client and all other parties or, if represented, their attorneys of record, is granted.

Specific Authority 440.45(1)(a), (4) Fla. Stat.

Law Implemented 440.45(1)(a), (4) Fla. Stat.

History: New 2-23-03, Amended 11-1-06.

60Q-6.105 Commencing a Case; Subsequent Petitions.

(1) An employee or claimant seeking an award of benefits commences a new case by filing a petition for benefits pursuant to Section 440.192, Florida Statutes, when there is not an existing case pertaining to the same employee and date of accident.

(2) When the employee and date of accident are the same as in an existing case, any subsequent petition for benefits or claim relating to that employee and date of accident shall be filed in the existing case.

(3) For any claim within the jurisdiction of the OJCC but not subject to a petition for benefits, the claimant shall file with the clerk of the OJCC the pleading setting forth the claim together with a request for assignment of case number.

(4) An employee or claimant who asserts he or she cannot provide a social security number or who asserts a legal basis for refusing to

provide one shall file a verified motion for assignment of substitute identification number along with the initial petition or request for assignment of case number.

(5) A claim for reimbursement from the Special Disability Trust Fund shall be made under the administrative rules promulgated by the division.

Specific Authority 440.45(1)(a), (4) Fla. Stat.

Law Implemented 440.192, 440.45(1)(a), (4) Fla. Stat.

History: New 2-23-03, 11-1-06.

60Q-6.106 Consolidation and Venue.

(1) The judge, on the judge's own initiative or on the motion of any party, may consolidate any claims or petitions, pending before the judge for the purpose of a hearing or for any other purpose, except for a claim for reimbursement from the Special Disability Trust Fund.

(2) Any motion to consolidate cases shall be filed in only the lowest-numbered case sought to be consolidated and shall be resolved by the judge to whom that case is assigned.

(3) A motion to change venue shall be filed with the judge and shall contain the signatures of all parties, or, if represented, their attorneys of record.

(4) When a judge assigned to a case determines that the case is proceeding in an incorrect venue, the judge may transfer the case to the proper venue.

(5) For accidents occurring outside of the state, the deputy chief judge's initial determination of venue may be changed by order of the assigned judge.

Specific Authority 440.45(1)(a), (4) Fla. Stat.

Law Implemented 440.25(4)(d), 440.45(1)(a), (4) Fla. Stat.

History: New 2-23-03, Amended 11-1-06.

60Q-6.107 Amendment and Dismissal of Petition for Benefits.

(1) A petition that does not contain the information required by Sections 440.192(2) through (4), Florida Statutes, shall be dismissed.

(2) A petition may only be amended by stipulation of the parties or by order of the judge, except that changes of addresses or phone numbers of parties or, if represented, their attorneys of record can be accomplished by filing a notice of change with the assigned judge.

Specific Authority 440.45(1)(a), (4) Fla. Stat.

Law Implemented 440.192, 440.45(1)(a), (4) Fla. Stat.

History: New 2-23-03, Amended 11-1-06.

60Q-6.108 Filing and Service.

(1) Filing.

(a) All petitions, amended petitions, responses to petitions, and requests for assignment of case number and initial pleadings relating thereto shall be filed with the OJCC. Except as otherwise provided in these rules, all motions, notices, pleadings, voluntary dismissals, any stipulations changing the issues pending in the case, or other documents shall be filed only with the judge.

(b) Any pleading or other paper filed in a proceeding shall be served on all other parties or, if represented, their attorneys of record at the time the document is filed.

(c) The following documents shall not be filed with the OJCC or with the judge unless relevant to an issue to be heard: requests or notices to produce and objections or responses thereto, deposition transcripts, correspondence between counsel or parties, subpoenas and returns of service.

(d) Facsimile or other electronic transmission of documents to the judge shall be used only when the judge authorizes such use for that document; otherwise, the document will not be considered.

(e) Any document, whether filed by electronic or other means, received by the OJCC or the judge after 5:00 p.m. shall be deemed filed as of 8:00 a.m. on the next regular business day.

(f) Any attorney, party, or other person who elects to file any document by electronic transmission shall be responsible for any delay, disruption, interruption of the electronic signals, and readability of the document, and accepts the full risk that the document may not be properly filed as a result.

(2) Service. Service is effectuated by:

(a) Handing it to the party or, if represented, the party's attorney of record;

(b) Leaving it at the attorney's office with a clerk or other person in charge or leaving it in a conspicuous place in the office;

(c) If the office is closed or the person to be served has no office, leaving it at the person's residence with a member of the person's family above 15 years of age and informing that person of the contents;

(d) Placing it in the United States mail; or

(e) Transmitting it by facsimile or by electronic transmission.

(3) Service by delivery, by facsimile transmission, or by electronic transmission after 5:00 p.m. shall be deemed to have been made on the next day that is not a Saturday, Sunday, or legal holiday.

(4) When service is made by mail, the copy shall be mailed by United States mail, postage prepaid, to the last known address of the party or, if represented, the party's attorney of record.

(5) Service by mail shall be complete upon mailing.

(6) When service of any pleading other than a petition is made by mail, 5 days shall be added to the time allowed for the performance of any act required to be done, or allowed to be done, within a certain time after service.

Specific Authority 440.45(1)(a), (4) Fla. Stat.

Law Implemented 440.192, 440.45(1)(a), (4) Fla. Stat.

History: New 2-23-03, Amended 11-1-06.

60Q-6.109. Computation of Time.

In computing any period of time prescribed or allowed by these rules, by order, or by applicable statute, the day of the act or event from which the designated period of time begins to run shall not be included. The last day of the period so computed shall be included. If any act required to be done, or allowed to be done, falls on a Saturday, Sunday, or legal holiday, performance of that act shall be required on the next regular working day. When the period of time allowed is less than seven days, intermediate Saturdays, Sundays, and legal holidays shall be excluded from the computation. As used in this rule, legal holiday means those days designated in Section 110.117, Florida Statutes.

Specific Authority 440.45(1)(a), (4) Fla. Stat.

Law Implemented 440.45(1)(a), (4) Fla. Stat.

History: New 2-23-03.

60Q-6.110 Mediation, Generally.

(1) All petitions and claims pending at the time a mediation conference is held are deemed consolidated and will be mediated at that conference.

(2) Parties who have agreed to private mediation or to re-schedule private mediation shall file with the judge at least 30 days prior to any scheduled mediation notice substituting private mediation for state mediation or re-scheduling private mediation. The notice shall include the name of the private mediator, along with the date and time of the private mediation and shall state that the private mediation meets the statutory deadline, unless the deadline is waived by all parties.

(3) The parties and private mediator shall be bound by the rules and statutes applicable to state mediation. If a notice and order regarding state mediation has been entered in the cause, the terms and requirements of the notice and order shall remain in full force and effect as to the substituted private mediation.

(4) If the parties settle all issues, or all issues except for attorney's fees, prior to the scheduled mediation conference, they shall immediately notify the mediator and the judge in writing.

(5) The following persons shall attend the mediation conference: the claimant; the claims representative of the carrier/servicing agent, which representative must have full authority to settle the issues; the employer, if uninsured; the insured or self-insured employer, if the

employer/servicing agent does not have full authority to settle the issues; and the attorneys for the parties. The appearance of an attorney for a party does not dispense with the required attendance of the party. No one may appear at the mediation conference by telephone unless such appearance is approved in advance by the mediator.

(6) Failure to attend the mediation conference without having shown good cause or failure to appear at the mediation conference with full authority to resolve the issues may subject the party or the attorney to sanctions.

(7) Immediately following the conclusion of the mediation conference, the mediator, whether state, adjunct, or private, shall prepare a report stating which issues or claims in dispute are resolved and which remain unresolved, and whether the parties completed a pretrial stipulation. The report shall identify by filing date each petition mediated. The claimant shall file with the judge within five days of the mediation conference the mediator's report and mediation settlement agreement, if any, together with any pretrial stipulation executed by the parties.

Specific Authority 440.45(1)(a), (4) Fla. Stat.

Law Implemented 440.25(1)-(4), 440.45(1)(a), (4) Fla. Stat.

History: New 2-23-03, Amended 11-1-06.

60Q-6.111 Authority and Duties of Mediator.

(1) Authority of Mediator.

(a) The mediator shall at all times be in control of the mediation and the procedures to be followed, subject to the direction of the judge.

(b) The mediator may meet and consult privately with any party or parties or their counsel during the mediation.

(c) The mediator shall have discretion to allow any party to appear at the mediation conference by telephone upon the party's written request furnished to the mediator and the opposing party or, if represented, the party's attorney of record no fewer than 5 days prior to the mediation conference.

(2) Duties of Mediator. The mediator shall inform the parties at the beginning of the mediation conference:

(a) Of the process of mediation;

(b) That the mediator is an impartial facilitator and is there to assist the parties in reaching, not to force them to reach, a voluntary settlement;

(c) Of the differences between mediation and a final hearing before the presiding judge;

(d) If applicable, of the costs of the mediation;

(e) That the mediation process is consensual in nature, and the parties retain their right to a final hearing if they do not reach agreement;

(f) Of the privileged and confidential nature of communications made during the mediation;

(g) That any agreement reached at the mediation conference will be by mutual consent of the parties reduced to writing and may be subject to the approval of the presiding judge; and

(h) That the mediator will timely determine when mediation should end.

(3) Disclosure. The mediator has a duty to be impartial and to advise all parties of any circumstances bearing on possible bias, prejudice, or partiality.

(4) Matters Beyond Mediator's Competence. A mediator shall decline appointment or withdraw when the mediator decides that a matter is beyond the mediator's competence.

Specific Authority 440.45(1)(a), (4) Fla. Stat.

Law Implemented 440.25(1)-(4), 440.45(1)(a), (4) Fla. Stat.

History: New 2-23-03, Amended 11-1-06.

60Q-6.112. Disqualification of Mediator.

Any party may, by motion, for good cause shown, request the judge to disqualify a mediator. The request must state with particularity the basis for disqualification. Any order disqualifying a mediator shall name a substitute mediator. Nothing in this rule shall preclude mediators from disqualifying themselves or refusing any assignment.

Specific Authority 440.45(1)(a), (4) Fla. Stat.

Law Implemented 440.45(1)(a), (4) Fla. Stat.

History: New 2-23-03.

60Q-6.113 Pretrial Procedure.

(1) A judge, on the judge's own initiative or on the motion of any party, may conduct status conferences or pre-hearing conferences.

(2) In pretrial stipulations and at any pretrial hearing, the parties shall:

(a) State and simplify the issues including bifurcation of compensability;

(b) Stipulate to such facts and the admissibility of documentary evidence as will avoid unnecessary proof;

(c) Examine and mark all exhibits (except for impeachment and rebuttal exhibits) for identification;

(d) Furnish the opposing party with the names and addresses of all witnesses (except for impeachment and rebuttal witnesses), identifying those who will testify by telephone;

(e) Exchange all available written reports of experts to be offered at trial; and

(f) Consider and determine such other matters as may aid in the disposition of the case.

(3) Where mediation has been waived by the deputy chief judge, the parties shall file a pretrial stipulation that conforms to the requirements of subsection (2) of this rule no later than 30 days following the waiver order.

(4) Witness lists, exhibit lists, supplements, and amendments served, and exhibits exchanged less than 30 days before the final hearing must be approved by the judge or stipulated to by the parties.

(5) The judge shall record the pretrial hearing by stenographic or electronic means at the request of any party.

Specific Authority 440.45(1)(a), (4) Fla. Stat.

Law Implemented 440.25(2)-(4), 440.29(2), 440.33(1), 440.45(1)(a), (4) Fla. Stat.

History: New 2-23-03, Amended 11-1-06.

60Q-6.114 Discovery.

(1) Any party may commence with discovery methods specifically authorized by statute, including depositions, issuance of subpoenas and requests for production, prior to invoking the jurisdiction of the judge.

(2) Depositions.

(a) Depositions of witnesses or parties may be taken and used in the same manner and for the same purposes as provided in the Florida Rules of Civil Procedure.

(b) Approval of the judge is not necessary to take a deposition by telephone. If a deposition is taken by telephone, the oath shall be administered in the physical presence of the witness by a notary public or other person authorized by law to administer oaths.

(3) Production and entry on land. Any party may seek production of documents or other tangible things from other parties or non-parties and may seek entry onto land or other property as provided in the Florida Rules of Civil Procedure.

(4) Responses and objections to depositions, production, or entry shall be made as provided in the Florida Rules of Civil Procedure.

(5) The judge may enter orders to effectuate discovery, including orders compelling discovery, protective orders, and orders imposing sanctions for failure to comply with or for using discovery methods not specifically authorized by statute. For good cause shown, the judge may enlarge or shorten applicable timeframes for complying with discovery.

Specific Authority 440.45(1)(a), (4) Fla. Stat.

Law Implemented 440.30, 440.33(1), 440.45(1)(a), (4) Fla. Stat.

History: New 2-23-03, Amended 11-1-06.

60Q-6.115 Motion Practice.

(1) Any request for an order or for other relief shall be by motion and shall have a title describing the relief requested. The judge may treat a non-standard request for relief from an

unrepresented party as a motion. All motions shall be in writing unless made on the record during a hearing and shall fully state the relief requested and the grounds relied upon.

(2) Except for motions to dismiss for lack of prosecution, prior to filing any motion, the movant shall personally confer with the opposing party or parties or, if represented, their attorneys of record to attempt to amicably resolve the subject matter of the motion. All motions shall include a statement that the movant has personally conferred or has used good-faith efforts to confer with all other parties or, if represented, their attorneys of record and shall state whether any party has an objection to the motion.

(3) A motion which is unopposed shall state why an order is necessary to execute the parties' agreement and, unless filed electronically, shall be accompanied by a proposed order which has a title describing the action being taken. The motion and proposed order shall specify the relief being requested or ordered in reasonable detail and not merely by reference to any other document.

(4) If the motion has not been amicably resolved, the movant shall file the motion, which shall include a statement as to whether a hearing on the motion is necessary and, if so, the basis for requesting a hearing. The other parties may, within ten days of service of the written motion, file a response in opposition, which shall include a statement as to whether a hearing on the motion is necessary and, if so, the basis for requesting a hearing. The judge may dispose of written motions without a hearing within ten days following the expiration of the time for service of a response by the other party or parties. If no order is entered within that ten-day period, the movant shall schedule a hearing time with the opposing party or parties or, if represented, their attorneys of record. If no hearing is scheduled within fourteen days following that ten-day period, the request for a hearing is deemed withdrawn. Motion hearings may be conducted either in person or telephonically as the judge deems necessary.

(5) Motions for extension of time shall be filed prior to the expiration of the deadline sought to be extended and shall state good cause for the request.

(6) Motions to expedite discovery or the final hearing shall set forth good cause and shall be served by facsimile transmission, hand delivery, or overnight delivery. Any opposition to the motion must be filed within four days from the date of the motion.

Specific Authority 440.25(4)(h), 440.45(1)(a), (4) Fla. Stat.

Law Implemented 440.25(4)(h), 440.45(1)(a), (4) Fla. Stat.

History: New 2-23-03, Amended 11-1-06.

60Q-6.116 Prosecution of Claim and Petition for Benefits.

(1) A request for a continuance shall be made by motion and shall specify the reason that the continuance is necessary.

(2) A claim or petition may be dismissed by the claimant or petitioner without an order by filing a notice of voluntary dismissal at any time before the conclusion of the final hearing. Unless otherwise stated in the notice, the dismissal is without prejudice, except that a second notice of voluntary dismissal shall operate as an adjudication of denial of any claim or petition for benefits previously the subject of a voluntary dismissal.

(3) The judge may conduct any proceedings by telephone conference. Testimony may be taken by telephone with the agreement of all parties or approval by the judge.

(4) In the event that testimony is taken by telephone, the oath shall be administered in the physical presence of the witness by a notary public or officer authorized to administer oaths.

(5) Except as authorized by statute, the judge may enter an order reflecting the terms of any written stipulation or agreement between the parties only where one of the parties to the stipulation or agreement alleges that another party has failed or refused to comply with the stipulation or agreement and an order is necessary for immediate enforcement; otherwise, the parties shall not request that the judge approve a

stipulation or agreement or reduce it to an order.

(6) Any attorney or unrepresented claimant who has filed a petition for benefits must file a pleading with the judge in order to cancel the corresponding final hearing. The pleading must be filed prior to the scheduled final hearing and shall indicate the manner in which each issue was resolved.

(7) At least two full business days prior to the final hearing, each party is required to file a brief memorandum consisting of a statement of relevant facts and written argument. All depositions a party intends to offer into evidence shall be filed with the memorandum.

Specific Authority 440.45(1)(a), (4) Fla. Stat.

Law Implemented 440.25(4), 440.29(2), 440.33(1), 440.45(1)(a), (4) Fla. Stat.

History: New 2-23-03, Amended 11-1-06.

60Q-6.117 Emergency Conferences.

(1) A written request for an emergency conference shall be filed with the judge and served on all other parties or, if represented, their attorneys of record. It shall set forth in detail the facts giving rise to the request, its legal basis, the factual or medical basis for the claim that there is a bona fide emergency involving the health, safety, or welfare of an employee, and the specific relief sought. Any documents relied upon should be specifically referenced and attached.

(2) After reviewing the merits of the request, the judge may summarily enter an order denying the request for an emergency conference or, after proper notice, conduct an evidentiary hearing to consider the request.

Specific Authority 440.45(1)(a), (4) Fla. Stat.

Law Implemented 440.25(4)(g), 440.45(1)(a), (4) Fla. Stat.

History: New 2-23-03, Amended 11-1-06.

60Q-6.118 Expedited Hearings.

(1) Scope. This rule applies in those cases deemed by the judge appropriate for expedited hearing pursuant to statute or by agreement of the parties.

(2) Discovery. The parties shall have at least 30 days to conduct discovery, which shall be completed 15 days before the hearing. The parties shall respond to requests for production within 10 days.

(3) No mediation conference and pretrial hearing shall be held unless requested in writing by a party within 10 days of service of the notice of expedited hearing.

(4) Stipulated Pretrial Outline. At least 15 days before the final hearing, a stipulated pretrial outline shall be filed and shall include the following:

(a) A concise statement of the nature of the controversy;

(b) A brief, general statement of each party's position;

(c) A list of all exhibits (except for impeachment and rebuttal exhibits) to be offered at the hearing, noting any objections thereto, and the grounds for each objection (no additional documentary evidence will be admitted at the hearing);

(d) A list of the names and addresses of all witnesses (except for impeachment and rebuttal witnesses) to be called at the hearing by each party, with expert witnesses being so designated, together with a summary of the expected testimony;

(e) A concise statement of those facts which are admitted and will require no proof at hearing, together with any reservations directed to any such admission; and

(f) A list of all pending motions or other matters which require action by the judge.

Specific Authority 440.25(4)(i), 440.45(1)(a), (4) Fla. Stat.

Law Implemented 440.25(4)(i), 440.45(1)(a), (4) Fla. Stat.

History: New 2-23-03, Amended 11-1-06.

60Q-6.119 Abbreviated Final Orders.

Any party may request that an abbreviated final order be vacated and that a final compensation order containing separate findings of fact and conclusions of law be entered. The request shall be made by motion and shall be filed within 10 days of the date of the abbreviated final order sought to be vacated.

Specific Authority 440.45(1)(a), (4) Fla. Stat.

Law Implemented 440.25(4)(d), 440.45(1)(a), (4) Fla. Stat.

History: New 2-23-03, Amended 11-1-06.

60Q-6.120 Summary Final Order.

(1) The judge may enter a summary final order when such an order would be dispositive of the issues raised by the subject petition. Issues that would be dispositive include, but are not limited to, whether there is coverage, whether the statute of limitations has run, whether the accident or occupational disease is compensable, whether the claim is barred by res judicata or a prior settlement, whether the judge has jurisdiction over the subject matter, whether the benefit sought has been paid, and whether the alleged employee is an independent contractor.

(2) Any party may file a motion for a summary final order when there is no genuine issue as to any material fact and the granting of the motion would be dispositive of the issues raised by the subject petition. A summary final order shall be rendered if the judge determines from the pleadings and depositions, together with affidavits, if any, that no genuine issue as to any material fact exists and that the moving party is entitled as a matter of law to the entry of a final order. A summary final order may be rendered on the issue of entitlement to a benefit alone although there is a genuine issue as to the amount of the benefits. No motion for summary final order may be filed less than 45 days prior to a scheduled final hearing.

(3) The opposing party shall file a response to motion for summary final order together with supporting depositions, affidavits and/or other documents within 30 days of service of the motion for summary final order. The judge shall grant an extension for good cause shown.

(4) When a motion for summary final order is denied, the judge shall impose sanctions pursuant to subsections 60Q-6.125(5) and (6), F.A.C., if the judge determines that the motion violates subsection 60Q-6.125(2), F.A.C.

(5) The motion is deemed denied if the judge has not ruled upon the motion by the commencement of the final hearing.

Specific Authority 440.45(1)(a), (4) Fla. Stat.

Law Implemented 440.25(4)(h), 440.45(1)(a), (4) Fla. Stat.

History: New 2-23-03, Amended 11-1-06.

60Q-6.121 Evidence.

(1) Evidence which has been offered but ruled inadmissible may be proffered but shall be clearly identified as such by the judge.

(2) An objection to the admissibility of evidence not ruled on by the judge is deemed adverse to the party making the objection.

(3) Legible copies may be substituted for original documents.

(4) Voluminous or cumbersome exhibits shall not be received in evidence unless their use is unavoidable.

(5) The judge may consider post-hearing evidence for good cause shown.

Specific Authority 440.45(1)(a), (4) Fla. Stat.

Law Implemented 440.45(1)(a), (4) Fla. Stat.

History: New 2-23-03, Amended 11-1-06.

60Q-6.122 Motion for Re-hearing and Amending or Vacating Order.

(1) A motion for re-hearing shall state specifically the grounds on which it is based and should not be used to re-argue issues already determined. A motion for re-hearing shall be filed and served within 10 days from the date of the order sought to be reviewed.

(2) The motion shall be limited to the following reasons:

(a) To challenge rulings that were outside the scope of the issues presented, or

(b) To seek clarification in matters of law or fact that the judge may have overlooked or misapprehended.

(3) A motion for re-hearing does not toll the

time within which an order becomes final or an appeal may be filed.

(4) Abbreviated final orders are not subject to a motion for re-hearing.

(5) A judge, on the judge's own initiative or on the motion of any party, may vacate or amend an order not yet final to correct clerical or technical errors, or where due consideration of a motion for re-hearing cannot be made before the order becomes final.

Specific Authority 440.45(1)(a), (4) Fla. Stat.

Law Implemented 440.45(1)(a), (4) Fla. Stat.

History: New 2-23-03, Amended 11-1-06.

60Q-6.123 Settlements Under Section 440.20(11), Florida Statutes.

(1) Settlements under Section 440.20(11)(a) or (b), F.S., involving unrepresented claimants.

(a) When a joint petition signed by the parties is filed pursuant to Section 440.20(11)(a) or (b), F.S., it shall be accompanied by:

1. The settlement stipulation executed by the attorneys of record and the employee or claimant;

2. A copy of any prior joint petition and order if indemnity benefits were previously settled, or, if unavailable, an affidavit from the claimant that indemnity was previously settled;

3. A summary or payout sheet indicating total indemnity and medical benefits previously paid, including impairment income benefits;

4. The employee's current work status and other sources of income, if not addressed in the joint stipulation;

5. A status statement from the Department of Revenue and a status statement from the Clerk of the Circuit and County Courts, Central Depository, as to whether the claimant has or owes any child support arrearage and, if so, the amount thereof;

6. A sworn statement by the employee that all existing child support obligations have been disclosed in the joint petition;

7. A letter from counsel stating that the carrier will issue a check in the amount of the arrearage or such other amount to be approved by the judge and that the check will be sent to the Department of Revenue or the Clerk of the Circuit and County Courts, Central Depository;

8. Any other documents in the possession of the parties or their attorneys, including any prior attorney's fee lien, that is material to the disposition of the settlement;

9. For settlements under Section 440.20(11)(a), F.S., the notice(s) of denial; and

10. For settlements under Section 440.20(11)(b), F.S., the required notice to the employer, a maximum medical improvement report establishing overall physical maximum medical improvement and psychiatric maximum medical improvement if the latter applies, available information concerning the need for future medical care or an explanation as to why the information cannot be reasonably obtained, and other essential medical information.

(b) The date and description of all accidents/injuries included in the settlement must be specified.

(c) Language regarding a general release of all liability or claims shall not be included, and no such general release or separate releases shall be attached.

(d) For settlements under Section 440.20(11)(a), F.S., and when a hearing is deemed necessary by the judge for settlements under Section 440.20(11)(b), Florida Statutes, the attorney for the employer/carrier shall contact the judge to schedule a hearing date and shall promptly notify the claimant of the hearing date, time, and location.

(2) Settlements under Sections 440.20(11)(c), (d), and (e), F.S..

(a) When a motion for approval of attorney's fees and child support allocation is filed pursuant to Section 440.20(11)(c), (d), or (e), F.S., it shall be signed by the claimant and the claimant's attorney, furnished to all other parties, and contain:

1. A statement that the parties have reached a

total settlement of the case;

2. The total monetary amount of the settlement payable by the employer/carrier;

3. The amount of attorney's fees and costs agreed to and payable by the claimant pursuant to the contract of representation and the net settlement proceeds to be disbursed to the claimant;

4. The amount of child support arrearages, if any, owed by the claimant, together with the amount of child support allocation the claimant requests be deducted from the settlement proceeds, after fees and costs, and remitted to the appropriate child support depository;

5. An attorney's fee data sheet setting forth the benefits obtained by claimant's counsel and the value of those benefits, and, depending upon the date of accident and the type of benefit involved, if the claimant's attorney seeks a fee in excess of the statutory percentage, an affidavit specifying the particular statutory criteria forming the basis for the variance; and

6. A status statement from the Department of Revenue and a status statement from the Clerk of the Circuit and County Courts, Central Depository, as to whether the claimant has an arrearage or owes past due child support and, if so, the amount thereof, and a letter from counsel stating that the carrier will issue a check in the amount of the arrearage and/or past due child support or such other amount to be approved by the judge or that claimant's counsel will deposit the settlement proceeds in a trust account and will issue a check in the amount of the arrearage and/ or past due child support or such other amount to be approved by the judge and that the check will be sent to the Department of Revenue or the Clerk of the Circuit and County Courts, Central Depository.

(b) No hearing shall be held except as deemed necessary by the judge.

(3) Settlement approval when more than one current support order exists. When more than one current support order exists, the judge may approve a proposed settlement only if it provides for an equitable share of settlement proceeds.

Specific Authority 440.45(1)(a), (4) Fla. Stat.

Law Implemented 440.20(11), 440.45(1)(a), (4) Fla. Stat.

History: New 2-23-03, Amended 11-1-06.

60Q-6.124 Payment of Attorney's Fees and Costs Other Than Pursuant to Section 440.20(11), Florida Statutes.

(1) Payment of Undisputed Attorney's Fees and Costs by Claimant. The claimant and his or her attorney may jointly move for the judge to approve the payment of an attorney's fee and reimbursement of costs. The motion shall be served on all parties and include a statement that claimant's counsel has not previously secured or received a fee on the benefits for which a fee is now being sought, the claimant's signature, and an attorney's fee data sheet setting forth the benefits secured by claimant's counsel and the value of the benefits.

(2) Payment of Undisputed Attorney's Fees and Costs by Employer/Carrier/Servicing Agent. The employee and the employer/carrier/servicing agent may stipulate to the payment of attorney's fees and costs. The stipulation submitted for the judge's approval shall be accompanied by an attorney's fee data sheet. If claimant's counsel is seeking payment of a fee from the employer/carrier which exceeds the statutory fee, counsel must submit an affidavit establishing the basis for approval of the fee. The claimant must be provided with notice of any stipulation providing for an employer/carrier-paid attorney's fee.

(3) Payment of Disputed Attorney's Fees and Costs.

(a) Any motion for attorney's fees and costs shall be filed and shall include:

1. A statement of the facts relied on in support of the motion,

2. The statutory and legal basis relied upon,

3. A recitation of all benefits secured for the claimant through the attorney's efforts, including projected future benefits reduced to present

value,

4. The statutory fee based on the benefit secured,

5. A detailed chronological listing of all time devoted to the claim, if applicable, and

6. A detailed list of all taxable costs advanced or incurred.

(b) Within 30 days after the motion is served, the opposing party or parties shall file a response to the motion, which includes a detailed recitation of all matters which are disputed in the form outlined in subparagraph (3)(a)1.-6. Failure to file a timely and specific response to a motion for attorney's fees and costs shall, absent good cause, result in acceptance of the allegations in the motion as true.

(c) If both entitlement and the amount of the fee are contested, the hearing may be bifurcated.

(d) Unless the judge orders otherwise, the parties shall exchange exhibit and witness lists no later than 10 days before the date of the attorney's fee hearing.

(e) The Statewide Uniform Guidelines for Taxation of Costs in Civil Actions shall be considered by the judge in determining the reasonableness of an award of cost reimbursement.

(4) No later than October 1 of each year, all self-insurers, third-party administrators, and carriers shall report by electronic transmission to the OJCC the amount of all attorney's fees paid to their defense attorneys in connection with workers' compensation claims during the prior July 1 through June 30 fiscal year.

Specific Authority 440.45(1)(a), (4) Fla. Stat.

Law Implemented 440.34, 440.45(1)(a), (4) Fla. Stat.

History: New 2-23-03, Amended 11-1-06.

60Q-6.125 Sanctions.

(1) Generally. Failure to comply with the provisions of these rules or any order of the judge may subject a party or attorney to one or more of the following sanctions: striking of claims, petitions, defenses, or pleadings; imposition of costs or attorney's fees; or such other sanctions as the judge may deem appropriate.

(2) Representations to the Judge. By filing a pleading or other document or presenting agurment before the judge at hearing, an attorney or unrepresented party is certifying to the best of that person's knowledge, information, and belief, formed after inquiry reasonable under the circumstances, that:

(a) It is not being presented for any improper purpose, such as to harass or to cause unnecessary delay or needless increase in the cost of litigation;

(b) The claims, defenses, and other legal contentions therein are warranted by existing law or by a non-frivolous argument for the extension, modification, or reversal of existing law or the establishment of a new law;

(c) The allegations and other factual contentions are true and have evidentiary support or, if specifically so identified, are likely to have evidentiary support after a reasonable opportunity for further investigation or discovery;

(d) The denials of factual contentions are true and warranted on the evidence or, if specifically so identified, are reasonably based on a lack of information or belief.

(3) Determination of Violation. If, after notice and a reasonable opportunity to respond, the judge determines that subsection (2) has been violated, the judge may impose an appropriate sanction.

(4) How Initiated.

(a) A motion for sanctions under this rule shall be made separately from other motions or requests and shall describe the specific conduct alleged to violate subsection (2). It shall be served but shall not be filed with or presented to the judge unless the challenged paper, claim, defense, allegation, or denial is not withdrawn or appropriately corrected within 21 days after service of the motion. If warranted, the judge may award to the party prevailing on the motion the cost of the proceeding and attorney's fees incurred in presenting or opposing the motion.

(b) On his or her own initiative, the judge may enter an order describing the specific conduct that appears to violate subsection (2) and directing an attorney or party to show cause why sanctions should not be imposed.

(5) Nature of Sanctions.

(a) A sanction imposed for violation of this rule shall be limited to what is sufficient to deter repetition of such conduct or comparable conduct by others similarly situated. Penalties, fees, and costs awarded under this provision may not be recouped from the party unless the party has committed the violation.

(b) Monetary sanctions may not be awarded against a represented party for a violation of paragraph (2)(b).

(6) Order. Any order imposing sanctions shall describe the conduct determined to constitute a violation of the rule and explain the basis for the sanction imposed.

Specific Authority 440.45(1)(a), (4) Fla. Stat.

Law Implemented 440.32, 440.33(1), (2), 440.45(1)(a), (4) Fla. Stat.

History: New 2-23-03, Amended 11-1-06.

60Q-6.126. Disqualification or Recusal of Judges.

(1) Any motion for disqualification of a judge shall be made and determined pursuant to Fla. R. Jud. Admin. 2.160.

(2) Upon entry of an order of disqualification or after the voluntary recusal of a judge, the deputy chief judge shall reassign the case to another judge.

Specific Authority 440.45(1)(a), (4) Fla. Stat.

Law Implemented 440.442, 440.45(1)(a), (4) Fla. Stat.

History: New 2-23-03.

60Q-6.127 Procedure for Relief from Appellate Filing Fee and Costs.

The procedure for relief from payment of the appellate filing fee and from the costs of the preparation of the record on appeal for the review of any order of a judge on the grounds of indigency shall be in accordance with Fla. R. App. P. 9.180.

Specific Authority 440.45(1)(a), (4) Fla Stat.

Law Implemented 440.271 Fla Stat.

History: New 11-1-06.

60Q-6.128 Destruction of Obsolete Records.

(1) All case files that have been closed and inactive for a period of two years are declared to be obsolete and may be destroyed. Designated personnel of the OJCC shall be responsible for the destruction of obsolete records and reports in accordance with applicable statutes and administrative rules.

(2) Recordings of hearings held before a judge shall become obsolete two years subsequent to the date of the hearing.

(3) Any forms, documents, reports or other records filed where this rule chapter specifically provides that filing is not required or requested shall be destroyed by the judge's office upon filing.

Specific Authority 440.44(7), 440.45(1)(a), (4) Fla. Stat.

Law Implemented 440.44(7) Fla. Stat.

History: New 11-1-06.

TITLE 69 DIVISION OF FINANCIAL SERVICES

CHAPTER 69L-3 Workers' Compensation Claims

69L-3.001. Purpose.

The purpose of this rule chapter is to establish the responsibilities of the employer and insurer to record and report workers' compensation accident information under Chapter 440, F.S., including the filing of claim forms with the Division, and to other affected parties. If an insurer contracts with another entity to handle claims on its behalf, the practices of the claims-handling entity in fulfilling the responsibilities under this chapter shall be deemed the practices of the insurer for the purposes of assessing penalties and fines against the insurer. These rules are intended to ensure the accurate and timely payment of compensation to the employee.

Specific Authority 440.591 Fla. Stat.

Law Implemented 440.20(8)(b), (15)(a), (20), 440.591 Fla Stat.

History: New 1-10-05.

69L-3.002. Definitions.

When used in this chapter, the following terms have the following meanings:

(1) "Average Weekly Temporary Total Disability Benefit" means the weekly average of all benefits paid pursuant to Sections 440.15(2)(a) and (b), F.S. The weekly average shall be determined by dividing the total amount of temporary total disability benefits paid to date, by the number of weeks and days paid as calculated pursuant to Section 440.14(1)(g), F.S. If no temporary total benefits were paid, the average weekly temporary total disability benefit shall be 66²/₃ % of the employee's average weekly wage, subject to the maximum compensation rate in accordance with Section 440.14, F.S.

(2) "Biweekly work week" means two consecutive 7-day periods coinciding with the post injury employer's work week. For the purposes of calculating Temporary Partial Benefits pursuant to Section 440.15(4), F.S., the first biweekly work week includes the week the employee returned to work.

(3) "Claims-handling Entity" means any insurer, service company/third-party administrator (Service Co/TPA), self-serviced self-insured employer or fund, or managing general agent and includes all claims office locations that will be responsible for adjusting and submitting workers' compensation claims to the Division.

(4) "Class Code" means the 4-digit code assigned by the National Council on Compensation Insurance (NCCI) for the particular occupation of the injured employee, as it exists in the NCCI Scopes Manual 2004 Edition, which is hereby incorporated by reference. A listing of Class Codes may be obtained by contacting NCCI's Customer Service Center at (800) 622-4123.

(5) "Compensation Rate" means 66²/₃ % of the employee's average weekly wage pursuant to Section 440.14, F.S., as calculated by the claims-handling entity, as ordered by a Judge of Compensation Claims, or to which the parties have stipulated.

(6) "Date Payment Mailed" means the date payment of a benefit left the control of the claims-handling entity (or the claims-handling entity's legal representative if delivery is made by the legal representative) for delivery to the employee or the employee's representative, whether by U.S. Postal Service or other delivery service, hand delivery, or deposit by electronic funds transfer.

(7) "Date Prepared" means the date the form was prepared by the adjuster or claims representative to be sent to the Division or other parties.

(8) "Days" means calendar days unless otherwise noted.

(9) "Denied Case" means any case for which the claims-handling entity has denied liability for all workers' compensation benefits.

(10) "Document" means any notice, form, or report which shall be submitted to the Division under this chapter or which the Division requests in connection with any matter covered by this chapter. Unless otherwise specified, this definition includes data submitted to the Division using Electronic Data Interchange (EDI) or another Division approved electronic format.

(11) "File" or "Filed" means a document has been received and accepted in accordance with Rule 69L-3.003, F.A.C., by the Division.

(12) "Filing Period for Supplemental Income Benefits" means a period of 13 consecutive weeks (approximately 3 months) for which the employee reports any earnings and files a claim for supplemental income benefits. The filing period shall represent a "quarter" as set out in Section 440.15(3)(b)7., F.S. (1994), which is incorporated herein by reference, except for the second filing period, which may consist of less than 13 weeks if the first payment period was pro-rated. The "initial filing period" is the filing period which occurs during the last 13 weeks of

impairment income benefits.

(13) "First Aid Case" means a work injury or illness which is treated at the work place, does not require medical treatment for which charges are incurred, and does not cause the employee to miss work for more than one day.

(14) "Full Salary in Lieu of Compensation" means the monies an employer paid the employee as salary, wage, or other remuneration for a period of disability for which the insurer would have otherwise been obligated to pay compensation benefits.

(15) "Full Salary End Date" means the date through which the employer paid full salary in lieu of compensation.

(16) "Indemnity Only Denied Case" means any case for which the claims-handling entity has denied all indemnity benefits at the time of the filing of the DFS-F2-DWC-1, however, compensability of the case is accepted and medical benefits will be provided.

(17) "Initial Payment of Supplemental Income Benefits" means payment of supplemental income benefits for the first whole or partial calendar month immediately following the expiration of the impairment income benefit period. The initial payment of supplemental income benefits shall cover the time beginning with the day after the expiration of impairment income benefits and ending with the last date in the initial calendar month pursuant to Section 440.15, F.S. (1994), which is incorporated herein by reference.

(18) "Insurer Code #" means the Division-assigned number for the insurer as defined in Section 440.02(38), F.S., which bears the financial risk of the claim.

(19) "Lost Time Case" means a work-related injury or illness, which has caused the employee to be disabled for more than 7 calendar days or for which indemnity benefits have been paid. Lost time cases shall also include compensable volunteer workers to whom no indemnity benefits will be paid, but who have been disabled for more than 7 calendar days from work; compensable death cases for which there are no known or confirmed dependents; and injuries which result in the disability of more than 7 calendar days for which the employer is continuing to pay full salary in lieu of compensation for any portion thereof. The 7 calendar days of disability do not have to be consecutive, but are cumulative and can occur over a period of time.

(20) "Medical Only Case" means a work-related injury or illness, which requires medical treatment for which charges will be incurred, but which does not cause the employee to be disabled for more than 7 calendar days.

(21) "Medical Only to Lost Time Case" means a work-related injury or illness, which initially did not result in disability of more than 7 calendar days but later resulted in a disability of more than 7 calendar days. Medical only to lost time cases shall include previous medical only cases in which Impairment Income Benefits are paid based on obtaining Maximum Medical Improvement with a Permanent Impairment Rating greater than zero (0) % and settlement only cases involving payment of indemnity benefits.

(22) "NAICS Code" means the code published in the North American Industry Classification System 2002 Edition, hereby incorporated by reference, that represents the nature of the employer's business. Classification information may be obtained by contacting the NAICS Association, 341 East James Circle, Sandy, Utah 84070, or visiting the website: www.naics.com.

(23) "Notification" or "Knowledge" means an entity's earliest receipt of information, including mail, telephone, facsimile, direct personal contact or electronic submission.

(24) "Overall Maximum Medical Improvement" means the date on which maximum medical improvement has been achieved with respect to all compensable medical or psychiatric conditions caused by a compensable injury or disease.

(25) "Payment Period for Supplemental Income Benefits" means the period of 3 consecutive calendar months immediately following the filing period The first payment period may consist of less than 3 full months if the first

monthly payment is pro-rated. The last payment period may consist of less than 3 full months if the employee has reached a maximum of 401 weeks of benefits. All other payment periods of supplemental income benefits shall be for 3 full calendar months, pursuant to Section 440.15, F.S.

(26) "Send" means to transmit a document to the party or parties intended to receive it, including by mail, hand delivery, or electronic transmission.

(27) "Service Co/TPA" means an entity, which has contracted with an insurer for the purpose of providing all services necessary to adjust workers' compensation claims on the insurer's behalf.

(28) "Service Co/TPA Code #" means the internal audit number assigned by the Division to a service company, adjusting company, managing general agent or third party administrator.

Specific Authority 440.20(3), 440.38(2), (6), 440.185(2), (6), (10), 440.591 Fla. Stat.

Law Implemented 440.13, 440.20(3), 440.38(2)(b), 440.185 Fla. Stat.

History: New 11-5-81, Formerly 38F-3.02, Amended 4-11-90, 1-30-91, 6-10-92, 11-8-94, Formerly 38F-3.002, 4L-3.002, Amended 1-10-05.

69L-3.003. Procedures for Filing Documents.

(1) Instructions on or pertaining to forms promulgated under this chapter, are also rules under this chapter and forms shall be completed in accordance with such instructions. When forms are reproduced, they shall be reproduced in their entirety, including instructions. The claims-handling entity shall ensure that all documents filed with the Division pursuant to this chapter are complete and legible. These documents shall be filed with the Florida Department of Financial Services, Division of Workers' Compensation, 200 East Gaines Street, Tallahassee, Florida 32399-4226, except as otherwise indicated. The Division shall return to the claims-handling entity any document on which the appropriate information required in subsection (3) of this section and paragraph 69L-3.0045(1)(d), F.A.C., does not appear, and will notify the claims-handling entity of its error or omission. If a document is not complete and legible, the Division will return it to the claims-handling entity's address as provided on the form for correction or completion. The claims-handling entity shall make the correction, include a revised "Sent to Division Date" and resubmit the document to the Division. The document will be considered completed and in compliance with this section when the corrected document is resent and accepted by the Division.

(2) Claims-handling entities shall respond to any written request for information by the Division no later than 14 days after receiving the request, except as otherwise provided in Chapter 69L-3, F.A.C.

(3) The claims-handling entity, where required, shall include on every document it submits to the Division the following information:

(a) The employee's name.

(b) The employee's social security number as assigned by the Social Security Administration. If the employee does not have a social security number, the claims-handling entity shall contact the Division following the instructions provided on the following website: www.fldfs.com/WC/organization/odqc.html (under Records Management — Division Assigned Numbers) to obtain a Division assigned number until the social security number is obtained. Upon receipt of the employee's social security number, the claims-handling entity shall file Form DFS-F2-DWC-4, as adopted in Rule 69L-3.025, F.A.C., with the Division in accordance with Rule 69L-3.0091, F.A.C.

(c) The month, day, and year of the employee's accident or illness, in the following order: mm-dd-yy or mm-dd-ccyy.

(d) The "Insurer Code #". A claims-handling entity adjusting claims for one or more insurers shall report the correct "Insurer Code #" for each specific claim.

(e) The "Service Co/TPA Code #". If a third-party administrator, servicing agent, or other claims-handling entity is servicing a claim for an insurer, self-insured employer or self-insurance fund, it shall include both the "Insurer Code #" and the "Service Co/TPA Code #" on any form.

(f) The "Claims-handling Entity File #". A claims-handling entity shall report its internal identification number assigned to a file on forms as required under this chapter.

(g) The name, address and telephone number of the claims-handling entity. When a "Service Co/TPA" is adjusting claims for an insurer, the name, address and telephone number of the "Service Co/TPA" in addition to the name of the insurer shall be provided. The telephone number provided shall enable a caller to readily contact the office handling the claim.

(h) The "Sent to Division Date".

(4) The insurer or the claims-handling entity shall provide a supply of Forms DFS-F2-DWC-1 and DFS-F2-DWC-1a, as adopted in Rule 69L-3.025, F.A.C., to the employer, unless an alternative electronic reporting arrangement with the claims-handling entity is in place. The name of the insurer and the claims-handling entity's name, address and telephone number shall be pre-printed or pre-stamped on each such form.

(5) All submissions of forms promulgated under this rule shall conform with the promulgated form in design, layout, field size, content and shall contain all data elements required by the promulgated form. If the Division finds that a computer-generated form is not the same as the promulgated form, the Division will return the form and the claims-handling entity shall make the correction, include a revised "Sent to Division Date" and resubmit a corrected form to the Division. The document will be considered completed and in compliance with this section when the corrected document is resent to the Division and is accepted.

(6) Any insurer or claims-handling entity failing to timely send documents promulgated under this chapter is subject to administrative fines assessed by the Division.

Specific Authority 440.185(2), (5), 440.20(3), 440.38(2), (5), 440.591 Fla. Stat.

Law Implemented 440.185, 440.20 Fla. Stat.

History: Originally numbered 38F-3.01, 3.02, 3.03, New 10-30-79, Amended 11-5-81, Formerly 38F-3.03, Amended 4-11-90, 1-30-91, 11-8-94, Formerly 38F-3.003, 4L-3.003, Amended 1-10-05.

69L-3.0033. Electronic Filing of Workers' Compensation Forms.

Forms DFS-F2-DWC-1 and DFS-F2-DWC-13, as incorporated in Rule 69L-3.025, F.A.C., may be alternatively reported to the Division using Electronic Data Interchange (EDI).

Specific Authority 440.185(2), 440.593 Fla. Stat.

Law Implemented 440.593 Fla Stat.

History: New 1-10-05.

69L-3.0035. Injured Worker Informational Brochure.

In accordance with Section 440.185(4), F.S., the carrier or its claims-handling entity on behalf of the carrier shall mail to the injured worker an informational brochure, Form DFS-F2-DWC-60, "Important Workers' Compensation Information For Florida's Workers" or Form DFS-F2-DWC-61, "Informacion Importante De Seguro De Indemnizacion Por Accidentes De Trabajo Para Los Trabajadores De La Florida", as adopted in Rule 69L-3.025, F.A.C., as applicable within 3 business days after notification of the injury or illness.

Specific Authority 440.185(4), 440.593 Fla Stat.

Law Implemented 440.593 Fla Stat.

History: New 1-10-05.

69L-3.0036. Employer Informational Brochure.

In accordance with Section 440.185(4), F.S., the carrier or its claims-handling entity on behalf of the carrier shall annually mail to the employer an informational brochure, Form DFS-F2-DWC-55, "Important Workers' Compensation Information For Florida's Employers" or Form DFS-F2-DWC-66, "Informacion Importante Del Seguro De Indemnizacion Por Accidentes De Trabajo Para Los Empleadores De La Florida", as adopted in Rule 69L-3.025, F.A.C., as applicable.

Specific Authority 440.185(4), 440.593 Fla Stat.

Law Implemented 440.593 Fla Stat.

History: New 1-10-05.

69L-3.004. First Report of Injury or Illness: Employer's Responsibility to Record and Report Accidents.

(1) An employer shall record all industrial injuries and diseases as follows:

(a) For a first aid case that is not required to be reported to the claims-handling entity, the employer shall maintain a record of the following information regarding the injury or illness:

1. The employee's name.

2. Social security number or other identifying number pursuant to paragraph 69L-3.003(3)(b), F.A.C.

3. Date and time of the accident or injury.

4. Occupation of the employee.

5. Who the injury was reported to and when.

6. Description of the accident or illness, including the cause of injury.

7. Injury or illness that occurred and affected body part.

8. Location address of the injury if different than the employer's address.

(b) For a medical only case, lost time case, or death case, the employer shall complete Form DFS-F2-DWC-1, as adopted in Rule 69L-3.025, F.A.C., or report the information regarding the injury or illness by other means as provided by the claims-handling entity.

(2) An employer shall report on Form DFS-F2-DWC-1, as adopted in Rule 69L-3.025, F.A.C., information concerning an industrial injury or disease to its claims-handling entity as follows:

(a) An employer shall report all cases, except first aid cases, to its claims-handling entity within 7 days after the employer's knowledge of an industrial injury or disease. The employer shall not delay reporting the injury or illness to the claims-handling entity because the employee's signature is unavailable.

(b) If a first aid case later becomes a medical only or lost time case, the employer shall report the injury or illness to the claims-handling entity within 7 days after the employer's knowledge of the change in status.

(c) When an employer submits to its claims-handling entity Form DFS-F2-DWC-1, the employer shall provide a copy of the form to the employee or the employee's estate. If the information required by Form DFS-F2-DWC-1, as adopted in Rule 69L-3.025, F.A.C., is reported to the claims-handling entity by other means the claims-handling entity shall provide the employee and the employer a completed Form DFS-F2-DWC-1, within three (3) business days of the claims-handling entity's notification of the injury or illness. Form IA-1 may be sent to the employee and employer, if the claims-handling entity is electronically sending the first report of injury information required in Rule 69L-3.0045, F.A.C., to the Division.

(d) In addition to the reporting requirements pursuant to paragraph 69L-3.004(2)(a), F.A.C., if an injury or illness results in the employee's death, the employer shall give notice by telephone or by other means to the Division of Workers' Compensation within 24 hours of the employer's knowledge of the death. The mailing address for reporting of death cases is: Department of Financial Services, Division of Workers' Compensation, Occupational Safety and Health Unit, 200 East Gaines Street, Tallahassee, Florida 32399-4222. The telephone number for reporting death cases is (800) 219-8953, (850) 413-1611 or by facsimile at (850) 922-0024.

(3) Employers shall retain a record of all information required under this section for not less than 2 years and 6 months after the date the injury or illness is reported to the employer.

Specific Authority 440.35, 440.14(3), 440.591, 440.185(2), (5), 440.19 Fla. Stat.

Law Implemented 440.14(3), 440.185(2), (3), (5), 440.35 Fla. Stat.

History: New 8-30-79, Amended 12-23-80, 11-5-81, 6-12-84, Formerly 38F-3.04, Amended 1-1-87, 4-11-90, 1-30-91, 11-8-94, Formerly 38F-3.004, 4L-3.004, Amended 1-10-05.

69L-3.0045. First Report of Injury or Illness:

Carrier's Responsibility to Record and Report Accidents.

(1) A claims-handling entity shall record all industrial injuries and diseases as follows:

(a) Upon receipt of a Form DFS-F2-DWC-1, as adopted in Rule 69L-3.025, F.A.C., the claims-handling entity shall legibly date stamp the form in the "Received by Claims-handling Entity" box. Upon notification of the injury by any other means, the claims-handling entity shall record the earliest date of notification in the file and on the Form DFS-F2-DWC-1.

(b) If the employer notifies the claims-handling entity of the injury by telephone or electronic data interchange, the claims-handling entity shall produce and mail to the employee and employer a paper copy of Form DFS-F2-DWC-1, as adopted in Rule 69L-3.025, F.A.C., within 3 business days of the claims-handling entity's knowledge of the injury. However, if the claims-handling is electronically sending the first report of injury information required in Rule 69L-3.0045, F.A.C., Form IA-1 may be sent to the employee and employer.

(c) The claims-handling entity shall make reasonable efforts to confirm that the following information on the Form DFS-F2-DWC-1 is correct:

1. Employee's name.

2. Social security number or other identifying number pursuant to paragraph 69L-3.003(3)(b), F.A.C.

3. Employee's address.

4. Employee's telephone number (if provided by the employee or employer).

5. Date (mm-dd-yy or mm-dd-ccyy) and time of accident.

6. Occupation of the employee.

7. Location of the accident.

8. Description of the accident, including the cause and nature of the injury, and part(s) of the body affected.

(d) The claims-handling entity shall complete the "Claims-handling Entity Information" section of Form DFS-F2-DWC-1 as follows:

1. "Insurer Code #".

2. "Service Co/TPA Code #", if applicable.

3. The "Insurer Name" and the "Claims-handling Entity Name, Address, & Telephone" as applicable. When a "Service Co/TPA" is adjusting claims for an insurer, the name, address and telephone number of the "Service Co/TPA" in addition to the name of the insurer shall be given. The telephone number provided shall enable a caller to readily contact the office handling the claim.

4. "Claims-handling Entity File #".

5. Indicate the status of the case by marking the appropriate box: "Denied Case", "Indemnity Only Denied Case", "Medical Only Which Became Lost Time Case", or "Lost Time Case". In addition, the following information is required:

a. "Denied Case": When the liability for the claim is being totally denied, Form DFS-F2-DWC-12, as adopted in Rule 69L-3.025, F.A.C., shall be filed with the Division at the same time as the Form DFS-F2-DWC-1 pursuant to Rule 69L-3.012, F.A.C.

b. "Indemnity Only Denied Case": When only indemnity benefits are being denied, a Form DFS-F2-DWC-12 shall be filed with the Division at the same time as the Form DFS-F2-DWC-1, pursuant to Rule 69L-3.012, F.A.C.

c. "Medical Only Which Became Lost Time Case":

i. Delayed disability cases: The fields for "First Date of Disability", "Date First Payment Mailed", "AWW", "Comp Rate", "Employee's 8th Day of Disability", the "Entity's Knowledge of the 8th Day of Disability" and the type of initial benefit paid shall be provided, except as indicated in subsubparagraph 69L-3.0045(1)(d)5.f, F.A.C.

ii. IB Only Cases: The "Date First Payment Mailed", "AWW", "Comp Rate", the type of initial benefit paid identified as "I.B.".

iii. Settlement Only Cases: The "Date First

Payment Mailed", the type of initial benefit paid identified, as "Settlement Only" shall be provided.

d. "Lost Time Cases": The "First Date of Disability", "Date First Payment Mailed", "AWW", "Comp Rate" and the type of initial benefit paid shall be provided except as indicated in subsubparagraph 69L-3.0045(1)(d)5.f., F.A.C.

e. "Full Salary End Date". If the employer paid full salary in lieu of compensation and the claims-handling entity has knowledge of the day the employer discontinued paying full salary, the "Full Salary In Lieu of Comp" box is to be checked "Yes" and the "Full Salary End Date" field on the DFS-F2-DWC-1 must be completed when the DFS-F2-DWC-1 is filed.

f. Exceptions to sub-subparagraphs 69L-3.0045(1)(d)5.c. and d., F.A.C. The following data fields are not required for the filing of Form DFS-F2-DWC-1:

i. If the employer is continuing full salary in lieu of compensation, the "Date First Payment Mailed", "AWW" and "Comp Rate" are not required.

ii. If a compensable volunteer has a lost time case, "Date First Payment Mailed", "AWW" and "Comp Rate" are not required unless the compensable volunteer meets statutory requirements to be paid for concurrent employment.

iii. If the employee's death is compensable and the employee has no known dependents, the "Date First Payment Mailed" is not required.

(e) The claims-handling entity shall report to the Division the "Employee's Class Code" based on the National Council on Compensation Insurance (NCCI) classification system (Scopes Manual), and the "Employers' NAICS Code" based on the North American Industrial Classification System (NAICS). The information shall be reported on Form DFS-F2-DWC-1 if the information is available at the time of filing with the Division. If either code is not available at time of filing, this information shall be filed on Form DFS-F2-DWC-4 pursuant to subsection 69L-3.0091(14), F.A.C.

(f) If the initial payment of compensation was not timely paid in accordance with Section 440.20, F.S., the claims-handling entity shall also report the following information, where applicable:

1. "Penalty Amount Paid in 1st Payment"; and

2. The "Interest Amount Paid in 1st Payment".

(2) The claims-handling entity shall report industrial injuries or illnesses to the Division as follows:

(a) When disability is immediate and continuous for 8 or more days, the claims-handling entity shall send a completed Form DFS-F2-DWC-1 within 14 days after the claims-handling entity's knowledge of the injury or illness for the following cases:

1. Initial lost time cases,

2. Death cases with or without dependents,

3. Lost time cases in which the employer continued full salary in lieu of compensation for 8 or more days,

4. Lost time cases for a compensable volunteer.

(b) When disability is not immediate and continuous but resulted in 8 or more days of disability, the claims-handling entity shall send a completed Form DFS-F2-DWC-1 within 6 days after the claims-handling entity's knowledge of the eighth day of disability for the following cases:

1. Medical only to lost time cases, delayed disability,

2. Cases involving multiple periods of disability,

3. Cases in which the employer continued full salary in lieu of compensation,

4. Lost time cases for a compensable volunteer.

(c) If the initial payment of indemnity benefits is for temporary partial, the claims-handling entity shall send to the Division a completed Form DFS-F2-DWC-1 within 14 days after the date payment mailed.

(d) If the initial payment of indemnity benefits is for impairment benefits, the claims-handling entity shall send to the Division a completed Form DFS-F2-DWC-1 within 14 days after the date payment mailed.

(e) When the initial payment of indemnity results from an agreement or order for indemnity benefits, and a Form DFS-F2-DWC-1 was not previously filed, the claims-handling entity shall send to the Division a completed Form DFS-F2-DWC-1 within 14 days after the date payment mailed.

(f) For all cases denied in their entirety, the claims-handling entity shall send to the Division completed Forms DFS-F2-DWC-1 and DFS-F2-DWC-12 within 14 days of its knowledge of the injury or illness.

(g) For cases where the claims-handling entity denied only indemnity benefits and is paying medical benefits for the employee, the claims-handling entity shall send to the Division completed Forms DFS-F2-DWC-1 and DFS-F2-DWC-12 within 14 days after denial of the indemnity benefits.

(h) Medical Only Cases shall not be sent to the Division unless the claims-handling entity has received a written request from the Division. The claims-handling entity shall send Form DFS-F2-DWC-1 within 14 days of receipt of the request. The notation "MO Filed Pursuant to Division Request" shall be provided in the "Remarks" field.

Specific Authority 440.185(2), (5), 440.20(3), 440.591 Fla. Stat.

Law Implemented 440.185(2), (5), 440.20(6) Fla. Stat.

History: New 4-11-90, Amended 1-30-91, 11-8-94, 12-5-96, Formerly 38F-3.0045, 4L-3.0045, Amended 1-10-05.

69L-3.0046. Wage Statement: Employer's and Claims-handling Entity's Responsibility to Record and Report Wages.

(1) Employer's responsibility: The employer shall report wage information to the claims-handling entity on Form DFS-F2-DWC-1a, as adopted in Rule 69L-3.025, F.A.C., pursuant to Section 440.14, F.S. The employer shall provide the claims-handling entity all required wage information within 14 days of the employer's knowledge of a "lost time" or a "medical only to lost time case".

(2) Claims-handling entity's responsibility: The claims-handling entity shall compare Forms DFS-F2-DWC-1 and DFS-F2-DWC-1a, as adopted in Rule 69L-3.025, F.A.C., to confirm that the employee name, social security number or other identifying information, and the date of injury on the two forms are consistent.

Specific Authority 440.14, 440.185(5), 440.591 Fla Stat.

Law Implemented 440.12(2), 440.185(5), (9) Fla Stat.

History: New 1-10-05.

69L-3.0047. Fraud Statement.

(1) An injured employee or any other party making a claim shall provide his or her personal signature attesting that they have reviewed, understand and acknowledge the fraud statement as specified in Section 440.105(7), F.S.

(2) A party who makes claims for services provided to the claims-handling entity on a recurring basis may make one personally signed attestation to the claims-handling entity as required by Section 440.105(7), F.S., which will satisfy the requirement for all claims submitted to the claims-handling entity for the calendar year in which the attestation is submitted.

Specific Authority 440.105(7), 440.591 Fla Stat.

Law Implemented 440.105(7) Fla Stat.

History: New 1-10-05.

69L-3.0085. Funeral Expense Bills.

Specific Authority 440.591 Fla. Stat.

Law Implemented 440.16, 440.20(2) Fla. Stat.

History: Formerly 38F-3.15, New 10-30-79, Amended 11-5-81, Formerly 38F-3.085, Amended 4-11-90, 1-30-91, 11-8-94, Formerly 38F-3.0085, 4L-3.0085, Repealed 4-14-04.

69L-3.0091. Notice of Action/Change.

The claims-handling entity shall send Form DFS-F2-DWC-4, as adopted in Rule 69L-3.025, F.A.C., to the Division as specified in this section for any industrial accident or injury filed for lost time cases as defined in subsection 69L-3.0045(2), F.A.C., within 14 days of the claims-handling entity's knowledge of the action or change which it is reporting. The claims-handling entity shall complete the applicable fields for each required Form DFS-F2-DWC-4; the "Remarks" section may only be used to supplement the information reported. The claims-handling entity shall send to the employee and the employer copies of Form DFS-F2-DWC-4, for each action or change required by this section within 14 days of the claims-handling entity's knowledge of the action or change which it is reporting to the Division.

(1) The claims-handling entity shall use the following codes to identify the "Disability Type" or the "Disability Type Adjusted" on Form DFS-F2-DWC-4.

"Disability Types":

(a) "TT" means temporary total disability benefits.

(b) "TTC" means increased temporary total disability benefits payable at 80% of the average weekly wage.

(c) "TTE" means temporary total compensation paid during training and education.

(d) "TP" means temporary partial disability benefits.

(e) "PI" means permanent impairment benefits for dates of accident prior to January 1, 1994.

(f) "IB" means impairment income benefits paid pursuant to Section 440.15(3), F.S. for dates of accident on or after January 1, 1994.

(g) "WL" means wage loss benefits for dates of accident prior to January 1, 1994.

(h) "SB" means supplemental income benefits paid pursuant to Section 440.15(3)(b), F.S. (1994) for dates of accident on or after January 1, 1994 through September 30, 2003.

(i) "PT" means permanent total disability benefits.

(j) "DB" means death benefits.

(2) If the claims-handling entity suspends benefits for any of the reasons stated in paragraphs (a)-(h) below, the claims-handling entity shall send the Division Form DFS-F2-DWC-4, and not Form DFS-F2-DWC-12, as adopted in Rule 69L-3.025, F.A.C. The claims-handling entity shall state the "Effective Date" of the suspension and the applicable suspension "Reason Code" in the applicable fields. The "Effective Date" of the suspension shall be the last date through which benefits were paid. The following "Suspension Reason Codes" shall be used to identify the reason for which all indemnity benefits have been suspended:

(a) "S1" means returned to work, or medically determined or qualified to return to work. All indemnity benefits have been suspended because the employee has returned to work, or has been medically released to return to work, and the claims-handling entity does not anticipate paying further indemnity benefits of any kind.

(b) "S2" means medical non-compliance. The employee failed to report for an independent medical examination pursuant to Section 440.13(5)(d), F.S., or failed to report for an evaluation by an expert medical advisor appointed by a Judge of Compensation Claims pursuant to Section 440.13(9)(c), F.S.

(c) "S3" means administrative non-compliance. The employee has failed to comply with one or more of the following statutory sections and any applicable rules:

1. Section 440.15(1)(e)3., F.S. (1994), which is incorporated herein by reference — employee in PT status failed to attend vocational evaluation or testing.

2. Section 440.15(1)(f)2.b., F.S. (1994), which is incorporated herein by reference — employee in PT status failed to report or apply for social security benefits.

3. Section 440.15(2)(d), F.S. (1994), which is incorporated herein by reference — employee in TT status failed or refused to complete and

return the Form DFS-F2-DWC-19.

4. Section 440.15(7), F.S. (1994), which is incorporated herein by reference — employee in TP status failed or refused to complete and return the Form DFS-F2-DWC-19.

5. Section 440.15(6), F.S. (2003), which is incorporated herein by reference — employee refused suitable employment.

6. Section 440.15(9), F.S. (2003), which is incorporated herein by reference employee failed or refused to sign and return the release for social security benefits earnings on the Form DFS-F2-DWC-14, or unemployment compensation earnings on Form DFS-F2-DWC-30, as adopted in Rule 69L-3.025, F.A.C.

7. Section 440.491(6)(b), F.S. (2003), which is incorporated herein by reference — employee failed or refused to accept vocational training or education.

8. Section 440.15(4)(d), F.S. (2003), which is incorporated herein by reference — employee in TP status failed to notify the claims-handling entity of the establishment of earnings capacity within 5 business days of returning to work.

9. Section 440.15(4)(e), F.S. (1994), which is incorporated herein by reference — employee in TP status terminated from post-injury employment due to the employee's misconduct.

10. Section 440.105(7), F.S. (2003), which is incorporated herein by reference — employee refused to sign and return the fraud statement.

(d) "S4" means employee death. This code is used if there are no known or confirmed dependents to whom death benefits must be paid or if the death was not compensable.

(e) "S5" means incarceration. The employee has become an inmate of a public institution and compensation benefits have been suspended because there are no known or confirmed dependents.

(f) "S6" means employee's whereabouts unknown. The claims-handling entity's good faith repeated attempts to locate and send compensation checks to the employee have been unsuccessful; or the employee has no known address, representative or guardian to whom the claims-handling entity can send compensation checks; or compensation checks have been returned to the claims-handling entity indicating that the employee has moved, with the address unknown, or does not reside at that address.

(g) "S7" means benefits exhausted, or entitlement to benefits exhausted, due to statutory limits. The employee is no longer eligible for or entitled to any indemnity benefits.

(h) "S8" means jurisdiction change. The employee elects to receive workers' compensation benefits under another state's law, or the claims-handling entity determines the claim is compensable under the Federal Employer's Liability Act, the Longshoremen's and Harbor Workers' Compensation Act, or the Jones Act.

(3) The claims-handling entity shall send Form DFS-F2-DWC-4 when it reinstates indemnity benefits after a suspension. It shall state the "Effective Date" of the "Indemnity Reinstated After Suspension" and the "Disability Type" of benefits being reinstated in the applicable fields.

(4) The claims-handling entity shall send Form DFS-F2-DWC-4 when the employee has resumed work, has been medically released to return to work, or to report the assignment of physical restrictions or the removal of all physical restrictions. The date the employee resumed work is the employee's actual return to work date and is to be reported in the "Actual Return To Work Date" field. The date the employee's medical release states that the employee may resume work is the employee's released to return to work date and is to be reported in the "Released To Return To Work Date" field. The claims-handling entity must indicate whether the employee was given any physical restrictions in the "Restrictions?" fields identified as either "Yes" or "No".

(5) The claims-handling entity shall send Form DFS-F2-DWC-4 reporting the date payment mailed resulting from a final order for indemnity benefits pursuant to Section 440.20(11), F.S. This date is to be placed in the "Date Final Settlement Mailed" field and shall not be reported as earlier than the date the

settlement was actually approved.

(6) The claims-handling entity shall send Form DFS-F2-DWC-4 when it is paying benefits to the employee after establishing the overall maximum medical improvement date and a permanent impairment rating to the body as a whole greater than zero. The date on which the overall maximum medical improvement is established is to be reported in the "MMI Date" field and the permanent impairment rating is to be reported in the "PI Rating" field.

(7) The claims-handling entity shall send Form DFS-F2-DWC-4 to report the date of the employee's death in the "Date of Death" field, whether or not the death is considered compensable.

(8) The claims-handling entity shall send Form DFS-F2-DWC-4 when it begins payment of impairment income benefits for dates of injury on and after January 1, 1994. It shall state the date the impairment income benefits were started in the "Start Date" field, the initial weekly rate at which the benefits will be paid in the "Weekly Rate" field, and the total number of weeks the employee is entitled to the benefits in the "Total Number of Weeks of Entitlement" field.

(9) The claims-handling entity shall send Form DFS-F2-DWC-4 when it amends either the employee's average weekly wage or the compensation rate. It shall state the previous average weekly wage in the "Previous AWW" field and previous compensation rate in the "Previous Comp Rate" field and the amended average weekly wage in the "Amended AWW" field and the amended compensation rate in the "Amended Comp Rate" field. It shall also indicate if the average weekly wage change was retroactive to the date of injury in the "Yes" or "No" boxes in the "Retroactive to D/A" field, and if not, the date on which the new average weekly wage was effective in the "If No, Give Effective Date" field.

(10)

(a) The claims-handling entity shall send Form DFS-F2-DWC-4 if the employee is permanently and totally disabled. The following information, when applicable, shall be provided:

1. The date on which the employee was accepted or adjudicated as permanently and totally disabled in the "Date Accepted/Adjudicated" field.

2. The claims-handling entity shall report any changes to the weekly rate at which the permanent total supplemental benefits will be paid, corresponding to the rate change in PT Supplemental Benefits, including the annual rate increases in the "Weekly PT Supplemental Rate" field.

3. The effective date of the change in the permanent total supplemental benefits rate, including the effective date for annual rate increases is to be reported in the "PT Supp Effective Date" field.

(b) If the employee's permanent total supplemental benefits are suspended because the employee has reached age 62 and is eligible for Social Security benefits, then the claims-handling entity reports $0 as the permanent total supplemental rate in the "Weekly PT Supplemental Rate" field. The effective date is the date on which permanent total supplemental benefits will no longer be paid and is to be reported in the "PT Supp Effective Date" field.

(11) The claims-handling entity shall send Form DFS-F2-DWC-4 when it adjusts or offsets the employee's weekly compensation rate. It shall include the Benefit Adjustment Code in the "Benefit Adjustment Code" section, the "Disability Type" in the "Disability Type Adjusted" field, the weekly amount by which the employee's payment is being reduced in the "Weekly Adj Amount" field, and the date the offset or adjustment is effective in the "Effective Date" field. If the offset or adjustment is temporary, the claims-handling entity shall send Form DFS-F2-DWC-4 when it resumes payment at the former rate to report the date the adjustment ends in the "Adjustment End Date" field.

(a) If the claims-handling entity sends Form DFS-F2-DWC-4 to report a change in the employee's weekly compensation rate due to a social security offset, it shall send a completed Form DFS-F2-DWC-14 when it submits Form

DFS-F2-DWC-4.

(b) The following codes shall be used to show that the rate of pay has been adjusted due to the corresponding reason(s), or that the rate of pay has been offset because of the below reason(s).

BENEFIT ADJUSTMENT CODES:

1. "A" means apportionment or contribution. The weekly benefit amount has been reduced for shared or partial liability(s).

2. "B" means subrogation or third party offset. The weekly benefit amount has been reduced for recovery from third party tort-feasor pursuant to Section 440.39(2), F.S.

3. "C" means overpayment credit. The weekly benefit amount has been reduced for benefits paid but not owed, pursuant to Section 440.15(12), F.S.

4. "H" means child support or alimony reduction. The weekly benefit amount has been reduced for income deduction orders, pursuant to Section 61.1301, F.S.

5. "N" means medical non-compliance offset. The weekly benefit amount has been reduced because the employee has failed to accept training and education pursuant to Section 440.491(6)(b), F.S., for dates of accident prior to October 1, 2003 or the employee has failed to timely cancel an independent medical examination pursuant to Section 440.13(5)(d), F.S.

6. "P" means advance recoupment. The weekly benefit amount has been reduced for reimbursement of benefit payments advanced pursuant to Section 440.20(13), F.S.

7. "R" means social security retirement offset. The weekly benefit amount has been reduced for retirement benefits paid under the Federal Old Age, Survivors, and Disability Insurance Act, pursuant to Section 440.15(9), F.S.

8. "S" means social security disability offset. The weekly benefit amount has been reduced for disability benefits paid under the Federal Old Age, Survivors, and Disability Insurance Act, pursuant to Section 440.15(9), F.S.

9. "U" means unemployment compensation offset. The weekly benefit amount has been reduced for unemployment compensation benefits, pursuant to Section 440.15(10), F.S.

10. "V" means safety violation offset. The weekly benefit amount has been reduced for safety violation(s) pursuant to Section 440.09(5), F.S.

11. "X" means death or dependent change. The weekly benefit amount has been adjusted because of a change in number or kind of dependents entitled to death benefits pursuant to Section 440.16, F.S.

(12) The claims-handling entity shall send Form DFS-F2-DWC-4, to report a correction in the employee's social security number in the "Social Security Number/Correct #" field, date of accident in the "Date of Accident/Correct Date" field, employee's name in the "Employee's Name/Correct Name" field, or the claims-handling entity handling the case in the "Claims-handling Entity" field. When reporting corrections to the employee's name, social security number, or date of accident, the claims-handling entity shall include the original (incorrect) information at the top of the form, and the corrected (new) information in the applicable field in the "Corrections Of" section. The claims-handling entity shall report these changes only for lost time cases as defined in subsection 69L-3.002(19), F.A.C.

(13) The claims-handling entity shall send Form DFS-F2-DWC-4 to report or change the class code of the employee in the "NAICS Code" field.

Specific Authority 440.185, 440.591, 440.20(3) Fla. Stat.

Law Implemented 440.185, 440.20 Fla. Stat.

History: New 1-30-91, Amended 11-8-94, Formerly 38F-3.0091, 4L-3.0091, Amended 1-10-05.

69L-3.012. Notice of Denial.

(1) If the claims-handling entity denies entitlement to any benefit, or subsequently rescinds that denial, it shall send a copy of Form DFS-F2-DWC-12, as adopted in Rule 69L-3.025, F.A.C., to the employee, employer and any additional party requesting payment or authorization. The Form DFS-F2-DWC-12 shall

be mailed within 14 days of the date the claims-handling entity decided to deny or rescind the denial of benefits.

(2) If the claims-handling entity initially denies the compensability of or coverage for a case, it shall send Form DFS-F2-DWC-12 to the Division within 14 days after the claims-handling entity receives notification of the injury, illness or death. The claims-handling entity shall also mark the "Denied Case" box on Form DFS-F2-DWC-1 pursuant to subsubparagraph 69L-3.0045(1)(d)5.a., F.A.C.

(3) If the claims-handling entity initially denies only the indemnity benefits of a claim, it shall send Form DFS-F2-DWC-12 to the Division within 14 days after the claims-handling entity's notification of the injury, illness or death. The claims-handling entity shall also mark the "Indemnity Only Denied Case" box on Form DFS-F2-DWC-1, as adopted in Rule 69L-3.025, F.A.C., pursuant to subsubparagraph 69L-3.0045(1)(d)5.b., F.A.C.

(4) When the claims-handling entity denies any subsequent indemnity benefit on a lost time case, it shall send Form DFS-F2-DWC-12. The Form DFS-F2-DWC-12 shall be sent to the Division within 14 days of the claims-handling entity's knowledge of the requested benefit being denied.

(5) If a Petition for Benefits is the claims-handling entity's first notification of an injury and the claims-handling entity denies the case in its entirety, it shall send Forms DFS-F2-DWC-12 and DFS-F2-DWC-1 to the Division within 14 days of the claims-handling entity's receipt of the Petition for Benefits.

(6) When the claims-handling entity has previously denied any indemnity benefits for a lost time case and has sent Form DFS-F2-DWC-12 to the Division, and then commences the payment of indemnity benefits, the claims-handling entity shall send Form DFS-F2-DWC-12 with the denial rescinded section completed. The "Date Denial Rescinded" is the date the claims-handling entity decided to rescind the denial. The Form DFS-F2-DWC-12 shall be sent to the Division within 14 days of the date that the denial was rescinded.

(7) When an employee requests wage loss benefits for dates of accident August 1, 1979 through December 31, 1993, by sending Form DFS-F2-DWC-3, as adopted in Rule 69L-3.025, F.A.C., to the claims-handling entity, and the wage loss calculation yields an amount of benefits payable, but the claims-handling entity denies or disputes the employee's eligibility for those benefits, the claims-handling entity shall, within 14 days of receipt of the Form DFS-F2-DWC-3:

(a) Send to the Division the following:

1. Form DFS-F2-DWC-3, completed by the employee and the claims-handling entity;

2. Form DFS-F2-DWC-12; and

3. A copy of any information or document relating to the employee's job search.

(b) Send to the employee the following:

1. Copies of the Forms DFS-F2-DWC-3; and

2. DFS-F2-DWC-12.

(8) When an employee files a Statement of Quarterly Earnings for Supplemental Income Benefits for Dates of Accident January 1, 1994 through September 30, 2003, Form DFS-F2-DWC-40, as adopted in Rule 69L-3.025, F.A.C., and the supplemental income benefit calculation yields an amount of benefits payable, but the claims-handling entity denies or disputes the employee's eligibility for those benefits, the claims-handling entity shall, within 14 days of receipt of the form:

(a) Send to the Division the following:

1. Form DFS-F2-DWC-40, completed by the employee and the claims-handling entity; and

2. Form DFS-F2-DWC-12.

(b) Send to the employee the following:

1. Copies of the Forms DFS-F2-DWC-40; and

2. DFS-F2-DWC-12.

Specific Authority440.20(3), 440.591 Fla. Stat.

Law Implemented 440.20(4), 440.192(8) Fla. Stat.

History: New 10-30-79, Amended 11-5-81, 5-30-82, 6-12-84, Formerly 38F-3.12, Amended 4-11-90, 1-30-91, 11-8-94, Formerly 38F-3.012, 4L-3.012, Amended 1-10-05.

69L-3.016. Claim Cost Report.

(1) The claims-handling entity shall send Form DFS-F2-DWC-13, as adopted in Rule 69L-3.025, F.A.C., to the Division for the following cases:

(a) Lost time cases as defined in subsection 69L-3.002(19), F.A.C., which include lost time cases in which no indemnity benefits have been paid for compensable volunteers pursuant to Section 440.02(15), F.S., and compensable death cases with no dependents.

(b) Lost time cases in which the employee has received full salary in lieu of compensation for 8 or more days of disability.

(c) Cases in which the only indemnity benefits paid were for impairment income benefits, a lump sum settlement or a final settlement.

(d) Denied cases in which indemnity benefits were paid.

(2) The claims-handling entity shall send Form DFS-F2-DWC-13, to the Division at the following times:

(a) Initial Claim Cost Report: The Form DFS-F2-DWC-13 shall reflect all cumulative claim costs paid within the first 6 months of the date of accident. This report shall be sent within 30 days after the 6-month anniversary of the date of accident. The initial claim cost report shall not be sent prior to the 6-month anniversary unless the case is closed. The claims-handling entity shall indicate the type of report as "Initial Report Summarizing First Six Months."

1. If the case status changed to lost time after the 6-month anniversary of the date of accident, the claims-handling entity shall submit Form DFS-F2-DWC-13, in accordance with paragraph 69L-3.016(2)(b), F.A.C. The claims-handling entity shall indicate the type of report as "Initial Report Summarizing First Six Months" and "Annual Report On Open Case."

2. If the case is closed within 6 months of the date of accident, the claims-handling entity shall submit Form DFS-F2-DWC-13 and indicate the type of report as "Initial Report Summarizing First Six Months" and "Final Report-Case Closed — No Activity in Past Year or Case Settled."

(b) Annual Claim Cost Report: The Form DFS-F2-DWC-13 shall reflect all cumulative claim costs paid on the case since the date of accident. The Form DFS-F2-DWC-13 shall be sent to the Division within 30 days after each annual anniversary of the date of accident for all open cases. The claims-handling entity shall indicate the type of report, as an "Annual Report On Open Case." The annual DFS-F2-DWC-13 filing shall not occur prior to the anniversary date of the date of accident unless the case is closed.

(c) Final Claim Cost Report:

1. The Form DFS-F2-DWC-13 shall reflect all cumulative claim costs paid on the case since the date of accident. The form shall be sent within 30 days after the annual anniversary of the date of accident for lost time cases closed since the last required filing of the Form DFS-F2-DWC-13. However, the claims-handling entity may send the Final Form DFS-F2-DWC-13 prior to the anniversary date if it has closed a case with respect to medical and indemnity benefits. The claims-handling entity shall indicate the type of report as a "Final Report-Case Closed — No Activity In Past Year Or Case Settled."

2. After filing a Final Claim Cost Report, if the claims-handling entity makes a subsequent payment for any category of benefits required to be reported on Form DFS-F2-DWC-13, the claims-handling entity shall send another Final Form DFS-F2-DWC-13 in accordance with subparagraph 69L-3.016(2)(c)1., F.A.C.

(3) The claims-handling entity shall complete Form DFS-F2-DWC-13 for all lost time cases, and shall include the following information, where applicable:

(a) The type of report being sent.

(b) The exact "Average Weekly Wage" and

"Compensation Rate" as of the date the report is sent, in dollars and cents.

(c) The "Full Salary End Date" for employees who receive full salary in lieu of compensation for any period after the date of accident. When the employer pays full salary in lieu of compensation through the time the form is sent, the claims-handling entity shall mark the "Full Salary In Lieu Of Compensation for Any Period Of Time" box "Yes" and leave the "Full Salary End Date" blank.

(d) The number of "Weeks" and "Days" for which a particular indemnity benefit was paid, except for statutory permanent impairment and wage loss benefits for dates of accident prior to January 1, 1994. Indemnity benefits are payable only for entire days and not fractions thereof.

(e) The exact cumulative total amount, in dollars and cents, of all benefits paid up to the date the form is sent, including amounts reported on previous Form DFS-F2-DWC-13 in the "Total (Paid To Date Columns I & II)" field.

(f) The cumulative total of any recoveries the claims-handling entity has obtained up to the filing of the form, except for recovery of overpayments. Totals entered as "Paid to Date" in Columns I and II are not reduced for recoveries, except for recovery of overpayment. Recovery of a deductible amount chargeable to an employer is reported in "All Other Recoveries Except Overpayments."

(g) The amount of money for indemnity and medical benefits settled and paid in a lump sum, or the amount paid to an employee as a lump sum settlement for medical benefits only, and the date payment mailed is to be reported in the "Date Payment Mailed" field for either settlement type as applicable. This latter settlement amount shall be reported only for lost time cases on Form DFS-F2-DWC-13 as "Medical Settlement Amt." For multiple settlements, the cumulative amount of the settlements and the latest date payment mailed shall be reported.

(h) In the event that claims are transferred from one claims-handling entity to another, the insurer shall provide cumulative totals by specific claim cost type for all applicable data elements on Form DFS-F2-DWC-13 on each transferred case to the acquiring claims-handling entity. All subsequent reporting on Form DFS-F2-DWC-13 shall include all historical data.

Specific Authority 440.185, 440.591 Fla. Stat.

Law Implemented 440.185 Fla. Stat.

History: New 10-30-79, Amended 11-5-81, Formerly 38F-3.16, Amended 4-11-90, 1-30-91, 11-8-94, Formerly 38F-3.016, 4L-3.016, Amended 1-10-05.

69L-3.018. Wage Loss Benefits Due to Permanent Impairment (Dates of Accident August 1, 1979 Through December 31, 1993).

(1) Employee's Responsibilities. During any 2 week period in which wage loss due to permanent impairment is suffered, the employee shall file a Form DFS-F2-DWC-3, as adopted in Rule 69L-3.025, F.A.C., with the claims-handling entity within 14 days of the end of that period. The employee shall complete the "Employee" portion of the Form DFS-F2-DWC-3 and the employee shall also fill out the back of the Form DFS-F2-DWC-3 thereby furnishing the claims-handling entity a "work search report" for the period during which wage loss benefits are claimed, including the name, address, telephone number, and person contacted at each business where the claimant applied for work during the period for which wage loss benefits are being claimed, the date the claimant applied for work at each business, and a description of the type of work or the specific job for which the claimant applied at each. The listing should also include any contacts with a public or private employment agency and the dates of such contacts. The employee shall sign and date the form with the signature authorizing the release of social security information and Unemployment Compensation wage and benefits information. The employee shall send the completed Form DFS-F2-DWC-3 to the claims-handling entity. A Form DFS-F2-DWC-3 without an original signature of the injured employee shall not be processed for payment by the claims-handling entity.

(2) Claims-handling entity's Responsibilities.

(a) Within 5 working days of its first knowledge of the date of maximum medical improvement, the claims-handling entity shall send to the employee an informational letter which explains the employee's possible eligibility for wage loss benefits, together with at least 4 copies of the Form DFS-F2-DWC-3. The letter to the employee must contain at least the following:

"Your treating physician has reported that you have reached maximum medical improvement and you may return to work but that you have a permanent impairment which has resulted in a work-related physical restriction which may affect your ability to perform the duties of your usual occupation or other appropriate employment. If this physical restriction causes you to lose wages, you may be entitled to additional benefit payments under the Florida Workers' Compensation Law.

If you lose wages, you must complete and send a REQUEST FOR WAGE LOSS/TEMPORARY PARTIAL BENEFITS Form (DFS-F2-DWC-3) to us within 14 days after the end of any 2 week period for which a loss of wages is claimed. If you fail to send the completed form within that 14-day period, you may be ineligible for wage loss benefits during that period.

In addition, to be eligible for wage loss benefits, you must demonstrate that you have made a valid effort to obtain suitable gainful employment and that your loss of wages is due to your work-related physical restriction and NOT due to economic conditions, the unavailability of jobs, your unemployment due to misconduct or your failure to accept employment within your capabilities.

To show that you have made a genuine effort to obtain employment, list the dates, names, addresses, type of work, person contacted and the telephone number of the places of employment that you have contacted on the reverse side of the REQUEST FOR WAGE LOSS/TEMPORARY PARTIAL BENEFITS form. You should also list the dates you make contact with any public or private employment agency.

Please note that the Florida Workers' Compensation Law allows us to evaluate your efforts to obtain gainful employment beginning with the 13th week after you have reached maximum medical improvement. If it can be shown that there are actual job openings within your geographical area and which are within your physical and vocational capabilities, the amount of earning you could have earned at those jobs can be deducted from your benefit payment.

Enclosed are REQUEST FOR WAGE LOSS/TEMPORARY PARTIAL BENEFITS forms for your use. Keep them with your other valuable documents until you either use them or your entitlement to these benefits expires. We are also reporting your permanent impairment to the Division of Workers' Compensation in Tallahassee.

If you desire further information regarding wage loss benefits, you may call the Employee Assistance and Ombudsman Office of the Division of Workers' Compensation at any of their local offices, or at 1(800)342-1741."

(b) The claims-handling entity shall date stamp the Form DFS-F2-DWC-3 upon receipt and within 14 days of receipt of the Form DFS-F2-DWC-3 from the employee, the claims-handling entity shall complete calculation of benefits due, make any payments due, and send copies of the completed form to the employee and the employer. The claims-handling entity shall also send the employee a blank Form DFS-F2-DWC-3. If the claims-handling entity is denying wage loss benefits, the claims-handling entity shall indicate in the claims-handling entity processing section of the Form DFS-F2-DWC-3 that wage loss benefits are being denied, complete a Form DFS-F2-DWC-12, as adopted in Rule 69L-3.025, F.A.C., and send both forms to the employee, employer, legal counsel, and the Division within 14 days of the claims-handling entity's receipt of Form DFS-F2-DWC-3.

(3) Calculation of Wage Loss Benefits. The first calendar week of eligibility for wage loss benefits may be a partial week since eligibility begins on the date of maximum medical improvement. All other weeks of eligibility shall be full calendar weeks. To determine the amount of wage loss benefits due for a partial week: divide the pre-injury average weekly wage by

the number of days employed per week, multiply by the number of days from date of maximum medical improvement through the last working day of that calendar week, multiply by 85% if the date of accident is before July 1, 1990 or by 80% if the date of accident is July 1, 1990 or later, insert the resulting figure on the DFS-F2-DWC-3 in the box labeled "ADJ. WW", and complete the calculations shown on that form.

Specific Authority 440.15(3)(b), 440.185(4), (10), 440.41, 440.591 Fla. Stat. (1993).

Law Implemented 440.15(3), 440.185(4), (10) Fla. Stat. (1993).

History: New 10-30-79, Amended 11-5-81, 5-30-82, 6-12-84, Formerly 38F-3.18, Amended 4-11-90, 1-30-91, 11-8-94, 11-11-96, Formerly 38F-3.018, 4L-3.018, Amended 1-10-05.

69L-3.019. Wage Loss Benefits for Temporary Partial Disability (Dates of Accident August 1, 1979 Through December 31, 1993).

(1) Employee's Responsibilities. During any 2 week period in which wage loss for temporary partial disability is suffered, the employee shall file a Form DFS-F2-DWC-3, as adopted in Rule 69L-3.025, F.A.C., with the claims-handling entity within 14 days. The employee shall complete the "Employee" portion of the Form DFS-F2-DWC-3 and the employee shall also fill out the back of the Form DFS-F2-DWC-3 thereby furnishing the claims-handling entity a "work search report" for the period for which temporary partial wage loss benefits are claimed, including the name, address, telephone number, and person contacted at each business where the claimant applied for work during the period for which temporary partial wage loss benefits are being claimed, the date the claimant applied for work at each business and a description of the type of work or the specific job for which the claimant applied at each. The listing should also include any contacts with a public or private employment agency and the dates of such contacts. The employee shall sign and date the form with the signature authorizing the release of Social Security information and Unemployment Compensation wage and benefit information. The employee shall file the completed Form DFS-F2-DWC-3 with the claims-handling entity. A Form DFS-F2-DWC-3 without an original signature of the injured employee shall not be processed for payment by the claims-handling entity.

(2) Claims-handling Entity's Responsibilities.

(a) Within 5 working days of its first knowledge of the date of temporary partial disability, the claims-handling entity shall mail to the employee an informational letter, which explains the employee's eligibility for temporary partial wage loss benefits, together with at least four (4) copies of the Form DFS-F2-DWC-3. The letter to the employee must at least contain the following: "Your treating physician has reported that you may return to limited duty work with some temporary physical restrictions. Your temporary total disability benefits have been suspended but you may be entitled to additional benefit payments under the Florida Workers' Compensation Law. If you lose wages, you must complete and send a REQUEST FOR WAGE LOSS/TEMPORARY PARTIAL BENEFITS Form (DFS-F2-DWC-3) to us within 14 days after the end of any two-week period for which a loss of wages is claimed. If you fail to send the completed form within that 14-day period, you may be ineligible for temporary partial wage loss benefits during that period. In addition, to be eligible for temporary partial wage loss benefits, you must demonstrate that you have made a valid effort to obtain suitable gainful employment and that your loss of wages is due to your work-related physical restriction and NOT due to economic conditions, the unavailability of jobs, your unemployment due to misconduct or your failure to accept employment within your capabilities.

To show that you have made a genuine effort to obtain employment, list the dates, names, addresses, type of work, person contacted and the telephone number of the places of employment that you have contacted on the reverse side of the REQUEST FOR WAGE LOSS/TEMPORARY PARTIAL BENEFITS form. You should also list the dates you make contact with any public or private employment agency.

Please note that the Florida Workers' Compensation Law allows us to evaluate your efforts to obtain gainful employment beginning with the 13th week after you have received the first payment of a temporary partial wage loss benefit. If it can be shown that there are actual job openings within your geographical area and which are within your physical and vocational capabilities, the amount of earnings you could have earned at those jobs can be deducted from your benefit payment.

Enclosed are REQUEST FOR WAGE LOSS/TEMPORARY PARTIAL BENEFITS forms for your use. Keep them with your other valuable documents until you either use them or your entitlement to these benefits expires. We are also reporting your status to the Division of Workers' Compensation in Tallahassee.

If you desire further information regarding Wage Loss benefits, you may call the Employee Assistance and Ombudsman Office (EAO) of the Division of Workers' Compensation at any of their local offices, or at 1 (800) 342-1741."

(b) The claims-handling entity shall date stamp the Form DFS-F2-DWC-3 upon receipt and within 14 days of receipt of the Form DFS-F2-DWC-3 from the employee, the claims-handling entity shall complete calculation of benefits due, make any payments due, and send copies of the completed form to the employee and the employer. The claims-handling entity shall also send the employee a blank Form DFS-F2-DWC-3. If the claims-handling entity is denying wage loss benefits for temporary partial disability, the claims-handling entity shall indicate in the claims-handling entity section of the Form DFS-F2-DWC-3 that wage loss benefits are being denied, complete a Form DFS-F2-DWC-12, as adopted in Rule 69L-3.025, F.A.C., and send both forms to the employee, employer, legal counsel, and the Division within 14 days of the claims-handling entity's receipt of Form DFS-F2-DWC-3.

(3) Calculation of Temporary Partial Wage Loss Benefits. The first calendar week of eligibility for temporary partial wage loss benefits may be a partial week since eligibility begins on the date of claimant's release to return to light duty work. All other weeks of eligibility shall be full calendar weeks. To determine the amount of benefits due for a partial week, divide the pre-injury average weekly wage by the number of days employed per week, multiply by the number of days from date of release to return to light duty work through the last working day of that calendar week, multiply by 85% if the date of accident is before July 1, 1990 or by 80% if the date of accident is July 1, 1990 or later, insert the resulting figure on Form DFS-F2-DWC-3 in the box labeled "ADJ.WW", and complete the calculations shown on that form.

Specific Authority 440.15(4)(a), 440.185(4), (10), 440.41, 440.591 Fla. Stat. (1993).

Law Implemented 440.15(4)(b), 440.185(4), (10), 440.20 Fla. Stat. (1993).

History: New 10-30-79, Amended 11-5-81, Formerly 38F-3.19, Amended 4-11-90, 1-30-91, 11-8-94, 11-11-96, Formerly 38F-3.019, 4L-3.019, Amended 1-10-05.

69L-3.0191. Temporary Disability Benefits (Dates of Accident January 1, 1994 through September 30, 2003).

(1) Temporary disability benefits include temporary total and temporary partial disability benefits and are payable for a maximum of 104 weeks. An employee's eligibility for temporary disability benefits ceases after the employee has received 104 weeks of temporary total disability benefits paid pursuant to Section 440.15(2)(a), F.S., or after the employee has received 104 weeks of temporary partial disability benefits paid pursuant to Section 440.15(4), F.S., or after the employee has received 104 weeks of any combination of these two benefits.

(2) An employee is eligible for temporary partial disability benefits if the employee has received a medical release to return to work, is unable to earn at least 80% of the employee's pre-injury average weekly wage, has not reached maximum medical improvement, and has not received payment for 104 weeks of temporary total or temporary partial disability benefits or any combination of the aforementioned benefits The Division does not require an employee to request temporary partial disability benefits by filing a form promulgated by the Division. The claims-handling entity shall not require the employee to demonstrate eligibility for temporary partial disability benefits by submitting documentation indicating the employee

has looked for work.

(3) Within five (5) days of its knowledge that the employee has been released to return to work, unless the employee's eligibility for temporary partial disability benefits has expired, the claims-handling entity shall mail to the employee an informational letter which explains the employee's eligibility for temporary partial disability benefits. The letter must advise the employee about the employee's obligation to report, at the claims-handling entity's request using Form DFS-F2-DWC-19, as adopted in Rule 69L-3.025, F.A.C., the employee's receipt of any and all of the following: salary, wages, unemployment compensation benefits, or Social Security benefits. The letter to the employee must contain at least the following:

"Your doctor has said that you are able to return to work, but you have not reached maximum medical improvement from your injury (maximum medical improvement is the date after which a doctor says you will not get any better from your injury). You are eligible for temporary partial disability benefits if you cannot make at least 80% of the wages you were making at the time of your accident after the doctor says you can return to work. These benefits will continue until one of the following happens:

(a) Your doctor says you have reached maximum medical improvement from your injury; or

(b) You have received 104 weeks of either temporary total or temporary partial disability benefits, or both combined; or

(c) You are making 80% or more of the wages you were making at the time of your accident. If you earn wages after the doctor says you can return to work, you must immediately contact this office and give us the name of your employer and the amount of money you are making. If you stop making at least 80% of the wages you were making at the time of your accident, you should also contact this office immediately. If you receive unemployment compensation benefits or Social Security benefits, you must immediately contact this office and tell us what kind of benefits you are getting and the amount of those benefits. If the form "Employee Earnings Report" (Form DFS-F2-DWC-19) was sent with this letter, you must fill it out, sign it and return it within 21 days after you received it. You may be asked to fill out one of these forms once a month. If you do not fill out, sign and return the form, your compensation benefits may be stopped until you return the form. If you turn down an offer of a job that you can do, your compensation benefits may be stopped. For more information about temporary partial disability benefits, please call the Employee Assistance and Ombudsman Office (EAO) of the Division of Workers' Compensation at any of its local offices listed in your "Important Workers' Compensation Information For Florida Workers" brochure, or at 1 (800) 342-1741."

(4) Calculations and payment of temporary partial disability benefits:Temporary partial disability benefits shall be calculated pursuant to Section 440.15(4)(a), F.S., even when the employee's earnings are $0. Temporary partial benefits calculated for any given week are subject to the maximum weekly compensation rate as defined by Section 440.12, F.S. The claims-handling entity shall investigate an employee's post-injury earnings, to determine the amount of temporary partial disability benefits for which the employee is entitled, and to ensure the timely payment of those benefits.

(a) No post-injury earnings — If the claims-handling entity has determined there are no earnings, the first installment of temporary partial disability benefits is due no later than 14 days after the date the employee's medical release states that the employee may resume work. The claims-handling entity shall pay temporary partial disability benefits to the employee based on $0 earnings. Subsequent payments of temporary partial disability benefits for any biweekly period is due no later than the last day of that biweekly period as long as the employee continues to be eligible.

(b) Post-injury earnings —

1. If re-employed and the employee or employer has notified the claims-handling entity within 5 business days after returning to work, the first installment is due within 7 days after the

last date of the post-injury employer's first biweekly work week as defined in subsection 69L-3.002(2), F.A.C. Subsequent payments of temporary partial disability benefits for any biweekly period are due no later than 7 days after the end of the last date of that biweekly period as long as the employee continues to be employed and eligible.

2. Once re-employed, the first week of temporary partial disability may be paid as a partial week in order to coincide with the post-injury employer's work week. To determine the amount of benefits due for a partial week:

a. Divide the pre-injury average weekly wage by the pre-injury number of days employed per week to calculate the daily rate;

b. Multiply this daily rate by the number of days the employee worked during the post injury employer's work week;

c. Multiply this amount by 80%;

d. Subtract the partial week's earnings; and

e. Multiply the difference by 80%, resulting in the temporary partial benefit due for this partial week.

(c) No confirmation of earnings — At any time the claims-handling entity is unable to confirm earnings information from the employee's post injury employer or employers, the claims-handling entity shall calculate benefits based on the last wage information submitted or obtained and continue to pay temporary partial disability benefits.

1. If the last known earnings are $0, payments of temporary partial disability benefits for any biweekly period are due no later than the last day of that biweekly period as long as the employee continues to be eligible.

2. If the last known earnings are greater than $0, payments of temporary partial disability benefits for any biweekly period are due no later than seven (7) days after the last day of that biweekly period as if the employee continues to be employed and eligible. If the employee does not timely return Form DFS-F2-DWC-19, the claims-handling entity may then suspend payment of the employee's temporary partial disability benefits until the claims-handling entity's receipt of the form in accordance with Rule 69L-3.021, F.A.C.

Specific Authority 440.15(2)(d), (4)(a), 440.185(4), (5), 440.20(3), 440.591 Fla. Stat.

Law Implemented 440.15(2), (4), 440.185(4), (5), 440.20(3) Fla. Stat.

History: New 11-8-94, Formerly 38F-3.0191, 4L-3.0191, Amended 1-10-05.

69L-3.01915. Temporary Partial Disability Benefits (Dates of Accident on or After October 1, 2003).

(1) Letter requirement — The claims-handling entity shall mail an informational letter to the employee and employer within 5 business days after the claims-handling entity's knowledge of the employee's release to restricted work. This letter shall explain the employee's eligibility for temporary partial disability benefits and the obligation to report earnings. These earnings would include the receipt of any of the following: salary, wages, unemployment compensation benefits, or Social Security benefits. The letter to the employee must contain at least the following:

"Your doctor has released you to return to work, but because of your work-related accident, you have been given restrictions on the type of work you can now do. Because you have not reached maximum medical improvement (the date after which your doctor says your injury will probably not get better), you may continue receiving workers' compensation benefits approximately every two weeks if you are not able to earn at least 80% of the weekly wages you were making before your injury.

(a) These benefits, called Temporary Partial Disability benefits, will be paid until:

1. You reach maximum medical improvement or can return to work without restrictions;

2. You receive the maximum of 104 weeks allowed by law for either Temporary Total Disability benefits, Temporary Partial Disability benefits or Training and Education Temporary Total benefits, or 104 weeks for the combined benefits; or

3. You earn 80% or more of the weekly wages you were making at the time of your accident.

(b) IMPORTANT: Temporary Partial Disability benefits may be stopped if:

1. You do not notify this office within five (5) business days after you return to work;

2. You are not working due to your own misconduct on the job;

3. You refuse suitable employment offered to you; or

4. You do not return, if requested, Form DFS-F2-DWC-19, "Employee Earnings Report", as adopted in Rule 69L-3.025, F.A.C., to this claims office within 21 days after you receive it and report the receipt of any earnings, including Unemployment Compensation or Social Security benefits. You may be asked to complete, sign, and return this form once a month.

You are to notify this office immediately if you stop making at least 80% of your pre-injury weekly wages. However, if you leave your job without just cause as determined by a judge, your temporary partial disability benefits will be paid based on the amount of money you would have earned had you not left work.

For more information about temporary partial disability benefits, please call the Employee Assistance Ombudsman Office (EAO) with the Division of Workers' Compensation at any of its local offices listed in your "Important Workers' Compensation Information For Florida Workers' brochure, or at 1 (800) 342-1741."

(2) Calculations and payment of temporary partial disability benefits:Temporary partial disability benefits shall be calculated pursuant to Section 440.15(4)(a), F.S., even when the employee's earnings are $0. Temporary partial benefits calculated for any given week are subject to the maximum weekly compensation rate as defined by Section 440.12, F.S. The claims-handling entity shall investigate an employee's post-injury earnings, to determine the amount of temporary partial disability benefits for which the employee is entitled, and to ensure the timely payment of those benefits.

(a) No post-injury earnings —If the claims-handling entity has determined there are no earnings, the first installment of temporary partial disability benefits is due no later than 14 days after the date the employee's medical release states that the employee may resume work. The claims-handling entity shall pay temporary partial disability benefits to the employee based on $0 earnings. Subsequent payments of temporary partial disability benefits for any biweekly period is due no later than the last day of that biweekly period as long as the employee continues to be eligible.

(b) Post-injury earnings —

1. If re-employed and the employee or employer has notified the claims-handling entity within 5 business days after returning to work, the first installment is due within 7 days after the last date of the post-injury employer's first biweekly work week, as defined in subsection 69L-3.002(2), F.A.C. Subsequent payments of temporary partial disability benefits for any biweekly period are due no later than 7 days after the end of the last date of that biweekly period as long as the employee continues to be employed and eligible.

2. Once re-employed, the first week of temporary partial disability may be paid as a partial week in order to coincide with the post-injury employer's work week. To determine the amount of benefits due for a partial week:

a. Divide the pre-injury average weekly wage by the pre-injury number of days employed per week to calculate the daily rate;

b. Multiply this daily rate by the number of days the employee worked during the post injury employer's work week;

c. Multiply this amount by 80%;

d. Subtract the partial week's earnings; and

e. Multiply the difference by 80 %, resulting in the temporary partial benefit due for this partial week.

(c) No confirmation of earnings — At any time the claims-handling entity is unable to confirm earnings information from the employee's post injury employer or employers, the claims-handling entity shall calculate benefits based on the last wage information submitted or obtained and continue to pay temporary partial disability benefits.

1. If the last known earnings are $0, payments of temporary partial disability benefits for any biweekly period are due no later than the last day of that biweekly period as long as the employee continues to be eligible.

2. If the last known earnings are greater than $0, payments of temporary partial disability benefits for any biweekly period are due no later than seven (7) days after the last day of that biweekly period as if the employee continues to be employed and eligible. If the employee does not timely return Form DFS-F2-DWC-19, the claims-handling entity may then suspend payment of the employee's temporary partial disability benefits until the claims-handling entity's receipt of the form in accordance with Rule 69L-3.021, F.A.C.

Specific Authority 440.15(4), 440.591 Fla Stat.

Law Implemented 440.15(4) Fla Stat.

History: New 1-10-05.

69L-3.0192 Impairment Income Benefits (Dates of Accident January 1, 1994 through September 30, 2003).

(1) (a) After the employee has reached maximum medical improvement, the claims-handling entity shall make the initial payment of impairment income benefits no later than the 20th day after the claims-handling entity has knowledge of the employee's permanent impairment rating; however this initial payment may be made before the 20th day. The initial payment of impairment income benefits must include payment for all full weeks of entitlement since the date of maximum medical improvement up to the time the initial payment is made. Impairment income benefits are payable whether the employee is working or not.

(b) Impairment income benefits may be paid in either weekly or biweekly installments. If the claims-handling entity pays benefits biweekly, it shall issue payment for both weeks at the end of the first week. To establish and maintain a biweekly installment schedule, the claims-handling entity shall issue the check for the first and second weeks of entitlement at the end of the first week, the third and fourth weeks of entitlement at the end of the third week, and so on.

(2) (a) Impairment income benefits are paid at a rate of 50% of the average weekly temporary total disability benefit, as defined in subsection 69L-3.002(1), F.A.C.

(b) If impairment income benefits are due and no previous temporary total disability benefits have been paid, the average weekly temporary total disability benefit shall be 66 $^{2}/_{3}$% of the employee's average weekly wage, up to the maximum compensation rate for the accident year.

(3) Impairment income benefits may not be offset by Social Security or unemployment compensation benefits received by the employee.

Specific Authority 440.591 FS.

Law Implemented 440.15(3) FS.

History: New 1-8-94, Formerly 38F-3.0192, 4L-3.0192, Amended 1-10-05.

69L-3.01925. Impairment Income Benefits (Dates of Accident on or After October 1, 2003).

(1) The initial payment of impairment income benefits shall include payment for all full weeks of entitlement since the date of maximum medical improvement up to the time the initial payment is made. After the employee has reached maximum medical improvement, the claims-handling entity shall make the initial payment of impairment income benefits no later than the 14th day after the claims-handling entity has knowledge of the employee's permanent impairment rating.

(2) Impairment income benefits shall be paid in biweekly installments pursuant to Sections 440.15(3)(c) and (g), F.S. (2003).

(3) Impairment income benefits may not be offset by social security or unemployment compensation benefits received by the employee.

Specific Authority 440.15(3)(f), 440.591 Fla Stat.

Law Implemented 440.15(3)(f) Fla Stat.

History: New 1-10-05.

69L-3.0193. Supplemental Income Benefits (Dates of Accident January 1, 1994 through September 30, 2003).

An employee may be eligible to receive Supplemental Income Benefits if an impairment rating of 20% or more has been assigned in accordance with Section 440.15(3)(b), F.S., (1994).

(1) Definitions: The following words and terms when used in this rule shall have the following meanings:

(a) "Filing Period for Supplemental Income Benefits" means a period of 13 consecutive weeks (approximately 3 months) for which the employee reports any earnings and files a claim for supplemental income benefits. The filing period shall represent a "quarter" as set out in Section 440.15(3)(b)7., F.S., (1994), except for the second filing period, which may consist of less than 13 weeks if the first payment period was pro-rated. The "initial filing period" is the filing period which occurs during the last 13 weeks of impairment income benefits.

(b) "Initial Payment of Supplemental Income Benefits" means payment of supplemental income benefits for the first whole or partial calendar month immediately following the expiration of the impairment income benefit period. The initial payment of supplemental income benefits shall cover the time beginning with the day after the expiration of impairment income benefits and ending with the last date in the initial calendar month.

(c) "Payment Period for Supplemental Income Benefits" means the period of 3 consecutive calendar months immediately following the filing period. The first payment period may consist of less than 3 full months if the first monthly payment is pro-rated. The last payment period may consist of less than 3 full months if the employee has reached a maximum of 401 weeks of benefits. All other payment periods of supplemental income benefits shall be for 3 full calendar months.

(2)

(a) No later than 15 weeks before the expiration of the impairment income benefit period, the claims-handling entity shall send by certified mail to each employee eligible for supplemental income benefits an informational letter substantially in conformance with subsection (7) of this rule section, and two copies of Form DFS-F2-DWC-40, as adopted in Rule 69L-3.025, F.A.C. The claims-handling entity shall fill out the first two lines on one of the Forms DFS-F2-DWC-40 before sending it to the employee and indicate the beginning and ending dates of the initial filing period. The second Form DFS-F2-DWC-40 should be left blank.

(b) If the claims-handling entity has knowledge that the employee is eligible for supplemental income benefits and fails to timely provide the employee with written notification and forms as required by this rule, the claims-handling entity shall pay supplemental income benefits for all months for which the employee was not provided a form. Payment shall be computed as if the employee had $0 earnings. The claims-handling entity may later obtain repayment of any overpayment in accordance with paragraph (3)(d) of this rule and pursuant to Section 440.15(12), F.S.

(c) For any filing period, the claims-handling entity shall add all earnings reported by the employee and divide by the total number of weeks in that filing period to yield a "current average weekly wage." The current average weekly wage shall include any weeks for which $0 earnings were reported.

(3) Payment of Supplemental Income Benefits:

(a) The claims-handling entity shall issue the initial payment (the first whole or partial calendar month) of supplemental income benefits by the 7th day after the expiration of impairment income benefits. The claims-handling entity shall make the first payment of supplemental income benefits with or without receipt of the employee's first Form DFS-F2-DWC-40. If the employee timely filed Form DFS-F2-DWC-40 with the claims-handling entity, the second and third months in the initial payment period shall be paid on the first (1st) day of each month in that payment period.

(b) To calculate benefits due for a partial month of the initial payment period: divide the monthly supplemental income benefit payment amount, computed from the "calculation" section on Form DFS-F2-DWC-40, by 4.3; divide that amount by 7 to yield the daily rate; multiply this daily rate by the number of days from the first day of eligibility for supplemental income benefits through the last day of the first calendar month in the payment period. Record this figure on Form DFS-F2-DWC-40 in the box labeled "Payment Amount for Initial Month."

(c) Except for the initial payment of supplemental income benefits, payments of additional monthly supplemental income benefits are contingent upon the employee having filed Form DFS-F2-DWC-40 with the claims-handling entity. Subsequent monthly payments of supplemental income benefits for which the claims-handling entity has received Form DFS-F2-DWC-40 shall be paid as follows:

1. The first month in the next payment period shall be paid within 7 days of the claims-handling entity's receipt of Form DFS-F2-DWC-40;

2. The second and third months of this payment period shall be paid on the first day of each month in that payment period. If Form DFS-F2-DWC-40 was not timely returned by the employee to allow the claims-handling entity to issue payment as per paragraphs (a) and (b) above, the claims-handling entity shall within 7 days of receipt of Form DFS-F2-DWC-40 pay any and all months of supplemental income benefits due and owing as of the date the form was received, subject to the information submitted by the employee on the form.

(d) If upon receipt of Form DFS-F2-DWC-40 it is determined that an overpayment of supplemental income benefits has occurred, the claims-handling entity may re-calculate the amount of supplemental income benefits due for the remaining months in that payment period or any subsequent payment periods and obtain repayment, subject to the provisions of Section 440.15(12), F.S. In no case shall the repayment amount be greater than 20% of the monthly supplemental income benefit payment amount.

(e) The monthly supplemental income benefit payable shall not exceed the maximum weekly benefit amount as set out in Section 440.12, F.S., multiplied by 4.3.

(4) Filing Requirements:

(a) The employee will not be entitled to supplemental income benefits for any filing period for which Form DFS-F2-DWC-40 has not been filed with the claims-handling entity by the seventh day after the expiration of the payment period associated with that filing period.

(b) Within 7 days after the claims-handling entity has made the first payment of supplemental income benefits in any payment period, the claims-handling entity shall send the completed Form DFS-F2-DWC-40 to the Division, the employee, the employer, and any other interested parties. If the claims-handling entity denies payment of supplemental income benefits for any payment period, the claims-handling entity must attach Form DFS-F2-DWC-12, as adopted in Rule 69L-3.025, F.A.C., to Form DFS-F2-DWC-40 and provide the reason(s) for the denial.

(c) The claims-handling entity shall provide the employee with at least two (2) additional Forms DFS-F2-DWC-40 upon payment of the first month for any payment period. The claims-handling entity shall indicate on one of the forms the beginning and ending dates of the employee's next filing period.

(5) The amount payable for supplemental income benefits shall be based on earnings information submitted by the employee for the previous filing period, and shall be paid monthly, with the exception of the initial payment which may be pro-rated. Once the employee has been determined to be eligible for supplemental income benefits for the filing period, the monthly benefit amounts shall be the same for each month of that filing period, unless it is the initial payment of supplemental income benefits for a partial month, or if an adjustment is being made for an overpayment, or if the final payment of

supplemental income benefits expires at the 401 week maximum.

(6) Supplemental income benefits may not be offset by social security or unemployment compensation benefits received by the employee.

(7) The informational letter to the employee referred to in subsection (2) of this rule must contain at least the following:

"Because your doctor found that you have a permanent impairment of 20% or more due to your work injury, you may be eligible to receive additional workers' compensation benefits, known as SUPPLEMENTAL INCOME BENEFITS. However, you must also meet the requirements below in order to receive payment for these benefits:"

1. You must be unable to earn at least 80% of what you earned before your injury for at least 90 days in a row, and

2. You must try in good faith to find a job that you are able to do and cooperate with any reemployment help offered by the employer, claims-handling entity or the Division of Workers' Compensation.

To get your first check for supplemental income benefits, you need to complete, sign and return the enclosed "Statement of Quarterly Earnings for Supplemental Benefits" Form (DFS-F2-DWC-40) to this office. We recommend you return the form no later than 7 days after the end of the filing period, shown in section "A" of the enclosed form. This should enable you to keep your payments coming about every 4 to 6 weeks. Report any wages you earn during the last 13 weeks that you are paid impairment income benefits. Do not include the amount paid to you for your impairment income benefits. Follow the filing instructions on the back of the form to make sure there will not be a break in your payments. Your supplemental income benefits will be calculated by a formula that is based on the wages you report for every filing period on each "Statement of Quarterly Earnings for Supplemental Income Benefits."

If you already know that you will not be eligible for payment of supplemental income benefits when your impairment income benefits end, keep this letter and the other blank form for possible future use, because you may later become eligible for supplemental benefits.

If you do not work during the filing period, it is suggested that you keep records of all the places you look for work, the dates you look, the type of work you are seeking, and the names of the people you contact.

If you turn down the offer of a job that you are able to do, your supplemental income benefits will be calculated on the basis of what that job would have paid you, for as long as the job offer remained open to you. Also, if you refuse to accept training or education offered by the employer, this office, or the Division, your supplemental income benefits may be reduced by one-half. If you have any questions, contact your claims representative at this office, at the address and telephone number listed in this letter. You may also call the Division of Workers' Compensation's Employee Assistance and Ombudsman Office (EAO) at any of its branch offices listed in your employee brochure, or at its toll-free telephone number in Tallahassee at 1 (800) 342-1741."

Specific Authority 440.15(3)(b)(5)., 440.591 Fla Stat.

Law Implemented 440.15(3), 440.20(3), 440.591 Fla Stat.

History: New 11-8-94, Formerly 38F-3.0193, 4L-3.0193, Amended 1-10-05.

69L-3.0194. Permanent Total and Permanent Total Supplemental Benefits for Dates of Accident Prior to October 1, 2003.

(1)

(a) Permanent total benefits paid for injuries occurring prior to July 1, 1955, shall not be made in excess of 700 weeks. Permanent total benefits paid for injuries occurring on or after July 1, 1955, shall continue during the continuance of the employee's entitlement.

(b) When a permanently and totally disabled employee re-establishes an earning capacity and undertakes a trial period of re-employment pursuant to Section 440.15(1)(d), F.S., the employee may be eligible for impairment income and supplemental benefits pursuant to Section

440.15(3), F.S.

(2) Permanently and totally disabled employees are entitled to permanent total disability supplemental benefits when the injury occurred subsequent to June 30, 1955, and the liability of the employer has not been discharged pursuant to Section 440.20(12), F.S. Such benefits shall be equal to 5% of the employee's weekly compensation rate which was in effect on the date of the employee's injury, multiplied by the number of calendar years since the date of injury.

(a) When the date of the employee's injury and acceptance or adjudication of permanent total disability is within the same calendar year, supplemental benefits are payable January 1st of the next calendar year.

(b) When acceptance or adjudication is in a calendar year other than the year of injury, supplemental benefits are payable as of the date the employee was accepted or adjudicated permanently and totally disabled.

(3)

(a) Permanent total supplemental benefits shall be paid by the Division, unless the claims-handling entity made an election to pay such benefits, to an injured employee whose accident occurred subsequent to June 30, 1955, and before July 1, 1984. Permanent total supplemental benefits are not payable for any period prior to October 1, 1974.

(b) Permanent total supplemental benefits shall be paid by the claims-handling entity for injury occurring on or after July 1, 1984. The claims-handling entity is not required to pay permanent total supplemental benefits for any period prior to October 1, 1974.

(c) An injured employee entitled to or receiving permanent total supplemental benefits shall have such benefits increased by 5% each January 1 after the commencement of such entitlement. However, when permanent total supplemental benefits are combined with the compensation rate, the combination of benefits shall not exceed the maximum compensation rate in effect for the year in which the combined benefits are being paid.

(d)

1. The injured employee is entitled to full permanent total supplemental and compensation benefits as of the employee's 62nd birthday for dates of accident prior to July 1, 1990. The employee's entitlement to permanent total supplemental benefits shall cease on the employee's 62nd birthday if the employee is eligible for social security benefits under 42 U.S.C. Sections 402 and 423, whether or not the employee has applied for benefits when the employee's date of accident occurred on or after July 1, 1990.

2. All permanent total benefits shall cease when the employee becomes an inmate of a public institution, unless the employee has dependents as defined in Chapter 440, F.S. Dependent benefits shall be determined for each dependent as though the employee were deceased.

3. When the injured employee receives a full or partial lump-sum advance of the employee's permanent total disability compensation benefits, the employee's permanent total supplemental benefits shall be computed on the employee's weekly compensation rate as reduced by the lump-sum advance.

4. Neither the claims-handling entity, employer, or Division of Workers' Compensation shall pay any permanent total benefits for as long as the injured employee willfully fails or refuses to file a completed Form DFS-F2-DWC-19, or Form DFS-F2-DWC-14, or Form DFS-F2-DWC-30, as adopted in Rule 69L-3.025, F.A.C., within 21 days after the employee received the request.

(4) The social security offset of permanent total disability benefits shall be calculated as follows:

(a) Convert monthly social security benefit to weekly benefit by dividing the monthly amount by 4.3 (monthly amount divided by 4.3).

(b) Add the Compensation Rate (CR) plus the Principal Insurance Amount (PIA) or the Maximum Family Benefits (MFB) if the employee has dependents plus 5% permanent total supplemental benefits due at the time of permanent total acceptance or adjudication.

(c) Subtract the greater of 80% of average weekly wage (AWW), or 80% of weekly average current earnings (ACE). The resulting difference is the offset amount.

(5)

(a) Neither the claims-handling entity nor the Division shall take the social security offset until after the Social Security Administration has removed its offset.

(b) Social security offset shall not be applied retroactively nor shall social security annual cost of living increases or initial lump-sum payments be included in any offset.

(c) The Division shall have priority over the claims-handling entity in taking any available social security offset on dates of accident prior to July 1, 1984.

(d) No social security offset shall be taken which is greater than the offset that would otherwise be taken by the Social Security Administration.

(e)

1. Within 14 days after request by the Division, the claims-handling entity shall file a completed Form DFS-F2-DWC-35, as adopted by reference in Rule 69L-3.025, F.A.C., with the Division's Permanent Total Section.

2. Within 14 days after request by the Division, the claims-handling entity shall file a completed Form DFS-F2-DWC-33, as adopted by reference in Rule 69L-3.025, F.A.C., with the Division's Permanent Total Section.

Specific Authority 440.15(3)(b)5., 440.591 Fla. Stat.

Law Implemented 440.15(3), 440.20(3), 440.491 Fla. Stat.

History: New 11-8-94, Formerly 38F-3.0193, 4L-3.0193, Amended 1-10-05.

69L-3.01945. Permanent Total and Permanent Total Supplemental Benefits for Dates of Accident on or After October 1, 2003.

(1) Permanent total benefits paid for injuries occurring on or after October 1, 2003, shall cease at age 75. If it is determined that the injury prevented the employee from working sufficient quarters to be eligible for social security benefits under 42 U.S.C. Section 402 or 423, benefits will continue to be paid in accordance with the requirements of Chapter 440, F.S. If the accident occurred on or after the employee reaches age 70, benefits shall be payable during the continuance of permanent total disability, not to exceed 5 years from the date of permanent total disability.

(2) Permanent total benefits paid for injuries occurring on or after October 1, 2003, shall continue during the continuance of the employee's entitlement.

(a) When a permanently and totally disabled employee re-establishes an earning capacity and undertakes a trial period of re-employment pursuant to Section 440.15(1)(d), F.S., the employee may be eligible for impairment income benefits pursuant to Section 440.15(3), F.S.

(3) Permanently and totally disabled employees are entitled to permanent total disability supplemental benefits, if the liability of the employer has not been discharged pursuant to Section 440.20(12), F.S. Such benefits shall be equal to 3% of the employee's weekly compensation rate which was in effect on the date of the employee's injury multiplied by the number of calendar years since the date of injury.

(a) When the date of the employee's injury and acceptance or adjudication of permanent total disability is within the same calendar year, supplemental benefits are payable January 1 of the next calendar year.

(b) When acceptance or adjudication is in a calendar year other than the year of injury, supplemental benefits are payable as of the date the employee was accepted or adjudicated permanently and totally disabled.

(4)

(a) Permanent total supplemental benefits shall be paid by the claims-handling entity.

(b) An injured employee entitled to or receiving permanent total supplemental benefits shall have such benefits increased by 3% each January 1 after the commencement of such entitlement. However, when the permanent total supplemental benefits are combined with the compensation rate, the combination of benefits shall not exceed the maximum compensation rate in effect for the year in which the combined benefits are being paid.

(c) For injuries occurring on or after October 1, 2003, the employee's entitlement to specific benefits shall cease when any of the following occurs:

1. Permanent total supplemental benefits shall cease on the employees 62nd birthday, regardless of whether the employee has applied for or is eligible to apply for social security benefits under 42 U.S.C., Section 402 or 423. If it is determined that the injury prohibited the employee from qualifying for social security benefits, supplemental benefits will continue to be paid as long as the employee remains eligible.

2. All permanent total benefits shall cease when the employee becomes an inmate of a public institution, unless the employee has dependents as defined in Chapter 440, F.S. Dependent benefits shall be determined for each dependent as though the employee were deceased.

3. When the injured employee receives a full or partial lump-sum advance of such employee's permanent total disability compensation benefits, the employee's permanent total supplemental benefits shall be computed on the employee's weekly compensation rate as reduced by the lump-sum advance.

4. Neither the claims-handling entity, employer, or Division of Workers' Compensation shall pay any permanent total benefits for as long as the injured employee willfully fails or refuses to file a completed Form DFS-F2-DWC-19, or Form DFS-F2-DWC-14, or Form DFS-F2-DWC-30, as adopted in Rule 69L-3.025, F.A.C., within 21 days after the employee receives the request.

(5) The social security offset of permanent total disability benefits shall be calculated as follows:

(a) Convert monthly social security benefit to weekly benefit by dividing the monthly amount by 4.3 (monthly amount divided by 4.3).

(b) Add the Compensation Rate (CR) + Principal Insurance Amount (PIA) or the Maximum Family Benefits (MFB) if the employee has dependents + 3% permanent total supplemental benefits due at the time of permanent total acceptance or adjudication.

(c) Subtract the greatest of 80% of average weekly wage (AWW), or 80% of weekly average current earnings (ACE). The resulting difference is the offset amount.

(6)

(a) Neither the claims-handling entity nor the Division shall take the social security offset until after the Social Security Administration has removed its offset.

(b) The social security offset shall not be applied retroactively nor shall social security annual cost of living increases or initial lump-sum payments be included in any offset.

(c) No social security offset shall be taken which is greater than the offset that would otherwise be taken by the Social Security Administration.

(d)

1. Within 14 days after request by the Division, the claims-handling entity shall file a completed Form DFS-F2-DWC-35, as adopted in Rule 69L-3.025, F.A.C., with the Division's Permanent Total Section.

2. Within 14 days after request by the Division, the claims-handling entity shall file a completed Form DFS-F2-DWC-33, as adopted in Rule 69L-3.025, F.A.C., with the Division's Permanent Total Section.

Specific Authority 440.15(1)(f)2.a., (2)(d), 440.591 Fla Stat.

Law Implemented 440.15(1) Fla Stat.

History: New 1-10-05.

69L-3.0195. Forms.

Specific Authority 440.13(11)(b), 440.591 Fla. Stat.

Law Implemented 440.13(11)(b), 440.15(1)(f)1., (10) Fla. Stat.

History: New 10-2-94, Amended 6-4-97, Formerly 38F-24.029, Formerly 38F-3.0195, 4L-3.0195, Repealed 4-18-04.

69L-3.021. Additional Income Source Reports.

(1) Within 21 days after the employee receives a request from either the Division or the claims-handling entity for either Form DFS-F2-DWC-14, or Form DFS-F2-DWC-30, as adopted in Rule 69L-3.025, F.A.C., the employee shall complete the form and return it to the party requesting the information. The employee shall renew the authorization each 12 months upon a request by the Division, employer or claims-handling entity.

(2) Upon request of the Division, employer, or claims-handling entity, any employee eligible for temporary total, temporary partial, permanent total disability or permanent total supplemental compensation shall complete, sign, and return Form DFS-F2-DWC-19, as adopted in Rule 69L-3.025, F.A.C., within 21 days after receiving it to report all earnings of any nature, including all social security benefits. The Division, employer, or claims-handling entity may require the employee to send Form DFS-F2-DWC-19 no more than once a month.

(3) If the employee refuses to report information requested in accordance with subsection (1) or (2) above within 21 days after receipt of the request, payments of workers' compensation disability benefits for temporary total, temporary partial, permanent total or permanent total supplemental compensation shall cease until such time as the employee furnishes the signed form.

(4) For dates of accident on or after October 1, 2003, upon the request of the claims-handling entity, any employee eligible for impairment income benefits shall complete, sign, and return Form DFS-F2-DWC-19 within 21 days after receiving it to report all earnings. The claims-handling entity may require the employee to send Form DFS-F2-DWC-19 no more than once a month. If the employee refuses to report earnings within 21 days after receipt of the request, payments of workers' compensation disability benefits for impairment income benefits shall cease until such time as the employee furnishes the signed form.

(5) The party requesting the employee's authorization for release of social security benefit information shall furnish the Form DFS-F2-DWC-14 to the employee. The requesting party shall be responsible for submitting the Request for Social Security Disability Benefit Information to the Social Security Administration office nearest to the employee's address. The requesting party must send a copy of the completed Form DFS-F2-DWC-14 to the Division within 14 days of the request.

(6) If the claims-handling entity changes the employee's compensation rate based on any offset, the claims-handling entity shall send to the Division, along with the appropriate income source report, Form DFS-F2-DWC-4, as adopted in Rule 69L-3.025, F.A.C., indicating the change in accordance with the provisions of Rule 69L-3.0091, F.A.C.

(7) If the employee's benefits have been suspended due to the employee's refusal to furnish a signed release, the claims-handling entity shall send to the Division Form DFS-F2-DWC-4 indicating the effective date and reason code for suspension of the benefits in accordance with the provisions of Rule 69L-3.0091, F.A.C.

Specific Authority 440.591, 440.15(1)(f)2.a., b., (2)(d) Fla. Stat.

Law Implemented 440.15(1), (2), (4), 440.185, 440.20(3) Fla. Stat.

History: New 10-30-79, Amended 11-5-81, Formerly 38F-3.021, Amended 4-11-90, 1-30-91, 6-10-92, 11-8-94, Formerly 38F-3.021, 4L-3.021, Amended 1-10-05.

69L-3.0212. Monthly Risk Class/SIC Code Report.

Specific Authority 440.591 Fla. Stat.

Law Implemented 440.59 Fla. Stat.

History: New 11-8-94, Formerly 38F-3.0212, 4L-3.0212, Repealed 4-18-05.

69L-3.0213. Aggregate Claims Administration Change Report.

(1) If the responsibility for handling claims files has changed due to a claims-handling entity taking over the claims from another claims-handling entity, the new claims-handling entity shall report this change to the Division. They may send Form DFS-F2-DWC-49, as adopted in Rule 69L-3.025, F.A.C., to report an aggregate listing of claims affected by the change in administration rather than sending an individual Form DFS-F2-DWC-4, as adopted in Rule 69L-3.025, F.A.C., on each claims file in accordance with the provisions of Rule 69L-3.0091, F.A.C.

(2) If the claims-handling entity chooses to send Form DFS-F2-DWC-49 in place of separate Forms DFS-F2-DWC-4 to report a claims administration change, the claims-handling entity shall send Form DFS-F2-DWC-49 to the Division within 30 days after the effective date of the change in the administration of claim files.

(3) If a claims-handling entity chooses to send Form DFS-F2-DWC-49 to report a claims administration change, the claims-handling entity must use a separate Form DFS-F2-DWC-49 for each claims office location handling those files.

(4) Any attachment(s) used to report additional information shall be in a format that contains all of the data fields identified on the Form DFS-F2-DWC-49.

Specific Authority 440.591 Fla. Stat.

Law Implemented 440.59 Fla. Stat.

History: New 11-8-94, Formerly 38F-3.0213, 4L-3.0213, Amended 1-10-05.

69L-3.0214. Aggregate Defense Attorney Fee Report.

Specific Authority 440.345 Fla. Stat.

Law Implemented 440.345 Fla. Stat.

History: New 11-25-96, Formerly 38F-3.0214, 4L-3.0214, Repealed 4-18-04.

69L-3.025. Forms.

(1) The following forms are to be used with this rule chapter and are hereby incorporated by reference:

(a)	Form DFS-F2-DWC-1	8/04	First Report of Injury or Illness
(b)	Form IA-1	11/02	Workers' Compensation — First Report of Injury or Illness — For use only by entities approved to transmit electronic First Reports of Injury to the Division
(c)	Form DFS-F2-DWC-1a	8/04	Wage Statement
(d)	Form DFS-F2-DWC-3	8/04	Request for Wage Loss/Temporary Partial Benefits
(e)	Form DFS-F2-DWC-4	8/04	Notice of Action/Change
(f)	Form DFS-F2-DWC-12	8/04	Notice of Denial
(g)	Form DFS-F2-DWC-13	8/04	Claim Cost Report
(h)	Form DFS-F2-DWC-14	8/04	Request for Social Security Disability Benefit Information
(i)	Form DFS-F2-DWC-19	8/04	Employee Earnings Report
(j)	Form DFS-F2-DWC-30	8/04	Authorization and Request for Unemployment Compensation Information

(k)	Form DFS-F2-DWC-33	8/04	Permanent Total Offset Worksheet
(l)	Form DFS-F2-DWC-35	8/04	Permanent Total Supplemental Worksheet
(m)	Form DFS-F2-DWC-40	8/04	Statement of Quarterly Earnings for Supplemental Income Benefits
(n)	Form DFS-F2-DWC-49	8/04	Aggregate Claims Administration Change Report
(o)	Form DFS-F2-DWC-60	8/04	Important Workers' Compensation Information for Florida's Workers
(p)	Form DFS-F2-DWC-61	8/04	Informacion Importante Del Seguro De Indemnizacion Por Accidentes De Trabajo Para Los Trabajadores De La Florida
(q)	Form DFS-F2-DWC-65	8/04	Important Workers' Compensation Information for Florida's Employers
(r)	Form DFS-F2-DWC-66	8/04	Informacion Importante Del Seguro De Indemnizacion Por Accidentes De Trabajo Para Los Empleadores De La Florida

(2) The Division will not supply the forms promulgated under this chapter, but will make sample forms available on the Division's web site: http://www.fldfs.com/wc.

(3) For a transitional period of 90 days from the effective date of this rule, an insurer or claims-handling entity may use forms identified and adopted in subsection 69L-3.025(1), F.A.C., or the corresponding form(s) in effect prior to the adoption of this rule. After the completion of the 90 day transitional period, only the forms adopted in this rule may be used.

Specific Authority 440.15, 440.185, 440.20, 440.345 Fla. Stat.

Law Implemented 440.15, 440.185, 440.20, 440.345 Fla. Stat.

History: New 4-11-90, Amended 1-30-91, 11-8-94, 11-11-96, 11-25-96, Formerly 38F-3.025, 4L-3.025, Amended 1-10-05.

CHAPTER 69L-5 Rules for Self-Insurers Under the Workers' Compensation Act

I. General Requirements

69L-5.101. Definitions.

When used in these rules, the following words or terms shall have the meaning as described in this section.

(1) "Actuarial Report"—Report written by an actuary who is a member of the Casualty Actuarial Society or the American Academy of Actuaries who has been approved by the Casualty Practice Council.

(2) "Division"—The Division of Worker's Compensation of the Florida Department of Financial Services.

(3) "Excess Insurance"—A policy providing "excess coverage" or "reinsurance" which must provide an actual transfer of risk to the reinsurer or excess carrier as defined in Financial Accounting Standards Board Statement 113 (FASB 113). FASB 113 which is hereby incorporated by reference into Rule Chapter 69L-5, F.A.C. The effective version of the statement identified by this rule shall bear the date December 1992. A copy of FASB 113 may be obtain from Financial Accounting Standards Board, 401

Merit 7, P.O. Box 5116, Norwalk, Connecticut 06856-5116, telephone 203-847-0700. A copy of FASB 113 may be viewed at the Division of Workers' Compensation, Bureau of Monitoring and Audit, Self-Insurance Section, 2012 Capital Circle, S.E., Hartman Building, Suite 200, Tallahassee, FL 32399-4224.

(4) "Financial Statement"—A presentation of financial data, including accompanying notes, dervied from accounting records that purports to show fiancial position and intended to communicate an entity's economic resources or obligations at a point in time, and the results of operations and cash flows for a period of time, in accordance with the Generally Accepted Accounting Principles.

(5) "Financial Summary" —As used within these rules indicates a summary of financial information consisting of at least: current assets, current liabilities, long term assets, all other liabilities, intangible assets (including deferred taxes), contingency liabilities, summary of cash flows and equity. The summary must contain generally accepted financial ratios, all footnotes, prepared in accordance with United States Generally Accepted Accounting Principles (see incorporation by reference in subsection 69L-5.101 (4)), F.A.C.) and contain an unqualified statement from a Certified Public Accountant attesting to its accuracy. All amounts in the financial summary shall be stated in United States Currency.

(6) "Generally Accepted Accounting Principles" —Accounting principles generally accepted in the United States of America in effect as of January 1, 2005, including, but not limited to, Accounting Principles Board Opinions Nos. 1 to 31 as published by the American Institute of Certified Public Accountants and statements of accounting standards and interpretations thereof, as published by the Financial Accounting Standards Board (FASB). The materials are entitled Original Pronouncements 2005/2006 Edition, Vols. I, II and III, dated June 1, 2005, and available from FASB, 401 Merritt 7, P.O. Box 5116, Norwalk, CT 06856-5116, (800) 748-0659, http://qqq.fasb.org.

(7) "Generally Accepted Auditing Standards" —Auditing standards generally accepted in the United States of America in effect as of January 1, 2005, including, but not limited to, general, field work and reporting standards approved and adopted by the membership of the American Institute of Certified Public Accountants (AICPA), as amended by the AICPA Auditing Standards Board (ASB), standards promulgated by the ASB in the form of Statements on Auditing Standards and standards promulgated by the Public Company Accounting Oversight Board (PCAOB). The AICPA materials are entitled Codification of Statements on Auditing Standards, dated January 1, 2005, available from the AICPA at http://www.pcaobus.org.

(8) "Incurred But Not Reported Reserves (IBNR)" —A reserve established by an actuary which estimates the incurred loss due to claims whose existence is unknown by the self-insurer or claims which have been reported but not recorded on the books of the self-insurer.

(9)

(a) "Premium, Manual"—Premium determined by multiplying the payroll (segregated into the proper workers' compensation job classifications) times the manual premium rates per $100 of payroll in effect at the start of the payroll period covered.

(b) "Premium, Normal"—Standard premium less allowed discount.

(c) "Premium, Standard"—Manual premium multiplied by the experience modification factor.

(10) "Security Deposit"—A security deposit conforming to the requirements of s. 440.38 (1)(b)4., Florida Statutes, in addition to any other deposit required of an individual self-insurer due to failure to comply with the requirements established pursuant to s. 440.38 (1)(b), Florida Statutes.

(11) "Self-Insurer"—This term shall include employers that self-fund their workers' compensation liabilities as prescribed in s. 440.38, Florida Statutes.

(12) "Service Company"—A business which has obtained Division approval to contract with

self-insurers for the purpose of providing all services necessary to plan and maintain an approved self-insurance program. The term "Service Agent" is synonymous with the term "Service Company" as used in these rules.

(13) "Surety Bond"—This term shall mean "indemnity bond" as used in s. 440.38 (1)(b)4.a., Chapter 624 and Chapter 627, Florida Statutes.

Specific Authority 440.38(1)(b), (2), 440.5705, 440.591 Fla. Stat.

Law Implemented 440.38(1)(b), (2), 440.57, 624.24 Fla. Stat.

History: New 10-1-82, Amended 12-17-85, Formerly 38F-5.30, Amended 3-11-87, 8-28-91, 12-19-93, Formerly 38F-5.030, Amended 5-19-97, Formerly 38-5.101, 4L-5.101, Amended 3-8-06.

II. Qualifying for Self-Insurance

69L-5.102 General Requirements.

(1) The state and its boards, bureaus, departments, and agencies and all of its political subdivisions which employ labor, and the state universities that are electing to self-insure pursuant to Section 440.38(6), F.S., shall submit to the Division for review at least 90 days prior to the preferred effective date of self insured status, the following information:

(a) Copy of document(s) through which the entity is organized or authorized to operate as a governmental entity, including articles of incorporation, grant of authority, or charter, if applicable;

(b) Notification By Governmental Entity To Self-Insure For Workers' Compensation, Form DFS-F2-SI-1G, incorporated by reference into rule (rev. 03/2006);

(c) Self-Insurance Estimated Payroll, Form DFS-F2-SI-EP, incorporated by reference into rule (rev. 03/2006);

(d) Certification of Servicing For Self-Insurers, Form SI-19, incorporated by reference into rule (rev. 09/1996); and

(e) Workers' Compensation Experience Rating For Self-Insurers worksheet, Form ERM-6, for the current and two preceding years, as set forth in the National Council on Compensation Insurance (NCCI) Experience Rating Plan Manual for Workers' Compensation and Employers Liability Insurance, incorporated by reference into rule (rev. 01/2002).

The notification and supporting documentation shall be submitted to the following address-:Division of Workers' CompensationBureau of Monitoring and Audit / Self-Insurance200 East Gaines StreetTallahassee, Florida 32399-4224

(2) Upon receipt of the notification and supporting documentation from an entity defined within the scope of Section 440.38(6), F.S., the Division shall provide to the entity the "Insurer Code #" pursuant to Rule Chapter 69L-3.002, F.A.C., prior to the effective date of self-insured status for compliance with filing requirements of Rule Chapters 69L-3 and 69L-7, F.A.C.

(3) All other individual employers not eligible under section (1) shall qualify for self-insurance under Section 440.38(1)(b), F.S., and must meet the following minimum requirements:

(a) Have and maintain a minimum net worth of $1,000,000 U.S.

(b) Have at least three (3) years' Financial Statements or Financial Summaries in the name of the applicant. The Financial Statements for the most recent year shall be audited in accordance with Generally Accepted Auditing Standards. If financial statements or financial summaries are prepared on a comparative basis, such statements shall be the most recent fiscal year ending statement and the preceding fiscal year ending statement. If the latest Financial Statement is over six (6) months old at the time of application, an interim statement up to, and including, their latest fiscal quarter must be included and must be certified by a corporate officer.

(c) If the name of the business has changed in the last three years, provide a copy of the Amended Articles of Incorporation.

(d) Have the financial strength to ensure the payment of current and estimated future compensation claims when due, as determined through review of their financial statement or summary by the division.

(4) An applicant which does not have three (3) years of financial statements or financial summaries in its own name due to recent purchase, may use the financial statements of the predecessor, provided there has been no change to the structure of the entity or the line of business which would adversely affect the financial condition.

(5) Forms adopted. The forms set forth in paragraphs (1)(b)-(e), as well as the accompanying instructions to the forms, are hereby adopted. Copies of the forms set forth in paragraphs (1)(b)-(d) are available from the Division of Workers' Compensation, Bureau of Monitoring and Audit, Self-insurance Section, 200 East Gaines Street, Tallahassee, FL 32399-4224. The form set forth in paragraph (1)(e) is found within the National Council on Compensation Insurance, Inc. (NCCI) Experience Rating Plan Manual for Workers' Compensation and Employers Liability Insurance. A copy of the Manual and a one year subscription to any and all updates may be obtained from the National Council on Compensation Insurance, Inc., 750 Commerce Drive, Boca Raton, FL 33487, telephone (800)622-4123, at a cost of $95. A copy of the Manual is also available for viewing at the Division of Workers' Compensation, Bureau of Monitoring and Audit, Self-Insurance Section, 2012 Capital Circle, S. E., Hartman Building, Suite 200, Tallahassee, FL 32399-4224.

Specific Authority 440.38(1)(b), (6) Fla. Stat.

Law Implemented 440.38(1)(b), (6) Fla. Stat.

History: New 5-19-97, Formerly 38F-5.102, 4L-5.102, Amended 3-8-06, 10-29-06.

69L-5.103. Application.

(1) Applications for self-insurance shall be considered for approval based upon the applicant having sufficient financial strength, as determined by a review of the financial statements, to ensure the payment of all current and estimated future claims when due.

(2) Applications for self-insurance shall be made in writing on Form SI-1 submitted in duplicate at least ninety (90) days prior to the desired effective date to allow for sufficient processing time. The application form, Form SI-1, is hereby incorporated by reference into Chapter 69L-5, F.A.C. The version of the form required by this rule shall bear the date September 1996 (9/96). A copy of Form SI-1 may be obtained from the Division of Workers' Compensation, Bureau of Monitoring and Audit, Self-Insurance Section, 2012 Captial Circle, S.E., Hartman Building, Suite 200, Tallahassee, FL 32399-4224. All effective dates will be the first day of the month following application approval, or the first day of a month selected by the applicant, providing their application has been approved, but on no occasion will the effective date be more than three months from the approval date. As a general guideline, applications submitted less than ninety (90) days in advance cannot be assured of being granted the requested effective date.

(3) Applications shall be accompanied by two copies of:

(a) The most recent past three years' financial statements in the name of the applicant. The Financial Statements for the most recent year shall be audited in accordance with the Generally Accepted Auditing Standards. If the Financial Statements for the two years prior to the most recent year have been audited in accordance with Generally Accepted Auditing Standards, the audit reports on these Financial Statements shall also be submitted.

(b) An outline of the proposed service program which complies with Rules 69L-5.112, 69L-5.113, and 69L-5.114, F.A.C.

(c) A list of all subsidiary companies which the applicant intends to include under its self-insurance privilege. The list shall include the percentage of the applicant's ownership interest in each subsidiary.

(d) Certification by a corporate officer stating that the applicant, at the time of application, and until approval of application, is in compliance with Section 440.38 (1), Florida Statutes.

(e) Experience modification work sheet for the current and two preceding years as set forth in the National Council on Compensation Insurance, Inc. (NCCI) Experience Rating Plan Manual for Workers' Compensation and Employers Liability Insurance, which is hereby incorporated by reference into Rule Chapter 69L-5, F.A.C. The Manual required by this rule shall bear the date September 1984, and shall include all issued updates. A copy of the Manual and a one-year subscription to any and all updates may be obtained from the National Council on Compensation Insurance, Inc., 750 Park of Commerce Drive, Boca Raton, FL 33487, telephone 1 (800) 622-4123, at a cost of $95. A copy of the Manual is also available for viewing at the Division of Workers' Compensation, Bureau of Monitoring and Audit, Self-Insurance Section, Forrest Building, 2012 Capitol Circle, S.E., Hartmen Building, Suite 200, Tallahassee, FL 32399-4224.

(f) A minimum initial security deposit, in addition to the security requirements for excess retention, of $100,000. If the last three years' losses not fully funded by insurance, reinsurance or subject to reimbursement exceed $100,000, a security deposit equal to those losses must be posted. (To be provided prior to issuance of certificate of self-insurance).

(g) Maximum excess insurance retention of $350,000 or 1% of tangible net worth, whichever is greater.

(4) Upon receipt of the application, the division shall review the application and request any additional information which may be necessary to render a decision on the application.

Specific Authority 440.38(1)(b), (6) Fla. Stat.

Law Implemented 440.38(1)(b), (6) Fla. Stat.

History: New 5-19-97, Formerly 38-5.103, 4L-5.103, Amended 3-8-06.

69L-5.104. Alternate Method of Application.

(1) In lieu of the requirements of paragraph (3)(a) above, entities with a tangible net worth in excess of $250 million, may submit, in duplicate, financial summaries in the name of the applicant and for the most recent three years consisting of at least: current assets, current liabilities, long term assets, all other liabilities, intangible assets (including deferred taxes), statement of cash flows and equity. In addition, an unqualified statement by a Certified Public Accountant attesting to the accuracy of such summaries along with the following ratios shall be required in duplicate:

(a) Current assets to current liabilities.

(b) Net income to net sales.

(c) Net income to tangible net worth.

(d) Net income to net working capital.

(e) Intangible assets to net worth.

(f) Net sales to net working capital.

(g) Net sales to inventory.

(h) Fixed assets to tangible net worth.

(i) Current liabilities to tangible net worth.

(j) Inventory to net working capital.

(k) Current liabilities to inventory.

(*l*) Total liabilities to tangible net worth.

(2) All other requirements as stated in the application process Rule 69L-5.103, F.A.C., above must be satisfied.

(3) The initial security deposit under this method shall be 150% of the total cumulative losses for the three years preceding application approval. For the first three years of self-insurance, security deposits will equal the greater of the initial security deposit or 150% of the actuarially computed cumulative loss reserves, and will be adjusted annually. Commencing with the fourth year of self-insurance, the security deposit shall equal 150% of the actuarially computed cumulative loss reserves adjusted annually. In no event will the security deposit be less than $100,000. Security deposit for this section shall be in the form of an irrevocable letter of credit assigned to the division.

Specific Authority 440.591, 440.38(2)(b) Fla. Stat.

Law Implemented 440.38(1)(b), (2)(b) Fla. Stat.

History: New 10-1-82, Amended 12-25-84, Formerly 38F-5.44, Amended 2-3-88, 6-12-91, 12-19-93, 5-14-96, Formerly 38F-5.044, Amended 5-19-97, Formerly 38F-5.104, 4L-5.104.

III. Retention, Revocation, and Withdrawal

69L-5.105. General Requirements.

(1) Employers approved for self-insurance privilege in accordance with Section 440.38, Florida Statutes, and these rules will be continuous unless and until voluntarily withdrawn or revoked.

(2) A review of all self-insurance programs will be made periodically. Deterioration in the financial strength as indicated in the financial statements or summaries which may affect their strength to pay current and estimated future claims when due or significant increases in losses detected as a result of such reviews, shall result in changes to the prior requirements to continue to be self-insured.

(3) Failure to comply with any of the rules herein or with any order of the division within the time prescribed shall be considered good cause for revocation or termination of the self-insurance privilege, within the meaning of Section 440.38 (3), Florida Statutes. Noncompliance with any of the provisions of the Workers' Compensation Law, Chapter 440, Florida Statutes, particularly those relating to time and method of compensation payments, the furnishing of medical treatment and filing of accident and compensation reports and failure to pay any assessment or penalty, shall likewise be deemed good cause.

(4) The division shall be given written notice of revocation or termination to the self-insurer. The self-insurer shall have fifteen (15) days from the date of receipt of the notice to request a hearing on the revocation or termination or to advise the division of the intent to submit an actuarial report and qualifying security deposit pursuant to Section 440.38 (1)(b)2., Florida Statutes. Failure to mail a request for hearing or to advise the division of the intent to submit an actuarial report and qualifying security deposit within the time prescribed shall result in the revocation or termination becoming effective thirty (30) days from the date of receipt of the original notice. If a hearing is requested, in no event shall any revocation or termination become effective prior to the date that a hearing on the question is scheduled. Such notice shall be served personally or by certified mail upon the self-insurer.

(5) A self-insurer who is a member of the Florida Self-Insurers Guaranty Association, Inc., and who voluntarily withdraws from self-insurance, on or after January 1, 1991, shall continue to file all reports required by this rule, in duplicate, with the division upon withdrawal, and at 12 month intervals thereafter until such time as the employer has satisfied the division that there is no remaining value to the claims incurred while the employer was self-insured. Should any of the financial statements so submitted fail to meet the financial standards set forth in Rule 69L-5.106, F.A.C., the self-insurer shall provide periodic actuarial studies and security deposits in the same manner as an employer whose self-insurance privilege has been revoked as set forth in Section 440.38 (1)(b)3., Florida Statutes.

Specific Authority 440.38(1)(b), (2)(b) Fla. Stat.

Law Implemented 440.38(1)(b), (2)(b) Fla. Stat.

History: New 5-19-97, Formerly 38F-5.105, 4L-5.105.

69L-5.106. Financial Statement or Financial Summary.

Failure to provide the following information in the name of the self-insurer when due shall be cause for revocation of privilege:

(1) Financial statement shall show, at all times, a net worth of at least $1,000,000 or a financial summary showing a minimum tangible net worth of $250,000,000 for those qualifying under the alternate method pursuant to Rule 69L-5.104, F.A.C. The financial statement or financial summary must demonstrate the self-insurer has the financial strength to ensure the payment of all current and estimated future compensation claims when due, as determined by the division. The statements and summaries must be submitted not later than four (4) months following the end of the self-insured employer's fiscal year.

(2) The following conditions shall apply to the financial statement or financial summary:

(a) The financial statement, or summary shall

be in the name of the business holding the self-insurance privilege;

(b) The financial statement, or financial summary shall be accompanied by a certification by an owner, partner or corporate officer that there has been no material adverse change in the financial condition of the self-insured since the date of the last financial statement or financial summary;

(c) The financial statement shall be audited in accordance with Generally Accepted Auditing Standards.

(d) Financial Statements submittted for employers currently authorized in self-insure under a privilege granted prior to January 1, 1997, are not required to be audited in accordance with Generally Accepted Auditing Standards.

(3) All separate legal entities which are included in the self-insurer's privilege shall submit financial statements in accordance with this rule. Separate financial statements shall be submitted for each entity unless consolidated or combined financial statements are submitted.

(4) If a self-insured entity is either purchased in whole or part by another company which is not self-insured in Florida, or is structurally separated as result of reorganization, their self-insurance privilege may continue provided the new owners submit Form SI-1a, Re-Application for Self-Insurance, their financial statements annually, and execute an indemnity agreement (Form SI-11) guaranteeing the performance of the original self-insurer. The re-application form, Form SI-1a, and the Idemnity Agreement, Form SI-11, are hereby incorporated by reference into Rule Chapter 69L-5, F.A.C. The version of the forms required by this rule shall bear the date September 1996 (9/96). Copies of both forms may be obtained from the Division of Workers' Compensation, Bureau of Monitoring and Audit, Self-Insurance Section, 2012 Capitol Circle, S.E., Hartmen Building, Suite 200, Tallahassee, FL 32399-4224.

(5) The division shall require additional financial information if it determines, based upon the self-insurer's financial statement or financial summary, that there has been or may be a significant change in the self-insurer's financial condition compared to the most recent financial statement.

(6) The division shall conduct an overall evaluation of the self-insurer's financial condition to determine if the self-insurer has the financial strength necessary to ensure the payment of all current and estimated future compensation benefits when due. Failure to maintain such financial strength shall constitute good cause for:

(a) Revocation of the self-insurance privilege

(b) Increasing The security deposit

(c) Requirement for quarterly financial filing, or

(d) A combination thereof. If the division has determined the self-insurer does not have the required financial strength and intends to revoke the self-insurance privilege, the self-insurer may elect to continue self-insuring pursuant to Section 440.38 (1)(b)2., Florida Statutes.

Specific Authority 440.591, 440.38(2)(b) Fla. Stat.

Law Implemented 440.38(1)(b), (2)(b) Fla. Stat.

History: New 10-1-82, Formerly 38F-5.47, Amended 6-12-91, 12-19-93, 5-14-96, Formerly 38F-5.047, Amended 5-19-97, Formerly 38F-5.106, 4L-5.106, Amended 3-8-06.

69L-5.107. Actuarial Reports.

(1) If the division determines the self-insurer does not have the required financial strength to ensure the payment of current and estimated future claims when due, the division shall require the submission of an actuarial report, accompanied by Form SI-26, Actuarial Report Checklist, prepared by a qualified actuary. Form SI-26 is hereby incorporated by reference into Rule Chapter 69L-5, F.A.C. The version of the form required by this rule shall bear the date September 1996 (9/96). A copy of the form may be obtained from the Division of Workers' Compensation, Bureau of Monitoring and Audit, Self-Insurance Section, 2012 Capitol Circle, S.E., Hartmen Building, Suite 200, Tallahassee, FL 32399-4224. The report shall evaluate the loss development of the company's operations in the state and shall evaluate the loss reserve

including loss adjustment expense and incurred but not reported (IBNR) reserves in Florida.

(2) Self-insurers qualifying under the alternate method identified in Rule 69L-5.104 are required to file an actuarial report and Form SI-26 annually in conjunction with their financial summary.

Specific Authority 440.38(1), (2) Fla. Stat.
Law Implemented 440.38(1), (2) Fla. Stat.

History: New 5-19-97, Formerly 38-5.107, 4L-5.107.

69L-5.108. Security Deposits.

(1) Each individually self-insured employer shall, as a condition for the approval and continuation of its self-insurance privilege, provide a qualifying security deposit to secure the payment of compensation. The qualifying security deposit shall be held by the division, or by a depository authorized by the division, exclusively for the benefit of workers' compensation claimants. The security shall not be subject to assignment, execution, attachment, or any legal process whatsoever, except as necessary to guarantee compensation under these rules.

(2) The surety bond or security deposit amount required of an individual self-insurer shall be a minimum of $100,000. This security deposit shall be in addition to any security deposit required pursuant to that required by paragraph 69L-5.109 (7)(a), F.A.C. If the division determines the self-insurer does not have the necessary financial strength to ensure the payment of current and estimated future claims when due, the division shall act in accordance with Section 440.38 (1)(b)1., Florida Statutes.

(3) Self-insured employers qualifying under the alternate financial summary method shall post a security deposit in the form of an irrevocable letter of credit, Form SI-6, in favor of the division drawn on a United States bank insured through the Federal Deposit Insurance Corporation Form SI-6, Irrevocable Letter of Credit, is hereby incorporated by reference in Rule Chapter 69L-5, F.A.C. The version of the form required by this rule shall bear the date September 1996 (9/96). A copy of Form SI-6 may be obtained from the Division of Workers' Compensation, Bureau of Monitoring and Audit, Self-Insurance Section, 2012 Capitol Circle, S.E., Hartmen Building, Suite 200, Tallahassee, FL 32399-4224. For the first three years of self-insurance such security deposit shall be equal to the greater of the initial security deposit or 150% of the actuarially computed cumulative loss reserve amount. Commencing with the fourth year of self-insurance the security deposit shall be equal to 150% of the actuarially computed cumulative loss reserve. Such security deposit shall be adjusted annually.

(4) If all or a portion of a self-insurer's outstanding workers' compensation liabilities are guaranteed by separate surety bonds or cash security deposits, then the amount so guaranteed may be deducted from the security deposit requirements. It shall be the responsibility of the self-insurer to request a reduction pursuant to this paragraph and to provide such documentation to the division as necessary to determine the amount of the reduction. Any security deposit maintained in accordance with Section 440.38 (1)(b)2., Florida Statutes, shall not be deducted from current requirements under this rule.

(5) Security deposits and surety bonds posted by self-insurers with no remaining unpaid liabilities resulting from injuries incurred prior to September 17, 1982, who are members of the Florida Self-Insurers Guaranty Association, Inc. shall provide that these bonds are payable directly to the Florida Self-Insurers Guaranty Association, Inc.

(6) The division is authorized to bring suit upon any surety bond posted to procure prompt payment of compensation benefits awarded or due under Chapter 440, Florida Statutes. In the event that the self-insurer is a member of the Florida Self-Insurers Guaranty Association, Inc., the Florida Self-Insurers Guaranty Association, Inc., shall be authorized to bring suit upon the surety bond.

(7) Any securities held by the division may be exchanged or replaced by the depositor with other securities of like nature and amount. Any surety bond may be exchanged or replaced with another surety bond, provided the required ninety (90) days notice of termination of liability is given to the division. Whenever an em-

ployer discontinues or desires to replace securities with a surety bond, it shall so notify the division and may recover the securities deposited with the division upon posting, in lieu thereof, a special release bond issued by a corporate surety in an amount equal to the total value of such securities. The special release bond shall cover all existing liabilities under the law and shall remain in force for a period in accordance with the statute of limitations in the Florida Workers' Compensation Law and until such time as all obligations under Chapter 440, Florida Statutes, have been fully discharged.

(8) All bonds or securities issued by the State of Florida or the U.S. Government which are posted as security deposits shall be reviewed annually by the division to determine market value in relation to the deposit requirement. In the event the market value is less than the deposit requirement, the division shall consider the self-insurer's financial condition, the amount that the market value is less than the deposit requirement, along with the likelihood that such securities will be needed to provide benefits, and act in accordance with Section 440.38 (1)(b)1, Florida Statutes.

(9) To be acceptable to the division, security deposits must conform with s. 440.38 (1)(b)4., Florida Statutes.

(10) Security deposits shall be assigned to the division in writing on Form SI-32, Assignment of Securities. Form SI-32 is hereby incorporated by reference into Rule Chapter 69L-5, F.A.C. The version of the form required by this rule shall bear the date September 1996 (9/96). A copy of Form SI-32 may be obtained from the Division of Workers' Compensation, Bureau of Monitoring and Audit, Self-Insurance Section, 2012 Capitol Circle, S.E., Hartmen Building, Suite 200, Tallahassee, FL 32399-4224. These assignments shall be kept on file with the division. Once the qualifying security deposit has been properly assigned to the division, the division shall file a Standard Form—Form UCC 1, State of Florida Financing Statement, with the Office of the Secretary of State in order to assist in the perfection of its security interest in the deposit. The UCC-1 is hereby incorporated by reference into Rule Chapter 69L-5, F.A.C. The version of the form required by this rule shall bear the year 1993. A copy of the form may be obtained from the Division of Workers' Compensation, Bureau of Monitoring and Audit, Self-Insurance Section, 2012 Capitol Circle, S.E., Hartmen Building, Suite 200, Tallahassee, FL 32399-4224. Any and all fees associated with the filing of the UCC 1 Form with the Office of the Secretary of State shall be assessed to the individual self-insurer posting the security deposit and must be paid prior to or in conjunction with the signing of the security agreement. Said fees are non-refundable. Nonpayment of fees in conjunction with the filing of the UCC 1 Form shall result in the denial of the application of the self-insurer by the division, or in revocation of the self-insurance privilege under Rule 69L-5.105, should that privilege already be in full force and effect.

Specific Authority 440.38(1)(b) Fla. Stat.

Law Implemented 440.38(1)(b) Fla. Stat.

History: New 5-19-97, Formerly 38F-5.108, 4L-5.108.

69L-5.109. Excess Insurance.

(1) Individual self-insurers, except those identified pursuant to Section 440.38 (6), Florida Statutes, and those with audited financial statements and a net worth in excess of $250,000,000, shall maintain specific excess insurance. Such specific excess insurance shall have a limit of not less than $1,000,000.

(2) To be acceptable to the division in fulfillment of the excess insurance requirements, worker' compensation excess policies shall be written by insurance companies licensed in Florida pursuant to Chapters 624, 628 or 629, Florida Statutes, and shall be subject to the protection afforded by the Florida Insurance Guaranty Association Act (Section 631.50, Florida Statutes). Policies issued without the protection of the Florida Insurance Guaranty Association Act shall be issued by insurance companies whose policyholders' and financial ratings as shown in the most current issue of A.M. BEST'S INSURANCE REPORTS, PROPERTY-LIABILITY, shall not be less than "A-" and "VII" respectively. A.M. BEST'S INSURANCE REPORTS, PROPERTY-

LIABILITY is hereby incorporated by reference into Rule Chapter 69L-5, F.A.C. The edition required by this rule shall bear the date September 1996 (9/96). Copies may be obtained from A.M. Best Company, Old Wick, New Jersey 08858, telephone 1 (800) 424-BEST. This report is published annually and the version of the report used should be the most current year. A copy is available for viewing at the Division of Workers' Compensation, Bureau of Monitoring and Audit, Self-Insurance Section, 2012 Capitol Circle, S.E., Hartmen Building, Suite 200, Tallahassee, FL 32399-4224.

(3) In the event an insurance company is not covered by the Florida Insurance Guaranty Association Act (Section 631.50, Florida Statutes) or not rated by BEST's, and adequate coverage is not available from either of the companies identified in subsection 69L-5.109 (2), F.A.C., above, then the division shall accept excess policies written by this company if the company is licensed in Florida pursuant to Chapters 624, 628, 629, Florida Statutes, or authorized to transact business in Florida by the Surplus Lines Law, Section 626.913, Florida Statutes, and provides security to the division for all policies issued which fulfill requirements under these rules. The division shall reject any insurer which:

(a) Does not pay its claims when due; or

(b) Is not in compliance with any requirement of Chapter 624, Florida Statutes.

(4) If an excess policy with a rated company cannot be secured by the self-insurer, the amount of security required shall be determined at policy effective date and shall equal 50 percent of all required aggregate limits and 25 percent of all required specific limits. Following the policy period end, the amount of security shall be redetermined by the division and shall be the amount of any future reimbursements due or payable from the excess policies. The amount of any reimbursements shall be calculated from an actuarially determined loss reserve including incurred but not reported (IBNR) loss.

(a) Excess recoveries not guaranteed by proper security shall become part of the self-insurer's security deposit requirement, even if a security deposit would not otherwise be required.

(b) The amount of security shall be redetermined by the division annually based on the most current actuarial analysis available. Security will be required to be maintained as long as any outstanding reimbursements remain on the excess policies in question.

(5) No contract or policy of excess liability shall be accepted by the division in consideration of the ability of an applicant to fulfill its financial obligations under Chapter 440, Florida Statutes, the Workers' Compensation Law, unless such contract or policy:

(a) Is issued by an insurance company conforming to the Rules for Self-Insurance and naming the Division as additional insured for the purposes of notification.

(b) Cannot be canceled except upon sixty (60) days' written notice by certified mail to the other party to the policy and to the division.

(c) Is automatically renewable at the expiration of the policy period unless written notice by certified mail is given to the other party to the policy and to the division, sixty (60) days prior to such expiration, by the party desiring to cancel or not to renew the policy.

(d) Provides that any commutation affected under a commutation clause shall not relieve the underwriter of further liability in respect to claims and expenses unknown at the time of such commutation. The underwriter shall not be relieved in regard to claims apparently closed but which may be subsequently revived, by or through a competent authority. In the event the underwriter proposes to redeem any future payments as compensation for accidents occurring during the term of the policy by the payment of a lump sum to be fixed as provided in the commutation clause of the policy, not less than 60 days prior to notice of such commutation shall be given to the division by certified mail by the underwriter or its agent.

(e) In the event any commutation is effected, the division shall have the right to direct that such sum either be placed in trust for the benefit of the injured employee or employees entitled to such future payments of compensation or be invested in approved securities and deposited with the division to insure such future payments of compensation to the employee or employees entitled thereto. Said commutation must contain a provision that the division may order that the monies due under the terms of an excess contract or policy be paid directly to the injured employee or such other party as the division may appoint. Such an action shall be ordered only if the division determines that it is necessary to insure continued benefits to the injured employee.

(f) Contains the provision that in the event of the insolvency of a member of the Florida Self-Insurers Guaranty Association, Inc. (FSIGA), that the policy will reimburse FSIGA for any monies expended on behalf of the member. Any reimbursement will be subject to the terms of the contract between the member and the insurer.

(6) No more than one named insured, which shall be defined as a principal named insured and its subsidiaries, shall be covered by any contract or policy of excess liability.

(7) The retention of specific excess policies shall be as follows:

(a) The maximum retention shall be no more than $350,000 or 1% of the self-insurers net worth, whichever is greater. The maximum retention so calculated shall be rounded to the nearest $50,000.

(b) Should a self-insurer purchase, after review by the division, a specific excess policy with a retention greater than the maximum specified in paragraph (7)(a), the higher retention may be allowed. If a higher retention is allowed, the self-insurer's security deposit requirement will be increased by an amount equal to twice the difference between the maximum retention allowed by subparagraph (7)(a) and the retention to be purchased by the self-insurer.

(c) The division shall determine retention levels for each self-insurer based on an evaluation of the self-insurer's financial condition, loss history, actuarial report, and exposure to future loss.

(8) Self-insurers with a financial net worth between $1,000,000 and $5,000,000 shall maintain aggregate excess insurance with a maximum retention of one hundred fifteen percent (115%) of estimated standard premium or 115% of manual premium, whichever is greater, for the term of the policy.

(9) All aggregate excess policies shall have a limit of at least fifty percent (50%) of the estimated standard premium for the term of the policy or $1,000,000, whichever is greater. Such policy shall only apply to the self-insurer's operations within the scope of Chapter 440, Florida Statutes.

Specific Authority 440.38(1)(b) Fla. Stat.

Law Implemented 440.38(1)(b) Fla. Stat.

History: New 10-1-82, Formerly 38F-5.36, Amended 2-3-88, 12-19-93, Formerly 38F-5.036, Amended 5-19-97, Formerly 38F-5.109, 4L-5.109.

69L-5.110. Experience Records.

(1) Employers individually self-insured under Section 440.38, Florida Statutes, shall be subject to the Experience Rating Plan (incorporated by reference in paragraph 69L-5.103 (3)(e), F.A.C.) and the payroll classification and premium determination system established by the National Council on Compensation Insurance (NCCI).

(2) An experience modification shall be determined annually or as otherwise provided by the Experience Rating Plan (incorporated by reference in paragraph 69L-5.103 (3)(e), F.A.C.) for each self-insurer qualified under Section 440.38, Florida Statutes. This experience modification shall be calculated on the same basis as if the employer were insured under the provisions of Section 440.38 (1)(a), Florida Statutes, and the modification shall be used for the determination of the employer's standard premium for the use in the calculation and collection of the administration (Section 440.51, Florida Statutes) and special disability (Section 440.49, Florida Statutes) trust fund assessments. Each employer, or each employer's service company, where requested in the servicing contract, shall be furnished a copy of the experience

rating calculations. Should an employer cease to be self-insured and purchase standard insurance coverage, Part II, Section C, Paragraph 5 of the Experience Rating Plan (incorporated by reference in paragraph 69L-5.103 (3)(e), F.A.C.) provides that self-insured experience may be used in the employer's future experience rating calculations. Loss experience tabulations will be furnished upon the request of the employer and a fee for such services shall be assessed in accordance with Section 119.07, Florida Statutes.

Specific Authority 440.38(1)(b), (2)(b), (3), 440.385 Fla. Stat.

Law Implemented 440.38(1)(b), (2)(b), (3), 440.385 Fla. Stat.

History: New 5-19-97, Formerly 38F-5.110, 4L-5.110.

69L-5.111. Late Reports; Penalties.

(1) Reports shall be submitted on paper in accordance with these rules unless an alternate method, i.e., electronic transfer, has been agreed upon.

(2) Reports submitted by a service company on behalf of the self-insurer shall be treated as if they were submitted by the self-insurer directly.

(3) If additional time is required to file a report, a request for an extension of time for filing financial statements or financial summaries shall be made in writing by the self-insurer or its service company and shall be postmarked or received no later than 15 days prior to the due date of the report. For all other reports, a request for extension must be postmarked on or before the due date of the report. Extensions will be granted by the division if proof is supplied by the self-insurer or service company that circumstances entirely beyond the control of the self-insurer or service company have made it impossible to file on a timely basis. Such circumstances shall include: (a) the destruction of the records of the self-insurer or service company; (b) failure of the division to provide proper forms; (c) delays caused by acts of God or nature or delays caused by other regulatory processes of the State of Florida or United States Government. Clerical errors, personnel turnover, accidental or intentional destruction of forms and records by employees of the self-insurer or service company or any delays caused by the incompetence of the employees of the self-insurer or service company shall not be grounds for an extension. Extensions shall be granted in writing and notice mailed to the self-insurer or service company. Such extension shall establish a new one-time due date subject to the same provision for late filing as heretofore provided.

(4) For purposes of this rule, the postmark date shall be considered the date of mailing. If a report is mailed by the due date, it shall be considered to be filed on a timely basis.

(5) Penalties shall be imposed pursuant to Section 440.38 (2)(b), Florida Statutes, for failure to comply with reporting requirements. Protests to such penalties may be made pursuant to Section 440.021, Florida Statutes.

(6) Each self-insurer shall submit payroll reports to determine the proper assessment to be paid as its proportionate share of the expense of administration. The rules, classifications and rates as set forth in the Basic Manual for Workers' Compensation and Employers' Liability Insurance and the SCOPES of basic Manual Classifications of the National Council on Compensation Insurance will govern the audits of payrolls and the adjustments of premiums. The NCCI Basic and SCOPES Manuals are hereby incorporated by reference into Rule Chapter 69L-5, F.A.C. The manual to be used in conjunction with these rules shall bear the date January 1997 reprint. The NCCI Basic Manual is updated periodically with the most recent edition bearing the year 1996. Both manuals may be purchased from the National Council on Compensation Insurance, Inc., 750 Park of Commerce Drive, Boca Raton, FL 33487, telephone (800) 622-4123. Copies of the manuals are also available for viewing at the Division of Workers' Compensation, Bureau of Operations Support, Self-Insurance Section, Forrest Building, 2728 Centerview Drive, Tallahassee, FL 32399-4002. Payroll reports shall be submitted in writing on Form SI-5 no later than sixty (60) days after the close of the audit period. Form SI-5, Payroll Report, is hereby incorporated by

reference into Rule Chapter 69L-5, F.A.C. The form required by this rule shall bear the date September 1996 (9/96). A copy of Form SI-5 is available from the Division of Workers' Compensation, Bureau of Monitoring and Audit, Self-Insurance Section, 2012 Capital Circle, S.E., Hartman Building, Suite 200, Tallahassee, FL 32399-4224. Each self-insurer shall maintain their payroll records in such manner that a true and accurate division by occupational classifications can readily be determined for proper rating. If such records are not maintained, then the entire payroll shall be presumed to be within the classification to which the highest insurance rate is applicable.

(7) Each self-insurer shall submit summary loss data to determine the proper assessment to be paid as its proportionate share of the expense of administration. The rules on evaluation dates and time of filing as set forth in the Workers' Compensation Statistical Plan Manual of the National Council on Compensation Insurance will govern the summary loss reporting and the manner in which the reports are prepared. The NCCI Workers' Compensation Statistical Plan Manual utilized within these rules shall bear the 1984 edition date and shall contain the most recent revisions. The manual may be purchased from the National Council on Compensation Insurance, Inc., 750 Park of Commerce Drive, Boca Raton, FL 33487, telephone (800) 622-4123, at a cost of $315. A copy of the manual is also available for viewing at the Division of Workers' Compensation, Bureau of Monitoring and Audit, Self-Insurance Section, 2012 Capitol Circle, S.E., Hartmen Building, Suite 200, Tallahassee, FL 32399-4224. Each self-insured employer shall maintain true and accurate loss records and summary loss data which shall be submitted to the division on Form SI-17, Unit Statistical Report, within sixty (60) days after the evaluation date of the losses being reported. Form SI-17 is hereby incorporated by reference into Rule Chapter 69L-5, F.A.C. The Form SI-17 required by this rule shall bear the date September 1996 (9/96). Copies of Form SI-17 may be obtained from the Division of Workers' Compensation, Bureau of Monitoring and Audit, Self-Insurance Section, 2012 Capitol Circle, S.E., Hartmen Building, Suite 200, Tallahassee, FL 32399-4224. The evaluation date shall be six (6) months after the end of the current report period unless otherwise established by the division in accordance with the Experience Rating Plan (incorporated in paragraph 69L-5.103 (3)(e), F.A.C.) established by the National Council on Compensation Insurance.

(8) Individual self-insurers required to post a security deposit or surety bond shall submit in duplicate Form SI-20, Report of Outstanding Workers' Compensation Liabilities on an annual basis along with, and at the same time as, the annual Summary Loss Reports. Such report shall include a reserve for losses incurred but not reported (IBNR). Form SI-20, Report of Outstanding Workers' Compensation Liabilities, is hereby incorporated by reference into Rule Chapter 69L-5, F.A.C. The form required by this rule shall bear the date September 1996 (9/96). Copies of Form SI-20 are available from the Division of Workers' Compensation, Bureau of Monitoring and Audit, Self-Insurance Section, 2012 Capitol Circle, S.E., Hartmen Building, Suite 200, Tallahassee, FL 32399-4224.

(9) Changes in the names and addresses of businesses owned in part or total by the self-insurer, and which are covered by the privilege, as well as changes in its structure with respect to divisions, subsidiaries and the like shall be reported to the division by letter within thirty (30) days of the effective date of the change.

(10) Individual self-insurers maintaining a Drug-Free Workplace Program pursuant to Section 440.102, Florida Statutes, shall qualify for premium discounts as set forth in Section 627.0915, Florida Statutes. Application for such credit shall be made to the division on NCCI Form 9 and filed prior to the effective date of credit and shall be refiled annually prior to self-insurers anniversary date. NCCI Form 9, Application for Credit for Drug Free Workplace, is hereby incorporated by reference into Rule Chapter 69L-5, F.A.C. The form required by this rule shall bear the date May 7, 1996 (5/7/96). Copies of the NCCI Form 9 are available from the Division of Workers' Compensation, Bureau of Monitoring and Audit, Self-Insurance Section, 2012 Capitol Circle, S.E., Hartmen Building, Suite 200, Tallahassee, FL 32399-4224.

(11) Copies of all new contracts or policies of excess insurance complete with all endorsements in the name of the insured shall be filed with the division in duplicate within ninety (90) days of the effective date of the policy. A binder issued by the excess carrier or its authorized agent providing for at least ninety (90) days coverage which specifies the terms of the policy shall be filed with the division within thirty (30) days after the effective date of the policy provided that this proof of excess is not being submitted in support of an application for self-insurance (SI-1, incorporated by reference in subsection 69L-5.103 (2)). Excess renewal endorsements specifying the terms of the policy submitted to the division within thirty (30) days after the renewal date satisfies this requirement. In the event of excess policy cancellation or non-renewal, it shall be necessary for the self-insurer to file proof of replacement excess coverage prior to the cancellation or non-renewal date.

Specific Authority 440.38(1)(b), (2)(b), 440.51(6)(b), 440.5705 Fla. Stat.

Law Implemented 440.38(1)(b), (2)(b), 440.51, 440.102, 624.24 Fla. Stat.

History: New 10-1-82, Formerly 38F-5.38, Amended 12-19-93, Formerly 38F-5.038, Amended 5-19-97, Formerly 38F-5.111, 4L-5.111.

IV. Servicing for Self-Insurers

69L-5.112. General Requirements.

(1) Each individual self-insurer, as a condition of approval to self-insure, shall be required to provide proof of compliance with the provisions of this section regarding the servicing requirements.

(a) It shall be the sole responsibility of each individual self-insurer to provide for competent persons to service its program in the areas of claims adjusting, underwriting, safety engineering and loss control. Should the individual self-insurer be unable or unwilling to provide any or all of these services through the use of its own employees, it shall contract with outside companies approved by the division to provide these services on a full-time basis.

(b) In the case where an individual self-insurer elects to contract with an approved service company, the division shall choose to use the service company as an intermediary in its dealings with the employer. The service company shall be used as an intermediary only if the division determines that this course of action will result in a more rapid and more accurate flow of information from the self-insurer and if this will assist the employer in being in compliance with these rules. In the case where no service company is used, the division shall only deal with the employer.

(2) All safety programs submitted in compliance with this section shall be approved pursuant to Section 627.0915, Florida Statutes.

(3) All self-insurers shall provide reemployment and rehabilitation services to their injured employees pursuant to s. 440.49 (1), Florida Statutes.

(4) It shall be the responsibility of the self-insurer to obtain written permission from the division before changing its method of fulfilling its servicing requirements from those previously approved by the division. Such approval will be granted only if the self-insurer provides for qualified personnel to service its program in the future.

Specific Authority 440.38(1)(b), (2), (4)(b), 440.49(1)(a), 440.56(4) Fla. Stat.

Law Implemented 440.20(16), 440.38(1)(b), (2), 440.49(1)(a), 440.56(4) Fla. Stat.

History: New 10-1-82, Formerly 38F-5.31, Amended 12-19-93, Formerly 38F-5.031, Amended 5-19-97, Formerly 38F-5.112, 4L-5.112.

69L-5.113. Application to Provide Servicing.

(1) Applications by businesses for approval to provide underwriting, claims adjusting, loss control, safety engineering services, and any other services for which the applicant has or intends to contract to provide to self-insurers pursuant to Section 440.38 (2)(a), Florida Statutes, shall be made on Form SI-22. Form SI-22, Service Company Application, is hereby incorporated by reference into Rule Chapter 69L-5, F.A.C. The form required by this rule shall bear the date September 1996 (9/96). A copy of Form

SI-22 is available from the Division of Workers' Compensation, Bureau of Monitoring and Audit, Self-Insurance Section, 2012 Capitol Circle, S.E., Hartmen Building, Suite 200, Tallahassee, FL 32399-4224. Applications shall be approved pursuant to Section 120.60, Florida Statutes, and the uniform rules of procedure.

(2) Any business desiring to become qualified as a service company for individual self-insurers must be approved before any contract for servicing shall be recognized.

(3) To satisfy application requirements, insurance companies licensed to write workers' compensation insurance by the Florida Department of Financial Services to operate within the State of Florida must submit a completed Form SI-22 (or a copy thereof), proof of the Certificate of Insurance, and a copy of the Division of Safety letter of approval for their safety program.

(4) Any business making application to qualify as a service company shall provide proof that it meets the following conditions before approval is to be granted:

(a) The ownership, control, and management is competent and trustworthy and possesses managerial experience that would make the proposed service company operation beneficial to the workers covered. Some examples as proof of competency shall be a history void of questionable claims handling techniques, questionable patterns of claims, repeated unreasonably controverted claims or poor payment practices. The division shall not grant or continue authority to transact the business of a service company in this state at any time during which the division has good reason to believe that the ownership, control, or management of the service company includes any person whose business practice or conduct is detrimental to the public, stockholders, or creditors. Each person listed above shall file a biographical statement, Form SI-27, and provide the division with an independent background investigation report. Form SI-27, Biographical Statement, is hereby incorporated by reference into Rule Chapter 69L-5, F.A.C. The form required by this rule shall bear the date September 1996 (9/96). A copy of Form SI-27 is available from the Division of Workers' Compensation, Bureau of Monitoring and Audit, Self-Insurance Section, 2012 Capitol Circle, S.E., Hartmen Building, Suite 200, Tallahassee, FL 32399-4224.

(b) A number of experienced and qualified claims personnel, licensed Florida worker' compensation claims adjusters, loss control and safety engineering personnel, as required in Section 626.897 (3)(b) and (c), Florida Statutes, employed on a full-time basis to meet the needs of all self-insurers with which it intends to contract.

(c) Experienced and qualified personnel, as required in Section 626.897 (3)(c), Florida Statutes, employed on a full-time basis in the area of underwriting to meet the needs of all self-insurers with which it intends to contract. In this context, underwriting includes coordinating of a self-insurance program, the ability to procure bonds and excess insurance, provide summary data regarding the self-insurer's cost of accidents, including the frequency and distribution, by type and cause, and the skill to make recommendations to self-insurers regarding the correction of any deficiencies that arise in the self-insurance program.

(d) Has, within the State of Florida, a person experienced and qualified in the field of workers' compensation authorized to act in all matters concerning the service company.

(e) That any rehabilitation services offered by, or under contract, to the service company shall be from the approved list of providers of such services maintained by the division pursuant to Section 440.49 (7), Florida Statutes.

(5) In support of its application, the business shall submit summary information concerning its organization, and detailed resumes of all staff with administrative or professional capacity in sufficient numbers to establish its ability to provide services to all self-insurers with which it intends to contract.

(6) Any service company which seeks authorization shall certify that they have sufficient record keeping capabilities.

Specific Authority 440.38(1)(b), (2), (4)(b), 440.56(4) Fla. Stat.

Law Implemented 440.38(1)(b), (2), (4)(b), 440.56(4) Fla. Stat.

History: New 10-1-82, Amended 12-25-84, Formerly 38F-5.40, Amended 12-19-93, Formerly 38F-5.040, Amended 5-19-97, Formerly 38F-5.113, 4L-5.113.

69L-5.114. Retaining Authorization as Service Company; Recertification.

(1) Each service company shall file with the division within thirty (30) days of entering into a contract for servicing, a copy of its service contract or Form SI-19. Form SI-19, Servicing Contract, is hereby incorporated by reference into Chapter 69L-5, F.A.C. The form required by this rule shall bear the date September 1996 (9/96). A copy of Form SI-19 is available from the Division of Workers' Compensation, Bureau of Monitoring and Audit, Self-Insurance Section, 2012 Capitol Circle, S.E., Hartmen Building, Suite 200, Tallahassee, FL 32399-4224.

(2) Each contract entered into by a service company, shall be available to the division for review at a mutually agreeable location, shall provide that all claims incurred during the contract period are handled until their conclusion, and shall contain the following provisions:

(a) Upon termination, the service company agrees it will continue to provide claims adjusting services on all claims incurred during the contract period for 90 days if requested to do so by the self-insurer. The service company shall be entitled to payment for its services at a rate agreed upon by the parties to the contract.

(b) In the event that claims files and claims servicing responsibilities are transferred to a new service company, the former service company will provide an accounting of all claims and claims activity sufficient to allow the new service company to establish its claims and accounting systems using accurate data.

(c) Paragraphs 69L-5.114 (2)(a) and (2)(b), F.A.C., notwithstanding, in the event of a self-insurer's insolvency, the service company will agree to provide claims adjusting services for 90 days or until relieved of this responsibility by the division, whichever occurs earlier. The service company shall be entitled to payment for its services at a rate agreed upon by the parties to the contract. Nothing in this subsection shall be construed to require the service company to pay claims or otherwise incur liabilities for unpaid claims due to the self-insurer's failure to fund claims payment.

(d) Files containing the records of the self-insurer's claims belong to the self-insurer, and upon cancellation or withdrawal of the service contract, are to be transferred to the new service company or to the self-insurer along with the responsibility for handling claims.

(3) Each service company shall file with the division no later than March 1 each year, an annual report on Form SI-23. Form SI-23, Service Company Recertification, is hereby incorporated by reference into Chapter 69L-5, F.A.C. The form required by this rule shall bear the date September 1995 (9/96). A copy of Form SI-23 is available from the Division of Workers' Compensation, Bureau of Monitoring and Audit, Self-Insurance Section, 2012 Capitol Circle, S.E., Hartmen Building, Suite 200. Tallahassee, FL 32399-4224. After an annual review for compliance with this rule, the division shall issue a recertification to each service company found to be in compliance. A service company which fails to demonstrate annually it is in compliance with this rule shall have its authorization as a service company withdrawn. Service companies which have received approval during the first two (2) months of the calendar year shall be exempt from recertification on March 1 of the year in which they qualified.

(4) Service companies are performing functions for self-insurers similar to those functions performed by a carrier for policyholders, and in place of functions normally required of the self-insurer itself and, therefore, shall be subject to the same Section 440.20 (15), Florida Statutes, compliance review as self-insurers. Certification by the division of questionable claims handling techniques, questionable patterns of claims, repeated unreasonably controverted claims or poor payment practices shall be considered good cause for the withdrawal of the authorization of the service company.

(5) Service companies shall maintain, within the State of Florida, copies of all records relating

to the self-insurers they service sufficient, in type and quantity, to verify the accuracy and completeness of all reports and documents submitted to the division. In the event that the service company has its records distributed in multiple locations, it shall inform the division of the location of each type of record.

(6) Records shall be open to inspection by representatives of the division during regular business hours. To ensure their availability for audit purposes, all records shall be retained for five years, a period similar to service company documents required by the Department of Financial Services pursuant to Section 626.898, Florida Statutes.

(7) Service companies shall be audited by the division periodically. Prior notice of the audit shall not be necessary. Written reports, which become part of the annual review, shall be prepared following each audit. Deficiencies cited in this report shall be considered during the recertification process. A copy of the audit report will be provided to the service company.

(8) Service companies are required to file, or ensure the self-insurers it services file, all required reports by the due dates established by these rules without prior notice from the division.

(9) Service companies shall be required to notify the division immediately upon becoming aware that a current or previous self-insured client has failed to provide the necessary funds for the timely payment of benefits.

Specific Authority 440.591, 440.38(2)(a) Fla. Stat.

Law Implemented 440.20(16), 440.38(1)(b), (2)(a), (b), (4)(b) Fla. Stat.

History: New 10-1-82, Amended 12-25-84, Formerly 38F-5.41, Amended 6-12-91, 12-19-93, Formerly 38F-5.041, Amended 5-19-97, Formerly 38F-5.114, 4L-5.114.

69L-5.115. Withdrawal of Authorization.

Failure to comply with these rules or order within the time prescribed shall be considered good cause for withdrawal of the certificate of approval. The division shall give prior written notice of such withdrawal served personally or by certified mail upon the service company with copies to each self-insurer serviced. The service company shall have fifteen (15) days from the date of mailing to request a hearing. Failure to request a hearing within the time prescribed shall result in the withdrawal becoming effective thirty (30) days from the date of mailing of the original notice. An approved service company which does not conduct any business under their certificate for 12 months shall be considered inactive.

Specific Authority 440.38(1)(b), (3)(b) Fla. Stat.

Law Implemented 440.38(2), (3) Fla. Stat.

History: New 10-1-82, Formerly 38F-5.42, Amended 12-19-93, Formerly 38F-5.042, Amended 5-19-97, Formerly 38F-5.115, 4L-5.115.

V. Payroll and Claims Records

69L-5.116. Review and Audit.

(1) All payroll and claims records shall be open to inspection during regular business hours. To ensure their availability for audit purposes, the records shall be retained for a period of five years. The location of these records shall be made known to the division upon the application for self-insurance and at such times thereafter. The audit is in addition to any audit performed in preparation of the financial reports required by these rules.

(2) Each individual self-insurer shall comply with the guidelines regarding questionable claims handling techniques, questionable patterns of claims, repeated unreasonably controverted claims or poor payment practices established pursuant to Section 440.20 (15), Florida Statutes.

(3) After each audit, a written report shall be prepared with a copy to the self-insurer; such report to be a part of the annual review for compliance with the "Rules for Self-Insurers." Any deficiencies cited by the audit report shall be considered on their merit in determining if there are grounds for the revocation of the self-insurance privilege pursuant to Sections 440.20 (15) and 440.38 (3), Florida Statutes.

(4) If any audit of a self-insurer's payroll records discloses an error which has resulted in the self-insurer making an underpayment of the

administration or special disability trust fund assessments, then the cost of such audit shall be paid by the self-insurer.

(5) The division shall audit compliance with all requirements of the Drug-Free Workplace Program.

Specific Authority 440.38(2)(b), 440.51(6)(b) Fla. Stat.

Law Implemented 440.20(16)(c), 440.38(1)(b), (2)(b) Fla. Stat.

History: New 10-1-82, Formerly 38F-5.51, Amended 12-19-93, Formerly 38F-5.051, Amended 5-19-97, Formerly 38F-5.116, 4L-5.116.

VI. Forms, Manuals, and Instructions

69L-5.117. Forms, Manuals, and Instructions.

(1) Forms adopted.The forms set forth in paragraphs (a) through (p) of this subsection, as well as the accompanying instructions to the forms, are hereby incorporated into Chapter 69L-5, F.A.C., by reference. Copies of the forms are available from the Division of Workers' Compensation, Bureau of Monitoring and Audit, Self-Insurance Section, 2012 Capitol Circle, S.E., Hartmen Building, Suite 200, Tallahassee, FL 32399-4224.

(a) Form SI-1, Application for Self-Insurance (Rev. 9/96).

(b) Form SI-1a, Re-Application for Self-Insurance (Rev. 9/96).

(c) Form SI-4, Revised Self-Insurers Surety Bond (Guaranty Fund Member) (Rev. 9/96).

(d) Form SI-4B, Self-Insurers Surety Bond (Rev. 9/96).

(e) Form SI-5, Payroll Report, and the accompanying instructions (Rev. 9/96).

(f) Form SI-6, Self-Insurance Letter of Credit (Rev. 9/96).

(g) Form SI-11, Indemnity Agreement (Rev. 9/96).

(h) Form SI-17, Unit Statistical Report, and the accompanying instructions (Rev. 9/96).

(i) Form SI-19, Certification of Servicing for Self-Insurance (Rev. 9/96).

(j) Form SI-20, Report of Workers Compensation Liabilities (Rev. 9/96).

(k) Form SI-22, Service Company Application (Rev. 9/96).

(*l*) Form SI-23, Service Company Annual Report Form (Rev. 9/96).

(m) Form SI-26, Actuarial Report Checklist (Rev. 9/96).

(n) Form SI-27, Biographical Statement (Rev. 9/96).

(o) Form SI-32, Assignment of Securities (Rev. 9/96).

(p) Form SI-206, Certificate of Self-Insurance, and the instructions (Rev. 9/96).

(q) NCCI Form 9, Drug-Free Workplace Credit (5/7/96).

(2) In addition to the forms incorporated in paragraph (1), the following manuals and forms are incorporated by reference:

(a) Best's Insurance Reports, Property—Liability (1996 edition).

(b) National Council on Compensation Insurance SCOPES of Basic Manual Classifications (January 1997 reprint).

(c) National Council on Compensation Insurance Basic Manual for Workers' Compensation and Employers Liability Insurance (1996 edition as revised).

(d) National Council on Compensation Insurance Statistical Plan Manual (1984 edition as revised).

(e) National Council on Compensation Insurance Experience Rating Plan Manual for Workers' Compensation and Employers Liability Insurance (9/84 as amended).

(f) UCC 1 Form, State of Florida Financing Statement (Rev. 1993).

(g) Financial Accounting Standards Board Statement 113 (eff. 12/92).

(h) GAAP Interpretation and Application of Generally Accepted Accounting Principles, copyright John Wiley & Sons, Inc., 1996.

Specific Authority 440.57, 440.5705, 440.591 Fla. Stat.

Law Implemented 440.381, 440.57, 440.5705, 624.316, 624.424 Fla. Stat.

History: New 5-19-97, Formerly 38F-5.117, 4L-5.117.

CHAPTER 69L-6 Workers' Compensation Compliance

69L-6.007. Compensation Notice.

(1) Upon issuance of an insurance policy or certificate of membership in a self-insurance fund or a renewal certificate thereof, the insurer or self-insurance servicing agent shall furnish the employer a sufficient number of typewritten or printed compensation notices, commonly referred to as the "broken arm poster." The compensation notice shall be printed on paper or cardboard stock 11 inches by 17 inches, and have the same form and content as Form DI4-1548,"Workers' Comp Works For You Poster", (Rev 12/02), which is incorporated herein by reference. As an alternative to having the Anti-Fraud Reward Program language in the poster itself, the employer may elect to attach the Anti-Fraud Reward Program Notice to the poster on a separate piece of paper, with the same form and contract as DI4-1549, "Anti-Fraud Reward Program Notice", (Rev 12/02), which is incorporated herein by reference.

(2) The following information shall, in addition to subsection (1) above, be included on the compensation notice if the employer is insured through a commercial insurer;

(a) The name and address of the employer; and

(b) The name and address of the insurer and the agent of record of the employer's current workers' compensation insurance policy and the policy number and effective date of coverage of that policy.

(3) The following information shall, in addition to subsection (1) above, be included on the compensation notice if the employer is self-insured through a self-insurance fund:

(a) The name and address of the employer;

(b) The name of self-insurers fund to which the employer belongs;

(c) The employer's membership number;

(d) The effective date of coverage; and

(e) The service agent employer's account number.

(4) The compensation notice may also include such other information, in addition to information required by subsections (1), (2), and (3) above, as the insurer or self-insurance fund may desire concerning accident reports, the names of physicians, or other pertinent information.

(5) Printers, insurers, self insurers or self insurer funds may obtain an electronic version of the art work for the compensation notices from:The Florida Division of Workers' CompensationCustomer Service Center200 East Gaines StreetTallahassee, FL 32399-4227

Specific Authority 440.40 Fla. Stat.

Law Implemented 440.40 Fla. Stat.

History: New 11-20-79, Amended 4-15-81, 1-2-86, Formerly 38F-6.07, Amended 2-2-00, Formerly 38F-6.007, Amended 3-26-03, 4L-6.007.

69L-6.008. Cancellation of Workers' Compensation Insurance by an Insurer.

Specific Authority 440.185(7), 440.42(3), 440.591, 440.593(5) Fla. Stat.

Law Implemented 440.185(7), 440.42(3), 440.593 Fla. Stat.

History: New 11-20-79, Amended 4-15-81, 1-2-86, Formerly 38F-6.08, Amended 12-28-97, 2-2-2000, 3-5-2002, Formerly 38F-6.008, 4L-6.008, Amended 3-11-04, Repealed 3-8-06.

69L-6.009 Forms and Instructions.

(1) The following forms are hereby adopted for use in connection with these rules:

(a) DWC 250 Notice of Election to be Exempt, (eff. 2/07); and instructions for same

(Instructions for Completing Notice of Election to be Exempt, (eff. 2/07).

(b) DWC 250-R Revocation of Election to be Exempt, revised 2/00.

(c) DWC 251 Notice of Election of Coverage, revised 2/00.

(d) DWC 251-R Revocation of Election of Coverage, revised 2/00.

(2) The forms may be obtained from any field office of the Division of Workers' Compensation, Bureau of Compliance.

(3) The field offices of the Division of Workers' Compensation, Bureau of Compliance, are:

921 North Davis Street, Building B
Suite 250
Jacksonville, FL 32209
Telephone (850) 798-5806

1111 N. E. 25th Avenue, Suite 403
Ocala, FL 34470
Telephone (352) 401-5350

2012 Capital Circle, S. E.
Suite 102, Hartman Bldg.
Tallahassee, FL 32399-2161
Telephone (850) 413-1609

610 East Burgess Road
Pensacola, FL 32504-6320
Telephone (850) 453-7804

3111 South Dixie Highway
Suite 123
West Palm Beach, FL 33405
Telephone (561) 837-5716

499 N.W. 70th Avenue
Suite 116
Plantation, FL 33317
Telephone (954) 321-2906

4415 Metro Parkway
Suite #300
Ft. Myers, FL 33916
Telephone (239) 938-1840

1313 North Tampa Street
Suite 503
Tampa, FL 33602
Telephone (813) 221-6506

1718 Main Street
Suite #201
Sarasota, FL 34236
Telephone (941) 361-6042

400 West Robinson Street
Suite N 512, North Tower
Orlando, FL 32801
Telephone (407) 835-4406

401 N.W. 2nd Avenue
South Tower, Suite 321
Miami, FL 33128
Telephone (305) 536-0306

Specific Authority 440.05, 440.591 FS.

Law Implemented 440.05 FS.

History: New 11-20-79, Amended 4-15-81, 1-2-86, Formerly 38F-6.09, Amended 5-28-91, 2-15-94, 2-2-00, 3-5-02, Formerly 38F-6.009, 4L-6.009, Amended 2-19-07.

69L-6.012 Notice of Election to be Exempt.

(1) (a) Only corporate officers of non-dissolved or active corporations who meet the conditions for the issuance of valid Certificates of Election to be Exempt as stated in Chapter 440, F.S., and implemented by this rule may file a Notice of Election to be Exempt. Only a business entity organized under Chapter 607 or 617, F.S., will qualify as a corporation for purposes of issuing a Certificate of Election to be Exempt to a corporate officer under this rule. While a limited liability company created and approved under Chapter 608, F.S., is not a corporation for purposes of Chapter 440, F.S., persons engaged in the construction industry

who are limited liability company members owning at least ten percent (10%) of the non-dissolved or active limited liability company qualify as a "corporate officer" and are eligible for the issuance of a Certificate of Election to be Exempt under this rule.

(b) The Department shall deny any Notice of Election to be Exempt filed by a corporate officer of a dissolved or inactive corporation or limited liability company. A new Notice of Election to be Exempt (DWC-250), as adopted in Rule 69L-6.009, must be filed by the corporate officer, and if the corporate officer is engaged in the construction industry, another $50.00 fee must be submitted with the Notice of Election to be Exempt.

(2) Any corporate officer engaged in the construction or non-construction industry, who elects to be exempt from the provisions of the workers' compensation law (Chapter 440, F.S.), shall file with the Department a Notice of Election to be Exempt (DWC-250). For purposes of this rule, an applicant is engaged in the "construction industry" when any portion of the applicant's business operations is described in the construction industry classification codes that are identified in Rule 69L-6.021, F.A.C.

(3) For a corporate officer engaged in the construction industry, the applicant shall attach to or, where appropriate, list on every Notice of Election to be Exempt (DWC-250) the following:

(a) A copy of an occupational license required by the jurisdiction in the state of Florida in which the business is located or has employees engaged in work, or a copy of the occupational license receipt that includes the occupational license number issued by the jurisdiction in the state of Florida in which the business is located or has employees engaged in work. If the applicant's business address, as listed on the Notice of Election to be Exempt, is outside the state of Florida, a copy of the occupational license issued by the jurisdiction outside the state of Florida in which the applicant's business is located is required, unless an occupational license is not required by the jurisdiction in which the applicant's business is located;

1. If the applicant is required to obtain a license issued pursuant to Chapter 489, F.S., the business name listed on the occupational license or occupational license receipt must match the name of the corporation or limited liability company listed on the Notice of Election to Be Exempt;

2. If the applicant is not required to obtain a license issued pursuant to Chapter 489, F.S., the business name listed on the occupational license or occupational license receipt must match the name of the corporation, limited liability company, or business listed on the Notice of Election to Be Exempt;

(b) The certified or registered license numbers held by the applicant issued pursuant to Chapter 489, F.S.; or the certified or registered license numbers held by the qualifier for the business listed on the Notice of Election to be Exempt (DWC-250) of which the applicant is a corporate officer;

(c) The Federal Employer Identification Number issued to the corporation or limited liability company, as applicable

(d) The Social Security Number or the individual taxpayer identification number of the applicant;

(e) The Florida Department of State, Division of Corporations, registration number of the corporation or limited liability company, as applicable, named on the Notice of Election to be Exempt;

(f) For corporate officers of a corporation, a copy of the stock certificate(s) issued to the applicant by the corporation named on the Notice of Election to be Exempt evidencing at least ten percent (10%) ownership of the named corporation by the applicant on the date that the Notice of Election to be Exempt is filed with the department;

1. The percent of ownership shall be calculated by dividing the number of shares issued to the applicant by the total number of shares issued by the corporation named on the stock certificate(s);

2. In addition to the ownership requirement

in paragraph (3)(f), the copy of the stock certificate(s) shall state, at a minimum, the name of the issuing corporation, the state in which the corporation is organized, the name of the person to whom the stock is issued. All stock certificate(s) must be signed by an officer or officers designated to do so in the bylaws or designated to do so by the board of directors;

(g) For members of a limited liability company, documentation establishing the number of units of membership, or a notarized statement reflecting that the applicant owns at least ten percent (10%) of the limited liability company named on the Notice of Election to be Exempt on the date that the Notice of Election to be Exempt is filed with the Department;

(h) The business(es) or trade(s) of the applicant;

(i) The applicant's corporate officer title or member status;

(j) The corporate name, Florida Department of State, Division of Corporations, registration number, and Federal Employer Identification Number of any other corporation(s) that is under the same or substantially the same ownership or control as the corporation named on the Notice of Election to be Exempt;

(k) The name of the corporation or limited liability company as registered with the Florida Department of State, Division of Corporations of which the applicant is a corporate officer or member.

(4) An applicant engaged in the construction industry must submit a $50.00 fee with each Notice of Election to be Exempt that is filed with the department. If an applicant's payment is returned to the department for non-sufficient funds, the Notice of Election to be Exempt is invalid and shall be denied. If a Certificate of Election to be Exempt was issued to the applicant and the applicant's payment was returned to the Department for non-sufficient funds, the Certificate of Election to be Exempt shall be revoked. In order for the department to process a new Notice of Election to be Exempt from an applicant who has had a payment returned for non-sufficient funds, the department must receive confirmation that the initial $50.00 payment and any associated service charge has been deposited into the Workers' Compensation Administration Trust Fund.

(5) For Notices of Election to be Exempt by a corporate officer or an officer of a corporation, as defined in Section 440.02(9), F.S., if the applicant is in the construction industry and the Department's records show three active Certificates of Election to be Exempt issued to corporate officers of a corporation or business entity or of any group of affiliated corporations or business entities, the Department shall deny any Notice of Election to be Exempt that would result in more than three corporate officers having active Certificates of Election to be Exempt for a corporation or business entity or any group of affiliated corporations or business entities.

(6) For a corporate officer not engaged in the construction industry, the applicant shall attach to or, where applicable, list on every Notice of Election to be Exempt (DWC-250) the following:

(a) A copy of an occupational license required by the jurisdiction in which the business is located or has employees engaged in work, or a copy of the occupational license receipt that includes the occupational license number issued by the jurisdiction in the state of Florida in which the business is located or has employees engaged in work. If the applicant's business address, as listed on the Notice of Election to be Exempt, is outside the state of Florida, a copy of the occupational license issued by the jurisdiction outside the state of Florida in which the applicant's business is located is required, unless an occupational license is not required by the jurisdiction in which the applicant's business is located;

The name of the corporation, limited liability company, or business listed on the Notice of Election to be Exempt must match the business name listed on the occupational license or on the occupational license receipt;

(b) The Federal Employer Identification Number issued to the corporation;

(c) The Social Security Number or the individual taxpayer identification number of the applicant;

(d) The Florida Department of State, Division of Corporations, registration number of the corporation named on the Notice of Election to be Exempt;

(e) The applicant's corporate officer title; and

(f) The corporate name, Florida Department of State, Division of Corporations, registration number, and Federal Employer Identification Number of any other corporation(s) in which the applicant has an ownership interest or serves as a corporate officer;

(g) The name of the corporation as registered with the Florida Department of State, Division of Corporations of which the applicant is a corporate officer.

(7) Incomplete Notices of Election to be Exempt, Issue Dates for Certificates of Election to be Exempt.

(a) An applicant shall have thirty days from the date his/her Notice of Election to be Exempt is mailed or otherwise returned by the Department to the applicant as incomplete in which to file documentation or information which completes the Notice of Election to be Exempt, at which time the Notice of Election to be Exempt shall be processed without any additional processing fee. The department shall deny the Notice of Election to be Exempt if the applicant fails to file with the department the documentation or information to complete the Notice of Election to be Exempt within 30 days of the date the Notice of Election to be Exempt was mailed or returned as incomplete. If the Notice of Election to be Exempt is denied, the applicant must submit a new Notice of Election to be Exempt and, if the applicant is engaged in the construction industry, another $50.00 fee is required.

(b) If the department receives a renewal Notice of Election to be Exempt that meets the eligibility requirements of Section 440.05, F.S. and this rule more than 90 days prior to the expiration date of the Certificate of Election to be Exempt, the issue date of the new Certificate of Election to be Exempt is the date the Certificate of Election to be Exempt is approved and saved to the Coverage and Compliance Automated System database of the department, and any duplicate Certificate of Election to be Exempt for the applicant of the same business shall be null and void as of the issue date of the new Certificate of Election to be Exempt.

(c) If the Department receives a renewal Notice of Election to be Exempt that meets the eligibility requirements of Section 440.05, F.S. and this rule more than 30 days but 90 days or less prior to the expiration date of the Certificate of Election to be Exempt, the issue date of the renewal Certificate of Election to be Exempt shall be the expiration date of the original Certificate of Election to be Exempt.

(d) Subject to the exceptions listed in Section 440.05(5), F.S., if the department receives a renewal Notice of Election to be Exempt that meets the eligibility requirements of Section 440.05, F.S. and this rule 30 days or less prior to the expiration date of the Certificate of Election to be Exempt, the issue date of the renewal Certificate of Election to be Exempt is the date the renewal Certificate of Election to be Exempt is approved and saved to the Coverage and Compliance Automated System database of the department, or 30 days after the date the renewal Notice of Election to be Exempt is received by the department, whichever is earlier. Any duplicate Certificate of Election to be Exempt for the applicant shall be null and void as of the issue date of the renewal Certificate of Election to be Exempt.

(e) Subject to the exceptions listed in Section 440.05(5), F.S., if the department receives a renewal Notice of Election to be Exempt after the expiration date of the Certificate of Election to be Exempt, the issue date of the renewal Certificate of Election to be Exempt is the date the renewal Certificate of Election to be Exempt is approved and saved to the Coverage and Compliance Automated System database of the department, or 30 days after the date the renewal Notice of Election to be Exempt is received by the department, whichever is earlier.

(f) Subject to the exceptions listed in Section 440.05(5), F.S., if the department receives a new Notice of Election to be Exempt, the issue date of the Certificate of Election to be Exempt is the date the Certificate of Election to be Exempt is approved and saved to the Coverage and Compliance Automated System database of the department, or 30 days after the date the Notice of Election to be Exempt is received by the department, whichever is earlier.

(8) Any Notice of Election to be Exempt which is returned to the applicant by the department within 30 days after receipt by the Department for failure to meet the eligibility requirements of Section 440.05, F.S. and this rule is not "received" for purposes of Section 440.05(5), F.S.

(9) Any corporate officer or member of a limited liability company engaged in the construction industry, or corporate officer engaged in the non-construction industry who has been issued a Certificate of Election to Be Exempt, may revoke such certificate by filing with the Department a Revocation of Election to be Exempt (DWC-250-R) as adopted in Rule 69L-6.009, F.A.C.

(10) A Revocation of Election to be Exempt (DWC-250-R) shall only be filed by the same person named on the Certificate of Election to be Exempt or by a corporate officer of the business named on the Certificate of Election to be Exempt and listed as a corporate officer with the Department of State, Division of Corporations.

(11) Payments made to the department under this rule shall be in a form made payable to DFS - Workers' Compensation Administration Trust Fund.

Specific Authority 440.05, 440.591 Fla. Stat.

Law Implemented 440.05 Fla. Stat.

History: New 5-28-91, Amended 2-15-94, 12-28-97, 2-2-00, 9-6-01, Formerly 38F-6.012, Amended 3-26-03, Formerly 4L-6.012, Amended 4-21-04, 10-30-06.

69L-6.014. Policy Information Electronic Filing Requirements for Insurers.

Specific Authority 440.185(7), (9), 440.42(3), 440.591, 440.593(5) Fla. Stat.

Law Implemented 440.185(7), (9), 440.42(3), 440.593 Fla. Stat.

History: New 2-2-2000, Amended 3-5-2002, Formerly 38F-6.014, 4L-6.014, Amended 3-11-04, Repealed 3-8-06.

69L-6.015. Record Maintenance and Production Requirements for Employers.

(1) Employers must at all times maintain the records required by this rule and must produce the records when requested by the division pursuant to Section 440.107, F.S.

(2) Identity, organizational, and occupational records. Every employer shall maintain the notice that assigns to the employer its Federal Employer Identification Number (IRS Form 575A); records that identify its business name, such as fictitious name registration; records that identify its business form, such as corporation, limited liability company, or partnership; and a copy of its articles of incorporation or organization, occupational licenses, trade licenses or certifications, and competency cards.

(3) Employment records. Every employer shall maintain employment records pertaining to every person to whom the employer paid or owes remuneration for the performance of any work or service in connection with any employment under any appointment or contract for hire or apprenticeship.

(a) The employment records required by this subsection shall indicate with regard to every such person:

1. Name of the person.

2. Social Security Number, Federal Employer Identification Number, or IRS Tax Identification Number of the person.

3. Each day, month, and year or pay period when the employer engaged the person in employment.

4. Amount of remuneration paid or owed by the employer for work or service performed by the person. Where remuneration is paid or owed on an hourly basis, the record shall indicate the day, month, and year of work or service and the

number of hours worked by the person during each pay period. Where remuneration is paid or owed on any basis other than hourly, the record shall specify the basis, such as competitive bid, piece rate, or task, and indicate the day, month, and year, when remuneration was earned.

(b) In addition, every employer shall maintain the following records for each such person:

1. All checks or other records provided to the person for salary, wage, or earned income.

2. All Form 1099 Miscellaneous Income and Form W-2 Wage and Tax Statements issued to the person.

3. All written contracts or agreements between the employer and the person that describe the terms of employment.

4. All employment and unemployment reports filed pursuant to Florida law.

(4) Tax records. Every employer shall maintain all forms, together with supporting records and schedules, filed with the Internal Revenue Service.

(5) Account records. Every employer shall maintain monthly, quarterly, or annual statements for all open or closed business accounts established by the employer or on its behalf with any credit card company or any financial institution, such as bank, savings bank, savings and loan association, credit union, or trust company.

(6) Disbursements. Every employer shall maintain a journal of its check and cash disbursements as well as a copy of each cashier's check, bank check, and money order, indicating chronologically the disbursement date, to whom the money was paid, the payment amount, and the purpose.

(7) Employee leasing company, labor pool, and temporary labor service records.

(a) Every employee leasing company licensed under Chapter 468, F.S., including a professional employer organization, shall maintain:

1. Records that indicate the Federal Employer Identification Number of each client company.

2. The application of each client company and contract between the employee leasing company and the client company whereby the employee leasing company assigned its employees to a client company.

3. Records that indicate the name, gross pay, deductions from gross pay, net pay, and rate of pay for every employee assigned to each client company.

(b) Every labor pool under Chapter 448, F.S., shall maintain:

1. The written itemized statement showing in detail the wages and each deduction made from wages paid to each day laborer.

2. The annual earnings summary provided to each day laborer.

(c) Every temporary labor service shall maintain records that identify the name, Social Security Number or IRS Tax Identification Number of each employee who the temporary labor service provided to a client, and the payments to and the pay period, type of service, and location of service performed by each such employee. In addition, the temporary labor service shall maintain records of payments that it received from the client.

(8) Subcontractor invoices. Every employer shall maintain all invoices received from a subcontractor for work or service performed by the subcontractor for the employer.

(9) Workers' compensation insurance and certificates of election to be exempt.

(a) Every employer shall maintain all workers' compensation insurance policies obtained by the employer or on the employer's behalf and all endorsements, declaration pages, certificates of workers' compensation insurance, notices of cancellation, notices of non-renewal, or notices of reinstatement of such policies.

(b) Every employer shall maintain all premium audit documents provided by the workers' compensation carrier to the employer and all premium self-audits, together with supporting documentation and correspondence provided by the employer to its workers' compensation carrier.

(c) Every contractor shall maintain evidence of workers' compensation insurance of every subcontractor and for every subcontractor that is a corporation or limited liability company that has an officer or a member who elects to be exempt from the coverage requirements of the workers' compensation law the contractor shall maintain a valid certificate of election to be exempt issued to the officer or member under Section 440.05, F.S.

(d) Every corporation that is actively engaged in the construction industry and has officers who possess valid certificates of election to be exempt issued under Section 440.05, F.S., shall maintain written statements of those exempt officers affirmatively acknowledging each such officer's exempt status. A written statement may be in the form of a copy of a completed DWC 250 (rev. 9/01) Notice of Election to be Exempt as adopted in paragraph 69L-6.009(1)(a), F.A.C.

(e) Every employer who claims that an employee or officer of a corporation is exempt from the coverage requirements of the workers' compensation law shall maintain a valid certificate of election to be exempt issued under Section 440.05, F.S., for that employee or officer of a corporation.

(10) Contracts. Each employer shall maintain:

(a) All complete executed written contracts between it and a general contractor, subcontractor, independent contractor, or employee leasing company licensed under Chapter 468, F.S., that specify the terms of reimbursement and performance of any work or service while engaged in any employment under any appointment or contract for hire or apprenticeship.

(b) Any records that establish the statutory elements of independent contractor prescribed in Section 440.02(15)(d), F.S., for each worker who claims to be or who the employer claims to be an independent contractor and not an employee under the workers' compensation law.

(11) Records retention. An employer under the workers' compensation law shall maintain the records specified in this rule for the current calendar year to date and for the preceding three calendar years, in original form, whether paper, film, machine readable electronic material, or other media. A legible copy of the original record is an acceptable substitute for the original.

(12) Records location. An employer shall maintain the records specified in this rule at the corporate registered office, principal place of business, or job site in Florida.

Specific Authority 440.107(2), 440.591 Fla. Stat.

Law Implemented 440.107(2), 440.591 Fla. Stat.

History: New 2-2-00, Formerly 38F-6.015, Amended 3-26-03, 4L-6.015, Amended 1-17-05.

69L-6.016. Definitions.

Specific Authority 440.185(7), 440.42(3), 440.591, 440.593 Fla. Stat.

Law Implemented 440.185(7), 440.42(3), 440.593 Fla. Stat.

History: New 3-5-2002, Formerly 38F-6.016, 4L-6.016, Repealed 3-8-06.

69L-6.018. Misclassification of Employees as Independent Contractors.

(1) An employer who fails to secure compensation as required by Sections 440.10(1) and 440.38(1), F.S., for each employee classified by the employer as an independent contractor but who does not meet the criteria of an independent contractor specified in Section 440.02, F.S., shall be assessed a penalty in the following amount:

(a) $2,500 per misclassified employee for the first two misclassified employees per site; and

(b) $5,000 per misclassified employee after the first two misclassified employees per site.

(2) The Division shall determine that an employer has misclassified an employee as an independent contractor if:

(a) The employer in any way reports that a worker who is an employee pursuant to Section 440.02(15), F.S., is an independent contractor;

(b) The employer maintains records identifying the worker as an independent contractor; or

(c) The employer holds out the employee as an independent contractor for federal tax purposes.

Specific Authority 440.10(1)(f), 440.591 Fla. Stat.
Law Implemented 440.10(1)(f) Fla. Stat.

History: New 3-26-03, 4L-6.018.

69L-6.019. Policies and Endorsements Covering Employees Engaged in Work in Florida.

(1) Every employer who is required to provide workers' compensation coverage for employees engaged in work in this state shall obtain a Florida policy or endorsement for such employees that utilizes Florida class codes, rates, rules and manuals that are in compliance with and approved under the provisions of Chapter 440, F.S., and the Florida Insurance Code, pursuant to Sections 440.10(1)(g) and 440.38(7), F.S.

(2) In order to comply with Sections 440.10(1)(g) and 440.38(7), F.S., any policy or endorsement presented by an employer as proof of workers' compensation coverage for employees engaged in work in this state must be issued by an insurer that holds a valid Certificate of Authority in the State of Florida.

(3) In order to comply with Sections 440.10(1)(g) and 440.38(7), F.S., for any workers' compensation policy or endorsement presented by an employer as proof of workers' compensation coverage for employees engaged in work in this state:

(a) The policy information page (NCCI form number WC 00 00 01 A) must list "Florida" in Item 3.A. and use Florida approved classification codes, rates, and estimated payroll in Item 4.

(b) The policy information page endorsement (NCCI form number WC 89 06 00 B) must list "Florida" in Item 3.A. and use Florida approved classification codes, rates, and estimated payroll in Item 4.

(4) A workers' compensation policy that lists "Florida" in Item 3.C. of the policy information page (NCCI form number WC 00 00 01 A) does not meet the requirements of Sections 440.10(1)(g) and 440.38(7), F.S., and is not valid proof of workers' compensation coverage for employees engaged in work in this state.

(5) Workers' Compensation and Employers Liability Insurance Policy Information Page, NCCI form numbers WC 00 00 01 A (rev. May 1, 1988) and Workers' Compensation and Employers Liability Insurance Policy–Policy Information Page Endorsement, WC 89 06 00 B (rev. July 7, 2001) are hereby adopted and incorporated herein by reference. These forms can be obtained from the Florida Department of Financial Services, Division of Workers' Compensation, 200 East Gaines Street, Tallahassee, FL 32399-4228.

(6) An employee of a construction industry employer headquartered outside the state of Florida is "engaged in work" in Florida if he or she participates in any one of the following activities in the state of Florida:

(a) The employee engages in new construction, alterations, or any job or any construction activities involving any form of the building, clearing, filling, excavation or improvement in the size or use of any structure or the appearance of any land as defined in Section 440.02(8), F.S., or performs any job duties or activities which would be subject to those contracting classifications identified in the Contracting Classification Premium Adjustment Program contained in the Florida State Special pages of the Basic Manual (as incorporated in Rule 69L-6.021, F.A.C.) within the borders of the state of Florida, regardless of whether an employee returns to his or her home state each night, or

(b) If the employer maintains a permanent staff of employees or superintendents and the staff employee or superintendent is assigned to construction activities in Florida for the duration of the job or any portion thereof, or

(c) If the employer hires employees in Florida for the specific purpose of completing all or any portion of construction contract work and related construction activities in the state of Florida.

Specific Authority 440.107(9), 440.591 Fla. Stat. Law Implemented 440.10(1)(g), 440.38(7) Fla. Stat. **History:** New 6-17-04, Amended 11-21-04.

69L-6.021 Construction Industry Classification Codes, Descriptions, and Operations Scope of Exemption.

(1) The Division adopts the classification codes and descriptions that are specified in the Florida Contracting Classification Premium Adjustment Program, and published in the Florida exception pages of the National Council on Compensation Insurance, Inc. (NCCI), Basic Manual (October 2005 ed.). For convenience, the Division lists here the classification codes and descriptions that are published in the Florida exception pages of the Basic Manual and adopted in this rule.

(a)	0042	Landscape Gardening and Drivers
(b)	0050	Farm Machinery Operation By Contractor and Drivers
(c)	1322	Oil or Gas Well: Cleaning or Swabbing of Old Wells Having Previously Produced Gas or Oil By Contractor No Drilling and Drivers
(d)	3365	Welding or Cutting NOC and Drivers
(e)	3719	Oil Still Erection or Repair
(f)	3724	Machinery or Equipment Erection or Repair NOC and Drivers
(g)	3726	Boiler Installation or Repair Steam
(h)	5020	Ceiling Installation Suspended Acoustical Grid Type
(i)	5022	Masonry NOC
(j)	5037	Painting: Metal Structures Over Two Stories in Height and Drivers
(k)	5040	Iron or Steel: Erection Frame Structures
(l)	5057	Iron or Steel: Erection NOC
(m)	5059	Iron or Steel: Erection Frame Structures Not Over Two Stories in Height
(n)	5069	Iron or Steel: Erection Construction of Dwellings Not Over Two Stories in Height
(o)	5102	Door, Door Frame or Sash Erection Metal or Metal Covered
(p)	5146	Furniture or Fixtures Installation Portable NOC
(q)	5160	Elevator Erection or Repair
(r)	5183	Plumbing NOC and Drivers
(s)	5188	Automatic Sprinkler Installation and Drivers
(t)	5190	Electrical Wiring Within Buildings and Drivers
(u)	5213	Concrete Construction NOC
(v)	5215	Concrete Work Incidental to the Construction of Private Residence
(w)	5221	Concrete or Cement Work Floors, Driveways, Yards, and Sidewalks and Drivers
(x)	5222	Concrete Construction in Connection with Bridges or Culverts
(y)	5223	Swimming Pool Construction Not Iron or Steel and Drivers
(z)	5348	Stone, Mosaic or Terrazzo or Ceramic Tile Work Inside
(aa)	5402	Hothouse Erection All Operations
(bb)	5403	Carpentry NOC
(cc)	5437	Carpentry Installation of Cabinet Work or Interior Trim
(dd)	5443	Lathing and Drivers
(ee)	5445	Wallboard Installation Within Buildings and Drivers
(ff)	5462	Glazier Away From Shop and Drivers

(gg)	5472	Asbestos Contractor Pipe and Boiler Work Exclusively and Drivers
(hh)	5473	Asbestos Contractor NOC and Drivers
(ii)	5474	Painting or Paperhanging NOC and Shop Operations, Drivers
(jj)	5478	Carpet, Linoleum, Vinyl, Asphalt, or Rubber Floor Tile Installation
(kk)	5479	Insulation Work NOC and Drivers
(ll)	5480	Plastering NOC and Drivers
(mm)	5491	Paperhanging and Drivers
(nn)	5506	Street or Road Construction: Paving or Repaving and Drivers
(oo)	5507	Street or Road Construction: Subsurface Work and Drivers
(pp)	5508	Street or Road Construction: Rock Excavation and Drivers
(qq)	5509	Street or Road Maintenance: County or State Department and Drivers
(rr)	5537	Heating, Ventilation, Air-Conditioning and Refrigeration Systems Installations, Service and Repair & Drivers
(ss)	5538	Sheet Metal Work Shop and Outside NOC and Drivers
(tt)	5551	Roofing All Kinds and Yard Employees, Drivers
(uu)	5606	Contractor Executive Supervisor or Construction Superintendent
(vv)	5610	Cleaner Debris Removal
(ww)	5613	Cleaner Debris Removal Temporary Labor Service
(xx)	5645	Carpentry Detached One or Two Family Dwellings
(yy)	5651	Carpentry Dwellings Three Stories or Less
(zz)	5703	Building Raising or Moving and Drivers
(aaa)	5705	Salvage Operation No Wrecking or Any Structural Operations
(bbb)	6004	Land Pile Driving
(ccc)	6006F	Marine Pile Driving, Dock & Seawall, Jetty or Breakwater, Dike or Revetment Construction — All Operations to Completion & Drivers
(ddd)	6017	Dam or Lock Construction: Concrete Work All Operations
(eee)	6018	Dam or Lock Construction: Earth Moving or Placing All Operations
(fff)	6045	Levee Construction All Operations to Completion and Drivers
(ggg)	6204	Drilling NOC and Drivers
(hhh)	6206	Oil or Gas Well: Cementing and Drivers
(iii)	6213	Oil or Gas Well: Specialty Tool Operation NOC By Contractor All Employees and Drivers
(jjj)	6214	Oil or Gas Well: Perforating of Casing All Employees and Drivers
(kkk)	6216	Oil or Gas Lease Work NOC By Contractor and Drivers
(lll)	6217	Excavation and Drivers
(mmm)	6229	Irrigation or Draining System Construction and Drivers
(nnn)	6233	Oil or Gas Pipeline Construction and Drivers
(ooo)	6235	Oil or Gas Well: Drilling or Redrilling and Drivers
(ppp)	6236	Oil or Gas Well: Installation or Recovery of Casing and Drivers
(qqq)	6237	Oil or Gas Well: Instrument Logging or Survey Work and Drivers
(rrr)	6251	Tunneling Not Pneumatic All Operations
(sss)	6252	Shaft Sinking All Operations
(ttt)	6260	Tunneling Pneumatic All Operations
(uuu)	6306	Sewer Construction All Operations and Drivers
(vvv)	6319	Gas Main or Connection Construction and Drivers
(www)	6325	Conduit Construction For Cable or Wires and Drivers

(xxx)	6400	Fence Erection Metal
(yyy)	7538	Electric Light or Power Line Construction and Drivers
(zzz)	7601	Telephone, Telegraph or Fire Alarm Construction and Drivers
(aaaa)	7605	Burglar Alarm Installation or Repair and Drivers
(bbbb)	7611	Telephone or Cable TV Line Installation Contractors, Underground and Drivers
(cccc)	7612	Telephone or Cable TV Line Installation Contractors, Overhead, and Drivers
(dddd)	7613	Telephone or Cable TV Line Installation Contractors, Service Lines and Connections and Drivers
(eeee)	7855	Railroad Construction: Laying or Relaying of Tracks or Maintenance of Way by Contractor No Work on Elevated Railroads and Drivers
(ffff)	8227	Construction or Erection Permanent Yard
(gggg)	9534	Mobile Crane and Hoisting Service Contractors NOC All Operations Including Yard Employees and Drivers
(hhhh)	9554	Sign Installation, Maintenance, Repair, Removal, or Replacement NOC & Drivers

(2) The Division adopts the definitions published by NCCI, SCOPES® of Basic Manual Classifications (October 2005) that correspond to the classification codes and descriptions adopted in subsection (1) above. The definitions identify the workplace operations that satisfy the criteria of the term "construction industry" as used in the workers' compensation law. The definitions are hereby incorporated by reference and can be obtained by writing to the Division of Workers' Compensation, Bureau of Compliance, 200 East Gaines Street, Tallahassee, Florida 32399-4228.

Specific Authority 440.02(8).

Law Implemented 440.02(8), Ch. 2003-412, Section 1, Laws of Florida (repealing parts of 440.02(15), Fla. Stat).

History: New 10-21-02, Formerly 4L-6.021, Amended 7-4-04, 3-15-06, 2-8-07.

69L-6.022. Confidentiality of Records Produced by the Division.

(1) Section 440.185(11), F.S., provides that any information in a report of injury or illness filed with the Division pursuant to Section 440.185, F.S., that would identify an ill or injured employee is confidential and exempt from the provisions of Section 119.07(1), F.S., and Section 24(a), Article I of the Constitution of the State of Florida. Section 440.125, F.S., provides in part that any information identifying an injured employee in medical bills which are provided to the Division pursuant to Section 440.13, F.S., is confidential and exempt from the provisions of Section 119.07(1), F.S., and Section 24(a), Article I of the Constitution of the State of Florida.

(2) For purposes of maintaining the confidentiality of information as required pursuant to Sections 440.125 and 440.185(11), F.S., the following constitutes information that would identify an ill or injured employee; the ill or injured employee's:

(a) Name or signature;

(b) Social security number;

(c) Business, residence, and mailing addresses; and

(d) Residence and business telephone number.

(3) In the Division's response to a public records request, information that would identify an ill or injured employee will be redacted from any report of injury or illness filed with the Division pursuant to Section 440.185, F.S., and from any medical bill provided to the Division pursuant to Section 440.13, F.S.

Specific Authority 440.185(10), 440.591 Fla. Stat.

Law Implemented 440.125, 440.185(11) Fla. Stat.

History: New 3-27-03, Formerly 4L-6.022.

69L-6.024. Subcontractors Requirement Regarding Proof of Coverage.

Under Section 440.05(14), F.S., an officer of a corporation who elects to be exempt from Chapter 440, F.S., may not recover benefits or compensation under Chapter 440, F.S., and a carrier may not consider any officer of a corporation who holds a valid certificate of election to be exempt for purposes of determining the appropriate premium for workers' compensation coverage. In order to be consistent with the provisions of Section 440.05(14), F.S., in instances where a subcontractor is a corporation and has an officer or officers who elect to be exempt, and the subcontractor provides a copy of the officer's or officers' certificate of election to be exempt to a contractor pursuant to Section 440.10(1)(c), F.S., the subcontractor is not required to also provide evidence of workers' compensation insurance to the contractor if the subcontractor has no employees who may recover benefits under Chapter 440, F.S., at any time during the life of the contract or project for which evidence of exemption or coverage is required. If a subcontractor hires one or more employees at any time during the life of a contract, that subcontractor must provide the contractor with evidence of workers' compensation insurance before any such employee or employees can perform any work related to that contract.

Specific Authority 440.05(9), 440.591 Fla Stat.

Law Implemented 440.02(15), 440.05(14), 440.10(1)(c) Fla Stat.

History: New 7-21-04.

69L-6.025 Conditional Release of Stop-Work Order and Periodic Payment Agreement.

(1) The requirements for issuance of an Order of Conditional Release From Stop-Work Order as provided for in Section 440.107, F.S., are:

(a) The employer has come into compliance with the coverage requirements of Chapter 440, F.S. Compliance with the coverage requirements of Chapter 440, F.S., includes demonstration by the employer that it is no longer failing to secure the payment of compensation within the meaning of Section 440.107, F.S.

(b) The employer and the Department have executed a Payment Agreement Schedule for Periodic Payment of Penalty, Form Number DFS-F4-1600 (rev. 7/04).

(c) The employer agrees to file probationary periodic reports with the Department for a time period that does not exceed 2 years that demonstrate the employer's continued compliance with Chapter 440, F.S. The probationary periodic reports shall be filed as a section of each monthly payment installment invoice pursuant to the Payment Agreement Schedule for Periodic Payment of Penalty.

(2) The terms and conditions of a Payment Agreement Schedule for Periodic Payment of Penalty shall be:

(a) The employer shall make a down payment on the total assessed penalty amount to the Department that is the greater of $1000.00 or at least 10% of the total assessed penalty amount. The amount constituting the total assessed penalty amount, less the down payment, shall be referred to as the "remaining penalty".

(b) Each monthly payment installment is due on the first day of the month in which it is due, and the employer is in violation of the Payment Agreement Schedule for Periodic Payment of Penalty if the full monthly payment installment is not received by the Department by the last day of the month in which the payment installment is due;

1. The employer shall pay the remaining penalty in up to sixty consecutive monthly installments.

2. The employer may at any time pre-pay the installments of the remaining penalty, which have not become due.

3. month of issuance of the Conditional Release From Stop-Work Order, Form Number DFS-F4-1602 (rev. 6/04), and each subsequent payment installment shall be due on the first day of each consecutive month.

(c) Monthly payment installments shall only be remitted to the Department's address designated in the Payment Agreement Schedule for Periodic Payment of Penalty.

(d) Monthly payment installments shall be in the form of a cashier's check or money order only, made payable to the DFS-Workers' Compensation Administration Trust Fund.

(e) If the employer is a corporation, only an officer of the corporation may execute the Payment Agreement Schedule For Periodic Payment of Penalty on behalf of the employer.

(f) If the employer is a business entity other than a corporation, any principal of the business entity may execute the Payment Agreement Schedule For Periodic Payment of Penalty on behalf of the employer.

(g) Failure by the employer to meet or violation of any term or condition of the Payment Agreement Schedule For Periodic Payment of Penalty shall constitute a default by the employer.

(3) The Payment Agreement Schedule For Periodic Payment of Penalty becomes effective when it is executed on behalf of the employer and by the Department. Upon execution of the Payment Agreement Schedule For Periodic Payment of Penalty, the Department will provide the employer with a Monthly Payment Installment Invoice, Form Number DFS-F4-1601 (rev. 8/04), which shall be submitted with each monthly payment installment. Each Monthly Payment Installment Invoice contains a probationary reporting section that shall be completed by the employer.

(4) If an employer defaults under any of its obligations under the Payment Agreement Schedule For Periodic Payment of Penalty, the Stop-Work Order to which the penalty applies shall be immediately reinstated and the entire unpaid balance of the remaining penalty shall immediately become due and payable. "Immediately reinstated" means twenty-one (21) calendar days after an Order Reinstating Stop-Work Order is executed by the Chief Financial Officer or his or her designee and has been filed with the agency clerk of the Department. Subsequent to the issuance of an Order Reinstating Stop-Work Order by the Department, the Department will rescind the Order Reinstating Stop-Work Order requiring the employer to adhere to the terms and conditions of its Payment Agreement Schedule For Periodic Payment of Penalty only if the Department receives from the employer all past due monthly payments prior to the expiration of the twenty-one day period. All past due monthly payments must be made by cashier check(s) or money order(s) made payable to DFS-Workers' Compensation Administration Trust Fund and be remitted to Department of Financial Services, Revenue Processing Section, Division of Workers' Compensation, P. O. Box 7900, Tallahassee, FL 32314-7900. The Department will not enter into another Payment Agreement Schedule For Periodic Payment of Penalty with an employer in a case where the employer has had its stop-work order immediately reinstated through an Order Reinstating Stop-Work Order, and in order to be released from a stop-work order that has been immediately reinstated the employer must pay the remainder of the entire penalty and show that it otherwise is in compliance with the coverage requirements of Chapter 440, F.S. The Department in any one case will not rescind an Order Reinstating Stop-Work Order more than twice.

(5) An employer that has entered into a Payment Agreement Schedule For Periodic Payment of Penalty with the Department currently in default of any of its obligations under such agreement or that has had its stop-work order immediately reinstated through an Order Reinstating Stop-Work Order is ineligible for conditional release from a stop-work order issued to it by the Department in a separate case.

(6) The Department hereby adopts and incorporates the following forms by reference. Copies of the forms can be obtained from the Division of Workers' Compensation's Bureau of Compliance, 200 East Gaines Street, Tallahassee, Florida 32399-4228, or from any field office identified in Rule 69L-6.009, F.A.C.

(a) DFS-F4-1600 Payment Agreement Schedule for Periodic Payment of Penalty rev. 7/04.

(b) DFS-F4-1601 Monthly Payment Installment Invoice rev. 8/04.

(c) DFS-F4-1602 Order of Conditional Release from Stop-Work Order rev. 6/04.

(7) Employers assessed penalties pursuant to Rule 69L-6.030, F.A.C. are eligible to enter into a Payment Agreement Schedule for Periodic Payment of Penalty with the Department.

(8) If an employer conducts business operations in violation of an Order Reinstating Stop-Work Order, a penalty shall be assessed against the employer pursuant to Section 440.107(7)(c), F.S. The number of days that the employer conducts business operations in violation of an Order Reinstating Stop-Work Order shall begin on the date the Order Reinstating Stop-Work Order is immediately reinstated.

Specific Authority 440.107(9), 440.591 Fla Stat.

Law Implemented 440.107(7)(a) Fla Stat.

History: New 4-6-05, Amended 7-20-05, 2-6-07.

69L-6.027. Penalty Calculation Worksheet.

(1) For purposes of calculating penalties to be assessed against employers pursuant to Section 440.107, F.S., the Division shall use form # DFS-F4-1595 (rev. 9/04) which is incorporated herein by reference.

(2) Copies of this form DFS-F4-1595 (rev. 9/04) are available from the Division of Workers' Compensation, Department of Financial Services, Larson Building, Tallahassee, Florida 32399-4226.

Specific Authority 440.107(9), 440.591 Fla Stat.

Law Implemented 440.107 Fla Stat.

History: New 12-29-04.

69L-6.028 Procedures for Imputing Payroll and Penalty Calculations.

(1) In the event an employer fails to provide business records sufficient for the department to determine the employer's payroll for the period requested for the calculation of the penalty pursuant to Section 440.107(7)(e), F.S., the department shall impute payroll at any time after the expiration of fifteen business days after receipt by the employer of a written request to produce such business records.

(2) When an employer fails to provide business records sufficient to enable the department to determine the employer's payroll for the period requested for purposes of calculating the penalty provided for in Section 440.107(7)(d), F.S., the imputed weekly payroll for each employee, corporate officer, sole proprietor or partner for the portion of the period of the employer's non-compliance occurring on or after October 1, 2003 shall be calculated as follows:

(a) For employees other than corporate officers, for each employee identified by the department as an employee of such employer at any time during the period of the employer's non-compliance, the imputed weekly payroll for each week of the employer's non-compliance for each such employee shall be the statewide average weekly wage as defined in Section 440.12(2), F.S., that is in effect at the time the stop work order was issued to the employer, multiplied by 1.5. Employees include sole proprietors and partners in a partnership.

(b) If the employer is a corporation, for each corporate officer of such employer identified as such on the records of the Division of Corporations at the time of issuance of the stop-work order, the imputed weekly payroll for each week of the employer's non-compliance for each such corporate officer shall be the statewide average weekly wage as defined in Section 440.12(2), F.S., that is in effect at the time the stop-work order was issued to the employer, multiplied by 1.5.

(c) If a portion of the period of non-compliance includes a partial week of non-compliance, the imputed weekly payroll for such partial week of non-compliance shall be prorated from the imputed weekly payroll for a full week.

(d) The imputed weekly payroll for each employee, corporate officer, sole proprietor, or partner shall be assigned to the highest rated workers' compensation classification code associated with the employer's business activities, unless the employer's business records demonstrate the assignment of an alternative workers' compensation classification code.

(3) If subsequent to imputation of weekly

payroll pursuant to subsection (2) herein, but before and only until the expiration of forty-five calendar days from the receipt by the employer of written request to produce business records, the employer provides business records sufficient for the department to determine the employer's payroll for the period requested for the calculation of the penalty pursuant to Section 440.107(7)(e), F.S., the department shall recalculate the employer's penalty to reflect the payroll information provided in such business records.

(4) Where periods of the employer's non-compliance occurred prior to October 1, 2003, and the employer fails to provide business records sufficient to enable the department to determine the employer's payroll for periods of non-compliance prior to October 1, 2003, for purposes of calculating the penalty to be assessed against the employer for periods of non-compliance prior to October 1, 2003, the department shall assess against the employer a penalty of $100 per day for each and every calendar day in the period of non-compliance occurring prior to October 1, 2003, the employer was not in compliance, pursuant to Section 440.107(5), F.S. (2002).

Specific Authority 440.107(9), 440.591 Fla. Stat.

Law Implemented 440.107(5) (2002), 440.107(7)(e) Fla. Stat.

History: New 7-12-05, Amended 8-31-06.

69L-6.029. Employer Worksites.

(1) "Worksite" for purposes of this rule means a place in Florida where an employer conducts business operations.

(2) Upon service of a stop work order on an employer, the stop work order shall be effective upon all employer worksites in the state for which the employer is not in compliance.

(3) The worksites for which an employer is not in compliance shall be determined as follows:

(a) If the employer failed to meet the coverage requirements of Chapter 440, F.S., and the Florida Insurance Code, all worksites of the employer in the state are not in compliance and the stop work order shall be in effect for all the employer's worksites requiring the cessation of all business operations for such employer in the state.

(b) If an out-of-state employer that is required to provide workers' compensation coverage for employees engaged in work in Florida, pursuant to Rule 69L-6.019, F.A.C., failed to obtain or maintain a Florida policy or endorsement that utilizes Florida class codes, rates, rules, and manuals that are in compliance with and approved under the provisions of Chapter 440, F.S., and the Florida Insurance Code, all worksites of the employer in the state are not in compliance and the stop work order shall be in effect for all the employer's worksites requiring the cessation of all business operations for such employer in the state.

(c) If the employer failed to produce the required business records within five business days after receipt of the written request of the department, all worksites of the employer in the state are not in compliance and the stop work order shall be in effect for all the employer's worksites requiring the cessation of all business operations for such employer in the state.

(d) If the employer has materially understated or concealed payroll, all worksites of the employer in the state are not in compliance and the stop work order shall be in effect for all the employer's worksites requiring the cessation of all business operations for such employer in the state.

(e) If the employer materially misrepresented or concealed employee duties so as to avoid proper classification for premium calculations, all worksites of the employer in the state are not in compliance and the stop work order shall be in effect for all the employer's worksites requiring the cessation of all business operations for such employer in the state.

(f) If the employer materially misrepresented or concealed information pertinent to the computation and application of an experience modification factor, all worksites of the employer in the state are not in compliance and the stop work order shall be in effect for the employer's worksites requiring the cessation of all business operations for such employer in the state.

(g) If the employer is a contractor that sublets any work at a particular worksite to a subcontractor and the contractor and subcontractor each failed to secure the payment of compensation for the subcontractor or the employees of the subcontractor engaged in work at the particular worksite, then a stop-work order issued to the contractor shall require the cessation of all business operations of the contractor at that particular worksite.

(4) A penalty assessed under Section 440.107(7)(d)1., F.S., that exceeds the statutory minimum penalty shall include the employer's payroll and any violations of Section 440.107, F.S., for all its worksites where the employer is not in compliance.

Specific Authority 440.107 Fla. Stat.

Law Implemented 440.107(7)(a), 440.107(7)(d)1. Fla. Stat.

History: New 1-11-06.

69L-6.030. Penalties for Employees Currently in Compliance Previously Failing to Secure the Payment of Compensation.

(1) When an investigation commenced by the department pursuant to Section 440.107, F.S., reflects that, on the date the investigation commences, the employer is failing to secure the payment of workers' compensation, is materially understating or concealing payroll, is materially understating or concealing employee duties so as to avoid proper classification for premium calculations, or is materially misrepresenting or concealing information pertinent to the computation and application of an experience rating modification factor, but the employer comes into compliance with the workers' compensation coverage requirements prior to the issuance of a stop work order, such employer shall be assessed a penalty pursuant to Section 440.107(7)(d)1., F.S., and a stop work order will not be issued for such violations.

(2) For purposes of this rule, an investigation commences on the date the department's compliance investigator conducts an on-site inspection of the employer's worksite or business location, or on the date the employer receives a written request to produce business records from the department pursuant to Section 440.107(7)(a), F.S., whichever is earlier.

Specific Authority 440.107(9) Fla. Stat.

Law Implemented 440.107(2) Fla Stat.

History: New 3-15-06.

69L-6.031. Stop Work Orders in Effect Against Successor Corporations or Business Entities.

(1) Under Section 440.107(7)(b), F.S., stop work orders or orders of penalty assessment issued against a corporation, partnership, or sole proprietorship shall be in effect against any successor corporation or business entity that has one or more of the same principals or officers as the predecessor corporation or business entity against which the stop work order was issued and are engaged in the same or equivalent trade or activity.

(a) For employers engaged in the construction industry, a corporation, partnership, or sole proprietorship and the successor corporation or business entity that has been issued a stop work order or order of penalty assessment, are engaged in the same or equivalent trade or activity if they each perform or have performed business operations that include operations described in at least one classification code listed in Rule 69L-6.021, F.A.C.

(b) For employers engaged in the non-construction industry, a corporation, partnership, or sole proprietorship and the successor corporation or business entity that has been issued a stop work order or order of penalty assessment, are engaged in the same or equivalent trade or activity if they each perform or have performed business operations that include operations described in at least one classification code that is in the manufacturing, goods and services, or the office and clerical industry group listed in subsection (6) of this rule.

(c) For employers that perform business operations described by one of the classification codes in the miscellaneous industry groups listed in subsection (6) of this rule, a corporation, partnership, or sole proprietorship and the successor corporation or business entity that has been issued a stop work order or order of penalty assessment, are engaged in the same or equivalent trade or activity if they each perform or have performed the same business operation described in one of the classification codes contained in the miscellaneous industry groups.

(2) A stop work order or order of penalty assessment issued against a corporation, partnership, or sole proprietorship becomes effective against a successor corporation or business entity that has one or more of the same principals, directors, officers, partners, or shareholders with a 10% or greater interest, including any "affiliated person" as defined in Section 440.05(15), F.S., in common with the predecessor corporation or business entity against which the original stop work order or order of penalty assessment was issued and is engaged in the same or equivalent trade or activity, through service on the successor corporation or business entity of an order applying a stop work order or order of penalty assessment to successor corporation or business entity. The order applying a stop work order or order of penalty assessment to successor corporation or business entity remains in effect until withdrawn by the department.

(3) In the event one of the following three criteria is satisfied, the department will withdraw an order applying a stop work order or order of penalty assessment:

(a) The department must have released the stop work order or order of penalty assessment in effect against the predecessor corporation, partnership, or sole proprietorship that has one or more of the same principals, officers, directors, partners, or shareholders with a 10% or greater interest, in common with the successor corporation or business entity.

(b) The principal, officer, director, partner, or a shareholder with a 10% or greater interest in the successor corporation or business entity against which the stop work order or order of penalty assessment has been served, must formally disassociate himself or herself from the predecessor corporation, partnership, or sole proprietorship by providing the department with the following:

1. Records obtained from the Florida Department of State. Division of Corporations, indicating that no person or entity affiliated with the successor corporation or business entity holds any position as an officer, director, or shareholder with a 10% or greater interest in the predecessor corporation or business entity.

2. A written statement from the current management of the predecessor corporation or business entity affirmatively acknowledging that no person affiliated with the successor corporation or business entity is engaged in any policy or decision-making capacity with the predecessor corporation or business entity.

3. Copies of the successor corporation or business entity's business records for review by the department.

(c) The successor corporation or business entity and the predecessor corporation, partnership, or sole proprietorship that has been issued a stop work order or order of penalty assessment, must no longer be engaged in the same or equivalent trade or activity, as determined by the department, pursuant to the codes from subsection (6) of this rule.

(4) An order applying a stop work order or order of penalty assessment shall take effect when served upon the employer or, for a particular worksite, when served at that worksite.

(5) Under Section 440.107(7)(c), F.S., the department shall assess a penalty of $1,000 per day against an employer for each day that the employer conducts business operations in violation of an orcer a applying a stop work order or order of penalty assessment.

(6) List of class codes, descriptions, and industry groups. A complete description of class codes is contained in the SCOPES® Manual Classifications (October 2005) published by the National Council on Compensation Insurance, Inc. (NCCI) and is available for viewing through the Division of Workers' Compensation, Bureau of Compliance, 2012 Capital Circle, S.E., Hartman Building, Tallahassee, Florida 32399-4228 or a copy is available, for a fee, by calling NCCI at 1(800)622-4123. The SCOPES® list of codes, descriptions and industry groups is as follows:

(a) Industry Group: Manufacturing

Class	Description
1. 1430	SMELTING, SINTERING OR REFINING — LEAD & DRIVERS
2. 1438	SMELTING, SINTERING OR REFINING — METALS — NOT IRON OR LEAD — NOC & DRIVERS
3. 1452	ORE MILLING & DRIVERS
4. 1463	ASPHALT WORKS OPERATED BY PAVING CONTRACTORS — PERMANENT LOCATION & DRIVERS
5. 1472	DISTILLATION — WOOD & DRIVERS
6. 1473	TURPENTINE OR RESIN MFG — STEAM OR NON-DESTRUCTIVE PROCESS & DRIVERS
7. 1642	LIME MFG
8. 1699	ROCK WOOL MFG
9. 1701	CEMENT MFG
10. 1741	FLINT OR SPAR GRINDING & DRIVERS
11. 1747	EMERY WORKS & DRIVERS
12. 1748	ABRASIVE WHEEL MFG & DRIVERS
13. 1803	STONE CUTTING OR POLISHING NOC & DRIVERS
14. 1852	ASBESTOS GOODS MFG
15. 1853	MICA GOODS MFG & MICA PREPARING
16. 1860	ABRASIVE PAPER OR CLOTH PREPARATION
17. 1924	WIRE DRAWING OR CABLE MFG — NOT IRON OR STEEL
18. 1925	DIE CASTING MFG
19. 2001	CRACKER MFG
20. 2002	MACARONI MFG
21. 2003	BAKERY & DRIVERS, ROUTE SUPERVISORS
22. 2014	GRAIN OR FEED MILLING
23. 2016	CEREAL OR BAR MFG
24. 2021	SUGAR REFINING
25. 2039	ICE CREAM MFG & DRIVERS
26. 2041	CANDY, CHOCOLATE, AND CONFECTION MFG
27. 2065	MILK PRODUCTS MFG NOC
28. 2070	CREAMERY OR DAIRY & ROUTE SUPERVISORS, DRIVERS
29. 2081	BUTCHERING
30. 2089	PACKING HOUSE — ALL OPERATIONS
31. 2095	MEAT PRODUCTS MFG NOC
32. 2105	FRUIT PACKING
33. 2110	PICKLE MFG
34. 2111	CANNERY NOC
35. 2112	FRUIT EVAPORATING OR PRESERVING
36. 2114	OYSTER PROCESSING
37. 2119	CITRUS PRODUCTS PROCESSING
38. 2121	BREWERY & DRIVERS
39. 2130	SPIRITUOUS LIQUOR DISTILLERY
40. 2131	SPIRITUOUS LIQUOR BOTTLING
41. 2150	ICE MFG OR ICE DEALERS
42. 2156	BOTTLING — NOT CARBONATED LIQUIDS — OR SPIRITUOUS LIQUORS & ROUTE SUPERVISORS
43. 2157	BOTTLING NOC & ROUTE SUPERVISORS, DRIVERS

Class	Description
44. 2172	CIGARETTE MFG
45. 2174	TOBACCO REHANDLING OR WAREHOUSING
46. 2211	COTTON BATTING, WADDING OR WASTE MFG
47. 2220	YARN OR THREAD MFG — COTTON
48. 2286	WOOL SPINNING AND WEAVING
49. 2288	FELTING MFG
50. 2300	PLUSH OR VELVET MFG
51. 2302	SILK THREAD OR YARN MFG
52. 2305	TEXTILE FIBER MFG — SYNTHETIC
53. 2361	HOSIERY MFG
54. 2362	KNIT GOODS MFG NOC
55. 2380	WEBBING MFG
56. 2386	LACE MFG
57. 2388	EMBROIDERY MFG
58. 2402	CARPET OR RUG MFG NOC
59. 2413	TEXTILE — BLEACHING, DYEING, MERCERIZING, FINISHING
60. 2416	YARN DYEING OR FINISHING
61. 2417	CLOTH PRINTING
62. 2501	CLOTH, CANVAS AND RELATED PRODUCTS MFG NOC
63. 2503	DRESSMAKING OR TAILORING — CUSTOM EXCLUSIVELY
64. 2534	FEATHER OR FLOWER MFG — ARTIFICIAL
65. 2570	MATTRESS OR BOX SPRING MFG
66. 2576	CANVAS GOODS, MTG. — NOC — SHOP
67. 2578	BAG OR SACK MFG — CLOTH
68. 2585	LAUNDRY NOC & ROUTE SUPERVISORS, DRIVERS
69. 2586	CLEANING OR DYEING & ROUTE SUPERVISORS DRIVERS
70. 2589	LAUNDRY AND DRY CLEANING STORE — RETAIL & ROUTE SUPERVISORS, DRIVERS
71. 2600	FUR MFG — PREPARING SKINS
72. 2623	LEATHER MFG — INCLUDING TANNING, LEATHER EMBOSSING, AND WOOL PULLING
73. 2651	SHOE STOCK MFG
74. 2660	BOOT OR SHOE MFG NOC
75. 2670	GLOVE MFG — LEATHER OR TEXTILE
76. 2683	LUGGAGE MFG
77. 2688	LEATHER GOODS MFG NOC
78. 2710	SAWMILL
79. 2714	VENEER MFG
80. 2731	PLANING OR MOLDING MILL
81. 2735	FURNITURE STOCK MFG
82. 2759	PALLET, BOX OR BOX SHOOK MFG WOODEN
83. 2790	PATTERN MAKING NOC
84. 2797	MOBILE OR TRAILER HOME MFG & DRIVERS
85. 2802	CARPENTRY — SHOP ONLY & DRIVERS
86. 2812	CABINET WORKS — WITH POWER MACHINERY
87. 2835	BRUSH OR BROOM ASSEMBLY
88. 2836	BRUSH OR BROOM MFG NOC
89. 2841	WOODENWARE MANUFACTURING NOC

Class	Description
90. 2881	FURNITURE ASSEMBLY — WOOD — FROM MANUFACTURED PARTS
91. 2883	FURNITURE MTG. — WOOD — NOC
92. 2913	RATTAN, WILLOW OR TWISTED FIBER PRODUCTS MFG
93. 2915	VENEER PRODUCTS MFG
94. 2916	VENEER PRODUCTS MFG — NO VENEER MFG
95. 2923	PIANO MFG
96. 2942	PENCIL, PENHOLDER OR CRAYON MFG
97. 2960	WOOD PRESERVING & DRIVERS
98. 3004	IRON OR STEEL: MANUFACTURING: STEEL MAKING & DRIVERS
99. 3018	IRON OR STEEL: MANUFACTURING: ROLLING MILL & DRIVERS
100. 3022	PIPE OR TUBE MFG NOC & DRIVERS
101. 3027	ROLLING MILL NOC & DRIVERS
102. 3028	PIPE OR TUBE MFG — IRON OR STEEL — & DRIVERS
103. 3030	IRON OR STEEL: FABRICATION: IRON OR STEEL WORKS — SHOP — STRUCTURAL & DRIVERS
104. 3040	IRON OR STEEL: FABRICATION: IRON WORKS — SHOP — ORNAMENTAL & DRIVERS
105. 3041	IRON OR STEEL: FABRICATION: IRON WORKS — SHOP — DECORATIVE OR ARTISTIC & FOUNDRIES & DRIVERS
106. 3042	ELEVATOR OR ESCALATOR MFG
107. 3064	SIGN MANUFACTURING — METAL
108. 3066	SHEET METAL WORK — SHOP
109. 3076	FIREPROOF EQUIPMENT MFG
110. 3081	FOUNDRY — FERROUS — NOC
111. 3082	FOUNDRY — STEEL CASTINGS
112. 3085	FOUNDRY — NON — FERROUS
113. 3110	FORGING WORK — DROP OR MACHINE
114. 3111	BLACKSMITH
115. 3113	TOOL MFG — NOT DROP OR MACHINE FORGED — NOC
116. 3114	TOOL MFG — DROP OR MACHINE FORGED — NOC: MACHINING OR FINISHING OF TOOLS OR DIE MAKING OPERATIONS
117. 3118	SAW MFG
118. 3119	NEEDLE MFG
119. 3122	CUTLERY MFG NOC
120. 3126	TOOL MFG — AGRICULTURAL, CONSTRUCTION, LOGGING, MINING, OIL OR ARTESIAN WELL
121. 3131	BUTTON OR FASTENER MFG — METAL
122. 3132	NUT OR BOLT MFG
123. 3145	SCREW MFG
124. 3146	HARDWARE MFG NOC
125. 3169	STOVE MFG
126. 3175	RADIATOR OR HEATER MFG
127. 3179	ELECTRICAL APPARATUS MFG NOC
128. 3180	ELECTRIC OR GAS LIGHTING FIXTURES MFG
129. 3188	PLUMBERS SUPPLIES MFG NOC
130. 3220	CAN MFG
131. 3223	LAMP OR PORTABLE LANTERN MFG
132. 3224	ENAMEL WARE MFG
133. 3227	ALUMINUM WARE MFG

Class	Description
134. 3240	WIRE ROPE MFG — IRON OR STEEL
135. 3241	WIRE DRAWING — IRON OR STEEL
136. 3255	WIRE CLOTH MFG
137. 3257	WIRE GOODS MFG NOC
138. 3270	EYELET MFG
139. 3300	BED SPRING OR WIRE MATTRESS MFG
140. 3303	SPRING MFG
141. 3307	HEAT — TREATING — METAL
142. 3315	BRASS OR COPPER GOODS MFG
143. 3334	TIN FOIL MFG
144. 3336	TYPE FOUNDRY
145. 3372	ELECTROPLATING
146. 3373	GALVANIZING OR TINNING — NOT ELECTROLYTIC
147. 3383	JEWELRY MFG
148. 3385	WATCH MFG
149. 3400	METAL STAMPED GOODS MFG NOC
150. 3507	CONSTRUCTION OR AGRICULTURAL MACHINERY MFG
151. 3515	TEXTILE MACHINERY MFG
152. 3548	PRINTING OR BOOKBINDING MACHINE MFG
153. 3559	CONFECTION MACHINE MFG
154. 3574	COMPUTING, RECORDING OR OFFICE MACHINE MFG NOC
155. 3581	FUEL INJECTION DEVICE MFG
156. 3612	PUMP MFG
157. 3620	BOILERMAKING
158. 3629	PRECISION MACHINED PARTS MFG NOC
159. 3632	MACHINE SHOP NOC
160. 3634	VALVE MFG
161. 3635	GEAR MFG OR GRINDING
162. 3638	BALL OR ROLLER BEARING MFG
163. 3642	BATTERY MFG — DRY
164. 3643	ELECTRIC POWER OR TRANSMISSION EQUIPMENT MFG
165. 3647	BATTERY MFG — STORAGE
166. 3648	AUTOMOTIVE LIGHTING, IGNITION OR STARTING APPARATUS MFG NOC
167. 3681	TELEVISION, RADIO, TELEPHONE OR TELECOMMUNICATION DEVICE MFG NOC
168. 3685	INSTRUMENT MFG NOC
169. 3803	AUTOMOBILE WHEEL MFG — METAL — NOT CAST
170. 3807	AUTOMOBILE RADIATOR MFG
171. 3808	AUTOMOBILE MFG OR ASSEMBLY
172. 3822	AUTOMOBILE, BUS, TRUCK OR TRAILER BODY MFG: DIE — PRESSED STEEL
173. 3824	AUTOMOBILE, BUS, TRUCK OR TRAILER BODY MFG: NOC
174. 3826	AIRCRAFT ENGINE MFG
175. 3827	AUTOMOBILE ENGINE MFG
176. 3830	AIRPLANE MFG
177. 3851	MOTORCYCLE MFG OR ASSEMBLY
178. 3865	BABY CARRIAGE MFG
179. 3881	CAR MFG — RAILROAD & DRIVERS
180. 4021	BRICK OR CLAY PRODUCTS MFG NOC & DRIVERS
181. 4024	REFRACTORY PRODUCTS MFG & DRIVERS

Class	Description
182. 4034	CONCRETE PRODUCTS MFG & DRIVERS
183. 4036	PLASTERBOARD OR PLASTER BLOCK MFG & DRIVERS
184. 4038	PLASTER STATUARY OR ORNAMENT MFG
185. 4053	POTTERY MFG: CHINA OR TABLEWARE
186. 4061	POTTERY MFG: EARTHENWARE — GLAZED OR PORCELAIN — HAND MOLDED OR CAST
187. 4062	POTTERY MFG: PORCELAIN WARE — MECHANICAL PRESS FORMING
188. 4101	GLASS MFG & DRIVERS
189. 4111	GLASSWARE MFG — NO AUTOMATIC BLOWING MACHINES
190. 4112	INCANDESCENT LAMP MFG
191. 4113	GLASS MFG — CUT
192. 4114	GLASSWARE MFG NOC
193. 4130	GLASS MERCHANT
194. 4131	MIRROR MFG
195. 4133	CATHEDRAL OR ART GLASS WINDOW MFG
196. 4150	OPTICAL GOODS MFG NOC
197. 4206	PULP MFG — GROUND WOOD PROCESS
198. 4207	PULP MFG — CHEMICAL PROCESS
199. 4239	PAPER MFG
200. 4240	BOX MFG — SET — UP PAPER
201. 4243	BOX MFG — FOLDING PAPER — NOC
202. 4244	CORRUGATED OR FIBER BOARD CONTAINER MFG
203. 4250	PAPER COATING
204. 4251	STATIONERY MFG
205. 4263	FIBER GOODS MFG
206. 4273	BAG MFG — PLASTIC OR PAPER
207. 4279	PAPER GOODS MFG NOC
208. 4282	DRESS PATTERN MFG — PAPER
209. 4283	BUILDING OR ROOFING PAPER OR FELT PREPARATION — NO INSTALLATION
210. 4299	PRINTING
211. 4304	NEWSPAPER PUBLISHING
212. 4307	BOOKBINDING
213. 4308	LINOTYPE OR HAND COMPOSITION
214. 4351	PHOTOENGRAVING
215. 4352	ENGRAVING
216. 4360	MOTION PICTURE: DEVELOPMENT OF NEGATIVES, PRINTING AND ALL SUBSEQUENT OPERATIONS
217. 4410	RUBBER GOODS MFG NOC
218. 4420	RUBBER TIRE NOC
219. 4431	PHONOGRAPH RECORD MFG MAGNETIC AND OPTICAL RECORDING & MEDIA MFG.
220. 4432	PEN MFG
221. 4439	LACQUER OR SPIRIT VARNISH MFG
222. 4452	PLASTICS MFG: FABRICATED PRODUCTS NOC
223. 4459	PLASTICS MFG: SHEETS, RODS, OR TUBES
224. 4470	CABLE MFG — INSULATED ELECTRICAL
225. 4484	PLASTICS MANUFACTURING: MOLDED PRODUCTS NOC
226. 4493	FABRIC COATING OR IMPREGNATING NOC

Class	Description
227. 4557	INK MFG
228. 4558	PAINT MFG
229. 4561	VARNISH MFG — OLEO — RESINOUS
230. 4568	SALT BORAX OR POTASH PRODUCING OR REFINING & DRIVERS
231. 4581	PHOSPHATE WORKS & DRIVERS
232. 4583	FERTILIZER MFG & DRIVERS
233. 4586	AMMONIUM NITRATE MFG
234. 4611	DRUG, MEDICINE OR PHARMACEUTICAL PREPARATION, COMPOUNDING, OR BLENDING — NO MTG. OF INGREDIENTS
235. 4635	OXYGEN OR HYDROGEN MFG & DRIVERS
236. 4653	GLUE MFG & DRIVERS
237. 4665	RENDERING WORKS NOC & DRIVERS
238. 4670	COTTONSEED OIL MFG — MECHANICAL & DRIVERS
239. 4683	OIL MFG — VEGETABLE — NOC
240. 4686	OIL MFG — VEGETABLE — SOLVENT EXTRACTION PROCESS
241. 4692	DENTAL LABORATORY
242. 4693	PHARMACEUTICAL OR SURGICAL GOODS MFG NOC
243. 4703	CORN PRODUCTS MFG
244. 4710	CANDLE MFG
245. 4717	BUTTER SUBSTITUTE MFG
246. 4720	SOAP OR SYNTHETIC DETERGENT MFG
247. 4740	OIL REFINING — PETROLEUM & DRIVERS
248. 4741	ASPHALT OR TAR DISTILLING OR REFINING & DRIVERS
249. 4751	SYNTHETIC RUBBER MFG
250. 4771	EXPLOSIVES OR AMMUNITION MFG: NOC & DRIVERS
251. 4777	EXPLOSIVES DISTRIBUTORS & DRIVERS
252. 4825	DRUG, MEDICINE OR PHARMACEUTICAL PREPARATION MFG & INCLUDES MFG OF INGREDIENTS
253. 4828	CHEMICAL BLENDING AND MIXING NOC — ALL OPERATIONS & DRIVERS
254. 4829	CHEMICAL MANUFACTURING NOC — ALL OPERATIONS & DRIVERS
255. 4830	CHEMICAL MIXING AND MANUFACT. NOC — ALL OPERATIONS & DRIVERS — FOR USE IN
256. 4902	SPORTING GOODS MFG NOC
257. 4923	PHOTOGRAPHIC SUPPLIES MFG
258. 5951	SERUM, ANTI — TOXIN OR VIRUS MFG & DRIVERS
259. 6504	FOOD SUNDRIES MFG NOC — NO CEREAL MILLING
260. 9501	PAINTING: SHOP ONLY & DRIVERS
261. 9505	PAINTING: AUTOMOBILE OR CARRIAGE BODIES
262. 9521	HOUSE FURNISHINGS INSTALLATION NOC & UPHOLSTERING
263. 9522	UPHOLSTERING
264. 9600	TAXIDERMIST

(b) Industry Group: Contracting

1. 0042	LANDSCAPE GARDENING & DRIVERS
2. 0050	FARM MACHINERY OPERATION — BY CONTRACTOR & DRIVERS
3. 1322	OIL OR GAS WELL: CLEANING OR SWABBING OF OLD WELLS HAVING PREVIOUSLY PRODUCED GAS OR OIL — BY CONTRACTOR — NO DRILLING & DRIVERS
4. 3365	WELDING OR CUTTING NOC & DRIVERS

5. 3719	OIL STILL ERECTION OR REPAIR
6. 3724	MACHINERY OR EQUIPMENT ERECTION OR REPAIR NOC & DRIVERS
7. 3726	BOILER INSTALLATION OR REPAIR — STEAM
8. 5020	CEILING INSTALLATION — SUSPENDED ACOUSTICAL GRID TYPE
9. 5022	MASONRY NOC
10. 5037	PAINTING: METAL STRUCTURES — OVER TWO STORIES IN HEIGHT & DRIVERS
11. 5040	IRON OR STEEL: ERECTION — FRAME STRUCTURES
12. 5057	IRON OR STEEL: ERECTION NOC
13. 5059	IRON OR STEEL: ERECTION — FRAME STRUCTURES NOT OVER TWO STORIES IN HEIGHT
14. 5069	IRON OR STEEL: ERECTION — CONSTRUCTION OF DWELLINGS NOT OVER TWO STORIES IN HEIGHT
15. 5102	DOOR, DOOR FRAME OR SASH ERECTION — METAL OR METAL COVERED
16. 5146	FURNITURE OR FIXTURES INSTALLATION — PORTABLE — NOC
17. 5160	ELEVATOR ERECTION OR REPAIR
18. 5183	PLUMBING NOC & DRIVERS
19. 5188	AUTOMATIC SPRINKLER INSTALLATION & DRIVERS
20. 5190	ELECTRICAL WIRING — WITHIN BUILDINGS & DRIVERS
21. 5213	CONCRETE CONSTRUCTION NOC
22. 5215	CONCRETE WORK — INCIDENTAL TO THE CONSTRUCTION OF PRIVATE RESIDENCE
23. 5221	CONCRETE OR CEMENT WORK — FLOORS, DRIVEWAYS, YARDS OR SIDEWALKS & DRIVERS
24. 5222	CONCRETE CONSTRUCTION IN CONNECTION WITH BRIDGES OR CULVERTS
25. 5223	SWIMMING POOL CONSTRUCTION, — NOT IRON OR STEEL & DRIVERS
26. 5348	TILE, STONE, MOSAIC OR TERRAZZO WORK — INSIDE CERAMIC TILE, INDOOR STONE, MARBLE, OR MOSAIC WORK
27. 5402	HOTHOUSE ERECTION — ALL OPERATIONS
28. 5403	CARPENTRY — NOC
29. 5437	CARPENTRY — INSTALLATION OF CABINET WORK OR INTERIOR TRIM
30. 5443	LATHING & DRIVERS
31. 5445	WALLBOARD INSTALLATION WITHIN BUILDINGS & DRIVERS
32. 5462	GLAZIER — AWAY FROM SHOP & DRIVERS
33. 5472	ASBESTOS REMOVAL OPERATIONS: CONTRACTOR — PIPE AND BOILER WORK EXCLUSIVELY & DRIVERS
34. 5473	ASBESTOS REMOVAL OPERATIONS: CONTRACTOR — NOC & DRIVERS
35. 5474	PAINTING OR PAPERHANGING NOC & SHOP OPERATIONS, DRIVERS
36. 5478	FLOOR COVERING INSTALLATION — RESILIENT FLOORING — CARPET AND LAMINATE FLOORING
37. 5479	INSULATION WORK NOC & DRIVERS
38. 5480	PLASTERING NOC & DRIVERS
39. 5491	PAPERHANGING & DRIVERS
40. 5506	STREET OR ROAD CONSTRUCTION: PAVING OR REPAVING & DRIVERS
41. 5507	STREET OR ROAD CONSTRUCTION: SUBSURFACE WORK & DRIVERS
42. 5508	STREET OR ROAD CONSTRUCTION: ROCK EXCAVATION & DRIVERS
43. 5509	STREET OR ROAD MAINTENANCE CONSTRUCTION, OR RECONSTRUCTION BY STATE, COUNTY OR MUNICIPALITY — ALL EMPLOYEES & DRIVERS
44. 5536	HEATING AND AIR CONDITIONING DUCT WORK — SHOP & OUTSIDE
45. 5537	HEATING, VENTILATION, AIR — CONDITIONING AND REFRIGERATION SYSTEM — INSTALLATION, SERVICE AND REPAIR & DRIVERS

46. 5538 SHEET METAL WORK — SHOP AND OUTSIDE — NOC & DRIVERS
47. 5551 ROOFING — ALL KINDS & DRIVERS
48. 5606 CONTRACTOR — PROJECT MANAGER, CONSTRUCTION EXECUTIVE, CONSTRUCTION MANAGER OR CONSTRUCTION SUPERINTENDENT
49. 5610 CLEANER — DEBRIS REMOVAL
50. 5613 CLEANER — DEBRIS REMOVAL — TEMPORARY LABOR SERVICE
51. 5645 CARPENTRY — DETACHED ONE OR TWO FAMILY DWELLINGS
52. 5651 CARPENTRY — DWELLINGS — THREE STORIES OR LESS
53. 5703 BUILDING RAISING OR MOVING
54. 5705 SALVAGE OPERATION — NO WRECKING OR ANY STRUCTURAL OPERATIONS
55. 6003 PILE DRIVING
56. 6005 JETTY OR BREAKWATER CONSTRUCTION — ALL OPERATIONS TO COMPLETION & DRIVERS
57. 6017 DAM OR LOCK CONSTRUCTION: CONCRETE WORK — ALL OPERATIONS
58. 6018 DAM OR LOCK CONSTRUCTION: EARTHMOVING OR PLACING — ALL OPERATIONS & DRIVERS
59. 6045 LEVEE CONSTRUCTION — ALL OPERATIONS TO COMPLETION & DRIVERS
60. 6204 DRILLING NOC & DRIVERS
61. 6206 OIL OR GAS WELL: CEMENTING & DRIVERS
62. 6213 OIL OR GAS WELL: SPECIALTY TOOL OPERATION NOC — BY CONTRACTOR — ALL EMPLOYEES & DRIVERS
63. 6214 OIL OR GAS WELL: PERFORATING OF CASING — ALL EMPLOYEES & DRIVERS
64. 6216 OIL OR GAS LEASE WORK NOC — BY CONTRACTOR & DRIVERS
65. 6217 EXCAVATION & DRIVERS NOC
66. 6229 IRRIGATION OR DRAINAGE SYSTEM CONSTRUCTION & DRIVERS
67. 6233 OIL OR GAS PIPELINE CONSTRUCTION & DRIVERS
68. 6235 OIL OR GAS WELL: DRILLING OR REDRILLING & DRIVERS
69. 6236 OIL OR GAS WELL: INSTALLATION OR RECOVERY OF CASING & DRIVERS
70. 6237 OIL OR GAS WELL: INSTRUMENT LOGGING OR SURVEY WORK & DRIVERS
71. 6251 TUNNELING — NOT PNEUMATIC — ALL OPERATIONS
72. 6252 SHAFT SINKING — ALL OPERATIONS
73. 6260 TUNNELING — PNEUMATIC — ALL OPERATIONS
74. 6306 SEWER CONSTRUCTION — ALL OPERATIONS & DRIVERS
75. 6319 GAS MAIN OR CONNECTION CONSTRUCTION & DRIVERS
76. 6325 CONDUIT CONSTRUCTION — FOR CABLES OR WIRES & DRIVERS
77. 6400 FENCE ERECTION — METAL
78. 7538 ELECTRIC LIGHT OR POWER LINE CONSTRUCTION & DRIVERS
79. 7601 TELEPHONE, TELEGRAPH OR FIRE ALARM LINE CONSTRUCTION & DRIVERS
80. 7605 BURGLAR ALARM INSTALLATION OR REPAIR & DRIVERS
81. 7611 TELEPHONE OR CABLE TV LINE INSTALLATION — CONTRACTORS, UNDERGROUND & DRIVERS
82. 7612 TELEPHONE OR CABLE TV LINE INSTALLATION — CONTRACTORS, OVERHEAD & DRIVERS
83. 7613 TELEPHONE OR CABLE TV LINE INSTALLATION — CONTRACTORS, SERVICE LINES AND CONNECTIONS & DRIVERS
84. 7855 RAILROAD CONSTRUCTION: LAYING OR RELAYING OF TRACKS OR MAINTENANCE OF WAY BY CONTRACTORS — NO WORK ON ELEVATED RAILROADS & DRIVERS
85. 8227 CONSTRUCTION OR ERECTION PERMANENT YARD
86. 9534 MOBILE CRANE AND HOISTING SERVICE CONTRACTORS — NOC — ALL OPERATIONS — INCLUDING YARD EMPLOYEES AND DRIVERS

87. 9554 SIGN INSTALLATION, MAINTENANCE, REPAIR, REMOVAL, OR REPLACEMENT — NOC & DRIVERS

(c) Industry Group: Office & Clerical

1. 4361 PHOTOGRAPHER — ALL EMPLOYEES & CLERICAL, SALESPERSONS, DRIVERS
2. 7610 RADIO OR TELEVISION BROADCASTING STATION — ALL EMPLOYEES & CLERICAL, DRIVERS
3. 8601 ARCHITECT OR ENGINEER — CONSULTING
4. 8721 REAL ESTATE APPRAISAL COMPANY —; OUTSIDE EMPLOYEES
5. 8742 SALESPERSONS OR COLLECTORS — OUTSIDE
6. 8748 AUTOMOBILE SALESPERSONS
7. 8755 LABOR UNION — ALL EMPLOYEES
8. 8800 MAILING OR ADDRESSING CO. & CLERICAL
9. 8803 AUDITORS, ACCOUNTANT OR FACTORY COST OR OFFICE SYSTEMATIZER —TRAVELING
10. 8810 CLERICAL OFFICE EMPLOYEES NOC
11. 8820 ATTORNEY — ALL EMPLOYEES & CLERICAL, MESSENGERS, DRIVERS
12. 8832 PHYSICIAN & CLERICAL
13. 8833 HOSPITAL: PROFESSIONAL EMPLOYEES
14. 8861 CHARITABLE OR WELFARE ORGANIZATION — PROFESSIONAL EMPLOYEES & CLERICAL
15. 8868 COLLEGE: PROFESSIONAL EMPLOYEES & CLERICAL
16. 8869 CHILD DAY CARE CENTER: PROFESSIONAL EMPLOYEES AND CLERICAL, SALESPERSONS
17. 8871 CLERICAL TELECOMMUTER EMPLOYEES
18. 8901 TELEPHONE OR TELEGRAPH CO.: OFFICE OR EXCHANGE EMPLOYEES & CLERICAL
19. 9012 BUILDINGS — OPERATION BY OWNER, LESSEE, OR REAL ESTATE MANAGEMENT FIRM: PROFESSIONAL EMPLOYEES, PROPERTY MANAGERS AND LEASING AGENTS & CLERICAL SALESPERSONS
20. 9156 THEATER NOC: PLAYERS, ENTERTAINERS OR MUSICIANS

(d) Industry Group: Goods & Services

1. 0005 FARM: NURSERY EMPLOYEES & DRIVERS
2. 0008 FARM: GARDENING — MARKET OR TRUCK & DRIVERS
3. 0016 FARM: ORCHARD & DRIVERS
4. 0030 SUGAR CANE PLANTATION & DRIVERS
5. 0034 FARM: POULTRY OR EGG PRODUCER & DRIVERS
6. 0035 FARM: FLORISTS & DRIVERS
7. 0036 FARM: DAIRY & DRIVERS
8. 0037 FARM: FIELD CROPS & DRIVERS
9. 0052 ORCHARD AND GROVE OWNERS AND OPERATORS — ALL OPERATIONS & DRIVERS
10. 0079 FARM: BERRY OR VINELAND & DRIVERS
11. 0083 FARM: CATTLE OR LIVESTOCK RAISING NOC & DRIVERS
12. 0113 FARM: FISH HATCHERY & DRIVERS
13. 0153 LAWN OR SHRUB SPRAYING & DRIVERS
14. 0170 FARM: ANIMAL RAISING & DRIVERS
15. 0173 BERRY FARM & DRIVERS
16. 0400 COTTON COMPRESSING & DRIVERS

17. 0401 COTTON GIN OPERATION & LOCAL MANAGERS, DRIVERS
18. 0908 DOMESTIC WORKERS — INSIDE — OCCASIONAL
19. 0909 DOMESTIC WORKERS — OUTSIDE — OCCASIONAL — INCLUDING OCCASIONAL PRIVATE CHAUFFEURS
20. 0912 DOMESTIC WORKERS — OUTSIDE — INCLUDING PRIVATE CHAUFFEURS
21. 0913 DOMESTIC WORKERS — INSIDE
22. 0917 DOMESTIC SERVICE CONTRACTOR — INSIDE
23. 2587 TOWEL OR TOILET SUPPLY CO. & ROUTE SUPERVISORS, DRIVERS
24. 3821 AUTOMOBILE RECYCLING & DRIVERS
25. 4362 MOTION PICTURE: FILM EXCHANGE & PROJECTION ROOMS, CLERICAL
26. 4511 ANALYTICAL CHEMIST
27. 5191 OFFICE MACHINE INSTALLATION, INSPECTION, ADJUSTMENT OR REPAIR
28. 5192 VENDING OR COIN OPERATED MACHINES — INSTALLATION, SERVICE OR REPAIR & SALESPERSON, DRIVERS
29. 7204 GREYHOUND BREEDING, TRAINING AND RACING & DRIVERS
30. 7390 BEER OR ALE DEALER — WHOLESALE & DRIVERS
31. 8001 STORE: FLORIST & DRIVERS
32. 8002 AUTOMOBILE RENTAL CO.: ALL OTHER EMPLOYEES & COUNTER PERSONNEL, DRIVERS
33. 8006 GASOLINE STATION: SELF — SERVICE AND CONVENIENCE/GROCERY — RETAIL
34. 8008 STORE: CLOTHING, WEARING APPAREL OR DRY GOODS — RETAIL
35. 8010 STORE: HARDWARE
36. 8013 STORE: JEWELRY
37. 8015 QUICK PRINTING — COPYING OR DUPLICATING SERVICE — ALL EMPLOYEES & CLERICAL, SALESPERSONS
38. 8017 STORE: RETAIL NOC
39. 8018 STORE: WHOLESALE NOC
40. 8021 STORE: MEAT, FISH OR POULTRY DEALER — WHOLESALE
41. 8031 STORE: MEAT, FISH OR POULTRY — RETAIL
42. 8032 STORE: CLOTHING, WEARING APPAREL OR DRY GOODS — WHOLESALE
43. 8033 STORE: MEAT, GROCERY AND PROVISIONS STORES COMBINED — RETAIL NOC
44. 8039 STORE: DEPARTMENT — RETAIL
45. 8044 STORE: FURNITURE & DRIVERS
46. 8045 STORE: DRUG — RETAIL
47. 8046 STORE: AUTOMOBILE PARTS AND ACCESSORIES — NOC & DRIVERS
48. 8047 STORE: DRUG — WHOLESALE
49. 8050 STORE: FIVE AND TEN CENT
50. 8058 BUILDING MATERIAL DEALER — NEW MATERIALS ONLY: STORE EMPLOYEES
51. 8061 GASOLINE STATION: SELF — SERVICE AND CONVENIENCE — RETAIL OR STORE
52. 8072 STORE: BOOK, RECORD, COMPACT DISC, SOFTWARE, VIDEO OR AUDIO CASSETTE — RETAIL
53. 9019 BRIDGE OR VEHICULAR TUNNEL OPERATION & DRIVERS
54. 8103 WOOL MERCHANT
55. 8105 STORE: HIDE OR LEATHER DEALER
56. 8106 IRON OR STEEL MERCHANT & DRIVERS
57. 8107 MACHINERY DEALER NOC — STORE OR YARD & DRIVERS
58. 8111 PLUMBERS SUPPLIES DEALER & DRIVERS
59. 8116 FARM MACHINERY DEALER — ALL OPERATIONS & DRIVERS

60. 8203	ICE MFG. OR DISTRIBUTION & DRIVERS
61. 8204	BUILDING MATERIAL YARD & LOCAL MANAGERS, DRIVERS
62. 8209	VEGETABLE PACKING & DRIVERS
63. 8215	FEED, FERTILIZER, HAY, OR GRAIN DEALER & LOCAL MANAGERS, DRIVERS — NO MFG
64. 8232	LUMBERYARD NEW MATERIALS ONLY: ALL OTHER EMPLOYEES & YARD, WAREHOUSE, DRIVERS
65. 8233	COAL MERCHANT & LOCAL MANAGERS, DRIVERS
66. 8235	SASH, DOOR OR ASSEMBLED MILLWORK DEALER & DRIVERS
67. 8263	JUNK DEALER & DRIVERS
68. 8264	BOTTLE DEALER — USED & DRIVERS
69. 8265	IRON OR STEEL SCRAP DEALER & DRIVERS
70. 8273	HORSE BREEDING INVOLVING STALLIONS & DRIVERS
71. 8274	HORSE BREEDING NOT INVOLVING STALLIONS & DRIVERS
72. 8279	STABLE OR BREEDING FARM & DRIVERS
73. 8288	LIVESTOCK DEALER OR COMMISSION MERCHANT & SALESPERSONS, DRIVERS
74. 8291	STORAGE WAREHOUSE — COLD
75. 8292	STORAGE WAREHOUSE NOC
76. 8293	STORAGE WAREHOUSE — FURNITURE & DRIVERS
77. 8304	GRAIN ELEVATOR OPERATION & LOCAL MANAGERS, DRIVERS
78. 8350	GASOLINE DEALER & DRIVERS
79. 8353	GAS DEALER — LPG & SALESPERSONS, DRIVERS
80. 8380	AUTOMOBILE SERVICE OR REPAIR CENTER & DRIVERS
81. 8381	GASOLINE STATION: SELF — SERVICE ONLY — RETAIL
82. 8385	BUS CO.: GARAGE EMPLOYEES
83. 8392	AUTOMOBILE STORAGE GARAGE, PARKING LOT OR PARKING STATION, VALET SERVICE, CASHIERS OR COUNTER PERSONNEL & DRIVERS
84. 8393	AUTOMOBILE BODY REPAIR
85. 8500	METAL SCRAP DEALER & DRIVERS
86. 8606	GEOPHYSICAL EXPLORATION — SEISMIC — ALL EMPLOYEES & DRIVERS
87. 8719	STEVEDORING: TALLIERS AND CHECKING CLERKS ENGAGED IN CONNECTION WITH STEVEDORE WORK
88. 8720	INSPECTION OF RISKS FOR INSURANCE OR VALUATION PURPOSES NOC
89. 8745	NEWS AGENT OR DISTRIBUTOR OF MAGAZINES OR OTHER PERIODICALS — NOT RETAIL DEALER & SALESPERSONS, DRIVERS
90. 8824	RETIREMENT LIVING CENTERS: HEALTH CARE EMPLOYEES
91. 8825	RETIREMENT LIVING CENTERS: FOOD SERVICE EMPLOYEES
92. 8826	RETIREMENT LIVING CENTERS: ALL OTHER EMPLOYEES, SALESPERSONS & DRIVERS
93. 8829	CONVALESCENT OR NURSING HOME — ALL EMPLOYEES
94. 8831	HOSPITAL — VETERINARY & DRIVERS
95. 8835	NURSING — HOME HEALTH, PUBLIC AND TRAVELING HEALTHCARE — ALL EMPLOYEES
96. 8841	NURSING HOME: PROFESSIONAL EMPLOYEES
97. 9000	JANITORIAL SERVICE BY CONTRACTOR: NO WINDOW CLEANING
98. 9001	JANITORIAL SERVICE BY CONTRACTOR: INCLUDES WINDOW CLEANING
99. 9014	BUILDINGS — OPERATION BY CONTRACTORS
100. 9015	BUILDINGS — OPERATION — BY OWNER, LESSEE, OR REAL ESTATE MANAGEMENT FIRM: ALL OTHER EMPLOYEES
101. 9016	AMUSEMENT PARK OR EXHIBITIONS OPERATIONS & DRIVERS

102.	9033	HOUSING AUTHORITY & CLERICAL, SALESPERSONS, DRIVERS
103.	9040	HOSPITAL: ALL OTHER EMPLOYEES
104.	9047	NURSING HOME: ALL OTHER EMPLOYEES
105.	9052	HOTEL: ALL OTHER EMPLOYEES & SALESPERSONS, DRIVERS
106.	9058	HOTEL: RESTAURANT EMPLOYEES
107.	9059	CHILD DAY CARE CENTER: ALL OTHER EMPLOYEES & DRIVERS
108.	9060	CLUB — COUNTRY, GOLF, FISHING OR YACHT & CLERICAL
109.	9061	CLUB NOC & CLERICAL
110.	9063	YMCA, YWCA, YMHA OR YWHA, INSTITUTION — ALL EMPLOYEES & CLERICAL
111.	9082	RESTAURANT NOC
112.	9083	RESTAURANT: FAST FOOD
113.	9084	BAR, DISCOTHEQUE, LOUNGE, NIGHT CLUB OR TAVERN
114.	9089	BILLIARD HALL
115	9093	BOWLING LANE
116.	9101	COLLEGE: ALL OTHER EMPLOYEES
117.	9110	CHARITABLE OR WELFARE ORGANIZATION — ALL OTHER EMPLOYEES & DRIVERS
118.	9220	CEMETERY OPERATIONS & DRIVERS
119.	9410	MUNICIPAL, TOWNSHIP, COUNTY OR STATE EMPLOYEE NOC
120.	9516	RADIO, TELEVISION, VIDEO, AND AUDIO EQUIPMENT INSTALLATION SERVICE OR REPAIR & DRIVERS
121.	9519	HOUSEHOLD AND COMMERCIAL APPLIANCES — ELECTRICAL — INSTALLATION, SERVICE OR REPAIR & DRIVERS
122.	9586	BARBERSHOP, BEAUTY PARLOR OR HAIRSTYLING SALON
123.	9620	FUNERAL DIRECTOR & DRIVERS

(e) Industry Group: Miscellaneous

1.	0106	TREE PRUNING, SPRAYING, REPAIRING — ALL OPERATIONS & DRIVERS
2.	0251	IRRIGATION WORKS OPERATION & DRIVERS
3.	1005	COAL MINING— SURFACE & DRIVERS
4.	1164	MINING NOC—; NOT COAL — UNDERGROUND & DRIVERS
5.	1165	MINING NOC — NOT COAL — SURFACE & DRIVERS
6.	1218	PHOSPHATE MINING & DRIVERS
7.	1320	OIL OR GAS LEASE OPERATOR — ALL OPERATIONS & DRIVERS
8.	1624	QUARRY NOC & DRIVERS
9.	1654	QUARRY — CEMENT ROCK — SURFACE & DRIVERS
10.	1655	LIME MFG — QUARRY —; SURFACE & DRIVERS
11.	1710	STONE CRUSHING & DRIVERS
12.	2702	LOGGING OR LUMBERING & DRIVERS
13.	4000	SAND OR GRAVEL DIGGING & DRIVERS
14.	6811	BOATBUILDING —; WOOD — NOC & DRIVERS
15.	6834	BOATBUILDING OR REPAIR & DRIVERS
16.	6836	MARINA & DRIVERS
17.	6838	BOATBUILDING OR REPAIR — FIBERGLASS ONLY & DRIVERS
18.	6854	SHIPBUILDING — IRON OR STEEL — NOC & DRIVERS
19.	6882	SHIP REPAIR CONVERSION — ALL OPERATIONS & DRIVERS
20.	6884	PAINTING: SHIP HULLS
21.	7133	RAILROAD OPERATION: NOC — ALL EMPLOYEES & DRIVERS

22.	7201	LIVERY OR BOARDING STABLE — NOT SALES STABLE & DRIVERS
23.	7205	HORSE TRAINING
24.	7219	TRUCKING: NOC — ALL EMPLOYEES & DRIVERS
25.	7222	TRUCKING: OIL FIELD EQUIPMENT — ALL EMPLOYEES & DRIVERS
26.	7230	TRUCKING: PARCEL OR PACKAGE DELIVERY — ALL EMPLOYEES & DRIVERS
27.	7231	TRUCKING: MAIL, PARCEL OR PACKAGE DELIVERY AND COURIER OR MESSENGER SERVICE COMPANIES — ALL EMPLOYEES & DRIVERS
28.	7232	TRUCKING: MAIL PARCEL OR PACKAGE DELIVERY —; UNDER CONTRACT WITH THE U.S. POSTAL SERVICE — ALL EMPLOYEES & DRIVERS
29.	7360	FREIGHT HANDLING NOC
30.	7370	TAXICAB CO.: ALL OTHER EMPLOYEES & DRIVERS
31.	7380	DRIVERS, CHAUFFEURS, MESSENGERS, & THEIR HELPERS NOC — COMMERCIAL
32.	7382	BUS CO.: ALL OTHER EMPLOYEES & DRIVERS
33.	7383	COLLEGE OR SCHOOL — SCHOOL BUS DRIVERS
34.	7403	AIRCRAFT OR HELICOPTER OPERATION: AIR CARRIER — SCHEDULED OR SUPPLEMENTAL: ALL OTHER EMPLOYEES & DRIVERS
35.	7405	AIRCRAFT OR HELICOPTER OPERATION: AIR CARRIER — SCHEDULED OR SUPPLEMENTAL: FLYING CREW
36.	7409	AIRCRAFT OR HELICOPTER OPERATION: AERIAL APPLICATION, SEEDING, HERDING OR SCINTILLOMETER SURVEYING: FLYING CREW
37.	7420	AIRCRAFT OR HELICOPTER OPERATION: PUBLIC EXHIBITION INVOLVING STUNT FLYING, RACING OR PARACHUTE JUMPING: FLYING CREW
38.	7421	AIRCRAFT OR HELICOPTER OPERATION: TRANSPORTATION OF PERSONNEL IN CONDUCT OF EMPLOYER'S BUSINESS: FLYING CREW
39.	7422	AIRCRAFT OR HELICOPTER OPERATION: NOC — OTHER THAN HELICOPTERS: FLYING CREW
40.	7423	AIRCRAFT OR HELICOPTER OPERATION: AIR CARRIER — COMMUTER: ALL OTHER EMPLOYEES & DRIVERS
41.	7425	AIRCRAFT OR HELICOPTER OPERATION: NOC — HELICOPTERS: FLYING CREW
42.	7431	AIRCRAFT OR HELICOPTER OPERATION: AIR CARRIER COMMUTER — FLYING CREW
43.	7502	GAS COMPANY: GAS CO. — NATURAL GAS — LOCAL DISTRIBUTION & DRIVERS
44.	7515	OIL OR GAS PIPELINE OPERATION & DRIVERS
45.	7520	WATERWORKS OPERATION & DRIVERS
46.	7539	ELECTRIC LIGHT OR POWER CO. NOC — ALL EMPLOYEES & DRIVERS
47.	7540	ELECTRIC LIGHT OR POWER COOPERATIVE — REA PROJECT ONLY — ALL EMPLOYEES & DRIVERS
48.	7580	SEWAGE DISPOSAL PLANT OPERATION & DRIVERS
49.	7590	GARBAGE WORKS
50.	7600	TELEPHONE OR TELEGRAPH CO.: ALL OTHER EMPLOYEES & DRIVERS
51.	7704	FIREFIGHTERS & DRIVERS
52.	7720	POLICE OFFICERS & DRIVERS
53.	9019	BRIDGE OR VEHICULAR TUNNEL OPERATION & DRIVERS
54.	9102	PARK NOC — ALL EMPLOYEES & DRIVERS
55.	9154	THEATER NOC: ALL OTHER EMPLOYEES
56.	9178	ATHLETIC TEAM OR PARK: NON — CONTACT SPORTS
57.	9179	ATHLETIC TEAM OR PARK: CONTACT SPORTS
58.	9180	AMUSEMENT DEVICE OPERATION NOC — NOT TRAVELING — & DRIVERS
59.	9182	ATHLETIC TEAM OR PARK: OPERATION & DRIVERS

60.	9186	CARNIVAL, CIRCUS OR AMUSEMENT DEVICE OPERATOR —; TRAVELING —ALL EMPLOYEES & DRIVERS
61.	9402	STREET CLEANING & DRIVERS
62.	9403	GARBAGE, ASHES OR REFUSE COLLECTION & DRIVERS

Specific Authority 440.107(9), 440.591 Fla. Stat

Law Implemented 440.107(7)(b) Fla. Stat.

History: New 10-29-06.

CHAPTER 69L-7 Workers' Compensation Medical Reimbursement and Utilization Review

69L-7.020. Florida Workers' Compensation Health Care Provider Reimbursement Manual.

(1) The Florida Workers' Compensation Health Care Provider Reimbursement Manual, 2006 Edition, is adopted by reference as part of this rule. The manual contains the Maximum Reimbursement Allowances determined by the Three-Member Panel, pursuant to Section 440.13(12), F.S., and establishes reimbursement policies, guidelines, codes and maximum reimbursement allowances for services and supplies provided by health care providers. Also, the manual includes reimbursement policies and payment methodologies for pharmacists and medical suppliers.

(2) The CPT® 2006 Current Procedural Terminology Professional Edition, Copyright 2005, American Medical Association; the Current Dental Terminology, CDT-2005, Copyright 2004, American Dental Association; and in part for D codes and for injectable J codes, and for other medical services and supply codes, the "Healthcare Common Procedure Coding System, Medicare's National Level II Codes, HCPCS 2006", American Medical Association, Eighteenth Edition, Copyright 2005, Ingenix Publishing Group, are adopted by reference as part of this rule. When a health care provider performs a procedure or service which is not listed in the Florida Workers' Compensation Health Care Provider Reimbursement Manual, 2006 Edition incorporated above, the provider must use a code contained in the CPT®-2006, CDT-2005 or HCPCS-2006 as specified in this section.

(3) The Florida Workers' Compensation Health Care Provider Reimbursement Manual, 2006 Edition incorporated above, is available for inspection during normal business hours at the Florida Department of Financial Services, Document Processing Section, 200 East Gaines Street, Tallahassee, Florida 32399-0311, or via the Department's web site at http://www.fldfs.com/wc.

Specific Authority 440.13(14)(b), 440.591 Fla. Stat.

Law Implemented 440.13(7), (12) and (14) Fla. Stat.

History: New 10-1-82, Amended 3-15-83, 11-6-83, 5-21-85, Formerly 38F-7.20, Amended 4-1-88, 7-20-88, 6-1-91, 4-29-92, 2-18-96, 9-1-97, 12-15-97, 9-17-98, 9-30-01, 7-7-02, Formerly 38F-7.020, 4L-7.020, Amended 12-4-03, 1-1-04, 7-4-04, 5-9-05, 9-4-05, 11-16-06.

69L-7.100. Florida Workers' Compensation Reimbursement Manual for Ambulatory Surgical Centers (ASCs).

(1) The Florida Workers' Compensation Reimbursement Manual for Ambulatory Surgical Centers, 2005 Edition, is adopted by reference as part of this rule. The manual contains reimbursement policies and maximum reimbursement allowances for ambulatory surgical facility services, which are items and services provided in connection with a surgical procedure. The manual contains basic instructions and information for all ambulatory surgical centers and insurers concerning reimbursement of claims for ambulatory surgical facilitiy services.

(2) The Division has incorporated in the Florida Workers' Compensation Reimbursement Manual for Ambulatory Surgical Centers, 2005 Edition, procedure codes consistent with the Physician's Current Procedural Terminology (CPT®), 2005 Professional Edition, Copyright 2004, American Medical Association. This publication is adopted by reference as part of this rule. When a procedure is performed which is not listed in the manual, the ambulatory surgical

center must use the appropriate code and descriptor contained in the Physicians' Current Procedural Technology (CPT®), 2005 Professional Edition, Copyright 2004, American Medical Association.

(3) The Florida Workers' Compensation Reimbursement Manual for Ambulatory Surgical Centers, 2005 Edition, incorporated above, is available for inspection during normal business hours at the Florida Department of Financial Services, Document Processing Section, 200 East Gaines Street, Tallahassee, Florida, 3239900311, or via the Department's web site at http://www.fldfs.com.

Specific Authority 440.13(14), 440.591 Fla. Stat.

Law Implemented 440.13(7), (12), (14), Fla. Stat.

History: New 8-7-91, Amended 12-31-92, Formerly 38F-7.100, 4L-7.100, Amended 9-4-05.

69L-7.501. Florida Workers' Compensation Reimbursement Manual for Hospitals.

(1) The Florida Workers' Compensation Reimbursement Manual for Hospitals, 2004 Second Edition is adopted by reference as part of this rule. The manual contains reimbursement policies and per diem rates for hospital services and supplies.

(2) Form DWC-90, Uniform Bill (rev. 1992), also known as the UB-92, or HCFA-1450, is hereby incorporated by reference as part of this rule. The Florida Workers' Compensation Health Care Provider Reimbursement Manual 2004, Second Edition is incorporated by reference as part of this rule also. The reimbursement policies, billing codes and maximum reimbursement allowances for physical therapy, occupational therapy, speech therapy, radiology and clinical laboratory services contained in the manual shall be applied to hospital services provided on an outpatient basis only.

(3) The Florida Workers' Compensation Reimbursement Manual for Hospitals, incorporated in subsection (1) above, and Form DWC-90 are available for inspection during normal business hours, at the State of Florida Department of Financial Services, Document Processing Section, 200 East Gaines Street, Tallahassee, Florida 32399-0311, or via the Department's website at http://www.fldfs.com.

Specific Authority 440.13(14), 440.591 Fla. Stat.

Law Implemented 440.13(7), (12), (14) Fla. Stat.

History: New 6-9-87, Amended 6-1-92, 10-27-99, 7-3-2001, Formerly 38F-7.501, 4L-7.501, Amended 12-04-03, 1-1-04, 7-4-04.

History: New 11-14-89, Formerly 38F-7.601, 4L-7.601.

69L-7.601 Copying Charges for Medical Records.

Health care providers and health care facilities shall upon demand furnish an injured employee or his attorney a copy of his office chart, records and reports. The health care provider or health care facility furnishing the records may charge the employee for copying the records up to $.50 per page or the actual direct cost to the health care provider or health care facility for x-rays, microfilm, or other non-paper records.

Specific Authority 440.13(2)(c) FS. (1988 Supp.).

Law Implemented 440.13(2)(c) FS. (1988 Supp.).

History: New 11-14-89, Formerly 38F-7.601, 4L-7.601.

69L-7.602 Florida Workers' Compensation Medical Services Billing, Filing and Reporting Rule.

(1) Definitions. As used in this rule:

(a) "Accurately Complete" or "Accurately Completed" means the form submitted contains the information necessary to meet the requirements of Chapter 440, F.S., and this rule.

(b) "Adjust" or "Adjusted" means payment is made with modification to the information provided on the bill.

(c) "Agency" means the Agency for Health Care Administration as defined in Section 440.02(3), F.S.

(d) "Ambulatory Surgical Center" is defined in Section 395.002(3), F.S.

(e) "Billing" means the process by which a health care provider submits a medical claim form or medical bill to an insurer, service company/third party administrator or any entity acting on behalf of the insurer, to receive reimbursement for medical services, goods or supplies provided to an injured employee.

(f) "Catastrophic Event" means the occurrence of an event outside the control of an insurer, submitter, service company/third party administrator or any entity acting on behalf of the insurer, such as an electronic data transmission failure due to a natural disaster or an act of terrorism (including but not limited to cyber terrorism), in which recovery time will prevent an insurer, submitter, service company/third party administrator or any entity acting on behalf of the insurer from meeting the filing and reporting requirements of Chapter 440, F.S., and this rule. Programming errors, system malfunctions or electronic data interchange transmission failures that are not a direct result of a catastrophic event are not considered to be a catastrophic event as defined in this rule. See subsection (6)(d) for requirements to request approval of an alternative method and timeline for medical report filing with the Division due to a catastrophic event.

(g) "Charges" means the dollar amount billed.

(h) "Charge Master" means for hospitals a comprehensive listing of all the goods and services for which the facility maintains a separate charge, with the facility's charge for each of the goods and services, regardless of payer type and means for ASCs a listing of the gross charge for each CPT® procedure for which an ASC maintains a separate charge, with the ASC's charge for each CPT® procedure, regardless of payer type.

(i) "Claims-Handling Entity File Number" means the number assigned to the claim file by the insurer or service company/third party administrator for purposes of internal tracking.

(j) "Current Dental Terminology" (CDT) means the American Dental Association's reference document containing descriptive terms to identify codes for billing and reporting dental procedures.

(k) "Current Procedural Terminology" (CPT®) means the American Medical Association's reference document (HCPCS Level I) containing descriptive terms to identify codes for billing and reporting medical procedures and services.

(l) "Date Insurer Paid" or "Date Insurer Paid, Adjusted, Disallowed or Denied" means the date the insurer, service company/third party administrator or any entity acting on behalf of the insurer mails, transfers or electronically transmits payment to the health care provider or the health care provider representative. If payment is disallowed or denied, "Date Insurer Paid" or "Date Insurer Paid, Adjusted, Disallowed or Denied" means the date the insurer, service company/third party administrator or any entity acting on behalf of the insurer mails, transfers or electronically transmits the appropriate notice of disallowance or denial to the health care provider or the health care provider representative. See paragraph (5)(l) for the requirement to accurately report the "date insurer paid".

(m) "Date Insurer Received" means the date that a Form DFS-F5-DWC-9, DFS-F5-DWC-10 (or insurer pre-approved alternate form), DFS-F5-DWC-11, DFS-F5-DWC-90 or the electronic form equivalent is in the possession of the insurer, service company/third party administrator or any entity acting on behalf of the insurer. See paragraph (5)(l) for the requirement to accurately report the "date insurer received". If a medical bill meets any of the critiera in paragraph (5)(j) of this rule and possession of the form is relinquished by the insurer, service company/TPA or any entity acting on behalf of the insurer by returning the medical bill to the provider with a written explanation for the insurer's reason for return, then "date insurer received" shall not apply to the medical bill as submitted.

(n) "Deny" or "Denied" means payment is not made because the service rendered is treatment for a non-compensable injury or illness.

(o) "Department" means Department of Financial Services (DFS) as defined in Section 440.02(12), F.S.

(p) "Disallow" or "Disallowed" means payment is not made because the service rendered has not been substantiated for reasons of medical necessity, insufficient documentation, lack of authorization or billing error.

(q) "Division" means the Division of Workers' Compensation (DWC) as defined in Section 440.02(14), F.S.

(r) "Electronic Filing" means the computer exchange of medical data from a submitter to the Division in the standardized format defined in the Florida Medical EDI Implementation Guide (MEIG).

(s) "Electronic Form Equivalent" means the format, provided in the Florida Medical EDI Implementation Guide (MEIG) to be used when a submitter electronically transmits required data to the Division. Electronic form equivalents do not include transmission by facsimile, data file(s) attached to electronic mail, or computer-generated paper-forms.

(t) "Electronically Filed with the Division" means the date an electronic filing has been received by the Division and has successfully passed structural and data-quality edits.

(u) "Entity" means any party involved in the provision of or the payment for medical services, care or treatment rendered to the injured employee, excluding the insurer, service company/third party administrator or health care provider as identified in this section.

(v) "Explanation of Bill Review" (EOBR) means the notice of payment or notice of adjustment, disallowance or denial sent by an insurer, service company/third party administrator or any entity acting on behalf of an insurer to a health care provider containing code(s) and code descriptor(s), in conformance with paragraph (5)(o) of this rule.

(w) "Florida Medical EDI Implementation Guide (MEIG)" is the Florida Division of Workers' Compensation's reference document containing the specific electronic formats and data elements required for insurer reporting of medical data to the Division.

(x) "Healthcare Common Procedure Coding System National Level II Codes (HCPCS)" (HCPCS) means the Centers for Medicare and Medicaid Services' (CMS) reference document listing descriptive codes for billing and reporting professional services, procedures, and supplies provided by health care providers.

(y) "Health Care Provider" is defined in Section 440.13(1)(h), F.S.

(z) "Hospital" is defined in Section 395.002(13), F.S.

(aa) "ICD-9-CM International Classification of Diseases" (ICD-9) is the U.S. Department of Health and Human Services' reference document listing the official diagnosis and inpatient-procedure code sets.

(bb) "Insurer" is defined in Section 440.02(38), F.S.

(cc) "Insurer Code Number" means the number the Division assigns to each individual insurer, self-insured employer or self-insured fund.

(dd) "Itemized Statement" means a detailed listing of goods, services and supplies provided to an injured employee, including the quantity and charges for each good, service or supply.

(ee) "Medical Bill" means the document or electronic equivalent submitted by a health care provider to an insurer, service company/TPA or any entity acting on behalf of the insurer for reimbursement for services or supplies (e.g. DFS-F5-DWC-9, DFS-F5-DWC-10, DFS-F5-DWC-11, DFS-F5-DWC-90 or the provider's usual invoice or business letterhead) as appropriate pursuant to paragraph (4)(b) of this rule.

(ff) "Medically Necessary" or "Medical Necessity" is defined in Section 440.13(1)(l), F.S.

(gg) "NDC Number" means the National Drug Code (NDC) number, assigned under Section 510 of the Federal Food, Drug, and Cosmetic Act, which identifies the drug product labeler/vendor, product, and trade package size. The NDC number is an eleven-digit number that is expressed in the universal 5-4-2 format and included on all applicable reports with each of the three segments separated by a dash (-).

(hh) "Pay" or "Paid" means payment is made applying the applicable reimbursement formula to the medical bill as submitted.

(ii) "Physician" is defined in Section 440.13(1)(q), F.S.

(jj) "Principal Physician" means the treating physician responsible for the oversight of medical care, treatment and attendance rendered to an injured employee, to include recommendation for appropriate consultations or referrals.

(kk) "Report" means any form related to medical services rendered, in relation to a workers' compensation injury, that is required to be filed with the Division under this rule.

(ll) "Service Company/Third Party Administrator (TPA)" means a party that has contracted with an insurer for the purpose of providing services necessary to adjust workers' compensation claims on the insurer's behalf.

(mm) "Service Company/Third Party Administrator (TPA) Code Number" means the number the Division assigns to a service company, adjusting company, managing general agent or third party administrator.

(nn) "Submitter" means an insurer, service company/TPA, entity or any other party acting as an agent on behalf of an insurer, service company/TPA or any entity to fulfill any insurer responsibility to electronically transmit required medical data to the Division.

(oo) "UB-92, National Uniform Billing Data Element Specifications as Adopted by the Florida State Uniform Billing Committee, November 2006" (UB-92 Manual) is the reference document providing billing and reporting completion instructions for the Form DFS-F5-DWC-90 (UB-92 HCFA-1450, Uniform Bill, Rev. 1992).

(pp) "UB 04 Manual" means the National Uniform Billing Committee Official UB-04 Data Specifications Manual 2007, which is the reference document providing billing and reporting completion instructions for the Form DFS-F5-DWC-90 (UB-04 CMS-1450, Uniform Bill, Rev. 2007).

(2) Forms Incorporated by Reference for Medical Billing, Filing and Reporting.

(a) 1. Form DFS-F5-DWC-9 (CMS-1500 Health Insurance Claim Form, Rev. 12/90); Form DFS-F5-DWC-9-A (Completion Instructions for Form DFS-F5-DWC-9: comprised of three sets of completion instructions for use by health care providers, ambulatory surgical centers, and work hardening and pain management programs), Rev. 5/26/05. Effective to bill for dates of service up to and including 03/31/07.

2. Form DFS-F5-DWC-9 (CMS-1500 Health Insurance Claim Form, Rev. 08/05); Form DFS-F5-DWC-9-B (Completion Instructions for Form DFS-F5-DWC-9: comprised of three sets of completion instructions for use by health care providers, ambulatory surgical centers, and work hardening and pain management programs), Rev. 1/1/07. May be used to bill for dates of service up to and including 3/31/07 and shall be used to bill for dates of service on and after 4/1/07.

(b) 1. Form DFS-F5-DWC-10 (Statement of Charges for Drugs and Medical Supplies Form), Rev. 2/14/06. Effective to bill for dates of service up to and including 3/31/07.

2. Form DFS-F5-DWC-10 (Statement of Charges for Drugs and Medical Supplies Form), Rev. 1/1/07. May be used to bill for dates of service up to and including 3/31/07 and shall be used to bill for dates of service on and after 4/1/07.

(c) 1. Form DFS-F5-DWC-11 (American Dental Association Dental Claim Form, Rev. 2002); Form DFS-F5-DWC-11-A (Completion Instructions for Form DFS-F5-DWC-11), Rev. 5/26/05. Effective to bill for dates of service up to and including 3/31/07.

2. Form DFS-F5-DWC-11 (American Dental Association Dental Claim Form, Rev. 2006); Form DFS-F5-DWC-11-B (Completion Instructions for Form DFS-F5-DWC-11), Rev. 1/1/07. May be used to bill for dates of service up to and including 3/31/07 and shall be used to bill for dates of service on and after 4/1/07.

(d) Form DFS-F5-DWC-25 (Florida Workers' Compensation Uniform Medical Treatment/Status Reporting Form), Rev. 2/14/06.

(e) 1. Form DFS-F5-DWC-90 (UB-92 HCFA-1450, Uniform Bill, Rev. 1992). Effective for submissions up to and including 5/22/07.

2. Form DFS-F5-DWC-90 (UB-04 CMS-1450, Uniform Bill, Rev. 2006); Form DFS-F5-DWC-90-B (Completion Instructions for Form DFS-F5-DWC-90), Rev. 1/1/07. May be used to bill for submissions between 3/1/07 and 5/22/07 and shall be used to bill for submissions on and after 5/23/07.

(f) Obtaining Copies of Forms and Instructions.

1. A copy of either revision of the Form DFS-F5-DWC-9 can be obtained from the CMS web site: http://www.cms.hhs.gov/forms/. Completion instructions for either revision of the form can be obtained from the Department of Financial Services/Division of Workers' Compensation (DFS/DWC) web site: http://www.fldfs.com/WC/forms.html#7.

2. A copy of either revision of the Form DFS-F5-DWC-10 and completion instructions for either revision of the form can be obtained from the DFS/DWC web site: http://www.fldfs.com/WC/forms.html#7.

3. A copy of either revision of the Form DFS-F5-DWC-11 can be obtained from the American Dental Association web site: http://www.ada.org/. Completion instructions for either revision of the form can be obtained from the DFS/DWC web site: http://www.fldfs.com/WC/forms.html#7.

4. A copy of the Form DFS-F5-DWC-25 and completion instructions can be obtained from the DFS/DWC web site: http://www.fldfs.com/WC/forms.html#7.

5. A copy of either revision of the Form DFS-F5-DWC-90 can be obtained from the CMS web site: http://www.cms.hhs.gov/forms/. Completion instructions for Form DFS-F5-DWC-90 (Rev. 1992) can be obtained from the UB-92, National Uniform Billing Data Element Specifications as Adopted by the Florida State Uniform Billing Committee (Rev. September 2006) and subparagraph (4)(b)4. of this rule. Completion instructions for Form DFS-F5-DWC-90 (Rev. 2006), Form DFS-F5-DWC-90-B (Rev. 1/1/07), can be obtained from the DFS/DWC web site: http://www.fldfs.com/WC/forms.html#7.

(g) In lieu of submitting a Form DFS-F5-DWC-10, when billing for drugs or medical supplies, alternate billing forms are acceptable if:

1. An insurer has approved the alternate billing form(s) prior to submission by a health care provider, and

2. The form provides all information required to be submitted to the Division, pursuant to the date-applicable Florida Medical EDI Implementation Guide (MEIG), on the Form DFS-F5-DWC-10. Form DFS-F5-DWC-9, DFS-F5-DWC-11 or DFS-F5-DWC-90 shall not be submitted as an alternate form.

(3) Materials Adopted by Reference. The following publications are incorporated by reference herein:

(a) UB-92, National Uniform Billing Data Element Specifications as Adopted by the Florida State Uniform Billing Committee (Rev. September 2006). A copy of this manual can be obtained from the Florida Hospital Association by calling (407) 841-6230.

(b) The Florida Medical EDI Implementation Guide (MEIG), 2006, applicable for data submission until 7/1/07. The Florida Medical EDI Implementation Guide (MEIG), 2006 can be obtained from the DFS/DWC web site: http://www.fldfs.com/WC/edi_med.html.

(c) The American Medical Association Healthcare Common Procedure Coding System, Medicare's National Level II Codes (HCPCS), as adopted in Rule 69L-7.020, F.A.C.

(d) The Current Procedural Terminology (CPT®), as adopted in Rule 69L-7.020, F.A.C.

(e) The Current Dental Terminology (CDT-2005), as adopted in Rule 69L-7.020, F.A.C.

(f) The 2007 ICD-9-CM Professional for Hospitals, Volumes 1, 2 and 3, International Classification of Diseases, 9th Revision, Clinical Modification, Copyright 2006, Ingenix, Inc. (American Medical Association).

(g) The Physician ICD-9-CM 2007, Volumes 1 & 2, International Classification of Diseases, 9th Revision, Clinical Modification, Copyright 2006, Ingenix, Inc. (American Medical Association).

(h) The American Medical Association's Guide to the Evaluation of Permanent Impairment, as adopted in Rule 69L-7.604, F.A.C.

(i) The Minnesota Department of Labor and Industry Disability Schedule, as adopted in Rule 69L-7.604, F.A.C.

(j) The Florida Impairment Rating Guide, as adopted in Rule 69L-7.604, F.A.C.

(k) The 1996 Florida Uniform Permanent Impairment Rating Schedule, as adopted in Rule 69L-7.604, F.A.C.

(l) National Uniform Billing Committee Official UB-04 Data Specifications Manual 2007, version 1.00, September 2006, as adopted by the National Uniform Billing Committee. A copy of this manual can be obtained from the National Uniform Billing Committee web site: http://www.nubc.org/UB-04%20SUBSCRIPTION%20ORDER%20FORM.doc

(m) The Florida Medical EDI Implementation Guide (MEIG), 2007, applicable for data submission on or after 4/2/07 and required for all data submission on or after 8/9/07. The Florida Medical EDI Implementation Guide (MEIG), 2007 can be obtained from the DFS/DWC web site: http://www.fldfs.com/WC/edi_med.html.

(n) Current Procedural Terminology (CPT®), 2007 Professional Edition, Copyright 2006, American Medical Association.

(4) Health Care Provider Responsibilities.

(a) Bill Submission/Filing and Reporting Requirements.

1. All health care providers are responsible for meeting their obligations, under this rule, regardless of any business arrangement with any entity under which claims are prepared, processed or submitted to the insurer.

2. Each health care provider is responsible for submitting any additional form completion information and supporting documentation requested, in writing, by the insurer at the time of authorization or at the time a reimbursement request is received.

3. Each health care provider shall resubmit a medical claim form or medical bill with insurer requested documentation when the EOBR provides an explanation for disallowance based on the lack of documentation submitted with the medical bill.

4. Insurers and health care providers shall utilize only the Form DFS-F5-DWC-25 for physician reporting of the injured employee's medical treatment/status. Any other reporting forms may not be used in lieu of or supplemental to the Form DFS-F5-DWC-25. Provider failure to accurately complete and submit the DFS-F5-DWC-25, in accordance with the Form DFS-F5-DWC-25 Completion/Submission Instructions adopted in this rule, may result in the Agency imposing sanctions or penalties pursuant to subsection 440.13(8), F.S. or subsection 440.13(11), F.S.

a. The Form DFS-F5-DWC-25 does not replace physician notes, medical records or Division-required medical reports.

b. All information submitted on physician notes, medical records or Division-required medical reports must be consistent with information documented on the Form DFS-F5-DWC-25.

5. All medical claim form(s) or medical bill(s) related to services rendered for a compensable injury shall be submitted by a health care provider to the insurer, service company/TFA or any entity acting on behalf of the insurer, as a requirement for billing.

6. Medical claim form(s) or medical bill(s) may be electronically filed or submitted via facsimile by a health care provider to the insurer, service company/TPA or any entity acting on behalf of the insurer, provided the insurer agrees.

7. When requested by the insurer, service company/TPA or any entity acting on behalf of the insurer, a health care provider shall send documentation that supports the medical necessity of the specific services rendered and any other required documentation pursuant to paragraph (4)(b) of this rule and the applicable reimbursement manual.

8. Each health care provider is responsible for correcting and resubmitting any billing forms returned by an insurer, service company/TPA or any entity acting on behalf of the insurer pursuant to paragraph (5)(j) of this rule.

9. Each hospital and ambulatory surgical center shall maintain its charge master and shall produce relevant portions when requested for the purpose of verifying its usual charges pursuant to Section 440.13(12)(d), F.S.

(b) Special Billing Requirements.

1. When anesthesia services are billed on a Form DFS-F5-DWC-9, completion of the form must include the CPT® code and the "P" code (physical status modifier), which correspond with the procedure performed, in Field 24D. Anesthesia health care providers shall enter the date of service and the 5-digit qualifying circumstance code, which correspond with the procedure performed, in Field 24D on the next line, if applicable.

2. When an Advanced Registered Nurse Practitioner (ARNP) provides services as a Certified Registered Nurse Anesthetist, the ARNP shall bill on a Form DFS-F5-DWC-9 for the services rendered and enter his/her Florida Department of Health ARNP license number in Field 33b, regardless of the employment arrangement under which the services were rendered, or the party submitting the bill.

3. Regardless of the employment arrangement under which the services are rendered or the party submitting the bill, the following health care providers, who render direct billable services for which reimbursement is sought from an insurer, service company/TPA or any entity acting on behalf of the insurer, service company/TPA, shall bill on a Form DFS-F5-DWC-9 and enter his/her Florida Department of Health license number in Field 33b on the Form DFS-F5-DWC-9:

a. Any licensed physician; or

b. Any non-physician health care provider, including a physician assistant or an ARNP (not providing an anesthesia-related service); or

c. Any licensed non-physician health care provider who is seeking reimbursement under his or her license number issued by the Florida Department of Health.

4. For hospital billing, the following special requirements apply:

a. Inpatient billing — Hospitals shall, in addition to filing a Form DFS-F5-DWC-90:

I. Attach an itemized statement with charges based on the facility's Charge Master; and

II. Submit all applicable documentation or certification required pursuant to Rule 69L-7.501, F.A.C.; and

III. Bill professional services provided by a physician, physician assistant, advanced registered nurse practitioner, or registered nurse first assistant on the Form DFS-F5-DWC-9, regardless of employment arrangement;

IV. When entering the CPT®, HCPCS or unique workers' compensation codes in Form Locator 44 on the Form DFS-F5-DWC-90, the hospital shall utilize CPT®, HCPCS or unique workers' compensation codes provided in the Florida Workers' Compensation Health Care Provider Reimbursement Manual adopted in Rule 69L-7.501, F.A.C.

b. Outpatient billing — Hospitals shall in addition to filing a Form DFS-F5-DWC-90:

I. Enter the CPT®, HCPCS or unique workers' compensation code (provided in the Florida Workers' Compensation Health Care Provider Reimbursement Manual as incorporated for reference in Rule 69L-7.501, F.A.C.) in Form Locator 44 on the Form DFS-F5-DWC-90, to bill outpatient radiology, clinical laboratory and physical, occupational or speech therapy charges; and

II. Make written entry "scheduled" or "non-scheduled" in Form Locator 84 of Form revision 1992 and in Form Locator 80 of Form revision 2006 — 'Remarks' on the DFS-F5-DWC-90, when billing outpatient surgery or outpatient surgical services; and

III. Make written entry "implant(s)" followed by the reimbursement calculation made pursuant to Rule 69L-7.501, F.A.C., in Form Locator 84 of Form revision 1992 and in Form Locator 80 of Form revision 2006 — 'Remarks' on the DFS-F5-DWC-90, directly after entry of "scheduled" or "non-scheduled", when present;

IV. Attach an itemized statement with charges based on the facility's Charge Master if there is no line item detail shown on the Form DFS-F5-DWC-90; and

V. Submit all applicable documentation or certification required pursuant to Rule 69L-7.501, F.A.C.;

VI. Bill professional services provided by a physician, physician assistant, advanced registered nurse practitioner, or registered nurse first assistant on the Form DFS-F5-DWC-9, regardless of employment arrangement;

5. A certified, licensed physician assistant, anesthesia assistant and registered nurse first assistant who provides services as a surgical assistant, in lieu of a second physician, shall bill on a Form DFS-F5-DWC-9 entering the CPT® code(s) plus modifier(s), which represent the service(s) rendered, in Field 24D, and must enter his/her Florida Department of Health license number in Field 33b.

6. Ambulatory Surgical Centers (ASCs) shall bill on a Form DFS-F5-DWC-9 using the American Medical Association's CPT® procedure codes, or using the unique workers' compensation procedure code 99070 and billing charges based on the ASC's Charge Master except when billing for procedure code 99070. ASC medical bills shall be accompanied by all applicable documentation required pursuant to Rule 69L-7.100, F.A.C.

7. Federal Facilities shall bill on their usual form.

8. Out-of-State health care providers shall bill on the applicable medical bill form pursuant to paragraph (4)(c) of this rule.

9. Dental Services.

a. Dentists shall bill for services on a Form DFS-F5-DWC-11.

b. Oral surgeons shall bill for oral and maxillofacial surgical services on a Form DFS-F5-DWC-9. Non-surgical dental services shall be billed on a Form DFS-F5-DWC-11.

10. Pharmaceutical(s), Durable Medical Equipment and Medical Supplies.

a. When dispensing commercially available medicinal drugs commonly known as legend or prescription drugs:

I. Pharmacists shall bill on Form DFS-F5-DWC-10 and shall enter the NDC number, in the universal 5-4-2 format, in Field 9, with each segment separated by a dash (-).

II. Physicians, physician assistants or ARNPs shall bill on Form DFS-F5-DWC-9 and shall enter the NDC number, in the universal 5-4-2 format, in Field 24D, with each segment separated by a dash (-). Optionally, the unique workers' compensation code 96370 may be entered in addition to the NDC number in Field 24D.

III. Hospitals shall bill on Form DFS-F5-DWC-90 using the appropriate revenue codes.

b. When dispensing medicinal drugs which are compounded and the prescribed formulation is not commercially available:

I. Pharmacists shall bill on Form DFS-F5-DWC-10 and shall enter the unique workers' compensation code 96371 in Field 9.

II. Physicians, physician assistants or ARNPs shall bill on Form DFS-F5-DWC-9 and shall enter the unique workers' compensation code 96371 in form Field 24D.

III. Hospitals shall bill on Form DFS-F5-DWC-90 using the appropriate revenue codes.

c. When dispensing over-the-counter drug products:

I. Pharmacists shall bill on Form DFS-F5-DWC-10 and shall enter the NDC number, in the universal 5-4-2 format in form Field 9, with each segment separated by a dash (-).

II. Physicians, physician assistants or ARNPs shall bill on Form DFS-F5-DWC-9, shall enter the NDC number in the universal 5-4-2 format, in Field 24D, with each segment separated by a dash (-). The requirement to enter the NDC number in Field 24D supersedes the instruction to enter 99070 in the Florida Workers' Compensation Health Care Provider Reimbursement Manual.

III. Hospitals shall bill on Form DFS-F5-DWC-90 using the appropriate revenue codes.

d. When administering or dispensing injectable drugs:

I. Pharmacists shall bill on Form DFS-F5-DWC-10 and shall enter the NDC number, in the universal 5-4-2 format, in form Field 9, with each segment separated by a dash (-).

II. Physicians, physician assistants or ARNPs shall bill on a Form DFS-F5-DWC-9 and enter the appropriate HCPCS "J" code in form Field 24D. When an appropriate HCPCS "J" code is not available for the injectable drug, enter the NDC number, in the universal 5-4-2 format in form Field 24D with each segment separated by a dash (-).

III. Hospitals shall bill on Form DFS-F5-DWC-90 using the appropriate revenue codes.

e. When dispensing durable medical equipment (DME):

I. Pharmacists shall bill on Form DFS-F5-DWC-10 and shall enter the applicable HCPCS code in Field 21 on form revision 2/14/06 and in Field 21 on form revision 1/1/07.

II. Physicians, physician assistants or ARNPs shall bill on Form DFS-F5-DWC-9, shall enter the applicable HCPCS code in Field 24D and attach documentation indicating the actual cost of the supply, including applicable manufacturer's shipping and handling.

III. Hospitals shall bill on Form DFS-F5-DWC-90 using the applicable revenue codes.

IV. Ambulatory Surgical Centers shall bill for these products on Form DFS-F5-DWC-9 using applicable HCPCS codes.

V. Medical Suppliers shall bill on Form DFS-F5-DWC-10 and shall enter the applicable HCPCS code in form Field 21 on form revision 2/14/06 and in Field 21 on form revision 1/1/07. The requirement to enter the HCPCS code when billing for medical equipment or supplies supersedes the instruction that "the medical supplier is not required to submit codes" in the Florida Workers' Compensation Health Care Provider Reimbursement Manual.

f. When dispensing medical supplies which are not incidental to a service or procedure:

I. Pharmacists shall bill on Form DFS-F5-DWC-10 and shall enter the applicable HCPCS code in Field 16 on form revision 2/14/06 and in Field 21 on form revision 1/1/07.

II. Physicians, physician assistants or ARNPs shall bill on Form DFS-F5-DWC-9, shall enter the applicable HCPCS code in Field 24D and attach documentation indicating the actual cost of the supply, including applicable manufacturer's shipping and handling. The requirement to enter the HCPCS code when billing for medical equipment or supplies supersedes the instruction "under the specific HCPCS code or 99070" in the Florida Workers' Compensation Health Care Provider Reimbursement Manual.

III. Hospitals shall bill on Form DFS-F5-DWC-90 under the applicable revenue codes.

IV. Ambulatory Surgical Centers shall bill separately for these products on Form DFS-F5-DWC-9 and shall enter the applicable CPT® code or HCPCS in Field 24D.

V. Medical Suppliers shall bill on Form DFS-F5-DWC-10 and shall enter the applicable HCPCS code in Field 16 on form revision 2/14/06 and in Field 19 on form revision 1/1/07. The requirement to enter the HCPCS code when billing for medical equipment or supplies supersedes the instruction that "the medical supplier is not required to submit codes" in the Florida Workers' Compensation Health Care Provider Reimbursement Manual.

g. Pharmacists who provide Medication Therapy Management Services shall bill for these services on a Form DFS-F5-DWC-9 by entering the appropriate CPT® code(s) 0115T, 0116T or 0117T that represent the service(s) rendered in form Field 24D, shall enter their Florida Department of Health license number in Field 33b and shall submit a copy of the physician's written prescription with the medical bill.

h. Pharmacists and medical suppliers may only bill on an alternate to Form DFS-F5-DWC-10 when an insurer has pre-approved use of the alternate form. Forms DFS-F5-DWC-9, DFS-F5-DWC-11 or DFS-F5-DWC-90 shall not be approved for use as the alternate form.

11. Physicians billing for a failed appointment for a scheduled independent medical examination (when the injured employee does not report to the physician office as scheduled) shall bill on their invoice or letterhead. The invoice shall not be a Form DFS-F5-DWC-9, DFS-F5-DWC-10, DFS-F5-DWC-11, or DFS-F5-DWC-90.

12. Health care providers receiving reimbursement under any payment plan (pre-payment, prospective pay, capitation, etc.) must accurately complete the Form DFS-F5-DWC-9 and submit the form to the insurer.

13. Health care providers and other insurer-authorized providers rendering services reimbursable under workers' compensation, whose billing requirements are not otherwise specified in this rule (e.g. home health agencies, independent, non-hospital based ambulance services, air- ambulance, emergency medical transportation, non-emergency transportation services, translation services, etc.) shall bill on their invoice or business letterhead. These providers shall not submit the Forms DFS-F5-DWC-9, DFS-F5-DWC-10, DFS-F5-DWC-11 or DFS-F5-DWC-90 as an invoice.

(c) Bill Completion.

1. Bills shall be legibly and accurately completed by all health care providers, regardless of location or reimbursement methodology, as set forth in this section and paragraph (4)(b) of this rule.

2. Billing elements required by the Division to be completed by a health care provider are identified in specific Form DFS-F5-DWC-9-A or Form DFS-F5-DWC-9-B (completion instructions), as appropriate for the date of the revised form, available at the following websites:

a. http://www.fldfs.com/wc/pdf/DWC-9instrHCP.pdf when submitted by Licensed Health Care Providers;

b. http://www.fldfs.com/wc/pdf/DWC-9instrASC.pdf when submitted by Ambulatory Surgical Centers;

c. http://www.fldfs.com/wc/pdf/DWC-9instrWHPM.pdf when submitted by Work Hardening and Pain Management Programs.

3. Billing elements required by the Division to be completed for Pharmaceutical or Medical Supplier Billing are identified in specific Form DFS-F5-DWC-10 (completion instructions), as appropriate for the date of the revised form, available at website: http://www.fldfs.com/WC/forms.html#7.

4. Billing elements required by the Division to be completed for Dental Billing are identified in specific Form DFS-F5-DWC-11-A or Form DFS-F5-DWC-9-B (completion instructions), as appropriate for the date of the revised form, available at website: http://www.fldfs.com/WC/forms.html#7.

5. Billing elements required by the Division to be completed for Hospital Billing are identified in the UB-92 Manual, the UB-04 Manual, Form DFS-F5-DWC-90-B (completion instructions) and subparagraph (4)(b)4. of this rule.

6. An insurer can require a health care provider to complete additional data elements that are not required by the Division on Form DFS-F5-DWC-9 or DFS-F5-DWC-11.

(5) Insurer Responsibilities.

(a) An insurer is responsible for meeting its obligations under this rule regardless of any business arrangements with any service company/TPA, submitter or any entity acting on behalf of an insurer under which claims are paid, adjusted and paid, disallowed, denied, or otherwise processed or submitted to the Division.

(b) At the time of authorization for medical service(s) or at the time a reimbursement request is received, an insurer shall notify each health care provider, in writing, of additional form completion requirements or supporting documentation that are necessary for reimbursement determinations.

(c) At the time of authorization for medical service(s), an insurer shall inform in-state and out-of-state health care providers of the specific reporting, billing and submission requirements of this rule and provide the specific address for submitting a reimbursement request.

(d) Insurers, service company/TPAs or entities acting on behalf of insurers and health care providers shall utilize only the Form DFS-F5-DWC-25 for physician reporting of an injured employee's medical treatment/status. Any other reporting forms may not be used in lieu of or supplemental to the Form DFS-F5-DWC-25.

(e) Required data elements on each Form DFS-F5-DWC-9, DFS-F5-DWC-10, DFS-F5-DWC-11, and DFS-F5-DWC-90, for both medical only and lost-time cases, shall be filed with the Division within 45-calendar days of when the medical bill is paid, adjusted, disallowed or denied by the insurer, service company/TPA or any entity acting on behalf of the insurer. The 45-calendar day filing requirement includes initial submission and correction and re-submission of all errors identified in the "Medical Claim Processing Report", as defined in the date-applicable Florida Medical EDI Implementation Guide (MEIG).

(f) An insurer shall be responsible for accurately completing required data filed with the Division, pursuant to the date-applicable Florida Medical EDI Implementation Guide (MEIG) and subparagraphs (4)(c)2.-5. of this rule.

(g) When an injured employee does not have a Social Security Number or division-assigned number, the insurer must contact the Division via information provided on the following web-site:
http://www.fldfs.com/WC/organization/odqc.html (under Records Management) to obtain a division-assigned number prior to submitting the medical report to the Division.

(h) An insurer, service company/TPA or any entity acting on behalf of an insurer must report to the Division the procedure code(s), number of line-items billed, diagnosis code(s), modifier code(s) and amount(s) charged, as billed by the health care provider when reporting these data to the Division. However, the insurer, service company/TPA or any entity acting on behalf of an insurer may correct the procedure code(s) or modifier code(s) to effect payment and shall report both the provider billed code(s) and insurer adjusted code(s) pursuant to the date-appropriate MEIG. The insurer, service company/TPA or any entity acting on behalf of an insurer shall utilize the EOBR code "80" to notify the health care provider concerning any such billing errors and shall transmit EOBR code "80", in instances when the carrier corrects the provider coding, when reporting to the Division.

(i) An insurer, service company/TPA or any entity acting on behalf of the insurer shall manually or electronically date stamp accurately completed Forms DFS-F5-DWC-9, DFS-F5-DWC-10 (or insurer pre-approved alternate form), DFS-F5-DWC-11, DFS-F5-DWC-90 or the electronic form equivalent on the "date insurer received" as defined in paragraph (1)(m) of this rule.

(j) 1. When a medical bill is submitted for reimbursement by a health care provider, the insurer, service company/TPA or entity acting on behalf of the insurer must review the medical bill to determine if any of the criteria in subparagraph (5)(j)5. of this rule are present. If a medical bill meets any of the criteria listed in subparagraph (5)(j)5. of this rule, the insurer, service company/TPA or entity acting on behalf of the insurer must either:

a. Secure and/or correct the information on the medical bill and proceed to make a reimbursement decision to pay, adjust, disallow or deny billed charges within 45-calendar days from the "date insurer received"; or

b. Return the medical bill to the provider with a written statement identifying the criteria under which the medical bill is being returned within twenty-one (21) days of the "Date Insurer Received". The written statement sent to the provider with the returned medical bill shall bear the following statement CAPITALIZED and in **BOLD** print: **"A HEALTH CARE PROVIDER MAY NOT BILL THE INJURED EMPLOYEE FOR SERVICES RENDERED FOR A COMPENSABLE WORK-RELATED INJURY".**

2. If the insurer returns a medical bill to the provider pursuant to subparagraph (5)(j)5. of this rule, the written statement must include all criteria upon which the return of the medical bill are based.

3. If the criterion upon which the return of the medical bill is based includes any of the criteria in sub-subparagraphs (5)(j)5.d.-f . of this rule, the written statement must identify the information that is illegible, incorrect, or omitted.

4. An insurer may return a medical bill to a provider without issuance of an EOBR only on the basis of the criteria set forth in subparagraph (5)(j)5. of this rule.

5. The criteria upon which a medical bill is to be reviewed by the insurer, service company/TPA or entity acting on behalf of the insurer for return to the provider pursuant to this sub-paragraph of paragraph (5)(j) of this rule are:

a. Services are billed on an incorrect medical billing form; or

b. The medical bill has been submitted to the incorrect insurer; or

c. The medical bill has been submitted to the incorrect service company/TPA or entity acting on behalf of the insurer; or

d. Claimant identification information required by this rule is illegible on the medical bill; or

e. Claimant identification information required by this rule is incorrect on the medical bill; or

f. Billing information required by this rule is omitted on the medical bill.

6. An insurer, service company/TPA or entity acting on behalf of the insurer shall establish and maintain a process by which medical bills that have been returned and written statements identifying the reason for return are compiled. The compiled information must be sufficiently detailed to allow verification and review by the Division.

(k) An insurer, service company/TPA or any entity acting on behalf of the insurer shall pay, adjust, disallow or deny billed charges within 45-calendar days from the date insurer received, pursuant to Section 440.20(2)(b), F.S.

(l) In the medical bill claims-handling process, the receipt of medical bills may be based upon receipt by the insurer or there may be an "entity" acting on behalf of an insurer for purposes of receipt of medical bills. Likewise, the payment of medical bills may be based upon payment by the insurer or there may be an "entity" acting on behalf of an insurer for purposes of payment of medical bills. Therefore, to properly reflect receipt date and payment date of medical bills, the medical bill reporting process must accommodate various receipt and payment options.

1. The receipt and payment option utilized by an insurer and reported to the Division must meet one of the following:

a. Both receipt and payment of medical bills are handled by the insurer. This option may be utilized only when the "date insurer received" is the date the insurer gained possession of the health care provider's medical bill, and the "date insurer paid" is the date the health care provider's payment is mailed, transferred or electronically transmitted by the insurer. This option may not be utilized when a health care provider is required by the insurer to submit medical billings to any "entity" other than the insurer.

b. Both receipt and payment of medical bills are handled by any "entity" acting on behalf of the insurer. This option may be utilized only when the "date insurer received" is the date the "entity" acting on behalf of the insurer gained possession of the health care provider's medical bill, and the "date insurer paid" is the date the health care provider's payment is mailed, transferred or electronically transmitted by the "entity" acting on behalf of the insurer. This option may not be utilized when a health care provider is required by the insurer to submit medical billings directly to the insurer.

c. Receipt of medical bills is handled by the insurer and payment of medical bills is handled by the "entity" acting on behalf of the insurer. This option may be utilized only when the "date insurer received" is the date the insurer gained possession of the health care provider's medical bill, and the "date insurer paid" is the date the health care provider's payment is mailed, transferred or electronically transmitted by the "entity" acting on behalf of the insurer. This option may not be utilized when a health care provider is required by the insurer to submit medical billings to any "entity" other than the insurer.

d. Receipt of medical bills is handled by any "entity" acting on behalf of the insurer and payment of medical bills is handled by the insurer. This option may be utilized only when the "date insurer received" is the date the "entity" acting on behalf of the insurer gained possession of the health care provider's medical bill, and the "date insurer paid" is the date the health care provider's payment is mailed, transferred or electronically transmitted by the insurer. This option may not be utilized when a health care provider is required by the insurer to submit medical billings directly to the insurer.

2. The insurer must:

a. Document the option(s) selected in subparagraph (5)(l)1. of this rule,

b. Document the specific effective date for each option selected,

c. Document the specific role of each "entity" acting on the insurers behalf in the option selected,

d. Make this written documentation available to the Division for audit purposes pursuant to Section 440.525, F.S.,

e. Maintain written documentation from the "entity" acknowledging its responsibilities concerning "date insurer received" and "date insurer paid" for each option when the insurer selects options b., c., or d. from subparagraph (5)(l)1. of this rule, and

f. Maintain written documentation identifying the applicability of the options selected in sufficient detail to allow verification of the coding of each medical bill under subparagraph (5)(l)4. of this rule.

3. An insurer and entity may select multiple options for medical bill claims handling between the insurer and the entity based on business practices or whether medical bills are submitted to the insurer electronically or on paper.

4. The option in subparagraph (5)(l)1. of this rule selected by the insurer must be identified on each medical report electronic submission to the Division and must utilize the following coding methodology:

a. If the "date insurer received" is the date the insurer gains possession of the health care provider's medical bill and the "date insurer paid" is the date the health care provider's payment is mailed, transferred or electronically transmitted by the insurer, then Payment Code "x" 1 must be transmitted on each individual form-type electronic submission. ("x" must equal 'R', 'M' or 'C' as denoted in Appendix D of the date-appropriate Florida Medical Implementation EDI Guide (MEIG).) When submitting Payment Code "x" 1 to the Division, the insurer is declaring that no "entity" as defined in paragraph (1)(u) of this rule is involved in the medical bill claims-handling processes related to "date insurer received" or "date insurer paid".

b. If the "date insurer received" is the date the "entity" acting on behalf of the insurer gains possession of the health care provider's medical bill and the "date insurer paid" is the date the health care provider's payment is mailed, transferred or electronically transmitted by the "entity" acting on behalf of the insurer, then Payment Code "x" 2 must be transmitted on each individual form-type electronic submission. ("x" must equal 'R', 'M' or 'C' as denoted in Appendix D of the date-appropriate Florida Medical Implementation EDI Guide (MEIG).) When submitting Payment Code "x" 2 to the Division, the insurer is declaring that the specified "entity" as defined in paragraph (1)(u) of this rule is acting on behalf of the insurer for purposes of the medical bill claims-handling processes related to "date insurer received" and "date insurer paid".

c. If the "date insurer received" is the date the insurer gains possession of the health care provider's medical bill and "date insurer paid" is the date the health care provider's payment is mailed, transferred or electronically transmitted by the "entity" acting on behalf of the insurer, then Payment Code "x" 3 must be transmitted on each individual form-type electronic submission. ("x" must equal 'R', 'M' or 'C' as denoted in Appendix D of the date-appropriate Florida Medical Implementation EDI Guide (MEIG).) When submitting Payment Code "x" 3 to the Division, the insurer is declaring that no "entity" as defined in paragraph (1)(u) of this rule is involved in the medical bill claims-handling process related to "date insurer received".

d. If the "date insurer received" is the date the "entity" acting on behalf of the insurer gains possession of the health care provider's medical bill and the "date insurer paid" is the date the health care provider's payment is mailed, transferred or electronically transmitted by the insurer, then Payment Code "x" 4 must be transmitted on each individual form-type electronic submission. ("x" must equal 'R', 'M' or 'C' as denoted in Appendix D of the date-appropriate Florida Medical Implementation EDI Guide (MEIG).) When submitting Payment Code "x" 4 to the Division, the insurer is declaring that no "entity" as defined in paragraph (1)(u) is involved in the medical bill claims-handling processes related to "date insurer paid".

(m) An insurer, service company/TPA or any entity acting on behalf of the insurer, when reporting paid medical claims data to the Division, shall report the dollar amount paid by the insurer or reimbursed to the employee, the employer or other insurer for healthcare service(s) or supply(ies). When reporting disallowed or denied charges, the dollar amount paid shall be reported as $0.00.

(n) An insurer, service company/TPA or any entity acting on behalf of the insurer is not required to report electronically as medical payment data to the Division, those payments made for failed appointments for scheduled independent medical examinations, for federal facilities billing on their usual form or for health care providers in subparagraph (4)(b)13. who bill on their invoice or letterhead.

(o) A submitter, filing electronically, shall submit to the Division the Explanation of Bill Review (EOBR) code(s), relating to the adjudication of each line item billed and:

1. Maintain the EOBR in a format that can be legibly reproduced, and

2. Use the EOBR codes and code descriptors as follows up through the date for reporting production data with the Medical Data System in the Claim Record Layout-Revision "D" as required in subparagraph (6)(f) of this rule:

a. 01 Services not authorized, as required.

b. 02 Services denied as not related to the compensable work injury.

c. 03 Services related to a denied work injury: Form DFS-F2-DWC-12 on file with the Division.

d. 04 Services billed are listed as not covered or non-covered ("NC") in the applicable reimbursement manual.

e. 05 Documentation does not support the level, intensity, frequency, duration or provision of service(s) billed. (Insurer must specify to the health care provider.)

f. 06 Location of service(s) is not consistent with the level of service(s) billed.

g. 07 Reimbursement equals the amount billed.

h. 08 Reimbursement is based on the applicable reimbursement fee schedule.

i. 09 Reimbursement is based on any contract.

j. 10 Reimbursement is based on charges exceeding the stop-loss point.

k. 11 Reimbursement is based on insurer re-coding. (Insurer must specify to the health care provider.)

l. 12 Charge(s) are included in the per diem reimbursement.

m. 13 Reimbursement is included in the allowance of another service. (Insurer must specify procedure to the health care provider.)

n. 14 Itemized statement not submitted with billing form.

o. 15 Invalid code. (Use only when other valid codes are present.)

p. 16 Documentation does not support that services rendered were medically necessary.

q. 17 Required supplemental documentation not filed with the bill. (Insurer must specify required documentation to the health care provider.)

r. 18 Duplicate Billing: Service previously paid, adjusted and paid, disallowed or denied on prior claim form or multiple billing of service(s) billed on same date of service.

s. 19 Required Form DFS-F5-DWC-25 not submitted within three business days of the first treatment pursuant to Section 440.13(4)(a), F.S.

t. 20 Other: Unique EOBR code descriptor. Use of EOBR code "20" is restricted to circumstances when an above-listed EOBR code does not explain the reason for payment, adjustment and payment, disallowance or denial of payment. When using EOBR code "20", an insurer must reflect code "20" and include the specific explanation of the code on the EOBR sent to the health care provider. The insurer, service company/TPA or any entity acting on behalf of the insurer must maintain a standardized EOBR code descriptor list.

3. When reporting production data with the Medical Data System in the Claim Record Layout-Revision "D" as required in subparagraph (6)(f) of this rule, the insurer shall comply with the following instructions pertaining to EOBRs: In completing an Explanation of Bill Review (EOBR) an insurer shall, for each line item billed, select the EOBR code(s) from the list below which identifies(y) the reason(s) for the insurer's reimbursement decision for each line item. The insurer may utilize up to three EOBR codes for each line item billed. When utilizing more than one EOBR, the insurer shall list the EOBR codes that describe the basis for its reimbursement decision in descending order of importance. An insurer, service company/TPA or any entity acting on behalf of the insurer shall submit to the Division the Explanation of Bill Review (EOBR) code, relating to the adjudication of each line item billed, in descending order of importance.

The EOBR code list is as follows:

10 — Payment denied: compensability: injury or illness for which service was rendered is not compensable.

21 — Payment disallowed: medical necessity: medical records reflect no physician's order was given for service rendered or supply provided.

22 — Payment disallowed: medical necessity: medical records reflect no physician's prescription was given for service rendered or supply provided.

23 — Payment disallowed: medical necessity: diagnosis does not support the service rendered.

24 — Payment disallowed: medical necessity: service rendered was not therapeutically appropriate.

25 — Payment disallowed: medical necessity: service rendered was experimental, investigative or research in nature.

26 — Payment disallowed: service rendered by healthcare practitioner outside scope of practitioner's licensure.

30 — Payment disallowed: lack of authorization: no authorization given for service rendered.

40 — Payment disallowed: insufficient documentation: documentation does not substantiate the service billed was rendered.

41 — Payment disallowed: insufficient documentation: level of evaluation and management service not supported by documentation.

42 — Payment disallowed: insufficient documentation: intensity of physical medicine and rehabilitation service not supported by documentation.

43 — Payment disallowed: insufficient documentation: frequency of service not supported by documentation.

44 — Payment disallowed: insufficient documentation: duration of service not supported by documentation.

45 — Payment disallowed: insufficient documentation: fraud statement not provided pursuant to Section 440.105(7), F.S.

46 — Payment disallowed: insufficient documentation: required itemized statement not submitted with the medical bill.

47 — Payment disallowed: insufficient documentation: invoice not submitted for implant.

48 — Payment disallowed: insufficient documentation: invoice not submitted for supplies.

49 — Payment disallowed: insufficient documentation: invoice not submitted for medication.

50 — Payment disallowed: insufficient documentation: requested documentation not submitted with the medical bill.

51 — Payment disallowed: insufficient documentation: required DFS-F5-DWC-25 not submitted.

52 — Payment disallowed: insufficient documentation: supply(ies) incidental to the procedure.

53 — Payment disallowed: insufficient documentation: required operative report not submitted with the medical bill.

54 — Payment disallowed: insufficient documentation: required narrative report not submitted with the medical bill.

60 — Payment disallowed: billing error: service previously billed and processed on prior medical bill.

61 — Payment disallowed: billing error: same service billed multiple times on same date of service.

62 — Payment disallowed: billing error: incorrect procedure, modifier or supply code.

63 — Payment disallowed: billing error: service billed is integral component of another procedure code.

64 — Payment disallowed: billing error: service "not covered" under applicable workers' compensation reimbursement manual.

65 — Payment disallowed: billing error: multiple providers billed on the same form.

71 — Payment adjusted: insufficient documentation: level of evaluation and management service not supported by documentation.

72 — Payment adjusted: insufficient documentation: intensity of physical medicine and rehabilitation service not supported by documentation.

73 — Payment adjusted: insufficient documentation: frequency of service not supported by documentation.

74 — Payment adjusted: insufficient documentation: duration of service not supported by documentation.

75 — Payment adjusted: insufficient documentation: requested documentation not submitted with the medical bill.

80 — Payment adjusted: billing error: cor-

rection of procedure, modifier or supply code.

81 — Payment adjusted: billing error: payment modified pursuant to a charge audit.

82 — Payment adjusted: payment modified pursuant to carrier charge analysis.

83 — Payment adjusted: medical benefits paid apportioning out the percentage of the need for such care attributable to preexisting condition (Section 440.15(5)(b), F.S.).

84 — Payment adjusted: co-payment applied pursuant to Section 440.13(14)(c), F.S.

90 — Paid: no modification to the information provided on the medical bill: payment made pursuant to Florida Workers' Compensation Health Care Provider Reimbursement Manual.

91 — Paid: no modification to the information provided on the medical bill: payment made pursuant to Florida Workers' Compensation Reimbursement Manual for Ambulatory Surgical Centers.

92 — Paid: no modification to the information provided on the medical bill: payment made pursuant to Florida Workers' Compensation Reimbursement Manual for Hospitals.

93 — Paid: no modification to the information provided on the medical bill: payment made pursuant to contractual arrangement.

94 — Paid: Out-of-State Provider: payment made pursuant to the Out-of-State Provider section of the applicable Florida reimbursement manual.

95 — Paid: Reimbursement Dispute Resolution: payment made pursuant to receipt of a Determination or Final Order on a Petition for Resolution of Reimbursement Dispute, pursuant to Section 440.13(7), F.S.

(p) An insurer, service company/TPA, submitter or any entity acting on behalf of the insurer shall make available to the Division and to the Agency, upon request and without charge, a legibly reproduced copy of the electronic form equivalents or Forms DFS-F5-DWC-9, DFS-F5-DWC-10 (or insurer pre-approved alternate form), DFS-F5-DWC-11, DFS-F5-DWC-25, DFS-F5-DWC-90, supplemental documentation, proof of payment, EOBR and the insurer written documentation required in subparagraphs (5)(j)6. and (5)(l)2. of this rule.

(q) An insurer, service company/TPA or any entity acting on behalf of the insurer to pay, adjust, disallow or deny a filed bill shall submit to the health care provider an Explanation of Bill Review, utilizing the EOBR codes and code descriptors, as set forth in paragraph (o) of this section, and shall include the insurer name and specific insurer contact information. An insurer, service company/TPA or any entity acting on behalf of the insurer shall notify the health care provider of notice of payment or notice of adjustment, disallowance or denial only through an EOBR. An EOBR shall specifically state that the EOBR constitutes notice of disallowance or adjustment of payment within the meaning of Section 440.13(7), F.S. An EOBR shall specifically identify the name and mailing address of the entity the carrier designates to receive service on behalf of the "carrier and all affected parties" for the purpose of receiving the petitioner's service of a copy of a petition for reimbursement dispute resolution by certified mail, pursuant to Section 440.13(7)(a), F.S.

(r) Copies of hospital medical records shall be subject to charges allowed pursuant to Section 395.3025, F.S. and Section 440.13, F.S.

(s) When an insurer, service company/TPA or any entity acting on behalf of the insurer renders reimbursement as pre-payment for medical services, goods or supplies, reimbursement of employee payment or payment for pharmacy first-fill services, the required data elements, optionally including the appropriate Pre-Payment/Employee Payment/First Fill Indicator as described in the MEIG, shall be submitted to the Division within 45 calendar days of the insurer, service company/TPA or any entity acting on behalf of the insurer receipt date of the medical billing form, regardless of the date of payment.

(t) When an insurer, service company/TPA or any entity acting on behalf of the insurer renders reimbursement following receipt of a Determination or Final Order in response to a petition to resolve a reimbursement dispute filed pursuant to Section 440.13(7), F.S., the insurer shall:

1. Submit the required data elements to the Division within 45 calendar days of rendering reimbursement; and

2. Submit the data as a replacement submission pursuant to the date-appropriate MEIG; and

3. Submit the cumulative, not the supplemental, payment information at the line-item level utilizing EOBR 95 for each line-item reflecting a payment amount differing from the payment amount reported on the original submission; and

4. Report the "date insurer received" as 22 days after the date the Determination was received by certified mail, in instances where the insurer has waived its rights under Section 120, F.S., or report the "date insurer received" as the date the carrier received the Final Order by certified mail, in instances where the insurer has invoked its rights pursuant to Section 120, F.S., whichever occurs first.

(u) When an insurer, service company/TPA, submitter or any entity acting on behalf of the insurer has reported medical claims data to the Division which was not required, the insurer shall withdraw the previously reported data as described in the MEIG.

(v) When an insurer, service company/TPA, any entity acting on behalf of the insurer renders reimbursement for multiple bills received from a health care provider, the insurer shall report required data elements to the Division for each individual bill, including "date insurer received" and "date insurer paid", submitted by the health care provider and shall not combine multiple bills received from a health care provider into a single medical bill data submission (i.e. a single bill equals a single datum transmission).

(6) Insurer Electronic Medical Report Filing to the Division.

(a) Effective 3/16/05, all required medical reports shall be electronically filed with the Division by all insurers.

(b) Required data elements shall be submitted in compliance with the instructions and formats as set forth in the date-appropriate Florida Medical EDI Implementation Guide (MEIG).

(c) The Division will notify the insurer on the "Medical Claim Processing Report" of the corrections necessary for rejected medical reports to be electronically re-filed with the Division. An insurer shall correct and re-file all rejected medical claim reports to meet the filing requirements of paragraph (5)(e) of this rule.

(d) Submitters who experience a catastrophic event resulting in the insurer's failure to meet the reporting requirements in paragraph (5)(e) of this rule, shall submit a written or electronic request within 15 business days after the catastrophic event to the Division for approval to submit in an alternative reporting method and an alternative filing timeline. The request shall contain a detailed explanation of the nature of the event, date of occurrence, and measures being taken to resume electronic submission. The request shall also provide an estimated date by which electronic submission of affected EDI filings will be resumed. Approval must be obtained from the Division's Office of Data Quality and Collection, 200 East Gaines Street, Tallahassee, Florida 32399-4226. Approval to submit in an alternative reporting method and an alternative filing timeline shall be granted by the Division if a catastrophic event prevents electronic submission.

(e) When filing any medical report that corrects a rejected medical bill or replaces a previously accepted medical bill, the submitter shall use the same control number as the original submission. The replacement submission shall contain all information necessary to process the medical bill including all services and charges from the claim as billed by the health care provider and all payments made by the insurer to the health care provider. Information contained on the original submission is deemed independent and is not considered as a supplement to information contained in the replacement submission.

(f) Additionally, an insurer shall be responsible for accurately completing the electronic record-layout programming requirements for the reporting of the Form DFS-F5-DWC-9 Claim Detail Record Layout — Revision "D", Form DFS-F5-DWC-10 Claim Detail Record Layout — Revision "D", Form DFS-F5-DWC-11 Claim Detail Record Layout — Revision "D" and Form DFS-F5-DWC-90 Claim Detail Record Layout — Revision "D" in accordance with the Florida Medical EDI Implementation Guide (MEIG), 2007, to the Division in accordance with the phase-in schedule as denoted below in subparagraphs 1., 2., and 3. of this section. The electronic record layout for Form DFS-F5-DWC-9 in the MEIG, 2007, adds the new fields for gender, date of birth, up to three new modifiers and a maximum of three EOBR codes per line item from the revised code set. The electronic record layout for Form DFS-F5-DWC-10 in the MEIG, 2007, adds the new fields for gender, date of birth, pharmacist's Florida Department of Health license number, and, medical supply and equipment HCPCS code(s), quantity, purchase or rental date, usual charge, amount paid, prescriber's license number and a maximum of three EOBR codes per line item from the revised code set. The electronic record layout for Form DFS-F5-DWC-11 in the MEIG, 2007, adds the new fields for gender, date of birth and a maximum of three EOBR codes per line item from the revised code set. The electronic record layout for Form DFS-F5-DWC-90 in the MEIG, 2007, adds the new form locators for gender, date of birth, designation of surgery as scheduled or unscheduled, implant amount, up to three External Cause of Injury codes, four additional ICD-9 diagnostic codes, four other procedure codes, operating physician's Florida DOH license number and a maximum of three EOBR codes per line item from the revised code set. The conversion implementation schedule is as follows:

1. Submitters who have been approved for reporting production data with the Medical Data System (Record Layout — Revision "C"), between 12/5/05 and 2/24/06 shall begin testing on 4/2/07 and shall complete the testing process with the new Revision "D" record layouts no later than 5/14/07.

2. Submitters who have been approved for reporting production data with the Medical Data System (Record Layout — Revision "C"), between 2/25/06 and 3/31/06 shall begin testing on 5/15/07 and shall complete the testing process with the new Revision "D" record layouts no later than 6/26/07.

3. Submitters who have been approved for reporting production data with the Medical Data System (Record Layout — Revision "C"), between 4/1/06 and the effective date of this rule shall begin testing on 6/27/07 and shall complete the testing process with the new Revision "D" record layouts no later than 8/8/07.

4. The Division will, resources permitting, allow submitters that volunteer to complete the test transmission processes earlier than the schedule denoted above. Each voluntary submitter shall have six weeks to complete test transmission to production transmission processes, for all electronic form equivalents, that comply with requirements set forth in the Florida Workers' Compensation Medical EDI Implementation Guide (MEIG), 2007.

(g) All submitters shall be in production with the new Revision "D" record layouts on 8/9/07. Optionally, after successful completion of the testing process and continuing up to and including 8/8/07, submitters may elect to submit all required medical reports as required in the new Revision "D" record layouts, as required in the current Revision "C" record layouts, or, as required in the Revision "C" record layouts for billings on the current medical claim forms and as required in the Revision "D" record layouts for billings on the new medical claim forms.

(h) Submitters who do not accurately complete and maintain electronic record-layout programming requirements of this rule shall not submit medical reports electronically until the submitter has been approved for reporting production data with the Medical Data System as necessary to meet the filing requirements of paragraph (5)(e) of this rule.

(7) Insurer Administrative Penalties and Administrative Fines for Untimely Health Care Provider-Payment or Disposition of Medical Bills.

(a) The Department shall impose insurer administrative penalties for failure to comply with the payment, adjustment, disallowance or denial requirements pursuant to Section 440.20(6)(b), F.S. Timely performance standards for timely payments, adjustments and payments, disallowances or denials, reported on Forms DFS-F5-DWC-9, DFS-F5-DWC-10, DFS-F5-DWC-11 and DFS-F5-DWC-90, shall be calculated and applied on a monthly basis for each separate form category that was received within a specific calendar month.

(b) Pursuant to Section 440.185(9), F.S., the Department shall impose insurer administrative fines for failure to comply with the submission, filing or reporting requirements of this rule. Insurer administrative fines shall be applied as follows:

1. Calculated on a monthly basis for each separate form category (Forms DFS-F5-DWC-9, DFS-F5-DWC-10, DFS-F5-DWC-11 and DFS-F5-DWC-90) received and accepted by the Division within a specific calendar month; and

2. Insurers are required to report all medical reports timely pursuant to paragraph (5)(e) of this rule. Insurers that fail to submit a minimum of 95% of all medical reports timely are subject to an administrative fine. Each untimely filed medical report which falls below the 95% requirement is subject to the following penalty schedule:

a. 1 - 30 calendar days late $5.00;

b. 31 - 60 calendar days late $10.00;

c. 61 - 90 calendar days late $25.00;

d. 91 or greater calendar days late $100.00.

3. Each medical report that does not pass the electronic reporting edits shall be rejected by the Division and considered not filed pursuant to paragraph (5)(e) of this rule. If the medical report remains rejected and not corrected, resubmitted and accepted by the Division for greater than 90 days, an administrative fine shall be assessed in the amount of $100.00 for each such medical report. Rejected and not resubmitted medical reports will not be included in the 95% timely reporting requirement.

4. Untimely filed medical reports for a given month will be excluded from the administrative fine set forth in subparagraph (7)(b)3. above as falling within the performance standard between 100% and 95% in the following order:

a. Medical Reports filed 1 - 30 calendar days late; then

b. Medical Reports filed 31 - 60 calendar days late; then

c. Medical Reports filed 61 - 90 calendar days late; then

d. Medical Reports filed 91+ calendar days late.

Specific Authority 440.13(4), 440.15(3)(b), (d), 440.185(5), 440.525(2), 440.591, 440.593(5) Fla. Stat.

Law Implemented 440.09, 440.13(2)(a), (3), (4), (6), (11), (2), (14), (16), 440.15(3)(b), (d), 440.185(5), (9), 440.20(6), 440.525(2), 440.593 Fla. Stat.

History: New 1-23-95, Formerly 38F-7.602, 4L-7.602, Amended 7-4-04, 10-20-05, 6-25-06, 3-8-07.

69L-7.603. Reporting Maximum Medical Improvement and Permanent Impairment.

Specific Authority 440.15(3)(a)4., 440.185, 440.591 Fla. Stat.

Law Implemented 440.15(2), (3) Fla. Stat.

History: New 8-22-95, Amended 1-6-97, Formerly 38F-7.603, 4L-7.603, Repealed 12-4-2005.

69L-7.604. Permanent Impairment.

(1) Determination of Physical Impairment Rating.The American Medical Association's Guide to the Evaluation of Permanent Impairment, 3rd Edition, (AMA Guide) (Copyright 1988 by the American Medical Association) is adopted as the schedule for determining the existence and degree of permanent impairment

for all injuries prior to July 1, 1990. For injuries occurring on or after July 1, 1990, but before the effective date of the Florida Impairment Rating Guide, the Minnesota Department of Labor and Industry Disability Schedule shall be used unless that schedule does not address an injury, in which case, the AMA Guide shall be used. For injuries occurring on or after its effective date, the Florida Impairment Rating Guide, which is adopted by reference as part of this rule, shall be used. The Florida Impairment Rating Guide shall also be known as the Florida Impairment Rating Schedule, which is the "uniform permanent impairment rating schedule" and the "uniform disability rating schedule" referenced in Section 440.15 (3)(a)2., Florida Statutes. The impairment rating must always be applied to the body as a whole.

(2) The 1996 Florida Uniform Permanent Impairment Rating Schedule is incorporated into this rule by reference and shall be used for injuries occurring on or after its effective date.

Specific Authority 440.15(3), 440.591 Fla. Stat.

Law Implemented 440.15(3), 440.185, 440.20 Fla. Stat.

History: New 10-30-79, Amended 11-5-81, 6-23-82, 6-12-84, Formerly 38F-3.17, Amended 4-11-90, 1-30-91, 6-21-93, 11-8-94, 6-15-95, 1-8-97, Formerly 38F-3.017, Formerly 38F-7.604, 4L-7.604.

CHAPTER 69L-9 Drug Testing Rule

69L-9.015. Drug Testing Criteria.

Chapter 59A-24, Florida Administrative Code, Drug-Free Workplace Standards, as adopted by the Agency for Health Care Administration, is hereby incorporated herein by reference, and shall be utilized for all drug testing pursuant to Chapter 440, Florida Statutes.

Specific Authority 440.09(7), 440.101, 440.102(10) Fla. Stat.

Law Implemented 440.09(7), 440.101, 440.102, 627.0915 Fla. Stat.

History: New 4-30-96, Formerly 38F-9.015, 4L-9.015.

CHAPTER 69L-10 Claim for Reimbursement Against the Special Disability Trust Fund

69L-10.006. Definitions.

(1) Claimant—an insurance carrier, self-insurance fund, or employer seeking reimbursement from the SDTF.

(2) Representative —a person representing a claimant such as an attorney or a service organization.

(3) Notice of Claim —The document[s] submitted by a claimant that places the SDTF on notice of the claim.

(4) Proof of Claim —The document[s] submitted by a claimant that includes a completely filled out DES Form SDF-1 (rev. 12/91) with all required documents attached to fully support the claim.

Specific Authority 440.49(2), 440.591 Fla. Stat.

Law Implemented 440.49 Fla. Stat.

History: New 4-19-92, Amended 8-18-93, Formerly 38F-10.006, 4L-10.006.

69L-10.0065. Filing; Facsimile Transmissions.

(1) All claims, notices, legal documents, forms, affidavits, reimbursement requests, and documentation shall be submitted by mail or in person at the Tallahassee office of the SDTF. The filing date shall be the date received.

(2) Documentation which is requested by the SDTF subsequent to receipt of the notice of claim and proof of claim may be submitted by facsimile transmission, provided there is a prior agreement between the sender and the SDTF regarding such specific transmission. The Fund will make the determination based on the urgency and volume of the transmission. All such facsimile transmissions shall be completed between the hours of 8:00 am and 5:00 pm EST or EDT.

(3) Any document which is required to be submitted by mail or in person may not be submitted by facsimile transmission and will not be accepted or effective until proper service is completed as set out in subsection (1).

Specific Authority 440.49(2)(g), 440.591 Fla. Stat.

Law Implemented 440.49(2) Fla. Stat.

History: New 8-18-93, Formerly 38F-10.0065, 4L-10.065.

69L-10.007. Notice of Claim.

A Notice Of Claim for reimbursement from the SDTF shall be filed with the SDTF, Division of Workers' Compensaion, 200 East Gaines Street, Tallahassee, FL, 32399-4223. The Notice Of Claim may be filed by letter form and shall include the following:

(1) Name and social security number of the employee;

(2) The name and address of the employer;

(3) The date of the accident;

(4) The name and address of the insurance carrier, self-insurance fund or employer on whose behalf the claim is made.

Specific Authority 440.49(2)(g) Fla. Stat.

Law Implemented 440.49(2) Fla. Stat.

History: New 4-19-92, Amended 8-18-93, Formerly 38F-10.007, 4L-10.007.

69L-10.009. Claimant's Representatives.

A Notice of Claim shall be filed by a claimant or its representative. Once a claimant is represented before the SDTF by an attorney or other representative, and then a substitute representative is employed by the claimant, the substitute representative must file, in letter form, a substitution of representation, with notice to the former representative.

Specific Authority 440.49(2)(g) Fla. Stat.

Law Implemented 440.49(2) Fla. Stat.

History: New 4-19-92, Formerly 38F-10.009, 4L-10.009.

69L-10.011. Informed Conclusion of Pre-Existing Conditions for Proof of Claim.

(1) Statements submitted to meet the proof requirement of this rule section and Section 440.49 (2)(f), F.S., shall be by deposition, as authorized by section 440.30, F.S., or by an original affidavit.

(2) Except as provided in Section 440.49 (2)(f), F.S., the claimant shall submit the sworn statement of the employer showing that the employer had reached an informed conclusion prior to the occurrence of the subsequent injury or occupational disease that the employee's pre-existing condition was permanent and was, or was likely to be, a hindrance or obstacle to employment. The employer's statement must fully explain the factual conditions under which the informed conclusion was made and further fully explain how the employer believed the pre-existing permanent condition was, or was likely to be, a hindrance or an obstacle to employment. The claimant shall support this statement with appropriate documentation, when possible.

(3) For those conditions or instances specified in Section 440.49 (2)(f), F.S., giving rise to the conclusive presumption, the claimant shall submit the sworn statement of the employer showing that the employer had knowledge of the condition prior to the occurrence of the subsequent injury or occupational disease. The claimant shall support this statement with all available documentation.

(4) Affidavits filed pursuant to this section shall include the following statement: "Under penalty of perjury, I declare that I have read the foregoing; that the facts as alleged are true, to the best of my knowledge and belief; and that a representative of the Special Disability Trust Fund is authorized to contact me to confirm the truthfulness of this statement." The affidavit will also include the address and telephone number of the affiant. This requirement shall apply to affidavits or depositions taken after July 19, 1992. Before any contact is made with any person who has made a sworn knowledge statement by affidavit or deposition, the SDTF shall first provide notice to the claimant's counsel of record that contact is desired.

Specific Authority 440.30, 440.49(2)(f), 440.591 Fla. Stat.

Law Implemented 440.49(2), 440.30 Fla. Stat

History: New 4-19-92, Amended 8-18-93, Formerly 38F-10.011, 4L-10.011.

69L-10.012. Review of Proof of Claim.

The SDTF will not consider a claim ripe, or mature, for review purposes, until a Proof of Claim is filed complete with all the necessary documents required by DES Form SDF-1 (Rev. 12/91). If a Proof of Claim is placed in line for review and it is discovered that certain documents or required information have not been provided by the claimant, the SDTF will advise the claimant in writing of the incomplete claim and will not review the claim until the missing information or document has been supplied by the claimant.

Specific Authority 440.49(2)(g) Fla. Stat.

Law Implemented 440.49(2) Fla. Stat.

History: New 4-19-92, Formerly 38F-10.012, 4L-10.012.

69L-10.013. Acknowledgements by SDTF.

The SDTF will only acknowledge in writing the filing of a Notice of Claim and a Proof of Claim. Any claimant who wishes the SDTF to acknowledge other documents must provide a self-addressed, stamped envelope and a copy of the document for acknowledgement.

Specific Authority 440.49(2)(g) Fla. Stat.

Law Implemented 440.49(2) Fla. Stat.

History: New 4-19-92, Formerly 38F-10.013, 4L-10.013.

69L-10.014. Procedure for Accepting an Offer of Reimbursement.

Acceptance of an offer of reimbursement by the Fund must be in writing and will be considered as acquiescing to all terms specified in the offer without modification.

Specific Authority 440.49(2)(g) Fla. Stat.

Law Implemented 440.49(2) Fla. Stat.

History: New 4-19-92, Formerly 38F-10.014, 4L-10.014.

69L-10.015. Deemed Denial—120 Day Time Period.

The 120 days that the SDTF has to accept a claim after it has been filed begins to run at the time the SDTF receives a fully completed Proof of Claim on DES Form SDF-1 (Rev. 12/91). Upon receipt of said form the SDTF shall notify the claimant within twenty-one (21) days of receipt that said form is complete and contains the required documents. If the form is complete the 120 days begins to run. If it is not complete and the SDTF notifies the claimant within the twenty-one (21) day period, then the 120 days from notice of claim does not begin to run until the claimant submits all the required documents necessary to support the claim.

Specific Authority 440.49(2)(g) Fla. Stat.

Law Implemented 440.49(2) Fla. Stat.

History: New 4-19-92, Formerly 38F-10.015, 4L-10.015.

69L-10.016. Documenting Expenditures for Purposes of Obtaining Reimbursement.

In order to obtain reimbursement after an offer of reimbursement has been extended by the Fund, an employer/carrier shall file with the Fund a Form SDF-2, as adopted in Rule 69L-10.019, F.A.C., with supporting schedules and documentation of expenditures as set forth below.

(1) Expenditures For Medical Benefits.Expenditures for medical benefits must be documented by the submission of applicable Division forms, as adopted in Rule 69L-3.025, F.A.C., showing compliance with the fee schedules adopted in Rule 69L-7.020, F.A.C., and applicable utilization review procedures such as medical bills marked "paid" or an EOB that was completed contemporaneously with the processing of the medical payments together with corroborating documentation of amount paid (e.g., computer printouts, ledger sheets, or copies of checks). The EOB shall be in the format prescribed by the Fund in DES form SDF-6, REV. 8/98, which form is hereby adopted by reference. DES form SDF-6 may be obtained from the SDTF at the address set out in Rule 69L-10.019, F.A.C. If the carrier is unable to provide the data on the forms adopted by this section they may submit their own version of an EOB provided that it contains all of the elements of the SDF-6. The SDTF shall request additional information documenting expenditures by health care providers if necessary to prove that the benefits requested for reimbursement are related to the injury and are required to be provided under Section 440.49, F.S. Computer printouts or ledger sheets are not acceptable forms of documenting expenditures for medical benefits unless accompanied by medical bills marked paid or an SDF-6 or its equivalent.

(2) Expenditures for Compensation Voluntarily Paid.

(a) When temporary or permanent disability compensation, permanent impairment benefits, or death benefits have been voluntarily paid, such benefits may be documented by Progress/Final Report, DES DWC-13 forms, as adopted in Rule 69L-3.025, F.A.C., which were prepared contemporaneously with payment, or by copies of checks. If the DWC-13 forms were not prepared contemporaneously with the payment of compensation, computer printouts or ledger sheets may be used to corroborate the payment. However, in regard to each of these classes of benefits, if the total payment listed on the DWC-13 form, printout, or ledger for a particular class is greater than the rate of compensation multiplied by the number of calendar weeks in the period, copies of checks must be supplied to document expenditures.

(b) When wage-loss benefits have been voluntarily paid, such benefits shall be documented only by copies of checks or by copies of fully completed Request for Wage Loss/Temporary Partial Benefits, DWC-3 forms, as adopted in Rule 69L-3.025, F.A.C.

(3) Expenditures for Compensation Pursuant to Order.

When temporary or permanent disability compensation, permanent impairment benefits, death benefits or wage-loss benefits have been paid pursuant to an order of the Judge of Compensation Claims, which has become final, payment can be documented by providing a copy of the order.

(4) Miscellaneous.

(a) Changes in the rate of compensation shall be established by Notice of Action/Change, DES DWC-4 forms and by DES DWC-13 forms, as adopted in Rule 69L-3.025, F.A.C., which set forth the number of weeks paid at each rate of compensation. If the DWC-13 forms were not prepared contemporaneously with payment, then computer printouts or ledger sheets may be used to corroborate the change in the compensation rate. Copies of checks are also a sufficient means of documenting changes in the rate of compensation.

(b) Changes in the class of benefits paid by the employer/carrier shall be documented by DES DWC-4 forms which set forth the date that a prior category of benefits was terminated, as well as the date that a subsequent class of benefits was first paid.

Specific Authority 440.49(2)(g), 440.591 Fla. Stat.

Law Implemented 440.49(2) Fla. Stat.

History: New 4-19-92, Amended 8-18-93, 12-8-98, Formerly 38F-10.016, 4L-10.016.

69L-10.0165. On-site Audit Criteria.

(1) On-site Audits will be conducted at the physical location of the entity being audited. The SDTF shall provide no less than thirty (30) days written notice that an audit will be conducted. The SDTF shall issue a written audit report within sixty (60) days after the conclusion of the on-site audit.

(2) All carriers, self-insurers, servicing agents, individuals or employers filing SDF-2's with the SDTF shall provide the SDTF with all information required by these rules for each claim for reimbursement and the SDTF indicators, to permit a complete review of the entity's operation and processes. Such information may be furnished through hard copy or through a computer format as long as the information is made available to the SDTF at the time of the audit. In the event the information is kept in a format other than hard copy, such format shall be accessible by the SDTF without unreasonable delay caused by access codes or the programming of access code for entry into the entity's database by the SDTF.

(3) SDTF indicators;

(a) Correct application of the offer;

(b) Properly filled out SDF-2;

(c) Actual payment of benefits claimed;

(d) Correct calculation of benefits paid;

(e) Reduction of medical charges in accordance with the fee schedule/reimbursement manual;

(f) Reduction of hospital charges in accordance with the fee schedule/reimbursement manual;

(g) Casual relation of benefits paid to the accident which formed the basis of the claim for reimbursement from the SDTF;

(h) Overpayments, underpayments or gratuitous payments made;

(i) Duplicate charges;

(j) Compliance with applicable statutes and rules governing managed care;

(k) Documentation as required by these rules;

(4) During an on-site audit, the entity being audited shall provide the following for review by the SDTF:

(a) The claims file subject to the limitations in section 381.004, F.S.;

(b) A list of authorized providers, including name, address, and provider license number;

(c) A medical bill, an SDF-6, or its equivalent for each medical payment claimed for reimbursement;

(d) The financial detail corroborating each payment made to the claimant or the provider;

(e) Information establishing that type of managed care arrangement being utilized;

(f) For managed care arrangements, provide methodology used to calculate payments to providers.

Specific Authority 440.49(7) Fla. Stat.

Law Implemented 440.49(7) Fla. Stat.

History: New 12-8-98, Formerly 38F-10.0165, 4L-10.165.

69L-10.017. Reimbursement to Subsequent Employer.

(1) An employer may seek reimbursement pursuant to the provisions of paragraph 440.49 (2)(k), Florida Statutes, which would reimburse the employer for hiring an employee who has incurred a permanent impairment from a Florida workers' compensation injury and has been unemployed as a result of his injury for two (2) consecutive years after the date of accident.

(2) Any employer seeking reimbursement shall file a Claim For Reimbursement for Salary on DES Form SDF-5 (12/91). The Claim for Reimbursement for Salary shall be filed within a six (6) month period from the date the employee is hired or the claim is forever barred.

(3) Any Claim for Reimbursement for Salary that is denied by the SDTF will be barred unless the claimant files an application for hearing with the Division within sixty (60) days after receipt of notice that their claim has been denied. The application for hearing shall be filed in the manner as provided by Section 440.49 (2)(g), Florida Statutes.

Specific Authority 440.49(2)(k) Fla. Stat.

Law Implemented 440.49(2) Fla. Stat.

History: New 4-19-92, Amended 8-18-93, 12-8-98, Formerly 38F-10.017, 4L-10.017.

69L-10.018. Attorneys' Fees, Costs, Penalties and Interest.

The SDTF will not reimburse any attorneys' fees, costs, penalties, supplemental permanent total disability benefits or interest paid by a carrier or a self insurance fund. Claimants shall disclose to the Special Disability Trust Fund any attorneys' fees, costs, penalties and interest paid in any settlement or in any claim to the SDTF whenever reimbursement is claimed.

Specific Authority 440.49(2)(f)2. Fla. Stat.

Law Implemented 440.49(2) Fla. Stat.

History: New 4-19-92, Formerly 38F-10.018, 4L-10.018.

69L-10.019. Forms.

The following forms are incorporated by reference into these rules and are available from and shall be filed with: SDTF, 535 John Knox Road, Tallahassee, FL 32399-4101.

(1) DES Form SDF-1—Proof of Claim (Rev. 12/91)

(2) DES Form SDF-2—Request For Reimbursement (Rev. 3/92)

(3) DES Form SDF-5—Claim For Reimbursement for Salary (9/91)

Specific Authority 440.49(2)(g), 440.30 Fla. Stat.

Law Implemented 440.49(2) Fla. Stat.

History: New 4-19-92, Amended 8-18-93, Formerly 38F-10.019, 4L-10.019.

CHAPTER 69L-11 Preferred Worker Program

69L-11.002. Definitions.

(1) "Regular employment" means a position with the same essential job duties as the preinjury position.

(2) "Qualified employee" means a person who has received a permanent impairment rating from a compensable accident occurring on or after January 1, 1994, and:

(a) is receiving supplemental income benefits payable pursuant to Section 440.15 (3)(b), F.S., for a rating of 20% or greater; or

(b) has received reemployment services as defined in section 440.491 (1)(e), F.S.

(3) "Identity Card" means the card issued by the Division showing that the person is a preferred worker.

(4) "Continuous employment" means uninterrupted employment with a single employer for at least six months.

(5) "Placement" means the hiring of a preferred worker who has obtained an identity card showing eligibility.

(6) "Certification of employment" means the Identity Card signed by both the employer and the preferred worker.

(7) "Premium" for purposes of reimbursement under this section means "net direct written premiums" as defined in Section 631.54 (8), F.S.

(8) "Hire" means placement on the payroll for the first time.

Specific Authority 440.49, 440.591 Fla. Stat.

Law Implemented 440.49 Fla. Stat.

History: New 11-29-94, Formerly 38F-11.002, 4L-11.002.

69L-11.003. Procedure for Obtaining Identity Card.

(1) The worker shall file a Request for Screening (DWC-23), adopted in Rule 69L-11.011, F.A.C., with the local district office of Rehabilitation and Medical Services.

(2) The district representative shall verify all of the following:

(a) A compensable accident occurring on or after January 1, 1994.

(b) A permanent impairment rating assigned for the compensable accident for which permanent benefits are being or have been provided.

(c) That the applicant has met all the criteria to be considered a qualified employee.

(3) The field office representative shall issue an Identity Card within 60 days of receipt of a completed Request for Screening (DWC-23).

Specific Authority 440.49, 440.591 Fla. Stat.

Law Implemented 440.49 Fla. Stat.

History: New 11-29-94, Formerly 38F-11.003, 4L-11.003.

69L-11.004. Time and Procedure for Notifying Injured Employees.

(1) Pursuant to Rule Chapter 69L-8.063, F.A.C., the carrier shall also notify the injured employee of benefits available under this rule chapter and application requirements specified in Section 440.49(8), F.S.

(2) The following suggested language may be used in making the required notification: "Under Section 440.49 (8) Florida Statutes you may be eligible for a preferred worker card. To apply for a card contact your local district office of Rehabilitation and Medical Services."

Specific Authority 440.49, 440.591 Fla. Stat.

Law Implemented 440.49 Fla. Stat.

History: New 11-29-94, Formerly 38F-11.004, 4L-11.004.

69L-11.005. Documentation of Placement of a Preferred Worker.

(1) Within 60 days of hire, the employer shall

send the Identity Card signed by both the Preferred Worker and the employer certifying date of hire to the Special Disability Trust Fund at Division of Workers' Compensation, 200 East Gaines Street, Tallahassee, FL 32399-4223.

(2) The three-year period of eligibility for reimbursement of premiums shall begin at the date of hire and run for three calendar years of continuous employment with the employer.

Specific Authority 440.49, 440.591 Fla. Stat.

Law Implemented 440.49 Fla. Stat.

History: New 11-29-94, Formerly 38F-11.005, 4L-11.005.

69L-11.006. Time for Filing Application for Identity Card.

An Application for Identity Card shall be filed within two years of the employee's original assignment of a permanent impairment rating.

Specific Authority 440.49, 440.591 Fla. Stat.

Law Implemented 440.49 Fla. Stat.

History: New 11-29-94, Formerly 38F-11.006, 4L-11.006.

69L-11.007. Documentation for Reimbursement of Premium.

In order to obtain reimbursement for premium after hiring a Preferred Worker, an employer shall file with the Fund a Form PW-2, as adopted in Rule 69L-11.011, F.A.C., with supporting documentation as set forth below:

(1) Copy of the UCT-6 or other acceptable documentation of payroll and job classification filed with the Division of Unemployment Compensation for all quarters for which reimbursement is requested;

(2) Copy of the Premium Calculation Sheet;

(3) Copy of the Premium Audit.

Specific Authority 440.49, 440.591 Fla. Stat.

Law Implemented 440.49 Fla. Stat.

History: New 11-29-94, Formerly 38F-11.007, 4L-11.007.

69L-11.008. Time for Requesting Reimbursement.

In order to obtain reimbursement, the employer must file a Form PW-2, as adopted in Rule 69L-11.011 F.A.C., with required documentation within six months of the end of the calendar year for which reimbursement is requested. Reimbursements shall be made annually.

Specific Authority 440.49, 440.591 Fla. Stat.

Law Implemented 440.49 Fla. Stat.

History: New 11-29-94, Formerly 38F-11.008, 4L-11.008.

69L-11.009. Procedure When Eligibility for a Card Is Denied.

When the district office determines the applicant is not a qualified employee and refuses to issue an Identity Card, such denial shall be in writing and shall be served on the employee by certified mail. This shall be considered final agency action subject to the procedures under Section 120.57, Florida Statutes.

Specific Authority 440.49, 440.591 Fla. Stat.

Law Implemented 440.49 Fla. Stat.

History: New 11-29-94, Formerly 38F-11.009, 4L-11.009.

69L-11.010. Procedure When Request for Reimbursement of Premium is Denied.

When the Fund determines that the employer is not eligible for reimbursement of premium, a written notice of such denial shall be in writing and served on the employer by certified mail. This shall be considered final agency action and subject to the procedures under Section 120.57, F.S.

Specific Authority 440.49, 440.591 Fla. Stat.

Law Implemented 440.49 Fla. Stat.

History: New 11-29-94, Formerly 38F-11.010, 4L-11.010.

69L-11.011. Forms.

The following forms are incorporated by reference into this rule chapter.

(1) DES Form DWC-23—Request for Screening, available from and shall be filed with, the district office of Rehabilitation and Medical Services.

(2) DES Form PW-1—Identity Card, to be

issued by the appropriate district office of Rehabilitation and Medical Services.

(3) DES Form PW-2—Request for Reimbursement of Premium, available from, and shall be filed with: SDTF, Division of Workers' Compensation, 200 East Gaines Street, Tallahassee, FL 32399-4223.

Specific Authority 440.49, 440.591 Fla. Stat.

Law Implemented 440.49 Fla. Stat.

History: New 11-29-94, Formerly 38F-11.011, 4L-11.011.

CHAPTER 69L-24 Insurers' Standards and Practices

69L-24.021. Minimum Performance Standards.

A ninety percent (90%) rate of compliance is the minimum standard of performance for carriers, self-insurers, employers and servicing agents in each of the following areas: timeliness in which they report and handle claims; promptness of payment of compensation benefits; and payment and disposition of medical bills. The 90% performance rate applies to all applicable carriers, self-insurers, employers, and servicing agents who are subject to the following rules: Chapter 69L-3; Chapter 69L-7; or Chapter 69L-8, F.A.C.

Specific Authority 440.20(8)(c), 440.13(11)(b), 440.591 Fla. Stat.

Law Implemented 440.20, 440.13(11) Fla. Stat.

History: New 8-29-94, Formerly 38F-24.021, 4L-24.021.

69L-24.0211. Monitoring.

(1) The Division shall continually monitor the performance of carriers, self-insurers, employers and servicing agents to ensure compliance with the performance standards prescribed in Rule 69L-24.021, F.A.C., and to assist these entities in improving their overall performance.

(2) Such monitoring will include the automated carrier performance system indicators as listed below:

(a) Timeliness and accuracy of all indemnity and medical payments;

(b) Timely and accurate reporting of required information;

(c) Volume and nature of employee complaints regarding the workers' compensation injury;

(d) Timeliness and accuracy of reporting coverage and changes in coverage;

(e) Compliance with rehabilitation status reviews and reporting requirements;

(f) Timeliness and accuracy of refunding overpayments;

(g) Effectiveness of utilization review program;

(h) Volume and cost of litigation in processing initial claims;

(i) Effectiveness in returning employees to work;

(j) Employee customer service ratings;

(k) Employer customer service ratings; and

(*l*) Amount of average medical costs and average total costs per claim. In addition to the data in the Automated Carrier Performance System, review will be based on data received on referrals of questionable carrier practices received from other units of the Division, governmental entities, the Department of Financial Services, claimants, and other interested parties.

Specific Authority 440.20(15)(f), 440.591 Fla. Stat.

Law Implemented 440.20(15) Fla. Stat.

History: New 8-29-94, Amended 5-14-95, Formerly 38F-24.0211, 4L-24.0211.

69L-24.022. Auditing.

(1) The audits by the Division will encompass all indicators covered by the Division's Automated Carrier Performance System as provided in Rule 69L-24.0211, F.AC. However, carriers, self-insurers or servicing agents shall not be penalized for performance below 90 percent based on the following Automated Carrier Performance System indicators:

(a) Volume and cost of litigation in processing initial claims;

(b) Effectiveness in returning employees to work;

(c) Employee customer service ratings;

(d) Employer customer service ratings;

(e) Amount of average medical costs and average total costs per claim; and

(f) Volume and nature of employee complaints regarding the workers' compensation injury. The Division will make recommendations to assist these entities to improve performance in the aforementioned areas for the specific purpose of rendering the Workers' Compensation system more effective and efficient.

(2) The Automated Carrier Performance System indicators and the other sources identified in this rule shall be reviewed by the Division to determine whether and how often to conduct audits of each carrier, self-insurer or servicing agent's practices. For purposes of this determination, substandard performance on any category outlined in Rule 69L-24.021, F.A.C., shall subject the entity to consideration for audit. No prior notice is required if the Division determines an audit is necessary. However, nothing set forth in these rules shall prohibit the Division from auditing all carriers, self-insurers and servicing agents at least once every three (3) years. Audits conducted under the three (3) year requirement shall cover the preceding three (3) fiscal years of the carrier, self-insurer or servicing agent's operation and must commence within twelve (12) months after the end of the most recent fiscal year being covered by the audit. The audit may cover any period of the entity's operations since the Division's last audit.

(3) If the Division conducts an on-site audit of any carrier's, self-insurer's or servicing agent's practices, the audit report shall be utilized to recommend changes in such entity's behavior and to ensure its continuing compliance with the minimum performance standards set forth in this rule.

(4) For purposes of this rule:

(a) On-Site audits will be conducted at the physical location of the entity being audited. The Division shall issue a written audit report within thirty (30) days after conclusion of an on-site audit conducted pursuant to this rule. This report shall include the Division's recommendations for improving the entity's overall performance in all categories as specified by the Automated Carrier Performance System.

(b) Desk audits will be conducted at the Division's office based on data reported to the Division. A written audit report shall be issued at any time the entity's performance is below the minimum performance standard.

(5) All carriers, self-insurers or servicing agents shall provide the Division with all information relevant to each case file and the Automated Carrier Performance System indicators, as needed, to permit a complete review of the entity's operations and processes during an audit. Such information may be furnished through hard copy or through a computerized format, as long as the information is made available to the Division at the time of the audit. In the event the information is kept in a format other than hard copy, such format shall be accessible by the Division without unreasonable delay caused by access codes or the programming of access codes for entry into the entity's database by the Division.

Specific Authority 440.13(11)(b), 440.20(8)(c), (17), 440.591 Fla. Stat.

Law Implemented 440.13(11), 440.20 Fla. Stat.

History: New 8-29-94, Amended 5-14-95, Formerly 38F-24.022, 4L-24.022.

69L-24.0222. Re-Audit and Certification for Noncompliance.

(1) Any carrier, self-insurer or servicing agent who fails to achieve at least 90 percent compliance on any initial audit shall be audited again within twelve (12) months of the date of the initial audit. During the re-audit, the Division shall examine the entity's performance based on the deficiencies identified in the initial audit report and the specific action proposed for eliminating the deficiencies in the entity's Statement of Objectives. Once the entity has been re-audited and determined not to satisfy the 90

percent compliance rate, that entity shall be subject to the following sanctions:

(a) If the entity's performance is below 90 percent compliance due to its failure to carry out the specific action proposed, it shall be certified to the Department of Financial Services or this Division, as applicable, under Section 440.20 (15)(a), Florida Statutes, in addition to any penalty or fine authorized under Rule 69L-24.0221, F.A.C.

(b) All carriers, self-insurers, or servicing agents failing to submit a Statement of Objectives and who do not achieve at least 90 percent compliance on re-audit shall be certified to the licensing authority, in addition to any penalty or fine authorized under Rule 69L-24.0221, F.A.C.

(2) Any carrier, self-insurer or servicing agent whose initial audit indicates a failure to achieve at least 50 percent compliance, shall be certified to the Department of Financial Services or this Division, as applicable, under section 440.20 (15)(a), Florida Statutes.

(3) Upon conclusion of any on-site audit, the Division's personnel conducting the audit shall review the preliminary findings of such audit with the claims manager or the individual in charge of the office being audited or his designee. Carriers that will be sanctioned under subsection (2) of this Rule may request that Division personnel hold, or cause to be held, a workshop which shall include, but not be limited to, the areas of deficiency identified in the audit.

(4) The Division shall not re-audit a carrier, self-insurer, or servicing agent for failure to achieve 90 percent compliance with the Automated Carrier Performance System indicators set forth in paragraphs 69L-24.0221 (1)(a)–(f), F.A.C.

Specific Authority 440.13(11)(b), 440.20(15)(f), 440.591 Fla. Stat.

Law Implemented 440.20 Fla. Stat.

History: New 8-29-94, Amended 5-14-95, Formerly 38F-24.0222, 4L-24.0222.

69L-24.0231. Benefits and Administration Trust Fund Penalties Improper Filing Practices.

(1)

(a) Failure to timely file by electronic or paper submission legible and complete forms, reports, or documents as required by Chapter 440, Florida Statutes, Chapter 69L-3, F.A.C., or other Division rules implementing Chapter 440, Florida Statutes, shall subject the party required to file such form, report, or document to assessment by the Division of an Administrative fine. For purposes of this rule, if disability is immediate and continuous for 8 or more calendar days after the injury an electronic equivalent of a First Report of Injury or Illness will be considered timely filed with the Division when it is received by the Division on or before the 21st day after the carrier's knowledge of the 8th day of disability and is assigned an acknowledgement code of Transaction Accepted (TA). Penalties shall be assessed as follows:

(b) DWC-1, First Report of Injury or Illness.Employers shall be penalized for each DWC-1 that is not timely filed with the carrier or servicing agent as follows:

1. $ 100 for one through seven days of untimely filing;

2. $ 200 for eight through 14 days of untimely filing;

3. $ 300 for 15 through 21 days of untimely filing;

4. $ 400 for 22 through 28 days of untimely filing; or

5. $ 500 for over 28 days of untimely filing.

(c) Carriers shall be penalized for each DWC-1 that is not timely filed with the Division as follows:

1. $ 100 for one through seven days of untimely filing;

2. $ 200 for eight through 14 days of untimely filing:

3. $ 300 for 15 through 21 days of untimely filing;

4. $ 400 for 22 through 28 days of untimely

filing; or

5. $ 500 for over 28 days of untimely filing.

(2) Improper Disposition of Medical Bill Penalties.Any penalty imposed on a carrier or self-insurer for the improper disposition of medical bills when such disposition is below 90 percent compliance, after 7-1-94, shall be assessed, per quarter, as follows:

80% through 89.99%	¼ percent of the prior year's assessment levied under s. 440.51 against the entity being fined.
70% through 79.99%	½ percent of the prior year's assessment levied under s. 440.51 against the entity being fined.
60% through 69.99%	¾ percent of the prior year's assessment levied under s. 440.51 against the entity being fined.
0% through 59.99%	1 percent of the prior year's assessment levied under s. 440.51 against the entity being fined.

(3) Penalty to the Administration Trust Fund.

(a) Any fine imposed on any carrier or servicing agent that is payable to the Administration Trust Fund for untimely payment of compensation benefits which were paid on or after 1-1-94 shall be as follows:

(b) $ 50 for each late payment of compensation which is below 90 percent compliance, not to exceed one percent of the prior year's assessment levied under Section 440.51, Florida Statutes;

(4) Benefit Penalty without an Award.Any penalty payable to the employee for the untimely payment of compensation benefits, on dates of accident on or after 1-1-94, payable without an award, shall be as follows:

(a) 20 percent on the first of any late installments of compensation not paid within seven days after it becomes due;

(b) $ 5 per subsequent installment of compensation not paid within seven days after it becomes due; and

(c) For dates of accident prior to 1-1-94, the penalty shall be the greater of 10 percent or $ 5 for any installment of compensation not paid within 14 days after it becomes due.

(5) Benefit Penalty with an Award.Any penalty for the untimely payment of compensation for dates of accident on or after 1-1-94 payable under the terms of an award shall be 20 percent of such unpaid compensation not paid within 37 days after the date the order is mailed to the parties, unless review of the compensation order making such award is taken as provided in Section 440.25, Florida Statutes. For dates of accidents prior to 1-1-94, the penalty shall be 20 percent of such unpaid compensation not paid within 60 days after the date the order is mailed to the parties, unless review of the compensation order making such award is taken as provided in Section 440.25, Florida Statutes.

(6) When a servicing agent is under contract with a carrier to fulfill the carrier's administrative responsibilities under this chapter, the payment practices of the servicing agent are deemed the payment practices of the carrier, in which case the carrier shall be the responsible party for any penalties assessed under this section.

Specific Authority 440.13(11)(b), 440.185, 440.591, 440.593(5) Fla. Stat.

Law Implemented 440.13(11)(b), 440.185(9), 440.20(8)(a) Fla. Stat.

History: New 8-29-94, Amended 5-14-95, 6-4-97, 11-28-2001, 1-8-2004, Formerly 38F-24.0231, 4L-24.0231.

69L-24.024. Medical Penalties.

(1) Penalty for Willful Refusal to Provide Medical Records or to Discuss Medical Condition.The Division, pursuant to Rule Chapter 69L-7, F.A.C., shall assess a penalty against a health care provider who willfully refuses to provide medical records or to discuss the medical condition of the injured employee, after a reasonable request is made by the Division, employer, carrier or attorney for either of them for such medical records or to discuss the medical condition of the injured employee.

(2) Failure to Timely Compensate a Certified Expert Medical Advisor.

(a) The Division shall assess a penalty which shall not exceed $500 against any carrier, self-insurer or servicing agent that fails to timely compensate a certified expert medical advisor for services rendered, pursuant to Section 440.13 (9), Florida Statutes. In accordance with Section 440.13 (9)(f), Florida Statutes, the Division establishes the following penalty schedule, with $500 being the maximum penalty for each failure to timely compensate such advisor.

(b) Payment by the carrier, self-insurer or servicing agent to a certified expert medical advisor is deemed timely when such payment is made within 45 calendar days after the date the carrier, self-insurer or servicing agent receives the expert medical advisor's bill for services rendered.

1. One through five calendar days of untimeliness in payment will result in a penalty of $200;

2. Six through ten calendar days of untimeliness in payment will result in a penalty of $400;

3. Over 10 calendar days of untimeliness in payment will result in a penalty of $500.

(3) Failure of Health Care Provider To Refund Overpayment Within 30 Days After Notification.The Division, pursuant to Chapter 69L-7, F.A.C, shall assess a penalty against any health care provider who fails to refund an overpayment made by the carrier, self-insurer or servicing agent within 30 days after receipt of written notification with substantiation of the overpayment by either the carrier, self-insurer, servicing agent or the Division of Workers' Compensation.

Specific Authority 440.13(11)(a), 440.20(8)(c), 440.591 Fla. Stat.

Law Implemented 440.13(9)(f), (11) Fla. Stat.

History: New 8-29-94, 5-14-95, Formerly 38F-24.024, 4L-24.024.

69L-24.0241. Employee Failure to Appear for Independent Medical Examination.

The carrier may contact the injured employee directly to schedule a reasonable time for an independent medical examination. The carrier has an obligation to confirm, in writing, the date and time of such examination to the injured employee within five days of the date and time the carrier and employee agreed to such examination. The carrier must also notify the injured employee's counsel, if any, of such examination no later than seven days prior to the date such examination is scheduled.

(1) For purposes of this section, "reasonable time" means a time acceptable to both parties.

(2) Injured employees are required to appear for all properly scheduled independent medical examinations, unless the injured employee can provide good cause for his absence. For purposes of this section, good cause can be established by showing that an immediate illness, injury, unforeseen event or intervening circumstances prevented the injured employee's appearance. An injured employee who does not properly provide at least 24-hours' notice of cancellation and cannot demonstrate good cause for his/her nonappearance for the independent medical examination shall not be excused from the sanctions of subsections (3) and (4) below.

(3) An injured employee who fails without good cause, as set forth above, to appear for the scheduled independent medical examination shall reimburse the carrier 50 percent of the cancellation or no-show fee. The carrier may withhold no more than 20 percent of each bi-weekly installment amount payable to the injured employee when recouping from the injured employee a cancellation or no-show fee that has been paid by the carrier. The carrier shall not recoup more than 50 percent of the actual cancellation or no-show fee.

(4) An injured employee who fails, without good cause as set forth in subsection (2), to appear for the scheduled independent medical examination is barred from recovering compensation for any period during which the injured employee has refused to submit to such examination. Compensation under this paragraph means indemnity benefits.

Specific Authority 440.591 Fla. Stat.

Law Implemented 440.13(5)(d) Fla. Stat.

History: New 8-29-94, Amended 5-14-95, Formerly 38F-24.0241, 4L-24.0241.

CHAPTER 69L-26 Employee Assistance and Ombudsman Office

69L-26.002. Definitions.

For the purposes of these rules, the following definitions shall apply:

(1) "Carrier" means any insurance carrier, or any individually self-insured employer licensed as such pursuant to Section 440.38, F.S., or group self-insurance fund licensed as such pursuant to Section 624.462, F.S., providing workers' compensation insurance and including the servicing agent and servicing company of any of the above.

(2) "Contact" as that term is used in Ch. 93-415, Section 24, Laws of Florida. [creating Section 440.191(2)(a), F.S.] means a party to a workers' compensation dispute has made "contact" with the EAO if he or she has done any of the following:

(a) Submitted to the EAO a Request for Assistance form (EAO-1, dated 6/17/94 and hereby incorporated by reference) which meets all the requirements set out in these rules; or

(b) Personally telephoned the EAO, spoken to an EAO representative, requested the assistance of the EAO, and as a result, the EAO has completed a Request for Assistance form (EAO-1) on behalf of the party so requesting.

(c) In the case of a minor or incompetent person, written or oral correspondence in accord with paragraph (2)(a) or (b), above requesting assistance from the EAO on behalf of the minor or incompetent person by his or her legally appointed guardian, shall constitute "contact" with the EAO for the purposes of these rules.

(d) In the case of a deceased person, written or oral correspondence in accord with paragraph (2)(a) or (b) above requesting assistance from the EAO on behalf of a deceased person by his or her personal representative shall constitute "contact" with the EAO for the purposes of these rules.

(e) The following will not be accepted by the EAO as a request for assistance and do not constitute "contact" with the EAO for purposes of these rules:

1. Written requests for assistance not submitted in accordance with these rules and on a Request for Assistance form (EAO-1); or

2. Written requests for assistance transmitted to the EAO by fax; or

3. Written requests for assistance not signed by the party to a workers' compensation dispute; or if the party to a dispute has retained an attorney, not signed by that attorney on behalf of the party; or if the party to a dispute is a minor or incompetent person, not signed by his or her legal guardian; or if the party to a dispute is deceased, not signed by his or her personal representative; or if the requestor is a health care provider that has provided authorized treatment to an injured worker, not signed by the health care provider; or

3. Telephone calls of an attorney to the EAO made on behalf of a party to a workers' compensation dispute, unless the attorney is the party to a dispute and is requesting assistance on his or her own behalf.

(3) "Division" means the Division of Workers' Compensation.

(4) "EAO" means the Employee Assistance and Ombudsman Office created by Ch. 93-415, Section 24, Laws of Florida [creating Section 440.191, F.S.]. Information or documentation requested or required by the EAO shall be submitted only to the address and during the regular business hours of the EAO as contained in this rule. The address for the EAO shall be as follows:

(a) For filing of Requests for Assistance: Post Office Box 8010, Tallahassee, Florida 32314-8010.

(b) For responding to requests for information by the EAO: To the address specified by the EAO in the request.

(c) For all other purposes: 200 East Gaines Street, Tallahassee, FL 32399-4224. The telephone number shall be (850) 488-5201 or (800) 342-1741. The normal business hours for the EAO shall be 8:00 a.m. to 5:00 p.m., Eastern Standard Time, Monday through Friday (working days).

(5) "Fax" or "Faxed" means any written communication transmitted by facsimile or telecopy machine.

(6) "Good Faith Effort" means cooperating with the division's efforts to resolve disagreements between the parties. The division shall consider the following factors in determining whether a party or party's attorney has cooperated with the division's efforts:

(a) Whether the party or the party's attorney has telephoned or written to the employer or carrier and communicated that party's complaint or disputed issue(s) to the employer or carrier before requesting assistance from the EAO with that (those) same issue(s).

(b) Whether a party or the party's attorney has provided complete and "specific" (as that term is defined herein) information on a Request for Assistance form (EAO-1), or by telephone, in the event the EAO has completed the form for a party pursuant to a telephoned request for assistance from that party to the EAO.

(c) Whether a party or the party's attorney has timely provided documents in his or her possession or under his or her control to the EAO. The production of documents shall be timely if any documents requested by the EAO which are in the possession or under the control of the party from whom they are requested are submitted to the EAO within five (5) working days of the EAO's request for the documents.

(d) Whether a party or the party's attorney has timely participated in a conference requested by the EAO. Timely means that if feasible and practical, the parties shall: participate in a telephone conference within three (3) working days of a request by the EAO for a telephone conference; or, the parties shall participate in an in-person conference within five (5) working days of a request by the EAO for an in-person conference.

(e) Whether the party or party's attorney has provided true and complete information to the best of his or her ability and knowledge. Every party and attorney participating in the EAO's dispute resolution proceedings shall have an affirmative obligation to correct errors or omissions in information he or she has provided when an error is discovered, and to update all receivers of previously submitted information as soon as it is discovered by the sender that the information previously submitted is no longer accurate or complete.

(7) "Informal Dispute Resolution" means the procedures established by these rules whereby the EAO, in response to a request for assistance in resolving a dispute regarding workers' compensation benefits, conducts an investigation and attempts to facilitate a resolution of any disputed issues.

(8) "JCC" means a Judge of Compensation Claims as that term is defined by Chapter 440, F.S.

(9) "Party" or "Person" includes individuals, children, firms, associations, joint ventures, partnerships, estates, trusts, business trusts, syndicates, fiduciaries, corporations, and all other groups or combinations.

(10) "Requestor" means the person requesting the assistance of the EAO. The requestor may be an actual party to a workers' compensation dispute, or an attorney representing a party to a workers' compensation dispute, or a legal guardian of an incompetent or minor person who is a party to a workers' compensation dispute or the personal representative of a deceased person who is a party to a workers' compensation dispute. The requestor may also be a health care provider that has provided treatment to an injured worker, where the employer or carrier has authorized the treatment by telephone or by fax and subsequently fails or refuses to pay for the treatment authorized.

(11) "Servicing Agent" or "Servicing Company" means any entity which has obtained approval pursuant to Florida law and administrative rule to contract with self-insurers for the purpose of providing all services necessary to

plan and maintain an approved self-insurance program.

(12) "Specific" means:

(a) If a disputed issue is indemnity benefits, then in order to make a "specific" request for assistance, the requestor must state on the Request for Assistance form (EAO-1) a classification for each benefit sought, such as: temporary total disability, temporary partial disability, wage loss, permanent total disability, impairment benefit, or supplemental benefits. The requestor must state for each benefit sought and allegedly not paid, the time period for which the injured worker asserts he was eligible to receive the benefits.

(b) If the disputed issue is authorization for a particular health care provider or a particular health care service, then in order to make a "specific" request for assistance, the requestor must state the type of service or name of the health care provider that has been requested, and a justification for any health care services requested and not provided.

(c) If the disputed issue is payment of health care bill(s), then in order to make a "specific" request for assistance, the requestor must state the name and address of the health care provider, the date(s) of service and the amount(s) of the bill(s) for which payment is sought; and, if the requestor is a health care provider, the requestor must provide evidence that the treatment was authorized by the employer or carrier, and that more than 45 days have elapsed since the bill(s) was (were) submitted for payment.

(d) If the disputed issue is mileage or prescription reimbursement, then in order to make a "specific" request for assistance, the requestor must state the drug or product prescribed, the name of the prescribing physician, the dollar amount requested and the date each reimbursement request was submitted to the employer or carrier. Legible copies of each mileage request or prescription, as applicable, must be attached to the Request for Assistance form (EAO-1) or timely provided to the EAO if requested by the EAO.

(13) "Working Day" means a day which is neither a Saturday, Sunday, or legal holiday observed by the State of Florida.

Specific Authority 440.591 Fla. Stat.

Law Implemented 440.191 Fla. Stat.

History: New 9-29-94, Amended 11-25-96, Formerly 38F-26.002, 4L-26.002, Amended 5-12-04.

69L-26.003. Computation of Time.

In computing any period of time prescribed or allowed by these rules, the day of the act from which the designated period of time begins to run shall not be included. The last day of the period shall be included unless it is a Saturday, Sunday, or legal holiday observed by the State of Florida, in which event, the period shall run until the end of the next day which is neither a Saturday, Sunday, or legal holiday observed by the State of Florida.

Specific Authority 440.591 Fla. Stat.

Law Implemented Chapter 93-415, Section 24, Laws of Florida [creating Section 440.191, Florida Statutes].

History: New 9-29-94, Formerly 38F-26.003, 4L-26.003.

69L-26.004. Requesting Assistance.

(1) An injured worker or any other party to a dispute involving a workers' compensation issue shall contact and request assistance from the EAO, and make a good faith effort to participate in the informal dispute resolution proceedings of the EAO.

(2) A request for assistance shall be accepted by the EAO and shall constitute contact with the EAO only if the request for assistance is submitted on a completed Request for Assistance form (EAO-1) and is otherwise in accordance with these rules.

Specific Authority 440.591 Fla. Stat.

Law Implemented 440.191 Fla. Stat.

History: New 9-29-94, Amended 11-25-96, Formerly 38F-26.004, 4L-26.004, Amended 5-12-04.

CHAPTER 69O-190 Rules for Self-Insurers Under the Workers' Compensation Act

69O-190.056. Application for Self-Insurers Fund.

(1) Licensing procedures pursuant to Section 120.60, Florida Statutes, and in accordance with the model rules of procedure shall apply to this application.

(2) All applications for a self-insurers fund shall be made in writing on OIR Form BSI-2.

(3) All applications shall be accompanied by:

(a) A properly completed indemnity agreement in accordance with Rule 69O-190.068, F.A.C.

(b) A properly executed Self-Insurer's Surety Bond on OIR Form BSI-4, pursuant to Rule 69O-190.032 and subsection 69O-190.060 (4), F.A.C., or proof of cash securities pursuant to Rule 69O-190.033 and in amounts pursuant to subsection 69O-190.060, F.A.C.

(c) Copies of acceptable excess insurance policies pursuant to Rule 69O-190.035 with limits and retentions pursuant to Rule 69O-190.061, F.A.C., and endorsements pursuant to Rule 69O-190.036, F.A.C.

(d) A fidelity bond or insurance policy pursuant to Rule 4-190.064 (5), F.A.C.

(e) A fidelity bond or insurance policy covering the service company pursuant to subsection 69O-190.064 (7), F.A.C.

(f) A certification from a designated depository attesting to sufficient monies on hand in order for the fund to meet initial obligations pursuant to paragraph 69O-190.056 (5)(c), F.A.C.

(g) Proof of servicing pursuant to Rule 69O-190.031, F.A.C.

(h) Copies of the fund by-laws or trust agreement and written policies pursuant to subsections 4-190.064 (2), (3), and (4), F.A.C.

(i) Membership applications executed on OIR Form BSI-3 or its equivalent complete with declarations and financial statements pursuant to Rule 69O-190.059. Funds must use the BSI-3 unless prior approval of the Office has been granted for use of an alternate form. Such alternate form must contain all information contained on the BSI-3, but may ask for additional information or use a different format. Approval will be granted if the alternate form contains all required information. OIR Form BSI-3, or its equivalent, shall be used for all new business. OIR Form BSI-3, or its equivalent, shall be used for all renewal business for twelve consecutive months. The use of this form for new and renewal business must commence within sixty (60) days of the date of this rule. A copy of this form may be obtained from the Bureau of P & L Insurer Solvency, Tallahassee, Florida.

(j) Proof that the initial membership of the fund have the combined financial conditions and combined premiums as specified in paragraph (m) of this section.

(k) The name of the attorney, certified public accountant, and actuary representing the fund.

(*l*) A completed Estimated Breakdown of Policy Year Expenses on OIR Form BSI-21.

(m) Each self-insurers fund shall submit a current financial statement on each member at the inception of the self-insurers fund showing the combined net worth of all members applying for coverage to be not less than $1,000,000, each member shall have a current ratio which is the median for the self-insureds standard industry code as published in the 1992 edition of the Robert Morris Associates Annual Statement Studies. An audited financial statement or a financial statement properly certified by an officer, owner or partner for all members joining the self-insurers fund after the inception date shall be submitted to the Office with the application for membership until such time as an audited financial statement is available for the self-insurers fund as a whole. In no event shall the cumulative net worth or current ratio of the combined assets and liabilities of all members be less than the minimum amounts currently required for a fund to qualify.

(n) Each applicant shall submit a feasibility study, prepared by an independent qualified actuary and an independent certified public accountant to satisfactorily address market potential, market penetration, market competition, operating expenses, gross revenues, net income total assets and liabilities, cash flow, and such other items as the division may require. The study shall be for the greater of 3 years or until the arrangement has been projected to be profitable for 12 consecutive months. The feasibility study must reflect and support all premium, reserve, and other financial requirements with which the fund must comply.

(4) Upon receipt of the application and other required materials, the Office will investigate the application and will request any additional information which is required in a letter to the applicant.

(5) The financial condition of the proposed fund shall be determined in light of the following:

(a) In considering the financial strength and liquidity of the group as evidence of ability to pay normal compensation claims promptly, the Office will take into consideration contracts or policies of aggregate excess liability insurance secured in accordance with Rule 60O-190.061, F.A.C.

(b) The trustees shall satisfy the Office that the normal premiums of the self-insurers fund will be at least $500,000 for the first and succeeding years of operation.

(c) The trustees shall submit at least ten (10) days prior to the proposed effective date, positive proof that the members have paid into a common claims fund in a designated depository, cash premiums in an amount of not less than $125,000 or twenty-five percent (25%) of the estimated annual standard premium of the members at inception, whichever amount is greater. The remainder of the deposit premiums shall be collected based on the schedule adopted by the trustees.

(6) If the initial contract for aggregate excess insurance contains a minimum loss fund or retention provision in excess of $70,000 then the trustees must submit with their initial filing, in addition to those of the members at inception, signed member agreements evidencing additional earned normal premium for the first year of operation sufficient to meet the minimum loss fund. These additional agreements may have varying effective dates.

(7) No applicant shall have an aggregate excess contract which provides for a minimum loss fund or retention greater than the product of the aggregate retention percentage and the normal premium of the members submitting signed agreements.

(8) Prior to making a final determination on the approval or denial of the application, the Office may schedule an informal conference in Tallahassee. In the event a meeting is scheduled, the board of trustees of the prospective fund, its administrator, a representative of the service company, its attorney, and its CPA shall meet with the representative of the Office to discuss any matters relevant to the qualification of the fund. A time and date that is mutually agreeable will be selected within the statutory time frame established by Chapter 120, F.S., for the approval and denial of the application.

Specific Authority 440.38(2)(b), 440.591, 624.4621(3) Fla. Stat.

Law Implemented 440.38(1)(b), (2)(b), 624.4621 Fla. Stat.

History: New 10-1-82, Amended 12-25-84, Formerly 38F-5.56, Amended 6-12-91, 12-19-93, Formerly 38F-5.056, 4L-190.056.

69O-190.057. Evaluation of Application for Self-Insurers Fund.

(1) The application will be evaluated and a determination will be made of:

(a) Whether the fund application, individual member applications and indemnity agreement are properly completed and that all required information is supplied.

(b) Whether the combined financial condition of the membership meets the criteria established in Rule 4-190.056, F.A.C.

(c) Whether or not the servicing program satisfied Rule 4-190.031, F.A.C.

(d) Whether the fidelity bonds or insurance policies for the administrator, service company, fiscal agent, and other individuals pursuant to subsection 69O-190.064 (5), F.A.C. are properly executed and in amounts sufficient to protect the fund against loss.

(e) Whether a sufficient amount of premium has been deposited pursuant to subsection 69O-190.056 (5).

(f) Whether the by-laws or trust agreement and written policies contain the items specified in subsections 4-190.064 (17), (18), and (19), F.A.C.

(g) Whether the surety bond is properly executed or the cash securities properly assigned and if they are in the proper amounts pursuant to Rules 69O-190.060, 69O-190.032 and 69O-190.033, F.A.C.

(h) Whether the excess contracts have proper endorsements and provide suitable coverage to the fund pursuant to Rules 69O-190.035 and 69O-190.036, F.A.C.

(i) Whether the excess coverages have limits and retentions pursuant to Rule 69O-190.061, F.A.C.

(j) Whether the combined annual normal premiums meet the criteria contained in subsection 4-190.056(5), F.A.C.

(k) Whether the proforma required in paragraph 69O-190.056 (3)(m), F.A.C., provides that the fund complies with all requirement of Chapter 440, F.S., and this rule for the period covered.

(2) Any deficiencies in the original filing will be noted in a letter to the applicant.

(3) The Office in evaluating the application shall review the financial condition of the fund and make the following determinations:

(a) Whether the operating budget of the fund as presented on OIR Form BSI-21 is adequate to meet the fund's needs.

(b) Whether the operating budget as presented on OIR Form BSI-21 contains reasonable estimates of the necessary expenses of the fund.

(c) Whether the fund will have sufficient income to pay for all necessary expenses.

(d) Whether the fund will be able to satisfy its minimum loss fund or retention requirements.

(e) Whether the applicant has demonstrated that it has the necessary financial strength and provides the necessary financial security to guarantee the payment of workers' compensation benefits.

(4) Failure to meet any of the criteria or provide the documentation contained in these rules shall be grounds for denial of the application.

(5) After completing its review of all required documentation contained in these rules, the Office shall issue its decision on the approval or denial of the application in accordance with the model rules of procedure.

Specific Authority 624.6241 Fla. Stat.

Law Implemented 624.6421 Fla. Stat.

History: New 10-1-82, Amended 12-25-84, Formerly 38F-5.57, Amended 12-19-93, Formerly 38F-5.057, 4L-190.057.

69O-190.058. Conditions for Retaining the Self-Insurance Privilege of Self-Insurers Funds.

(1) The self-insurance privilege of a self-insurers fund is granted continuously until revoked.

(2) A review of all self-insurers fund programs will be made annually. As a result of such reviews, changes in the prior requirements to self-insure or the imposition of additional requirements in order to continue to be self-insured may be made pursuant to Rules 69O-190.060 and 69O-190.061, F.A.C.

(3) In addition to complying with the continuing requirements for self-insurance, all self-insurers funds shall be required to submit the following documents and reports on a continuing basis:

(a) Annual financial statements, audited financial statements, and actuarial reports pursuant to Rule 69O-190.059, F.A.C.

(b) Annual Summary Loss Reports on each member pursuant to paragraph 69O-4-190.062 (1)(a), F.A.C.

(c) Annual Payroll Reports on each member pursuant to Rule 69O-190.062 (1)(b), F.A.C.

(d) Quarterly Financial Statements pursuant to Rule 69O-190.059, F.A.C., and Status Reports pursuant to paragraph 69O-190.062 (1)(c), F.A.C.

(e) Proof of servicing pursuant to Rule 69O-190.031, F.A.C.

(f) Proof of excess coverage pursuant to Rules 69O-190.061 and 69O-190.035, F.A.C.

(g) Copies of endorsements to excess policies pursuant to Rule 69O-190.036, F.A.C.

(h) Copies of surety bonds or riders pursuant to Rules 69O-190.060 and 69O-190.032, F.A.C.

(i) Proof of cash securities pursuant to Rule 69O-190.032.

(j) Reporting changes in coverage of the membership pursuant to subsection 69O-190.062 (3), F.A.C.

(k) Changes in by-laws or trust agreement and written policies pursuant to subsection 69O-190.064 (20), F.A.C.

(*l*) Fidelity bonds, riders, insurance policies or endorsements pursuant to subsection 69O-190.064 (5), F.A.C.

(m) Copies of new member applications pursuant to subsection 69O-190.062 (2), F.A.C.

(n) Estimated Breakdown of Policy Year Expenses pursuant to subsection 69O-190.059 (6), F.A.C.

(4) Whenever the Office determines that the fund has knowingly submitted an application containing false or misleading information, the Division may proceed with revocation of the self-insurer status of the fund.

(5) If any fund intentionally submits any false or misleading document or report required by these rules, the Office may proceed with revocation of the self-insurer status of the fund.

Specific Authority440.39(1)(b), (2)(b), 624.4621 Fla. Stat.

Law Implemented440.39(1)(b), (2)(b), 624.4621 Fla. Stat.

History: New 10-1-82, Amended 12-25-84, Formerly 38F-5.58, Amended 12-19-93, Formerly 38F-5.058, 4L-190.058.

69O-190.059. Financial and Actuarial Reports for Self-Insurers Funds.

(1) Each fund shall file with the Office quarterly financial statements on OIR Form BSI-28 or the 1992 National Association of Insurance Commissioners (NAIC) Quarterly Statement, Fire and Casualty Companies Association Edition in its entirety.

(2) Each fund shall file with the Office an annual financial statement on OIR Form BSI-29 or the following portions of the 1992 National Association of Insurance Commissioners Annual Statement, Fire and Casualty Companies Association Edition: Jurat Page; Statutory Balance Sheet; Underwriting and Investment Exhibit—Income Statement; Cash Flow; Underwriting and Investment Exhibit Part 1, Part 1A, Part 2, Part 2A, Part 3, Part 3A, and Part 4; Exhibit 1—Analysis of Assets; Exhibit 2—Analysis of Non-Admitted Assets; Notes to Financial Statements; Five Year Historical Data (NOTE: funds shall complete this form on a going forward basis); Schedule of Special Deposits; Schedule A Part 1; Schedule B; Schedule BA; Schedule C; Schedule D Part 1, Part 1A, Part 3, Part 4 and Part 5 (NOTE: only 4th quarter transactions need to be reported); Schedule DA Part 1; Schedule F—Part 1A (NOTE: any amounts in dispute must be disclosed); Schedule M; Schedule N; Schedule P, Part 1 Summary, Part 2 Summary, Part 3 Summary, Part 5 Summary, interrogatories; Schedule X; Schedule Y.

(a) As part of its annual financial statement each fund shall file with the Office an Estimated Breakdown of Policy Year Expenses on OIR Form BSI-21 within 60 days after the beginning of each policy year. The projection of its anticipated income and expenses, shall also include the comparable, actual results for the immediate preceding year.

(3) The quarterly and annual financial statements, required by subsections 69O-190.059 (1) and 69O-190.059 (2), F.A.C., shall be prepared in accordance with the NAIC's Annual Statement Instructions, Property and Casualty, 1993 edition, and the NAIC's Accounting Practices and Procedures Manual for Property and Casu-

alty Insurance Companies, 1993 edition. The NAIC's Accounting Practices and Procedures Manual for Property and Casualty Insurance Companies applies to the preparation of all statements required by this rule, except that the following shall be admitted assets:

(a) Prepaid expenses which have a liquidation value.

(b) Equipment, furniture and fixtures depreciated using a 5-year useful life.

(c) Deferred taxes when the deferred tax asset is created by timing differences in the treatment of bad debt reserves, unearned premiums, and accrued dividends. Such timing differences shall reverse within two years in order to be eligible, and the fund shall provide to the division a statement from the fund's Certified Public Accountant or Tax Attorney that in the event of the insolvency of the fund, these deferred tax assets will generate a refund of prior years' taxes to the estate of the fund. The fund shall also provide upon request from the division a detailed disclosure of the components of the deferred tax asset deemed by the fund to be an admitted asset. This provision shall become inoperative as of December 31, 1995, and deferred taxes shall be deemed nonadmitted assets for all fiscal years beginning after December 31, 1995.

(d) An aggregate write-in on the balance sheet of the annual statement for assets and policy holder's surplus, an entry for future investment income on losses and allocated loss adjustment expense reserves and unallocated loss adjustment expense reserves shall be reflected. Future investment income shall be calculated as follows:

$$A + B + C - D$$

A = Losses and Allocated Loss Adjustment Expense Reserves. B = Unallocated Loss Adjustment Expense Reserves. C = Excess of Statutory Reserves over Statement Reserves. D = The present value of A + B + C. Present value of Unallocated Loss Adjustment Expense Reserves, Present Value of Loss and Allocated Loss Adjustment Expense Reserves, or Present Value of Excess of Statutory Reserves over Statement Reserves means reserves discounted to present value using the most recent United States Internal Revenue Service present value factors.

(4) Each fund shall file with the Office an annual audited financial statement prepared in accordance with the NAIC's Accounting Practices and Procedures Manual for Property and Casualty Insurance Companies, 1993 edition.

(a) Annual audited financial statements shall disclose audited premiums based on the audit of the payrolls of fund members who represent at least 90 percent of the fund's annual normal premium. The type of payroll audit is set forth in Rule 69O-190.073, F.A.C. Nothing in this rule prohibits a fund from doing interim payroll audits, as allowed in Rule 69O-190.073, F.A.C., when the fund determines it must do so to comply with this rule.

(b) The annual audited financial statement shall include the following:

1. Report of an independent certified public accountant. If the report is qualified by the independent certified public accountant the Office shall require the fund to provide a plan to correct the deficiencies noted in the report.

2. Balance sheet reporting admitted assets, liabilities, capital and surplus.

3. Statement of operations.

4. Statement of cash flows.

5. Statement of changes in capital and surplus.

6. The notes to financial statements shall be those required by the NAIC's Annual Statement Instructions, Property and Casualty, 1992 edition, and any other notes required by generally accepted accounting principles. The notes shall also include a reconciliation of differences, if any, between the annual audited financial statement required by subsection 69O-190.059 (4), F.A.C., and the annual financial statement required by subsection 69O-190.059 (2), F.A.C., with a written description of the nature of these differences.

7. The annual audited financial statement required by subsection 69O-190.059 (4), F.A.C. shall be prepared in a form and using substan-

tially the same language and groupings substantially the same as the relevant sections of the annual financial statement of the fund required by subsection 69O-190.059 (2), F.A.C. The annual audited financial statement shall be comparative, presenting the amounts as of the end of the current fiscal year and the amounts as of the immediately preceding fiscal year. However, in the first year in which a fund is required to file an annual audited financial statement, the comparative data may be omitted. The fund may submit an audited form BSI-29 if it so chooses, providing the independent certified public accountant report is provided as an addendum to the form.

8. The annual audited financial statement shall reflect, at a minimum, the reserves which have been deemed appropriate by the funds actuaries in the actuarial certification. If the certified public accountant discovers information which may alter the reserves determined by the actuary, they shall notify both the Office and the actuary. If the Office and the actuary concur that this information will materially alter the reserves as determined by the actuary and the report cannot be timely filed, the Office may waive the requirements in subsection 69O-190.038(3), F.A.C., for filing a request for extension. In no event shall the extension be granted for more than 30 days.

9. OIR Form BSI 30, report on Preferred Payment Plans.

10. A copy of the management letter as prepared by the certified public accountant in conjunction with the audit of the fund.

11. A list of the current trustees of the fund along with their business affiliation, the business address, and business phone number.

(5) Each fund shall file with the Division at the same time as the fund's annual audited financial statement an actuarial report prepared by a qualified actuary. The actuarial report shall evaluate the loss development of the fund and estimate the loss reserve including allocated and unallocated loss adjustment expenses and incurred but not reported reserves.

(a) A completed OIR Form BSI-26, Checklist for the Submission of Loss Reserve Reports, shall accompany each actuarial report submitted pursuant to this rule. Actuarial reports shall contain, at a minimum, summaries of the computations and methodologies used to estimate the fund's loss reserves. These reports shall include loss development triangles for all funds with 5 or more years experience. These loss triangles shall include, paid losses, incurred losses, and number of open claims.

(b) Loss reserves in the actuarial report:

1. Shall be calculated in accordance with section 625.091, F.S., except that Section 625.091 (2)(a), F.S., the discount factor shall be 0%.

2. Shall not contain subrogation awards except for those amounts which have been awarded in a court of law.

(6) Quarterly or annual financial statements or actuarial reports shall contain loss reserves which have not been adjusted to reflect recoveries from the Special Disability Trust Fund (SDTF) except for:

(a) Those recoveries which have been approved by the Special Disability Trust Fund, awarded by a Judge of Compensation Claims, or awarded by a ruling of the First District Court of Appeals.

(b) The prohibition and limitations in this rule against adjustment of loss reserves for anticipated SDTF recoveries does not preclude the use of historical data pertaining to the fund's actual recoveries by actuaries in computations and methodologies implicitly used to develop ultimate reserves.

(7) Any fund whose financial condition is shown to be deficient in the financial statements required by this rule shall be allowed to file a corrective action plan to correct any deficiency. Such corrective action plan shall disclose what specific areas of the fund operations will be addressed, and the time table for taking such actions. If the corrective action plan encompasses more than one reporting (calendar or fiscal) year, the Office shall require that the corrective action plan be revised at the end of

each fiscal year if the actual performance of the fund for that reporting year varies more than 10% from the corrective action plan. Such corrective action plan shall be submitted within sixty days of the receipt of notification from the Office. Extensions shall be granted for good cause.

(8) Each fund shall make a copy of its quarterly financial statement, annual financial statement, annual audited financial statement, and actuarial report available to members of the fund upon request. This requirement may be satisfied by making available annually to new and renewal members an extract of the statements or report; the form of such extract shall be approved by the Office in advance of distribution. Such approval shall be given if the Office determines that the extracted information fairly and accurately represents the financial condition of the fund, and discloses any material footnote information disclosed in the filings with the Office. In lieu of Office approval, the fund's certified public accountant and qualified actuary from whose reports the extracts are derived, may file a statement with the Office that they have reviewed the extract and have no objections to it. Such a statement shall contain a copy of the extract for the Office's file.

(9) Due date of quarterly, annual and audited financial statements. Each fund shall submit four (4) quarterly statements which shall be due 45 days after the end of the fund's fiscal quarter. The annual statement and audited annual report shall be due on or before the last day of the sixth month after the end of the fund's fiscal year.

(10) Effective Date.All funds shall comply with this rule for fiscal years beginning after December 31, 1993, and each year thereafter.

(11) Requests for an extension of time to file quarterly, annual, and audited financial statements must be received in writing at least 15 days before the date the report is due. The request must include the reason the extension is requested. Any request received 14 days or less before the date the report is due will be denied except for, but not limited to, death of key management personnel, destruction of records or facilities by fire, flood, hurricane, or some other natural disaster, or act not under control of the management.

Specific Authority 440.5705, 440.591, 624.4621 Fla. Stat.

Law Implemented 624.316, 624.424, 624.4621 Fla. Stat.

History: New 10-1-82, Amended 12-25-84, 12-17-85, Formerly 38F-5.59, Amended 3-11-87, 3-11-90, 12-19-93, Formerly 38F-5.059, 4L-190.059.

69O-190.0591. Independent Certified Public Accountants.

(1) Designation of Independent Certified Public Accountant.

(a) Each fund required by subsection 4-190.059 (4), F.A.C., to file an annual audited financial statement shall, by the end of the fiscal year subject to audit, notify the Office in writing of the name and address of the fund's independent certified public accountant or accounting firm (generally referred to in this rule as the "accountant") retained to conduct the annual audit required by subsection 69O-190.059 (4), F.A.C.

(b) The fund shall obtain a letter from the accountant, and file a copy with the Office, stating that the accountant is aware of the provisions of the Florida Statutes which relate to the financial reporting and operation of the fund and the Rules and of the Office, and affirming that he will express his opinion on the financial statements in terms of their conformity to the NAIC's Accounting Practices and Procedures Manual for Property and Casualty Insurance Companies, 1993 edition, specifying the exceptions as he may believe appropriate.

(c) If an accountant who was the accountant for the immediately preceding filed annual audited financial statement is dismissed or resigns, the fund shall within five (5) business days notify the Office of this event. The fund shall also furnish the Office with a separate letter within ten (10) business days of the above notification stating whether in the twenty-four (24) months preceding that event there were any disagreements with the former accountant on any matter of accounting principles or practices, financial statement disclosure, or auditing scope or procedure; which disagreements, if not resolved to the satisfaction of the former accountant, would have caused him to make reference to the subject matter of the disagreement in connection with his opinion. The disagreements required to be reported in response to this section include both those resolved to the former accountant's satisfaction and those not resolved to the former accountant's satisfaction.

(d) Disagreements contemplated by this section are those that occur at the decision-making level, i.e., between personnel of the fund responsible for presentation of its financial statements and personnel of the accounting firm responsible for rendering its report. The fund shall also in writing request the former accountant to furnish a letter addressed to the fund stating whether the accountant agrees with the statements contained in the fund's letter, and if not, stating the reasons for which he does not agree; and the fund shall furnish the responsive letter from the former accountant to the Office together with its own.

(e) The reporting requirements in paragraphs (c) and (d) above shall also apply to the fund's qualified actuary.

(2) Qualifications of Independent Certified Public Accountant.

(a) The Office shall not recognize any person or firm as a qualified independent certified public accountant that is not in good standing with the licensing authority or accrediting authority for certified public accountants in the State of Florida.

(b) Except as otherwise provided herein, an independent certified public accountant shall be recognized as qualified as long as he or she prepares reports, filings, and statements as required by Florida Statutes, and conforms to the standards of his or her profession as contained in the Rules and Regulations and Code of Ethics and Rules of Professional Conduct of the Florida Board of Public Accountancy, or similar code.

(3) Scope of Examination and Report of Independent Certified Public Accountant.Annual audited financial statements required by subsection 69O-190.059 (4), F.A.C., shall be examined by an independent certified public accountant in accordance with generally accepted auditing standards. Consideration should also be given to the procedures set forth in the Financial Condition Examiner's Handbook of the National Association of Insurance Commissioners, 1993 edition.

(4) Notification of Adverse Financial Condition.

(a) Each fund shall require the independent certified public accountant to report, in writing, within five (5) business days to the board of trustees and its audit committee any determination by the independent certified public accountant that the fund has materially misstated its financial condition as reported to the Office as of the balance sheet date currently under examination. A fund which has received a report pursuant to this paragraph shall forward a copy of the report to the Office within five (5) business days of receipt of said report and shall provide the independent certified public accountant making the report with evidence of the report being furnished to the Office. If the independent certified public accountant fails to receive the evidence within the required five (5) business day period, the independent certified public accountant shall furnish to the Office a copy of its report within the next five (5) business days.

(b) An independent certified public accountant shall not be liable in any manner to any person for any statement made in connection with the paragraph 69O-190.0591 (4)(a), F.A.C., if the statement is made in good faith in compliance with paragraph 69O-190.0591 (4)(a), F.A.C.

(c) If the accountant, subsequent to the date of the annual audited financial statement filed pursuant to subsection 69O-190.059 (4)(a), F.A.C., becomes aware of facts which might have affected his report, the accountant shall report those facts to the Office and the fund within seven (7) business days of discovery.

(5) Report on Significant Deficiencies in Internal Controls.In addition to the annual audited financial statement required by subsection 69O-190.059 (4), F.A.C., each fund shall file with the

Office with a written report prepared by the accountant describing significant deficiencies in the fund's internal control structure noted by the accountant during the audit. The report on significant deficiencies in internal controls of the fund shall be filed with the annual audited financial statement. The report on significant deficiencies in internal controls may be filed as part of the management letter, or may be a separate report. The fund is required to provide a description of remedial actions taken or proposed to correct significant deficiencies, if said actions are not described in the accountant's report.

(6) Definition, Availability, and Maintenance of CPA Workpapers.

(a) Every fund shall require the accountant to make available for review by Division examiners all workpapers prepared in the conduct of his examination, and any communications related to the audit between the accountant and the fund at the offices of the fund, the offices of the certified public accountant, or at any other reasonable place agreed to by the Office. The fund shall require that the accountant retain the audit workpapers and communications until the Office has filed a report on examination covering the period of the audit, but no less than seven (7) years from the date of the audit reports.

(7) Funds shall be subject to examination pursuant to Section 624.316, Florida Statutes-.Funds shall reimburse the Office for actual expenses incurred for the examination pursuant to sections 624.316 and 624.320, Florida Statutes.

Specific Authority 440.5705, 624.4621 Fla. Stat.

Law Implemented 624.316, 624.424, 624.4621 Fla. Stat.

History: New 12-19-93, Formerly 38F-5.0591, 4L-190.0591.

69O-190.060. Security Deposits or Bonds for Self-Insurers Fund.

(1) Pursuant to Section 624.4621, Florida Statutes, each self-insurers fund shall deposit with the Office acceptable securities or post a surety bond issued by a corporate surety authorized to do business in the State of Florida or make provisions as otherwise provided in these rules.

(2) The security deposit or bond required of a self-insurers fund providing coverage under Section 624.4621, Florida Statutes, shall be equal to the greater of:

(a) $250,000

(b) 10% of the normal premium, and

(c) 10% of the total loss reserves. The amount of the security deposit or bond shall be determined at least annually based on data submitted by the self-insurers fund to the Office for the previous fiscal year end. Documents assigning investment assets to the division shall be filed with the division within 90 days of the effective date of these rules. Extensions may be granted for good cause.

(3) The security deposit requirement shall be satisfied by one of the following means:

(a) Self-insurers funds, upon application and during the first 24 months of operation, may post a surety bond to satisfy the security deposit requirement.

(b) All other funds shall satisfy the security deposit requirement by allocation of general investment assets of the fund to the division. No monies may be allocated from surplus in the loss fund in a given fund year until at least 12 months after the close of the fund year.

(c) If assets are not available, then the fund may post a surety bond in the amount of the difference between the amount of the security deposit requirement and the amount of assets available.

(d) The amount of the surety bond posted shall be considered a contingent liability. The necessity of the surety bond shall be eliminated before any dividends from premiums or investment income will be approved. If the deficiency is not completely eliminated within 12 months after the Office notifies the fund that a deficiency exists, then the failure to eliminate the deficiency shall be evidence of the fund's failure to satisfy the mandatory reserve requirements. Such failure shall be good cause for the revocation of the fund's self-insurance privilege and for the ordering of the assessment of the membership.

(4) Any surety bond posted by a self-insurers fund shall contain the provision that the surety agrees to provide reimbursements under the terms of the bond immediately upon failure or refusal of the self-insurers fund to meet any of its obligations under the Law.

Specific Authority 440.38(2)(b), 624.4621 Fla. Stat.

Law Implemented 440.38(2)(b), (3), 624.4621 Fla. Stat.

History: New 10-1-82, Amended 12-25-84, Formerly 38F-5.60, Amended 12-19-93, Formerly 38F-5.060, 4L-190.060.

69O-190.061. Excess Insurance Requirements—Self-Insurers Funds.

(1) When used in this rule, the following words or terms shall have the meaning as described herein:

(a) Loss fund—the retention under the terms of an aggregate excess contract, or if no aggregate excess is purchased, the amount remaining from normal premium in each fund year after all necessary expenses are paid. For the purposes of paragraphs 69O-190.061 (8)(b) and (c), F.A.C., no loss fund shall be less than 70 percent of earned normal premium without the approval of the Office.

(b) Aggregate loss—the amount of all claims incurred, including reserves for loss development and IBNR, which exceeds the loss fund.

(2) All self-insurers funds shall maintain specific excess insurance with a limit or not less than $1,000,000 or 5 times the policy retention whichever is greater. This amount shall not include the retention amount. Self-insurers funds containing businesses with a high risk of multiple injury from a single accident may be required to maintain higher limits. In determining whether to require such higher limits, the Office shall consider the likelihood of serious multiple injuries occurring in a single accident and the financial condition of the fund.

(3) The maximum retention allowed for a fund's specific excess policy shall be in accordance with the following schedule unless a waiver is granted pursuant to subsections (4), (5), (6) and (7):

(a) For funds with a loss fund of less than $3,000,000 the maximum retention shall be $225,000.

(b) For funds with a loss fund greater than or equal to $3,000,000 and less than $4,000,000, the maximum retention shall be $230,000.

(c) For funds with a loss fund greater than or equal to $4,000,000 and less than $5,000,000, the maximum retention shall be $240,000.

(d) For funds with a loss fund greater than or equal to $5,000,000 and less than $6,000,000, the maximum retention shall be $250,000.

(e) For funds with a loss fund greater than or equal to $6,000,000, and less than $7,000,000, the maximum retention shall be $260,000.

(f) For funds with a loss fund greater than or equal to $7,000,000 and less than $8,000,000, the maximum retention shall be $270,000.

(g) For funds with a loss fund greater than or equal to $8,000,000 and less than $9,000,000, the maximum retention shall be $280,000.

(h) For funds with a loss fund greater than or equal to $9,000,000 and less than $10,000,000, the maximum retention shall be $290,000.

(i) For funds with a loss fund greater than or equal to $10,000,000 and less than $50,000,000, the maximum retention shall be 3 percent of the fund's loss fund.

(j) For funds with a loss fund greater than or equal to $50,000,000 and less than $100,000,000, the maximum retention shall be 3.5 percent of the fund's loss fund.

(k) For funds with a loss fund greater than or equal to $100,000,000 the maximum retention shall be 4 percent of the fund's loss fund.

(*l*) Regardless of any maximum contained in this paragraph, no fund shall secure a retention which is not actuarially sound. Upon the request of the Office, a fund shall submit evidence of the actuarial soundness of its desired retention in a report prepared by its actuary. In the event that the fund does not have its own actuary, the Office shall prepare its own report on the actuarial soundness of the retention. After evaluating all evidence the Office shall determine if the desired retention is actuarially sound. In the event the desired retention is not actuarially sound, the Office shall not approve the desired retention.

(4) If a fund wishes to secure a specific excess policy with a retention greater than the maximum allowed by subsection (3), then the fund shall comply with the procedure described in subsections (5), (6) and (7).

(5) Funds which have been in operation at least 60 months may request permission to secure a retention higher than that authorized by subsection (3). A fund shall submit a feasibility study prepared by a qualified actuary which analyzes the impact on the fund of the higher retention. The study shall be in writing and shall be submitted to the Division at least 90 days prior to the beginning of the fund year for which the higher retention is requested. The Division shall advise the fund of its decision on allowing the higher retention no later than 45 days prior to the beginning of the fund year in question. If the fund has elected to make application for establishing an aggregate reserve, the specific excess feasibility study may be combined with the aggregate excess feasibility study. If the two studies are combined, the actuary shall specify the intent for the report to satisfy both requirements.

(6) The specific excess study shall analyze the past 5 fund years and illustrate the effect on the fund had the higher retention been in place during the past 5 fund years. The study shall also examine the impact of the higher retention on the fund for the next fund year. The report of the actuary shall also describe the method by which the additional reserves due to the higher retention will be funded. Monies used to fund the higher retentions shall be allocated from premium earned during the year the loss was incurred, from investment earnings from the year in which the loss was incurred or from future investment earnings on the specific loss reserve.

(7) The Office shall deny the use of a higher retention if it finds that the higher retention will adversely affect fund solvency or if the fund is unable to establish reserves using monies authorized by subsection (6).

(8) Each self-insurers fund shall provide security for liabilities in excess of its loss fund in each fund year by selecting one of the following alternatives:

(a) Purchasing an acceptable aggregate excess policy as defined in Rules 69O-190.035, 69O-190.036 and 69O-190.061, F.A.C.,

(b) Upon approval by the Office, pursuant to subsection 69O-190.061 (12), post a separate cash security deposit in the amount of $1,000,000 or 20 percent (20%) of annual standard premium, whichever is greater, or

(c) Upon written approval of the Office, pursuant to subsection 69O-190.061 (13), (14), and (15), F.A.C., establish a reserve for aggregate excess losses in accordance with this rule. A fund shall have been in operation for at least 60 months before this option may be selected.

(9) The insured aggregate limit for a self-insurers fund shall not be less than $1,000,000. Subject to this minimum, the self-insurers fund shall secure an aggregate limit of at least 20 percent (20%) of the annual standard premium of the fund for the term of the policy. The limit so determined shall be rounded to the nearest $100,000. The retention of an aggregate policy is limited to the highest retention that can be funded from normal premium in the fund year without developing a contingent liability. A higher retention than can be funded from normal premium may be allowed by the Division if the resulting contingent liability can be guaranteed by a cash security deposit.

(10) If the option in paragraph 69O-190.061 (8)(a), F.A.C., is selected, the self-insurers fund, upon written approval of the Office, may self-insure part of its aggregate limit by posting as a separate cash security deposit for the amount which is self-insured. The procedures set out in 4-190.061 (8)(b) and 4-190.061 (12) shall be used by the Office to determine whether the aggregate may be partially funded by posting a

cash security.

(11) No aggregate excess policy shall be acceptable if it contains a provision for a minimum retention or loss fund which is greater than the product of the aggregate excess retention percentage and the fund's estimated annual normal premium for the term of the policy, unless the fund has sufficient unencumbered surplus to guarantee the resulting contingent liability.

(12) The Office shall grant permission to post the cash security deposit in lieu of the fund purchasing an aggregate excess policy, if the Office determines that based upon a comparison of the assets and liabilities of the fund, the fund has a surplus equal to or greater than the total security deposits required by Rule 69O-190.060, F.A.C., including the cash security to be posted in lieu of purchase of the aggregate excess policy.

(13) If the option in paragraph 69O-190.061 (8)(c), F.A.C., is selected, the fund shall make application to the Office, in the manner prescribed herein, at least 90 days prior to the beginning of the first fund year for which permission is requested to establish an aggregate reserve to provide security for aggregate losses. The Office shall render a decision on the application no less than 45 days prior to the beginning of that first fund year. Thereafter, application shall be filed as set out at paragraph 69O-190.061 (16)(a), F.A.C., for each year for which permission is sought to establish an aggregate reserve. The time periods set out in this rule shall not apply to applications submitted within the first 90 days after the effective date of this rule.

(14) An application under paragraph 69O-190.061 (8)(c), F.A.C., shall be in writing and shall include the following information:

(a) A plan for the first year of operation with a reserve account which establishes the proposed funding of the reserve account. The plan shall set forth the assumptions upon which the funding of the aggregate reserve is based. The plan shall use current rate levels and reasonable estimates of premium income, expenses, and investment rates of return. The plan may also include alternative analyses using anticipated rate level changes, and various assumptions regarding premium income, investment income, and expenses.

(b) A feasibility study by a qualified actuary which evaluates the last 5 fund years. This study must illustrate the effect of using the assumptions contained in the plan applied to the past 5 fund years. In making this study, the rules, as hereinafter provided, governing the funding of the aggregate reserve account shall be used in determining the feasibility of the plan.

(c) A statement by the actuary that, in his opinion, the proposed plan is an actuarially sound method of providing security for aggregate losses on a retrospective and prospective basis. Furthermore, the actuary shall state that the report is complete and accurate and that, in his opinion, the techniques and assumptions used are reasonable and meet the requirements and intent of this rule.

(15) The application shall be rejected if the Office determines that the proposed plan to fund aggregate losses does not comply with this rule.

(16) If a fund receives permission to fund its aggregate losses by establishing an aggregate reserve, the fund shall comply with the following requirements:

(a) At least 60 days prior to the beginning of each policy year for which an aggregate reserve will be established, the fund shall submit a plan for that year as prescribed in paragraphs 69O-190.061 (14) (a) and (c), F.A.C. Written approval of the plan by the Office shall be required before an aggregate reserve may be established for the next policy year.

(b) Within 6 months after the end of each fund year, the fund shall submit an actuarial report, by a qualified actuary, of its aggregate reserve for each fund year whose aggregate losses are guaranteed by the reserve. Fund years more than 4 years old may be consolidated for the report. All other years must be evaluated separately.

(c) The actuarial report shall evaluate the losses, estimate loss development and establish a reserve for losses incurred but not reported (IBNR). The report shall provide a single best estimate of ultimate loss for each year evaluated separately and a single best estimate for all years more than 4 years old which are grouped together.

(d) Along with the actuarial report, the fund shall provide financial information which sets forth the financial position of the aggregate reserve. The financial report shall indicate whether the reserve account, including reserves for losses, loss development and IBNR, can be funded from the premium income of the fund. If the monies allocated to the loss fund are insufficient to satisfy the requirements of the aggregate reserve, then the fund shall provide a plan for funding the amounts necessary to make the aggregate reserve actuarially sound.

(e) In developing a plan for funding the aggregate reserve, the actuary shall estimate the amount of time it will take for the fund to pay out the cash currently remaining in its loss fund in each fund year. The plan shall set forth an actuarially sound procedure for allocating money to the aggregate reserve to insure that the fund will have, at any point in the future, sufficient money to meet all its claims payments. At a point in time no later than 4 years from the end of each fund year, the fund shall have fully funded the aggregate reserve for that year, so that taking into account investment earnings, no further contributions will be necessary to fund all future claims liabilities. Failure to meet the requirement for having made all necessary contributions within 4 years shall be good cause for finding that the aggregate reserve is actuarially unsound for purposes of paragraph 69O-190.039(2)(a), F.A.C.

(f) The actuarial report shall also estimate the unfunded liability for each year with an aggregate reserve requirement and determine the ability of the fund to pay its future liabilities under the assumption that no further premium income will be available after the end of the current fund year. The financial report shall review the fund's liquidity and determine if the fund will have sufficient cash available under the assumption that no further premium income will be earned after the end of the current fund year. Failure to demonstrate that the fund will have sufficient cash to meet its claims obligations or eliminate its unfunded liability without the contribution of additional earned premium from subsequent fund years shall be good cause for finding that the aggregate reserve is actuarially unsound for purposes of paragraph 69O-190.039(2)(a), F.A.C.

(g) In actuarially determining the amount of ultimate loss, the fund and its actuary may take into account current or future recoveries from any aggregate or specific excess contract, if such contract complies with these rules.

(h) Any fund with an approved preferred payment plan shall have its actuary determine the necessary amount of additional premium to be paid by the preferred payment plan participants so that all potential funding deficits in the loss fund will be eliminated. Funds which charge this additional premium shall be excused from the requirement to allocate surplus to the loss fund to fund the deficit as required by paragraph 69O-190.066 (8)(k), F.A.C.

(17) The Office shall:

(a) Reject an actuarial report or financial report which does not comply with the requirements of subsection 69O-190.061 (16), F.A.C. If this occurs, the Office shall conduct its own actuarial or financial review or upon request of the fund allow the fund to submit another actuarial or financial report within sixty (60) days subject to the Office's approval of the party preparing the report.

(b) For good cause, order a fund to cease using an aggregate reserve for securing its aggregate losses. Good cause shall include a finding that the aggregate reserve is actuarially unsound, that the fund is insolvent, that the fund will lack sufficient liquidity to run off its claims without reliance on future premium income, or that the fund has failed to comply with the provisions of this rule.

(c) In the event that the fund's aggregate reserve, or reserves, is actuarially unsound, order the fund to take such corrective action as necessary to make the reserve actuarially sound.

(18) In consideration of approval of its plan to use an aggregate reserve to fund its aggregate losses, the fund agrees to the following:

(a) Payment of dividends from premium in a fund year shall not be requested or approved for that fund year as long as any claims reserves, reserves for loss development or reserves for IBNR are unfunded by actual cash reserves.

(b) No dividends shall be requested or approved from investment earnings unless the aggregate reserves for all years are actuarially sound, taking into account future contributions.

(c) That advance premium discounts and all expenses unnecessary for the fund to meet its obligations under the law will be reduced or eliminated, if necessary, to provide funds to make an aggregate reserve actuarially sound.

(d) That the amounts actuarially determined to be necessary for the reserves for loss development shall be in addition to the fund's security deposit requirement as specified in Rule 69O-190.060, F.A.C.

(e) That no premium from a year prior to the year for which the aggregate reserve is established may be allocated to fund an aggregate reserve until 12 months after the close of the prior year.

Specific Authority 440.38(2)(b), 624.4621 Fla. Stat.

Law Implemented 440.38(2)(b), (3), 624.4621 Fla. Stat.

History: New 10-1-82, Amended 12-25-84, 12-17-85, Formerly 38F-5.61, Amended 3-11-87, 2-3-88, 12-19-93, Formerly 38F-5.061, 4L-190.061.

69O-190.062. Filing Reports—Self-Insurers Funds.

(1) Reports as to payroll records, coverage, accident experience and compensation payment and such periodic reports as are required to be filed with the Office shall be made as follows:

(a) Summary loss data shall be filed with the Office on each fund member within 60 days after the evaluation date of the losses being reported on OIR Form BSI-17. Procedures for reporting losses as specified in subsection 69O-190.050(3), F.A.C., shall apply.

(b) Properly classified and audited payrolls on each fund member shall be submitted to the Office on OIR Form BSI-5 within 60 days after the evaluation date of the summary loss information required in paragraph (a) above. The classification and audit procedures specified in subsection 69O-190.050(1), F.A.C., shall apply.

(c) Quarterly Status Reports submitted on OIR Form BSI-24 (Revised 3-11-87), which accurately reflect the financial condition of each open fund year shall be filed with the Division within thirty (30) days after the close of each fund year quarter and signed by the chairman of the board of trustees or authorized self-insurers fund administrator. A fund year is considered open as long as one claim from that fund year remains unsettled.

(2) After the inception date of the fund, prospective new members of the self-insurers fund shall submit an application for membership to the board of trustees or its administrator on OIR Form BSI-3 or its equivalent. The trustees or administrator must approve the application for membership in accordance with these rules and the terms of the indemnity agreement for the application to be binding upon the self-insurers fund and the prospective member. A copy of the application for membership shall be filed with the Office along with a properly completed OIR Form BSI-206 within twenty-one (21) days after the effective date of membership.

(3) It shall be the responsibility of each self-insurers fund member to notify the fund to which it belongs or its service company of any changes in the names, addresses, structure and composition of all businesses or subsidiaries which participate in the self-insurers fund. It shall also be the responsibility of the fund member to notify the fund or service company of any additions or deletions in the business or subsidiaries participating in the fund. These changes include changes in majority ownership interest in any business or subsidiary that is covered or that will be covered by the fund. All such changes shall be reported to the fund or its service company within 30 days after the effective date of the change. Each self-insurers fund or service company shall notify the Office, by written endorsement, of any such changes re-

ported to it by its members within 30 days after it has first knowledge of the change. Repeated failure to file the required endorsements within the time prescribed shall result in civil penalties being assessed pursuant to Rule 69O-190.038, F.A.C. If the Office determines the self-insurers fund members made the late reporting, then the penalty shall be assessed against the member; otherwise, the penalty shall be assessed against the self-insurers fund.

Specific Authority 440.38(2)(b), 3 Fla. Stat.

Law Implemented 440.38(1)(b), (2)(b), 440.51, 624.4621 Fla. Stat.

History: New 10-1-82, Amended 12-25-84, Formerly 38F-5.62, Amended 3-11-87, 2-3-88, 12-19-93, Formerly 38F-5.062, 4L-190.062.

69O-190.063. Annual Review and Examination—Self-Insurers Funds.

(1) All bonds or securities issued by the State of Florida or the United States Government which are posted as security deposits shall be reviewed annually by the Office to determine market value. In the event market value is less than the deposit requirement, the Office may require that additional securities be posted by the self-insurer. In making such a determination, the Office shall consider the self-insurer's financial condition, the amount that market value is less than the deposit requirement and the likelihood that such securities will be needed to provide benefits.

(2) All self-insurers funds shall maintain at a central location within the State of Florida such records as are necessary to verify the accuracy and completeness of all reports submitted to the Office pursuant to these rules as well as all reports necessary to establish the financial solvency of the self-insurers fund. Furthermore, the central location shall be the office of the administrator or fiscal agent of the self-insurers fund. However, the self-insurers fund shall be authorized to transfer its financial records to the offices of the Certified Public Accountant for the self-insurers fund upon the written permission of the Office. In addition, if the self-insurers fund has contracted with a service company for claims handling, then the claims files and related records may be located at the offices of the service company as long as they are within the State of Florida.

(3) All records as herein required shall be open to inspection by authorized representatives of the Office during regular business hours. Records shall be retained for a period of time sufficient to ensure their availability for audit purposes. In the absence of other guidelines, the records shall be retained according to the schedule adopted by the Office for similar records. The location of these records shall be made known to the Office upon the application for self-insurance and at such times thereafter sufficient to keep the Office informed of their location.

(4) The fund, in any agreement or contract with the administrator or fiscal agent, shall require that the records of the administrator or fiscal agent which pertain to fund operations, assets or liabilities under Chapter 440, Florida Statutes, shall be open to inspection by authorized representatives of the Office during regular business hours.

(5) Each self-insurers fund's records shall be examined in accordance with section 624.316, Florida Statutes, by representatives of the Office at such time as may be determined by the Office. Prior notice of the audit shall not be required. This audit is in addition to any audit performed in preparation of the financial reports required by these rules.

(6) Each self-insurers fund shall comply with the guidelines regarding questionable claims handling techniques, questionable patterns of claims, repeated unreasonably controverted claims or poor payment practices established pursuant to Section 440.20 (16), Florida Statutes.

(7) After each audit, a written report shall be prepared with a copy to the self-insurers fund; such report to be a part of the annual review for compliance with these rules. Any deficiencies cited by this report shall be considered on their merit in determining if there are grounds for revocation of the self-insurance privilege or the imposition of penalties pursuant to subsection (9). Within 45 days after the receipt of an audit

report which contains findings that the fund violated a rule contained in Rule Chapter 69O-190, F.A.C., the trustees shall convene a meeting to discuss the report. The discussion of the report shall be noted in the minutes of the meeting.

(8) As part of its annual review and audit, the Office shall determine if the self-insurers fund has a contingent liability. In the event the fund is found to have a contingent liability, the Office shall inform the fund and order that this liability be funded in accordance with subsections 69O-190.060 (2) and 69O-190.065 (5), F.A.C.

(9) In addition to the penalties prescribed in Rule 69O-190.038, F.A.C., the Office may impose civil penalties not to exceed $100 for each violation of the Law or these rules. Penalties shall be imposed pursuant to Section 440.021, Florida Statutes.

Specific Authority 440.38(2)(b), (3), 624.4621 Fla. Stat.

Law Implemented 440.38(2)(b), 624.4621 Fla. Stat.

History: New 10-1-82, Amended 12-25-84, Formerly 38F-5.63, Amended 3-11-87, 12-19-93, Formerly 38F-5.063, 4L-190.063.

69O-190.064. Trustees' Responsibilities.

(1) The board of trustees shall have complete authority over and shall retain ultimate control of the assets of the fund and shall be responsible for all operations of the fund.

(2) The trustees shall have the authority to approve applications for membership in the fund. The trustees may delegate this authority to the administrator.

(3) The composition of the board of trustees shall be as follows:

(a) A majority of the board shall be owners, officers, directors, partners or employees of one or more members of the fund.

(b) A trustee, or relative of the trustee, shall not be an owner, officer, director, partner or employee of the fund's service company. This does not apply to employment of a relative of the trustee in which the relative's duties are of a clerical, or non-managerial nature. Non-managerial being a position which cannot affect the financial standing of a self-insurer, or the benefits to which an injured employee is entitled under Chapter 440, Florida Statutes.

(4) The trustees shall act in a prudent and responsible manner in safeguarding the assests of the fund. The trustees may designate a fiscal agent to oversee, invest and disburse the fund's assets on a day-to-day basis. The trustees may designate an administrator to handle the management of the fund on a day-to-day basis. The administrator may also be delegated the responsibilities of a fiscal agent.

(5) The administrator, fiscal agent or any other individual with authority to disburse funds shall furnish a fidelity bond or insurance policy payable to the trustees in an amount sufficient to protect the fund's assets against misappropriation or misuse. The amount of the bond shall an amount equal to not less than 10 percent of the funds handled annually and issued in the name of the fund covering its trustees, employees, administrator, or other individuals managing or handling the funds or assets of the fund. In no case may such bond be less than $1,000 or more than $500,000, except that the division may for good cause prescribe an amount in excess of $500,000, subject to the 10-percent limitation of the preceding sentence.

(6) The fiscal agent, or administrator, or service company shall be subject to the following conditions:

(a) A fiscal agent or administrator shall be an employee of or under contract to the fund.

(b) The administrator may provide some or all of the services required by the rules.

(c) In delegating authority to the administrator, fiscal agent or service company, the trustees shall insure that no conflict of interest exists between the interests of the fund and that of the administrator, fiscal agent, or service company. In the event that fiscal authority is delegated, the trustees shall insure that adequate division of responsibility exists and that satisfactory internal fiscal controls are established to safeguard the fund's assets.

(d) If the administrator provides claims adjusting services to the fund, the trustees shall not delegate any fiscal authority to the administrator except for control of the claims revolving fund.

(e) If the administrator or its representative, or any officer, director, partner, or management of the service company has a business or financial relationship with a business providing goods or services to the fund, then:

1. Such relationship shall be disclosed by the administrator or service company in writing to the trustees and to the audit committee, and

2. All business transactions between the fund and the business providing goods or services shall be conducted so that said business or financial relationship will not influence the outcome of the transactions, and

3. The trustees shall exercise all reasonable precautions so that the business providing goods or services is not unjustly enriched due to the business or financial relationship with the administrator or service company.

(f) Upon receipt of notification as required by subparagraph (e)1. above, the minutes of the next Trustee's meeting shall reflect the discussion of the notification and the action taken by the trustees. The fund shall also maintain a file of the written notices for review by the division.

(g) The trustees shall establish an audit committee subject to the following conditions:

1. The committee shall be independent of the control of the administrator and the service company and shall report directly to the trustees.

2. The committee shall be responsible on a continuing basis for determining that the fund has instituted and is complying with satisfactory internal fiscal controls in order to protect the fund's assets.

3. The committee shall investigate all potential conflicts of interest involving the administrator or service company. It shall report in writing to the trustees all cases of actual conflict of interest.

4. The committee shall work closely with the fund's certified public accountants to verify the accuracy and completeness of the fund's financial records and reports.

5. The management of the fund, the administrator, or officer, stockholder, owner, management of the service company shall not be represented on the committee.

6. The committee shall make at least one written report to the trustees per year detailing its activities and findings.

7. All committee reports shall be reviewed by the trustees and such reviews shall be noted in the minutes of the meeting at which the review was discussed.

8. All written reports by the committee shall be made available for review by authorized representatives of the Office as part of the audit of the fund.

(7) The trustees may establish a revolving fund for the use of the service company for the payment of claims and related expenses, subject to the following:

(a) The service company shall furnish a fidelity bond or insurance policy covering its officers and employees, payable to the trustees of the fund in an amount sufficient to protect all monies placed in the revolving fund. The amount shall be no less than the one months average receipts deposited into the revolving fund. Average receipts shall be the total deposits made during the previous fund year divided by twelve (12).

(b) If the bond or policy required pursuant to subsection 69O-190.064 (5), F.A.C., also covers the monies in the revolving fund, a separate bond or policy shall not be required from the service company.

(8) All fidelity bonds or insurance policies required by subsection 69O-190.064 (5), F.A.C., and paragraph 69O-190.064 (7)(a), F.A.C., may provide for a deductible of not more than $5,000.

(9) The trustees shall maintain up-to-date, accurate, and complete records of the fund's finances. The accounts and records of the fund shall be audited at least annually and at any

other time necessary to determine the financial condition of the fund.

(10) The trustees shall obtain audits of the fund and disclose the financial condition of the fund as indicated below.

(a) Audits shall be made by a certified public accountant. Audits may also be made by authorized representatives of the Office.

(b) The Office shall prescribe a standard report of financial condition to be used by all self-insurers funds pursuant to Rule 4-190.059, F.A.C.

(c) The Office reserves the right to prescribe the types of audits to be performed to determine fund solvency.

(d) The reserves for losses and loss development shall be reviewed annually pursuant to Rule 4-190.059 to determine the adequacy of these reserves.

(e) Copies of all audits and financial reports required pursuant to Rule 4-190.059, F.A.C., and prepared by personnel other than Office personnel shall be filed with the Office pursuant to Rule 4-190.059, F.A.C.

(11) Subject to the terms and conditions indicated below, the trustees may establish a penalty rate to produce premium in excess of standard premium for any class of employers with unfavorable loss experience.

(a) The trustees shall submit to the Office a justification for the application of the penalty rate as well as a description of how it will be applied.

(b) Approval by the Office shall be required prior to implementation of the penalty rate.

(c) Employers subject to a penalty rate shall be notified in writing prior to the effective date of the penalty rate.

(12) The trustees, fiscal agent, or administrator shall not utilize any of the money collected as premium from members for any purpose other than those specifically authorized by these rules or the fund's indemnity agreement.

(13) The trustees shall be prohibited from borrowing money from the fund or in the name of the fund without obtaining prior approval from the Office. Approval shall be granted only if:

(a) The loan is for a productive purpose, and

(b) It is consistent with the fund's purpose, and

(c) It does not impair the financial solvency of the fund.

(14) The trustees shall be authorized to invest the fund's assets only in the manner prescribed by Rule 4-190.071.

(15) The safety of any investment shall be the responsibility of the trustees.

(16) The trustees shall be prohibited from making any type of investment as authorized by these rules with the intent to trade, dispose or sell the security in any manner other than redeeming it at maturity. Therefore, it shall be the responsibility of the trustees to purchase securities in such denominations and with dates of maturity to ensure that these securities shall be redeemable at the same time and in the same amounts as the self-insurers fund's current and long-term liabilities.

(17) The trustees of each authorized self-insurers fund shall cause to be adopted a set of by-laws or shall enter into a trust agreement which shall govern the operation of the fund. These by-laws or trust agreement shall contain, but not be limited to the following subjects:

(a) Qualifications for self-insurers fund membership including underwriting considerations.

(b) The method for selecting the trustees, including the term of office.

(c) The method of amending the by-laws.

(d) Employer's Liability Limit provided by the self-insurers fund.

(e) The amount of the trustees' remuneration which is in excess of actual expenses incurred.

(18) In addition to the above by-laws, the trustees shall adopt written policies on the following subjects, such policies shall be recorded

in the minutes of the meeting at which they were adopted and shall be binding on the administrator and service company:

(a) Investment of surplus monies and claims reserves in accordance with Chapter 440, F.S., and Chapter 69O-190, F.A.C.

(b) Frequency and extent of loss control and safety engineering service to members.

(c) The size of the revolving claims fund.

(d) A schedule for payment and collection of premiums including a definition of delinquent premium.

(e) Cancellation procedures, including cancellation for non-payment of premium and cancellation for excessive losses.

(f) Delineation of authority granted to the administrator or fiscal agent.

(g) Delineation of authority granted to the service company.

(h) A penalty program for surcharging members with excessive losses.

(i) Procedures for handling disputes regarding premium paid by members.

(j) Dividend policies including underwriting criteria.

(19) The trustees shall review at least annually the following items for the purpose of determining whether these areas of concern are being adequately provided for and the findings of such review shall be recorded in the minutes of the meeting at which they were discussed:

(a) Service company performance.

(b) Loss control and safety engineering.

(c) Investment policies.

(d) Collection of bad debt.

(e) Cancellation procedures.

(f) Initial member review.

(g) Administrator performance.

(h) Dividend policies.

(20) All self-insurers shall file copies of the current by-laws or trust agreement and required written policies with the Division. Any changes in the by-laws, trust agreement or written policies shall be filed with the Office no later than ten (10) days after their taking effect. The Office reserves the right to order the self-insurers fund to rescind or revoke any by-law or policy if it is in violation of these rules or the Law.

(21) The board of trustees of a self-insurers fund shall meet from time to time as needed to conduct the business of the fund. However, the trustees shall meet at least four (4) times per fund year and written minutes of each meeting shall be kept. The minutes shall be signed and dated by the chairman or secretary of the board of trustees. Such minutes shall be open to inspection by the Office.

Specific Authority 624.4621 Fla. Stat.

Law Implemented624.4621 Fla. Stat.

History: New 1C-1-82, Amended 12-25-84, Formerly 38F-5.64, Amended 3-11-87, 12-19-93, Formerly 38F-5.064, 4L-190.064.

69O-190.065. Distribution of Surplus Monies by Self-Insurers Funds.

(1) Any surplus monies for a fund year in excess of the amount necessary to fulfill all obligations under the Law for that fund year may be declared refundable to members by the trustees at any time. The amount of such declaration shall be a liability of the fund at the time of the declaration. Date of payment shall be as agreed by the trustees and the Division subject to this section.

(2) Distribution of dividends are subject to the following conditions:

(a) Dividends of surplus premium (i.e., underwriting profit) shall be payable only to employers who paid premium to the fund during the year the underwriting profit occurred.

(b) Dividends of surplus investment or miscellaneous income may be paid to any member who meets the criteria established by the fund pursuant to Rule paragraph 69O-190.065 (2)(c), F.A.C. Payment of any such dividend shall be subject to a plan filed with and approved in writing by the Division. Any such plan shall comply with Rule 69O-190.072, F.A.C.

(c) Eligibility for dividends pursuant to paragraphs (a) and (b) shall be based on criteria which meet the following conditions:

1. The criteria shall be objective and measurable such as an employer's accident record, the amount of premium paid, or any other criteria which encourages workplace safety or cost containment.

2. The criteria shall only apply to fund membership, and

3. The amount of dividend otherwise earned shall be prorated based upon the length of membership of the member in the fund.

(d) All dividends from policy years beginning on or after October 1, 1989, whether from premium, investment income or miscellaneous income, shall be payable to employers who were members of the fund at the end of the policy year in question but have since left the fund and are otherwise entitled to receive a dividend according to the criteria established by the trustees.

(e) No fund shall offer to provide a dividend or seek to enlist a new member based upon the promise of payment of a dividend. No fund may promise, or make any representation of, a specific amount of dividend for which a potential member may become eligible. A fund may disclose in its solicitation of new members, the formula which it intends to use to calculate a member's future dividend pursuant to paragraph (2)(c).

(3) A request to the Division for authorization to disburse a declared refund shall be made in writing to the Office by the fund administrator or trustees. A request for permission to pay a dividend shall be in accordance with Section 440.57(5), F.S. Such request shall include a current financial statement and an actuarial report regarding the adequacy of the reserves for all fund years. Such request shall be delivered to the Division in such manner that a signed receipt is provided to the sender.

(4) Before approving any refund distribution request, the Division shall determine that such refund will not impair the financial solvency of the self-insurers fund. In any given fund year, the monies allocated to the loss fund shall not be used for any purpose other than paying claims and authorized expenses until such time as surplus monies are eligible to be refunded. The intent of these rules is to ensure that sufficient monies are retained so that total assets are greater than total liabilities in each fund year.

(5) In the event of a deficit or contingent liability in any fund year, such deficit shall be funded immediately, either from surplus from a fund year other than the current fund year or from trustee' funds or by assessment of the membership, if ordered by the Division, or by such alternate method as the Division may approve. An alternate method shall not increase the liability of the fund. Alternate methods may include, but are not limited to, capital contributions by a sponsoring association, capital contributions from a trustee or member, sale of a fixed asset by the fund, or by disallowing or reducing an advance premium discount to members. The Division shall be notified prior to any transfer of surplus funds.

(6) When a dividend is disbursed, it shall be the responsibility of the fund to ensure that dividends are paid to employers eligible for a dividend including those who are no longer members of the fund. The fund shall give each member, upon joining the fund, written notice that dividends may be payable to a member after leaving the fund. Such notice shall also instruct the member to keep the fund informed of any changes in address after leaving the fund.

(7) When disbursing a dividend, the fund shall make a reasonable effort to locate all former members of the fund who are eligible for a dividend. Reasonable effort shall include:

(a) Mailing the dividend payment to the last known address of the member according to the records of the fund,

(b) For dividends in excess of $500, if the member is not located at the last known address, the fund shall make an attempt to locate the former member through the member's insurance agent, association or through sources of information available to the general public.

Specific Authority 440.591, 624.4621 Fla. Stat.

Law Implemented 624.4621 Fla. Stat.

History: New 10-1-82, Amended 12-25-84, Formerly 38F-5.65, Amended 3-11-90, 6-12-91, 8-28-91, 12-19-93, Formerly 38F-5.065, 4L-190.065.

69O-190.066. Premium Billing and Collection.

(1) The trustees shall not allow a premium discount to any member for the period beginning on September 1, 1990 and ending on December 31, 1991. Beginning on January 1, 1992, if a self-insurer's fund allows premium discounts to its members, the trustees shall allow a premium discount to each member as follows: First $5,000 of standard premium 0% Next 95,000 of standard premium 10.9% Next 400,000 of standard premium 12.6% Over 500,000 of standard premium 14.4% It is the intention of the Office that these discounts be identical to the rates approved by the Office of Insurance for voluntary stock premium discounts. The trustees may not authorize a discount in excess of that allowed by the fund's excess insurer in determining the excess policies' premium and retention.

(2) In no event shall a fund using a dividend to offset billed premium make any representation to a member or a potential member that this dividend constitutes an additional advance discount. Premium reported to the Division shall be normal premium.

(3) If in any given fund year, the self-insurers fund will have an unfunded contingent liability, then no advance discount to members shall be allowed that year until the liability is funded.

(4) In determining "net premiums" on which Administrative and Special Disability Assessments are computed pursuant to Sections 440.49 (2)(h) and 440.51, Florida Statutes, self-insurers funds shall use amounts collected after both advance discounts and refunds. In no event shall the fund be allowed to deduct more than 15 percent from standard premium when calculating net premium.

(5) The trustees shall make all reasonable efforts to collect delinquent premiums. The trustees shall establish premium payment schedules which provide for premium payment dates, corresponding amounts due, and a basis for determining when unpaid premiums are to be considered delinquent. Copies of all payment schedules shall be filed with the Office within 30 days after implementation.

(6) The trustees at their discretion may establish any payment schedule that adequately provides for sufficient cash flow and that gives proper consideration for the potential adverse effects of delinquent premium on fund solvency. Payment schedules, other than preferred payment plans, shall require that a member's annual pro-rata normal premium is payable in full upon presentation of the final annual billing. Such billings shall include credits for amounts already paid and may include credits for any dividend or administrative savings allowed. The Office reserves the right to order modification of any payment schedule contrary to these rules or which it determines will adversely affect the fund's liquidity or solvency.

(7) The trustees may establish preferred payment plans for certain members which allow these members to pay a premium other than normal premium. Each member participating in a preferred payment plan shall enter into a contract or agreement which sets forth the terms and conditions of the plan. Such payment plans shall be subject to the following conditions:

(a) All proposed plans including the proposed contract or agreement shall be submitted to and approved by the Office prior to implementation. In approving or disapproving a plan, the Office shall determine if the plan complies with this rule. Additionally, all revisions to the approved plan, contract, or agreement shall be submitted to the Office and approved prior to implementation.

(b) The plan shall establish a minimum normal premium that a member must pay to qualify for participation in the plan.

(c) The fund shall conduct a reasonable financial review of any employer desiring to participate in the plan for the purpose of determining that the member is financially sound. A description of the financial review shall be part of the plan. Only financially sound employers may participate in these plans.

(d) The plan and contract or agreement shall require that each participant shall pay to the fund a portion of the total fixed expenses for the fund. At the beginning of each policy year in which the plan is offered, the fixed expenses associated with the fund's operation shall be calculated.

1. The minimum fixed expense shall be based upon the portion of the fund's estimated annual normal premium in excess of the aggregate retention or loss fund. The percentage of the estimated annual normal premium determined by the fixed expenses of the fund shall be applied to the estimated annual normal premium of each member in the plan to determine the minimum pro-rata fixed expenses to be paid to the fund by each participant.

2. The fixed expenses owed by each participant may be greater than the minimum but shall be fixed at policy inception and adjusted on final audit only to reflect changes in the member's audited normal premium. Expenses which are allowable charges to the aggregate excess contract loss fund may be deducted from the member's claims deposit.

3. Each fund shall adopt a fixed expense charge which it shall apply to all members of the preferred payment plan during a given fund year. The fund may elect to apply an expense charge which is greater than the actual expense factor of the fund but this charge shall be uniformly applied to all preferred payment plan members in a given year.

(e) If the plan allows the member to pay less than the earned normal premium upon final audit, then the plan shall require, at a minimum, that the member provide security to the fund for the difference between the premium actually paid and the member's annual normal premium. After the end of the policy year, the security may be reduced to the amount of the member's outstanding claims reserves. Such security may be surety bonds, cash security, letters of credit, or other methods approved by the Office. This security shall be adjusted annually to reflect current incurred loss, claims payments, and lump sum settlements. The fund shall establish a reserve for the amount of the outstanding claims reserves.

(f) The plan shall establish a minimum and maximum premium that each member shall be subject to for each policy period in the plan.

1. The minimum premium shall be greater than or equal to the sum of the fixed expenses established pursuant to paragraph 69O-190.066 (8)(d), F.A.C., and the cost of all claims incurred net of excess recoveries.

2. The maximum premium shall not be less than 115% of the member's standard premium. The maximum premium established by the fund shall be the most any member shall be required to pay the fund for coverage except for assessments made pursuant to the fund's indemnity agreement.

3. The fund shall collect a deposit premium which shall be at least equal to the amount of the claims deposit plus a pro-rata portion of the expense charge. This deposit premium shall be paid prior to the beginning of the member's participation in the plan in a given year.

(g) The plan shall require that the member forfeit any dividends paid by the fund for the period the member participated in the plan.

(h) The participation in the plan by a member shall be terminated by the fund if the member's financial condition deteriorates to the point where its ability to meet future financial obligations is in doubt. The fund shall maintain a file for each participant, and such file shall be made available to Office personnel upon request. Each file shall contain, but shall not be limited to, financial statements or audited financial statements for each member's three (3) most recent fiscal years.

(i) The plan shall provide that the member provide a cash deposit out of which the fund will pay the member's claims. Such deposit shall be reviewed by the fund at least quarterly and increased or decreased to reflect the actual claims paid by the fund on behalf of the member.

1. Each member shall be billed monthly for any claims paid by the fund during the previous month. It is the intent of this rule that funds should use only the preferred payment plan claims deposits or collateral to pay preferred payment plan claims.

2. Cash claims deposits shall be treated as a liability for accounting purposes and payments made from cash deposits shall be accounted for separately by fund year.

3. A fund may elect to use a loss conversion factor or factors when billing members for reimbursement of the cash claims deposit. These factors will require that the members reimburse the fund for the actual amount of claims paid plus an additional fixed percentage of the amount paid. The loss conversion factors shall be a part of the plan and shall be fixed for any given policy year. If more than one factor is to be used by the fund, the plan shall explicitly state the criteria for applying a specific factor to an individual member.

4. The fund may limit the liability of a member to reimburse the fund for actual claims payments by capping the cost associated with a given claim at the fund's specific excess retention. No other limit shall be used to cap the members' liability to reimburse the fund on individual claims. If the contract period for a member's participation in the preferred payment plan includes two or more specific retentions, then the contract shall be amended to reflect the actual specific retentions in effect during the preferred payment plan contract period. The loss limits specified in this paragraph shall not affect or amend the maximum premium required in paragraph (f).

(j) The plan shall provide that any claims reserves, less specific excess recoveries, outstanding when a member leaves the fund, shall be paid in full by the member or shall be guaranteed by security acceptable to the Office.

(k) The fund's aggregate excess policy shall provide that the retention be determined by using the premium paid or if normal premium is used, then the fund shall establish a reserve funded from surplus in the amount of the difference between normal premium and premium paid.

(*l*) The fund shall limit the participation in the plan to insure that it has adequate liquidity. In no event shall the fund allow more than 25 percent of its premium in these plans. Such percentage shall be determined by calculating the participating members' normal premium and expressing this amount as a percentage of the fund's total normal premium.

(m) The fund shall report to theOffice, as part of its Quarterly Status Reports or annual financial statement, the number of employers participating in the plan, their equivalent normal fund premium, the amount of premium paid in, the amount of claims paid, the amount of reserves outstanding and the amount of any delinquent premium. The Preferred Payment Plan Quarterly Status Reports shall be filed on OIR Form BSI-30.

(n) The fund shall pay its assessments on the basis of normal premium for any employers participating in the plan.

(o) The Office reserves the right to order the preferred payment plans terminated if it determines that the continuation of the plan would adversely affect the solvency of the fund or if the fund fails to comply with the provisions of this rule. All approvals for preferred payment plans shall be for a single fund year only. Plans or any amendments to previously filed plans shall be filed annually and be subject to approval of the Office in the same manner as and according to the same criteria used for approving new plans. If a fund wishes to continue a plan with no changes from the previous year, then the fund may advise the Office in writing and the fund need not make any additional filing for that year.

(p) Any claims remaining open two years after the end of the policy period in which they were incurred may be commuted into a lump sum payment by the employer at the request of the fund or at the request of the employer and with the concurrence of the fund.

(8) Funds may be allowed to offer retrospectively rated plans to their members. Funds may request permission to use plans filed by the National Council on Compensation Insurance (NCCI) with the Department of Insurance or funds may develop their own plans.

(a) Funds shall obtain the approval of the Office prior to offering any retrospectively rated plans.

(b) Funds shall adopt explicit underwriting criteria which shall be submitted to the Office along with the actual plan. The fund shall also submit with the request an actuarial analysis of the impact of the plan on the solvency and liquidity of the fund.

(c) The Office may approve the use of a plan if the offering of a plan does not adversely affect fund solvency and liquidity. In approving a plan, the Office may limit the participation in the plan to a fixed percentage of fund premium when such limit is necessary to assure fund solvency and liquidity.

(d) Funds may submit their own retrospectively rated plans which have been developed by a qualified actuary. These plans shall address the same issues as are contained in the NCCI plans. Any plan which allows a minimum premium of less than standard premium shall have a maximum premium which is in excess of standard premium. The fund's actuary shall attest that the plan is actuarially sound.

(e) All plans shall be reviewed annually by the fund's actuary. The review shall include an analysis of the actuarial soundness of the plan and the effect of the plan on fund solvency and liquidity.

(f) Changes in a plan must be filed with and approved by the Office prior to implementation. All changes must be reviewed by the fund's actuary and included in the actuary's annual analysis of the plan and in its impact on the fund's financial condition.

(g) The Office may withdraw the authorization of a fund to offer a retrospectively rated plan if the office determines that the continuation of the plan would adversely affect fund solvency and liquidity.

Specific Authority 440.591, 440.51(6)(b), 624.4621 Fla. Stat.

Law Implemented 440.51(6)(b), 624.4621 Fla. Stat.
History: New 10-1-82, Amended 12-25-84, Formerly 38F-5.66, Amended 3-11-87, 1-8-91, 6-12-91, 8-28-91, 3-16-92, 12-19-93, Formerly 38F-5.066, 4L-190.066.

69O-190.067. Member's Qualifications and Responsibilities.

(1) All members of a self-insurers fund shall have common interest. Different businesses which are owned or controlled by the same interests shall be eligible for membership in a self-insurers fund provided one of them is eligible.

(2) Unless the context clearly indicates to the contrary, the requirements imposed by these rules shall apply to the self-insurer as defined by Section 440.02 (7)(b)3., Florida Statutes. The duties, responsibilities and requirements of the members as defined by Section 440.02 (7)(b)2., Florida Statutes, are as provided by the indemnity agreement as specified in Rule 69O-190.068, F.A.C.

(3) Self-insurers funds are authorized only to accept liability and extend coverage for injuries under Chapter 440, Florida Statutes. No fund shall accept as a member any employer who is known to have United States Longshoremen and Harbor Workers Act or Jones Act exposure for which the fund may be liable. Whenever a fund determines that a member has United States Longshoremen and Harbor Workers Act or Jones Act exposure for which the fund was or may be liable, then that member shall be issued a notice of termination by the fund unless such exposure was a one time occurrence and will not be repeated or unless the member secures acceptable insurance coverage for the continuing United States Longshoremen and Harbor Workers Act or Jones Act exposure.

(4) Self-insurers funds shall use form BSI-31 to assure itself that any person claiming exemption from Chapter 440, Florida Statutes, pursuant to Section 440.05, Florida Statutes, is en-

titled to such an exemption.

Specific Authority 624.4621 Fla. Stat.

Law Implemented 440.05, 440.09(2), 624.4621 Fla. Stat.

History: New 10-1-82, Amended 12-25-84, Formerly 38F-5.67, Amended 12-19-93, Formerly 38F-5.067, 4L-190.067.

69O-190.068. Indemnity Agreement.

(1) Each self-insurers fund member shall enter into an indemnity agreement jointly and severally binding the self-insurers fund and each member thereof to comply with the provisions of the Florida Workers' Compensation Law and rules of the Office. Employers in the public sector who are legally unable to enter into a joint and several liability indemnity agreement with private employers shall be ineligible to participate in a self-insurers fund with members who are private employers. Self-insurers funds composed entirely of public employers may be authorized and must qualify in the same manner and be subject to the same regulations as all other self-insurers funds.

(2) The indemnity agreement required pursuant to paragraph 69O-190.056 (3)(a), F.A.C., shall conform to the form of the indemnity agreement hereinafter set forth and shall contain all its provisions but may also contain other provisions not inconsistent with these rules or with the required provisions. "Administrator" or "Fiscal Agent" may be substituted as may be necessary to reflect the respective authority, responsibility and duties of these agents, consistent with these rules.

INDEMNITY AGREEMENT

THIS INDENTURE, made and entered into this__________day of__________, A. D., 19______, by and between all the parties who are now or may hereafter become members of the__________ Self-Insurers Fund, acting by and through a Board of Trustees of their own selection.

WITNESSETH

WHEREAS, the undersigned persons, firms and corporations, hereinafter referred to as "Members," have applied to the Office of Employment Regulation, hereinafter referred to as the "Office," for authority to pool our liabilities pursuant to the terms of the Florida Workers' Compensation Law and specifically as provided by Section 624.6421, Florida Statutes, and WHEREAS, the said members have organized and formed a fund pursuant to said section, which fund shall be known as __________ Self-Insurers Fund, herein referred to as the "Fund," and WHEREAS, the Office of said Fund have designated __________ as its first Board of Trustees to direct the affairs of said Fund and to pass on the admissability of future members of the Fund until the members select succeeding Trustees for said Fund, and WHEREAS, the said Trustees have designated__________ as Service Agent for said Fund, and WHEREAS, the Office, upon petition of the group, has made its order approving said application, but upon the following conditions, to-wit:

I

The group shall, before being issued a certificate, post either a corporate surety bond or securities acceptable to the Office in the aggregate sum of__________ dollars ($) to secure performance of any awards which might be made against the Fund or any member thereof, and keep said bond or securities posted as long as may be required by the Office. The Trustees shall from time to time be entitled to receive all interest accruing on any negotiable securities posted, provided that the Fund is not in default in payment of compensation benefits or of any assessment levied by the Office in accordance with Sections 440.20 (9), 440.49 and 440.51, Florida Statutes.

II

That the members of said Fund execute a covenant or agreement whereby in addition to the collateral just above mentioned, the Fund and its members will jointly and severally covenant to assume and discharge, by payment, any lawful awards entered by the Office against any member of the group, which awards shall have been sustained by the courts where an appeal by either party is taken.

III

That the members of the Fund execute a covenant or agreement whereby the Fund and each member thereof will jointly and severally covenant and agree to pay premiums and assessments, based upon appropriate classifications and rates, into a designated cash reserve fund out of which lawful and proper claims and awards are to be paid, and further, that the group will jointly and severally covenant and agree there will be no disbursements out of this fund by way of dividends or distribution of accumulated reserves to the respective members, except at the direction of the Trustees after application to and approval by the Office. AND WHEREAS, the members of said fund, through their designated Trustees, have elected to comply with said conditions and become self-insurers, and to execute the other covenants required; NOW, THEREFORE, for and in consideration of the mutual covenants, promises and obligations herein contained, which are given to and accepted by each member hereof to the other, the parties to this instrument covenant, stipulate and and agree as follows:

1. The Fund hereby agrees either to file with the Office a corporate surety bond in the principal sum of______________ dollars ($) or to deposit______________ dollars ($) in acceptable securities with the Office to secure performance by the Fund of payment of all lawful awards made by the Office against any member or members of the group, predicated on a claim or claims by an employee or employees of any member of the Fund arising out of and in the course of such claimant's employment, and which awards shall have been sustained by the courts where an appeal by either party is taken; and upon condition that said member through which such claim originated shall not have been suspended from, resigned from, or expelled from the Fund after thirty (30) days' notice to the Division of such suspension, resignation, or expulsion, and which notice to the Office shall have been given thirty (30) days prior to the accident complained of.

2. The members of this Fund do jointly and severally covenant and agree that they will pay any such award as would otherwise be a claim against the aforesaid surety bond or securities as soon as the same shall become payable under the laws of the State of Florida; and the group agrees to pay to the Office for the administration of the law such assessments as may be ordered by said Office in accordance with Sections 440.20 (9), 440.49 and 440.51, Florida Statutes.

3. The members intend this agreement as a mutual covenant of assumption and not as a partnership, but should any court of competent jurisdiction construe same to be a partnership, then it is the intention of the parties that such partnership be limited in scope to the uses for which this contract is executed and no other.

4. That, subject to the approval of the Office, the Trustees of the Fund shall set up, operate, and enforce its own administrative rules, regulations and by-laws as between the individual members of the Fund.

5. The members ratify and confirm appointment by the Trustees of______________ as Service Agent for the Fund and its members, individually and collectively. The Service Agent shall determine all sums due the Fund from the members, pay all approved items of expense as directed by the Trustees, and give a monthly account of all monies so handled. For handling the administrative and servicing functions of the Fund, the Service Agent shall receive a fee which shall be negotiated from time to time by the Trustees. This fee shall be in consideration of all services and expenses contracted for with the Fund, which services or expenses may include the collecting, disbursing, and account&hardhyph; ing for monies collected, counseling with members as to safety hazards, claims handling and investigation, and providing for excess insurance coverage. The Service Agent's books and records are to be open to inspection by the Office and by the Trustees or their agents at all reasonable times.

6. The Service Agent shall deposit to the account of the Trustees, at any bank or banks designated by the Trustees, all premiums as and when collected, and said monies shall be disbursed only as provided by (1) the rules, regulations and by-laws of the Trustees, (2) the Agreement between the Trustees and the Service Agent, and (3) the Rules of the Commission pertaining to self-insurers funds.

7. The Trustees are authorized and directed to

take all reasonable precaution to protect the members from losses and shall provide for excess insurance coverage designed to protect said members against excess losses. The contracts for coverage shall be governed by the Rules of the Commission pertaining to self-insurers.

8. All members of the Fund hereby agree that the Trustees may admit as members of this Fund only acceptable and financially sound employers in the State of Florida who have common interest as defined in the Rules of the Commission pertaining to self-insurers, and that, subject to the approval of the Office, the Trustees shall be sole judge of whether or not any applying business shall be admitted to membership; and further, that a member may be suspended or expelled from the Fund after thirty (30) days' notice has been given to him and the Office, and that no liability shall accrue to the Fund or its members for any accident to an employee of the suspended or expelled member occurring after thirty (30) days' notice has been given to him and the Office as above provided.

9. The rules and regulations for the administering of the Fund and the admission and expulsion or suspension of members shall be promulgated by the Trustees. However, each member of the Fund agrees to abide by the following rules and regulations:

(a) The member agrees to follow the safety recommendations of the Trustees and the Service Agent in order to give his employees the maximum in safe and sanitary working conditions, and to follow the general recommendations of the Fund in this field to promote the general welfare of his employees.

(b) In the event of an accident or a reported claim, to make immediate provision for remedial care for his employees, and to give immediate notification of said accident to the Service Agent on the prescribed forms.

(c) The members shall make prompt payment of all premiums and assessments as required by the Trustees, said premiums to be determined by applying applicable experience modification to the standard rates for the exposure to risk, said standard rates to be as compiled by the National Council on Compensation Insurance and approved by the Office of Insurance Regulation. Further, said premium shall include loss and expense constants and minimum premiums, where applicable. Finally, said premium may be reduced by any discount allowed by the Trustees as long as such discount does not exceed the amount permitted by the Rules of the Commission pertaining to self-insurers.

(d) The member hereby appoints the Service Agent of this Fund as his agent and attorney-in-fact to act in his behalf and to execute all contracts and reports, waivers, agreements, excess insurance contracts, and service contracts; to make or arrange for payment of claims, medical expenses, and all other things required or necessary insofar as they affect his workers' compensation and/or employer's liability under Florida law and as covered by the terms of this Fund Agreement and the rules and regulations as now provided or as hereafter promulgated by the Trustees and the Division.

(e) The member agrees that in the event of the payment of any loss by the Fund under this contract, the Fund shall be subrogated to the extent of such payment to all the rights of the member against any person or other entity legally responsible for damages for said loss, and in such event the member hereby agrees to render all reasonable assistance, other than pecuniary, to effect recovery.

(f) The Fund is to defend in the name of and on behalf of the member any suits or other proceedings which may at any time be instituted against him on account of injuries or death within the purview of the Florida Workers' Compensation Law or on the basis of employer's liability, including suits or other proceedings alleging such injuries and demanding damages or compensation therefor, although such suits, other proceedings, allegations or demands are wholly groundless, false, or fraudulent, and to pay all costs taxed against this member in any legal proceeding defended by the company, all interest accruing after entry of judgment and all expenses incurred for investigation, negotiation or defense.

(g) Liability of the Fund to the employees of any employer is specifically limited to such obligations as are imposed by Florida law against the employer for workers' compensation and/or employer's liability.

(h) The Trustees of the Fund, the Service Agent, and any of their agents, servants, employees or attorneys shall be permitted at all reasonable times to inspect the work places, plants, works, machinery and appliances covered by this agreement, and shall be permitted at all reasonable times and within two years after the final termination of the membership to examine members' books, vouchers, contracts, documents, and records of any and every kind which show or tend to show or verify the premium which is payable under the terms hereof.

(i) The coverage of the Fund does not apply to punitive or exemplary damages on account of such injuries to any employee or employer in violation of law.

(j) Coverage by the Fund under the terms of this agreement shall expire and be cancelled automatically for nonpayment of premium, and a member may be expelled and dropped from the Fund upon thirty (30) days written notice by the Trustees or the Service Agent of the Fund to the member stating when, no less than thirty (30) days thereafter, cancellation shall be effective.

(k) The Fund shall not be liable for any additional compensation imposed by Section 440.54, Florida Statutes.

10. The Trustees are authorized to set aside from the premiums collected a reasonable sum for the operating expenses or administrative expenses of the Fund. All remaining funds coming into their hands during any one fiscal year of the Fund shall be set aside and shall be used only for the following purposes:

(a) Fee for the Service Agent for said Fund as provided in paragraph 5, supra.

(b) Payments for medical, surgical, hospital and nursing expense, and payments of compensation to employees covered by this contract, including settlements, awards, judgments, legal fees, and costs in all contest cases.

(c) Payment of Administrative, Special Disability Fund, and other assessments as required by the Office.

(d) Payment of cost of all bonds and auditing expenses required of the Fund or its agents or employees by the Office.

(e) Distribution to members in such manner as the Trustees shall deem to be equitable of any excess monies remaining after payment of claims and claims expenses and after provision has been made for open claims and outstanding reserves; provided, however, that no such distributions shall be made prior to the approval of the Office, and after complying with the applicable law and rules; provided, further, that undistributed excess funds from previous Fund Years may be distributed at any time if not required for reserves and if approved for distribution by the Office.

11. The Fund shall operate on a fiscal year from 12:01 a.m._______________ first to midnight of the last day in_______________ of the succeeding year. Application for continuing membership, when approved in writing by the Trustees or their designee, shall constitute a continuing contract for each succeeding fiscal period unless cancelled by the Office or the fund, or unless the member shall have resigned or withdrawn from said Fund by written notice.

12. The members jointly and severally covenant and agree that there will be no disbursement out of this Fund by way of dividends or distribution of accumulated reserve to members until after provision has been made for all obligations under the Workers' Compensation Law against said Fund and except at the discretion of the Trustees, upon application to and approval by the Division.

13. Any member who formally applies for membership in this Fund and is accepted by the Trustees shall thereupon become a party to this agreement and be bound by all of the terms and conditions hereof, and said approved application shall constitute a counterpart of this agreement.

IN WITNESS WHEREOF, the members of____________ Self-Insurers Fund have caused these presents to be signed by their duly authorized Chairman of the Board of Trustees and have had this agreement attested by its duly authorized secretary.

______________________ Self-Insurers Fund

By______________________

CHAIRMAN

ATTEST:

____

Secretary of Board of Trustees

Signed, sealed and delivered in the presence of:

____

We, the undersigned_ do hereunto set our hands and seals to certify our acceptance of our duties as Service Agent for_ Self-Insurers Fund this_ day of_ A.D., 19_.

By______________________

Attest______________________

Its Secretary

Signed, sealed and delivered in the presence of:

____

____

Specific Authority 440.591, 440.38(*l*)(b)1., 624.4621 Fla. Stat.

Law Implemented 624.4621 Fla. Stat.

History: New 10-1-82, Formerly 38F-5.68, Amended 3-11-90, Formerly 38F-5.068, 4L-190.068.

69O-190.069. Self-Insurers Fund Member Experience Records.

(1) Employers participating in a self-insurers fund under the provisions of Section 624.4621, Florida Statutes, shall be subject to the Experience Rating Plan and the payroll classification and premium determination system established by the National Council on Compensation Insurance (NCCI).

(2) The Office shall determine an experience modification for each qualified member of a self-insurers fund annually, or as otherwise provided, on the same basis as if the employer were insured under the provisions of Section 440.38 (1)(a), Florida Statutes, and such modification is to be used to determine the employer's standard premium as provided by these rules and the indemnity agreement. Funds shall submit only those members who qualify for experience rating in accordance with the NCCI Experience Rating Plan Manual.

(3) For any fund member who's experience must be combined with the experience modification factor of an insured group because of ownership requirements under the NCCI Experience Rating Plan, the fund must provide its experience to NCCI and have a combined experience modification factor calculated by NCCI. Any expenses of this transaction shall be the responsibility of the fund.

(4) Each self-insurers fund administrator and each self-insurers fund service company, if applicable, may be furnished a copy of the experience rating calculations.

(5) Should a member cease to participate in a self-insurers fund and purchase standard insurance coverage, the Experience Rating Plan provides that self-insured experience may be used in the employer's future experience rating calculation.

(6) Loss experience tabulations will be furnished upon request of the employer and a fee for such services may be assessed to defray preparing such tabulations, such cost to be

actual reimbursement to the Office.

Specific Authority 440.38(2)(b), 624.4621 Fla. Stat.
Law Implemented 440.49(7)(h)2., 440.51, 624.4621 Fla. Stat.

History: New 10-1-82, Formerly 38F-5.69, Amended 12-19-93, Formerly 38F-5.069, 4L-190.069.

69O-190.071. Authorized Investments for Self-Insurers Funds.

(1) The trustees of a fund are authorized to invest the assets of the fund only in the manner prescribed by these rules.

(2) Monies allocated to claims reserves net of excess recoveries for all policy years prior to the current year, the current year loss fund, all security deposits, and encumbered miscellaneous income shall be invested only in the following manner:

(a) Bankers acceptances from Prime Money Center Banks located within the United States and purchased through authorized financial institutions as defined in this rule.

(b) Savings accounts, checking accounts, money market accounts, certificates of deposit and fully collateralized repurchase agreements in financial institutions authorized pursuant to this rule.

(c) U.S. Treasury notes, bonds, and bills.

(d) Any security issued by the U.S. government or government agency and backed by the full faith and credit of the U.S. government.

(e) Any security which is a general obligation of the U.S. government or U.S. government agency.

(f) Securities issued by the State of Florida, or any agency or political subdivision which are backed by the full faith and credit of the State of Florida.

(g) Mutual funds which invest 100% in U.S. government or U.S. governments agency securities and whose published management policy limits the risk to principal amount invested. Funds must maintain current prospectuses on all mutual funds in which they invest.

(h) Annuities issued by insurers licensed by the State of Florida and whose policies are subject to the protection of the Florida Life and Health Insurance Guaranty Association. Investments in annuities are subject to the following limitations:

1. At least 30 days prior to the fund purchasing its first annuity, and annually thereafter, a fund shall submit an actuarial review by a qualified actuary examining the impact on the fund's present and future financial condition of purchasing annuities and foregoing the earning of investment income on the amounts invested in the annuities. The actuarial review shall take into account all aggregate reserve requirements and shall estimate the percent of the fund's reserves which may safely be invested in annuities. This percentage shall be the maximum amount allowable for investment in annuities subject to subsequent annual reviews by the fund's actuary. For purposes of this paragraph only, the actuary may be a member of the Society of Actuaries, American Academy of Actuaries or Casualty Actuarial Society.

2. Annuities shall be single premium annuities and shall be purchased only for the purpose of providing a payment stream for a given claim. Claims eligible for annuity funding shall be those claims with specific periodic benefit payments and with payments expected to continue for at least 61 months.

3. All annuities purchased shall have the fund as beneficiary. The fund may instruct the insurer to pay benefits directly to the claimant. The policy shall provide that the sum of the periodic benefit payments paid plus the cash value of the policy shall be greater than or equal to the amount of premium paid.

4. All annuities shall be tied to the claimant's life span.

5. If the cash value of the annuity exceeds $100,000 or the estimated benefits payable under the terms of the annuity, including cash value, exceeds $300,000, then the annuity shall be purchased only from a licensed insurer with a rating from the most recent edition of the A. M. BEST INSURANCE REPORTS, LIFE-HEALTH, of at least "A". The annuity policy

shall also be subject to the protection of the Florida Life and Health Insurance Guaranty Association.

6. The rules contained in paragraph (f) relating to the purchase of annuities shall not apply to annuities purchased for a claim settlement pursuant to an order of a Deputy Commissioner.

(i) Land and existing buildings used or acquired for use as its principal home office and for use by its service company, if any, when conducting business involving the fund. Prior to investing in land and buildings, the fund shall submit to the Office the following items:

1. An appraisal of the building and land showing that the market value of the building and land is greater than or equal to the principal amount of the investment. The appraisal shall be prepared in accordance with the Uniform Standards of Professional Appraisal Practice. The Uniform Standards of Professional Appraisal Practice of the Society of Real Estate Appraisers (effective July 1, 1987) are hereby adopted by reference and made a part of this rule by reference.

2. An analysis by the fund's actuary on the impact of the investment on the liquidity of the fund for claims payment purposes.

3. A financial analysis using generally accepted accounting principles showing that the proposed investment will decrease the expense overhead of the fund compared to acquiring office space through renting commercial property.

4. A certified resolution of the board of trustees stating that the investment is intended solely for reducing the overhead expense of the fund and that the investment is not for purposes of speculation or resale.

(j) If the building or land purchased requires modification or renovation in order to make it suitable for the fund's use, then the total cost of purchase of the building and land plus the cost of renovation or modification shall not exceed the 5 percent limit imposed by paragraph (n).

(k) If, instead of buying an existing building, a fund wishes to purchase land and construct a building on the land, then the following conditions shall be met in addition to those imposed by paragraph (i):

1. Land acquired for use in the construction of a building may be held for no longer than 18 months before construction shall begin. If construction is not begun within 18 months, then the fund may request a one time extension period to begin construction. An extension shall be granted upon submission of evidence that the fund has made a reasonable effort to begin construction within the time prescribed and that construction will begin before the end of the extension. If no extension is granted or if construction does not begin by the end of the extension then the land shall be sold.

2. All contracts awarded to the prime contractor shall contain a maximum fixed cost. The fund shall secure a performance bond in the amount of the contract from the prime contractor.

3. The total cost of acquiring the land, improving the land and construction of the building shall not exceed the 5 percent limit imposed by paragraph (n).

(*l*) The fund shall be the sole owner or mortgagee of the land and building, and no sale of real property for a price less than the original cost of the land and building shall take place without the written consent of the Office. The Office shall approve the sale unless the sale impairs the ability of the fund to meet its financial obligations.

(m) Investment in land or building pursuant to paragraphs (i) and (k) shall be subject to the approval of the Office. In approving this investment, the Division shall consider the impact of the investment on fund liquidity and solvency, the percent of net claims reserves invested and the amount of fund overhead expenses reduced by the investment. All books and records of the fund relating to acquiring land and acquiring or constructing a building shall be open to inspection by the Office.

(n) In no event shall the amount invested in land or building exceed 5 percent of the fund's claims reserves, net of excess recoveries.

1. If the cost of purchasing land, purchasing or constructing a building, renovating a building or improving the land exceeds the 5 percent limit imposed by paragraph (n), then the fund shall allocate all its unencumbered surplus until an amount equal to the portion of the cost in excess of 5 percent is transferred to claims reserves.

2. If the Office subsequently determines that the investment endangers fund solvency or liquidity, or if the original cost of purchasing land, purchasing or constructing a building, renovating a building or improving the land ever exceeds 10 percent of loss reserves as defined by subsection 69O-190.059 (3), F.A.C., the fund shall sell the land or building, obtain a mortgage on the property or allocate unappropriated surplus in order to provide sufficient liquidity to meet its obligations.

3. The fund shall allocate an amount each year to claims reserves equal to the amount of depreciation taken on the land and building.

(3) Investments pursuant to subsection (2), paragraphs (a) through (f), shall have maturity dates of not more than 10 years from the date of purchase. Furthermore, all investments shall be made in such a manner that dates of maturity of investments shall coincide with the claim payment needs of the fund. The Commission shall adopt as a rule a schedule which may be amended from time to time and which is based on the analysis of the payment patterns of all active self-insurers funds. Such schedule shall be used by all funds to determine the maturity dates for investments so that the claim payment needs of each fund are satisfied. If a fund submits to the Office an analysis by a qualified actuary which demonstrates the fund's payment pattern is substantially different from the schedule published by the Office, the Office shall authorize the fund to purchase its investments based on the payment pattern of the fund rather than on the published schedule.

(4) No fund shall invest so that more than 10 percent of the fund's assets are invested in a single financial institution unless such investment is fully insured by an agency of the United States government or satisfactorily collateralized pursuant to the conditions contained in subsection (7).

(5) All monies, other than those specified in subsection (2), held by a fund shall be invested in any manner authorized in subsection (2) and for any period of maturity.

(6) Investments pursuant to subsection (4) may be purchased with maturity dates subject to the discretion of the trustees. All such investments shall be purchased through financial institutions within the State of Florida.

(7) The trustees, upon approval by the Office, are authorized to enter into repurchase agreements subject to the following conditions:

(a) The agreement is with a financial institution within the State of Florida.

(b) The fund secures collateral for the agreement in the form of specific securities pledged to the fund whose market value is no less than the amount of the agreement.

(c) All securities pledged as collateral shall be acceptable pursuant to the restrictions imposed by subsections (2), (3) and (4). Upon receipt of proof of compliance with these conditions the Office shall approve the repurchase agreements.

(8) Authorized securities may be purchased through authorized financial institutions. For the purposes of this section, authorized financial institutions shall mean:

(a) Banks, savings and loan associations, and credit unions operating within the State of Florida and licensed by the State of Florida, the U.S. government or authorized under the Reciprocal Regional Banking Act of 1984 and whose accounts are insured by an agency of the U.S. government and,

(b) Investment brokerage firms licensed by the Securities and Exchange Commission and insured by an agency of the U.S. government and operating within the State of Florida.

(9) The Office shall prohibit a fund from investing in, or order the liquidation of, an otherwise authorized investment upon a finding, based on reasonable cause, that a specific invest-

ment has become unsafe or that a specific financial institution is or may become insolvent.

Specific Authority 624.4621 Fla. Stat.

Law Implemented 624.4621 Fla. Stat.

History: New 12-25-84, Amended 12-17-85, Formerly 38F-5.71, Amended 12-3-87, 7-20-88, 12-19-93, Formerly 38F-5.071, 4L-190.071.

69O-190.072. Miscellaneous Income of a Self-Insurers Fund.

(1) Miscellaneous income is all income received by a fund other than premium paid by members.

(2) If the Office determines that a fund shall allocate miscellaneous income to fund a deficit or contingent liability, then the amount allocated shall be part of the fund's security deposit and shall be encumbered for use only as specified by the Division.

(3) All unencumbered miscellaneous income may be disbursed at the discretion of the trustees in any manner not contrary to the rules or to the purpose for which the fund was established.

(4) Investment income earned after the end of the last policy year shall be disbursed only for essential fund operating expenses and dividends pursuant to subsection 69O-190.065 (6), F.A.C. These expenses shall include payment of claims and claims expenses, service fees, administrative overhead, marketing costs, promotional costs, commissions, and other expenses related to the direct operating costs of the fund. Essential fund operating expenses shall not include refunds, dividends, bonuses, or other similar expenses.

Specific Authority 624.4621 Fla. Stat.

Law Implemented 624.4621 Fla. Stat.

History: New 12-25-84, Formerly 38F-5.72, Amended 12-19-93, Formerly 38F-5.072, 4L-190.072.

69O-190.073. Premium Audit.

(1) All self-insurers funds shall determine the normal premium due from each member in each policy year based on actual audited payroll. Audits shall consist of physical, on-site audits or mail self-audits. The requirements set forth in this rule shall apply to the fund and its present or former members. Funds shall be responsible for the compliance with this rule of contracted audit personnel or firms.

(2) Physical, on-site audits shall be required for all members who meet one of the following conditions:

(a) New members (new businesses or members who had coverage with another fund or carrier when they joined the current fund) who are eligible for experience rating at policy inception.

(b) New members in the construction industry. Any employer with classification codes subject to the Florida Contractors Classification Premium Adjustment program shall be deemed to be in the construction industry.

(c) All renewal members (members who were in the same fund for the new and prior policy period) who are eligible for experience rating at policy renewal

(d) Any member may be audited at the discretion of the fund.

(3) Mail self-audits will be allowed for all new and renewal accounts not required to have a physical, on-site audit. However, any member shall have the right to request a physical, on-site audit when such a request is made on reasonable grounds.

(4) Each member shall be notified in writing by the fund of the audit requirements and penalties set forth in these rules. Such notice in plain language shall be mailed to the member at least 45 days prior to the end of each policy year.

(5) Each member shall be notified by the fund, either in person, by telephone or in writing prior to date that the physical audit is to be made.

(6) The following procedures shall govern the scheduling of physical, on-site audits:

(a) The fund shall make at least two separate good faith attempts to schedule a physical, on-site audit at a date and time mutually agreeable to the member and the fund.

(b) The fund shall keep a written record of the

time and date of each attempt.

(c) After two attempts, if the fund is unable to establish, with the member, a mutually agreeable date for an audit, then the fund shall give the member notice by certified mail of the date of the fund's choice on which an audit is to be performed. The fund may, at this time, issue a notice of termination to the member. This procedure is also applicable if the member cancels, with sufficient notice, two different appointments for a mutually agreed upon audit.

(d) Such notice shall include, in plain language, the statutory penalties for the member's failure to give the fund access to the member's records and for the member's failure to allow the fund to complete its audit.

(7) All funds shall complete audits (both physical or mail) on 90% of its premium within 5 months after the end of the policy year.

(8) If a new member meets one or more of the following criteria then a preliminary, on-site audit should be performed within 6 months of the beginning of the policy year:

(a) Payroll contained on the UCT-6 forms or the monthly application updates is inconsistent with the member's estimated annual premium.

(b) Information contained on the monthly application updates (OIR Form BSI-3A) is inconsistent with the member's estimated annual premium.

(c) Construction risks with estimated annual premium in excess of $10,000.

(d) Any trucking or employee leasing business.

(e) Any business with over $50,000 in estimated annual premium.

(9) A physical on-site audit shall be performed on all members who terminate during their first year of membership. Such audit shall be scheduled within 30 days after the termination date and completed within 60 days after the termination date. Procedures applicable to year ending physical audits shall also apply to audits of terminated members.

(10) The following procedures and standards shall apply to all physical, on-site audits performed by the fund:

(a) The audit shall include a review of the member's records and such review shall be sufficient to determine the actual premium owed to the fund and shall include an inspection of the member's premises sufficient to determine the correctness of classification assignments, if such inspection has not previously been performed.

(b) If all of a member's records are not maintained at one location, then an audit shall be performed at each location containing records.

(c) If a member's estimated annual premium is in excess of $100,000, then an inspection of the member's premises at all locations shall be part of the audit. Locations which were inspected during the expiring policy period by the fund's safety personnel or which were the subject of a classification inspection during the same period need not be visited again during the audit.

(11) The following records are to be audited on-site, as applicable to the individual member:

(a) Payroll records.

(b) Ledgers or journals.

(c) UCT-6 reports.

(d) Checking accounts.

(e) Certificates of insurance for subcontractors.

(f) Form 1099's.

(g) Claims history.

(h) Any other pertinent records.

(12) All audit reports, both physical and mail, shall include a summary of the correct audited payroll by classification, payrolls and classifications previously reported by the member, the calculation of the difference in payroll and a determination of the under or over payment of premium. The fund shall retain the audit report for at least 2 years and the audit workpapers for at least one year.

(13) When a fund schedules a mutually

agreed upon audit, the member shall provide the name and title of the person who will represent the member at the time of the audit. If the agreed upon audit is more than 7 working days from the date the appointment was made, the fund shall confirm the appointment in writing and include the name of person designated to represent the member at the audit. The confirmation should include a statement that the member is to notify the fund by telephone immediately if the appointment cannot be kept.

(14) The fund shall make at least two good faith attempts to obtain the return of a mail audit before any penalties may be applied.

(15) If the fund attempts to complete a mutually agreed upon audit and cannot complete the audit because the member failed to give the fund access to the necessary records, the fund shall select a new date and time at least 2 weeks in advance. The fund shall send a notice to the member by certified mail advising the member of the audit and of the penalties for failure to allow the fund to complete the scheduled audit. Denial of access of records by the member's agent or representative shall be considered the same as a denial by the member.

(16) If a member disputes the findings of a physical audit or the fund's premium determination based on a mail audit, the following procedures shall apply:

(a) The member shall have 30 days from the date the audit results were mailed to file a written response to the fund. The response shall contain the specific facts in dispute as well as any documents which are pertinent to the dispute.

(b) Upon receipt of a timely notice of the dispute, the fund shall investigate the matter and render a written decision. A written decision shall be rendered on at least 75% of disputed audits within 30 days after the response was mailed by the member.

(c) If the fund does not agree with the member's position, the fund may schedule another audit in the same manner as the original audit.

(d) Any reaudit scheduled shall be used to determine the member's premium and the fund is not obligated to perform any further audit unless there is substantial evidence that both the original audit and the reaudit were incorrectly performed.

(e) The dispute shall be resolved in accordance with the dispute resolution procedure adopted by the fund pursuant to Rule 69O-190.064, F.A.C.

(f) Failure of the member or the fund to comply with the timeframes contained in paragraphs (a) and (b) without reasonable cause shall result in the matter being resolved in favor of the other party.

(17) Any overpayment of premium shall be refunded to the member within 60 days after the completion of any undisputed audit. Refunds of overpayment of premium shall be refunded within 30 days after the resolution of any dispute. The fund shall have the right to apply any overpayment of premium to any unpaid premium.

(18) A member may be fined $500 by a fund for failure to allow access to essential records during the course of a physical audit subject to the following conditions:

(a) The member has failed to allow the completion of a prior physical audit, when such audit was scheduled on a date and time mutually agreeable to the fund and the member, or

(b) The member has canceled two previous appointments for a physical audit, and

(c) The fund has notified the member by certified mail of the date and time of the next scheduled audit and such notice shall include the penalties for failure to complete the next audit, and

(d) The fund incurred time and travel expenses in attempting to complete the next audit.

(19) If the fund cannot complete an audit because the employer failed to maintain essential records then the member shall be subject to a $500 fine in the same manner and under the same conditions as if the member denied the fund access to his records.

(20) The $500 fine imposed by the fund shall become a part of the premium owed the fund and shall be collected in the same manner and at the same time as other premium. The $500 fine may be deducted from any premium overpayment owed to the member.

(21) If the failure to complete a physical audit or to return a mail audit results in the fund's inability to determine an accurate final premium, the fund may arbitrarily determine payroll and charge up to a maximum of three times the most recent estimated annual premium in accordance with Section 440.381 (8), F.S.

(22) If the member intentionally understates payroll or misrepresents employee duties on the Application for membership or on the monthly updates and this results in an underpayment of premium, the member shall pay 12 percent simple interest to the fund on the amount of underpaid premium. The fund shall not be eligible to collect interest on the underpayment if the understatement of payroll or misrepresentation of employee duties could have been determined from a review of the monthly updates or UCT-6 forms.

(23) If the fund determines that a member has deliberately filed an Application for Membership or monthly updates containing false, misleading or incomplete information for the purpose of avoiding or reducing the amount of premium owed, then the fund shall notify the office and the Bureau of Worker' Compensation Insurance Fraud of the name of the member as well as all supporting documents.

Specific Authority 440.591, 440.51(6)(b), 440.381(3) Fla. Stat.

Law Implemented 440.51(6)(b), 440.381 Fla. Stat. **History:** New 6-12-91, Amended 12-19-93, Formerly 38F-5.073, 4L-190.073.

69O-190.074. Forms, Manuals and Instructions Adopted.

(1) OIR forms adopted.The OIR forms set forth in paragraphs (a) through (aa) of this subsection, as well as the accompanying instructions to the forms, are hereby incorporated into Rule Chapter 69O-190, F.A.C., by reference. Copies of the forms are available from the Bureau of P & L Insurer Solvency, Office of Insurance Regulation, Tallahassee, Florida 32399-0300.

(a) OIR Form BSI-1, Application for Self-Insurance.

(b) OIR Form BSI-2, Employer Application for Group Coverage.

(c) OIR Form BSI-3, Membership Application.

(d) OIR Form BSI-3A, Self-Insurers Fund Member Application Monthly Change Sheet.

(e) OIR Form BSI-4, Revised Self-Insurers Surety Bond (Guaranty Fund Member).

(f) OIR Form BSI-4A, Self-Insurers Surety Bond (Guaranty Fund Non-Member).

(g) OIR Form BSI-4B, Self-Insurers Surety Bond.

(h) OIR Form BSI-5, Payroll Report, and the accompanying instructions.

(i) OIR Form BSI-6, Self-Insurance Letter of Credit.

(j) OIR Form BSI-11, Indemnity Agreement.

(k) OIR Form BSI-12, Drug-Free Workplace Program.

(*l*) OIR Form BSI-17, Unit Statistical Report, and the accompanying instructions.

(m) OIR Form BSI-19, Certification of Servicing for Self-Insurance.

(n) OIR Form BSI-20, Report of Workers' Compensation Liabilities.

(o) OIR Form BSI-21, Breakdown of Policy Year Expenses.

(p) OIR Form BSI-22, Service Company Application.

(q) OIR Form BSI-23, Service Company Annual Report Form.

(r) OIR Form BSI-24, Quarterly Status Report.

(s) OIR Form BSI-24A, Preferred Payment Plan Quarterly Report.

(t) OIR Form BSI-26, Checklist for the Submission of Loss Reserve Reports.

(u) OIR Form BSI-27, Biographical Statement.

(v) OIR Form BSI-28, Quarterly Financial Statement.

(w) OIR Form BSI-29, Annual Financial Statement.

(x) OIR Form BSI-30, Report on Preferred Payment Plan.

(y) OIR Form BSI-31, Audit Procedures for Contractor/Independent Contractor Relationship.

(z) OIR Form BCM 201, Notice of Termination.

(aa) OIR Form BSI 206, Certificate of Self-Insurance, and the accompanying instructions.

(2) NAIC forms, instructions and manuals adopted.The NAIC forms, instructions and manual set forth in subparagraphs (a) through (e) of this subsection are hereby incorporated into Rule Chapter 69O-190, F.A.C., by reference. Copies of the forms are available from the National Association of Insurance Commissioners, 120 West 12th Street, Suite 1100, Kansas City, Missouri 64105, and are available for inspection during regular business hours at the Bureau P & L Insurer Solvency, Tallahassee, Florida 32399-0300.

(a) The 1992 National Association of Insurance Commissioners Quarterly Statement, Fire and Casualty Companies Association Edition.

(b) The Jurat Page; Statutory Balance Sheet; Underwriting and Investment Exhibit—Income Statement; Cash Flow; Underwriting and Investment Exhibit Part 1, Part 1A, Part 2, Part 2A, Part 3, Part 3A and Part 4; Exhibit 1—Analysis of Assets; Exhibit 2—Analysis of Non-Admitted Assets; Notes to Financial Statements; Five Year Historical Data (NOTE: funds shall complete this form on a going forward basis); Schedule of Special Deposits; Schedule A Part 1; Schedule B; Schedule BA; Schedule C; Schedule D Part 1, Part 1A, Part 3, Part 4 and Part 5 (NOTE: only 4th quarter transactions need to be reported); Schedule DA Part 1; Schedule E—Part 1A (NOTE: any amounts in dispute must be disclosed), Schedule M; Schedule N; Schedule P, Part 1 Summary, Part 2 Summary, Part 3 Summary, Part 5 Summary, Interrogatories; Schedule X; Schedule Y of the 1992 National Association of Insurance Commissioners Annual Statement, Fire and Casualty Companies Association Edition.

(c) The NAIC's Annual Statement Instructions, Property and Casualty, 1993 edition.

(d) The NAIC's Accounting Practices and Procedures Manual for Property and Casualty Insurance Companies, 1993 edition.

(e) The NAIC's Financial Condition Examiner's Handbook, 1993 edition.

Specific Authority 440.5705, 440.591, 624.4621 Fla. Stat.

Law Implemented 440.381, 440.5705, 624.316, 624.424, 614.4621 Fla. Stat.

History: New 12-19-93, Formerly 38F-5.074, 4L-190.074.

CHAPTER 69O-220 Adjusters

69O-220.001. Pre-Qualification and Licensure of Emergency Adjusters.

(1) Purpose.This rule sets forth office policy and procedure for licensure of emergency adjusters under Section 626.874, Florida Statutes.

(2) Scope.Each emergency is unique and the terms, conditions, and other provisions of emergency licensure for particular emergencies must often be tailored by emergency rule to the scope and nature of the particular emergency. This rule sets out what are essentially default licensure provisions which are effective for emergency licensure unless and to the extent the department issues emergency rules modifying, supplementing, or replacing this rule. Where not expressly modified or replaced by emergency rule regarding a particular emergency, the provisions of this rule shall apply.

(3) Definitions.For purposes of this rule, the following definitions shall apply.

(a) "Office" means the Office of Insurance

Regulation.

(b) "Licensed adjuster" and similar terms, refer to and include only persons actually currently licensed in good standing by this department as a public adjuster, company adjuster, or independent adjuster, whether the licensure be permanent resident licensure, or emergency licensure pursuant to this rule, and whether limited licensure or unlimited licensure. The terms do not include persons licensed as an adjuster or public adjuster by states other than the State of Florida.

(c) "Emergency" and "Catastrophe." These two terms as used in Section 626.874, Florida Statutes, are synonymous, and no separate treatment is afforded catastrophe over emergency adjusters.

(d) "Emergency adjuster" when used in this rule without further specification, includes emergency company adjusters, emergency independent adjusters, and emergency public adjusters.

(e) "Public adjuster" when used in this rule without further specification, includes both permanent resident licensed public adjusters and emergency public adjusters.

(f) "Unlicensed persons" as used in this rule means and refers to persons who are not actually currently licensed in good standing by this department as an adjuster, whether the licensure be permanent resident licensure or emergency licensure pursuant to this rule.

(4) General Provisions Applicable to All Emergency Adjusters.

(a) Declaration of Emergency; Determination that Emergency Exists.

1. The department does not issue proclamations or other formal declarations of emergency. Instead, any person believing that an emergency exists and desiring licensure under Section 626.874, Florida Statutes, shall apply or cause application to be made to the department for such licensure.

2. For purposes of Section 626.874, Florida Statutes, an emergency exists when, due to a specific, infrequent, and sudden natural or man-made disaster or phenomenon, there have arisen losses to property in Florida that are covered by insurance, and the losses are so numerous and severe that resolution of claims related to such covered property losses will not occur expeditiously without the licensing of emergency adjusters due to the magnitude of the catastrophic damage.

3. A failure of claims to be resolved expeditiously shall exist upon an insurer's filing with the Office a written statement that one of the following conditions exists:

a. The insurer expects to incur at least 500 claims as a result of the event; or

b. The magnitude of the event is expected to generate twice the mean number of claims for one month for the affected area.

4. Requests for emergency adjuster licensure as an independent adjuster must be accompanied by the same statement from an insurer who requires such services.

5. If the Office determines that an emergency exists, public adjusters seeking emergency licensure shall upon request be granted licensure pursuant to the provisions of this rule.

(b) Licenses Valid for 180 Days.

1. Emergency adjuster licenses are valid for 180 days from the date of issuance of the emergency license, unless a shorter period of time is specified in the license as issued. Because emergency licensure is an extraordinary deviation from regular licensing procedures, it is department policy to specify, as the duration of emergency licensure, the shortest possible time in each particular emergency.

2. The department shall grant an extension of emergency licensure if the conditions set forth in subparagraph (4)(a)2. of this rule still exist. Each extension will last for a period of up to an additional 180 days.

a. To apply for an extension of licensure as an emergency company or independent adjuster, the licensee shall execute Form OIR-396E, "Application for Extension of License and Appointment as an Emergency Adjuster," rev. 10/95, which is hereby adopted and incorporated by reference, and shall submit to the department the applicable fee, as specified in Form DI4-396E, for each extension.

b. To apply for an extension of licensure as an emergency public adjuster the licensee shall execute Form DI4-AAS-1E, "Application for Extension of License and Appointment as an Emergency Public Adjuster," rev. 10/95, which is hereby adopted and incorporated by reference, and shall submit the fee specified in Form OIR-AAS-1E, for each extension.

c. These forms may be obtained at the Bureau of Licensing, Office of Insurance Regulation, 200 E. Gaines Street, Tallahassee, Florida 32399-0319.

d. Only the licensure type and class which the licensee holds at the time of application for extension may be extended.

(c) "Temporary Licenses." The provisions of Section 626.872, Florida Statutes, regarding "Temporary Licenses" are not applicable to licensing persons temporarily for catastrophe or emergency situations.

(d) Emergency-Related Losses Only.Licensure as an emergency adjuster may be used only for adjustment of losses directly resulting from the emergency regarding which the license was issued.

(e) Natural Persons Only.The department issues emergency adjuster licenses only to natural persons.

(f) Address For Department.Unless a different address is specified herein, any notice or other item to be provided to the department, shall be addressed as follows: Bureau of Agent/Adjuster Licensing, Florida Department of Insurance, 200 East Gaines Street, Tallahassee, FL 32399-0319. If the communication is from or on behalf of a licensee, it shall not be deemed effectively received unless it shows the licensee's full name, license number, address, and phone number.

(g) Administrative Jurisdiction.By applying for pre-qualification determination or licensure as an emergency adjuster the applicant agrees that:

1. The applicant is subject to all the disciplinary provisions and penalties of the Florida Insurance Code and the administrative procedures set forth in the Florida Statutes for the routine processing of such charges;

2. Jurisdiction for acts committed prior to licensure or while licensed continues after the emergency licensure expires or is terminated;

3. If after the licensure expires or is terminated, the department has reason to believe there was a violation of any provision of the Florida Insurance Code by the former licensee while licensed, the department is not precluded from filing administrative action against the former licensee, and from serving the charges by certified mail to the licensee, or by publication of notice of action in the legal notices section of a newspaper of general circulation in or near the city or county of permanent residence or place of business as shown on the licensee's application for emergency licensure if certified mail service is unsuccessful;

4. The former licensee will respond to and defend the charges in Florida, or be defaulted;

5. The former licensee will not assert lack of jurisdiction; and

6. The former licensee believes that the preceding provisions satisfy minimum due process requirements of all state and federal constitutions.

(h) Civil Jurisdiction; Service of Process.By the act of applying for pre-qualification determination or licensure as emergency public adjuster, the applicant irrevocably:

1. Agrees and submits to the jurisdiction of the courts of Florida concerning civil liability for all acts in any way related to the licensee's activities under licensure in Florida;

2. Designates the Chief Financial Officer as the applicant's agent for service of all process in any way related to the applicant's activities licensed as an emergency public adjuster; and

3. Agrees that these provisions shall survive

the expiration or termination of pre-qualification or licensure.

(5) Emergency Company and Independent Adjusters.The provisions of this subsection apply only to emergency company and emergency independent adjusters, and not to licensure of emergency public adjusters.

(a) All Florida-licensed insurers, independent adjusters, and general lines agents, shall use the following procedures to utilize emergency company or independent adjusters. The entities or persons listed in the preceding sentence may immediately and without advance paperwork to this office, engage and cause commencement of catastrophe adjusting work for themselves, by any persons, whether on their staff, or hired by them, or engaged by them as independent contractors or as employees of a contractor engaged by them, which persons they determine to be qualified to do such adjusting work, and even though the person is not currently licensed as an adjuster in Florida. Within 30 calendar days after adjusting work has begun, the appropriate entity official must execute and submit to the department Form OIR-396, "Application for License and Appointment as a Catastrophe or Emergency Adjuster," rev. 7/94, which is hereby adopted and incorporated by reference, and shall attach a check for applicable fee per applicant, as specified in Form OIR-396, payable to the Office of Insurance Regulation. Form OIR-396 is available at all office consumer service offices or from office headquarters. The application and check shall be submitted to: Bureau of Licensing, P. O. Box 6000, Tallahassee, FL 32314-6000, or by overnight courier to: Bureau of Licensing, 200 East Gaines Street, Tallahassee, FL 32399-0319. One check may be used to pay the fees for multiple applications submitted together.

(b) Within 3 days of when an emergency adjuster begins work, the insurance company, independent adjuster, or general lines agent that is using the emergency adjuster must fax to the Bureau of Licensing the name of the emergency adjuster and his/her social security number. The fax must be on the letterhead of the insurance company, general lines agent, or independent adjuster/firm, and shall include the name and phone number of the contact person regarding emergency adjuster licensing. Contact should be made with the department for the appropriate fax numbers.

(c) The insurance company representative, general lines agent, or independent adjuster who signs Form OIR-396 to certify that the applicant is qualified (referred to herein as the "certifier"), thereby appoints the applicant to represent that company, agent, or independent adjuster; and once the license is issued, the certifier is bound by the acts of the applicant as in the case of any regular licensed (non-Temporary or non-Catastrophic) adjuster licensed pursuant to Chapter 626, Florida Statutes, appointed by that company, agent, or independent adjuster. Such responsibility continues until such time as said certifier shall notify the department in writing that the certifier desires to terminate the certification, at which time the emergency license is cancelled automatically, until such time as the applicant can obtain another certifier.

(d) The insurer, general lines agent, or independent adjuster who certifies to the office that the applicant is qualified, is responsible for assuring, by due diligence inquiry, that the applicant is in fact qualified to adjust claims and is of good and honest character.

(e) There is an affirmative duty on the insurance company, general lines agent, or independent adjuster signing Form OIR-396, to provide continuing and significant supervision to the applicant after licensure.

(f) Nonresident Company Adjusters.Persons employed by insurers and licensed by the office as non-resident company adjusters may temporarily come into Florida and work out of Florida offices as emergency adjusters for their employing insurance company without further licensure from the office, for 180 days or such shorter time as the office may by emergency rule specify as the maximum duration of emergency licensure for that particular emergency, and will not be deemed to have a Florida office such as would disqualify them from holding non-resident licensure or be held violative of their non-resident license status; provided, their employing insurance company shall before allowing such persons to adjust emergency losses while physically in Florida, provide the office with a listing of the names and adjuster license numbers of all such persons, and shall obtain from the office written acknowledgment that an emergency exists, specifying the emergency.

(g) Application for Emergency Adjuster Licensure as a Company or Independent Adjuster-.Application for licensure as an Emergency Adjuster shall be made on Form OIR-396, "Application for Licensure and Appointment as Emergency Adjuster," rev. 10/95, which is hereby adopted and incorporated by reference.

(6) Emergency Public Adjusters: General Provisions.This subsection pertains only to licensure of emergency public adjusters.

(a) Advance Approval Required.

1. No person may commence work as an emergency public adjuster until notified in writing by the office that the department:

a. Has received an application and made an affirmative pre-qualification determination and issued a letter so indicating, or

b. Has been approved for licensure if no pre-qualification determination was requested in advance.

2. If the pre-qualification method is used, the subject of the pre-qualification must request licensure pursuant to paragraph (7)(b) of this rule in order to commence work.

(b) Background Checking; Grounds for Denial.As to all applications for licensure as an emergency public adjuster, the office shall conduct such background inquiry as is necessary to determine the applicant's fitness and character. Adverse information noted in any area will be grounds for denial of application. The inquiry is limited to:

1. Inquiry of state or federal regulatory authorities in other states where the applicant has resided or done business;

2. Checking references provided;

3. Inquiry of criminal databases and law enforcement authorities; and

4. Checking for judgments and other adverse credit references.

(c) Bond Required.No person will be licensed as an emergency public adjuster unless the applicant has supplied to the office the $5,000 bond required by Section 626.865(2), Florida Statutes. Applications for licensure will be received and preliminarily processed without the bond, but no licensure shall be issued until the bond is received in good and proper form.

(d) Policy Regarding Licensing Threshold.It is office policy and finding that a substantially higher threshold of certainty regarding fitness and character is appropriate and required for licensure as an emergency public adjuster, as compared to licensure as an emergency company or independent adjuster. This is because if a company or independent adjuster proves dishonest or incompetent, there is generally a regulated insurance company that may be required to make good that adjuster's misconduct. However, regarding a public adjuster, there is no such safeguard for consumers.

(e) Records To Be Kept.

1. All emergency public adjusters shall at all times while licensed and for 30 days thereafter maintain in Florida an office and keep their records or copies of all records relating to all Florida losses being adjusted or previously adjusted under said emergency licensure. All emergency public adjusters licensed under this rule shall designate their Florida office location to the department within 72 hours after becoming licensed, and shall notify the office in writing within 24 hours of any change in said office location. Failure to designate such an office or to timely update the office as to its location is grounds for immediate termination of licensure. The address of this office shall appear on all contracts, literature, etc., used by the public adjuster. This office shall be open and staffed at least six hours of every day, between the hours of 8 a.m. and 5 p.m., Monday through Friday, public holidays excluded.

2. The records and offices of all emergency public adjusters shall be subject to inspection by the office without notice at any time.

(f) Advertising.All emergency public adjusters are strictly prohibited from advertising. Advertising means promotions, statements of availability, qualifications, and other similar statements, appearing on or in television, radio, newspapers, or magazines; and flyers, brochures, adhesive stickers affixed to any structure showing the adjusters name, address, phone number, and other similar information. Emergency public adjusters shall not use the services of any person or firm, who advertises for the emergency public adjuster, or who is directly or indirectly compensated for referring potential clients to the emergency public adjuster. The following do not constitute prohibited advertising:

1. The emergency public adjuster personally handing to any claimant or potential claimant brochures or other descriptive materials as to the public adjusting function, the public adjuster's qualifications, fees, and other similar information.

2. Solicitation (as defined herein) of work, by the emergency public adjuster in person, wherein the solicitation is made to the loss claimant, and subject to other limitations in this rule concerning solicitation; provided, limited emergency public adjusters may not solicit work on any premises which are not clearly commercial premises.

(g) Advising Claimants and Others.The advising of insureds, claimants, potential claimants, or other persons as to the role, value, or usefulness of public adjusters is deemed to be a material part of the business of public adjusting, and therefore requires licensure as a public adjuster under the laws of Florida and this rule, and may be engaged in only by persons licensed by this office as permanent or emergency public adjusters. Unlicensed persons may not engage in such activity even under the supervision of a licensed public adjuster.

(h) Certain Contracts Unenforceable.It is department policy that contracts engaging the services of a public adjuster, entered into in violation of any provisions of this rule or any emergency rule, shall be declared unenforceable on the part of any public adjuster, as violative of public policy.

(i) Photo ID Required.No emergency public adjuster, once approved for licensure by the department, shall be licensed or commence work, until obtaining from the department a photo identification card, paying in connection therewith the applicable fee as specified in Forms OIR-AAS-1 and OIR-AAS-3.

(7) Emergency Public Adjuster Applicants.

(a) To apply for licensure as an emergency public adjuster, the applicant shall execute Form OIR-AAS-1, "Application for License and Appointment as an Emergency Public Adjuster," rev. 3/96 which is hereby adopted and incorporated by reference, and shall submit the fee specified in Form OIR-AAS-1.

(b) To apply for pre-qualification determination for licensure as an emergency public adjuster, the applicant shall execute Form OIR-1199 "Application for Pre-qualification for Licensure as An Emergency Public Adjuster" Rev. 6/96 which is hereby adopted and incorporated by reference, and shall submit the fee specified in Form OIR-1199.

(c)

1. Pre-Qualification Determination is not required for licensure as an Emergency Public Adjuster. However, persons are urged to pre-qualify prior to a disaster in order to expedite the emergency licensure process.

2. Pre-Qualification Determination requests will be considered between January 1 and April 30 of each year.

3. Any Pre-Qualification Determination made will be valid for a period of two years.

(d)

1. Persons may apply for pre-qualification determination or licensure as an emergency public adjuster if they are currently licensed as a public adjuster in their home state for the type or kinds of insurance for which they intend to adjust claims in this state.

2. Applicants must be in good standing in all

states where so licensed.

3. Evidence of good standing must be in the form of a current original Letter of Certification from the applicable state insurance department(s). The letter shall not be older than 90 days when submitted in connection with the application for licensure or pre-qualification determination.

(e) The application form must be signed by three persons:

1. The person to receive emergency licensure;

2. A regularly licensed (non-Temporary, non-Catastrophic) public adjuster who will supervise the emergency public adjuster (the supervising public adjuster); and

3. One of the following persons (the certifying person):

a. An officer of a Florida-licensed or admitted insurance company; or

b. A Florida-licensed independent adjuster in good standing; or

c. A Florida-licensed resident general lines insurance agent in good standing.

(f) The application forms may be obtained at all department consumer service offices or from department headquarters in Tallahassee and must be sent, with a check for the applicable fee, as specified in Form OIR-AAS-1 or OIR-1199, to: Office of Insurance Regulation, P. O. Box 6000, Tallahassee, FL 32314-6000; or the applicant may contact the department for an address for use of overnight courier service.

(g) Supervising Public Adjuster.Licensees who are licensed under this subsection must be supervised by a regularly licensed (non-Temporary, non-Catastrophic) resident public adjuster in good standing while they are performing work under their emergency public adjuster licensure. The emergency licensure automatically terminates if the supervising public adjuster ceases to supervise the emergency adjuster. The emergency adjuster will be deemed to be an appointee of the supervising public adjuster. The supervising public adjuster is under an affirmative duty to provide continuing, significant supervision to the emergency public adjuster whose application he/she signed. The supervising public adjuster may prospectively terminate this duty at any time by notifying the department by certified mail, return receipt requested, or by overnight courier, that he/she will no longer be supervising the emergency public adjuster as of a date specified in said letter. Such a notice is not effective until actually received by the department.

(8) Non-Resident Public and Independent Adjusters.Non-Resident Public and Independent Adjusters are required to annually execute Form OIR-1297, "Affidavit of Insurance For Non-Resident Public and Independent Adjusters", rev. 10/02 which is hereby adopted and incorporated by reference. A copy of Form OIR-1297 may be obtained from the State of Florida, Office of Insurance Regulation, Bureau of Agent and Agency Licensing, 200 East Gaines Street, Tallahassee Florida 32399-0319, phone (850) 413-3137.

Specific Authority 624.308(1) Fla. Stat.

Law Implemented 624.307(1), 626.8732, 626.8734 Fla. Stat.

History: New 2-25-93, Amended 8-18-94, 1-7-97, 10-20-97, 1-9-03, Formerly 4-220.001.

69O-220.051. Conduct of Public Adjusters.

(1) Purpose and Scope.This rule sets forth Office policy as to certain matters generally affecting public adjusters. Procedures regarding application for licensure are not dealt with in this rule. Ethical provisions are not dealt with in this rule.

(2) Definitions.The following definitions shall apply for purposes of this rule.

(a) "Compensation" means anything of value, whether received directly or indirectly.

(b) "Office" means the Office of Insurance Regulation.

(c) "Licensed public adjuster" and "public adjuster" refer to and include only persons actually currently licensed in good standing by the Office as public adjusters, whether the licensure is resident licensure under Section 626.865, Florida Statutes, or emergency licensure under

Section 626.874, Florida Statutes, and whether the licensure is limited or unlimited. The phrase does not include persons licensed as public adjusters by other states but not by the State of Florida.

(d) "Resident public adjuster" and references thereto refers to a public adjuster not licensed on an emergency basis as contemplated by Section 626.874, Florida Statutes, and Rule 69O-220.001, F.A.C., and who is a bona fide resident of this state.

(e) "Unlicensed persons," as used in this rule, means and refers to persons who are not actually currently licensed in good standing by this Office as resident or emergency public adjusters.

(3) Communications Concerning Public Adjuster Services.

(a) Solicitation.The solicitation of public adjusting business for compensation is deemed to be a material part of the business of public adjusting and, therefore, requires licensure as a public adjuster under the laws of Florida and the rules of the Office, and shall be engaged in only by persons licensed by this Office as public adjusters. Unlicensed persons shall not engage in such activity even under the supervision of a licensed public adjuster. The phrase "solicitation of public adjusting business" and similar phrases as used in this rule means, for compensation, initiating contact with any person, whether in person, by mail, by telephone, or otherwise, and therein seeking, causing, urging, advising, or attempting:

1. To have any person enter into any agreement engaging the services of a public adjuster in any capacity; or

2. To have any person subsequently speak or meet with a licensed public adjuster for the purpose of engaging the services of a public adjuster in any capacity or for the purpose of being advised by a public adjuster in any regard.

(b) Answering Telephone Calls.The answering of incoming telephone calls by unlicensed persons, at the place of business of a public adjuster, is not violative of this rule so long as the unlicensed persons engage in purely administrative matters and not in judgment or interpretation with regard to any insurance contract, claim, or potential claim.

(4) Advertising.

(a) As with all forms of advertising concerning the business of insurance, public adjusters shall not falsely inform or advertise as set forth in Section 626.9541(1)(b), Florida Statutes, as well as any other section within the Insurance Code which relates to advertising.

(b) Only Licensed Adjusters to Advertise.No person or entity shall in any way advertise services as a public adjuster in this state, unless licensed as a resident public adjuster or a member of the Florida Bar.

(c) Advertisements to Show Licensee's Full Name.Any advertisement by a resident public adjuster shall state the full name as specified in Department records of the public adjuster who has caused the advertisement to appear. Where a firm containing multiple licensed public adjusters is causing the advertisement to appear, the firm shall designate one of said licensees whose full name as specified in Department records shall appear in the advertisement.

1. Print Advertisements.In print advertisements the public adjuster's full name as specified in Department records shall be in typeface no smaller than the typeface of the main body of text in the advertisement. Print advertisements include newspapers, magazines, flyers, brochures, business cards, adhesive and magnetic publication, and similar printed materials. If the material is already printed when this rule takes effect, the required public adjuster's full name shall be added by means of rubber stamp, adhesive label, or other means.

2. Television Advertisements.In television advertisements the public adjuster's full name as specified in Department records shall be made to appear on the screen for a period reasonably calculated to allow a viewer to write the name down.

3. Radio Advertisements.In radio advertisements, the public adjuster's full name as specified in Department records shall be read during

the advertisement, and at a speed reasonably calculated to allow an average listener to note the name of the licensee as it appears on his or her licensure.

(d) Responsibility of Advertising Licensee.The licensed adjuster whose name appears in the advertisement is responsible for personally reviewing the content of the advertisement and assuring that the advertisement complies with the rules of the Office and the Insurance Code and is in all regards fair, accurate, and in no way misleading.

(5) It is an affirmative duty of every resident public adjuster to supervise their business affairs and their staff to ensure to the extent it is within the public adjuster's power that this rule is not violated.

(6) All contracts for public adjuster services must be in writing. The contract must be signed by the public adjuster who solicited the contract. If the public adjuster is licensed by the Office as an emergency public adjuster, the contract shall show the public adjuster's permanent home address and home phone number, and permanent home state business address and phone number and Florida Office license number.

(7) No public adjuster may settle a claim unless the terms and conditions of settlement are approved by the insured.

Specific Authority 624.308(1), 626.9611 Fla. Stat. Law Implemented 624.307(1), 626.112(1), 626.865(2), 626.874, 626.9541(1)(b), (i) Fla. Stat. **History:** New 4-26-94, Amended 12-18-2001, Formerly 4-220.051.

69O-220.201. Ethical Requirements.

(1) Purpose.This rule sets forth the various ethical considerations and constraints for various classes of insurance adjusters.

(2) Definitions.The following definitions shall apply for purposes of this rule.

(a) "Adjuster," when used without further specification, refers to and includes all types and classes of insurance adjusters, (company, independent, and public), subject to Chapter 626, Florida Statutes, and regardless whether resident or nonresident, and whether permanent, temporary, or emergency licensees.

(b) "Client" refers to and includes both clients and potential clients; and means any person who consults with or hires an adjuster to provide adjusting services.

(c) "Office" refers to the Florida Office of Insurance.

(d) "Person" includes natural persons and legal entities.

(3) Violation.Violation of any provision of this rule shall constitute grounds for administrative action against the licensee, upon grounds, that include but are not limited to, that the violation demonstrates a lack of fitness to engage in the business of insurance. Additionally, a breach of any provision of this rule constitutes an unfair claims settlement practice.

(4) Code of Ethics.The work of adjusting insurance claims engages the public trust. An adjuster must put the duty for fair and honest treatment of the claimant above the adjuster's own interests. in every instance. The following are standards of conduct that define ethical behavior.

(a) An adjuster shall disclose all financial interest in any direct or indirect aspect of an adjusting transaction. For example: an adjuster shall not directly or indirectly refer or steer any claimant needing repairs or other services in connection with a loss to any person with whom the adjuster has an undisclosed financial interest, or which person will or is reasonably anticipated to provide the adjuster any direct or indirect compensation for the referral or for any resulting business.

(b) An adjuster shall treat all claimants equally. An adjuster shall not provide favored treatment to any claimant. An adjuster shall adjust all claims strictly in accordance with the insurance contract.

(c) An adjuster shall never approach investigations, adjustments, and settlements in a manner prejudicial to the insured.

(d) An adjuster shall make truthful and unbiased reports of the facts after making a complete investigation.

(e) An adjuster shall handle every adjustment and settlement with honesty and integrity and allow a fair adjustment or settlement to all parties without any remuneration to himself except that to which he is legally entitled.

(f) An adjuster, upon undertaking the handling of a claim, shall act with dispatch and due diligence in achieving a proper disposition thereof.

(g) An adjuster shall promptly report to the Office any conduct by any licensed insurance representative of this state, which conduct violates any insurance law or Office rule or order.

(h) An adjuster shall exercise extraordinary care when dealing with elderly clients, to assure that they are not disadvantaged in their claims transactions by failing memory or impaired cognitive processes.

(i) An adjuster shall not negotiate or effect settlement directly or indirectly with any third-party claimant represented by an attorney, if said adjuster has knowledge of such representation, except with the consent of the attorney. For purposes of this subsection, the term "third-party claimant" does not include the insured or the insured's resident relatives.

(j) An adjuster is permitted to interview any witness, or prospective witness, without the consent of opposing counsel or party. In doing so, however, the adjuster shall scrupulously avoid any suggestion calculated to induce a witness to suppress or deviate from the truth, or in any degree affect their appearance or testimony at the trial or on the witness stand. If any witness making or giving a signed or recorded statement so requests, the witness shall be given a copy thereof.

(k) An adjuster shall not advise a claimant to refrain from seeking legal advice, nor advise against the retention of counsel to protect the claimant's interest.

(*l*) An adjuster shall not attempt to negotiate with or obtain any statement from a claimant or witness at a time that the claimant or witness is, or would reasonably be expected to be, in shock or serious mental or emotional distress as a result of physical, mental, or emotional trauma associated with a loss. Further, the adjuster shall not conclude a settlement when such settlement would be disadvantageous or to the detriment of a claimant who is in the traumatic or distressed state described above.

(m) An adjuster shall not knowingly fail to advise a claimant of their claim rights in accordance with the terms and conditions of the contract and of the applicable laws of this state. An adjuster shall exercise care not to engage in the unlicensed practice of law as prescribed by the Florida Bar.

(n) A company or independent adjuster shall not draft, unless approved in writing in advance by the insurer and such written communication can be demonstrated to the Office, special releases called for by the unusual circumstances of any settlement or otherwise draft any form of release. Except as provided above, a company or independent adjuster is only permitted to fill in the blanks in a release form approved by the insurer they represent.

(5) Public Adjusters, Other Ethical Constraints.In addition to considerations set out above for adjusters, the following ethical considerations are specific to public adjusters.

(a) A public adjuster shall advise the insured and claimant in advance of their right to choice of counsel to represent the insured or claimant, and that such choice is to be made solely by the insured or claimant.

(b) The public adjuster shall notify the insured or claimant in advance of the name and location of any proposed contractor, architect, engineer, or similar professional, before any bid or proposal by any of these persons may be used by the public adjuster in estimating the loss or negotiating settlement, and the insured or claimant may exercise veto power of any of these persons in which case that person shall not be used in estimating costs.

(c) The public adjuster shall ensure that if a contractor, architect, engineer, or other licensed professional is used in formulating estimates or otherwise participates in the adjustment of the claim, the professional must be licensed by the Florida Department of Business and Professional Regulation.

(d) A public adjuster shall not prevent, or attempt to dissuade or prevent, a claimant from speaking privately with the insurer, company or independent adjuster, attorney, or any other person, regarding the settlement of the claim.

(e) A public adjuster shall not acquire any interest in salvaged property, except with the written consent and permission of the insured.

(f) A public adjuster shall not accept referrals of business from any person with whom the public adjuster may conduct business where there is any form or manner of agreement to compensate the person, whether directly or indirectly, for referring business to the public adjuster. Except as between licensed public adjusters, or licensed public adjusters and members of the Florida Bar, no public adjuster may compensate any person, whether directly or indirectly, for the principal purpose of referring business to the public adjuster.

Specific Authority 624.308, 626.878, 626.9611 Fla. Stat.

Law Implemented 624.307(1), 626.611, 626.621, 626.865(2), 626.878, 626.9541(1)(i) Fla. Stat.

History: New 6-2-93, Amended 12-18-2001, Formerly 4-220.201.

PART VII

FLORIDA CODE OF JUDICIAL CONDUCT

SYNOPSIS

Judicial Conduct

FLORIDA CODE OF JUDICIAL CONDUCT

Preamble

Our legal system is based on the principle that an independent, fair and competent judiciary will interpret and apply the laws that govern us. The role of the judiciary is central to American concepts of justice and the rule of law. Intrinsic to all sections of this Code are the precepts that judges, individually and collectively, must respect and honor the judicial office as a public trust and strive to enhance and maintain confidence in our legal system. The judge is an arbiter of facts and law for the resolution of disputes and a highly visible symbol of government under the rule of law.

The Code of Judicial Conduct establishes standards for ethical conduct of judges. It consists of broad statements called Canons, specific rules set forth in Sections under each Canon, a Definitions Section, an Application Section and Commentary. The text of the Canons and the Sections, including the Definitions and Application Sections, is authoritative. The Commentary, by explanation and example, provides guidance with respect to the purpose and meaning of the Canons and Sections. The Commentary is not intended as a statement of additional rules. When the text uses "shall" or "shall not," it is intended to impose binding obligations the violation of which, if proven, can result in disciplinary action. When "should" or "should not" is used, the text is intended as hortatory and as a statement of what is or is not appropriate conduct but not as a binding rule under which a judge may be disciplined. When "may" is used, it denotes permissible discretion or, depending on the context, it refers to action that is not covered by specific proscriptions.

The Canons and Sections are rules of reason. They should be applied consistent with constitutional requirements, statutes, other court rules and decisional law and in the context of all relevant circumstances. The Code is not to be construed to impinge on the essential independence of judges in making judicial decisions.

The Code is designed to provide guidance to judges and candidates for judicial office and to provide a structure for regulating conduct through disciplinary agencies. It is not designed or intended as a basis for civil liability or criminal prosecution. Furthermore, the purpose of the Code would be subverted if the Code were invoked by lawyers for mere tactical advantage in a proceeding.

The text of the Canons and Sections is intended to govern conduct of judges and to be binding upon them. It is not intended, however, that every transgression will result in disciplinary action. Whether disciplinary action is appropriate, and the degree of discipline to be imposed, should be determined through a reasonable and reasoned application of the text and should depend on such factors as the seriousness of the transgression, whether there is a pattern of improper activity and the effect of the improper activity on others or on the judicial system.

The Code of Judicial Conduct is not intended as an exhaustive guide for the conduct of judges. They should also be governed in their judicial and personal conduct by general ethical standards. The Code is intended, however, to state basic standards which should govern the conduct of all judges and to provide guidance to assist judges in establishing and maintaining high standards of judicial and personal conduct.

Definitions

"Appropriate authority" denotes the authority with responsibility for initiation of disciplinary process with respect to the violation to be reported. **"Candidate."** A candidate is a person seeking selection for or retention in judicial office by election or appointment. A person becomes a candidate for judicial office as soon as he or she makes a public announcement of candidacy, opens a campaign account as defined by Florida law, declares or files as a candidate with the election or appointment authority, or authorizes solicitation or acceptance of contributions or support. The term "candidate" has the same meaning when applied to a judge seeking election or appointment to nonjudicial office. **"Court personnel"** does not include the lawyers in a proceeding before a judge. **"De minimis"** denotes an insignificant interest that could not raise reasonable question as to a judge's impartiality. **"Economic interest"** denotes ownership of a more than de minimis legal or equitable interest, or a relationship as officer, director, advisor, or other active participant in the affairs of a party, except that:

(i) ownership of an interest in a mutual or common investment fund that holds securities is not an economic interest in such securities unless the judge participates in the management of the fund or a proceeding pending or impending before the judge could substantially affect the value of the interest;

(ii) service by a judge as an officer, director, advisor, or other active participant in an educational, religious, charitable, fraternal, sororal, or civic organization, or service by a judge's spouse, parent, or child as an officer, director, advisor, or other active participant in any organization does not create an economic interest in securities held by that organization;

(iii) a deposit in a financial institution, the proprietary interest of a policy holder in a mutual insurance company, of a depositor in a mutual savings association, or of a member in a credit union, or a similar proprietary interest, is not an economic interest in the organization unless a proceeding pending or impending before the judge could substantially affect the value of the interest;

(iv) ownership of government securities is not an economic interest in the issuer unless a proceeding pending or impending before the judge could substantially affect the value of the securities. **"Fiduciary"** includes such relationships as personal representative, administrator, trustee, guardian, and attorney in fact. **"Impartiality"** or "impartial" denotes absence of bias or prejudice in favor of, or against, particular parties, as well as maintaining an open mind in considering issues that may come before the judge. **"Judge."** When used herein this term means Article V, Florida Constitution judges and, where applicable, those persons performing judicial functions under the direction or supervision of an Article V judge. **"Knowingly," "knowledge," "known," or "knows"** denotes actual knowledge of the fact in question. A person's knowledge may be inferred from circumstances. **"Law"** denotes court rules as well as statutes, constitutional provisions, and decisional law. **"Member of the candidate's family"** denotes a spouse, child, grandchild, parent, grandparent, or other relative or person with whom the candidate maintains a close familial relationship. **"Member of the judge's family"** denotes a spouse, child, grandchild, parent, grandparent, or other relative or person with whom the judge maintains a close familial relationship. **"Member of the judge's family residing in the judge's household"** denotes any relative of a judge by blood or marriage, or a person treated by a judge as a member of the judge's family, who resides in the judge's household. **"Nonpublic information"** denotes information that, by law, is not available to the public. Nonpublic information may include but is not limited to: information that is sealed by statute or court order, impounded or communicated in camera; and information offered in grand jury proceedings, presentencing reports, dependency cases, or psychiatric reports. **"Political organization"** denotes a political party or other group, the principal purpose of which is to further the election or appointment of candidates to political office. **"Public election."** This term includes primary and general elections; it includes partisan elections, nonpartisan elections, and retention elections. **"Require."** The rules prescribing that a judge "require" certain conduct of others are, like all of the rules in this Code, rules of reason. The use of the term "require" in that context means a judge is to exercise reasonable direction and control over the conduct of those persons subject to the judge's direction and control. **"Third degree of relationship."** The following persons are relatives within the third degree of relationship: great-grandparent, grandparent, parent, uncle, aunt, brother, sister, child, grandchild, great-grandchild, nephew, or niece.

Canon 1. A Judge Shall Uphold the Integrity and Independence of the Judiciary

An independent and honorable judiciary is indispensable to justice in our society. A judge should participate in establishing, maintaining, and enforcing high standards of conduct, and shall personally observe those standards so that the integrity and independence of the judiciary

Judicial Conduct

may be preserved. The provisions of this Code should be construed and applied to further that objective.

COMMENTARY

Deference to the judgments and rulings of courts depends upon public confidence in the integrity and independence of judges. The integrity and independence of judges depend in turn upon their acting without fear or favor. Although judges should be independent, they must comply with the law, including the provisions of this Code. Public confidence in the impartiality of the judiciary is maintained by the adherence of each judge to this responsibility. Conversely, violation of this Code diminishes public confidence in the judiciary and thereby does injury to the system of government under law.

Canon 2. A Judge Shall Avoid Impropriety and the Appearance of Impropriety in all of the Judge's Activities

A. A judge shall respect and comply with the law and shall act at all times in a manner that promotes public confidence in the integrity and impartiality of the judiciary.

B. A judge shall not allow family, social, political or other relationships to influence the judge's judicial conduct or judgment. A judge shall not lend the prestige of judicial office to advance the private interests of the judge or others; nor shall a judge convey or permit others to convey the impression that they are in a special position to influence the judge. A judge shall not testify voluntarily as a character witness.

C. A judge should not hold membership in an organization that practices invidious discrimination on the basis of race, sex, religion, or national origin. Membership in a fraternal, sororal, religious, or ethnic heritage organization shall not be deemed to be a violation of this provision.

COMMENTARY

Canon 2A. Irresponsible or improper conduct by judges erodes public confidence in the judiciary. A judge must avoid all impropriety and appearance of impropriety. A judge must expect to be the subject of constant public scrutiny. A judge must therefore accept restrictions on the judge's conduct that might be viewed as burdensome by the ordinary citizen and should do so freely and willingly. Examples are the restrictions on judicial sppech imposed by Sections 3B(9) are (10) that are indispensable to the maintenance of integrity, impartiality and independence of the judiciary.

The prohibition against behaving with impropriety or the appearance of impropriety applies to both the professional and personal conduct of a judge. Because it is not practicable to list all prohibited acts, the proscription is necessarily cast in general terms that extend to conduct by judges that is harmful although not specifically mentioned in the Code. Actual improprieties under this standard include violations of law, court rules, or other specific provisions of this Code. The test for appearance of impropriety is whether the conduct would create in reasonable minds, with knowledge of all the relevant circumstances that a reasonable inquiry would disclose, a perception that the judge's ability to carry out judicial responsibilities with integrity, impartiality, and competence is impaired.

See also Commentary under Section 2C.

Canon 2B. Maintaining the prestige of judicial office is essential to a system of government in which the judiciary functions independently of the executive and legislative branches. Respect for the judicial office facilitates the orderly conduct of legitimate judicial functions. Judges should distinguish between proper and improper use of the prestige of office in all of their activities. For example, it would be improper for a judge to allude to his or her judgeship to gain a personal advantage such as deferential treatment when stopped by a police officer for a traffic offense. Similarly, judicial letterhead must not be used for conducting a judge's personal business, although a judge may use judicial letterhead to write character reference letters when such letters are otherwise permitted under this Code.

A judge must avoid lending the prestige of judicial office for the advancement of the private interests of others. For example, a judge must not use the judge's judicial position to gain advantage in a civil suit involving a member of the judge's family. In contracts for publication of a judge's writings, a judge should retain control over the advertising to avoid exploitation of the judge's office. As to the acceptance of awards, see Section 5D(5) and Commentary.

Although a judge should be sensitive to possible abuse of the prestige of office, a judge may, based on the judge's personal knowledge, serve as a reference or provide a letter of recommendation. However, a judge must not initiate the communication of information to a sentencing judge or a probation or corrections officer but may provide to such persons information for the record in response to a formal request.

Judges may participate in the process of judicial selection by cooperating with appointing authorities and screening committees seeking names for consideration, and by responding to official inquiries concerning a person being considered for a judgeship. See also Canon 7 regarding use of a judge's name in political activities.

A judge must not testify voluntarily as a character witness because to do so may lend the prestige of the judicial office in support of the party for whom the judge testifies. Moreover, when a judge testifies as a witness, a lawyer who regularly appears before the judge may be placed in the awkward position of cross-examining the judge. A judge may, however, testify when properly summoned. Except in unusual circumstances where the demands of justice require, a judge should discourage a party from requiring the judge to testify as a character witness.

Canon 2C. Florida Canon 2C is derived from a recommendation by the American Bar Association and from the United States Senate Committee Resolution, 101st Congress, Second Session, as adopted by the United States Senate Judiciary Committee on August 2, 1990.

Membership of a judge in an organization that practices invidious discrimination gives rise to perceptions that the judge's impartiality is impaired. Whether an organization practices invidious discrimination is often a complex question to which judges should be sensitive. The answer cannot be determined from a mere examination of an organization's current membership rolls but rather depends on the history of the organization's selection of members and other relevant factors, such as that the organization is dedicated to the preservation of religious, ethnic, or cultural values of legitimate common interest to its members, or that it is in fact and effect an intimate, purely private organization whose membership limitations could not be constitutionally prohibited. See New York State Club Ass'n Inc. v. City of New York, 487 U.S. 1, 108 S.Ct. 2225, 101 L.Ed.2d 1 (1988); Board of Directors of Rotary International v. Rotary Club of Duarte, 481 U.S. 537, 107 S.Ct. 1940, 95 L.Ed.2d 474 (1987); Roberts v. United States Jaycees, 468 U.S. 609, 104 S.Ct. 3244, 82 L.Ed.2d 462 (1984). Other relevant factors include the size and nature of the organization and the diversity of persons in the locale who might reasonably be considered potential members. Thus the mere absence of diverse membership does not by itself demonstrate a violation unless reasonable persons with knowledge of all the relevant circumstances would expect that the membership would be diverse in the absence of invidious discrimination. Absent such factors, an organization is generally said to discriminate invidiously if it arbitrarily excludes from membership on the basis of race, religion, sex, or national origin persons who would otherwise be admitted to membership.

This Canon is not intended to prohibit membership in religious and ethnic clubs, such as Knights of Columbus, Masons, B'nai B'rith, and Sons of Italy; civic organizations, such as Rotary, Kiwanis and The Junior League; young people's organizations, such as Boy Scouts, Girl Scouts, Boy's Clubs, and Girl's Clubs; and charitable organizations, such as United Way and Red Cross.

Although Section 2C relates only to membership in organizations that invidiously discriminate on the basis of race, sex, religion or national origin, a judge's membership in an organization that engages in any discriminatory membership practices prohibited by the law of the jurisdiction also violates Canon 2 and Section 2A and gives the appearance of impropriety. In addition, it would be a violation of Canon 2 and Section 2A for a judge to arrange a meeting at a club that the judge knows practices invidious discrimination on the basis of race, sex, religion or national origin in its membership or other policies, or for the judge to regularly use such a club. Moreover, public manifestation by a judge of the judge's knowing approval of invidious discrimination on any basis gives the appearance of impropriety under Canon 2 and diminishes public confidence in the integrity and impartiality of the judiciary, in violation of Section 2A.

When a person who is a judge on the date this Code becomes effective learns that an organization to which the judge belongs engages in invidious discrimination that would preclude membership under Section 2C or under Canon 2 and Section 2A, the judge is permitted, in lieu of resigning, to make immediate efforts to have the organization discontinue its invidiously discriminatory practices, but is required to suspend participation in any other activities of the organization. If the organization fails to discontinue its invidiously discriminatory practices as promptly as possible (and in all events within a year of the judge's first learning of the practices), the judge is required to resign immediately from the organization.

Canon 3. A Judge Shall Perform the Duties of Judicial Office Impartially and Diligently

A. Judicial Duties in General The judicial duties of a judge take precedence over all the judge's other activities. The judge's judicial duties include all the duties of the judge's office prescribed by law. In the performance of these duties, the specific standards set forth in the following sections apply.

B. Adjudicative Responsibilities.

(1) A judge shall hear and decide matters assigned to the judge except those in which disqualification is required.

(2) A judge shall be faithful to the law and maintain professional competence in it. A judge shall not be swayed by partisan interests, public clamor, or fear of criticism.

(3) A judge shall require order and decorum in proceedings before the judge.

(4) A judge shall be patient, dignified, and courteous to litigants, jurors, witnesses, lawyers, and others with whom the judge deals in an official capacity, and shall require similar conduct of lawyers, and of staff, court officials, and others subject to the judge's direction and control.

(5) A judge shall perform judicial duties without bias or prejudice. A judge shall not, in the performance of judicial duties, by words or conduct manifest bias or prejudice, including but not limited to bias or prejudice based upon race, sex, religion, national origin, disability, age, sexual orientation, or socioeconomic status, and shall not permit staff, court officials, and others subject to the judge's direction and control to do so. This section does not preclude the consideration of race, sex, religion, national origin, disability, age, sexual orientation, socioeconomic status, or other similar factors when they are issues in the proceeding.

(6) A judge shall require lawyers in proceedings before the judge to refrain from manifesting, by words, gestures, or other conduct, bias or prejudice based upon race, sex, religion, national origin, disability, age, sexual orientation, or socioeconomic status, against parties, witnesses, counsel, or others. This Section 3B(6) does not preclude legitimate advocacy when race, sex, religion, national origin, disability, age, sexual orientation, socioeconomic status, or other similar factors are issues in the proceeding.

(7) A judge shall accord to every person who has a legal interest in a proceeding, or that person's lawyer, the right to be heard according to law. A judge shall not initiate, permit, or consider ex parte communications, or consider other communications made to the judge outside the presence of the parties concerning a pending or impending proceeding except that:

(a) Where circumstances require, ex parte communications for scheduling, administrative purposes, or emergencies that do not deal with substantive matters or issues on the merits are authorized, provided:

(i) the judge reasonably believes that no party will gain a procedural or tactical advantage as a result of the ex parte communication, and

(ii) the judge makes provision promptly to notify all other parties of the substance of the ex parte communication and allows an opportunity to respond.

(b) A judge may obtain the advice of a disinterested expert on the law applicable to a proceeding before the judge if the judge gives notice to the parties of the person consulted and the substance of the advice and affords the parties reasonable opportunity to respond.

(c) A judge may consult with other judges or with court personnel whose function is to aid the judge in carrying out the judge's adjudicative responsibilities.

(d) A judge may, with the consent of the parties, confer separately with the parties and their lawyers in an effort to mediate or settle matters pending before the judge.

(e) A judge may initiate or consider any ex parte communications when expressly authorized by law to do so.

(8) A judge shall dispose of all judicial matters promptly, efficiently, and fairly.

(9) A judge shall not, while a proceeding is pending or impending in any court, make any public comment that might reasonably be expected to affect its outcome or impair its fairness or make any nonpublic comment that might

substantially interfere with a fair trial or hearing. The judge shall require similar abstention on the part of court personnel subject to the judge's direction and control. This Section does not prohibit judges from making public statements in the course of their official duties or from explaining for public information the procedures of the court. This Section does not apply to proceedings in which the judge is a litigant in a personal capacity.

(10) A judge shall not, with respect to parties or classes of parties, cases, controversies or issues likely to come before the court, amke pledges, promises, or commitments that are inconsistent with the impartial performance of the adjudicative duties of the office.

(11) A judge shall not, with respect to parties or classes of parties, cases, controversies or issues likely to come before the court, make pledges, promises or commitments that are inconsistent with the impartial performance of the adjudicative duties of the office.

(12) A judge shall not disclose or use, for any purpose unrelated to judicial duties, nonpublic information acquired in a judicial capacity.

C. Administrative Responsibilities.

(1) A judge shall diligently discharge the judge's administrative responsibilities without bias or prejudice and maintain professional competence in judicial administration, and should cooperate with other judges and court officials in the administration of court business.

(2) A judge shall require staff, court officials, and others subject to the judge's direction and control to observe the standards of fidelity and diligence that apply to the judge and to refrain from manifesting bias or prejudice in the performance of their official duties.

(3) A judge with supervisory authority for the judicial performance of other judges shall take reasonable measures to assure the prompt disposition of matters before them and the proper performance of their other judicial responsibilities.

(4) A judge shall not make unnecessary appointments. A judge shall exercise the power of appointment impartially and on the basis of merit. A judge shall avoid nepotism and favoritism. A judge shall not approve compensation of appointees beyond the fair value of services rendered.

D. Disciplinary Responsibilities.

(1) A judge who receives information or has actual knowledge that substantial likelihood exists that another judge has committed a violation of this Code shall take appropriate action.

(2) A judge who receives information or has actual knowledge that substantial likelihood exists that a lawyer has committed a violation of the Rules Regulating The Florida Bar shall take appropriate action.

(3) Acts of a judge, in the discharge of disciplinary responsibilities, required or permitted by Sections 3D(1) and 3D(2) are part of a judge's judicial duties and shall be absolutely privileged, and no civil action predicated thereon may be instituted against the judge.

E. Disqualification.

(1) A judge shall disqualify himself or herself in a proceeding in which the judge's impartiality might reasonably be questioned, including but not limited to instances where:

(a) the judge has a personal bias or prejudice concerning a party or a party's lawyer, or personal knowledge of disputed evidentiary facts concerning the proceeding;

(b) the judge served as a lawyer or was the lower court judge in the matter in controversy, or a lawyer with whom the judge previously practiced law served during such association as a lawyer concerning the matter, or the judge has been a material witness concerning it;

(c) the judge knows that he or she individually or as a fiduciary, or the judge's spouse, parent, or child wherever residing, or any other member of the judge's family residing in the judge's household has an economic interest in the subject matter in controversy or in a party to the proceeding or has any other more than de minimis interest that could be substantially affected by the proceeding;

Judicial Conduct

(d) the judge or the judge's spouse, or a person within the third degree of relationship to either of them, or the spouse of such a person:

(i) is a party to the proceeding, or an officer, director, or trustee of a party;

(ii) is acting as a lawyer in the proceeding;

(iii) is known by the judge to have a more than de minimus interest that could be substantially affected by the proceeding;

(iv) is to the judge's knowledge likely to be a material witness in the proceeding;

(e) the judge's spouse or a person within the third degree of relationship to the judge participated as a lower court judge in a decision to be reviewed by the judge;

(f) the judge, while a judge or candidate, for judicial office, has made a public statement that commits, or appears to commit, the judge with respect to:

(i) parties or classes of parties in the proceeding;

(ii) an issue in the proceeding; or

(iii) the controversy in the proceeding.

(2) A judge should keep informed about the judge's personal and fiduciary economic interests, and make a reasonable effort to keep informed about the economic interests of the judge's spouse and minor children residing in the judge's household.

F. Remittal of Disqualification.A judge disqualified by the terms of Section 3E may disclose on the record the basis of the judge's disqualification and may ask the parties and their lawyers to consider, out of the presence of the judge, whether to waive disqualification. If following disclosure of any basis for disqualification other than personal bias or prejudice concerning a party, the parties and lawyers, without participation by the judge, all agree the judge should not be disqualified, and the judge is then willing to participate, the judge may participate in the proceeding. The agreement shall be incorporated in the record of the proceeding.

COMMENTARY

Canon 3B(4). The duty to hear all proceedings fairly and with patience is not inconsistent with the duty to dispose promptly of the business of the court. Judges can be efficient and business-like while being patient and deliberate.

Canon 3B(5). A judge must refrain from speech, gestures or other conduct that could reasonably be perceived as sexual harassment and must require the same standard of conduct of others subject to the judge's direction and control.

A judge must perform judicial duties impartially and fairly. A judge who manifests bias on any basis in a proceeding impairs the fairness of the proceeding and brings the judiciary into disrepute. Facial expression and body language, in addition to oral communication, can give to parties or lawyers in the proceeding, jurors, the media and others an appearance of judicial bias. A judge must be alert to avoid behavior that may be perceived as prejudicial.

Canon 3B(7). The proscription against communications concerning a proceeding includes communications from lawyers, law teachers, and other persons who are not participants in the proceeding, except to the limited extent permitted.

To the extent reasonably possible, all parties or their lawyers shall be included in communications with a judge.

Whenever presence of a party or notice to a party is required by Section 3B(7), it is the party's lawyer, or if the party is unrepresented, the party who is to be present or to whom notice is to be given.

An appropriate and often desirable procedure for a court to obtain the advice of a disinterested expert on legal issues is to invite the expert to file a brief as amicus curiae.

Certain ex parte communication is approved by Section 3B(7) to facilitate scheduling and other administrative purposes and to accommodate emergencies. In general, however, a judge must discourage ex parte communication and allow it only if all the criteria stated in Section 3B(7) are clearly met. A judge must disclose to all parties all ex parte communications described in Sections 3B(7)(a) and 3B(7)(b) regarding a proceeding pending or impending before the judge.

A judge must not independently investigate facts in a case and must consider only the evidence presented.

A judge may request a party to submit proposed findings of fact and conclusions of law, so long as the other parties are apprised of the request and are given an opportunity to respond to the proposed findings and conclusions.

A judge must make reasonable efforts, including the provision of appropriate supervision, to ensure that Section 3B(7) is not violated through law clerks or other personnel on the judge's staff.

If communication between the trial judge and the appellate court with respect to a proceeding is permitted, a copy of any written communication or the substance of any oral communication should be provided to all parties.

Canon 3B(8). In disposing of matters promptly, efficiently, and fairly, a judge must demonstrate due regard for the rights of the parties to be heard and to have issues resolved without unnecessary cost or delay. Containing costs while preserving fundamental rights of parties also protects the interests of witnesses and the general public. A judge should monitor and supervise cases so as to reduce or eliminate dilatory practices, avoidable delays, and unnecessary costs. A judge should encourage and seek to facilitate settlement, but parties should not feel coerced into surrendering the right to have their controversy resolved by the courts.

Prompt disposition of the court's business requires a judge to devote adequate time to judicial duties, to be punctual in attending court and expeditious in determining matters under submission, and to insist that court officials, litigants, and their lawyers cooperate with the judge to that end.

Canon 3B(9) and 3B(10). Sections 3B(9) and (10) restrictions on judicial speech are essential to the maintenence of the integrity, impartiality, and the independence of the judiciary.

A pending proceeding is one that has begun but not yet reached final disposition. An impending proceeding is one that is anticipated but not yet begun. The requirement that judges abstain from public comment regarding a pending or impending proceeding continues during any appellate process and until final disposition. Sections 3B(9) and (10) do not prohibit a judge from commenting on proceedings in which the judge is a litigant in a personal capacity, but in cases such as a writ of mandamus where the judge is a litigant in an official capacity, the judge must not comment publicly. The conduct of lawyers relating to trial publicity is governed by Rule 4-3.6 of the Rules Regulating The Florida Bar.

Canon 3B(10). Commending or criticizing jurors for their verdict may imply a judicial expectation in future cases and may impair a juror's ability to be fair and impartial in a subsequent case.

Canon 3C(4). Appointees of a judge include assigned counsel, officials such as referees, commissioners, special magistrates, receivers, mediators, arbitrators, and guardians and personnel such as clerks, secretaries, and bailiffs. Consent by the parties to an appointment or an award of compensation does not relieve the judge of the obligation prescribed by Section 3C(4). See also Fla.Stat § 112.3135 (1991).

Canon 3D. Appropriate action may include direct communication with the judge or lawyer who has committed the violation, other direct action if available, or reporting the violation to the appropriate authority or other agency. If the conduct is minor, the Canon allows a judge to address the problem solely by direct communication with the offender. A judge having knowledge, however, that another judge has committed a violation of this Code that raises a substantial question as to that other judge's fitness for office or has knowledge that a lawyer has committed a violation of the Rules of Professional Conduct that raises a substantial question as to the lawyer's honesty, trustworthiness or fitness as a lawyer in other respects, is required under this Canon to inform the appropriate authority. While worded differently, this Code provision has the identical purpose as the related Model Code provisions.

Canon 3E(1). Under this rule, a judge is disqualified whenever the judge's impartiality might reasonably be questioned, regardless of whether any of the specific rules in Section 3E(1) apply. For example, if a judge were in the process of negotiating for employment with a law firm, the judge would be disqualified from any matters in which that law firm appeared, unless the disqualification was waived by the parties after disclosure by the judge.

A judge should disclose on the record information that the judge believes the parties or their lawyers might consider relevant to the question of disqualification, even if the judge believes there is no real basis for disqualification. The fact that the judge conveys this information does not automatically require the judge to be disqualified upon a request by either party, but the issue should be resolved on a case-by-case basis. Similarly, if a lawyer or party has previously filed a complaint against the judge with the Judicial Qualifications Commission, that the fact does not automatically require disqualification of the judge. Such disqualification should be on a case-by-case basis.

By decisional law, the rule of necessity may override the rule of disqualification. For example, a judge might be required to participate in judicial review of a judicial salary statute, or might be the only judge available in a matter requiring immediate judicial action, such as a hearing on probable cause or a temporary restraining order. In the latter case, the judge must disclose on the record the basis for possible disqualification and use reasonable efforts to transfer the matter to another judge as soon as practicable.

Canon 3E(1)(b). A lawyer in a government agency does not ordinarily have an association with other lawyers employed by that agency within the meaning of Section 3E(1)(b); a judge formerly employed by a government agency, however, should disqualify himself or herself in a proceeding if the judge's impartiality might reasonably be questioned because of such association.

Canon 3E(1)(d). The fact that a lawyer in a proceeding is affiliated with a law firm with which a relative of the judge is affiliated does not of itself disqualify the judge. Under appropriate circumstances, the fact that "the judge's impartiality might reasonably be questioned" under Section 3E(1), or that the relative is known by the judge to have an interest in the law firm that could be "substantially affected by the outcome of the proceeding" under Section 3E(1)(d)(iii) may require the judge's disqualification.

Canon 3E(1)(e). It is not uncommon for a judge's spouse or a person within the third degree of relationship to a judge to also serve as a judge in either the trial or appellate courts. However, when a judge exercises appellate authority over another judge, and that other judge is either a spouse or a relationship within the third degree, then this Code requires disqualification of the judge that is exercising appellate authority. This Code, under these circumstances, precludes the appellate judge from participating in the review of the spouse's or relation's case.

Canon 3F. A remittal procedure provides the parties an opportunity to proceed without delay if they wish to waive the disqualification. To assure that consideration of the question of remittal is made independently of the judge, a judge must not solicit, seek, or hear comment on possible remittal or waiver of the disqualification unless the lawyers jointly propose remittal after consultation as provided in the rule. A party may act through counsel if counsel represents on the record that the party has been consulted and consents. As a practical matter, a judge may wish to have all parties and their lawyers sign the remittal agreement.

Commentary amended June 15, 1995, effective Nov. 9, 1995 (656 So.2d 926); Aug. 24, 1995 (659 So.2d 692).

Canon 4. A Judge is Encouraged to Engage in Activities to Improve the Law, the Legal System, and the Administration of Justice

A. A judge shall conduct all of the judge's quasi-judicial activities so that they do not:

(1) cast reasonable doubt on the judge's capacity to act impartially as a judge;

(2) demean the judicial office; or

(3) interfere with the proper performance of judicial duties.

B. A judge is encouraged to speak, write, lecture, teach and participate in other quasi-judicial activities concerning the law, the legal system, the administration of justice, and the role of the juduciary as an independent branch within our system of government, subject to the requirements of this Code.

C. A judge shall not appear at a public hearing before, or otherwise consult with, an executive or legislative body or official except on matters concerning the law, the legal system or the administration of justice or except when acting pro se in a matter involving the judge or the judge's interests.

D. A judge is encouraged to serve as a member, officer, director, trustee or non-legal advisor of an organization or governmental agency devoted to the improvement of the law, the legal system, the judicial branch, or the administration of justice, subject to the following limitations and the other requirements of this Code.

(1) A judge shall not serve as an officer, director, trustee or non-legal advisor if it is likely that the organization

(a) will be engaged in proceedings that would ordinarily come before the judge, or

(b) will be engaged frequently in adversary proceedings in the court of which the judge is a member or in any court subject to the appellate jurisdiction of the court of which the judge is a member.

(2) A judge as an officer, director, trustee or non-legal advisor, or as a member or otherwise:

(a) may assist such an organization in planning fund-raising and may participate in the management and investment of the organization's funds, but shall not personally participate in the solicitation of funds or other fund-raising activities, except that a judge may solicit funds from other judges over whom the judge does not exercise supervisory or appellate authority;

(b) may make recommendations to public and private fund-granting organizations on projects and programs concerning the law, the legal system or the administration of justice;

(c) shall not personally participate in membership solicitation if the solicitation might reasonably be perceived as coercive or, except as permitted in Section 4D(2)(a), if the membership solicitation is essentially a fund-raising mechanism;

(d) shall not use or permit the use of the prestige of judicial office for fund-raising or membership solicitation.

COMMENTARY

Canon 4A. A judge is encouraged to participate in activities designed to improve the law, the legal system, and the administration of justice. In doing so, however, it must be understood that expressions of bias or prejudice by a judge, even outside the judge's judicial activities, may cast reasonable doubt on the judge's capacity to act impartially as a judge. Expressions which may do so include jokes or other remarks demeaning individuals on the basis of their race, sex, religion, national origin, disability, age, sexual orientation or socioeconomic status. See Section 2C and accompanying Commentary.

Canon 4B. This canon is clarified in order to encourage judges to engage in activities to improve the law, the legal system, and the administration of justice. As a judicial officer and person specially learned in the law, a judge is in a unique position to contribute to the improvement of the law, the legal system, and the administration of justice, including, but not limited to, the improvement of the role of the judiciary as an independent branch of government, the revision of substantive and procedural law, the improvement of criminal and juvenile justice, and the improvement of justice in the areas of civil, criminal, family, domestic violence, juvenile delinquency, juvenile dependency, probate and motor vehicle law. To the extent that time permits, a judge is encouraged to do so, either independently or through a bar association, judicial conference or other organization dedicated to the improvement of the law. Support of pro bono legal services by members of the bench is an activity that relates to improvement of the administration of justice. Accordingly, a judge may engage in activities intended to encourage attorneys to perform pro bono services, including, but not limited to: participating in events to recognize attorneys who do pro bono work, establishing general procedural or scheduling accomodations for pro bono attorneys as feasible, and acting in an advisory capacity to pro bono programs. Judges are encouraged to participate in efforts to promote the fair administration of justice, the independence of the judiciary and the integrity of the legal profession, which may include the expression of opposition to the persecution of lawyers and judges in other countries.

The phrase "subject to the requirements of this Code" is included to remind judges that the use of permissive language in various Sections of the Code does not relieve a judge from the other requirements of the Code that apply to the specific conduct.

Canon 4C. See Section 2B regarding the obligation to avoid improper influence.

Canon 4D(1). The changing nature of some organizations and of their relationship to the law makes it necessary for a judge regularly to reexamine the activities of each organization with which the judge is affiliated to determine if it is proper for the judge to continue the affiliation. For example, the boards of some legal aid organizations now make policy decisions that may have political significance or imply commitment to causes that may come before the courts for adjudication.

Canon 4D(2). A judge may solicit membership or endorse or encourage membership efforts for an organization devoted to the improvement of the law, the legal system or the administration of justice as long as the solicitation cannot reasonably be perceived as coercive and is not essentially a fund-raising mechanism. Solicitation of funds for an organization and solicitation of memberships similarly involve the danger that the person solicited will feel obligated to respond favorably to the solicitor if the solicitor is in a position of influence or control. A judge must not engage in direct, individual solicitation of funds or memberships in person, in writing or by telephone except in the following cases: 1) a judge may solicit for funds or memberships other judges over whom the judge does not exercise supervisory or appellate authority, 2) a judge may solicit other persons for membership in the organizations described above if neither those persons nor persons with whom they are affiliated are likely ever to appear before the court on which the judge serves and 3) a judge who is an officer of such an organization may send a general membership solicitation mailing over the judge's signature.

Use of an organization letterhead for fund-raising or membership solicitation does not violate Section

Judicial Conduct

4D(2) provided the letterhead lists only the judge's name and office or other position in the organization, and, if comparable designations are listed for other persons, the judge's judicial designation. In addition, a judge must also make reasonable efforts to ensure that the judge's staff, court officials and others subject to the judge's direction and control do not solicit funds on the judge's behalf for any purpose, charitable or otherwise.

A judge must not be a speaker or guest of honor at an organization's fund-raising event, but mere attendance at such an event is permissible if otherwise consistent with this Code.

Canon 5. A Judge Shall Regulate Extrajudicial Activities to Minimize the Risk of Conflict With Judicial Duties

A. Extrajudicial Activities in General.A judge shall conduct all of the judge's extra-judicial activities so that they do not:

(1) cast reasonable doubt on the judge's capacity to act impartially as a judge;

(2) demean the judicial office; or

(3) interfere with the proper performance of judicial duties.

B. Avocational Activities.A judge is encouraged to speak, write, lecture, teach and participate in other extrajudicial activities concerning non-legal subjects, subject to the requirements of this Code.

C. Governmental, Civic or Charitable Activities.

(1) A judge shall not appear at a public hearing before, or otherwise consult with, an executive or legislative body or official except on matters concerning the law, the legal system or the administration of justice or except when acting pro se in a matter involving the judge or the judge's interests.

(2) A judge shall not accept appointment to a governmental committee or commission or other governmental position that is concerned with issues of fact or policy on matters other than the improvement of the law, the legal system, the judicial branch, or the administration of justice. A judge may, however, represent a country, state or locality on ceremonial occasions or in connection with historical, educational or cultural activities.

(3) A judge may serve as an officer, director, trustee or non-legal advisor of an educational, religious, charitable, fraternal, sororal or civic organization not conducted for profit, subject to the following limitations and the other requirements of this Code.

(a) A judge shall not serve as an officer, director, trustee or non-legal advisor if it is likely that the organization

(i) will be engaged in proceedings that would ordinarily come before the judge, or

(ii) will be engaged frequently in adversary proceedings in the court of which the judge is a member or in any court subject to the appellate jurisdiction of the court of which the judge is a member.

(b) A judge as an officer, director, trustee or non-legal advisor, or as a member or otherwise:

(i) may assist such an organization in planning fund-raising and may participate in the management and investment of the organization's funds, but shall not personally participate in the solicitation of funds or other fund-raising activities, except that a judge may solicit funds from other judges over whom the judge does not exercise supervisory or appellate authority;

(ii) shall not personally participate in membership solicitation if the solicitation might reasonably be perceived as coercive or, except as permitted in Section 5C(3)(b)(i), if the membership solicitation is essentially a fund-raising mechanism;

(iii) shall not use or permit the use of the prestige of judicial office for fund-raising or membership solicitation.

D. Financial Activities.

(1) A judge shall not engage in financial and business dealings that

(a) may reasonably be perceived to exploit the judge's judicial position, or

(b) involve the judge in frequent transactions or continuing business relationships with those lawyers or other persons likely to come before the court on which the judge serves.

(2) A judge may, subject to the requirements of this Code, hold and manage investments of the judge and members of the judge's family, including real estate, and engage in other remunerative activity.

(3) A judge shall not serve as an officer, director, manager, general partner, advisor or employee of any business entity except that a judge may, subject to the requirements of this Code, manage and participate in:

(a) a business closely held by the judge or members of the judge's family, or

(b) a business entity primarily engaged in investment of the financial resources of the judge or members of the judge's family.

(4) A judge shall manage the judge's investments and other financial interests to minimize the number of cases in which the judge is disqualified. As soon as the judge can do so without serious financial detriment, the judge shall divest himself or herself of investments and other financial interests that might require frequent disqualification.

(5) A judge shall not accept, and shall urge members of the judge's family residing in the judge's household not to accept, a gift, bequest, favor or loan from anyone except for:

(a) a gift incident to a public testimonial, books, tapes and other resource materials supplied by publishers on a complimentary basis for official use, or an invitation to the judge and the judge's spouse or guest to attend a bar-related function or an activity devoted to the improvement of the law, the legal system or the administration of justice;

(b) a gift, award or benefit incident to the business, profession or other separate activity of a spouse or other family member of a judge residing in the judge's household, including gifts, awards and benefits for the use of both the spouse or other family member and the judge (as spouse or family member), provided the gift, award or benefit could not reasonably be perceived as intended to influence the judge in the performance of judicial duties;

(c) ordinary social hospitality;

(d) a gift from a relative or friend, for a special occasion, such as a wedding, anniversary or birthday, if the gift is fairly commensurate with the occasion and the relationship;

(e) a gift, bequest, favor or loan from a relative or close personal friend whose appearance or interest in a case would in any event require disqualification under Canon 3E;

(f) a loan from a lending institution in its regular course of business on the same terms generally available to persons who are not judges;

(g) a scholarship or fellowship awarded on the same terms and based on the same criteria applied to other applicants; or

(h) any other gift, bequest, favor or loan, only if: the donor is not a party or other person who has come or is likely to come or whose interests have come or are likely to come before the judge; and, if its value, or the aggregate value in a calendar year of such gifts, bequests, favors, or loans from a single source, exceeds $100.00, the judge reports it in the same manner as the judge reports gifts under Section 6B(2).

E. Fiduciary Activities.

(1) A judge shall not serve as executor, administrator or other personal representative, trustee, guardian, attorney in fact or other fiduciary, except for the estate, trust or person of a member of the judge's family, and then only if such service will not interfere with the proper performance of judicial duties.

(2) A judge shall not serve as a fiduciary if it is likely that the judge as a fiduciary will be engaged in proceedings that would ordinarily come before the judge, or if the estate, trust or ward becomes involved in adversary proceedings in the court on which the judge serves or one under its appellate jurisdiction.

(3) The same restrictions on financial activities that apply to a judge personally also apply to the judge while acting in a fiduciary capacity.

Judicial Conduct

F. Service as Arbitrator or Mediator.A judge shall not act as an arbitrator or mediator or otherwise perform judicial functions in a private capacity unless expressly authorized by law or Court rule. A judge may, however, take the necessary educational and training courses required to be a qualified and certified arbitrator or mediator, and may fulfill the requirements of observing and conducting actual arbitration or mediation proceedings as part of the certification process, provided such program does not, in any way, interfere with the performance of the judge's judicial duties.

G. Practice of Law.A judge shall not practice law. Notwithstanding this prohibition, a judge may act pro se and may, without compensation, give legal advice to and draft or review documents for a member of the judge's family.

COMMENTARY

Canon 5A. Complete separation of a judge from extra-judicial activities is neither possible nor wise; a judge should not become isolated from the community in which the judge lives. For that reason, judges are encouraged to participate in extrajudicial community activities.

Expressions of bias or prejudice by a judge, even outside the judge's judicial activities, may cast reasonable doubt on the judge's capacity to act impartially as a judge. Expressions which may do so include jokes or other remarks demeaning individuals on the basis of their race, sex, religion, national origin, disability, age, sexual orientation or socioeconomic status. See Section 2C and accompanying Commentary.

Canon 5B. In this and other Sections of Canon 5, the phrase "subject to the requirements of this Code" is used, notably in connection with a judge's governmental, civic or charitable activities. This phrase is included to remind judges that the use of permissive language in various Sections of the Code does not relieve a judge from the other requirements of the Code that apply to the specific conduct.

Canon 5C(1). See Section 2B regarding the obligation to avoid improper influence.

Canon 5C(2). Section 5C(2) prohibits a judge from accepting any governmental position except one relating to the law, legal system or administration of justice as authorized by Section 4D. The appropriateness of accepting extra-judicial assignments must be assessed in light of the demands on judicial resources created by crowded dockets and the need to protect the courts from involvement in extra-judicial matters that may prove to be controversial. Judges should not accept governmental appointments that are likely to interfere with the effectiveness and independence of the judiciary.

Section 5C(2) does not govern a judge's service in a nongovernmental position. See Section 5C(3) permitting service by a judge with educational, religious, charitable, fraternal, sororal or civic organizations not conducted for profit. For example, service on the board of a public educational institution, unless it were a law school, would be prohibited under Section 5C(2), but service on the board of a public law school or any private educational institution would generally be permitted under Section 5C(3).

Canon 5C(3). Section 5C(3) does not apply to a judge's service in a governmental position unconnected with the improvement of the law, the legal system or the administration of justice; see Section 5C(2).

See Commentary to Section 5B regarding use of the phrase "subject to the following limitations and the other requirements of this Code." As an example of the meaning of the phrase, a judge permitted by Section 5C(3) to serve on the board of a fraternal institution may be prohibited from such service by Sections 2C or 5A if the institution practices invidious discrimination or if service on the board otherwise casts reasonable doubt on the judge's capacity to act impartially as a judge.

Service by a judge on behalf of a civic or charitable organization may be governed by other provisions of Canon 5 in addition to Section 5C. For example, Section 5G prohibits a judge from serving as a legal advisor to a civic or charitable organization.

Canon 5C(3)(a). The changing nature of some organizations and of their relationship to the law makes it necessary for a judge to regularly reexamine the activities of each organization with which the judge is affiliated in order to determine if it is proper for the judge to continue the affiliation. For example, in many jurisdictions charitable hospitals are now more frequently in court than in the past.

Canon 5C(3)(b). A judge may solicit membership or endorse or encourage membership efforts for a nonprofit educational, religious, charitable, fraternal, sororal or civic organization as long as the solicitation cannot reasonably be perceived as coercive and is not essentially a fund-raising mechanism. Solicitation of funds for an organization and solicitation of memberships similarly involve the danger that the person solicited will feel obligated to respond favorably to the solicitor if the solicitor is in a position of influence or control. A judge must not engage in direct, individual solicitation of funds or memberships in person, in writing or by telephone except in the following cases: 1) a judge may solicit for funds or memberships other judges over whom the judge does not exercise supervisory or appellate authority, 2) a judge may solicit other persons for membership in the organizations described above if neither those persons nor persons with whom they are affiliated are likely ever to appear before the court on which the judge serves and 3) a judge who is an officer of such an organization may send a general membership solicitation mailing over the judge's signature.

Use of an organization letterhead for fund-raising or membership solicitation does not violate Section 5C(3)(b) provided the letterhead lists only the judge's name and office or other position in the organization, and, if comparable designations are listed for other persons, the judge's judicial designation. In addition, a judge must also make reasonable efforts to ensure that the judge's staff, court officials and others subject to the judge's direction and control do not solicit funds on the judge's behalf for any purpose, charitable or otherwise.

A judge must not be a speaker or guest of honor at an organization's fund-raising event, but mere attendance at such an event is permissible if otherwise consistent with this Code.

Canon 5D(1). When a judge acquires in a judicial capacity information, such as material contained in filings with the court, that is not yet generally known, the judge must not use the information for private gain. See Section 2B; see also Section 3B(11).

A judge must avoid financial and business dealings that involve the judge in frequent transactions or continuing business relationships with persons likely to come either before the judge personally or before other judges on the judge's court. In addition, a judge should discourage members of the judge's family from engaging in dealings that would reasonably appear to exploit the judge's judicial position. This rule is necessary to avoid creating an appearance of exploitation of office or favoritism and to minimize the potential for disqualification. With respect to affiliation of relatives of the judge with law firms appearing before the judge, see Commentary to Section 3E(1) relating to disqualification.

Participation by a judge in financial and business dealings is subject to the general prohibitions in Section 5A against activities that tend to reflect adversely on impartiality, demean the judicial office, or interfere with the proper performance of judicial duties. Such participation is also subject to the general prohibition in Canon 2 against activities involving impropriety or the appearance of impropriety and the prohibition in Section 2B against the misuse of the prestige of judicial office. In addition, a judge must maintain high standards of conduct in all of the judge's activities, as set forth in Canon 1. See Commentary for Section 5B regarding use of the phrase "subject to the requirements of this Code."

Canon 5D(2). This Section provides that, subject to the requirements of this Code, a judge may hold and manage investments owned solely by the judge, investments owned solely by a member or members of the judge's family, and investments owned jointly by the judge and members of the judge's family.

Canon 5D(3). Subject to the requirements of this Code, a judge may participate in a business that is closely held either by the judge alone, by members of the judge's family, or by the judge and members of the judge's family.

Although participation by a judge in a closely-held family business might otherwise be permitted by Section 5D(3), a judge may be prohibited from participation by other provisions of this Code when, for example, the business entity frequently appears before the judge's court or the participation requires significant time away from judicial duties. Similarly, a judge must avoid participating in a closely-held family business if the judge's participation would involve misuse of the prestige of judicial office.

Canon 5D(5). Section 5D(5) does not apply to contributions to a judge's campaign for judicial office, a matter governed by Canon 7.

Because a gift, bequest, favor or loan to a member of the judge's family residing in the judge's household might be viewed as intended to influence the judge, a judge must inform those family members of the relevant ethical constraints upon the judge in this regard and discourage those family members from violating them A judge cannot, however, reasonably be expected to know or control all of the financial or business activities of all family members residing in the judge's household.

Canon 5D(5)(a). Acceptance of an invitation to a law-related function is governed by Section 5D(5)(a); acceptance of an invitation paid for by an individual lawyer or group of lawyers is governed by Section 5D(5)(h).

A judge may accept a public testimonial or a gift incident thereto only if the donor organization is not an organization whose members comprise or frequently represent the same side in litigation, and the testimonial and gift are otherwise in compliance with

Judicial Conduct

other provisions of this Code. See Sections 5A(1) and 2B.

Canon 5D(5)(d). A gift to a judge, or to a member of the judge's family living in the judge's household, that is excessive in value raises questions about the judge's impartiality and the integrity of the judicial office and might require disqualification of the judge where disqualification would not otherwise be required. See, however, Section 5D(5)(e).

Canon 5D(5)(h). Section 5D(5)(h) prohibits judges from accepting gifts, favors, bequests or loans from lawyers or their firms if they have come or are likely to come before the judge; it also prohibits gifts, favors, bequests or loans from clients of lawyers or their firms when the clients' interests have come or are likely to come before the judge.

Canon 5E(3). The restrictions imposed by this Canon may conflict with the judge's obligation as a fiduciary. For example, a judge should resign as trustee if detriment to the trust would result from divestiture of holdings the retention of which would place the judge in violation of Section 5D(4).

Canon 5F. Section 5F does not prohibit a judge from participating in arbitration, mediation or settlement conferences performed as part of judicial duties. An active judge may take the necessary education and training programs to be certified or qualified as a mediator or arbitrator, but this shall not be a part of the judge's judicial duties. While such a course will allow a judge to have a better understanding of the arbitration and mediation process, the certification and qualification of a judge as a mediator or arbitrator is primarily for the judge's personal benefit. While actually participating in the mediation and arbitration training activities, care must be taken in the selection of both cases and locations so as to guarantee that there is no interference or conflict between the training and the judge's judicial responsibilities. Indeed, the training should be conducted in such a manner as to avoid the involvement of persons likely to appear before the judge in legal proceedings.

Canon 5G. This prohibition refers to the practice of law in a representative capacity and not in a pro se capacity. A judge may act for himself or herself in all legal matters, including matters involving litigation and matters involving appearances before or other dealings with legislative and other governmental bodies. However, in so doing, a judge must not abuse the prestige of office to advance the interests of the judge or the judge's family. See Section 2B.

The Code allows a judge to give legal advice to and draft legal documents for members of the judge's family, so long as the judge receives no compensation. A judge must not, however, act as an advocate or negotiator for a member of the judge's family in a legal matter.

Canon 6. Fiscal Matters of a Judge Shall be Conducted in a Manner That Does Not Give the Appearance of Influence or Impropriety; a Judge Shall Regularly File Public Reports as Required by Article II, Section 8, of the Constitution of Florida, and Shall Publicly Report Gifts; Additional Financial Information Shall be Filed With the Judicial Qualifications Commission to Ensure Full Financial Disclosure

A. Compensation for Quasi-Judicial and Extrajudicial Services and Reimbursement of Expenses.A judge may receive compensation and reimbursement of expenses for the quasi-judicial and extrajudicial activities permitted by this Code, if the source of such payments does not give the appearance of influencing the judge in the performance of judicial duties or otherwise give the appearance of impropriety, subject to the following restrictions:

(1) Compensation.Compensation shall not exceed a reasonable amount nor shall it exceed what a person who is not a judge would receive for the same activity.

(2) Expense Reimbursement.Expense reimbursement shall be limited to the actual cost of travel, food, and lodging reasonably incurred by the judge and, where appropriate to the occasion, to the judge's spouse. Any payment in excess of such an amount is compensation.

B. Public Financial Reporting.

(1) Income and Assets.A judge shall file such public report as may be required by law for all public officials to comply fully with the provisions of Article II, Section 8, of the Constitution of Florida. The form for public financial disclosure shall be that recommended or adopted by the Florida Commission on Ethics for use by all public officials. The form shall be filed with the Florida Commission on Ethics on the date prescribed by law, and a copy shall be filed simultaneously with the Judicial Qualifications Commission.

(2) Gifts.A judge shall file a public report of all gifts which are required to be disclosed under Canon 5D(5)(h) of the Code of Judicial Conduct. The report of gifts received in the preceding calendar year shall be filed with the Florida Commission on Ethics on or before July 1 of each year. A copy shall be filed simultaneously with the Judicial Qualifications Commission.

(3) Disclosure of Financial Interests Upon Leaving Office.A judge shall file a final disclosure statement within 60 days after leaving office, which report shall cover the period between January 1 of the year in which the judge leaves office and his or her last day of office, unless, within the 60-day period, the judge takes another public position requiring financial disclosure under Article II, Section 8, of the Constitution of Florida, or is otherwise required to file full and public disclosure for the final disclosure period. The form for disclosure of financial interests upon leaving office shall be that recommended or adopted by the Florida Commission on Ethics for use by all public officials. The form shall be filed with the Florida Commission on Ethics and a copy shall be filed simultaneously with the Judicial Qualifications Commission.

C. Confidential Financial Reporting to the Judicial Qualifications Commission.To ensure that complete financial information is available for all judicial officers, there shall be filed with the Judicial Qualifications Commission on or before July 1 of each year, if not already included in the public report to be filed under Canon 6B(1) and (2), a verified list of the names of the corporations and other business entities in which the judge has a financial interest as of December 31 of the preceding year, which shall be transmitted in a separate sealed envelope, placed by the Commission in safekeeping, and not be opened or the contents thereof disclosed except in the manner hereinafter provided.

At any time during or after the pendency of a cause, any party may request information as to whether the most recent list filed by the judge or judges before whom the cause is or was pending contains the name of any specific person or corporation or other business entity which is a party to the cause or which has a substantial direct or indirect financial interest in its outcome. Neither the making of the request nor the contents thereof shall be revealed by the chair to any judge or other person except at the instance of the individual making the request. If the request meets the requirements hereinabove set forth, the chair shall render a prompt answer thereto and thereupon return the report to safekeeping for retention in accordance with the provisions hereinabove stated. All such requests shall be verified and transmitted to the chair of the Commission on forms to be approved by it.

D. Limitation of Disclosure.Disclosure of a judge's income, debts, investments or other assets is required only to the extent provided in this Canon and in Sections 3E and 3F, or as otherwise required by law.

COMMENTARY

Canon 6A. See Section 5D(5)(a)-(h) regarding reporting of gifts, bequests and loans.

The Code does not prohibit a judge from accepting honoraria or speaking fees provided that the compensation is reasonable and commensurate with the task performed. A judge should ensure, however, that no conflicts are created by the arrangement. Judges must not appear to trade on the judicial position for personal advantage. Nor should a judge spend significant time away from court duties to meet speaking or writing commitments for compensation. In addition, the source of the payment must not raise any question of undue influence or the judge's ability or willingness to be impartial.

Canon 6C. Subparagraph A prescribes guidelines for additional compensation and the reimbursement of expense funds received by a judge.

Subparagraphs B and C prescribe the three types of financial disclosure reports required of each judicial officer.

The first is the Ethics Commission's constitutionally required form pursuant to Article II, Section 8, of the Constitution. It must be filed each year as prescribed by law. The financial reporting period is for the previous calendar year. A final disclosure statement generally is required when a judge leaves office. The filing of the income tax return is a permissible alternative.

The second is a report of gifts received during the preceding calendar year to be filed publicly with the Florida Commission on Ethics. The gifts to be reported are in accordance with Canon 5D(5)(h). This

Judicial Conduct

reporting is in lieu of that prescribed by statute as stated in the Supreme Court's opinion rendered in In re Code of Judicial Conduct, 281 So.2d 21 (Fla.1973). The form for this report is as follows:

Form 6A. Gift Disclosure

All judicial officers must file with the Florida Commission on Ethics a list of all gifts received during the preceding calendar year of a value in excess of $100.00 as provided in Canon 5D(5) and Canon 6B(2) of the Code of Judicial Conduct.

Name: ____________________
Telephone: ____________________
Address: ____________________
Position Held: ____________________

Please identify all gifts you received during the preceding calendar year of a value in excess of $100.00, as required by Canon 5D(5) and Canon 6B(2) of the Code of Judicial Conduct.

____

____

____

____

OATH
State of Florida
County of ____________________

I, ______________, the public official filing this disclosure statement, being first duly sworn, do depose on oath and say that the facts set forth in the above statement are true, correct, and complete to the best of my knowledge and belief.

____
(Signature of Reporting Official)

____
(Signature of Officer Authorized to Administer Oaths)

My Commission expires ______________.

Sworn to and subscribed before me this ______________ day of ______________, 20 ______.

The third financial disclosure report is prescribed in subparagraph C. This provision ensures that there will be complete financial information for all judicial officers available with the Judicial Qualifications Commission by requiring that full disclosure be filed confidentially with the Judicial Qualifications Commission in the event the limited disclosure alternative is selected under the provisions of Article II, Section 8.

The amendment to this Canon requires in 6B(2) a separate gift report to be filed with the Florida Commission on Ethics on or before July 1 of each year. The form to be used for that report is included in the commentary to Canon 6. It should be noted that Canon 5, as it presently exists, restricts and prohibits the receipt of certain gifts. This provision is not applicable to other public officials.

With reference to financial disclosure if the judge chooses the limited disclosure alternative available under the provision of Article II, Section 8, of the Constitution of Florida, without the inclusion of the judge's Federal Income Tax Return, then the judge must file with the Commission a list of the names of corporations or other business entities in which the judge has a financial interest even though the amount is less than $1,000. This information remains confidential until a request is made by a party to a cause before the judge. This latter provision continues to ensure that complete financial information for all judicial officers is available with the Judicial Qualifications Commission and that parties who are concerned about a judge's possible financial interest have a means of obtaining that information as it pertains to a particular cause before the judge.

Canon 6D. Section 3E requires a judge to disqualify himself or herself in any proceeding in which the judge has an economic interest. See "economic interest" as explained in the Definitions Section. Section 5D requires a judge to refrain from engaging in business and from financial activities that might interfere with the impartial performance of judicial duties; Section 6B requires a judge to report all compensation the judge received for activities outside judicial office. A judge has the rights of any other citizen, including the right to privacy of the judge's financial affairs, except to the extent that limitations established by law are required to safeguard the proper performance of the judge's duties.

Canon 7. A Judge or Candidate for Judicial Office Shall Refrain From Inappropriate Political Activity

A. All Judges and Candidates.

(1) Except as authorized in Sections 7B(2), 7C(2) and 7C(3), a judge or a candidate for election or appointment to judicial office shall not:

(a) act as a leader or hold an office in a political organization;

(b) publicly endorse or publicly oppose another candidate for public office;

(c) make speeches on behalf of a political organization;

(d) attend political party functions; or

(e) solicit funds for, pay an assessment to or make a contribution to a political organization or candidate, or purchase tickets for political party dinners or other functions.

(2) A judge shall resign from judicial office upon becoming a candidate for a non-judicial office either in a primary or in a general election, except that the judge may continue to hold judicial office while being a candidate for election to or serving as a delegate in a state constitutional convention if the judge is otherwise permitted by law to do so.

(3) A candidate for a judicial office:

(a) shall maintain the dignity appropriate to judicial office and act in a manner consistent with the integrity and independence of the judiciary, and shall encourage members of the candidate's family to adhere to the same standards of political conduct in support of the candidate as apply to the candidate;

(b) shall prohibit employees and officials who serve at the pleasure of the candidate, and shall discourage other employees and officials subject to the candidate's direction and control from doing on the candidate's behalf what the candidate is prohibited from doing under the Sections of this Canon;

(c) except to the extent permitted by Section 7C(1), shall not authorize or knowingly permit any other person to do for the candidate what the candidate is prohibited from doing under the Sections of this Canon;

(d) shall not:

(i) with respect to parties or classes of parties, cases, controversies, or issues that are likely to come before the court, make pledges, promises or commitments that are inconsistent with the impartial performance of the adjudicative duties of the office; or

(ii) knowingly misrepresent the identity, qualifications, present position or other fact concerning the candidate or an opponent.

(iii) while a proceeding is pending or impending in any court, make any public comment that might reasonably be expected to affect its outcome or impair its fairness or make any nonpublic comment that might substantially interfere with a fair trial or hearing. This section does not apply to proceedings in which the judicial candidate is a litigant in a personal capacity.

(e) may respond to personal attacks or attacks on the candidate's record as long as the response does not violate Section 7A(3)(d).

B. Candidates Seeking Appointment to Judicial or Other Governmental Office.

(1) A candidate for appointment to judicial office or a judge seeking other governmental office shall not solicit or accept funds, personally or through a committee or otherwise, to support his or her candidacy.

(2) A candidate for appointment to judicial office or a judge seeking other governmental office shall not engage in any political activity to secure the appointment except that:

(a) such persons may:

(i) communicate with the appointing authority, including any selection or nominating commission or other agency designated to screen candidates;

(ii) seek support or endorsement for the appointment from organizations that regularly make recommendations for reappointment or appointment to the office, and from individuals; and

(iii) provide to those specified in Sections 7B(2)(a)(i) and 7B(2)(a)(ii) information as to his or her qualifications for the office;

(b) a non-judge candidate for appointment to judicial office may, in addition, unless otherwise prohibited by law:

(i) retain an office in a political organization,

(ii) attend political gatherings, and

(iii) continue to pay ordinary assessments and ordinary contributions to a political organization or candidate and purchase tickets for political party dinners or other functions.

Judicial Conduct

C. Judges and Candidates Subject to Public Election.

(1) A candidate, including an incumbent judge, for a judicial office that is filled by public election between competing candidates shall not personally solicit campaign funds, or solicit attorneys for publicly stated support, but may establish committees of responsible persons to secure and manage the expenditure of funds for the candidate's campaign and to obtain public statements of support for his or her candidacy. Such committees are not prohibited from soliciting campaign contributions and public support from any person or corporation authorized by law. A candidate shall not use or permit the use of campaign contributions for the private benefit of the candidate or members of the candidate's family.

(2) A candidate for merit retention in office may conduct only limited campaign activities until such time as the judge certifies that the judge's candidacy has drawn active opposition. Limited campaign activities shall only include the conduct authorized by subsection C(1), interviews with reporters and editors of the print, audio and visual media, and appearances and speaking engagements before public gatherings and organizations. Upon mailing a certificate in writing to the Secretary of State, Division of Elections, with a copy to the Judicial Qualifications Commission, that the judge's candidacy has drawn active opposition, and specifying the nature thereof, a judge may thereafter campaign in any manner authorized by law, subject to the restrictions of subsection A(3).

(3) A judicial candidate involved in an election or re-election, or a merit retention candidate who has certified that he or she has active opposition, may attend a political party function to speak in behalf of his or her candidacy or on a matter that relates to the law, the improvement of the legal system, or the administration of justice. The function must not be a fund raiser, and the invitation to speak must also include the other candidates, if any, for that office. The candidate should refrain from commenting on the candidate's affiliation with any political party or other candidate, and should avoid expressing a position on any political issue. A judicial candidate attending a political party function must avoid conduct that suggests or appears to suggest support of or opposition to a political party, a political issue, or another candidate. Conduct limited to that described above does not constitute participation in a partisan political party activity.

D. Incumbent Judges.A judge shall not engage in any political activity except (i) as authorized under any other Section of this Code, (ii) on behalf of measures to improve the law, the legal system or the administration of justice, or (iii) as expressly authorized by law.

E. Applicability.Canon 7 generally applies to all incumbent judges and judicial candidates. A successful candidate, whether or not an incumbent, is subject to judicial discipline for his or her campaign conduct; an unsuccessful candidate who is a lawyer is subject to lawyer discipline for his or her campaign conduct. A lawyer who is a candidate for judicial office is subject to Rule 4-8.2(b) of the Rules Regulating The Florida Bar.

COMMENTARY

Canon 7A(1). A judge or candidate for judicial office retains the right to participate in the political process as a voter.

Where false information concerning a judicial candidate is made public, a judge or another judicial candidate having knowledge of the facts is not prohibited by Section 7A(1) from making the facts public.

Section 7A(1)(a) does not prohibit a candidate for elective judicial office from retaining during candidacy a public office such as county prosecutor, which is not "an office in a political organization."

Section 7A(1)(b) does not prohibit a judge or judicial candidate from privately expressing his or her views on judicial candidates or other candidates for public office.

A candidate does not publicly endorse another candidate for public office by having that candidate's name on the same ticket.

Canon 7A(3)(a). Although a judicial candidate must encourage members of his or her family to adhere to the same standards of political conduct in support of the candidate that apply to the candidate, family members are free to participate in other political activity.

Canon 7A(3)(d). Section 7A(3)(d) prohibits a candidate for judicial office from making statements that commit the candidate regarding cases, controversies or issues likely to come before the court. As a corollary, a candidate should emphasize in any public statement the candidate's duty to uphold the law regardless of his or her personal views. Section 7A(3)(d) does not prohibit a candidate from making pledges or promises respecting improvements in court administration. Nor does this Section prohibit an incumbent judge from making private statements to other judges or court personnel in the performance of judicial duties. This Section applies to any statement made in the process of securing judicial office, such as statements to commissions charged with judicial selection and tenure and legislative bodies confirming appointment.

Canon 7B(2). Section 7B(2) provides a limited exception to the restrictions imposed by Sections 7A(1) and 7D. Under Section 7B(2), candidates seeking reappointment to the same judicial office or appointment to another judicial office or other governmental office may apply for the appointment and seek appropriate support.

Although under Section 7B(2) non-judge candidates seeking appointment to judicial office are permitted during candidacy to retain office in a political organization, attend political gatherings and pay ordinary dues and assessments, they remain subject to other provisions of this Code during candidacy. See Sections 7B(1), 7B(2)(a), 7E and Application Section.

Canon 7C. The term "limited campaign activities" is not intended to permit the use of common forms of campaign advertisement which include, but are not limited to, billboards, bumperstickers, media commercials, newspaper advertisements, signs, etc. Informational brochures about the merit retention system, the law, the legal system or the administration of justice, and neutral, factual biographical sketches of the candidates do not violate this provision.

Active opposition is difficult to define but is intended to include any form of organized public opposition or an unfavorable vote on a bar poll. Any political activity engaged in by members of a judge's family should be conducted in the name of the individual family member, entirely independent of the judge and without reference to the judge or to the judge's office.

Canon 7D. Neither Section 7D nor any other section of the Code prohibits a judge in the exercise of administrative functions from engaging in planning and other official activities with members of the executive and legislative branches of government. With respect to a judge's activity on behalf of measures to improve the law, the legal system and the administration of justice, see Commentary to Section 4B and Section 4C and its Commentary.

Application

This Code applies to justices of the Supreme Court and judges of the District Courts of Appeal, Circuit Courts, and County Courts. Anyone, whether or not a lawyer, who performs judicial functions, including but not limited to a civil traffic infraction hearing officer, court commissioner, general or special magistrate, domestic relations commissioner, child support hearing officer, or judge of compensation claims, shall, while performing judicial functions, conform with Canons 1, 2A, and 3, and such other provisions of this Code that might reasonably be applicable depending on the nature of the judicial function performed. Any judge responsible for a person who performs a judicial function should require compliance with the applicable provisions of this Code. If the hiring or appointing authority for persons who perform a judicial function is not a judge then that authority should adopt the applicable provisions of this Code.

A. Civil Traffic Infraction Hearing Officer. A civil traffic infraction hearing officer:

(1) is not required to comply with Sections 5C(2), 5D(2) and (3), 5E, 5F, and 5G, and Sections 6B and 6C.

(2) should not practice law in the civil or criminal traffic court in any county in which the civil traffic infraction hearing officer presides.

B. Retired/Senior JudgeA judge who has retired from judicial service and who has complied with the procedures established by the Supreme Court of Florida so as to be eligible for recall to judicial service should comply with all the provisions of this Code except Sections 5C(2), 5E, 5F, and 6A. A retired judge who is subject to recall shall not practice law and shall refrain from accepting any assignment in any cause in which the judge's present financial business dealings, investments, or other extrajudicial activities might be directly or indirectly affected. A retired judge who is subject to recall may serve as a mediator, may place his or her name on the mediator master list maintained by the chief judge, and may be associated with

Judicial Conduct

entities that are solely engaged in offering mediation or other alternative dispute resolution services but that are not otherwise engaged in the practice of law. However, such judge may in no other way advertise, solicit business, associate with a law firm, or participate in any other activity that directly or indirectly promotes his or her mediation services. A retired judge assigned to adjudicate a case shall disclose any negotiations or agreements for the provision of mediation services between the judge and any of the parties or counsel to the case. The purpose of these admonitions is to ensure that the judge's impartiality is not subject to question.

If a retired justice or judge does not desire to be assigned to judicial service, such justice or judge who is a member of The Florida Bar may engage in the practice of law and still be entitled to receive retirement compensation. The justice or judge shall then be entitled to all the rights of an attorney-at-law and no longer be subject to this Code.

PART VIII

TABLES

SYNOPSIS

Tables

Table 1 STATEWIDE AVERAGE WEEKLY WAGE—MAXIMUM COMPENSATION RATE

The maximum weekly compensation is an amount equal to the statewide average weekly wage for the year of the injured worker's injury. The Florida Department of Labor calculates the statewide average weekly wage every year. Injured workers are entitled to receive the calculated compensation rate or the maximum, whichever is less [§ 440.12(2), Fla. Stat.; *see* Ch. 12, *Calculating Indemnity Benefits, Average Weekly Wage, Penalties, and Offsets*]. The statewide average weekly wage, and therefore the maximum compensation rates, for the years since 1980 are as follows:

1980	$211
1981	$228
1982	$253
1983	$271
1984	$288
1985	$307
1986	$315
1987	$330
1988	$344
1989	$362
1990	$382
1991	$392
1992	$409
1993	$425
1994	$444
1995	$453
1996	$465
1997	$479
1998	$494
1999	$522
2000	$541
2001	$571
2002	$594
2003	$608
2004	$626
2005	$651
2006	$683
2007	$724

Table 2 WAGE LOSS DISCOUNT FACTOR

For accidents occurring through December 31, 1993, carriers must increase wage loss benefits beginning with the 25th month after maximum medical improvement. The increase is by a factor of 5 percent compounded annually and 5 percent after that [§ 440.15(3)(b)(8), Fla. Stat.].

How does the calculation work? Simply multiply the injured worker's weekly earnings by the discount factor found in the tables that the Division provides and as listed below. For example, assume the injured worker's 25th month after maximum medical improvement occurs in 1995, and reported earnings are $80 in a given week in 1995. Multiply the $80 by the 1995 discount factor of .9737. The result is ($80 x .9737 = $77.89)]. This reduces the reported earnings, thus increasing the wage loss benefit. Note that this provision is of no benefit to an injured worker who has no earnings. This is because such an injured worker will already be at the maximum rate.

For further discussion, see Ch. 14, *Temporary Partial and Permanent Partial Disability Benefits,* § 14.06[5][a].

1. WHEN THE 25TH MONTH OCCURS IN 1983

Calendar Payment Year	Discount Factor
1983	0.9625
1984	0.9274
1985	0.8919
1986	0.8598
1987	0.8504
1988	0.8147
1989	0.7802
1990	0.7455
1991	0.7100
1992	0.6889
1993	0.6695
1994	0.6519
1995	0.6348
1996	0.6193
1997	0.5995
1998	0.5895
1999	0.5802
2000	0.5649
2001	0.5459
2002	0.5373
2003	0.5246
2004	0.5148
2005	0.4984
2006	0.4811

Tables

Calendar Payment Year	Discount Factor
2007	0.4694

2. WHEN THE 25TH MONTH OCCURS IN 1984

Calendar Payment Year	Discount Factor
1984	0.9635
1985	0.9266
1986	0.8933
1987	0.8836
1988	0.8465
1989	0.8107
1990	0.7747
1991	0.7378
1992	0.7159
1993	0.6957
1994	0.6774
1995	0.6596
1996	0.6435
1997	0.6229
1998	0.6125
1999	0.5802
2000	0.5649
2001	0.5673
2002	0.5584
2003	0.5453
2004	0.5351
2005	0.5180
2006	0.5000
2007	0.4878

3. WHEN THE 25TH MONTH OCCURS IN 1985

Calendar Payment Year	Discount Factor
1985	0.9617
1986	0.9271
1987	0.9170
1988	0.8785
1989	0.8413
1990	0.8039
1991	0.7656
1992	0.7429
1993	0.7219

Calendar Payment Year	Discount Factor
1994	0.7030
1995	0.6845
1996	0.6678
1997	0.6465
1998	0.6357
1999	0.6257
2000	0.6092
2001	0.5887
2002	0.5795
2003	0.5659
2004	0.5553
2005	0.5376
2006	0.5189
2007	0.5062

4. WHEN THE 25TH MONTH OCCURS IN 1986

Calendar Payment Year	Discount Factor
1986	0.9640
1987	0.9535
1988	0.9135
1989	0.8748
1990	0.8359
1991	0.7961
1992	0.7725
1993	0.7507
1994	0.7310
1995	0.7118
1996	0.6944
1997	0.6722
1998	0.6610
1999	0.6506
2000	0.6335
2001	0.6121
2002	0.6025
2003	0.5884
2004	0.5774
2005	0.5590
2006	0.5396
2006	0.5264

Tables

5. WHEN THE 25TH MONTH OCCURS IN 1987

Calendar Payment Year	Discount Factor
1987	0.9891
1988	0.9476
1989	0.9075
1990	0.8672
1991	0.8259
1992	0.8014
1993	0.7788
1994	0.7583
1995	0.7384
1996	0.7204
1997	0.6974
1998	0.6857
1999	0.6749
2000	0.6571
2001	0.6418
2002	0.6317
2003	0.6104
2004	0.5990
2005	0.5799
2006	0.5597
2007	0.5460

6. WHEN THE 25TH MONTH OCCURS IN 1988

Calendar Payment Year	Discount Factor
1988	0.9580
1989	0.9174
1990	0.8766
1991	0.8349
1992	0.8101
1993	0.7872
1994	0.7666
1995	0.7464
1996	0.7282
1997	0.7049
1998	0.6931
1999	0.6822
2000	0.6643
2001	0.6418
2002	0.6317

Calendar Payment Year	Discount Factor
2003	0.6169
2004	0.6054
2005	0.5861
2006	0.5657
2007	0.5519

7. WHEN THE 25TH MONTH OCCURS IN 1989

Calendar Payment Year	Discount Factor
1989	0.9577
1990	0.9151
1991	0.8715
1992	0.8456
1993	0.8218
1994	0.8002
1995	0.7792
1996	0.7602
1997	0.7359
1998	0.7236
1999	0.7122
2000	0.6935
2001	0.6701
2002	0.6596
2003	0.6441
2004	0.6321
2005	0.6119
2006	0.5906
2007	0.5762

8. WHEN THE 25TH MONTH OCCURS IN 1990

Calendar Payment Year	Discount Factor
1990	0.9556
1991	0.9101
1992	0.8831
1993	0.8582
1994	0.8356
1995	0.8136
1996	0.7938
1997	0.7684
1998	0.7556
1999	0.7437

Tables

Calendar Payment Year	Discount Factor
2000	0.7241
2001	0.6997
2002	0.6887
2003	0.6726
2004	0.6601
2005	0.6390
2006	0.6168
2007	0.6018

9. WHEN THE 25TH MONTH OCCURS IN 1991

Calendar Payment Year	Discount Factor
1991	0.9524
1992	0.9241
1993	0.8981
1994	0.8745
1995	0.8515
1996	0.8307
1997	0.8042
1998	0.7908
1999	0.7783
2000	0.7578
2001	0.7322
2002	0.7207
2003	0.7038
2004	0.6907
2005	0.6686
2006	0.6454
2006	0.6297

10. WHEN THE 25TH MONTH OCCURS IN 1992

Calendar Payment Year	Discount Factor
1992	0.9703
1993	0.9430
1994	0.9182
1995	0.8941
1996	0.8723
1997	0.8444
1998	0.8303
1999	0.8172
2000	0.7557

Calendar Payment Year	Discount Factor
2001	0.7688
2002	0.7800
2003	0.7390
2004	0.7252
2005	0.7020
2006	0.6776
2006	0.6611

11. WHEN THE 25TH MONTH OCCURS IN 1993

Calendar Payment Year	Discount Factor
1993	0.9718
1994	0.9463
1995	0.9214
1996	0.8989
1997	0.8702
1998	0.8557
1999	0.8422
2000	0.8201
2001	0.9724
2002	0.7800
2003	0.7617
2004	0.7475
2005	0.7236
2006	0.6985
2006	0.6815

12. WHEN THE 25TH MONTH OCCURS IN 1994

Calendar Payment Year	Discount Factor
1994	0.9737
1995	0.9481
1996	0.9250
1997	0.8954
1998	0.8804
1999	0.8665
2000	0.8437
2001	0.8152
2002	0.8024
2003	0.7836
2004	0.7690
2005	0.7444

Tables

Calendar Payment Year	Discount Factor
2006	0.7185
2007	0.7010

13. WHEN THE 25TH MONTH OCCURS IN 1995

Calendar Payment Year	Discount Factor
1995	0.9737
1996	0.9500
1997	0.9197
1998	0.9043
1999	0.8901
2000	0.8667
2001	0.8375
2002	0.8244
2003	0.8051
2004	0.7900
2005	0.7648
2006	0.7382
2007	0.7202

14. WHEN THE 25TH MONTH OCCURS IN 1996

Calendar Payment Year	Discount Factor
1996	0.9756
1997	0.9444
1998	0.9286
1999	0.9140
2000	0.8900
2001	0.8599
2002	0.8464
2003	0.8266
2004	0.8112
2005	0.7853
2006	0.7580
2007	0.7395

15. WHEN THE 25TH MONTH OCCURS IN 1997

Calendar Payment Year	Discount Factor
1997	0.9681
1998	0.9519

Calendar Payment Year	Discount Factor
1999	0.9140
2000	0.8900
2001	0.8815
2002	0.8677
2003	0.8474
2004	0.8316
2005	0.8050
2006	0.7770
2007	0.7580

16. WHEN THE 25TH MONTH OCCURS IN 1998

Calendar Payment Year	Discount Factor
1998	0.9833
1999	0.9678
2000	0.9424
2001	0.9105
2002	0.8962
2003	0.8752
2004	0.8589
2005	0.8315
2006	0.8026
2007	0.7830

17. WHEN THE 25TH MONTH OCCURS IN 1999

Calendar Payment Year	Discount Factor
2001	0.9269
2002	0.9123
2003	0.8909
2004	0.8743
2005	0.8464
2006	0.8170
2007	0.7971

18. WHEN THE 25TH MONTH OCCURS IN 2000

Calendar Payment Year	Discount Factor
2001	0.9417
2002	0.9269
2003	0.9052

Tables

Calendar Payment Year	Discount Factor
2004	0.8883
2005	0.8599
2006	0.8300
2007	0.8098

19. WHEN THE 25TH MONTH OCCURS IN 2001

Calendar Payment Year	Discount Factor
2001	0.9671
2002	0.9519
2003	0.9296
2004	0.9123
2005	0.8832
2006	0.8525
2007	0.8317

20. WHEN THE 25TH MONTH OCCURS IN 2002

Calendar Payment Year	Discount Factor
2002	0.9843
2003	0.9612
2004	0.9433
2005	0.9132
2006	0.8815
2007	0.8600

21. WHEN THE 25TH MONTH OCCURS IN 2003

Calendar Payment Year	Discount Factor
2003	0.9766
2004	0.9584
2005	0.9278
2006	0.8956
2007	0.8738

22. WHEN THE 25TH MONTH OCCURS IN 2004

Calendar Payment Year	Discount Factor
2004	0.9814
2005	0.9500
2006	0.9170

Calendar Payment Year	Discount Factor
2007	0.8946

23. WHEN THE 25TH MONTH OCCURS IN 2005

Calendar Payment Year	Discount Factor
2005	0.9681
2006	0.9345
2007	0.9117

24. WHEN THE 25TH MONTH OCCURS IN 2006

Calendar Payment Year	Discount Factor
2006	0.9653
2007	0.9418

25. WHEN THE 25TH MONTH OCCURS IN 2007

Calendar Payment Year	Discount Factor
2007	0.9761

Tables

Table 3 CODES RELATING TO DWC-4: NOTICE OF ACTION/CHANGE

Title 3–1 DISABILITY TYPE CODES

Use the Disability Type Codes when completing the DWC-4 form [Fla. Admin. Code R. 4L-3.0091(4) (11/8/94); *see* Ch. 2, *Reporting: Employee, Employer, and Carrier.* § 2.08[10]].

TT	Temporary Total
TTC	Catastrophic Temporary Total
TTE	Retraining Temporary Total
TP	Temporary Partial
PI	Permanent Impairment: Old Law
IB	Impairment Income: New Law
WL	Wage Loss: Old Law
SB	Supplemental Income: New Law
PT	Permanent Total
DB	Death

Table 3–2 BENEFIT SUSPENSION, REASON, AND AUTHORITY CODES

Use the Benefit Suspension, Reason, and Authority Codes when completing the DWC-4 form [Fla. Admin. Code R. 4L-3.0091(5) (11/8/94); *see* Ch. 2, *Reporting: Employee, Employer, and Carrier,* § 2.08[10]].

BENEFIT SUSPENSION CODES

S1	Returned or Able to Work (Benefits Suspended)
S2	Medical Non Compliance: (e.g. no show for IME)
S3	Administrative Non Compliance *See Table 3-3, below
S4	Claimant Died. (No Dependents & Benefits Suspended)
S5	Claimant Incarcerated. (No Dependents)
S6	Claimant Whereabouts Unknown
S7	Benefits Exhausted
S8	Jurisdiction Change: Other State, Federal Law, Etc.

Table 3–3 CODE S3

Carriers may suspend benefits for administrative non-compliance under code S3 for specified reasons [Fla. Admin. Code R. 4L-3.0091(5) (11/8/94); *see* Ch. 2, *Reporting: Employee, Employer, and Carrier.* § 2.08[10]].

S3 REASON	AUTHORITY
Refusing to Appear for Vocational Testing	§ 440.15(1)(e)3, Fla. Stat. (1/1/94)
Failure to File Employee Earnings Report (PTD)	§ 440.15(1)(f)2.b., Fla. Stat. (1/1/94)
Failure to File Employee Earnings Report (TTD)	§ 440.15(2)(d), Fla. Stat. (1/1/94)
Refusing Job (Supp. Benefits)	§ 440.15(7), Fla. Stat. (1/1/94)
Earnings Exceed 80% (Supp. Benefits)	§ 440.15(8), Fla. Stat. (1/1/94)
Refusal to Apply for S.A. Disability Benefits (PTD)	§ 440.15(1)(c), Fla. Stat. (1/1/94)

Table 3–4 BENEFIT ADJUSTMENT CODES

When carriers adjust benefits, they must report the reason to the Division on form DWC-4 [Fla. Admin. Code R. 4L-3.0091(15)(b) (11/3/94); *see* Ch. 2, *Reporting: Employee, Employer, and Carrier.* § 2.08[10]].

BENEFIT ADJUSTMENT CODES

CODE	REASON
A	Apportionment or Contribution.
B	Subrogation Offset.
C	Overpayment Credit.
H	Child Support or Alimony.
N	Refused Training under 440.491(6)(b), Fla. Stat., Or Failed to Cancel an IME.
P	Advanced Payment Recoupment.
R	Social Security Retirement Offset
S	Social Security Disability Offset.
U	Unemployment Compensation Offset.
V	Safety Violation Offset.
X	Dependents Change.

Tables

Table 4 U.S. LIFE EXPECTANCY TABLE

Catastrophic or lifetime disability cases, such as paraplegia, are easily recognized but can be difficult to reserve since most adjusters' experience with them is infrequent. Indemnity reserves are not too difficult to estimate. The first step is to estimate the injured worker's life expectancy. Once determined, simply multiply the compensation rate by the number of weeks of life expectancy. Be sure to use the most current life expectancy tables. Also be sure these tables consider the differences in life expectancy between males and females and also among races. Also, remember the standard tables are based on the life expectancy of relatively healthy persons of a given age. By definition the injured worker is not a normal healthy person. Carefully examine the medical records. Find out if the results of the injury, or unrelated medical or lifestyle problems, will likely produce a reduction in life expectancy. The impact of these factors is not always obvious so a medical consultant may be helpful. For further discussion of life expectancy tables, see Ch. 11, *Reserves,* § 11.07.

Age	All races			White			All other					
							Total			Black		
	Both sexes	Male	Female	Both sexes	Male	Female	Both sexes	Male	Female	Both sexes	Male	Female
0	75.8	72.3	79.1	76.5	73.2	79.8	71.8	67.7	75.7	69.6	65.0	73.9
1	75.4	72.0	78.7	76.1	72.8	79.3	71.8	67.7	75.7	69.7	65.2	74.1
2	74.5	71.1	77.8	75.1	71.8	78.3	70.9	66.8	74.8	68.8	64.3	73.1
3	73.5	70.1	76.8	74.1	70.9	77.3	69.9	65.9	73.8	67.9	63.4	72.2
4	72.5	69.1	75.8	73.2	69.9	76.3	69.0	64.9	72.9	66.9	62.4	71.2
5	71.6	68.1	74.8	72.2	68.9	75.4	68.0	63.9	71.9	65.9	61.4	70.3
6	70.6	67.2	73.9	71.2	67.9	74.4	67.0	62.9	70.9	65.0	60.5	69.3
7	69.6	66.2	72.9	70.2	66.9	73.4	66.1	62.0	69.9	64.0	59.5	68.3
8	68.6	65.2	71.9	69.2	65.9	72.4	65.1	61.0	68.9	63.0	58.5	67.3
9	67.6	64.2	70.9	68.2	65.0	71.4	64.1	60.0	68.0	62.0	57.5	66.3
10	66.6	63.2	69.9	67.2	64.0	70.4	63.1	59.0	67.0	61.0	56.5	65.4
11	65.6	62.2	68.9	66.3	63.0	69.4	62.1	58.0	66.0	60.1	55.5	64.4
12	64.6	61.2	67.9	65.3	62.0	68.4	61.1	57.0	65.0	59.1	54.6	63.4
13	63.7	60.3	66.9	64.3	61.0	67.4	60.1	56.1	64.0	58.1	53.6	62.4
14	62.7	59.3	65.9	63.3	60.0	66.5	59.2	55.1	63.0	57.1	52.6	61.4
15	61.7	58.3	65.0	62.3	59.1	65.5	58.2	54.1	62.0	56.1	51.7	60.4
16	60.7	57.4	64.0	61.4	58.1	64.5	57.2	53.2	61.1	55.2	50.7	59.5
17	59.8	56.4	63.0	60.4	57.2	63.5	56.3	52.3	60.1	54.3	49.8	58.5
18	58.8	55.5	62.0	59.4	56.2	62.5	55.4	51.4	59.1	53.3	48.9	57.5
19	57.9	54.6	61.1	58.5	55.3	61.6	54.4	50.5	58.1	52.4	48.1	56.6
20	56.9	53.7	60.1	57.5	54.3	60.6	53.5	49.6	57.2	51.5	47.2	55.6
21	56.0	52.7	59.1	56.6	53.4	59.6	52.6	48.7	56.2	50.6	46.3	54.6
22	55.1	51.8	58.2	55.6	52.5	58.7	51.7	47.9	55.3	49.7	45.5	53.7
23	54.1	50.9	57.2	54.7	51.6	57.7	50.8	47.0	54.3	48.8	44.6	52.7
24	53.2	50.0	56.2	53.7	50.6	56.7	49.9	46.1	53.3	47.9	43.8	51.8
25	52.2	49.1	55.2	52.8	49.7	55.7	49.0	45.2	52.4	47.0	42.9	50.8
26	51.3	48.2	54.3	51.8	48.8	54.8	48.0	44.4	51.4	46.1	42.1	49.9
27	50.4	47.2	53.3	50.9	47.8	53.8	47.1	43.5	50.5	45.2	41.2	48.9
28	49.4	46.3	52.3	49.9	46.9	52.8	46.2	42.6	49.5	44.3	40.4	48.0
29	48.5	45.4	51.4	49.0	46.0	51.8	45.3	41.8	48.6	43.4	39.5	47.1
30	47.5	44.5	50.4	48.1	45.1	50.9	44.4	40.9	47.7	42.5	38.7	46.1
31	46.6	43.6	49.4	47.1	44.1	49.9	43.5	40.0	46.7	41.7	37.8	45.2
32	45.7	42.7	48.5	46.2	43.2	48.9	42.6	39.2	45.8	40.8	37.0	44.3
33	44.7	41.8	47.5	45.2	42.3	48.0	41.7	38.3	44.9	39.9	36.2	43.4
34	43.8	40.9	46.6	44.3	41.4	47.0	40.8	37.4	43.9	39.0	35.3	42.4
35	42.9	40.0	45.6	43.4	40.5	46.0	40.0	36.6	43.0	38.2	34.5	41.5
36	42.0	39.1	44.7	42.4	39.6	45.1	39.1	35.8	42.1	37.3	33.7	40.6
37	41.0	38.2	43.7	41.5	38.7	44.1	38.2	34.9	41.2	36.5	32.9	39.7
38	40.1	37.3	42.8	40.6	37.8	43.2	37.3	34.1	40.3	35.6	32.1	38.8
39	39.2	36.4	41.8	39.6	36.9	42.2	36.5	33.3	39.3	34.8	31.3	37.9

Tables

40	38.3	35.5	40.9	38.7	36.0	41.2	35.6	32.4	38.4	34.0	30.5	37.1
41	37.4	34.6	39.9	37.8	35.1	40.3	34.8	31.6	37.5	33.1	29.7	36.2
42	36.5	33.7	39.0	36.9	34.2	39.3	33.9	30.8	36.6	32.3	28.9	35.3
43	35.6	32.8	38.0	35.9	33.3	38.4	33.1	30.0	35.8	31.5	28.2	34.4
44	34.7	32.0	37.1	35.0	32.4	37.5	32.2	29.2	34.9	30.7	27.4	33.6
45	33.8	31.1	36.2	34.1	31.5	36.5	31.4	28.4	34.0	29.9	26.7	32.7
46	32.9	30.2	35.3	33.2	30.6	35.6	30.5	27.6	33.1	29.1	25.9	31.9
47	32.0	29.4	34.3	32.3	29.7	34.7	29.7	26.8	32.2	28.3	25.2	31.0
48	31.1	28.5	33.4	31.4	28.8	33.7	28.9	26.0	31.4	27.5	24.4	30.2
49	30.2	27.6	32.5	30.5	28.0	32.8	28.1	25.3	30.5	26.7	23.7	29.3
50	29.3	26.8	31.6	29.6	27.1	31.9	27.3	24.5	29.6	25.9	23.0	28.5
51	28.5	25.9	30.7	28.8	26.3	31.0	26.5	23.7	28.8	25.2	22.3	27.7
52	27.6	25.1	29.8	27.9	25.4	30.1	25.7	23.0	28.0	24.4	21.5	26.8
53	26.8	24.3	29.0	27.0	24.6	29.2	24.9	22.2	27.1	23.6	20.8	26.0
54	25.9	23.5	28.1	26.2	23.7	28.3	24.1	21.5	26.3	22.9	20.1	25.3
55	25.1	22.7	27.2	25.3	22.9	27.5	23.4	20.8	25.5	22.2	19.5	24.5
56	24.3	21.9	26.4	24.5	22.1	26.6	22.6	20.1	24.7	21.5	18.8	23.7
57	23.5	21.1	25.5	23.7	21.3	25.7	21.9	19.4	23.9	20.8	18.2	23.0
58	22.7	20.4	24.7	22.9	20.6	24.9	21.2	18.8	23.2	20.1	17.6	22.2
59	21.9	19.6	23.9	22.1	19.8	24.1	20.5	18.1	22.4	19.5	16.9	21.5
60	21.1	18.9	23.1	21.3	19.1	23.2	19.8	17.5	21.7	18.8	16.3	20.8
61	20.4	18.2	22.3	20.6	18.3	22.4	19.1	16.8	20.9	18.2	15.8	20.1
62	19.7	17.5	21.5	19.8	17.6	21.6	18.4	16.2	20.2	17.5	15.2	19.4
63	18.9	16.8	20.7	19.1	16.9	20.8	17.8	15.6	19.5	16.9	14.6	18.7
64	18.2	16.1	19.9	18.3	16.2	20.0	17.1	15.0	18.8	16.3	14.1	18.0
65	17.5	15.4	19.2	17.6	15.5	19.3	16.5	14.4	18.1	15.7	13.5	17.4
66	16.8	14.8	18.4	16.9	14.9	18.5	15.9	13.9	17.4	15.1	13.0	16.7
67	16.1	14.2	17.7	16.2	14.3	17.8	15.3	13.3	16.7	14.5	12.5	16.1
68	15.5	13.5	16.9	15.5	13.6	17.0	14.7	12.8	16.1	14.0	12.0	15.5
69	14.8	12.9	16.2	14.9	13.0	16.3	14.1	12.2	15.4	13.4	11.5	14.9
70	14.2	12.4	15.5	14.2	12.4	15.6	13.5	11.7	14.8	12.9	11.0	14.3
71	13.5	11.8	14.8	13.6	11.8	14.9	12.9	11.2	14.2	12.4	10.5	13.7
72	12.9	11.2	14.1	13.0	11.3	14.2	12.4	10.8	13.6	11.9	10.1	13.1
73	12.3	10.7	13.5	12.4	10.7	13.5	11.9	10.3	13.0	11.4	9.7	12.5
74	11.7	10.1	12.8	11.8	10.2	12.9	11.3	9.8	12.4	10.9	9.3	11.9
75	11.2	9.6	12.2	11.2	9.6	12.2	10.8	9.4	11.8	10.4	8.9	11.4
76	10.6	9.1	11.6	10.6	9.1	11.6	10.3	8.9	11.2	9.9	8.4	10.8
77	10.0	8.6	10.9	10.1	8.6	11.0	9.8	8.5	10.6	9.4	8.0	10.3
78	9.5	8.1	10.3	9.5	8.1	10.4	9.3	8.1	10.0	8.9	7.6	9.7
79	9.0	7.7	9.7	9.0	7.7	9.8	8.8	7.6	9.5	8.4	7.2	9.2
80	8.5	7.2	9.2	8.5	7.2	9.2	8.3	7.2	8.9	8.0	6.8	8.6
81	8.0	6.8	8.6	8.0	6.8	8.6	7.8	6.8	8.4	7.5	6.4	8.1
82	7.5	6.4	8.1	7.5	6.4	8.1	7.3	6.4	7.9	7.1	6.1	7.6
83	7.1	6.0	7.6	7.0	6.0	7.6	6.9	6.0	7.4	6.7	5.7	7.2
84	6.6	5.6	7.1	6.6	5.6	7.1	6.5	5.7	6.9	6.3	5.4	6.7
85	6.2	5.3	6.6	6.2	5.3	6.6	6.1	5.4	6.5	5.9	5.1	6.3

Table 5 EIGHT PERCENT PRESENT VALUE

The following table may be used when figuring present value of a series of future payments. An 8 percent discount rate is referenced in § 440.20, Fla. Stat.

Procedure for Using Table

Determine the number of weeks which is to be computed. Find the present worth factor corresponding to that number of weeks. Multiply the weekly compensation rate by that present worth factor.

AN EXAMPLE: Assume you want to find the present value of a weekly compensation rate of $80 for 200 weeks. From the table we find the present worth factor of 172.9882 corresponding to 200 weeks. Now multiply the weekly compensation rate ($80) by that present worth factor. Thus, 80 times 172.9882 or, 13,839.06.

Weeks	Present Worth	Weeks	Present Worth	Weeks	Present Worth
0		50	48.1591	100	92.8831
1	.9985	51	49.0864	101	93.7442
2	1.9956	52	50.0123	102	94.6041
3	2.9911	53	50.9369	103	95.4627
4	3.9852	54	51.8601	104	96.3201
5	4.9779	55	52.7819	105	971761
6	5.9690	56	53.7024	106	98.0309
7	6.9587	57	54.6215	107	98.8845
8	7.9469	58	55.5392	108	99.7368
9	8.9337	59	56.4556	109	100.5878
10	9.9190	60	57.3706	110	101.4375
11	10.9029	61	58.2843	111	102.2860
12	11.8853	62	59.1966	112	103.1333
13	12.8662	63	60.1076	113	103.9793
14	13.8457	64	61.0172	114	104.8240
15	14.8237	65	61.9255	115	105.6675
16	15.8003	66	62.8324	116	106.5098
17	16.7755	67	63.7380	117	107.3508
18	17.7492	68	64.6423	118	108.1905
19	18.7215	69	65.5452	119	109.0290
20	19.6923	70	66.4468	120	109.8663
21	20.6617	71	67.3471	121	110.7024
22	21.6297	72	68.2460	122	111.5372
23	22.5962	73	69.1436	123	112.3707
24	23.5613	74	70.0398	124	113.2031
25	24.5250	75	70.9348	125	114.0342
26	25.4872	76	71.8284	126	114.8640
27	26.4481	77	72.7207	127	115.6927
28	27.4075	78	73.6116	128	116.5201
29	28.3655	79	74.5013	129	117.3463
30	29.3220	80	75.3896	130	118.1713
31	30.2772	81	76.2767	131	118.9950
32	31.2309	82	77.1624	132	119.8176
33	32.1833	83	78.0468	133	120.6389
34	33.1342	84	78.9299	134	121.4590
35	34.0837	85	79.8117	135	122.2779
36	35.0318	86	80.6921	136	123.0956
37	35.9785	87	81.5713	137	123.9120
38	36.9238	88	82.4492	138	124.7273
39	37.8678	89	83.3258	139	125.5414
40	38.8103	90	84.2011	140	126.3542
41	39.7514	91	85.0751	141	127.1659
42	40.6911	92	85.9478	142	127.9763
43	41.6295	93	86.8192	143	128.7856
44	42.5664	94	87.6893	144	129.5936
45	43.5020	95	88.5582	145	130.4005
46	44.4362	96	89.4257	146	131.2062
47	45.3690	97	90.2920	147	132.0106
48	46.3004	98	91.1570	148	132.8139
49	47.2305	99	92.0207	149	133.6160

Weeks	Present Worth	Weeks	Present Worth	Weeks	Present Worth
150	*134.4169*	**200**	*172.9882*	**250**	*208.8082*
151	*135.2167*	**201**	*173.7309*	**251**	*209.4979*
152	*136.0152*	**202**	*174.4725*	**252**	*210.1866*
153	*136.8126*	**203**	*175.2130*	**253**	*210.8743*
154	*137.6088*	**204**	*175.9523*	**254**	*211.5609*
155	*138.4038*	**205**	*176.6906*	**255**	*212.2466*
156	*139.1976*	**206**	*177.4279*	**256**	*212.9312*
157	*139.9903*	**207**	*178.1640*	**257**	*213.6148*
158	*140.7817*	**208**	*178.8990*	**258**	*214.2974*
159	*141.5721*	**209**	*179.6329*	**259**	*214.9790*
160	*142.3612*	**210**	*180.3658*	**260**	*215.6595*
161	*143.1492*	**211**	*181.0976*	**261**	*216.3391*
162	*143.9360*	**212**	*181.8283*	**262**	*217.0177*
163	*144.7216*	**213**	*182.5579*	**263**	*217.6953*
164	*145.5061*	**214**	*183.2864*	**264**	*218.3719*
165	*146.2895*	**215**	*184.0139*	**265**	*219.0474*
166	*147.0716*	**216**	*184.7402*	**266**	*219.7220*
167	*147.8526*	**217**	*185.4655*	**267**	*220.3956*
168	*148.6325*	**218**	*186.1898*	**268**	*221.0681*
169	*149.4112*	**219**	*186.9129*	**269**	*221.7397*
170	*150.1888*	**220**	*187.6350*	**270**	*222.4103*
171	*150.9652*	**221**	*188.3561*	**271**	*222.0799*
172	*151.7404*	**222**	*189.0760*	**272**	*223.7485*
173	*152.5145*	**223**	*189.7949*	**273**	*224.4161*
174	*153.2875*	**224**	*190.5127*	**274**	*225.0827*
175	*154.0593*	**225**	*191.2295*	**275**	*225.7844*
176	*154.8300*	**226**	*191.9452*	**276**	*226.4130*
177	*155.5995*	**227**	*192.6599*	**277**	*227.0767*
178	*156.3679*	**228**	*193.3734*	**278**	*227.7394*
179	*157.1352*	**229**	*194.0860*	**279**	*228.4011*
180	*157.9013*	**230**	*194.7975*	**280**	*229.0618*
181	*158.6663*	**231**	*195.5079*	**281**	*229.7216*
182	*159.4302*	**232**	*196.2173*	**282**	*230.3804*
183	*160.1929*	**233**	*196.9256*	**283**	*231.0382*
184	*160.9545*	**234**	*197.6329*	**284**	*231.6950*
185	*161.7150*	**235**	*198.3391*	**285**	*232.3509*
186	*162.4744*	**236**	*199.0443*	**286**	*233.0058*
187	*163.2326*	**237**	*199.7485*	**287**	*233.6597*
188	*163.9897*	**238**	*200.4516*	**288**	*234.3126*
189	*164.7457*	**239**	*201.1536*	**289**	*234.9646*
190	*165.5006*	**240**	*201.8547*	**290**	*235.6157*
191	*166.2543*	**241**	*202.5547*	**291**	*236.2657*
192	*167.0070*	**242**	*203.2536*	**292**	*236.9148*
193	*167.7585*	**243**	*203.9515*	**293**	*237.5630*
194	*168.5089*	**244**	*204.6484*	**294**	*238.2101*
195	*169.2582*	**245**	*205.3443*	**295**	*238.8564*
196	*170.0064*	**246**	*206.0391*	**296**	*239.5016*
197	*170.7535*	**247**	*206.7329*	**297**	*240.1460*
198	*171.4995*	**248**	*207.4257*	**298**	*240.7893*
199	*172.2444*	**249**	*208.1175*	**299**	*241.4317*

Tables

Weeks	Present Worth	Weeks	Present Worth	Weeks	Present Worth
300	242.0732	350	272.9654	400	301.6541
301	242.7137	351	273.5602	401	302.2065
302	243.3533	352	274.1542	402	302.7581
303	243.9919	353	274.7473	403	303.3089
304	244.6296	354	275.3394	404	303.8588
305	245.2663	355	275.9308	405	304.4079
306	245.9021	356	276.5212	406	304.9563
307	246.5369	357	277.1108	407	305.5038
308	247.1708	358	277.6995	408	306.0505
309	247.8038	359	278.2873	409	306.5964
310	248.4359	360	278.8742	410	307.1415
311	249.0670	361	279.4603	411	307.6858
312	249.6971	362	280.0455	412	308.2292
313	250.3264	363	280.6299	413	308.7719
314	250.9547	364	281.2134	414	309.3138
315	251.5821	365	281.7960	415	309.8548
316	252.2085	366	282.3778	416	310.3951
317	252.8340	367	282.9587	417	310.9346
318	253.4586	368	283.5387	418	311.4733
319	254.0823	369	284.1179	419	312.0111
320	254.7051	370	284.6963	420	312.5482
321	255.3269	371	285.2737	421	313.0845
322	255.9478	372	285.8504	422	313.6200
323	256.5678	373	286.4261	423	314.1547
324	257.1869	374	287.0010	424	314.6886
325	257.8050	375	287.5751	425	315.2217
326	258.4223	376	288.1483	426	315.7540
327	259.0386	377	288.7207	427	316.2856
328	259.6540	378	289.2922	428	316.8163
329	260.2685	379	289.8629	429	317.3463
330	260.8821	380	290.4327	430	317.8755
331	261.4948	381	291.0017	431	318.4039
332	262.1066	382	291.5699	432	318.9315
333	262.7175	383	292.1372	433	319.4584
334	263.3275	384	292.7037	434	319.9845
335	263.9366	385	293.2693	435	320.5097
336	264.5448	386	293.8341	436	321.0343
337	265.1520	387	294.3981	437	321.5580
338	265.7584	388	294.9612	438	322.0809
339	266.3639	389	295.5235	439	322.6031
340	266.9685	390	296.0849	440	323.1246
341	267.5722	391	296.6456	441	323.6452
342	268.1750	392	297.2054	442	324.1651
343	268.7769	393	297.7644	443	324.6842
344	269.3779	394	298.3225	444	325.2025
345	269.9780	395	298.8798	445	325.7201
346	270.5773	396	299.4363	446	326.2369
347	271.1756	397	299.9920	447	326.7529
348	271.7731	398	300.5469	448	327.2682
349	272.3697	399	301.1009	449	327.7827

Weeks	Present Worth	Weeks	Present Worth	Weeks	Present Worth
450	*328.2965*	**500**	*353.0385*	**550**	*376.0156*
451	*328.8095*	**501**	*353.5149*	**551**	*376.4580*
452	*329.3217*	**502**	*353.9906*	**552**	*376.8998*
453	*329.8332*	**503**	*354.4656*	**533**	*377.3409*
454	*330.3439*	**504**	*354.9398*	**554**	*377.7814*
455	*330.8539*	**505**	*355.4134*	**555**	*378.2212*
456	*331.3631*	**506**	*355.8863*	**556**	*378.6604*
457	*331.8715*	**507**	*356.3585*	**557**	*379.0989*
458	*332.3793*	**508**	*356.8300*	**558**	*379.5367*
459	*332.8862*	**509**	*357.3008*	**559**	*379.9739*
460	*333.3924*	**510**	*357.7709*	**560**	*380.4105*
461	*333.8979*	**511**	*358.2403*	**561**	*380.8464*
462	*334.4026*	**512**	*358.7090*	**562**	*381.2817*
463	*334.9066*	**513**	*359.1770*	**563**	*381.7163*
464	*335.4098*	**514**	*359.6444*	**564**	*382.1503*
465	*335.9122*	**515**	*360.1110*	**565**	*382.5837*
466	*336.4140*	**516**	*360.5769*	**566**	*383.0164*
467	*336.9150*	**517**	*361.0422*	**567**	*383.4485*
468	*337.4152*	**518**	*361.5068*	**568**	*383.8799*
469	*337.9147*	**519**	*361.9706*	**569**	*384.3107*
470	*338.4135*	**520**	*362.4338*	**570**	*384.7408*
471	*338.9115*	**521**	*362.8964*	**571**	*385.1703*
472	*339.4088*	**522**	*363.3582*	**572**	*385.5992*
473	*339.9054*	**523**	*363.8193*	**573**	*386.0275*
474	*340.4012*	**524**	*364.2798*	**574**	*386.4551*
475	*340.8963*	**525**	*364.7396*	**575**	*386.8821*
476	*341.3907*	**526**	*365.1987*	**576**	*387.3084*
477	*341.8843*	**527**	*365.6571*	**577**	*387.7342*
478	*342.3772*	**528**	*366.1148*	**578**	*388.1592*
479	*342.8694*	**529**	*366.5719*	**579**	*388.5837*
480	*343.3608*	**530**	*367.0283*	**580**	*389.0075*
481	*343.8515*	**531**	*367.4840*	**581**	*389.4307*
482	*344.3415*	**532**	*367.9390*	**582**	*389.8533*
483	*344.8308*	**533**	*368.3934*	**583**	*390.2753*
484	*345.3193*	**534**	*368.8471*	**584**	*390.6966*
485	*345.8071*	**535**	*369.3001*	**585**	*391.1173*
486	*346.2942*	**536**	*369.7525*	**586**	*391.5374*
487	*346.7806*	**537**	*370.2041*	**587**	*391.9569*
488	*347.2663*	**538**	*370.6552*	**588**	*392.3757*
489	*347.7512*	**539**	*371.1055*	**589**	*392.7940*
490	*348.2354*	**540**	*371.5552*	**590**	*393.2116*
491	*348.7189*	**541**	*372.0042*	**591**	*393.6286*
492	*349.2017*	**542**	*372.4526*	**592**	*394.0449*
493	*349.6838*	**543**	*372.9003*	**593**	*394.4607*
494	*350.1652*	**544**	*373.3473*	**594**	*394.8758*
495	*350.6458*	**545**	*373.7937*	**595**	*395.2904*
496	*351.1258*	**546**	*374.2394*	**596**	*395.7043*
497	*351.6050*	**547**	*374.6844*	**597**	*396.1176*
498	*352.0835*	**548**	*375.1288*	**598**	*396.5303*
499	*352.5614*	**549**	*375.5725*	**599**	*396.9424*

Tables

Weeks	Present Worth	Weeks	Present Worth	Weeks	Present Worth
600	*397.3538*	**650**	*417.1700*	**700**	*435.5727*
601	*397.7647*	**651**	*417.5516*	**701**	*435.9270*
602	*398.1749*	**652**	*417.9325*	**702**	*436.2809*
603	*398.5846*	**653**	*418.3130*	**703**	*436.6342*
604	*398.9936*	**654**	*418.6928*	**704**	*436.9869*
605	*399.4021*	**655**	*419.0722*	**705**	*437.3392*
606	*399.8099*	**656**	*419.4509*	**706**	*437.6909*
607	*400.2171*	**657**	*419.8291*	**707**	*438.0421*
608	*400.6238*	**658**	*420.2067*	**708**	*438.3928*
609	*401.0298*	**659**	*420.5838*	**709**	*438.7430*
610	*401.4352*	**660**	*420.9603*	**710**	*439.0926*
611	*401.8401*	**661**	*421.3362*	**711**	*439.4418*
612	*402.2443*	**662**	*421.7116*	**712**	*439.7904*
613	*402.6479*	**663**	*422.0865*	**713**	*440.1385*
614	*403.0510*	**664**	*422.4608*	**714**	*440.4861*
615	*403.4534*	**665**	*422.8345*	**715**	*440.8331*
616	*403.8552*	**666**	*423.2077*	**716**	*441.1797*
617	*404.2565*	**667**	*423.5803*	**717**	*441.5258*
618	*404.6571*	**668**	*423.9524*	**718**	*441.8713*
619	*405.0572*	**669**	*424.3239*	**719**	*442.2163*
620	*405.4567*	**670**	*424.6949*	**720**	*442.5608*
621	*405.8556*	**671**	*425.0653*	**721**	*442.9048*
622	*406.2539*	**672**	*425.4352*	**722**	*443.2483*
623	*406.6516*	**673**	*425.8045*	**723**	*443.5913*
624	*407.0487*	**674**	*426.1733*	**724**	*443.9338*
625	*407.4452*	**675**	*426.5416*	**725**	*444.2758*
626	*407.8411*	**676**	*426.9093*	**726**	*444.6173*
627	*408.2365*	**677**	*427.2764*	**727**	*444.9582*
628	*408.6313*	**678**	*427.6430*	**728**	*445.2987*
629	*409.0254*	**679**	*428.0091*	**729**	*445.6386*
630	*409.4190*	**680**	*428.3746*	**730**	*445.9781*
631	*409.8121*	**681**	*428.7396*	**731**	*446.3171*
632	*410.2045*	**682**	*429.1040*	**732**	*446.6555*
633	*410.5964*	**683**	*429.4680*	**733**	*446.9935*
634	*410.9876*	**684**	*429.8313*	**734**	*447.3309*
635	*411.3784*	**685**	*430.1942*	**735**	*447.6679*
636	*411.7685*	**686**	*430.5565*	**736**	*448.0043*
637	*412.1580*	**687**	*430.9182*	**737**	*448.3403*
638	*412.5470*	**688**	*431.2794*	**738**	*448.6757*
639	*412.9354*	**689**	*431.6401*	**739**	*449.0107*
640	*413.3232*	**690**	*432.0003*	**740**	*449.3452*
641	*413.7104*	**691**	*432.3599*	**741**	*449.6791*
642	*414.0971*	**692**	*432.7190*	**742**	*450.0126*
643	*414.4832*	**693**	*433.0776*	**743**	*450.3456*
644	*414.8688*	**694**	*433.4356*	**744**	*450.6781*
645	*415.2537*	**695**	*433.7931*	**745**	*451.0101*
646	*415.6381*	**696**	*434.1501*	**746**	*451.3416*
647	*416.0219*	**697**	*434.5065*	**747**	*451.6726*
648	*416.4052*	**698**	*434.8624*	**748**	*452.0032*
649	*416.7879*	**699**	*435.2178*	**749**	*452.3332*

Weeks	Present Worth	Weeks	Present Worth	Weeks	Present Wcrth
750	452.6627	800	468.5338	850	483.2727
751	452.9918	801	468.8394	851	483.5565
752	453.3204	802	469.1445	852	483.8399
753	453.6485	803	469.4492	853	484.1229
754	453.9761	804	469.7534	854	484.4054
755	454.3032	805	470.0572	855	484.6873
756	454.6299	806	470.3606	856	484.9692
757	454.9560	807	470.6635	857	485.2505
758	455.2817	808	470.9659	858	485.5314
759	455.6069	809	471.2679	859	485.8119
760	455.9316	810	471.5695	860	486.0919
761	456.2558	811	471.8706	861	486.3715
762	456.5796	812	472.1712	862	486.6507
763	456.9029	813	472.4714	863	486.9295
764	457.2257	814	472.7712	864	487.2079
765	457.5480	815	473.0705	865	487.4859
766	457.8698	816	473.3694	866	487.7635
767	458.1912	817	473.6679	867	488.0406
768	458.5121	818	473.9659	868	488.3174
769	458.8325	819	474.2634	869	488.5937
770	459.1524	820	474.5606	870	488.8696
771	459.4719	821	474.8572	871	489.1451
772	459.7909	822	474.1535	872	489.4203
773	460.1094	823	475.4493	873	489.6950
774	460.4275	824	475.7446	874	489.9693
775	460.7451	825	476.0396	875	490.2432
776	461.0622	826	476.3341	876	490.5166
777	461.3788	827	476.6281	877	490.7897
778	461.6950	828	476.9218	878	491.0624
779	462.0107	829	477.2149	879	491.3347
780	462.3259	830	477.5077	880	491.6066
781	462.6407	831	477.8000	881	491.8780
782	462.9550	832	478.0919	882	492.1491
783	463.2689	833	478.3834	883	492.4198
784	463.5823	834	478.6744	884	492.6900
785	463.8952	835	478.9650	885	492.9599
786	464.2076	836	479.2552	886	493.2294
787	464.5196	837	479.5449	887	493.4984
788	464.8311	838	479.8342	888	493.7671
789	465.1422	839	480.1231	889	494.0354
790	465.4528	840	480.4115	890	494.3033
791	465.7630	841	480.6996	891	494.5708
792	466.0727	842	480.9872	892	494.8378
793	466.3819	843	481.2744	893	495.1045
794	466.6907	844	481.5611	894	495.3708
795	466.9990	845	481.8474	895	495.6367
796	467.3069	846	482.1333	896	495.9023
797	467.6143	847	482.4188	897	496.1674
798	467.9212	848	482.7039	898	496.4321
799	468.2277	849	482.9885	899	496.6964

Weeks	Present Worth	Weeks	Present Worth	Weeks	Present Worth
900	*496.9604*	**950**	*509.6717*	**1000**	*521.4763*
901	*497.2239*	**951**	*509.9164*	**1001**	*521.7036*
902	*497.4871*	**952**	*510.1608*	**1002**	*521.9306*
903	*497.7499*	**953**	*510.4049*	**1003**	*522.1572*
904	*498.0123*	**954**	*510.6485*	**1004**	*522.3835*
905	*498.2743*	**955**	*510.8919*	**1005**	*522.6094*
906	*498.5359*	**956**	*511.1348*	**1006**	*522.8351*
907	*498.7971*	**957**	*511.3774*	**1007**	*523.0604*
908	*499.0579*	**958**	*511.6196*	**1008**	*523.2853*
909	*499.3184*	**959**	*511.8615*	**1009**	*523.5099*
910	*499.5784*	**960**	*512.1030*	**1010**	*523.7342*
911	*499.8381*	**961**	*512.3442*	**1011**	*523.9582*
912	*500.0974*	**962**	*512.5850*	**1012**	*524.1818*
913	*500.3563*	**963**	*512.8254*	**1013**	*524.4051*
914	*500.6149*	**964**	*513.0655*	**1014**	*524.6281*
915	*500.8730*	**965**	*513.3052*	**1015**	*524.8507*
916	*501.1308*	**966**	*513.5446*	**1016**	*525.0730*
917	*501.3882*	**967**	*513.7837*	**1017**	*525.2950*
918	*501.6452*	**968**	*514.0223*	**1018**	*525.5166*
919	*501.9018*	**969**	*514.2606*	**1019**	*525.7379*
920	*502.1580*	**970**	*514.4986*	**1020**	*525.9589*
921	*502.4139*	**971**	*514.7362*	**1021**	*526.1796*
922	*502.6694*	**972**	*514.9735*	**1022**	*526.3999*
923	*502.9245*	**973**	*515.2104*	**1023**	*526.6200*
924	*503.1792*	**974**	*515.4470*	**1024**	*526.8397*
925	*503.4336*	**975**	*515.6832*	**1025**	*527.0590*
926	*503.6876*	**976**	*516.9191*	**1026**	*527.2781*
927	*503.9412*	**977**	*516.1546*	**1027**	*527.4968*
928	*504.1944*	**978**	*516.3897*	**1028**	*527.7152*
929	*504.4473*	**979**	*516.6246*	**1029**	*527.9332*
930	*504.6998*	**980**	*516.8590*	**1030**	*528.1510*
931	*504.9519*	**981**	*517.0931*	**1031**	*528.3684*
932	*505.2036*	**982**	*517.3269*	**1032**	*528.5855*
933	*505.4550*	**983**	*517.5604*	**1033**	*528.8023*
934	*505.7060*	**984**	*517.7934*	**1034**	*529.0188*
935	*505.9566*	**985**	*518.0262*	**1035**	*529.2349*
936	*506.2068*	**986**	*518.2586*	**1036**	*529.4507*
937	*506.4567*	**987**	*518.4906*	**1037**	*529.6662*
938	*506.7062*	**988**	*518.7224*	**1038**	*529.8814*
939	*506.9553*	**989**	*518.9537*	**1039**	*530.0963*
940	*507.2041*	**990**	*519.1848*	**1040**	*530.3108*
941	*507.4525*	**991**	*519.4154*	**1041**	*530.5250*
942	*507.7006*	**992**	*519.6458*	**1042**	*530.7390*
943	*507.9482*	**993**	*519.8758*	**1043**	*530.9526*
944	*508.1955*	**994**	*520.1055*	**1044**	*531.1658*
945	*508.4425*	**995**	*520.3348*	**1045**	*531.3788*
946	*508.6890*	**996**	*520.5638*	**1046**	*531.5915*
947	*508.9353*	**997**	*520.7924*	**1047**	*531.8038*
948	*509.1811*	**998**	*521.0207*	**1048**	*532.0158*
949	*509.4266*	**999**	*521.2487*	**1049**	*532.2275*

Weeks	Present Worth	Weeks	Present Worth	Weeks	Present Worth
1050	532.4389	1100	542.6196	1150	552.0741
1051	532.6500	1101	542.8156	1151	552.2561
1052	532.8608	1102	543.0113	1152	552.4379
1053	533.0712	1103	543.2068	1153	552.6194
1054	533.2814	1104	543.4020	1154	552.8006
1055	533.4912	1105	543.5968	1155	552.9816
1056	533.7008	1106	543.7914	1156	553.1623
1057	533.9100	1107	543.9857	1157	553.3427
1058	534.1189	1108	544.1797	1158	553.5229
1059	534.3275	1109	544.3734	1159	553.7028
1060	534.5358	1110	544.5669	1160	553.8824
1061	534.7438	1111	544.7600	1161	554.0618
1062	534.9514	1112	544.9529	1162	554.2409
1063	535.1588	1113	545.1454	1163	554.4198
1064	535.3659	1114	545.3377	1164	554.5983
1065	535.5726	1115	545.5297	1165	554.7766
1066	535.7791	1116	545.7215	1166	554.9547
1067	535.9852	1117	545.9129	1167	555.1325
1068	536.1910	1118	546.1041	1168	555.3100
1069	536.3966	1119	546.2949	1169	555.4873
1070	536.6018	1120	546.4855	1170	555.6642
1071	536.8067	1121	546.6758	1171	555.8410
1072	537.0114	1122	546.8659	1172	556.0175
1073	537.2157	1123	547.0556	1173	556.1937
1074	537.4197	1124	547.2451	1174	556.3696
1075	537.6234	1125	547.4343	1175	556.5453
1076	537.8268	1126	547.6232	1176	556.7207
1077	538.0299	1127	547.8118	1177	556.8959
1078	538.2328	1128	548.0001	1178	557.0708
1079	538.4353	1129	548.1882	1179	557.2455
1080	538.6375	1130	548.3760	1180	557.4199
1081	538.8394	1131	548.5635	1181	557.5940
1082	539.0410	1132	548.7508	1182	557.7679
1083	539.2423	1133	548.9377	1883	557.9415
1084	539.4434	1134	549.1244	1184	558.1149
1085	539.6441	1135	549.3018	1185	558.2880
1086	539.8445	1136	549.4969	1186	558.4609
1087	540.0447	1137	549.6828	1187	558.6335
1088	540.2445	1138	549.8684	1188	558.8058
1089	540.4440	1139	550.0537	1189	558.9779
1090	540.6433	1140	550.2387	1190	559.1497
1091	540.8422	1141	550.4235	1191	559.3213
1092	541.0409	1142	550.6080	1192	559.4926
1093	541.2392	1143	550.7922	1193	559.6637
1094	541.4373	1144	550.9761	1194	559.8345
1095	541.6351	1145	551.1598	1195	560.0051
1096	541.8326	1146	551.3432	1196	560.1754
1097	542.0298	1147	551.5263	1197	560.3455
1098	542.2267	1148	551.7092	1198	560.5153
1099	542.4233	1149	551.8917	1199	560.6848

Weeks	Present Worth	Weeks	Present Worth	Weeks	Present Worth
1200	560.8542	1250	569.0080	1300	576.5802
1201	561.0232	1251	569.1650	1301	576.7260
1202	561.1920	1252	569.3218	1302	576.8716
1203	561.3606	1253	569.4783	1303	577.0169
1204	561.5289	1254	569.6346	1304	577.1621
1205	561.6970	1255	569.7907	1305	577.3070
1206	561.8648	1256	569.9465	1306	577.4518
1207	562.0323	1257	570.1021	1307	577.5963
1208	562.1996	1258	570.2575	1308	577.7406
1209	562.3667	1259	570.4126	1309	577.8847
1210	562.5335	1260	570.5676	1310	578.0285
1211	562.7001	1261	570.7223	1311	578.1722
1212	562.8664	1262	570.8767	1312	578.3156
1213	563.0325	1263	571.0310	1313	578.4589
1214	563.1984	1264	571.1850	1314	578.6019
1215	563.3640	1265	571.3388	1315	578.7447
1216	563.5293	1266	571.4923	1316	578.8873
1217	563.6944	1267	571.6456	1317	579.0297
1218	563.8593	1268	571.7987	1318	579.1719
1219	564.0239	1269	571.9516	1319	579.3139
1220	564.1883	1270	572.1043	1320	579.4556
1221	564.3524	1271	572.2567	1321	579.5972
1222	564.5163	1272	572.4089	1322	579.7385
1223	564.6799	1273	572.5608	1323	579.8796
1224	564.8433	1274	572.7126	1324	580.0206
1225	565.0065	1275	572.8641	1325	580.1613
1226	565.1694	1276	573.0154	1326	580.3018
1227	565.3321	1277	573.1665	1327	580.4421
1228	565.4945	1278	573.3173	1328	580.5822
1229	565.6567	1279	573.4680	1329	580.7220
1230	565.8187	1280	573.6184	1330	580.8617
1231	565.9804	1281	573.7685	1331	581.0012
1232	566.1419	1282	573.9185	1332	581.1405
1233	566.3031	1283	574.0682	1333	581.2795
1234	566.4641	1284	574.2178	1334	581.4184
1235	566.6249	1285	574.3671	1335	581.5570
1236	566.7854	1286	574.5161	1336	581.6955
1237	566.9457	1287	574.6650	1337	581.8337
1238	567.1057	1288	574.8136	1338	581.9717
1239	567.2655	1289	574.9620	1339	582.1096
1240	567.4251	1290	575.1102	1340	582.2472
1241	567.5845	1291	575.2582	1341	582.3846
1242	567.7436	1292	575.4060	1342	582.5218
1243	567.9024	1293	575.5535	1343	582.6588
1244	568.0611	1294	575.7008	1344	582.7956
1245	568.2195	1295	575.8479	1345	582.9323
1246	568.3776	1296	575.9948	1346	583.0687
1247	568.5356	1297	576.1415	1347	583.2049
1248	568.6933	1298	576.2879	1348	583.3409
1249	568.8507	1299	576.4342	1349	583.4767

Weeks	Present Worth	Weeks	Present Worth	Weeks	Present Worth
1350	583.6123	1400	590.1428	1450	596.2075
1351	583.7477	1401	590.2685	1451	596.3242
1352	583.8829	1402	590.3941	1452	596.4408
1353	584.0179	1403	590.5194	1453	596.5573
1354	584.1527	1404	590.6446	1454	596.6735
1355	584.2873	1405	590.7696	1455	596.7896
1356	584.4217	1406	590.8945	1456	596.9055
1357	584.5559	1407	591.0191	1457	597.0213
1358	584.6899	1408	591.1435	1458	597.1368
1359	584.8237	1409	591.2678	1459	597.2522
1360	584.9573	1410	591.3919	1460	597.3675
1361	585.0907	1411	591.5158	1461	597.4825
1362	585.2239	1412	591.6395	1462	597.5974
1363	585.3570	1413	591.7630	1463	597.7121
1364	585.4898	1414	591.8864	1464	597.8267
1365	585.6224	1415	592.0096	1465	597.9411
1366	585.7548	1416	592.1325	1466	598.0553
1367	585.8871	1417	592.2553	1467	598.1693
1368	586.0191	1418	592.3779	1468	598.2832
1369	586.1510	1419	592.5004	1469	598.3969
1370	586.2826	1420	592.6226	1470	598.5104
1371	586.4141	1421	592.7447	1471	598.6238
1372	586.5453	1422	592.8666	1472	598.7370
1373	586.6764	1423	592.9883	1473	598.8500
1374	586.8072	1424	593.1099	1474	598.9629
1375	586.9379	1425	593.2312	1475	599.0756
1376	587.0684	1426	593.3524	1476	599.1881
1377	587.1987	1427	593.4734	1477	599.3005
1378	587.3288	1428	593.5942	1478	599.4127
1379	587.4587	1429	593.7148	1479	599.5247
1380	587.5884	1430	593.8353	1480	599.6366
1381	587.7179	1431	593.9556	1481	599.7483
1382	587.8473	1432	594.0757	1482	599.8598
1383	587.9764	1433	594.1956	1483	599.9712
1384	588.1054	1434	594.3154	1484	600.0824
1385	588.2341	1435	594.4349	1485	600.1935
1386	588.3627	1436	594.5543	1486	600.3043
1387	588.4911	1437	594.6736	1487	600.4151
1388	588.6192	1438	594.7926	1488	600.5256
1389	588.7472	1439	594.9115	1489	600.6360
1390	588.8750	1440	595.0302	1490	600.7462
1391	589.0027	1441	595.1487	1491	600.8563
1392	589.1301	1442	595.2670	1492	600.9662
1393	589.2573	1443	595.3852	1493	601.0759
1394	589.3844	1444	595.5032	1494	601.1855
1395	589.5113	1445	595.6210	1495	601.2949
1396	589.6379	1446	595.7386	1496	601.4042
1397	589.7644	1447	595.8561	1497	601.5132
1398	589.8907	1448	595.9734	1498	601.6222
1399	590.0168	1449	596.0905	1499	601.7309

Tables

Weeks	Present Worth	Weeks	Present Worth	Weeks	Present Worth
1500	*601.8395*	**1550**	*607.0699*	**1600**	*611.9272*
1501	*601.9480*	**1551**	*607.1706*	**1601**	*612.0207*
1502	*602.0563*	**1552**	*607.2712*	**1602**	*612.1141*
1503	*602.1644*	**1553**	*607.3716*	**1603**	*612.2074*
1504	*602.2724*	**1554**	*607.4719*	**1604**	*612.3005*
1505	*602.3802*	**1555**	*607.5720*	**1605**	*612.3934*
1506	*602.4878*	**1556**	*607.6719*	**1606**	*612.4863*
1507	*602.5953*	**1557**	*607.7718*	**1607**	*612.5790*
1508	*602.7026*	**1558**	*607.8714*	**1608**	*612.6715*
1509	*602.8098*	**1559**	*607.9710*	**1609**	*612.7640*
1510	*602.9168*	**1560**	*608.0703*	**1610**	*612.8563*
1511	*603.0237*	**1561**	*608.1696*	**1611**	*612.9484*
1512	*603.1304*	**1562**	*608.2686*	**1612**	*613.0404*
1513	*603.2369*	**1563**	*608.3676*	**1613**	*613.1323*
1514	*603.3433*	**1564**	*608.4664*	**1614**	*613.2240*
1515	*603.4495*	**1565**	*608.5650*	**1615**	*613.3157*
1516	*603.5556*	**1566**	*608.6635*	**1616**	*613.4071*
1517	*603.6615*	**1567**	*608.7619*	**1617**	*613.4985*
1518	*603.7672*	**1568**	*608.8601*	**1618**	*613.5897*
1519	*603.8728*	**1569**	*608.9581*	**1619**	*613.6807*
1520	*603.9782*	**1570**	*609.0561*	**1620**	*613.7717*
1521	*604.0835*	**1571**	*609.1538*	**1621**	*613.8625*
1522	*604.1887*	**1572**	*609.2515*	**1622**	*613.9531*
1523	*604.2936*	**1573**	*609.3489*	**1623**	*614.0437*
1524	*604.3984*	**1574**	*609.4463*	**1624**	*614.1341*
1525	*604.5031*	**1575**	*609.5435*	**1625**	*614.2243*
1526	*604.6076*	**1576**	*609.6405*	**1626**	*614.3145*
1527	*604.7120*	**1577**	*609.7374*	**1627**	*614.4044*
1528	*604.8162*	**1578**	*609.8342*	**1628**	*614.4943*
1529	*604.9202*	**1579**	*609.9308*	**1629**	*614.5840*
1530	*605.0241*	**1580**	*610.0273*	**1630**	*614.6736*
1531	*605.1278*	**1581**	*610.1236*	**1631**	*614.7631*
1532	*605.2314*	**1582**	*610.2198*	**1632**	*614.8524*
1533	*605.3348*	**1583**	*610.3159*	**1633**	*614.9416*
1534	*605.4381*	**1584**	*610.4118*	**1634**	*615.0307*
1535	*605.5412*	**1585**	*610.5076*	**1635**	*615.1196*
1536	*605.6442*	**1586**	*610.6032*	**1636**	*615.2084*
1537	*605.7470*	**1587**	*610.6987*	**1637**	*615.2971*
1538	*605.8497*	**1588**	*610.7940*	**1638**	*615.3857*
1539	*605.9522*	**1589**	*610.8892*	**1639**	*615.4741*
1540	*606.0546*	**1590**	*610.9843*	**1640**	*615.5624*
1541	*606.1568*	**1591**	*611.0792*	**1641**	*615.6505*
1542	*606.2588*	**1592**	*611.1740*	**1642**	*615.7385*
1543	*606.3608*	**1593**	*611.2686*	**1643**	*615.8264*
1544	*606.4625*	**1594**	*611.3631*	**1644**	*615.9142*
1545	*606.5641*	**1595**	*611.4575*	**1645**	*616.0018*
1546	*606.6656*	**1596**	*611.5517*	**1646**	*616.0893*
1547	*606.7669*	**1597**	*611.6458*	**1647**	*616.1767*
1548	*606.8680*	**1598**	*611.7397*	**1648**	*616.2639*
1549	*606.9691*	**1599**	*611.8335*	**1649**	*616.3510*

Weeks	Present Worth	Weeks	Present Worth	Weeks	Present Worth
1650	616.4380	1700	620.6271	1750	624.5173
1651	616.5249	1701	620.7077	1751	624.5922
1652	616.6116	1702	620.7883	1752	624.6670
1653	616.6982	1703	620.8687	1753	624.7417
1654	616.7847	1704	620.9490	1754	624.8163
1655	616.8710	1705	621.0292	1755	624.8908
1656	616.9572	1706	621.1092	1756	624.9651
1657	617.0433	1707	621.1892	1757	625.0394
1658	617.1293	1708	621.2690	1758	625.1135
1659	617.2151	1709	621.3487	1759	625.1875
1660	617.3008	1710	621.4283	1760	625.2614
1661	617.3864	1711	621.5078	1761	625.3352
1662	617.4718	1712	621.5872	1762	625.4089
1663	617.5572	1713	621.6664	1763	625.4825
1664	617.6424	1714	621.7455	1764	625.5560
1665	617.7274	1715	621.8245	1765	625.6294
1666	617.8124	1716	621.9034	1766	625.7026
1667	617.8972	1717	621.9822	1767	625.7758
1668	617.9819	1718	622.0608	1768	625.8488
1669	618.0665	1719	622.1394	1769	625.9218
1670	618.1509	1720	622.2178	1770	625.9946
1671	618.2352	1721	622.2961	1771	626.0673
1672	618.3194	1722	622.3743	1772	626.1399
1673	618.4035	1723	622.4524	1773	626.2124
1674	618.4875	1724	622.5303	1774	626.2848
1675	618.5713	1725	622.6082	1775	626.3571
1676	618.6550	1726	622.6859	1776	626.4293
1677	618.7386	1727	622.7635	1777	626.5014
1678	618.8220	1728	622.8410	1778	626.5734
1679	618.9053	1729	622.9184	1779	626.6452
1680	618.9886	1730	622.9957	1780	626.7170
1681	619.0716	1731	623.0728	1781	626.7886
1682	619.1546	1732	623.1499	1782	626.8602
1683	619.2374	1733	623.2268	1783	626.9316
1684	619.3201	1734	623.3036	1784	627.0030
1685	619.4027	1735	623.3803	1785	627.0742
1686	619.4852	1736	623.4569	1786	627.1453
1687	619.5676	1737	623.5334	1787	627.2163
1688	619.6498	1738	623.6098	1788	627.2873
1689	619.7319	1739	623.6860	1789	627.3581
1690	619.8139	1740	623.7621	1790	627.4288
1691	619.8957	1741	623.8382	1791	627.4994
1692	619.9775	1742	623.9141	1792	627.5699
1693	620.0591	1743	623.9899	1793	627.6403
1694	620.1406	1744	624.0656	1794	627.7106
1695	620.2220	1745	624.1411	1795	627.7807
1696	620.3032	1746	624.2166	1796	627.8508
1697	620.3844	1747	624.2919	1797	627.9208
1698	620.4654	1748	624.3672	1798	627.9907
1699	620.5463	1749	624.4423	1799	628.0604

Tables

Weeks	Present Worth	Weeks	Present Worth	Weeks	Present Worth
1800	*628.1301*	**1850**	*631.4852*	**1900**	*634.6009*
1801	*628.1997*	**1851**	*631.5498*	**1901**	*634.6609*
1802	*628.2691*	**1852**	*631.6143*	**1902**	*634.7208*
1803	*628.3385*	**1853**	*631.6787*	**1903**	*634.7807*
1804	*628.4077*	**1854**	*631.7430*	**1904**	*634.8404*
1805	*628.4769*	**1855**	*631.8072*	**1905**	*634.9000*
1806	*628.5459*	**1856**	*631.8714*	**1906**	*634.9596*
1807	*628.6149*	**1857**	*631.9354*	**1907**	*635.0190*
1808	*628.6837*	**1858**	*631.9993*	**1908**	*635.0784*
1809	*628.7525*	**1859**	*632.0632*	**1909**	*635.1377*
1810	*628.8211*	**1860**	*632.1269*	**1910**	*635.1969*
1811	*628.8897*	**1861**	*632.1906*	**1911**	*635.2560*
1812	*628.9581*	**1862**	*632.2541*	**1912**	*635.3150*
1813	*629.0264*	**1863**	*632.3176*	**1913**	*635.3740*
1814	*629.0947*	**1864**	*632.3810*	**1914**	*635.4328*
1815	*629.1628*	**1865**	*632.4442*	**1915**	*635.4916*
1816	*629.2309*	**1866**	*632.5074*	**1916**	*635.5503*
1817	*629.2988*	**1867**	*632.5705*	**1917**	*635.6089*
1818	*629.3666*	**1868**	*632.6335*	**1918**	*635.6674*
1819	*629.4344*	**1869**	*632.6964*	**1919**	*635.7258*
1820	*629.5020*	**1870**	*632.7592*	**1920**	*635.7841*
1821	*629.5695*	**1871**	*632.8219*	**1921**	*635.8423*
1822	*629.6370*	**1872**	*632.8846*	**1922**	*635.9005*
1823	*629.7043*	**1873**	*632.9471*	**1923**	*635.9586*
1824	*629.7715*	**1874**	*633.0095*	**1924**	*636.0166*
1825	*629.8387*	**1875**	*633.0719*	**1925**	*636.0745*
1826	*629.9057*	**1876**	*633.1341*	**1926**	*636.1323*
1827	*629.9726*	**1877**	*633.1963*	**1927**	*636.1900*
1828	*630.0395*	**1878**	*633.2584*	**1928**	*636.2476*
1829	*630.1062*	**1879**	*633.3203*	**1929**	*636.3052*
1830	*630.1729*	**1880**	*633.3822*	**1930**	*636.3627*
1831	*630.2394*	**1881**	*633.4440*	**1931**	*636.4201*
1832	*630.3059*	**1882**	*633.5057*	**1932**	*636.4774*
1833	*630.3722*	**1883**	*633.5673*	**1933**	*636.5346*
1834	*630.4384*	**1884**	*633.6289*	**1934**	*636.5917*
1835	*630.5046*	**1885**	*633.6903*	**1935**	*636.6488*
1836	*630.5706*	**1886**	*633.7516*	**1936**	*636.7057*
1837	*630.6366*	**1887**	*633.8129*	**1937**	*636.7626*
1838	*630.7025*	**1888**	*633.8740*	**1938**	*636.8194*
1839	*630.7682*	**1889**	*633.9351*	**1939**	*636.8761*
1840	*630.8339*	**1890**	*633.9961*	**1940**	*636.9328*
1841	*630.8994*	**1891**	*634.0570*	**1941**	*636.9893*
1842	*630.9649*	**1892**	*634.1178*	**1942**	*637.0458*
1843	*631.0303*	**1893**	*634.1785*	**1943**	*637.1021*
1844	*631.0956*	**1894**	*634.2391*	**1944**	*637.1584*
1845	*631.1607*	**1895**	*634.2996*	**1945**	*637.2146*
1846	*631.2258*	**1896**	*634.3601*	**1946**	*637.2708*
1847	*631.2908*	**1897**	*634.4204*	**1947**	*637.3268*
1848	*631.3557*	**1898**	*634.4807*	**1948**	*637.3828*
1849	*631.4205*	**1899**	*634.5409*	**1949**	*637.4387*

Weeks	Present Worth	Weeks	Present Worth	Weeks	Present Worth
1950	*637.4945*	**2000**	*640.1816*	**2050**	*642.6770*
1951	*637.5502*	**2001**	*640.2333*	**2051**	*642.7251*
1952	*637.6058*	**2002**	*640.2850*	**2052**	*642.7731*
1953	*637.6614*	**2003**	*640.3366*	**2053**	*642.8210*
1954	*637.7168*	**2004**	*640.3881*	**2054**	*642.8688*
1955	*637.7722*	**2005**	*640.4395*	**2055**	*642.9166*
1956	*637.8275*	**2006**	*640.4909*	**2056**	*642.9643*
1957	*637.8827*	**2007**	*640.5422*	**2057**	*643.0119*
1958	*637.9379*	**2008**	*640.5934*	**2058**	*643.0594*
1959	*637.9929*	**2009**	*640.6445*	**2059**	*643.1069*
1960	*638.0479*	**2010**	*640.6956*	**2060**	*643.1543*
1961	*638.1028*	**2011**	*640.7465*	**2061**	*643.2017*
1962	*638.1576*	**2012**	*640.7974*	**2062**	*643.2490*
1963	*638.2123*	**2013**	*640.8483*	**2063**	*643.2962*
1964	*638.2670*	**2014**	*640.8990*	**2064**	*643.3433*
1965	*638.3216*	**2015**	*640.9497*	**2065**	*643.3904*
1966	*638.3761*	**2016**	*641.0003*	**2066**	*643.4374*
1967	*638.4305*	**2017**	*641.0508*	**2067**	*643.4843*
1968	*638.4848*	**2018**	*641.1013*	**2068**	*643.5311*
1969	*638.5391*	**2019**	*641.1517*	**2069**	*643.5779*
1970	*638.5932*	**2020**	*641.2020*	**2070**	*643.6246*
1971	*638.6473*	**2021**	*641.2522*	**2071**	*643.6713*
1972	*638.7013*	**2022**	*641.3024*	**2072**	*643.7179*
1973	*638.7553*	**2023**	*641.3524*	**2073**	*643.7644*
1974	*638.8091*	**2024**	*641.4025*	**2074**	*643.8108*
1975	*638.8629*	**2025**	*641.4524*	**2075**	*643.8572*
1976	*638.9166*	**2026**	*641.5022*	**2076**	*643.9035*
1977	*638.9702*	**2027**	*641.5520*	**2077**	*643.9497*
1978	*638.0237*	**2028**	*641.6017*	**2078**	*643.9959*
1979	*639.0772*	**2029**	*641.6514*	**2079**	*644.0420*
1980	*639.1305*	**2030**	*641.7010*	**2080**	*644.0880*
1981	*639.1838*	**2031**	*641.7504*	**2081**	*644.1340*
1982	*639.2370*	**2032**	*641.7999*	**2082**	*644.1799*
1983	*639.2902*	**2033**	*641.8492*	**2083**	*644.2257*
1984	*639.3432*	**2034**	*641.8985*	**2084**	*644.2715*
1985	*639.3962*	**2035**	*641.9477*	**2085**	*644.3172*
1986	*639.4491*	**2036**	*641.9968*	**2086**	*644.3628*
1987	*639.5019*	**2037**	*642.0459*	**2087**	*644.4083*
1988	*639.5547*	**2038**	*642.0949*	**2088**	*644.4538*
1989	*639.6074*	**2039**	*642.1438*	**2089**	*644.4993*
1990	*639.6599*	**2040**	*642.1926*	**2090**	*644.5446*
1991	*639.7125*	**2041**	*642.2414*	**2091**	*644.5899*
1992	*639.7649*	**2042**	*642.2901*	**2092**	*644.6351*
1993	*639.8172*	**2043**	*642.3387*	**2093**	*644.6803*
1994	*639.8695*	**2044**	*642.3872*	**2094**	*644.7254*
1995	*639.9217*	**2045**	*642.4357*	**2095**	*644.7704*
1996	*639.9739*	**2046**	*642.4841*	**2096**	*644.8153*
1997	*640.0259*	**2047**	*642.5325*	**2097**	*644.8602*
1998	*640.0779*	**2048**	*642.5807*	**2098**	*644.9050*
1999	*640.1298*	**2049**	*642.6289*	**2099**	*644.9498*

Tables

Weeks	Present Worth	Weeks	Present Worth	Weeks	Present Worth
2100	644.9945	2150	647.1466	2200	649.1453
2101	645.0391	2151	647.1881	2201	649.1838
2102	645.0837	2152	647.2295	2202	649.2222
2103	645.1282	2153	647.2708	2203	649.2606
2104	645.1726	2154	647.3120	2204	649.2989
2105	645.2169	2155	647.3532	2205	649.3371
2106	645.2612	2156	647.3944	2206	649.3753
2107	645.3055	2157	647.4354	2207	649.4135
2108	645.3496	2158	647.4764	2208	649.4516
2109	645.3937	2159	647.5174	2209	649.4896
2110	645.4377	2160	647.5583	2210	649.5276
2111	645.4817	2161	647.5991	2211	649.5655
2112	645.5256	2162	647.6399	2212	649.6033
2113	645.5695	2163	647.6806	2213	649.6411
2114	645.6132	2164	647.7212	2214	649.6789
2115	645.6569	2165	647.7618	2215	649.7166
2116	645.7006	2166	647.8024	2216	649.7542
2117	645.7442	2167	647.8428	2217	649.7918
2118	645.7877	2168	647.8832	2218	649.8293
2119	645.8311	2169	647.9236	2219	649.8668
2120	645.8745	2170	647.9639	2220	649.9042
2121	645.9178	2171	648.0041	2221	649.9416
2122	645.9611	2172	648.0443	2222	649.9789
2123	646.0043	2173	648.0844	2223	650.0161
2124	646.0474	2174	648.1244	2224	650.0533
2125	646.0905	2175	648.1644	2225	650.0905
2126	646.1335	2176	648.2044	2226	650.1276
2127	646.1764	2177	648.2443	2227	650.1646
2128	646.2193	2178	648.2841	2228	650.2016
2129	646.2621	2179	648.3238	2229	650.2385
2130	646.3048	2180	648.3635	2230	650.2754
2131	646.3475	2181	648.4032	2231	650.3122
2132	646.3901	2182	648.4427	2232	650.3489
2133	646.4327	2183	648.4823	2233	650.3856
2134	646.4752	2184	648.5217	2234	650.4223
2135	646.5176	2185	648.5611	2235	650.4589
2136	646.5600	2186	648.6005	2236	650.4954
2137	646.6023	2187	648.6398	2237	650.5319
2138	646.6446	2188	648.6790	2238	650.5683
2139	646.6867	2189	648.7182	2239	650.6047
2140	646.7289	2190	648.7573	2240	650.6410
2141	646.7709	2191	648.7964	2241	650.6773
2142	646.8129	2192	648.8353	2242	650.7135
2143	646.8548	2193	648.8743	2243	650.7497
2144	646.8967	2194	648.9132	2244	650.7858
2145	646.9385	2195	648.9520	2245	650.8219
2146	646.9803	2196	648.9908	2246	650.8579
2147	647.0220	2197	649.0295	2247	650.8938
2148	647.0636	2198	649.0681	2248	650.9297
2149	647.1051	2199	649.1067	2249	650.9656

Weeks	Present Worth	Weeks	Present Worth	Weeks	Present Worth
2250	*651.0014*	**2300**	*652.7250*	**2350**	*654.3258*
2251	*651.0371*	**2301**	*652.7582*	**2351**	*654.3566*
2252	*651.0728*	**2302**	*652.7914*	**2352**	*654.3874*
2253	*651.1084*	**2303**	*652.8245*	**2353**	*654.4181*
2254	*651.1440*	**2304**	*652.8575*	**2354**	*654.4488*
2255	*651.1795*	**2305**	*652.8905*	**2355**	*654.4794*
2256	*651.2150*	**2306**	*652.9234*	**2356**	*654.5100*
2257	*651.2504*	**2307**	*652.9563*	**2357**	*654.5406*
2258	*651.2858*	**2308**	*652.9892*	**2358**	*654.5711*
2259	*651.3211*	**2309**	*653.0220*	**2359**	*654.6015*
2260	*651.3564*	**2310**	*653.0547*	**2360**	*654.6320*
2261	*651.3916*	**2311**	*653.0874*	**2361**	*654.6623*
2262	*651.4267*	**2312**	*653.1201*	**2362**	*654.6926*
2263	*651.4619*	**2313**	*653.1527*	**2363**	*654.7229*
2264	*651.4969*	**2314**	*653.1853*	**2364**	*654.7532*
2265	*651.5319*	**2315**	*653.2178*	**2365**	*654.7834*
2266	*651.5669*	**2316**	*653.2502*	**2366**	*654.8135*
2267	*651.6018*	**2317**	*653.2826*	**2367**	*654.8436*
2268	*651.6366*	**2318**	*653.3150*	**2368**	*654.8737*
2269	*651.6714*	**2319**	*653.3473*	**2369**	*654.9037*
2270	*651.7062*	**2320**	*653.3796*	**2370**	*654.9336*
2271	*651.7409*	**2321**	*653.4118*	**2371**	*654.9636*
2272	*651.7755*	**2322**	*653.4440*	**2372**	*654.9934*
2273	*651.8101*	**2323**	*653.4761*	**2373**	*655.0233*
2274	*651.8446*	**2324**	*653.5082*	**2374**	*655.0531*
2275	*651.8791*	**2325**	*653.5402*	**2375**	*655.0828*
2276	*651.9136*	**2326**	*653.5722*	**2376**	*655.1125*
2277	*651.9480*	**2327**	*653.6041*	**2377**	*655.1422*
2278	*651.9823*	**2328**	*653.6360*	**2378**	*655.1718*
2279	*652.0166*	**2329**	*653.6679*	**2379**	*655.2014*
2280	*652.0508*	**2330**	*653.6997*	**2380**	*655.2309*
2281	*652.0850*	**2331**	*653.7314*	**2381**	*655.2604*
2282	*652.1192*	**2332**	*653.7631*	**2382**	*655.2898*
2283	*652.1532*	**2333**	*653.7948*	**2383**	*655.3192*
2283	*652.1873*	**2334**	*653.8264*	**2384**	*655.3486*
2285	*652.2213*	**2335**	*653.8579*	**2385**	*655.3779*
2286	*652.2552*	**2336**	*653.8894*	**2386**	*655.4071*
2287	*652.2891*	**2337**	*653.9209*	**2387**	*655.4364*
2288	*652.3229*	**2338**	*653.9523*	**2388**	*655.4655*
2289	*652.3567*	**2339**	*653.9837*	**2389**	*655.4947*
2290	*652.3904*	**2340**	*654.0150*	**2390**	*655.5238*
2291	*652.4241*	**2341**	*654.0463*	**2391**	*655.5528*
2292	*652.4578*	**2342**	*654.0776*	**2392**	*655.5818*
2293	*652.4913*	**2343**	*654.1087*	**2393**	*655.6108*
2294	*652.5249*	**2344**	*654.1399*	**2394**	*655.6397*
2295	*652.5584*	**2345**	*654.1710*	**2395**	*655.6686*
2296	*652.5918*	**2346**	*654.2020*	**2396**	*655.6974*
2297	*652.6252*	**2347**	*654.2330*	**2397**	*655.7262*
2298	*652.6585*	**2348**	*654.2640*	**2398**	*655.7550*
2299	*652.6918*	**2349**	*654.2949*	**2399**	*655.7837*

Tables

Weeks	Present Worth	Weeks	Present Worth	Weeks	Present Worth
2400	655.8123	2450	657.1929	2500	658.4749
2401	655.8410	2451	657.2194	2501	658.4996
2402	655.8695	2452	657.2460	2502	658.5242
2403	655.8981	2453	657.2725	2503	658.5489
2404	655.9266	2454	657.2990	2504	658.5734
2405	655.9550	2455	657.3254	2505	658.5980
2406	655.9834	2456	657.3518	2506	658.6225
2407	656.0118	2457	657.3781	2507	658.6469
2408	656.0401	2458	657.4044	2508	658.6714
2409	656.0684	2459	657.4307	2509	658.6958
2410	656.0967	2460	657.4569	2510	658.7201
2411	656.1249	2461	657.4831	2511	658.7445
2412	656.1530	2462	657.5093	2512	658.7687
2413	656.1812	2463	657.5354	2513	658.7930
2414	656.2092	2464	657.5614	2514	658.8172
2415	656.2373	2465	657.5875	2515	658.8414
2416	656.2653	2466	657.6135	2516	658.8655
2417	656.2932	2467	657.6394	2517	658.8896
2418	656.3211	2468	657.6654	2518	658.9137
2419	656.3490	2469	657.6912	2519	658.9377
2420	656.3768	2470	657.7171	2520	658.9617
2421	656.4046	2471	657.7429	2521	658.9857
2422	656.4324	2472	657.7687	2522	659.0096
2423	656.4601	2473	657.7944	2523	659.0335
2424	656.4877	2474	657.8201	2524	659.0574
2425	656.5154	2475	657.8457	2525	659.0812
2426	656.5429	2476	657.8714	2526	659.1050
2427	656.5705	2477	657.8969	2527	659.1288
2428	656.5980	2478	657.9225	2528	659.1525
2429	656.6255	2479	657.9480	2529	659.1762
2430	656.6529	2480	657.9734	2530	659.1998
2431	656.6803	2481	657.9989	2531	659.2234
2432	656.7076	2482	658.0243	2532	659.2470
2433	656.7349	2483	658.0496	2533	659.2706
2434	656.7622	2484	658.0749	2534	659.2941
2435	656.7894	2485	658.1002	2535	659.3175
2436	656.8166	2486	658.1254	2536	659.3410
2437	656.8437	2487	658.1506	2537	659.3644
2438	656.8708	2488	658.1758	2538	659.3878
2439	656.8978	2489	658.2009	2539	659.4111
2440	656.9249	2490	658.2260	2540	659.4344
2441	656.9518	2491	658.2511	2541	659.4577
2442	656.9788	2492	658.2761	2542	659.4809
2443	657.0057	2493	658.3011	2543	659.5041
2444	657.0325	2494	658.3260	2544	659.5272
2445	657.0594	2495	658.3509	2545	659.5504
2446	657.0861	2496	658.3758	2546	659.5735
2447	657.1129	2497	658.4006	2547	659.5965
2448	657.1396	2498	658.4254	2548	659.6196
2449	657.1662	2499	658.4502	2549	659.6426

Weeks	Present Worth	Weeks	Present Worth	Weeks	Present Worth
2550	*659.6655*	**2600**	*660.7712*	**2650**	*661.7980*
2551	*659.6884*	**2601**	*660.7925*	**2651**	*661.8178*
2552	*659.7113*	**2602**	*660.8137*	**2652**	*661.8375*
2553	*659.7342*	**2603**	*660.8350*	**2653**	*661.8572*
2554	*659.7570*	**2604**	*660.8562*	**2654**	*661.8769*
2555	*659.7798*	**2605**	*660.8773*	**2655**	*661.8966*
2556	*659.8026*	**2606**	*660.8985*	**2656**	*661.9162*
2557	*659.8253*	**2607**	*660.9196*	**2657**	*661.9358*
2558	*659.8480*	**2608**	*660.9406*	**2658**	*661.9554*
2559	*659.8706*	**2609**	*660.9617*	**2659**	*661.9749*
2560	*659.8932*	**2610**	*660.9827*	**2660**	*661.9944*
2561	*659.9158*	**2611**	*661.0037*	**2661**	*662.0139*
2562	*659.9384*	**2612**	*661.0246*	**2662**	*662.0333*
2563	*659.9609*	**2613**	*661.0455*	**2663**	*662.0528*
2564	*659.9834*	**2614**	*661.0664*	**2664**	*662.0722*
2565	*660.0058*	**2615**	*661.0873*	**2665**	*622.0915*
2566	*660.0283*	**2616**	*661.1081*	**2666**	*662.1109*
2567	*660.0507*	**2617**	*661.1289*	**2667**	*662.1302*
2568	*660.0730*	**2618**	*661.1496*	**2668**	*662.1494*
2569	*660.0953*	**2619**	*661.1704*	**2669**	*662.1687*
2570	*660.1176*	**2620**	*661.1911*	**2670**	*662.1879*
2571	*660.1399*	**2621**	*661.2117*	**2671**	*662.2071*
2572	*660.1621*	**2622**	*661.2324*	**2672**	*662.2263*
2573	*660.1843*	**2623**	*661.2530*	**2673**	*662.2454*
2574	*660.2065*	**2624**	*661.2735*	**2674**	*662.2645*
2575	*660.2286*	**2625**	*661.2941*	**2675**	*662.2836*
2576	*660.2507*	**2626**	*661.3146*	**2676**	*662.3027*
2577	*660.2727*	**2627**	*661.3351*	**2677**	*662.3217*
2578	*660.2948*	**2628**	*661.3556*	**2678**	*662.3407*
2579	*660.3168*	**2629**	*661.3760*	**2679**	*662.3596*
2580	*660.3387*	**2630**	*661.3694*	**2680**	*662.3786*
2581	*660.3606*	**2631**	*661.4167*	**2681**	*662.3975*
2582	*660.3825*	**2632**	*661.4371*	**2682**	*662.4164*
2583	*660.4044*	**2633**	*661.4574*	**2683**	*662.4352*
2584	*660.4262*	**2634**	*661.4777*	**2684**	*662.4541*
2585	*660.4480*	**2635**	*661.4979*	**2685**	*662.4729*
2586	*660.4698*	**2636**	*661.5181*	**2686**	*662.4916*
2587	*660.4915*	**2637**	*661.5383*	**2687**	*662.5104*
2588	*660.5132*	**2638**	*661.5585*	**2688**	*662.5291*
2589	*660.5349*	**2639**	*661.5786*	**2689**	*662.5478*
2590	*660.5566*	**2640**	*661.5987*	**2690**	*662.5665*
2591	*660.5782*	**2641**	*661.6187*	**2691**	*662.5851*
2592	*660.5997*	**2642**	*661.6388*	**2692**	*662.6037*
2593	*660.6213*	**2643**	*661.6588*	**2693**	*662.6223*
2594	*660.6428*	**2644**	*661.6788*	**2694**	*662.6408*
2595	*660.6643*	**2645**	*661.6987*	**2695**	*662.6594*
2596	*660.6857*	**2646**	*661.7186*	**2696**	*662.6779*
2597	*660.7071*	**2647**	*661.7385*	**2697**	*662.6963*
2598	*660.7285*	**2648**	*661.7584*	**2698**	*662.7148*
2599	*660.7499*	**2649**	*661.7782*	**2699**	*662.7332*

Tables

Weeks	Present Worth	Weeks	Present Worth	Weeks	Present Worth
2700	*662.7515*	**2750**	*663.6371*	**2800**	*664.4595*
2701	*662.7699*	**2751**	*663.6542*	**2801**	*664.4753*
2702	*662.7883*	**2752**	*663.6712*	**2802**	*664.4912*
2703	*662.8066*	**2753**	*663.6882*	**2803**	*664.5069*
2704	*662.8249*	**2754**	*663.7052*	**2804**	*664.5227*
2705	*662.8431*	**2755**	*663.7221*	**2805**	*664.5385*
2706	*662.8613*	**2756**	*663.7391*	**2806**	*664.5542*
2707	*662.8795*	**2757**	*663.7560*	**2807**	*664.5699*
2708	*662.8977*	**2758**	*663.7728*	**2808**	*664.5855*
2709	*662.9158*	**2759**	*663.7897*	**2809**	*664.6012*
2711	*662.9340*	**2760**	*663.8065*	**2810**	*664.6168*
2711	*662.9521*	**2761**	*663.8233*	**2811**	*664.6324*
2712	*662.9701*	**2762**	*663.8401*	**2812**	*664.6480*
2713	*662.9882*	**2763**	*663.8568*	**2813**	*664.6635*
2714	*663.0062*	**2764**	*663.8736*	**2814**	*664.6791*
2715	*663.0242*	**2765**	*663.8903*	**2815**	*664.6946*
2716	*663.0421*	**2766**	*663.9069*	**2816**	*664.7101*
2717	*663.0600*	**2767**	*663.9236*	**2817**	*664.7255*
2718	*663.0779*	**2768**	*663.9402*	**2818**	*664.7410*
2719	*663.0958*	**2769**	*663.9568*	**2819**	*664.7564*
2720	*663.1137*	**2770**	*663.9734*	**2820**	*664.7718*
2721	*663.1315*	**2771**	*663.9900*	**2821**	*664.7872*
2722	*663.1493*	**2772**	*664.0065*	**2822**	*664.8025*
2723	*663.1671*	**2773**	*664.0230*	**2823**	*664.8178*
2724	*663.1848*	**2774**	*664.0395*	**2824**	*664.8332*
2725	*663.2025*	**2775**	*664.0559*	**2825**	*664.8484*
2726	*663.2202*	**2776**	*664.0724*	**2826**	*664.8637*
2727	*663.2379*	**2777**	*664.0888*	**2827**	*664.8789*
2728	*663.2555*	**2778**	*664.1051*	**2828**	*664.8941*
2729	*663.2732*	**2779**	*664.1215*	**2829**	*664.9093*
2730	*663.2907*	**2780**	*664.1378*	**2830**	*664.9245*
2731	*663.3083*	**2781**	*664.1541*	**2831**	*664.9397*
2732	*663.3258*	**2782**	*664.1704*	**2832**	*664.9548*
2733	*663.3434*	**2783**	*664.1867*	**2833**	*664.9699*
2734	*663.3608*	**2784**	*664.2029*	**2834**	*664.9850*
2735	*663.3783*	**2785**	*664.2192*	**2835**	*665.0000*
2736	*663.3957*	**2786**	*664.2353*	**2836**	*665.0151*
2737	*663.4131*	**2787**	*664.2515*	**2837**	*665.0301*
2738	*663.4305*	**2788**	*664.2677*	**2838**	*665.0451*
2739	*663.4479*	**2789**	*664.2838*	**2839**	*665.0600*
2740	*663.4652*	**2790**	*664.2999*	**2840**	*665.0750*
2741	*663.4852*	**2791**	*664.3159*	**2841**	*665.0899*
2742	*663.4998*	**2792**	*664.3320*	**2842**	*665.1048*
2743	*663.5171*	**2793**	*662.3480*	**2843**	*665.1197*
2744	*663.5343*	**2794**	*664.3640*	**2844**	*665.1345*
2745	*663.5515*	**2795**	*664.3800*	**2845**	*665.1494*
2746	*663.5687*	**2796**	*664.3959*	**2846**	*665.1642*
2747	*663.5858*	**2797**	*664.4119*	**2847**	*665.1790*
2748	*663.6029*	**2798**	*664.4278*	**2848**	*665.1938*
2749	*663.6200*	**2799**	*664.4437*	**2849**	*665.2085*

Weeks	Present Worth	Weeks	Present Worth	Weeks	Present Worth
2850	*665.2232*	**2900**	*665.9325*	**2950**	*666.5911*
2851	*665.2379*	**2901**	*665.9461*	**2951**	*666.6038*
2852	*665.2526*	**2902**	*665.9598*	**2952**	*666.6165*
2853	*665.2673*	**2903**	*665.9734*	**2953**	*666.6291*
2854	*665.2819*	**2904**	*665.9870*	**2954**	*666.6418*
2855	*665.2965*	**2905**	*666.0006*	**2955**	*666.6544*
2856	*665.3111*	**2906**	*666.0141*	**2956**	*666.6670*
2857	*665.3257*	**2907**	*666.0277*	**2957**	*666.6795*
2858	*665.3403*	**2908**	*666.0412*	**2958**	*666.6921*
2859	*665.3548*	**2909**	*666.0547*	**2959**	*666.7046*
2860	*665.3693*	**2910**	*666.0681*	**2960**	*666.7171*
2861	*665.3838*	**2911**	*666.0816*	**2961**	*666.7296*
2862	*665.3983*	**2912**	*666.0950*	**2962**	*666.7421*
2863	*665.4127*	**2913**	*666.1085*	**2963**	*666.7546*
2864	*665.4271*	**2914**	*666.1218*	**2964**	*666.7670*
2865	*665.4415*	**2915**	*666.1352*	**2965**	*666.7794*
2866	*665.4559*	**2916**	*666.1486*	**2966**	*666.7918*
2867	*665.4703*	**2917**	*666.1619*	**2967**	*666.8042*
2868	*665.4846*	**2918**	*666.1752*	**2968**	*666.8166*
2869	*665.4990*	**2919**	*666.1885*	**2969**	*666.8289*
2870	*665.5132*	**2920**	*666.2018*	**2970**	*666.8413*
2871	*665.5275*	**2921**	*666.2151*	**2971**	*666.8536*
2872	*665.5418*	**2922**	*666.2283*	**2972**	*666.8659*
2873	*665.5560*	**2923**	*666.2415*	**2973**	*666.8781*
2874	*665.5702*	**2924**	*666.2547*	**2974**	*666.8904*
2875	*665.5844*	**2925**	*666.2679*	**2975**	*666.9026*
2876	*665.5986*	**2926**	*666.2811*	**2976**	*666.9149*
2877	*665.6127*	**2927**	*666.2942*	**2977**	*666.9271*
2878	*665.6269*	**2928**	*666.3073*	**2978**	*666.9393*
2879	*665.6410*	**2929**	*666.3204*	**2979**	*666.9514*
2880	*665.6551*	**2930**	*666.3335*	**2980**	*666.9636*
2881	*665.6691*	**2931**	*666.3466*	**2981**	*666.9757*
2882	*665.6832*	**2932**	*666.3596*	**2982**	*666.9878*
2883	*665.6972*	**2933**	*666.3726*	**2983**	*666.9999*
2884	*665.7112*	**2934**	*666.3857*	**2984**	*667.0120*
2885	*665.7252*	**2935**	*666.3986*	**2985**	*667.0240*
2886	*665.7392*	**2936**	*666.4116*	**2986**	*667.0361*
2887	*665.7531*	**2937**	*666.4246*	**2987**	*667.0481*
2888	*665.7670*	**2938**	*666.4375*	**2988**	*667.0601*
2889	*665.7809*	**2939**	*666.4504*	**2989**	*667.0721*
2890	*665.7948*	**2940**	*666.4633*	**2990**	*667.0841*
2891	*665.8087*	**2941**	*666.4762*	**2991**	*667.0960*
2892	*665.8225*	**2942**	*666.4890*	**2992**	*667.1080*
2893	*665.8363*	**2943**	*666.5018*	**2993**	*667.1199*
2894	*665.8501*	**2944**	*666.5147*	**2994**	*667.1318*
2895	*665.8539*	**2945**	*666.5275*	**2995**	*667.1437*
2896	*665.8777*	**2946**	*666.5402*	**2996**	*667.1555*
2897	*665.8914*	**2947**	*666.5530*	**2997**	*667.1674*
2898	*665.9051*	**2948**	*666.5657*	**2998**	*667.1792*
2899	*665.9188*	**2949**	*666.5784*	**2999**	*667.1910*

Tables

Weeks	Present Worth	Weeks	Present Worth	Weeks	Present Worth
3000	*667.2028*	**3050**	*667.7709*	**3100**	*668.2984*
3001	*667.2146*	**3051**	*667.7818*	**3101**	*668.3086*
3002	*667.2264*	**3052**	*667.7927*	**3102**	*668.3187*
3003	*667.2381*	**3053**	*667.8036*	**3103**	*668.3288*
3004	*667.2498*	**3054**	*667.8145*	**3104**	*668.3389*
3005	*667.2615*	**3055**	*667.8254*	**3105**	*668.3490*
3006	*667.2732*	**3056**	*667.8363*	**3106**	*668.3591*
3007	*667.2849*	**3057**	*667.8471*	**3107**	*668.3692*
3008	*667.2966*	**3058**	*667.8579*	**3108**	*668.3792*
3009	*667.3082*	**3059**	*667.8687*	**3109**	*668.3893*
3010	*667.3198*	**3060**	*667.8795*	**3110**	*668.3993*
3011	*667.3314*	**3061**	*667.8903*	**3111**	*668.4093*
3012	*667.3430*	**3062**	*667.9011*	**3112**	*668.4193*
3013	*667.3546*	**3063**	*667.9118*	**3113**	*668.4293*
3014	*337.3661*	**3064**	*667.9225*	**3114**	*668.4392*
3015	*667.3777*	**3065**	*667.9332*	**3115**	*668.4492*
3016	*667.3892*	**3066**	*667.9439*	**3116**	*668.4591*
3017	*667.4007*	**3067**	*667.9546*	**3117**	*668.4690*
3018	*667.4122*	**3068**	*667.9653*	**3118**	*668.4790*
3019	*667.4236*	**3069**	*667.9759*	**3119**	*668.4888*
3020	*667.4351*	**3070**	*667.9866*	**3120**	*668.4987*
3021	*667.4465*	**3071**	*667.9972*		
3022	*667.4580*	**3072**	*668.0078*		
3023	*667.4694*	**3073**	*668.0184*		
3024	*667.4807*	**3074**	*668.0290*		
3025	*667.4921*	**3075**	*668.0395*		
3026	*667.5035*	**3076**	*668.0501*		
3027	*667.5148*	**3078**	*668.0606*		
3028	*667.5261*	**3077**	*668.0711*		
3029	*667.5374*	**3079**	*668.0816*		
3030	*667.5487*	**3080**	*668.0921*		
3031	*667.5599*	**3081**	*668.1025*		
3032	*667.5712*	**3082**	*668.1130*		
3033	*667.5824*	**3083**	*668.1234*		
3034	*667.5936*	**3084**	*668.1338*		
3035	*667.6048*	**3085**	*668.1442*		
3036	*667.6160*	**3086**	*668.1546*		
3037	*667.6272*	**3087**	*668.1650*		
3038	*667.6383*	**3088**	*668.1753*		
3039	*667.6495*	**3089**	*668.1857*		
3040	*667.6606*	**3090**	*668.1960*		
3041	*667.6717*	**3091**	*668.2063*		
3042	*667.6828*	**3092**	*668.2166*		
3043	*667.6939*	**3093**	*668.2269*		
3044	*667.7049*	**3094**	*668.2371*		
3045	*667.7159*	**3095**	*668.2474*		
3046	*667.7270*	**3096**	*668.2576*		
3047	*667.7380*	**3097**	*668.2678*		
3048	*667.7489*	**3098**	*668.2780*		
3049	*667.7599*	**3099**	*668.2882*		

Table 6 GLOSSARY OF ABBREVIATIONS AND JARGON FREQUENTLY USED IN "COMP"

ADA	Americans With Disabilities Act
AHCA	Agency for Health Care Administration
App.	Appellate
AWW	Average weekly wage
C/O	Complain of
CCM	Catastrophic case manager
Ceding Company	The primary insurer
CFS	Chronic fatigue syndrome
cir.	Federal Circuit Court
CM	Case manager
CR	Compensation rate
CT	Cumulative trauma
D/A	Date of accident or injury
dba	Doing business as
DCA	District Court of Appeal
div	Division
DLES	Department of Labor and Employment Security
DOI	Department of Insurance
DOL	Department of Labor
DWC	Division of Workers' Compensation
Dx	Diagnosis
EAO	Employee Assistance Office
E/C	Employer/Carrier
EMA	Expert medical advisor
ERISA	Employment Retirement Income Security Act
Experience rating	An adjustment in manual premium based on an employer's individual loss history
FCE	Functional capacity evaluation
FECA	Federal Employees Compensation Act
FELA	Federal Employees Liability Act
Fla. Stat.	Florida Statutes
FWCIGA	Florida Workers' Compensation Insurance Guaranty Association
HB	House bill
HIV	Human Immunodeficiency Virus
Hx	History
IB	Impairment Income Benefits
IME	Independent medical examination
IV	Intravenous
JCC	Judge of Compensation Claims

Tables

Larson's	LARSON'S WORKERS' COMPENSATION, DESK EDITION (Matthew Bender)
LDP	Last day paid
LDW	Last day worked
LHWCA	Longshore and Harbor Workers'Compensation Act
LT	Lost time
Manual Premium	Premium rates derived from the Manual on Compensation for individual occupational classes
MCA	Managed care arrangement
MCC	Medical care coordinator
MMI	Maximum medical improvement
MO	Medical only
MOD	Premium modification factor
NLT	No lost time
NOI	Notice of injury
OSHA	Occupational Safety and Health Act
OT	Occupational therapy
OV	Office visit
PD	Permanent disability
PFB	Petition for benefits
PPD	Permanent Partial Disability
Primary Insurer	The reinsured party to a policy of reinsurance
PT	Physical therapy
PTD	Permanent total disability
PV	Present value
Rehab	Vocational rehabilitation
RFA	Request for assistance
RRTW	Released to return to work
RRTWLD	Released to return to work light duty
RTP	Request to produce
SB	Senate bill
SDTF	Special Disability Trust Fund
SI	Self-insured
SSA	Social Security Administration
SSD	Social Security Disability
Subro	Subrogation
Super Doc	Expert medical advisor or EMA
TD	Temporary disability
TPD	Temporary partial disability
TTD	Temporary total disability
VA	Veterans Administration
WL	Wage loss
WO	Wash out settlement

WS Wage statement

Table 7 Bibliography of LexisNexis Medical Publications

A complete, up to date list of LexisNexis Medical Publications can be found on the Internet at http://www.lexisnexis.com.

ATTORNEYS' DICTIONARY OF MEDICINE

The best medical dictionary designed for attorneys. Medical jargon is explained in a plain English that juries can understand. The dictionary includes over 57,000 definitions of medical terms, with examples and practical analogies as well as the unique Reversicon which converts lay words into the correct medical terms. There are over 700 illustrations of anatomical features, body movements, medical equipment, injuries, and more. Also included are a key to abbreviations used in medical records and a simplified guide to correct pronunciation.

ATTORNEYS' TEXTBOOK OF MEDICINE

Written in language the practicing lawyer can understand, backed by hundreds of illustrations, diagrams, charts, tables, and checklists, this classic research aide is essential for any attorney trying a medico-legal case. It provides quick access to explanations of every compensable injury and a wide range of disease conditions, including AIDS and Blood Transfusion Reactions. It includes the background information needed to confidently prepare complex cases, evaluate injuries and disabilities, present evidence to jurors in language they can understand, and effectively examine and cross-examine medical witnesses. The extensive medico-legal annotations include: concise descriptions, nature of the accident, diagnosis of the injury, prognosis, extent of disability, monetary awards held excessive or not, and full case data. In addition, there are three volumes of full color transparencies correlated to the text which detail anatomy and injuries. Included also is an evaluation of permanent physical impairment by the AMA which explains all standards for testing and evaluating injuries.

ATTORNEYS' TEXTBOOK OF MEDICINE: MANUAL OF TRAUMATIC INJURIES

An ideal, quick reference for attorneys preparing cases involving physical injuries, for rehabilitation specialists seeking background on the cause of injuries, and for insurance company employees handling medical claims. It contains concise coverage of the mechanism of injury, signs and symptoms, diagnosis, treatment, and frequent complications. Also included are chapter bibliographies, a glossary of medical terms in each chapter, and medical illustrations that help clarify many diagnostic procedures and treatment methods.

CANCER (COURTROOM MEDICINE SERIES)

This most comprehensive guide to cancer as the subject of litigation covers etiology, epidemiology, anatomic site, histology, metastasis, relation to various industrial exposures, occupations subject to exposures, and the relationship of cancer to various carcinogenic agents such as diethylstilbesterol (DES), Agent Orange, and asbestos. Each cancer that is related to an industrial setting is discussed in terms of latency period, signs and symptoms of exposure, diagnosis, treatment and prognosis. Federal rules and regulations, an index, specific damage awards, trial testimony, a glossary, and bibliography are also included.

CHEST, HEART AND LUNGS (COURTROOM MEDICINE SERIES)

Full medical and legal coverage of heart disease, lung cancer and occupational diseases of the lungs (asbestosis, silicosis, etc.), diagnosic tests and procedures, disability standards, and evaluation. Also included are illustrations, diagrams, charts, case annotations, bibliography, glossary, and index.

COMMON DIAGNOSTIC PROCEDURES: ORTHOPEDICS AND NEUROLOGY

This deskbook of medical tests and findings helps you successfully present evidence of injury for settlement or trial. Each test-specific chapter presents easy-to-understand coverage of the diagnostic procedures you're researching. Among the many features you'll find throughout this indispensable volume are: detailed illustrations; a handy scope box for every chapter; chapter-by-chapter bibliographies; a useful glossary of terms, defining difficult medico-legal terminology.

CROSS-EXAMINATION OF MEDICAL EXPERTS

Renowned medico-legal authority Marshall Houts analyzes the cross-examination of leading practitioners which illustrate: the impeachment of an expert witness; proving a case through cross-examination of an adverse witness; refuting negative test results by establishing the importance of subjective symptoms; and many other crucial issues.

DEATH (COURTROOM MEDICINE SERIES)

Examines the medical facts of death and the techniques of prosecuting or defending resulting actions. It discusses cause (legal causation), determination (brain death), time (survivorship determinations), and provides full explanations of autopsy procedures, exhumation, the death certificate, and laboratory and toxicological procedures. Also examined is the relationship of death to intervening factors of medical treatment or disease. Annotations, bibliography, illustrations, and an index are provided.

ELBOW AND SHOULDER PAIN, SECOND EDITION

Elbow and Shoulder Pain addresses the medical issues involved in obtaining fair compensation for injuries that result in loss of work or diminished earning capacity: what caused the pain; how severe is the pain; what treatment is most effective yet cost efficient; what is the percentage of permanent disability; how much work can the injured person perform? *Elbow and Shoulder Pain* offers a standardized and objective method for determining the extent of impairment. Based on a survey of medical specialists, an easy-to-read table provides the percentage of permanent partial physical impairment for a range of diagnoses, along with the corresponding standard level of work medically permitted. This valuable book presents a practical treatment protocol in algorithmic format for a full range of conservative and surgical treatments.

THE EYE (COURTROOM MEDICINE SERIES)

Details chemical, thermal and radiation injuries, blunt trauma, penetrating injuries, foreign body injuries cararacts, glaucoma, and retinal detachment. It discusses the problems associated with medications and drugs, contact lenses, and intraocular implants, and explains eye examinations the evaluation of visual capability and disability, and the treatment and prognosis of various forms of eye injury. Illustrations, case annotations, examples of expert testimony, bibliography, and index are included.

HEAD AND BRAIN (COURTROOM MEDICINE SERIES)

Provides a clear explanation of the various types of head injuries, their diagnosis and treatment, and the consequences of trauma. It discusses the possible sequelae of head and brain injury-epilepsy; loss of vision or hearing; amnesia; and other conditions. The underlying medical considerations of neuro-anatomy and physiology are carefully detailed, and facial and eye injuries are fully discussed. Annotations, glossary, bibliography, illustrations, and index are provided.

HEAD AND BRAIN, NECK AND LOW BACK (COURTROOM MEDICINE SERIES) (CD-ROM)

This comprehensive set — written by medical experts specifically for attorneys — covers all injuries, illnesses, diseases and syndromes related to three common areas of injury — the head, neck, and low back. With information on current medications and the latest medical procedures, as well as the most recent medical-legal case annotations, Courtroom Medicine gives you everything you need to practice with complete confidence.

HIP AND THIGH (COURTROOM MEDICINE SERIES)

Gives a detailed explanation of injuries and diseases of this area including total hip replacement, diagnosis, differential diagnosis, causation, disability evaluation, complications, rehabilitation, and surgical procedures. It covers techniques of examination and cross-examination as well as pertinent case annotations and authoritative medical statements. Bibliography, illustrations, and index are included.

KNEE AND ITS RELATED STRUCTURES (COURTROOM MEDICINE SERIES)

Explains diagnostic methods, causation, complications, and treatment of injuries to the knee, lower leg, ankle, foot, and toes, including a discussion of fractures, dislocations, and amputations. Techniques of examination and cross-examination of medical experts are covered as is disability evaluation, complications, and differential diagnosis. Annotations, bibliography, authoritative statements, illustrations, and index are provided.

LAWYERS GUIDE TO MEDICAL PROOF

Provides practical, down-to-earth advice on the psychology of a personal injury trial, effective dramatic advocacy, and impeachment of expert's testimony, demonstrated by cross-examinations drawn from actual cases. Medical terminology, procedures, and technology are clearly explained. How medical evidence becomes an instrument of jury-convincing courtroom proof is shown through actual court records.

LAWYERS' MEDICAL CYCLOPEDIA, FOURTH EDITION

Lawyers' Medical Cyclopedia is the authoritative reference for attorneys involved in personal injury, medical malpractice, workers' compensation, social security, disability income, and health insurance cases. First published 40 years ago, this 10-volume reference is now in its fourth edition. *Lawyers' Medical Cyclopedia* offers in-depth information and case law on hundreds of medical and surgical specialties. It includes an extensive bibliography of references to medical journals, law review articles, and American Law Reports, as well as summaries of state and federal appellate opinions. Written by physicians skilled at translating complex anatomy, physiology, and medical treatment into clear language that is easy for you to understand, it provides quick, accurate insight into medical issues. *Lawyers' Medical Cyclopedia* keeps you up-to-date on the latest medical and legal developments with annual supplementation written by specialists in both medicine and the law. It saves you valuable research time by emphasizing medical and medicolegal issues most likely to be the subject of litigation and focusing on information most useful to busy practitioners.

THE LOW BACK (COURTROOM MEDICINE SERIES)

These volumes provide extensive coverage of intervertebral disc injuries, fractures and dislocations of the thoracic and lumbar spines, fractures of the sacrum and coccyx, congenital anomalies and developmental defects, arthritic conditions, metabolic bone disease and many others. In addition, these volumes provide analysis of the extent, causes, diagnostic procedures, treatments, and possible prognosis of back injuries. Amounts of awards, examples of expert testimony, and selected cases are provided as well.

MEDICAL MALPRACTICE

An essential treatise and complete litigation guide to proving or defending against malpractice charges. It covers: determining whether to bring an action for tort or breach of implied contract; a physicians liability for the negligence of other medical personnel; a physician's duty to obtain informed consent; malpractice by specific health care providers, such as nurses, psychiatrists and dentists; circumventing the "Conspiracy of Silence" (winning without an expert witness). Charles Kramer examines the litigation process step-by-step. Strategies are illustrated by transcripts with commentary.

MEDICAL MALPRACTIDCE: GUIDE TO MEDICAL ISSUES

Find out how to recognize departures from standard of care and distinquish errors in clinical judgement with this seven-volume treatise, which provides the medical background you need to handle malpractice cases. Each chapter contains extensive medical information, including standards of care and potential causes of medical malpractice actions.

MEDICAL MALPRACTICE REPORTS

These reports provide all the facts, background information, and expert analysis needed to keep on top of new legislation, new theories of liability, and the impact of new medical technology. Each monthly issue contains news affecting those persons in the field--personal injury attorneys or attorneys representing medical professions, hospital administrators and in-house counsel, and health care administrators and providers. Each month an article is highlighted to point out the most important development of the month. Case summaries, taken from every jurisdiction, complete with descriptive headings, are topically organized. Also included are summaries from recent law reviews and legislative developments.

THE NECK (COURTROOM MEDICINE SERIES)

Complete coverage of whiplash, cervical cord injuries, fractures, and dislocations of the vertebrae. Also covers injuries to larynx, vocal cords, trachea, blood vessels, intervertebral disc disease and injury, and TMJ disorders. The cause, mechanism, and effect of injury are discussed. Diagnostic and treatment procedures are covered as well. Illustrations, glossary, bibliography, annotations, and index are included.

OCCUPATIONAL INJURIES AND ILLNESSES

This authoritative resource provides the medical information needed to prove, refute, or prevent allegations of occupational injury and illnesses. Each chapter contains the AMA evaluation of impairment.

ORTHOPEDIC, NEUROLOGICAL AND CHIROPRACTICE PHYSICAL EXAMINATIONS: TECHNIQUE AND SIGNIFICANCE

Written in non-technical language to assist the plaintiff's bar in understanding medical reports and examinations relating to personal injuries, this book includes an alphabetical listing of the various types of examinations, a summary of different conditions and the examinations that might be performed to detect them, and a diagram setting out the planes of the body.

PAIN AND SUFFERING (COURTROOM MEDICINE SERIES)

This publication covers every anatomic site, source and condition associated with pain, examination of expert medico-legal witnesses, legal aspects of recovery for pain and suffering, recovery for loss of enjoyment of life, psychiatric aspects of pain, chronic pain syndromes, methods of treating pain syndromes, basic principles for proof and securing proper compensation, annotations on major legal issues, bibliography, glossary, aphorisms, and index.

PROVING MEDICAL DIAGNOSIS AND PROGNOSIS

Gives complete, authoritative guidance on orthopedic, neurological, and laboratory tests. Provides in-depth discussion of medical records, and nine steps for measuring the examining doctor's performance in every primary medical test. Included are: anatomy and physiology--the medical background to each test results to the injury. Also covered are direct and cross-examinations using techniques form actual court transcripts. Numerous charts, tables, illustrations, and a detailed index are included.

PSYCHIC INJURIES (COURTROOM MEDICINE SERIES)

Covers three areas essential to understanding psychic injuries: adaption to physical disabilities, types of trauma associated with psychological sequelae, and maladaptive reactions to trauma. A chapter on pharmacological agents used in the treatment of psychic disorders is included. Also covered is the examination of expert witnesses, including material on elements of recovery for psychic injuries. Glossary of psychiatric terms, annotations, aphorisms, and an index are provided.

SHOULDER AND ELBOW (COURTROOM MEDICINE SERIES)

All types of fractures and dislocations of the shoulder, elbow, arm, wrist, and hand, as well as blood vessel injuries, nerve injuries, and arthritic conditions are discussed. The volumes also explain diagnostic methods, disability evaluation causation, complications, and treatment. Case annotations, bibliography, illustrative cases, glossary, authoritative quotes, and index are provided.

TRAUMATIC BRAIN INJURY: EVALUATION AND LITIGATION

This volume provides a detailed and practical guide for litigating brain injury cases. Written by an experienced trial lawyer, a neuropsychologist, and a neuropsychiatrist/neurologist, *Traumatic Brain Injury: Evaluation and Litigation* includes a detailed bibliography, comprehensive checklists, and many useful forms. The book covers the medical and neuropsychological analysis of brain injury, including its causes and effects; the process of case investigation, including evaluation of liability and damages; and trial techniques, including settlement considerations.

Table 8 Bibliography of LexisNexis Workers' Compensation Related Publications

The following are LexisNexis workers' compensation related print publications. For a complete listing of CD-ROM and online products, or to order any of these publications, please call Customer Service at 1-800-223-1940:

National Treatises

Larson's Workers' Compensation Law

Larson's Workers' Compensation, Desk Edition

Workers' Compensation for Employers

Workers' Compensation: The Survival Guide for Business

International Employment Law

Labor and Employment in California: A Guide to Employment Laws, Regulations and Practices

Labor and Employment in Connecticut: A Guide to Employment Laws, Regulations and Practices

Employment in Florida: A Guide to Employment Laws, Regulations and Practices

Labor and Employment in Georgia: A Guide to Employment Laws, Regulations and Practices

Illinois Jurisprudence: Labor and Employment Law

Labor and Employment in Louisiana: A Guide to Employment Laws, Regulations and Practices

Labor and Employment in Massachusetts: A Guide to Employment Laws, Regulations and Practices

Labor and Employment in Nebraska: A Guide to Employment Laws, Regulations and Practices

Labor and Employment in New Hampshire: A Guide to Employment Laws, Regulations and Practices

Labor and Employment in New Jersey: A Guide to Employment Laws, Regulations and Practices

Employment in Ohio: A Guide to Employment Laws, Regulations and Practices

Labor and Employment in Pennsylvania: A Guide to Employment Laws, Regulations and Practices

Labor and Employment in Rhode Island: A Guide to Employment Laws, Regulations and Practices

Employment in Texas: A Guide to Employment Laws, Regulations and Practices

Employment in Washington: A Guide to Employment Laws, Regulations and Practices

Tables

<u>State Workers' Compensation Treatises, Guidebooks, Case Finders</u>

Alabama Workers' Compensation Law and Handbook

California Law of Employee Injuries and Workers' Compensation

California Workers' Compensation Handbook

California Workers' Compensation Law

Florida Workers' Compensation Handbook

Attorney's Fees in Florida: Insurance, Workers' Compensation, Administrative, Government

Georgia Workers' Compensation Law

Illinois Workers' Compensation Handbook

Kentucky Workers' Compensation

Louisiana Workers' Compensation

Maryland Workers' Compensation Handbook

Nebraska Legal Forms: Workers' Compensation

New Hampshire Workers' Compensation Manual

New York Workers' Compensation Handbook

Ohio Workers' Compensation Law

Texas Workers' Compensation Law: A Guide to Practice Before Commission & Court

Virginia Workers' Compensation: Law and Practice

Virginia Workers' Compensation Case Finder

<u>State Workers' Compensation Reporters</u>

Benefits Review Board Service—Longshore Reporter

California Compensation Cases

Massachusetts Workers' Compensation Reports

<u>State Workers' Compensation Codes</u>

Alabama Workers' Compensation Law Annotated

Alaska Workers' Compensation Laws and Regulations Annotated

Arizona Workers' Compensation Laws and Rules Annotated

Arkansas Workers' Compensation Law and Rules Annotated

Parker's California Labor Code

Workers' Compensation Laws of California

State of Connecticut Workers' Compensation

Florida Rules of Workers' Compensation Procedure (A Florida Bar CLE Publication)

Georgia Workers' Compensation Laws, Rules and Regulations Annotated

Hawaii Workers' Compensation Laws

Idaho Workers' Compensation Laws Annotated

Illinois Workers' Compensation Laws Annotated

Indiana Workers' Compensation Laws and Rules Annotated

Kentucky Workers' Compensation Laws Annotated

Maryland Workers' Compensation Law

Mississippi Workers' Compensation Laws and Rules Annotated

Nebraska Workers' Compensation Laws and Rules Annotated

New Mexico Workers' Compensation Laws and Regulations Annotated

New York State Workers' Compensation Law Annotated

North Carolina Workers' Compensation Law Annotated

North Dakota Workers' Compensation Law

Ohio Workers' Compensation Law Handbook

Rhode Island Workers' Compensation Law

Tennessee Workers' Compensation Laws Annotated

Utah Workers' Compensation Laws and Rules Annotated

The Virginia Workers' Compensation Act Annotated

West Virginia Workers' Compensation and Unemployment Compensation Laws

Wyoming Workers' Compensation Act

<u>Social Security Disability Treatise</u>

Social Security Practice Guide

INDEX

References in regular type are to text sections.
References in **boldface** type are to the following:

ABBREVIATIONS

AC . . . . Part VI: Florida Administrative Code
CJC . . . . Part VII: Code Of Judicial Conduct
CS . . . . Part II: Case Summaries
C&T . . . . Part VIII: Tables
RAP . . . . Part V: Florida Rules of Appellate Procedure
RAP–F . . . . Part V: Rules of Appellate Procedure–Forms
RPWCA . . . . Part IV: Florida Rules of Procedure for Workers' Compensation Adjudications
Stats . . . . Part III: Florida Statutes

A

Index

Index

Index

Index

Index

Index

Index

Index

Index

Index

B

Index

C

Index

Index

Index

D

Index

Index

Index

Index

Index

Index

Index

F

Index

Index

Index

Index

Index

J

Index

Index

Index

K

L

Index

Index

Index

Index

Index

Index

Index

Index

Index

Index

Index

Index

Index

Index

Index

Index

S

Index

Index

Index

Index

Index

Index

Index

Index

Index

Index

T

Index

Index

Index

Index

Index